IMMIGRATION LAW HANDBOOK

Eighth Edition

MARGARET PHELAN

Barrister

AND

JAMES GILLESPIE

Barrister (retired)

OXFORD

UNIVERSITY PRESS

OXFORD
UNIVERSITY PRESS

Great Clarendon Street, Oxford, OX2 6DP,
United Kingdom

Oxford University Press is a department of the University of Oxford.
It furthers the University's objective of excellence in research, scholarship,
and education by publishing worldwide. Oxford is a registered trade mark of
Oxford University Press in the UK and in certain other countries

© Margaret Phelan and James Gillespie, 2013

The moral rights of the authors have been asserted

First Edition published in 1997
Eighth Edition published in 2013

Impression: 1

British Library Cataloguing in Publication Data

Data available

ISBN 978–0–19–965970–8

Printed in Italy by
L.E.G.O. S.p.A.— Lavis TN

CONTENTS

IMMIGRATION RULES

STATUTORY INSTRUMENTS

EUROPEAN MATERIALS

INTERNATIONAL MATERIALS

PREFACE

The changes have been coming thick and fast, with some 21 sets of changes in immigration rules since June 2010 when the last edition was prepared.

Domestic immigration law is increasingly complicated and user unfriendly, lacking transparency and accessibility. The courts have repeatedly complained about the complexity of the Immigration Rules and "the absolute whirlwind which litigants and judges now feel themselves in due to the speed with which the law, practice and policy change in this field of law". These problems have worsened since the last edition.

Many amendments made to existing statutes have never come into force, leading to a parallel system of old laws not repealed and new laws not commenced.

We do not have the space to include both the new and old in our book. Our system is prospective, we insert changes to statutes as Parliament legislates. We cannot second guess what will or will not ever come into force.

The decision of the Supreme Court in the case of *Alvi* has resulted in an enormous expansion in length of the Immigration Rules. These important changes (which include numerous drafting errors) have been incorporated, including the rule changes published on 5 September 2012.

EU and international law remains relatively stable.

We do thank Julia Gasparro, Helen Leadbeater, Colin Yeo and Renaissance Chambers for their help.

And UNHCR for kind permission to use the Handbook. Save where otherwise indicated in the text statutory provisions have been included and annotated to reflect the law at 1 July 2012. The Immigration Rules incorporate all changes up to and including those published on 5 September 2012. Subsequent changes in HC 760 and HC 820 were published too late for inclusion in this edition.

Margaret Phelan
James Gillespie
December 2012

STATUTES

Immigration Act 1971
(1971, c. 77)

Arrangement of Sections

PART IV. SUPPLEMENTARY

SCHEDULES

An Act to amend and replace the present immigration laws, to make certain related changes in the citizenship law and enable help to be given to those wishing to return abroad, and for purposes connected therewith.   [28 October 1971]

PART I
REGULATION OF ENTRY INTO AND STAY IN UNITED KINGDOM

1. General principles

(1) All those who are in this Act expressed to have the right of abode in the United Kingdom shall be free to live in and to come and go into and from, the United Kingdom

without let or hindrance except such as may be required under and in accordance with this Act to enable their right to be established or as may be otherwise lawfully imposed on any person.

(2) Those not having that right may live, work and settle in the United Kingdom by permission and subject to such regulation and control of their entry into, stay in and departure from the United Kingdom as is imposed by this Act; and indefinite leave to enter or remain in the United Kingdom shall, by virtue of this provision, be treated as having been given under this Act to those in the United Kingdom at its coming into force, if they are then settled there (and not exempt under this Act from the provisions relating to leave to enter or remain).

(3) Arrival in and departure from the United Kingdom on a local journey from or to any of the Islands (that is to say, the Channel Islands and Isle of Man) or the Republic of Ireland shall not be subject to control under this Act, nor shall a person require leave to enter the United Kingdom on so arriving, except in so far as any of those places is for any purpose excluded from this subsection under the powers conferred by this Act; and in this Act the United Kingdom and those places, or such of them as are not so excluded, are collectively referred to as 'the common travel area'.

(4) The rules laid down by the Secretary of State as to the practice to be followed in the administration of this Act for regulating the entry into and stay in the United Kingdom of persons not having the right of abode shall include provision for admitting (in such cases and subject to such restrictions as may be provided by the rules, and subject or not to conditions as to length of stay or otherwise) persons coming for the purpose of taking employment, or for purposes of study, or as visitors, or as dependants of persons lawfully in or entering the United Kingdom.

(5) ...

Note: Section 1(5) repealed by Immigration Act 1988, s 1.

[2. Statement of right of abode in United Kingdom

(1) A person is under this Act to have the right of abode in the United Kingdom if—
   (a) he is a British citizen; or
   (b) he is a Commonwealth citizen who—
      (i) immediately before the commencement of the British Nationality Act 1981 was a Commonwealth citizen having the right of abode in the United Kingdom by virtue of section 2(1)(d) or section 2(2) of this Act as then in force; and
      (ii) has not ceased to be a Commonwealth citizen in the meanwhile.

(2) In relation to Commonwealth citizens who have the right of abode in the United Kingdom by virtue of subsection (1)(b) above, this Act, except this section and [section 5(2)], shall apply as if they were British citizens; and in this Act (except as aforesaid) 'British citizen' shall be construed accordingly.]

Note: Section 2 substituted by British Nationality Act 1981, s 39(2). Words in square brackets in s 2(2) substituted by the Immigration Act 1988, s 3(3).

[2A. Deprivation of right of abode

(1) The Secretary of State may by order remove from a specified person a right of abode in the United Kingdom which he has under section 2(1)(b).

(2) The Secretary of State may make an order under subsection (1) in respect of a person only if the Secretary of State thinks that it would be conducive to the public good for the person to be excluded or removed from the United Kingdom.

(3) An order under subsection (1) may be revoked by order of the Secretary of State.

(4) While an order under subsection (1) has effect in relation to a person—
   (a) section 2(2) shall not apply to him, and
   (b) any certificate of entitlement granted to him shall have no effect.]

Note: Section 2A inserted by Immigration, Asylum and Nationality Act 2006, s 57(1) from 16 June 2006 (SI 2006/1497).

3. General provisions for regulation and control

(1) Except as otherwise provided by or under this Act, where a person is not [a British citizen]—
   (a) he shall not enter the United Kingdom unless given leave to do so in accordance with [the provisions of, or made under,] this Act;
   (b) he may be given leave to enter the United Kingdom (or, when already there, leave to remain in the United Kingdom) either for a limited or for an indefinite period);
   [(c) if he is given limited leave to enter or remain in the United Kingdom, it may be given subject to all or any of the following conditions, namely—
      (i) a condition restricting his employment or occupation in the United Kingdom;
      [(ia) a condition restricting his studies in the United Kingdom;]
      (ii) a condition requiring him to maintain and accommodate himself, and any dependants of his, without recourse to public funds;...
      (iii) a condition requiring him to register with the police.
      {(iv) a condition requiring him to report to an immigration officer or the Secretary of State; and
      (v) a condition about residence.}]

(2) The Secretary of State shall from time to time (and as soon as may be) lay before Parliament statements of the rules, or of any changes in the rules, laid down by him as to the practice to be followed in the administration of this Act for regulating the entry into and stay in the United Kingdom of persons required by this Act to have leave to enter, including any rules as to the period for which leave is to be given and the conditions to be attached in different circumstances; and section 1(4) above shall not be taken to require uniform provision to be made by the rules as regards admission of persons for a purpose or in a capacity specified in section 1(4) (and in particular, for this as well as other purposes of this Act, account may be taken of citizenship or nationality).

   If a statement laid before either House of Parliament under this subsection is disapproved by a resolution of that House passed within the period of forty days beginning with the date of laying (and exclusive of any period during which Parliament is dissolved or prorogued or during which both Houses are adjourned for more than four days), then the Secretary of State shall as soon as may be make such changes or further changes in the rules as appear to him to be required in the circumstances, so that the statement of those changes be laid before Parliament at latest by the end of the period of forty days beginning with the date of the resolution (but exclusive as aforesaid).

(3) In the case of a limited leave to enter or remain in the United Kingdom,—

(a) a person's leave may be varied, whether by restricting, enlarging or removing the limit on its duration, or by adding, varying or revoking conditions, but if the limit on its duration is removed, any conditions attached to the leave shall cease to apply; and

(b) the limitation on and any conditions attached to a person's leave [(whether imposed originally or on a variation) shall], if not superseded, apply also to any subsequent leave he may obtain after an absence from the United Kingdom within the period limited for the duration of the earlier leave.

(4) A person's leave to enter or remain in the United Kingdom shall lapse on his going to a country or territory outside the common travel area (whether or not he lands there), unless within the period for which he had leave he returns to the United Kingdom in circumstances in which he is not required to obtain leave to enter; but, if he does so return, his previous leave (and any limitation on it or conditions attached to it) shall continue to apply.

[(5) A person who is not a British citizen is liable to deportation from the United Kingdom if—

(a) the Secretary of State deems his deportation to be conducive to the public good; or

(b) another person to whose family he belongs is or has been ordered to be deported.]

(6) Without prejudice to the operation of subsection (5) above, a person who is not [a British citizen] shall also be liable to deportation from the United Kingdom if, after he has attained the age of seventeen, he is convicted of an offence for which he is punishable with imprisonment and on his conviction is recommended for deportation by a court empowered by this Act to do so.

(7) Where it appears to Her Majesty proper so to do by reason of restrictions or conditions imposed on [British citizens, British Dependent Territories citizens or British Overseas citizens] when leaving or seeking to leave any country or the territory subject to the government of any country, Her Majesty may by Order in Council make provision for prohibiting persons who are nationals or citizens of that country and are not [British citizens] from embarking in the United Kingdom, or from doing so elsewhere than at a port of exit, or for imposing restrictions or conditions on them when embarking or about to embark in the United Kingdom; and Her Majesty may also make provision by Order in Council to enable those who are not [British citizens] to be, in such cases as may be prescribed by the Order, prohibited in the interests of safety from so embarking on a ship or aircraft specified or indicated in the prohibition.

Any Order in Council under this subsection shall be subject to annulment in pursuance of a resolution of either House of Parliament.

(8) When any question arises under this Act whether or not a person is [a British citizen], or is entitled to any exemption under this Act, it shall lie on the person asserting it to prove that he is.

[(9) A person seeking to enter the United Kingdom and claiming to have the right of abode there shall prove it by means of—

(a) a United Kingdom passport describing him as a British citizen,

(b) a United Kingdom passport describing him as a British subject with the right of abode in the United Kingdom, {or}

(c) ...

(d) ...

(e) a certificate of entitlement.]

Note: Section 3(1)(c) substituted by Asylum and Immigration Act 1996 from 1 November 1996. Words in square brackets in s 3(6)–(8) and first square brackets in s 3(1) substituted by British Nationality Act 1981. Words in square brackets in s 3(3) substituted by Immigration Act 1988. Words in square brackets in s 3(1)(a) inserted by Immigration and Asylum Act 1999 from 14 February 2000. Section 3(5) substituted by Immigration and Asylum Act 1999 from 2 October 2000. Section 3(9) substituted by Immigration, Asylum and Nationality Act 2006, s 30 from 16 June 2006 (SI 2006/1497). Subsection (1)(c)(iv) and (v) inserted by UK Borders Act 2007, s 16 from 31 January 2008 (SI 2008/99). Subsection (1)(c)(ia) inserted by Borders, Citizenship and Immigration Act 2009, s 50(1) from 21 July 2009. Subsections (9)(c) and (d) omitted by Identity Documents Act 2010, Schedule, para 1 from 21 January 2011 (s 14). Section 3 has effect in a form modified by and in circumstances specified by the Channel Tunnel (International Arrangements) Order (SI 1993/1813) as amended by SIs 1994/1405, 2000/913, 2001/178, 2001/3707, 2006/1003 and 2007/3759.

[3A. Further provision as to leave to enter

(1) The Secretary of State may by order make further provision with respect to the giving, refusing or varying of leave to enter the United Kingdom.

(2) An order under subsection (1) may, in particular, provide for—

(a) leave to be given or refused before the person concerned arrives in the United Kingdom;

(b) the form or manner in which leave may be given, refused or varied;

(c) the imposition of conditions;

(d) a person's leave to enter not to lapse on his leaving the common travel area.

(3) The Secretary of State may by order provide that, in such circumstances as may be prescribed—

(a) an entry visa, or

(b) such other form of entry clearance as may be prescribed, is to have effect as leave to enter the United Kingdom.

(4) An order under subsection (3) may, in particular—

(a) provide for a clearance to have effect as leave to enter—

(i) on a prescribed number of occasions during the period for which the clearance has effect;

(ii) on an unlimited number of occasions during that period;

(iii) subject to prescribed conditions; and

(b) provide for a clearance which has the effect referred to in paragraph (a)(i) or (ii) to be varied by the Secretary of State or an immigration officer so that it ceases to have that effect.

(5) Only conditions of a kind that could be imposed on leave to enter given under section 3 may be prescribed.

(6) In subsections (3), (4) and (5) 'prescribed' means prescribed in an order made under subsection (3).

(7) The Secretary of State may, in such circumstances as may be prescribed in an order made by him, give or refuse leave to enter the United Kingdom.

(8) An order under subsection (7) may provide that, in such circumstances as may be prescribed by the order, paragraphs 2, 4, 6, 7, 8, 9 and 21 of Part I of Schedule 2 to this Act are to be read, in relation to the exercise by the Secretary of State of functions which he

has as a result of the order, as if references to an immigration officer included references to the Secretary of State.

(9) Subsection (8) is not to be read as affecting any power conferred by subsection (10).

(10) An order under this section may—

(a) contain such incidental, supplemental, consequential and transitional provision as the Secretary of State considers appropriate; and

(b) make different provision for different cases.

(11) This Act and any provision made under it has effect subject to any order made under this section.

(12) An order under this section must be made by statutory instrument.

(13) But no such order is to be made unless a draft of the order has been laid before Parliament and approved by a resolution of each House.]

Note: Section 3A inserted by Immigration and Asylum Act 1999 from 14 February 2000.

[3B. Further provision as to leave to remain

(1) The Secretary of State may by order make further provision with respect to the giving, refusing or varying of leave to remain in the United Kingdom.

(2) An order under subsection (1) may, in particular, provide for—

(a) the form or manner in which leave may be given, refused or varied;

(b) the imposition of conditions;

(c) a person's leave to remain in the United Kingdom not to lapse on his leaving the common travel area.

(3) An order under this section may—

(a) contain such incidental, supplemental, consequential and transitional provision as the Secretary of State considers appropriate; and

(b) make different provision for different cases.

(4) This Act and any provision made under it has effect subject to any order made under this section.

(5) An order under this section must be made by statutory instrument.

(6) But no such order is to be made unless a draft of the order has been laid before Parliament and approved by a resolution of each House.]

Note: Section 3B inserted by Immigration and Asylum Act 1999 from 14 February 2000.

[3C. Continuation of leave pending variation decision

(1) This section applies if—

(a) a person who has limited leave to enter or remain in the United Kingdom applies to the Secretary of State for variation of the leave,

(b) the application for variation is made before the leave expires, and

(c) the leave expires without the application for variation having been decided.

(2) The leave is extended by virtue of this section during any period when—

(a) the application for variation is neither decided nor withdrawn,

(b) an appeal under section 82(1) of the Nationality, Asylum and Immigration Act 2002 could be brought [, while the appellant is in the United Kingdom] against the decision on the application for variation (ignoring any possibility of an appeal out of time with permission), or

(c) an appeal under that section against that decision [, brought while the appellant is in the United Kingdom,] is pending (within the meaning of section 104 of that Act).

(3) Leave extended by virtue of this section shall lapse if the applicant leaves the United Kingdom.

(4) A person may not make an application for variation of his leave to enter or remain in the United Kingdom while that leave is extended by virtue of this section.

(5) But subsection (4) does not prevent the variation of the application mentioned in subsection (1)(a).

[(6) The Secretary of State may make regulations determining when an application is decided for the purposes of this section; and the regulations—

(a) may make provision by reference to receipt of a notice,

(b) may provide for a notice to be treated as having been received in specified circumstances,

(c) may make different provision for different purposes or circumstances,

(d) shall be made by statutory instrument, and

(e) shall be subject to annulment in pursuance of a resolution of either House of Parliament.]]

Note: Section 3C substituted by Nationality, Immigration and Asylum Act 2002, s 118 from 1 April 2003 (SI 2003/754). Transitional provisions set out in SI 2003/754. Words added to sub-s (2)(b) and (c) and sub-s (6) substituted by Immigration, Nationality and Asylum Act 2006, s 11 from 31 August 2006 (SI 2006/2226), applying to applications made before that date in respect of which no decision has been made, as it applies to applications made on or after that date.

[3D. Continuation of leave following revocation

(1) This section applies if a person's leave to enter or remain in the United Kingdom—

(a) is varied with the result that he has no leave to enter or remain in the United Kingdom, or

(b) is revoked.

(2) The person's leave is extended by virtue of this section during any period when—

(a) an appeal under section 82(1) of the Nationality, Immigration and Asylum Act 2002 could be brought, while the person is in the United Kingdom, against the variation or revocation (ignoring any possibility of an appeal out of time with permission), or

(b) an appeal under that section against the variation or revocation, brought while the appellant is in the United Kingdom, is pending (within the meaning of section 104 of that Act).

(3) A person's leave as extended by virtue of this section shall lapse if he leaves the United Kingdom.

(4) A person may not make an application for variation of his leave to enter or remain in the United Kingdom while that leave is extended by virtue of this section.]

Note: Section 3D inserted by Immigration, Asylum and Nationality Act 2006, s 11 from 31 August 2006 (SI 2006/2226), only in relation to a decision made on or after that date.

4. Administration of control

(1) The power under this Act to give or refuse leave to enter the United Kingdom shall be exercised by immigration officers, and the power to give leave to remain in the United Kingdom, or to vary any leave under section 3(3)(a) (whether as regards duration or conditions), shall be exercised by the Secretary of State; and, unless otherwise [allowed by or under] this Act, those powers shall be exercised by notice in writing given to the person affected, except that the powers under section 3(3)(a) may be exercised generally in respect of any class of persons by order made by statutory instrument.

(2) The provisions of Schedule 2 to this Act shall have effect with respect to—

(a) the appointment and powers of immigration officers and medical inspectors for purposes of this Act;

(b) the examination of persons arriving in or leaving the United Kingdom by ship or aircraft, and the special powers exercisable in the case of those who arrive as, or with a view to becoming, members of the crews of ships and aircraft; and

(c) the exercise by immigration officers of their powers in relation to entry into the United Kingdom, and the removal from the United Kingdom of persons refused leave to enter or entering or remaining unlawfully; and

(d) the detention of persons pending examination or pending removal from the United Kingdom;

and for other purposes supplementary to the foregoing provisions of this Act.

(3) The Secretary of State may by regulations made by statutory instrument, which shall be subject to annulment in pursuance of a resolution of either House of Parliament, make provision as to the effect of a condition under this Act requiring a person to register with the police; and the regulations may include provision—

(a) as to the officers of police by whom registers are to be maintained, and as to the form and content of the registers;

(b) as to the place and manner in which anyone is to register and as to the documents and information to be furnished by him, whether on registration or on any change of circumstances;

(c) as to the issue of certificates of registration and as to the payment of fees for certificates of registration;

and the regulations may require anyone who is for the time being subject to such a condition to produce a certificate of registration to such persons and in such circumstances as may be prescribed by the regulations.

(4) The Secretary of State may by order made by statutory instrument, which shall be subject to annulment in pursuance of a resolution of either House of Parliament, make such provision as appears to him to be expedient in connection with this Act for records to be made and kept of persons staying at hotels and other premises where lodging or sleeping accommodation is provided, and for persons (whether [British citizens] or not) who stay at any such premises to supply the necessary information.

Note: Words in square brackets in s 4(4) substituted by British Nationality Act 1981, s 39(6). Words in square brackets in s 4(1) substituted by Immigration and Asylum Act 1999 from 14 February 2000. Section 4 has effect in a form modified by and in circumstances specified by the Channel Tunnel (International Arrangements) Order (SI 1993/1813) as amended by SIs 1994/1405, 2000/913, 2001/178, 2001/3707, 2006/1003 and 2007/3759.

5. Procedure for, and further provisions as to, deportation

(1) Where a person is under section 3(5) or (6) above liable to deportation, then subject to the following provisions of this Act the Secretary of State may make a deportation order against him, that is to say an order requiring him to leave and prohibiting him from entering the United Kingdom; and a deportation order against a person shall invalidate any leave to enter or remain in the United Kingdom given him before the order is made or while it is in force.

(2) A deportation order against a person may at any time be revoked by a further order of the Secretary of State, and shall cease to have effect if he becomes [a British citizen].

(3) A deportation order shall not be made against a person as belonging to the family of another person if more than eight weeks have elapsed since the other person left the United Kingdom after the making of the deportation order against him; and a deportation order made against a person on that ground shall cease to have effect if he ceases to belong to the family of the other person, or if the deportation order made against the other person ceases to have effect.

(4) For purposes of deportation the following shall be those who are regarded as belonging to another person's family—

(a) where that other person is a man, his wife [or civil partner,] and his or her children under the age of eighteen; and

[(b) where that other person is a woman, her husband [or civil partner,] and her or his children under the age of eighteen;]

and for purposes of this subsection an adopted child, whether legally adopted or not, may be treated as the child of the adopter and, if legally adopted, shall be regarded as the child only of the adopter; an illegitimate child (subject to the foregoing rule as to adoptions) shall be regarded as the child of the mother; and 'wife' includes each of two or more wives.

(5) The provisions of Schedule 3 to this Act shall have effect with respect to the removal from the United Kingdom of persons against whom deportation orders are in force and with respect to the detention or control of persons in connection with deportation.

(6) Where a person is liable to deportation under section [3(5)] or (6) above but, without a deportation order being made against him, leaves the United Kingdom to live permanently abroad, the Secretary of State may make payments of such amounts as he may determine to meet that person's expenses in so leaving the United Kingdom, including travelling expenses for members of his family or household.

Note: Words in square brackets in s 5(2) substituted by British Nationality Act 1981, s 39(6). Figures in square brackets in s 5(6) substituted by Immigration Act 1988, s 10. Section 5(4)(b) substituted by Asylum and Immigration Act 1996 from 1 October 1996. Transitional provisions set out in SI 2003/754. Words in square brackets in sub-s (4) inserted by Sch 27 Civil Partnership Act 2004 from 5 December 2005 (SI 2005/3175).

6. Recommendations by court for deportation

(1) Where under section 3(6) above a person convicted of an offence is liable to deportation on the recommendation of a court, he may be recommended for deportation by any court having power to sentence him for the offence unless the court commits him to be sentenced or further dealt with for that offence by another court:

Provided that in Scotland the power to recommend a person for deportation shall be exercisable only by the sheriff or the High Court of Justiciary, and shall not be exercisable by the latter on an appeal unless the appeal is against a conviction on indictment or against a sentence upon such a conviction.

(2) A court shall not recommend a person for deportation unless he has been given not less than seven days notice in writing stating that a person is not liable to deportation if he is [a British citizen] describing the persons who are [British citizens] and stating (so far as material) the effect of section 3(8) above and section 7 below; but the powers of adjournment conferred by [section 10(3) of the Magistrates' Courts Act 1980], [section 179 or 380 of the Criminal Procedure (Scotland) Act 1975] or any corresponding enactment for the time being in force in Northern Ireland shall include power to adjourn, after convicting an offender, for the purpose of enabling a notice to be given to him under this subsection or, if a notice was so given to him less than seven days previously, for the purpose of enabling the necessary seven days to elapse.

(3) For purposes of section 3(6) above—

(a) a person shall be deemed to have attained the age of seventeen at the time of his conviction if, on consideration of any available evidence, he appears to have done so to the court making or considering a recommendation for deportation; and

(b) the question whether an offence is one for which a person is punishable with imprisonment shall be determined without regard to any enactment restricting the imprisonment of young offenders or [persons who have not previously been sentenced to imprisonment]; and for purposes of deportation a person who on being charged with an offence is found to have committed it shall, notwithstanding any enactment to the contrary and notwithstanding that the court does not proceed to conviction, be regarded as a person convicted of the offence, and references to conviction shall be construed accordingly.

(4) Notwithstanding any rule of practice restricting the matters which ought to be taken into account in dealing with an offender who is sentenced to imprisonment, a recommendation for deportation may be made in respect of an offender who is sentenced to imprisonment for life.

(5) Where a court recommends or purports to recommend a person for deportation, the validity of the recommendation shall not be called in question except on an appeal against the recommendation or against the conviction on which it is made; but—

(a) the recommendation shall be treated as a sentence for the purpose of any enactment providing an appeal against sentence;

(b) ...

(6) A deportation order shall not be made on the recommendation of a court so long as an appeal or further appeal is pending against the recommendation or against the conviction on which it was made; and for this purpose an appeal or further appeal shall be treated as pending (where one is competent but has not been brought) until the expiration of the time for bringing that appeal or, in Scotland, until expiration of twenty-eight days from the date of the recommendation.

(7) For the purpose of giving effect to any of the provisions of this section in its application to Scotland, the High Court of Justiciary shall have power to make rules by act of adjournal.

Note: Words in first and second square brackets in s 6(2) substituted by British Nationality Act 1981, s 39(6). Words in third square brackets in s 6(2) substituted by Magistrates' Courts Act 1980, s 154. Words in fourth square brackets in s 6(2) substituted by Criminal Procedure (Scotland) Act

1975, s 461. Words in square brackets in s 6(3)(b) substituted (E.W.) by Criminal Justice Act 1972, s 64(1). Words omitted from s 6(5) repealed by Criminal Justice (Scotland) Act 1980, s 83(3) and Criminal Justice Act 1982, ss 77, 78.

7. Exemption from deportation for certain existing residents

(1) Notwithstanding anything in section 3(5) or (6) above but subject to the provisions of this section, a Commonwealth citizen or citizen of the Republic of Ireland who was such a citizen at the coming into force of this Act and was then ordinarily resident in the United Kingdom—

(a) ...

[(b) shall not be liable to deportation under section 3(5) if at the time of the Secretary of State's decision he had for the last five years been ordinarily resident in the United Kingdom and Islands;] and

(c) shall not on conviction of an offence be recommended for deportation under section 3(6) if at the time of the conviction he had for the last five years been ordinarily resident in the United Kingdom and Islands.

(2) A person who has at any time become ordinarily resident in the United Kingdom or in any of the Islands shall not be treated for the purposes of this section as having ceased to be so by reason only of his having remained there in breach of the immigration laws.

(3) The 'last five years' before the material time under subsection (1)(b) or (c) above is to be taken as a period amounting in total to five years exclusive of any time during which the person claiming exemption under this section was undergoing imprisonment or detention by virtue of a sentence passed for an offence on a conviction in the United Kingdom and Islands, and the period for which he was imprisoned or detained by virtue of the sentence amounted to six months or more.

(4) For purposes of subsection (3) above—

(a) 'sentence' includes any order made on conviction of an offence; and

(b) two or more sentences for consecutive (or partly consecutive) terms shall be treated as a single sentence; and

(c) a person shall be deemed to be detained by virtue of a sentence—

(i) at any time when he is liable to imprisonment or detention by virtue of the sentence, but is unlawfully at large; and

(ii) (unless the sentence is passed after the material time) during any period of custody by which under any relevant enactment the term to be served under the sentence is reduced.

In paragraph (c)(ii) above 'relevant enactment' means [section 240{, 240A or 240ZA} of the Criminal Justice Act 2003] (or, before that section operated, section 17(2) of the Criminal Justice Administration Act 1962) and any similar enactment which is for the time being or has (before or after the passing of this Act) been in force in any part of the United Kingdom and Islands.

(5) Nothing in this section shall be taken to exclude the operation of section 3(8) above in relation to an exemption under this section.

Note: Subsection (1)(a) repealed by Nationality, Immigration and Asylum Act 2002, s 75 from 10 February 2003 (SI 2003/1). Subsection (1)(b) substituted by Nationality, Immigration and Asylum Act 2003, s 75 from 10 February 2003 (SI 2003/1). Words in square brackets in sub-s 4 substituted by

Sch 32 Criminal Justice Act 2003 from 4 April 2005 (SI 2005/950). Words in curly brackets in sub-s 4 inserted by Legal Aid, Sentencing and Punishment of Offenders Act 2012, Sch 13, para 7, from a date to be appointed.

8. Exceptions for seamen, aircrews and other special cases

(1) Where a person arrives at a place in the United Kingdom as a member of the crew of a ship or aircraft under an engagement requiring him to leave on that ship as a member of the crew, or to leave within seven days on that or another aircraft as a member of its crew, then unless either—

(a) there is in force a deportation order made against him; or

(b) he has at any time been refused leave to enter the United Kingdom and has not since then been given leave to enter or remain in the United Kingdom; or

(c) an immigration officer requires him to submit to examination in accordance with Schedule 2 to this Act;

he may without leave enter the United Kingdom at that place and remain until the departure of the ship or aircraft on which he is required by his engagement to leave.

(2) The Secretary of State may by order exempt any person or class of persons, either unconditionally or subject to such conditions as may be imposed by or under the order, from all or any of the provisions of this Act relating to those who are not [British citizens].

An order under this subsection, if made with respect to a class of persons, shall be made by statutory instrument, which shall be subject to annulment in pursuance of a resolution of either House of Parliament.

(3) [Subject to subsection 3A below,] the provisions of this Act relating to those who are not [British citizens] shall not apply to any person so long as he is a member of a mission (within the meaning of the Diplomatic Privileges Act 1964), a person who is a member of the family and forms part of the household of such a member, or a person otherwise entitled to the like immunity from jurisdiction as is conferred by that Act on a diplomatic agent.

[(3A) For the purposes of subsection (3), a member of a mission other than diplomatic agent (as defined by the 1964 Act) is not to count as a member of a mission unless—

(a) he was resident outside the United Kingdom, and was not in the United Kingdom, when he was offered a post as such a member; and

(b) he has not ceased to be such a member after having taken up the post.]

(4) The provisions of this Act relating to those who are not [British citizens], other than the provisions relating to deportation, shall also not apply to any person so long as either—

(a) he is subject, as a member of the home forces, to service law; or

(b) being a member of a Commonwealth force or of a force raised under the law of any ..., colony, protectorate or protected state, is undergoing or about to undergo training in the United Kingdom with any body, contingent or detachment of the home forces; or

(c) he is serving or posted for service in the United Kingdom as a member of a visiting force or of any force raised as aforesaid or as a member of an international headquarters or defence organisation designated for the time being by an Order in Council under section 1 of the International Headquarters and Defence Organisations Act 1964.

(5) Where a person having a limited leave to enter or remain in the United Kingdom becomes entitled to an exemption under this section, that leave shall continue to apply

after he ceases to be entitled to the exemption, unless it has by then expired; and a person is not to be regarded for purposes of this Act as having been [settled in the United Kingdom at any time when he was entitled under the former immigration laws to any exemption corresponding to any of those afforded by subsection (3) or (4)(b) or (c) above or by any order under subsection (2) above].

[(5A) An order under subsection (2) above may, as regards any person or class of persons to whom it applies, provide for that person or class to be in specified circumstances regarded (notwithstanding the order) as settled in the United Kingdom for the purposes of section 1(1) of the British Nationality Act 1981.]

(6) In this section 'the home forces' means any of Her Majesty's forces other than a Commonwealth force or a force raised under the law of any associated state, colony, protectorate or protected state; 'Commonwealth force' means a force of any country to which provisions of the Visiting Forces Act 1952 apply without an Order in Council under section 1 of the Act; and 'visiting force' means a body, contingent or detachment of the forces of a country to which any of those provisions apply, being a body, contingent or detachment for the time being present in the United Kingdom on the invitation of Her Majesty's Government in the United Kingdom.

Note: Section 8(3A) inserted by Immigration and Asylum Act 1999 from 1 March 2000. First words in square brackets in s 8(3) inserted by Immigration Act 1988. Other words in square brackets in s 8(2), (3), (4) and (5) substituted and s 8(5A) inserted by British Nationality Act 1981. Section 8(3A) inserted by Immigration and Asylum Act 1999 from 1 March 2000. Section 8 has effect in a form modified by and in circumstances specified by the Channel Tunnel (International Arrangements) Order (SI 1993/1813) as amended by SIs 1994/1405, 2000/913, 2001/178, 2001/3707, 2006/1003 and 2007/3759.

[8A. Persons ceasing to be exempt

(1) A person is exempt for the purposes of this section if he is exempt from provisions of this Act as a result of section 8(2) or (3).

(2) If a person who is exempt—

(a) ceases to be exempt, and

(b) requires leave to enter or remain in the United Kingdom as a result, he is to be treated as if he had been given leave to remain in the United Kingdom for a period of 90 days beginning on the day on which he ceased to be exempt.

(3) If—

(a) a person who is exempt ceases to be exempt, and

(b) there is in force in respect of him leave for him to enter or remain in the United Kingdom which expires before the end of the period mentioned in subsection (2), his leave is to be treated as expiring at the end of that period.]

Note: Section 8A inserted by Immigration and Asylum Act 1999 from 1 March 2000.

[8B. Persons excluded from the United Kingdom under international obligations

(1) An excluded person must be refused—

(a) leave to enter the United Kingdom;

(b) leave to remain in the United Kingdom.

(2) A person's leave to enter or remain in the United Kingdom is cancelled on his becoming an excluded person.

(3) A person's exemption from the provisions of this Act as a result of section 8(1), (2) or (3) ceases on his becoming an excluded person.

(4) 'Excluded person' means a person—

    (a) named by or under, or

    (b) of a description specified in, a designated instrument.

(5) The Secretary of State may by order designate an instrument if it is a resolution of the Security Council of the United Nations or an instrument made by the Council of the European Union and it—

    (a) requires that a person is not to be admitted to the United Kingdom (however that requirement is expressed); or

    (b) recommends that a person should not be admitted to the United Kingdom (however that recommendation is expressed).

(6) Subsections (1) to (3) are subject to such exceptions (if any) as may be specified in the order designating the instrument in question.

(7) An order under this section must be made by statutory instrument.

(8) Such a statutory instrument shall be laid before Parliament without delay.]

Note: Section 8B inserted by Immigration and Asylum Act 1999 from 1 March 2000.

9. Further provisions as to common travel area

(1) Subject to subsection (5) below, the provisions of Schedule 4 to this Act shall have effect for the purpose of taking account in the United Kingdom of the operation in any of the Islands of the immigration laws there.

(2) Persons who lawfully enter the United Kingdom on a local journey from a place in the common travel area after having either—

    (a) entered any of the Islands or the Republic of Ireland on coming from a place outside the common travel area; or

    (b) left the United Kingdom while having a limited leave to enter or remain which has since expired;

if they are not [British citizens] (and are not to be regarded under Schedule 4 to this Act as having leave to enter the United Kingdom), shall be subject in the United Kingdom to such restrictions on the period for which they may remain, and such conditions restricting their employment or occupation or requiring them to register with the police or both, as may be imposed by an order of the Secretary of State and may be applicable to them.

(3) Any provision of this Act applying to a limited leave or to conditions attached to a limited leave shall, unless otherwise provided, have effect in relation to a person subject to any restriction or condition by virtue of an order under subsection (2) above as if the provisions of the order applicable to him were terms on which he had been given leave under this Act to enter the United Kingdom.

(4) Section 1(3) above shall not be taken to affect the operation of a deportation order; and, subject to Schedule 4 to this Act, a person who is not [a British citizen] may not by virtue of section 1(3) enter the United Kingdom without leave on a local journey from a place in the common travel area if either—

    (a) he is on arrival in the United Kingdom given written notice by an immigration officer stating that, the Secretary of State having issued directions for him not to be given entry to the United Kingdom on the ground that his exclusion is conducive to the public good as being in the interests of national security, he is accordingly refused leave to enter the United Kingdom; or

(b) he has at any time been refused leave to enter the United Kingdom and has not since then been given leave to enter or remain in the United Kingdom.

(5) If it appears to the Secretary of State necessary so to do by reason of differences between the immigration laws of the United Kingdom and any of the Islands, he may by order exclude that island from section 1(3) above for such purposes as may be specified in the order, and references in this Act to the Islands...shall apply to an island so excluded so far only as may be provided by order of the Secretary of State.

(6) The Secretary of State shall also have power by order to exclude the Republic of Ireland from section 1(3) for such purposes as may be specified in the order.

(7) An order of the Secretary of State under this section shall be made by statutory instrument, which shall be subject to annulment in pursuance of a resolution of either House of Parliament.

Note: Words in square brackets in s 9(2) and (4) substituted by British Nationality Act 1981, s 39(6). Words omitted from s 9(5) repealed by British Nationality Act 1981, s 52(8).

10. Entry otherwise than by sea or air

(1) Her Majesty may by Order in Council direct that any of the provisions of this Act shall have effect in relation to persons entering or seeking to enter the United Kingdom on arrival otherwise than by ship or aircraft as they have effect in the case of a person arriving by ship or aircraft;...

[(1A) Her Majesty may by Order in Council direct that paragraph 27B or 27C of Schedule 2 shall have effect in relation to trains or vehicles as it has effect in relation to ships or aircraft.

(1B) Any Order in Council under this section may make—
    (a) such adaptations or modifications of the provisions concerned, and
    (b) such supplementary provisions,
as appear to Her Majesty to be necessary or expedient for the purposes of the Order.]

(2) The provision made by an Order in Council under [subsection (1)] may include provision for excluding the Republic of Ireland from section 1(3) of this Act either generally or for any specified purposes.

(3) No recommendation shall be made to Her Majesty to make an Order in Council under this section unless a draft of the Order has been laid before Parliament and approved by a resolution of each House of Parliament.

Note: Words omitted from s 10(1), s 10(1A), 10(1B) and words in square brackets in s 10(2) substituted by Immigration and Asylum Act 1999, Sch 14 from a date to be appointed.

11. Construction of references to entry and other phrases relating to travel

(1) A person arriving in the United Kingdom by ship or aircraft shall for purposes of this Act be deemed not to enter the United Kingdom unless and until he disembarks, and on disembarkation at a port shall further be deemed not to enter the United Kingdom

so long as he remains in such area (if any) at the port as may be approved for this purpose by an immigration officer; and a person who has not otherwise entered the United Kingdom shall be deemed not to do so as long as he is detained, or temporarily admitted or released while liable to detention, under the powers conferred by Schedule 2 to this Act [or by Part III of the Immigration and Asylum Act 1999] [or section 62 of the Nationality, Immigration and Asylum Act 2002] [or by section 68 of the Nationality, Immigration and Asylum Act 2002].

[**1A** ...]

(2) In this Act 'disembark' means disembark from a ship or aircraft, and 'embark' means embark in a ship or aircraft; and, except in subsection (1) above,—

(a) references to disembarking in the United Kingdom do not apply to disembarking after a local journey from a place in the United Kingdom or elsewhere in the common travel area; and

(b) references to embarking in the United Kingdom do not apply to embarking for a local journey to a place in the United Kingdom or elsewhere in the common travel area.

(3) Except in so far as the context otherwise requires, references in this Act to arriving in the United Kingdom by ship shall extend to arrival by any floating structure, and 'disembark' shall be construed accordingly; but the provisions of this Act specially relating to members of the crew of a ship shall not by virtue of this provision apply in relation to any floating structure not being a ship.

(4) For purposes of this Act 'common travel area' has the meaning given by section 1(3), and a journey is, in relation to the common travel area, a local journey if but only if it begins and ends in the common travel area and is not made by a ship or aircraft which—

(a) in the case of a journey to a place in the United Kingdom, began its voyage from, or has during its voyage called at, a place not in the common travel area; or

(b) in the case of a journey from a place in the United Kingdom, is due to end its voyage in, or call in the course of its voyage at, a place not in the common travel area.

(5) A person who enters the United Kingdom lawfully by virtue of section 8(1) above, and seeks to remain beyond the time limited by section 8(1), shall be treated for purposes of this Act as seeking to enter the United Kingdom.

Note: Words in first square brackets in sub-s (1) inserted by Immigration and Asylum Act 1999, Sch 14, para 48 from a date to be appointed. Words in second square brackets in sub-s (1) inserted by Nationality, Immigration and Asylum Act 2002, s 62 from 10 February 2003 (SI 2003/1). Words in third square brackets inserted by SI 2003/1016 from 4 April 2003. Sub-s (1A) repealed from 2 August 1993 (SI 1993/1813). Section 11 has effect in a form modified by and in circumstances specified by the Channel Tunnel (International Arrangements) Order (SI 1993/1813) as amended by SIs 1994/1405, 2000/913, 2001/178, 2001/3707, 2006/1003 and 2007/3759. Sub-s.(1A) deleted from 5 November 1993 (SI 1993/1813).

PART II

APPEALS

...

Note: Part II repealed by Immigration and Asylum Act 1999 from 2 October 2000 (SI 2000/2444). Transitional provisions set out in SI 2003/754.

PART III

CRIMINAL PROCEEDINGS

24. Illegal entry and similar offences

(1) A person who is not [a British citizen] shall be guilty of an offence punishable on summary conviction with a fine of not more than [level 5] on the standard scale or with imprisonment for not more than six months, or with both, in any of the following cases:—

(a) if contrary to this Act he knowingly enters the United Kingdom in breach of a deportation order or without leave;

(aa) ...

(b) if, having only a limited leave to enter or remain in the United Kingdom, he knowingly either—

(i) remains beyond the time limited by the leave; or

(ii) fails to observe a condition of the leave;

(c) if, having lawfully entered the United Kingdom without leave by virtue of section 8(1) above, he remains without leave beyond the time allowed by section 8(1);

(d) if, without reasonable excuse, he fails to comply with any requirement imposed on him under Schedule 2 to this Act to report to a medical officer of health, or to attend, or submit to a test or examination, as required by such an officer;

(e) if, without reasonable excuse, he fails to observe any restriction imposed on him under Schedule 2 or 3 to this Act as to residence, [as to his employment or occupation] or as to reporting to the police [, to an immigration officer or to the Secretary of State];

(f) if he disembarks in the United Kingdom from a ship or aircraft after being placed on board under Schedule 2 or 3 to this Act with a view to his removal from the United Kingdom;

(g) if he embarks in contravention of a restriction imposed by or under an Order in Council under section 3(7) of this Act.

[(1A) A person commits an offence under subsection (1)(b)(i) above on the day when he first knows that the time limited by his leave has expired and continues to commit it throughout any period during which he is in the United Kingdom thereafter; but a person shall not be prosecuted under that provision more than once in respect of the same limited leave.]

(2) ...

(3) The extended time limit for prosecutions which is provided for by section 28 below shall apply to offences under [subsection (1)(a) and (c)] above.

(4) In proceedings for an offence against subsection (1)(a) above of entering the United Kingdom without leave,—

(a) any stamp purporting to have been imprinted on a passport or other travel document by an immigration officer on a particular date for the purpose of giving leave shall be presumed to have been duly so imprinted, unless the contrary is proved;

(b) proof that a person had leave to enter the United Kingdom shall lie on the defence if, but only if, he is shown to have entered within six months before the date when the proceedings were commenced.

Note: Words in first square brackets in s 24(1) substituted by British Nationality Act 1981. Words in second square brackets in s 24(1) substituted by Asylum and Immigration Act 1996 from 1 October 1996. Words in first square brackets in s 24(1)(e) added by and words in square brackets in s 24(3) substituted by Immigration Act 1988. Words in second square brackets in sub-s 24(1)(e) substituted by Nationality, Immigration and Asylum Act 2002, s 62, from 10 February 2003 (SI 2003/1).

Section 24(1A) added by Immigration Act 1988, s 6, except in relation to persons whose leave had expired before 10 July 1988. Sections 24(1)(aa) and 24(2) omitted by Immigration and Asylum Act 1999 from 14 February 2000. Sub-s (1)(d) applies in Scotland in modified form (1972 c 58, Sch 6). Section 24 has effect in a form modified by and in circumstances specified by the Channel Tunnel (International Arrangements) Order (SI 1993/1813) as amended by SIs 1994/1405, 2000/913, 2001/178, 2001/3707, 2006/1003 and 2007/3759.

[24A. Deception

(1) A person who is not a British citizen is guilty of an offence if, by means which include deception by him—

(a) he obtains or seeks to obtain leave to enter or remain in the United Kingdom; or

(b) he secures or seeks to secure the avoidance, postponement or revocation of enforcement action against him.

(2) 'Enforcement action', in relation to a person, means—

(a) the giving of directions for his removal from the United Kingdom ('directions') under Schedule 2 to this Act or section 10 of the Immigration and Asylum Act 1999;

(b) the making of a deportation order against him under section 5 of this Act; or

(c) his removal from the United Kingdom in consequence of directions or a deportation order.

(3) A person guilty of an offence under this section is liable—

(a) on summary conviction, to imprisonment for a term not exceeding six months or to a fine not exceeding the statutory maximum, or to both; or

(b) on conviction on indictment, to imprisonment for a term not exceeding two years or to a fine, or to both.

(4) ...]

Note: Section 24A inserted by Immigration and Asylum Act 1999 from 14 February 2000. Section 24A(4) repealed by Nationality, Immigration and Asylum Act 2002, s 156 from 10 February 2003 (SI 2003/1).

[25. Assisting unlawful immigration to Member State

(1) A person commits an offence if he—

(a) does an act which facilitates the commission of a breach of immigration law by an individual who is not a citizen of the European Union,

(b) knows or has reasonable cause for believing that the act facilitates the commission of a breach of immigration law by the individual, and

(c) knows or has reasonable cause for believing that the individual is not a citizen of the European Union.

(2) In subsection (1) 'immigration law' means a law which has effect in a member State and which controls, in respect of some or all persons who are not nationals of the State, entitlement to—

(a) enter the State,

(b) transit across the State, or

(c) be in the State.

(3) A document issued by the government of a member State certifying a matter of law in that State—

(a) shall be admissible in proceedings for an offence under this section, and

(b) shall be conclusive as to the matter certified.

[(**4**) Subsection (1) applies to things done whether inside or outside the United Kingdom.]

(**5**) …

(**6**) A person guilty of an offence under this section shall be liable—

(a) on conviction on indictment, to imprisonment for a term not exceeding 14 years, to a fine or to both, or

(b) on summary conviction, to imprisonment for a term not exceeding six months, to a fine not exceeding the statutory maximum or to both.]

[(**7**) In this section—

(a) a reference to a member State includes a reference to a State on a list prescribed for the purposes of this section by order of the Secretary of State (to be known as the 'Section 25 List of Schengen Acquis States'), and

(b) a reference to a citizen of the European Union includes a reference to a person who is a national of a State on that list.

(**8**) An order under subsection (7)(a)—

(a) may be made only if the Secretary of State thinks it necessary for the purpose of complying with the United Kingdom's obligations under the {EU} Treaties,

(b) may include transitional, consequential or incidental provision,

(c) shall be made by statutory instrument, and

(d) shall be subject to annulment in pursuance of a resolution of either House of Parliament.]

Note: Section 25 substituted by Nationality, Immigration and Asylum Act 2002, s 143, from 10 February 2003 (SI 2003/1). Subsections (7) and (8) inserted by Asylum and Immigration Act 2004, s 1 from 1 October 2004. Subsection (4) substituted and sub-s (5) deleted by UK Borders Act 2007 (s 30) from 31 January 2008 (SI 2008/99). The term 'EU' substituted from 22 April 2011 (SI 2011/1043). Section 25 has effect in a form modified by and in circumstances specified by the Channel Tunnel (International Arrangements) Order (SI 1993/1813) as amended by SIs 1994/1405, 2000/913, 2001/178, 2001/3707, 2006/1003 and 2007/3759.

[25A. Helping asylum-seeker to enter United Kingdom

(**1**) A person commits an offence if—

(a) he knowingly and for gain facilitates the arrival in [, or the entry into,] the United Kingdom of an individual, and

(b) he knows or has reasonable cause to believe that the individual is an asylum-seeker.

(**2**) In this section 'asylum-seeker' means a person who intends to claim that to remove him from or require him to leave the United Kingdom would be contrary to the United Kingdom's obligations under—

(a) the Refugee Convention (within the meaning given by section 167(1) of the Immigration and Asylum Act 1999 (c. 33) (interpretation)), or

(b) the Human Rights Convention (within the meaning given by that section).

(**3**) Subsection (1) does not apply to anything done by a person acting on behalf of an organisation which—

(a) aims to assist asylum-seekers, and

(b) does not charge for its services.

(**4**) [Subsections (4) and (6)] of section 25 apply for the purpose of the offence in subsection (1) of this section as they apply for the purpose of the offence in subsection (1) of that section.]

Note: Section 25A inserted by Nationality, Immigration and Asylum Act 2002, s 143 from 10 February 2003 (SI 2003/1). Words in square brackets in subsections (1)(a) and (4) inserted by UK Borders Act 2007, ss 29-30 from 31 January 2008 (SI 2008/99).

[25B. Assisting entry to United Kingdom in breach of deportation or exclusion order

(1) A person commits an offence if he—

(a) does an act which facilitates a breach of a deportation order in force against an individual who is a citizen of the European Union, and

(b) knows or has reasonable cause for believing that the act facilitates a breach of the deportation order.

(2) Subsection (3) applies where the Secretary of State personally directs that the exclusion from the United Kingdom of an individual who is a citizen of the European Union is conducive to the public good.

(3) A person commits an offence if he—

(a) does an act which assists the individual to arrive in, enter or remain in the United Kingdom,

(b) knows or has reasonable cause for believing that the act assists the individual to arrive in, enter or remain in the United Kingdom, and

(c) knows or has reasonable cause for believing that the Secretary of State has personally directed that the individual's exclusion from the United Kingdom is conducive to the public good.

(4) [Subsections (4) and (6)] of section 25 apply for the purpose of an offence under this section as they apply for the purpose of an offence under that section.]

Note: Section 25B inserted by Nationality, Immigration and Asylum Act 2002, s 143 from 10 February 2003 (SI 2003/1). Words in square brackets in sub-s (4) substituted by UK Borders Act 2007, s 30 from 31 January 2008 (SI 2008/99).

[25C. Forfeiture of vehicle, ship or aircraft

(1) This section applies where a person is convicted on indictment of an offence under section 25, 25A or 25B.

(2) The court may order the forfeiture of a vehicle used or intended to be used in connection with the offence if the convicted person—

(a) owned the vehicle at the time the offence was committed,

(b) was at that time a director, secretary or manager of a company which owned the vehicle,

(c) was at that time in possession of the vehicle under a hire-purchase agreement,

(d) was at that time a director, secretary or manager of a company which was in possession of the vehicle under a hire-purchase agreement, or

(e) was driving the vehicle in the course of the commission of the offence.

(3) The court may order the forfeiture of a ship or aircraft used or intended to be used in connection with the offence if the convicted person—

(a) owned the ship or aircraft at the time the offence was committed,

(b) was at that time a director, secretary or manager of a company which owned the ship or aircraft,

(c) was at that time in possession of the ship or aircraft under a hire-purchase agreement,

(d) was at that time a director, secretary or manager of a company which was in possession of the ship or aircraft under a hire-purchase agreement,

(e) was at that time a charterer of the ship or aircraft, or

(f) committed the offence while acting as captain of the ship or aircraft.

(4) But in a case to which subsection (3)(a) or (b) does not apply, forfeiture may be ordered only—

(a) in the case of a ship, if subsection (5) or (6) applies;

(b) in the case of an aircraft, if subsection (5) or (7) applies.

(5) This subsection applies where—

(a) in the course of the commission of the offence, the ship or aircraft carried more than 20 illegal entrants, and

(b) a person who, at the time the offence was committed, owned the ship or aircraft or was a director, secretary or manager of a company which owned it, knew or ought to have known of the intention to use it in the course of the commission of an offence under section 25, 25A or 25B.

(6) This subsection applies where a ship's gross tonnage is less than 500 tons.

(7) This subsection applies where the maximum weight at which an aircraft (which is not a hovercraft) may take off in accordance with its certificate of airworthiness is less than 5,700 kilogrammes.

(8) Where a person who claims to have an interest in a vehicle, ship or aircraft applies to a court to make representations on the question of forfeiture, the court may not make an order under this section in respect of the ship, aircraft or vehicle unless the person has been given an opportunity to make representations.

(9) In the case of an offence under section 25, the reference in subsection (5)(a) to an illegal entrant shall be taken to include a reference to—

(a) an individual who seeks to enter a member State in breach of immigration law [(for which purpose 'member State' and 'immigration law' have the meanings given by section 25(2) and (7))] and

(b) an individual who is a passenger for the purpose of section 145 of the Nationality, Immigration and Asylum Act 2002 (traffic in prostitution) [or section 4 of the Asylum and Immigration (Treatment of Claimants, etc.) Act 2004 (trafficking people for exploitation)].

(10) In the case of an offence under section 25A, the reference in subsection (5)(a) to an illegal entrant shall be taken to include a reference to—

(a) an asylum-seeker (within the meaning of that section), and

(b) an individual who is a passenger for the purpose of section 145(1) of the Nationality, Immigration and Asylum Act 2002 [or section 4 of the Asylum and Immigration (Treatment of Claimants, etc.) Act 2004 (trafficking people for exploitation)].

(11) In the case of an offence under section 25B, the reference in subsection (5)(a) to an illegal entrant shall be taken to include a reference to an individual who is a passenger for the purpose of section 145(1) of the Nationality, Immigration and Asylum Act 2002 [or section 4 of the Asylum and Immigration (Treatment of Claimants, etc.) Act 2004 (trafficking people for exploitation)].

Note: Section 25C inserted by Nationality, Immigration and Asylum Act 2002, s 143 from 10 February 2003 (SI 2003/1). Words in square brackets in sub-s 9(a) substituted by Asylum and

Immigration (Treatment of Claimants etc.) Act 2004, s 1 from 1 October 2004. Other words in square brackets inserted by Asylum and Immigration (Treatment of Claimants etc.) Act 2004, s 5 from 1 December 2004 (SI 2004/2999; SSI 2004/494).

[25D. Detention of ship, aircraft or vehicle

(1) If a person has been arrested for an offence under section 25[, 25A or 25B], a senior officer or a constable may detain a relevant ship, aircraft or vehicle—

(a) until a decision is taken as to whether or not to charge the arrested person with that offence; or

(b) if the arrested person has been charged—

(i) until he is acquitted, the charge against him is dismissed or the proceedings are discontinued; or

(ii) if he has been convicted, until the court decides whether or not to order forfeiture of the ship, aircraft or vehicle.

(2) A ship, aircraft or vehicle is a relevant ship, aircraft or vehicle, in relation to an arrested person, if it is one which the officer or constable concerned has reasonable grounds for believing could, on conviction of the arrested person for the offence for which he was arrested, be the subject of an order for forfeiture made under [section 25C].

(3) [A person (other than the arrested person) may apply to the court for the release of a ship, aircraft or vehicle on the grounds that—

(a) he owns the ship, aircraft or vehicle,

(b) he was, immediately before the detention of the ship, aircraft or vehicle, in possession of it under a hire-purchase agreement, or

(c) he is a charterer of the ship or aircraft.]

(4) The court to which an application is made under subsection (3) may, on such security or surety being tendered as it considers satisfactory, release the ship, aircraft or vehicle on condition that it is made available to the court if—

(a) the arrested person is convicted; and

(b) an order for its forfeiture is made under [section 25C].

(5) In the application to Scotland of subsection (1), for paragraphs (a) and (b) substitute—

'(a) until a decision is taken as to whether or not to institute criminal proceedings against the arrested person for that offence; or

(b) if criminal proceedings have been instituted against the arrested person—

(i) until he is acquitted or, under section 65 or 147 of the Criminal Procedure (Scotland) Act 1995, discharged or liberated or the trial diet is deserted simpliciter;

(ii) if he has been convicted, until the court decides whether or not to order forfeiture of the ship, aircraft or vehicle, and for the purposes of this subsection, criminal proceedings are instituted against a person at whichever is the earliest of his first appearance before the sheriff on petition, or the service on him of an indictment or complaint.'

(6) 'Court' means—

(a) in England and Wales—

[(ia) if the arrested person has not been charged, or he has been charged but proceedings for the offence have not begun to be heard, a magistrates' court;]

(iii) if he has been charged and proceedings for the offence are being heard, the court hearing the proceedings;

(b) in Scotland, the sheriff; and

(c) in Northern Ireland—

(i) if the arrested person has not been charged, the magistrates' court for the county court division in which he was arrested;

(ii) if he has been charged but proceedings for the offence have not begun to be heard, the magistrates' court for the county court division in which he was charged;

(iii) if he has been charged and proceedings for the offence are being heard, the court hearing the proceedings.

(7) ...

(8) 'Senior officer' means an immigration officer not below the rank of chief immigration officer.]

Note: Section 25D (previously s 25A) renumbered by Nationality, Immigration and Asylum Act 2002 from 10 February 2003 (SI 2003/1) and inserted by Immigration and Asylum Act 1999 from 2 October 2000. Words in square brackets in sub-s (2) substituted by and sub-s (3) inserted by Nationality, Immigration and Asylum Act 2002, s 144 from 10 February 2003 (SI 2003/1). Words in square brackets in sub-s (4)(b) substituted by and sub-s (7) omitted by Nationality, Immigration and Asylum Act 2002, s 144 from 10 February 2003 (SI 2003/1). Words in square brackets in sub-s (6)(a)(ia) substituted for original (6)(a) (i) and (ii) by Sch 8 Courts Act 2003 from 1 April 2005 (SI 2005/190).

26. General offences in connection with administration of Act

(1) A person shall be guilty of an offence punishable on summary conviction with a fine of not more than [level 5 on the standard scale] or with imprisonment for not more than six months, or with both, in any of the following cases—

(a) if, without reasonable excuse, he refuses or fails to submit to examination under Schedule 2 of this Act;

(b) if, without reasonable excuse, he refuses or fails to furnish or produce any information in his possession, or any documents in his possession or control, which he is on an examination under that Schedule required to furnish or produce;

(c) if on any such examination or otherwise he makes or causes to be made to an immigration officer or other person lawfully acting in the execution of [a relevant enactment] a return, statement or representation which he knows to be false or does not believe to be true;

(d) if, without lawful authority, he alters any [certificate of entitlement], entry clearance, work permit or other document issued or made under or for the purposes of this Act, or uses for the purposes of this Act, or has in his possession for such use, any passport, [certificate of entitlement], entry clearance, work permit or other document which he knows or has reasonable cause to believe to be false;

(e) if, without reasonable excuse, he fails to complete and produce a landing or embarkation card in accordance with any order under Schedule 2 of this Act;

(f) if, without reasonable excuse, he fails to comply with any requirement of regulations under section 4(3) or of an order under section 4(4) above;

(g) if, without reasonable excuse, he obstructs an immigration officer or other person lawfully acting in the execution of this Act.

(2) The extended time limit for prosecutions which is provided for by section 28 below shall apply to offences under subsection (1)(c) and (d) above.

[(3) 'Relevant enactment' means—

(a) this Act;

(b) the Immigration Act 1988;

(c) the Asylum and Immigration Appeals Act 1993 (apart from section 4 or 5); ...

(d) the Immigration and Asylum Act 1999 (apart from Part VI)]; [or

(e) the Nationality, Immigration and Asylum Act 2002 (apart from Part 5).]

Note: Words in first square brackets in s 26(1) substituted by virtue of Criminal Justice Act 1982, and amended by Asylum and Immigration Act 1996 from 1 October 1996. Words in square brackets in s 26(1)(d) substituted by British Nationality Act 1981, s 39(6). Words in square brackets in s 26(1) (c) and sub-s (3) inserted by Immigration and Asylum Act 1999 from 14 February 2000. Subsection 3(e) inserted by and words in sub-s 3(c) omitted by Nationality, Immigration and Asylum Act 2002, s 151 from 10 February 2003 (SI 2003/1).

[26A. Registration card

(1) In this section 'registration card' means a document which—

(a) carries information about a person (whether or not wholly or partly electronically), and

[(b) is issued by the Secretary of State to the person wholly or partly in connection with—

(i) a claim for asylum (whether or not made by that person), or

(ii) a claim for support under section 4 of the Immigration and Asylum Act 1999 (whether or not made by that person).]

(2) In subsection (1) 'claim for asylum' has the meaning given by section 18 of the Nationality, Immigration and Asylum Act 2002.

(3) A person commits an offence if he—

(a) makes a false registration card,

(b) alters a registration card with intent to deceive or to enable another to deceive,

(c) has a false or altered registration card in his possession without reasonable excuse,

(d) uses or attempts to use a false registration card for a purpose for which a registration card is issued,

(e) uses or attempts to use an altered registration card with intent to deceive,

(f) makes an article designed to be used in making a false registration card,

(g) makes an article designed to be used in altering a registration card with intent to deceive or to enable another to deceive, or

(h) has an article within paragraph (f) or (g) in his possession without reasonable excuse.

(4) In subsection (3) 'false registration card' means a document which is designed to appear to be a registration card.

(5) A person who is guilty of an offence under subsection (3)(a), (b), (d), (e), (f) or (g) shall be liable—

(a) on conviction on indictment, to imprisonment for a term not exceeding ten years, to a fine or to both, or

(b) on summary conviction, to imprisonment for a term not exceeding six months, to a fine not exceeding the statutory maximum or to both.

(6) A person who is guilty of an offence under subsection (3)(c) or (h) shall be liable—

(a) on conviction on indictment, to imprisonment for a term not exceeding two years, to a fine or to both, or

(b) on summary conviction, to imprisonment for a term not exceeding six months, to a fine not exceeding the statutory maximum or to both.

(7) The Secretary of State may by order—

(a) amend the definition of 'registration card' in subsection (1);

(b) make consequential amendment of this section.

(8) An order under subsection (7)—

(a) must be made by statutory instrument, and

(b) may not be made unless a draft has been laid before and approved by resolution of each House of Parliament.]

Note: Section 26A inserted by Nationality, Immigration and Asylum Act 2002, s 148 from 10 February 2003 (SI 2003/1). Subsection (1)(b) substituted by The Immigration (Registration Card) Order 2008 (SI 2008/1693) from 27 June 2008.

[26B. Possession of immigration stamp

(1) A person commits an offence if he has an immigration stamp in his possession without reasonable excuse.

(2) A person commits an offence if he has a replica immigration stamp in his possession without reasonable excuse.

(3) In this section—

(a) 'immigration stamp' means a device which is designed for the purpose of stamping documents in the exercise of an immigration function,

(b) 'replica immigration stamp' means a device which is designed for the purpose of stamping a document so that it appears to have been stamped in the exercise of an immigration function, and

(c) 'immigration function' means a function of an immigration officer or the Secretary of State under the Immigration Acts.

(4) A person who is guilty of an offence under this section shall be liable—

(a) on conviction on indictment, to imprisonment for a term not exceeding two years, to a fine or to both, or

(b) on summary conviction, to imprisonment for a term not exceeding six months, to a fine not exceeding the statutory maximum or to both.]

Note: Section 26B inserted by Nationality, Immigration and Asylum Act 2002, s 148 from 10 February 2003 (SI 2003/1).

27. Offences by persons connected with ships or aircraft or with ports

A person shall be guilty of an offence punishable on summary conviction with a fine of not more than [level 5 on the standard scale] or with imprisonment for not more than six months, or with both, in any of the following cases—

(a) if, being the captain of a ship or aircraft,—

(i) he knowingly permits a person to disembark in the United Kingdom when required under Schedule 2 or 3 to this Act to prevent it, or fails without reasonable excuse to take any steps he is required by or under Schedule 2 to take in connection with the disembarkation or examination of passengers or for furnishing a passenger list or particulars of members of the crew; or

(ii) he fails, without reasonable excuse, to comply with any directions given him under Schedule 2 or 3 [or under the Immigration and Asylum Act 1999] with respect to the removal of a person from the United Kingdom;

(b) if, as owner or agent of a ship or aircraft,—

(i) he arranges, or is knowingly concerned in any arrangements, for the ship or aircraft to call at a port other than a port of entry contrary to any provision of Schedule 2 to this Act; or

(ii) he fails, with reasonable excuse, to take any steps required by an order under Schedule 2 for the supply to passengers of landing or embarkation cards; or

(iii) he fails, without reasonable excuse, to make arrangements for [or in connection with] the removal of a person from the United Kingdom when required to do so by directions given under Schedule 2 or 3 to this Act [or under the Immigration and Asylum Act 1999; or

(iv) he fails, without reasonable excuse, to comply with [a requirement imposed by or under Schedule 2]

(c) if, as a person concerned in the management of a port, he fails, without reasonable excuse, to take any steps required by Schedule 2 in relation to the embarkation or disembarkation of passengers where a control area is designated.

Note: Words in first square brackets in s 27 substituted by virtue of Criminal Justice Act 1982, and amended by Asylum and Immigration Act 1996 from 1 October 1996. Words in square brackets in sub-s (b)(iv) substituted and words omitted from sub-s (c) by Immigration, Asylum and Nationality Act 2006, s 31 from 1 March 2008 (SI 2007/3138 as amended by SI 2007/3580). Other words in square brackets inserted by Immigration and Asylum Act 1999 from 2 October 2000. Section 27 has effect in a form modified by and in circumstances specified by the Channel Tunnel (International Arrangements) Order (SI 1993/1813) as amended by SIs 1994/1405, 2000/913, 2001/178, 2001/3707, 2006/1003 and 2007/3759.

28. Proceedings

(1) Where the offence is one to which, under section 24, [...] or 26 above, an extended time limit for prosecutions is to apply, then—

(a) an information relating to the offence may in England and Wales be tried by a magistrates' court if it is laid within six months after the commission of the offence, or if it is laid within three years after the commission of the offence and not more than two months after the date certified by [an officer of police above the rank of chief superintendent] to be the date on which evidence sufficient to justify proceedings came to the notice of an officer of [the police force to which he belongs] and;

(b) summary proceedings for the offence may in Scotland be commenced within six months after the commission of the offence, or within three years after the commission of the offence and not more than two months after the date on which evidence sufficient in the opinion of the Lord Advocate to justify proceedings came to his knowledge; and

(c) a complaint charging the commission of the offence may in Northern Ireland be heard and determined by a magistrates' court if it is made within six months after the commission of the offence, or if it is made within three years after the commission of the offence and not more than two months after the date certified by an officer of police not below the rank of assistant chief constable to be the date on which evidence sufficient to justify the proceedings came to the notice of the police in Northern Ireland.

(2) For purposes of subsection (1)(b) above proceedings shall be deemed to be commenced on the date on which a warrant to apprehend or to cite the accused is granted, if such warrant is executed without undue delay; and a certificate of the Lord Advocate as to the date on which such evidence as is mentioned in subsection (1)(b) came to his knowledge shall be conclusive evidence.

(3) For the purposes of the trial of a person for an offence under this Part of this Act, the offence shall be deemed to have been committed either at the place at which it actually was committed or at any place at which he may be.

(4) Any powers exercisable under this Act in the case of any person may be exercised notwithstanding that proceedings for an offence under this Part of this Act have been taken against him.

Note: Words omitted from sub-s (1) by Nationality, Immigration and Asylum Act 2002, s 156 from 10 February 2003 (SI 2003/1). Words in square brackets in s 28(1)(a) substituted by Immigration Act 1988.

[28A. Arrest without warrant

(1) [An] immigration officer may arrest without warrant a person—
    (a) who has committed or attempted to commit an offence under section 24 or 24A; or
    (b) whom he has reasonable grounds for suspecting has committed or attempted to commit such an offence.

(2) But subsection (1) does not apply in relation to an offence under section 24(1)(d).

(3) An immigration officer may arrest without warrant a person—
    (a) who has committed an offence under section [25, 25A or 25B]; or
    (b) whom he has reasonable grounds for suspecting has committed that offence.

(4) ...

(5) An immigration officer may arrest without warrant a person ('the suspect') who, or whom he has reasonable grounds for suspecting—
    (a) has committed or attempted to commit an offence under section 26(1)(g); or
    (b) is committing or attempting to commit that offence.

(6) The power conferred by subsection (5) is exercisable only if either the first or the second condition is satisfied.

(7) The first condition is that it appears to the officer that service of a summons (or, in Scotland, a copy complaint) is impracticable or inappropriate because—
    (a) he does not know, and cannot readily discover, the suspect's name;
    (b) he has reasonable grounds for doubting whether a name given by the suspect as his name is his real name;
    (c) the suspect has failed to give him a satisfactory address for service; or
    (d) he has reasonable grounds for doubting whether an address given by the suspect is a satisfactory address for service.

(8) The second condition is that the officer has reasonable grounds for believing that arrest is necessary to prevent the suspect—
    (a) causing physical injury to himself or another person;
    (b) suffering physical injury; or
    (c) causing loss of or damage to property.

(9) For the purposes of subsection (7), an address is a satisfactory address for service if it appears to the officer—
    (a) that the suspect will be at that address for a sufficiently long period for it to be possible to serve him with a summons (or copy complaint); or
    (b) that some other person specified by the suspect will accept service of a summons (or copy complaint) for the suspect at that address.

[(**9A**) [An] immigration officer may arrest without warrant a person—

(a) who has committed an offence under section 26A or 26B; or

(b) who he has reasonable grounds for suspecting has committed an offence under section 26A or 26B.]

(**10**) In relation to the exercise of the powers conferred by subsections (3)(b) ... and (5), it is immaterial that no offence has been committed.

(**11**) In Scotland the powers conferred by subsections (3) ... and (5) may also be exercised by a constable.]

Note: Section 28A inserted by Immigration and Asylum Act 1999 from 14 February 2000. Words in square brackets in sub-s (3)(a) substituted by and sub-s (4) omitted by Nationality, Immigration and Asylum Act 2002, s 144 from 10 February 2003 (SI 2003/1). Subsection (9A) inserted by Nationality, Immigration and Asylum Act 2002, s 150 from 10 February 2003 (SI 2003/1). Words omitted from sub-ss (10) and (11) by Nationality, Immigration and Asylum Act 2002, s 144 from 10 February 2003 (SI 2003/1). Words in square brackets in sub-ss (1) and (9A) substituted (England and Wales) by Serious Organised Crime and Police Act 2005, Schedule 7 para 53 from 1 April 2006 (SI 2006/378).

[28AA. Arrest with warrant

(**1**) This section applies if on an application by an immigration officer a justice of the peace is satisfied that there are reasonable grounds for suspecting that a person has committed an offence under—

(a) section 24(1)(d), or

[(b) section 21(1) of the Immigration, Asylum and Nationality Act 2006.]

(**2**) The justice of the peace may grant a warrant authorising any immigration officer to arrest the person.

(**3**) In the application of this section to Scotland a reference to a justice of the peace shall be treated as a reference to the sheriff or a justice of the peace.]

Note: Section 28AA inserted by Nationality, Immigration and Asylum Act 2002, s 152 from 10 February 2003 (SI 2003/1). Subsection (1)(b) substituted by UK Borders Act 2007, s 27 from 29 February 2008 (SI 2008/309).

[28B. Search and arrest by warrant

(**1**) Subsection (2) applies if a justice of the peace is, by written information on oath, satisfied that there are reasonable grounds for suspecting that a person ('the suspect') who is liable to be arrested for a relevant offence is to be found on any premises.

(**2**) The justice may grant a warrant authorising any immigration officer or constable to enter, if need be by force, the premises named in the warrant for the purpose of searching for and arresting the suspect.

(**3**) Subsection (4) applies if in Scotland the sheriff or a justice of the peace is by evidence on oath satisfied as mentioned in subsection (1).

(**4**) The sheriff or justice may grant a warrant authorising any immigration officer or constable to enter, if need be by force, the premises named in the warrant for the purpose of searching for and arresting the suspect.

(**5**) 'Relevant offence' means an offence under section 24(1)(a), (b), (c), (d), (e) or (f), [24A, 26A or 26B].]

Note: Section 28B inserted by Immigration and Asylum Act 1999 from 14 February 2000. Words in square brackets in sub-s (5) substituted by Nationality, Immigration and Asylum Act 2002, ss 144, 150 from 10 February 2003 (SI 2003/1).

[28C. Search and arrest without warrant

(1) An immigration officer may enter and search any premises for the purpose of arresting a person for an offence under [section 25, 25A or 25B].

(2) The power may be exercised—

(a) only to the extent that it is reasonably required for that purpose; and

(b) only if the officer has reasonable grounds for believing that the person whom he is seeking is on the premises.

(3) In relation to premises consisting of two or more separate dwellings, the power is limited to entering and searching—

(a) any parts of the premises which the occupiers of any dwelling comprised in the premises use in common with the occupiers of any such other dwelling; and

(b) any such dwelling in which the officer has reasonable grounds for believing that the person whom he is seeking may be.

(4) The power may be exercised only if the officer produces identification showing that he is an immigration officer (whether or not he is asked to do so).]

Note: Section 28C inserted by Immigration and Asylum Act 1999 from 14 February 2000. Words in square brackets in sub-s (1) substituted by Nationality, Immigration and Asylum Act 2002, s 144 from 10 February 2003 (SI 2003/1).

[28CA. Business premises: entry to arrest

(1) A constable or immigration officer may enter and search any business premises for the purpose of arresting a person—

(a) for an offence under section 24,

(b) for an offence under section 24A, or

(c) under paragraph 17 of Schedule 2.

(2) The power under subsection (1) may be exercised only—

(a) to the extent that it is reasonably required for a purpose specified in subsection (1),

(b) if the constable or immigration officer has reasonable grounds for believing that the person whom he is seeking is on the premises,

(c) with the authority of the Secretary of State (in the case of an immigration officer) or a Chief Superintendent (in the case of a constable), and

(d) if the constable or immigration officer produces identification showing his status.

(3) Authority for the purposes of subsection (2)(c)—

(a) may be given on behalf of the Secretary of State only by a civil servant of the rank of at least Assistant Director, and

(b) shall expire at the end of the period of seven days beginning with the day on which it is given.

(4) Subsection (2)(d) applies—

(a) whether or not a constable or immigration officer is asked to produce identification, but

(b) only where premises are occupied.

(5) Subsection (6) applies where a constable or immigration officer—

(a) enters premises in reliance on this section, and

(b) detains a person on the premises.

(6) A detainee custody officer may enter the premises for the purpose of carrying out a search.

(7) In subsection (6)—

'detainee custody officer' means a person in respect of whom a certificate of authorisation is in force under section 154 of the Immigration and Asylum Act 1999 (c. 33) (detained persons: escort and custody), and

'search' means a search under paragraph 2(1)(a) of Schedule 13 to that Act (escort arrangements: power to search detained person).]

Note: Section 28CA inserted by Nationality, Immigration and Asylum Act 2002, s 153 from 10 February 2003 (SI 2003/1).

[28D. Entry and search of premises

(1) If, on an application made by an immigration officer, a justice of the peace is satisfied that there are reasonable grounds for believing that—

(a) a relevant offence has been committed,

(b) there is material on premises specified in the application which is likely to be of substantial value (whether by itself or together with other material) to the investigation of the offence,

(c) the material is likely to be relevant evidence,

(d) the material does not consist of or include items subject to legal privilege, excluded material or special procedure material, and

(e) any of the conditions specified in subsection (2) applies, he may issue a warrant authorising an immigration officer to enter and search the premises.

(2) The conditions are that—

(a) it is not practicable to communicate with any person entitled to grant entry to the premises;

(b) it is practicable to communicate with a person entitled to grant entry to the premises but it is not practicable to communicate with any person entitled to grant access to the evidence;

(c) entry to the premises will not be granted unless a warrant is produced;

(d) the purpose of a search may be frustrated or seriously prejudiced unless an immigration officer arriving at the premises can secure immediate entry to them.

(3) An immigration officer may seize and retain anything for which a search has been authorised under subsection (1).

(4) 'Relevant offence' means an offence under section 24(1)(a), (b), (c), (d), (e) or (f), [24A, 25, 25A, 25B, 26A or 26B].

(5) In relation to England and Wales, expressions which are given a meaning by the Police and Criminal Evidence Act 1984 have the same meaning when used in this section.

(6) In relation to Northern Ireland, expressions which are given a meaning by the Police and Criminal Evidence (Northern Ireland) Order 1989 have the same meaning when used in this section.

(7) In the application of subsection (1) to Scotland—

(a) read the reference to a justice of the peace as a reference to the sheriff or a justice of the peace; and

(b) in paragraph (d), omit the reference to excluded material and special procedure material.]

Note: Section 28D inserted by Immigration and Asylum Act 1999 from 14 February 2000. Words in square brackets in sub-s (4) substituted by Nationality, Immigration and Asylum Act 2002, ss 144, 150 from 10 February 2003 (SI 2003/1).

[28E. Entry and search of premises following arrest

(1) This section applies if a person is arrested for an offence under this Part at a place other than a police station.

(2) An immigration officer may enter and search any premises—

(a) in which the person was when arrested, or

(b) in which he was immediately before he was arrested, for evidence relating to the offence for which the arrest was made ('relevant evidence').

(3) The power may be exercised—

(a) only if the officer has reasonable grounds for believing that there is relevant evidence on the premises; and

(b) only to the extent that it is reasonably required for the purpose of discovering relevant evidence.

(4) In relation to premises consisting of two or more separate dwellings, the power is limited to entering and searching—

(a) any dwelling in which the arrest took place or in which the arrested person was immediately before his arrest; and

(b) any parts of the premises which the occupier of any such dwelling uses in common with the occupiers of any other dwellings comprised in the premises.

(5) An officer searching premises under subsection (2) may seize and retain anything he finds which he has reasonable grounds for believing is relevant evidence.

(6) Subsection (5) does not apply to items which the officer has reasonable grounds for believing are items subject to legal privilege.]

Note: Section 28E inserted by Immigration and Asylum Act 1999 from 14 February 2000.

[28F. Entry and search of premises following arrest under section 25, 25A or 25B

(1) An immigration officer may enter and search any premises occupied or controlled by a person arrested for an offence under [section 25, 25A, 25B.]

(2) The power may be exercised—

(a) only if the officer has reasonable grounds for suspecting that there is relevant evidence on the premises;

(b) only to the extent that it is reasonably required for the purpose of discovering relevant evidence; and

(c) subject to subsection (3), only if a senior officer has authorised it in writing.

(3) The power may be exercised—

(a) before taking the arrested person to a place where he is to be detained; and

(b) without obtaining an authorisation under subsection (2)(c), if the presence of that person at a place other than one where he is to be detained is necessary for the effective investigation of the offence.

(4) An officer who has relied on subsection (3) must inform a senior officer as soon as is practicable.

(5) The officer authorising a search, or who is informed of one under subsection (4), must make a record in writing of—

(a) the grounds for the search; and

(b) the nature of the evidence that was sought.

(6) An officer searching premises under this section may seize and retain anything he finds which he has reasonable grounds for suspecting is relevant evidence.

(7) 'Relevant evidence' means evidence, other than items subject to legal privilege, that relates to the offence in question.

(8) 'Senior officer' means an immigration officer not below the rank of chief immigration officer.]

Note: Section 28F inserted by Immigration and Asylum Act 1999 from 14 February 2000. Words in square brackets in sub-s (1) substituted by Nationality, Immigration and Asylum Act 2002, s 144 from 10 February 2003 (SI 2003/1).

[28FA. Search for personnel records: warrant unnecessary

(1) This section applies where—

(a) a person has been arrested for an offence under section 24(1) or 24A(1),

(b) a person has been arrested under paragraph 17 of Schedule 2,

(c) a constable or immigration officer reasonably believes that a person is liable to arrest for an offence under section 24(1) or 24A(1), or

(d) a constable or immigration officer reasonably believes that a person is liable to arrest under paragraph 17 of Schedule 2.

(2) A constable or immigration officer may search business premises where the arrest was made or where the person liable to arrest is if the constable or immigration officer reasonably believes—

(a) that a person has committed an immigration employment offence in relation to the person arrested or liable to arrest, and

(b) that employee records, other than items subject to legal privilege, will be found on the premises and will be of substantial value (whether on their own or together with other material) in the investigation of the immigration employment offence.

(3) A constable or officer searching premises under subsection (2) may seize and retain employee records, other than items subject to legal privilege, which he reasonably suspects will be of substantial value (whether on their own or together with other material) in the investigation of—

(a) an immigration employment offence, or

(b) an offence under section 105 or 106 of the Immigration and Asylum Act 1999 (c. 33) (support for asylum-seeker: fraud).

(4) The power under subsection (2) may be exercised only—

(a) to the extent that it is reasonably required for the purpose of discovering employee records other than items subject to legal privilege,

(b) if the constable or immigration officer produces identification showing his status, and

(c) if the constable or immigration officer reasonably believes that at least one of the conditions in subsection (5) applies.

(5) Those conditions are—

(a) that it is not practicable to communicate with a person entitled to grant access to the records,

(b) that permission to search has been refused,

(c) that permission to search would be refused if requested, and

(d) that the purpose of a search may be frustrated or seriously prejudiced if it is not carried out in reliance on subsection (2).

(6) Subsection (4)(b) applies—

(a) whether or not a constable or immigration officer is asked to produce identification, but

(b) only where premises are occupied.

(7) In this section 'immigration employment offence' means [an offence under section 21 of the Immigration, Asylum and Nationality Act 2006] (employment).]

Note: Section 28FA inserted by Nationality, Immigration and Asylum Act 2002, s 154 from 10 February 2003 (SI 2003/1). Words in square brackets in subsection (7) substituted by UK Borders Act 2007 s 28 from 29 February 2008 (SI 2008/309).

[28FB. Search for personnel records: with warrant

(1) This section applies where on an application made by an immigration officer in respect of business premises a justice of the peace is satisfied that there are reasonable grounds for believing—

(a) that an employer has provided inaccurate or incomplete information under section 134 of the Nationality, Immigration and Asylum Act 2002 (compulsory disclosure by employer),

(b) that employee records, other than items subject to legal privilege, will be found on the premises and will enable deduction of some or all of the information which the employer was required to provide, and

(c) that at least one of the conditions in subsection (2) is satisfied.

(2) Those conditions are—

(a) that it is not practicable to communicate with a person entitled to grant access to the premises,

(b) that it is not practicable to communicate with a person entitled to grant access to the records,

(c) that entry to the premises or access to the records will not be granted unless a warrant is produced, and

(d) that the purpose of a search may be frustrated or seriously prejudiced unless an immigration officer arriving at the premises can secure immediate entry.

(3) The justice of the peace may issue a warrant authorising an immigration officer to enter and search the premises.

(4) Subsection (7)(a) of section 28D shall have effect for the purposes of this section as it has effect for the purposes of that section.

(5) An immigration officer searching premises under a warrant issued under this section may seize and retain employee records, other than items subject to legal privilege, which he reasonably suspects will be of substantial value (whether on their own or together with other material) in the investigation of—

(a) an offence under section 137 of the Nationality, Immigration and Asylum Act 2002 (disclosure of information: offences) in respect of a requirement under section 134 of that Act, or

(b) an offence under section 105 or 106 of the Immigration and Asylum Act 1999 (c. 33) (support for asylum-seeker: fraud).]

Note: Section 28FB inserted by Nationality, Immigration and Asylum Act 2002, s 154 from 10 February 2003 (SI 2003/1).

[28G. Searching arrested persons

(1) This section applies if a person is arrested for an offence under this Part at a place other than a police station.

(2) An immigration officer may search the arrested person if he has reasonable grounds for believing that the arrested person may present a danger to himself or others.

(3) The officer may search the arrested person for—
(a) anything which he might use to assist his escape from lawful custody; or
(b) anything which might be evidence relating to the offence for which he has been arrested.

(4) The power conferred by subsection (3) may be exercised—
(a) only if the officer has reasonable grounds for believing that the arrested person may have concealed on him anything of a kind mentioned in that subsection; and
(b) only to the extent that it is reasonably required for the purpose of discovering any such thing.

(5) A power conferred by this section to search a person is not to be read as authorising an officer to require a person to remove any of his clothing in public other than an outer coat, jacket or glove; but it does authorise the search of a person's mouth.

(6) An officer searching a person under subsection (2) may seize and retain anything he finds, if he has reasonable grounds for believing that that person might use it to cause physical injury to himself or to another person.

(7) An officer searching a person under subsection (3) may seize and retain anything he finds, if he has reasonable grounds for believing—
(a) that that person might use it to assist his escape from lawful custody; or
(b) that it is evidence which relates to the offence in question.

(8) Subsection (7)(b) does not apply to an item subject to legal privilege.]

Note: Section 28G inserted by Immigration and Asylum Act 1999 from 14 February 2000.

[28H. Searching persons in police custody

(1) This section applies if a person—
(a) has been arrested for an offence under this Part; and
(b) is in custody at a police station or in police detention at a place other than a police station.

(2) An immigration officer may at any time, search the arrested person in order to see whether he has with him anything—

    (a) which he might use to—

        (i) cause physical injury to himself or others;

        (ii) damage property;

        (iii) interfere with evidence; or

        (iv) assist his escape; or

    (b) which the officer has reasonable grounds for believing is evidence relating to the offence in question.

(3) The power may be exercised only to the extent that the custody officer concerned considers it to be necessary for the purpose of discovering anything of a kind mentioned in subsection (2).

(4) An officer searching a person under this section may seize anything he finds, if he has reasonable grounds for believing that—

    (a) that person might use it for one or more of the purposes mentioned in subsection (2)(a); or

    (b) it is evidence relating to the offence in question.

(5) Anything seized under subsection (4)(a) may be retained by the police.

(6) Anything seized under subsection (4)(b) may be retained by an immigration officer.

(7) The person from whom something is seized must be told the reason for the seizure unless he is—

    (a) violent or appears likely to become violent; or

    (b) incapable of understanding what is said to him.

(8) An intimate search may not be conducted under this section.

(9) The person carrying out a search under this section must be of the same sex as the person searched.

(10) 'Custody officer'—

    (a) in relation to England and Wales, has the same meaning as in the Police and Criminal Evidence Act 1984;

    (b) in relation to Scotland, means the officer in charge of a police station; and

    (c) in relation to Northern Ireland, has the same meaning as in the Police and Criminal Evidence (Northern Ireland) Order 1989.

(11) 'Intimate search'—

    (a) in relation to England and Wales, has the meaning given by section 65 of the Act of 1984;

    (b) in relation to Scotland, means a search which consists of the physical examination of a person's body orifices other than the mouth; and

    (c) in relation to Northern Ireland, has the same meaning as in the 1989 Order.

(12) 'Police detention'—

    (a) in relation to England and Wales, has the meaning given by section 118(2) of the 1984 Act; and

    (b) in relation to Northern Ireland, has the meaning given by Article 2 of the 1989 Order.

(13) In relation to Scotland, a person is in police detention if—

    (a) he has been taken to a police station after being arrested for an offence; or

(b) he is arrested at a police station after attending voluntarily at the station, accompanying a constable to it or being detained under section 14 of the Criminal Procedure (Scotland) Act 1995, and is detained there or is detained elsewhere in the charge of a constable, but is not in police detention if he is in court after being charged.]

Note: Section 28H inserted by Immigration and Asylum Act 1999 from 14 February 2000.

[28I. Seized material: access and copying

(1) If a person showing himself—
  (a) to be the occupier of the premises on which seized material was seized, or
  (b) to have had custody or control of the material immediately before it was seized,

asks the immigration officer who seized the material for a record of what he seized, the officer must provide the record to that person within a reasonable time.

(2) If a relevant person asks an immigration officer for permission to be granted access to seized material, the officer must arrange for him to have access to the material under the supervision—
  (a) in the case of seized material within subsection (8)(a), of an immigration officer;
  (b) in the case of seized material within subsection (8)(b), of a constable.

(3) An immigration officer may photograph or copy, or have photographed or copied, seized material.

(4) If a relevant person asks an immigration officer for a photograph or copy of seized material, the officer must arrange for—
  (a) that person to have access to the material for the purpose of photographing or copying it under the supervision—
    (i) in the case of seized material within subsection (8)(a), of an immigration officer;
    (ii) in the case of seized material within subsection (8)(b), of a constable; or
  (b) the material to be photographed or copied.

(5) A photograph or copy made under subsection (4)(b) must be supplied within a reasonable time.

(6) There is no duty under this section to arrange for access to, or the supply of a photograph or copy of, any material if there are reasonable grounds for believing that to do so would prejudice—
  (a) the exercise of any functions in connection with which the material was seized; or
  (b) an investigation which is being conducted under this Act, or any criminal proceedings which may be brought as a result.

(7) 'Relevant person' means—
  (a) a person who had custody or control of seized material immediately before it was seized, or
  (b) someone acting on behalf of such a person.

(8) 'Seized material' means anything—
  (a) seized and retained by an immigration officer, or
  (b) seized by an immigration officer and retained by the police, under this Part.]

Note: Section 28I inserted by Immigration and Asylum Act 1999 from 14 February 2000.

[28J. Search warrants: safeguards

(1) The entry or search of premises under a warrant is unlawful unless it complies with this section and section 28K.

(2) If an immigration officer applies for a warrant, he must—

(a) state the ground on which he makes the application and the provision of this Act under which the warrant would be issued;

(b) specify the premises which it is desired to enter and search; and

(c) identify, so far as is practicable, the persons or articles to be sought.

(3) In Northern Ireland, an application for a warrant is to be supported by a complaint in writing and substantiated on oath.

(4) Otherwise, an application for a warrant is to be made ex parte and supported by an information in writing or, in Scotland, evidence on oath.

(5) The officer must answer on oath any question that the justice of the peace or sheriff hearing the application asks him.

(6) A warrant shall authorise an entry on one occasion only.

(7) A warrant must specify—

(a) the name of the person applying for it;

(b) the date on which it is issued;

(c) the premises to be searched; and

(d) the provision of this Act under which it is issued.

(8) A warrant must identify, so far as is practicable, the persons or articles to be sought.

(9) Two copies of a warrant must be made.

(10) The copies must be clearly certified as copies.

(11) 'Warrant' means a warrant to enter and search premises issued to an immigration officer under this Part or under paragraph 17(2) of Schedule 2.]

Note: Section 28J inserted by Immigration and Asylum Act 1999 from 14 February 2000.

[28K. Execution of warrants

(1) A warrant may be executed by any immigration officer.

(2) A warrant may authorise persons to accompany the officer executing it.

(3) Entry and search under a warrant must be—

(a) within one month from the date of its issue; and

(b) at a reasonable hour, unless it appears to the officer executing it that the purpose of a search might be frustrated.

(4) If the occupier of premises which are to be entered and searched is present at the time when an immigration officer seeks to execute a warrant, the officer must—

(a) identify himself to the occupier and produce identification showing that he is an immigration officer;

(b) show the occupier the warrant; and

(c) supply him with a copy of it.

(5) If—

(a) the occupier is not present, but

(b) some other person who appears to the officer to be in charge of the premises is present,

subsection (4) has effect as if each reference to the occupier were a reference to that other person.

(6) If there is no person present who appears to the officer to be in charge of the premises, the officer must leave a copy of the warrant in a prominent place on the premises.

(7) A search under a warrant may only be a search to the extent required for the purpose for which the warrant was issued.

(8) An officer executing a warrant must make an endorsement on it stating—
  (a) whether the persons or articles sought were found; and
  (b) whether any articles, other than articles which were sought, were seized.

(9) A warrant which has been executed, or has not been executed within the time authorised for its execution, must be returned—
  [(a) if issued by a justice of the peace in England and Wales, to the designated officer for the local justice area in which the justice was acting when he issued the warrant;]
  (b) if issued by a justice of the peace in Northern Ireland, to the clerk of petty sessions for the petty sessions district in which the premises are situated;
  (c) if issued by a justice of the peace in Scotland, to the clerk of the district court for the commission area for which the justice of the peace was appointed;
  (d) if issued by the sheriff, to the sheriff clerk.

(10) A warrant returned under subsection (9)(a) must be retained for 12 months by the [designated officer].

(11) A warrant issued under subsection (9)(b) or (c) must be retained for 12 months by the clerk.

(12) A warrant returned under subsection (9)(d) must be retained for 12 months by the sheriff clerk.

(13) If during that 12-month period the occupier of the premises to which it relates asks to inspect it, he must be allowed to do so.

(14) 'Warrant' means a warrant to enter and search premises issued to an immigration officer under this Part or under paragraph 17(2) of Schedule 2.]

Note: Section 28K inserted by Immigration and Asylum Act 1999 from 14 February 2000. Words in square brackets in sub-ss (9) and (10) substituted by Sch 8 Courts Act 2003 from 1 April 2005 (SI 2005/910).

[28L. Interpretation of Part III

[(1)] In this Part, 'premises' and 'items subject to legal privilege' have the same meaning—
  (a) in relation to England and Wales, as in the Police and Criminal Evidence Act 1984;
  (b) in relation to Northern Ireland, as in the Police and Criminal Evidence (Northern Ireland) Order 1989; and
  (c) in relation to Scotland, as in {section 412 of the Proceeds of Crme Act 2002}.

[(2) In this Part 'business premises' means premises (or any part of premises) not used as a dwelling.

(3) In this Part 'employee records' means records which show an employee's—

    (a) name,

    (b) date of birth,

    (c) address,

    (d) length of service,

    (e) rate of pay, or

    (f) nationality or citizenship.

(4) The Secretary of State may by order amend section 28CA(3)(a) to reflect a change in nomenclature.

(5) An order under subsection (4)—

    (a) must be made by statutory instrument, and

    (b) shall be subject to annulment in pursuance of a resolution of either House of Parliament.]

Note: Section 28L inserted by Immigration and Asylum Act 1999 from 14 February 2000. Words in curly brackets in sub-s (1) substituted from 24 February 2003 by Proceeds of Crime Act 2002 Sch 11. Subsections (2)–(5) inserted by Nationality, Immigration and Asylum Act 2002, s 155 from 10 February 2003 (SI 2003/1).

PART IV
SUPPLEMENTARY

29. ...

Note: Repealed by Nationality, Immigration and Asylum Act 2002, s 58 and Sch 9 from 1 April 2003 (SI 2003/754).

30. ...

Note: Repealed by British Nationality Act 1981, s 52(8) and Mental Health (Scotland) Act 1984, s 127(2).

31. Expenses

There shall be defrayed out of moneys provided by Parliament any expenses incurred [by the Lord Chancellor under Schedule 5 to this Act or] by a Secretary of State under or by virtue of this Act—

    (a) by way of administrative expenses ...; or

    (b) in connection with the removal of any person from the United Kingdom under Schedule 2 or 3 to this Act or the departure with him of his dependants, or his or their maintenance pending departure; or

    (c) ...

    (d) ...

Note: Words in square brackets in s 31 inserted and s 31(c) repealed by SI 1987/465. Words omitted from s 31(a) repealed by British Nationality Act 1981, s 52(8). Section 31(d) repealed by Nationality, Immigration and Asylum Act 2002, s 58 and Sch 9 from 1 April 2003 (SI 2003/754).

[31A. Procedural requirements as to applications

...]

Note: Section 31A repealed by Immigration, Asylum and Nationality Act 2006, s 50 from 29 February 2008 (SI 2008/310).

32. General provisions as to Orders in Council, etc.

(1) Any power conferred by Part I of this Act to make an Order in Council or order (other than a deportation order) or to give any directions includes power to revoke or vary the Order in Council, order or directions.

(2) Any document purporting to be an order, notice or direction made or given by the Secretary of State for the purposes of [the Immigration Acts] and to be signed by him or on his behalf, and any document purporting to be a certificate of the Secretary of State so given and to be signed by him [or on his behalf] shall be received in evidence, and shall, until the contrary is proved, be deemed to be made or issued by him.

(3) Prima facie evidence of any such order, notice, direction or certificate as afore-said may, in any legal proceedings or [other proceedings under the Immigration Acts], be given by the production of a document bearing a certificate purporting to be signed by or on behalf of the Secretary of State and stating that the document is a true copy of the order, notice, direction or certificate.

(4) Where an order under section 8(2) above applies to persons specified in a schedule to the order, or any directions of the Secretary of State given for the purposes of [the Immigration Acts] apply to persons specified in a schedule to the directions, prima facie evidence of the provisions of the order or directions other than the schedule and of any entry contained in the schedule may, in any legal proceedings or [other proceedings under the Immigration Acts], be given by the production of a document purporting to be signed by or on behalf of the Secretary of State and stating that the document is a true copy of the said provisions and of the relevant entry.

(5) ...

Note: Words in square brackets in sub-ss (2), (3) and (4) inserted by Immigration and Asylum Act 1999 from 6 December 1999. Subsection (5) substituted by Nationality, Immigration and Asylum Act 2002, s 158 from 10 February 2003 (SI 2003/1). Subsection (5) ceased to have effect by Immigration, Asylum and Nationality Act 2006, s 61 and Sch 3 from 30 March 2006 (Royal Assent).

33. Interpretation

(1) For purposes of this Act, except in so far as the context otherwise requires—
'aircraft' includes hovercraft, 'airport' includes hoverport and 'port' includes airport;
'captain' means master (of a ship) or commander (of an aircraft);
['certificate of entitlement' means a certificate under section 10 of the Nationality, Immigration and Asylum Act 2002 that a person has the right of abode in the United Kingdom];
['Convention adoption' has the same meaning as in the Adoption Act 1976 and {the Adoption and Children (Scotland) Act 2007} {or in the Adoption and Children Act 2002};]

'crew', in relation to a ship or aircraft, means all persons actually employed in the working or service of the ship or aircraft, including the captain, and 'member of the crew' shall be construed accordingly;

['entrant' means a person entering or seeking to enter the United Kingdom and 'illegal entrant' means a person—

(a) unlawfully entering or seeking to enter in breach of a deportation order or of the immigration laws, or

(b) entering or seeking to enter by means which include deception by another person, and includes also a person who has entered as mentioned in paragraph (a) or (b) above;]

'entry clearance' means a visa, entry certificate or other document which, in accordance with the immigration rules, is to be taken as evidence [or the requisite evidence] of a person's eligibility, though not [a British citizen], for entry into the United Kingdom (but does not include a work permit);

'immigration laws' means this Act and any law for purposes similar to this Act which is for the time being or has (before or after the passing of this Act) been in force in any part of the United Kingdom and Islands;

'immigration rules' means the rules for the time being laid down as mentioned in section 3(2) above;

'the Islands' means the Channel Islands and the Isle of Man, and 'the United Kingdom and Islands' means the United Kingdom and the Islands taken together;

'legally adopted' means adopted in pursuance of an order made by any court in the United Kingdom and Islands [under a Convention adoption] or by any adoption specified as an overseas adoption by order of the Secretary of State under [section 72(2) the Adoption Act 1976] {or by regulations made by the Scottish Ministers under section 67(1) of the Adoption and Children (Scotland) Act 2007};

'limited leave' and 'indefinite leave' mean respectively leave under this Act to enter or remain in the United Kingdom which is, and one which is not, limited as to duration;

'settled' shall be construed in accordance with [subsection (2A) below];

'ship' includes every description of vessel used in navigation;

['United Kingdom passport' means a current passport issued by the Government of the United Kingdom, or by the Lieutenant-Governor of any of the Islands or by the Government of any territory which is for the time being a dependent territory within the meaning of the British Nationality Act 1981;]

'work permit' means a permit indicating, in accordance with the immigration rules, that a person named in it is eligible, though not [a British citizen], for entry into the United Kingdom for the purpose of taking employment.

(1A) A reference to being the owner of a vehicle, ship or aircraft includes a reference to being any of a number of persons who jointly own it.

(2) It is hereby declared that, except as otherwise provided in this Act, a person is not to be treated for the purposes of any provision of this Act as ordinarily resident in the United Kingdom or in any of the Islands at a time when he is there in breach of the immigration laws.

(2A) Subject to section 8(5) above, references to a person being settled in the United Kingdom are references to his being ordinarily resident there without being subject under the immigration laws to any restriction on the period for which he may remain.]

(3) The ports of entry for purposes of this Act, and the ports of exit for purposes of any Order in Council under section 3(7) above, shall be such ports as may from time to time be designated for the purpose by order of the Secretary of State made by statutory instrument.

[(4) For the purposes of this Act, the question of whether an appeal is pending shall be determined {in accordance with section 104 of the Nationality, Immigration and Asylum Act 2002 (pending appeals)}.]

(5) This Act shall not be taken to supersede or impair any power exercisable by Her Majesty in relation to aliens by virtue of Her prerogative.

Note: Definition of certificate of entitlement in s 33(1) substituted by Nationality, Immigration and Asylum Act 2002, s 10 from 21 December 2006 (SI 2006/3144). Definition of 'Convention adoption' and amendment to definition of 'legally adopted' inserted by Adoption (Intercountry Aspects) Act 1999, Sch 2 from 1 June 2003 (SI 2003/362) and amended by Adoption and Children Act 2002 and further amended from 14 July 2011 by the Adoption and Children (Scotland) Act 2007 (Consequential Modifications) Order 2007 (SI 2011/1740). Definition of 'entrant' in s 33(1) substituted by Asylum and Immigration Act 1996 from 1 October 1996. Words in fifth square brackets in s 33(1) substituted by Adoption Act 1976. Other words in square brackets in s 33(1) substituted by British Nationality Act 1981. Subsection (1A) inserted by Nationality, Immigration and Asylum Act 2002, s 144 from 10 February 2003 (SI 2003/1). Subsection (2A) inserted by British Nationality Act 1981. Subsection (4) substituted by Immigration and Asylum Act 1999 from 2 October 2000. Words in curly brackets in sub-s (4) substituted by Sch 7 Nationality, Immigration and Asylum Act 2002 from 1 April 2003 (SI 2003/754). Section 33 has effect in a form modified by and in circumstances specified by the Channel Tunnel (International Arrangements) Order (SI 1993/1813) as amended by SIs 1994/1405, 2000/913, 2001/178, 2001/3707, 2006/1003 and 2007/3759.

34. Repeal, transitional and temporary

(1) Subject to the following provisions of this section, the enactments mentioned in Schedule 6 to this Act are hereby repealed, as from the coming into force of this Act, to the extent mentioned in column 3 of the Schedule; and—

(a) this Act, as from its coming into force, shall apply in relation to entrants or others arriving in the United Kingdom at whatever date before or after it comes into force; and

(b) after this Act comes into force anything done under or for the purposes of the former immigration laws shall have effect, in so far as any corresponding action could be taken under or for the purposes of this Act, as if done by way of action so taken, and in relation to anything so done this Act shall apply accordingly.

(2) Without prejudice to the generality of subsection (1)(a) and (b) above, a person refused leave to land by virtue of the Aliens Restriction Act 1914 shall be treated as having been refused leave to enter under this Act, and a person given leave to land by virtue of that Act shall be treated as having been given leave to enter under this Act; and similarly with the Commonwealth Immigrants Acts 1962 and 1968.

(3) A person treated in accordance with subsection (2) above as having leave to enter the United Kingdom—

(a) shall be treated as having an indefinite leave, if he is not at the coming in to force of this Act subject to a condition limiting his stay in the United Kingdom; and

(b) shall be treated, if he is then subject to such a condition, as having a limited leave of such duration, and subject to such conditions (capable of being attached to leave under this Act), as correspond to the conditions to which he is then subject, but not to conditions not capable of being so attached.

This subsection shall have effect in relation to any restriction or requirement imposed by Order in Council under the Aliens Restriction Act 1914 as if it had been imposed by way of a landing condition.

(4) Notwithstanding anything in the foregoing provisions of this Act, the former immigration laws shall continue to apply, and this Act shall not apply,—

(a) in relation to the making of deportation orders and matters connected therewith in any case where a decision to make the order has been notified to the person concerned before the coming into force of this Act;

(b) in relation to removal from the United Kingdom and matters connected therewith (including detention pending removal or pending the giving of directions for removal) in any case where a person is to be removed in pursuance of a decision taken before the coming into force of this Act or in pursuance of a deportation order to the making of which paragraph (a) above applies;

(c) in relation to appeals against any decision taken or other thing done under the former immigration laws, whether taken or done before the coming into force of this Act or by virtue of this subsection.

(5) Subsection (1) above shall not be taken as empowering a court on appeal to recommend for deportation a person whom the court below could not recommend for deportation, or as affecting any right of appeal in respect of a recommendation for deportation made before this Act comes into force, or as enabling a notice given before this Act comes into force and not complying with section 6(2) to take the place of the notice required by section 6(2) to be given before a person is recommended for deportation.

(6) ...

Note: Section 34(6) repealed by Statute Law (Repeals) Act 1993, s 1.

35. Commencement, and interim provisions

(1) Except as otherwise provided by this Act, Parts I to III of this Act shall come into force on such day as the Secretary of State may appoint by order made by statutory instrument; and references to the coming into force of this Act shall be construed as references to the beginning of the day so appointed.

(2) Section 25 above, except section 25(2), and section 28 in its application to offences under section 25(1) shall come into force at the end of one month beginning with the date this Act is passed.

(3) ...
(4) ...
(5) ...

Note: Section 35(3)–(5) repealed by Statute Law (Repeals) Act 1986.

36. Power to extend to Islands

Her Majesty may by Order in Council direct that any of the provisions of this Act shall extend, with such exceptions, adaptations and modifications, if any, as may be specified in the Order, to any of the Islands; and any Order in Council under this subsection may be varied or revoked by a further Order in Council.

Note: Part 1, Part 3 and Part 4 (except for ss 29–30, 34–36) extended to the Isle of Man with modifications: see SI 2008/680 as amended by SI 2011/1408.

37. Short title and extent

(1) This Act may be cited as the Immigration Act 1971.

(2) It is hereby declared that this Act extends to Northern Ireland, and (without prejudice to any provision of Schedule 1 to this Act as to the extent of that Schedule) where an enactment repealed by this Act extends outside the United Kingdom, the repeal shall be of like extent.

SCHEDULES

SCHEDULE 1

Note: Repealed by British Nationality Act 1981, s 52(8).

Section 4   SCHEDULE 2

ADMINISTRATIVE PROVISIONS AS TO CONTROL ON ENTRY ETC.

PART I GENERAL PROVISIONS

Immigration officers and medical inspectors

1.—(1) Immigration officers for the purposes of this Act shall be appointed by the Secretary of State, and he may arrange with the Commissioners of Customs and Excise for the employment of officers of customs and excise as immigration officers under this Act.

(2) Medical inspectors for the purposes of this Act may be appointed by the Secretary of State or, in Northern Ireland, by the Minister of Health and Social Services or other appropriate Minister of the Government of Northern Ireland in pursuance of arrangements made between that Minister and the Secretary of State, and shall be fully qualified medical practitioners.

[(2A) The Secretary of State may direct that his function of appointing medical inspectors under sub-paragraph (2) is also to be exercisable by such persons specified in the direction who exercise functions relating to health in England or Wales.]

(3) In the exercise of their functions under this Act immigration officers shall act in accordance with such instructions (not inconsistent with the immigration rules) as may be given them by the Secretary of State, and medical inspectors shall act in accordance with such instructions as may be given them by the Secretary of State or, in Northern Ireland, as may be given in pursuance of the arrangements mentioned in sub-paragraph (2) above by the Minister making appointments of medical inspectors in Northern Ireland.

(4) An immigration officer or medical inspector may board any ship [or aircraft] for the purpose of exercising his functions under this Act.

(5) An immigration officer, for the purpose of satisfying himself whether there are persons he may wish to examine under paragraph 2 below, may search any ship [or aircraft] and anything on board it, or any vehicle taken off a ship or aircraft on which it has been brought to the United Kingdom.

Note: Words in square brackets in sub-paras (4) and (5) substituted by SI 1993/1813. Sub-paragraph (2A) inserted by Health Protection Agency Act 2004, s 12(3) and Sch 3 from 22 September 2004. Paragraph 1 has effect in a form modified by and in circumstances specified by the Channel Tunnel (International Arrangements) Order (SI 1993/1813) as amended by SIs 1994/1405, 2000/913, 2001/178, 2001/3707, 2006/1003 and 2007/3759.

Examination by immigration officers, and medical examination

2.—(1) An immigration officer may examine any persons who have arrived in the United Kingdom by ship [or aircraft] (including transit passengers, members of the crew and others not seeking to enter the United Kingdom) for the purpose of determining—

(a) whether any of them is or is not [a British citizen]; and

(b) whether, if he is not, he may or may not enter the United Kingdom without leave; and

[(c) whether, if he may not—

(i) he has been given leave which is still in force,

(ii) he should be given leave and for what period or on what conditions (if any), or

(iii) he should be refused leave.]

(2) Any such person, if he is seeking to enter the United Kingdom, may be examined also by a medical inspector or by any qualified person carrying out a test or examination required by a medical inspector.

(3) A person, on being examined under this paragraph by an immigration officer or medical inspector, may be required in writing by him to submit to further examination; but a requirement under this sub-paragraph shall not prevent a person who arrives as a transit passenger, or as a member of the crew of a ship or aircraft, or for the purpose of joining a ship or aircraft as a member of the crew, from leaving by his intended ship or aircraft.

Note: Words in first square brackets substituted by SI 1993/1813. Words in square brackets in sub-para (1)(a) substituted by British Nationality Act 1981, s 39(6). Sub-paragraph (1)(c) substituted by Immigration and Asylum Act 1999 from 14 February 2000. Paragraph 2 has effect in a form modified by and in circumstances specified by the Channel Tunnel (International Arrangements) Order (SI 1993/1813) as amended by SIs 1994/1405, 2000/913, 2001/178, 2001/3707, 2006/1003 and 2007/3759.

[Examination of persons who arrive with continuing leave

2A.—(1) This paragraph applies to a person who has arrived in the United Kingdom with leave to enter which is in force but which was given to him before his arrival.

(2) He may be examined by an immigration officer for the purpose of establishing—

(a) whether there has been such a change in the circumstances of his case, since that leave was given, that it should be cancelled;

(b) whether that leave was obtained as a result of false information given by him or his failure to disclose material facts; or

(c) whether there are medical grounds on which that leave should be cancelled.

[**(2A)** Where the person's leave to enter derives, by virtue of section 3A(3), from an entry clearance, he may also be examined by an immigration officer for the purpose of establishing whether the leave should be cancelled on the grounds that the person's purpose in arriving in the United Kingdom is different from the purpose specified in the entry clearance.]

(3) He may also be examined by an immigration officer for the purpose of determining whether it would be conducive to the public good for that leave to be cancelled.

(4) He may also be examined by a medical inspector or by any qualified person carrying out a test or examination required by a medical inspector.

(5) A person examined under this paragraph may be required by the officer or inspector to submit to further examination.

(6) A requirement under sub-paragraph (5) does not prevent a person who arrives—

(a) as a transit passenger,

(b) as a member of the crew of a ship or aircraft, or

(c) for the purpose of joining a ship or aircraft as a member of the crew, from leaving by his intended ship or aircraft.

(7) An immigration officer examining a person under this paragraph may by notice suspend his leave to enter until the examination is completed.

(8) An immigration officer may, on the completion of any examination of a person under this paragraph, cancel his leave to enter.

(9) Cancellation of a person's leave under sub-paragraph (8) is to be treated for the purposes of this Act and [Part 5 of the Nationality, Immigration and Asylum Act 2002 (immigration and asylum appeals)] as if he had been refused leave to enter at a time when he had a current entry clearance.

(10) A requirement imposed under sub-paragraph (5) and a notice given under sub-paragraph (7) must be in writing.]

Note: Paragraph 2A inserted by Immigration and Asylum Act 1999 from 14 February 2000. Words in square brackets in para 2A(9) substituted by Sch 7 Nationality, Immigration and Asylum Act 2002 from 1 April 2003 (SI 2003/754). Sub-para (2A) inserted by Asylum and Immigration Act 2004, s 18 from 1 October 2004 (SI 2004/2523).

3.—(1) An immigration officer may examine any person who is embarking or seeking to embark in the United Kingdom for the purpose of determining whether he is [a British citizen] [and, if he is not a British citizen, for the purpose of establishing—

    (a) his identity;

    (b) whether he entered the United Kingdom lawfully;

    (c) whether he has complied with any conditions of leave to enter or remain in the United Kingdom;

    (d) whether his return to the United Kingdom is prohibited or restricted.

(1A) An immigration officer who examines a person under sub-paragraph (1) may require him, by notice in writing, to submit to further examination for a purpose specified in that sub-paragraph.]

(2) So long as any Order in Council is in force under section 3(7) of this Act, an immigration officer may examine any person who is embarking or seeking to embark in the United Kingdom for the purpose of determining—

    (a) whether any of the provisions of the Order apply to him; and

    (b) whether, if so, any power conferred by the Order should be exercised in relation to him and in what way.

Note: Words in first square brackets in sub-para (1) substituted by British Nationality Act 1981. Other words in square brackets substituted by Immigration, Asylum and Nationality Act 2006, s 42 from 31 August 2006 (SI 2006/2226). Paragraph 3 has effect in a form modified by and in circumstances specified by the Channel Tunnel (International Arrangements) Order (SI 1993/1813) as amended by SIs 1994/1405, 2000/913, 2001/178, 2001/3707, 2006/1003 and 2007/3759.

Information and documents

4.—(1) It shall be the duty of any person examined under paragraph 2, [2A] or 3 above to furnish to the person carrying out the examination all such information in his possession as that person may require for the purpose of his functions under that paragraph.

(2) A person on his examination under paragraph 2, [2A] or 3 above by an immigration officer shall, if so required by the immigration officer—

    (a) produce either a valid passport with photograph or some other document satisfactorily establishing his identity and nationality or citizenship; and

    (b) declare whether or not he is carrying or conveying [, or has carried or conveyed] documents of any relevant description specified by the immigration officer, and produce any documents of that description which he is carrying or conveying.

In paragraph (b), 'relevant description' means any description appearing to the immigration officer to be relevant for the purposes of the examination.

(3) Where under sub-paragraph (2)(b) above a person has been required to declare whether or not he is carrying or conveying [or has carried or conveyed,] documents of any description.

[(a) he and any baggage or vehicle belonging to him or under his control; and

(b) any ship, aircraft or vehicle in which he arrived in the United Kingdom,]; may be searched with a view to ascertaining whether he is doing, [or, as the case may be, has done], so by the immigration officer or a person acting under the directions of the officer:

Provided that no woman or girl shall be searched except by a woman.

[(4) Where a passport or other document is produced or found in accordance with this paragraph an immigration officer may examine it and detain it—

(a) for the purpose of examining it, for a period not exceeding 7 days;

(b) for any purpose, until the person to whom the document relates is given leave to enter the United Kingdom or is about to depart or be removed following refusal of leave or until it is decided that the person does not require leave to enter;

(c) after a time described in paragraph (b), while the immigration officer thinks that the document may be required in connection with proceedings in respect of an appeal under the Immigration Acts or in respect of an offence.

(5) For the purpose of ascertaining that a passport or other document produced or found in accordance with this paragraph relates to a person examined under paragraph 2, 2A or 3 above, the person carrying out the examination may require the person being examined to provide information (whether or not by submitting to a process by means of which information is obtained or recorded) about his external physical characteristics (which may include, in particular, fingerprints or features of the iris or any other part of the eye).]

Note: Words in square brackets in para 4(1) and (2) inserted by Immigration and Asylum Act 1999 from 14 February 2000. Sub-paragraph (2A) ceased to have effect and sub-para 4 substituted by Immigration, Asylum and Nationality Act 2006, s 27 from 31 August 2006 (SI 2006/2226). Where, immediately before that date, a passport or other document produced or found in accordance with para 4 is being examined or detained by an immigration officer under para 4(2A) or para 4(4), para 4(4) shall apply to the examination or detention of those documents on or after 31 August 2006 as if it had been in force on the date on which the passport or other document was produced or found, and para 4(2A) shall cease to have effect. Paragraph 4(5) shall apply only where the examination under para 2, 2A or 3 of that Schedule begins on or after 31 August 2006.

5.   The Secretary of State may by order made by statutory instrument make provision for requiring passengers disembarking or embarking in the United Kingdom, or any class of such passengers, to produce to an immigration officer, if so required, landing or embarkation cards in such form as the Secretary of State may direct, and for requiring the owners or agents of ships and aircraft to supply such cards to those passengers.

Note: Paragraph 5 has effect in a form modified by and in circumstances specified by the Channel Tunnel (International Arrangements) Order (SI 1993/1813) as amended by SIs 1994/1405, 2000/913, 2001/178, 2001/3707, 2006/1003 and 2007/3759.

Notice of leave to enter or of refusal of leave

6.—(1) Subject to sub-paragraph (3) below, where a person examined by an immigration officer under paragraph 2 above is to be given a limited leave to enter the United Kingdom or is to be refused leave, the notice giving or refusing leave shall be given not later than [twenty four] hours after the conclusion of his examination (including any further examination) in pursuance of that paragraph; and if notice giving or refusing leave is not given him before the end of those [twenty four] hours, he shall (if not [a British citizen]) be deemed to have been given [leave to enter the United Kingdom for a period of six months subject to a condition prohibiting his taking employment] and the immigration officer shall as soon as may be given him written notice of that leave.

(2) Where on a person's examination under paragraph 2 above he is given notice of leave to enter the United Kingdom, then at any time before the end of [twenty four hours] from the conclusion of the examination he may be given a further notice in writing by an immigration officer cancelling the earlier notice and refusing him leave to enter.

(3) Where in accordance with this paragraph a person is given notice refusing him leave to enter the United Kingdom, that notice may at any time be cancelled by notice in writing given him by an immigration officer; and where a person is given a notice of cancellation under this sub-paragraph, [and the immigration officer does not at the same time give him indefinite or limited leave to enter {or require him to submit to further examination}, he shall be deemed to have been given leave to enter for a period of six months subject to a condition prohibiting his taking employment and the immigration officer shall as soon as may be give him written notice of that leave.]

(4) Where an entrant is a member of a party in charge of a person appearing to the immigration officer to be a responsible person, any notice to be given in relation to that entrant in accordance with this paragraph shall be duly given if delivered to the person in charge of the party.

Note: Words in third square brackets substituted by British Nationality Act 1981, s 39(6); other words in square brackets substituted by Immigration Act 1988, s 10. Words in curly brackets in para 6(3) inserted by Nationality, Immigration and Asylum Act 2002, s 119 from 8 January 2003 (SI 2002/2811).

[Power to require medical examination after entry

7.—(1) This paragraph applies if an immigration officer examining a person under paragraph 2 decides—
   (a) that he may be given leave to enter the United Kingdom; but
   (b) that a further medical test or examination may be required in the interests of public health.

(2) This paragraph also applies if an immigration officer examining a person under paragraph 2A decides—
   (a) that his leave to enter the United Kingdom should not be cancelled; but
   (b) that a further medical test or examination may be required in the interests of public health.

(3) The immigration officer may give the person concerned notice in writing requiring him—
   (a) to report his arrival to such medical officer of health as may be specified in the notice; and
   (b) to attend at such place and time and submit to such test or examination (if any), as that medical officer of health may require.

(4) In reaching a decision under paragraph (b) of sub-paragraph (1) or (2), the immigration officer must act on the advice of—
   (a) a medical inspector; or
   (b) if no medical inspector is available, a fully qualified medical practitioner.]

Note: Paragraph 7 substituted by Immigration and Asylum Act 1999 from 14 February 2000.

Removal of persons refused leave to enter and illegal entrants

8.—(1) Where a person arriving in the United Kingdom is refused leave to enter, an immigration officer may, subject to sub-paragraph (2) below—
   (a) give the captain of the ship or aircraft in which he arrives directions requiring the captain to remove him from the United Kingdom in that ship or aircraft; or

(b) give the owners or agents of that ship or aircraft directions requiring them to remove him from the United Kingdom in any ship or aircraft specified or indicated in the directions, being a ship or aircraft of which they are the owners or agents; or

(c) give those owners or agents directions requiring them to make arrangements for his removal from the United Kingdom in any ship or aircraft specified or indicated in the directions to a country or territory so specified, being either—

    (i) a country of which he is a national or citizen; or

    (ii) a country or territory in which he has obtained a passport or other document of identity; or

    (iii) a country or territory in which he embarked for the United Kingdom; or

    (iv) a country or territory to which there is reason to believe that he will be admitted.

(2) No directions shall be given under this paragraph in respect of anyone after the expiration of two months beginning with the date on which he was refused leave to enter the United Kingdom [(ignoring any period during which an appeal by him under the Immigration Acts is pending)] [except that directions may be given under sub-paragraph (1)(b) or (c) after the end of that period if the immigration officer has within that period given written notice to the owners or agents in question of his intention to give directions to them in respect of that person].

Note: Words in first square brackets in sub-para (2) inserted by Sch 7 Nationality, Immigration and Asylum Act 2002 from 1 April 2003 (SI 2003/754). Words in second square brackets in sub-para (2) added by Immigration Act 1988, s 10. Paragraph 8 modified in relation to certain persons entering or seeking to enter through Republic of Ireland with effect from 17 July 2002: see the Immigration (Entry otherwise than by Sea or Air) Order 2002 (SI 2002/1832). Paragraph 8 has effect in a form modified by and in circumstances specified by the Channel Tunnel (International Arrangements) Order (SI 1993/1813) as amended by SIs 1994/1405, 2000/913, 2001/178, 2001/3707, 2006/1003 and 2007/3759.

9.—(1) Where an illegal entrant is not given leave to enter or remain in the United Kingdom, an immigration officer may give any such directions in respect of him as in a case within paragraph 8 above are authorised by paragraph 8(1).

[(2) Any leave to enter the United Kingdom which is obtained by deception shall be disregarded for the purposes of this paragraph.]

Note: Paragraph 9(2) added by Asylum and Immigration Act 1996 from 1 October 1996. Sub-paragraph (1) modified in relation to certain persons entering or seeking to enter through Republic of Ireland with effect from 17 July 2002: see the Immigration (Entry otherwise than by Sea or Air) Order 2002 (SI 2002/1832). Paragraph 9 has effect in a form modified by and in circumstances specified by the Channel Tunnel (International Arrangements) Order (SI 1993/1813) as amended by SIs 1994/1405, 2000/913, 2001/178, 2001/3707, 2006/1003 and 2007/3759.

10.—(1) Where it appears to the Secretary of State either—

(a) that directions might be given in respect of a person under paragraph 8 or 9 above, but that it is not practicable for them to be given or that, if given, they would be ineffective; or

(b) that directions might have been given in respect of a person under paragraph 8 above [but that the requirements of paragraph 8(2) have not been complied with];

then the Secretary of State may give to the owners or agents of any ship or aircraft any such directions in respect of that person as are authorised by paragraph 8(1)(c).

(2) Where the Secretary of State may give directions for a person's removal in accordance with sub-paragraph (1) above, he may instead give directions for his removal in accordance with arrangements to be made by the Secretary of State to any country or territory to which he could be removed under sub-paragraph (1).

(3) The costs of complying with any directions given under this paragraph shall be defrayed by the Secretary of State.

Note: Paragraph 10 has effect in a form modified by and in circumstances specified by the Channel Tunnel (International Arrangements) Order (SI 1993/1813) as amended by SIs 1994/1405, 2000/913, 2001/178, 2001/3707, 2006/1003 and 2007/3759.

[10A Where directions are given in respect of a person under any of paragraphs 8 to 10 above, directions to the same effect may be given under that paragraph in respect of a member of the person's family].

Note: Paragraph 10A inserted by Nationality, Immigration and Asylum Act 2002 from 10 February 2003 (SI 2003/1).

11.   A person in respect of whom directions are given under any of paragraphs 8 to 10 above may be placed, under the authority of an immigration officer, on board any ship or aircraft in which he is to be removed in accordance with the directions.

Note: Paragraph 11 modified in relation to certain persons entering or seeking to enter through Republic of Ireland with effect from 17 July 2002: see the Immigration (Entry otherwise than by Sea or Air) Order 2002 (SI 2002/1832). Paragraph 11 has effect in a form modified by and in circumstances specified by the Channel Tunnel (International Arrangements) Order (SI 1993/1813) as amended by SIs 1994/1405, 2000/913, 2001/178, 2001/3707, 2006/1003 and 2007/3759.

Seamen and aircrews

12.—(1) If, on a person's examination by an immigration officer under paragraph 2 above, the immigration officer is satisfied that he has come to the United Kingdom for the purpose of joining a ship or aircraft as a member of the crew, then the immigration officer may limit the duration of any leave he gives that person to enter the United Kingdom by requiring him to leave the United Kingdom in a ship or aircraft specified or indicated by the notice giving leave.

(2) Where a person (not being [a British citizen]) arrives in the United Kingdom for the purpose of joining a ship or aircraft as a member of the crew and, having been given leave to enter as mentioned in sub-paragraph (1) above, remains beyond the time limited by that leave, or is reasonably suspected by an immigration officer of intending to do so, an immigration officer may—

(a) give the captain of that ship or aircraft directions requiring the captain to remove him from the United Kingdom in that ship or aircraft; or

(b) give the owners or agents of that ship or aircraft directions requiring them to remove him from the United Kingdom in any ship or aircraft specified or indicated in the directions, being a ship or aircraft of which they are the owners or agents; or

(c) give those owners or agents directions requiring them to make arrangements for his removal from the United Kingdom in any ship or aircraft specified or indicated in the directions to a country or territory so specified, being either—

(i) a country of which he is a national or citizen; or

(ii) a country or territory in which he has obtained a passport or other document of identity; or

(iii) a country or territory in which he embarked for the United Kingdom; or

(iv) a country or territory where he was engaged as a member of the crew of the ship or aircraft which he arrived in the United Kingdom to join; or

(v) a country or territory to which there is reason to believe that he will be admitted.

Note: Words in square brackets substituted by British Nationality Act 1981, s 39(6).

13.—(1) Where a person being a member of the crew of a ship or aircraft is examined by an immigration officer under paragraph 2 above, the immigration officer may limit the duration of any leave he gives that person to enter the United Kingdom—

(a) in the manner authorised by paragraph 12(1) above; or

(b) if that person is to be allowed to enter the United Kingdom in order to receive hospital treatment, by requiring him, on completion of that treatment, to leave the United Kingdom in accordance with arrangements to be made for his repatriation; or

(c) by requiring him to leave the United Kingdom within a specified period in accordance with arrangements to be made for his repatriation.

(2) Where a person (not being [a British citizen]) arrives in the United Kingdom as a member of the crew of a ship or aircraft, and either—

(A) having lawfully entered the United Kingdom without leave by virtue of section 8(1) of this Act, he remains without leave beyond the time allowed by section 8(1), or is reasonably suspected by an immigration officer of intending to do so; or

(B) having been given leave limited as mentioned in sub-paragraph (1) above, he remains beyond the time limited by that leave, or is reasonably suspected by an immigration officer of intending to do so;

an immigration officer may—

(a) give the captain of the ship or aircraft in which he arrived directions requiring the captain to remove him from the United Kingdom in that ship or aircraft; or

(b) give the owners or agents of that ship or aircraft directions requiring them to remove him from the United Kingdom in any ship or aircraft specified or indicated in the directions, being a ship or aircraft of which they are the owners or agents; or

(c) give those owners or agents directions requiring them to make arrangements for his removal from the United Kingdom in any ship or aircraft specified or indicated in the directions to a country or territory so specified, being either—

(i) a country of which he is a national or citizen; or

(ii) a country or territory in which he has obtained a passport or other document of identity; or

(iii) a country in which he embarked for the United Kingdom; or

(iv) a country or territory in which he was engaged as a member of the crew of the ship or aircraft in which he arrived in the United Kingdom; or

(v) a country or territory to which there is reason to believe that he will be admitted.

Note: Words in square brackets substituted by British Nationality Act 1981, s 39(6). Paragraph 13 has effect in a form modified by and in circumstances specified by the Channel Tunnel (International Arrangements) Order (SI 1993/1813) as amended by SIs 1994/1405, 2000/913, 2001/178, 2001/3707, 2006/1003 and 2007/3759.

14.—(1) Where it appears to the Secretary of State that directions might be given in respect of a person under paragraph 12 or 13 above, but that it is not practicable for them to be given or that, if given, they would be ineffective, then the Secretary of State may give to the owners or agents of any ship or aircraft any such directions in respect of that person as are authorised by paragraph 12(2)(c) or 13(2)(c).

(2) Where the Secretary of State may give directions for a person's removal in accordance with sub-paragraph (1) above, he may instead give directions for his removal in accordance with arrangements to be made by the Secretary of State to any country or territory to which he could be removed under sub-paragraph (1).

(3) The costs of complying with any directions given under this paragraph shall be defrayed by the Secretary of State.

15. A person in respect of whom directions are given under any of paragraphs 12 to 14 above may be placed, under the authority of an immigration officer, on board any ship or aircraft in which he is to be removed in accordance with the directions.

Note: Paragraph 15 has effect in a form modified by and in circumstances specified by the Channel Tunnel (International Arrangements) Order (SI 1993/1813) as amended by SIs 1994/1405, 2000/913, 2001/178, 2001/3707, 2006/1003 and 2007/3759.

Detention of persons liable to examination or removal

16.—(1) A person who may be required to submit to examination under paragraph 2 above may be detained under the authority of an immigration officer pending his examination and pending a decision to give or refuse him leave to enter.

[(**1A**) A person whose leave to enter has been suspended under paragraph 2A may be detained under the authority of an immigration officer pending—
   (a) completion of his examination under that paragraph; and
   (b) a decision on whether to cancel his leave to enter.]

[(**1B**) A person who has been required to submit to further examination under paragraph 3(1A) may be detained under the authority of an immigration officer, for a period not exceeding 12 hours, pending the completion of the examination.]

[(**2**) If there are reasonable grounds for suspecting that a person is someone in respect of whom directions may be given under any of paragraphs [8 to 10A] or 12 to 14, that person may be detained under the authority of an immigration officer pending—
   (a) a decision whether or not to give such directions;
   (b) his removal in pursuance of such directions.]

(3) A person on board a ship or aircraft may, under the authority of an immigration officer, be removed from the ship or aircraft for detention under this paragraph; but if an immigration officer so requires the captain of a ship or aircraft shall prevent from disembarking in the United Kingdom any person who has arrived in the United Kingdom in the ship or aircraft and been refused leave to enter, and the captain may for that purpose detain him in custody on board the ship or aircraft.

(4) The captain of a ship or aircraft, if so required by an immigration officer, shall prevent from disembarking in the United Kingdom or before the directions for his removal have been fulfilled any person placed on board the ship or aircraft under paragraph 11 or 15 above, and the captain may for that purpose detain him in custody on board the ship or aircraft.

Note: Sub-paragraph (1A) inserted by Immigration and Asylum Act 1999 from 14 February 2000, sub-para (2) substituted by Immigration and Asylum Act 1999. Words in square brackets substituted by Nationality, Immigration and Asylum Act 2002 from 10 February 2003 (SI 2003/1). Sub-paragraph (1B) inserted by Immigration, Asylum and Nationality Act 2006, s 42 from 31 August 2006 (SI 2006/2226). Paragraph 16 has effect in a form modified by and in circumstances specified by the Channel Tunnel (International Arrangements) Order (SI 1993/1813) as amended by SIs 1994/1405, 2000/913, 2001/178, 2001/3707, 2006/1003 and 2007/3759.

17.—(1) A person liable to be detained under paragraph 16 above may be arrested without warrant by a constable or by an immigration officer.

(2) If—
   (a) a justice of the peace is by written information on oath satisfied that there is reasonable ground for suspecting that a person liable to be arrested under this paragraph is to be found on any premises; or
   (b) in Scotland, a sheriff, or a ... justice of the peace, having jurisdiction in the place where the premises are situated is by evidence on oath so satisfied; he may grant a warrant [authorising any immigration officer or constable to enter], [if need be by reasonable force], the premises named in the warrant for the purpose of searching for and arresting that person.

[(3) Sub-paragraph (4) applies where an immigration officer or constable—
   (a) enters premises in reliance on a warrant under sub-paragraph (2), and
   (b) detains a person on the premises.

(4) A detainee custody officer may enter the premises, if need be by reasonable force, for the purpose of carrying out a search.

(5) In sub-paragraph (4)—

'detainee custody officer' means a person in respect of whom a certificate of authorisation is in force under section 154 of the Immigration and Asylum Act 1999 (c. 33) (detained persons: escort and custody), and

'search' means a search under paragraph 2(1)(a) of Schedule 13 to that Act (escort arrangements: power to search detained person).]

Note: Words omitted from (2)(b) repealed by Asylum and Immigration Act 1996 from 1 October 1996; other words omitted by Police and Criminal Evidence Act 1984, s 119(2). Words in first square brackets in (2)(b) substituted by Immigration and Asylum Act 1999, s 140(2); words in second square brackets substituted by Nationality, Immigration and Asylum Act 2002 from 10 February 2003 (SI 2003/1).

18.—(1) Persons may be detained under paragraph 16 above in such places as the Secretary of State may direct (when not detained in accordance with paragraph 16 on board a ship or aircraft).

(2) Where a person is detained under paragraph 16, any immigration officer, constable or prison officer, or any other person authorised by the Secretary of State, may take all such steps as may be reasonably necessary for photographing, measuring or otherwise identifying him.

[(**2A**) The power conferred by sub-paragraph (2) includes power to take fingerprints.]

(3) Any person detained under paragraph 16 may be taken in the custody of a constable, or of any person acting under the authority of an immigration officer, to and from any place where his attendance is required for the purpose of ascertaining his citizenship or nationality or of making arrangements for his admission to a country or territory other than the United Kingdom, or where he is required to be for any other purpose connected with the operation of this Act.

(4) A person shall be deemed to be in legal custody at any time when he is detained under paragraph 16 or is being removed in pursuance of sub-paragraph (3) above.

Note: Sub-paragraph (2A) inserted by Immigration and Asylum Act 1999 from 11 December 1999 (SI 2000/3099).

19.—(1) Where a person is refused leave to enter the United Kingdom and directions are given in respect of him under paragraph 8 or 10 above, then subject to the provisions of this paragraph the owners or agents of the ship or aircraft in which he arrived shall be liable to pay the Secretary of State on demand any expenses incurred by the latter in respect of the custody, accommodation or maintenance of that person [for any period (not exceeding 14 days)] after his arrival while he was detained or liable to be detained under paragraph 16 above.

(2) Sub-paragraph (1) above shall not apply to expenses in respect of a person who, when he arrived in the United Kingdom, held a [certificate of entitlement] or a current entry clearance or was the person named in a current work permit; and for this purpose a document purporting to be a [certificate of entitlement], entry clearance or work permit is to be regarded as being one unless its falsity is reasonably apparent.

(3) If, before the directions for a person's removal under paragraph 8 or 10 above have been carried out, he is given leave to enter the United Kingdom, or if he is afterwards given that leave in consequence of the determination in his favour of an appeal under this Act (being an appeal against a refusal of leave to enter by virtue of which the directions were given), or it is determined on an appeal under this Act that he does not require leave to enter (being an appeal occasioned by such a refusal), no sum shall be demanded under sub-paragraph (1) above for expenses incurred in respect of that person and any sum already demanded and paid shall be refunded.

(4) Sub-paragraph (1) above shall not have effect in relation to directions which in consequence of an appeal under this Act, have ceased to have effect or are for the time being of no effect; and the expenses to which that sub-paragraph applies include expenses in conveying the person in

question to and from the place where he is detained or accommodated unless the journey is made for the purpose of attending an appeal by him under this Act.

Note: Words in square brackets in sub-para (1) substituted by Asylum and Immigration Act 1996 from 1 October 1996. Words in square brackets in sub-para (2) substituted by British Nationality Act 1981, s 39(6). Paragraph 19 has effect in a form modified by and in circumstances specified by the Channel Tunnel (International Arrangements) Order (SI 1993/1813) as amended by SIs 1994/1405, 2000/913, 2001/178, 2001/3707, 2006/1003 and 2007/3759.

20.—(1) Subject to the provisions of this paragraph, in either of the following cases, that is to say,—

(a) where directions are given in respect of an illegal entrant under paragraph 9 or 10 above; and

(b) where a person has lawfully entered the United Kingdom without leave by virtue of section 8(1) of this Act, but directions are given in respect of him under paragraph 13(2)(A) above or, in a case within paragraph 13(2)(A), under paragraph 14; the owners or agents of the ship or aircraft in which he arrived in the United Kingdom shall be liable to pay the Secretary of State on demand any expenses incurred by the latter in respect of the custody, accommodation or maintenance of that person [for any period (not exceeding 14 days)] after his arrival while he was detained or liable to be detained under paragraph 16 above.

[(1A) Sub-paragraph (1) above shall not apply to expenses in respect of an illegal entrant if he obtained leave to enter by deception and the leave has not been cancelled under paragraph 6(2) above.]

(2) If, before the directions for a person's removal from the United Kingdom have been carried out, he is given leave to remain in the United Kingdom, no sum shall be demanded under sub-paragraph (1) above for expenses incurred in respect of that person and any sum already demanded and paid shall be refunded.

(3) Sub-paragraph (1) above shall not have effect in relation to directions which, in consequence of an appeal under this Act, are for the time being of no effect; and the expenses to which that sub-paragraph applies include expenses in conveying the person in question to and from the place where he is detained or accommodated unless the journey is made for the purpose of attending an appeal by him under this Act.

Note: Words in square brackets substituted and (1A) inserted by Asylum and Immigration Act 1996 from 1 October 1996. Paragraph 20 has effect in a form modified by and in circumstances specified by the Channel Tunnel (International Arrangements) Order (SI 1993/1813) as amended by SIs 1994/1405, 2000/913, 2001/178, 2001/3707, 2006/1003 and 2007/3759.

Temporary admission of persons liable to detention

21.—(1) A person liable to detention or detained under paragraph 16 [(1), (1A) or (2)] above may, under the written authority of an immigration officer, be temporarily admitted to the United Kingdom without being detained or be released from detention; but this shall not prejudice a later exercise of the power to detain him.

(2) So long as a person is at large in the United Kingdom by virtue of this paragraph, he shall be subject to such restrictions as to residence [, as to his employment or occupation] and as to reporting to the police or an immigration officer as may from time to time be notified to him in writing by an immigration officer.

[(2A) The provisions that may be included in restrictions as to residence imposed under sub-paragraph (2) include provisions of such a description as may be prescribed by regulations made by the Secretary of State.

(2B) The regulations may, among other things, provide for the inclusion of provisions—

(a) prohibiting residence in one or more particular areas;

(b) requiring the person concerned to reside in accommodation provided under section 4 of the Immigration and Asylum Act 1999 and prohibiting him from being absent from that accommodation except in accordance with the restrictions imposed on him.

(2C) The regulations may provide that a particular description of provision may be imposed only for prescribed purposes.

(2D) The power to make regulations conferred by this paragraph is exercisable by statutory instrument and includes a power to make different provision for different cases.

(2E) But no regulations under this paragraph are to be made unless a draft of the regulations has been laid before Parliament and approved by a resolution of each House.]

[(3) Sub-paragraph (4) below applies where a person who is at large in the United Kingdom by virtue of this paragraph is subject to a restriction as to reporting to an immigration officer with a view to the conclusion of his examination under paragraph 2 [or 2A] above.

(4) If the person fails at any time to comply with that restriction—
(a) an immigration officer may direct that the person's examination shall be treated as concluded at that time; but
(b) nothing in paragraph 6 above shall require the notice giving or refusing him leave to enter the United Kingdom to be given within twenty-four hours after that time.]

Note: Words in square brackets in sub-paragraph (1) inserted by Immigration, Asylum and Nationality Act 2006, s 42 from 31 August 2006 (SI 2006/2226). Words in square brackets in sub-para (2) inserted by Immigration Act 1988, s 10; sub-paras (3) and (4) inserted by Asylum and Immigration Act 1996 from 1 October 1996. Sub-paras (2A), (2B), (2C), (2D) and (2E) inserted by Immigration and Asylum Act 1999 from 11 November 1999, other words in square brackets inserted and words in sub-para (4)(a) omitted by Immigration and Asylum Act 1999 from 14 February 2000.

Temporary release of persons liable to detention

22.—[(1) The following, namely—
(a) a person detained under paragraph 16(1) above pending examination;
[(aa) a person detained under paragraph 16(1A) above pending completion of his examination or a decision on whether to cancel his leave to enter;] and
(b) a person detained under paragraph 16(2) above pending the giving of directions,
may be released on bail in accordance with this paragraph.

(1A) An immigration officer not below the rank of chief immigration officer or [the First-tier Tribunal] may release a person so detained on his entering into a recognizance or, in Scotland, bail bond conditioned for his appearance before an immigration officer at a time and place named in the recognizance or bail bond or at such other time and place as may in the meantime be notified to him in writing by an immigration officer.

(1B) Sub-paragraph (1)(a) above shall not apply unless seven days have elapsed since the date of the person's arrival in the United Kingdom.]

(2) The conditions of a recognizance or bail bond taken under this paragraph may include conditions appearing to the [immigration officer or [the First-tier Tribunal]] to be likely to result in the appearance of the person bailed at the required time and place; and any recognizance shall be with or without sureties as the [officer or [the First-tier Tribunal]] may determine.

(3) In any case in which an [immigration officer or [the First-tier Tribunal]] has power under this paragraph to release a person on bail, the [officer or [the First-tier Tribunal]] may, instead of taking the bail, fix the amount and conditions of the bail (including the amount in which any sureties are to be bound) with a view to its being taken subsequently by any such person as may be specified by the [officer or [the First-tier Tribunal]]; and on the recognizance or bail bond being so taken the person to be bailed shall be released.

Note: Subparagraphs (1)-(1B) substituted by Asylum and Immigration Act 1996 from 1 October 1996 and subparagraphs (2) and (3) amended by the same Act from 1 September 1996 (SI 1996/2053). Sub-paragraph (1)(aa) inserted by Immigration and Asylum Act 1999 from 14 February 2000. Words "the First-tier Tribunal" substituted from 15 February 2010 (SI 2010/21).

23.—(1) Where a recognizance entered into under paragraph 22 above appears to [the First-tier Tribunal] to be forfeited, [the First-tier Tribunal] may by order declare it to be forfeited and adjudge the persons bound thereby, whether as principal or sureties, or any of them, to pay the sum in which they are respectively bound or such part of it, if any, as [the First-tier Tribunal] thinks fit; and an order under this sub-paragraph shall specify a magistrates' court or, in Northern Ireland, court of summary jurisdiction, and—

   (a) the recognizance shall be treated for the purposes of collection, enforcement and remission of the sum forfeited as having been forfeited by the court so specified; and

   (b) [the First-tier Tribunal] shall, as soon as practicable, give particulars of the recognizance to the [proper officer] of that court.

[(1A) In sub-paragraph (3) "proper officer" means—

   (a) in relation to a magistrates' court in England and Wales, the [designated officer] for the court; and

   (b) in relation to a court of summary jurisdiction in Northern Ireland, the clerk of the court.]

(2) Where a person released on bail under paragraph 22 above as it applies in Scotland fails to comply with the terms of his bail bond, [the First-tier Tribunal] may declare the bail to be forfeited, and any bail so forfeited shall be transmitted by [the First-tier Tribunal] to the sheriff court having jurisdiction in the area where the proceedings took place, and shall be treated as having been forfeited by that court.

(3) Any sum the payment of which is enforceable by a magistrates' court in England or Wales by virtue of this paragraph shall be treated for the [purposes of section 38 of the Courts Act 2003 (application of receipts of designated officers) as being] due under a recognizance forfeited by such a court ...

(4) Any sum the payment of which is enforceable by virtue of this paragraph by a court of summary jurisdiction in Northern Ireland shall, for the purposes of section 20(5) of the Administration of Justice Act (Northern Ireland) 1954, be treated as a forfeited recognizance.

Note: Words in square brackets in sub-para 3 substituted by Justices of the Peace Act 1979; words omitted repealed by Criminal Justice Act 1972. Sub-paragraph (1A) inserted by and words in brackets in sub-para (1) substituted by Access to Justice Act 1999, Sch 13 para 70 from 1 April 2001 (SI 2001/916). Words in square brackets in sub-para (1A)((a) and sub-para (3) substituted by Sch 8 Courts Act 2003 from 1 April 2005 (SI 2005/910).). Words "the First-tier Tribunal" substituted from 15 February 2010 (SI 2010/21). Other words in square brackets substituted by Sch 2 Asylum and Immigration (Treatment of Claimants etc.) Act 2004 from 4 April 2005 (SI 2005/565).

24.—(1) An immigration officer or constable may arrest without warrant a person who has been released by virtue of paragraph 22 above—

   (a) if he has reasonable grounds for believing that that person is likely to break the condition of his recognizance or bail bond that he will appear at the time and place required or to break any other condition of it, or has reasonable ground to suspect that the person is breaking or has broken any such other condition; or

   (b) if, a recognizance with sureties having been taken, he is notified in writing by any surety of the surety's belief that that person is likely to break the first-mentioned condition, and of the surety's wish for that reason to be relieved of his obligations as a surety; and paragraph 17(2) above shall apply for the arrest of a person under this paragraph as it applies for the arrest of a person under paragraph 17.

(2) A person arrested under this paragraph—

    (a) if not required by a condition on which he was released to appear before an immigration officer within twenty-four hours after the time of his arrest, shall as soon as practicable be brought before [the First-tier Tribunal] or, if that is not practicable within those twenty-four hours, before {in England and Wales, a justice of the peace, in Northern Ireland,} a justice of the peace acting for the petty sessions area in which he is arrested or, in Scotland, the sheriff; and

    (b) if required by such a condition to appear within those twenty-four hours before an immigration officer, shall be brought before that officer.

(3) [Where a person is brought before the First-tier Tribunal, a justice of the peace or the sheriff by virtue of sub-paragraph (2)(a), the Tribunal, justice of the peace or sheriff]—

    (a) if of the opinion that that person has broken or is likely to break any condition on which he was released, may either—

       (i) direct that he be detained under the authority of the person by whom he was arrested; or

      (ii) release him, on his original recognizance or on a new recognizance, with or without sureties, or, in Scotland, on his original bail or on new bail; and

    (b) if not of that opinion, shall release him on his original recognizance or bail.

Note: Words in square brackets substituted by Sch 2 Asylum and Immigration (Treatment of Claimants etc.) Act 2004 from 4 April 2005 (SI 2005/565). Words in curly brackets in sub-para (2) inserted by Courts Act 2003 from 1 April 2005. Words "the First-tier Tribunal" substituted from 15 February 2010 (SI 2010/21).

[25. Tribunal Procedure Rules may make provision with respect to applications to the First-tier Tribunal under paragraphs 22 to 24 and matters arising out of such applications.]

Note: Paragraph 25 substituted by SI 2010/21 from 15 February 2010.

[Entry and search of premises

25A.—(1) This paragraph applies if—

    (a) a person is arrested under this Schedule; or

    (b) a person who was arrested by a constable (other than under this Schedule) is detained by an immigration officer under this Schedule.

(2) An immigration officer may enter and search any premises—

    (a) occupied or controlled by the arrested person, or

    (b) in which that person was when he was arrested, or immediately before he was arrested, for relevant documents.

(3) The power may be exercised—

    (a) only if the officer has reasonable grounds for believing that there are relevant documents on the premises;

    (b) only to the extent that it is reasonably required for the purpose of discovering relevant documents; and

    (c) subject to sub-paragraph (4), only if a senior officer has authorised its exercise in writing.

(4) An immigration officer may conduct a search under sub-paragraph (2)—

    (a) before taking the arrested person to a place where he is to be detained; and

    (b) without obtaining an authorisation under sub-paragraph (3)(c), if the presence of that person at a place other than one where he is to be detained is necessary to make an effective search for any relevant documents.

(5) An officer who has conducted a search under sub-paragraph (4) must inform a senior officer as soon as is practicable.

(6) The officer authorising a search, or who is informed of one under sub-paragraph (5), must make a record in writing of—

    (a) the grounds for the search; and

(b) the nature of the documents that were sought.

(7) An officer searching premises under sub-paragraph (2)—
  (a) may seize and retain any documents he finds which he has reasonable grounds for believing are relevant documents; but
  (b) may not retain any such document for longer than is necessary in view of the purpose for which the person was arrested.

(8) But sub-paragraph (7)(a) does not apply to documents which the officer has reasonable grounds for believing are items subject to legal privilege.

(9) 'Relevant documents' means any documents which might—
  (a) establish the arrested person's identity, nationality or citizenship; or
  (b) indicate the place from which he has travelled to the United Kingdom or to which he is proposing to go.

(10) 'Senior officer' means an immigration officer not below the rank of chief immigration officer.]

Note: Paragraph 25A inserted by Immigration and Asylum Act 1999 from 14 February 2000.

[Searching persons arrested by immigration officers

25B.—(1) This paragraph applies if a person is arrested under this Schedule.

(2) An immigration officer may search the arrested person if he has reasonable grounds for believing that the arrested person may present a danger to himself or others.

(3) The officer may search the arrested person for—
  (a) anything which he might use to assist his escape from lawful custody; or
  (b) any document which might—
    (i) establish his identity, nationality or citizenship; or
    (ii) indicate the place from which he has travelled to the United Kingdom or to which he is proposing to go.

(4) The power conferred by sub-paragraph (3) may be exercised—
  (a) only if the officer has reasonable grounds for believing that the arrested person may have concealed on him anything of a kind mentioned in that sub-paragraph; and
  (b) only to the extent that it is reasonably required for the purpose of discovering any such thing.

(5) A power conferred by this paragraph to search a person is not to be read as authorising an officer to require a person to remove any of his clothing in public other than an outer coat, jacket or glove; but it does authorise the search of a person's mouth.

(6) An officer searching a person under sub-paragraph (2) may seize and retain anything he finds, if he has reasonable grounds for believing that the person searched might use it to cause physical injury to himself or to another person.

(7) An officer searching a person under sub-paragraph (3)(a) may seize and retain anything he finds, if he has reasonable grounds for believing that he might use it to assist his escape from lawful custody.

(8) An officer searching a person under sub-paragraph (3)(b) may seize and retain anything he finds, other than an item subject to legal privilege, if he has reasonable grounds for believing that it might be a document falling within that sub-paragraph.

(9) Nothing seized under sub-paragraph (6) or (7) may be retained when the person from whom it was seized—
  (a) is no longer in custody, or
  (b) is in the custody of a court but has been released on bail.]

Note: Paragraph 25B inserted by Immigration and Asylum Act 1999 from 14 February 2000.

[Searching persons in police custody

25C.—(1) This paragraph applies if a person—
  (a) has been arrested under this Schedule; and
  (b) is in custody at a police station.

(2) An immigration officer may, at any time, search the arrested person in order to ascertain whether he has with him—
  (a) anything which he might use to—
      (i) cause physical injury to himself or others;
      (ii) damage property;
      (iii) interfere with evidence; or
      (iv) assist his escape; or
  (b) any document which might—
      (i) establish his identity, nationality or citizenship; or
      (ii) indicate the place from which he has travelled to the United Kingdom or to which he is proposing to go.

(3) The power may be exercised only to the extent that the officer considers it to be necessary for the purpose of discovering anything of a kind mentioned in sub-paragraph (2).

(4) An officer searching a person under this paragraph may seize and retain anything he finds, if he has reasonable grounds for believing that—
  (a) that person might use it for one or more of the purposes mentioned in sub-paragraph (2)(a); or
  (b) it might be a document falling within sub-paragraph (2)(b).

(5) But the officer may not retain anything seized under sub-paragraph (2)(a)—
  (a) for longer than is necessary in view of the purpose for which the search was carried out; or
  (b) when the person from whom it was seized is no longer in custody or is in the custody of a court but has been released on bail.

(6) The person from whom something is seized must be told the reason for the seizure unless he is—
  (a) violent or appears likely to become violent; or
  (b) incapable of understanding what is said to him.

(7) An intimate search may not be conducted under this paragraph.

(8) The person carrying out a search under this paragraph must be of the same sex as the person searched.

(9) 'Intimate search' has the same meaning as in section 28H(11).]

Note: Paragraph 25C inserted by Immigration and Asylum Act 1999 from 14 February 2000.

[Access and copying

25D.—(1) If a person showing himself—
  (a) to be the occupier of the premises on which seized material was seized, or
  (b) to have had custody or control of the material immediately before it was seized, asks the immigration officer who seized the material for a record of what he seized, the officer must provide the record to that person within a reasonable time.

(2) If a relevant person asks an immigration officer for permission to be granted access to seized material, the officer must arrange for that person to have access to the material under the supervision of an immigration officer.

(3) An immigration officer may photograph or copy, or have photographed or copied, seized material.

(4) If a relevant person asks an immigration officer for a photograph or copy of seized material, the officer must arrange for—

    (a) that person to have access to the material under the supervision of an immigration officer for the purpose of photographing or copying it; or

    (b) the material to be photographed or copied.

(5) A photograph or copy made under sub-paragraph (4)(b) must be supplied within a reasonable time.

(6) There is no duty under this paragraph to arrange for access to, or the supply of a photograph or copy of, any material if there are reasonable grounds for believing that to do so would prejudice—

    (a) the exercise of any functions in connection with which the material was seized; or

    (b) an investigation which is being conducted under this Act, or any criminal proceedings which may be brought as a result.

(7) 'Relevant person' means—

    (a) a person who had custody or control of seized material immediately before it was seized, or

    (b) someone acting on behalf of such a person.

(8) 'Seized material' means anything which has been seized and retained under this Schedule.]

Note: Paragraph 25D inserted by Immigration and Asylum Act 1999 from 14 February 2000.

[**25E.** Section 28L applies for the purposes of this Schedule as it applies for the purposes of Part III.]

Note: Paragraph 25E inserted by Immigration and Asylum Act 1999 from 14 February 2000.

Supplementary duties of those connected with ships or aircraft or with ports

26.—(1) The owners or agents of a ship or aircraft employed to carry passengers for reward shall not, without the approval of the Secretary of State, arrange for the ship or aircraft to call at a port in the United Kingdom other than a port of entry for the purpose of disembarking passengers, if any of the passengers on board may not enter the United Kingdom without leave, or for the purpose of embarking passengers unless the owners or agents have reasonable cause to believe all of them to be [British citizens].

[(**1A**) Sub-paragraph (1) does not apply in such circumstances, if any, as the Secretary of State may by order prescribe.]

(2) The Secretary of State may from time to time give written notice to the owners or agents of any ships or aircraft designating control areas for the embarkation or disembarkation of passengers in any port in the United Kingdom, and specifying the conditions and restrictions (if any) to be observed in any control area; and where by notice given to any owners or agents a control area is for the time being designated for the embarkation or disembarkation of passengers at any port, the owners or agents shall take all reasonable steps to secure that, in the case of their ships or aircraft, passengers do not embark or disembark, as the case may be, at the port outside the control area and that any conditions or restrictions notified to them are observed.

(3) The Secretary of State may also from time to time give to any persons concerned with the management of a port in the United Kingdom written notice designating control areas in the port and specifying conditions or restrictions to be observed in any control area; and any such person shall take all reasonable steps to secure that any conditions or restrictions as notified to him are observed.

[(**3A**) The power conferred by sub-paragraph (1A) is exercisable by statutory instrument; and any such instrument shall be subject to annulment by a resolution of either House of Parliament.]

Note: Words in square brackets substituted by British Nationality Act 1981. Words omitted from para 26(1) and paras 26(1A) and 26(3A) inserted by Immigration and Asylum Act 1999 from 14

February 2000. Paragraph 26 has effect in a form modified by and in circumstances specified by the Channel Tunnel (International Arrangements) Order (SI 1993/1813) as amended by SIs 1994/1405, 2000/913, 2001/178, 2001/3707, 2006/1003 and 2007/3759.

27.—(1) The captain of a ship or aircraft arriving in the United Kingdom—

    (a) shall take such steps as may be necessary to secure that persons on board do not disembark there unless either they have been examined by an immigration officer, or they disembark in accordance with arrangements approved by an immigration officer, or they are members of the crew who may lawfully enter the United Kingdom without leave by virtue of section 8(1) of this Act; and

    (b) where the examination of persons on board is to be carried out on the ship or aircraft, shall take such steps as may be necessary to secure that those to be examined are presented for the purpose in an orderly manner.

[(**2**) The Secretary of State may by order require, or enable an immigration officer to require, a responsible person in respect of a ship or aircraft to supply—

    (a) a passenger list showing the names and nationality or citizenship of passengers arriving or leaving on board the ship or aircraft;

    (b) particulars of members of the crew of the ship or aircraft.

(3) An order under sub-paragraph (2) may relate—

    (a) to all ships or aircraft arriving or expected to arrive in the United Kingdom;

    (b) to all ships or aircraft leaving or expected to leave the United Kingdom;

    (c) to ships or aircraft arriving or expected to arrive in the United Kingdom from or by way of a specified country;

    (d) to ships or aircraft leaving or expected to leave the United Kingdom to travel to or by way of a specified country;

    (e) to specified ships or specified aircraft.

(**4**) For the purposes of sub-paragraph (2) the following are responsible persons in respect of a ship or aircraft—

    (a) the owner or agent, and

    (b) the captain.

(5) An order under sub-paragraph (2)—

    (a) may specify the time at which or period during which information is to be provided,

    (b) may specify the form and manner in which information is to be provided,

    (c) shall be made by statutory instrument, and

    (d) shall be subject to annulment in pursuance of a resolution of either House of Parliament.]

Note: Sub-paragraph (2) substituted (from 5 November 2007 (SI 2007/3138)) and sub-paras (3)-(5) inserted (from 1 March 2008 (SI 2007/3138 as amended by SI 2007/3580)) by Immigration, Asylum and Nationality Act 2006, s 31. Paragraph 27 has effect in a form modified by and in circumstances specified by the Channel Tunnel (International Arrangements) Order (SI 1993/1813) as amended by SIs 1994/1405, 2000/913, 2001/178, 2001/3707, 2006/1003 and 2007/3759.

27A...

[Passenger information

27B.—(1) This paragraph applies to ships or aircraft—

    (a) which have arrived, or are expected to arrive, in the United Kingdom; or

    (b) which have left, or are expected to leave, the United Kingdom.

(**2**) If an immigration officer asks the owner or agent ('the carrier') of a ship or aircraft for passenger information [or service information], the carrier must provide that information to the officer.

(3) The officer may ask for passenger information [or service information] relating to—

    (a) a particular ship or particular aircraft of the carrier;

    (b) particular ships or aircraft (however described) of the carrier; or

    (c) all of the carrier's ships or aircraft.

(4) The officer may ask for—

    (a) all passenger information [or service information] in relation to the ship or aircraft concerned; or

    (b) particular passenger information [or service information] in relation to that ship or aircraft.

[(4A) The officer may ask the carrier to provide a copy of all or part of a document that relates to a passenger and contains passenger information [or service information].]

(5) A request under sub-paragraph (2)—

    (a) must be in writing;

    (b) must state the date on which it ceases to have effect; and

    (c) continues in force until that date, unless withdrawn earlier by written notice by an immigration officer.

(6) The date may not be later than six months after the request is made.

(7) The fact that a request under sub-paragraph (2) has ceased to have effect as a result of sub-paragraph (5) does not prevent the request from being renewed.

(8) The information must be provided—

    (a) in such form and manner as the Secretary of State may direct; and

    (b) at such time as may be stated in the request.

(9) 'Passenger information' [or service information] means such information relating to the passengers carried, or expected to be carried, by the ship or aircraft as may be specified.

[(9A) 'Service information' means such information relating to the voyage or flight undertaken by the ship or aircraft as may be specified.]

(10) 'Specified' means specified in an order made by statutory instrument by the Secretary of State.

(11) Such an instrument shall be subject to annulment in pursuance of a resolution of either House of Parliament.]

Note: Paragraph 27B inserted by Immigration and Asylum Act 1999 from 3 April 2000. Sub-paragraph 4A inserted by Asylum and Immigration (Treatment of Claimants etc.) Act 2004, s 16 from a date to be appointed. Words in square brackets and sub-para (9A) inserted by Immigration, Asylum and Nationality Act 2006, s 31 from 5 November 2007 (SI 2007/3138). Paragraph 27(B2) modified in its extension to Guernsey by Art 6, Sch 3, SI 2011/2444.

[Notification of non-EEA arrivals

27C.—(1) If a senior officer, or an immigration officer authorised by a senior officer, gives written notice to the owner or agent ('the carrier') of a ship or aircraft, the carrier must inform a relevant officer of the expected arrival in the United Kingdom of any ship or aircraft—

    (a) of which he is the owner or agent; and

    (b) which he expects to carry a person who is not an EEA national.

(2) The notice may relate to—

    (a) a particular ship or particular aircraft of the carrier;

    (b) particular ships or aircraft (however described) of the carrier; or

    (c) all of the carrier's ships or aircraft.

(3) The notice—

    (a) must state the date on which it ceases to have effect; and

    (b) continues in force until that date, unless withdrawn earlier by written notice given by a senior officer.

(4) The date may not be later than six months after the notice is given.

(5)   The fact that a notice under sub-paragraph (1) has ceased to have effect as a result of sub-paragraph (3) does not prevent the notice from being renewed.

(6)   The information must be provided—
  (a) in such form and manner as the notice may require; and
  (b) before the ship or aircraft concerned departs for the United Kingdom.

(7)   If a ship or aircraft travelling to the United Kingdom stops at one or more places before arriving in the United Kingdom, it is to be treated as departing for the United Kingdom when it leaves the last of those places.

(8)   'Senior officer' means an immigration officer not below the rank of chief immigration officer.

(9)   'Relevant officer' means—
  (a) the officer who gave the notice under sub-paragraph (1); or
  (b) any immigration officer at the port at which the ship or aircraft concerned is expected to arrive.

(10) 'EEA national' means a national of a State which is a Contracting Party to the Agreement on the European Economic Area signed at Oporto on 2nd May 1992 as it has effect for the time being.]

Note: Paragraph 27C inserted by Immigration and Asylum Act 1999 from 3 April 2000.

Part II

Effect of Appeals

Stay on directions for removal

28.   ...

Note: Paragraph 28 omitted by Immigration and Asylum Act 1999 from 2 October 2000. Transitional provisions set out in SI 2003/754.

Grant of bail pending appeal

29.—(1) Where a person (in the following provisions of this Schedule referred to as 'an appellant') has an appeal pending under [Part 5 of the Nationality, Immigration and Asylum Act 2002] and is for the time being detained under Part I of this Schedule, he may be released on bail in accordance with this paragraph.

(2)   An immigration officer not below the rank of chief immigration officer or a police officer not below the rank of inspector may release an appellant on his entering into a recognizance or, in Scotland, bail bond conditioned for his appearance before [the First-tier Tribunal] at a time and place named in the recognizance or bail bond.

(3)   [the First-tier Tribunal] may release an appellant on his entering into a recognizance or, in Scotland, bail bond conditioned for his appearance before [the Tribunal] at a time and place named in the recognizance or bail bond; ...

(4)   ...

(5)   The conditions of a recognizance or bail bond taken under this paragraph may include conditions appearing to the person fixing the bail to be likely to result in the appearance of the appellant at the time and place named; and any recognizance shall be with or without sureties as that person may determine.

(6)   In any case in which [the First-tier Tribunal] has power or is required by this paragraph to release an appellant on bail, [the Tribunal] may, instead of taking the bail, fix the amount and conditions of the bail (including the amount in which any sureties are to be bound) with a view to its being taken subsequently by any such person as may be specified by [the Tribunal]; and on the recognizance or bail bond being so taken the appellant shall be released.

Note: Words in first square brackets substituted by Sch 7 Nationality, Immigration and Asylum Act 2002 from 1 April 2003 (SI 2003/754). Transitional provisions regarding sub-para (1) set out in SI 2003/754. Words "the First-tier Tribunal" substituted from 15 February 2010 (SI 2010/21). Other words in square brackets substituted by and words omitted by Sch 2 Asylum and Immigration (Treatment of Claimants etc.) Act 2004 from 4 April 2005 (SI 2005/565).

Restrictions on grant of bail

30.—(1) An appellant shall not be released under paragraph 29 above without the consent of the Secretary of State if directions for the removal of the appellant from the United Kingdom are for the time being in force, or the power to give such directions is for the time being exercisable.

(2) Notwithstanding paragraph 29(3) or (4) above, [the Tribunal] shall not be obliged to release an appellant unless the appellant enters into a proper recognizance, with sufficient and satisfactory sureties if required, or in Scotland sufficient and satisfactory bail is found if so required; and [the Tribunal] shall not be obliged to release an appellant if it appears to [the Tribunal]—

  (a) that the appellant, having on any previous occasion been released on bail (whether under paragraph 24 or under any other provision), has failed to comply with the conditions of any recognizance or bail bond entered into by him on that occasion;

  (b) that the appellant is likely to commit an offence unless he is retained in detention;

  (c) that the release of the appellant is likely to cause danger to public health;

  (d) that the appellant is suffering from mental disorder and that his continued detention is necessary in his own interests or for the protection of any other person; or

  (e) that the appellant is under the age of seventeen, that arrangements ought to be made for his care in the event of his release and that no satisfactory arrangements for that purpose have been made.

Note: Words in square brackets substituted by Sch 2 Asylum and Immigration Act 2004 from 4 April 2005 (SI 2005/565).

Forfeiture of recognizances

31.—(1) Where under paragraph 29 above (as it applies in England and Wales or in Northern Ireland) a recognizance is entered into conditioned for the appearance of an appellant, [before the Tribunal], and it appears to [the Tribunal] to be forfeited, [the Tribunal] may by order declare it to be forfeited and adjudge the persons bound thereby, whether as principal or sureties, or any of them, to pay the sum in which they are respectively bound or such part of it, if any, as [the Tribunal] thinks fit.

(2) An order under this paragraph shall, for the purposes of this sub-paragraph, specify a magistrates' court or, in Northern Ireland, court of summary jurisdiction; and the recognizance shall be treated for the purposes of collection, enforcement and remission of the sum forfeited as having been forfeited by the court so specified.

(3) Where [the Tribunal] makes an order under this paragraph [the Tribunal] shall, as soon as practicable, give particulars of the recognizance to the [proper officer] of the court specified in the order in pursuance of sub-paragraph (2) above.

[(3A) In sub-paragraph (3) "proper officer" means—

  (a) in relation to a magistrates' court in England and Wales, the {designated officer} for the court; and

  (b) in relation to a court of summary jurisdiction in Northern Ireland, the clerk of the court.]

(4) Any sum the payment of which is enforceable by a magistrates' court in England or Wales by virtue of this paragraph shall be treated for the purposes of the [Justices of the Peace Act 1979

and, in particular, section 61 thereof] as being due under a recognizance forfeited by such a court ...

(5) Any sum the payment of which is enforceable by virtue of this paragraph by a court of summary jurisdiction in Northern Ireland shall, for the purposes of section 20(5) of the Administration of Justice Act (Northern Ireland) 1954, be treated as a forfeited recognizance.

Note: Words in square brackets in sub-para (4) substituted by Justices of the Peace Act 1979, s 71; words omitted by Criminal Justice Act 1972, s 64a. Other words in square brackets substituted by Sch 2 Asylum and Immigration Act 2004 from 4 April 2005, (SI 2005/565). Sub-paragraph (3A) inserted by and words in brackets in sub-para (3) substituted by Access to Justice Act 1999, Sch 13 para 70 from 1 April 2001 (SI 2001/916). Words substituted in sub-para (3A)(a) by Courts Act 2003 from 1 April 2005.

32.   Where under paragraph 29 above (as it applies in Scotland) a person released on bail fails to comply with the terms of a bail bond conditioned for his appearance [before the Tribunal], [the Tribunal] may declare the bail to be forfeited, and any bail so forfeited shall be transmitted by [the Tribunal] to the sheriff court having jurisdiction in the area where the proceedings took place, and shall be treated as having been forfeited by that court.

Note: Words in square brackets substituted by Sch 2 Asylum and Immigration Act 2004 from 4 April 2005 (SI 2005/565).

Arrest of appellants released on bail

33.—(1) An immigration officer or constable may arrest without warrant a person who has been released by virtue of this Part of this Schedule—

(a) if he has reasonable grounds for believing that that person is likely to break the condition of his recognizance or bail bond that he will appear at the time and place required or to break any other condition of it, or has reasonable ground to suspect that that person is breaking or has broken any such other condition; or

(b) if, a recognizance with sureties having been taken, he is notified in writing by any surety of the surety's belief that that person is likely to break the first-mentioned condition, and of the surety's wish for that reason to be relieved of his obligations as a surety; and paragraph 17(2) above shall apply for the arrest of a person under this paragraph as it applies for the arrest of a person under paragraph 17.

(2) A person arrested under this paragraph—

(a) if not required by a condition on which he was released to appear [before the Tribunal] within twenty-four hours after the time of his arrest, shall as soon as practicable be brought [before the Tribunal], or, if that is not practicable within those twenty-four hours, before {in England and Wales, a justice of the peace, in Northern Ireland,} a justice of the peace acting for the petty sessions area in which he is arrested or, in Scotland, the sheriff; and

(b) if required by such a condition to appear within those twenty-four hours [before the Tribunal] shall be brought [before it].

(3) [Where a person is brought before the First-tier Tribunal, a justice of the peace or the sheriff by virtue of sub-paragraph (2)(a), the Tribunal, justice of the peace or sheriff—]

(a) if of the opinion that that person has broken or is likely to break any condition on which he was released, may either—
(i) direct that he be detained under the authority of the person by whom he was arrested; or
(ii) release him on his original recognizance or on a new recognizance, with or without sureties, or, in Scotland, on his original bail or on new bail; and

(b) if not of that opinion, shall release him on his original recognizance or bail.

Note: Words in square brackets substituted by Sch 2 Asylum and Immigration Act 2004 from 4 April 2005 (SI 2005/565). Words inserted in sub-para (2)(a) by Courts Act 2003 from 1 April 2005. Words "the First-tier Tribunal" substituted from 15 February 2010 (SI 2010/21).

Grant of bail pending removal

[**34.**—(**1**) Paragraph 22 above shall apply in relation to a person—
  (a) directions for whose removal from the United Kingdom are for the time being in force; and
  (b) who is for the time being detained under Part I of this Schedule, as it applies in relation to a person detained under paragraph 16(1) above pending examination [, detained under paragraph 16(1A) above pending completion of his examination or a decision on whether to cancel his leave to enter] or detained under paragraph 16(2) above pending the giving of directions.

(**2**) Paragraphs 23 to 25 above shall apply as if any reference to paragraph 22 above included a reference to that paragraph as it applies by virtue of this paragraph.]

Note: Paragraph 34 inserted by Asylum and Immigration Act 1996 from 1 October 1996. Words in square brackets inserted by Immigration and Asylum Act 1999 from 2 October 2000.

Section 5   **SCHEDULE 3**

SUPPLEMENTARY PROVISIONS AS TO DEPORTATION

Removal of persons liable to deportation

1.—(**1**) Where a deportation order is in force against any person, the Secretary of State may give directions for his removal to a country or territory specified in the directions being either—
  (a) a country of which he is a national or citizen; or
  (b) a country or territory to which there is reason to believe that he will be admitted.

(**2**) The directions under sub-paragraph (1) above may be either—
  (a) directions given to the captain of a ship or aircraft about to leave the United Kingdom requiring him to remove the person in question in that ship or aircraft; or
  (b) directions given to the owners or agents of any ship or aircraft requiring them to make arrangements for his removal in a ship or aircraft specified or indicated in the directions; or
  (c) directions for his removal in accordance with arrangements to be made by the Secretary of State.

(**3**) In relation to directions given under this paragraph, paragraphs 11 and 16(4) of Schedule 2 to this Act shall apply, with the substitution of references to the Secretary of State for references to an immigration officer, as they apply in relation to directions for removal given under paragraph 8 of that Schedule.

(**4**) The Secretary of State, if he thinks fit, may apply in or towards payment of the expenses of or incidental to the voyage from the United Kingdom of a person against whom a deportation order is in force, or the maintenance until departure of such a person and his dependants, if any, any money belonging to that person; and except so far as they are paid as aforesaid, those expenses shall be defrayed by the Secretary of State.

Detention or control pending deportation

2.—(**1**) Where a recommendation for deportation made by a court is in force in respect of any person, [and that person is not detained in pursuance of the sentence or order of any court] he shall, unless the court by which the recommendation is made otherwise directs, [or a direction is given under sub-paragraph (1A) below,] be detained pending the making of a deportation order in pursuance of the recommendation, unless the Secretary of State directs him to be released pending further consideration of his case [or he is released on bail].

[(**1A**) Where—

    (a) a recommendation for deportation made by a court on a conviction of a person is in force in respect of him; and

    (b) he appeals against his conviction or against that recommendation, the powers that the court determining the appeal may exercise include power to direct him to be released without setting aside the recommendation.]

(**2**) Where notice has been given to a person in accordance with regulations under [section 105 of the Nationality, Immigration and Asylum Act 2002 (notice of decision)] of a decision to make a deportation order against him, [and he is not detained in pursuance of the sentence or order of a court], he may be detained under the authority of the Secretary of State pending the making of the deportation order.

(**3**) Where a deportation order is in force against any person, he may be detained under the authority of the Secretary of State pending his removal or departure from the United Kingdom (and if already detained by virtue of sub-paragraph (1) or (2) above when the order is made, shall continue to be detained unless [he is released on bail or] the Secretary of State directs otherwise).

(**4**) In relation to detention under sub-paragraph (2) or (3) above, paragraphs 17 [,18 and 25A to 25E] of Schedule 2 to this Act shall apply as they apply in relation to detention under paragraph 16 of that Schedule [; and for that purpose the reference in paragraph 17(1) to a person liable to detention includes a reference to a person who would be liable to detention upon receipt of a notice which is ready to be given to him.]

[(**4A**) Paragraphs 22 to 25 of Schedule 2 to this Act apply in relation to a person detained under sub-paragraph (1), (2) or (3) as they apply in relation to a person detained under paragraph 16 of that Schedule.]

[(**5**) A person to whom this sub-paragraph applies shall be subject to such restrictions as to residence, [as to his employment or occupation] and as to reporting to the police [or an immigration officer] as may from time to time be notified to him in writing by the Secretary of State.

(**6**) The persons to whom sub-paragraph (5) above applies are—

    (a) a person liable to be detained under sub-paragraph (1) above, while by virtue of a direction of the Secretary of State he is not so detained; and

    (b) a person liable to be detained under sub-paragraph (2) or (3) above, while he is not so detained.]

Effect of appeals

[**3**. So far as they relate to an appeal under section 82(1) of the Nationality, Immigration and Asylum Act 2002 against a decision of the kind referred to in section 82(2)(j) or (k) of that Act (decision to make a deportation order and refusal to revoke deportation order), paragraphs 29 to 33 to this Act shall apply for the purposes of this schedule as if the reference in paragraph 29(1) to Part 1 of that Schedule were a reference to this Schedule.]

[*Powers of courts pending deportation*

4. Where the release of a person recommended for deportation is directed by a court, he shall be subject to such restrictions as to residence [as to his employment or occupation] and as to reporting to the police as the court may direct.

5.—(1) On an application made—

    (a) by or on behalf of a person recommended for deportation whose release was so directed; or

    (b) by a constable; or

    (c) by an Immigration Officer,

the appropriate court shall have the powers specified in sub-paragraph (2) below.

(2) The powers mentioned in sub-paragraph (1) above are—

    (a) if the person to whom the application relates is not subject to any such restrictions imposed by a court as are mentioned in paragraph 4 above, to order that he shall be subject to any such restrictions as the court may direct; and

    (b) if he is subject to restrictions imposed by a court by virtue of that paragraph or this paragraph—

        (i) to direct that any of them shall be varied or shall cease to have effect; or

        (ii) to give further directions as to his residence and reporting.

6.—(1) In this Schedule 'the appropriate court' means, except in a case to which sub-paragraph (2) below applies, the court which directed release.

(2) This sub-paragraph applies where the court which directed release was—

    (a) the Crown Court;

    (b) the Court of Appeal;

    (c) the High Court of Justiciary;

    (d) the Crown Court in Northern Ireland; or

    (e) the Court of Appeal in Northern Ireland.

[(2A) Where the Crown Court directed release, the appropriate court is that court or a magistrates' court]

(3) Where…the Crown Court or the Crown Court in Northern Ireland directed release, the appropriate court is—

    (a) the court that directed release; or

    (b) a magistrates' court acting for the … county court division where the person to whom the application relates resides.

(4) Where the Court of Appeal or the Court of Appeal in Northern Ireland gave the direction, the appropriate court is the Crown Court or the Crown Court in Northern Ireland, as the case may be.

(5) Where the High Court of Justiciary directed release, the appropriate court is—

    (a) that court; or

    (b) in a case where release was directed by that court on appeal, the court from which the appeal was made.

7.—(1) A constable or immigration officer may arrest without warrant any person who is subject to restrictions imposed by a court under this Schedule and who at the time of the arrest is in the relevant part of the United Kingdom—

    (a) if he has reasonable grounds to suspect that that person is contravening or has contravened any of those restrictions; or

    (b) if he has reasonable grounds for believing that that person is likely to contravene any of them.

(2) In sub-paragraph (2) above 'the relevant part of the United Kingdom' means—

    (a) England and Wales, in a case where a court with jurisdiction in England or Wales imposed the restrictions;

    (b) Scotland, in a case where a court with jurisdiction in Scotland imposed them; and

    (c) Northern Ireland, in a case where a court in Northern Ireland imposed them.

8.—(1) A person arrested in [England or Wales in pursuance of paragraph 7 above shall be brought as soon as practicable and in any event within twenty-four hours after his arrest before a justice of the peace in England or Wales, and a person arrested in Northern Ireland in pursuance of paragraph 7 above shall be brought as soon as practicable and in any event within 24 hours after his arrest before a justice of the peace for the petty sessions … district in which he was arrested.

(2) In reckoning for the purposes of this paragraph any period of 24 hours, no account shall be taken of Christmas Day, Good Friday or any Sunday.

9.—(1) A person arrested in Scotland in pursuance of paragraph 7 above shall wherever practicable be brought before the appropriate court not later than in the course of the first day after his arrest, such day not being a Saturday, a Sunday or a court holiday prescribed for that court under section 10 of the Bail etc. (Scotland) Act 1980.

(2) Nothing in this paragraph shall prevent a person arrested in Scotland being brought before a court on a Saturday, a Sunday or such a court holiday as is mentioned in sub-paragraph (1) above where the court is, in pursuance of section 10 of the said Act of 1980, sitting on such day for the disposal of criminal business.

10. Any justice of the peace or court before whom a person is brought by virtue of paragraph 8 or 9 above—

(a) if of the opinion that that person is contravening, has contravened or is likely to contravene any restriction imposed on him by a court under this Schedule, may direct—

(i) that he be detained; or

(ii) that he be released subject to such restrictions as to his residence and reporting to the police as the court may direct; and

(b) if not of that opinion, shall release him without altering the restrictions as to his residence and his reporting to the police.]

Note: Paragraph 1: has effect in a form modified by and in circumstances specified by the Channel Tunnel (International Arrangements) Order (SI 1993/1813) as amended by SIs 1994/1405, 2000/913, 2001/178, 2001/3707, 2006/1003 and 2007/3759. Paragraph 2: words in second square brackets in para 2(1) and paras 2(1A), (5) and (6) added by Criminal Justice Act 1982. Words in first square brackets in para 2(2) substituted by Sch 7 Nationality, Immigration and Asylum Act 2002 from 1 April 2003 (SI 2003/754). Other words in square brackets in paras 2(1) and (2) substituted by Sch 2 Asylum and Immigration (Treatment of Claimants, etc.) Act 2004 from 4 April 2005 (SI 2005/565). Other words in square brackets in para 2(2) and para 2(4A) inserted by Immigration and Asylum Act 1999, s 54 from 10 February 2003 (SI 2003/2). Words in first square brackets in para 2(5) added by Immigration Act 1988, s 10, other words in square brackets inserted by Asylum and Immigration Act 1996 from 1 October 1996. Words in last square brackets in para 2(4) inserted by Immigration, Asylum and Nationality Act 2006 from 31 August 2006 (SI 2006/2226). Paragraph 3 substituted by Sch 7 Nationality, Immigration and Asylum Act 2002 from 1 April 2003 (SI 2003/754, which sets out transitional provisions). Paragraphs 4–10: added by Criminal Justice Act 1982. Paragraph 4: words in square brackets added by Immigration Act 1988, s 10. Paragraph 6: sub-para (2A) inserted and words omitted from sub-para (3) by Courts Act 2003, Sch 8 para 150 from 1 April 2005 (SI 2005/910). Paragraph 8: words substituted in and omitted from sub-para (1) by Courts Act 2003, Sch para 150 from 1 April 2005 (SI 2005/910).

Section 9   SCHEDULE 4

INTEGRATION WITH UNITED KINGDOM LAW OF
IMMIGRATION LAW OF ISLANDS
Leave to enter

1.—(1) Where under the immigration laws of any of the Islands a person is or has been given leave to enter or remain in the island, or is or has been refused leave, this Act shall have effect in relation to him, if he is not [a British citizen], as if the leave were leave (of like duration) given under this Act to enter or remain in the United Kingdom, or, as the case may be, as if he had under this Act been refused leave to enter the United Kingdom.

(2) Where under the immigration laws of any of the Islands a person has a limited leave to enter or remain in the island subject to any such conditions as are authorised in the United Kingdom by section 3(1) of this Act (being conditions imposed by notice given to him, whether the notice of

leave or a subsequent notice), then on his coming to the United Kingdom this Act shall apply, if he is not [a British citizen], as if those conditions related to his stay in the United Kingdom and had been imposed by notice under this Act.

(3) Without prejudice to the generality of sub-paragraphs (1) and (2) above, anything having effect in the United Kingdom by virtue of either of those sub-paragraphs may in relation to the United Kingdom be varied or revoked under this Act in like manner, and subject to the like appeal (if any), as if it had originated under this Act as mentioned in that sub-paragraph.

(4) Where anything having effect in the United Kingdom by virtue of sub-paragraph (1) or (2) above ceases to have effect or is altered in effect as mentioned in sub-paragraph (3) or otherwise by anything done under this Act, sub-paragraph (1) or (2) shall not thereafter apply to it or, as the case may be, shall apply to it as so altered in effect.

(5) Nothing in this paragraph shall be taken as conferring on a person a right of appeal under this Act against any decision or action taken in any of the Islands.

2. Notwithstanding section 3(4) of this Act, leave given to a person under this Act to enter or remain in the United Kingdom shall not continue to apply on his return to the United Kingdom after an absence if he has during that absence entered any of the Islands in circumstances in which he is required under the immigration laws of that island to obtain leave to enter.

Deportation

[3.—(1) This Act has effect in relation to a person who is subject to an Islands deportation order as if the order were a deportation order made against him under this Act.

(2) Sub-paragraph (1) does not apply if the person concerned is—
 (a) a British citizen;
 (b) an EEA national;
 (c) a member of the family of an EEA national; or
 (d) a member of the family of a British citizen who is neither such a citizen nor an EEA national.

(3) The Secretary of State does not, as a result of sub-paragraph (1), have power to revoke an Islands deportation order.

(4) In any particular case, the Secretary of State may direct that paragraph (b), (c) or (d) of sub-paragraph (2) is not to apply in relation to the Islands deportation order.

(5) Nothing in this paragraph makes it unlawful for a person in respect of whom an Islands deportation order is in force in any of the Islands to enter the United Kingdom on his way from that island to a place outside the United Kingdom.

(6) 'Islands deportation order' means an order made under the immigration laws of any of the Islands under which a person is, or has been, ordered to leave the island and forbidden to return.

(7) Subsections (10) and (12) to (14) of section 80 of the Immigration and Asylum Act 1999 apply for the purposes of this section as they apply for the purposes of that section.]

Illegal entrants

4. Notwithstanding anything in section 1(3) of this Act, it shall not be lawful for a person who is not [a British citizen] to enter the United Kingdom from any of the Islands where his presence was unlawful under the immigration laws of that island, unless he is given leave to enter.

Note: Words in square brackets substituted by British Nationality Act 1981, s 39(6). Paragraph 3 substituted by Immigration and Asylum Act 1999 from 2 October 2000.

SCHEDULE 5

Note: Schedule 5 repealed by Immigration and Asylum Act 1999 from 14 February 2000.

Section 34

SCHEDULE 6

...

REPEALS

British Nationality Act 1981
(1981, c. 61)

Arrangement of Sections

PART I. BRITISH CITIZENSHIP

Acquisition after commencement

PART II. [BRITISH OVERSEAS TERRITORIES] CITIZENSHIP
Acquisition after commencement

SCHEDULES

An Act to make fresh provision about citizenship and nationality, and to amend the Immigration Act 1971 as regards the right of abode in the United Kingdom.

[30 October 1981]

PART I

BRITISH CITIZENSHIP

Acquisition after commencement

1. Acquisition by birth or adoption

(1) A person born in the United Kingdom after commencement [, or in a qualifying territory on or after the appointed day,] shall be a British citizen if at the time of the birth his father or mother is—

(a) a British citizen; or

(b) settled in the United Kingdom [or that territory].

[(1A) A person born in the United Kingdom or a qualifying territory on or after the relevant day shall be a British citizen if at the time of the birth his father or mother is a member of the armed forces.]

(2) A new-born infant who, after commencement, is found abandoned in the United Kingdom [, or on or after the appointed day is found abandoned in a qualifying territory,] shall, unless the contrary is shown, be deemed for the purposes of subsection (1)—

(a) to have been born in the United Kingdom after commencement; [or in that territory on or after the appointed day] and

(b) to have been born to a parent who at the time of the birth was a British citizen or settled in the United Kingdom [or that territory].

(3) A person born in the United Kingdom after commencement who is not a British citizen by virtue of subsection (1)[, (1A) or (2) shall be entitled to be registered as a British citizen if, while he is a minor—

(a) his father or mother becomes a British citizen or becomes settled in the United Kingdom; and

(b) an application is made for his registration as a British citizen.

[(3A) A person born in the United Kingdom on or after the relevant day who is not a British citizen by virtue of subsection (1), (1A) or (2) shall be entitled to be registered as a British citizen if, while he is a minor—

(a) his father or mother becomes a member of the armed forces; and

(b) an application is made for his registration as a British citizen.]

(4) A person born in the United Kingdom after commencement who is not a British citizen by virtue of subsection (1) [,(1A)] or (2) shall be entitled, on an application for his registration as a British citizen made at any time after he has attained the age of ten years, to be registered as such a citizen if, as regards each of the first ten years of that person's life, the number of days on which he was absent from the United Kingdom in that year does not exceed 90.

[(5) Where—

(a) any court in the United Kingdom [or, on or after the appointed day, any court in a qualifying territory] makes an order authorising the adoption of a minor who is not a British citizen; or

(b) a minor who is not a British citizen is adopted under a Convention adoption, that minor shall, if the requirements of subsection (5A) are met, be a British citizen as from the date on which the order is made or the Convention adoption is effected, as the case may be {effected under the law of a country or territory outside the United Kingdom}.

(5A) Those requirements are that on the date on which the order is made or the Convention adoption is effected (as the case may be)—

(a) the adopter or, in the case of a joint adoption, one of the adopters is a British citizen; and

(b) in a case within subsection (5)(b), the adopter or, in the case of a joint adoption, both of the adopters are habitually resident in the United Kingdom {or in a designated territory}.]

(6) Where an order [or a Convention adoption] in consequence of which any person became a British citizen by virtue of subsection (5) ceases to have effect, whether on annulment or otherwise, the cesser shall not effect the status of that person as a British citizen.

(7) If in the special circumstances of any particular case the Secretary of State thinks fit, he may for the purposes of subsection (4) treat the person to whom the application relates as fulfilling the requirement specified in that subsection although, as regards any one or more of the first ten years of that person's life, the number of days on which he was absent from the United Kingdom in that year or each of the years in question exceeds 90.

(8) In this section and elsewhere in this Act 'settled' has the meaning given by section 50 ...

[(9) The relevant day for the purposes of subsection (1A) or (3A) is the day appointed for the commencement of section 42 of the Borders, Citizenship and Immigration Act 2009 (which inserted those subsections)].

Note: Subsection (5) substituted and words in square brackets in sub-s (6) inserted by Adoption (Intercountry Aspects) Act 1999, s 7 from 1 June 2003 (SI 2003/362). Subsections (1A), (3A) and (9) and words in square brackets in sub-ss (3)–(4) inserted by s 42 Borders Citizenship and Immigration Act 2009 from 13 January 2010 (SI 2009/2731). Other words in square brackets inserted by Sch 1 British Overseas Territories Act 2002, from 21 May 2002 (SI 2002/1252). The reference in subsection (5)(a) to an order authorising the adoption of a minor is to be read as including a reference to a parental order in respect of a minor and the reference in subsection (5A) (a) to the adopter or, in the case of a joint adoption, one of the adopters is to be read as including a reference to one of the persons who obtained the parental order (SI 2010/985). Words in curly brackets inserted and words omitted from sub-s (8) by Adoption and Children Act 2002 from 30 December 2005.

2. Acquisition by descent

(1) A person born outside the United Kingdom [and the qualifying territories] after commencement shall be a British citizen if at the time of the birth his father or mother—

(a) is a British citizen otherwise than by descent; or

(b) is a British citizen and is serving outside the United Kingdom [and the qualifying territories] in service to which this paragraph applies, his or her recruitment for that service having taken place in the United Kingdom [or a qualifying territory]; or

(c) is a British citizen and is serving outside the United Kingdom [and the qualifying territories] in service under a {EU} institution, his or her recruitment for that service having taken place in a country which at the time of the recruitment was a member of the {European Union}.

(2) Paragraph (b) of subsection (1) applies to—

(a) Crown service under the government of the United Kingdom [or of a qualifying territory]; and

(b) service of any description for the time being designated under subsection (3).

(3) For the purposes of this section the Secretary of State may by order made by statutory instrument designate any description of service which he considers to be closely associated with the activities outside the United Kingdom [and the qualifying territories] of Her Majesty's government in the United Kingdom [or in a qualifying territory].

(4) Any order made under subsection (3) shall be subject to annulment in pursuance of a resolution of either House of Parliament.

Note: Words in square brackets inserted by Sch 1 British Overseas Territories Act 2002 from 21 May 2002 (SI 2002/1252), but without effect to the operation of this section in relation to persons born before that date.

3. Acquisition by registration: minors

(1) If while a person is a minor an application is made for his registration as a British citizen, the Secretary of State may, if he thinks fit, cause him to be registered as such a citizen.

(2) A person born outside the United Kingdom [and the qualifying territories] shall be entitled, on an application for his registration as a British citizen made [while he is a minor], to be registered as such a citizen if the requirements specified in subsection (3) or, in the case of a person born stateless, the requirements specified in paragraphs (a) and (b) of that subsection, are fulfilled in the case of either that person's father or his mother ('the parent in question').

(3) The requirements referred to in subsection (2) are—

(a) that the parent in question was a British citizen by descent at the time of the birth; and

(b) that the father or mother of the parent in question—

(i) was a British citizen otherwise than by descent at the time of the birth of the parent in question; or

(ii) became a British citizen otherwise than by descent at commencement, or would have become such a citizen otherwise than by descent at commencement but for his or her death; and

(c) that, as regards some period of three years ending with a date not later than the date of the birth—

(i) the parent in question was in the United Kingdom [or a qualifying territory] at the beginning of that period; and

(ii) the number of days on which the parent in question was absent from the United Kingdom [and the qualifying territories] in that period does not exceed 270.

(4) ...

(5) A person born outside the United Kingdom [and the qualifying territories] shall be entitled, on an application for his registration as a British citizen made while he is a minor, to be registered as such a citizen if the following requirements are satisfied, namely—

(a) that at the time of that person's birth his father or mother was a British citizen by descent; and

(b) subject to subsection (6), that that person and his father and mother were in the United Kingdom [or a qualifying territory] at the beginning of the period of three years ending with the date of the application and that, in the case of each of them, the number of days on which the person in question was absent from the United Kingdom [and the qualifying territories] in that period does not exceed 270; and

(c) subject to subsection (6), that the consent of his father and mother to the registration has been signified in the prescribed manner.

(6) In the case of an application under subsection (5) for the registration of a person as a British citizen—

(a) if his father or mother dies, or their marriage [or civil partnership] was terminated, on or before the date of the application, or his father and mother were legally separated on that date, the references to his father and mother in paragraph (b) of that subsection shall be read either as references to his father or as references to his mother; [and]

(b) if his father or mother died on or before that date, the reference to his father and mother in paragraph (c) of that subsection shall be read as a reference to either of them; [. . .]

(c) [. . .]

Note: Last word in square brackets in sub-s (6)(a) inserted and words deleted from sub-ss (6)(b) and (c) by, Nationality, Immigration and Asylum Act 2002, s 9 from 7 November 2002, with effect in relation to children born on or after a date to be appointed. Other words in square brackets inserted by Sch 1 British Overseas Territories Act 2002, from 21 May 2002 (SI 2002/1252) but without effect to the operation of this section in relation to persons born before that date. Words in first square brackets in sub-s (6)(a) inserted by Sch 27 Civil Partnership Act 2004 from 5 December 2005 (SI 2005/3175). Words in 2nd square brackets in sub-s (2) substituted and sub-s (4) revoked by s 43 Borders, Citizenship and Immigration Act 2009 from 13 January 2010 (SI 2009/2731).

4. Acquisition by registration: [British overseas territories] citizens etc

(1) This section applies to any person who is a [British overseas territories] citizen, [a British National (Overseas)] a British Overseas citizen, a British subject under this Act or a British protected person.

(2) A person to whom this section applies shall be entitled, on an application for his registration as a British citizen, to be registered as such a citizen if the following requirements are satisfied in the case of that person, namely—

(a) subject to subsection (3), that he was in the United Kingdom at the beginning of the period of five years ending with the date of the application and that the number of days on which he was absent from the United Kingdom in that period does not exceed 450; and

(b) that the number of days on which he was absent from the United Kingdom in the period of twelve months so ending does not exceed 90; and

(c) that he was not at any time in the period of twelve months so ending subject under the immigration law to any restriction on the period for which he might remain in the United Kingdom; and

(d) that he was not at any time in the period of five years so ending in the United Kingdom in breach of the immigration laws.

(3) So much of subsection (2)(a) as requires the person in question to have been in the United Kingdom at the beginning of the period there mentioned shall not apply in relation to a person who was settled in the United Kingdom immediately before commencement.

(4) If in the special circumstances of any particular case the Secretary of State thinks fit, he may for the purposes of subsection (2) do all or any of the following things, namely—

(a) treat the person to whom the application relates as fulfilling the requirement specified in subsection (2)(a) or subsection (2)(b), or both, although the number of days on which he was absent from the United Kingdom in the period there mentioned exceeds the number there mentioned;

(b) disregard any such restriction as is mentioned in subsection (2)(c), not being a restriction to which that person was subject on the date of the application;

(c) treat that person as fulfilling the requirement specified in subsection (2)(d) although he was in the United Kingdom in breach of the immigration laws in the period there mentioned.

(5) If, on an application for registration as a British citizen made by a person to whom this section applies, the Secretary of State is satisfied that the applicant has at any time served in service to which this subsection applies, he may, if he thinks fit in the special circumstances of the applicant's case, cause him to be registered as such a citizen.

(6) Subsection (5) applies to—

(a) Crown service under the government of a [British overseas territory]; and

(b) paid or unpaid service (not falling within paragraph (a)) as a member of any body established by law in a [British overseas territory] members of which are appointed by or on behalf of the Crown.

Note: Words in second square brackets in s 4(1) inserted by SI 1986/948. Dependent territories became British overseas territories from 26 February 2002, British Overseas Territories Act 2002, s 1.

[4A. Acquisition by registration: further provision for British overseas territories citizens

(1) If an application is made to register as a British citizen a person who is a British overseas territories citizen, the Secretary of State may if he thinks fit cause the person to be so registered.

(2) Subsection (1) does not apply in the case of a British overseas territories citizen who—

(a) is such a citizen by virtue only of a connection with the Sovereign Base Areas of Akrotiri and Dhekelia; or

(b) has ceased to be a British citizen as a result of a declaration of renunciation.]

Note: Section 4A inserted by British Overseas Territories Act, s 4 from 21 May 2002 (SI 2002/1252).

[4B. Acquisition by registration: certain persons without other citizenship

(1) This section applies to a person who has the status of—

(a) British Overseas citizen,

(b) British subject under this Act, …

(c) British protected person [, or

(d) British National (Overseas).]

(2) A person to whom this section applies shall be entitled to be registered as a British citizen if—

(a) he applies for registration under this section,

(b) the Secretary of State is satisfied that the person does not have, apart from the status mentioned in subsection (1), any citizenship or nationality, and

(c) the Secretary of State is satisfied that the person has not after [the relevant day] renounced, voluntarily relinquished or lost through action or inaction any citizenship or nationality.]

[(3) For the purposes of subsection (2)(c), the "relevant day" means—

(a) in the case of a person to whom this section applies by virtue of subsection (1)(d) only, 19 March 2009, and

(b) in any other case, 4 July 2002.]

Note: Section 4B inserted by Nationality, Immigration and Asylum Act 2002, s 12 from 30 April 2003 (SI 2003/754). Sub-ss (1)(d) and (3) inserted and words in square brackets in sub-s (2)(c) substituted by s 44 Borders, Citizenship and Immigration Act 2009 from 13 January 2010 (SI 2009/2731).

[4C. Acquisition by registration: certain persons born between 1961 and 1983

(1) A person is entitled to be registered as a British citizen if—

(a) he applies for registration under this section, and

(b) he satisfies each of the following conditions.

(**2**) The first condition is that the applicant was born [...] before 1 January 1983.

[(**3**) The second condition is that the applicant would at some time before 1 January 1983 have become a citizen of the United Kingdom and Colonies—

(a) under section 5 of, or paragraph 3 of Schedule 3 to, the 1948 Act if assumption A had applied,

(b) under section 12(3), (4) or (5) of that Act if assumption B had applied and as a result of its application the applicant would have been a British subject immediately before 1st January 1949, or

(c) under section 12(2) of that Act if one or both of the following had applied—

(i) assumption A had applied;

(ii) assumption B had applied and as a result of its application the applicant would have been a British subject immediately before 1st January 1949.

(**3A**) Assumption A is that—

(a) section 5 or 12(2) of, or paragraph 3 of Schedule 3 to, the 1948 Act (as the case may be) provided for citizenship by descent from a mother in the same terms as it provided for citizenship by descent from a father, and

(b) references in that provision to a father were references to the applicant's mother.

(**3B**) Assumption B is that—

(a) a provision of the law at some time before 1st January 1949 which provided for a nationality status to be acquired by descent from a father provided in the same terms for its acquisition by descent from a mother, and

(b) references in that provision to a father were references to the applicant's mother.

(**3C**) For the purposes of subsection (3B), a nationality status is acquired by a person ("P") by descent where its acquisition—

(a) depends, amongst other things, on the nationality status of one or both of P's parents, and

(b) does not depend upon an application being made for P's registration as a person who has the status in question.

(**3D**) For the purposes of subsection (3), it is not to be assumed that any registration or other requirements of the provisions mentioned in that subsection or in subsection (3B) were met.]

(**4**) The third condition is that immediately before 1st January 1983 the applicant would have had the right of abode in the United Kingdom by virtue of section 2 of the Immigration Act 1971 (c. 77) had he become a citizen of the United Kingdom and Colonies as described in subsection (3) above.]

[(**5**) For the purposes of the interpretation of section 5 of the 1948 Act in its application in the case of assumption A to a case of descent from a mother, the reference in the proviso to subsection (1) of that section to "a citizen of the United Kingdom and Colonies by descent only" includes a reference to a female person who became a citizen of the United Kingdom and Colonies by virtue of—

(a) section 12(2), (4) or (6) only of the 1948 Act,

(b) section 13(2) of that Act,

(c) paragraph 3 of Schedule 3 to that Act, or

(d) section 1(1)(a) or (c) of the British Nationality (No. 2) Act 1964.]

Note: Section 4C inserted by Nationality, Immigration and Asylum Act 2002, s 13 from 30 April 2003 (SI 2003/754). Words omitted in sub-ss (2), sub-ss (3) substituted and sub-ss (5) inserted by s 45 Borders, Citizenship and Immigration Act 2009 from 13 January 2010 (SI 2009/2731).

4D. Acquisition by registration: children of members of the armed forces

(1) A person ('P') born outside the United Kingdom and the qualifying territories on or after the relevant day is entitled to be registered as a British citizen if—
   (a) an application is made for P's registration under this section; and
   (b) each of the following conditions is satisfied.

(2) The first condition is that, at the time of P's birth, P's father or mother was—
   (a) a member of the armed forces; and
   (b) serving outside the United Kingdom and the qualifying territories.

(3) The second condition is that, if P is a minor on the date of the application, the consent of P's father and mother to P's registration as a British citizen has been signified in the prescribed manner.

(4) But if P's father or mother has died on or before the date of the application, the reference in subsection (3) to P's father and mother is to be read as a reference to either of them.

(5) The Secretary of State may, in the special circumstances of a particular case, waive the need for the second condition to be satisfied.

(6) The relevant day for the purposes of this section is the day appointed for the commencement of section 46 of the Borders, Citizenship and Immigration Act 2009 (which inserted this section).

Note: Section 4D inserted by s 46 Borders, Citizenship and Immigration Act 2009 from 13 January 2010 (SI 2009/2731).

5. Acquisition by registration: nationals for purposes of the [EU] Treaties

A [British overseas territories] citizen who falls to be treated as a national of the United Kingdom for the purposes of the [EU] Treaties shall be entitled to be registered as a British citizen if an application is made for his registration as such a citizen.

Note: British dependent territories became British overseas territories from 26 February 2002, British Overseas Territories Act 2002, s 1.

6. Acquisition by naturalisation

(1) If, on an application for naturalisation as a British citizen made by a person of full age and capacity, the Secretary of State is satisfied that the applicant fulfils the requirements of Schedule 1 for naturalisation as such a citizen under this subsection, he may, if he thinks fit, grant to him a certificate of naturalisation as such a citizen.

(2) If, on an application for naturalisation as a British citizen made by a person of full age and capacity who on the date of the application [has a relevant family association], the Secretary of State is satisfied that the applicant fulfils the requirements of Schedule 1 for naturalisation as such a citizen under this subsection, he may, if he thinks fit, grant to him a certificate of naturalisation as such a citizen.

[(3) For the purposes of this section and Schedule 1, a person ("A") has a relevant family association if A has a connection of a prescribed description to a person of a prescribed description.

(4) If in the special circumstances of any particular case the Secretary of State thinks fit, the Secretary of State may for the purposes of subsection (3) treat A as having a relevant family association on the date of the application although the relevant family association ceased to exist before that date.]

Note: Words in square brackets substituted and sub-ss(3)–(4) inserted by s 40 Borders, Citizenship and Immigration Act 2009 from a date to be appointed.

Acquisition after commencement: special cases

7. ...

Note: Section 7 repealed by Sch 2 of Nationality, Immigration and Asylum Act 2002 from 1 April 2003 (SI 2003/754).

8. ...

Note: Section 8 repealed by Sch 2 of Nationality, Immigration and Asylum Act 2002 from 1 April 2003 (SI 2003/754).

9. ...

Note: Section 9 repealed by Sch 2 of Nationality, Immigration and Asylum Act 2002 from 1 April 2003 (SI 2003/754).

10. Registration following renunciation of citizenship of UK and Colonies

(1) Subject to subsection (3), a person shall be entitled, on an application for his registration as a British citizen, to be registered as such a citizen if immediately before commencement he would (had he applied for it) have been entitled under section 1(1) of the British Nationality Act 1964 (resumption of citizenship) to be registered as a citizen of the United Kingdom and Colonies by virtue of having an appropriate qualifying connection with the United Kingdom or, [. . .] by virtue of having been married before commencement to a person who has, or would if living have, such a connection.

(2) On an application for his registration as a British citizen made by a person of full capacity who had before commencement ceased to be a citizen of the United Kingdom and Colonies as a result of a declaration of renunciation, the Secretary of State may, if he thinks fit, cause that person to be registered as a British citizen if that person—

(a) has an appropriate qualifying connection with the United Kingdom; or

(b) [...] has been married to [, or has been the civil partner of,] a person who has, or would if living have, such a connection.

(3) A person shall not be entitled to registration under subsection (1) on more than one occasion.

(4) For the purposes of this section a person shall be taken to have an appropriate qualifying connection with the United Kingdom if he, his father or his father's father—

(a) was born in the United Kingdom; or

(b) is or was a person naturalised in the United Kingdom; or

(c) was registered as a citizen of the United Kingdom and Colonies in the United Kingdom or in a country which at the time was mentioned in section 1(3) of the 1948 Act.

Note: The words deleted from sub-ss (1) and (2) repealed by Nationality, Immigration and Asylum Act 2002, s 5 from 7 November 2002 in relation to applications made after that date or not yet decided before that date (s 162(3)). Words in square brackets in sub-s (2) inserted by Sch 27 Civil Partnership Act 2004 from 5 December 2005 (SI 2005/3175).

Acquisition at commencement

11. Citizens of UK and Colonies who are to become British citizens at commencement

(1) Subject to subsection (2), a person who immediately before commencement—

(a) was a citizen of the United Kingdom and Colonies; and

(b) had the right of abode in the United Kingdom under the Immigration Act 1971 as then in force,

shall at commencement become a British citizen.

(2) A person who was registered as a citizen of the United Kingdom and Colonies under section 1 of the British Nationality (No. 2) Act 1964 (stateless persons) on the ground mentioned in subsection (1)(a) of that section (namely that his mother was a citizen of the United Kingdom and Colonies at the time when he was born) shall not become a British citizen under subsection (1) unless—

(a) his mother becomes a British citizen under subsection (1) or would have done so but for her death; or

(b) immediately before commencement he had the right of abode in the United Kingdom by virtue of section 2(1)(c) of the Immigration Act 1971 as then in force (settlement in United Kingdom, combined with five or more years' ordinary residence there as a citizen of the United Kingdom and Colonies).

(3) A person who—

(a) immediately before commencement was a citizen of the United Kingdom and Colonies by virtue of having been registered under subsection (6) of section 12 of the 1948 Act (British subjects before commencement of 1948 Act becoming citizens of United Kingdom and Colonies) under arrangements made by virtue of subsection (7) of that section (registration in independent Commonwealth country by United Kingdom High Commissioner); and

(b) was so registered on an application under the said subsection (6) based on the applicant's descent in the male line from a person ('the relevant person') possessing one of the qualifications specified in subsection (1)(a) and (b) of that section (birth or naturalisation in the United Kingdom and Colonies),

shall at commencement become a British citizen if the relevant person was born or naturalised in the United Kingdom.

Renunciation and resumption

12. Renunciation

(1) If any British citizen of full age and capacity makes in the prescribed manner a declaration of renunciation of British citizenship, then, subject to subsections (3) and (4), the Secretary of State shall cause the declaration to be registered.

(2) On the registration of a declaration made in pursuance of this section the person who made it shall cease to be a British citizen.

(3) A declaration made by a person in pursuance of this section shall not be registered unless the Secretary of State is satisfied that the person who made it will after the registration have or acquire some citizenship or nationality other than British citizenship; and if that person does not have any such citizenship or nationality on the date of registration and does not acquire some such citizenship or nationality within six months from that date, he shall be, and be deemed to have remained, a British citizen notwithstanding the registration.

(4) The Secretary of State may withhold registration of any declaration made in pursuance of this section if it is made during any war in which Her Majesty may be engaged in right of Her Majesty's government in the United Kingdom.

(5) For the purposes of this section any person who has been married [or has formed a civil partnership] shall be deemed to be of full age.

Note: Words in square brackets in sub-s (5) inserted by Sch 27 Civil Partnership Act 2004 from 5 December 2005 (SI 2005/3175).

13. Resumption

(1) Subject to subsection (2), a person who has ceased to be a British citizen as a result of a declaration of renunciation shall be entitled, on an application for his registration as a British citizen, to be registered as such a citizen if—

(a) he is of full capacity; and

(b) his renunciation of British citizenship was necessary to enable him to retain or acquire some other citizenship or nationality.

(2) A person shall not be entitled to registration under subsection (1) on more than one occasion.

(3) If a person of full capacity who has ceased to be a British citizen as a result of a declaration of renunciation (for whatever reason made) makes an application for his registration as such a citizen, the Secretary of State may, if he thinks fit, cause him to be registered as such a citizen.

Supplementary

14. Meaning of British citizen 'by descent'

(1) For the purposes of this Act a British citizen is a British citizen 'by descent' if and only if—

(a) he is a person born outside the United Kingdom after commencement who is a British citizen by virtue of section 2(1)(a) only or by virtue of registration under section 3(2) or 9; or

(b) subject to subsection (2), he is a person born outside the United Kingdom before commencement who became a British citizen at commencement and immediately before commencement—

(i) was a citizen of the United Kingdom and Colonies by virtue of section 5 of the 1948 Act (citizenship by descent); or

(ii) was a person who, under any provision of the British Nationality Acts 1948 to 1965, was deemed for the purposes of the proviso to section 5(1) of the 1948 Act to be a citizen of the United Kingdom and Colonies by descent only, or would have been so deemed if male; or

(iii) had the right of abode in the United Kingdom by virtue only of paragraph (b) of subsection (1) of section 2 of the Immigration Act 1971 as then in force (connection with United Kingdom through parent or grandparent), or by virtue only of that paragraph and paragraph (c) of that subsection (settlement in United Kingdom with five years' ordinary residence there), or by virtue only of being or having been the wife of a person who immediately before commencement had that right by virtue only of the said paragraph (b) or the said paragraphs (b) and (c); or

(iv) being a woman, was a citizen of the United Kingdom and Colonies as a result of her registration as such a citizen under section 6(2) of the 1948 Act by virtue of having been married to a man who at commencement became a British citizen by descent or would have done so but for his having died or ceased to be a citizen of the United Kingdom and Colonies as a result of a declaration of renunciation; or

(c) he is a British citizen by virtue of registration under section 3(1) and either—

(i) his father or mother was a British citizen at the time of the birth; or

(ii) his father or mother was a citizen of the United Kingdom and Colonies at that time and became a British citizen at commencement, or would have done so but for his or her death; or

(d) he is a British citizen by virtue of registration under [section 4B [4C] or 5]; or

(e) subject to subsection (2), being a woman born outside the United Kingdom before commencement, she is a British citizen as a result of her registration as such a citizen under section 8 by virtue of being or having been married to a man who at commencement became a British citizen by descent or would have done so but for his having died or ceased to be a citizen of the United Kingdom and Colonies as a result of a declaration of renunciation; or

(f) he is a British citizen by virtue of registration under section 10 who, having before commencement ceased to be a citizen of the United Kingdom and Colonies as a result of a declaration of renunciation, would, if he had not so ceased, have at commencement become a British citizen by descent by virtue of paragraph (b); or

(g) he is a British citizen by virtue of registration under section 13 who, immediately before he ceased to be a British citizen as a result of a declaration of renunciation, was such a citizen by descent; or

(h) he is a person born in a [British overseas territory] after commencement who is a British citizen by virtue of paragraph 2 of Schedule 2.

(2) A person born outside the United Kingdom before commencement is not a British citizen 'by descent' by virtue of subsection (1)(b) or (e) if his father was at the time of his birth serving outside the United Kingdom—

(a) in service of a description mentioned in subsection (3), his recruitment for the service in question having taken place in the United Kingdom; or

(b) in service under a [EU] institution, his recruitment for that service having taken place in a country which at the time of the recruitment was a member of the [European Union].

(3) The descriptions of service referred to in subsection (2) are—

(a) Crown service under the government of the United Kingdom; and

(b) service of any description at any time designated under section 2(3).

Note: First words in square brackets in sub-s (1)(d) substituted by Nationality, Immigration and Asylum Act 2002, s 12 from 30 April 2003 (SI 2003/754). Second words in square brackets in sub-s (1)(d) inserted by Nationality, Immigration and Asylum Act 2002, s 13 from 30 April 2003 (SI 2003/754). British dependent territories became British overseas territories from 26 February 2002, British Overseas Territories Act 2002, s 1.

PART II

[British Overseas Territories] Citizenship

Acquisition after commencement

15. Acquisition by birth or adoption

(1) A person born in a [British overseas territory] after commencement shall be a [British overseas territories] citizen if at the time of the birth his father or mother is—

(a) a [British overseas territories] citizen; or

(b) settled in a [British overseas territory].

(2) A new-born infant who, after commencement, is found abandoned in a [British overseas territory] shall, unless the contrary is shown, be deemed for the purposes of subsection (1)—

(a) to have been born in that territory after commencement; and

(b) to have been born to a parent who at the time of the birth was a [British over-seas territories] citizen or settled in a [British overseas territory].

(3) A person born in a [British overseas territory] after commencement who is not a [British overseas territories] citizen by virtue of subsection (1) or (2) shall be entitled to be registered as such a citizen if, while he is a minor—

(a) his father or mother becomes such a citizen or becomes settled in a [British overseas territory]; and

(b) an application is made for his registration as such a citizen.

(4) A person born in a [British overseas territory] after commencement who is not a [British overseas territories] citizen by virtue of subsection (1) or (2) shall be entitled, on an application for his registration as a [British overseas territories] citizen made at any time after he has attained the age of ten years, to be registered as such a citizen if, as regards each of the first ten years of that person's life, the number of days on which he was absent from that territory in that year does not exceed 90.

(5) Where after commencement an order authorising the adoption of a minor who is not a [British overseas territories] citizen is made by a court in any [British overseas territory], he shall be a [British overseas territories] citizen as from the date on which the order is made if the adopter or, in the case of a joint adoption, one of the adopters, is a [British overseas territories] citizen on that date.

[(5A) Where—

(a) a minor who is not a British overseas territories citizen is adopted under a Convention adoption,

(b) on the date on which the adoption is effected—

(i) the adopter or, in the case of a joint adoption, one of the adopters is a British overseas territories citizen, and

(ii) the adopter or, in the case of a joint adoption, both of the adopters are habitually resident in a designated territory, and

(c) the Convention adoption is effected under the law of a country or territory outside the designated territory,

the minor shall be a British overseas territories citizen as from that date.]

(6) Where an order [or a Convention adoption] in consequence of which any person became a [British overseas territories] citizen by virtue of subsection (5) ceases to have effect, whether on annulment or otherwise, the cesser shall not affect the status of that person as such a citizen.

(7) If in the special circumstances of any particular case the Secretary of State thinks fit, he may for the purposes of subsection (4) treat the person to whom the application relates as fulfilling the requirements specified in that subsection although, as regards any one or more of the first ten years of that person's life, the number of days on which he was absent from the [British overseas territory] there mentioned in that year or each of the years in question exceeds 90.

Note: British dependent territories became British overseas territories from 26 February 2002, British Overseas Territories Act 2002, s 1. Sub-s (5A) and words in sub-s (6) inserted from 30 December 2005 by Adoption and Children Act 2002.

16. Acquisition by descent

(1) A person born outside the [British overseas territories] after commencement shall be a [British overseas territories] citizen if at the time of the birth his father or mother—
    (a) is such a citizen otherwise than by descent; or
    (b) is such a citizen and is serving outside the [British overseas territories] in service to which this paragraph applies, his or her recruitment for that service having taken place in a [British overseas territory].

(2) Paragraph (b) of subsection (1) applies to—
    (a) Crown service under the government of a [British overseas territory]; and
    (b) service of any description for the time being designated under subsection (3).

(3) For the purposes of this section the Secretary of State may by order made by statutory instrument designate any description of service which he considers to be closely associated with the activities outside the [British overseas territories] of the government of any [British overseas territory].

(4) Any order made under subsection (3) shall be subject to annulment in pursuance of a resolution of either House of Parliament.

Note: British dependent territories became British overseas territories from 26 February 2002, British Overseas Territories Act 2002, s 1.

17. Acquisition by registration: minors

(1) If while a person is a minor an application is made for his registration as a [British overseas territories] citizen the Secretary of State may, if he thinks fit, cause him to be registered as such a citizen.

(2) A person born outside the [British overseas territories] shall be entitled, on an application for his registration as a [British overseas territories] citizen made within the period of twelve months from the date of the birth, to be registered as such a citizen if the requirements specified in subsection (3) or, in the case of a person born stateless, the

requirements specified in paragraphs (a) and (b) of that subsection, are fulfilled in the case of either that person's father or his mother ('the parent in question').

(3) The requirements referred to in subsection (2) are—

(a) that the parent in question was a [British overseas territories] citizen by descent at the time of the birth; and

(b) that the father or mother of the parent in question—

(i) was a [British overseas territories] citizen otherwise than by descent at the time of the birth of the parent in question; or

(ii) became a [British overseas territories] citizen otherwise than by descent at commencement, or would have become such a citizen otherwise than by descent at commencement but for his or her death; and

(c) that, as regards some period of three years ending with a date not later than the date of the birth—

(i) the parent in question was in a [British overseas territory] at the beginning of that period; and

(ii) the number of days on which the parent in question was absent from that territory in that period does not exceed 270.

(4) If in the special circumstances of any particular case the Secretary of State thinks fit, he may treat subsection (2) as if the reference to twelve months were a reference to six years.

(5) A person born outside the [British overseas territories] shall be entitled, on an application for his registration as a [British overseas territories citizen] made while he is a minor, to be registered as such a citizen if the following requirements are satisfied, namely—

(a) that at the time of that person's birth his father or mother was a [British overseas territories] citizen by descent; and

(b) subject to subsection (6), that that person and his father and mother were in one and the same [British overseas territory] (no matter which) at the beginning of the period of three years ending with the date of the application and that, in the case of each of them, the number of days on which the person in question was absent from the last-mentioned territory in that period does not exceed 270; and

(c) subject to subsection (6), that the consent of his father and mother to the registration has been signified in the prescribed manner.

(6) In the case of an application under subsection (5) for the registration of a person as a [British overseas territories] citizen—

(a) if his father or mother died, or their marriage [or civil partnership] was terminated, on or before the date of the application, or his father and mother were legally separated on that date, the references to his father and mother in paragraph (b) of that subsection shall be read either as references to his father or as references to his mother; [and]

(b) if his father or mother died on or before that date, the reference to his father and mother in paragraph (c) of that subsection shall be read as a reference to either of them; [...

(c) ...]

Note: Last word in square brackets in sub-s (6)(a) inserted, and words deleted from sub-ss (6)(b) and (c) by Nationality, Immigration and Asylum Act 2002, s 9 from 7 November 2002, in relation to children born on or after a date to be appointed. British dependent territories became British overseas territories from 26 February 2002, British Overseas Territories Act 2002, s 1. Words in first square brackets in sub-s (6)(a) inserted by Sch 27 Civil Partnership Act 2004 from 5 December 2005 (SI 2005/3175).

18. Acquisition by naturalisation

(1) If, on an application for naturalisation as a [British overseas territories] citizen made by a person of full age and capacity, the Secretary of State is satisfied that the applicant fulfils the requirements of Schedule 1 for naturalisation as such a citizen under this subsection, he may, if he thinks fit, grant to him a certificate of naturalisation as such a citizen.

(2) If, on an application for naturalisation as a [British overseas territories] citizen made by a person of full age and capacity who on the date of the application is married to such a citizen [or is the civil partner of such a citizen] the Secretary of State is satisfied that the applicant fulfils the requirements of Schedule 1 for naturalisation as such a citizen under this subsection, he may, if he thinks fit, grant to him a certificate of naturalisation as such a citizen.

(3) Every application under this section shall specify the [British overseas territory] which is to be treated as the relevant territory for the purposes of that application; and, in relation to any such application, references in Schedule 1 to the relevant territory shall be construed accordingly.

Note: British dependent territories became British overseas territories from 26 February 2002, British Overseas Territories Act 2002, s 1. Words in square brackets in sub-s (2) inserted by Sch 27 Civil Partnership Act 2004 from 5 December 2005 (SI 2005/3175).

Acquisition after commencement: special cases

19. ...

Note: Section 19 repealed by Sch 2 Nationality, Immigration and Asylum Act 2002 from 1 April 2003 (SI 2003/754).

20. ...

Note: Section 20 repealed by Sch 2 Nationality, Immigration and Asylum Act 2002 from 1 April 2003 (SI 2003/754).

21. ...

Note: Section 21 repealed by Sch 2 Nationality, Immigration and Asylum Act 2002 from 1 April 2003 (SI 2003/754).

22. Right to registration replacing right to resume citizenship of UK and Colonies

(1) Subject to subsection (3), a person shall be entitled, on an application for his registration as a [British overseas territories] citizen, to be registered as such a citizen if immediately before commencement he would (had he applied for it) have been entitled under section 1(1) of the British Nationality Act 1964 (resumption of citizenship) to be registered as a citizen of the United Kingdom and Colonies by virtue of having an appropriate qualifying connection with a [British overseas territory] or, [...,] by virtue of having been married before commencement to a person who has, or would if living have, such a connection.

(2) On an application for his registration as a [British overseas territories] citizen made by a person of full capacity who had before commencement ceased to be a citizen of the United Kingdom and Colonies as a result of a declaration of renunciation, the Secretary

of State may, if he thinks fit, cause that person to be registered as a [British overseas territories] citizen if that person—

(a) has an appropriate qualifying connection with a [British overseas territory]; or

(b) [. . .] has been married to [or has been the civil partner of,] a person who has, or would if living have, such a connection.

(3) A person shall not be entitled to registration under subsection (1) on more than one occasion.

(4) For the purposes of this section a person shall be taken to have an appropriate qualifying connection with a [British overseas territory] if he, his father or his father's father—

(a) was born in that territory; or

(b) is or was a person naturalised in that territory; or

(c) was registered as a citizen of the United Kingdom and Colonies in that territory; or

(d) became a British subject by reason of the annexation of any territory included in that territory.

Note: The words deleted from sub-ss (1) and (2) cease to have effect with regard to applications made after 7 November 2002, or applications not determined before that date: Nationality, Immigration and Asylum Act 2002, s 5. British dependent territories became British overseas territories from 26 February 2002, British Overseas Territories Act 2002, s 1. Words in square brackets in sub-s (2)(b) inserted by Sch 27 Civil Partnership Act 2004 from 5 December 2005 (SI 2005/3175).

Acquisition at commencement

23. Citizens of UK and Colonies who are to become [British overseas territories] citizens at commencement

(1) A person shall at commencement become a [British overseas territories] citizen if—

(a) immediately before commencement he was a citizen of the United Kingdom and Colonies who had that citizenship by his birth, naturalisation or registration in a [British overseas territory]; or

(b) he was immediately before commencement a citizen of the United Kingdom and Colonies, and was born to a parent—

(i) who at the time of the birth ('the material time') was a citizen of the United Kingdom and Colonies; and

(ii) who either had that citizenship at the material time by his birth, naturalisation or registration in a [British overseas territory] or was himself born to a parent who at the time of that birth so had that citizenship; or

(c) being a woman, she was immediately before commencement a citizen of the United Kingdom and Colonies and either was then, or had at any time been, the wife of a man who under paragraph (a) or (b) becomes a [British overseas territories] citizen at commencement or would have done so but for his death.

(2) A person shall at commencement become a [British overseas territories] citizen if—

(a) immediately before commencement he was a citizen of the United Kingdom and Colonies by virtue of registration under section 7 of the 1948 Act (minor children) or section 1 of the British Nationality (No. 2) Act 1964 (stateless persons); and

(b) he was so registered otherwise than in a [British overseas territory]; and

(c) his father or mother (in the case of a person registered under the said section 7) or his mother (in the case of a person registered under the said section 1)—

(i) was a citizen of the United Kingdom and Colonies at the time of the registration or would have been such a citizen at that time but for his or her death; and

(ii) becomes a [British overseas territories] citizen at commencement or would have done so but for his or her death.

(3) A person who—

(a) immediately before commencement was a citizen of the United Kingdom and Colonies by virtue of having been registered under subsection (6) of section 12 of the 1948 Act (British subjects before commencement of 1948 Act becoming citizens of United Kingdom and Colonies) otherwise than in a [British overseas territory]; and

(b) was so registered on an application under that subsection based on the applicant's descent in the male line from a person ('the relevant person') possessing one of the qualifications specified in subsection (1) of that section (birth or naturalisation in the United Kingdom and Colonies, or acquisition of the status of British subject by reason of annexation of territory),

shall at commencement become a [British overseas territories] citizen if the relevant person—

(i) was born or naturalised in a [British overseas territory]; or

(ii) became a British subject by reason of the annexation of any territory included in a [British overseas territory].

(4) A person who—

(a) immediately before commencement was a citizen of the United Kingdom and Colonies by virtue of registration under section 1 of the British Nationality Act 1964 (resumption of citizenship); and

(b) was so registered otherwise than in a [British overseas territory]; and

(c) was so registered by virtue of having an appropriate qualifying connection with a [British overseas territory] or, if a woman, by virtue of having been married to a person who at the time of the registration had or would, if then living, have had such a connection,

shall at commencement become a [British overseas territories] citizen.

(5) For the purposes of subsection (4) a person shall be taken to have an appropriate qualifying connection with a [British overseas territory] if he, his father or his father's father—

(a) was born in a [British overseas territory]; or

(b) is or was a person naturalised in a [British overseas territory]; or

(c) was registered as a citizen of the United Kingdom and Colonies in a [British overseas territory]; or

(d) became a British subject by reason of the annexation of any territory included in a [British overseas territory].

(6) For the purposes of subsection (1)(b) references to citizenship of the United Kingdom and Colonies shall, in relation to a time before the year 1949, be construed as references to British nationality.

Note: British dependent territories became British overseas territories from 26 February 2002, British Overseas Territories Act 2002, s 1.

Renunciation and resumption

24. Renunciation and resumption

The provisions of sections 12 and 13 shall apply in relation to [British overseas territories] citizens and [British Overseas Territories] citizenship as they apply in relation to British citizens and British citizenship.

Note: British dependent territories became British overseas territories from 26 February 2002, British Overseas Territories Act 2002, s 1.

Supplementary

25. Meaning of [British overseas territories] citizen 'by descent'

(1) For the purposes of this Act a [British overseas territories] citizen is such a citizen 'by descent' if and only if—

(a) he is a person born outside the [British overseas territories] after commencement who is a [British overseas territories] citizen by virtue of section 16(1)(a) only or by virtue of registration under section 17(2) or 21; or

(b) subject to subsection (2), he is a person born outside the [British overseas territories] before commencement who became a [British overseas territories] citizen at commencement and immediately before commencement—

(i) was a citizen of the United Kingdom and Colonies by virtue of section 5 of the 1948 Act (citizenship by descent); or

(ii) was a person who, under any provision of the British Nationality Acts 1948 to 1965, was deemed for the purposes of the proviso to section 5(1) of the 1948 Act to be a citizen of the United Kingdom and Colonies by descent only, or would have been so deemed if male; or

(c) he is a [British overseas territories] citizen by virtue of registration under section 17(1) and either—

(i) his father or mother was a [British overseas territories] citizen at the time of the birth; or

(ii) his father or mother was a citizen of the United Kingdom and Colonies at that time and became a [British overseas territories] citizen at commencement, or would have done so but for his or her death; or

(d) subject to subsection (2), he is a person born outside the [British overseas territories] before commencement who became a [British overseas territories] citizen at commencement under section 23(1)(b) only; or

(e) subject to subsection (2), being a woman, she became a [British overseas territories] citizen at commencement under section 23(1)(c) only, and did so only by virtue of having been, immediately before commencement or earlier, the wife of a man who immediately after commencement was, or would but for his death have been, a [British overseas territories] citizen by descent by virtue of paragraph (b) or (d) of this subsection; or

(f) subject to subsection (2), being a woman born outside the [British overseas territories] before commencement, she is a [British overseas territories] citizen as a result of her registration as such a citizen under section 20 by virtue of being or having been married to a man who at commencement became such a citizen by descent or would have done so but for his having died or ceased to be a citizen of the United Kingdom and Colonies as a result of a declaration of renunciation; or

(g) he is a [British overseas territories] citizen by virtue of registration under section 22 who, having before commencement ceased to be a citizen of the United Kingdom and Colonies as a result of a declaration of renunciation, would, if he had not so ceased, have at commencement become a [British overseas territories] citizen by descent by virtue of paragraph (b), (d) or (e);

(h) he is a [British overseas territories] citizen by virtue of registration under section 13 (as applied by section 24) who, immediately before he ceased to be a [British overseas territories] citizen as a result of a declaration of renunciation, was such a citizen by descent; or

(i) he is a person born in the United Kingdom after commencement who is a [British overseas territories] citizen by virtue of paragraph 1 of Schedule 2.

(2) A person born outside the [British overseas territories] before commencement is not a [British overseas territories] citizen 'by descent' by virtue of subsection (1)(b), (d), (e) or (f) if his father was at the time of his birth serving outside the [British overseas territories] in service of a description mentioned in subsection (3), his recruitment for the service in question having taken place in a [British overseas territory].

(3) The descriptions of service referred to in subsection (2) are—

   (a) Crown service under the government of a [British overseas territory]; and

   (b) service of any description at any time designated under section 16(3).

Note: British dependent territories became British overseas territories from 26 February 2002, British Overseas Territories Act 2002, s 1.

PART III
BRITISH OVERSEAS CITIZENSHIP

26. Citizens of UK and Colonies who are to become British Overseas citizens at commencement

Any person who was a citizen of the United Kingdom and Colonies immediately before commencement and who does not at commencement become either a British citizen or a [British overseas territories] citizen shall at commencement become a British Overseas citizen.

Note: British dependent territories became British overseas territories from 26 February 2002, British Overseas Territories Act 2002, s 1.

27. Registration of minors

(1) If while a person is a minor an application is made for his registration as a British Overseas citizen, the Secretary of State may, if he thinks fit, cause him to be registered as such a citizen.

(2) . . .

Note: Section 27(2) repealed by Sch 2 Nationality, Immigration and Asylum Act 2002 from 1 April 2003 (SI 2003/754).

28. . . .

Note: Section 28 repealed by Sch 2 Nationality, Immigration and Asylum Act 2002 from 1 April 2003 (SI 2003/754).

29. Renunciation

The provisions of section 12 shall apply in relation to British Overseas citizens and British Overseas citizenship as they apply in relation to British citizens and British citizenship.

PART IV
BRITISH SUBJECTS

30. Continuance as British subjects of existing British subjects of certain descriptions

A person who immediately before commencement was—

(a) a British subject without citizenship by virtue of section 13 or 16 of the 1948 Act; or

(b) a British subject by virtue of section 1 of the British Nationality Act 1965 (registration of alien women who have been married to British subjects of certain descriptions),

shall as from commencement be a British subject by virtue of this section.

31. Continuance as British subjects of certain former citizens of Eire

(1) A person is within this subsection if immediately before 1st January 1949 he was both a citizen of Eire and a British subject.

(2) A person within subsections (1) who immediately before commencement was a British subject by virtue of section 2 of the 1948 Act (continuance of certain citizens of Eire as British subjects) shall as from commencement be a British subject by virtue of this subsection.

(3) If at any time after commencement a citizen of the Republic of Ireland who is within subsection (1) but is not a British subject by virtue of subsection (2) gives notice in writing to the Secretary of State claiming to remain a British subject on either or both of the following grounds, namely—

(a) that he is or has been in Crown Service under the government of the United Kingdom; and

(b) that he has associations by way of descent, residence or otherwise with the United Kingdom or with any [British overseas territory], he shall as from that time be a British subject by virtue of this subsection.

(4) A person who is a British subject by virtue of subsection (2) or (3) shall be deemed to have remained a British subject from 1 January 1949 to the time when (whether already a British subject by virtue of the said section 2 or not) he became a British subject by virtue of that subsection.

Note: British dependent territories became British overseas territories from 26 February 2002, British Overseas Territories Act 2002, s 1.

32. Registration of minors

If while a person is a minor an application is made for his registration as a British subject, the Secretary of State may, if he thinks fit, cause him to be registered as a British subject.

33. . . .

Note: Section 33 repealed by Sch 2 Nationality, Immigration and Asylum Act 2002 from 1 April 2003 (SI 2003/754).

34. Renunciation

The provisions of section 12 shall apply in relation to British subjects and the status of a British subject as they apply in relation to British citizens and British citizenship.

35. Circumstances in which British subjects are to lose that status

A person who under this Act is a British subject otherwise than by virtue of section 31 shall cease to be such a subject if, in whatever circumstances and whether under this Act or otherwise, he acquires any other citizenship or nationality whatever.

Part V
Miscellaneous and Supplementary

36. Provisions for reducing statelessness

The provisions of Schedule 2 shall have effect for the purpose of reducing statelessness.

37. Commonwealth citizenship

(1) Every person who—

(a) under [the British Nationality Acts 1981 and 1983] [or the British Overseas Territories Act 2002] is a British citizen, a [British overseas territories] citizen, [a British National (Overseas),] a British Overseas citizen or a British subject; or

(b) under any enactment for the time being in force in any country mentioned in Schedule 3 is a citizen of that country,

shall have the status of a Commonwealth citizen.

(2) Her Majesty may by Order in Council amend Schedule 3 by the alteration of any entry, the removal of any entry, or the insertion of any additional entry.

(3) Any Order in Council made under this section shall be subject to annulment in pursuance of a resolution of either House of Parliament.

(4) After commencement no person shall have the status of a Commonwealth citizen or the status of a British subject otherwise than under this Act.

Note: Words in first square brackets in sub-s (1) substituted by British Nationality (Falkland Islands) Act 1983. Words in second square brackets inserted by Sch 1 British Overseas Territories Act 2002 from 21 May 2002 (SI 2002/1252). Words in 4th square brackets in sub-s (1) inserted by SI 1986/948. British dependent territories became British overseas territories from 26 February 2002, British Overseas Territories Act 2002, s 1.

38. British protected persons

(1) Her Majesty may by Order in Council made in relation to any territory which was at any time before commencement—

(a) a protectorate or protected state for the purposes of the 1948 Act; or

(b) a United Kingdom trust territory within the meaning of that Act,

declare to be British protected persons for the purposes of this Act any class of persons who are connected with that territory and are not citizens of any country mentioned in Schedule 3 which consists of or includes that territory.

(2) Any Order in Council made under this section shall be subject to annulment in pursuance of a resolution of either House of Parliament.

39. Amendment of Immigration Act 1971

(1) ...

(2) ...

(3) ...

(4) ...

(5) ...

(6) ...

(7) ...

(8) A certificate of patriality issued under the Immigration Act 1971 and in force immediately before commencement shall have effect after commencement as if it were a certificate of entitlement issued under that Act [as in force after commencement] unless at commencement the holder ceases to have the right of abode in the United Kingdom.

Note: Section 39(1), (2), (4), (6) amend Immigration Act 1971. Section 39(3), (5) repealed, and words in square brackets in sub-s (8) substituted by Immigration Act 1988, s 3. Section 39(7) amended Mental Health Act 1959, Mental Health (Scotland) Act 1960.

[40. Deprivation of citizenship

(1) In this section a reference to a person's 'citizenship status' is a reference to his status as—

   (a) a British citizen,

   (b) a British overseas territories citizen,

   (c) a British Overseas citizen,

   (d) a British National (Overseas),

   (e) a British protected person, or

   (f) a British subject.

[(2) The Secretary of State may by order deprive a person of a citizenship status if the Secretary of State is satisfied that deprivation is conducive to the public good.]

(3) The Secretary of State may by order deprive a person of a citizenship status which results from his registration or naturalisation if the Secretary of State is satisfied that the registration or naturalisation was obtained by means of—

   (a) fraud,

   (b) false representation, or

   (c) concealment of a material fact.

(4) The Secretary of State may not make an order under subsection (2) if he is satisfied that the order would make a person stateless.

(5) Before making an order under this section in respect of a person the Secretary of State must give the person written notice specifying—

   (a) that the Secretary of State has decided to make an order,

   (b) the reasons for the order, and

   (c) the person's right of appeal under section 40A(1) or under section 2B of the Special Immigration Appeals Commission Act 1997 (c. 68).

(6) Where a person acquired a citizenship status by the operation of a law which applied to him because of his registration or naturalisation under an enactment having effect before commencement, the Secretary of State may by order deprive the person of the citizenship status if the Secretary of State is satisfied that the registration or naturalisation was obtained by means of—

(a) fraud,

(b) false representation, or

(c) concealment of a material fact.

Note: Section 40 substituted by Nationality, Immigration and Asylum Act 2002, s 4 from 1 April 2003 (SI 2003/754). Subsection (2) substituted by Immigration, Asylum and Nationality Act 2006, s 56 from 16 June 2006 (SI 2006/1498).

40A. Deprivation of citizenship: appeal

(1) A person who is given notice under section 40(5) of a decision to make an order in respect of him under section 40 may appeal against the decision to [the First-tier Tribunal].

(2) Subsection (1) shall not apply to a decision if the Secretary of State certifies that it was taken wholly or partly in reliance on information which in his opinion should not be made public—

(a) in the interests of national security,

(b) in the interests of the relationship between the United Kingdom and another country, or

(c) otherwise in the public interest.

[(3) The following provisions of the Nationality, Immigration and Asylum Act 2002 (c. 41) shall apply in relation to an appeal under this section as they apply in relation to an appeal under section 82 [,83 or 83A] of that Act—

(a) section 87 (successful appeal: direction) (for which purpose a direction may, in particular, provide for an order under section 40 above to be treated as having had no effect),

(b) ...

(c) section 106 (rules),

(d) section 107 (practice directions)] [, and

(e) section 108 (forged document: proceedings in private).]

(6) ...

(7) ...

(8) ...

Note: Section 40A inserted by Nationality, Immigration and Asylum Act 2002, s 4 from 1 April 2003 (SI 2003/754). Words in first square brackets substituted and sub-ss (3)(b) revoked from 15 February 2010 (SI 2010/21). Words in other square brackets substituted by and sub-ss (6)–(8) omitted by Sch 2 Asylum and Immigration (Treatment of Claimants etc.) Act 2004 from 4 April 2005 (SI 2005/565). Words in square brackets in sub-s (3) and sub-s (3)(e) inserted by Immigration, Asylum and Nationality Act 2006, s 56 from 16 June 2006 (SI 2006/1498).

41. Regulations and Orders in Council

(1) The Secretary of State may by regulations make provision generally for carrying into effect the purposes of this Act, and in particular provision—

(a) for prescribing anything which under this Act is to be prescribed;

(b) for prescribing the manner in which, and the persons to and by whom, applications for registration or naturalisation under any provision of this Act may or must be made;

[(ba) for determining whether a person has sufficient knowledge of a language for the purpose of an application for naturalisation;

(bb) for determining whether a person has sufficient knowledge about life in the United Kingdom for the purpose of an application for naturalisation;]

[(bc) for amending paragraph 4B(3)(a) or (b) or (4)(a) or (b) of Schedule 1 to substitute a different number for the number for the time being specified there;

(bd) for determining whether a person has, for the purposes of an application for naturalisation under section 6, participated in activities prescribed for the purposes of paragraph 4B(5)(a) of Schedule 1;

(be) for determining whether a person is to be treated for the purposes of such an application as having so participated;]

(c) for the registration of anything required or authorised by or under this Act to be registered;

[(d) for the time within which an obligation to make a citizenship oath and pledge at a citizenship ceremony must be satisfied;

(da) for the time within which an obligation to make a citizenship oath or pledge must be satisfied;

(db) for the content and conduct of a citizenship ceremony;

(dc) for the administration and making of a citizenship oath or pledge;

(dd) for the registration and certification of the making of a citizenship oath or pledge;

(de) for the completion and grant of a certificate of registration or naturalisation;]

(e) for the giving of any notice required or authorised to be given to any person under this Act;

(f) for the cancellation of the registration of, and the cancellation and amendment of certificates of naturalisation relating to, persons deprived of citizenship [or of the status of a British National (overseas)] under this Act, and for requiring such certificates to be delivered up for those purposes;

(g) for the births and deaths of persons of any class or description born or dying in a country mentioned in Schedule 3 to be registered there by the High Commissioner for Her Majesty's government in the United Kingdom or by members of his official staff;

(h) for the births and deaths of persons of any class or description born or dying in a foreign country to be registered there by consular officers or other officers in the service of Her Majesty's government in the United Kingdom;

(i) for enabling the births and deaths of British citizens, [British overseas territories citizens], [British Nationals (Overseas),] British Overseas citizens, British subjects and British protected persons born or dying in any country in which Her Majesty's government in the United Kingdom has for the time being no diplomatic or consular representatives to be registered—

(i) by persons serving in the diplomatic, consular or other foreign service of any country which, by arrangement with Her Majesty's government in the United Kingdom, has undertaken to represent that government's interest in that country, or

(ii) by a person authorised in that behalf by the Secretary of State.

[(j) as to the consequences of failure to comply with provision made under any of paragraphs (a) to (i).]

[**(1A)** Regulations under subsection (1)(ba) or (bb) may, in particular—

(a) make provision by reference to possession of a specified qualification;

(b) make provision by reference to possession of a qualification of a specified kind;

(c) make provision by reference to attendance on a specified course;

(d) make provision by reference to attendance on a course of a specified kind;

(e) make provision by reference to a specified level of achievement;

(f) enable a person designated by the Secretary of State to determine sufficiency of knowledge in specified circumstances;

(g) enable the Secretary of State to accept a qualification of a specified kind as evidence of sufficient knowledge of a language].

[**(1B)** Regulations under subsection (1)(bc) may make provision so that—

(a) the number specified in sub-paragraph (3)(a) of paragraph 4B of Schedule 1 is the same as the number specified in sub-paragraph (4)(a) of that paragraph;

(b) the number specified in sub-paragraph (3)(b) of that paragraph is the same as the number specified in sub-paragraph (4)(b) of that paragraph.

(**1C**) Regulations under subsection (1)(bd) or (be)—

(a) may make provision that applies in relation to time before the commencement of section 41 of the Borders, Citizenship and Immigration Act 2009;

(b) may enable the Secretary of State to make arrangements for such persons as the Secretary of State thinks appropriate to determine whether, in accordance with those regulations, a person has, or (as the case may be) is to be treated as having, participated in an activity.]

(**2**) . . .

(**3**) Regulations under subsection (1) . . . may make different provision for different circumstances; and—

(a) regulations under subsection (1) may provide for the extension of any time-limit for the [making of oaths and pledges of citizenship]; and

. . .

[(**3A**) Regulations under subsection (1)(d) to (de) may, in particular—

(a) enable the Secretary of State to designate or authorise a person to exercise a function (which may include a discretion) in connection with a citizenship ceremony or a citizenship oath or pledge;

(b) require, or enable the Secretary of State to require, a local authority to provide specified facilities and to make specified arrangements in connection with citizenship ceremonies;

(c) impose, or enable the Secretary of State to impose, a function (which may include a discretion) on a local authority or on a registrar.

[(**3B**) In subsection (3A)—

'local authority' means—

(a) in relation to England and Wales, a county council, a county borough council, a metropolitan district council, a London Borough Council and the Common Council of the City of London, and

(b) in relation to Scotland, a council constituted under section 2 of the Local Government etc. (Scotland) Act 1994 (c. 39), and

'registrar' means—

(a) in relation to England and Wales, a superintendent registrar of births, deaths and marriages (or, in accordance with section 8 of the Registration Service Act 1953 (c. 37), a deputy superintendent registrar), and

(b) in relation to Scotland, a district registrar within the meaning of section 7(12) of the Registration of Births, Deaths and Marriages (Scotland) Act 1965 (c. 49).]

(4) Her Majesty may by Order in Council provide for any Act or Northern Ireland legislation to which this subsection applies to apply, with such adaptations and modifications as appear to Her necessary, to births and deaths registered—

(a) in accordance with regulations made in pursuance of subsection (1)(g) to (i) of this section or subsection (1)(f) and (g) of section 29 of the 1948 Act; or

(b) at a consulate of Her Majesty in accordance with regulations made under the British Nationality and Status of Aliens Acts 1914 to 1943 or in accordance with instructions of the Secretary of State; or

(c) by a High Commissioner for Her Majesty's government in the United Kingdom or members of his official staff in accordance with instructions of the Secretary of State; and an Order in Council under this subsection may exclude, in relation to births and deaths so registered, any of the provisions of section 45.

(5) Subsection (4) applies to—

(a) the Births and Deaths Registration Act 1953, the Registration Service Act 1953 and the Registration of Births, Deaths and Marriages (Scotland) Act 1965; and

(b) so much of any Northern Ireland legislation for the time being in force (whether passed or made before or after commencement) as relates to the registration of births and deaths.

(6) The power to make regulations under subsection (1) or (2) shall be exercisable by statutory instrument.

(7) Any regulations or Order in Council made under this section [(other than regulations referred to in subsection (8))] shall be subject to annulment in pursuance of a resolution of either House of Parliament.

[(8) Any regulations (whether alone or with other provision)—

(a) under subsection (1)(a) for prescribing activities for the purposes of paragraph 4B(5)(a) of Schedule 1; or

(b) under subsection (1)(bc), (bd) or (be), may not be made unless a draft has been laid before and approved by a resolution of each House of Parliament.]

Note: Words in square brackets in sub-ss (1)(f), (1)(i), inserted by SI 1986/948. Subsections (1) (ba), (bb) inserted by Nationality, Immigration and Asylum Act 2002, s 1 from 6 July 2004 (SI 2004/1707) and s 1A inserted by s 1 of that Act from 1 November 2005 (SI 2005/2782). Section 41(1) (d) substituted by para 4, Sch 1 Nationality, Immigration and Asylum Act 2002 from 1 January 2004 (SI 2003/3156). Words in square brackets in sub-ss (3)(a) substituted by para 5, Sch 1 of the Nationality, Immigration and Asylum Act 2002 from 1 January 2004 (SI 2003/3156). Subsections (3A) and (3B) inserted by para 7, Sch 1, Nationality, Immigration and Asylum Act 2002 from 1 January 2004 (SI 2003/3156). British dependent territories became British overseas territories from 26 February 2002, British Overseas Territories Act 2002, s 1. Subsection (1)(j) inserted and sub-ss (2), (3)(b) and words in (3)(a) omitted by Sch 2 Immigration, Asylum and Nationality Act 2006 from 1 April 2003 (SI 2003/754). Sub-ss (1)(bc)–(be), (1B)–(1C), (8) and words in square brackets in sub-s (7) inserted by s 41 Borders, Citizenship and Immigration Act 2009 from a date to be appointed.

[41A. Registration: requirement to be of good character

(1) An application for registration of an adult or young person as a British citizen under section 1(3), (3A) or (4), 3(1), (2) or (5), 4(2) or (5), 4A, 4C, 4D, 5, 10(1) or (2) or 13(1) or (3) must not be granted unless the Secretary of State is satisfied that the adult or young person is of good character.

(2) An application for registration of an adult or young person as a British overseas territories citizen under section 15(3) or (4), 17(1) or (5), 22(1) or (2) or 24 must not be granted unless the Secretary of State is satisfied that the adult or young person is of good character.

(3) An application for registration of an adult or young person as a British Overseas citizen under section 27(1) must not be granted unless the Secretary of State is satisfied that the adult or young person is of good character.

(4) An application for registration of an adult or young person as a British subject under section 32 must not be granted unless the Secretary of State is satisfied that the adult or young person is of good character.

(5) In this section, "adult or young person" means a person who has attained the age of 10 years at the time when the application is made.]

Note: Section 41A inserted by s 47 Borders, Citizenship and Immigration Act 2009 from 13 January 2010 (SI 2001/2731).

[42. Registration and naturalisation: citizenship ceremony, oath and pledge

(1) A person of full age shall not be registered under this Act as a British citizen unless he has made the relevant citizenship oath and pledge specified in Schedule 5 at a citizenship ceremony.

(2) A certificate of naturalisation as a British citizen shall not be granted under this Act to a person of full age unless he has made the relevant citizenship oath and pledge specified in Schedule 5 at a citizenship ceremony.

(3) A person of full age shall not be registered under this Act as a British overseas territories citizen unless he has made the relevant citizenship oath and pledge specified in Schedule 5.

(4) A certificate of naturalisation as a British overseas territories citizen shall not be granted under this Act to a person of full age unless he has made the relevant citizenship oath and pledge specified in Schedule 5.

(5) A person of full age shall not be registered under this Act as a British Overseas citizen or a British subject unless he has made the relevant citizenship oath specified in Schedule 5.

(6) Where the Secretary of State thinks it appropriate because of the special circumstances of a case he may—

(a) disapply any of subsections (1) to (5), or
(b) modify the effect of any of those subsections.

(7) Sections 5 and 6 of the Oaths Act 1978 (c. 19) (affirmation) apply to a citizenship oath; and a reference in this Act to a citizenship oath includes a reference to a citizenship affirmation.]

Note: Section 42 substituted by para 1, Sch 1 Nationality, Immigration and Asylum Act 2002 from 1 January 2004 (SI 2003/3156).

[42A.

Note: Section 42A inserted by para 1, Sch 1 Nationality, Immigration and Asylum Act 2002 from 1 January 2004 (SI 2003/3156). Ceases to have effect from 2 April 2007, Sch 3 Immigration, Asylum and Nationality Act 2006 (SI 2007/1109).

[42B. Registration and naturalisation: timing

(1) A person who is registered under this Act as a citizen of any description or as a British subject shall be treated as having become a citizen or subject—

(a) immediately on making the required citizenship oath and pledge in accordance with section 42, or

(b) where the requirement for an oath and pledge is disapplied, immediately on registration.

(2) A person granted a certificate of naturalisation under this Act as a citizen of any description shall be treated as having become a citizen—

(a) immediately on making the required citizenship oath and pledge in accordance with section 42, or

(b) where the requirement for an oath and pledge is disapplied, immediately on the grant of the certificate.

(3) In the application of subsection (1) to registration as a British Overseas citizen or as a British subject the reference to the citizenship oath and pledge shall be taken as a reference to the citizenship oath.]

Note: Section 42B inserted by para 1, Sch 1 Nationality, Immigration and Asylum Act 2002 from January 2004 (SI 2003/3156).

43. Exercise of functions of Secretary of State by Governors and others

(1) Subject to subsection (3), the Secretary of State may in the case of any of his functions under this Act with respect to any of the matters mentioned in subsection (2), make arrangements for that function to be exercised—

(a) in any of the Islands, by the Lieutenant-Governor in cases concerning British citizens or British citizenship;

(b) in any [British overseas territory] [. . .], by the Governor in cases concerning [British overseas territories] citizens or [British overseas territories] citizenship [and in cases concerning British National (Overseas) or the status of a British National (Overseas)];

(2) The said matters are—

(a) registration and naturalisation; and

(b) renunciation, resumption and deprivation of British citizenship or [British overseas territories] citizenship.

[(c) renunciation and deprivation of the status of a British National (Overseas).]

(3) Nothing in this section applies in the case of any power to make regulations or rules conferred on the Secretary of State by this Act.

(4) Arrangements under subsection (1) may provide for any such function as is there mentioned to be exercisable only with the approval of the Secretary of State.

Note: Words in fifth square brackets in sub-s (1)(b) and sub-s (2)(c) added by SI 1986/948. British dependent territories became British overseas territories from 26 February 2002, British Overseas Territories Act 2002, s 1.

44. Decisions involving exercise of discretion

(1) Any discretion vested by or under this Act in the Secretary of State, a Governor or a Lieutenant-Governor shall be exercised without regard to the race, colour or religion of any person who may be affected by its exercise.

(2) . . .

(3) . . .

Note: Subsections (2) and (3) cease to have effect from 7 November 2002, Nationality, Immigration and Asylum Act 2002, s 7.

[44A. Waiver of requirement for full capacity

Where a provision of this Act requires an applicant to be of full capacity, the Secretary of State may waive the requirement in respect of a specified applicant if he thinks it in the applicant's best interests.]

Note: Section 44A inserted by Immigration, Asylum and Nationality Act 2006, s 49 from 31 August 2006 (SI 2006/2226, which contains transitional provisions).

45. Evidence

(1) Every document purporting to be a notice, certificate, order or declaration, or an entry in a register, or a subscription of an oath of allegiance, given, granted or made under this Act or any of the former nationality Acts shall be received in evidence and shall, unless the contrary is proved, be deemed to have been given, granted or made by or on behalf of the person by whom or on whose behalf it purports to have been given, granted or made.

(2) Prima facie evidence of any such document may be given by the production of a document purporting to be certified as a true copy of it by such person and in such manner as may be prescribed.

(3) Any entry in a register made under this Act or any of the former nationality Acts shall be received as evidence (and in Scotland as sufficient evidence) of the matters stated in the entry.

(4) A certificate given by or on behalf of the Secretary of State that a person was at any time in Crown service under the government of the United Kingdom or that a person's recruitment for such service took place in the United Kingdom shall, for the purposes of this Act, be conclusive evidence of that fact.

46. Offences and proceedings

(1) Any person who for the purpose of procuring anything to be done or not to be done under this Act—

   (a) makes any statement which he knows to be false in a material particular; or

   (b) recklessly makes any statement which is false in a material particular, shall be liable on summary conviction in the United Kingdom to imprisonment for a term not exceeding three months or to a fine not exceeding [level 5 on the standard scale], or both.

(2) Any person who without reasonable excuse fails to comply with any requirement imposed on him by regulations made under this Act with respect to the delivering up of certificates of naturalisation shall be liable on summary conviction in the United Kingdom to a fine not exceeding [level 4 on the standard scale].

(3) In the case of an offence under subsection (1)—

(a) any information relating to the offence may in England and Wales be tried by a magistrates' court if it is laid within six months after the commission of the offence, or if it is laid within three years after the commission of the offence and not more than two months after the date certified by a chief officer of police to be the date on which evidence sufficient to justify proceedings came to the notice of an officer of his police force; and

(b) summary proceedings for the offence may in Scotland be commenced within six months after the commission of the offence, or within three years after the commission of the offence and not more than two months after the date on which evidence sufficient in the opinion of the Lord Advocate to justify proceedings came to his knowledge; and

(c) a complaint charging the commission of the offence may in Northern Ireland be heard and determined by a magistrates' court if it is made within six months after the commission of the offence, or if it is made within three years after the commission of the offence and not more than two months after the date certified by an officer of police not below the rank of assistant chief constable to be the date on which evidence sufficient to justify the proceedings came to the notice of the police in Northern Ireland.

(4) For the purposes of subsection (3)(b) proceedings shall be deemed to be commenced on the date on which a warrant to apprehend or to cite the accused is granted, if such warrant is executed without undue delay; and a certificate of the Lord Advocate as to the date on which such evidence as is mentioned in subsection (3)(b) came to his knowledge shall be conclusive evidence.

(5) For the purposes of the trial of a person for an offence under subsection (1) or (2), the offence shall be deemed to have been committed either at the place at which it actually was committed or at any place at which he may be.

(6) In their application to the Bailiwick of Jersey subsections (1) and (2) shall have effect with the omission of the words 'on summary conviction'.

Note: Words in square brackets in s 46(1), (2), substituted by virtue of Criminal Justice Act 1982, s 46.

47. ...

Note: Section 47 ceases to have effect in relation to a child born on or after 1 July 2006, Nationality, Immigration and Asylum Act 2002, s 9(SI 2006/1498).

48. Posthumous children

Any reference in this Act to the status of description of the father or mother of a person at the time of that person's birth shall, in relation to a person born after the death of his father or mother, be construed as a reference to the status or description of the parent in question at the time of that parent's death; and where that death occurred before, and the birth occurs after, commencement, the status or description which would have been applicable to the father or mother had he or she died after commencement shall be deemed to be the status or description applicable to him or her at the time of his or her death.

49. Registration and naturalisation under British Nationality Acts 1948 to 1965

...

Note: Section 49 repealed by s 52(8) and Sch 9 of this Act.

50. Interpretation

(1) In this Act, unless the context otherwise requires—

'the 1948 Act' means the British Nationality Act 1948;

'alien' means a person who is neither a Commonwealth citizen nor a British protected person nor a citizen of the Republic of Ireland;

['appointed day' means the day appointed by the Secretary of State under section 8 of the British Overseas Territories Act 2002 for the commencement of Schedule 1 to that Act;]

'association' means an unincorporated body of persons;

['British National (Overseas)' means a person who is a British National (Overseas) under the Hong Kong (British Nationality) Order 1986, and 'status of a British National (Overseas)' shall be construed accordingly;

'British Overseas citizen' includes a person who is a British Overseas citizen under the Hong Kong (British Nationality) Order 1986.]

'British protected person' means a person who is a member of any class of persons declared to be British protected persons by an Order in Council for the time being in force under section 38 or is a British protected person by virtue of the Solomon Islands Act 1978;

'commencement', without more, means the commencement of this Act;

'Commonwealth citizen' means a person who has the status of a Commonwealth citizen under this Act;

'company' means a body corporate;

['Convention adoption' means an adoption effected under the law of a country or territory in which the Convention is in force, and certified in pursuance of Article 23(1) of the Convention;]

'Crown service' means the service of the Crown, whether within Her Majesty's dominions or elsewhere;

'Crown service under the government of the United Kingdom' means Crown service under Her Majesty's government in the United Kingdom or under Her Majesty's government in Northern Ireland [or under the Scottish Administration] [or under the Welsh Assembly Government];

['designated territory' means a qualifying territory, or the Sovereign Base Areas of Akrotiri and Dhekelia, which is designated by Her Majesty by Order in Council under subsection (14)]

[. . .]

'enactment' includes an enactment comprised in Northern Ireland legislation;

'foreign country' means a country other than the United Kingdom, a [British overseas territory], a country mentioned in Schedule 3 and the Republic of Ireland;

'the former nationality Acts' means—

(a) the British Nationality Acts 1948 to 1965;

(b) the British Nationality and Status of Aliens Acts 1914 to 1943; and

(c) any Act repealed by the said Acts of 1914 to 1943 or by the Naturalization Act 1870;

'Governor', in relation to a [British overseas territory], includes the officer for the time being administering the government of that territory;

'High Commissioner' includes an acting High Commissioner;

'immigration laws'—

(a) in relation to the United Kingdom, means the Immigration Act 1971 and any law for purposes similar to that Act which is for the time being or has at any time been in force in any part of the United Kingdom;

(b) in relation to a [British overseas territory], means any law for purposes similar to the Immigration Act 1971 which is for the time being or has at any time been in force in that territory;

'the Islands' means the Channel Islands and the Isle of Man;

'minor' means a person who has not attained the age of eighteen years;

'prescribed' means prescribed by regulations made under section 41;

['qualifying territory' means a British overseas territory other than the Sovereign Base Areas of Akrotiri and Dhekelia;]

'settled' shall be construed in accordance with subsections (2) to (4);

'ship' includes a hovercraft;

'statutory provision' means any enactment or any provision contained in—

(a) subordinate legislation (as defined in section 21(1) of the Interpretation Act 1978); or

(b) any instrument of a legislative character made under any Northern Ireland legislation;

'the United Kingdom' means Great Britain, Northern Ireland and the Islands, taken together;

'United Kingdom consulate' means the office of a consular officer of Her Majesty's government in the United Kingdom where a register of births is kept or, where there is no such office, such office as may be prescribed.

[(**1A**) Subject to subsection (1B), references in this Act to being a member of the armed forces are references to being—

(a) a member of the regular forces within the meaning of the Armed Forces Act 2006, or

(b) a member of the reserve forces within the meaning of that Act subject to service law by virtue of paragraph (a), (b) or (c) of section 367(2) of that Act.

(**1B**) A person is not to be regarded as a member of the armed forces by virtue of subsection (1A) if the person is treated as a member of a regular or reserve force by virtue of—

(a) section 369 of the Armed Forces Act 2006, or

(b) section 4(3) of the Visiting Forces (British Commonwealth) Act 1933.]

(**2**) Subject to subsection (3), references in this Act to a person being settled in the United Kingdom or in a [British overseas territory] are references to his being ordinarily resident in the United Kingdom or, as the case may be, in that territory without being subject under the immigration laws to any restriction on the period for which he may remain.

(**3**) Subject to subsection (4), a person is not to be regarded for the purposes of this Act—

(a) as having been settled in the United Kingdom at any time when he was entitled to an exception under section 8(3) or (4)(b) or (c) of the Immigration Act 1971 or, unless the order under section 8(2) of that Act conferring the exemption in question provides otherwise, to an exemption under the said section 8(2), or to any corresponding exemption under the former immigration laws; or

(b) as having been settled in a [British overseas territory] at any time when he was under the immigration laws entitled to any exemption corresponding to any such exemption as is mentioned in paragraph (a) (that paragraph being for the purposes of this paragraph read as if the words from 'unless' to 'otherwise' were omitted).

(4) A person to whom a child is born in the United Kingdom after commencement is to be regarded for the purposes of section 1(1) as being settled in the United Kingdom at the time of the birth if—

(a) he would fall to be so regarded but for his being at that time entitled to an exemption under section 8(3) of the Immigration Act 1971; and

(b) immediately before he became entitled to that exemption he was settled in the United Kingdom; and

(c) he was ordinarily resident in the United Kingdom from the time when he became entitled to that exemption to the time of the birth;

but this subsection shall not apply if at the time of the birth the child's father or mother is a person on whom any immunity from jurisdiction is conferred by or under the Diplomatic Privileges Act 1964.

(5) It is hereby declared that a person is not to be treated for the purpose of any provision of this Act as ordinarily resident in the United Kingdom or in a [British overseas territory] at a time when he is in the United Kingdom or, as the case may be, in that territory in breach of the immigration laws.

(6) For the purposes of this Act—

(a) a person shall be taken to have been naturalised in the United Kingdom if, but only if, he is—

(i) a person to whom a certificate of naturalisation was granted under any of the former nationality Acts by the Secretary of State or, in any of the Islands, by the Lieutenant-Governor; or

(ii) a person who by virtue of section 27(2) of the British Nationality and Status of Aliens Act 1914 was deemed to be a person to whom a certificate of naturalisation was granted, if the certificate of naturalisation in which his name was included was granted by the Secretary of State; or

(iii) a person who by virtue of section 10(5) of the Naturalisation Act 1870 was deemed to be a naturalised British subject by reason of his residence with his father or mother;

(b) a person shall be taken to have been naturalised in a [British overseas territory] if, but only if, he is—

(i) a person to whom a certificate of naturalisation was granted under any of the former nationality Acts by the Governor of that territory or by a person for the time being specified in a direction given in relation to that territory under paragraph 4 of Schedule 3 to the West Indies Act 1967 or for the time being holding an office so specified; or

(ii) a person who by virtue of the said section 27(2) was deemed to be a person to whom a certificate of naturalisation was granted, if the certificate of naturalisation in which his name was included was granted by the Governor of that territory; or

(iii) a person who by the law in force in that territory enjoyed the privileges of naturalisation within that territory only;

and references in this Act to naturalisation in the United Kingdom or in a [British overseas territory] shall be construed accordingly.

(7) For the purposes of this Act a person born outside the United Kingdom aboard a ship or aircraft—

(a) shall be deemed to have been born in the United Kingdom if—

(i) at the time of the birth his father or mother was a British citizen; or

(ii) he would, but for this subsection, have been born stateless,

and (in either case) at the time of the birth the ship or aircraft was registered in the United Kingdom or was an unregistered ship or aircraft of the government of the United Kingdom; but

(b) subject to paragraph (a), is to be regarded as born outside the United Kingdom, whoever was the owner of the ship or aircraft at that time, and irrespective of whether or where it was then registered.

[(7A) For the purposes of this Act a person born outside a qualifying territory aboard a ship or aircraft—

(a) shall be deemed to have been born in that territory if—

(i) at the time of the birth his father or mother was a British citizen or a British overseas territories citizen; or

(ii) he would, but for this subsection, have been born stateless,

and (in either case) at the time of the birth the ship or aircraft was registered in that territory or was an unregistered ship or aircraft of the government of that territory; but

(b) subject to paragraph (a), is to be regarded as born outside that territory, whoever was the owner of the ship or aircraft at the time, and irrespective of whether or where it was then registered.

(7B) For the purposes of this Act a person born outside a British overseas territory, other than a qualifying territory, aboard a ship or aircraft—

(a) shall be deemed to have been born in that territory if—

(i) at the time of the birth his father or mother was a British overseas territories citizen; or

(ii) he would, but for this subsection, have been born stateless,

and (in either case) at the time of the birth the ship or aircraft was registered in that territory or was an unregistered ship or aircraft of the government of that territory; but

(b) subject to paragraph (a), is to be regarded as born outside that territory, whoever was the owner of the ship or aircraft at the time, and irrespective of whether or where it was then registered.]

(8) For the purposes of this Act an application under any provision thereof shall be taken to have been made at the time of its receipt by a person authorised to receive it on behalf of the person to whom it is made; and references in this Act to the date of such an application are references to the date of its receipt by a person so authorised.

[(9) For the purposes of this Act a child's mother is the woman who gives birth to the child.

(9A) For the purposes of this Act a child's father is—

(a) the husband, at the time of the child's birth, of the woman who gives birth to the child, or

[(b) where a person is treated as the father of the child under section 28 of the Human Fertilisation and Embryology Act 1990 or section 35 or 36 of the Human Fertilisation and Embryology Act 2008, that person, or

(ba) where a person is treated as a parent of the child under section 42 or 43 of the Human Fertilisation and Embryology Act 2008, that person, or

(c) where none of paragraphs (a) to (ba) applies, a person who satisfies prescribed requirements as to proof of paternity.]

(b) where a person is treated as the father of the child under section 28 of the Human Fertilisation and Embryology Act 1990 (c. 37) (father), that person, or

(c) where neither paragraph (a) nor paragraph (b) applies, any person who satisfies prescribed requirements as to proof of paternity.

(9B) In subsection (9A)(c) 'prescribed' means prescribed by regulations of the Secretary of State; and the regulations—

(a) may confer a function (which may be a discretionary function) on the Secretary of State or another person,

(b) may make provision which applies generally or only in specified circumstances,

(c) may make different provision for different circumstances,

(d) must be made by statutory instrument, and

(e) shall be subject to annulment in pursuance of a resolution of either House of Parliament.

(9C) The expressions 'parent', 'child' and 'descended' shall be construed in accordance with subsections (9) and (9A).]

(10) For the purposes of this Act—

(a) a period 'from' or 'to' a specified date includes that date; and

(b) any reference to a day on which a person was absent from the United Kingdom or from a [British overseas territory] or from the [British overseas] territories is a reference to a day for the whole of which he was so absent.

(11) For the purposes of this Act—

(a) a person is of full age if he has attained the age of eighteen years, and of full capacity if he is not of unsound mind; and

(b) a person attains any particular age at the beginning of the relevant anniversary of the date of his birth.

(12) References in this Act to any country mentioned in Schedule 3 include references to the dependencies of that country.

(13) Her Majesty may by Order in Council subject to annulment in pursuance of a resolution of either House of Parliament amend Schedule 6 in any of the following circumstances, namely—

(a) where the name of any territory mentioned in it is altered; or

(b) where any territory mentioned in it is divided into two or more territories.

(14) For the purposes of the definition of "designated territory" in subsection (1), an Order in Council may—

(a) designate any qualifying territory, or the Sovereign Base Areas of Akrotiri and Dhekelia, if the Convention is in force there, and

(b) make different designations for the purposes of section 1 and section 15; and, for the purposes of this subsection and the definition of "Convention adoption" in subsection (1), "the Convention" means the Convention on the Protection of Children and Co-operation in respect of Intercountry Adoption, concluded at the Hague on 29th May 1993.

An Order in Council under this subsection shall be subject to annulment in pursuance of a resolution of either House of Parliament.]

Note: Words in second square brackets in s 50(1) inserted by SI 1986/948. "Scottish Administration" inserted from 6 May 1999 (SI 1999/1042). "Welsh Assembly" inserted from 6 November 2009 (SI 2009/2958). Other words in square brackets inserted in sub-s 1 and sub-ss (7A) and (7B) substituted by Sch 1 British Overseas Territories Act from 21 May 2002 (SI 2002/1252). Subsection (9) substituted by Nationality, Immigration and Asylum Act 2002, s 9, from 7 November 2002, with effect in relation to children born on or after 1 July 2006 (SI 2006/1498). British dependent territories became British overseas territories from 26 February 2002, British Overseas Territories Act 2002, s 1. Definitions of 'Convention adoption' and 'designated territory' inserted and sub-s (14) inserted by Adoption and Children Act 2002, s 137 and Schedule 4 from 30 December 2005 (SI 2005/2213). Subsection (1A)–(1B) inserted by s 59 Borders, Citizenship and Immigration Act 2009 from 13 January 2010 (SI 2009/2731). Subsections 9A(b)–(c) substituted by Sch 6 Human Fertilisation and Embryology Act 2008 from 6 April 2010 (SI 2010/987).

[50A Meaning of references to being in breach of immigration laws

(1) This section applies for the construction of a reference to being in the United Kingdom "in breach of the immigration laws" in—

(a) section 4(2) or (4);

(b) section 50(5); or

(c) Schedule 1.

(2) It applies only for the purpose of determining on or after the relevant day—

(a) whether a person born on or after the relevant day is a British citizen under section 1(1),

(b) whether, on an application under section 1(3) or 4(2) made on or after the relevant day, a person is entitled to be registered as a British citizen, or

(c) whether, on an application under section 6(1) or (2) made on or after the relevant day, the applicant fulfils the requirements of Schedule 1 for naturalisation as a British citizen under section 6(1) or (2).

(3) But that is subject to section 48(3)(d) and (4) of the Borders, Citizenship and Immigration Act 2009 (saving in relation to section 11 of the Nationality, Immigration and Asylum Act 2002).

(4) A person is in the United Kingdom in breach of the immigration laws if (and only if) the person—

(a) is in the United Kingdom;

(b) does not have the right of abode in the United Kingdom within the meaning of section 2 of the Immigration Act 1971;

(c) does not have leave to enter or remain in the United Kingdom (whether or not the person previously had leave);

(d) does not have a qualifying CTA entitlement;

(e) is not entitled to reside in the United Kingdom by virtue of any provision made under section 2(2) of the European Communities Act 1972 (whether or not the person was previously entitled);

(f) is not entitled to enter and remain in the United Kingdom by virtue of section 8(1) of the Immigration Act 1971 (crew) (whether or not the person was previously entitled); and

(g) does not have the benefit of an exemption under section 8(2) to (4) of that Act (diplomats, soldiers and other special cases) (whether or not the person previously had the benefit of an exemption).

(5) For the purposes of subsection (4)(d), a person has a qualifying CTA entitlement if the person—

(a) is a citizen of the Republic of Ireland,

(b) last arrived in the United Kingdom on a local journey (within the meaning of the Immigration Act 1971) from the Republic of Ireland, and

(c) on that arrival, was a citizen of the Republic of Ireland and was entitled to enter without leave by virtue of section 1(3) of the Immigration Act 1971 (entry from the common travel area).

(6) Section 11(1) of the Immigration Act 1971 (person deemed not to be in the United Kingdom before disembarkation, while in controlled area or while under immigration control) applies for the purposes of this section as it applies for the purposes of that Act.

(7) This section is without prejudice to the generality of—

(a) a reference to being in a place outside the United Kingdom in breach of immigration laws, and

(b) a reference in a provision other than one specified in subsection (1) to being in the United Kingdom in breach of immigration laws.

(8) The relevant day for the purposes of subsection (2) is the day appointed for the commencement of section 48 of the Borders, Citizenship and Immigration Act 2009 (which inserted this section).]

Note: Section 50A inserted by s 48 Borders, Citizenship and Immigration Act 2009 from 13 January 2010 (SI 2009/2731).

51. Meaning of certain expressions relating to nationality to other Acts and instruments

(1) Without prejudice to subsection (3)(c), in any enactment or instrument whatever passed or made before commencement 'British subject' and 'Commonwealth citizen' have the same meaning, that is—

(a) in relation to any time before commencement—

(i) a person who under the 1948 Act was at that time a citizen of the United Kingdom and Colonies or who, under any enactment then in force in a country mentioned in section 1(3) of that Act as then in force, was at that time a citizen of that country; and

(ii) any other person who had at that time the status of a British subject under that Act or any other enactment then in force;

(b) in relation to any time after commencement, a person who has the status of a Commonwealth citizen under this Act.

(2) In any enactment or instrument whatever passed or made after commencement—

'British subject' means a person who has the status of a British subject under this Act;

'Commonwealth citizen' means a person who has the status of a Commonwealth citizen under this Act.

(3) In any enactment or instrument whatever passed or made before commencement—

(a) 'citizen of the United Kingdom and Colonies'—

(i) in relation to any time before commencement, means a person who under the 1948 Act was at that time a citizen of the United Kingdom and Colonies;

(ii) in relation to any time after commencement, means a person who under [the British Nationality Acts 1981 and 1983] [or the British Overseas Territories Act 2002] is a British citizen, a [British overseas territories] citizen or a British Overseas citizen [or who under the Hong Kong (British Nationality) Order 1986 is a British National (Overseas)];

(b) any reference to ceasing to be a citizen of the United Kingdom and Colonies shall, in relation to any time after commencement, be construed as a reference to becoming a person who is neither a British citizen nor a [British overseas territories] citizen [nor a British National (Overseas)] nor a British Overseas citizen;

(c) any reference to a person who is a British subject (or a British subject without citizenship) by virtue of section 2, 13, or 16 of the 1948 Act or by virtue of, or of section 1 of, the British Nationality Act 1965 shall, in relation to any time after commencement, be construed as a reference to a person who under this Act is a British subject.

(4) In any statutory provision, whether passed or made before or after commencement, and in any other instrument whatever made after commencement 'alien', in relation to any

time after commencement, means a person who is neither a Commonwealth citizen nor a British protected person nor a citizen of the Republic of Ireland.

(5) The preceding provisions of this section—

(a) shall not apply in cases where the context otherwise requires; and

(b) shall not apply to this Act or to any instrument made under this Act.

Note: Words in first square brackets in s 51(3) substituted by British Nationality (Falkland Islands) Act 1983. Words in second square brackets inserted by Sch 1 British Overseas Territories Act 2002 from 21 May 2002 (SI 2002/1252). Words at end of sub-s (3)(a)(ii) and in second square brackets in sub-s (3)(b) inserted by SI 1986/948. British dependent territories became British overseas territories from 26 February 2002, British Overseas Territories Act 2002, s 1.

52. Consequential amendments, transitional provisions, repeals and savings

(1) In any enactment or instrument whatever passed or made before commencement, for any reference to section 1(3) of the 1948 Act (list of countries whose citizens are Commonwealth citizens under that Act) there shall be substituted a reference to Schedule 3 to this Act, unless the context makes that substitution inappropriate.

(2) Subject to subsection (3), Her Majesty may by Order in Council make such consequential modifications of—

(a) any enactment of the Parliament of the United Kingdom passed before commencement;

(b) any provision contained in any Northern Ireland legislation passed or made before commencement; or

(c) any instrument made before commencement under any such enactment or provision, as appear to Her necessary or expedient for preserving after commencement the substantive effect of that enactment, provision or instrument.

(3) Subsection (2) shall not apply in relation to—

(a) the Immigration Act 1971; or

(b) any provision of this Act not contained in Schedule 7.

(4) Any Order in Council made under subsection (2) shall be subject to annulment in pursuance of a resolution of either House of Parliament.

(5) Any provision made by Order in Council under subsection (2) after commencement may be made with retrospective effect as from commencement or any later date.

(6) The enactments specified in Schedule 7 shall have effect subject to the amendments there specified, being amendments consequential on the provisions of this Act.

(7) This Act shall have effect subject to the transitional provisions contained in Schedule 8.

(8) The enactments mentioned in Schedule 9 are hereby repealed to the extent specified in the third column of that Schedule.

(9) Without prejudice to section 51, nothing in this Act affects the operation, in relation to any time before commencement, of any statutory provision passed or made before commencement.

(10) Nothing in this Act shall be taken as prejudicing the operation of sections 16 and 17 of the Interpretation Act 1978 (which relate to the effect of repeals).

(11) In this section 'modifications' includes additions, omissions and alterations.

53. Citation, commencement and extent

(1) This Act may be cited as the British Nationality Act 1981.

(2) This Act, except the provisions mentioned in subsection (3), shall come into force on such day as the Secretary of State may by order made by statutory instrument appoint; and references to the commencement of this Act shall be construed as references to the beginning of that day.

(3) Section 49 and this section shall come into force on the passing of this Act.

(4) This Act extends to Northern Ireland.

(5) The provisions of this Act, except those mentioned in subsection (7), extend to the Islands and all [British overseas territories]; and section 36 of the Immigration Act 1971 (power to extend provisions of that Act to Islands) shall apply to the said excepted provisions as if they were provisions of that Act.

(6) ...

(7) The provisions referred to in subsections (5)... are—
    (a) section 39 and Schedule 4;
    (b) section 52(7) and Schedule 8 so far as they relate to the Immigration Act 1971; and
    (c) section 52(8) and Schedule 9 so far as they relate to provisions of the Immigration Act 1971 other than Schedule 1.

Note: Sub-s (6) and words in sub-s 7 repealed by Statute Law Repeals Act 1995 Schedule 1, Pt. II. British dependent territories became British overseas territories from 26 February 2002, British Overseas Territories Act 2002, s 1.

SCHEDULES

Sections 6 and 18	SCHEDULE 1

REQUIREMENTS FOR NATURALISATION
Naturalisation as a British citizen under section 6(1)

1.—(1) Subject to paragraph 2, the requirements for naturalisation as a British citizen under section 6(1) are, in the case of any person who applies for it—
    (a) the requirements specified in sub-paragraph (2) of this paragraph, [...]; and
    (b) that he is of good character; and
    (c) that he has a sufficient knowledge of the English, Welsh or Scottish Gaelic language; and
    [(ca) that he has sufficient knowledge about life in the United Kingdom; and]
    (d) that either—
        (i) his intentions are such that, in the event of a certificate of naturalisation as a British citizen being granted to him, his home or (if he has more than one) his principal home will be in the United Kingdom; or
        (ii) he intends, in the event of such a certificate being granted to him, to enter into, or continue in, Crown service under the government of the United Kingdom, or service under an international organisation of which the United Kingdom or Her Majesty's government therein is a member, or service in the employment of a company or association established in the United Kingdom.

[(2) The requirements referred to in sub-paragraph (1)(a) of this paragraph are—

(a) that the applicant ("A") was in the United Kingdom at the beginning of the qualifying period;

(b) that the number of days on which A was absent from the United Kingdom in each year of the qualifying period does not exceed 90;

(c) that A had a qualifying immigration status for the whole of the qualifying period;

(d) that on the date of the application A has probationary citizenship leave, permanent residence leave, a qualifying CTA entitlement, a Commonwealth right of abode or a permanent EEA entitlement;

(e) that, where on the date of the application A has probationary citizenship leave granted for the purpose of taking employment in the United Kingdom, A has been in continuous employment since the date of the grant of that leave; and

(f) that A was not at any time in the qualifying period in the United Kingdom in breach of the immigration laws.]

(3) ...

Note: Words omitted from sub-paragraph (1)(a), sub-paragraph (2) substituted and sub-paragraph (3) revoked by s 39 Borders, Citizenship and Immigration Act 2009 from a date to be appointed. Sub-paragraph (1)(ca) inserted by s 1 Nationality, Immigration and Asylum Act 2002, from 1 November 2005 (SI 2005/2782).

2.—[(1)] If in the special circumstances of any particular case the Secretary of State thinks fit, he may for the purposes of paragraph 1 do all or any of the following things, namely—

[(a) treat the applicant as fulfilling the requirement specified in paragraph 1(2)(b) although the number of days on which the applicant was absent from the United Kingdom in a year of the qualifying period exceeds 90;]

(b) treat the applicant as having been in the United Kingdom for the whole or any part of any period during which he would otherwise fall to be treated under paragraph 9(1) as having been absent;

[(ba) treat the applicant as fulfilling the requirement specified in paragraph 1(2)(c) where the applicant has had a qualifying immigration status for only part of the qualifying period;

(bb) treat the applicant as fulfilling the requirement specified in paragraph 1(2)(d) where the applicant has had probationary citizenship leave but it expired in the qualifying period;]

(c) ...

[(ca) treat the applicant as fulfilling the requirement specified in paragraph 1(2)(e) although the applicant has not been in continuous employment since the date of the grant mentioned there;]

(d) treat the applicant as fulfilling the requirement specified in paragraph [1(2)(f)] although he was in the United Kingdom in breach of the immigration laws in the [qualifying period] there mentioned;

(e) waive the need to fulfil [either or both of the requirements specified in paragraph 1(1)(c) and (ca)] if he considers that because of the applicant's age or physical or mental condition it would be unreasonable to [expect him to fulfil that requirement or those requirements].

[(2) If in the special circumstances of a particular case that is an armed forces case or an exceptional Crown service case the Secretary of State thinks fit, the Secretary of State may for the purposes of paragraph 1 waive the need to fulfil all or any of the requirements specified in paragraph 1(2).

(3) An armed forces case is a case where, on the date of the application, the applicant is or has been a member of the armed forces.

(4) An exceptional Crown service case is a case where—

(a) the applicant is, on the date of the application, serving outside the United Kingdom in Crown service under the government of the United Kingdom; and

(b) the Secretary of State considers the applicant's performance in the service to be exceptional.]

[(5) In paragraph 1(2)(e) and sub-paragraph (1)(ca) of this paragraph, "employment" includes self-employment.]

Note: Sub-paragraph (1)(a) and words in square brackets in sub-paragraph (1)(d) substituted, sub-paragraph (1)(c) revoked and sub-paragraphs (1)(ba)–(bb), (ca), (2)–(5) inserted by s 39 Borders, Citizenship and Immigration Act 2009 from a date to be appointed. Words in square brackets in paragraph 2(e) substituted by s 1 Nationality, Immigration and Asylum Act 2002, from 1 November 2005 (SI 2005/2782).

[**2A.**—(1) A person has a qualifying immigration status for the purposes of paragraph 1(2) if the person has—
(a) qualifying temporary residence leave;
(b) probationary citizenship leave;
(c) permanent residence leave;
(d) a qualifying CTA entitlement;
(e) a Commonwealth right of abode; or
(f) a temporary or permanent EEA entitlement.

(2) A person who is required for those purposes to have a qualifying immigration status for the whole of the qualifying period need not have the same qualifying immigration status for the whole of that period.]

Note: Paragraph 2A inserted by s 39 Borders, Citizenship and Immigration Act 2009 from a date to be appointed.

Naturalisation as a British citizen under section 6(2)

[**3(1)** Subject to paragraph 4, the requirements for naturalisation as a British citizen under section 6(2) are, in the case of any person ("A") who applies for it—
(a) the requirements specified in sub-paragraph (2) of this paragraph;
(b) the requirement specified in sub-paragraph (3) of this paragraph;
(c) that A is of good character;
(d) that A has a sufficient knowledge of the English, Welsh or Scottish Gaelic language; and
(e) that A has sufficient knowledge about life in the United Kingdom.

(2) The requirements referred to in sub-paragraph (1)(a) are—
(a) that A was in the United Kingdom at the beginning of the qualifying period;
(b) that the number of days on which A was absent from the United Kingdom in each year of the qualifying period does not exceed 90;
(c) that, subject to sub-paragraph (5)—
   (i) A had a relevant family association for the whole of the qualifying period, and
   (ii) A had a qualifying immigration status for the whole of that period;
(d) that on the date of the application—
   (i) A has probationary citizenship leave, or permanent residence leave, based on A's having the relevant family association referred to in section 6(2), or
   (ii) A has a qualifying CTA entitlement or a Commonwealth right of abode; and
(e) that A was not at any time in the qualifying period in the United Kingdom in breach of the immigration laws.

(3) The requirement referred to in sub-paragraph (1)(b) is—
(a) that A's intentions are such that, in the event of a certificate of naturalisation as a British citizen being granted to A, A's home or (if A has more than one) A's principal home will be in the United Kingdom;
(b) that A intends, in the event of such a certificate being granted to A, to enter into, or continue in, service of a description mentioned in sub-paragraph (4); or
(c) that, in the event of such a certificate being granted to A—
   (i) the person with whom A has the relevant family association referred to in section 6(2) ("B") intends to enter into, or continue in, service of a description mentioned in sub-paragraph (4); and
   (ii) A intends to reside with B for the period during which B is in the service in question.

(4) The descriptions of service referred to in sub-paragraph (3) are—

  (a) Crown service under the government of the United Kingdom;

  (b) service under an international organisation of which the United Kingdom, or Her Majesty's government in the United Kingdom, is a member; or

  (c) service in the employment of a company or association established in the United Kingdom.

(5) Where the relevant family association referred to in section 6(2) is (in accordance with regulations under section 41(1)(a)) that A is the partner of a person who is a British citizen or who has permanent residence leave—

  (a) the requirement specified in sub-paragraph (2)(c)(i) is fulfilled only if A was that person's partner for the whole of the qualifying period, and

  (b) for the purposes of sub-paragraph (2)(c)(ii), A can rely upon having a qualifying immigration status falling within paragraph 4A(1)(a), (b) or (c) only if that partnership is the relevant family association upon which the leave to which the status relates is based.

(6) For the purposes of sub-paragraph (5), A is a person's partner if—

  (a) that person is A's spouse or civil partner or is in a relationship with A that is of a description that the regulations referred to in that sub-paragraph specify, and

  (b) the marriage, civil partnership or other relationship satisfies the conditions (if any) that those regulations specify.

(7) For the purposes of sub-paragraph (5), the relationship by reference to which A and the other person are partners need not be of the same description for the whole of the qualifying period.]

Note: Paragraph 3 substituted by s 40 Borders, Citizenship and Immigration Act 2009 from a date to be appointed.

[4. If in the special circumstances of any particular case the Secretary of State thinks fit, the Secretary of State may for the purposes of paragraph 3 do all or any of the following, namely—

  (a) treat A as fulfilling the requirement specified in paragraph 3(2)(b), although the number of days on which A was absent from the United Kingdom in a year of the qualifying period exceeds 90;

  (b) treat A as having been in the United Kingdom for the whole or any part of any period during which A would otherwise fall to be treated under paragraph 9(1) as having been absent;

  (c) treat A as fulfilling the requirement specified in paragraph 3(2)(c)(i) (including where it can be fulfilled only as set out in paragraph 3(5)) where a relevant family association of A's has ceased to exist;

  (d) treat A as fulfilling the requirement specified in paragraph 3(2)(c)(ii) (including where it can be fulfilled only as set out in paragraph 3(5)) where A has had a qualifying immigration status for only part of the qualifying period;

  (e) treat A as fulfilling the requirement specified in paragraph 3(2)(d) where A has had probationary citizenship leave but it expired in the qualifying period;

  (f) treat A as fulfilling the requirement specified in paragraph 3(2)(e) although A was in the United Kingdom in breach of the immigration laws in the qualifying period;

  (g) waive the need to fulfil either or both of the requirements specified in paragraph 3(1)(d) and (e) if the Secretary of State considers that because of A's age or physical or mental condition it would be unreasonable to expect A to fulfil that requirement or those requirements;

  (h) waive the need to fulfil all or any of the requirements specified in paragraph 3(2)(a), (b), (c) or (d) (including where paragraph 3(2)(c) can be fulfilled only as set out in paragraph 3(5)) if—

    (i) on the date of the application, the person with whom A has the relevant family association referred to in section 6(2) is serving in service to which section 2(1)(b) applies, and

    (ii) that person's recruitment for that service took place in the United Kingdom.]

Note: Paragraph 4 substituted by s 40 Borders, Citizenship and Immigration Act 2009 from a date to be appointed.

[4A.—(1) Subject to paragraph 3(5), a person has a qualifying immigration status for the purposes of paragraph 3 if the person has—

(a) qualifying temporary residence leave based on a relevant family association;

(b) probationary citizenship leave based on a relevant family association;

(c) permanent residence leave based on a relevant family association;

(d) a qualifying CTA entitlement; or

(e) a Commonwealth right of abode.

(2) For the purposes of paragraph 3 and this paragraph, the leave mentioned in sub-paragraph (1)(a), (b) or (c) is based on a relevant family association if it was granted on the basis of the person having a relevant family association.

(3) A person who is required for the purposes of paragraph 3 to have, for the whole of the qualifying period, a qualifying immigration status and a relevant family association need not, for the whole of that period—

(a) have the same qualifying immigration status; or

(b) (subject to paragraph 3(5)) have the same relevant family association.

(4) Where, by virtue of sub-paragraph (3)(a), a person relies upon having more than one qualifying immigration status falling within sub-paragraph (1)(a), (b) or (c)—

(a) subject to paragraph 3(5), it is not necessary that the leave to which each status relates is based on the same relevant family association, and

(b) in a case where paragraph 3(5) applies, the relationship by reference to which the persons referred to in paragraph 3(5) are partners need not be of the same description in respect of each grant of leave.]

Note: Paragraph 4A inserted by s 40 Borders, Citizenship and Immigration Act 2009 from a date to be appointed.

[The qualifying period for naturalisation as a British citizen under section 6

4B.—(1) The qualifying period for the purposes of paragraph 1 or 3 is a period of years which ends with the date of the application in question.

(2) The length of the period is determined in accordance with the following provisions of this paragraph.

(3) In the case of an applicant who does not meet the activity condition, the number of years in the period is—

(a) 8, in a case within paragraph 1;

(b) 5, in a case within paragraph 3.

(4) In the case of an applicant who meets the activity condition, the number of years in the period is—

(a) 6, in a case within paragraph 1;

(b) 3, in a case within paragraph 3.

(5) The applicant meets the activity condition if the Secretary of State is satisfied that the applicant—

(a) has participated otherwise than for payment in prescribed activities; or

(b) is to be treated as having so participated.]

Note: Paragraph 4B inserted by s 41 Borders, Citizenship and Immigration Act 2009 from a date to be appointed.

Naturalisation as a [British overseas territories] citizen under section 18(1)

5.—(1) Subject to paragraph 6, the requirements for naturalisation as a [British overseas territories] citizen under section 18(1) are, in the case of any person who applies for it—

(a) the requirements specified in sub-paragraph (2) of this paragraph, or the alternative requirement specified in sub-paragraph (3) of this paragraph; and

(b) that he is of good character; and

(c) that he has a sufficient knowledge of the English language or any other language recognised for official purposes in the relevant territory; and

(d) that either—

    (i) his intentions are such that, in the event of a certificate of naturalisation as a [British overseas territories] citizen being granted to him, his home or (if he has more than one) his principal home will be in the relevant territory; or

    (ii) he intends, in the event of such a certificate being granted to him, to enter into, or continue in, Crown service under the government of that territory, or service under an international organisation of which that territory or the government of that territory is a member, or service in the employment of a company or association established in that territory.

(2) The requirements referred to in sub-paragraph (1)(a) of this paragraph are—

(a) that he was in the relevant territory at the beginning of the period of five years ending with the date of the application, and that the number of days on which he was absent from that territory in that period does not exceed 450; and

(b) that the number of days on which he was absent from that territory in the period of twelve months so ending does not exceed 90; and

(c) that he was not at any time in the period of twelve months so ending subject under the immigration laws to any restriction on the period for which he might remain in that territory; and

(d) that he was not at any time in the period of five years so ending in that territory in breach of the immigration laws.

(3) The alternative requirement referred to in sub-paragraph (1)(a) of this paragraph is that on the date of the application he is serving outside the relevant territory in Crown service under the government of that territory.

6. If in the special circumstances of any particular case the Secretary of State thinks fit, he may for the purposes of paragraph 5 do all or any of the following things, namely—

(a) treat the applicant as fulfilling the requirement specified in paragraph 5(2)(a) or paragraph 5(2)(b), or both, although the number of days on which he was absent from the relevant territory in the period there mentioned exceeds the number there mentioned;

(b) treat the applicant as having been in the relevant territory for the whole or any part of any period during which he would otherwise fall to be treated under paragraph 9(2) as having been absent;

(c) disregard any such restriction as is mentioned in paragraph 5(2)(c), not being a restriction to which the applicant was subject on the date of the application;

(d) treat the applicant as fulfilling the requirement specified in paragraph 5(2)(d) although he was in the relevant territory in breach of the immigration laws in the period there mentioned;

(e) waive the need to fulfil the requirement specified in paragraph 5(1)(c) if he considers that because of the applicant's age or physical or mental condition it would be unreasonable to expect him to fulfil it.

Naturalisation as a [British overseas territories] citizen under section 18(2)

7. Subject to paragraph 8, the requirements for naturalisation as a [British overseas territories] citizen under section 18(2) are, in the case of any person who applies for it—

(a) that he was in the relevant territory at the beginning of the period of three years ending with the date of the application, and that the number of days on which he was absent from that territory in that period does not exceed 270; and

(b) that the number of days on which he was absent from that territory in the period of twelve months so ending does not exceed 90; and

(c) that on the date of the application he was not subject under the immigration laws to any restriction on the period for which he might remain in that territory; and

(d) that he was not at any time in the period of three years ending with the date of the application in that territory in breach of the immigration laws; and

(e) the [requirements specified in paragraph 5(1)(b) and (c)].

Note: Words in square brackets in sub-paragraph (e) substituted by s 2 of Nationality, Immigration and Asylum Act 2002, from 1 November 2005 (SI 2005/2782).

8. Paragraph 6 shall apply in relation to paragraph 7 with the following modifications, namely—
  (a) the reference to the purposes of paragraph 5 shall be read as a reference to the purposes of paragraph 7;
  (b) the references to paragraphs 5(2)(a), 5(2)(b) and 5(2)(d) shall be read as references to paragraphs 7(a), 7(b) and 7(d) respectively;
  (c) paragraph 6(c) [. . .] shall be omitted; and
  (d) after paragraph (e) there shall be added—
  '(f) waive the need to fulfil all or any of the requirements specified in paragraph 7(a) and (b) if on the date of the application the person to whom the applicant is married [, or of whom the applicant is the civil partner,] is serving in service to which section 16(1)(b) applies, that person's recruitment for that service having taken place in a [British overseas territory]'.

Note: Words in square brackets in para 8(c) omitted by Nationality, Immigration and Asylum Act 2002, s 2 from 1 November 2005 (SI 2005/2782). Words in square brackets in sub-para 8(d) inserted by Sch 27 Civil Partnerships Act 2004 from 5 December 2005 (SI 105/3175).

Periods to be treated as periods of absence from UK or a [British overseas territory]

9.—(1) For the purposes of this Schedule a person shall (subject to [paragraph 2(1)(b) or 4(b)]) be treated as having been absent from the United Kingdom during any of the following periods, that is to say—
  (a) any period when he was in the United Kingdom and either was entitled to an exemption under section 8(3) or (4) of the Immigration Act 1971 (exemptions for diplomatic agents etc. and members of the forces) or was a member of the family and formed part of the household of a person so entitled;
  (b) any period when he was detained—
    (i) in any place of detention in the United Kingdom in pursuance of a sentence passed on him by a court in the United Kingdom or elsewhere for any offence;
    (ii) in any hospital in the United Kingdom under a hospital order made under [Part III of the Mental Health Act 1983] or section 175 or 376 of the Criminal Procedure (Scotland) Act 1975 or Part III of the Mental Health [(Northern Ireland) Order 1986], being an order made in connection with his conviction of an offence; or
    (iii) under any power of detention conferred by the immigration laws of the United Kingdom;
  (c) any period when, being liable to be detained as mentioned in paragraph (b)(i) or (ii) of this sub-paragraph, he was unlawfully at large or absent without leave and for that reason liable to be arrested or taken into custody;
  (d) any period when, his actual detention under any such power as is mentioned in paragraph (b)(iii) of this sub-paragraph being required or specifically authorised, he was unlawfully at large and for that reason liable to be arrested.
(2) For the purposes of this Schedule a person shall (subject to paragraph 6(b)) be treated as having been absent from any particular [British overseas territory] during any of the following periods, that is to say—
  (a) any period when he was in that territory and either was entitled to an exemption under the immigration laws of that territory corresponding to any such exemption as is mentioned in sub-paragraph (1)(a) or was a member of the family and formed part of the household of a person so entitled;
  (b) any period when he was detained—

(i) in any place of detention in the relevant territory in pursuance of a sentence passed on him by a court in that territory or elsewhere for any offence;

(ii) in any hospital in that territory under a direction (however described) made under any law for purposes similar to [Part III of the Mental Health Act 1983] which was for the time being in force in that territory, being a direction made in connection with his conviction of an offence and corresponding to a hospital order under that Part; or

(iii) under any power of detention conferred by the immigration laws of that territory;

(c) any period when, being liable to be detained as mentioned in paragraph (b)(i) or (ii) of this sub-paragraph, he was unlawfully at large or absent without leave and for that reason liable to be arrested or taken into custody;

(d) any period when, his actual detention under any such power as is mentioned in paragraph (b)(iii) of this sub-paragraph being required or specifically authorised, he was unlawfully at large and for that reason liable to be arrested.

Note: Words in first square brackets in sub-paras (1)(b) and 9(2)(b) substituted by Mental Health Act 1983, s 148. Words in second square brackets in sub-para (1)(b) substituted by SI 1956/596. Words in first square brackets in paragraph 9 substituted by s 49 Borders, Citizenship and Immigration Act 2009 from 13 January 2010 (SI 2009/2731).

Interpretation

10. In this Schedule 'the relevant territory' has the meaning given by section 18(3).

[**11.—(1)** This paragraph applies for the purposes of this Schedule.

(2) A person has qualifying temporary residence leave if—
 (a) the person has limited leave to enter or remain in the United Kingdom, and
 (b) the leave is granted for a purpose by reference to which a grant of probationary citizenship leave may be made.

(3) A person has probationary citizenship leave if—
 (a) the person has limited leave to enter or remain in the United Kingdom, and
 (b) the leave is of a description identified in rules under section 3 of the Immigration Act 1971 as "probationary citizenship leave", and the reference in sub-paragraph (2) to a grant of probationary citizenship leave is to be construed accordingly.

(4) A person has permanent residence leave if the person has indefinite leave to enter or remain in the United Kingdom.

(5) A person has a qualifying CTA entitlement if the person—
 (a) is a citizen of the Republic of Ireland,
 (b) last arrived in the United Kingdom on a local journey (within the meaning of the Immigration Act 1971) from the Republic of Ireland, and
 (c) on that arrival, was a citizen of the Republic of Ireland and was entitled to enter without leave by virtue of section 1(3) of the Immigration Act 1971 (entry from the common travel area).

(6) A person has a Commonwealth right of abode if the person has the right of abode in the United Kingdom by virtue of section 2(1)(b) of the Immigration Act 1971.

(7) A person has a permanent EEA entitlement if the person is entitled to reside in the United Kingdom permanently by virtue of any provision made under section 2(2) of the European Communities Act 1972.

(8) A person has a temporary EEA entitlement if the person does not have a permanent EEA entitlement but is entitled to reside in the United Kingdom by virtue of any provision made under section 2(2) of the European Communities Act 1972.

(9) A reference in this paragraph to having leave to enter or remain in the United Kingdom is to be construed in accordance with the Immigration Act 1971.]

Note: Paragraph 11 inserted by s 49 Borders, Citizenship and Immigration Act 2009 from 13 January 2010 (SI 2009/2731).

Section 36   SCHEDULE 2

PROVISIONS FOR REDUCING STATELESSNESS

Persons born in the United Kingdom after commencement

1.—(1) Where a person born in the United Kingdom after commencement would, but for this paragraph, be born stateless, then, subject to sub-paragraph (3)—

(a) if at the time of the birth his father or mother is a citizen or subject of a description mentioned in sub-paragraph (2), he shall be a citizen or subject of that description; and accordingly

(b) [. . .] at the time of the birth each of his parents is a citizen or subject of a different description so mentioned, he shall be a citizen or subject of the same description so mentioned as each of them is respectively at that time.

(2) The descriptions referred to in sub-paragraph (1) are a [British overseas territories] citizen, a British Overseas citizen and a British subject under this Act.

(3) A person shall not be a British subject by virtue of this paragraph if by virtue of it he is a citizen of a description mentioned in sub-paragraph (2).

Note: British dependent territories became British overseas territories from 26 February 2002, British Overseas Territories Act 2002, s 1. Words deleted from paras 1(1)(b) cease to have effect in relation to children born on or after 1 July 2006 (SI 2006/1498).

Persons born in a [British overseas territory] after commencement

2.—(1) Where a person born in a [British overseas territory] after commencement would, but for this paragraph, be born stateless, then, subject to sub-paragraph (3)—

(a) if at the time of the birth his father or mother is a citizen or subject of a description mentioned in sub-paragraph (2), he shall be a citizen or subject of that description; and accordingly

(b) [. . .] at the time of the birth each of his parents is a citizen or subject of a different description so mentioned, he shall be a citizen or subject of the same description so mentioned as each of them is respectively at that time.

(2) The descriptions referred to in sub-paragraph (1) are a British citizen, a British Overseas citizen and a British subject under this Act.

(3) A person shall not be a British subject by virtue of this paragraph if by virtue of it he is a citizen of a description mentioned in sub-paragraph (2).

Note: British dependent territories became British overseas territories from 26 February 2002, British Overseas Territories Act 2002, s 1. Words deleted from para 2(1)(b) cease to have effect in relation to children born on or after 1 July 2006 (SI 2006/1498).

Persons born in the United Kingdom or a [British overseas territory] after commencement

3.—(1) A person born in the United Kingdom or a [British overseas territory] after commencement shall be entitled, on an application for his registration under this paragraph, to be so registered if the following requirements are satisfied in his case, namely—

(a) that he is and always has been stateless; and

(b) that on the date of the application he [. . .] was under the age of twenty-two; and

(c) that he was in the United Kingdom or a [British overseas territory] (no matter which) at the beginning of the period of five years ending with that date and that (subject to paragraph 6) the number of days on which he was absent from both the United Kingdom and the [British overseas territories] in that period does not exceed 450.

(2) A person entitled to registration under this paragraph—

(a) shall be registered under it as a British citizen if, in the period of five years mentioned in sub-paragraph (1), the number of days wholly or partly spent by him in the United Kingdom exceeds the number of days wholly or partly spent by him in the [British overseas territories];

(b) in any other case, shall be registered under it as a [British overseas territories] citizen.

Note: British dependent territories became British overseas territories from 26 February 2002, British Overseas Territories Act 2002, s 1. Words deleted from para 3(1)(b) cease to have effect in relation to an application made on or after 1 April 2003 or an application not determined by that date, Nationality, Immigration and Asylum Act 2002, s 8 and SI 2003/754.

Persons born outside the United Kingdom and the [British Overseas Territories]
after commencement

4.—(1) A person born outside the United Kingdom and the [British overseas territories] after commencement shall be entitled, on an application for his registration under this paragraph, to be so registered if the following requirements are satisfied, namely—
   (a) that that person is and always has been stateless; and
   (b) that at the time of that person's birth his father or mother was a citizen or subject of a description mentioned in sub-paragraph (4); and
   (c) that that person was in the United Kingdom or a [British overseas territory] (no matter which) at the beginning of the period of three years ending with the date of the application and that (subject to paragraph 6) the number of days on which he was absent from both the United Kingdom and the [British overseas territories] in that period does not exceed 270.

(2) A person entitled to registration under this paragraph—
   (a) shall be registered under it as a citizen or subject of a description available to him in accordance with sub-paragraph (3); and
   (b) if more than one description is so available to him, shall be registered under this paragraph as a citizen of whichever one or more of the descriptions so available to him is or are stated in the application under this paragraph to be wanted.

(3) For the purposes of this paragraph the descriptions of citizen or subject available to a person entitled to registration under this paragraph are—
   (a) in the case of a person whose father or mother was at the time of that person's birth a citizen of a description mentioned in sub-paragraph (4), any description of citizen so mentioned which applied to his father or mother at that time;
   (b) in any case, a British subject under this Act.

(4) The description referred to in sub-paragraphs (1) to (3) are a British citizen, a [British overseas territories] citizen, a British Overseas citizen and a British subject under this Act.

Note: British dependent territories became British overseas territories from 26 February 2002, British Overseas Territories Act 2002, s 1.

Persons born stateless before commencement

5.—(1) A person born before commencement shall be entitled, on an application for his registration under this paragraph, to be so registered if the circumstances are such that, if—
   (a) this Act had not been passed, and the enactments repealed or amended by this Act had continued in force accordingly; and
   (b) an application for the registration of that person under section 1 of the British Nationality (No. 2) Act 1964 (stateless persons) as a citizen of the United Kingdom and Colonies had been made on the date of the application under this paragraph, that person would have been entitled under that section to be registered as such a citizen.

(2) A person entitled to registration under this paragraph shall be registered under it as such a citizen as he would have become at commencement if, immediately before commencement, he had been registered as a citizen of the United Kingdom and Colonies under section 1 of the British Nationality (No. 2) Act 1964 on whichever of the grounds mentioned in subsection (1)(a) to (c) of that section he would have been entitled to be so registered on in the circumstances described in sub-paragraph (1)(a) and (b) of this paragraph.

Supplementary

6. If in the special circumstances of any particular case the Secretary of State thinks fit, he
   may for the purposes of paragraph 3 or 4 treat the person who is the subject of the application as fulfilling the requirement specified in sub-paragraph (1)(c) of that paragraph
   although the number of days on which he was absent from both the United Kingdom and
   the [British overseas territories] in the period there mentioned exceeds the number there
   mentioned.

Note: British dependent territories became British overseas territories from 26 February 2002,
British Overseas Territories Act 2002, s 1.

Section 37   SCHEDULE 3
COUNTRIES WHOSE CITIZENS ARE COMMONWEALTH CITIZENS

Antigua and Barbuda	Papua New Guinea
Australia	[Saint Christopher and Nevis]
The Bahamas	Saint Lucia
Bangladesh	Saint Vincent and the Grenadines
Barbados	Republic of Cyprus
Belize	Dominica
Botswana	Fiji
[Brunei]	The Gambia
[Cameroon]	Ghana
Canada	Grenada
Kenya	Guyana
Kiribati	India
Lesotho	Jamaica
Malawi	Seychelles
Malaysia	Sierra Leone
[Maldives]	Singapore
Malta	Solomon Islands
Mauritius	Sri Lanka
[Mozambique]	Swaziland
Nauru	Tanzania
New Zealand	Tonga
Nigeria	Trinidad and Tobago
[Pakistan]	Tuvalu
[Rwanda]	Zambia
Uganda	Zimbabwe
Vanuatu	[Namibia]
Western Samoa	

Note: 'Brunei' inserted by SI 1983/1699; 'Maldives' inserted by Brunei and Maldives Act 1985;
'Pakistan' inserted by SI 1989/1331; 'Saint Christopher and Nevis' inserted by SI 1983/882;
'Namibia' inserted by SI 1990/1502. 'Cameroon' and 'Mozambique' inserted by SI 1998/3161 from
25 January 1999. 'Rwanda' inserted from 10 March 2010 (SI 2010/246).

SCHEDULE 4

Note: Schedule 4 amends Immigration Act 1971, ss 3–6, 8, 9, 13, 14, 22, 24–26, 29, 33, Schs 2, 4.

. . .

Section 42(1) [SCHEDULE 5

CITIZENSHIP OATH AND PLEDGE

1. The form of citizenship oath and pledge is as follows for registration of or naturalisation as a British citizen—

OATH

'I, [name], swear by Almighty God that, on becoming a British citizen, I will be faithful and bear true allegiance to Her Majesty Queen Elizabeth the Second, Her Heirs and Successors according to law.'

PLEDGE

'I will give my loyalty to the United Kingdom and respect its rights and freedoms. I will uphold its democratic values. I will observe its laws faithfully and fulfil my duties and obligations as a British citizen.'

2. The form of citizenship oath and pledge is as follows for registration of or naturalisation as a British overseas territories citizen—

OATH

'I, [name], swear by Almighty God that, on becoming a British overseas territories citizen, I will be faithful and bear true allegiance to Her Majesty Queen Elizabeth the Second, Her Heirs and Successors according to law.'

PLEDGE

'I will give my loyalty to [name of territory] and respect its rights and freedoms. I will uphold its democratic values. I will observe its laws faithfully and fulfil my duties and obligations as a British overseas territories citizen.'

3. The form of citizenship oath is as follows for registration of a British Overseas citizen—

'I, [name], swear by Almighty God that, on becoming a British Overseas citizen, I will be faithful and bear true allegiance to Her Majesty Queen Elizabeth the Second, Her Heirs and Successors according to law.'

4. The form of citizenship oath is as follows for registration of a British subject—

'I, [name], swear by Almighty God that, on becoming a British subject, I will be faithful and bear true allegiance to Her Majesty Queen Elizabeth the Second, Her Heirs and Successors according to law.']

Note: Schedule 5 substituted by Nationality, Immigration and Asylum Act 2002, Sch 1, para 2, from 1 January 2004 (SI 2003.3156).

Section 50(1) SCHEDULE 6

[BRITISH OVERSEAS TERRITORIES]

Anguilla
Bermuda
British Antarctic Territory
British Indian Ocean Territory

Cayman Islands
Falkland Islands [. . .]
Gibraltar
. . .
Montserrat
Pitcairn, Henderson, Ducie and Oeno Islands
. . .
[St Helena, Ascension and Tristan da Cunha]
[South Georgia and the South Sandwich Islands]
The Sovereign Base Areas of Akrotiri and Dhekelia (that is to say the areas mentioned in section
2(1) of the Cyprus Act 1960)
Turks and Caicos Islands
Virgin Islands

> **Note:** British dependent territories became British overseas territories from 26 February 2002,
> British Overseas Territories Act 2002, s 1. First words omitted in Sch 6 repealed by SI 2002/3497.
> Second words omitted repealed by SI 1986/948. Third words omitted repealed by SI 1983/893.
> Words in first square brackets substituted from 14 November 2009 (SI 2009/2744), words in second
> square brackets inserted by SI 2001/3497 from 4 December 2001.

Senior Courts Act

(1981, c.54)

> **Note:** Citation of Act altered to Senior Courts Act (formerly Supreme Court Act) by Constitutional
> Reform Act 2005 Schedule 11 from 1 October 2009 (SI 2009/1604)

31A. Transfer of judicial review applications to Upper Tribunal

(1) This section applies where an application is made to the High Court—
  (a) for judicial review, or
  (b) for permission to apply for judicial review.

(2) If Conditions 1, 2, 3 and 4 are met, the High Court must by order transfer the application to the Upper Tribunal.

[(2A)If Conditions 1, 2, 3 and 5 are met, but Condition 4 is not, the High Court must by order transfer the application to the Upper Tribunal.]

(3) If Conditions 1, 2 and 4 are met, but Condition 3 is not, the High Court may by order transfer the application to the Upper Tribunal if it appears to the High Court to be just and convenient to do so.

(4) Condition 1 is that the application does not seek anything other than—
  (a) relief under section 31(1)(a) and (b);
  (b) permission to apply for relief under section 31(1)(a) and (b);
  (c) an award under section 31(4);
  (d) interest;
  (e) costs.

(5) Condition 2 is that the application does not call into question anything done by the
Crown Court.

(6) Condition 3 is that the application falls within a class specified under section 18(6) of the Tribunals, Courts and Enforcement Act 2007.

(7) Condition 4 is that the application does not call into question any decision made under—

   (a) the Immigration Acts,

   (b) the British Nationality Act 1981 (c. 61),

   (c) any instrument having effect under an enactment within paragraph (a) or (b), or

   (d) any other provision of law for the time being in force which determines British citizenship, British overseas territories citizenship, the status of a British National (Overseas) or British Overseas citizenship.

[(8) Condition 5 is that the application calls into question a decision of the Secretary of State not to treat submissions as an asylum claim or a human rights claim within the meaning of Part 5 of the Nationality, Immigration and Asylum Act 2002 wholly or partly on the basis that they are not significantly different from material that has previously been considered (whether or not it calls into question any other decision).]

Note: Section 31A inserted by Tribunal, Courts and Enforcement Act 2007, s 19 from 3 November 2008 (SI 2008/2696). Sub-sections (2A) and (8) inserted by Borders, Citizenship and Immigration Act 2009, s 53 from 8 August 2011 (SI 2011/1741).

Immigration Act 1988
(1988, c. 14)

An Act to make further provision for the regulation of immigration into the United Kingdom; and for connected purposes.   [10 May 1988]

1. Termination of saving in respect of Commonwealth citizens settled before 1973

...

Note: Section 1 repeals Immigration Act 1971, s 1(5).

2. Restriction on exercise of right of abode in cases of polygamy

(1) this section applies to any woman who—

(a) has the right of abode in the United Kingdom under section 2(1)(b) of the principal Act as, or as having been, the wife of a man ('the husband')—

(i) to whom she is or was polygamously married; and

(ii) who is or was such a citizen of the United Kingdom and Colonies, Commonwealth citizen or British subject as is mentioned in section 2(2)(a) or (b) of that Act as in force immediately before the commencement of the British Nationality Act 1981; and

(b) has not before the coming into force of this section and since her marriage to the husband been in the United Kingdom.

(2) A woman to whom this section applies shall not be entitled to enter the United Kingdom in the exercise of the right of abode mentioned in subsection (1)(a) above or to be granted a certificate of entitlement in respect of that right if there is another woman living (whether or not one to whom this section applies) who is the wife or widow of the husband and who—

(a) is, or at any time since her marriage to the husband has been, in the United Kingdom; or

(b) has been granted a certificate of entitlement in respect of the right of abode mentioned in subsection (1)(a) above or an entry clearance to enter the United Kingdom as the wife of the husband.

(3) So long as a woman is precluded by subsection (2) above from entering the United Kingdom in the exercise of her right of abode or being granted a certificate of entitlement in respect of that right the principal Act shall apply to her as it applies to a person not having a right of abode.

(4) Subsection (2) above shall not preclude a woman from re-entering the United Kingdom if since her marriage to the husband she has at any time previously been in the United Kingdom and there was at that time no such other woman living as is mentioned in that subsection.

(5) Where a woman claims that this section does not apply to her because she had been in the United Kingdom before the coming into force of this section and since her marriage to the husband it shall be for her to prove that fact.

(6) For the purposes of this section a marriage may be polygamous although at its inception neither party has any spouse additional to the other.

(7) For the purposes of subsection (1)(b), (2)(a), (4) and (5) above there shall be disregarded presence in the United Kingdom as a visitor or an illegal entrant and presence in circumstances in which a person is deemed by section 11(1) of the principal Act not to have entered the United Kingdom.

(8) In subsection (2)(b) above the reference to a certificate of entitlement includes a reference to a certificate treated as such a certificate by virtue of section 39(8) of the British Nationality Act 1981.

(9) No application by a woman for a certificate of entitlement in respect of such a right of abode as is mentioned in subsection (1)(a) above or for an entry clearance shall be granted if another application for such a certificate or clearance is pending and that application is made by a woman as the wife or widow of the same husband.

(10) For the purposes of subsection (9) above an application shall be regarded as pending so long as it and any appeal proceedings relating to it have not been finally determined.

3. Proof of right of abode

. . .

Note: Amends Immigration Act 1971, ss 3(9), 13(3), 2(2); British Nationality Act 1981, s 39.

4. Members of diplomatic missions

. . .

Note: Amends Immigration Act 1971, s 8.

5. . . .

Note: Section 5 repealed by Immigration and Asylum Act 1999 from 2 October 2000, transitional provisions set out in SI 2003/754.

6. Knowingly overstaying limited leave

(1) . . .

(2) . . .

(3) These amendments do not apply in relation to a person whose leave has expired before the coming into force of this section.

Note: Section 6(1) and (2) amend Immigration Act 1971, s 24.

7. Persons exercising Community rights and nationals of member States

(1) A person shall not under the principal Act require leave to enter or remain in the United Kingdom in any case in which he is entitled to do so by virtue of an enforceable [EU] right or of any provision made under section 2(2) of the European Communities Act 1972.

(2) The Secretary of State may by order made by statutory instrument give leave to enter the United Kingdom for a limited period to any class of persons who are nationals of member States but who are not entitled to enter the United Kingdom as mentioned in subsection (1) above; and any such order may give leave subject to such conditions as may be imposed by the order.

(3) References in the principal Act to limited leave shall include references to leave given by an order under subsection (2) above and a person having leave by virtue of such an order shall be treated as having been given that leave by a notice given to him by an immigration officer within the period specified in paragraph 6(1) of Schedule 2 to that Act.

Note: 'EU' substituted from 22 April 2011 (SI 2011/1043).

8. ...

Note: Section 8 repealed by Sch 14 Immigration and Asylum Act 1999 from a date to be notified.

9. ...

Note: Section 9 repealed by Sch 14 Immigration and Asylum Act 1999 from 30 June 2003, (SI 2003/1469).

10. Miscellaneous minor amendments

The principal Act shall have effect with the amendments specified in the Schedule to this Act.

11. Expenses and receipts

(1) There shall be paid out of money provided by Parliament any expenses incurred by the Secretary of State in consequences of this Act.

(2) Any sums received by the Secretary of State by virtue of this Act shall be paid into the Consolidated Fund.

12. Short title, interpretation, commencement and extent

(1) This Act may be cited as the Immigration Act 1988.

(2) In this Act 'the principal Act' means the Immigration Act 1971 and any expression which is also used in that Act has the same meaning as in that Act.

(3) Except as provided in subsection (4) below this Act shall come into force at the end of the period of two months beginning with the day on which it is passed.

(4) Sections 1, 2, 3, 4, 5 and 7(1) and paragraph 1 of the Schedule shall come into force on such day as may be appointed by the Secretary of State by an order made by statutory instrument; and such an order may appoint different days for different provisions and contain such transitional provisions and savings as the Secretary of State thinks necessary or expedient in connection with any provision brought into force.

(5) This Act extends to Northern Ireland and section 36 of the principal Act (power to extend any of its provisions to the Channel Islands or the Isle of Man) shall apply also to the provisions of this Act.

Section 10

SCHEDULE

MINOR AMENDMENTS

...

Asylum and Immigration Appeals Act 1993
(1993, c. 23)

An Act to make provision about persons who claim asylum in the United Kingdom and their dependants; to amend the law with respect to certain rights of appeal under the Immigration Act 1971; and to extend the provisions of the Immigration (Carriers' Liability) Act 1987 to transit passengers. [1 July 1993]

Introductory

1. Interpretation

In this Act—

'the 1971 Act' means the Immigration Act 1971;

'claim for asylum' means a claim made by a person (whether before or after the coming into force of this section) that it would be contrary to the United Kingdom's obligations under the Convention for him to be removed from, or required to leave, the United Kingdom; and

'the Convention' means the Convention relating to the Status of Refugees done at Geneva on 28 July 1951 and the Protocol to that Convention.

2. Primacy of Convention

Nothing in the immigration rules (within the meaning of the 1971 Act) shall lay down any practice which would be contrary to the Convention.

Treatment of persons who claim asylum

3. ...

Note: Section 3 repealed by Immigration and Asylum Act 1999 from 11 December 2000.

4. ...

Note: Section 4 repealed by Immigration and Asylum Act 1999 from 3 April 2000.

5. ...

Note: Section 5 repealed by Immigration and Asylum Act 1999 from 3 April 2000.

6. ...

Note: Section 6 repealed by Immigration and Asylum Act 1999 from 11 November 1999, with effect from 26 July 1993.

7. ...

Note: Section 7 repealed by Immigration and Asylum Act 1999 from 2 October 2000.

8. ...

Note: Section 8 repealed by Immigration and Asylum Act 1999 from 2 October 2000, transitional provisions set out in SI 2003/754.

9. ...

Note: Section 9 repealed by Immigration and Asylum Act 1999 from 2 October 2000.

[9A. ...

Note: Section 9A repealed by Sch 2 Asylum and Immigration Act 2004 from 4 April 2005 (SI 2005/565).

10. Visitors, short-term and prospective students and their dependants

...

Note: Section 10 repealed by Immigration and Asylum Act 1999 from 2 October 2000.

11. Refusals which are mandatory under immigration rules

...

Note: Section 11 repealed by Immigration and Asylum Act 1999 from 2 October 2000.

12. ...

Note: Section 12 repealed by Immigration and Asylum Act 1999.

Supplementary

13. Financial provision

(1) There shall be paid out of money provided by Parliament—
    (a) any expenditure incurred by the Secretary of State under this Act; and
    (b) any increase attributable to this Act in the sums payable out of such money under any other enactment.

(2) Any sums received by the Secretary of State by virtue of this Act shall be paid into the Consolidated Fund.

14. Commencement

(1) Sections 4 to 11 above (and section 1 above so far as it relates to those sections) shall not come into force until such day as the Secretary of State may by order appoint, and different days may be appointed for provisions or for different purposes.

(2) An order under subsection (1) above—

(a) shall be made by statutory instrument; and

(b) may contain such transitional and supplemental provisions as the Secretary of State thinks necessary or expedient.

(3) Without prejudice to the generality of subsections (1) and (2) above, with respect to any provision of section 4 above an order under subsection (1) above may appoint different days in relation to different descriptions of asylum-seekers and dependants of asylum-seekers; and any such descriptions may be framed by reference to nationality, citizenship, origin or other connection with any particular country or territory, but not by reference to race, colour or religion.

15. Extent

(1) Her Majesty may by Order in Council direct that any of the provisions of this Act shall extend, with such modifications as appear to Her Majesty to be appropriate, to any of the Channel Islands or the Isle of Man.

(2) This Act extends to Northern Ireland.

16. Short title

This Act may be cited as the Asylum and Immigration Appeals Act 1993.

SCHEDULES
SCHEDULE 1

...

Note: Schedule 1 repealed by Immigration and Asylum Act 1999 from 3 April 2000.

Section 8(6)   SCHEDULE 2

Note: Schedule 2 repealed by Immigration and Asylum Act 1999 from 2 October 2000.

Special Immigration Appeals Commission Act 1997
(1997, c. 68)

An Act to establish the Special Immigration Appeals Commission; to make provision with respect to its jurisdiction; and for connected purposes   [17 December 1997]

1. Establishment of the commission

(1) There shall be a commission, known as the Special Immigration Appeals Commission, for the purpose of exercising the jurisdiction conferred by this Act.

(2) Schedule 1 to this Act shall have effect in relation to the Commission.

[(3) The Commission shall be a superior court of record.

(4) A decision of the Commission shall be questioned in legal proceedings only in accordance with—

    (a) section 7, or

    (b) ...]

Note: Words in square brackets inserted by Anti-terrorism, Crime and Security Act 2001, s 35 from 13 December 2001. Subsection 4(b) repealed by Prevention of Terrorism Act 2005, s 16 from 14 March 2005.

[2. Jurisdiction: appeals

(1) A person may appeal to the Special Immigration Appeals Commission against a decision if—

    (a) he would be able to appeal against the decision under section 82(1) [83(2) or 83A(2)] of the Nationality, Immigration and Asylum Act 2002 but for a certificate of the Secretary of State under section 97 of that Act (national security &c.), or

    (b) an appeal against the decision under section 82(1) [83(2) or 83A(2)] of that Act lapsed under section 99 of that Act by virtue of a certificate of the Secretary of State under section 97 of that Act.

(2) The following provisions shall apply, with any necessary modifications, in relation to an appeal against an immigration decision under this section as they apply in relation to an appeal under section 82(1) of the Nationality, Immigration and Asylum Act 2002—

    (a) section 3C [or 3D] of the Immigration Act 1971 (c. 77) [continuation of leave],

    (b) section 78 of the Nationality, Immigration and Asylum Act 2002 (no removal while appeal pending),

    (c) section 79 of that Act (deportation order: appeal),

    (d) section 82(3) of that Act (variation or revocation of leave to enter or remain: appeal),

    (e) section 84 of that Act (grounds of appeal),

    (f) section 85 of that Act (matters to be considered),

    (g) section 86 of that Act (determination of appeal),

    (h) section 87 of that Act (successful appeal: direction),

    (i) section 96 of that Act (earlier right of appeal),

    (j) section 104 of that Act (pending appeal),

   (k) section 105 of that Act (notice of immigration decision), and

   (l) section 110 of that Act (grants).

(3) The following provisions shall apply, with any necessary modifications, in relation to [an appeal against a decision other than an immigration decision] under this section as they apply in relation to an appeal under section 83(2) [or 83A(2)] of the Nationality, Immigration and Asylum Act 2002—

   (a) section 85(4) of that Act (matters to be considered),

   (b) section 86 of that Act (determination of appeal),

   (c) section 87 of that Act (successful appeal direction), and

   (d) section 110 of that Act (grants).

(4) An appeal against the rejection of a claim for asylum under this section shall be treated as abandoned if the appellant leaves the United Kingdom.

(5) A person may bring or continue an appeal against an immigration decision under this section while he is in the United Kingdom only if he would be able to bring or continue the appeal while he was in the United Kingdom if it were an appeal under section 82(1) of that Act.

(6) In this section 'immigration decision' has the meaning given by section 82(2) of the Nationality, Immigration and Asylum Act 2002.]

[**2A.** . . . .]

[**2B.** A person may appeal to the Special Immigration Appeals Commission against a decision to make an order under section 40 of the British Nationality Act 1981 (c. 61) (deprivation of citizenship) if he is not entitled to appeal under section 40A(1) of that Act because of a certificate under section 40A(2)] [and section 40A(3)(a) shall have effect in relation to appeals under this section.]

Note: Section 2 substituted and s 2A ceased to have effect by Sch 7 Nationality, Immigration and Asylum Act 2002 from 1 April 2003 (SI 2003/754). Words in square brackets in s 2 inserted or substituted by Sch 1 Immigration, Asylum and Nationality Act 2006 from 31 August 2006 (SI 2006/2226). Section 2B inserted by Nationality, Immigration and Asylum Act 2002, s 4 from 1 April 2003 (SI 2003/754). Transitional provisions set out in SI 2003/754. Words in second square brackets in s 2B inserted by Sch 2 Asylum and Immigration Act 2004 from 4 April 2004 (SI 2005/565).

3. Jurisdiction: bail

(1) In the case of a person to whom subsection (2) below applies, the provisions of Schedule 2 to the Immigration Act 1971 specified in Schedule 3 to this Act shall have effect with the modifications set out there.

(2) This subsection applies to a person who is detained under the Immigration Act 1971 [or the Nationality, Immigration and Asylum Act 2002] if—

   (a) the Secretary of State certifies that his detention is necessary in the interests of national security,

   (b) he is detained following a decision to refuse him leave to enter the United Kingdom on the ground that his exclusion is in the interests of national security, or

   (c) he is detained following a decision to make a deportation order against him on the ground that his deportation is in the interests of national security.

Note: Words in square brackets inserted from 4 April 2003 (SI 2003/1016).

4. ...

Note: Section 4 ceased to have effect from 1 April 2003 (SI 2003/754), Sch 7 Nationality, Immigration and Asylum Act 2002. Transitional provisions set out in SI 2003/754.

5. Procedure in relation to jurisdiction under sections 2 and 3

(1) The Lord Chancellor may make rules—

(a) for regulating the exercise of the rights of appeal conferred by section 2 [or 2B]...above,

(b) for prescribing the practice and procedure to be followed on or in connection with appeals under [section 2 [or 2B]...] above, including the mode and burden of proof and admissibility of evidence on such appeals, and

(c) for other matters preliminary or incidental to or arising out of such appeals, including proof of the decisions of the Special Immigration Appeals Commission.

(2) Rules under this section shall provide that an appellant has the right to be legally represented in any proceedings before the Commission on an appeal under section 2 [or 2B] [...] above, subject to any power conferred on the Commission by such rules.

[(2A) Rules under this section may, in particular, do anything which may be done by [Tribunal Procedure Rules].

(3) Rules under this section may, in particular—

(a) make provision enabling proceedings before the Commission to take place without the appellant being given full particulars of the reasons for the decision which is the subject of the appeal,

(b) make provision enabling the Commission to hold proceedings in the absence of any person, including the appellant and any legal representative appointed by him,

(c) make provision about the functions in proceedings before the Commission of persons appointed under section 6 below, and

(d) make provision enabling the Commission to give the appellant a summary of any evidence taken in his absence.

(4) Rules under this section may also include provision—

(a) enabling any functions of the Commission which relate to matters preliminary or incidental to an appeal, or which are conferred by Part II of Schedule 2 to the Immigration Act 1971, to be performed by a single member of the Commission, or

(b) conferring on the Commission such ancillary powers as the Lord Chancellor thinks necessary for the purposes of the exercise of its functions.

(5) The power to make rules under this section shall include power to make rules with respect to applications to the Commission under paragraphs 22 to 24 of Schedule 2 to the Immigration Act 1971 and matters arising out of such applications.

(6) In making rules under this section, the Lord Chancellor shall have regard, in particular, to—

(a) the need to secure that decisions which are the subject of appeals are properly reviewed, and

(b) the need to secure that information is not disclosed contrary to the public interest.

(7) ...

(8) The power to make rules under this section shall be exercisable by statutory instrument.

(9) No rules shall be made under this section unless a draft of them has been laid before and approved by resolution of each House of Parliament.

Note: Subsection (7) omitted by Sch 5 Regulation of Investigatory Powers Act 2000 from 2 October 2002 (SI 2000/2543). Words deleted from and words in square brackets in sub-ss 5(1) and 5(2), and sub-s 5(2A) inserted by Sch 7 Nationality, Immigration and Asylum Act 2002 from 1 April 2003 (SI 2003/754, which sets out transitional provisions). Words in square brackets in sub-s (2A) substituted from 15 February 2010 (SI 2010/21).

6. Appointment of person to represent the appellant's interests

(1) The relevant law officer may appoint a person to represent the interests of an appellant in any proceedings before the Special Immigration Appeals Commission from which the appellant and any legal representative of his are excluded.

(2) For the purposes of subsection (1) above, the relevant law officer is—

(a) in relation to proceedings before the Commission in England and Wales, the Attorney General,

(b) in relation to proceedings before the Commission in Scotland, the Lord Advocate, and

(c) in relation to proceedings before the Commission in Northern Ireland, the Attorney General for Northern Ireland.

(3) A person appointed under subsection (1) above—

(a) if appointed for the purposes of proceedings in England and Wales, shall have a general qualification for the purposes of section 71 of the Courts and Legal Services Act 1990,

(b) if appointed for the purposes of proceedings in Scotland, shall be—

(i) an advocate, or

(ii) a solicitor who has by virtue of section 25A of the Solicitors (Scotland) Act 1980 rights of audience in the Court of Session and the High Court of Justiciary, and

(c) if appointed for the purposes of proceedings in Northern Ireland, shall be a member of the Bar of Northern Ireland.

(4) A person appointed under subsection (1) above shall not be responsible to the person whose interests he is appointed to represent.

7. Appeals from the Commission

(1) Where the Special Immigration Appeals Commission has made a final determination of an appeal, any party to the appeal may bring a further appeal to the appropriate appeal court on any question of law material to that determination.

(2) An appeal under this section may be brought only with the leave of the Commission or, if such leave is refused, with the leave of the appropriate appeal court.

(3) In this section 'the appropriate appeal court' means—

(a) in relation to a determination made by the Commission in England and Wales, the Court of Appeal,

(b) in relation to a determination made by the Commission in Scotland, the Court of Session, and

(c) in relation to a determination made by the Commission in Northern Ireland, the Court of Appeal in Northern Ireland.

(4) ...

[7A. ...]

Note: Section 7(4) omitted and s 7A inserted by Immigration and Asylum Act 1999 from 2 October 2000. Section 7A ceased to have effect from 1 April 2003 (SI 2003/754), Sch 7 Nationality, Immigration and Asylum Act 2002. SI 2003/754 sets out transitional provisions.

8. Procedure on applications to the Commission for leave to appeal

(1) The Lord Chancellor may make rules regulating, and prescribing the procedure to be followed on, applications to the Special Immigration Appeals Commission for leave to appeal under section 7 above.

(2) Rules under this section may include provision enabling an application for leave to appeal to be heard by a single member of the Commission.

(3) The power to make rules under this section shall be exercisable by statutory instrument.

(4) No rules shall be made under this section unless a draft of them has been laid before and approved by resolution of each House of Parliament.

9. Short title, commencement and extent

(1) This Act may be cited as the Special Immigration Appeals Commission Act 1997.

(2) This Act, except for this section, shall come into force on such day as the Secretary of State may by order made by statutory instrument appoint; and different days may be so appointed for different purposes.

(3) Her Majesty may by Order in Council direct that any of the provisions of this Act shall extend, with such modifications as appear to Her Majesty to be appropriate, to any of the Channel Islands or the Isle of Man.

(4) This Act extends to Northern Ireland.

Note: Commencement: s 9 on 17 December 1997, ss 5 and 8 on 11 June 1998, remainder of Act on 3 August 1998.

SCHEDULES

Section 1

SCHEDULE 1

THE COMMISSION

Members

1.—(1) The Special Immigration Appeals Commission shall consist of such number of members appointed by the Lord Chancellor as he may determine.

(2) A member of the Commission shall hold and vacate office in accordance with the terms of his appointment and shall, on ceasing to hold office, be eligible for reappointment.

(3)   A member of the Commission may resign his office at any time by notice in writing to the Lord Chancellor.

Chairman

2.   The Lord Chancellor shall appoint one of the members of the Commission to be its chairman.

Payments to members

3.—(1)   The Lord Chancellor may pay to the members of the Commission such remuneration and allowances as he may determine.

(2)   The Lord Chancellor may, if he thinks fit in the case of any member of the Commission, pay such pension, allowance or gratuity to or in respect of the member, or such sums towards the provision of such pension, allowance or gratuity, as he may determine.

(3)   If a person ceases to be a member of the Commission and it appears to the Lord Chancellor that there are special circumstances which make it right that the person should receive compensation, he may pay to that person a sum of such amount as he may determine.

Proceedings

4.   The Commission shall sit at such times and in such places as the Lord Chancellor may direct and may sit in two or more divisions.

5.   The Commission shall be deemed to be duly constituted if it consists of three members of whom—
   (a)   at least one holds or has held high judicial office (within the meaning of the Appellate Jurisdiction Act 1876), and
   [(b)   at least one is or has been [a judge of the First-tier Tribunal, or of the Upper Tribunal, who is assigned to a chamber with responsibility for immigration and asylum matters].

Note: Paragraph 5(b) substituted by Sch 2 Asylum and Immigration Act 2004 from 4 April 2005 (SI 2005/565). Words in square brackets substituted from 15 February 2010 (SI 2010/21).

6.   The chairman or, in his absence, such other member of the Commission as he may nominate, shall preside at sittings of the Commission and report its decisions.

Staff

7.   The Lord Chancellor may appoint such officers and servants for the Commission as he thinks fit.

Expenses

8.   The Lord Chancellor shall defray the remuneration of persons appointed under paragraph 7 above and such expenses of the Commission as he thinks fit.

Section 2   SCHEDULE 2

APPEALS: SUPPLEMENTARY

. . .

Note: Schedule 2 ceased to have effect from 1 April 2003 (SI 2003/754), Sch 7 Nationality, Immigration and Asylum Act 2002. SI 2003/754 sets out transitional provisions.

Section 3   SCHEDULE 3

BAIL: MODIFICATIONS OF SCHEDULE 2 TO THE IMMIGRATION ACT 1971

1.—(1) Paragraph 22 shall be amended as follows.

(2) In sub-paragraph (1A), for the words from the beginning to ['Tribunal'] there shall be substituted 'The Special Immigration Appeals Commission'.

(3) In sub-paragraph (2)—
    (a) for the words 'immigration officer or [the First-tier Tribunal] there shall be substituted 'Special Immigration Appeals Commission', and
    (b) for the words 'officer or [the First-tier Tribunal]' there shall be substituted 'Commission'.

(4) In sub-paragraph (3)—
    (a) for 'an immigration officer or [the First-tier Tribunal] there shall be substituted 'the Special Immigration Appeals Commission', and
    (b) for 'officer or [the First-tier Tribunal]', in both places, there shall be substituted 'Commission'.

Note: Words in first square brackets substituted by Sch 2 Asylum and Immigration Act 2004 from 4 April 2005 (SI 2005/565). Words in other square brackets substituted from 15 February 2010 (SI 2010/21).

2.—(1) Paragraph 23 shall be amended as follows.

(2) In sub-paragraph (1)—
    (a) for ['the First-tier Tribunal'] there shall be substituted 'the Special Immigration Appeals Commission', and
    (b) for ['the First-tier Tribunal'], in each place, there shall be substituted 'the Commission'.

(3) In sub-paragraph (2)—
    (a) for ['the First-tier Tribunal'] there shall be substituted 'the Special Immigration Appeals Commission', and
    (b) for ['the First-tier Tribunal'] there shall be substituted 'the Commission'.

Note: Words in square brackets substituted from 15 February 2010 (SI 2010/21).

3.—(1) Paragraph 24 shall be amended as follows.

(2) For sub-paragraph (2), there shall be substituted—
    '(2) A person arrested under this paragraph shall be brought before the Special Immigration Appeals Commission within twenty-four hours.'

(3) In sub-paragraph (3), for the words from the beginning to 'above' there shall be substituted 'Where a person is brought before the Special Immigration Appeals Commission by virtue of sub-paragraph (2) above, the Commission—'.

4.—(1) Paragraph 29 shall be amended as follows.

(2) For sub-paragraphs (2) to (4) there shall be substituted—
    '(2) The Special Immigration Appeals Commission may release an appellant on his entering into a recognizance or, in Scotland, bail bond conditioned for his appearance before the Commission at a time and place named in the recognizance or bail bond.'

(3) For sub-paragraph (6) there shall be substituted—
    '(6) In any case in which the Special Immigration Appeals Commission has power to release an appellant on bail, the Commission may, instead of taking the bail, fix the amount and conditions of the bail (including the amount in which any sureties are to be bound) with a view to its being taken subsequently by any such person as may be specified by the Commission; and on the recognizance or bail bond being so taken the appellant shall be released.'

5. Paragraph 30(2) shall be omitted.

6.—(1) Paragraph 31 shall be amended as follows.

(2) In sub-paragraph (1)—
- (a) for ['the Tribunal'] there shall be substituted 'the Special Immigration Appeals Commission',
- (b) for ['the Tribunal'] there shall be substituted 'the Commission', and
- (c) for ['the Tribunal'], in both places, there shall be substituted 'the Commission'.

(3) In sub-paragraph (3)—
- (a) for ['the Tribunal'] there shall be substituted 'the Special Immigration Appeals Commission,' and
- (b) for ['the Tribunal'] there shall be substituted 'it'.

7. Paragraph 32 shall be amended as follows—
- (a) for ['the Tribunal'] there shall be substituted 'the Special Immigration Appeals Commission',
- (b) for ['the Tribunal'] there shall be substituted 'the Commission', and
- (c) for ['the Tribunal'] there shall be substituted 'the Commission'.

Note : Words in square brackets substituted by Sch 2 Asylum and Immigration Act 2004 from 4 April 2005 (SI 2005/565).

8.—(1) Paragraph 33 shall be amended as follows.

(2) For sub-paragraph (2), there shall be substituted—
'(2) A person arrested under this paragraph shall be brought before the Special Immigration Appeals Commission within twenty-four hours.'

(3) In sub-paragraph (3), for the words from the beginning to 'above' there shall be substituted 'Where a person is brought before the Special Immigration Appeals Commission by virtue of sub-paragraph (2) above, the Commission—'.

Note: Extends jurisdiction of Tribunal to Special Immigration Appeals Commission in paras 22–24, 29, 31–33.

Crime (Sentences) Act 1997

(1997, c. 43)

32A. Removal of prisoners liable to removal from United Kingdom

(1) Where P—
- (a) is a life prisoner in respect of whom a minimum term order has been made, and
- (b) is liable to removal from the United Kingdom,

the Secretary of State may remove P from prison under this section at any time after P has served the relevant part of the sentence (whether or not the Parole Board has directed P's release under section 28).

(2) But if P is serving two or more life sentences—

(a) this section does not apply to P unless a minimum term order has been made in respect of each of those sentences; and

(b) the Secretary of State may not remove P from prison under this section until P has served the relevant part of each of them.

(3) If P is removed from prison under this section—

(a) P is so removed only for the purpose of enabling the Secretary of State to remove P from the United Kingdom under powers conferred by—

(i) Schedule 2 or 3 to the Immigration Act 1971, or

(ii) section 10 of the Immigration and Asylum Act 1999, and

(b) so long as remaining in the United Kingdom, P remains liable to be detained in pursuance of the sentence.

(4) So long as P, having been removed from prison under this section, remains in the United Kingdom but has not been returned to prison, any duty or power of the Secretary of State under section 28 or 30 is exercisable in relation to P as if P were in prison.

(5) In this section—

'liable to removal from the United Kingdom' has the meaning given by section 259 of the Criminal Justice Act 2003;

'the relevant part' has the meaning given by section 28.

Note: Sections 32A and 32B inserted from a date to be appointed by the Legal Aid, Sentencing and Punishment of Offenders Act 2012, s 119.

32B. Re-entry into United Kingdom of offender removed from prison

(1) This section applies if P, having been removed from prison under section 32A, is removed from the United Kingdom.

(2) If P enters the United Kingdom—

(a) P is liable to be detained in pursuance of the sentence from the time of P's entry into the United Kingdom;

(b) if no direction was given by the Parole Board under subsection (5) of section 28 before P's removal from prison, that section applies to P;

(c) if such a direction was given before that removal, P is to be treated as if P had been recalled to prison under section 32.

(3) A person who is liable to be detained by virtue of subsection (2)(a) is, if at large, to be taken for the purposes of section 49 of the Prison Act 1952 (persons unlawfully at large) to be unlawfully at large.

(4) Subsection (2)(a) does not prevent P's further removal from the United Kingdom.

Note: Sections 32A and 32B inserted from a date to be appointed by the Legal Aid, Sentencing and Punishment of Offenders Act 2012, s 119.

Human Rights Act 1998
(1998, c. 42)

Arrangement of Sections

Introduction

Legislation

Public authorities

Remedial action

Other rights and proceedings

Derogations and reservations

Judges of the European Court of Human Rights

Parliamentary procedure

An Act to give further effect to rights and freedoms guaranteed under the European Convention on Human Rights; to make provision with respect to holders of certain judicial offices who become judges of the European Court of Human Rights; and for connected purposes. [9 November 1998]

Introduction

1. The Convention Rights

(1) In this Act 'the Convention rights' means the rights and fundamental freedoms set out in—

(a) Articles 2 to 12 and 14 of the Convention,

(b) Articles 1 to 3 of the First Protocol, and

(c) [Article 1 of the Thirteenth Protocol] as read with Articles 16 to 18 of the Convention.

(2) Those Articles are to have effect for the purposes of this Act subject to any designated derogation or reservation (as to which see sections 14 and 15).

(3) The Articles are set out in Schedule 1.

(4) The [Secretary of State] may by order make such amendments to this Act as he considers appropriate to reflect the effect, in relation to the United Kingdom, of a protocol.

(5) In subsection (4) 'protocol' means a protocol to the Convention—

(a) which the United Kingdom has ratified; or

(b) which the United Kingdom has signed with a view to ratification.

(6) No amendment may be made by an order under subsection (4) so as to come into force before the protocol concerned is in force in relation to the United Kingdom.

Note: Commencement 2 October 2000. Words in square brackets in sub-s (1)(c) substituted from 22 June 2004 (SI 2004/1574). Words in square brackets in sub-s (4) substituted from 19 August 2003 (SI 2003/1887).

2. Interpretation of Convention rights

(1) A court or tribunal determining a question which has arisen in connection with a Convention right must take into account any—

(a) judgment, decision, declaration or advisory opinion of the European Court of Human Rights,

(b) opinion of the Commission given in a report adopted under Article 31 of the Convention,

(c) decision of the Commission in connection with Article 26 or 27(2) of the Convention, or

(d) decision of the Committee of Ministers taken under Article 46 of the Convention,

whenever made or given, so far as, in the opinion of the court or tribunal, it is relevant to the proceedings in which that question has arisen.

(2) Evidence of any judgment, decision, declaration or opinion of which account may have to be taken under this section is to be given in proceedings before any court or tribunal in such manner as may be provided by rules.

(3) In this section 'rules' means rules of court or, in the case of proceedings before a tribunal, rules made for the purposes of this section—

(a) by [the Lord Chancellor or] the Secretary of State, in relation to any proceedings outside Scotland;

(b) by the Secretary of State, in relation to proceedings in Scotland; or

(c) by a Northern Ireland department, in relation to proceedings before a tribunal in Northern Ireland—

(i) which deals with transferred matters; and

(ii) for which no rules made under paragraph (a) are in force.

Note: Commencement 2 October 2000. Words in square brackets in sub-s (3)(a) omitted from 19 August 2003 (SI 2003/1887), re-inserted from 12 January 2006 (SI 2005/3429).

Legislation

3. Interpretation of legislation

(1) So far as it is possible to do so, primary legislation and subordinate legislation must be read and given effect in a way which is compatible with the Convention rights.

(2) This section—

(a) applies to primary legislation and subordinate legislation whenever enacted;

(b) does not affect the validity, continuing operation or enforcement of any incompatible primary legislation; and

(c) does not affect the validity, continuing operation or enforcement of any incompatible subordinate legislation if (disregarding any possibility of revocation) primary legislation prevents removal of the incompatibility.

Note: Commencement 2 October 2000.

4. Declaration of incompatibility

(1) Subsection (2) applies in any proceedings in which a court determines whether a provision of primary legislation is compatible with a Convention right.

(2) If the court is satisfied that the provision is incompatible with a Convention right, it may make a declaration of that incompatibility.

(3) Subsection (4) applies in any proceedings in which a court determines whether a provision of subordinate legislation, made in the exercise of a power conferred by primary legislation, is compatible with a Convention right.

(4) If the court is satisfied—

(a) that the provision is incompatible with a Convention right, and

(b) that (disregarding any possibility of revocation) the primary legislation concerned prevents removal of the incompatibility, it may make a declaration of that incompatibility.

(5) In this section 'court' means—

[(a) the Supreme Court;]

(b) the Judicial Committee of the Privy Council;

(c) the [Court Martial Appeal Court];

(d) in Scotland, the High Court of Justiciary sitting otherwise than as a trial court or the Court of Session;

(e) in England and Wales or Northern Ireland, the High Court or the Court of Appeal.

[(f) the Court of Protection, in any matter being dealt with by the President of the Family Division, the Vice-Chancellor or a puisne judge of the High Court.]

(6) A declaration under this section ('a declaration of incompatibility')—

(a) does not affect the validity, continuing operation or enforcement of the provision in respect of which it is given; and

(b) is not binding on the parties to the proceedings in which it is made.

Note: Commencement 2 October 2000. Subsection (5)(a) substituted by the Constitutional Reform Act 2005 Sch 9 from 1 October 2009 (SI 2009/1604). Words substituted in subsection (5)(c) by Armed Forces Act 2006 Sch. 16 from 28 March 2009 (for certain purposes) (SI 2009/812) and from 31 October 2009 otherwise (SI 2009/1167). Subsection (5)(f) inserted by Mental Capacity Act 2005 Sch 6 from 1 October 2007 (SI 2007/1897).

5. Right of Crown to intervene

(1) Where a court is considering whether to make a declaration of incompatibility, the Crown is entitled to notice in accordance with rules of court.

(2) In any case to which subsection (1) applies—

(a) a Minister of the Crown (or a person nominated by him),

(b) a member of the Scottish Executive,

(c) a Northern Ireland Minister,

(d) a Northern Ireland department, is entitled, on giving notice in accordance with rules of court, to be joined as a party to the proceedings.

(3) Notice under subsection (2) may be given at any time during the proceedings.

(4) A person who has been made a party to criminal proceedings (other than in Scotland) as the result of a notice under subsection (2) may, with leave, appeal to [the Supreme Court] against any declaration of incompatibility made in the proceedings.

(5) In subsection (4)—

'criminal proceedings' includes all proceedings before the [Court-Martial Appeal Court]; and 'leave' means leave granted by the court making the declaration of incompatibility or by [the Supreme Court].

Note: Commencement 2 October 2000. Words 'the Supreme Court' substituted by the Constitutional Reform Act 2005 Sch 9 from 1 October 2009 (SI 2009/1604). Words 'Court Martial Appeal Court' substituted by Armed Forces Act 2006 Sch 16 from 28 March 2009 (for certain purposes) (SI 2009/812) and from 31 October 2009 otherwise (SI 2009/1167).

Public authorities

6. Acts of public authorities

(1) It is unlawful for a public authority to act in a way which is incompatible with a Convention right.

(2) Subsection (1) does not apply to an act if—

(a) as the result of one or more provisions of primary legislation, the authority could not have acted differently; or

(b) in the case of one or more provisions of, or made under, primary legislation which cannot be read or given effect in a way which is compatible with the Convention rights, the authority was acting so as to give effect to or enforce those provisions.

(3) In this section 'public authority' includes—

(a) a court or tribunal, and

(b) any person certain of whose functions are functions of a public nature, but does not include either House of Parliament or a person exercising functions in connection with proceedings in Parliament.

(4) ...

(5) In relation to a particular act, a person is not a public authority by virtue only of subsection (3)(b) if the nature of the act is private.

(6) 'An act' includes a failure to act but does not include a failure to—

(a) introduce in, or lay before, Parliament a proposal for legislation; or

(b) make any primary legislation or remedial order.

Note: Commencement 2 October 2000. Sub-section (4) deleted by the Constitutional Reform Act 2005 Sch 9 from 1 October 2009 (SI 2009/1604).

7. Proceedings

(1) A person who claims that a public authority has acted (or proposes to act) in a way which is made unlawful by section 6(1) may—

(a) bring proceedings against the authority under this Act in the appropriate court or tribunal, or

(b) rely on the Convention right or rights concerned in any legal proceedings, but only if he is (or would be) a victim of the unlawful act.

(2) In subsection (1)(a) 'appropriate court or tribunal' means such court or tribunal as may be determined in accordance with rules; and proceedings against an authority include a counterclaim or similar proceeding.

(3) If the proceedings are brought on an application for judicial review, the applicant is to be taken to have a sufficient interest in relation to the unlawful act only if he is, or would be, a victim of that act.

(4) If the proceedings are made by way of a petition for judicial review in Scotland, the applicant shall be taken to have title and interest to sue in relation to the unlawful act only if he is, or would be, a victim of that act.

(5) Proceedings under subsection (1)(a) must be brought before the end of—

(a) the period of one year beginning with the date on which the act complained of took place; or

(b) such longer period as the court or tribunal considers equitable having regard to all the circumstances, but that is subject to any rule imposing a stricter time limit in relation to the procedure in question.

(6) In subsection (1)(b) 'legal proceedings' includes—

(a) proceedings brought by or at the instigation of a public authority; and

(b) an appeal against the decision of a court or tribunal.

(7) For the purposes of this section, a person is a victim of an unlawful act only if he would be a victim for the purposes of Article 34 of the Convention if proceedings were brought in the European Court of Human Rights in respect of that act.

(8) Nothing in this Act creates a criminal offence.

(9) In this section 'rules' means—

(a) in relation to proceedings before a court or tribunal outside Scotland, rules made by [the Lord Chancellor or] the Secretary of State for the purposes of this section or rules of court,

(b) in relation to proceedings before a court or tribunal in Scotland, rules made by the Secretary of State for those purposes,

(c) in relation to proceedings before a tribunal in Northern Ireland—

(i) which deals with transferred matters; and

(ii) for which no rules made under paragraph (a) are in force, rules made by a Northern Ireland department for those purposes, and includes provision made by order under section 1 of the Courts and Legal Services Act 1990.

(10) In making rules, regard must be had to section 9.

(11) The Minister who has power to make rules in relation to a particular tribunal may, to the extent he considers it necessary to ensure that the tribunal can provide an appropriate remedy in relation to an act (or proposed act) of a public authority which is (or would be) unlawful as a result of section 6(1), by order add to—

(a) the relief or remedies which the tribunal may grant; or

(b) the grounds on which it may grant any of them.

(12) An order made under subsection (11) may contain such incidental, supplemental, consequential or transitional provision as the Minister making it considers appropriate.

(13) 'The Minister' includes the Northern Ireland department concerned.

Note: Commencement 2 October 2000. Words in square brackets in sub-s (9)(a) omitted from 19 August 2003 (SI 2003/1887), re-inserted from 12 January 2006 (SI 2005/3429).

8. Judicial remedies

(1) In relation to any act (or proposed act) of a public authority which the court finds is (or would be) unlawful, it may grant such relief or remedy, or make such order, within its powers as it considers just and appropriate.

(2) But damages may be awarded only by a court which has power to award damages, or to order the payment of compensation, in civil proceedings.

(3) No award of damages is to be made unless, taking account of all the circumstances of the case, including—

(a) any other relief or remedy granted, or order made, in relation to the act in question (by that or any other court), and

(b) the consequences of any decision (of that or any other court) in respect of that act, the court is satisfied that the award is necessary to afford just satisfaction to the person in whose favour it is made.

(4) In determining—

(a) whether to award damages, or

(b) the amount of an award, the court must take into account the principles applied by the European Court of Human Rights in relation to the award of compensation under Article 41 of the Convention.

(5) A public authority against which damages are awarded is to be treated—

(a) in Scotland, for the purposes of section 3 of the Law Reform (Miscellaneous Provisions) (Scotland) Act 1940 as if the award were made in an action of damages in which the authority has been found liable in respect of loss or damage to the person to whom the award is made;

(b) for the purposes of the Civil Liability (Contribution) Act 1978 as liable in respect of damage suffered by the person to whom the award is made.

(6) In this section—

'court' includes a tribunal;

'damages' means damages for an unlawful act of a public authority; and

'unlawful' means unlawful under section 6(1).

Note: Commencement 2 October 2000.

9. Judicial acts

(1) Proceedings under section 7(1)(a) in respect of a judicial act may be brought only—

(a) by exercising a right of appeal;

(b) on an application (in Scotland a petition) for judicial review; or

(c) in such other forum as may be prescribed by rules.

(2) That does not affect any rule of law which prevents a court from being the subject of judicial review.

(3) In proceedings under this Act in respect of a judicial act done in good faith, damages may not be awarded otherwise than to compensate a person to the extent required by Article 5(5) of the Convention.

(4) An award of damages permitted by subsection (3) is to be made against the Crown; but no award may be made unless the appropriate person, if not a party to the proceedings, is joined.

(5) In this section—

'appropriate person' means the Minister responsible for the court concerned, or a person or government department nominated by him;

'court' includes a tribunal;

'judge' includes a member of a tribunal, a justice of the peace [(or, in Northern Ireland, a lay magistrate)] and a clerk or other officer entitled to exercise the jurisdiction of a court;

'judicial act' means a judicial act of a court and includes an act done on the instructions, or on behalf, of a judge; and

'rules' has the same meaning as in section 7(9).

Note: Commencement 2 October 2000. Words in square brackets in subsection (5) inserted (NI) by Justice (Northern Ireland) Act 2002 Sch 4 from 1 April 2005 (SR 2005/109).

Remedial action

10. Power to take remedial action

(1) This section applies if—

(a) a provision of legislation has been declared under section 4 to be incompatible with a Convention right and, if an appeal lies—

(i) all persons who may appeal have stated in writing that they do not intend to do so;

(ii) the time for bringing an appeal has expired and no appeal has been brought within that time; or

(iii) an appeal brought within that time has been determined or abandoned; or

(b) it appears to a Minister of the Crown or Her Majesty in Council that, having regard to a finding of the European Court of Human Rights made after the coming into force of this section in proceedings against the United Kingdom, a provision of legislation is incompatible with an obligation of the United Kingdom arising from the Convention.

(2) If a Minister of the Crown considers that there are compelling reasons for proceeding under this section, he may by order make such amendments to the legislation as he considers necessary to remove the incompatibility.

(3) If, in the case of subordinate legislation, a Minister of the Crown considers—

(a) that it is necessary to amend the primary legislation under which the subordinate legislation in question was made, in order to enable the incompatibility to be removed, and

(b) that there are compelling reasons for proceeding under this section, he may by order make such amendments to the primary legislation as he considers necessary.

(4) This section also applies where the provision in question is in subordinate legislation and has been quashed, or declared invalid, by reason of incompatibility with a Convention right and the Minister proposes to proceed under paragraph 2(b) of Schedule 2.

(5) If the legislation is an Order in Council, the power conferred by subsection (2) or (3) is exercisable by Her Majesty in Council.

(6) In this section 'legislation' does not include a Measure of the Church Assembly or of the General Synod of the Church of England.

(7) Schedule 2 makes further provision about remedial orders.

Note: Commencement 2 October 2000.

Other rights and proceedings

11. Safeguard for existing human rights

A person's reliance on a Convention right does not restrict—

(a) any other right or freedom conferred on him by or under any law having effect in any part of the United Kingdom; or

(b) his right to make any claim or bring any proceedings which he could make or bring apart from sections 7 to 9.

Note: Commencement 2 October 2000.

12. Freedom of expression

(1) This section applies if a court is considering whether to grant any relief which, if granted, might affect the exercise of the Convention right to freedom of expression.

(2) If the person against whom the application for relief is made ('the respondent') is neither present nor represented, no such relief is to be granted unless the court is satisfied—
    (a) that the applicant has taken all practicable steps to notify the respondent; or
    (b) that there are compelling reasons why the respondent should not be notified.

(3) No such relief is to be granted so as to restrain publication before trial unless the court is satisfied that the applicant is likely to establish that publication should not be allowed.

(4) The court must have particular regard to the importance of the Convention right to freedom of expression and, where the proceedings relate to material which the respondent claims, or which appears to the court, to be journalistic, literary or artistic material (or to conduct connected with such material), to—
    (a) the extent to which—
      (i) the material has, or is about to, become available to the public; or
      (ii) it is, or would be, in the public interest for the material to be published;
    (b) any relevant privacy code.

(5) In this section—
'court' includes a tribunal; and
'relief' includes any remedy or order (other than in criminal proceedings).

Note: Commencement 2 October 2000.

13. Freedom of thought, conscience and religion

(1) If a court's determination of any question arising under this Act might affect the exercise by a religious organisation (itself or its members collectively) of the Convention right to freedom of thought, conscience and religion, it must have particular regard to the importance of that right.

(2) In this section 'court' includes a tribunal.

Note: Commencement 2 October 2000.

Derogations and reservations

14. Derogations

(1) In this Act 'designated derogation' means [...] any derogation by the United Kingdom from an Article of the Convention, or of any protocol to the Convention, which is designated for the purposes of this Act in an order made by the [Secretary of State].

(2) ...

(3) If a designated derogation is amended or replaced it ceases to be a designated derogation.

(4) But subsection (3) does not prevent the Secretary of State from exercising his power under subsection (1)[...] to make a fresh designation order in respect of the Article concerned.

(5) The Secretary of State must by order make such amendments to Schedule 3 as he considers appropriate to reflect—
    (a) any designation order; or
    (b) the effect of subsection (3).

(6) A designation order may be made in anticipation of the making by the United Kingdom of a proposed derogation.

Note: Commencement 2 October 2000. Words omitted from 1 April 2001 (SI 2001/1216). Words in square brackets in sub-s (4) substituted from 19 August 2003 (SI 2003/1887).

15. Reservations

(1) In this Act 'designated reservation' means—
    (a) the United Kingdom's reservation to Article 2 of the First Protocol to the Convention; and
    (b) any other reservation by the United Kingdom to an Article of the Convention, or of any protocol to the Convention, which is designated for the purposes of this Act in an order made by the [Secretary of State].

(2) The text of the reservation referred to in subsection (1)(a) is set out in Part II of Schedule 3.

(3) If a designated reservation is withdrawn wholly or in part it ceases to be a designated reservation.

(4) But subsection (3) does not prevent the [Secretary of State] from exercising his power under subsection (1)(b) to make a fresh designation order in respect of the Article concerned.

(5) The [Secretary of State] must by order make such amendments to this Act as he considers appropriate to reflect—
    (a) any designation order; or
    (b) the effect of subsection (3).

Note: Commencement 2 October 2000. Words in square brackets substituted from 19 August 2003 (SI 2003/1887).

16. Period for which designated derogations have effect

(1) If it has not already been withdrawn by the United Kingdom, a designated derogation ceases to have effect for the purposes of this Act—
    [...] at the end of the period of five years beginning with the date on which the order designation was made.

(2) At any time before the period—
    (a) fixed by subsection (1)..., or
    (b) extended by an order under this subsection, comes to an end, the [Secretary of State] may by order extend it by a further period of five years.

(3) An order under section 14(1)…ceases to have effect at the end of the period for consideration, unless a resolution has been passed by each House approving the order.

(4) Subsection (3) does not affect—

(a) anything done in reliance on the order; or

(b) the power to make a fresh order under section 14(1)[…].

(5) In subsection (3) 'period for consideration' means the period of forty days beginning with the day on which the order was made.

(6) In calculating the period for consideration, no account is to be taken of any time during which—

(a) Parliament is dissolved or prorogued; or

(b) both Houses are adjourned for more than four days.

(7) If a designated derogation is withdrawn by the United Kingdom, the [Secretary of State] must by order make such amendments to this Act as he considers are required to reflect that withdrawal.

Note: Commencement 2 October 2000. Words omitted from 1 April 2001 (SI 2001/1216). Words in square brackets substituted from 19 August 2003 (SI 2003/1887),

17. Periodic review of designated reservations

(1) The appropriate Minister must review the designated reservation referred to in section 15(1)(a)—

(a) before the end of the period of five years beginning with the date on which section 1(2) came into force; and

(b) if that designation is still in force, before the end of the period of five years beginning with the date on which the last report relating to it was laid under subsection (3).

(2) The appropriate Minister must review each of the other designated reservations (if any)—

(a) before the end of the period of five years beginning with the date on which the order designating the reservation first came into force; and

(b) if the designation is still in force, before the end of the period of five years beginning with the date on which the last report relating to it was laid under subsection (3).

(3) The Minister conducting a review under this section must prepare a report on the result of the review and lay a copy of it before each House of Parliament.

Note: Commencement 2 October 2000.

Judges of the European Court of Human Rights

18. Appointment to European Court of Human Rights

(1) In this section 'judicial office' means the office of—

(a) Lord Justice of Appeal, Justice of the High Court or Circuit judge, in England and Wales;

(b) judge of the Court of Session or sheriff, in Scotland;

(c) Lord Justice of Appeal, judge of the High Court or county court judge, in Northern Ireland.

(2) The holder of a judicial office may become a judge of the European Court of Human Rights ('the Court') without being required to relinquish his office.

(3) But he is not required to perform the duties of his judicial office while he is a judge of the Court.

(4) In respect of any period during which he is a judge of the Court—

(a) a Lord Justice of Appeal or Justice of the High Court is not to count as a judge of the relevant court for the purposes of section 2(1) or 4(1) of the [the Senior Courts Act 1981] (maximum number of judges) nor as a judge of the [Senior Courts] for the purposes of section 12(1) to (6) of that Act (salaries etc.);

(b) a judge of the Court of Session is not to count as a judge of that court for the purposes of section 1(1) of the Court of Session Act 1988 (maximum number of judges) or of section 9(1)(c) of the Administration of Justice Act 1973 ('the 1973 Act') (salaries etc.);

(c) a Lord Justice of Appeal or judge of the High Court in Northern Ireland is not to count as a judge of the relevant court for the purposes of section 2(1) or 3(1) of the Judicature (Northern Ireland) Act 1978 (maximum number of judges) nor as a judge of the [Court of Judicature] of Northern Ireland for the purposes of section 9(1)(d) of the 1973 Act (salaries etc.);

(d) a Circuit judge is not to count as such for the purposes of section 18 of the Court Act 1971 (salaries etc.);

(e) a sheriff is not to count as such for the purposes of section 14 of the Sheriff Courts (Scotland) Act 1907 (salaries etc.);

(f) a county court judge of Northern Ireland is not to count as such for the purposes of section 106 of the County Courts Act (Northern Ireland) 1959 (salaries etc.).

(5) If a sheriff principal is appointed a judge of the Court, section 11(1) of the Sheriff Courts (Scotland) Act 1971 (temporary appointment of sheriff principal) applies, while he holds that appointment, as if his office is vacant.

(6) Schedule 4 makes provision about judicial pensions in relation to the holder of a judicial office who serves as a judge of the Court.

(7) The Lord Chancellor or the Secretary of State may by order make such transitional provision (including, in particular, provision for a temporary increase in the maximum number of judges) as he considers appropriate in relation to any holder of a judicial office who has completed his service as a judge of the Court.

[(7A) The following paragraphs apply to the making of an order under subsection (7) in relation to any holder of a judicial office listed in subsection (1)(a)—

(a) before deciding what transitional provision it is appropriate to make, the person making the order must consult the Lord Chief Justice of England and Wales;

(b) before making the order, that person must consult the Lord Chief Justice of England and Wales.

(7B) The following paragraphs apply to the making of an order under subsection (7) in relation to any holder of a judicial office listed in subsection (1)(c)—

(a) before deciding what transitional provision it is appropriate to make, the person making the order must consult the Lord Chief Justice of Northern Ireland;

(b) before making the order, that person must consult the Lord Chief Justice of Northern Ireland.

(7C) The Lord Chief Justice of England and Wales may nominate a judicial office holder (within the meaning of section 109(4) of the Constitutional Reform Act 2005) to exercise his functions under this section.

(7D) The Lord Chief Justice of Northern Ireland may nominate any of the following to exercise his functions under this section—

(a) the holder of one of the offices listed in Schedule 1 to the Justice (Northern Ireland) Act 2002;

(b) a Lord Justice of Appeal (as defined in section 88 of that Act).]

Note: Commencement 9 November 1998. Subsections (7A)-(7D) inserted by Sch 4 Constitutional Reform Act from 3 April 2006 (SI 2006/1014). Words in sub-section (4) substituted by Constitutional Reform Act 2005 Sch 11 from 1 October 2009 (SI 2009/1604).

Parliamentary procedure

19. Statements of compatibility

(1) A Minister of the Crown in charge of a Bill in either House of Parliament must, before Second Reading of the Bill—

(a) make a statement to the effect that in his view the provisions of the Bill are compatible with the Convention rights ('a statement of compatibility'); or

(b) make a statement to the effect that although he is unable to make a statement of compatibility the government nevertheless wishes the House to proceed with the Bill.

(2) The statement must be in writing and be published in such manner as the Minister making it considers appropriate.

Note: Commencement 24 November 1998.

Supplemental

20. Orders etc. under this Act

(1) Any power of a Minister of the Crown to make an order under this Act is exercisable by statutory instrument.

(2) The power of [the Lord Chancellor or] the Secretary of State to make rules (other than rules of court) under section 2(3) or 7(9) is exercisable by statutory instrument.

(3) Any statutory instrument made under section 14, 15 or 16(7) must be laid before Parliament.

(4) No order may be made by [the Lord Chancellor or] the Secretary of State under section 1(4), 7(11) or 16(2) unless a draft of the order has been laid before, and approved by, each House of Parliament.

(5) Any statutory instrument made under section 18(7) or Schedule 4, or to which sub-section (2) applies, shall be subject to annulment in pursuance of a resolution of either House of Parliament.

(6) The power of a Northern Ireland department to make—

(a) rules under section 2(3)(c) or 7(9)(c), or

(b) an order under section 7(11), is exercisable by statutory rule for the purposes of the Statutory Rules (Northern Ireland) Order 1979.

(7) Any rules made under section 2(3)(c) or 7(9)(c) shall be subject to negative resolution; and section 41(6) of the Interpretation Act (Northern Ireland) 1954 (meaning of 'subject to negative resolution') shall apply as if the power to make the rules were conferred by an Act of the Northern Ireland Assembly.

(8) No order may be made by a Northern Ireland department under section 7(11) unless a draft of the order has been laid before, and approved by, the Northern Ireland Assembly.

Note: Commencement 9 November 1998. Words in square brackets omitted from 19 August 2003 (SI 2003/1887), re-inserted from 12 January 2006 (SI 2005/3429).

21. Interpretation, etc

(1) In this Act—

'amend' includes repeal and apply (with or without modifications);

'the appropriate Minister' means the Minister of the Crown having charge of the appropriate authorised government department (within the meaning of the Crown Proceedings Act 1947);

'the Commission' means the European Commission of Human Rights;

'the Convention' means the Convention for the Protection of Human Rights and Fundamental Freedoms, agreed by the Council of Europe at Rome on 4 November 1950 as it has effect for the time being in relation to the United Kingdom;

'declaration of incompatibility' means a declaration under section 4;

'Minister of the Crown' has the same meaning as in the Ministers of the Crown Act 1975;

'Northern Ireland Minister' includes the First Minister and the deputy First Minister in Northern Ireland;

'primary legislation' means any—

- (a) public general Act;
- (b) local and personal Act;
- (c) private Act;
- (d) Measure of the Church Assembly;
- (e) Measure of the General Synod of the Church of England;
- (f) Order in Council—
  - (i) made in exercise of Her Majesty's Royal Prerogative;
  - (ii) made under section 38(1)(a) of the Northern Ireland Constitution Act 1973 or the corresponding provision of the Northern Ireland Act 1998; or
  - (iii) amending an Act of a kind mentioned in paragraph (a), (b) or (c); and

includes an order or other instrument made under primary legislation (otherwise than by the [Welsh Ministers, the First Minister for Wales, the Counsel General to the Welsh Assembly Government,] a member of the Scottish Executive, a Northern Ireland Minister or a Northern Ireland department) to the extent to which it operates to bring one or more provisions of that legislation into force or amends any primary legislation;

'the First Protocol' means the protocol to the Convention agreed at Paris on 20 March 1952;

...

'the Eleventh Protocol' means the protocol to the Convention (restructuring the control machinery established by the Convention) agreed at Strasbourg on 11 May 1994;

['the Thirteenth Protocol' means the protocol to the Convention (concerning the abolition of the death penalty in all circumstances) agreed at Vilnius on 3 May 2002;]

'remedial order' means an order under section 10;

'subordinate legislation' means any—

- (a) Order in Council other than one—
  - (i) made in exercise of Her Majesty's Royal Prerogative;
  - (ii) made under section 38(1)(a) of the Northern Ireland Constitution Act 1973 or the corresponding provision of the Northern Ireland Act 1998; or

(iii) amending an Act of a kind mentioned in the definition of primary legislation;

(b) Act of the Scottish Parliament;

[(ba) Measure of the National Assembly for Wales;

(bb) Act of the National Assembly for Wales;]

(c) Act of the Parliament of Northern Ireland;

(d) Measure of the Assembly established under section 1 of the Northern Ireland Assembly Act 1973;

(e) Act of the Northern Ireland Assembly;

(f) order, rules, regulations, scheme, warrant, byelaw or other instrument made under primary legislation (except to the extent to which it operates to bring one or more provisions of that legislation into force or amends any primary legislation);

(g) order, rules, regulations, scheme, warrant, byelaw or other instrument made under legislation mentioned in paragraph (b), (c), (d) or (e) or made under an Order in Council applying only to Northern Ireland;

(h) order, rules, regulations, scheme, warrant, byelaw or other instrument made by a member of the Scottish Executive, [Welsh Ministers, the First Minister for Wales, the Counsel General to the Welsh Assembly Government,] a Northern Ireland Minister or a Northern Ireland department in exercise of prerogative or other executive functions of Her Majesty which are exercisable by such a person on behalf of Her Majesty;

'transferred matters' has the same meaning as in the Northern Ireland Act 1998; and

'tribunal' means any tribunal in which legal proceedings may be brought.

(2) The references in paragraphs (b) and (c) of section 2(1) to Articles are to Articles of the Convention as they had effect immediately before the coming into force of the Eleventh Protocol.

(3) The reference in paragraph (d) of section 2(1) to Article 46 includes a reference to Articles 32 and 54 of the Convention as they had effect immediately before the coming into force of the Eleventh Protocol.

(4) The references in section 2(1) to a report or decision of the Commission or a decision of the Committee of Ministers include references to a report or decision made as provided by paragraphs 3, 4 and 6 of Article 5 of the Eleventh Protocol (transitional provisions).

(5) Any liability under the Army Act 1955, the Air Force Act 1955 or the Naval Discipline Act 1957 to suffer death for an offence is replaced by a liability to imprisonment for life or any less punishment authorised by those Acts; and those Acts shall accordingly have effect with the necessary modifications.

Note: Commencement of s 21(5) on 9 November 1998, remainder of s 21 on 2 October 2000. Words omitted and second words in square brackets in sub-s (1) substituted by SI 2004/1574 from 22 June 2004. Other words in square brackets substituted from 4 May 2007, Government of Wales Act 2006, s 160.

22. Short title, commencement, application and extent

(1) This Act may be cited as the Human Rights Act 1998.

(2) Sections 18, 20 and 21(5) and this section come into force on the passing of this Act.

(3) The other provisions of this Act come into force on such day as the Secretary of State may by order appoint; and different days may be appointed for different purposes.

(4) Paragraph (b) of subsection (1) of section 7 applies to proceedings brought by or at the instigation of a public authority whenever the act in question took place; but otherwise that subsection does not apply to an act taking place before the coming into force of that section.

(5) This Act binds the Crown.

(6) This Act extends to Northern Ireland.

(7) ...

Note: Commencement 9 November 1998. Sub-section (7) deleted by Armed Forces Act 2006 Sch 16 from 28 March 2009 (for certain purposes) (SI 2009/812) and from 31 October 2009 otherwise (SI 2009/1167).

SCHEDULES

Section 1(3)

SCHEDULE 1
THE ARTICLES
PART I
THE CONVENTION
RIGHTS AND FREEDOMS

Article 2 *Right to life*

1. Everyone's right to life shall be protected by law. No one shall be deprived of his life intentionally save in the execution of a sentence of a court following his conviction of a crime for which this penalty is provided by law.

2. Deprivation of life shall not be regarded as inflicted in contravention of this Article when it results from the use of force which is no more than absolutely necessary:
   (a) in defence of any person from unlawful violence;
   (b) in order to effect a lawful arrest or to prevent the escape of a person lawfully detained;
   (c) in action lawfully taken for the purpose of quelling a riot or insurrection.

Article 3 *Prohibition of torture*

No one shall be subjected to torture or to inhuman or degrading treatment or punishment.

Article 4 *Prohibition of slavery and forced labour*

1. No one shall be held in slavery or servitude.

2. No one shall be required to perform forced or compulsory labour.

3. For the purpose of this Article the term 'forced or compulsory labour' shall not include:
   (a) any work required to be done in the ordinary course of detention imposed according to the provisions of Article 5 of this Convention or during conditional release from such detention;
   (b) any service of a military character or, in case of conscientious objectors in countries where they are recognised, service exacted instead of compulsory military service;

(c) any service exacted in case of an emergency or calamity threatening the life or well-being of the community;

(d) any work or service which forms part of normal civic obligations.

Article 5   *Right to liberty and security*

1. Everyone has the right to liberty and security of person. No one shall be deprived of his liberty save in the following cases and in accordance with a procedure prescribed by law:

   (a) the lawful detention of a person after conviction by a competent court;

   (b) the lawful arrest or detention of a person for non-compliance with the lawful order of a court or in order to secure the fulfilment of any obligation prescribed by law;

   (c) the lawful arrest or detention of a person effected for the purpose of bringing him before the competent legal authority on reasonable suspicion of having committed an offence or when it is reasonably considered necessary to prevent his committing an offence or fleeing after having done so;

   (d) the detention of a minor by lawful order for the purpose of educational supervision or his lawful detention for the purpose of bringing him before the competent legal authority;

   (e) the lawful detention of persons for the prevention of the spreading of infectious diseases, of persons of unsound mind, alcoholics or drug addicts or vagrants;

   (f) the lawful arrest or detention of a person to prevent his effecting an unauthorised entry into the country or of a person against whom action is being taken with a view to deportation or extradition.

2. Everyone who is arrested shall be informed promptly, in a language which he understands, of the reasons for his arrest and of any charge against him.

3. Everyone arrested or detained in accordance with the provisions of paragraph 1(c) of this Article shall be brought promptly before a judge or other officer authorised by law to exercise judicial power and shall be entitled to trial within a reasonable time or to release pending trial. Release may be conditioned by guarantees to appear for trial.

4. Everyone who is deprived of his liberty by arrest or detention shall be entitled to take proceedings by which the lawfulness of his detention shall be decided speedily by a court and his release ordered if the detention is not lawful.

5. Everyone who has been the victim of arrest or detention in contravention of the provisions of this Article shall have an enforceable right to compensation.

Article 6   *Right to a fair trial*

1. In the determination of his civil rights and obligations or of any criminal charge against him, everyone is entitled to a fair and public hearing within a reasonable time by an independent and impartial tribunal established by law. Judgment shall be pronounced publicly but the press and public may be excluded from all or part of the trial in the interest of morals, public order or national security in a democratic society, where the interests of juveniles or the protection of the private life of the parties so require, or to the extent strictly necessary in the opinion of the court in special circumstances where publicity would prejudice the interests of justice.

2. Everyone charged with a criminal offence shall be presumed innocent until proved guilty according to law.

3. Everyone charged with a criminal offence has the following minimum rights:

   (a) to be informed promptly, in a language which he understands and in detail, of the nature and cause of the accusation against him;

   (b) to have adequate time and facilities for the preparation of his defence;

   (c) to defend himself in person or through legal assistance of his own choosing or, if he has not sufficient means to pay for legal assistance, to be given it free when the interests of justice so require;

(d) to examine or have examined witnesses against him and to obtain the attendance and examination of witnesses on his behalf under the same conditions as witnesses against him;

(e) to have the free assistance of an interpreter if he cannot understand or speak the language used in court.

Article 7 *No punishment without law*

1. No one shall be held guilty of any criminal offence on account of any act or omission which did not constitute a criminal offence under national or international law at the time when it was committed. Nor shall a heavier penalty be imposed than the one that was applicable at the time the criminal offence was committed.

2. This Article shall not prejudice the trial and punishment of any person for any act or omission which, at the time when it was committed, was criminal according to the general principles of law recognised by civilised nations.

Article 8 *Right to respect for private and family life*

1. Everyone has the right to respect for his private and family life, his home and his correspondence.

2. There shall be no interference by a public authority with the exercise of this right except such as is in accordance with the law and is necessary in a democratic society in the interests of national security, public safety or the economic well being of the country, for the prevention of disorder or crime, for the protection of health or morals, or for the protection of the rights and freedoms of others.

Article 9 *Freedom of thought, conscience and religion*

1. Everyone has the right to freedom of thought, conscience and religion; this right includes freedom to change his religion or belief and freedom, either alone or in community with others and in public or private, to manifest his religion or belief, in worship, teaching, practice and observance.

2. Freedom to manifest one's religion or beliefs shall be subject only to such limitations as are prescribed by law and are necessary in a democratic society in the interests of public safety, for the protection of public order, health or morals, or for the protection of the rights and freedoms of others.

Article 10 *Freedom of expression*

1. Everyone has the right to freedom of expression. This right shall include freedom to hold opinions and to receive and impart information and ideas without interference by public authority and regardless of frontiers. This Article shall not prevent States from requiring the licensing of broadcasting, television or cinema enterprises.

2. The exercise of these freedoms, since it carries with it duties and responsibilities, may be subject to such formalities, conditions, restrictions or penalties as are prescribed by law and are necessary in a democratic society, in the interests of national security, territorial integrity or public safety, for the prevention of disorder or crime, for the protection of health or morals, for the protection of the reputation or rights of others, for preventing the disclosure of information received in confidence, or for maintaining the authority and impartiality of the judiciary.

Article 11 *Freedom of assembly and association*

1. Everyone has the right to freedom of peaceful assembly and to freedom of association with others, including the right to form and to join trade unions for the protection of his interests.

2. No restrictions shall be placed on the exercise of these rights other than such as are prescribed by law and are necessary in a democratic society in the interests of national security or public safety, for the prevention of disorder or crime, for the protection of health or morals or for the protection of the rights and freedoms of others. This Article shall not prevent the imposition of lawful restrictions on the exercise of these rights by members of the armed forces, of the police or of the administration of the State.

Article 12   *Right to marry*

Men and women of marriageable age have the right to marry and to found a family, according to the national laws governing the exercise of this right.

Article 14   *Prohibition of discrimination*

The enjoyment of the rights and freedoms set forth in this Convention shall be secured without discrimination on any ground such as sex, race, colour, language, religion, political or other opinion, national or social origin, association with a national minority, property, birth or other status.

Article 16   *Restrictions on political activity of aliens*

Nothing in Articles 10, 11 and 14 shall be regarded as preventing the High Contracting Parties from imposing restrictions on the political activity of aliens.

Article 17   *Prohibition of abuse of rights*

Nothing in this Convention may be interpreted as implying for any State, group or person any right to engage in any activity or perform any act aimed at the destruction of any of the rights and freedoms set forth herein or at their limitation to a greater extent than is provided for in the Convention.

Article 18   *Limitation on use of restrictions on rights*

The restrictions permitted under this Convention to the said rights and freedoms shall not be applied for any purpose other than those for which they have been prescribed.

PART II
THE FIRST PROTOCOL

Article 1   *Protection of property*

Every natural or legal person is entitled to the peaceful enjoyment of his possessions. No one shall be deprived of his possessions except in the public interest and subject to the conditions provided for by law and by the general principles of international law.

The preceding provisions shall not, however, in any way impair the right of a State to enforce such laws as it deems necessary to control the use of property in accordance with the general interest or to secure the payment of taxes or other contributions or penalties.

Article 2   *Right to education*

No person shall be denied the right to education. In the exercise of any functions which it assumes in relation to education and to teaching, the State shall respect the right of parents to ensure such education and teaching in conformity with their own religious and philosophical convictions.

Article 3   *Right to free elections*

The High Contracting Parties undertake to hold free elections at reasonable intervals by secret ballot, under conditions which will ensure the free expression of the opinion of the people in the choice of the legislature.

[PART III

ARTICLE 1 OF THE THIRTEENTH PROTOCOL

Abolition of the death penalty

The death penalty shall be abolished. No one shall be condemned to such penalty or executed.]

Note: Part 3 substituted from 22 June 2004 (SI 2004/1574).

Section 10   SCHEDULE 2

REMEDIAL ORDERS

Orders

1.—(1) A remedial order may—
  (a) contain such incidental, supplemental, consequential or transitional provision as the person making it considers appropriate;
  (b) be made so as to have effect from a date earlier than that on which it is made;
  (c) make provision for the delegation of specific functions;
  (d) make different provision for different cases.

(2) The power conferred by sub-paragraph (1)(a) includes—
  (a) power to amend primary legislation (including primary legislation other than that which contains the incompatible provision); and
  (b) power to amend or revoke subordinate legislation (including subordinate legislation other than that which contains the incompatible provision).

(3) A remedial order may be made so as to have the same extent as the legislation which it affects.

(4) No person is to be guilty of an offence solely as a result of the retrospective effect of a remedial order.

Procedure

2. No remedial order may be made unless—
  (a) a draft of the order has been approved by a resolution of each House of Parliament made after the end of the period of 60 days beginning with the day on which the draft was laid; or
  (b) it is declared in the order that it appears to the person making it that, because of the urgency of the matter, it is necessary to make the order without a draft being so approved.

Orders laid in draft

3.—(1) No draft may be laid under paragraph 2(a) unless—
  (a) the person proposing to make the order has laid before Parliament a document which contains a draft of the proposed order and the required information; and
  (b) the period of 60 days, beginning with the day on which the document required by this sub-paragraph was laid, has ended.

(2) If representations have been made during that period, the draft laid under paragraph 2(a) must be accompanied by a statement containing—

(a) a summary of the representations; and

(b) if, as a result of the representations, the proposed order has been changed, details of the changes.

Urgent cases

4.—(1) If a remedial order ('the original order') is made without being approved in draft, the person making it must lay it before Parliament, accompanied by the required information, after it is made.

(2) If representations have been made during the period of 60 days beginning with the day on which the original order was made, the person making it must (after the end of that period) lay before Parliament a statement containing—

(a) a summary of the representations; and

(b) if, as a result of the representations, he considers it appropriate to make changes to the original order, details of the changes.

(3) If sub-paragraph (2)(b) applies, the person making the statement must—

(a) make a further remedial order replacing the original order; and

(b) lay the replacement order before Parliament.

(4) If, at the end of the period of 120 days beginning with the day on which the original order was made, a resolution has not been passed by each House approving the original or replacement order, the order ceases to have effect (but without that affecting anything previously done under either order or the power to make a fresh remedial order).

Definitions

5. In this Schedule—

'representations' means representations about a remedial order (or proposed remedial order) made to the person making (or proposing to make) it and includes any relevant Parliamentary report or resolution; and

'required information' means—

(a) an explanation of the incompatibility which the order (or proposed order) seeks to remove, including particulars of the relevant declaration, finding or order; and

(b) a statement of the reasons for proceeding under section 10 and for making an order in those terms.

Calculating periods

6. In calculating any period for the purposes of this Schedule, no account is to be taken of any time during which—

(a) Parliament is dissolved or prorogued; or

(b) both Houses are adjourned for more than four days.

[7. — (1) This paragraph applies in relation to–

(a) any remedial order made, and any draft of such an order proposed to be made,

(i) by the Scottish Ministers; or

(ii) within devolved competence (within the meaning of the Scotland Act 1998) by Her Majesty in Council; and

(b) any document or statement to be laid in connection with such an order (or proposed order).

(2) This Schedule has effect in relation to any such order (or proposed order), document or statement subject to the following modifications.

(3) Any reference to Parliament, each House of Parliament or both Houses of Parliament shall be construed as a reference to the Scottish Parliament.

(4) Paragraph 6 does not apply and instead, in calculating any period for the purposes of this Schedule, no account is to be taken of any time during which the Scottish Parliament is dissolved or is in recess for more than four days.]

Note: Paragraph (7) inserted from 27 July 2000 (SI 2000/2040).

Section 14 and 15   SCHEDULE 3
                      DEROGATION AND RESERVATION

                              PART II
                           RESERVATION

At the time of signing the present (First) Protocol, I declare that, in view of certain provisions of the Education Acts in the United Kingdom, the principle affirmed in the second sentence of Article 2 is accepted by the United Kingdom only so far as it is compatible with the provision of efficient instruction and training, and the avoidance of unreasonable public expenditure.

Dated 20 March 1952. Made by the United Kingdom Permanent Representative to the Council of Europe.

Note: Part 1 repealed from 1 April 2001 (SI 2001/1216), new Part 1 inserted from 20 December 2001 (SI 2001/4032), and repealed from 8 April 2005 (SI 2005/1071).

Section 18(6)   SCHEDULE 4
                          JUDICIAL PENSIONS

Immigration and Asylum Act 1999
(1999, c. 33)

Arrangement of Sections

PART I. IMMIGRATION: GENERAL

Leave to enter, or remain in, the United Kingdom

SCHEDULES

An Act to make provision about immigration and asylum; provision about procedures in connection with marriage on superintendent registrar's certificate; and for connected purposes. [11 November 1999]

PART I

IMMIGRATION: GENERAL

Leave to enter, or remain in, the United Kingdom

1. . . .

   Note: Amends Immigration Act 1971, s 3A.

2. . . .

   Note: Amends Immigration Act 1971, s 3B.

3. . . .

   Note: Amends Immigration Act 1971, s 3C.

4. Accommodation

(1) The Secretary of State may provide, or arrange for the provision of, facilities for the accommodation of persons—

(a) temporarily admitted to the United Kingdom under paragraph 21 of Schedule 2 to the 1971 Act;

(b) released from detention under that paragraph; or

(c) released on bail from detention under any provision of the Immigration Acts.

[(2) The Secretary of State may provide, or arrange for the provision of, facilities for the accommodation of a person if—

(a) he was (but is no longer) an asylum-seeker, and

(b) his claim for asylum was rejected.

(3) The Secretary of State may provide, or arrange for the provision of, facilities for the accommodation of a dependant of a person for whom facilities may be provided under subsection (2).

(4) The following expressions have the same meaning in this section as in Part VI of this Act (as defined in section 94)—

(a) asylum-seeker,

(b) claim for asylum, and

(c) dependant.]

[(5) The Secretary of State may make regulations specifying criteria to be used in determining—

(a) whether or not to provide accommodation, or arrange for the provision of accommodation, for a person under this section;

(b) whether or not to continue to provide accommodation, or arrange for the provision of accommodation, for a person under this section.

(6) The regulations may, in particular—

(a) provide for the continuation of the provision of accommodation for a person to be conditional upon his performance of or participation in community activities in accordance with arrangements made by the Secretary of State;

(b) provide for the continuation of the provision of accommodation to be subject to other conditions;

(c) provide for the provision of accommodation (or the continuation of the provision of accommodation) to be a matter for the Secretary of State's discretion to a specified extent or in a specified class of case.

(7) For the purposes of subsection (6)(a)—

(a) 'community activities' means activities that appear to the Secretary of State to be beneficial to the public or a section of the public, and

(b) the Secretary of State may, in particular—

(i) appoint one person to supervise or manage the performance of or participation in activities by another person;

(ii) enter into a contract (with a local authority or any other person) for the provision of services by way of making arrangements for community activities in accordance with this section;

(iii) pay, or arrange for the payment of, allowances to a person performing or participating in community activities in accordance with arrangements under this section.

(8) Regulations by virtue of subsection (6)(a) may, in particular, provide for a condition requiring the performance of or participation in community activities to apply to a person only if the Secretary of State has made arrangements for community activities in an area that includes the place where accommodation is provided for the person.

(9) A local authority or other person may undertake to manage or participate in arrangements for community activities in accordance with this section.]

[(10) The Secretary of State may make regulations permitting a person who is provided with accommodation under this section to be supplied also with services or facilities of a specified kind.

(11) Regulations under subsection (10)—

(a) may, in particular, permit a person to be supplied with a voucher which may be exchanged for goods or services,

(b) may not permit a person to be supplied with money,

(c) may restrict the extent or value of services or facilities to be provided, and

(d) may confer a discretion.]

Note: Commencement 11 November 1999. Heading substituted and sub-s (2) inserted by Nationality, Immigration and Asylum Act 2002, s 49 from 7 November 2002. Subsections (5)– (9) inserted by Asylum and Immigration Act 2004, s 10 from 1 December 2004 (SI 2004/2999). Subsections (10)–(11) inserted by Immigration, Asylum and Nationality Act 2006, s 43 from 16 June 2006 (SI 2006/1497).

5. . . .

Note: Ceased to have effect from 2 April 2007, Sch 2 Immigration, Asylum and Nationality Act 2006 (SI 2007/1109).

Exemption from immigration control

6. . . .

Note: Amends Immigration Act 1971, s 8.

7. . . .

Note: Amends Immigration Act 1971, s 8.

8. . . .

Note: Amends Immigration Act 1971, s 8.

Removal from the United Kingdom

9. Treatment of certain overstayers

(1) During the regularisation period overstayers may apply, in the prescribed manner, for leave to remain in the United Kingdom.

(2) The regularisation period begins on the day prescribed for the purposes of this subsection and is not to be less than three months.

(3) The regularisation period ends—

(a) on the day prescribed for the purposes of this subsection; or

(b) if later, on the day before that on which section 65 comes into force.

(4) Section 10 and paragraph 12 of Schedule 15 come into force on the day after that on which the regularisation period ends.

(5) The Secretary of State must publicise the effect of this section in the way appearing to him to be best calculated to bring it to the attention of those affected.

(6) 'Overstayer' means a person who, having only limited leave to enter or remain in the United Kingdom, remains beyond the time limited by the leave.

Note: Commencement 11 November 1999, s 170.

10. Removal of certain persons unlawfully in the United Kingdom

(1) A person who is not a British citizen may be removed from the United Kingdom, in accordance with directions given by an immigration officer, if—

(a) having only a limited leave to enter or remain, he does not observe a condition attached to the leave or remains beyond the time limited by the leave;

[(b) he uses deception in seeking (whether successfully or not) leave to remain;

(ba) his indefinite leave to enter or remain has been revoked under section 76(3) of the Nationality, Immigration and Asylum Act 2002 (person ceasing to be refugee);] or

(c) directions [. . .] have been given for the removal, under this section, of a person [. . .] to whose family he belongs.

(2) Directions may not be given under subsection (1)(a) if the person concerned has made an application for leave to remain in accordance with regulations made under section 9.

[(3) Directions for the removal of a person may not be given under subsection (1)(c) unless the Secretary of State has given the person written notice of the intention to remove him.

(4) A notice under subsection (3) may not be given if—

(a) the person whose removal under subsection (1)(a) or (b) is the cause of the proposed directions under subsection (1)(c) has left the United Kingdom, and

(b) more than eight weeks have elapsed since that person's departure.

(5) If a notice under subsection (3) is sent by first class post to a person's last known address, that subsection shall be taken to be satisfied at the end of the second day after the day of posting.

(5A) Directions for the removal of a person under subsection (1)(c) cease to have effect if he ceases to belong to the family of the person whose removal under subsection (1)(a) or (b) is the cause of the directions under subsection (1)(c).]

(6) Directions under this section—

(a) may be given only to persons falling within a prescribed class;

(b) may impose any requirements of a prescribed kind.

(7) In relation to any such directions, paragraphs 10, 11, 16 to 18, 21 and 22 to 24 of Schedule 2 to the 1971 Act (administrative provisions as to control of entry), apply as they apply in relation to directions given under paragraph 8 of that Schedule.

[(8) When a person is notified that a decision has been made to remove him in accordance with this section, the notification invalidates any leave to enter or remain in the United Kingdom previously given to him.]

(9) The costs of complying with a direction given under this section (so far as reasonably incurred) must be met by the Secretary of State.

[(**10**) A person shall not be liable to removal from the United Kingdom under this section at a time when section 7(1)(b) of the Immigration Act 1971 (Commonwealth and Irish citizens ordinarily resident in United Kingdom) would prevent a decision to deport him.]

Note: Section 10(6) commenced 22 May 2000, SI 2000/282, remainder of s 10 on 2 October 2000, SI 2000/244. Subsection (1)(b) substituted by and sub-s (1)(ba) inserted by Nationality, Immigration and Asylum Act 2002, ss 74 and 76 from 10 February 2003 (SI 2003/1). Subsections (3)–(5A) substituted by Nationality, Immigration and Asylum Act 2002 from 10 February 2003 (SI 2003/1). Subsection (10) inserted by Nationality, Immigration and Asylum Act 2002, s 75 from 10 February 2003 (SI 2003/1). Transitional provisions set out in SI 2003/754. Subsection (8) substituted by Immigration, Asylum and Nationality Act 2006, s 48 from 16 June 2006 (SI 2006/1497).

11. . . .

Note: Section 11 ceased to have effect from 1 October 2004, Asylum and Immigration Act 2004, s 33 (SI 2004/2523).

12. . . .

Note: Section 12 ceased to have effect from 1 October 2004, Asylum and Immigration Act 2004, s 33 (SI 2004/2523).

13. Proof of identity of persons to be removed or deported

(**1**) This section applies if a person—

(a) is to be removed from the United Kingdom to a country of which he is a national or citizen; but

(b) does not have a valid passport or other document establishing his identity and nationality or citizenship and permitting him to travel.

(**2**) If the country to which the person is to be removed indicates that he will not be admitted to it unless identification data relating to him are provided by the Secretary of State, he may provide them with such data.

(**3**) In providing identification data, the Secretary of State must not disclose whether the person concerned has made a claim for asylum.

(**4**) For the purposes of paragraph 4(1) of Schedule 4 to the Data Protection Act 1998, the provision under this section of identification data is a transfer of personal data which is necessary for reasons of substantial public interest.

(**5**) 'Identification data' means—

(a) fingerprints taken under section 141; or

(b) data collected in accordance with regulations made under section 144.

(**6**) 'Removed' means removed as a result of directions given under section 10 or under Schedule 2 or 3 to the 1971 Act.

Note: Commenced 11 December 2000, SI 2000/3099.

14. Escorts for persons removed from the United Kingdom under directions

(**1**) Directions for, or requiring arrangements to be made for, the removal of a person from the United Kingdom may include or be amended to include provision for the person who is to be removed to be accompanied by an escort consisting of one or more persons specified in the directions.

(2) The Secretary of State may by regulations make further provision supplementing subsection (1).

(3) The regulations may, in particular, include provision—

(a) requiring the person to whom the directions are given to provide for the return of the escort to the United Kingdom;

(b) requiring him to bear such costs in connection with the escort (including, in particular, remuneration) as may be prescribed;

(c) as to the cases in which the Secretary of State is to bear those costs;

(d) prescribing the kinds of expenditure which are to count in calculating the costs incurred in connection with escorts.

Note: Commencement 1 March 2000 (SI 2000/168).

15. . . .

Note: Section 15 repealed by Nationality, Immigration and Asylum Act 2002, s 77 from 1 April 2003 (SI 2003/754).

Provision of financial security

16. Security on grant of entry clearance

(1) In such circumstances as may be specified, the Secretary of State may require security to be given, with respect to a person applying for entry clearance, before clearance is given.

(2) In such circumstances as may be specified—

(a) the Secretary of State may accept security with respect to a person who is applying for entry clearance but for whom security is not required; and

(b) in determining whether to give clearance, account may be taken of any security so provided.

(3) 'Security' means—

(a) the deposit of a sum of money by the applicant, his agent or any other person, or

(b) the provision by the applicant, his agent or any other person of a financial guarantee of a specified kind, with a view to securing that the applicant will, if given leave to enter the United Kingdom for a limited period, leave the United Kingdom at the end of that period.

(4) Immigration rules must make provision as to the circumstances in which a security provided under this section—

(a) is to be repaid, released or otherwise cancelled; or

(b) is to be forfeited or otherwise realised by the Secretary of State.

(5) No security provided under this section may be forfeited or otherwise realised unless the person providing it has been given an opportunity, in accordance with immigration rules, to make representations to the Secretary of State.

(6) Immigration rules may, in particular—

(a) fix the maximum amount that may be required, or accepted, by way of security provided under this section;

(b) specify the form and manner in which such a security is to be given or may be accepted;

(c) make provision, where such a security has been forfeited or otherwise realised, for the person providing it to be reimbursed in such circumstances as may be specified;

(d) make different provision for different cases or descriptions of case.

(7) 'Specified' means specified by immigration rules.

(8) Any security forfeited or otherwise realised by the Secretary of State under this section must be paid into the Consolidated Fund.

Note: Commencement on a date to be appointed.

17. Provision of further security on extension of leave

(1) This section applies if security has been provided under section 16(1) or (2) with respect to a person who, having entered the United Kingdom (with leave to do so), applies—

(a) to extend his leave to enter the United Kingdom; or

(b) for leave to remain in the United Kingdom for a limited period.

(2) The Secretary of State may refuse the application if security of such kind as the Secretary of State considers appropriate is not provided, or continued, with respect to the applicant.

(3) Immigration rules must make provision as to the circumstances in which a security provided under this section—

(a) is to be repaid, released or otherwise cancelled; or

(b) is to be forfeited or otherwise realised by the Secretary of State.

(4) No security provided under this section may be forfeited or otherwise realised unless the person providing it has been given an opportunity, in accordance with immigration rules, to make representations to the Secretary of State.

(5) Subsection (7) of section 16 applies in relation to this section as it applies in relation to that section.

(6) Any security forfeited or otherwise realised by the Secretary of State under this section must be paid into the Consolidated Fund.

Note: Commencement on a date to be appointed.

Information

18. ...

Note: Amends para 27B, Sch 2 Immigration Act 1971.

19. ...

Note: Amends para 27C, Sch 2 Immigration Act 1971.

20. Supply of information to Secretary of State

(1) This section applies to information held by—

(a) a chief officer of police;

[(b) the Serious Organised Crime Agency;]

(c) ...

(d) ...

(e) a person with whom the Secretary of State has made a contract or other arrangements under section 95 or 98 or a sub-contractor of such a person; or

(f) any specified person, for purposes specified in relation to that person.

[(1A) This section also applies to a document or article which—

(a) comes into the possession of a person listed in subsection (1) or someone acting on his behalf, or

(b) is discovered by a person listed in subsection (1) or someone acting on his behalf.]

(2) The information [, document or article] may be supplied to the Secretary of State for use for immigration purposes.

[(2A) The Secretary of State may—

(a) retain for immigration purposes a document or article supplied to him under subsection (2), and

(b) dispose of a document or article supplied to him under subsection (2) in such manner as he thinks appropriate (and the reference to use in subsection (2) includes a reference to disposal).]

(3) 'Immigration purposes' means any of the following—

(a) the administration of immigration control under the Immigration Acts;

(b) the prevention, detection, investigation or prosecution of criminal offences under those Acts;

(c) the imposition of penalties or charges under Part II;

(d) the provision of support for asylum-seekers and their dependants under Part VI;

(e) such other purposes as may be specified.

(4) 'Chief officer of police' means—

(a) the chief officer of police for a police area in England and Wales;

(b) the chief constable of a police force maintained under the Police (Scotland) Act 1967;

(c) the [Chief Constable of the Police Service of Northern Ireland].

(5) 'Specified' means specified in an order made by the Secretary of State.

(6) This section does not limit the circumstances in which information [, documents or articles] may be supplied apart from this section.

Note: Commencement 1 January 2000 (SI 1999/3190). Subsection (1)(b) substituted by Sch 4 Serious Organised Crime and Police Act 2005 from 1 April 2006 (SI 2006/378). Subsection (1)(d) omitted from 31 January 2008, (Schedule, UK Borders Act 2007). Subsection (1A) and sub-s (2A) inserted by Nationality, Immigration and Asylum Act 2002, s 132 from 10 February 2003 (SI 2003/1). Words in square brackets in sub-ss (2) and (6) inserted by Nationality, Immigration and Asylum Act 2002, s 132 from 10 February 2003 (SI 2003/1). Words in square brackets in sub-s (4)(c) substituted from 4 November 2001, s 78 Police (Northern Ireland) Act 2000 (SR 2001/396).

21. Supply of information by Secretary of State

(1) This section applies to information held by the Secretary of State in connection with the exercise of functions under any of the Immigration Acts.

(2) The information may be supplied to—

(a) a chief officer of police, for use for police purposes;

[(b) the Serious Organised Crime Agency, for use for SOCA purposes;]

(c) . . .

(d) the Commissioners of Customs and Excise, or a person providing services to them, for use for customs purposes; or

(e) any specified person, for use for purposes specified in relation to that person.

(3) 'Police purposes' means any of the following—

(a) the prevention, detection, investigation or prosecution of criminal offences;

(b) safeguarding national security;

(c) such other purposes as may be specified.

[(4) 'SOCA purposes' means any of the functions of the Serious Organised Crime Agency mentioned in section 2, 3 or 5 of the Serious Organised Crime and Police Act 2005].

(6) 'Customs purposes' means any of the Commissioners' functions in relation to—

(a) the prevention, detection, investigation or prosecution of criminal offences;

(b) the prevention, detection or investigation of conduct in respect of which penalties which are not criminal penalties are provided for by or under any enactment;

(c) the assessment or determination of penalties which are not criminal penalties;

(d) checking the accuracy of information relating to, or provided for purposes connected with, any matter under the care and management of the Commissioners or any assigned matter (as defined by section 1(1) of the Customs and Excise Management Act 1979);

(e) amending or supplementing any such information (where appropriate);

(f) legal or other proceedings relating to anything mentioned in paragraphs (a) to (e);

(g) safeguarding national security; and

(h) such other purposes as may be specified.

(7) 'Chief officer of police' and 'specified' have the same meaning as in section 20.

(8) This section does not limit the circumstances in which information may be supplied apart from this section.

Note: Commencement 1 January 2000 (SI 1999/3190). Words in square brackets substituted from 1 April 2006, Sch 4 Serious Organised Crime and Police Act 2005 (SI 2006/378).

22. . . .

Note: Amends Asylum and Immigration Act 1996, s 8A.

Monitoring entry clearance

23. Monitoring refusals of entry clearance

[(1) The Secretary of State must appoint a person to monitor, in such manner as the Secretary of State may determine, refusals of entry clearance in cases where, as a result of section 88A of the Nationality, Immigration and Asylum Act 2002 (c. 41)(entry clearance: non-family visitors and students), an appeal under section 82(1) of that Act may be brought only on the grounds referred to in section 84(1)(b) and (c) of that Act (racial discrimination and human rights).]

(2) But the Secretary of State may not appoint a member of his staff.

(3) The monitor must make an annual report on the discharge of his functions to the Secretary of State.

(4) The Secretary of State must lay a copy of any report made to him under subsection (3) before each House of Parliament.

(5) The Secretary of State may pay to the monitor such fees and allowances as he may determine.

Note: Commencement 2 October 2000 (SI 2000/2444). Subsection (1) substituted with effect to applications to be considered under the 'Points Based System' from 1 April 2008 (SI 2008/310).

Reporting suspicious marriages

24. Duty to report suspicious marriages

(1) Subsection (3) applies if—

(a) a superintendent registrar to whom a notice of marriage has been given under section 27 of the Marriage Act 1949,

(b) any other person who, under section 28(2) of that Act, has attested a declaration accompanying such a notice,

(c) a district registrar to whom a marriage notice or an approved certificate has been submitted under section 3 of the Marriage (Scotland) Act 1977, or

(d) a registrar or deputy registrar to whom notice has been given under section 13 of the Marriages (Ireland) Act 1844 or section 4 of the Marriage Law (Ireland) Amendment Act 1863,

has reasonable grounds for suspecting that the marriage will be a sham marriage.

(2) Subsection (3) also applies if—

(a) a marriage is solemnized in the presence of a registrar of marriages or, in relation to Scotland, an authorised registrar (within the meaning of the Act of 1977); and

(b) before, during or immediately after solemnization of the marriage, the registrar has reasonable grounds for suspecting that the marriage will be, or is, a sham marriage.

(3) The person concerned must report his suspicion to the Secretary of State without delay and in such form and manner as may be prescribed by regulations.

(4) The regulations are to be made—

(a) in relation to England and Wales, by the Registrar General for England and Wales with the approval of [the Secretary of State];

(b) in relation to Scotland, by the Secretary of State after consulting the Registrar General of Births, Deaths and Marriages for Scotland;

(c) in relation to Northern Ireland, by the Secretary of State after consulting the Registrar General in Northern Ireland.

(5) 'Sham marriage' means a marriage (whether or not void)—

(a) entered into between a person ('A') who is neither a British citizen nor a national of an EEA State other than the United Kingdom and another person (whether or not such a citizen or such a national); and

(b) entered into by A for the purpose of avoiding the effect of one or more provisions of United Kingdom immigration law or the immigration rules.

Note: Commencement 1 January 2001 (SI 2000/2698). Words in square brackets in sub-section (4) (a) substituted by SI 2008/678 from 3 April 2008.

[24A. Duty to report suspicious civil partnerships

(1) Subsection (3) applies if—

(a) a registration authority to whom a notice of proposed civil partnership has been given under section 8 of the Civil Partnership Act 2004,

(b) any person who, under section 8 of the 2004 Act, has attested a declaration accompanying such a notice,

(c) a district registrar to whom a notice of proposed civil partnership has been given under section 88 of the 2004 Act, or

(d) a registrar to whom a civil partnership notice has been given under section 139 of the 2004 Act,

has reasonable grounds for suspecting that the civil partnership will be a sham civil partnership.

(2) Subsection (3) also applies if—

(a) two people register as civil partners of each other under Part 2, 3 or 4 of the 2004 Act in the presence of the registrar, and

(b) before, during or immediately after they do so, the registrar has reasonable grounds for suspecting that the civil partnership will be, or is, a sham civil partnership.

(3) The person concerned must report his suspicion to the Secretary of State without delay and in such form and manner as may be prescribed by regulations.

(4) The regulations are to be made—

(a) in relation to England and Wales, by the Registrar General for England and Wales with the approval of[the Secretary of State];

(b) in relation to Scotland, by the Secretary of State after consulting the Registrar General of Births, Deaths and Marriages for Scotland;

(c) in relation to Northern Ireland, by the Secretary of State after consulting the Registrar General in Northern Ireland.

(5) 'Sham civil partnership' means a civil partnership (whether or not void)—

(a) formed between a person ('A') who is neither a British citizen nor a national of an EEA State other than the United Kingdom and another person (whether or not such a citizen or such a national), and

(b) formed by A for the purpose of avoiding the effect of one or more provisions of United Kingdom immigration law or the immigration rules.

(6) 'The registrar' means—

(a) in relation to England and Wales, the civil partnership registrar acting under Part 2 of the 2004 Act;

(b) in relation to Scotland, the authorised registrar acting under Part 3 of the 2004 Act;

(c) in relation to Northern Ireland, the registrar acting under Part 4 of the 2004 Act.]

Note: Section 24A inserted by Sch 27 Civil Partnership Act 2004 from 15 April 2004 for the purposes of making regulations (SI 2005/1112), remainder 5 December 2005 (SI 2005/3175). Words in square brackets in sub-section (4)(a) substituted by SI 2008/678 from 3 April 2008.

Immigration control: facilities and charges

25. Provision of facilities for immigration control at ports

(1) The person responsible for the management of a control port ('the manager') must provide the Secretary of State free of charge with such facilities at the port as the Secretary

of State may direct as being reasonably necessary for, or in connection with, the operation of immigration control there.

(2) Before giving such a direction, the Secretary of State must consult such persons likely to be affected by it as he considers appropriate.

(3) If the Secretary of State gives such a direction, he must send a copy of it to the person appearing to him to be the manager.

(4) If the manager persistently fails to comply with the direction (or part of it), the Secretary of State may—

(a) in the case of a control port which is not a port of entry, revoke any approval in relation to the port given under paragraph 26(1) of Schedule 2 to the 1971 Act;

(b) in the case of a control port which is a port of entry, by order revoke its designation as a port of entry.

(5) A direction under this section is enforceable, on the application of the Secretary of State—

(a) by injunction granted by a county court; or

(b) in Scotland, by an order under section 45 of the Court of Session Act 1988.

(6) 'Control port' means a port in which a control area is designated under paragraph 26(3) of Schedule 2 to the 1971 Act.

(7) 'Facilities' means accommodation, facilities, equipment and services of a class or description specified in an order made by the Secretary of State.

Note: Commenced on 17 February 2003 for the purpose of enabling the Secretary of State to exercise power to make subordinate legislation; otherwise commenced on 1 April 2003 (SI 2003/2).

26. Charges: immigration control

(1) The Secretary of State may, at the request of any person and in consideration of such charges as he may determine, make arrangements—

(a) for the provision at any control port of immigration officers or facilities in addition to those (if any) needed to provide a basic service at the port;

(b) for the provision of immigration officers or facilities for dealing with passengers of a particular description or in particular circumstances.

(2) 'Control port' has the same meaning as in section 25.

(3) 'Facilities' includes equipment.

(4) 'Basic service' has such meaning as may be prescribed.

Note: Commenced on 5 June 2003 for purpose of enabling Secretary of State to make subordinate legislation; remainder commenced on 30 June 2003 (SI 2003/1469).

Charges: travel documents

27. . . .

Note: Repealed 2 April 2007 Sch 2 Immigration, Asylum and Nationality Act 2006 (SI 2007/1109).

Offences

28. ...

Note: Amends Immigration Act 1971, s 24A.

29. ...

Note: Repealed by Sch 9 Nationality, Immigration and Asylum Act 2002 from 1 April 2003 (SI 2003/754).

30. ...

Note: Amends Immigration Act 1971, s 26.

31. Defences based on Article 31(1) of the Refugee Convention

(1) It is a defence for a refugee charged with an offence to which this section applies to show that, having come to the United Kingdom directly from a country where his life or freedom was threatened (within the meaning of the Refugee Convention), he—

(a) presented himself to the authorities in the United Kingdom without delay;

(b) showed good cause for his illegal entry or presence; and

(c) made a claim for asylum as soon as was reasonably practicable after his arrival in the United Kingdom.

(2) If, in coming from the country where his life or freedom was threatened, the refugee stopped in another country outside the United Kingdom, subsection (1) applies only if he shows that he could not reasonably have expected to be given protection under the Refugee Convention in that other country.

(3) In England and Wales and Northern Ireland the offences to which this section applies are any offence, and any attempt to commit an offence, under—

(a) Part I of the Forgery and Counterfeiting Act 1981 (forgery and connected offences);

[(aa) section 4 or 6 of the Identity Documents Act 2010;]

(b) section 24A of the 1971 Act (deception); or

(c) section 26(1)(d) of the 1971 Act (falsification of documents).

(4) In Scotland, the offences to which this section applies are those—

(a) of fraud,

(b) of uttering a forged document,

[(ba) under section 4 or 6 of the Identity Documents Act 2010;]

(c) under section 24A of the 1971 Act (deception), or

(d) under section 26(1)(d) of the 1971 Act (falsification of documents), and any attempt to commit any of those offences.

(5) A refugee who has made a claim for asylum is not entitled to the defence provided by subsection (1) in relation to any offence committed by him after making that claim.

(6) 'Refugee' has the same meaning as it has for the purposes of the Refugee Convention.

(7) If the Secretary of State has refused to grant a claim for asylum made by a person who claims that he has a defence under subsection (1), that person is to be taken not to be a refugee unless he shows that he is.

(8) A person who—

(a) was convicted in England and Wales or Northern Ireland of an offence to which this section applies before the commencement of this section, but

(b) at no time during the proceedings for that offence argued that he had a defence based on Article 31(1), may apply to the Criminal Cases Review Commission with a view to his case being referred to the Court of Appeal by the Commission on the ground that he would have had a defence under this section had it been in force at the material time.

(9) A person who—

(a) was convicted in Scotland of an offence to which this section applies before the commencement of this section, but

(b) at no time during the proceedings for that offence argued that he had a defence based on Article 31(1), may apply to the Scottish Criminal Cases Review Commission with a view to his case being referred to the High Court of Justiciary by the Commission on the ground that he would have had a defence under this section had it been in force at the material time.

(10) The Secretary of State may by order amend—

(a) subsection (3), or

(b) subsection (4), by adding offences to those for the time being listed there.

(11) Before making an order under subsection (10)(b), the Secretary of State must consult the Scottish Ministers.

Note: Commencement 11 November 1999, s 170. Subsections (3)(aa) and (4)(ba) substituted by Identity Documents Act 2010, Schedule, para 10 from 21 January 2011 (s 14).

Part II
Carriers' Liability

Clandestine entrants

32. Penalty for carrying clandestine entrants

(1) A person is a clandestine entrant if—

(a) he arrives in the United Kingdom concealed in a vehicle, ship or aircraft,

[(aa) he arrives in the United Kingdom concealed in a rail freight wagon,]

(b) he passes, or attempts to pass, through immigration control concealed in a vehicle, or

(c) he arrives in the United Kingdom on a ship or aircraft, having embarked—

(i) concealed in a vehicle; and

(ii) at a time when the ship or aircraft was outside the United Kingdom, and claims, or indicates that he intends to seek, asylum in the United Kingdom or evades, or attempts to evade, immigration control.

[(2) The Secretary of State may require a person who is responsible for a clandestine entrant to pay—

(a) a penalty in respect of the clandestine entrant;

(b) a penalty in respect of any person who was concealed with the clandestine entrant in the same transporter.]

[(**2A**) In imposing a penalty under subsection (2) the Secretary of State—

(a) must specify an amount which does not exceed the maximum prescribed for the purpose of this paragraph,

(b) may, in respect of a clandestine entrant or a concealed person, impose separate penalties on more than one of the persons responsible for the clandestine entrant, and

(c) may not impose penalties in respect of a clandestine entrant or a concealed person which amount in aggregate to more than the maximum prescribed for the purpose of this paragraph.]

(**3**) A penalty imposed under this section must be paid to the Secretary of State before the end of the prescribed period.

[(**4**) Where a penalty is imposed under subsection (2) on the driver of a vehicle who is an employee of the vehicle's owner or hirer—

(a) the employee and the employer shall be jointly and severally liable for the penalty imposed on the driver (irrespective of whether a penalty is also imposed on the employer), and

(b) a provision of this Part about notification, objection or appeal shall have effect as if the penalty imposed on the driver were also imposed on the employer (irrespective of whether a penalty is also imposed on the employer in his capacity as the owner or hirer of the vehicle).]

[(**4A**) In the case of a detached trailer, subsection (4) shall have effect as if a reference to the driver were a reference to the operator.]

(**5**) In the case of a clandestine entrant to whom subsection (1)(a) applies, each of the following is a responsible person—

(a) if the transporter is a ship or aircraft, the owner [and] captain;

(b) if it is a vehicle (but not a detached trailer), the owner, hirer [and] driver of the vehicle;

(c) if it is a detached trailer, the owner, hirer [and] operator of the trailer.

[(**5A**) In the case of a clandestine entrant to whom subsection (1)(aa) applies, the responsible person is—

(a) where the entrant arrived concealed in a freight train, the train operator who, at the train's last scheduled stop before arrival in the United Kingdom, was responsible for certifying it as fit to travel to the United Kingdom, or

(b) where the entrant arrived concealed in a freight shuttle wagon, the operator of the shuttle-train of which the wagon formed part.]

(**6**) In the case of a clandestine entrant to whom subsection (1)(b) or (c) applies, each of the following is a responsible person—

(a) if the transporter is a detached trailer, the owner, hirer [and] operator of the trailer;

(b) if it is not, the owner, hirer [and] driver of the vehicle.

[(**6A**) Where a person falls within the definition of responsible person in more than one capacity, a separate penalty may be imposed on him under subsection (2) in respect of each capacity.]

(**7**) Subject to any defence provided by section 34, it is immaterial whether a responsible person knew or suspected—

(a) that the clandestine entrant was concealed in the transporter; or

(b) that there were one or more other persons concealed with the clandestine entrant in the same transporter.

(8) Subsection (9) applies if a transporter ('the carried transporter') is itself being carried in or on another transporter.

(9) If a person is concealed in the carried transporter, the question whether any other person is concealed with that person in the same transporter is to be determined by reference to the carried transporter and not by reference to the transporter in or on which it is carried.

(10) 'Immigration control' means United Kingdom immigration control and includes any United Kingdom immigration control operated in a prescribed control zone outside the United Kingdom.

Note: Sections 32(2)(a), 32(3) and 32(10) commenced 6 December 1999 (SI 1999/3190), remainder on 3 April 2000 (SI 2000/464). Subsections (1)(aa), (2A), (4A), (5A) and (6A) inserted and sub-ss (2) and (4) substituted by and words in square brackets in sub-ss (5) and (6) inserted by Sch 8 Nationality, Immigration and Asylum Act 2002 from 8 December 2002 (SI 2002/2811) for certain purposes; from 11 May 2012 for other purposes (SI 2012/1263).

[32A. Level of penalty: code of practice

(1) The Secretary of State shall issue a code of practice specifying matters to be considered in determining the amount of a penalty under section 32.

(2) The Secretary of State shall have regard to the code (in addition to any other matters he thinks relevant)—
    (a) when imposing a penalty under section 32, and
    (b) when considering a notice of objection under section 35(4).

(3) Before issuing the code the Secretary of State shall lay a draft before Parliament.

(4) After laying the draft code before Parliament the Secretary of State may bring the code into operation by order.

(5) The Secretary of State may from time to time revise the whole or any part of the code and issue the code as revised.

(6) Subsections (3) and (4) also apply to a revision or proposed revision of the code.]

Note: Section 32A inserted by Sch 8 Nationality, Immigration and Asylum Act 2002 from 14 November 2002 for the purpose of enabling the Secretary of State to exercise the power under s 32A(1), (3) and (4); otherwise takes effect from 8 December 2002 (SI 2002/2811) for certain purposes and from 11 May 2012 for other purposes (SI 2012/1263).

33. [Prevention of clandestine entrants: code of practice]

(1) The Secretary of State must issue a code of practice to be followed by any person operating a system for preventing the carriage of clandestine entrants.

(2) Before issuing the code, the Secretary of State must—
    (a) consult such persons as he considers appropriate; and
    (b) lay a draft before . . . Parliament.

(3) The requirement of subsection (2)(a) may be satisfied by consultation before the passing of this Act.

(4) After laying the draft code before Parliament, the Secretary of State may bring the code into operation by an order.

(5) The Secretary of State may from time to time revise the whole or any part of the code and issue the code as revised.

(6) Subsections (2) and (4) also apply to any revision, or proposed revision, of the code.

Note: Commenced 6 December 1999 (SI 1999/3190). Heading substituted and words omitted from sub-s (2)(b) by Sch 8 Nationality, Immigration and Asylum Act 2002 from 8 December 2002 (SI 2002/2811) for certain purposes and for other purposes from 11 May 2012 (SI 2012/1263).

34. Defences to claim that penalty is due under section 32

[(1) A person ('the carrier') shall not be liable to the imposition of a penalty under section 32(2) if he has a defence under this section.]

(2) It is a defence for the carrier to show that he, or an employee of his who was directly responsible for allowing the clandestine entrant to be concealed, was acting under duress.

(3) It is also a defence for the carrier to show that—

(a) he did not know, and had no reasonable grounds for suspecting, that a clandestine entrant was, or might be, concealed in the transporter;

(b) an effective system for preventing the carriage of clandestine entrants was in operation in relation to the transporter; and

(c) . . . on the occasion in question the person or persons responsible for operating that system did so properly.

[(3A) It is also a defence for the carrier to show that—

(a) he knew or suspected that a clandestine entrant was or might be concealed in a rail freight wagon, having boarded after the wagon began its journey to the United Kingdom;

(b) he could not stop the train or shuttle-train of which the wagon formed part without endangering safety;

(c) an effective system for preventing the carriage of clandestine entrants was in operation in relation to the train or shuttle-train; and

(d) on the occasion in question the person or persons responsible for operating the system did so properly.]

(4) In determining, for the purposes of this section, whether a particular system is effective, regard is to be had to the code of practice issued by the Secretary of State under section 33.

(5) . . .

[(6) Where a person has a defence under subsection (2) in respect of a clandestine entrant, every other responsible person in respect of the clandestine entrant is also entitled to the benefit of the defence.]

Note: Commencement 3 April 2000 (SI 2000/464). Subsections (1) and (6) substituted by and sub-s (3A) inserted by and words in sub-s (3)(c) omitted by and sub-s (5) omitted by Sch 8 Nationality, Immigration and Asylum Act 2002 from 8 December 2002 (SI 2002/2811) for certain purposes and from 11 May 2012 for other purposes (SI 2012/1263).

35. Procedure

(1) If the Secretary of State decides that a person ('P') is liable to one or more penalties under section 32, he must notify P of his decision.

(2) A notice under subsection (1) (a 'penalty notice') must—

(a) state the Secretary of State's reasons for deciding that P is liable to the penalty (or penalties);

(b) state the amount of the penalty (or penalties) to which P is liable;

(c) specify the date before which, and the manner in which, the penalty (or penalties) must be paid; and

(d) include an explanation of the steps—

(i) that P [may] take if he objects to the penalty;

(ii) that the Secretary of State may take under this Part to recover any unpaid penalty.

[(3) Subsection (4) applies where a person to whom a penalty notice is issued objects on the ground that—

(a) he is not liable to the imposition of a penalty, or

(b) the amount of the penalty is too high.

(4) The person may give a notice of objection to the Secretary of State.

(5) A notice of objection must—

(a) be in writing,

(b) give the objector's reasons, and

(c) be given before the end of such period as may be prescribed.

(6) Where the Secretary of State receives a notice of objection to a penalty in accordance with this section he shall consider it and—

(a) cancel the penalty,

(b) reduce the penalty,

(c) increase the penalty, or

(d) determine to take no action under paragraphs (a) to (c).

(7) Where the Secretary of State considers a notice of objection under subsection (6) he shall—

(a) inform the objector of his decision before the end of such period as may be prescribed or such longer period as he may agree with the objector,

(b) if he increases the penalty, issue a new penalty notice under subsection (1), and

(c) if he reduces the penalty, notify the objector of the reduced amount.]

(8) . . .

(9) The Secretary of State may by regulations provide, in relation to detached trailers, for a penalty notice which is [issued] in such manner as may be prescribed to have effect as a penalty notice properly [issued to] the responsible person or persons concerned under this section.

(10) Any sum payable to the Secretary of State as a penalty under section 32 may be recovered by the Secretary of State as a debt due to him.

[(11) In proceedings for enforcement of a penalty under subsection (10) no question may be raised as to—

(a) liability to the imposition of the penalty, or

(b) its amount.

(12) A document which is to be issued to or served on a person outside the United Kingdom for the purpose of subsection (1) or (7) or in the course of proceedings under subsection (10) may be issued or served—

(a) in person,

(b) by post,

(c) by facsimile transmission, or

(d) in another prescribed manner.

(13) The Secretary of State may by regulations provide that a document issued or served in a manner listed in subsection (12) in accordance with the regulations is to be taken to have been received at a time specified by or determined in accordance with the regulations.]

Note: Section 35(7)–(9) commenced 6 December 1999 (SI 1999/3190), remainder 3 April 2000 (SI 2000/464). Subsections (3)–(7) substituted by and sub-s (8) omitted by and sub-ss (11)–(13) inserted by and words in square brackets in sub-s (2) and (9) substituted by Sch 8 Nationality, Immigration and Asylum Act 2002 from 8 December 2002 (SI 2002/2811) for certain purposes and from 11 May 2012 for other purposes (SI 2012/1263).

[35A. Appeal

(1) A person may appeal to the court against a penalty imposed on him under section 32 on the ground that—

(a) he is not liable to the imposition of a penalty, or

(b) the amount of the penalty is too high.

(2) On an appeal under this section the court may—

(a) allow the appeal and cancel the penalty,

(b) allow the appeal and reduce the penalty, or

(c) dismiss the appeal.

(3) An appeal under this section shall be a re-hearing of the Secretary of State's decision to impose a penalty and shall be determined having regard to—

(a) any code of practice under section 32A which has effect at the time of the appeal,

(b) the code of practice under section 33 which had effect at the time of the events to which the penalty relates, and

(c) any other matters which the court thinks relevant (which may include matters of which the Secretary of State was unaware).

(4) Subsection (3) has effect despite any provision of Civil Procedure Rules.

(5) An appeal may be brought by a person under this section against a penalty whether or not—

(a) he has given notice of objection under section 35(4);

(b) the penalty has been increased or reduced under section 35(6).]

Note: Section 35A inserted by Sch 8 Nationality, Immigration and Asylum Act 2002 from 8 December 2002 (SI 2002/2811) for certain purposes and from 11 May 2012 for other purposes (SI 2012/1263).

36. Power to detain vehicles etc. in connection with penalties under section 32

(1) If a penalty notice has been [issued] under section 35, a senior officer may detain any relevant—

(a) vehicle,

(b) small ship, . . .

(c) small aircraft, . . . [or

(d) rail freight wagon,] until all penalties to which the notice relates, and any expenses reasonably incurred by the Secretary of State in connection with the detention, have been paid.

(2) That power—

(a) may be exercised only if, in the opinion of the senior officer concerned, there is a significant risk that the penalty (or one or more of the penalties) will not be paid before the end of the prescribed period if the transporter is not detained; and

(b) may not be exercised if alternative security which the Secretary of State considers is satisfactory, has been given.

[(2A) A vehicle may be detained under subsection (1) only if—

(a) the driver of the vehicle is an employee of its owner or hirer,

(b) the driver of the vehicle is its owner or hirer, or

(c) a penalty notice is issued to the owner or hirer of the vehicle.

(2B) A senior officer may detain a relevant vehicle, small ship, small aircraft or rail freight wagon pending—

(a) a decision whether to issue a penalty notice,

(b) the issue of a penalty notice, or

(c) a decision whether to detain under subsection (1).

(2C) That power may not be exercised in any case—

(a) for longer than is necessary in the circumstances of the case, or

(b) after the expiry of the period of 24 hours beginning with the conclusion of the first search of the vehicle, ship, aircraft or wagon by an immigration officer after it arrived in the United Kingdom.]

(3) If a transporter is detained under this section, the owner, consignor or any other person who has an interest in any freight or other thing carried in or on the transporter may remove it, or arrange for it to be removed, at such time and in such way as is reasonable.

(4) The detention of a transporter under this section is lawful even though it is subsequently established that the penalty notice on which the detention was based was ill-founded in respect of all or any of the penalties to which it related.

(5) But subsection (4) does not apply if the Secretary of State was acting unreasonably in issuing the penalty notice.

Note: Section 36(2)(a) commenced 6 December 1999 (SI 1999/3190), remainder 3 April 2000 (SI 2000/464). Subsections (2A), (2B) and (2C) inserted by and words in square brackets in sub-s (1) substituted by Sch 8 Nationality Immigration and Asylum Act 2002 from 8 December 2002 (SI 2002/2811) for certain purposes and from 11 May 2012 for other purposes (SI 2012/1263).

[36A. Detention in default of payment

(1) This section applies where a person to whom a penalty notice has been issued under section 35 fails to pay the penalty before the date specified in accordance with section 35(2)(c).

(2) The Secretary of State may make arrangements for the detention of any vehicle, small ship, small aircraft or rail freight wagon which the person to whom the penalty notice was issued uses in the course of a business.

(3) A vehicle, ship, aircraft or wagon may be detained under subsection (2) whether or not the person to whom the penalty notice was issued owns it.

(4) But a vehicle may be detained under subsection (2) only if the person to whom the penalty notice was issued—

(a) is the owner or hirer of the vehicle, or

(b) was an employee of the owner or hirer of the vehicle when the penalty notice was issued.

(5) The power under subsection (2) may not be exercised while an appeal against the penalty under section 35A is pending or could be brought (ignoring the possibility of an appeal out of time with permission).

(6) The Secretary of State shall arrange for the release of a vehicle, ship, aircraft or wagon detained under this section if the person to whom the penalty notice was issued pays—

(a) the penalty, and

(b) expenses reasonably incurred in connection with the detention.]

Note: Section 36A inserted by Sch 8 Nationality, Immigration and Asylum Act 2002 from 8 December 2002 (SI 2002/2811) for certain purposes and from 11 May 2012 for other purposes (SI 2012/1263).

37. Effect of detention

(1) This section applies if a transporter is detained under [section 36(1)].

(2) The person to whom the penalty notice was addressed, or the owner or any other person [whose interests may be affected by detention of the transporter], may apply to the court for the transporter to be released.

(3) The court may release the transporter if it considers that—

(a) satisfactory security has been tendered in place of the transporter for the payment of the penalty alleged to be due and connected expenses;

(b) there is no significant risk that the penalty (or one or more of the penalties) and any connected expenses will not be paid; or

(c) there is a significant doubt as to whether the penalty is payable. . . .

[(3A) The court may also release the transporter on the application of the owner of the transporter under subsection (2) if—

(a) a penalty notice was not issued to the owner or an employee of his, and

(b) the court considers it right to release the transporter.

(3B) In determining whether to release a transporter under subsection (3A) the court shall consider—

(a) the extent of any hardship caused by detention,

(b) the extent (if any) to which the owner is responsible for the matters in respect of which the penalty notice was issued, and

(c) any other matter which appears to the court to be relevant (whether specific to the circumstances of the case or of a general nature).]

(4) If the court has not ordered the release of the transporter, the Secretary of State may sell it if the penalty in question and connected expenses are not paid before the end of the period of 84 days beginning with the date on which the detention began.

(5) 'Connected expenses' means expenses reasonably incurred by the Secretary of State in connection with the detention.

[(5A) The power of sale under subsection (4) may be exercised only when no appeal against the imposition of the penalty is pending or can be brought (ignoring the possibility of an appeal out of time with permission).

(5B) The power of sale under subsection (4) shall lapse if not exercised within a prescribed period.]

(6) Schedule 1 applies to the sale of transporters under this section.

[(7) This section applies to a transporter detained under section 36A as it applies to a transporter detained under section 36(1); but for that purpose—

(a) the court may release the transporter only if the court considers that the detention was unlawful or under subsection (3A) (and subsection (3) shall not apply), and

(b) the reference in subsection (4) to the period of 84 days shall be taken as a reference to a period prescribed for the purpose of this paragraph.]

Note: Section 37(6) commenced 6 December 1999 (SI 1999/3190), remainder 3 April 2000 (SI 2000/464). Subsections (3A)–(3B), (5A)–(5B) and (7) inserted by Sch 8 Nationality, Immigration and Asylum Act 2002 from 8 December 2002 (SI 2002/2811). Words in square brackets in sub-ss (1) and (2) and words in sub-s (3)(c) omitted by Sch 8 Nationality, Immigration and Asylum Act 2002 from 8 December 2002 (SI 2002/2811) for certain purposes and from 11 May 2012 for other purposes (SI 2012/1263).

38. Assisting illegal entry and harbouring

. . .

Note: Inserts s 25A of Immigration Act 1971 from 3 April 2000. Subsections (1) and (3) repealed by Sch 9 Nationality, Immigration and Asylum Act 2002 from a date to be appointed.

39. . . .

Note: Section 39 repealed by Sch 8 Nationality, Immigration and Asylum Act 2002 from 8 December 2002 (SI 2002/2811).

Passengers without proper documents

[40. Charge in respect of passenger without proper documents

(1) This section applies if an individual requiring leave to enter the United Kingdom arrives in the United Kingdom by ship or aircraft and, on being required to do so by an immigration officer, fails to produce—

(a) an immigration document which is in force and which satisfactorily establishes his identity and his nationality or citizenship, and

(b) if the individual requires a visa, a visa of the required kind.

(2) The Secretary of State may charge the owner of the ship or aircraft; in respect of the individual, the sum of £2,000.

(3) The charge shall be payable to the Secretary of State on demand.

(4) No charge shall be payable in respect of any individual who is shown by the owner to have produced the required document or documents to the owner or his employee or agent when embarking on the ship or aircraft for the voyage or flight to the United Kingdom.

(5) For the purpose of subsection (4) an owner shall be entitled to regard a document as—

(a) being what it purports to be unless its falsity is reasonably apparent, and

(b) relating to the individual producing it unless it is reasonably apparent that it does not relate to him.

(6) For the purposes of this section an individual requires a visa if—

(a) under the immigration rules he requires a visa for entry into the United Kingdom, or

(b) as a result of section 41 he requires a visa for passing through the United Kingdom.

(**7**) The Secretary of State may by order amend this section for the purpose of applying it in relation to an individual who—

(a) requires leave to enter the United Kingdom, and

(b) arrives in the United Kingdom by train.

(**8**) An order under subsection (7) may provide for the application of this section—

(a) except in cases of a specified kind;

(b) subject to a specified defence.

(**9**) In this section 'immigration document' means—

(a) a passport, and

(b) a document which relates to a national of a country other than the United Kingdom and which is designed to serve the same purpose as a passport.

(**10**) The Secretary of State may by order substitute a sum for the sum in subsection (2).]

Note: Section 40 substituted by Sch 8 Nationality, Immigration and Asylum Act 2002 from 8 December 2002 (SI 2003/2811).

40A. Notification and objection

(**1**) If the Secretary of State decides to charge a person under section 40, the Secretary of State must notify the person of his decision.

(**2**) A notice under subsection (1) (a 'charge notice') must—

(a) state the Secretary of State's reasons for deciding to charge the person,

(b) state the amount of the charge,

(c) specify the date before which, and the manner in which, the charge must be paid,

(d) include an explanation of the steps that the person may take if he objects to the charge, and

(e) include an explanation of the steps that the Secretary of State may take under this Part to recover any unpaid charge.

(**3**) Where a person on whom a charge notice is served objects to the imposition of the charge on him, he may give a notice of objection to the Secretary of State.

(**4**) A notice of objection must—

(a) be in writing,

(b) give the objector's reasons, and

(c) be given before the end of such period as may be prescribed.

(**5**) Where the Secretary of State receives a notice of objection to a charge in accordance with this section, he shall—

(a) consider it, and

(b) determine whether or not to cancel the charge.

(**6**) Where the Secretary of State considers a notice of objection, he shall inform the objector of his decision before the end of—

(a) such period as may be prescribed, or

(b) such longer period as he may agree with the objector.

(7) Any sum payable to the Secretary of State as a charge under section 40 may be recovered by the Secretary of State as a debt due to him.

(8) In proceedings for enforcement of a charge under subsection (7) no question may be raised as to the validity of the charge.

(9) Subsections (12) and (13) of section 35 shall have effect for the purpose of this section as they have effect for the purpose of section 35(1), (7) and (10).]

Note: Section 40A inserted by Sch 8 Nationality, Immigration and Asylum Act 2002 from 8 December 2002 (SI 2002/2811).

40B. Appeal

(1) A person may appeal to the court against a decision to charge him under section 40.

(2) On an appeal under this section the court may—
    (a) allow the appeal and cancel the charge, or
    (b) dismiss the appeal.

(3) An appeal under this section—
    (a) shall be a re-hearing of the Secretary of State's decision to impose a charge, and
    (b) may be determined having regard to matters of which the Secretary of State was unaware.

(4) Subsection (3)(a) has effect despite any provision of Civil Procedure Rules.

(5) An appeal may be brought by a person under this section against a decision to charge him whether or not he has given notice of objection under section 40A(3).

Note: Section 40B inserted by Sch 8 Nationality, Immigration and Asylum Act 2002 from 8 December 2002 (SI 2002/2811).

41. Visas for transit passengers

(1) The Secretary of State may by order require transit passengers to hold a transit visa.

(2) 'Transit passengers' means persons of any description specified in the order who on arrival in the United Kingdom pass through to another country without entering the United Kingdom; and 'transit visa' means a visa for that purpose.

(3) The order—
    (a) may specify a description of persons by reference to nationality, citizenship, origin or other connection with any particular country but not by reference to race, colour or religion;
    (b) may not provide for the requirement imposed by the order to apply to any person who under the 1971 Act has the right of abode in the United Kingdom;
    (c) may provide for any category of persons of a description specified in the order to be exempt from the requirement imposed by the order;
    (d) may make provision about the method of application for visas required by the order.

Note: Commenced 8 December 2002 (SI 2002/2815).

42. . . .

Note: Section 42 repealed by Sch 8 Nationality, Immigration and Asylum Act from 8 December 2002 (SI 2002/2811).

Interpretation

43. Interpretation of Part II

[(**1**)] In this Part—

'aircraft' includes hovercraft;

'captain' means the master of a ship or commander of an aircraft;

'concealed' includes being concealed in any freight, stores or other thing carried in or on the vehicle, ship [, aircraft or rail freight wagon] concerned;

. . .

'detached trailer' means a trailer, semi-trailer, caravan or any other thing which is designed or adapted for towing by a vehicle but which has been detached for transport—

    (a) in or on the vehicle concerned; or

    (b) in the ship or aircraft concerned (whether separately or in or on a vehicle);

'equipment', in relation to an aircraft, includes—

    (a) any certificate of registration, maintenance or airworthiness of the aircraft;

    (b) any log book relating to the use of the aircraft; and

    (c) any similar document;

['freight shuttle wagon' means a wagon which—

    (a) forms part of a shuttle-train, and

    (b) is designed to carry commercial goods vehicles;

'freight train' means any train other than—

    (a) a train engaged on a service for the carriage of passengers, or

    (b) a shuttle-train;]

'hirer', in relation to a vehicle, means any person who has hired the vehicle from another person;

'operating weight', in relation to an aircraft, means the maximum total weight of the aircraft and its contents at which the aircraft may take off anywhere in the world, in the most favourable circumstances, in accordance with the certificate of airworthiness in force in respect of the aircraft;

'owner' includes—

    (a) in relation to a ship or aircraft, the agent or operator of the ship or aircraft;

    . . .

    (b) . . . and in relation to a transporter which is the subject of a hire- purchase agreement, includes the person in possession of it under that agreement;

'penalty notice' has the meaning given in section 35(2);

['rail freight wagon' means—

    (a) any rolling stock, other than a locomotive, which forms part of a freight train, or

    (b) a freight shuttle wagon, and for the purpose of this definition, 'rolling stock' and 'locomotive' have the meanings given by section 83 of the Railways Act 1993 (c.43);]

'senior officer' means an immigration officer not below the rank of chief immigration officer;

'ship' includes every description of vessel used in navigation;

['shuttle-train' has the meaning given by section 1(9) of the Channel Tunnel Act 1987 (c. 53);]

'small aircraft' means an aircraft which has an operating weight of less than 5,700 kilogrammes;

'small ship' means a ship which has a gross tonnage of less than 500 tonnes;

'train' means a train which—

(a) is engaged on an international service as defined by section 13(6) of the Channel Tunnel Act 1987; but

(b) is not a shuttle train as defined by section 1(9) of that Act;

'train operator', in relation to a person arriving in the United Kingdom on a train, means the operator of trains who embarked that person on that train for the journey to the United Kingdom;

'transporter' means a vehicle, ship, [aircraft or rail freight wagon] together with—

(a) its equipment; and

(b) any stores for use in connection with its operation;

'vehicle' includes a trailer, semi-trailer, caravan or other thing which is designed or adapted to be towed by another vehicle.

[(2) A reference in this Part to 'the court' is a reference—

(a) in England and Wales, to a county court,

(b) in Scotland, to the sheriff, and

(c) in Northern Ireland, to a county court.

(3) But—

(a) a county court may transfer proceedings under this Part to the High Court, and

(b) the sheriff may transfer proceedings under this Part to the Court of Session.]

Note: Commenced 6 December 1999 (SI 1999/3190). Subsections (2) and (3) and words in square brackets in sub-s (1) inserted by and words in sub-s (1) omitted by Sch 8 Nationality, Immigration and Asylum Act from 8 December 2002 (SI 2002/2811).

PART III

BAIL

Routine bail hearings

. . .

44–52. . . .

Note: Sections 44 to 52 repealed by the Nationality, Immigration and Asylum Act 2002, s 68 from 10 February 2003 (SI 2003/1).

Bail hearings under other enactments

53. Applications for bail in immigration cases

(1) The Secretary of State may by regulations make new provision in relation to applications for bail by persons detained under the 1971 Act [or under section 62 of the Nationality, Immigration and Asylum Act 2002].

(**2**) The regulations may confer a right to be released on bail in prescribed circumstances.

(**3**) The regulations may, in particular, make provision—

(a) creating or transferring jurisdiction to hear an application for bail by a person detained under the 1971 Act [or under section 62 of the Nationality, Immigration and Asylum Act 2002];

(b) as to the places in which such an application may be held;

(c) as to the procedure to be followed on, or in connection with, such an application;

(d) as to circumstances in which, and conditions (including financial conditions) on which, an applicant may be released on bail;

(e) amending or repealing any enactment so far as it relates to such an application.

(**4**) The regulations must include provision for securing that an application for bail made by a person who has brought an appeal under any provision of [the Nationality, Immigration and Asylum Act 2002] or the Special Immigration Appeals Commission Act 1997 is heard by the appellate authority hearing that appeal.

(**5**) . . .

(**6**) Regulations under this section require the approval of the Lord Chancellor.

[(**6A**) In so far as regulations under this section relate to England and Wales, the Lord Chancellor must consult the Lord Chief Justice of England and Wales before giving his approval.

(**6B**) In so far as regulations under this section relate to Northern Ireland, the Lord Chancellor must consult the Lord Chief Justice of Northern Ireland before giving his approval.]

(**7**) In so far as regulations under this section relate to the sheriff or the Court of Session, the Lord Chancellor must obtain the consent of the Scottish Ministers before giving his approval.

[(**8**) The Lord Chief Justice of England and Wales may nominate a judicial office holder (as defined in section 109(4) of the Constitutional Reform Act 2005) to exercise his functions under this section.

(**9**) The Lord Chief Justice of Northern Ireland may nominate any of the following to exercise his functions under this section—

(a) the holder of one of the offices listed in Schedule 1 to the Justice (Northern Ireland) Act 2002;

(b) a Lord Justice of Appeal (as defined in section 88 of that Act).]

Note: Section 53 commenced 10 February 2003 (SI 2003/2). Words in square brackets in sub-ss (1) and (3) inserted by and sub-s (5) omitted by Nationality, Immigration and Asylum Act 2002, ss 62, 68 from 10 February 2003 (SI 2003/1). Words in square brackets in sub-s (4) substituted by Sch 7 Nationality, Immigration and Asylum Act 2002 from 1 April 2003 (SI 2003/754). Subsections (6A), (8)–(9) inserted by Sch 4 Constitutional Reform Act 2005 from 3 April 2006 (SI 2006/1014). Any function of the Lord Chancellor under sub-s (6) to become a protected function from a date to be appointed, Sch 7 Constitutional Reform Act 2005.

54. Extension of right to apply for bail in deportation cases

Note: Amends para 2, Sch 3 Immigration Act 1971.

Grants

55. ...

Note: Section 55 ceased to have effect from 10 February 2003, Nationality, Immigration and Asylum Act 2002, s 68.

PART IV
APPEALS

...

Note: Part IV repealed by the Nationality, Immigration and Asylum Act 2002, s 114 and Sch 9 from 1 April 2003 (SI 2003/754, which sets out transitional provisions).

PART V

IMMIGRATION ADVISERS AND IMMIGRATION SERVICE PROVIDERS

Interpretation

82. Interpretation of Part V

(1) In this Part—

'claim for asylum' means a claim that it would be contrary to the United Kingdom's obligations under—

(a) the Refugee Convention, or

(b) Article 3 of the Human Rights Convention, for the claimant to be removed from, or required to leave, the United Kingdom;

'the Commissioner' means the Immigration Services Commissioner;

'the complaints scheme' means the scheme established under paragraph 5(1) of Schedule 5;

'designated judge' has the same meaning as in section 119(1) of the Courts and Legal Services Act 1990;

'designated professional body' has the meaning given by section 86;

['designated qualifying regulator' has the meaning given by section 86A;]

'immigration advice' means advice which—

(a) relates to a particular individual;

(b) is given in connection with one or more relevant matters;

(c) is given by a person who knows that he is giving it in relation to a particular individual and in connection with one or more relevant matters; and

(d) is not given in connection with representing an individual before a court in criminal proceedings or matters ancillary to criminal proceedings;

'immigration services' means the making of representations on behalf of a particular individual—

(a) in civil proceedings before a court, tribunal or adjudicator in the United Kingdom, or

(b) in correspondence with a Minister of the Crown or government department, in connection with one or more relevant matters;

'Minister of the Crown' has the same meaning as in the Ministers of the Crown Act 1975;

'qualified person' means a person who is qualified for the purposes of section 84;

'registered person' means a person who is registered with the Commissioner under section 85;

'relevant matters' means any of the following—

(a) a claim for asylum;

(b) an application for, or for the variation of, entry clearance or leave to enter or remain in the United Kingdom;

[(ba) an application for an immigration employment document;]

(c) unlawful entry into the United Kingdom;

(d) nationality and citizenship under the law of the United Kingdom;

(e) citizenship of the European Union;

(f) admission to Member States under [EU] law;

(g) residence in a Member State in accordance with rights conferred by or under [EU] law;

(h) removal or deportation from the United Kingdom;

(i) an application for bail under the Immigration Acts or under the Special Immigration Appeals Commission Act 1997;

(j) an appeal against, or an application for judicial review in relation to, any decision taken in connection with a matter referred to in paragraphs (a) to (i).

[. . .]

(2) In this Part, references to the provision of immigration advice or immigration services are to the provision of such advice or services by a person—

(a) in the United Kingdom (regardless of whether the persons to whom they are provided are in the United Kingdom or elsewhere); and

(b) in the course of a business carried on (whether or not for profit) by him or by another person.

[(3) In the definition of 'relevant matters' in subsection (1) 'immigration employment document' means—

(a) a work permit (within the meaning of section 33(1) of the Immigration Act 1971 (interpretation)), and

(b) any other document which relates to employment and is issued for a purpose of immigration rules or in connection with leave to enter or remain in the United Kingdom.]

Note: Commenced 22 May 2000 (SI 2000/1282). First words in square brackets in sub-s (1) inserted Sch 18 Legal Services Act 2007 from 1 April 2011 (SI 2011/720). Second words in square brackets in sub-s (1) and sub-s (3) inserted by Nationality, Immigration and Asylum Act 2002, s 123 from 1 April 2004 (SI 2003/2993). Words omitted from sub-s (1) from 18 January 2010 (SI 2010/22).

The Immigration Services Commissioner

83. The Commissioner

(1) There is to be an Immigration Services Commissioner (referred to in this Part as 'the Commissioner').

(2) The Commissioner is to be appointed by the Secretary of State after consulting the Lord Chancellor and the Scottish Ministers.

(3) It is to be the general duty of the Commissioner to promote good practice by those who provide immigration advice or immigration services.

(4) In addition to any other functions conferred on him by this Part, the Commissioner is to have the regulatory functions set out in Part I of Schedule 5.

(5) The Commissioner must exercise his functions so as to secure, so far as is reasonably practicable, that those who provide immigration advice or immigration services—

(a) are fit and competent to do so;

(b) act in the best interests of their clients;

(c) do not knowingly mislead any court, tribunal or adjudicator in the United Kingdom;

(d) do not seek to abuse any procedure operating in the United Kingdom in connection with immigration or asylum (including any appellate or other judicial procedure);

(e) do not advise any person to do something which would amount to such an abuse.

(6) The Commissioner—

(a) must arrange for the publication, in such form and manner and to such extent as he considers appropriate, of information about his functions and about matters falling within the scope of his functions; and

(b) may give advice about his functions and about such matters.

[(6A) The duties imposed on the Commissioner by subsections (3) and (5) apply in relation to persons within section 84(2)(ba) only to the extent that those duties have effect in relation to the Commissioner's functions under section 92 or 92A.]

(7) Part II of Schedule 5 makes further provision with respect to the Commissioner.

Note: Section 83(4) and (5) commenced 22 May 2000 for the purposes of Sch 5, and 30 October 2000 (SI 2000/1985). Subsection (6A) inserted by Sch 18 Legal Services Act 2007 from 1 April 2011 (SI 2011/720).

The general prohibition

84. Provision of immigration services

(1) No person may provide immigration advice or immigration services unless he is a qualified person.

[(2) A person is a qualified person if he is—

(a) a registered person,

(b) authorised by a designated professional body to practise as a member of the profession whose members the body regulates,

[(ba) a person authorised to provide immigration advice or immigration services by a designated qualifying regulator,]

(c) the equivalent in an EEA State of—

(i) a registered person, or

(ii) a person within paragraph (b) [or (ba)],

(d) a person permitted, by virtue of exemption from a prohibition, to provide in an EEA State advice or services equivalent to immigration advice or services, or

(e) acting on behalf of, and under the supervision of, a person within any of paragraphs (a) to (d) (whether or not under a contract of employment).

(3) Subsection (2)(a) and (e) are subject to any limitation on the effect of a person's registration imposed under paragraph 2(2) of Schedule 6.]

[(**3A**) A person's entitlement to provide immigration advice or immigration services by virtue of subsection (2)(ba)—

(a) is subject to any limitation on that person's authorisation imposed by the regulatory arrangements of the designated qualifying regulator in question, and

(b) does not extend to the provision of such advice or services by the person other than in England and Wales (regardless of whether the persons to whom they are provided are in England and Wales or elsewhere).

(**3B**) In subsection (3A) 'regulatory arrangements' has the same meaning as in the Legal Services Act 2007 (see section 21 of that Act).]

(**4**) Subsection (1) does not apply to a person who—

(a) is certified by the Commissioner as exempt ('an exempt person');

(b) is employed by an exempt person;

(c) works under the supervision of an exempt person or an employee of an exempt person; or

(d) who falls within a category of person specified in an order made by the Secretary of State for the purposes of this subsection.

(**5**) A certificate under subsection (4)(a) may relate only to a specified description of immigration advice or immigration services.

(**6**) Subsection (1) does not apply to a person—

(a) holding an office under the Crown, when acting in that capacity;

(b) employed by, or for the purposes of, a government department, when acting in that capacity;

(c) acting under the control of a government department; or

(d) otherwise exercising functions on behalf of the Crown.

(**7**) An exemption given under subsection (4) may be withdrawn by the Commissioner.

Note: Subsections (4)(a) and (d), (5) and (7) commenced 30 October 2000 (SI 2000/1985), remainder on 30 April 2001 (SI 2001/1394). Subsections (2) and (3) substituted by Asylum and Immigration (Treatment of Claimants etc.) Act 2004, s 37 from 1 October 2004 (SI 2004/2523). Subsections (2) (ba), (3A) and (3B) and words in square brackets in sub-s (2)(c)(ii) inserted by Sch 18 Legal Services Act 2007 from 1 April 2011 (SI 2011/720).

85. Registration and exemption by the Commissioner

(**1**) The Commissioner must prepare and maintain a register for the purposes of section 84(2)(a) . . .

(**2**) The Commissioner must keep a record of the persons to whom he has issued a certificate of exemption under section 84(4)(a).

(**3**) Schedule 6 makes further provision with respect to registration.

Note: Subsection (3) commenced 1 August 2000, remainder 30 October 2000 (SI 2000/1985). Words omitted from sub-s (1) by Asylum and Immigration (Treatment of Claimants etc.) Act 2004, s 37 from 1 October 2004 (SI 2004/2523).

86. Designated professional bodies

(**1**) 'Designated professional body' means—

(a) The Law Society;

(b) The Law Society of Scotland;

(c) The Law Society of Northern Ireland;

(d) . . .

(e) . . .

(f) The Faculty of Advocates; or

(g) The General Council of the Bar of Northern Ireland.

[(2) The Secretary of State may by order remove a body from the list in subsection (1) if he considers that the body—

(a) has failed to provide effective regulation of its members in their provision of immigration advice or immigration services, or

(b) has failed to comply with a request of the Commissioner for the provision of information (whether general or in relation to a particular case or matter).]

(3) If a designated professional body asks the Secretary of State to amend subsection (1) so as to remove its name, the Secretary of State may by order do so.

(4) If the Secretary of State is proposing to act under subsection (2) he must, before doing so—

(a) consult the Commissioner;

(b) . . .

(c) consult the [Scottish Legal Complaints Commission], if the proposed order would affect a designated professional body in Scotland;

(d) consult the lay observers appointed under Article 42 of the Solicitors (Northern Ireland) Order 1976, if the proposed order would affect a designated professional body in Northern Ireland;

(e) notify the body concerned of his proposal and give it a reasonable period within which to make representations; and

(f) consider any representations so made.

(5) An order under subsection (2) requires the approval of—

(a) the Lord Chancellor, if it affects a designated professional body in . . . Northern Ireland;

(b) the Scottish Ministers, if it affects a designated professional body in Scotland.

(6) Before deciding whether or not to give his approval under subsection (5)(a), the Lord Chancellor must consult—

(a) . . .

(b) the Lord Chief Justice of Northern Ireland, if [the order] affects a designated professional body in Northern Ireland.

(7) Before deciding whether or not to give their approval under subsection (5)(b), the Scottish Ministers must consult the Lord President of the Court of Session.

(8) If the Secretary of State considers that a body [(other than a body in England and Wales] which—

(a) is concerned (whether wholly or in part) with regulating the legal profession, or a branch of it, in an EEA State,

(b) is not a designated professional body, and

(c) is capable of providing effective regulation of its members in their provision of immigration advice or immigration services, ought to be designated, he may by order amend subsection (1) to include the name of that body.

(9) The Commissioner must—

(a) keep under review the list of designated professional bodies set out in subsection (1); and

[(b) report to the Secretary of State if the Commissioner considers that a designated professional body—

(i) is failing to provide effective regulation of its members in their provision of immigration advice or immigration services, or

(ii) has failed to comply with a request of the Commissioner for the provision of information (whether general or in relation to a particular case or matter).]

[(**9A**) A designated professional body shall comply with a request of the Commissioner for the provision of information (whether general or in relation to a specified case or matter).]

(**10**) For the purpose of meeting the costs incurred by the Commissioner in discharging his functions under this Part, each designated professional body must pay to the Commissioner, in each year and on such date as may be specified, such fee as may be specified.

(**11**) Any unpaid fee for which a designated professional body is liable under subsection (10) may be recovered from that body as a debt due to the Commissioner.

(**12**) 'Specified' means specified by an order made by the Secretary of State.

Note: Subsections (1)–(9) commenced 22 May 2000 (SI 2000/1282), remainder 30 October 2000 (SI 2000/1985). Words in square brackets substituted by Asylum and Immigration (Treatment of Claimants etc.) Act 2004, s 41 from 1 October 2004 (SI 2004/2523). Words in square brackets in sub-s (4)(c) substituted by s 196 Legal Services Act 2007 from 1 October 2008 (SI 2008/1436). Subsections (1)(a), (d) and (e), (4)(b) and (6)(a) omitted and words in sub-s (5)(a) omitted and words in sub-s (6)(b) substituted by Schs 18 and 23 Legal Services Act 2007 from 1 April 2011 (SI 2011/720).

[86A Designated qualifying regulators

(**1**) 'Designated qualifying regulator' means a body which is a qualifying regulator and is listed in subsection (2).

(**2**) The listed bodies are—
(a) the Law Society;
(b) the Institute of Legal Executives;
(c) the General Council of the Bar.

(**3**) The Secretary of State may by order remove a body from the list in subsection (2) if the Secretary of State considers that the body has failed to provide effective regulation of relevant authorised persons in their provision of immigration advice or immigration services.

(**4**) If a designated qualifying regulator asks the Secretary of State to amend subsection (2) so as to remove its name, the Secretary of State may by order do so.

(**5**) Where, at a time when a body is listed in subsection (2), the body ceases to be a qualifying regulator by virtue of paragraph 8(1)(a) of Schedule 18 to the Legal Services Act 2007 (loss of approved regulator status), the Secretary of State must, by order, remove it from the list.

(**6**) If the Secretary of State considers that a body which—
(a) is a qualifying regulator,
(b) is not a designated qualifying regulator, and

(c) is capable of providing effective regulation of relevant authorised persons in their provision of immigration advice or immigration services, ought to be designated, the Secretary of State may, by order, amend the list in subsection (2) to include the name of that body.

(7) If the Secretary of State is proposing to act under subsection (3) or (6), the Secretary of State must, before doing so, consult the Commissioner.

(8) If the Secretary of State is proposing to act under subsection (3), the Secretary of State must, before doing so, also —

(a) notify the body concerned of the proposal and give it a reasonable period within which to make representations, and

(b) consider any representations duly made.

(9) An order under subsection (3) or (6) requires the approval of the Lord Chancellor.

(10) If the Legal Services Board considers that a designated qualifying regulator is failing to provide effective regulation of relevant authorised persons in their provision of immigration advice or immigration services, the Legal Services Board must make a report to this effect to—

(a) the Secretary of State, and

(b) the Lord Chancellor.

(11) In this section—

'qualifying regulator' means a body which is a qualifying regulator for the purposes of this Part of this Act by virtue of Part 1 of Schedule 18 to the Legal Services Act 2007 (approved regulators approved by the Legal Services Board in relation to immigration matters);

'relevant authorised persons', in relation to a designated qualifying regulator, means persons who are authorised by the designated qualifying regulator to provide immigration advice or immigration services.]

Note: Section 86A inserted by Sch 18 Legal Services Act 2007 from 1 April 2011 (SI 2011/720).

[Appeals to the First-tier Tribunal]

87. **[Appeals to the First-tier Tribunal]**

(1) . . .

(2) Any person aggrieved by a relevant decision of the Commissioner may appeal to the [First-tier Tribunal] against the decision.

(3) 'Relevant decision' means a decision—

(a) to refuse an application for registration made under paragraph 1 of Schedule 6;

(b) to withdraw an exemption given under section 84(4)(a);

(c) under paragraph 2(2) of that Schedule to register with limited effect;

(d) to refuse an application for continued registration made under paragraph 3 of that Schedule;

(e) to vary a registration on an application under paragraph 3 of that Schedule;

[(ea) to vary a registration under paragraph 3A of that Schedule;] or

(f) . . .

[(3A) A relevant decision of the Commissioner is not to have effect while the period within which an appeal may be brought against the decision is running.

(3B) In the case of an appeal under this section, Tribunal Procedure Rules may include provision permitting the First-tier Tribunal to direct that while the appeal is being dealt with—

(a) no effect is to be given to the decision appealed against; or

(b) only such limited effect is to be given to it as may be specified in the direction.

(3C) If provision is made in Tribunal Procedure Rules by virtue of subsection (3B), the rules must also include provision requiring the First-tier Tribunal to consider applications by the Commissioner for the cancellation or variation of directions given by virtue of that subsection;]

[(4) For a further function of the First-tier Tribunal under this Part, see paragraph 9(1)(e) of Schedule 5 (disciplinary charges laid by the Commissioner).]

(5) ...

Note: Subsection (5) commenced 1 August 2000, remainder 30 October 2000 (SI 2000/1985). Words in square brackets inserted by Nationality, Immigration and Asylum Act 2002, s 140 from 8 January 2003 (SI 2003/1). Heading, words in square brackets in sub-s (2) and sub-s (4) substituted; sub-ss (3A)–(3C) inserted and sub-ss (1) and (5) revoked from 18 January 2010 (SI 2010/22).

88. Appeal upheld by the [First-tier Tribunal]

(1) This section applies if the [First-tier Tribunal] allows an appeal under section 87.

(2) If the [First-tier Tribunal] considers it appropriate, it may direct the Commissioner—

(a) to register the applicant or to continue the applicant's registration;

(b) to make or vary the applicant's registration so as to have limited effect in any of the ways mentioned in paragraph 2(2) of Schedule 6;

(c) to restore an exemption granted under section 84(4)(a); or

(d) to quash a decision recorded under paragraph 9(1)(a) of Schedule 5 and the record of that decision.

Note: Commenced 30 October 2000 (SI 2000/1985). Words in square brackets substituted from 18 January 2010 (SI 2010/22).

89. Disciplinary charge upheld by the [First-tier Tribunal]

(1) This section applies if the [First-tier Tribunal] upholds a disciplinary charge laid by the Commissioner under paragraph 9(1)(e) of Schedule 5 against a person ('the person charged').

[(2) If the person charged is a registered person or acts on behalf of a registered person, the [First-tier Tribunal] may—

(a) direct the Commissioner to record the charge and the [First-tier Tribunal's] decision for consideration in connection with the registered person's next application for continued registration;

(b) direct the registered person to apply for continued registration as soon as is reasonably practicable.]

(4) If the person charged is certified by the Commissioner as exempt under section 84(4)(a), the [First-tier Tribunal] may direct the Commissioner to consider whether to withdraw his exemption.

(5) If the person charged is found to have charged unreasonable fees for immigration advice or immigration services, the [First-tier Tribunal] may direct him to repay to the clients concerned such portion of those fees as it may determine.

(6) The [First-tier Tribunal] may direct the person charged to pay a penalty to the Commissioner of such sum as it considers appropriate.

(7) A direction given by the [First-tier Tribunal] under subsection (5) (or under subsection (6)) may be enforced by the clients concerned (or by the Commissioner)—

(a) as if it were an order of a county court; or

(b) in Scotland, as if it were an extract registered decree arbitral bearing a warrant for execution issued by the sheriff court of any sheriffdom in Scotland.

(8) The [First-tier Tribunal] may direct that the person charged or any person [acting on his behalf or] under his supervision is to be—

(a) subject to such restrictions on the provision of immigration advice or immigration services as the [First-tier Tribunal] considers appropriate;

(b) suspended from providing immigration advice or immigration services for such period as the [First-tier Tribunal] may determine; or

(c) prohibited from providing immigration advice or immigration services indefinitely.

(9) The Commissioner must keep a record of the persons against whom there is in force a direction given by the [First-tier Tribunal] under subsection (8).

Note: Commenced 30 October 2000 (SI 2000/1985). 'First-tier Tribunal' substituted from 18 January 2010 (SI 2010/22). Words in other square brackets substituted for (2) and (3) by Asylum and Immigration (Treatment of Claimants etc.) Act 2004, s 37 from 1 October 2004 (SI 2004/2523).

90. Orders by disciplinary bodies

(1) A disciplinary body may make an order directing that a person subject to its jurisdiction is to be—

(a) subject to such restrictions on the provision of immigration advice or immigration services as the body considers appropriate;

(b) suspended from providing immigration advice or immigration services for such period as the body may determine; or

(c) prohibited from providing immigration advice or immigration services indefinitely.

(2) 'Disciplinary body' means any body—

[(a) appearing to the Secretary of State to be established for the purpose of hearing disciplinary charges against—

(i) members of a designated professional body, or

(ii) persons regulated by designated qualifying regulators; and]

(b) specified in an order made by the Secretary of State.

(3) The Secretary of State must consult the designated professional body [or designated qualifying regulator] concerned before making an order under subsection (2)(b).

(4) For the purposes of this section, a person is subject to the jurisdiction of a disciplinary body if he is an authorised person or [acting on his behalf or] an authorised person.

(5) 'Authorised person' means [—

(a)] , a person who is authorised by the designated professional body concerned to practise as a member of the profession whose members are regulated by that body [, or

(b) a person who is authorised by the designated qualifying regulator concerned to provide immigration advice or immigration services.]

Note: Commenced 1 August 2000 (SI 2000/1985). Words in square brackets in sub-s (4) substituted by Asylum and Immigration (Treatment of Claimants etc.) Act 2004, s 37 from 1 October 2004 (SI 2004/2523). Others words in square brackets inserted and substituted by Sch 18 Legal Services Act 2007 from a date to be appointed.

Enforcement

91. Offences

(1) A person who provides immigration advice or immigration services in contravention of section 84 or of a restraining order is guilty of an offence and liable—

(a) on summary conviction, to imprisonment for a term not exceeding six months or to a fine not exceeding the statutory maximum, or to both; or

(b) on conviction on indictment, to imprisonment for a term not exceeding two years or to a fine, or to both.

(2) 'Restraining order' means—

(a) a direction given by the [First-tier Tribunal] under section 89(8) or paragraph 9(3) of Schedule 5; or

(b) an order made by a disciplinary body under section 90(1).

(3) If an offence under this section committed by a body corporate is proved—

(a) to have been committed with the consent or connivance of an officer, or

(b) to be attributable to neglect on his part, the officer as well as the body corporate is guilty of the offence and liable to be proceeded against and punished accordingly.

(4) 'Officer', in relation to a body corporate, means a director, manager, secretary or other similar officer of the body, or a person purporting to act in such a capacity.

(5) If the affairs of a body corporate are managed by its members, subsection (3) applies in relation to the acts and defaults of a member in connection with his functions of management as if he were a director of the body corporate.

(6) If an offence under this section committed by a partnership in Scotland is proved—

(a) to have been committed with the consent or connivance of a partner, or

(b) to be attributable to neglect on his part, the partner as well as the partnership is guilty of the offence and liable to be proceeded against and punished accordingly.

(7) 'Partner' includes a person purporting to act as a partner.

Note: Commenced 30 April 2001 (SI 2001/1394). Words in square brackets in sub-s (2) substituted from 18 January 2010 (SI 2010/22).

92. Enforcement

(1) If it appears to the Commissioner that a person—

(a) is providing immigration advice or immigration services in contravention of section 84 or of a restraining order, and

(b) is likely to continue to do so unless restrained, the Commissioner may apply to a county court for an injunction, or to the sheriff for an interdict, restraining him from doing so.

(2) If the court is satisfied that the application is well-founded, it may grant the injunction or interdict in the terms applied for or in more limited terms.

(3) 'Restraining order' has the meaning given by section 91.

Note: Commenced 30 April 2001 (SI 2001/1394).

[92A. Investigation of offence: power of entry

(1) On an application made by the Commissioner a justice of the peace may issue a warrant authorising the Commissioner to enter and search premises.

(2) A justice of the peace may issue a warrant in respect of premises only if satisfied that there are reasonable grounds for believing that—

(a) an offence under section 91 has been committed,

(b) there is material on the premises which is likely to be of substantial value (whether by itself or together with other material) to the investigation of the offence, and

(c) any of the conditions specified in subsection (3) is satisfied.

(3) Those conditions are—

(a) that it is not practicable to communicate with a person entitled to grant entry to the premises,

(b) that it is not practicable to communicate with a person entitled to grant access to the evidence,

(c) that entry to the premises will be prevented unless a warrant is produced, and

(d) that the purpose of a search may be frustrated or seriously prejudiced unless the Commissioner can secure immediate entry on arrival at the premises.

(4) The Commissioner may seize and retain anything for which a search is authorised under this section.

(5) A person commits an offence if without reasonable excuse he obstructs the Commissioner in the exercise of a power by virtue of this section.

(6) A person guilty of an offence under subsection (5) shall be liable on summary conviction to—

(a) imprisonment for a term not exceeding six months,

(b) a fine not exceeding level 5 on the standard scale, or

(c) both.

(7) In this section—

(a) a reference to the Commissioner includes a reference to a member of his staff authorised in writing by him,

(b) a reference to premises includes a reference to premises used wholly or partly as a dwelling, and

(c) a reference to material—

(i) includes material subject to legal privilege within the meaning of the Police and Criminal Evidence Act 1984 (c. 60),

(ii) does not include excluded material or special procedure material,

(iii) includes material whether or not it would be admissible in evidence at a trial.

(8) In the application of this section to Scotland—

(a) a reference to a justice of the peace shall be taken as a reference to the sheriff,

(b) for sub-paragraph (i) of subsection (7)(c) there is substituted—

'(i) includes material comprising items subject to legal privilege (as defined by section 412 of the Proceeds of Crime Act 2002 (c. 29)),' and

(c) sub-paragraph (ii) of subsection (7)(c) shall be ignored.

(9) In the application of this section to Northern Ireland the reference to the Police and Criminal Evidence Act 1984 shall be taken as a reference to the Police and Criminal Evidence (Northern Ireland) Order 1989 (S.I. 1989/1341 (N.I. 12)).]

Note: Section 92A inserted by Asylum and Immigration (Treatment of Claimants etc.) Act 2004, s 38 from 1 October 2004 (SI 2004/2523).

[92B. Advertising

(1) A person commits an offence if—

(a) he offers to provide immigration advice or immigration services, and

(b) provision by him of the advice or services would constitute an offence under section 91.

(2) For the purpose of subsection (1) a person offers to provide advice or services if he—

(a) makes an offer to a particular person or class of person,

(b) makes arrangements for an advertisement in which he offers to provide advice or services, or

(c) makes arrangements for an advertisement in which he is described or presented as competent to provide advice or services.

(3) A person guilty of an offence under this section shall be liable on summary conviction to a fine not exceeding level 4 on the standard scale.

(4) Subsections (3) to (7) of section 91 shall have effect for the purposes of this section as they have effect for the purposes of that section.

(5) An information relating to an offence under this section may in England and Wales be tried by a magistrates' court if—

(a) it is laid within the period of six months beginning with the date (or first date) on which the offence is alleged to have been committed, or

(b) it is laid—

(i) within the period of two years beginning with that date, and

(ii) within the period of six months beginning with a date certified by the Immigration Services Commissioner as the date on which the commission of the offence came to his notice.

(6) In Scotland, proceedings for an offence under this section may be commenced—

(a) at any time within the period of six months beginning with the date (or first date) on which the offence is alleged to have been committed, or

(b) at any time within both—

(i) the period of two years beginning with that date, and

(ii) the period of six months beginning with a date specified, in a certificate signed by or on behalf of the procurator fiscal, as the date on which evidence sufficient in his opinion to warrant such proceedings came to his knowledge, any such certificate purporting to be so signed shall be deemed so signed unless the contrary is proved and be conclusive as to the facts stated in it.

(7) Subsection (3) of section 136 of the Criminal Procedure (Scotland) Act 1995 (c. 46) (date on which proceedings are deemed commenced) has effect to the purposes of subsection (6) as it has effect for the purposes of that section.

(8) A complaint charging the commission of an offence under this section may in Northern Ireland be heard and determined by a magistrates' court if—

(a) it is made within the period of six months beginning with the date (or first date) on which the offence is alleged to have been committed, or

(b) it is made—

(i) within the period of two years beginning with that date, and

(ii) within the period of six months beginning with a date certified by the Immigration Services Commissioner as the date on which the commission of the offence came to his notice.]

Note: Section 92B inserted by Asylum and Immigration (Treatment of Claimants etc.) Act 2004, s 39 from 1 October 2004 (SI 2004/2523).

Miscellaneous

93. Information

(1) No enactment or rule of law prohibiting or restricting the disclosure of information prevents a person from—

(a) giving the Commissioner information which is necessary for the discharge of his functions; or

(b) giving the [First-tier Tribunal] information which is necessary for the discharge of its functions.

(2) No relevant person may at any time disclose information which—

(a) has been obtained by, or given to, the Commissioner under or for purposes of this Act,

(b) relates to an identified or identifiable individual or business, and

(c) is not at that time, and has not previously been, available to the public from other sources,

unless the disclosure is made with lawful authority.

(3) For the purposes of subsection (2), a disclosure is made with lawful authority only if, and to the extent that—

(a) it is made with the consent of the individual or of the person for the time being carrying on the business;

(b) it is made for the purposes of, and is necessary for, the discharge of any of the Commissioner's functions under this Act or any [EU] obligation of the Commissioner;

(c) it is made for the purposes of any civil or criminal proceedings arising under or by virtue of this Part, or otherwise; or

(d) having regard to the rights and freedoms or legitimate interests of any person, the disclosure is necessary in the public interest.

(4) A person who knowingly or recklessly discloses information in contravention of subsection (2) is guilty of an offence and liable—

(a) on summary conviction, to a fine not exceeding the statutory maximum; or

(b) on conviction on indictment, to a fine.

(5) 'Relevant person' means a person who is or has been—

(a) the Commissioner;

(b) a member of the Commissioner's staff; or

(c) an agent of the Commissioner.

Note: Commenced 22 May 2000 (SI 2000/1282). Words in square brackets in sub-s (1)(b) substituted from 18 January 2010 (SI 2010/22). The term 'EU' substituted from 22 April 2011 (SI 2011/1043).

PART VI

SUPPORT FOR ASYLUM-SEEKERS

Interpretation

94. Interpretation of Part VI

(**1**) In this Part—

[. . .];

['asylum-seeker' means a person—

(a) who is at least 18 years old,

(b) who is in the United Kingdom,

(c) who has made a claim for asylum at a place designated by the Secretary of State,

(d) whose claim has been recorded by the Secretary of State, and

(e) whose claim has not been determined;]

'claim for asylum' means a claim that it would be contrary to the United Kingdom's obligations under the Refugee Convention, or under Article 3 of the Human Rights Convention, for the claimant to be removed from, or required to leave, the United Kingdom;

'the Department' means the Department of Health and Social Services for Northern Ireland;

['dependant' in relation to an asylum-seeker or a supported person means a person who—

(a) is in the United Kingdom, and

(b) is within a prescribed class;]

'the Executive' means the Northern Ireland Housing Executive;

'housing accommodation' includes flats, lodging houses and hostels;

'local authority' means—

(a) in England and Wales, a county council, a county borough council, a district council, a London borough council, the Common Council of the City of London or the Council of the Isles of Scilly;

(b) in Scotland, a council constituted under section 2 of the Local Government etc. (Scotland) Act 1994;

['Northern Ireland authority' has the meaning given by section 110(9).]

'supported person' means—

(a) an asylum-seeker, or

(b) a dependant of an asylum-seeker,

who has applied for support and for whom support is provided under section 95.

(**2**) References in this Part to support provided under section 95 include references to support which is provided under arrangements made by the Secretary of State under that section.

[(3) A claim for asylum shall be treated as determined for the purposes of subsection (1) at the end of such period as may be prescribed beginning with—

(a) the date on which the Secretary of State notifies the claimant of his decision on the claim, or

(b) if the claimant appeals against the Secretary of State's decision, the date on which the appeal is disposed of.

(3A) A person shall continue to be treated as an asylum-seeker despite paragraph (e) of the definition of 'asylum-seeker' in subsection (1) while—

(a) his household includes a dependant child who is under 18, and

(b) he does not have leave to enter or remain in the United Kingdom.]

(4) An appeal is disposed of when it is no longer pending for the purposes of the Immigration Acts or the Special Immigration Appeals Commission Act 1997.

(5) . . .

(6) . . .

(7) For the purposes of this Part, the Secretary of State may inquire into, and decide, the age of any person.

(8) A notice under subsection (3) must be given in writing.

(9) If such a notice is sent by the Secretary of State by first class post, addressed—

(a) to the asylum-seeker's representative, or

(b) to the asylum-seeker's last known address,

it is to be taken to have been received by the asylum-seeker on the second day after the day on which it was posted.

Note: Commenced 11 November 1999, s 170. Words in first and second square brackets in sub-s (1) substituted by Nationality, Immigration and Asylum Act 2002, s 44 from a date to be appointed and words in third square brackets in sub-s (1) inserted by the same Act, s 60 from 10 February 2003 (SI 2003/1). Subsection (3) substituted by and sub-s (3A) inserted by and sub-ss (5) and (6) omitted by Nationality, Immigration and Asylum Act 2002, s 44 from a date to be appointed. Definition of 'asylum-seeker' modified in relation to ss 110 and 111 from 11 November 2002 so as not to exclude persons under 18 (Nationality, Immigration and Asylum Act 2002, s 48). Words omitted in sub-s (1) from 3 November 2008 (SI 2008/2833).

Provision of support

95. Persons for whom support may be provided

(1) The Secretary of State may provide, or arrange for the provision of, support for—

(a) asylum-seekers, or

(b) dependants of asylum-seekers, who appear to the Secretary of State to be destitute or to be likely to become destitute within such period as may be prescribed.

[(2) Where a person has dependants, he and his dependants are destitute for the purpose of this section if they do not have and cannot obtain both—

(a) adequate accommodation, and

(b) food and other essential items.

(3) Where a person does not have dependants, he is destitute for the purpose of this section if he does not have and cannot obtain both—

(a) adequate accommodation, and

(b) food and other essential items.

(4) In determining whether accommodation is adequate for the purposes of subsection (2) or (3) the Secretary of State must have regard to any matter prescribed for the purposes of this subsection.

(5) In determining whether accommodation is adequate for the purposes of subsection (2) or (3) the Secretary of State may not have regard to—

    (a) whether a person has an enforceable right to occupy accommodation,

    (b) whether a person shares all or part of accommodation,

    (c) whether accommodation is temporary or permanent,

    (d) the location of accommodation, or

    (e) any other matter prescribed for the purposes of this subsection.

(6) The Secretary of State may by regulations specify items which are or are not to be treated as essential items for the purposes of subsections (2) and (3).

(7) The Secretary of State may by regulations—

    (a) provide that a person is not to be treated as destitute for the purposes of this Part in specified circumstances;

    (b) enable or require the Secretary of State in deciding whether a person is destitute to have regard to income which he or a dependant of his might reasonably be expected to have;

    (c) enable or require the Secretary of State in deciding whether a person is destitute to have regard to support which is or might reasonably be expected to be available to the person or a dependant of his;

    (d) enable or require the Secretary of State in deciding whether a person is destitute to have regard to assets of a prescribed kind which he or a dependant of his has or might reasonably be expected to have;

    (e) make provision as to the valuation of assets.]

(9) Support may be provided subject to conditions.

[(9A) A condition imposed under subsection (9) may, in particular, relate to—

    (a) any matter relating to the use of the support provided, or

    (b) compliance with a restriction imposed under paragraph 21 of Schedule 2 to the 1971 Act (temporary admission or release from detention) or paragraph 2 or 5 of Schedule 3 to that Act (restriction pending deportation).]

(10) The conditions must be set out in writing.

(11) A copy of the conditions must be given to the supported person.

(12) Schedule 8 gives the Secretary of State power to make regulations supplementing this section.

(13) Schedule 9 makes temporary provision for support in the period before the coming into force of this section.

Note: Commenced in part 11 November 1999 and 6 December 1999, remainder 1 January 2000 (SI 1999/3190). Subsections (2)–(8) substituted by Nationality, Immigration and Asylum Act 2002, s 44 from a date to be appointed and sub-s 9A inserted by Nationality, Immigration and Asylum Act 2002, s 50 from 7 November 2002.

96. Ways in which support may be provided

(1) Support may be provided under section 95—

(a) by providing accommodation appearing to the Secretary of State to be adequate for the needs of the supported person and his dependants (if any);

[(b) by providing the supported person and his dependants (if any) with food or other essential items;]

(c) to enable the supported person (if he is the asylum-seeker) to meet what appear to the Secretary of State to be expenses (other than legal expenses or other expenses of a prescribed description) incurred in connection with his claim for asylum;

(d) to enable the asylum-seeker and his dependants to attend bail proceedings in connection with his detention under any provision of the Immigration Acts; or

(e) to enable the asylum-seeker and his dependants to attend bail proceedings in connection with the detention of a dependant of his under any such provision.

(2) If the Secretary of State considers that the circumstances of a particular case are exceptional, he may provide support under section 95 in such other ways as he considers necessary to enable the supported person and his dependants (if any) to be supported.

(3) . . . . . .

(4) . . .

(5) . . .

(6) . . .

Note: Commenced 3 April 2000 (SI 2000/464). Subsection 1(b) substituted by Nationality, Immigration and Asylum Act 2002, s 45 from a date to be appointed. Subsection (3) repealed from 8 April 2002 (SI 2002/782). Subsections (4)–(6) repealed by the same Act, s 61 from 7 November 2002.

97. Supplemental

(1) When exercising his power under section 95 to provide accommodation, the Secretary of State must have regard to—

(a) the fact that the accommodation is to be temporary pending determination of the asylum-seeker's claim;

(b) the desirability, in general, of providing accommodation in areas in which there is a ready supply of accommodation; and

(c) such other matters (if any) as may be prescribed.

(2) But he may not have regard to—

(a) any preference that the supported person or his dependants (if any) may have as to the locality in which the accommodation is to be provided; or

(b) such other matters (if any) as may be prescribed.

(3) The Secretary of State may by order repeal all or any of the following—

(a) subsection (1)(a);

(b) subsection (1)(b);

(c) subsection (2)(a).

(4) When exercising his power under section 95 to provide [food and other essential items], the Secretary of State—

(a) must have regard to such matters as may be prescribed for the purposes of this paragraph; but

(b) may not have regard to such other matters as may be prescribed for the purposes of this paragraph.

(5) In addition, when exercising his power under section 95 to provide [food and other essential items], the Secretary of State may limit the overall amount of the expenditure which he incurs in connection with a particular supported person—

[(a) to such portion of the applicable amount in respect of an income-based job-seeker's allowance provided under section 4 of the Jobseekers Act 1995, or]

(b) to such portion of any components of that amount, as he considers appropriate having regard to the temporary nature of the support that he is providing.

(6) For the purposes of subsection (5), any support of a kind falling within section 96(1) (c) is to be treated as if it were the provision of essential [items].

(7) In determining how to provide, or arrange for the provision of, support under section 95, the Secretary of State may disregard any preference which the supported person or his dependants (if any) may have as to the way in which the support is to be given.

Note: Commenced for the purposes of enabling subordinate legislation 1 January 2000 (SI 1999/3190), remainder 3 April 2000 (SI 2000/464). Words in square brackets substituted by Nationality, Immigration and Asylum Act 2002, s 45 from a date to be appointed. Sub-s (5)(a) substituted by Sch 2 Welfare Reform Act 2009 from a date to be appointed.

98. Temporary support

(1) The Secretary of State may provide, or arrange for the provision of, support for—
(a) asylum-seekers, or
(b) dependants of asylum-seekers, who it appears to the Secretary of State may be destitute.

(2) Support may be provided under this section only until the Secretary of State is able to determine whether support may be provided under section 95.

(3) Subsections (2) to (11) of section 95 apply for the purposes of this section as they apply for the purposes of that section.

Note: Subsection (3) commenced for the purposes of enabling subordinate legislation 1 March 2000, remainder 3 April 2000 (SI 2000/464).

Support and assistance by local authorities etc.

99. Provision of support by local authorities

(1) A local authority [or Northern Ireland authority] may provide support for [persons] in accordance with arrangements made by the Secretary of State under section [4,] 95 [or 98].

(2) Support may be provided by an authority in accordance with arrangements made with the authority or with another person.

(3) Support may be provided by an authority in accordance with arrangements made under section 95 only in one or more of the ways mentioned in section 96(1) and (2).

(4) [An authority] may incur reasonable expenditure in connection with the preparation of proposals for entering into arrangements under section [4,] 95 [or 98].

(5) The powers conferred on [an authority] by this section include power to—
(a) provide services outside their area;
(b) provide services jointly with one or more [other bodies];
(c) form a company for the purpose of providing services;
(d) tender for contracts (whether alone or with any other person).

Note: Subsections (1)–(3) commenced 3 April 2000 (SI 2000/464). Subsections (4) and (5) commenced 11 November 1999, s 170. Words in second and third square brackets in sub-s (1) and second square brackets in sub-s (4) substituted by Immigration, Nationality and Asylum Act 2006, s 43 from 16 June 2006 (SI 2006/1497). Subsections (2) and (3) substituted by and other words in square brackets substituted by Nationality, Immigration and Asylum Act 2002, s 56 from 7 November 2002.

100. Local authority and other assistance for Secretary of State

(1) This section applies if the Secretary of State asks—

(a) a local authority,

(b) a registered social landlord,

(c) a registered housing association in Scotland or Northern Ireland, or

(d) the Executive, to assist him to exercise his power under section 95 to provide accommodation.

(2) The person to whom the request is made must co-operate in giving the Secretary of State such assistance in the exercise of that power as is reasonable in the circumstances.

(3) Subsection (2) does not require a registered social landlord to act beyond its powers.

(4) A local authority must supply to the Secretary of State such information about their housing accommodation (whether or not occupied) as he may from time to time request.

(5) The information must be provided in such form and manner as the Secretary of State may direct.

(6) 'Registered social landlord' has the same meaning as in Part I of the Housing Act 1996.

(7) 'Registered housing association' has the same meaning—

(a) in relation to Scotland, as in the Housing Associations Act 1985; and

(b) in relation to Northern Ireland, as in Part II of the Housing (Northern Ireland) Order 1992.

Note: Commenced 3 April 2000 (SI 2000/464).

101. Reception zones

(1) The Secretary of State may by order designate as reception zones—

(a) areas in England and Wales consisting of the areas of one or more local authorities;

(b) areas in Scotland consisting of the areas of one or more local authorities;

(c) Northern Ireland.

(2) Subsection (3) applies if the Secretary of State considers that—

(a) a local authority whose area is within a reception zone has suitable housing accommodation within that zone; or

(b) the Executive has suitable housing accommodation.

(3) The Secretary of State may direct the local authority or the Executive to make available such of the accommodation as may be specified in the direction for a period so specified—

(a) to him for the purpose of providing support under section 95; or

(b) to a person with whom the Secretary of State has made arrangements under section 95.

(4) A period specified in a direction under subsection (3)—

(a) begins on a date so specified; and

(b) must not exceed five years.

(5) A direction under subsection (3) is enforceable, on an application made on behalf of the Secretary of State, by injunction or in Scotland an order under section 45(b) of the Court of Session Act 1988.

(6) The Secretary of State's power to give a direction under subsection (3) in respect of a particular reception zone must be exercised by reference to criteria specified for the purposes of this subsection in the order designating that zone.

(7) The Secretary of State may not give a direction under subsection (3) in respect of a local authority in Scotland unless the Scottish Ministers have confirmed to him that the criteria specified in the designation order concerned are in their opinion met in relation to that authority.

(8) Housing accommodation is suitable for the purposes of subsection (2) if it—

(a) is unoccupied;

(b) would be likely to remain unoccupied for the foreseeable future if not made available; and

(c) is appropriate for the accommodation of persons supported under this Part or capable of being made so with minor work.

(9) If housing accommodation for which a direction under this section is, for the time being, in force—

(a) is not appropriate for the accommodation of persons supported under this Part, but

(b) is capable of being made so with minor work, the direction may require the body to whom it is given to secure that that work is done without delay.

(10) The Secretary of State must make regulations with respect to the general management of any housing accommodation for which a direction under subsection (3) is, for the time being, in force.

(11) Regulations under subsection (10) must include provision—

(a) as to the method to be used in determining the amount of rent or other charges to be payable in relation to the accommodation;

(b) as to the times at which payments of rent or other charges are to be made;

(c) as to the responsibility for maintenance of, and repairs to, the accommodation;

(d) enabling the accommodation to be inspected, in such circumstances as may be prescribed, by the body to which the direction was given;

(e) with respect to the condition in which the accommodation is to be returned when the direction ceases to have effect.

(12) Regulations under subsection (10) may, in particular, include provision—

(a) for the cost, or part of the cost, of minor work required by a direction under this section to be met by the Secretary of State in prescribed circumstances;

(b) as to the maximum amount of expenditure which a body may be required to incur as a result of a direction under this section.

(13) The Secretary of State must by regulations make provision ('the dispute resolution procedure') for resolving disputes arising in connection with the operation of any regulations made under subsection (10).

(14) Regulations under subsection (13) must include provision—

(a) requiring a dispute to be resolved in accordance with the dispute resolution procedure;

(b) requiring the parties to a dispute to comply with obligations imposed on them by the procedure; and

(c) for the decision of the person resolving a dispute in accordance with the procedure to be final and binding on the parties.

(15) Before—

(a) designating a reception zone in Great Britain,

(b) determining the criteria to be included in the order designating the zone, or

(c) making regulations under subsection (13),

the Secretary of State must consult such local authorities, local authority associations and other persons as he thinks appropriate.

(16) Before—

(a) designating Northern Ireland as a reception zone, or

(b) determining the criteria to be included in the order designating Northern Ireland, the Secretary of State must consult the Executive and such other persons as he thinks appropriate.

(17) Before making regulations under subsection (10) which extend only to Northern Ireland, the Secretary of State must consult the Executive and such other persons as he thinks appropriate.

(18) Before making any other regulations under subsection (10), the Secretary of State must consult—

(a) such local authorities, local authority associations and other persons as he thinks appropriate; and

(b) if the regulations extend to Northern Ireland, the Executive.

Note: Commenced 3 April 2000 (SI 2000/464).

Appeals

102. . . .

Note: Commenced 3 April 2000 (SI 2000/464). Revoked from 3 November 2008 (SI 2008/2833).

[103. Appeals: general

[(1) This section applies where a person has applied for support under all or any of the following provisions—

(a) section 4,

(b) section 95, and

(c) section 17 of the Nationality, Immigration and Asylum Act 2002]

(2) The person may appeal to [the First-tier Tribunal] against a decision that the person is not qualified to receive the support for which he has applied.

(3) The person may also appeal to [the First-tier Tribunal] against a decision to stop providing support under a provision mentioned in subsection (1).

(4) But subsection (3) does not apply—

(a) to a decision to stop providing support under one of the provisions mentioned in subsection (1) if it is to be replaced immediately by support under [another of those provisions], or

(b) to a decision taken on the ground that the person is no longer an asylum-seeker or the dependant of an asylum-seeker.

(5) On an appeal under this section [the First-tier Tribunal] may—

(a) require the Secretary of State to reconsider a matter;

(b) substitute [its] decision for the decision against which the appeal is brought;

(c) dismiss the appeal.

(6) . . . .

(7) If an appeal under this section is dismissed the Secretary of State shall not consider any further application by the appellant for support under a provision mentioned in [subsection (1)] unless the Secretary of State thinks there has been a material change in circumstances.

(8) An appeal under this section may not be brought or continued by a person who is outside the United Kingdom.]

Note: Section 103 substituted by Nationality, Immigration and Asylum Act 2002, s 53 from a date to be appointed. Subsection (1) and words in square brackets in sub-s (7) substituted by Asylum and Immigration (Treatment of Claimants etc.) Act 2004, s 10 from 31 March 2005 (SI 2005/372). Other words in square brackets substituted from 3 November 2008 (SI 2008/2833).

[103A. Appeals: location of support under [section 4 or 95]

(1) The Secretary of State may by regulations provide for a decision as to where support provided under [section 4 or 95] is to be provided to be appealable to [the First-tier Tribunal] under this Part.

(2) Regulations under this section may provide for a provision of section 103 to have effect in relation to an appeal under the regulations with specified modifications.

Note: Section 103A inserted by Nationality, Immigration and Asylum Act 2002, s 53 from a date to be appointed. Words in first square brackets inserted by Asylum and Immigration (Treatment of Claimants etc.) Act 2004, s 10 from 31 March 2005 (SI 2005/372). Other words in square brackets substituted from 3 November 2008 (SI 2008/2833).

103B. Appeals: travelling expenses

The Secretary of State may pay reasonable travelling expenses incurred by an appellant in connection with attendance for the purposes of an appeal under or by virtue of section 103 or 103A.]

Note: Section 103B inserted by Nationality, Immigration and Asylum Act 2002, s 53 from a date to be appointed.

104. . . . .

Note: Commenced 1 January 2000 (SI 1999/3190). Revoked from 3 November 2008 (SI 2008/2833).

Offences

105. False representations

(1) A person is guilty of an offence if, with a view to obtaining support for himself or any other person under any provision made by or under this Part, he—

(a) makes a statement or representation which he knows is false in a material particular;

(b) produces or gives to a person exercising functions under this Part, or knowingly causes or allows to be produced or given to such a person, any document or information which he knows is false in a material particular;

(c) fails, without reasonable excuse, to notify a change of circumstances when required to do so in accordance with any provision made by or under this Part; or

(d) without reasonable excuse, knowingly causes another person to fail to notify a change of circumstances which that other person was required to notify in accordance with any provision made by or under this Part.

(2) A person guilty of an offence under this section is liable on summary conviction to imprisonment for a term not exceeding [51 weeks] or to a fine not exceeding level 5 on the standard scale, or to both.

Note: Commenced 11 November 1999, s 170. Words in square brackets in sub-s (2) substituted by Sch 26 Criminal Justice Act 2003, from a date to be appointed.

106. Dishonest representations

(1) A person is guilty of an offence if, with a view to obtaining any benefit or other payment or advantage under this Part for himself or any other person, he dishonestly—

(a) makes a statement or representation which is false in a material particular;

(b) produces or gives to a person exercising functions under this Part, or causes or allows to be produced or given to such a person, any document or information which is false in a material particular;

(c) fails to notify a change of circumstances when required to do so in accordance with any provision made by or under this Part; or

(d) causes another person to fail to notify a change of circumstances which that other person was required to notify in accordance with any provision made by or under this Part.

(2) A person guilty of an offence under this section is liable—

(a) on summary conviction, to imprisonment for a term not exceeding six months or to a fine not exceeding the statutory maximum, or to both; or

(b) on conviction on indictment, to imprisonment for a term not exceeding seven years or to a fine, or to both.

(3) In the application of this section to Scotland, in subsection (1) for 'dishonestly' substitute 'knowingly'.

Note: Commenced 11 November 1999, s 170.

107. Delay or obstruction

(1) A person is guilty of an offence if, without reasonable excuse, he—

(a) intentionally delays or obstructs a person exercising functions conferred by or under this Part; or

(b) refuses or neglects to answer a question, give any information or produce a document when required to do so in accordance with any provision made by or under this Part.

(2) A person guilty of an offence under subsection (1) is liable on summary conviction to a fine not exceeding level 3 on the standard scale.

Note: Commenced 11 November 1999, s 170.

108. Failure of sponsor to maintain

(1) A person is guilty of an offence if, during any period in respect of which he has given a written undertaking in pursuance of the immigration rules to be responsible for the maintenance and accommodation of another person—

(a) he persistently refuses or neglects, without reasonable excuse, to maintain that person in accordance with the undertaking; and

(b) in consequence of his refusal or neglect, support under any provision made by or under this Part is provided for or in respect of that person.

(2) A person guilty of an offence under this section is liable on summary conviction to imprisonment for a term not exceeding [51 weeks] or to a fine not exceeding level 4 on the standard scale, or to both.

(3) For the purposes of this section, a person is not to be taken to have refused or neglected to maintain another person by reason only of anything done or omitted in furtherance of a trade dispute.

Note: Commenced 11 November 1999, s 170. Words in square brackets in sub-s (2) substituted by Sch 26 Criminal Justice Act 2003, from a date to be appointed.

109. Supplemental

(1) If an offence under section 105, 106, 107 or 108 committed by a body corporate is proved—

(a) to have been committed with the consent or connivance of an officer, or

(b) to be attributable to neglect on his part,

the officer as well as the body corporate is guilty of the offence and liable to be proceeded against and punished accordingly.

(2) 'Officer', in relation to a body corporate, means a director, manager, secretary or other similar officer of the body, or a person purporting to act in such a capacity.

(3) If the affairs of a body corporate are managed by its members, subsection (1) applies in relation to the acts and defaults of a member in connection with his functions of management as if he were a director of the body corporate.

(4) If an offence under section 105, 106, 107 or 108 committed by a partnership in Scotland is proved—

(a) to have been committed with the consent or connivance of a partner, or

(b) to be attributable to neglect on his part,

the partner as well as the partnership is guilty of the offence and liable to be proceeded against and punished accordingly.

(5) 'Partner' includes a person purporting to act as a partner.

Note: Commenced 11 November 1999, s 170.

[109A. Arrest

An immigration officer may arrest without warrant a person whom the immigration officer reasonably suspects has committed an offence under section 105 or 106.

Note: Section 109A inserted from 31 January 2008, (SI 2008/99).

109B. Entry, search and seizure

(1) An offence under section 105 or 106 shall be treated as—

(a) a relevant offence for the purposes of sections 28B and 28D of the Immigration Act 1971, and

(b) an offence under Part 3 of that Act (criminal proceedings) for the purposes of sections 28(4), 28E, 28G and 28H (search after arrest, &c.) of that Act.

(2) The following provisions of the Immigration Act 1971 (c. 77) shall have effect in connection with an offence under section 105 or 106 of this Act as they have effect in connection with an offence under that Act—

(a) section 28I (seized material: access and copying),

(b) section 28J (search warrants: safeguards),

(c) section 28K (execution of warrants), and

(d) section 28L(1) (interpretation).]

Note: Section 109B inserted from 31 January 2008, (SI 2008/99).

Expenditure

110. Payments to local authorities

(1) The Secretary of State may from time to time pay to any local authority or Northern Ireland authority such sums as he considers appropriate in respect of expenditure incurred, or to be incurred, by the authority in connection with—

(a) persons who are, or have been, asylum-seekers; and

(b) their dependants.

(2) The Secretary of State may from time to time pay to any—

(a) local authority,

(b) local authority association, or

(c) Northern Ireland authority,

such sums as he considers appropriate in respect of services provided by the authority or association in connection with the discharge of functions under this Part.

(3) The Secretary of State may make payments to any local authority towards the discharge of any liability of supported persons or their dependants in respect of council tax payable to that authority.

(4) The Secretary of State must pay to a body to which a direction under section 101(3) is given such sums as he considers represent the reasonable costs to that body of complying with the direction.

(5) The Secretary of State must pay to a directed body sums determined to be payable in relation to accommodation made available by that body under section 101(3)(a).

(6) The Secretary of State may pay to a directed body sums determined to be payable in relation to accommodation made available by that body under section 101(3)(b).

(7) In subsections (5) and (6)—

'determined' means determined in accordance with regulations made by virtue of sub-section (11)(a) of section 101, and

'directed body' means a body to which a direction under subsection (3) of section 101 is given.

(8) Payments under subsection (1), (2) or (3) may be made on such terms, and subject to such conditions, as the Secretary of State may determine.

(9) 'Northern Ireland authority' means—

(a) the Executive; or

(b) a Health and Social Services Board established under Article 16 of the Health and Personal Social Services (Northern Ireland) Order 1972 [; or

(c) a Health and Social Services trust established under the Health and Personal Social Services (Northern Ireland) Order 1991 (S.I. 1991/194 (N.I. 1).]

Note: Subsections (1), (2) and (8) commenced 11 November 1999, s 170, sub-s (9) 6 December 1999 (SI 1999/3190), remainder 3 April 2000 (SI 2000/464). Subsection (9)(c) inserted by Nationality, Immigration and Asylum Act 2002, s 60 from 7 November 2002.

111. Grants to voluntary organisations

(1) The Secretary of State may make grants of such amounts as he thinks appropriate to voluntary organisations in connection with—

(a) the provision by them of support (of whatever nature) to persons who are, or have been, asylum-seekers and to their dependants; and

(b) connected matters.

(2) Grants may be made on such terms, and subject to such conditions, as the Secretary of State may determine.

Note: Commenced 11 November 1999, s 170.

112. Recovery of expenditure on support: misrepresentation etc.

(1) This section applies if, on an application made by the Secretary of State, the court determines that—

(a) a person ('A') has misrepresented or failed to disclose a material fact (whether fraudulently or otherwise); and

(b) as a consequence of the misrepresentation or failure, support has been provided under section 95 or 98 (whether or not to A).

(2) If the support was provided by the Secretary of State, the court may order A to pay to the Secretary of State an amount representing the monetary value of the support which would not have been provided but for A's misrepresentation or failure.

(3) If the support was provided by another person ('B') in accordance with arrangements made with the Secretary of State under section 95 or 98, the court may order A to pay to the Secretary of State an amount representing the payment to B which would not have been made but for A's misrepresentation or failure.

(4) 'Court' means a county court or, in Scotland, the sheriff.

Note: Commenced 3 April 2000 (SI 2000/464).

113. Recovery of expenditure on support from sponsor

(1) This section applies if—

(a) a person ('the sponsor') has given a written undertaking in pursuance of the immigration rules to be responsible for the maintenance and accommodation of another person; and

(b) during any period in relation to which the undertaking applies, support under section 95 is provided to or in respect of that other person.

(2) The Secretary of State may make a complaint against the sponsor to a magistrates' court for an order under this section.

(3) The court—

(a) must have regard to all the circumstances (and in particular to the sponsor's income); and

(b) may order him to pay to the Secretary of State such sum (weekly or otherwise) as it considers appropriate.

(4) But such a sum is not to include any amount attributable otherwise than to support provided under section 95.

(5) In determining—

(a) whether to order any payments to be made in respect of support provided under section 95 for any period before the complaint was made, or

(b) the amount of any such payments, the court must disregard any amount by which the sponsor's current income exceeds his income during that period.

(6) An order under this section is enforceable as a magistrates' court maintenance order within the meaning of section 150(1) of the Magistrates' Courts Act 1980.

(7) In the application of this section to Scotland—

(a) omit subsection (6);

(b) for references to a complaint substitute references to an application; and

(c) for references to a magistrates' court substitute references to the sheriff.

(8) In the application of this section to Northern Ireland, for references to a magistrates' court substitute references to a court of summary jurisdiction and for subsection (6) substitute—

'(6) An order under this section is an order to which Article 98(11) of the Magistrates' Courts (Northern Ireland) Order 1981 applies.'

Note: Commenced 3 April 2000 (SI 2000/464).

114. Overpayments

(1) Subsection (2) applies if, as a result of an error on the part of the Secretary of State, support has been provided to a person under section 95 or 98.

(2) The Secretary of State may recover from a person who is, or has been, a supported person an amount representing the monetary value of support provided to him as a result of the error.

(3) An amount recoverable under subsection (2) may be recovered as if it were a debt due to the Secretary of State.

(4) The Secretary of State may by regulations make provision for other methods of recovery, including deductions from support provided under section 95.

Note: Commenced 1 January 2000 for the purposes of enabling subordinate legislation (SI 1999/3190), otherwise commenced on 3 April 2000 (SI 2000/464).

Exclusions

115. Exclusion from benefits

(1) No person is entitled to income-based jobseeker's allowance under the Jobseekers Act 1995 [or to state pension credit under the State Pension Credit Act 2002] [or to income-related allowance under Part 1 of the Welfare Reform Act 2007 (employment and support allowance)] or to—

(a) attendance allowance,

(b) severe disablement allowance,

(c) [carer's allowance],

(d) disability living allowance,

(e) . . .

(f) . . .

(g) . . .

(h) a social fund payment,

[(ha) health in pregnancy grant,]

(i) child benefit,

(j) housing benefit, or

(k) council tax benefit, under the Social Security Contributions and Benefits Act 1992 while he is a person to whom this section applies.

(2) No person in Northern Ireland is entitled to [state pension credit under the State Pension Credit Act (Northern Ireland) 2002, or to]—

(a) income-based jobseeker's allowance under the Jobseekers (Northern Ireland) Order 1995, or

(b) any of the benefits mentioned in paragraphs (a) to (j) of subsection (1), under the Social Security Contributions and Benefits (Northern Ireland) Act 1992 while he is a person to whom this section applies.

(3) This section applies to a person subject to immigration control unless he falls within such category or description, or satisfies such conditions, as may be prescribed.

(4) Regulations under subsection (3) may provide for a person to be treated for prescribed purposes only as not being a person to whom this section applies.

(5) In relation to [health in pregnancy grant or] [child benefit], 'prescribed' means prescribed by regulations made by the Treasury.

(6) In relation to the matters mentioned in subsection (2) (except so far as it relates to [health in pregnancy grant or] [child benefit]), 'prescribed' means prescribed by regulations made by the Department.

(7) Section 175(3) to (5) of the Social Security Contributions and Benefits Act 1992 (supplemental powers in relation to regulations) applies to regulations made by the Secretary of State or the Treasury under subsection (3) as it applies to regulations made under that Act.

(8) Sections 133(2), 171(2) and 172(4) of the Social Security Contributions and Benefits (Northern Ireland) Act 1992 apply to regulations made by the Department under subsection (3) as they apply to regulations made by the Department under that Act.

(9) 'A person subject to immigration control' means a person who is not a national of an EEA State and who—

(a) requires leave to enter or remain in the United Kingdom but does not have it;

(b) has leave to enter or remain in the United Kingdom which is subject to a condition that he does not have recourse to public funds;

(c) has leave to enter or remain in the United Kingdom given as a result of a maintenance undertaking; or

(d) has leave to enter or remain in the United Kingdom only as a result of paragraph 17 of Schedule 4.

(10) 'Maintenance undertaking', in relation to any person, means a written undertaking given by another person in pursuance of the immigration rules to be responsible for that person's maintenance and accommodation.

Note: Commenced for the purposes of enabling subordinate legislation 1 January 2000 (SI 1999/3190), remainder 3 April 2000 (SI 2000/464). First words in square brackets in sub-s (1) inserted by s 4 State Pension Credit Act 2002, from 6 October 2003 (SI 2003/1766). Second words in square brackets in sub-s (1) inserted by Sch 3 Welfare Reform Act 2007 from 27 October 2008 (SI 2008/787). Subsection (1)(c) substituted from 1 April 2003 (SI 2002/1457). Words in square brackets in sub-s (2) substituted by s 4 State Pension Credit Act (Northern Ireland) 2002 from 2 December 2002 (SI 2002/366). Subsection (1)(ha) inserted and words in first square brackets in sub-ss (5) and (6) substituted by s 138 Health and Social Care Act 2008 from 1 January 2009 (SI 2009/2994). Words in second square brackets in sub-ss (5) and (6) substituted by Sch 4 Tax Credits Act 2002 from 7 April 2003 (SI 2003/392). Subsection (1)(e) revoked by Schedule 7 Welfare Reform Act 2009 from a date to be appointed.

116. ...

Note: Amends National Assistance Act 1948, s 21.

117. ...

Note: Amends Health Services and Public Health Act 1968, s 4; Sch 8 National Health Service Act 1977; and Housing Act 1996, ss 161, 185–187.

118. Housing authority accommodation

(1) Each housing authority must secure that, so far as practicable, a tenancy of, or licence to occupy, housing accommodation provided under the accommodation provisions is not granted to a person subject to immigration control unless—

(a) he is of a class specified in an order made by the Secretary of State; or

(b) the tenancy of, or licence to occupy, such accommodation is granted in accordance with arrangements made under section [4, 95 or 98].

(2) 'Housing authority' means—

(a) in relation to England and Wales, a local housing authority within the meaning of the Housing Act 1985;

(b) in relation to Scotland, a local authority within the meaning of the Housing (Scotland) Act 1987; and

(c) in relation to Northern Ireland, the Executive.

(3) 'Accommodation provisions' means—

(a) in relation to England and Wales, Part II of the Housing Act 1985;

(b) in relation to Scotland, Part I of the Housing (Scotland) Act 1987;

(c) in relation to Northern Ireland, Part II of the Housing (Northern Ireland) Order 1981.

(4) 'Licence to occupy', in relation to Scotland, means a permission or right to occupy.

(5) 'Tenancy', in relation to England and Wales, has the same meaning as in the Housing Act 1985.

(6) 'Person subject to immigration control' means a person who under the 1971 Act requires leave to enter or remain in the United Kingdom (whether or not such leave has been given).

(7) This section does not apply in relation to any allocation of housing to which Part VI of the Housing Act 1996 (allocation of housing accommodation) applies.

Note: Commenced 1 January 2000 for purposes of enabling subordinate legislation (SI 1999/3190), remainder 1 March 2000 (SI 2000/464). Words in square brackets in sub-s (1)(b) substituted by Immigration, Nationality and Asylum Act 2006, s 43 from 16 June 2006 (SI 2006/1497).

119. Homelessness: Scotland and Northern Ireland

(1) A person subject to immigration control—

(a) is not eligible for accommodation or assistance under the homelessness provisions, and

(b) is to be disregarded in determining for the purposes of those provisions, whether [a person falling within subsection (1A)] —

(i) is homeless or is threatened with homelessness, or

(ii) has a priority need for accommodation, unless he is of a class specified in an order made by the Secretary of State.

[(1A) A person falls within this subsection if the person—

(a) falls within a class specified in an order under subsection (1); but

(b) is not a national of an EEA State or Switzerland.]

(2) An order under subsection (1) may not be made so as to include in a specified class any person to whom section 115 applies.

(3) 'The homelessness provisions' means—

(a) in relation to Scotland, Part II of the Housing (Scotland) Act 1987; and

(b) in relation to Northern Ireland, Part II of the Housing (Northern Ireland) Order 1988.

(4) 'Person subject to immigration control' has the same meaning as in section 118.

Note: Commenced 1 January 2000 for purposes of enabling subordinate legislation, remainder 1 March 2000 (SI 2000/464). Words in square brackets substituted and s 1A inserted by Sch 15 Housing and Regeneration Act 2008 from 2 March 2009 in relation to applications (a) for accommodation or assistance in obtaining accommodation under Part I (provision of housing) or Part II (homeless persons) of the Housing (Scotland) Act 1987, or (b) for housing assistance under Part II (housing the homeless) of the Housing (Northern Ireland) Order 1988, made on or after 2 March 2009 (SI 2009/415).

120. . . .

Note: Amends Social Work (Scotland) Act 1968, ss 2 and 13, Mental Health (Scotland) Act 1984, ss 7–8 and Asylum and Immigration Appeals Act 1993, ss 4–5 and Sch 1.

121. . . .

Note: Amends Health and Personal Social Services (Northern Ireland) Order 1972.

[122. Family with children

(1) This section applies where a person ('the asylum-seeker') applies for support under section 95 of this Act or section 17 of the Nationality, Immigration and Asylum Act 2002 (accommodation centres) if—

(a) the Secretary of State thinks that the asylum-seeker is eligible for support under either or both of those sections, and

(b) the asylum-seeker's household includes a dependant child who is under 18.

(2) The Secretary of State must offer the provision of support for the child, as part of the asylum-seeker's household, under one of the sections mentioned in subsection (1).

(3) A local authority (or, in Northern Ireland, an authority) may not provide assistance for a child if—

(a) the Secretary of State is providing support for the child in accordance with an offer under subsection (2),

(b) an offer by the Secretary of State under subsection (2) remains open in respect of the child, or

(c) the Secretary of State has agreed that he would make an offer in respect of the child under subsection (2) if an application were made as described in subsection (1).

(4) In subsection (3) 'assistance' means assistance under—

(a) section 17 of the Children Act 1989 (c. 41) (local authority support),

(b) section 22 of the Children (Scotland) Act 1995 (c. 36) (similar provision for Scotland), or

(c) Article 18 of the Children (Northern Ireland) Order 1995 (similar provision for Northern Ireland).

(5) The Secretary of State may by order disapply subsection (3) in specified circumstances.

(6) Where subsection (3) ceases to apply to a child because the Secretary of State stops providing support, no local authority may provide assistance for the child except the authority for the area within which the support was provided.]

Note: Section 122 substituted by Nationality, Immigration and Asylum Act 2002, s 47 from a date to be appointed.

123. Back-dating of benefits where person recorded as refugee

. . .

Note: Section 123 ceased to have effect from 30 April 2003 Asylum and Immigration Act 2004, s 12.

Miscellaneous

124. Secretary of State to be corporation sole for purposes of Part VI

(1) For the purpose of exercising his functions under this Part, the Secretary of State is a corporation sole.

(2) Any instrument in connection with the acquisition, management or disposal of property, real or personal, heritable or moveable, by the Secretary of State under this Part may be executed on his behalf by a person authorised by him for that purpose.

(3) Any instrument purporting to have been so executed on behalf of the Secretary of State is to be treated, until the contrary is proved, to have been so executed on his behalf.

Note: Commenced 11 November 1999, s 170.

125. Entry of premises

(1) This section applies in relation to premises in which accommodation has been provided under section 95 or 98 for a supported person.

(2) If, on an application made by a person authorised in writing by the Secretary of State, a justice of the peace is satisfied that there is reason to believe that—

(a) the supported person or any dependants of his for whom the accommodation is provided is not resident in it,

(b) the accommodation is being used for any purpose other than the accommodation of the asylum-seeker or any dependant of his, or

(c) any person other than the supported person and his dependants (if any) is residing in the accommodation, he may grant a warrant to enter the premises to the person making the application.

(3) A warrant granted under subsection (2) may be executed—

(a) at any reasonable time;

(b) using reasonable force.

(4) In the application of subsection (2) to Scotland, read the reference to a justice of the peace as a reference to the sheriff or a justice of the peace.

Note: Commenced 3 April 2000 (SI 2000/464).

126. Information from property owners

(1) The power conferred by this section is to be exercised with a view to obtaining information about premises in which accommodation is or has been provided for supported persons.

(2) The Secretary of State may require any person appearing to him—

(a) to have any interest in, or

(b) to be involved in any way in the management or control of,

such premises, or any building which includes such premises, to provide him with such information with respect to the premises and the persons occupying them as he may specify.

(3) A person who is required to provide information under this section must do so in accordance with such requirements as may be prescribed.

(4) Information provided to the Secretary of State under this section may be used by him only in the exercise of his functions under this Part.

Note: Commenced 3 April 2000 (SI 2000/464).

127. Requirement to supply information about redirection of post

(1) The Secretary of State may require any person conveying postal packets to supply redirection information to the Secretary of State—

(a) for use in the prevention, detection, investigation or prosecution of criminal offences under this Part;

(b) for use in checking the accuracy of information relating to support provided under this Part; or

(c) for any other purpose relating to the provision of support to asylum-seekers.

(2) The information must be supplied in such manner and form, and in accordance with such requirements, as may be prescribed.

(3) The Secretary of State must make payments of such amount as he considers reasonable in respect of the supply of information under this section.

(4) 'Postal packet' has the same meaning as in the [Postal Services Act 2000].

(5) 'Redirection information' means information relating to arrangements made with any person conveying postal packets for the delivery of postal packets to addresses other than those indicated by senders on the packets.

Note: Commenced 3 April 2000 (SI 2000/464). Words in square brackets in sub-s (4) substituted from 26 March 2001 (SI 2001/1149).

PART VII

POWER TO ARREST, SEARCH AND FINGERPRINT

Power to arrest

128. . . .

Note: Amends Immigration Act 1971, s 28.

Power to search and arrest

129. . . .

Note: Amends Immigration Act 1971, s 28.

130. . . .

Note: Amends Immigration Act 1971, s 28.

Power to enter and search premises

131. . . .

Note: Amends Immigration Act 1971, s 28.

132. . . .

Note: Amends Immigration Act 1971, s 28 and Sch 2, para 25.

133. . . .

Note: Amends Immigration Act 1971, s 28.

Power to search persons

134. . . .

Note: Amends Immigration Act 1971, s 28 and Sch 2, para 25.

135. . . .

Note: Amends Immigration Act 1971, s 28 and Sch 2, para 25.

Seized material: access and copying

136. . . .

Note: Amends Immigration Act 1971, s 28 and Sch 2, para 25.

Search warrants

137. . . .

Note: Amends Immigration Act 1971, s 28.

138. . . .

Note: Amends Immigration Act 1971, s 28.

139. . . .

Note: Amends Immigration Act 1971, s 28 and Sch 2, para 25.

Detention

140. . . .

Note: Amends Immigration Act 1971, Sch 2, paras 16–17.

Fingerprinting

141. Fingerprinting

(1) Fingerprints may be taken by an authorised person from a person to whom this section applies.

(2) Fingerprints may be taken under this section only during the relevant period.

(3) Fingerprints may not be taken under this section from a person under the age of sixteen ('the child') except in the presence of a person of full age who is—

(a) the child's parent or guardian; or

(b) a person who for the time being takes responsibility for the child.

(4) The person mentioned in subsection (3)(b) may not be—

(a) an officer of the Secretary of State who is not an authorised person;

(b) an authorised person.

(5) 'Authorised person' means—

(a) a constable;

(b) an immigration officer;

(c) a prison officer;

(d) an officer of the Secretary of State authorised for the purpose; or

(e) a person who is employed by a contractor in connection with the discharge of the contractor's duties under a [removal centre] contract.

(6) In subsection (5)(e) 'contractor' and '[removal centre] contract' have the same meaning as in Part VIII.

(7) This section applies to—

(a) any person ('A') who, on being required to do so by an immigration officer on his arrival in the United Kingdom, fails to produce a valid passport with photograph or some other document satisfactorily establishing his identity and nationality or citizenship;

(b) any person ('B') who has been refused leave to enter the United Kingdom but has been temporarily admitted under paragraph 21 of Schedule 2 to the 1971 Act if an immigration officer reasonably suspects that B might break any condition imposed on him relating to residence or as to reporting to the police or an immigration officer;

[(c) any person ('C') in respect of whom a relevant immigration decision has been made;]

(d) any person ('D') who has been [detained under paragraph 16 of Schedule 2 to the 1971 Act or arrested under paragraph 17 of that Schedule;]

(e) any person ('E') who has made a claim for asylum;

(f) any person ('F') who is a dependant of any of those persons [, other than a dependant of a person who falls within paragraph (c) by reason of a relevant immigration decision within subsection (16)(b) having been made in respect of that person.]

(8) 'The relevant period' begins—

(a) for A, on his failure to produce the passport or other document;

(b) for B, on the decision to admit him temporarily;

[(c) for C, on the service on him of notice of the relevant immigration decision by virtue of section 105 of the Nationality, Immigration and Asylum Act 2002 (c. 41);]

　　(d) for D, on his [detention or arrest;]

　　(e) for E, on the making of his claim for asylum; and

　　(f) for F, at the same time as for the person whose dependant he is.

(9) 'The relevant period' ends on the earliest of the following—

　　(a) the grant of leave to enter or remain in the United Kingdom;

　　(b) for A, B, C or D, his removal or deportation from the United Kingdom;

　　[(c) for C—

　　　　(i) the time when the relevant immigration decision ceases to have effect, whether as a result of an appeal or otherwise, or

　　　　(ii) if a deportation order has been made against him, its revocation or its otherwise ceasing to have effect;]

　　(d) for D, his release if he is no longer liable to be detained under paragraph 16 of Schedule 2 to the 1971 Act;

　　(e) for E, the final determination or abandonment of his claim for asylum; and

　　(f) for F, at the same time as for the person whose dependant he is.

(10) No fingerprints may be taken from A if the immigration officer considers that A has a reasonable excuse for the failure concerned.

(11) No fingerprints may be taken from B unless the decision to take them has been confirmed by a chief immigration officer.

(12) An authorised person may not take fingerprints from a person under the age of sixteen unless his decision to take them has been confirmed—

　　(a) if he is a constable, by a person designated for the purpose by the chief constable of his police force;

　　(b) if he is a person mentioned in subsection (5)(b) or (e), by a chief immigration officer;

　　(c) if he is a prison officer, by a person designated for the purpose by the governor of the prison;

　　(d) if he is an officer of the Secretary of State, by a person designated for the purpose by the Secretary of State.

(13) Neither subsection (3) nor subsection (12) prevents an authorised person from taking fingerprints if he reasonably believes that the person from whom they are to be taken is aged sixteen or over.

(14) For the purposes of subsection (7)(f), a person is a dependant of another person if—

　　(a) he is that person's spouse or child under the age of eighteen; and

　　(b) he does not have a right of abode in the United Kingdom or indefinite leave to enter or remain in the United Kingdom.

(15) 'Claim for asylum' has the same meaning as in Part VI.

[(16) 'Relevant immigration decision' means [—]

　　[(a)] a decision of the kind mentioned in section 82(2)(g), (h), (i), (j) or (k) of the Nationality, Immigration and Asylum Act 2002 (c. 41).][, or

　　(b) a decision that section 32(5) of the UK Borders Act 2007 applies (whether made before, or on or after, the day appointed for the commencement of section 51 of the Borders, Citizenship and Immigration Act 2009 which inserted this paragraph)].

[**(17)** Section 157(1) applies to this section (in so far as it relates to removal centres by virtue of subsection (5)(e)) as it applies to Part VIII.]

Note: Commenced 11 December 2000 (SI 2000/3099). Words in first and second square brackets substituted by Nationality, Immigration and Asylum Act 2002, s 66 from 10 February 2003 (SI 2003/1). Words in square brackets in sub-ss (7)(c), (8)(c) and (9)(c) substituted and sub-s (16) added by Asylum and Immigration (Treatment of Claimants etc.) Act 2004, s 15 from 1 October 2004 (SI 2004/2523). Words in square brackets in sub-ss (7)(d) and (8)(d) substituted and sub-s (17) added by Immigration, Asylum and Nationality Act 2006, s 28 from 31 August 2006 (SI 2006/2226). Words in square brackets in sub-ss (7)(f) and (16) inserted by s 51 Borders, Citizenship and Immigration Act 2009 from 15 November 2009 (SI 2009/2731).

142. Attendance for fingerprinting

(1) The Secretary of State may, by notice in writing, require a person to whom section 141 applies to attend at a specified place for fingerprinting.

[(2) In the case of a notice given to a person of a kind specified in section 141(7)(a) to (d) or (f) (in so far as it applies to a dependant of a person of a kind specified in section 141(7)(a) to (d)), the notice—

(a) must require him to attend during a specified period of at least seven days beginning with a day not less than seven days after the date given in the notice as its date of issue, and

(b) may require him to attend at a specified time of day or during specified hours.

(2A) In the case of a notice given to a person of a kind specified in section 141(7)(e) or (f) (in so far as it applies to a dependant of a person of a kind specified in section 141(7) (e)), the notice—

(a) may require him to attend during a specified period beginning with a day not less than three days after the date given in the notice as its date of issue,

(b) may require him to attend on a specified day not less than three days after the date given in the notice as its date of issue, and

(c) may require him to attend at a specified time of day or during specified hours.]

(3) A constable or immigration officer may arrest without warrant a person who has failed to comply with a requirement imposed on him under this section (unless the requirement has ceased to have effect).

(4) Before a person arrested under subsection (3) is released—

(a) he may be removed to a place where his fingerprints may conveniently be taken; and

(b) his fingerprints may be taken (whether or not he is so removed).

(5) A requirement imposed under subsection (1) ceases to have effect at the end of the relevant period (as defined by section 141).

Note: Commenced 11 December 2000 (SI 2000/3099). Subsection (2) substituted and sub-s 2A inserted by Immigration, Asylum and Nationality Act 2006, s 29 from 31 August 2006 (SI 2006/2226).

143. Destruction of fingerprints

(1) If they have not already been destroyed, fingerprints must be destroyed before the end of the specified period beginning with the day on which they were taken.

(2) If a person from whom fingerprints were taken proves that he is—

(a) a British citizen, or

(b) a Commonwealth citizen who has a right of abode in the United Kingdom as a result of section 2(1)(b) of the 1971 Act, the fingerprints must be destroyed as soon as reasonably practicable.

(3) . . .

(4) . . .

(5) . . .

(6) . . .

(7) . . .

(8) . . .

(9) Fingerprints taken from F [within the meaning of section 141(7)] must be destroyed when fingerprints taken from the person whose dependant he is have to be destroyed.

(10) The obligation to destroy fingerprints under this section applies also to copies of fingerprints.

(11) The Secretary of State must take all reasonably practicable steps to secure—

(a) that data which are held in electronic form and which relate to fingerprints which have to be destroyed as a result of this section are destroyed or erased; or

(b) that access to such data is blocked.

(12) The person to whom the data relate is entitled, on request, to a certificate issued by the Secretary of State to the effect that he has taken the steps required by subsection (11).

(13) A certificate under subsection (12) must be issued within three months of the date of the request for it.

(14) . . .

(15) 'Specified period' means—

(a) such period as the Secretary of State may specify by order;

(b) if no period is so specified, ten years.

Note: Commenced 11 December 2000 (SI 2000/3099). Subsections (3)–(8) and (14) cease to have effect and words in square brackets in sub-s (9) inserted by Anti-terrorism, Crime and Security Act 2001, s 36 14 December 2001 with effect to fingerprints whether taken before or after 14 December 2001. Those fingerprints which were required by s 143 to be destroyed before 14 December 2001 shall be treated as though these amendments had effect before the requirement arose.

144. Other methods of collecting data about physical characteristics

[(1)] The Secretary of State may make regulations containing provisions equivalent to sections 141, 142 and 143 in relation to such other methods of collecting data about external physical characteristics as may be prescribed.

[(2) In subsection (1) 'external physical characteristics' includes, in particular, features of the iris or any other part of the eye.]

Note: Commenced 11 December 2000 (SI 2000/3099). Subsection (2) inserted by Nationality, Immigration and Asylum Act 2002, s 128 from 10 February 2003 (SI 2003/1).

Codes of practice

145. Codes of practice

(1) An immigration officer exercising any specified power to—

(a) arrest, question, search or take fingerprints from a person,

(b) enter and search premises, or

(c) seize property found on persons or premises,

must have regard to such provisions of a code as may be specified.

(2) Subsection (1) also applies to an authorised person exercising the power to take fingerprints conferred by section 141.

[(2A) A person exercising a power under regulations made by virtue of section 144 must have regard to such provisions of a code as may be specified.]

(3) Any specified provision of a code may have effect for the purposes of this section subject to such modifications as may be specified.

(4) 'Specified' means specified in a direction given by the Secretary of State.

(5) 'Authorised person' has the same meaning as in section 141.

(6) 'Code' means—

(a) in relation to England and Wales, any code of practice for the time being in force under the Police and Criminal Evidence Act 1984;

(b) in relation to Northern Ireland, any code of practice for the time being in force under the Police and Criminal Evidence (Northern Ireland) Order 1989.

(7) This section does not apply to any person exercising powers in Scotland.

Note: Commenced 11 November 1999, s 170. Subsection (2A) inserted by Nationality, Immigration and Asylum Act 2002, s 128 from 10 February 2003 (SI 2003/1).

Use of force

146. Use of force

(1) An immigration officer exercising any power conferred on him by the 1971 Act or this Act may, if necessary, use reasonable force.

[(2) A person exercising a power under any of the following may if necessary use reasonable force—

(a) section 28CA, 28FA or 28FB of the 1971 Act (business premises: entry to arrest or search),

(b) section 141 or 142 of this Act, and

(c) regulations under section 144 of this Act.]

Note: Commenced 1 November 1999, s 170 (Royal Assent). Subsection (2) substituted by Nationality, Immigration and Asylum Act 2002, s 153 from 8 January 2003 (SI 2003/1).

PART VIII
[REMOVAL CENTRES] AND DETAINED PERSONS

Interpretation

147. Interpretation of Part VIII

In this Part—

'certificate of authorisation' means a certificate issued by the Secretary of State under section 154;

'certified prisoner custody officer' means a prisoner custody officer certified under section 89 of the Criminal Justice Act 1991, or section 114 of the Criminal Justice and Public Order Act 1994, to perform custodial duties;

'contract monitor' means a person appointed by the Secretary of State under section 149(4);

'contracted out [removal centre]' means a [removal centre] in relation to which a [removal centre] contract is in force;

'contractor', in relation to a [removal centre] which is being run in accordance with a [removal centre] contract, means the person who has contracted to run it;

'custodial functions' means custodial functions at a [removal centre];

'detained persons' means persons detained or required to be detained under the 1971 Act [or under section 62 of the Nationality, Immigration and Asylum Act 2002 (detention by Secretary of State);]

'detainee custody officer' means a person in respect of whom a certificate of authorisation is in force;

. . .

'[removal centre] contract' means a contract entered into by the Secretary of State under section 149;

'[removal] centre rules' means rules made by the Secretary of State under section 153;

'directly managed [removal centre]' means a [removal centre] which is not a contracted out [removal centre];

'escort arrangements' means arrangements made by the Secretary of State under section 156;

'escort functions' means functions under escort arrangements;

'escort monitor' means a person appointed under paragraph 1 of Schedule 13;

'prisoner custody officer'—

(a) in relation to England and Wales, has the same meaning as in the Criminal Justice Act 1991;

(b) in relation to Scotland, has the meaning given in section 114(1) of the Criminal Justice and Public Order Act 1994;

(c) in relation to Northern Ireland, has the meaning given in section 122(1) of that Act of 1994;

['removal centre' means a place which is used solely for the detention of detained persons but which is not a short-term holding facility, a prison or part of a prison;]

'short-term holding facility' means a place used

[–(a) solely for the detention of detained persons for a period of not more than seven days or for such other period as may be prescribed [, or

(b) for the detention of—

(i) detained persons for a period of not more than seven days or for such other period as may be prescribed, and

(ii) persons other than detained persons for any period].

Note: Commenced 1 August 2000 (SI 2000/1985). Definition of removal centre inserted by Nationality, Immigration and Asylum Act 2002, s 66 from 10 February 2003 (SI 2003/1). Definition of detained persons amended by Nationality, Immigration and Asylum Act 2002, s 62 from 10

February 2003 (SI 2003/1). Definition of 'short term holding facility' amended by s 25 Borders, Citizenship and Immigration Act 2009 from 21 July 2009 (s 57). Other words in square brackets inserted by Nationality, Immigration and Asylum Act 2002, s 66 from 10 February 2003 (SI 2003/1).

[Removal centres]

148. Management of [removal centres]

(1) A manager must be appointed for every [removal centre].

(2) In the case of a contracted out [removal centre], the person appointed as manager must be a detainee custody officer whose appointment is approved by the Secretary of State.

(3) The manager of a [removal centre] is to have such functions as are conferred on him by [removal centre] rules.

(4) The manager of a contracted out [removal centre] may not—

   (a) enquire into a disciplinary charge laid against a detained person;

   (b) conduct the hearing of such a charge; or

   (c) make, remit or mitigate an award in respect of such a charge.

(5) The manager of a contracted out [removal centre] may not, except in cases of urgency, order—

   (a) the removal of a detained person from association with other detained persons;

   (b) the temporary confinement of a detained person in special accommodation; or

   (c) the application to a detained person of any other special control or restraint (other than handcuffs).

Note: Subsection (3) commenced 1 August 2000 (SI 2000/1985). Remainder commenced 2 April 2001 (SI 2001/239). Words in square brackets substituted by Nationality, Immigration and Asylum Act 2002, s 66 from 10 February 2003 (SI 2003/1).

149. Contracting out of certain [removal centres]

(1) The Secretary of State may enter into a contract with another person for the provision or running (or the provision and running) by him, or (if the contract so provides) for the running by sub-contractors of his, of any [removal centre] or part of a [removal centre].

(2) While a [removal centre] contract for the running of a [removal centre] or part of a [removal centre] is in force—

   (a) the [removal centre] or part is to be run subject to and in accordance with the provisions of or made under this Part; and

   (b) in the case of a part, that part and the remaining part are to be treated for the purposes of those provisions as if they were separate [removal centres].

(3) If the Secretary of State grants a lease or tenancy of land for the purposes of a detention centre contract, none of the following enactments applies to the lease or tenancy—

   (a) Part II of the Landlord and Tenant Act 1954 (security of tenure);

   (b) section 146 of the Law of Property Act 1925 (restrictions on and relief against forfeiture);

   (c) section 19(1), (2) and (3) of the Landlord and Tenant Act 1927 and the Landlord and Tenant Act 1988 (covenants not to assign etc.);

(d) the Agricultural Holdings Act 1986;

(e) sections 4 to 7 of the Law Reform (Miscellaneous Provisions) (Scotland) Act 1985 (irritancy clauses);

(f) the Agricultural Holdings (Scotland) Act 1991 [and the Agricultural Holdings (Scotland) Act 2003 (asp 11)];

(g) section 14 of the Conveyancing Act 1881;

(h) the Conveyancing and Law of Property Act 1892;

(i) the Business Tenancies (Northern Ireland) Order 1996.

(4) The Secretary of State must appoint a contract monitor for every contracted out [removal centre].

(5) A person may be appointed as the contract monitor for more than one [removal centre].

(6) The contract monitor is to have—

(a) such functions as may be conferred on him by [removal centre] rules;

(b) the status of a Crown servant.

(7) The contract monitor must—

(a) keep under review, and report to the Secretary of State on, the running of a [removal centre] for which he is appointed; and

(b) investigate, and report to the Secretary of State on, any allegations made against any person performing custodial functions at that centre.

(8) The contractor, and any sub-contractor of his, must do all that he reasonably can (whether by giving directions to the officers of the [removal centre] or otherwise) to facilitate the exercise by the contract monitor of his functions.

(9) 'Lease or tenancy' includes an underlease, sublease or sub-tenancy.

(10) In relation to a [removal centre] contract entered into by the Secretary of State before the commencement of this section, this section is to be treated as having been in force at that time.

Note: Subsections (1), (3), (6)(a) and (9) commenced 1 August 2000 (SI 2000/1985). Remainder commenced 2 April 2001, s 66 (SI 2001/239). Words in square brackets substituted by Nationality, Immigration and Asylum Act 2002, s 66 from 10 February 2003 (SI 2003/1). Words in square brackets in sub-s (3)(f) inserted by Agricultural Holdings (Scotland) Act 2003 (asp 11) Schedule para 52 from 27 November 2003 (SSI 2003/511).

150. Contracted out functions at directly managed [removal centres]

(1) The Secretary of State may enter into a contract with another person—

(a) for functions at, or connected with, a directly managed [removal centre] to be performed by detainee custody officers provided by that person; or

(b) for such functions to be performed by certified prisoner custody officers who are provided by that person.

(2) For the purposes of this section '[removal centre]' includes a short-term holding facility.

Note: Commenced 2 April 2001 (SI 2001/239). Words in square brackets substituted by Nationality, Immigration and Asylum Act 2002, s 66 from 10 February 2003 (SI 2003/1).

151. Intervention by Secretary of State

(1) The Secretary of State may exercise the powers conferred by this section if it appears to him that—

(a) the manager of a contracted out [removal centre] has lost, or is likely to lose, effective control of the centre or of any part of it; or

(b) it is necessary to do so in the interests of preserving the safety of any person, or of preventing serious damage to any property.

(2) The Secretary of State may appoint a person (to be known as the Controller) to act as manager of the [removal centre] for the period—

(a) beginning with the time specified in the appointment; and

(b) ending with the time specified in the notice of termination under subsection (5).

(3) During that period—

(a) all the functions which would otherwise be exercisable by the manager or the contract monitor are to be exercisable by the Controller;

(b) the contractor and any sub-contractor of his must do all that he reasonably can to facilitate the exercise by the Controller of his functions; and

(c) the staff of the detention centre must comply with any directions given by the Controller in the exercise of his functions.

(4) The Controller is to have the status of a Crown servant.

(5) If the Secretary of State is satisfied that a Controller is no longer needed for a particular detention centre, he must (by giving notice to the Controller) terminate his appointment at a time specified in the notice.

(6) As soon as practicable after making an appointment under this section, the Secretary of State must give notice of the appointment to those entitled to notice.

(7) As soon as practicable after terminating an appointment under this section, the Secretary of State must give a copy of the notice of termination to those entitled to notice.

(8) Those entitled to notice are the contractor, the manager, the contract monitor and the Controller.

Note: Commenced 2 April 2001 (SI 2001/239). Words in square brackets substituted by Nationality, Immigration and Asylum Act 2002, s 66 from 10 February 2003 (SI 2003/1).

152. Visiting Committees and inspections

(1) The Secretary of State must appoint a committee (to be known as the Visiting Committee) for each detention centre.

(2) The functions of the Visiting Committee for a [removal centre] are to be such as may be prescribed by the [removal centre] rules.

(3) Those rules must include provision—

(a) as to the making of visits to the centre by members of the Visiting Committee;

(b) for the hearing of complaints made by persons detained in the centre;

(c) requiring the making of reports by the Visiting Committee to the Secretary of State.

(4) Every member of the Visiting Committee for a [removal centre] may at any time enter the centre and have free access to every part of it and to every person detained there.

(5) . . .

Note: Sub-sections (2) and (3) commenced for the purposes of enabling subordinate legislation 1 August 2000 (SI 2000/1985). Otherwise commenced 2 April 2001 (SI 2001/239). Sub-section (5) amends the Prison Act 1952, s 5A. Words in square brackets substituted by Nationality, Immigration and Asylum Act 2002, s 66 from 10 February 2003 (SI 2003/1).

153. [Removal centre] rules

(1) The Secretary of State must make rules for the regulation and management of [removal centres].

(2) [Removal centre] rules may, among other things, make provision with respect to the safety, care, activities, discipline and control of detained persons.

Note: Commenced for the purposes of enabling subordinate legislation 1 August 2000 (SI 2000/1985). Otherwise commenced 2 April 2001 (SI 2001/239). Words in square brackets substituted by Nationality, Immigration and Asylum Act 2002, s 66 from 10 February 2003 (SI 2003/1).

[153A. Detained persons: national minimum wage

A detained person does not qualify for the national minimum wage in respect of work which he does in pursuance of removal centre rules.]

Note: Inserted by Immigration, Asylum and Nationality Act 2006, s 59 from 31 August 2006 (SI 2006/2226).

Custody and movement of detained persons

154. Detainee custody officers

(1) On an application made to him under this section, the Secretary of State may certify that the applicant—

    (a) is authorised to perform escort functions; or

    (b) is authorised to perform both escort functions and custodial functions.

(2) The Secretary of State may not issue a certificate of authorisation unless he is satisfied that the applicant—

    (a) is a fit and proper person to perform the functions to be authorised; and

    (b) has received training to such standard as the Secretary of State considers appropriate for the performance of those functions.

(3) A certificate of authorisation continues in force until such date, or the occurrence of such event, as may be specified in the certificate but may be suspended or revoked under paragraph 7 of Schedule 11.

(4) A certificate which authorises the performance of both escort functions and custodial functions may specify one date or event for one of those functions and a different date or event for the other.

[(5) The Secretary of State may confer functions of detainee custody officers on prison officers or prisoner custody officers.]

(6) A prison officer acting under arrangements made under subsection (5) has all the powers, authority, protection and privileges of a constable.

(7) Schedule 11 makes further provision about detainee custody officers.

Note: Commenced 2 April 2001 (SI 2001/239). Subsection (5) substituted by Nationality, Immigration and Asylum Act 2002, s 65 from 10 February 2003 (SI 2003/1).

155. Custodial functions and discipline etc. at [removal centres]

(1) Custodial functions may be discharged at a [removal centre] only by—

(a) a detainee custody officer authorised, in accordance with section 154(1), to perform such functions; or

(b) a prison officer, or a certified prisoner custody officer, exercising functions in relation to the [removal centre]—

 (i) in accordance with arrangements made under section 154(5); or

 (ii) as a result of a contract entered into under section 150(1)(b).

(2) Schedule 12 makes provision with respect to discipline and other matters at [removal centres] and short-term holding facilities.

Note: Sub-section (2) commenced 1 August 2000 (SI 2000/1985). Remainder commenced 2 April 2001 (SI 2001/239). Words in square brackets substituted by Nationality, Immigration and Asylum Act 2002, s 66 from 10 February 2003 (SI 2003/1).

156. Arrangements for the provision of escorts and custody

(1) The Secretary of State may make arrangements for—

(a) the delivery of detained persons to premises in which they may lawfully be detained;

(b) the delivery of persons from any such premises for the purposes of their removal from the United Kingdom in accordance with directions given under the 1971 Act or this Act;

(c) the custody of detained persons who are temporarily outside such premises;

(d) the custody of detained persons held on the premises of any court.

(2) Escort arrangements may provide for functions under the arrangements to be performed, in such cases as may be determined by or under the arrangements, by detainee custody officers.

(3) 'Court' includes—

[(a) the First-tier Tribunal;

(b) the Upper Tribunal; and]

(c) the Commission.

(4) Escort arrangements may include entering into contracts with other persons for the provision by them of—

(a) detainee custody officers; or

(b) prisoner custody officers who are certified under section 89 of the Criminal Justice Act 1991, or section 114 or 122 of the Criminal Justice and Public Order Act 1994, to perform escort functions.

(5) Schedule 13 makes further provision about escort arrangements.

(6) A person responsible for performing a function of a kind mentioned in subsection (1), in accordance with a transfer direction, complies with the direction if he does all that he reasonably can to secure that the function is performed by a person acting in accordance with escort arrangements.

(7) 'Transfer direction' means a transfer direction given under—

(a) section 48 of the Mental Health Act 1983 or section 71 of the Mental Health (Scotland) Act 1984 (removal to hospital of, among others, persons detained under the 1971 Act); or

(b) in Northern Ireland, article 54 of the Mental Health (Northern Ireland) Order 1986 (provision corresponding to section 48 of the 1983 Act).

Note: Subsection (5) commenced 1 August 2000 (SI 2000/1985). Remainder commenced 2 April 2001 (SI 2001/239). Words in square brackets substituted from 15 February 2010 (SI 2010/21).

157. Short-term holding facilities

(1) The Secretary of State may by regulations extend any provision made by or under this Part in relation to [removal centres] (other than one mentioned in subsection (2)) to short-term holding facilities.

(2) Subsection (1) does not apply to section 150.

(3) The Secretary of State may make rules for the regulation and management of short-term holding facilities.

Note: Commenced for the purposes of enabling subordinate legislation 1 August 2000 (SI 2000/1985). Otherwise commenced 2 April 2001 (SI 2001/239). Words in square brackets substituted by Nationality, Immigration and Asylum Act 2002, s 66 from 10 February 2003 (SI 2003/1).

Miscellaneous

158. Wrongful disclosure of information

(1) A person who is or has been employed (whether as a detainee custody officer, prisoner custody officer or otherwise)—

(a) in accordance with escort arrangements,

(b) at a contracted out [removal centre], or

(c) to perform contracted out functions at a directly managed detention centre, is guilty of an offence if he discloses, otherwise than in the course of his duty or as authorised by the Secretary of State, any information which he acquired in the course of his employment and which relates to a particular detained person.

(2) A person guilty of such an offence is liable—

(a) on conviction on indictment, to imprisonment for a term not exceeding two years or to a fine or to both;

(b) on summary conviction, to imprisonment for a term not exceeding six months or to a fine not exceeding the statutory maximum or to both.

(3) 'Contracted out functions' means functions which, as the result of a contract entered into under section 150, fall to be performed by detainee custody officers or certified prisoner custody officers.

Note: Commenced 2 April 2001 (SI 2001/239). Words in square brackets substituted by Nationality, Immigration and Asylum Act 2002, s 66 from 10 February 2003 (SI 2003/1).

159. Power of constable to act outside his jurisdiction

(1) For the purpose of taking a person to or from a [removal centre] under the order of any authority competent to give the order, a constable may act outside the area of his jurisdiction.

(2) When acting under this section, the constable concerned retains all the powers, authority, protection and privileges of his office.

Note: Commenced 2 April 2001 (SI 2001/239). Words in square brackets substituted by Nationality, Immigration and Asylum Act 2002, s 66 from 10 February 2003 (SI 2003/1).

PART IX
REGISTRAR'S CERTIFICATES: PROCEDURE

160. ...

Note: Amends Marriage Act 1949, ss 26–7, 31.

161. ...

Note: Amends the Marriage Act 1949, ss 26–7 and the Marriage Law (Ireland) Amendment Act 1863, s 2.

162. ...

Note: Amends the Marriage Act 1949, s 28 and the Marriage Law (Ireland) Amendment Act 1863 s 3.

163. ...

Note: Amends the Marriage Act 1949, s 31 and the Marriages (Ireland) Act 1844, s 16.

PART X
MISCELLANEOUS AND SUPPLEMENTAL

164. ...

Note: Amends the Prosecution of Offences Act 1985, s 3.

165. ...

Note: Amends Immigration Act 1971, s 31.

166. Regulations and orders

(1) Any power to make rules, regulations or orders conferred by this Act is exercisable by statutory instrument.

(2) But subsection (1) does not apply in relation to [orders made under section 90(1),] rules made under paragraph 1 of Schedule 5 or immigration rules.

(3) Any statutory instrument made as a result of subsection (1) may—

(a) contain such incidental, supplemental, consequential and transitional provision as the person making it considers appropriate;

(b) make different provision for different cases or descriptions of case; and

(c) make different provision for different areas.

(4) No order is to be made under—

(a) section 20,

(b) section 21,

(c) section 31(10),

[(da) section 86A(3)]

(d) section 86(2),

(e) ...

(f) section 97(3),

(g) section 143(15), or

(h) paragraph 4 of Schedule 5, unless a draft of the order has been laid before Parliament and approved by a resolution of each House.

(5) No regulations are to be made under—

[(za) section 4(5),]

(a) section 9,

(b) section 46(8);

(c) section 53, or

(d) section 144,

unless a draft of the regulations has been laid before Parliament and approved by a resolution of each House.

(6) Any statutory instrument made under this Act, apart from one made—

(a) under any of the provisions mentioned in subsection (4) or (5), or

(b) under section 24(3) [, 24A(3)] or 170(4) or (7), shall be subject to annulment by a resolution of either House of Parliament.

Note: Commencement 11 November 1999, s 170. Subsection (4)(e) omitted by Nationality, Immigration and Asylum Act 2002, s 61 from 7 November 2002. Words in square brackets in sub-s (2) inserted by Asylum and Immigration Act 2004, s 41 from 1 October 2004 (SI 2004/2523). Subsection (4)(da) inserted by Sch 18 Legal Services Act from 1 April 2011 (SI 2011/720). Subsection (5)(za) inserted by Asylum and Immigration Act 2004, s 10 from 1 December 2004 (SI 2004/2999). Words in square brackets in sub-s 6(b) inserted by Civil Partnership Act 2004 Schedule 27 from 15 April 2005 SI 2005/1112.

167. Interpretation

(1) In this Act—

'the 1971 Act' means the Immigration Act 1971;

'adjudicator' (except in Part VI) means an adjudicator appointed under section 57;

'Chief Adjudicator' means the person appointed as Chief Adjudicator under section 57(2);

'claim for asylum' (except in Parts V and VI and section 141) means a claim that it would be contrary to the United Kingdom's obligations under the Refugee Convention for the claimant to be removed from, or required to leave, the United Kingdom;

'the Commission' means the Special Immigration Appeals Commission;

'country' includes any territory;

'EEA State' means a State which is a Contracting Party to the Agreement on the European Economic Area signed at Oporto on 2nd May 1992 as it has effect for the time being;

'the Human Rights Convention' means the Convention for the Protection of Human Rights and Fundamental Freedoms, agreed by the Council of Europe at Rome on 4 November 1950 as it has effect for the time being in relation to the United Kingdom;

. . . . .

'prescribed' means prescribed by regulations made by the Secretary of State;

'the Refugee Convention' means the Convention relating to the Status of Refugees done at Geneva on 28 July 1951 and the Protocol to the Convention;

'voluntary organisations' means bodies (other than public or local authorities) whose activities are not carried on for profit.

(2) The following expressions have the same meaning as in the 1971 Act—

'certificate of entitlement';

'entry clearance';

'illegal entrant';

'immigration officer';

'immigration rules';

'port';

'United Kingdom passport';

'work permit'.

Note: Commencement 11 November 1999, s 170. Words omitted ceased to have effect from 30 March 2006, s 64 Immigration, Asylum and Nationality Act 2006 (Royal Assent).

168. Expenditure and receipts

(1) There is to be paid out of money provided by Parliament—

(a) any expenditure incurred by the Secretary of State or the Lord Chancellor in consequence of this Act; and

(b) any increase attributable to this Act in the sums so payable by virtue of any other Act.

(2) Sums received by the Secretary of State under section 5, 32, 40, 112 or 113 or by the Lord Chancellor under section 48(4) or 49(4) must be paid into the Consolidated Fund.

Note: Commencement 11 November 1999, s 170.

169. Minor and consequential amendments, transitional provisions and repeals

(1) Schedule 14 makes minor and consequential amendments.

(2) Schedule 15 contains transitional provisions and savings.

(3) The enactments set out in Schedule 16 are repealed.

170. Short title, commencement and extent

(1) This Act may be cited as the Immigration and Asylum Act 1999.

(2) Subsections (1) and (2) of section 115 come into force on the day on which the first regulations made under Schedule 8 come into force.

(3) The following provisions come into force on the passing of this Act—

(a) section 4;

(b) section 9;

(c) section 15;

(d) section 27;

(e) section 31;

(f) section 94;

(g) section 95(13);

(h) section 99(4) and (5);

(i) sections 105 to 109;

(j) section 110(1), (2) and (8) (so far as relating to subsections (1) and (2));

(k) section 111;

(l) section 124;

(m) section 140;

(n) section 145;

(o) section 146(1);

(p) sections 166 to 168;

(q) this section;

(r) Schedule 9;

(s) paragraphs 62(2), 73, 78, 79, 81, 82, 87, 88 and 102 of Schedule 14;

(t) paragraph 2 and 13 of Schedule 15.

(4) The other provisions of this Act, except section 10 and paragraph 12 of Schedule 15 (which come into force in accordance with section 9), come into force on such day as the Secretary of State may by order appoint.

(5) Different days may be appointed for different purposes.

(6) This Act extends to Northern Ireland.

(7) Her Majesty may by Order in Council direct that any of the provisions of this Act are to extend, with such modifications (if any) as appear to Her Majesty to be appropriate, to any of the Channel Islands or the Isle of Man.

Note: Commenced 11 November 1999.

SCHEDULES

Sections 37(6) and 42(8)   SCHEDULE 1

SALE OF TRANSPORTERS

. . .

Section 56(2)   SCHEDULE 2

THE IMMIGRATION APPEAL TRIBUNAL

. . .

Note: Schedule 2 repealed by Sch 9 Nationality, Immigration and Asylum Act 2002 from 1 April 2003 (SI 2003/754, which sets out transitional provisions).

Schedule 3

Adjudicators

...

Note: Schedule 3 repealed by Sch 9 Nationality, Immigration and Asylum Act 2002 from 1 April 2003 (SI 2003/754, which sets out transitional provisions).

Schedule 4

Appeals

...

Note: Schedule 4 repealed by Sch 9 Nationality, Immigration and Asylum Act 2002 from 1 April 2003 (SI 2003/754, which sets out transitional provisions).

Section 83

Schedule 5

The Immigration Services Commissioner

Part I

Regulatory Functions

The Commissioner's rules

1.—(1) The Commissioner may make rules regulating any aspect of the professional practice, conduct or discipline of—

(a) registered persons, and

[(b) those acting on behalf of registered persons.]

(2) Before making or altering any rules, the Commissioner must consult such persons appearing to him to represent the views of persons engaged in the provision of immigration advice or immigration services as he considers appropriate.

(3) In determining whether a registered person is competent or otherwise fit to provide immigration advice or immigration services, the Commissioner may take into account any breach of the rules by—

(a) that person; and

[(b) any person acting on behalf of that person.]

(4) The rules may, among other things, make provision requiring the keeping of accounts or the obtaining of indemnity insurance.

Note Subparagraphs (1)(b) and (3)(b) substituted by s 37 Asylum and Immigration (Treatment of Claimants) Act 2004 from 1 October 2004 (SI 2004/2523).

2.—(1) The Commissioner's rules must be made or altered by an instrument in writing.

(2) Such an instrument must specify that it is made under this Schedule.

(3) Immediately after such an instrument is made, it must be printed and made available to the public.

(4) The Commissioner may charge a reasonable fee for providing a person with a copy of the instrument.

(5) A person is not to be taken to have contravened a rule made by the Commissioner if he shows that at the time of the alleged contravention the instrument containing the rule had not been made available in accordance with this paragraph.

(6) The production of a printed copy of an instrument purporting to be made by the Commissioner on which is endorsed a certificate signed by an officer of the Commissioner authorised by him for that purpose and stating—

(a) that the instrument was made by the Commissioner,

(b) that the copy is a true copy of the instrument, and

(c) that on a specified date the instrument was made available to the public in accordance with this paragraph, is evidence (or in Scotland sufficient evidence) of the facts stated in the certificate.

(7) A certificate purporting to be signed as mentioned in sub-paragraph (6) is to be treated as having been properly signed unless the contrary is shown.

(8) A person who wishes in any legal proceedings to rely on an instrument containing the Commissioner's rules may require him to endorse a copy of the instrument with a certificate of the kind mentioned in sub-paragraph (6).

Code of Standards

3.—(1) The Commissioner must prepare and issue a code setting standards of conduct which those to whom the code applies are expected to meet.

(2) The code is to be known as the Code of Standards but is referred to in this Schedule as 'the Code'.

(3) The Code is to apply to any person providing immigration advice or immigration services other than—

(a) a person who is authorised by a designated professional body to practise as a member of the profession whose members are regulated by that body;

[(aa) a person who is authorised by a designated qualifying regulator to provide immigration advice or immigration services;]

[(b) a person who is acting on behalf of a person who is within paragraph (a), [or (aa)]];

(4) It is the duty of any person to whom the Code applies to comply with its provisions in providing immigration advice or immigration services.

(5) If the Commissioner alters the Code, he must re-issue it.

(6) Before issuing the Code or altering it, the Commissioner must consult—

(a)   each of the designated professional bodies;

[(aa) each of the designated qualifying regulators;]

(b)   . . .

(c)   the Lord President of the Court of Session;

(d)   the Lord Chief Justice of Northern Ireland; and

(e)   such other persons appearing to him to represent the views of persons engaged in the provision of immigration advice or immigration services as he considers appropriate.

(7) The Commissioner must publish the Code in such form and manner as the Secretary of State may direct.

Note: Subparagraphs (3)(aa), (6)(aa) and first words in square brackets in sub-para (3)(b) inserted by Sch 18 Legal Services Act 2007 from 1 April 2011 (SI 2011/720). Subparagraph (3)(b) substituted by s 37 Asylum and Immigration (Treatment of Claimants) Act 2004 from 1 October 2004 (SI 2004/2523).

Extension of scope of the Code

4.—(1) The Secretary of State may by order provide for the provisions of the Code, or such provisions of the Code as may be specified by the order, to apply to—

(a) persons authorised by any designated professional body to practise as a member of the profession whose members are regulated by that body; and

[(b) persons acting on behalf of persons who are within paragraph (a)].

(2) If the Secretary of State is proposing to act under sub-paragraph (1) he must, before doing so, consult—

    (a) the Commissioner;

    (b) ...

    (c) the [Scottish Legal Complaints Commission], if the proposed order would affect a desig-nated professional body in Scotland;

    (d) the lay observers appointed under Article 42 of the Solicitors (Northern Ireland) Order 1976, if the proposed order would affect a designated professional body in Northern Ireland.

(3) An order under sub-paragraph (1) requires the approval of—

    (a) the Lord Chancellor, if it affects a designated professional body in ... Northern Ireland;

    (b) the Scottish Ministers, if it affects a designated professional body in Scotland.

(4) Before deciding whether or not to give his approval under sub-paragraph (3)(a), the Lord Chancellor must consult—

    (a) ...

    (b) the Lord Chief Justice of Northern Ireland, if it affects a designated professional body in Northern Ireland.

(5) Before deciding whether or not to give their approval under sub-paragraph (3)(b), the Scottish Ministers must consult the Lord President of the Court of Session.

Note: Sub-paragraph (1)(b) substituted by s 37 Asylum and Immigration (Treatment of Claimants) Act 2004 from 1 October 2004 (SI 2004/2523). Sub-paragraphs (2)(b), (4)(a), and words in (3)(a) omitted, words in square brackets in (2)(c) substituted by Sch 18 Legal Services Act 2007 from 1 April 2011 (SI 2011/720).

Investigation of complaints

5.—(1) The Commissioner must establish a scheme ('the complaints scheme') for the investigation by him of relevant complaints made to him in accordance with the provisions of the scheme.

(2) Before establishing the scheme or altering it, the Commissioner must consult—

    (a) each of the designated professional bodies; and

    (b) such other persons appearing to him to represent the views of persons engaged in the pro-vision of immigration advice or immigration services as he considers appropriate.

(3) A complaint is a relevant complaint if it relates to—

    (a) the competence or fitness of a person to provide immigration advice or immigration services,

    (b) the competence or fitness of a person [acting on behalf of] a person providing immigration advice or immigration services,

    (c) an alleged breach of the Code,

    (d) an alleged breach of one or more of the Commissioner's rules by a person to whom they apply, or

    [(e) an alleged breach of a rule of a relevant regulatory body.]

    [but not if the complaint is excluded by sub-paragraph (3A).]

[(3A) A complaint is excluded if—

    (a) it relates to a person who is excluded from the application of subsection (1) of section 84 by subsection (6) of that section, or

    (b) it relates to a person within section 84(2)(ba).]

(4) The Commissioner may, on his own initiative, investigate any matter which he would have power to investigate on a complaint made under the complaints scheme.

(5) In investigating any such matter on his own initiative, the Commissioner must proceed as if his investigation were being conducted in response to a complaint made under the scheme.

Note: Words in square brackets in subparagraphs (3)(b) and (e) substituted by s 37 Asylum and Immigration (Treatment of Claimants) Act 2004 from 1 October 2004 (SI 2004/2523). Other words in square brackets in sub-para (3) and (3A) inserted by Sch 18 Legal Services Act 2007 from 1 April 2011 (SI 2011/720).

6.—**(1)** The complaints scheme must provide for a person who is the subject of an investigation under the scheme to be given a reasonable opportunity to make representations to the Commissioner.

(2) Any person who is the subject of an investigation under the scheme must—

(a) take such steps as are reasonably required to assist the Commissioner in his investigation; and

(b) comply with any reasonable requirement imposed on him by the Commissioner.

(3) If a person fails to comply with sub-paragraph (2)(a) or with a requirement imposed under sub-paragraph (2)(b) the Commissioner may—

(a) in the ease of a registered person, cancel his registration;

(b) in the case of a person certified by the Commissioner as exempt under section 84(4)(a), withdraw his exemption; or

[(c) in any other case, refer the matter to any relevant regulatory body.]

Note: Subparagraph (3)(c) substituted by s 37 Asylum and Immigration (Treatment of Claimants) Act 2004 from 1 October 2004 (SI 2004/2523).

Power to enter premises

7.—**(1)** This paragraph applies if—

(a) the Commissioner is investigating a complaint under the complaints scheme;

(b) the complaint falls within paragraph 5(3)(a), (b), [(c)] or (d); and

(c) there are reasonable grounds for believing that particular premises are being used in connection with the provision of immigration advice or immigration services by a [registered or exempt person.]

[**(1A)** This paragraph also applies if the Commissioner is investigating a matter under paragraph 5(5) and—

(a) the matter is of a kind described in paragraph 5(3)(a), (b), [(c)] or (d) (for which purpose a reference to an allegation shall be treated as a reference to a suspicion of the Commissioner), and

(b) there are reasonable grounds for believing that particular premises are being used in connection with the provision of immigration advice or immigration services by a [registered or exempt person.]

(2) The Commissioner, or a member of his staff authorised in writing by him, may enter the premises at reasonable hours.

(3) Sub-paragraph (2) does not apply to premises to the extent to which they constitute a private residence.

(4) A person exercising the power given by sub-paragraph (2) ('the investigating officer') may—

(a) take with him such equipment as appears to him to be necessary;

(b) require any person on the premises—

(i) to produce any document which he considers relates to any matter relevant to the investigation; and

(ii) if the document is produced, to provide an explanation of it;

(c) require any person to state, to the best of his knowledge and belief, where any such document is to be found;

(d) take copies of, or extracts from, any document which is produced;

(e) require any information which is held in a computer and is accessible from the premises and which the investigating officer considers relates to any matter relevant to the investigation, to be produced in a form—

(i) in which it can be taken away; and

(ii) in which it is visible and legible.

(5) Instead of exercising the power under sub-paragraph (2), the Commissioner may require such person as he may determine ('his agent') to make a report on the provision of immigration advice or immigration services from the premises.

(6) If the Commissioner so determines, his agent may exercise the power conferred by sub-paragraph (2) as if he were a member of the Commissioner's staff appropriately authorised.

(7) If a registered person fails without reasonable excuse to allow access under sub-paragraph (2) or (6) to any premises under his occupation or control, the Commissioner may cancel his registration.

(8) The Commissioner may also cancel the registration of a registered person who—

(a) without reasonable excuse fails to comply with a requirement imposed on him under sub-paragraph (4);

(b) intentionally delays or obstructs any person exercising functions under this paragraph; or

(c) fails to take reasonable steps to prevent an employee of his from obstructing any person exercising such functions.

[(9) Sub-paragraphs (7) and (8) shall apply to an exempt person as they apply to a registered person, but with a reference to cancellation of registration being treated as a reference to withdrawal of exemption.

(10) In this paragraph 'exempt person' means a person certified by the Commissioner as exempt under section 84(4)(a).]

Note: Words in square brackets in sub-paras (1)(b), (c) and (1A)(a) substituted and sub-paras (9) and (10) inserted by s 38 Asylum and Immigration (Treatment of Claimants) Act 2004 from 1 October 2004 (SI 2004/2523). Paragraph 7(1A) inserted by Nationality, Immigration and Asylum Act 2002, s 140 from 8 January 2003 (SI 2003/1).

Determination of complaints

8.—(1) On determining a complaint under the complaints scheme, the Commissioner must give his decision in a written statement.

(2) The statement must include the Commissioner's reasons for his decision.

(3) A copy of the statement must be given by the Commissioner to—

(a) the person who made the complaint; and

(b) the person who is the subject of the complaint.

9.—(1) On determining a complaint under the complaints scheme, the Commissioner may—

(a) if the person to whom the complaint relates is a registered person [or is acting on behalf of] a registered person, record the complaint and the decision on it for consideration when that registered person next applies for his registration to be continued;

(b) if the person to whom the complaint relates is a registered person [or is acting on behalf of] a registered person and the Commissioner considers the matter sufficiently serious to require immediate action, require that registered person to apply for continued registration without delay;

[(c) refer the complaint and his decision on it to a relevant regulatory body;]

(d) if the person to whom the complaint relates is certified by the Commissioner as exempt under section 84(4)(a) or is employed by, or working under the supervision of, such a person, consider whether to withdraw that person's exemption;

(e) lay before the [First-tier Tribunal] a disciplinary charge against a relevant person.

(2) Sub-paragraph (3) applies if—

(a) the [First-tier Tribunal] is considering a disciplinary charge against a relevant person; and

(b) the Commissioner asks it to exercise its powers under that subparagraph.

(3) The [First-tier Tribunal] may give directions (which are to have effect while it is dealing with the charge)—

[(a) imposing restrictions on the provision of immigration advice or immigration services by the relevant person or by a person acting on his behalf or under his supervision;

(b) prohibiting the provision of immigration advice or immigration services by the relevant person or a person acting on his behalf or under his supervision.]

(4) 'Relevant person' means a person providing immigration advice or immigration services who is—

(a) a registered person;

[(b) a person acting on behalf of a registered person;]

(e) a person certified by the Commissioner as exempt under section 84(4)(a);

(f) a person to whom section 84(4)(d) applies; or

(g) a person employed by, or working under the supervision of, a person to whom paragraph (e) or (f) applies.

Note: Words in first and second square brackets substituted by s 37 Asylum and Immigration (Treatment of Claimants) Act 2004 from 1 October 2004 (SI 2004/2523). Other words in square brackets substituted from 6 April 2010 (SI 2010/22).

Complaints referred to designated professional bodies

10.—**(1)** This paragraph applies if the Commissioner refers a complaint to a designated professional body under paragraph 9(1)(c).

(2) The Commissioner may give directions setting a timetable to be followed by the designated professional body—

(a) in considering the complaint; and

(b) if appropriate, in taking disciplinary proceedings in connection with the complaint.

(3) In making his annual report to the Secretary of State under paragraph 21, the Commissioner must take into account any failure of a designated professional body to comply (whether wholly or in part) with directions given to it under this paragraph.

(4) Sub-paragraph (5) applies if the Commissioner or the Secretary of State considers that a designated professional body has persistently failed to comply with directions given to it under this paragraph.

(5) The Commissioner must take the failure into account in determining whether to make a report under section 86(9)(b) and the Secretary of State must take it into account in determining whether to make an order under section 86(2).

PART II

COMMISSIONER'S STATUS, REMUNERATION AND STAFF ETC

. . .

Section 85(3)   SCHEDULE 6

REGISTRATION

Applications for registration

1.—**(1)** An application for registration under section 84(2)(a) . . . must—

(a) be made to the Commissioner in such form and manner, and

(b) be accompanied by such information and supporting evidence, as the Commissioner may from time to time determine.

(2) When considering an application for registration, the Commissioner may require the applicant to provide him with such further information or supporting evidence as the Commissioner may reasonably require.

Registration

2.—(1) If the Commissioner considers that an applicant for registration is competent and otherwise fit to provide immigration advice and immigration services, he must register the applicant.

(2) Registration may be made so as to have effect—
   (a) only in relation to a specified field of advice or services;
   (b) only in relation to the provision of advice or services to a specified category of person;
   (c) only in relation to the provision of advice or services to a member of a specified category of person; or
   (d) only in specified circumstances.

Review of qualifications

3.—(1) At such intervals as the Commissioner may determine, each registered person must submit an application for his registration to be continued.

(2) Different intervals may be fixed by the Commissioner in relation to different registered persons or descriptions of registered person.

(3) An application for continued registration must—
   (a) be made to the Commissioner in such form and manner, and
   (b) be accompanied by such information and supporting evidence, as the Commissioner may from time to time determine.

(4) When considering an application for continued registration, the Commissioner may require the applicant to provide him with such further information or supporting evidence as the Commissioner may reasonably require.

(5) If the Commissioner considers that an applicant for continued registration is no longer competent or is otherwise unfit to provide immigration advice or immigration services, he must cancel the applicant's registration.

(6) Otherwise, the Commissioner must continue the applicant's registration but may, in doing so, vary the registration—
   (a) so as to make it have limited effect in any of the ways mentioned in paragraph 2(2); or
   (b) so as to make it have full effect.

(7) If a registered person fails, without reasonable excuse—
   (a) to make an application for continued registration as required by subparagraph (1) or by a direction given by the [First-tier Tribunal] under [section 89(2)(b)], or
   (b) to provide further information or evidence under sub-paragraph (4),

the Commissioner may cancel the person's registration as from such date as he may determine.

[Variation of registration

3A. The Commissioner may vary a person's registration—
   (a) so as to make it have limited effect in any of the ways mentioned in paragraph 2(2); or
   (b) so as to make it have full effect.]

Disqualification of certain persons

4. A person convicted of an offence under section 25 or 26(1)(d) or (g) of the 1971 Act is disqualified for registration under paragraph 2 or for continued registration under paragraph 3.

Fees

5.—(1) The Secretary of State may by order specify fees for the registration or continued registration of persons on the register.

(2) No application under paragraph 1 or 3 is to be entertained by the Commissioner unless it is accompanied by the specified fee.

Open registers

6.—(1) The register must be made available for inspection by members of the public in a legible form at reasonable hours.

(2) A copy of the register or of any entry in the register must be provided—

    (a) on payment of a reasonable fee;

    (b) in written or electronic form; and

    (c) in a legible form.

(3) Sub-paragraphs (1) and (2) also apply to—

    (a) the record kept by the Commissioner of the persons to whom he has issued a certificate of exemption under section 84(4)(a); and

    (b) the record kept by the Commissioner of the persons against whom there is in force a direction given by the [First-tier Tribunal] under section 89(8).

Note: Words omitted from sub-para (1), by s 37 Asylum and Immigration (Treatment of Claimants) Act 2004 from 1 October 2004 (SI 2004/2523). Words in second square brackets in sub-para (3)(7) substituted by s 37 Asylum and Immigration (Treatment of Claimants) Act 2004 from 1 October 2004 (SI 2004/2523). Paragraph 3A inserted by Nationality, Immigration and Asylum Act 2002, s 140 from 8 January 2003 (SI 2003/1). Other words in square brackets substituted from 6 April 2010 (SI 2010/22).

Section 87(5)   SCHEDULE 7

Note : Revoked from 6 April 2010 (SI 2010/22).

Section 95(12)   SCHEDULE 8

PROVISION OF SUPPORT: REGULATIONS

. . .

Section 95(13)   SCHEDULE 9

ASYLUM SUPPORT: INTERIM PROVISIONS

. . .

Section 102(3)   SCHEDULE 10

ASYLUM SUPPORT ADJUDICATORS

Note : Revoked from 3 November 2008 (SI 2008/2833) . . .

Section 154(7)   SCHEDULE 11

DETAINEE CUSTODY OFFICERS

. . .

Section 155(2)   SCHEDULE 12
DISCIPLINE ETC. AT [REMOVAL CENTRES]

. . .

Section 156(5)   SCHEDULE 13
ESCORT ARRANGEMENTS

. . .

Section 169(1)   SCHEDULE 14
CONSEQUENTIAL AMENDMENTS

. . .

Section 169(2)   SCHEDULE 15
TRANSITIONAL PROVISIONS AND SAVINGS

Leave to enter or remain

1.—(1) An order made under section 3A of the 1971 Act may make provision with respect to leave given before the commencement of section 1.

(2) An order made under section 3B of the 1971 Act may make provision with respect to leave given before the commencement of section 2.

Section 2 of the Asylum and Immigration Act 1996

2.—(1) This paragraph applies in relation to any time before the commencement of the repeal by this Act of section 2 of the Asylum and Immigration Act 1996.

(2) That section has effect, and is to be deemed always to have had effect, as if the reference to section 6 of the Asylum and Immigration Appeals Act 1993 were a reference to section 15, and any certificate issued under that section is to be read accordingly.

Adjudicators and the Tribunal

3. . . .

References to justices' chief executive

4. . . .

Duties under National Assistance Act 1948

5. . . .

Duties under Health Services and Public Health Act 1968

6. . . .

Duties under Social Work (Scotland) Act 1968

7. . . .

Duties under Health and Personal Social Services (Northern Ireland) Order 1972

8. . . .

Duties under National Health Service Act 1977

9. . . .

Duties under Mental Health (Scotland) Act 1984

10. . . .

Appeals relating to deportation orders

11. Section 15 of the 1971 Act, section 5 of the Immigration Act 1988 and the Immigration (Restricted Right of Appeal against Deportation) (Exemption) Order 1993 are to continue to have effect in relation to any person on whom the Secretary of State has, before the commencement of the repeal of those sections, served a notice of his decision to make a deportation order.

12.—(1) Sub-paragraph (2) applies if, on the coming into force of section 10, sections 15 of the 1971 Act and 5 of the Immigration Act 1988 have been repealed by this Act.

(**2**) Those sections are to continue to have effect in relation to any person—
  (a) who applied during the regularisation period fixed by section 9, in accordance with the regulations made under that section, for leave to remain in the United Kingdom, and
  (b) on whom the Secretary of State has since served a notice of his decision to make a deportation order.

Assistance under Part VII of the Housing Act 1996

13. . . .

Provision of support

14. . . .

Section 169(3)   SCHEDULE 16
                                         REPEALS

. . .

British Overseas Territories Act 2002
(2002, c. 8)

An Act to make provision about the name 'British overseas territories' and British citizenship so far as relating to the British overseas territories. [26 February 2002]

Change of names

1. British overseas territories

(1) As the territories mentioned in Schedule 6 to the British Nationality Act 1981 (c. 61) are now known as 'British overseas territories'—

    (a) ...

    (b) ...

    (c) ...

(2) In any other enactment passed or made before the commencement of this section (including an enactment comprised in subordinate legislation), any reference to a dependent territory within the meaning of the British Nationality Act 1981 shall be read as a reference to a British overseas territory.

(3) ...

Note: Subsection (1)(a)–(c) amends British Nationality Act 1981, sub-s (3) amends Sch 1 Interpretation Act 1978. Commenced 26 February 2002.

2. British overseas territories citizenship

(1) Pursuant to section 1, British Dependent Territories citizenship is renamed 'British overseas territories citizenship'; and a person having that citizenship is a 'British overseas territories citizen'.

(2) ...

(3) In any other enactment passed or made before the commencement of this section (including an enactment comprised in subordinate legislation), any reference to British Dependent Territories citizenship, or a British Dependent Territories citizen, shall be read as a reference to British overseas territories citizenship, or a British overseas territories citizen.

Note: Subsection (2) amends British Nationality Act 1981. Commenced 26 February 2002.

British citizenship

3. Conferral on British overseas territories citizens

(1) Any person who, immediately before the commencement of this section, is a British overseas territories citizen shall, on the commencement of this section, become a British citizen.

(2) Subsection (1) does not apply to a person who is a British overseas territories citizen by virtue only of a connection with the Sovereign Base Areas of Akrotiri and Dhekelia.

(3) A person who is a British citizen by virtue of this section is a British citizen by descent for the purposes of the British Nationality Act 1981 if, and only if—

(a) he was a British overseas territories citizen by descent immediately before the commencement of this section, and

(b) if at that time he was a British citizen as well as a British overseas territories citizen, he was a British citizen by descent.

Note: Commenced 21 May 2002 (SI 2002/1252).

4. Acquisition by British overseas territories citizens by registration

...

Note: Amends British Nationality Act1981, s 4.

5. Acquisition by reference to the British overseas territories

Schedule 1 (which makes provision about the acquisition of British citizenship by reference to the British overseas territories) has effect.

Note: Commenced 21 May 2002 (SI 2002/1252).

Supplementary

6. The Ilois: citizenship

(1) A person shall become a British citizen on the commencement of this section if—

(a) he was born on or after 26 April 1969 and before 1 January 1983,

(b) he was born to a woman who at the time was a citizen of the United Kingdom and Colonies by virtue of her birth in the British Indian Ocean Territory, and

(c) immediately before the commencement of this section he was neither a British citizen nor a British overseas territories citizen.

(2) A person who is a British citizen by virtue of subsection (1) is a British citizen by descent for the purposes of the British Nationality Act 1981 (c. 61).

(3) A person shall become a British overseas territories citizen on the commencement of this section if—

(a) subsection (1)(a) and (b) apply in relation to him, and

(b) immediately before the commencement of this section he was not a British overseas territories citizen.

(4) A person who is a British overseas territories citizen by virtue of subsection (3) is such a citizen by descent for the purposes of the British Nationality Act 1981.

Note: Commenced 21 May 2002 (SI 2002/1252).

7. Repeals

The enactments mentioned in Schedule 2 (which include some which are spent or effectively superseded) are repealed to the extent specified there.

Note: Commenced 26 February 2002, save in relation to the British Nationality (Falkland Islands) Act 1983, where commencement was 21 May 2002 (SI 2002/1252).

8. Short title, commencement and extent

(1) This Act may be cited as the British Overseas Territories Act 2002.

(2) The following provisions of this Act are to come into force on such day as the Secretary of State may by order made by statutory instrument appoint—

    (a) sections 3 to 5 and Schedule 1,

    (b) section 6, and

    (c) section 7 and Schedule 2, so far as relating to the British Nationality (Falkland Islands) Act 1983 (c. 6).

(3) An order under subsection (2) may—

    (a) appoint different days for different purposes, and

    (b) include such transitional provision as the Secretary of State considers expedient.

(4) This Act extends to—

    (a) the United Kingdom,

    (b) the Channel Islands and the Isle of Man, and

    (c) the British overseas territories.

SCHEDULES

SCHEDULE 1
BRITISH CITIZENSHIP AND THE BRITISH OVERSEAS TERRITORIES

Birth or adoption

1. …

Descent

2. …

Registration of minors

3. …

Commonwealth citizens

4. …

Interpretation

5. …

6. …

Note: Amends British Nationality Act 1981, ss 1, 2, 3, 37(1)(a), 50 and 51(3)(a) from 21 May 2002 (SI 2002/1252).

SCHEDULE 2
REPEALS

...

Note: Commencement 26 February 2002.

Nationality, Immigration and Asylum Act 2002
(2002, c. 41)

Arrangement of Sections

Part I. Nationality

Part II. Accommodation Centres

Establishment

Use of centres

Operation of centres

PART V. IMMIGRATION AND ASYLUM APPEALS

Appeal to Tribunal

Exceptions and limitations

PART VI. IMMIGRATION PROCEDURE

Applications

Work permit

Authority-to-carry scheme

Procedure

152.–156. ...

An Act to make provision about nationality, immigration and asylum; to create offences in connection with international traffic in prostitution; to make provision about international projects connected with migration; and for connected purposes. [7 November 2002]

PART I

NATIONALITY

1. Naturalisation: knowledge of language and society

...

Note: Amends British Nationality Act 1981, s 41 and Sch 1.

2. Naturalisation: spouse of citizen

...

Note: Amends Sch 1 British Nationality Act 1981.

3. Citizenship ceremony, oath and pledge

Schedule 1 (which makes provision about citizenship ceremonies, oaths and pledges) shall have effect.

Note: Commencement 1 January 2004 (SI 2003/3516).

4. Deprivation of citizenship

(1) . . .

> **Note:** Amends British Nationality Act 1981, s 40.

(2) . . .

> **Note:** Amends Special Immigration Appeals Commission Act 1997, s 2.

(3) . . .

> **Note:** Amends Special Immigration Appeals Commission Act 1997, s 5.

(4) In exercising a power under section 40 of the British Nationality Act 1981 after the commencement of subsection (1) above the Secretary of State may have regard to anything which—

(a) occurred before commencement, and

(b) he could have relied on (whether on its own or with other matters) in making an order under section 40 before commencement.

Note: Commencement from 1 April 2003 (SI 2003/754).

5. Resumption of citizenship

. . .

> **Note:** Amends British Nationality Act 1981, ss 10, 22.

6. Nationality decision: discrimination

. . .

> **Note:** Amends Race Relations Act 1976, ss 19 and 71. Subsections (1)–(4) omitted from 4 April 2011 (SI 2011/1060).

7. Nationality decision: reasons and review

(1) . . .

> **Note:** Amends British Nationality Act 1981, s 44.

(2) . . .

> **Note:** Amends British Nationality (Hong Kong) Act 1990, s 1.

8. Citizenship: registration

. . .

> **Note:** Amends para 3, Sch 2 British Nationality Act 1981.

9. Legitimacy of child

(1) ...

Note: Amends British Nationality Act 1981, s 50(9).

(2) ...

Note: Amends British Nationality Act 1981, s 3(6).

(3) ...

Note: Amends British Nationality Act 1981, s 17(6).

(4) ...

Note: Amends British Nationality Act 1981, s 47.

(5) ...

Note: Amends paras 1, 2, Sch 2 British Nationality Act 1981.

10. Right of abode: certificate of entitlement

(1) The Secretary of State may by regulations make provision for the issue to a person of a certificate that he has the right of abode in the United Kingdom.

(2) The regulations may, in particular—

(a) specify to whom an application must be made;

(b) specify the place (which may be outside the United Kingdom) to which an application must be sent;

(c) provide that an application must be [accompanied by specified information;]

(d) provide that an application must be accompanied by specified documents;

(e) ...

(f) specify the consequences of failure to comply with a requirement under any of paragraphs [(a) to (d)] above;

(g) provide for a certificate to cease to have effect after a period of time specified in or determined in accordance with the regulations;

(h) make provision about the revocation of a certificate.

(3) The regulations may—

(a) make provision which applies generally or only in specified cases or circumstances;

(b) make different provision for different purposes;

(c) include consequential, incidental or transitional provision.

(4) The regulations—

(a) must be made by statutory instrument, and

(b) shall be subject to annulment in pursuance of a resolution of either House of Parliament.

(5) ...

(6) Regulations under this section may, in particular, include provision saving, with or without modification, the effect of a certificate which—

(a) is issued before the regulations come into force, and

(b) is a certificate of entitlement for the purposes of sections 3(9) and 33(1) of the Immigration Act 1971 as those sections have effect before the commencement of subsection (5) above.

Note: Subsection (5) amends Immigration Act 1971, ss 3, 33. Subsections (1)–(4) and (6) commenced on 7 November 2002, s 162. Subsection (2)(e) deleted by Immigration, Asylum and Nationality Act 2006, s 52 and Sch 2 from 2 April 2007 (SI 2007/182). Words in square brackets in sub-s (2) substituted by Immigration, Asylum and Nationality Act 2006, s 50 from 5 November 2007 (SI 2007/3138).

11. Unlawful presence in United Kingdom

. . .

Note: Commenced 7 November 2002, s 162. Revoked by s 48 Borders, Citizenship and Immigration Act 2009 from 13 January 2010 (SI 2009/2731), with transitional provisions.

12. British citizenship: registration of certain persons without other citizenship

Note: Amends British Nationality Act 1981, ss 4, 14.

13. British citizenship: registration of certain persons born between 1961 and 1983

Note: Amends British Nationality Act 1981, ss 4, 14.

14. Hong Kong

A person may not be registered as a British overseas territories citizen under a provision of the British Nationality Act 1981 (c. 61) by virtue of a connection with Hong Kong.

Note: Commencement from 1 January 2004 (SI 2003/3156).

15. Repeal of spent provisions

Schedule 2 (which repeals spent provisions) shall have effect.

Note: Commencement 7 November 2002, s 162.

PART II
ACCOMMODATION CENTRES
Establishment

16. Establishment of centres

(1) The Secretary of State may arrange for the provision of premises for the accommodation of persons in accordance with this Part.

(2) A set of premises provided under this section is referred to in this Act as an 'accommodation centre'.

(3) The Secretary of State may arrange for—

(a) the provision of facilities at or near an accommodation centre for sittings of adjudicators appointed for the purpose of Part 5 in accordance with a determination . . . under paragraph 2 of Schedule 4;

(b) the provision of facilities at an accommodation centre for the taking of steps in connection with the determination of claims for asylum (within the meaning of section 18(3)).

Note: Commencement 7 November 2002, s 162. Words deleted by Sch 18 Constitutional Reform Act 2005 from 3 April 2006 (SI 2006/1014).

Use of centres

17. Support for destitute asylum-seeker

(1) The Secretary of State may arrange for the provision of accommodation for a person in an accommodation centre if—

(a) the person is an asylum-seeker or the dependant of an asylum-seeker, and

(b) the Secretary of State thinks that the person is destitute or is likely to become destitute within a prescribed period.

(2) The Secretary of State may make regulations about procedure to be followed in respect of the provision of accommodation under this section.

(3) The regulations may, in particular, make provision—

(a) specifying procedure to be followed in applying for accommodation in an accommodation centre;

(b) providing for an application to be combined with an application under or in respect of another enactment;

(c) requiring an applicant to provide information;

(d) specifying circumstances in which an application may not be considered (which provision may, in particular, provide for an application not to be considered where the Secretary of State is not satisfied that the information provided is complete or accurate or that the applicant is co-operating with enquiries under paragraph (e));

(e) about the making of enquiries by the Secretary of State;

(f) requiring a person to notify the Secretary of State of a change in circumstances.

(4) Sections 18 to 20 define the following expressions for the purpose of this Part—

(a) asylum-seeker,

(b) dependant, and

(c) destitute.

Note: Commencement from a date to be appointed.

18. Asylum-seeker: definition

(1) For the purposes of this Part a person is an 'asylum-seeker' if—

(a) he is at least 18 years old,

(b) he is in the United Kingdom,

(c) a claim for asylum has been made by him at a place designated by the Secretary of State,

(d) the Secretary of State has recorded the claim, and

(e) the claim has not been determined.

(2) A person shall continue to be treated as an asylum-seeker despite subsection (1)(e) while—

(a) his household includes a dependent child who is under 18, and

(b) he does not have leave to enter or remain in the United Kingdom.

(3) A claim for asylum is a claim by a person that to remove him from or require him to leave the United Kingdom would be contrary to the United Kingdom's obligations under—

(a) the Convention relating to the Status of Refugees done at Geneva on 28 July 1951 and its Protocol, or

(b) Article 3 of the Convention for the Protection of Human Rights and Fundamental Freedoms agreed by the Council of Europe at Rome on 4 November 1950.

Note: Commenced for the purposes of ss 55(9), 70(3) and para 17(1)(b) of Sch 3 on 8 January 2003 (SI 2003/1). For the purposes of Immigration Act 1971, s 26A(2) and this Act, s 71(5), 10 February 2003 (SI 2003/01).

19. Destitution: definition

(1) Where a person has dependants, he and his dependants are destitute for the purpose of this Part if they do not have and cannot obtain both—

(a) adequate accommodation, and

(b) food and other essential items.

(2) Where a person does not have dependants, he is destitute for the purpose of this Part if he does not have and cannot obtain both—

(a) adequate accommodation, and

(b) food and other essential items.

(3) In determining whether accommodation is adequate for the purposes of subsection (1) or (2) the Secretary of State must have regard to any matter prescribed for the purposes of this subsection.

(4) In determining whether accommodation is adequate for the purposes of subsection (1) or (2) the Secretary of State may not have regard to—

(a) whether a person has an enforceable right to occupy accommodation,

(b) whether a person shares all or part of accommodation,

(c) whether accommodation is temporary or permanent,

(d) the location of accommodation, or

(e) any other matter prescribed for the purposes of this subsection.

(5) The Secretary of State may by regulations specify items which are or are not to be treated as essential items for the purposes of subsections (1) and (2).

(6) The Secretary of State may by regulations—

(a) provide that a person is not to be treated as destitute for the purposes of this Part in specified circumstances;

(b) enable or require the Secretary of State in deciding whether a person is destitute to have regard to income which he or a dependant of his might reasonably be expected to have;

(c) enable or require the Secretary of State in deciding whether a person is destitute to have regard to support which is or might reasonably be expected to be available to the person or a dependant of his;

(d) enable or require the Secretary of State in deciding whether a person is destitute to have regard to assets of a prescribed kind which he or a dependant of his has or might reasonably be expected to have;

(e) make provision as to the valuation of assets.

Note: Commencement at a date to be appointed.

20. Dependant: definition

For the purposes of this Part a person is a 'dependant' of an asylum-seeker if (and only if) that person—

(a) is in the United Kingdom, and

(b) is within a prescribed class.

Note: Commencement at a date to be appointed.

21. Sections 17 to 20: supplementary

(1) This section applies for the purposes of sections 17 to 20.

(2) The Secretary of State may inquire into and decide a person's age.

(3) A claim for asylum shall be treated as determined at the end of such period as may be prescribed beginning with—

(a) the date on which the Secretary of State notifies the claimant of his decision on the claim, or

(b) if the claimant appeals against the Secretary of State's decision, the date on which the appeal is disposed of.

(4) A notice under subsection (3)(a)—

(a) must be in writing, and

(b) if sent by first class post to the claimant's last known address or to the claimant's representative, shall be treated as being received by the claimant on the second day after the day of posting.

(5) An appeal is disposed of when it is no longer pending for the purpose of—

(a) Part 5 of this Act, or

(b) the Special Immigration Appeals Commission Act 1997 (c. 68).

Note: Commencement at a date to be appointed.

22. Immigration and Asylum Act 1999, s 95

The Secretary of State may provide support under section 95 of the Immigration and Asylum Act 1999 (c. 33) (destitute asylum-seeker) by arranging for the provision of accommodation in an accommodation centre.

Note: Commencement at a date to be appointed.

23. Person subject to United Kingdom entrance control

(1) A residence restriction may include a requirement to reside at an accommodation centre.

(2) In subsection (1) 'residence restriction' means a restriction imposed under—

(a) paragraph 21 of Schedule 2 to the Immigration Act 1971 (c. 77) (temporary admission or release from detention), or

(b) paragraph 2(5) of Schedule 3 to that Act (control pending deportation).

(3) Where a person is required to reside in an accommodation centre by virtue of subsection (1) the Secretary of State must arrange for the provision of accommodation for the person in an accommodation centre.

(4) But if the person is required to leave an accommodation centre by virtue of section 26 or 30 he shall be treated as having broken the residence restriction referred to in subsection (1).

(5) The Secretary of State may provide support under section 4 of the Immigration and Asylum Act 1999 (persons subject to entrance control) (including that section as amended by section 49 of this Act) by arranging for the provision of accommodation in an accommodation centre.

Note: Commencement at a date to be appointed.

24. Provisional assistance

(1) If the Secretary of State thinks that a person may be eligible for the provision of accommodation in an accommodation centre under section 17, he may arrange for the provision for the person, pending a decision about eligibility, of—

    (a) accommodation in an accommodation centre, or

    (b) other support or assistance (of any kind).

(2) Section 99 of the Immigration and Asylum Act 1999 (c. 33) (provision of support by local authority) shall have effect in relation to the provision of support for persons under subsection (1) above as it has effect in relation to the provision of support for asylum-seekers under sections 95 and 98 of that Act.

Note: Commencement at a date to be appointed.

25. Length of stay

(1) The Secretary of State may not arrange for the provision of accommodation for a person in an accommodation centre if he has been a resident of an accommodation centre for a continuous period of six months.

(2) But—

    (a) subsection (1) may be disapplied in respect of a person, generally or to a specified extent, by agreement between the Secretary of State and the person, and

    (b) if the Secretary of State thinks it appropriate in relation to a person because of the circumstances of his case, the Secretary of State may direct that subsection (1) shall have effect in relation to the person as if the period specified in that subsection were the period of nine months.

(3) Section 51 is subject to this section.

(4) The Secretary of State may by order amend subsection (1) or (2)(b) so as to substitute a shorter period for a period specified.

Note: Commencement at a date to be appointed.

26. Withdrawal of support

(1) The Secretary of State may stop providing support for a person under section 17 or 24 if—

    (a) the Secretary of State suspects that the person or a dependant of his has committed an offence by virtue of section 35, or

(b) the person or a dependant of his has failed to comply with directions of the Secretary of State as to the time or manner of travel to accommodation provided under section 17 or 24.

(2) The Secretary of State may by regulations specify other circumstances in which he may stop providing support for a person under section 17 or 24.

(3) In determining whether or not to provide a person with support or assistance under section 17 or 24 of this Act or section 4, 95 or 98 of the Immigration and Asylum Act 1999 (asylum-seeker) the Secretary of State may take into account the fact that—

(a) he has withdrawn support from the person by virtue of this section or section 30(4) or (5), or

(b) circumstances exist which would have enabled the Secretary of State to withdraw support from the person by virtue of this section had he been receiving support.

(4) This section is without prejudice to section 103 of the Immigration and Asylum Act 1999 (c. 33) (appeal against refusal to support).

Note: Commencement at a date to be appointed.

Operation of centres

27. Resident of centre

A reference in this Part to a resident of an accommodation centre is a reference to a person for whom accommodation in the centre is provided—

(a) under section 17,

(b) by virtue of section 22,

(c) by virtue of section 23, or

(d) under section 24.

Note: Commencement at a date to be appointed.

28. Manager of centre

A reference in this Part to the manager of an accommodation centre is a reference to a person who agrees with the Secretary of State to be wholly or partly responsible for the management of the centre.

Note: Commencement at a date to be appointed.

29. Facilities

(1) The Secretary of State may arrange for the following to be provided to a resident of an accommodation centre—

(a) food and other essential items;

(b) money;

(c) assistance with transport for the purpose of proceedings under the Immigration Acts or in connection with a claim for asylum;

(d) transport to and from the centre;

(e) assistance with expenses incurred in connection with carrying out voluntary work or other activities;

(f) education and training;

    (g) facilities relating to health;

    (h) facilities for religious observance;

    (i) anything which the Secretary of State thinks ought to be provided for the purpose of providing a resident with proper occupation and for the purpose of maintaining good order;

    (j) anything which the Secretary of State thinks ought to be provided for a person because of his exceptional circumstances.

(2) The Secretary of State may make regulations specifying the amount or maximum amount of money to be provided under subsection (1)(b).

(3) The Secretary of State may arrange for the provision of facilities in an accommodation centre for the use of a person in providing legal advice to a resident of the centre.

(4) The Secretary of State shall take reasonable steps to ensure that a resident of an accommodation centre has an opportunity to obtain legal advice before any appointment made by an immigration officer or an official of the Secretary of State for the purpose of obtaining information from the resident to be used in determining his claim for asylum.

(5) The Secretary of State may by order amend subsection (1) so as to add a reference to facilities which may be provided.

Note: Commencement at a date to be appointed.

30. Conditions of residence

(1) The Secretary of State may make regulations about conditions to be observed by residents of an accommodation centre.

(2) Regulations under subsection (1) may, in particular, enable a condition to be imposed in accordance with the regulations by—

    (a) the Secretary of State, or

    (b) the manager of an accommodation centre.

(3) A condition imposed by virtue of this section may, in particular—

    (a) require a person not to be absent from the centre during specified hours without the permission of the Secretary of State or the manager;

    (b) require a person to report to an immigration officer or the Secretary of State.

(4) If a resident of an accommodation centre breaches a condition imposed by virtue of this section, the Secretary of State may—

    (a) require the resident and any dependant of his to leave the centre;

    (b) authorise the manager of the centre to require the resident and any dependant of his to leave the centre.

(5) If a dependant of a resident of an accommodation centre breaches a condition imposed by virtue of this section, the Secretary of State may—

    (a) require the resident and any dependant of his to leave the centre;

    (b) authorise the manager of the centre to require the resident and any dependant of his to leave the centre.

(6) Regulations under this section must include provision for ensuring that a person subject to a condition is notified of the condition in writing.

(7) A condition imposed by virtue of this section is in addition to any restriction imposed under paragraph 21 of Schedule 2 to the Immigration Act 1971 (c. 77) (control of entry to United Kingdom) or under paragraph 2(5) of Schedule 3 to that Act (control pending deportation).

(8) A reference in this Part to a condition of residence is a reference to a condition imposed by virtue of this section.

Note: Commencement at a date to be appointed.

31. Financial contribution by resident

(1) A condition of residence may, in particular, require a resident of an accommodation centre to make payments to—

(a) the Secretary of State, or

(b) the manager of the centre.

(2) The Secretary of State may make regulations enabling him to recover sums representing the whole or part of the value of accommodation and other facilities provided to a resident of an accommodation centre if—

(a) accommodation is provided for the resident in response to an application by him for support,

(b) when the application was made the applicant had assets which were not capable of being realised, and

(c) the assets have become realisable.

(3) In subsection (2) 'assets' includes assets outside the United Kingdom.

(4) An amount recoverable by virtue of regulations made under subsection (2) may be recovered—

(a) as a debt due to the Secretary of State;

(b) by another prescribed method (which may include the imposition or variation of a residence condition).

Note: Commencement at a date to be appointed.

32. Tenure

(1) A resident of an accommodation centre shall not be treated as acquiring a tenancy of or other interest in any part of the centre (whether by virtue of an agreement between the resident and another person or otherwise).

(2) Subsection (3) applies where—

(a) the Secretary of State decides to stop arranging for the provision of accommodation in an accommodation centre for a resident of the centre, or

(b) a resident of an accommodation centre is required to leave the centre in accordance with section 30.

(3) Where this subsection applies—

(a) the Secretary of State or the manager of the centre may recover possession of the premises occupied by the resident, and

(b) the right under paragraph (a) shall be enforceable in accordance with procedure prescribed by regulations made by the Secretary of State.

(4) Any licence which a resident of an accommodation centre has to occupy premises in the centre shall be an excluded licence for the purposes of the Protection from Eviction Act 1977 (c. 43).

(5) . . .

(6) . . .

(7) In this section a reference to an accommodation centre includes a reference to premises in which accommodation is provided under section 24(1)(b).

Note: Subsection (5) amends Protection from Eviction Act 1977, s 3A(7A), sub-s (6) amends Rent (Scotland) Act 1984, s 23A(5A). Commencement at a date to be appointed.

33. Advisory Groups

(1) The Secretary of State shall appoint a group (to be known as an Accommodation Centre Advisory Group) for each accommodation centre.

(2) The Secretary of State may by regulations—
(a) confer functions on Advisory Groups;
(b) make provision about the constitution and proceedings of Advisory Groups.

(3) Regulations under subsection (2)(a) must, in particular, provide for members of an accommodation centre's Advisory Group—
(a) to visit the centre;
(b) to hear complaints made by residents of the centre;
(c) to report to the Secretary of State.

(4) The manager of an accommodation centre must permit a member of the centre's Advisory Group on request—
(a) to visit the centre at any time;
(b) to visit any resident of the centre at any time, provided that the resident consents.

(5) A member of an Advisory Group shall hold and vacate office in accordance with the terms of his appointment (which may include provision about retirement, resignation or dismissal).

(6) The Secretary of State may—
(a) defray expenses of members of an Advisory Group;
(b) make facilities available to members of an Advisory Group.

Note: Commencement at a date to be appointed.

General

34. . . .

Note: Section 34 deleted by UK Borders Act 2007 s 54 from 1 April 2008 (SI 2008/309).

35. Ancillary provisions

(1) The following provisions of the Immigration and Asylum Act 1999 (c. 33) shall apply for the purposes of this Part as they apply for the purposes of Part VI of that Act (support for asylum-seeker)—
(a) section 105 (false representation),
(b) section 106 (dishonest representation),
(c) section 107 (delay or obstruction),
(d) section 108 (failure of sponsor to maintain),

    (e) section 109 (offence committed by body),

    (f) section 112 (recovery of expenditure),

    (g) section 113 (recovery of expenditure from sponsor),

    (h) section 124 (corporation sole), and

    (i) section 127 (redirection of post).

(2) In the application of section 112 a reference to something done under section 95 or 98 of that Act shall be treated as a reference to something done under section 17 or 24 of this Act.

(3) In the application of section 113 a reference to section 95 of that Act shall be treated as a reference to section 17 of this Act.

Note: Subsection (1)(h) commenced on 7 November 2002, s 162. Remainder to commence on a date to be appointed.

36. Education: general

(1) For the purposes of section 13 of the Education Act 1996 (c. 56) (general responsibility of [local authority]) a resident of an accommodation centre shall not be treated as part of the population of a [local authority's] area.

(2) A child who is a resident of an accommodation centre may not be admitted to a maintained school or a maintained nursery (subject to section 37).

(3) But subsection (2) does not prevent a child's admission to a school which is—

    (a) a community special school or a foundation special school, and

    (b) named in a statement in respect of the child under section 324 of the Education Act 1996 (c. 56) (special educational needs).

(4) In subsections (2) and (3)—

    (a) 'maintained school' means a maintained school within the meaning of section 20(7) of the School Standards and Framework Act 1998 (c. 31) (definition), and

    (b) 'maintained nursery' means a facility for nursery education, within the meaning of section 117 of that Act, provided by a [local authority].

(5) The following shall not apply in relation to a child who is a resident of an accommodation centre (subject to section 37)—

    (a) section 86(1) and (2) of the School Standards and Framework Act 1998 (parental preference),

    (b) section 94 of that Act (appeal),

    (c) section 19 of the Education Act 1996 (education out of school),

    (d) section 316(2) and (3) of that Act (child with special educational needs to be educated in mainstream school), and

    (e) paragraphs 3 and 8 of Schedule 27 to that Act (special education needs: making of statement: parental preference).

(6) The power of the [First-tier Tribunal or the Special Educational Needs Tribunal for Wales] under section 326(3) of the Education Act 1996 (appeal against content of statement) is subject to subsection (2) above.

(7) A person exercising a function under this Act or the Education Act 1996 shall (subject to section 37) secure that a child who is a resident of an accommodation centre and who has special educational needs shall be educated by way of facilities provided under section 29(1)(f) of this Act unless that is incompatible with—

(a) his receiving the special educational provision which his learning difficulty calls for,

(b) the provision of efficient education for other children who are residents of the centre, or

(c) the efficient use of resources.

(8) A person may rely on subsection (7)(b) only where there is no action—

(a) which could reasonably be taken by that person or by another person who exercises functions, or could exercise functions, in respect of the accommodation centre concerned, and

(b) as a result of which subsection (7)(b) would not apply.

(9) An accommodation centre is not a school within the meaning of section 4 of the Education Act 1996 (definition); but—

(a) [Part 1 of the Education Act 2005 (school inspections)] shall apply to educational facilities provided at an accommodation centre as if the centre were a school (for which purpose a reference to the appropriate authority shall be taken as a reference to the person (or persons) responsible for the provision of education at the accommodation centre),

(b) section 329A of the Education Act 1996 (review or assessment of educational needs at request of responsible body) shall have effect as if—

(i) an accommodation centre were a relevant school for the purposes of that section,

(ii) a child for whom education is provided at an accommodation centre under section 29(1)(f) were a registered pupil at the centre, and

(iii) a reference in section 329A to the responsible body in relation to an accommodation centre were a reference to any person providing education at the centre under section 29(1)(f), and

(c) section 140 of the Learning and Skills Act 2000 (c. 21) (learning difficulties: assessment of post-16 needs) shall have effect as if an accommodation centre were a school.

(10) Subsections (1), (2) and (5) shall not apply in relation to an accommodation centre if education is not provided for children who are residents of the centre under section 29(1)(f).

(11) An expression used in this section and in the Education Act 1996 (c. 56) shall have the same meaning in this section as in that Act.

Note: Commencement at a date to be appointed. Words in square brackets in sub-s (9) substituted by Education Act 2005, s 61 and Sch 9 from 1 September 2005 (SI 2005/2034) and from 1 September 2006 (W) (SI 2006/1338). Words in square brackets in sub-s (6) substituted from 3 November 2008 (SI 2008/2833). Term 'local authority' substituted from 5 April 2010 (SI 2010/1158).

37. Education: special cases

(1) This section applies to a child if a person who provides education to residents of an accommodation centre recommends in writing to the [local authority] for the area in which the centre is that this section should apply to the child on the grounds that his special circumstances call for provision that can only or best be arranged by the authority.

(2) A [local authority] may—

(a) arrange for the provision of education for a child to whom this section applies;

(b) disapply a provision of section 36 in respect of a child to whom this section applies.

(3) In determining whether to exercise a power under subsection (2) in respect of a child a [local authority] shall have regard to any relevant guidance issued by the Secretary of State.

(4) The governing body of a maintained school shall comply with a requirement of the [local authority] to admit to the school a child to whom this section applies.

(5) Subsection (4) shall not apply where compliance with a requirement would prejudice measures taken for the purpose of complying with a duty arising under section 1(6) of the School Standards and Framework Act 1998 (c. 31) (limit on infant class size).

(6) A [local authority] may not impose a requirement under subsection (4) in respect of a school unless the authority has consulted the school in accordance with regulations made by the Secretary of State.

(7) In the case of a maintained school for which the [local authority] are the admission authority, the authority may not arrange for the admission of a child to whom this section applies unless the authority has notified the school in accordance with regulations made by the Secretary of State.

(8) In this section—

(a) 'maintained school' means a maintained school within the meaning of section 20(7) of the School Standards and Framework Act 1998 (definition), and

(b) an expression which is also used in the Education Act 1996 (c. 56) shall have the same meaning as it has in that Act.

Note: Commencement at a date to be appointed. Term 'local authority' substituted from 5 April 2010 (SI 2010/1158).

38. Local authority

(1) A local authority may in accordance with arrangements made by the Secretary of State—

(a) assist in arranging for the provision of an accommodation centre;
(b) make premises available for an accommodation centre;
(c) provide services in connection with an accommodation centre.

(2) In particular, a local authority may—

(a) incur reasonable expenditure;
(b) provide services outside its area;
(c) provide services jointly with another body;
(d) form a company;
(e) tender for or enter into a contract;
(f) do anything (including anything listed in paragraphs (a) to (e)) for a preparatory purpose.

(3) In this section 'local authority' means—

(a) a local authority within the meaning of section 94 of the Immigration and Asylum Act 1999 (c. 33), and

(b) a Northern Ireland authority within the meaning of section 110 of that Act and an Education and Library Board established under Article 3 of the Education and Libraries (Northern Ireland) Order 1986 (SI 1986/594 (N.I. 3)).

Note: Commenced 7 November 2002, s 162.

39. 'Prescribed': orders and regulations

(1) In this Part 'prescribed' means prescribed by the Secretary of State by order or regulations.

(2) An order or regulations under this Part may—

(a) make provision which applies generally or only in specified cases or circumstances (which may be determined wholly or partly by reference to location);

(b) make different provision for different cases or circumstances;

(c) include consequential, transitional or incidental provision.

(3) An order or regulations under this Part must be made by statutory instrument.

(4) An order or regulations under any of the following provisions of this Part shall be subject to annulment in pursuance of a resolution of either House of Parliament—

(a) section 17,

(b) section 19,

(c) section 20,

(d) section 21,

(e) section 26,

(f) section 29,

(g) section 31,

(h) section 32,

(i) section 33,

(j) section 37,

(k) section 40, and

(l) section 41.

(5) An order under section 25 or regulations under section 30 may not be made unless a draft has been laid before and approved by resolution of each House of Parliament.

Note: Commencement at a date to be appointed.

40. Scotland

(1) The Secretary of State may not make arrangements under section 16 for the provision of premises in Scotland unless he has consulted the Scottish Ministers.

(2) The Secretary of State may by order make provision in relation to the education of residents of accommodation centres in Scotland.

(3) An order under subsection (2) may, in particular—

(a) apply, disapply or modify the effect of an enactment (which may include a provision made by or under an Act of the Scottish Parliament);

(b) make provision having an effect similar to the effect of a provision of section 36 or 37.

Note: Subsection (1) commenced on 7 November 2002, s 162. Remainder at a date to be appointed.

41. Northern Ireland

(1) The Secretary of State may not make arrangements under section 16 for the provision of premises in Northern Ireland unless he has consulted the First Minister and the deputy First Minister.

(2) The Secretary of State may by order make provision in relation to the education of residents of accommodation centres in Northern Ireland.

(3) An order under subsection (2) may, in particular—

(a) apply, disapply or modify the effect of an enactment (which may include a provision made by or under Northern Ireland legislation);

(b) make provision having an effect similar to the effect of a provision of section 36 or 37.

Note: Subsection (1) commenced on 7 November 2002, s 162. Remainder at a date to be appointed.

42. Wales

The Secretary of State may not make arrangements under section 16 for the provision of premises in Wales unless he has consulted the National Assembly for Wales.

Note: Commenced 7 November 2002, s 162.

PART III
OTHER SUPPORT AND ASSISTANCE

43. Asylum-seeker: form of support

(1) The Secretary of State may make an order restricting the application of section 96(1)(b) of the Immigration and Asylum Act 1999 (c. 33) (support for asylum-seeker: essential living needs)—

(a) in all circumstances, to cases in which support is being provided under section 96(1)(a) (accommodation), or

(b) in specified circumstances only, to cases in which support is being provided under section 96(1)(a).

(2) An order under subsection (1)(b) may, in particular, make provision by reference to—

(a) location;

(b) the date of an application.

(3) An order under subsection (1) may include transitional provision.

(4) An order under subsection (1)—

(a) must be made by statutory instrument, and

(b) may not be made unless a draft has been laid before and approved by resolution of each House of Parliament.

Note: Commenced 7 November 2002, s 162.

44. Destitute asylum-seeker

Note: Amends Immigration and Asylum Act 1999, ss 94, 95 (c. 33).

45. Section 44: supplemental

(1) . . .

Note: Amends Immigration and Asylum Act 1999, s 96.

(2) ...

Note: Amends Immigration and Asylum Act 1999, s 97.

(3) ...

Note: Amends Immigration and Asylum Act 1999, Sch 8, paras 2, 6.

(4) ...

Note: Amends para 3, Sch 9 Immigration and Asylum Act 1999.

(5) ...

Note: Amends National Assistance Act 1948, s 21(1B) (c. 29).

(6) ...

Note: Amends Health Services and Public Health Act 1968, s 45(4B).

(7) ...

Note: Amends para 2(2B), Sch 8 National Health Service Act 1977.

46. Section 44: supplemental: Scotland and Northern Ireland

(1–3) ...

Note: Amends the Social Work (Scotland) Act 1968.

(4–5) ...

Note: Amends the Mental Health (Scotland) Act 1984.

(6–7) ...

Note: Amends the Health and Personal Social Services (Northern Ireland) Order 1972 (SI 1972/1265 (NI 14)).

47. Asylum-seeker: family with children

Note: Amends Immigration and Asylum Act 1999, s 122.

48. Young asylum-seeker

The following provisions of the Immigration and Asylum Act 1999 (c. 33) shall have effect as if the definition of asylum-seeker in section 94(1) of that Act did not exclude persons who are under 18—

(a) section 110 (local authority expenditure on asylum-seekers), and

(b) section 111 (grants to voluntary organisations).

Note: Commenced on 7 November 2002, s 162.

49. Failed asylum-seeker

Note: Amends Immigration and Asylum Act 1999, s 4.

50. Conditions of support

Note: Amends Immigration and Asylum Act 1999, s 95 and Sch 9.

51. Choice of form of support

(1) The Secretary of State may refuse to provide support for a person under a provision specified in subsection (2) on the grounds that an offer has been made to the person of support under another provision specified in that subsection.

(2) The provisions are—

(a) sections 17 and 24 of this Act,

(b) section 4 of the Immigration and Asylum Act 1999 (accommodation for person temporarily admitted or released from detention), and

(c) sections 95 and 98 of that Act (support for destitute asylum-seeker).

(3) In deciding under which of the provisions listed in subsection (2) to offer support to a person the Secretary of State may—

(a) have regard to administrative or other matters which do not concern the person's personal circumstances;

(b) regard one of those matters as conclusive;

(c) apply different criteria to different persons for administrative reasons (which may include the importance of testing the operation of a particular provision).

Note: Commencement at a date to be appointed.

52. Back-dating of benefit for refugee

Note: Amends Immigration and Asylum Act 1999, s 123.

53. Asylum-seeker: appeal against refusal to support

Note: Amends Immigration and Asylum Act 1999, s 103.

54. Withholding and withdrawal of support

Schedule 3 (which makes provision for support to be withheld or withdrawn in certain circumstances) shall have effect.

Note: Commenced for the purpose of making subordinate legislation 8 December 2002. Remainder commenced 8 January 2003 (SI 2002/2811).

55. Late claim for asylum: refusal of support

(1) The Secretary of State may not provide or arrange for the provision of support to a person under a provision mentioned in subsection (2) if—

(a) the person makes a claim for asylum which is recorded by the Secretary of State, and

(b) the Secretary of State is not satisfied that the claim was made as soon as reasonably practicable after the person's arrival in the United Kingdom.

(2) The provisions are—

(a) sections 4, 95 and 98 of the Immigration and Asylum Act 1999 (c. 33) (support for asylum-seeker, &c.), and

(b) sections 17 and 24 of this Act (accommodation centre).

(3) An authority may not provide or arrange for the provision of support to a person under a provision mentioned in subsection (4) if—

(a) the person has made a claim for asylum, and

(b) the Secretary of State is not satisfied that the claim was made as soon as reasonably practicable after the person's arrival in the United Kingdom.

(4) The provisions are—

(a) section 29(1)(b) of the Housing (Scotland) Act 1987 (c. 26) (accommodation pending review),

(b) section 188(3) or 204(4) of the Housing Act 1996 (c. 52) (accommodation pending review or appeal), and

(c) section 2 of the Local Government Act 2000 (c. 22) (promotion of well-being) [and.

[(d) section 1 of the Localism Act 2011 (local authority's general power of competence)].

(5) This section shall not prevent—

(a) the exercise of a power by the Secretary of State to the extent necessary for the purpose of avoiding a breach of a person's Convention rights (within the meaning of the Human Rights Act 1998 (c. 42)),

(b) the provision of support under section 95 of the Immigration and Asylum Act 1999 (c. 33) or section 17 of this Act in accordance with section 122 of that Act (children), or

(c) the provision of support under section 98 of the Immigration and Asylum Act 1999 or section 24 of this Act (provisional support) to a person under the age of 18 and the household of which he forms part.

(6) An authority which proposes to provide or arrange for the provision of support to a person under a provision mentioned in subsection (4)—

(a) must inform the Secretary of State if the authority believes that the person has made a claim for asylum,

(b) must act in accordance with any guidance issued by the Secretary of State to determine whether subsection (3) applies, and

(c) shall not be prohibited from providing or arranging for the provision of support if the authority has complied with paragraph (a) and (b) and concluded that subsection (3) does not apply.

(7) The Secretary of State may by order—

(a) add, remove or amend an entry in the list in subsection (4);

(b) provide for subsection (3) not to have effect in specified cases or circumstances.

(8) An order under subsection (7)—

(a) may include transitional, consequential or incidental provision,

(b) must be made by statutory instrument, and

(c) may not be made unless a draft has been laid before and approved by resolution of each House of Parliament.

(9) For the purposes of this section 'claim for asylum' has the same meaning as in section 18.

(10) A decision of the Secretary of State that this section prevents him from providing or arranging for the provision of support to a person is not a decision that the person does not qualify for support for the purpose of section 103 of the Immigration and Asylum Act 1999 (appeals).

(11) This section does not prevent a person's compliance with a residence restriction imposed in reliance on section 70 (induction).

Note: Commenced 8 January 2003 (SI 2002/2811). Sub-s (4)(d) inserted from 28 March 2012 (SI 2012/961).

56. Provision of support by local authority

. . .

Note: Amends Immigration and Asylum Act 1999, s 99.

57. Application for support: false or incomplete information

. . .

Note: Amends para 12, Sch 8 Immigration and Asylum Act 1999.

58. Voluntary departure from United Kingdom

(1) A person is a 'voluntary leaver' for the purposes of this section if—

(a) he is not a British citizen or an EEA national,

(b) he leaves the United Kingdom for a place where he hopes to take up permanent residence (his 'new place of residence'), and

(c) the Secretary of State thinks that it is in the person's interest to leave the United Kingdom and that the person wishes to leave.

(2) The Secretary of State may make arrangements to—

(a) assist voluntary leavers;

(b) assist individuals to decide whether to become voluntary leavers.

(3) The Secretary of State may, in particular, make payments (whether to voluntary leavers or to organisations providing services for them) which relate to—

(a) travelling and other expenses incurred by or on behalf of a voluntary leaver, or a member of his family or household, in leaving the United Kingdom;

(b) expenses incurred by or on behalf of a voluntary leaver, or a member of his family or household, on or shortly after arrival in his new place of residence;

(c) the provision of services designed to assist a voluntary leaver, or a member of his family or household, to settle in his new place of residence;

(d) expenses in connection with a journey undertaken by a person (with or without his family or household) to prepare for, or to assess the possibility of, his becoming a voluntary leaver.

(4) In subsection (1)(a) 'EEA national' means a national of a State which is a contracting party to the Agreement on the European Economic Area signed at Oporto on 2nd May 1992 (as it has effect from time to time).

(5) . . .

Note: Subsection (5) repeals Immigration Act 1971, ss 29 and 31(d). Commenced 7 November 2002, s 162.

59. International projects

(1) The Secretary of State may participate in a project which is designed to—

(a) reduce migration,

(b) assist or ensure the return of migrants,

(c) facilitate co-operation between States in matters relating to migration,

(d) conduct or consider research about migration, or

(e) arrange or assist the settlement of migrants (whether in the United Kingdom or elsewhere).

(2) In particular, the Secretary of State may—

(a) provide financial support to an international organisation which arranges or participates in a project of a kind described in subsection (1);

(b) provide financial support to an organisation in the United Kingdom or another country which arranges or participates in a project of that kind;

(c) provide or arrange for the provision of financial or other assistance to a migrant who participates in a project of that kind;

(d) participate in financial or other arrangements which are agreed between Her Majesty's Government and the government of one or more other countries and which are or form part of a project of that kind.

(3) In this section—

(a) 'migrant' means a person who leaves the country where he lives hoping to settle in another country (whether or not he is a refugee within the meaning of any international Convention), and

(b) 'migration' shall be construed accordingly.

(4) Subsection (1) does not—

(a) confer a power to remove a person from the United Kingdom, or

(b) affect a person's right to enter or remain in the United Kingdom.

Note: Commenced 7 November 2002, s 162.

60. Northern Ireland authorities

. . .

Note: Amends Immigration and Asylum Act 1999, ss 94 and 110.

61. Repeal of spent provisions

. . .

Note: Repeals Immigration and Asylum Act 1999, ss 96(4)–(6), 166(4)(e).

PART IV
DETENTION AND REMOVAL

Detention

62. Detention by Secretary of State

(1) A person may be detained under the authority of the Secretary of State pending—

(a) a decision by the Secretary of State whether to give directions in respect of the person under paragraph 10, 10A or 14 of Schedule 2 to the Immigration Act 1971 (c. 77) (control of entry: removal), or

(b) removal of the person from the United Kingdom in pursuance of directions given by the Secretary of State under any of those paragraphs.

(2) Where the Secretary of State is empowered under section 3A of that Act (powers of Secretary of State) to examine a person or to give or refuse a person leave to enter the United Kingdom, the person may be detained under the authority of the Secretary of State pending—

(a) the person's examination by the Secretary of State,

(b) the Secretary of State's decision to give or refuse the person leave to enter,

(c) a decision by the Secretary of State whether to give directions in respect of the person under paragraph 8 or 9 of Schedule 2 to that Act (removal), or

(d) removal of the person in pursuance of directions given by the Secretary of State under either of those paragraphs.

(3) A provision of Schedule 2 to that Act about a person who is detained or liable to detention under that Schedule shall apply to a person who is detained or liable to detention under this section: and for that purpose—

(a) a reference to paragraph 16 of that Schedule shall be taken to include a reference to this section,

(b) a reference in paragraph 21 of that Schedule to an immigration officer shall be taken to include a reference to the Secretary of State, and

(c) a reference to detention under that Schedule or under a provision or Part of that Schedule shall be taken to include a reference to detention under this section.

(4) In the case of a restriction imposed under paragraph 21 of that Schedule by virtue of this section—

(a) a restriction imposed by an immigration officer may be varied by the Secretary of State, and

(b) a restriction imposed by the Secretary of State may be varied by an immigration officer.

(5) In subsection (1) the reference to paragraph 10 of that Schedule includes a reference to that paragraph as applied by virtue of section 10 of the Immigration and Asylum Act 1999 (c. 33) (persons unlawfully in United Kingdom: removal).

(6) Subsection (5) is without prejudice to the generality of section 159.

(7) A power under this section which is exercisable pending a decision of a particular kind by the Secretary of State is exercisable where the Secretary of State has reasonable grounds to suspect that he may make a decision of that kind.

(8–16) . . .

Note: Subsections 8–16 amend Immigration Act 1971, ss 11, 24; Mental Health Act 1983, ss 48, 53; Mental Health (Scotland) Act 1984, ss 71, 74; Mental Health (Northern Ireland) Order 1986, Arts 54, 59; Immigration and Asylum Act 1999, ss 53, 147; Anti-terrorism, Crime and Security Act 2001, ss 23, 24. Commencement 10 February 2003 (SI 2003/1). Subsections (15)-(16) repealed by Prevention of Terrorism Act 2005, section 16(2) from 14 March 2005. Prevention of Terrorism Act, section 26(3)).

63. Control of entry to United Kingdom, &c.: use of force

. . .

Note: Amends para 17(2), Sch 2 Immigration Act 1971.

64. Escorts

. . .

Note: Amends para 17, Sch 2 Immigration Act 1971.

65. Detention centres: custodial functions

. . .

Note: Amends Immigration and Asylum Act 1999, s 154 and Sch 11.

66. Detention centres: change of name

(1)–(3) . . .

(4) A reference in an enactment or instrument to a detention centre within the meaning of Part VIII of the Immigration and Asylum Act 1999 (c. 33) shall be construed as a reference to a removal centre within the meaning of that Part.

Note: Subsections (1)–(3) amend Immigration and Asylum Act 1999, ss 141, 147–53, 155, 157–9 and Schs 11–13 and Prison Act 1952, s 5A and Sch 4A Water Industry Act 1991.

67. Construction of reference to person liable to detention

(1) This section applies to the construction of a provision which—

(a) does not confer power to detain a person, but

(b) refers (in any terms) to a person who is liable to detention under a provision of the Immigration Acts.

(2) The reference shall be taken to include a person if the only reason why he cannot not be detained under the provision is that—

(a) he cannot presently be removed from the United Kingdom, because of a legal impediment connected with the United Kingdom's obligations under an international agreement,

(b) practical difficulties are impeding or delaying the making of arrangements for his removal from the United Kingdom, or

(c) practical difficulties, or demands on administrative resources, are impeding or delaying the taking of a decision in respect of him.

(3) This section shall be treated as always having had effect.

Note: Commenced 7 November 2002, s 162.

Temporary release

68. Bail

(1) This section applies in a case where an immigration officer not below the rank of chief immigration officer has sole or shared power to release a person on bail in accordance with—

(a) a provision of Schedule 2 to the Immigration Act 1971 (c. 77) (control of entry) (including a provision of that Schedule applied by a provision of that Act or by another enactment), or

(b) section 9A of the Asylum and Immigration Appeals Act 1993 (c. 23) (pending appeal from Immigration Appeal Tribunal).

(2) In respect of an application for release on bail which is instituted after the expiry of the period of eight days beginning with the day on which detention commences, the power to release on bail—

(a) shall be exercisable by the Secretary of State (as well as by any person with whom the immigration officer's power is shared under the provision referred to in subsection (1)), and

(b) shall not be exercisable by an immigration officer (except where he acts on behalf of the Secretary of State).

(3) In relation to the exercise by the Secretary of State of a power to release a person on bail by virtue of subsection (2), a reference to an immigration officer shall be construed as a reference to the Secretary of State.

(4) The Secretary of State may by order amend or replace subsection (2) so as to make different provision for the circumstances in which the power to release on bail may be exercised by the Secretary of State and not by an immigration officer.

(5) An order under subsection (4)—

(a) may include consequential or transitional provision,

(b) must be made by statutory instrument, and

(c) may not be made unless a draft has been laid before and approved by resolution of each House of Parliament.

(6) . . .

Note: Subsection (6) repeals Immigration and Asylum Act 1999, ss 44–52, 53(5) and 55, from 10 February 2003 (SI 2003/1). Remainder of s 68 commenced 1 April 2003 (SI 2003/754).

69. Reporting restriction: travel expenses

(1) The Secretary of State may make a payment to a person in respect of travelling expenses which the person has incurred or will incur for the purpose of complying with a reporting restriction.

(2) In subsection (1) 'reporting restriction' means a restriction which—

(a) requires a person to report to the police, an immigration officer or the Secretary of State, and

(b) is imposed under a provision listed in subsection (3).

(3) Those provisions are—

(a) paragraph 21 of Schedule 2 to the Immigration Act 1971 (c. 77) (temporary admission or release from detention),

(b) paragraph 29 of that Schedule (bail), and

(c) paragraph 2 or 5 of Schedule 3 to that Act (pending deportation).

Note: Commenced 7 November 2002, s 162.

70. Induction

(1) A residence restriction may be imposed on an asylum-seeker or a dependant of an asylum-seeker without regard to his personal circumstances if—

(a) it requires him to reside at a specified location for a period not exceeding 14 days, and

(b) the person imposing the residence restriction believes that a programme of induction will be made available to the asylum-seeker at or near the specified location.

(2) In subsection (1) 'residence restriction' means a restriction imposed under—

(a) paragraph 21 of Schedule 2 to the Immigration Act 1971 (temporary admission or release from detention), or

(b) paragraph 2(5) of Schedule 3 to that Act (control pending deportation).

(3) In this section—

'asylum-seeker' has the meaning given by section 18 of this Act but disregarding section 18(1)(a),

'dependant of an asylum-seeker' means a person who appears to the Secretary of State to be making a claim or application in respect of residence in the United Kingdom by virtue of being a dependant of an asylum-seeker, and

'programme of induction' means education about the nature of the asylum process.

(4) Regulations under subsection (3)—

(a) may make different provision for different circumstances,

(b) must be made by statutory instrument, and

(c) shall be subject to annulment in pursuance of a resolution of either House of Parliament.

(5) Subsection (6) applies where the Secretary of State arranges for the provision of a programme of induction (whether or not he also provides other facilities to persons attending the programme and whether or not all the persons attending the programme are subject to residence restrictions).

(6) A local authority may arrange for or participate in the provision of the programme or other facilities.

(7) In particular, a local authority may—

(a) incur reasonable expenditure;

(b) provide services outside its area;

(c) provide services jointly with another body;

(d) form a company;

(e) tender for or enter into a contract;

(f) do anything (including anything listed in paragraphs (a) to (e)) for a preparatory purpose.

(8) In this section 'local authority' means—

(a) a local authority within the meaning of section 94 of the Immigration and Asylum Act 1999 (c. 33), and

(b) a Northern Ireland authority within the meaning of section 110 of that Act.

Note: Commenced 7 November 2002, s 162.

71. Asylum-seeker: residence, &c. restriction

(1) This section applies to—

(a) a person who makes a claim for asylum at a time when he has leave to enter or remain in the United Kingdom, and

(b) a dependant of a person within paragraph (a).

(2) The Secretary of State or an immigration officer may impose on a person to whom this section applies any restriction which may be imposed under paragraph 21 of Schedule

2 to the Immigration Act 1971 (c. 77) (control of entry: residence, reporting and occupation restrictions) on a person liable to detention under paragraph 16 of that Schedule.

(3) Where a restriction is imposed on a person under subsection (2)—

(a) the restriction shall be treated for all purposes as a restriction imposed under paragraph 21 of that Schedule, and

(b) if the person fails to comply with the restriction he shall be liable to detention under paragraph 16 of that Schedule.

(4) A restriction imposed on a person under this section shall cease to have effect if he ceases to be an asylum-seeker or the dependant of an asylum-seeker.

(5) In this section—

'asylum-seeker' has the same meaning as in section 70,

'claim for asylum' has the same meaning as in section 18, and

'dependant' means a person who appears to the Secretary of State to be making a claim or application in respect of residence in the United Kingdom by virtue of being a dependant of another person.

(6) Regulations under subsection (5)—

(a) may make different provision for different circumstances,

(b) must be made by statutory instrument, and

(c) shall be subject to annulment in pursuance of a resolution of either House of Parliament.

Note: Commenced 10 February 2003 (SI 2003/1).

Removal

72. Serious criminal

(1) This section applies for the purpose of the construction and application of Article 33(2) of the Refugee Convention (exclusion from protection).

(2) A person shall be presumed to have been convicted by a final judgment of a particularly serious crime and to constitute a danger to the community of the United Kingdom if he is—

(a) convicted in the United Kingdom of an offence, and

(b) sentenced to a period of imprisonment of at least two years.

(3) A person shall be presumed to have been convicted by a final judgment of a particularly serious crime and to constitute a danger to the community of the United Kingdom if—

(a) he is convicted outside the United Kingdom of an offence,

(b) he is sentenced to a period of imprisonment of at least two years, and

(c) he could have been sentenced to a period of imprisonment of at least two years had his conviction been a conviction in the United Kingdom of a similar offence.

(4) A person shall be presumed to have been convicted by a final judgment of a particularly serious crime and to constitute a danger to the community of the United Kingdom if—

(a) he is convicted of an offence specified by order of the Secretary of State, or

(b) he is convicted outside the United Kingdom of an offence and the Secretary of State certifies that in his opinion the offence is similar to an offence specified by order under paragraph (a).

(5) An order under subsection (4)—

(a) must be made by statutory instrument, and

(b) shall be subject to annulment in pursuance of a resolution of either House of Parliament.

(6) A presumption under subsection (2), (3) or (4) that a person constitutes a danger to the community is rebuttable by that person.

(7) A presumption under subsection (2), (3) or (4) does not apply while an appeal against conviction or sentence—

(a) is pending, or

(b) could be brought (disregarding the possibility of appeal out of time with leave).

(8) Section 34(1) of the Anti-terrorism, Crime and Security Act 2001 (c. 24) (no need to consider gravity of fear or threat of persecution) applies for the purpose of considering whether a presumption mentioned in subsection (6) has been rebutted as it applies for the purpose of considering whether Article 33(2) of the Refugee Convention applies.

(9) Subsection (10) applies where—

(a) a person appeals under section 82, 83 [, 83A] or 101 of this Act or under section 2 of the Special Immigration Appeals Commission Act 1997 (c. 68) wholly or partly on the ground that to remove him from or to require him to leave the United Kingdom would breach the United Kingdom's obligations under the Refugee Convention, and

(b) the Secretary of State issues a certificate that presumptions under subsection (2), (3) or (4) apply to the person (subject to rebuttal).

(10) The [. . .] Tribunal or Commission hearing the appeal—

(a) must begin substantive deliberation on the appeal by considering the certificate, and

(b) if in agreement that presumptions under subsection (2), (3) or (4) apply (having given the appellant an opportunity for rebuttal) must dismiss the appeal in so far as it relies on the ground specified in subsection (9)(a).

[(10A) Subsection (10) also applies in relation to the Upper Tribunal when it acts under section 12(2)(b)(ii) of the Tribunals, Courts and Enforcement Act 2007.]

(11) For the purposes of this section—

(a) 'the Refugee Convention' means the Convention relating to the Status of Refugees done at Geneva on 28 July 1951 and its Protocol, and

(b) a reference to a person who is sentenced to a period of imprisonment of at least two years—

(i) does not include a reference to a person who receives a suspended sentence [(unless a court subsequently orders that the sentence or any part of it is to take effect)],

[(ia) does not include a reference to a person who is sentenced to a period of imprisonment of at least two years only by virtue of being sentenced to consecutive

sentences which amount in aggregate to more than two years,]

(ii) includes a reference to a person who is sentenced to detention, or ordered or directed to be detained, in an institution other than a prison (including, in particular, a hospital or an institution for young offenders), and

(iii) includes a reference to a person who is sentenced to imprisonment or detention, or ordered or directed to be detained, for an indeterminate period (provided that it may last for two years).

Note: Subsections (1)–(8) and (11) commenced 10 February 2003 (SI 2003/1), remainder on 1 April 2003 (SI 2003/754). Word in subsection (10) omitted by Sch 2 Asylum and Immigration (Treatment of Claimants etc.) Act 2004 from 4 April 2005 (SI 2005/565). Serious offences for the purposes of sub-s (4)(a) set out in SI 2004/1910. Words in square brackets in sub-s (9) inserted by Sch 1 Immigration, Asylum and Nationality Act 2006 from 31 August 2006 (SI 2006/2226). Words in subsection (11)(b)(i) substituted and subsection (11)(b)(ia) inserted by UK Borders Act 2007, s 39 from 1 August 2008 (SI 2008/1818). Subsection (10A) inserted from 15 February 2010 (SI 2010/21).

73. Family

. . .

Note: Amends Sch 2 Immigration Act 1971 (c. 77); Immigration and Asylum Act 1999, s 10.

74. Deception

. . .

Note: Amends Immigration and Asylum Act 1999, s 10(1).

75. Exemption from deportation

. . .

Note: Amends Immigration Act 1971, s 7; Immigration and Asylum Act 1999, s 10.

76. Revocation of leave to enter or remain

(1) The Secretary of State may revoke a person's indefinite leave to enter or remain in the United Kingdom if the person—

(a) is liable to deportation, but

(b) cannot be deported for legal reasons.

(2) The Secretary of State may revoke a person's indefinite leave to enter or remain in the United Kingdom if—

(a) the leave was obtained by deception,

(b) the person would be liable to removal because of the deception, but

(c) the person cannot be removed for legal or practical reasons.

(3) The Secretary of State may revoke a person's indefinite leave to enter or remain in the United Kingdom if the person, or someone of whom he is a dependant, ceases to be a refugee as a result of—

(a) voluntarily availing himself of the protection of his country of nationality,

(b) voluntarily re-acquiring a lost nationality,

(c) acquiring the nationality of a country other than the United Kingdom and availing himself of its protection, or

(d) voluntarily establishing himself in a country in respect of which he was a refugee.

(4) In this section—

'indefinite leave' has the meaning given by section 33(1) of the Immigration Act 1971 (c. 77) (interpretation),

'liable to deportation' has the meaning given by section 3(5) and (6) of that Act (deportation),

'refugee' has the meaning given by the Convention relating to the Status of Refugees done at Geneva on 28 July 1951 and its Protocol, and

'removed' means removed from the United Kingdom under—

(a) paragraph 9 or 10 of Schedule 2 to the Immigration Act 1971 (control of entry: directions for removal), or

(b) section 10(1)(b) of the Immigration and Asylum Act 1999 (c. 33) (removal of persons unlawfully in United Kingdom: deception).

(5) A power under subsection (1) or (2) to revoke leave may be exercised—

(a) in respect of leave granted before this section comes into force;

(b) in reliance on anything done before this section comes into force.

(6) A power under subsection (3) to revoke leave may be exercised—

(a) in respect of leave granted before this section comes into force, but

(b) only in reliance on action taken after this section comes into force.

(7) . . .

Note: Subsection (7) amends Immigration and Asylum Act 1999, s 10(1). Commencement 10 February 2003 (SI 2003/1).

77. No removal while claim for asylum pending

(1) While a person's claim for asylum is pending he may not be—

(a) removed from the United Kingdom in accordance with a provision of the Immigration Acts, or

(b) required to leave the United Kingdom in accordance with a provision of the Immigration Acts.

(2) In this section—

(a) 'claim for asylum' means a claim by a person that it would be contrary to the United Kingdom's obligations under the Refugee Convention to remove him from or require him to leave the United Kingdom, and

(b) a person's claim is pending until he is given notice of the Secretary of State's decision on it.

(3) In subsection (2) 'the Refugee Convention' means the Convention relating to the Status of Refugees done at Geneva on 28 July 1951 and its Protocol.

(4) Nothing in this section shall prevent any of the following while a claim for asylum is pending—

(a) the giving of a direction for the claimant's removal from the United Kingdom,

(b) the making of a deportation order in respect of the claimant, or

(c) the taking of any other interim or preparatory action.

(5) . . .

Note: Subsection (5) repeals Immigration and Asylum Act 1999, s 15. Commencement 1 April 2003 (SI 2003/754). Has effect in relation to a claim for asylum pending on 31 March 2003 as it has effect in relation to claims pending under the 2002 Act (SI 2003/754).

78. No removal while appeal pending

(1) While a person's appeal under section 82(1) is pending he may not be—

(a) removed from the United Kingdom in accordance with a provision of the Immigration Acts, or

(b) required to leave the United Kingdom in accordance with a provision of the Immigration Acts.

(2) In this section 'pending' has the meaning given by section 104.

(3) Nothing in this section shall prevent any of the following while an appeal is pending—

(a) the giving of a direction for the appellant's removal from the United Kingdom,

(b) the making of a deportation order in respect of the appellant (subject to section 79), or

(c) the taking of any other interim or preparatory action.

(4) This section applies only to an appeal brought while the appellant is in the United Kingdom in accordance with section 92.

Note: Commencement 1 April 2003 (SI 2003/754). Has effect in relation to appeals pending under the old appeal provisions as it has effect in relation to an appeal pending under s 82(1) of the 2002 Act.

79. Deportation order: appeal

(1) A deportation order may not be made in respect of a person while an appeal under section 82(1) against the decision to make the order—

(a) could be brought (ignoring any possibility of an appeal out of time with permission), or

(b) is pending.

(2) In this section 'pending' has the meaning given by section 104.

[(3) This section does not apply to a deportation order which states that it is made in accordance with section 32(5) of the UK Borders Act 2007.]

[(4) But a deportation order made in reliance on subsection (3) does not invalidate leave to enter or remain, in accordance with section 5(1) of the Immigration Act 1971, if and for so long as section 78 above applies.]

Note: Commencement 1 April 2003 (SI 2003/754). Has effect in relation to an appeal pending under the old appeals provisions as it has effect in relation to an appeal pending under s 82(1) of the 2002 Act. Subsections (3) and (4) inserted by UK Borders Act 2007, s 35 from 1 August 2008 (SI 2008/1818).

80. Removal of asylum-seeker to third country

. . .

Note: Amends Immigration and Asylum Act 1999, s 11.

PART V
IMMIGRATION AND ASYLUM APPEALS

[Appeal to Tribunal

[**Meaning of 'the Tribunal'**

81.

. . .

In this Part 'the Tribunal' means the First-tier Tribunal.]

Note: Section 81 substituted from 15 February 2010 (SI 2010/21).

82. Right of appeal: general

(1) Where an immigration decision is made in respect of a person he may appeal [to the Tribunal].

(2) In this Part 'immigration decision' means—

(a) refusal of leave to enter the United Kingdom,

(b) refusal of entry clearance,

(c) refusal of a certificate of entitlement under section 10 of this Act,

(d) refusal to vary a person's leave to enter or remain in the United Kingdom if the result of the refusal is that the person has no leave to enter or remain,

(e) variation of a person's leave to enter or remain in the United Kingdom if when the variation takes effect the person has no leave to enter or remain,

(f) revocation under section 76 of this Act of indefinite leave to enter or remain in the United Kingdom,

(g) a decision that a person is to be removed from the United Kingdom by way of directions under [section 10(1)(a), (b), (ba) or (c)] of the Immigration and Asylum Act 1999 (c. 33) (removal of person unlawfully in United Kingdom),

(h) a decision that an illegal entrant is to be removed from the United Kingdom by way of directions under paragraphs 8 to 10 of Schedule 2 to the Immigration Act 1971 (c. 77) (control of entry: removal),

[(ha) a decision that a person is to be removed from the United Kingdom by way of directions under section 47 of the Immigration, Asylum and Nationality Act 2006 (removal: persons with statutorily extended leave),]

(i) a decision that a person is to be removed from the United Kingdom by way of directions given by virtue of paragraph 10A of that Schedule (family),

[(ia) a decision that a person is to be removed from the United Kingdom by way of directions under paragraph 12(2) of Schedule 2 to the Immigration Act 1971 (c. 77) (seamen and aircrews),]

[(ib) a decision to make an order under section 2A of that Act (deprivation of right of abode),]

(j) a decision to make a deportation order under section 5(1) of that Act, and

(k) refusal to revoke a deportation order under section 5(2) of that Act.

(3) . . .

[(3A) Subsection (2)(j) does not apply to a decision to make a deportation order which states that it is made in accordance with section 32(5) of the UK Borders Act 2007; but—

(a) a decision that section 32(5) applies is an immigration decision for the purposes of this Part, and

(b) a reference in this Part to an appeal against an automatic deportation order is a reference to an appeal against a decision of the Secretary of State that section 32(5) applies.]

(4) The right of appeal under subsection (1) is subject to the exceptions and limitations specified in this Part.

Note: Commencement from 1 April 2003 (SI 2003/754, which sets out transitional provisions). Words in square brackets in sub-s (1) substituted by Asylum and Immigration (Treatment of Claimants, etc.) Act 2004, s 26 from 4 April 2005 (SI 2005/565). Subsection (2)(ia) inserted by Asylum and Immigration Act 2004, s 26 from 4 April 2005 (SI 2005/565). Words in square brackets in sub-s (2)(g) substituted by Immigration Asylum and Nationality Act 2006, s 2 from 31 August 2006 (SI 2006/2226) in respect of decisions made on or after that date. Subsection (2)(ha) inserted by s 47 of that Act from 1 April 2007 (SI 2008/310). Subsection (2)(ib) inserted by Immigration, Asylum and Nationality Act 2006, s 57 from 16 June 2006 (SI 2006/1497). Subsection (3) ceased to have effect from 31 August 2006 (SI 2006/2226), Immigration, Asylum and Nationality Act 2006, s 11, but continues to have effect in relation to decisions made before that date. Subsection (3A) inserted by UK Borders Act 2007, s 35 from 1 August 2008 (SI 2008/1818).

83. Appeal: asylum claim

(1) This section applies where a person has made an asylum claim and—

(a) his claim has been rejected by the Secretary of State, but

(b) he has been granted leave to enter or remain in the United Kingdom for a period exceeding one year (or for periods exceeding one year in aggregate).

(2) The person may appeal [to the Tribunal] against the rejection of his asylum claim.

Note: Commencement from 1 April 2003 (SI 2003/754, which sets out transitional provisions). Words in square brackets in sub-s (2) substituted by Asylum and Immigration Act 2004, s 26 from 4 April 2005 (SI 2005/565).

[83A. Appeal: variation of limited leave

(1) This section applies where—

(a) a person has made an asylum claim,

(b) he was granted limited leave to enter or remain in the United Kingdom as a refugee within the meaning of the Refugee Convention,

(c) a decision is made that he is not a refugee, and

(d) following the decision specified in paragraph (c) he has limited leave to enter or remain in the United Kingdom otherwise than as a refugee.

(2) The person may appeal to the Tribunal against the decision to curtail or to refuse to extend his limited leave.]

Note: Section 83A inserted by Immigration, Asylum and Nationality Act 2006, s 1 from 31 August 2006 (SI 2006/2226) in respect of decisions made on or after that date.

84. Grounds of appeal

(1) An appeal under section 82(1) against an immigration decision must be brought on one or more of the following grounds—

(a) that the decision is not in accordance with immigration rules;

(b) that the decision is unlawful by virtue of ... [Article 20A of the Race Relations (Northern Ireland) Order 1976] (discrimination by public authorities);

(c) that the decision is unlawful under section 6 of the Human Rights Act 1998 (c. 42) (public authority not to act contrary to Human Rights Convention) as being incompatible with the appellant's Convention rights;

(d) that the appellant is an EEA national or a member of the family of an EEA national and the decision breaches the appellant's rights under the Community Treaties in respect of entry to or residence in the United Kingdom;

(e) that the decision is otherwise not in accordance with the law;

(f) that the person taking the decision should have exercised differently a discretion conferred by immigration rules;

(g) that removal of the appellant from the United Kingdom in consequence of the immigration decision would breach the United Kingdom's obligations under the Refugee Convention or would be unlawful under section 6 of the Human Rights Act 1998 as being incompatible with the appellant's Convention rights.

(2) In subsection (1)(d) 'EEA national' means a national of a State which is a contracting party to the Agreement on the European Economic Area signed at Oporto on 2 May 1992 (as it has effect from time to time).

(3) An appeal under section 83 must be brought on the grounds that removal of the appellant from the United Kingdom would breach the United Kingdom's obligations under the Refugee Convention.

[(4) An appeal under section 83A must be brought on the grounds that removal of the appellant from the United Kingdom would breach the United Kingdom's obligations under the Refugee Convention.]

Note: Commencement from 1 April 2003 (SI 2003/754, which sets out transitional provisions). Subsection (4) inserted by Immigration, Asylum and Nationality Act 2006, s 3 from 31 August 2006 (SI 2006/2226) in respect of decisions made on or after that date. Words inserted in sub-s (1) (b) from 19 July 2003 (SR (N.I.) 2003/341). Words omitted from sub-s (1)(b) from 4 April 2011 (SI 2011/1060).

85. Matters to be considered

(1) An appeal under section 82(1) against a decision shall be treated by [the Tribunal] as including an appeal against any decision in respect of which the appellant has a right of appeal under section 82(1).

(2) If an appellant under section 82(1) makes a statement under section 120, [the Tribunal] shall consider any matter raised in the statement which constitutes a ground of appeal of a kind listed in section 84(1) against the decision appealed against.

(3) Subsection (2) applies to a statement made under section 120 whether the statement was made before or after the appeal was commenced.

(4) On an appeal under section 82(1) [, 83(2) or 83A(2)] against a decision [the Tribunal] may consider evidence about any matter which [it] thinks relevant to the substance of the decision, including evidence which concerns a matter arising after the date of the decision.

[(5) But subsection (4) is subject to the exceptions in section 85A.]

Note: Commencement from 1 April 2003 (SI 2003/754, which sets out transitional provisions). First words in square brackets in sub-s (4) substituted by Sch 1 Immigration, Asylum and Nationality Act 2006 from 31 August 2006 (SI 2006/2226). Other words in square brackets substituted by Sch 2 Asylum and Immigration (Treatment of Claimants, etc.) Act 2004 from 4 April 2005 (SI 2005/565). Subsection (5) substituted by UK Borders Act 2007, s 19 from 23 May 2011 (SI 2011/1293, which contains transitional provisions).

[85A Matters to be considered: new evidence: exceptions

(1) This section sets out the exceptions mentioned in section 85(5).

(2) Exception 1 is that in relation to an appeal under section 82(1) against an immigration decision of a kind specified in section 82(2)(b) or (c) the Tribunal may consider only the circumstances appertaining at the time of the decision.

(3) Exception 2 applies to an appeal under section 82(1) if—

(a) the appeal is against an immigration decision of a kind specified in section 82(2) (a) or (d),

(b) the immigration decision concerned an application of a kind identified in immigration rules as requiring to be considered under a 'Points Based System', and

(c) the appeal relies wholly or partly on grounds specified in section 84(1)(a), (e) or (f).

(4) Where Exception 2 applies the Tribunal may consider evidence adduced by the appellant only if it—

(a) was submitted in support of, and at the time of making, the application to which the immigration decision related,

(b) relates to the appeal in so far as it relies on grounds other than those specified in subsection (3)(c),

(c) is adduced to prove that a document is genuine or valid, or

(d) is adduced in connection with the Secretary of State's reliance on a discretion under immigration rules, or compliance with a requirement of immigration rules, to refuse an application on grounds not related to the acquisition of 'points' under the 'Points Based System'.]

[(5) Tribunal Procedure Rules may make provision, for the purposes of subsection (4) (a), about the circumstances in which evidence is to be treated, or not treated, as submitted in support of, and at the time of making, an application.]

Note: Section 85A inserted by UK Borders Act 2007, s 19 from 23 May 2011 (SI 2011/1293) subject to transitional provisions set out in Art 3 of SI 2011/1293. Subsection (5) inserted from 15 February 2010 (SI 2010/21).

86. Determination of appeal

(1) This section applies on an appeal under section 82(1) [, 83 or 83A.]

(2) [the Tribunal] must determine—

(a) any matter raised as a ground of appeal (whether or not by virtue of section 85(1)), and

(b) any matter which section 85 requires [it] to consider.

(3) [the Tribunal] must allow the appeal in so far as [it] thinks that—

(a) a decision against which the appeal is brought or is treated as being brought was not in accordance with the law (including immigration rules), or

(b) a discretion exercised in making a decision against which the appeal is brought or is treated as being brought should have been exercised differently.

(4) For the purposes of subsection (3) a decision that a person should be removed from the United Kingdom under a provision shall not be regarded as unlawful if it could have been lawfully made by reference to removal under another provision.

(5) In so far as subsection (3) does not apply, [the Tribunal] shall dismiss the appeal.

(6) Refusal to depart from or to authorise departure from immigration rules is not the exercise of a discretion for the purposes of subsection (3)(b).

Note: Commencement from 1 April 2003 (SI 2003/754, which sets out transitional provisions). Words in square brackets in sub-s (1) substituted by Sch 1 Immigration, Asylum and Nationality Act 2006 from 31 August 2006 (SI 2006/2226). Other words in square brackets substituted by Sch 2 Asylum and Immigration (Treatment of Claimants, etc.) Act 2004 from 4 April 2005 (SI 2005/565).

87. Successful appeal: direction

(1) If [the Tribunal] allows an appeal under section 82 [, 83 or 83A] [it] may give a direction for the purpose of giving effect to [its] decision.

(2) A person responsible for making an immigration decision shall act in accordance with any relevant direction under subsection (1).

[(3) But a direction under this section shall not have effect while—

(a) an application for permission to appeal under section 11 or 13 of the Tribunals, Courts and Enforcement Act 2007 could be made or is awaiting determination,

(b) permission to appeal to the Upper Tribunal or a court under either of those sections has been granted and the appeal is awaiting determination, or

(c) an appeal has been remitted under section 12 or 14 of that Act and is awaiting determination.]

(4) A direction under subsection (1) shall be treated [as part of the Tribunal's decision on the appeal for the purposes of section [11 of the Tribunals, Courts and Enforcement Act 2007]].

Note: Commencement from 1 April 2003 (SI 2003/754, which sets out transitional provisions). Second words in square brackets in sub-s (1) substituted by Sch 1 Immigration, Asylum and Nationality Act 2006 from 31 August 2006 (SI 2006/2226). Subsection (3) and words in 2nd square brackets in sub-s (4) substituted from 15 February 2010 (SI 2010/21). Other words in square brackets substituted by Sch 2 Asylum and Immigration (Treatment of Claimants, etc.) Act 2004 from 4 April 2005 (SI 2005/565).

Exceptions and limitations

88. Ineligibility

(1) This section applies to an immigration decision of a kind referred to in section 82(2) (a), (b), (d) or (e).

(2) A person may not appeal under section 82(1) against an immigration decision which is taken on the grounds that he or a person of whom he is a dependant—

(a) does not satisfy a requirement as to age, nationality or citizenship specified in immigration rules,

(b) does not have an immigration document of a particular kind (or any immigration document),

[(ba) has failed to supply a medical report or a medical certificate in accordance with a requirement of immigration rules,]

(c) is seeking to be in the United Kingdom for a period greater than that permitted in his case by immigration rules, or

(d) is seeking to enter or remain in the United Kingdom for a purpose other than one for which entry or remaining is permitted in accordance with immigration rules.

(3) In subsection (2)(b) 'immigration document' means—

(a) entry clearance,

(b) a passport,

(c) a work permit or other immigration employment document within the meaning of section 122, and

(d) a document which relates to a national of a country other than the United Kingdom and which is designed to serve the same purpose as a passport.

(4) Subsection (2) does not prevent the bringing of an appeal on any or all of the grounds referred to in section 84(1)(b), (c) and (g).

Note: Commencement from 1 April 2003 (SI 2003/754, which sets out transitional provisions). Subsection (2)(ba) inserted by Immigration, Asylum and Nationality Act 2006, s 5 from 31 August 2006 (SI 2006/2226) in respect of decisions made on or after that date.

[88A. Entry clearance

(1) A person may not appeal under section 82(1) against refusal of an application for entry clearance unless the application was made for the purpose of—

(a) visiting a person of a class or description prescribed by regulations for the purpose of this subsection, or

(b) entering as the dependant of a person in circumstances prescribed by regulations for the purpose of this subsection.

(2) Regulations under subsection (1) may, in particular—

(a) make provision by reference to whether the applicant is a member of the family (within such meaning as the regulations may assign) of the person he seeks to visit;

(b) provide for the determination of whether one person is dependent on another;

(c) make provision by reference to the circumstances of the applicant, of the person whom the applicant seeks to visit or on whom he depends, or of both (and the regulations may, in particular, include provision by reference to—

(i) whether or not a person is lawfully settled in the United Kingdom within such meaning as the regulations may assign;

(ii) the duration of two individuals' residence together);

(d) make provision by reference to an applicant's purpose in entering as a dependant;

(e) make provision by reference to immigration rules;

(f) confer a discretion.

(3) Subsection (1)—

(a) does not prevent the bringing of an appeal on either or both of the grounds referred to in section 84(1)(b) and (c), and

(b) is without prejudice to the effect of section 88 in relation to an appeal under section 82(1) against refusal of entry clearance.]

Note: Section 88A substituted for ss 88A, 90 and 91 by Immigration, Asylum and Nationality Act 2006, s 4 from 1 April 2008 subject to savings and transitional provisions: see SI 2008/310. There is a further saving in respect of applications for entry clearance made before 9 July 2012: see SI 2012/1531.

[89. Refusal of leave to enter

(1) A person may not appeal under section 82(1) against refusal of leave to enter the United Kingdom unless—

(a) on his arrival in the United Kingdom he had entry clearance, and

(b) the purpose of entry specified in the entry clearance is the same as that specified in his application for leave to enter.

(2) Subsection (1) does not prevent the bringing of an appeal on any or all of the grounds referred to in section 84(1)(b), (c) and (g).]

Note: Section 89 substituted by Immigration, Asylum and Nationality Act 2006, s 6 from 31 August 2006 (SI 2006/2226), without effect in relation to decisions made before that date.

90. . . .

Note: See note to s 88A above.

91. . . .

Note: See note to s 88A above.

92. Appeal from within United Kingdom: general

(**1**) A person may not appeal under section 82(1) while he is in the United Kingdom unless his appeal is of a kind to which this section applies.

(**2**) This section applies to an appeal against an immigration decision of a kind specified in section 82(2)(c), (d), (e), (f) [, (ha)] and (j).

[(**3**) This section also applies to an appeal against refusal of leave to enter the United Kingdom if—
> (a) at the time of the refusal the appellant is in the United Kingdom, and
> (b) on his arrival in the United Kingdom the appellant had entry clearance.

(**3A**) But this section does not apply by virtue of subsection (3) if subsection (3B) or (3C) applies to the refusal of leave to enter.

(**3B**) This subsection applies to a refusal of leave to enter which is a deemed refusal under paragraph 2A(9) of Schedule 2 to the Immigration Act 1971 (c. 77) resulting from cancellation of leave to enter by an immigration officer—
> (a) under paragraph 2A(8) of that Schedule, and
> (b) on the grounds specified in paragraph 2A(2A) of that Schedule.

(**3C**) This subsection applies to a refusal of leave to enter which specifies that the grounds for refusal are that the leave is sought for a purpose other than that specified in the entry clearance.

(**3D**) This section also applies to an appeal against refusal of leave to enter the United Kingdom if at the time of the refusal the appellant—
> (a) is in the United Kingdom,
> (b) has a work permit, and
> (c) is any of the following (within the meaning of the British Nationality Act 1981 (c. 61))—
>> (i) a British overseas territories citizen,
>> (ii) a British Overseas citizen,
>> (iii) a British National (Overseas),
>> (iv) a British protected person, or
>> (v) a British subject.]

(**4**) This section also applies to an appeal against an immigration decision if the appellant—
> (a) has made an asylum claim, or a human rights claim, while in the United Kingdom, or
> (b) is an EEA national or a member of the family of an EEA national and makes a claim to the Secretary of State that the decision breaches the appellant's rights under the Community Treaties in respect of entry to or residence in the United Kingdom.

Note: Commencement from 1 April 2003 (SI 2003/754, which sets out transitional provisions). Subsections (3)-(3D) substituted by Asylum and Immigration (Treatment of Claimants, etc.) Act 2004, s 28 from 1 October 2004 (SI 2004/2523). Words in square brackets in sub-s (2) substituted by Immigration, Asylum and Nationality Act 2006, s 47 from 1 April 2008 (SI 2008/310).

93. Appeal from within United Kingdom: 'third country' removal

. . .

Note: Section 93 ceased to have effect from 1 October 2004, Asylum and Immigration Act 2004, s 33 (SI 2004/2523).

94. Appeal from within United Kingdom: unfounded human rights or asylum claim

(1) This section applies to an appeal under section 82(1) where the appellant has made an asylum claim or a human rights claim (or both).

[(1A) A person may not bring an appeal against an immigration decision of a kind specified in section 82(2)(c), (d) [, (e) or (ha)] in reliance on section 92(2) if the Secretary of State certifies that the claim or claims mentioned in subsection (1) above is or are clearly unfounded.]

(2) A person may not bring an appeal to which this section applies [in reliance on section 92(4)(a)] if the Secretary of State certifies that the claim or claims mentioned in subsection (1) is or are clearly unfounded.

(3) If the Secretary of State is satisfied that an asylum claimant or human rights claimant is entitled to reside in a State listed in subsection (4) he shall certify the claim under subsection (2) unless satisfied that it is not clearly unfounded.

(4) Those States are—
    (a)–(j) . . .
    [(k)   the Republic of Albania,
    (l)   . . .
    (m)   . . .
    (n)   Jamaica,
    (o)   Macedonia,
    (p)   the Republic of Moldova, and
    (q)   . . .]
    [(r)   . . .
    (s)   Bolivia,
    (t)   Brazil,
    (u)   Ecuador,
    (v)   . . .
    (w)   South Africa, and
    (x)   Ukraine.]
    (y)   India,
    [(z)   Mongolia,
    (aa)   Ghana (in respect of men),
    (bb)   Nigeria (in respect of men).]
    [(cc)   Bosnia-Herzegovina,

  (dd)   Gambia (in respect of men),
  (ee)   Kenya (in respect of men),
  (ff)   Liberia (in respect of men),
  (gg)   Malawi (in respect of men),
  (hh)   Mali (in respect of men),
  (ii)   Mauritius,
  (jj)   Montenegro,
  (kk)   Peru,
  (ll)   Serbia,
  (mm) Sierra Leone (in respect of men)]
  [(nn)   Kosovo,
  (oo)   South Korea]

(5) The Secretary of State may by order add a State, or part of a State, to the list in subsection (4) if satisfied that—

  (a) there is in general in that State or part no serious risk of persecution of persons entitled to reside in that State or part, and

  (b) removal to that State or part of persons entitled to reside there will not in general contravene the United Kingdom's obligations under the Human Rights Convention.

[(5A) If the Secretary of State is satisfied that the statements in subsection (5)(a) and (b) are true of a State or part of a State in relation to a description of person, an order under subsection (5) may add the State or part to the list in subsection (4) in respect of that description of person.

(5B) Where a State or part of a State is added to the list in subsection (4) in respect of a description of person, subsection (3) shall have effect in relation to a claimant only if the Secretary of State is satisfied that he is within that description (as well as being satisfied that he is entitled to reside in the State or part).

(5C) A description for the purposes of subsection (5A) may refer to—

  (a) gender,
  (b) language,
  (c) race,
  (d) religion,
  (e) nationality,
  (f) membership of a social or other group,
  (g) political opinion, or
  (h) any other attribute or circumstance that the Secretary of State thinks appropriate.]

[(5D) In deciding whether the statements in subsection (5)(a) and (b) are true of a State
or part of a State, the Secretary of State—

  (a) shall have regard to all the circumstances of the State or part (including its laws and how they are applied), and

  (b) shall have regard to information from any appropriate source (including other member States and international organisations).]

[(6) The Secretary of State may by order amend the list in subsection (4) so as to omit a State or part added under subsection (5); and the omission may be—

  (a) general, or
  (b) effected so that the State or part remains listed in respect of a description of person.]

[(**6A**) Subsection (3) shall not apply in relation to an asylum claimant or human rights claimant who—

(a) is the subject of a certificate under section 2 or 70 of the Extradition Act 2003 (c. 41),

(b) is in custody pursuant to arrest under section 5 of that Act,

(c) is the subject of a provisional warrant under section 73 of that Act,

(d) is the subject of an authority to proceed under section 7 of the Extradition Act 1989 (c. 33) or an order under paragraph 4(2) of Schedule 1 to that Act, or

(e) is the subject of a provisional warrant under section 8 of that Act or of a warrant under paragraph 5(1)(b) of Schedule 1 to that Act.]

[(**6B**) A certificate under subsection (1A) or (2) may not be issued (and subsection (3) shall not apply) in relation to an appeal under section 82(2)(d) or (e) against a decision relating to leave to enter or remain in the United Kingdom, where the leave was given in circumstances specified for the purposes of this subsection by order of the Secretary of State.]

(7) A person may not bring an appeal to which this section applies in reliance on section 92(4) if the Secretary of State certifies that—

(a) it is proposed to remove the person to a country of which he is not a national or citizen, and

(b) there is no reason to believe that the person's rights under the Human Rights Convention will be breached in that country.

(8) In determining whether a person in relation to whom a certificate has been issued under subsection (7) may be removed from the United Kingdom, the country specified in the certificate is to be regarded as—

(a) a place where a person's life and liberty is not threatened by reason of his race, religion, nationality, membership of a particular social group, or political opinion, and

(b) a place from which a person will not be sent to another country otherwise than in accordance with the Refugee Convention.

(9) Where a person in relation to whom a certificate is issued under this section subsequently brings an appeal under section 82(1) while outside the United Kingdom, the appeal shall be considered as if he had not been removed from the United Kingdom.

Note: Subsection (5) commenced 10 February 2003 for the purposes of enabling subordinate legislation (SI 2003/249), remainder from 1 April 2003 (SI 2003/754, which sets out transitional provisions). Words in square brackets in sub-s (1A) substituted by Immigration, Asylum and Nationality Act 2006, s 47 from 1 April 2008 (SI 2008/310). Subsection (6B) inserted by Immigration, Asylum and Nationality Act 2006, s 13 from a date to be appointed. Subsection 4: words in first square brackets added by SI 2003/970 from 1 April 2003, words in second square brackets added by SI 2003/1919 from 23 July 2003, Bangladesh omitted and last words in square brackets inserted from December 2005 (SI 2005/3306). First words omitted and other words in square brackets substituted or added by Asylum and Immigration (Treatment of Claimants etc.) Act 2004, s 27 from 1 October 2004 (SI 2004/2523). Other words omitted from 22 April 2005 (SI 2005/1016). Subsection (5D) inserted by SI 2007/3187 from 1 December 2007. India inserted from 15 February 2005 (SI 2005/330). Serbia and Montenegro omitted from subsection (4) and (cc)-(mm) inserted from 27 July 2007 (SI 2007/2221). Sri Lanka omitted from subsection (4) from 13 December 2006 (SI 2006/3275). Bulgaria and Romania omitted from sub-section (4) from 1 January 2007 (SI 2006/3215). Kosovo and South Korea inserted from 3 March 2010, but without effect to asylum claims made before that date, (SI 2010/561).

[94A European Common List of Safe Countries of Origin

(1) The Secretary of State shall by order prescribe a list of States to be known as the 'European Common List of Safe Countries of Origin'.

(2) Subsections (3) and (4) apply where a person makes an asylum claim or a human rights claim (or both) and that person is—

(a) a national of a State which is listed in the European Common List of Safe Countries of Origin, or

(b) a Stateless person who was formerly habitually resident in such a State.

(3) The Secretary of State shall consider the claim or claims mentioned in subsection (2) to be unfounded unless satisfied that there are serious grounds for considering that the State in question is not safe in the particular circumstances of the person mentioned in that subsection.

(4) The Secretary of State shall also certify the claim or claims mentioned in subsection

(2) under section 94(2) unless satisfied that the claim or claims is or are not clearly unfounded.

(5) An order under subsection (1) –

(a) may be made only if the Secretary of State thinks it necessary for the purpose of complying with the United Kingdom's obligations under Community law,

(b) may include transitional, consequential or incidental provision,

(c) shall be made by statutory instrument, and

(d) shall be subject to annulment in pursuance of a resolution of either House of Parliament.]

Note: Section 94A inserted by SI 2007/3187 from 1 December 2007.

95. Appeal from outside United Kingdom: removal

A person who is outside the United Kingdom may not appeal under section 82(1) on the ground specified in section 84(1)(g) (except in a case to which section 94(9) applies).

Note: Commencement from 1 April 2003 (SI 2003/754, which sets out transitional provisions).

96. Earlier right of appeal

[(1) An appeal under section 82(1) against an immigration decision ('the new decision') in respect of a person may not be brought if the Secretary of State or an immigration officer certifies—

(a) that the person was notified of a right of appeal under that section against another immigration decision ('the old decision') (whether or not an appeal was brought and whether or not any appeal brought has been determined),

(b) that the claim or application to which the new decision relates relies on a matter that could have been raised in an appeal against the old decision, and

(c) that, in the opinion of the Secretary of State or the immigration officer, there is no satisfactory reason for that matter not having been raised in an appeal against the old decision.

(2) An appeal under section 82(1) against an immigration decision ('the new decision') in respect of a person may not be brought if the Secretary of State or an immigration officer certifies—

(a) that the person received a notice under section 120 by virtue of an application other than that to which the new decision relates or by virtue of a decision other than the new decision,

(b) that the new decision relates to an application or claim which relies on a matter that should have been, but has not been, raised in a statement made in response to that notice, and

(c) that, in the opinion of the Secretary of State or the immigration officer, there is no satisfactory reason for that matter not having been raised in a statement made in response to that notice.]

(4) In subsection (1) 'notified' means notified in accordance with regulations under section 105.

(5) [Subsections (1) and (2) apply to prevent] a person's right of appeal whether or not he has been outside the United Kingdom since an earlier right of appeal arose or since a requirement under section 120 was imposed.

(6) In this section a reference to an appeal under section 82(1) includes a reference to an appeal under section 2 of the Special Immigration Appeals Commission Act 1997 (c. 68) which is or could be brought by reference to an appeal under section 82(1).

[(7) A certificate under subsection (1) or (2) shall have no effect in relation to an appeal instituted before the certificate is issued.]

Note: Commencement from 1 April 2003 (SI 2003/754, which sets out transitional provisions). Words in square brackets substituted and sub-s (7) added by Asylum and Immigration (Treatment of Claimants, etc.) Act 2004, s 30 from 1 October 2004 (SI 2004/2523).

97. National security, &c.

(1) An appeal under section 82(1) [, 83(2) or 83A(2)] against a decision in respect of a person may not be brought or continued if the Secretary of State certifies that the decision is or was taken—

(a) by the Secretary of State wholly or partly on a ground listed in subsection (2), or

(b) in accordance with a direction of the Secretary of State which identifies the person to whom the decision relates and which is given wholly or partly on a ground listed in subsection (2).

(2) The grounds mentioned in subsection (1) are that the person's exclusion or removal from the United Kingdom is—

(a) in the interests of national security, or

(b) in the interests of the relationship between the United Kingdom and another country.

(3) An appeal under section 82(1) [, 83(2) or 83A(2)] against a decision may not be brought or continued if the Secretary of State certifies that the decision is or was taken wholly or partly in reliance on information which in his opinion should not be made public—

(a) in the interests of national security,

(b) in the interests of the relationship between the United Kingdom and another country, or

(c) otherwise in the public interest.

(4) In subsections (1)(a) and (b) and (3) a reference to the Secretary of State is to the Secretary of State acting in person.

Note: Commencement from 1 April 2003 (SI 2003/754, which sets out transitional provisions). Words in square brackets in sub-ss (1) and (3) substituted by Sch 1 Immigration, Asylum and Nationality Act 2006 from 31 August 2006 (SI 2006/2226).

[97A. National security: deportation

(1) This section applies where the Secretary of State certifies that the decision to make a deportation order in respect of a person was taken on the grounds that his removal from the United Kingdom would be in the interests of national security.

(2) Where this section applies—

(a) section 79 shall not apply,

(b) the Secretary of State shall be taken to have certified the decision to make the deportation order under section 97, and

(c) for the purposes of section 2(5) of the Special Immigration Appeals Commission Act 1997 (c. 68) (appeals from within United Kingdom) it shall be assumed that section 92 of this Act—

(i) would not apply to an appeal against the decision to make the deportation order by virtue of section 92(2) to (3D),

(ii) would not apply to an appeal against that decision by virtue of section 92(4)(a) in respect of an asylum claim, and

(iii) would be capable of applying to an appeal against that decision by virtue of section 92(4)(a) in respect of a human rights claim unless the Secretary of State certifies that the removal of the person from the United Kingdom would not breach the United Kingdom's obligations under the Human Rights Convention.

(3) A person in respect of whom a certificate is issued under subsection (2)(c)(iii) may appeal to the Special Immigration Appeals Commission against the issue of the certificate; and for that purpose the Special Immigration Appeals Commission Act 1997 shall apply as to an appeal against an immigration decision to which section 92 of this Act applies.

(4) The Secretary of State may repeal this section by order.]

Note: Section 97A inserted by Immigration, Asylum and Nationality Act 2006, s 7 from 31 August 2006 (SI 2006/2226).

98. Other grounds of public good

(1) This section applies to an immigration decision of a kind referred to in section 82(2)(a) or (b).

(2) An appeal under section 82(1) against an immigration decision may not be brought or continued if the Secretary of State certifies that the decision is or was taken—

(a) by the Secretary of State wholly or partly on the ground that the exclusion or removal from the United Kingdom of the person to whom the decision relates is conducive to the public good, or

(b) in accordance with a direction of the Secretary of State which identifies the person to whom the decision relates and which is given wholly or partly on that ground.

(3) In subsection (2)(a) and (b) a reference to the Secretary of State is to the Secretary of State acting in person.

(4) Subsection (2) does not prevent the bringing of an appeal on either or both of the grounds referred to in section 84(1)(b) and (c).

(5) Subsection (2) does not prevent the bringing of an appeal against an immigration decision of the kind referred to in section 82(2)(a) on the grounds referred to in section 84(1)(g).

Note: Commencement from 1 April 2003 (SI 2003/754, which sets out transitional provisions).

99. Sections 96 to 98: appeal in progress

(1) This section applies where a certificate is issued under section 96(1) or (2), 97 or 98 in respect of a pending appeal.

(2) The appeal shall lapse.

Note: Commencement from 1 April 2003 (SI 2003/754, which sets out transitional provisions).

Appeal from adjudicator

100. Immigration Appeal Tribunal

. . .

Note: Section 100 ceased to have effect, Asylum and Immigration (Treatment of Claimants, etc.) Act 2004, s 26 from 4 April 2005 (SI 2005/565).

101. Appeal to Tribunal

. . .

Note: Section 101 ceased to have effect, Asylum and Immigration (Treatment of Claimants, etc.) Act 2004, s 26 from 4 April 2005 (SI 2005/565).

102. Decision

. . .

Note: Section 102 ceased to have effect from 4 April 2005 (SI 2005/565), Asylum and Immigration (Treatment of Claimants, etc.) Act 2004, s 26.

103. Appeal from Tribunal

. . .

Note: Section 103 ceased to have effect from 4 April 2005 (SI 2005/565), Asylum and Immigration (Treatment of Claimants, etc.) Act 2004, s 26.

[103A.–103E.]

Note: Sections 103A–E inserted by Asylum and Immigration (Treatment of Claimants, etc.) Act 2004, s 26 from 4 April 2005 (SI 2005/565). Revoked from 15 February 2010 (SI 2010/21).

Procedure

104. Pending appeal

(1) An appeal under section 82(1) is pending during the period—
(a) beginning when it is instituted, and
(b) ending when it is finally determined, withdrawn or abandoned (or when it lapses under section 99).

[(2) An appeal under section 82(1) is not finally determined for the purpose of subsection (1)(b) while—

(a) an application for permission to appeal under section 11 or 13 of the Tribunals, Courts and Enforcement Act 2007 could be made or is awaiting determination,

(b) permission to appeal under either of those sections has been granted and the appeal is awaiting determination, or

(c) an appeal has been remitted under section 12 or 14 of that Act and is awaiting determination.]

(3) . . .

[(4) An appeal under section 82(1) brought by a person while he is in the United Kingdom shall be treated as abandoned if the appellant leaves the United Kingdom.

(4A) An appeal under section 82(1) brought by a person while he is in the United Kingdom shall be treated as abandoned if the appellant is granted leave to enter or remain in the United Kingdom (subject to subsections (4B) and (4C)).

(4B) Subsection (4A) shall not apply to an appeal in so far as it is brought on the ground relating to the Refugee Convention specified in section 84(1)(g) where the appellant—

(a) is granted leave to enter or remain in the United Kingdom for a period exceeding 12 months, and

(b) gives notice, in accordance with [Tribunal Procedure Rules], that he wishes to pursue the appeal in so far as it is brought on that ground.

(4C) Subsection (4A) shall not apply to an appeal in so far as it is brought on the ground specified in section 84(1)(b) where the appellant gives notice, in accordance with [Tribunal Procedure Rules] any relevant procedural rules (which may include provision about timing), that he wishes to pursue the appeal in so far as it is brought on that ground.]

(5) An appeal under section 82(2)(a), (c), (d), (e) or (f) shall be treated as finally determined if a deportation order is made against the appellant.

Note: Commencement from 1 April 2003 (SI 2003/754). Subsection (3) omitted by Sch 2 Asylum and Immigration (Treatment of Claimants, etc.) Act 2004 from 4 April 2005 (SI 2005/565). Sub-section (4) substituted and sub-ss (4A)–(4C) inserted by Immigration, Asylum and Nationality Act 2006, s 9 from 13 November 2006 (SI 2006/2838). Subsection (2) and words in square brackets in sub-ss (4B)(b) and (4C) substituted from 15 February 2010 (SI 2010/21).

105. Notice of immigration decision

(1) The Secretary of State may make regulations requiring a person to be given written notice where an immigration decision is taken in respect of him.

(2) The regulations may, in particular, provide that a notice under subsection (1) of a decision against which the person is entitled to appeal under section 82(1) must state—

(a) that there is a right of appeal under that section, and

(b) how and when that right may be exercised.

(3) The regulations may make provision (which may include presumptions) about service.

Note: Commencement from 1 April 2003 (SI 2003/754).

106. Rules

(1) . . .

[(1A) . . .

(2) ...

[**(3)** In the case of an appeal under section 82, 83 or 83A or by virtue of section 109, Tribunal Procedure Rules may enable the Tribunal to certify that the appeal had no merit (and shall make provision for the consequences of the issue of a certificate).]

(4) A person commits an offence if without reasonable excuse he fails to comply with a requirement imposed in accordance with [Tribunal Procedure Rules in connection with proceedings under section 82, 83 or 83A or by virtue of section 109] to attend before ... the Tribunal—

    (a) to give evidence, or

    (b) to produce a document.

(5) A person who is guilty of an offence under subsection (4) shall be liable on summary conviction to a fine not exceeding level 3 on the standard scale.

Note: Commencement from 1 April 2003 (SI 2003/754). Subsections (1), (1A) and (2) revoked, sub-s (3) and words in square brackets in sub-s (4) substituted from 15 February 2010 (SI 2010/21).

107. Practice directions

(1) ...

[**(1A)** ...

(2) ...

[**(3)** In the case of proceedings under section 82, 83 or 83A or by virtue of section 109, or proceedings in the Upper Tribunal arising out of such proceedings, practice directions under section 23 of the Tribunals, Courts and Enforcement Act 2007—

    (a) may require the Tribunal to treat a specified decision of the Tribunal or Upper Tribunal as authoritative in respect of a particular matter; and

    (b) may require the Upper Tribunal to treat a specified decision of the Tribunal or Upper Tribunal as authoritative in respect of a particular matter.]

[**(3A)** In subsection (3) the reference to a decision of the Tribunal includes—

    (a) a decision of the Asylum and Immigration Tribunal, and

    (b) a decision of the Immigration Appeal Tribunal.]

[**(4)** ...

(5) ......

(6) ....

(7) ....

Note: Commencement from 1 April 2003 (SI 2003/754). Subsections (1), (1A) and (4)—(7) revoked and subs (3) substituted and (3A) inserted from 15 February 2010 (SI 2010/21).

108. Forged document: proceedings in private

(1) This section applies where it is alleged—

    (a) that a document relied on by a party to an appeal under section 82 [, 83 or 83A] is a forgery, and

    (b) that disclosure to that party of a matter relating to the detection of the forgery would be contrary to the public interest.

(2) [The Tribunal]

(a) must investigate the allegation in private, and

(b) may proceed in private so far as necessary to prevent disclosure of the matter referred to in subsection (1)(b).

Note: Commencement from 1 April 2003 (SI 2003/754). Amended by Sch 2 Asylum and Immigration (Treatment of Claimants, etc.) Act 2004, from 4 April 2005 (SI 2005/565). Words in square brackets in sub-s (1)(a) substituted by Sch 1 Immigration, Asylum and Nationality Act 2006 from 31 August 2006 (SI 2006/2226).

General

109. European Union and European economic area

(1) Regulations may provide for, or make provision about, an appeal against an immigration decision taken in respect of a person who has or claims to have a right under any of the Community Treaties.

(2) The regulations may—

(a) apply a provision of this Act or the Special Immigration Appeals Commission Act 1997 (c. 68) with or without modification;

(b) make provision similar to a provision made by or under this Act or that Act;

(c) disapply or modify the effect of a provision of this Act or that Act.

(3) In subsection (1) 'immigration decision' means a decision about—

(a) a person's entitlement to enter or remain in the United Kingdom, or

(b) removal of a person from the United Kingdom.

Note: Commencement from 1 April 2003 (SI 2003/754).

110. Grants

Note: Commencement from 1 April 2003 (SI 2003/754). Ceased to have effect from 16 June 2006, Immigration, Asylum and Nationality Act 2006, s 10 (SI 2006/1497).

111. ...

Note: Section 111 deleted by UK Borders Act 2007 s 54(c) from 1 April 2008 (SI 2008/309).

112. Regulations, &c.

(1) Regulations under this Part shall be made by the Secretary of State.

(2) Regulations . . . under this Part . . . —

(a) must be made by statutory instrument, and

(b) shall be subject to annulment in pursuance of a resolution of either House of Parliament.

(3) Regulations . . . under this Part—

(a) may make provision which applies generally or only in a specified case or in specified circumstances,

(b) may make different provision for different cases or circumstances,

(c) may include consequential, transitional or incidental provision, and

(d) may include savings.

[(3A) An order under section 88A—

(a) must be made by statutory instrument,

(b) may not be made unless a draft has been laid before and approved by resolution of each House of Parliament, and

(c) may include transitional provision.]

(4) An order under section 94(5) or 115(8)—

(a) must be made by statutory instrument,

(b) may not be made unless a draft has been laid before and approved by resolution of each House of Parliament, and

(c) may include transitional provision.

(5) An order under section [94(6) or (6B)] or 115(9)—

(a) must be made by statutory instrument,

(b) shall be subject to annulment in pursuance of a resolution of either House of Parliament, and

(c) may include transitional provision.

[(5A) If an instrument makes provision under section 94(5) and 94(6)—

(a) subsection (4)(b) above shall apply, and

(b) subsection (5)(b) above shall not apply.]

[(5B) An order under section 97A(4)—

(a) must be made by statutory instrument,

(b) shall be subject to annulment in pursuance of a resolution of either House of Parliament, and

(c) may include transitional provision.]

[(6) . . .

(7) . . .]

Note: Commenced 10 February 2003 (SI 2003/249). Subsection (3A) and (5A) inserted by Asylum and Immigration (Treatment of Claimants, etc.) Act 2004, ss 29 and 27 respectively from 1 October 2004 (SI 2004/2523). Words in square brackets in sub-s (5) substituted and sub-s (5B) inserted by Immigration, Asylum and Nationality Act 2006, ss 7, 14, 62 and Sch 1 from 31 August 2006 (SI 2006/2226). Words omitted from sub-ss (2) and (3) and sub-ss (6)–(7) revoked from 15 February 2010 (SI 2010/21, which contains savings).

113. Interpretation

(1) In this Part, unless a contrary intention appears—

['asylum claim'—

(a) means a claim made by a person that to remove him from or require him to leave the United Kingdom would breach the United Kingdom's obligations under the Refugee Convention, but

(b) does not include a claim which, having regard to a former claim, falls to be disregarded for the purposes of this Part in accordance with immigration rules,]

'entry clearance' has the meaning given by section 33(1) of the Immigration Act 1971 (c. 77) (interpretation),

['human rights claim'—

(a) means a claim made by a person that to remove him from or require him to leave the United Kingdom would be unlawful under section 6 of the Human Rights Act 1998 (c. 42) (public authority not to act contrary to Convention) as being incompatible with his Convention rights, but

(b) does not include a claim which, having regard to a former claim, falls to be disregarded for the purposes of this Part in accordance with immigration rules,]

'the Human Rights Convention' has the same meaning as 'the Convention' in the Human Rights Act 1998 and 'Convention rights' shall be construed in accordance with section 1 of that Act,

'illegal entrant' has the meaning given by section 33(1) of the Immigration Act 1971,

'immigration rules' means rules under section 1(4) of that Act (general immigration rules),

'prescribed' means prescribed by regulations,

'the Refugee Convention' means the Convention relating to the Status of Refugees done at Geneva on 28 July 1951 and its Protocol,

'visitor' means a visitor in accordance with immigration rules, and

'work permit' has the meaning given by section 33(1) of the Immigration Act 1971 (c. 77) (interpretation).

(2) A reference to varying leave to enter or remain in the United Kingdom does not include a reference to adding, varying or revoking a condition of leave.

Note: Commenced 10 February 2003 (SI 2003/249). Definitions of asylum claim and human rights claim substituted by Immigration, Asylum and Nationality Act 2006, s 12 from a date to be appointed.

114. Repeal

(1) ...

(2) Schedule 6 (which makes transitional provision in connection with the repeal of Part IV of that Act and its replacement by this Part) shall have effect.

(3) Schedule 7 (consequential amendments) shall have effect.

Note: Subsection (1) repeals Part IV of the Immigration and Asylum Act 1999. Subsection (3) Commenced 10 February 2003 (SI 2003/1). Remainder from 1 April 2003 (SI 2003/754).

115. Appeal from within United Kingdom: unfounded human rights or asylum claim: transitional provision

(1) A person may not bring an appeal under section 65 or 69 of the Immigration and Asylum Act 1999 (human rights and asylum) while in the United Kingdom if—

(a) the Secretary of State certifies that the appeal relates to a human rights claim or an asylum claim which is clearly unfounded, and

(b) the person does not have another right of appeal while in the United Kingdom under Part IV of that Act.

(2) A person while in the United Kingdom may not bring an appeal under section 69 of that Act, or raise a question which relates to the Human Rights Convention under section 77 of that Act, if the Secretary of State certifies that—

(a) it is proposed to remove the person to a country of which he is not a national or citizen, and

(b) there is no reason to believe that the person's rights under the Human Rights Convention will be breached in that country.

(3) A person while in the United Kingdom may not bring an appeal under section 65 of that Act (human rights) if the Secretary of State certifies that—

(a) it is proposed to remove the person to a country of which he is not a national or citizen, and

(b) there is no reason to believe that the person's rights under the Human Rights Convention will be breached in that country.

(4) In determining whether a person in relation to whom a certificate has been issued under subsection (2) or (3) may be removed from the United Kingdom, the country specified in the certificate is to be regarded as—

(a) a place where a person's life and liberty is not threatened by reason of his race, religion, nationality, membership of a particular social group, or political opinion, and

(b) a place from which a person will not be sent to another country otherwise than in accordance with the Refugee Convention.

(5) Where a person in relation to whom a certificate is issued under this section subsequently brings an appeal or raises a question under section 65, 69 or 77 of that Act while outside the United Kingdom, the appeal or question shall be considered as if he had not been removed from the United Kingdom.

(6) If the Secretary of State is satisfied that a person who makes a human rights claim or an asylum claim is entitled to reside in a State listed in subsection (7), he shall issue a certificate under subsection (1) unless satisfied that the claim is not clearly unfounded.

(7) Those States are—
    (a) the Republic of Cyprus,
    (b) the Czech Republic,
    (c) the Republic of Estonia,
    (d) the Republic of Hungary,
    (e) the Republic of Latvia,
    (f) the Republic of Lithuania,
    (g) the Republic of Malta,
    (h) the Republic of Poland,
    (i) the Slovak Republic, and
    (j) the Republic of Slovenia.
    [(k) the Republic of Albania,
    (l) Bulgaria,
    (m) Serbia and Montenegro,
    (n) Jamaica,
    (o) Macedonia,
    (p) the Republic of Moldova, and
    (q) Romania.]

(8) The Secretary of State may by order add a State, or part of a State, to the list in subsection (7) if satisfied that—

(a) there is in general in that State or part no serious risk of persecution of persons entitled to reside in that State or part, and

(b) removal to that State or part of persons entitled to reside there will not in general contravene the United Kingdom's obligations under the Human Rights Convention.

(9) The Secretary of State may by order remove from the list in subsection (7) a State or part added under subsection (8).

(10) In this section 'asylum claim' and 'human rights claim' have the meanings given by section 113 but—

(a) a reference to a claim in that section shall be treated as including a reference to an allegation, and

(b) a reference in that section to making a claim at a place designated by the Secretary of State shall be ignored.

Note: Commenced 7 November 2002, s 162. Continues to have effect in relation to any person who made an asylum or human rights claim (as defined in sub-s (10)) on or after 1 April 2003. Words in square brackets added by SI 2003/970 from 1 April 2003.

116. Special Immigration Appeals Commission: Community Legal Service

. . .

Note: Amends para 2(1), Sch 2 Access to Justice Act 1999. Repealed by Legal Aid, Sentencing and Punishment of Offenders Act 2012, Sch 5, Part 2 from a date to be appointed.

117. Northern Ireland appeals: legal aid

. . .

Note: Amends Part 1, Sch 1 Legal Aid, Advice and Assistance (Northern Ireland) Order 1981.

PART VI

IMMIGRATION PROCEDURE

Applications

118. Leave pending decision on variation application

. . .

Note: Amends Immigration Act 1971, s 3C.

119. Deemed leave on cancellation of notice

. . .

Note: Amends para 6(3), Sch 2 Immigration Act 1971.

120. Requirement to state additional grounds for application

(1) This section applies to a person if—

(a) he has made an application to enter or remain in the United Kingdom, or

(b) an immigration decision within the meaning of section 82 has been taken or may be taken in respect of him.

(2) The Secretary of State or an immigration officer may by notice in writing require the person to state—

(a) his reasons for wishing to enter or remain in the United Kingdom,

(b) any grounds on which he should be permitted to enter or remain in the United Kingdom, and

(c) any grounds on which he should not be removed from or required to leave the United Kingdom.

(3) A statement under subsection (2) need not repeat reasons or grounds set out in—

(a) the application mentioned in subsection (1)(a), or

(b) an application to which the immigration decision mentioned in subsection (1)(b) relates.

Note: Commencement from 1 April 2003 (SI 2003/754).

121. Compliance with procedure

. . .

Note: Amends Immigration Act 1971, s 31A.

Work permit

122. . . .

Note: Commenced 10 February 2003 (SI 2003/1). Ceased to have effect by Sch 2 Immigration, Asylum and Nationality Act 2006 from 2 April 2007 (SI 2007/1109).

123. Advice about work permit, &c.

. . .

Note: Amends Immigration and Asylum Act 1999, s 82.

Authority-to-carry scheme

124. Authority to carry

(1) Regulations made by the Secretary of State may authorise him to require a person (a 'carrier') to pay a penalty if the carrier brings a passenger to the United Kingdom and—

(a) the carrier was required by an authority-to-carry scheme to seek authority under the scheme to carry the passenger, and

(b) the carrier did not seek authority before the journey to the United Kingdom commenced or was refused authority under the scheme.

(2) An 'authority-to-carry scheme' is a scheme operated by the Secretary of State which requires carriers to seek authority to bring passengers to the United Kingdom.

(3) An authority-to-carry scheme must specify—

(a) the class of carrier to which it applies (which may be defined by reference to a method of transport or otherwise), and

(b) the class of passenger to which it applies (which may be defined by reference to nationality, the possession of specified documents or otherwise).

(4) The Secretary of State may operate different authority-to-carry schemes for different purposes.

(5) Where the Secretary of State makes regulations under subsection (1) he must—

(a) identify in the regulations the authority-to-carry scheme to which they refer, and

(b) lay the authority-to-carry scheme before Parliament.

(6) Regulations under subsection (1) may, in particular—

(a) apply or make provision similar to a provision of sections 40 to 43 of and Schedule 1 to the Immigration and Asylum Act 1999 (c. 33) (charge for passenger without document);

(b) do anything which may be done under a provision of any of those sections;

(c) amend any of those sections.

(7) Regulations by virtue of subsection (6)(a) may, in particular—

(a) apply a provision with modification;

(b) apply a provision which confers power to make legislation.

(8) The grant or refusal of authority under an authority-to-carry scheme shall not be taken to determine whether a person is entitled or permitted to enter the United Kingdom.

(9) Regulations under this section—

(a) must be made by statutory instrument, and

(b) may not be made unless a draft has been laid before and approved by resolution of each House of Parliament.

Note: Commencement at a date to be appointed.

Evasion of procedure

125. Carriers' liability

Schedule 8 (which amends Part II of the Immigration and Asylum Act 1999 (carriers' liability)) shall have effect.

Note: Commencement 14 November 2002 for the purpose of enabling subordinate legislation; 8 December 2002 for certain purposes (SI 2002/2811) and 11 May 2012 for certain other purposes (2012/1263).

Provision of information by traveller

126. Physical data: compulsory provision

(1) The Secretary of State may by regulations—

(a) require an immigration application to be accompanied by specified information about external physical characteristics of the applicant;

(b) enable an authorised person to require an individual who makes an immigration application to provide information about his external physical characteristics;

(c) enable an authorised person to require an entrant to provide information about his external physical characteristics.

(2) In subsection (1) 'immigration application' means an application for—

(a) entry clearance,

(b) leave to enter or remain in the United Kingdom, or

(c) variation of leave to enter or remain in the United Kingdom.

(3) Regulations under subsection (1) may not—

(a) impose a requirement in respect of a person to whom section 141 of the Immigration and Asylum Act 1999 (c. 33) (fingerprinting) applies, during the relevant period within the meaning of that section, or

(b) enable a requirement to be imposed in respect of a person to whom that section applies, during the relevant period within the meaning of that section.

(4) Regulations under subsection (1) may, in particular—

(a) require, or enable an authorised person to require, the provision of information in a specified form;

(b) require an individual to submit, or enable an authorised person to require an individual to submit, to a specified process by means of which information is obtained or recorded;

(c) make provision about the effect of failure to provide information or to submit to a process (which may, in particular, include provision for an application to be disregarded or dismissed if a requirement is not satisfied);

(d) confer a function (which may include the exercise of a discretion) on an authorised person;

(e) require an authorised person to have regard to a code (with or without modification);

(f) require an authorised person to have regard to such provisions of a code (with or without modification) as may be specified by direction of the Secretary of State;

(g) make provision about the use and retention of information provided (which may include provision permitting the use of information for specified purposes which do not relate to immigration);

(h) make provision which applies generally or only in specified cases or circumstances;

(i) make different provision for different cases or circumstances.

(5) Regulations under subsection (1) must—

(a) include provision about the destruction of information obtained or recorded by virtue of the regulations,

(b) require the destruction of information at the end of the period of ten years beginning with the day on which it is obtained or recorded in a case for which destruction at the end of another period is not required by or in accordance with the regulations, and

(c) include provision similar to section 143(2) and (10) to (13) of the Immigration and Asylum Act 1999 (c. 33) (fingerprints: destruction of copies and electronic data).

(6) In so far as regulations under subsection (1) require an individual under the age of 16 to submit to a process, the regulations must make provision similar to section 141(3) to (5) and (13) of the Immigration and Asylum Act 1999 (fingerprints: children).

(7) In so far as regulations under subsection (1) enable an authorised person to require an individual under the age of 16 to submit to a process, the regulations must make provision similar to section 141(3) to (5), (12) and (13) of that Act (fingerprints: children).

(8) Regulations under subsection (1)—

(a) must be made by statutory instrument, and

(b) shall not be made unless a draft of the regulations has been laid before and approved by resolution of each House of Parliament.

(9) In this section—

'authorised person' has the meaning given by section 141(5) of the Immigration and Asylum Act 1999 (authority to take fingerprints),

'code' has the meaning given by section 145(6) of that Act (code of practice),

'entrant' has the meaning given by section 33(1) of the Immigration Act 1971 (c. 77) (interpretation), 'entry clearance' has the meaning given by section 33(1) of that Act, and

'external physical characteristics' includes, in particular, features of the iris or any other part of the eye.

Note: Commencement from 1 April 2003 (SI 2003/754).

127. Physical data: voluntary provision

(1) The Secretary of State may operate a scheme under which an individual may supply, or submit to the obtaining or recording of, information about his external physical characteristics to be used (wholly or partly) in connection with entry to the United Kingdom.

(2) In particular, the Secretary of State may—

(a) require an authorised person to use information supplied under a scheme;

(b) make provision about the collection, use and retention of information supplied under a scheme (which may include provision requiring an authorised person to have regard to a code);

(c) charge for participation in a scheme.

(3) In this section the following expressions have the same meaning as in section 126—

(a) 'authorised person',

(b) 'code', and

(c) 'external physical characteristics'.

Note: Commencement from 10 December 2004 (SI 2004/2998).

128. Data collection under Immigration and Asylum Act 1999

Note: Amends Immigration and Asylum Act 1999, ss 144, 145.

Disclosure of information by public authority

129. Local authority

(1) The Secretary of State may require a local authority to supply information for the purpose of establishing where a person is if the Secretary of State reasonably suspects that—

(a) the person has committed an offence under section 24(1)(a), (b), (c), (e) or (f), 24A(1) or 26(1)(c) or (d) of the Immigration Act 1971 (c. 77) (illegal entry, deception, &c.), and

(b) the person is or has been resident in the local authority's area.

(2) A local authority shall comply with a requirement under this section.

(3) In the application of this section to England and Wales 'local authority' means—

(a) a county council,

(b) a county borough council,

(c) a district council,

(d) a London borough council,

(e) the Common Council of the City of London, and

(f) the Council of the Isles of Scilly.

(4) In the application of this section to Scotland 'local authority' means a council constituted under section 2 of the Local Government etc. (Scotland) Act 1994 (c. 39).

(5) In the application of this section to Northern Ireland—

(a) a reference to a local authority shall be taken as a reference to the Northern Ireland Housing Executive, and

(b) the reference to a local authority's area shall be taken as a reference to Northern Ireland.

Note: Commencement from 30 July 2003 (SI 2003/1747).

130. . . .

Note: Section 130 deleted by UK Borders Act 2007, ss 40(6)(b), 58 and Schedule from 31 January 2008 (SI 2008/99).

131. Police, &c.

Information may be supplied under section 20 of the Immigration and Asylum Act 1999 (c. 33) (supply of information to Secretary of State) for use for the purpose of—

[(a) determining whether an applicant for naturalisation under the British Nationality Act 1981 is of good character;

[(b) determining whether, for the purposes of an application referred to in section 41A of the British Nationality Act 1981, the person for whose registration the application is made is of good character;

(ba) determining whether, for the purposes of an application under section 1 of the Hong Kong (War Wives and Widows) Act 1996, the woman for whose registration the application is made is of good character;

(bb) determining whether, for the purposes of an application under section 1 of the British Nationality (Hong Kong) Act 1997 for the registration of an adult or young person within the meaning of subsection (5A) of that section, the person is of good character;]

(c) determining whether to make an order in respect of a person under section 40 of the British Nationality Act 1981.]

Note: Commencement 10 February 2003 (SI 2001/1). Words in square brackets substituted by UK Borders Act 2007, s 43 from 31 January 2008 (SI 2008/99). Subsections (b)–(bb) substituted by s 47 Borders, Citizenship and Immigration Act 2009 from 13 January 2010 (SI 2009/2731).

132. Supply of document, &c. to Secretary of State

. . .

Note: Amends Immigration and Asylum Act 1999, s 20.

133. Medical inspectors

(1) This section applies to a person if an immigration officer acting under Schedule 2 to the Immigration Act 1971 (c. 77) (control on entry, &c.) has brought the person to the attention of—

(a) a medical inspector appointed under paragraph 1(2) of that Schedule, or

(b) a person working under the direction of a medical inspector appointed under that paragraph.

(2) A medical inspector may disclose to a health service body—

(a) the name of a person to whom this section applies,

(b) his place of residence in the United Kingdom,

(c) his age,

(d) the language which he speaks,

(e) the nature of any disease with which the inspector thinks the person may be infected,

(f) relevant details of the person's medical history,

(g) the grounds for an opinion mentioned in paragraph (e) (including the result of any test or examination which has been carried out), and

(h) the inspector's opinion about action which the health service body should take.

(3) A disclosure may be made under subsection (2) only if the medical inspector thinks it necessary for the purpose of—

(a) preventative medicine,

(b) medical diagnosis,

(c) the provision of care or treatment, or

(d) the management of health care services.

(4) For the purposes of this section 'health service body' in relation to a person means a body which carries out functions in an area which includes his place of residence and which is—

(a) in relation to England—

(i) a Primary Care Trust established under [section 18 of the National Health Service Act 2006],

(ii) a National Health Service Trust established under [section 25 of the National Health Service Act 2006 or section 18 of the National Health Service (Wales) Act 2006],

{(iia) an NHS foundation trust,}

(iii) a Strategic Health Authority established under [section 13 of the National Health Service Act],

(iv) a Special Health Authority established under [section 28 of that Act or section 22 of the National Health Service (Wales) Act 2006], or

(v) the Public Health Laboratory Service Board,

[or

(vi) the Health Protection Agency.]

(b) in relation to Wales—

[(i) a Local Health Board established under section 11 of the National Health Service (Wales) Act 2006],

(ii) a National Health Service Trust established under [section 25 of the National Health Service Act 2006 or section 18 of the National Health Service (Wales) Act 2006], or

(iii) the Public Health Laboratory Service Board,—

[or

(iv) the Health Protection Agency.]

(c) in relation to Scotland—

(i) a Health Board, Special Health Board or National Health Service Trust established under section 2 or 12A of the National Health Service (Scotland) Act 1978 (c. 29), …

(ii) the Common Services Agency for the Scottish Health Service established under section 10 of that Act, or

[(iia) Healthcare Improvement Scotland established under section 10A of the 1978 Act, or] [(iii) the Health Protection Agency, or]

(d) in relation to Northern Ireland—

(i) a Health and Social Services Board established under the Health and Personal Social Services (Northern Ireland) Order 1972 (S.I. 1972/1265 (N.I. 14)),

(ii) a Health and Social Services Trust established under the Health and Personal Social Services (Northern Ireland) Order 1991 (S.I. 1991/194 (N.I. 1)), . . .

(iii) the Department of Health, Social Services and Public Safety,

[or

(iv) the Health Protection Agency.]

Note: Commencement 10 February 2003 (SI 2003/1). Words in square brackets inserted and words omitted by Sch 3 Health Protection Agency Act 2004 from 1 April 2005 (SI 2005/121). Words in square brackets in subsection (4)(a)(i)-(iv) and (4)(b)(i) and (ii) substituted by National Health Service (Consequential Provisions) Act Sch 1 para 228 from 1 March 2007. Subsection ((4)(a)(iia) inserted by Health and Social Care (Community Health and Standards) Act 2003 Sch 4 from 1 April 2004 (SI 2004/759). Subsection (4)(c)(iia) inserted from 28 October 2011 (SI 2011/2581).

Disclosure of information by private person

134. Employer

(1) The Secretary of State may require an employer to supply information about an employee whom the Secretary of State reasonably suspects of having committed an offence under—

(a) section 24(1)(a), (b), (c), (e) or (f), 24A(1) or 26(1)(c) or (d) of the Immigration Act 1971 (c. 77) (illegal entry, deception, &c.),

(b) section 105(1)(a), (b) or (c) of the Immigration and Asylum Act 1999 (c. 33) (support for asylum-seeker: fraud), or

(c) section 106(1)(a), (b) or (c) of that Act (support for asylum-seeker: fraud).

(2) The power under subsection (1) may be exercised to require information about an employee only if the information—

(a) is required for the purpose of establishing where the employee is, or

(b) relates to the employee's earnings or to the history of his employment.

(3) In this section a reference to an employer or employee—

(a) includes a reference to a former employer or employee, and

(b) shall be construed in accordance with section 8(8) of the Asylum and Immigration Act 1996 (c. 49) (restrictions on employment).

(4) Where—

(a) a business (the 'employment agency') arranges for one person (the 'worker') to provide services to another (the 'client'), and

(b) the worker is not employed by the employment agency or the client, this section shall apply as if the employment agency were the worker's employer while he provides services to the client.

Note: Commencement from 30 July 2003 (SI 2003/1747).

135. Financial institution

(1) The Secretary of State may require a financial institution to supply information about a person if the Secretary of State reasonably suspects that—

(a) the person has committed an offence under section 105(1)(a), (b) or (c) or 106(1) (a), (b) or (c) of the Immigration and Asylum Act 1999 (c. 33) (support for asylum-seeker: fraud),

(b) the information is relevant to the offence, and

(c) the institution has the information.

(2) In this section 'financial institution' means—

(a) a person who has permission under Part 4 of the Financial Services and Markets Act 2000 (c. 8) to accept deposits, and

(b) a building society (within the meaning given by the Building Societies Act 1986 (c. 53)).

Note: Commencement from 30 July 2003 (SI 2003/1747).

136. Notice

(1) A requirement to provide information under section 134 or 135 must be imposed by notice in writing specifying—

(a) the information,

(b) the manner in which it is to be provided, and

(c) the period of time within which it is to be provided.

(2) A period of time specified in a notice under subsection (1)(c)—

(a) must begin with the date of receipt of the notice, and

(b) must not be less than ten working days.

(3) A person on whom a notice is served under subsection (1) must provide the Secretary of State with the information specified in the notice.

(4) Information provided under subsection (3) must be provided—

(a) in the manner specified under subsection (1)(b), and

(b) within the time specified under subsection (1)(c).

(5) In this section 'working day' means a day which is not—

(a) Saturday,

(b) Sunday,

(c) Christmas Day,

(d) Good Friday, or

(e) a day which is a bank holiday under the Banking and Financial Dealings Act 1971 (c. 80) in any part of the United Kingdom.

Note: Commencement from 30 July 2003 (SI 2003/1747).

137. Disclosure of information: offences

(1) A person commits an offence if without reasonable excuse he fails to comply with section 136(3).

(2) A person who is guilty of an offence under subsection (1) shall be liable on summary conviction to—

(a) imprisonment for a term not exceeding three months,

(b) a fine not exceeding level 5 on the standard scale, or

(c) both.

Note: Commencement from 30 July 2003 (SI 2003/1747).

138. Offence by body

(1) Subsection (2) applies where an offence under section 137 is committed by a body corporate and it is proved that the offence—

(a) was committed with the consent or connivance of an officer of the body, or

(b) was attributable to neglect on the part of an officer of the body.

(2) The officer, as well as the body, shall be guilty of the offence.

(3) In this section a reference to an officer of a body corporate includes a reference to—

(a) a director, manager or secretary,

(b) a person purporting to act as a director, manager or secretary, and

(c) if the affairs of the body are managed by its members, a member.

(4) Where an offence under section 137 is committed by a partnership (other than a limited partnership), each partner shall be guilty of the offence.

(5) Subsection (1) shall have effect in relation to a limited partnership as if—

(a) a reference to a body corporate were a reference to a limited partnership, and

(b) a reference to an officer of the body were a reference to a partner.

Note: Commencement from 30 July 2003 (SI 2003/1747).

139. Privilege against self-incrimination

(1) Information provided by a person pursuant to a requirement under section 134 or 135 shall not be admissible in evidence in criminal proceedings against that person.

(2) This section shall not apply to proceedings for an offence under section 137.

Note: Commencement from 30 July 2003 (SI 2003/1747).

Immigration services

140. Immigration Services Commissioner

. . .

Note: Amends, Immigration and Asylum Act 1999 s 87(3), Sch 5, para 7 and Sch 6, para 3.

Immigration control

141. EEA ports: juxtaposed controls

(1) The Secretary of State may by order make provision for the purpose of giving effect to an international agreement which concerns immigration control at an EEA port (whether or not it also concerns other aspects of frontier control at the port).

(2) An order under this section may make any provision which appears to the Secretary of State—

(a) likely to facilitate implementation of the international agreement (including those aspects of the agreement which relate to frontier control other than immigration control), or

(b) appropriate as a consequence of provision made for the purpose of facilitating implementation of the agreement.

(3) In particular, an order under this section may—

(a) provide for a law of England and Wales to have effect, with or without modification, in relation to a person in a specified area or anything done in a specified area;

(b) provide for a law of England and Wales not to have effect in relation to a person in a specified area or anything done in a specified area;

(c) provide for a law of England and Wales to be modified in its effect in relation to a person in a specified area or anything done in a specified area;

(d) disapply or modify an enactment in relation to a person who has undergone a process in a specified area;

(e) disapply or modify an enactment otherwise than under paragraph (b), (c) or (d);

(f) make provision conferring a function (which may include—

(i) provision conferring a discretionary function;

(ii) provision conferring a function on a servant or agent of the government of a State other than the United Kingdom);

(g) create or extend the application of an offence;

(h) impose or permit the imposition of a penalty;

(i) require the payment of, or enable a person to require the payment of, a charge or fee;

(j) make provision about enforcement (which may include—

(i) provision conferring a power of arrest, detention or removal from or to any place;

(ii) provision for the purpose of enforcing the law of a State other than the United Kingdom);

(k) confer jurisdiction on a court or tribunal;

(l) confer immunity or provide for indemnity;

(m) make provision about compensation;

(n) impose a requirement, or enable a requirement to be imposed, for a person to co-operate with or to provide facilities for the use of another person who is performing a function under the order or under the international agreement (which may include a requirement to provide facilities without charge);

(o) make provision about the disclosure of information.

(4) An order under this section may—

(a) make provision which applies generally or only in specified circumstances;

(b) make different provision for different circumstances;

(c) amend an enactment.

(5) An order under this section—

(a) must be made by statutory instrument,

(b) may not be made unless the Secretary of State has consulted with such persons as appear to him to be appropriate, and

(c) may not be made unless a draft has been laid before and approved by resolution of each House of Parliament.

(6) In this section—

'EEA port' means a port in an EEA State from which passengers are commonly carried by sea to or from the United Kingdom,

'EEA State' means a State which is a contracting party to the Agreement on the European Economic Area signed at Oporto on 2 May 1992 (as it has effect from time to time),

'frontier control' means the enforcement of law which relates to, or in so far as it relates to, the movement of persons or goods into or out of the United Kingdom or another State, 'immigration control' means arrangements made in connection with the movement of persons into or out of the United Kingdom or another State,

'international agreement' means an agreement made between Her Majesty's Government and the government of another State, and

'specified area' means an area (whether of the United Kingdom or of another State) specified in an international agreement.

Note: Commenced 8 January 2003 (SI 2002/2811).

Country information

142 ...

Note: Section 142 deleted by UK Borders Act 2007, s 54 from 1 April 2008 (SI 2008/309).

PART VII
OFFENCES
Substance

143. Assisting unlawful immigration, &c.

...

Note: Amends Immigration Act 1971, s 25.

144. Section 143: consequential amendments

...

Note: Amends Immigration Act 1971, ss 25A, 28A, 28B, 28C, 28D, 28F and 33.

145. Traffic in prostitution

(1) A person commits an offence if he arranges or facilitates the arrival in the United Kingdom of an individual (the 'passenger') and—

(a) he intends to exercise control over prostitution by the passenger in the United Kingdom or elsewhere, or

(b) he believes that another person is likely to exercise control over prostitution by the passenger in the United Kingdom or elsewhere.

(2) A person commits an offence if he arranges or facilitates travel within the United Kingdom by an individual (the 'passenger') in respect of whom he believes that an offence under subsection (1) may have been committed and—

(a) he intends to exercise control over prostitution by the passenger in the United Kingdom or elsewhere, or

(b) he believes that another person is likely to exercise control over prostitution by the passenger in the United Kingdom or elsewhere.

(3) A person commits an offence if he arranges or facilitates the departure from the United Kingdom of an individual (the 'passenger') and—

(a) he intends to exercise control over prostitution by the passenger outside the United Kingdom, or

(b) he believes that another person is likely to exercise control over prostitution by the passenger outside the United Kingdom.

(4) For the purposes of subsections (1) to (3) a person exercises control over prostitution by another if for purposes of gain he exercises control, direction or influence over the prostitute's movements in a way which shows that he is aiding, abetting or compelling the prostitution.

(5) A person guilty of an offence under this section shall be liable—

(a) on conviction on indictment, to imprisonment for a term not exceeding 14 years, to a fine or to both, or

(b) on summary conviction, to imprisonment for a term not exceeding six months, to a fine not exceeding the statutory maximum or to both.

Note: Commenced 10 February 2003 (SI 2003/1). Repealed by Sexual Offences Act 2003, Sch 6 from 1 May 2004 (SI 2004/874).

146. Section 145: supplementary

(1) Subsections (1) to (3) of section 145 apply to anything done—

(a) in the United Kingdom,

(b) outside the United Kingdom by an individual to whom subsection (2) applies, or

(c) outside the United Kingdom by a body incorporated under the law of a part of the United Kingdom.

(2) This subsection applies to—

(a) a British citizen,

(b) a British overseas territories citizen,

(c) a British National (Overseas),

(d) a British Overseas citizen,

(e) a person who is a British subject under the British Nationality Act 1981 (c. 61), and

(f) a British protected person within the meaning of that Act.

(3) Sections 25C and 25D of the Immigration Act 1971 (c. 77) (forfeiture or detention of vehicle, &c.) shall apply in relation to an offence under section 145 of this Act as they apply in relation to an offence under section 25 of that Act.

(4) . . .

Note: Subsection (4) amends para 2, Sch 4 Criminal Justice and Court Services Act 2000. Commenced 10 February 2003 (SI 2003/1). Repealed by Sexual Offences Act 2003, Sch 6 from 1 May 2004 (SI 2004/874).

147. Employment

Note: Amends Asylum and Immigration Act 1996, s 8.

148. Registration card

Note: Amends Immigration Act 1971, s 26.

149. Immigration stamp

Note: Inserts s 26B into the Immigration Act 1971.

150. Sections 148 and 149: consequential amendments

Note: Amends Immigration Act 1971, ss 28A, 28B and 28D.

151. False information

Note: Amends Immigration Act 1971, s 26(3).

Procedure

152. Arrest by immigration officer

. . .

Note: Inserts s 28AA into the Immigration Act 1971.

153. Power of entry

. . .

Note: Inserts s 28CA into the Immigration Act 1971; amends Immigration and Asylum Act 1999, s 146.

154. Power to search for evidence

. . .

Note: Inserts ss 28FA, 28FB into the Immigration Act 1971.

155. Sections 153 and 154: supplemental

. . .

Note: Amends Immigration Act 1971, s 28L.

156. Time limit on prosecution

. . .

Note: Amends Immigration Act 1971, ss 24A, 28(1).

PART VIII
GENERAL

157. Consequential and incidental provision

(1) The Secretary of State may by order make consequential or incidental provision in connection with a provision of this Act.

(2) An order under this section may, in particular—

  (a) amend an enactment;

(b) modify the effect of an enactment.

(3) An order under this section must be made by statutory instrument.

(4) An order under this section which amends an enactment shall not be made unless a draft has been laid before and approved by resolution of each House of Parliament.

(5) Any other order under this section shall be subject to annulment pursuant to a resolution of either House of Parliament.

Note: Commenced 7 November 2002, s 162.

158. Interpretation: 'the Immigration Acts'

Note: Ceased to have effect by Immigration, Asylum and Nationality Act 2006, s 64 from 30 March 2006 (Royal Assent).

159. Applied provision

(1) Subsection (2) applies where this Act amends or refers to a provision which is applied by, under or for purposes of—
   (a) another provision of the Act which contains the provision, or
   (b) another Act.

(2) The amendment or reference shall have effect in relation to the provision as applied.

(3) Where this Act applies a provision of another Act, a reference to that provision in any enactment includes a reference to the provision as applied by this Act.

Note: Commenced 10 February 2003 (SI 2003/1).

160. Money

(1) Expenditure of the Secretary of State or the Lord Chancellor in connection with a provision of this Act shall be paid out of money provided by Parliament.

(2) An increase attributable to this Act in the amount payable out of money provided by Parliament under another enactment shall be paid out of money provided by Parliament.

(3) A sum received by the Secretary of State or the Lord Chancellor in connection with a provision of this Act shall be paid into the Consolidated Fund.

Note: Commenced 7 November 2002, s 162.

161. Repeals

The provisions listed in Schedule 9 are hereby repealed to the extent specified.

Note: Commenced 8 December 2002 (SI 2002/2811) and 10 February 2003 (SI 2003/1).

162. Commencement

(1) Subject to subsections (2) to (5), the preceding provisions of this Act shall come into force in accordance with provision made by the Secretary of State by order.

(**2**) The following provisions shall come into force on the passing of this Act—

    (a)   section 6,

    (b)   section 7,

    (c)   section 10(1) to (4) and (6),

    (d)   section 11,

    (e)   section 15 (and Schedule 2),

    (f)   section 16,

    (g)   section 35(1)(h),

    (h)   section 38,

    (i)   section 40(1),

    (j)   section 41(1),

    (k)   section 42,

    (l)   section 43,

    (m)   section 48,

    (n)   section 49,

    (o)   section 50,

    (p)   section 56,

    (q)   section 58,

    (r)   section 59,

    (s)   section 61,

    (t)   section 67,

    (u)   section 69,

    (v)   section 70,

    (w)   section 115 and paragraph 29 of Schedule 7 (and the relevant entry in Schedule 9),

    (x)   section 157, and

    (y)   section 160.

(**3**) Section 5 shall have effect in relation to—

    (a) an application made after the passing of this Act, and

    (b) an application made, but not determined, before the passing of this Act.

(**4**) Section 8 shall have effect in relation to—

    (a) an application made on or after a date appointed by the Secretary of State by order, and

    (b) an application made, but not determined, before that date.

(**5**) Section 9 shall have effect in relation to a child born on or after a date appointed by the Secretary of State by order.

(**6**) An order under subsection (1) may—

    (a) make provision generally or for a specified purpose only (which may include the purpose of the application of a provision to or in relation to a particular place or area);

    (b) make different provision for different purposes;

    (c) include transitional provision;

    (d) include savings;

    (e) include consequential provision;

    (f) include incidental provision.

(**7**) An order under this section must be made by statutory instrument.

Note: Commenced 7 November 2002 (Royal Assent). The date appointed for the purpose of sub-s (5) is 1 July 2006 (SI 2006/1498).

163. Extent

(1) A provision of this Act which amends or repeals a provision of another Act or inserts a provision into another Act has the same extent as the provision amended or repealed or as the Act into which the insertion is made (ignoring, in any case, extent by virtue of an Order in Council).

(2) Sections 145 and 146 extend only to—

(a) England and Wales, and

(b) Northern Ireland.

(3) A provision of this Act to which neither subsection (1) nor subsection (2) applies extends to—

(a) England and Wales,

(b) Scotland, and

(c) Northern Ireland.

(4) Her Majesty may by Order in Council direct that a provision of this Act is to extend, with or without modification or adaptation, to—

(a) any of the Channel Islands;

(b) the Isle of Man.

(5) Subsection (4) does not apply in relation to the extension to a place of a provision which extends there by virtue of subsection (1).

164. Short title

This Act may be cited as the Nationality, Immigration and Asylum Act 2002.

SCHEDULES

Section 3   SCHEDULE 1

CITIZENSHIP CEREMONY, OATH AND PLEDGE

1.—7. ...

8. The Secretary of State may make a payment to a local authority in respect of anything done by the authority in accordance with regulations made by virtue of section 41(3A) of the British Nationality Act 1981 (c. 61).

9.—(1) A local authority must—

(a) comply with a requirement imposed on it by regulations made by virtue of that section, and

(b) carry out a function imposed on it by regulations made by virtue of that section.

(2) A local authority on which a requirement or function is imposed by regulations made by virtue of that section—

(a) may provide facilities or make arrangements in addition to those which it is required to provide or make, and

(b) may make a charge for the provision of facilities or the making of arrangements under paragraph (a) which does not exceed the cost of providing the facilities or making the arrangements.

Note: Paragraphs 1–7 amend the British Nationality Act 1981. Commencement 1 January 2004 (SI 2003/3156).

Section 15   SCHEDULE 2

NATIONALITY: REPEAL OF SPENT PROVISIONS

1. . . .

2 Nothing in this Schedule has any effect in relation to a registration made under a provision before its repeal.

Note: Paragraph 1 repeals parts of British Nationality Act 1981. Commencement from 1 January 2004 (SI 2003/3156).

Section 54   SCHEDULE 3

WITHHOLDING AND WITHDRAWAL OF SUPPORT

Ineligibility for support

1.—**(1)** A person to whom this paragraph applies shall not be eligible for support or assistance under—

(a) section 21 or 29 of the National Assistance Act 1948 (c. 29) (local authority: accommodation and welfare),

(b) section 45 of the Health Services and Public Health Act 1968 (c. 46) (local authority: welfare of elderly),

(c) section 12 or 13A of the Social Work (Scotland) Act 1968 (c. 49) (social welfare services),

(d) Article 7 or 15 of the Health and Personal Social Services (Northern Ireland) Order 1972 (S.I. 1972/1265 (N.I. 14)) (prevention of illness, social welfare, &c.),

(e) section 21 of and Schedule 8 to the National Health Service Act 1977 (c. 49) (social services),

(f) section 29(1)(b) of the Housing (Scotland) Act 1987 (c. 26) (interim duty to accommodate in case of apparent priority need where review of a local authority decision has been requested),

(g) section 17, 23C, [23CA,] 24A or 24B of the Children Act 1989 (c. 41) (welfare and other powers which can be exercised in relation to adults),

(h) Article 18, 35 or 36 of the Children (Northern Ireland) Order 1995 (SI 1995/ 755 (N.I. 2)) (welfare and other powers which can be exercised in relation to adults),

(i) sections 22, 29 and 30 of the Children (Scotland) Act 1995 (c. 36) (provisions analogous to those mentioned in paragraph (g)),

(j) section 188(3) or 204(4) of the Housing Act 1996 (c. 52) (accommodation pending review or appeal),

(k) section 2 of the Local Government Act 2000 (c. 22) (promotion of well-being),

(l) a provision of the Immigration and Asylum Act 1999 (c. 33), or

(m) a provision of this Act.

(2) A power or duty under a provision referred to in sub-paragraph (1) may not be exercised or performed in respect of a person to whom this paragraph applies (whether or not the person has previously been in receipt of support or assistance under the provision).

(3) An approval or directions given under or in relation to a provision referred to in sub-paragraph (1) shall be taken to be subject to sub-paragraph (2).

Exceptions

2.—**(1)** Paragraph 1 does not prevent the provision of support or assistance—

(a) to a British citizen, or

(b) to a child, or

(c) under or by virtue of regulations made under paragraph 8, 9 or 10 below, or

(d) in a case in respect of which, and to the extent to which, regulations made by the Secretary of State disapply paragraph 1, or

(e) in circumstances in respect of which, and to the extent to which, regulations made by the Secretary of State disapply paragraph 1.

(2) Regulations under sub-paragraph (1)(d) may confer a discretion on the Secretary of State.

(3) Regulations under sub-paragraph (1)(e) may, in particular, disapply paragraph 1 to the provision of support or assistance by a local authority to a person where the authority—

(a) has taken steps in accordance with guidance issued by the Secretary of State to determine whether paragraph 1 would (but for the regulations) apply to the person, and

(b) has concluded on the basis of those steps that there is no reason to believe that paragraph 1 would apply.

(4) Regulations under sub-paragraph (1)(d) or (e) may confer a discretion on an authority.

(5) A local authority which is considering whether to give support or assistance to a person under a provision listed in paragraph 1(1) shall act in accordance with any relevant guidance issued by the Secretary of State under sub-paragraph (3)(a).

(6) A reference in this Schedule to a person to whom paragraph 1 applies includes a reference to a person in respect of whom that paragraph is disapplied to a limited extent by regulations under sub-paragraph (1)(d) or (e), except in a case for which the regulations provide otherwise.

3. Paragraph 1 does not prevent the exercise of a power or the performance of a duty if, and to the extent that, its exercise or performance is necessary for the purpose of avoiding a breach of—

(a) a person's Convention rights, or

(b) a person's rights under the Community Treaties.

First class of ineligible person: refugee status abroad

4.—(1) Paragraph 1 applies to a person if he—

(a) has refugee status abroad, or

(b) is the dependant of a person who is in the United Kingdom and who has refugee status abroad.

(2) For the purposes of this paragraph a person has refugee status abroad if—

(a) he does not have the nationality of an EEA State, and

(b) the government of an EEA State other than the United Kingdom has determined that he is entitled to protection as a refugee under the Refugee Convention.

Second class of ineligible person: citizen of other EEA State

5. Paragraph 1 applies to a person if he—

(a) has the nationality of an EEA State other than the United Kingdom, or

(b) is the dependant of a person who has the nationality of an EEA State other than the United Kingdom.

Third class of ineligible person: failed asylum-seeker

6.—(1) Paragraph 1 applies to a person if—

(a) he was (but is no longer) an asylum-seeker, and

(b) he fails to cooperate with removal directions issued in respect of him.

(2) Paragraph 1 also applies to a dependant of a person to whom that paragraph applies by virtue of sub-paragraph (1).

Fourth class of ineligible person: person unlawfully in United Kingdom

7. Paragraph 1 applies to a person if—

(a) he is in the United Kingdom in breach of the immigration laws within the meaning of [section 50A of the British Nationality Act 1981], and

(b) he is not an asylum-seeker.

Fifth class of ineligible person: failed asylum-seeker with family

[**7A.**—(1) Paragraph 1 applies to a person if—

(a) he—

(i) is treated as an asylum-seeker for the purposes of Part VI of the Immigration and Asylum Act 1999 (c. 33) (support) by virtue only of section 94(3A) (failed asylum-seeker with dependent child), or

(ii) is treated as an asylum-seeker for the purposes of Part 2 of this Act by virtue only of section 18(2),

(b) the Secretary of State has certified that in his opinion the person has failed without reasonable excuse to take reasonable steps—

(i) to leave the United Kingdom voluntarily, or

(ii) to place himself in a position in which he is able to leave the United Kingdom voluntarily,

(c) the person has received a copy of the Secretary of State's certificate, and

(d) the period of 14 days, beginning with the date on which the person receives the copy of the certificate, has elapsed.

(2) Paragraph 1 also applies to a dependant of a person to whom that paragraph applies by virtue of sub-paragraph (1).

(3) For the purpose of sub-paragraph (1)(d) if the Secretary of State sends a copy of a certificate by first class post to a person's last known address, the person shall be treated as receiving the copy on the second day after the day on which it was posted.

(4) The Secretary of State may by regulations vary the period specified in sub-paragraph (1)(d).]

Travel assistance

8. The Secretary of State may make regulations providing for arrangements to be made enabling a person to whom paragraph 1 applies by virtue of paragraph 4 or 5 to leave the United Kingdom.

Temporary accommodation

9.—(1) The Secretary of State may make regulations providing for arrangements to be made for the accommodation of a person to whom paragraph 1 applies pending the implementation of arrangements made by virtue of paragraph 8.

(2) Arrangements for a person by virtue of this paragraph—

(a) may be made only if the person has with him a dependent child, and

(b) may include arrangements for a dependent child.

10.—(1) The Secretary of State may make regulations providing for arrangements to be made for the accommodation of a person if—

(a) paragraph 1 applies to him by virtue of paragraph 7, and

(b) he has not failed to cooperate with removal directions issued in respect of him.

(2) Arrangements for a person by virtue of this paragraph—

(a) may be made only if the person has with him a dependent child, and

(b) may include arrangements for a dependent child.

Assistance and accommodation: general

11. Regulations under paragraph 8, 9 or 10 may—

(a) provide for the making of arrangements under a provision referred to in paragraph 1(1) or otherwise;

(b) confer a function (which may include the exercise of a discretion) on the Secretary of State, a local authority or another person;

(c) provide that arrangements must be made in a specified manner or in accordance with specified principles;

(d) provide that arrangements may not be made in a specified manner;

(e) require a local authority or another person to have regard to guidance issued by the Secretary of State in making arrangements;

(f) require a local authority or another person to comply with a direction of the Secretary of State in making arrangements.

12.—(1) Regulations may, in particular, provide that if a person refuses an offer of arrangements under paragraph 8 or fails to implement or cooperate with arrangements made for him under that paragraph—

(a) new arrangements may not be made for him under paragraph 8, but

(b) new arrangements may not be made for him under paragraph 9.

(2) Regulations by virtue of this paragraph may include exceptions in the case of a person who—

(a) has a reason of a kind specified in the regulations for failing to implement or cooperate with arrangements made under paragraph 8, and

(b) satisfies any requirements of the regulations for proof of the reason.

Offences

13.—(1) A person who leaves the United Kingdom in accordance with arrangements made under paragraph 8 commits an offence if he—

(a) returns to the United Kingdom, and

(b) requests that arrangements be made for him by virtue of paragraph 8, 9 or 10.

(2) A person commits an offence if he—

(a) requests that arrangements be made for him by virtue of paragraph 8, 9 or 10, and

(b) fails to mention a previous request by him for the making of arrangements under any of those paragraphs.

(3) A person who is guilty of an offence under this paragraph shall be liable on summary conviction to imprisonment for a term not exceeding six months.

Information

14.—(1) If it appears to a local authority that paragraph 1 applies or may apply to a person in the authority's area by virtue of [paragraph 6, 7 or 7A], the authority must inform the Secretary of State.

(2) A local authority shall act in accordance with any relevant guidance issued by the Secretary of State for the purpose of determining whether paragraph 1 applies or may apply to a person in the authority's area by virtue of [paragraph 6, 7 or 7A].

Power to amend Schedule

15. The Secretary of State may by order amend this Schedule so as—

(a) to provide for paragraph 1 to apply or not to apply to a class of person;

(b) to add or remove a provision to or from the list in paragraph 1(1);

(c) to add, amend or remove a limitation of or exception to paragraph 1.

Orders and regulations

16.—(1) An order or regulations under this Schedule must be made by statutory instrument.

(2) An order or regulations under this Schedule may—

(a) make provision which applies generally or only in specified cases or circumstances or only for specified purposes;

(b) make different provision for different cases, circumstances or purposes;

(c) make transitional provision;

(d) make consequential provision (which may include provision amending a provision made by or under this or another Act).

(3) An order under this Schedule, regulations under paragraph 2(1)(d) or (e) or other regulations which include consequential provision amending an enactment shall not be made unless a draft has been laid before and approved by resolution of each House of Parliament.

(4) Regulations under this Schedule to which sub-paragraph (3) does not apply shall be subject to annulment in pursuance of a resolution of either House of Parliament.

Interpretation

17.—(1) In this Schedule—

'asylum-seeker' means a person—

(a) who is at least 18 years old,

(b) who has made a claim for asylum (within the meaning of section 18(3)), and

(c) whose claim has been recorded by the Secretary of State but not determined,

'Convention rights' has the same meaning as in the Human Rights Act 1998 (c. 42),

'child' means a person under the age of eighteen,

'dependant' and 'dependent' shall have such meanings as may be prescribed by regulations made by the Secretary of State,

'EEA State' means a State which is a contracting party to the Agreement on the European Economic Area signed at Oporto on 2 May 1992 (as it has effect from time to time),

'local authority'—

(a) in relation to England and Wales, has the same meaning as in section 129(3),

(b) in relation to Scotland, has the same meaning as in section 129(4), and

(c) in relation to Northern Ireland, means a health service body within the meaning of section 133(4)(d) and the Northern Ireland Housing Executive (for which purpose a reference to the authority's area shall be taken as a reference to Northern Ireland),

'the Refugee Convention' means the Convention relating to the status of Refugees done at Geneva on 28 July 1951 and its Protocol, and

'removal directions' means directions under Schedule 2 to the Immigration Act 1971 (c. 77) (control of entry, &c.), under Schedule 3 to that Act (deportation) or under section 10 of the Immigration and Asylum Act 1999 (c. 33) (removal of person unlawfully in United Kingdom).

(2) For the purpose of the definition of 'asylum-seeker' in sub-paragraph (1) a claim is determined if—

(a) the Secretary of State has notified the claimant of his decision,

(b) no appeal against the decision can be brought (disregarding the possibility of an appeal out of time with permission), and

(c) any appeal which has already been brought has been disposed of.

(3) For the purpose of sub-paragraph (2)(c) an appeal is disposed of when it is no longer pending for the purpose of—

(a) Part 5 of this Act, or

(b) the Special Immigration Appeals Commission Act 1997 (c. 68).

(4) The giving of directions in respect of a person under a provision of the Immigration Acts is not the provision of assistance to him for the purposes of this Schedule.

Note: Paragraphs 2, 8, 9, 10, 11, 12, 15 and 16 commenced on 8 December 2002, for the purpose of enabling subordinate legislation. Remainder of Schedule commenced 8 January 2003 (SI 2002/2811). Paragraph (7A) inserted and words in square brackets in para 14 substituted by Asylum and Immigration Act 2004, s 9 from 1 December 2004 (SI 2004/2999). Words in square brackets in paragraph 7(a) substituted by Borders Citizenship and Immigration Act 2009, s 48 from 13 January 2010 (SI 2009/2731). Words in square brackets in paragraph 1(1)(g) inserted by Children and Young Persons Act 2008 s 22 from 1 April 2011 (SI 2010/2981).

Section 81   [SCHEDULE 4

. . .]

Note: Schedule 4 revoked from 15 February 2010 (SI 2010/21).

Section 100   SCHEDULE 5

THE IMMIGRATION APPEAL TRIBUNAL

. . .

Note: Schedule 5 ceased to have effect from 4 April 2005, subject to savings (SI 2005/565), Asylum and Immigration Act 2004, s 26.

Section 114   SCHEDULE 6

IMMIGRATION AND ASYLUM APPEALS: TRANSITIONAL PROVISION

'Commencement'

1. In this Schedule 'commencement' means the coming into force of Part 5 this Act.

Adjudicator

2. Where a person is an adjudicator under section 57 of the Immigration and Asylum Act 1999 (c. 33) immediately before commencement his appointment shall have effect after commencement as if made under section 81 of this Act.

Tribunal

3.—(1) Where a person is a member of the Immigration Appeal Tribunal immediately before commencement his appointment shall have effect after commencement as if made under Schedule 5.

(2) Where a person is a member of staff of the Immigration Appeal Tribunal immediately before commencement his appointment shall have effect after commencement as if made under Schedule 5.

Earlier appeal

4. In the application of section 96—

(a) a reference to an appeal or right of appeal under a provision of this Act includes a reference to an appeal or right of appeal under the Immigration and Asylum Act 1999,

(b) a reference to a requirement imposed under this Act includes a reference to a requirement of a similar nature imposed under that Act,

(c) a reference to a statement made in pursuance of a requirement imposed under a provision of this Act includes a reference to anything done in compliance with a requirement of a similar nature under that Act, and

(d) a reference to notification by virtue of this Act includes a reference to notification by virtue of any other enactment.

Saving

5.—(1) This Schedule is without prejudice to the power to include transitional provision in an order under section 162.

(2) An order under that section may, in particular, provide for a reference to a provision of Part 5 of this Act to be treated as being or including a reference (with or without modification) to a provision of the Immigration and Asylum Act 1999 (c. 33).

Note: Commencement from 1 April 2003 (SI 2003/754).

Section 114	SCHEDULE 7

IMMIGRATION AND ASYLUM APPEALS: CONSEQUENTIAL AMENDMENTS

. . .

Section 125	SCHEDULE 8

CARRIERS' LIABILITY

. . .

Note: Amends the Immigration and Asylum Act 1999.

Section 161	SCHEDULE 9

REPEALS

. . .

Asylum and Immigration (Treatment of Claimants, etc.) Act 2004
(2004, c. 19)

Arrangement of Sections

Offences

Treatment of claimants

Enforcement powers

Procedure for marriage

Appeals

An Act to make provision about asylum and immigration.

[22 July 2004]

Offences

1. Assisting unlawful immigration

...

Note: Amends Immigration Act 1971, ss 25 and 25C.

2. Entering United Kingdom without passport, &c.

(1) A person commits an offence if at a leave or asylum interview he does not have with him an immigration document which—

(a) is in force, and

(b) satisfactorily establishes his identity and nationality or citizenship.

(2) A person commits an offence if at a leave or asylum interview he does not have with him, in respect of any dependent child with whom he claims to be travelling or living, an immigration document which—

(a) is in force, and

(b) satisfactorily establishes the child's identity and nationality or citizenship.

(3) But a person does not commit an offence under subsection (1) or (2) if—

(a) the interview referred to in that subsection takes place after the person has entered the United Kingdom, and

(b) within the period of three days beginning with the date of the interview the person provides to an immigration officer or to the Secretary of State a document of the kind referred to in that subsection.

(4) It is a defence for a person charged with an offence under subsection (1)—

(a) to prove that he is an EEA national,

(b) to prove that he is a member of the family of an EEA national and that he is exercising a right under the Community Treaties in respect of entry to or residence in the United Kingdom,

(c) to prove that he has a reasonable excuse for not being in possession of a document of the kind specified in subsection (1),

(d) to produce a false immigration document and to prove that he used that document as an immigration document for all purposes in connection with his journey to the United Kingdom, or

(e) to prove that he travelled to the United Kingdom without, at any stage since he set out on the journey, having possession of an immigration document.

(5) It is a defence for a person charged with an offence under subsection (2) in respect of a child—

(a) to prove that the child is an EEA national,

(b) to prove that the child is a member of the family of an EEA national and that the child is exercising a right under the Community Treaties in respect of entry to or residence in the United Kingdom,

(c) to prove that the person has a reasonable excuse for not being in possession of a document of the kind specified in subsection (2),

(d) to produce a false immigration document and to prove that it was used as an immigration document for all purposes in connection with the child's journey to the United Kingdom, or

(e) to prove that he travelled to the United Kingdom with the child without, at any stage since he set out on the journey, having possession of an immigration document in respect of the child.

(6) Where the charge for an offence under subsection (1) or (2) relates to an interview which takes place after the defendant has entered the United Kingdom—

(a) subsections (4)(c) and (5)(c) shall not apply, but

(b) it is a defence for the defendant to prove that he has a reasonable excuse for not providing a document in accordance with subsection (3).

(7) For the purposes of subsections (4) to (6)—

(a) the fact that a document was deliberately destroyed or disposed of is not a reasonable excuse for not being in possession of it or for not providing it in accordance with subsection (3), unless it is shown that the destruction or disposal was—

(i) for a reasonable cause, or

(ii) beyond the control of the person charged with the offence, and

(b) in paragraph (a)(i) 'reasonable cause' does not include the purpose of—

(i) delaying the handling or resolution of a claim or application or the taking of a decision,

(ii) increasing the chances of success of a claim or application, or

(iii) complying with instructions or advice given by a person who offers advice about, or facilitates, immigration into the United Kingdom, unless in the circumstances of the case it is unreasonable to expect non-compliance with the instructions or advice.

(8) A person shall be presumed for the purposes of this section not to have a document with him if he fails to produce it to an immigration officer or official of the Secretary of State on request.

(9) A person guilty of an offence under this section shall be liable—

(a) on conviction on indictment, to imprisonment for a term not exceeding two years, to a fine or to both, or

(b) on summary conviction, to imprisonment for a term not exceeding twelve months, to a fine not exceeding the statutory maximum or to both.

(10) If [an] immigration officer reasonably suspects that a person has committed an offence under this section he may arrest the person without warrant.

(11) An offence under this section shall be treated as—

(a) a relevant offence for the purposes of sections 28B and 28D of the Immigration Act 1971 (c. 77) (search, entry and arrest), and

(b) an offence under Part III of that Act (criminal proceedings) for the purposes of sections 28(4), 28E, 28G and 28H (search after arrest, &c.) of that Act.

(12) In this section—

'EEA national' means a national of a State which is a contracting party to the Agreement on the European Economic Area signed at Oporto on 2 May 1992 (as it has effect from time to time),

'immigration document' means—

(a) a passport, and

(b) a document which relates to a national of a State other than the United Kingdom and which is designed to serve the same purpose as a passport, and

'leave or asylum interview' means an interview with an immigration officer or an official of the Secretary of State at which a person—

(a) seeks leave to enter or remain in the United Kingdom, or

(b) claims that to remove him from or require him to leave the United Kingdom would breach the United Kingdom's obligations under the Refugee Convention or would be unlawful under section 6 of the Human Rights Act 1998 (c. 42) as being incompatible with his Convention rights.

(13) For the purposes of this section—

(a) a document which purports to be, or is designed to look like, an immigration document, is a false immigration document, and

(b) an immigration document is a false immigration document if and in so far as it is used—

   (i) outside the period for which it is expressed to be valid,

   (ii) contrary to provision for its use made by the person issuing it, or

   (iii) by or in respect of a person other than the person to or for whom it was issued.

(14) Section 11 of the Immigration Act 1971 (c. 77) shall have effect for the purpose of the construction of a reference in this section to entering the United Kingdom.

(15) In so far as this section extends to England and Wales, subsection (9)(b) shall, until the commencement of section 154 of the Criminal Justice Act 2003 (c. 44) (increased limit on magistrates' power of imprisonment), have effect as if the reference to twelve months were a reference to six months.

(16) In so far as this section extends to Scotland, subsection (9)(b) shall have effect as if the reference to twelve months were a reference to six months.

(17) In so far as this section extends to Northern Ireland, subsection (9)(b) shall have effect as if the reference to twelve months were a reference to six months.

Note: Commenced 22 September 2004, s 48. Word in square brackets in sub-s (10) substituted by Sch 7 Serious Organised Crime and Police Act 2005 from 1 January 2006 (SI 2005/3495).

3. Immigration documents: forgery

. . .

Note: Section 3 repealed from 7 June 2006, Identity Cards Act 2006, s 44 and Sch 2.

4. Trafficking people for exploitation

(1) A person commits an offence if he arranges or facilitates the arrival in [, or the entry into,] the United Kingdom of an individual (the 'passenger') and—

  (a) he intends to exploit the passenger in the United Kingdom or elsewhere, or

  (b) he believes that another person is likely to exploit the passenger in the United Kingdom or elsewhere.

(2) A person commits an offence if he arranges or facilitates travel within the United Kingdom by an individual (the 'passenger') in respect of whom he believes that an offence under subsection (1) may have been committed and—

  (a) he intends to exploit the passenger in the United Kingdom or elsewhere, or

  (b) he believes that another person is likely to exploit the passenger in the United Kingdom or elsewhere.

(3) A person commits an offence if he arranges or facilitates the departure from the United Kingdom of an individual (the 'passenger') and—

  (a) he intends to exploit the passenger outside the United Kingdom, or

  (b) he believes that another person is likely to exploit the passenger outside the United Kingdom.

(4) For the purposes of this section a person is exploited if (and only if)—

  (a) he is the victim of behaviour that contravenes Article 4 of the Human Rights Convention (slavery and forced labour),

  (b) he is encouraged, required or expected to do anything as a result of which he or another person would commit an offence under the Human Organ Transplants Act 1989 (c. 31) or [under section 32 or 33 of the Human Tissue Act 2004],

(c) he is subjected to force, threats or deception designed to induce him—

    (i) to provide services of any kind,

    (ii) to provide another person with benefits of any kind, or

    (iii) to enable another person to acquire benefits of any kind, or

[(d) a person uses or attempts to use him for any purpose within sub-paragraph (i), (ii) or (iii) of paragraph (c), having chosen him for that purpose on the grounds that—

    (i) he is mentally or physically ill or disabled, he is young or he has a family relationship with a person, and

    (ii) a person without the illness, disability, youth or family relationship would be likely to refuse to be used for that purpose.]

(5) A person guilty of an offence under this section shall be liable—

(a) on conviction on indictment, to imprisonment for a term not exceeding 14 years, to a fine or to both, or

(b) on summary conviction, to imprisonment for a term not exceeding twelve months, to a fine not exceeding the statutory maximum or to both.

Note: Commencement 1 December 2004 (SI 2004/2999). Words in square brackets in sub-s (1) inserted by s 31 UK Borders Act 2007 from 31 January 2008 (SI 2008/99). Words in square brackets in sub-s (4) (b) substituted by Sch 6 Human Tissue Act 2004 from 1 September 2006 (SI 2006/1997). Subsection (4)(d) substituted by s 54 Borders, Citizenship and Immigration Act 2009 from 10 November 2009 (SI 2009/2731). Amended in relation to Scotland by the Criminal Justice and Licensing (Scotland) Act 2010 (asp). There are prospective amendments to sub-s (4): see Protection of Freedoms Act 2012, s 110.

5. Section 4: supplemental

[(1) Subsections (1) to (3) of section 4 apply to anything done whether inside or outside the United Kingdom.]

(2) . . .

(3) In section 4(4)(a) 'the Human Rights Convention' means the Convention for the Protection of Human Rights and Fundamental Freedoms agreed by the Council of Europe at Rome on 4 November 1950.

(4) Section 25C and 25D of the Immigration Act 1971 (c. 77) (forfeiture or detention of vehicle, &c.) shall apply in relation to an offence under section 4 of this Act as they apply in relation to an offence under section 25 of that Act.

(5) . . .

Note: Amends Immigration Act 1971, s 25C(9)(b), (10)(b) and (11).

(6) . . .

Note: Amends para 2, Sch 4 Criminal Justice and Court Services Act 2000.

(7) . . .

Note: Amends para 4, Sch 2 Proceeds of Crime Act 2002.

(8) . . .

Note: Amends para 4, Sch 4 Proceeds of Crime Act 2002.

(9) . . .

Note: Amends para 4, Sch 5 Proceeds of Crime Act 2002.

(10). . . .

Note: Amends para 2(1), Sch Protection of Children and Vulnerable Adults (Northern Ireland) Order 2003.

(11) In so far as section 4 extends to England and Wales, subsection (5)(b) shall, until the commencement of section 154 of the Criminal Justice Act 2003 (c. 44) (increased limit on magistrates' power of imprisonment), have effect as if the reference to twelve months were a reference to six months.

(12) In so far as section 4 extends to Scotland, subsection (5)(b) shall have effect as if the reference to twelve months were a reference to six months.

(13) In so far as section 4 extends to Northern Ireland, subsection (5)(b) shall have effect as if the reference to twelve months were a reference to six months.

Note: Commenced 1 December 2004 (SI 2004/2999). Subsections (1) – (2) substituted by s 31 UK Borders Act 2007 from 31 January 2008 (SI 2008/99). Amended in relation to Scotland by the Criminal Justice and Licensing (Scotland) Act 2010 (asp). There are prospective amendments to this section: see Protection of Freedoms Act 2012, s 110, Schedules 9, 10.

6. Employment

. . .

Note: Amends Asylum and Immigration Act 1996, s 8.

7. Advice of Director of Public Prosecutions

. . .

Note: Amends Prosecution of Offences Act 1985, s 3(2).

Treatment of claimants

8. Claimant's credibility

(1) In determining whether to believe a statement made by or on behalf of a person who makes an asylum claim or a human rights claim, a deciding authority shall take account, as damaging the claimant's credibility, of any behaviour to which this section applies.

(2) This section applies to any behaviour by the claimant that the deciding authority thinks—

(a) is designed or likely to conceal information,

(b) is designed or likely to mislead, or

(c) is designed or likely to obstruct or delay the handling or resolution of the claim or the taking of a decision in relation to the claimant.

(3) Without prejudice to the generality of subsection (2) the following kinds of behaviour shall be treated as designed or likely to conceal information or to mislead—

(a) failure without reasonable explanation to produce a passport on request to an immigration officer or to the Secretary of State,

(b) the production of a document which is not a valid passport as if it were,

(c) the destruction, alteration or disposal, in each case without reasonable explanation, of a passport,

(d) the destruction, alteration or disposal, in each case without reasonable explanation, of a ticket or other document connected with travel, and

(e) failure without reasonable explanation to answer a question asked by a deciding authority.

(4) This section also applies to failure by the claimant to take advantage of a reasonable opportunity to make an asylum claim or human rights claim while in a safe country.

(5) This section also applies to failure by the claimant to make an asylum claim or human rights claim before being notified of an immigration decision, unless the claim relies wholly on matters arising after the notification.

(6) This section also applies to failure by the claimant to make an asylum claim or human rights claim before being arrested under an immigration provision, unless—

(a) he had no reasonable opportunity to make the claim before the arrest, or

(b) the claim relies wholly on matters arising after the arrest.

(7) In this section—

'asylum claim' has the meaning given by section 113(1) of the Nationality, Immigration and Asylum Act 2002 (c. 41) (subject to subsection (9) below),

'deciding authority' means—

(a) an immigration officer,

(b) the Secretary of State,

(c) [the First-tier Tribunal] or

(d) the Special Immigration Appeals Commission,

'human rights claim' has the meaning given by section 113(1) of the Nationality, Immigration and Asylum Act 2002 (subject to subsection (9) below),

'immigration decision' means—

(a) refusal of leave to enter the United Kingdom,

(b) refusal to vary a person's leave to enter or remain in the United Kingdom,

(c) grant of leave to enter or remain in the United Kingdom,

(d) a decision that a person is to be removed from the United Kingdom by way of directions under section 10(1)(a), (b), (ba) or (c) of the Immigration and Asylum Act 1999 (c. 33) (removal of persons unlawfully in United Kingdom),

(e) a decision that a person is to be removed from the United Kingdom by way of directions under paragraphs 8 to 12 of Schedule 2 to the Immigration Act 1971 (c. 77) (control of entry: removal),

(f) a decision to make a deportation order under section 5(1) of that Act, and

(g) a decision to take action in relation to a person in connection with extradition from the United Kingdom,

'immigration provision' means—

(a) sections 28A, 28AA, 28B, 28C and 28CA of the Immigration Act 1971 (immigration offences: enforcement),

(b) paragraph 17 of Schedule 2 to that Act (control of entry),

(c) section 14 of this Act, and

(d) a provision of the Extradition Act 1989 (c. 33) or 2003 (c. 41),

'notified' means notified in such manner as may be specified by regulations made by the Secretary of State,

'passport' includes a document which relates to a national of a country other than the United Kingdom and which is designed to serve the same purpose as a passport, and

'safe country' means a country to which Part 2 of Schedule 3 applies.

(8) A passport produced by or on behalf of a person is valid for the purposes of subsection (3)(b) if it—

(a) relates to the person by whom or on whose behalf it is produced,

(b) has not been altered otherwise than by or with the permission of the authority who issued it, and

(c) was not obtained by deception.

(9) In subsection (4) a reference to an asylum claim or human rights claim shall be treated as including a reference to a claim of entitlement to remain in a country other than the United Kingdom made by reference to the rights that a person invokes in making an asylum claim or a human rights claim in the United Kingdom.

[(9A) In paragraph (c) of the definition of a "deciding authority" in subsection (7) the reference to the First-tier Tribunal includes a reference to the Upper Tribunal when acting under section 12(2)(b)(ii) of the Tribunals, Courts and Enforcement Act 2007.]

(10) Regulations under subsection (7) specifying a manner of notification may, in particular—

(a) apply or refer to regulations under section 105 of the Nationality, Immigration and Asylum Act 2002 (c. 41) (notice of immigration decisions);

(b) make provision similar to provision that is or could be made by regulations under that section;

(c) modify a provision of regulations under that section in its effect for the purpose of regulations under this section;

(d) provide for notice to be treated as received at a specified time if sent to a specified class of place in a specified manner.

(11) Regulations under subsection (7) specifying a manner of notification—

(a) may make incidental, consequential or transitional provision,

(b) shall be made by statutory instrument, and

(c) shall be subject to annulment in pursuance of a resolution of either House of Parliament.

(12) This section shall not prevent a deciding authority from determining not to believe a statement on the grounds of behaviour to which this section does not apply.

(13) . . .

Note: Commencement 1 January 2005 (SI 2004/3398). Words in square brackets in sub-s (7)(c) substituted, sub-s (9A) inserted and sub-s (13) revoked from 15 February 2010 (SI 2010/21).

9. Failed asylum seekers: withdrawal of support

(1) . . .

Note: Amends Sch 3 Nationality, Immigration and Asylum Act 2002.

(2) . . .

Note: Amends Sch 3 Nationality, Immigration and Asylum Act 2002.

(3) No appeal may be brought under section 103 of the Immigration and Asylum Act 1999 (asylum support appeal) against a decision—

(a) that by virtue of a provision of Schedule 3 to the Nationality, Immigration and Asylum Act 2002 (c. 41) other than paragraph 7A a person is not qualified to receive support, or

(b) on the grounds of the application of a provision of that Schedule other than paragraph 7A, to stop providing support to a person.

(4) On an appeal under section 103 of the Immigration and Asylum Act 1999 (c. 33) against a decision made by virtue of paragraph 7A of Schedule 3 to the Nationality, Immigration and Asylum Act 2002 the [First-tier Tribunal] may, in particular—

(a) annul a certificate of the Secretary of State issued for the purposes of that paragraph;

(b) require the Secretary of State to reconsider the matters certified.

(5) An order under section 48 providing for this section to come into force may, in particular, provide for this section to have effect with specified modifications before the coming into force of a provision of the Nationality, Immigration and Asylum Act 2002.

Note: Commencement 1 December 2004 (SI 2004/2999). Words in square brackets in sub-s (4) substituted from 3 November 2008 (SI 2008/2833).

10. Failed asylum seekers: accommodation

(1) . . .

Note: Amends Immigration and Asylum Act 1999, s 4.

(2) . . .

Note: Amends Immigration and Asylum Act 1999, s 166(5).

(3) . . .

Note: Amends Immigration and Asylum Act 1999, s 103.

(4) . . .

Note: Amends Immigration and Asylum Act 1999, s 103.

(5) . . .

Note: Amends Immigration and Asylum Act 1999, s 103A.

(6) In an amendment made by this section a reference to providing accommodation includes a reference to arranging for the provision of accommodation.

(7) Regulations under section 4(5)(b) of the Immigration and Asylum Act 1999 (c. 33) (as inserted by subsection (1) above) may apply to persons receiving support under section 4 when the regulations come into force.

Note: Subsections (1), (2), (6) and (7) commenced 1 December 2004 (SI 2004/2999), remainder 31 March 2005 (SI 2005/372).

11. Accommodation for asylum seekers: local connection

(1) . . .

Note: Amends Housing Act 1996, s 199.

(2) Subsection (3) applies where—

(a) a local housing authority would (but for subsection (3)) be obliged to secure that accommodation is available for occupation by a person under section 193 of the Housing Act 1996 (homeless persons),

(b) the person was (at any time) provided with accommodation in a place in Scotland under section 95 of the Immigration and Asylum Act 1999 (support for asylum seekers),

(c) the accommodation was not provided in an accommodation centre by virtue of section 22 of the Nationality, Immigration and Asylum Act 2002 (use of accommodation centres for section 95 support), and

(d) the person has neither—

(i) a local connection with the district of a local housing authority (in England or Wales) within the meaning of section 199 of the Housing Act 1996 as amended by subsection (1) above, nor

(ii) a local connection with a district (in Scotland) within the meaning of section 27 of the Housing (Scotland) Act 1987 (c. 26).

(3) Where this subsection applies—

(a) the duty of the local housing authority under section 193 of the Housing Act 1996 in relation to the person shall not apply, but

(b) the local housing authority—

(i) may secure that accommodation is available for occupation by the person for a period giving him a reasonable opportunity of securing accommodation for his occupation, and

(ii) may provide the person (or secure that he is provided with) advice and assistance in any attempts he may make to secure that accommodation becomes available for his occupation.

Note: Commenced 4 January 2005 (SI 2004/2999).

12. Refugee: back-dating of benefits

(1) . . .

Note: Repeals Immigration and Asylum Act 1999, s 123.

(2) . . .

Note: Amends SI 1987/1967, SR 1987/459, SI 1987/1968, SR 1987/465, SI 1987/1971, SR 1987/461, SI 1992/1814.

(3) . . .

Note: Amends SI 2000/636.

(4) . . .

Note: Amends SR 2000/71.

(5) An order under section 48 bringing this section into force may, in particular, provide for this section to have effect in relation to persons recorded as refugees after a specified date (irrespective of when the process resulting in the record was begun).

Note: Commencement 14 June 2007, but not with effect to a person recorded as a refugee on or before that date (SI 2007/1602), which sets out transitional provision.

13. [Integration loans for refugees]

(1) The Secretary of State may make regulations enabling him to make loans [—

(a) to refugees, and

(b) to such other classes of person, or to persons other than refugees in such circumstances, as the regulations may prescribe.]

(2) A person is a refugee for the purpose of subsection (1) if the Secretary of State has—

(a) recorded him as a refugee within the meaning of the Convention relating to the Status of Refugees done at Geneva on 28 July 1951, and

(b) [granted him leave to enter or remain] in the United Kingdom (within the meaning of section 33(1) of the Immigration Act 1971 (c. 77)).

(3) Regulations under subsection (1)—

(a) shall specify matters which the Secretary of State shall, in addition to other matters appearing to him to be relevant, take into account in determining whether or not to make a loan (and those matters may, in particular, relate to—

(i) a person's income or assets,

(ii) a person's likely ability to repay a loan, or

(iii) the length of time since a person was recorded as a refugee [or since some other event)],

(b) shall enable the Secretary of State to specify (and vary from time to time) a minimum and a maximum amount of a loan,

(c) shall prevent a person from receiving a loan if—

(i) he is under the age of 18,

(ii) he is insolvent, within a meaning given by the regulations, or

(iii) he has received a loan under the regulations,

(d) shall make provision about repayment of a loan (and may, in particular, make provision—

(i) about interest;

(ii) for repayment by deduction from a social security benefit or similar payment due to the person to whom the loan is made),

(e) shall enable the Secretary of State to attach conditions to a loan (which may include conditions about the use of the loan),

(f) shall make provision about—

(i) the making of an application for a loan, and

(ii) the information, which may include information about the intended use of a loan, to be provided in or with an application,

(g) may make provision about steps to be taken by the Secretary of State in establishing an applicant's likely ability to repay a loan,

(h) may make provision for a loan to be made jointly to more than one refugee, and

(i) may confer a discretion on the Secretary of State.

(4) Regulations under this section—

(a) shall be made by statutory instrument, and

(b) may not be made unless a draft has been laid before and approved by resolution of each House of Parliament.

Note: Commencement 29 June 2006 (SI 2006/1517). Words in square brackets substituted from 30 June 2006, Immigration, Nationality and Asylum Act 2006, s 45 (SI 2006/1497).

Enforcement powers

14. Immigration officer: power of arrest

(1) Where an immigration officer in the course of exercising a function under the Immigration Acts forms a reasonable suspicion that a person has committed or attempted to commit an offence listed in subsection (2), he may arrest the person without warrant.

(2) Those offences are—

(a) the offence of conspiracy at common law (in relation to conspiracy to defraud),

(b) at common law in Scotland, any of the following offences—

(i) fraud,

(ii) conspiracy to defraud,

(iii) uttering and fraud,

(iv) bigamy,

(v) theft, and

(vi) reset,

(c) an offence under section 57 of the Offences against the Person Act 1861 (c. 100) (bigamy),

(d) an offence under section 3 or 4 of the Perjury Act 1911 (c. 6) (false statements),

(e) an offence under section 7 of that Act (aiding, abetting &c.) if it relates to an offence under section 3 or 4 of that Act,

(f) an offence under section 53 of the Registration of Births, Deaths and Marriages (Scotland) Act 1965 (c. 49) (knowingly giving false information to district registrar, &c.),

(g) an offence under any of the following provisions of the Theft Act 1968 (c. 60)—

(i) . . . section 1 (theft),

(ii) . . .

(iii) . . .

(iv) section 17 (false accounting), and

(v) section 22 (handling stolen goods),

(h) an offence under section 1, . . . 17 or 21 of the Theft Act (Northern Ireland) 1969 (c. 16) (N.I.),

[(ha) an offence under either of the following provisions of the Fraud Act 2006—

(i) section 1 (fraud);

(ii) section 11 (obtaining services dishonestly),]

(i) . . .

(j) . . .

(k) an offence under Article 8 or 9 of the Perjury (Northern Ireland) Order 1979 (S.I. 1979/1714 (N.I. 19)),

(l) an offence under Article 12 of that Order if it relates to an offence under Article 8 or 9 of that Order,

(m) an offence under any of the following provisions of the Forgery and Counterfeiting Act 1981 (c. 45)—

(i) section 1 (forgery),

(ii) section 2 (copying false instrument),

(iii) section 3 (using false instrument),

(iv) section 4 (using copy of false instrument), and

(v) section 5(1) and (3) (false documents),

(n) an offence under any of sections 57 to 59 of the Sexual Offences Act 2003 (c. 42) (trafficking for sexual exploitation),

(o) an offence under section 22 of the Criminal Justice (Scotland) Act 2003 (asp 7) (trafficking in prostitution), . . .

(p) an offence under section 4 of this Act.

[(q) an offence under any of sections 4 to 6 of the Identity Documents Act 2010].

(3) The following provisions of the Immigration Act 1971 (c. 77) shall have effect for the purpose of making, or in connection with, an arrest under this section as they have effect for the purpose of making, or in connection with, arrests for offences under that Act—

(a) section 28C (entry and search before arrest),

(b) sections 28E and 28F (entry and search after arrest),

(c) sections 28G and 28H (search of arrested person), and

(d) section 28I (seized material).

(4) . . .

Note: Commencement 1 December 2004 (SI 2004/2999). Subsection (4) amends Race Relations Act 1976, s 19D. Words in sub-s 14(2)(o) omitted from 7 June 2006, Identity Cards Act 2006, s 30 and Sch 2, (SI 2006/1439). Subsections (2)(g), (ii)-(iii), (2)(i)-(j) omitted and words omitted in sub-s (2) (h), sub-s(2)(ha) inserted by Sch 1 Fraud Act 2006 from 15 January 2007 (SI 2006/3200). Subsection (2)(q) substituted by Identity Documents Act 2010, Schedule, para 18 from 21 January 2011. There is a prospective amendment to sub-s (2)(n): see Protection of Freedoms Act 2012 Sch 9.

15. Fingerprinting

. . .

Note: Amends Immigration and Asylum Act 1999, s 141.

16. Information about passengers

. . .

Note: Amends para 27B, Sch 2 Immigration Act 1971.

17. Retention of documents

Where a document comes into the possession of the Secretary of State or an immigration officer in the course of the exercise of an immigration function, the Secretary of State or an immigration officer may retain the document while he suspects that—

(a) a person to whom the document relates may be liable to removal from the United Kingdom in accordance with a provision of the Immigration Acts, and

(b) retention of the document may facilitate the removal.

Note: Commencement 1 December 2004 (SI 2004/2999).

18. Control of entry

. . .

Note: Amends para 2A, Sch 2 Immigration Act 1971.

Procedure for marriage

19. England and Wales

(1) This section applies to a marriage—

(a) which is to be solemnised on the authority of certificates issued by a superintendent registrar under Part III of the Marriage Act 1949 (c. 76), and

(b) a party to which is subject to immigration control.

(2) In relation to a marriage to which this section applies, the notices under section 27 of the Marriage Act 1949—

(a) shall be given to the superintendent registrar of a registration district specified for the purpose of this paragraph by regulations made by the Secretary of State,

(b) shall be delivered to the superintendent registrar in person by the two parties to the marriage,

(c) may be given only if each party to the marriage has been resident in a registration district for the period of seven days immediately before the giving of his or her notice (but the district need not be that in which the notice is given and the parties need not have resided in the same district), and

(d) shall state, in relation to each party, the registration district by reference to which paragraph (c) is satisfied.

(3) . . .

(4) For the purposes of this section—

(a) a person is subject to immigration control if—

(i) he is not an EEA national, and

(ii) under the Immigration Act 1971 (c. 77) he requires leave to enter or remain in the United Kingdom (whether or not leave has been given),

(b) 'EEA national' means a national of a State which is a contracting party to the Agreement on the European Economic Area signed at Oporto on 2 May 1992 (as it has effect from time to time),

(c) . . .

(d) . . .

Note: Commencement 1 February 2005 (SI 2004/3398). Subsections (3) and (4)(c) and (d) repealed from 9 May 2011 (SI 2011/1158).

20. England and Wales: supplemental

(1) The Marriage Act 1949 (c. 76) shall have effect in relation to a marriage to which section 19 applies—

(a) subject to that section, and

(b) with any necessary consequential modification.

(2) In particular—

(a) section 28(1)(b) of that Act (declaration: residence) shall have effect as if it required a declaration that—

(i) the notice of marriage is given in compliance with section 19(2) above, . . .

(b) section 48 of that Act (proof of certain matters not essential to validity of marriage) shall have effect as if the list of matters in section 48(1)(a) to (e) included compliance with section 19 above.

(3) [Regulations under section 19(2(a)—

    (a) may make transitional provision,

    (b) shall be made by statutory instrument, and

    (c) shall be subject to annulment in pursuance of a resolution of either House of Parliament.

(4) Before making regulations under section 19(2)(a) the Secretary of State shall consult the Registrar General.

(5) An expression used in section 19 or this section and in Part III of the Marriage Act 1949 (c. 76) has the same meaning in section 19 or this section as in that Part.

(6) . . .

Note: Commenced 1 February 2005 (SI 2004/3398). Subsection (6) repealed from 8 January 2007, ss 30, 33 Legislative and Regulatory Reform Act 2006. Words omitted from sub-s (2) and words substituted in sub-s (3) from 9 May 2011 (SI 2011/1158).

21. Scotland

(1) This section applies to a marriage—

    (a) which is intended to be solemnised in Scotland, and

    (b) a party to which is subject to immigration control.

(2) In relation to a marriage to which this section applies, notice under section 3 of the Marriage (Scotland) Act 1977 (c. 15)—

    (a) may be submitted to the district registrar of a registration district prescribed for the purposes of this section, and

    (b) may not be submitted to the district registrar of any other registration district.

(3) . . .

(4) Where the district registrar to whom notice is submitted by virtue of subsection (2) (here the 'notified registrar') is not the district registrar for the registration district in which the marriage is to be solemnised (here the 'second registrar')—

    (a) the notified registrar shall . . . send the notices and any fee, certificate or declaration [submitted in pursuance of section 3 of the Marriage (Scotland) Act 1977 (c. 15) in relation to the marriage], to the second registrar, and

    (b) the second registrar shall be treated as having received the notices from the parties to the marriage on the dates on which the notified registrar received them.

(5) Subsection (4) of section 19 applies for the purposes of this section as it applies for the purposes of that section.

Note: Commenced 1 February 2005 (SI 2004/3398). Words in square brackets in sub-section (4)(a) substituted by s 59 Local Electoral Administration and Registration Services (Scotland) Act 2006 (asp) from 1 January 2007 (SSI 2006/469). Subsection (3) repealed and words omitted from sub-ss (4) and (5) from 9 May 2011 (SI 2011/1158).

22. Scotland: supplemental

(1) The Marriage (Scotland) Act 1977 shall have effect in relation to a marriage to which section 21 applies—

    (a) subject to that section, and

    (b) with any necessary consequential modification.

(2) In subsection (2)(a) of that section 'prescribed' means prescribed by regulations made by the Secretary of State after consultation with the Registrar General for Scotland; and other expressions used in subsections (1) to (4) of that section and in the Marriage (Scotland) Act 1977 have the same meaning in those subsections as in that Act.

(3) Regulations made by the Secretary of State under subsection (2)(a) ... of that section—

(a) may make transitional provision,

(b) shall be made by statutory instrument, and

(c) shall be subject to annulment in pursuance of a resolution of either House of Parliament.

Note: Commenced 1 February 2005 (SI 2004/3398). Words omitted from sub-s (3) from 9 May 2011 (SI 2011/1158).

23. Northern Ireland

(1) This section applies to a marriage—

(a) which is intended to be solemnised in Northern Ireland, and

(b) a party to which is subject to immigration control.

(2) In relation to a marriage to which this section applies, the marriage notices—

(a) shall be given only to a prescribed registrar, and

(b) shall, in prescribed cases, be given by both parties together in person at a prescribed register office.

(3) ...

(4) ... if the prescribed registrar is not the registrar for the purposes of Article 4 of that Order, the prescribed registrar shall send him the marriage notices and he shall be treated as having received them from the parties to the marriage on the dates on which the prescribed registrar received them.

(5) ...

(6) For the purposes of this section—

(a) a person is subject to immigration control if—

(i) he is not an EEA national, and

(ii) under the Immigration Act 1971 (c. 77) he requires leave to enter or remain in the United Kingdom (whether or not leave has been given),

(b) 'EEA national' means a national of a State which is a contracting party to the Agreement on the European Economic Area signed at Oporto on 2 May 1992 (as it has effect from time to time),

(c) ...

(d) ...

Note: Commenced 1 February 2005 (SI 2004/3398). Subsections (3), (5) and (6)(c) and (d) repealed and words omitted from sub-s (4) from 9 May 2011 (SI 2011/1158).

24. Northern Ireland: supplemental

(1) The Marriage (Northern Ireland) Order 2003 (SI 2003/413 (N.I.3)) shall have effect in relation to a marriage to which section 23 applies—

(a) subject to section 23, and

(b) with any necessary consequential modification.

(2) In section 23 'prescribed' means prescribed for the purposes of that section by regulations made by the Secretary of State after consulting the Registrar General for Northern Ireland and other expressions used in that section or this section and the Marriage (Northern Ireland) Order 2003 have the same meaning in section 23 or this section as in that Order.

(3) Section 18(3) of the Interpretation Act (Northern Ireland) 1954 (c.33 (N.I.)) (provisions as to holders of offices) shall apply to section 23 as if that section were an enactment within the meaning of that Act.

(4) Regulations of the Secretary of State under section 23—
    (a) may make transitional provision,
    (b) shall be made by statutory instrument, and
    (c) shall be subject to annulment in pursuance of a resolution of either House of Parliament.

Note: Commenced 1 February 2005 (SI 2004/3398).

25. Application for permission under section 19(3)(b), 21(3)(b) or 23(3)(b)

Note: Repealed by s 50 Immigration, Asylum and Nationality Act 2006 from 30 April 2007 subject to savings (SI 2007/1109), and repealed for all remaining purposes from 9 May 2011 (SI 2011/1158).

Appeals

26. Unification of appeal system

(1) . . .

Note: Amends Nationality, Immigration and Asylum Act 2002, s 81.

(2) . . .

Note: Amends Nationality, Immigration and Asylum Act 2002, s 82(1).

(3) . . .

Note: Amends Nationality, Immigration and Asylum Act 2002, s 83(2).

(4) . . .

(5) . . .

Note: Amends Nationality, Immigration and Asylum Act 2002, ss 100–103 and Sch 5.

(6) . . .

(7) Schedule 2 (which makes amendments consequential on this section, and transitional provision) shall have effect.

(8) . . .

(9) . . .

(10) . . .

Note: Commenced 4 April 2005 (SI 2005/565). Subsections (4), (6), (8)–(10) revoked from 15 February 2010 (SI 2010/21).

27. Unfounded human rights or asylum claim

. . .

Note: Amends Nationality, Immigration and Asylum Act 2002, ss 94 and 112 from 1 October 2004 (SI 2004/2523).

28. Appeal from within United Kingdom

. . .

Note: Amends Nationality, Immigration and Asylum Act 2002, s 92(3) from 1 October 2004 (SI 2004/2523).

29. Entry clearance

. . .

Note: Amends Nationality, Immigration and Asylum Act 2002, ss 88 and 112 from 1 October 2004 (SI 2004/2523).

30. Earlier right of appeal

. . .

Note: Amends Nationality, Immigration and Asylum Act 2002, s 96 from 1 October 2004 (SI 2004/2523).

31. Seamen and aircrews: right of appeal

. . .

Note: Amends Nationality, Immigration and Asylum Act 2002, s 82 from 1 October 2004 (SI 2004/2523).

32. Suspected international terrorist: bail

. . .

Note: Section 32 repealed from 14 March 2005, Prevention of Terrorism Act 2005, s 16(2).

Removal and detention

33. Removing asylum seeker to safe country

(1) Schedule 3 (which concerns the removal of persons claiming asylum to countries known to protect refugees and to respect human rights) shall have effect.

(2) . . .

Note: Repeals Immigration and Asylum Act 1999, ss 11 and 12.

(3) ...

Note: Repeals Nationality, Immigration and Asylum Act 2002, ss 80 and 93. Commencement 1 October 2004 (SI 2004/2523).

34. Detention pending deportation

. . .

Note: Amends para 2, Sch 3 Immigration Act 1971 from 1 October 2004 (SI 2004/2523).

35. Deportation or removal: cooperation

(1) The Secretary of State may require a person to take specified action if the Secretary of State thinks that—

(a) the action will or may enable a travel document to be obtained by or for the person, and

(b) possession of the travel document will facilitate the person's deportation or removal from the United Kingdom.

(2) In particular, the Secretary of State may require a person to—

(a) provide information or documents to the Secretary of State or to any other person;

(b) obtain information or documents;

(c) provide fingerprints, submit to the taking of a photograph or provide information, or submit to a process for the recording of information, about external physical characteristics (including, in particular, features of the iris or any other part of the eye);

(d) make, or consent to or cooperate with the making of, an application to a person acting for the government of a State other than the United Kingdom;

(e) cooperate with a process designed to enable determination of an application;

(f) complete a form accurately and completely;

(g) attend an interview and answer questions accurately and completely;

(h) make an appointment.

(3) A person commits an offence if he fails without reasonable excuse to comply with a requirement of the Secretary of State under subsection (1).

(4) A person guilty of an offence under subsection (3) shall be liable—

(a) on conviction on indictment, to imprisonment for a term not exceeding two years, to a fine or to both, or

(b) on summary conviction, to imprisonment for a term not exceeding twelve months, to a fine not exceeding the statutory maximum or to both.

(5) If [an] immigration officer reasonably suspects that a person has committed an offence under subsection (3) he may arrest the person without warrant.

(6) An offence under subsection (3) shall be treated as—

(a) a relevant offence for the purposes of sections 28B and 28D of the Immigration Act 1971 (c. 77) (search, entry and arrest), and

(b) an offence under Part III of that Act (criminal proceedings) for the purposes of sections 28(4), 28E, 28G and 28H (search after arrest, &c.) of that Act.

(7) In subsection (1)—

'travel document' means a passport or other document which is issued by or for Her Majesty's Government or the government of another State and which enables or facilitates travel from the United Kingdom to another State, and

'removal from the United Kingdom' means removal under—

(a) Schedule 2 to the Immigration Act 1971 (control on entry) (including a provision of that Schedule as applied by another provision of the Immigration Acts),

(b) section 10 of the Immigration and Asylum Act 1999 (c. 33) (removal of person unlawfully in United Kingdom), or

(c) Schedule 3 to this Act.

(8) While sections 11 and 12 of the Immigration and Asylum Act 1999 continue to have effect, the reference in subsection (7)(c) above to Schedule 3 to this Act shall be treated as including a reference to those sections.

(9) In so far as subsection (3) extends to England and Wales, subsection (4)(b) shall, until the commencement of section 154 of the Criminal Justice Act 2003 (c. 44) (increased limit on magistrates' power of imprisonment), have effect as if the reference to twelve months were a reference to six months.

(10) In so far as subsection (3) extends to Scotland, subsection (4)(b) shall have effect as if the reference to twelve months were a reference to six months.

(11) In so far as subsection (3) extends to Northern Ireland, subsection (4)(b) shall have effect as if the reference to twelve months were a reference to six months.

Note: Commencement 1 October 2004 (s 48). Word in square bracket in sub-s (5) substituted by Sch 7 Serious Organised Crime and Police Act 2005 from 1 January 2006 (SI 2005/3495) and from 1 March 2007 (NI) (SI 2007/288 NI 2).

36. Electronic monitoring

(1) In this section—

(a) 'residence restriction' means a restriction as to residence imposed under—

(i) paragraph 21 of Schedule 2 to the Immigration Act 1971 (c. 77) (control on entry) (including that paragraph as applied by another provision of the Immigration Acts), or

(ii) Schedule 3 to that Act (deportation),

(b) 'reporting restriction' means a requirement to report to a specified person imposed under any of those provisions,

(c) 'employment restriction' means a restriction as to employment or occupation imposed under any of those provisions, and

(d) 'immigration bail' means—

(i) release under a provision of the Immigration Acts on entry into a recognizance or bail bond,

(ii) bail granted in accordance with a provision of the Immigration Acts by a court, a justice of the peace, the sheriff, [the First-tier Tribunal], the Secretary of State or an immigration officer (but not by a police officer), and

(iii) bail granted by the Special Immigration Appeals Commission.

(2) Where a residence restriction is imposed on an adult—

(a) he may be required to cooperate with electronic monitoring, and

(b) failure to comply with a requirement under paragraph (a) shall be treated for all purposes of the Immigration Acts as failure to observe the residence restriction.

(3) Where a reporting restriction could be imposed on an adult—

(a) he may instead be required to cooperate with electronic monitoring, and

(b) the requirement shall be treated for all purposes of the Immigration Acts as a reporting restriction.

(4) Immigration bail may be granted to an adult subject to a requirement that he cooperate with electronic monitoring; and the requirement may (but need not) be imposed as a condition of a recognizance or bail bond.

(5) In this section a reference to requiring an adult to cooperate with electronic monitoring is a reference to requiring him to cooperate with such arrangements as the person imposing the requirement may specify for detecting and recording by electronic means the location of the adult, or his presence in or absence from a location—

(a) at specified times,

(b) during specified periods of time, or

(c) throughout the currency of the arrangements.

(6) In particular, arrangements for the electronic monitoring of an adult—

(a) may require him to wear a device;

(b) may require him to make specified use of a device;

(c) may prohibit him from causing or permitting damage of or interference with a device;

(d) may prohibit him from taking or permitting action that would or might prevent the effective operation of a device;

(e) may require him to communicate in a specified manner and at specified times or during specified periods of time;

(f) may involve the performance of functions by persons other than the person imposing the requirement to cooperate with electronic monitoring (and those functions may relate to any aspect or condition of a residence restriction, of a reporting restriction, of an employment restriction, of a requirement under this section or of immigration bail).

(7) In this section 'adult' means an individual who is at least 18 years old.

(8) The Secretary of State—

(a) may make rules about arrangements for electronic monitoring for the purposes of this section, and

(b) when he thinks that satisfactory arrangements for electronic monitoring are available in respect of an area, shall notify persons likely to be in a position to exercise power under this section in respect of the area.

(9) Rules under subsection (8)(a) may, in particular, require that arrangements for electronic monitoring impose on a person of a specified description responsibility for specified aspects of the operation of the arrangements.

(10) A requirement to cooperate with electronic monitoring—

(a) shall comply with rules under subsection (8)(a), and

(b) may not be imposed in respect of an adult who is or is expected to be in an area unless the person imposing the requirement has received a notification from the Secretary of State under subsection (8)(b) in respect of that area.

(11) Rules under subsection (8)(a)—

(a) may include incidental, consequential or transitional provision,

(b) may make provision generally or only in relation to specified cases, circumstances or areas,

(c) shall be made by statutory instrument, and

(d) shall be subject to annulment in pursuance of a resolution of either House of Parliament.

(12) . . . . . .

Note: Commencement 1 October 2004 (SI 2004/2523). Words in square brackets in sub-s (1)(d) substituted and sub-s (12) revoked from 15 February 2010 (SI 2010/21).

Immigration services

37. Provision of immigration services

Note: Amends Immigration and Asylum Act 1999, ss 84, 85, 89, 90 and Sch 5 and 6.

38. Immigration Services Commissioner: power of entry

. . .

Note: Amends Immigration and Asylum Act 1999, s 92 and Sch 5, para 7.

39. Offence of advertising services

. . .

Note: Amends Immigration and Asylum Act 1999, s 92.

40. Appeal to Immigration Services Tribunal

. . .

Note: Repeals Immigration and Asylum Act 1999, s 87(3)(f).

41. Professional bodies

. . .

Note: Amends Immigration and Asylum Act 1999, ss 86, 166 and Sch 5, para 21.

Fees

42. Amount of fees

(1) [In prescribing a fee under section 51 of the Immigration, Asylum and Nationality Act 2006 (fees) in connection with a matter specified in subsection (2)] the Secretary of State may, . . . prescribe an amount which is intended to—

(a) exceed the administrative costs of determining the application or undertaking the process, and

(b) reflect benefits that the Secretary of State thinks are likely to accrue to the person who makes the application, to whom the application relates or by or for whom the process is undertaken, if the application is successful or the process is completed.

[(**2**) Those matters are—

(a) anything done under, by virtue of or in connection with a provision of the British Nationality Act 1981 (c. 61) or of the former nationality Acts (within the meaning given by section 50(1) of that Act),

(b) an application for leave to remain in the United Kingdom,

(c) an application for the variation of leave to enter, or remain in, the United Kingdom,

(d) section 10 of the Nationality, Immigration and Asylum Act 2002 (c. 41) (right of abode: certificate of entitlement),

[(da) an application or process in connection with sponsorship of persons seeking leave to enter or remain in the United Kingdom,]

(e) a work permit, and

(f) any other document which relates to employment and is issued for a purpose of immigration rules or in connection with leave to enter or remain in the United Kingdom.]

[(**2A**) Regulations under section 51(3) of the Immigration, Asylum and Nationality Act 2006, specifying the amount of a fee for a claim, application, service, process or other matter in respect of which an order has been made under section 51(1) or (2), may specify an amount which reflects (in addition to any costs referable to the claim, application, service, process or other matter) costs referable to—

(a) any other claim, application, service, process or matter in respect of which the Secretary of State has made an order under section 51(1) or (2),

(b) the determination of applications for entry clearances (within the meaning given by section 33(1) of the Immigration Act 1971),

(c) the determination of applications for transit visas under section 41 of the Immigration and Asylum Act 1999, or

(d) the determination of applications for certificates of entitlement to the right of abode in the United Kingdom under section 10 of the Nationality, Immigration and Asylum Act 2002.]

(**3**) An Order in Council under section 1 of the Consular Fees Act 1980 (c. 23) (fees) which prescribes a fee in relation to an application for the issue of a certificate under section 10 of the Nationality, Immigration and Asylum Act 2002 (right of abode: certificate of entitlement) may prescribe an amount which is intended to—

(a) exceed the administrative costs of determining the application, and

(b) reflect benefits that in the opinion of Her Majesty in Council are likely to accrue to the applicant if the application is successful.

[(3A) The amount of a fee under section 1 of the Consular Fees Act 1980 in respect of a matter specified in subsection (2A)(b) to (d) above may be set so as to reflect costs referable to any claim, application, service, process or other matter in respect of which the Secretary of State has made an order under section 51(1) or (2) of the Immigration, Asylum and Nationality Act 2006.]

(**4**) Where an instrument prescribes a fee in reliance on this section it may include provision for the refund, where an application is unsuccessful or a process is not completed, of that part of the fee which is intended to reflect the matters specified in subsection (1)(b) or (3)(b).

(**5**) Provision included by virtue of subsection (4)—

(a) may determine, or provide for the determination of, the amount to be refunded;

(b) may confer a discretion on the Secretary of State or another person (whether in relation to determining the amount of a refund or in relation to determining whether a refund should be made).

(6) An instrument may not be made in reliance on this section unless the Secretary of State has consulted with such persons as appear to him to be appropriate.

(7) An instrument may not be made in reliance on this section unless a draft has been laid before and approved by resolution of each House of Parliament (and any provision making the instrument subject to annulment in pursuance of a resolution of either House of Parliament shall not apply).

(8) This section is without prejudice to the power to make an order under section 102 of the Finance (No. 2) Act 1987 (c. 51) (government fees and charges) in relation to a power under a provision specified in this section.

Note: Commencement 1 October 2004 (SI 2004/2523). Words omitted from and words in square brackets in sub-s (1) and sub-s (2) substituted by para 6, Sch 2 Asylum, Immigration and Nationality Act 2006 from 7 March 2007 (SI 2007/467). Subsections (2)(da), (2A) and (3A) inserted by s 20 UK Borders Act 2007 from 31 January 2008 (SI 2008/99).

43. Transfer of leave stamps

. . .

Note: Amends Immigration and Asylum Act 1999, s 5.

General

44.

. . .

Note: Section 44 repealed by Immigration, Asylum and Nationality Act 2006, s 64(3) from 30 March 2006 (Royal Assent).

45. Interpretation: immigration officer

In this Act 'immigration officer' means a person appointed by the Secretary of State as an immigration officer under paragraph 1 of Schedule 2 to the Immigration Act 1971.

Note: Commencement 1 October 2004 (SI 2004/2523).

46. Money

There shall be paid out of money provided by Parliament—

(a) any expenditure incurred by a Minister of the Crown in connection with this Act, and

(b) any increase attributable to this Act in the sums payable under any other enactment out of money provided by Parliament.

Note: Commencement 1 October 2004 (SI 2004/2523).

47. Repeals

. . .

48. Commencement

(1) Sections 2, 32(2) and 35 shall come into force at the end of the period of two months beginning with the date on which this Act is passed.

(2) Section 32(1) shall have effect in relation to determinations of the Special Immigration Appeals Commission made after the end of the period of two months beginning with the date on which this Act is passed.

(3) The other preceding provisions of this Act shall come into force in accordance with provision made—

(a) in the case of section 26 or Schedule 1 or 2, by order of the Lord Chancellor,

(b) in the case of sections 4 and 5 in so far as they extend to Scotland, by order of the Scottish Ministers, and

(c) in any other case, by order of the Secretary of State.

(4) An order under subsection (3)—

(a) may make transitional or incidental provision,

(b) may make different provision for different purposes, and

(c) shall be made by statutory instrument.

(5) Transitional provision under subsection (4)(a) in relation to the commencement of section 26 may, in particular, make provision in relation to proceedings which, immediately before commencement—

(a) are awaiting determination by an adjudicator appointed, or treated as if appointed, under section 81 of the Nationality, Immigration and Asylum Act 2002 (c. 41),

(b) are awaiting determination by the Immigration Appeal Tribunal,

(c) having been determined by an adjudicator could be brought before the Immigration Appeal Tribunal,

(d) are awaiting the determination of a further appeal brought in accordance with section 103 of that Act,

(e) having been determined by the Immigration Appeal Tribunal could be brought before another court by way of further appeal under that section,

(f) are or could be made the subject of an application under section 101 of that Act (review of decision on permission to appeal to Tribunal), or

(g) are or could be made the subject of another kind of application to the High Court or the Court of Session.

(6) Provision made under subsection (5) may, in particular—

(a) provide for the institution or continuance of an appeal of a kind not generally available after the commencement of section 26,

(b) provide for the termination of proceedings, or

(c) make any other provision that the Lord Chancellor thinks appropriate.

49. Extent

(1) This Act extends (subject to subsection (2)) to—

(a) England and Wales,

(b) Scotland, and

(c) Northern Ireland.

(2) An amendment effected by this Act has the same extent as the enactment, or as the relevant part of the enactment, amended (ignoring extent by virtue of an Order in Council).

(3) Her Majesty may by Order in Council direct that a provision of this Act is to extend, with or without modification or adaptation, to—

(a) any of the Channel Islands;

(b) the Isle of Man.

50. Short title

This Act may be cited as the Asylum and Immigration (Treatment of Claimants, etc.) Act 2004.

SCHEDULES
SCHEDULE 1

. . .

Note: Schedule 1 amends Nationality, Immigration and Asylum Act 2002.

Section 26   SCHEDULE 2

ASYLUM AND IMMIGRATION TRIBUNAL:
CONSEQUENTIAL AMENDMENTS AND TRANSITIONAL PROVISION

PART 1
CONSEQUENTIAL AMENDMENTS

. . .

PART 2
TRANSITIONAL PROVISION

26. In this Part 'commencement' means the coming into force of section 26.

27. A person who immediately before commencement is, or is to be treated as, an adjudicator appointed under section 81 of the Nationality, Immigration and Asylum Act 2002 (c. 41) (appeals) (as it has effect before commencement) shall be treated as having been appointed as a member of the Asylum and Immigration Tribunal under paragraph 1 of Schedule 4 to that Act (as it has effect after commencement) immediately after commencement.

28. Where immediately before commencement a person is a member of the Immigration Appeal Tribunal—

(a) he shall be treated as having been appointed as a member of the Asylum and Immigration Tribunal under paragraph 1 of Schedule 4 to that Act immediately after commencement, and

(b) if he was a legally qualified member of the Immigration Appeal Tribunal (within the meaning of Schedule 5 to that Act) he shall be treated as having been appointed as a legally qualified member of the Asylum and Immigration Tribunal.

29. A person who immediately before commencement is a member of staff of adjudicators appointed or treated as appointed under section 81 of the Nationality, Immigration and Asylum Act 2002 (c. 41) or of the Immigration Appeal Tribunal shall be treated as having been appointed as a member of the staff of the Asylum and Immigration Tribunal under

paragraph 9 of Schedule 4 to the Nationality, Immigration and Asylum Act 2002 immediately after commencement.

30. ....

Note: Commencement 4 April 2005 (SI 2005/565). Paragraph 30 revoked from 15 February 2010 (SI 2010/21).

Section 33

SCHEDULE 3

REMOVAL OF ASYLUM SEEKER TO SAFE COUNTRY

PART 1

INTRODUCTORY

1.—(1) In this Schedule—
'asylum claim' means a claim by a person that to remove him from or require him to leave the United Kingdom would breach the United Kingdom's obligations under the Refugee Convention,
'Convention rights' means the rights identified as Convention rights by section 1 of the Human Rights Act 1998 (c. 42) (whether or not in relation to a State that is a party to the Convention),
'human rights claim' means a claim by a person that to remove him from or require him to leave the United Kingdom would be unlawful under section 6 of the Human Rights Act 1998 (public authority not to act contrary to Convention) as being incompatible with his Convention rights,
'immigration appeal' means an appeal under section 82(1) of the Nationality, Immigration and Asylum Act 2002 (c. 41) (appeal against immigration decision), and
'the Refugee Convention' means the Convention relating to the Status of Refugees done at Geneva on 28 July 1951 and its Protocol.

(2) In this Schedule a reference to anything being done in accordance with the Refugee Convention is a reference to the thing being done in accordance with the principles of the Convention, whether or not by a signatory to it.

PART 2

FIRST LIST OF SAFE COUNTRIES (REFUGEE CONVENTION AND HUMAN RIGHTS (1))

2. This Part applies to—
  (a)   Austria,
  (b)   Belgium,
  [(ba) Bulgaria,]
  (c)   Republic of Cyprus,
  (d)   Czech Republic,
  (e)   Denmark,
  (f)   Estonia,
  (g)   Finland,
  (h)   France,
  (i)   Germany,
  (j)   Greece,
  (k)   Hungary,
  (l)   Iceland,

(m)	Ireland,
(n)	Italy,
(o)	Latvia,
(p)	Lithuania,
(q)	Luxembourg,
(r)	Malta,
(s)	Netherlands,
(t)	Norway,
(u)	Poland,
(v)	Portugal,
[(va)	Romania,]
(w)	Slovak Republic,
(x)	Slovenia,
(y)	Spain, . . .
(z)	Sweden.
{(z1)	Switzerland}

Note: Words in square brackets inserted from 1 January 2007 (SI 2006/3393). Switzerland added from 20 November 2010 (SI 2010/2802); the amendment adding Switzerland (a) applies in relation to asylum and human rights claims made before 20 November 2010 (as well as those made after), but (b) does not apply in relation to an asylum or human rights claim if, before 20 November 2010, a decision is made to refuse the claimant leave to enter the United Kingdom or to remove the claimant from the United Kingdom: see Art 1(3) SI 2010/2802.

3.—(1) This paragraph applies for the purposes of the determination by any person, tribunal or court whether a person who has made an asylum claim or a human rights claim may be removed—
(a) from the United Kingdom, and
(b) to a State of which he is not a national or citizen.

(2) A State to which this Part applies shall be treated, in so far as relevant to the question mentioned in sub-paragraph (1), as a place—
(a) where a person's life and liberty are not threatened by reason of his race, religion, nationality, membership of a particular social group or political opinion,
(b) from which a person will not be sent to another State in contravention of his Convention rights, and
(c) from which a person will not be sent to another State otherwise than in accordance with the Refugee Convention.

4. Section 77 of the Nationality, Immigration and Asylum Act 2002 (c. 41) (no removal while claim for asylum pending) shall not prevent a person who has made a claim for asylum from being removed—
(a) from the United Kingdom, and
(b) to a State to which this Part applies;
provided that the Secretary of State certifies that in his opinion the person is not a national or citizen of the State.

5.—(1) This paragraph applies where the Secretary of State certifies that—
(a) it is proposed to remove a person to a State to which this Part applies, and
(b) in the Secretary of State's opinion the person is not a national or citizen of the State.

(2) The person may not bring an immigration appeal by virtue of section 92(2) or (3) of that Act (appeal from within United Kingdom: general).

(3) The person may not bring an immigration appeal by virtue of section 92(4)(a) of that Act (appeal from within United Kingdom: asylum or human rights) in reliance on—
(a) an asylum claim which asserts that to remove the person to a specified State to which this Part applies would breach the United Kingdom's obligations under the Refugee Convention, or

(b) a human rights claim in so far as it asserts that to remove the person to a specified State to which this Part applies would be unlawful under section 6 of the Human Rights Act 1998 because of the possibility of removal from that State to another State.

(4) The person may not bring an immigration appeal by virtue of section 92(4)(a) of that Act in reliance on a human rights claim to which this sub-paragraph applies if the Secretary of State certifies that the claim is clearly unfounded; and the Secretary of State shall certify a human rights claim to which this sub-paragraph applies unless satisfied that the claim is not clearly unfounded.

(5) Sub-paragraph (4) applies to a human rights claim if, or in so far as, it asserts a matter other than that specified in sub-paragraph (3)(b).

6. A person who is outside the United Kingdom may not bring an immigration appeal on any ground that is inconsistent with treating a State to which this Part applies as a place—

(a) where a person's life and liberty are not threatened by reason of his race, religion, nationality, membership of a particular social group or political opinion,

(b) from which a person will not be sent to another State in contravention of his Convention rights, and

(c) from which a person will not be sent to another State otherwise than in accordance with the Refugee Convention.

PART 3

SECOND LIST OF SAFE COUNTRIES (REFUGEE CONVENTION AND HUMAN RIGHTS (2))

7.—(1) This Part applies to such States as the Secretary of State may by order specify.

(2) An order under this paragraph—

(a) shall be made by statutory instrument, and

(b) shall not be made unless a draft has been laid before and approved by resolution of each House of Parliament.

8.—(1) This paragraph applies for the purposes of the determination by any person, tribunal or court whether a person who has made an asylum claim may be removed—

(a) from the United Kingdom, and

(b) to a State of which he is not a national or citizen.

(2) A State to which this Part applies shall be treated, in so far as relevant to the question mentioned in sub-paragraph (1), as a place—

(a) where a person's life and liberty are not threatened by reason of his race, religion, nationality, membership of a particular social group or political opinion, and

(b) from which a person will not be sent to another State otherwise than in accordance with the Refugee Convention.

9. Section 77 of the Nationality, Immigration and Asylum Act 2002 (c. 41) (no removal while claim for asylum pending) shall not prevent a person who has made a claim for asylum from being removed—

(a) from the United Kingdom, and

(b) to a State to which this Part applies;

provided that the Secretary of State certifies that in his opinion the person is not a national or citizen of the State.

10.—(1) This paragraph applies where the Secretary of State certifies that—

(a) it is proposed to remove a person to a State to which this Part applies, and

(b) in the Secretary of State's opinion the person is not a national or citizen of the State.

(2) The person may not bring an immigration appeal by virtue of section 92(2) or (3) of that Act (appeal from within United Kingdom: general).

(3) The person may not bring an immigration appeal by virtue of section 92(4)(a) of that Act (appeal from within United Kingdom: asylum or human rights) in reliance on an asylum claim which asserts that to remove the person to a specified State to which this Part applies would breach the United Kingdom's obligations under the Refugee Convention.

(4) The person may not bring an immigration appeal by virtue of section 92(4)(a) of that Act in reliance on a human rights claim if the Secretary of State certifies that the claim is clearly unfounded; and the Secretary of State shall certify a human rights claim where this paragraph applies unless satisfied that the claim is not clearly unfounded.

11. A person who is outside the United Kingdom may not bring an immigration appeal on any ground that is inconsistent with treating a State to which this Part applies as a place—
   (a) where a person's life and liberty are not threatened by reason of his race, religion, nationality, membership of a particular social group or political opinion, and
   (b) from which a person will not be sent to another State otherwise than in accordance with the Refugee Convention.

PART 4
THIRD LIST OF SAFE COUNTRIES (REFUGEE CONVENTION ONLY)

12.—(1) This Part applies to such States as the Secretary of State may by order specify.

(2). An order under this paragraph—
   (a) shall be made by statutory instrument, and
   (b) shall not be made unless a draft has been laid before and approved by resolution of each House of Parliament.

13.—(1) This paragraph applies for the purposes of the determination by any person, tribunal or court whether a person who has made an asylum claim may be removed—
   (a) from the United Kingdom, and
   (b) to a State of which he is not a national or citizen.

(2) A State to which this Part applies shall be treated, in so far as relevant to the question mentioned in sub-paragraph (1), as a place—
   (a) where a person's life and liberty are not threatened by reason of his race, religion, nationality, membership of a particular social group or political opinion, and
   (b) from which a person will not be sent to another State otherwise than in accordance with the Refugee Convention.

14. Section 77 of the Nationality, Immigration and Asylum Act 2002 (c. 41) (no removal while claim for asylum pending) shall not prevent a person who has made a claim for asylum from being removed—
   (a) from the United Kingdom, and
   (b) to a State to which this Part applies;
provided that the Secretary of State certifies that in his opinion the person is not a national or citizen of the State.

15.—(1) This paragraph applies where the Secretary of State certifies that—
   (a) it is proposed to remove a person to a State to which this Part applies, and
   (b) in the Secretary of State's opinion the person is not a national or citizen of the State.

(2) The person may not bring an immigration appeal by virtue of section 92(2) or (3) of that Act (appeal from within United Kingdom: general).

(3) The person may not bring an immigration appeal by virtue of section 92(4)(a) of that Act (appeal from within United Kingdom: asylum or human rights) in reliance on an asylum

claim which asserts that to remove the person to a specified State to which this Part applies would breach the United Kingdom's obligations under the Refugee Convention.

(4) The person may not bring an immigration appeal by virtue of section 92(4)(a) of that Act in reliance on a human rights claim if the Secretary of State certifies that the claim is clearly unfounded.

16. A person who is outside the United Kingdom may not bring an immigration appeal on any ground that is inconsistent with treating a State to which this Part applies as a place—
   (a) where a person's life and liberty are not threatened by reason of his race, religion, nationality, membership of a particular social group or political opinion, and
   (b) from which a person will not be sent to another State otherwise than in accordance with the Refugee Convention.

Part 5

Countries Certified as Safe for Individuals

17. This Part applies to a person who has made an asylum claim if the Secretary of State certifies that—
   (a) it is proposed to remove the person to a specified State,
   (b) in the Secretary of State's opinion the person is not a national or citizen of the specified State, and
   (c) in the Secretary of State's opinion the specified State is a place—
      (i) where the person's life and liberty will not be threatened by reason of his race, religion, nationality, membership of a particular social group or political opinion, and
      (ii) from which the person will not be sent to another State otherwise than in accordance with the Refugee Convention.

18. Where this Part applies to a person section 77 of the Nationality, Immigration and Asylum Act 2002 (c. 41) (no removal while claim for asylum pending) shall not prevent his removal to the State specified under paragraph 17.

19. Where this Part applies to a person—
   (a) he may not bring an immigration appeal by virtue of section 92(2) or (3) of that Act (appeal from within United Kingdom: general),
   (b) he may not bring an immigration appeal by virtue of section 92(4)(a) of that Act (appeal from within United Kingdom: asylum or human rights) in reliance on an asylum claim which asserts that to remove the person to the State specified under paragraph 17 would breach the United Kingdom's obligations under the Refugee Convention,
   (c) he may not bring an immigration appeal by virtue of section 92(4)(a) of that Act in reliance on a human rights claim if the Secretary of State certifies that the claim is clearly unfounded, and
   (d) he may not while outside the United Kingdom bring an immigration appeal on any ground that is inconsistent with the opinion certified under paragraph 17(c).

Part 6

Amendment of Lists

20.—(1) The Secretary of State may by order add a State to the list specified in paragraph 2.

(2) The Secretary of State may by order—
   (a) add a State to a list specified under paragraph 7 or 12, or
   (b) remove a State from a list specified under paragraph 7 or 12.

21.—(1) An order under paragraph 20(1) or (2)(a)—

(a) shall be made by statutory instrument,

(b) shall not be made unless a draft has been laid before and approved by resolution of each House of Parliament, and

(c) may include transitional provision.

(2) An order under paragraph 20(2)(b)—

(a) shall be made by statutory instrument,

(b) shall be subject to annulment in pursuance of a resolution of either House of Parliament, and

(c) may include transitional provision.

Note: Commencement 1 October 2004 (SI 2004/2523).

Section 47   SCHEDULE 4

                                          REPEALS

· · ·

Immigration, Asylum and Nationality Act 2006
(2006, c. 13)

Contents

SCHEDULES

An Act to make provision about immigration, asylum and nationality; and for connected purposes.

[30 March 2006]

Appeals

1. Variation of leave to enter or remain

. . .

Note: Amends Nationality, Immigration and Asylum Act 2002, s 83.

2. Removal

. . .

Note: Amends Nationality, Immigration and Asylum Act 2002, s 82(2).

3. Grounds of appeal

. . .

Note: Amends Nationality, Immigration and Asylum Act 2002, s 84(3).

4. Entry clearance

(1) . . .

(2) . . .

(3) Within the period of three years beginning with the commencement (for any purpose) of subsection (1), the Secretary of State shall lay before Parliament a report about the effect of that subsection; and the report—

(a) must specify the number of applications for entry clearance made during that period,

(b) must specify the number of those applications refused,

(c) must specify the number of those applications granted, after an initial indication to the applicant of intention to refuse the application, as a result of further consideration in accordance with arrangements established by the Secretary of State,

(d) must describe those arrangements,

(e) must describe the effect of regulations made under section 88A(1)(a) or (b) as substituted by subsection (1) above,

(f) may include other information about the process and criteria used to determine applications for entry clearance, and

(g) may record opinions.

Note: Subsection(1) amends Nationality, Immigration and Asylum Act 2002, s 88A, sub-s (2) amends Immigration and Asylum Act 1999, s 23. Commencement 1 April 2008 (SI 2008/310).

5. Failure to provide documents

. . .

Note: Amends Nationality, Immigration and Asylum Act 2002, s 88(2).

6. Refusal of leave to enter

. . .

Note: Amends Nationality, Immigration and Asylum Act 2002, s 89.

7. Deportation

. . .

Note: Amends Nationality, Immigration and Asylum Act 2002, ss 97, 112.

8. Legal aid

. . .

Note: Amends Nationality, Immigration and Asylum Act 2002, s 103D.

9. Abandonment of appeal

. . .

Note: Amends Nationality, Immigration and Asylum Act 2002, s 104(4).

10. Grants

. . .

Note: Amends Nationality, Immigration and Asylum Act 2002, s 110.

11. Continuation of leave

. . .

Note: Amends Immigration Act 1971, s 3C and Nationality, Immigration and Asylum Act 2002, s 82(3).

12. Asylum and human rights claims: definition

. . .

Note: Amends Nationality, Immigration and Asylum Act 2002, s 113.

13. Appeal from within United Kingdom: certification of unfounded claim

. . .

Note: Amends Nationality, Immigration and Asylum Act 2002, s 94.

14. Consequential amendments

Schedule 1 (which makes amendments consequential on the preceding provisions of this Act) shall have effect.

Note: Commencement 31 August 2006 (SI 2006/2226).

Employment

15. Penalty

(1) It is contrary to this section to employ an adult subject to immigration control if—

(a) he has not been granted leave to enter or remain in the United Kingdom, or

(b) his leave to enter or remain in the United Kingdom—

(i) is invalid,

(ii) has ceased to have effect (whether by reason of curtailment, revocation, cancellation, passage of time or otherwise), or

(iii) is subject to a condition preventing him from accepting the employment.

(2) The Secretary of State may give an employer who acts contrary to this section a notice requiring him to pay a penalty of a specified amount not exceeding the prescribed maximum.

(3) An employer is excused from paying a penalty if he shows that he complied with any prescribed requirements in relation to the employment.

(4) But the excuse in subsection (3) shall not apply to an employer who knew, at any time during the period of the employment, that it was contrary to this section.

(5) The Secretary of State may give a penalty notice without having established whether subsection (3) applies.

(6) A penalty notice must—

(a) state why the Secretary of State thinks the employer is liable to the penalty,

(b) state the amount of the penalty,

(c) specify a date, at least 28 days after the date specified in the notice as the date on which it is given, before which the penalty must be paid,

(d) specify how the penalty must be paid,

(e) explain how the employer may object to the penalty, and

(f) explain how the Secretary of State may enforce the penalty.

(7) An order prescribing requirements for the purposes of subsection (3) may, in particular—

(a) require the production to an employer of a document of a specified description;

(b) require the production to an employer of one document of each of a number of specified descriptions;

(c) require an employer to take specified steps to verify, retain, copy or record the content of a document produced to him in accordance with the order;

(d) require action to be taken before employment begins;

(e) require action to be taken at specified intervals or on specified occasions during the course of employment.

Note: Commencement for the purposes of making an order under sub-ss (2), (3) and (7), 5 November 2007 (SI 2007/3138), remainder 29 February 2008, but without effect on employment which commenced before that date (SI 2008/310, which sets out transitional provisions).

16. Objection

(1) This section applies where an employer to whom a penalty notice is given objects on the ground that—

(a) he is not liable to the imposition of a penalty,

(b) he is excused payment by virtue of section 15(3), or

(c) the amount of the penalty is too high.

(2) The employer may give a notice of objection to the Secretary of State.

(3) A notice of objection must—

(a) be in writing,

(b) give the objector's reasons,

(c) be given in the prescribed manner, and

(d) be given before the end of the prescribed period.

(4) Where the Secretary of State receives a notice of objection to a penalty he shall consider it and—

(a) cancel the penalty,

(b) reduce the penalty,

(c) increase the penalty, or

(d) determine to take no action.

(5) Where the Secretary of State considers a notice of objection he shall—

(a) have regard to the code of practice under section 19 (in so far as the objection relates to the amount of the penalty),

(b) inform the objector of his decision before the end of the prescribed period or such longer period as he may agree with the objector,

(c) if he increases the penalty, issue a new penalty notice under section 15, and

(d) if he reduces the penalty, notify the objector of the reduced amount.

Note: Commencement for the purposes of making an order under sub-ss (3) and (5), 5 November 2007 (SI 2007/3138), remainder 29 February 2008, but without effect on employment which commenced before that date (SI 2008/310, which sets out transitional provisions).

17. Appeal

(1) An employer to whom a penalty notice is given may appeal to the court on the ground that—

(a) he is not liable to the imposition of a penalty,

(b) he is excused payment by virtue of section 15(3), or

(c) the amount of the penalty is too high.

(2) The court may—

(a) allow the appeal and cancel the penalty,

(b) allow the appeal and reduce the penalty, or

(c) dismiss the appeal.

(3) An appeal shall be a re-hearing of the Secretary of State's decision to impose a penalty and shall be determined having regard to—

(a) the code of practice under section 19 that has effect at the time of the appeal (in so far as the appeal relates to the amount of the penalty),

and

(b) any other matters which the court thinks relevant (which may include matters of which the Secretary of State was unaware);

and this subsection has effect despite any provision of rules of court.

(4) An appeal must be brought within the period of 28 days beginning with—

(a) the date specified in the penalty notice as the date upon which it is given, or

(b) if the employer gives a notice of objection and the Secretary of State reduces the penalty, the date specified in the notice of reduction as the date upon which it is given, or

(c) if the employer gives a notice of objection and the Secretary of State determines to take no action, the date specified in the notice of that determination as the date upon which it is given.

(5) An appeal may be brought by an employer whether or not—
  (a) he has given a notice of objection under section 16;
  (b) the penalty has been increased or reduced under that section.

(6) In this section 'the court' means—
  (a) where the employer has his principal place of business in England and Wales, a county court,
  (b) where the employer has his principal place of business in Scotland, the sheriff, and
  (c) where the employer has his principal place of business in Northern Ireland, a county court.

Note: Commencement 29 February 2008, but without effect on employment which commenced before that date (SI 2008/310, which sets out transitional provisions).

18. Enforcement

(1) A sum payable to the Secretary of State as a penalty under section 15 may be recovered by the Secretary of State as a debt due to him.

(2) In proceedings for the enforcement of a penalty no question may be raised as to—
  (a) liability to the imposition of the penalty,
  (b) the application of the excuse in section 15(3), or
  (c) the amount of the penalty.

(3) Money paid to the Secretary of State by way of penalty shall be paid into the Consolidated Fund.

Note: Commencement 29 February 2008, but without effect on employment which commenced before that date (SI 2008/310, which sets out transitional provisions).

19. Code of practice

(1) The Secretary of State shall issue a code of practice specifying factors to be considered by him in determining the amount of a penalty imposed under section 15.

(2) The code—
  (a) shall not be issued unless a draft has been laid before Parliament, and
  (b) shall come into force in accordance with provision made by order of the Secretary of State.

(3) The Secretary of State shall from time to time review the code and may revise and re-issue it following a review; and a reference in this section to the code includes a reference to the code as revised.

Note: Commencement 31 August 2006 (SI 2006/2226).

20. Orders

(1) An order of the Secretary of State under section 15, 16 or 19—
  (a) may make provision which applies generally or only in specified circumstances,
  (b) may make different provision for different circumstances,

    (c) may include transitional or incidental provision, and

    (d) shall be made by statutory instrument.

(2) An order under section 15(2) may not be made unless a draft has been laid before and approved by resolution of each House of Parliament.

(3) Any other order shall be subject to annulment in pursuance of a resolution of either House of Parliament.

Note: Commencement 5 November 2007 (SI 2007/3138).

21. Offence

(1) A person commits an offence if he employs another ('the employee') knowing that the employee is an adult subject to immigration control and that—

    (a) he has not been granted leave to enter or remain in the United Kingdom, or

    (b) his leave to enter or remain in the United Kingdom—

        (i) is invalid,

        (ii) has ceased to have effect (whether by reason of curtailment, revocation, cancellation, passage of time or otherwise), or

        (iii) is subject to a condition preventing him from accepting the employment.

(2) A person guilty of an offence under this section shall be liable—

    (a) on conviction on indictment—

        (i) to imprisonment for a term not exceeding two years,

        (ii) to a fine, or

        (iii) to both, or

    (b) on summary conviction—

        (i) to imprisonment for a term not exceeding 12 months in England and Wales or 6 months in Scotland or Northern Ireland,

        (ii) to a fine not exceeding the statutory maximum, or

        (iii) to both.

(3) An offence under this section shall be treated as—

    (a) a relevant offence for the purpose of sections 28B and 28D of the Immigration Act 1971 (c. 77) (search, entry and arrest), and

    (b) an offence under Part III of that Act (criminal proceedings) for the purposes of sections 28E, 28G and 28H (search after arrest).

(4) In relation to a conviction occurring before the commencement of section 154(1) of the Criminal Justice Act 2003 (c. 44) (general limit on magistrates' powers to imprison) the reference to 12 months in subsection (2)(b)(i) shall be taken as a reference to 6 months.

Note: Commencement 29 February 2008, but without effect on employment which commenced before that date (SI 2008/310, which sets out transitional provisions).

22. Offence: bodies corporate, &c.

(1) For the purposes of section 21(1) a body (whether corporate or not) shall be treated as knowing a fact about an employee if a person who has responsibility within the body for an aspect of the employment knows the fact.

(2) If an offence under section 21(1) is committed by a body corporate with the consent or connivance of an officer of the body, the officer, as well as the body, shall be treated as having committed the offence.

(3) In subsection (2) a reference to an officer of a body includes a reference to—
    (a) a director, manager or secretary,
    (b) a person purporting to act as a director, manager or secretary, and
    (c) if the affairs of the body are managed by its members, a member.

(4) Where an offence under section 21(1) is committed by a partnership (whether or not a limited partnership) subsection (2) above shall have effect, but as if a reference to an officer of the body were a reference to—
    (a) a partner, and
    (b) a person purporting to act as a partner.

Note: Commencement 29 February 2008, but without effect on employment which commenced before that date (SI 2008/310, which sets out transitional provisions).

23. Discrimination: code of practice

(1) The Secretary of State shall issue a code of practice specifying what an employer should or should not do in order to ensure that, while avoiding liability to a penalty under section 15 and while avoiding the commission of an offence under section 21, he also avoids contravening—
    (a) [the Equality Act 2010, so far as relating to race], or
    (b) the Race Relations (Northern Ireland) Order 1997 (S.I. 869 (N.I. 6)).

(2) Before issuing the code the Secretary of State shall—
    (a) consult—
        (i) the Commission for Equality and Human Rights,
        (ii) the Equality Commission for Northern Ireland,
        (iii) such bodies representing employers as he thinks appropriate, and
        (iv) such bodies representing workers as he thinks appropriate,
    (b) publish a draft code (after that consultation),
    (c) consider any representations made about the published draft, and
    (d) lay a draft code before Parliament (after considering representations under paragraph (c) and with or without modifications to reflect the representations).

(3) The code shall come into force in accordance with provision made by order of the Secretary of State; and an order—
    (a) may include transitional provision,
    (b) shall be made by statutory instrument, and
    (c) shall be subject to annulment in pursuance of a resolution of either House of Parliament.

(4) A breach of the code—
    (a) shall not make a person liable to civil or criminal proceedings, but
    (b) may be taken into account by a court or tribunal.

(5) The Secretary of State shall from time to time review the code and may revise and re-issue it following a review; and a reference in this section to the code includes a reference to the code as revised.

(**6**) Until the dissolution of the Commission for Racial Equality, the reference in sub-section (2)(a)(i) to the Commission for Equality and Human Rights shall be treated as a reference to the Commission for Racial Equality.

Note: Commencement 31 August 2006 (SI 2006/2226). Words substituted in sub-s (1)(a) from 1 October 2010 by the Equality Act 2010, Sch 26, para 86 as inserted by SI 2010/2279.

24. Temporary admission, &c.

Where a person is at large in the United Kingdom by virtue of paragraph 21(1) of Schedule 2 to the Immigration Act 1971 (c. 77) (temporary admission or release from detention)—

(a) he shall be treated for the purposes of sections 15(1) and 21(1) as if he had been granted leave to enter the United Kingdom, and

(b) any restriction as to employment imposed under paragraph 21(2) shall be treated for those purposes as a condition of leave.

Note: Commencement 29 February 2008, but without effect on employment which commenced before that date (SI 2008/310, which sets out transitional provisions).

25. Interpretation

In sections 15 to 24—

(a) 'adult' means a person who has attained the age of 16,

(b) a reference to employment is to employment under a contract of service or apprenticeship, whether express or implied and whether oral or written,

(c) a person is subject to immigration control if under the Immigration Act 1971 he requires leave to enter or remain in the United Kingdom, and

(d) 'prescribed' means prescribed by order of the Secretary of State.

Note: Commencement 5 November 2007 (SI 2007/3138), but without effect on employment which commenced before 29 February 2008 (SI 2008/310, which sets out transitional provisions).

26. Repeal

. . .

Note: Repeals Asylum and Immigration Act 1996, ss 8 and 8A, but without effect on employment which commenced before 29 February 2008 (SI 2008/310), which sets out transitional provisions).

Information

27. Documents produced or found

. . .

Note: Amends para 4, Sch 2 Immigration Act 1971.

28. Fingerprinting

. . .

Note: Amends Immigration and Asylum Act 1999, s 141.

29. Attendance for fingerprinting

. . .

Note: Amends Immigration and Asylum Act 1999, s 142(2).

30. Proof of right of abode

. . .

Note: Amends Immigration Act 1971, s 3(9).

31. Provision of information to immigration officers

. . .

Note: Subsections (1)–(3) amend para 27, Sch 2 Immigration Act 1971, sub-s (4) amends s 27 of that Act.

32. Passenger and crew information: police powers

(1) This section applies to ships and aircraft which are—

[(a) arriving, or expected to arrive, at any place in the United Kingdom (whether from a place in the United Kingdom or from outside the United Kingdom), or

(b) leaving, or expected to leave, from any place in the United Kingdom (whether for a place in the United Kingdom or for outside the United Kingdom).]

(2) The owner or agent of a ship or aircraft shall comply with any requirement imposed by a constable of the rank of superintendent or above to provide passenger or service information.

(3) A passenger or member of crew shall provide to the owner or agent of a ship or aircraft any information that he requires for the purpose of complying with a requirement imposed by virtue of subsection (2).

(4) A constable may impose a requirement under subsection (2) only if he thinks it necessary—

(a) in the case of a constable in England, Wales or Northern Ireland, for police purposes, or

(b) in the case of a constable in Scotland, for police purposes which are or relate to reserved matters.

(5) In this section—

(a) 'passenger or service information' means information which is of a kind specified by order of the Secretary of State and which relates to—

(i) passengers,

(ii) members of crew, or

(iii) a voyage or flight,

(b) 'police purposes' has the meaning given by section 21(3) of the Immigration and Asylum Act 1999 (c. 33) (disclosure by Secretary of State), . . .

(c) 'reserved matters' has the same meaning as in the Scotland Act 1998 (c. 46)[, and

(d) 'ship' includes—

(i) every description of vessel used in navigation, and

(ii) hovercraft.]

(6) A requirement imposed under subsection (2)—

    (a) must be in writing,

    (b) may apply generally or only to one or more specified ships or aircraft,

    (c) must specify a period, not exceeding six months and beginning with the date on which it is imposed, during which it has effect,

    (d) must state—

        (i) the information required, and

        (ii) the date or time by which it is to be provided.

(7) The Secretary of State may make an order specifying a kind of information under subsection (5)(a) only if satisfied that the nature of the information is such that there are likely to be circumstances in which it can be required under subsection (2) without breaching Convention rights (within the meaning of the Human Rights Act 1998 (c. 42)).

(8) An order under subsection (5)(a)—

    (a) may apply generally or only to specified cases or circumstances,

    (b) may make different provision for different cases or circumstances,

    (c) may specify the form and manner in which information is to be provided,

    (d) shall be made by statutory instrument, and

    (e) shall be subject to annulment in pursuance of a resolution of either House of Parliament.

Note: Commencement for the purposes of making an order under sub-s (5)(a), 5 November 2007 (SI 2007/3138), remainder 1 March 2008 (SI 2007/3580). Sub-s (1)(a) and (b) substituted and sub-s (5)(d) inserted and word omitted from sub-s (5)(c) by Police and Justice Act 2006, s 14, Schedule 15 from a date to be appointed. Section 32 has effect in a form modified by and in circumstances specified by the Channel Tunnel (International Arrangements) Order (SI 1993/1813) as amended by SIs 1994/1405, 2000/913, 2001/178, 2001/3707, 2006/1003 and 2007/3759.

33. Freight information: police powers

(1) This section applies to ships, aircraft and vehicles which are—

    (a) arriving, or expected to arrive, in the United Kingdom, or

    (b) leaving, or expected to leave, the United Kingdom.

(2) If a constable of the rank of superintendent or above requires a person specified in subsection (3) to provide freight information he shall comply with the requirement.

(3) The persons referred to in subsection (2) are—

    (a) in the case of a ship or aircraft, the owner or agent,

    (b) in the case of a vehicle, the owner or hirer, and

    (c) in any case, persons responsible for the import or export of the freight into or from the United Kingdom.

(4) A constable may impose a requirement under subsection (2) only if he thinks it necessary—

    (a) in the case of a constable in England, Wales or Northern Ireland, for police purposes, or

    (b) in the case of a constable in Scotland, for police purposes which are or relate to reserved matters.

(5) In this section—

    (a) 'freight information' means information which is of a kind specified by order of the Secretary of State and which relates to freight carried,

(b) 'police purposes' has the meaning given by section 21(3) of the Immigration and Asylum Act 1999 (c. 33) (disclosure by Secretary of State), and

(c) 'reserved matters' has the same meaning as in the Scotland Act 1998 (c. 46). . .[ ) [, and

(d) 'ship' includes—

(i) every description of vessel used in navigation, and

(ii) hovercraft.]

(**6**) A requirement imposed under subsection (2)—

(a) must be in writing,

(b) may apply generally or only to one or more specified ships, aircraft or vehicles,

(c) must specify a period, not exceeding six months and beginning with the date on which it is imposed, during which it has effect, and

(d) must state—

(i) the information required, and

(ii) the date or time by which it is to be provided.

(**7**) The Secretary of State may make an order specifying a kind of information under subsection (5)(a) only if satisfied that the nature of the information is such that there are likely to be circumstances in which it can be required under subsection (2) without breaching Convention rights (within the meaning of the Human Rights Act 1998 (c. 42)).

(**8**) An order under subsection (5)(a)—

(a) may apply generally or only to specified cases or circumstances,

(b) may make different provision for different cases or circumstances,

(c) may specify the form and manner in which the information is to be provided,

(d) shall be made by statutory instrument, and

(e) shall be subject to annulment in pursuance of a resolution of either House of Parliament.

Note: Commencement for the purposes of making an order under sub-s (5)(a) 1 April 2008 (SI 2008/310). Sub-s (5)(d) inserted and word omitted from sub-s (5)(c) by Police and Justice Act 2006 s 14, Schedule 15 from a date to be appointed.

34. Offence

(**1**) A person commits an offence if without reasonable excuse he fails to comply with a requirement imposed under section 32(2) or (3) or 33(2).

(**2**) But—

(a) a person who fails without reasonable excuse to comply with a requirement imposed under section 32(2) or 33(2) by a constable in England and Wales or Northern Ireland otherwise than in relation to a reserved matter (within the meaning of the Scotland Act 1998 (c. 46)) shall not be treated as having committed the offence in Scotland (but has committed the offence in England and Wales or Northern Ireland), and

(b) a person who fails without reasonable excuse to comply with a requirement which is imposed under section 32(3) for the purpose of complying with a requirement to which paragraph (a) applies—

(i) shall not be treated as having committed the offence in Scotland, but

(ii) shall be treated as having committed the offence in England and Wales or Northern Ireland.

(3) A person who is guilty of an offence under subsection (1) shall be liable on summary conviction to—

    (a) imprisonment for a term not exceeding 51 weeks in England and Wales or 6 months in Scotland or Northern Ireland,

    (b) a fine not exceeding level 4 on the standard scale, or

    (c) both.

(4) In relation to a conviction occurring before the commencement of section 281(5) of the Criminal Justice Act 2003 (c. 44) (51 week maximum term of sentences) the reference to 51 weeks in subsection (2)(a) shall be taken as a reference to three months.

Note: Commencement 1 March 2008 (SI 2007/3580). Section 34 has effect in a form modified by and in circumstances specified by the Channel Tunnel (International Arrangements) Order (SI 1993/1813) as amended by SIs 1994/1405, 2000/913, 2001/178, 2001/3707, 2006/1003 and 2007/3759.

35. Power of Revenue and Customs to obtain information

. . .

Note: Amends Customs and Excise Management Act 1979, s 35.

36. Duty to share information

(1) This section applies to—

    [(a) designated customs officials,

    (aa) immigration officers,

    (ab) the Secretary of State in so far as the Secretary of State has general customs functions,

    (ac) the Secretary of State in so far as the Secretary of State has functions relating to immigration, asylum or nationality,

    (ad) the Director of Border Revenue and any person exercising functions of the Director,]

    (b) a chief officer of police, and

    (c) Her Majesty's Revenue and Customs.

(2) The persons specified in subsection (1) shall share information to which subsection (4) applies and which is obtained or held by them in the course of their functions to the extent that the information is likely to be of use for—

    (a) immigration purposes,

    (b) police purposes, or

    (c) Revenue and Customs purposes.

(3) But a chief officer of police in Scotland shall share information under subsection (2) only to the extent that it is likely to be of use for—

    (a) immigration purposes,

    (b) police purposes, in so far as they are or relate to reserved matters within the meaning of the Scotland Act 1998, or

    (c) Revenue and Customs purposes other than the prosecution of crime.

(4) This subsection applies to information which—

    (a) is obtained or held in the exercise of a power specified by the Secretary of State and the Treasury jointly by order and relates to—

        (i) passengers on a ship or aircraft,

        (ii) crew of a ship or aircraft,

      (iii) freight on a ship or aircraft, or

      (iv) flights or voyages, or

   (b) relates to such other matters in respect of travel or freight as the Secretary of State and the Treasury may jointly specify by order.

(5) The Secretary of State and the Treasury may make an order under subsection (4) which has the effect of requiring information to be shared only if satisfied that—

   (a) the sharing is likely to be of use for—

      (i) immigration purposes,

      (ii) police purposes, or

      (iii) Revenue and Customs purposes, and

   (b) the nature of the information is such that there are likely to be circumstances in which it can be shared under subsection (2) without breaching Convention rights (within the meaning of the Human Rights Act 1998 (c. 42)).

(6) Information shared in accordance with subsection (2)—

   (a) shall be made available to each of the persons [or descriptions of persons] specified in subsection (1), and

   (b) may be used for immigration purposes, police purposes or Revenue and Customs purposes (regardless of its source).

(7) An order under subsection (4) may not specify—

   (a) a power of Her Majesty's Revenue and Customs if or in so far as it relates to a matter to which section 7 of the Commissioners for Revenue and Customs Act 2005 (c. 11) (former Inland Revenue matters) applies, or

   (b) a matter to which that section applies.

(8) An order under subsection (4)—

   (a) shall be made by statutory instrument, and

   (b) may not be made unless a draft has been laid before and approved by resolution of each House of Parliament.

(9) In this section—

'chief officer of police' means—

   (a) in England and Wales, the chief officer of police for a police area specified in section 1 of the Police Act 1996 (c. 16),

   (b) in Scotland, the chief constable of a police force maintained under the Police (Scotland) Act 1967 (c. 77), and

   (c) in Northern Ireland, the chief constable of the Police Service of Northern Ireland,

['designated customs official' and 'general customs function' have the meanings given by Part 1 of the Borders, Citizenship and Immigration Act 2009,]

'immigration purposes' has the meaning given by section 20(3) of the Immigration and Asylum Act 1999 (c. 33) (disclosure to Secretary of State),

'police purposes' has the meaning given by section 21(3) of that Act (disclosure by Secretary of State), and

'Revenue and Customs purposes' means those functions of Her Majesty's Revenue and Customs specified in section 21(6) of that Act.

(10) This section has effect despite any restriction on the purposes for which information may be disclosed or used.

Note: Commencement for the purposes of making an order under sub-s (4), 5 November 2007 (SI 2007/3138), remainder 1 March 2008 (SI 2007/3580). Subsection (1)(a) substituted and words in square brackets in sub-ss (6) and (9) inserted by s 21 Borders, Citizenship and Immigration Act 2009 from a date to be appointed (SI 2009/2731). There is a prospective insertion of a definition, the definition of 'ship': see Police and Justice Act 2006 s 14(4). Section 36 has effect in a form modified by and in circumstances specified by the Channel Tunnel (International Arrangements) Order (SI 1993/1813) as amended by SIs 1994/1405, 2000/913, 2001/178, 2001/3707, 2006/1003 and 2007/3759.

37. Information sharing: code of practice

(1) The Secretary of State and the Treasury shall jointly issue one or more codes of practice about—

(a) the use of information shared in accordance with section 36(2), and

(b) the extent to which, or form or manner in which, shared information is to be made available in accordance with section 36(6).

(2) A code—

(a) shall not be issued unless a draft has been laid before Parliament, and

(b) shall come into force in accordance with provision made by order of the Secretary of State and the Treasury jointly.

(3) The Secretary of State and the Treasury shall jointly from time to time review a code and may revise and re-issue it following a review; and subsection (2) shall apply to a revised code.

(4) An order under subsection (2)—

(a) shall be made by statutory instrument, and

(b) shall be subject to annulment in pursuance of a resolution of either House of Parliament.

Note: Commencement for the purposes of laying a draft code before Parliament and making an order under sub-s (2), 5 November 2007 (SI 2007/3138), remainder 1 March 2008 (SI 2007/3580). Section 37 has effect in a form modified by and in circumstances specified by the Channel Tunnel (International Arrangements) Order (SI 1993/1813) as amended by SIs 1994/1405, 2000/913, 2001/178, 2001/3707, 2006/1003 and 2007/3759.

38. . . .

Note: Commencement for the purposes of making an order under sub-s (4) 5 November 2007 (SI 2007/3138), remainder 1 March 2008 (SI 2007/3580). Revoked by Sch 1 Counter-Terrorism Act 2008 from a date to be appointed.

39. Disclosure to law enforcement agencies

(1) A chief officer of police may disclose information obtained in accordance with section 32 or 33 to—

(a) the States of Jersey police force;

(b) the salaried police force of the Island of Guernsey;

(c) the Isle of Man constabulary;

(d) any other foreign law enforcement agency.

(2) In subsection (1) 'foreign law enforcement agency' means a person outside the United Kingdom with functions similar to functions of—

(a) a police force in the United Kingdom, or

(b) the Serious Organised Crime Agency.

(3) In subsection (1) 'chief officer of police' means—

(a) in England and Wales, the chief officer of police for a police area specified in section 1 of the Police Act 1996,

(b) in Scotland, the chief constable of a police force maintained under the Police (Scotland) Act 1967, and

(c) in Northern Ireland, the chief constable of the Police Service of Northern Ireland.

Note: Commencement 1 March 2008 (SI 2007/3580). Section 39 has effect in a form modified by and in circumstances specified by the Channel Tunnel (International Arrangements) Order (SI 1993/1813) as amended by SIs 1994/1405, 2000/913, 2001/178, 2001/3707, 2006/1003 and 2007/3759.

40. Searches: contracting out

(1) An authorised person may, in accordance with arrangements made under this section, search a searchable ship, aircraft, vehicle or other thing for the purpose of satisfying himself whether there are individuals whom an immigration officer might wish to examine under paragraph 2 of Schedule 2 to the Immigration Act 1971 (c. 77) (control of entry: administrative provisions).

(2) For the purposes of subsection (1)—

(a) 'authorised' means authorised for the purpose of this section by the Secretary of State, and

(b) a ship, aircraft, vehicle or other thing is 'searchable' if an immigration officer could search it under paragraph 1(5) of that Schedule.

(3) The Secretary of State may authorise a specified class of constable for the purpose of this section.

(4) The Secretary of State may, with the consent of the Commissioners for Her Majesty's Revenue and Customs, authorise a specified class of officers of Revenue and Customs for the purpose of this section.

(5) The Secretary of State may authorise a person other than a constable or officer of Revenue and Customs for the purpose of this section only if—

(a) the person applies to be authorised, and

(b) the Secretary of State thinks that the person is—

(i) fit and proper for the purpose, and

(ii) suitably trained.

(6) The Secretary of State—

(a) may make arrangements for the exercise by authorised constables of the powers under subsection (1),

(b) may make arrangements with the Commissioners for Her Majesty's Revenue and Customs for the exercise by authorised officers of Revenue and Customs of the powers under subsection (1), and

(c) may make arrangements with one or more persons for the exercise by authorised persons other than constables and officers of Revenue and Customs of the power under subsection (1).

(7) Where in the course of a search under this section an authorised person discovers an individual whom he thinks an immigration officer might wish to examine under paragraph 2 of that Schedule, the authorised person may—

(a) search the individual for the purpose of discovering whether he has with him anything of a kind that might be used—

(i) by him to cause physical harm to himself or another,

(ii) by him to assist his escape from detention, or

(iii) to establish information about his identity, nationality or citizenship or about his journey;

(b) retain, and as soon as is reasonably practicable deliver to an immigration officer, anything of a kind described in paragraph (a) found on a search under that paragraph;

(c) detain the individual, for a period which is as short as is reasonably necessary and which does not exceed three hours, pending the arrival of an immigration officer to whom the individual is to be delivered;

(d) take the individual, as speedily as is reasonably practicable, to a place for the purpose of delivering him to an immigration officer there;

(e) use reasonable force for the purpose of doing anything under paragraphs (a) to (d).

(8) Despite the generality of subsection (7)—

(a) an individual searched under that subsection may not be required to remove clothing other than an outer coat, a jacket or a glove (but he may be required to open his mouth), and

(b) an item may not be retained under subsection (7)(b) if it is subject to legal privilege—

(i) in relation to a search carried out in England and Wales, within the meaning of the Police and Criminal Evidence Act 1984 (c. 60),

(ii) in relation to a search carried out in Scotland, within the meaning of section 412 of the Proceeds of Crime Act 2002 (c. 29), and

(iii) in relation to a search carried out in Northern Ireland, within the meaning of the Police and Criminal Evidence (Northern Ireland) Order 1989 (SI 1989/1341 (N.I. 12)).

Note: Commencement 31 August 2006 (SI 2006/2226).

41. Section 40: supplemental

(1) Arrangements under section 40(6)(c) must include provision for the appointment of a Crown servant to—

(a) monitor the exercise of powers under that section by authorised persons (other than constables or officers of Revenue and Customs),

(b) inspect from time to time the way in which the powers are being exercised by authorised persons (other than constables or officers of Revenue and Customs), and

(c) investigate and report to the Secretary of State about any allegation made against an authorised person (other than a constable or officer of Revenue and Customs) in respect of anything done or not done in the purported exercise of a power under that section.

(2) The authorisation for the purpose of section 40 of a constable or officer of Revenue and Customs or of a class of constable or officer of Revenue and Customs—

(a) may be revoked, and

(b) shall have effect, unless revoked, for such period as shall be specified (whether by reference to dates or otherwise) in the authorisation.

(3) The authorisation of a person other than a constable or officer of Revenue and Customs for the purpose of section 40—

(a) may be subject to conditions,

(b) may be suspended or revoked by the Secretary of State by notice in writing to the authorised person, and

(c) shall have effect, unless suspended or revoked, for such period as shall be specified (whether by reference to dates or otherwise) in the authorisation.

(4) A class may be specified for the purposes of section 40(3) or (4) by reference to—

(a) named individuals,

(b) the functions being exercised by a person,

(c) the location or circumstances in which a person is exercising functions, or

(d) any other matter.

(5) An individual or article delivered to an immigration officer under section 40 shall be treated as if discovered by the immigration officer on a search under Schedule 2 to the Immigration Act 1971 (c. 77).

(6) A person commits an offence if he—

(a) absconds from detention under section 40(7)(c),

(b) absconds while being taken to a place under section 40(7)(d) or having been taken to a place in accordance with that paragraph but before being delivered to an immigration officer,

(c) obstructs an authorised person in the exercise of a power under section 40, or

(d) assaults an authorised person who is exercising a power under section 40.

(7) But a person does not commit an offence under subsection (6) by doing or failing to do anything in respect of an authorised person who is not readily identifiable—

(a) as a constable or officer of Revenue and Customs, or

(b) as an authorised person (whether by means of a uniform or badge or otherwise).

(8) A person guilty of an offence under subsection (6) shall be liable on summary conviction to—

(a) imprisonment for a term not exceeding 51 weeks, in the case of a conviction in England and Wales, or six months, in the case of a conviction in Scotland or Northern Ireland,

(b) a fine not exceeding level 5 on the standard scale, or

(c) both.

(9) In relation to a conviction occurring before the commencement of section 281(5) of the Criminal Justice Act 2003 (c. 44) (51 week maximum term of sentences) the reference in subsection (8)(a) to 51 weeks shall be treated as a reference to six months.

Note: Commencement 31 August 2006 (SI 2006/2226).

42. Information: embarking passengers

. . .

Note: Amends Sch 2 Immigration Act 1971 (c. 77).

Claimants and applicants

43. Accommodation

(1) . . .

(2) . . .

(3) . . .

(4) . . .

(5) A tenancy is not a Scottish secure tenancy (within the meaning of the Housing (Scotland) Act 2001 (asp 10)) if it is granted in order to provide accommodation under section 4 of the Immigration and Asylum Act 1999 (accommodation).

(6) A tenancy which would be a Scottish secure tenancy but for subsection (4) becomes a Scottish secure tenancy if the landlord notifies the tenant that it is to be regarded as such.

(7) . . .

Note: Subsections (1) and (2) amend Immigration and Asylum Act 1999, s 99. Subsection (3) amends s 118 and sub-s 7 amends s 4 of that Act. Subsection (4) amends Protection from Eviction Act 1977, s 3A; para 3A, Sch 2 Housing (Northern Ireland Order 1983 (SI 1983/1118, NI 15); Rent (Scotland) Act 1984, s 23A; para 4A, Sch 1 Housing Act 1985; para 1B, Sch 4 Housing (Scotland) Act 1988; para 12A, Sch 1 Housing Act 1988. Commenced 16 June 2006 (SI 2006/1497).

44. Failed asylum-seekers: withdrawal of support

(1) The Secretary of State may by order provide for paragraph 7A of Schedule 3 to the Nationality, Immigration and Asylum Act 2002 (c. 41) (failed asylum seeker with family: withdrawal of support) to cease to have effect.

(2) An order under subsection (1) shall also provide for the following to cease to have effect—

    (a) section 9(1), (2) and (4) of the Asylum and Immigration (Treatment of Claimants, etc.) Act 2004 (c. 19) (which insert paragraph 7A of Schedule 3 and make consequential provision), and

    (b) in section 9(3)(a) and (b) of that Act, the words 'other than paragraph 7A.'

(3) An order under subsection (1)—

    (a) may include transitional provision,

    (b) shall be made by statutory instrument, and

    (c) shall be subject to annulment in pursuance of a resolution of either House of Parliament.

Note: Commencement at a date to be appointed.

45. Integration loans

. . .

Note: Amends Asylum and Immigration (Treatment of Claimants, etc.) Act 2004, s 13.

46. Inspection of detention facilities

. . .

Note: Amends Prison Act 1952, ss 5 and 5A.

47. Removal: persons with statutorily extended leave

(1) Where a person's leave to enter or remain in the United Kingdom is extended by section 3C(2)(b) or 3D(2)(a) of the Immigration Act 1971 (c. 77) (extension pending appeal), the Secretary of State may decide that the person is to be removed from the United Kingdom, in accordance with directions to be given by an immigration officer if and when the leave ends.

(2) Directions under this section may impose any requirements of a kind prescribed for the purpose of section 10 of the Immigration and Asylum Act 1999 (c. 33) (removal of persons unlawfully in United Kingdom).

(3) In relation to directions under this section, paragraphs 10, 11, 16 to 18, 21 and 22 to 24 of Schedule 2 to the Immigration Act 1971 (administrative provisions as to control of entry) apply as they apply in relation to directions under paragraph 8 of that Schedule.

(4) The costs of complying with a direction given under this section (so far as reasonably incurred) must be met by the Secretary of State.

(5) A person shall not be liable to removal from the United Kingdom under this section at a time when section 7(1)(b) of the Immigration Act 1971 (Commonwealth and Irish citizens ordinarily resident in United Kingdom) would prevent a decision to deport him.

(6) ...

(7) ...

(8) ...

Note: Subsection (6) amends Nationality, Immigration and Asylum Act 2002, s 82, sub-s (7) amends s 92 and sub-s (8) amends s 94(1A) of that Act. Commenced 1 April 2008 (SI 2008/310).

48. Removal: cancellation of leave

...

Note: Amends Immigration and Asylum Act 1999, s 10(8).

49. Capacity to make nationality application

...

Note: Amends British Nationality Act 1981, s 44.

50. Procedure

(1) Rules under section 3 of the Immigration Act 1971 (c. 77)—

(a) may require a specified procedure to be followed in making or pursuing an application or claim (whether or not under those rules or any other enactment),

(b) may, in particular, require the use of a specified form and the submission of specified information or documents,

(c) may make provision about the manner in which a fee is to be paid, and

(d) may make provision for the consequences of failure to comply with a requirement under paragraph (a), (b) or (c).

(2) In respect of any application or claim in connection with immigration (whether or not under the rules referred to in subsection (1) or any other enactment) the Secretary of State—

    (a) may require the use of a specified form,

    (b) may require the submission of specified information or documents, and

    (c) may direct the manner in which a fee is to be paid; and the rules referred to in subsection (1) may provide for the consequences of failure to comply with a requirement under paragraph (a), (b) or (c).

(3) ...

(4) ...

(5) ...

(6) ...

Note: Subsection (3) repeals Immigration Act 1971, s 31A and Asylum and Immigration (Treatment of Claimants etc) Act 2004, s 25. Subsection (4) amends British Nationality Act 1981, s 41. Subsection (5) amends Nationality, Immigration and Asylum Act 2002, s 10. Subsection (6) repeals para 2(3), Sch 23 Civil Partnership Act 2004. Commencement 31 January 2007 (SI 2007/182).

51. Fees

(1) The Secretary of State may by order require an application or claim in connection with immigration or nationality (whether or not under an enactment) to be accompanied by a specified fee.

(2) The Secretary of State may by order provide for a fee to be charged by him, by an immigration officer or by another specified person in respect of—

    (a) the provision on request of a service (whether or not under an enactment) in connection with immigration or nationality,

    (b) a process (whether or not under an enactment) in connection with immigration or nationality,

    (c) the provision on request of advice in connection with immigration or nationality, or

    (d) the provision on request of information in connection with immigration or nationality.

(3) Where an order under this section provides for a fee to be charged, regulations made by the Secretary of State—

    (a) shall specify the amount of the fee,

    (b) may provide for exceptions,

    (c) may confer a discretion to reduce, waive or refund all or part of a fee,

    (d) may make provision about the consequences of failure to pay a fee,

    (e) may make provision about enforcement, and

    (f) may make provision about the time or period of time at or during which a fee may or must be paid.

(4) Fees paid by virtue of this section shall—

    (a) be paid into the Consolidated Fund, or

    (b) be applied in such other way as the relevant order may specify.

Note: Commencement 31 January 2007 (SI 2007/182).

52. Fees: supplemental

(1) A fee imposed under section 51 may relate to a thing whether or not it is done wholly or partly outside the United Kingdom; but that section is without prejudice to—

  (a) section 1 of the Consular Fees Act 1980 (c. 23), and

  (b) any other power to charge a fee.

(2) Section 51 is without prejudice to the application of section 102 of the Finance (No. 2) Act 1987 (c. 51) (government fees and charges); and an order made under that section in respect of a power repealed by Schedule 2 to this Act shall have effect as if it related to the powers under section 51 above in so far as they relate to the same matters as the repealed power.

(3) An order or regulations under section 51—

  (a) may make provision generally or only in respect of specified cases or circumstances,

  (b) may make different provision for different cases or circumstances,

  (c) may include incidental, consequential or transitional provision, and

  (d) shall be made by statutory instrument.

(4) An order under section 51—

  (a) may be made only with the consent of the Treasury, and

  (b) may be made only if a draft has been laid before and approved by resolution of each House of Parliament.

(5) Regulations under section 51—

  (a) may be made only with the consent of the Treasury, and

  (b) shall be subject to annulment in pursuance of a resolution of either House of Parliament.

(6) A reference in section 51 to anything in connection with immigration or nationality includes a reference to anything in connection with an enactment (including an enactment of a jurisdiction outside the United Kingdom) that relates wholly or partly to immigration or nationality.

(7) Schedule 2 (consequential amendments) shall have effect.

Note: Subsections (1)-(6) commenced 31 January 2007, (SI 2007/182), remainder 2 April 2007 (SI 2007/1109).

Miscellaneous

53. Arrest pending deportation

. . .

Note: Amends para 2(4), Sch 3 Immigration Act 1971.

54. Refugee Convention: construction

(1) In the construction and application of Article 1(F)(c) of the Refugee Convention the reference to acts contrary to the purposes and principles of the United Nations shall be taken as including, in particular—

  (a) acts of committing, preparing or instigating terrorism (whether or not the acts amount to an actual or inchoate offence), and

(b) acts of encouraging or inducing others to commit, prepare or instigate terrorism (whether or not the acts amount to an actual or inchoate offence).

(2) In this section—

'the Refugee Convention' means the Convention relating to the Status of Refugees done at Geneva on 28 July 1951, and

'terrorism' has the meaning given by section 1 of the Terrorism Act 2000 (c. 11).

Note: Commencement 31 August 2006 (SI 2006/2226).

55. Refugee Convention: certification

(1) This section applies to an asylum appeal where the Secretary of State issues a certificate that the appellant is not entitled to the protection of Article 33(1) of the Refugee Convention because—

(a) Article 1(F) applies to him (whether or not he would otherwise be entitled to protection), or

(b) Article 33(2) applies to him on grounds of national security (whether or not he would otherwise be entitled to protection).

(2) In this section—

(a) 'asylum appeal' means an appeal—

(i) which is brought under section 82, 83 or 101 of the Nationality, Immigration and Asylum Act 2002 (c. 41) or section 2 of the Special Immigration Appeals Commission Act 1997 (c. 68), and

(ii) in which the appellant claims that to remove him from or require him to leave the United Kingdom would be contrary to the United Kingdom's obligations under the Refugee Convention, and

(b) 'the Refugee Convention' means the Convention relating to the Status of Refugees done at Geneva on 28 July 1951.

(3) The [First-tier Tribunal] or the Special Immigration Appeals Commission must begin substantive deliberations on the asylum appeal by considering the statements in the Secretary of State's certificate.

(4) If the Tribunal or Commission agrees with those statements it must dismiss such part of the asylum appeal as amounts to an asylum claim (before considering any other aspect of the case).

(5) Section 72(10)(a) of the Nationality, Immigration and Asylum Act 2002 (serious criminal: Tribunal or Commission to begin by considering certificate) shall have effect subject to subsection (3) above.

[(5A) Subsections (3) and (4) also apply in relation to the Upper Tribunal when it acts under section 12(2)(b)(ii) of the Tribunals, Courts and Enforcement Act 2007.]

(6) . . .

Note: Subsection (6) repeals Anti-terrorism, Crime and Security Act 2001, s 33. Commencement 31 August 2006 (SI 2006/2226). Words in square brackets in sub-s (3) substituted and sub-s (5A) inserted from 15 February 2010 (SI 2010/21).

56. Deprivation of citizenship

(1) . . .

(2) . . .

Note: Subsection (1) amends the British Nationality Act 1981, s 42(2) sub-s (2) amends s 40A of that Act.

57. Deprivation of right of abode

(1) . . .

(2) . . .

Note: Subsection (1) amends Immigration Act 1971, s 2 sub-s (2) amends Nationality, Immigration and Asylum Act 2002, s 82.

58. . . .

Note: Commencement from 4 December 2006, but without effect in relation to any application under the provisions listed in sub-s (2) which was made before that date (SI 2006/2838). Section 50(8) of the British Nationality Act 1981 applies for the purpose of this section. Revoked by Schedule Borders, Citizenship and Immigration Act 2009 from 13 January 2010 (SI 2009/2731).

59. Detained persons: national minimum wage

(1) . . .

(2) . . .

Note: Subsection (1) amends Immigration and Asylum Act 1999, s 153. Sub-section (2) amends National Minimum Wage Act 1998, s 45A.

General

60. Money

There shall be paid out of money provided by Parliament—
  (a) any expenditure of the Secretary of State in connection with this Act, and
  (b) any increase attributable to this Act in sums payable under another enactment out of money provided by Parliament.

Note: Commenced 16 June 2006 (SI 2006/1497).

61. Repeals

Schedule 3 (repeals) shall have effect.

Note: Commenced with regard to British Nationality Act 1981, s 40A(3) 16 June 2006 (SI 2006/1497). Remainder from 31 August 2006 (SI 2006/2226).

62. Commencement

(1) The preceding provisions of this Act shall come into force in accordance with provision made by order of the Secretary of State.

(2) An order under subsection (1)—
  (a) may make provision generally or only for specified purposes,
  (b) may make different provision for different purposes,
  (c) may include transitional or incidental provision or savings, and
  (d) shall be made by statutory instrument.

63. Extent

(1) This Act extends to—
  (a) England and Wales,
  (b) Scotland, and
  (c) Northern Ireland.

(2) But—
  (a) an amendment by this Act of another Act has the same extent as that Act or as the relevant part of that Act (ignoring extent by virtue of an Order in Council), and
  (b) a provision of this Act shall, so far as it relates to nationality, have the same extent as the British Nationality Act 1981 (c. 61) (disregarding excepted provisions under section 53(7) of that Act).

(3) Her Majesty may by Order in Council direct that a provision of this Act is to extend, with or without modification or adaptation, to—
  (a) any of the Channel Islands;
  (b) the Isle of Man.

[(3A) In subsection (3), the reference to this Act includes—
  (a) a reference to this Act as it has effect with the amendments and repeals made in it by the Police and Justice Act 2006, and
  (b) a reference to this Act as it has effect without those amendments and repeals.]

(4) Subsection (3) does not apply in relation to the extension to a place of a provision which extends there by virtue of subsection (2)(b).

Note: Commencement 30 March 2006, s 62 (Royal Assent). Sub-s (3A) inserted by Police and Justice Act 2006 s54 from 8 November 2006 (Royal Assent).

64. Citation

(1) This Act may be cited as the Immigration, Asylum and Nationality Act 2006.

(2) . . .

(3) . . .

(4) . . .

Note: Subsection (2) repealed from 30 October 2007 (s 61 UK Borders Act 2007). Subsection (3) repeals the definition of the Immigration Acts in Immigration Act 1971, s 32(5) Immigration and Asylum Act 1999, s 167(1) Nationality, Immigration and Asylum Act 2002, s 158 and Asylum and Immigration (Treatment of Claimants, etc) Act 2004, s 44. Subsection (4) amends Sch 1 Interpretation Act 1978. Commencement 30 March 2006, s 62 (Royal Assent).

SCHEDULES

UK Borders Act 2007
(2007, c. 30)

Contents

Detention at ports

Biometric registration

Treatment of claimants

Enforcement

Deportation of criminals

Information

Border and Immigration Inspectorate

General

Schedule – Repeals

---

*An Act to make provision about immigration and asylum; and for connected
purposes.*

[30 October 2007]

Detention at ports

1. Designated immigration officers

(1) The Secretary of State may designate immigration officers for the purposes of section 2.

(2) The Secretary of State may designate only officers who the Secretary of State thinks are—

(a) fit and proper for the purpose, and

(b) suitably trained.

(3) A designation—

(a) may be permanent or for a specified period, and

(b) may (in either case) be revoked.

Note: Commencement 31 January 2008 (SI 2008/99).

2. Detention

(1) A designated immigration officer at a port in England, Wales or Northern Ireland may detain an individual if the immigration officer thinks that the individual—

(a) may be liable to arrest by a constable under section 24(1), (2) or (3) of the Police and Criminal Evidence Act 1984 or Article 26(1), (2) or (3) of the Police and Criminal Evidence (Northern Ireland) Order 1989 (S.I. 1989/1341 (N.I. 12)), or

(b) is subject to a warrant for arrest.

[(1A) A designated immigration officer at a port in Scotland may detain an individual if the immigration officer thinks that the individual is subject to a warrant for arrest.]

(2) A designated immigration officer who detains an individual—

(a) must arrange for a constable to attend as soon as is reasonably practicable,

(b) may search the individual for, and retain, anything that might be used to assist escape or to cause physical injury to the individual or another person,

(c) must retain anything found on a search which the immigration officer thinks may be evidence of the commission of an offence, and

(d) must, when the constable arrives, deliver to the constable the individual and anything retained on a search.

(3) An individual may not be detained under this section for longer than three hours.

(4) A designated immigration officer may use reasonable force for the purpose of exercising a power under this section.

(5) Where an individual whom a designated immigration officer has detained or attempted to detain under this section leaves the port, a designated immigration officer may—

(a) pursue the individual, and

(b) return the individual to the port.

(6) Detention under this section shall be treated as detention under the Immigration Act 1971 for the purposes of Part 8 of the Immigration and Asylum Act 1999 (detained persons).

Note: Commencement 31 January 2008 (SI 2008/99). Subsection (1A) inserted by s 52 Borders, Citizenship and Immigration Act 2009 from a date to be appointed.

3. Enforcement

(**1**) An offence is committed by a person who—
(a) absconds from detention under section 2,
(b) assaults an immigration officer exercising a power under section 2, or
(c) obstructs an immigration officer in the exercise of a power under section 2.

(**2**) A person guilty of an offence under subsection (1)(a) or (b) shall be liable on summary conviction to—
(a) imprisonment for a term not exceeding 51 weeks,
(b) a fine not exceeding level 5 on the standard scale, or
(c) both.

(**3**) A person guilty of an offence under subsection (1)(c) shall be liable on summary conviction to—
(a) imprisonment for a term not exceeding 51 weeks,
(b) a fine not exceeding level 3 on the standard scale, or
(c) both.

(**4**) In the application of this section to Northern Ireland—
(a) the reference in subsection (2)(a) to 51 weeks shall be treated as a reference to six months, and
(b) the reference in subsection (3)(a) to 51 weeks shall be treated as a reference to one month.

[(**4A**) In the application of this section to Scotland, the references in subsections (2)(a) and (3)(a) to 51 weeks shall be treated as references to 12 months.]

(**5**) In relation to an offence committed before the commencement of section 281(5) of the Criminal Justice Act 2003 (51 week maximum term of sentences)—
(a) the reference in subsection (2)(a) to 51 weeks shall be treated as a reference to six months, and
(b) the reference in subsection (3)(a) to 51 weeks shall be treated as a reference to one month.

Note: Commencement 31 January 2008 (SI 2008/99). Subsection (4A) inserted by s 52 Borders, Citizenship and Immigration Act 2009 from a date to be appointed.

4. Interpretation: 'port'

(**1**) In section 2 'port' includes an airport and a hoverport.

(**2**) A place shall be treated for the purposes of that section as a port in relation to an individual if a designated immigration officer believes that the individual—
(a) has gone there for the purpose of embarking on a ship or aircraft, or
(b) has arrived there on disembarking from a ship or aircraft.

Note: Commencement 31 January 2008 (SI 2008/99).

Biometric registration

5. Registration regulations

(**1**) The Secretary of State may make regulations—
(a) requiring a person subject to immigration control to apply for the issue of a document recording biometric information (a 'biometric immigration document');

(b) requiring a biometric immigration document to be used—

    (i) for specified immigration purposes,

    (ii) in connection with specified immigration procedures, or

    (iii) in specified circumstances, where a question arises about a person's status in relation to nationality or immigration;

(c) requiring a person who produces a biometric immigration document by virtue of paragraph (b) to provide information for comparison with information provided in connection with the application for the document.

(2) Regulations under subsection (1)(a) may, in particular—

(a) apply generally or only to a specified class of persons subject to immigration control (for example, persons making or seeking to make a specified kind of application for immigration purposes);

(b) specify the period within which an application for a biometric immigration document must be made;

(c) make provision about the issue of biometric immigration documents;

(d) make provision about the content of biometric immigration documents (which may include non-biometric information);

(e) make provision permitting a biometric immigration document to be combined with another document;

(f) make provision for biometric immigration documents to begin to have effect, and cease to have effect, in accordance with the regulations;

(g) require a person who acquires a biometric immigration document, without the consent of the person to whom it relates or of the Secretary of State, to surrender it to the Secretary of State as soon as is reasonably practicable;

(h) permit the Secretary of State to require the surrender of a biometric immigration document in other specified circumstances;

    (i) permit the Secretary of State on issuing a biometric immigration document to require the surrender of other documents connected with immigration or nationality.

(3) Regulations under subsection (1)(a) may permit the Secretary of State to cancel a biometric immigration document—

(a) if the Secretary of State thinks that information provided in connection with the document was or has become false, misleading or incomplete,

(b) if the Secretary of State thinks that the document has been lost or stolen,

(c) if the Secretary of State thinks that the document (including any information recorded in it) has been altered, damaged or destroyed (whether deliberately or not),

(d) if the Secretary of State thinks that an attempt has been made (whether successfully or not) to copy the document or to do anything to enable it to be copied,

(e) if the Secretary of State thinks that a person has failed to surrender the document in accordance with subsection (2)(g) or (h),

(f) if the Secretary of State thinks that the document should be re-issued (whether because the information recorded in it requires alteration or for any other reason),

(g) if the Secretary of State thinks that the holder is to be given leave to enter or remain in the United Kingdom,

(h) if the Secretary of State thinks that the holder's leave to enter or remain in the United Kingdom is to be varied, cancelled or invalidated or to lapse,

    (i) if the Secretary of State thinks that the holder has died,

(j) if the Secretary of State thinks that the holder has been removed from the United Kingdom (whether by deportation or otherwise),

(k) if the Secretary of State thinks that the holder has left the United Kingdom without retaining leave to enter or remain, and

(l) in such other circumstances as the regulations may specify.

(4) Regulations under subsection (1)(a) may require notification to be given to the Secretary of State by the holder of a biometric immigration document—

(a) who knows or suspects that the document has been lost or stolen,

(b) who knows or suspects that the document has been altered or damaged (whether deliberately or not),

(c) who knows or suspects that information provided in connection with the document was or has become false, misleading or incomplete,

(d) who was given leave to enter or remain in the United Kingdom in accordance with a provision of rules under section 3 of the Immigration Act 1971 (immigration rules) and knows or suspects that owing to a change of the holder's circumstances the holder would no longer qualify for leave under that provision, or

(e) in such other circumstances as the regulations may specify.

(5) Regulations under subsection (1)(a) may require a person applying for the issue of a biometric immigration document to provide information (which may include biographical or other non-biometric information) to be recorded in it or retained by the Secretary of State; and, in particular, the regulations may—

(a) require, or permit an authorised person to require, the provision of information in a specified form;

(b) require an individual to submit, or permit an authorised person to require an individual to submit, to a specified process by means of which biometric information is obtained or recorded;

(c) confer a function (which may include the exercise of a discretion) on an authorised person;

(d) permit the Secretary of State, instead of requiring the provision of information, to use or retain information which is (for whatever reason) already in the Secretary of State's possession.

(6) Regulations under subsection (1)(b) may, in particular, require the production or other use of a biometric immigration document that is combined with another document . . .

(7) Regulations under subsection (1)(b) may not make provision the effect of which would be to require a person to carry a biometric immigration document at all times.

(8) Regulations under subsection (1)(c) may, in particular, make provision of a kind specified in subsection (5)(a) or (b).

(9) Rules under section 3 of the Immigration Act 1971 may require a person applying for the issue of a biometric immigration document to provide non-biometric information to be recorded in it or retained by the Secretary of State.

(10) Subsections (5) to (9) are without prejudice to the generality of section 50 of the Immigration, Asylum and Nationality Act 2006 (procedure).

Note: Commencement 31 January 2008 (SI 2008/99). Words omitted from sub-s (6) by the Identity Documents Act 2010, Schedule, para 19 from 21 January 2011 (s 14(2)).

6. Regulations: supplemental

(1) This section applies to regulations under section 5(1).

(2) Regulations amending or replacing earlier regulations may require a person who holds a biometric immigration document issued under the earlier regulations to apply under the new regulations.

(3) In so far as regulations require an individual under the age of 16 to submit to a process for the recording of biometric information, or permit an authorised person to require an individual under the age of 16 to submit to a process of that kind, the regulations must make provision similar to section 141(3) to (5) and (13) of the Immigration and Asylum Act 1999 (fingerprints: children).

(4) Rules under section 3 of the Immigration Act 1971 (immigration rules) may make provision by reference to compliance or non-compliance with regulations.

(5) Information in the Secretary of State's possession which is used or retained in accordance with regulations under section 5(5)(d) shall be treated, for the purpose of requirements about treatment and destruction, as having been provided in accordance with the regulations at the time at which it is used or retained in accordance with them.

(6) Regulations—

(a) may make provision having effect generally or only in specified cases or circumstances,

(b) may make different provision for different cases or circumstances,

(c) may include incidental, consequential or transitional provision,

(d) shall be made by statutory instrument, and

(e) may not be made unless a draft has been laid before and approved by resolution of each House of Parliament.

Note: Commencement 31 January 2008 (SI 2008/99).

7. Effect of non-compliance

(1) Regulations under section 5(1) must include provision about the effect of failure to comply with a requirement of the regulations.

(2) In particular, the regulations may—

(a) require or permit an application for a biometric immigration document to be refused;

(b) require or permit an application or claim in connection with immigration to be disregarded or refused;

(c) require or permit the cancellation or variation of leave to enter or remain in the United Kingdom;

(d) require the Secretary of State to consider giving a notice under section 9;

(e) provide for the consequence of a failure to be at the discretion of the Secretary of State.

(3) The regulations may also permit the Secretary of State to designate an adult as the person responsible for ensuring that a child complies with requirements of the regulations; and for that purpose—

(a) 'adult' means an individual who has attained the age of 18,

(b) 'child' means an individual who has not attained the age of 18, and

(c) sections 9 to 13 shall apply (with any necessary modifications) to a designated adult's failure to ensure compliance by a child with a requirement of regulations as they apply to a person's own failure to comply with a requirement.

Note: Commencement 31 January 2008 (SI 2008/99).

8. Use and retention of information

(1) Regulations under section 5(1) must make provision about the use and retention by the Secretary of State of biometric information provided in accordance with the regulations.

(2) The regulations may include provision permitting the use of information—
    (a) in connection with the exercise of a function by virtue of the Immigration Acts,
    (b) in connection with control of the United Kingdom's borders,
    (c) in connection with the exercise of a function in relation to nationality,
    (d) in connection with the prevention, investigation or prosecution of an offence,
    (e) for a purpose which appears to the Secretary of State to be required in order to protect national security, and
    (f) for such other purposes (whether in connection with functions under an enactment or otherwise) as the regulations may specify.

(3) Regulations under section 5(1)—
    (a) must include provision about the destruction of biometric information held by the Secretary of State having been obtained or recorded by virtue of the regulations,
    (b) must, in particular, require the destruction of biometric information held by the Secretary of State if the Secretary of State thinks that it is no longer likely to be of use in accordance with provision made by virtue of subsection (1) above, and
    (c) must, in particular, include provision similar to section 143(2) and (10) to (13) of the Immigration and Asylum Act 1999 (fingerprints: destruction of copies and electronic data).

(4) But a requirement to destroy information shall not apply if and in so far as the information is retained in accordance with and for the purposes of another enactment.

Note: Commencement 31 January 2008 (SI 2008/99).

9. Penalty

(1) The Secretary of State may by notice require a person to pay a penalty for failing to comply with a requirement of regulations under section 5(1).

(2) The notice must—
    (a) specify the amount of the penalty,
    (b) specify a date before which the penalty must be paid to the Secretary of State,
    (c) specify methods by which the penalty may be paid,
    (d) explain the grounds on which the Secretary of State thinks the person has failed to comply with a requirement of the regulations, and
    (e) explain the effect of sections 10 to 12.

(3) The amount specified under subsection (2)(a) may not exceed £1,000.

(4) The date specified under subsection (2)(b) must be not less than 14 days after the date on which the notice is given.

(5) A person who has been given a notice under subsection (1) for failing to comply with regulations may be given further notices in the case of continued failure; but a person may not be given a new notice—

(a) during the time available for objection or appeal against an earlier notice, or

(b) while an objection or appeal against an earlier notice has been instituted and is neither withdrawn nor determined.

(6) The Secretary of State may by order amend subsection (3) to reflect a change in the value of money.

Note: Commencement 25 November 2009 (SI 2008/2822).

10. Penalty: objection

(1) A person (P) who is given a penalty notice under section 9(1) may by notice to the Secretary of State object on the grounds—

(a) that P has not failed to comply with a requirement of regulations under section 5(1),

(b) that it is unreasonable to require P to pay a penalty, or

(c) that the amount of the penalty is excessive.

(2) A notice of objection must—

(a) specify the grounds of objection and P's reasons,

(b) comply with any prescribed requirements as to form and content, and

(c) be given within the prescribed period.

(3) The Secretary of State shall consider a notice of objection and—

(a) cancel the penalty notice,

(b) reduce the penalty by varying the penalty notice,

(c) increase the penalty by issuing a new penalty notice, or

(d) confirm the penalty notice.

(4) The Secretary of State shall act under subsection (3) and notify P—

(a) in accordance with any prescribed requirements, and

(b) within the prescribed period or such longer period as the Secretary of State and P may agree.

Note: Commencement for the purposes of making an order under sub-ss (2) and (4) 31 January 2008 (SI 2008/99), remainder 25 November 2008 (SI 2008/2822).

11. Penalty: appeal

(1) A person (P) who is given a penalty notice under section 9(1) may appeal to—

(a) a county court, in England and Wales or Northern Ireland, or

(b) the sheriff, in Scotland.

(2) An appeal may be brought on the grounds—

(a) that P has not failed to comply with a requirement of regulations under section 5(1),

(b) that it is unreasonable to require P to pay a penalty, or

(c) that the amount of the penalty is excessive.

(3) The court or sheriff may—

(a) cancel the penalty notice,

(b) reduce the penalty by varying the penalty notice,

(c) increase the penalty by varying the penalty notice (whether because the court or sheriff thinks the original amount insufficient or because the court or sheriff thinks that the appeal should not have been brought), or

(d) confirm the penalty notice.

(4) An appeal may be brought—

(a) whether or not P has given a notice of objection, and

(b) irrespective of the Secretary of State's decision on any notice of objection.

(5) The court or sheriff may consider matters of which the Secretary of State was not and could not have been aware before giving the penalty notice.

(6) Rules of court may make provision about the timing of an appeal under this section.

Note: Commencement for the purposes of making rules under subs (6) 31 January 2008 (SI 2008/99), remainder 25 November 2008 (SI 2008/2822).

12. Penalty: enforcement

(1) Where a penalty has not been paid before the date specified in the penalty notice in accordance with section 9(2)(b), it may be recovered as a debt due to the Secretary of State.

(2) Where a notice of objection is given in respect of a penalty notice, the Secretary of State may not take steps to enforce the penalty notice before—

(a) deciding what to do in response to the notice of objection, and

(b) informing the objector.

(3) The Secretary of State may not take steps to enforce a penalty notice while an appeal under section 11—

(a) could be brought (disregarding any possibility of an appeal out of time with permission), or

(b) has been brought and has not been determined or abandoned.

(4) In proceedings for the recovery of a penalty no question may be raised as to the matters specified in sections 10 and 11 as grounds for objection or appeal.

(5) Money received by the Secretary of State in respect of a penalty shall be paid into the Consolidated Fund.

Note: Commencement 25 November 2008 (SI 2008/2822).

13. Penalty: code of practice

(1) The Secretary of State shall issue a code of practice setting out the matters to be considered in determining—

(a) whether to give a penalty notice under section 9(1), and

(b) the amount of a penalty.

(2) The code may, in particular, require the Secretary of State to consider any decision taken by virtue of section 7.

(3) A court or the sheriff shall, when considering an appeal under section 11, have regard to the code.

(4) The Secretary of State may revise and re-issue the code.

(5) Before issuing or re-issuing the code the Secretary of State must—
  (a) publish proposals,
  (b) consult members of the public, and
  (c) lay a draft before Parliament.

(6) The code (or re-issued code) shall come into force at the prescribed time.

Note: Commencement for the purposes of issuing a code of practice under sub-s (1) and making an order under sub-s (6) 31 January 2008 (SI 2008/99), remainder 25 November 2008 (SI 2008/2822).

14. Penalty: prescribed matters

(1) In sections 10 to 13 'prescribed' means prescribed by the Secretary of State by order.

(2) An order under subsection (1) or under section 9(6)—
  (a) may make provision generally or only for specified purposes,
  (b) may make different provision for different purposes,
  (c) shall be made by statutory instrument, and
  (d) shall be subject to annulment in pursuance of a resolution of either House of Parliament.

(3) But the first order under section 13(6) shall not be made unless a draft has been laid before and approved by resolution of each House of Parliament (and shall not be subject to annulment).

Note: Commencement 31 January 2008 (SI 2008/99).

15. Interpretation

(1) For the purposes of section 5—
  (a) 'person subject to immigration control' means a person who under the Immigration Act 1971 requires leave to enter or remain in the United Kingdom (whether or not such leave has been given),
  (b) 'biometric information' means information about external physical characteristics,
  (c) 'external physical characteristics' includes, in particular—
    (i) fingerprints, and
    (ii) features of the iris or any other part of the eye,
  (d) 'document' includes a card or sticker and any other method of recording information (whether in writing or by the use of electronic or other technology or by a combination of methods),
  (e) 'authorised person' has the meaning given by section 141(5) of the Immigration and Asylum Act 1999 (authority to take fingerprints),
  (f) 'immigration' includes asylum, and
  (g) regulations permitting something to be done by the Secretary of State may (but need not) permit it to be done only where the Secretary of State is of a specified opinion.

(2) An application for a biometric immigration document is an application in connection with immigration for the purposes of—
  (a) section 50(1) and (2) of the Immigration, Asylum and Nationality Act 2006 (procedure), and

(b) section 51 of that Act (fees);

and in the application of either of those sections to an application for a biometric immigration document, the prescribed consequences of non-compliance may include any of the consequences specified in section 7(2) above.

Note: Commencement 31 January 2008 (SI 2008/99).

Treatment of claimants

16. Conditional leave to enter or remain

Note: Amends s 3(1)(c) Immigration Act 1971.

17. Support for failed asylum-seekers

(1) This section applies for the purposes of—

(a) Part 6 (and section 4) of the Immigration and Asylum Act 1999 (support and accommodation for asylum-seekers),

(b) Part 2 of the Nationality, Immigration and Asylum Act 2002 (accommodation centres), and

(c) Schedule 3 to that Act (withholding and withdrawal of support).

(2) A person (A-S) remains (or again becomes) an asylum-seeker, despite the fact that the claim for asylum made by A-S has been determined, during any period when—

(a) A-S can bring an in-country appeal against an immigration decision under section 82 of the 2002 Act or section 2 of the Special Immigration Appeals Commission Act 1997, or

(b) an in-country appeal, brought by A-S under either of those sections against an immigration decision, is pending (within the meaning of section 104 of the 2002 Act).

(3) For the purposes of subsection (2)—

(a) 'in-country' appeal means an appeal brought while the appellant is in the United Kingdom, and

(b) the possibility of an appeal out of time with permission shall be ignored.

(4) For the purposes of the provisions mentioned in subsection (1)(a) and (b), a person's status as an asylum-seeker by virtue of subsection (2)(b) continues for a prescribed period after the appeal ceases to be pending.

(5) In subsection (4) 'prescribed' means prescribed by regulations made by the Secretary of State; and the regulations—

(a) may contain incidental or transitional provision,

(b) may make different provision for different classes of case,

(c) shall be made by statutory instrument, and

(d) shall be subject to annulment in pursuance of a resolution of either House of Parliament.

(6) This section shall be treated as always having had effect.

Note: The prescribed period for the purposes of sub-s (4) is 28 days where an appeal has been disposed of by being allowed, and 21 days in all other cases (SI 2007/3102). Commencement 30 October 2007, s 59 (Royal Assent).

18. Support for asylum-seekers: enforcement

Note: Amends s 109 Immigration and Asylum Act 1999.

19. Points-based applications: no new evidence on appeal

Note: Amends ss 85 and 106 of the Nationality, Immigration and Asylum Act 2002.

20. Fees

Note: Amends s 42 of the Asylum and Immigration (Treatment of Claimants, etc.) Act 2004

21. Children

. . .

Note: Revoked by s 55 Borders, Citizenship and Immigration Act 2009 from 2 November 2009 (SI 2009/2731).

Enforcement

22. Assaulting an immigration officer: offence

(1) A person who assaults an immigration officer commits an offence.

(2) A person guilty of an offence under this section shall be liable on summary conviction to—
  (a) imprisonment for a period not exceeding 51 weeks,
  (b) a fine not exceeding level 5 on the standard scale, or
  (c) both.

(3) In the application of this section to Northern Ireland the reference in subsection (2)(a) to 51 weeks shall be treated as a reference to 6 months.

(4) In the application of this section to Scotland the reference in subsection (2)(a) to 51 weeks shall be treated as a reference to 12 months.

(5) In relation to an offence committed before the commencement of section 281(5) of the Criminal Justice Act 2003 (51 week maximum term of sentences) the reference in subsection (2)(a) to 51 weeks shall be treated as a reference to 6 months.

Note: Commencement 31 January 2008 (SI 2008/99).

23. Assaulting an immigration officer: powers of arrest, &c.

(1) An immigration officer may arrest a person without warrant if the officer reasonably suspects that the person has committed or is about to commit an offence under section 22.

(2) An offence under section 22 shall be treated as—
  (a) a relevant offence for the purposes of sections 28B and 28D of the Immigration Act 1971 (search, entry and arrest), and

(b) an offence under Part 3 of that Act (criminal proceedings) for the purposes of sections 28(4), 28E, 28G and 28H (search after arrest, &c.) of that Act.

(3) The following provisions of the Immigration Act 1971 shall have effect in connection with an offence under section 22 of this Act as they have effect in connection with an offence under that Act—

(a) section 28I (seized material: access and copying),

(b) section 28J (search warrants: safeguards),

(c) section 28K (execution of warrants), and

(d) section 28L(1) (interpretation).

Note: Commencement 31 January 2008 (SI 2008/99).

24. Seizure of cash

(1) Chapter 3 of Part 5 of the Proceeds of Crime Act 2002 (recovery of cash) shall apply in relation to an immigration officer as it applies in relation to a constable.

(2) For that purpose—

(a) 'unlawful conduct', in or in relation to section 289, means an offence under the Immigration Acts,

(b) 'unlawful conduct', in or in relation to other provisions, means an offence—

(i) under the Immigration Acts, or

(ii) listed in section 14(2) of the Asylum and Immigration (Treatment of Claimants, etc.) Act 2004,

(c) 'senior officer' in [sections 290 and 297A] means an official of the Secretary of State who is a civil servant of the rank of at least Assistant Director,

(d) in section 292 the words '(in relation to England and Wales and Northern Ireland)' shall be disregarded,

(e) section 293 shall not apply,

(f) an application for an order under section 295(2) must be made—

(i) in relation to England and Wales or Northern Ireland, by an immigration officer, and

(ii) in relation to Scotland, by the Scottish Ministers in connection with their functions under section 298 or by a procurator fiscal,

(g) an application for forfeiture under section 298 must be made—

(i) in relation to England and Wales or Northern Ireland, by an immigration officer, and

(ii) in relation to Scotland, by the Scottish Ministers, and

(h) any compensation under section 302 shall be paid by the Secretary of State.

(3) The Secretary of State may by order amend subsection (2)(c) to reflect a change in nomenclature; and an order—

(a) shall be made by statutory instrument, and

(b) shall be subject to annulment in pursuance of a resolution of either House of Parliament.

Note: Commencement 1 April 2010 (SI 2010/606). Words in square brackets substituted by para 113 Sch 7 Policing and Crime Act 2009 from a date to be appointed.

25. Forfeiture of detained property

(1) A court making a forfeiture order about property may order that the property be taken into the possession of the Secretary of State (and not of the police).

(2) An order may be made under subsection (1) only if the court thinks that the offence in connection with which the order is made—

(a) related to immigration or asylum, or

(b) was committed for a purpose connected with immigration or asylum.

(3) In subsection (1) 'forfeiture order' means an order under—

(a) section 143 of the Powers of Criminal Courts (Sentencing) Act 2006 or

(b) Article 11 of the Criminal Justice (Northern Ireland) Order 1994 (S.I. 1994/2795 (N.I. 15)).

Note: Commencement 31 March 2008 (SI 2008/309).

26. Disposal of property

(1) In this section 'property' means property which—

(a) has come into the possession of an immigration officer, or

(b) has come into the possession of the Secretary of State in the course of, or in connection with, a function under the Immigration Acts.

(2) A magistrates' court may, on the application of the Secretary of State or a claimant of property—

(a) order the delivery of property to the person appearing to the court to be its owner, or

(b) if its owner cannot be ascertained, make any other order about property.

(3) An order shall not affect the right of any person to take legal proceedings for the recovery of the property, provided that the proceedings are instituted within the period of six months beginning with the date of the order.

(4) An order may be made in respect of property forfeited under section 25, or under section 25C of the Immigration Act 1971 (vehicles, &c.), only if—

(a) the application under subsection (2) above is made within the period of six months beginning with the date of the forfeiture order, and

(b) the applicant (if not the Secretary of State) satisfies the court—

(i) that the applicant did not consent to the offender's possession of the property, or

(ii) that the applicant did not know and had no reason to suspect that the property was likely to be used, or was intended to be used, in connection with an offence.

(5) The Secretary of State may make regulations for the disposal of property—

(a) where the owner has not been ascertained,

(b) where an order under subsection (2) cannot be made because of subsection (4)(a), or

(c) where a court has declined to make an order under subsection (2) on the grounds that the court is not satisfied of the matters specified in subsection (4)(b).

(6) The regulations may make provision that is the same as or similar to provision that may be made by regulations under section 2 of the Police (Property) Act 1897 (or any similar enactment applying in relation to Scotland or Northern Ireland); and the regulations—

(a) may apply, with or without modifications, regulations under that Act,

(b) may, in particular, provide for property to vest in the Secretary of State,

(c) may make provision about the timing of disposal (which, in particular, may differ from provision made by or under the Police (Property) Act 1897),

(d) shall have effect only in so far as not inconsistent with an order of a court (whether or not under subsection (2) above),

(e) shall be made by statutory instrument, and

(f) shall be subject to annulment in pursuance of a resolution of either House of Parliament.

(7) For the purposes of subsection (1) it is immaterial whether property is acquired as a result of forfeiture or seizure or in any other way.

(8) In the application of this section to Scotland a reference to a magistrates' court is a reference to the sheriff.

Note: Commencement for the purposes of making regulations under sub-s (5) 31 January 2008 (SI 2008/99). Remainder from 1 April 2008 (SI 2008/309) which sets out transitional provisions.

27. Employment: arrest

Note: Amends s 28AA of the Immigration Act 1971.

28. Employment: search for personnel records

Note: Amends s 28FA(7) of the Immigration Act 1971.

29. Facilitation: arrival and entry

Note: Amends s 25A(1)(a) of the Immigration Act 1971.

30. Facilitation: territorial application

Note: Amends ss 25, 25A and 25B of the Immigration Act 1971.

31. People trafficking

Note: Amends ss 4 and 5 of the Asylum and Immigration (Treatment of Claimants, etc.) Act 2004, ss 57 and 60 of the Sexual Offences Act 2003.

Deportation of criminals

32. Automatic deportation

(1) In this section 'foreign criminal' means a person—

(a) who is not a British citizen,

(b) who is convicted in the United Kingdom of an offence, and

(c) to whom Condition 1 or 2 applies.

(2) Condition 1 is that the person is sentenced to a period of imprisonment of at least 12 months.

(3) Condition 2 is that—

(a) the offence is specified by order of the Secretary of State under section 72(4)(a) of the Nationality, Immigration and Asylum Act 2002 (serious criminal), and

(b) the person is sentenced to a period of imprisonment.

(4) For the purpose of section 3(5)(a) of the Immigration Act 1971 (c. 77), the deportation of a foreign criminal is conducive to the public good.

(5) The Secretary of State must make a deportation order in respect of a foreign criminal (subject to section 33).

(6) The Secretary of State may not revoke a deportation order made in accordance with subsection (5) unless—

(a) he thinks that an exception under section 33 applies,

(b) the application for revocation is made while the foreign criminal is outside the United Kingdom, or

(c) section 34(4) applies.

(7) Subsection (5) does not create a private right of action in respect of consequences of non-compliance by the Secretary of State.

Note: Commencement in respect of a person for whom condition 1 applies, if the person has not been served with a notice of intention to make a deportation order before 1 August 2008, is in custody on, or has a suspended sentence at 1 August 2008 (SI 2008/1818), which sets out transitional provisions.

33. Exceptions

(1) Section 32(4) and (5)—

(a) do not apply where an exception in this section applies (subject to subsection (7) below), and

(b) are subject to sections 7 and 8 of the Immigration Act 1971 (Commonwealth citizens, Irish citizens, crew and other exemptions).

(2) Exception 1 is where removal of the foreign criminal in pursuance of the deportation order would breach—

(a) a person's Convention rights, or

(b) the United Kingdom's obligations under the Refugee Convention.

(3) Exception 2 is where the Secretary of State thinks that the foreign criminal was under the age of 18 on the date of conviction.

(4) Exception 3 is where the removal of the foreign criminal from the United Kingdom in pursuance of a deportation order would breach rights of the foreign criminal under the [EU] treaties.

(5) Exception 4 is where the foreign criminal—

(a) is the subject of a certificate under section 2 or 70 of the Extradition Act 2003,

(b) is in custody pursuant to arrest under section 5 of that Act,

(c) is the subject of a provisional warrant under section 73 of that Act,

(d) is the subject of an authority to proceed under section 7 of the Extradition Act 1989 or an order under paragraph 4(2) of Schedule 1 to that Act, or

(e) is the subject of a provisional warrant under section 8 of that Act or of a warrant under paragraph 5(1)(b) of Schedule 1 to that Act.

(6) Exception 5 is where any of the following has effect in respect of the foreign criminal—

(a) a hospital order or guardianship order under section 37 of the Mental Health Act 1983,

(b) a hospital direction under section 45A of that Act,

(c) a transfer direction under section 47 of that Act,

(d) a compulsion order under section 57A of the Criminal Procedure (Scotland) Act 1995,

(e) a guardianship order under section 58 of that Act,

(f) a hospital direction under section 59A of that Act,

(g) a transfer for treatment direction under section 136 of the Mental Health (Care and Treatment) (Scotland) Act 2003, or

(h) an order or direction under a provision which corresponds to a provision specified in paragraphs (a) to (g) and which has effect in relation to Northern Ireland.

[(6A) Exception 6 is where the Secretary of State thinks that the application of section 32(4) and (5) would contravene the United Kingdom's obligations under the Council of Europe Convention on Action against Trafficking in Human Beings (done at Warsaw on 16 May 2005).]

(7) The application of an exception—

(a) does not prevent the making of a deportation order;

(b) results in it being assumed neither that deportation of the person concerned is conducive to the public good nor that it is not conducive to the public good; but section 32(4) applies despite the application of Exception 1 or 4.

Note: Commencement in respect of a person for whom condition 1 of s 32 applies, 1 August 2008 (SI 2008/1818), which sets out transitional provisions. Subsection (6A) inserted by s 146 Criminal Justice and Immigration Act 2008 from 1 April 2009 (SI 2009/860). Term 'EU' substituted from 22 April 2011 (SI 2011/1043).

34. Timing

(1) Section 32(5) requires a deportation order to be made at a time chosen by the Secretary of State.

(2) A deportation order may not be made under section 32(5) while an appeal or further appeal against the conviction or sentence by reference to which the order is to be made—

(a) has been instituted and neither withdrawn nor determined, or

(b) could be brought.

(3) For the purpose of subsection (2)(b)—

(a) the possibility of an appeal out of time with permission shall be disregarded, and

(b) a person who has informed the Secretary of State in writing that the person does not intend to appeal shall be treated as being no longer able to appeal.

(4) The Secretary of State may withdraw a decision that section 32(5) applies, or revoke a deportation order made in accordance with section 32(5), for the purpose of—

(a) taking action under the Immigration Acts or rules made under section 3 of the Immigration Act 1971 (immigration rules), and

(b) subsequently taking a new decision that section 32(5) applies and making a deportation order in accordance with section 32(5).

Note: Commencement in respect of a person for whom condition 1 of s 32 applies, 1 August 2008 (SI 2008/1818) which sets out transitional provisions.

35. Appeal

Note: Amends ss 79 and 82 of the Nationality, Immigration and Asylum Act 2002.

36. Detention

(1) A person who has served a period of imprisonment may be detained under the authority of the Secretary of State—

(a) while the Secretary of State considers whether section 32(5) applies, and

(b) where the Secretary of State thinks that section 32(5) applies, pending the making of the deportation order.

(2) Where a deportation order is made in accordance with section 32(5) the Secretary of State shall exercise the power of detention under paragraph 2(3) of Schedule 3 to the Immigration Act 1971 (detention pending removal) unless in the circumstances the Secretary of State thinks it inappropriate.

(3) A court determining an appeal against conviction or sentence may direct release from detention under subsection (1) or (2).

(4) Provisions of the Immigration Act 1971 which apply to detention under paragraph 2(3) of Schedule 3 to that Act shall apply to detention under subsection (1) (including provisions about bail).

(5) Paragraph 2(5) of Schedule 3 to that Act (residence, occupation and reporting restrictions) applies to a person who is liable to be detained under subsection (1).

Note: Commencement in respect of a person for whom condition 1 of s 32 applies, 1 August 2008 (SI 2008/1818) which sets out transitional provisions.

37. Family

(1) Where a deportation order against a foreign criminal states that it is made in accordance with section 32(5) ('the automatic deportation order') this section shall have effect in place of the words from 'A deportation order' to 'after the making of the deportation order against him' in section 5(3) of the Immigration Act 1971 (period during which family members may also be deported).

(2) A deportation order may not be made against a person as belonging to the family of the foreign criminal after the end of the relevant period of 8 weeks.

(3) In the case of a foreign criminal who has not appealed in respect of the automatic deportation order, the relevant period begins when an appeal can no longer be brought (ignoring any possibility of an appeal out of time with permission).

(4) In the case of a foreign criminal who has appealed in respect of the automatic deportation order, the relevant period begins when the appeal is no longer pending (within the meaning of section 104 of the Nationality, Immigration and Asylum Act 2002.

Note: Commencement in respect of a person for whom condition 1 of s 32 applies, 1 August 2008 (SI 2008/1818) which sets out transitional provisions.

38. Interpretation

(1) In section 32(2) the reference to a person who is sentenced to a period of imprisonment of at least 12 months—

(a) does not include a reference to a person who receives a suspended sentence (unless a court subsequently orders that the sentence or any part of it (of whatever length) is to take effect),

(b) does not include a reference to a person who is sentenced to a period of imprisonment of at least 12 months only by virtue of being sentenced to consecutive sentences amounting in aggregate to more than 12 months,

(c) includes a reference to a person who is sentenced to detention, or ordered or directed to be detained, in an institution other than a prison (including, in particular, a hospital or an institution for young offenders) for at least 12 months, and

(d) includes a reference to a person who is sentenced to imprisonment or detention, or ordered or directed to be detained, for an indeterminate period (provided that it may last for 12 months).

(2) In section 32(3)(b) the reference to a person who is sentenced to a period of imprisonment—

(a) does not include a reference to a person who receives a suspended sentence (unless a court subsequently orders that the sentence or any part of it is to take effect), and

(b) includes a reference to a person who is sentenced to detention, or ordered or directed to be detained, in an institution other than a prison (including, in particular, a hospital or an institution for young offenders).

(3) For the purposes of section 32 a person subject to an order under section 5 of the Criminal Procedure (Insanity) Act 1964 (insanity, &c.) has not been convicted of an offence.

(4) In sections 32 and 33—

(a) 'British citizen' has the same meaning as in section 3(5) of the Immigration Act 1971 (and section 3(8) (burden of proof) shall apply),

(b) 'Convention rights' has the same meaning as in the Human Rights Act 1998,

(c) 'deportation order' means an order under section 5, and by virtue of section 3(5), of the Immigration Act 1971, and

(d) 'the Refugee Convention' means the Convention relating to the Status of Refugees done at Geneva on 28 July 1951 and its Protocol.

Note: Commencement in respect of a person for whom condition 1 of s 32 applies, 1 August 2008 (SI 2008/1818) which sets out transitional provisions.

39. Consequential amendments

Note: Amends s 72(11) of the Nationality, Immigration and Asylum Act 2002.

Information

40. Supply of Revenue and Customs information

(1) Her Majesty's Revenue and Customs (HMRC) and the Revenue and Customs Prosecutions Office (the RCPO) may each supply the Secretary of State with information for use for the purpose of—

(a) administering immigration control under the Immigration Acts;

(b) preventing, detecting, investigating or prosecuting offences under those Acts;

(c) determining whether to impose, or imposing, penalties or charges under Part 2 of the Immigration and Asylum Act 1999 (carriers' liability);

(d) determining whether to impose, or imposing, penalties under section 15 of the Immigration, Asylum and Nationality Act 2006 (restrictions on employment);

(e) providing facilities, or arranging for the provision of facilities, for the accommodation of persons under section 4 of the Immigration and Asylum Act 1999;

(f) providing support for asylum-seekers and their dependants under Part 6 of that Act;

(g) determining whether an applicant for naturalisation under the British Nationality Act 1981 is of good character;

[(h) determining whether, for the purposes of an application referred to in section 41A of the British Nationality Act 1981, the person for whose registration the application is made is of good character;

(ha) determining whether, for the purposes of an application under section 1 of the Hong Kong (War Wives and Widows) Act 1996, the woman for whose registration the application is made is of good character;

(hb) determining whether, for the purposes of an application under section 1 of the British Nationality (Hong Kong) Act 1997 for the registration of an adult or young person within the meaning of subsection (5A) of that section, the person is of good character;]

(i) determining whether to make an order in respect of a person under section 40 of the British Nationality Act 1981 (deprivation of citizenship);

(j) doing anything else in connection with the exercise of immigration and nationality functions.

(2) This section applies to a document or article which comes into the possession of, or is discovered by, HMRC or the RCPO, or a person acting on behalf of HMRC or the RCPO, as it applies to information.

(3) The Secretary of State—

(a) may retain for a purpose within subsection (1) a document or article supplied by virtue of subsection (2);

(b) may dispose of a document or article supplied by virtue of subsection (2).

(4) In subsection (1) 'immigration and nationality functions' means functions exercisable by virtue of—

(a) the Immigration Acts,

(b) the British Nationality Act 1981,

(c) the Hong Kong Act 1985,

(d) the Hong Kong (War Wives and Widows) Act 1996, or

(e) the British Nationality (Hong Kong) Act 1997.

(5) A power conferred by this section on HMRC or the RCPO may be exercised on behalf of HMRC or the RCPO by a person who is authorised (generally or specifically) for the purpose.

(6) . . .

Note: Subsection (6) amends s 20(1)(d) of the Immigration and Asylum Act 1999, s 130 of the Nationality, Immigration and Asylum Act 2002 and paras 17 and 20 of Sch 2 to the Commissioners for Revenue and Customs Act 2005. Commencement 31 January 2008 (SI 2008/99). Subsections (1)(h)–(hb) substituted by s 47 Borders, Citizenship and Immigration Act 2009 from 13 January 2010 (SI 2009/2731).

41. Confidentiality

(1) A person to whom relevant information is supplied (whether before or after the commencement of this section) may not disclose that information.

(2) Information is relevant information if it is supplied by or on behalf of HMRC or the RCPO under—

(a) section 20 of the Immigration and Asylum Act 1999,

(b) section 130 of the Nationality, Immigration and Asylum Act 2002,

(c) section 36 of the Immigration, Asylum and Nationality Act 2006 (except in so far as that section relates to information supplied to a chief officer of police), or

(d) section 40 of this Act.

(3) But subsection (1) does not apply to a disclosure—

(a) which is made for a purpose within section 40(1),

(b) which is made for the purposes of civil proceedings (whether or not within the United Kingdom) relating to an immigration or nationality matter,

(c) which is made for the purposes of a criminal investigation or criminal proceedings (whether or not within the United Kingdom) relating to an immigration or nationality matter,

(d) which is made in pursuance of an order of a court,

(e) which is made with the consent (which may be general or specific) of HMRC or the RCPO, depending on by whom or on whose behalf the information was supplied, or

(f) which is made with the consent of each person to whom the information relates.

(4) Subsection (1) is subject to any other enactment permitting disclosure.

(5) The reference in subsection (1) to a person to whom relevant information is supplied includes a reference to a person who is or was acting on behalf of that person.

(6) The reference in subsection (2) to information supplied under section 40 of this Act includes a reference to documents or articles supplied by virtue of subsection (2) of that section.

(7) In subsection (3) 'immigration or nationality matter' means a matter in respect of which the Secretary of State has immigration and nationality functions (within the meaning given in section 40(4)).

(8) In subsection (4) 'enactment' does not include—

(a) an Act of the Scottish Parliament,

(b) an Act of the Northern Ireland Assembly, or

(c) an instrument made under an Act within paragraph (a) or (b).

Note: Commencement 31 January 2008 (SI 2008/1999).

[41A. Supply of information to UK Border Agency

(1) HMRC and the RCPO may each supply a person to whom this section applies with information for use for the purpose of the customs functions exercisable by that person.

(2) This section applies to—

(a) a designated customs official,

(b) the Secretary of State by whom general customs functions are exercisable,

(c) the Director of Border Revenue, and

(d) a person acting on behalf of a person mentioned in paragraphs (a) to (c).

(3) This section applies to a document or article which comes into the possession of, or is discovered by, HMRC or the RCPO, or a person acting on behalf of HMRC or the RCPO, as it applies to information.

(4) A person to whom this section applies—

(a) may retain for a purpose within subsection (1) a document or article supplied by virtue of subsection (3);

(b) may dispose of a document or article supplied by virtue of subsection (3).

(5) A power conferred by this section on HMRC or the RCPO may be exercised on behalf of HMRC or the RCPO by a person who is authorised (generally or specifically) for the purpose.

(6) In this section and section 41B "customs function" and "general customs function" have the meanings given by Part 1 of the Borders, Citizenship and Immigration Act 2009.

41B. UK Border Agency: onward disclosure

(1) A person to whom information is supplied under section 41A may not disclose that information.

(2) But subsection (1) does not apply to a disclosure—

(a) which is made for the purpose of a customs function, where the disclosure does not contravene any restriction imposed by the Commissioners for Her Majesty's Revenue and Customs;

(b) which is made for the purposes of civil proceedings (whether or not within the United Kingdom) relating to a customs function;

(c) which is made for the purpose of a criminal investigation or criminal proceedings (whether or not within the United Kingdom);

(d) which is made in pursuance of an order of a court;

(e) which is made with the consent (which may be general or specific) of HMRC or the RCPO, depending on by whom or on whose behalf the information was supplied;

(f) which is made with the consent of each person to whom the information relates.

(3) Subsection (1) is subject to any other enactment permitting disclosure.

(4) The reference in subsection (1) to information supplied under section 41A includes a reference to documents or articles supplied by virtue of subsection (3) of that section.

(5) The reference in that subsection to a person to whom information is supplied includes a reference to a person who is or was acting on behalf of that person.

(6) In subsection (3) "enactment" does not include—

(a) an Act of the Scottish Parliament,

(b) an Act of the Northern Ireland Assembly, or

(c) an instrument made under an Act within paragraph (a) or (b).]

Note : Sections 41A and 41B inserted by s 20 Borders, Citizenship and Immigration Act 2009 from 21 July 2009 (s 58).

42. Wrongful disclosure

(1) An offence is committed by a person who contravenes section 41 [or 41B] by disclosing information relating to a person whose identity—

(a) is specified in the disclosure, or

(b) can be deduced from it.

(2) Subsection (1) does not apply to the disclosure of information about internal administrative arrangements of HMRC or the RCPO (whether relating to Commissioners, officers, members of the RCPO or others).

(3) It is a defence for a person (P) charged with an offence under this section of disclosing information to prove that P reasonably believed—

(a) that the disclosure was lawful, or

(b) that the information had already and lawfully been made available to the public.

(4) A person guilty of an offence under this section shall be liable—

(a) on conviction on indictment, to imprisonment for a term not exceeding two years, to a fine or to both, or

(b) on summary conviction, to imprisonment for a term not exceeding 12 months, to a fine not exceeding the statutory maximum or to both.

(5) The reference in subsection (4)(b) to 12 months shall be treated as a reference to six months—

(a) in the application of this section to Northern Ireland;

(b) in the application of this section to England and Wales, in relation to an offence under this section committed before the commencement of section 282 of the Criminal Justice Act 2003 (imprisonment on summary conviction for certain offences in England and Wales);

(c) in the application of this section to Scotland, until the commencement of section 45(1) of the Criminal Proceedings etc. (Reform) (Scotland) Act 2007 (corresponding provision in Scotland).

(6) A prosecution for an offence under this section may be instituted—

(a) in England and Wales, only with the consent of the Director of Public Prosecutions;

(b) in Northern Ireland, only with the consent of the Director of Public Prosecutions for Northern Ireland.

Note: Commencement 31 January 2008 (SI 2008/1999). Words in square brackets in sub-s (1) inserted by s 20 Borders, Citizenship and Immigration Act 2009 from 21 July 2009 (s 58).

43. Supply of police information, etc.

. . .

Note: Amends s 131 of the Nationality, Immigration and Asylum Act 2002.

44. Search for evidence of nationality

(1) This section applies where an individual has been arrested on suspicion of the commission of an offence and an immigration officer or a constable suspects—

(a) that the individual may not be a British citizen, and

(b) that nationality documents relating to the individual may be found on—

(i) premises occupied or controlled by the individual,

(ii) premises on which the individual was arrested, or

(iii) premises on which the individual was, immediately before being arrested.

(2) The immigration officer or constable may enter and search the premises for the purpose of finding those documents.

(3) The power of search may be exercised only with the written authority of a senior officer; and for that purpose—

(a) 'senior officer' means—

(i) in relation to an immigration officer, an immigration officer of at least the rank of chief immigration officer, and

(ii) in relation to a constable, a constable of at least the rank of inspector, and

(b) a senior officer who gives authority must arrange for a written record to be made of—

(i) the grounds for the suspicions in reliance on which the power of search is to be exercised, and

(ii) the nature of the documents sought.

(4) The power of search may not be exercised where the individual has been released without being charged with an offence.

(5) In relation to an individual 'nationality document' means a document showing—

(a) the individual's identity, nationality or citizenship,

(b) the place from which the individual travelled to the United Kingdom, or

(c) a place to which the individual is proposing to go from the United Kingdom.

Note: Commencement 29 February 2008 (SI 2008/309), which sets out transitional provisions.

45. Search for evidence of nationality: other premises

(1) This section applies where an individual—

(a) has been arrested on suspicion of the commission of an offence, and

(b) has not been released without being charged with an offence.

(2) If, on an application made by an immigration officer or a constable, a justice of the peace is satisfied that there are reasonable grounds for believing that—

(a) the individual may not be a British citizen,

(b) nationality documents relating to the individual may be found on premises specified in the application,

(c) the documents would not be exempt from seizure under section 46(2), and

(d) any of the conditions in subsection (3) below applies,

the justice of the peace may issue a warrant authorising an immigration officer or constable to enter and search the premises.

(3) The conditions are that—

(a) it is not practicable to communicate with any person entitled to grant entry to the premises;

(b) it is practicable to communicate with a person entitled to grant entry to the premises but it is not practicable to communicate with any person entitled to grant access to the nationality documents;

(c) entry to the premises will not be granted unless a warrant is produced;

(d) the purpose of a search may be frustrated or seriously prejudiced unless an immigration officer or constable arriving at the premises can secure immediate entry.

(4) Sections 28J and 28K of the Immigration Act 1971 (warrants: application and execution) apply, with any necessary modifications, to warrants under this section.

(5) In the application of this section to Scotland a reference to a justice of the peace shall be treated as a reference to the sheriff or a justice of the peace.

Note: Commencement 29 February 2008 (SI 2008/309), which sets out transitional provisions.

46. Seizure of nationality documents

(1) An immigration officer or constable searching premises under section 44 or 45 may seize a document which the officer or constable thinks is a nationality document in relation to the arrested individual.

(2) Subsection (1) does not apply to a document which—

(a) in relation to England and Wales or Northern Ireland, is subject to legal professional privilege, or

(b) in relation to Scotland, is an item subject to legal privilege within the meaning of section 412 of the Proceeds of Crime Act 2002.

(3) An immigration officer or constable may retain a document seized under subsection (1) while the officer or constable suspects that—

(a) the individual to whom the document relates may be liable to removal from the United Kingdom in accordance with a provision of the Immigration Acts, and

(b) retention of the document may facilitate the individual's removal.

(4) Section 28I of the Immigration Act 1971 (seized material: access and copying) shall have effect in relation to a document seized and retained by an immigration officer.

(5) Section 21 of the Police and Criminal Evidence Act 1984 or Article 23 of the Police and Criminal Evidence (Northern Ireland) Order 1989 (S.I. 1989/1341 (N.I. 12)) (seized material: access and copying) shall have effect in relation to a document seized and retained by a constable in England and Wales or Northern Ireland.

Note: Commencement 29 February 2008 (SI 2008/309), which sets out transitional provisions.

47. Police civilians

. . .

Note: Amends Schedule 4 to the Police Reform Act 2002.

Border and Immigration Inspectorate

48. Establishment

(1) The Secretary of State shall appoint a person as Chief Inspector of [the UK Border Agency].

[(1A) The Chief Inspector shall monitor and report on the efficiency and effectiveness of the performance of functions by the following—

(a) designated customs officials, and officials of the Secretary of State exercising customs functions;

(b) immigration officers, and officials of the Secretary of State exercising functions relating to immigration, asylum or nationality;

(c) the Secretary of State in so far as the Secretary of State has general customs functions;

(d) the Secretary of State in so far as the Secretary of State has functions relating to immigration, asylum or nationality;

(e) the Director of Border Revenue and any person exercising functions of the Director.

(1B) The Chief Inspector shall monitor and report on the efficiency and effectiveness of the services provided by a person acting pursuant to arrangements relating to the discharge of a function within subsection (1A).]

(2) . . .; in particular, the Chief Inspector shall consider and make recommendations about—

(a) consistency of approach [among the persons listed in subsections (1A) and (1B) (the 'listed persons')],

(b) the practice and performance of [the listed persons] compared to other persons doing similar things,

(c) practice and procedure in making decisions,

(d) the treatment of claimants and applicants,

(e) certification under section 94 of the Nationality, Immigration and Asylum Act 2002 (unfounded claim),

(f) compliance with law about discrimination in the exercise of functions, including reliance on paragraph 17 of Schedule 3 of the Equality Act 2010 (exception for immigration functions),

(g) practice and procedure in relation to the exercise of enforcement powers (including powers of arrest, entry, search and seizure),

[(ga) practice and procedure in relation to the prevention, detection and investigation of offences,

(gb) practice and procedure in relation to the conduct of criminal proceedings,

(gc) whether customs functions have been appropriately exercised by the Secretary of State and the Director of Border Revenue,]

(h) the provision of information,

(i) the handling of complaints, and

(j) the content of information about conditions in countries outside the United Kingdom which the Secretary of State compiles and makes available, for purposes connected with immigration and asylum, to immigration officers and other officials.

[(2A) Unless directed to do so by the Secretary of State, the Chief Inspector shall not monitor and report on the exercise by the listed persons of—

(a) functions at removal centres and short term holding facilities, and under escort arrangements, in so far as Her Majesty's Chief Inspector of Prisons has functions under section 5A of the Prison Act 1952 in relation to such functions, and

(b) functions at detention facilities, in so far as Her Majesty's Inspectors of Constabulary, the Scottish inspectors or the Northern Ireland inspectors have functions by virtue of section 29 of the Borders, Citizenship and Immigration Act 2009 in relation to such functions.]

(3) . . .

[(3A) In this section "customs function", "designated customs official" and "general customs function" have the meanings given by Part 1 of the Borders, Citizenship and Immigration Act 2009.]

(4) The Chief Inspector shall not aim to investigate individual cases (although this subsection does not prevent the Chief Inspector from considering or drawing conclusions

about an individual case for the purpose of, or in the context of, considering a general issue).

Note: Commencement 1 April 2008 (SI 2008/309). Words in square brackets in sub-s (1)–(2), sub-ss (1A), (1B), (2)(ga)–(gc), (2A) and (3A) inserted and words in sub-s (2) and (3) omitted by s 28 Borders, Citizenship and Immigration Act 2009 from 21 July 2009 (s 58). Words substituted in sub-s (2)(f) from 1 October 2010 by the Equality Act 2010, Sch 26, para 86 as inserted by SI 2010/2279.

49. Chief Inspector: supplemental

(1) The Secretary of State shall pay remuneration and allowances to the Chief Inspector.

(2) The Secretary of State—

(a) shall before the beginning of each financial year specify a maximum sum which the Chief Inspector may spend on functions for that year,

(b) may permit that to be exceeded for a specified purpose, and

(c) shall defray the Chief Inspector's expenditure for each financial year subject to paragraphs (a) and (b).

(3) The Chief Inspector shall hold and vacate office in accordance with terms of appointment (which may include provision about retirement, resignation or dismissal).

(4) The Chief Inspector may appoint staff.

(5) A person who is employed by or in any of the following may not be appointed as Chief Inspector—

(a) a government department,

(b) the Scottish Administration,

(c) the National Assembly for Wales, and

(d) a department in Northern Ireland.

Note: Commencement 1 April 2008 (SI 2008/309).

50. Reports

(1) The Chief Inspector shall report in writing to the Secretary of State—

(a) once each calendar year, in relation to the performance of the functions under section 48 generally, and

(b) at other times as requested by the Secretary of State in relation to specified matters.

(2) The Secretary of State shall lay before Parliament a copy of any report received under subsection (1).

(3) But a copy may omit material if the Secretary of State thinks that its publication—

(a) is undesirable for reasons of national security, or

(b) might jeopardise an individual's safety.

Note: Commencement 1 April 2008 (SI 2008/309).

51. Plans

(1) The Chief Inspector shall prepare plans describing the objectives and terms of reference of proposed inspections.

(2) Plans shall be prepared—

(a) at prescribed times and in respect of prescribed periods, and

(b) at such other times, and in respect of such other periods, as the Chief Inspector thinks appropriate.

(3) A plan must—

(a) be in the prescribed form, and

(b) contain the prescribed information.

(4) In preparing a plan the Chief Inspector shall consult—

(a) the Secretary of State, and

(b) prescribed persons.

(5) As soon as is reasonably practicable after preparing a plan the Chief Inspector shall send a copy to—

(a) the Secretary of State, and

(b) each prescribed person.

(6) The Chief Inspector and a prescribed person may by agreement disapply a requirement—

(a) to consult the person, or

(b) to send a copy of a plan to the person.

(7) Nothing in this section prevents the Chief Inspector from doing anything not mentioned in a plan.

Note: Commencement for the purposes of making an order under sub-ss (2)-(6) 1 April 2008 (SI 2008/309).

52. Relationship with other bodies: general

(1) The Chief Inspector shall cooperate with prescribed persons in so far as the Chief Inspector thinks it consistent with the efficient and effective performance of the functions under section 48.

(2) The Chief Inspector may act jointly with prescribed persons where the Chief Inspector thinks it in the interests of the efficient and effective performance of the functions under section 48.

(3) The Chief Inspector may assist a prescribed person.

(4) The Chief Inspector may delegate a specified aspect of the functions under section 48 to a prescribed person.

Note: Commencement for the purposes of making an order under these provisions 1 April 2008 (SI 2008/309).

53. Relationship with other bodies: non-interference notices

(1) Subsection (2) applies if the Chief Inspector believes that—

(a) a prescribed person proposes to inspect any aspect of the work of [a person listed in section 48(1A) or (1B)], and

(b) the inspection may impose an unreasonable burden on [such a person].

(2) The Chief Inspector may give the prescribed person a notice prohibiting a specified inspection.

(3) The prescribed person shall comply with the notice, unless the Secretary of State cancels it on the grounds that the inspection would not impose an unreasonable burden on [a person listed in section 48(1A) or (1B)].

(4) A notice must—
  (a) be in the prescribed form, and
  (b) contain the prescribed information.

(5) The Secretary of State may by order make provision about—
  (a) the timing of notices;
  (b) the publication of notices;
  (c) the revision or withdrawal of notices.

Note: Commencement for the purposes of making an order under these provisions 1 April 2008 (SI 2008/309). Words in square brackets in sub-ss (1) and (3) substituted by s 28 Borders, Citizenship and Immigration Act 2009 from 21 July 2009 (s 58).

54. Abolition of other bodies

Note: Amends s 19E of the Race Relations Act 1976, ss 34, 111, 142 of the Nationality, Immigration and Asylum Act 2002.

55. Prescribed matters

(1) In sections 48 to 53 'prescribed' means prescribed by order of the Secretary of State.

(2) An order under any of those sections—
  (a) may make provision generally or only for specified purposes,
  (b) may make different provision for different purposes, and
  (c) may include incidental or transitional provision.

(3) An order under any of those sections prescribing a person may specify—
  (a) one or more persons, or
  (b) a class of person.

(4) An order under any of those sections—
  (a) shall be made by statutory instrument, and
  (b) shall be subject to annulment in pursuance of a resolution of either House of Parliament.

Note: Commencement 1 April 2008 (SI 2008/309).

56. Senior President of Tribunals

(1) . . .

(2) In exercising the function under section 43 of the Tribunals, Courts and Enforcement Act 2007 the Senior President of Tribunals shall have regard to—
  (a) the functions of the Chief Inspector of [the UK Border Agency], and
  (b) in particular, the Secretary of State's power to request the Chief Inspector to report about specified matters.

Note: Subsection (1) amends s 43(3) of the Tribunals, Courts and Enforcement Act 2007. Commencement 1 April 2008 (SI 2008/309). Words in square brackets substituted by s 28 Borders, Citizenship and Immigration Act 2009 from 21 July 2009 (s 58).

General

56A. No rehabilitation for certain immigration or nationality purposes

(1) Section 4(1), (2) and (3) of the Rehabilitation of Offenders Act 1974 (effect of rehabilitation) do not apply—

(a) in relation to any proceedings in respect of a relevant immigration decision or a relevant nationality decision, or

(b) otherwise for the purposes of, or in connection with, any such decision.

(2) In this section—

'immigration officer' means a person appointed by the Secretary of State as an immigration officer under paragraph 1 of Schedule 2 to the Immigration Act 1971,

'relevant immigration decision' means any decision, or proposed decision, of the Secretary of State or an immigration officer under or by virtue of the Immigration Acts, or rules made under section 3 of the Immigration Act 1971 (immigration rules), in relation to the entitlement of a person to enter or remain in the United Kingdom (including, in particular, the removal of a person from the United Kingdom, whether by deportation or otherwise),

'relevant nationality decision' means any decision, or proposed decision, of the Secretary of State under or by virtue of—

(a) the British Nationality Act 1981,

(b) the British Nationality (Hong Kong) Act 1990, or

(c) the Hong Kong (War Wives and Widows) Act 1996,

in relation to the good character of a person.

(3) The references in subsection (2) to the Immigration Acts and to the Acts listed in the definition of 'relevant nationality decision' include references to any provision made under section 2(2) of the European Communities Act 1972, or of EU law, which relates to the subject matter of the Act concerned.]

Note: Section 56A inserted from a date to be appointed by the Legal Aid, Sentencing and Punishment of Offenders Act 2012, s 140, subject to transitional and consequential provisions set out in s 141(7)–(9) of that Act.

57. Money

The following shall be paid out of money provided by Parliament—

(a) any expenditure of a Minister of the Crown in consequence of this Act, and

(b) any increase attributable to this Act in sums payable out of money provided by Parliament under another enactment.

Note: Commencement at a date to be appointed.

58. Repeals

. . .

59. Commencement

(1) Section 17 comes into force on the day on which this Act is passed.

(2) The other preceding provisions of this Act shall come into force in accordance with provision made by the Secretary of State by order.

(3) An order—

    (a) may make provision generally or only for specified purposes,

    (b) may make different provision for different purposes, and

    (c) may include incidental, consequential or transitional provision.

(4) In particular, transitional provision—

    (a) in the case of an order commencing section 16, may permit the adding of a condition to leave given before the passing of this Act;

    (b) in the case of an order commencing section 25, may permit an order to be made in proceedings instituted before the passing of this Act;

    (c) in the case of an order commencing section 26, may permit an order or regulations to have effect in relation to property which came into the possession of an immigration officer or the Secretary of State before the passing of this Act;

    (d) in the case of an order commencing section 32—

        (i) may provide for the section to apply to persons convicted before the passing of this Act who are in custody at the time of commencement or whose sentences are suspended at the time of commencement;

        (ii) may modify the application of the section in relation to those persons so as to disapply, or apply only to a specified extent, Condition 2.

(5) An order shall be made by statutory instrument.

Note: Commencement 30 October 2007 (s 59, Royal Assent).

60. Extent

(1) Sections. . .25 and 31(1) and (2) extend to—

    (a) England and Wales, and

    (b) Northern Ireland.

(2) Other provisions of this Act extend (subject to subsection (3)) to—

    (a) England and Wales,

    (b) Scotland, and

    (c) Northern Ireland.

(3) A provision of this Act which amends another Act shall (subject to subsection (1)) have the same extent as the relevant part of the amended Act (ignoring extent by virtue of an Order in Council).

(4) Her Majesty may by Order in Council direct that a provision of this Act is to extend, with or without modification or adaptation, to—

    (a) any of the Channel Islands;

    (b) the Isle of Man.

Note: Commencement 30 October 2007 (s 59, Royal Assent). Numbers in sub-s (1) omitted by s 52 Borders, Citizenship and Immigration Act 2009 from a date to be appointed.

61. Citation

(1) This Act may be cited as the UK Borders Act 2007.

(2) A reference (in any enactment, including one passed or made before this Act) to 'the Immigration Acts' is to—

(a) the Immigration Act 1971,

(b) the Immigration Act 1988,

(c) the Asylum and Immigration Appeals Act 1993,

(d) the Asylum and Immigration Act 1996,

(e) the Immigration and Asylum Act 1999,

(f) the Nationality, Immigration and Asylum Act 2002,

(g) the Asylum and Immigration (Treatment of Claimants, etc.) Act 2004,

(h) the Immigration, Asylum and Nationality Act 2006, and

(i) this Act.

(3) . . . Section 64(2) (meaning of 'Immigration Acts') shall cease to have effect.

(4) . . .

Note: Subsection (3) repeals s 64(2) of the Immigration, Asylum and Nationality Act 2006. Subsection (4) amends Sch 1 of the Interpretation Act 1978. Commencement 30 October 2007, (s 59 Royal Assent).

SCHEDULE

REPEALS

Tribunals, Courts and Enforcement Act 2007
(2007 c. 15)

Chapter 2 First-tier Tribunal and Upper Tribunal

Establishment

3. The First-tier Tribunal and the Upper Tribunal

(1) There is to be a tribunal, known as the First-tier Tribunal, for the purpose of exercising the functions conferred on it under or by virtue of this Act or any other Act.

(2) There is to be a tribunal, known as the Upper Tribunal, for the purpose of exercising the functions conferred on it under or by virtue of this Act or any other Act.

(3) Each of the First-tier Tribunal, and the Upper Tribunal, is to consist of its judges and other members.

(4) The Senior President of Tribunals is to preside over both of the First-tier Tribunal and the Upper Tribunal.

(5) The Upper Tribunal is to be a superior court of record.

Note: Commenced 3 November 2008 (SI 2008/2696).

Members and composition of tribunals

4. Judges and other members of the First-tier Tribunal

(1) A person is a judge of the First-tier Tribunal if the person—
(a) is a judge of the First-tier Tribunal by virtue of appointment under paragraph 1(1) of Schedule 2,
(b) is a transferred-in judge of the First-tier Tribunal (see section 31(2)),
(c) is a judge of the Upper Tribunal,
(d) . . . or
(e) is a member of a panel of chairmen of employment tribunals.

(2) A person is also a judge of the First-tier Tribunal, but only as regards functions of the tribunal in relation to appeals such as are mentioned in subsection (1) of section 5 of the Criminal Injuries Compensation Act 1995 (c. 53), if the person is an adjudicator appointed under that section by the Scottish Ministers.

(3) A person is one of the other members of the First-tier Tribunal if the person—
(a) is a member of the First-tier Tribunal by virtue of appointment under paragraph 2(1) of Schedule 2,
(b) is a transferred-in other member of the First-tier Tribunal (see section 31(2)),
(c) is one of the other members of the Upper Tribunal, or
(d) is a member of a panel of members of employment tribunals that is not a panel of chairmen of employment tribunals.

(4) Schedule 2—
contains provision for the appointment of persons to be judges or other members of the First-tier Tribunal, and
makes further provision in connection with judges and other members of the First-tier Tribunal.

Note: Commenced 3 November 2008 (SI 2008/2696). Subsection (1)(d) omitted from 15 February 2010 (SI 2010/21).

5. Judges and other members of the Upper Tribunal

(1) A person is a judge of the Upper Tribunal if the person—

(a) is the Senior President of Tribunals,

(b) is a judge of the Upper Tribunal by virtue of appointment under paragraph 1(1) of Schedule 3, [or]

(c) is a transferred-in judge of the Upper Tribunal (see section 31(2)),

(d) . . .

(f) is a Social Security Commissioner appointed under section 50(2) of that Act (deputy Commissioners),

(g) is within section 6(1),

(h) is a deputy judge of the Upper Tribunal (whether under paragraph 7 of Schedule 3 or under section 31(2)), or

(i) is a Chamber President or a Deputy Chamber President, whether of a chamber of the Upper Tribunal or of a chamber of the First-tier Tribunal, and does not fall within any of paragraphs (a) to (h).

(2) A person is one of the other members of the Upper Tribunal if the person—

(a) is a member of the Upper Tribunal by virtue of appointment under paragraph 2(1) of Schedule 3,

(b) is a transferred-in other member of the Upper Tribunal (see section 31(2)), [or]

(c) is a member of the Employment Appeal Tribunal appointed under section 22(1) (c) of the Employment Tribunals Act 1996 (c. 17),. . .

(d) . . .

(3) Schedule 3—

contains provision for the appointment of persons to be judges (including deputy judges), or other members, of the Upper Tribunal, and

makes further provision in connection with judges and other members of the Upper Tribunal.

Note: Commenced 3 November 2008 (SI 2008/2696). Subsections (1)(d) and 2(d) omitted from 15 February 2010 (SI 2010/21).

6. Certain judges who are also judges of First-tier Tribunal and Upper Tribunal

(1) A person is within this subsection (and so, by virtue of sections 4(1)(c) and 5(1)(g), is a judge of the First-tier Tribunal and of the Upper Tribunal) if the person—

(a) is an ordinary judge of the Court of Appeal in England and Wales (including the vice-president, if any, of either division of that Court),

(b) is a Lord Justice of Appeal in Northern Ireland,

(c) is a judge of the Court of Session,

(d) is a puisne judge of the High Court in England and Wales or Northern Ireland,

(e) is a circuit judge,

(f) is a sheriff in Scotland,

(g) is a county court judge in Northern Ireland,

(h) is a district judge in England and Wales or Northern Ireland, or

(i) is a District Judge (Magistrates' Courts).

(**2**) References in subsection (1)(c) to (i) to office-holders do not include deputies or temporary office-holders.

Note: Commenced 3 November 2008 (SI 2008/2696).

7. Chambers: jurisdiction and Presidents

(**1**) The Lord Chancellor may, with the concurrence of the Senior President of Tribunals, by order make provision for the organisation of each of the First-tier Tribunal and the Upper Tribunal into a number of chambers.

(**2**) There is—
  (a) for each chamber of the First-tier Tribunal, and
  (b) for each chamber of the Upper Tribunal,
  to be a person, or two persons, to preside over that chamber.

(**3**) A person may not at any particular time preside over more than one chamber of the First-tier Tribunal and may not at any particular time preside over more than one chamber of the Upper Tribunal (but may at the same time preside over one chamber of the First-tier Tribunal and over one chamber of the Upper Tribunal).

(**4**) A person appointed under this section to preside over a chamber is to be known as a Chamber President.

(**5**) Where two persons are appointed under this section to preside over the same chamber, any reference in an enactment to the Chamber President of the chamber is a reference to a person appointed under this section to preside over the chamber.

(**6**) The Senior President of Tribunals may (consistently with subsections (2) and (3)) appoint a person who is the Chamber President of a chamber to preside instead, or to preside also, over another chamber.

(**7**) The Lord Chancellor may (consistently with subsections (2) and (3)) appoint a person who is not a Chamber President to preside over a chamber.

(**8**) Schedule 4 (eligibility for appointment under subsection (7), appointment of Deputy Chamber Presidents and Acting Chamber Presidents, assignment of judges and other members of the First-tier Tribunal and Upper Tribunal, and further provision about Chamber Presidents and chambers) has effect.

(**9**) Each of the Lord Chancellor and the Senior President of Tribunals may, with the concurrence of the other, by order—
  (a) make provision for the allocation of the First-tier Tribunal's functions between its chambers;
  (b) make provision for the allocation of the Upper Tribunal's functions between its chambers;
  (c) amend or revoke any order made under this subsection.

Note: Subsections (1) and (9) in force from 19 September 2007 (SI 2007/2709). Remainder in force from 3 November 2008 (SI 2008/2696).

8. Senior President of Tribunals: power to delegate

(**1**) The Senior President of Tribunals may delegate any function he has in his capacity as Senior President of Tribunals—
  (a) to any judge, or other member, of the Upper Tribunal or First-tier Tribunal;
  (b) to staff appointed under section 40(1).

(2) Subsection (1) does not apply to functions of the Senior President of Tribunals under section 7(9).

(3) A delegation under subsection (1) is not revoked by the delegator's becoming incapacitated.

(4) Any delegation under subsection (1) that is in force immediately before a person ceases to be Senior President of Tribunals continues in force until varied or revoked by a subsequent holder of the office of Senior President of Tribunals.

(5) The delegation under this section of a function shall not prevent the exercise of the function by the Senior President of Tribunals.

Note: Commenced 3 November 2008 (SI 2008/2696).

Review of decisions and appeals

9. Review of decision of First-tier Tribunal

(1) The First-tier Tribunal may review a decision made by it on a matter in a case, other than a decision that is an excluded decision for the purposes of section 11(1) (but see subsection (9)).

(2) The First-tier Tribunal's power under subsection (1) in relation to a decision is exercisable—

(a) of its own initiative, or

(b) on application by a person who for the purposes of section 11(2) has a right of appeal in respect of the decision.

(3) Tribunal Procedure Rules may—

(a) provide that the First-tier Tribunal may not under subsection (1) review (whether of its own initiative or on application under subsection (2)(b)) a decision of a description specified for the purposes of this paragraph in Tribunal Procedure Rules;

(b) provide that the First-tier Tribunal's power under subsection (1) to review a decision of a description specified for the purposes of this paragraph in Tribunal Procedure Rules is exercisable only of the tribunal's own initiative;

(c) provide that an application under subsection (2)(b) that is of a description specified for the purposes of this paragraph in Tribunal Procedure Rules may be made only on grounds specified for the purposes of this paragraph in Tribunal Procedure Rules;

(d) provide, in relation to a decision of a description specified for the purposes of this paragraph in Tribunal Procedure Rules, that the First-tier Tribunal's power under subsection (1) to review the decision of its own initiative is exercisable only on grounds specified for the purposes of this paragraph in Tribunal Procedure Rules.

(4) Where the First-tier Tribunal has under subsection (1) reviewed a decision, the First-tier Tribunal may in the light of the review do any of the following—

(a) correct accidental errors in the decision or in a record of the decision;

(b) amend reasons given for the decision;

(c) set the decision aside.

(5) Where under subsection (4)(c) the First-tier Tribunal sets a decision aside, the First-tier Tribunal must either—

(a) re-decide the matter concerned, or

(b) refer that matter to the Upper Tribunal.

(6) Where a matter is referred to the Upper Tribunal under subsection (5)(b), the Upper Tribunal must re-decide the matter.

(7) Where the Upper Tribunal is under subsection (6) re-deciding a matter, it may make any decision which the First-tier Tribunal could make if the First-tier Tribunal were re-deciding the matter.

(8) Where a tribunal is acting under subsection (5)(a) or (6), it may make such findings of fact as it considers appropriate.

(9) This section has effect as if a decision under subsection (4)(c) to set aside an earlier decision were not an excluded decision for the purposes of section 11(1), but the First-tier Tribunal's only power in the light of a review under subsection (1) of a decision under subsection (4)(c) is the power under subsection (4)(a).

(10) A decision of the First-tier Tribunal may not be reviewed under subsection (1) more than once, and once the First-tier Tribunal has decided that an earlier decision should not be reviewed under subsection (1) it may not then decide to review that earlier decision under that subsection.

(11) Where under this section a decision is set aside and the matter concerned is then re-decided, the decision set aside and the decision made in re-deciding the matter are for the purposes of subsection (10) to be taken to be different decisions.

Note: Subsection (3) in force from 19 September 2007 (SI 2007/2709). Remainder in force from 3 November 2008 (SI 2008/2696).

10. Review of decision of Upper Tribunal

(1) The Upper Tribunal may review a decision made by it on a matter in a case, other than a decision that is an excluded decision for the purposes of section 13(1) (but see subsection (7)).

(2) The Upper Tribunal's power under subsection (1) in relation to a decision is exercisable—

(a) of its own initiative, or

(b) on application by a person who for the purposes of section 13(2) has a right of appeal in respect of the decision.

(3) Tribunal Procedure Rules may—

(a) provide that the Upper Tribunal may not under subsection (1) review (whether of its own initiative or on application under subsection (2)(b)) a decision of a description specified for the purposes of this paragraph in Tribunal Procedure Rules;

(b) provide that the Upper Tribunal's power under subsection (1) to review a decision of a description specified for the purposes of this paragraph in Tribunal Procedure Rules is exercisable only of the tribunal's own initiative;

(c) provide that an application under subsection (2)(b) that is of a description specified for the purposes of this paragraph in Tribunal Procedure Rules may be made only on grounds specified for the purposes of this paragraph in Tribunal Procedure Rules;

(d) provide, in relation to a decision of a description specified for the purposes of this paragraph in Tribunal Procedure Rules, that the Upper Tribunal's power under subsection (1) to review the decision of its own initiative is exercisable only on grounds specified for the purposes of this paragraph in Tribunal Procedure Rules.

(4) Where the Upper Tribunal has under subsection (1) reviewed a decision, the Upper Tribunal may in the light of the review do any of the following—

(a) correct accidental errors in the decision or in a record of the decision;

(b) amend reasons given for the decision;

(c) set the decision aside.

(5) Where under subsection (4)(c) the Upper Tribunal sets a decision aside, the Upper Tribunal must re-decide the matter concerned.

(6) Where the Upper Tribunal is acting under subsection (5), it may make such findings of fact as it considers appropriate.

(7) This section has effect as if a decision under subsection (4)(c) to set aside an earlier decision were not an excluded decision for the purposes of section 13(1), but the Upper Tribunal's only power in the light of a review under subsection (1) of a decision under subsection (4)(c) is the power under subsection (4)(a).

(8) A decision of the Upper Tribunal may not be reviewed under subsection (1) more than once, and once the Upper Tribunal has decided that an earlier decision should not be reviewed under subsection (1) it may not then decide to review that earlier decision under that subsection.

(9) Where under this section a decision is set aside and the matter concerned is then re-decided, the decision set aside and the decision made in re-deciding the matter are for the purposes of subsection (8) to be taken to be different decisions.

Note: Subsection (3) in force from 19 September 2007 (SI 2007/2709). Remainder in force from 3 November 2008 (SI 2008/2696).

11. Right to appeal to Upper Tribunal

(1) For the purposes of subsection (2), the reference to a right of appeal is to a right to appeal to the Upper Tribunal on any point of law arising from a decision made by the First-tier Tribunal other than an excluded decision.

(2) Any party to a case has a right of appeal, subject to subsection (8).

(3) That right may be exercised only with permission (or, in Northern Ireland, leave).

(4) Permission (or leave) may be given by—

(a) the First-tier Tribunal, or

(b) the Upper Tribunal, on an application by the party.

(5) For the purposes of subsection (1), an "excluded decision" is—

(a) any decision of the First-tier Tribunal on an appeal made in exercise of a right conferred by the Criminal Injuries Compensation Scheme in compliance with section 5(1)(a) of the Criminal Injuries Compensation Act 1995 (c. 53) (appeals against decisions on reviews),

[(aa) any decision of the First-tier Tribunal on an appeal made in exercise of a right conferred by the Victims of Overseas Terrorism Compensation Scheme in compliance with section 52(3) of the Crime and Security Act 2010,]

(b) any decision of the First-tier Tribunal on an appeal under section 28(4) or (6) of the Data Protection Act 1998 (c. 29) (appeals against national security certificate),

(c) any decision of the First-tier Tribunal on an appeal under section 60(1) or (4) of the Freedom of Information Act 2000 (c. 36) (appeals against national security certificate),

(d) a decision of the First-tier Tribunal under section 9—

(i) to review, or not to review, an earlier decision of the tribunal,

(ii) to take no action, or not to take any particular action, in the light of a review of an earlier decision of the tribunal,

(iii) to set aside an earlier decision of the tribunal, or

(iv) to refer, or not to refer, a matter to the Upper Tribunal,

(e) a decision of the First-tier Tribunal that is set aside under section 9 (including a decision set aside after proceedings on an appeal under this section have been begun), or

(f) any decision of the First-tier Tribunal that is of a description specified in an order made by the Lord Chancellor.

(6) A description may be specified under subsection (5)(f) only if—

(a) in the case of a decision of that description, there is a right to appeal to a court, the Upper Tribunal or any other tribunal from the decision and that right is, or includes, something other than a right (however expressed) to appeal on any point of law arising from the decision, or

(b) decisions of that description are made in carrying out a function transferred under section 30 and prior to the transfer of the function under section 30(1) there was no right to appeal from decisions of that description.

(7) Where—

(a) an order under subsection (5)(f) specifies a description of decisions, and

(b) decisions of that description are made in carrying out a function transferred under section 30, the order must be framed so as to come into force no later than the time when the transfer under section 30 of the function takes effect (but power to revoke the order continues to be exercisable after that time, and power to amend the order continues to be exercisable after that time for the purpose of narrowing the description for the time being specified).

(8) The Lord Chancellor may by order make provision for a person to be treated as being, or to be treated as not being, a party to a case for the purposes of subsection (2).

Note: Subsection (5)(f) and (6)–(8) in force from 19 September 2007 (SI 2007/2709). Remainder in force from 3 November 2008 (SI 2008/2696). Application of s 11 modified by SI 2010/22 Sch 5, para 5(a) from 18 January 2010. Subsection (5)(aa) inserted from 8 April 2010 by Crime and Security Act 2010. There are other modifications/exclusions not relevant to immigration law.

12. Proceedings on appeal to Upper Tribunal

(1) Subsection (2) applies if the Upper Tribunal, in deciding an appeal under section 11, finds that the making of the decision concerned involved the making of an error on a point of law.

(2) The Upper Tribunal—

(a) may (but need not) set aside the decision of the First-tier Tribunal, and

(b) if it does, must either—

(i) remit the case to the First-tier Tribunal with directions for its reconsideration, or

(ii) re-make the decision.

(3) In acting under subsection (2)(b)(i), the Upper Tribunal may also—

(a) direct that the members of the First-tier Tribunal who are chosen to reconsider the case are not to be the same as those who made the decision that has been set aside;

(b) give procedural directions in connection with the reconsideration of the case by the First-tier Tribunal.

(4) In acting under subsection (2)(b)(ii), the Upper Tribunal—

(a) may make any decision which the First-tier Tribunal could make if the First-tier Tribunal were re-making the decision, and

(b) may make such findings of fact as it considers appropriate.

Note: Commenced 3 November 2008 (SI 2008/2696).

13. Right to appeal to Court of Appeal etc.

(1) For the purposes of subsection (2), the reference to a right of appeal is to a right to appeal to the relevant appellate court on any point of law arising from a decision made by the Upper Tribunal other than an excluded decision.

(2) Any party to a case has a right of appeal, subject to subsection (14).

(3) That right may be exercised only with permission (or, in Northern Ireland, leave).

(4) Permission (or leave) may be given by—

(a) the Upper Tribunal, or

(b) the relevant appellate court, on an application by the party.

(5) An application may be made under subsection (4) to the relevant appellate court only if permission (or leave) has been refused by the Upper Tribunal.

(6) The Lord Chancellor may, as respects an application under subsection (4) that falls within subsection (7) and for which the relevant appellate court is the Court of Appeal in England and Wales or the Court of Appeal in Northern Ireland, by order make provision for permission (or leave) not to be granted on the application unless the Upper Tribunal or (as the case may be) the relevant appellate court considers—

(a) that the proposed appeal would raise some important point of principle or practice, or

(b) that there is some other compelling reason for the relevant appellate court to hear the appeal.

(7) An application falls within this subsection if the application is for permission (or leave) to appeal from any decision of the Upper Tribunal on an appeal under section 11.

(8) For the purposes of subsection (1), an "excluded decision" is—

(a) any decision of the Upper Tribunal on an appeal under section 28(4) or (6) of the Data Protection Act 1998 (c. 29) (appeals against national security certificate),

(b) any decision of the Upper Tribunal on an appeal under section 60(1) or (4) of the Freedom of Information Act 2000 (c. 36) (appeals against national security certificate),

(c) any decision of the Upper Tribunal on an application under section 11(4)(b) (application for permission or leave to appeal),

(d) a decision of the Upper Tribunal under section 10—

(i) to review, or not to review, an earlier decision of the tribunal,

(ii) to take no action, or not to take any particular action, in the light of a review of an earlier decision of the tribunal, or

(iii) to set aside an earlier decision of the tribunal,

(e) a decision of the Upper Tribunal that is set aside under section 10 (including a decision set aside after proceedings on an appeal under this section have been begun), or

(f) any decision of the Upper Tribunal that is of a description specified in an order made by the Lord Chancellor.

(9) A description may be specified under subsection (8)(f) only if—

(a) in the case of a decision of that description, there is a right to appeal to a court from the decision and that right is, or includes, something other than a right (however expressed) to appeal on any point of law arising from the decision, or

(b) decisions of that description are made in carrying out a function transferred under section 30 and prior to the transfer of the function under section 30(1) there was no right to appeal from decisions of that description.

(10) Where—

(a) an order under subsection (8)(f) specifies a description of decisions, and

(b) decisions of that description are made in carrying out a function

transferred under section 30, the order must be framed so as to come into force no later than the time when the transfer under section 30 of the function takes effect (but power to revoke the order continues to be exercisable after that time, and power to amend the order continues to be exercisable after that time for the purpose of narrowing the description for the time being specified).

(11) Before the Upper Tribunal decides an application made to it under subsection (4), the Upper Tribunal must specify the court that is to be the relevant appellate court as respects the proposed appeal.

(12) The court to be specified under subsection (11) in relation to a proposed appeal is whichever of the following courts appears to the Upper Tribunal to be the most appropriate—

(a) the Court of Appeal in England and Wales;

(b) the Court of Session;

(c) the Court of Appeal in Northern Ireland.

(13) In this section except subsection (11), "the relevant appellate court", as respects an appeal, means the court specified as respects that appeal by the Upper Tribunal under subsection (11).

(14) The Lord Chancellor may by order make provision for a person to be treated as being, or to be treated as not being, a party to a case for the purposes of subsection (2).

(15) Rules of court may make provision as to the time within which an application under subsection (4) to the relevant appellate court must be made.

Note: Subsections (6), (8)(f), (9), (10), (14) and (15) in force from 19 September 2007 (SI 2007/2709). Remainder in force from 3 November 2008 (SI 2008/2696). Application of s 11 modified by SI 2010/22 Sch 5, para 5(a) from 18 January 2010.

14. Proceedings on appeal to Court of Appeal etc.

(1) Subsection (2) applies if the relevant appellate court, in deciding an appeal under section 13, finds that the making of the decision concerned involved the making of an error on a point of law.

(2) The relevant appellate court—

(a) may (but need not) set aside the decision of the Upper Tribunal, and

(b) if it does, must either—

(i) remit the case to the Upper Tribunal or, where the decision of the Upper Tribunal was on an appeal or reference from another tribunal or some other person, to the Upper Tribunal or that other tribunal or person, with directions for its reconsideration, or

  (ii) re-make the decision.

  (3) In acting under subsection (2)(b)(i), the relevant appellate court may also—

  (a) direct that the persons who are chosen to reconsider the case are not to be the same as those who—

    (i) where the case is remitted to the Upper Tribunal, made the decision of the Upper Tribunal that has been set aside, or

    (ii) where the case is remitted to another tribunal or person, made the decision in respect of which the appeal or reference to the Upper Tribunal was made;

  (b) give procedural directions in connection with the reconsideration of the case by the Upper Tribunal or other tribunal or person.

  (4) In acting under subsection (2)(b)(ii), the relevant appellate court—

  (a) may make any decision which the Upper Tribunal could make if the Upper Tribunal were re-making the decision or (as the case may be) which the other tribunal or person could make if that other tribunal or person were re-making the decision, and

  (b) may make such findings of fact as it considers appropriate.

  (5) Where—

  (a) under subsection (2)(b)(i) the relevant appellate court remits a case to the Upper Tribunal, and

  (b) the decision set aside under subsection (2)(a) was made by the Upper Tribunal on an appeal or reference from another tribunal or some other person,

  the Upper Tribunal may (instead of reconsidering the case itself) remit the case to that other tribunal or person, with the directions given by the relevant appellate court for its reconsideration.

  (6) In acting under subsection (5), the Upper Tribunal may also—

  (a) direct that the persons who are chosen to reconsider the case are not to be the same as those who made the decision in respect of which the appeal or reference to the Upper Tribunal was made;

  (b) give procedural directions in connection with the reconsideration of the case by the other tribunal or person.

  (7) In this section "the relevant appellate court", as respects an appeal under section 13, means the court specified as respects that appeal by the Upper Tribunal under section 13(11).

Note: Commenced 3 November 2008 (SI 2008/2696).

Judicial review

15. Upper Tribunal's "judicial review" jurisdiction

  (1) The Upper Tribunal has power, in cases arising under the law of England and Wales or under the law of Northern Ireland, to grant the following kinds of relief—

  (a) a mandatory order;

  (b) a prohibiting order;

  (c) a quashing order;

  (d) a declaration;

  (e) an injunction.

(2) The power under subsection (1) may be exercised by the Upper Tribunal if—

(a) certain conditions are met (see section 18), or

(b) the tribunal is authorised to proceed even though not all of those conditions are met (see section 19(3) and (4)).

(3) Relief under subsection (1) granted by the Upper Tribunal—

(a) has the same effect as the corresponding relief granted by the High Court on an application for judicial review, and

(b) is enforceable as if it were relief granted by the High Court on an application for judicial review.

(4) In deciding whether to grant relief under subsection (1)(a), (b) or (c), the Upper Tribunal must apply the principles that the High Court would apply in deciding whether to grant that relief on an application for judicial review.

(5) In deciding whether to grant relief under subsection (1)(d) or (e), the Upper Tribunal must—

(a) in cases arising under the law of England and Wales apply the principles that the High Court would apply in deciding whether to grant that relief under section 31(2) of the Supreme Court Act 1981 (c. 54) on an application for judicial review, and

(b) in cases arising under the law of Northern Ireland apply the principles that the High Court would apply in deciding whether to grant that relief on an application for judicial review.

(6) For the purposes of the application of subsection (3)(a) in relation to cases arising under the law of Northern Ireland—

(a) a mandatory order under subsection (1)(a) shall be taken to correspond to an order of mandamus,

(b) a prohibiting order under subsection (1)(b) shall be taken to correspond to an order of prohibition, and

(c) a quashing order under subsection (1)(c) shall be taken to correspond to an order of certiorari.

Note: Commenced 3 November 2008 (SI 2008/2696).

16. Application for relief under section 15(1)

(1) This section applies in relation to an application to the Upper Tribunal for relief under section 15(1).

(2) The application may be made only if permission (or, in a case arising under the law of Northern Ireland, leave) to make it has been obtained from the tribunal.

(3) The tribunal may not grant permission (or leave) to make the application unless it considers that the applicant has a sufficient interest in the matter to which the application relates.

(4) Subsection (5) applies where the tribunal considers—

(a) that there has been undue delay in making the application, and

(b) that granting the relief sought on the application would be likely to cause substantial hardship to, or substantially prejudice the rights of, any person or would be detrimental to good administration.

(5) The tribunal may—

(a) refuse to grant permission (or leave) for the making of the application;

(b) refuse to grant any relief sought on the application.

(6) The tribunal may award to the applicant damages, restitution or the recovery of a sum due if—

(a) the application includes a claim for such an award arising from any matter to which the application relates, and

(b) the tribunal is satisfied that such an award would have been made by the High Court if the claim had been made in an action begun in the High Court by the applicant at the time of making the application.

(7) An award under subsection (6) may be enforced as if it were an award of the High Court.

(8) Where—

(a) the tribunal refuses to grant permission (or leave) to apply for relief under section 15(1),

(b) the applicant appeals against that refusal, and

(c) the Court of Appeal grants the permission (or leave),

the Court of Appeal may go on to decide the application for relief under section 15(1).

(9) Subsections (4) and (5) do not prevent Tribunal Procedure Rules from limiting the time within which applications may be made.

Note: Commenced 3 November 2008 (SI 2008/2696).

17. Quashing orders under section 15(1): supplementary provision

(1) If the Upper Tribunal makes a quashing order under section 15(1)(c) in respect of a decision, it may in addition—

(a) remit the matter concerned to the court, tribunal or authority that made the decision, with a direction to reconsider the matter and reach a decision in accordance with the findings of the Upper Tribunal, or

(b) substitute its own decision for the decision in question.

(2) The power conferred by subsection (1)(b) is exercisable only if—

(a) the decision in question was made by a court or tribunal,

(b) the decision is quashed on the ground that there has been an error of law, and

(c) without the error, there would have been only one decision that the court or tribunal could have reached.

(3) Unless the Upper Tribunal otherwise directs, a decision substituted by it under subsection (1)(b) has effect as if it were a decision of the relevant court or tribunal.

Note: Commenced 3 November 2008 (SI 2008/2696).

18. Limits of jurisdiction under section 15(1)

(1) This section applies where an application made to the Upper Tribunal seeks (whether or not alone)—

(a) relief under section 15(1), or

(b) permission (or, in a case arising under the law of Northern Ireland, leave) to apply for relief under section 15(1).

(2) If Conditions 1 to 4 are met, the tribunal has the function of deciding the application.

(3) If the tribunal does not have the function of deciding the application, it must by order transfer the application to the High Court.

(4) Condition 1 is that the application does not seek anything other than—

(a) relief under section 15(1);

(b) permission (or, in a case arising under the law of Northern Ireland, leave) to apply for relief under section 15(1);

(c) an award under section 16(6);

(d) interest;

(e) costs.

(5) Condition 2 is that the application does not call into question anything done by the Crown Court.

(6) Condition 3 is that the application falls within a class specified for the purposes of this subsection in a direction given in accordance with Part 1 of Schedule 2 to the Constitutional Reform Act 2005 (c. 4).

(7) The power to give directions under subsection (6) includes—

(a) power to vary or revoke directions made in exercise of the power, and

(b) power to make different provision for different purposes.

(8) Condition 4 is that the judge presiding at the hearing of the application is either—

(a) a judge of the High Court or the Court of Appeal in England and Wales or Northern Ireland, or a judge of the Court of Session, or

(b) such other persons as may be agreed from time to time between the Lord Chief Justice, the Lord President, or the Lord Chief Justice of Northern Ireland, as the case may be, and the Senior President of Tribunals.

(9) Where the application is transferred to the High Court under subsection (3)—

(a) the application is to be treated for all purposes as if it—

(i) had been made to the High Court, and

(ii) sought things corresponding to those sought from the tribunal, and

(b) any steps taken, permission (or leave) given or orders made by the tribunal in relation to the application are to be treated as taken, given or made by the High Court.

(10) Rules of court may make provision for the purpose of supplementing subsection (9).

(11) The provision that may be made by Tribunal Procedure Rules about amendment of an application for relief under section 15(1) includes, in particular, provision about amendments that would cause the application to become transferrable under subsection (3).

(12) For the purposes of subsection (9)(a)(ii), in relation to an application transferred to the High Court in Northern Ireland—

(a) an order of mandamus shall be taken to correspond to a mandatory order under section 15(1)(a),

(b) an order of prohibition shall be taken to correspond to a prohibiting order under section 15(1)(b), and

(c) an order of certiorari shall be taken to correspond to a quashing order under section 15(1)(c).

Note: Subsections (10) and (11) in force from 19 September 2007 (SI 2007/2709). Remainder in force from 3 November 2008 (SI 2008/2696).

19. Transfer of judicial review applications from High Court

(1) ...

(2) ...

(3) Where an application is transferred to the Upper Tribunal under 31A of the Supreme Court Act 1981 (c. 54) or section 25A of the Judicature (Northern Ireland) Act 1978 (transfer from the High Court of judicial review applications)—

    (a) the application is to be treated for all purposes as if it—

        (i) had been made to the tribunal, and

        (ii) sought things corresponding to those sought from the High Court,

    (b) the tribunal has the function of deciding the application, even if it does not fall within a class specified under section 18(6), and

    (c) any steps taken, permission given, leave given or orders made by the High Court in relation to the application are to be treated as taken, given or made by the tribunal.

(4) Where—

    (a) an application for permission is transferred to the Upper Tribunal under section 31A of the Supreme Court Act 1981 (c. 54) and the tribunal grants permission, or

    (b) an application for leave is transferred to the Upper Tribunal under section 25A of the Judicature (Northern Ireland) Act 1978 (c. 23) and the tribunal grants leave, the tribunal has the function of deciding any subsequent application brought under the permission or leave, even if the subsequent application does not fall within a class specified under section 18(6).

(5) Tribunal Procedure Rules may make further provision for the purposes of supplementing subsections (3) and (4).

(6) For the purposes of subsection (3)(a)(ii), in relation to an application transferred to the Upper Tribunal under section 25A of the Judicature (Northern Ireland) Act 1978—

    (a) a mandatory order under section 15(1)(a) shall be taken to correspond to an order of mandamus,

    (b) a prohibiting order under section 15(1)(b) shall be taken to correspond to an order of prohibition, and

    (c) a quashing order under section 15(1)(c) shall be taken to correspond to an order of certiorari.

Note: Commenced 3 November 2008 (SI 2008/2696). Subsection (1) amends the Supreme Court Act 1981. Subsection (2) amends the Judicature (Northern Ireland) Act 1978.

20. Transfer of judicial review applications from the Court of Session

(1) Where an application is made to the supervisory jurisdiction of the Court of Session, the Court—

    (a) must, if Conditions 1, 2 and 4 are met, and

    (b) may, if Conditions 1, 3 and 4 are met, but Condition 2 is not, by order transfer the application to the Upper Tribunal.

(2) Condition 1 is that the application does not seek anything other than an exercise of the supervisory jurisdiction of the Court of Session.

(3) Condition 2 is that the application falls within a class specified for the purposes of this subsection by act of sederunt made with the consent of the Lord Chancellor.

(4) Condition 3 is that the subject matter of the application is not a devolved Scottish matter.

(5) Condition 4 is that the application does not call into question any decision made under—

(a) the Immigration Acts,

(b) the British Nationality Act 1981 (c. 61),

(c) any instrument having effect under an enactment within paragraph (a) or (b), or

(d) any other provision of law for the time being in force which determines British citizenship, British overseas territories citizenship, the status of a British National (Overseas) or British Overseas citizenship.

(6) There may not be specified under subsection (3) any class of application which includes an application the subject matter of which is a devolved Scottish matter.

(7) For the purposes of this section, the subject matter of an application is a devolved Scottish matter if it—

(a) concerns the exercise of functions in or as regards Scotland, and

(b) does not relate to a reserved matter within the meaning of the Scotland Act 1998 (c. 46).

(8) In subsection (2), the reference to the exercise of the supervisory jurisdiction of the Court of Session includes a reference to the making of any order in connection with or in consequence of the exercise of that jurisdiction.

Note: Subsections (3), (6) and (7) in force from 19 September 2007 (SI 2007/2709). Remainder in force from 3 November 2008 (SI 2008/2696).

21. Upper Tribunal's "judicial review" jurisdiction: Scotland

(1) The Upper Tribunal has the function of deciding applications transferred to it from the Court of Session under section 20(1).

(2) The powers of review of the Upper Tribunal in relation to such applications are the same as the powers of review of the Court of Session in an application to the supervisory jurisdiction of that Court.

(3) In deciding an application by virtue of subsection (1), the Upper Tribunal must apply principles that the Court of Session would apply in deciding an application to the supervisory jurisdiction of that Court.

(4) An order of the Upper Tribunal by virtue of subsection (1)—

(a) has the same effect as the corresponding order granted by the Court of Session on an application to the supervisory jurisdiction of that Court, and

(b) is enforceable as if it were an order so granted by that Court.

(5) Where an application is transferred to the Upper Tribunal by virtue of section 20(1), any steps taken or orders made by the Court of Session in relation to the application (other than the order to transfer the application under section 20(1)) are to be treated as taken or made by the tribunal.

(6) Tribunal Procedure Rules may make further provision for the purposes of supplementing subsection (5).

Note: Subsection (6) in force from 19 September 2007 (SI 2007/2709). Remainder in force from 3 November 2008 (SI 2008/2696).

Miscellaneous

22. Tribunal Procedure Rules

(1) There are to be rules, to be called "Tribunal Procedure Rules", governing—

(a) the practice and procedure to be followed in the First-tier Tribunal, and

(b) the practice and procedure to be followed in the Upper Tribunal.

(2) Tribunal Procedure Rules are to be made by the Tribunal Procedure Committee.

(3) In Schedule 5—

Part 1 makes further provision about the content of Tribunal Procedure Rules,

Part 2 makes provision about the membership of the Tribunal Procedure Committee,

Part 3 makes provision about the making of Tribunal Procedure Rules by the Committee, and

Part 4 confers power to amend legislation in connection with Tribunal Procedure Rules.

(4) Power to make Tribunal Procedure Rules is to be exercised with a view to securing—

(a) that, in proceedings before the First-tier Tribunal and Upper Tribunal, justice is done,

(b) that the tribunal system is accessible and fair,

(c) that proceedings before the First-tier Tribunal or Upper Tribunal are handled quickly and efficiently,

(d) that the rules are both simple and simply expressed, and

(e) that the rules where appropriate confer on members of the First-tier Tribunal, or Upper Tribunal, responsibility for ensuring that proceedings before the tribunal are handled quickly and efficiently.

(5) In subsection (4)(b) "the tribunal system" means the system for deciding matters within the jurisdiction of the First-tier Tribunal or the Upper Tribunal.

Note: Commenced 19 September 2007 (SI 2007/2709).

23. Practice directions

(1) The Senior President of Tribunals may give directions—

(a) as to the practice and procedure of the First-tier Tribunal;

(b) as to the practice and procedure of the Upper Tribunal.

(2) A Chamber President may give directions as to the practice and procedure of the chamber over which he presides.

(3) A power under this section to give directions includes—

(a) power to vary or revoke directions made in exercise of the power, and

(b) power to make different provision for different purposes (including different provision for different areas).

(4) Directions under subsection (1) may not be given without the approval of the Lord Chancellor.

(5) Directions under subsection (2) may not be given without the approval of—

(a) the Senior President of Tribunals, and

(b) the Lord Chancellor.

(6) Subsections (4) and (5)(b) do not apply to directions to the extent that they consist of guidance about any of the following—

(a) the application or interpretation of the law;

(b) the making of decisions by members of the First-tier Tribunal or Upper Tribunal.

(7) Subsections (4) and (5)(b) do not apply to directions to the extent that they consist of criteria for determining which members of the First-tier Tribunal or Upper Tribunal may be chosen to decide particular categories of matter; but the directions may, to that extent, be given only after consulting the Lord Chancellor.

Note: Commenced 3 November 2008 (SI 2008/2696).

24. Mediation

(1) A person exercising power to make Tribunal Procedure Rules or give practice directions must, when making provision in relation to mediation, have regard to the following principles—

(a) mediation of matters in dispute between parties to proceedings is to take place only by agreement between those parties;

(b) where parties to proceedings fail to mediate, or where mediation between parties to proceedings fails to resolve disputed matters, the failure is not to affect the outcome of the proceedings.

(2) Practice directions may provide for members to act as mediators in relation to disputed matters in a case that is the subject of proceedings.

(3) The provision that may be made by virtue of subsection (2) includes provision for a member to act as a mediator in relation to disputed matters in a case even though the member has been chosen to decide matters in the case.

(4) Once a member has begun to act as a mediator in relation to a disputed matter in a case that is the subject of proceedings, the member may decide matters in the case only with the consent of the parties.

(5) Staff appointed under section 40(1) may, subject to their terms of appointment, act as mediators in relation to disputed matters in a case that is the subject of proceedings.

(6) In this section—

'member' means a judge or other member of the First-tier Tribunal or a judge or other member of the Upper Tribunal;

'practice direction' means a direction under section 23(1) or (2);

'proceedings' means proceedings before the First-tier Tribunal or proceedings before the Upper Tribunal.

25. Supplementary powers of Upper Tribunal

(1) In relation to the matters mentioned in subsection (2), the Upper Tribunal—

(a) has, in England and Wales or in Northern Ireland, the same powers, rights, privileges and authority as the High Court, and

(b) has, in Scotland, the same powers, rights, privileges and authority as the Court of Session.

(2) The matters are—

    (a) the attendance and examination of witnesses,

    (b) the production and inspection of documents, and

    (c) all other matters incidental to the Upper Tribunal's functions.

(3) Subsection (1) shall not be taken—

    (a) to limit any power to make Tribunal Procedure Rules;

    (b) to be limited by anything in Tribunal Procedure Rules other than an express limitation.

(4) A power, right, privilege or authority conferred in a territory by subsection (1) is available for purposes of proceedings in the Upper Tribunal that take place outside that territory (as well as for purposes of proceedings in the tribunal that take place within that territory).

Note: Commenced 3 November 2008 (SI 2008/2696).

26. First-tier Tribunal and Upper Tribunal: sitting places

Each of the First-tier Tribunal and the Upper Tribunal may decide a case—

    (a) in England and Wales,

    (b) in Scotland, or

    (c) in Northern Ireland, even though the case arises under the law of a territory other than the one in which the case is decided.

Note: Commenced 3 November 2008 (SI 2008/2696).

27. Enforcement

(1) A sum payable in pursuance of a decision of the First-tier Tribunal or Upper Tribunal made in England and Wales—

    (a) shall be recoverable as if it were payable under an order of a county court in England and Wales;

    (b) shall be recoverable as if it were payable under an order of the High Court in England and Wales.

(2) An order for the payment of a sum payable in pursuance of a decision of the First-tier Tribunal or Upper Tribunal made in Scotland (or a copy of such an order certified in accordance with Tribunal Procedure Rules) may be enforced as if it were an extract registered decree arbitral bearing a warrant for execution issued by the sheriff court of any sheriffdom in Scotland.

(3) A sum payable in pursuance of a decision of the First-tier Tribunal or Upper Tribunal made in Northern Ireland—

    (a) shall be recoverable as if it were payable under an order of a county court in Northern Ireland;

    (b) shall be recoverable as if it were payable under an order of the High Court in Northern Ireland.

(4) This section does not apply to a sum payable in pursuance of—

    (a) an award under section 16(6), or

    (b) an order by virtue of section 21(1).

(5) The Lord Chancellor may by order make provision for subsection (1) or (3) to apply in relation to a sum of a description specified in the order with the omission of one (but not both) of paragraphs (a) and (b).

(6) Tribunal Procedure Rules—

(a) may make provision as to where, for purposes of this section, a decision is to be taken to be made;

(b) may provide for all or any of subsections (1) to (3) to apply only, or not to apply except, in relation to sums of a description specified in Tribunal Procedure Rules. Tribunals, Courts and Enforcement Act 2007 (c. 15).

Note: Subsections (5) and (6) in force from 19 September 2007 (SI 2007/2709). Remainder in force from 3 November 2008 (SI 2008/2696).

28. Assessors

(1) If it appears to the First-tier Tribunal or the Upper Tribunal that a matter before it requires special expertise not otherwise available to it, it may direct that in dealing with that matter it shall have the assistance of a person or persons appearing to it to have relevant knowledge or experience.

(2) The remuneration of a person who gives assistance to either tribunal as mentioned in subsection (1) shall be determined and paid by the Lord Chancellor.

(3) The Lord Chancellor may—

(a) establish panels of persons from which either tribunal may (but need not) select persons to give it assistance as mentioned in subsection (1);

(b) under paragraph (a) establish different panels for different purposes;

(c) after carrying out such consultation as he considers appropriate, appoint persons to a panel established under paragraph (a);

(d) remove a person from such a panel.

Note: Commenced 3 November 2008 (SI 2008/2696).

29. Costs or expenses

(1) The costs of and incidental to—

(a) all proceedings in the First-tier Tribunal, and

(b) all proceedings in the Upper Tribunal, shall be in the discretion of the Tribunal in which the proceedings take place.

(2) The relevant Tribunal shall have full power to determine by whom and to what extent the costs are to be paid.

(3) Subsections (1) and (2) have effect subject to Tribunal Procedure Rules.

(4) In any proceedings mentioned in subsection (1), the relevant Tribunal may—

(a) disallow, or

(b) (as the case may be) order the legal or other representative concerned to meet, the whole of any wasted costs or such part of them as may be determined in accordance with Tribunal Procedure Rules.

(5) In subsection (4) "wasted costs" means any costs incurred by a party—

(a) as a result of any improper, unreasonable or negligent act or omission on the part of any legal or other representative or any employee of such a representative, or

(b) which, in the light of any such act or omission occurring after they were incurred, the relevant Tribunal considers it is unreasonable to expect that party to pay.

(6) In this section "legal or other representative", in relation to a party to proceedings, means any person exercising a right of audience or right to conduct the proceedings on his behalf.

(7) In the application of this section in relation to Scotland, any reference in this section to costs is to be read as a reference to expenses.

Note: Commenced 3 November 2008 (SI 2008/2696).

Criminal Justice and Immigration Act 2008
(2008, c. 4)

130. Designation

(1) The Secretary of State may designate a person who satisfies Condition 1 or 2 (subject to subsections (4) and (5)).

(2) Condition 1 is that the person
(a) is a foreign criminal within the meaning of section 131, and
(b) is liable to deportation, but cannot be removed from the United Kingdom because of section 6 of the Human Rights Act 1998 (c. 42) (public authority not to act contrary to Convention).

(3) Condition 2 is that the person is a member of the family of a person who satisfies Condition 1.

(4) A person who has the right of abode in the United Kingdom may not be designated.

(5) The Secretary of State may not designate a person if the Secretary of State thinks that an effect of designation would breach—
(a) the United Kingdom's obligations under the Refugee Convention, or
(b) the person's rights under the Community treaties.

Note: Commencement at a date to be appointed.

131. 'Foreign criminal'

(1) For the purposes of section 130 'foreign criminal' means a person who—
(a) is not a British citizen, and
(b) satisfies any of the following Conditions.

(2) Condition 1 is that section 72(2)(a) and (b) or (3)(a) to (c) of the Nationality, Immigration and Asylum Act 2002 (c. 41) applies to the person (Article 33(2) of the Refugee Convention: imprisonment for at least two years).

(3) Condition 2 is that—
(a) section 72(4)(a) or (b) of that Act applies to the person (person convicted of specified offence), and
(b) the person has been sentenced to a period of imprisonment.

(**4**) Condition 3 is that Article 1F of the Refugee Convention applies to the person (exclusions for criminals etc.).

(**5**) Section 72(6) of that Act (rebuttal of presumption under section 72(2) to (4)) has no effect in relation to Condition 1 or 2.

(**6**) Section 72(7) of that Act (non-application pending appeal) has no effect in relation to Condition 1 or 2.

Note: Commencement at a date to be appointed.

132. Effect of designation

(**1**) A designated person does not have leave to enter or remain in the United Kingdom.

(**2**) For the purposes of a provision of the Immigration Acts and any other enactment which concerns or refers to immigration or nationality (including any provision which applies or refers to a provision of the Immigration Acts or any other enactment about immigration or nationality) a designated person—

 (a) is a person subject to immigration control,

 (b) is not to be treated as an asylum-seeker or a former asylum-seeker, and

 (c) is not in the United Kingdom in breach of the immigration laws.

(**3**) Despite subsection (2)(c), time spent in the United Kingdom as a designated person may not be relied on by a person for the purpose of an enactment about nationality.

(**4**) A designated person—

 (a) shall not be deemed to have been given leave in accordance with paragraph 6 of Schedule 2 to the Immigration Act 1971 (c. 77) (notice of leave or refusal), and

 (b) may not be granted temporary admission to the United Kingdom under paragraph 21 of that Schedule.

(**5**) Sections 134 and 135 make provision about support for designated persons and their dependants.

Note: Commencement at a date to be appointed.

133. Conditions

(**1**) The Secretary of State or an immigration officer may by notice in writing impose a condition on a designated person.

(**2**) A condition may relate to—

 (a) residence,

 (b) employment or occupation, or

 (c) reporting to the police, the Secretary of State or an immigration officer.

(**3**) Section 36 of the Asylum and Immigration (Treatment of Claimants, etc.) Act 2004 (c. 19) (electronic monitoring) shall apply in relation to conditions imposed under this section as it applies to restrictions imposed under paragraph 21 of Schedule 2 to the Immigration Act 1971 (with a reference to the Immigration Acts being treated as including a reference to this section).

(4) Section 69 of the Nationality, Immigration and Asylum Act 2002 (c. 41) (reporting restrictions: travel expenses) shall apply in relation to conditions imposed under subsection (2)(c) above as it applies to restrictions imposed under paragraph 21 of Schedule 2 to the Immigration Act 1971.

(5) A person who without reasonable excuse fails to comply with a condition imposed under this section commits an offence.

(6) A person who is guilty of an offence under subsection (5) shall be liable on summary conviction to—

   (a) a fine not exceeding level 5 on the standard scale,
   (b) imprisonment for a period not exceeding 51 weeks, or
   (c) both.

(7) A provision of the Immigration Act 1971 (c. 77) which applies in relation to an offence under any provision of section 24(1) of that Act (illegal entry etc.) shall also apply in relation to the offence under subsection (5) above.

(8) In the application of this section to Scotland or Northern Ireland the reference in subsection (6)(b) to 51 weeks shall be treated as a reference to six months.

Note: Commencement at a date to be appointed. In the application of this section in England and Wales to offences committed before the commencement of s 281(5) of the Criminal Justice Act 2003, the maximum term of sentence in sub-s (6)(b) shall be read as 6 months, Sch 27 para 36.

134. Support

(1) Part VI of the Immigration and Asylum Act 1999 (c. 33) (support for asylum seekers) shall apply in relation to designated persons and their dependants as it applies in relation to asylum-seekers and their dependants.

(2) But the following provisions of that Part shall not apply—

   (a) section 96 (kinds of support),
   (b) section 97(1)(b) (desirability of providing accommodation in well-supplied area),
   (c) section 100 (duty to cooperate in providing accommodation),
   (d) section 101 (reception zones),
   (e) section 108 (failure of sponsor to maintain),
   (f) section 111 (grants to voluntary organisations), and
   (g) section 113 (recovery of expenditure from sponsor).

(3) Support may be provided under section 95 of the 1999 Act as applied by this section—

   (a) by providing accommodation appearing to the Secretary of State to be adequate for a person's needs;
   (b) by providing what appear to the Secretary of State to be essential living needs;
   (c) in other ways which the Secretary of State thinks necessary to reflect exceptional circumstances of a particular case.

(4) Support by virtue of subsection (3) may not be provided wholly or mainly by way of cash unless the Secretary of State thinks it appropriate because of exceptional circumstances.

(5) Section 4 of the 1999 Act (accommodation) shall not apply in relation to designated persons.

(6) . . .

Note: Commencement at a date to be appointed. Subsection (6) repealed by Housing and Regeneration Act 2008 Sch 15 para 24 from 2 March 2009 (SI 2009/415).

135. Support: supplemental

(1) A reference in an enactment to Part VI of the 1999 Act or to a provision of that Part includes a reference to that Part or provision as applied by section 134 above; and for that purpose—

(a) a reference to section 96 shall be treated as including a reference to section 134(3) above,

(b) a reference to a provision of section 96 shall be treated as including a reference to the corresponding provision of section 134(3), and

(c) a reference to asylum-seekers shall be treated as including a reference to designated persons.

(2) A provision of Part VI of the 1999 Act which requires or permits the Secretary of State to have regard to the temporary nature of support shall be treated, in the application of Part VI by virtue of section 134 above, as requiring the Secretary of State to have regard to the nature and circumstances of support by virtue of that section.

(3) . . .

(4) Any . . . instrument under Part VI of the 1999 Act—

(a) may make provision in respect of that Part as it applies by virtue of section 134 above, as it applies otherwise than by virtue of that section, or both, and

(b) may make different provision for that Part as it applies by virtue of section 134 above and as it applies otherwise than by virtue of that section.

(5) In the application of paragraph 9 of Schedule 8 to the 1999 Act (regulations: notice to quit accommodation) the reference in paragraph (2)(b) to the determination of a claim for asylum shall be treated as a reference to ceasing to be a designated person.

(6) The Secretary of State may by order repeal, modify or disapply (to any extent) section 134(4).

(7) . . .

Note: Commencement at a date to be appointed. Subsection (3) omitted and words omitted from subsection (4) by The Transfer of Tribunal Functions (Lands Tribunal and Miscellaneous Amendments) Order 2009 Sch 1 para 288(a) from 1 June 2009 (SI 2009/1307). Subsection (7) repealed by Housing and Regeneration Act 2008 Sch 15 para 25 from 2 March 2009 (SI 2009/415).

136. End of designation

(1) Designation lapses if the designated person—

(a) is granted leave to enter or remain in the United Kingdom,

(b) is notified by the Secretary of State or an immigration officer of a right of residence in the United Kingdom by virtue of the Community treaties,

(c) leaves the United Kingdom, or

(d) is made the subject of a deportation order under section 5 of the Immigration Act 1971 (c. 77).

(2) After designation lapses support may not be provided by virtue of section 134, subject to the following exceptions.

(3) Exception 1 is that, if designation lapses under subsection (1)(a) or (b), support may be provided in respect of a period which—

(a) begins when the designation lapses, and

(b) ends on a date determined in accordance with an order of the Secretary of State.

(4) Exception 2 is that, if designation lapses under subsection (1)(d), support may be provided in respect of—

(a) any period during which an appeal against the deportation order may be brought (ignoring any possibility of an appeal out of time with permission),

(b) any period during which an appeal against the deportation order is pending, and

(c) after an appeal ceases to be pending, such period as the Secretary of State may specify by order.

Note: Commencement at a date to be appointed.

137. Interpretation: general

(1) This section applies to sections 130 to 136.

(2) A reference to a designated person is a reference to a person designated under section 130.

(3) 'Family' shall be construed in accordance with section 5(4) of the Immigration Act 1971 (c. 77) (deportation: definition of 'family').

(4) 'Right of abode in the United Kingdom' has the meaning given by section 2 of that Act.

(5) 'The Refugee Convention' means the Convention relating to the Status of Refugees done at Geneva on 28 July 1951 and its Protocol.

(6) 'Period of imprisonment' shall be construed in accordance with section 72(11)(b)(i) and (ii) of the Nationality, Immigration and Asylum Act 2002 (c. 41).

(7) A voucher is not cash.

(8) A reference to a pending appeal has the meaning given by section 104(1) of that Act.

(9) A reference in an enactment to the Immigration Acts includes a reference to sections 130 to 136.

Note: Commencement at a date to be appointed.

Borders, Citizenship and Immigration Act 2009
(2009, c. 11)

Contents

PART 4. MISCELLANEOUS AND GENERAL

Judicial review

Trafficking people for exploitation

Children

General

SCHEDULE
REPEALS

An Act to provide for customs functions to be exercisable by the Secretary of State, the Director of Border Revenue and officials designated by them; to make provision about the use and disclosure of customs information; to make provision for and in connection with the exercise of customs functions and functions relating to immigration, asylum or nationality; to make provision about citizenship and other nationality matters; to make further provision about immigration and asylum; and for connected purposes. [21 July 2009] BE IT ENACTED by the Queen's Most Excellent Majesty, by and with the advice and consent of the Lords Spiritual and Temporal, and Commons, in this present Parliament assembled, and by the authority of the same, as follows:—

PART 1

BORDER FUNCTIONS

Note: Part 1 makes provision relating to the exercise of customs functions and related matters and only the sections below are reproduced. Sections are also identified that amend or repeal statutory provisions that appear elsewhere in this book.

20. Supply of Revenue and Customs information

Note: Inserts sections 41A and 41B and amends section 42(1) of the UK Borders Act 2007.

21. Duty to share information

Note: Amends section 36 of the Immigration Asylum and Nationality Act 2006.

25. Short-term holding facilities

Note: Amends section 147 of the Immigration and Asylum Act 1999.

Inspection and oversight

28. Inspections by the Chief Inspector of the UK Border Agency

(1)–(6)) ...

(7)–(8)) ...

(9) ...

(10)   The person holding the office of the Chief Inspector of the Border and Immigration Agency immediately before the day on which this section comes into force is to be treated, on and after that day, as if appointed as the Chief Inspector of the UK Border Agency under section 48(1) of the UK Borders Act 2007 (c. 30).

Note: Commenced 21 July 2009 (s 58). Subsections (1)–(6) amend section 48 of the UK Borders Act 2007. Subsections (7)–(8) amend section 53 of the UK Borders Act 2007. Subsection (9) amends section 56(2)(a) of the UK Borders Act 2007.

34. Children

(1)–(5)) ...

(6) This section ceases to have effect on the coming into force of section 55 (duty regarding welfare of children).

Note: Commenced 21 July 2009 (s 58). Subsections (1)–(5) amend section 21 of the UK Borders Act 2007.

PART 2

CITIZENSHIP

Acquisition of British citizenship by naturalisation

39. Application requirements: general

...

Note: Amends paragraphs 1 and 2 and inserts paragraph 2A of Schedule 1 of the British Nationality Act 1981.

40. Application requirements: family members etc.

(1)–(2)) . . .

(3)–(5)) . . .

Note: Subsections (1)–(2) amends section 6 of the British Nationality Act 1981. Subsections (3)–(5) amend paragraph 3 and 4 and inserts paragraph 4A of Schedule 1 of the British Nationality Act 1981.

41. The qualifying period

(1)) . . .

(2)–(5)) . . .

Note: Subsection (1) inserts paragraph 4B of Schedule 1 to the British Nationality Act 1981. Subsections (2)–(5) amend section 41 of the British nationality Act 1981.

Acquisition of British citizenship by birth

42. Children born in UK etc. to members of the armed forces

Note: Amends section 1 of the British Nationality Act 1981.

Acquisition of British citizenship etc. by registration

43. Minors

Note: Amends section 3 of the British Nationality Act 1981.

44. British Nationals (Overseas) without other citizenship

Note: Amends section 4B of the British Nationality Act 1981.

45. Descent through the female line

Note: Amends section 4C of the British Nationality Act 1981.

46. Children born outside UK etc. to members of the armed forces

Note: Inserts section 4D of the British Nationality Act 1981.

47. Good character requirement

(1) . . .

(2)) . . .

(3)) . . .

(4)) . . .

(5)) . . .

Note: Subsection (1) inserts section 41A of the British Nationality Act 1981. Subsection (2) amends section 1 of the Hong Kong (War Wives and Widows) Act 1996. Subsection (3) amends section 1 of the British Nationality (Hong Kong) Act 1997. Subsection (4) amends section 131 of the Nationality, Immigration and Asylum Act 2002. Subsection (5) amends section 40 of the UK Borders Act 2007.

Interpretation etc.

48. Meaning of references to being in breach of immigration laws

(1) ...

(2) ...

(3) Notwithstanding its repeal, section 11 of the 2002 Act is to continue to have effect for the purpose of determining on or after the relevant day—

(a) whether a person born before the relevant day is a British citizen under section 1(1) of the British Nationality Act 1981 (c. 61),

(b) whether, on an application under section 1(3) or 4(2) of that Act made but not determined before the relevant day, a person is entitled to be registered as a British citizen,

(c) whether, on an application under section 6(1) or (2) of that Act made but not determined before the relevant day, the applicant fulfils the requirements of Schedule 1 for naturalisation as a British citizen under section 6(1) or (2) of that Act, or

(d) whether, in relation to an application under section 1(3) or 6(1) or (2) of that Act made on or after the relevant day, a person was in the United Kingdom "in breach of the immigration laws" at a time before 7 November 2002 (the date of commencement of section 11 of the 2002 Act).

(4) Where section 11 of the 2002 Act continues to have effect by virtue of paragraph (d) of subsection (3) for the purpose of determining on or after the relevant day the matter mentioned in that paragraph, section 50A of the British Nationality Act 1981 is not to apply for the purpose of determining that matter.

(5) The relevant day for the purposes of subsection (3) is the day appointed for the commencement of this section.

(6) ...

Note: Commenced 13 January 2010 (SI 2009/2731). Subsection (1) inserts section 50A of the British Nationality Act 1981. Subsection (2) repeals section 11 of the Nationality, Immigration and Asylum Act 2002, subject to subsection (3). Subsection (6) amends paragraph 7(a) of Schedule 3 to the Nationality, Immigration and Asylum Act 2002.

49. Other interpretation etc.

(1) ...

(2) ...

(3) ...

Note: Subsection (1) commenced 13 January 2010 (SI 2009/2731), remainder on a date to be appointed. Subsection (1) amends section 50 of the British Nationality Act 1981. Subsection (2) amends Schedule 1 to the British Nationality Act 1981. Subsection (3) inserts paragraph 11 of Schedule 1 to the British Nationality Act 1981.

PART 3

IMMIGRATION

Studies

50. Restriction on studies

(1) ...

(2) A condition under section 3(1)(c)(ia) of that Act may be added as a condition to leave given before the passing of this Act (as well as to leave given on or after its passing).

Note: Commenced 21 July 2009 (s 58). Subsection (1) amends section 3(1)(c) of the Immigration Act 1971.

Fingerprinting

51. Fingerprinting of foreign criminals liable to automatic deportation

...

Note: Amends section 141 of the Immigration and Asylum Act 1999.

Detention at ports in Scotland

52. Extension of sections 1 to 4 of the UK Borders Act 2007 to Scotland

(1)–(2)) ...

(3) ...

Note: Subsections (1) and (2) amend sections 2 and 3 of the UK Borders Act 2007. Subsection (3) amends section 60(1) of the UK Borders Act 2007.

PART 4

MISCELLANEOUS AND GENERAL

Judicial review

53. Transfer of certain immigration judicial review applications

(1) ...

(2) ...

(3) ...

Note: Subsection (1) amends section 31A of the Supreme Court Act 1981. Subsection (2) amends section 25A of the Judicature (Northern Ireland) Act 1978. Subsection (3) amends section 20 of the Tribunals, Courts and Enforcement Act 2007.

Trafficking people for exploitation

54. Trafficking people for exploitation

Note: Amends section 4(4) of the Asylum and Immigration (Treatment of Claimants, etc.) Act 2004.

Children

55. Duty regarding the welfare of children

(1) The Secretary of State must make arrangements for ensuring that—

(a) the functions mentioned in subsection (2) are discharged having regard to the need to safeguard and promote the welfare of children who are in the United Kingdom; and

(b) any services provided by another person pursuant to arrangements which are made by the Secretary of State and relate to the discharge of a function mentioned in subsection (2) are provided having regard to that need.

(2) The functions referred to in subsection (1) are—

(a) any function of the Secretary of State in relation to immigration, asylum or nationality;

(b) any function conferred by or by virtue of the Immigration Acts on an immigration officer;

(c) any general customs function of the Secretary of State; and

(d) any customs function conferred on a designated customs official.

(3) A person exercising any of those functions must, in exercising the function, have regard to any guidance given to the person by the Secretary of State for the purpose of subsection (1).

(4) The Director of Border Revenue must make arrangements for ensuring that—

(a) the Director's functions are discharged having regard to the need to safeguard and promote the welfare of children who are in the United Kingdom; and

(b) any services provided by another person pursuant to arrangements made by the Director in the discharge of such a function are provided having regard to that need.

(5) A person exercising a function of the Director of Border Revenue must, in exercising the function, have regard to any guidance given to the person by the Secretary of State for the purpose of subsection (4).

(6) In this section—

'children' means persons who are under the age of 18;

'customs function', 'designated customs official' and 'general customs function' have the meanings given by Part 1.

(7) A reference in an enactment (other than this Act) to the Immigration Acts includes a reference to this section.

(8) ...

Note: Commenced 2 November 2009 (SI 2009/2731). Subsection (8) repeals section 21 of the UK Borders Act 2007.

General

56. Repeals

The Schedule contains repeals.

Note: Commenced 2 November 2009 (SI 2009/2731).

57. Extent

(1) Subject to the following provisions of this section, this Act extends to—

    (a) England and Wales,

    (b) Scotland, and

    (c) Northern Ireland.

(2) Sections 22 (application of the PACE orders) and 23 (investigations and detention: England and Wales and Northern Ireland) extend to England and Wales and Northern Ireland only.

(3) An amendment, modification or repeal by this Act has the same extent as the enactment or relevant part of the enactment to which it relates (ignoring extent by virtue of an Order in Council under any of the Immigration Acts).

(4) Subsection (3) does not apply to—

    (a) the amendments made by section 52 (detention at ports in Scotland);

    (b) the amendment made by section 54 (trafficking people for exploitation), which extends to England and Wales and Northern Ireland only.

(5) Her Majesty may by Order in Council provide for any of the provisions of this Act, other than any provision of Part 1 (border functions) or section 53 (transfer of certain immigration judicial review applications), to extend, with or without modifications, to any of the Channel Islands or the Isle of Man.

(6) Subsection (5) does not apply in relation to the extension to a place of a provision which extends there by virtue of subsection (3).

Note: Commenced 21 July 2009 (s 58).

58. Commencement

(1) Part 1 (border functions) comes into force on the day this Act is passed.

(2) The provisions of Part 2 (citizenship) come into force on such day as the Secretary of State may by order appoint.

(3) In Part 3 (immigration)—

    (a) section 50 (restriction on studies) comes into force on the day this Act is passed;

    (b) sections 51 (fingerprinting of foreign criminals) and 52 (detention at ports in Scotland) come into force on such day as the Secretary of State may by order appoint.

(4) In this Part—

    (a) section 53 (transfer of certain immigration judicial review applications) comes into force on such day as the Lord Chancellor may by order appoint;

    (b) sections 54 (trafficking people for exploitation) and 55 (duty regarding the welfare of children) come into force on such day as the Secretary of State may by order appoint.

(5) Any repeal in the Schedule (and section 56 so far as relating to the repeal) comes into force in the same way as the provisions of this Act to which the repeal relates.

(6) The other provisions of this Part come into force on the day this Act is passed.

(7) An order under this section must be made by statutory instrument.

(8) An order under this section—

    (a) may appoint different days for different purposes;

(b) may include transitional or incidental provision or savings.

(9) An order commencing sections 39 to 41 (acquisition of British citizenship by naturalisation) must include provision that the amendments made by those sections do not have effect in relation to an application for naturalisation as a British citizen if—

(a) the date of the application is before the date on which those sections come into force in accordance with the order ("the date of commencement"), or

(b) the date of the application is before the end of the period of 24 months beginning with the date of commencement and the application is made by a person who falls within subsection (10) or (11).

(10) A person falls within this subsection if on the date of commencement the person has indefinite leave to remain in the United Kingdom.

(11) A person falls within this subsection if the person is given indefinite leave to remain in the United Kingdom on an application—

(a) the date of which is before the date of commencement, and

(b) which is decided after the date of commencement.

(12) The reference in subsection (9) to an order commencing sections 39 to 41 does not include an order commencing those sections for the purpose only of enabling regulations to be made under the British Nationality Act 1981 (c. 61).

(13) In the case of an order commencing sections 39 to 41, transitional provision may, in particular—

(a) provide that the qualifying period for the purposes of paragraph 1 or 3 of Schedule 1 to the British Nationality Act 1981 includes time before that commencement;

(b) provide for leave to enter or remain in the United Kingdom granted before that commencement to be treated as qualifying temporary residence leave or probationary citizenship leave for the purposes of that Schedule.

(14) In the case of an order commencing section 45 (acquisition of British citizenship through the female line), transitional provision may, in particular, provide that section 45 is to apply to an application made, but not determined, under section 4C of the British Nationality Act 1981 before that commencement.

(15) No order may be made commencing section 52 (detention at ports in Scotland) unless the Secretary of State has consulted the Scottish Ministers.

(16) No order may be made commencing section 53 (transfer of certain immigration judicial review applications) unless the functions of the Asylum and Immigration Tribunal in relation to appeals under Part 5 of the Nationality, Immigration and Asylum Act 2002 (c. 41) have been transferred under section 30(1) of the Tribunals, Courts and Enforcement Act 2007 (c. 15).

Note: Commenced 21 July 2009 (s 58).

59. Short title

This Act may be cited as the Borders, Citizenship and Immigration Act 2009.

Note: Commenced 21 July 2009 (s 58).

Section 56   SCHEDULE

Note: The Schedule sets out repeals of provisions of the UK Borders Act 2007, British Nationality Act 1981, Hong Kong (War Wives and Widows) Act 1996, Nationality, Asylum and Immigration Act 2002, and the Immigration, Asylum and Nationality Act 2006.

PROCEDURE RULES AND PRACTICE DIRECTIONS

The Asylum and Immigration Tribunal (Procedure) Rules 2005
(SI 2005, No. 230)

Arrangement of Rules

Part 1

Introduction

Part 2

Appeals to the Tribunal

Part 3

Appeals to the Upper Tribunal

PART 4

Bail

PART 5

General Provisions

PART 6

Revocation and Transitional Provisions

PART I

Introduction

Citation and commencement

1. These Rules may be cited as the Asylum and Immigration Tribunal (Procedure) Rules 2005 and shall come into force on 4 April 2005.

Interpretation

2. In these Rules—

'the 2002 Act' means the Nationality, Immigration and Asylum Act 2002;

'the 2004 Act' means the Asylum and Immigration (Treatment of Claimants, etc.) Act 2004;

["appeal to the Upper Tribunal" means the exercise of a right of appeal on a point of law under section 11 of the Tribunals, Courts and Enforcement Act 2007;]

'appellant' means a person who has given a notice of appeal to the Tribunal against a relevant decision in accordance with these Rules;

. . .

'asylum claim' has the meaning given in section 113(1) of the 2002 Act;

'business day' means any day other than a Saturday or Sunday, a bank holiday, 25 to 31 December or Good Friday;

['certificate of fee satisfaction' means a certificate of fee satisfaction issued by the Lord Chancellor under article 8 of the Fees Order;]

'determination', in relation to an appeal, means a decision by the Tribunal in writing to allow or dismiss the appeal, and does not include a procedural, ancillary or preliminary decision;

['the Fees Order' means the First-tier Tribunal (Immigration and Asylum Chamber) Fees Order 2011;]

'the Immigration Acts' means the Acts referred to in section 44(1) of the 2004 Act;

'immigration decision' means a decision of a kind listed in section 82(2) of the 2002 Act;

'immigration rules' means the rules referred to in section 1(4) of the Immigration Act 1971;

. . .

'relevant decision' means a decision against which there is an exercisable right of appeal to the Tribunal;

'respondent' means the decision maker specified in the notice of decision against which a notice of appeal has been given;

. . .

'Tribunal' means the [First-tier Tribunal];

'United Kingdom Representative' means the United Kingdom Representative of the United Nations High Commissioner for Refugees.

Note: Third words omitted from 13 November 2006 (SI 2006/2788). Other words omitted, inserted and definition of Tribunal substituted from 15 February 2010 (SI 2010/21). Definitions of 'certificate of fee satisfaction' and 'the Fees Order' inserted from 19 December 2011 (SI 2011/2840).

[**Scope of these Rules**

[3. These Rules apply to proceedings before the Immigration and Asylum Chamber of the First-tier Tribunal.]

Note: Rule 3 substituted from 29 November 2010 (SI 2010/2653).

Overriding objective

4. The overriding objective of these Rules is to secure that proceedings before the Tribunal are handled as fairly, quickly and efficiently as possible; and, where appropriate, that members of the Tribunal have responsibility for ensuring this, in the interests of the parties to the proceedings and in the wider public interest.

PART 2

Appeals to the Tribunal

Scope of this Part

5. This Part applies to appeals to the Tribunal.

Giving notice of appeal

6.—(1) An appeal to the Tribunal may only be instituted by giving notice of appeal against a relevant decision in accordance with these Rules.

(2) Subject to [paragraph (3)], notice of appeal must be given by filing it with the Tribunal in accordance with rule 55(1).

(3) A person who is in detention under the Immigration Acts may give notice of appeal [to the Tribunal] either—

(a) in accordance with paragraph (2); or

(b) by serving it on the person having custody of him.

(4) ...

(5) Where a notice of appeal is served on a custodian under paragraph (3)(b), that person must—

(a) endorse on the notice the date that it is served on him; and

(b) forward it to the Tribunal within 2 days.

(6) ...

Note: Words substituted in para (2), words inserted in para (3) and paras (4) and (6) omitted from 19 December 2011 (SI 2011/2840).

Time limit for appeal

7.—(1) A notice of appeal by a person who is in the United Kingdom must be given—

(a) if the person is in detention under the Immigration Acts when he is served with notice of the decision against which he is appealing, not later than 5 days after he is served with that notice; and

(b) in any other case, not later than 10 days after he is served with notice of the decision.

(2) A notice of appeal by a person who is outside the United Kingdom must be given—

(a) if the person—

(i) was in the United Kingdom when the decision against which he is appealing was made; and

(ii) may not appeal while he is the United Kingdom by reason of a provision of the 2002 Act,

not later than 28 days after his departure from the United Kingdom; or

(b) in any other case, not later than 28 days after he is served with notice of the decision.

(3) Where a person—

(a) is served with notice of a decision to reject an asylum claim; and

(b) on the date of being served with that notice does not satisfy the condition in section 83(1)(b) of the 2002 Act, but later satisfies that condition,

paragraphs (1) and (2)(b) apply with the modification that the time for giving notice of appeal under section 83(2) runs from the date on which the person is served with notice of the decision to grant him leave to enter or remain in the United Kingdom by which he satisfies the condition in section 83(1)(b).

Form and contents of notice of appeal

8.—(1) The notice of appeal must be [made on a form approved for the purpose by the {Senior President *of Tribunals*]} and must—

(a) state the name and address of the appellant; and

(b) state whether the appellant has authorised a representative to act for him in the appeal and, if so, give the representative's name and address;

(c) set out the grounds for the appeal;

(d) give reasons in support of those grounds;

(e) so far as reasonably practicable, list any documents which the appellant intends to rely upon as evidence in support of the appeal; [and

(f) state whether the appellant consents to the appeal being determined without a hearing].

[(2) The notice of appeal must be accompanied by—

{(a) the notice of decision against which the appellant is appealing or, if it is not practicable to include the notice of decision, the reasons why it is not practicable; and

(b) an application for the Lord Chancellor to issue a certificate of fee satisfaction]}.

(3) The notice of appeal must be signed by the appellant or his representative, and dated.

(4) If a notice of appeal is signed by the appellant's representative, the representative must certify in the notice of appeal that he has completed it in accordance with the appellant's instructions.

Note: Words in square brackets substituted in para (1) from 13 November 2006 (SI 2006/2788). Paragraph (2) substituted from 12 May 2008 (SI 2008/1088). Words in curly brackets in paragraph (1) substituted from 15 February 2010 (SI 2010/21). Italicised words in para (1), sub-para (1)(f) inserted and sub-paras (2)(a) and (b) substituted from 19 December 2011 (SI 2011/2840).

[Where the Tribunal may not accept a notice of appeal]

9.—[(1) Where a person has given a notice of appeal to the Tribunal and the circumstances in paragraph (1A) apply, the Tribunal may not accept the notice of appeal.

(1A) The circumstances referred to in paragraph (1) are that—

(a) there is no relevant decision;

(b) the notice of appeal concerns the refusal of an application for entry clearance which was not made for a purpose falling within section 88A(1)(a) or (b) of the 2002 Act, and the notice of appeal does not rely on either of the grounds specified in section 88A(3)(a) of the 2002 Act;] [or

(c) the Lord Chancellor has refused to issue a certificate of fee satisfaction.]

(2) Where the Tribunal does not accept a notice of appeal, it must—

(a) notify the person giving the notice of appeal and the respondent; and

(b) take no further action [on that notice of appeal].

Note: Paragraphs (1) and (1A) amended from 12 May 2008 (SI 2008/1088). Subparagraph (1A)(c) inserted and words inserted in sub-para 2(b) from 19 December 2011 (SI 2011/2840).

Late notice of appeal

10.—(1) If a notice of appeal is given outside the applicable time limit, it must include an application for an extension of time for appealing, which must—

(a) include a statement of the reasons for failing to give the notice within that period; and

(b) be accompanied by any written evidence relied upon in support of those reasons.

(2) If a notice of appeal appears to the Tribunal to have been given outside the applicable time limit but does not include an application for an extension of time, unless the Tribunal extends the time for appealing of its own initiative, it must notify the person giving notice of appeal in writing that it proposes to treat the notice of appeal as being out of time.

(3) Where the Tribunal gives notification under paragraph (2), if the person giving notice of appeal contends that—

(a) the notice of appeal was given in time, or

(b) there were special circumstances for failing to give the notice of appeal in time which could not reasonably have been stated in the notice of appeal,

he may file with the Tribunal written evidence in support of that contention.

(4) Written evidence under paragraph (3) must be filed—

(a) if the person giving notice of appeal is in the United Kingdom, not later than 3 days; or

(b) if the person giving notice of appeal is outside the United Kingdom, not later than 10 days,

after notification is given under paragraph (2).

(5) Where the notice of appeal was given out of time, the Tribunal may extend the time for appealing if satisfied that by reason of special circumstances it would be unjust not to do so.

(6) The Tribunal must decide any issue as to whether a notice of appeal was given in time, or whether to extend the time for appealing, as a preliminary decision without a hearing, and in doing so may only take account of—

(a) the matters stated in the notice of appeal;

(b) any evidence filed by the person giving notice of appeal in accordance with paragraph (1) or (3); and

(c) any other relevant matters of fact within the knowledge of the Tribunal.

[(6A) Where the Tribunal makes a decision under this rule it must give written notice of its decision, including its reasons which may be in summary form.]

(7) Subject to paragraphs (8) and (9), the Tribunal must serve [the] written notice [given under paragraph (6A)] on the parties.

(8) Where—

(a) a notice of appeal under section 82 of the 2002 Act which relates in whole or in part to an asylum claim was given out of time;

(b) the person giving notice of appeal is in the United Kingdom; and

(c) the Tribunal refuses to extend the time for appealing,

the Tribunal must serve written notice of its decision on the respondent, which must—

(i) serve the notice of decision on the person giving notice of appeal not later than 28 days after receiving it from the Tribunal; and

(ii) as soon as practicable after serving the notice of decision, notify the Tribunal on what date and by what means it was served.

(9) Where paragraph (8) applies, if the respondent does not give the Tribunal notification under sub-paragraph (ii) within 29 days after the Tribunal serves the notice of decision on it, the Tribunal must serve the notice of decision on the person giving notice of appeal as soon as reasonably practicable thereafter.

Note: Paragraph 6A and words in square brackets in para (7) inserted from 13 November 2006 (SI 2006/2788).

Special provisions for imminent removal cases

11.—(1) This rule applies in any case in which the respondent notifies the Tribunal that removal directions have been issued against a person who has given notice of appeal, pursuant to which it is proposed to remove him from the United Kingdom within 5 calendar days of the date on which the notice of appeal was given.

(2) The Tribunal must, if reasonably practicable, make any preliminary decision under rule 10 before the date and time proposed for his removal.

(3) Rule 10 shall apply subject to the modifications that the Tribunal may—

(a) give notification under rule 10(2) orally, which may include giving it by telephone;

(b) shorten the time for giving evidence under rule 10(3); and

(c) direct that any evidence under rule 10(3) is to be given orally, which may include requiring the evidence to be given by telephone, and hold a hearing or telephone hearing for the purpose of receiving such evidence.

Service of notice of appeal on respondent

12.—(1) ... when the Tribunal receives a notice of appeal it shall serve a copy upon the respondent as soon as reasonably practicable.

(2) ...

Note: Words omitted from para (1) and para (2) omitted from 19 December 2011 (SI 2011/2840).

Filing of documents by respondent

13.—(1) When the respondent is served with a copy of a notice of appeal, it must ... file with the Tribunal a copy of—

(a) the notice of the decision to which the notice of appeal relates, and any other document served on the appellant giving reasons for that decision;

(b) any—

(i) statement of evidence form completed by the appellant; and

(ii) record of an interview with the appellant,

in relation to the decision being appealed;

(c) any other unpublished document which is referred to in a document mentioned in sub-paragraph (a) or relied upon by the respondent; and

(d) the notice of any other immigration decision made in relation to the appellant in respect of which he has a right of appeal under section 82 of the 2002 Act.

(2) Subject to paragraph (3), the respondent must file the documents listed in paragraph (1)—

(a) in accordance with any directions given by the Tribunal; and

(b) if no such directions are given, as soon as reasonably practicable and in any event not later than 2.00 p.m. on the business day before the earliest date appointed for any hearing of or in relation to the appeal.

(3) If the Tribunal considers the timeliness of a notice of appeal as a preliminary issue under rule 10, the respondent must file the documents listed in paragraph (1) as soon as reasonably practicable after being served with a decision of the Tribunal allowing the appeal to proceed, and in any event not later than 2.00 p.m. on the business day before the earliest date appointed for any hearing of or in relation to the appeal following that decision.

(4) The respondent must, at the same time as filing them, serve on the appellant a copy of all the documents listed in paragraph (1), except for documents which the respondent has already sent to the appellant.

Note: Words omitted from para (1) from 19 December 2011 (SI 2011/2840).

Variation of grounds of appeal

14. Subject to section 85(2) of the 2002 Act, the appellant may vary his grounds of appeal only with the permission of the Tribunal.

Method of determining appeal

15.—(1) Every appeal must be considered by the Tribunal at a hearing, except where—

(a) the appeal—

    (i) lapses pursuant to section 99 of the 2002 Act;

    (ii) is treated as abandoned pursuant to section 104(4) of the 2002 Act;

    (iii) is treated as finally determined pursuant to section 104(5) of the 2002 Act; or

    (iv) is withdrawn by the appellant or treated as withdrawn in accordance with rule 17;

  (b) paragraph (2) of this rule applies; or

  (c) any other provision of these Rules or of any other enactment permits or requires the Tribunal to dispose of an appeal without a hearing.

  (2) The Tribunal may determine an appeal without a hearing if—

  (a) all the parties to the appeal consent;

  [(aa) the appellant has not consented to the appeal being determined without a hearing but the Lord Chancellor has refused to issue a certificate of fee satisfaction for the fee payable for a hearing;]

  [(b) the appellant is outside the United Kingdom and does not have a representative who has an address for service in the United Kingdom.]

  (ba) ...(c) a party has failed to comply with a provision of these Rules or a direction of the Tribunal [, or to provide a satisfactory explanation under rule 8(2)(b)], and the Tribunal is satisfied that in all the circumstances, including the extent of the failure and any reasons for it, it is appropriate to determine the appeal without a hearing;

  (d) subject to paragraph (3), the Tribunal is satisfied, having regard to the material before it and the nature of the issues raised, that the appeal can be justly determined without a hearing; [or

  (e) it is impracticable to give the appellant notice of the hearing].

  (3) Where paragraph (2)(d) applies, the Tribunal must not determine the appeal without a hearing without first giving the parties notice of its intention to do so, and an opportunity to make written representations as to whether there should be a hearing.

Note: Sub-paragraph (2)(aa) inserted, sub-para(2)(b) substituted, sub-para (2)(ba) omitted and sub-para (2)(e) inserted from 19 December 2011 (SI 2011/2840).

Certification of pending appeal

  16.—(1) If the Secretary of State or an immigration officer issues a certificate under section 97 or 98 of the 2002 Act which relates to a pending appeal, he must file notice of the certification with the Tribunal.

  (2) Where a notice of certification is filed under paragraph (1), the Tribunal must—

  (a) notify the parties; and

  (b) take no further action in relation to the appeal.

Withdrawal of appeal

  17.—(1) An appellant may withdraw an appeal—

  (a) orally, at a hearing; or

  (b) at any time, by filing written notice with the Tribunal.

  (2) An appeal shall be treated as withdrawn if the respondent notifies the Tribunal that the decision (or, where the appeal relates to more than one decision, all of the decisions) to which the appeal relates has been withdrawn.

[(**2A**) Where an appellant dies before his appeal has been determined by the Tribunal, the Tribunal may direct that—

(a) the appeal shall be treated as withdrawn; or (b) where the Tribunal considers it necessary, the personal representative of the appellant may continue the proceedings in the place of the appellant.]

(**3**) If an appeal is withdrawn or treated as withdrawn, the Tribunal must serve on the parties a notice that the appeal has been recorded as having been withdrawn.

Note: Paragraph (2A) inserted from 13 November 2006 (SI 2006/2788).

Striking out an appeal for non-payment of fee

[**17A** Where the Tribunal is notified by the Lord Chancellor that a certificate of fee satisfaction has been revoked the appeal will automatically be struck out without order of the Tribunal and the Tribunal must notify each party that the appeal has been struck out. Reinstatement of an appeal struck out for non-payment of fee.]

Note: Paragraph 17A inserted from 19 December 2011 (SI 2011/2840).

17B Where an appeal has been struck out in accordance with rule 17A, the appeal may be reinstated if—

(a) the appellant applies to have the appeal reinstated; and

(b) the Lord Chancellor has issued a new certificate of fee satisfaction.

Note: Paragraph 17B inserted from 19 December 2011 (SI 2011/2840).

Abandonment of appeal

18.—(1) Any party to a pending appeal must notify the Tribunal if they are aware that an event specified in—

(a) section 104(4) [,(4A)] or (5) of the 2002 Act; or

(b) regulation 33(1A) of the Immigration (European Economic Area) Regulations 2000 ('the 2000 Regulations'), [or, on or after 30 April 2006, paragraph 4(2) of Schedule 2 to the Immigration (European Economic Area) Regulations 2006 ('the 2006 Regulations')], has taken place.

[(**1A**) Where section 104(4A) of the 2002 Act applies and the appellant wishes to pursue his appeal, the appellant must file a notice with the Tribunal—

(a) where section 104(4B) of the 2002 Act applies, within 28 days of the date on which the appellant received notice of the grant of leave to enter or remain in the United Kingdom for a period exceeding 12 months; or (b) where section 104(4C) of the 2002 Act applies, within 28 days of the date on which the appellant received notice of the grant of leave to enter or remain in the United Kingdom.

(**1B**) Where the appellant does not comply with the time limits specified in paragraph (1A) the appeal will be treated as abandoned in accordance with section 104(4) of the 2002 Act.

(**1C**) At the same time as filing the notice under paragraph (1A), the appellant must serve a copy of the notice on the respondent.

(**1D**) Where section 104(4B) of the 2002 Act applies, the notice filed under paragraph (1A) must state—

(a) the appellant's full name and date of birth;

(b) the Tribunal's reference number;

(c) the Home Office reference number, if applicable;

(d) the Foreign and Commonwealth Office reference number, if applicable;

(e) the date on which the appellant was granted leave to enter or remain in the United Kingdom for a period exceeding 12 months; and

(f) that the appellant wishes to pursue the appeal in so far as it is brought on the ground specified in section 84(1)(g) of the 2002 Act which relates to the Refugee Convention.

(1E) Where section 104(4C) of the 2002 Act applies, the notice filed under paragraph (1A) must state—

(a) the appellant's full name and date of birth;

(b) the Tribunal's reference number;

(c) the Home Office reference number, if applicable;

(d) the Foreign and Commonwealth Office reference number, if applicable;

(e) the date on which the appellant was granted leave to enter or remain in the United Kingdom; and

(f) that the appellant wishes to pursue the appeal in so far as it is brought on the ground specified in section 84(1)(b) of the 2002 Act which relates to section 19B of the Race Relations Act 1976.

(1F) Where an appellant has filed a notice under paragraph (1A) the Tribunal will notify the appellant of the date on which it received the notice.

(1G) The Tribunal will send a copy of the notice issued under paragraph (1F) to the respondent.]

(2) Where an appeal is treated as abandoned pursuant to section 104(4) [or (4A)] of the 2002 Act or regulation 33(1A) of the 2000 Regulations, [or paragraph 4(2) of Schedule 2 to the 2006 Regulations], or finally determined pursuant to section 104(5) of the 2002 Act, the Tribunal must—

(a) serve on the parties a notice informing them that the appeal is being treated as abandoned or finally determined; and

(b) take no further action in relation to the appeal.

Note: Words in second square brackets in paragraph (1) inserted from 30 April 2006 (SI 2006/1003). Other words in square brackets inserted from 13 November 2006 (SI 2006/2788).

Hearing appeal in absence of a party

19.—(1) The Tribunal [may] hear an appeal in the absence of a party or his representative, if satisfied that—

(a) [the party or his representative] has been given notice of the date, time and place of the hearing, and

[(b) there is no good reason for such absence].

(2) Where paragraph (1) does not apply, the Tribunal may hear an appeal in the absence of a party if satisfied that—

(a) a representative of the party is present at the hearing;

(b) the party is outside the United Kingdom;

(c) the party is suffering from a communicable disease or there is a risk of him behaving in a violent or disorderly manner;

(d) the party is unable to attend the hearing because of illness, accident or some other good reason;

(e) the party is unrepresented and it is impracticable to give him notice of the hearing; or

(f) the party has notified the Tribunal that he does not wish to attend the hearing.

Note: Words in square brackets in sub-para (2)(a) inserted and sub-para (2)(b) substituted from 10 April 2007 (SI 2007/835).

Hearing two or more appeals together

20. Where two or more appeals are pending at the same time, the Tribunal may direct them to be heard together if it appears that—

(a) some common question of law or fact arises in each of them;

(b) they relate to decisions or action taken in respect of persons who are members of the same family; or

(c) for some other reason it is desirable for the appeals to be heard together.

Adjournment of appeals

21.—(1) Where a party applies for an adjournment of a hearing of an appeal, he must—

(a) if practicable, notify all other parties of the application;

(b) show good reason why an adjournment is necessary; and

(c) produce evidence of any fact or matter relied upon in support of the application.

(2) The Tribunal must not adjourn a hearing of an appeal on the application of a party, unless satisfied that the appeal cannot otherwise be justly determined.

(3) The Tribunal must not, in particular, adjourn a hearing on the application of a party in order to allow the party more time to produce evidence, unless satisfied that—

(a) the evidence relates to a matter in dispute in the appeal;

(b) it would be unjust to determine the appeal without permitting the party a further opportunity to produce the evidence; and

(c) where the party has failed to comply with directions for the production of the evidence, he has provided a satisfactory explanation for that failure.

(4) Where the hearing of an appeal is adjourned, the Tribunal will fix a new hearing date which—

(a) shall be not more than 28 days after the original hearing date, unless the Tribunal is satisfied that because of exceptional circumstances the appeal cannot justly be heard within that time; and

(b) shall in any event be not later than is strictly required by the circumstances necessitating the adjournment.

Giving of determination

22.—(1) Except in cases to which rule 23 applies, where the Tribunal determines an appeal it must serve on every party a written determination containing its decision and the reasons for it.

(2) The Tribunal must send its determination—

(a) if the appeal is considered at a hearing, not later than 10 days after the hearing finishes; or

(b) if the appeal is determined without a hearing, not later than 10 days after it is determined.

Special procedures and time limits in asylum appeals

23.—(1) This rule applies to appeals under section 82 of the 2002 Act where—

(a) the appellant is in the United Kingdom; and

(b) the appeal relates, in whole or in part, to an asylum claim.

(2) Subject to paragraph (3)—

(a) where an appeal is to be considered by the Tribunal at a hearing, the hearing must be fixed for a date not more than [35] days after the later of—

(i) the date on which the Tribunal receives the notice of appeal; or

(ii) if the Tribunal makes a preliminary decision under rule 10 (late notice of appeal), the date on which notice of that decision is served on the appellant; and

(b) where an appeal is to be determined without a hearing, the Tribunal must determine it not more than [35] days after the later of those dates.

(3) If the respondent does not file the documents specified in rule 13(1) within the time specified in rule 13 or directions given under that rule—

(a) paragraph (2) does not apply; and

(b) the Tribunal may vary any hearing date that it has already fixed in accordance with paragraph (2)(a), if it is satisfied that it would be unfair to the appellant to proceed with the hearing on the date fixed.

(4) The Tribunal must serve its determination on the respondent—

(a) if the appeal is considered at a hearing, by sending it not later than 10 days after the hearing finishes; or

(b) if the appeal is determined without a hearing, by sending it not later than 10 days after it is determined.

(5) The respondent must—

(a) serve the determination on the appellant—

[(i) if the respondent makes an application for permission to appeal against a decision of the Tribunal, by sending, delivering or personally serving the determination not later than the date on which the respondent makes that application;]

(ii) otherwise, not later than 28 days after receiving the determination from the Tribunal; and

(b) as soon as practicable after serving the determination, notify the Tribunal on what date and by what means it was served.

(6) If the respondent does not give the Tribunal notification under paragraph (5)(b) within 29 days after the Tribunal serves the determination on it, the Tribunal must serve the determination on the appellant as soon as reasonably practicable thereafter.

(7) In paragraph (2) of this rule, references to a hearing do not include a case management review hearing or other preliminary hearing.

Note: Numbers in square brackets substituted from 13 November 2006 (SI 2006/2788). Paragraph (5)(a)(i) substituted from 15 February 2010 (SI 2010/21).

[Costs

23A {(1) Except as provided for in paragraph (2)}, the Tribunal may not make any order in respect of costs (or, in Scotland, expenses) pursuant to section 29 of the Tribunals, Courts and Enforcement Act 2007 (power to award costs).

{(2) If the Tribunal allows an appeal, it may order the respondent to pay to the appellant an amount no greater than—

    (a) any fee paid under the Fees Order that has not been refunded; and

    (b) any fee which the appellant is or may be liable to pay under that Order.}]

Note: Rule 23A inserted from 15 February 2010 (SI 2010/21). Heading amended, words inserted in para (1) and para (2) inserted from 19 December 2011 (SI 2011/2840).

[PART 3

Appeals to the Upper Tribunal

Application for permission to appeal to the Upper Tribunal

24.—(1) A party seeking permission to appeal to the Upper Tribunal must make a written application to the Tribunal for permission to appeal.

[(2) Subject to paragraph (3), an application under paragraph (1) must be sent or delivered to the Tribunal so that it is received no later than 5 days after the date on which the party making the application is deemed to have been served with written reasons for the decision.]

(3) Where an appellant is outside the UK, the time limit for [that person] sending or delivering an application under paragraph (1) is 28 days.

(4) If a person makes an application under paragraph (1) later than the time required by paragraph (2)—

    (a) the Tribunal may extend the time for appealing if satisfied that by reason of special circumstances it would be unjust not to do so; and

    (b) unless the Tribunal extends time under sub-paragraph (a), the Tribunal must not admit the application.

(5) An application under paragraph (1) must—

    (a) identify the decision of the Tribunal to which it relates;

    (b) identify the alleged error or errors of law in the decision; and

    (c) state the result the party making the application is seeking.

Note: Rule 24 substituted from 15 February 2010, (SI 2010/21). Paragraph (2) substituted and words in square brackets in paragraph (3) inserted from 15 February 2010 (SI 2010/44).

Tribunal's consideration of an application for permission to appeal to the Upper Tribunal

25.—(1) On receiving an application for permission to appeal the Tribunal must first consider whether to review the decision in accordance with rule 26.

(2) If the Tribunal decides not to review the decision, or reviews the decision and decides to take no action in relation to the decision, or part of it, the Tribunal must consider whether to give permission to appeal in relation to the decision or that part of it.

(3) The Tribunal must make a decision under paragraph (1) and, where relevant, paragraph (2), no later than 10 days after receiving the application.

[(**4**) Subject to rule 27, the Tribunal must send to the parties—

(a) written reasons for a decision under this rule; and

(b) if the application is refused, notification of the right to make an application to the Upper Tribunal for permission to appeal and the time within which, and the method by which, such application must be made.]

(**5**) The Tribunal may give permission to appeal on limited grounds, but must comply with paragraph (4) in relation to any grounds on which it has refused permission.

Note: Rule 25 substituted from 15 February 2010, (SI 2010/21). Paragraph (5) substituted from 15 February 2010 (SI 2010/44).

Review of a decision

26.—(**1**) The Tribunal may only undertake a review of a decision pursuant to rule 25(2) if it is satisfied that there was an error of law in the decision.

(**2**) Subject to rule 27, the Tribunal must notify the parties in writing of the outcome of any review, and of any right of appeal in relation to the outcome.

(**3**) If the Tribunal takes any action in relation to a decision following a review without first giving every party an opportunity to make representations, the notice under paragraph (2) must state that any party that did not have an opportunity to make representations may apply for such action to be set aside and for the decision to be reviewed again.

Note: Rule 26 substituted from 15 February 2010, (SI 2010/21).

Special procedure for providing notice of a decision relating to an asylum case

27.—(**1**) This Rule applies to an application to the Tribunal for permission to appeal to the Upper Tribunal where—

(a) the appellant is in the United Kingdom at the time the application is made; and

(b) the appeal relates, in whole or in part, to an asylum claim.

(**2**) In cases to which this paragraph applies—

(a) the Tribunal must send the documents mentioned in rule 25(4), or, where appropriate, rule 26(2), to the Secretary of State for the Home Department;

(b) the Secretary of State for the Home Department must serve those documents on the appellant not later than 28 days after receiving them from the Tribunal;

(c) the Secretary of State for the Home Department must, as soon as practicable after serving the documents mentioned in sub-paragraph (b), notify the Tribunal on what date and by what means they were served; and

(d) if the Secretary of State for the Home Department does not give the Tribunal notification under sub-paragraph (c) within 29 days after the Tribunal sends the documents mentioned in rule 25(4), or, where appropriate, rule 26(2) on it, the Tribunal must serve those documents on the appellant as soon as reasonably practicable thereafter.]

Note: Rule 27 substituted from 15 February 2010, (SI 2010/21).

PART 4

Bail

Scope of this Part and interpretation

37.—(1) This Part applies to applications under the Immigration Acts to the Tribunal, by persons detained under those Acts, to be released on bail.

(2) In this Part, 'applicant' means a person applying to the Tribunal to be released on bail.

(3) The parties to a bail application are the applicant and the Secretary of State.

Applications for bail

38.—(1) An application to be released on bail must be made by filing with the Tribunal an application notice in [a form approved for the purpose by the {Senior President *of Tribunals*}.]

(2) The application notice must contain the following details—
    (a) the applicant's—
      (i) full name;
     (ii) date of birth; and
     (iii) date of arrival in the United Kingdom;
    (b) the address of the place where the applicant is detained;
    (c) whether an appeal by the applicant to the Tribunal is pending;
    (d) the address where the applicant will reside if his application for bail is granted, or, if he is unable to give such an address, the reason why an address is not given;
    (e) where the applicant is aged 18 or over, whether he will, if required, agree as a condition of bail to co-operate with electronic monitoring under section 36 of the 2004 Act;
    (f) the amount of the recognizance in which he will agree to be bound;
    (g) the full names, addresses, occupations and dates of birth of any persons who have agreed to act as sureties for the applicant if bail is granted, and the amounts of the recognizances in which they will agree to be bound;
    (h) the grounds on which the application is made and, where a previous application has been refused, full details of any change in circumstances which has occurred since the refusal; and
    (i) whether an interpreter will be required at the hearing, and in respect of what language or dialect.

(3) The application must be signed by the applicant or his representative or, in the case of an applicant who is a child or is for any other reason incapable of acting, by a person acting on his behalf.

Note: Words in square brackets substituted from 13 November 2006 (SI 2006/2788). Words in curly brackets substituted from 15 February 2010 (SI 2010/21). Italicised words in para (1) inserted from 19 December 2011 (SI 2011/2840).

Bail hearing

39.—(1) Where an application for bail is filed, the Tribunal must—
    (a) as soon as reasonably practicable, serve a copy of the application on the Secretary of State; and
    (b) fix a hearing.

(2) If the Secretary of State wishes to contest the application, he must file with the Tribunal and serve on the applicant a written statement of his reasons for doing so—

    (a) not later than 2.00 p.m. on the business day before the hearing; or

    (b) if he was served with notice of the hearing less than 24 hours before that time, as soon as reasonably practicable.

(3) The Tribunal must serve written notice of its decision on—

    (a) the parties; and

    (b) the person having custody of the applicant.

(4) Where bail is granted, the notice must include—

    (a) the conditions of bail; and

    (b) the amount in which the applicant and any sureties are to be bound.

(5) Where bail is refused, the notice must include reasons for the refusal.

Recognizances

40.—(1) The recognizance of an applicant or a surety must be in writing and must state—

    (a) the amount in which he agrees to be bound; and

    (b) that he has read and understood the bail decision and that he agrees to pay that amount of money if the applicant fails to comply with the conditions set out in the bail decision.

(2) The recognizance must be—

    (a) signed by the applicant or surety; and

    (b) filed with the Tribunal.

Release of applicant

41. The person having custody of the applicant must release him upon—

    (a) being served with a copy of the decision to grant bail; and

    (b) being satisfied that any recognizances required as a condition of that decision have been entered into.

Application of this Part to Scotland

42. This Part applies to Scotland with the following modifications—

    (a) in rule 38, for paragraph (2)(f) and (g) substitute—

    '(f) the amount, if any, to be deposited if bail is granted;

    (g) the full names, addresses and occupations of any persons offering to act as cautioners if the application for bail is granted;'

    (b) in rule 39, for paragraph (4)(b) substitute—

    '(b) the amount (if any) to be deposited by the applicant and any cautioners.';

    (c) rule 40 does not apply; and

    (d) in rule 41, for sub-paragraph (b) substitute—

    '(b) being satisfied that the amount to be deposited, if any, has been deposited.'

PART 5

General Provisions

Conduct of appeals and applications

43.—(1) The Tribunal may, subject to these Rules, decide the procedure to be followed in relation to any appeal or application.

(2) Anything of a formal or administrative nature which is required or permitted to be done by the Tribunal under these Rules may be done by a member of the Tribunal's staff.

[(3) Staff appointed under section 40(1) of the Tribunals, Courts and Enforcement Act 2007 (tribunal staff and services) may, with the approval of the Senior President of Tribunals, carry out functions of a judicial nature permitted or required to be done by the Tribunal.

(4) The approval referred to at paragraph (3) may apply generally to the carrying out of specified functions by members of staff of a specified description in specified circumstances.

(5) Within 14 days after the date on which the Tribunal sends notice of a decision made by a member of staff under paragraph (3) to a party, that party may apply in writing to the Tribunal for that decision to be considered afresh by a judge.]

Note: Paragraphs (3)–(5) inserted from 19 December 2011 (SI 2011/2840).

44. . . .

Note: Rule 44 revoked from 15 February 2010 (SI 2010/21).

Directions

45.—(1) The Tribunal may give directions to the parties relating to the conduct of any appeal or application.

(2) The power to give directions is to be exercised subject to any specific provision of these Rules.

(3) Directions must be given orally or in writing to every party.

(4) Directions of the Tribunal may, in particular—

  (a) relate to any matter concerning the preparation for a hearing;

  (b) specify the length of time allowed for anything to be done;

  (c) vary any time limit in these Rules or in directions previously given by the Tribunal for anything to be done by a party [(including, where the Tribunal considers that there are exceptional reasons for doing so, extending a time limit which has expired)];

  (d) provide for—

    (i) a particular matter to be dealt with as a preliminary issue;

    (ii) a case management review hearing to be held;

    (iii) a party to provide further details of his case, or any other information which appears to be necessary for the determination of the appeal;

    (iv) the witnesses, if any, to be heard;

    (v) the manner in which any evidence is to be given (for example, by directing that witness statements are to stand as evidence in chief);

(e) require any party to file and serve—

    (i) statements of the evidence which will be called at the hearing;

    (ii) a paginated and indexed bundle of all the documents which will be relied on at the hearing;

    (iii) a skeleton argument which summarises succinctly the submissions which will be made at the hearing and cites all the authorities which will be relied on, identifying any particular passages to be relied on;

    (iv) a time estimate for the hearing;

    (v) a list of witnesses whom any party wishes to call to give evidence;

    (vi) a chronology of events; and

    (vii) details of whether an interpreter will be required at the hearing, and in respect of what language and dialect;

(f) limit—

    (i) the number or length of documents upon which a party may rely at a hearing;

    (ii) the length of oral submissions;

    (iii) the time allowed for the examination and cross-examination of witnesses; and

    (iv) the issues which are to be addressed at a hearing; and

(g) require the parties to take any steps to enable two or more appeals to be heard together under rule 20.

(h) provide for a hearing to be conducted or evidence given or representations made by video link or by other electronic means; and

(i) make provision to secure the anonymity of a party or a witness.

(5) The Tribunal must not direct an unrepresented party to do something unless it is satisfied that he is able to comply with the direction.

(6) The [Tribunal] may direct that, in individual cases or in such classes of case as he shall specify, any time period in these Rules for the Tribunal to do anything shall be extended by such period as he shall specify.

Note: Words in square brackets inserted from 12 May 2008 (SI 2008/1088). Word in square brackets in paragraph (6) substituted from 15 February 2010 (SI 2010/21).

Notification of hearings

46.—(1) When the Tribunal fixes a hearing it must serve notice of the date, time and place of the hearing on every party.

(2) The Tribunal may vary the date of a hearing, but must serve notice of the new date, time and place of the hearing on every party.

Adjournment

47. Subject to any provision of these Rules, the Tribunal may adjourn any hearing.

Representation

48.—(1) An appellant or applicant for bail may act in person or be represented by any person not prohibited from representing him by section 84 of the Immigration and Asylum Act 1999.

(2) A respondent to an appeal, the Secretary of State or the United Kingdom Representative may be represented by any person authorised to act on his behalf.

(3) If a party to whom paragraph (1) applies is represented by a person not permitted by that paragraph to represent him, any determination given or other step taken by the Tribunal in the proceedings shall nevertheless be valid.

(4) Where a representative begins to act for a party, he must immediately notify the Tribunal and the other party of that fact.

[(4A) Where a notice of appeal, or an application for bail under rule 38, is signed by a representative, the representative will be deemed to have notified the Tribunal and the other party that he is acting for a party in accordance with paragraph (4).

(4B) Where a notice of appeal, or an application for bail under rule 38, is not signed by a representative, the representative must file a separate notice with the Tribunal and serve it on the other party to comply with his obligations under paragraph (4).]

(5) Where a representative is acting for a party, he may on behalf of that party do anything that these Rules require or permit that party to do.

(6) Where a representative is acting for an appellant, the appellant is under a duty—
    (a) to maintain contact with his representative until the appeal is finally determined; and
    (b) to notify the representative of any change of address.

(7) Where a representative ceases to act for a party, the representative and the party must immediately notify the Tribunal and the other party [in writing] of that fact, and of the name and address of any new representative (if known).

(8) Notification under paragraph (4) —
    (a) [where a representative is appointed to act for a party on the day of a hearing,] may be given orally at [that] hearing to the Tribunal and to any other party present at that hearing; but
    (b) must otherwise be given in writing.

(9) Until the Tribunal is notified that a representative has ceased to act for a party, any document served on that representative shall be deemed to be properly served on the party he was representing.

Note: Words in square brackets inserted from 13 November 2006 (SI 2006/2788).

United Kingdom Representative

49.—(1) The United Kingdom Representative may give notice to the Tribunal that he wishes to participate in any proceedings where the appellant has made an asylum claim.

(2) Where the United Kingdom Representative has given notice under paragraph (1)—
    (a) rules 54(6) and 55(7) shall apply; and
    (b) the Tribunal must permit him to make representations in the proceedings if he wishes to do so, and may give directions for that purpose.

[Interpreters

49A. An appellant is entitled to the services of an interpreter—
    (a) when giving evidence; and
    (b) in such other circumstances as the Tribunal considers necessary.]

Note: Rule 49A inserted from 1 December 2007 (SI 2007/3170).

Summoning of witnesses

50.—(1) The Tribunal may, by issuing a summons ('a witness summons'), require any person in the United Kingdom—

(a) to attend as a witness at the hearing of an appeal; and

(b) subject to rule 51(2), at the hearing to answer any questions or produce any documents in his custody or under his control which relate to any matter in issue in the appeal.

(2) A person is not required to attend a hearing in obedience to a witness summons unless—

(a) the summons is served on him; and

(b) the necessary expenses of his attendance are paid or tendered to him.

(3) If a witness summons is issued at the request of a party, that party must pay or tender the expenses referred to in paragraph (2)(b).

Evidence

51.—(1) The Tribunal may allow oral, documentary or other evidence to be given of any fact which appears to be relevant to an appeal or an application for bail, even if that evidence would be inadmissible in a court of law.

(2) The Tribunal may not compel a party or witness to give any evidence or produce any document which he could not be compelled to give or produce at the trial of a civil claim in the part of the United Kingdom in which the hearing is taking place.

(3) The Tribunal may require the oral evidence of a witness to be given on oath or affirmation.

(4) Where the Tribunal has given directions setting time limits for the filing and serving of written evidence, it must not consider any written evidence which is not filed or served in accordance with those directions unless satisfied that there are good reasons to do so.

(5) Where a party seeks to rely upon a copy of a document as evidence, the Tribunal may require the original document to be produced.

(6) In an appeal to which section 85(5) of the 2002 Act applies, the Tribunal must only consider evidence relating to matters which it is not prevented by that section from considering.

(7) Subject to section 108 of the 2002 Act, the Tribunal must not take account of any evidence that has not been made available to all the parties.

Language of documents

52.—(1) Subject to paragraph (2)—

(a) any notice of appeal or application notice filed with the Tribunal must be completed in English; and

(b) any other document filed with the Tribunal must be in English, or accompanied by a translation into English signed by the translator to certify that the translation is accurate.

(2) In proceedings in or having a connection with Wales, a document may be filed with the Tribunal in Welsh.

(3) The Tribunal shall be under no duty to consider a document which is not in English (or, where paragraph (2) applies, in Welsh), or accompanied by a certified translation.

Burden of proof

53.—(1) If an appellant asserts that a relevant decision ought not to have been taken against him on the ground that the statutory provision under which that decision was taken does not apply to him, it is for that party to prove that the provision does not apply to him.

(2) If—

(a) an appellant asserts any fact; and

(b) by virtue of an Act, statutory instrument or immigration rules, if he had made such an assertion to the Secretary of State, an immigration officer or an entry clearance officer, it would have been for him to satisfy the Secretary of State or officer that the assertion was true,

it is for the appellant to prove that the fact asserted is true.

Admission of public to hearings

54.—(1) Subject to the following provisions of this rule, every hearing before the Tribunal must be held in public.

(2) Where the Tribunal is considering an allegation referred to in section 108 of the 2002 Act—

(a) all members of the public must be excluded from the hearing, and

(b) any party or representative of a party may be excluded from the hearing.

(3) The Tribunal may exclude any or all members of the public from any hearing or part of a hearing if it is necessary—

(a) in the interests of public order or national security; or

(b) to protect the private life of a party or the interests of a minor.

(4) The Tribunal may also, in exceptional circumstances, exclude any or all members of the public from any hearing or part of a hearing to ensure that publicity does not prejudice the interests of justice, but only if and to the extent that it is strictly necessary to do so.

(5) A member of the Council on Tribunals or of its Scottish Committee acting in that capacity is entitled to attend any hearing and may not be excluded pursuant to paragraph (2), (3) or (4) of this rule.

(6) The United Kingdom Representative, where he has given notice to the Tribunal under rule 49, is entitled to attend any hearing except where paragraph (2) applies, and may not be excluded pursuant to paragraph (3) or (4) of this rule.

Filing and service of documents

55.—(1) Any document which is required or permitted by these Rules or by a direction of the Tribunal to be filed with the Tribunal, or served on any person may be—

(a) delivered, or sent by post, to an address;

(b) sent via a document exchange to a document exchange number or address;

(c) sent by fax to a fax number;

(d) sent by e-mail to an e-mail address; or

[(e) sent or delivered by any other method.]

specified for that purpose by the Tribunal or person to whom the document is directed.

(2) A document to be served on an individual may be served personally by leaving it with that individual.

(3) Where a person has notified the Tribunal that he is acting as the representative of an appellant and has given an address for service, if a document is served on the appellant, a copy must also at the same time be sent to the appellant's representative.

(4) If any document is served on a person who has notified the Tribunal that he is acting as the representative of a party, it shall be deemed to have been served on that party.

(5) Subject to paragraph (6), any document that is served on a person in accordance with this rule shall, unless the contrary is proved, be deemed to be served—

(a) where the document is sent by post or document exchange from and to a place within the United Kingdom, on the second day after it was sent;

(b) where the document is sent by post or document exchange from or to a place outside the United Kingdom, on the twenty-eighth day after it was sent; and

(c) in any other case, on the day on which the document was sent or delivered to, or left with, that person.

(6) Any notice of appeal which is served on a person under rule 6(3)(b) or 6(4)(b) shall be treated as being served on the day on which it is received by that person.

(7) Where the United Kingdom Representative has given notice to the Tribunal under rule 49 in relation to any proceedings, any document which is required by these Rules or by a direction of the Tribunal to be served on a party in those proceedings must also be served on the United Kingdom Representative.

Note: Sub-paragraph (1)(e) inserted from 19 December 2011 (SI 2011/2840).

Address for service

56.—(1) Every party, and any person representing a party, must notify the Tribunal in writing of a postal address at which documents may be served on him and of any changes to that address.

(2) Until a party or representative notifies the Tribunal of a change of address, any document served on him at the most recent address which he has notified to the Tribunal shall be deemed to have been properly served on him.

[(3) If the respondent knows that the appellant has changed the address referred to in paragraph (1), he must notify the Tribunal in writing of that fact and, if he is aware of it, the new address.]

Note: Paragraph (3) inserted from 12 May 2008 (SI 2008/1088).

Calculation of time

57.—(1) Where a period of time for doing any act is specified by these Rules or by a direction of the Tribunal, that period is to be calculated—

(a) excluding the day on which the period begins; and

(b) where the period is 10 days or less, excluding any day which is not a business day (unless the period is expressed as a period of calendar days).

(2) Where the time specified by these Rules or by a direction of the Tribunal for doing any act ends on a day which is not a business day, that act is done in time if it is done on the next business day.

Signature of documents

58. Any requirement in these Rules for a document to be signed by a party or his representative shall be satisfied, in the case of a document which is filed or served electronically in accordance with these rules, by the person who is required to sign the document typing his name or producing it by computer or other mechanical means.

Errors of procedure

59.—(1) Where, before the Tribunal has determined an appeal or application, there has been an error of procedure such as a failure to comply with a rule—

(a) subject to these Rules, the error does not invalidate any step taken in the proceedings, unless the Tribunal so orders; and

(b) the Tribunal may make any order, or take any other step, that it considers appropriate to remedy the error.

(2) In particular, any determination made in an appeal or application under these Rules shall be valid notwithstanding that—

(a) a hearing did not take place; or

(b) the determination was not made or served,

within a time period specified in these Rules.

Correction of orders and determinations

60.—(1) The Tribunal may at any time amend an order, notice of decision or determination to correct a clerical error or other accidental slip or omission.

[(1A) The [Tribunal] may, either of [its] own motion or on application, review any order, notice of decision or determination made by the Tribunal and, after consulting all the parties to the appeal, may set it aside and direct that the relevant proceedings be dealt with again by the Tribunal, on the ground that it was wrongly made as the result of an administrative error on the part of the Tribunal or its staff.

(1B) An application under paragraph (1A) must be filed—

(a) if the party making the application is in the United Kingdom, within 10 days; or (b) if the party making the application is outside the United Kingdom, within 28 days, of the date on which the party is served with the order, notice of decision or determination.

(1C) At the same time as filing an application under paragraph (1A), the party making the application must serve a copy on the other party to the appeal.

(2) Where an order, notice of decision or determination is amended under this rule—

(a) the Tribunal must serve an amended version on the party or parties on whom it served the original; and

(b) if rule 10(8) and (9), [rule 23(5) and (6)] applied in relation to the service of the original, it shall also apply in relation to the service of the amended version.

(3) The time within which a party may apply for permission to appeal against, or for a review of, an amended determination runs from the date on which the party is served with the amended determination.

Note: Paragraphs (1A)–(1D) inserted from 13 November 2006 (SI 2006/2788), paragraph 1D revoked and words in square brackets substituted from 15 February 2010 (SI 2010/21).

PART 6

Note: Part 6 revoked from 15 February 2010 (SI 2010/21).

The Asylum and Immigration Tribunal (Fast Track Procedure) Rules 2005

(SI 2005, No. 560 [L.12])

ARRANGEMENT OF RULES

PART 1

Introduction

PART 2

Appeals to the Tribunal

PART 3

Appeals to the Upper Tribunal

PART 1

Introduction

Citation and commencement

1. These Rules may be cited as the Asylum and Immigration Tribunal (Fast Track Procedure) Rules 2005 and shall come into force on 4 April 2005.

Interpretation

2.—(1) In these Rules, 'the Principal Rules' means the Asylum and Immigration Tribunal (Procedure) Rules 2005.

(2) Subject to paragraph (3), words and expressions used in these Rules which are defined in rule 2 of the Principal Rules have the same meaning in these Rules as in the Principal Rules.

(3) In these Rules, and in any provision of the Principal Rules which applies by virtue of these Rules, 'business day' means any day other than a Saturday or Sunday, a bank holiday, 24 to 31 December, Maundy Thursday, Good Friday or the Tuesday after the last Monday in May.

(5) Where a provision of the Principal Rules applies by virtue of these Rules—

(a) any reference in that provision to the Principal Rules is to be interpreted as including a reference to these Rules; and

(b) any reference in that provision to a specific Part or rule in the Principal Rules is to be interpreted as including a reference to any equivalent Part or rule in these Rules.

Note: Paragraph (4) omitted from 13 November 2006 (SI 2006/2789).

Scope of these Rules

3.—(1) Part 2 of these Rules applies to appeals to the Tribunal in the circumstances specified in rule 5.

[(2) Part 3 applies to applications to appeal to the Upper Tribunal in the circumstances specified in rule 15.]

(3) Part 4 applies to proceedings before the Tribunal to which Part 2 or 3 applies.

(4) Part 5 applies to proceedings before the Tribunal to which Part 2 or 3 applies or has applied.

(5) For the purpose of rules 5 and 15, a party does not cease to satisfy a condition that he must have been continuously in detention under the Immigration Acts at a place or places specified in Schedule 2 to these Rules by reason only of—

(a) being transported from one place of detention specified in that Schedule to another place which is so specified; or

(b) leaving and returning to such a place of detention for any purpose between the hours of 6 a.m. and 10 p.m.

Note: Paragraph (2) substituted from 15 February 2010 (SI 2010/21).

Application of the Principal Rules

4.—(1) Rule 4 of the Principal Rules (Overriding objective) applies to these Rules.

(2) Where Part 2 or 3 of these Rules applies to proceedings before the Tribunal, the Principal Rules also apply to the extent specified in rules 6, 16, [. . .] and 27 of these Rules.

Note: Numbers omitted from 15 February 2010 (SI 2010/21).

PART 2
Appeals to the Tribunal

Scope of this Part

5.—(1) This Part applies to an appeal to the Tribunal where the person giving notice of appeal—

(a) was in detention under the Immigration Acts at a place specified in Schedule 2 when he was served with notice of the immigration decision against which he is appealing; and

(b) has been continuously in detention under the Immigration Acts at a place or places specified in Schedule 2 since that notice was served on him.

(2) This Part shall cease to apply if the Tribunal makes an order under rule 30(1).

Application of Part 2 of the Principal Rules

6. Where this Part applies to an appeal, the following provisions of Part 2 of the Principal Rules apply—

(a) rule 6(1) to (3), omitting the reference to rule 6(4) in rule 6(2);

(b) rule 8;

(c) rule 10(1);

(d) rule 13(1) and (4);

(e) rule 14;

(f) rules 17 to [19;]

[(g) rule 20, provided that this Part applies to all of the appeals proposed to be heard together.]

[(h) rule 23A].

Note: Paragraph (g) inserted from 12 May 2008 (SI 2008/1089). Paragraph (h) inserted from 15 February 2010 (SI 2010/21).

Giving notice of appeal

7. Where a notice of appeal is served on a custodian under rule 6(3)(b) of the Principal Rules, the custodian must—

(a) endorse on the notice the date that it is served on him; and

(b) forward it to the Tribunal immediately.

Time limit

8.—(1) A person who wishes to appeal must give a notice of appeal not later than 2 days after the day on which he is served with notice of the immigration decision against which he is appealing.

(2) Where a notice of appeal is given outside the time limit in paragraph (1), the Tribunal must not extend the time for appealing unless it is satisfied that, because of circumstances outside the control of the person giving notice of appeal or his representative, it was not practicable for the notice of appeal to be given within that time limit.

Service of notice of appeal on respondent

9. When the Tribunal receives a notice of appeal it shall immediately serve a copy upon the respondent.

Filing of documents by respondent

10. The respondent must file the documents listed in rule 13(1) of the Principal Rules not later than 2 days after the day on which the Tribunal serves the respondent with the notice of appeal.

Listing

11.—(1) The Tribunal shall fix a hearing date which is—

(a) not later than 2 days after the day on which the respondent files the documents under rule 10; or

(b) if the Tribunal is unable to arrange a hearing within that time, as soon as practicable thereafter.

(2) The Tribunal must serve notice of the date, time and place of the hearing on every party as soon as practicable, and in any event not later than noon on the business day before the hearing.

Deciding timeliness issues

12.—(1) The Tribunal shall consider any issue as to—

(a) whether a notice of appeal was given outside the applicable time limit; and

(b) whether to extend the time for appealing where the notice of appeal was given outside that time limit,

as a preliminary issue at the hearing fixed under rule 11, subject to paragraph (2) of this rule.

(2) Rule 13 applies to the consideration and decision of such an issue as it applies to the consideration and determination of an appeal.

(3) Where the notice of appeal was given outside the applicable time limit and the Tribunal does not grant an extension of time, the Tribunal must take no further action in relation to the notice of appeal, except that it must serve [on every party] written notice of its decision under this rule [, including its reasons which may be in summary form] not later than 1 day after the day on which that decision is made.

Note: Words in square brackets inserted from 13 November 2006 (SI 2006/2789).

Method of determining appeal

13. **(1)** The Tribunal must consider the appeal at the hearing fixed under rule 11 except where—

(a) the appeal—

(i) lapses pursuant to section 99 of the 2002 Act;

(ii) is treated as abandoned pursuant to section 104(4) [or (4A)] of the 2002 Act;

(iii) is treated as finally determined pursuant to section 104(5) of the 2002 Act; or

(iv) is withdrawn by the appellant or treated as withdrawn in accordance with rule 17 of the Principal Rules;

(b) the Tribunal adjourns the hearing under rule 28 or 30(2)(a) of these Rules; or

(c) all of the parties to the appeal consent to the Tribunal determining the appeal without a hearing.

[(2) The Tribunal may consider an appeal without a hearing where—

(a) the person giving notice of appeal fails to comply with rule 8(2) of the Principal Rules; or

(b) the Tribunal does not consider that the reasons given under rule 8(2)(b) of those Rules are satisfactory.]

Note: Words in square brackets in paragraph (1) inserted from 13 November 2006 (SI 2006/1279). Paragraph (2) inserted from 12 May 2008 (SI 2008/1089).

Giving of determination

14.—(1) Where the Tribunal determines an appeal, it must give a written determination containing its decision and the reasons for it.

(2) The Tribunal must serve its determination on every party to the appeal—

(a) if the appeal is considered at a hearing, not later than 2 days after the day on which the hearing of the appeal finishes; or

(b) if the appeal is determined without a hearing, not later than 2 days after the day on which it is determined.

[PART 3

Appeals to the Upper Tribunal

Scope of this Part

15.—(1)) This Part applies to applications for permission to appeal to the Upper Tribunal made pursuant to rule 25 of the Principal Rules, where—

(a) Part 2 of these Rules applied at all times to the appeal to the Tribunal; and

(b) the appellant has been continuously in detention under the Immigration Acts at a place or places specified in Schedule 2 to these Rules since being served with notice of the immigration decision that is the subject of the appeal.

(2) This Part shall cease to apply if the Tribunal makes an order under rule 30(1).

Application of the Principal Rules to this Part

16. The following provisions of the Principal Rules apply to proceedings to which this Part applies—

(a) rule 24 except for [paragraphs (2) and (4)]; and

(b) rule 25 except for paragraph (1).

Note: Words in square brackets substituted from 15 February 2010 (SI 2010/44).

Time limits for making an application for permission to appeal

[17.—(1) An application under rule 24(1) of the Principal Rules must be sent or delivered to the Tribunal so that it is received no later than 2 days after the date on which the party is served with written reasons for the decision.

(2) If a person makes an application under rule 24(1) of the Principal Rules later than the time required by paragraph (1)—

(a) the Tribunal may extend the time for appealing if satisfied that by reason of special circumstances it would be unjust not to do so; and

(b) unless the Tribunal extends time under sub-paragraph (a), the Tribunal must not admit the application.]

Note: Rule 17 substituted from 15 February 2010 (SI 2010/44).

Service of permission application decision

18. The Tribunal must send to the parties written reasons for its decision in relation to an application for permission to appeal not later than 1 business day after the application was received by the Tribunal.]

Note: Part 3 substituted from 15 February 2010 (SI 2010/21).

PART 4

General Provisions

Application of Part 5 of the Principal Rules

27. Where this Part applies, Part 5 of the Principal Rules applies, except that—

(a) rule 47 applies subject to rule 28 of these Rules; and

(b) rule 60(2) does not apply.

Adjournment

28. The Tribunal may only adjourn a hearing where—

(a) it is necessary to do so because there is insufficient time to hear the appeal or application which is before the Tribunal;

(b) a party has not been served with notice of the hearing in accordance with these Rules;

(c) the Tribunal is satisfied by evidence filed or given by or on behalf of a party that—

(i) the appeal or application cannot be justly determined on the date on which it is listed for hearing; and

(ii) there is an identifiable future date, not more than 10 days after the date on which the appeal or application is listed for hearing, by which it can be justly determined; or

(d) the Tribunal makes an order under rule 30.

Correction of orders and determinations

29. Where an order, notice of decision or determination is amended under rule 60(1) of the Principal Rules, the Tribunal must, not later than 1 day after making the amendment, serve an amended version on every party on whom it served the original. [Correction of administrative errors

29A Where an order, notice of decision or determination is set aside and the [Tribunal] orders that the relevant proceedings be dealt with again by the Tribunal under rule 60(1A) of the Principal Rules, the Tribunal must, not later than 1 day after making the order, notify every party of its decision.]

Note: Rule 29A inserted from 13 November 2006 (SI 2006/2789). Word in square brackets substituted from 15 February 2010 (SI 2010/21).

PART 5
Removal of Pending Proceedings from Fast Track

Transfer out of fast track procedure

30.—(1) Where Part 2 or 3 of these Rules applies to an appeal or application, the Tribunal must order that that Part shall cease to apply—

(a) if all the parties consent;

(b) if it is satisfied by evidence filed or given by or on behalf of a party that there are exceptional circumstances which mean that the appeal or application cannot otherwise be justly determined; or

(c) if—

(i) the respondent to the appeal has failed to comply with a provision of these Rules, or the Principal Rules as applied by these Rules, or a direction of the Tribunal; and

(ii) the Tribunal is satisfied that the appellant would be prejudiced by that failure if the appeal or application were determined in accordance with these Rules.

(**2**) When making an order under paragraph (1), the Tribunal may—
  (a) adjourn any hearing of the appeal or application; and
  (b) give directions relating to the further conduct of the appeal or application.

(**3**) Where the Tribunal adjourns a hearing under paragraph (2)(a)—
  (a) it must fix a new date, time and place for the hearing; and
  (b) in the case of an adjournment of an appeal, rule 21(4) of the Principal Rules shall apply.

Application of the Principal Rules on transfer out of fast track

31.—(**1**) This rule applies where Part 2 or 3 of these Rules ceases to apply to an appeal or application because—
  (a) the conditions in rule 5 or 15 cease to apply; or
  (b) the Tribunal makes an order under rule 30(1).

(**2**) Subject to paragraph (3), the Principal Rules shall apply to the appeal or application from the date on which these Rules cease to apply.

(**3**) Where—
  (a) a period of time for doing something has started to run under a provision of these Rules; and
  (b) that provision ceases to apply, if the Principal Rules contain a time limit for doing the same thing, the time limit in the Principal Rules shall apply, and the relevant period of time shall be treated as running from the date on which the period of time under these Rules started to run.

PART 6

Note: Part 6 revoked from 15 February 2010 (SI 2010/21).

| Rules 5 and 15 | SCHEDULE 2 |

SPECIFIED PLACES OF DETENTION

Harmondsworth Immigration Removal Centre, Harmondsworth, Middlesex
[Oakington Reception Centre, Longstanton, Cambridgeshire]
Campsfield House Immigration Removal Centre, Kidlington, Oxfordshire
Colnbrook House Immigration Removal Centre, Harmondsworth, Middlesex
Yarls Wood Immigration Removal Centre, Clapham, Bedfordshire

Note: Words in square brackets inserted from 12 May 2008 (SI 2008/1089).

The Tribunal Procedure (Upper Tribunal) Rules 2008
(SI 2008 No. 2698 [L. 15])

Contents

PART 4
Judicial review proceedings in the Upper Tribunal

PART 5
Hearings

PART 6
Decisions

PART 7
Correcting, setting aside, reviewing and appealing decisions of the Upper Tribunal

SCHEDULES

PART I

Introduction

Citation, commencement, application and interpretation

1.—(1) These Rules may be cited as the Tribunal Procedure (Upper Tribunal) Rules 2008 and came into force on 3rd November 2008.

(2) These Rules apply to proceedings before the Upper Tribunal [except proceedings in the Lands Chamber].

(3) In these Rules—
'the 2007 Act' means the Tribunals, Courts and Enforcement Act 2007;
['appellant' means—
(a) a person who makes an appeal, or applies for permission to appeal, to the Upper Tribunal;
(b) in proceedings transferred or referred to the Upper Tribunal from the First-tier Tribunal, a person who started the proceedings in the First-tier Tribunal; or
(c) a person substituted as an appellant under rule 9(1) (substitution and addition of parties);]
['applicant' means—
(a) a person who applies for permission to bring, or does bring, judicial review proceedings before the Upper Tribunal and, in judicial review proceedings transferred to the Upper Tribunal from a court, includes a person who was a claimant or petitioner in the proceedings immediately before they were transferred; or
(b) a person who refers a financial services case to the Upper Tribunal;]
['appropriate national authority' means, in relation to an appeal, the Secretary of State, the Scottish Ministers[, the Department of the Environment in Northern Ireland] or the Welsh Ministers, as the case may be;

['asylum case' means proceedings before the Upper Tribunal on appeal against a decision in proceedings under section 82, 83 or 83A of the Nationality, Immigration and Asylum Act 2002 in which a person claims that removal from, or a requirement to leave, the United Kingdom would breach the United Kingdom's obligations under the Convention relating to the Status of Refugees done at Geneva on 28 July 1951 and the Protocol to the Convention;]

['authorised person' means—
(a) an examiner appointed by the Secretary of State under section 66A of the Road Traffic Act 1988;
(b) an examiner appointed by the Department of the Environment in Northern Ireland under Article 74 of the Road Traffic (Northern Ireland) Order 1995; or
(c) any person authorised in writing by the Department of the Environment in Northern Ireland for the purposes of the Goods Vehicles (Licensing of Operators) Act (Northern

Ireland) 2010; and includes a person acting under the direction of such an examiner or other authorised person, who has detained the vehicle to which an appeal relates;]…

'dispose of proceedings' includes, unless indicated otherwise, disposing of a part of the proceedings;

'document' means anything in which information is recorded in any form, and an obligation under these Rules or any practice direction or direction to provide or allow access to a document or a copy of a document for any purpose means, unless the Upper Tribunal directs otherwise, an obligation to provide or allow access to such document or copy in a legible form or in a form which can be readily made into a legible form;

'fast-track case' means an asylum case or an immigration case where the person who appealed to the First-tier Tribunal—

(a) was detained under the Immigration Acts at a place specified in Schedule 2 to the Asylum and Immigration Tribunal (Fast-track Procedure) Rules 2005 when the notice of decision that was the subject of the appeal to the First-tier Tribunal was served on the appellant;

(b) remains so detained; and

(c) the First-tier Tribunal or the Upper Tribunal has not directed that the case cease to be treated as a fast-track case;]

['financial services case' means a reference to the Upper Tribunal in respect of—

(a) a decision of the Financial Services Authority;

(b) a decision of the Bank of England;

(c) a decision of the Pensions Regulator; or

(d) a decision of a person relating to the assessment of any compensation or consideration under the Banking (Special Provisions) Act 2008 or the Banking Act 2009;] or

[(e) any determination, calculation or dispute which may be referred to the Upper Tribunal under the Financial Services and Markets Act 2000 (Contribution to Costs of Special Resolution Regime) Regulations 2010(b) (and in these Rules a decision in respect of which a reference has been made to the Upper Tribunal in a financial services case includes any such determination, calculation or, except for the purposes of rule 5(5), dispute relating to the making of payments under the Regulations);]

['fresh claim proceedings' means judicial review proceedings which call into question a decision of the Secretary of State not to treat submissions as an asylum claim or a human rights claim within the meaning of Part 5 of the Nationality, Immigration and Asylum Act 2002(a) wholly or partly on the basis that they are not significantly different from material that has previously been considered, and which have been begun in or transferred to the Upper Tribunal pursuant to a direction made by the Lord Chief Justice of England and Wales for the purposes of section 18(6) of the 2007 Act;]

'hearing' means an oral hearing and includes a hearing conducted in whole or in part by video link, telephone or other means of instantaneous two-way electronic communication;

['immigration case' means proceedings before the Upper Tribunal on appeal against a decision in proceedings under section 40A of the British Nationality Act 1981, section 82 of the Nationality, Immigration and Asylum Act 2002, or regulation 26 of the Immigration (European Economic Area) Regulations 2006 that are not an asylum case;]

'interested party' means—

(a) a person who is directly affected by the outcome sought in judicial review proceedings, and has been named as an interested party under rule 28 or 29 (judicial review), or has been substituted or added as an interested party under rule 9 [(addition, substitution and removal of parties)];

(b) in judicial review proceedings transferred to the Upper Tribunal under section 25A(2) or (3) of the Judicature (Northern Ireland) Act 1978 or section 31A(2) or (3) of the Supreme Court Act 1981, a person who was an interested party in the proceedings immediately before they were transferred to the Upper Tribunal;

[and

(c) in a financial services case, any person other than the applicant who could have referred the case to the Upper Tribunal and who has been added or substituted as an interested party under rule 9 (addition, substitution and removal of parties);]

'judicial review proceedings' means proceedings within the jurisdiction of the Upper Tribunal pursuant to section 15 or 21 of the 2007 Act, whether such proceedings are started in the Upper Tribunal or transferred to the Upper Tribunal;

...

'mental health case' means proceedings before the Upper Tribunal on appeal against a decision in proceedings under the Mental Health Act 1983 or paragraph 5(2) of the Schedule to the Repatriation of Prisoners Act 1984;

['national security certificate appeal' means an appeal under section 28 of the Data Protection Act 1998 or section 60 of the Freedom of Information Act 2000 (including that section as applied and modified by regulation 18 of the Environmental Information Regulations 2004);]

'party' means a person who is an appellant, an applicant, a respondent or an interested party in proceedings before the Upper Tribunal, a person who has referred a question [or matter] to the Upper Tribunal or, if the proceedings have been concluded, a person who was an appellant, an applicant, a respondent or an interested party when the Tribunal finally disposed of all issues in the proceedings;

'permission' includes leave in cases arising under the law of Northern Ireland;

'practice direction' means a direction given under section 23 of the 2007 Act;

['reference', in a financial services case, includes an appeal;]

['relevant minister' means the Minister or designated person responsible for the signing of the certificate to which a national security certificate appeal relates;]

'respondent' means—

(a) in an appeal, or application for permission to appeal, against a decision of another tribunal, any person other than the appellant who—

(i) was a party before that other tribunal;

(ii) ...

(iii) otherwise has a right of appeal against the decision of the other tribunal and has given notice to the Upper Tribunal that they wish to be a party to the appeal;

(b) in an appeal [other than a road transport case], the person who made the decision;

(c) in judicial review proceedings—

(i) in proceedings started in the Upper Tribunal, the person named by the applicant as the respondent;

(ii) in proceedings transferred to the Upper Tribunal under section 25A(2) or (3) of the Judicature (Northern Ireland) Act 1978 or section 31A(2) or (3) of the Supreme Court Act 1981, a person who was a defendant in the proceedings immediately before they were transferred;

(iii) in proceedings transferred to the Upper Tribunal under section 20(1) of the 2007 Act, a person to whom intimation of the petition was made before the proceedings were transferred, or to whom the Upper Tribunal has required intimation to be made.

[(ca) in proceedings transferred or referred to the Upper Tribunal from the First-tier Tribunal, a person who was a respondent in the proceedings in the First-tier Tribunal;]

(d) in a reference under the Forfeiture Act 1982, the person whose eligibility for a benefit or advantage is in issue;

[(da) in a financial services case, the maker of the decision in respect of which a reference has been made; or]

(e) a person substituted or added as a respondent under rule 9 (substitution and addition of parties);

['road transport case' means an appeal against a decision of a traffic commissioner or the Department of the Environment in Northern Ireland;]

['tribunal' does not include a traffic commissioner;]

...

'working day' means any day except a Saturday or Sunday, Christmas Day, Good Friday or a bank holiday under section 1 of the Banking and Financial Dealings Act 1971.

Note: Words in square brackets in paragraph (2), definitions of 'appropriate national authority', 'authorised person' and 'tribunal' and words in square brackets in sub-paragraph (b) of definition of respondent inserted from 1 September 2009 (SI 2009/1975). Definition of appellant substituted, definitions of 'disability discrimination in schools cases', 'legal representative', 'special education needs case' omitted and in definition of respondent subparagraph (a)(ii) omitted and (ca) inserted from 1 April 2009 (SI 2009/274). Definitions of 'national security certificate appeal' and 'relevant minister' inserted from 18 January 2010 (SI 2010/43). Definitions of 'asylum case', 'immigration case' and 'fast-track case' inserted from 15 February 2010 (SI 2010/44). Definition of 'applicant' and words in square brackets in sub-para (a) of definition of interested party substituted; definitions of 'financial services case' and 'reference', sub-para (c) of definition of interested party. Words in square brackets in definition of party and sub-para (da) in definition of respondent inserted from 6 April 2010 (SI 2010/747). Sub-paragraph (e) in definition of 'financial services case' inserted from 1 April 2011 (SI 2011/651). Definition of 'fresh claim proceedings' inserted from 17 October 2011 (SI 2011/2343). Words inserted in the definition of 'appropriate national authority', definition of 'authorised person' substituted, definition of 'respondent' further amended and definition of 'road transport case' inserted from 1 July 2012 (SI 2012/1363).

Overriding objective and parties' obligation to co-operate with the Upper Tribunal

2.—(1) The overriding objective of these Rules is to enable the Upper Tribunal to deal with cases fairly and justly.

(2) Dealing with a case fairly and justly includes—

(a) dealing with the case in ways which are proportionate to the importance of the case, the complexity of the issues, the anticipated costs and the resources of the parties;

(b) avoiding unnecessary formality and seeking flexibility in the proceedings;

(c) ensuring, so far as practicable, that the parties are able to participate fully in the proceedings;

(d) using any special expertise of the Upper Tribunal effectively; and

(e) avoiding delay, so far as compatible with proper consideration of the issues.

(3) The Upper Tribunal must seek to give effect to the overriding objective when it—

(a) exercises any power under these Rules; or

(b) interprets any rule or practice direction.

(4) Parties must—

(a) help the Upper Tribunal to further the overriding objective; and

(b) co-operate with the Upper Tribunal generally.

Alternative dispute resolution and arbitration

3.—(1) The Upper Tribunal should seek, where appropriate—

(a) to bring to the attention of the parties the availability of any appropriate alternative procedure for the resolution of the dispute; and

(b) if the parties wish and provided that it is compatible with the overriding objective, to facilitate the use of the procedure.

(2) Part 1 of the Arbitration Act 1996 does not apply to proceedings before the Upper Tribunal.

PART 2
General powers and provisions

Delegation to staff

4.—(1) Staff appointed under section 40(1) of the 2007 Act (tribunal staff and services) may, with the approval of the Senior President of Tribunals, carry out functions of a judicial nature permitted or required to be done by the Upper Tribunal.

(2) The approval referred to at paragraph (1) may apply generally to the carrying out of specified functions by members of staff of a specified description in specified circumstances.

(3) Within 14 days after the date on which the Upper Tribunal sends notice of a decision made by a member of staff under paragraph (1) to a party, that party may apply in writing to the Upper Tribunal for that decision to be considered afresh by a judge.

Case management powers

5.—(1) Subject to the provisions of the 2007 Act and any other enactment, the Upper Tribunal may regulate its own procedure.

(2) The Upper Tribunal may give a direction in relation to the conduct or disposal of proceedings at any time, including a direction amending, suspending or setting aside an earlier direction.

(3) In particular, and without restricting the general powers in paragraphs (1) and (2), the Upper Tribunal may—

(a) extend or shorten the time for complying with any rule, practice direction or direction;

(b) consolidate or hear together two or more sets of proceedings or parts of proceedings raising common issues, or treat a case as a lead case;

(c) permit or require a party to amend a document;

(d) permit or require a party or another person to provide documents, information, evidence or submissions to the Upper Tribunal or a party;

(e) deal with an issue in the proceedings as a preliminary issue;

(f) hold a hearing to consider any matter, including a case management issue;

(g) decide the form of any hearing;

(h) adjourn or postpone a hearing;

(i) require a party to produce a bundle for a hearing;

(j) stay (or, in Scotland, sist) proceedings;

(k) transfer proceedings to another court or tribunal if that other court or tribunal has jurisdiction in relation to the proceedings; and—

(i) because of a change of circumstances since the proceedings were started, the Upper Tribunal no longer has jurisdiction in relation to the proceedings; or

(ii) the Upper Tribunal considers that the other court or tribunal is a more appropriate forum for the determination of the case;

(l) suspend the effect of its own decision pending an appeal or review of that decision;

(m) in an appeal, or an application for permission to appeal, against the decision of another tribunal, suspend the effect of that decision pending the determination of the application for permission to appeal, and any appeal;

[(n) require any person, body or other tribunal whose decision is the subject of proceedings before the Upper Tribunal to provide reasons for the decision, or other information or documents in relation to the decision or any proceedings before that person, body or tribunal.]

[(4) The Upper Tribunal may direct that a fast -track case cease to be treated as a fast-track case if—

(a) all the parties consent;

(b) the Upper Tribunal is satisfied that there are exceptional circumstances which suggest that the appeal or application could not be justly determined if it were treated as a fast -track case; or

(c) the Secretary of State for the Home Department has failed to comply with a provision of these Rules or a direction of the First-tier Tribunal or the Upper Tribunal, and the Upper Tribunal is satisfied that the other party would be prejudiced if the appeal or application were treated as a fast -track case.]

[(5) In a financial services case, the Upper Tribunal may direct that the effect of the decision in respect of which the reference has been made is to be suspended pending the determination of the reference, if it is satisfied that to do so would not prejudice—

(a) the interests of any persons (whether consumers, investors or otherwise) intended to be protected by that notice; or

(b) the smooth operation or integrity of any market intended to be protected by that notice.

(6) Paragraph (5) does not apply in the case of a reference in respect of a decision of the Pensions Regulator.].

Note: Paragraph (3)(n) substituted from 1 September 2009 (SI 2009/1975). Paragraph (4) inserted from 15 February 2010 (SI 2010/44). Paragraph (5) inserted from 6 April 2010 (SI 2010/747).

Procedure for applying for and giving directions

6.—(1) The Upper Tribunal may give a direction on the application of one or more of the parties or on its own initiative.

(2) An application for a direction may be made—

    (a) by sending or delivering a written application to the Upper Tribunal; or

    (b) orally during the course of a hearing.

(3) An application for a direction must include the reason for making that application.

(4) Unless the Upper Tribunal considers that there is good reason not to do so, the Upper Tribunal must send written notice of any direction to every party and to any other person affected by the direction.

(5) If a party or any other person sent notice of the direction under paragraph (4) wishes to challenge a direction which the Upper Tribunal has given, they may do so by applying for another direction which amends, suspends or sets aside the first direction.

Failure to comply with rules etc.

7.—(1) An irregularity resulting from a failure to comply with any requirement in these Rules, a practice direction or a direction, does not of itself render void the proceedings or any step taken in the proceedings.

(2) If a party has failed to comply with a requirement in these Rules, a practice direction or a direction, the Upper Tribunal may take such action as it considers just, which may include—

    (a) waiving the requirement;

    (b) requiring the failure to be remedied;

    (c) exercising its power under rule 8 (striking out a party's case); or

    (d) except in [a mental health case, an asylum case or an immigration case], restricting a party's participation in the proceedings.

(3) Paragraph (4) applies where the First-tier Tribunal has referred to the Upper Tribunal a failure by a person to comply with a requirement imposed by the First-tier Tribunal—

    (a) to attend at any place for the purpose of giving evidence;

    (b) otherwise to make themselves available to give evidence;

    (c) to swear an oath in connection with the giving of evidence;

    (d) to give evidence as a witness;

    (e) to produce a document; or

    (f) to facilitate the inspection of a document or any other thing (including any premises).

(4) The Upper Tribunal may exercise its power under section 25 of the 2007 Act (supplementary powers of the Upper Tribunal) in relation to such non-compliance as if the requirement had been imposed by the Upper Tribunal.

Note: Words in square brackets in paragraph (2)(d) inserted from 15 February 2010 (SI 2010/44).

Striking out a party's case

8.—[(1A) Except for paragraph (2), this rule does not apply to an asylum case or an immigration case.]

[(1) The proceedings, or the appropriate part of them, will automatically be struck out—

(a) if the appellant or applicant has failed to comply with a direction that stated that failure by the appellant or applicant to comply with the direction would lead to the striking out of the proceedings or part of them; or

(b) when a fee has not been paid upon the grant of permission in fresh claim proceedings as required.]

(2) The Upper Tribunal must strike out the whole or a part of the proceedings if the Upper Tribunal—

(a) does not have jurisdiction in relation to the proceedings or that part of them; and

(b) does not exercise its power under rule 5(3)(k)(i) (transfer to another court or tribunal) in relation to the proceedings or that part of them.

(3) The Upper Tribunal may strike out the whole or a part of the proceedings if—

(a) the appellant or applicant has failed to comply with a direction which stated that failure by the appellant or applicant to comply with the direction could lead to the striking out of the proceedings or part of them;

(b) the appellant or applicant has failed to co-operate with the Upper Tribunal to such an extent that the Upper Tribunal cannot deal with the proceedings fairly and justly; or

(c) in proceedings which are not an appeal from the decision of another tribunal or judicial review proceedings, the Upper Tribunal considers there is no reasonable prospect of the appellant's or the applicant's case, or part of it, succeeding.

(4) The Upper Tribunal may not strike out the whole or a part of the proceedings under paragraph (2) or (3)(b) or (c) without first giving the appellant or applicant an opportunity to make representations in relation to the proposed striking out.

(5) If the proceedings have been struck out under paragraph (1) or (3)(a), the appellant or applicant may apply for the proceedings, or part of them, to be reinstated.

(6) An application under paragraph (5) must be made in writing and received by the Upper Tribunal within 1 month after the date on which the Upper Tribunal sent notification of the striking out to the appellant or applicant.

(7) This rule applies to a respondent [or an interested party] as it applies to an appellant or applicant except that—

(a) a reference to the striking out of the proceedings is to be read as a reference to the barring of the respondent [or interested party] from taking further part in the proceedings; and

(b) a reference to an application for the reinstatement of proceedings which have been struck out is to be read as a reference to an application for the lifting of the bar on the respondent [or interested party] ... taking further part in the proceedings.

(8) If a respondent [or an interested party] has been barred from taking further part in proceedings under this rule and that bar has not been lifted, the Upper Tribunal need not consider any response or other submission made by that respondent [or interested party, and may summarily determine any or all issues against that respondent or interested party].

Note: Paragraph (1A) inserted from 15 February 2010 (SI 2010/44). Words in square brackets in paragraphs (7)–(8) inserted from 1 April 2009 (SI 2009/274). Paragraph 1 substituted from 17 October 2011 (SI 2011/2343).

[Addition, substitution and removal of parties

9.—(1) The Upper Tribunal may give a direction adding, substituting or removing a party as an appellant, a respondent or an interested party.

(2) If the Upper Tribunal gives a direction under paragraph (1) it may give such consequential directions as it considers appropriate.

(3) A person who is not a party may apply to the Upper Tribunal to be added or substituted as a party.

(4) If a person who is entitled to be a party to proceedings by virtue of another enactment applies to be added as a party, and any conditions applicable to that entitlement have been satisfied, the Upper Tribunal must give a direction adding that person as a respondent or, if appropriate, as an appellant.]

[(5) In an asylum case, the United Kingdom Representative of the United Nations High Commissioner for Refugees ('the United Kingdom Representative') may give notice to the Upper Tribunal that the United Kingdom Representative wishes to participate in the proceedings.

(6) If the United Kingdom Representative gives notice under paragraph (5)—

(i) the United Kingdom Representative is entitled to participate in any hearing; and

(ii) all documents which are required to be sent or delivered to parties must be sent or delivered to the United Kingdom Representative.]

Note: Rule 9 substituted from 1 September 2009 (SI 2009/1975). Paragraph (5) inserted from 15 February 2010 (SI 2010/44).

[Orders for costs

10.—(1) The Upper Tribunal may not make an order in respect of costs (or, in Scotland, expenses) in proceedings [transferred or referred by, or on appeal from,] another tribunal except—

[(aa) in a national security certificate appeal, to the extent permitted by paragraph (1A);]

(a) in proceedings [transferred by, or on appeal from,] the Tax Chamber of the First-tier Tribunal; or

(b) to the extent and in the circumstances that the other tribunal had the power to make an order in respect of costs (or, in Scotland, expenses).

[(1A) In a national security certificate appeal—

(a) the Upper Tribunal may make an order in respect of costs or expenses in the circumstances described at paragraph (3)(c) and (d);

(b) if the appeal is against a certificate, the Upper Tribunal may make an order in respect of costs or expenses against the relevant Minister and in favour of the appellant if the Upper Tribunal allows the appeal and quashes the certificate to any extent or the Minister withdraws the certificate;

(c) if the appeal is against the application of a certificate, the Upper Tribunal may make an order in respect of costs or expenses—

(i) against the appellant and in favour of any other party if the Upper Tribunal dismisses the appeal to any extent; or

(ii) in favour of the appellant and against any other party if the Upper Tribunal allows the appeal to any extent.]

(2) The Upper Tribunal may not make an order in respect of costs or expenses under section 4 of the Forfeiture Act 1982.

(3) In other proceedings, the Upper Tribunal may not make an order in respect of costs or expenses except—

(a) in judicial review proceedings;

(b) ...;

(c) under section 29(4) of the 2007 Act (wasted costs);

(d) if the Upper Tribunal considers that a party or its representative has acted unreasonably in bringing, defending or conducting the proceedings [; or

(e) if, in a financial services case, the Upper Tribunal considers that the decision in respect of which the reference was made was unreasonable.]

(4) The Upper Tribunal may make an order for costs (or, in Scotland, expenses) on an application or on its own initiative.

(5) A person making an application for an order for costs or expenses must—

(a) send or deliver a written application to the Upper Tribunal and to the person against whom it is proposed that the order be made; and

(b) send or deliver with the application a schedule of the costs or expenses claimed sufficient to allow summary assessment of such costs or expenses by the Upper Tribunal.

6) An application for an order for costs or expenses may be made at any time during the proceedings but may not be made later than 1 month after the date on which the Upper Tribunal sends—

(a) a decision notice recording the decision which finally disposes of all issues in the proceedings; or

(b) notice of a withdrawal under rule 17 which ends the proceedings.

7) The Upper Tribunal may not make an order for costs or expenses against a person (the 'paying person') without first—

(a) giving that person an opportunity to make representations; and

(b) if the paying person is an individual and the order is to be made under paragraph (3)(a), (b) or (d), considering that person's financial means.

8) The amount of costs or expenses to be paid under an order under this rule may be ascertained by—

(a) summary assessment by the Upper Tribunal;

(b) agreement of a specified sum by the paying person and the person entitled to receive the costs or expenses ('the receiving person'); or

(c) assessment of the whole or a specified part of the costs or expenses incurred by the receiving person, if not agreed.

9) Following an order for assessment under paragraph (8)(c), the paying person or the receiving person may apply—

(a) in England and Wales, to the High Court or the Costs Office of the Supreme Court (as specified in the order) for a detailed assessment of the costs on the standard basis or, if specified in the order, on the indemnity basis; and the Civil Procedure Rules 1998 shall apply, with necessary modifications, to that application and assessment as if the proceedings in the tribunal had been proceedings in a court to which the Civil Procedure Rules 1998 apply;

(b) in Scotland, to the Auditor of the Court of Session for the taxation of the expenses according to the fees payable in that court; or

(c) in Northern Ireland, to the Taxing Office of the High Court of Northern Ireland for taxation on the standard basis or, if specified in the order, on the indemnity basis.]

Note: Rule 10 substituted from 1 April 2009 (SI 2009/274). Words in square brackets in paragraph (1) and (1)(a) substituted and paragraph (3)(a) omitted from 1 September 2009 (SI 2009/1975). Paragraph(1)(aa) and (1A) inserted from 18 January 2010 (SI 2010/43). Paragraph (3)(e) inserted from 6 April 2010 (SI 2010/747).

Representatives

11.—(1) [Subject to paragraph 5A] a party may appoint a representative (whether a legal representative or not) to represent that party in the proceedings [save that a party in an asylum or immigration case may not be represented by any person prohibited from representing by section 84 of the Immigration and Asylum Act 1999].

(2) If a party appoints a representative, that party (or the representative if the representative is a legal representative) must send or deliver to the Upper Tribunal ... written notice of the representative's name and address.

[(2A) If the Upper Tribunal receives notice that a party has appointed a representative under paragraph (2), it must send a copy of that notice to each other party.]

(3) Anything permitted or required to be done by a party under these Rules, a practice direction or a direction may be done by the representative of that party, except signing a witness statement.

(4) A person who receives due notice of the appointment of a representative—

(a) must provide to the representative any document which is required to be provided to the represented party, and need not provide that document to the represented party; and

(b) may assume that the representative is and remains authorised as such until they receive written notification that this is not so from the representative or the represented party.

(5) [Subject to paragraph (5B)] At a hearing a party may be accompanied by another person whose name and address has not been notified under paragraph (2) but who, subject to paragraph (8) and with the permission of the Upper Tribunal, may act as a representative or otherwise assist in presenting the party's case at the hearing.

[(5A) In fresh claim proceedings, a party may appoint as a representative only a person authorised under the Legal Services Act 2007(c) to undertake the conduct of litigation in the High Court.]

[(5B) At a hearing of fresh claim proceedings, rights of audience before the Upper Tribunal are restricted to persons authorised to exercise those rights in the High Court under the Legal Services Act 2007.]

(6) Paragraphs (2) to (4) do not apply to a person who accompanies a party under paragraph (5).

(7) In a mental health case if the patient has not appointed a representative the Upper Tribunal may appoint a legal representative for the patient where—

(a) the patient has stated that they do not wish to conduct their own case or that they wish to be represented; or

(b) the patient lacks the capacity to appoint a representative but the Upper Tribunal believes that it is in the patient's best interests for the patient to be represented.

(8) In a mental health case a party may not appoint as a representative, or be represented or assisted at a hearing by—

(a) a person liable to be detained or subject to guardianship or after-care under supervision, or who is a community patient, under the Mental Health Act 1983; or

(b) a person receiving treatment for mental disorder at the same hospital [or] home as the patient.

[(9) In this rule 'legal representative' means [a person who, for the purposes of the Legal Services Act 2007, is an authorised person in relation to an activity which constitutes the exercise of a right of audience or the conduct of litigation within the meaning of that Act] [a qualified person as defined in section 84(2) of the Immigration and Asylum Act 1999,] an advocate or solicitor in Scotland or a barrister or solicitor in Northern Ireland.]

[(10) In an asylum case or an immigration case, an appellant's representative before the First-tier Tribunal will be treated as that party's representative before the Upper Tribunal, unless the Upper Tribunal receives notice—

(a) of a new representative under paragraph (2) of this rule; or

(b) from the appellant stating that they are no longer represented.]

Note: Words omitted from paragraph (2), paragraphs (2A) and (9) inserted from 1 April 2009 (SI 2009/274). Word in square brackets in paragraph (8)(b) inserted from 1 September 2009 (SI 2009/275). Words in first square brackets in paragraph (9) substituted from 18 January 2010 (SI 2010/43). Paragraph (10), words in square brackets in paragraph (1) and second square brackets in paragraph (9) inserted from 15 February 2010 (SI 2010/44). Words inserted in paragraphs (1) and (5) and paragraphs (5A) and (5B) inserted from 17 October 2011 (SI 2011/2343).

Calculating time

12.—(1) An act required by these Rules, a practice direction or a direction to be done on or by a particular day must be done by 5pm on that day.

(2) If the time specified by these Rules, a practice direction or a direction for doing any act ends on a day other than a working day, the act is done in time if it is done on the next working day.

(3) In a special educational needs case or a disability discrimination in schools case, the following days must not be counted when calculating the time by which an act must be done—

(a) 25th December to 1st January inclusive; and

(b) any day in August.

[(3A) In an asylum case or an immigration case, when calculating the time by which an act must be done, in addition to the days specified in the definition of 'working days' in rule 1 (interpretation), the following days must also not be counted as working days—

(a) 27th to 31st December inclusive; and

(b) in a fast-track case, 24th December, Maundy Thursday or the Tuesday after the last Monday in May.]

(4) Paragraph (3) [or (3A)] does not apply where the Upper Tribunal directs that an act must be done by or on a specified date.

[(5) In this rule—

'disability discrimination in schools case' means proceedings concerning disability discrimination in the education of a child or related matters; and

'special educational needs case' means proceedings concerning the education of a child who has or may have special educational needs.]

Note: Paragraph (5) inserted from 1 April 2009 (SI 2009/274). Paragraph (3A) and words in square brackets in paragraph (4) inserted from 15 February 2010 (SI 2010/44).

Sending and delivery of documents

13.—(1) Any document to be provided to the Upper Tribunal under these Rules, a practice direction or a direction must be—

(a) sent by pre-paid post or [by document exchange, or delivered by hand,] to the address specified for the proceedings;

(b) sent by fax to the number specified for the proceedings; or

(c) sent or delivered by such other method as the Upper Tribunal may permit or direct.

(2) Subject to paragraph (3), if a party provides a fax number, email address or other details for the electronic transmission of documents to them, that party must accept delivery of documents by that method.

(3) If a party informs the Upper Tribunal and all other parties that a particular form of communication, other than pre-paid post or delivery by hand, should not be used to provide documents to that party, that form of communication must not be so used.

(4) If the Upper Tribunal or a party sends a document to a party or the Upper Tribunal by email or any other electronic means of communication, the recipient may request that the sender provide a hard copy of the document to the recipient. The recipient must make such a request as soon as reasonably practicable after receiving the document electronically.

(5) The Upper Tribunal and each party may assume that the address provided by a party or its representative is and remains the address to which documents should be sent or delivered until receiving written notification to the contrary.

[(6) Subject to paragraph (7), if a document submitted to the Upper Tribunal is not written in English, it must be accompanied by an English translation.

(7) In proceedings that are in Wales or have a connection with Wales, a document or translation may be submitted to the Tribunal in Welsh.]

Note: Words in square brackets in paragraph (1)(a) substituted from 1 April 2009 (SI 2009/274). Paragraphs (6) and (7) inserted from 15 February 2010 (SI 2010/44).

Use of documents and information

14.—(1) The Upper Tribunal may make an order prohibiting the disclosure or publication of—

(a) specified documents or information relating to the proceedings; or

(b) any matter likely to lead members of the public to identify any person whom the Upper Tribunal considers should not be identified.

(2) The Upper Tribunal may give a direction prohibiting the disclosure of a document or information to a person if—

(a) the Upper Tribunal is satisfied that such disclosure would be likely to cause that person or some other person serious harm; and

(b) the Upper Tribunal is satisfied, having regard to the interests of justice, that it is proportionate to give such a direction.

(3) If a party ('the first party') considers that the Upper Tribunal should give a direction under paragraph (2) prohibiting the disclosure of a document or information to another party ('the second party'), the first party must—

(a) exclude the relevant document or information from any documents that will be provided to the second party; and

(b) provide to the Upper Tribunal the excluded document or information, and the reason for its exclusion, so that the Upper Tribunal may decide whether the document or information should be disclosed to the second party or should be the subject of a direction under paragraph (2).

(4) ...

(5) If the Upper Tribunal gives a direction under paragraph (2) which prevents disclosure to a party who has appointed a representative, the Upper Tribunal may give a direction that the documents or information be disclosed to that representative if the Upper Tribunal is satisfied that—

    (a) disclosure to the representative would be in the interests of the party; and

    (b) the representative will act in accordance with paragraph (6).

(6) Documents or information disclosed to a representative in accordance with a direction under paragraph (5) must not be disclosed either directly or indirectly to any other person without the Upper Tribunal's consent.

(7) Unless the Upper Tribunal gives a direction to the contrary, information about mental health cases and the names of any persons concerned in such cases must not be made public.

[(8) The Upper Tribunal may, on its own initiative or on the application of a party, give a direction that certain documents or information must or may be disclosed to the Upper Tribunal on the basis that the Upper Tribunal will not disclose such documents or information to other persons, or specified other persons.

(9) A party making an application for a direction under paragraph (8) may withhold the relevant documents or information from other parties until the Upper Tribunal has granted or refused the application.

(10) In a case involving matters relating to national security, the Upper Tribunal must ensure that information is not disclosed contrary to the interests of national security.

(11) The Upper Tribunal must conduct proceedings and record its decision and reasons appropriately so as not to undermine the effect of an order made under paragraph (1), a direction given under paragraph (2) or (8) or the duty imposed by paragraph (10).]

Note: Paragraph (4) omitted and paragraphs (8)–(11) inserted from 1 September 2009 (2009/1975).

Evidence and submissions

15.—(1) Without restriction on the general powers in rule 5(1) and (2) (case management powers), the Upper Tribunal may give directions as to—

    (a) issues on which it requires evidence or submissions;

    (b) the nature of the evidence or submissions it requires;

    (c) whether the parties are permitted or required to provide expert evidence, and if so whether the parties must jointly appoint a single expert to provide such evidence;

    (d) any limit on the number of witnesses whose evidence a party may put forward, whether in relation to a particular issue or generally;

    (e) the manner in which any evidence or submissions are to be provided, which may include a direction for them to be given—

        (i) orally at a hearing; or

        (ii) by written submissions or witness statement; and

    (f) the time at which any evidence or submissions are to be provided.

(2) The Upper Tribunal may—

   (a) admit evidence whether or not—

     (i) the evidence would be admissible in a civil trial in the United Kingdom; or

     (ii) the evidence was available to a previous decision maker; or

   (b) exclude evidence that would otherwise be admissible where—

     (i) the evidence was not provided within the time allowed by a direction or a practice direction;

     (ii) the evidence was otherwise provided in a manner that did not comply with a direction or a practice direction; or

     (iii) it would otherwise be unfair to admit the evidence.

[(2A) In an asylum case or an immigration case—

   (a) if a party wishes the Upper Tribunal to consider evidence that was not before the First-tier Tribunal, that party must send or deliver a notice to the Upper Tribunal and any other party—

     (i) indicating the nature of the evidence; and

     (ii) explaining why it was not submitted to the First-tier Tribunal; and

   (b) when considering whether to admit evidence that was not before the First-tier Tribunal, the Upper Tribunal must have regard to whether there has been unreasonable delay in producing that evidence.]

(3) The Upper Tribunal may consent to a witness giving, or require any witness to give, evidence on oath, and may administer an oath for that purpose.

Note: Paragraph 2A inserted from 15 February 2010 (SI 2010/44).

Summoning or citation of witnesses and orders to answer questions or produce documents

16.—(1) On the application of a party or on its own initiative, the Upper Tribunal may—

   (a) by summons (or, in Scotland, citation) require any person to attend as a witness at a hearing at the time and place specified in the summons or citation; or

   (b) order any person to answer any questions or produce any documents in that person's possession or control which relate to any issue in the proceedings.

(2) A summons or citation under paragraph (1)(a) must—

   (a) give the person required to attend 14 days' notice of the hearing or such shorter period as the Upper Tribunal may direct; and

   (b) where the person is not a party, make provision for the person's necessary expenses of attendance to be paid, and state who is to pay them.

(3) No person may be compelled to give any evidence or produce any document that the person could not be compelled to give or produce on a trial of an action in a court of law in the part of the United Kingdom where the proceedings are due to be determined.

[(4) A person who receives a summons, citation or order may apply to the Upper Tribunal for it to be varied or set aside if they did not have an opportunity to object to it before it was made or issued.

(5) A person making an application under paragraph (4) must do so as soon as reasonably practicable after receiving notice of the summons, citation or order.

(6) A summons, citation or order under this rule must—

(a) state that the person on whom the requirement is imposed may apply to the Upper Tribunal to vary or set aside the summons, citation or order, if they did not have an opportunity to object to it before it was made or issued; and

(b) state the consequences of failure to comply with the summons, citation or order.]

Note: Paragraph (4) substituted from 1 April 2009 (SI 2009/274).

Withdrawal

17.—**(1)** Subject to paragraph (2), a party may give notice of the withdrawal of its case, or any part of it—

(a) at any time before a hearing to consider the disposal of the proceedings (or, if the Upper Tribunal disposes of the proceedings without a hearing, before that disposal), by sending or delivering to the Upper Tribunal a written notice of withdrawal; or

(b) orally at a hearing.

(2) Notice of withdrawal will not take effect unless the Upper Tribunal consents to the withdrawal except in relation to an application for permission to appeal.

(3) A party which has withdrawn its case may apply to the Upper Tribunal for the case to be reinstated.

(4) An application under paragraph (3) must be made in writing and be received by the Upper Tribunal within 1 month after—

(a) the date on which the Upper Tribunal received the notice under paragraph (1)(a); or

(b) the date of the hearing at which the case was withdrawn orally under paragraph (1)(b).

(5) The Upper Tribunal must notify each party in writing of a withdrawal under this rule.

[**(6)** Paragraph (3) does not apply to a financial services case other than a reference against a penalty.]

Note: Paragraph (6) inserted from 6 April 2010 (SI 2010/747).

[Appeal treated as abandoned or finally determined in an asylum case or an immigration case

17A.—**(1)** A party to an asylum case or an immigration case before the Upper Tribunal must notify the Tribunal if they are aware that—

(a) the appellant has left the United Kingdom;

(b) the appellant has been granted leave to enter or remain in the United Kingdom;

(c) a deportation order has been made against the appellant; or

(d) a document listed in paragraph 4(2) of Schedule 2 to the Immigration (European Economic Area) Regulations 2006 has been issued to the appellant.

(2) Where an appeal is treated as abandoned pursuant to section 104(4) or (4A) of the Nationality, Immigration and Asylum Act 2002 or paragraph 4(2) of Schedule 2 to the Immigration (European Economic Area) Regulations 2006, or as finally determined pursuant to section 104(5) of the Nationality, Immigration and Asylum Act 2002, the Upper

Tribunal must send the parties a notice informing them that the appeal is being treated as abandoned or finally determined.

(3) Where an appeal would otherwise fall to be treated as abandoned pursuant to section 104(4A) of the Nationality, Immigration and Asylum Act 2002, but the appellant wishes to pursue their appeal, the appellant must send or deliver a notice, which must comply with any relevant practice directions, to the Upper Tribunal and the respondent so that it is received within thirty days of the date on which the notice of the grant of leave to enter or remain in the United Kingdom was sent to the appellant.

(4) Where a notice of grant of leave to enter or remain is sent electronically or delivered personally, the time limit in paragraph (3) is twenty eight days.

(5) Notwithstanding rule 5(3)(a) (case management powers) and rule 7(2) (failure to comply with rules etc.), the Upper Tribunal must not extend the time limits in paragraph (3) and (4).]

Note: Rule 17A inserted from 15 February 2010 (SI 2010/44).

Notice of funding of legal services

18. If a party is granted funding of legal services at any time, that party must as soon as practicable—

(a)(i) if funding is granted by the Legal Services Commission or the Northern Ireland Legal Services Commission, send a copy of the funding notice to the Upper Tribunal; or

(ii) if funding is granted by the Scottish Legal Aid Board, send a copy of the legal aid certificate to the Upper Tribunal; and

(b) notify every other party in writing that funding has been granted.

Confidentiality in child support or child trust fund cases

19.—(1) Paragraph (3) applies to an appeal against a decision of the First-tier Tribunal in proceedings under the Child Support Act 1991 in the circumstances described in paragraph (2), other than an appeal against a reduced benefit decision (as defined in section 46(10)(b) of the Child Support Act 1991, as that section had effect prior to the commencement of section 15(b) of the Child Maintenance and Other Payments Act 2008).

(2) The circumstances referred to in paragraph (1) are that—

(a) in the proceedings in the First-tier Tribunal in respect of which the appeal has been brought, there was an obligation to keep a person's address confidential; or

(b) a person whose circumstances are relevant to the proceedings would like their address (or, in the case of the person with care of the child, the child's address) to be kept confidential and has given notice to that effect—

(i) to the Upper Tribunal in an application for permission to appeal or notice of appeal;

(ii) to the Upper Tribunal within 1 month after an enquiry by the Upper Tribunal; or

(iii) to the Secretary of State, the Child Maintenance and Enforcement Commission or the Upper Tribunal when notifying a change of address after proceedings have been started.

(3) Where this paragraph applies, the Secretary of State, the Child Maintenance and Enforcement Commission and the Upper Tribunal must take appropriate steps to secure

the confidentiality of the address, and of any information which could reasonably be expected to enable a person to identify the address, to the extent that the address or that information is not already known to each other party.

(4) Paragraph (6) applies to an appeal against a decision of the First-tier Tribunal in proceedings under the Child Trust Funds Act 2004 in the circumstances described in paragraph (5).

(5) The circumstances referred to in paragraph (4) are that—

(a) in the proceedings in the First-tier Tribunal in respect of which the appeal has been brought, there was an obligation to keep a person's address confidential; or

(b) a person whose circumstances are relevant to the proceedings would like their address (or, in the case of the person with care of the eligible child, the child's address) to be kept confidential and has given notice to that effect—

(i) to the Upper Tribunal in an application for permission to appeal or notice of appeal;

(ii) to the Upper Tribunal within 1 month after an enquiry by the Upper Tribunal; or

(iii) to HMRC or the Upper Tribunal when notifying a change of address after proceedings have been started.

(6) Where this paragraph applies, HMRC and the Upper Tribunal must take appropriate steps to secure the confidentiality of the address, and of any information which could reasonably be expected to enable a person to identify the address, to the extent that the address or that information is not already known to each other party.

(7) In this rule—

'eligible child' has the meaning set out in section 2 of the Child Trust Funds Act 2004; and

'HMRC' means Her Majesty's Revenue and Customs.

Power to pay expenses and allowances

20.—(1) In proceedings brought under section 4 of the Safeguarding Vulnerable Groups Act 2006 ..., the Secretary of State may pay such allowances for the purpose of or in connection with the attendance of persons at hearings as the Secretary of State may, with the consent of the Treasury, determine.

(2) Paragraph (3) applies to proceedings on appeal from a decision of—

(a) the First-tier Tribunal in proceedings under the Child Support Act 1991, section 12 of the Social Security Act 1998 or paragraph 6 of Schedule 7 to the Child Support, Pensions and Social Security Act 2000;

(b) the First-tier Tribunal in a war pensions and armed forces case (as defined in the Tribunal Procedure (First-tier Tribunal) (War Pensions and Armed Forces Compensation Chamber) Rules 2008; or

(c) a Pensions Appeal Tribunal for Scotland or Northern Ireland.

(3) The Lord Chancellor (or, in Scotland, the Secretary of State) may pay to any person who attends any hearing such travelling and other allowances, including compensation for loss of remunerative time, as the Lord Chancellor (or, in Scotland, the Secretary of State) may determine.

Note: Words omitted from paragraph (1) from 1 April 2009 (SI 2009/274).

[Procedure for applying for a stay of a decision pending an appeal

20A.—(1) This rule applies where another enactment provides in any terms for the Upper Tribunal to stay or suspend, or to lift a stay or suspension of, a decision which is or may be the subject of an appeal to the Upper Tribunal ('the substantive decision') pending such appeal.

(2) A person who wishes the Upper Tribunal to decide whether the substantive decision should be stayed or suspended must make a written application to the Upper Tribunal which must include—

(a) the name and address of the person making the application;

(b) the name and address of any representative of that person;

(c) the address to which documents for that person should be sent or delivered;

(d) the name and address of any person who will be a respondent to the appeal;

(e) details of the substantive decision and any decision as to when that decision is to take effect, and copies of any written record of, or reasons for, those decisions; and

(f) the grounds on which the person making the application relies.

(3) In the case of an application under paragraph (2) [in a road transport case]—

(a) the person making the application must notify the [decision maker] when making the application;

(b) within 7 days of receiving notification of the application the [decision maker] must send or deliver written reasons for refusing or withdrawing the stay—

(i) to the Upper Tribunal; and

(ii) to the person making the application, if the [decision maker] has not already done so.

(4) If the Upper Tribunal grants a stay or suspension following an application under this rule—

(a) the Upper Tribunal may give directions as to the conduct of the appeal of the substantive decision; and

(b) the Upper Tribunal may, where appropriate, grant the stay or suspension subject to conditions.

(5) Unless the Upper Tribunal considers that there is good reason not to do so, the Upper Tribunal must send written notice of any decision made under this rule to each party.]

Note: Rule 20A inserted from 1 September 2009 (SI 2009/1975). Para (3) amended from 1 July 2012 (SI 2012/1363).

PART 3

[Procedure for cases in] the Upper Tribunal

Application to the Upper Tribunal for permission to appeal

21.—(1) ...

(2) A person may apply to the Upper Tribunal for permission to appeal to the Upper Tribunal against a decision of another tribunal only if—

(a) they have made an application for permission to appeal to the tribunal which made the decision challenged; and

(b) that application has been refused or has not been admitted.

(3) An application for permission to appeal must be made in writing and received by the Upper Tribunal no later than—

(a) in the case of an application under section 4 of the Safeguarding Vulnerable Groups Act 2006, 3 months after the date on which written notice of the decision being challenged was sent to the appellant;

[(aa) subject to paragraph (3A), in an asylum case or an immigration case where the appellant is in the United Kingdom at the time that the application is made—

(i) seven working days after the date on which notice of the First-tier Tribunal's refusal of permission was sent to the appellant; or

(ii) if the case is a fast-track case, four working days after the date on which notice of the First-tier Tribunal's refusal of permission was sent to the appellant;

(ab) subject to paragraph (3A), in an asylum case or an immigration case where the appellant is outside the United Kingdom at the time that the application is made, fifty six days after the date on which notice of the First-tier Tribunal's refusal of permission was sent to the appellant; or]

(b) otherwise, a month after the date on which the tribunal that made the decision under challenge sent notice of its refusal of permission to appeal, or refusal to admit the application for permission to appeal, to the appellant.

[(3A) Where a notice of decision is sent electronically or delivered personally, the time limits in paragraph (3)(aa) and (ab) are—

(a) in sub-paragraph (aa)(i), five working days;

(b) in sub-paragraph (aa)(ii), two working days; and

(c) in sub-paragraph (ab), twenty eight days.]

(4) The application must state—

(a) the name and address of the appellant;

(b) the name and address of the representative (if any) of the appellant;

(c) an address where documents for the appellant may be sent or delivered;

(d) details (including the full reference) of the decision challenged;

(e) the grounds on which the appellant relies; and

(f) whether the appellant wants the application to be dealt with at a hearing.

(5) The appellant must provide with the application a copy of—

(a) any written record of the decision being challenged;

(b) any separate written statement of reasons for that decision; and

(c) if the application is for permission to appeal against a decision of another tribunal, the notice of refusal of permission to appeal, or notice of refusal to admit the application for permission to appeal, from that other tribunal.

(6) If the appellant provides the application to the Upper Tribunal later than the time required by paragraph (3) or by an extension of time allowed under rule 5(3)(a) (power to extend time)—

(a) the application must include a request for an extension of time and the reason why the application was not provided in time; and

(b) unless the Upper Tribunal extends time for the application under rule 5(3)(a) (power to extend time) the Upper Tribunal must not admit the application.

(7) If the appellant makes an application to the Upper Tribunal for permission to appeal against the decision of another tribunal, and that other tribunal refused to admit the appellant's application for permission to appeal because the application for permission or for a written statement of reasons was not made in time—

(a) the application to the Upper Tribunal for permission to appeal must include the reason why the application to the other tribunal for permission to appeal or for a written statement of reasons, as the case may be, was not made in time; and

(b) the Upper Tribunal must only admit the application if the Upper Tribunal considers that it is in the interests of justice for it to do so.

Note: Paragraph (1) omitted from 1 September 2009 (SI 2009/1975). Paragraphs (3)(aa)–(ab) and (3A) inserted from 15 February 2010 (SI 2010/44).

Decision in relation to permission to appeal

22.—(1) If the Upper Tribunal refuses permission to appeal, it must send written notice of the refusal and of the reasons for the refusal to the appellant.

(2) If the Upper Tribunal gives permission to appeal—

(a) the Upper Tribunal must send written notice of the permission, and of the reasons for any limitations or conditions on such permission, to each party;

(b) subject to any direction by the Upper Tribunal, the application for permission to appeal stands as the notice of appeal and the Upper Tribunal must send to each respondent a copy of the application for permission to appeal and any documents provided with it by the appellant; and

(c) the Upper Tribunal may, with the consent of the appellant and each respondent, determine the appeal without obtaining any further response.

[(3) Paragraph (4) applies where the Upper Tribunal, without a hearing, determines an application for permission to appeal—

(a) against a decision of—

  (i) the Tax Chamber of the First-tier Tribunal;

  (ii) the Health, Education and Social Care Chamber of the First-tier Tribunal;

  [(iia) the General Regulatory Chamber of the First-tier Tribunal;]

  (iii) the Mental Health Review Tribunal for Wales; or

  (iv) the Special Educational Needs Tribunal for Wales; or

(b) under section 4 of the Safeguarding Vulnerable Groups Act 2006.]

(4) In the circumstances set out at paragraph (3) the appellant may apply for the decision to be reconsidered at a hearing if the Upper Tribunal—

(a) refuses permission to appeal; or

(b) gives permission to appeal on limited grounds or subject to conditions.

(5) An application under paragraph (4) must be made in writing and received by the Upper Tribunal within 14 days after the date on which the Upper Tribunal sent written notice of its decision regarding the application to the appellant.

Note: Paragraph (3) substituted from 1 April 2009 (SI 2009/274). Paragraph (3)(a)(ii) inserted from 1 September 2009 (SI 2009/1975).

Notice of appeal

23.— [(1) This rule applies—

(a) to proceedings on appeal to the Upper Tribunal for which permission to appeal is not required, except proceedings to which rule 26A [or (26B)] applies;

(b) if another tribunal has given permission for a party to appeal to the Upper Tribunal; or

(c) subject to any other direction by the Upper Tribunal, if the Upper Tribunal has given permission to appeal and has given a direction that the application for permission to appeal does not stand as the notice of appeal.

[(**1A**) In an asylum case or an immigration case in which the First-tier Tribunal has given permission to appeal, subject to any direction of the First-tier Tribunal or the Upper Tribunal, the application for permission to appeal sent or delivered to the First-tier Tribunal stands as the notice of appeal and accordingly paragraphs (2) to (6) of this rule do not apply.]

(**2**) The appellant must provide a notice of appeal to the Upper Tribunal so that it is received within 1 month after—

(a) the date that the tribunal that gave permission to appeal sent notice of such permission to the appellant; or

(b) if permission to appeal is not required, the date on which notice of decision to which the appeal relates was sent to the appellant.]

(**3**) The notice of appeal must include the information listed in rule 21(4)(a) to (e) (content of the application for permission to appeal) and, where the Upper Tribunal has given permission to appeal, the Upper Tribunal's case reference.

(**4**) If another tribunal has granted permission to appeal, the appellant must provide with the notice of appeal a copy of—

(a) any written record of the decision being challenged;

(b) any separate written statement of reasons for that decision; and

(c) the notice of permission to appeal.

(**5**) If the appellant provides the notice of appeal to the Upper Tribunal later than the time required by paragraph (2) or by an extension of time allowed under rule 5(3)(a) (power to extend time)—

(a) the notice of appeal must include a request for an extension of time and the reason why the notice was not provided in time; and

(b) unless the Upper Tribunal extends time for the notice of appeal under rule 5(3)(a) (power to extend time) the Upper Tribunal must not admit the notice of appeal.

[(**6**) When the Upper Tribunal receives the notice of appeal it must send a copy of the notice and any accompanying documents—

(a) to each respondent; or

[(b) in a road transport case, to—

(i) the decision maker;

(ii) the appropriate national authority; and

(iii) in a case relating to the detention of a vehicle, the authorised person.]

Note: Paragraphs (1), (2) and (6) substituted from 1 September 2009 (SI 2009/1975). Paragraph (1A) inserted from 15 February 2010 (SI 2010/44). Number in square brackets in paragraph (1)(a) inserted from 6 April 2010 (SI 2010/747). Para 6(b) substituted from 1 July 2012 (SI 2012/1363).

Response to the notice of appeal

24.—[(1) This rule and rule 25 do not apply to {a road transport case}, in respect of which Schedule 1 makes alternative provision.

(1A) Subject to any direction given by the Upper Tribunal, a respondent may provide a response to a notice of appeal.]

(2) Any response provided under paragraph [(1A)] must be in writing and must be sent or delivered to the Upper Tribunal so that it is received—

[(a) if an application for permission to appeal stands as the notice of appeal, no later than one month after the date on which the respondent was sent notice that permission to appeal had been granted;]

[(aa) in a fast-track case, one day before the hearing of the appeal; or].

(b) in any other case, no later than 1 month after the date on which the Upper Tribunal sent a copy of the notice of appeal to the respondent.

(3) The response must state—

(a) the name and address of the respondent;

(b) the name and address of the representative (if any) of the respondent;

(c) an address where documents for the respondent may be sent or delivered;

(d) whether the respondent opposes the appeal;

(e) the grounds on which the respondent relies, including [(in the case of an appeal against the decision of another tribunal)], any grounds on which the respondent was unsuccessful in the proceedings which are the subject of the appeal, but intends to rely in the appeal; and

(f) whether the respondent wants the case to be dealt with at a hearing.

(4) If the respondent provides the response to the Upper Tribunal later than the time required by paragraph (2) or by an extension of time allowed under rule 5(3)(a) (power to extend time), the response must include a request for an extension of time and the reason why the [response] was not provided in time.

(5) When the Upper Tribunal receives the response it must send a copy of the response and any accompanying documents to the appellant and each other party.

Note: Paragraph (1) substituted and words in square brackets in paragraph (3)(e) substituted from 1 September 2009 (SI 2009/1975). Words in curly brackets in para 1 substituted from 1 July 2012 (SI 2012/1363). Paragraph (2)(a) substituted and (2)(aa) inserted from 15 February 2010 (SI 2010/44). Word in square bracket in paragraph (4) substituted from 1 April 2009 (SI 2009/274).

Appellant's reply

25.—(1) Subject to any direction given by the Upper Tribunal, the appellant may provide a reply to any response provided under rule 24 (response to the notice of appeal).

(2) [Subject to paragraph (2A), any] reply provided under paragraph (1) must be in writing and must be sent or delivered to the Upper Tribunal so that it is received within one month after the date on which the Upper Tribunal sent a copy of the response to the appellant.

[(2A) In an asylum case or an immigration case, the time limit in paragraph (2) is—

(a) one month after the date on which the Upper Tribunal sent a copy of the response to the appellant, or five days before the hearing of the appeal, whichever is the earlier; and

(b) in a fast-track case, the day of the hearing.]

(3) When the Upper Tribunal receives the reply it must send a copy of the reply and any accompanying documents to each respondent.

Note: Words in square brackets in paragraph (2) substituted and (2A) inserted from 15 February 2010 (SI 2010/44).

References under the Forfeiture Act 1982

26.—(1) If a question arises which is required to be determined by the Upper Tribunal under section 4 of the Forfeiture Act 1982, the person to whom the application for the relevant benefit or advantage has been made must refer the question to the Upper Tribunal.

(2) The reference must be in writing and must include—

(a) a statement of the question for determination;

(b) a statement of the relevant facts;

(c) the grounds upon which the reference is made; and

(d) an address for sending documents to the person making the reference and each respondent.

(3) When the Upper Tribunal receives the reference it must send a copy of the reference and any accompanying documents to each respondent.

(4) Rules 24 (response to the notice of appeal) and 25 (appellant's reply) apply to a reference made under this rule as if it were a notice of appeal.

[Cases transferred or referred to the Upper Tribunal, applications made directly to the Upper Tribunal and proceedings without notice to a respondent

26A.—[(1) Paragraphs (2) and (3) apply to—

(a) a case transferred or referred to the Upper Tribunal from the First-tier Tribunal; or

(b) a case, other than an appeal or a case to which rule 26 (references under the Forfeiture Act 1982) applies, which is started by an application made directly to the Upper Tribunal.]

(2) In a case to which this paragraph applies—

(a) the Upper Tribunal must give directions as to the procedure to be followed in the consideration and disposal of the proceedings;

[(aa) in a reference under Schedule 1D of the Charities Act 1993, the Upper Tribunal may give directions providing for an application to join the proceedings as a party and the time within which it may be made; and]

(b) the preceding rules in this Part will only apply to the proceedings to the extent provided for by such directions.

(3) If a case or matter to which this paragraph applies is to be determined without notice to or the involvement of a respondent—

(a) any provision in these Rules requiring a document to be provided by or to a respondent; and

(b) any other provision in these Rules permitting a respondent to participate in the proceedings

does not apply to that case or matter.]

[(4) Schedule 2 makes further provision for national security certificate appeals transferred to the Upper Tribunal.]

Note: Rule 26A inserted from 1 April 2009 (SI 2009/274). Paragraph (1) substituted from 1 September 2009 (SI 2009/1975). Paragraph (4) inserted from 18 January 2010 (SI 2010/43). Subparagraph (2) (aa) inserted from 6 April 2012 (SI 2012/500).

[Financial services cases

26B. Schedule 3 makes provision for financial services cases.]

Note: Rule 26B inserted from 6 April 2010 (SI 2010/747).

PART 4

Judicial review proceedings in the Upper Tribunal

Application of this Part to judicial review proceedings transferred to the Upper Tribunal

27.—(1) When a court transfers judicial review proceedings to the Upper Tribunal, the Upper Tribunal—

(a) must notify each party in writing that the proceedings have been transferred to the Upper Tribunal; and

(b) must give directions as to the future conduct of the proceedings.

(2) The directions given under paragraph (1)(b) may modify or disapply for the purposes of the proceedings any of the provisions of the following rules in this Part.

(3) In proceedings transferred from the Court of Session under section 20(1) of the 2007 Act, the directions given under paragraph (1)(b) must—

(a) if the Court of Session did not make a first order specifying the required intimation, service and advertisement of the petition, state the Upper Tribunal's requirements in relation to those matters;

(b) state whether the Upper Tribunal will consider summary dismissal of the proceedings; and

(c) where necessary, modify or disapply provisions relating to permission in the following rules in this Part.

Applications for permission to bring judicial review proceedings

28.—(1) A person seeking permission to bring judicial review proceedings before the Upper Tribunal under section 16 of the 2007 Act must make a written application to the Upper Tribunal for such permission.

(2) Subject to paragraph (3), an application under paragraph (1) must be made promptly and, unless any other enactment specifies a shorter time limit, must be sent or delivered to the Upper Tribunal so that it is received no later than 3 months after the date of the decision[, action or omission] to which the application relates.

(3) An application for permission to bring judicial review proceedings challenging a decision of the First-tier Tribunal may be made later than the time required by paragraph (2) if it is made within 1 month after the date on which the First-tier Tribunal sent—

(a) written reasons for the decision; or

(b) notification that an application for the decision to be set aside has been unsuccessful, provided that that application was made in time.

(4) The application must state—

(a) the name and address of the applicant, the respondent and any other person whom the applicant considers to be an interested party;

(b) the name and address of the applicant's representative (if any);

(c) an address where documents for the applicant may be sent or delivered;

(d) details of the decision challenged (including the date, the full reference and the identity of the decision maker);

(e) that the application is for permission to bring judicial review proceedings;

(f) the outcome that the applicant is seeking; and

(g) the facts and grounds on which the applicant relies.

(5) If the application relates to proceedings in a court or tribunal, the application must name as an interested party each party to those proceedings who is not the applicant or a respondent.

(6) The applicant must send with the application—

(a) a copy of any written record of the decision in the applicant's possession or control; and

(b) copies of any other documents in the applicant's possession or control on which the applicant intends to rely.

(7) If the applicant provides the application to the Upper Tribunal later than the time required by paragraph (2) or (3) or by an extension of time allowed under rule 5(3)(a) (power to extend time)—

(a) the application must include a request for an extension of time and the reason why the application was not provided in time; and

(b) unless the Upper Tribunal extends time for the application under rule 5(3)(a) (power to extend time) the Upper Tribunal must not admit the application.

(8) [Except where rule 28A(2)(a) (special provisions for fresh claim proceedings) applies,] when the Upper Tribunal receives the application it must send a copy of the application and any accompanying documents to each person named in the application as a respondent or interested party.

Note: Words in square brackets in paragraph (2) inserted from 1 April 2009 (SI 2009/274). Words inserted in paragraph (8) from 17 October 2011 (SI 2011/2343).

[Special provisions for fresh claim proceedings

28A.—(1) The Upper Tribunal must not accept an application for permission to bring fresh claim proceedings unless it is either accompanied by any required fee or the Upper Tribunal accepts an undertaking that the fee will be paid.

(2) Within 9 days of making an application referred to in paragraph (1), an applicant must provide—

(a) a copy of the application and any accompanying documents to each person named in the application as a respondent or an interested party; and

(b) the Upper Tribunal with a written statement of when and how this was done.]

Note: Rule 28A inserted from 17 October 2011 (SI 2011/2343).

Acknowledgment of service

29.—(1) A person who is sent [or provided with] a copy of an application for permission under rule 28(8) (application for permission to bring judicial review proceedings) [or rule 28A(2)(a) (special provisions for fresh claim proceedings)] and wishes to take part in the proceedings must [provide] to the Upper Tribunal an acknowledgment of service so that it is received no later than 21 days after the date on which the Upper Tribunal sent, [or in fresh claim proceedings the applicant provided,] a copy of the application to that person.

(2) An acknowledgment of service under paragraph (1) must be in writing and state—

(a) whether the person intends to [support or] oppose the application for permission;

(b) their grounds for any [support or] opposition under sub-paragraph (a), or any other submission or information which they consider may assist the Upper Tribunal; and

(c) the name and address of any other person not named in the application as a respondent or interested party whom the person providing the acknowledgment considers to be an interested party.

[(**2A**) In fresh claim proceedings, a person who provides an acknowledgement of service under paragraph (1) must also provide a copy to—

(a) the applicant; and

(b) any other person named in the application under rule 28(4)(a) or acknowledgement of service under paragraph (2)(c) no later than the time specified in paragraph (1).]

(**3**) A person who is {provided with} a copy of an application for permission under rule 28(8) [or 28A(2)(a)] but does not provide an acknowledgment of service [to the Upper Tribunal] may not take part in the application for permission {unless allowed to do so by the Upper Tribunal}, but may take part in the subsequent proceedings if the application is successful.

Note: Word in square brackets in paragraph (2) inserted from 1 April 2009 (SI 2009/274). Words in curly brackets in paragraph (3) inserted from 1 April 2011 (SI 2011/651). Words inserted/substituted in paragraph (1), paragraph (2A) inserted and words in square brackets in paragraph (3) inserted/substituted from 17 October 2011 (SI 2011 2343).

Decision on permission or summary dismissal, and reconsideration of permission or summary dismissal at a hearing

30.—(1) The Upper Tribunal must send to the applicant, each respondent and any other person who provided an acknowledgment of service to the Upper Tribunal, and may send to any other person who may have an interest in the proceedings, written notice of—

(a) its decision in relation to the application for permission; and

(b) the reasons for any refusal of the application, or any limitations or conditions on permission.

(**2**) In proceedings transferred from the Court of Session under section 20(1) of the 2007 Act, where the Upper Tribunal has considered whether summarily to dismiss of the proceedings, the Upper Tribunal must send to the applicant and each respondent, and may send to any other person who may have an interest in the proceedings, written notice of—

(a) its decision in relation to the summary dismissal of proceedings; and

(b) the reasons for any decision summarily to dismiss part or all of the proceedings, or any limitations or conditions on the continuation of such proceedings.

(**3**) Paragraph (4) applies where the Upper Tribunal, without a hearing—

(a) determines an application for permission to bring judicial review proceedings and either refuses permission, or gives permission on limited grounds or subject to conditions; or

(b) in proceedings transferred from the Court of Session, summarily dismisses part or all of the proceedings, or imposes any limitations or conditions on the continuation of such proceedings.

(**4**) In the circumstances specified in paragraph (3) the applicant may apply for the decision to be reconsidered at a hearing.

(5) An application under paragraph (4) must be made in writing and must be sent or delivered to the Upper Tribunal so that it is received within 14 days, [or in fresh claim proceedings 9 days,] after the date on which the Upper Tribunal sent written notice of its decision regarding the application to the applicant.

Note: Words inserted in paragraph (5) from 17 October 2011 (SI 2011/2343).

Responses

31.—(1) Any person to whom the Upper Tribunal has sent notice of the grant of permission under rule 30(1) (notification of decision on permission), and who wishes to contest the application or support it on additional grounds, must provide detailed grounds for contesting or supporting the application to the Upper Tribunal.

(2) Any detailed grounds must be provided in writing and must be sent or delivered to the Upper Tribunal so that they are received not more than 35 days after the Upper Tribunal sent notice of the grant of permission under rule 30(1).

Applicant seeking to rely on additional grounds

32. The applicant may not rely on any grounds, other than those grounds on which the applicant obtained permission for the judicial review proceedings, without the consent of the Upper Tribunal.

Right to make representations

33. Each party and, with the permission of the Upper Tribunal, any other person, may—

    (a) submit evidence, except at the hearing of an application for permission;

    (b) make representations at any hearing which they are entitled to attend; and

    (c) make written representations in relation to a decision to be made without a hearing.

[Amendments and additional grounds resulting in transfer of proceedings to the High Court in England and Wales

33A.—(1) This rule applies only to judicial review proceedings arising under the law of England and Wales.

(2) In relation to such proceedings—

    (a) the powers of the Upper Tribunal to permit or require amendments under rule 5(3)(c) extend to amendments which would, once in place, give rise to an obligation or power to transfer the proceedings to the High Court in England and Wales under section 18(3) of the 2007 Act or paragraph (3);

    (b) except with the permission of the Upper Tribunal, additional grounds may not be advanced, whether by an applicant or otherwise, if they would give rise to an obligation or power to transfer the proceedings to the High Court in England and Wales under section 18(3) of the 2007 Act or paragraph (3).

(3) Where the High Court in England and Wales has transferred judicial review proceedings to the Upper Tribunal under any power or duty and subsequently the proceedings are amended or any party advances additional grounds—

(a) if the proceedings in their present form could not have been transferred to the Upper Tribunal under the relevant power or duty had they been in that form at the time of the transfer, the Upper Tribunal must transfer the proceedings back to the High Court in England and Wales;

(b) subject to sub-paragraph, where the proceedings were transferred to the Upper Tribunal under section 31A(3) of the Senior Courts Act 1981 (power to transfer judicial review proceedings to the Upper Tribunal), the Upper Tribunal may transfer proceedings back to the High Court in England and Wales if it appears just and convenient to do so.]

Note: Rule 33A inserted from 17 October 2011 (SI 2011/2343).

Part 5
Hearings

Decision with or without a hearing

34.—(1) Subject to paragraph (2), the Upper Tribunal may make any decision without a hearing.

(2) The Upper Tribunal must have regard to any view expressed by a party when deciding whether to hold a hearing to consider any matter, and the form of any such hearing.

Entitlement to attend a hearing

35.— [(1)] Subject to rule 37(4) (exclusion of a person from a hearing), each party is entitled to attend a hearing.

[(2) In a national security certificate appeal the relevant Minister is entitled to attend any hearing.]

Note: Paragraph (2) inserted from 18 January 2010 (SI 2010/43).

Notice of hearings

36.—(1) The Upper Tribunal must give each party entitled to attend a hearing reasonable notice of the time and place of the hearing (including any adjourned or postponed hearing) and any change to the time and place of the hearing.

(2) The period of notice under paragraph (1) must be at least 14 days except that—

(a) in applications for permission to bring judicial review proceedings, the period of notice must be at least 2 working days;

[(aa) in a fast-track case the period of notice must be at least one working day; and]

(b) [in any case other than a fast-track case] the Upper Tribunal may give shorter notice—

(i) with the parties' consent; or

(ii) in urgent or exceptional cases.

Note: Words in square brackets inserted from 15 February 2010 (SI 2010/44).

[Special time limits for hearing an appeal in a fast-track case

36A.—(**1**) Subject to rule 36(2)(aa) (notice of hearings) and paragraph (2) of this rule, where permission to appeal to the Upper Tribunal has been given in a fast-track case, the Upper Tribunal must start the hearing of the appeal not later than—

(a) four working days after the date on which the First-tier Tribunal or the Upper Tribunal sent notice of its grant of permission to appeal to the appellant; or

(b) where the notice of its grant of permission to appeal is sent electronically or delivered personally, two working days after the date on which the First-tier Tribunal or the Upper Tribunal sent notice of its grant of permission to appeal to the appellant.

(**2**) If the Upper Tribunal is unable to arrange for the hearing to start within the time specified in paragraph (1), it must set a date for the hearing as soon as is reasonably practicable.]

Note: Rule 36A inserted from 15 February 2010 (SI 2010/44).

Public and private hearings

37.—(**1**) Subject to the following paragraphs, all hearings must be held in public.

(**2**) The Upper Tribunal may give a direction that a hearing, or part of it, is to be held in private.

[(**2A**) In a national security certificate appeal, the Upper Tribunal must have regard to its duty under rule 14(10) (no disclosure of information contrary to the interests of national security) when considering whether to give a direction that a hearing, or part of it, is to be held in private.]

(**3**) Where a hearing, or part of it, is to be held in private, the Upper Tribunal may determine who is entitled to attend the hearing or part of it.

(**4**) The Upper Tribunal may give a direction excluding from any hearing, or part of it—

(a) any person whose conduct the Upper Tribunal considers is disrupting or is likely to disrupt the hearing;

(b) any person whose presence the Upper Tribunal considers is likely to prevent another person from giving evidence or making submissions freely;

(c) any person who the Upper Tribunal considers should be excluded in order to give effect to [the requirement at rule 14(11) (prevention of disclosure or publication of documents and information)];

(d) any person where the purpose of the hearing would be defeated by the attendance of that person [; or

(e) a person under the age of eighteen years.].

(**5**) The Upper Tribunal may give a direction excluding a witness from a hearing until that witness gives evidence.

Note: Paragraph (2A) inserted from 18 January 2010 (SI 2010/43).). Words in square brackets in paragraph (4)(c) substituted from 1 September 2009 (SI 2009/1975). Paragraph (4)(e) inserted from 1 April 2009 (SI 2009/274).

Hearings in a party's absence

38. If a party fails to attend a hearing, the Upper Tribunal may proceed with the hearing if the Upper Tribunal—

(a) is satisfied that the party has been notified of the hearing or that reasonable steps have been taken to notify the party of the hearing; and

(b) considers that it is in the interests of justice to proceed with the hearing.

PART 6
Decisions

Consent orders

39.—(1) The Upper Tribunal may, at the request of the parties but only if it considers it appropriate, make a consent order disposing of the proceedings and making such other appropriate provision as the parties have agreed.

(2) Notwithstanding any other provision of these Rules, the Tribunal need not hold a hearing before making an order under paragraph (1)…

Note: Words omitted from paragraph (2) from 1 April 2009 (SI 2009/274).

Decisions

40.—(1) The Upper Tribunal may give a decision orally at a hearing.

(2) [Except where rule 40A (special procedure for providing notice of a decision relating to an asylum case) applies,] the Upper Tribunal must provide to each party as soon as reasonably practicable after making a decision which finally disposes of all issues in the proceedings (except a decision under Part 7)—

(a) a decision notice stating the Tribunal's decision; and

(b) notification of any rights of review or appeal against the decision and the time and manner in which such rights of review or appeal may be exercised.

(3) [Subject to rule [14(11) (prevention of disclosure or publication of documents and information)] the Upper Tribunal must provide written reasons for its decision with a decision notice provided under paragraph (2)(a) unless—

(a) the decision was made with the consent of the parties; or

(b) the parties have consented to the Upper Tribunal not giving written reasons.

(4) The [Upper] Tribunal may provide written reasons for any decision to which paragraph (2) does not apply.

[(5) In a national security certificate appeal, when the Upper Tribunal provides a notice or reasons to the parties under this rule, it must also provide the notice or reasons to the relevant Minister and the Information Commissioner, if they are not parties.]

Note: Words in square brackets in paragraph (2) inserted from 15 February 2010 (SI 2010/44). Words in square brackets in paragraphs (3) substituted and in (4) inserted from 1 September 2009 (SI 2009/1975). Paragraph (5) inserted from 18 January 2010 (SI 2010/43).

[Special procedure for providing notice of a decision relating to an asylum case

40A.—(1) This rule applies to an appeal before the Upper Tribunal under section 11 of the 2007 Act in an asylum case where—

(a) the person who appealed to the First-tier Tribunal is in the United Kingdom; and

(b) the case is not a fast-track case.

(2) The Upper Tribunal must provide to the Secretary of State for the Home Department as soon as reasonably practicable—

(a) a decision notice stating the Upper Tribunal's decision; and

(b) a statement of any right of appeal against the decision and the time and manner in which such a right of appeal may be exercised.

(3) The Secretary of State must, subject to paragraph (5)—

(a) send the documents listed in paragraph (2) to the other party not later than 30 days after the Upper Tribunal sent them to the Secretary of State for the Home Department; and

(b) as soon as practicable after sending the documents listed in paragraph (2), notify the Upper Tribunal on what date and by what means they were sent.

(4) If the Secretary of State does not notify the Upper Tribunal under paragraph (3)(b) within 31 days after the documents listed in paragraph (2) were sent, the Upper Tribunal must send the notice of decision to the other party as soon as reasonably practicable.

(5) If the Secretary of State applies for permission to appeal under section 13 of the 2007 Act, the Secretary of State must send the documents listed in paragraph (2) to the other party no later than the date on which the application for permission is sent to the Upper Tribunal.]

Note: Rule 40A inserted from 15 February 2010 (SI 2010/44).

PART 7
*Correcting, setting aside, reviewing and appealing decisions of the
Upper Tribunal*

Interpretation

41. In this Part—

'appeal' [, except in rule 44(2) (application for permission to appeal),] means the exercise of a right of appeal under section 13 of the 2007 Act; and

'review' means the review of a decision by the Upper Tribunal under section 10 of the 2007 Act.

Note: Words in square brackets inserted from 1 April 2009 (SI 2009/274).

Clerical mistakes and accidental slips or omissions

42. The Upper Tribunal may at any time correct any clerical mistake or other accidental slip or omission in a decision or record of a decision by—

(a) sending notification of the amended decision, or a copy of the amended record, to all parties; and

(b) making any necessary amendment to any information published in relation to the decision or record.

Setting aside a decision which disposes of proceedings

43.—(1) The Upper Tribunal may set aside a decision which disposes of proceedings, or part of such a decision, and re-make the decision or the relevant part of it, if—

(a) the Upper Tribunal considers that it is in the interests of justice to do so; and

(b) one or more of the conditions in paragraph (2) are satisfied.

(2) The conditions are—

(a) a document relating to the proceedings was not sent to, or was not received at an appropriate time by, a party or a party's representative;

(b) a document relating to the proceedings was not sent to the Upper Tribunal at an appropriate time;

(c) a party, or a party's representative, was not present at a hearing related to the proceedings; or

(d) there has been some other procedural irregularity in the proceedings.

(3) [Except where paragraph (4) applies,] a party applying for a decision, or part of a decision, to be set aside under paragraph (1) must make a written application to the Upper Tribunal so that it is received no later than 1 month after the date on which the Tribunal sent notice of the decision to the party.

[(4) In an asylum case or an immigration case, the written application referred to in paragraph (3) must be sent or delivered so that it is received by the Upper Tribunal—

(a) where the person who appealed to the First-tier Tribunal is in the United Kingdom at the time that the application is made, no later than twelve days after the date on which the Upper Tribunal or, as the case may be in an asylum case, the Secretary of State for the Home Department, sent notice of the decision to the party making the application; or

(b) where the person who appealed to the First-tier Tribunal is outside the United Kingdom at the time that the application is made, no later than thirty eight days after the date on which the Upper Tribunal sent notice of the decision to the party making the application.

(5) Where a notice of decision is sent electronically or delivered personally, the time limits in paragraph (4) are ten working days.].

Note: Paragraph (4) and words in square brackets in paragraph (3) inserted from 15 February 2010 (SI 2010/44).

Application for permission to appeal

44.—(1) A person seeking permission to appeal must make a written application to the Upper Tribunal for permission to appeal.

(2) Paragraph (3) applies to an application under paragraph (1) in respect of a decision—

(a) on an appeal against a decision in a social security and child support case (as defined in the Tribunal Procedure (First-tier Tribunal) (Social Entitlement Chamber) Rules 2008);

(b) on an appeal against a decision in proceedings in the War Pensions and Armed Forces Compensation Chamber of the First-tier Tribunal;

[(ba) on an appeal against a decision of a Pensions Appeal Tribunal for Scotland or Northern Ireland; or]

(c) in proceedings under the Forfeiture Act 1982.

(3) Where this paragraph applies, the application must be sent or delivered to the Upper Tribunal so that it is received within 3 months after the date on which the Upper Tribunal sent to the person making the application—

(a) written notice of the decision;

(b) notification of amended reasons for, or correction of, the decision following a review; or

(c) notification that an application for the decision to be set aside has been unsuccessful.

[(3A) An application under paragraph (1) in respect of a decision in an asylum case or an immigration case must be sent or delivered to the Upper Tribunal so that it is received within the appropriate period after the Upper Tribunal or, as the case may be in an asylum case, the Secretary of State for the Home Department, sent any of the documents in paragraph (3) to the party making the application.

(3B) The appropriate period referred to in paragraph (3A) is as follows—

(a) where the person who appealed to the First-tier Tribunal is in the United Kingdom at the time that the application is made—

(i) [twelve working days]; or

(ii) if the party making the application is in detention under the Immigration Acts, seven working days; and

(b) where the person who appealed to the First-tier Tribunal is outside the United Kingdom at the time that the application is made, thirty-eight days.

(3C) Where a notice of decision is sent electronically or delivered personally, the time limits in paragraph (3B) are—

(a) in sub-paragraph (a)(i), ten working days;

(b) in sub-paragraph (a)(ii), five working days; and

(c) in sub-paragraph (b), ten working days.]

[(3D) An application under paragraph (1) in respect of a decision in a financial services case must be sent or delivered to the Upper Tribunal so that it is received within 14 days after the date on which the Upper Tribunal sent to the person making the application—

(a) written notice of the decision;

(b) notification of amended reasons for, or correction of, the decision following a review; or

(c) notification that an application for the decision to be set aside has been unsuccessful.]

(4) Where paragraph (3)[, (3A) or (3D)] does not apply, an application under paragraph (1) must be sent or delivered to the Upper Tribunal so that it is received within 1 month after the latest of the dates on which the Upper Tribunal sent to the person making the application—

(a) written reasons for the decision;

(b) notification of amended reasons for, or correction of, the decision following a review; or

(c) notification that an application for the decision to be set aside has been unsuccessful.

(5) The date in paragraph (3)(c) or (4)(c) applies only if the application for the decision to be set aside was made within the time stipulated in rule 43 (setting aside a decision which disposes of proceedings) or any extension of that time granted by the Upper Tribunal.

(6) If the person seeking permission to appeal provides the application to the Upper Tribunal later than the time required by paragraph (3)[, [3A]{, 3D}] or (4), or by any extension of time under rule 5(3)(a) (power to extend time)—

(a) the application must include a request for an extension of time and the reason why the application notice was not provided in time; and

(b) unless the Upper Tribunal extends time for the application under rule 5(3)(a) (power to extend time) the Upper Tribunal must refuse the application.

(7) An application under paragraph (1) must—

(a) identify the decision of the Tribunal to which it relates;

(b) identify the alleged error or errors of law in the decision; and

(c) state the result the party making the application is seeking.

Note: Paragraph (2)(ba) inserted from 1 April 2009 (SI 2009/274). Paragraphs (3A)–(3C) and numbers in square brackets in paragraph (6) inserted from 15 February 2010 (SI 2010/44). Paragraph (3D) and numbers in curly brackets in paragraph (6) inserted and numbers in square brackets in paragraph (4) substituted from 6 April 2010 (SI 2010/747). Subparagraph (3B)(a)(i) amended from 1 April 2011 (SI 2011/651).

Upper Tribunal's consideration of application for permission to appeal

45.—(1) On receiving an application for permission to appeal the Upper Tribunal may review the decision in accordance with rule 46 (review of a decision), but may only do so if—

(a) when making the decision the Upper Tribunal overlooked a legislative provision or binding authority which could have had a material effect on the decision; or

(b) since the Upper Tribunal's decision, a court has made a decision which is binding on the Upper Tribunal and which, had it been made before the Upper Tribunal's decision, could have had a material effect on the decision.

(2) If the Upper Tribunal decides not to review the decision, or reviews the decision and decides to take no action in relation to the decision or part of it, the Upper Tribunal must consider whether to give permission to appeal in relation to the decision or that part of it.

(3) The Upper Tribunal must send a record of its decision to the parties as soon as practicable.

(4) If the Upper Tribunal refuses permission to appeal it must send with the record of its decision—

(a) a statement of its reasons for such refusal; and

(b) notification of the right to make an application to the relevant appellate court for permission to appeal and the time within which, and the method by which, such application must be made.

(5) The Upper Tribunal may give permission to appeal on limited grounds, but must comply with paragraph (4) in relation to any grounds on which it has refused permission.

[Setting aside] of a decision

46.—[(1) The Upper Tribunal may only undertake a review of a decision pursuant to rule 45(1) (review on an application for permission to appeal).]

(2) The Upper Tribunal must notify the parties in writing of the outcome of any review and of any rights of review or appeal in relation to the outcome.

(3) If the Upper Tribunal decides to take any action in relation to a decision following a review without first giving every party an opportunity to make representations, the notice under paragraph (2) must state that any party that did not have an opportunity to make representations may apply for such action to be set aside and for the decision to be reviewed again.

Note: Paragraph (1) substituted from 17 October 2011 (SI 2011/2343).

Review of a decision in proceedings under the Forfeiture Act 1982

47.—(1) A person who referred a question to the Upper Tribunal under rule 26 (references under the Forfeiture Act 1982) must refer the Upper Tribunal's previous decision in relation to the question to the Upper Tribunal if they—

(a) consider that the decision should be[set aside and re-made under this rule]; or

(b) have received a written application for the decision to be [set aside and re-made under this rule] from the person to whom the decision related.

(2) The Upper Tribunal may [set aside the decision, either in whole or in part, and re-make it] if—

(a) ...

(b) the decision was made in ignorance of, or was based on a mistake as to, some material fact; or

(c) there has been a relevant change in circumstances since the decision was made.

[(3) Rule 26(2) to (4), Parts 5 and 6 and this Part apply to a reference under this rule as they apply to a reference under rule 26(1).]

(4) ...

(5) ...

Note: Words inserted/substituted in paras (1) and (2), sub-para 2(a) omitted, para (3) substituted and paras (4) and (5) omitted from 17 October 2011 (SI 2011/2343).

[Power to treat an application as a different type of application

48. The Tribunal may treat an application for a decision to be corrected, set aside or reviewed, or for permission to appeal against a decision, as an application for any other one of those things.]

Note: Rule 48 inserted from 29 November 2010 (SI 2010/2653).

[SCHEDULE 1

Procedure after the notice of appeal in appeals against decisions of traffic commissioners]

...

RULE 26A(4)

[SCHEDULE 2
ADDITIONAL PROCEDURE IN NATIONAL SECURITY CERTIFICATE CASES

SCHEDULE 3
PROCEDURE IN FINANCIAL SERVICES CASES]

PRACTICE DIRECTION
IMMIGRATION AND ASYLUM CHAMBERS OF THE FIRST-TIER TRIBUNAL AND
THE UPPER TRIBUNAL

Contents

PART I

Preliminary

PART 2

*Practice Directions for the Immigration and Asylum Chamber
of The First-Tier Tribunal*

PART 3

*Practice Directions for the Immigration and Asylum Chamber
of The Upper Tribunal*

PART 4

*Practice Directions for the Immigration and Asylum Chamber of the
First-Tier Tribunal and The Upper Tribunal*

PART 1

PRELIMINARY

1. *Interpretation, etc.*

1.1 In these Practice Directions:-
"the 2002 Act" means the Nationality, Immigration and Asylum Act 2002;
"the 2007 Act" means the Tribunals, Courts and Enforcement Act 2007;

"adjudicator" means an adjudicator appointed, or treated as appointed, under section 81 of the 2002 Act (as originally enacted);

"AIT" means the Asylum and Immigration Tribunal;

"CMR hearing" means a case management review hearing;

"fast track appeal" means an appeal to which Part 2 of the Fast Track Rules applies;

"Fast Track Rules" means the Asylum and Immigration Tribunal (Fast Track Procedure) Rules 2005;

"First-tier rule", followed by a number, means the rule bearing that number in the Asylum and Immigration Tribunal (Procedure) Rules 2005;

"IAT" means the Immigration Appeal Tribunal;

"Practice Statements" means the Practice Statements - *Immigration and Asylum Chambers of the First-tier Tribunal and the Upper Tribunal* (dated 10 February 2010); and "Practice Statement", followed by a number, means the Statement bearing that number in the Practice Statements;

"Transfer of Functions Order" means the Transfer of Functions of the Asylum and Immigration Tribunal Order 2010 (SI/2010/21);

"The Tribunal" means the Immigration and Asylum Chamber of the First-tier Tribunal or of the Upper Tribunal, as the case may be;

"UT rule", followed by a number, means the rule bearing that number in the Tribunal Procedure (Upper Tribunal) Rules 2008.

1.2 Except where expressly stated to the contrary, any reference in these Practice Directions to an enactment is a reference to that enactment as amended by or under any other enactment.

1.3 Other expressions in these Practice Statements have the same meanings as in the 2007 Act.

1.4 These Practice Directions come into force on 15 February 2010.

1.5 These Practice Directions apply, as appropriate, in relation to transitional cases to which Schedule 4 to the Transfer of Functions Order applies; and references to the First-tier Tribunal and the Upper Tribunal shall be construed accordingly.

PART 2

PRACTICE DIRECTIONS FOR THE IMMIGRATION AND ASYLUM CHAMBER OF THE FIRST-TIER TRIBUNAL

2. *Standard directions in fast track appeals*

2.1 In the case of a fast track appeal, the parties must respectively serve the material specified in Practice Direction 7.5(a) and (b) either at the hearing or, if practicable, on the business day immediately preceding the date of the hearing.

2.2 Subject to the exception mentioned in Practice Direction 7.7, witness statements served in pursuance of paragraph 2.1 shall stand as evidence-in-chief at the hearing.

PART 3

PRACTICE DIRECTIONS FOR THE IMMIGRATION AND ASYLUM CHAMBER OF THE UPPER TRIBUNAL

3. *Procedure on appeal*

3.1 Where permission to appeal to the Upper Tribunal has been granted, then, unless and to the extent that they are directed otherwise, for the purposes of preparing for a hearing in the Upper Tribunal the parties should assume that:-

(a) the Upper Tribunal will decide whether the making of the decision of the First-tier Tribunal involved the making of an error on a point of law, such that the decision should be set aside under section 12(2)(a) of the 2007 Act;

(b) except as specified in Practice Statement 7.2 (disposal of appeals by Upper Tribunal), the Upper Tribunal will proceed to re-make the decision under section 12(2)(b)(ii), if satisfied that the original decision should be set aside; and

(c) in that event, the Upper Tribunal will consider whether to re-make the decision by reference to the First-tier Tribunal's findings of fact and any new documentary evidence submitted under UT rule 15(2A) which it is reasonably practicable to adduce for consideration at that hearing.

3.2 The parties should be aware that, in the circumstances described in paragraph 3.1(c), the Upper Tribunal will generally expect to proceed, without any further hearing, to re-make the decision, where this can be undertaken without having to hear oral evidence. In certain circumstances, the Upper Tribunal may give directions for the giving of oral evidence at the relevant hearing, where it appears appropriate to do so. Such directions may be given before or at that hearing.

3.3 In a case where no oral evidence is likely to be required in order for the Upper Tribunal to re-make the decision, the Upper Tribunal will therefore expect any documentary evidence relevant to the re-making of the decision to be adduced in accordance with Practice Direction 4 so that it may be considered at the relevant hearing; and, accordingly, the party seeking to rely on such documentary evidence will be expected to show good reason why it is not reasonably practicable to adduce the same in order for it to be considered at that hearing.

3.4 If the Upper Tribunal nevertheless decides that it cannot proceed as described in paragraph 3.1(c) because findings of fact are needed which it is not in a position to make, the Upper Tribunal will make arrangements for the adjournment of the hearing, so that the proceedings may be completed before the same constitution of the Tribunal; or, if that is not reasonably practicable, for their transfer to a different constitution, in either case so as to enable evidence to be adduced for that purpose.

3.5 Where proceedings are transferred in the circumstances described in paragraph 3.4, any documents sent to or given by the Tribunal from which the proceedings are transferred shall be deemed to have been sent to or given by the Tribunal to which those proceedings are transferred.

3.6 Where such proceedings are transferred, the Upper Tribunal shall prepare written reasons for finding that the First-tier Tribunal made an error of law, such that its decision fell to be set aside, and those written reasons shall be sent to the parties before the next hearing.

3.7 The written reasons shall be incorporated **in full** in, and form part of, the determination of the Upper Tribunal that re-makes the decision. Only in very exceptional cases can the decision contained in those written reasons be departed from or varied by the Upper Tribunal which re-makes the decision under section 12(2)(b)(ii) of the 2007 Act.

3.8 Unless directed otherwise, the parties to any fast track appeal which is before the Upper Tribunal will be expected to attend with all necessary witnesses and evidence that may be required if the Upper Tribunal should decide that it is necessary to set aside the decision of the First-tier Tribunal and re-make the decision. It will be unusual for the Upper Tribunal to adjourn or transfer, but, if it does so, paragraph 3.6 and 3.7 will, so far as appropriate, apply.

3.9 In this Practice Direction and Practice Direction 4, 'the relevant hearing' means a hearing fixed by the Upper Tribunal at which it will consider if the First-tier Tribunal made an error of law.

3.10 Without prejudice to the generality of paragraph 1.5, where, by virtue of any transitional provisions in Schedule 4 to the Transfer of Functions Order, the Upper Tribunal is undertaking the reconsideration of a decision of the AIT, references in this Practice Direction and Practice Direction 4 to the First-tier Tribunal shall be construed as references to the AIT.

4. *Evidence*

4.1 UT rule 15(2A) imposes important procedural requirements where the Upper Tribunal is asked to consider evidence that was not before the First-tier Tribunal. UT rule 15(2A) must be complied with in **every case** where permission to appeal is granted and a party wishes the Upper Tribunal to consider such evidence. Notice under rule 15(2A)(a), indicating the nature of the evidence and explaining why it was not submitted to the First-tier Tribunal, must be filed with the Upper Tribunal and served on the other party within the time stated in any specific directions given by the Upper Tribunal; or, if no such direction has been given, as soon as practicable after permission to appeal has been granted.

4.2 A party who wishes the Upper Tribunal to consider any evidence that was not before the First-tier Tribunal must indicate in the notice whether the evidence is sought to be adduced:-
  (a) in connection with the issue of whether the First-tier Tribunal made an error of law, requiring its decision to be set aside; or
  (b) in connection with the re-making of the decision by the Upper Tribunal, in the event of the First-tier Tribunal being found to have made such an error.

4.3 The notice must clearly indicate whether the party concerned wishes the evidence to be considered at the relevant hearing and state whether the evidence is in oral or documentary form.

4.4 Where a party wishes, in the circumstances described in paragraph 4.2(b), to adduce only documentary evidence, Practice Direction 3.3 will apply.

4.5 Where a party wishes, in the circumstances described in paragraph 4.2(b), to adduce oral evidence at the relevant hearing, the notice must explain why it is considered desirable to proceed in such a manner and give details of the oral evidence and a time estimate.

4.6 Where the Upper Tribunal acts under Practice Direction 3 to adjourn or transfer the hearing, it shall consider any notice given under UT rule 15(2A) and give any directions arising therefrom, if and to the extent that this has not already been done.

4.7 This Practice Direction does not apply in the case of a fast track appeal (as to which, see Practice Direction 3.8).

5. *Pursuing appeal after grant of leave*

5.1 This Practice Direction applies where:-
   (a) an appeal would otherwise fall to be treated as abandoned pursuant to section 104(4A) of the 2002 Act because the appellant is granted leave to remain in the United Kingdom; but
   (b) the appellant wishes, in pursuance of section 104(4B) or (4C), to pursue the appeal, insofar as it is brought on asylum grounds or on grounds of unlawful discrimination.

5.2 Where this Practice Direction applies, the appellant must comply with the following requirements (which are the relevant practice directions for the purposes of UT rule 17A(3)).

5.3 Where section 104(4B) of the 2002 Act (asylum grounds) applies, the notice required by UT rule 17A(3) to be sent or delivered to the Upper Tribunal must state:-
   (a) the appellant's full name and date of birth;
   (b) the Tribunal's reference number;
   (c) the Home Office reference number, if applicable;
   (d) the Foreign and Commonwealth Office reference number, if applicable;
   (e) the date on which the appellant was granted leave to enter or remain in the United Kingdom for a period exceeding 12 months; and
   (f) that the appellant wishes to pursue the appeal in so far as it is brought on the ground specified in section 84(1)(g) of the 2002 Act which relates to the Refugee Convention.

5.4 Where section 104(4C) of the 2002 Act (grounds of unlawful discrimination) applies, the notice required by UT rule 17A(3) to be sent or delivered to the Upper Tribunal must state:-
   (a) the appellant's full name and date of birth;
   (b) the Tribunal's reference number;
   (c) the Home Office reference number, if applicable;
   (d) the Foreign and Commonwealth Office reference number, if applicable;
   (e) the date on which the appellant was granted leave to enter or remain in the United Kingdom; and
   (f) that the appellant wishes to pursue the appeal in so far as it is brought on the ground specified in section 84(1)(b) of the 2002 Act which relates to section 19B of the Race Relations Act 1976 (discrimination by public authorities).

5.5 Where an appellant has sent or delivered a notice under UT rule 17A(3), the Upper Tribunal will notify the appellant of the date on which it received the notice.

5.6 The Upper Tribunal will send a copy of the notice issued under paragraph 5.5 to the respondent.

5.7 In this Practice Direction:-

"appellant" means the party who was the appellant before the First- tier Tribunal; and

"respondent" means the party who was the respondent before the First-tier Tribunal.

PART 4
PRACTICE DIRECTIONS FOR THE IMMIGRATION AND ASYLUM CHAMBER OF THE FIRST-TIER TRIBUNAL AND THE UPPER TRIBUNAL

6. *Form of notice of appeal etc.*

6.1 The form of notice approved for the purpose of:-
   (a) First-tier rule 8 (notice of appeal);

(b) First-tier rule 24 (application for permission to appeal to the Upper Tribunal);

(c) First-tier rule 38 (application for bail); and

(d) UT rule 21 (application to the Upper Tribunal for permission to appeal).

as the case may be, is the appropriate form as displayed on the Tribunal's website at the time when the notice is given, or that form with any variations that circumstances may require.

7. *Case management review hearings and directions*

7.1 Where the Tribunal so directs, a CMR hearing will be held in the case of an appeal where the party who is or was the appellant before the First-tier Tribunal:-

(a) is present in the United Kingdom; and

(b) has a right of appeal whilst in the United Kingdom.

7.2 It is important that the parties and their representatives understand that a CMR hearing is a hearing in the appeal and that the appeal may be determined under the relevant Procedure Rules if a party does not appear and is not represented at that hearing.

7.3 In addition to any information required by First-tier rule 8 (form of contents and notice of appeal), the appellant before the First-tier Tribunal must provide that Tribunal and the respondent at the CMR hearing with:-

(a) particulars of any application for permission to vary the grounds of appeal;

(b) particulars of any amendments to the reasons in support of the grounds of appeal;

(c) particulars of any witnesses to be called or whose written statement or report is proposed to be relied upon at the full hearing; and

(d) the draft of any directions that the appellant is requesting the Tribunal to make at the CMR hearing.

7.4 In addition to any documents required by relevant Procedure Rules, the party who is or was the respondent before the First-tier Tribunal must provide the Tribunal and the other party at the CMR hearing with:-

(a) any amendment that has been made or is proposed to be made to the notice of decision to which the appeal relates or to any other document served on the person concerned giving reasons for that decision; and

(b) a draft of any directions that the Tribunal is requested to make at the CMR hearing.

7.5 In most cases, including those appeals where a CMR hearing is to be held, the Tribunal will normally have given to the parties the following directions with the notice of hearing:-

(a) not later than 5 working days before the full hearing (or 10 days in the case of an out-of-country appeal) the appellant shall serve on the Tribunal and the respondent:

(i) witness statements of the evidence to be called at the hearing, such statements to stand as evidence in chief at the hearing;

(ii) a paginated and indexed bundle of all the documents to be relied on at the hearing with a schedule identifying the essential passages;

(iii) a skeleton argument, identifying all relevant issues including human rights claims and citing all the authorities relied upon; and

(iv) a chronology of events;

(b) not later than 5 working days before the full hearing, the respondent shall serve on the Tribunal and the appellant a paginated and indexed bundle of all the documents to be relied upon at the hearing, with a schedule identifying the relevant passages, and a list of any authorities relied upon.

7.6 At the end of the CMR hearing, the Tribunal will give the parties any further written directions relating to the conduct of the appeal.

7.7 Although in normal circumstances a witness statement should stand as evidence-in-chief, there may be cases where it will be appropriate for appellants or witnesses to have the opportunity of adding to or supplementing their witness statements.

7.8 In addition to the directions referred to above, at the end of the CMR hearing the Tribunal will also give to the parties written confirmation of:-

(a) any issues that have been agreed at the CMR hearing as being relevant to the determination of the appeal; and

(b) any concessions made at the CMR hearing by a party.

8. *Trial bundles*

8.1 The parties must take all reasonably practicable steps to act in accordance with paragraph 8.2 to 8.6 in the preparation of trial bundles for hearings before the Tribunal.

8.2 The best practice for the preparation of bundles is as follows:-

(a) all documents must be relevant, be presented in logical order and be legible;

(b) where the document is not in the English language, a typed translation of the document signed by the translator, and certifying that the translation is accurate, must be inserted in the bundle next to the copy of the original document, together with details of the identity and qualifications of the translator;

(c) if it is necessary to include a lengthy document, that part of the document on which reliance is placed should, unless the passages are outlined in any skeleton argument, be highlighted or clearly identified by reference to page and/or paragraph number;

(d) bundles submitted must have an index showing the page numbers of each document in the bundle;

(e) the skeleton argument or written submission should define and confine the areas at issue in a numbered list of brief points and each point should refer to any documentation in the bundle on which the appellant proposes to rely (together with its page number);

(f) where reliance is placed on a particular case or text, photocopies of the case or text must be provided in full for the Tribunal and the other party; and

(g) large bundles should be contained in a ring binder or lever arch file, capable of lying flat when opened.

8.3 The Tribunal recognises the constraints on those representing the parties in appeals in relation to the preparation of trial bundles and this Practice Direction does not therefore make it mandatory in every case that bundles in exactly the form prescribed must be prepared. Where the issues are particularly complex it is of the highest importance that comprehensive bundles are prepared. If parties to appeals fail in individual cases to present documentation in a way which complies with the direction, it will be for the Tribunal to deal with any such issue.

8.4 Much evidence in immigration and asylum appeals is in documentary form. Representatives preparing bundles need to be aware of the position of the Tribunal, which may be coming to the case for the first time. The better a bundle has been prepared, the greater it will assist the Tribunal. Bundles should contain all the documents that the Tribunal will require to enable it to reach a decision without the need to refer to any other file or document. The Tribunal will not be assisted by repetitious, outdated or irrelevant material.

8.5 It may not be practical in many appeals to require there to be an agreed trial bundle but it nevertheless remains vital that the parties inform each other at an early stage of all and any documentation upon which they intend to rely.

8.6 The parties cannot rely on the Tribunal having any prior familiarity with any country information or background reports in relation to the case in question. If either party wishes to rely on such country or background information, copies of the relevant documentation must be provided.

9. *Adjournments*

9.1 Applications for the adjournment of appeals (other than fast track appeals) listed for hearing before the Tribunal must be made not later than 5.00p.m. one clear working day before the date of the hearing.

9.2 For the avoidance of doubt, where a case is listed for hearing on, for example, a Friday, the application must be received by 5.00p.m. on the Wednesday.

9.3 The application for an adjournment must be supported by full reasons and must be made in accordance with relevant Procedure Rules.

9.4 Any application made later than the end of the period mentioned in paragraph 9.1 must be made to the Tribunal at the hearing and will require the attendance of the party or the representative of the party seeking the adjournment.

9.5 It will be only in the most exceptional circumstances that a late application for an adjournment will be considered without the attendance of a party or representative.

9.6 Parties must not assume that an application, even if made in accordance with paragraph 9.1, will be successful and they must always check with the Tribunal as to the outcome of the application.

9.7 Any application for the adjournment of a fast track appeal must be made to the Tribunal at the hearing and will be considered by the Tribunal in accordance with relevant Procedure Rules.

9.8 If an adjournment is not granted and the party fails to attend the hearing, the Tribunal may in certain circumstances proceed with the hearing in that party's absence.

10. *Expert evidence*

10.1 A party who instructs an expert must provide clear and precise instructions to the expert, together with all relevant information concerning the nature of the appellant's case, including the appellant's immigration history, the reasons why the appellant's claim or application has been refused by the respondent and copies of any relevant previous reports prepared in respect of the appellant.

10.2 It is the duty of an expert to help the Tribunal on matters within the expert's own expertise. This duty is paramount and overrides any obligation to the person from whom the expert has received instructions or by whom the expert is paid.

10.3 Expert evidence should be the independent product of the expert uninfluenced by the pressures of litigation.

10.4 An expert should assist the Tribunal by providing objective, unbiased opinion on matters within his or her expertise, and should not assume the role of an advocate.

10.5 An expert should consider all material facts, including those which might detract from his or her opinion.

10.6 An expert should make it clear:-
  (a) when a question or issue falls outside his or her expertise; and
  (b) when the expert is not able to reach a definite opinion, for example because of insufficient information.

10.7 If, after producing a report, an expert changes his or her view on any material matter, that change of view should be communicated to the parties without delay, and when appropriate to the Tribunal.

10.8 An expert's report should be addressed to the Tribunal and not to the party from whom the expert has received instructions.

10.9 An expert's report must be:-
(a) give details of the expert's qualifications;
(b) give details of any literature or other material which the expert has relied on in making the report;
(c) contain a statement setting out the substance of all facts and instructions given to the expert which are material to the opinions expressed in the report or upon which those opinions are based;
(d) make clear which of the facts stated in the report are within the expert's own knowledge;
(e) say who carried out any examination, measurement or other procedure which the expert has used for the report, give the qualifications of that person, and say whether or not the procedure has been carried out under the expert's supervision;
(f) where there is a range of opinion on the matters dealt with in the report:
   (i) summarise the range of opinion, so far as reasonably practicable, and
   (ii) give reasons for the expert's own opinion;
(g) contain a summary of the conclusions reached;
(h) if the expert is not able to give an opinion without qualification, state the qualification; and
(j) contain a statement that the expert understands his or her duty to the Tribunal, and has complied and will continue to comply with that duty.

10.10 An expert's report must be verified by a Statement of Truth as well as containing the statements required in paragraph 10.9(h) and (j).

10.11 The form of the Statement of Truth is as follows:-
"I confirm that insofar as the facts stated in my report are within my own knowledge I have made clear which they are and I believe them to be true, and that the opinions I have expressed represent my true and complete professional opinion".

10.12 The instructions referred to in paragraph 10.9(c) are not protected by privilege but cross-examination of the expert on the contents of the instructions will not be allowed unless the Tribunal permits it (or unless the party who gave the instructions consents to it). Before it gives permission the Tribunal must be satisfied that there are reasonable grounds to consider that the statement in the report or the substance of the instructions is inaccurate or incomplete. If the Tribunal is so satisfied, it will allow the cross-examination where it appears to be in the interests of justice to do so.

10.13 In this Practice Direction:-
"appellant" means the party who is or was the appellant before the First-tier Tribunal; and
"respondent" means the party who is or was the respondent before the First-tier Tribunal.

11. *Citation of unreported determinations*

11.1 A determination of the Tribunal which has not been reported may not be cited in proceedings before the Tribunal unless:-
(a) the person who is or was the appellant before the First-tier Tribunal, or a member of that person's family, was a party to the proceedings in which the previous determination was issued; or
(b) the Tribunal gives permission.

11.2 An application for permission to cite a determination which has not been reported must:-
(a) include a **full** transcript of the determination;
(b) identify the proposition for which the determination is to be cited; and
(c) certify that the proposition is not to be found in any reported determination of the Tribunal, the IAT or the AIT and had not been superseded by the decision of a higher authority.

11.3 Permission under paragraph 11.1 will be given only where the Tribunal considers that it would be materially assisted by citation of the determination, as distinct from the adoption in argument of the reasoning to be found in the determination. Such instances are likely to be rare; in particular, in the case of determinations which were unreportable (see Practice Statement 11 (reporting of determinations)). It should be emphasised that the Tribunal will not exclude good arguments from consideration but it will be rare for such an argument to be capable of being made only by reference to an unreported determination.

11.4 The provisions of paragraph 11.1 to 11.3 apply to unreported and unreportable determinations of the AIT, the IAT and adjudicators, as those provisions apply respectively to unreported and unreportable determinations of the Tribunal.

11.5 A party citing a determination of the IAT bearing a neutral citation number prior to [2003] (including all series of "bracket numbers") must be in a position to certify that the matter or proposition for which the determination is cited has not been the subject of more recent, reported, determinations of the IAT, the AIT or the Tribunal.

11.6 In this Practice Direction and Practice Direction 12, "determination" includes any decision of the AIT or the Tribunal.

12.   *Starred and Country Guidance determinations*

12.1 Reported determinations of the Tribunal, the AIT and the IAT which are "starred" shall be treated by the Tribunal as authoritative in respect of the matter to which the "starring" relates, unless inconsistent with other authority that is binding on the Tribunal.

12.2 A reported determination of the Tribunal, the AIT or the IAT bearing the letters "CG" shall be treated as an authoritative finding on the country guidance issue identified in the determination, based upon the evidence before the members of the Tribunal, the AIT or the IAT that determine the appeal. As a result, unless it has been expressly superseded or replaced by any later "CG" determination, or is inconsistent with other authority that is binding on the Tribunal, such a country guidance case is authoritative in any subsequent appeal, so far as that appeal:-

(a) relates to the country guidance issue in question; and
(b) depends upon the same or similar evidence.

12.3 A list of current CG cases will be maintained on the Tribunal's website. Any representative of a party to an appeal concerning a particular country will be expected to be conversant with the current "CG" determinations relating to that country.

12.4 Because of the principle that like cases should be treated in like manner, any failure to follow a clear, apparently applicable country guidance case or to show why it does not apply to the case in question is likely to be regarded as grounds for appeal on a point of law.

13.   *Bail applications*

13.1 An application for bail must if practicable be listed for hearing within three working days of receipt by the Tribunal of the notice of application.

13.2 Any such notice which is received by the Tribunal after 3.30p.m. on a particular day will be treated for the purposes of this paragraph as if it were received on the next business day.

13.3 An Upper Tribunal judge may exercise bail jurisdiction under the Immigration Act 1971 by reason of being also a First-tier judge.

13.4 Notwithstanding paragraph 13.3, it will usually be appropriate for a bail application to be made to an Upper Tribunal judge only where the appeal in question is being heard by the Upper Tribunal, or where a hearing before the Upper Tribunal is imminent. In case of doubt, a potential applicant should consult the bails section of the First-tier Tribunal.

14 This Practice Direction is made by the Senior President of Tribunals with the agreement of
the Lord Chancellor. It is made in the exercise of powers conferred by the Tribunals, Courts and
Enforcement Act 2007.

Practice Direction

Fresh Claim Judicial Review in the Immigration and Asylum Chamber of The Upper Tribunal

Contents

Part 1

Preliminary

Part 2
Scope

Part 3
General Provisions

The application to bring judicial review proceedings

The substantive hearing

PART 4
Urgent Applications for Permission to Bring Judicial Review Proceedings

11. Request for Urgent Consideration
12. Notifying the other parties
13. Consideration by Tribunal

PART 5
Applications which Challenge Removal

14. General
15. Special requirements regarding the application
16. Referral in case of non-compliance
17. Application clearly without merit

PART 1
PRELIMINARY

1. *Interpretation*

1.1 In these Practice Directions:-
"applicant" has the same meaning as in the UT Rules;

"the application" means the written application under rule 28 for permission to bring judicial review proceedings;

"fresh claim proceedings" has the same meaning as in the UT Rules;

"party" has the same meaning as in the UT Rules;

"respondent" has the same meaning as in the UT Rules;

"the Tribunal" means the Immigration and Asylum Chamber of the Upper Tribunal;

"UKBA" means the UK Border Agency of the Home Office;

"UT Rules" means the Tribunal Procedure (Upper Tribunal) Rules 2008 and "rule", followed by a number, means the rule bearing that number in the UT Rules.

PART 2
SCOPE

2. *Scope*

2.1 Parts 3 and 4 of these Practice Directions apply to fresh claim proceedings.

2.2 Part 5 of these Practice Directions applies to proceedings to which Part 3 applies, where:-
   (a) a person has been served with a copy of directions for that person's removal from the United Kingdom by UKBA and notified that Part 5 applies; and

   (b) that person makes an application to the Tribunal or a court for permission to bring judicial review proceedings or to apply for judicial review, before the removal takes effect.

2.3 In the case of proceedings transferred to the Tribunal by a court, the Tribunal will expect the applicant to have complied with all relevant Practice Directions of that court that applied up to the point of transfer. In the event of non-compliance, the Tribunal will make such directions pursuant to rule 27(1)(b) as are necessary and which may, in particular, include applying provisions of these Practice Directions.

PART 3

GENERAL PROVISIONS

The application to bring judicial review proceedings

3. *Form of application*

3.1 The application must be made using the form displayed on the Upper Tribunal's website at the time the application is made.

4. *Additional materials to be filed with the application*

4.1 Without prejudice to rule 28, the application must be accompanied by:-
   (a) any written evidence on which it is intended to rely (but see paragraph 4.2 below);
   (b) copies of any relevant statutory material; and
   (c) a list of essential documents for advance reading by the Tribunal (with page references to the passages relied on).

4.2 The applicant may rely on the matters set out in the application as evidence under this Practice Direction if the application is verified by a statement of truth.

5. *Bundle of documents to be sent etc. with the application*

5.1 The applicant must file two copies of a paginated and indexed bundle containing all the documents required by rule 28 and these Practice Directions to be sent or delivered with the application.

6. *Permission without a hearing*

6.1 The Tribunal will generally, in the first instance, consider the question of permission without a hearing.

The substantive hearing

7. *Additional grounds at the substantive hearing*

7.1 Where an applicant who has been given permission to bring judicial review proceedings intends to apply under rule 32 to rely on additional grounds at the substantive hearing, the applicant must give written notice to the Tribunal and to any other person served with the application, not later than 7 working days before that hearing.

8. *Skeleton arguments for the substantive hearing*

8.1 The applicant must serve a skeleton argument on the Tribunal and on any other person served with the application, not later than 21 days before the substantive hearing.

8.2 The respondent and any other party wishing to make representations at the hearing must serve a skeleton argument on the Tribunal and on the applicant, not later than 14 days before the hearing.

8.3 Skeleton arguments must contain:-
   (a) a time estimate for the complete hearing, including the giving of the decision by the Tribunal;
   (b) a list of issues;
   (c) a list of the legal points to be taken (together with any relevant authorities with page references to the passages relied on);
   (d) a chronology of events (with page references to the bundle of documents (see Practice Direction 9 below);
   (e) a list of essential documents for the advance reading of the Tribunal (with page references to the passages relied on) (if different from that served with the application) and a time estimate for that reading; and
   (f) a list of persons referred to.

9. *Bundle of documents for the substantive hearing*

9.1 The applicant must serve on the Tribunal and any other person served with the application a paginated and indexed bundle of all relevant documents required for the substantive hearing, when the applicant's skeleton argument is served.

9.2 The bundle must also include those documents required by the respondent and any other person who is expected to make representations at the hearing.

10. *Agreed final order*

10.1 If the parties agree about the final order to be made, the applicant must file at the Tribunal a document (with 2 copies) signed by all the parties setting out the terms of the proposed agreed order, together with a short statement of the matters relied on as justifying the proposed agreed order and copies of any authorities or statutory provisions relied on.

10.2 The Tribunal will consider the documents referred to in paragraph 10.1 above and will make the order if satisfied that the order should be made.

10.3 If the Tribunal is not satisfied that the order should be made, a hearing date will be set.

PART 4
URGENT APPLICATIONS FOR PERMISSION TO BRING JUDICIAL REVIEW PROCEEDINGS

11. *Request for Urgent Consideration*

11.1 Where it is intended to request the Tribunal to deal urgently with the application or where an interim injunction is sought, the applicant must serve with the application a written "Request for Urgent Consideration", in the form displayed on the Upper Tribunal's website at the time the application is made, which states:

   (a) the need for urgency;

   (b) the timescale sought for the consideration of the application (eg. within 72 hours or sooner if necessary); and

   (c) the date by which the substantive hearing should take place.

11.2 Where an interim injunction is sought, the applicant must, in addition, provide:

   (a) the draft order; and

   (b) the grounds for the injunction.

12. *Notifying the other parties*

12.1 The applicant must serve (by fax and post) the application form and the Request for Urgent Consideration on the respondent and interested parties, advising them of the application and that they may make representations.

12.2 Where an interim injunction is sought, the applicant must serve (by fax and post) the draft order and grounds for the injunction on the respondent and interested parties, advising them of the application and that they may make representations.

13. *Consideration by Tribunal*

13.1 The Tribunal will consider the application within the time requested and may make such order as it considers appropriate.

13.2 If the Tribunal specifies that a hearing shall take place within a specified time, the representatives of the parties must liaise with the Tribunal and each other to fix a hearing of the application within that time.

PART 5

APPLICATIONS WHICH CHALLENGE REMOVAL

14 *General*

14.1 The requirements contained in this Part are additional to those contained in Part 3 and (where applicable) Part 4 of these Practice Directions.

14.2 Nothing in these Practice Directions prevents a person from making the application after that person has been removed from the United Kingdom.

15 *Special requirements regarding the application*

15.1 Without prejudice to rule 28, the application must:-

   (a) indicate on its face that this Part of these Practice Directions applies; and

   (b) be accompanied by:-

     (i) a copy of the removal directions and the decisions to which the application relates; and

     (ii) any document served with the removal directions including any document which contains UKBA's factual summary of the case; and

   (c) contain or be accompanied by the detailed statement of the applicant's grounds for making the application.

15.2 If the applicant is unable to comply with paragraph 15.1(b) or (c) above, the application must contain or be accompanied by a statement of the reasons why.

15.3 Notwithstanding rule 28A, immediately upon issue of the application, the applicant must send copies of the issued application form and accompanying documents to the address specified by the United Kingdom Border Agency.

16 *Referral in case of non-compliance*

16.1 Where the applicant has not complied with Practice Direction 15.1(b) or (c) above and has provided reasons for not complying, and the Tribunal has issued the application form, the Tribunal's staff will:-

(a) refer the matter to a Judge for consideration as soon as practicable; and

(b) notify the parties that they have done so.

17 *Application clearly without merit*

17.1 If, upon a refusal to grant permission to bring judicial review proceedings, the Tribunal indicates that the application is clearly without merit, that indication will be included in the order refusing permission.

These Practice Directions are made by the Senior President of Tribunals with the agreement of the Lord Chancellor. They are made in the exercise of powers conferred by the Tribunals, Courts and Enforcement Act 2007.

LORD JUSTICE CARNWATH SENIOR PRESIDENT OF
TRIBUNALS 17 OCTOBER 2011

...

IMMIGRATION RULES

Immigration Rules
(HC 395)

Laid before Parliament on 23 May 1994 under section 3(2) of the Immigration Act 1971

Arrangement of Rules

PART 2. PERSONS SEEKING TO ENTER OR REMAIN IN THE UNITED KINGDOM FOR VISITS

PART 3. PERSONS SEEKING TO ENTER OR REMAIN IN THE UNITED KINGDOM FOR STUDIES

PART 4. PERSONS SEEKING TO ENTER OR REMAIN IN THE UNITED KINGDOM IN AN 'AU PAIR' PLACEMENT, AS A WORKING HOLIDAYMAKER, OR FOR TRAINING OR WORK EXPERIENCE

PART 5. PERSONS SEEKING TO ENTER OR REMAIN IN THE UNITED KINGDOM FOR EMPLOYMENT

PART 6. PERSONS SEEKING TO ENTER OR REMAIN IN THE UNITED KINGDOM AS A BUSINESSMAN, SELF-EMPLOYED PERSON, INVESTOR, WRITER, COMPOSER OR ARTIST

PART 6A. POINTS-BASED SYSTEM

INTRODUCTION

1. The Home Secretary has made changes in the Rules laid down by him as to the practice to be followed in the administration of the Immigration Acts for regulating entry into and the stay of persons in the United Kingdom and contained in the statement laid before Parliament on 23 March 1990 (HC 251) (as amended). This statement contains the Rules as changed and replaces the provisions of HC 251 (as amended).

2. Immigration Officers, Entry Clearance Officers and all staff of the Home Office Immigration and Nationality [Directorate] will carry out their duties without regard to the race, colour or religion of persons seeking to enter or remain in the United Kingdom [and in compliance with the provisions of the Human Rights Act 1998].

Note: Words in square brackets inserted from 2 October 2000 (Cm 4851).

3. In these Rules words importing the masculine gender includes the feminine unless the contrary intention appears.

Implementation and transitional provisions

4. These Rules come into effect on 1 October 1994 and will apply to all decisions taken on or after that date save that any application made before 1 October 1994 for entry clearance, leave to enter or remain or variation of leave to enter or remain [other than an application for leave by a person seeking asylum,] shall be decided under the provisions of HC 251, as amended, as if these Rules had not been made.

Note: Inserted from 1 September 1996 (Cm 3365).

Application

[5. Save where expressly indicated, these Rules do not apply to those persons who are entitled to enter or remain in the United Kingdom by virtue of the provisions of {the 2006 EEA Regulations}. But any person who is not entitled to rely on the provisions of those Regulations is covered by these Rules.]

Note: Substituted from 2 October 2000 (Cm 4851). Words in curly brackets substituted from 30 April 2006 (HC 1053).

Interpretation

6. In these Rules the following interpretations apply:

['Immigration Acts' has the same meaning as it has in the Interpretation Act 1978.]

'the 1993 Act' is the Asylum and Immigration Appeals Act 1993.

['the 1996 Act' is the Asylum and Immigration Act 1996.]

['the 2006 EEA Regulations' means the Immigration (European Economic Area) Regulations 2006.]

['adoption' unless the contrary intention appears, includes a de facto adoption in accordance with the requirements of paragraph 309A of these Rules, and 'adopted' and 'adoptive parent' should be construed accordingly.]

[In Appendix FM references to 'application for leave to remain' include an application for variation of leave to enter or remain of a person in the UK.]

['Approved Destination Status Agreement with China' means the Memorandum of Understanding on visa and related issues concerning tourist groups from the People's Republic of China to the United Kingdom as an approved destination, signed on 21 January 2005.]

['a bona fide private education institution' is a private education institution which:

(a) maintains satisfactory records of enrolment and attendance of students, and supplies these to the Border and Immigration Agency when requested;

(b) provides courses which involve a minimum of 15 hours organised daytime study per week;

(c) ensures a suitably qualified tutor is present during the hours of study to offer teaching and instruction to the students;

(d) offers courses leading to qualifications recognised by the appropriate accreditation bodies;

(e) employs suitably qualified staff to provide teaching, guidance and support to the students;

(f) provides adequate accommodation, facilities, staffing levels and equipment to support the numbers of students enrolled at the institution; and

(g) if it offers tuition support to external students at degree level, ensures that such students are registered with the UK degree awarding body.]

['Business day' means any day other than Saturday or Sunday, a day which is a bank holiday under the Banking and Financial Dealings Act 1971 in the part of the United Kingdom to which the notice is sent, Christmas Day or Good Friday.]

['civil partner' means a civil partnership which exists under or by virtue of the Civil Partnership Act 2004 (and any reference to a civil partner is to be read accordingly);]

['conviction' means conviction for a criminal offence in the UK or any other country.]

['degree level study' means a course which leads to a recognised United Kingdom degree at bachelor's level or above, or an equivalent qualification at level 6 or above of the revised National Qualifications Framework, or levels 9 or above of the Scottish Credit and Qualifications Framework;]

[Under Part 8 of these rules, 'post-graduate level study' means a course at level 7 or above of the revised National Qualifications Framework or Qualifications and Credit Framework, or level 11 or above of the Scottish Credit and Qualifications Framework, which leads to a recognised United Kingdom postgraduate degree at Master's level or above, or an equivalent qualification at the same level.]

['foundation degree' means a programme of study which leads to a qualification awarded by an English higher education institution with degree awarding powers which is at a minimum of level 5 on the revised National Qualifications Framework, or awarded on a directly equivalent basis in the devolved administrations.]

[A 'UK recognised body' is an institution that has been granted degree-awarding powers by either a Royal Charter, an Act of Parliament or the Privy Council.][For the purposes of these rules we will consider the Foundation Programme Office and the Yorkshire and Humber Strategic Health Authority as equivalent to UK recognised bodies.]

[A 'UK listed body' is an institution that is not a UK recognised body but which provides full courses that lead to the award of a degree by a UK recognised body.]

['EEA national' has the meaning given in regulation 2(1) of the 2006 EEA Regulations.]

['an external student' is a student studying for a degree from a UK degree awarding body without any requirement to attend the UK degree awarding body's premises or a UK Listed Body's premises for lectures and tutorials.]

'United Kingdom passport' bears the meaning it has in the Immigration Act 1971.

['a UK Bachelors degree' means–

(a) a programme of study or research which leads to the award, by or on behalf of a university, college or other body which is authorised by Royal Charter or by or under an Act of Parliament to grant degrees, of a qualification designated by the awarding institution to be of Bachelors degree level; or

(b) a programme of study or research, which leads to a recognised award for the purposes of section 214(2)(c) of the Education Reform Act 1988, of a qualification designated by the awarding institution to be of Bachelors degree level.]

'Immigration Officer' includes a Customs Officer acting as an Immigration Officer.

['Multiple Entry work permit employment' is work permit employment where the person concerned does not intend to spend a continuous period in the United Kingdom in work permit employment.]

['public funds' means—

(a) housing under Part VI or VII of the Housing Act 1996 and under Part II of the Housing Act 1985, Part I or II of the Housing (Scotland) Act 1987, Part II of the Housing (Northern Ireland) Order 1981 or Part II of the Housing (Northern Ireland) Order 1988;

(b) attendance allowance, severe disablement allowance, {carer's allowance} and disability living allowance under Part III of the Social Security Contribution and Benefits Act 1992; income support, . . . council tax benefit, . . . and housing benefit under Part VII of that Act; a social fund payment under Part VIII of that Act; child benefit under Part IX of that Act; income based jobseeker's allowance under the Jobseekers Act 1995; [income related allowance under Part 1 of the Welfare Reform Act 2007 (employment and support allowance)]{; state pension credit under the State Pension Credit Act 2002; or child tax credit and working tax credit under Part 1 of the Tax Credits Act 2002.}

(c) attendance allowance, severe disablement allowance, {carer's allowance} and disability living allowance under Part III of the Social Security Contribution and Benefits (Northern Ireland) Act 1992; income support, . . . council tax benefit, [and] . . . housing benefit under Part VII of that Act; a social fund payment under Part VIII of that Act; child benefit under Part IX of that Act; .. income based jobseeker's allowance under the Jobseekers (Northern Ireland) Order 1995 [or income related allowance under Part 1 of the Welfare Reform Act (Northern Ireland) 2007].

(d) . . .]

'settled in the United Kingdom' means that the person concerned:

(a) is free from any restriction on the period for which he may remain save that a person entitled to an exemption under Section 8 of the Immigration Act 1971 otherwise than as a member of the home forces) is not to be regarded as settled in the United Kingdom except in so far as Section 8(5A) so provides; and

(b) is either:

(i) ordinarily resident in the United Kingdom without having entered or remained in breach of the immigration laws; or

(ii) despite having entered or remained in breach of the immigration laws, has subsequently entered lawfully or has been granted leave to remain and is ordinarily resident.

'a parent' includes

(a) the stepfather of a child whose father is dead [(and the reference to a stepfather includes a relationship arising through civil partnership)];

(b) the stepmother of a child whose mother is dead; [(and the reference to a stepmother includes a relationship arising through civil partnership)];

(c) the father as well as the mother of an illegitimate child where he is proved to be the father;

(d) an adoptive parent, where a child was adopted in accordance with a decision taken by the competent administrative authority or court in a country whose adoption orders are recognised by the United Kingdom or where a child is the subject of a de facto adoption in accordance with the requirements of paragraph 309A of these Rules (except that an adopted child or child who is the subject of a de facto adoption may not make an application for leave to enter or remain in order to accompany, join or remain with an adoptive parent under paragraphs 297 to 303);

(e) in the case of a child born in the United Kingdom who is not a British citizen, a person to whom there has been a genuine transfer of parental responsibility on the ground of the original parent(s)' inability to care for the child.

['date of application' means the date of application determined in accordance with paragraph 30 or 34G of these rules as appropriate.]

['a valid application' means an application made in accordance with the requirements of Part 1 of these Rules.]

['refugee leave' means limited leave granted pursuant to paragraph 334 or 335 of these rules and has not been revoked pursuant to paragraph 339A or 339B of these rules.]

['humanitarian protection' means limited leave granted pursuant to paragraph 339C of these rules and has not been revoked pursuant to paragraph 339G or 339H of these rules.]

['a period of imprisonment' referred to in these rules has the same meaning as set out in section 38(2) of the UK Borders Act 2007.]

['Overstayed' or 'Overstaying' means the applicant has stayed in the UK beyond the latest of:

(i) the time limit attached to the last period of leave granted, or

(ii) beyond the period that his leave was extended under sections 3C or 3D of the Immigration Act 1971, or

(iii) the date that an applicant receives the notice of invalidity declaring that an application for leave to remain is not a valid application, provided the application was submitted before the time limit attached to the last period of leave expired.]

['intention to live permanently with the other' means an intention to live together, evidenced by a clear commitment from both parties that they will live together permanently in the United Kingdom immediately following the outcome of the application in question or as soon as circumstances permit thereafter, [and intend to live together permanently.]

['present and settled' means that the person concerned is settled in the United Kingdom, and, at the time that an application under these Rules is made, is physically present here or is coming here with or to join the applicant and intends to make the United Kingdom their home with the applicant if the application is successful;] [For the purposes of Appendix FM a member of HM Forces serving overseas, or a permanent member of HM Diplomatic Service, or a comparable UK-based staff member of the British Council on a tour of duty abroad, or a staff member of the Department for International Development or the Home Office, who is a British Citizen or settled in the UK, is to be regarded as present and settled in the UK.]

['sponsor' means the person in relation to whom an applicant is seeking leave to enter or remain as their {spouse, fiancé, civil partner, proposed civil partner, unmarried partner, same-sex partner} or dependent relative, as the case may be, under paragraphs 277 to 295O or 317 to 319;] [or the person in relation to whom an applicant is seeking entry clearance or leave as their partner or dependent relative under Appendix FM.]

['prohibited degree of relationship' has the same meaning as in the Marriage Act 1949, the Marriage (Prohibited Degrees of Relationship) Act 1986 and the Civil Partnership Act 2004.]

['overcrowded' means overcrowded within the meaning of the Housing Act 1985, the Housing (Scotland) Act 1987 or the Housing (Northern Ireland) Order 1988 (as appropriate).]

['working illegally' means working in breach of conditions of leave or working when in the UK without valid leave where such leave is required.]

['in breach of immigration laws' means without valid leave where such leave is required, or in breach of the conditions of leave.]

['adequate' and 'adequately' in relation to a maintenance and accommodation requirement shall mean that, after income tax, [national insurance contributions] and housing costs have been deducted, there must be available to the family the level of income that would be available to them if the family was in receipt of income support.]

['occupy exclusively' in relation to accommodation shall mean that part of the accommodation must be for the exclusive use of the [family].]

['must not be leading an independent life' means that the applicant does not have a partner as defined in Appendix FM; is living with their parents (except where they are at boarding school, [college or university] as part of their full-time education); is not employed full-time (unless aged 18 years or over); is wholly or mainly dependent upon their parents for financial support (unless aged 18 years or over); and is wholly or mainly dependent upon their parents for emotional support.]

['visa nationals' are the persons specified in Appendix 1 to these Rules who need a visa for the United Kingdom.]

['Non-visa nationals' are persons who are not specified in Appendix 1 to the Rules.]

['specified national' is a person specified in Appendix 3 to the Rules who seeks leave to enter the United Kingdom for a period of more that 6 months.]

'employment', unless the contrary intention appears, includes paid and unpaid employment, [paid and unpaid work placements undertaken as part of a course or period of study,] self-employment and engaging in business or any professional activity.

['the Human Rights Convention' means the Convention for the Protection of Human Rights and Fundamental Freedoms, agreed by the Council of Europe at Rome on 4 November 1950 as it has effect for the time being in relation to the United Kingdom.]

['Immigration employment document' means a work permit or any other document which relates to employment and is issued for the purpose of these Rules or in connection with leave to enter or remain in the United Kingdom.]

['Employment as a doctor or dentist in training' means employment in a medical post or training programme which has been approved by the Postgraduate Medical Education and Training Board, or employment in a postgraduate training programme in dentistry.]

'these Rules' means these immigration rules (HC 395) made under section 3(2) of the Immigration Act 1971.

['A refugee' is a refugee as defined in regulation 2 of the Refugee or Person in Need of International Protection (Qualification) Regulation 2006.]

[In part 6A of these Rules, 'relevant grant allocation period' means a specified period of time, which will be published by the Secretary of State on the UK Border Agency website, during which applications for entry clearance or leave to enter in respect of a particular route may be granted subject to the grant allocation for that period;]

[In part 6A of these Rules, 'grant allocation' means a limit, details of which will be published by the Secretary of State on the UK Border Agency website, on the number of grants of entry clearance or leave to enter which may be granted in respect of a particular route during the relevant grant allocation period;]

Under Part 6A of these Rules, 'Highly Skilled Migrant' means a migrant {granted leave under paragraphs 135A to 135G of the Rules in force before 30 June 2008}.

Under Part 6A of these Rules, 'Highly Skilled Migrant Programme Approval Letter' means a letter issued by the Home Office confirming that the applicant meets the criteria specified by the Secretary of State for entry to or stay in the UK under the Highly Skilled Migrant Programme.

Under Part 6A of these Rules, 'Innovator' means a migrant {granted leave under 210A-210F of the Rules in force before 30 June 2008}.

Under Part 6A of these Rules, 'Lawfully' means with valid leave.

Under Part 6A of these Rules, 'Participant in the Fresh Talent Working in Scotland Scheme' means a migrant {granted leave under paragraphs 143A to 143F of the Rules in force before 30 June 2008}.

Under Part 6A of these Rules, 'Participant in the International Graduates Scheme' means a migrant {granted leave under paragraphs 135O to 135T of the Rules in force before 30 June 2008}.

Under Part 6A of these Rules, 'Postgraduate Doctor or Dentist' means a migrant who is granted leave under paragraphs 70 to 75 of these Rules.

Under Part 6A of these Rules, 'Self-Employed' means an applicant is registered as self-employed with HM Revenue & Customs, or is employed by a company of which the applicant is a controlling shareholder.

Under Part 6A of these Rules, 'Student' means a migrant who is granted leave under paragraphs 57 to 62 of these Rules.

Under Part 6A of these Rules, 'Student Nurse' means a migrant who is granted leave under paragraphs 63 to 69 of these Rules.

Under Part 6A of these Rules, 'Student Re-Sitting an Examination' means a migrant who is granted leave under paragraphs 69A to 69F of these Rules.

Under Part 6A of these Rules, 'Student Writing-Up a Thesis' means a migrant who is granted leave under paragraphs 69G to 69L of these Rules.

Under Part 6A of these Rules, 'Work Permit Holder' means a migrant who is granted leave under paragraphs 128 to 133 of these Rules.]

Under Part 6A of these Rules, 'Prospective student' means a migrant who is granted leave under paragraphs 82 to 87 of these Rules.

Under Part 6A of these Rules, an 'A-rated sponsor' is a sponsor which is recorded as being 'A-rated' on the register of licensed sponsors maintained by the United Kingdom Border Agency.

[Under Part 6A and Appendix A of these rules, a 'B-rated Sponsor' is a sponsor which is recorded as being 'B-rated' on the register of licensed sponsors maintained by the United Kingdom Border Agency.]

Under Part 6A of these Rules, 'Highly Trusted Sponsor' means a sponsor which is recorded as being 'highly trusted' on the register of licensed sponsors maintained by the United Kingdom Border Agency.

[Under paragraph 34K of these Rules, a 'Premium Sponsor' is a Sponsor which is recorded as holding Premium status on the register of licensed Sponsors maintained by the United Kingdom Border Agency.]

Under Part 6A of these Rules, 'Certificate of Sponsorship' means an authorisation issued by the Secretary of State to a sponsor in respect of one or more applications, or potential applications, for entry clearance, leave to enter or remain {as a Tier 2 migrant or a Tier 5 migrant} in accordance with these Rules.

[Under Part 6A and Appendix A of these rules, 'Confirmation of Acceptance for Studies' means a unique reference number electronically issued by a sponsor via the Sponsor Management system to an applicant for entry clearance, leave to enter or remain as a Tier 4 Migrant in accordance with these rules.]

Under Part 6A of these Rules, 'Certificate of Sponsorship Checking Service' means a computerised interface with the Points Based System computer database which allows a United Kingdom Border Agency caseworker or entry clearance officer assessing a migrant's application for entry clearance, leave to enter or leave to remain to access and review details of the migrant's Certificate of Sponsorship, including details of the migrant's Sponsor, together with details of the job … and other details associated with the circumstances in which the Certificate of Sponsorship was issued.

[Under Part 6A and Appendix A of these Rules, 'length of the period of engagement' is the period beginning with the employment start date as recorded on the Certificate of Sponsorship Checking service entry which relates to the Certificate of Sponsorship reference number for which the migrant was awarded points under Appendix A and ending on the employment end date as recorded in the same entry.

Under Part 6A and Appendix A of these rules, 'working for the same employer' includes working for the business or concern in respect of which employment the earlier grant of leave was granted where that business or concern has, since that date, merged with, or been taken over by, another entity.

Under Part 6A and Appendix A of these rules, 'Designated Competent Body' means an organisation which has been approved by the UK Border Agency to endorse applicants as a Tier 1 (Exceptional Talent) Migrant.]

[Under Part 6A and Appendix A of these Rules, 'Tier 1 (Exceptional Talent) Unique Reference Number' means a unique reference number issued for the purposes of managing the Tier 1 (Exceptional Talent) Limit and provided by the UK Border Agency to an applicant prior to making his application as a Tier 1 (Exceptional Talent) Migrant.]

[For the purpose of paragraph 320(7B) of these rules 'Removal Decision' means

(a) a decision to remove in accordance with section 10 of the Immigration and Asylum Act 1999;

(b) a decision to remove an illegal entrant by way of directions under paragraphs 8 to 10 of Schedule 2 to the Immigration Act 1971; or

(c) a decision to remove in accordance with section 47 of the Immigration, Asylum and Nationality Act 2006.

'Pending appeal' has the same meaning as in section 104 of the Nationality, Immigration and Asylum Act 2002.]

Under Part 6A of these Rules, 'Confirmation of Acceptance for Studies Checking Service' means a computerised interface with the Points Based System computer database which allows a United Kingdom Border Agency caseworker or entry clearance officer assessing a migrant's application for entry clearance, leave to enter or leave to remain as a Tier 4 migrant under these Rules to access and review details of the migrant's Confirmation of Acceptance for Studies, including details of the migrant's sponsor, together with details of the course of study and other details associated with the circumstances in which the Confirmation of Acceptance for Studies was issued.

Under Part 6A of these Rules, 'established entertainer' means an applicant who is applying for leave to remain as a Tier 2 (General) Migrant or a Tier 2 (Intra-Company Transfer) Migrant in respect of whom the following conditions are satisfied:

(a) the Certificate of Sponsorship Checking Service entry to which the applicant's Certificate of Sponsorship reference number relates, records that the applicant is being sponsored in an occupation which is defined in the United Kingdom Border Agency's Transitional Guidance as being a job in the entertainment sector,

(b) the applicant has, or has previously had, entry clearance, leave to enter or leave to remain in the UK as a work permit holder, and the work permit that led to that grant was issued in the sports and entertainment category to enable him to work in the occupation in which he is, at the date of the application for leave to remain, currently being sponsored,

[(c) the applicant's last grant of leave was:

(i) as a Work Permit Holder in the sports and entertainment category, provided the work permit on the basis of which that leave was granted was issued in the sports and entertainment category to enable him to work either in the occupation in which he is, at the date of the current application for leave to remain, currently being sponsored, or in another occupation which is defined in the UK Border Agency's Transitional Guidance as being a job in the entertainment sector, or

(ii) leave to remain as a Tier 2 (General) Migrant or a Tier 2 (Intra-Company Transfer) Migrant, provided (in either case):

(1) he previously had leave as a Work Permit Holder in the sports and entertainment category to work as described in (i) above,

(2) he has not been granted entry clearance in this or any other route since his last grant of leave as a Work Permit Holder, and

(3) his last grant of leave was made to enable him to work either in the occupation in which he is, at the date of the current application for leave to remain, currently being sponsored or in another occupation which is defined in the UK Border Agency's Transitional Guidance as being a job in the entertainment sector,]

(d) the Certificate of Sponsorship Checking Service entry to which the applicant's Certificate of Sponsorship reference number relates records:

(i) that the applicant will be paid a salary for the job that is at or above the appropriate entertainments industry rate, as listed in the United Kingdom Border Agency's Transitional Guidance; and

(ii) that before agreeing to employ the applicant, the sponsor consulted with such bodies as the United Kingdom Border Agency's Transitional Guidance indicates that it should consult with before employing someone in this capacity.

(e) the applicant has not spent a period of 5 years or more in the UK, beginning with the last grant of entry clearance, as a Qualifying Work Permit Holder, Tier 2 (General) Migrant or Tier 2 (Intra- Company Transfer) Migrant, or in any combination of these.

Under Part 6A of these Rules, 'Qualifying Work Permit Holder' means a Work Permit Holder who was issued a work permit in the business and commercial or sports and entertainment work permit categories.

Under Part 6A of these Rules, 'Senior Care Worker' means an applicant who is applying for leave to remain as a Tier 2 (General) Migrant or a Tier 2 (Intra-Company Transfer) Migrant in respect of whom the following conditions are satisfied:

[(a) the Certificate of Sponsorship Checking Service entry to which the applicant's Certificate of Sponsorship reference number relates, records that the applicant is being sponsored in an occupation which is defined in the codes of practice for Tier 2 sponsors published by the UK Border Agency as being a Senior Care Worker role, (b) the applicant's last grant of leave was:

(i) as a Qualifying Work Permit Holder, or

(ii) leave to remain as a Tier 2 (General) Migrant or a Tier 2 (Intra-Company Transfer) Migrant, provided (in either case):

(1) he previously had leave as a Qualifying Work Permit Holder, and

(2) he has not been granted entry clearance in this or any other route since his last grant of leave as a Qualifying Work Permit Holder.]

(c) the work permit or Certificate of Sponsorship that led to the last grant of leave was issued to enable the applicant to work as a senior care worker, and

(d) the applicant has not spent a period of 5 years or more in the UK, beginning with the last grant of entry clearance, as a Qualifying Work Permit Holder, Tier 2 (General) Migrant or Tier 2 (Intra- Company Transfer) Migrant, or in any combination of these.

Under Part 6A of these Rules, 'sponsor' means the person or Government that the Certificate of Sponsorship Checking Service or {Confirmation of Acceptance for Studies Checking Service} records as being the Sponsor for a migrant.

Under Part 6A of these Rules, a reference to a 'sponsor licence' means a licence granted by the Secretary of State to a person who, by virtue of such a grant, is licensed as a Sponsor under Tiers 2, 4 or 5 of the Points Based System.

[In Part 6A and Appendices A and J of these Rules, 'settled worker' means a person who:

(i) is a national of the UK,

(ii) is a national of the European Economic Area or Switzerland who is exercising a Treaty Right in the UK,

(iii) is a British overseas territories citizen, except those from Sovereign Base Areas in Cyprus,

(iv) is a Commonwealth citizen with leave to enter or remain granted on the basis of UK Ancestry (paragraphs 186 to 193 of these Rules), or

(v) has settled status in the UK within the meaning of the Immigration Act 1971, as amended by the Immigration and Asylum Act 1999, and the Nationality, Immigration and Asylum Act 2002.]

Under Part 6A of these Rules, 'supplementary employment' means other employment in the same profession and at the same professional level as that which the migrant is being sponsored to do provided that:

(a) the migrant remains working for the sponsor in the employment that the Certificate of Sponsorship Checking Service records that the migrant is being sponsored to do,

(b) the other employment does not exceed 20 hours per week and takes place outside of the hours when the migrant is contracted to work for the sponsor in the employment the migrant is being sponsored to do.

[Under Part 6A and Appendix A of these Rules, 'overseas higher education institution' means an institution which holds overseas accreditation confirmed by UK NARIC as offering degree programmes which are equivalent to UK degree level qualifications, and which teach no more than half of a degree programme in the UK as a study abroad programme.]

'Business person' means a migrant granted leave under paragraphs 200 to 208 of the Rules in force before 30 June 2008.

'Investor' means a migrant granted leave under paragraphs 224 to 229 of the Rules in force before 30 June 2008.

'Self-employed lawyer' means a migrant granted entry clearance, or leave to enter or remain, outside the Rules under the concession for Self-employed lawyers that formerly appeared in Chapter 6, Section 1 Annex D of the Immigration Directorate instructions.

['Points Based System Migrant' means a migrant applying for or granted leave as a Tier 1 Migrant, a Tier 2 Migrant, a Tier 4 Migrant or a Tier 5 Migrant.

'Tier 1 Migrant' means a migrant who is granted leave as a Tier 1 (Exceptional Talent) Migrant, a Tier 1 (General) Migrant, a Tier 1 (Entrepreneur) Migrant, a Tier 1 (Investor) Migrant, a Tier 1 (Graduate Entrepreneur) Migrant or a Tier 1 (Post-Study Work) Migrant.

'Tier 1 (Exceptional Talent) Migrant' means a migrant who is granted leave under paragraphs 245B to 245BF of these Rules.

'Tier 1 (General) Migrant' means a migrant who is granted leave under paragraphs 245C to 245CE of these Rules.

'Tier 1 (Entrepreneur) Migrant' means a migrant who is granted leave under paragraphs 245D to 245DF of these Rules.

'Tier 1 (Investor) Migrant' means a migrant who is granted leave under paragraphs 245E to 245EF of these Rules.

'Tier 1 (Graduate Entrepreneur) Migrant' means a migrant who is granted leave under paragraphs 245F to 245FB of these Rules in place on or after 6 April 2012.

'Tier 1 (Post-Study Work) Migrant' means a migrant who is granted leave under paragraphs 245F to 245FE of the Rules in place before 6 April 2012.

'Tier 2 Migrant' means a migrant who is granted leave as a Tier 2 (Intra-Company Transfer) Migrant, a Tier 2 (General) Migrant, a Tier 2 (Minister of Religion) Migrant or a Tier 2 (Sportsperson) Migrant.

'Tier 2 (Intra-Company Transfer) Migrant' means a migrant granted leave under paragraphs 245G to 245GF of these Rules.

'Tier 2 (General) Migrant' means a migrant granted leave under paragraphs 245H to 245HF of these Rules and who obtains points under paragraphs 76 to 84A of Appendix A.

'Tier 2 (Minister of Religion) Migrant' means a migrant granted leave under paragraphs 245H to 245HF of these Rules and who obtains points under paragraphs 85 to 92 of Appendix A.

'Tier 2 (Sportsperson) Migrant' means a migrant granted leave under paragraphs 245H to 245HF of these Rules and who obtains points under paragraphs 93 to 100 of Appendix A.]

'Tier 4 (General) Student' means a migrant granted leave under paragraphs 245ZT to 245ZY of these Rules.

'Tier 4 (Child) Student' means a migrant granted leave under paragraphs 245ZZ to 245ZZD of these Rules.

'Tier 4 Migrant' means a Tier 4 (General) Student or a Tier 4 (Child) Student.

'Tier 5 (Youth Mobility) Temporary Migrant' means a migrant granted leave under paragraphs 245ZI to 245ZL of these Rules.

['Deemed sponsorship status' means that the country or territory is not required to issue its nationals or passport holders with a Certificate of Sponsorship in order to enable a successful application under the Tier 5 Youth Mobility Scheme and is held by a country or territory listed as such at Appendix G of these Rules.]

'Tier 5 (Temporary Worker) Migrant' means a migrant granted leave under paragraphs 245ZM to 245ZS of these Rules.

'Tier 5 Migrant' means a migrant who is either a Tier 5 (Temporary Worker) Migrant or a Tier 5 (Youth Mobility) Temporary Migrant.

[Under Part 6A of these Rules 'Government Authorised Exchange Scheme' means a scheme under the Tier 5 (Temporary Worker) Government Authorised Exchange sub-category which is endorsed by a Government Department in support of Government objectives and provides temporary work in an occupation which appears on the list of occupations skilled to National Qualifications Framework level 3, as stated in the codes of practice for Tier 2 Sponsors published by the UK Border Agency, and where the migrant will be supernumerary.

Under Part 6A of these Rules 'Work Experience Programme' means work experience including volunteering and job-shadowing, internships and work exchange programmes under a Government Authorised Exchange Scheme.

Under Part 6A of these Rules 'Research Programme' means research programmes and fellowships under a Government Authorised Exchange Scheme where the migrant is working on a scientific, academic, medical, or government research project/s at either a UK Higher Education Institution or another research institution operating under the authority and/or financial sponsorship of a relevant Government Department.

Under Part 6A of these Rules 'Training Programme' means a training programme under a Government Authorised Exchange Scheme where the migrant either receives formal, practical training in the fields of science and/or medicine or meets the requirements of paragraph 245ZQ(b)(vi)(2) to (4).

Under Part 6A of these Rules, 'Temporary Engagement as a Sports Broadcaster' means providing guest expert commentary on a particular sporting event.]

'Jewish Agency Employee' means a migrant granted leave outside of these Rules under the concession that formerly appeared in Chapter 17 Section 5 Part 2 of the Immigration Directorate Instructions.

'Member of the Operational Ground Staff of an Overseas-owned Airline' means a migrant granted leave under paragraphs 178 to 185 of the Rules in force before 27 November 2008.

'Minister of Religion, Missionary or Member of a Religious Order' means a migrant granted leave under paragraphs 170 to 177A of the Rules in force before 27 November 2008.

'Overseas qualified nurse or midwife' means a migrant granted leave under paragraphs 69M to 69R of the Rules in force before 27 November 2008.

'Participant in the Science and Engineering Graduates Scheme' means a migrant granted leave under paragraphs 135O to 135T of the Rules in force before 1 May 2007.

'Representative of an overseas newspaper, news agency or broadcasting organisation' means a migrant granted leave under paragraphs 136 to 143 of the Rules in force before 27 November 2008.

'Student union sabbatical officer' means a migrant granted leave under paragraphs 87A to 87F of the Rules in force before 27 November 2008.

'Working holidaymaker' means a migrant granted leave under paragraphs 95 to 97 of the Rules in force before 27 November 2008.

A 'business visitor' is a person granted leave to enter or remain in the UK under paragraphs 46G-46L, 75A-F or 75G-M of these Rules.

An 'academic visitor' is a person who is from an overseas academic institution or who is highly qualified within his own field of expertise seeking leave to enter the UK to carry out research and associated activities for his own purposes.

A 'visiting professor' is a person who is seeking leave to enter the UK as an academic professor to accompany students who are studying here on Study Abroad Programmes.

A 'sports visitor' is a person granted leave to enter or remain in the UK under paragraphs 46M–46R of these Rules.

An 'amateur' is a person who engages in a sport or creative activity solely for personal enjoyment and who is not seeking to derive a living from the activity.

A 'series of events' is two or more linked events, such as a tour, or rounds of a competition, which do not add up to a league or a season.

An 'entertainer visitor' is a person granted leave to enter or remain in the UK under paragraphs 46S–46X of these Rules.

A 'special visitor' is a person granted leave for a short-term visit in the following circumstances:

(a) A person granted leave to enter or remain in the UK as a visitor for private medical treatment under paragraphs 51–56 of these Rules.

(b) A person granted leave to enter or remain in the UK for the purpose of marriage or to enter into civil partnership under paragraphs 56D–56F of these Rules.

(c) A person granted leave to enter or remain in the UK as a Parent of a child at school under paragraphs 56A–56C of these Rules.

(d) A person granted leave to enter or remain in the UK as a Child Visitor under paragraphs 46A–46F of these Rules.

(e) A person granted leave to enter or remain in the UK as a Student Visitor under paragraphs 56K–56M of these Rules.

(f) A person granted leave to enter or remain in the UK as a Prospective Student under paragraphs 82–87 of these Rules.

(g) A person granted leave to enter the UK as a visitor in transit under paragraphs 47–50 of these Rules [, or

(h) a person granted entry clearance, leave to enter or leave to remain in the UK as a Prospective Entrepreneur under paragraphs 56N–56Q of these Rules.]

['A visitor undertaking permitted paid engagements' is someone who is granted leave to enter under paragraphs 56X–56Z of these Rules.]

'Writer, composer or artist' means a migrant granted leave under paragraphs 232 to 237 of the Rules in force before 30 June 2008.

[In paragraph 320(7B) {and paragraph 320(11)} of these Rules:

'Deception' means making false representations or submitting false documents (whether or not material to the application), or failing to disclose material facts.

'Illegal Entrant' has the same definition as in section 33(1) of the Immigration Act 1971.

[In paragraph 320(22) and 322(12) of these Rules: 'relevant NHS body' means—

  (a) in relation to England—

    (i) a National Health Service Trust established under section 25 of the National Health Service Act 2006,

    (ii) a NHS foundation trust.

  (b) in relation to Wales—

    (i) a Local Health Board established under section 11 of the National Health Service (Wales) Act 2006,

    (ii) a National Health Service Trust established under section 18 of the National Health Service (Wales) Act 2006,

    (iii) a Special Health Authority established under [section] 22 of the National Health Service (Wales) Act 2006.

  (c) in relation to Scotland—

    (i) a Health Board or Special Health Board established under section 2 of the National Health Service (Scotland) Act 1978 (c. 29),

    (ii) the Common Services Agency for the Scottish Health Service established under section 10 of that Act,

    (iii) Healthcare Improvement Scotland established under section 10A of that Act.

  (d) in relation to Northern Ireland—

    (i) the Regional Health and Social Care Board established under the Health and Social Care (Reform) Act (Northern Ireland) 2009,

    (ii) a Health and Social Care trust established under the Health and Personal Social Services (Northern Ireland) Order 1991 (S.I. 1991/194 (N.I. 1)) and renamed under the Health and Social Care (Reform) Act (Northern Ireland) 2009.

'relevant NHS regulations' means—

    (i) The National Health Service (Charges to Overseas Visitors) (Amendment) (Wales) Regulations 2004 (2004 No 1433);

    (ii) The National Health Service (Charges to Overseas Visitors) (Scotland) Regulations 1989 as amended (1989 No 364);

    (iii) The Health and Personal Social Services (Provision of Health Services to Persons not Ordinarily Resident) Regulations (Northern Ireland) 2005 (2005 No 551); or

    (iv) The National Health Service (Charges to Overseas Visitors) Regulations (2011 No 1556).]

[For the purposes of an application as a fiancé(e) or proposed civil partner under Appendix FM, an EEA national who holds a registration certificate or a document certifying permanent residence issued under the 2006 EEA Regulations (including an EEA national who holds a residence permit issued under the Immigration (European Economic Area) Regulations 2000 which is treated as if it were such a certificate or document by virtue of Schedule 4 to the 2006 EEA Regulations) is to be regarded as present and settled in the United Kingdom.]

Note: Definition of 'the 2000 EEA Regulations' and 'the Human Rights Convention' inserted from 2 October 2000 (Cm 4851). Definition of 'the 1996 Act' inserted from 1 September 1996 (HC 31). Definition of 'visa nationals' substituted from 11 November 1998 (Cm 3953). Definition of 'public funds' substituted from and definition of 'immigration employment document' inserted from 18 September 2002 (Cm 5597). Definition of 'adoption' substituted from 1 April 2003 (HC

538). Definition of 'parent' amended from 1 April 2003 (HC 538). Definitions of 'intention to live permanently with the other', 'present and settled' inserted from 1 April 2003 (HC 538). Definition of 'specified national' inserted from 13 November 2003 (HC 1224). Definition of 'degree level study' inserted from 1 October 2004 (Cm 6339). Definition of 'sponsor' substituted from 1 October 2004 (Cm 6339). Definition of 'Accession State National' inserted from 1 May 2004 (HC 523). Paragraphs 6(b) and 6(c) amended and para 6(d) deleted from 15 March 2005 (HC 346). Definition of 'Approved Destination Status Agreement with China' inserted from 5 April 2005 (HC 486). Definition of 'civil partner' inserted and definition of 'parent' and 'sponsor' amended from 14 November 2005 (HC 582). Definition of 'non-visa national' inserted from 3 April 2006 (HC 1016). Definition of 'the 2006 EEA Regulations' inserted and definition of 'EEA national' substituted from 30 April 2006 (HC 1053). Further definitions and amendments made by HC 321 (29 February and 1 April 2008). HC 607 (30 June 2008), HC 40 (30 November 2007), Cm 7074 (19 April 2007), HC 439 (6 April 2010), HC 1113 (27 November 2008), Cm 7701 (1 October 2009), HC 314 (31 March 2009), HC 367 (3 March 2010), HC 59 (19 July 2010), Cm 7944 (22 October 2010), HC 698 (23 December 2010), HC 863 (6 April 2012), HC 908 (21 April 2011), HC 1436 (9 August 2011), HC 1511 (31 October 2011), HC 1693 (1 January 2012), HC 1888 (6 April 2012), Cm 8423 (20 July 2012), HC 565 (6 September 2012).

[**6A.** For the purpose of these Rules, a person (P) is not to be regarded as having (or potentially having) recourse to public funds merely because P is (or will be) reliant in whole or in part on public funds provided to P's sponsor unless, as a result of P's presence in the United Kingdom, the sponsor is (or would be) entitled to increased or additional public funds (save where such entitlement to increased or additional public funds is by virtue of P and the sponsor's joint entitlement to benefits under the regulations referred to in paragraph 6B).]

Note: Paragraph 6A substituted from 31 March 2009 (HC 314).

[**6B.** Subject to paragraph 6C, a person (P) shall not be regarded as having recourse to public funds if P is entitled to benefits specified under section 115 of the Immigration and Asylum Act 1999 by virtue of regulations made under sub-sections (3) and (4) of that section or section 42 of the Tax Credits Act 2002.]

Note: Paragraph 6B substituted from 31 March 2009 (HC 314).

[**6C.** A person (P) making an application from outside the United Kingdom will be regarded as having recourse to public funds where P relies upon the future entitlement to any public funds that would be payable to P or to P's sponsor as a result of P's presence in the United Kingdom, (including those benefits to which P or the sponsor would be entitled as a result of P's presence in the United Kingdom under the regulations referred to in to paragraph 6B).]

Note: Paragraph 6C inserted from 31 March 2009 (HC 314).

PART I
GENERAL PROVISIONS REGARDING LEAVE TO ENTER
OR REMAIN IN THE UNITED KINGDOM

Leave to enter the United Kingdom

7. [A person who is neither a British citizen nor a Commonwealth citizen with the right of abode nor a person who is entitled to enter or remain in the United Kingdom by virtue of the provisions of {the 2006 EEA Regulations} requires leave to enter the United Kingdom.]

Note: Substituted from 2 October 2000 (Cm 4851). Words in curly brackets substituted from 30 April 2006 (HC 1053).

[8. Under Sections 3 and 4 of the Immigration Act 1971 an Immigration Officer when admitting to the United Kingdom a person subject to immigration control under that Act may give leave to enter for a limited period and, if he does, may impose all or any of the following conditions:

(i) a condition restricting employment or occupation in the United Kingdom;

(ii) a condition requiring the person to maintain and accommodate himself, and any dependants of his, without recourse to public funds; and

(iii) a condition requiring the person to register with the police.

He may also require him to report to the appropriate Medical Officer of Environmental Health. Under Section 24 of the 1971 Act it is an offence knowingly to remain beyond the time limit or fail to comply with such a condition or requirement.]

Note: Paragraph 8 substituted from 1 November 1996 (Cm 3365).

[9. The time limit and any conditions attached will normally be made known to the person concerned either:

(i) by written notice given to him or endorsed by the immigration officer in his passport or travel document; or

(ii) in any other manner permitted by the Immigration (Leave to Enter and Remain) Order 2000.]

Note: Substituted from 30 July 2000 (HC 704).

[Exercise of the power to refuse leave to enter the United Kingdom or to cancel leave to enter or remain which is in force]

10. The power to refuse leave to enter the United Kingdom [or to cancel leave to enter or remain which is already in force] is not to be exercised by an Immigration Officer acting on his own. The authority of a Chief Immigration Officer or of an Immigration Inspector must always be obtained.

Note: Words in square brackets inserted from 30 July 2000 (HC 704).

[Suspension of leave to enter or remain in the United Kingdom

10A. Where a person has arrived in the United Kingdom with leave to enter or remain which is in force but which was given to him before his arrival he may be examined by an Immigration Officer under paragraph 2A of Schedule 2 to the Immigration Act 1971. An Immigration Officer examining a person under paragraph 2A may suspend that person's leave to enter or remain in the United Kingdom until the examination is completed.

Cancellation of leave to enter or remain in the United Kingdom

10B. Where a person arrives in the United Kingdom with leave to enter or remain in the United Kingdom which is already in force, an Immigration Officer may cancel that leave.]

Note: Paragraphs 10A and 10B inserted from 30 July 2000 (HC 704).

Requirement for persons arriving in the United Kingdom or seeking entry through the Channel Tunnel to produce evidence of identity and nationality

11. A person must, on arrival in the United Kingdom or when seeking entry through the Channel Tunnel, produce on request by the Immigration Officer:

(i) a valid national passport or other document satisfactorily establishing his identity and nationality; and

(ii) such information as may be required to establish whether he requires leave to enter the United Kingdom and, if so, whether and on what terms leave to enter should be given.

Requirement for a person not requiring leave to enter the United Kingdom to prove that he has the right of abode

12. A person claiming to be a British citizen must prove that he has the right of abode in the United Kingdom by producing either:

(i) a United Kingdom passport describing him as a British citizen or as a citizen of the United Kingdom and Colonies having the right of abode in the United Kingdom; or

(ii) a certificate of entitlement duly issued by or on behalf of the Government of the United Kingdom certifying that he has the right of abode.

13. A person claiming to be a Commonwealth citizen with the right of abode in the United Kingdom must prove that he has the right of abode by producing a certificate of entitlement duly issued to him by or on behalf of the Government of the United Kingdom certifying that he has the right of abode.

14. A Commonwealth citizen who has been given limited leave to enter the United Kingdom may later claim to have the right of abode. The time limit on his stay may be removed if he is able to establish a claim to the right of abode, for example by showing that:

(i) immediately before the commencement of the British Nationality Act 1981 he was a Commonwealth citizen born to or legally adopted by a parent who at the time of the birth had citizenship of the United Kingdom and Colonies by his birth in the United Kingdom or any of the Islands; and

(ii) he has not ceased to be a Commonwealth citizen in the meanwhile.

Common travel area

15. The United Kingdom, the Channel Islands, the Isle of Man and the Republic of Ireland collectively form a common travel area. A person who has been examined for the purpose of immigration control at the point at which he entered the area does not normally require leave to enter any other part of it. However certain persons subject to the Immigration (Control of Entry through the Republic of Ireland) Order 1972 (as amended) who enter the United Kingdom through the Republic of Ireland do require leave to enter. This includes:

(i) those who merely passed through the Republic of Ireland;

(ii) persons requiring visas;

(iii) persons who entered the Republic of Ireland unlawfully;

(iv) persons who are subject to directions given by the Secretary of State for their exclusion from the United Kingdom on the ground that their exclusion is conducive to the public good;

(v) persons who entered the Republic of Ireland from the United Kingdom and Islands after entering there unlawfully or overstaying their leave.

Admission of certain British passport holders

16. A person in any of the following categories may be admitted freely to the United Kingdom on production of a United Kingdom passport issued in the United Kingdom and Islands or the Republic of Ireland prior to 1 January 1973, unless his passport has been endorsed to show that he was subject to immigration control:

 (i) a British Dependent Territories citizen;

 (ii) a British National (Overseas);

 (iii) a British Overseas citizen;

 (iv) a British protected person;

 (v) a British subject by virtue of Section 30(a) of the British Nationality Act 1981, (who, immediately before the commencement of the 1981 Act, would have been a British subject not possessing citizenship of the United Kingdom and Colonies or the citizenship of any other Commonwealth country or territory).

17. British Overseas citizens who hold United Kingdom passports wherever issued and who satisfy the Immigration Officer that they have, since 1 March 1968, been given indefinite leave to enter or remain in the United Kingdom may be given indefinite leave to enter.

[Persons outside the United Kingdom

17A. Where a person is outside the United Kingdom but wishes to travel to the United Kingdom an Immigration Officer may give or refuse him leave to enter. An Immigration Officer may exercise these powers whether or not he is, himself, in the United Kingdom. However, an Immigration Officer is not obliged to consider an application for leave to enter from a person outside the United Kingdom.

17B. Where a person, having left the common travel area, has leave to enter the United Kingdom which remains in force under article 13 of the Immigration (Leave to Enter and Remain) Order 2000, an Immigration Officer may cancel that leave. An Immigration Officer may exercise these powers whether or not he is, himself, in the United Kingdom. If a person outside the United Kingdom has leave to remain in the United Kingdom which is in force in this way, the Secretary of State may cancel that leave.]

Note: Paragraphs 17A and 17B inserted from 30 July 2000 (HC 704).

Returning residents

18. A person seeking leave to enter the United Kingdom as a returning resident may be admitted for settlement provided the Immigration Officer is satisfied that the person concerned:

 (i) had indefinite leave to enter or remain in the United Kingdom when he last left; and

(ii) has not been away from the United Kingdom for more than 2 years; and

(iii) did not receive assistance from public funds towards the cost of leaving the United Kingdom; and

(iv) now seeks admission for the purpose of settlement.

19. A person who does not benefit from the preceding paragraph by reason only of having been away from the United Kingdom too long may nevertheless be admitted as a returning resident if, for example, he has lived here for most of his life.

[**19A**. Where a person who has indefinite leave to enter or remain in the United Kingdom accompanies, on a tour of duty abroad, a {spouse, civil partner, unmarried partner or same-sex partner} who is a member of HM Forces serving overseas, or a permanent member of HM Diplomatic Service, or a comparable United Kingdom-based staff member of the British Council, or a staff member of the Department for International Development who is a British Citizen or is settled in the United Kingdom, sub-paragraphs (ii) and (iii) of paragraph 18 shall not apply.]

Note: Paragraph 19A substituted from 18 September 2002 (Cm 5597). Words in curly brackets substituted from 5 December 2005 (HC 582).

20. The leave of a person whose stay in the United Kingdom is subject to a time limit lapses on his going to a country or territory outside the common travel area [if the leave was given for a period of six months or less or conferred by a visit visa. In other cases, leave lapses on the holder remaining outside the United Kingdom for a continuous period of more than two years]. [A person whose leave has lapsed and] who returns after a temporary absence abroad within the period of this earlier leave has no claim to admission as a returning resident. His application to re-enter the United Kingdom should be considered in the light of all the relevant circumstances. The same time limit and any conditions attached will normally be reimposed if he meets the requirements of these Rules, unless he is seeking admission in a different capacity from the one in which he was last given leave to enter or remain.

Note: Amended from 30 July 2000 (HC 704).

[Non-lapsing leave

20A. Leave to enter or remain in the United Kingdom will usually lapse on the holder going to a country or territory outside the common travel area. However, under article 13 of the Immigration (Leave to Enter and Remain) Order 2000 such leave will not lapse where it was conferred by means of an entry clearance (other than a visit visa).]

Note: Inserted from 30 July 2000 (HC704).

Holders of restricted travel documents and passports

21. The leave to enter or remain in the United Kingdom of the holder of a passport or travel document whose permission to enter another country has to be exercised before a given date may be restricted so as to terminate at least 2 months before that date.

22. If his passport or travel document is endorsed with a restriction on the period for which he may remain outside his country of normal residence, his leave to enter or remain in the United Kingdom may be limited so as not to extend beyond the period of authorised absence.

23. The holder of a travel document issued by the Home Office should not be given leave to enter or remain for a period extending beyond the validity of that document. This paragraph and paragraphs 21–22 do not apply to a person who is eligible for admission for settlement or to a spouse [or civil partner] who is eligible for admission under paragraph 282 or to a person who qualifies for the removal of the time limit on his stay.

Note: Words in square brackets inserted from 5 December 2005 (HC 582).

[Leave to enter granted on arrival in the United Kingdom

[**23A.** A person who is not a visa national and who is seeking leave to enter on arrival in the United Kingdom for a period not exceeding 6 months for a purpose for which prior entry clearance is not required under these Rules may be granted such leave, for a period not exceeding 6 months.

[This paragraph does not apply where the person is a British National (Overseas), a British overseas territories citizen, a British Overseas citizen, a British protected person, or a person who under the British Nationality Act 1981 is a British subject.]

Note: Paragraph 23A substituted from 13 November 2005 (HC 645).

[**23B.** A person who is a British National (Overseas), a British overseas territories citizen, a British Overseas citizen, a British protected person, or a person who under the British Nationality Act 1981 is a British subject, and who is seeking leave to enter on arrival in the United Kingdom for a purpose for which prior entry clearance is not required under these Rules may be granted such leave, irrespective of the period of time for which he seeks entry, for a period not exceeding 6 months.]

Note: Paragraph 23B inserted from 13 November 2005 (HC 645).

Entry clearance

[**24.** The following must produce to the Immigration Officer a valid Passport or other identity document endorsed with a United Kingdom entry clearance issued to him for the purpose for which he seeks entry:
    (i) a visa national;
    (ii) any other person (other than British Nationals (Overseas), a British overseas territories citizen, a British Overseas citizen, a British protected person or a person who under the British Nationality Act 1981 is a British subject) who is seeking entry for a period exceeding six months or is seeking entry for a purpose for which prior entry clearance is required under these Rules.

Such a person will be refused leave to enter if he has no such current entry clearance. Any other person who wishes to ascertain in advance whether he is eligible for admission to the United Kingdom may apply for the issue of an entry clearance.]

Note: Paragraph 24 substituted from 13 November 2005 (HC 645).

25. Entry clearance takes the form of a visa (for visa nationals) or an entry certificate (for non-visa nationals). These documents are to be taken as evidence of the holder's eligibility for entry into the United Kingdom, and accordingly accepted as 'entry clearances' within the meaning of the Immigration Act 1971.

25A. An entry clearance which satisfies the requirements set out in article 3 of the Immigration (Leave to Enter and Remain) Order 2000 will have effect as leave to enter the United Kingdom. The requirements are that the entry clearance must specify the purpose for which the holder wishes to enter the United Kingdom and should be endorsed with the conditions to which it is subject or with a statement that it has effect as indefinite leave to enter the United Kingdom. The holder of such an entry clearance will not require leave to enter on arrival in the United Kingdom and, for the purposes of these Rules, will be treated as a person who has arrived in the United Kingdom with leave to enter the United Kingdom which is in force but which was given to him before his arrival.]

Note: Paragraph 25A inserted from 30 July 2000 (HC 704).

26. An application for entry clearance will be considered in accordance with the provisions in these Rules governing the grant or refusal of leave to enter. Where appropriate, the term 'Entry Clearance Officer' should be substituted for 'Immigration Officer'.

27. An application for entry clearance is to be decided in the light of the circumstances existing at the time of the decision, except that an applicant will not be refused an entry clearance where entry is sought in one of the categories contained in paragraphs 296–316 [or paragraph EC-C of Appendix FM] solely on account of his attaining the age of 18 years between receipt of his application and the date of the decision on it.

Note: Words in square brackets inserted from 9 July 2012 with savings for applications made but not decided before that date (HC 194).

28. An applicant for an entry clearance must be outside the United Kingdom and Islands at the time of the application. An applicant for an entry clearance who is seeking entry as a visitor must apply to a post designated by the Secretary of State to accept applications for entry clearance for that purpose and from that category of applicant. [Subject to paragraph 28A, any other application] must be made to the post in the country or territory where the applicant is living which has been designated by the Secretary of State to accept applications for entry clearance for that purpose and from that category of applicant. Where there is no such post the applicant must apply to the appropriate designated post outside the country or territory where he is living.

Note: Amended from 27 November 2008 (HC 1113).

[**28A.**

(a) An application for entry clearance as a Tier 5 (Temporary Worker) Migrant in the creative and sporting sub-category of Tier 5 may also be made at the post in the country or territory where the applicant is situated at the time of the application, provided that:

(i) the post has been designated by the Secretary of State to accept applications for entry clearance for that purpose and from that category of applicant,

(ii) the applicant is in that country or territory for a similar purpose to the activity he proposes to undertake in the UK, and

(iii) the applicant is able to demonstrate to the Entry Clearance Officer that he has authority to be living in that country or territory in accordance with its immigration laws. Those applicants who are known to the authorities of that country or territory but who have not been given permission to live in that country or territory will not be eligible to make an application.

(b) An application for entry clearance as a Tier 5 (Youth Mobility Scheme) Temporary Migrant may also be made at the post in the country or territory where the applicant is situated at the time of the application, provided that:

(i) the post has been designated by the Secretary of State to accept applications for entry clearance for that purpose and from that category of applicant, and

(ii) the applicant is able to demonstrate to the Entry Clearance Officer that he has authority to be living in that country or territory in accordance with its immigration laws and that when he was given authority to live in that country or territory he was given authority to live in that country or territory for a period of more than 6 months. Those applicants who are known to the authorities of that country or territory but who have not been given permission to live in that country or territory will not be eligible to make an application.]

Note: Paragraph 28A inserted from 27 November 2008 (HC 1113).

29. For the purposes of paragraph 28 [and 28A] 'post' means a British Diplomatic Mission, British Consular post or the office of any person outside the United Kingdom and Islands who has been authorised by the Secretary of State to accept applications for entry clearance. A list of designated posts is published by the Foreign and Commonwealth Office.

Note: Words inserted from 27 November 2008 (HC 1113).

30. An application for an entry clearance is not made until any fee required to be paid under the Consular Fees Act 1980 (including any Regulations or Orders made under that Act) has been paid.

[**30A.** An entry clearance may be revoked if the Entry Clearance Officer is satisfied that:

(i) whether or not to the holder's knowledge, false representations were employed or material facts were not disclosed, either in writing, or orally for the purpose of obtaining the entry clearance; or

(ii) a change of circumstances since the entry clearance was issued has removed the basis of the holder's claim to be admitted to the United Kingdom, except where the change of circumstances amounts solely to his exceeding the age for entry in one of the categories contained in paragraphs 296–316 of these Rules since the issue of the entry clearance; or

(iii) the holder's exclusion from the United Kingdom would be conducive to the public good.]

Note: Paragraph 30A inserted from 1 November 1996 (HC 31).

[**30B.** An entry clearance shall cease to have effect where the entry clearance has effect as leave to enter and an Immigration Officer cancels that leave in accordance with paragraph 2A(8) of Schedule 2 to the Immigration Act 1971.

30C. An Immigration Officer may cancel an entry clearance which is capable of having effect as leave to enter if the holder arrives in the United Kingdom before the day on which the entry clearance becomes effective or if the holder seeks to enter the United Kingdom for a purpose other than the purpose specified in the entry clearance.]

Note: Paragraph 30B and 30C inserted from 30 July 2000 (HC 704).

Variation of leave to enter or remain in the United Kingdom

31. Under Section 3(3) of the 1971 Act a limited leave to enter or remain in the United Kingdom may be varied by extending or restricting its duration, by adding, varying or revoking conditions or by removing the time limit (whereupon any condition attached to the leave ceases to apply). When leave to enter or remain is varied an entry is to be made in the applicant's passport or travel document (and his registration certificate where appropriate) or the decision may be made known in writing in some other appropriate way.

[**31A.** Where a person has arrived in the United Kingdom with leave to enter or remain in the United Kingdom which is in force but was given to him before his arrival, he may apply, on arrival at a port of entry in the United Kingdom, for variation of that leave. An Immigration Officer acting on behalf of the Secretary of State may vary the leave at the port of entry but is not obliged to consider an application for variation made at the port of entry. If an Immigration Officer acting on behalf of the Secretary of State has declined to consider an application for variation of leave at a port of entry but the leave has not been cancelled under paragraph 2A(8) of Schedule 2 to the Immigration Act 1971, the person seeking variation should apply to the Home Office under paragraph 32.]

Note: Paragraph 31A inserted from 30 July 2000 (HC 704).
Note: Paragraphs 32–33 deleted from 29 February 2008 (HC 321).

[**33A.** Where a person, having left the common travel area, has leave to enter or remain in the United Kingdom which remains in force under article 13 of the Immigration (Leave to Enter and Remain) Order 2000, his leave may be varied (including any conditions to which it is subject) in such form and manner as permitted for the giving of leave to enter. However, the Secretary of State is not obliged to consider an application for variation of leave to enter or remain from a person outside the United Kingdom.]

Note: Inserted from 30 July 2000 (HC 704).

Knowledge of language and life in the United Kingdom

[**33B.** A person has sufficient knowledge of the English language and sufficient knowledge about life in the United Kingdom for the purpose of an application for indefinite leave to remain under these rules [(unless paragraph 33BA applies)] if—

[(a)

    (i) he has attended an ESOL course at an accredited college;

    (ii) the course used teaching materials derived from the document entitled 'Citizenship Materials for ESOL Learners' (ISBN 1-84478-5424);

    (iii) he has demonstrated relevant progress in accordance with paragraph 33F; and

    (iv) he has attained a relevant qualification.

(b) he has passed the test known as the 'Life in the UK Test' administered by [learndirect ltd or if taken in the Isle of Man, the test known as the "Life in the UK Test" or if taken in the Bailiwick of Guernsey or the Bailiwick of Jersey, the test known as the "Citizenship Test" administered by an educational institution or other person approved for this purpose by the Lieutenant Governor]; or

(c) in the case of a person who is the spouse or civil partner or unmarried or same sex partner of:

    (i) a permanent member of HM Diplomatic Service; or

(ii) a comparable UK-based staff member of the British Council on a tour of duty abroad; or

(iii) a staff member of the Department for International Development who is a British citizen or is settled in the UK,

a person designated by the Secretary of State certifies in writing that he has sufficient knowledge of the English language and sufficient knowledge about life in the United Kingdom for this purpose.]

Note: Paragraph 33B inserted from 2 April 2007 (HC 398). Paragraph 33B(a) substituted from 7 April 2010 with savings for applications made before 6 April 2010 (HC 439). Words in first square brackets inserted from 6 April 2011, but not in relation to applications made but not decided before that date (HC 863). Words substituted in para (b) from 6 September 2012 (HC 565).

[**33BA.**

(a) Subject to sub-paragraph (b), for the purposes of an application for indefinite leave to remain under these rules, where a person is making an application for indefinite leave to remain as:

(i) a work permit holder under paragraph 134;

(ii) a Highly Skilled Migrant under paragraph 135G;

(iii) a representative of an overseas newspaper, news agency or broadcasting organisation under paragraph 142;

(iv) a representative of an overseas business under paragraph 150;

(v) an overseas government employee under paragraph 167;

(vi) a Minister of religion, religious missionary, or member of a religious order under paragraph 176;

(vii) an airport based operational ground staff of an overseas-owned airline under paragraph 184;

(viii) a person established in business under paragraph 209;

(ix) an innovator under paragraph 210G;

(x) a person established in business under the provisions of EC Association Agreements under paragraph 222;

(xi) an investor under paragraph 230;

(xii) a writer, composer or artist under paragraph 238;

(xiii) a Tier 1 (Exceptional Talent) Migrant under paragraph 245BF;

(xiv) a Tier 1 (General) Migrant under paragraph 245CD;

(xv) a Tier 1 (Entrepreneur) Migrant under paragraph 245DF;

(xvi) a Tier 1 (Investor) Migrant under paragraph 245EF;

(xvii) a Tier 2 (Intra-Company Transfer) under paragraph 245GF;

(xviii) a Tier 2 (General), Tier 2 (Minister of religion) and Tier 2 (Sportsperson) Migrant under paragraph 245HF.

that person has sufficient knowledge of the English language and sufficient knowledge about life in the United Kingdom, only if they have passed the test known as the 'Life in the UK Test' administered by [learndirect ltd or if taken in the Isle of Man, the test known as the 'Life in the UK Test' or if taken in the Bailiwick of Guernsey or the Bailiwick of Jersey, the test known as the 'Citizenship Test' administered by an educational institution or other person approved for this purpose by the Lieutenant Governor.]

(b) This sub-paragraph makes provision for transitional arrangements with regards to the requirement to pass the life in the UK Test for those people applying for indefinite leave to remain in one of the categories listed in 33BA(i)–(xviii):

(i) where an applicant enrolled on an ESOL course or gained an ESOL qualification prior to 23rd November 2010, that applicant will be able to rely on an ESOL qualification to meet the requirement to demonstrate sufficient knowledge of the English language and sufficient knowledge about life in the United Kingdom for any future application for indefinite leave to remain under one of the categories listed in 33BA;

(ii) an applicant who enrolled on an ESOL course after 23rd November 2010 and applies for indefinite leave to remain in one of the categories listed in 33BA after 6th April 2011 will have to pass the life in the UK Test;

(iii) an applicant who enrolled on an ESOL course after 23rd November 2010 and who gains an ESOL qualification can continue to use that qualification in an application for indefinite leave to remain in one of the categories listed in 33BA if that application was made before 6th April 2011.]

Note: Paragraph 33BA inserted from 6 April 2011, but not in relation to applications made but not decided before that date, HC 863. Words inserted at the end of para (a) from 6 September 2012 (HC 565).

[33C. In these Rules, an 'accredited college' is:

(a) a publicly funded college that is subject to inspection by the Office for Standards in Education, Children's Services and Skills (if situated in England), the Education and Training Inspectorate (if situated in Northern Ireland), [Education Scotland] (if situated in Scotland), Estyn (if situated in Wales); or an inspection programme that has been approved by the Island's Government (if situated in the Channel Islands or Isle of Man); or

(b) a private college that has been accredited by Accreditation UK, The British Accreditation Council (BAC), the Accreditation Body for Language Services (ABLS), the Accreditation Service for International Colleges (ASIC).]

Note: Paragraph 33C substituted from 7 April 2010 with savings for applications made before 6 April 2010 (HC 413). Words in square brackets substituted from 31 October 2011, and applicable to applications made but undecided before that date, HC 1511.

[33D. In these rules, a 'relevant qualification' is—

(a) an ESOL qualification in speaking and listening which is awarded or authenticated by a body which is recognised by the Office of Qualifications and Examinations Regulation (Ofqual) under section 132 of the Apprenticeships, Skills, Children and Learning Act 2009 and is determined by Ofqual as being at Entry Level; or

(b) one National Qualifications Unit in ESOL at Access 2, Access 3 or Intermediate 1 Level approved by the Scottish Qualifications Authority.]

Note: Paragraph 33D inserted from 7 April 2010 with savings for applications made before 6 April 2010 (HC 439).

[33E In these rules, a 'suitably qualified person' is a person who is deemed suitably qualified by the institution in which the assessment is undertaken.]

Note: Paragraph 33E inserted from 7 April 2010 with savings for applications made before 6 April 2010 (HC 439). Previous paragraph 33E deleted from 31 March 2009 (HC 314).

[33F An applicant has 'demonstrated relevant progress' if he meets the requirements of paragraphs 33F (a) or (b).

(a) The requirements in respect of a relevant qualification awarded or authenticated by a body which is recognised by Ofqual under section 132 of the Apprenticeships, Skills,

Children and Learning Act 2009, are that the applicant provides evidence to the Secretary of State that –

(i) prior to his commencing a course of study leading to a relevant qualification an ESOL assessment was undertaken by a suitably qualified person to assess his level of English language ability; and

(ii) he has successfully completed a course of study leading to a relevant qualification; and

(iii) having been assessed in accordance with paragraph (i) as being below Entry 1, he has attained a relevant qualification at Entry 1, 2 or 3; or

(iv) having been assessed in accordance with paragraph (i) as being at Entry 1, he has attained a relevant qualification at Entry 2 or 3; or

(v) having been assessed in accordance with paragraph (i) as being at Entry 2, he has attained a relevant qualification at Entry 3.

(b) The requirements in respect of a relevant qualification approved by the Scottish Qualifications Authority are that the applicant provides evidence to the Secretary of State that —

(i) prior to his commencing a course of study leading to a relevant qualification an ESOL assessment was undertaken by a suitably qualified person to assess his level of English language ability; and

(ii) he has successfully completed a course of study leading to a relevant qualification; and

(iii) having been assessed in accordance with paragraph (i) as being below Access 2, he has attained a relevant qualification at Access 2 or 3 or at Intermediate 1 level; or

(iv) having been assessed in accordance with paragraph (i) at Access 2, he has attained a relevant qualification at Access 3 or Intermediate 1 level; or

(v) having been assessed in accordance with paragraph (i) at Access 3, he has attained a relevant qualification at Intermediate 1 level.]

[(c) An applicant must provide evidence including:

(i) their original certificate and/or unit transcript awarded or authenticated by a body which is recognised by Ofqual under section 132 of the Apprenticeships, Skills, Children and Learning Act 2009 or awarded or authenticated by the Scottish Qualifications' Authority that shows they have gained a relevant qualification; and

(ii) a letter on official headed notepaper from the college at which they studied for their ESOL qualification, dated and signed by an official of the college, and including the following information:

aa) the applicant's name;

bb) title of the qualification that applicant has gained;

cc) name of the awarding body;

dd) confirmation that the course used teaching materials derived from the document entitled 'Citizenship Materials for ESOL Learners' produced by NIACE/LLU+;

ee) confirmation that that applicant was assessed at the beginning of the course by a suitably qualified teacher;

ff) the level at which that applicant was initially assessed;

gg) the level to which that applicant has progressed;

hh) the duration of the course attended by that applicant; and

ii) information demonstrating that the college meets the definition of an 'accredited college' in paragraph 33C.]

Note: Paragraph 33F inserted from 7 April 2010 with savings for applications made before 6 April 2010 (HC 439). Previous paragraph 33F deleted from 31 March 2009. Sub-paragraph (c) inserted from 6 September 2012 (HC 565).

[**33G.** If in the special circumstances of any particular case the Secretary of State thinks fit, he may waive the need to fulfil the requirement to have sufficient knowledge of the English language and sufficient knowledge about life in the United Kingdom if he considers that, because of the applicant's physical or mental condition, it would be unreasonable to expect him to fulfil that requirement.]

Note: Paragraph 33G inserted from 2 April 2007 (HC 398) and renumbered from 7 April 2010 (HC 439).

Specified forms and procedures for applications or claims in connection with immigration

[**A34.** An application for leave to remain in the United Kingdom as a Tier 2 Migrant or a Tier 5 Migrant under Part 6A of these Rules, or the family member of a Tier 2 or Tier 5 Migrant under Part 8 of these Rules, must be made either by completing the relevant online application process in accordance with paragraph A34(iii) or by using the specified application form in accordance with paragraphs 34A to 34D.

(i) 'The relevant online application process' means the application process accessible via the website of the United Kingdom Border Agency and identified there as relevant for applications for leave to remain as a Tier 2 Migrant, Tier 5 Migrant or family member of a Tier 2 or Tier 5 Migrant.

(ii) 'Specified' in relation to the relevant online application process means specified in the online guidance accompanying that process.

(iii) When the application is made via the relevant online application process:

(a) any specified fee in connection with the application must be paid in accordance with the method specified;

(b) if the online application process requires the applicant to provide biometric information that information must be provided as specified;

(c) if the online application process requires supporting documents to be submitted by post then any such documents specified as mandatory must be submitted in the specified manner within 15 working days of submission of the online application;

(d) if the online application process requires the applicant to make an appointment to attend a public enquiry office of the United Kingdom Border Agency the applicant must, within 45 working days of submission of the online application, make and attend that appointment; and comply with any specified requirements in relation to the provision of biometric information and documents specified as mandatory.]

Note: Paragraph A34 inserted from 13 February 2012, HC 1733.

[**34.** An application form is specified when:

(i) it is posted on the website of the [United Kingdom Border Agency] of the Home Office,

(ii) it is marked on the form that it is a specified form for the purpose of the immigration rules,

(iii) it comes into force on the date specified on the form and/or in any accompanying announcement.]

Note: Paragraph 34 substituted from 29 February 2008 (HC 321). Words substituted from 27 November 2008 (HC 1113).

[**34A.** Where an application form is specified, the application or claim must also comply with the following requirements:

(i) [Subject to paragraph A34] the application or claim must be made using the specified form,

(ii) any specified fee in connection with the application or claim must be paid in accordance with the method specified in the application form, separate payment form and/or related guidance notes, as applicable,

(iii) any section of the form which is designated as mandatory in the application form and/or related guidance notes must be completed as specified,

(iv) if the application form and/or related guidance notes require the applicant to provide biographical . . . information, such information must be provided as specified,

(v) an appointment for the purposes stated in subparagraph (iv) must be made and must take place by the dates specified in any subsequent notification by the Secretary of State following receipt of the application, or as agreed by the Secretary of State,

(vi) where the application or claim is made by post or courier, or submitted in person:

(a) the application or claim must be accompanied by the photographs and documents specified as mandatory in the application form and/or related guidance notes,...

[(ab) those photographs must be in the same format specified as mandatory in the application form and/or related guidance notes, and]

(b) the form must be signed by the applicant, and where applicable, the applicant's spouse, civil partner, same-sex partner or unmarried partner, save that where the applicant is under the age of eighteen, the form may be signed by the parent or legal guardian of the applicant on his behalf,

...

Note: Paragraph 34A inserted from 29 February 2008 (HC 321). Words deleted from sub-para (iv), (vi)(a) and sub-paras (vi)(ab) and (vii)(ab) inserted from 25 November 2008 (HC 1113). Words in square brackets in sub-para (i) inserted and sub-para (vii) deleted from 13 February 2012, HC 1733.

[**34B.** Where an application form is specified, it must be sent by prepaid post to the [United Kingdom Border Agency] of the Home Office, or submitted in person at a public enquiry office of the Border and Immigration Agency of the Home Office, save for the following exceptions:

(i) an application may not be submitted at a public enquiry office of the [United Kingdom Border Agency] of the Home Office if it is an application for:

(a) limited or indefinite leave to remain as a . . . sole representative, retired person of independent means, . . .

[(ba) limited or indefinite leave to remain as a [Tier 1 (Exceptional Talent) Migrant, Tier 1 (Entrepreneur) Migrant, Tier 1 (Investor) Migrant or Tier 1 (Graduate Entrepreneur) Migrant,]

(b) indefinite leave to remain as a victim of domestic violence,

(c) a certificate of approval for a marriage or civil partnership, . . .

(d) a Tier 2, Tier 4 or Tier 5 (Temporary Worker) sponsorship licence

[(e) indefinite leave to remain as a businessperson, investor or innovator, or]

[f] an extension of stay or indefinite leave to remain on the basis of long residence in the United Kingdom.

(ii) an application may be sent by courier to the Border and Immigration Agency of the Home Office if it is an application for:

(a) limited or indefinite leave to remain as a . . . sole representative, retired person of independent means, . . . or as a [Tier 1 Migrant or Tier 2 Migrant], . . .

(b) limited leave to remain for work permit employment, as a seasonal agricultural worker, for the purpose of employment under the Sectors-Based Scheme, . . .

[(c) indefinite leave to remain as a businessperson, investor or innovator]

[(d) limited leave to remain as a Tier 5 (Temporary Worker).]

[(iii) [an applicant may submit an application online where this option is available on the United Kingdom Border Agency's website]

[(iv) an application may not be sent by pre-paid post, and must be made online, if it is an application for a Tier 2, Tier 4 or Tier 5 (Temporary Worker) sponsorship licence.]]

Note: Paragraph 34B inserted from 29 February 2008 (HC 321). Sub-para (i)(e) inserted from 30 June 2008 (HC 607). References to United Kingdom Border Agency substituted from 27 November 2008 (HC 1113). Sub-para (i)(ba) inserted from 31 March 2009 (HC 314). Sub-paragraph (i)(f) inserted from 1 January 2010 (HC 120). Words in square brackets in sub-para (ii)(a) substituted from 27 November 2008 (HC 1113). Words omitted from sub-para (ii)(b) from 27 November 2008 (HC 1113). Sub-paragraphs (ii)(d) and (iii) inserted from 27 November 2008 (HC 1113). Sub-paragraph (iii) renumbered as (iv) and text of sub-para (iii) substituted from 22 October 2010, with savings for applications made before that date (Cm 7944).

[34C. Where an application or claim in connection with immigration for which an application form is specified does not comply with the requirements in paragraph 34A, such application or claim will be invalid and will not be considered.] [Notice of invalidity will be given in writing and deemed to be received on the date it is given, except where it is sent by post, in which case it will be deemed to be received on the second day after it was posted excluding any day which is not a business day.]

Note: Paragraph 34C inserted from 29 February 2008 (HC 321). Words in square brackets inserted from 9 July 2012 with savings for applications made but not decided before that date (HC 194).

[34CA. Where an application for leave to remain in the United Kingdom as a Tier 2 Migrant or a Tier 5 Migrant under Part 6A of these Rules, or the family member of a Tier 2 or Tier 5 Migrant under Part 8 of these Rules, is made by completing the relevant online application process the application will be invalid if it does not comply with the requirements of paragraph A34 and will not be considered.] [Notice of invalidity will be given in writing and deemed to be received on the date it is given, except where it is sent by post, in which case it will be deemed to be received on the second day after it was posted excluding any day which is not a business day.]

Note: Paragraph 34CA inserted from 13 February 2012, HC 1733. Words in second square brackets inserted from 9 July 2012 with savings for applications made but not decided before that date (HC 194).

[34D. Where the main applicant wishes to include applications or claims by any members of his family as his dependants on his own application form, the applications or claims of the dependants must meet the following requirements or they will be invalid and will not be considered:

(i) the application form must expressly permit the applications or claims of dependants to be included, and

(ii) such dependants must be the spouse, civil partner, unmarried or same-sex partner and/or children under the age of 18 of the main applicant.]

Note: Paragraph 34D inserted from 29 February 2008 (HC 321).

Variation of Applications or Claims for Leave to Remain

[**34E.** If a person wishes to vary the purpose of an application or claim for leave to remain in the United Kingdom and an application form is specified for such new purpose [, or paragraph A34 applies], the variation must comply with the requirements of paragraph 34A [or paragraph A34] (as they apply at the date the variation is made) as if the variation were a new application or claim, or the variation will be invalid and will not be considered.]

Note: Paragraph 34E inserted from 29 February 2008 (HC 321). Words in square brackets inserted from 13 February 2012, HC 1733.

[**34F.** Any valid variation of a leave to remain application will be decided in accordance with the immigration rules in force at the date such variation is made.]

Note: Paragraph 34F inserted from 29 February 2008 (HC 321).

Determination of the date of an application or claim (or variation of an application or claim) in connection with immigration

[**34G.** For the purposes of these rules, the date on which an application or claim (or a variation in accordance with paragraph 34E) is made is as follows:
(i) where the application form is sent by post, the date of posting,
(ii) where the application form is submitted in person, the date on which it is accepted by a public enquiry office of the [United Kingdom Border Agency] of the Home Office,
(iii) where the application form is sent by courier, the date on which it is delivered to the [United Kingdom Border Agency] of the Home Office, or
[(iv) where the application is made via the online application process, on the date on which the online application is submitted.]

Note: Paragraph 34G inserted from 29 February 2008 (HC 321). References to United Kingdom Border agency substituted from 27 November 2008 (HC 1113). Sub-paragraph (iv) substituted from 13 February 2012, HC 1733.

[**34H.** Applications or claims for leave to remain made before 29 February 2008 for which a form was prescribed prior to 29 February 2008 shall be subject to the forms and procedures as in force on the date on which the application or claim was made.]

Note: Paragraph 34H inserted from 29 February 2008 (HC 321).

[**34I.** Where an application or claim is made no more than 21 days after the date on which a form is specified under the immigration rules and on a form that was permitted for such application or claim immediately prior to the date of such specification, the application or claim shall be deemed to have been made on the specified form.]

Note: Paragraph 34I inserted from 29 February 2008 (HC 321).

Withdrawn applications or claims for leave to remain in the United Kingdom

[**34J**. Where a person whose application or claim for leave to remain is being considered requests the return of his passport for the purpose of travel outside the common travel area, the application for leave shall, provided it has not already been determined, be treated as withdrawn as soon as the passport is returned in response to that request.]

Note: Paragraph 34J inserted from 29 February 2008 (HC 321).

[**34K**. Paragraph 34J does not apply to an applicant who is applying as a Tier 2 Migrant or a Tier 5 Migrant and whose application is supported by a Certificate of Sponsorship from a Premium Sponsor.]

Note: Paragraph 34K inserted from 6 April 2012 except for applications made but not decided before that date (HC 1888).

Undertakings

35. A sponsor of a person seeking leave to enter ... or remain in the United Kingdom may be asked to give an undertaking in writing to be responsible for that person's [maintenance, accommodation and (as appropriate) personal care] for the period of any leave granted, including any further variation[, or for a period of 5 years from date of grant where indefinite leave to enter or remain is granted]. Under the Social Security Administration Act 1992 and the Social Security Administration (Northern Ireland) Act 1992, the Department of Social Security or, as the case may be, the Department of Health and Social Services in Northern Ireland may seek to recover from the person giving such an undertaking any income support paid to meet the needs of the person in respect of whom the undertaking has been given.

[Under the Immigration and Asylum Act 1999 the Home Office may seek to recover from the person giving such an undertaking amounts attributable to any support provided under section 95 of the Immigration and Asylum Act 1999 (support for asylum seekers) to, or in respect of, the person in respect of whom the undertaking has been given. Failure by the sponsor to maintain that person in accordance with the undertaking, may also be an offence under section 105 of the Social Security Administration Act 1992 and/or under section 108 of the Immigration and Asylum Act 1999 if, as a consequence, asylum support and/or income support is provided to, or in respect of, that person.]

Note: Words in square brackets in second paragraph inserted from 2 October 2000 (Cm 4851). Words omitted, substituted and inserted in first sentence from 9 July 2012 with savings for applications made but not decided before that date (HC 194).

Medical

36. A person who intends to remain in the United Kingdom for more than 6 months should normally be referred to the Medical Inspector for examination. If he produces a medical certificate he should be advised to hand it to the Medical Inspector. Any person seeking entry who mentions health or medical treatment as a reason for his visit, or who appears not to be in good mental or physical health, should also be referred to the Medical Inspector; and the Immigration Officer has discretion, which should be exercised sparingly, to refer for examination in any other case.

37. Where the Medical Inspector advises that a person seeking entry is suffering from a specified disease or condition which may interfere with his ability to support himself or his dependants, the Immigration Officer should take account of this, in conjunction with other factors, in deciding whether to admit that person. The Immigration Officer should also take account of the Medical Inspector's assessment of the likely course of treatment in deciding whether a person seeking entry for private medical treatment has sufficient means at his disposal.

38. A returning resident should not be refused leave to enter [or have existing leave to enter or remain cancelled] on medical grounds. But where a person would be refused leave to enter [or have existing leave to enter or remain cancelled] on medical grounds if he were not a returning resident, or in any case where it is decided on compassionate grounds not to exercise the power to refuse leave to enter [or to cancel have existing leave to enter or remain], or in any other case where the Medical Inspector so recommends, the Immigration Officer should give the person concerned a notice requiring him to report to the Medical Officer of Environmental Health designated by the Medical Inspector with a view to further examination and any necessary treatment.

Note: Words in square brackets inserted from 30 July 2000 (HC 704).

A39. Any person making an application for entry clearance to come to the UK for more than six months from a country listed in Appendix T Part 1 must present at the time of application a valid medical certificate issued by a medical practitioner listed in Appendix T Part 2 confirming that they have undergone screening for active pulmonary tuberculosis and that this tuberculosis is not present in the applicant.

Note: Paragraphs A39 and B39 inserted from 6 April 2012 (HC 565).

B39. Applicants seeking leave to enter as a returning resident under paragraph 19 of these rules, having been absent from the United Kingdom for more than two years are also subject to the requirements in paragraph A39.

Note: Paragraphs A39 and B39 inserted from 6 April 2012 (HC 565).

39. The Entry Clearance Officer has the same discretion as an Immigration Officer to refer applicants for entry clearance for medical examination and the same principles will apply to the decision whether or not to issue an entry clearance.

[Students

39A. An application for a variation of leave to enter or remain made by a student who is sponsored by a government or international sponsorship agency may be refused if the sponsor has not given written consent to the proposed variation.]

Note: Paragraph 39A inserted from 4 April 1996 (HC 329).

[Specified Documents

39B.

(a) Where these Rules state that specified documents must be provided, that means documents specified in these Rules as being specified documents for the route under which the applicant is applying. If the specified documents are not provided, the applicant will not meet the requirement for which the specified documents are required as evidence.

(b) Where these Rules specify documents that are to be provided, those documents are considered to be specified documents, whether or not they are named as such, and as such are subject to the requirements in (c) to (f) below.

(c) If the Entry Clearance Officer or Secretary of State has reasonable cause to doubt the genuineness of any document submitted by an applicant which is, or which purports to be, a specified document under these Rules, and having taken reasonable steps to verify the document is unable to verify that it is genuine, the document will be discounted for the purposes of this application.

(d) Specified documents must be originals, not copies, except where stated otherwise.

(e) Specified documents must contain, or the applicant must provide, full contact details to allow each document to be verified.

(f) Where any specified documents provided are not in English or Welsh, the applicant must provide the original and a full translation that can be independently verified by the UK Border Agency. The translation must:

    (i) include details of the translator's credentials,

    (ii) confirm that it is an accurate translation of the original document,

    (iii) be dated, and

    (iv) include the original signature of the translator.]

Note: Paragraph 39B inserted from 20 July 2012 (Cm 8423).

PART 2
PERSONS SEEKING TO ENTER OR REMAIN IN THE UNITED KINGDOM FOR VISITS
Visitors

[**Requirements for leave to enter as a general visitor**

40. For the purposes of paragraphs 41–46 a general visitor includes a person living and working outside the United Kingdom who comes to the United Kingdom as a tourist. A person seeking leave to enter the United Kingdom as a business visitor, which includes academic visitors, must meet the requirements of paragraph 46G. A person seeking entry as a sports visitor must meet the requirements of paragraph 46M. A person seeking entry as an entertainer visitor must meet the requirements of paragraph 46S. {A visitor seeking leave to enter for the purpose of marriage or to enter into a civil partnership must meet the requirements of paragraph 56D}.]

Note: Paragraph 40 including the heading substituted from 27 November 2008 (HC 1113). The final sentence of para 40 inserted from 6 April 2009 (HC 314). Note that para 7 of HC 314 expresses this insertion as a substitution for words that had already been deleted by HC 1113.

41. The requirements to be met by a person seeking leave to enter the United Kingdom as a [general visitor] are that he:

    (i) is genuinely seeking entry as a [general visitor] for a limited period as stated by him, not exceeding 6 months; {or not exceeding 12 months in the case of a person seeking entry to accompany an academic visitor, provided in the latter case the visitor accompanying the academic visitor has entry clearance}; and

(ii) intends to leave the United Kingdom at the end of the period of the visit as stated by him; and

(iii) does not intend to take employment in the United Kingdom; and

(iv) does not intend to produce goods or provide services within the United Kingdom, including the selling of goods or services direct to members of the public; and

(v) does not intend to [undertake a course of study]; and

(vi) will maintain and accommodate himself and any dependants adequately out of resources available to him without recourse to public funds or taking employment; or will, with any dependants, be maintained and accommodated adequately by relatives or friends; and

(vii) can meet the cost of the return or onward journey; [and

[(viii) is not a child under the age of 18]; and]

[(ix) does not intend to do any of the activities provided for in paragraphs 46G(iii), 46M(iii) or 46S(iii); and

(x) does not, during his visit, intend to marry or form a civil partnership, or to give notice of marriage or civil partnership; and

(xi) does not intend to receive private medical treatment during his visit; and

(xii) is not in transit to a country outside the common travel area.]

[(xiii) where he is seeking leave to enter as a general visitor to take part in archaeological excavations, provides a letter from the director or organiser of the excavation stating the length of their visit and, where appropriate, what arrangements have been made for their accommodation and maintenance.]

Note: Sub-paragraph (viii) inserted from 12 February 2006 (HC 819). Sub-paragraph (v) amended from 1 September 2007 (Cm 7074). References to 'general visitor' substituted from 27 November 2008 (HC 1113). Words in curly brackets in sub-para (i) inserted from 6 April 2009 (HC 314). Sub-paras (ix)–(xii) inserted from 27 November 2008 (HC 1113). Sub-paragraph (xiii) inserted from 20 July 2012 (Cm 8423).

Leave to enter as a general visitor

[**42.** A person seeking leave to enter to the United Kingdom as a general visitor may be admitted for a period not exceeding 6 months {or not exceeding 12 months in the case of a person accompanying an academic visitor}, subject to a condition prohibiting employment, [study and recourse to public funds], provided the Immigration Officer is satisfied that each of the requirements of paragraph 41 is met.]

Note: Paragraph 42 substituted from 27 November 2008 (HC 1113). Amendment in curly brackets inserted from 6 April 2009 (HC 314). Amendment in square brackets inserted from 6 September 2012 (HC 565)

Refusal of leave to enter as a general visitor

[**43.** Leave to enter as a general visitor is to be refused if the Immigration Officer is not satisfied that each of the requirements of paragraph 41 is met.]

Note: Paragraph 43 substituted from 27 November 2008 (HC 1113).

Requirements for an extension of stay as a general visitor

[**44.** Six months is the maximum permitted leave which may be granted to a general visitor. The requirements for an extension of stay as a general visitor are that the applicant:

    (i) meets the requirements of paragraph 41 (ii)–(vii) and (ix)–(xii); and

    (ii) has not already spent, or would not as a result of an extension of stay spend, more than 6 months in total in the United Kingdom {or not more than 12 months in the case of a person accompanying an academic visitor} as a general visitor. Any periods spent as a child visitor are to be counted as a period spent as a general visitor; and

    (iii) has, or was last granted, entry clearance, leave to enter or leave to remain as a general visitor or as a child visitor][; and

    (iv) must not be in the UK in breach of immigration laws except that any period of overstaying for a period of 28 days or less will be disregarded.]

Note: Paragraph 44 substituted from 27 November 2008 (HC 1113). Amendment in curly brackets inserted from 31 March 2009 (HC 314). Sub-paragraph (iv) inserted from 1 October 2012 with savings for applications made but not decided before 9 July 2012 (HC 194).

Extension of stay as a general visitor

[**45.** An extension of stay as a general visitor may be granted, subject to a condition prohibiting employment, [study and recourse to public funds] provided the Secretary of State is satisfied that each of the requirements of paragraph 44 is met.]

Note: Paragraph 45 substituted from 27 November 2008 (HC 1113). Words inserted from 6 April 2012 (HC 565).

Refusal of extension of stay as a general visitor

[**46.** An extension of stay as a general visitor is to be refused if the Secretary of State is not satisfied that each of the requirements of paragraph 44 is met.]

Note: Paragraph 46 substituted from 27 November 2008 (HC 1113).

Child visitors

Requirements for leave to enter as a child visitor

[**46A.** The requirements to be met by a person seeking leave to enter the United Kingdom as a child visitor are that the applicant:

    (i) is genuinely seeking entry as a child visitor for a limited period as stated, not exceeding 6 months or not exceeding 12 months to accompany an academic visitor, provided in the latter case the applicant has entry clearance; and

    (ii) meets the requirements of paragraph 41 (ii)–(iv), (vi)–(vii) and (x)–(xii); and

    (iii) is under the age of 18; and

    (iv) can demonstrate that suitable arrangements have been made for their travel to, and reception and care in the United Kingdom; [and]

    (v) has a parent or guardian in their home country or country of habitual residence who is responsible for their care and who confirms that they consent to the arrangements for the applicant's travel, reception and care in the United Kingdom; and

(vi) if a visa national:

(a) the applicant holds a valid United Kingdom entry clearance for entry as an accompanied child visitor and is travelling in the company of the adult identified on the entry clearance, who is on the same occasion being admitted to the United Kingdom; or

(b) the applicant holds a valid United Kingdom entry clearance for entry as an unaccompanied child visitor; and

(vii) if the applicant has been accepted for a course of study, this is to be provided by an institution which is outside the maintained sector and is:

(a) the holder of a Sponsor Licence for Tier 4 of the Points Based System, or

(b) the holder of valid accreditation from [Accreditation UK; the Accreditation Body for Language Services (ABLS); the British Accreditation Council (BAC) or the Accreditation Service for International Colleges (ASIC), or]

[(c) the holder of a valid and satisfactory full institutional inspection, review or audit by one of the following bodies: the Bridge Schools Inspectorate; the Education and Training Inspectorate; Estyn; Education Scotland; the Independent Schools Inspectorate; Office for Standards in Education; the Schools Inspection Service or the Education and Training Inspectorate Northern Ireland.]

[(viii) if the applicant is undertaking an exchange or educational visit only, this is to be provided by one of the following schools:

(a) For England and Wales, maintained schools as defined under section 20(7) of the School Standards and Framework Act 1998; non-maintained special schools approved under section 342 of the Education Act 1996; independent schools as defined under section 463 of the Education Act 1996 and registered independent schools entered on the register of independent schools maintained under section 158 of the Education Act 2002; academies as defined in section 1(10) of the Academies Act 2010; city technology colleges and city colleges for technology of the arts as established under the Education Act 1996 and treated as academies under section 15(4) of the Academies Act.

(b) For Scotland, state-maintained schools, grant-aided schools and independent fee paying schools as defined under Section 135 of the Education (Scotland) Act 1980.

(c) For Northern Ireland, grant-aided schools as defined under Articles 10 and 11 of and Schedules 4 to 7 to the Education and Libraries (NI) Order in Council 1986; grant maintained integrated schools as defined under Article 69 of and Schedule 5 to the Education Reform (NI) Order 1989; independent fee paying schools as defined under Article 38 of the Education and Libraries (NI) Order 1986.]

Note: Paragraph 46A substituted from 1 January 2010 (HC 120). Sub-paragraph (iv) amended from 20 July 2012 (Cm 8423) and then further amended from 6 September 2012 (HC 565). Words substituted in sub-para (vii)(b), words substituted in sub-para (vii)(c) and sub-para (viii) substituted from 6 September 2012 (HC 565).

Leave to enter as a child visitor

[**46B**. {An applicant} seeking leave to enter the United Kingdom as a child visitor may be admitted for a period not exceeding 6 months, [or not exceeding 12 months in the case of a child visitor accompanying an academic visitor] subject to a condition prohibiting employment [and recourse to public funds], providing that the Immigration Officer is satisfied that each of the requirements of paragraph 46A is met.]

Note: Paragraph 46B inserted from 12 February 2006 (HC 819). Words in curly brackets substituted from 1 January 2010 (HC 120). First words in square brackets inserted from 31 March 2009 (HC 314). Words in second square brackets inserted from 6 September 2012 (HC 565).

Refusal of leave to enter as a child visitor

[46C. Leave to enter as a child visitor is to be refused if the Immigration Officer is not satisfied that each of the requirements of paragraph 46A is met.]

Note: Paragraph 46C inserted from 12 February 2006 (HC 819).

Requirements for an extension of stay as a child visitor

[46D. Six months is the maximum permitted leave which may be granted to a child visitor. The requirements for an extension of stay as a child visitor are that the applicant:

(i) [(i) meets the requirements of paragraph 41 (ii)–(vii) and (x)–(xii);] [and]

(ii) is under the age of 18; and

(iii) can demonstrate that there are suitable arrangements for his care in the United Kingdom and

(iv) has a parent or guardian in his home country or country of habitual residence who is responsible for his care [and who confirms that they consent to the arrangements for the applicant's travel, reception and care in the United Kingdom]; and

(v) has not already spent, or would not as a result of an extension of stay spend, more than 6 months in total in the United Kingdom [or not more than 12 months in total in the case of a child visitor accompanying an academic visitor] as a child visitor; and

[(vi) has, or was last granted, entry clearance, leave to enter or leave to remain as a child visitor]] [; and

(vii) must not be in the UK in breach of immigration laws except that any period of overstaying for a period of 28 days or less will be disregarded.]

Note: Paragraph 46D inserted from 12 February 2006 (HC 819). Sub-para (i) substituted from 31 March 2009 (HC 314) and amended from 1 January 2010 (HC 120). Words inserted in sub-paras (iii) and (iv) from 1 January 2010 (HC 120). Paragraph (vi) inserted from 27 November 2008 (HC 1113). Sub-paragraph (vii) inserted from 1 October 2012 with savings for applications made but not decided before 9 July 2012. Words in square brackets in sub-para (iii) substituted from 20 July 2012 (Cm 8423).

Extension of stay as a child visitor

[46E. An extension of stay as a child visitor may be granted, subject to a condition prohibiting employment {and recourse to public funds}, provided the Secretary of State is satisfied that each of the requirements of paragraph 46D is met.]

Note: Paragraph 46E inserted from 12 February 2006 (HC 819). Words in curly brackets inserted from 6 September 2012 (HC 565).

Refusal of extension of stay as a child visitor

[46F. An extension of stay as a child visitor is to be refused if the Secretary of State is not satisfied that each of the requirements of paragraph 46D is met.]

Note: Paragraph 46F inserted from 12 February 2006 (HC 819).

Business visitors

Requirements for leave to enter as a Business Visitor

46G. The requirements to be met by a person seeking leave to enter the United Kingdom as a business visitor are that he:

(i) is genuinely seeking entry as a business visitor for a limited period as stated by him:

(a) not exceeding 6 months; or

(b) not exceeding 12 months if seeking entry as an academic visitor

(ii) meets the requirements of paragraphs 41(ii)–(viii) and (x)–(xii)

(iii) intends to do one or more of the following during his visit:

[(a) to carry out one of the following activities;

(i) to attend meetings, conferences and interviews, provided they were arranged before arrival in the UK and, if the applicant is a board-level director attending board meetings in the UK, provided they are not employed by a UK company (although they may be paid a fee for attending the meeting);

(ii) to attend trade fairs for promotional work only, provided they are not directly selling;

(iii) to arrange deals, or negotiating or signing trade agreements or contracts;

(iv) to carry out fact-finding missions;

(v) to conduct site visits;

(vi) to work as a driver on a genuine international route delivering goods or passengers from abroad;

(vii) to work as a tour group courier, providing the applicant is contracted to a firm with headquarters outside the UK, is seeking entry to accompany a tour group, and will depart with that tour, or another tour organised by the same company;

(viii) to speak at a one-off conference which is not organised as a commercial concern, and is not making a profit for the organiser;

(ix) to represent a foreign manufacturer by:

(i) carrying out installing, debugging or enhancing work for computer software companies,

(ii) servicing or repairing the manufacturer's products within the initial guarantee period, or

(iii) being briefed on the requirements of a UK customer, provided this is limited to briefing and does not include work involving use of the applicant's expertise to make a detailed assessment of a potential customer's requirements;

(x) to represent a foreign machine manufacturer, as part of the contract of purchase and supply, in erecting and installing machinery too heavy to be delivered in one piece;

(xi) to act as an interpreter or translator for visiting business people, provided they are all employed by, and doing the business of, the same overseas company;

(xii) to erect, dismantle, install, service, repair or advise on the development of foreign-made machinery, provided they will only do so in the UK for up to six months.]

(b) to take part in a location shoot as a member of a film crew [meaning he is a film actor, producer, director or technician paid or employed by an overseas firm other than one established in the UK and is coming to the UK for location sequences only for an overseas film];

(c) to represent overseas news media including as a journalist, correspondent, producer or cameraman provided he is employed or paid by an overseas company and is gathering information for an overseas publication;

(d) to act as an academic visitor but only if [:

(1) he is an academic who is:

(a) on sabbatical leave from an overseas academic institution to carry out research;

(b) taking part in formal exchange arrangements with UK counterparts (including doctors);

(c) coming to share knowledge or experience, or to hold informal discussions with their UK counterparts, or

(d) taking part in a single conference or seminar that is not a commercial or non-profit venture;

(e) an eminent senior doctor or dentist taking part in research, teaching or clinical practice; and

(2) he has been working as an academic in an institution of higher education over-seas or in the field of their academic expertise immediately prior to seeking entry;]

(e) to act as a visiting professor [subject to undertaking only a small amount of teaching for the institution hosting the students he is supervising, being employed and paid by the overseas academic institution and not intending to base himself or seek employment in the UK];

[(f) To be a secondee to a UK company which is directly contracted with the visitor's overseas company, with which it has no corporate relationship, to provide goods or services, provided the secondee remains employed and paid by the overseas company throughout the secondee's visit;]

(g) to undertake some preaching or pastoral work as a religious worker, provided his base is abroad and he is not taking up an office, post or appointment;

[(h) To act as an adviser, consultant, trainer or trouble shooter, to the UK branch of the same group of companies as the visitor's overseas company, provided the visitor remains employed and paid by the overseas company and does not undertake work, paid or unpaid with the UK company's clients;]

[(i) Specific, one-off training on techniques and work practices used in the UK where:

(a) the training is to be delivered by the UK branch of the same group of companies to which the individual's employer belongs; or

(b) the training is to be provided by a UK company contracted to provide goods or services to the overseas company; or

(c) a UK company is contracted to provide training facilities only, to an overseas company][or

(d) the training is corporate training which is being delivered by an outside provider to overseas and UK employees of the same group of companies.]

Note: Paragraph 46G inserted from 27 November 2008 (HC 1113). Sub-paras (iii)(f), (h) and (i) substituted from 31 March 2009 (HC 314). Words in square brackets in sub-paras (iii)(b), (d) and (e) inserted from 20 July 2012 (Cm 8423). Sub-paragraph (iii)(a) substituted and sub-para (iii)(i)(d) inserted from 6 September 2012 (HC 565).

Leave to enter as a business visitor

46H. A person seeking leave to enter to the United Kingdom as a business visitor may be admitted for a period not exceeding 6 months, subject to a condition prohibiting employment, [study and recourse to public funds] provided the Immigration Officer is satisfied that each of the requirements of paragraph 46G is met. A person seeking leave to enter the United Kingdom as an academic visitor who does not have entry clearance may, if otherwise eligible, be admitted for a period not exceeding 6 months, subject to a condition prohibiting employment, [study and recourse to public funds] provided the Immigration Officer is satisfied that each of the requirements of paragraph 46G are met. An academic visitor who has entry clearance may be admitted for up to 12 months subject to a condition prohibiting employment [, study and recourse to public funds].

Note: Paragraph 46H inserted from 27 November 2008 (HC 1113). Words inserted from 6 September 2012 (HC 565).

Refusal of leave to enter as a business visitor

46I. Leave to enter as a business visitor is to be refused if the Immigration Officer is not satisfied that each of the requirements of paragraph 46G is met.

Note: Paragraph 46I inserted from 27 November 2008 (HC 1113).

Requirements for an extension of stay as a business visitor

46J. Twelve months is the maximum permitted leave which may be granted to an academic visitor and six months is the maximum that may be granted to any other form of business visitor. The requirements for an extension of stay as a business visitor are that the applicant:

   (i) meets the requirements of paragraph 46G(ii)–(iii); and

   (ii) if he is a business visitor other than an academic visitor, has not already spent, or would not as a result of an extension of stay spend, more than 6 months in total in the United Kingdom as a business visitor; and

   (iii) if he is an academic visitor, has not already spent, or would not as a result of an extension of stay spend, more than 12 months in total in the United Kingdom as a business visitor; and

   (iv) has, or was last granted, entry clearance, leave to enter or leave to remain as a business visitor[; and

   (v) must not be in the UK in breach of immigration laws except that any period of overstaying for a period of 28 days or less will be disregarded.]

Note: Paragraph 46J inserted from 27 November 2008 (HC 1113). Sub-paragraph (v) inserted from 1 October 2012 with savings for applications made but not decided before 9 July 2012 (HC 194).

Extension of stay as a business visitor

46K. An extension of stay as a business visitor may be granted, subject to a condition prohibiting employment [, study and recourse to public funds], provided the Secretary of State is satisfied that each of the requirements of paragraph 46J is met.

Note: Paragraph 46K inserted from 27 November 2008 (HC 1113). Words inserted from 6 September 2012 (HC 565).

Refusal of extension of stay as a business visitor

46L An extension of stay as a business visitor is to be refused if the Secretary of State is not satisfied that each of the requirements of paragraph 46J is met.

Note: Paragraph 46L inserted from 27 November 2008 (HC 1113).

Sports visitors

Requirements for leave to enter as a sports visitor

46M. The requirements to be met by a person seeking leave to enter the United Kingdom as a sports visitor are that he:

(i) is genuinely seeking entry as a sports visitor for a limited period as stated by him, not exceeding six months; and

(ii) meets the requirements of paragraphs 41(ii)–(viii) and (x)–(xii); and

(iii) intends to do one or more of the following during his visit:

[(a) to take part in a sports tournament, a particular sporting event or series of sporting events in which the applicant is either:

(i) taking part, either as an individual or as part of a team;

(ii) making personal appearances and promotions, such as book signings, television interviews, guest commentaries, negotiating contracts, or to discuss sponsorship deals;

(iii) taking part in 'trials', providing it is not in front of an audience, either paying or non-paying;

(iv) undertaking short periods of training, either as an individual or as part of a team, providing the applicant is not intending to settle in the UK, being paid by a UK sporting body, or joining a UK team where they are involved in friendly or exhibition matches.]

(b) To take part in a specific one off charity sporting event, provided no payment is received other than for travelling and other expenses;

(c) To join, as an amateur, a wholly or predominantly amateur team provided no payment is received other than for board and lodging and reasonable expenses;

(d) To serve as a member of the technical or personal staff, or as an official, attending the same event as a visiting sportsperson coming for one or more of the purposes listed in (a), (b) or (c) [, or attending the same event as a sportsperson carrying out permitted paid engagements as a visitor].

Note: Paragraph 46M inserted from 27 November 2008 (HC 1113). Words in square brackets in (d) inserted from 6 April 2012 except for applications made but not decided before that date (HC 1888). Sub-paragraph (iii)(a) substituted from 6 September 2012 (HC 565).

Leave to enter as a sports visitor

46N. A person seeking leave to enter to the United Kingdom as a sports visitor may be admitted for a period not exceeding 6 months, subject to a condition prohibiting employment [, study and recourse to public funds], provided the Immigration Officer is satisfied that each of the requirements of paragraph 46M is met.

Note: Paragraph 46N inserted from 27 November 2008 (HC 1113). Words inserted from 6 September 2012 (HC 565).

Refusal of leave to enter as a sports visitor

46O. Leave to enter as a sports visitor is to be refused if the Immigration Officer is not satisfied that each of the requirements of paragraph 46M is met.

Note: Paragraph 46O inserted from 27 November 2008 (HC 1113).

Requirements for an extension of stay as a sports visitor

46P. Six months is the maximum permitted leave which may be granted to a sports visitor. The requirements for an extension of stay as a sports visitor are that the applicant:

(i) meets the requirements of paragraph 46M (ii)–(iii); and

(ii) has not already spent, or would not as a result of an extension of stay spend, more than 6 months in total in the United Kingdom as a sports visitor; and

(iii) has, or was last granted, entry clearance, leave to enter or leave to remain as a sports visitor [; and (iv) must not be in the UK in breach of immigration laws except that any period of overstaying for a period of 28 days or less will be disregarded.]

Note: Paragraph 46P inserted from 27 November 2008 (HC 1113). Sub-paragraph (iv) inserted from 1 October 2012 with savings for applications made but not decided before 9 July 2012 (HC 194).

Extension of stay as a sports visitor

46Q. An extension of stay as a sports visitor may be granted, subject to a condition prohibiting employment [, study and recourse to public funds] provided the Secretary of State is satisfied that each of the requirements of paragraph 46P is met.

Note: Paragraph 46Q inserted from 27 November 2008 (HC 1113). Words inserted from 6 September 2012 (HC 565).

Refusal of extension of stay as a sports visitor

46R. An extension of stay as a sports visitor is to be refused if the Secretary of State is not satisfied that each of the requirements of paragraph 46P is met.

Note: Paragraph 46R inserted from 27 November 2008 (HC 1113).

Entertainer visitors

Requirements for leave to enter as an entertainer visitor

46S. The requirements to be met by a person seeking leave to enter the United Kingdom as an entertainer visitor are that he:

(i) is genuinely seeking entry as an entertainer visitor for a limited period as stated by him, not exceeding 6 months; and

(ii) meets the requirements of paragraphs 41 (ii)–(viii) and (x)–(xii); and

(iii) intends to do one or more of the following during his visit:

(a) to take part as a professional entertainer in one or more music competitions; and/or

(b) to fulfil one or more specific engagements as either an individual amateur entertainer or as an amateur group; and/or [(c) to take part, as an amateur or professional entertainer, in one or more cultural events or festivals on the list of permit free festivals at Appendix R to these Rules.]

(d) to serve as a member of the technical or personal staff, or of the production team, of an entertainer coming for one or more of the purposes listed in (a), (b), or (c) [, or attending the same event as an entertainer carrying out permitted paid engagements as a visitor].

Note: Paragraph 46S inserted from 27 November 2008 (HC 1113). Words in square brackets in (iii) (d) inserted from 6 April 2012 with savings for applications made but not decided before that date (HC 1888). Sub-paragraph (iii)(c) substituted from 6 September 2012 (HC 565).

Leave to enter as an entertainer visitor

46T. A person seeking leave to enter to the United Kingdom as an entertainer visitor may be admitted for a period not exceeding 6 months, subject to a condition prohibiting employment [, study and recourse to public funds], provided the Immigration Officer is satisfied that each of the requirements of paragraph 46S is met.

Note: Paragraph 46T inserted from 27 November 2008 (HC 1113). Words inserted from 6 September 2012 (HC 565).

Refusal of leave to enter as an entertainer visitor

46U. Leave to enter as an entertainer visitor is to be refused if the Immigration Officer is not satisfied that each of the requirements of paragraph 46S is met.

Note: Paragraph 46U inserted from 27 November 2008 (HC 1113).

Requirements for an extension of stay as an entertainer visitor

46V. Six months is the maximum permitted leave which may be granted to an entertainer visitor. The requirements for an extension of stay as an entertainer visitor are that the applicant:

(i) meets the requirements of paragraph 46S (ii)–(iii); and

(ii) has not already spent, or would not as a result of an extension of stay spend, more than 6 months in total in the United Kingdom as an entertainer visitor; and

(iii) has, or was last granted, entry clearance, leave to enter or leave to remain as an entertainer visitor [; and

(iv) must not be in the UK in breach of immigration laws except that any period of overstaying for a period of 28 days or less will be disregarded.]

Note: Paragraph 46V inserted from 27 November 2008 (HC 1113). Sub-paragraph (iv) inserted from 9 October 2012 with savings for applications made but not decided before 9 July 2012 (HC 194).

Extension of stay as an entertainer visitor

46W. An extension of stay as an entertainer visitor may be granted, subject to a condition prohibiting employment [, study and recourse to public funds], provided the Secretary of State is satisfied that each of the requirements of paragraph 46V is met.

Note: Paragraph 46W inserted from 27 November 2008 (HC 1113). Words inserted from 6 September 2012 (HC 565).

Refusal of extension of stay as an entertainer visitor

46X. An extension of stay as an entertainer visitor is to be refused if the Secretary of State is not satisfied that each of the requirements of paragraph 46V is met.

Note: Paragraph 46X inserted from 27 November 2008 (HC 1113).

Visitors in transit

Requirements for admission as a visitor in transit to another country

47. The requirements to be met by a person (not being a member of the crew of a ship, aircraft, hovercraft, hydrofoil or train) seeking leave to enter the United Kingdom as a visitor in transit to another country are that he:

   (i) is in transit to a country outside the common travel area; and

  (ii) has both the means and the intention of proceeding at once to another country; and

 (iii) is assured of entry there; and

 (iv) intends and is able to leave the United Kingdom within 48 hours.

Leave to enter as a visitor in transit

48. A person seeking leave to enter the United Kingdom as a visitor in transit may be admitted for a period not exceeding 48 hours with a prohibition on employment [, study and recourse to public funds] provided the Immigration Officer is satisfied that each of the requirements of paragraph 47 is met.

Note: Words inserted from 6 September 2012 (HC 565).

Refusal of leave to enter as a visitor in transit

49. Leave to enter as a visitor in transit is to be refused if the Immigration Officer is not satisfied that each of the requirements of paragraph 47 is met.

Extension of stay as a visitor in transit

50. The maximum permitted leave which may be granted to a visitor in transit is 48 hours. An application for an extension of stay beyond 48 hours from a person admitted in this category is to be refused.

Visitors seeking to enter or remain for private medical treatment

Requirements for leave to enter as a visitor for private medical treatment

51. The requirements to be met by a person seeking leave to enter the United Kingdom as a visitor for private medical treatment are that he:

[(i) meets the requirements set out in paragraph 41 (iii)–(vii), (ix)–(x) and (xii) for entry as a general visitor; and]

(ii) in the case of a person suffering from a communicable disease, has satisfied the Medical Inspector that there is no danger to public health; and

(iii) can show, if required to do so, that any proposed course of treatment is of finite duration; and

(iv) intends to leave the United Kingdom at the end of his treatment; and

(v) can produce satisfactory evidence, if required to do so, of:

(a) the medical condition requiring consultation or treatment; and

(b) satisfactory arrangements for the necessary consultation or treatment at his own expense; and

(c) the estimated costs of such consultation or treatment; and

(d) the likely duration of his visit; and

(e) sufficient funds available to him in the United Kingdom to meet the estimated costs and his undertaking to do so.

Note: Sub-paragraph (i) substituted from 27 November 2008 (HC 1113).

Leave to enter as a visitor for private medical treatment

52. A person seeking leave to enter the United Kingdom as a visitor for private medical treatment may be admitted for a period not exceeding 6 months, subject to a condition prohibiting employment [, study and recourse to public funds], provided the Immigration Officer is satisfied that each of the requirements of paragraph 51 is met.

Note: Words inserted from 6 September 2012 (HC 565).

Refusal of leave to enter as a visitor for private medical treatment

53. Leave to enter as a visitor for private medical treatment is to be refused if the Immigration Officer is not satisfied that each of the requirements of paragraph 51 is met.

Requirements for an extension of stay as a visitor for private medical treatment

54. The requirements for an extension of stay as a visitor to undergo or continue private medical treatment are that the applicant:

[(i) meets the requirements set out in paragraph 41(iii)–(vii), (ix)–(x) and (xii) and paragraph 51 (ii)–(v); and]

[(ii) has produced evidence [in the form of a letter on headed notepaper giving a private practice or hospital address] from a registered medical practitioner who holds an NHS consultant post or who appears in the Specialist Register of the General Medical Council of [that provides full details of the:

(a) nature of the illness;

(b) proposed or continuing treatment;

(c) frequency of consultations;

(d) probable duration of the treatment;

(e) details of the cost of treatment and confirmation that all expenses are being met; and

(f) where treatment amounts to private visits to a consultant for a relatively minor ailment, details of the progress being made]; and]

(iii) [has provided evidence that] that he has met, out of the resources available to him, any costs and expenses incurred in relation to his treatment in the United Kingdom; and

(iv) has [provided evidence that he has] sufficient funds available to him in the United Kingdom [, or if relying on funds from abroad has provided evidence that those funds are fully transferable to the United Kingdom,] to meet the likely costs of his treatment and intends to meet those costs [; and

(v) was not last admitted to the United Kingdom under the Approved Destination Status Agreement with China][; and

(vi) must not be in the UK in breach of immigration laws except that any period of overstaying for a period of 28 days or less will be disregarded.]

Note: Paragraph 54(ii) substituted from 2 October 2000 (Cm 4851). Paragraph 54(v) inserted from 5 April 2005 (HC 486). Paragraph 54(i) substituted from 27 November 2008 (HC 1113). Sub-paragraph (vi) inserted from 1 October 2012 with savings for applications made but not decided before 9 July 2012 (HC 194). Words in first square brackets in sub-para (ii) and square brackets in (iv) inserted and other words in square brackets in (ii) and (iii) substituted from 20 July 2012 (Cm 8423).

Extension of a stay as a visitor for private medical treatment

55. An extension of stay to undergo or continue private medical treatment may be granted, with a prohibition on employment [, study and recourse to public funds], provided the Secretary of State is satisfied that each of the requirements of paragraph 54 is met.

Note: Words inserted from 6 September 2012 (HC 565).

Refusal of extension of stay as a visitor for private medical treatment

56. An extension of stay as a visitor to undergo or continue private medical treatment is to be refused if the Secretary of State is not satisfied that each of the requirements of paragraph 54 is met.

[Parent of a Child at School

Requirements for leave to enter or remain as the parent of a child at school

56A. The requirements to be met by a person seeking leave to enter or remain in the United Kingdom as the parent of a child at school are that:

[(i) the parent meets the requirements set out in paragraph 41 (ii)–(xii); and]

[(ii) (1) if the child has leave under paragraphs 57 to 62 of these Rules, the child is attending an independent fee- paying day school and meets the requirements set out in paragraph 57 (i)–(ix), or

(2) if the child is a Tier 4 (Child) Student, the child is attending an independent fee- paying day school and meets the requirements set out in paragraph 245ZZA (if seeking leave to enter) or 245ZZC (if seeking leave to remain); and]

(iii) the child is under 12 years of age; and

(iv) the parent can provide satisfactory evidence of adequate and reliable funds for maintaining a second home in the United Kingdom; and

(v) the parent is not seeking to make the United Kingdom his main home [; and

(vi) the parent was not last admitted to the United Kingdom under the Approved Destination Status Agreement with China][; and

(vii) if seeking leave to remain must not be in the UK in breach of immigration laws except that any period of overstaying for a period of 28 days or less will be disregarded.]

Note: Paragraphs 56A–C inserted from 2 October 2000 (CM 4851). Sub-paragraph (i) substituted from 27 November 2008 (HC 1113) and '41' inserted from 31 March 2009 (HC 314). Sub-para (ii) substituted from 31 March 2009 (HC 314). Paragraph 56A (vi) inserted from 5 April 2005 (HC 486). Sub-paragraph (vii) inserted from 1 October 2012 with savings for applications made but not decided before 9 July 2102 (HC 194).

Leave to enter or remain as the parent of a child at school

56B. A person seeking leave to enter or remain in the United Kingdom as the parent of a child at school may be admitted or allowed to remain for a period not exceeding 12 months, subject to a condition prohibiting employment [, study and recourse to public funds], provided the Immigration Officer or, in the case of an application for limited leave to remain, the Secretary of State is satisfied that each of the requirements of paragraph 56A is met.

Note: Paragraphs 56A–C inserted from 2 October 2000 (CM 4851). Words inserted from 6 September 2012 (HC 565).

Refusal of leave to enter or remain as the parent of a child at school

56C. Leave to enter or remain in the United Kingdom as the parent of a child at school is to be refused if the Immigration Officer or, in the case of an application for limited leave to remain, the Secretary of State is not satisfied that each of the requirements of paragraph 56A is met.]

Note: Paragraphs 56A–C inserted from 2 October 2000 (CM 4851).

*Visitors seeking to enter for the purposes of marriage or to enter
into a civil partnership*

Requirements for leave to enter as a visitor for marriage or to enter into a civil partnership

[**56D.** The requirements to be met by a person seeking leave to enter the United Kingdom as a visitor for marriage [or civil partnership] are that he:

(i) meets the requirements set out in paragraph 41 [(i)–(ix) and (xi)–((xii)]; and

(ii) can show that he intends to give notice of marriage [or civil partnership], or marry [or form a civil partnership], in the United Kingdom within the period for which entry is sought; and

(iii) can produce satisfactory evidence, if required to do so, of the arrangements for giving notice of marriage [or civil partnership], or for his wedding [or civil partnership] . . . to take place, in the United Kingdom during the period for which entry is sought; and

(iv) holds a valid United Kingdom entry clearance for entry in this capacity.]

Note: Headings substituted from 31 March 2009 (HC 314). Paragraph 56D inserted from 15 March 2005 (HC 346). References to civil partnership inserted from 14 November 2005 (HC 582). Sub-paragraph (i) amended from 31 March 2008 (HC 314). Word omitted from sub-para (iii) from 31 March 2009 (HC 314).

Leave to enter as a visitor for marriage [or civil partnership]

[**56E.** A person seeking leave to enter the United Kingdom as a visitor for marriage [or civil partnership] may be admitted for a period not exceeding 6 months, subject to a condition prohibiting employment [, study and recourse to public funds], provided the Immigration Officer is satisfied that each of the requirements of paragraph 56D is met.]

Note: Paragraph 56E inserted from 15 March 2005 (HC 346). References to civil partnership inserted from 14 November 2005 (HC 582). Words inserted from 6 September 2012 (HC 565).

Refusal of leave to enter as a visitor for marriage [or civil partnership]

[**56F.** Leave to enter as a visitor for marriage [or civil partnership] is to be refused if the Immigration Officer is not satisfied that each of the requirements of paragraph 56D is met.]

Note: Paragraph 56F inserted from 15 March 2005 (HC 346). References to civil partnership inserted from 14 November 2005 (HC 582).

[*Visitors Seeking Leave to Enter Under the Approved Destination Status (ADS) Agreement with China*

Requirements for leave to enter as a visitor under the Approved Destination Status Agreement with China ('ADS Agreement')

56G. The requirements to be met by a person seeking leave to enter the United Kingdom as a visitor under the ADS Agreement with China are that he:
    [(i) meets the requirements set out in paragraph (ii)–(xii); and]
    (ii) is a national of the People's Republic of China; and
    (iii) is genuinely seeking entry as a visitor for a limited period as stated by him, not exceeding 30 days; and
    (iv) intends to enter, leave and travel within the territory of the United Kingdom as a member of a tourist group under the ADS Agreement; and
    (v) holds a valid ADS Agreement visit visa.

Note: Paragraphs 56G–56J inserted from 5 April 2005 (HC 486). Sub-paragraph (i) substituted from 27 November 2008 (HC 1113). Note that the substitution appearing in the text reflects the wording of para 37 of HC 1113; it is believed that '(ii)–(xii)' is intended to refer to sub-paras of para 41.

Leave to enter as a visitor under the ADS Agreement with China

56H. A person seeking leave to enter the United Kingdom as a visitor under the ADS Agreement may be admitted for a period not exceeding 30 days, subject to a condition prohibiting employment [, study and recourse to public funds], provided they hold an ADS Agreement visit visa.

Note: Paragraphs 56G–56J inserted from 5 April 2005 (HC 486). Words inserted from 6 September 2012 (HC 565).

Refusal of leave to enter as a visitor under the ADS Agreement with China

56I. Leave to enter as a visitor under the ADS Agreement with China is to be refused if the person does not hold an ADS Agreement visit visa.

Note: Paragraphs 56G–56J inserted from 5 April 2005 (HC 486).

Extension of stay as a visitor under the ADS Agreement with China

56J. Any application for an extension of stay as a visitor under the ADS Agreement with China is to be refused.]

Note: Paragraphs 56G–56J inserted from 5 April 2005 (HC 486).

[Student visitors]

Requirements for leave to enter as a student visitor

[**56K.** The requirements to be met by a person seeking leave to enter the United Kingdom as a student visitor are that he:

    (i) is genuinely seeking entry as a student visitor for a limited period as stated by him, not exceeding six months; and

    [(ii) has been accepted on a course of study which is to be provided by an institution which is:

        (a) the holder of a sponsor licence for Tier 4 of the Points Based System, or

        (b) the holder of valid accreditation from[Accreditation UK, the Accreditation Body for Language Services (ABLS), the British Accreditation Council (BAC) or the Accreditation Service for International Colleges (ASIC)], or

        [(c) the holder of a valid and satisfactory full institutional inspection, review or audit by one of the following bodies: Bridge Schools Inspectorate; the Education and Training Inspectorate; Estyn; Education Scotland; the Independent Schools Inspectorate; Office for Standards in Education; the Quality Assurance Agency for Higher Education; the Schools Inspection Service or the Education and Training Inspectorate Northern Ireland, or]

        (d) an overseas Higher Education Institution offering only part of their programmes in the United Kingdom, holding its own national accreditation and offering programmes that are an equivalent level to a United Kingdom degree, and.]

    (iii) intends to leave the United Kingdom at the end of his visit as stated by him; and

    (iv) does not intend to take employment in the United Kingdom; and

    (v) does not intend to engage in business, to produce goods or provide services within the United Kingdom, including the selling of goods or services direct to members of the public; and

    (vi) does not intend to study at a maintained school; and

    (vii) will maintain and accommodate himself and any dependants adequately out of resources available to him without recourse to public funds or taking employment; or will, with any dependants, be maintained and accommodated adequately by relatives or friends; and

    (viii) can meet the cost of the return or onward journey; and

    (ix) is not a child under the age of 18.]

[(x) meets the requirements set out in paragraph 41 (ix)–(xii).]

Note: Paragraph 56K inserted from 1 September 2007 (Cm 7074). Sub-paragraph (ii) substituted from 22 February 2010 subject to savings for applications made before that date (HC 120). Sub-paragraph (x) inserted from 31 March 2009 (HC 314). Words substituted in sub-para (ii)(b) and sub-para (ii)(c) substituted from 6 September 2012 (HC 565).

Leave to enter as a student visitor

[**56L.** A person seeking leave enter the United Kingdom as a student visitor may be admitted for a period not exceeding 6 months, subject to a condition prohibiting employment [, study and recourse to public funds], provided the Immigration Officer is satisfied that each of the requirements of paragraph 56K is met.]

Note: Paragraph 56L inserted from 1 September 2007 (Cm 7074). Words inserted from 6 September 2012 (HC 565).

Refusal of leave to enter as a student visitor

[**56M.** Leave to enter as a student visitor is to be refused if the Immigration Officer is not satisfied that each of the requirements of paragraph 56K is met.]

Note: Paragraph 56M inserted from 1 September 2007 (Cm 7074).

[Prospective Entrepreneurs

Purpose

56N. This Special Visitor route is to enable individuals who are at the time of applying for leave under this route in discussions with:

    (i) one or more registered venture capitalist firms regulated by the Financial Services Authority, and/or

    (ii) one or more UK entrepreneurial seed funding competitions which is listed as endorsed on the UK Trade & Investment website, and/or

    (iii) one or more UK Government Departments,

    to secure funding in order to join, set up or take over, and be actively involved in the running of, a business in the UK.]

Note: Paragraph 56N inserted from 6 April 2011 (HC 863).

Requirements for leave to enter as a Prospective Entrepreneur

56O. The requirements to be met by a person seeking leave to enter the United Kingdom as a Prospective Entrepreneur are that:

    (a) The applicant must provide an original letter on headed paper [signed by an authorized official of that institution] supporting the application from:

    (i) one or more registered venture capitalist firms regulated by the Financial Services Authority,

    (ii) one or more UK entrepreneurial seed funding competitions which is listed as endorsed on the UK Trade & Investment website, or

    (iii) one or more UK Government Departments;

(b) The letter referred to in (a) must be dated no earlier than three months before the date of the application, be signed by an authorised official, and contain:

(i) a description of the nature of the individual(s) and/or organisation(s) supporting the application;

(ii) a description of the background and nature of the proposed business;

(iii) a description of the applicant's suitability to be involved with the proposed business;

(iv) a commitment by the individual(s) and/or organisation(s) supporting the applicant [to make a decision whether to provide a minimum of £50,000 funding] for the proposed business within 6 months of the applicant entering the UK (if more than one individual and/or organisation is supporting the applicant, each amount proposed may be less than £50k, provided that the total amount is a minimum of £50k);

(v) a commitment by the individual(s) or organisation(s) supporting the applicant that the proposed business will be set up and run from the UK;

(vi) details of a contact name, telephone number and e-mail address for the individual(s) and/or organisation(s) supporting the applicant; and

(vii) confirmation that the individual(s) and/or organisation(s) supporting the applicant is content to be contacted about the applicant;

(c) The applicant's primary intention in applying as a Prospective Entrepreneur is to secure funding in order to join, set up or take over, and be actively involved in the running of a business in the UK;

(d) The applicant intends to carry out one of the activities as listed [in paragraph 56O(d)(i)], specifying the activities that a Prospective Entrepreneur may undertake during a visit to the UK;

[56O(d)(i). The permitted activities are:

(1) attending meetings, including meetings arranged while in the UK, interviews arranged before arriving in the UK and conferences;

(2) attending trade fairs provided this is restricted to promotional work and does not involve selling directly to members of the public;

(3) arranging deals and negotiating or signing trade agreements and contracts;

(4) conducting site visits;

(5) speaking at a one-off conference which is not organised as a commercial concern;

(6) undertaking fact finding missions;

(7) purchasing, checking the details of or examining goods;

(8) recruiting staff for the proposed business activity which is the object of the visa;]

(e) The applicant intends to leave the United Kingdom at the end of the period of the visit as stated by him, unless he makes a successful application for leave to remain as a Tier 1 (Entrepreneur) Migrant before the end of the period of the visit;

(f) The applicant will maintain and accommodate himself and any dependants adequately out of resources available to him without recourse to public funds or taking employment; or will, with any dependants, be maintained and accommodated adequately by relatives or friends;

(g) The applicant does not intend during his visit to:

(i) take employment in the United Kingdom;

(ii) produce goods or provide services within the United Kingdom, including the selling of goods or services direct to members of the public;

(iii) undertake a course of study;

(iv) marry or form a civil partnership, or to give notice of marriage or civil partnership; or

(v) receive private medical treatment.

(h) The applicant is not under the age of 18;

(i) The applicant is not in transit to a country outside the common travel area; and

(j) The applicant holds a valid United Kingdom entry clearance for entry in this capacity.

Note: Paragraphs 56O inserted from 6 April 2011 (HC 863). Words in square brackets in sub-para (b)(iv) substituted from 21 April 2011 except for applications made but not decided before that date (HC) 908. Words in square brackets in sub-para (a) and (d) and 56O(d)(i) inserted from 20 July 2012 (Cm 8423).

Leave to enter as a Prospective Entrepreneur

56P. A person seeking leave to enter to the United Kingdom as a Prospective Entrepreneur may be admitted for a period not exceeding 6 months, subject to a condition prohibiting employment [, study and recourse to public funds], provided the Secretary of State is satisfied that each of the requirements of paragraph 56O is met.

Note: Paragraph 56P inserted from 6 April 2011 (HC 863). Words inserted from 6 September 2012 (HC 565).

Refusal of leave to enter as a Prospective Entrepreneur

56Q. Leave to enter as a Prospective Entrepreneur is to be refused if the Secretary of State is not satisfied that each of the requirements of paragraph 56O is met.

Note: Paragraph 56Q inserted from 6 April 2011 (HC 863).

[Olympic or Paralympic Games Family Member Visitor Requirements for leave to enter or remain as an Olympic or Paralympic Games Family Member Visitor

56R. The requirements to be met by a person seeking leave to enter or remain as an Olympic or Paralympic Games Family Member Visitor are that the applicant:

(i) is genuinely seeking leave to enter or remain as an Olympic or Paralympic Games Family Member Visitor; and

(ii) is accredited by the London Organising Committee of the Olympic Games and Paralympic Games Limited for the 2012 London Olympic and Paralympic Games and that accreditation has not been revoked by the International Olympic Committee or the International Paralympic Committee; and

(iii) is not accredited for the 2012 London Olympic and Paralympic Games in accreditation category codes OCOG, S or X; and

(iv) when seeking leave to enter or remain presents an Olympic Identity and Accreditation Card or a Paralympic Identity and Accreditation Card issued by the London Organising Committee of the Olympic Games and Paralympic Games Limited; and

(v) is seeking leave to enter or remain during the period commencing on 30 March 2012 and ending on 8 November 2012; and

(vi) if seeking leave to enter or remain during the period commencing on 30 March 2012 and ending on 8 May 2012 is seeking leave for a period not exceeding

6 months; or if seeking leave to enter or remain during the period commencing on 9 May 2012 and ending on 8 November 2012 is not seeking leave beyond 8 November 2012; and

(vii) if seeking leave to enter or remain on or after 13 August 2012 and presents an Olympic Identity and Accreditation Card must have held leave to enter, leave to remain or entry clearance at any time during the period commencing on 30 March 2012 and ending on 12 August 2012; or if seeking leave to enter or remain on or after 10 September 2012 and presents a Paralympic Identity and Accreditation Card must have held leave to enter, leave to remain or entry clearance at any time during the period commencing on 30 March 2012 and ending on 9 September 2012; and

(viii) if intending to take employment, takes employment only related to the Olympic and Paralympic Games; and

(ix) will maintain and accommodate himself and any dependents adequately out of resources available to him without recourse to public funds; or will, with any dependents, be maintained and accommodated adequately by relatives, friends, or associates; and

(x) does not intend to undertake a course of study; and

(xi) does not, during his visit, intend to marry or form a civil partnership, or to give notice of marriage or civil partnership; and

(xii) can meet the cost of the return or onward journey; and

(xiii) intends to leave the United Kingdom by or on 8 November 2012; and

(xiv) is not a child under the age of 18.

Note: Paragraph 56R inserted from 30 March 2012 with effect until 9 November 2012 (HC 1511).

Leave to enter or remain as an Olympic or Paralympic Games Family Member Visitor

56S. A person seeking leave to enter or remain in the United Kingdom as an Olympic or Paralympic Games Family Member Visitor during the period commencing on 30 March 2012 and ending on 8 May 2012 may be admitted or allowed to stay in the United Kingdom for up to 6 months subject to a condition prohibiting recourse to public funds and restricting employment to employment only related to the Olympic or Paralympic Games, provided the Immigration Officer is satisfied that each of the requirements of paragraph 56R is met. A person seeking leave to enter or remain in the United Kingdom as an Olympic or Paralympic Games Family Member Visitor during the period commencing on 9 May 2012 and ending on 8 November 2012 may be admitted or allowed to stay in the United Kingdom until 8 November 2012 subject to a condition prohibiting recourse to public funds and restricting employment to employment only related to the Olympic and Paralympic Games provided the Immigration Officer is satisfied that each of the requirements of paragraph 56R is met.

Note: Paragraph 56S inserted from 30 March 2012 with effect until 9 November 2012 (HC 1511).

Refusal of leave to enter or remain as an Olympic or Paralympic Games Family Member Visitor

56T. Leave to enter or remain as an Olympic or Paralympic Games Family Member Visitor is to be refused if the Immigration Officer is not satisfied that each of the requirements of paragraph 56R is met.

Note: Paragraph 56T inserted from 30 March 2012 with effect until 9 November 2012 (HC 1511).

Olympic or Paralympic Games Family Member Child Visitor
Requirements for leave to enter or remain as an Olympic or Paralympic Games Family Member Child Visitor

56U. The requirements to be met by a person seeking leave to enter or remain as an Olympic or Paralympic Games Family Member Child Visitor are that the applicant—

(i)   is genuinely seeking leave to enter or remain as an Olympic or Paralympic Games Family Member Child Visitor; and

(ii) meets the requirements of paragraph 56R (ii) to (xiii); and

(iii) is under the age of 18; and

(iv) can demonstrate that suitable arrangements have been made for their travel to, and reception and care in the United Kingdom; and

(v)   can demonstrate that their parent or guardian in their home country or country of habitual residence who is responsible for their care consents to arrangements for applicant's travel, reception and care in the United Kingdom.

Note: Paragraph 56U inserted from 30 March 2012 with effect until 9 November 2012 (HC 1511).

Leave to enter or remain as an Olympic or Paralympic Games Family Member Child Visitor

56V. A person seeking leave to enter or remain in the United Kingdom as an Olympic or Paralympic Games Family Member Child Visitor during the period commencing on 30 March 2012 and ending on 8 May 2012 may be admitted or allowed to stay in the United Kingdom for up to 6 months subject to a condition prohibiting recourse to public funds and restricting employment to employment only related to the Olympic or Paralympic Games, provided the Immigration Officer is satisfied that each of the requirements of paragraph 56U is met. A person seeking leave to enter or remain in the United Kingdom as an Olympic or Paralympic Games Family Member Child Visitor during the period commencing on 9 May 2012 and ending on 8 November 2012 may be admitted or allowed to stay in the United Kingdom until 8 November 2012 subject to a condition prohibiting recourse to public funds and restricting employment to employment only related to the Olympic and Paralympic Games providing the Immigration Officer is satisfied that each of the requirements of paragraph 56U is met.

Note: Paragraph 56V inserted from 30 March 2012 with effect until 9 November 2012 (HC 1511).

Refusal of leave to enter or remain as an Olympic or Paralympic Games Family Member Child Visitor

56W. Leave to enter or remain as an Olympic or Paralympic Games Family Member Child Visitor is to be refused if the Immigration Officer is not satisfied that each of the requirements of paragraph 56U is met.]

Note: Paragraph 56W inserted from 30 March 2012 with effect until 9 November 2012 (HC 1511).

[Visitors undertaking permitted paid engagements Requirements for leave to enter as a visitor undertaking permitted paid engagements

56X. The requirements to be met by a person seeking leave to enter the United Kingdom as a visitor undertaking permitted paid engagements are that the applicant:

(i) is genuinely seeking entry as a visitor undertaking a permitted paid engagement for a limited period, not exceeding one month; and

(ii) meets the requirements of paragraphs 41(ii), (v), (vii), (viii), (x)–(xii); and

(iii) intends to do one of the following pre-arranged permitted paid engagements which can be evidenced by a formal invitation, and can show that the engagement relates to his or her area of expertise and/or qualifications, and full time occupation overseas:

(a) examine students and/or participate in or chair selection panels as a visiting academic, who is highly qualified within his or her own field of expertise, invited by a United Kingdom Higher Education Institution or a United Kingdom based research or arts organisation as part of that institution or organisation's quality assurance processes;

(b) give one or more lectures in his or her field of expertise as a visiting lecturer, invited by a United Kingdom Higher Education Institution or a United Kingdom based research or arts organisation [, provided this is not in a formal teaching role];

(c) as an overseas designated pilot examiner, assess United Kingdom based pilots to ensure they meet the national aviation regulatory requirements of other countries, by invitation of an approved training organisation based in the United Kingdom that is regulated by the United Kingdom Civil Aviation Authority for that purpose;

(d) provide advocacy in a particular area of law as a qualified lawyer for the purposes of a court or tribunal hearing, arbitration or other form of alternative dispute resolution for legal proceedings within the United Kingdom, at the invitation of a client in the United Kingdom or foreign based client;

(e) undertake an activity relating to the arts, entertainment or sporting professions, by invitation of an arts or sports organisation or broadcaster based in the United Kingdom; and

(iv) does not intend to take employment, produce goods or provide services within the United Kingdom, including the selling of goods or services direct to members of the public other than as permitted for by the pre-arranged paid engagement; and

(v) will maintain and accommodate him or herself adequately out of resources available to the applicant without recourse to public funds or taking employment; or will be maintained and accommodated adequately by relatives or friends.

Note: Paragraph 56X inserted from 6 April 2012 except for applications made but not decided before that date (HC 1888). Words inserted from 6 September 2012 (HC 565).

Leave to enter as a visitor undertaking permitted paid engagements

56Y. A person seeking leave to enter the United Kingdom as a visitor undertaking permitted paid engagements may be admitted for a single entry and for a period not exceeding 1 month [with a condition prohibiting study and recourse to public funds], provided the Immigration Officer is satisfied that each of the requirements of paragraph 56X are met.

Note: Paragraph 56Y inserted from 6 April 2012 except for applications made but not decided before that date (HC 1888). Words inserted from 6 September 2012 (HC 565).

Refusal of leave to enter as a visitor undertaking permitted paid engagements

56Z. Leave to enter as a visitor undertaking permitted paid engagements is to be refused if the Immigration Officer is not satisfied that each of the requirements at paragraph 56X are met.]

Note: Paragraph 56Z inserted from 6 April 2012 except for applications made but not decided before that date (HC 1888).

PART 3

PERSONS SEEKING TO ENTER OR REMAIN IN THE
UNITED KINGDOM FOR STUDIES

Students

Requirements for leave to enter as a student

57–62 ...

Note: Paragraphs 57–62 deleted from 31 March 2009 (HC 314). However, if an applicant has made an application for leave before 31 March 2009 under any of these paragraphs and the application has not been decided before that date, it will be decided in accordance with the Rules in force on 30 March 2009 as set out in Appendix F: see introduction to HC 314.

Student nurses

63–69 ...

Note: Paragraphs 63–69 deleted from 31 March 2009 (HC 314). However, if an applicant has made an application for leave before 31 March 2009 under any of these paragraphs and the application has not been decided before that date, it will be decided in accordance with the Rules in force on 30 March 2009 as set out in Appendix F: see introduction to HC 314.

Re-sits of examinations

69A–69F ...

Note: Paragraphs 69A–69F deleted from 31 March 2009 (HC 314). However, if an applicant has made an application for leave before 31 March 2009 under any of these paragraphs and the application has not been decided before that date, it will be decided in accordance with the Rules in force on 30 March 2009 as set out in Appendix F: see introduction to HC 314.

Writing up a thesis

69G–69L ...

Note: Paragraphs 69G–69L deleted from 31 March 2009 (HC 314). However, if an applicant has made an application for leave before 31 March 2009 under any of these and the application has not been decided before that date, it will be decided in accordance with the Rules in force on 30 March 2009 as set out in Appendix F: see introduction to HC 314.

Requirements for leave to enter as an overseas qualified nurse or midwife

[**69M–69R** ...

Note: Paragraphs 69M–69R deleted from 6 April 2012 except for applications made but not decided before that date (HC 1888).

Requirements for leave to enter the United Kingdom as a postgraduate doctor or dentist]

[70–75 ...

Note: Paragraphs 70–75 deleted from 31 March 2008 (HC 314). However, if an applicant has made an application for leave before 31 March 2009 under any of these and the application has not been decided before that date, it will be decided in accordance with the Rules in force on 30 March 2009 as set out in Appendix F: see introduction to HC 314.

Requirements for leave to enter the United Kingdom to take the PLAB Test

[75A. The requirements to be met by a person seeking leave to enter in order to take the PLAB Test are that the applicant:

(i) is a graduate from a medical school and intends to take the PLAB Test in the United Kingdom; and

(ii) can provide documentary evidence of a confirmed test date or of his eligibility to take the PLAB Test [by way of a letter or email from the General Medical Council or a test admission card]; and

(iii) meets the requirements of paragraph 41 (iii)–(vii) for entry as a visitor; and

[(iv) intends to leave the United Kingdom at the end of the leave granted under this paragraph unless he is successful in the PLAB Test and granted leave to remain to undertake a clinical attachment in accordance with paragraphs 75G to 75M of these Rules.]

. . .

Note: Paragraph 75A inserted from 15 March 2005 (HC 364). Sub-paragraph (iv) substituted from 31 March 2009 (HC 314). Words inserted in sub-para (ii) from 6 September 2012 (HC 565).

Leave to enter to take the PLAB Test

[75B. A person seeking leave to enter the United Kingdom to take the PLAB Test may be admitted for a period not exceeding 6 months [subject to a condition prohibiting employment, study and recourse to public funds], provided the Immigration Officer is satisfied that each of the requirements of paragraph 75A is met.]

Note: Paragraph 75B inserted from 15 March 2005 (HC 364). Words inserted from 6 September 2012 (HC 565).

Refusal of leave to enter to take the PLAB Test

[75C. Leave to enter the United Kingdom to take the PLAB Test is to be refused if the Immigration Officer is not satisfied that each of the requirements of paragraph 75A is met.]

Note: Paragraph 75C inserted from 15 March 2005 (HC 364).

Requirements for an extension of stay in order to take the PLAB Test

[75D. The requirements for an extension of stay in the United Kingdom in order to take the PLAB Test are that the applicant:

(i) was given leave to enter the United Kingdom for the purposes of taking the PLAB Test in accordance with paragraph 75B of these Rules; and

(ii) intends to take the PLAB Test and can provide documentary evidence of a confirmed test date [by way of a letter or email from the General Medical Council or a test admission card]; and

(iii) meets the requirements set out in paragraph 41 (iii)–(vii); and

[(iv) intends to leave the United Kingdom at the end of the leave granted under this paragraph unless he is successful in the PLAB Test and granted leave to remain to undertake a clinical attachment in accordance with paragraphs 75G to 75M of these Rules; and]

(v) would not as a result of an extension of stay spend more than 18 months in the United Kingdom for the purpose of taking the PLAB Test][; and

(vi) must not be in the UK in breach of immigration laws except that any period of overstaying for a period of 28 days or less will be disregarded.]

Note: Paragraph 75D inserted from 15 March 2005 (HC 364). Sub-paragraph (iv) substituted from 31 March 2009 (HC 314). Words inserted in sub-para (ii) from 6 September 2012 (HC 565). Sub-paragraph (vi) inserted from 1 October 2012 with savings for applications made but not decided before 9 July 2012 (HC 194).

Extension of stay to take the PLAB Test

[75E. A person seeking leave to remain in the United Kingdom to take the PLAB Test may be granted an extension of stay for a period not exceeding 6 months [subject to a condition prohibiting employment, study and recourse to public funds], provided the Secretary of State is satisfied that each of the requirements of paragraph 75D is met.]

Note: Paragraph 75E inserted from 15 March 2005 (HC 364). Words inserted from 6 September 2012 (HC 565).

Refusal of extension of stay to take the PLAB Test

[75F. Leave to remain in the United Kingdom to take the PLAB Test is to be refused if the Secretary of State is not satisfied that each of the requirements of paragraph 75D is met.]

Note: Paragraph 75F inserted from 15 March 2005 (HC 364).

Requirements for leave to enter to undertake a clinical attachment or dental observer post

[75G. The requirements to be met by a person seeking leave to enter to undertake a clinical attachment or dental observer post are that the applicant:

(i) is a graduate from a medical or dental school and intends to undertake a clinical attachment or dental observer post in the United Kingdom; and

(ii) can provide documentary evidence of the clinical attachment or dental observer post which will:

(a) be unpaid; and

(b) only involve observation, not treatment, of patients; and

(iii) meets the requirements of paragraph 41 (iii)–(vii) of these Rules; and

[(iv) intends to leave the United Kingdom at the end of the leave granted under this paragraph;]

(v) if he has previously been granted leave in this category, is not seeking leave to enter which, when amalgamated with those previous periods of leave, would total more than 6 months.}]

Note: Paragraph 75G inserted from 15 March 2005 (HC 364). Sub-paragraph (v) inserted from 3 April 2006 (HC 1016). Sub-paragraph (iv)(c) deleted from 29 February 2008 (HC 321). Sub-paragraph (iv) substituted from 31 March 2009 (HC 314).

Leave to enter to undertake a clinical attachment or dental observer post

[75H. A person seeking leave to enter the United Kingdom to undertake a clinical attachment or dental observer post may be admitted for the period of the clinical attachment or dental observer post {up to a maximum of 6 weeks at a time or 6 months in total in this capacity [subject to a condition prohibiting employment, study and recourse to public funds]}, provided the Immigration Officer is satisfied that each of the requirements of paragraph 75G is met.]

Note: Paragraph 75H inserted from 15 March 2005 (HC 364). Words in curly brackets substituted from 3 April 2006 (HC 1016). Words in square brackets inserted from 6 September 2012 (HC 565).

Refusal of leave to enter to undertake a clinical attachment or dental observer post

[75J. Leave to enter the United Kingdom to undertake a clinical attachment or dental observer post is to be refused if the Immigration Officer is not satisfied that each of the requirements of paragraph 75G is met.]

Note: Paragraph 75J inserted from 15 March 2005 (HC 364).

Requirements for an extension of stay in order to undertake a clinical attachment or dental observer post

[75K. The requirements to be met by a person seeking an extension of stay to undertake a clinical attachment or dental observer post are that the applicant:

(i) was given leave to enter or remain in the United Kingdom to undertake a clinical attachment or dental observer post or:

(a) for the purposes of taking the PLAB Test in accordance with paragraphs 75A to 75F and has passed both parts of the PLAB Test;

(b) as a postgraduate doctor, dentist or trainee general practitioner in accordance with paragraphs 70 to 75; or

(c) as a work permit holder for employment in the UK as a doctor or dentist in accordance with paragraphs 128 to 135; and

(ii) is a graduate from a medical or dental school and intends to undertake a clinical attachment or dental observer post in the United Kingdom; and

(iii) can provide documentary evidence of the clinical attachment or dental observer post which will:

(a) be unpaid; and

(b) only involve observation, not treatment, of patients; and

[(iv) intends to leave the United Kingdom at the end of the leave granted under this paragraph; and]

(v) meets the requirements of paragraph 41 (iii)–(vii) of these Rules;] {and

(vi) if he has previously been granted leave in this category, is not seeking an extension of stay which, when amalgamated with those previous periods of leave, would total more than 6 months.}][; and

(vii) must not be in the UK in breach of immigration laws except that any period of overstaying for a period of 28 days or less will be disregarded.]

Note: Paragraph 75K inserted from 15 March 2005 (HC 364). Words in curly brackets inserted from 3 April 2006 (HC 1016). Sub-paragraph (iv)(c) deleted from 29 February 2008. Sub-paragraph (iv) substituted from 31 March 2009 (HC 314). Sub-paragraph (vii) inserted from 1 October 2012 with savings for applications made before 9 July 2012 (HC 194).

Extension of stay to undertake a clinical attachment or dental observer post

[**75L.** A person seeking leave to remain in the United Kingdom to undertake a clinical attachment or dental observer post may be granted an extension of stay for the period of their clinical attachment or dental observer post {up to a maximum of 6 weeks at a time or 6 months in total in this category [subject to a condition prohibiting employment, study and recourse to public funds]}, provided that the Secretary of State is satisfied that each of the requirements of paragraph 75K is met.]

Note: Paragraph 75L inserted from 15 March 2005 (HC 364). Words in curly brackets inserted from 3 April 2006 (HC 1016). Words in square brackets inserted from 6 September 2012 (HC 565).

Refusal of extension of stay to undertake a clinical attachment or dental observer post

[**75M.** Leave to remain in the United Kingdom to undertake a clinical attachment or dental observer post is to be refused if the Secretary of State is not satisfied that each of the requirements of paragraph 75K is met.]

Note: Paragraph 75M inserted from 15 March 2005 (HC 364).

Spouses or civil partners of students or prospective students granted leave under this part of the Rules

Note: Heading substituted from 31 March 2009 (HC 314).

Requirements for leave to enter or remain as the spouse [or civil partner] of a student

76. The requirements to be met by a person seeking leave to enter or remain in the United Kingdom as the spouse [or civil partner] of a student are that:

(i) the applicant is married to [or the civil partner of] a person admitted to or allowed to remain in the United Kingdom under paragraphs 57–75 [or 82–87F]; and

(ii) each of the parties intends to live with the other as his or her spouse [or civil partner] during the applicant's stay and the marriage [or civil partnership] is subsisting; and

(iii) there will be adequate accommodation for the parties and any dependants without recourse to public funds; and

(iv) the parties will be able to maintain themselves and any dependants adequately without recourse to public funds; and

(v) the applicant does not intend to take employment except as permitted under paragraph 77 below; and

(vi) the applicant intends to leave the United Kingdom at the end of any period of leave granted to him [; and

(vii) if seeking leave to remain must not be in the UK in breach of immigration laws except that any period of overstaying for a period of 28 days or less will be disregarded.]

Note: Words in square brackets substituted from 30 November 2007 (HC 40). References to civil partnership inserted from 5 December 2005 (HC 582). Sub-paragraph (vii) inserted from 1 October 2012 with savings for applications made but not decided before 9 July 2012 (HC 194).

Leave to enter or remain as the spouse [or civil partner] of a student [or prospective student]

[77. A person seeking leave to enter or remain in the United Kingdom as the spouse [or civil partner] of a student [or a prospective student] may be admitted or allowed to remain for a period not in excess of that granted to the student [or prospective student] provided the Immigration Officer or, in the case of an application for limited leave to remain, the Secretary of State is satisfied that each of the requirements of paragraph 76 is met. Employment may be permitted where the period of leave granted [to the student or prospective student] is, or was, 12 months or more.]

Note: Words in square brackets inserted from 1 November 1996 (HC 31). Paragraph 77 substituted from 2 October 2000 (Cm 4851). References to civil partnership inserted from 5 December 2005 (HC 582).

Refusal of leave to enter or remain as the spouse [or civil partner] of a student [or prospective student]

78. Leave to enter or remain as the spouse [or civil partner] of a student [or prospective student] is to be refused if the Immigration Officer or, in the case of an application for a limited leave to remain, the Secretary of State is not satisfied that each of the requirements of paragraph 76 is met.

Note: Words in square brackets inserted from 1 November 1996 (HC 31). References to civil partnership inserted from 5 December 2005 (HC 582).

Children of students or prospective students granted leave under this part of the Rules

Note: Heading amended from 31 March 2009 (HC 314).

Requirements for leave to enter or remain as the child of a student [or prospective student]

79. The requirements to be met by a person seeking leave to enter or remain in the United Kingdom as the child of a student [or prospective student] are that he:

(i) is the child of a parent admitted to or allowed to remain in the United Kingdom as a student [or prospective student] under paragraphs 57–75 [or 82–87F]; and

(ii) is under the age of 18 or has current leave to enter or remain in this capacity; and

(iii) [is not married or in a civil partnership,] has not formed an independent family unit and is not leading an independent life; and

(iv) can, and will, be maintained and accommodated adequately without recourse to public funds; and

(v) will not stay in the United Kingdom beyond any period of leave granted to his parent; and

[(vi) meets the requirements of paragraph 79A][; and

(vii) if seeking leave to remain must not be in the UK in breach of immigration laws except that any period of overstaying for a period of 28 days or less will be disregarded.]

Note: Words in square brackets in sub-para (i) inserted from 30 November 2007 (HC 40). Sub-paragraph (vi) inserted from 31 March 2009 (HC 314). Words in square brackets in sub-para (iii) inserted from 6 April 2012 except for applications made but not decided before that date (HC 1888). Sub-paragraph (vii) inserted from 1 October 2012 with savings for applications made but not decided before 9 July 2012 (HC 194).

[**79A.** Both of the applicant's parents must either be lawfully present in the UK, or being granted entry clearance or leave to remain at the same time as the applicant, [or one parent must be lawfully present in the UK and the other being granted entry clearance or leave to remain at the same time as the applicant,] unless:

(i) the student or prospective student is the applicant's sole surviving parent, or

(ii) the student or prospective student parent has and has had sole responsibility for the applicant's upbringing, or

(iii) there are serious or compelling family or other considerations which would make it desirable not to refuse the application and suitable arrangements have been made in the UK for the applicant's care.]

Note: Paragraph 79A inserted from 31 March 2009 (HC 314). Words in square brackets inserted from 6 April 2012 except for applications made but not decided before that date (HC 1888).

Leave to enter or remain as the child of a student [or prospective student]

[**80.** A person seeking leave to enter or remain in the United Kingdom as the child of a student [or prospective student] may be admitted to remain for a period not in excess of that granted to the student [or prospective student] provided the Immigration Officer or, in the case of an application for limited leave to remain, the Secretary of State is satisfied that each of the requirements of paragraph 79 is met. Employment may be permitted where the period of leave granted to the student is or was 12 months or more.]

Note: Substituted from 2 October 2000 (Cm 4851).

Refusal of leave to enter or remain as the child of a student [or prospective student]

81. Leave to enter or remain in the United Kingdom as the child of a student [or prospective student] is to be refused if the Immigration Officer or, in the case of an application for limited leave to remain, the Secretary of State is not satisfied that each of the requirements of paragraph 79 is met.

Prospective students

Requirements for leave to enter as a prospective student

82. The requirements to be met by a person seeking leave to enter the United Kingdom as a prospective student are that he:

[(i) can demonstrate a genuine and realistic intention of undertaking, within 6 months of his date of entry:

(a) a course of study which would meet the requirements for an extension of stay as a student under {paragraph 245 ZX or paragraph 245 ZZC; and}

[(ii) intends to leave the United Kingdom on completion of his studies or on the expiry of his leave to enter if he is not able to meet the requirements for an extension of stay:

(a) as a student in accordance with {paragraph 245 ZX or paragraph 245 ZZC; and}

(iii) is able without working or recourse to public funds to meet the costs of his intended course and accommodation and the maintenance of himself and any dependants while making arrangements to study and during the course of his studies [; and

(iv) holds a valid United Kingdom entry clearance for entry on this capacity.]

Note: Sub-paragraphs (i) and (ii) substituted from 30 November 2005 (HC 645). Sub-paragraph (iv) inserted from 1 September 2007 (Cm 7074). Sub-paragraphs (i)(a) and (ii)(a) amended and sub-paragraphs (i)(b) and (ii)(b) deleted from 31 March 2009 (HC 314).

Leave to enter as a prospective student

[83. A person seeking leave to enter the United Kingdom as a prospective student may be admitted for a period not exceeding 6 months with a condition prohibiting employment, provided he is able to produce to the Immigration Officer on arrival a valid United Kingdom entry clearance for entry in this capacity.]

Note: Paragraph 83 substituted from 1 September 2007 (Cm 7074).

Refusal of leave to enter as a prospective student

84. Leave to enter as a prospective student is to be refused if the Immigration Officer is not satisfied that each of the requirements of paragraph 82 is met.

Requirements for extension of stay as a prospective student

85. Six months is the maximum permitted leave which may be granted to a prospective student. The requirements for an extension of stay as a prospective student are that the applicant:

(i) was admitted to the United Kingdom with a valid prospective student entry clearance . . . ; and

(ii) meets the requirements of paragraph 82; and

(iii) would not, as a result of an extension of stay, spend more than 6 months in the United Kingdom [; and

(iv) must not be in the UK in breach of immigration laws except that any period of overstaying for a period of 28 days or less will be disregarded.]

Note: Words omitted from sub-para (i) from 1 September 2007 (Cm 7074).

Extension of stay as a prospective student

86. An extension of stay as a prospective student may be granted, with a prohibition on employment, provided the Secretary of State is satisfied that each of the requirements of paragraph 85 is met.

Refusal of extension of stay as a prospective student

87. An extension of stay as a prospective student is to be refused if the Secretary of State is not satisfied that each of the requirements of paragraph 85 is met.

[Students' unions sabbatical officers

87A–87F . . .

Note: Paragraphs 87A–87F deleted from 31 March 2009 (HC 314). However, if an applicant has made an application for leave before 31 March 2009 under any of these and the application has not been decided before that date, it will be decided in accordance with the Rules in force on 30 March 2009 as set out in Appendix F: see introduction to HC 314.

PART 4
PERSONS SEEKING TO ENTER OR REMAIN IN THE UNITED KINGDOM IN AN 'AU PAIR' PLACEMENT, AS A WORKING HOLIDAYMAKER, OR FOR TRAINING OR WORK EXPERIENCE

'Au pair' placements

Note: Paragraphs 88–94 deleted from 27 November 2008, subject to savings for applications for leave made before 27 November 2008 and undecided by that date: see introduction to HC 1113.

Working holidaymakers

Note: Paragraphs 95–97 deleted from 27 November 2008, subject to savings for applications for leave made before 27 November 2008 and undecided by that date: see introduction to HC 1113.

Children of working holidaymakers

Note: Paragraphs 101–103 deleted from 27 November 2008, subject to savings for applications for leave made before 27 November 2008 and undecided by that date: see introduction to HC 1113.

Seasonal workers at agricultural camps

Note: Paragraphs 104–109 deleted from 6 April 2012 except for applications made but not decided before that date (HC 1888).

Teachers and language assistants coming to the United Kingdom under approved exchange schemes

Note: Paragraphs 110–115 deleted from 27 November 2008, subject to savings for applications for leave made before 27 November 2008 and undecided by that date: see introduction to HC 1113.

[Home Office] approved training or work experience

Note: Paragraphs 116–121 deleted from 27 November 2008, subject to savings for applications for leave made before 27 November 2008 and undecided by that date: see introduction to HC 1113.

Spouses [or civil partners] of persons with limited leave to enter or remain under paragraphs 110–121

Requirements for leave to enter or remain as the spouse [or civil partner] of a person with limited leave to enter or remain in the United Kingdom under paragraphs 110–121

122. The requirements to be met by a person seeking leave to enter or remain in the United Kingdom as the spouse [or civil partner] of a person with limited leave to enter or remain in the United Kingdom under paragraphs 110–121 are that:

    (i) the applicant is married to [or the civil partner of] a person with limited leave to enter or remain in the United Kingdom under paragraphs 110–121; and

    (ii) each of the parties intends to live with the other as his or her spouse [or civil partner] during the applicant's stay and the marriage [or civil partnership] is subsisting; and

    (iii) there will be adequate accommodation for the parties and any dependants without recourse to public funds in accommodation which they own or occupy exclusively; and

    (iv) the parties will be able to maintain themselves and any dependants adequately without recourse to public funds; and

    (v) the applicant does not intend to stay in the United Kingdom beyond any period of leave granted to his spouse [or civil partner]; and

    (vi) if seeking leave to enter, the applicant holds a valid United Kingdom entry clearance for entry in this capacity or, if seeking leave to remain, was admitted with a valid United Kingdom entry clearance for entry in this capacity [; or

    (vii) if seeking leave to remain, must not be in the UK in breach of immigration laws except that any period of overstaying for a period of 28 days or less will be disregarded.]

Note: References to civil partnership inserted from 5 December 2005 (HC 582). Sub-paragraph (vii) inserted from 1 October 2012 with savings for applications made but not decided before 9 July 2012 (HC 194).

Leave to enter or remain as the spouse [or civil partner] of a person with limited leave to enter or remain in the United Kingdom under paragraphs 110–121

123. A person seeking leave to enter or remain in the United Kingdom as the spouse [or civil partner] of a person with limited leave to enter or remain in the United Kingdom under paragraphs 110–121 may be given leave to enter or remain in the United Kingdom for a period of leave not in excess of that granted to the person with limited leave to enter or remain under paragraphs 110–121 provided that, in relation to an application for leave to enter, he is able, on arrival, to produce to the Immigration Officer a valid United Kingdom entry clearance for entry in this capacity or, in the case of an application for limited leave to remain, was admitted with a valid United Kingdom entry clearance for entry in this capacity and is able to satisfy the Secretary of State that each of the requirements of paragraph 122(i)–(v) [and (vii)] is met.

Note: References to civil partnership inserted from 5 December 2005 (HC 582). Words in square brackets in final sentence inserted from 1 October 2012 with savings for applications made but not decided before 9 July 2012 (HC 194).

**Refusal of leave to enter or remain as the spouse [or civil partner]
of a person with limited leave to enter or remain in the United Kingdom
under paragraphs 110–121**

124. Leave to enter or remain in the United Kingdom as the spouse [or civil partner] of a person with limited leave to enter or remain in the United Kingdom under paragraphs 110–121 is to be refused if, in relation to an application for leave to enter, a valid United Kingdom entry clearance for entry in this capacity is not produced to the Immigration Officer on arrival or, in the case of an application for limited leave to remain, if the applicant was not admitted with a valid United Kingdom entry clearance for entry in this capacity or is unable to satisfy the Secretary of State that each of the requirements of paragraph 112(i)–(v) [and (vii)] is met.

> **Note:** References to civil partnership inserted from 5 December 2005 (HC 582). Words in square brackets in final line inserted from 1 October 2012 with savings for applications made but not decided before 9 July 2012 (HC 194).

Children of persons admitted or allowed to remain under paragraphs 110–121

**Requirements for leave to enter or remain as the child of a person
with limited leave to enter or remain in the United Kingdom under
paragraphs 110–121**

125. The requirements to be met by a person seeking leave to enter or remain in the United Kingdom as the child of a person with limited leave to enter or remain in the United Kingdom under paragraphs 110–121 are that:

    (i) he is the child of a parent who has limited leave to enter or remain in the United Kingdom under paragraphs 110–121; and

    (ii) he is under the age of 18 or has current leave to enter or remain in this capacity; and

    (iii) he is unmarried [and is not a civil partner], has not formed an independent family unit and is not leaving an independent life; and

    (iv) he can, and will, be maintained and accommodated adequately without recourse to public funds in accommodation which his parent(s) own or occupy exclusively; and

    (v) he will not stay in the United Kingdom beyond any period of leave granted to his parent(s); and

    (vi) both parents are being or have been admitted to or allowed to remain in the United Kingdom save where:

    (a) the parent he is accompanying or joining is his sole surviving parent: or

    (b) the parent he is accompanying or joining has had sole responsibility for his upbringing; or

    (c) there are serious and compelling family or other considerations which make exclusion from the United Kingdom undesirable and suitable arrangements have been made for his care; and

    (vii) if seeking leave to enter, he holds a valid United Kingdom entry clearance for entry in this capacity or, if seeking leave to remain, was admitted with a valid United Kingdom entry clearance for entry in this capacity [; or

    (viii) if seeking leave to remain, must not be in the UK in breach of immigration laws except that any period of overstaying for a period of 28 days or less will be disregarded.]

Note: Words in square brackets in sub-para (iii) inserted from 5 December 2005 (HC 582). Sub-paragraph (viii) inserted from 1 October 2012 with savings for applications made but not decided before 9 July 2012 (HC 194).

Leave to enter or remain as the child of a person with limited leave to enter or remain in the United Kingdom under paragraphs 110–121

126. A person seeking leave to enter or remain in the United Kingdom as the child of a person with limited leave to enter or remain in the United Kingdom under paragraphs 110–121 may be given leave to enter or remain in the United Kingdom for a period of leave not in excess of that granted to the person with limited leave to enter or remain under paragraphs 110–121 provided that, in relation to an application for leave to enter, he is able, on arrival, to produce to the Immigration Officer a valid United Kingdom entry clearance for entry in this capacity or, in the case of an application for limited leave to remain, he was admitted with a valid United Kingdom entry clearance for entry in this capacity and is able to satisfy the Secretary of State that each of the requirements of paragraph 125(i)–(vi) [and (viii)] is met.

Note: Words in square brackets inserted from 1 October 2012 with savings for applications made but not decided before 9 July 2012.

Refusal of leave to enter or remain as the child of a person with limited leave to enter or remain in the United Kingdom under paragraphs 110–121

127. Leave to enter or remain in the United Kingdom as the child of a person with limited leave to enter or remain in the United Kingdom under paragraphs 110–121 is to be refused if, in relation to an application for leave to enter, a valid United Kingdom entry clearance for entry in this capacity is not produced to the Immigration Officer on arrival or, in the case of an application for limited leave to remain, if the applicant was not admitted with a valid United Kingdom entry clearance for entry in this capacity or is unable to satisfy the Secretary of State that each of the requirements of paragraph 125(i)–(vi) [and (viii)] is met.

Note: Words in square brackets inserted from 1 October 2012 with savings for applications made but not decided before 9 July 2012.

PART 5
PERSONS SEEKING TO ENTER OR REMAIN IN THE UNITED KINGDOM FOR EMPLOYMENT
Work permit employment

Requirements for leave to enter the United Kingdom for work permit employment

[128. A person coming to the UK to seek or take employment must be otherwise eligible for admission under these Rules or eligible for admission as a seaman under contract to join a ship due to leave British waters.

The requirements for applications for work permit employment set out in paragraphs 128 to 133 of these Rules were deleted on 6 April 2012 by Statement of Changes HC 1888 except insofar as relevant to paragraphs 134 to 135.]

Note: Paragraphs 128–133 deleted and para 128 substituted from 6 April 2012, except for applications made but not decided before that date (HC 1888).

Indefinite leave to remain as a work permit holder

[**134.** Indefinite leave to remain may be granted on application to a person provided:

(i) he has spent a continuous period of 5 years lawfully in the UK, of which the most recent period must have been spent with leave as a work permit holder (under paragraphs 128 to 133 of these rules), and the remainder must be made up of [any combination of] leave as a work permit holder or leave as a highly skilled migrant (under paragraphs 135A to 135F of these rules) [or leave as a self-employed lawyer (under the concession that appeared in chapter 6, Section 1 Annex D of the Immigration Directorate Instructions), or leave as a writer, composer or artist (under paragraphs 232 to 237 of these rules)];

(ii) he has met the requirements of paragraph 128(i) to (v) throughout his leave as a work permit holder, and has met the requirements of paragraph 135G(ii) throughout any leave as a highly skilled migrant;

(iii) he is still required for the employment in question, as certified by his employer;

[(iv) his employer certifies that he is paid at or above the appropriate rate for the job as stated in [the Codes of Practice in Appendix J], and

[(v) the applicant provides [the specified documents in paragraph 134-SD] to evidence the employer's certification in sub-section (iv), and]

[(vi)] he has sufficient knowledge of the English language and sufficient knowledge about life in the United Kingdom, in accordance with paragraph 33BA of these Rules, unless he is under the age of 18 or aged 65 or over at the date of his application;

[(vii)] he does not have one or more unspent convictions within the meaning of the Rehabilitation of Offenders Act 1974] [; and

(viii) must not be in the UK in breach of immigration laws except that any period of overstaying for a period of 28 days or less will be disregarded.]

Note: Paragraph 134 inserted from 29 February 2008 (HC 321). Words in square brackets in sub-para (i) inserted from 30 June 2008 (HC 607). Sub-paragraph (iv) substituted from 6 April 2011 (HC 863). New sub-para (v) inserted and subsequent sub-paras renumbered from 31 October 2011, except for applications made but not decided before that date (HC 1511). Sub-paragraph (viii) inserted from 1 October 2012 with savings for applications made but not decided before 9 July 2012 (HC 194). Words in square brackets in sub-paras (iv) and (v) substituted from 20 July 2012 (Cm 8423).

[**134-SD** Specified documents

The specified documents referred to in paragraph 134(v) are either a payslip and a personal bank or building society statement, or a payslip and a building society pass book.

(a) Payslips must be:

(i) the applicant's most recent payslip,

(ii) dated no earlier than one calendar month before the date of the application, and

(iii) either:

(1) an original payslip,

(2) on company-headed paper, or

(3) accompanied by a letter from the applicant's Sponsor, on company headed paper and signed by a senior official, confirming the payslip is authentic.

(b) Personal bank or building society statements must:

(i) be the most applicant's most recent statement,

(ii) be dated no earlier than one calendar month before the date of the application,

    (iii) clearly show:
        (1) the applicant's name,
        (2) the applicant's account number,
        (3) the date of the statement,
        (4) the financial institution's name,
        (5) the financial institution's logo, and
        (6) transactions by the Sponsor covering the period no earlier than one calendar month before the date of the application,
    (iv) be either:
        (1) printed on the bank's or building society's letterhead,
        (2) electronic bank or building society statements from an online account, accompanied by a supporting letter from the bank or building society, on company headed paper, confirming the statement provided is authentic, or
        (3) electronic bank or building society statements from an online account, bearing the official stamp of the bank or building society on every page,
    and
    (v) not be mini-statements from automatic teller machines (ATMs).
  (c) Building society pass books must
    (i) clearly show:
        (1) the applicant's name,
        (2) the applicant's account number,
        (3) the financial institution's name,
        (4) the financial institution's logo, and
        (5) transactions by the sponsor covering the period no earlier than one calendar month before the date of the application,
    and
    (ii) be either:
        (1) the original pass book, or
        (2) a photocopy of the pass book which has been certified by the issuing building society on company headed paper, confirming the statement provided is authentic.]

Note: Paragraph 134-SD inserted from 20 July 2012 (Cm 8423).

Refusal of indefinite leave to remain for a work permit holder

135. Indefinite leave to remain in the United Kingdom for a work permit holder is to be refused if the Secretary of State is not satisfied that each of the requirements of paragraph 134 is met.

Highly skilled migrants

135A–135C

Note: Paragraphs 135A–135C deleted from 30 June 2008 (HC 607).

Requirements for an extension of stay as a highly skilled migrant

135D–135F

Note: Paragraphs 135D–135F deleted from 29 February 2008 (HC 321).

Requirements for indefinite leave to remain as a highly skilled migrant

[135G. The requirements for indefinite leave to remain for a person who has been granted leave as a highly skilled migrant are that the applicant:

(i) has spent a continuous period of 5 years [(or four years where the applicant is applying under the terms {set out in Appendix S})] lawfully in the United Kingdom, of which the most recent period must have been spent with leave as a highly skilled migrant (in accordance with paragraphs 135A to 135F of these Rules), and the remainder must be made up of leave as a highly skilled migrant, leave as a work permit holder (under paragraphs 128 to 133 of these Rules), or leave as an Innovator (under paragraphs 210A to 210F of these Rules); and

(ii) throughout the five years [(or four years where the applicant is applying under the terms {set out in Appendix S})] spent in the United Kingdom has been able to maintain and accommodate himself and any dependants adequately without recourse to public funds; and

(iii) is lawfully economically active in the United Kingdom in employment, self-employment or a combination of both; [and

(iv) has sufficient knowledge of the English language and sufficient knowledge about life in the United Kingdom, [in accordance with paragraph 33BA of these Rules] unless he is under the age of 18 or aged 65 or over at the time he makes his application [or the applicant is applying under the terms {set out in Appendix S}]] [; and

(v) unless the applicant is applying under the terms {set out in Appendix S}, does not have one or more unspent convictions within the meaning of the Rehabilitation of Offenders Act 1974] [; and

(vi) unless the applicant is applying under the terms of the HSMP ILR Judicial Review Policy Document, must not be in the UK in breach of immigration laws except that any period of overstaying for a period of 28 days or less will be disregarded.]

Note: Paragraph 135G substituted from 5 December 2006 (HC 1702). Sub-paragraph (iv) inserted from 2 April 2007 (HC 398). Words in square brackets in sub-paras (i), (ii) and (iv) inserted from 1 October 2009 (HC 7701). Sub-paragraph (v) and words in square brackets in sub-para (iv) inserted from 6 April 2011 (HC 863). Sub-paragraph (vi) inserted from 1 October 2012 with savings for applications made but not decided before 9 July 2012 (HC 194). Words in curly brackets in sub-paras (i), (ii), (iv) and (v) inserted from 6 September 2012 (HC 565).

Indefinite leave to remain as a highly skilled migrant

[135GA. Indefinite leave to remain may be granted provided that the Secretary of State is satisfied that each of the requirements of paragraph 135G is met and that the application does not fall for refusal under paragraph 135HA.]

Note: Paragraph 135GA substituted from 5 December 2006 (HC 1702).

Refusal of indefinite leave to remain as a highly skilled migrant

[135H. Indefinite leave to remain in the United Kingdom is to be refused if the Secretary of State is not satisfied that each of the requirements of paragraph 135G is met or if the application falls for refusal under paragraph 135HA.]

Note: Paragraph 135H substituted from 5 December 2006 (HC 1702).

Additional grounds for refusal for highly skilled migrants

[**135HA.** An application under paragraphs 135A–135C or 135G–135H of these Rules is to be refused, even if the applicant meets all the requirements of those paragraphs, if the Immigration Officer or Secretary of State has cause to doubt the genuineness of any document submitted by the applicant and, having taken reasonable steps to verify the document, has been unable to verify that it is genuine.]

Note: Paragraph 135HA substituted from 29 February 2009 (HC 321).

Sectors-Based Scheme

Note: Paragraphs 135I–135N deleted from 31 March 2009 (HC 314). However, if an applicant has made an application for leave before 31 March 2009 under any of these and the application has not been decided before that date, it will be decided in accordance with the Rules in force on 30 March 2009 as set out in Appendix F: see introduction to HC 314.

Representatives of overseas newspapers, news agencies and broadcasting organisations

136. The requirements to be met by a person seeking leave to enter the United Kingdom as a representative of an overseas newspaper, news agency or broadcasting organisation are that he:

(i) has been engaged by that organisation outside the United Kingdom and is being posted to the United Kingdom on a long-term assignment as a representative; and

(ii) intends to work full-time as a representative of that overseas newspaper, news agency or broadcasting organisation; and

(iii) does not intend to take employment except within the terms of this paragraph; and

(iv) can maintain and accommodate himself and any dependants adequately without recourse to public funds; and

(v) holds a valid United Kingdom entry clearance for entry in this capacity.

Note: Paragraph 136 deleted from 27 November 2008 save insofar as relates to paras 142–143: see HC 1113, para 39; Deletion subject to savings for applications for leave made before 27 November 2008 and undecided by that date: see introduction to HC 1113.

Leave to enter as a representative of an overseas newspaper, news agency or broadcasting organisation

137. A person seeking leave to enter the United Kingdom as a representative of an overseas newspaper, news agency or broadcasting organisation may be admitted for a period not exceeding [2 years] provided he is able to produce to the Immigration Officer, on arrival, a valid United Kingdom entry clearance for entry in this capacity.

Note: Paragraph 137 deleted from 27 November 2008 save in so far as it relates to paras 142–143: see HC 1113, para 39; Deletion subject to savings for applications for leave made before 27 November 2008 and undecided by that date: see introduction to HC 1113. Words in square brackets substituted from 3 April 2006 (HC 1016).

Refusal of leave to enter as a representative of an overseas newspaper, news agency or broadcasting organisation

138. Leave to enter as a representative of an overseas newspaper, news agency or broadcasting organisation is to be refused if a valid United Kingdom entry clearance for entry in this capacity is not produced to the Immigration Officer on arrival.

Note: Paragraph 138 deleted from 27 November 2008 save in so far as it relates to paras 142–143: see HC 1113, para 39; Deletion subject to savings for applications for leave made before 27 November 2008 and undecided by that date: see introduction to HC 1113.

Requirements for an extension of stay as a representative of an overseas newspaper, news agency or broadcasting organisation

139. The requirements for an extension of stay as a representative of an overseas newspaper, news agency or broadcasting organisation are that the applicant:

(i) entered the United Kingdom with a valid United Kingdom entry clearance as a representative of an overseas newspaper, news agency or broadcasting organisation; and

(ii) is still engaged in the employment for which his entry clearance was granted; and

(iii) is still required for the employment in question, as certified by his employer; and

(iv) meets the requirements of paragraph 136(ii)–(iv).

Note: Paragraph 139 deleted from 27 November 2008 save insofar as it relates to paras 142–143: see HC 1113, para 39; Deletion subject to savings for applications for leave made before 27 November 2008 and undecided by that date: see introduction to HC 1113.

Extension of stay as a representative of an overseas newspaper, news agency or broadcasting organisation

140. An extension of stay as a representative of an overseas newspaper, news agency or broadcasting organisation may be granted for a period not exceeding 3 years provided the Secretary of State is satisfied that each of the requirements of paragraph 139 is met.

Note: Paragraph 140 deleted from 27 November 2008 save insofar as it relates to paras 142–143: see HC 1113, para 39.; Deletion subject to savings for applications for leave made before 27 November 2008 and undecided by that date: see introduction to HC 1113.

Refusal of extension of stay as a representative of an overseas newspaper, news agency or broadcasting organisation

141. An extension of stay as a representative of an overseas newspaper, news agency or broadcasting organisation is to be refused if the Secretary of State is not satisfied that each of the requirements of paragraph 139 is met.

Note: Paragraph 141 deleted from 27 November 2008 save in so far as it relates to paras 142–143: see HC 1113, para 39; Deletion subject to savings for applications for leave made before 27 November 2008 and undecided by that date: see introduction to HC 1113.

Indefinite leave to remain for a representative of an overseas newspaper, news agency or broadcasting organisation

142. Indefinite leave to remain may be granted, on application, to a representative of an overseas newspaper, news agency or broadcasting organisation provided:

(i) he has spent a continuous period of [5 years] in the United Kingdom in this capacity; and

(ii) he has met the requirements of paragraph 139 throughout the [5 year] period; and

(iii) he is still required for the employment in question, as certified by his employer [; and

(iv) he has sufficient knowledge of the English language and sufficient knowledge about life in the United Kingdom, [in accordance with paragraph 33BA of these Rules] unless he is under the age of 18 or aged 65 or over at the time he makes his application][, and

(v) he does not have one or more unspent convictions within the meaning of the Rehabilitation of Offenders Act 1974] [and;

(vi) he is not in the UK in breach of immigration laws except that any period of over-staying for a period of 28 days or less will be disregarded.]

Note: Words in square brackets in sub-paras (i) and (ii) substituted from 3 April 2006 (HC 1016). Sub-paragraph (iv) inserted from 2 April 2007 (HC 398). Sub-paragraph (v) and words in square brackets in sub-para (iv) inserted from 6 April 2011 except for applications made but not decided before that date (HC 863). Sub-paragraph (vi) inserted from 1 October 2012 with savings for applications made before 9 July 2012 (HC 194).

Refusal of indefinite leave to remain for a representative of an overseas newspaper, news agency or broadcasting organisation

143. Indefinite leave to remain in the United Kingdom for a representative of an overseas newspaper, news agency or broadcasting organisation is to be refused if the Secretary of State is not satisfied that each of the requirements of paragraph 142 is met.

143A–143F.

Note: Paragraphs 143A–143F deleted from 30 June 2008 (HC 607).

Representatives of overseas businesses

Requirements for leave to enter as a representative of an overseas business

144. The requirements to be met by a person seeking leave to enter the United Kingdom as a representative of an overseas business are that he:

(i) has been recruited and taken on as an employee outside the United Kingdom of a business which has its headquarters and principal place of business outside the United Kingdom . . . ; and

(ii) is seeking entry to the United Kingdom:

(a) as a senior employee [of an overseas business which has no branch, subsidiary or other representative in the United Kingdom] with full authority to take operational decisions on behalf of the overseas business for the purpose of representing it in the United Kingdom by establishing and operating a registered branch or wholly owned subsidiary of that overseas business, the branch or subsidiary of which will be concerned with same type of business activity as the overseas business; or

(b) as an employee of an overseas newspaper, news agency or broadcasting organisation being posted on a long-term assignment as a representative of their overseas employer.

(iii) where entry is sought under (ii)(a), the person:

(a) will be the sole representative of the employer present in the United Kingdom under the terms of this paragraph;

(b) intends to be employed full time as a representative of that overseas business; and

(c) is not a majority shareholder in that overseas business.

(iv) where entry is sought under (ii)(b), the person intends to work full-time as a representative of their overseas employer.

(v) does not intend to take employment except within the terms of this paragraph; and

(vi) has competence in the English language to the required standard on the basis that

[(a) the applicant is a national of one of the following countries: Antigua and Barbuda; Australia; the Bahamas; Barbados; Belize; Canada; Dominica; Grenada; Guyana; Jamaica; New Zealand; St Kitts and Nevis; St Lucia; St Vincent and the Grenadines; Trinidad and Tobago; United States of America; [and provides the specified documents in paragraph 144-SD(a)] or

(b) [the applicant has a knowledge of English equivalent to level A1 or above of the Council of Europe's Common European Framework for Language Learning, and]

(1) provides an original English language test certificate from an English language test provider approved by the Secretary of State for these purposes, [as listed in Appendix O] which clearly shows the applicant's name, the qualification obtained (which must meet or exceed [the standard described above] and the date of the award, or

[(2) has obtained an academic qualification (not a professional or vocational qualification) which is deemed by UK NARIC to meet the recognised standard of a Bachelor's degree in the UK, and

(i) provides [the specified documents in paragraph 144-SD(b)] to show he has the qualification, and

(ii) UK NARIC has confirmed that the qualification was taught or researched in English to level C1 of the Council of Europe's Common European Framework for Language learning or above, or

(3) has obtained an academic qualification (not a professional or vocational qualification) which is deemed by UK NARIC to meet or exceed the recognised standard of a Bachelor's or Master's degree in the UK, and provides [the specified documents in paragraph 144-SD(c)] to show that:

(i) he has the qualification, and

(ii) the qualification was taught or researched in English][, or

(4) has obtained an academic qualification (not a professional or vocational qualification), which is deemed by UK NARIC to meet the recognised standard of a Bachelor's or Master's degree or PhD in the UK, from an educational establishment in one of the following countries: Antigua and Barbuda; Australia; The Bahamas; Barbados; Belize; Dominica; Grenada; Guyana; Ireland; Jamaica; New Zealand; St Kitts and Nevis; St Lucia; St Vincent and The Grenadines; Trinidad and Tobago; the UK; the USA; and provides [the specified documents in paragraph 144-SD(b).]]

(vii) can maintain and accommodate himself and any dependants adequately without recourse to public funds; and

(viii) holds a valid United Kingdom entry clearance for entry in this capacity.

Note: Paragraph 144 substituted from 1 October 2009 (HC 7701). Heading amended and words omitted from sub-para (i) and words inserted in sub-para (ii)(a) from 6 April 2010 (HC 439). Sub-paragraph (vi)(b)(2) substituted from 6 April 2011 except for applications made but not decided before that date (HC 863). Sub-paragraph (vi)(a) and words in square brackets in sub-para (vi)(b) substituted and sub-para (vi)(b)(3)(ii) inserted from 6 April 2012 except for applications made but not decided before that date (HC 1888). Words in square brackets in sub-para (vi)(a) and first square brackets in (vi)(b) inserted and other words in square brackets in sub-para (vi) substituted from 20 July 2012 (Cm 8423).

[144-SD. Specified documents

(a) The specified documents in paragraph 144(vi)(a) as evidence of nationality are the applicant's current valid original passport or travel document. If the applicant is unable to provide these, the UK Border Agency may exceptionally consider this requirement to have been met where the applicant provides full reasons in the passport section of the application form, and either:

(1) a current national identity document, or

(2) an original letter from his home government or embassy, on the letter-headed paper of the government or embassy, which has been issued by an authorised official of that institution and confirms the applicant's full name, date of birth and nationality.

(b) The specified documents in paragraph 144(vi)(b)(2)(i) and paragraph 144(vi)(4) as evidence of qualifications taught in English are:

(1) the original certificate of the award, or

(2) if the applicant is awaiting graduation having successfully completed the qualification, or no longer has the certificate and the awarding institution is unable to provide a replacement, an academic transcript (or original letter in the case of a PhD qualification) from the awarding institution on its official headed paper, which clearly shows:

(a) the applicant's name,

(b) the name of the awarding institution,

(c) the title of the award,

(d) confirmation that the qualification has been or will be awarded, and

(e) the date that the certificate will be issued (if the applicant has not yet graduated) or confirmation that the institution is unable to reissue the original certificate or award.

(c) The specified documents in paragraph 144(vi)(b)(3)(i) as evidence of qualifications taught in English are:

(1) the specified documents in (b) above, and

(2) an original letter from the awarding institution on its official headed paper, which clearly shows:

(a) the applicant's name,

(b) the name of the awarding institution,

(c) the title of the award,

(d) the date of the award, and

(e) confirmation that the qualification was taught in English.]

Note: Paragraph 144-SD inserted from 20 July 2012 (Cm 8423).

Leave to enter as a representative of an overseas business

[**145.** A person seeking leave to enter the United Kingdom as a representative of an overseas business may be admitted for a period not exceeding 3 years provided he is able to produce to the Immigration Officer, on arrival, a valid United Kingdom entry clearance for entry in this capacity, and his leave may be subject to the following conditions:

(i) no recourse to public funds,

(ii) registration with the police, if this is required by paragraph 326 of these Rules, and

(iii) no employment other than working for the business which the applicant has been admitted to represent.]

Note: Paragraph 145 substituted from 1 October 2009 (HC 7701).

Refusal of leave to enter as a representative of an overseas business

[**146.** Leave to enter as a representative of an overseas business is to be refused if a valid United Kingdom entry clearance for entry in this capacity is not produced to the Immigration Officer on arrival.]

Note: Paragraph 146 substituted from 1 October 2009 (HC 7701).

Requirements for an extension of stay as a representative of an overseas business

[**147.** The requirements for an extension of stay as a representative of an overseas business are that the applicant:

(i) entered the United Kingdom with a valid United Kingdom entry clearance as:

(a) a sole representative of an overseas business, including entry under the rules providing for the admission of sole representatives in force prior to 1 October 2009; or

(b) a representative of an overseas newspaper, news agency or broadcasting organisation;

(ii) the person was admitted in accordance with paragraph 144(ii)(a) and can show that:

(a) the overseas business still has its headquarters and principal place of business outside the United Kingdom; and

(b) he is employed full time as a representative of that overseas business and has established and is in charge of its registered branch or wholly owned subsidiary; and

(c) he is still required for the employment in question, as certified by his employer;

(iii) the person was admitted in accordance with paragraph 144(ii)(b) and can show that:

(a) he is still engaged in the employment for which the entry clearance was granted; and

(b) he is still required for the employment in question, as certified by his employer.

(iv) does not intend to take employment except within the terms of this paragraph; and

(v) can maintain and accommodate himself and any dependants adequately without recourse to public funds] [; and

(vi) must not be in the UK in breach of immigration laws except that any period of overstaying for a period of 28 days or less will be disregarded.

Note: Paragraph 147 substituted from 1 October 2009 (HC 7701). Sub-paragraph (vi) inserted from 1 October 2012 with savings for applications made before 9 July 2012 (HC 194).

Extension of stay as a representative of an overseas business

[148. An extension of stay as a representative of an overseas business may be granted provided the Secretary of State is satisfied that each of the requirements of paragraph 147 is met. The extension of stay will be granted for:

(i) a period not exceeding 2 years, unless paragraph (ii) applies.

(ii) a period not exceeding 3 years, if the applicant was last granted leave prior to 1 October 2009, and will be subject to the following conditions:

(i) no recourse to public funds,

(ii) registration with the police, if this is required by paragraph 326 of these Rules, and

(iii) no employment other than working for the business which the applicant has been admitted to represent.]

Note: Paragraph 148 substituted from 1 October 2009 (HC 7701).

Refusal of extension of stay as a representative of an overseas business

[149. An extension of stay as a representative of an overseas business is to be refused if the Secretary of State is not satisfied that each of the requirements of paragraph 147 is met.]

Note: Paragraph 149 substituted from 1 October 2009 (HC 7701).

Indefinite leave to remain for a representative of an overseas business

[150. Indefinite leave to remain may be granted, on application, to a representative of an overseas business provided:

(i) he has spent a continuous period of 5 years in the United Kingdom in this capacity; and

(ii) he has met the requirements of paragraph 147 throughout the 5 year period; and

(iii) he is still required for the employment in question, as certified by his employer; and

(iv) he has sufficient knowledge of the English language and sufficient knowledge about life in the United Kingdom, [in accordance with paragraph 33BA of these Rules] unless he is under the age of 18 or aged 65 or over at the time he makes his application] [; and

(v) he does not have one or more unspent convictions within the meaning of the Rehabilitation of Offenders Act 1974] [; and

(vi) he is not in the UK in breach of immigration laws except that any period of overstaying for a period of 28 days or less will be disregarded.]

Note: Paragraph 150 substituted from 1 October 2009 (HC 7701). Sub-paragraph (v) and words in square brackets in sub-para (iv) inserted from 6 April 2011 (HC 863). Sub-paragraph (vi) inserted from 1 October 2012 with savings for applications made but not decided before 9 July 2012 (HC 194).

Refusal of indefinite leave to remain for a sole representative of an overseas business

[**151.** Indefinite leave to remain in the United Kingdom for a representative of an overseas business is to be refused if the Secretary of State is not satisfied that each of the requirements of paragraph 150 is met.]

Note: Paragraph 151 substituted from 1 October 2009 (HC 7701).

Private servants in diplomatic households

Requirements for leave to enter as a private servant in a diplomatic household

152. The requirements to be met by a person seeking leave to enter the United Kingdom as a private servant in a diplomatic household are that he:

(i)   is aged 18 or over; and

(ii) is employed as a private servant in the household of a member of staff of a diplomatic or consular mission who enjoys diplomatic privileges and immunity within the meaning of the Vienna Convention on Diplomatic and Consular Relations or a member of the family forming part of the household of such a person; and

(iii) intends to work full-time as a private servant within the terms of this paragraph; and

(iv) does not intend to take employment except within the terms of this paragraph; and

(v)   can maintain and accommodate himself and any dependants adequately without recourse to public funds; and

(vi) holds a valid United Kingdom entry clearance for entry in this capacity.

Note: Paragraph 152 deleted from 27 November 2008 save in so far as it relates to paras 158–159: see HC 1113, para 39. Deletion subject to savings for applications for leave made before 27 November 2008 and undecided by that date: see introduction to HC 1113.

Leave to enter as a private servant in a diplomatic household

153. A person seeking leave to enter the United Kingdom as a private servant in a diplomatic household may be given leave to enter for a period not exceeding 12 months provided he is able to produce to the Immigration Officer, on arrival, a valid United Kingdom entry clearance for entry in this capacity.

Note: Paragraph 153 deleted from 27 November 2008 save in so far as it relates to paras 158–159: see HC 1113, para 39. Deletion subject to savings for applications for leave made before 27 November 2008 and undecided by that date: see introduction to HC 1113.

Refusal of leave to enter as a private servant in a diplomatic household

154. Leave to enter as a private servant in a diplomatic household is to be refused if a valid United Kingdom entry clearance for entry in this capacity is not produced to the Immigration Officer on arrival.

Note: Paragraph 154 deleted from 27 November 2008 save insofar as it relates to paras 158–159: see HC 1113, para 39. Deletion subject to savings for applications for leave made before 27 November 2008 and undecided by that date: see introduction to HC 1113.

Requirements for an extension of stay as a private servant in a diplomatic household

155. The requirements for an extension of stay as a private servant in a diplomatic household are that the applicant:

(i)   entered the United Kingdom with a valid United Kingdom entry clearance as a private servant in a diplomatic household; and

(ii) is still engaged in the employment for which his entry clearance was granted; and

(iii) is still required for the employment in question, as certified by the employer; and

(iv) meets the requirements of paragraph 152(iii)–(v).

Note: Paragraph 155 deleted from 27 November 2008 save in so far as it relates to paras 158–159: see HC 1113, para 39. Deletion subject to savings for applications for leave made before 27 November 2008 and undecided by that date: see introduction to HC 1113.

Extension of stay as a private servant in a diplomatic household

156. An extension of stay as a private servant in a diplomatic household may be granted for a period not exceeding 12 months [at a time] provided the Secretary of State is satisfied that each of the requirements of paragraph 155 is met.

Note: Paragraph 156 deleted from 27 November 2008 save insofar as it relates to paras 158–159: see HC 1113, para 39. Deletion subject to savings for applications for leave made before 27 November 2008 and undecided by that date: see introduction to HC 1113. Words in square brackets inserted from 3 April 2006 (HC 1016).

Refusal of extension of stay as a private servant in a diplomatic household

157. An extension of stay as a private servant in a diplomatic household is to be refused if the Secretary of State is not satisfied that each of the requirements of paragraph 155 is met.

Note: Paragraph 157 deleted from 27 November 2008 save insofar as it relates to paras 158–159: see HC 1113, para 39. Deletion subject to savings for applications for leave made before 27 November 2008 and undecided by that date: see introduction to HC 1113.

Indefinite leave to remain for a servant in a diplomatic household

158. Indefinite leave to remain may be granted, on application, to a private servant in a diplomatic household provided:

(i)   he has spent a continuous period of [5 years] in the United Kingdom in this capacity; and

(ii) he has met the requirements of paragraph 155 throughout the [5 year] period; and

(iii) he is still required for the employment in question, as certified by his employer [; and

(iv) he has sufficient knowledge of the English language and sufficient knowledge about life in the United Kingdom [in accordance with paragraph 33B of these Rules], unless he is under the age of 18 or aged 65 or over at the time he makes his application] [; and

(v)   he does not have one or more unspent convictions within the meaning of the Rehabilitation of Offenders Act 1974] [; and

(vi) he is not in the UK in breach of immigration laws except that any period of over-staying for a period of 28 days or less will be disregarded.]

Note: Words in square brackets in sub-paras (i) and (ii) inserted from 3 April 2006 (HC 1016). Sub-paragraph (iv) inserted from 2 April 2007 (HC 398). Sub-paragraph (v) inserted from 6 April 2011 (HC 863). Words in square brackets in sub-para (iv) inserted from 6 April 2012 except for applications made but not decided before that date (HC 1888). Sub-paragraph (vi) inserted from 1 October 2012 with savings for applications made but not decided before 9 July 2012.

Refusal of indefinite leave to remain for a servant in a diplomatic household

159. Indefinite leave to remain in the United Kingdom for a private servant in a diplomatic household is to be refused if the Secretary of State is not satisfied that each of the requirements of paragraph 158 is met.

Domestic Workers in Private Households

Requirements for leave to enter as a domestic worker in a private household

[159A. The requirements to be met by a person seeking leave to enter the United Kingdom as a domestic worker in a private household are that the applicant:

(i) is aged 18–65 inclusive; and

(ii) has been employed as a domestic worker for one year or more immediately prior to the application for entry clearance under the same roof as the employer or in a household that the employer uses for himself on a regular basis and where evidence . . . is produced to demonstrate the connection between employer and employee [in the form of;

(a) a letter from the employer confirming that the domestic worker has been employed by them in that capacity for the twelve months immediately prior to the date of application; and

(b) one of the following documents covering the same period of employment as that in (a):

(i) pay slips or bank statements showing payment of salary;

(ii) confirmation of tax paid;

(iii) confirmation of health insurance paid;

(iv) contract of employment;

(v) work visa, residence permit or equivalent passport endorsement for the country in which the domestic worker has been employed by that employer; or

(vi) visas or equivalent passport endorsement to confirm that the domestic worker has travelled with the employer]; and

(iii) intends to work for the employer whilst the employer is in the United Kingdom and intends to travel in the company of either;

(a) a British or EEA national employer, or that employer's British or EEA national spouse, civil partner or child, where the employer's usual place of residence is outside the UK and where the employer does not intend to remain in the UK beyond six months; or

(b) a British or EEA national employer's foreign national spouse, civil partner or child where the employer does not intend to remain in the UK beyond six months; or

(c) a foreign national employer or the employer's spouse, civil partner or child where the employer is seeking or has been granted entry clearance or leave to enter under Part 2 of these Rules; and

(iv) intends to leave the UK at the end of six months in the United Kingdom or at the same time as the employer, whichever is the earlier; and

(v) has agreed in writing terms and conditions of employment in the UK with the employer, . . . including specifically that the applicant will be paid in accordance with the National Minimum Wage Act 1998 and any Regulations made under it, and provides [evidence of this in the form set out in Appendix 7] this {sic} with the entry clearance application; and

(vi) will not take employment other than within the terms of this paragraph to work full time as a domestic worker for the employer in a household that the employer intends to live in; and

(vii) can maintain and accommodate him or herself adequately without recourse to public funds; and

(viii) holds a valid entry clearance for entry in this capacity.]

Note: Paragraph 159A inserted from 18 September 2002 (Cm 5597) and substituted from 6 April 2012 except for applications made but not decided before that date (HC 1888). Words deleted from sub-paras (ii) and (v) and words inserted in sub-paras (ii) and (v) from 6 September 2012 (HC 565).

Leave to enter as a domestic worker in a private household

[**159B.** A person seeking leave to enter the United Kingdom as a domestic worker in a private household may be given leave to enter for that purpose for a period not exceeding [6] months provided he is able to produce to the Immigration Officer, on arrival, a valid United Kingdom entry clearance for entry in this capacity.]

Note: Paragraph 159B inserted from 18 September 2002 (Cm 5597). Number in square brackets substituted from 6 April 2012 except for applications made but not decided before that date (HC 1888).

Refusal of leave to enter as a domestic worker in a private household

[**159C.** Leave to enter as a domestic worker in a private household is to be refused if a valid United Kingdom entry clearance for entry in this capacity is not produced to the Immigration Officer on arrival.]

Note: Paragraph 159C inserted from 18 September 2002 (Cm 5597).

[Requirements for extension of stay as a domestic worker in a private household

159D. The requirements for an extension of stay as a domestic worker in a private household are that the applicant:

(i) entered the United Kingdom with a valid entry clearance as a domestic worker in a private household; and

(ii) was granted less than 6 months leave to enter in this capacity; and

(iii) has continued to be employed for the duration of leave granted as a domestic worker in the private household of the employer with whom the applicant entered or joined in the UK; and

(iv) continues to be required for employment for the period of the extension sought as a domestic worker in a private household that the employer lives in [where there is evidence of this in the form of written terms and conditions of employment in the UK as set out in Appendix 7 and evidence that the employer is living in the UK]; and

(v) does not intend to take employment except as a domestic worker in the private household of the employer; and

(vi) meets the requirements of paragraph 159A (iv) and (vii)] [; and

(vii) must not be in the UK in breach of immigration laws except that any period of overstaying for a period of 28 days or less will be disregarded.]

Note: Paragraph 159D inserted from 18 September 2002 (Cm 5597), substituted from 6 April 2012 except for applications made but not decided before that date (HC 1888). Sub-paragraph (vii) inserted from 1 October 2012 with savings for applications made but not decided before 9 July 2012 (HC 194). Words inserted in sub-para (iv) from 6 September 2012 (HC 565).

[Extension of stay as a domestic worker in a private household

159E. An extension of stay as a domestic worker in a private household may be granted for a period of six months less the period already spent in the UK in this capacity.

Note: Paragraph 159E inserted from 18 September 2002 (Cm 5597), substituted from 6 April 2012 except for applications made but not decided before that date (HC 1888).

Requirements for extension of stay as a domestic worker in a private household for applicants who entered the United Kingdom under the Rules in place before 6 April 2012

159EA. The requirements for an extension of stay as a domestic worker in a private household for applicants who entered the United Kingdom under Rules in place before 6 April 2012 are that the applicant:

(i) entered the UK with a valid entry clearance as a domestic worker in a private household under Rules in place before 6 April 2012; and

(ii) has continued to be employed for the duration of leave granted as a domestic worker in a private household; and

(iii) continues to be required for employment for the period of the extension sought as a domestic worker in a private household under the same roof as the employer or in the same household that the employer has lived in and where [evidence of this in the form of written terms and conditions of employment in the UK as set out in Appendix 7 and evidence that the employer resides in the UK]; and

(iv) does not intend to take employment except as a domestic worker in a private household; and

(v) meets the requirements of paragraph 159A(i) and (vii) [; and

(vi) must not be in the UK in breach of immigration laws except that any period of overstaying for a period of 28 days or less will be disregarded.]]

Note: Paragraph 159EA inserted from 6 April 2012 subject to savings for applications made but not decided before that date (HC 1888). Sub-paragraph (vi) inserted from 1 October 2012 with savings for applications made but not decided before 9 July 2012 (HC 194).Words substituted in sub-para (iii) from 6 September 2012 (HC 565).

Extension of stay as a domestic worker in a private household for applicants who entered the United Kingdom under the Rules in place before 6 April 2012

[**159EB.** An extension of stay as a domestic worker in a private household may be granted for a period not exceeding 12 months at a time provided the Secretary of State is satisfied that each of the requirements of paragraph 159EA are met.]

Note: Paragraph 159EB inserted from 6 April 2012 subject to savings for applications made but not decided before that date (HC 1888).

Refusal of extension of stay as a domestic worker in a private household

[159F. An extension of stay as a domestic worker may be refused if the Secretary of State is not satisfied that each of the requirements of [either paragraph 159D or, where applicable, paragraph 159EA, is met.]

Note: Paragraph 159F inserted from 18 September 2002 (Cm 5597). Words in square brackets substituted from 6 April 2012 except for applications made but not decided before that date (HC 1888).

Indefinite leave to remain for a domestic worker in a private household

[159G. The requirements for indefinite leave to remain as a domestic worker in a private household are that the applicant:

    (i) entered the United Kingdom with a valid entry clearance as a domestic worker in a private household under the Rules in place before 6 April 2012; and

    (ii) has spent a continuous period of 5 years in the United Kingdom employed in this capacity; and

    (iii) has met the requirements of paragraph 159A (vi) and (vii) throughout the 5 year period; and

    (iv) continues to be required for employment as a domestic worker in a private household as certified by the current employer; and

    (v) has sufficient knowledge of the English language and sufficient knowledge about life in the United Kingdom, in accordance with paragraph 33B of these Rules, unless they are under 18 or over 65 at the time the application is made; and

    (vi) does not have one or more unspent convictions within the meaning of the Rehabilitation of Offenders Act 1974] [; and

    (vii) must not be in the UK in breach of immigration laws except that any period of overstaying for a period of 28 days or less will be disregarded.]

Note: Paragraph 159G inserted from 18 September 2002 (Cm 5597) and substituted from 6 April 2012 except for applications made before that date (HC 1888). Sub-paragraph (vii) inserted from 1 October 2012 with savings for applications made but not decided before 9 July 2012 (HC 194).

Refusal of indefinite leave to remain for a domestic worker in a private household

[159H. Indefinite leave to remain in the United Kingdom for a domestic worker in a private household is to be refused if the Secretary of State is not satisfied that each of the requirements of paragraph 159G is met.]

Note: Paragraph 159H inserted from 18 September 2002 (Cm 5597).

Overseas government employees

Requirements for leave to enter as an overseas government employee

160. For the purposes of these Rules an overseas government employee means a person coming for employment by an overseas government or employed by the United Nations Organisation or other international organisation of which the United Kingdom is a member.

Note: Paragraph 160 deleted from 27 November 2008 save in so far as it relates to paras 167–168: see HC 1113, para 39. Deletion subject to savings for applications for leave made before 27 November 2008 and undecided by that date: see introduction to HC 1113.

161. The requirements to be met by a person seeking leave to enter the United Kingdom as an overseas government employee are that he:

(i) is able to produce either a valid United Kingdom entry clearance for entry in this capacity or satisfactory documentary evidence of his status as an overseas government employee; and

(ii) intends to work full time for the government or organisation concerned; and

(iii) does not intend to take employment except within the terms of this paragraph; and

(iv) can maintain and accommodate himself and any dependants adequately without recourse to public funds.

Note: Paragraph 161 deleted from 27 November 2008 save in so far as it relates to paras 167–168: see HC 1113, para 39. Deletion subject to savings for applications for leave made before 27 November 2008 and undecided by that date: see introduction to HC 1113.

Leave to enter as an overseas government employee

162. A person seeking leave to enter the United Kingdom as an overseas government employee may be given leave to enter for a period not exceeding [2 years], provided he is able, on arrival, to produce to the Immigration Officer a valid United Kingdom entry clearance for entry in this capacity or satisfy the Immigration Officer that each of the requirements of paragraph 161 is met.

Note: Paragraph 162 deleted from 27 November 2008 save insofar as it relates to paras 167–168: see HC 1113, para 39. Deletion subject to savings for applications for leave made before 27 November 2008 and undecided by that date: see introduction to HC 1113. Words in square brackets substituted from 3 April 2006 (HC 1016).

Refusal of leave to enter as an overseas government employee

163. Leave to enter as an overseas government employee is to be refused if a valid United Kingdom entry clearance for entry in this capacity is not produced to the Immigration Officer on arrival or if the Immigration Officer is not satisfied that each of the requirements of paragraph 161 is met.

Note: Paragraph 163 deleted from 27 November 2008 save insofar as it relates to paras 167–168: see HC 1113, para 39. Deletion subject to savings for applications for leave made before 27 November 2008 and undecided by that date: see introduction to HC 1113.

Requirements for an extension of stay as an overseas government employee

164. The requirements to be met by a person seeking an extension of stay as an overseas government employee are that the applicant:

(i) was given leave to enter the United Kingdom under paragraph 162 as an overseas government employee; and

(ii) is still engaged in the employment in question; and

(iii) is still required for the employment in question, as certified by the employer; and

(iv) meets the requirements of paragraph 161(ii)–(iv).

Note: Paragraph 164 deleted from 27 November 2008 save in so far as it relates to paras 167–168: see HC 1113, para 39. Deletion subject to savings for applications for leave made before 27 November 2008 and undecided by that date: see introduction to HC 1113.

Extension of stay as an overseas government employee

165. An extension of stay as an overseas government employee may be granted for a period not exceeding 3 years provided the Secretary of State is satisfied that each of the requirements of paragraph 164 is met.

Note: Paragraph 165 deleted from 27 November 2008 save in so far as it relates to paras 167–168: see HC 1113, para 39. Deletion subject to savings for applications for leave made before 27 November 2008 and undecided by that date: see introduction to HC 1113.

Refusal of extension of stay as an overseas government employee

166. An extension of stay as an overseas government employee is to be refused if the Secretary of State is not satisfied that each of the requirements of paragraph 164 is met.

Note: Paragraph 166 deleted from 27 November 2008 save insofar as it relates to paras 167–168: see HC 1113, para 39. Deletion subject to savings for applications for leave made before 27 November 2008 and undecided by that date: see introduction to HC 1113.

Indefinite leave to remain for an overseas government employee

167. Indefinite leave to remain may be granted, on application, to an overseas government employee provided:

    (i) he has spent a continuous period of [5 years] in the United Kingdom in this capacity; and

    (ii) he has met the requirements of paragraph 164 throughout the [5 year] period; and

    (iii) he is still required for the employment in question, as certified by his employer [; and

    (iv) he has sufficient knowledge of the English language and sufficient knowledge about life in the United Kingdom, [in accordance with paragraph 33BA of these Rules] unless he is under the age of 18 or aged 65 or over at the time he makes his application] [; and

    (v) he does not have one or more unspent convictions within the meaning of the Rehabilitation of Offenders Act 1974] [; and

    (vi) he is not in the UK in breach of immigration laws except that any period of overstaying for a period of 28 days or less will be disregarded.]

Note: Words in square brackets in sub-paras (i) and (ii) substituted from 3 April 2006 (HC 1016). Sub-paragraph (iv) inserted from 2 April 2007 (HC 398). Sub-paragraph (v) and words in square brackets in sub-para (iv) inserted from 6 April 2011 except for applications made but not decided before that date (HC 863). Sub-paragraph (vi) inserted from 1 October 2012 with savings for applications made before 9 July 2012 (HC 194).

Refusal of indefinite leave to remain for an overseas government employee

168. Indefinite leave to remain in the United Kingdom for an overseas government employee is to be refused if the Secretary of State is not satisfied that each of the requirements of paragraph 167 is met.

Ministers of religion, missionaries and members of religious orders

169. For the purposes of these Rules:

(i) a minister of religion means a religious functionary whose main regular duties comprise the leading of a congregation in performing the rites and rituals of the faith and in preaching the essentials of the creed;

(ii) a missionary means a person who is directly engaged in spreading a religious doctrine and whose work is not in essence administrative or clerical;

(iii) a member of a religious order means a person who is coming to live in a community run by that order.

Requirements for leave to enter as a minister of religion, missionary or member of a religious order

170. The requirements to be met by a person seeking leave to enter the United Kingdom as a minister of religion, missionary or member of a religious order are that he:

(i) (a) if seeking leave to enter as a minister of religion has either been working for at least one year as a minister of religion [in any of the 5 years immediately prior to the date on which the application is made] or, where ordination is prescribed by a religious faith as the sole means of entering the ministry, has been ordained as a minister or religion following at least one year's full-time or two years' part-time training for the ministry; or

(b) if seeking leave to enter as a missionary has been trained as a missionary or has worked as a missionary and is being sent to the United Kingdom by an overseas organisation; or

(c) if seeking leave to enter as a member of a religious order is coming to live in a community maintained by the religious order of which he is a member and, if intending to teach, does not intend to do so save at an establishment maintained by his order; and

(ii) intends to work full-time as a minister of religion, missionary or for the religious order of which he is a member; and

(iii) does not intend to take employment except within the terms of this paragraph; and

(iv) can maintain and accommodate himself and any dependants adequately without recourse to public funds; and

[(iva) if seeking leave as a Minister of Religion can produce an International English Language Testing System certificate issued to him to certify that he has achieved level 6 competence in spoken and written English and that it is dated not more than two years prior to the date on which the application is made; and]

(v) holds a valid United Kingdom entry clearance for entry in this capacity.

Note: Paragraph 170 deleted from 27 November 2008 save insofar as it relates to paras 176–177: see HC 1113, para 39. Deletion subject to savings for applications for leave made before 27 November 2008 and undecided by that date: see introduction to HC 1113. Words in square brackets in sub-para (i)(a) inserted from 23 August 2004 (Cm 6297). Sub-paragraph (iva) substituted from 19 April 2007 (Cm 7074).

Leave to enter as a minister of religion, missionary or member of a religious order

171. A person seeking leave to enter the United Kingdom as a minister of religion, missionary or member of a religious order may be admitted for a period not exceeding

[2 years] provided he is able to produce to the Immigration Officer, on arrival, a valid United Kingdom entry clearance for entry in this capacity.

Note: Paragraph 171 deleted from 27 November 2008 save insofar as it relates to paras 176–177: see HC 1113, para 39. Deletion subject to savings for applications for leave made before 27 November 2008 and undecided by that date: see introduction to HC 1113. Words in square brackets substituted from 3 April 2006 (HC 1016).

Refusal of leave to enter as a minister of religion, missionary or member of a religious order

172. Leave to enter as a minister or religion, missionary or member of a religious order is to be refused if a valid United Kingdom entry clearance for entry in this capacity is not produced to the Immigration Officer on arrival.

Note: Paragraph 172 deleted from 27 November 2008 save insofar as it relates to paras 176–177: see HC 1113, para 39. Deletion subject to savings for applications for leave made before 27 November 2008 and undecided by that date: see introduction to HC 1113.

[Requirements for an extension of stay as a minister of religion where entry to the United Kingdom was granted in that capacity]

173. The requirements for an extension of stay as a minister of religion [where entry to the United Kingdom was granted in that capacity,] missionary or member of a religion order are that the applicant:

(i) entered the United Kingdom with a valid United Kingdom entry clearance as a minister of religion, missionary or member of a religious order; and

(ii) is still engaged in the employment for which his entry clearance was granted; and

(iii) is still required for the employment in question as certified by the leadership of his congregation, his employer or the head of his religious order; and

[(iv) (a) if he entered the United Kingdom as a minister of religion, missionary or member of a religious order in accordance with sub-paragraph (i) prior to 23 August 2004 meets the requirements of paragraph 170 (ii)–(iv); or

(b) if he entered the United Kingdom as a minister of religion, missionary or member of a religious order in accordance with sub-paragraph (i), on or after 23 August 2004 but prior to 19 April 2007, or was granted leave to remain in accordance with paragraph 174B between those dates, meets the requirements of paragraph 170 (ii)–(iv), and if a minister of religion met the requirement to produce an International English Language Testing System certificate certifying that he achieved level 4 competence in spoken English at the time he was first granted leave in this capacity; or

(c) if he entered the United Kingdom as a minister of religion, missionary or member of a religious order in accordance with sub-paragraph (i) on or after 19 April 2007, or was granted leave to remain in accordance with paragraph 174B on or after that date, meets the requirements of paragraph 170 (ii)-(iv), and if a minister of religion met the requirement to produce an International English Language Testing System certificate certifying that he achieved level 6 competence in spoken and written English at the time he was first granted leave in this capacity.]

Note: Paragraph 173 deleted from 27 November 2008 save insofar as it relates to paras 176–177: see HC 1113, para 39. Deletion subject to savings for applications for leave made before 27 November

2008 and undecided by that date: see introduction to HC 1113. Heading substituted, and words inserted, from 23 August 2004 (Cm 6297). Sub-paragraph (iv) substituted from 19 April 2007 (Cm 7074).

Extension of stay as a minister of religion, missionary or member of a religious order

174. An extension of stay as a minister of religion, missionary or member of a religious order may be granted for a period not exceeding 3 years provided the Secretary of State is satisfied that each of the requirements of paragraph 173 is met.

Note: Paragraph 174 deleted from 27 November 2008 save insofar as it relates to paras 176–177: see HC 1113, para 39. Deletion subject to savings for applications for leave made before 27 November 2008 and undecided by that date: see introduction to HC 1113.

[Requirements for an extension of stay as a minister of religion where entry to the United Kingdom was not granted in that capacity]

[174A. The requirements for an extension of stay as a minister of religion for an applicant who did not enter the United Kingdom in that capacity are that he:

(i) entered the United Kingdom, or was given an extension of stay, in accordance with these Rules, except as a minister of religion or as a visitor under paragraphs 40–56 of these Rules, and has spent a continuous period of at least 12 months here pursuant to that leave immediately prior to the application being made; and

(ii) has either been working for at least one year as a minister of religion in any of the 5 years immediately prior to the date on which the application is made (provided that, when doing so, he was not in breach of a condition of any subsisting leave to enter or remain) or, where ordination is prescribed by a religious faith as the sole means of entering the ministry, has been ordained as a minister of religion following at least one year's full-time or two years' part-time training for the ministry; and

(iii) is imminently to be appointed, or has been appointed, to a position as a minister of religion in the United Kingdom and is suitable for such a position, as certified by the leadership of his prospective congregation; and

(iv) meets the requirements of paragraph 170(ii)-(iva).]

Note: Paragraph 174A inserted from 23 August 2004 (Cm 7074) and deleted from 27 November 2008 save insofar as it relates to paras 176–177: see HC 1113, para 39. Deletion subject to savings for applications for leave made before 27 November 2008 and undecided by that date: see introduction to HC 1113.

[Extension of stay as a minister of religion where leave to enter was not granted in that capacity]

[174B. An extension of stay as a minister of religion may be granted for a period not exceeding {3 years at a time} provided the Secretary of State is satisfied that each of the requirements of paragraph 174A is met.]

Note: Paragraph 174B inserted from 23 August 2004 (Cm 6297) and deleted from 27 November 2008 save insofar as it relates to paras 176–177: see HC 1113, para 39. Deletion subject to savings for applications for leave made before 27 November 2008 and undecided by that date: see introduction to HC 1113. Words in curly brackets inserted from 3 April 2006 (HC 1016).

Refusal of extension of stay as a minister of religion, missionary or member of a religious order

175. An extension of stay as a minister of religion, missionary or member of a religious order is to be refused if the Secretary of State is not satisfied that each of the requirements of paragraph 173 [or 174A] is met.

Note: Paragraph 172 deleted from 27 November 2008 save insofar as it relates to paras 176–177: see HC 1113, para 39. Deletion subject to savings for applications for leave made before 27 November 2008 and undecided by that date: see introduction to HC 1113. Words in square brackets inserted from 23 August 2004 (Cm 6297).

Indefinite leave to remain for a minister of religion, missionary or member of a religious order

176. Indefinite leave to remain may be granted, on application, to a person admitted as a minister of religion, missionary or member of a religious order provided:

    (i) he has spent a continuous period of {5 years} in the United Kingdom in this capacity; and

    (ii) he has met the requirements of paragraph 173 [or 174A] throughout the {5 year} period; and

    (iii) he is still required for the employment in question as certified by the leadership of his congregation, his employer or the head of the religious order to which he belongs [; and

    (iv) he has sufficient knowledge of the English language and sufficient knowledge about life in the United Kingdom, [in accordance with paragraph 33BA of these Rules,] unless he is under the age of 18 or aged 65 or over at the time he makes his application] [; and

    (v) he does not have one or more unspent convictions within the meaning of the Rehabilitation of Offenders Act 1974] [; and

    (vi) he is not in the UK in breach of immigration laws except that any period of overstaying for a period of 28 days or less will be disregarded.]

Note: Words in square brackets in sub-paras (i) and (ii) inserted from 23 August 2004 (Cm 6297). Words in curly brackets in sub-para (i) substituted from 3 April (HC 1016). Sub-paragraph (iv) inserted from 2 April 2007 (HC 398). Sub-paragraph (v) and words in square brackets in sub-para (iv) inserted from 6 April except for applications made but not decided before that date 2011 (HC 863). Sub-paragraph (vi) inserted from 1 October 2012 with savings for applications made but not decided before 9 July 2012 (HC 194).

Refusal of indefinite leave to remain for a minister of religion, missionary or member of a religious order

177. Indefinite leave to remain in the United Kingdom for a minister of religion, missionary or member of a religious order is to be refused if the Secretary of State is not satisfied that each of the requirements of paragraph 176 is met.

177A–177G.

Note: Paragraphs 177A–177G deleted from 27 November 2008 (HC 1113), subject to savings for applications for leave made before 27 November 2008 and undecided by that date: see introduction to HC 1113.

Airport-based operational ground staff of overseas-owned airlines

Requirements for leave to enter the United Kingdom as a member of the operational ground staff of an overseas-owned airline

178. The requirements to be met by a person seeking leave to enter the United Kingdom as a member of the operational ground staff of an overseas-owned airline are that he:

(i) has been transferred to the United Kingdom by an overseas-owned airline operating services to and from the United Kingdom to take up duty at an international airport as station manager, security manager or technical manager; and

(ii) intends to work full-time for the airline concerned; and

(iii) does not intend to take employment except within the terms of this paragraph; and

(iv) can maintain and accommodate himself and any dependants without recourse to public funds; and

(v) holds a valid United Kingdom entry clearance for entry in this capacity.

Note: Paragraph 178 deleted from 27 November 2008 save insofar as it relates to paras 184–185: see HC 1113, para 39. Deletion subject to savings for applications for leave made before 27 November 2008 and undecided by that date: see introduction to HC 1113.

Leave to enter as a member of the operational ground staff of an overseas-owned airline

179. A person seeking leave to enter the United Kingdom as a member of the operational ground staff of an overseas-owned airline may be given leave to enter for a period not exceeding [2 years], provided he is able to produce to the Immigration Officer, on arrival, a valid United Kingdom entry clearance for entry in this capacity.

Note: Paragraph 179 deleted from 27 November 2008 save insofar as it relates to paras 184–185: see HC 1113, para 39. Deletion subject to savings for applications for leave made before 27 November 2008 and undecided by that date: see introduction to HC 1113. Words in square brackets substituted from 3 April 2006 (HC 1016).

Refusal of leave to enter as a member of the operational ground staff of an overseas-owned airline

180. Leave to enter as a member of the operational ground staff of an overseas-owned airline is to be refused if a valid United Kingdom entry clearance for entry in this capacity is not produced to the Immigration Officer on arrival.

Note: Paragraph 180 deleted from 27 November 2008 save insofar as it relates to paras 184–185: see HC 1113, para 39. Deletion subject to savings for applications for leave made before 27 November 2008 and undecided by that date: see introduction to HC 1113.

Requirements for an extension of stay as a member of the operational ground staff of an overseas-owned airline

181. The requirements to be met by a person seeking an extension of stay as a member of the operational ground staff of an overseas-owned airline are that the applicant:

(i) entered the United Kingdom with a valid United Kingdom entry clearance as a member of the operational ground staff of an overseas-owned airline; and

(ii) is still engaged in the employment for which entry was granted; and

(iii) is still required for the employment in question, as certified by the employer; and

(iv) meets the requirements of paragraph 178(ii)–(iv).

Note: Paragraph 181 deleted from 27 November 2008 save insofar as it relates to paras 184–185: see HC 1113, para 39. Deletion subject to savings for applications for leave made before 27 November 2008 and undecided by that date: see introduction to HC 1113.

Extension of stay as a member of the operational ground staff of an overseas-owned airline

182. An extension of stay as a member of the operational ground staff of an overseas-owned airline may be granted for a period not exceeding 3 years, provided the Secretary of State is satisfied that each of the requirements of paragraph 181 is met.

Note: Paragraph 182 deleted from 27 November 2008 save insofar as it relates to paras 184–185: see HC 1113, para 39. Deletion subject to savings for applications for leave made before 27 November 2008 and undecided by that date: see introduction to HC 1113.

Refusal of extension of stay as a member of the operational ground staff of an overseas-owned airline

183. An extension of stay as a member of the operational ground staff of an overseas-owned airline is to be refused if the Secretary of State is not satisfied that each of the requirements of paragraph 181 is met.

Note: Paragraph 183 deleted from 27 November 2008 save insofar as it relates to paras 184–185: see HC 1113, para 39. Deletion subject to savings for applications for leave made before 27 November 2008 and undecided by that date: see introduction to HC 1113.

Indefinite leave to remain for a member of the operational ground staff of an overseas-owned airline

184. Indefinite leave to remain may be granted, on application, to a member of the operational ground staff of an overseas-owned airline provided:

(i) he has spent a continuous period of [5 years] in the United Kingdom in this capacity; and

(ii) he has met the requirements of paragraph 181 throughout the [5 year] period; and

(iii) he is still required for the employment in question, as certified by the employer [; and

(iv) he has sufficient knowledge of the English language and sufficient knowledge about life in the United Kingdom, [in accordance with paragraph 33BA of these Rules] unless he is under the age of 18 or aged 65 or over at the time he makes his application.] [; and

(v) he does not have one or more unspent convictions within the meaning of the Rehabilitation of Offenders Act 1974] [; and

(vi) he is not in the UK in breach of immigration laws except that any period of overstaying for a period of 28 days or less will be disregarded.]

Note: Words in square brackets in sub-paras (i) and (ii) substituted from 3 April 2006 (HC 1016). Sub-paragraph (iv) inserted from 2 April 2007 (HC 398). Sub-paragraph (v) and words in square brackets in sub-para (iv) inserted from 6 April 2011 except for applications made but not decided before that date (HC 863). Sub-paragraph (vi) inserted from 1 October 2012 with savings for applications made but not decided before 9 July 2012 (HC 194).

Refusal of indefinite leave to remain for a member of the operational ground staff of an overseas-owned airline

185. Indefinite leave to remain in the United Kingdom for a member of the operational ground staff of an overseas-owned airline is to be refused if the Secretary of State is not satisfied that each of the requirements of paragraph 184 is met.

Persons with United Kingdom ancestry

Requirements for leave to enter on the grounds of United Kingdom ancestry

186. The requirements to be met by a person seeking leave to enter the United Kingdom on the grounds of his United Kingdom ancestry are that he:
    (i) is a Commonwealth citizen; and
    (ii) is aged 17 or over; and
    (iii) is able to provide proof that one of his grandparents was born in the United Kingdom and Islands [and that any such grandparent is the applicant's blood grandparent or grandparent by reason of an adoption recognised by the laws of the United Kingdom relating to adoption]; and
    (iv) is able to work and intends to take or seek employment in the United Kingdom; and
    (v) will be able to maintain and accommodate himself and any dependants adequately without recourse to public funds; and
    (vi) holds a valid United Kingdom entry clearance for entry in this capacity.

Note: Words in square brackets in para 186(iii) inserted from 25 August 2003 (Cm 5949).

Leave to enter the United Kingdom on the grounds of United Kingdom ancestry

187. A person seeking leave to enter the United Kingdom on the grounds of his United Kingdom ancestry may be given leave to enter for a period not exceeding [5 years] provided he is able to produce to the Immigration Officer, on arrival, a valid United Kingdom entry clearance for entry in this capacity.

Note: Words in square brackets substituted from 3 April 2006 (HC 1016).

Refusal of leave to enter on the grounds of United Kingdom ancestry

188. Leave to enter the United Kingdom on the grounds of United Kingdom ancestry is to be refused if a valid United Kingdom entry clearance for entry in this capacity is not produced to the Immigration Officer on arrival.

Requirements for an extension of stay on the grounds of United Kingdom ancestry

[189. The requirements to be met by a person seeking an extension of stay on the grounds of United Kingdom ancestry are that:

    (i) he is able to meet each of the requirements of paragraph 186 (i)–(v); and

    (ii) he was admitted to the United Kingdom on the grounds of United Kingdom ancestry in accordance with paragraphs 186 to 188 or has been granted an extension of stay in this capacity] [; and

    (iii) he is not in the UK in breach of immigration laws except that any period of over-staying for a period of 28 days or less will be disregarded.]

Note: Paragraph 189 substituted from 25 October 2004 (Cm 1112). Sub-paragraph (iii) inserted from 1 October 2012 with savings for applications made but not decided before 9 July 2012 (HC 194).

Extension of stay on the grounds of United Kingdom ancestry

190. An extension of stay on the grounds of United Kingdom ancestry may be granted for a period not exceeding {5 years} provided the Secretary of State is satisfied that each of the requirements of paragraph [189] is met.

Note: Words in square brackets substituted from 25 October 2004 (Cm 1112). Words in curly brackets substituted from 3 April 2006 (HC 1016).

Refusal of extension of stay on the grounds of United Kingdom ancestry

191. An extension of stay on the grounds of United Kingdom ancestry is to be refused if the Secretary of State is not satisfied that each of the requirements of paragraph [189] is met.

Note: Words in square brackets substituted from 25 October 2004 (Cm 1112).

Indefinite leave to remain on the grounds of United Kingdom ancestry

192. Indefinite leave to remain may be granted, on application, to a Commonwealth citizen with a United Kingdom born grandparent provided:

    (i) he meets the requirements of paragraph 186(i)–(v); and

    (ii) he has spent a continuous period of [5 years] in the United Kingdom in this capacity [; and

    (iii) he has sufficient knowledge of the English language and sufficient knowledge about life in the United Kingdom, unless he is under the age of 18 or aged 65 or over at the time he makes his application] [; and

    (iv) he does not have one or more unspent convictions within the meaning of the Rehabilitation of Offenders Act 1974] [; and

    (v) he is not in the UK in breach of immigration laws except that any period of over-staying for a period of 28 days or less will be disregarded.]

Note: Words in square brackets in sub-para (ii) substituted from 3 April 2006 (HC 1016). Sub-paragraph (iii) inserted from 2 April 2007 (HC 398). Sub-paragraph (iv) inserted from 6 April 2011 except for applications made but not decided before that date (HC 863). Sub-paragraph (v) inserted from 1 October 2012 with savings for applications made but not decided before 9 July 2012 (HC 194).

Refusal of indefinite leave to remain on the grounds of United Kingdom ancestry

193. Indefinite leave to remain in the United Kingdom on the grounds of a United Kingdom born grandparent is to be refused if the Secretary of State is not satisfied that each of the requirements of paragraph 192 is met.

Spouses or civil partners of persons who have or have had leave to enter or remain under paragraphs 128–193 (but not paragraphs 135I–135K)

[**193A.** Nothing in paragraphs 194–196F is to be construed as allowing a person to be granted entry clearance, leave to enter, leave to remain or variation of leave as a spouse or civil partner of a person granted entry clearance or leave to enter under paragraph 159A where that entry clearance or leave to enter was granted under 159A on or after 6 April 2012.]

Note: Paragraph 193A inserted from 6 April 2012 except for applications made but not decided before that date (HC 1888).

Requirements for leave to enter as the spouse or civil partner of a person with limited leave to enter or remain in the United Kingdom under paragraphs 128–193 (but not paragraphs 135I–135K)

[**194.** The requirements to be met by a person seeking leave to enter the United Kingdom as the spouse or civil partner of a person with limited leave to enter or remain in the United Kingdom under paragraphs 128–193 (but not paragraphs 135I-135K) are that:

(i) the applicant is married to or a civil partner of a person with limited leave to enter the United Kingdom under paragraphs 128–193 (but not paragraphs 135I–135K); and

(ii) each of the parties intends to live with the other as his or her spouse or civil partner during the applicant's stay and the marriage or civil partnership is subsisting; and

(iii) there will be adequate accommodation for the parties and any dependants without recourse to public funds in accommodation which they own or occupy exclusively; and

(iv) the parties will be able to maintain themselves and any dependants adequately without recourse to public funds; and

(v) the applicant does not intend to stay in the United Kingdom beyond any period of leave granted to his spouse; and

(vi) the applicant holds a valid United Kingdom entry clearance for entry in this capacity.]

Note: Paragraph 194 substituted from 2 April 2007 (HC 398).

Leave to enter as the spouse or civil partner of a person with limited leave to enter or remain in the United Kingdom under paragraphs 128–193 (but not paragraphs 135I-135K)

[**195.** A person seeking leave to enter the United Kingdom as the spouse or civil partner of a person with limited leave to enter or remain in the United Kingdom under paragraphs 128–193 (but not paragraphs 135I–135K) may be given leave to enter for a period not in excess of that granted to the person with limited leave to enter or remain under paragraphs 128–193 (but not paragraphs 135I–135K) provided the Immigration Officer is satisfied that each of the requirements of paragraph 194 is met. [If the person is seeking leave to enter as the spouse or civil partner of a Highly Skilled Migrant, leave which is granted will be subject to a condition {prohibiting employment as a doctor or dentist in training, unless the applicant has obtained a degree in medicine or dentistry at bachelor's level or above from a UK institution that is a UK recognised or listed body, or which holds a sponsor licence under Tier 4 of the Points Based System}]][, and provides evidence of this degree.]

> **Note:** Paragraph 195 substituted from 2 April 2007 (HC 398). Final sentence inserted from 29 February 2008 (HC 321) and subsequently amended from 6 April 2010 (HC 439) subject to a saving for applications for leave made before 6 April 2010 and not decided by that date: see introduction to HC 439. Final words inserted from 20 July 2012 (Cm 8423).

Refusal of leave to enter as the spouse or civil partners of a person with limited leave to enter or remain in the United Kingdom under paragraphs 128–193 (but not paragraphs 135I–135K)

196. Leave to enter the United Kingdom as the spouse or civil partner of a person with limited leave to enter or remain in the United Kingdom under paragraphs 128–193 (but not paragraphs 135I–135K) is to be refused if the Immigration Officer is not satisfied that each of the requirements of paragraph 194 is met.

> **Note:** Paragraph 196 substituted from 2 April 2007 (HC 398).

Requirements for extension of stay as the spouse or civil partner of a person who has or has had leave to enter or remain in the United Kingdom under paragraphs 128–193 (but not paragraphs 135I–135K)

196A. The requirements to be met by a person seeking an extension of stay in the United Kingdom as the spouse or civil partner of a person who has or has had leave to enter or remain in the United Kingdom under paragraphs 128–193 (but not paragraphs 135I–135K) are that the applicant:

(i) is married to or civil partner of a person with limited leave to enter or remain in the United Kingdom under paragraphs 128–193 (but not paragraphs 135I–135K); or

(ii) is married to or civil partner of a person who has limited leave to enter or remain in the United Kingdom under paragraphs 128–193 (but not paragraphs 135I–135K) and who is being granted indefinite leave to remain at the same time; or

(iii) is married to or a civil partner of a person who has indefinite leave to remain in the United Kingdom and who had limited leave to enter or remain in the United Kingdom under paragraphs 128–193 (but not paragraphs 135I–135K) immediately before being granted indefinite leave to remain; and

(iv) meets the requirements of paragraph 194(ii)–(v); and

(v) was admitted with a valid United Kingdom entry clearance for entry in this capacity] [; and

(vi) must not be in the UK in breach of immigration laws except that any period of overstaying for a period of 28 days or less will be disregarded.]

> **Note:** Paragraph 196A inserted from 2 April 2007 (HC 398). Sub-paragraph (vi) inserted from 1 October 2012 with savings for applications made but not decided before 9 July 2012 (HC 194).

Extension of stay as the spouse or civil partner of a person who has or has had leave to enter or remain in the United Kingdom under paragraphs 128–193 (but not paragraphs 135I–135K)

[**196B.** An extension of stay in the United Kingdom as:

(i) the spouse or civil partner of a person who has limited leave to enter or remain under paragraphs 128–193 (but not paragraphs 135I–135K) may be granted for a period not in excess of that granted to the person with limited leave to enter or remain; or

(ii) the spouse or civil partner of a person who is being admitted at the same time for settlement, or the spouse or civil partner of a person who has indefinite leave to remain, may be granted for a period not exceeding 2 years, in both instances, provided the Secretary of State is satisfied that each of the requirements of paragraph 196A is met.

[If the person is seeking an extension of stay as the spouse or civil partner, of a Highly Skilled Migrant, leave which is granted will be subject to a condition prohibiting Employment as a Doctor or Dentist in Training, unless the applicant:

(1) has obtained a [primary degree] in medicine or dentistry at bachelor's level or above from a UK institution that is a UK recognised or listed body, or which holds a sponsor licence under Tier 4 of the Points Based System; or]

[(2) has, or has last been granted, entry clearance, leave to enter or leave to remain that was not subject to any condition restricting him from taking employment as a Doctor in Training, and has been employed during that leave as a Doctor in Training; or

(3) has, or has last been granted, entry clearance, leave to enter or leave to remain that was not subject to any condition restricting him from taking employment as a Dentist in Training, and has been employed during that leave as a Dentist in Training.]

> Note: Paragraph 196B inserted from 2 April 2007 (HC 398). Final sentence para (ii) substituted from 6 April 2010 (HC 439) subject to a saving for applications for leave made before 6 April 2010 and not decided by that date: see introduction to HC 439. Sub-paragraph (2) and words in square brackets in sub-para (1) substituted from 6 April 2011 except for applications made but not decided before that date (HC 863).

Refusal of extension of stay as the spouse or civil partner of a person who has or has had leave to enter or remain in the United Kingdom under paragraphs 128–193 (but not paragraphs 135I–135K)

[**196C.** An extension of stay in the United Kingdom as the spouse or civil partner of a person who has or has had leave to enter or remain in the United Kingdom under paragraphs 128–193 (but not paragraphs 135I–135K) is to be refused if the Secretary of State is not satisfied that each of the requirements of paragraph 196A is met.]

> Note: Paragraph 196C inserted from 2 April 2007 (HC 398).

Requirements for indefinite leave to remain for the spouse or civil partner of a person who has or has had leave to enter or remain in the United Kingdom under paragraphs 128–193 (but not paragraphs 135I–135K)

[**196D.** The requirements to be met by a person seeking indefinite leave to remain in the United Kingdom as the spouse or civil partner of a person who has or has had leave to enter or remain in the United Kingdom under paragraphs 128–193 (but not paragraphs 135I–135K) are that the applicant:

(i) is married to or civil partner of a person who has limited leave to enter or remain in the United Kingdom under paragraphs 128–193 (but not paragraphs 135I–135K) and who is being granted indefinite leave to remain at the same time; or

(ii) is married to or a civil partner of a person who has indefinite leave to remain in the United Kingdom and who had limited leave to enter or remain in the United Kingdom under paragraphs 128–193 (but not paragraphs 135I–135K) immediately before being granted indefinite leave to remain; and

(iii) meets the requirements of paragraph 194(ii)–(v); and

(iv) has sufficient knowledge of the English language and sufficient knowledge about life in the United Kingdom, unless he is under the age of 18 or aged 65 or over at the time he makes his application; and

(v) was admitted with a valid United Kingdom entry clearance for entry in this capacity][; and

(vi) does not have one or more unspent convictions within the meaning of the Rehabilitation of Offenders Act 1974] [; and

(vii) must not be in the UK in breach of immigration laws except that any period of overstaying for a period of 28 days or less will be disregarded.]

Note: Paragraph 196D inserted from 2 April 2007 (HC 398). Sub-paragraph (vi) inserted from 6 April 2011 except for applications made but not decided before that date (HC 863). Sub-paragraph (vii) inserted from 1 October 2012 with savings for applications made but not decided before 9 July 2012 (HC 194).

Indefinite leave to remain as the spouse or civil partner of a person who has or has had leave to enter or remain in the United Kingdom under paragraphs 128-193 (but not paragraphs 135I-135K)

[196E. Indefinite leave to remain in the United Kingdom for the spouse or civil partner of a person who has or has had leave to enter or remain in the United Kingdom under paragraphs 128–193 (but not paragraphs 135I–135K) may be granted provided the Secretary of State is satisfied that each of the requirements of paragraph 196D is met.

Note: Paragraph 196E inserted from 2 April 2007 (HC 398).

Refusal of indefinite leave to remain as the spouse or civil partner of a person who has or has had leave to enter or remain in the United Kingdom under paragraphs 128–193 (but not paragraphs 135I–135K)

[196F. Indefinite leave to remain in the United Kingdom for the spouse or civil partner of a person who has or has had limited leave to enter or remain in the United Kingdom under paragraphs 128–193 (but not paragraphs 135I–135K) is to be refused if the Secretary of State is not satisfied that each of the requirements of [paragraph 194D] is met.]

Note: Paragraph 196F inserted from 2 April 2007 (HC 398). Words in square brackets substituted from 22 October 2010 with savings for applications made before that date (Cm 7944).

[196G. Nothing in paragraphs 197–199 is to be construed as allowing a person to be granted entry clearance, leave to enter, leave to remain or variation of leave as the child of a person granted entry clearance or leave to enter under paragraph 159A where that entry clearance or leave to enter was granted under 159A on or after 6 April 2012.]

Note: Paragraph 196G inserted from 6 April 2012 except for applications made before that date (HC 1888).

Children of persons with limited leave to enter or remain in the United Kingdom under paragraphs 128–193

Requirements for leave to enter or remain as the child of a person with limited leave to enter or remain in the United Kingdom under paragraphs 128–193 [(but not paragraphs 135I–135K)]

197. The requirements to be met by a person seeking leave to enter or remain in the United Kingdom as a child of a person with limited leave to enter or remain in the United Kingdom under paragraphs 128–193 [but not paragraphs 135I–135K] are that:

(i) he is the child of a parent with limited leave to enter or remain in the United Kingdom under paragraphs 128–193 [but not paragraphs 135I–135K]; and

(ii) he is under the age of 18 or has current leave to enter or remain in this capacity; and

(iii) he is unmarried [and is not a civil partner], has not formed an independent family unit and is not leading an independent life; and

(iv) he can and will be maintained and accommodated adequately without recourse to public funds in accommodation which his parent(s) own or occupy exclusively; and

(v) he will not stay in the United Kingdom beyond any period of leave granted to his parent(s); and

(vi) both parents are being or have been admitted to or allowed to remain in the United Kingdom save where:

(a) the parent he is accompanying or joining is his sole surviving parent; or

(b) the parent he is accompanying or joining has had sole responsibility for his upbringing; or

(c) there are serious and compelling family or other considerations which make exclusion from the United Kingdom undesirable and suitable arrangements have been made for his care; and

(vii) if seeking leave to enter, he holds a valid United Kingdom entry clearance for entry in this capacity or, if seeking leave to remain, was admitted with a valid United Kingdom entry clearance for entry in this capacity [; or

(viii) if seeking leave to remain, must not be in the UK in breach of immigration laws except that any period of overstaying for a period of 28 days or less will be disregarded.]

Note: Words in square brackets inserted from 30 May 2003 (Cm 5829). Words in square brackets in sub-para (iii) inserted from 5 December 2006 (HC 582). Sub-paragraph (viii) inserted from 1 October 2012 with savings for applications made but not decided before 9 July 2012 (HC 194).

Leave to enter or remain as the child of a person with limited leave to enter or remain in the United Kingdom under paragraphs 128–193 [(but not paragraphs 135I–135K)]

198. A person seeking leave to enter or remain in the United Kingdom as the child of a person with limited leave to enter or remain in the United Kingdom under paragraphs

128–193 [but not paragraphs 135I–135K] may be given leave to enter or remain in the United Kingdom for a period of leave not in excess of that granted to the person with limited leave to enter or remain under paragraphs 128–193 [but not paragraphs 135I–135K] provided that, in relation to an application for leave to enter, he is able to produce to the Immigration Officer, on arrival, a valid United Kingdom entry clearance for entry in this capacity or, in the case of an application for limited leave to remain, he was admitted with a valid United Kingdom entry clearance for entry in this capacity and is able to satisfy the Secretary of State that each of the requirements of paragraph 197(i)–(vi) [and (viii)] is met. An application for indefinite leave to remain in this category may be granted provided the applicant was admitted with a valid United Kingdom entry clearance for entry in this capacity and is able to satisfy the Secretary of State that each of the requirements of paragraph 197(i)–(vi) [and (viii)] is met and provided indefinite leave to remain is, at the same time, being granted to the person with limited leave to enter or remain under paragraphs 128–193 [but not paragraphs 135I–135K].

> **Note:** References to paragraphs 135I–135K inserted from 30 May 2003 (Cm 5829). Other words in square brackets inserted from 1 October 2012 with savings for applications made but not decided before 9 July 2012 (HC 194).

Refusal of leave to enter or remain as the child of a person with limited leave to enter or remain in the United Kingdom under paragraphs 128–193 [(but not paragraphs 135I–135K)]

199. Leave to enter or remain in the United Kingdom as the child of a person with limited leave to enter or remain in the United Kingdom under paragraphs 128–193 [but not paragraphs 135I–135K] is to be refused if, in relation to an application for leave to enter, a valid United Kingdom entry clearance for entry in this capacity is not produced to the Immigration Officer on arrival or, in the case of an application for limited leave to remain, if the applicant was not admitted with a valid United Kingdom entry clearance for entry in this capacity or is unable to satisfy the Secretary of State that each of the requirements of paragraph 197(i)–(vi) [and (viii)] is met. An application for indefinite leave to remain in this category is to be refused if the applicant was not admitted with a valid United Kingdom entry clearance for entry in this capacity or is unable to satisfy the Secretary of State that each of the requirements of paragraph 197(i)–(vi) [and (viii)] is met or if indefinite leave to remain is not, at the same time, being granted to the person with limited leave to enter or remain under paragraphs 128–193 [but not paragraphs 135I–135K].

> **Note:** References to paragraphs 135I–135K inserted from 30 May 2003 (Cm 5829). Other words in square brackets inserted from 1 October 2012 with savings for applications made but not decided before 9 July 2012 (HC 194).

Multiple entry work permit employment

> **Note:** Paragraphs 199A–199C deleted from 6 April 2012 except for applications made but not decided before that date (HC 1888). See Appendix F for the wording where relevant.

PART 6
PERSONS SEEKING TO ENTER OR REMAIN IN THE UNITED KINGDOM AS A BUSINESSMAN, SELF-EMPLOYED PERSON, INVESTOR, WRITER, COMPOSER OR ARTIST
Persons intending to establish themselves in business

200–208

Note: Paragraphs 200–208 deleted from 30 June 2008 (HC 607) save as relevant to para 209. See Appendix F for wording where relevant.

Indefinite leave to remain for a person established in business

209. Indefinite leave to remain may be granted, on application, to a person established in business provided he:

(i) has spent a continuous period of [5 years] in the United Kingdom in this capacity and is still engaged in the business in question; and

(ii) has met the requirements of paragraph 206 throughout the [5 year] period; and

[(iii) submits audited accounts for the first 4 years of trading and management accounts for the 5th year] {; and

(iv) has sufficient knowledge of the English language and sufficient knowledge about life in the United Kingdom, [in accordance with paragraph 33BA of these Rules,] unless he is under the age of 18 or aged 65 or over at the time he makes his application} [; and

(v) does not have one or more unspent convictions within the meaning of the Rehabilitation of Offenders Act 1974] [; and

(vi) must not be in the UK in breach of immigration laws except that any period of overstaying for a period of 28 days or less will be disregarded.]

Note: Words in square brackets in sub-paras (i) and (ii) substituted and sub-para (iii) inserted from 3 April 2006 (HC 1016). Sub-paragraph (iv) inserted from 2 April 2007. Sub-paragraph (v) and words in square brackets in sub-para (iv) inserted from 6 April 2011 except for applications made but not decided before that date (HC 863). Sub-paragraph (vi) inserted from 1 October 2012 with savings for applications made but not decided before 9 July 2012 (HC 194).

Refusal of indefinite leave to remain for a person established in business

210. Indefinite leave to remain in the United Kingdom for a person established in business is to be refused if the Secretary of State is not satisfied that each of the requirements of paragraph 209 is met.

Innovators

210A–210F.

Note: Paragraphs 210A–210F deleted from 30 June 2008 (HC 607) save as relevant to para 210G. See Appendix F for wording where relevant.

[Indefinite leave to remain for an innovator

210G. Indefinite leave to remain may be granted, on application, to a person currently with leave as an innovator provided that he:

(i) has spent a continuous period of at least {5 years} leave in the United Kingdom in this capacity; and

(ii) has met the requirements of paragraph 210D throughout the {5 year} period; [and

(iii) he has sufficient knowledge of the English language and sufficient knowledge about life in the United Kingdom, [in accordance with paragraph 33BA of these Rules,] unless he is under the age of 18 or aged 65 or over at the time he makes his application]] [; and

(iv) he does not have one or more unspent convictions within the meaning of the Rehabilitation of Offenders Act 1974] [; and

(v) he is not in the UK in breach of immigration laws except that any period of overstaying for a period of 28 days or less will be disregarded.]

Note: Paragraph 210G inserted from 1 April 2003 (HC 538). Words in curly brackets substituted from 3 April 2006 (HC 1016). Sub-paragraph (iii) inserted from 2 April 2007 (HC 398). Sub-paragraph (iv) and words in square brackets in sub-para (iii) inserted from 6 April 2011 except for applications made but not decided before that date (HC 863). Sub-paragraph (v) inserted from 1 October 2012 with savings for applications made but not decided before 9 July 2012 (HC 194).

[Refusal of indefinite leave to remain as an innovator

210H. Indefinite leave to remain in the United Kingdom as a person currently with leave as a innovator is to be refused if the Secretary of State is not satisfied that each of the requirements of paragraph 210G is met.]

Note: Paragraph 210H inserted from 1 April 2003 (HC 538).

Persons intending to establish themselves in business under provisions of EC Association Agreements

211–221.

Note: Paragraphs 211–221 deleted from 1 January 2007 (HC 130).

Indefinite leave to remain for a person established in business under the provisions of an EC Association Agreement

[**222.** Indefinite leave to remain may be granted, on application, to a person established in business provided he—

(i) is a national of Bulgaria or Romania; and

(ii) entered the United Kingdom with a valid United Kingdom entry clearance as a person intending to establish himself in business under the provisions of an EC Association Agreement; and

(iii) was granted an extension of stay before 1 January 2007 in order to remain in business under the provisions of the Agreement; and

(iv) established himself in business in the United Kingdom, spent a continuous period of 5 years in the United Kingdom in this capacity and is still so engaged; and

(v) met the requirements of paragraph 222A throughout the period of 5 years; and

(vi) submits audited accounts for the first 4 years of trading and management accounts for the 5th year [and

(vii) he has sufficient knowledge of the English language and sufficient knowledge about life in the United Kingdom,[in accordance with paragraph 33BA of these Rules] unless he is under the age of 18 or aged 65 or over at the time he makes his application]] [; and

(viii) does not have one or more unspent convictions within the meaning of the Rehabilitation of Offenders Act 1974] [; and

(ix) must not be in the UK in breach of immigration laws except that any period of overstaying for a period of 28 days or less will be disregarded.]

Note: Paragraph 222 substituted from 1 January 2007 (HC 130). Sub-paragraph (vii) inserted from 2 April 2007 (HC 398). Sub-paragraph (viii) and words in square brackets in sub-para (vii) inserted from 6 April 2011 except for applications made but not decided before that date (HC 863). Sub-paragraph (ix) inserted from 1 October 2012 with savings for applications made but not decided before 9 July 2012 (HC 194).

[**222A.** The requirements mentioned in paragraph 222(v) are that throughout the period of 5 years—

(i) the applicant's share of the profits of the business has been sufficient to maintain and accommodate himself and any dependants without recourse to employment (other than his work for the business) or to public funds; and

(ii) he has not supplemented his business activities by taking or seeking employment in the United Kingdom (other than his work for the business); and

(iii) he has satisfied the requirements in paragraph 222B or 222C.]

Note: Paragraph 222A substituted from 1 January 2007 (HC 130).

[**222B.** Where the applicant has established himself in a company in the United Kingdom which he effectively controls, the requirements for the purpose of paragraph 222A(iii) are that—

(i) the applicant has been actively involved in the promotion and management of the company; and

(ii) he has had a controlling interest in the company; and

(iii) the company was registered in the United Kingdom and has been trading or providing services in the United Kingdom; and

(iv) the company owned the assets of the business.]

Note: Paragraph 222B substituted from 1 January 2007 (HC 130).

[**222C.** Where the applicant has established himself as a sole trader or in a partnership in the United Kingdom, the requirements for the purpose of paragraph 222A(iii) are that—

(i) the applicant has been actively involved in trading or providing services on his own account or in a partnership in the United Kingdom; and

(ii) the applicant owned, or together with his partners owned, the assets of the business; and

(iii) in the case of a partnership, the applicant's part in the business did not amount to disguised employment.]

Note: Paragraph 222C substituted from 1 January 2007 (HC 130).

Refusal of indefinite leave to remain for a person established in business under the provision of an EC Association Agreement

223. Indefinite leave to remain in the United Kingdom for a person established in business is to be refused if the Secretary of State is not satisfied that each of the requirements of paragraph 222 is met.

[**223A.** Notwithstanding paragraph 5, paragraphs 222 to 223 shall apply to a person who is entitled to remain in the United Kingdom by virtue of the provisions of the 2006 EEA Regulations.]

Note: Paragraph 223A inserted from 1 January 2007 (HC 130).

Investors

Requirements for leave to enter the United Kingdom as an investor

224–229.

Note: Paragraphs 224–229 deleted from 30 June 2008 (HC 607) save as relevant to para 230. See Appendix F for wording where relevant.

Indefinite leave to remain for an investor

230. Indefinite leave to remain may be granted, on application, to a person admitted as an investor provided he:

(i) has spent a continuous period of [5 years] in the United Kingdom in this capacity; and

(ii) has met the requirements of paragraph 227 throughout the [5 year] period including the requirement as to the investment of £750,000 and continues to do so [; and

(iii) has sufficient knowledge of the English language and sufficient knowledge about life in the United Kingdom, [in accordance with paragraph 33BA of these Rules,]unless he is under the age of 18 or aged 65 or over at the time he makes his application [; and

(iv) does not have one or more unspent convictions within the meaning of the Rehabilitation of Offenders Act 1974] [; and

(v) must not be in the UK in breach of immigration laws except that any period of overstaying for a period of 28 days or less will be disregarded.]

Note: Words in square brackets in sub-paras (i) and (ii) substituted from 3 April 2006 (HC 1016). Sub-paragraph (iii) inserted from 2 April 2007 (HC 398). Sub-paragraph (iv) and words in square brackets in sub-para (iii) inserted from 6 April 2011 except for applications made but not decided before that date (HC 863). Sub-paragraph (v) inserted from 1 October 2012 with savings for applications made before 9 July 2012 (HC 194).

Refusal of indefinite leave to remain for an investor

231. Indefinite leave to remain in the United Kingdom for an investor is to be refused if the Secretary of State is not satisfied that each of the requirements of paragraph 230 is met.

Writers, composers and artists

Note: Paragraphs 232–237 deleted from 30 June 2008 (HC 607) save as relevant to para 238. See Appendix F for wording where relevant.

Indefinite leave to remain for a writer, composer or artist

238. Indefinite leave to remain may be granted, on application, to a person admitted as a writer, composer or artist provided he:

(i) has spent a continuous period of [5 years] in the United Kingdom in this capacity; and

(ii) has met the requirements of paragraph 235 throughout the [5 year] period [; and

(iii) he has sufficient knowledge of the English language and sufficient knowledge about life in the United Kingdom, [in accordance with paragraph 33BA of these Rules,] unless he is under the age of 18 or aged 65 or over at the time he makes his application [; and

(iv) does not have one or more unspent convictions within the meaning of the Rehabilitation of Offenders Act 1974] [; and

(v) must not be in the UK in breach of immigration laws except that any period of overstaying for a period of 28 days or less will be disregarded.]

Note: Words in square brackets in sub-paras (i) and (ii) substituted from 3 April 2006 (HC 1016). Sub-paragraph (iii) inserted from 2 April 2007 (HC 398). Sub-paragraph (iv) and words in square brackets in sub-para (iii) inserted from 6 April 2011 except for applications made but not decided before that date (HC 863). Sub-paragraph (v) inserted from 1 October 2012 with savings for applications made but not decided before 9 July 2012 (HC 194).

Refusal of indefinite leave to remain for a writer, composer or artist

239. Indefinite leave to remain for a writer, composer or artist is to be refused if the Secretary of State is not satisfied that each of the requirements of paragraph 238 is met.

Spouses or civil partners of persons who have or have had limited leave to enter or remain under paragraphs 200–239

Requirements for leave to enter as the spouse or civil partner of a person with limited leave to enter or remain under paragraphs 200–239

[**240.** The requirements to be met by a person seeking leave to enter the United Kingdom as the spouse or civil partner of a person with limited leave to enter or remain in the United Kingdom under paragraphs 200–239 are that:

(i) the applicant is married to or the civil partner of a person with limited leave to enter or remain in the United Kingdom under paragraphs 200–239; and

(ii) each of the parties intends to live with the other as his or her spouse or civil partner during the applicant's stay and the marriage or civil partnership is subsisting; and

(iii) there will be adequate accommodation for the parties and any dependants without recourse to public funds in accommodation which they own or occupy exclusively; and

(iv) the parties will be able to maintain themselves and any dependants adequately without recourse to public funds; and

(v) the applicant does not intend to stay in the United Kingdom beyond any period of leave granted to his spouse or civil partner; and

(vi) the applicant holds a valid United Kingdom entry clearance for entry in this capacity.]

Note: Paragraph 240 substituted from 2 April 2007 (HC 398).

Leave to enter as the spouse or civil partner of a person with limited leave to enter or remain in the United Kingdom under paragraphs 200–239

[241. A person seeking limited leave to enter the United Kingdom as the spouse or civil partner of a person with limited leave to enter or remain in the United Kingdom under paragraphs 200–239 may be given leave to enter for a period not in excess of that granted to the person with limited leave to enter or remain under paragraphs 200–239 provided the Immigration Officer is satisfied that each of the requirements of paragraph 240 is met.]

Note: Paragraph 241 substituted from 2 April 2007 (HC 398).

Refusal of leave to enter as the spouse or civil partner of a person with limited leave to enter or remain in the United Kingdom under paragraphs 200–239

[242. Leave to enter the United Kingdom as the spouse or civil partner of a person with limited leave to enter or remain in the United Kingdom under paragraphs 200–239 is to be refused if the Immigration Officer is not satisfied that each of the requirements of paragraph 240 is met.]

Note: Paragraph 242 substituted from 2 April 2007 (HC 398).

Requirements for extension of stay as the spouse or civil partner of a person who has or has had leave to enter or remain in the United Kingdom under paragraphs 200–239

[242A. The requirements to be met by a person seeking an extension of stay in the United Kingdom as the spouse or civil partner of a person who has or has had leave to enter or remain under paragraphs 200–239 are that the applicant:

(i) is married to or the civil partner of a person with limited leave to enter or remain in the United Kingdom under paragraphs 200–239; or

(ii) is married to or civil partner of a person who has limited leave to enter or remain in the United Kingdom under paragraphs 200–239 and who is being granted indefinite leave to remain at the same time; or

(iii) is married to or civil partner of a person who has indefinite leave to remain in the United Kingdom and who had limited leave to enter or remain in the United Kingdom under paragraphs 200–239 immediately before being granted indefinite leave to remain; and

(iv) meets the requirements of paragraph 240(ii)–(v); and

(v) was admitted with a valid United Kingdom entry clearance for entry in this capacity] [; and

(vi) must not be in the UK in breach of immigration laws except that any period of overstaying for a period of 28 days or less will be disregarded.]

Note: Paragraph 242A inserted from 2 April 2007 (HC 398). Sub-paragraph (vi) inserted from 1 October 2012 with savings for applications made but not decided before 9 July 2012 (HC 194).

Extension of stay as the spouse or civil partner of a person who has or has had leave to enter or remain in the United Kingdom under paragraphs 200–239

[**242B.** An extension of stay in the United Kingdom as:
(i) the spouse or civil partner of a person who has limited leave to enter or remain under paragraphs 200–239 may be granted for a period not in excess of that granted to the person with limited leave to enter or remain; or
(ii) the spouse or civil partner of a person who is being admitted at the same time for settlement or the spouse or civil partner of a person who has indefinite leave to remain may be granted for a period not exceeding 2 years, in both instances, provided the Secretary of State is satisfied that each of the requirements of paragraph 242A is met.]

Note: Paragraph 242B inserted from 2 April 2007 (HC 398).

Refusal of extension of stay as the spouse or civil partner of a person who has or has had leave to enter or remain in the United Kingdom under paragraphs 200–239

[**242C.** An extension of stay in the United Kingdom as the spouse or civil partner of a person who has or has had leave to enter or remain under paragraphs 200–239 is to be refused if the Secretary of State is not satisfied that each of the requirements of paragraph 242A is met.]

Note: Paragraph 242C inserted from 2 April 2007 (HC 398).

Requirements for indefinite leave to remain as the spouse or civil partner of a person who has or has had leave to enter or remain in the United Kingdom under paragraphs 200–239

[**242D.** The requirements to be met by a person seeking indefinite leave to remain in the United Kingdom as the spouse or civil partner of a person who has or has had leave to enter or remain in the United Kingdom under paragraphs 200–239 are that the applicant:
(i) is married to or civil partner of a person who has limited leave to enter or remain in the United Kingdom under paragraphs 200–239 and who is being granted indefinite leave to remain at the same time; or
(ii) is married to or civil partner of a person who has indefinite leave to remain in the United Kingdom and who had limited leave to enter or remain under paragraphs 200–239 immediately before being granted indefinite leave to remain; and
(iii) meets the requirements of paragraph 240 (ii) to (v);
(iv) has sufficient knowledge of the English language and sufficient knowledge about life in the United Kingdom, unless the applicant is under the age of 18 or aged 65 or over at the time he makes his application; and

(v) was admitted with a valid United Kingdom entry clearance for entry in this capacity [; and

(vi) does not have one or more unspent convictions within the meaning of the Rehabilitation of Offenders Act 1974] [; and

(vii) must not be in the UK in breach of immigration laws except that any period of overstaying for a period of 28 days or less will be disregarded.

Note: Paragraph 242D inserted from 2 April 2007 (HC 398). Sub-paragraph (vi) inserted from 6 April 2011 except for applications made but not decided before that date (HC 863). Sub-paragraph (vii) inserted from 1 October 2012 with savings for applications made but not decided before 9 July 2012 (HC 194).

Indefinite leave to remain as the spouse or civil partner of a person who has or has had leave to enter or remain in the United Kingdom under paragraphs 200–239.]

[242E. Indefinite leave to remain in the United Kingdom as the spouse or civil partner of a person who has or has had limited leave to enter or remain in the United Kingdom under paragraphs 200–239 may be granted provided the Secretary of State is satisfied that each of the requirements of paragraph 242D is met.]

Note: Paragraph 242E inserted from 2 April 2007 (HC 398).

Refusal of indefinite leave to remain as the spouse or civil partner of a person who has or has had leave to enter or remain in the United Kingdom under paragraphs 200–239

[242F. Indefinite leave to remain in the United Kingdom as the spouse or civil partner of a person who has or has had limited leave to enter or remain in the United Kingdom under paragraphs 200–239 is to be refused if the Secretary of State is not satisfied that each of the requirements of paragraph 242D is met.]

Note: Paragraph 242F inserted from 2 April 2007 (HC 398).

Children of persons with limited leave to enter or remain under paragraphs 200–239

Requirements for leave to enter or remain as the child of a person with limited leave to enter or remain in the United Kingdom under paragraphs 200–239

243. The requirements to be met by a person seeking leave to enter or remain in the United Kingdom as a child of a person with limited leave to enter or remain in the United Kingdom under paragraphs 200–239 are that:

(i) he is the child of a parent who has leave to enter or remain in the United Kingdom under paragraphs 200–239; and

(ii) he is under the age of 18 or has current leave to enter or remain in this capacity; and

(iii) he is unmarried [and is not a civil partner], has not formed an independent family unit and is not leading an independent life; and

(iv) he can and will be maintained and accommodated adequately without recourse to public funds in accommodation which his parent(s) own or occupy exclusively; and

(v) he will not stay in the United Kingdom beyond any period of leave granted to his parent(s); and

(vi) both parents are being or have been admitted to or allowed to remain in the United Kingdom save where:

(a) the parent he is accompanying or joining is his sole surviving parent; or

(b) the parent he is accompanying or joining has had sole responsibility for his upbringing; or

(c) there are serious and compelling family or other considerations which make exclusion from the United Kingdom undesirable and suitable arrangements have been made for his care; and

(vii) if seeking leave to enter, he holds a valid United Kingdom entry clearance for entry in this capacity or, if seeking leave to remain, was admitted with a valid United Kingdom entry clearance for entry in this capacity [; or

(viii) if seeking leave to remain, must not be in the UK in breach of immigration laws except that any period of overstaying for a period of 28 days or less will be disregarded.]

Note: Words in square brackets in sub-para (iii) inserted from 5 December 2005 (HC 582). Sub-paragraph (viii) inserted from 1 October 2012 with savings for applications made but not decided before 9 July 2012 (HC 194).

Leave to enter or remain as the child of a person with limited leave to enter or remain in the United Kingdom under paragraphs 200–239

244. A person seeking leave to enter or remain in the United Kingdom as the child of a person with limited leave to enter or remain in the United Kingdom under paragraphs 200–239 may be admitted to or allowed to remain in the United Kingdom for the same period of leave as that granted to the person given limited leave to enter or remain under paragraphs 200–239 provided that, in relation to an application for leave to enter, he is able to produce to the Immigration Officer, on arrival, a valid United Kingdom entry clearance for entry in this capacity or, in the case of an application for limited leave to remain, he was admitted with a valid United Kingdom entry clearance for entry in this capacity and is able to satisfy the Secretary of State that each of the requirements of paragraph 243(i)–(vi) [and (viii)] is met. An application for indefinite leave to remain in this category may be granted provided the applicant was admitted with a valid United Kingdom entry clearance for entry in this capacity and is able to satisfy the Secretary of State that each of the requirements of paragraph 243(i)–(vi) [and (viii)] is met and provided indefinite leave to remain is, at the same time, being granted to the person with limited leave to remain under paragraphs 200–239.

Note: Words in square brackets inserted from 1 October 2012 with savings for applications made but not decided before 9 July 2012 (HC 194).

Refusal of leave to enter or remain as the child of a person with limited leave to enter or remain in the United Kingdom under paragraphs 200–239

245. Leave to enter or remain in the United Kingdom as the child of a person with limited leave to enter or remain in the United Kingdom under paragraphs 200–239 is to be

refused if, in relation to an application for leave to enter, a valid United Kingdom entry clearance for entry in this capacity is not produced to the Immigration Officer on arrival or, in the case of an application for limited leave to remain, if the applicant was not admitted with a valid United Kingdom entry clearance for entry in this capacity or is unable to satisfy the Secretary of State that each of the requirements of paragraph 243(i)–(vi) [and (viii)] is met. An application for indefinite leave to remain in this capacity is to be refused if the applicant was not admitted with a valid United Kingdom entry clearance for entry in this capacity or is unable to satisfy the Secretary of State that each of the requirements of paragraph 243(i)–(vi) [and (viii)] is met or if indefinite leave to remain is not, at the same time, being granted to the person with limited leave to remain under paragraphs 200–239.

Note: Words in square brackets inserted from 1 October 2012 with savings for applications made but not decided before 9 July 2012 (HC 194).

Part 6A
Points-Based System

Note: Part 6A inserted from 29 February 2008 (HC 321) with transitional provisions and then substituted from 1 April 2008 (HC 321).

[245AA. Documents not submitted with applications

(a) Where Part 6A or any appendices referred to in Part 6A state that specified documents must be provided, the UK Border Agency will only consider documents that have been submitted with the application, and will only consider documents submitted after the application where subparagraph (b) applies.

(b) The sub-paragraph applies if the applicant has submitted:

(i) a sequence of documents and some of the documents in the sequence have been omitted (for example, if one bank statement from a series is missing);

(ii) a document in the wrong format; or

(iii) a document that is a copy and not an original document, the UK Border Agency will contact the applicant or his representative in writing, and request the correct documents. The requested documents must be received by the UK Border Agency at the address specified in the request within 7 working days of the date of the request.

(c) The UK Border Agency will not request documents where a specified document has not been submitted (for example an English language certificate is missing), or where the UK Border Agency does not anticipate that addressing the omission or error referred to in sub-paragraph (b) will lead to a grant because the application will be refused for other reasons.]

Note: New para 245AA inserted from 6 September 2012 (HC 565).

[245A. Specified documents for students previously sponsored by an overseas government or international scholarship agency

Where Part 6A of these Rules state that specified documents must be provided to show that a sponsoring government or international scholarship agency has provided its unconditional written consent to the application, the specified documents are original letters, on the official letter-headed paper or stationery of the organisation(s), bearing the official stamp of that organisation and issued by an authorised official of that organisation. The documents must confirm that the organisation gives the applicant unconditional consent to remain in or re-enter the UK for an unlimited time.]   ,

Note: Paragraph 245AA inserted from 30 June 2008 (HC 607) and sub-para (a) amended from 27 November 2008 (HC 1113). Sub-paragraph (c) inserted from 6 April 2010 (HC 439) subject to savings for applications made before 6 April 2010 and not decided before that date: see introduction to HC 439. Renumbered as para 245A from 6 April 2011 except for applications made but not decided before that date (HC 863). Paragraph 245A substituted from 20 July 2012 (Cm 8423).

[Tier 1 (Exceptional Talent) Migrants

[245B. Purpose

This route is for exceptionally talented individuals in the fields of science, humanities, engineering and the arts, who wish to work in the UK. These individuals are those who are already internationally recognised at the highest level as world leaders in their particular field, or who have already demonstrated exceptional promise [in the fields of science, humanities and engineering] and are likely to become world leaders in their particular area.]

Note: Previous paragraphs 245A to 245E deleted and paras 245B, 245BA, 245BB, 245BC, 245BD, 245BE, 245BF and 245C, 245CA, 245CB, 245CD inserted from 6 April 2011 except for applications made but not decided before that date (HC 863). Paragraph 245B substituted from 9 August 2011 (HC 1436) and words inserted from 1 October 2012 (HC 565).

245BA. Entry to the UK

All migrants arriving in the UK and wishing to enter as a Tier 1 (Exceptional Talent) Migrant must have a valid entry clearance for entry under this route. If they do not have a valid entry clearance, entry will be refused.

Note: Previous paragraphs 245A–245E deleted and paras 245B, 245BA, 245BB, 245BC, 245 BD, 245BE, 245BF and 245C, 245CA, 245CB, 245CD inserted from 6 April 2011 except for applications made but not decided before that date (HC 863).

245BB. Requirements for entry clearance

To qualify for entry clearance as a Tier 1 (Exceptional Talent) Migrant, an applicant must meet the requirements listed below. If the applicant meets these requirements, entry clearance will be granted. If the applicant does not meet these requirements, the application will be refused.

Requirements:

(a) The applicant must not fall for refusal under the general grounds for refusal.

[(c)] The applicant must have a minimum of 75 points under paragraphs 1 to 6 of Appendix A.

[(d)] an applicant who has, or was last granted, leave as a Student or a Postgraduate Doctor or Dentist, a Student Nurse, a Student Writing-Up a Thesis, a Student Re-Sitting an Examination or as a Tier 4 Migrant and:

(i) is currently being sponsored by a government or international scholarship agency, or

(ii) was being sponsored by a government or international scholarship agency, and that sponsorship came to an end 12 months ago or less,

must provide the unconditional written consent of the sponsoring Government or agency to the application and must provide [the specified documents as set out in paragraph 245A above], to show that this requirement has been met.

Note: Previous paras 245A–245E deleted and paras 245B, 245BA, 245BB, 245BC, 245BD, 245BE, 245BF and 245C, 245CA, 245CB, 245CD inserted from 6 April 2011 except for applications made but not decided before that date (HC 863). New sub-para (b) inserted and subsequent sub-paras renumbered from 9 August 2011 (HC 1436). Sub-para (b) then deleted from 1 October 2012 (HC 565). Words in square brackets in sub-para (d) substituted from 20 July 2012 (Cm 8423)

245BC. Period and conditions of grant

Entry clearance will be granted for a period of 3 years and 4 months and will be subject to the following conditions:

(i) no recourse to public funds,

(ii) registration with the police, if this is required by paragraph 326,

(iii) no employment as a Doctor or Dentist in Training, and

(iv) no employment as a professional sportsperson (including as a sports coach).

Note: Previous paras 245A–245E deleted and paras 245B, 245BA, 245BB, 245BC, 245BD, 245BE, 245BF and 245C, 245CA, 245CB, 245CD inserted from 6 April 2011 except for applications made but not decided before that date (HC 863).

245BD. Requirements for leave to remain

To qualify for leave to remain as a Tier 1 (Exceptional Talent) Migrant, an applicant must meet the requirements listed below. If the applicant meets these requirements, leave to remain will be granted. If the applicant does not meet these requirements, the application will be refused.

Requirements:

(a) The applicant must not fall for refusal under the general grounds for refusal, and must not be an illegal entrant.

(b) The applicant must have a minimum of 75 points under paragraphs 1 to 6 of Appendix A.

[(c) If the applicant has, or was last granted, leave as a Tier 1 (Exceptional Talent) Migrant, the applicant must have a minimum of 10 points under paragraphs 1 to 15 of Appendix B.]

[(d) The applicant must have, or have last been granted, entry clearance, leave to enter or remain as:

(i) a Tier 1 (Exceptional Talent) Migrant,

(ii) a Tier 2 (General) Migrant, or

(iii) as a Tier 5 (Temporary Worker) Migrant, sponsored in the Government Authorised Exchange sub-category in an exchange scheme for sponsored researchers.]

[(e) The applicant must not be in the UK in breach of immigration laws except that any period of overstaying for a period of 28 days or less will be disregarded.]

Note: Previous paras 245A–245E deleted and paras 245B, 245BA, 245BB, 245BC, 245BD, 245BE, 245BF and 245C, 245CA, 245CB, 245CD inserted from 6 April 2011 except for applications made but not decided before that date (HC 863). Sub-paragraph (c) substituted from 9 August 2011 (HC 1436). Sub-paragraph (c) substituted from 1 October 2012 (HC 565). Sub-paragraph (e) inserted from 1 October 2012 with savings for applications made but not decided before 9 July 2012 (HC 194). Sub-paragraph (d) substituted from 1 October 2012 (HC 565).

245BE. Period and conditions of grant

Leave to remain will be granted for a period of 2 years and will be subject to the following conditions:

  (i) no recourse to public funds,

  (ii) registration with the police, if this is required by paragraph 326,

  (iii) no employment as a Doctor or Dentist in Training, and

  (iv) no employment as a professional sportsperson (including as a sports coach).

Note: Previous paras 245A–245E deleted and paras 245B, 245BA, 245BB, 245BC, 245BD, 245BE, 245BF and 245C, 245CA, 245CB, 245CD inserted from 6 April 2011 except for applications made but not decided before that date (HC 863).

245BF. Requirements for indefinite leave to remain

To qualify for indefinite leave to remain, a Tier 1 (Exceptional Talent) Migrant must meet the requirements listed below. If the applicant meets these requirements, indefinite leave to remain will be granted. If the applicant does not meet these requirements, the application will be refused.

Requirements:

(a) The applicant must not have one or more unspent convictions within the meaning of the Rehabilitation of Offenders Act 1974.

(b) The applicant must not fall for refusal under the general grounds for refusal, and must not be an illegal entrant.

(c) The applicant must have spent a continuous period of 5 years lawfully in the UK with leave as a Tier 1 (Exceptional Talent) Migrant.

(d) The applicant must have a minimum of 75 points under paragraphs 1 to 6 of Appendix A.

(e) The applicant must have sufficient knowledge of the English language and sufficient knowledge about life in the United Kingdom, in accordance with paragraph 33BA of these Rules, unless the applicant is under the age of 18 or aged 65 or over at the date the application is made.

[(f) The applicant must not be in the UK in breach of immigration laws except that any period of overstaying for a period of 28 days or less will be disregarded.]

Note: Previous paras 245A–245E deleted and paras 245B, 245BA, 245BB, 245BC, 245BD, 245BE, 245BF and 245C, 245CA, 245CB, 245CD inserted from 6 April 2011 except for applications made but not decided before that date (HC 863). Sub-paragraph (f) inserted from 1 October 2012 with savings for applications made but not decided before 9 July 2012 (HC 194).

Tier 1 (General) Migrants

245C. Purpose

This route is for highly skilled migrants who wish to work, or become self-employed, to extend their stay in the UK.

Note: Previous paras 245A–245E deleted and paras 245B, 245BA, 245BB, 245BC, 245BD, 245BE, 245BF and 245C, 245CA, 245CB, 245CD inserted from 6 April 2011 except for applications made but not decided before that date (HC 863).

245CA. Requirements for leave to remain

To qualify for leave to remain as a Tier 1 (General) Migrant, an applicant must meet the requirements listed below. If the applicant meets these requirements, leave to remain will be granted. If the applicant does not meet these requirements, the application will be refused.

Requirements:

(a) The applicant must not fall for refusal under the general grounds for refusal, and must not be an illegal entrant.

(b) If the applicant has, or has had, leave as a Highly Skilled Migrant, as a Writer, Composer or Artist, Self-Employed Lawyer, or as a Tier 1 (General) Migrant under the Rules in place before 19 July 2010, and has not been granted leave in any categories other than these under the rules in place since 19 July 2010, the applicant must have 75 points under paragraphs 7 to 34 of Appendix A.

(c) In all cases other than those referred to in (b) above, the applicant must have 80 points under paragraphs 7 to 34 of Appendix A.

(d) The applicant must have 10 points under paragraphs [1 to 15] of Appendix B.

(e) The applicant must have 10 points under paragraphs 1 to 3 of Appendix C.

(f) The applicant must have, or have last been granted, entry clearance, leave to enter or remain:

    (i) as a Tier 1 (General) Migrant,

    (ii) as a Highly Skilled Migrant,

    (iii) as a Writer, Composer or Artist, or

    (iv) as a Self-Employed Lawyer.

[(g) The applicant must not be in the UK in breach of immigration laws except that any period of overstaying for a period of 28 days or less will be disregarded.]

Note: Previous paras 245A–245E deleted and paras 245B, 245BA, 245BB, 245BC, 245BD, 245BE, 245BF and 245C, 245CA, 245CB, 245CD inserted from 6 April 2011 except for applications made but not decided before that date (HC 863). Words in square brackets in sub-para (d) substituted from 6 April 2012 except for applications made but not decided before that date (HC 1888). Sub-paragraph (g) inserted from 1 October 2012 with savings for applications made but not decided before 9 July 2012 (HC 194).

245CB. Period and conditions of grant

(a) Leave to remain will be granted for a period of 2 years, to an applicant who has, or was last granted, leave as a Tier 1 (General) Migrant under the Rules in place before 6 April 2010.

(b) in all other cases, leave to remain will be granted for a period of 3 years.

(c) leave to remain under this route will be subject to the following conditions:

    (i) no recourse to public funds,

    (ii) registration with the police, if this is required by paragraph 326, and

    [(iii) no Employment as a Doctor or Dentist in Training, unless the applicant:

        (1) has obtained a primary degree in medicine or dentistry at bachelor's level or above from a UK institution that is a UK recognised or listed body, or which holds a sponsor licence under Tier 4 of the Points Based System, and provides evidence of this degree; or

        (2) has, or has last been granted, entry clearance, leave to enter or leave to remain that was not subject to any condition restricting him from taking employment as a Doctor in Training, has been employed during that leave as a Doctor in Training, and provides a letter from the Postgraduate Deanery or NHS Trust employing them which confirms that they have been working in a post or programme that has been approved by the Postgraduate Medical Education and Training Board as a training programme or post; or

        (3) has, or has last been granted, entry clearance, leave to enter or leave to remain that was not subject to any condition restricting him from taking employment as a Dentist in Training, has been employed during that leave as a Dentist in Training, and provides a letter from the Postgraduate Deanery or NHS Trust employing them which confirms that they have been working in a post or programme that has been approved by the Postgraduate Medical Education and Training Board as a training programme or post.]

    (iv) no employment as a professional sportsperson (including as a sports coach).

Note: Previous paras 245A–245E deleted and paras 245B, 245BA, 245BB, 245BC, 245BD, 245BE, 245BF and 245C, 245CA, 245CB, 245CD inserted from 6 April 2011 except for applications made but not decided before that date (HC 863). Sub-paragraph (c)(iii) substituted from 20 July 2012 (Cm 8423).

245CD. Requirements for indefinite leave to remain

To qualify for indefinite leave to remain, a Tier 1 (General) Migrant must meet the requirements listed below. If the applicant meets these requirements, indefinite leave to remain will be granted. If the applicant does not meet these requirements, the application will be refused.

Requirements:

(a) The applicant must not have one or more unspent convictions within the meaning of the Rehabilitation of Offenders Act 1974 [unless the applicant is applying under the terms {set out In Appendix S}].

(b) The applicant must not fall for refusal under the general grounds for refusal, and must not be an illegal entrant.

(c) Unless the application is being made under the terms{set out In Appendix S}, the applicant must have spent a continuous period of 5 years lawfully in the UK, of which the most recent period must have been spent with leave as a Tier 1 (General) Migrant, in any combination of the following categories:

    (i) as a Tier 1 (General) Migrant,

    (ii) as a Highly Skilled Migrant,

    (iii) as a Work Permit Holder,

    (iv) as an Innovator,

    (v) as a Self-Employed Lawyer,

    (vi) as a Writer, Composer or Artist,

(vii) as a Tier 2 (General) Migrant, a Tier 2 (Minister of Religion) Migrant or a Tier 2 (Sportsperson) Migrant, or

(viii) as a Tier 2 (Intra-Company Transfer) Migrant, provided the continuous period of 5 years spent lawfully in the UK includes a period of leave as a Tier 2 (Intra-Company Transfer) Migrant granted under the Rules in place before 6 April 2010.

(d) if the applicant has or has had leave as a Highly Skilled Migrant, a Writer, Composer or Artist, a Self- Employed Lawyer or as a Tier 1 (General) Migrant under the Rules in place before 19 July 2010, and has not been granted leave in any categories other than these under the rules in place since 19 July 2010, the applicant must have 75 points under paragraphs 7 to 34 of Appendix A.

(e) Where the application is being made under the terms {set out In Appendix S}, the applicant must have a continuous period of 4 years lawful leave in the UK, [or 5 years lawful leave in the UK if the applicant applied to the HSMP between 3 April 2006 and 7 November 2006, received an approval letter and came to or stayed in the United Kingdom on the basis of that letter,] of which the most recent must have been spent with leave as a Tier 1 (General) Migrant, in any combination of the following categories:

(i) as a Tier 1 (General) Migrant;

(ii) as a Highly Skilled Migrant;

(iii) as a Work Permit Holder; or

(iv) as an Innovator.

(f) Where the application is being made under the terms{set out In Appendix S}, the applicant must be economically active in the UK, in employment or self-employment or both.

(g) In all other cases than those referred to in (d) or (e) above, the applicant must have 80 points under paragraphs 7 to 34 of Appendix A.

(h) The applicant must have sufficient knowledge of the English language and sufficient knowledge about life in the United Kingdom, in accordance with paragraph 33BA, unless the applicant is under the age of 18 or aged 65 or over at the time the application is made or the applicant is applying under the terms{set out In Appendix S}.

[(i) The applicant must not be in the UK in breach of immigration laws except that any period of overstaying for a period of 28 days or less will be disregarded.]

Note: Previous paras 245A–245E deleted and paras 245B, 245BA, 245BB, 245BC, 245BD, 245BE, 245BF and 245C, 245CA, 245CB, 245CD inserted from 6 April 2011 except for applications made but not decided before that date (HC 863). Words in square brackets in para 245CD(a) and (e) inserted from 6 April 2011 except for applications made but not decided before that date (HC 908). Sub-paragraph (i) inserted from 1 October 2012 with savings for applications made but not decided before 9 July 2012 (HC 194). Words in curly brackets in sub-paras (a), (c), (e), (f) and (h) substituted from 6 September 2012 (HC 565).

[[245CE]. Transitional arrangements

This paragraph makes special provision for applicants who on 29 February 2008 are in the UK, or on 1 April are in India, and who are in the process of applying to become a Highly Skilled Migrant. It will also be relevant to applicants who have, or have last been granted, leave to remain as a Highly Skilled Migrant, …, and who fall within subparagraph (c) below.

(a) If an applicant has made an application for entry clearance in India as a Highly Skilled Migrant before 1 April 2008, and the application has not been decided before that date, it will be decided in accordance with the Rules in force on 31 March 2008 as set out in Appendix D.

(b) If an applicant has made an application for limited leave to remain as a Highly Skilled Migrant before 29 February 2008, and the application has not been decided before that date, it will be decided in accordance with these Rules in force on 28 February 2008 as set out in Appendix D.

(c) If an applicant has made an application in India for entry clearance on or after 1 April 2008, or has made an application in the UK for limited leave to remain on or after 29 February 2008, and has submitted with that application a valid Highly Skilled Migrant Programme Approval Letter, the applicant will be automatically awarded 75 points under Appendix A and 10 points under Appendix B. [The applicant must separately score 10 points under Appendix C.]

[(ca) If an applicant has made an application other than in India for entry clearance on or after 30 June 2008, and has submitted with that application a valid Highly Skilled Migrant Programme Approval Letter, the applicant will be automatically awarded 75 points under Appendix A and 10 points under Appendix B.] [The applicant must separately score 10 points under Appendix C.]

(d) ...

[(iia) The applicant must not be in the UK in breach of immigration laws except that any period of overstaying for a period of 28 days or less will be disregarded.

[(d) The applicant must not fall for refusal under the general grounds for refusal, and must not be an illegal entrant.

(e) If the requirements are met, leave to remain as a Tier 1 (General) Migrant will be granted for a period of 3 years, subject to the conditions in paragraph 245CB(c) above.]

Note: Sub-paragraph (ca) inserted from 30 June 2008 (HC 607). Sub-para (d) deleted from 27 November 2008 (HC 1113). Previously para 245F, renumbered as 245CE from 6 April 2011, except for applications made but not decided before that date (HC 863). Sub-paragraph (d)(iia) inserted from 1 October 2012 with savings for applications made but not decided before 9 July 2012 (HC 194). Sub-paragraphs (d) and (e) substituted from 20 July 2012 (Cm 8423).

Tier 1 (Entrepreneur) Migrants

[245D]. Purpose of this route and meaning of 'business'

(a) This route is for migrants who wish to establish, join or take over one or more businesses in the UK.

(b) For the purpose of [paragraphs 245D–245DF] and [paragraphs 35 to 53 of Appendix A] 'business' means an enterprise as:

    (i) a sole trader,

    (ii) a partnership, or

    (iii) a company registered in the UK.

Note: Paragraph 245H inserted from 30 June 2008 (HC 607). Renumbered as para 245D and words in square brackets substituted from 6 April 2011 except for applications made but not decided before that date (HC 836).

[245DA]. Entry to the UK

All migrants arriving in the UK and wishing to enter as a Tier 1 (Entrepreneur) Migrant must have a valid entry clearance for entry under this route. If they do not have a valid entry clearance, entry will be refused.

Note: Paragraph 245I inserted from 30 June 2008 (HC 607), renumbered as para 245DA from 6 April 2011 except for applications made but not decided before that date (HC 836).

[245DB]. Requirements for entry clearance

To qualify for entry clearance as a Tier 1 (Entrepreneur) Migrant, an applicant must meet the requirements listed below. If the applicant meets these requirements, entry clearance will be granted. If the applicant does not meet these requirements, the application will be refused.

Requirements:

(a) The applicant must not fall for refusal under the general grounds for refusal.

(b) The applicant must have a minimum of 75 points under [paragraphs 35 to 53 of Appendix A].

(c) The applicant must have a minimum of 10 points under [paragraphs 1 to 15 of] Appendix B.

(d) The applicant must have a minimum of 10 points under [paragraphs 1 to 2 of] Appendix C.

[(e) An applicant who has, or was last granted, leave as a Student or a Postgraduate Doctor or Dentist, a Student Nurse, a Student Writing up a Thesis, {a Student Re-Sitting an Examination or as a Tier 4 Migrant} and:

(i) is currently being sponsored by a government or international scholarship agency, or

(ii) was being sponsored by a government or international scholarship agency, and that sponsorship came to an end 12 months ago or less must provide the unconditional written consent of the sponsoring government or agency to the application and must provide the specified documents [as set out in paragraph 245A above] to show that this requirement has been met.]

Note: Paragraph 245J inserted from 30 June 2008 (HC 607). Words inserted in sub-paras (c) and (d) from 27 November 2008 (HC 1113), and words in (c) then substituted from 6 April 2012 except for applications made but not decided before that date (HC 1888). Sub-paragraph (e) inserted from 27 November 2008 (HC 1113) and amended from 31 March 2009 (HC 314). Renumbered as para 245DB and words in square brackets in sub-para (b) substituted from 6 April 2011, except for applications made but not decided before that date (HC 836). Words in square brackets in sub-para (e) inserted from 20 July 2012 (Cm 8423).

[245DC]. Period and conditions of grant

(a) Entry clearance will be granted for a period of 3 years [and four months] and will be subject to the following conditions:

(i) no recourse to public funds,

(ii) registration with the police, if this is required by paragraph 326 of these Rules, and

(iii) no employment other than working for the business(es) the applicant has established, joined or taken over [, and

(iv) no employment as a professional sportsperson (including as a sports coach).]

Note: Paragraph 245K inserted from 30 June 2008 (HC 607), renumbered as para 245DC and words in square brackets inserted from 6 April 2011 (HC 863).

[245DD]. Requirements for leave to remain

To qualify for leave to remain as a Tier 1 (Entrepreneur) Migrant under this rule, an applicant must meet the requirements listed below. If the applicant meets these requirements, leave to remain will be granted. If the applicant does not meet these requirements, the application will be refused.

Requirements:

(a) The applicant must not fall for refusal under the general grounds for refusal, and must not be an illegal entrant.

(b) The applicant must have a minimum of 75 points under [paragraphs 35 to 53 of Appendix A].

(c) The applicant must have a minimum of 10 points under [paragraphs 1 to 15 of] Appendix B.

(d) The applicant must have a minimum of 10 points under [paragraphs 1 to 2 of] Appendix C.

(e) The applicant who is applying for leave to remain must have, or have last been granted, entry clearance, leave to enter or remain:

    (i) as a Highly Skilled Migrant,

    (ii) as a Tier 1 (General) Migrant,

    (iii) as a Tier 1 (Entrepreneur) Migrant,

    (iv) as a Tier 1 (Investor) Migrant,

    [(v) as a Tier 1 (Graduate Entrepreneur) Migrant]

    [(vi)] as a Tier 1 (Post-Study Work) Migrant,

    [(vii)] as a Businessperson,

    [(viii)] as an Innovator,

    [(ix)] as an Investor,

    [(x)] as a Participant in the Fresh Talent: Working in Scotland Scheme,

    [(xi)] as a Participant in the International Graduates Scheme (or its predecessor, the Science and Engineering Graduates Scheme),

    [(xii)] as a Postgraduate Doctor or Dentist,

    [(xiii)] as a Self-employed Lawyer,

    [(xiv)] as a Student,

    [(xv)] as a Student Nurse,

    [(xvi)] as a Student Re-Sitting an Examination,

    [(xvii)] as a Student Writing Up a Thesis,

    [(xviii)] as a Work Permit Holder, or

    [(xix)] as a Writer, Composer or Artist.

    [(xx)] as a Tier 2 Migrant,]

    [(xxi)] as a Tier 4 Migrant][, or

    [(xxii)] as a Prospective Entrepreneur].

(f) An applicant who has, or was last granted, leave as a Student or a Postgraduate Doctor or Dentist [Student Nurse, Student Re-Sitting an Examination, {a Student Writing Up a Thesis or as a Tier 4 Migrant}] and:

(i) is currently being sponsored by a government or international scholarship agency, or

(ii) was being sponsored by a government or international scholarship agency, and that sponsorship came to an end 12 months ago or less, must provide the [unconditional] written consent of the sponsoring Government or agency to the application [and must provide the specified documents [as set out in paragraph 245A above] to show that this requirement has been met.]

[(g) The applicant must not be in the UK in breach of immigration laws except that any period of overstaying for a period of 28 days or less will be disregarded.]

Note: Paragraph 245L inserted from 30 June 2008 (HC 607). Words inserted in sub-paras (c) and (d) from 27 November 2008 (HC 1113), and words substituted in sub-para (c) from 6 April 2012 except for applications made but not decided before that date (HC 1888). Sub-paragraph (e) (xix) inserted from 27 November 2008 (HC 1113). Sub-paragraph (e)(xix)–(xx) inserted from 31 March 2009 (HC 314). Words in first and second square brackets inserted in sub-para. (f) from 27 November 2008 (HC 1113) and said insertion then amended from 31 March 2009 (HC 314). Words inserted into sub-para (f)(ii) from 27 November 2008 (HC 1113). Paragraph 245L renumbered as para 245DD, and sub-para (xxi) inserted from 6 April 2011 except for applications made but not decided before that date (HC 836). Sub-paragraph (v) inserted and subsequent sub-paras renumbered from (vi)–(xxii) from 6 April 2012 except for applications made but not decided before that date (HC 1888). Sub-paragraph (g) inserted from 1 October 2012 with savings for applications made but not decided before 9 July 2012 (HC 194). Words in third square brackets in sub-para (f) inserted from 20 July 2012 (Cm 8423).

[245DE]. Period, conditions and curtailment of grant

(a) Leave to remain will be granted:

(i) for a period of 2 years, to an applicant who has, or was last granted, leave as a Tier 1 (Entrepreneur) Migrant,

(ii) for a period of 3 years, to any other applicant.

(b) Leave to remain under this route will be subject to the following conditions:

(i) no recourse to public funds,

(ii) registration with the police, if this is required by paragraph 326 of these Rules, and

(iii) no employment, other than working for the business or businesses which he has established, joined or taken over [, and

(iv) no employment as a professional sportsperson (including as a sports coach).]

[(c) Without prejudice to the grounds for curtailment in paragraph 323 of these rules, leave to enter or remain granted to a Tier 1 (Entrepreneur) Migrant may be curtailed if, within [6 months] of the date specified in paragraph (d), the applicant has not done one or more of the following things:

(i) registered with HM Revenue and Customs as self-employed,

(ii) registered a new business in which he is a director, or

(iii) registered as a director of an existing business.

(d) The date referred to in paragraph (c) is:

(i) the date of the applicant's entry to the UK, in the case of an applicant granted entry clearance as a Tier 1 (Entrepreneur) Migrant where there is evidence to establish the applicant's date of entry to the UK,

(ii) the date of the grant of entry clearance to the applicant, in the case of an applicant granted entry clearance as a Tier 1 (Entrepreneur) Migrant where there is no evidence to establish the applicant's date of entry to the UK, or

(iii) the date of the grant of leave to remain to the applicant, in any other case.

(e) [Paragraph 245DE(c)] does not apply where the applicant's last grant of leave prior to the grant of the leave that he currently has was as a Tier 1 (Entrepreneur) Migrant, a Businessperson or an innovator.

Note: Paragraph 245M inserted from 30 June 2008 (HC 607). Heading amended and sub-paras (c)–(e) inserted from 27 November 2008 (HC 1113). Paragraph renumbered as 245DE; sub-para (b)(iv) inserted and words in square brackets in (c) and (e) substituted from 6 April 2011 except for applications made but decided before that date (HC 836).

[245DF. Requirements for Indefinite Leave to Remain

To qualify for indefinite leave to remain as a Tier 1 (Entrepreneur) Migrant, an applicant must meet the requirements listed below. If the applicant meets these requirements, indefinite leave to remain will be granted. If the applicant does not meet these requirements, the application will be refused.

Requirements:

(a) The applicant must not have one or more unspent convictions within the meaning of the Rehabilitation of Offenders Act 1974.

(b) The applicant must not fall for refusal under the general grounds for refusal, and must not be an illegal entrant.

(c) The applicant must have a minimum of 75 points under paragraphs 35 to 53 of Appendix A.

(d) The applicant must have sufficient knowledge of the English language and sufficient knowledge about life in the United Kingdom, in accordance with paragraph 33BA, unless the applicant is under the age of 18 or aged 65 or over at the date the application is made.]

[(e) The applicant must not be in the UK in breach of immigration laws except that any period of overstaying for a period of 28 days or less will be disregarded.]

Note: Paragraph 245N inserted from 30 June 2008 (HC 607), deleted and substituted and renumbered as para 245DF from 6 April 2011 except for applications made but not decided before that date (HC 245). Sub-paragraph (e) inserted from 1 October 2012 with savings for applications made but not decided before 9 July 2012 (HC 194).

Tier 1 (Investor) Migrants

[245E]. Purpose

This route is for high net worth individuals making a substantial financial investment to the UK.

Note: Paragraph 245O inserted from 30 June 2008 (HC 607), renumbered as para 245E from 6 April 2011 except for applications made but not decided before that date (HC 863).

[245EA]. Entry to the UK

All migrants arriving in the UK and wishing to enter as a Tier 1 (Investor) Migrant must have a valid entry clearance for entry under this route. If they do not have a valid entry clearance, entry will be refused.

Note: Paragraph 245P inserted from 30 June 2008 (HC 607), renumbered as para 245EA from 6 April 2011 except for applications made but not decided before that date (HC 863).

[245EB]. Requirements for entry clearance

To qualify for entry clearance or leave to remain as a Tier 1 (Investor) Migrant, an applicant must meet the requirements listed below. If the applicant meets these requirements, entry clearance will be granted. If the applicant does not meet these requirements, the application will be refused.

Requirements:

(a) The applicant must not fall for refusal under the general grounds for refusal.

(b) The applicant must have a minimum of 75 points under [paragraphs 54 to 65 of Appendix A].

[(c) An applicant who has, or was last granted, leave as a Student or a Postgraduate Doctor or Dentist, a Student Nurse, {a Student Re-Sitting an Examination, a Student Writing Up a Thesis or as a Tier 4 Migrant} and:

(i) is currently being sponsored by a government or international scholarship agency, or

(ii) was being sponsored by a government or international scholarship agency, and that sponsorship came to an end 12 months ago or less

must provide the unconditional written consent of the sponsoring government or agency to the application and must provide the specified documents [as set out in paragraph 245A above] to show that this requirement has been met.]

Note: Paragraph 245Q inserted from 30 June 2008 (HC 607). Sub-para (c) inserted from 27 November 2008 (HC 1113) and amended from 31 March 2009 (HC 314). Words in square brackets in sub-para (b) substituted and para renumbered as 245EB from 6 April 2011 except for applications made but not decided before that date (HC 863). Words inserted in sub-para (c) from 20 July 2012 (Cm 8423).

[245EC]. Period and conditions of grant

(a) Entry clearance will be granted for a period of 3 years [and four months] and will be subject to the following conditions:

(i) no recourse to public funds,

(ii) registration with the police, if this is required by paragraph 326 of these Rules, and

(iii) no employment as a doctor or dentist in training, unless the applicant has obtained a [primary degree] in medicine or dentistry at bachelor's level or above from a UK institution that is a UK recognised or listed body, or which holds a sponsor licence under Tier 4 of the Points Based System.]

Note: Paragraph 245R inserted from 30 June 2008 (HC 607). Sub-para (iii) substituted from 6 April 2010 (HC 439). Words in square brackets inserted and para renumbered as 245EC from 6 April 2011 except for applications made but not decided before that date (HC 863).

[245ED]. Requirements for leave to remain

To qualify for leave to remain as a Tier 1 (Investor) Migrant, an applicant must meet the requirements listed below. If the applicant meets these requirements, leave to remain will be granted. If the applicant does not meet these requirements, the application will be refused.

Requirements:

(a) The applicant must not fall for refusal under the general grounds for refusal, and must not be an illegal entrant.

(b) The applicant must have a minimum of 75 points under [paragraphs 54 to 65 of Appendix A].

(c) The applicant must have, or have last been granted, entry clearance, leave to enter or remain:

(i) as a Highly Skilled Migrant,

(ii) as a Tier 1 (General) Migrant,

(iii) as a Tier 1 (Entrepreneur) Migrant,

(iv) as a Tier 1 (Investor) Migrant,

(v) as a Tier 1 (Post-Study Work) Migrant,

(vi) as a Businessperson,

(vii) as an Innovator,

(viii) as an Investor,

(ix) as a Student,

(x) as a Student Nurse,

(xi) as a Student Re-Sitting an Examination,

(xii) as a Student Writing Up a Thesis,

(xiii) as a Work Permit Holder,

(xiv) as a Writer, Composer or Artist.

[(xv) as a Tier 2 Migrant, or]

[(xvi) as a Tier 4 Migrant.]

(d) An applicant who has, or was last granted, leave as a Student, [Student Nurse, Student Re-Sitting an Examination, {Student Writing Up a Thesis or as a Tier 4 Migrant}] and:

(i) is currently being sponsored by a government or international scholarship agency, or

(ii) was being sponsored by a government or international scholarship agency, and that sponsorship came to an end 12 months ago or less, must provide the [unconditional] written consent of the sponsoring government or agency to the application [and must provide the specified documents [as set out in paragraph 245A above] to show that this requirement has been met.]

[(e) The applicant must not be in the UK in breach of immigration laws except that any period of overstaying for a period of 28 days or less will be disregarded.]

Note: Paragraph 245S inserted from 30 June 2008 (HC 607). Sub-para (c)(xv) inserted from 27 November 2008 (HC 1113). Sub-para (xvi) inserted from 31 March 2009 (HC 314). Words inserted in sub-para (d) from 27 November 2008 (HC 1113) and inserted words amended from 31 March 2009 (HC 314). Words inserted in sub-para (d)(ii) from 27 November 2008 (HC 1113). Paragraph renumbered as para 245ED and words in square brackets in sub-para (b) inserted from 6 April except for applications made but not decided before that date 2011 (HC 836). Sub-paragraph (e) inserted from 1 October 2012 with savings for applications made but not decided before 9 July 2012 (HC 194). Words in fourth square brackets in sub-para (d) inserted from 20 July 2012 (Cm 8423).

[245EE]. Period, conditions and curtailment of grant

(a) Leave to remain will be granted:

(i) for a period of 2 years, to an applicant who has, or was last granted, leave as a Tier 1 (Investor) Migrant,

(ii) for a period of 3 years, to any other applicant.

(b) Leave to remain under this route will be subject to the following conditions:

(i) no recourse to public funds,

(ii) registration with the police, if this is required by paragraph 326 of these Rules, and

[(iii) no Employment as a Doctor or Dentist in Training, unless the applicant:

(1) has obtained a primary degree in medicine or dentistry at bachelor's level or above from a UK institution that is a UK recognised or listed body, or which holds a sponsor licence under Tier 4 of the Points Based System, and provides evidence of this degree; or

(2) has, or has last been granted, entry clearance, leave to enter or leave to remain that was not subject to any condition restricting him from taking employment as a Doctor in Training, has been employed during that leave as a Doctor in Training, and provides a letter from the Postgraduate Deanery or NHS Trust employing them which confirms that they have been working in a post or programme that has been approved by the Postgraduate Medical Education and Training Board as a training programme or post; or

(3) has, or has last been granted, entry clearance, leave to enter or leave to remain that was not subject to any condition restricting him from taking employment as a Dentist in Training, has been employed during that leave as a Dentist in Training, and provides a letter from the Postgraduate Deanery or NHS Trust employing them which confirms that they have been working in a post or programme that has been approved by the Postgraduate Medical Education and Training Board as a training programme or post.]

[(c) Without prejudice to the grounds for curtailment in paragraph 323 of these Rules, leave to enter or remain as a Tier 1 (Investor) Migrant may be curtailed if within 3 months of the date specified in paragraph (d), the applicant has not invested, or had invested on his behalf, at least £750,000 of his capital in the UK by way of UK Government bonds, share capital or loan capital in active and trading UK registered companies other than those principally engaged in property investment.

(d) The date referred to in paragraph (c) is:

(i) the date of the applicant's entry to the UK, in the case of an applicant granted entry clearance as a Tier 1 (Investor) Migrant where there is evidence to establish the applicant's date of entry to the UK,

(ii) the date of the grant of entry clearance to the applicant, in the case of an applicant granted entry clearance as a Tier 1 (Investor) Migrant where there is no evidence to establish the applicant's date of entry to the UK, or

(iii) the date of the grant of leave to remain to the applicant, in any other case.

(e) Paragraph [245EE(c)] does not apply where the applicant's last grant of leave prior to the grant of the leave that he currently has was as a Tier 1 (Investor) Migrant or as an Investor.

Note: Paragraph 245T inserted from 30 June 2008 (HC 607). Heading substituted from 27 November 2008 (HC 1113). Sub-paragraphs (b)(iii) substituted from 27 November 2008 (HC 1113). Sub-paragraphs (c)–(e) inserted from 27 November 2009 (HC 1113). Paragraph renumbered as 245EE, sub-para (b)(ii) and words in square brackets in sub-para (e) substituted from 6 April 2011 except for applications made but not decided before that date (HC 863). Sub-paragraph (b)(iii) substituted from 20 July 2012 (Cm 8423).

245EF. Requirements for indefinite leave to remain

To qualify for indefinite leave to remain, a Tier 1 (Investor) Migrant must meet the requirements listed below. If the applicant meets these requirements, indefinite leave to remain will be granted. If the applicant does not meet these requirements, the application will be refused.

Requirements:

(a) The applicant must not have one or more unspent convictions within the meaning of the Rehabilitation of Offenders Act 1974.

(b) The applicant must not fall for refusal under the general grounds for refusal, and must not be an illegal entrant.

(c) The applicant must have a minimum of 75 points under paragraphs 54 to 65 of Appendix A.

(d) The applicant must have sufficient knowledge of the English language and sufficient knowledge about life in the United Kingdom, in accordance with paragraph 33BA, unless the applicant is under the age of 18 or aged 65 or over at the date the application is made.]

[(e) The applicant must not be in the UK in breach of immigration laws except that any period of overstaying for a period of 28 days or less will be disregarded.]

Note: Paragraph 245U deleted and substituted and renumbered as para 245EF from 6 April 2011 except for applications made but not decided before that date (HC 836). Sub-paragraph (e) inserted from 9 July 2012 with savings for applications made but not decided before 9 July 2012 (HC 194).

[Tier 1 (Graduate Entrepreneur) Migrants

245F. Purpose of the route and meaning of business

(a) This route is for graduates who have been identified by Higher Education Institutions as having developed world class innovative ideas or entrepreneurial skills to extend their stay in the UK after graduation to establish one or more businesses in the UK.

(b) For the purpose of paragraphs 245F to 245FB and paragraphs 66 to 72 of Appendix A a 'business' means an enterprise as:

  (i) a sole trader,
  (ii) a partnership, or
  (iii) a company registered in the UK.

Note: Paragraph 245F substituted from 6 April 2012 except for applications made but not decided before that date (HC 1888).

245FA. Requirements for leave to remain

To qualify for leave to remain as a Tier 1 (Graduate Entrepreneur) Migrant, an applicant must meet the requirements listed below. If the applicant meets these requirements, leave to remain will be granted. If the applicant does not meet these requirements, the application will be refused.

Requirements:

(a) The applicant must not fall for refusal under the general grounds for refusal, and must not be an illegal entrant.

(b) The applicant must have a minimum of 75 points under paragraphs 66 to 72 of Appendix A.

(c) The applicant must have a minimum of 10 points under paragraph 9 of Appendix B.

(d) The applicant must have a minimum of 10 points under paragraphs 1 to 2 of Appendix C.

(e) The applicant must have, or have last been granted, entry clearance, leave to enter or remain:

    (i) as a Tier 4 Migrant,

    (ii) as a Student,

    (iii) as a Student Nurse,

    (iv) as a Student Re-sitting an Examination,

    (v) as a Student Writing Up a Thesis,

    (vi) as a Postgraduate Doctor or Dentist, or

    (vii) as a Tier 1 (Graduate Entrepreneur) Migrant.

(f) The applicant must not have previously been granted entry clearance, leave to enter or remain as a Tier 1 (Post-Study Work) Migrant, a Participant in the Fresh Talent: Working in Scotland Scheme, or a Participant in the International Graduates Scheme (or its predecessor, the Science and Engineering Graduates Scheme).

(g) The applicant must not previously have been granted leave as a Tier 1 (Graduate Entrepreneur) Migrant on more than 1 occasion.

(h) An applicant who does not have, or was not last granted, leave to remain as a Tier 1 (Graduate Entrepreneur) Migrant and:

    (i) is currently being sponsored in his studies by a government or international scholarship agency, or

    (ii) was being sponsored in his studies by a government or international scholarship agency, and that sponsorship came to an end 12 months ago or less,

    must provide the unconditional written consent of the sponsoring government or agency to the application and must provide the specified documents [as set out in paragraph 245A above,] to show that this requirement has been met.

[(i) The applicant must not be in the UK in breach of immigration laws except that any period of overstaying for a period of 28 days or less will be disregarded.]

Note: Paragraph 245FA substituted from 6 April 2012 except for applications made but not decided before that date (HC 1888). Sub-paragraph (i) inserted from 1 October 2012 with savings for applications made but not decided before 9 July 2012 (HC 194). Words inserted in sub-para (h) from 20 July 2012 (Cm 8423).

245FB. Period and conditions of grant

Leave to remain will be granted for a period of 1 year and will be subject to the following conditions:

    (i) no recourse to public funds,

    (ii) registration with the police, if this is required by paragraph 326 of these Rules,

    (iii) no employment except: (1) working for the business(es) the applicant has established and (2) other employment of no more than 20 hours per week,

    (iv) no employment as a Doctor or Dentist in Training, and

    (v) no employment as a professional sportsperson (including as a sports coach).

Note: Paragraph 245FB substituted from 6 April 2012 except for applications made but not decided before that date (HC 1888).

Tier 2 Migrants

[Tier 2 (Intra-Company Transfer) Migrants

245G. Purpose of this route and definitions

This route enables multinational employers to transfer their existing employees from outside the EEA to their UK branch for training purposes or to fill a specific vacancy that cannot be filled by a British or EEA worker. There are four sub-categories in this route:

(i) Short Term Staff: for established employees of multi-national companies who are being transferred to a skilled job in the UK for 12 months or less that could not be carried out by a new recruit from the resident workforce;

(ii) Long Term Staff: for established employees of multi-national companies who are being transferred to a skilled job in the UK which will, or may, last for more than 12 months and could not be carried out by a new recruit from the resident workforce;

(iii) Graduate Trainee: for recent graduate recruits of multi-national companies who are being transferred to the UK branch of the same organisation as part of a structured graduate training programme, which clearly defines progression towards a managerial or specialist role;

(iv) Skills Transfer: for overseas employees of multi-national companies who are being transferred to the UK branch of the same organisation in a graduate occupation to learn the skills and knowledge they will need to perform their jobs overseas, or to impart their specialist skills to the UK workforce.

Note: Previous paras 245ZB–245ZH deleted and substituted by paras 245G–245HF from 6 April 2011 except for applications made but not decided before that date (HC 863).

245GA. Entry clearance

All migrants arriving in the UK and wishing to enter as a Tier 2 (Intra-Company Transfer) Migrant must have a valid entry clearance for entry under this route. If they do not have a valid entry clearance, entry will be refused.

Note: Previous paras 245ZB–245ZH deleted and substituted by paras 245G–245HF from 6 April 2011 except for applications made but not decided before that date (HC 863).

245GB. Requirements for entry clearance

To qualify for entry clearance as a Tier 2 (Intra-Company Transfer) Migrant, an applicant must meet the requirements listed below. If the applicant meets these requirements, entry clearance will be granted. If the applicant does not meet these requirements, the application will be refused.

Requirements:

(a) The applicant must not fall for refusal under the general grounds for refusal.

(b) The applicant must have a minimum of 50 points under paragraphs 73 to 75E of Appendix A.

(c) The applicant must have a minimum of 10 points under paragraphs 4 to 5 of Appendix C.

(d) The applicant must not have had entry clearance or leave to remain as a [Tier 2 Migrant] at any time during the 12 months immediately before the date of the application, regardless of whether he was in the UK during that time, unless paragraph (e) below applies.

(e) Paragraph (d) above does not apply to an applicant who is applying under the Long Term Staff sub-category and who has, or last had entry clearance or leave to remain as a Tier 2 (Intra-Company Transfer) Migrant in the Short Term Staff, Graduate Trainee or Skills Transfer sub-categories, or under the Rules in place before 6 April 2011.

(f) An applicant who has, or was last granted, leave as a Student, a Student Nurse, a Student Re-Sitting an Examination, a Student Writing-Up a Thesis, a Postgraduate Doctor or Dentist or a Tier 4 Migrant and:

   (i) is currently being sponsored by a government or international scholarship agency, or

   (ii) was being sponsored by a government or international scholarship agency, and that sponsorship came to an end 12 months ago or less,

   must provide the unconditional written consent of the sponsoring Government or agency to the application and must provide the specified documents [as set out in paragraph 245A above,] to show that this requirement has been met.

(g) The applicant must be at least 16 years old.

(h) Where the applicant is under 18 years of age, the application must be supported by the applicant's parents or legal guardian, or by one parent if that parent has sole legal responsibility for the child.

(i) Where the applicant is under 18 years of age, the applicant's parents or legal guardian, or just one parent if that parent has sole responsibility for the child, must confirm that they consent to the arrangements for the applicant's travel to, and reception and care in, the UK.

Note: Previous paras 245ZB–245ZH deleted and substituted by paras 245G–245HF from 6 April 2011 except for applications made but not decided before that date (HC 863). Words in square brackets in (d) substituted from 6 April 2012 except for applications made but not decided before that date (HC 1888). Words inserted in (f) from 20 July 2012 (Cm 8423).

245GC. Period and conditions of grant

(a) If the applicant is applying as a Tier 2 (Intra-Company Transfer) Migrant in either of the Short Term Staff or Graduate Trainee sub-categories, entry clearance will be granted for:

   (i) a period equal to the length of the period of engagement plus 1 month, or

   (ii) a period of 1 year, whichever is the shorter.

(b) if the applicant is applying as a Tier 2 (Intra-Company Transfer) Migrant in the Skills Transfer sub-category, entry clearance will be granted for:

   (i) a period equal to the length of the period of engagement plus 1 month, or

   (ii) a period of 6 months, whichever is the shorter.

(c) if the applicant is applying as a Tier 2 (Intra-Company Transfer) Migrant in the Long Term Staff sub-category, entry clearance will be granted for:

   (i) a period equal to the length of the period of engagement plus 1 month, or

   (ii) a period of 3 years and 1 month, whichever is the shorter.

(d) Entry clearance will be granted with effect from 14 days before the date that the Certificate of Sponsorship Checking Service records as the start date for the applicant's employment in the UK, unless entry clearance is being granted less than 14 days before that date, in which case it will be granted with immediate effect.

(e) Entry clearance will be subject to the following conditions:

(i) no recourse to public funds,

(ii) registration with the police, if this is required by paragraph 326, and

(iii) no employment except:

(1) working for the Sponsor in the employment that the Certificate of Sponsorship Checking Service records that the migrant is being sponsored to do, [subject to any notification of a change to the details of that employment, other than prohibited changes as defined in paragraph 323AA,]

(2) supplementary employment, and

(3) voluntary work.

Note: Previous paras 245ZB–245ZH deleted and substituted by paras 245G–245HF from 6 April 2011 except for applications made but not decided before that date (HC 863). Words substituted in sub-para (e)(iii)(1) from 20 July 2012 (Cm 8423).

245GD. Requirements for leave to remain

To qualify for leave to remain as a Tier 2 (Intra-Company Transfer) Migrant under this rule, an applicant must meet the requirements listed below. If the applicant meets these requirements, leave to remain will be granted. If the applicant does not meet these requirements, the application will be refused.

Requirements:

(a) The applicant must not fall for refusal under the general grounds for refusal, and must not be an illegal entrant.

(b) If the applicant is applying for leave to remain as a Tier 2 (Intra-Company Transfer) Migrant in the Long Term staff sub-category:

(i) the applicant must have, or have last been granted, entry clearance, leave to enter or leave to remain as either:

(1) a Tier 2 (Intra-Company Transfer) Migrant in the Long Term Staff sub-category, or

(2) a Tier 2 (Intra-Company Transfer) Migrant in the Established Staff sub-category under the Rules in place before 6 April 2011, or

(3) a Tier 2 (Intra-Company Transfer) Migrant granted under the Rules in place before 6 April 2010, or

(4) a Qualifying Work Permit Holder, provided that the work permit was granted because the applicant was the subject of an intra-company transfer, or

(5) as a Representative of an Overseas Business, and

(ii) the applicant must still be working for the same employer as he was at the time of that earlier grant of leave.

(c) if the applicant is applying for leave to remain as a Tier 2 (Intra-Company Transfer) Migrant in the Short Term Staff sub-category:

(i) the applicant must have, or have last been granted, entry clearance, leave to enter or leave to remain as a Tier 2 (Intra-Company Transfer) Migrant in the short Term Staff sub-category, and

(ii) the applicant must still be working for the same employer as he was at the time of that earlier grant of leave.

(d) if the applicant is applying for leave to remain as a Tier 2 (Intra-Company Transfer) Migrant in the Graduate Trainee sub-category:

(i) the applicant must have, or have last been granted, entry clearance, leave to enter or leave to remain as a Tier 2 (Intra-Company Transfer) Migrant in the Graduate Trainee sub-category, and

(ii) the applicant must still be working for the same employer as he was at the time of that earlier grant of leave.

(e) if the applicant is applying for leave to remain as a Tier 2 (Intra-Company Transfer) Migrant in the Skills Transfer sub-category:

(i) the applicant must have, or have last been granted, entry clearance, leave to enter or leave to remain as a Tier 2 (Intra-Company Transfer) Migrant in the Skills Transfer sub-category, and

(ii) the applicant must still be working for the same employer as he was at the time of that earlier grant of leave.

(f) In all cases the applicant must have a minimum of 50 points under paragraphs 73 to 75E of Appendix A.

(g) If the applicant is seeking a grant of leave to remain that would extend his total stay as a Tier 2 (Intra-Company Transfer) Migrant beyond 3 years, the applicant must have a minimum of 10 points under [paragraphs 1 to 16] of Appendix B.

(h) The applicant must have a minimum of 10 points under paragraphs 4 to 5 of appendix C.

(i) The applicant must be at least 16 years old.

(j) Where the applicant is under 18 years of age, the application must be supported by the applicant's parents or legal guardian, or by one parent if that parent has sole legal responsibility for the child.

(k) Where the applicant is under 18 years of age, the applicant's parents or legal guardian, or one parent if that parent has sole legal responsibility for the child, must confirm that they consent to the arrangements for the applicant's care in the UK.

[(l) The applicant must not be in the UK in breach of immigration laws except that any period of overstaying for a period of 28 days or less will be disregarded.]

Note: Previous paras 245ZB–245ZH deleted and substituted by paras 245G–245HF from 6 April 2011 except for applications made but not decided before that date (HC 863). Words in square brackets in sub-para (g) substituted from 6 April 2012 except for applications made but not decided before that date (HC 1888). Sub-paragraph (l) inserted from 1 October 2012 with savings for applications made but not decided before 9 July 2012 (HC 194).

245GE. Period and conditions of grant

(a) If the applicant is applying for leave to remain as a Tier 2 (intra-Company Transfer) Migrant in either the Short Term Staff or Graduate Trainee sub-categories, leave to remain will be granted for:

(i) the length of the period of engagement plus 14 days, or

(ii) the difference between the period of leave that the applicant has already been granted, beginning with his last grant of entry clearance as a Tier 2 (Intra-Company Transfer) Migrant, and 12 months,

whichever is the shorter. If the calculation of period of leave comes to zero or a negative number, leave to remain will be refused.

(b) If the applicant is applying for leave to remain as a Tier 2 (Intra-Company Transfer) Migrant in the Skills Transfer sub-category, leave to remain will be granted for:

(i) the length of the period of engagement plus 14 days, or

(ii) the difference between the period of leave that the applicant has already been granted, beginning with his last grant of entry clearance as a Tier 2 (Intra-Company Transfer) Migrant, and 6 months,

whichever is the shorter. If the calculation of period of leave comes to zero or a negative number, leave to remain will be refused.

[(c) In the cases set out in paragraph (d) below, leave to remain will be granted for:

(i) a period equal to the length of the period of engagement plus 14 days, or

(ii) a period of 3 years plus 14 days,

whichever is the shorter.]

(d) The cases referred to in paragraph (c) are those where the applicant is applying for leave to remain as a Tier 2 (Intra-Company Transfer) Migrant in the Long Term Staff sub-category, and was last granted:

(i) entry clearance, leave to enter or leave to remain as a Qualifying Work Permit Holder, or

(ii) leave to remain as a Tier 2 (Intra-Company Transfer) Migrant, provided:

(1) he previously had leave as a Qualifying Work Permit Holder,

(2) at some time during that period of leave as a Qualifying Work Permit Holder he was granted leave to remain as a Tier 2 (Intra-Company Transfer) Migrant,

(3) he has not been granted entry clearance in this or any other route since his last grant of leave as a Qualifying Work Permit Holder, and

(4) he is still working for the same employer named on the Work Permit document which led to his last grant of leave as a Qualifying Work Permit Holder.

(e) In the cases set out in paragraph (f) below, leave to remain will be granted for:

(i) a period equal to the length of the period of engagement plus 14 days, or

(ii) a period of 2 years,

whichever is the shorter.

[[(f) The cases referred to in paragraph (e) are those where:

(i) the applicant is applying for leave to remain as a Tier 2 (Intra-Company Transfer) Migrant in the Long Term Staff sub-category, and

(ii) the applicant previously had leave as a Tier 2 (Intra-Company Transfer) Migrant under the rules in place before 6 April 2011; and

(iii) the applicant has not been granted entry clearance in this or any other route since the grant of leave referred to in (ii) above; and

(iv) paragraphs (c) to (d) do not apply.]

(g) if the applicant is applying for leave to remain as a Tier 2 (Intra-Company Transfer) Migrant in the Long Term Staff sub-category and [paragraphs (c) to (f)] do not apply, leave to remain will be granted for:

(i) a period equal to the length of the period of engagement plus 14 days, or

(ii) a period of 2 years,

(iii) the difference between the period that the applicant has already spent in the UK since his last grant of entry clearance as a Tier 2 (Intra-Company Transfer) Migrant and 5 years, whichever is the shorter. If the calculation of period of leave comes to zero or a negative number, leave to remain will be refused.

(h) In addition to the periods in [paragraphs (a) to (g)], leave to remain will be granted for the period between the date that the application is decided and the date that the Certificate of Sponsorship Checking Service records as the start date of employment in the UK, provided this is not a negative value.

(i) Leave to remain will be granted subject to the following conditions:

(i) no recourse to public funds,

(ii) registration with the police, if this is required by paragraph 326, and

(iii) no employment except:

(1) working for the Sponsor in the employment that the Certificate of Sponsorship Checking Service records that the migrant is being sponsored to do, [subject to any notification of a change to the details of that employment, other than prohibited changes as defined in paragraph 323AA,]

(2) supplementary employment, and

(3) voluntary work.

Note: Previous paras 245ZB–245ZH deleted and substituted by paras 245G–245HF from 6 April 2011 except for applications made but not decided before that date (HC 863). Words in square brackets in sub-paras (g) and (h) substituted from 21 April 2011 except for applications made but not decided before that date (HC 908). Sub-paragraph (f) substituted from 4 July 2011 except for applications made but not decided before that date (HC 1148). Sub-paragraph (c) substituted from 6 April 2012 except for applications made but not decided before that date (HC 1888). Words substituted in sub-para (h)(iii)(1) form 20 July 2012 (Cm 8423).

245GF. Requirements for indefinite leave to remain

To qualify for indefinite leave to remain as a Tier 2 (Intra-Company Transfer) Migrant, an applicant must meet the requirements listed below. If the applicant meets these requirements, indefinite leave to remain will be granted. If the applicant does not meet these requirements, the application will be refused.

Requirements:

(a) The applicant must not have one or more unspent convictions within the meaning of the Rehabilitation of Offenders Act 1974.

(b) The applicant must not fall for refusal under the general grounds for refusal, and must not be an illegal entrant.

(c) The applicant must have spent a continuous period of 5 years lawfully in the UK, of which the most recent period must have been spent with leave as a Tier 2 (Intra-Company Transfer) Migrant, in any combination of the following categories:

(i) as a Tier 2 (Intra-Company Transfer) Migrant,

(ii) as a Qualifying Work Permit Holder, or

(iii) as a Representative of an Overseas Business.

(d) The continuous period of 5 years referred to in paragraph (b) must include a period of leave as:

(i) a Tier 2 (Intra-Company Transfer) Migrant granted under the Rules in place before 6 April 2010, or

(ii) a Qualifying Work Permit Holder, provided that the work permit was granted because the applicant was the subject of an intra-company transfer.

(e) The Sponsor that issued the Certificate of Sponsorship that led to the applicant's last grant of leave must certify in writing that:

(i) he still requires the applicant for the employment in question, and

(ii) [.......] he is paid at or above the appropriate rate for the job as stated in [the Codes of Practice in Appendix J].

[(f) The applicant provides [the specified documents in paragraph 245GF-SD] to evidence the sponsor's certification in subsection (e)(ii)]

[(g)] The applicant must have sufficient knowledge of the English language and sufficient knowledge about life in the United Kingdom, in accordance with paragraph 33BA of these Rules, unless the applicant is under the age of 18 or aged 65 or over at the date the application is made.

[(h) The applicant must not be in the UK in breach of immigration laws except that any period of overstaying for a period of 28 days or less will be disregarded.]

Note: Previous paras 245ZB–245ZH deleted and substituted by paras 245G–245HF from 6 April 2011 except for applications made but not decided before that date (HC 863). Sub-paragraph (f) inserted and subsequent sub-para renumbered as (g), words omitted from (e)(ii) from 31 October

2011 except for applications made but not decided before that date (HC 1551). Sub-paragraph (h) inserted from 1 October 2012 with savings for applications made but not decided before 9 July 2012 (HC 194). Words substituted in sub-paras (e)(ii) and (f) from 20 July 2012 (Cm 8423).

[245GF-SD. Specified documents

The specified documents referred to in paragraph 245GF(f) are either a payslip and a personal bank or building society statement, or a payslip and a building society pass book.

(a) Payslips must be:
   (i) the applicant's most recent payslip,
  (ii) dated no earlier than one calendar month before the date of the application, and
  (iii) either:
     (1) an original payslip,
     (2) on company-headed paper, or
     (3) accompanied by a letter from the applicant's Sponsor, on company headed paper and signed by a senior official, confirming the payslip is authentic.

(b) Personal bank or building society statements must:
   (i) be the most applicant's most recent statement,
  (ii) be dated no earlier than one calendar month before the date of the application,
  (iii) clearly show:
     (1) the applicant's name,
     (2) the applicant's account number,
     (3) the date of the statement,
     (4) the financial institution's name,
     (5) the financial institution's logo, and
     (6) transactions by the Sponsor covering the period no earlier than one calendar month before the date of the application,
  (iv) be either:
     (1) printed on the bank's or building society's letterhead,
     (2) electronic bank or building society statements from an online account, accompanied by a supporting letter from the bank or building society, on company headed paper, confirming the statement provided is authentic, or
     (3) electronic bank or building society statements from an online account, bearing the official stamp of the bank or building society on every page, and
   (v) not be mini-statements from automatic teller machines (ATMs).

(c) Building society pass books must:
   (i) clearly show:
     (1) the applicant's name,
     (2) the applicant's account number,
     (3) the financial institution's name,
     (4) the financial institution's logo, and
     (5) transactions by the sponsor covering the period no earlier than one calendar month before the date of the application,
   and
  (ii) be either:
     (1) the original pass book, or
     (2) a photocopy of the pass book which has been certified by the issuing building society on company headed paper, confirming the statement provided is authentic.]

Note: Paragraph 245GF–SD inserted from 20 July 2012 (Cm 8423).

Tier 2 (General) Migrants, Tier 2 (Minister of Religion) Migrants and Tier 2
(Sportsperson) Migrants

245H. Purpose of these routes and definitions

These routes enable UK employers to recruit workers from outside the EEA to fill a particular vacancy that cannot be filled by a British or EEA worker.

Note: Previous paras 245ZB–245ZH deleted and substituted by paras 245G–245HF from 6 April
2011 except for applications made but not decided before that date (HC 863).

245HA. Entry clearance

All migrants arriving in the UK and wishing to enter as a Tier 2 (General) Migrant, Tier 2
(Minister of Religion) Migrant or Tier 2 (Sportsperson) Migrant must have a valid entry
clearance for entry under the relevant one of these routes. If they do not have a valid entry
clearance, entry will be refused.

Note: Previous paras 245ZB–245ZH deleted and substituted by paras 245G–245HF from 6 April
2011 except for applications made but not decided before that date (HC 863).

245HB. Requirements for entry clearance

To qualify for entry clearance as a Tier 2 (General) Migrant, Tier 2 (Minister of
Religion) Migrant or Tier 2 (Sportsperson) Migrant, an applicant must meet the
requirements listed below. If the applicant meets these requirements, entry clearance
will be granted. If the applicant does not meet these requirements, the application will
be refused.

Requirements:

(a) The applicant must not fall for refusal under the general grounds for refusal.

(b) If applying as a Tier 2 (General) Migrant, the applicant must have a minimum of 50
points under paragraphs 76 to 84A of Appendix A.

(c) If applying as a Tier 2 (Minister of Religion) Migrant, the applicant must have a
minimum of 50 points under paragraphs 85 to 92 of Appendix A.

(d) If applying as a Tier 2 (Sportsperson) Migrant, the applicant must have a minimum
of 50 points under paragraphs 93 to 100 of Appendix A.

(e) The applicant must have a minimum of 10 points under [paragraphs 1 to 18] of
Appendix B.

(f) The applicant must have a minimum of 10 points under paragraphs 4 to 5 of
Appendix C.

[(g) The applicant must not have had entry clearance or leave to remain as a Tier 2
Migrant at any time during the 12 months immediately before the date of the application,
regardless of whether he was in the UK during that time.]

[(h)] an applicant who has, or was last granted, leave as a Student, a Student Nurse,
a Student Re-Sitting an Examination, a Student Writing-Up a Thesis, a Postgraduate
Doctor or Dentist or a Tier 4 Migrant and:

(i) is currently being sponsored by a government or international scholarship
agency, or

(ii) was being sponsored by a government or international scholarship agency, and
that sponsorship came to an end 12 months ago or less

must provide the unconditional written consent of the sponsoring Government or agency to the application and must provide the specified documents [as set out in paragraph 245A above] to show that this requirement has been met.

[(i)] The applicant must be at least 16 years old.

[(j)] Where the applicant is under 18 years of age, the application must be supported by the applicant's parents or legal guardian, or by one parent if that parent has sole legal responsibility for the child.

[(k)] Where the applicant is under 18 years of age, the applicant's parents or legal guardian, or one parent if that parent has sole responsibility for the child, must confirm that they consent to the arrangements for the applicant's travel to, and reception and care in, the UK.

[(l)] If the sponsor is a limited company, the applicant must not own more than 10% of its shares.

Note: Previous paras 245ZB–245ZH deleted and substituted by paras 245G–245HF from 6 April 2011 except for applications made but not decided before that date (HC 863). Words in square brackets in sub-para (e) substituted, subsequent sub-paras renumbered as (h)–(l), and sub-para (g) inserted from 6 April 2012 except for applications made but not decided before that date (HC 1888). Words inserted in (h) from 20 July 2012 (Cm 8423).

245HC. Period and conditions of grant

(a) Entry clearance will be granted for:
  (i) a period equal to the length of the period of engagement plus 1 month, or
  (ii) a period of 3 years and 1 month,
  whichever is the shorter.

(d) entry clearance will be granted with effect from 14 days before the date that the Certificate of Sponsorship Checking Service records as the start date for the applicant's employment in the UK, unless entry clearance is being granted less than 14 days before that date, in which case it will be granted with immediate effect.

(e) entry clearance will be subject to the following conditions:
  (i) no recourse to public funds,
  (ii) registration with the police, if this is required by paragraph 326 of these Rules, and
  (iii) no employment except:
    (1) working for the Sponsor in the employment that the Certificate of Sponsorship Checking service records that the migrant is being sponsored to do, [subject to any notification of a change to the details of that employment, other than prohibited changes as defined in paragraph 323AA,]
    (2) supplementary employment,
    (3) voluntary work, and
    (4) if the applicant is applying as a Tier 2 (Sportsperson) Migrant, employment as a sportsperson for his national team while his national team is in the UK.

(f) (i) applicants who meet the requirements for entry clearance and who obtain points under paragraphs 76 to 79D of Appendix A shall be granted entry clearance as a Tier 2 (General) Migrant.

  (ii) applicants who meet the requirements for entry clearance and who obtain points under paragraphs 85 to 92 of Appendix A shall be granted entry clearance as a Tier 2 (Minister of Religion) Migrant.

  (iii) applicants who meet the requirements for entry clearance and who obtain points under paragraphs 93 to 100 of Appendix A shall be granted entry clearance as a Tier 2 (Sportsperson) Migrant.

Note: Previous paras 245ZB–245ZH deleted and substituted by paras 245G–245HF from 6 April 2011 except for applications made but not decided before that date (HC 863). Words substituted in sub-para (e)(iii)(1) from 20 July 2012 (Cm 8423).

245HD. Requirements for leave to remain

To qualify for leave to remain as a Tier 2 (General) Migrant, Tier 2 (Minister of Religion) Migrant or Tier 2 (Sportsperson) Migrant under this rule, an applicant must meet the requirements listed below. If the applicant meets these requirements, leave to remain will be granted. If the applicant does not meet these requirements, the application will be refused.

Requirements:

(a) The applicant must not fall for refusal under the general grounds for refusal, and must not be an illegal entrant.

[(b) the applicant must:

(i) have, or have last been granted, entry clearance, leave to enter or leave to remain as:

(1) a Tier 1 Migrant,

(2) a Tier 2 Migrant,

(3) a Highly Skilled Migrant,

(4) an Innovator,

(5) a Jewish Agency Employee,

(6) a Member of the Operational Ground Staff of an Overseas-owned Airline,

(7) a Minister of Religion, Missionary or Member of a Religious Order,

(8) a Participant in the Fresh Talent: Working in Scotland Scheme,

(9) a Participant in the International Graduates Scheme (or its predecessor, the Science and Engineering Graduates Scheme),

(10) a Qualifying Work Permit Holder,

(11) a Representative of an Overseas Business

(12) a Representative of an Overseas Newspaper, News Agency or Broadcasting Organisation,

(13) a Tier 5 (Temporary Worker) Migrant, or

(14) the partner of a Relevant Points Based System Migrant if the relevant Points Based System Migrant is a Tier 4 Migrant, or

(ii) have current entry clearance, leave to enter or leave to remain which has not expired, as:

(1) a Tier 4 Migrant,

(2) a Student,

(3) a Student Nurse,

(4) a Student Re-Sitting an Examination,

(5) a Person Writing Up a Thesis,

(6) an Overseas Qualified Nurse or Midwife,

(7) a Postgraduate Doctor or Dentist, or

(8) a Student Union Sabbatical Officer.]

[(c) An applicant who has, or was last granted leave as a Tier 2 (Intra-Company Transfer) Migrant must:

(i) have previously had leave as a Tier 2 (Intra-Company Transfer) Migrant under the Rules in place before 6 April 2010, or in the Established Staff sub-category under the Rules in place before 6 April 2011,

(ii) not have been granted entry clearance in this or any other route since the grant of leave referred to in (i) above; and

(iii) not be applying to work for the same Sponsor as sponsored him when he was last granted leave.]

[(d) An applicant under the provisions in (b)(ii) above must meet the following requirements:

(i) The applicant must have completed and passed:

(1) a UK recognised bachelor or postgraduate degree (not a qualification of equivalent level which is not a degree),

(2) a UK Postgraduate Certificate in Education or Professional Graduate Diploma of Education (not a qualification of equivalent level), or the applicant must have completed a minimum of 12 months study in the UK towards a UK PhD.

(ii) The applicant must have studied for the course in (d)(i) at a UK institution that is a UK recognised or listed body, or which holds a sponsor licence under Tier 4 of the Points Based System.

(iii) The applicant must have studied the course referred to in (d)(i) during:

(1) his last grant of leave, or

(2) a period of continuous leave which includes his last grant of leave.

(iv) The applicant's periods of UK study and/or research towards the course in (i) must have been undertaken whilst he had entry clearance, leave to enter or leave to remain in the UK that was not subject to a restriction preventing him from undertaking that course of study and/or research.

(v) If the institution studied at is removed from the Tier 4 Sponsor Register, the applicant's qualification must not have been obtained on or after the date of removal from the Sponsor Register.

(vi) If the applicant:

(1) is currently being sponsored by a government or international scholarship agency, or

(2) was being sponsored by a government or international scholarship agency, and that sponsorship came to an end 12 months ago or less, the applicant must provide the unconditional written consent of the sponsoring Government or agency to the application and must provide the specified documents [as set out in paragraph 245A above] to show that this requirement has been met.

[(vii) The applicant must provide an original degree certificate, academic transcript or an academic reference on official headed paper of the institution, which clearly shows:

(1) The applicant's name,

(2) the course title/award,

(3) the course duration, and

(4) unless the course is a PhD course, the date of course completion and pass.]

[(e) An applicant who was last granted leave as a Tier 5 (Temporary Worker) Migrant must have been granted such leave in the Creative and Sporting sub-category of Tier 5 in order to allow the applicant to work as a professional footballer, … [, and the applicant must be applying for leave to remain as a Tier 2 (Sportsperson) Migrant].

[(f)] If applying as a Tier 2 (General) Migrant, the applicant must have a minimum of 50 points under paragraphs 76 to 79D of Appendix A.

[(g)] If applying as a Tier 2 (Minister of Religion) Migrant, the applicant must have a minimum of 50 points under paragraphs 85 to 92 of Appendix A.

[(h)] If applying as a Tier 2 (Sportsperson) Migrant, the applicant must have a minimum of 50 points under paragraphs 93 to 100 of Appendix A.

[(i)] The applicant must have a minimum of 10 points under [paragraphs 1 to 16] of Appendix B.

[(j)] The applicant must have a minimum of 10 points under paragraphs 4 to 5 of Appendix C.

[(k) Unless the applicant's last grant of leave was as a Tier 2 Migrant, the applicant must not have had entry clearance or leave to remain as a Tier 2 Migrant at any time during the 12 months immediately before the date of the application, regardless of whether he was in the UK during that time.]

[(l)] The applicant must be at least 16 years old.

[(m)] Where the applicant is under 18 years of age, the application must be supported by the applicant's parents or legal guardian, or by just one parent if that parent has sole legal responsibility for the child.

[(n)] Where the applicant is under 18 years of age, the applicant's parents or legal guardian, or just one parent if that parent has sole legal responsibility for the child, must confirm that they consent to the arrangements for the applicant's care in the UK.

[(o)] If the Sponsor is a limited company, the applicant must not own more than 10% of its shares.

[(p) The applicant must not be in the UK in breach of immigration laws except that any period of overstaying for a period of 28 days or less will be disregarded.]

Note: Previous paras 245ZB–245ZH deleted and substituted by paras 245G–245HF from 6 April 2011 except for applications made but not decided before that date (HC 863). Sub-paragraphs (b), (d), words in square brackets in sub-para (i) substituted; sub-paras (c) and (k) and words in square brackets in (e) inserted and other sub-paras renumbered from 6 April 2012 except for applications made but not decided before that date (HC 1888). Sub-paragraph (p) inserted from 1 October 2012 with savings for applications made but not decided before 9 July 2012 (HC 194). Words inserted in sub-para (d)(vi) deleted from (e) and (d)(vii) substituted from 20 July 2012 (Cm 8432).

245HE. Period and conditions of grant

[(a) If the applicant:

(i) previously had leave under the Rules in place before 6 April 2011 as:

(1) a Tier 2 (General) Migrant,

(2) a Tier 2 (Minister of Religion) Migrant,

(3) a Tier 2 (Sportsperson) Migrant,

(4) a Jewish Agency Employee,

(5) a Member of the Operational Ground Staff of an Overseas-owned Airline,

(6) a Minister of Religion, Missionary or Member of a Religious Order,

(7) a Qualifying Work Permit Holder, or

(8) a Representative of an Overseas Newspaper, News Agency or Broadcasting Organisation, and

(ii) has not been granted entry clearance as a Tier 2 (General) Migrant, Tier 2 (Minister of Religion) Migrant or Tier 2 (Sportsperson) Migrant under the Rules in place from 6 April 2011, and

(iii) has not been granted entry clearance, leave to enter or leave to remain in any other category since the grant of leave referred to in (i) above, leave to remain will be granted as set out in paragraph (d) below.

(b) In all other cases, leave to remain will be granted as set out in paragraph (e) below.

(c) In paragraph (e) below, X refers to the continuous period of time, during which the applicant:

(i) has had entry clearance, leave to enter or leave to remain as a Tier 2 (General) Migrant, Tier 2 (Minister of Religion) Migrant or Tier 2 (Sportsperson) Migrant; or

(ii) has been in the UK without leave following leave in one of these categories.

(d) in the cases set out in paragraph (a) above, leave to remain will be granted for:

(i) the length of the period of engagement plus 14 days, or

(ii) a period of 3 years plus 14 days,

whichever is the shorter.

(e) If paragraph (a) does not apply, leave to remain will be granted for:

(i) the length of the period of engagement plus 14 days,

(ii) a period of 3 years plus 14 days, or

(iii) a period equal to 6 years less X,

whichever is the shorter. If the calculation of the period of leave comes to zero or a negative number, leave to remain will be refused.]

(f) in addition to the periods in paragraphs [...], (d) and (e), leave to remain will be granted for the period between the date that the application is decided and the date that the Certificate of Sponsorship Checking Service records as the start date of employment in the UK, provided this is not a negative value.

(g) Leave to remain will be granted subject to the following conditions:

(i) no recourse to public funds,

(ii) registration with the police, if this is required by paragraph 326 of these rules, and

(iii) no employment except:

(1) working for the Sponsor in the employment that the Certificate of Sponsorship Checking Service records that the migrant is being sponsored to do, [subject to any notification of a change to the details of that employment, other than prohibited changes as defined in paragraph 323AA,]

(2) supplementary employment,

(3) voluntary work,

[(4) until the start date of the period of engagement, any employment which the applicant was lawfully engaged in on the date of his application, and]

[(5)] if the applicant is applying as a Tier 2 (Sportsperson) Migrant, employment as a sportsperson for his national team while his national team is in the UK.

(h) (i) Applicants who meet the requirements for leave to remain and who obtain points under paragraphs 76 to 79D of Appendix A shall be granted leave to remain as a Tier 2 (General) Migrant.

(ii) Applicants who meet the requirements for leave to remain and who obtain points under paragraphs 85 to 92 of Appendix A shall be granted leave to remain as a Tier 2 (Minister of Religion) Migrant.

(iii) Applicants who meet the requirements for leave to remain and who obtain points under paragraphs 93 to 100 of Appendix A shall be granted leave to remain as a Tier 2 (Sportsperson) Migrant.

Note: Previous paras 245ZB–245ZH deleted and substituted by paras 245G–245HF from 6 April 2011 except for applications made but not decided before that date (HC 863). Paragraphs (a)–(e) substituted; sub-para (g)(iii)(4) inserted and (5) renumbered from 6 April 2012 except for applications made but not decided before that date (HC 1888). Words substituted in sub-para (g) from 20 July 2012 (Cm 8423).

245HF. Requirements for indefinite leave to remain

To qualify for indefinite leave to remain as a Tier 2 (General) Migrant, Tier 2 (Minister of Religion) Migrant or Tier 2 (Sportsperson) Migrant, an applicant must meet the requirements listed below. If the applicant meets these requirements, indefinite leave to remain will be granted. If the applicant does not meet these requirements, the application will be refused.

(a) The applicant must not have one or more unspent convictions within the meaning of the Rehabilitation of Offenders Act 1974.

(b) The applicant must not fall for refusal under the general grounds for refusal, and must not be an illegal entrant.

(c) The applicant must have spent a continuous period of 5 years lawfully in the UK, of which the most recent period must have been spent with leave as a Tier 2 Migrant, in any combination of the following categories:

(i) as a Member of the Operational Ground Staff of an Overseas-owned Airline,

(ii) as a Minister of Religion, Missionary or Member of a Religious Order,

(iii) as a Qualifying Work Permit Holder,

(iv) as a Representative of an Overseas Business,

(v) as a Representative of an Overseas Newspaper, News Agency or Broadcasting Organisation,

(vi) as a Tier 1 Migrant, other than a Tier 1 (Post Study Work) Migrant,

(vii) as a Highly Skilled Migrant,

(viii) as an Innovator,

(ix) as a Tier 2 (General) Migrant, a Tier 2 (Minister of Religion) Migrant or a Tier 2 (Sportsperson) Migrant, or

(x) as a Tier 2 (Intra-Company Transfer) Migrant, provided the continuous period of 5 years spent lawfully in the UK includes a period of leave as:

(1) a Tier 2 (Intra-Company Transfer) Migrant granted under the rules in place before 6 April 2010, or

(2) a Qualifying Work Permit Holder, provided that the work permit was granted because the applicant was the subject of an intra-company transfer.

(d) The Sponsor that issued the Certificate of Sponsorship that led to the applicant's last grant of leave must certify in writing that:

(i) he still requires the applicant for the employment in question, and

(ii) in the case of a Tier 2 (General) Migrant applying for settlement, that they are paid at or above the appropriate rate for the job as stated in[the Codes of Practice in Appendix J].

[(e) The applicant provides [the specified documents in paragraph 245HF-SD] to evidence the sponsor's certification in sub-section (d)(ii)].

[(f)] The applicant must have sufficient knowledge of the English language and sufficient knowledge about life in the United Kingdom, in accordance with paragraph 33BA of these Rules, unless the applicant is under the age of 18 or aged 65 or over at the time the application is made.]

[(g) The applicant must not be in the UK in breach of immigration laws except that any period of overstaying for a period of 28 days or less will be disregarded.]

Note: Previous paras 245ZB–245ZH deleted and substituted by paras 245G–245HF from 6 April 2011 except for applications made but not decided before that date (HC 863). Sub-paragraph (e) inserted and subsequent sub-para renumbered (f) from 31 October 2011 except for applications made but not determined before that date (HC 1511). Sub-paragraph (g) inserted from 1 October 2012 with savings for applications made but not decided before 9 July 2012 (HC 194) Words substituted in sub-para (e) from 20 July 2012 (Cm 8423). Words substituted in sub-para (d)(ii) from 6 September 2012 (HC 565).

[245HF-SD. Specified documents

The specified documents referred to in paragraph 245HF(e) are either a payslip and a personal bank or building society statement, or a payslip and a building society pass book.

(a) Payslips must be:

(i) the applicant's most recent payslip,

(ii) dated no earlier than one calendar month before the date of the application, and

(iii) either:

(1) an original payslip,

(2) on company-headed paper, or

(3) accompanied by a letter from the applicant's Sponsor, on company headed paper and signed by a senior official, confirming the payslip is authentic.

(b) Personal bank or building society statements must:

(i) be the most applicant's most recent statement,

(ii) be dated no earlier than one calendar month before the date of the application,

(iii) clearly show:

(1) the applicant's name,

(2) the applicant's account number,

(3) the date of the statement,

(4) the financial institution's name,

(5) the financial institution's logo, and

(6) transactions by the Sponsor covering the period no earlier than one calendar month before the date of the application,

(iv) be either:

(1) printed on the bank's or building society's letterhead,

(2) electronic bank or building society statements from an online account, accompanied by a supporting letter from the bank or building society, on company headed paper, confirming the statement provided is authentic, or

(3) electronic bank or building society statements from an online account, bearing the official stamp of the bank or building society on every page, and

(v) not be mini-statements from automatic teller machines (ATMs).

(c) Building society pass books must

(i) clearly show:

(1) the applicant's name,

(2) the applicant's account number,

(3) the financial institution's name,

(4) the financial institution's logo, and

(5) transactions by the sponsor covering the period no earlier than one calendar month before the date of the application, and

(ii) be either:
    (1) the original pass book, or
    (2) a photocopy of the pass book which has been certified by the issuing building
society on company headed paper, confirming the statement provided is authentic.]

Note: Paragraph 245HF–SD inserted from 20 July 2012 (Cm 8423).

Tier 5 (Youth Mobility Scheme) Temporary Migrants

245ZI. Purpose of this route

This route is for sponsored young people from participating countries [and territories]
who wish to live and work temporarily in the UK.

Note: Paragraph 245I inserted from 27 November 2008 (HC 1113). Words in square brackets
inserted from 1 January 2012 (HC 1693).

245ZJ. Entry clearance

All migrants arriving in the UK and wishing to enter as a Tier 5 (Youth Mobility Scheme)
Temporary Migrant must have a valid entry clearance for entry under this route. [If a
migrant does not] have a valid entry clearance, entry will be refused.

Note: Paragraph 245ZJ inserted from 27 November 2008 (HC 1113). Words in square brackets
inserted from 1 January 2012 (HC 1693).

245ZK. Requirements for entry clearance

To qualify for entry clearance as a Tier 5 (Youth Mobility Scheme) Temporary Migrant,
an applicant must meet the requirements listed below. However, whether or not the
requirements listed below are met, if a citizen of a country [or the rightful holder of a
passport issued by a territory] listed in Appendix G makes an application for entry clearance which, if granted, would mean that the annual allocation of places under this route
[as specified in Appendix G for citizens of that country or rightful holders of passports
issued by that territory would be exceeded, the application will be refused]. The applicant
will also be refused if the requirements listed below are not met.
  Requirements:
    (a) The applicant must not fall for refusal under the general grounds for refusal[; and]
    (b) The applicant must be:
    (i) a citizen of a country [or rightful holder of a passport issued by a territory] listed
in Appendix G to these Rules, or
    (ii) a British Overseas Citizen, British Overseas Territories Citizen or British
National (Overseas), as defined by the British Nationality Act 1981 and must provide
[a valid passport] to show that this requirement has been met[; and]
    [(c) The applicant must be sponsored by his country of citizenship or the territory of
which he is a rightful passport holder as follows:
    (i) If the applicant is a citizen of a country or the rightful holder of a passport issued
by a territory that does not have Deemed Sponsorship Status, the applicant must hold
a valid Certificate of Sponsorship issued by that country or territory and must use that
Certificate of Sponsorship in support of an application lodged in the country or territory
of issue; or

(ii) If the applicant is a citizen of a country or the rightful holder of a passport issued by a territory that has Deemed Sponsorship Status, his valid passport issued by the country or territory holding such status will stand as evidence of sponsorship and the application for leave may be made at any post worldwide; and]

[(d)] The applicant must have a minimum of 40 points under paragraphs 101 to 104 of Appendix A[; and]

[(e)] The applicant must have a minimum of 10 points under paragraphs 6 to 7 of Appendix C[; and]

[(f)] The applicant must have no children under the age of 18 who are either living with him or for whom he is financially responsible[; and]

[(g)] The applicant must not previously have spent time in the UK as a Working Holidaymaker or a Tier 5 (Youth Mobility Scheme) Temporary Migrant.

Note: Paragraph 245ZK inserted from 27 November 2008 (HC 1113). Sub-paragraph (c) inserted, subsequent sub-para numbers and words in square brackets substituted from 1 January 2012 (HC 1693). Words in square brackets in sub-para (b)(ii) substituted from 20 July 2012 (Cm 8423).

245ZL. Period and conditions of grant

Entry clearance will be granted for a period of 2 years subject to the following conditions:

(a) no recourse to public funds,

(b) registration with the police, if this is required by paragraph 326 of these Rules,

(c) no employment as a professional sportsperson (including as a sports coach), ... and

[(d) no employment as a Doctor or Dentist in Training, unless the applicant has obtained a degree in medicine or dentistry at bachelor's level or above from a UK institution that is a UK recognised or listed body, or which holds a sponsor licence under Tier 4 of the Points Based System, [and provides evidence of this degree], and]

(e) no self employment, except where the following conditions are met:

(i) the migrant has no premises which he owns, other than his home, from which he carries out his business,

(ii) the total value of any equipment used in the business does not exceed £5,000, and

(iii) the migrant has no employees.

Note: Paragraph 245ZL inserted from 27 November 2008 (HC 1113). Words omitted from sub-para (c), sub-para (d) inserted and sub-para (e) renumbered from 6 April 2010 (HC 439). Words inserted in (d) from 20 July 2012 (Cm 8423).

Tier 5 (Temporary Worker) Migrants

245ZM. Purpose of this route and definitions

(a) This route is for certain types of temporary worker whose entry helps to satisfy cultural, charitable, religious or international objectives [including volunteering and job shadowing].

(b) For the purposes of paragraphs 245ZM to [245ZS] and paragraphs 105 to [112] of Appendix A: a migrant has 'consecutive engagements' if:

(i) more than one Certificate of Sponsorship reference number has been allocated in respect of the migrant,

(ii) there is no gap of more than 14 days between any of the periods of engagement, and

(iii) all the Certificate of Sponsorship Checking Service references record that the migrant is being sponsored in the creative and sporting subcategory of the Tier 5 (Temporary Worker) Migrant route.

'Period of engagement' means a period beginning with the employment start date as recorded on the Certificate of Sponsorship Checking Service entry which relates to the Certificate of Sponsorship reference number for which the migrant was awarded points under paragraphs 105 to 111 of Appendix A, and ending on the employment end date as recorded in the same entry.

Note: Paragraph 245ZM inserted from 27 November 2008 (HC 1113). Words substituted in sub-para (b) from 31 March 2009 (HC 314). Words inserted in sub-para (a) from 6 April 2012 except for applications made but not decided before that date (HC 1888).

245ZN. Entry clearance

(a) Subject to paragraph (b), all migrants arriving in the UK and wishing to enter as a Tier 5 (Temporary Worker) Migrant must have a valid entry clearance for entry under this route. If they do not have a valid entry clearance, entry will be refused.

(b) A migrant arriving in the UK and wishing to enter as a Tier 5 (Temporary Worker) Migrant who does not have a valid entry clearance will not be refused entry if the following conditions are met:

(i) the migrant is not a visa national,

(ii) the Certificate of Sponsorship reference number provided by the migrant leading to points being obtained under Appendix A links to an entry in the Certificate of Sponsorship Checking Service recording that their Sponsor has sponsored them in the creative and sporting subcategory of the Tier 5 (Temporary Worker) Migrant route,

(iii) if the migrant has consecutive engagements, the total length of all the periods of engagement, together with any gap between those engagements, is 3 months or less,

(iv) if the migrant does not have consecutive engagements, the total length of the period of engagement is 3 months or less, and

(v) the migrant meets the requirements in paragraph 245ZO below.

Note: Paragraph 245ZN inserted from 27 November 2008 (HC 1113).

245ZO. Requirements for entry clearance or leave to enter

To qualify for entry clearance or, as the case may be, leave to enter, as a Tier 5 (Temporary Worker) Migrant, an applicant must meet the requirements listed below. If the applicant meets these requirements, entry clearance will be granted. If the applicant does not meet these requirements, the application will be refused.

Requirements:

(a) The applicant must not fall for refusal under the general grounds for refusal.

(b) The applicant must have a minimum of 30 points under paragraphs 105 to [112] of Appendix A.

(c) The applicant must have a minimum of 10 points under paragraphs 8 to 9 of Appendix C.

(d) Where the applicant is under 18 years of age, the application must be supported by the applicant's parents or legal guardian, or by just one parent if that parent has sole legal responsibility for the child.

(e) Where the applicant is under 18 years of age, the applicant's parents or legal guardian, or just one parent if that parent has sole responsibility for the child, must confirm that they consent to the arrangements for the applicant's travel to, and reception and care in, the UK.

[(f) An applicant being sponsored in the international agreement sub-category of Tier 5 (Temporary Workers) as a private servant in a diplomatic household must:

(i) be no less than 18 years of age at the time of application, and

(ii) provide evidence of agreed written terms and conditions of employment in the UK with his employer {including specifically that the applicant will be paid in accordance with the National Minimum Wage Act 1998 and regulations made under that Act, in the form set out in Appendix Q}.]

Note: Paragraph 245ZO inserted from 27 November 2008 (HC 1113). Words substituted in sub-para (b) from 31 March 2009 (HC 314). Sub-paragraph (f) inserted from 6 April 2012 except for applications made but not decided before that date. Words deleted from (f) from 20 July 2012 (Cm 8423). Words in curly brackets in sub-para (f)(ii) inserted from 6 September 2012 (HC 565).

245ZP. Period and conditions of grant

(a) Where paragraph 245ZN(b) applies and the applicant has consecutive engagements, leave to enter will be granted for:

(i) a period commencing not more than 14 days before the beginning of the first period of engagement and ending 14 days after the end of the last period of engagement, or

(ii) 3 months,

whichever is the shorter.

(b) Where paragraph 245ZN(b) applies and the applicant does not have consecutive engagements, leave to enter will be granted for:

(i) a period commencing not more than 14 days before the beginning of the period of engagement and ending 14 days after the end of that period of engagement, or

(ii) 3 months, whichever is the shorter.

(c) Where paragraph 245ZN(b) does not apply and the Certificate of Sponsorship Checking Service reference number for which the applicant was awarded points under Appendix A records that the applicant is being [sponsored in the Creative and Sporting subcategory, the Government Authorised Exchange subcategory for a Work Experience Programme, or the Charity Workers sub-category of the Tier 5 (Temporary Worker) Migrant route, entry clearance or leave to enter will be granted for:]

(i) a period commencing 14 days before the beginning of the period of engagement (or of the first period of engagement, where the applicant has consecutive engagements) and ending 14 days after the end of that period of engagement (or of the last period of engagement, where the applicant has consecutive engagements), or

(ii) 12 months,

whichever of (i) or (ii) is the shorter.

[(d) Where paragraph 245ZN(b) does not apply and the Certificate of Sponsorship Checking Service reference number for which the applicant was awarded points under Appendix A records that the applicant is being sponsored in the Religious Workers sub-category, the Government Authorised Exchange subcategory for a Research Programme or Training Programme or the International Agreement subcategory of the Tier 5 (Temporary Worker) Migrant route, entry clearance will be granted for:

    (i) a period commencing 14 days before the beginning of the period of engagement and ending 14 days after the end of that period of engagement, or

    (ii) 2 years,

  whichever is the shorter.]

  (e) Leave to enter and entry clearance will be granted subject to the following conditions:

    (i) no recourse to public funds,

    (ii) registration with the police if this is required by paragraph 326 of these Rules, and

  [(iii) no employment except:

    (1) unless paragraph (2) applies, working for the person who for the time being is the sponsor in the employment that the Certificate of Sponsorship Checking Service records that the migrant is being sponsored to do for that Sponsor,

    [(2) in the case of a migrant whom the Certificate of Sponsorship Checking Service records as being sponsored in the Government Authorised Exchange subcategory of Tier 5 (Temporary Workers), the work, volunteering or job shadowing authorised by the Sponsor and that the Certificate of Sponsorship Checking Service records that the migrant is being sponsored to do,

    (3) supplementary employment, [except in the case of a migrant whom the Certificate of Sponsorship Checking Service records as being sponsored in the international agreement sub-category, to work as a private servant in a diplomatic household, and

    (4) in the case of a migrant whom the Certificate of Sponsorship Checking Service records as being sponsored in the creative and sporting subcategory of Tier 5 (Temporary Workers), employment as a sportsperson for his national team while his national team is in the UK [and Temporary Engagement as a Sports Broadcaster].]

  [(iv) in the case of an applicant whom the Certificate of Sponsorship Checking Service records as being sponsored in the international agreement sub-category of Tier 5 (Temporary Workers), to work as a private servant in a diplomatic household, the employment in (iii)(1) above means working only in the household of the employer recorded by the Certificate of Sponsorship Checking Service.]

Note: Paragraph 245ZP inserted from 27 November 2008 (HC 1113). Sub-paragraph (e)(iii) substituted from 6 April 2010 (HC 439). Sub-paragraphs (d), (e)(iii)(2) and words in square brackets in sub-paras (c) and (e)(iii)(4) substituted and sub-para (e)(iv) and words in square brackets in (e)(iii)(3) inserted from 6 April 2012 except for applications made but not decided before that date (HC 1888).

245ZQ. Requirements for leave to remain

To qualify for leave to remain as a Tier 5 (Temporary Worker) Migrant under this rule, an applicant must meet the requirements listed below. Subject to paragraph 245ZR(a), if the applicant meets these requirements, leave to remain will be granted. If the applicant does not meet these requirements, the application will be refused.

Requirements:

  (a) The applicant must not fall for refusal under the general grounds for refusal, and must not be an illegal entrant.

  (b) [The applicant must have, or have last been granted;]:

    [(i) entry clearance or leave to remain as a Tier 5 (Temporary Worker) Migrant, or

    (ii) [entry clearance, leave to enter or leave to remain as] a Sports Visitor or Entertainer Visitor, provided:

(1) the Certificate of Sponsorship Checking Service reference for which he is being awarded points in this application shows that he is being sponsored in the creative and sporting subcategory; and

(2) the Certificate of Sponsorship reference number was allocated to the applicant before he entered the UK as a Sports Visitor or Entertainer Visitor, or

(iii) [entry clearance, leave to enter or leave to remain as] an Overseas Government Employee, provided:

(a) the Certificate of Sponsorship Checking Service reference for which he is being awarded points in this application shows he is being sponsored in the international agreement sub-category, and

(b) the applicant is continuing employment with the same overseas government or international organisation for which earlier leave was granted, or

(iv) [entry clearance, leave to enter or leave to remain as] a Qualifying Work Permit Holder, provided:

(a) the applicant was previously issued with a work permit for the purpose of employment by an overseas government, and

(b) the Certificate of Sponsorship Checking Service reference for which he is being awarded points in this application shows he is being sponsored in the international agreement sub-category, and

(c) the applicant is continuing employment with the same overseas government or international organisation for which earlier leave was granted[, or]

[(v) [entry clearance, leave to enter or leave to remain as] a Qualifying Work Permit Holder, provided

(1) the applicant was previously issued with a work permit for the purpose of employment as a sponsored researcher, and

(2) the Certificate of Sponsorship Checking Service reference for which he is being awarded points in this application shows he is being sponsored in the government authorised exchange sub-category, and

(3) the applicant is continuing employment with the same organisation for which his most recent period of leave was granted] [or

[(vi) entry clearance, leave to enter or leave to remain as a Student, a Student Re-Sitting an Examination, a Person Writing Up a Thesis, a Postgraduate Doctor or Dentist, a Student Nurse, a Student Union Sabbatical Officer, or a Tier 4 (General) Migrant, provided the Certificate of Sponsorship Checking Service reference for which he is being awarded points in this application confirms:

(1) he is being sponsored in the government authorised exchange sub-category, and

(2) he lawfully obtained a UK recognised bachelor or postgraduate degree (not a qualification of equivalent level which is not a degree) during his last grant of leave, and

(3) he is being sponsored to undertake a period of postgraduate professional training or work experience which is required to obtain a professional qualification or professional registration in the same professional field as the qualification in (2) above, and

(4) that he will not be filling a permanent vacancy, such that the employer he is directed to work for by the Sponsor does not intend to employ him in the UK once the training or work experience for which he is being sponsored has concluded.]

(c) The applicant must have a minimum of 30 points under paragraphs 105 to [112] of Appendix A.

(d) The applicant must have a minimum of 10 points under paragraphs 8 to 9 of Appendix C.

[(e) The Certificate of Sponsorship Checking Service entry to which the Certificate of Sponsorship reference number for which points under Appendix A were awarded relates must:

(i) record that the applicant is being sponsored in the same subcategory of the Tier 5 (Temporary Worker) Migrant route as the one in which he was being sponsored to work for when he was last granted entry clearance or leave to remain as a Tier 5 (Temporary Worker) Migrant, and

(ii) in the case of an applicant who the Certificate of Sponsorship Checking Service records as being sponsored in the international agreement sub-category of Tier 5 (Temporary Workers), to work as a private servant in a diplomatic household, who entered the UK with a valid entry clearance in that capacity under the Rules in place from 6 April 2012, record that the applicant is being sponsored to work for the same employer he was being sponsored to work for when he was last granted entry clearance or leave to remain as a Tier 5 (Temporary Worker) Migrant, and the applicant must have continued to work for that employer throughout his period of leave and must provide evidence of agreed written terms and conditions of employment in the UK with his employer {in the form set out in Appendix Q}...]

[(f) Where the applicant is under 18 years of age, the application must be supported by the applicant's parents or legal guardian, or by just one parent if that parent has sole legal responsibility for the child.]

[(g) Where the applicant is under 18 years of age, the applicant's parents or legal guardian, or just one parent if that parent has sole legal responsibility for the child, must confirm that they consent to the arrangements for the applicant's care in the UK.]

[(h) An applicant who has, or was last granted, leave as a Student, a Student Re-Sitting an Examination, a Person Writing Up a Thesis, a Postgraduate Doctor or Dentist, a Student Nurse, a Student Union Sabbatical Officer, or a Tier 4 (General) Migrant and:

(i) is currently being sponsored by a government or international scholarship agency, or

(ii) was being sponsored by a government or international scholarship agency, and that sponsorship came to an end 12 months ago or less must provide the unconditional written consent of the sponsoring Government or agency to the application and must provide the specified documents [as set out in paragraph 245A above] to show that this requirement has been met.]

[(i) The applicant must not be in the UK in breach of immigration laws except that any period of overstaying for a period of 28 days or less will be disregarded.]

Note: Paragraph 245ZQ inserted from 27 November 2008 (HC 1113). Words substituted in sub-para (c) from 31 March 2009 (HC 314). Sub-paragraphs (b)(iii) to (iv) inserted from 1 January 2010 (HC 120). Sub-paragraphs (b)(v), (f) and (g) inserted from 6 April 2010 (HC 439). Words in square brackets in sub-para (b) substituted from 6 April 2011 (HC 863). Sub-paragraphs (b)(vi) and (h) inserted and (e) substituted from 6 April 2012 except for applications made but not decided before that date (HC 1888). Sub-paragraph (i) inserted from 1 October 2012 with savings for applications made but not decided before that date (HC 194). Words deleted from sub-para (e)(ii) and inserted in (h)(ii) from 20 July 2012 (Cm 8423). Words in curly brackets in sub-para (e)(ii) inserted from 6 September 2012 (HC 565).

245ZR. Period and conditions of grant

(a) If any calculation of period of leave comes to zero or a negative number, leave to remain will be refused.

(b) Subject to paragraphs (c) to (f) below, leave to remain will be granted for:

(i) the length of the period of engagement, as recorded in the Certificate of Sponsorship Checking Service entry, plus 14 days (or, where the applicant has consecutive engagements, a period beginning on the first day of the first period of engagement and ending 14 days after the last day of the last period of engagement) or

[(ii) the difference between the period that the applicant has already spent in the UK since his last grant of entry clearance or leave to enter as a Tier 5 (Temporary Worker) Migrant and:

(1) 12 months, if he is being sponsored in the Government Authorised exchange sub-category for a Work Experience Programme where the initial grant of leave was granted under the Rules in place from 6 April 2012, the Creative and Sporting subcategory, or the Charity Workers subcategory, or

(2) 2 years, if he is being sponsored in the Government Authorised Exchange subcategory where the initial grant of leave was made under the Rules in place before 6 April 2012 or for a Research Programme or Training Programme, the Religious Workers subcategory, or the International Agreement subcategory,]

whichever of (i) or (ii) is the shorter.

(c) Where the provisions in paragraph 245ZQ(b)(ii) apply, the migrant will be granted leave to remain for:

(i) the period of engagement plus 14 days (or, where the applicant has consecutive engagements, a period beginning on the first day of the first period of engagement and ending 14 days after the last day of the last period of engagement), or

(ii) 12 months,

whichever of (i) or (ii) is the shorter.

(d) Where the Certificate of Sponsorship Checking Service reference records that the migrant is being sponsored in the international agreement subcategory of the Tier 5 (Temporary Worker) Migrant route as an overseas government employee or a private servant in a diplomatic household, [where in the case of the latter he entered the UK with a valid entry clearance in that capacity under the Rules in place before 6 April 2012,] leave to remain will be granted for:

(i) the period of engagement plus 14 days, or

(ii) 12 months,

whichever of (i) or (ii) is the shorter, unless at the date of the application for leave to remain the applicant has spent more than 5 years continuously in the UK with leave as a Tier 5 (Temporary Worker) Migrant, in which case leave to remain will be granted for:

(iii) the period of engagement plus 14 days, or

(iv) a period equal to 6 years less X, where X is the period of time, beginning with the date on which the applicant was last granted entry clearance or leave to enter as a Tier 5 (Temporary Worker) Migrant, that the applicant has already spent in the UK as a Tier 5 (Temporary Worker) Migrant,

whichever of (iii) or (iv) is the shorter.

[(e) Where the Certificate of Sponsorship Checking Service reference records that the applicant is being sponsored in the international agreement sub-category of the Tier 5 (Temporary Worker) Migrant route as a private servant in a diplomatic household to work in a domestic capacity in the household of a named individual and where he entered the UK with a valid entry clearance in that capacity under the Rules in place from 6 April 2012, leave to remain will be granted for:

(i) the period of engagement plus 14 days, or

(ii) 12 months,

whichever of (i) or (ii) is the shorter, unless at the date of the application the applicant has spent more than 4 years continuously in the UK with leave as a Tier 5 (Temporary Worker) migrant, in which case leave will be granted for:

(iii) the period of engagement plus 14 days, or

(iv) a period equal to 5 years less X, where X is the period of time, beginning with the date on which the applicant was first granted entry clearance as a Tier 5 (Temporary

Worker) Migrant, that the applicant has already spent in the UK as a Tier 5 (Temporary Worker) Migrant whichever of (iii) or (iv) is the shorter. Where the calculation at (iv) above results in zero or a negative number, the application for leave to remain will be refused.]

[(f)] Where:

(i) the Certificate of Sponsorship Checking Service reference number records that the applicant is being sponsored in the creative and sporting subcategory of the Tier 5 (Temporary Worker) Migrant route as a creative worker, and

(ii) the sponsor is the sponsor who sponsored the applicant when he received his last grant of leave to remain will be granted for the period set out in paragraph (f) below.

[(g)] Where the conditions in paragraph (e) above are met, leave to remain will be granted for:

(i) the period of engagement plus 14 days (or, where the applicant has consecutive engagements, a period beginning on the first day of the first period of engagement and ending 14 days after the last day of the last period of engagement), or

(ii) 12 months,

whichever of (i) or (ii) is the shorter, unless the applicant has spent more than 1 year continuously in the UK with leave as a Tier 5 (Temporary Worker) Migrant, in which case leave to remain will be granted for:

(iii) the period of engagement plus 14 days (or, where the applicant has consecutive engagements, a period beginning on the first day of the first period of engagement and ending 14 days after the last day of the last period of engagement), or

(iv) a period equal to 2 years less X, where X is the period of time, beginning with the date on which the applicant was last granted entry clearance or leave to enter as a Tier 5 (Temporary Worker) Migrant, that the applicant has already spent in the UK as a Tier 5 (Temporary Worker) Migrant,

whichever of (iii) or (iv) is the shorter.

[(h)] Leave to remain will be granted subject to the following conditions:

(i) no recourse to public funds,

(ii) registration with the police if this is required by paragraph 326 of these Rules, and

[(iii) no employment except:

(1) unless paragraph (2) applies, working for the person who for the time being is the sponsor in the employment that the Certificate of Sponsorship Checking Service records that the migrant is being sponsored to do for that Sponsor,

[(2) in the case of a migrant whom the Certificate of Sponsorship Checking Service records as being sponsored in the government authorised exchange sub-category of Tier 5 (Temporary Workers), the work, volunteering or job shadowing authorised by the Sponsor and that the Certificate of Sponsorship Checking Service records that the migrant is being sponsored to do,]

(3) supplementary employment, and

(4) in the case of a migrant whom the Certificate of Sponsorship Checking Service records as being sponsored in the creative and sporting subcategory of Tier 5 (Temporary Workers), employment as a sportsperson for his national team while his national team is in the UK [and Temporary Engagement as a Sports Broadcaster.]]

[(iv) in the case of a migrant whom the Certificate of Sponsorship Checking Service records as being sponsored in the international agreement sub-category of Tier 5 (Temporary Workers), to work as a private servant in a diplomatic household, the employment in (iii)(1) above means working only in the household of the employer recorded by the Certificate of Sponsorship Checking Service.]

Note: Paragraph 245ZR inserted from 27 November 2008 (HC 1113). Sub-paragraph (g)(iii) substituted from 6 April 2010 (HC 439). Sub-paragraph (b)(ii), (h)(iii)(2), substituted; para (e) and words in square brackets in (d) and (h)(iii)(4) inserted; paras renumbered as (f)–(h) from 6 April 2012 except for applications made but not decided before that date (HC 1888).

245ZS. Requirements for indefinite leave to remain

To qualify for indefinite leave to remain as a Tier 5 (Temporary Worker) Migrant, an applicant must meet the requirements listed below. If the applicant meets these requirements, indefinite leave to remain will be granted. If the applicant does not meet these requirements, the application will be refused.

Requirements:

[(aa) The applicant must not have one or more unspent convictions within the meaning of the Rehabilitation of Offenders Act 1974.]

(a) The applicant must not fall for refusal under the general grounds for refusal and must not be an illegal entrant.

(b) The applicant must have spent a continuous period of 5 years lawfully in the UK with leave in the international agreement sub-category of Tier 5 and working as a private servant in a diplomatic household [and have last been granted entry clearance in this capacity under the Rules in place before 6 April 2012].

(c) The applicant must have sufficient knowledge of the English language and sufficient knowledge about life in the United Kingdom, with reference to paragraphs 33B to 33D of these Rules, unless the applicant is under the age of 18 or aged 65 or over at the time the application is made.

[(d) The applicant must not be in the UK in breach of immigration laws except that any period of overstaying for a period of 28 days or less will be disregarded.]

Note: Paragraph 245ZS inserted from 31 March 2009 (HC 314). Sub-paragraph (aa) inserted from 6 April 2011 (HC 863). Words inserted into sub-para (c) from 6 April 2012 except for applications made before that date (HC 1888). Sub-paragraph (d) inserted from 1 October 2012 with savings for applications made but not decided before 9 July 2012 (HC 194).

Tier 4 (General) Student

245ZT. Purpose of this route

This route is for migrants aged 16 or over who wish to study in the UK.

Note: Paragraph 245ZT inserted from 31 March 2009 (HC 314).

245ZU. Entry clearance

All migrants arriving in the UK and wishing to enter as a Tier 4 (General) Student must have a valid entry clearance for entry under this route. If they do not have a valid entry clearance, entry will be refused.

Note: Paragraph 245ZU inserted from 31 March 2009 (HC 314).

245ZV. Requirements for entry clearance

To qualify for entry clearance as a Tier 4 (General) Student, an applicant must meet the requirements listed below. If the applicant meets these requirements, entry clearance will be granted. If the applicant does not meet these requirements, the application will be refused.

Requirements:

(a) The applicant must not fall for refusal under the General Grounds for Refusal.

(b) The applicant must have a minimum of 30 points under [paragraphs 113 to 120] of Appendix A.

(c) The applicant must have a minimum of 10 points under paragraphs 10 to [14] of Appendix C.

[(ca) [...] The applicant must, if required to do so on examination or interview, be able to demonstrate without the assistance of an interpreter English language proficiency of a standard to be expected from an individual who has reached the standard specified in a Confirmation of Acceptance for Studies assigned in accordance with Appendix A paragraph 118(c) (for the avoidance of doubt, the applicant will not be subject to a test at the standard set out in Appendix A, paragraph 118(c)).]

[(da) if the applicant wishes to undertake a course [...] which is:

(i) undergraduate or postgraduate studies leading to a Doctorate or Masters degree by research in one of the disciplines listed in paragraph 1 of Appendix 6 of these Rules, or

(ii) undergraduate or postgraduate studies leading to a taught Masters degree or other postgraduate qualification in one of the disciplines listed in paragraph 2 of Appendix 6 of these Rules, or

(iii) a period of study or research in excess of 6 months in one of the disciplines listed in paragraphs 1 or 2 of Appendix 6 of these rules at an institution of higher education where this forms part of an overseas postgraduate qualification

the applicant must hold a valid Academic Technology Approval Scheme clearance certificate from the Counter-Proliferation Department of the Foreign and Commonwealth Office which relates to the course, or area of research, that the applicant will be taking and at the institution at which the applicant wishes to undertake it and must provide [a print-out of his Academic Technology Approval Scheme clearance certificate] to show that these requirements have been met.

(e) If the applicant wishes to be a postgraduate doctor or dentist on a recognised Foundation Programme:

(i) the applicant must have successfully completed a recognised UK degree in medicine or dentistry from:

(1) an institution with a Tier 4 General Sponsor Licence,

(2) a UK publicly funded institution of further or higher education, or

(3) a UK bona fide private education institution which maintains satisfactory records of enrolment and attendance,

(ii) the applicant must have previously been granted leave:

(1) as a Tier 4 (General) Student, or as a Student, for the final academic year of the studies referred to in paragraph (i) above, and

(2) as a Tier 4 (General) Student, or as a Student, for at least one other academic year (aside from the final year) of the studies referred to in paragraph (i) above,

(iii) if the applicant has previously been granted leave as a Postgraduate Doctor or Dentist, the applicant must not be seeking entry clearance or leave to enter or remain to a date beyond 3 years from the date on which he was first granted leave to enter or remain in that category, and

(iv) if the applicant has previously been granted leave as a Tier 4 (General) Student to undertake a course as a postgraduate doctor or dentist, the applicant must not be seeking entry clearance or leave to enter or remain to a date beyond 3 years from the date on which the applicant was first granted leave to undertake such a course.

(f) If the applicant is currently being sponsored by a Government or international scholarship agency, or within the last 12 months has come to the end of such a period of sponsorship, the applicant must provide the written consent of the sponsoring Government or agency to the application and must provide the specified documents [as set out in paragraph 245A above] to show that this requirement has been met.

[(g) If the course is below degree level the grant of entry clearance the applicant is seeking must not lead to the applicant having spent more than 3 years in the UK as a Tier 4 Migrant since the age of 18 studying courses that did not consist of degree level study.[...]]

[(ga) If the course is at degree level or above, the grant of entry clearance the applicant is seeking must not lead to the applicant having spent more than 5 years in the UK as a Tier 4 (General) Migrant, or as a Student, studying courses at degree level or above unless:

(i) the applicant has successfully completed a course at degree level in the UK of a minimum duration of 4 academic years, and will follow a course of study at Master's degree level sponsored by a Sponsor that is a Recognised Body or a body in receipt of public funding as a higher education institution from the Department of Employment and Learning in Northern Ireland, the Higher Education Funding Council for England, the Higher Education Funding Council for Wales or the Scottish Funding Council, and the grant of entry clearance must not lead to the applicant having spent more than 6 years in the UK as a Tier 4 (General) Migrant[, or as a Student] studying courses at degree level or above; or

(ii) the grant of entry clearance is to follow a course leading to the award of a PhD, and the applicant is sponsored by a Sponsor that is a Recognised Body or a body in receipt of public funding as a higher education institution from the Department of Employment and Learning in Northern Ireland, the Higher Education Funding Council for England, the Higher Education Funding Council for Wales or the Scottish Funding Council; or

(iii) the applicant is following a course of study in;

(1) Architecture;

(2) Medicine;

(3) Dentistry;

(4) Law, where the applicant has completed a course at degree level in the UK and is progressing to:

      a. the Common Professional Examination;

      b. the Graduate Diploma in Law and Legal Practice Course; or

      c. the Bar Professional Training Course.

(5) Veterinary Medicine & Science; or

(6) Music at a music college that is a member of Conservatoires UK (CUK).

(gb) If the applicant has completed a course leading to the award of a PhD in the UK, the grant of entry clearance the applicant is seeking must not lead to the applicant having spent more than 8 years in the UK as a Tier 4 (General) Migrant [, or as a Student.]]

(h) The applicant must be at least 16 years old.

(i) Where the applicant is under 18 years of age, the application must be supported by the applicant's parents or legal guardian, or by just one parent if that parent has sole legal responsibility for the child.

(j) Where the applicant is under 18 years of age, the applicant's parents or legal guardian, or just one parent if that parent has sole responsibility for the child, must confirm that they consent to the arrangements for the applicant's travel to, and reception and care in, the UK.

[(k) The Entry Clearance Officer must be satisfied that the applicant is a genuine student.

245ZV(k) will not be applied to a national or the rightful holder of a qualifying passport issued by one of the relevant competent authorities listed in Appendix H.]

Note: Paragraph 245ZV inserted from 31 March 2009 (HC 314). Sub-paragraph (g) substituted from 6 April 2010. Words substituted in sub-paragraph (b) from 1 October 2009 (HC 7701). Number in sub-para (c) substituted and sub-para (ca) inserted from 21 April 2011 except for applications made but not decided before that date (HC 908). Words in square brackets in sub-para (d) and sub-para (da) inserted from 1 October 2011 except for applications made but not decided before that date (HC 1148). Words omitted from sub-para (g) from 4 July 2011 except for applications made but not decided before that date (HC 1148). Paragraph (d), words in sub-paras (ca), (da) deleted and (ga)–(gb) inserted from 6 April 2012 except for applications made but not decided before that date (HC 1888). Words in square brackets in (ga)(i) and (gb) inserted from 6 April 2012 except for applications made but not decided before that date (Cm 8337). Sub-paragraph (k) inserted from 30 July 2012 except for applications made but not decided before that date (HC 514). Words in square brackets in sub-para (da) substituted and (f) inserted from 20 July 2012 (Cm 8423).

245ZW. Period and conditions of grant

(a) Subject to paragraph (b), entry clearance will be granted for the duration of the course.

(b) In addition to the period of entry clearance granted in accordance with paragraph (a), entry clearance will also be granted for the periods set out in the following table. Notes to accompany the table appear below the table.

Type of course	Period of leave to remain to be granted before the course starts	Period of leave to remain to be granted after the course ends
12 months or more	1 month	4 months
6 months or more but less than 12 months	1 month	2 months
Pre-sessional course of less than 6 months	1 month	1 month
Course of less than 6 months that is not a pre-sessional course	7 days	7 days
Postgraduate doctor or dentist	1 month	1 month

Notes

(i) If the grant of entry clearance is made less than 1 month or, in the case of a course of less than 6 months that is not a pre-sessional course, less than 7 days before the start of the course, entry clearance will be granted with immediate effect.

(ii) A pre-sessional course is a course which prepares a student for the student's main course of study in the UK.

[(iii) The additional periods of entry clearance granted further to the table above will be disregarded for the purposes of calculating whether a migrant has exceeded the limits specified at 245ZV(g) to 245ZV(gb)],

(c) Entry clearance will be granted subject to the following conditions:

(i) no recourse to public funds,

(ii) registration with the police, if this is required by paragraph 326 of these Rules,

(iii) no employment except:

[(1) employment during term time of no more than 20 hours per week and employment (of any duration) during vacations, where the student is following a course of degree level study and is either:

(a) sponsored by a Sponsor that is a Recognised Body or a body in receipt of public funding as a higher education institution from the Department of Employment and Learning in Northern Ireland, the Higher Education Funding Council for England, the Higher Education Funding Council for Wales or the Scottish Funding Council; or

(b) sponsored by an overseas higher education institution to undertake a short-term Study Abroad Programme in the United Kingdom.

(2) employment during term time of no more than 10 hours per week and employment (of any duration) during vacations, where the student is following a course of below degree level study and is sponsored by a Sponsor that is a Recognised Body or a body in receipt of public funding as a higher education institution from the Department of Employment and Learning in Northern Ireland, the Higher Education Funding Council for England, the Higher Education Funding Council for Wales or the Scottish Funding Council,

(3) employment during term time of no more than 10 hours per week and employment (of any duration) during vacations, where the student is following a course of study at any academic level and is sponsored by a Sponsor that is a publicly funded further education college,]

(4) employment as part of a course-related work placement which forms an assessed part of the applicant's course and provided that any period that the applicant spends on that placement does not exceed [one third] of the total length of the course undertaken in the UK [except [:

(i) where it is a United Kingdom statutory requirement that the placement should exceed one third of the total length of the course; or

(ii) where the placement does not exceed one half of the total length of the course undertaken in the UK and the student is following a course of degree level study and is either:

(a) sponsored by a Sponsor that is a Recognised Body or a body in receipt of public funding as a higher education institution from the Department of Employment and Learning in Northern Ireland, the Higher Education Funding Council for England, the Higher Education Funding Council for Wales or the Scottish Funding Council; or

(b) sponsored by an overseas higher education institution to undertake a short-term Study Abroad Programme in the United Kingdom.]

(5) employment as a Student Union Sabbatical Officer, for up to 2 years, provided the post is elective and is at the institution which is the applicant's Sponsor.

(6) employment as a postgraduate doctor or dentist on a recognised Foundation Programme; and

[(7) until such time as a decision is received from the UK Border Agency on an application which is supported by a Certificate of Sponsorship assigned by a licensed Tier 2 Sponsor and which is made following successful completion of course at degree level or above at a Sponsor that is a Recognised Body or a body in receipt of public funding as a higher education institution from the Department of Employment and Learning in Northern Ireland, the Higher Education Funding Council for England, the Higher

Education Funding Council for Wales or the Scottish Funding Council and while the applicant has extant leave, and any appeal against that decision has been determined, employment with the Tier 2 Sponsor, in the role for which they assigned the Certificate of Sponsorship to the Tier 4 migrant.]

Provided that the migrant is not self employed, or [employed as a Doctor or Dentist in Training unless the course that the migrant is being sponsored to do (as recorded by the Confirmation of Acceptance for Studies Checking Service) is a recognised Foundation Programme] [or professional sportsperson (including a sports coach) or an entertainer, and provided that the migrant's employment would not fill a [permanent] full time vacancy other than [under the conditions of (7) above] a vacancy on a recognised Foundation Programme][or as a sabbatical officer]; and

　　[(iv) no study except:

　　(1) study at the institution that the Confirmation of Acceptance for Studies Checking Service records as the migrant's Sponsor, or where the migrant was awarded points for a visa letter [unless the migrant is studying at an institution which is a partner institution of the migrant's Sponsor], study at the institution which issued that visa letter,]

　　[(2) until such time as a decision is received from the UK Border Agency on an application which is supported by a Confirmation of Acceptance for Studies assigned by a Highly Trusted Sponsor and which is made while the applicant has extant leave, and any appeal against that decision has been determined, study at the Highly Trusted Sponsor institution which the Confirmation of Acceptance for Studies Checking Service records as having assigned a Confirmation of Acceptance for Studies to the Tier 4 migrant; and

　　(3) supplementary study.]

> **Note:** Paragraph 245ZW inserted from 31 March 2009 (HC 314). Sub-paragraphs (c)(iii)(1) and (2) substituted/inserted from 3 March 2010 (HC 367); however, if an applicant has made an application for entry clearance or leave to enter or remain before 3 March 2010 and the application has not been decided before that date, it will be decided in accordance with the Rules in force on 2 March 2010 and the conditions applicable to any leave granted will be those in force on 2 March 2010: see introduction to HC 367. Words in 1st square brackets in sub-para (c)(iii)(6) substituted from 6 April 2010 (HC 439). Words inserted in sub-paras (c)(iii)(4) and words in 2nd and 3rd square brackets in (c)(iii)(6) inserted from 1 October 2009 (Cm 7701). Sub-paragraph (c)(iv) inserted from 1 October 2009 (HC 7701). Sub-paragraph (iv)(2) substituted from 23 July 2010, HC 382. Words in square brackets in sub-para (c)(iv)(1) inserted from 21 April 2011 except for applications made but not decided before that date (HC 908). Sub-paragraphs (c)(iii)(1)–(3) substituted from 4 July 2011 except for applications made but not decided before that date (HC 1148). Sub-paragraph (iii) in 'notes' section, and sub-para (iii)(7) inserted, sub-paras (c)(iii)(4)(i) and words in square brackets in (c)(iii) substituted from 6 April 2012 except for applications made but not decided before that date (HC 1888).

245ZX. Requirements for leave to remain

To qualify for leave to remain as a Tier 4 (General) Student under this rule, an applicant must meet the requirements listed below. If the applicant meets these requirements, leave to remain will be granted. If the applicant does not meet these requirements, the applicant will be refused.

Requirements:

(a) The applicant must not fall for refusal under the general grounds for refusal and must not be an illegal entrant.

(b) The applicant must have, or have last been granted, entry clearance, leave to enter or leave to remain:

　　(i) as a Tier 4 (General) Student,

(ii) as a Tier 4 (Child) Student,

(iii) as a Tier 1 (Post-study Work) Migrant,

(iv) as a Tier 2 Migrant,

(v) as a Participant in the International Graduates Scheme (or its predecessor, the Science and Engineering Graduates Scheme),

(vi) as a Participant in the Fresh Talent: Working in Scotland Scheme,

(vii) as a Postgraduate Doctor or Dentist,

(viii) as a Prospective Student,

(ix) as a Student,

(x) as a Student Nurse,

(xi) as a Student Re-sitting an Examination,

(xii) as a Student Writing-Up a Thesis,

(xiii) as a Student Union Sabbatical Officer, or

(xiv) as a Work Permit Holder.

(c) The applicant must have a minimum of 30 points under [paragraphs 113 to 120] of Appendix A.

(d) The applicant must have a minimum of 10 points under paragraphs 10 to [14] of Appendix C.

[(ea) if the applicant wishes to undertake a course [...] which is:

(i) undergraduate or postgraduate studies leading to a doctorate or Masters degree by research in one of the disciplines listed in paragraph 1 of Appendix 6 of these Rules, or

(ii) undergraduate or postgraduate studies leading to a taught Masters degree or other postgraduate qualification in one of the disciplines listed in paragraph 2 of Appendix 6 of these Rules, or

(iii) a period of study or research in excess of 6 months in one of the disciplines listed in paragraphs 1 or 2 of Appendix 6 of these Rules at an institution of higher education where this forms part of an overseas postgraduate qualification.

The applicant must hold a valid Academic Technology Approval Scheme clearance certificate from the Counter-Proliferation Department of the Foreign and Commonwealth Office which relates to the course, or area of research, that the applicant will be taking and at the institution at which the applicant wishes to undertake it and must provide [a print-out of his Academic Technology Approval Scheme clearance certificate] to show that these requirements have been met.

(f) If the applicant wishes to be a postgraduate doctor or dentist on a recognised Foundation Programme:

(i) the applicant must have successfully completed a recognised UK degree in medicine or dentistry from:

(1) an institution with a Tier 4 General Sponsor Licence,

(2) a UK publicly funded institution of further or higher education, or

(3) a UK bona fide private education institution which maintains satisfactory records of enrolment and attendance,

(ii) the applicant must have previously been granted leave:

(1) as a Tier 4 (General) Student, or as a Student, for the final academic year of the studies referred to in paragraph (i) above, and

(2) as a Tier 4 (General) Student, or as a Student, for at least one other academic year (aside from the final year) of the studies referred to in paragraph (i) above,

(iii) if the applicant has previously been granted leave as a Postgraduate Doctor or Dentist the applicant must not be seeking entry clearance or leave to enter or remain to a date beyond 3 years from the date on which he was first granted leave to enter or remain in that category, and

(iv) if the applicant has previously been granted leave as a Tier 4 (General) Student to undertake a course as a postgraduate doctor or dentist, the applicant must not be seeking entry clearance or leave to enter or remain to a date beyond 3 years from the date on which he was first granted leave to undertake such a course.

(g) If the applicant is currently being sponsored by a government or international scholarship agency, or within the last 12 months has come to the end of such a period of sponsorship, the applicant must provide the unconditional written consent of the sponsoring government or agency to the application and must provide the specified documents [as set out in paragraph 245A above] to show that this requirement has been met.

[(h) If the course is below degree level the grant of leave to remain the applicant is seeking must not lead to the applicant having spent more than 3 years in the UK as a Tier 4 Migrant since the age of 18 studying courses that did not consist of degree level study, [...]

[(ha) If the course is at degree level or above, the grant of leave to remain the applicant is seeking must not lead to the applicant having spent more than 5 years in the UK as a Tier 4 (General) Migrant, or as a Student, studying courses at degree level or above unless:

(i) the applicant has successfully completed a course at degree level in the UK of a minimum duration of 4 academic years, and will follow a course of study at Master's degree level sponsored by a Sponsor that is a Recognised Body or a body in receipt of public funding as a higher education institution from the Department of Employment and Learning in Northern Ireland, the Higher Education Funding Council for England, the Higher Education Funding Council for Wales or the Scottish Funding Council, and the grant of leave to remain must not lead to the applicant having spent more than 6 years in the UK as a Tier 4 (General) Migrant [, or as a Student] studying courses at degree level or above; or

(ii) the grant of leave to remain is to follow a course leading to the award of a PhD and the applicant is sponsored by a Sponsor that is a Recognised Body or a body in receipt of public funding as a higher education institution from the Department of Employment and Learning in Northern Ireland, the Higher Education Funding Council for England, the Higher Education Funding Council for Wales or the Scottish Funding Council; or

(iii) the applicant is following a course of study in;

    (1) Architecture;

    (2) Medicine;

    (3) Dentistry;

    (4) Law, where the applicant has completed a course at degree level in the UK and is progressing to:

        a. the Common Professional Examination:

        b. the Graduate Diploma in Law and Legal Practice Course; or

        c. the Bar Professional Training Course.

    (5) Veterinary Medicine & Science; or

    (6) Music at a music college that is a member of Conservatoires UK (CUK).

(hb) If the applicant has completed a course leading to the award of a PhD in the UK, the grant of leave to remain the applicant is seeking must not lead to the applicant having spent more than 8 years in the UK as a Tier 4 (General) Migrant[, or as a Student].]

(i) The applicant must be at least 16 years old.

(j) Where the applicant is under 18 years of age, the application must be supported by the applicant's parents or legal guardian, or by just one parent if that parent has sole legal responsibility for the child.

(k) Where the applicant is under 18 years of age, the applicant's parents or legal guardian, or just one parent if that parent has sole legal responsibility for the child, must confirm that they consent to the arrangements for the applicant's care in the UK.

(l) The applicant must be applying for leave to remain for the purpose of studies which commence within 28 days of the expiry of the applicant's current leave to enter or remain or, where the applicant has overstayed, within 28 days of when that period of overstaying began.]

[(m) The applicant must not be in the UK in breach of immigration laws except that any period of overstaying for a period of 28 days or less will be disregarded.]

Note: Paragraph 245ZX inserted from 31 March 2009 (HC 314). Sub-paragraph (h) substituted from 6 April 2010 (HC 439). Words in sub-para (c) substituted from 1 October 2009 (HC7711). Number in sub-para (d) inserted from 21 April 2011 except for applications made but not decided before that date. Sub-paragraph (ea) inserted from 1 October 2011 except for applications made but not decided before that date; and words deleted from (h) from 4 July 2011 except for applications made but not decided before that date (HC 1148). Sub-paragraph (e) deleted and words deleted from (ea), sub-paras (ha) and (hb) inserted from 6 April 2012 except for applications made but not decided before that date (HC 1888). Words in square brackets inserted in sub-paras (ha)(i) and (hb) from 6 April 2012 except for applications made but not decided before that date (Cm 8337). Paragraph 245ZX(l) substituted and (m) inserted from 1 October 2012 with savings for applications made but not decided before 9 July 2012 (HC 194). Words substituted in sub-para (ea)(iii) and inserted in (g) from 20 July 2012 (Cm 8423).

245ZY. Period and conditions of grant

(a) Subject to paragraphs (b) and (c) below, leave to remain will be granted for the duration of the course.

(b) In addition to the period of leave to remain granted in accordance with paragraph (a), leave to remain will also be granted for the periods set out in the following table. Notes to accompany the table appear below the table.

Type of course	Period of leave to remain to be granted before the course starts	Period of leave to remain to be granted after the course ends
12 months or more	1 month	4 months
6 months or more but less than 12 months	1 month	2 months
Pre-sessional course of less than 6 months	1 month	1 month
Course of less than 6 months that is not a pre-sessional course	7 days	7 days
Postgraduate doctor or dentist	1 month	1 month

Notes

(i) If the grant of leave to remain is being made less than 1 month or, in the case of a course of less than 6 months that is not a pre-sessional course, less than 7 days before the start of the course, leave to remain will be granted with immediate effect.

(ii) A pre-sessional course is a course which prepares a student for the student's main course of study in the UK.

[(iii) The additional periods of entry clearance granted further to the table above will be disregarded for the purposes of calculating whether a migrant has exceeded the limits specified at 245ZX(h) to 245ZX(hb).]

(c) Leave to remain will be granted subject to the following conditions:

(i) no recourse to public funds,

(ii) registration with the police, if this is required by paragraph 326 of these Rules,

(iii) no employment except:

[(1) employment during term time of no more than 20 hours per week and employment (of any duration) during vacations, where the student is following a course of degree level study and is either:

(a) sponsored by a Sponsor that is a Recognised Body or a body in receipt of public funding as a higher education institution from the Department of Employment and Learning in Northern Ireland, the Higher Education Funding Council for England, the Higher Education Funding Council for Wales or the Scottish Funding Council; or

(b) sponsored by an overseas higher education institution to undertake a short-term Study Abroad Programme in the United Kingdom.

(2) employment during term time of no more than 10 hours per week and employment (of any duration) during vacations, where the student is following a course of below degree level study and is sponsored by a Sponsor that is a Recognised Body or a body in receipt of public funding as a higher education institution from the Department of Employment and Learning in Northern Ireland, the Higher Education Funding Council for England, the Higher Education Funding Council for Wales or the Scottish Funding Council,

(3) employment during term time of no more than 10 hours per week and employment (of any duration) during vacations, where the student is following a course of study at any academic level and is sponsored by a Sponsor that is a publicly funded further education college,]

(4) employment as part of a course-related work placement which forms an assessed part of the applicant's course and provided that any period that the applicant spends on that placement does not exceed [one third] of the total length of the course undertaken in the UK except [:

(i) where it is a United Kingdom statutory requirement that the placement should exceed one third of the total length of the course; or

(ii) where the placement does not exceed one half of the total length of the course undertaken in the UK and the student is following a course of degree level study and is either:

(a) sponsored by a Sponsor that is a Recognised Body or a body in receipt of public funding as a higher education institution from the Department of Employment and Learning in Northern Ireland, the Higher Education Funding Council for England, the Higher Education Funding Council for Wales or the Scottish Funding Council; or

  (b) sponsored by an overseas higher education institution to undertake a short-term Study Abroad Programme in the United Kingdom.]

  (5) employment as a Student Union Sabbatical Officer for up to 2 years provided the post is elective and is at the institution which is the applicant's sponsor,

  (6) employment as a postgraduate doctor or dentist on a recognised Foundation Programme,

  (7) until such time as a decision is received from the UK Border Agency on an application which is supported by a Certificate of Sponsorship assigned by a licensed Tier 2 Sponsor and which is made following successful completion of course at degree level or above at a Sponsor that is a Recognised Body or a body in receipt of public funding as a higher education institution from the Department of Employment and Learning in Northern Ireland, the Higher Education Funding Council for England, the Higher Education Funding Council for Wales or the Scottish Funding Council and while the applicant has extant leave, and any appeal against that decision has been determined, employment with the Tier 2 Sponsor institution, in the role for which they assigned the Certificate of Sponsorship to the Tier 4 migrant,]

  provided that the migrant is not self-employed, [or [employed as a Doctor or Dentist in Training unless the course that the migrant is being sponsored to do (as recorded by the Confirmation of Acceptance for Studies Checking Service) is a recognised Foundation Programme], a professional sportsperson (including a sports coach) or an entertainer, and provided that the migrant's employment would not fill a permanent full time vacancy other than [under the conditions of (7) above, or] a vacancy on a recognised Foundation Programme or as a sabbatical officer].

  (iv) no study except:

  (1) study at the institution that the Confirmation of Acceptance for Studies Checking Service records as the migrant's Sponsor, or where the migrant was awarded points for a visa letter, [unless the migrant is studying at an institution which is a partner institution of the migrant's Sponsor], study at the institution which issued that visa letter;

  [(2) until such time as a decision is received from the UK Border Agency on an application which is supported by a Confirmation of Acceptance for Studies assigned by a Highly Trusted Sponsor and which is made while the applicant has extant leave, and any appeal against that decision has been determined, study at the Highly Trusted Sponsor Institution which the Confirmation of Acceptance for Studies Checking Service records as having assigned a Confirmation of Acceptance for studies to the Tier 4 migrant; and

  (3) supplementary study.]

Note: Paragraph 245ZY inserted from 31 March 2009 (HC 314). Sub-paragraphs (c)(iii)(1) and (2) substituted from 3 March 2010 (HC 367); however, if an applicant has made an application for entry clearance or leave to enter or remain before 3 March 2010 and the application has not been decided before that date, it will be decided in accordance with the Rules in force on 2 March 2010 and the conditions applicable to any leave granted will be those in force on 2 March 2010: see introduction to HC 367. Words in square brackets in sub-para (c)(iii)(6) substituted from 6 April 2010 (HC 439). Sub-paragraph (iv)(2) substituted from 23 July 2010 (HC 382). Words in square brackets in sub-para (c)(iv)(1) inserted from 21 April 2011 with savings for applications made but undecided before that date. Sub-paragraphs (c)(iii)(1)–(3) substituted from 4 July 2011 except for applications made before that date (HC 1148). Other amendments from 6 April 2012 except for applications made but not decided by that date (HC 1888).

Tier 4 (Child) Student

245ZZ. Purpose of route

This route is for children at least 4 years old and under the age of 18 who wish to be educated in the UK.

Note: Paragraph 245ZZ inserted from 31 March 2009 (HC 314).

245ZZA. Entry clearance

All migrants arriving in the UK and wishing to enter as a Tier 4 (Child) Student must have a valid entry clearance for entry under this route. If they do not have a valid entry clearance, entry will be refused.

Requirements:

(a) The applicant must not fall for refusal under the general grounds for refusal.

(b) The applicant must have a minimum of 30 points under [paragraphs 121 to 126] of Appendix A.

(c) The applicant must have a minimum of 10 points under paragraphs [15 to 22] of Appendix C.

(d) The applicant must be at least 4 years old and under the age of 18.

(e) The applicant must have no children under the age of 18 who are either living with the applicant or for whom the applicant is financially responsible.

[(f) If a foster carer or a relative (not a parent or guardian) of the applicant will be responsible for the care of the applicant:

(i) the arrangements for the care of the applicant by the foster carer or relative must meet the requirements in paragraph 245ZZE and the applicant must provide the specified documents in paragraph 245ZZE to show that this requirement has been met, and

(ii) the applicant must provide details of the care arrangements as specified in paragraph 245ZZE.]

(g) The application must be supported by the applicant's parents or legal guardian, or by just one parent if that parent has sole legal responsibility for the child.

(h) The applicant's parents or legal guardian, or just one parent if that parent has sole responsibility for the child, must confirm that they consent to the arrangements for the applicant's travel to, and reception and care in, the UK.

(i) If the applicant is currently being sponsored by a Government or international scholarship agency, or within the last 12 months has come to the end of such a period of sponsorship, the applicant must provide the written consent of the sponsoring Government or agency to the application and must provide the specified documents [as set out in paragraph 245A above) to show that this requirement has been met.

Note: Paragraph 245ZZA inserted from 31 March 2009 (HC 314). Words inserted in sub-para (b) and sub-para (i) inserted from 1 October 2009 (HC 7701). Numbers in sub-para (c) substituted from 21 April 2011 with savings for applications made but not decided before that date (HC 908). Sub-paragraph (f) substituted and words inserted in (i) from 20 July 2012 (Cm 8423).

245ZZB. Period and conditions of grant

(a) Where the applicant is under the age of 16, entry clearance will be granted for:

   (i) a period of no more than 1 month before the course starts, plus

   (ii) a period:

     (1) requested by the applicant,

     (2) equal to the length of the programme the applicant is following, or

     (3) of 6 years,

    whichever is the shorter, plus:

   (iii) 4 months.

(b) Where the applicant is aged 16 or over, entry clearance will be granted for:

   (i) a period of no more than 1 month before the course starts, plus

   (ii) a period:

     (1) requested by the applicant,

     (2) equal to the length of the programme the applicant is following, or

     (3) of [3] years, whichever is the shorter, plus:

   (iii) 4 months.

(c) Entry clearance will be granted subject to the following conditions:

   (i) no recourse to public funds,

   (ii) registration with the police, if this is required by paragraph 326 of these Rules,

   (iii) no employment whilst the migrant is aged under 16,

   (iv) no employment whilst the migrant is aged 16 or over except:

     (1) employment during term time of no more than [10] hours per week,

     (2) employment (of any duration) during vacations,

     (3) employment as part of a course-related work placement which forms an assessed part of the applicant's course and provided that any period that the applicant spend on that placement does not exceed half of the total length of the course undertaken in the UK [except where it is a United Kingdom statutory requirement that the placement should exceed half the total length of the course],

     (4) employment as a Student Union Sabbatical Officer for up to 2 years provided the post is elective and is at the institution which is the applicant's Sponsor provided that the migrant is not self employed, or employed as a Doctor in Training, a professional sportsperson (including a sports coach) or an entertainer, and provided that the migrant's employment would not fill a [permanent full time vacancy other than a vacancy as a sabbatical officer.]

   (v) no study except:

     (1) study at the institution that the Confirmation of Acceptance for Studies Checking Service records as the migrant's Sponsor, or where the migrant was awarded points for a visa letter, study at the institution which issued that visa letter [unless the migrant is studying at an institution which is a partner institution of the migrant's Sponsor],

     [(2) until such time as a decision is received from the UK Border agency on an application which is supported by a Confirmation of Acceptance for Studies assigned by a Highly Trusted Sponsor and which is made while the applicant has extant leave, and any appeal against that decision has been determined, study at the Highly Trusted Sponsor institution which the Confirmation of Acceptance for Studies Checking Service records as having assigned a Confirmation of Acceptance for Studies to the Tier 4 migrant; and

     (3) supplementary study].

Note: Paragraph 245ZZB inserted from 31 March 2009 (HC 314). Words inserted in sub-para (c)(iv)(3), words substituted in sub-para (c)(iv)(4) and sub-para (v) inserted from 1 October 2009 (HC 7701). Words inserted in sub-para (c)(iv)(1) from 3 March 2010 (HC 367); however, if an applicant has made an application for entry clearance or leave to enter or remain before 3 March 2010 and the application has not been decided before that date, it will be decided in accordance with the Rules in force on 2 March 2010 and the conditions applicable to any leave granted will be those in force on 2 March 2010: see introduction to HC 367. Words substituted in sub-para (b)(ii)(3) from 6 April 2010 (HC 439). Sub-paragraph (c)(v) (2) substituted from 23 July 2010 (HC 382). Words in square brackets in sub-para (c)(v)(1) inserted from 4 July 2011 with savings for applications made but not decided before that date (HC 1148).

245ZZC. Requirements for leave to remain

To qualify for leave to remain as a Tier 4 (Child) Student under this rule, an applicant must meet the requirements listed below. If the applicant meets these requirements, leave to remain will be granted. If the applicant does not meet these requirements, leave to remain will be refused.

Requirements:

(a) The applicant must not fall for refusal under the general grounds for refusal and must not be an illegal entrant.

(b) The applicant must have, or have last been granted, entry clearance, leave to enter or leave to remain:

(i) as a Tier 4 [Migrant],

(ii) as a Student, or

(iii) as a Prospective Student.

(c) The applicant must have a minimum of 30 points under [paragraphs 121 to 126] of Appendix A.

(d) The applicant must have a minimum of 10 points under paragraphs [15 to 22] of Appendix C.

(e) The applicant must be under the age of 18.

(f) The applicant must have no children under the age of 18 who are either living with the applicant or for whom the applicant is financially responsible.

[(g) If a foster carer or a relative (not a parent or guardian) of the applicant will be responsible for the care of the applicant:

(i) the arrangements for the care of the applicant by the foster carer or relative must meet the requirements in paragraph 245ZZE and the applicant must provide the specified documents in paragraph 245ZZE to show that this requirement has been met, and

(ii) the applicant must provide details of the care arrangements as specified in paragraph 245ZZE.]

(h) The application must be supported by the applicant's parents or legal guardian, or by just one parent if that parent has sole legal responsibility for the child.

(i) The applicant's parents or legal guardian, or just one parent if that parent has sole legal responsibility for the child, must confirm that they consent to the arrangements for the applicant's care in the UK.

[(j) The applicant must be applying for leave to remain for the purpose of studies which commence within 28 days of the expiry of the applicant's current leave to enter or remain or, where the applicant has overstayed, within 28 days of when that period of overstaying began.]

[(k) If the applicant is currently being sponsored by a Government or international scholarship agency, or within the last 12 months has come to the end of such a period of sponsorship, the applicant must provide the written consent of the sponsoring Government or agency to the application and must provide the specified documents [as set out in paragraph 245A above] to show that this requirement has been met.]

[(l) The applicant must not be in the UK in breach of immigration laws except that any period of overstaying for a period of 28 days or less will be disregarded.]

Note: Paragraph 245ZZC inserted from 31 March 2009 (HC 314). Sub-paragraph (k) inserted from 1 October 2009 (HC 7701). Words substituted in sub-para (c) from 1 October 2009 (HC 7711). Words in square brackets in sub-para (f) substituted from 22 October 2010, with savings for applications made but undecided before that date. Words in square brackets in (b)(i) and (d) substituted from 21 April 2011 with savings for applications made but undecided before that date (HC 908). Sub-paragraph (j) substituted and sub-para (l) inserted from 1 October 2012, with savings for applications made but not decided before 9 July 2012 (HC 194). Sub-paragraph (g) substituted and words in square brackets in (k) inserted from 20 July 2012 (Cm 8423).

245ZZD. Period and conditions of grant

(a) Where the applicant is under the age of 16, leave to remain will be granted for:
  (i) a period of no more than 1 month before the course starts, plus
  (ii) a period:
    (1) requested by the applicant,
    (2) equal to the length of the programme the applicant is following, or
    (3) of 6 years,
  whichever is the shorter, plus:
  (iii) 4 months.

(b) Where the applicant is aged 16 or over, leave to remain will be granted for:
  (i) a period of no more than 1 month before the course starts, plus
  (ii) a period:
    (1) requested by the applicant,
    (2) equal to the length of the programme the applicant is following, or
    (3) of [3] years,
  whichever is the shorter, plus:
  (iii) 4 months.

(c) Leave to remain will be granted subject to the following conditions:
  (i) no recourse to public funds,
  (ii) registration with the police, if this is required by paragraph 326 of these Rules,
  (iii) no employment whilst the migrant is aged under 16,
  (iv) no employment whilst the migrant is aged 16 or over except:
    (1) employment during term time of no more than [10] hours per week,
    (2) employment (of any duration) during vacations,
    (3) employment as part of a course-related work placement which forms an assessed part of the applicant's course, and provided that any period that the applicant spend on that placement does not exceed half of the total length of the course undertaken in the UK [except where it is a United Kingdom statutory requirement that the placement should exceed half the total length of the course,]
    (4) employment as a Student Union Sabbatical Officer for up to 2 years provided the post is elective and is at the institution which is the applicant's Sponsor, provided that

the migrant is not self-employed, or employed as a Doctor in Training, a professional sportsperson (including a sports coach) or an entertainer, and provided that the migrant's employment would not fill a [permanent full time vacancy other than a vacancy as a sabbatical officer.]

[(v) no study except:

(1) study at the institution that the Confirmation of Acceptance for Studies Checking Service records as the migrant's Sponsor, or where the migrant was awarded points for a visa letter, study at the institution which issued that visa letter [unless the migrant is studying at an institution which is a partner institution of the migrant's Sponsor],

[(2) until such time as a decision is received from the UK Border Agency on an application which is supported by a Confirmation of Acceptance for Studies assigned by a Highly Trusted Sponsor and which is made while the applicant has extant leave, and any appeal against that decision has been determined, study at the Highly Trusted Sponsor institution which the Confirmation of Acceptance for Studies Checking Service records as having assigned a Confirmation of Acceptance for Studies to the Tier 4 migrant; and

(3) supplementary study.]

Note: Paragraph 245ZZD inserted from 31 March 2009 (HC 314). Words inserted in sub-para (c)(iv)(3), words substituted in sub-para (c)(iv)(4) and sub-para (v) inserted from 1 October 2009 (HC 7701). Words inserted in sub-para (c)(iv)(1) from 3 March 2010 (HC 367); however, if an applicant has made an application for entry clearance or leave to enter or remain before 3 March 2010 and the application has not been decided before that date, it will be decided in accordance with the Rules in force on 2 March 2010 and the conditions applicable to any leave granted will be those in force on 2 March 2010: see introduction to HC 367. Words substituted in sub-para (b)(ii)(3) from 6 April 2010 (HC 439). Sub-paragraph (c)(v)(2) substituted from 23 July 2010 (HC 382). Words in square brackets in sub-para (c)(v)(1) inserted from 4 July 2011 except for applications made but not decided before that date (HC 1148).

[245ZZE. Specified documents, details and requirements of care arrangements

The specified documents, details and requirements of care arrangements referred to in paragraph 245ZZA(f) and paragraph 245ZZC(g) are:

(i) The applicant must provide a written letter of undertaking from the intended carer confirming the care arrangement, which shows:

(1) the name, current address and contact details of the intended carer,

(2) the address where the carer and the Tier 4 (Child) student will be living in the UK if different from the intended carer's current address,

(3) confirmation that the accommodation offered to the Tier 4 (Child) student is a private address, and not operated as a commercial enterprise, such as a hotel or a youth hostel,

(4) the nature of the relationship between the Tier 4 (Child) student's parent(s) or legal guardian and the intended carer,

(5) that the intended carer agrees to the care arrangements for the Tier 4 (Child) student,

(6) that the intended carer has at least £500 per month (up to a maximum of nine months) available to look after and accommodate the Tier 4 (Child) student for the length of the course,

(7) a list of any other people that the intended carer has offered support to, and

(8) the signature and date of the undertaking.

(ii) The applicant must provide a letter from his parent(s) or legal guardian confirming the care arrangement, which shows:

(1) the nature of their relationship with the intended carer,

(2) the address in the UK where the Tier 4 (Child) student and the Tier 4 (Child) student's intended carer will be living,

(3) that the parent(s) or legal guardian support the application, and authorise the intended carer to take responsibility for the care of the Tier 4 (Child) student during his stay in the UK,

(4) the intended carer's current passport, travel document or certificate of naturalisation, confirming that they are lawfully allowed to be in the UK. The UK Border Agency will accept a notarised copy of the original passport or travel document, but reserves the right to request the original.

(iii) If the applicant will be staying in a private foster care arrangement, he must receive permission from the private foster carer's UK local authority, as set out in the Children (Private Arrangements for Fostering) Regulations 2005.

(iv) If the applicant will be staying in a private foster care arrangement and is under 16 years old, he must provide:

(1) a copy of the letter of notification from his parent(s), legal guardian or intended carer to the UK local authority, which confirms that the applicant will be in the care of a private foster carer while in the UK, and

(2) the UK local authority's confirmation of receipt, which confirms that the local authority has received notification of the foster care arrangement.]

Note: Paragraph 245ZZE inserted from 20 July 2012 (Cm 8423).

PART 7
OTHER CATEGORIES

[Requirements for leave to enter the United Kingdom as a person exercising rights of access to a child resident in the United Kingdom

[A246. Paragraphs 246 to 248F apply only to a person who has made an application before 9 July 2012 for leave to enter or remain or indefinite leave to remain as a person exercising rights of access to a child resident in the UK[, or who before 9 July 2012 has been granted leave to enter or remain as a person exercising rights of access to a child resident in the UK.]]

Note: Paragraphs A246 and AB246 inserted with effect from 9 July 2012 (HC 194). Words in square brackets in para A246 inserted from 6 September 2012 (HC 565).

[AB246. Where an application for leave to enter or remain is made on or after 9 July 2012 as a person exercising rights of access to a child resident in the UK Appendix FM will apply.]

Note: Paragraphs A246 and AB246 inserted with effect from 9 July 2012 (HC 194).

246. The requirements to be met by a person seeking leave to enter the United Kingdom to exercise access rights to a child resident in the United Kingdom are that:

(i) the applicant is the parent of a child who is resident in the United Kingdom; and

(ii) the parent or carer with whom the child permanently resides is resident in the United Kingdom; and

(iii) the applicant produces evidence that he has access rights to the child in the form of:

(a) a Residence Order or a Contact Order granted by a Court in the United Kingdom; or

(b) a certificate issued by a district judge confirming the applicant's intention to maintain contact with the child; and

(iv) the applicant intends to continue to take an active role in the child's upbringing; and

(v) the child is under the age of 18; and

(vi) there will be adequate accommodation for the applicant and any dependants without recourse to public funds in accommodation which the applicant owns or occupies exclusively; and

(vii) the applicant will be able to maintain himself and any dependants adequately without recourse to public funds; and

(viii) the applicant holds a valid United Kingdom entry clearance for entry in this capacity.]

Note: Substituted from 2 October 2000 (Cm 4851).

[Leave to enter the United Kingdom as a person exercising rights of access to a child resident in the United Kingdom

247. Leave to enter as a person exercising access rights to a child resident in the United Kingdom may be granted for 12 months in the first instance, provided that a valid United Kingdom entry clearance for entry in this capacity is produced to the Immigration Officer on arrival.]

Note: Substituted from 2 October 2000 (Cm 4851).

[Refusal of leave to enter the United Kingdom as a person exercising rights of access to a child resident in the United Kingdom

248. Leave to enter as a person exercising rights of access to a child resident in the United Kingdom is to be refused if a valid United Kingdom entry clearance for entry in this capacity is not produced to the Immigration Officer on arrival.]

Note: Substituted from 2 October 2000 (Cm 4851).

[Requirements for leave to remain in the United Kingdom as a person exercising rights of access to a child resident in the United Kingdom

248A. The requirements to be met by a person seeking leave to remain in the United Kingdom to exercise access rights to a child resident in the United Kingdom are that:

(i) the applicant is the parent of a child who is resident in the United Kingdom; and

(ii) the parent or carer with whom the child permanently resides is resident in the United Kingdom; and

(iii) the applicant produces evidence that he has access rights to the child in the form of:

(a) a Residence Order or a Contact Order granted by a Court in the United Kingdom; or

(b) a certificate issued by a district judge confirming the applicant's intention to maintain contact with the child; or

(c) a statement from the child's other parent (or, if contact is supervised, from the supervisor) that the applicant is maintaining contact with the child; and

(iv) the applicant takes and intends to continue to take an active role in the child's upbringing; and

(v) the child visits or stays with the applicant on a frequent and regular basis and the applicant intends this to continue; and

(vi) the child is under the age of 18; and

(vii) the applicant has limited leave to remain in the United Kingdom as the [spouse, civil partner, unmarried partner or same-sex partner] of a person present and settled in the United Kingdom who is the other parent of the child; and

(viii) the applicant has not remained in breach of the immigration laws; and

(ix) there will be adequate accommodation for the applicant and any dependants without recourse to public funds in accommodation which the applicant owns or occupies exclusively; and

(x) the applicant will be able to maintain himself and any dependants adequately without recourse to public funds.

Note: Words in square brackets substituted from 5 December 2005 (HC 582).

Leave to remain in the United Kingdom as a person exercising rights of access to a child resident in the United Kingdom

248B. Leave to remain as a person exercising access rights to a child resident in the United Kingdom may be granted for 12 months in the first instance, provided the Secretary of State is satisfied that each of the requirements of paragraph 248A is met.

Refusal of leave to remain in the United Kingdom as a person exercising rights of access to a child resident in the United Kingdom

248C. Leave to remain as a person exercising rights of access to a child resident in the United Kingdom is to be refused if the Secretary of State is not satisfied that each of the requirements of paragraph 248A is met.

Indefinite leave to remain in the United Kingdom as a person exercising rights of access to a child resident in the United Kingdom

248D. The requirements for indefinite leave to remain in the United Kingdom as a person exercising rights of access to a child resident in the United Kingdom are that:

(i) the applicant was admitted to the United Kingdom or granted leave to remain in the United Kingdom for a period of 12 months as a person exercising rights of access to a child and has completed a period of 12 months as a person exercising rights of access to a child; and

(ii) the applicant takes and intends to continue to take an active role in the child's upbringing; and

(iii) the child visits or stays with the applicant on a frequent and regular basis and the applicant intends this to continue; and

(iv) there will be adequate accommodation for the applicant and any dependants without recourse to public funds in accommodation which the applicant owns or occupies exclusively; and

(v) the applicant will be able to maintain himself and any dependants adequately without recourse to public funds; and

(vi) the child is under 18 years of age [; and

(vi) the applicant has sufficient knowledge of the English language and sufficient knowledge about life in the United Kingdom, unless he is under the age of 18 or aged 65 or over at the time he makes his application] [and]

(vii) the applicant does not have one or more unspent convictions within the meaning of the Rehabilitation of Offenders Act 1974.].

Note: Second sub-para (vii) inserted from 2 April 2007 (HC 398). Sub-paragraph (vii) inserted from 6 April 2011 except for applications made but not decided before that date (HC 863).

Indefinite leave to remain as a person exercising rights of access to a child resident in the United Kingdom

248E. Indefinite leave to remain as a person exercising rights of access to a child may be granted provided the Secretary of State is satisfied that each of the requirements of paragraph 248D is met.

Refusal of indefinite leave to remain in the United Kingdom as a person exercising rights of access to a child resident in the United Kingdom

248F. Indefinite leave to remain as a person exercising rights of access to a child is to be refused if the Secretary of State is not satisfied that each of the requirements of paragraph 248D is met.]

Note: Paragraphs 248A–F inserted from 2 October 2000 (Cm 4851).

Holders of special *vouchers*

Note: Paragraphs 249–54 deleted from 18 September 2002 (Cm 5597).

EEA nationals and their families

255.–255B....

Note: Paragraphs 255–255B deleted from 30 April 2006, subject to transitional provisions (HC 1053).

256. ...

Note: Deleted from 2 October 2000 (Cm 4851).

257.–257B. …

Note: Paragraphs 257, 257A and 257B deleted from 30 April 2006, subject to transitional provisions (HC 1053).

Requirements for leave to enter or remain as the primary carer or relative of an EEA national self-sufficient child

[257C. The requirements to be met by a person seeking leave to enter or remain as the primary carer or relative of an EEA national self-sufficient child are that the applicant:
  (i) is:
    (a) the primary carer; or
    (b) the parent; or
    (c) the sibling,of an EEA national under the age of 18 who has a right of residence in the United Kingdom under [the 2006 EEA Regulations] as a self-sufficient person; and
  (ii) is living with the EEA national or is seeking entry to the United Kingdom in order to live with the EEA national; and
  (iii) in the case of a sibling of the EEA national:
    (a) is under the age of 18 or has current leave to enter or remain in this capacity; and
    (b) is unmarried [and is not a civil partner], has not formed an independent family unit and is not leading an independent life; and
  (iv) can, and will, be maintained and accommodated without taking employment or having recourse to public funds; and
  (v) if seeking leave to enter, holds a valid United Kingdom entry clearance for entry in this capacity.
  In this paragraph, 'sibling' includes a half-brother or half-sister and a stepbrother or stepsister.]

Note: Paragraph 257C inserted from 1 January 2005 (HC 164). Words in square brackets in sub-para (i)(c) substituted from 30 April 2006 (HC 1053). Words in square brackets in sub-para (iii) inserted from 5 December 2005 (HC 582).

Leave to enter or remain as the primary carer or relative of an EEA national self-sufficient child

[257D. Leave to enter or remain in the United Kingdom as the primary carer or relative of an EEA national self-sufficient child may be granted for a period not exceeding five years or the remaining period of validity of any residence permit held by the EEA national under the 2006 EEA Regulations, whichever is the shorter, provided that, in the case of an application for leave to enter, the applicant is able to produce to the Immigration Officer, on arrival, a valid entry clearance for entry in this capacity or, in the case of an application for leave to remain, the applicant is able to satisfy the Secretary of State that each of the requirements of paragraph 257C(i) to (iv) is met. Leave to enter or remain is to be subject to a condition prohibiting employment and recourse to public funds.]

Note: Paragraph 257D inserted from 1 January 2005 (HC 164). Reference to 2006 regulations inserted from 30 April 2006 (HC1053).

Refusal of leave to enter or remain as the primary carer or relative of an EEA national self-sufficient child

[**257E**. Leave to enter or remain in the United Kingdom as the primary carer or relative of an EEA national self-sufficient child is to be refused if, in the case of an application for leave to enter, the applicant is unable to produce to the Immigration Officer on arrival a valid United Kingdom entry clearance for entry in this capacity or, in the case of an application for leave to remain, if the applicant is unable to satisfy the Secretary of State that each of the requirements of paragraph 257C(i) to (iv) is met.]

Note: Paragraph 257C inserted from 1 January 2005 (HC 164).

258–261....

Note: Paragraphs 258–261 deleted from 2 October 2000 (Cm 4851).

Registration with the police for family members of EEA nationals

262....

Note: Deleted from 11 May 1998 (Cm 3953).

Retired persons of independent means

Requirements for leave to enter the United Kingdom as a retired person of independent means

263.–265.

Note: Paragraphs 263 to 265 deleted from 27 November 2008 (HC 1113) subject to a saving for applications for leave made before 27 November 2008 and not decided by that date, in which case the Rules as in force on 26 November 2008 as set out in Appendix F apply: see introduction to HC 1113.

Requirements for an extension of stay as a retired person of independent means

266. The requirements for an extension of stay as a retired person of independent means are that the applicant:

(i) entered the United Kingdom with a valid United Kingdom entry clearance as a retired person of independent means; and

(ii) meets the following requirements:

(a) has under his control and disposable in the United Kingdom an income of his own of not less than £25,000 per annum; and

(b) is able and willing to maintain and accommodate himself and any dependants indefinitely in the United Kingdom from his own resources with no assistance from any other person and without taking employment or having recourse to public funds; and

(c) can demonstrate a close connection with the United Kingdom; and

(iii) has made the United Kingdom his main home[; and

(iv) must not be in the UK in breach of immigration laws, except that any period of overstaying for a period of 28 days or less will be disregarded.]

Note: Paragraph 266 substituted from 27 November 2008 (HC 1113). Sub-paragraph (iv) inserted from 1 October 2012 with savings for applications made but not decided before 9 July 2012 (HC 194).

[266A.–266E.

Note: Paragraphs 266A to 266E deleted from 27 November 2008 (HC 1113) subject to a saving for applications for leave made before 27 November 2008 and not decided by that date, in which case the Rules as in force on 26 November 2008 as set out in Appendix F apply: see introduction to HC 1113.

Extension of stay as a retired person of independent means

[267. An extension of stay as a retired person of independent means, with a prohibition on the taking of employment, may be granted so as to bring the person's stay in this category up to a maximum of 5 years in aggregate, provided the Secretary of State is satisfied that each of the requirements of paragraph 266 is met.]

Note: Paragraph 267 substituted from 27 November 2008 (HC 1113).

Refusal of extension of stay as a retired person of independent means

[268. An extension of stay as a retired person of independent means is to be refused if the Secretary of State is not satisfied that each of the requirements of paragraph 266 is met.]

Note: Paragraph 268 substituted from 27 November 2008 (HC 1113).

Indefinite leave to remain for a retired person of independent means

269. Indefinite leave to remain may be granted, on application, to a person admitted as a retired person of independent means provided he:

(i) has spent a continuous period of [5 years] in the United Kingdom in this capacity; and

(ii) has met the requirements of paragraph 266 throughout the [5 year] period and continues to do so[; and

(iii) does not have one or more unspent convictions within the meaning of the Rehabilitation of Offenders Act 1974] [; and

(iv) must not be in the UK in breach of immigration laws, except that any period of overstaying for a period of 28 days or less will be disregarded.]

Note: Words in square brackets substituted from 3 April 2006 (HC 1016). Sub-paragraph (iii) inserted from 6 April 2011 except for applications made but not decided before that date (HC 863). Sub-paragraph (iv) inserted from 1 October 2012 with savings for applications made but not decided before 9 July 2012 (HC 194).

Refusal of indefinite leave to remain for a retired person of independent means

270. Indefinite leave to remain in the United Kingdom for a retired person of independent means is to be refused if the Secretary of State is not satisfied that each of the requirements of paragraph [269] is met.

Note: Number in square brackets substituted from 1 September 1996 (Cm 3365).

Spouses [or civil partners] of persons with limited leave to enter or remain in the United Kingdom as retired persons of independent means

Spouses or civil partners of persons who have or have had leave to enter or remain in the United Kingdom as retired persons of independent means

Requirements for leave to enter as the spouse or civil partner of a person with limited leave to enter or remain in the United Kingdom as a retired person of independent means

[271. The requirements to be met by a person seeking leave to enter the United Kingdom as the spouse or civil partner of a person with limited leave to enter or remain in the United Kingdom as a retired person of independent means are that:

(i) the applicant is married to or the civil partner of a person with limited leave to enter or remain in the United Kingdom as a retired person of independent means; and

(ii) each of the parties intends to live with the other as his or her spouse or civil partners during the applicant's stay and the marriage or civil partnership is subsisting; and

(iii) there will be adequate accommodation for the parties and any dependants without recourse to public funds in accommodation which they own or occupy exclusively; and

(iv) the parties will be able to maintain themselves and any dependants adequately without recourse to public funds; and

(v) the applicant does not intend to stay in the United Kingdom beyond any period of leave granted to his spouse or civil partner; and

(vi) the applicant holds a valid United Kingdom entry clearance for entry in this capacity.]

Note: Paragraph 271 substituted from 2 April 2007 (HC 398).

Leave to enter as the spouse or civil partner of a person with limited leave to enter or remain in the United Kingdom as a retired person of independent means

[272. A person seeking leave to enter the United Kingdom as the spouse or civil partner of a person with limited leave to enter or remain in the United Kingdom as a retired person of independent means may be given leave to enter for a period not in excess of that granted to the person with limited leave to enter or remain as a retired person of independent means, provided the Immigration Officer is satisfied that each of the requirements of paragraph 271 is met.]

Note: Paragraph 272 substituted from 2 April 2007 (HC 398).

Refusal of leave to enter as the spouse or civil partner of a person with limited leave to enter or remain in the United Kingdom as a retired person of independent means

[273. Leave to enter as the spouse or civil partner of a person with limited leave to enter or remain in the United Kingdom as a retired person of independent means is to be refused if the Immigration Officer is not satisfied that each of the requirements of paragraph 271 is met.]

Note: Paragraph 273 substituted from 2 April 2007 (HC 398).

Requirements for extension of stay as the spouse or civil partner of a person who has or has had leave to enter or remain in the United Kingdom as a retired person of independent means

[**273A.** The requirements to be met by a person seeking an extension of stay in the United Kingdom as the spouse or civil partner of a person who has or has had leave to enter or remain in the United Kingdom as a retired person of independent means are that the applicant:

(i) is married to or the civil partner of a person with limited leave to enter or remain in the United Kingdom as a retired person of independent means; or

(ii) is married to or the civil partner of a person who has limited leave to enter or remain in the United Kingdom as a retired person of independent means and who is being granted indefinite leave to remain at the same time; or

(iii) is married to or the civil partner of a person who has indefinite leave to remain in the United Kingdom and who had limited leave to enter or remain as a retired person of independent means immediately before being granted indefinite leave to remain; and

(iv) meets the requirements of paragraph 271 (ii)–(v); and

(v) was admitted with a valid United Kingdom entry clearance for entry in this capacity[; and (vi) must not be in the UK in breach of immigration laws, except that any period of overstaying for a period of 28 days or less will be disregarded.]

Note: Paragraph 273A inserted from 2 April 2007 (HC 398). Sub-paragraph (vi) inserted from 1 October 2012 with savings for applications made but not decided before 9 July 2012 (HC 194).

Extension of stay as the spouse or civil partner of a person who has or has had leave to enter or remain in the United Kingdom as a retired person of independent means

[**273B.** An extension of stay in the United Kingdom as:

(i) the spouse or civil partner of a person who has limited leave to enter or remain as a retired person of independent means may be granted for a period not in excess of that granted to the person with limited leave to enter or remain; or

(ii) the spouse or civil partner of a person who is being admitted at the same time for settlement or the spouse or civil partner of a person who has indefinite leave to remain may be granted for a period not exceeding 2 years, in both instances, provided the Secretary of State is satisfied that each of the requirements of paragraph 273A is met.]

Note: Paragraph 273B inserted from 2 April 2007 (HC 398).

Refusal of extension of stay as the spouse or civil partner of a person who has or has had leave to enter or remain in the United Kingdom as a retired person of independent means

[**273C.** An extension of stay in the United Kingdom as the spouse or civil partner of a person who has or has had leave to enter or remain in the United Kingdom as a retired person of independent means is to be refused if the Secretary of State is not satisfied that each of the requirements of paragraph 273A is met.

Note: Paragraph 273C inserted from 2 April 2007 (HC 398).

Requirements for indefinite leave to remain for the spouse or civil partner of a person who has or has had leave to enter or remain in the United Kingdom as a retired person of independent means

[273D. The requirements to be met by a person seeking indefinite leave to remain in the United Kingdom as the spouse or civil partner of a person who has or has had leave to enter or remain in the United Kingdom as a retired person of independent means are that the applicant:

(i) is married to or the civil partner of a person who has limited leave to enter or remain in the United Kingdom as a retired person of independent means and who is being granted indefinite leave to remain at the same time; or

(ii) is married to or the civil partner of a person who has indefinite leave to remain in the United Kingdom and who had limited leave to enter or remain as a retired person of independent means immediately before being granted indefinite leave to remain; and

(iii) meets the requirements of paragraph 271 (ii)–(v); and

(iv) has sufficient knowledge of the English language and sufficient knowledge about life in the United Kingdom, unless he is under the age of 18 or aged 65 or over at the time he makes his application; and

(v) was admitted with a valid United Kingdom entry clearance for entry in this capacity [, and

(vi) does not have one or more unspent convictions within the meaning of the Rehabilitation of Offenders Act 1974 [; and

(vii) must not be in the UK in breach of immigration laws, except that any period of overstaying for a period of 28 days or less will be disregarded.]

Note: Paragraph 273D inserted from 2 April 2007 (HC 398). Sub-paragraph (vi) inserted from 6 April 2011 except for applications made but not decided before that date (HC 863). Sub-paragraph (vii) inserted from 1 October 2012 with savings for applications made but not decided before 9 July 2012 (HC 194).

Indefinite leave to remain as the spouse or civil partner of a person who has or has had leave to enter or remain in the United Kingdom as a retired person of independent means

[273E. Indefinite leave to remain in the United Kingdom for the spouse or civil partner of a person who has or has had leave to enter or remain in the United Kingdom as a retired person of independent means may be granted provided the Secretary of State is satisfied that each of the requirements of paragraph 273D is met.]

Note: Paragraph 273E inserted from 2 April 2007 (HC 398).

Refusal of indefinite leave to remain as the spouse or civil partner of a person who has or has had leave to enter or remain in the United Kingdom as a retired person of independent means

[273F. Indefinite leave to remain in the United Kingdom for the spouse or civil partner of a person who has or has had leave to enter or remain in the United Kingdom as a retired person of independent means is to be refused if the Secretary of State is not satisfied that each of the requirements of paragraph 273D is met.]

Note: Paragraph 273F inserted from 2 April 2007 (HC 398).

Children of persons with limited leave to enter or remain in the
United Kingdom as retired persons of independent means

Requirements for leave to enter or remain as the child of a person with limited leave to enter or remain in the United Kingdom as a retired person of independent means

274. The requirements to be met by a person seeking leave to enter or remain in the United Kingdom as the child of a person with limited leave to enter or remain in the United Kingdom as a retired person of independent means are that:

(i) he is the child of a parent who has been admitted to or allowed to remain in the United Kingdom as a retired person of independent means; and

(ii) he is under the age of 18 or has current leave to enter or remain in this capacity; and

(iii) he is unmarried [and is not a civil partner], has not formed an independent family unit and is not leading an independent life; and

(iv) he can, and will, be maintained and accommodated adequately without recourse to public funds in accommodation which his parent(s) own or occupy exclusively; and

(v) he will not stay in the United Kingdom beyond any period of leave granted to his parent(s); and

(vi) both parents are being or have been admitted to or allowed to remain in the United Kingdom save where:

(a) the parent he is accompanying or joining is his sole surviving parent; or

(b) the parent he is accompanying or joining has had sole responsibility for his upbringing; or

(c) there are serious and compelling family or other considerations which make exclusion from the United Kingdom undesirable and suitable arrangements have been made for his care; and

(vii) if seeking leave to enter, he holds a valid United Kingdom entry clearance for entry in this capacity or, if seeking leave to remain, was admitted with a valid United Kingdom entry clearance for entry in this capacity [; or

(viii) if seeking leave to remain, must not be in the UK in breach of immigration laws except that any period of overstaying for a period of 28 days or less will be disregarded.]

Note: Words in square brackets in sub-para (iii) inserted from 5 December 2005 (HC 582). Sub-paragraph (viii) inserted from 1 October 2012 with savings for applications made but not decided before 9 July 2012 (HC 194).

Leave to enter or remain as the child of a person with limited leave to enter or remain in the United Kingdom as a retired person of independent means

275. A person seeking leave to enter or remain in the United Kingdom as the child of a person with limited leave to enter or remain in the United Kingdom as a retired person of independent means may be given leave to enter or remain in the United Kingdom for

a period of leave not in excess of that granted to the person with limited leave to enter or remain as a retired person of independent means provided that, in relation to an application for leave to enter, he is able to produce to the Immigration Officer, on arrival, a valid United Kingdom entry clearance for entry in this capacity or, in the case of an application for limited leave to remain, he was admitted with a valid United Kingdom entry clearance for entry in this capacity and is able to satisfy the Secretary of State that each of the requirements of paragraph 274(i)–(vi) [and (viii)] is met. An application for indefinite leave to remain in this category may be granted provided the applicant was admitted to the United Kingdom with a valid United Kingdom entry clearance for entry in this capacity and is able to satisfy the Secretary of State that each of the requirements of paragraph 274(i)–(vi) [and (viii)] is met and provided indefinite leave to remain is, at the same time, being granted to the person with limited leave to enter or remain as a retired person of independent means. Leave to enter or remain is to be subject to a condition prohibiting employment except in relation to the grant of indefinite leave to remain.

Note: Words in square brackets inserted from 1 October 2012 with savings for applications made but not decided before 9 July 2012 (HC 194).

Refusal of leave to enter or remain as the child of a person with limited leave to enter or remain in the United Kingdom as a retired person of independent means

276. Leave to enter or remain in the United Kingdom as the child of a person with limited leave to enter or remain in the United Kingdom as a retired person of independent means is to be refused if, in relation to an application for leave to enter, a valid United Kingdom entry clearance for entry in this capacity is not produced to the Immigration Officer on arrival, or in the case of an application for limited leave to remain, if the applicant was not admitted with a valid United Kingdom entry clearance for entry in this capacity or is unable to satisfy the Secretary of State that each of the requirements of paragraph 274(i)–(vi) [and (viii)] is met. An application for indefinite leave to remain in this category is to be refused if the applicant was not admitted with a valid United Kingdom entry clearance for entry in this capacity or is unable to satisfy the Secretary of State that each of the requirements of paragraph 274(i)–(vi) [and (viii)] is met or if indefinite leave to remain is not, at the same time, being granted to the person with limited leave to enter or remain as a retired person of independent means.

Note: Words in square brackets inserted from 1 October 2012 with savings for applications made but not decided before 9 July 2012 (HC 194).

Long residence

[Long residence in the United Kingdom

276A. For the purposes of paragraphs 276B to 276D[, 276ADE and 399A]:

(a) 'continuous residence' means residence in the United Kingdom for an unbroken period, and for these purposes a period shall not be considered to have been broken where an applicant is absent from the United Kingdom for a period of 6 months or less at any one time, provided that the applicant in question has existing limited leave to enter or remain upon their departure and return, but shall be considered to have been broken if the applicant:

(i) has been removed under Schedule 2 of the 1971 Act, section 10 of the 1999 Act, has been deported or has left the United Kingdom having been refused leave to enter or remain here; or

(ii) has left the United Kingdom and, on doing so, evidenced a clear intention not to return; or

(iii) left the United Kingdom in circumstances in which he could have had no reasonable expectation at the time of leaving that he would lawfully be able to return; or

(iv) has been convicted of an offence and was sentenced to a period of imprisonment or was directed to be detained in an institution other than a prison (including, in particular, a hospital or an institution for young offenders), provided that the sentence in question was not a suspended sentence; or

(v) has spent a total of more than 18 months absent from the United Kingdom during the period in question.

(b) 'lawful residence' means residence which is continuous residence pursuant to:

(i) existing leave to enter or remain; or

(ii) temporary admission within section 11 of the 1971 Act where leave to enter or remain is subsequently granted; or

(iii) an exemption from immigration control, including where an exemption ceases to apply if it is immediately followed by a grant of leave to enter or remain.]

[(c) 'lived continuously' and 'living continuously' mean 'continuous residence', except that paragraph 276A(a)(iv) shall not apply.]

Note: Paragraph 276A inserted from 1 April 2003 (HC 538). Words in square brackets at end of first line substituted from 6 September 2012 (HC 565) replacing previous words which were inserted from 9 July 2012 with savings for applications made but not decided before that date (HC 194). Sub-paragraph (c) inserted from 6 September 2012 (HC 565).

Requirements for an extension of stay on the ground of long residence in the United Kingdom

[**276A1.** The requirement to be met by a person seeking an extension of stay on the ground of long residence in the United Kingdom is that the applicant meets each of the requirements in paragraph 276B(i)–(ii) [and (v)].]

Note: Paragraph 276A1 inserted from 2 April 2007 (HC 398), substituted from 6 April 2012 except for applications made but not decided before that date (HC 1888). Words in square brackets at end inserted from 1 October 2012 with savings for applications made but not decided before 9 July 2012 (HC 194).

Extension of stay on the ground of long residence in the United Kingdom

[**276A2.** An extension of stay on the ground of long residence in the United Kingdom may be granted for a period not exceeding 2 years provided that the Secretary of State is satisfied that the requirement in paragraph 276A1 is met[, and a person granted such an extension of stay following an application made before 9 July 2012 will remain subject to the rules in force on 8 July 2012.]]

Note: Paragraph 276A2 inserted from 2 April 2007 (HC 398). Words inserted from 6 September 2012 (HC 565).

Conditions to be attached to extension of stay on the ground of long residence in the United Kingdom

[276A3. Where an extension of stay is granted under paragraph 276A2:

(i) if the applicant has spent less than [20] years in the UK, the grant of leave should be subject to the same conditions attached to his last period of lawful leave, or

(ii) if the applicant has spent [20] years or more in the UK, the grant of leave should not contain any restriction on employment.]

Note: Paragraph 276A3 inserted from 2 April 2007 (HC 398). Numbers in square brackets inserted from 9 July 2012 with savings for applications made but not decided before that date (HC 194).

Refusal of extension of stay on the ground of long residence in the United Kingdom

[276A4. An extension of stay on the ground of long residence in the United Kingdom is to be refused if the Secretary of State is not satisfied that the requirement in paragraph 276A1 is met.]

Note: Paragraph 276A4 inserted from 2 April 2007 (HC 398).

[Requirements for indefinite leave to remain on the ground of long residence in the United Kingdom

276B. The requirements to be met by an applicant for indefinite leave to remain on the ground of long residence in the United Kingdom are that:

(i) (a) he has had at least 10 years continuous lawful residence in the United Kingdom[.]

(ii) having regard to the public interest there are no reasons why it would be undesirable for him to be given indefinite leave to remain on the ground of long residence, taking into account his:

(a) age; and

(b) strength of connections in the United Kingdom; and

(c) personal history, including character, conduct, associations and employment record; and

(d) domestic circumstances; ... and

[(e)] compassionate circumstances; and

[(f)] any representations received on the person's behalf [; and

(iii) the applicant does not have one or more unspent convictions within the meaning of the Rehabilitation of Offenders Act 1974.]

[(iv)] the applicant has sufficient knowledge of the English language and sufficient knowledge about life in the United Kingdom, unless he is under the age of 18 or aged 65 or over at the time he makes his application.]]

[(v) the applicant must not be in the UK in breach of immigration laws except that any period of overstaying for a period of 28 days or less will be disregarded.]

Note: Paragraph 276B inserted from 1 April 2003 (HC 538). Sub-paragraph (i)(b) substituted from 1 October 2004 (Cm 6339). Sub-paragraph (iii) inserted from 2 April 2007 (HC 398).

Sub-paragraphs (e), (f) and (iv) renumbered and new sub-para (iii) inserted from 6 April 2011 except for applications made but not decided before that date (HC 863). Sub-paragraph (i)(b) deleted from 9 July 2012 with savings for applications made but not decided before that date and sub-para (v) inserted from 1 October 2012 with savings for applications made but not decided before 9 July 2012 (HC 194).

[Indefinite leave to remain on the ground of long residence in the United Kingdom

276C. Indefinite leave to remain on the ground of long residence in the United Kingdom may be granted provided that the Secretary of State is satisfied that each of the requirements of paragraph 276B is met.]

Note: Paragraph 276C inserted from 1 April 2003 (HC 538).

[Refusal of indefinite leave to remain on the ground of long residence in the United Kingdom

276D. Indefinite leave to remain on the ground of long residence in the United Kingdom is to be refused if the Secretary of State is not satisfied that each of the requirements of paragraph 276B is met.]

Note: Paragraph 276D inserted from 1 April 2003 (HC 538).

[Private life

Requirements to be met by an applicant for leave to remain on the grounds of private life

276ADE. The requirements to be met by an applicant for leave to remain on the grounds of private life in the UK are that at the date of application, the applicant:

(i) does not fall for refusal under any of the grounds in Section S-LTR 1.2 to S-LTR {2.3 and S-LTR 3.1.} in Appendix FM; and

(ii) ...

(iii) has lived continuously in the UK for at least 20 years (discounting any period of imprisonment); or

(iv) is under the age of 18 years and has lived continuously in the UK for at least 7 years (discounting any period of imprisonment); or

(v) is aged 18 years or above and under 25 years and has spent at least half of his life {living}continuously in the UK (discounting any period of imprisonment); or

(vi) is aged 18 years or above, has lived continuously in the UK for less than 20 years (discounting any period of imprisonment) but has no ties (including social, cultural or family) with the country to which he would have to go if required to leave the UK.]

...

Note: Paragraph 276ADE inserted from 9 July 2012 with savings for applications made but not decided before that date (HC 194). words in curly brackets in sub-paras (i) and (v) substituted, sub-para (ii) and words at the end of para 276ADE deleted from 6 September 2012 (HC 565).

[Leave to remain on the grounds of private life in the UK

276BE. Limited leave to remain on the grounds of private life in the UK may be granted for a period not exceeding 30 months provided that the Secretary of State is satisfied that the requirements in paragraph 276ADE are met [or, in respect of the requirements in paragraph 276ADE(iv) and (v), were met in a previous application which led to a grant of limited leave to remain under paragraph 276BE.] Such leave shall be given subject to such conditions as the Secretary of State deems appropriate.]

Note: Paragraph 276BE inserted from 9 July 2012 with savings for applications made but not decided before that date (HC 194). Words inserted from 6 September 2012 (HC 565).

[Refusal of limited leave to remain on the grounds of private life in the UK

276CE. Limited leave to remain on the grounds of private life in the UK is to be refused if the Secretary of State is not satisfied that the requirements in paragraph 276ADE are met.]

Note: Paragraph 276CE inserted from 9 July 2012 with savings for applications made but not decided before that date (HC 194).

[Requirements for indefinite leave to remain on the grounds of private life in the UK

276DE. The requirements to be met for the grant of indefinite leave to remain on the grounds of private life in the UK are that:

(a) the applicant has been in the UK with continuous leave on the grounds of private life for a period of at least 120 months;

(b) the applicant meets the requirements of paragraph 276ADE;

(c) the applicant has no unspent convictions;

(d) the applicant has sufficient knowledge of the English language and sufficient knowledge about life in the UK unless the applicant is under the age of 18 or aged 65 or over at the time the applicant makes the application; and

(e) there are no reasons why it would be undesirable to grant the applicant indefinite leave to remain based on the applicant's conduct, character or associations or because the applicant represents a threat to national security.]

Note: Paragraph 276DE inserted from 9 July 2012 with savings for applications made but not decided before that date (HC 194).

[Indefinite leave to remain on the grounds of private life in the UK

276DF. Indefinite leave to remain on the grounds of private life in the UK may be granted provided that the Secretary of State is satisfied that each of the requirements of paragraph 276DE is met.]

Note: Paragraph 276DF inserted from 9 July 2012 with savings for applications made but not decided before that date (HC 194).

[**276DG.** If the applicant does not meet the requirements for indefinite leave to remain on the grounds of private life in the UK only for one or both of the following reasons-

(a) the applicant has an unspent conviction;

(b) the applicant has not met the requirements of paragraphs 33B to 33G of these Rules,

the applicant may be granted further limited leave to remain on the grounds of private life in the UK for a period not exceeding 30 months, and subject to such conditions as the Secretary of State deems appropriate.]

Note: Paragraph 276DG inserted from 9 July 2012 with savings for applications made but not decided before that date (HC 194).

[Refusal of indefinite leave to remain on the grounds of private life in the UK

276DH. Indefinite leave to remain on the grounds of private life in the UK is to be refused if the Secretary of State is not satisfied that each of the requirements of paragraph 276DE is met, subject to paragraph 276DG.]

Note: Paragraph 276DH inserted from 9 July 2012 with savings for applications made but not decided before that date (HC 194).

HM Forces

Definition of Gurkha

[**276E.** For the purposes of these Rules the term 'Gurkha' means a citizen or national of Nepal who has served in the Brigade of Gurkhas of the British Army under the Brigade of Gurkhas' terms and conditions of service.]

Note: Paragraph 276E inserted from 25 October 2004 (Cm 1112).

Leave to enter or remain in the United Kingdom as a Gurkha discharged from the British Army

Requirements for indefinite leave to enter the United Kingdom as a Gurkha discharged from the British Army

[**276F.** The requirements for indefinite leave to enter the United Kingdom as a Gurkha discharged from the British Army are that:

(i) the applicant has completed at least four years' service as a Gurkha with the British Army; and

(ii) was discharged from the British Army in Nepal on completion of engagement on or after 1 July 1997; and

(iii) was not discharged from the British Army more than 2 years prior to the date on which the application is made; and

(iv) holds a valid United Kingdom entry clearance for entry in this capacity] [, and

(v) does not have one or more unspent convictions within the meaning of the Rehabilitation of Offenders Act 1974.]

Note: Paragraph 276F inserted from 25 October 2004 (Cm 1112). Sub-paragraph (v) inserted from 6 April 2011 except for applications made but not decided before that date (HC 863).

Indefinite leave to enter the United Kingdom as a Gurkha discharged from the British Army

[**276G.** A person seeking indefinite leave to enter the United Kingdom as a Gurkha discharged from the British Army may be granted indefinite leave to enter provided a valid United Kingdom entry clearance for entry in this capacity is produced to the Immigration Officer on arrival.]

Note: Paragraph 276G inserted from 25 October 2004 (Cm 1112).

Refusal of indefinite leave to enter the United Kingdom as a Gurkha discharged from the British Army

276H. Indefinite leave to enter the United Kingdom as a Gurkha discharged from the British Army is to be refused if a valid United Kingdom entry clearance for entry in this capacity is not produced to the Immigration Officer on arrival.

Note: Paragraph 276H inserted from 25 October 2004 (Cm 1112).

Requirements for indefinite leave to remain in the United Kingdom as a Gurkha discharged from the British Army

[**276I.** The requirements for indefinite leave to remain in the United Kingdom as a Gurkha discharged from the British Army are that:

(i)   the applicant has completed at least four years' service as a Gurkha with the British Army; and

(ii)   was discharged from the British Army in Nepal on completion of engagement on or after 1 July 1997; and

(iii)   was not discharged from the British Army more than 2 years prior to the date on which the application is made; and

(iv)   [is not in the UK in breach of immigration laws except that any period of overstaying for a period of 28 days or less will be disregarded] [, and

(v)   does not have one or more unspent convictions within the meaning of the Rehabilitation of Offenders Act 1974.]

Note: Paragraph 276I inserted from 25 October 2004 (Cm 1112). Sub-paragraph (v) inserted from 6 April 2011 except for applications made but not decided before that date (HC863). Sub-paragraph (iv) substituted from 1 October 2012 with savings for applications made but not decided before 9 July 2012 (HC 194).

Indefinite leave to remain in the United Kingdom as a Gurkha discharged from the British Army

[**276J.** A person seeking indefinite leave to remain in the United Kingdom as a Gurkha discharged from the British Army may be granted indefinite leave to remain provided the Secretary of State is satisfied that each of the requirements of paragraph 276I is met.]

Note: Paragraph 276J inserted from 25 October 2004 (Cm 1112).

Refusal of indefinite leave to remain in the United Kingdom as a Gurkha discharged from the British Army

[**276K.** Indefinite leave to remain in the United Kingdom as a Gurkha discharged from the British Army is to be refused if the Secretary of State is not satisfied that each of the requirements of paragraph 276I is met.]

Note: Paragraph 276K inserted from 25 October 2004 (Cm 1112).

Leave to enter or remain in the United Kingdom as a foreign or Commonwealth citizen discharged from HM forces

Requirements for indefinite leave to enter the United Kingdom as a foreign or Commonwealth citizen discharged from HM Forces

[**276L.** The requirements for indefinite leave to enter the United Kingdom as a foreign or Commonwealth citizen discharged from HM Forces are that:
   (i) the applicant has completed at least four years' service with HM Forces; and
   (ii) was discharged from HM Forces on completion of engagement; and
   (iii) was not discharged from HM Forces more than 2 years prior to the date on which the application is made; and
   (iv) holds a valid United Kingdom entry clearance for entry in this capacity.] [, and
   (v) does not have one or more unspent convictions within the meaning of the Rehabilitation of Offenders Act 1974.]

Note: Paragraph 276L inserted from 25 October 2004 (Cm 1112). Subparagraph (v) inserted from 6 April 2011 except for applications made but not decided before that date (HC 863).

Indefinite leave to enter the United Kingdom as a foreign or Commonwealth citizen discharged from HM Forces

[**276M.** A person seeking indefinite leave to enter the United Kingdom as a foreign or Commonwealth citizen discharged from HM Forces may be granted indefinite leave to enter provided a valid United Kingdom entry clearance for entry in this capacity is produced to the Immigration Officer on arrival.]

Note: Paragraph 276M inserted from 25 October 2004 (Cm 1112).

Refusal of indefinite leave to enter the United Kingdom as a foreign or Commonwealth citizen discharged from HM Forces

[**276N.** Indefinite leave to enter the United Kingdom as a foreign or Commonwealth citizen discharged from HM Forces is to be refused if a valid United Kingdom entry clearance for entry in this capacity is not produced to the Immigration Officer on arrival.]

Note: Paragraph 276N inserted from 25 October 2004 (Cm 1112).

Requirements for indefinite leave to remain in the United Kingdom as a foreign or Commonwealth citizen discharged from HM Forces

[276O. The requirements for indefinite leave to remain in the United Kingdom as a foreign or Commonwealth citizen discharged from HM Forces are that:

    (i) the applicant has completed at least four years' service with HM Forces; and

    (ii) was discharged from HM Forces on completion of engagement; and

    (iii) was not discharged from HM Forces more than 2 years prior to the date on which the application is made; and

    (iv) [is not in the UK in breach of immigration laws except that any period of overstaying for a period of 28 days or less will be disregarded][, and

    (v) does not have one or more unspent convictions within the meaning of the Rehabilitation of Offenders Act 1974.]

Note: Paragraph 276O inserted from 25 October 2004 (Cm 1112). Sub-paragraph (v) inserted from 6 April 2011 except for applications made but not decided before that date (HC 863). Sub-paragraph (iv) substituted from 1 October 2012 with savings for applications made but not decided before 9 July 2012 (HC 194).

Indefinite leave to remain in the United Kingdom as a foreign or Commonwealth citizen discharged from HM Forces

[276P. A person seeking indefinite leave to remain in the United Kingdom as a foreign or Commonwealth citizen discharged from HM Forces may be granted indefinite leave to remain provided the Secretary of State is satisfied that each of the requirements of paragraph 276O is met.]

Note: Paragraph 276P inserted from 25 October 2004 (Cm 1112).

Refusal of indefinite leave to remain in the United Kingdom as a foreign or Commonwealth citizen discharged from HM Forces

[276Q. Indefinite leave to remain in the United Kingdom as a foreign or Commonwealth citizen discharged from HM Forces is to be refused if the Secretary of State is not satisfied that each of the requirements of paragraph 276O is met.]

Note: Paragraph 276Q inserted from 25 October 2004 (Cm 1112).

Spouses, civil partners, unmarried or same-sex partners of persons settled or seeking settlement in the United Kingdom in accordance with paragraphs 276E to 276Q (HM Forces rules) or of members of HM Forces who are exempt from immigration control under section 8(4)(a) of the Immigration Act 1971 and have at least 5 years' continuous service

Leave to enter or remain in the UK as the spouse, civil partner, unmarried or same-sex partner of a person present and settled in the United Kingdom or being granted settlement on the same occasion in accordance with paragraphs 276E to 276Q or of a member of HM Forces who is exempt from immigration control under section 8(4)(a) of the Immigration Act 1971 and has at least 5 years' continuous service.

Requirements for indefinite leave to enter the United Kingdom as the spouse, civil partner, unmarried or same-sex partner of a person present and settled in the United Kingdom
or being admitted on the same occasion for settlement under paragraphs 276E to 276Q or
of a member of HM Forces who is exempt from immigration control under section 8(4)(a)
of the Immigration Act 1971 and has at least 5 years' continuous service.

276R. The requirements to be met by a person seeking indefinite leave to enter the
United Kingdom as the spouse, civil partner, unmarried or same-sex partner of a person
present and settled in the United Kingdom or being admitted on the same occasion for settlement in accordance with paragraphs 276E to 276Q or of a member of HM Forces who
is exempt from immigration control under section 8(4)(a) of the Immigration Act 1971
and has at least 5 years' continuous service are that:

    (i) the applicant is married to, or the civil partner, unmarried or same-sex partner
of, a person present and settled in the United Kingdom or who is being admitted on the
same occasion for settlement in accordance with paragraphs 276E to 276Q or of a member of HM Forces who is exempt from immigration control under section 8(4)(a) of the
Immigration Act 1971 and has at least 5 years' continuous service; and

    (ii) the parties to the marriage, or civil partnership or relationship akin to marriage
or civil partnership have met; and

    (iii) the parties were married or formed a civil partnership or a relationship akin to
marriage or civil partnership at least 2 years ago; and

    (iv) each of the parties intends to live permanently with the other as his or her
spouse, civil partner, unmarried or same-sex partner; and

    (v) the marriage, civil partnership or relationship akin to marriage or civil partner-
ship is subsisting; and

    (vi) the applicant holds a valid United Kingdom entry clearance for entry in this
capacity [, and

    (vii) does not have one or more unspent convictions within the meaning of the
Rehabilitation of Offenders Act 1974.]

Note: Paragraph 276R substituted from 31 March 2009 (HC 314). Sub-paragraph (vii) inserted
from 6 April 2011 except for applications made but not decided before that date (HC 863).

**Indefinite leave to enter the United Kingdom as the spouse, civil partner,
unmarried or same-sex partner of a person present and settled in the United
Kingdom or being admitted on the same occasion for settlement in accordance
with paragraphs 276E to 276Q or of a member of HM Forces who is exempt from
immigration control under section 8(4)(a) of the Immigration Act 1971 and has at
least 5 years' continuous service**

276S. A person seeking leave to enter the United Kingdom as the spouse, civil partner,
unmarried or same-sex partner of a person present and settled in the United Kingdom or
being admitted on the same occasion for settlement in accordance with paragraphs 276E
to 276Q or of a member of HM Forces who is exempt from immigration control under
section 8(4)(a) of the Immigration Act 1971 and has at least 5 years' continuous service
may be granted indefinite leave to enter provided a valid United Kingdom entry clearance
for entry in this capacity is produced to the Immigration Officer on arrival.

Note: Paragraph 276S substituted from 31 March 2009 (HC 314).

Refusal of indefinite leave to enter the United Kingdom as the spouse, civil partner, unmarried or same-sex partner of a person present and settled in the UK or being admitted on the same occasion for settlement in accordance with paragraphs 276E to 276Q or of a member of HM Forces who is exempt from immigration control under section 8(4)(a) of the Immigration Act 1971 and has at least 5 years' continuous service

276T. Leave to enter the United Kingdom as the spouse, civil partner, unmarried or same-sex partner of a person present and settled in the United Kingdom or being admitted on the same occasion for settlement in accordance with paragraphs 276E to 276Q or of a member of HM Forces who is exempt from immigration control under section 8(4)(a) of the Immigration Act 1971 and has at least 5 years' continuous service is to be refused if a valid United Kingdom entry clearance for entry in this capacity is not produced to the Immigration Officer on arrival.

Note: Paragraph 276T substituted from 31 March 2009 (HC 314).

Requirement for indefinite leave to remain in the United Kingdom as the spouse, civil partner, unmarried or same-sex partner of a person present and settled in the United Kingdom under paragraphs 276E to 276Q or being granted settlement on the same occasion in accordance with paragraphs 276E to 276Q or of a member of HM Forces who is exempt from immigration control under section 8(4)(a) of the Immigration Act 1971 and has at least 5 years' continuous service

276U. The requirements to be met by a person seeking indefinite leave to remain in the United Kingdom as the spouse, civil partner, unmarried or same-sex partner of a person present and settled in the United Kingdom or being granted settlement on the same occasion in accordance with paragraphs 276E to 276Q or of a member of HM Forces who is exempt from immigration control under section 8(4)(a) of the Immigration Act 1971 and has at least 5 years' continuous service are that:

(i) the applicant is married to or the civil partner or unmarried or same-sex partner of a person present and settled in the United Kingdom or being granted settlement on the same occasion in accordance with paragraphs 276E to 276Q or of a member of HM Forces who is exempt from immigration control under section 8(4)(a) of the Immigration Act 1971 and has at least 5 years' continuous service; and

(ii) the parties to the marriage, civil partnership or relationship akin to marriage or civil partnership have met; and

(iii) the parties were married or formed a civil partnership or relationship akin to marriage or civil partnership at least 2 years ago; and

(iv) each of the parties intends to live permanently with the other as his or her spouse, civil partner, unmarried or same-sex partner; and

(v) the marriage, civil partnership or relationship akin to marriage or civil partnership is subsisting; and

(vi) has, or has last been granted, leave to enter or remain in the United Kingdom as the spouse, civil partner, unmarried or same-sex partner. [, and

(vii) the applicant does not have one or more unspent convictions within the meaning of the Rehabilitation of Offenders Act 1974.]

Note: Paragraph 276U substituted from 31 March 2009 (HC 314). Sub-paragraph (vii) inserted from 6 April 2011 except for applications made but not decided before that date (HC 863).

Indefinite leave to remain in the United Kingdom as the spouse, civil partner, unmarried or same-sex partner of a person present and settled in the United Kingdom or being granted settlement on the same occasion in accordance with paragraphs 276E to 276Q or of a member of HM Forces who is exempt from immigration control under section 8(4)(a) of the Immigration Act 1971 and has at least 5 years' continuous service

276V. Indefinite leave to remain in the United Kingdom as the spouse, civil partner, unmarried or same-sex partner of a person present and settled in the United Kingdom or being granted settlement on the same occasion in accordance with paragraphs 276E to 276Q or of a member of HM Forces who is exempt from immigration control under section 8(4)(a) of the Immigration Act 1971 and has at least 5 years' continuous service may be granted provided the Secretary of State is satisfied that each of the requirements of paragraph 276U is met.

Note: Paragraph 276V substituted from 31 March 2009 (HC 314).

Refusal of indefinite leave to remain in the United Kingdom as the spouse, civil partner, unmarried or same-sex partner of a person present and settled in the United Kingdom or being granted settlement on the same occasion in accordance with paragraphs 276E to 276Q or of a member of HM Forces who is exempt from immigration control under section 8(4)(a) of the Immigration Act 1971 and has at least 5 years' continuous service

276W. Indefinite leave to remain in the United Kingdom as the spouse, civil partner, unmarried or same-sex partner of a person present and settled in the United Kingdom or being granted settlement on the same occasion in accordance with paragraphs 276E to 276Q or of a member of HM Forces who is exempt from immigration control under section 8(4)(a) of the Immigration Act 1971 and has at least 5 years' continuous service is to be refused if the Secretary of State is not satisfied that each of the requirements of paragraph 276U is met.

Note: Paragraph 276W substituted from 31 March 2009 (HC 314).

Children of a parent, parents or a relative settled or seeking settlement in the United Kingdom under paragraphs 276E to 276Q (HM Forces rules) or of members of HM Forces who are exempt from immigration control under section 8(4)(a) of the Immigration Act 1971 and have at least 5 years' continuous service

Leave to enter or remain in the United Kingdom as the child of a parent, parents or a relative present and settled in the United Kingdom or being granted settlement on the same occasion in accordance with paragraphs 276E to 276Q or of a member of HM Forces who is exempt from immigration control under section 8(4)(a) of the Immigration Act 1971 and has at least 5 years' continuous service.

Requirements for indefinite leave to enter the United Kingdom as the child of a parent, parents or a relative present and settled in the United Kingdom or being admitted for settlement on the same occasion in accordance with paragraphs 276E to 276Q or of a member of HM Forces who is exempt from immigration control under section 8(4)(a) of the Immigration Act 1971 and has at least 5 years' continuous service

276X. The requirements to be met by a person seeking indefinite leave to enter the United Kingdom as the child of a parent, parents or a relative present and settled in the United Kingdom or being admitted for settlement on the same occasion in accordance with paragraphs 276E to 276Q or of a member of HM Forces who is exempt from immigration control under section 8(4)(a) of the Immigration Act 1971 and has at least 5 years' continuous service are that:

(i) the applicant is seeking indefinite leave to enter to accompany or join a parent, parents or a relative in one of the following circumstances:

(a) both parents are present and settled in the United Kingdom; or

(b) both parents are being admitted on the same occasion for settlement; or

(c) one parent is present and settled in the United Kingdom or is a member of HM Forces who is exempt from immigration control under section 8(4)(a) of the Immigration Act 1971 and has at least 5 years' continuous service and the other is being admitted on the same occasion for settlement or is a member of HM Forces who is exempt from immigration control under section 8(4)(a) of the Immigration Act 1971 and has at least 5 years' continuous service; or

(d) one parent is present and settled in the United Kingdom or being admitted on the same occasion for settlement or is a member of HM Forces who is exempt from immigration control under section 8(4)(a) of the Immigration Act 1971 and has at least 5 years' continuous service and the other parent is dead; or

(e) one parent is present and settled in the United Kingdom or being admitted on the same occasion for settlement or is a member of HM Forces who is exempt from immigration control under section 8(4)(a) of the Immigration Act 1971 and has at least 5 years' continuous service and has had sole responsibility for the child's upbringing; or

(f) one parent or a relative is present and settled in the United Kingdom or being admitted on the same occasion for settlement or is a member of HM Forces who is exempt from immigration control under section 8(4)(a) of the Immigration Act 1971 and has at least 5 years' continuous service and there are serious and compelling family or other considerations which make exclusion of the child undesirable and suitable arrangements have been made for the child's care; and

(ii) is under the age of 18; and

(iii) is not leading an independent life, is unmarried and is not a civil partner, and has not formed an independent family unit; and

(iv) holds a valid United Kingdom entry clearance for entry in this capacity. [, and

(v) the applicant does not have one or more unspent convictions within the meaning of the Rehabilitation of Offenders Act 1974.]

Note: Paragraph 276W substituted from 31 March 2009 (HC 314). Sub-paragraph (v) inserted from 6 April 2011 except for applications made but not decided before that date (HC 863).

Indefinite leave to enter the United Kingdom as the child of a parent, parents or a relative present and settled in the United Kingdom or being admitted for settlement on the same occasion in accordance with paragraphs 276E to 276Q or of a member of HM Forces who is exempt from immigration control under section 8(4)(a) of the Immigration Act 1971 and has at least 5 years' continuous service

276Y. Indefinite leave to enter the United Kingdom as the child of a parent, parents or a relative present and settled in the United Kingdom or being admitted for settlement on the same occasion in accordance with paragraphs 276E to 276Q or of a member of HM Forces who is exempt from immigration control under section 8(4)(a) of the Immigration Act 1971 and has at least 5 years' continuous service may be granted provided a valid United Kingdom entry clearance for entry in this capacity is produced to the Immigration Officer on arrival.

Note: Paragraph 276Y substituted from 31 March 2009 (HC 314).

Refusal of indefinite leave to enter the United Kingdom as the child of a parent, parents or a relative present and settled in the United Kingdom or being admitted for settlement on the same occasion in accordance with paragraphs 276E to 276Q or of a member of HM Forces who is exempt from immigration control under section 8(4)(a) of the Immigration Act 1971 and has at least 5 years' continuous service

276Z. Indefinite leave to enter the United Kingdom as the child of a parent, parents, or a relative present and settled in the United Kingdom or being admitted for settlement on the same occasion in accordance with paragraphs 276E to 276Q or of a member of HM Forces who is exempt from immigration control under section 8(4)(a) of the Immigration Act 1971 and has at least 5 years' continuous service is to be refused if a valid United Kingdom entry clearance for entry in this capacity is not produced to the Immigration Officer on arrival.

Note: Paragraph 276Z substituted from 31 March 2009 (HC 314).

Requirements for indefinite leave to remain in the United Kingdom as the child of a parent, parents or a relative present and settled in the United Kingdom or being granted settlement on the same occasion in accordance with paragraphs 276E to 276Q or of a member of HM Forces who is exempt from immigration control under section 8(4)(a) of the Immigration Act 1971 and has at least 5 years' continuous service

276AA. The requirements to be met by a person seeking indefinite leave to remain in the United Kingdom as the child of a parent, parents or a relative present and settled in the United Kingdom or being granted settlement on the same occasion in accordance with paragraphs 276E to 276Q or of a member of HM Forces who is exempt from immigration control under section 8(4)(a) of the Immigration Act 1971 and has at least 5 years' continuous service are that:

(i) the applicant is seeking indefinite leave to remain with a parent, parents or a relative in one of the following circumstances:

(a) both parents are present and settled in the United Kingdom or being granted settlement on the same occasion; or

(ab) one parent is present and settled in the United Kingdom or is a member of HM Forces who is exempt from immigration control under section 8(4)(a) of the Immigration Act 1971 and has at least 5 years' continuous service and the other is being granted settlement on the same occasion or is a member of HM Forces who is exempt from immigration control under section 8(4)(a) of the Immigration Act 1971 and has at least 5 years' continuous service; or

(b) one parent is present and settled in the United Kingdom or being granted settlement on the same occasion or is a member of HM Forces who is exempt from immigration control under section 8(4)(a) of the Immigration Act 1971 and has at least 5 years' continuous service and the other parent is dead; or

(c) one parent is present and settled in the United Kingdom or being granted settlement on the same occasion or is a member of HM Forces who is exempt from immigration control under section 8(4)(a) of the Immigration Act 1971 and has at least 5 years' continuous service and has had sole responsibility for the child's upbringing; or

(d) one parent or a relative is present and settled in the United Kingdom or being granted settlement on the same occasion or is a member of HM Forces who is exempt from immigration control under section 8(4)(a) of the Immigration Act 1971 and has at least 5 years' continuous service and there are serious and compelling family or other considerations which make exclusion of the child undesirable and suitable arrangements have been made for the child's care; and

(ii) is under the age of 18; and

(iii) is not leading an independent life, is unmarried and is not a civil partner, and has not formed an independent family unit; and

(iv) [is not in the UK in breach of immigration laws except that any period of overstaying for a period of 28 days or less will be disregarded] [, and

(v) the applicant does not have one or more unspent convictions within the meaning of the Rehabilitation of Offenders Act 1974.]

Note: Paragraph 276AA substituted from 31 March 2009 (HC 314). Sub-paragraph (v) inserted from 6 April 2011 except for applications made but not decided before that date (HC 863). Sub-paragraph (iv) substituted from 1 October 2012 with savings for applications made but not decided before t9 July 2012 (HC 194).

Indefinite leave to remain in the United Kingdom as the child of a parent, parents or a relative present and settled in the United Kingdom or being granted settlement on the same occasion in accordance with paragraphs 276E to 276Q or of a member of HM Forces who is exempt from immigration control under section 8(4)(a) of the Immigration Act 1971 and has at least 5 years' continuous service

276AB. Indefinite leave to remain in the United Kingdom as the child of a parent, parents or a relative present and settled in the United Kingdom or being granted settlement on the same occasion in accordance with paragraphs 276E to 276Q or of a member of HM Forces who is exempt from immigration control under section 8(4)(a) of the Immigration Act 1971 and has at least 5 years' continuous service may be granted if the Secretary of State is satisfied that each of the requirements of paragraph 276AA is met.

Note: Paragraph 276AB substituted from 31 March 2009 (HC 314).

Refusal of indefinite leave to remain in the United Kingdom as the child of a parent, parents or a relative present and settled in the United Kingdom or being granted settlement on the same occasion in accordance with paragraphs 276E to 276Q or of a member of HM Forces who is exempt from immigration control under section 8(4)(a) of the Immigration Act 1971 and has at least 5 years' continuous service.

276AC. Indefinite leave to remain in the United Kingdom as the child of a parent, parents or a relative present and settled in the United Kingdom or being granted settlement on the same occasion in accordance with paragraphs 276E to 276Q or of a member of HM Forces who is exempt from immigration control under section 8(4)(a) of the Immigration Act 1971 and has at least 5 years' continuous service is to be refused if the Secretary of State is not satisfied that each of the requirements of paragraph 276AA is met.

Note: Paragraph 276AC substituted from 31 March 2009 (HC 314).

Spouses, civil partners, unmarried or same-sex partners of armed forces members who are exempt from immigration control under section 8(4) of the Immigration Act 1971

Requirements for leave to enter or remain as the spouse, civil partner, unmarried or same-sex partner of an armed forces member who is exempt from immigration control under section 8(4) of the Immigration Act 1971

276AD. The requirements to be met by a person seeking leave to enter or remain in the United Kingdom as the spouse, civil partner, unmarried or same-sex partner of an armed forces member who is exempt from immigration control under section 8(4) of the Immigration Act 1971 are that:

(i) the applicant is married to or the civil partner, unmarried or same-sex partner of an armed forces member who is exempt from immigration control under section 8(4) of the Immigration Act 1971; and

(ii) each of the parties intends to live with the other as his or her spouse or civil partner, unmarried or same-sex partner during the applicant's stay and the marriage, civil partnership, or relationship akin to a marriage or civil partnership is subsisting; and

(iii) there will be adequate accommodation for the parties and any dependants without recourse to public funds in accommodation which they own or occupy exclusively; and

(iv) the parties will be able to maintain themselves and any dependants adequately without recourse to public funds;

(v) the applicant does not intend to stay in the United Kingdom beyond his or her spouse's, civil partner's, unmarried or same-sex partner's enlistment in the home forces, or period of posting or training in the United Kingdom; and

(vi) where the applicant is the unmarried or same-sex partner of an armed forces member who is exempt from immigration control under section 8(4) of the Immigration Act 1971, the following requirements are also met:

(a) any previous marriage or civil partnership or relationship akin to a marriage by the applicant or the exempt armed forces member must have permanently broken down,

(b) the applicant and the exempt armed forces member must not be so closely related that they would be prohibited from marrying each other in the UK, and

(c) the applicant and the exempt armed forces member must have been living together in a relationship akin to marriage or civil partnership for a period of at least 2 years.

Note: Paragraph 276AD substituted from 31 March 2009 (HC 314).

Leave to enter or remain as the spouse, civil partner, unmarried or same-sex partner of an armed forces member who is exempt from immigration control under section 8(4) of the Immigration Act 1971

276AE. A person seeking leave to enter or remain in the United Kingdom as the spouse, civil partner, unmarried or same-sex partner of an armed forces member who is exempt from immigration control under section 8(4) of the Immigration Act 1971 may be given leave to enter or remain in the United Kingdom for a period not exceeding 4 years or the expected duration of the enlistment, posting or training of his or her spouse, civil partner, unmarried or same-sex partner, whichever is shorter, provided that the Immigration Officer, or in the case of an application for leave to remain, the Secretary of State, is satisfied that each of the requirements of paragraph 276AD (i)–(vi) is met.

Note: Paragraph 276AE substituted from 31 March 2009 (HC 314).

Refusal of leave to enter or remain as the spouse, civil partner, unmarried or same-sex partner of an armed forces member who is exempt from immigration control under section 8(4) of the Immigration Act 1971.

276AF. Leave to enter or remain in the United Kingdom as the spouse, civil partner, unmarried or same-sex partner of an armed forces member who is exempt from immigration control under section 8(4) of the Immigration Act 1971 is to be refused if the Immigration Officer, or in the case of an application for leave to remain, the Secretary of State, is not satisfied that each of the requirements of paragraph 276AD (i)–(vi) is met.

Note: Paragraph 276AF substituted from 31 March 2009 (HC 314).

Children of Armed Forces members who are exempt from immigration control under section 8(4) of the Immigration Act 1971

Requirements for leave to enter or remain as the child of an armed forces member exempt from immigration control under section 8(4) of the Immigration Act 1971

[**276AG.** The requirements to be met by a person seeking leave to enter or remain in the United Kingdom as the child of an armed forces member exempt from immigration control under section 8(4) of the Immigration Act 1971 are that:

(i) he is the child of a parent who is an armed forces member exempt from immigration control under section 8(4) of the Immigration Act 1971; and

(ii) he is under the age of 18 or has current leave to enter or remain in this capacity; and

(iii) he is unmarried [and is not a civil partner], has not formed an independent family unit, and is not leading an independent life; and

(iv) he can and will be maintained and accommodated adequately without recourse to public funds in accommodation which his parent(s) own or occupy exclusively; and

(v) he will not stay in the United Kingdom beyond the period of his parent's enlistment in the home forces, or posting or training in the United Kingdom; and

(vi) his other parent is being or has been admitted to or allowed to remain in the United Kingdom save where:

(a) the parent he is accompanying or joining is his sole surviving parent; or

(b) the parent he is accompanying or joining has had sole responsibility for his upbringing; or

(c) there are serious and compelling family or other considerations which make exclusion from the United Kingdom undesirable and suitable arrangements have been made for his care.]

Note: Paragraph 276AG inserted from 15 March 2005 (HC 346). Reference to civil partner inserted from 5 December 2005 (HC 582).

Leave to enter or remain as the child of an armed forces member exempt from immigration control under section 8(4) of the Immigration Act 1971

[**276AH.** A person seeking leave to enter or remain in the United Kingdom as the child of an armed forces member exempt from immigration control under section 8(4) of the Immigration Act 1971 may be given leave to enter or remain in the United Kingdom for a period not exceeding 4 years or the duration of the enlistment, posting or training of his parent, whichever is the shorter, provided that the Immigration Officer, or in the case of an application for leave to remain, the Secretary of State, is satisfied that each of the requirements of 276AG (i)–(vi) is met.]

Note: Paragraph 276AH inserted from 15 March 2005 (HC 346).

Refusal of leave to enter or remain as the child of an armed forces member exempt from immigration control under section 8(4) of the Immigration Act 1971

[**276AI.** Leave to enter or remain in the United Kingdom as the child of an armed forces member exempt from immigration control under section 8(4) of the Immigration Act 1971 is to be refused if the Immigration Officer, or in the case of an application for leave to remain, the Secretary of State, is not satisfied that each of the requirements of paragraph 276AG (i)–(vi) is met.]

Note: Paragraph 276AI inserted from 15 March 2005 (HC 346).

PART 8
FAMILY MEMBERS

[**Transitional provisions and interaction between Part 8{, Appendix FM and Appendix FM-SE}**

Note: Heading amended from 6 September 2012.

[**A277.** From 9 July 2012 Appendix FM will apply to all applications to which Part 8 of these rules applied on or before 8 July 2012 except where the provisions of Part 8 are preserved and continue to apply, as set out in paragraph A280.]

Note: Paragraph A277 inserted from 9 July 2012 (HC 194).

[**A277A.** Where the Secretary of State is considering an application for indefinite leave to remain to which Part 8 of these rules continues to apply (excluding an application from a family member of a Relevant Points Based System Migrant), and where the applicant:

(a) does not meet the requirements of Part 8 for indefinite leave to remain, and

(b) continues to meet the requirements for limited leave to remain on which the applicant's last grant of limited leave to remain under Part 8 was based, further limited leave to remain under Part 8 may be granted of such a period and subject to such conditions as the Secretary of State deems appropriate.]

Note: Paragraphs A277A–A277C inserted from 6 September 2012 (HC 565).

[**A277B.** Where the Secretary of State is considering an application for indefinite leave to remain to which Part 8 of these rules continues to apply (excluding an application from a family member of a Relevant Points Based System Migrant) and where the application does not meet the requirements of Part 8 for indefinite leave to remain or limited leave to remain:

(a) the application will also be considered under paragraphs R-LTRP.1.1.(a), (b) and (d), R-LTRPT.1.1.(a), (b) and (d) and EX.1. of Appendix FM (family life) and paragraphs 276ADE to 276DH (private life) of these rules;

(b) if the applicant meets the requirements for leave under those paragraphs of Appendix FM or paragraphs 276ADE to 276DH (except the requirement for a valid application under that route), the applicant will be granted leave under those provisions; and

(c) if the applicant is granted leave under those provisions, the period of the applicant's continuous leave under Part 8 at the date of application will be counted towards the period of continuous leave which must be completed before the applicant can apply for indefinite leave to remain under those provisions.]

Note: Paragraphs A277A–A277C inserted from 6 September 2012 (HC 565).

[**A277C.** Subject to paragraphs A277 to A280 and paragraph GEN.1.9. of Appendix FM of these rules, where the Secretary of State is considering any application to which the provisions of Appendix FM (family life) and paragraphs 276ADE to 276DH (private life) of these rules do not already apply, she will also do so in line with those provisions.]

Note: Paragraphs A277A–A277C inserted from 6 September 2012 (HC 565).

A278. The requirements to be met under Part 8 after 9 July 2012 may be modified or supplemented by the requirements in Appendix FM [and Appendix FM-SE.]]

Note: Paragraph A278 inserted from 9 July 2012 (HC 194).

A279. The requirements of sections 'S-EC: Suitability – entry clearance' and 'S-LTR: Suitability – leave to remain' of Appendix FM shall apply to all applications made under Part 8 and paragraphs 276A–276D[;] and paragraphs 398–399A shall apply to all immigration decisions made further to applications under Part 8 and paragraphs 276A–276D where a decision is made on or after 9 July 2012, irrespective of the date the application was made.

Note: Paragraph A279 inserted from 9 July 2012 (HC 194). Punctuation amended from 6 September 2012 (HC 565).

A280. The following provisions of Part 8 apply in the manner and circumstances specified:

(a) The following paragraphs apply in respect of all applications made under Part 8 [and Appendix FM], irrespective of the date of application or decision:
277–280
289AA
295AA
296

(b) The following paragraphs of Part 8 continue to apply to all applications made on or after 9 July 2012. The paragraphs apply in their current form unless an additional requirement by reference to Appendix FM is specified:

Paragraph number	Additional requirement
295J	None
297–300	None
304-309	None
309[A]–316F	Where the applicant: • falls under paragraph 314(i)(a); • or falls under paragraph 316A(i)(d) or (e); and • is applying on or after 9 July 2012 the application must also meet the requirements of paragraphs E-ECC 2.1–2.3 (entry clearance applications) or E-LTRC 2.1–2.3 (leave to remain applications) of Appendix FM. Where the applicant: • falls under paragraph 314(i)(d); • is applying on or after 9 July 2012; and • has two parents or prospective parents and one of the applicant's parents or prospective parents does not have right of abode, indefinite leave to enter or remain, is not present and settled in the UK or being admitted for settlement on the same occasion as the applicant is seeking admission the application must also meet the requirements of paragraphs E-ECC 2.1–2.3 (entry clearance applications) or E-LTRC 2.1–2.3 (leave to remain applications) of Appendix FM.
319X	None

(c) The following provisions of Part 8 continue to apply ... on or after 9 July 2012, and are not subject to any additional requirement listed in (b) above:

(i) [to] persons who have made an application before 9 July 2012 under Part 8 which was not decided as at 9 July 2012; and

(ii) [to] applications made] by persons who have been granted entry clearance or limited leave to enter or remain under Part 8 before 9 July 2012 [and this leave to enter or limited leave to remain is extant]:

281–289
289A–289C
290–295
295A–295O
297–316F
317–319
319L–319U
319V–319Y

(d) The following provisions of Part 8 continue to apply to applications made on or after 9 July 2012, and are not subject to any additional requirement listed in (b) above, by persons who have made an application for entry clearance, leave to enter or remain as the fiancé(e), proposed civil partner, spouse, civil partner, unmarried partner, same sex partner, or child or other dependant relative of a British citizen or settled person who is a full-time member of HM Forces:

281–289
289A–289C
290–295
295A–295O
297–316F
317–319

(e) The following provisions of Part 8 shall continue to apply to applications made on or after 9 July 2012, and are not subject to any additional requirement listed in (b) above, by a spouse, civil partner, unmarried partner or same sex partner who was admitted to the UK before 9 July 2012 further to paragraph 282(c) or 295B(c) of these Rules who has not yet applied for indefinite leave to remain:

284–286
287(a)(i)(c)
287(a)(ii)–(vii)
287(b)
288–289
289A–289C
295D–295F
295G(i)(c)
295G(ii)–(vii)
295H-295I]

[(f) Paragraphs 301-303F continue to apply to applications made under this route on or after 9 July 2012, and are not subject to any additional requirement listed in (b) above, by a child of a person to whom those paragraphs relate who has been granted limited leave to enter or remain or an extension of stay following an application made before 9 July 2012,] [(g) For the avoidance of doubt, notwithstanding the introduction of Appendix FM, paragraphs 319AA - 319J of Part 8 continue to apply, and are not subject to any additional requirement listed in paragraph (b) above, to applications for entry clearance or leave to enter or remain as the spouse, civil partner, unmarried partner, same sex partner, or child of a Relevant Points Based System Migrant.]

Note: Paragraph A280 inserted from 9 July 2012 (HC 194). Sub-paragraphs (a)–(c) amended and sub-paras (e) and (f) inserted from 6 September 2012 (HC 565).

[**A281.** In Part 8 'specified' means specified in Appendix FM-SE, unless otherwise stated, and 'English language test provider approved by the Secretary of State' means a provider specified in Appendix O.]

Note: Paragraph A281 inserted from 6 September 2012 (HC 565).

Spouses [and civil partners]

277. Nothing in these Rules shall be construed as permitting a person to be granted entry clearance, leave to enter, leave to remain or variation of leave as a spouse {or civil partner} of another if [either the applicant] [or the sponsor will be aged under [18]] {...} on the date of arrival in the United Kingdom or (as the case may be) on the date on which the leave to remain or variation of leave would be granted. [In these rules the term 'sponsor' includes 'partner' as defined in GEN 1.2 of Appendix FM.]

Note: Words in 1st square brackets substituted from 21 December 2004 (HC 164) and words in 2nd square brackets inserted from 1 April 2003 (HC 538). References to civil partners inserted from 5 December 2005 (HC 582). Words in 1st curly brackets substituted from 27 November 2008 (HC 1113). Words in 2nd curly brackets inserted from 6 April 2010 (HC 439), and omitted from 28 November 2011 (HC 1682). Number in square brackets substituted from 28 November 2011 (HC 1622). Words in last square brackets inserted from 9 July 2012 with savings for applications made but not decided before that date (HC 194).

[**278.** Nothing in these Rules shall be construed as allowing a person to be granted entry clearance, leave to enter, leave to remain or variation of leave as the spouse of a man or woman (the sponsor) if:
   (i) his or her marriage to the sponsor is polygamous; and
   (ii) there is another person living who is the husband or wife of the sponsor and who:
      (a) is, or at any time since his or her marriage to the sponsor has been, in the United Kingdom; or
      (b) has been granted a certificate of entitlement in respect of the right of abode mentioned in Section 2(1)(a) of the Immigration Act 1988 or an entry clearance to enter the United Kingdom as the husband or wife of the sponsor.
For the purpose of this paragraph a marriage may be polygamous although at its inception neither party had any other spouse.]

Note: Substituted from 2 October 2000 (Cm 4851).

[**279.** Paragraph 278 does not apply to any person who seeks entry clearance, leave to enter, leave to remain or variation of leave where:
   (i) he or she has been in the United Kingdom before 1 August 1988 having been admitted for the purpose of settlement as the husband or wife of the sponsor; or

(ii) he or she has, since their marriage to the sponsor, been in the United Kingdom at any time when there was no such other spouse living as is mentioned in paragraph 278(ii).

But where a person claims that paragraph 278 does not apply to them because they have been in the United Kingdom in circumstances which cause them to fall within sub-paragraphs (i) or (ii) of that paragraph, it shall be for them to prove that fact.]

Note: Substituted from 2 October 2000 (Cm 4851).

[**280.** For the purposes of paragraphs 278 and 279 the presence of any wife or husband in the United Kingdom in any of the following circumstances shall be disregarded:

(i) as a visitor; or

(ii) as an illegal entrant; or

(iii) in circumstances whereby a person is deemed by virtue of Section 11(1) of the Immigration Act 1971 not to have entered the United Kingdom.]

Note: Substituted from 2 October 2000 (Cm 4851).

Spouses [or civil partners] of persons present and settled in the United Kingdom or being admitted on the same occasion for settlement

Requirements for leave to enter the United Kingdom with a view to settlement as the spouse [or civil partner] of a person present and settled in the United Kingdom or being admitted on the same occasion for settlement

[**281.** The requirements to be met by a person seeking leave to enter the United Kingdom with a view to settlement as the spouse [or civil partner] of a person present and settled in the United Kingdom or who is on the same occasion being admitted for settlement are that:

{(i) (a)(i) the applicant is married to [, or the civil partner of] a person present and settled in the United Kingdom or who is on the same occasion being admitted for settlement; [and]}

[(ii) the applicant provides an original English language test certificate in speaking and listening from an English language test provider approved by the Secretary of State for these purposes, which clearly shows the applicant's name and the qualification obtained (which must meet or exceed level A1 of the Common European Framework of Reference) unless:

(a) the applicant is aged 65 or over at the time he makes his application; or

(b) [...] the applicant has a physical or mental condition that would prevent him from meeting the requirement; or;

(c) [...] there are exceptional compassionate circumstances that would prevent the applicant from meeting the requirement; or

(iii) the applicant is a national of one of the following countries: Antigua and Barbuda; Australia; the Bahamas; Barbados; Belize; Canada; Dominica; Grenada; Guyana; Jamaica; New Zealand; St Kitts and Nevis; St Lucia; St Vincent and the Grenadines; Trinidad and Tobago; United States of America; or

(iv) the applicant has obtained an academic qualification (not a professional or vocational qualification), which is deemed by UK NARIC to meet the recognised standard of a Bachelor's [or Master's] degree [or PhD] in the UK, from an educational establishment in one of the following countries: Antigua and Barbuda; Australia; The Bahamas; Barbados;

Belize; Dominica; Grenada; Guyana; Ireland; Jamaica; New Zealand; St Kitts and Nevis; St Lucia; St Vincent and The Grenadines; Trinidad and Tobago; the UK; the USA; and provides the specified documents; or

    (v) the applicant has obtained an academic qualification (not a professional or vocational qualification) which is deemed by UK NARIC to meet the recognised standard of a Bachelor's [or Master's] degree [or PhD] in the UK, and

       (1) provides the specified evidence to show he has the qualification, and

       (2) UK NARIC has confirmed that the [qualification] was taught or researched in English,

      or

    (vi) has obtained an academic qualification (not a professional or vocational qualification) which is deemed by UK NARIC to meet the recognised standard of a Bachelor's [or Master's] degree [or PhD] in the UK, and provides the specified evidence to show:

       (1) he has the qualification, and

       (2) that the qualification was taught or researched in English,

      or]

       [(b) (i) the applicant is married to or the civil partner of a person who has a right of abode in the United Kingdom or indefinite leave to enter or remain in the United Kingdom and is on the same occasion seeking admission to the United Kingdom for the purposes of settlement and the parties were married or formed a civil partnership at least 4 years ago, since which time they have been living together outside the United Kingdom; and

         (ii) the applicant has sufficient knowledge of the English language and sufficient knowledge about life in the United Kingdom, unless he is under the age of 18 or aged 65 or over at the time he makes his application; and]

         (iii) the applicant does not have one or more unspent convictions within the meaning of the Rehabilitation of Offenders Act 1974; and]

    (ii) the parties to the marriage [or civil partnership] have met; and

    (iii) each of the parties intends to live permanently with the other as his or her spouse [or civil partner] and the marriage [or civil partnership] is subsisting; and

    (iv) there will be adequate accommodation for the parties and any dependants without recourse to public funds in accommodation which they own or occupy exclusively; and

    (v) the parties will be able to maintain themselves and any dependants adequately without recourse to public funds; and

    (vi) the applicant holds a valid United Kingdom entry clearance for entry in this capacity.]

[For the purposes of this paragraph and paragraphs 282–289 a member of HM Forces serving overseas, or a permanent member of HM Diplomatic Service or a comparable UK-based staff member of the British Council on a tour of duty abroad, or a staff member of the Department for International Development who is a British citizen or is settled in the United Kingdom, is to be regarded as present and settled in the United Kingdom.]

Note: Paragraph 281 substituted from 5 June 1997 (HC 26). Words following sub-para (vi) substituted from 18 September 2002 (Cm 5597). Words in curly brackets substituted from 1 April 2003 (HC 358). References to civil partnership inserted from 5 December 2005 (HC 582). Sub-paragraph (i)(b)(i) substituted and sub-para (i)(b)(ii) inserted from 2 April 2007 (HC 398). Sub-paragraph (i) (a) renumbered as sub-para (i)(a)(i) and sub-paras (i)(a)(ii)–(v) inserted from 29 November 2010, with savings for applications made but not decided before that date (Cm 7944). Sub-paragraph

(vii) inserted from 6 April 2011 (HC 863), deleted from 6 April 2011, and sub-para (b)(iii) inserted from 6 April 2011 except for applications made but undecided before that date (HC 908). Words in square brackets in sub-paras (i)(a)(iv)–(v) inserted and words deleted from sub-paras (i)(a)(ii)(b)–(c) from 4 July 2011 except for applications made but not decided before that date (HC 1148).

Leave to enter as the spouse {or civil partner} of a person present and settled in the United Kingdom or being admitted for settlement on the same occasion

[282. A person seeking leave to enter the United Kingdom as the spouse or civil partner of a person present and settled in the United Kingdom or who is on the same occasion being admitted for settlement may:

(a) in the case of a person [who meets the requirements of paragraph 281(i)(a)(i) and one of the requirements of paragraph 281(i)(a)(ii)–(vi)], be admitted for an initial period not exceeding [27 months], or

(b) in the case of a person who meets [all] of the requirements in paragraph 281(i)(b), be granted indefinite leave to enter, or

(c) in the case of a person who meets the requirement in paragraph 281(i)(b)(i), but not the requirement in paragraph 281(i)(b)(ii) to have sufficient knowledge of the English language and about life in the United Kingdom, be admitted for an initial period not exceeding [27 months], in all cases provided the Immigration Officer is satisfied that each of the relevant requirements of paragraph 281 is met.]

Note: Paragraph 282 substituted from 2 April 2007 (HC 398). Words in first square brackets in sub-para (a) substituted from 29 November 2010, with savings for applications made but not decided before that date (Cm 7944). Other words in square brackets in sub-paras (a) and (c) substituted from 22 July 2008 (HC 971). Word in square brackets in (c) substituted from 6 April 2011 with savings for applications made but not decided on that date (HC908).

Refusal of leave to enter as the spouse [or civil partner] of a person present and settled in the United Kingdom or being admitted on the same occasion for settlement

283. Leave to enter the United Kingdom as the spouse [or civil partner] of a person present and settled in the United Kingdom or who is on the same occasion being admitted for settlement is to be refused [if the immigration officer is not satisfied that each of the requirements of paragraph 281 is met.]

Note: Words in square brackets at end of paragraph 283 substituted from 2 April 2007 (HC 398).

Requirements for an extension of stay as the spouse [or civil partner] of a person present and settled in the United Kingdom

[284. The requirements for an extension of stay as the spouse [or civil partner] of a person present and settled in the United Kingdom are that:

(i) the applicant has limited leave to enter or remain in the United Kingdom {which was given in accordance with any of the provisions of these Rules} other than where as a result of that leave he would not have been in the United Kingdom beyond 6 months from the date on which he was admitted to the United Kingdom on this occasion in accordance with these Rules, unless] [:

(a) the leave in question is limited leave to enter as a fiancé or proposed civil partner; or

(b) the leave in question was granted to the applicant as the spouse, civil partner, unmarried or same-sex partner of a Relevant Points Based System Migrant and that spouse or partner is the same person in relation to whom the applicant is applying for an extension of stay under this rule; and]

(ii) is married to [, or the civil partner of] a person present and settled in the United Kingdom; and

(iii) the parties to the marriage [or civil partnership] have met; and

(iv) the applicant has not remained in breach of the immigration laws; and

(v) the marriage [or civil partnership] has not taken place after a decision has been made to deport the applicant or he has been recommended for deportation or been given notice under Section 6(2) of the Immigration Act 1971 [or been given directions for his removal under section 10 of the Immigration and Asylum Act 1999]; and

(vi) each of the parties intends to live permanently with the other as his or her spouse [or civil partner] and the marriage [or civil partnership] is subsisting; and

(vii) there will be adequate accommodation for the parties and any dependants without recourse to public funds in accommodation which they own or occupy exclusively; and

(viii) the parties will be able to maintain themselves and any dependants adequately without recourse to public funds[, and]]

[(ix) (a) the applicant provides an original English language test certificate in speaking and listening from an English language test provider approved by the Secretary of State for these purposes, which clearly shows the applicant's name and the qualification obtained (which must meet or exceed level A1 of the Common European Framework of Reference) unless:

(i) the applicant is aged 65 or over at the time he makes his application; or

(ii) [...] the applicant has a physical or mental condition that would prevent him from meeting the requirement; or

(iii) [...] there are exceptional compassionate circumstances that would prevent the applicant from meeting the requirement; or

(ix) (b) the applicant is a national of one of the following countries: Antigua and Barbuda; Australia; the Bahamas; Barbados; Belize; Canada; Dominica; Grenada; Guyana; Jamaica; New Zealand; St Kitts and Nevis; St Lucia; St Vincent and the Grenadines; Trinidad and Tobago; United States of America; or

(ix) (c) the applicant has obtained an academic qualification (not a professional or vocational qualification), which is deemed by UK NARIC to meet the recognised standard of a Bachelor's [or Master's] degree [or PhD] in the UK, from an educational establishment in one of the following countries: Antigua and Barbuda; Australia; The Bahamas; Barbados; Belize; Dominica; Grenada; Guyana; Ireland; Jamaica; New Zealand; St Kitts and Nevis; St Lucia; St Vincent and The Grenadines; Trinidad and Tobago; the UK; the USA; and provides the specified documents; or

(ix) (d) the applicant has obtained an academic qualification (not a professional or vocational qualification) which is deemed by UK NARIC to meet the recognised standard of a Bachelor's [or Master's] degree [or PhD] in the UK, and

(1) provides the specified evidence to show he has the qualification, and

(2) UK NARIC has confirmed that the [qualification] degree was taught or researched in English, or

(ix)(e) has obtained an academic qualification (not a professional or vocational qualification) which is deemed by UK NARIC to meet the recognised standard of a Bachelor's [or Master's] degree [or PhD] in the UK, and provides the specified evidence to show:

    (1) he has the qualification, and

    (2) that the qualification was taught or researched in English.]

Note: Substituted from 5 June 1997 (HC 26). Sub-paragraph (i) substituted from 25 August 2003 (Cm 5949). Words in first curly brackets in sub-para (i) inserted from 1 October 2004 (Cm 6339). Other references to civil partnership inserted from 5 December 2005 (HC 582). Words in square brackets in sub-para (v) inserted from 22 July 2008 (HC 971). Sub-paragraph (ix) inserted from 29 November 2010 except for applications made but not decided before that date (Cm 7944). Words deleted from sub-para (i) from 6 April 2011 except for applications made but not decided before that date (HC 863). Words in square brackets in sub-paras (ix)(c)–(e) inserted and words deleted from sub-paras (ix)(a)(ii)–(iii) from 4 July 2011 except for applications made but not decided before that date (HC 1148). Words in square brackets in sub-para (i) substituted from 31 October 2011 except for applications made but not decided before that date (HC 1511).

Extension of stay as the spouse {or civil partner} of a person present and settled in the United Kingdom

285. An extension of stay as the spouse {or civil partner} of a person present and settled in the United Kingdom may be granted for a period of [2 years] in the first instance, provided the Secretary of State is satisfied that each of the requirements of paragraph 284 is met.

Note: Words in square brackets substituted from 1 April 2003 (HC 538). References to civil partners inserted from 5 December 2005 (HC 582).

Refusal of extension of stay as the spouse [or civil partner] of a person present and settled in the United Kingdom

286. An extension of stay as the spouse [or civil partner] of a person present and settled in the United Kingdom is to be refused if the Secretary of State is not satisfied that each of the requirements of paragraph 284 is met.

Requirements for indefinite leave to remain for the spouse {or civil partner} of a person present and settled in the United Kingdom

[**287.**—(a) The requirements for indefinite leave to remain for the spouse {or civil partner} of a person present and settled in the United Kingdom are that:

    [(i) (a) the applicant was admitted to the United Kingdom for a period not exceeding 27 months or given an extension of stay for a period of 2 years in accordance with paragraphs 281 to 286 of these Rules and has completed a period of 2 years as the spouse or civil partner of a person present and settled in the United Kingdom; or]

    [(b) the applicant was admitted to the United Kingdom for a period not exceeding 27 months or given an extension of stay for a period of 2 years in accordance with paragraphs 295AA to 295F of these Rules and during that period married or formed a civil partnership with the person whom he or she was admitted or granted an extension of stay to join and has completed a period of 2 years as the unmarried or same-sex partner and then the spouse or civil partner of a person present and settled in the United Kingdom; or] [(c) was admitted to the United Kingdom in accordance with leave granted under paragraph 282(c) of these rules[; and]]

[(d) the applicant was admitted to the UK or given an extension of stay as the spouse or civil partner of a [Relevant Points Based System Migrant], and then obtained an extension of stay under paragraphs 281 to 286 of these Rules and has completed a period of 2 years as the spouse or civil partner of the person who is now present and settled here; or]

[(e) the applicant was admitted to the UK or given an extension of stay as the unmarried or same-sex partner of a [Relevant Points Based System Migrant] and during that period married or formed a civil partnership with the person whom he or she was admitted or granted an extension of stay to join and has completed a period of 2 years as the unmarried or same-sex partner and then the spouse or civil partner of the person who is now present and settled in the UK[; or]

[(f) the applicant was admitted into the UK in accordance with paragraph 319L and has completed a period of 2 years limited leave as the spouse or civil partner of a refugee or beneficiary of humanitarian protection who is now present and settled in the UK or as the spouse or civil partner of a former refugee or beneficiary of humanitarian protection who is now a British Citizen;]

(ii) the applicant is still the spouse {or civil partner} of the person he or she was admitted or granted an extension of stay to join and the marriage {or civil partnership} is subsisting; and

(iii) each of the parties intends to live permanently with the other as his or her spouse {or civil partner}; and

(iv) there will be adequate accommodation for the parties and any dependants without recourse to public funds in accommodation which they own or occupy exclusively; and

(v) the parties will be able to maintain themselves and any dependants adequately without recourse to public funds [; and

(vi) the applicant has sufficient knowledge of the English language and sufficient knowledge about life in the United Kingdom, unless he is under the age of 18 or aged 65 or over at the time he makes his application[; and

(vii) the applicant does not have one or more unspent convictions within the meaning of the Rehabilitation of Offenders Act 1974.]

(b) The requirements for indefinite leave to remain for the bereaved spouse {or civil partner} of a person who was present and settled in the United Kingdom are that:

[(i) (a) the applicant was admitted to the United Kingdom for a period not exceeding 27 months or given an extension of stay for a period of 2 years as the spouse or civil partner of a person present and settled in the United Kingdom in accordance with paragraphs 281 to 286 of these Rules; or]

[(b) the applicant was admitted to the United Kingdom for a period not exceeding 27 months or given an extension of stay for a period of 2 years as the unmarried or same-sex partner of a person present and settled in the United Kingdom in accordance with paragraphs 295AA to 295F of these Rules and during that period married or formed a civil partnership with the person whom he or she was admitted or granted an extension of stay to join; and]

(ii) the person whom the applicant was admitted or granted an extension of stay to join died during that . . . period; and

(iii) the applicant was still the spouse {or civil partner} of the person he or she was admitted or granted an extension of stay to join at the time of the death; and

(iv) each of the parties intended to live permanently with the other as his or her spouse {or civil partner} and the marriage [or civil partnership] was subsisting at the time of the death [; and

(vii) the applicant does not have one or more unspent convictions within the meaning of the Rehabilitation of Offenders Act 1974.]]

Note: Substituted from 2 October 2000 (Cm 4851). Sub-paragraphs (a)(i)(a), (a)(i)(b) and (b)(i)(a) and (b)(i)(b) substituted from 22 July 2008 (HC 971). Words omitted from sub-para (b)(ii) from 22 July 2008 (HC 971). Sub-paragraph (a)(i)(c) inserted from 2 April 2007 (HC 398). References to civil partnership inserted from 5 December 2005 (HC 582). Sub-paragraph (a)(vi) inserted from 2 April 2007(HC 398). Sub-paragraphs (a)(i)(d) and (e) inserted from 29 February 2008 (HC 321). Words in square brackets in sub-paras (c), (d), (e) and sub-para (f) inserted from 6 April 2011 (HC 863). Sub-paragraphs (a)(vii) and (b)(v) inserted from 6 April 2011 except for applications made but not decided before that date (HC 908).

Indefinite leave to remain for the spouse [or civil partner] of a person present and settled in the United Kingdom

288. Indefinite leave to remain for the spouse [or civil partner] of a person present and settled in the United Kingdom may be granted provided the Secretary of State is satisfied that each of the requirements of paragraph 287 is met.

Refusal of indefinite leave to remain for the spouse [or civil partner] of a person present and settled in the United Kingdom

289. Indefinite leave to remain for the spouse [or civil partner] of a person present and settled in the United Kingdom is to be refused if the Secretary of State is not satisfied that each of the requirements of paragraph 287 is met.

Note: References to civil partners inserted from 5 December 2005 (HC 582).

[Requirements for indefinite leave to remain in the United Kingdom as the victim of domestic violence

289A. The requirements to be met by a person who is the victim of domestic violence and who is seeking indefinite leave to remain in the United Kingdom are that the applicant:

[(i) was admitted to the United Kingdom for a period not exceeding 27 months or given an extension of stay for a period of 2 years as the spouse or civil partner of a person present and settled here; or]

[(ii) was admitted to the United Kingdom for a period not exceeding 27 months or given an extension of stay for a period of 2 years as the unmarried or same-sex partner of a person present and settled here; and]

(iii) the relationship with their [spouse, civil partner, unmarried partner or same-sex partner], as appropriate, was subsisting at the beginning of the relevant period of leave or extension of stay referred to in (i) or (ii) above; and

(iv) is able to produce ... evidence ... to establish that the relationship was caused to permanently break down before the end of that period as a result of domestic violence] [; and

(v) the applicant does not have one or more unspent convictions within the meaning of the Rehabilitation of Offenders Act 1974.]

Note: Paragraph 289A inserted from 18 December 2002 (HC 104). Words in square brackets in sub-para (iii) inserted from 5 December 2005 (HC 582). Sub-paragraphs (i) and (ii) substituted from 22 July 2008 (HC 971). Sub-paragraph (v) inserted from 6 April 2011 except for applications made but not decided before that date (HC 908). Words deleted from sub-para (iv) from 6 September 2012 (HC 565).

[Indefinite leave to remain as the victim of domestic violence

289B. Indefinite leave to remain as the victim of domestic violence may be granted provided the Secretary of State is satisfied that each of the requirements of paragraph 289A is met.]

Note: Paragraph 289B inserted from 1 April 2003 (HC 538).

[Refusal of indefinite leave to remain as the victim of domestic violence

289C. Indefinite leave to remain as the victim of domestic violence is to be refused if the Secretary of State is not satisfied that each of the requirements of paragraph 289A is met.]

Note: Paragraph 289C inserted from 1 April 2003 (HC 538).

Fiancé(e)s [and proposed civil partners]

[289AA. Nothing in these Rules shall be construed as permitting a person to be granted entry clearance, leave to enter or variation of leave as a fiancé(e) [or proposed civil partner] if {either the applicant} or the sponsor will be aged under [18] [...]on the date of arrival of the applicant in the United Kingdom or (as the case may be) on the date on which the leave to enter or variation of leave would be granted.]

Note: Paragraph 289AA inserted from 1 April 2003 (HC 538). Words in 1st curly brackets inserted from 21 December 2004 (HC 164). References to civil partnership inserted from 5 December 2005 (HC 582). Words in 2nd square brackets inserted from 6 April 2010 (HC 439). Number in square brackets substituted and words deleted from 28 November 2011 (HC 1622).

Requirements for leave to enter the United Kingdom as a fiancé(e) [or proposed civil partner] (ie with a view to marriage and permanent settlement in the United Kingdom)

[290. The requirements to be met by a person seeking leave to enter the United Kingdom as a fiancé(e) [or proposed civil partner] are that:
    (i) the applicant is seeking leave to enter the United Kingdom for marriage [or civil partnership] to a person present and settled in the United Kingdom or who is on the same occasion being admitted for settlement; and
    (ii) the parties to the proposed marriage [or civil partnership] have met; and
    (iii) each of the parties intends to live permanently with the other as his or her spouse [or civil partner] after the marriage [or civil partnership]; and
    (iv) adequate maintenance and accommodation without recourse to public funds will be available for the applicant until the date of the marriage [or civil partnership]; and

(v) there will, after the marriage [or civil partnership], be adequate accommodation for the parties and any dependants without recourse to public funds in accommodation which they own or occupy exclusively; and

(vi) the parties will be able after the marriage [or civil partnership] to maintain
themselves and any dependants adequately without recourse to public funds; and

[(vii) (a) the applicant provides an original English language test certificate in speaking and listening from an English language test provider approved by the Secretary of
State for these purposes, which clearly shows the applicant's name and the qualification
obtained (which must meet or exceed level A1 of the Common European Framework of
Reference) unless:

(i) the applicant is aged 65 or over at the time he makes his application; or

(ii) [...] the applicant has a physical or mental condition that would prevent him
from meeting the requirement; or

(iii) [...] there are exceptional compassionate circumstances that would prevent
the applicant from meeting the requirement; or

(vii)(b) the applicant is a national of one of the following countries: Antigua and
Barbuda; Australia; the Bahamas; Barbados; Belize; Canada; Dominica; Grenada; Guyana;
Jamaica; New Zealand; St Kitts and Nevis; St Lucia; St Vincent and the Grenadines;
Trinidad and Tobago; United States of America; or

(vii)(c) the applicant has obtained an academic qualification (not a professional or
vocational qualification), which is deemed by UK NARIC to meet the recognised standard of a Bachelor's [or Master's] degree [or PhD] in the UK, from an educational establishment in one of the following countries: Antigua and Barbuda; Australia; The Bahamas;
Barbados; Belize; Dominica; Grenada; Guyana; Ireland; Jamaica; New Zealand; St Kitts
and Nevis; St Lucia; St Vincent and The Grenadines; Trinidad and Tobago; the UK; the
USA; and provides the specified documents; or

(vii)(d) the applicant has obtained an academic qualification (not a professional or
vocational qualification) which is deemed by UK NARIC to meet the recognised standard
of a Bachelor's [or Master's] degree [or PhD] in the UK, and

(1) provides the specified evidence to show he has the qualification, and

(2) UK NARIC has confirmed that the [qualification] was taught or researched in
English, or

(vii)(e) has obtained an academic qualification (not a professional or vocational
qualification) which is deemed by UK NARIC to meet the recognised standard of a
Bachelor's [or Master's] degree [or PhD] in the UK, and provides the specified evidence
to show:

(1) he has the qualification, and

(2) that the qualification was taught or researched in English, and]

[(viii) the applicant holds a valid United Kingdom entry clearance for entry in this
capacity.]]

Note: Substituted from 5 June 1997 (HC 26). References to civil partnership inserted from 5
December 2005 (HC 582). Sub-paragraph (vii) substituted and sub-para (viii) inserted from
29 November 2010 with saving for applications made but not decided before that date (Cm
7944). Words in square brackets in sub-paras (vii)(c)–(e) inserted and words deleted from
sub-paras(vii)(a)(ii)–(iii) from 4 July 2011 except for applications made but not decided before
that date (HC 1148).

[**290A.** For the purposes of paragraph 290 and paragraphs 291–295, an EEA national who holds a registration certificate or a document certifying permanent residence issued under the 2006 EEA Regulations (including an EEA national who holds a residence permit issued under the Immigration (European Economic Area) Regulations 2000 which is treated as if it were such a certificate or document by virtue of Schedule 4 to the 2006 EEA Regulations) is to be regarded as present and settled in the United Kingdom.]

Note: Paragraph 290A substituted from 30 April 2006 (HC 1053).

Leave to enter as a fiancé(e) [or proposed civil partner]

291. A person seeking leave to enter the United Kingdom as a fiancé(e) [or proposed civil partner] may be admitted, with a prohibition on employment, for a period not exceeding 6 months to enable the marriage [or civil partnership] to take place provided a valid United Kingdom entry clearance for entry in this capacity is produced to the Immigration Officer on arrival.

Note: References to civil partnership inserted from 5 December 2005 (HC 582).

Refusal of leave to enter as a fiancé(e) [or proposed civil partner]

292. Leave to enter the United Kingdom as a fiancé(e) [or proposed civil partner] is to be refused if a valid United Kingdom entry clearance for entry in this capacity is not produced to the Immigration Officer on arrival.

Note: References to civil partnership inserted from 5 December 2005 (HC 582).

Requirements for an extension of stay as a fiancé(e) [or proposed civil partner]

293. The requirements for an extension of stay as a fiancé(e) [or proposed civil partner] are that:

(i) the applicant was admitted to the United Kingdom with a valid United Kingdom entry clearance as a fiancé(e) [or proposed civil partner]; and

(ii) good cause is shown why the marriage [or civil partnership] did not take place within the initial period of leave granted under paragraph 291; and

(iii) there is satisfactory evidence that the marriage [or civil partnership] will take place at an early date; and

[(iv) the requirements of [paragraph 290(ii)–(vii) are met.]]

Note: Sub-paragraph (iv) substituted from 5 June 1997 (HC 26), words in square brackets in sub-para (iv) substituted from 29 November 2010 except for applications made before that date (Cm 7944).

Extension of stay as a fiancé(e) [or proposed civil partner]

294. An extension of stay as a fiancé(e) [or proposed civil partner] may be granted for an appropriate period with a prohibition on employment to enable the marriage [or civil partnership] to take place provided the Secretary of State is satisfied that each of the requirements of paragraph 293 is met.

Note: References to civil partnership inserted from 5 December 2005 (HC 582).

Refusal of extension of stay as a fiancé(e) [or proposed civil partner]

295. An extension of stay is to be refused if the Secretary of State is not satisfied that each of the requirements of paragraph 293 is met.

[Leave to enter as the unmarried [or same-sex] partner of a person present and settled in the United Kingdom or being admitted on the same occasion for settlement

[**295AA.** Nothing in these Rules shall be construed as permitting a person to be granted entry clearance, leave to enter or variation of leave as an unmarried [or same-sex] partner if {either the applicant} or the sponsor will be aged under [18] [...] on the date of arrival of the applicant in the United Kingdom or (as the case may be) on the date on which the leave to enter or variation of leave would be granted.]

Note: Paragraph 295AA inserted from 1 April 2003 (HC 538). Words in 1st curly brackets inserted from 21 December 2004 (HC 164). References to same-sex partners inserted from 5 December 2005 (HC 582). Number in square brackets and words omitted from 28 November 2011 (HC 1622).

[Requirements for leave to enter the United Kingdom with a view to settlement as the unmarried [or same-sex] partner of a person present and settled in the United Kingdom or being admitted on the same occasion for settlement

295A. The requirements to be met by a person seeking leave to enter the United Kingdom with a view to settlement as the unmarried [or same-sex] partner of a person present and settled in the United Kingdom or being admitted on the same occasion for settlement, are that:

[(i) (a)(i) the applicant is the unmarried [or same-sex] partner of a person present and settled in the United Kingdom or who is on the same occasion being admitted for settlement and the parties have been living together in a relationship akin to marriage which has subsisted for two years or more; [and]]

[(ii) the applicant provides an original English language test certificate in speaking and listening from an English language test provider approved by the Secretary of State for these purposes, which clearly shows the applicant's name and the qualification obtained (which must meet or exceed level A1 of the Common European Framework of Reference) unless:

(a) the applicant is aged 65 or over at the time he makes his application; or

(b) [...] the applicant has a physical or mental condition that would prevent him from meeting the requirement; or

(c) [...] there are exceptional compassionate circumstances that would prevent the applicant from meeting the requirement; or

(iii) the applicant is a national of one of the following countries: Antigua and Barbuda; Australia; the Bahamas; Barbados; Belize; Canada; Dominica; Grenada; Guyana; Jamaica; New Zealand; St Kitts and Nevis; St Lucia; St Vincent and the Grenadines; Trinidad and Tobago; United States of America; or

(iv) the applicant has obtained an academic qualification (not a professional or vocational qualification), which is deemed by UK NARIC to meet the recognised standard of a Bachelor's [or Master's] degree [or PhD] in the UK, from an educational establishment in one of the following countries: Antigua and Barbuda; Australia; The Bahamas; Barbados;

Belize; Dominica; Grenada; Guyana; Ireland; Jamaica; New Zealand; St Kitts and Nevis; St Lucia; St Vincent and The Grenadines; Trinidad and Tobago; the UK; the USA; and provides the specified documents; or

(v) the applicant has obtained an academic qualification (not a professional or vocational qualification) which is deemed by UK NARIC to meet the recognised standard of a Bachelor's [or Master's] degree [or PhD] in the UK, and

(1) provides the specified evidence to show he has the qualification, and

(2) UK NARIC has confirmed that the [qualification] was taught or researched in English, or

(vi) has obtained an academic qualification (not a professional or vocational qualification) which is deemed by UK NARIC to meet the recognised standard of a Bachelor's [or Master's] degree [or PhD] in the UK, and provides the specified evidence to show:

(1) he has the qualification, and

(2) that the qualification was taught or researched in English.

or]

[(b) (i) the applicant is the unmarried or same-sex partner of a person who has a right of abode in the United Kingdom or indefinite leave to enter or remain in the United Kingdom and is on the same occasion seeking admission to the United Kingdom for the purposes of settlement and the parties have been living together outside the United Kingdom in a relationship akin to marriage which has subsisted for 4 years or more; and

(b) (ii) the applicant has sufficient knowledge of the English language and sufficient knowledge about life in the United Kingdom, unless he is under the age of 18 or aged 65 or over at the time he makes his application; and]

[(b)(iii) the applicant does not have one or more unspent convictions within the meaning of the Rehabilitation of Offenders Act 1974; and]

(ii) any previous marriage [or civil partnership] (or similar relationship) by either partner has permanently broken down; and

[(iii) the parties are not involved in a consanguineous relationship with one another; and]

(iv) ...

(v) there will be adequate accommodation for the parties and any dependants without recourse to public funds in accommodation which they own or occupy exclusively; and

(vi) the parties will be able to maintain themselves and any dependants adequately without recourse to public funds; and

(vii) the parties intend to live together permanently: and

(viii) the applicant holds a valid United Kingdom entry clearance for entry in this capacity.

[For the purpose of this paragraph and paragraphs 295B–295I, a member of HM Forces serving overseas, or a permanent member of HM Diplomatic Service or a comparable UK-based staff member of the British Council on a tour of duty abroad, or a staff member of the Department for International Development who is a British citizen or is settled in the United Kingdom, is to be regarded as present and settled in the United Kingdom.]]

Note: Paragraph 295A inserted from 2 October 2000 (Cm 4581). Sub-paragraph (i) substituted and sub-para (iv) deleted from 1 April 2003 (HC 538). Words in square brackets at the end of sub-para (viii) inserted from 18 September 2002 (Cm 5597). Sub-paragraph (iii) inserted from 25 August 2003 (Cm 5949). References to same-sex partners inserted from 5 December 2005 (HC 582). Sub-paragraphs (i)(b)(i) and (i)(b)(ii) substituted from 2 April 2007 (HC 398). Sub-paragraph (i)

(a) renumbered as (i)(a)(i) and sub-paras (i)(a)(ii)–(vi) inserted from 29 November 2010 except for applications made but not decided before that date (Cm 7944). Sub-paragraph (i)(b)((iii) inserted from 6 April 2011 except for applications made but not decided before that date (HC 908). Words in square brackets in sub-paras (i)(a)(iv)–(vi) inserted and words deleted from sub-paras (i)(a)(ii) (b)–(c) from 4 July 2011 except for applications made but not decided before that date (HC 1148).

[Leave to enter the United Kingdom with a view to settlement as the unmarried [or same-sex] partner of a person present and settled in the United Kingdom or being admitted on the same occasion for settlement

[295B. A person seeking leave to enter the United Kingdom as the unmarried or same-sex partner of a person present and settled in the United Kingdom or who is on the same occasion being admitted for settlement may:

(a) in the case of a person [who meets the requirements of paragraph 295A(i)(a)(i), and one of the requirements of paragraph 295A(i)(a)(ii)–(vi)]], be admitted for an initial period not exceeding [27 months], or

(b) in the case of a person who meets [all] of the requirements in paragraph 295A(i) (b), be granted indefinite leave to enter, or

(c) in the case of a person who meets the requirement in paragraph 295A(i)(b)(i), but not the requirement in paragraph 295A(i)(b)(ii) to have sufficient knowledge of the English language and about life in the United Kingdom, be admitted for an initial period not exceeding [27 months], in all cases provided the Immigration Officer is satisfied that each of the relevant requirements of paragraph 295A is met.]

Note: Paragraph 295B substituted from 2 April 2007 (HC 398). Words in first square brackets in sub-para (a) substituted from 29 November 2010 with savings for applications made but not decided before that date (Cm 7944). Words in other square brackets in sub-paras (a) and (c) substituted from 22 July 2008 (HC 971). Word in square brackets in (b) substituted from 6 April 2011 with savings for applications made but not decided before that date (HC 908).

[Refusal of leave to enter the United Kingdom with a view to settlement as the unmarried [or same-sex] partner of a person present and settled in the United Kingdom or being admitted on the same occasion for settlement

295C. Leave to enter the United Kingdom with a view to settlement as the unmarried [or same-sex] partner of a person present and settled in the United Kingdom or being admitted on the same occasion for settlement, is to be refused {if the immigration officer is not satisfied that each of the requirements of paragraph 295A are met}]

Note: Paragraph 295C inserted from 2 October 2000 (Cm 4581). References to same-sex partners inserted from 5 December 2005 (HC 582). Words in curly brackets substituted from 2 April 2007 (HC 398).

Leave to remain as the unmarried [or same-sex] partner of a person present and settled in the United Kingdom

[Requirements for leave to remain as the unmarried [or same-sex] partner of a person present and settled in the United Kingdom

295D. The requirements to be met by a person seeking leave to remain as the unmarried [or same-sex] partner of a person present and settled in the United Kingdom are that:

(i) the applicant has limited leave to [enter or] remain in the United Kingdom [which was given in accordance with any of the provisions of these Rules] [, other than where as a result of that leave he would not have been in the United Kingdom beyond 6 months from the date on which he was admitted to the United Kingdom on this occasion in accordance with these rules]; and

(ii) any previous marriage [or civil partnership] (or similar relationship) by either partner has permanently broken down; and

(iii) the applicant is the unmarried [or same-sex] partner of a person who is present and settled in the United Kingdom; and

(iv) the applicant has not remained in breach of the immigration laws; and

[(v) the parties are not involved in a consanguineous relationship with one another; and]

(vi) the parties have been living together in a relationship akin to marriage which has subsisted for two years or more; and

(vii) the parties' relationship pre-dates any decision to deport the applicant, recommend him for deportation, give him notice under Section 6(2) of the Immigration Act 1971, or give directions for his removal under section 10 of the Immigration and Asylum Act 1999; and

(viii) there will be adequate accommodation for the parties and any dependants without recourse to public funds in accommodation which they own or occupy exclusively; and

(ix) the parties will be able to maintain themselves and any dependants adequately without recourse to public funds; and

(x) the parties intend to live together permanently[, and]]

[(xi) (a) the applicant provides an original English language test certificate in speaking and listening from an English language test provider approved by the Secretary of State for these purposes, which clearly shows the applicant's name and the qualification obtained (which must meet or exceed level A1 of the Common European Framework of Reference) unless:

(i) the applicant is aged 65 or over at the time he makes his application; or

(ii) [...] the applicant has a physical or mental condition that would prevent him from meeting the requirement; or

(iii) [...] there are exceptional compassionate circumstances that would prevent the applicant from meeting the requirement; or

(xi) (b) the applicant is a national of one of the following countries: Antigua and Barbuda; Australia; the Bahamas; Barbados; Belize; Canada; Dominica; Grenada; Guyana; Jamaica; New Zealand; St Kitts and Nevis; St Lucia; St Vincent and the Grenadines; Trinidad and Tobago; United States of America; or

(xi) (c) the applicant has obtained an academic qualification (not a professional or vocational qualification), which is deemed by UK NARIC to meet the recognised standard of a Bachelor's [or Master's] degree [or PhD] in the UK, from an educational establishment in one of the following countries: Antigua and Barbuda; Australia; The Bahamas; Barbados; Belize; Dominica; Grenada; Guyana; Ireland; Jamaica; New Zealand; St Kitts and Nevis; St Lucia; St Vincent and The Grenadines; Trinidad and Tobago; the UK; the USA; and provides the specified documents; or

(xi) (d) the applicant has obtained an academic qualification (not a professional or vocational qualification) which is deemed by UK NARIC to meet the recognised standard of a Bachelor's [or Master's] degree [or PhD] in the UK, and

(1) provides the specified evidence to show he has the qualification, and

(2) UK NARIC has confirmed that the [qualification] was taught or researched in English, or

(xi)(e) has obtained an academic qualification (not a professional or vocational qualification) which is deemed by UK NARIC to meet the recognised standard of a Bachelor's [or Master's] degree [or PhD] in the UK, and provides the specified evidence to show:
    (1) he has the qualification, and
    (2) that the qualification was taught or researched in English.]

Note: Paragraph 295D inserted from 2 October 2000 (Cm 4581). Sub-paragraph (v) inserted from 25 August 2003 (Cm 5949). Words in second square brackets in sub-para (i) inserted from 1 October 2004 (Cm 6339). References to same-sex partners inserted from 5 December 2005 (HC 582). Sub-paragraph (xi) inserted from 29 November 2010 with savings for applications made before that date (Cm 7944). Words in square brackets in sub-paras (xi)(c)–(e) inserted and words deleted from sub-paras (xi)(a)(ii)–(iii) from 4 July 2011 with savings for applications made but not decided before that date (HC 1148). Words in first and third square brackets in sub-para (i) inserted from 31 October 2011 except for applications made but not decided before that date (HC 1511).

[Leave to remain as the unmarried [or same-sex] partner of a person present and settled in the United Kingdom

295E. Leave to remain as the unmarried [or same-sex] partner of a person present and settled in the United Kingdom may be granted for a period of 2 years in the first instance provided that the Secretary of State is satisfied that each of the requirements of paragraph 295D is met.]

Note: Paragraph 295E inserted from 2 October 2000 (Cm 4581). References to same-sex partners inserted from 5 December 2005 (HC 582).

[Refusal of leave to remain as the unmarried [or same-sex] partner of a person present and settled in the United Kingdom

295F. Leave to remain as the unmarried [or same-sex] partner of a person present and settled in the United Kingdom is to be refused if the Secretary of State is not satisfied that each of the requirements of paragraph 295D is met.]

Note: Paragraph 295F inserted from 2 October 2000 (Cm 4581). References to same-sex partners inserted from 5 December 2005 (HC 582).

Indefinite leave to remain as the unmarried [or same-sex] partner of a person present and settled in the United Kingdom

[Requirements for indefinite leave to remain as the unmarried [or same-sex] partner of a person present and settled in the United Kingdom

295G. The requirements to be met by a person seeking indefinite leave to remain as the unmarried [or same-sex] partner of a person present and settled in the United Kingdom are that:

[(i) (a) the applicant was admitted to the United Kingdom {for a period not exceeding 27 months} or given an extension of stay for a period of 2 years in accordance with paragraphs 295AA to 295F of these Rules and has completed a period of 2 years as the unmarried or same-sex partner of a person present and settled here; or

(b) the applicant was admitted to the United Kingdom or given an extension of stay as the unmarried or same-sex partner of a [Relevant Points Based System Migrant], and then obtained an extension of stay under paragraphs 295AA to 295F of these Rules and has completed a period of 2 years as the unmarried or same-sex partner of the person who is now present and settled here; or

(c) the applicant was admitted to the United Kingdom in accordance with leave granted under paragraph 295B(c) of these rules; [or]

[(d) the applicant was admitted into the UK in accordance with paragraph 319O and has completed a period of 2 years limited leave as the unmarried or same-sex partner of a refugee or beneficiary of humanitarian protection who is now present and settled in the UK or as the unmarried or same-sex partner of a former refugee or beneficiary of humanitarian protection who is now a British Citizen;]

(ii) the applicant is still the unmarried [or same-sex] partner of the person he was admitted or granted an extension of stay to join and the relationship is still subsisting; and

(iii) each of the parties intends to live permanently with the other as his partner; and

(iv) there will be adequate accommodation for the parties and any dependants without recourse to public funds in accommodation which they own or occupy exclusively; and

(v) the parties will be able to maintain themselves and any dependants adequately without recourse to public funds [; and

(vi) the applicant has sufficient knowledge of the English language and sufficient knowledge about life in the United Kingdom, unless he is under the age of 18 or aged 65 or over at the time he makes his application]][; and

(vii) the applicant does not have one or more unspent convictions within the meaning of the Rehabilitation of Offenders Act 1974.]

Note: Paragraph 295G inserted from 2 October 2000 (Cm 4581). Words in square brackets in sub-para (i) inserted from 1 October 2004 (Cm 6339). References to same-sex partners inserted from 5 December 2005 (HC 582). Words in curly brackets in sub-para (i)(a) inserted from 22 July 2008 (HC 971). Sub-paragraph (vi) inserted from 2 April 2007 (HC 398). Sub-paragraph (i) substituted from 7 April 2008 (HC 420). Words in square brackets in sub-paragraph (i)(b) substituted and sub-paras (i)(d) and (vii) inserted from 6 April 2011 except for applications made but not decided before that date (HC 863).

[Indefinite leave to remain as the unmarried [or same-sex] partner of a person present and settled in the United Kingdom

295H. Indefinite leave to remain as the unmarried [or same-sex] partner of a person present and settled in the United Kingdom may be granted provided that the Secretary of State is satisfied that each of the requirements of paragraph 295G is met.]

Note: Paragraph 295H inserted from 2 October 2000 (Cm 4581). References to same-sex partners inserted from 5 December 2005 (HC 582).

[Refusal of indefinite leave to remain as the unmarried [or same-sex] partner of a person present and settled in the United Kingdom

295I. Indefinite leave to remain as the unmarried [or same-sex] partner of a person present and settled in the United Kingdom is to be refused if the Secretary of State is not satisfied that each of the requirements of paragraph 295G is met.]

Note: Paragraph 295I inserted from 2 October 2000 (Cm 4581). References to same-sex partners inserted from 5 December 2005 (HC 582).

Leave to enter or remain as the unmarried [or same-sex] partner of a person with limited leave to enter or remain in the United Kingdom under paragraphs 128–193; 200–239; or 263–270

[Requirements for leave to enter or remain as the unmarried [or same-sex] partner of a person with limited leave to enter or remain in the United Kingdom under paragraphs 128–193; 200–239; or 263–270

295J. The requirements to be met by a person seeking leave to enter or remain as the unmarried [or same-sex] partner of a person with limited leave to enter or remain in the United Kingdom under paragraphs 128–193; 200–239; or 263–270; are that:

(i) the applicant is the unmarried [or same-sex] partner of a person who has limited leave to enter or remain in the United Kingdom under paragraphs 128–193; 200–239; or 263–270; and

(ii) any previous marriage [or civil partnership] (or similar relationship) by either partner has permanently broken down; and

[(iii) the parties are not involved in a consanguineous relationship with one another; and]

(iv) the parties have been living together in a relationship akin to marriage [or civil partnership] which has subsisted for 2 years or more; and

(v) each of the parties intends to live with the other as his partner during the applicant's stay; and

(vi) there will be adequate accommodation for the parties and any dependants without recourse to public funds in accommodation which they own or occupy exclusively; and

(vii) the parties will be able to maintain themselves and any dependants adequately without recourse to public funds; and

(viii) the applicant does not intend to stay in the United Kingdom beyond any period of leave granted to his partner; and

(ix) if seeking leave to enter, the applicant holds a valid United Kingdom entry clearance for entry in this capacity or, if seeking leave to remain, was admitted with a valid United Kingdom entry clearance for entry in this capacity.

Note: Paragraph 295J inserted from 2 October 2000 (Cm 4581). Sub-paragraph (iii) inserted from 25 August 2003 (Cm 5949). References to same-sex partners inserted from 5 December 2005 (HC 582).

[Leave to enter or remain as the unmarried [or same-sex] partner of a person with limited leave to enter or remain in the United Kingdom under paragraphs 128–193; 200–239; or 263–270

295K. Leave to enter as the unmarried [or same-sex] partner of a person with limited leave to enter or remain in the United Kingdom under paragraphs 128–193; 200–239; or 263–270; may be granted provided that a valid United Kingdom entry clearance for entry in this capacity is produced to the Immigration Officer on arrival. Leave to remain as the unmarried [or same-sex] partner of a person with limited leave to enter or remain in the United Kingdom under paragraphs 128–193; 200–239; or 263–270; may be granted provided that the Secretary of State is satisfied that each of the requirements of paragraph 295J is met. {If the applicant is seeking leave to enter or remain as the unmarried or same-sex partner of a Highly Skilled Migrant, any leave which is granted will be subject to a condition prohibiting Employment as a Doctor or Dentist in Training, unless the applicant:

[(1) has obtained a primary degree in medicine or dentistry at bachelor's level or above from a UK institution that is a UK recognised or listed body, or which holds a sponsor licence under Tier 4 of the Points Based System, and provides evidence of this degree; or

(2) is applying for leave to remain and has, or has last been granted, entry clearance, leave to enter or leave to remain that was not subject to any condition restricting him from taking employment as a Doctor in Training, has been employed during that leave as a Doctor in Training, and provides a letter from the Postgraduate Deanery or NHS Trust employing them which confirms that they have been working in a post or programme that has been approved by the Postgraduate Medical Education and Training Board as a training programme or post; or

(3) is applying for leave to remain and has, or has last been granted, entry clearance, leave to enter or leave to remain that was not subject to any condition restricting him from taking employment as a Dentist in Training, has been employed during that leave as a Dentist in Training, and provides a letter from the Postgraduate Deanery or NHS Trust employing them which confirms that they have been working in a post or programme that has been approved by the Postgraduate Medical Education and Training Board as a training programme or post.]

Note: Paragraph 295K inserted from 2 October 2000 (Cm 4581). References to same-sex partners inserted from 5 December 2005 (HC 582). Words in curly brackets substituted from 6 April 2010 (HC 439). Sub-paragraphs (1) to (3) substituted from 20 July 2012 (Cm 8423).

[Refusal of leave to enter or remain as the unmarried [or same-sex] partner of a person with limited leave to enter or remain in the United Kingdom under paragraphs 128–193; 200–239; or 263–270

295L. Leave to enter as the unmarried [or same-sex] partner of a person with limited leave to enter or remain in the United Kingdom under paragraphs 128–193; 200–239; or 263–270; is to be refused if a valid United Kingdom entry clearance for entry in this capacity is not produced to the Immigration Officer on arrival. Leave to remain as the unmarried [or same-sex] partner of a person with limited leave to enter or remain in the United Kingdom under paragraphs 128–193; 200–239; or 263–270; is to be refused if the Secretary of State is not satisfied that each of the requirements of paragraph 295J is met.]

Note: Paragraph 295L inserted from 2 October 2000 (Cm 4581). References to same-sex partners inserted from 5 December 2005 (HC 582).

Indefinite leave to remain for the bereaved unmarried [or same-sex] partner of a person present and settled in the United Kingdom

[Requirements for indefinite leave to remain for the bereaved unmarried [or same-sex] partner of a person present and settled in the United Kingdom

295M. The requirements to be met by a person seeking indefinite leave to remain as the bereaved unmarried [or same-sex] partner of a person present and settled in the United Kingdom, are that:

(i) the applicant was admitted to the United Kingdom {for a period not exceeding 27 months} or given an extension of stay for a period of 2 years [in accordance with paragraphs 295AA to 295F of these Rules] as the unmarried [or same-sex] partner of a person present and settled in the United Kingdom; and

(ii) the person whom the applicant was admitted or granted an extension of stay to join died during that {period of leave}; and

(iii) the applicant was still the unmarried [or same-sex] partner of the person he was admitted or granted an extension of stay to join at the time of the death; and

(iv) each of the parties intended to live permanently with the other as his partner and the relationship was subsisting at the time of the death] [; and

(v) the applicant does not have one or more unspent convictions within the meaning of the Rehabilitation of Offenders Act 1974.]

> **Note:** Paragraph 295M inserted from 2 October 2000 (Cm 4581). Words in square brackets in sub-para (i) inserted from 1 October 2004 (Cm 6339). References to same-sex partners inserted from 5 December 2005 (HC 582). Words in curly brackets in sub-paras (i) and (ii) substituted from 22 July 2008 (HC 971). Sub-paragraph (v) inserted from 6 April 2011 except for applications made but not decided before that date (HC 863).

[Indefinite leave to remain for the bereaved unmarried [or same-sex] partner of a person present and settled in the United Kingdom

295N. Indefinite leave to remain for the bereaved unmarried [or same-sex] partner of a person present and settled in the United Kingdom, may be granted provided that the Secretary of State is satisfied that each of the requirements of paragraph 295M is met.]

> **Note:** Paragraph 295N inserted from 2 October 2000 (Cm 4581). References to same-sex partners inserted from 5 December 2005 (HC 582).

[Refusal of indefinite leave to remain for the bereaved unmarried [or same-sex] partner of a person present and settled in the United Kingdom

295O. Indefinite leave to remain for the bereaved unmarried [or same-sex] partner of a person present and settled in the United Kingdom, is to be refused if the Secretary of State is not satisfied that each of the requirements of paragraph 295M is met.]

> **Note:** Paragraph 295O inserted from 2 October 2000 (Cm 4581). References to same-sex partners inserted from 5 December 2005 (HC 582).

Children

[**296.** Nothing in these Rules shall be construed as permitting a child to be granted entry clearance, leave to enter or remain, or variation of leave where his parent is party to a polygamous marriage [or civil partnership] and any application by that parent for admission or leave to remain for settlement or with a view to settlement would be refused pursuant to paragraphs 278 or 278A.]

> **Note:** Substituted from 2 October 2000 (Cm 4851).

Leave to enter or remain in the United Kingdom as the child of a parent,
parents or a relative present and settled or being admitted for settlement in
the United Kingdom

Requirements for indefinite leave to enter the United Kingdom as the child of a parent, parents or a relative present and settled or being admitted for settlement in the United Kingdom

297. The requirements to be met by a person seeking indefinite leave to enter the United Kingdom as the child of a parent, parents or a relative present and settled or being admitted for settlement in the United Kingdom are that he:

(i) is seeking leave to enter to accompany or join a parent, parents or a relative in one of the following circumstances:

(a) both parents are present and settled in the United Kingdom; or

(b) both parents are being admitted on the same occasion for settlement; or

(c) one parent is present and settled in the United Kingdom and the other is being admitted on the same occasion for settlement; or

(d) one parent is present and settled in the United Kingdom or being admitted on the same occasion for settlement and the other parent is dead; or

(e) one parent is present and settled in the United Kingdom or being admitted on the same occasion for settlement and has had sole responsibility for the child's upbringing; or

(f) one parent or a relative is present and settled in the United Kingdom or being admitted on the same occasion for settlement and there are serious and compelling family or other considerations which make exclusion of the child undesirable and suitable arrangements have been made for the child's care; and

(ii) is under the age of 18; and

(iii) is not leading an independent life, is unmarried [and is not a civil partner], and has not formed an independent family unit; and

[(iv) can, and will, be accommodated adequately by the parent, parents or relative the child is seeking to join without recourse to public funds in accommodation which the parent, parents or relative the child is seeking to join, own or occupy exclusively; and

(v) can, and will, be maintained adequately by the parent, parents or relative the child is seeking to join, without recourse to public funds; and

(vi) holds a valid United Kingdom entry clearance for entry in this capacity][; and

(vii) does not have one or more unspent convictions within the meaning of the Rehabilitation of Offenders Act 1974.]

Note: Sub-paragraphs (iv)–(vi) substituted from 2 October 2000 (Cm 4851). Words in square brackets in sub-para (iii) inserted from 5 December 2005 (HC 582). Sub-paragraph (vii) inserted from 6 April 2011 except for applications made but not decided before that date (HC 863).

Requirements for indefinite leave to remain in the United Kingdom as the child of a parent, parents or a relative present and settled or being admitted for settlement in the United Kingdom

298. The requirements to be met by a person seeking indefinite leave to remain in the United Kingdom as the child of a parent, parents or a relative present and settled in the United Kingdom are that he:

(i) is seeking to remain with a parent, parents or a relative in one of the following circumstances:

(a) both parents are present and settled in the United Kingdom; or

(b) one parent is present and settled in the United Kingdom and the other parent is dead; or

(c) one parent is present and settled in the United Kingdom and has had sole responsibility for the child's upbringing; or

(d) one parent or a relative is present and settled in the United Kingdom and there are serious and compelling family or other considerations which make exclusion of the child undesirable and suitable arrangements have been made for the child's care; and

(ii) has limited leave to enter or remain in the United Kingdom, and

(a) is under the age of 18; or

(b) was given leave to enter or remain with a view to settlement under paragraph 302 [or appendix FM][; or

[(c) was admitted into the UK in accordance with paragraph 319R and has completed a period of 2 years limited leave as the child of a refugee or beneficiary of humanitarian protection who is now present and settled in the UK or as the child of a former refugee or beneficiary of humanitarian protection who is now a British Citizen][,or]

[(d) the applicant [has limited leave to enter or remain in] the United Kingdom in accordance with paragraph 319X, as the child of a relative with limited leave to remain as a refugee or beneficiary of humanitarian protection in the United Kingdom and who is now present and settled here;]

(iii) is not leading an independent life, is unmarried [and is not a civil partner], and has not formed an independent family unit; and

[(iv) can, and will, be accommodated adequately by the parent, parents or relative the child was admitted to join without recourse to public funds in accommodation which the parent, parents or relative the child was admitted to join, own or occupy exclusively; and

(v) can, and will, be maintained adequately by the parent, parents or relative the child was admitted to join, without recourse to public funds] [; and

(vi) does not have one or more unspent convictions within the meaning of the Rehabilitation of Offenders Act 1974.]

Note: Sub-paragraphs (iv) and (v) substituted from 2 October 2000 (Cm 4851). Words in square brackets in sub-para (iii) inserted from 5 December 2005 (HC 582). Sub-paragraphs (ii)(c) and (vi) inserted from 6 April 2011 (HC 863). Sub-paragraph (ii)(d) inserted from 4 July 2011 with savings made for applications made but not decided before that date (HC 1148). Words in square brackets in sub-para (ii)(d) substituted from 31 October 2011 with savings for applications made but not determined before that date (HC 1511). Words inserted in sub-para (ii)(b) from 6 September 2012 (HC 565).

Indefinite leave to enter or remain in the United Kingdom as the child of a parent, parents or a relative present and settled or being admitted for settlement in the United Kingdom

299. Indefinite leave to enter the United Kingdom as the child of a parent, parents or a relative present and settled or being admitted for settlement in the United Kingdom may be granted provided a valid United Kingdom entry clearance for entry in this capacity is produced to the Immigration Officer on arrival. Indefinite leave to remain in the United Kingdom as the child of a parent, parents or a relative present and settled in the United Kingdom may be granted provided the Secretary of State is satisfied that each of the requirements of paragraph 298 is met.

Refusal of indefinite leave to enter or remain in the United Kingdom as the child of a parent, parents or a relative present and settled or being admitted for settlement in the United Kingdom

300. Indefinite leave to enter the United Kingdom as the child of a parent, parents or a relative present and settled or being admitted for settlement in the United Kingdom is to be refused if a valid United Kingdom entry clearance for entry in this capacity is not produced to the Immigration Officer on arrival. Indefinite leave to remain in the United Kingdom as the child of a parent, parents or a relative present and settled in the United Kingdom is to be refused if the Secretary of State is not satisfied that each of the requirements of paragraph 298 is met.

Requirements for limited leave to enter or remain in the United Kingdom with a view to settlement as the child of a parent or parents given limited leave to enter or remain in the United Kingdom with a view to settlement

301. The requirements to be met by a person seeking limited leave to enter or remain in the United Kingdom with a view to settlement as the child of a parent or parents given limited leave to enter or remain in the United Kingdom with a view to settlement are that he:

(i) is seeking leave to enter to accompany or join or remain with a parent or parents in one of the following circumstances:

(a) one parent is present and settled in the United Kingdom or being admitted on the same occasion for settlement and the other parent is being or has been given limited leave to enter or remain in the United Kingdom with a view to settlement; or

(b) one parent is being or has been given limited leave to enter or remain in the United Kingdom with a view to settlement and has had sole responsibility for the child's upbringing; or

(c) one parent is being or has been given limited leave to enter or remain in the United Kingdom with a view to settlement and there are serious and compelling family or other considerations which make exclusion of the child undesirable and suitable arrangements have been made for the child's care; and

(ii) is under the age of 18; and

(iii) is not leading an independent life, is unmarried [and is not a civil partner], and has not formed an independent family unit; and

[(iv) can, and will, be accommodated adequately without recourse to public funds, in accommodation which the parent or parents own or occupy exclusively; and

(iva) can, and will, be maintained adequately by the parent or parents without recourse to public funds; and]

[(ivb) does not qualify for limited leave to enter as a child of a parent or parents given limited leave to enter or remain as a refugee or beneficiary of humanitarian protection under paragraph 319R; and]

(v) (where an application is made for limited leave to remain with a view to settlement) has limited leave to enter or remain in the United Kingdom; and

(vi) if seeking leave to enter, holds a valid United Kingdom entry clearance for entry in this capacity or, if seeking leave to remain, was admitted with a valid United Kingdom entry clearance for entry in this capacity.

Note: Sub-paragraph (iv) substituted and sub-para (iva) inserted from 2 October 2000 (Cm 4851). Words in square brackets in sub-para (iii) inserted from 5 December 2005 (HC 582).

Sub-paragraph (ivb) inserted from 6 April 2011 except for applications made but not decided before that date (HC 863).

Limited leave to enter or remain in the United Kingdom with a view to settlement as the child of a parent or parents given limited leave to enter or remain in the United Kingdom with a view to settlement

302. A person seeking limited leave to enter the United Kingdom with a view to settlement as the child of a parent or parents given limited leave to enter or remain in the United Kingdom with a view to settlement may be admitted for a period not exceeding [27 months] provided he is able, on arrival, to produce to the Immigration Officer a valid United Kingdom entry clearance for entry in this capacity. A person seeking limited leave to remain in the United Kingdom with a view to settlement as the child of a parent or parents given limited leave to enter or remain in the United Kingdom with a view to settlement may be given limited leave to remain for a period not exceeding [27 months] provided the Secretary of State is satisfied that each of the requirements of paragraph 301(i)–(v) is met.

Note: Words in square brackets substituted from 22 July 2008 (HC 971).

Refusal of limited leave to enter or remain in the United Kingdom with a view to settlement as the child of a parent or parents given limited leave to enter or remain in the United Kingdom with a view to settlement

303. Limited leave to enter the United Kingdom with a view to settlement as the child of a parent or parents given limited leave to enter or remain in the United Kingdom with a view to settlement is to be refused if a valid United Kingdom entry clearance for entry in this capacity is not produced to the Immigration Officer on arrival. Limited leave to remain in the United Kingdom with a view to settlement as the child of a parent or parents given limited leave to enter or remain in the United Kingdom with a view to settlement is to be refused if the Secretary of State is not satisfied that each of the requirements of paragraph 301(i)–(v) is met.

[Leave to enter and extension of stay in the United Kingdom as the child of a parent who is being, or has been admitted to the United Kingdom as a fiancé(e) [or proposed civil partner]

Requirements for limited leave to enter the United Kingdom as the child of a fiancé(e) [or proposed civil partner]

303A. The requirements to be met by a person seeking limited leave to enter the United Kingdom as the child of a fiancé(e) [or proposed civil partner], are that:

(i) he is seeking to accompany or join a parent who is, on the same occasion that the child seeks admission, being admitted as a fiancé(e) [or proposed civil partner], or who has been admitted as a fiancé(e) [or proposed civil partner]; and

(ii) he is under the age of 18; and

(iii) he is not leading an independent life, is unmarried [and is not a civil partner], and has not formed an independent family unit; and

(iv) he can, and will, be maintained and accommodated adequately without recourse to public funds with the parent admitted or being admitted as a fiancé(e) [or proposed civil partner]; and

(v) there are serious and compelling family or other considerations which make the child's exclusion undesirable, that suitable arrangements have been made for his care in the United Kingdom, and there is no other person outside the United Kingdom who could reasonably be expected to care for him; and

(vi) he holds a valid United Kingdom entry clearance for entry in this capacity.]

Note: Paragraph 303A inserted from 2 October 2000 (Cm 4851). References to civil partnership inserted from 5 December 2005 (HC 582).

Limited leave to enter the United Kingdom as the child of a parent who is being, or has been admitted to the United Kingdom as a fiancé(e) [or proposed civil partner]

[303B. A person seeking limited leave to enter the United Kingdom as the child of a fiancé(e) [or proposed civil partner], may be granted limited leave to enter the United Kingdom for a period not in excess of that granted to the fiancé(e) [or proposed civil partner], provided that a valid United Kingdom entry clearance for entry in this capacity is produced to the Immigration Officer on arrival. Where the period of limited leave granted to a fiancé(e) [or proposed civil partner] will expire in more than 6 months, a person seeking limited leave to enter as the child of the fiancé(e) [or proposed civil partner] should be granted leave for a period not exceeding six months.]

Note: Paragraph 303B inserted from 2 October 2000 (Cm 4851). References to civil partnership inserted from 5 December 2005 (HC 582).

Refusal of limited leave to enter the United Kingdom as the child of a parent who is being, or has been admitted to the United Kingdom as a fiancé(e) [or proposed civil partner]

[303C. Limited leave to enter the United Kingdom as the child of a fiancé(e) [or proposed civil partner], is to be refused if a valid United Kingdom entry clearance for entry in this capacity is not produced to the Immigration Officer on arrival.]

Note: Paragraph 303C inserted from 2 October 2000 (Cm 4851). References to civil partnership inserted from 5 December 2005 (HC 582).

Requirements for an extension of stay in the United Kingdom as the child of a fiancé(e) [or proposed civil partner]

[303D. The requirements to be met by a person seeking an extension of stay in the United Kingdom as the child of a fiancé(e) [or proposed civil partner] are that:

(i) the applicant was admitted with a valid United Kingdom entry clearance as the child of a fiancé(e) [or proposed civil partner]; and

(ii) the applicant is the child of a parent who has been granted limited leave to enter, or an extension of stay, as a fiancé(e) [or proposed civil partner]; and

(iii) the requirements of paragraph 303A (ii)–(v) are met.]

Note: Paragraph 303D inserted from 2 October 2000 (Cm 4851). References to civil partnership inserted from 5 December 2005 (HC 582).

Extension of stay in the United Kingdom as the child of a fiancé(e) [or proposed civil partner]

[303E. An extension of stay as the child of a fiancé(e) [or proposed civil partner] may be granted provided that the Secretary of State is satisfied that each of the requirements of paragraph 303D is met.]

Note: Paragraph 303E inserted from 2 October 2000 (Cm 4851). References to civil partnership inserted from 5 December 2005 (HC 582).

Refusal of an extension of stay in the United Kingdom as the child of a fiancé(e) [or proposed civil partner]

[303F. An extension of stay as the child of a fiancé(e) [or proposed civil partner] is to be refused if the Secretary of State is not satisfied that each of the requirements of paragraph 303D is met.]

Note: Paragraph 303F inserted from 2 October 2000 (Cm 4851). References to civil partnership inserted from 5 December 2005 (HC 582).

Children born in the United Kingdom who are not British citizens

304. This paragraph and paragraphs 305–309 apply only to [. . .] dependent children under 18 years of age [who are unmarried and are not civil partners and] who were born in the United Kingdom on or after 1 January 1983 (when the British Nationality Act 1981 came into force) but who, because neither of their parents was a British citizen or settled in the United Kingdom at the time of their birth, are not British citizens and are therefore subject to immigration control. Such a child requires leave to enter where admission to the United Kingdom is sought, and leave to remain where permission is sought for the child to be allowed to stay in the United Kingdom. If he qualifies for entry clearance, leave to enter or leave to remain under any other part of these Rules, a child who was born in the United Kingdom but is not a British citizen may be granted entry clearance, leave to enter or leave to remain in accordance with the provisions of that other part.

Note: Words deleted and words in square brackets inserted from 5 December 2005 (HC 582).

Requirements for leave to enter or remain in the United Kingdom as the child of a parent or parents given leave to enter or remain in the United Kingdom

305. The requirements to be met by a child born in the United Kingdom who is not a British citizen who seeks leave to enter or remain in the United Kingdom as the child of a parent or parents given leave to enter or remain in the United Kingdom are that he:

(i) (a) is accompanying or seeking to join or remain with a parent or parents who have, or are given, leave to enter or remain in the United Kingdom; or

(b) is accompanying or seeking to join or remain with a parent or parents one of whom is a British citizen or has the right of abode in the United Kingdom; or

(c) is a child in respect of whom the parental rights and duties are vested solely in a local authority; and

(ii) is under the age of 18; and

(iii) was born in the United Kingdom; and

(iv) is not leading an independent life, is unmarried [and is not a civil partner], and has not formed an independent family unit; and

(v) (where an application is made for leave to enter) has not been away from the United Kingdom for more than 2 years.

Note: Words in square brackets in sub-para (iv) inserted from 5 December 2005 (HC 582).

Leave to enter or remain in the United Kingdom

306. A child born in the United Kingdom who is not a British citizen and who requires leave to enter or remain in the circumstances set out in paragraph 304 may be given leave to enter for the same period as his parent or parents where paragraph 305(i)(a) applies, provided the Immigration Officer is satisfied that each of the requirements of paragraph 305(ii)–(v) is met. Where leave to remain is sought, the child may be granted leave to remain for the same period as his parent or parents where paragraph 305(i)(a) applies, provided the Secretary of State is satisfied that each of the requirements of paragraph 305(ii)–(iv) is met. Where the parent or parents have or are given periods of leave of different duration, the child may be given leave to whichever period is longer except that if the parents are living apart the child should be given leave for the same period as the parent who has day to day responsibility for him.

307. If a child does not qualify for leave to enter or remain because neither of his parents has a current leave (and neither of them is a British citizen or has the right of abode), he will normally be refused leave to enter or remain, even if each of the requirements of paragraph 305 (ii)–(v) has been satisfied. However, he may be granted leave to enter or remain for a period not exceeding 3 months if both of his parents are in the United Kingdom and it appears unlikely that they will be removed in the immediate future, and there is no other person outside the United Kingdom who could reasonably be expected to care for him.

308. A child born in the United Kingdom who is not a British citizen and who requires leave to enter or remain in the United Kingdom in the circumstances set out in paragraph 304 may be given indefinite leave to enter where paragraph 305(i)(b) or (i)(c) applies provided the Immigration Officer is satisfied that each of the requirements of paragraph 305(ii)–(v) is met. Where an application is for leave to remain, such a child may be granted indefinite leave to remain where paragraph 305(i)(b) or (i)(c) applies, provided the Secretary of State is satisfied that each of the requirements of paragraph 305(ii)–(iv) is met.

Refusal of leave to enter or remain in the United Kingdom

309. Leave to enter the United Kingdom where the circumstances set out in paragraph 304 apply is to be refused if the Immigration Officer is not satisfied that each of the requirements of paragraph 305 is met. Leave to remain for such a child is to be refused if the Secretary of State is not satisfied that each of the requirements of paragraph 305(i)–(iv) is met.

Adopted children

[**309A**. For the purposes of adoption under paragraphs 310–316C a de facto adoption shall be regarded as having taken place if:

(a) at the time immediately preceding the making of the application for entry clearance under these Rules the adoptive parent or parents have been living abroad (in applications involving two parents both must have lived abroad together) for at least a period of time equal to the first period mentioned in sub-paragraph (b)(i) and must have cared for the child for at least a period of time equal to the second period material in that sub-paragraph; and

(b) during their time abroad, the adoptive parent or parents have:

(i) lived together for a minimum period of 18 months, of which the 12 months immediately preceding the application for entry clearance must have been spent living together with the child; and

(ii) have assumed the role of the child's parents, since the beginning of the 18 month period, so that there has been a genuine transfer of parental responsibility.]

Note: Paragraph 309A inserted from 1 April 2003 (HC 538).

[**309B**. Inter-country adoptions which are not a de facto adoption under paragraph 309A are subject to the Adoption and Children Act 2002 and the Adoptions with a Foreign Element Regulations 2005. As such all prospective adopters must be assessed as suitable to adopt by a competent authority in the UK, and obtain a Certificate of Eligibility from the Department for Education, before travelling abroad to identify a child for adoption. This Certificate of Eligibility must be provided with all entry clearance adoption applications under paragraphs 310–316F.]

Note: Paragraph 309B inserted from 6 September 2012 (HC 565).

Requirements for indefinite leave to enter the United Kingdom as the adopted child of a parent or parents present and settled or being admitted for settlement in the United Kingdom

310. The requirements to be met in the case of a child seeking indefinite leave to enter the United Kingdom as the adopted child of a parent or parents present and settled or being admitted for settlement in the United Kingdom are that he:

(i) is seeking leave to enter to accompany or join an adoptive parent or parents in one of the following circumstances;

(a) both parents are present and settled in the United Kingdom; or

(b) both parents are being admitted on the same occasion for settlement; or

(c) one parent is present and settled in the United Kingdom and the other is being admitted on the same occasion for settlement; or

(d) one parent is present and settled in the United Kingdom or being admitted on the same occasion for settlement and the other parent is dead; or

(e) one parent is present and settled in the United Kingdom or being admitted on the same occasion for settlement and has had sole responsibility for the child's upbringing; or

(f) one parent is present and settled in the United Kingdom or being admitted on the same occasion for settlement and there are serious and compelling family or other considerations which make exclusion of the child undesirable and suitable arrangements have been made for the child's care; [or]

[(g) in the case of a de facto adoption one parent has a right of abode in the United Kingdom or indefinite leave to enter or remain in the United Kingdom and is seeking admission to the United Kingdom on the same occasion for the purposes of settlement; and]

(ii) is under the age of 18; and

(iii) is not leading an independent life, is unmarried [and is not a civil partner], and has not formed an independent family unit; and

[(iv) can, and will, be accommodated {and maintained} adequately without recourse to public funds in accommodation which the adoptive parent or parents own or occupy exclusively; and]

(v) . . .

[(vi) (a) was adopted in accordance with a decision taken by the competent administrative authority or court in his country of origin or the country in which he is resident, being a country whose adoption orders are recognised by the United Kingdom; or

(b) is the subject of a de facto adoption; and]

(vii) was adopted at a time when:

(a) both adoptive parents were resident together abroad; or

(b) either or both adoptive parents were settled in the United Kingdom; and

(viii) has the same rights and obligations as any other child of the [adoptive parent's or parents' family]; and

(ix) was adopted due to the inability of the original parent(s) or current carer(s) to care for him and there has been a genuine transfer of parental responsibility to the adoptive parents; and

(x) has lost or broken his ties with his family of origin; and

(xi) was adopted, but the adoption is not one of convenience arranged to facilitate his admission to or remaining in the United Kingdom; and

(xii) holds a valid United Kingdom entry clearance for entry in this capacity[; and

(xiii) does not have one or more unspent convections within the meaning of the Rehabilitation of Offenders Act 1974.]

Note: Sub-paragraph (iv) substituted from 2 October 2000 (Cm 4851). Sub-paragraph (i)(g) inserted and words in curly brackets in sub-para (iv) substituted from 1 April 2003 (HC 538). Sub-paragraph (v) deleted from 1 April 2003 (HC 538). Sub-paragraph (vi) and words in square brackets in sub-para (i)(f) and (viii) substituted from 1 April 2003 (HC 538). Words in square brackets in sub-para (iii) inserted from 5 December 2005 (HC 582). Sub-paragraph (xiii) inserted from 6 April 2011 except for applications made but not decided before that date (HC 863).

Requirements for indefinite leave to remain in the United Kingdom as the adopted child of a parent or parents present and settled in the United Kingdom

311. The requirements to be met in the case of a child seeking indefinite leave to remain in the United Kingdom as the adopted child of a parent or parents present and settled in the United Kingdom are that he:

(i) is seeking to remain with an adoptive parent or parents in one of the following circumstances:

(a) both parents are present and settled in the United Kingdom; or

(b) one parent is present and settled in the United Kingdom and the other parent is dead; or

(c) one parent is present and settled in the United Kingdom and has had sole responsibility for the child's upbringing; or

(d) one parent is present and settled in the United Kingdom and there are serious and compelling family or other considerations which make exclusion of the child undesirable and suitable arrangements have been made for the child's care; [or]

[(e) in the case of a de facto adoption one parent has a right of abode in the United Kingdom or indefinite leave to enter or remain in the United Kingdom and is seeking admission to the United Kingdom on the same occasion for the purpose of settlement; and]

(ii) has limited leave to enter or remain in the United Kingdom, and

(a) is under the age of 18; or

(b) was given leave to enter or remain with a view to settlement under paragraph 315 [or paragraph 316B]; and

(iii) is not leading an independent life, is unmarried [and is not a civil partner], and has not formed an independent family unit; and

[(iv) can, and will, be accommodated {and maintained} adequately without recourse to public funds in accommodation which the adoptive parent or parents own or occupy exclusively; and]

(v) . . .

[(vi) (a) was adopted in accordance with a decision taken by the competent administrative authority or court in his country of origin or the country in which he is resident, being a country whose adoption orders are recognised by the United Kingdom; or

(b) is the subject of a de facto adoption; and]

(vii) was adopted at a time when:

(a) both adoptive parents were resident together abroad; or

(b) either or both adoptive parents were settled in the United Kingdom; and

(viii) has the same rights and obligations as any other child of the [adoptive parent's or parents' family]; and

(ix) was adopted due to the inability of the original parent(s) or current carer(s) to care for him and there has been a genuine transfer of parental responsibility to the adoptive parents; and

(x) has lost or broken his ties with his family of origin; and

(xi) was adopted, but the adoption is not one of convenience arranged to facilitate his admission to or remaining in the United Kingdom [; and

(xii) does not have one or more unspent convections within the meaning of the Rehabilitation of Offenders Act 1974.]

Note: Sub-paragraph (iv) substituted from 2 October 2000 (Cm 4851). Sub-paragraph (i) (e) inserted, sub-para (v) deleted and sub-para (vi) substituted from 1 April 2003 (HC 538). Words in square brackets in sub-para (i)(d) substituted, words in curly brackets in sub-para (iv) inserted and words in square brackets in sub-para (viii) substituted from 1 April 2003 (HC 538). Words in square brackets in sub-para (iii) inserted from 5 December 2005 (HC 582). Sub-paragraph (xii) inserted from 6 April 2011 except for applications made but not decided before that date (HC 863).

Indefinite leave to enter or remain in the United Kingdom as the adopted child of a parent or parents present and settled or being admitted for settlement in the United Kingdom

312. Indefinite leave to enter the United Kingdom as the adopted child of a parent or parents present and settled or being admitted for settlement in the United Kingdom may be granted provided a valid United Kingdom entry clearance for entry in this capacity is produced to the Immigration Officer on arrival. Indefinite leave to remain in the United Kingdom as the adopted child of a parent or parents present and settled in the United Kingdom may be granted provided the Secretary of State is satisfied that each of the requirements of paragraph 311 is met.

Refusal of indefinite leave to enter or remain in the United Kingdom as the adopted child of a parent or parents present and settled or being admitted for settlement in the United Kingdom

313. Indefinite leave to enter the United Kingdom as the adopted child of a parent or parents present and settled or being admitted for settlement in the United Kingdom is to be refused if a valid United Kingdom entry clearance for entry in this capacity is not produced to the Immigration Officer on arrival. Indefinite leave to remain in the United Kingdom as the adopted child of a parent or parents present and settled in the United Kingdom is to be refused if the Secretary of State is not satisfied that each of the requirements of paragraph 311 is met.

Requirements for limited leave to enter or remain in the United Kingdom with a view to settlement as the adopted child of a parent or parents given limited leave to enter or remain in the United Kingdom with a view to settlement

314. The requirements to be met in the case of a child seeking limited leave to enter or remain in the United Kingdom with a view to settlement as the adopted child of a parent or parents given limited leave to enter or remain in the United Kingdom with a view to settlement are that he:

(i) is seeking leave to enter to accompany or join or remain with a parent or parents in one of the following circumstances:

(a) one parent is present and settled in the United Kingdom or being admitted on the same occasion for settlement and the other parent is being or has been given limited leave to enter or remain in the United Kingdom with a view to settlement; or

(b) one parent is being or has been given limited leave to enter or remain in the United Kingdom with a view to settlement and has had sole responsibility for the child's upbringing; or

(c) one parent is being or has been given limited leave to enter or remain in the United Kingdom with a view to settlement and there are serious and compelling family or other considerations which make exclusion of the child undesirable and suitable arrangements have been made for the child's care; and

[{(d)} in the case of a de facto adoption one parent has a right of abode in the United Kingdom or indefinite leave to enter or remain in the United Kingdom and is seeking admission to the United Kingdom on the same occasion for the purpose of settlement; and]

(ii) is under the age of 18; and

(iii) is not leading an independent life, is unmarried [and is not a civil partner], and has not formed an independent family unit; and

[(iv) can, and will, be accommodated {and maintained} adequately without recourse to public funds in accommodation which the adoptive parent or parents own or occupy exclusively; and

[(v) (a) was adopted in accordance with a decision taken by the competent administrative authority or court in his country of origin or the country in which he is resident, being a country whose adoption orders are recognised by the United Kingdom; or

(b) is the subject of a de facto adoption; and]

(vi) was adopted at a time when:

(a) both adoptive parents were resident together abroad; or

(b) either or both adoptive parents were settled in the United Kingdom; and

(vii) has the same rights and obligations as any other child of the [adoptive parent's or parents' family]; and

(viii) was adopted due to the inability of the original parent(s) or current carer(s) to care for him and there has been a genuine transfer of parental responsibility to the adoptive parents; and

(ix) has lost or broken ties with his family of origin; and

(x) was adopted, but the adoption is not one of convenience arranged to facilitate his admission to the United Kingdom; and

(xi) (where an application is made for limited leave to remain with a view to settlement) has limited leave to enter or remain in the United Kingdom; and

(xii) if seeking leave to enter, holds a valid United Kingdom entry clearance for entry in this capacity.

Note: Sub-paragraph (iv) substituted from 2 October 2000 (Cm 4851). Sub-paragraph (i)(d) inserted, sub-para (iva) deleted and sub-para (v) substituted from 1 April 2003 (HC 538). Words in curly brackets in sub-para (iv) inserted and words in square brackets in sub-para (vii) substituted from 1 April 2003 (HC 538). Words in curly brackets in sub-para (i)(d) substituted from 30 May 2003 (Cm 5829). Words in square brackets in sub-para (iii) inserted from 5 December 2005 (HC 582).

Limited leave to enter or remain in the United Kingdom with a view to settlement as the adopted child of a parent or parents given limited leave to enter or remain in the United Kingdom with a view to settlement

315. A person seeking limited leave to enter the United Kingdom with a view to settlement as the adopted child of a parent or parents given limited leave to enter or remain in the United Kingdom with a view to settlement may be admitted for a period not exceeding 12 months provided he is able, on arrival, to produce to the Immigration Officer a valid United Kingdom entry clearance for entry in this capacity. A person seeking limited leave to remain in the United Kingdom with a view to settlement as the adopted child of a parent or parents given limited leave to enter or remain in the United Kingdom with a view to settlement may be granted limited leave for a period not exceeding 12 months provided the Secretary of State is satisfied that each of the requirements of paragraph 314(i)–(xi) is met.

Refusal of limited leave to enter or remain in the United Kingdom with a view to settlement as the adopted child of a parent or parents given limited leave to enter or remain in the United Kingdom with a view to settlement

316. Limited leave to enter the United Kingdom with a view to settlement as the adopted child of a parent or parents given limited leave to enter or remain in the United Kingdom with a view to settlement is to be refused if a valid United Kingdom entry clearance for entry in this capacity is not produced to the Immigration Officer on arrival. Limited leave to remain in the United Kingdom with a view to settlement as the adopted child of a parent or parents given limited leave to enter or remain in the United Kingdom with a view to settlement is to be refused if the Secretary of State is not satisfied that each of the requirements of paragraph 314(i)–(xi) is met.

[Requirements for limited leave to enter the United Kingdom with a view to settlement as a child for adoption

316A. The requirements to be satisfied in the case of a child seeking limited leave to enter the United Kingdom for the purpose of being adopted {(which, for the avoidance of doubt, does not include a de facto adoption)} in the United Kingdom are that he:

(i) is seeking limited leave to enter to accompany or join a person or persons who wish to adopt him in the United Kingdom (the 'prospective parent(s)'), in one of the following circumstances:

(a) both prospective parents are present and settled in the United Kingdom; or

(b) both prospective parents are being admitted for settlement on the same occasion that the child is seeking admission; or

(c) one prospective parent is present and settled in the United Kingdom and the other is being admitted for settlement on the same occasion that the child is seeking admission; or

(d) one prospective parent is present and settled in the United Kingdom and the other is being given limited leave to enter or remain in the United Kingdom with a view to settlement on the same occasion that the child is seeking admission, or has previously been given such leave; or

(e) one prospective parent is being admitted for settlement on the same occasion that the other is being granted limited leave to enter with a view to settlement, which is also on the same occasion that the child is seeking admission; or

(f) one prospective parent is present and settled in the United Kingdom or is being admitted for settlement on the same occasion that the child is seeking admission, and has had sole responsibility for the child's upbringing; or

(g) one prospective parent is present and settled in the United Kingdom or is being admitted for settlement on the same occasion that the child is seeking admission, and there are serious and compelling family or other considerations which would make the child's exclusion undesirable, and suitable arrangements have been made for the child's care; and

(ii) is under the age of 18; and

(iii) is not leading an independent life, is unmarried [and is not a civil partner], and has not formed an independent family unit; and

(iv) can, and will, be maintained and accommodated adequately without recourse to public funds in accommodation which the prospective parent or parents own or occupy exclusively; and

(v) will have the same rights and obligations as any other child of the marriage [or civil partnership]; and

(vi) is being adopted due to the inability of the original parent(s) or current carer(s) (or those looking after him immediately prior to him being physically transferred to his prospective parent or parents) to care for him, and there has been a genuine transfer of parental responsibility to the prospective parent or parents; and

(vii) has lost or broken or intends to lose or break his ties with his family of origin; and

(viii) will be adopted in the United Kingdom by his prospective parent or parents [in accordance with the law relating to adoption in the United Kingdom], but the proposed adoption is not one of convenience arranged to facilitate his admission to the United Kingdom.

Note: Paragraph 316A inserted from 2 October 2000 (Cm 4851). Words in curly brackets and words in square brackets inserted from 1 April 2003 (HC 538). Words in square brackets in sub-para (iii) inserted from 5 December 2005 (HC 582).

Limited leave to enter the United Kingdom with a view to settlement as a child for adoption

316B. A person seeking limited leave to enter the United Kingdom with a view to settlement as a child for adoption may be admitted for a period not exceeding [24 months] provided he is able, on arrival, to produce to the Immigration Officer a valid United Kingdom entry clearance for entry in this capacity.

Note: Paragraph 316B inserted from 2 October 2000 (Cm 4851). Words in square brackets substituted from 30 May 2003 (Cm 5829).

Refusal of limited leave to enter the United Kingdom with a view to settlement as a child for adoption

316C. Limited leave to enter the United Kingdom with a view to settlement as a child for adoption is to be refused if a valid United Kingdom entry clearance for entry in this capacity is not produced to the Immigration Officer on arrival.]

Note: Paragraph 316C inserted from 2 October 2000 (Cm 4851).

Requirements for limited leave to enter the United Kingdom with a view to settlement as a child for adoption under the Hague Convention

[**316D.** The requirements to be satisfied in the case of a child seeking limited leave to enter the United Kingdom for the purpose of being adopted in the United Kingdom under the Hague Convention are that he:

(i) is seeking limited leave to enter to accompany one or two people each of whom is habitually resident in the United Kingdom and wishes to adopt him under the Hague Convention ('the prospective parents');

(ii) is the subject of an agreement made under Article 17(c) of the Hague Convention; and

(iii) has been entrusted to the prospective parents by the competent administrative authority of the country from which he is coming to the United Kingdom for adoption under the Hague Convention; and

(iv) is under the age of 18; and

(v) can, and will, be maintained and accommodated adequately without recourse to public funds in accommodation which the prospective parent or parents own or occupy exclusively; and

(vi) holds a valid United Kingdom entry clearance for entry in this capacity.

Note: Inserted from 30 May 2003 (Cm 5829).

Limited leave to enter the United Kingdom with a view to settlement as a child for adoption under the Hague Convention

316E. A person seeking limited leave to enter the United Kingdom with a view to settlement as a child for adoption under the Hague Convention may be admitted for a period not exceeding 24 months provided he is able, on arrival, to produce to the Immigration Officer a valid United Kingdom entry clearance for entry in this capacity.

Note: Inserted from 30 May 2003 (Cm 5829).

Refusal of limited leave to enter the United Kingdom with a view to settlement as a child for adoption under the Hague Convention

316F. Limited leave to enter the United Kingdom with a view to settlement as a child for adoption under the Hague Convention is to be refused if a valid United Kingdom entry clearance for entry in this capacity is not produced to the Immigration Officer on arrival.]

Note: Inserted from 30 May 2003 (Cm 5829).

Parents, grandparents and other dependent relatives of persons present and settled in the United Kingdom

Requirements for indefinite leave to enter or remain in the United Kingdom as the parent, grandparent or other dependent relative of a person present and settled in the United Kingdom

317. The requirements to be met by a person seeking indefinite leave to enter or remain in the United Kingdom as the parent, grandparent or other dependent relative of a person present and settled in the United Kingdom are that the person:

(i) is related to a person present and settled in the United Kingdom in one of the following ways:

(a) [parent or grandparent who is divorced, widowed, single or separated] aged 65 years or over; or

[(b)] parent or grandparents travelling together of whom at least one is aged 65 or over; or

[[(c)] a parent or grandparent aged 65 or over who has entered into a second relationship of marriage or civil partnership but cannot look to the spouse, civil partner or children of that second relationship for financial support; and where the person settled in the United Kingdom is able and willing to maintain the parent or grandparent and any spouse or civil partner or child of the second relationship who would be admissible as a dependant;]

[(d)] a parent or grandparent under the age of 65 if living alone outside the United Kingdom in the most exceptional compassionate circumstances [...]; or [(e) parents or grandparents travelling together who are both under the age of 65 if living in the most exceptional compassionate circumstances; or]

(f) the son, daughter, sister, brother, uncle or aunt over the age of 18 if living alone outside the United Kingdom in the most exceptional compassionate circumstances [...]; and

(ii) is joining or accompanying a person who is present and settled in the United Kingdom or who is on the same occasion being admitted for settlement; and

(iii) is financially wholly or mainly dependent on the relative present and settled in the United Kingdom; and

[(iv) can, and will, be accommodated adequately, together with any dependants, without recourse to public funds, in accommodation which the sponsor owns or occupies exclusively; and

(iva) can, and will, be maintained adequately, together with any dependants, without recourse to public funds; and]

(v) has no other close relatives in his own country to whom he could turn for financial support; and

(vi) if seeking leave to enter, holds a valid United Kingdom entry clearance for entry in this capacity[; and

(vii) does not have one or more unspent convections within the meaning of the Rehabilitation of Offenders Act 1974.]

Note: Sub-paragraph (iv) and (iva) substituted from 2 October 2000 (Cm 4851). Sub-paragraph (i) (d) substituted from 5 December 2005 (HC 582). Sub-paragraph (vii) inserted from 6 April 2011 (HC 863). Words in square brackets in sub-para (i)(a) substituted, sub-paras (b)–(d) renumbered, words omitted from (d) and (f) and sub-para (e) inserted from 31 October 2011 with savings for applications made but not decided before that date (HC 1511).

Indefinite leave to enter or remain as the parent, grandparent or other dependent relative of a person present and settled in the United Kingdom

318. Indefinite leave to enter the United Kingdom as the parent, grandparent or other dependent relative of a person present and settled in the United Kingdom may be granted provided a valid United Kingdom entry clearance for entry in this capacity is produced to the Immigration Officer on arrival. Indefinite leave to remain in the United Kingdom as the parent, grandparent or other dependent relative of a person present and settled in the United Kingdom may be granted provided the Secretary of State is satisfied that each of the requirements of paragraph 317(i)–(v) is met.

Refusal of indefinite leave to enter or remain in the United Kingdom as the parent, grandparent or other dependent relative of a person present and settled in the United Kingdom

319. Indefinite leave to enter the United Kingdom as the parent, grandparent or other dependent relative of a person settled in the United Kingdom is to be refused if a valid United Kingdom entry clearance for entry in this capacity is not produced to the Immigration Officer on arrival. Indefinite leave to remain in the United Kingdom as the parent, grandparent or other dependent relative of a person present and settled in the United Kingdom is to be refused if the Secretary of State is not satisfied that each of the requirements of paragraph 317(i)–(v) is met.

Family members of Relevant Points Based System Migrants

Partners of Relevant Points Based System Migrants

General Note: "Relevant Points Based System Migrant" substituted for "Tier 1 Migrant" wherever occurring in Paragraphs 319A to 319J from 27 November 2008 (HC 1113).

319AA. In paragraphs 319A to 319K and Appendix E "Relevant Points Based System Migrant" means a migrant granted leave as a Tier 1 Migrant, a Tier 2 Migrant, [[a Tier 4 (General) Student] Migrant or a Tier 5 (Temporary Worker) Migrant.]

Note: Paragraph 319AA inserted from 27 November 2008 (HC 1113). Words in square brackets substituted from 31 March 2009 (HC 314). Words in square brackets substituted from 21 April 2011 with savings for applications made but not decided by that date (HC 908).

[319A. Purpose

This route is for the spouse, civil partner, unmarried or same-sex partner of a [Relevant Points Based System Migrant] (Partner of a [Relevant Points Based System Migrant]). Paragraphs 277 to 280 of these Rules apply to spouses [or civil partners] of [Relevant Points Based System Migrant]s; paragraph 277 of these Rules applies to civil partners of [Relevant Points Based System Migrants]; and paragraph 295AA of these Rules applies to unmarried and same-sex partners of [Relevant Points Based System Migrants].

Note: Paragraph 319A inserted from 29 February 2008 (HC 321).

[319B. Entry to the UK

[(a) Subject to paragraph (b), all migrants] arriving in the UK and wishing to enter as the Partner of a [Relevant Points Based System Migrant] must have a valid entry clearance for entry under this route. If they do not have a valid entry clearance, entry will be refused.]

[(b) A migrant arriving in the UK, and wishing to enter as a Partner of a Tier 5 (Temporary Worker) Migrant, who does not have a valid entry clearance will not be refused entry if the following conditions are met:

(i) the migrant wishing to enter as a Partner is not a visa national,

(ii) the migrant wishing to enter as a Partner is accompanying an applicant who at the same time is being granted leave to enter under paragraph 245ZN(b), and

(iii) the migrant wishing to enter as a Partner meets the requirements of entry clearance in paragraph 319C.]

Note: Paragraph 319B inserted from 29 February 2008 (HC 321). Words substituted and sub-para (b) inserted from 27 November 2008 (HC 1113).

[319C. Requirements for entry clearance or leave to remain

To qualify for entry clearance or leave to remain as the Partner of a [Relevant Points Based System Migrant], an applicant must meet the requirements listed below. If the applicant meets these requirements, entry clearance or leave to remain will be granted. If the applicant does not meet these requirements, the application will be refused.

Requirements:

(a) The applicant must not fall for refusal under the general grounds for refusal, and if applying for leave to remain, must not be an illegal entrant.

(b) The applicant must be the spouse or civil partner, unmarried or same-sex partner of a person who:

    (i) has valid leave to enter or remain as a [Relevant Points Based System Migrant], or

    (ii) is, at the same time, being granted entry clearance or leave to remain as a [Relevant Points Based System Migrant], [or

    [(iii) has indefinite leave to remain as a Relevant Points Based System Migrant, or is, at the same time being granted indefinite leave to remain as a Relevant Points Based System Migrant, where the applicant is applying for further leave to remain and was last granted leave:

    (1) as the partner of that same Relevant Points Based System Migrant; or

    (2) as the spouse or civil partner, unmarried or same-sex partner of that person at a time when that person had leave under another category of these Rules; or

    (iv) has become a British Citizen where prior to that they held indefinite leave to Remain as a Relevant Points Based System Migrant and where the applicant is applying for further leave to remain and was last granted leave:

    (1) as the partner of that same Relevant Points Based System Migrant, or

    (2) as the spouse or civil partner, unmarried or same-sex partner of that person at a time when that person had leave under another category of these Rules.]

(c) An applicant who is the unmarried or same-sex partner of a [Relevant Points Based System Migrant] must also meet the following requirements:

    (i) any previous marriage or similar relationship by the applicant or the [Relevant Points Based System Migrant] with another person must have permanently broken down,

    (ii) the applicant and the [Relevant Points Based System Migrant] must not be so closely related that they would be prohibited from marrying each other in the UK, and

    (iii) the applicant and the [Relevant Points Based System Migrant] must have been living together in a relationship similar to marriage or civil partnership for a period of at least 2 years.

(d) The marriage or civil partnership, or relationship similar to marriage or civil partnership, must be subsisting at the time the application is made.

(e) The applicant and the [Relevant Points Based System Migrant] must intend to live with the other as their spouse or civil partner, unmarried or same-sex partner throughout the applicant's stay in the UK.

(f) The applicant must not intend to stay in the UK beyond any period of leave granted to the [Relevant Points Based System Migrant].

(g) [Unless the [Relevant Points Based System Migrant] is a Tier 1 (Investor) Migrant [or a Tier 1 Exceptional Talent) Migrant], there] must be a sufficient level of funds available to the applicant, as set out in Appendix E.

(h) An applicant who is applying for leave to remain, must have, or have last been granted, leave:

    (i) as the Partner of a [Relevant Points Based System Migrant],

    (ii) as the spouse or civil partner, unmarried or same-sex partner of a person with leave under another category of these Rules who has since been granted, or is, at the same time, being granted leave to remain as a [Relevant Points Based System Migrant], or]

    [(iii) in any other category of these Rules, provided the Relevant Points Based System Migrant has, or is being granted, leave to remain as a Tier 5 (Temporary Worker) Migrant in the creative and sporting subcategory on the basis of having met the requirement at paragraph 245ZQ(b)(ii).]

[(i) If the Relevant Points Based System Migrant is a [Tier 4 (General) Student],

[(1) the Relevant Points Based System Migrant must be applying for a course of study of more than six months duration and must have or have last had entry clearance, leave to enter or leave to remain as a Tier 4 (General) Student or Student for a course of more than six months duration within the three months immediately preceding the date of the application; and

(2) the Partner must have or have last had entry clearance, leave to enter or leave to remain as the Partner of a Tier 4 (General) Student or Student with leave for a course of more than six months duration within the three months immediately preceding the date of the application; and

(3) the relevant Points Based System Migrant and Partner must be applying at the same time; or

(4) the relevant Points Based System Migrant must be a Government Sponsored student who is applying for or has entry clearance or leave to remain for a course of study that is longer than six months; or

(5) the relevant Points Based System Migrant must be undertaking a course which is 12 months or longer in duration, and is of post-graduate level study, sponsored by a Sponsor which is a Recognised Body or a body in receipt of funding as a higher education institution from the Department for Employment and Learning in Northern Ireland, the Higher Education Funding Council for England, the Higher Education Funding Council for Wales or the Scottish Funding Council.]

[(j) The applicant must not be in the UK in breach of immigration laws except that any period of overstaying for a period of 28 days will be disregarded.]

Note: Paragraph 319C inserted from 29 February 2008 (HC 321). Sub-paragraph (h)(iii) inserted from 31 March 2009 (HC 314). Sub-para. (i) inserted from 3 March 2010 (HC 367); however, if an applicant has made an application for entry clearance or leave to enter or remain before 3 March 2010 and the application has not been decided before that date, it will be decided in accordance with the Rules in force on 2 March 2010 and the conditions applicable to any leave granted will be those in force on 2 March 2010: see introduction to HC 367. Sub-paragraph (i) substituted from 4 July 2011 with savings for applications made but not decided before that date, (HC 1148). Words in second square brackets in (g) inserted from 6 April 2012 except for applications made but not decided before that date (HC 1888). Sub-paragraph (j) inserted from 1 October 2012 with savings for applications made but not decided before 9 July 2012 (HC 194). Sub-paragraphs (b)(iii) and (iv) inserted from 6 September 2012 (HC 565).

[319D. Period and conditions of grant

[(a)(i) Entry clearance or limited leave to remain will be granted for a period which expires on the same day as the leave granted to the Relevant Points Based System Migrant, or

(ii) If the Relevant Points-Based System Migrant has indefinite leave to remain as a Relevant Points Based System Migrant, or is, at the same time being granted indefinite leave to remain as a Relevant Points Based System Migrant, or where the Relevant Points-Based System Migrant has since become a British Citizen, leave to remain will be granted to the applicant for a period of three years.]

(b) Entry clearance and leave to remain under this route will be subject to the following conditions:

(i) no recourse to public funds,

(ii) registration with the police, if this is required under paragraph 326 of these Rules,

[(iii) no Employment as a Doctor or Dentist in Training, unless the applicant:

(1) has obtained a primary degree in medicine or dentistry at bachelor's level or above from a UK institution that is a UK recognised or listed body, or which holds a sponsor licence under Tier 4 of the Points Based System, and provides evidence of this degree; or

(2) is applying for leave to remain and has, or has last been granted, entry clearance, leave to enter or leave to remain that was not subject to any condition restricting him from taking employment as a Doctor in Training, has been employed during that leave as a Doctor in Training, and provides a letter from the Postgraduate Deanery or NHS Trust employing them which confirms that they have been working in a post or programme that has been approved by the Postgraduate Medical Education and Training Board as a training programme or post; or

(3) is applying for leave to remain and has, or has last been granted, entry clearance, leave to enter or leave to remain that was not subject to any condition restricting him from taking employment as a Dentist in Training, has been employed during that leave as a Dentist in Training, and provides a letter from the Postgraduate Deanery or NHS Trust employing them which confirms that they have been working in a post or programme that has been approved by the Postgraduate Medical Education and Training Board as a training programme or post.]

[(iv) if the relevant Points Based System Migrant is a Tier 4 (General) student and the Partner meets the requirements of paragraphs 319C(i)(1), (2) and (3) and:

(1) the relevant Points Based System Migrant is a Tier 4 (General) student applying for leave for less than 12 months, no employment, or

(2) the relevant Points Based System Migrant is a Tier 4 (General) student who is following a course of below degree level study, no employment.

Note: Paragraph 319D inserted from 29 February 2008 (HC 321). Sub-paragraph (b) (iii) substituted from 6 April 2010 (HC 439). Sub-paragraph (b)(iv) inserted from 31 March 2009 (HC 314). Sub-paragraph (b)(v) inserted from 3 March 2010 (HC 367); however, if an applicant has made an application for entry clearance or leave to enter or remain before 3 March 2010 and the application has not been decided before that date, it will be decided in accordance with the Rules in force on 2 March 2010 and the conditions applicable to any leave granted will be those in force on 2 March 2010: see introduction to HC 367. Sub-paragraphs (b)(iv)–(v) substituted from 4 July 2011 with savings for applications made but not decided before that date (HC 1148). Sub-paragraph (b)(iii) substituted from 20 July 2012 (Cm 8423). Sub-paragraph (a) substituted from 6 September 2012 (HC 565).

[319E. Requirements for indefinite leave to remain

To qualify for indefinite leave to remain as the Partner of a [Relevant Points Based System Migrant], an applicant must meet the requirements listed below. If the applicant meets these requirements, indefinite leave to remain will be granted. If the applicant does not meet these requirements, the application will be refused ...

Requirements:

(a) The applicant must not fall for refusal under the general grounds for refusal, and must not be an illegal entrant.

[(b) The applicant must be the spouse or civil partner, unmarried or same-sex partner of a person who:

(i) has indefinite leave to remain as a Relevant Points Based System Migrant; or

(ii) is, at the same time being granted indefinite leave to remain as a Relevant Points Based System Migrant, or

(iii) has become a British Citizen where prior to that they held indefinite leave to remain as a Relevant Points Based System Migrant.

(c) The applicant must have, or have last been granted, leave as the partner of the Relevant Points Based System Migrant who:

(i) has indefinite leave to remain as a Relevant Points Based System Migrant; or

(ii) is, at the same time being granted indefinite leave to remain as a Relevant Points Based System Migrant, or

(iii) has become a British Citizen where prior to that they held indefinite leave to remain as a Relevant Points Based System Migrant.

(d) The applicant and the Relevant Points Based System Migrant must have been living together in the UK in a marriage or civil partnership, or in a relationship similar to marriage or civil partnership, for at least the period specified in (i) or (ii):

(i) If the applicant was granted leave as:

(a) the Partner of that Relevant Points Based System Migrant, or

(b) the spouse or civil partner, unmarried or same-sex partner of that person at a time when that person had leave under another category of these Rules

under the Rules in place before 9 July 2012, and since then has had continuous leave as the Partner of that Relevant Points based System Migrant, the specified period is 2 years.

(ii) If (i) does not apply, the specified period is 5 years, during which the applicant must:

(a) have been in a relationship with the same Relevant Points Based System Migrant for this entire period,

(b) have spent the most recent part of the 5 year period with leave as the Partner of that Relevant Points Based System Migrant, and during that part of the period have met all of the requirements of paragraph 319C(a) to (e), and

(c) have spent the remainder of the 5 year period, where applicable, as the spouse or civil partner, unmarried or same-sex partner of that person at a time when that person had leave under another category of these Rules.]

(e) The marriage or civil partnership, or relationship similar to marriage or civil partnership, must be subsisting at the time the application is made.

(f) The applicant and the [Relevant Points Based System Migrant] must intend to live permanently with the other as their spouse or civil partner, unmarried or same-sex partner.

(g) The applicant must have sufficient knowledge of the English language and sufficient knowledge about life in the United Kingdom, with reference to paragraphs 33B to 33F of these Rules, unless the applicant is aged 65 or over at the time this application is made[.]

(h) The applicant does not have one or more unspent convictions within the meaning of the Rehabilitation of Offenders Act 1974][;and

(i) The applicant must not be in the UK in breach of immigration laws except that any period of overstaying for a period of 28 days will be disregarded.]

Note: Paragraph 319E inserted from 29 February 2008 (HC 321). Words omitted from 7 April 2010 (HC 439); however, if an applicant has made an application for entry clearance or leave to enter or remain before 6 April and the application has not been decided before that date, it will be decided in accordance with the Rules in force on 6 April 2010: see introduction to HC 439. Sub-paragraph (h) inserted from 6 April 2011 except for applications made but not decided before that date (HC 863). Sub-paragraphs (b)–(d) substituted from 5 September 2012 (HC 565). Sub-paragraph (i) inserted from 1 October 2012 with savings for applications made but not decided before 9 July 2012 (HC 194).

Children of [Relevant Points Based System Migrant]s

[319F. Purpose

This route is for the children of {a} [Relevant Points Based System Migrant]s who are under the age of 18 when they apply to enter under this route. Paragraph 296 of these Rules applies to children of Tier 1 (General) Migrants.]

Note: Paragraph 319F inserted from 29 February 2008 (HC 321).

[319G. Entry to the UK

[(a) Subject to paragraph (b), all migrants arriving] in the UK and wishing to enter as the Child of a [Relevant Points Based System Migrant] must have a valid entry clearance for entry under this route. If they do not have a valid entry clearance, entry will be refused.]

[(b) A migrant arriving in the UK and wishing to enter as the child of a Tier 5 (Temporary Worker) Migrant who does not have a valid entry clearance will not be refused entry if the following conditions are met:

(i) the migrant wishing to enter as {a}[*sic*] the child is not a visa national,

(ii) the migrant wishing to enter as the child is accompanying an applicant who at the same time is being granted leave to enter under 245ZN(b), and

(iii) the migrant wishing to enter as the child meets the requirements of entry clearance in paragraph 319H.]

Note: Paragraph 319G inserted from 29 February 2008 (HC 321). Words in square brackets in sub-para (a) substituted and sub-para (b) inserted from 27 November 2008 (HC 1113). Word inserted in sub-para (b)(i) from 6 September 2012 (HC 565).

[319H. Requirements for entry clearance or leave to remain

To qualify for entry clearance or leave to remain under this route, an applicant must meet the requirements listed below. If the applicant meets these requirements, entry clearance or leave to remain will be granted. If the applicant does not meet these requirements, the application will be refused.

Requirements:

(a) The applicant must not fall for refusal under the general grounds for refusal, and if applying for leave to remain, must not be an illegal entrant.

[(b) The applicant must be the child of either—

(i) one parent who has valid leave to enter or remain as a Relevant Points Based System Migrant, or is, at the same time, being granted entry clearance or leave to remain as a Relevant Points Based System Migrant where:

(a) that parent is the applicant's sole surviving parent, or

(b) that parent has and has had sole responsibility for the applicant's upbringing, or

(c) There are serious and compelling family or other considerations which would make it desirable not to refuse the application and suitable arrangements have been made for the applicant's care, or

(ii) parents-

(a) one of whom has valid leave to enter or remain as a Relevant Points Based System Migrant and one of whom has leave as the partner of a Relevant Points Based System Migrant, or

(b) who are at the same being granted entry clearance or leave to remain as a Relevant Points Based System Migrant and as the partner of a Relevant Points Based System Migrant, or

(c) where one parent has valid leave to enter or remain as the partner of a person who has either limited leave to enter or remain as a Relevant Points Based System Migrant, indefinite leave to remain as a Relevant Points Based System Migrant, or who has become a British Citizen where immediately prior to that they had indefinite leave to remain as a Relevant Points Based System Migrant.]

(c) The applicant must be under the age of 18 on the date the application is made, or if over 18 and applying for leave to remain, must have, or have last been granted, leave as the Child of a [Relevant Points Based System Migrant] or as the child of a parent who had leave under another category of these Rules and who has since been granted, or is at the time being granted, leave to remain as a Relevant Points Based System Migrant.}

(d) The applicant must not be married or in a civil partnership, must not have formed an independent family unit, and must not be leading an independent life.

(e) The applicant must not intend to stay in the UK beyond any period of leave granted to the [Relevant Points Based System Migrant] parent.

(f)

(g) [Unless the {Relevant Points Based System Migrant} is [Tier 1 (Investor) Migrant or a Tier 1 (Exceptional Talent) Migrant], there] must be a sufficient level of funds available to the applicant, as set out in Appendix E.

[(h) an applicant who is applying for leave to remain must have, or have last been granted leave as the child of, [,or have been born in the United Kingdom to] a parent who had leave under any category of these rules.]

[(i) If the Relevant Points Based System Migrant is a [Tier 4 (General) Student],

[(1) the Relevant Points Based System Migrant must be applying for a course of study of more than six months duration and must have or have last had entry clearance, leave to enter or leave to remain as a Tier 4 (General) Student or Student for a course of more than six months duration within the three months immediately preceding the date of the application; and

(2) the Child must have or last have had entry clearance, leave to enter or leave to remain as the Child of a Tier 4 (General) Student or Student with leave for a course of more than six months duration within the three months immediately preceding the date of the application; and

(3) the Relevant Points Based System Migrant and Child must be applying at the same time; or

(4) the Relevant Points Based System Migrant must be a Government Sponsored Student who is applying for or has entry clearance or leave to remain for a course of study that is longer than six months; or

(5) the Relevant Points Based System Migrant must be undertaking a course which is 12 months or longer in duration, and is of post-graduate level study, sponsored by a Sponsor which is a Recognised Body or a body in receipt of funding as a higher education institution from the Department for Employment and Learning in Northern Ireland, the

Higher Education Funding Council for England, the Higher Education Funding Council for Wales or the Scottish Funding Council.

(j) a Child whose parent is a Relevant Points Based System Migrant, who is a Tier 4 (General) Student or Student, and who does not otherwise meet the requirements of paragraph 319H(i):

(1) must have been born during the Relevant Points Based System Migrant's most recent grant of entry clearance, leave to enter or leave to remain as a Tier 4 (General) Student or Student with leave for a course of more than six months duration; or

(2) where the Relevant Points Based System Migrant's most recent grant of entry clearance, leave to enter or leave to remain was to re-sit examinations or repeat a module of a course, must either have been born during a period of leave granted for the purposes of re-sitting examinations or repeating a module of a course or during the Relevant Points Based System Migrant's grant of leave for a course of more than six months, where that course is the same as the one for which the most recent grant of leave was to re-sit examinations or repeat a module; or

(3) must have been born no more than three months after the expiry of that most recent grant of leave; and

(4) must be applying for entry clearance.]

[(k) If the applicant is a child born in the UK to a Relevant Points Based System migrant and their partner, the applicant must provide a full UK birth certificate showing the names of both parents.

(l) All arrangements for the child's care and accommodation in the UK must comply with relevant UK legislation and regulations.]

[(k) The applicant must not be in the UK in breach of immigration laws except that any period of overstaying for a period of 28 days will be disregarded.]

Note: Paragraph 319H inserted from 29 February 2008 (HC 321). Words in square brackets in sub-para (g) substituted from 30 June 2008 (HC 607). Sub-para (h)(iii) inserted from 31 March 2009 (HC 314). Sub-paragraph (h)(iii) inserted from 31 March 2009 (HC 314). Sub-paragraph (i) inserted from 3 March 2010 (HC 367); however, if an applicant has made an application for entry clearance or leave to enter or remain before 3 March 2010 and the application has not been decided before that date, it will be decided in accordance with the Rules in force on 2 March 2010 and the conditions applicable to any leave granted will be those in force on 2 March 2010: see introduction to HC 367. Words in square brackets in sub-para (i) substituted from 21 April 2011 with savings for applications made but not decided before that date (HC 908). Sub-paragraphs (i) (1)–(5) and (j) substituted from 4 July 2011 (HC 1148). Words in first square brackets in sub-para (f) and second square brackets in (h) inserted and in second square brackets in (g) substituted from 6 April 2012 except for applications made but not decided before that date (HC 1888). Words in square brackets in sub-para (f)(iii) substituted from 9 July 2012 with savings for applications made but not decided before that date and sub-para (k) inserted from 1 October 2012 with savings for applications made but not decided before 9 July 2012 (HC 194). Sub-paragraphs (k) and (l) inserted from 20 July 2012 (Cm 8423). Subparagraph (b) substituted and sub-para (f) deleted from 6 September 2012 (HC 565).

[319I. Period and conditions of grant

(a) Entry clearance and leave to remain will be granted for a period which expires on the same day as the leave granted to the [Relevant Points Based System Migrant] parent [or, where paragraph 319H (b) (ii) applies, for a period which expires on the same day as the leave granted to the parent who has valid leave to enter or remain as the partner of a person who has either limited leave to enter or remain as a Relevant Points Based System Migrant, indefinite leave to remain as a Relevant Points Based System Migrant, or who has become a British Citizen where prior to that they held indefinite leave to remain as a Relevant Points Based System Migrant.]

(b) Entry clearance and leave to remain under this route will be subject to the following conditions:

(i) no recourse to public funds,

(ii) registration with the police, if this is required under paragraph 326 of these Rules, and

[(iii) if the Relevant Points Based System Migrant is a Tier 4 (General) Student and the Child meets the requirements of paragraphs 319H(i)(1), (2) and (3) or 319H(j) and:

(1) the Relevant Points Based System Migrant is a Tier 4 (General) Student applying for leave for less than 12 months, no employment, or

(2) the Relevant Points Based System Migrant is a Tier 4 (General) Student who is following a course of below degree level study, no employment.]]

Note: Paragraph 319I inserted from 29 February 2008 (HC 321). Sub-paragraph (iii) inserted from 31 March 2009 (HC314). Sub-paragraph (b)(iv) inserted from 3 March 2010 (HC 367); however, if an applicant has made an application for entry clearance or leave to enter or remain before 3 March 2010 and the application has not been decided before that date, it will be decided in accordance with the Rules in force on 2 March 2010 and the conditions applicable to any leave granted will be those in force on 2 March 2010: see introduction to HC 367. Sub-paragraphs (b)(iii)–(iv) substituted from 4 July 2011 with savings for applications made but not decided before that date (HC1148). Words in sub-para (a) inserted from 6 September 2012 (HC 565).

[319J. Requirements for indefinite leave to remain

To qualify for indefinite leave to remain under this route, an applicant must meet the requirements listed below. If the applicant meets these requirements, indefinite leave to remain will be granted. If the applicant does not meet these requirements, the application will be refused.

Requirements:

(a) The applicant must not fall for refusal under the general grounds for refusal, and must not be an illegal entrant.

(b) [The applicant must be the child of a parent in one of the circumstances specified in (i) or (ii) below:

(i) if the applicant was granted leave as the child of a Relevant Points Based System Migrant under rules in place prior to 9 July 2012 the applicant must be the child of a parent who is, at the same time, being granted indefinite leave to remain as a Points Based System Migrant; or

(ii) ..., the applicant must be the child of

(a) a parent who has been granted or is at the same time being granted indefinite leave to remain as a Relevant Points Based System Migrant where:

(i) that parent is the applicant's sole surviving parent, or

(ii) that parent has and has had sole responsibility for the applicant's upbringing, or

(iii) there are serious and compelling family or other considerations which would make it desirable not to refuse the application and suitable arrangements have been made for the applicant's care; or

(b) a parent who is at the same time being granted indefinite leave to remain as the partner of a person who has indefinite leave to remain as a Relevant Points Based System

Migrant, or who has become a British Citizen where immediately prior to that they had indefinite leave to remain as a Relevant Points Based System Migrant.]

(c) The applicant must have, or have last been granted, leave as the Child of[, or have been born in the United Kingdom to,] the [Relevant Points Based System Migrant] who is being granted indefinite leave to remain.

(d) The applicant must not be married or in a civil partnership, must not have formed an independent family unit, and must not be leading an independent life.

(e) Both of an applicant's parents must either be lawfully present in the UK, or being granted entry clearance, limited leave to remain, or indefinite leave to remain at the same time as the applicant, unless:

(i) The [Relevant Points Based System Migrant] is the applicant's sole surviving parent, or

(ii) The [Relevant Points Based System Migrant] parent has and has had sole responsibility for the applicant's upbringing, or

(iii) there are [serious and compelling] family or other considerations which would make it desirable not to refuse the application and suitable arrangements have been made for the applicant's care.

(f) The applicant must have sufficient knowledge of the English language and sufficient knowledge about life in the United Kingdom, with reference to paragraphs 33B to 33F of these Rules, unless the applicant is under the age of 18 at the time this application is made][.]

(g) The applicant does not have one or more unspent convictions within the meaning of the Rehabilitation of Offenders Act 1974.]

[(h) If the applicant is a child born in the UK to a Relevant Points Based System migrant and their partner, the applicant must provide a full UK birth certificate showing the names of both parents.

(i) All arrangements for the child's care and accommodation in the UK must comply with relevant UK legislation and regulations.]

[(h) The applicant must not be in the UK in breach of immigration laws except that any period of overstaying for a period of 28 days will be disregarded.]

Note: Paragraph 319J inserted from 29 February 2008 (HC 321). Words deleted from 7 April 2010 (HC 439); however, if an applicant has made an application for entry clearance or leave to enter or remain before 6 April and the application has not been decided before that date, it will be decided in accordance with the Rules in force on 6 April 2010. Sub-paragraph (g) inserted from 6 April 2011 (HC 863). Words in first square brackets in sub-para (c) inserted from 6 April 2012 except for applications made but not decided before that date (HC 1888). Words in square brackets in sub-para (e) substituted from 9 July 2012 with savings made but not decided before that date and sub-para (h) inserted from 1 October 2012 with savings for applications made but not decided before 9 July 2012 (HC 194). A second sub-para (h) and sub-para (i) inserted from 20 July 2012 (Cm 8423). Words substituted in sub-para (b) from 6 September 2012 (HC 565).

[319K. ....

Note: Paragraph 319K inserted from 29 February 2008 (HC 321), deleted from 20 July 2012 (Cm 8423).

[Other family members of persons with limited leave to enter or remain in the United Kingdom as a refugee or beneficiary of humanitarian protection

Note: Heading inserted from 6 April 2011 (HC 863).

[Requirements for leave to enter the United Kingdom as the spouse or civil partner of a person with limited leave to enter or remain in the United Kingdom as a refugee or beneficiary of humanitarian protection.

319L The requirements to be met by a person seeking leave to enter the United Kingdom as the spouse or civil partner of a person with limited leave to enter or remain in the United Kingdom as a refugee or beneficiary of humanitarian protection, are that:

(i) (a) the applicant is married to or the civil partner of a person who has limited leave to enter or remain in the United Kingdom as a refugee or beneficiary of humanitarian protection granted such status under the immigration rules and the parties are married or have formed a civil partnership after the person granted asylum or humanitarian protection left the country of his former habitual residence in order to seek asylum or humanitarian protection; and

(b) the applicant provides an original English language test certificate in speaking and listening from an English language test provider approved by the Secretary of State for these purposes, which clearly shows the applicant's name and the qualification obtained (which must meet or exceed level A1 of the Common European Framework of Reference) unless:

(i) the applicant is aged 65 or over at the date he makes his application; or

(ii) the Secretary of State or Entry Clearance Officer considers that the applicant has a physical or mental condition that would prevent him from meeting the requirement; or

(iii) the Secretary of State or Entry Clearance Officer considers there are exceptional compassionate circumstances that would prevent the applicant from meeting the requirement; or

(iv) the applicant is a national of one of the following countries: Antigua and Barbuda; Australia; the Bahamas; Barbados; Belize; Canada; Dominica; Grenada; Guyana; Jamaica; New Zealand; St Kitts and Nevis; St Lucia; St Vincent and the Grenadines; Trinidad and Tobago; USA; or

(v) the applicant has obtained an academic qualification (not a professional or vocational qualification), which is deemed by UK NARIC to meet the recognised standard of a Bachelor's or Masters degree or PhD in the UK, from an educational establishment in one of the following countries: Antigua and Barbuda; Australia; The Bahamas; Barbados; Belize; Dominica; Grenada; Guyana; Ireland; Jamaica; New Zealand; St Kitts and Nevis; St Lucia; St Vincent and The Grenadines; Trinidad and Tobago; the UK; the USA; and provides the specified documents; or

(vi) the applicant has obtained an academic qualification (not a professional or vocational qualification) which is deemed by UK NARIC to meet the recognised standard of a Bachelor's or Masters degree or PhD in the UK, and

(1) provides the specified evidence to show he has the qualification, and

(2) UK NARIC has confirmed that the degree was taught or researched in English, or

(vii) has obtained an academic qualification (not a professional or vocational qualification) which is deemed by UK NARIC to meet the recognised standard of a Bachelor's or Masters degree or PhD in the UK, and provides the specified evidence to show:

(1) he has the qualification, and

(2) that the qualification was taught or researched in English; and

(ii) the parties to the marriage or civil partnership have met; and

(iii) each of the parties intends to live permanently with the other as his or her spouse or civil partner and the marriage or civil partnership is subsisting; and

(iv) there will be adequate accommodation for the parties and any dependants without recourse to public funds in accommodation which they own or occupy exclusively; and

(v) the parties will be able to maintain themselves and any dependants adequately without recourse to public funds; and

(vi) the applicant holds a valid United Kingdom entry clearance for entry in this capacity.

Note: Paragraph 319L inserted from 6 April 2011 except for applications made but not decided before that date (HC 863).

319M. Leave to enter the United Kingdom as the spouse or civil partner of a refugee or beneficiary of humanitarian protection may be granted for 63 months provided the Immigration Officer is satisfied that each of the requirements of paragraph 319L (i)–(vi) are met.

Note: Paragraph 319M inserted from 6 April 2011 except for applications made but not decided before that date (HC 863).

319N. Leave to enter the United Kingdom as the spouse or civil partner of a refugee or beneficiary of humanitarian protection is to be refused if the immigration officer is not satisfied that each of the requirements of paragraph [319L(i)–(vi)] are met.

Note: Paragraph 319N inserted from 6 April 2011 except for applications made but not decided before that date (HC 863). Words in square brackets substituted from 4 July 2011 with savings for applications made but not decided before that date (HC 1148).

Requirements for leave to enter the United Kingdom as the unmarried or same-sex partner of a person with limited leave to enter or remain in the United Kingdom as a refugee or beneficiary of humanitarian protection.

319O. The requirements to be met by a person seeking leave to enter the United Kingdom as the unmarried or same-sex partner of a person with limited leave to enter or remain in the United Kingdom as a refugee or beneficiary of humanitarian protection, are that:

(i) (a) the applicant is the unmarried or same-sex partner of a person who has limited leave to enter or remain in the United Kingdom as a refugee or beneficiary of humanitarian protection granted such status under the immigration rules, and the parties have been living together in a relationship akin to either a marriage or civil partnership subsisting for two years or more after the person granted asylum or humanitarian protection left the country of his former habitual residence in order to seek asylum or humanitarian protection; and

(b) the applicant provides an original English language test certificate in speaking and listening from an English language test provider approved by the Secretary of State for these purposes, which clearly shows the applicant's name and the qualification obtained (which must meet or exceed level A1 of the Common European Framework of Reference) unless:

(i) the applicant is aged 65 or over at the time he makes his application;

(ii) the Secretary of State or Entry Clearance Officer considers that the applicant has a physical or mental condition that would prevent him from meeting the requirement;

(iii) the Secretary of State or Entry Clearance Officer considers there are exceptional compassionate circumstances that would prevent the applicant from meeting the requirement;

(iv) the applicant is a national of one of the following countries: Antigua and Barbuda; Australia; the Bahamas; Barbados; Belize; Canada; Dominica; Grenada; Guyana; Jamaica; New Zealand; St Kitts and Nevis; St Lucia; St Vincent and the Grenadines; Trinidad and Tobago; USA;

(v) the applicant has obtained an academic qualification (not a professional or vocational qualification), which is deemed by UK NARIC to meet the recognised standard of a Bachelor's or Masters degree or PhD in the UK, from an educational establishment in one of the following countries: Antigua and Barbuda; Australia; The Bahamas; Barbados; Belize; Dominica; Grenada; Guyana; Ireland; Jamaica; New Zealand; St Kitts and Nevis; St Lucia; St Vincent and The Grenadines; Trinidad and Tobago; the UK; the USA; and provides the specified documents; or

(vi) the applicant has obtained an academic qualification (not a professional or vocational qualification) which is deemed by UK NARIC to meet the recognised standard of a Bachelor's or Masters degree or PhD in the UK, and

(1) provides the specified evidence to show he has the qualification, and

(2) UK NARIC has confirmed that the degree was taught or researched in English, or

(vii) has obtained an academic qualification (not a professional or vocational qualification) which is deemed by UK NARIC to meet the recognised standard of a Bachelor's or Masters degree or PhD in the UK, and provides the specified evidence to show:

(1) he has the qualification, and

(2) that the qualification was taught or researched in English; and

(ii) any previous marriage or civil partnership (or similar relationship) by either partner has permanently broken down; and

(iii) the parties are not involved in a consanguineous relationship with one another; and

(iv) there will be adequate accommodation for the parties and any dependants without recourse to public funds in accommodation which they own or occupy exclusively; and

(v) the parties will be able to maintain themselves and any dependants adequately without recourse to public funds; and

(vi) the parties intend to live together permanently; and

(vii) the applicant holds a valid United Kingdom entry clearance for entry in this capacity.

Note: Paragraph 319O inserted from 6 April 2011 except for applications made but not decided before that date (HC 863).

319P. Leave to enter the United Kingdom as the unmarried or same-sex partner of a refugee or beneficiary of humanitarian protection may be granted for 63 months provided the Immigration Officer is satisfied that each of the requirements of paragraph 319O(i)–(vii) are met.

Note: Paragraph 319P inserted from 6 April 2011 except for applications made but not decided before that date (HC 863).

319Q. Leave to enter the United Kingdom as the unmarried or same-sex partner of a refugee or beneficiary of humanitarian protection is to be refused if the Immigration Officer is not satisfied that each of the requirements of paragraph 319O(i)–(vii) are met.

Note: Paragraph 319Q inserted from 6 April 2011 except for applications made but not decided before that date (HC 863).

Requirements for leave to enter the United Kingdom as the child of a parent or parents given limited leave to enter or remain in the United Kingdom as a refugee or beneficiary of humanitarian protection

319R. The requirements to be met by a person seeking leave to enter the United Kingdom as the child of a parent or parents given limited leave to enter or remain in the United Kingdom as a refugee or beneficiary of humanitarian protection, are that the applicant:

(i) is the child of a parent or parents granted limited leave to enter or remain as a refugee or beneficiary of humanitarian protection granted as such under the immigration rules; and

(ii) is under the age of 18, and

(iii) is not leading an independent life, is unmarried, is not in a civil partnership, and has not formed an independent family unit; and

(iv) was conceived after the person granted asylum or humanitarian protection left the country of his habitual residence in order to seek asylum in the UK; and

(v) can, and will, be accommodated adequately by the parent or parents the child is seeking to join without recourse to public funds in accommodation which the parent or parents the child is seeking to join, own or occupy exclusively; and

(vi) can, and will, be maintained adequately by the parent or parents the child is seeking to join, without recourse to public funds; and

(vii) if seeking leave to enter, holds a valid United Kingdom entry clearance for entry in this capacity.

Note: Paragraph 319R inserted from 6 April 2011 except for applications made but not decided before that date (HC 863).

319S. Limited leave to enter the United Kingdom as the child of a refugee or beneficiary of humanitarian protection may be granted for 63 months provided the Immigration Officer is satisfied that each of the requirements in paragraph 319R (i)–(vii) are met.

Note: Paragraph 319S inserted from 6 April 2011 except for applications made but not decided before that date (HC 863).

319T. Limited leave to enter the United Kingdom as the child of a refugee or beneficiary humanitarian protection is to be refused if the Immigration Officer is not satisfied that each of the requirements in paragraph 319R (i)–(vii) are met.

Note: Paragraph 319T inserted from 6 April 2011 except for applications made but not decided before that date (HC 863).

Requirements for indefinite leave to remain in the United Kingdom as the spouse or civil partner, unmarried or same-sex partner or child of a refugee or beneficiary of humanitarian protection present and settled in the United Kingdom

319U. To qualify for indefinite leave to remain in the UK, an applicant must meet the requirements set out in paragraph 287 if the applicant is a spouse or civil partner, paragraph 295G if they are an unmarried or same-sex partner, or 298 if the applicant is a child and the sponsor must be present and settled in the United Kingdom at the time the application is made. If an applicant meets the requirements as set out in the relevant paragraphs, indefinite leave to remain will be granted. If the applicant does not meet these requirements, the application will be refused.]

Note: Paragraph 319U inserted from 6 April 2011 except for applications made but not decided before that date (HC 863).

[Parents, grandparents and other dependent relatives of persons with limited leave to enter or remain in the United Kingdom as a refugee or beneficiary of humanitarian protection]

Note: Heading inserted from 4 July 2011 with savings for applications made but not decided before that date (HC 1148).

[Requirements for leave to enter or remain in the United Kingdom as the parent, grandparent or other dependent relative of a person with limited leave to enter or remain in the United Kingdom as a refugee or beneficiary of humanitarian protection

319V. The requirements to be met by a person seeking leave to enter or remain in the United Kingdom as the parent, grandparent or other dependent relative of a person with limited leave to enter or remain in the United Kingdom as a refugee or beneficiary of humanitarian protection are that the person:

(i) is related to a refugee or beneficiary of humanitarian protection with limited leave to enter or remain in the United Kingdom in one of the following ways:

(a) [parent or grandparent who is divorced, widowed, single or separated] aged 65 years or over; or

[(b)] parents or grandparents travelling together of whom at least one is aged 65 or over; or

[(c)] a parent or grandparent aged 65 or over who has entered into a second relationship of marriage or civil partnership but cannot look to the spouse, civil partner or children of that second relationship for financial support; and where the person with limited leave to enter or remain in the United Kingdom is able and willing to maintain the parent or grandparent and any spouse or civil partner or child of the second relationship who would be admissible as a dependant; or

[(d)] a parent or grandparent under the age of 65 if living alone outside the United Kingdom in the most exceptional compassionate circumstances [...]; or

[(e)] parents or grandparents travelling together who are both under the age of 65 if living in the most exceptional compassionate circumstances; or]

(f) the son, daughter, sister, brother, uncle or aunt over the age of 18 if living alone outside the United Kingdom in the most exceptional compassionate circumstances [...]; and

(ii) is joining a refugee or beneficiary of humanitarian protection with limited leave to enter or remain in the United Kingdom; and

(iii) is financially wholly or mainly dependent on the relative who has limited leave to enter or remain as a refugee or beneficiary of humanitarian protection in the United Kingdom; and

(iv) can, and will, be accommodated adequately, together with any dependants, without recourse to public funds, in accommodation which the sponsor owns or occupies exclusively; and

(v) can, and will, be maintained adequately, together with any dependants, without recourse to public funds; and

(vi) has no other close relatives in his own country to whom he could turn for financial support; and

(vii) if seeking leave to enter, holds a valid United Kingdom entry clearance for entry in this capacity [or, if seeking leave to remain, holds valid leave to remain in another capacity.]

Note: Paragraphs 319V inserted from 4 July 2011 except for applications made but not decided before that date (HC 1148). Words in square brackets in sub-para (i)(a) substituted; sub-paras (b)–(d) renumbered, sub-para (viii) and words in (d) and (f) omitted; sub-para (e) and words in square brackets in sub-para (vii) inserted from 31 October 2011 except for applications made but not decided before that date (HC 1511).

319VA. Limited leave to enter the United Kingdom as the parent, grandparent or other dependent relative of a refugee or beneficiary of humanitarian protection with limited leave to enter or remain in the United Kingdom may be granted for 5 years provided a valid United Kingdom entry clearance for entry in this capacity is produced to the Immigration Officer on arrival. Limited leave to remain in the United Kingdom as the parent, grandparent or other dependent relative of a refugee or beneficiary of humanitarian protection with limited leave to enter or remain in the United Kingdom may be granted provided the Secretary of State is satisfied that each of the requirements of paragraph [319V (i)–(vii)] is met.

Note: Paragraphs 319VA inserted from 4 July 2011 except for applications made but not decided before that date (HC 1148). Numbers in square brackets substituted from 31 October 2011 with savings for applications made but not decided before that date (HC 1511).

319VB. Limited leave to enter the United Kingdom as the parent, grandparent or other dependent relative of a refugee or beneficiary of humanitarian protection with limited leave to enter or remain in the United Kingdom is to be refused if a valid United Kingdom entry clearance for entry in this capacity is not produced to the Immigration Officer on arrival. Limited leave to remain in the United Kingdom as the parent, grandparent or other dependent relative of a refugee or beneficiary of humanitarian protection with limited leave to enter or remain in the United Kingdom is to be refused if the Secretary of State is not satisfied that each of the requirements of paragraph [319V (i)–(vii)] is met.

Note: Paragraphs 319VB inserted from 4 July 2011 except for applications made but not decided before that date (HC 1148). Numbers in square brackets substituted from 31 October 2011 with savings for applications made but not decided before that date (HC 1511).

Requirements for indefinite leave to remain in the United Kingdom as the parent, grandparent or other dependent relative of a refugee or beneficiary of humanitarian protection who is present and settled in the United Kingdom or of a former refugee or beneficiary humanitarian protection, who is now a British Citizen

319W. The requirements for indefinite leave to remain in the United Kingdom as the parent, grandparent or other dependent relative of a refugee or beneficiary of humanitarian protection who is now present and settled in the United Kingdom or who is now a British Citizen are that:

(i) the applicant [has limited leave to enter or remain in] the United Kingdom in accordance with paragraph 319V as a dependent relative of a refugee or beneficiary of humanitarian protection with limited leave to enter or remain in the United Kingdom; and

(ii) the sponsor the applicant was admitted to join is now present and settled in the United Kingdom, or is now a British Citizen; and

(iii) the applicant is financially wholly or mainly dependent on the relative who is present and settled in the United Kingdom; and

(iv) the applicant can, and will, be accommodated adequately, together with any dependants, without recourse to public funds, in accommodation which the sponsor owns or occupies exclusively; and

(v) the applicant can, and will, be maintained adequately, together with any dependants, without recourse to public funds; and

(vi) the applicant has no other close relatives in their country of former habitual residence to whom he could turn for financial support; and

(vii) does not have one or more unspent convictions within the meaning of the Rehabilitation of Offenders Act 1974.

Note: Paragraphs 319W inserted from 4 July 2011 except for applications made but not decided before that date (HC 1151). Words in square brackets in sub-para (i) substituted from 31 October 2011 except for applications made but not decided before that date (HC 1511).

319WA. Indefinite leave to remain in the United Kingdom as the parent, grandparent or other dependent relative of a refugee or beneficiary of humanitarian protection who is present and settled in the United Kingdom, or who is now a British Citizen may be granted provided the Secretary of State is satisfied that each of the requirements of paragraph 319W(i)–(vii) is met.

Note: Paragraphs 319WA inserted from 4 July 2011 except for applications made but not decided before that date (HC 1148).

319WB. Indefinite leave to remain in the United Kingdom as the parent, grandparent or other dependent relative of a person present and settled in the United Kingdom is to be refused if the secretary of state is not satisfied that each of the requirements of paragraph 319W (i)–(vii) is met.

Note: Paragraphs 319WB inserted from 4 July 2011 except for applications made but not decided before that date (HC 1148).

Requirements for leave to enter or remain in the United Kingdom as the child of a relative with limited leave to enter or remain in the United Kingdom as a refugee or beneficiary of humanitarian protection

319X. The requirements to be met by a person seeking leave to enter or remain in the United Kingdom as the child of a relative with limited leave to remain as a refugee or beneficiary of humanitarian protection in the United Kingdom are that:

(i) the applicant is seeking leave to enter [or remain] to [...] join a relative with limited leave to enter or remain as a refugee or person with humanitarian protection; and:

(ii) the relative has limited leave in the United Kingdom as a refugee or beneficiary of humanitarian protection and there are serious and compelling family or other considerations which make exclusion of the child undesirable and suitable arrangements have been made for the child's care; and

(iii) the relative is not the parent of the child who is seeking leave to enter or remain in the United Kingdom; and

(iv) the applicant is under the age of 18; and

(v) the applicant is not leading an independent life, is unmarried and is not a civil partner, and has not formed an independent family unit; and

(vi) the applicant can, and will, be accommodated adequately by the relative the child is seeking to join without recourse to public funds in accommodation which the relative in the United Kingdom owns or occupies exclusively; and

(vii) the applicant can, and will, be maintained adequately by the relative in the United Kingdom without recourse to public funds; and

(viii) [if seeking leave to enter, the applicant holds a valid United Kingdom entry clearance for entry in this capacity or, if seeking leave to remain, holds valid leave to remain in another capacity.]

Note: Paragraphs 319X inserted from 4 July 2011 except for applications made but not decided before that date (HC 1148). Words in square brackets in sub-para (i) inserted and other word in (i) omitted; words in square brackets in (viii) substituted and (ix) deleted from 31 October 2011, except for applications made but not decided before that date (HC 1511).

319XA. Limited leave to enter the United Kingdom as the child of a relative with limited leave to enter or remain as a refugee or beneficiary of humanitarian protection in the United Kingdom may be granted for 5 years provided a valid United Kingdom entry clearance for entry in this capacity is produced to the immigration officer on arrival. Limited leave to remain in the United Kingdom as the child of a relative with limited leave to enter or remain as a refugee or beneficiary of humanitarian protection in the United Kingdom may be granted provided the Secretary of State is satisfied that each of the requirements of paragraph [319X (i)–(viii)] is met.

Note: Paragraphs 319XA inserted from 4 July 2011 except for applications made but not decided before that date (HC 1148). Numbers in square brackets substituted from 31 October 2011 except for applications made but not decided before that date (HC 1511).

319XB. Limited leave to enter the United Kingdom as the child of a relative with limited leave to enter or remain as a refugee or beneficiary of humanitarian protection in the United Kingdom is to be refused if a valid United Kingdom entry clearance for entry in this capacity is not produced to the Immigration Officer on arrival. Limited leave to remain in the United Kingdom as the child of a relative with limited leave to enter or remain as a refugee or beneficiary of humanitarian protection in the United Kingdom is to be refused if the Secretary of State is not satisfied that each of the requirements of paragraph [319X (i)–(viii)] is met.

Note: Paragraphs 319XB inserted from 4 July 2011 except for applications made but not decided before that date (HC 1148). Numbers in square brackets substituted from 31 October 2011 with savings for applications made but not decided before that date (HC 1511).

Requirements for indefinite leave to remain in the United Kingdom as the child of a relative who is present and settled in the United Kingdom or as a former refugee or beneficiary of humanitarian protection who is now a British Citizen

319Y. To qualify for indefinite leave to remain as the child of a relative who is present and settled in the United Kingdom, an applicant must meet the requirements set out in paragraph [298].]

Note: Paragraph 319Y inserted from 4 July 2011 except for applications made but not decided before that date (HC 1148). Numbers in square brackets substituted from 31 October 2011 except for applications made but not decided before that date (HC 1511).

PART 9

GENERAL GROUNDS FOR THE REFUSAL OF ENTRY CLEARANCE, LEAVE TO ENTER, LEAVE TO REMAIN, VARIATION OF LEAVE TO ENTER OR REMAIN AND CURTAILMENT OF LEAVE IN THE UNITED KINGDOM

Note: Heading substituted from 12 August 2010 (HC 382).

[**A320.** Paragraphs 320 (except subparagraph (3), (10) and (11)) and 322 do not apply to an application for entry clearance, leave to enter or leave to remain as a Family Member under Appendix FM[, and Part 9 (except for paragraph 322(1)) does not apply to an application for leave to remain on the grounds of private life under paragraphs 276ADE-276DH.]]

Note: Paragraph A320 inserted from 9 July 2012 with savings for applications made but not decided before that date (HC 194). Words inserted from 6 September 2012 (HC 565).

Refusal of entry clearance or leave to enter the United Kingdom

320. In addition to the grounds for refusal of entry clearance or leave to enter set out in Parts 2–8 of these Rules, and subject to paragraph 321 below, the following grounds for the refusal of entry clearance or leave to enter apply:

Grounds on which entry clearance or leave to enter the United Kingdom is to be refused

(1) the fact that entry is being sought for a purpose not covered by these Rules;

(2) the fact that the person seeking entry to the United Kingdom is currently the subject of a deportation order;

(3) failure by the person seeking entry to the United Kingdom to produce to the Immigration Officer a valid national passport or other document satisfactorily establishing his identity and nationality;

(4) failure to satisfy the Immigration Officer, in the case of a person arriving in the United Kingdom or seeking entry through the Channel Tunnel with the intention of entering any other part of the common travel area, that he is acceptable to the immigration authorities there;

(5) failure, in the case of a visa national, to produce to the Immigration Officer a passport or other identity document endorsed with a valid and current United Kingdom entry clearance issued for the purpose for which entry is sought;

(6) where the Secretary of State has personally directed that the exclusion of a person from the United Kingdom is conducive to the public good;

(7) save in relation to a person settled in the United Kingdom or where the Immigration Officer is satisfied that there are strong compassionate reasons justifying admission, confirmation from the Medical Inspector that, for medical reasons, it is undesirable to admit a person seeking leave to enter the United Kingdom;

[(7A) where false representations have been made or false documents [or information] have been submitted (whether or not material to the application, and whether or not to the applicant's knowledge), or material facts have not been disclosed, in relation to the application [, or in order to obtain documents from the Secretary of State or a third party required in support of the application];]

[(7B) [where the applicant has previously breached the UK's immigration laws (and was over 18 at the time of his most recent breach) by];

(a) Overstaying,

(b) breaching a condition attached to his leave,

(c) being an Illegal Entrant,

(d) using Deception in an application for entry clearance, leave to enter or remain[, or in order to obtain documents from the Secretary of State or a third party required in support of the application] (whether successful or not),

unless the applicant:

(i) Overstayed for [90] days or less and left the UK voluntarily, not at the expense (directly or indirectly) of the Secretary of State,

(ii) used Deception in an application for entry clearance more than 10 years ago,

(iii) left the UK voluntarily, not at the expense (directly or indirectly) of the Secretary of State, more than 12 months ago,

[(iv) left the UK voluntarily, at the expense (directly or indirectly) of the Secretary of State, more than 2 years ago; and the date the person left the UK was no more than 6 months after the date on which the person was given notice of the removal decision, or no more than 6 months after the date on which the person no longer had a pending appeal; whichever is the later;

(v) left the UK voluntarily, at the expense (directly or indirectly) of the Secretary of State, more than 5 years ago; or

(vi) was removed or deported from the UK more than 10 years ago.]

Where more than one breach of the UK's immigration laws has occurred, only the breach which leads to the longest period of absence from the UK will be relevant under this paragraph;

[(7C) ...

[(7D) failure, without providing a reasonable explanation, to comply with a request made on behalf of the Entry Clearance Officer to attend for interview.]

Grounds on which entry clearance or leave to enter the United Kingdom should normally be refused

(8) failure by a person arriving in the United Kingdom to furnish the Immigration Officer with such information as may be required for the purpose of deciding whether he requires leave to enter and, if so, whether and on what terms leave should be given;

[(8A) where the person seeking leave is outside the United Kingdom, failure by him to supply any information, documents, copy documents or medical report requested by an Immigration Officer;]

(9) failure by a person seeking leave to enter as a returning resident to satisfy the Immigration Officer that he meets the requirements of paragraph 18 of these Rules [or that he seeks leave to enter for the same purpose as that for which his earlier leave was granted;]

(10) production by the person seeking leave to enter the United Kingdom of a national passport or travel document issued by a territorial entity or authority which is not recognised by Her Majesty's Government as a state or is not dealt with as a government by them, or which does not accept valid United Kingdom passports for the purpose of its own immigration control; or a passport or travel document which does not comply with international passport practice;

[(11) where the applicant has previously contrived in a significant way to frustrate the intentions of the Rules by:

(i) overstaying; or

(ii) breaching a condition attached to his leave; or

(iii) being an illegal entrant; or

(iv) using deception in an application for entry clearance, leave to enter or remain or in order to obtain documents from the Secretary of State or a third party required in support of the application (whether successful or not); and

there are other aggravating circumstances, such as absconding, not meeting temporary admission/reporting restrictions or bail conditions, using an assumed identity or multiple identities, switching nationality, making frivolous applications or not complying with the re-documentation process.]

(12) . . .

(13) failure, except by a person eligible for admission to the United Kingdom for settlement, ...to satisfy the Immigration Officer that he will be admitted to another country after a stay in the United Kingdom;

(14) refusal by a sponsor of a person seeking leave to enter the United Kingdom to give, if requested to do so, an undertaking in writing to be responsible for that person's maintenance and accommodation for the period of any leave granted.

(15) ...

(16) failure, in the case of a child under the age of 18 years seeking leave to enter the United Kingdom otherwise than in conjunction with an application made by his parent(s) or legal guardian, to provide the Immigration Officer, if required to do so, with written consent to the application from his parent(s) or legal guardian; save that the requirement as to written consent does not apply in the case of a child seeking admission to the United Kingdom as an asylum seeker;

(17) save in relation to a person settled in the United Kingdom, refusal to undergo a medical examination when required to do so by the Immigration Officer;

(18) save where the Immigration Officer is satisfied that admission would be justified for strong compassionate reasons, conviction in any country including the United Kingdom of an offence which, if committed in the United Kingdom, is punishable with imprisonment for a term of 12 months or any greater punishment or, if committed outside the United Kingdom, would be so punishable if the conduct constituting the offence had occurred in the United Kingdom;

(19) where, from information available to the Immigration Officer, it seems right to refuse leave to enter on the ground that exclusion from the United Kingdom is conducive to the public good; if, for example, in the light of the character, conduct or associations of the person seeking leave to enter it is undesirable to give him leave to enter;

[(20) failure by the person seeking entry into the United Kingdom to comply with a requirement relating to the provision of physical data to which he is subject by regulations made under section 126 of the Nationality, Immigration and Asylum Act 2002;]

(21) ...

[(22) Where one or more relevant NHS body has notified the Secretary of State that the person seeking entry or leave to enter has failed to pay a charge or charges with a total value of at least £1000 in accordance with the relevant NHS regulations on charges to overseas visitors.]

Note: Words in square brackets in sub-para (9) inserted from 1 November 1996 (HC 31). Sub-paragraph 8A inserted from 30 July 2000 (HC 704). Sub-paragraph (20) inserted from 27 February 2004 (HC 370). Words in square brackets in sub-para (15) substituted from 1 October 2004 (Cm 6339). Words in square brackets in sub-para (13) inserted from 5 December 2005 (HC 582). Sub-paragraph (7A) inserted from 29 February 2008 (HC 321). Sub-paragraph (21) deleted from 29 February 2008 (HC 321). Sub-paragraph (7B) inserted from 1 April 2008 (HC 321). Sub-paragraphs (11) and (12) deleted from 1 April 2008 (HC 321). New sub-para (11) inserted from 30 June 2008

(HC 607) and then substituted from 6 September 2012 (HC 565). Sub-paragraph 320(7C) inserted from 30 June 2008 (HC 607), deleted from 9 July 2012 with savings for applications made but not decided before that date (HC 194). Words inserted in sub-para (7A) from 27 November 2008 (HC 1113). Sub-paragraphs (7B)(iv) and (v) substituted from 6 April 2011 (HC 863). Sub-paragraph (22) inserted from 31 October 2011 except for applications made but not decided before that date (HC 1511). Words in second square brackets in sub-para (7A), square brackets in (7B)(d) inserted and (15) deleted from 6 April 2012 except for applications made but not decided before that date (HC 1888). Number in square brackets in sub-para (7B)(d)(i) substituted from 1 October 2012 with savings for applications made but not decided before 9 July 2012 (HC 194). Words in first square brackets in sub-para 7B substituted and words deleted from sub-para 13 from 9 July 2012 with savings for applications made but not decided before that date (HC 194). Sub-paragraph 7D inserted from 30 July 2012 with savings for applications made but not decided before that date (HC 514).

Refusal of leave to enter in relation to a person in possession of an entry clearance

321. A person seeking leave to enter the United Kingdom who holds an entry clearance which was duly issued to him and is still current may be refused leave to enter only where the Immigration Officer is satisfied that:

[(i) False representations were made or false documents {or information} were submitted (whether or not material to the application, and whether or not to the holder's knowledge), or material facts were not disclosed, in relation to the application for entry clearance[, or in order to obtain documents from the Secretary of State or a third party required in support of the application]; or]

(ii) a change of circumstances since it was issued has removed the basis of the holder's claim to admission, except where the change of circumstances amounts solely to the person becoming over age for entry in one of the categories contained in paragraphs 296–316 of these Rules since the issue of the entry clearance; or

(iii) refusal is justified on grounds of restricted returnability; on medical grounds; on grounds of criminal record; because the person seeking leave to enter is the subject of a deportation order or because exclusion would be conducive to the public good.

Note: Sub-paragraph (i) substituted from 29 February 2008 (HC 321). First words inserted in sub-para (i) from 27 November 2008 (HC 1113), second words inserted in sub-para (i) from 6 April 2012 except for applications made but not decided before that date (HC 1888).

[Grounds on which leave to enter or remain which is in force is to be cancelled at port or while the holder is outside the United Kingdom

321A. The following grounds for the cancellation of a person's leave to enter or remain which is in force on his arrival in, or whilst he is outside, the United Kingdom apply:

(1) there has been such a change in the circumstances of that person's case, since the leave was given, that it should be cancelled; or

[(2) false representations were made or false documents were submitted (whether or not material to the application, and whether or not to the holder's knowledge), or material facts were not disclosed, in relation to the application for leave[, or in order to obtain documents from the Secretary of State or a third party required in support of the application]; or]

(3) save in relation to a person settled in the United Kingdom or where the Immigration Officer or the Secretary of State is satisfied that there are strong compassionate reasons

justifying admission, where it is apparent that, for medical reasons, it is undesirable to admit that person to the United Kingdom; or

(4) where the Secretary of State has personally directed that the exclusion of that person from the United Kingdom is conducive to the public good; or

(5) where from information available to the Immigration Officer or the Secretary of State, it seems right to cancel leave on the ground that exclusion from the United Kingdom is conducive to the public good; if, for example, in the light of the character, conduct or associations of that person it is undesirable for him to have leave to enter the United Kingdom; or

(6) where that person is outside the United Kingdom, failure by that person to supply any information, documents, copy documents or medical report requested by an Immigration Officer or the Secretary of State.]

Note: Paragraph 321A inserted from 30 July 2000 (HC 704). Sub-paragraph (2) substituted from 29 February 2008 (HC 321). Words inserted into sub-para (2) from 6 April 2012 except for applications made but not decided before that date (HC 1888).

[Refusal of leave to remain, variation of leave to enter or remain or curtailment of leave]

322. In addition to the grounds for refusal of extension of stay set out in Parts 2–8 of these Rules, the following provisions apply in relation to the refusal of an application for [leave to remain,] variation of leave to enter or remain or, where appropriate, the curtailment of leave:

[Grounds on which leave to remain and variation of leave to enter or remain in the United Kingdom are to be refused]

(1) the fact that variation of leave to enter or remain is being sought for a purpose not covered by these Rules.

[(1A) where false representations have been made or false documents {or information} have been submitted (whether or not material to the application, and whether or not to the applicant's knowledge), or material facts have not been disclosed, in relation to the application[, or in order to obtain documents from the Secretary of State or a third party required in support of the application].]

[Grounds on which leave to remain and variation of leave to enter or remain in the United Kingdom should normally be refused]

(2) the making of false representations or the failure to disclose any material fact for the purpose of obtaining leave to enter or a previous variation of leave[, or in order to obtain documents from the Secretary of State or a third party required in support of the application for leave to enter or a previous variation of leave];

(3) failure to comply with any conditions attached to the grant of leave to enter or remain;

(4) failure by the person concerned to maintain or accommodate himself and any dependants without recourse to public funds;

(5) the undesirability of permitting the person concerned to remain in the United Kingdom in the light of his character, conduct or associations or the fact that he represents a threat to national security;

(6) refusal by a sponsor of the person concerned to give, if requested to do so, an undertaking in writing to be responsible for his maintenance and accommodation in the United Kingdom or failure to honour such an undertaking once given;

(7) failure by the person concerned to honour any declaration or undertaking given orally or in writing as to the intended duration and/or purpose of his stay;

(8) failure, except by a person who qualifies for settlement in the United Kingdom or by the spouse [or civil partner] of a person settled in the United Kingdom, to satisfy the Secretary of State that he will be returnable to another country if allowed to remain in the United Kingdom for a further period;

[(9) failure by an applicant to produce within a reasonable time information, documents or other evidence required by the Secretary of State to establish his claim to remain under these Rules;]

(10) failure, without providing a reasonable explanation, to comply with a request made on behalf of the Secretary of State to attend for interview;

(11) failure, in the case of a child under the age of 18 years seeking a variation of his leave to enter or remain in the United Kingdom otherwise than in conjunction with an application by his parent(s) or legal guardian, to provide the Secretary of State, if required to do so, with written consent to the application from his parent(s) or legal guardian; save that the requirement as to written consent does not apply in the case of a child who has been admitted to the United Kingdom as an asylum seeker;

[(12) Where one or more relevant NHS body has notified the Secretary of State that the person seeking leave to remain or a variation of leave to enter or remain has failed to pay a charge or charges with a total value of at least £1000 in accordance with the relevant NHS regulations on charges to overseas visitors.]

Note: Sub-paragraph (9) substituted from 6 July 2005 (HC 104). Sub-paragraph (1A) inserted from 29 February 2008 (HC 321). Words inserted in sub-para (1A) from 27 November 2008 (HC 1113). Headings substituted and words in first square brackets inserted from 12 August 2010 (HC 382). Sub-paragraph (12) inserted from 31 October 2011 except for applications made but not decided before that date (HC 1511). Words in square brackets in (1A) and (2) inserted from 6 April 2012 except for applications made but not decided before that date (HC 1888).

Grounds on which leave to enter or remain may be curtailed

[**323.** A person's leave to enter or remain may be curtailed:

    (i) on any of the grounds set out in paragraph 322(2)–(5) above; or

    (ii) if he ceases to meet the requirements of the Rules under which his leave to enter or remain was granted; or

    (iii) if he is the dependant, or is seeking leave to remain as the dependant, of an asylum applicant whose claim has been refused and whose leave has been curtailed under section 7 of the 1993 Act, and he does not qualify for leave to remain in his own right;]

    [(iv) on any of the grounds set out in paragraph 339A(i)–(vi) and paragraph (i)–(vi).]

Note: Paragraph 323 substituted from 1 September 1996 (Cm 3365). Sub-paragraph (iv) inserted from 9 October 2006 (Cm 6918).

Curtailment of leave or alteration of duration of leave in relation to a Tier 2 Migrant, a Tier 5 Migrant [or a Tier 4 Migrant]

[323A. In addition to the grounds specified in paragraph 323, the leave to enter or remain of a Tier 2 Migrant, a Tier 4 Migrant or a Tier 5 Migrant:

  (a) is to be curtailed, or its duration varied, if:

    (i) in the case of a Tier 2 Migrant or a Tier 5 Migrant:

      (1) the migrant fails to commence working for the Sponsor, or

      (2) the migrant ceases to be employed by the Sponsor.

    (ii) in the case of a Tier 4 Migrant:

      (1) the migrant fails to commence studying with the Sponsor, or

      (2) the migrant has been excluded or withdrawn from the course of studies.

  (b) may be curtailed, or its duration varied, if:

    (i) the migrant's Sponsor ceases to have a sponsor licence (for whatever reason); or

    (ii) the migrant's Sponsor transfers the business for which the migrant works, or at which the migrant is studying, to another person; and

      (1) that person does not have a sponsor licence; and

      (2) fails to apply for a sponsor licence within 28 days of the date of the transfer of the business; or

      (3) applies for a sponsor licence but is refused; or

      (4) makes a successful application for a sponsor licence, but the Sponsor licence granted is not in a category that would allow the Sponsor to issue a Certificate of Sponsorship to the migrant;

    [(iii) in the case of a Tier 2 Migrant or a Tier 5 Migrant, if the employment that the Certificate of Sponsorship Checking Service records that the migrant is being sponsored to do undergoes a prohibited change as specified in paragraph 323AA;

    ((iv) paragraph (a) above applies but:

      (1) the migrant is under the age of 18;

      (2) the migrant has a dependant child under the age of 18;

      (3) leave is to be varied such that when the variation takes effect the migrant will have leave to enter or remain and the migrant has less than 60 days extant leave remaining;

      (4) the migrant has been granted leave to enter or remain with another Sponsor or under another immigration category; or

      (5) the migrant has a pending application for leave to remain, or variation of leave, with the UK Border Agency, or has a pending appeal under Section 82 of the Nationality, Immigration and Asylum Act 2002.]

Note: Paragraph 323A inserted from 27 November 2008 (HC 1113), substituted from 6 April 2012 except for applications made but not decided before that date (HC 1888). Words inserted in heading from 31 March 2009 (HC 314). Sub-paragraph (iii) substituted from 20 July 2012 (Cm 8423).

[323AA. Prohibited changes to employment for Tier 2 Migrants and Tier 5 Migrants

The following are prohibited changes, unless a further application for leave to remain is granted which expressly permits:

  (a) The migrant continues to be employed by, but ceases working for and being remunerated by, the Sponsor for a period of one calendar month or more, unless the period is due solely to:

    (i) maternity leave,

    (ii) paternity leave,

    (iii) adoption leave, or

    (iv) sick leave.

(b) The employment changes such that the migrant is working for a different employer or Sponsor, unless:

    (i) the migrant is a Tier 5 (Temporary Worker) Migrant in the Government Authorised Exchange sub-category and the change of employer is authorised by the Sponsor and under the terms of the work, volunteering or job shadowing that the Certificate of Sponsorship Checking Service records that the migrant is being sponsored to do, or

    (ii) the migrant is working for a different Sponsor under arrangements covered by the Transfer of Undertakings (Protection of Employment) Regulations 2006 or similar protection to continue in the same job.

(c) The employment changes to a job in a different Standard Occupational Classification code to that recorded by the Certificate of Sponsorship Checking Service.

(d) If the migrant is a Tier 2 (Intra-Company Transfer) Migrant or a Tier 2 (General) Migrant, the employment changes to a different job in the same Standard Occupational Classification code to that recorded by the Certificate of Sponsorship Checking Service, and the gross annual salary (including such allowances as are specified as acceptable for this purpose in Appendix A) is:

    (i) below the appropriate salary rate for that job as specified in the Codes of Practice in Appendix J, or

    (ii) higher than the appropriate salary rate for that job as specified in the Codes of Practice in Appendix J, but lower than the rate recorded by the Certificate of Sponsorship Checking Service for the previous job.

(e) If the Standard Occupational Classification code recorded by the Certificate of Sponsorship Checking Service appears in Table 4 of the Codes of Practice in Appendix J, the employment changes from a job which is skilled to National Qualifications Framework level 3 or above to a job which is at a lower skill level.

(f) If the migrant is a Tier 2 (Intra-Company Transfer) Migrant or a Tier 2 (General) migrant and leave was first granted under the Rules in place on 6 April 2011 and the Standard Occupational Classification code recorded by the Certificate of Sponsorship Checking Service appears in Table 3 of the Codes of Practice in Appendix J, the employment changes from a job which is skilled to a lower skill level.

(g) If the migrant is a Tier 2 (Intra-Company Transfer) Migrant or a Tier 2 (General) migrant and leave was first granted under the Rules in place on 6 April 2012 and the Standard Occupational Classification code recorded by the Certificate of Sponsorship Checking Service appears in Table 2 of the Codes of Practice in Appendix J, the employment changes from a job which is skilled to a lower skill level.

(h) If the migrant is a Tier 2 (General) Migrant and scored points from the shortage occupation provisions of Appendix A, the employment changes to a job which does not appear in the Shortage Occupation List in Appendix K.

(i) The gross annual salary (including such allowances as are specified as acceptable for this purpose in Appendix A) reduces below that recorded by the Certificate of Sponsorship Checking Service unless the reduction coincides with a period of:

    (i) maternity leave,

    (ii) paternity leave,

    (iii) adoption leave,

    (iv) long term sick leave of one calendar month or more, or

    (v) reduced working hours for a temporary period, where:

(1) the reduced working hours are part of a company-wide policy to avoid redundancies,

(2) under this policy, the Sponsor is not treating the migrant more, or less, favourably than settled workers,

(3) the migrant's pay and working hours do not reduce by more than 30%,

(4) the reduction in pay is proportionate to the reduction in working hours,

(5) the arrangements will not be in place for more than one year, and

(6) the migrant's pay will return to at least the level recorded by the Certificate of Sponsorship Checking Service immediately after that period ends.]

Note: Paragraph 323AA inserted from 20 July 2012 (Cm 8423).

[Curtailment of leave in relation to a Tier 1 (Exceptional Talent) Migrant

323B. In addition to the grounds specified in paragraph 323, the leave to enter or remain of a Tier 1 (Exceptional Talent) Migrant may be curtailed if the Designated Competent Body that endorsed the application which led to the migrant's current grant of leave withdraws its endorsement of the migrant.]

Note: Paragraph 323B inserted from 9 August 2011 (HC 1436).

[Curtailment of leave in relation to a Tier 1 (Graduate Entrepreneur) Migrant

323C. In addition to the grounds specified in paragraph 323, the leave to enter or remain of a Tier 1 (Graduate Entrepreneur) Migrant may be curtailed if the Higher Education Institution that endorsed the application which led to the migrant's current grant of leave:

(a) loses its status as an endorsing institution for Tier 1 (Graduate Entrepreneur) Migrants,

(b) loses its status as a Highly Trusted Sponsor under Tier 4 of the Points-Based System (for whatever reason),

(c) ceases to be an A-rated Sponsor under Tier 2 or Tier 5 of the Points-Based System because its Tier 2 or Tier 5 Sponsor licence is downgraded or revoked by the UK Border Agency, or

(d) withdraws its endorsement of the migrant.]

Note: Paragraph 323C inserted from 6 April 2012 except for applications made but not decided before that date (HC 1888).

Crew members

324. A person who has been given leave to enter to join a ship, aircraft, hovercraft, hydrofoil or international train service as a member of its crew, or a crew member who has been given leave to enter for hospital treatment, repatriation or transfer to another ship, aircraft, hovercraft, hydrofoil or international train service in the United Kingdom, is to be refused leave to remain unless an extension of stay is necessary to fulfil the purpose for which he was given leave to enter or unless he meets the requirements for an extension of stay as a spouse [or proposed civil partner] in paragraph 284.

Note: Words in square brackets inserted from 5 December 2005 (HC 582).

PART 10

REGISTRATION WITH THE POLICE

Note: Paragraph 324A deleted from 4 February 2005 (HC 194).

[**325.** For the purposes of paragraph 326, a 'relevant foreign national' is a person aged 16 or over who is:

    (i) a national or citizen of a country or territory listed in Appendix 2 to these Rules;

    (ii) a stateless person; or

    (iii) a person holding a non-national travel document.]

Note: Paragraph 325 substituted from 4 February 2005 (HC 194).

[**326.**—(1) Subject to sub-paragraph (2) below, a condition requiring registration with the police should normally be imposed on any relevant foreign national who is:

    (i) given limited leave to enter the United Kingdom for longer than six months; or

    (ii) given limited leave to remain which has the effect of allowing him to remain in the United Kingdom for longer than six months, reckoned from the date of his arrival (whether or not such a condition was imposed when he arrived).

(2) Such a condition should not normally be imposed where the leave is given:

    (i) as a seasonal agricultural worker;

    (ii) as [Tier 5 (Temporary Worker) Migrant, provided the Certificate of Sponsorship Checking System reference for which points were awarded records that the applicant is being sponsored as an overseas government employee or a private servant in a diplomatic household;]

    (iii) as a [Tier 2 (Minister of Religion) Migrant;]

    (iv) on the basis of marriage to [or civil partnership with] a person settled in the UK or as the unmarried [or same-sex] partner of a person settled in the UK;

    (v) as a person exercising access rights to a child resident in the United Kingdom;

    (vi) as the parent of a child at school; or

    (vii) following the grant of asylum.

(3) Such a condition should also be imposed on any foreign national given limited leave to enter the United Kingdom where, exceptionally, the Immigration Officer considers it necessary to ensure that he complies with the terms of the leave.]

Notes: Paragraph 326 substituted from 4 February 2005 (HC 194). Words in square brackets in sub-para (iv) inserted from 5 December 2005 (HC 582). Sub-paragraph (2)(iv) substituted from 30 November 2007 (HC 40). Words substituted in sub-paras (2)(ii) and (iii) from 27 November 2008 (HC 1113).

PART 11

ASYLUM

Procedure

[**326A.** The procedures set out in these Rules shall apply to the consideration of asylum and humanitarian protection.]

Note: Paragraph 326A inserted from 1 December 2007 (HC 82).

[**326B.** Where the Secretary of State is considering a claim for asylum or humanitarian protection under this Part, she will consider any Article 8 elements of that claim in line with the provisions of Appendix FM (family life) and paragraphs 276ADE to 276DH (private life) of these Rules.]

Note: Paragraph 326B inserted from 9 July 2012 with savings for applications made but not decided before that date (HC 194).

Definition of asylum applicant

[**327.** Under the Rules an asylum applicant is a person who either

(a) makes a request to be recognised as a refugee under the Geneva Convention on the basis that it would be contrary to the United Kingdom's obligations under the Geneva Convention for him to be removed from or required to leave the United Kingdom, {or

(b) otherwise makes a request for international protection. 'Application for asylum' shall be construed accordingly.}]

Note: Paragraph 327 substituted from 9 October 2006 (Cm 6918). Words in curly brackets inserted from 1 December 2007 (HC 82).

[**327A.** Every person has the right to make an application for asylum on his own behalf.]

Note: Paragraph 327A inserted from 1 December 2007 (HC 82).

Applications for asylum

328. All asylum applications will be determined by the Secretary of State in accordance with the United Kingdom's obligations under the [Geneva Convention]. Every asylum application made by a person at a port or airport in the United Kingdom will be referred by the Immigration Officer for determination by the Secretary of State in accordance with these Rules.

Note: Words in square brackets substituted from 9 October 2006 (Cm 6918).

[**328A.** The Secretary of State shall ensure that authorities which are likely to be addressed by someone who wishes to make an application for asylum are able to advise that person how and where such an application may be made.]

Note: Paragraph 328A inserted from 1 December 2007 (HC 82).

[**329.** Until an asylum application has been determined by the Secretary of State or the Secretary of State has issued a certificate under Part 2, 3, 4 or 5 of Schedule 3 to the Asylum and Immigration (Treatment of Claimants, etc.) Act 2004 no action will be taken to require the departure of the asylum applicant or his dependants from the United Kingdom.]

Note: Paragraph 329 substituted from 25 October 2004 (Cm 1112).

330. If the Secretary of State decides to grant asylum and the person has not yet been given leave to enter, the Immigration Officer will grant limited leave to enter.

[**331.** [If a person seeking leave to enter is refused asylum {or their application for asylum is withdrawn or treated as withdrawn under paragraph 333C of these Rules}, the Immigration Officer will consider whether or not he is in a position to decide to give or refuse leave to enter without interviewing the person further. If the Immigration Officer decides that a further interview is not required he may serve the notice giving or refusing leave to enter by post. If the Immigration Officer decides that a further interview is required, he will then resume his examination to determine whether or not to grant the person] leave to enter under any other provision of these Rules. If the person fails at any time to comply with a requirement to report to an Immigration Officer for examination, the Immigration officer may direct that the person's examination shall be treated as concluded at that time. The Immigration Officer will then consider any outstanding applications for entry on the basis of any evidence before him.]

Note: Paragraph 331 substituted from 1 September 1996 (Cm 3365). Words in square brackets substituted from 28 July 2000 (HC 704). Words in curly brackets inserted from 7 April 2008 (HC 420).

332. If a person who has been refused leave to enter applies for asylum and that application is refused {or withdrawn or treated as withdrawn under paragraph 333C of these Rules}, leave to enter will again be refused unless the applicant qualifies for admission under any other provision of these Rules.

Note: Words in curly brackets inserted from 7 April 2008 (HC 420).

[**333.** Written notice of decisions on applications for asylum shall be given in reasonable time. Where the applicant is legally represented, notice may instead be given to the representative. Where the applicant has no legal representative and free legal assistance is not available, he shall be informed of the decision on the application for asylum and, if the application is rejected, how to challenge the decision, in a language that he may reasonably be supposed to understand.]

Note: Paragraph 333 deleted from 2 October 2000 (Cm 4851). New paragraph 333 inserted from 1 December 2007 (HC 82).

[**333A.** The Secretary of State shall ensure that a decision is taken by him on each application for asylum as soon as possible, without prejudice to an adequate and complete examination. Where a decision on an application for asylum cannot be taken within six months of the date it was recorded, the Secretary of State shall either:

(a) inform the applicant of the delay; or

(b) if the applicant has made a specific written request for it, provide information on the timeframe within which the decision on his application is to be expected. The provision of such information shall not oblige the Secretary of State to take a decision within the stipulated time-frame.]

Note: Paragraph 333A inserted from 1 December 2007 (HC 82).

[**333B.** Applicants for asylum shall be allowed an effective opportunity to consult, at their own expense or at public expense in accordance with provision made for this by the Legal Services Commission or otherwise, a person who is authorised under Part V of the Immigration and Asylum Act 1999 to give immigration advice. This paragraph shall also apply where the Secretary of State is considering revoking a person's refugee status in accordance with these Rules.]

Note: Paragraph 333B inserted from 1 December 2007 (HC 82).

[**333C.** If an application for asylum is withdrawn either explicitly or implicitly, consideration of it may be discontinued. An application will be treated as explicitly withdrawn if the applicant signs the relevant form provided by the Secretary of State. An application may be treated as impliedly withdrawn if an applicant fails to attend the personal interview as provided in paragraph 339NA of these Rules unless the applicant demonstrates within a reasonable time that that failure was due to circumstances beyond his or her control. The Secretary of State will indicate on the applicant's asylum file that the application for asylum has been withdrawn and consideration of it has been discontinued.]

Note: Paragraph 333C substituted from 7 April 2008 (HC 420).

Grant of asylum

[334. An asylum applicant will be granted asylum in the United Kingdom if the Secretary of State is satisfied that:

(i) he is in the United Kingdom or has arrived at a port of entry in the United Kingdom;

(ii) he is a refugee, as defined in regulation 2 of The Refugee or Person in Need of International Protection (Qualification) Regulations 2006;

(iii) there are no reasonable grounds for regarding him as a danger to the security of the United Kingdom;

(iv) he does not, having been convicted by a final judgment of a particularly serious crime, constitute danger to the community of the United Kingdom; and

(v) refusing his application would result in him being required to go (whether immediately or after the time limited by any existing leave to enter or remain) in breach of the Geneva Convention, to a country in which his life or freedom would be threatened on account of his race, religion, nationality, political opinion or membership of a particular social group.]

Note: Paragraph 334 substituted from 9 October 2006 (Cm 6918).

335. If the Secretary of State decides to grant asylum to a person who has been given leave to enter (whether or not the leave has expired) or a person who has entered without leave, the Secretary of State will vary the existing leave or grant limited leave to remain.

Refusal of asylum

336. An application which does not meet the criteria set out in paragraph 334 will be refused. [Where an application for asylum is refused, the reasons in fact and law shall be stated in the decision and information provided in writing on how to challenge the decision.]

Note: Words in square brackets inserted from 1 December 2007 (HC 82).

337. . . .

Note: Paragraph 337 deleted from 1 September 1996 (Cm 3365).

338. When a person in the United Kingdom is {notified that his asylum application has been refused} he may, if he is liable to removal as an illegal entrant [, removal under section 10 of the Immigration and Asylum Act 1999] or to deportation, at the same time be notified of removal directions, served with a notice of intention to make a deportation order, or served with a deportation order, as appropriate.

Note: Words in square brackets inserted from 2 October 2000 (Cm 4851). Words in curly brackets substituted from 9 October 2006 (Cm 6918).

[339. ....

Note: Paragraph 339 deleted from 2 October 2000 (Cm 4851).

Revocation or refusal to renew a grant of asylum

[339A. A person's grant of asylum under paragraph 334 will be revoked or not renewed if the Secretary of State is satisfied that:

(i) he has voluntarily re-availed himself of the protection of the country of nationality;

(ii) having lost his nationality, he has voluntarily re-acquired it; or

(iii) he has acquired a new nationality, and enjoys the protection of the country of his new nationality;

(iv) he has voluntarily re-established himself in the country which he left or outside which he remained owing to a fear of persecution;

(v) he can no longer, because the circumstances in connection with which he has been recognised as a refugee have ceased to exist, continue to refuse to avail himself of the protection of the country of nationality;

(vi) being a stateless person with no nationality, he is able, because the circumstances in connection with which he has been recognised as a refugee have ceased to exist, to return to the country of former habitual residence;

(vii) he should have been or is excluded from being a refugee in accordance with regulation 7 of The Refugee or Person in Need of International Protection (Qualification) Regulations 2006;

(viii) his misrepresentation or omission or facts, including the use of false documents, were decisive for the grant of asylum;

(ix) there are reasonable grounds for regarding him as a danger to the security of the United Kingdom; or

(x) having been convicted by a final judgment of a particularly serious crime he constitutes danger to the community of the United Kingdom.

In considering (v) and (vi), the Secretary of State shall have regard to whether the change of circumstances is of such a significant and non-temporary nature that the refugee's fear of persecution can no longer be regarded as well-founded.

Where an application for asylum was made on or after 21 October 2004, the Secretary of State will revoke or refuse to renew a person's grant of asylum where he is satisfied that at least one of the provisions in sub-paragraph (i)–(vi) apply.]

Note: Paragraph 339A inserted from 9 October 2006 (Cm 6918).

[339B. When a person's grant of asylum is revoked or not renewed any limited leave which they have may be curtailed.]

Note: Paragraph 339B inserted from 9 October 2006 (Cm 6918).

[339BA. Where the Secretary of State is considering revoking refugee status in accordance with these Rules, the person concerned shall be informed in writing that the Secretary of State is reconsidering his qualification for refugee status and the reasons for the reconsideration. That person shall be given the opportunity to submit, in a personal interview or in a written statement, reasons as to why his refugee status should not be revoked. If there is a personal interview, it shall be subject to the safeguards set out in these Rules.] [However, where a person acquires British citizenship status, his refugee status is automatically revoked in accordance with paragraph 339A(iii) upon acquisition of that status without the need to follow the procedure set out above.]

Note: Paragraph 333BA inserted from 1 December 2007 (HC 82). Final sentence inserted from 22 October 2010 with savings for applications for leave made before that date (Cm 7944).

Grant of humanitarian protection

[**339C.** A person will be granted humanitarian protection in the United Kingdom if the Secretary of State is satisfied that:

(i) he is in the United Kingdom or has arrived at a port of entry in the United Kingdom;

(ii) he does not qualify as a refugee as defined in regulation 2 of The Refugee or Person in Need of International Protection (Qualification) Regulations 2006;

(iii) substantial grounds have been shown for believing that the person concerned, if he returned to the country of return, would face a real risk of suffering serious harm and is unable, or, owing to such risk, unwilling to avail himself of the protection of that country; and

(iv) he is not excluded from a grant of humanitarian protection.

Serious harm consists of:

(i) the death penalty or execution;

(ii) unlawful killing;

(iii) torture or inhuman or degrading treatment or punishment of a person in the country of return; or

(iv) serious and individual threat to a civilian's life or person by reason of indiscriminate violence in situations of international or internal armed conflict.]

Note: Paragraph 339C inserted from 9 October 2006 (Cm 6918).

Exclusion from humanitarian protection

[**339D.** A person is excluded from a grant of humanitarian protection under paragraph 339C (iv) where the Secretary of State is satisfied that:

(i) there are serious reasons for considering that he has committed a crime against peace, a war crime, a crime against humanity, or any other serious crime or instigated or otherwise participated in such crimes;

(ii) there are serious reasons for considering that he is guilty of acts contrary to the purposes and principles of the United Nations or has committed, prepared or instigated such acts or encouraged or induced others to commit, prepare or instigate such acts;

(iii) there are serious reasons for considering that he constitutes a danger to the community or to the security of the United Kingdom; and

(iv) prior to his admission to the United Kingdom the person committed a crime outside the scope of (i) and (ii) that would be punishable by imprisonment were it committed in the United Kingdom and the person left his country of origin solely in order to avoid sanctions resulting from the crime.]

Note: Paragraph 339D inserted from 9 October 2006 (Cm 6918).

[**339E.** If the Secretary of State decides to grant humanitarian protection and the person has not yet been given leave to enter, the Secretary of State or an Immigration Officer will grant limited leave to enter. If the Secretary of State decides to grant humanitarian protection to a person who has been given limited leave to enter (whether or not that leave has expired) or a person who has entered without leave, the Secretary of State will vary the existing leave or grant limited leave to remain.]

Note: Paragraph 339E inserted from 9 October 2006 (Cm 6918).

Refusal of humanitarian protection

[**339F.** Where the criteria set out in paragraph 339C is not met humanitarian protection will be refused.]

Note: Paragraph 339F inserted from 9 October 2006 (Cm 6918).

Revocation of humanitarian protection

[**339G.** A person's humanitarian protection granted under paragraph 339C will be revoked or not renewed if the Secretary of State is satisfied that at least one of the following applies:

(i) the circumstances which led to the grant of humanitarian protection have ceased to exist or have changed to such a degree that such protection is no longer required;

(ii) the person granted humanitarian protection should have been or is excluded from humanitarian protection because there are serious reasons for considering that he has committed a crime against peace, a war crime, a crime against humanity, or any other serious crime or instigated or otherwise participated in such crimes;

(iii) the person granted humanitarian protection should have been or is excluded from humanitarian protection because there are serious reasons for considering that he is guilty of acts contrary to the purposes and principles of the United Nations or has committed, prepared or instigated such acts or encouraged or induced others to commit, prepare or instigate such acts;

(iv) the person granted humanitarian protection should have been or is excluded from humanitarian protection because there are serious reasons for considering that he constitutes a danger to the community or to the security of the United Kingdom;

(v) the person granted humanitarian protection misrepresented or omitted facts, including the use of false documents, which were decisive to the grant of humanitarian protection; or

(vi) the person granted humanitarian protection should have been or is excluded from humanitarian protection because prior to his admission to the United Kingdom the person committed a crime outside the scope of (ii) and (iii) that would be punishable by imprisonment had it been committed in the United Kingdom and the person left his country of origin solely in order to avoid sanctions resulting from the crime.

In applying (i) the Secretary of State shall have regard to whether the change of circumstances is of such a significant and non-temporary nature that the person no longer faces a real risk of serious harm.]

Note: Paragraph 339G inserted from 9 October 2006 (Cm 6918).

[**339H.** When a person's humanitarian protection is revoked or not renewed any limited leave which they have may be curtailed.]

Note: Paragraph 339H inserted from 9 October 2006 (Cm 6918).

Consideration of applications

[**339HA.** The Secretary of State shall ensure that the personnel examining applications for asylum and taking decisions on his behalf have the knowledge with respect to relevant standards applicable in the field of asylum and refugee law.]

Note: Paragraph 333HA inserted from 1 December 2007 (HC 82).

[**339I.** When the Secretary of State considers a person's asylum claim, eligibility for a grant of humanitarian protection or human rights claim it is the duty of the person to submit to the Secretary of State as soon as possible all material factors needed to substantiate the asylum claim or establish that he is a person eligible for humanitarian protection or substantiate the human rights claim, which the Secretary of State shall assess in cooperation with the person.

The material factors include:

(i) the person's statement on the reasons for making an asylum claim or on eligibility for a grant of humanitarian protection or for making a human rights claim;

(ii) all documentation at the person's disposal regarding the person's age, background (including background details of relevant relatives), identity, nationality(ies), country(ies) and place(s) of previous residence, previous asylum applications, travel routes; and

(iii) identity and travel documents.]

Note: Paragraph 339I inserted from 9 October 2006 (Cm 6918).

[**339IA.** For the purposes of examining individual applications for asylum

(i) information provided in support of an application and the fact that an application has been made shall not be disclosed to the alleged actor(s) of persecution of the applicant, and

(ii) information shall not be obtained from the alleged actor(s) of persecution that would result in their being directly informed that an application for asylum has been made by the applicant in question and would jeopardise the physical integrity of the applicant and his dependants, or the liberty and security of his family members still living in the country of origin.

This paragraph shall also apply where the Secretary of State is considering revoking a person's refugee status in accordance with these Rules.]

Note: Paragraph 333IA inserted from 1 December 2007 (HC 82).

[**339J.** The assessment by the Secretary of State of an asylum claim, eligibility for a grant of humanitarian protection or a human rights claim will be carried out on an individual {, objective and impartial} basis. This will include taking into account in particular:

(i) all relevant facts as they relate to the country of origin or country of return at the time of taking a decision on the grant; including laws and regulations of the country of origin or country of return and the manner in which they are applied;

(ii) relevant statements and documentation presented by the person including information on whether the person has been or may be subject to persecution or serious harm;

(iii) the individual position and personal circumstances of the person, including factors such as background, gender and age, so as to assess whether, on the basis of the person's personal circumstances, the acts to which the person has been or could be exposed would amount to persecution or serious harm;

(iv) whether the person's activities since leaving the country of origin or country of return were engaged in for the sole or main purpose of creating the necessary conditions for making an asylum claim or establishing that he is a person eligible for humanitarian protection or a human rights claim, so as to assess whether these activities will expose the person to persecution or serious harm if he returned to that country; and

(v) whether the person could reasonably be expected to avail himself of the protection of another country where he could assert citizenship.]

Note: Paragraph 339J inserted from 9 October 2006 (Cm 6918). Words in curly brackets inserted from 1 December 2007 (HC 82).

[**339JA.** Reliable and up-to-date information shall be obtained from various sources as to the general situation prevailing in the countries of origin of applicants for asylum and, where necessary, in countries through which they have transited. Such information shall be made available to the personnel responsible for examining applications and taking decisions and may be provided to them in the form of a consolidated country information report. This paragraph shall also apply where the Secretary of State is considering revoking a person's refugee status in accordance with these Rules.]

Note: Paragraph 339JA inserted from 1 December 2007 (HC 82).

[**339K.** The fact that a person has already been subject to persecution or serious harm, or to direct threats of such persecution or such harm, will be regarded as a serious indication of the person's well-founded fear of persecution or real risk of suffering serious harm, unless there are good reasons to consider that such persecution or serious harm will not be repeated.]

Note: Paragraph 339K inserted from 9 October 2006 (Cm 6918).

[**339L.** It is the duty of the person to substantiate the asylum claim or establish that he is a person eligible for humanitarian protection or substantiate his human rights claim. Where aspects of the person's statements are not supported by documentary or other evidence, those aspects will not need confirmation when all of the following conditions are met:

(i) the person has made a genuine effort to substantiate his asylum claim or establish that he is a person eligible for humanitarian protection or substantiate his human rights claim;

(ii) all material factors at the person's disposal have been submitted, and a satisfactory explanation regarding any lack of other relevant material has been given;

(iii) the person's statements are found to be coherent and plausible and do not run counter to available specific and general information relevant to the person's case;

(iv) the person has made an asylum claim or sought to establish that he is a person eligible for humanitarian protection or made a human rights claim at the earliest possible time, unless the person can demonstrate good reason for not having done so; and

(v) the general credibility of the person has been established.]

Note: Paragraph 339L inserted from 9 October 2006 (Cm 6918).

[**339M.** The Secretary of State may consider that a person has not substantiated his asylum claim or established that he is a person eligible for humanitarian protection or substantiated his human rights claim, {and thereby reject his application for asylum, determine that he is not eligible for humanitarian protection or reject his human rights claim,} if he fails, without reasonable explanation, to make a prompt and full disclosure of material facts, either orally or in writing, or otherwise to assist the Secretary of State in establishing the facts of the case; this includes, for example,... failure to report to a designated place to be fingerprinted, failure to complete an asylum questionnaire or failure to comply with a requirement to report to an immigration officer for examination.]

Note: Paragraph 339M inserted from 9 October 2006 (Cm 6918). Words in curly brackets inserted from 1 December 2007 (HC 82). Words omitted from 7 April 2008 (HC 420).

[**339MA.** Applications for asylum shall be neither rejected nor excluded from examination on the sole ground that they have not been made as soon as possible.]

Note: Paragraph 333MA inserted from 1 December 2007 (HC 82).

[**339N.** In determining whether the general credibility of the person has been established the Secretary of State will apply the provisions in s 8 of the Asylum and Immigration (Treatment of Claimants, etc.) Act 2004.]

Note: Paragraph 339N inserted from 9 October 2006 (Cm 6918).

Personal interview

[**339NA.** Before a decision is taken on the application for asylum, the applicant shall be given the opportunity of a personal interview on his application for asylum with a representative of the Secretary of State who is legally competent to conduct such an interview.

The personal interview may be omitted where:

(i) the Secretary of State is able to take a positive decision on the basis of evidence available;

(ii) the Secretary of State has already had a meeting with the applicant for the purpose of assisting him with completing his application and submitting the essential information regarding the application;

(iii) the applicant, in submitting his application and presenting the facts, has only raised issues that are not relevant or of minimal relevance to the examination of whether he is a refugee, as defined in regulation 2 of the Refugee or Person in Need of International Protection (Qualification) Regulations 2006;

(iv) the applicant has made inconsistent, contradictory, improbable or insufficient representations which make his claim clearly unconvincing in relation to his having been the object of persecution;

(v) the applicant has submitted a subsequent application which does not raise any relevant new elements with respect to his particular circumstances or to the situation in his country of origin;

(vi) the applicant is making an application merely in order to delay or frustrate the enforcement of an earlier or imminent decision which would result in his removal; and

(vii) it is not reasonably practicable, in particular where the Secretary of State is of the opinion that the applicant is unfit or unable to be interviewed owing to enduring circumstances beyond his control.

The omission of a personal interview shall not prevent the Secretary of State from taking a decision on the application.

Where the personal interview is omitted, the applicant and dependants shall be given a reasonable opportunity to submit further information.]

Note: Paragraph 339NA inserted from 1 December 2007 (HC 82).

[**339NB.** (i) The personal interview mentioned in paragraph 339NA above shall normally take place without the presence of the applicant's family members unless the Secretary of State considers it necessary for an appropriate examination to have other family members present.

(ii) The personal interview shall take place under conditions which ensure appropriate confidentiality.]

Note: Paragraph 339NB inserted from 1 December 2007 (HC 82).

[**339NC.** (i) A written report shall be made of every personal interview containing at least the essential information regarding the asylum application as presented by the applicant in accordance with paragraph 339I of these Rules.

(ii) The Secretary of State shall ensure that the applicant has timely access to the report of the personal interview and that access is possible as soon as necessary for allowing an appeal to be prepared and lodged in due time.

(iii) ...

(iv) ...

Note: Paragraph 339NC inserted from 1 December 2007 (HC 82). Sub-paragraphs (iii) and (iv) deleted from 6 April 2010 (HC 439); however, if an applicant has made an application for entry clearance or leave to enter or remain before 6 April and the application has not been decided before that date, it will be decided in accordance with the Rules in force on 5 April 2010: see introduction to HC 439.

[**339ND.** The Secretary of State shall provide at public expense an interpreter for the purpose of allowing the applicant to submit his case, wherever necessary. The Secretary of State shall select an interpreter who can ensure appropriate communication between the applicant and the representative of the Secretary of State who conducts the interview.]

Note: Paragraph 339ND inserted from 1 December 2007 (HC 82).

Internal relocation

[**339O.**—(i) The Secretary of State will not make:

(a) a grant of asylum if in part of the country of origin a person would not have a well-founded fear of being persecuted, and the person can reasonably be expected to stay in that part of the country; or

(b) a grant of humanitarian protection if in part of the country of return a person would not face a real risk of suffering serious harm, and the person can reasonably be expected to stay in that part of the country.

(ii) In examining whether a part of the country of origin or country of return meets the requirements in (i) the Secretary of State, when making his decision on whether to grant asylum or humanitarian protection, will have regard to the general circumstances prevailing in that part of the country and to the personal circumstances of the person.

(iii) (i) applies notwithstanding technical obstacles to return to the country of origin or country of return.]

Note: Paragraph 339O inserted from 9 October 2006 (Cm 6918).

Sur place claims

[339P. A person may have a well-founded fear of being persecuted or a real risk of suffering serious harm based on events which have taken place since the person left the country of origin or country of return and/or activities which have been engaged in by a person since he left the country of origin or country of return, in particular where it is established that the activities relied upon constitute the expression and continuation of convictions or orientations held in the country of origin or country of return.]

Note: Paragraph 339P inserted from 9 October 2006 (Cm 6918).

Residence Permits

[339Q.—(i) The Secretary of State will issue to a person granted asylum in the United Kingdom a United Kingdom Residence Permit (UKRP) as soon as possible after the grant of asylum. The UKRP will be valid for five years and renewable, unless compelling reasons of national security or public order otherwise require or where there are reasonable grounds for considering that the applicant is a danger to the security of the UK or having been convicted by a final judgment of a particularly serious crime, the applicant constitutes a danger to the community of the UK.]

(ii) The Secretary of State will issue to a person granted humanitarian protection in the United Kingdom a UKRP as soon as possible after the grant of humanitarian protection. The UKRP will be valid for five years and renewable, unless compelling reasons of national security or public order otherwise require or where there are reasonable grounds for considering that the person granted humanitarian protection is a danger to the security of the UK or having been convicted by a final judgment of a serious crime, this person constitutes a danger to the community of the UK.

(iii) The Secretary of State will issue a UKRP to a family member of a person granted asylum or humanitarian protection where the family member does not qualify for such status. A UKRP will be granted for a period of five years. The UKRP is renewable on the terms set out in (i) and (ii) respectively. ['Family member' for the purposes of this sub-paragraph refers only to those who are treated as dependants for the purposes of paragraph 349.]]

(iv) The Secretary of State may revoke or refuse to renew a person's UKRP where their grant of asylum or humanitarian protection is revoked under the provisions in the immigration rules.]

Note: Paragraph 339Q inserted from 9 October 2006 (Cm 6918). Words inserted in paragraph 339Q (iii) from 8 November 2007 (HC 28).

340.–341.

Note: Paragraphs 340–341 deleted from 9 October 2006 (Cm 6918).

342. The actions of anyone acting as an agent of the asylum applicant or human rights claimant may also be taken into account in regard to the matters set out in paragraphs 340 and 341.

343.–344.

Note: Paragraphs 343-344 deleted from 9 October 2006 (Cm 6918).

Travel documents

[344A.—(i) After having received a complete application for a travel document, the Secretary of State will issue to a person granted asylum in the United Kingdom and their family members travel documents, in the form set out in the Schedule to the Geneva Convention, for the purpose of travel outside the United Kingdom, unless compelling reasons of national security or public order otherwise require.

(ii) After having received a complete application for a travel document, the Secretary of State will issue travel documents to a person granted humanitarian protection in the United Kingdom where that person is unable to obtain a national passport or other identity documents which enable him to travel, unless compelling reasons of national security or public order otherwise require.

(iii) Where the person referred to in (ii) can obtain a national passport or identity documents but has not done so, the Secretary of State will issue that person with a travel document where he can show that he has made reasonable attempts to obtain a national passport or identity document and there are serious humanitarian reasons for travel.]

Note: Paragraph 344A inserted from 9 October 2006 (Cm 6918).

Access to Employment

[344B. The Secretary of State will not impose conditions restricting the employment or occupation in the United Kingdom of a person granted asylum or humanitarian protection.]

Note: Paragraph 344B inserted from 9 October 2006 (Cm 6918).

Information

[344C. A person who is granted asylum or humanitarian protection will be provided with access to information in a language that they may reasonably be supposed to understand which sets out the rights and obligations relating to that status. The Secretary of State will provide the information as soon as possible after the grant of asylum or humanitarian protection.]

Note: Paragraph 344C inserted from 9 October 2006 (Cm 6918).

Third country cases

[345.—(1) In a case where the Secretary of State is satisfied that the conditions set out in Paragraphs 4 and 5(1), 9 and 10(1), 14 and 15(1) or 17 of Schedule 3 to the Asylum and Immigration (Treatment of Claimants, etc.) Act 2004 are fulfilled, he will normally decline to examine the asylum application substantively and issue a certificate under Part 2, 3, 4 or 5 of Schedule 3 to the Asylum and Immigration (Treatment of Claimants, etc.) Act 2004 as appropriate.

(2) The Secretary of State shall not issue a certificate under Part 2, 3, 4 or 5 of Schedule 3 to the Asylum and Immigration (Treatment of Claimants, etc.) Act 2004 unless:

(i) the asylum applicant has not arrived in the United Kingdom directly from the country in which he claims to fear persecution and has had an opportunity at the border or within the third country or territory to make contact with the authorities of that third country or territory in order to seek their protection; or

(ii) there is other clear evidence of his admissibility to a third country or territory.

Provided that he is satisfied that a case meets these criteria, the Secretary of State is under no obligation to consult the authorities of the third country or territory before the removal of an asylum applicant to that country or territory.

[(2A) Where a certificate is issued under Part 2, 3, 4 or 5 of Schedule 3 to the Asylum and Immigration (Treatment of Claimants, etc.) Act 2004 the asylum applicant shall:

(i) be informed in a language that he may reasonably be expected to understand regarding his removal to a safe third country;

(ii) be provided with a document informing the authorities of the safe third country, in the language of that country, that the asylum application has not been examined in substance by the authorities in the United Kingdom;

(iii) sub-paragraph 345(2A)(ii) shall not apply if removal takes place with reference to the arrangements set out in Regulation (EC) No. 343/2003 (the Dublin Regulation); and

(iv) if an asylum applicant removed under this paragraph is not admitted to the safe third country (not being a country to which the Dublin Regulation applies as specified in paragraph 345(2A)(iii)), subject to determining and resolving the reasons for his non-admission, the asylum applicant shall be admitted to the asylum procedure in the UK.]

(3) Where a certificate is issued under Part 2, 3, 4 or 5 of Schedule 3 to the Asylum and Immigration (Treatment of Claimants, etc.) Act 2004 in relation to the asylum claim and the person is seeking leave to enter, the Immigration Officer will consider whether or not he is in a position to decide to give or refuse leave to enter without interviewing the person further. If the Immigration Officer decides that a further interview is not required he may serve the notice giving or refusing leave to enter by post. If the Immigration Officer decides that a further interview is required, he will then resume his examination to determine whether or not to grant the person leave to enter under any other provision of these Rules. If the person fails at any time to comply with a requirement to report to an Immigration Officer for examination, the Immigration Officer may direct that the person's examination shall be treated as concluded at that time. The Immigration Officer will then consider any outstanding applications for entry on the basis of any evidence before him.

(4) Where a certificate is issued under Part 2, 3, 4 or 5 of Schedule 3 to the Asylum and Immigration (Treatment of Claimants, etc.) Act 2004 the person may, if liable to removal as an illegal entrant, or removal under section 10 of the Immigration and Asylum Act 1999 or to deportation, at the same time be notified of removal directions, served with a notice of intention to make a deportation order, or served with a deportation order, as appropriate.]

Note: Paragraph 345 substituted from 25 October 2004 (Cm 1112). Sub-paragraph (2A) inserted from 1 December 2007 (HC 82).

346. ....

Note: Paragraph 346 deleted from 25 October 2004 (Cm 1112).

347. . . .

Note: Paragraph 347 deleted from 1 September 1996 (Cm 3365).

Rights of appeal

348. . . .

Note: Deleted from 2 October 2000 (Cm 4851).

Dependants

[349. A spouse, civil partner, unmarried or same-sex partner, or minor child accompanying a principal applicant may be included in his application for asylum as his dependant, {provided, in the case of an adult dependant with legal capacity, the dependant consents to being treated as such at the time the application is lodged.} A spouse, civil partner, unmarried or same-sex partner, or minor child may also claim asylum in his own right. If the principal applicant is granted asylum [{or humanitarian protection}] and leave to enter or remain any spouse, civil partner, unmarried or same-sex partner, or minor child will be granted leave to enter or remain for the same duration. The case of any dependant who claims asylum in his own right will be {also} considered individually in accordance with paragraph 334 above. An applicant under this paragraph, including an accompanied child, may be interviewed where he makes a claim as a dependant or in his own right.

If the spouse, civil partner, unmarried or same-sex partner, or minor child in question has a claim in his own right, that claim should be made at the earliest opportunity. Any failure to do so will be taken into account and may damage credibility if no reasonable explanation for it is given. Where an asylum [or humanitarian protection] application is unsuccessful, at the same time that asylum [or humanitarian protection] is refused the applicant may be notified of removal directions or served with a notice of the Secretary of State's intention to deport him, as appropriate. In this paragraph and paragraphs 350–352 a child means a person who is under 18 years of age or who, in the absence of documentary evidence establishing age, appears to be under that age. An unmarried or same-sex partner for the purposes of this paragraph, is a person who has been living together with the principal applicant in a subsisting relationship akin to marriage or a civil partnership for two years or more.]

Note: Paragraph 349 substituted from 9 October 2006 (Cm 6918). Words 'or humanitarian protection' inserted from 8 November (HC 28). Words in curly brackets inserted from 1 December 2007 (HC 82).

Unaccompanied children

350. Unaccompanied children may also apply for asylum and, in view of their potential vulnerability, particular priority and care is to be given to the handling of their cases.

351. A person of any age may qualify for refugee status under the Convention and the criteria in paragraph 334 apply to all cases. However, account should be taken of the applicant's maturity and in assessing the claim of a child more weight should be given to objective indications of risk than to the child's state of mind and understanding of his situation. An asylum application made on behalf of a child should not be refused

solely because the child is too young to understand his situation or to have formed a well-founded fear of persecution. Close attention should be given to the welfare of the child at all times.

[352. Any child over the age of 12 who has claimed asylum in his own right shall be interviewed about the substance of his claim unless the child is unfit or unable to be interviewed. When an interview takes place it shall be conducted in the presence of a parent, guardian, representative or another adult independent of the Secretary of State who has responsibility for the child. The interviewer shall have specialist training in the interviewing of children and have particular regard to the possibility that a child will feel inhibited or alarmed. The child shall be allowed to express himself in his own way and at his own speed. If he appears tired or distressed, [the interview will be suspended. The interviewer should then consider whether it would be appropriate for the interview to be resumed the same day or on another day.]

Note: Paragraph 352 substituted from 1 December 2007 (HC 82). Words substituted from 6 April 2010 (HC 439); however, if an applicant has made an application for entry clearance or leave to enter or remain before 6 April and the application has not been decided before that date, it will be decided in accordance with the Rules in force on 5 April 2010.

[352ZA. The Secretary of State shall as soon as possible after an unaccompanied child makes an application for asylum take measures to ensure that a representative represents and/or assists the unaccompanied child with respect to the examination of the application and ensure that the representative is given the opportunity to inform the unaccompanied child about the meaning and possible consequences of the interview and, where appropriate, how to prepare himself for the interview. The representative shall have the right to be present at the interview and ask questions and make comments in the interview, within the framework set by the interviewer.]

Note: Paragraph 352ZA inserted from 1 December 2007 (HC 82).

[352ZB. The decision on the application for asylum shall be taken by a person who is trained to deal with asylum claims from children.]

Note: Paragraph 352ZB inserted from 1 December 2007 (HC 82).

[352A. The requirements to be met by a person seeking leave to enter or remain in the United Kingdom as the spouse {or civil partner} of a refugee are that:
  (i) the applicant is married to {or the civil partner of} a person [who is currently a refugee granted status as such under the immigration rules] in the United Kingdom; and
  (ii) the marriage {or civil partnership} did not take place after the person granted asylum left the country of his former habitual residence in order to seek asylum; and
  (iii) the applicant would not be excluded from protection by virtue of article 1F of the United Nations Convention and Protocol relating to the Status of Refugees if he were to seek asylum in his own right; and
  [(iv) each of the parties intends to live permanently with the other as his or her spouse {or civil partner} and the marriage {or civil partnership} is subsisting; and]
  (v) if seeking leave to enter, the applicant holds a valid United Kingdom entry clearance for entry in this capacity.]

Note: Paragraph 352(iv) inserted from 18 September 2002 (Cm 5597). Words in curly brackets inserted from 5 December 2005 (HC 582). Words in square brackets in sub-para (i) substituted from 22 October 2010 with savings for applications for leave made before that date (Cm 7944).

[**352AA.** The requirements to be met by a person seeking leave to enter or remain in the United Kingdom as the unmarried or the same-sex partner of a refugee are that:

[(i)] the applicant is the unmarried or same-sex partner of a person [who is currently a refugee granted status as such under the immigration rules in the United Kingdom and was granted that status] on or after 9 October 2006; and

[(ii)] the parties have been living together in a relationship akin to either a marriage or a civil partnership which has subsisted for two years or more; and

[(iii)] the relationship existed before the person granted asylum left the country of his former habitual residence in order to seek asylum; and

[(iv)] the applicant would not be excluded from protection by virtue of paragraph 334(iii) or (iv) of these Rules or article 1F of the Geneva Convention if he were to seek asylum in his own right; and

[(v)] each of the parties intends to live permanently with the other as his or her unmarried or same-sex partner and the relationship is subsisting; and

[(vi) the parties are not involved in a consanguineous relationship with one another; and]

[(vii)] if seeking leave to enter, the applicant holds a valid United Kingdom entry clearance for entry in this capacity.]

Note: Paragraph 352AA inserted from 9 October 2006 (Cm 6918). Words in square brackets in sub-para (i) substituted from 22 October 2010 with savings for applications for leave made before that date (Cm 7944). Sub-paragraphs renumbered and new sub-para (vi) inserted from 6 April 2011 except for applications made but not decided before that date (HC 863).

[**352B.** Limited leave to enter the United Kingdom as the spouse {or civil partner} of a refugee may be granted provided a valid United Kingdom entry clearance for entry in this capacity is produced to the Immigration Officer on arrival. Limited leave to remain in the United Kingdom as the spouse {or civil partner} of a refugee may be granted provided the Secretary of State is satisfied that each of the requirements of paragraph [352A (i)–(v)] is met.]

Note: Numbers in square brackets substituted from 6 April 2011 except for applications made but not decided before that date (HC 863).

[**352BA.** Limited leave to enter the United Kingdom as the unmarried or same-sex partner of a refugee may be granted provided a valid United Kingdom entry clearance for entry in this capacity is produced to the Immigration Officer on arrival. Limited leave to remain in the United Kingdom as the unmarried or same-sex partner of a refugee may be granted provided the Secretary of State is satisfied that each of the requirements of paragraph [352AA (i)–(vii)] is met.]

Note: Paragraph 352BA inserted from 9 October 2006 (Cm 6918). Numbers in square brackets substituted from 6 April 2011 except for applications made but not decided before that date (HC 863).

[**352C.** Limited leave to enter the United Kingdom as the spouse [or civil partner] of a refugee is to be refused if a valid United Kingdom entry clearance for entry in this capacity is not produced to the Immigration Officer on arrival. Limited leave to remain as the spouse [or civil partner] of a refugee is to be refused if the Secretary of State is not satisfied that each of the requirements of paragraph [352A (i)–(v)] is met.]

Note: Numbers in square brackets substituted from 6 April 2011 except for applications made but not decided before that date (HC 863).

[**352CA.** Limited leave to enter the United Kingdom as the unmarried or same-sex partner of a refugee is to be refused if a valid United Kingdom entry clearance for entry in this capacity is not produced to the Immigration Officer on arrival. Limited leave to remain as the unmarried or same-sex partner of a refugee is to be refused if the Secretary of State is not satisfied that each of the requirements of paragraph [352AA (i)–(vi)] is met.]

Note: Paragraph 352CA inserted from 9 October 2006 (Cm 6918). Numbers in square brackets inserted from 6 April 2011 except for applications made but not decided before that date (HC 863).

[**352D.** The requirements to be met by a person seeking leave to enter or remain in the United Kingdom [in order to join or remain with the parent [who is currently a refugee granted status as such under the immigration rules] in the United Kingdom] are that the applicant:

(i) is the child of a parent [who is currently a refugee granted status as such under the immigration rules] in the United Kingdom; and

(ii) is under the age of 18, and

(iii) is not leading an independent life, is unmarried {and is not a civil partner}, and has not formed an independent family unit; and

(iv) was part of the family unit of the person granted asylum at the time that the person granted asylum left the country of his habitual residence in order to seek asylum; and

(v) would not be excluded from protection by virtue of article 1F of the United Nations Convention and Protocol relating to the Status of Refugees if he were to seek asylum in his own right; and

(vi) if seeking leave to enter, holds a valid United Kingdom entry clearance for entry in this capacity.]

Note: Words in square brackets substituted from 18 September 2002 (Cm 5597). Words in second square brackets and in sub-para (i) substituted from 22 October 2010 except for applications made but not decided before that date (Cm 7944).

[**352E.** Limited leave to enter the United Kingdom as the child of a refugee may be granted provided a valid United Kingdom entry clearance for entry in this capacity is produced to the Immigration Officer on arrival. Limited leave to remain in the United Kingdom as the child of a refugee may be granted provided the Secretary of State is satisfied that each of the requirements of paragraph 352D (i)–(v) is met.]

[**352F.** Limited leave to enter the United Kingdom as the child of a refugee is to be refused if a valid United Kingdom entry clearance for entry in this capacity is not produced to the Immigration Officer on arrival. Limited leave to remain as the child of a refugee is to be refused if the Secretary of State is not satisfied that each of the requirements of paragraph 352D (i)–(v) is met.]

Note: Paragraph 352F inserted from 2 October 2000 (Cm 4851).

[**352FA.** The requirements to be met by a person seeking leave to enter or remain in the United Kingdom as the spouse or civil partner of a person [who is currently a beneficiary of humanitarian protection granted under the immigration rules in the United Kingdom and was granted that status] on or after 30 August 2005 are that:

(i) the applicant is married to or the civil partner of a person [who is currently a beneficiary of humanitarian protection granted under the immigration rules and was granted that status] on or after 30 August 2005; and

(ii) the marriage or civil partnership did not take place after the person granted humanitarian protection left the country of his former habitual residence in order to seek asylum in the UK; and

(iii) the applicant would not be excluded from a grant of humanitarian protection for any of the reasons in paragraph 339D; and

(iv) each of the parties intends to live permanently with the other as his or her spouse or civil partner and the marriage or civil partnership is subsisting; and

(v) if seeking leave to enter, the applicant holds a valid United Kingdom entry clearance for entry in this capacity.]

Note: Paragraph 352FA inserted from 8 November 2007 (HC 28). Words in square brackets substituted from 22 October 2010 with savings for applications for leave made before that date (Cm 7944).

[**352FB.** Limited leave to enter the United Kingdom as the spouse or civil partner of a person granted humanitarian protection may be granted provided a valid United Kingdom entry clearance for entry in this capacity is produced to the Immigration Officer on arrival. Limited leave to remain in the United Kingdom as the spouse or civil partner of a person granted humanitarian protection may be granted provided the Secretary of State is satisfied that each of the requirements in subparagraphs 352FA(i)–(iv) is met.]

Note: Paragraph 352FB inserted from 8 November 2007 (HC 28).

[**352FC.** Limited leave to enter the United Kingdom as the spouse or civil partner of a person granted humanitarian protection is to be refused if a valid United Kingdom entry clearance for entry in this capacity is not produced to the Immigration Officer on arrival. Limited leave to remain as the spouse or civil partner of a person granted humanitarian protection is to be refused if the Secretary of State is not satisfied that each of the requirements in subparagraphs 352FA (i)–(iv) is met.]

Note: Paragraph 352FC inserted from 8 November 2007 (HC 28).

[**352FD.** The requirements to be met by a person seeking leave to enter or remain in the United Kingdom as the unmarried or same-sex partner of a person [who is currently a beneficiary of humanitarian protection granted under the immigration rules] in the United Kingdom are that:

[(i)] the applicant is the unmarried or same-sex partner of a person [who is currently a beneficiary of humanitarian protection granted under the immigration rules and was granted that status] on or after 9 October 2006; and

[(ii)] the parties have been living together in a relationship akin to either a marriage or a civil partnership which has subsisted for two years or more; and

[(iii)] the relationship existed before the person granted humanitarian protection left the country of his former habitual residence in order to seek asylum; and

[(iv)] the applicant would not be excluded from a grant of humanitarian protection for any of the reasons in paragraph 339D; and

[(v)] each of the parties intends to live permanently with the other as his or her unmarried or same-sex partner and the relationship is subsisting; and

[(vi)] the parties are not involved in a consanguineous relationship with one another; and]

[(vii)] if seeking leave to enter, the applicant holds a valid United Kingdom entry clearance for entry in this capacity.]

Note: Paragraph 352FD inserted from 8 November 2007 (HC 28). Words in square brackets substituted from 22 October 2010 with savings for applications for leave made before that date (Cm 7944). Sub-paragraphs renumbered and new sub-para (vi) inserted from 6 April 2011 (HC 395).

[**352FE.** Limited leave to enter the United Kingdom as the unmarried or same-sex partner of a person granted humanitarian protection may be granted provided a valid United Kingdom entry clearance for entry in this capacity is produced to the Immigration Officer on arrival. Limited leave to remain in the United Kingdom as the unmarried or same sex partner of a person granted humanitarian protection may be granted provided the Secretary of State is satisfied that each of the requirements in subparagraphs [352FD (i)-(vi)] is met.]

Note: Paragraph 352FE inserted from 8 November 2007 (HC 28). Numbers in square brackets substituted from 6 April 2011 except for applications made but not decided before that date (HC 863).

[**352FF.** Limited leave to enter the United Kingdom as the unmarried or same-sex partner of a person granted humanitarian protection is to be refused if a valid United Kingdom entry clearance for entry in this capacity is not produced to the Immigration Officer on arrival. Limited leave to remain as the unmarried or same-sex partner of a person granted humanitarian protection is to be refused if the Secretary of State is not satisfied that each of the requirements in subparagraphs [352FD(i)–(vi)] is met.]

Note: Paragraph 352FF inserted from 8 November 2007 (HC 28). Numbers in square brackets substituted from 6 April 2011 except for applications made but not decided before that date (HC 863).

[**352FG.** The requirements to be met by a person seeking leave to enter or remain in the United Kingdom in order to join or remain with their parent [who is currently a beneficiary of humanitarian protection granted under the immigration rules in the United Kingdom and was granted that status] on or after 30 August 2005 are that the applicant:

(i) is the child of a parent [who is currently a beneficiary of humanitarian protection granted under the immigration rules in the United Kingdom and was granted that status] on or after 30 August 2005; and

(ii) is under the age of 18, and

(iii) is not leading an independent life, is unmarried or is not in a civil partnership, and has not formed an independent family unit; and

(iv) was part of the family unit of the person granted humanitarian protection at the time that the person granted humanitarian protection left the country of his habitual residence in order to seek asylum in the UK; and

(v) would not be excluded from a grant of humanitarian protection for any of the reasons in paragraph 339D; and

(vi) if seeking leave to enter, holds a valid United Kingdom entry clearance for entry in this capacity.]

Note: Paragraph 352FG inserted from 8 November 2007 (HC 28). Words in square brackets substituted from 22 October 2010 with savings for applications for leave made before that date (Cm 7944).

[**352FH.** Limited leave to enter the United Kingdom as the child of a person granted humanitarian protection may be granted provided a valid United Kingdom entry clearance for entry in this capacity is produced to the Immigration Officer on arrival. Limited leave to remain in the United Kingdom as the child of a person granted humanitarian protection may be granted provided the Secretary of State is satisfied that each of the requirements in subparagraphs 352FG(i)-(v) is met.]

Note: Paragraph 352FH inserted from 8 November 2007 (HC 28).

[**352FI.** Limited leave to enter the United Kingdom as the child of a person granted humanitarian protection is to be refused if a valid United Kingdom entry clearance for entry in this capacity is not produced to the Immigration Officer on arrival. Limited leave to remain as the child of a person granted humanitarian protection is to be refused if the Secretary of State is not satisfied that each of the requirements in sub paragraphs 352FG(i)-(v) is met.]

Note: Paragraph 352FI inserted from 8 November 2007 (HC 28).

[**352FJ.** Nothing in paragraphs 352A–352FI shall allow a person to be granted leave to enter or remain in the United Kingdom as the spouse or civil partner, unmarried or same-sex partner or child of a refugee, or of a person granted humanitarian protection under the immigration rules in the United Kingdom on or after 30 August 2005, if the refugee or, as the case may be, person granted humanitarian protection, is a British Citizen.]

Note: Paragraph 352FJ inserted from 22 October 2010 with savings for applications for leave made before that date (Cm 7944).

Interpretation

[**352G.** For the purposes of this Part:

(a) 'Geneva Convention' means the United Nations Convention and Protocol relating to the Status of Refugees;

(b) 'Country of return' means a country or territory listed in paragraph 8(c) of Schedule 2 of the Immigration Act 1971;

(c) 'Country of origin' means the country or countries of nationality or, for a stateless person, or [sic] former habitual residence.]

Note: Paragraph 352G inserted from 9 October 2006 (Cm 6918).

PART 11A
TEMPORARY PROTECTION

Definition of Temporary Protection Directive

[**354.** For the purposes of paragraphs 355 to 356B, 'Temporary Protection Directive' means Council Directive 2001/55/EC of 20 July 2001 regarding the giving of temporary protection by Member States in the event of a mass influx of displaced persons.]

Note: Paragraph 354 inserted from 1 January 2004 (HC 164).

Grant of temporary protection

[**355.** An applicant for temporary protection will be granted temporary protection if the Secretary of State is satisfied that:

(i) the applicant is in the United Kingdom or has arrived at a port of entry in the United Kingdom; and

(ii) the applicant is a person entitled to temporary protection as defined by, and in accordance with, the Temporary Protection Directive; and

(iii) the applicant does not hold an extant grant of temporary protection entitling him to reside in another Member State of the European Union. This requirement is subject to the provisions relating to dependants set out in paragraphs 356 to 356B and to any agreement to the contrary with the Member State in question; and

(iv) the applicant is not excluded from temporary protection under the provisions in paragraph 355A.]

Note: Paragraph 355 inserted from 1 January 2004 (HC 164).

[355A. An applicant or a dependant may be excluded from temporary protection if:

(i) there are serious reasons for considering that:

(a) he has committed a crime against peace, a war crime, or a crime against humanity, as defined in the international instruments drawn up to make provision in respect of such crimes; or

(b) he has committed a serious non-political crime outside the United Kingdom prior to his application for temporary protection; or

(c) he has committed acts contrary to the purposes and principles of the United Nations, or

(ii) there are reasonable grounds for regarding the applicant as a danger to the security of the United Kingdom or, having been convicted by a final judgment of a particularly serious crime, to be a danger to the community of the United Kingdom.

Consideration under this paragraph shall be based solely on the personal conduct of the applicant concerned. Exclusion decisions or measures shall be based on the principle of proportionality.]

Note: Paragraph 355A inserted from 1 January 2004 (HC 164).

[355B. If temporary protection is granted to a person who has been given leave to enter or remain (whether or not the leave has expired) or to a person who has entered without leave, the Secretary of State will vary the existing leave or grant limited leave to remain.]

Note: Paragraph 355B inserted from 1 January 2004 (HC 164).

[355C. A person to whom temporary protection is granted will be granted limited leave to enter or remain, which is not to be subject to a condition prohibiting employment, for a period not exceeding 12 months. On the expiry of this period, he will be entitled to apply for an extension of this limited leave for successive periods of 6 months thereafter.]

Note: Paragraph 355C inserted from 1 January 2004 (HC 164).

[355D. A person to whom temporary protection is granted will be permitted to return to the United Kingdom from another Member State of the European Union during the period of a mass influx of displaced persons as established by the Council of the European Union pursuant to Article 5 of the Temporary Protection Directive.]

Note: Paragraph 355D inserted from 1 January 2004 (HC 164).

[355E. A person to whom temporary protection is granted will be provided with a document in a language likely to be understood by him in which the provisions relating to temporary protection and which are relevant to him are set out. A person with temporary protection will also be provided with a document setting out his temporary protection status.]

Note: Paragraph 355E inserted from 1 January 2004 (HC 164).

[355F. The Secretary of State will establish and maintain a register of those granted temporary protection. The register will record the name, nationality, date and place of birth and marital status of those granted temporary protection and their family relationship to any other person who has been granted temporary protection.]

Note: Paragraph 355F inserted from 1 January 2004 (HC 164).

[355G. If a person who makes an asylum application is also eligible for temporary protection, the Secretary of State may decide not to consider the asylum application until the applicant ceases to be entitled to temporary protection.]

Note: Paragraph 355G inserted from 1 January 2004 (HC 164).

Dependants

[356. In this part:
'dependant' means a family member or a close relative.
'family member' means:
(i) the spouse {or civil partner} of an applicant for, or a person who has been granted, temporary protection; or
(ii) the unmarried {or same-sex} partner of an applicant for, or a person who has been granted, temporary protection where the parties have been living together in a relationship akin to marriage {or civil partnership} which has subsisted for 2 years or more; or
(iii) the {minor child (who is unmarried and not a civil partner)} of an applicant for, or a person who has been granted, temporary protection or his spouse,
who lived with the principal applicant as part of the family unit in the country of origin immediately prior to the mass influx.

'close relative' means:
(i) the {adult child (who is unmarried and not a civil partner)} [parent or grandparent] of an applicant for, or person who has been granted, temporary protection; or
(ii) the {sibling (who is unmarried and not a civil partner)} or the uncle or aunt of an applicant for, or person who has been granted, temporary protection, who lived with the principal applicant as part of the family unit in the country of origin immediately prior to the mass influx and was wholly or mainly dependent upon the principal applicant at that time, and would face extreme hardship if reunification with the principal applicant did not take place.]

Note: Paragraph 356 inserted from 1 January 2004 (HC 164). Words in curly brackets inserted from 5 December 2005 (HC 582).

[356A. A dependant may apply for temporary protection. Where the dependant falls within paragraph 356 and does not fall to be excluded under paragraph 355A, he will be granted temporary protection for the same duration and under the same conditions as the principal applicant.]

Note: Paragraph 356A inserted from 1 January 2004 (HC 164).

[**356B.** When considering any application by a dependent child, the Secretary of State shall take into consideration the best interests of that child.]

Note: Paragraph 356B inserted from 1 January 2004 (HC 164).

PART 11B
ASYLUM
Reception conditions for non-EU asylum applicants

[**357.** Part 11B only applies to asylum applicants (within the meaning of these Rules) who are not nationals of a member State.]

Note: Paragraph 357 inserted from 4 February 2005 (HC 194).

Information to be provided to asylum applicants

[**357A.** The Secretary of State shall inform asylum applicants in a language they may reasonably be supposed to understand and within a reasonable time after their claim for asylum has been recorded of the procedure to be followed, their rights and obligations during the procedure, and the possible consequences of non-compliance and non-cooperation. They shall be informed of the likely timeframe for consideration of the application and the means at their disposal for submitting all relevant information.]

Note: Paragraph 357A inserted from 1 December 2007 (HC 82).

[**358.** The Secretary of State shall inform asylum applicants within a reasonable time not exceeding fifteen days after their claim for asylum has been recorded of the benefits and services that they may be eligible to receive and of the rules and procedures with which they must comply relating to them. The Secretary of State shall also provide information on non-governmental organisations and persons that provide legal assistance to asylum applicants and which may be able to help asylum applicants or provide information on available benefits and services.]

Note: Paragraph 358 inserted from 4 February 2005 (HC 194).

[**358A.** The Secretary of State shall ensure that the information referred to in paragraph 358 is available in writing and, to the extent possible, will provide the information in a language that asylum applicants may reasonably be supposed to understand. Where appropriate, the Secretary of State may also arrange for this information to be supplied orally.]

Note: Paragraph 358A inserted from 4 February 2005 (HC 194).

Information to be provided by asylum applicants
[**358B.** An asylum applicant must notify the Secretary of State of his current address and of any change to his address or residential status. If not notified beforehand, any change must be notified to the Secretary of State without delay after it occurs.]

Note: Paragraph 358B inserted from 4 February 2005 (HC 194).

The United Nations High Commissioner for Refugees

[358C. A representative of the United Nations High Commissioner for Refugees (UNHCR) or an organisation working in the United Kingdom on behalf of the UNHCR pursuant to an agreement with the government shall:

(a) have access to applicants for asylum, including those in detention;

(b) have access to information on individual applications for asylum, on the course of the procedure and on the decisions taken on applications for asylum, provided that the applicant for asylum agrees thereto;

(c) be entitled to present his views, in the exercise of his supervisory responsibilities under Article 35 of the Geneva Convention, to the Secretary of State regarding individual applications for asylum at any stage of the procedure. This paragraph shall also apply where the Secretary of State is considering revoking a person's refugee status in accordance with these Rules.]

Note: Paragraph 358C inserted from 1 December 2007 (HC 82).

Documentation

[359. The Secretary of State shall ensure that, within three working days of recording an asylum application, a document is made available to that asylum applicant, issued in his own name, certifying his status as an asylum applicant or testifying that he is allowed to remain in the United Kingdom while his asylum application is pending. For the avoidance of doubt, in cases where the Secretary of State declines to examine an application it will no longer be pending for the purposes of this rule.]

Note: Paragraph 359 inserted from 4 February 2005 (HC 194).

[359A. The obligation in paragraph 359 above shall not apply where the asylum applicant is detained under the Immigration Acts, the Immigration and Asylum Act 1999 or the Nationality, Immigration and Asylum Act 2002.]

Note: Paragraph 359A inserted from 4 February 2005 (HC 194).

[359B. A document issued to an asylum applicant under paragraph 359 does not constitute evidence of the asylum applicant's identity.]

Note: Paragraph 359B inserted from 4 February 2005 (HC 194).

[359C. In specific cases the Secretary of State or an Immigration Officer may provide an asylum applicant with evidence equivalent to that provided under rule 359. This might be, for example, in circumstances in which it is only possible or desirable to issue a time-limited document.]

Note: Paragraph 359C inserted from 4 February 2005 (HC 194).

Right to request permission to take up employment

[360. An asylum applicant may apply to the Secretary of State for permission to take up employment if a decision at first instance has not been taken on the applicant's asylum application within one year of the date on which it was recorded. The Secretary of State shall only consider such an application if, in the Secretary of State's opinion, any delay in reaching a decision at first instance cannot be attributed to the applicant.

360A. If permission to take up employment is granted under paragraph 360, that permission will be subject to the following restrictions:

(i) employment may only be taken up in a post which is, at the time an offer of employment is accepted, included on the list of shortage occupations published by the United Kingdom Border Agency (as that list is amended from time to time);

(ii) no work in a self-employed capacity; and

(iii) no engagement in setting up a business.

360B. If an asylum applicant is granted permission to take up employment under paragraph 360 this shall only be until such time as his asylum application has been finally determined.

360C. Where an individual makes further submissions which raise asylum grounds and which fall to be considered under paragraph 353 of these Rules, that individual may apply to the Secretary of State for permission to take up employment if a decision pursuant to paragraph 353 of these Rules has not been taken on the further submissions within one year of the date on which they were recorded. The Secretary of State shall only consider such an application if, in the Secretary of State's opinion, any delay in reaching a decision pursuant to paragraph 353 of these Rules cannot be attributed to the individual.

360D. If permission to take up employment is granted under paragraph 360C, that permission will be subject to the following restrictions:

(i) employment may only be taken up in a post which is, at the time an offer of employment is accepted, included on the list of shortage occupations published by the United Kingdom Border Agency (as that list is amended from time to time);

(ii) no work in a self-employed capacity; and

(iii) no engagement in setting up a business.

360E. Where permission to take up employment is granted pursuant to paragraph 360C, this shall only be until such time as:

(i) a decision has been taken pursuant to paragraph 353 that the further submissions do not amount to a fresh claim; or

(ii) where the further submissions are considered to amount to a fresh claim for asylum pursuant to paragraph 353, all rights of appeal from the immigration decision made in consequence of the rejection of the further submissions have been exhausted.]

Note: Paragraph 360 and 360A inserted from 4 February 2005 (HC 194), substituted from 9 September 2010 with savings for asylum applicants who have been granted permission to take employment before that date or who have applied for permission to take up employment before that date and the previous paras 360–360A would have applied (Cm 7929). The savings do not apply to those who have made further submissions on asylum grounds which fall to be considered in para 353, and previous paras 360–360A would not have applied. See introduction to Cm 7929.

Interpretation

[**361.** For the purposes of this Part—

(a) 'working day' means any day other than a Saturday or Sunday, a bank holiday, Christmas day or Good Friday;

(b) 'member State' has the same meaning as in Schedule 1 to the European Communities Act 1972.]

Note: Paragraph 361 inserted from 4 February 2005 (HC 194).

PART 12
PROCEDURE AND RIGHTS OF APPEAL

Fresh claims

[353. When a human rights or asylum claim has been refused {or withdrawn or treated as withdrawn under paragraph 333C of these Rules} and any appeal relating to that claim is no longer pending, the decision maker will consider any further submissions and, if rejected, will then determine whether they amount to a fresh claim. The submissions will amount to a fresh claim if they are significantly different from the material that has previously been considered. The submissions will only be significantly different if the content:

(i) had not already been considered; and

(ii) taken together with the previously considered material, created a realistic prospect of success, notwithstanding its rejection.

This paragraph does not apply to claims made overseas.]

Note: Paragraph 353 inserted from 25 October 2004 (Cm 1112). Words in curly brackets inserted from 7 April 2008 (HC 420).

[353A. Consideration of further submissions shall be subject to the procedures set out in these Rules. An applicant who has made further submissions shall not be removed before the Secretary of State has considered the submissions under paragraph 353 or otherwise. This paragraph does not apply to submissions made overseas.]

Note: Paragraph 353A inserted from 1 December 2007 (HC 82).

[Exceptional Circumstances

353B. Where further submissions have been made and the decision maker has established whether or not they amount to a fresh claim under paragraph 353 of these Rules, or in cases with no outstanding further submissions whose appeal rights have been exhausted and which are subject to a review, the decision maker will also have regard to the migrant's:

(i) character, conduct and associations including any criminal record and the nature of any offence of which the migrant concerned has been convicted;

(ii) compliance with any conditions attached to any previous grant of leave to enter or remain and compliance with any conditions of temporary admission or immigration bail where applicable;

(iii) length of time spent in the United Kingdom spent for reasons beyond the migrant's control after the human rights or asylum claim has been submitted or refused;

in deciding whether there are exceptional circumstances which mean that removal from the United Kingdom is no longer appropriate.]

[This paragraph does not apply where the person is liable to deportation.]

Note: Paragraph 353B inserted from 13 February 2012 (HC 1733). Final sentence inserted from 9 July 2012 with savings for applications made but not decided before that date (HC 194).

PART 13

DEPORTATION (AND ADMINISTRATIVE REMOVAL
UNDER SECTION 10 OF THE 1999 ACT)

A deportation order

[**A362.** Where Article 8 is raised in the context of deportation under Part 13 of these Rules, the claim under Article 8 will only succeed where the requirements of these rules as at 9 July 2012 are met, regardless of when the notice of intention to deport or the deportation order, as appropriate, was served.]

Note: Paragraph A362 inserted from 9 July 2012 with savings for applications made but not decided before that date (HC 194).

362. A deportation order requires the subject to leave the United Kingdom and authorises his detention until he is removed. It also prohibits him from re-entering the country for as long as it is in force and invalidates any leave to enter or remain in the United Kingdom given him before the order was made or while it is in force.

[**363.** The circumstances in which a person is liable to deportation include:

(i) where the Secretary of State deems the person's deportation to be conducive to the public good;

(ii) where the person is the spouse [or civil partner] or child under 18 of a person ordered to be deported; and

(iii) where a court recommends deportation in the case of a person over the age of 17 who has been convicted of an offence punishable with imprisonment.]

Note: Paragraph 363 substituted from 2 October 2000 (Cm 4851). Words in square brackets in sub-para (ii) inserted from 5 December 2005 (HC 582).

[**363A.** Prior to 2 October 2000, a person would have been liable to deportation in certain circumstances in which he is now liable to administrative removal. These circumstances are listed in paragraph 394B below. However, such a person remains liable to deportation, rather than administrative removal where:

(i) a decision to make a deportation order against him was taken before 2 October 2000; or

(ii) the person has made a valid application under the Immigration (Regulation Period for Overstayers) Regulations 2000.]

Note: Paragraph 363A inserted from 2 October 2000 (Cm 4851).

[**364.** ...

Note: Paragraph 364 deleted from 9 July 2012 with savings for applications made before that date (HC 194).

364A. ...

Note: Paragraph 364A deleted from 9 July 2012 with savings for applications made before that date (HC 194).

Deportation of family members

[**365.** Section 5 of the Immigration Act 1971 gives the Secretary of State power in certain circumstances to make a deportation order against the {spouse, civil partner or child} of a person against whom a deportation order has been made. The Secretary of State will not normally decide to deport the spouse {or civil partner} of a deportee where:

    (i) he has qualified for settlement in his own right; or

    (ii) he has been living apart from the deportee.]

Note: Paragraph 365 substituted from 1 October 1996 (Cm 3365). Words in curly brackets inserted from 5 December 2005 (HC 582).

[**366.** The Secretary of State will not normally decide to deport the child of a deportee where:

    (i) he and his mother or father are living apart from the deportee; or

    (ii) he has left home and has established himself on an independent basis; or

    (iii) he married {or formed a civil partnership} before deportation came into prospect.]

Note: Paragraph 366 substituted from 1 October 1996 by (Cm 3365). Words in curly brackets inserted from 5 December 2005 (HC 582).

[**367.** ...

Note: Paragraph 367 deleted from 9 July 2012 with savings for applications made before that date (HC 194).

368. Where the Secretary of State decides that it would be appropriate to deport a member of a family as such, the decision, and the right of appeal, will be notified and it will at the same time be explained that it is open to the member of the family to leave the country voluntarily if he does not wish to appeal or if he appeals and his appeal is dismissed.

Note: Paragraph 369–377 deleted from 2 October 2000 (Cm 4851).

[**378.** A deportation order may not be made while it is still open to the person to appeal against the Secretary of State's decision, or while an appeal is pending [except where the Secretary of State must make the deportation order in respect of a foreign criminal under section 32(5) of the UK Borders Act 2007.] There is no appeal within the immigration appeal system against the making of a deportation order on the recommendation of a court; but there is a right of appeal to a higher court against the recommendation itself. A deportation order may not be made while it is still open to the person to appeal against the relevant conviction, sentence or recommendation, or while such an appeal is pending.

Note: Substituted from 2 October 2000 (Cm 4851). Words in square brackets inserted from 1 August 2008 (HC 951). Paragraphs 379 and 379A deleted from 2 October 2000 (Cm 4851).

380. ...

Note: Paragraph 380 deleted from 9 July 2012 with savings for applications made before that date (HC 194).

Procedure

381. When a decision to make a deportation order has been taken (otherwise than on the recommendation of a court) a notice will be given to the person concerned informing him of the decision and of his right of appeal....

Note: Words omitted from 2 October 2000 (Cm 4851).

382. [Following the issue of such a notice the Secretary of State may authorise detention or make an order restricting a person as to residence, employment or occupation and requiring him to report to the police, pending the making of a deportation order.]

Note: Substituted from 2 October 2000 (Cm 4851).

383. ...

Note: Deleted from 2 October 2000 (Cm 4851).

384. If a notice of appeal is given within the period allowed, a summary of the facts of the case on the basis of which the decision was taken will be sent to the [appropriate] appellate authorities, who will notify the appellant of the arrangements for the appeal to be heard.

Note: Word in square brackets inserted from 2 October 2000 (Cm 4851).

Arrangements for removal

385. A person against whom a deportation order has been made will normally be removed from the United Kingdom. The power is to be exercised so as to secure the person's return to the country of which he is a national, or which has most recently provided him with a travel document, unless he can show that another country will receive him. In considering any departure from the normal arrangements, regard will be had to the public interest generally, and to any additional expense that may fall on public funds.

386. The person will not be removed as the subject of a deportation order while an appeal may be brought against the removal directions or such an appeal is pending.

Supervised departure

387. ...

Note: Deleted from 2 October 2000 (Cm 4851).

Returned deportees

388. Where a person returns to this country when a deportation order is in force against him, he may be deported under the original order. The Secretary of State will consider every such case in the light of all the relevant circumstances before deciding whether to enforce the order.

Returned family members

389. Persons deported in the circumstances set out in paragraph 365–368 above (deportation of family members) may be able to seek re-admission to the United Kingdom under the Immigration Rules where:

(i) a child reaches 18 (when he ceases to be subject to the deportation order); or

(ii) in the case of a spouse or civil partner, the marriage or civil partnership comes to an end.]

Note: Sub-paragraph (iii) substituted from 5 December 2005 (HC 582).

Revocation of deportation order

390. An application for revocation of a deportation order will be considered in the light of all the circumstances including the following:

    (i) the grounds on which the order was made;

    (ii) any representations made in support of revocation;

    (iii) the interests of the community, including the maintenance of an effective immigration control;

    (iv) the interests of the applicant, including any compassionate circumstances.

[**390A.** Where paragraph 398 applies the Secretary of State or Entry Clearance Officer assessing the application will consider whether paragraph 399 or 399A applies and, if it does not, it will only be in exceptional circumstances that the public interest in maintaining the deportation order will be outweighed by other factors.]

Note: Paragraph 390A inserted from 9 July 2012 with savings for applications made before that date (HC 194).

391. In the case of an applicant . . . [who has been deported following a criminal offence] continued exclusion . . .

    [(i) in the case of a conviction which is capable of being spent under the Rehabilitation of Offenders Act 1974, unless the conviction is spent within the meaning of that Act or, if the conviction is spent in less than 10 years, 10 years have elapsed since the making of the deportation order; or

    (ii) in the case of a conviction not capable of being spent under that Act, at any time, unless refusal to revoke the deportation order would be contrary to the Human Rights Convention or the Convention and Protocol Relating to the Status of Refugees.]
will normally be the proper course. In other cases revocation of the order will not normally be authorised unless the situation has been materially altered, either by a change of circumstances since the order was made, or by fresh information coming to light which was not before . . . or the appellate authorities, or the Secretary of State. The passage of time since the person was deported may also in itself amount to such a change of circumstances as to warrant revocation of the order . . .

Note: Words deleted and words in square brackets inserted from 30 June 2008 (HC 607).

392. Revocation of a deportation order does not entitle the person concerned to re-enter the United Kingdom; it renders him eligible to apply for admission under the Immigration Rules. Application for revocation of the order may be made to the Entry Clearance Officer or direct to the Home Office.

Rights of appeal in relation to a decision not to revoke a deportation order

    393. . . .

    394. . . .

Note: Paragraphs 393–394 deleted from 2 October 2000 (Cm 4851).

395. [There may be a right of appeal against refusal to revoke a deportation order.] Where an appeal does lie the right of appeal will be notified at the same time as the decision to refuse to revoke the order.

Note: Words in square brackets in para 395 inserted F inserted from 2 October 2000 (Cm 4851). Paragraphs 395A–F deleted from 13 February 2012 (HC 1733).

[**396.** Where a person is liable to deportation the presumption shall be that the public interest requires deportation. It is in the public interest to deport where the Secretary of State must make a deportation order in accordance with section 32 of the UK Borders Act 2007.]

Note: Paragraph 396 inserted from 9 July 2012 with savings for applications made before that date (HC 194).

[**397.** A deportation order will not be made if the person's removal pursuant to the order would be contrary to the UK's obligations under the Refugee Convention or the Human Rights Convention. Where deportation would not be contrary to these obligations, it will only be in exceptional circumstances that the public interest in deportation is outweighed.]

Note: Paragraph 397 inserted from 9 July 2012 with savings for applications made before that date (HC 194).

[**398.** Where a person claims that their deportation would be contrary to the UK's obligations under Article 8 of the Human Rights Convention, and

(a) the deportation of the person from the UK is conducive to the public good because they have been convicted of an offence for which they have been sentenced to a period of imprisonment of at least 4 years;

(b) the deportation of the person from the UK is conducive to the public good because they have been convicted of an offence for which they have been sentenced to a period of imprisonment of less than 4 years but at least 12 months; or

(c) the deportation of the person from the UK is conducive to the public good because, in the view of the Secretary of State, their offending has caused serious harm or they are a persistent offender who shows a particular disregard for the law, the Secretary of State in assessing that claim will consider whether paragraph 399 or 399A applies and, if it does not, it will only be in exceptional circumstances that the public interest in deportation will be outweighed by other factors.]

Note: Paragraph 398 inserted from 9 July 2012 with savings for applications made before that date (HC 194).

[**399.** This paragraph applies where paragraph 398 (b) or (c) applies if –

(a) the person has a genuine and subsisting parental relationship with a child under the age of 18 years who is in the UK, and

(i) the child is a British Citizen; or

(ii) the child has lived in the UK continuously for at least the 7 years immediately preceding the date of the immigration decision; and in either case

(a) it would not be reasonable to expect the child to leave the UK; and

(b) there is no other family member who is able to care for the child in the UK; or

(b) the person has a genuine and subsisting relationship with a partner who is in the UK and is a British Citizen, settled in the UK, or in the UK with refugee leave or humanitarian protection, and

(i) the person has lived in the UK with valid leave continuously for at least the 15 years immediately preceding the date of the immigration decision (discounting any period of imprisonment); and

(ii) there are insurmountable obstacles to family life with that partner continuing outside the UK.]

Note: Paragraph 399 inserted from 9 July 2012 with savings for applications made before that date (HC 194).

[**399A.** This paragraph applies where paragraph 398(b) or (c) applies if –

(a) the person has lived continuously in the UK for at least 20 years immediately preceding the date of the immigration decision (discounting any period of imprisonment) and he has no ties (including social, cultural or family) with the country to which he would have to go if required to leave the UK; or

(b) the person is aged under 25 years, he has spent at least half of his life living continuously in the UK immediately preceding the date of the immigration decision (discounting any period of imprisonment) and he has no ties (including social, cultural or family) with the country to which he would have to go if required to leave the UK.]

Note: Paragraph 399A inserted from 9 July 2012 with savings for applications made before that date (HC 194).

[**399B.** Where paragraph 399 or 399A applies limited leave may be granted for a period not exceeding 30 months. Such leave shall be given subject to such conditions as the Secretary of State deems appropriate.]

Note: Paragraph 399B inserted from 9 July 2012 with savings for applications made before that date (HC 194).

[**399C.** Where limited leave has been granted under paragraph 399B, the person may qualify for further limited leave, subject to such conditions as the Secretary of State deems appropriate. The requirements for further leave are that the applicant continues to meet the criteria set out in paragraph 399 or 399A.]

Note: Paragraph 399C inserted from 9 July 2012 with savings for applications made before that date (HC 194).

[**400.** Where a person claims that their removal under paragraphs 8 to 10 of Schedule 2 to the Immigration Act 1971, section 10 of the Immigration and Asylum Act 1999 or section 47 of the Immigration, Asylum and Nationality Act 2006 would be contrary to the UK's obligations under Article 8 of the Human Rights Convention, the Secretary of State may require an application under paragraph 276ADE (private life) or Appendix FM (family life) of these rules. Where an application is not required, in assessing that claim the Secretary of State or an immigration officer will, subject to paragraph 353, consider that claim against the requirements to be met under paragraph 276ADE or Appendix FM and if appropriate the removal decision will be cancelled.]

Note: Paragraph 400 inserted from 9 July 2012 with savings for applications made before that date (HC 194).

Appendix 1

Visa Requirements for the United Kingdom

1. Subject to paragraph 2 below the following persons need a visa for the United Kingdom:

 (a) Nationals or citizens of the following countries or territorial entities:

Afghanistan
Albania
Algeria
Angola
Armenia
Azerbaijan
Bahrain
Bangladesh
Belarus
Benin
Bhutan
Bolivia [*from 18 May 2009*]
Bosnia-Herzegovina
Burkina Faso
Burma
Burundi
Cambodia
Cameroon
Cape Verde
Central African Republic
Chad
[People's Republic of China (except for those referred to in subparagraphs 2(d) and (e) of this Appendix)]
[Colombia]
Comoros
Congo
Cuba
[Democratic Republic of Congo]
Djibouti
Dominican Republic
[Ecuador]
Egypt
Equatorial Guinea
Eritrea

Ethiopia
Fiji
Gabon
Gambia
Georgia
Ghana
Guinea
Guinea-Bissau
Guyana
Haiti
India
Indonesia
Iran
Iraq
Ivory Coast
[Jamaica]
Jordan
Kazakhstan
Kenya
Kirgizstan
Korea (North)
Kuwait
Laos
Lebanon
Lesotho [*from 1 July 2009*]
Liberia
Libya
Macedonia
Madagascar
[Malawi]
Mali
Mauritania
Moldova
Mongolia
Morocco
Mozambique
Nepal
Niger
Nigeria

Oman (except those referred to in sub-paragraph 2(j) of this Appendix)
Pakistan
Peru
Philippines
Qatar (except those referred to in sub-paragraph 2(k) of this Appendix)
Russia
Rwanda
Sao Tome e Principe
Saudi Arabia
Senegal
Serbia
Sierra Leone
Somalia
South Africa [*from 3 March 2009 subject to an exception that was deleted on 1 July 2009*]
[South Sudan]
Sri Lanka
Sudan
Surinam
Swaziland [*from 1 July 2009*]
Syria
Taiwan (except those referred to in sub paragraph 2(h) of this Appendix) [*from 18 May 2009*]
Tajikistan
Tanzania
Thailand

Togo	Ukraine	sub-paragraph 2(i) of
Tunisia	United Arab Emirates	this Appendix) [*from 18*
Turkey (except those	[(except those referred	*May 2009*]
referred to in	to in sub-paragraph 2(j)	Vietnam
sub-paragraph 2(q) of	of this Appendix)]	Yemen
this Appendix)	Uzbekistan	Zambia
Turkmenistan	Venezuela (except	[Zimbabwe]
Uganda	those referred to in	

The territories formerly comprising the Socialist Federal Republic of Yugoslavia excluding Croatia and Slovenia.

(b) Persons who hold passports or travel documents issued by the former Soviet Union or by the former Socialist Federal Republic of Yugoslavia.

(c) Stateless persons.

(d) Persons who hold non-national documents.

2. The following persons do not need a visa for the United Kingdom:

(a) those who qualify for admission to the United Kingdom as returning residents in accordance with paragraph 18;

[(b) those who seek leave to enter the United Kingdom within the period of their earlier leave and for the same purpose as that for which leave was granted, unless it—

(i) was for a period of six months or less, or

(ii) was extended by statutory instrument] [or by section 3C of the Immigration Act 1971 (inserted by section 3 of the Immigration and Asylum Act 1999)];

(c) . . .

[(d) those nationals or citizens of the People's Republic of China holding passports issued by Hong Kong Special Administrative Region; or

(e) those nationals or citizens of the People's Republic of China holding passports issued by Macao Special Administrative Region.]

[(f) those who arrive in the United Kingdom with leave to enter which is in force but which was given before arrival so long as those in question arrive within the period of their earlier leave and for the same purpose as that for which leave was granted, unless that leave—

(i) was for a period of six months or less, or

(ii) was extended by statutory instrument or by section 3C of the Immigration Act 1971 (inserted by section 3 of the Immigration and Asylum Act 1999).]

(g) . . .

[(h) those nationals or citizens of Taiwan who hold a passport issued by Taiwan that includes the number of the identification card issued by the competent authority in Taiwan in it.]

[(i) those nationals or citizens of Venezuela who hold a passport issued by the Republic of Venezuela that contains biometric information held in an electronic chip.]

[(j) those nationals or citizens of Oman, who hold diplomatic and special passports issued by Oman when travelling to the UK for the purpose of a general visit in accordance with paragraph 41;

(k) those nationals or citizens of Qatar who hold diplomatic and special passports issued by Qatar when travelling to the UK for the purpose of a general visit in accordance with paragraph 41;

(l) those nationals or citizens of the United Arab Emirates who hold diplomatic and special passports issued by the United Arab Emirates when travelling to the UK for the purpose of a general visit in accordance with paragraph 41;]

[(m) during the period commencing on 30 March 2012 up to and including 12 August 2012 those nationals or citizens of all the countries or territorial entities listed in paragraph 1 of Appendix 1 who hold an Olympic Identity and Accreditation Card issued by the London Organising Committee of the Olympic Games and Paralympic Games Limited unless that card has the accreditation category code OCOG, S or X;

(n) during the period commencing on 13 August 2012 up to and including 8 November 2012 those nationals or citizens of all the countries or territorial entities listed in paragraph 1 of Appendix 1 who hold an Olympic Identity and Accreditation Card issued by the London Organising Committee of the Olympic Games and Paralympic Games Limited unless—

(i) that card has the accreditation category code OCOG, S or X; or

(ii) the holder had not held leave to enter, leave to remain or entry clearance at any time during the period commencing on 30 March 2012 and ending on 12 August 2012;

(o) during the period commencing on 30 March 2012 up to and including 9 September 2012 those nationals or citizens of all the countries or territorial entities listed in paragraph 1 of Appendix 1 who hold an Paralympic Identity and Accreditation Card issued by the London Organising Committee of the Olympic Games and Paralympic Games Limited unless that card has the accreditation category code OCOG, S or X;

(p) during the period commencing on 10 September 2012 up to and including the 8 November 2012 those nationals or citizens of all the countries or territorial entities listed in paragraph 1 of Appendix 1 who hold the Paralympic Identity and Accreditation Card issued by the London Organising Committee of the Olympic Games and Paralympic Games Limited unless—

(i) that card has the accreditation category code OCOG, S or X; or

(ii) the holder had not held leave to enter, leave to remain or entry clearance at any time during the period commencing on 30 March 2012 and ending on 9 September 2012.]

[(q) those nationals or citizens of Turkey, who hold diplomatic passports issued by Turkey when travelling to the UK for the purpose of a general visit in accordance with paragraph 41.]

Note: Appendix substituted from 4 April 1996 (HC 329); para 2(b) substituted from 1 November 1996 (HC 31); words in square brackets at the end of 2(b)(ii) inserted from 18 December 2002 (HC 104); paras 2(d) and (e) inserted from 17 April 2002 (HC 735); para 2(c) deleted from 11 February 2003 (HC 389); para 2(f) inserted from 18 December 2002 (HC104). Transitional provisions apply to certain nationals of Malawi: see HC 949 (March 2006). Sub-paragraph 2(g) deleted and sub-paras 2(h) and 2(i) inserted from 1 July 2009 (HC 413). Entries for Oman, Qatar and United Arab Emirates qualified and paras 2(j)–(l) inserted from 6 April 2011 (HC 863). Sub-paragraphs (m)–(p) inserted from 30 March 2012, and cease to have effect on 9 November 2012 (HC 1511) .South Sudan and words in square brackets in Turkey entry in para 1(a) and sub-para (q) inserted from 9 January 2012 (HC 1719).

Paragraph 324A.

[APPENDIX 2
COUNTRIES OR TERRITORIES WHOSE NATIONALS OR CITIZENS ARE
RELEVANT FOREIGN NATIONALS FOR THE PURPOSES OF
PART 10 OF THESE RULES (REGISTRATION WITH THE POLICE)

Afghanistan	Iran	Peru
Algeria	Iraq	Qatar
Argentina	Israel	Russia
Armenia	Jordan	Saudi Arabia
Azerbaijan	Kazakhstan	Sudan
Bahrain	Kirgizstan	Syria
Belarus	Kuwait	Tajikistan
Bolivia	Lebanon	Tunisia
Brazil	Libya	Turkey
China	Moldova	Turkmenistan
Colombia	Morocco	United Arab Emirates
Cuba	North Korea	Ukraine
Egypt	Oman	Uzbekistan
Georgia	Palestine	Yemen]

Note: Appendix 2 inserted from 11 May 1998 (Cm 3953).

APPENDIX 3

Note: Appendix 3 deleted from 13 November 2005 (HC 645).

[*List of countries participating in the Working Holidaymaker Scheme*

Antigua and Barbuda	India	Papua New Guinea
Australia	Jamaica	Republic of Tonga
Bangladesh	Kenya	Seychelles
Barbados	Kiribati	Sierra Leone
Belize	Malawi	Singapore
Botswana	Malaysia	Solomon Islands
Brunei Darussalam	Maldives	Saint Christopher and
Canada	Mauritius	Nevis
Cameroon	Mozambique	South Africa
Dominica	Namibia	Sri Lanka
Fiji Islands	Nauru	Saint Vincent and
Ghana	New Zealand	the Grenadines
Grenada	Nigeria	Tuvalu
Guyana	Pakistan	Tanzania, United

Trinidad and Tobago	Uganda	Zambia
The Gambia	Vanuatu	Zimbabwe]
The Bahamas	Western Samoa	

Note: List of countries participating in the Working Holidaymaker Scheme inserted from 8 February 2005 (HC 302).

APPENDIX 4

Note: Appendix 4 Deleted from 29 February 2008 (HC 321).

APPENDIX 5

Note: Appendix 5 Deleted from 29 February 2008 (HC 321).

[APPENDIX 6

Disciplines for which an Academic Technology Approval Scheme certificate from the Counter-Proliferation Department of the Foreign and Commonwealth Office is required for the purposes of [Tier 4 of the Points Based System] of these Rules:

1. Doctorate or Masters by research:

Subjects allied to Medicine:

JACs codes beginning:
- B1 – Anatomy, Physiology and Pathology
- B2 – Pharmacology, Toxicology and Pharmacy
- B9 – Others in subjects allied to Medicine

Biological Sciences:

JACs codes beginning:
- C1 – Biology
- C2 – Botany
- C4 – Genetics
- C5 – Microbiology
- C7 – Molecular Biology, Biophysics and Biochemistry
- C9 – Others in Biological Sciences

Veterinary Sciences, Agriculture and related subjects:

JACs codes beginning:
- D3 – Animal Science
- D9 – Others in Veterinary Sciences, Agriculture and related subjects

Physical Sciences:

JACs codes beginning:
  F1 – Chemistry
  F2 – Materials Science
  F3 – Physics
  F5 – Astronomy
  F8 – Physical and Terrestrial Geographical and Environmental Sciences
  F9 – Others in Physical Sciences

Mathematical and Computer Sciences:

JACs codes beginning:
  G1 – Mathematics
  G2 – Operational Research
  G4 – Computer Science
  G7 – Artificial Intelligence
  G9 – Others in Mathematical and Computing Sciences

Engineering:

JACs codes beginning:
  H1 – General Engineering
  H2 – Civil Engineering
  H3 – Mechanical Engineering
  H4 – Aerospace Engineering
  H5 – Naval Architecture
  H6 – Electronic and Electrical Engineering
  H7 – Production and Manufacturing Engineering
  H8 – Chemical, Process and Energy Engineering
  H9 – Others in Engineering

Technologies:

JACs codes beginning:
  J2 – Metallurgy
  J4 – Polymers and Textiles
  J5 – Materials Technology not otherwise specified
  J7 – Industrial Biotechnology
  J9 – Others in Technology

2. Taught Masters:

  F2 – Materials Science

  F3 – Physics (including Nuclear Physics)

  H3 – Mechanical Engineering

  H4 – Aerospace Engineering

  J5 – Materials Technology/Materials Science not otherwise specified]

[For courses commencing on or after 1 January 2012:

1. Doctorate or Masters by Research

JACs codes beginning:

  G0 – Mathematical and Computer Sciences

  I1 – Computer Science

  I4 – Artificial Intelligence

  I9 – Others in Computer Sciences

2. Taught Masters:

  H8 – Chemical, Process and Energy Engineering]

Note: Appendix 6 inserted from 30 November 2007 (HC 40). Words in square brackets in introduction substituted from 31 March 2009 (HC 314). Final words in square brackets substituted from 1 October 2011 except for applications made but not decided before that date (HC 1148).

Appendix 7

Statement of Written Terms and Conditions of employment required in paragraph 159A (v) and paragraph 159D (iv)

Statement of the terms and conditions of employment of an overseas domestic worker in a private household in the United Kingdom

This form must be completed and signed by the employer, signed by the overseas domestic worker and submitted with the entry clearance application or with the leave to remain application as required by paragraphs 159a (v) and 159d (iv) of the Immigration Rules.

  Please complete this form in capitals

  Name of employee:

  Name of employer:

  1. Job Title:

  2. Duties/Responsibilities:

  3. Date of start of employment in the UK:

  4. Employer's address in the UK:

5. Employee's address in the UK (if different from 4 please explain):

6. Employee's place of work in the UK (if different from 4 please explain):

7. Rate of Pay per week/month:

Note: By signing this document, the employer is declaring that the employee will be paid in accordance with the National Minimum Wage Act 1998 and any Regulations made under it for the duration of the employment.

8. Hours of work per day/week:

Free periods per day:
Free periods per week:

9. Details of sleeping accommodation:

10. Details of Holiday entitlement:

11. Ending the employment:

Employee must give_____weeks notice if he/she decides to leave his/her job.

Employee is entitled to_____weeks notice if the employer decides to dismiss him/her.

Employee is employed on a fixed-term contract until (date) [if applicable].

Signed_____Date_____(Employer)

I confirm that the above reflects my conditions of employment:

Signed_____Date_____(Employee)**Note:** Appendix 7 inserted from 6 September 2012 (HC 565).

Appendix A
Attributes

[Attributes for Tier 1 (Exceptional Talent) Migrants

1. An applicant applying for entry clearance, leave to remain or indefinite leave to remain as a Tier 1 (Exceptional Talent) Migrant must score 75 points for attributes.

Note: Paragraphs 1–65 and Tables 1–9 substituted from 6 April 2011 (HC 863).

2. Available points are shown in Table 1.

Note: Paragraphs 1–65 and Tables 1–9 substituted from 6 April 2011 (HC 863).

3. Notes to accompany the table are shown below the table.

Note: Paragraphs 1–65 and Tables 1–9 substituted from 6 April 2011 (HC 863). Words in square brackets inserted from 9 August 2011 (HC 1436), substituted from 20 July 2012 (Cm 8423).

Table 1

All applications for entry clearance and applications for leave to remain where the applicant has, or last had leave that was not leave as a Tier 1 (Exceptional Talent) Migrant

Criterion	Points
Endorsed by Designated Competent Body according to that Body's criteria as set out in Appendix L.	75

All other applications for leave to remain and applications for indefinite leave to remain

Criterion	Points
(i) During his most recent period of leave as a Tier 1 (Exceptional Talent) Migrant, the applicant has earned money in the UK as a result of employment or self-employment in his expert field as previously endorsed by a Designated Competent Body; and	75
(ii) That Designated Competent Body has not withdrawn its endorsement of the applicant.	

Notes

[Tier 1 (Exceptional Talent) Limit

4. (a) The Secretary of State shall be entitled to limit the total number of Tier 1 (Exceptional Talent) endorsements Designated Competent Bodies may make in support of successful applications in a particular period, to be referred to as the Tier 1 (Exceptional Talent) Limit.

(b) The Tier 1 (Exceptional Talent) Limit for [each of the periods 6 April 2012 to 5 April 2013 and 6 April 2013 to 5 April 2014] is 1,000 endorsements in total, which will be allocated to the Designated Competent Bodies as follows:

(i) 300 endorsements to The Arts Council for the purpose of endorsing applicants with exceptional talent in the fields of arts and culture;

(ii) 300 endorsements to The Royal Society for the purpose of endorsing applicants with exceptional talent in the fields of natural sciences and medical science research;

(iii) 200 endorsements to The Royal Academy of Engineering for the purpose of endorsing applicants with exceptional talent in the field of engineering; and

(iv) 200 endorsements to The British Academy for the purpose of endorsing applicants with exceptional talent in the fields of humanities and social sciences.

[(c) The Tier 1 (Exceptional Talent) Limit will be operated according to the practice set out in paragraph 5 below.]

(d) If a Designated Competent Body chooses to transfer part of its unused allocation of endorsements to another Designated Competent Body by mutual agreement of both bodies and the Secretary of State, the allocations of both bodies will be adjusted accordingly and the adjusted allocations will be published on the UK Border Agency website.

Note: Paragraphs 1–65 and Tables 1–9 substituted from 6 April 2011 (HC 863). Words in square brackets in sub-para (b) substituted from 6 April 2012 except for applications made but not decided before that date (HC 1888). Sub-para (c) substituted from 1 October 2012 (HC 565).

[5. (a) An applicant must state which Designated Competent Body he wishes to endorse his application.

(b) A number of endorsements will be made available for each Designated Competent Body, as follows:

(i) From 6 April to 30 September each year, half that body's allocated endorsements under paragraph 4 above.

(ii) From 1 October to 5 April each year, that body's remaining unused allocated endorsements under paragraph 4 above.

(c) Unused endorsements will not be carried over from one year to the next.

(d) If a Designated Competent Body endorses an application, that application is refused, and that refusal is not subsequently overturned, the used endorsement will be returned to the number of endorsements available for the relevant Designated Competent Body.

(e) No points will be awarded for an endorsement if the Designated Competent Body has exceeded the number of endorsements available to it.]

Note: Paragraph 5 substituted from 1 October 2012 (HC 565).

Endorsement by the relevant Designated Competent Body

6. Points will only be awarded for an endorsement from the relevant Designated Competent Body if the endorsement has not been withdrawn by the relevant Designated Competent Body at the time the application for Entry Clearance is considered by the UK Border Agency.]

Note: Paragraphs 1–65 and Tables 1–9 substituted from 6 April 2011 (HC 863). Paragraphs 4–6 substituted from 9 August 2011 (HC 1436).

[Money earned in the UK

6A Points will only be awarded for money earned in the UK if the applicant provides the following specified documents:

(a) If the applicant is a salaried employee, the specified documents are at least one of the following:

(i) payslips confirming his earnings, which must be either:

(1) original payslips on company-headed paper,

(2) stamped and signed by the applicant's employer, or

(3) accompanied by a letter from the applicant's employer, on company headed paper and signed by a senior official, confirming the payslips are authentic;

or

(ii) personal bank statements on official bank stationery, showing the payments made to the applicant;

or

(iii) electronic bank statements from an online account (defined as one that operates solely over the internet and sends their bank statements to their customers electronically), which either:

(1) are accompanied by a supporting letter from the bank on company headed paper confirming that the documents are authentic, or

(2) bear the official stamp of the issuing bank on every page of the document;

or

(iv) an official tax document produced by HM Revenue & Customs or the applicant's employer, which shows earnings on which tax has been paid or will be paid in a tax year, and is either:

(1) a document produced by HM Revenue & Customs that shows details of declarable taxable income on which tax has been paid or will be paid in a tax year, such as a tax refund letter or tax demand,

(2) a P60 document produced by an employer as an official return to HM Revenue & Customs, showing details of earnings on which tax has been paid in a tax year, or

(3) a document produced by a person, business, or company as an official return to HM Revenue & Customs, showing details of earnings on which tax has been paid or will be paid in a tax year, and which has been approved, registered, or stamped by HM Revenue & Customs;

or

(v) Dividend vouchers, confirming the gross and net dividend paid by a company to the applicant, normally from its profits. The applicant must provide a separate dividend voucher or payment advice slip for each dividend payment.

(b) If the applicant has worked in a self-employed capacity, the specified documents are at least one of the following:

(i) A letter from the applicant's accountant (who must be either a fully qualified chartered accountant or a certified accountant who is a member of a registered body in the UK), on headed paper, which shows a breakdown of the gross and net earnings. The letter should give a breakdown of salary, dividends, profits, tax credits and dates of net payments earned. If the applicant's earnings are a share of the net profit of the company, the letter should also explain this; or

(ii) Company or business accounts that meet statutory requirements and clearly show:

(1) the net profit of the company or business made over the earnings period to be assessed,

(2) both a profit and loss account (or income and expenditure account if the organisation is not trading for profit), and

(3) a balance sheet signed by a director;

or

(iii) If the applicant has worked as a sponsored researcher, a letter on official headed paper to the applicant from the institution providing the funding, which confirms:

(1) the applicant's name,

(2) the name of the sponsoring institution providing the funding,

(3) the name of the host institution where the applicant's sponsored research is based,

(4) the title of the post, and

(5) details of the funding provided.

(c) All applicants must also provide at least one of the following specified documents:

(i) A contract of service or work between the applicant and a UK employer or UK institution which indicates the field of work he has undertaken; or

(ii) A letter from a UK employer or UK institution on its official headed paper, confirming that the applicant has earned money in his expert field.]

Note: Paragraph 6A inserted from 1 October 2012 (HC 565).

Attributes for Tier 1 (General) Migrants

7. An applicant applying for leave to remain or indefinite leave to remain as a Tier 1 (General) Migrant must score 75 points for attributes, if the applicant has, or has had, leave as a Highly Skilled Migrant, as a Writer, Composer or Artist, Self-employed Lawyer, or as a Tier 1 (General) Migrant under the rules in place before 19 July 2010, and has not been granted leave in any categories other than these under the rules in place since 19 July 2010.

Note: Paragraphs 1–65 and Tables 1–9 substituted from 6 April 2011 (HC 863).

8. An applicant applying for leave to remain or indefinite leave to remain as a Tier 1 (General) Migrant who does not fall within the scope of paragraph 7 above or paragraph 9 below must score 80 points for attributes.

Note: Paragraphs 1–65 and Tables 1–9 substituted from 6 April 2011 (HC 863).

9. An applicant applying for indefinite leave to remain as a Tier 1 (General) Migrant whose application is being made under terms [set out in Appendix S] is not required to score points for attributes.

Note: Paragraphs 1–65 and Tables 1–9 substituted from 6 April 2011 (HC 863). Words substituted in para 9 from 6 September 2012 (HC 565).

10. Available points are shown in Table 2 and Table 3 below. Only one set of points will be awarded per column in each table. For example, points will only be awarded for one qualification.

Note: Paragraphs 1–65 and Tables 1–9 substituted from 6 April 2011 (HC 863).

11. Notes to accompany Table 2 and Table 3 appear below Table 3.

Note: Paragraphs 1–65 and Tables 1–9 substituted from 6 April 2011 (HC 863).

Table 2 – applications for leave to remain and indefinite leave to remain where the applicant has, or has had, leave as a Highly Skilled Migrant, as a Writer, Composer or Artist, Self-Employed Lawyer, or as a Tier 1 (General) Migrant under the rules in place before 6 April 2010, and has not been granted leave in any categories other than these since 6 April 2010

Qualification	Points	Previous earnings	Points	UK Experience	Points	Age (at date of application for first grant)	Points
Bachelor's Degree (see paragraph 13 below)	30	£16,000-£17,999.99 (see paragraph 18 below)	5	If £16,000 or more of the previous earnings for which points are claimed were earned in the UK	5	Under 28 years of age	20
Master's degree	35	£18,000 £19,999.99 (see paragraph 18 below)	10			28 or 29 years of age	10
PhD	50	£20,000– £22,999.99	15			30 or 31 years of age	5
		£23,000– £25,999.99	20				
		£26,000– £28,999.99	25				
		£29,000– £31,999.99	30				
		£32,000– £34,999.99	35				
		£35,000– £39,999.99	40				
		£40,000 or more	45				

Table 3 – All other applications for leave to remain and indefinite leave to remain

Qualification	Points	Previous earnings	Points	UK Experience	Points	Age (at date of application for first grant)	Points
Bachelor's Degree (see paragraph 13 below)	30	£25,000-£29,999.99 (see paragraph 18 below)	5	If £25,000 or more of the previous earnings for which points are claimed were earned in the UK	5	Under 30 years of age	20
Master's degree	35	£30,000–£34,999.99	15			30 to 34 years of age	10
PhD	50	£35,000–£39,999.99	20			35 to 39 years of age	5
		£40,000–£49,999.99	25				
		£50,000–£54,999.99	30				
		£55,000–£64,999.99	35				
		£65,000–£74,999.99	40				
		£75,000–£149,999.99	45				
		£150,000 or more	80				

Notes

12. Qualifications and/or earnings will not be taken into account if the applicant was in breach of the UK's immigration laws at the time those qualifications were studied for or those earnings were made.

Note: Paragraphs 1–65 and Tables 1–9 substituted from 6 April 2011 (HC 863).

Qualifications: notes

13. An applicant will be awarded no points for a Bachelor's degree if:

(a) his last grant of entry clearance was as a Tier 1 (General) Migrant under the rules in place between 31 March 2009 and 5 April 2010, or

(b) (i) he has had leave to remain as a Tier 1 (General) Migrant under the rules in place between 31 March 2009 and 5 April 2010, and

(ii) his previous entry clearance, leave to enter or leave to remain before that leave was not as a Highly Skilled Migrant, as a Writer, Composer or Artist, as a Self-employed Lawyer, or as a Tier 1 (General) Migrant.

14. [The specified documents in paragraph 14-SD must be provided] as evidence of the qualification, unless the applicant has, or was last granted, leave as a Highly Skilled Migrant or a Tier 1 (General) Migrant and previously scored points for the same qualification in respect of which points are being claimed in this application.

Note: Paragraphs 1–65 and Tables 1–9 substituted from 6 April 2011 (HC 863). Words in square brackets in para 14 substituted from 20 July 2012 (Cm 8423).

[14-SD. (a) The specified documents in paragraph 14 are:

(i) The original certificate of award of the qualification, which clearly shows the:

    (1) applicant's name,

    (2) title of the award,

    (3) date of the award, and

    (4) name of the awarding institution,

or

(ii) if:

    (1) the applicant is awaiting graduation having successfully completed his degree, or

    (2) the applicant no longer has the certificate and the institution who issued the certificate is unable to produce a replacement,

an original academic reference from the institution that is awarding the degree together with an original academic transcript, unless (d) applies.

(b) The academic reference referred to in (a)(ii) must be on the official headed paper of the institution and clearly show the:

    (1) applicant's name,

    (2) title of award,

    (3) date of award, confirming that it has been or will be awarded, and

    (4) either the date that the certificate will be issued (if the applicant has not yet graduated) or confirmation that the institution is unable to re-issue the original certificate or award.

(c) The academic transcript referred to in (a)(ii) must be on the institution's official paper and must show the:

    (1) applicant's name,

    (2) name of the academic institution,

    (3) course title, and

    (4) confirmation of the award.

(d) If the applicant cannot provide his original certificate for one of the reasons given in (a)(ii) and is claiming points for a qualification with a significant research bias, such as a doctorates, an academic transcript is not required, providing the applicant provides an academic reference which includes all the information detailed in (b) above.

(e) Where an applicant cannot find details of his academic qualification on the points based calculator on the UK Border Agency website, he must, in addition to the document or documents in (a), provide an original letter or certificate from UK NARIC confirming the equivalency of the level of his qualification.

(f) Where an applicant cannot find details of his professional or vocational qualification on the points based calculator, he must, in addition to the document or documents in (a), provide an original letter from the appropriate UK professional body confirming the equivalence to UK academic levels of his qualification, which clearly shows:

(1) the name of the qualification, including the country and awarding body, and

(2) confirmation of which UK academic level this qualification is equivalent to.]

Note: Paragraph 14-SD inserted from 20 July 2012 (Cm 8423).

15. Points will only be awarded for an academic qualification if an applicant's qualification is deemed by the National Academic Recognition Information Centre for the United Kingdom (UK NARIC) to meet or exceed the recognised standard of a Bachelor's or Master's degree or a PhD, as appropriate, in the UK.

Note: Paragraphs 1–65 and Tables 1–9 substituted from 6 April 2011 (HC 863).

16. Points will also be awarded for vocational and professional qualifications that are deemed by UK NARIC or the appropriate UK professional body to be equivalent to a Bachelor's or Master's degree or a PhD in the UK.

Note: Paragraphs 1–65 and Tables 1–9 substituted from 6 April 2011 (HC 863).

17. If the applicant has, or was last granted, leave as a Tier 1 (General) Migrant or a Highly Skilled Migrant and the qualification for which points are now claimed was, in the applicant's last successful application for leave or for a Highly Skilled Migrant Programme Approval Letter, assessed to be of a higher level than now indicated by UK NARIC, the higher score of points will be awarded in this application too.

Note: Paragraphs 1–65 and Tables 1–9 substituted from 6 April 2011 (HC 863).

Previous earnings: notes

18. An applicant will be awarded no points for previous earnings of less than £20,000 if:

(a) his last grant of entry clearance was as a Tier 1 (General) Migrant under the Rules in place between 31 March 2009 and 5 April 2010, or

(b) (i) he has had leave to remain as a Tier 1 (General) Migrant under the rules in place between 31 March 2009 and 5 April 2010, and

(ii) his previous entry clearance, leave to enter or leave to remain before that leave was not as a Highly Skilled Migrant, as a Writer, Composer or Artist, as a Self-employed Lawyer, or as a Tier 1 (General) Migrant.

Note: Paragraphs 1–65 and Tables 1–9 substituted from 6 April 2011 (HC 863).

[19. (a) In all cases, the applicant must provide at least two different types of the specified documents in paragraph 19-SD(a) from two or more separate sources as evidence for each source of previous earnings.

(b) If the applicant is claiming points for self-employed earnings made in the UK, he must also provide the specified documents in paragraph 19-SD(b) to show that:

(i) he is registered as self-employed,

(ii) he was registered as self-employed during the period(s) of self-employment used to claim points, and

(iii) he was paying Class 2 National Insurance contributions during the period(s) of self-employment used to claim points.

(c) Each piece of supporting evidence must support all the other evidence and, where appropriate, be accompanied by any information or explanation of the documents submitted, including further documents such as a letter of explanation from the applicant's accountant, so that together the documents clearly prove the earnings claimed.

(d) Full contact details must be provided for each supporting document for verification purposes.

(e) Where an applicant is providing bank statements as evidence, the bank statements provided must:

(i) be on official bank stationery, and must show each of the payments that the applicant is claiming, or

(ii) electronic bank statements from an online account (defined as one that operates solely over the internet and sends their bank statements to their customers electronically), which either:

(1) are accompanied by a supporting letter from the bank on company headed paper confirming that the documents are authentic, or

(2) bear the official stamp of the issuing bank on every page of the statement.

(f) Where an applicant is providing official tax documents as evidence, the documents must be:

(i) a document produced by a tax authority that shows details of declarable taxable income on which tax has been paid or will be paid in a tax year (for example a tax refund letter or tax demand),

(ii) a document produced by an employer as an official return to a tax authority, showing details of earnings on which tax has been paid in a tax year (for example a P60 in the United Kingdom), or

(iii) a document produced by a person, business, or company as an official return to a tax authority, showing details of earnings on which tax has been paid or will be paid in a tax year, and which has been approved, registered, or stamped by the tax authority.

g) (i) Where an applicant is providing evidence from an accountant or accountancy firm, the accountant must be either a fully qualified chartered accountant or a certified accountant who is a member of a registered body.

(ii) If the earnings were for work done while the applicant was in the UK, such evidence must come from an accountant or accountancy firm in the UK who is a member of one of the following recognised supervisory bodies:

(1) The Institute of Chartered Accountants in England and Wales (ICAEW),

(2) The Institute of Chartered Accountants in Scotland (ICAS),

(3) The Institute of Chartered Accountants in Ireland (ICAI),

(4) The Association of Chartered Certified Accountants (ACCA),

(5) The Chartered Institute of Public Finance and Accountancy (CIPFA),

(6) The Institute of Financial Accountants (IFA), or

(7) The Chartered Institute of Management Accountants (CIMA).

(iii) If the earnings were made while the applicant was not in the UK, the evidence must come from an accountant or accountancy firm which meets the requirements in (ii) or appears on the list of full members given on the website of the International Federation of Accountants.

19-SD. (a) The specified documents in paragraph 19(a) are:

(i) Formal payslips covering the whole period claimed, which must be on company headed paper or stamped and signed as authentic by the employer;

(ii) Personal bank statements showing the payments made to the applicant;

(iii) A letter from the applicant's employer(s) during the period claimed (or in the case of winnings, the relevant awarding body), on company headed paper, which:

(1) is dated after the period for which earnings are being claimed, and

(2) clearly confirms the applicant's gross and net earnings during the period claimed, and the date and amount of each payment;

(iv) Official tax document produced by the relevant tax authority or employer, showing earnings on which tax has been paid or will be paid in a tax year;

(v) Dividend vouchers which show the amount of money paid by the company to the applicant, normally from its profits, and which confirm both the gross and net dividend paid. The applicant must provide a separate dividend voucher or payment advice slip for each dividend payment, to cover the whole period claimed;

(vi) If the applicant is claiming points for self-employed earnings, a letter from his accountant on headed paper, confirming that the applicant received the exact amount he is claiming, or the net profit to which he is entitled. This is a letter from the applicant's accountant on headed paper confirming the gross and net pay for the period claimed. The letter should give a breakdown of salary, dividends, profits, tax credits and dates of net payments earned. If the applicant's earnings are a share of the net profit of the company, the letter should also explain this;

(vii) Invoice explanations or payment summaries from the applicant's accountant, which include a breakdown of the gross salary, tax deductions and dividend payments made to the applicant, and which enable the UK Border Agency to check that the total gross salary and dividend payments correspond with the net payments into the applicant's personal bank account.

(viii) Company or business accounts that meet statutory requirements and clearly show:

(1) the net profit of the company or business made over the earnings period to be assessed,

(2) both a profit and loss account (or income and expenditure account if the organisation is not trading for profit), and

(3) a balance sheet signed by a director;

(ix) Business bank statements showing the payments made to the applicant;

(x) If the applicant provides a combination of bank statements and a letter or invoice summary from his accountant, he must also provide any invoices generated during the period for which earnings are being claimed.

(b) The specified documents in paragraph 19(b) are:

(i) If the applicant's National Insurance is paid by bill, the original bill from the billing period immediately before the application.

(ii) If the applicant's National Insurance is paid by direct debit, the most recent bank statement issued before the application, showing the direct debit payment of National Insurance to HM Revenue & Customs.

(iii) If the applicant has low earnings, an original small earnings exception certificate issued by HM Revenue & Customs for the most recent return date.

(iv) If the applicant has not yet received the documents in (i) to (iii), the original, dated welcome letter from HM Revenue & Customs containing the applicant's unique taxpayer reference number.]

Note: Paragraph 19 substituted from 20 July 2012 (Cm 8423)

Period for assessment

20. Applicants should indicate in the application form for which 12-month period their earnings should be assessed.

Note: Paragraphs 1–65 and Tables 1–9 substituted from 6 April 2011 (HC 863).

21. (a) For all applicants the period for assessment of earnings must:
  (i) consist of no more than 12 months which must run consecutively, and
  (ii) fall within the 15 months immediately preceding the application.
 (b) if the applicant:
  (i) has been on maternity or adoption leave at some point within the 12 months preceding the application, and
  (ii) has provided the specified documents [in paragraph 21-SD], or where due to exceptional circumstances the specified documents are not available, has provided alternative documents which show that the circumstances provided for in (i) apply,
  the applicant may choose for a period of no more than 12 months spent on maternity or adoption leave to be disregarded when calculating both the 12-month and 15-month period.

Note: Paragraphs 1–65 and Tables 1–9 substituted from 6 April 2011 (HC 863). Words in square brackets inserted from 20 July 2012 (Cm 8423)

[21-SD. (a) Where paragraph 21(b)(ii) states that specified documents must be provided, the applicant must provide:
  (i) The document in (b) below, if it has been issued, and
  (ii) If the document in (b) has been issued and is provided, the documents in either (c)(i) or (c)(ii) below, or
  (iii) If the document in (b) has not been issued, the documents in both (c)(i) and (ii) below, or
  (iv) If the applicant is unable to satisfy (ii) or (iii) above:
    (1) the documents in either (b) or (c)(i) or (c)(ii),
    (2) a satisfactory explanation as to why the other types of document cannot be provided, and
    (3) one of the types of documents in (d) below. The specified documents are:
 (b) The original full birth certificate or original full certificate of adoption (as appropriate), containing the names of parents or adoptive parents of the child for whom the period of maternity or adoption-related absence was taken;
 (c) (i) An original letter from the applicant's employer, on the company headed paper, which confirms the start and end dates of the period of maternity or adoption-related absence;
  (ii) Original payslips or other payment or remittance documents, on the official letter-headed paper of the issuing authority, and covering the entire period for which the maternity or adoption-related absence is being claimed and showing the statutory maternity or adoption payments to the applicant;

(d) One of the following documents, from an official source and which is independently verifiable:

 (i) official adoption papers issued by the relevant authority;

 (ii) any relevant medical documents

 (iii) a relevant extract from a register of birth accompanied by an original letter from the issuing authority.]

Note: Paragraph 21-SD inserted from 20 July 2012 (Cm 8423).

22. If the applicant has not indicated a period for assessment of earnings, or has indicated a period which does not meet the conditions [in paragraph 21 above], their earnings will be assessed against the 12-month period immediately preceding their application, assuming the specified documents [in paragraph 19-SD above] have been provided. Where the specified documents [in paragraph 19-SD above] have not been provided, points will not be awarded for previous earnings.

Note: Paragraphs 1–65 and Tables 1–9 substituted from 6 April 2011 (HC 863). Words in first square brackets substituted and other words inserted from 20 July 2012 (Cm 8423).

Earnings

23. Earnings include, but are not limited to:
 (a) salaries (includes full-time, part-time and bonuses),
 (b) earnings derived through self-employment,
 (c) earnings derived through business activities,
 (d) statutory and contractual maternity pay, statutory and contractual adoption pay,
 (e) allowances (such as accommodation, schooling or car allowances) which form part of an applicant's remuneration package and are specified in the applicant's payslips,
 (f) dividends paid by a company in which the applicant is active in the day-to-day management, or where the applicant receives the dividend as part or all of their remuneration package,
 (g) property rental income, where this constitutes part of the applicant's business, and
 (h) payments in lieu of notice.

Note: Paragraphs 1–65 and Tables 1–9 substituted from 6 April 2011 (HC 863).

24. Where the earnings take the form of a salary or wages, they will be assessed before tax (i.e. gross salary).

Note: Paragraphs 1–65 and Tables 1–9 substituted from 6 April 2011 (HC 863).

25. Where the earnings are the profits of a business derived through self-employment or other business activities:
 (a) the earnings that will be assessed are the profits of the business before tax. Where the applicant only has a share of the business, the earnings that will be assessed are the profits of the business before tax to which the applicant is entitled, and
 (b) the applicant must be registered as self-employed in the UK, and must provide the specified evidence.

Note: Paragraphs 1–65 and Tables 1–9 substituted from 6 April 2011 (HC 863).

26. Earnings do not include unearned sources of income, such as:

(a) allowances (such as accommodation, schooling or car allowances) which are paid as reimbursement for monies the applicant has previously paid,

(b) any other allowances, unless part of the applicant's remuneration package and specified in the applicant's payslips,

(c) dividends, unless paid by a company in which the applicant is active in the day-to-day management, or unless the applicant receives the dividend as part or all of their remuneration package,

(d) property rental income, unless this constitutes part of the applicant's business,

(e) interest on savings and investments,

(f) funds received through inheritance,

(g) monies paid to the applicant as a pension,

(h) expenses where the payment constitutes a reimbursement for monies the applicant has previously outlaid,

(i) redundancy payment,

(j) sponsorship for periods of study,

(k) state benefits, or

(l) prize money or competition winnings, other than where they are directly related to the applicant's main profession or occupation.

Note: Paragraphs 1–65 and Tables 1–9 substituted from 6 April 2011 (HC 863).

Converting foreign currencies

27. Earnings in a foreign currency will be converted to pound sterling (£) using the closing spot exchange rate for the last day of the period for which the applicant has claimed earnings in that currency.

Note: Paragraphs 1–65 and Tables 1–9 substituted from 6 April 2011 (HC 863).

28. If the applicant's earnings fall either side of a period of maternity or adoption leave, earnings in a foreign currency will be converted to pounds sterling (£) using the closing spot exchange rate which exists:

(a) for the earnings earned before maternity or adoption leave, on the last day of the period before maternity leave, and

(b) for the earnings earned after maternity or adoption leave, on the last day of the period after maternity leave.

Note: Paragraphs 1–65 and Tables 1–9 substituted from 6 April 2011 (HC 863).

29. The spot exchange rate which will be used is that which appears on www.oanda. com*

Note: Paragraphs 1–65 and Tables 1–9 substituted from 6 April 2011 (HC 863).

30. Where the previous earnings claimed are in different currencies, any foreign currencies will be converted before being added together, and then added to any UK earnings, to give a total amount.

Note: Paragraphs 1–65 and Tables 1–9 substituted from 6 April 2011 (HC 863).

UK experience: notes

31. Previous earnings will not be taken into account for the purpose of awarding points for UK experience if the applicant was not physically present in the UK at the time those earnings were made.

Note: Paragraphs 1–65 and Tables 1–9 substituted from 6 April 2011 (HC 863).

32. Previous earnings will not be taken into account for the purpose of awarding points for UK experience if the applicant was physically present in the Isle of Man or the Channel Islands at the time those earnings were made.

Note: Paragraphs 1–65 and Tables 1–9 substituted from 6 April 2011 (HC 863).

Age: notes

33. If the applicant was first granted leave in the categories of Highly Skilled Migrant, Writer, Composer or Artist, Self-employed lawyer or Tier 1 (General) Migrant and has not been granted leave in any category other than those listed here since the first grant of leave, points will be awarded based on the applicant's age at the date of the application for that first grant of leave. If the applicant has been granted leave since his first grant of leave in a category not listed in this paragraph, points will be awarded based on his age at the date of application for a grant of leave in a category listed in this paragraph where leave has not been granted in any category not listed in this paragraph between that grant of leave and the current application.

Note: Paragraphs 1–65 and Tables 1–9 substituted from 6 April 2011 (HC 863).

34. [The specified documents in paragraph 34-SD must be provided] as evidence of age.

Note: Paragraphs 1–65 and Tables 1–9 substituted from 6 April 2011 (HC 863). Words in square brackets substituted from 20 July 2012 (Cm 8423).

[34-SD. The specified documents in paragraph 34 are:
    (i) The applicant's Biometric Residence Permit, which contains the date of approval of the last grant of leave and the age of the applicant; or
    (ii) The applicant's current valid original passport or travel document containing the last visa granted to the applicant.]

Note : Paragraph 34-SD inserted from 20 July 2012 (Cm 8423).

Attributes for Tier 1 (Entrepreneur) Migrants

35. An applicant applying for entry clearance, leave to remain or indefinite leave to remain as a Tier 1 (Entrepreneur) Migrant must score 75 points for attributes.

Note: Paragraphs 1–65 and Tables 1–9 substituted from 6 April 2011 (HC 863).

36. Subject to paragraph 37, available points for applications for entry clearance or leave to remain are shown in Table 4.

Note: Paragraphs 1–65 and Tables 1–9 substituted from 6 April 2011 (HC 863).

[37. Available points are shown in Table 5 for an applicant who:

(a) has had entry clearance, leave to enter or leave to remain as a Tier 1 (Entrepreneur) Migrant, a Businessperson or an Innovator in the 12 months immediately before the date of application, or

(b) is applying for leave to remain and has, or was last granted, entry clearance, leave to enter or leave to remain as a Tier 1 (Entrepreneur) Migrant, a Businessperson or an Innovator.

Note: Paragraphs 1–65 and Tables 1–9 substituted from 6 April 2011 (HC 863). Subparagraph (b) substituted from 6 April 2012 except for applications made but not decided before that date (HC 1888).

38. Available points for applications for indefinite leave to remain are shown in Table 6.

Note: Paragraphs 1–65 and Tables 1–9 substituted from 6 April 2011 (HC 863).

39. (a) notes to accompany Table 4 appear below Table 4.

[(b) Notes to accompany Tables 4, 5 and 6 appear below Table 6.]

Note: Paragraphs 1–65 and Tables 1–9 substituted from 6 April 2011 (HC 863). Sub-paragraph (b) substituted from 6 April 2012 except for applications made but not decided before that date (HC 1888).

[Table 4:

Investment and business activity	Points
(a) The applicant has access to not less than £200,000, or	25
(b) The applicant has access to not less than £50,000 from:	
(i) one or more registered venture capitalist firms regulated by the Financial Services Authority,	
(ii) one or more UK Entrepreneurial seed funding competitions which is listed as endorsed on the UK Trade & Investment website, or	
(iii) one or more UK Government Departments, and made available by the Department(s) for the specific purpose of establishing or expanding a UK business, or	
(c) The applicant:	
(i) is applying for leave to remain,	
(ii) has, or was last granted, leave as a Tier 1 (Graduate Entrepreneur) Migrant, and	
(iii) has access to not less than £50,000, or	
(d) The applicant:	
(i) is applying for leave to remain,	
(ii) has, or was last granted, leave as a Tier 1 (Post-Study Work) Migrant	
(iii) was, on a date falling within the three months immediately prior to the date of application,	
(1) registered with HM Revenue and Customs as self-employed, or	
(2) registered a new business in which he is a director, or	
(3) registered as a director of an existing business,	

Investment and business activity	Points

(iv) is engaged in business activity, other than the work necessary to administer his business, in an occupation which appears on the list of occupations skilled to National Qualifications Framework level 4 or above, as stated in [the Codes of Practice in Appendix J, and provides the specified evidence in paragraph 41-SD],

and

(v) has access to not less than £50,000.

The money is held in one or more regulated financial institutions	25
The money is disposable in the UK	25

Note: Paragraphs 1–65 and Tables 1–9 substituted from 6 April 2011 (HC 863). Table 4 substituted from 6 April 2012 except for applications made but not decided before that date (HC 1118). Words in square brackets substituted from 20 July 2012 (Cm 8423).

Investment: notes

[40. DELETED.]

Note: Paragraphs 1–65 and Tables 1–9 substituted from 6 April 2011 (HC 863). Paragraph 40 deleted from 20 July 2012 (Cm 8423).

41. An applicant will only be considered to have access to funds if:

(a) [The specified documents in paragraph 41-SD are provided] to show cash money to the amount required (this must not be in the form of assets);

(b) [The specified documents in paragraph 41-SD are provided] to show that the applicant has permission to use the money to invest in a business in the UK; and

(c) The money is either held in a UK regulated financial institution or is transferable to the UK.

Note: Paragraphs 1–65 and Tables 1–9 substituted from 6 April 2011 (HC 863) Words in square brackets substituted from 20 July 2012 (Cm 8423).

[41-SD. The specified documents in Table 4 and paragraph 41 are as follows:

(a) The specified documents to show evidence of the money available to invest are one or more of the following specified documents:

(i) A letter from each financial institution holding the funds, to confirm the amount of money available to the applicant (or the entrepreneurial team if applying under the provisions in paragraph 52 of this Appendix). Each letter must:

(1) be an original document and not a copy,

(2) be on the institution's official headed paper,

(3) have been issued by an authorised official of that institution,

(4) have been produced within the three months immediately before the date of your application,

(5) confirm that the institution is regulated by the appropriate body,

(6) state the applicant's name, and his team partner's name if the applicant is applying under the provisions in paragraph 52 of this Appendix,

(7) state the date of the document,

(8) confirm the amount of money available from the applicant's own funds (if applicable) that are held in that institution,

(9) confirm the amount of money provided to the applicant from any third party (if applicable) that is held in that institution,

(10) confirm the name of each third party and their contact details, including their full address including postal code, landline phone number and any email address, and

(11) confirm that if the money is not in an institution regulated by the FSA, the money can be transferred into the UK;

   or

(ii) For money held in the UK only, a recent personal bank or building society statement from each UK financial institution holding the funds, which confirms the amount of money available to the applicant (or the entrepreneurial team if applying under the provisions in paragraph 52 of this Appendix). The statements must satisfy the following requirements:

(1) The statements must be original documents and not copies;

(2) The bank or building society holding the money must be based in the UK and regulated by the Financial Services Authority;

(3) The money must be in cash in the account, not Individual Savings Accounts or assets such as stocks and shares;

(4) The account must be in the applicant's own name only (or both names for an entrepreneurial team), not in the name of a business or third party;

(5) Each bank or building society statement must be on the institution's official stationary and confirm the applicant's name and, where relevant, the applicant's entrepreneurial team partner's name, the account number, the date of the statement, and the financial institution's name and logo;

(6) The bank or building society statement must have been issued by an authorised official of that institution and produced within the three months immediately before the date of the application; and

(7) If the statements are printouts of electronic statements from an online account, they must either be accompanied by a supporting letter from the bank, on company headed paper, confirming the authenticity of the statements, or bear the official stamp of the bank in question on each page of the statement;

   or

(iii) For £50,000 from a Venture Capital firm, Seed Funding Competition or UK Government Department only, a recent letter from an accountant, who is a member of a recognised UK supervisory body, confirming the amount of money made available to the applicant (or the entrepreneurial team if applying under the provisions in paragraph 52 of this Appendix). Each letter must:

(1) be an original document and not a copy,

(2) be on the institution's official headed paper,

(3) have been issued by an accountant engaged by the Venture Capital firm, Seed funding competition or UK Government Department to provide the information,

(4) have been produced within the three months immediately before the date of the application,

(5) state the applicant's name, and his team partner's name if the applicant is applying under the provisions in paragraph 52 of this Appendix,

(6) state the date of the document,

(7) confirm the amount of money available to the applicant or the applicant's business from the Venture Capital firm, Seed funding competition or UK Government Department, and

(8) confirm the name of the Venture Capital firm, Seed funding competition or UK Government Department and the contact details of an official of that organisation, including their full address, postal code, landline phone number and any email address,

(b) If the applicant is applying using money from a third party, he must provide all of the following specified documents:

(i) An original declaration from every third party that they have made the money available for the applicant to invest in a business in the United Kingdom, containing:

(1) the names of the third party and the applicant (and his team partner's name if the applicant is applying under the provisions in paragraph 52 of this Appendix),

(2) the date of the declaration;

(3) the applicant's signature and the signature of the third party (and the signature of the applicant's team partner if the applicant is applying under the provisions in paragraph 52 of this Appendix),

(4) the amount of money available to the applicant from the third party in pounds sterling,

(5) the relationship(s) of the third party to the applicant,

(6) if the third party is a venture capitalist firm, confirmation of whether this body is an Financial Services Authority-registered venture capital firm, in the form of a document confirming the award and the amount of money, and including the Financial Services Authority registration number that the firm's permission to operate as a Venture Capital firm is listed as permitted under,

(7) if the third party is a UK entrepreneurial seed funding competition, a document confirming that the applicant has been awarded money and that the competition is listed as endorsed on the UK Trade & Investment website, together with the amount of the award and naming the applicant as a winner,

(8) if the third party is a UK Government Department, a document confirming that it has made money available to the applicant for the specific purpose of establishing or expanding a UK business, and the amount.

and

(ii) A letter from a legal representative confirming the validity of signatures on each third-party declaration provided, which confirms that the declaration(s) from the third party/parties contains the signatures of the people stated. It can be a single letter covering all third-party permissions, or several letters from several legal representatives. It must be an original letter and not a copy, and it must be from a legal representative permitted to practise in the country where the third party or the money is. The letter must clearly show the following:

(1) the name of the legal representative confirming the details,

(2) the registration or authority of the legal representative to practise legally in the country in which the permission or permissions was/were given,

(3) the date of the confirmation letter,

(4) the applicant's name (and the name of the applicant's team partner if the applicant is applying under the provisions in paragraph 52 of this Appendix),

(5) the third party's name,

(6) that the declaration from the third party is signed and valid, and

(7) if the third party is not a venture capitalist firm, seed funding competition or UK Government Department, the number of the third party's identity document (such as a passport or national identity card), the place of issue and dates of issue and expiry.

(c) If the applicant is applying under the provisions in (d) in Table 4, he must provide:

(i) his job title,

(ii) confirmation that his job appears on the list of occupations skilled to National Qualifications Framework level 4 or above, as stated in the Codes of Practice in Appendix J,

(iii) one or more of the following specified documents:

(1) Advertising or marketing material, including printouts of online advertising, that has been published locally or nationally, showing the applicant's name (and the name of the business if applicable) together with the business activity,

(2) Article(s) or online links to article(s) in a newspaper or other publication showing the applicant's name (and the name of the business if applicable) together with the business activity,

(3) Information from a trade fair(s), at which the applicant has had a stand or given a presentation to market his business, showing the applicant's name (and the name of the business if applicable) together with the business activity, or

(4) Personal registration with a trade's body linked to the applicant's occupation.

and

(iii) one or more contracts showing trading. If a contract is not an original the applicant must sign each page of the contract. The contract must show:

(1) the applicant's name and the name of the business,

(2) the service provided by the applicant's business; and

(3) the name of the other party or parties involved in the contract and their contact details, including their full address, postal code, landline phone number and any email address.]

Note: Paragraph 41-SD inserted from 20 July 2012 (Cm 8423).

42. Points will only be awarded to an applicant to whom Table 4, paragraph (b) applies if the total sum of those funds derives from one or more of the sources listed in (b)(i) to (iii) in Table 4.

Note: Paragraphs 1–65 and Tables 1–9 substituted from 6 April 2011 (HC 863).

43. A regulated financial institution is one which is regulated by the appropriate regulatory body for the country in which the financial institution operates.

Note: Paragraphs 1–65 and Tables 1–9 substituted from 6 April 2011 (HC 863).

44. Money is disposable in the UK if all of the money is held in a UK based financial institution or if the money is freely transferable to the UK and convertible to sterling. Funds in a foreign currency will be converted to pounds sterling (£) using the spot exchange rate which appeared on www.oanda.com* on the date on which the application was made.

Note: Paragraphs 1–65 and Tables 1–9 substituted from 6 April 2011 (HC 863).

45. If the applicant has invested the money referred to in Table 4 in the UK before the date of the application, points will be awarded for funds available as if the applicant had not yet invested the funds, providing the investment was made no more than 12 months before the date of the application [and the specified documents in paragraph 46-SD are provided.]

Note: Paragraphs 1–65 and Tables 1–9 substituted from 6 April 2011 (HC 863). Words in square brackets inserted from 20 July 2012 (Cm 8423).

Table 5: Applications for leave to remain referred to in paragraph 37

Investment and business activity	Points
The applicant has invested, or had invested on his behalf, not less than £200,000 (or £50,000) if, in his last grant of leave, he was awarded points for funds of £50,000 [as set out in Table 4 above] in cash directly into one or more businesses in the UK.	20
The applicant has: (a) registered with HM revenue and Customs as self-employed, or (b) registered a new business in which he is a director, or (c) registered as a director of an existing business. Where the applicant's last grant of entry clearance, leave to enter or leave to remain was as a Tier 1 (Entrepreneur) Migrant, the above condition must have been met within 6 months of his entry to the UK (if he was granted entry clearance as a Tier 1 (Entrepreneur) Migrant and there is evidence to establish his date of arrival to the UK), or, in any other case, the date of the grant of leave to remain.	20
On a date no earlier than three months prior to the date of application, the applicant was: (a) registered with HM revenue and Customs as self-employed, or (b) registered a new business in which he is a director, or (c) registered as a director of an existing business.	15
The applicant has: (a) established a new business or businesses that has or have created the equivalent of at least two new full time jobs for persons settled in the UK, or (b) taken over or invested in an existing business or businesses and his services or investment have resulted in a net increase in the employment provided by the business or businesses for persons settled in the UK by creating the equivalent of at least two new full time jobs. Where the applicant's last grant of entry clearance or leave to enter or remain was as a Tier 1 (entrepreneur) Migrant, the jobs must have existed for at least 12 months of the period for which the previous leave was granted.	20

Note: Paragraphs 1–65 and Tables 1–9 substituted from 6 April 2011 (HC 863). Words in square brackets substituted from 6 April 2012 except for applications made but not decided before that date (HC 1888).

Table 6: Applications for indefinite leave to remain as referred to in paragraph 38

Row	Investment and business activity	Points
1.	On a date no earlier than three months prior to the date of application, the applicant was:	20
	(a) registered with HM revenue and Customs as self-employed, or	
	(b) registered a new business in which he is a director, or	
	(c) registered as a director of an existing business.	
2.	The applicant has:	20
	(a) established a new UK business or businesses that has or have created the equivalent of X new full time jobs for persons settled in the UK, or	
	(b) taken over or invested in an existing UK business or businesses and his services or investment have resulted in a net increase in the employment provided by the business or businesses for persons settled in the UK by creating the equivalent of X new full time jobs where X is at least 2.	
	Where the applicant's last grant of entry clearance or leave to enter or remain was as a Tier 1 (Entrepreneur) Migrant, the jobs must have existed for at least 12 months of the period for which the previous leave was granted.	
3.	The applicant has spent the specified continuous period lawfully in the UK, with absences from the UK of no more than 180 days in any 12 calendar months during that period.	35
	The specified period must have been spent with leave as a Tier 1 (Entrepreneur) Migrant, as a Businessperson and/or as an Innovator, of which the most recent period must have been spent with leave as a Tier (1) (Entrepreneur) Migrant.	
	The specified continuous period is:	
	(a) 3 years if the number of new full time jobs, X, referred to in row 2 above is at least 10,	
	(b) 3 years if the applicant has:	
	(i) established a new UK business that has had an income from business activity of at least £5 million during a 3 year period in which the applicant has had leave as a Tier 1 (Entrepreneur) Migrant, or	
	(ii) taken over or invested in an existing UK business and his services or investment have resulted in a net increase in income from business activity to that business of £5 million during a 3 year period in which the applicant has had leave as a Tier 1 (Entrepreneur) Migrant, when compared to the immediately preceding 3 year period, or (c) 5 years in all other cases.	

Note: Paragraphs 1–65 and Tables 1–9 substituted from 6 April 2011 (HC 863).

Investment and business activity: notes

[46. Documentary evidence must be provided in all cases. The specified documents in paragraph 46-SD must be provided as evidence of any investment and business activity that took place when the applicant had leave as a Tier 1 (Entrepreneur) Migrant or a Tier 1 (Post-Study Work) Migrant, and any investment made no more than 12 months before the date of the application for which the applicant is claiming points.]

Note: Paragraph 46 substituted from 20 July 2012 (Cm 8423).

[46-SD. The specified documents in paragraphs 45 and 46 are as follows:

(a) The applicant must provide all the appropriate specified documents needed to establish the amount of money he has invested from the following list:

(i) If the applicant's business is a registered company that is required to produce audited accounts, the audited accounts must be provided;

(ii) If the applicant's business is not required to produce audited accounts, unaudited accounts and an accountant's certificate of confirmation, from an accountant who is a member of a UK Recognised Supervisory Body (as defined in the Companies Act 2006), must be provided;

(iii) If the applicant has made the investment in the form of a director's loan, it must be shown in the relevant set of accounts provided, and the applicant must also provide a legal agreement, between the applicant (in the name that appears on his application) and the company, showing:

(1) the terms of the loan,

(2) any interest that is payable,

(3) the period of the loan, and

(4) that the loan is unsecured and subordinated in favour of third-party creditors.

(b) Audited or unaudited accounts must show the investment in money made directly by the applicant, in his own name. If he has invested by way of share capital the business accounts must show the shareholders, the amount and value of the shares (on the date of purchase) in the applicant's name as it appears on his application. If the value of the applicant's share capital is not shown in the accounts, then share certificates must be submitted as documentary evidence. The accounts must clearly show the name of the accountant, the date the accounts were produced, and how much the applicant has invested in the business.

(c) The applicant must provide the following specified documents to show that he has established a UK business:

(i) Evidence that the business has business premises in the United Kingdom:

(1) If the applicant is self employed, his registration with HM Revenue and Customs to show that the business is based in the UK, or

(2) If the applicant is a director, printout of a Companies House document showing the address of the registered office in the UK, or head office in the UK if it has no registered office, and the applicant's name, as it appears on the application form, as a director,

and

(ii) Evidence that the business has a UK bank account:

(1) If the applicant is self employed, a personal bank statement showing transactions for his business, or a business bank statement, or a letter from a UK bank confirming that he has a business and acts through that bank, or

(2) If the applicant is a director, a company bank statement showing that the company has a UK account, or a letter from a UK bank confirming that the company has a bank account,

and

(iii) Evidence that the business is subject to UK taxation:

(1) If the applicant is self-employed, he must be registered as self-employed for National Insurance assessment and provide either the welcome letter from HM Revenue & Customs, the Small Earnings Exception certificate, a copy of the National Insurance bill from HM Revenue & Customs, or

the applicant's bank statement showing that National Insurance is taken by HM Revenue & Customs by direct debit, or

(2) If the applicant is a director of a business, the business must be registered for corporation tax and the applicant must provide either a copy of form CT41G from HM Revenue & Customs, which is completed and shows the date of registration of the company with HM Revenue & Customs and the HM Revenue & Customs unique reference number, or a completed HM Revenue & Customs tax return document showing the tax reference number for the company.

(d) If the applicant has bought property that includes residential accommodation the value of this part of the property will not be counted towards the amount of the business investment. The applicant must provide an estimate of the value of the living accommodation if it is part of the premises also used for the business, from a surveyor who is a member of the Royal Institution of Chartered Surveyors. This valuation must be produced in the three months prior to the date of application.

(e) If some of the money has been invested into a business in the UK, the balance of funds must be held in a regulated financial institution and disposable in the UK, and the applicant must provide the specified documents required in paragraph 41-SD for the previous investment of money together with the specified documents required in paragraph 41-SD required for his access to the balance of sufficient funds.

(f) Where Table 5 applies and the applicant's last grant of entry clearance, leave to enter or leave to remain was as a Tier 1 (Entrepreneur) Migrant, he must provide the following specified documents as evidence of his registration as self-employed or as a director within the 6 months after the specified date in the second row of Table 5:

(i) If the applicant was self-employed, he must provide one of the following:

(1) an original, dated welcome letter from HM Revenue & Customs containing the applicant's unique taxpayer reference number,

(2) an original Exception Certificate from HM Revenue & Customs, dated no more than 8 months from the specified date in the second row of Table 5,

(3) an original National Insurance bill from the HM Revenue & Customs dated during the 6 months after the specified date in the second row of Table 5, or

(4) a bank statement dated in the 6 months after the specified date in the second row of Table 5, showing the direct debit payment of National Insurance to HM Revenue & Customs.

(ii) If the applicant was a director of a new or existing company, he must provide a Current Appointment Report from Companies House, listing the applicant as the Director of the company and the date of his appointment, which must be no more than 8 months after the specified date in the second row of Table 5.

(g) The applicant must provide the following specified documents as evidence of his current registration as self-employed or as a director:

(i) If the applicant is claiming points for being currently self-employed, he must provide the following specified documents to show that he is paying Class 2 National Insurance contributions:

(1) the original bill from the billing period immediately before the application, if his Class 2 National Insurance is paid by quarterly bill,

(2) the most recent bank statement issued before the application, showing the direct debit payment of National Insurance to HM Revenue & Customs, if his National Insurance is paid by direct debit,

(3) an original small earnings exception certificate issued by HM Revenue & Customs for the most recent return date, if he has low earnings, or

(4) the original, dated welcome letter from HM Revenue & Customs containing the applicant's unique taxpayer reference number, if he has not yet received the documents in (1) to (3).

(ii) If the applicant is claiming points for currently being a director of a UK company, he must provide a printout of a Current Appointment Report from Companies House, dated no earlier than three months before the date of the application, listing the applicant as a director of the company, and confirming the date of his appointment. The company must be actively trading and not struck-off, or dissolved or in liquidation on the date that the printout was produced. Directors who are on the list of disqualified Directors provided by Companies House will not be awarded points.

(h) If the applicant is required to score points for creating the net increase in employment in Table 5 or Table 6, he must provide the following information and specified documents:

(i) A HM Revenue & Customs P11 form (also called the Employee Payment Record), showing details of the earnings for the settled worker for each week that he worked for the applicant, and signed and dated by the applicant;

(ii) If the date of the start of the employment is not shown in the form P11, an original HM Revenue & Customs form P45 or form P46 (also called a Full Payment Submission) for the settled worker, showing the starting date of the employment;

(iii) If the employer is taking part in the Real Time Initiative pilot, printouts of the Full Payment Submission, sent to HM Revenue & Customs, which include the start date of the settled worker and are initialled by the applicant;

(iv) Duplicate payslips or wage slips for each settled worker for whom points are being claimed, covering the full period of the employment for which points are being claimed;

(v) Confirmation of the hourly rate for each settled worker used to claim points, including any changes in the hourly rate and the dates of the changes, enabling calculation of the hours of work created for each settled worker;

(vi) Documents which show that the employment was created for settled workers, such as the passport pages from a UK passport that contain the employee's personal details, and the page containing the UK Government stamp or endorsement, if appropriate, or the worker's full birth certificate, showing the name of at least one parent;

vii) If the applicant was a director of a company, the information from the Companies House Current Appointment Report to confirm that he was a Director of the company that employed the settled worker at the time that he was employed;

(viii) If the applicant was self-employed, the specified documents in (c) above showing the dates that the applicant became self-employed, the names on the P11 and bank account, and the address of the business;

(ix) If the applicant took over or joined a business that employed workers before he joined it, he must also provide one of the following types of payroll documentation:

(1) a duplicate HM Revenue & Customs form P35 for the year before the jobs were created and the year that the jobs were created, showing the net increase in employment, and signed and dated by the applicant (If the posts were created too recently for a P35 to have been produced, the applicant must provide a draft copy), or

(2) a printout of the information sent to HM Revenue & Customs, initialled by the applicant, if the employer is taking part in the Real Time Initiative pilot;

(x) If the applicant took over or joined a business that employed workers before he joined it, he must also provide an original accountant's letter verifying the net increase in employment and confirming the number of posts. The accountant must be a member of the Institute of Chartered Accountants in England and Wales, the Institute of Chartered Accountants in Scotland, the Institute of Chartered Accountants in Ireland, the Association of Chartered Certified Accountants, or the Association of Authorised Public Accountants. The letter must contain:

(1) the name and contact details of the business,

(2) the applicant's status in the business,

(3) the number of posts created in the business and the hours worked,

(4) the dates of the employment created,

(5) the registration or permission of the accountant to operate in the United Kingdom,

(6) the date that the accountant created the letter on the applicant's behalf, and

(7) that the accountant will confirm the content of the letter to the UK Border Agency on request.]

Note: Paragraph 46-SD inserted from 20 July 2012 (Cm 8423).

47. For the purposes of tables 4, 5 and 6, 'investment' does not include the value of any residential accommodation, property development or property management and must not be in the form of a director's loan, unless it is unsecured and subordinated in favour of the business.

Note: Paragraphs 1–65 and Tables 1–9 substituted from 6 April 2011 (HC 863).

48. Points will only be awarded in respect of a UK business or businesses. A business will be considered to be in the UK if:

(i) it is trading within the UK economy, and

(ii) it has a registered office in the UK, except where the applicant is registered with HM Revenue & Customs as self-employed and does not have a business office, and

(iii) it has a UK bank account, and

(iv) it is subject to UK taxation.

Multinational companies that are registered as UK companies with either a registered office or head office in the UK are considered to be UK businesses for the purposes of tables 4, 5 and 6.

Note: Paragraphs 1–65 and Tables 1–9 substituted from 6 April 2011 (HC 863).

49. A full time job is one involving at least 30 hours' of work a week. Two or more part time jobs that add up to 30 hours a week will count as one full time job but one full time job of more than 30 hours work a week will not count as more than one full time job.

Note: Paragraphs 1–65 and Tables 1–9 substituted from 6 April 2011 (HC 863).

50. Where the applicant's last grant of entry clearance or leave was as a Tier 1 (Entrepreneur) Migrant, the jobs must have existed for a total of at least 12 months during the period in which the migrant had leave in that category. This need not consist of 12 consecutive months and the jobs need not exist at the date of application, provided they existed for at least 12 months during the period in which the migrant had leave as a Tier 1 (Entrepreneur) Migrant.

Note: Paragraphs 1–65 and Tables 1–9 substituted from 6 April 2011 (HC 863).

51. The jobs must comply with all relevant UK legislation including, but not limited to, the National Minimum Wage and the Working Time Directive.

Note: Paragraphs 1–65 and Tables 1–9 substituted from 6 April 2011 (HC 863).

Entrepreneurial teams: Notes

52. Two applicants may claim points for the same investment and business activity in Tables 4, 5 or 6 providing the following requirements are met.

Requirements:

(a) The applicants have equal level of control over the funds and/or the business or businesses in question;

(b) The applicants are both shown by name in each other's applications and in the specified evidence required in the relevant table; and

(c) neither applicant has previously been granted leave as a Tier 1 (Entrepreneur) Migrant on the basis of investment and/or business activity linked in this way with any applicant other than each other if the same funds are being relied on as in a previous application.

Note: Paragraphs 1–65 and Tables 1–9 substituted from 6 April 2011 (HC 863).

[53. DELETED]

Note: Paragraph 53 deleted from 6 April 2012 except for applications made but not decided before that date (HC 1888).

Attributes for Tier 1 (Investor) Migrants

54. An applicant applying for entry clearance, leave to remain or indefinite leave to remain as a Tier 1 (Investor) Migrant must score 75 points for attributes.

Note: Paragraphs 1–65 and Tables 1–9 substituted from 6 April 2011 (HC 863).

55. Subject to paragraph 56, available points for applications for entry clearance or leave to remain are shown in Table 7.

Note: Paragraphs 1–65 and Tables 1–9 substituted from 6 April 2011 (HC 863).

[56. Available points are shown in Table 8 for an applicant who:

(a) has had entry clearance, leave to enter or leave to remain as a Tier 1 (Investor) Migrant or an Investor in the 12 months immediately before the date of application, or

(b) is applying for leave to remain and has, or was last granted, entry clearance, leave to enter or leave to remain as a Tier 1 (Investor) Migrant or an Investor.]

Note: Paragraphs 1–65 and Tables 1–9 substituted from 6 April 2011 (HC 863). Paragraph 56 substituted from 6 April 2012 except for applications made but not decided before that date (HC 1888).

57. Available points for applications for indefinite leave to remain are shown in Table 9.

Note: Paragraphs 1–65 and Tables 1–9 substituted from 6 April 2011 (HC 863).

58. Notes to accompany Table 7, Table 8 and Table 9 appear below Table 9.

Note: Paragraphs 1–65 and Tables 1–9 substituted from 6 April 2011 (HC 863).

Table 7: Applications for entry clearance or leave to remain referred to in [paragraph 55]

Assets	Points
The applicant:	75
(a) has money of his own under his control held in a regulated financial institution and disposable in the UK amounting to not less than £1 million; or	
(b) (i) owns personal assets which, taking into account any liabilities to which they are subject, have a value exceeding £2 million, and	
(ii) has money under his control held in a regulated financial institution and disposable in the UK amounting to not less than £1 million which has been loaned to him by a UK regulated financial institution.	

Note: Paragraphs 1–65 and Tables 1–9 substituted from 6 April 2011 (HC 863). Words in square brackets in header substituted from 6 April 2012 except for applications made but not decided before that date (HC 1888).

Table 8: Applications for leave to remain referred to in [paragraph 56]

Assets and investment	Points
The applicant:	30
(a) has money of his own under his control in the UK amounting to not less than £1 million, or	
(b) (i) owns personal assets which, taking into account any liabilities to which they are subject, have a value of not less than £2 million, and	
(ii) has money under his control and disposable in the UK amounting to not less than £1 million which has been loaned to him by a UK regulated financial institution.	
The applicant has invested not less than £750,000 of his capital in the UK by way of UK Government bonds, share capital or loan capital in active and trading UK registered companies, subject to the restrictions set out in paragraph 65 below and has invested the remaining balance of £1,000,000 in the UK by the purchase of assets or by maintaining the money on deposit in a UK regulated financial institution.	30

The investment referred to above was made within 3 months of his entry to the   15
UK (if he was granted entry clearance as a as a Tier 1 (Investor) Migrant and
there is evidence to establish his date of arrival to the UK), or the date of the
grant of entry clearance as a Tier 1 (Investor) Migrant (if there is no evidence
to establish his date of arrival to the UK), or, in any other case, the date of the
grant of leave to remain as a Tier 1 (Investor) Migrant and in each case the
investment has been maintained for the whole of the remaining period of that
leave; or

The migrant has, or was last granted, entry clearance, leave to enter or leave to
remain as an Investor.

Note: Paragraphs 1–65 and Tables 1–9 substituted from 6 April 2011 (HC 863). Words in square
brackets in header substituted from 6 April 2012 except for applications made but not decided
before that date (HC 1888).

Table 9: Applications for indefinite leave to remain

Row	Assets and investment	Points
1.	The applicant:	20
	(a) (i) has money of his own under his control in the UK amounting to not less than £10 million, or	
	(ii) (1) owns personal assets which, taking into account any liabilities to which they are subject, have a value of not less than £20 million, and	
	(2) has money under his control and disposable in the UK amounting to not less than £10 million which has been loaned to him by a UK regulated financial institution, or	
	(b)(i) has money of his own under his control in the UK amounting to not less than £5 million, or	
	(ii) (1) owns personal assets which, taking into account any liabilities to which they are subject, have a value of not less than £10 million, and	
	(2) has money under his control and disposable in the UK amounting to not less than £5 million which has been loaned to him by a UK regulated financial institution,	
	(c) (i) has money of his own under his control in the UK amounting to not less than £1 million, or	
	(ii) (1) owns personal assets which, taking into account any liabilities to which they are subject, have a value of not less than £2 million, and	
	(2) has money under his control and disposable in the UK amounting to not less than £1 million which has been loaned to him by a UK regulated financial institution,	

2. The applicant has invested not less than 75% of the specified invested   20
amount of his capital in the UK by way of UK Government bonds,
share capital or loan capital in active and trading UK registered
companies, subject to the restrictions set out in paragraph 65 below,
and has invested the remaining balance of the specified invested
amount in the UK by the purchase of assets or by maintaining the
money on deposit in a UK regulated financial institution.

The specified invested amount is:

(a) £10,000,000 if the applicant scores points from row 1(a) above,

(b) £5,000,000 if the applicant scores points from row 1(b) above, or

(c) £1,000,000 if the applicant scores points from row 1(c) above.

3. The applicant has spent the specified continuous period lawfully in the   20
UK, with absences from the UK of no more than 180 days in any 12
calendar months during that period. The specified continuous period
must have been spent with leave as a Tier 1 (Investor) Migrant and/or
as an Investor, of which the most recent period must have been spent
with leave as a Tier 1 (Investor) Migrant.

The specified continuous period is:

(a) 2 years if the applicant scores points from row 1(a) above,

(b) 3 years if the applicant scores points from row 1(b) above, or

(c) 5 years if the applicant scores points from row 1(c) above.

4. The applicant has maintained the full specified invested amount   15
referred to in the relevant part of row 2 throughout the relevant
specified continuous period referred to in row 3, other than in the first
3 months of that period and, in relation to time spent with leave as a
Tier 1 (Investor) Migrant, has provided specified documents to show
that this requirement has been met.

When calculating the specified continuous period, the first day of that
period will be taken to be the day 3 months before the full specified
amount is invested.

Note: Paragraphs 1–65 and Tables 1–9 substituted from 6 April 2011 (HC 863).

Assets and investment: notes

[59. DELETED]

Note: Paragraph 59 deleted from 20 July 2012 (Cm 8423)

60. Money is disposable in the UK if all of the money is held in a UK based financial institution or if the money is freely transferable to the UK and convertible to sterling. Funds in a foreign currency will be converted to pounds sterling (£) using the spot exchange rate which appeared on www.oanda.com* on the date on which the application was made.

Note: Paragraphs 1–65 and Tables 1–9 substituted from 6 April 2011 (HC 863).

61. 'Money of his own', 'personal assets' and 'his capital' include money or assets belonging to the applicant's spouse, civil partner or unmarried or same-sex partner, provided that:

(a) the applicant's spouse, civil partner or unmarried or same-sex partner meets the requirements of [paragraphs 319C(c) and (d)] of these Rules, [and the specified documents in paragraph 61-SD are provided,] and

(b) specified documents [in paragraph 61-SD] are provided to show that the money or assets are under the applicant's control and that he is free to invest them.

Note: Paragraphs 1–65 and Tables 1–9 substituted from 6 April 2011 (HC 863). Words in 1st square brackets in sub-para (a) substituted from 6 April 2012 except for applications made but not decided before that date (HC 1888). Words in other square brackets inserted from 20 July 2012 (HC 8423)

[61-SD. The specified documents in paragraph 61, as evidence of the relationship and to show that the money or assets are under the applicant's control and that he is free to invest them, are as follows:

(a) The applicant must provide:

(i) The original certificate of marriage or civil partnership, to confirm the relationship, which includes the name of the applicant and the husband, wife or civil partner, or

(ii) At least three of the following types of specified documents to demonstrate a relationship similar in nature to marriage or civil partnership, including unmarried and same-sex relationships, covering a full two-year period immediately before the date of the application:

(1) a bank statement or letter from a bank confirming a joint bank account held in both names,

(2) an official document such as a mortgage agreement showing a joint mortgage,

(3) official documents such as deeds of ownership or a mortgage agreement showing a joint investment, such as in property or business,

(4) a joint rent (tenancy) agreement,

(5) any other official correspondence linking both partners to the same address, such as example bills for council tax or utilities,

(6) a life insurance policy naming the other partner as beneficiary,

(7) birth certificates of any children of the relationship, showing both partners as parents, or

(8) any other evidence that adequately demonstrates the couple's long-term commitment to one another.

(b) The applicant must provide an original declaration from the applicant's husband, wife, civil partner, or unmarried or same-sex partner that he will permit all joint or personal money used to claim points for the application to be under the control of the applicant in the UK, known as a gift of beneficial ownership of the money while retaining the legal title, which clearly shows:

(1) the names of husband, wife, civil partner, or unmarried or same-sex partner and the applicant,

(2) the date of the declaration,

(3) the signatures of the husband, wife, civil partner, or unmarried or same- sex partner and applicant,

(4) the amount of money available, and

(5) a statement that the husband, wife, civil partner, or unmarried or same- sex partner agrees that the applicant has sole control over the money.

(c) The applicant must provide a letter, from a legal adviser who is permitted to practise in the country where the declaration was made, confirming that the declaration is valid and which clearly shows:

(1) the name of the legal adviser confirming that the declaration is valid,

(2) the registration or authority of the legal adviser to practise legally in the country in which the document was drawn up,

(3) the date of the confirmation of the declaration,

(4) the names of the applicant and husband, wife, civil partner, or unmarried or same-sex partner, and

(5) that the declaration is signed and valid according to the laws of the country in which it was made.]

Note: Paragraph 61-SD inserted from 20 July 2012 (Cm 8423).

62. 'Regulated financial institution' is defined in paragraph 43, Appendix A.

Note: Paragraphs 1–65 and Tables 1–9 substituted from 6 April 2011 (HC 863).

[62A 'Active and trading UK registered companies' means companies which: (a) have a registered office or head office in the UK; (b) have a UK bank account showing current business transactions; and (c) are subject to UK taxation.]

Note: Paragraph 62A inserted from 20 July 2012 (Cm 8423).

63. In the case of an application where Table 7 applies, where the money or assets referred to in Table 7 have already been invested in the UK before the date of application, points will only be awarded if they were invested in the UK no more than 12 months before the date of application.

Note: Paragraphs 1–65 and Tables 1–9 substituted from 6 April 2011 (HC 863).

64. In the case of an application where Table 7 applies, points will only be awarded if the applicant:

(a) has had the money or assets referred to in Table 7 for a consecutive 90-day period of time, ending no earlier than one calendar month before the date of application, [and provides the specified documents in paragraph 64-SD]; or

(b) [provides the additional specified documents in paragraph 64A-SD] of the source of the money or assets.

Note: Paragraphs 1–65 and Tables 1–9 substituted from 6 April 2011 (HC 863). Words in square brackets substituted from 20 July 2012 (Cm 8423).

[64-SD. The specified document requirements in paragraph 64(a), as evidence of having held the money or assets for the specified 90-day period, are as follows:

(a) If the applicant is claiming points from (a) in the first row of Table 7, he must provide:

(i) A portfolio report produced by a UK regulated financial institution, or a breakdown of investments in an original letter produced by a UK regulated financial institution, on the official letter-headed paper of the institution, issued by an authorised official of that institution. The portfolio report or letter must cover the three consecutive months before the date of application. The report must be no more than one calendar month old at the time of application. The portfolio report or letter must confirm all the following:

(1) the amount of the money held in the investments,

(2) the beneficial owner of the funds,

(3) the date of the investment period covered,

(4) that the institution is a UK regulated financial institution, with the details of the registration shown on the documentation, and

(5) that the money can be transferred into the UK should the application be successful, if it is held abroad, or that the money has already been invested in the UK in the form of UK Government bonds, share capital or loan capital in active and trading UK registered companies, and the dates of these investments;

(ii) If the applicant manages his own investments, or has a portfolio manager who does not operate in the UK and is not therefore regulated by the Financial Services Authority, he must provide one or more of the documents from the list below, as relevant to their type of investments, covering the three consecutive months in the period immediately before the date of application:

(1) certified copies of bond documents showing the value of the bonds, the date of purchase and the owner;

(2) share documents showing the value of the shares, the date of purchase and the owner,

(3) the latest audited annual accounts of the organisation in which the investment has been made, clearly showing the amount of money held in the investments, the name of the applicant (or applicant and/or husband, wife, civil partner, or unmarried or same-sex partner), and the date of investment, or, if no accounts have been produced, a certificate from an accountant showing the amount of money held in the investments, and

(4) original trust fund documents from a legal adviser showing the amount of money in the fund, the date that the money is available and the beneficial owner, and including the name and contact details of the legal adviser and at least one of the trustees;

(iii) Original personal bank statements on the official bank stationery from a bank that is regulated by the official regulatory body for the country in which the institution operates and the funds are located, showing the amount of money available in the name of the applicant (or applicant and/or husband, wife, civil partner, or unmarried or same-sex partner), covering the three full consecutive months before the date of application. The most recent statement must be no more than one calendar month old at the date of application. Electronic bank statements from an online account must be accompanied by a supporting letter from the bank on the institution's official headed paper, issued by an authorising official of that institution, confirming the content and that the document is genuine;

(iv) If the applicant cannot provide bank statements, an original letter from a bank that is regulated by the official regulatory body for the country in which the institution operates and the funds are located, on the institution's official headed paper, issued by an authorised official of that institution, stating that the account has held the required amount of money on the day the letter was produced and for the three full consecutive months immediately before the date of the letter. The letter must be dated no more than one calendar month before the date of application. The letter must confirm:

(1) the name of the applicant (or applicant and/or husband, wife, civil partner, or unmarried or same-sex partner), and that the money is available in their name(s),

(2) that the bank is regulated by the official regulatory body for the country in which the institution operates and the funds are located,

(3) the dates of the period covered, including both the day the letter was produced and three full consecutive months immediately before the date of the letter, and

(4) the balance of the account to cover the amount claimed as a credit balance on the date of the letter and the three full consecutive months before the date of the letter;

(v) If the funds are not held in the UK, the applicant must provide an original letter from a bank or financial institution that is regulated by the official regulatory body for the country in which the institution operates and the funds are located, on the institution's official headed paper, issued by an authorised official of that institution, which confirms:

(1) the name of the beneficial owner, which should be the applicant (or applicant and/or husband, wife, civil partner, or unmarried or same-sex partner),

(2) the date of the letter,

(3) the amount of money to be transferred,

(4) that the money can be transferred to the UK if the application is successful, and

(5) that the institution will confirm the content of the letter to the UK Border Agency on request.

(b) If the applicant is claiming points from (b) in the first row of Table 7, he must provide an original letter of confirmation produced by a UK regulated financial institution, on the official letter-headed paper of the institution, issued by an authorised official of that institution, which confirms:

(1) that not less than £1 million are available for the applicant to borrow,

(2) that the money is available on the date that the letter is issued,

(3) that the institution is a UK regulated financial institution,

(4) that the applicant's personal net worth is at least £2 million, and

(5) that the institution will confirm the content of the letter to the UK Border Agency on request.

(c) If specified documents are provided from accountants, the accountant must:

(i) if based in the UK, be a member of the Institute of Chartered Accountants in England and Wales, the Institute of Chartered Accountants in Scotland, the Institute of Chartered Accountants in Ireland, the Association of Chartered Certified Accountants, or the Association of Authorised Public Accountants, or

(ii) if not based in the UK, be a member of an equivalent, appropriate supervisory or regulatory body in the country in which they operate.

Note: Paragraph 64-SD inserted from 20 July 2012 (Cm 8423).

64A-SD. Where paragraph 64(b) states that specified documents are required as evidence that the money or assets are under the applicant's control and that he is free to invest them, the applicant must provide all the specified documents from the following list, with contact details that enable verification:

(a) Original documents in the form of:

(i) Money given to the applicant (or applicant and/or husband, wife, civil partner, or unmarried or same-sex partner) within the three months immediately before the application must be shown in an irrevocable memorandum of gift, which clearly shows:

(1) the name and signature of the person receiving the gift,

(2) the name and signature of the person giving the gift,

(3) the date of the memorandum,

(4) the amount of money being given,

(5) a statement that the legal ownership of the gift is transferred and that the document is the memorandum of transfer,

(6) a clear description of the gift, and

(7) a statement that the gift is irrevocable;

(ii) If a memorandum of gift in (i) is provided, it must be accompanied by an original confirmation letter from a legal adviser permitted to practise in the country where the gift was made, which clearly shows:

(1) the name of the legal adviser who is confirming the details,

(2) the registration or authority of the legal adviser to practise legally in the country in which the gift was made,

(3) the date of the confirmation of the memorandum,

(4) the names of the person giving the gift and the person receiving it,

(5) the amount of money given,

(6) the date that the money was transferred to the applicant, or to the husband, wife, civil partner, or unmarried partner or same-sex partner of the applicant,

(7) that the memorandum is signed and valid,

(8) that the gift is irrevocable, and

(9) that the memorandum is binding according to the laws of the country in which it was made;

(iii) Deeds of sale of assets such as business or property, if the applicant has generated these funds within the three months immediately before the date of application, which meet the relevant legal requirements of the country of sale and clearly show:

(1) the name of the applicant (or applicant and/or husband, wife, civil partner, or unmarried or same-sex partner),

(2) the amount of money raised, and

(3) the date of the sale;

(iv) If a deed of sale in (iii) is provided, it must be accompanied by an original confirmation letter from a legal adviser permitted to practise in the country where the sale was made, which clearly shows:

(1) the name of the legal adviser confirming the details,

(2) the registration or authority of the legal adviser to practise legally in the country in which the sale was made,

(3) the date of the sale,

(4) the date of production of the letter confirming the sale,

(5) the details of what was sold and the amount of money received from the sale,

(6) the name of the person receiving the money from the sale,

(7) the date that the money was transferred, and

(8) that the sale was valid according to the laws of the country in which it was made;

(v) If the funds are currently held in the applicant's business (or the business of the applicant and/or the applicant's husband, wife, civil partner, or unmarried or same-sex partner), the applicant must provide business accounts, which:

(1) are profit and loss accounts (or income and expenditure accounts if the organisation is not trading for profit),

(2) are prepared and signed off in accordance with statutory requirements, and

(3) clearly show the amount of money available for investment;

(vi) If business accounts in (v) are provided, they must be accompanied by an original letter from a legal adviser who is permitted to practise in the country where business was operating, confirming that the applicant (or applicant and/or husband, wife, civil partner, or unmarried or same-sex partner) can lawfully extract the money from the business, which clearly shows:

(1) the name of the legal adviser who is confirming the details,

(2) the registration or authority of the legal adviser to practise legally in the country in which the business is operating,

(3) the date on which the details are confirmed, and

(4) that the applicant (or applicant and/or husband, wife, civil partner, or unmarried or same-sex partner) can lawfully extract the money from the business in question;

(vii) If the applicant (or applicant and/or husband, wife, civil partner, or unmarried or same sex partner) has been the beneficiary of a will within the three months before making the application, and has received money as a result, the applicant must provide a notarised copy of the will. If the applicant (or applicant and/or husband, wife, civil partner, or unmarried or same-sex partner) has received possessions or assets, rather than money, then the applicant (or applicant and/or husband, wife, civil partner, or unmarried or same-sex partner) may not use estimates of the value of the items as evidence of funds for investment. The notarised copy of the will must clearly show:

(1) the date of the will,

(2) the beneficiary of the will (this should be the applicant or applicant and/or husband, wife, civil partner, or unmarried or same-sex partner),

(3) the amount of money that the applicant (or applicant and/or husband, wife, civil partner, or unmarried or same-sex partner) has inherited, and

(4) the names of any executors, plus any codicils (additions) to the will that affect the amount of money that was received;

(viii) If a notarised copy of a will in (vii) is provided, it must be accompanied by an original confirmation letter from a legal adviser who is permitted to practise in the country where will was made, confirming the validity of the will, which clearly shows:

(1) the name of the legal adviser confirming the details,

(2) the registration or authority of the legal adviser to practise legally in the country in which the will was made,

(3) the date of the document produced by the legal adviser confirming the will,

(4) the date that the applicant received the money as a result of the settlement of the will,

(5) the names of the person making the will and the beneficiary,

(6) confirmation of the amount of money received by the applicant (or applicant and/or husband, wife, civil partner, or unmarried or same-sex partner).

(7) that the will is signed and valid, and

(8) that the will is valid according to the laws of the country in which it was made;

(ix) If the applicant (or applicant and/or husband, wife, civil partner, or unmarried or same sex partner) has obtained money as a result of a divorce settlement within the three months immediately before the date of application, the applicant must provide a notarised copy of a financial agreement following a divorce. If the applicant (or applicant and/or husband, wife, civil partner, or unmarried or same- sex partner) has received possessions or assets, rather than money, estimates of the value of the items will not be accepted as evidence of money for investment.

(x) If a divorce settlement in (ix) is provided, it must be accompanied by an original confirmation letter from a legal adviser who is permitted to practise in the country where the divorce took place, which clearly shows:

(1) the name of the legal adviser confirming the details,

(2) the registration or authority of the legal adviser to practise legally in the country in which the divorce took place,

(3) the date of the document produced by the legal adviser confirming the divorce settlement,

(4) the date that the applicant received the money as a result of the settlement,

(5) the names of the persons who are divorced,

(6) confirmation of the amount of money received by the applicant (or applicant and/or husband, wife, civil partner, or unmarried or same-sex partner,

(7) that the divorce settlement is complete and valid, and

(8) that the divorce settlement is valid according to the laws of the country in which it was made;

(xi) If the applicant is relying on a financial award or winnings as a source of funds, he must provide an original letter from the organisation issuing the financial award or winnings, which clearly shows:

(1) the name of the applicant (or applicant and/or husband, wife, civil partner, or unmarried or same-sex partner),

(2) the date of the award,

(3) the amount of money won,

(4) the winnings are genuine, and

(5) the contact details for the organisation issuing the award or winnings;

(xii) If a letter showing a financial award or winnings in (xi) is provided, it must be accompanied by an original confirmation letter from a legal adviser who is permitted to practise in the country where the award was made, which clearly shows:

(1) the name of the legal adviser confirming the details,

(2) the registration or authority of the legal adviser to practise legally in the country in which the award was made,

(3) the date of the letter of confirmation,

(4) the date of the award,

(5) the name of the recipient of the award,

(6) the amount of the winnings,

(7) the source of the winnings, and

(8) the date that the money was transferred to the applicant, or husband, wife, civil partner, or unmarried or same-sex partner;

(xiii) If the applicant (or applicant and/or husband, wife, civil partner, or unmarried or same-sex partner) has received money from a source not listed above, the applicant must provide relevant original documentation as evidence of the source of the money, together with independent supporting evidence, which both clearly confirm:

(1) the amount of money received,

(2) the date that the money was received,

(3) the source of the money, and

(4) that the applicant (or applicant and/or husband, wife, civil partner, or unmarried or same-sex partner) was the legal recipient of the money.]

Note: Paragraph 64A-SD inserted from 20 July 2012 (Cm 8423).

65. Investment excludes investment by the applicant by way of:

(a) an offshore company or trust,

(b) open-ended investment companies, investment trust companies or pooled investment vehicles,

(c) companies mainly engaged in property investment, property management or property development,

(d) deposits with a bank, building society or other enterprise whose normal course of business includes the acceptance of deposits,

(e) ISAs, premium bonds and saving certificates issued by the National Savings and Investment Agency (NS&I), for an applicant who has, or last had leave as a Tier 1 (Investor) Migrant, or

(f) leveraged investment funds.]

Note: Paragraphs 1–65 and Tables 1–9 substituted from 6 April 2011 (HC 863). A new para 65 has been inserted from 20 July 2012 (see below) but the original para 65 has not been deleted.

[65-SD. The following specified documents must be provided as evidence of investment:

(a) The applicant must provide a portfolio of investments certified as correct by a UK regulated financial institution, which must:

(i) Cover the required period, beginning no later than the end of the 3 month timescale specified in the third row of Table 8;

(ii) Continue to the last reporting date of the most recent billing period of the year directly before the date of the application;

(iii) Include the value of the investments;

(iv) Show that any shortfall in investments below the specified investment amount was made up by the next reporting period;

(v) Show the dates that the investments were made;

(vi) Show the destination of the investments;

(vii) Include, for investments made as loan funds to companies, audited accounts or unaudited accounts with an accountant's certificate for the investments made, giving the full details of the applicant's investment. The accountant must be a member of the Institute of Chartered Accountants in England and Wales, the Institute of Chartered Accountants in Scotland, the Institute of Chartered Accountants in Ireland, the Association of Chartered Certified Accountants, or the Association of Authorised Public Accountants;

(viii) Show the name and contact details of the financial institution that has certified the portfolio as correct, and confirmation that this institution is regulated by the Financial Services Authority;

(ix) Show that the investments were made in the applicant's name and/or that of his spouse, civil partner, unmarried or same-sex partner and not in the name of an offshore company or trust even if this is wholly owned by the applicant;

(x) include the date that the portfolio was certified by the financial institution; and

(xi) state that the institution will confirm the content of the letter to the UK Border Agency on request.

(b) Where the applicant previously had leave as an Investor and is unable to provide the evidence listed above because he manages his own investments, or has a portfolio manager who does not operate in the UK and is therefore not regulated by the Financial Services Authority, the applicant must provide the following specified documents showing his holdings used to claim points, as relevant to the type of investment:

(i) Certified copies of bond documents showing the value of the bonds, the date of purchase and the owner;

(ii) Share documents showing the value of the shares, the date of purchase and the owner;

(iii) The latest audited annual accounts of the organisation in which the investment has been made, which clearly show:

(1) the amount of money held in the investments,

(2) the name of the applicant (or applicant and/or husband, wife, civil partner, or unmarried or same-sex partner), and

(3) the date of investment.

(iv) If the organisation in (iii) is not required to produce accounts, the applicant must provide a certificate showing the amount of money held in the investments, from an accountant who is a member of the Institute of Chartered Accountants in England and Wales, the Institute of Chartered Accountants in Scotland, the Institute of Chartered Accountants in Ireland, the Association of Chartered Certified Accountants, or the Association of Authorised Public Accountants.

(c) Where the applicant has invested at least 75% of the specified investment amount but less than 100%, he must provide one or more of the following specified documents as evidence of the balance of the funds required to bring his total investment in the UK up to the specified investment amount:

(i) Documents confirming the purchase of assets in the UK, showing the assets purchased, the value of these assets and the dates of purchase. When using property only the unmortgaged portion of the applicant's own home can be considered and the valuation must be provided on a report issued by a surveyor (who is a member of the Royal Institution of Chartered Surveyors) in the six months prior to the date of application;

(ii) If the applicant maintained money on deposit in the UK, a statement or statements of account on the official stationery of the institution that holds the funds. These statements must be in the name of the applicant (or applicant and/or the husband, wife, civil partner, or unmarried or same-sex partner of the applicant) and confirm the dates and amount of money held. The applicant must ensure that the institution will confirm the content of the statement to the UK Border Agency on request;

(iii) An original letter from the financial institution that holds the cash on deposit, on the institution's official headed paper, issued by an authorised official of that institution, which confirms the dates and amount of money held and that the institution will confirm the content of the letter to the UK Border Agency on request.

(d) If the applicant wishes the start of the 3 month timescale specified in the third row of Table 8 to be taken as the date he entered the UK, he must provide evidence which proves this date, such as a stamp in the applicant's passport, or an aircraft boarding card.

(e) Evidence of the investment having been maintained, from the date that the funds were invested for the full period of remaining leave, will be determined using the portfolio provided in (a).]

Note: This para inserted from 20 July 2012 (Cm 8423) and renumbered as para 65-SD from 6 September 2012 (HC 565).

[Attributes for Tier 1 (Graduate Entrepreneur) Migrants

66. An applicant applying for leave to remain as a Tier 1 (Graduate Entrepreneur) Migrant must score 75 points for attributes.

67. Available points are shown in Table 10.

68. Notes to accompany the table appear below the table.

Note: Paragraphs 66–72 and Table 10 substituted from 6 April 2012, except for applications made but not decided before that date (HC 1888).

Table 10

Criterion	Points
The applicant has been endorsed by a UK Higher Education Institution which:	25
(a) has Highly Trusted Sponsor status under Tier 4 of the Points-Based System,	
(b) is an A-rated Sponsor under Tier 2 of the Points-Based System if a Tier 2 licence is held,	
(c) is an A-rated Sponsor under Tier 5 of the Points-Based System if a Tier 5 licence is held, and	
(d) has established processes and competence for identifying, nurturing and developing entrepreneurs among its undergraduate and postgraduate population.	
(a) If the applicant's previous grant of leave was not as a Tier 1 (Graduate Entrepreneur) Migrant, the endorsement confirms that, within the 12 months immediately before the date of the endorsement, the institution has awarded the applicant a UK recognised Bachelor degree, Masters degree or PhD (not a qualification of equivalent level which is not a degree), or	25
(b) If the applicant's previous grant of leave was as a Tier 1 (Graduate Entrepreneur) Migrant, the endorsement is from the same institution which provided the endorsement for that previous grant of leave.	
The endorsement must confirm that the institution has assessed the applicant and considers that	25
(a) the applicant has a genuine, credible and innovative business idea, and	
(b) the applicant will spend the majority of his working time on developing business ventures, and	
(c) if the applicant's previous grant of leave was as a Tier 1 (Graduate Entrepreneur), he has made satisfactory progress in developing his business since that leave was granted and will, on the balance of probabilities, qualify for leave to remain as a Tier 1 (Entrepreneur) Migrant within the next 12 months.	

Note: Paragraphs 66–72 and Table 10 substituted from 6 April 2012, except for applications made but not decided before that date (HC 1888).

Notes

Tier 1 (Graduate Entrepreneur) Limit

69. (a) The Secretary of State shall be entitled to limit the total number of Tier 1 (Graduate Entrepreneur) endorsements qualifying Higher Education Institutions may make in support of successful applications in a particular period, to be referred to as the Tier 1 (Graduate Entrepreneur) Limit.

(b) The Tier 1 (Graduate Entrepreneur) Limit for each of the periods 6 April 2012 to 5 April 2013 and 6 April 2013 to 5 April 2014 is 1,000 endorsements, which will be allocated to qualifying Higher Education Institutions as follows:

(i) The UK Border Agency will invite all UK Higher Education Institutions which meet the requirements in (a) to (c) in the first row of Table 10 above to take part as endorsing institutions, with responses required by 4 May 2012 for the period 6 April 2012 to 5 April 2013, and by 5 April 2013 for the period 6 April 2013 to 5 April 2014;

(ii) Subject to the limit, the endorsements will be divided equally between all invited institutions who confirm that:

(1) they wish to take part, and

(2) they meet the requirement in (c) in the first row of Table 10 above, up to a maximum of 10 endorsements per institution;

(iii) Where the resulting allocation for each institution is not an integer, the allocations will be rounded down to the next lowest integer;

(iv) If the result of (ii) or (iii) above is that the total number of allocated endorsements is less than 1,000, the remaining places in the Tier 1 (Graduate Entrepreneur) Limit will not be allocated.

(c) If:

(i) an applicant does not make a valid application within 3 months of the date of his endorsement, or

(ii) an application is refused, and that refusal is not subsequently overturned, the endorsement used in that application will be cancelled and the relevant institution's unused allocation of endorsements will be increased by one.

(d) The Tier 1 (Graduate Entrepreneur) limit will not apply to applications for leave to remain where the applicant has, or last had, leave to remain as a Tier 1 (Graduate Entrepreneur).

Note: Paragraphs 66–72 and Table 10 substituted from 6 April 2012, except for applications made but not decided before that date (HC 1888).

Endorsement

70. Points will only be awarded for an endorsement if:

(a) the endorsement was issued to the applicant no more than 3 months before the date of application,

(b) the endorsement has not been withdrawn by the relevant Higher Education Institution at the time the application is considered by the UK Border Agency, and

[(c) the applicant provides an original endorsement from the relevant UK Higher Education Institution, which shows:

(i) the endorsement reference number,

(ii) the date of issue (including a statement on how long the letter is valid for),

    (iii) the applicant's name,

    (iv) the applicant's date of birth,

    (v) the applicant's nationality,

    (vi) the applicant's current passport number,

    (vii) details of any dependants of the applicant who are already in the UK or who the applicant intends to bring to the UK,

    (viii) the name of the endorsing UK Higher Education Institution,

    (ix) the name and contact details of the authorising official of the endorsing UK Higher Education Institution,

    (x) the name, level and date of award of the applicant's qualification, unless the applicant was last granted leave as a Tier 1 (Graduate Entrepreneur) Migrant,

    (xi) the applicant's intended business sector or business intention, (xii)what has led the UK Higher Education Institution to endorse the application, and

    (xiii) if the applicant was last granted leave as a Tier 1 (Graduate Entrepreneur) Migrant, confirmation that the UK Higher Education Institution is satisfied that he has made satisfactory progress and on the balance of probabilities will qualify for a Tier 1 (Entrepreneur) visa within the next 12 months.]

Note: Paragraphs 66–72 and Table 10 substituted from 6 April 2012, except for applications made but not decided before that date (HC 1888). Sub-paragraph (c) substituted from 20 July 2012 (Cm 8423).

[Qualifications

71. Points will only be awarded for a qualification awarded by the endorsing Higher Education Institution if the endorsement in paragraph 70(c) contains the specified details of the qualification, as set out in paragraph 70(c)]

Note: Paragraph 71 substituted from 20 July 2012 (Cm 8423).

[Attributes for Tier 2 (Intra-Company Transfer) Migrants

73. An applicant applying for entry or leave to remain as a Tier 2 (Intra-Company Transfer) Migrant must score 50 points for attributes.

73A. Available points for entry clearance or leave to remain are shown in Table 11.

73B. Notes to accompany Table 11 appear below the table.

Table 11

Criterion	Points
Certificate of Sponsorship	30
Appropriate salary	20

Notes

Certificate of Sponsorship

74. In order to obtain points for a Certificate of Sponsorship, the applicant must provide a valid Certificate of Sponsorship reference number.

74A. A Certificate of Sponsorship reference number will only be considered to be valid if:

(a) the number supplied links to a Certificate of Sponsorship Checking Service entry that names the applicant as the migrant and confirms that the Sponsor is sponsoring him as a Tier 2 (Intra-Company Transfer) Migrant and specifies the sub-category of Tier 2 (Intra-Company Transfer) under which he is applying,

(b) the Sponsor assigned the Certificate of Sponsorship reference number to the migrant no more than 3 months before the application for entry clearance or leave to remain is made,

(c) the application for entry clearance or leave to remain is made no more than 3 months before the start of the employment as stated on the Certificate of Sponsorship,

(d) the migrant must not previously have applied for entry clearance, leave to enter or leave to remain using the same Certificate of Sponsorship reference number, if that application was either approved or refused (not rejected as an invalid application[, declared void] or withdrawn),

(e) that reference number must not have been withdrawn or cancelled by the Sponsor or by the UK Border Agency since it was assigned, including where it has been cancelled by the UK Border Agency due to having been used in a previous application [, and

(f) the sponsor is an A-rated Sponsor, unless the application is for leave to remain and the applicant has, or was last granted, leave as a Tier 2 (Intra-Company) Migrant or a Qualifying Work Permit Holder.]

> **Note:** Sub-paragraph (f) inserted from 21 April 2011 with savings for applications made before that date (HC 908). Words in square brackets in sub-para (d) inserted from 6 April 2012 with savings for applications made before that date (HC 1888).

[74B. No points will be awarded for a Certificate of Sponsorship unless:

(a) the job that the Certificate of Sponsorship Checking Service entry records that the person is being sponsored to do appears on:

(i) the list of occupations skilled to National Qualifications Framework level 6 or above, as stated in [the Codes of Practice in Appendix J], or

[(ii) one of the following creative sector occupations skilled to National Qualifications Framework level 4 or above:

(1) 3411 Artists,

(2) 3412 Authors, writers,

(3) 3413 Actors, entertainers,

(4) 3414 Dancers and choreographers, or

(5) 3422 Designers, product, clothing-related,

or

(b) (i) the applicant is applying for leave to remain,

(ii) the applicant previously had leave as a Tier 2 (Intra-Company Transfer) Migrant under the Rules in place between 6 April 2011 and 5 April 2012, and has not since been granted leave to remain in any other route, or entry clearance or leave to enter in any route, and

(iii) the job that the Certificate of Sponsorship Checking Service entry records that the person is being sponsored to do appears on the list of occupations skilled to National Qualifications Framework level 4 or above, as stated in [the Codes of Practice in Appendix J],

or

(c) (i) the applicant is applying for leave to remain as a Tier 2 (Intra-Company Transfer) Migrant in the Long Term Staff sub-category,

(ii) the applicant previously had leave as:

(1) a Tier 2 (Intra-Company Transfer) Migrant under the rules in place before 6 April 2011, or

(2) a Qualifying Work Permit Holder,

and has not since been granted leave to remain in any other route, or entry clearance or leave to enter in any route, and

(iii) the job that the Certificate of Sponsorship Checking Service entry records that the person is being sponsored to do appears on the list of occupations skilled to National Qualifications Framework level 3 or above, as stated in [the Codes of Practice in Appendix J], or the applicant is a Senior Care Worker or an Established Entertainer as defined in paragraph 6 of these Rules.]

Note: Paragraph 74B substituted from 14 June 2012 except for applications made but not decided before that date (Cm 8337). Words in square brackets substituted from 20 July 2012 (Cm 8423).

74C. (a) If the applicant is applying as a Tier 2 (Intra-Company Transfer) Migrant in either the Short Term Staff or Long Term Staff sub-categories, no points will be awarded for a Certificate of Sponsorship unless:

(i) the applicant has been working for the Sponsor for the specified period in paragraph (b) below,

(ii) the applicant has been working for the Sponsor outside the UK and/or in the UK, provided he had leave to work for the Sponsor as:

(1) a Tier 2 (Intra-Company Transfer) Migrant in either of the Short Term Staff or Long Term Staff sub-categories,

(2) a Tier 2 (Intra-Company Transfer) Migrant in the Established Staff sub-category under the Rules in place before 6 April 2011,

(3) a Tier 2 (Intra-Company Transfer) Migrant under the Rules in place before 6 April 2010,

(4) a Qualifying Work Permit Holder (provided that the work permit was granted because the holder was the subject of an intra-company transfer), and/or

(5) as a Representative of an Overseas Business, and

[(iii) the applicant provides the specified documents as set out in paragraph 74C-SD(a) below, unless he was last granted leave in the same sub-category as he is currently applying under.]

(b) The specified period referred to in paragraph (a)(i) above is:

(i) a continuous period of 12 months immediately prior to the date of application, or

(ii) if at some point within the 12 months preceding the date of application, the applicant has been:

(1) on maternity, paternity or adoption leave,

(2) on long-term sick leave lasting one month or longer, or

(3) working for the sponsor in the UK as a Tier 2 (Intra-Company Transfer) Migrant in either of the Graduate Trainee or skills Transfer sub-categories,

[and provides the specified documents as set out in paragraph 74C-SD(c) below] an aggregated period of at least 12 months within the 24 month period immediately prior to the date of application.

Note: Words in square brackets inserted from 20 July 2012 (Cm 8423).

[74C-SD. (a) The specified documents in paragraph 74C(a) are:

(i) Formal payslips on company-headed paper covering the full specified period (The most recent payslip must be dated no earlier than 31 days before the date of the application);

(ii) Payslips that are on un-headed paper or are printouts of online payslips covering the full specified period (The most recent payslip must be dated no earlier than 31 days before the date of the application), accompanied by a letter from the Sponsor, on company headed paper and signed by a senior official, confirming the authenticity of the payslips;

(iii) Personal bank or building society statements covering the full specified period, which clearly show:

(1) the applicant's name,

(2) the account number,

(3) the date of the statement (The most recent statement must be dated no earlier than 31 days before the date of the application),

(4) the financial institution's name and logo, and

(5) transactions by the Sponsor covering the full specified period;

(iv) A building society pass book, which clearly shows:

(1) the applicant's name,

(2) the account number,

(3) the financial institution's name and logo, and

(4) transactions by the Sponsor covering the full specified period.

(b) If the applicant provides the bank or building society statements in (a)(iii):

(i) The statements must:

(1) be printed on paper bearing the bank or building society's letterhead,

(2) bear the official stamp of the bank on every page, or

(3) be accompanied by a supporting letter from the issuing bank or building society, on company headed paper, confirming the authenticity of the statements provided;

(ii) The statements must not be mini-statements obtained from an Automated Teller Machine.

(c) The specified documents as evidence of periods of maternity, paternity or adoption leave, as required in paragraph 74C(b), are:

(i) The original full birth certificate or original full certificate of adoption (as appropriate) containing the names of the parents or adoptive parents of the child for whom the leave was taken, if this is available; and

(ii) At least one (or both, if the document in (i) is unavailable) of the following, if they are available:

(1) An original letter from the applicant and his sponsor, on company headed paper, confirming the start and end dates of the applicant's leave,

(2) One of the types of documents set out in (a) above, covering the entire period of leave, and showing the maternity, paternity or adoption payments.

and

(iii) If the applicant cannot provide two of the types of specified document in (i) and (ii), at least one of the types of specified documents in either (i) or (ii), a full explanation of why the other documents cannot be provided, and at least one of the following specified documents, from an official source and which is independently verifiable:

    (1) official adoption papers issued by the relevant authority,

    (2) any relevant medical documents, or

    (3) a relevant extract from a register of birth which is accompanied by an original letter from the issuing authority.

(d) The specified documents as evidence of periods of long term sick leave, as required in paragraph 74C(b), are:

    (i) An original letter from the applicant's Sponsor, on company headed paper, confirming the start and end dates of the applicant's leave, if this is available;

    (ii) One of the types of documents set out in (a) above, covering the entire period of leave, and showing the statutory sick pay and/or sick pay from health insurance, if these documents are available; and

    (iii) If the applicant cannot provide the specified documents in both (i) and (ii), the specified documents in either (i) or (ii), a full explanation of why the other documents cannot be provided, and any relevant medical documents, from an official source and which are independently verifiable.]

Note: Paragraph74C-SD(a) inserted from 20 July 2012 (Cm 8423).

74D. If the applicant is applying as a Tier 2 (Intra-Company Transfer) Migrant in the Graduate Trainee sub-category, no points will be awarded for a Certificate of Sponsorship unless:

(a) the job that the Certificate of Sponsorship Checking Service entry records that the person is being sponsored to do is part of a structured graduate training programme [with clearly defined progression towards a managerial or specialist role within the organisation,]

(b) The Sponsor has assigned Certificates of Sponsorship to 5 applicants or fewer, including the applicant in question, under the Graduate Trainee sub-category in the current year, [beginning 6 April and ending 5 April each year], and

(c) the applicant has been working for the Sponsor outside the UK for a continuous period of 3 months immediately prior to the date of application, and must provide the specified documents [in paragraph 74C-SD(a) above] to prove this,

Note: Words in square brackets in (b) substituted from 6 April 2012 except for applications made but not decided before that date (Cm 8337). Words in square brackets in (a) substituted and (c) inserted from 20 July 2012 (Cm 8423).

74E. If the applicant is applying as a Tier 2 (Intra-Company Transfer) Migrant in the Skills Transfer subcategory, no points will be awarded for a Certificate of Sponsorship unless the job that the Certificate of Sponsorship Checking Service entry records that the person is being sponsored to do is for the sole purpose of transferring skills to or from the Sponsor's UK work environment. The appointment must be additional to staffing requirements, that is the role in the UK would not exist but for the need for skills transfer.

74F. An applicant cannot score points for a Certificate of Sponsorship from Table 11 if the job that the Certificate of sponsorship Checking service entry records that he is being sponsored to do is as a Sports person or a Minister of Religion.

Appropriate salary

75. The points awarded for appropriate salary will be based on the applicant's gross annual salary to be paid by the Sponsor, as recorded in the Certificate of Sponsorship Checking service entry to which the applicant's Certificate of Sponsorship reference number relates, subject to the following conditions:

(i) Points will be awarded based on basic pay (excluding overtime);

(ii) Allowances will be included in the salary for the awarding of points where they are part of the guaranteed salary package and:

(1) would be paid to a local settled worker in similar circumstances, or

(2) are paid to cover the additional cost of living in the UK;

(iii) Where allowances are made available solely for the purpose of accommodation, they will only be included up to a value of:

(1) 40% of the total salary package for which points are being awarded, if the applicant is applying in either the Short Term Staff, Graduate Trainee or Skills Transfer sub-categories, or

(2) 30% of the total salary package for which points are being awarded, if the applicant is applying in the Long Term Staff sub-category;

(iv) Allowances to cover business expenses, including (but not limited to) travel to and from the sending country, will not be included.

75A. No points will be awarded if the salary referred to in paragraph 75 above is less than £40,000 per year where the applicant is applying in the Long Term Staff sub-category, unless the applicant is applying for leave to remain and has, or last had entry clearance, leave to enter or leave to remain as:

(i) a Qualifying Work Permit Holder, or

(ii) a Tier 2 (Intra-Company Transfer) Migrant under the rules in place before 6 April 2011.

75B. No points will be awarded if the salary referred to in paragraph 75 above is less than £24,000 per year where the applicant is applying in the Short Term Staff, Graduate Trainee or Skills Transfer sub-categories, unless the applicant is applying for leave to remain and has, or last had entry clearance, leave to enter or leave to remain as a Tier 2 (Intra-Company Transfer) Migrant under the Rules in place before 6 April 2011.

75C. No points will be awarded if the salary referred to in paragraph 75 above is less than the appropriate rate for the job as stated in [the Codes of Practice in Appendix J], unless the applicant is an Established Entertainer as defined in paragraph 6 of these Rules.

Note : Words in square brackets substituted from 20 July 2012 (Cm 8423)

75D. Where the applicant is paid hourly, the appropriate salary consideration will be based on earnings up to a maximum of 48 hours a week, even if the applicant works for longer than this. for example, an applicant who works 60 hours a week for £8 per hour be considered to have a salary of £19,968 (8x48x52) and not £25,960 (8x60x52), and will therefore not be awarded points for appropriate salary.

75E. No points will be awarded for appropriate salary if the applicant does not provide a valid Certificate of Sponsorship reference number with his application.

Attributes for Tier 2 (General) Migrants

76. An applicant applying for entry or leave to remain as a Tier 2 (General) Migrant must score 50 points for attributes.

76A. Available points for entry clearance or leave to remain are shown in Table 11a.

76B. Notes to accompany Table 11a appear below the table.

Table 11A

Certificate of Sponsorship	Points	Appropriate salary	Points
Shortage occupation	30	Appropriate salary	20
Job offer with a salary of £150,000 or more	30		
Job offer passes Resident Labour Market Test [or an exemption applies]	30		
Post-Study Work	30		
Continuing to work in the same job for the same Sponsor	30		

Note: Words in square brackets inserted from 6 April 2011 with savings for applications made before that date (HC 1888).

Notes

Certificate of Sponsorship

77. Points may only be scored for one entry in the Certificate of Sponsorship column.

77A. In order to obtain points for a Certificate of Sponsorship, the applicant must provide a valid Certificate of Sponsorship reference number.

77B. The only Certificates of Sponsorship to be allocated to Sponsors for applicants to be sponsored as Tier 2 (General) Migrants during the period [6 April 2012 to 5 April 2014] are:

(a) Certificates of Sponsorship to be assigned to applicants [. . .] as a Tier 2 (General) Migrant, as allocated to Sponsors under the Tier 2 (General) limit, which is set out in paragraphs 80 to 84A below.

(b) Certificates of Sponsorship to be assigned to [specified applicants for leave to remain as a Tier 2 (General) Migrant, as set out in paragraph 77D of Appendix A,]

(c) Certificates of Sponsorship to be assigned to an applicant to do a job for which the gross annual salary (including such allowances as are specified as acceptable for this purpose in guidance issued by the UK Border Agency) is £150,000 or higher, and

Note: Words in square brackets substituted and words omitted from 6 April 2012 except for applications made but not decided before that date (Cm 8337).

77C. A Certificate of Sponsorship reference number will only be considered to be valid if:

(a) the number supplied links to a Certificate of Sponsorship Checking Service entry that names the applicant as the migrant and confirms that the Sponsor is sponsoring him as a Tier 2 (General) Migrant,

(b) the Sponsor assigned that reference number to the migrant no more than 3 months after the Sponsor was allocated the Certificate of Sponsorship, if the Certificate of Sponsorship was allocated to the Sponsor under the Tier 2 (General) limit,

(c) the Sponsor assigned that reference number to the migrant no more than 3 months before the application for entry clearance or leave to remain is made,

(d) the application for entry clearance or leave to remain is made no more than 3 months before the start of the employment as stated on the Certificate of Sponsorship,

[(e) The migrant must not previously have applied for entry clearance, leave to enter or leave to remain using the same Certificate of Sponsorship reference number, if that application was either approved or refused (not rejected as an invalid application, declared void or withdrawn),]

(f) that reference number must not have been withdrawn or cancelled by the Sponsor or by the UK Border Agency since it was assigned, including where it has been cancelled by the UK Border Agency due to having been used in a previous application[, and

(g) the Sponsor is an A-rated Sponsor, unless:

(1) the application is for leave to remain, and

(2) the applicant has, or was last granted, leave as a Tier 2 (General) Migrant, a Jewish Agency Employee, a Member of the Operational Ground Staff of an Overseas-owned Airline, a Representative of an Overseas Newspaper, News Agency or Broadcasting Organisation, or a Qualifying Work Permit Holder, and

(3) the applicant is applying to work for the same employer named on the Certificate of Sponsorship or Work Permit document which led to his last grant of leave or, in the case of an applicant whose last grant of leave was as a Jewish Agency Employee, a Member of the Operational Ground Staff of an Overseas-owned Airline, a Representative of an Overseas Newspaper, News Agency or Broadcasting Organisation, the same employer for whom the applicant was working or stated he was intending to work when last granted leave.]

Note: Sub-paragraph (e) substituted from 6 April 2012 with savings for applications made before that date (HC 1888).

77D. No points will be awarded for a Certificate of Sponsorship unless:

(a) in the case of a Certificate of Sponsorship which was allocated to the Sponsor under the Tier 2 (General) limit, the number supplied links to a Certificate of Sponsorship Checking Service entry which contains the same job and at least the same salary details as stated in the Sponsor's application for that Certificate of Sponsorship,

(b) in the case of a Certificate of Sponsorship which was not allocated to the Sponsor under the Tier 2 (General) limit:

[(i) the applicant is applying for leave to remain unless the applicant has, or was last granted entry clearance, leave to enter or leave to remain as the partner of a Relevant Points Based System Migrant, or]

(ii) the number supplied links to a Certificate of Sponsorship Checking Service entry which shows that the applicant's gross annual salary (including such allowances as are specified as acceptable for this purpose in paragraph 79 of this appendix) to be paid by the Sponsor is £150,000 or higher.

Note: Sub-paragraph 77D(b)(i) substituted from 6 April 2012 except for applications made but not decided before that date (Cm 8337).

[77E. No points will be awarded for a Certificate of Sponsorship unless:

(a) the job that the Certificate of Sponsorship Checking Service entry records that the person is being sponsored to do appears on:

(i) the list of occupations skilled to National Qualifications Framework level 6 or above, as stated in [the Codes of Practice in Appendix J], or

[(ii) one of the following creative sector occupations skilled to National Qualifications Framework level 4 or above:

(1) 3411 Artists,

(2) 3412 Authors, writers,

(3) 3413 Actors, entertainers,

(4) 3414 Dancers and choreographers, or

(5) 3422 Designers, product, clothing-related,

or]

(b) the job that the Certificate of Sponsorship Checking Service entry records that the person is being sponsored to do is skilled to National Qualifications Framework level 4 or above, and appears on [the Shortage Occupation List in Appendix K,] or

(c)(i) the applicant is applying for leave to remain,

(ii) the applicant previously had leave as a Tier 2 (General) Migrant or a Qualifying Work Permit Holder, and has not since been granted leave to remain in any other route, or entry clearance or leave to enter in any route,

(iii) at the time a Certificate of Sponsorship or Work Permit which led to a grant of leave in (ii) was issued, the job referred to in that Certificate of Sponsorship or Work Permit appeared on [the Shortage Occupation List in Appendix K,]

and

(iv) the job that the Certificate of Sponsorship Checking service entry records that the person is being sponsored to do in his current application is the same as the job referred to in (iii), for either the same or a different employer, or

(d)(i) the applicant is applying for leave to remain,

(ii) the applicant previously had leave as a Tier 2 (General) Migrant under the Rules in place between 6 April 2011 and 5 April 2012, and has not since been granted leave to remain in any other route, or entry clearance or leave to enter in any route, and

(iii) the job that the Certificate of Sponsorship Checking Service entry records that the person is being sponsored to do appears on the list of occupations skilled to National Qualifications Framework level 4 or above, as stated in [the Codes of Practice in Appendix J], or

(e)(i) the applicant is applying for leave to remain,

(ii) the applicant previously had leave as:

(1) a Tier 2 (General) Migrant under the rules in place before 6 April 2011,

(2) a Qualifying Work Permit Holder,

(3) a Representative of an Overseas Newspaper, News Agency or Broadcasting Organisation,

(4) a Member of the Operational Ground Staff of an Overseas-owned Airline,

(5) a Jewish Agency Employee,

and has not since been granted leave to remain in any other route, or entry clearance or leave to enter in any route, and

(iii) the job that the Certificate of Sponsorship Checking Service entry records that the person is being sponsored to do appears on the list of occupations skilled to National Qualifications Framework level 3 or above, as stated in [the Codes of Practice in Appendix J], or the applicant is a Senior Care Worker or an Established Entertainer as defined in paragraph 6 of these Rules.]

Note: Paragraph 77E substituted from 14 June 2012 except for applications made but not decided before that date (Cm 8337). Words in square brackets substituted from 20 July 2012 (Cm 8423).

77F. An applicant cannot score points for a Certificate of Sponsorship from Table 11A if the job that the Certificate of Sponsorship Checking Service entry records that he is being sponsored to do is as a Sports person or a Minister of Religion.

Shortage occupation

78. In order for the applicant to be awarded points for a job offer in a shortage occupation:

(a) the job must, at the time the Certificate of Sponsorship was assigned to the applicant, have appeared on [the Shortage Occupation List in Appendix K,]

(b) in all cases, contracted working hours must be for at least 30 hours a week, and

(c) in all cases, if the UK Border Agency list of shortage occupations indicates that the job appears on the 'Scotland only' shortage occupation list, the job offer must be for employment in which the applicant will be working at a location in Scotland.

Note: Words in square brackets substituted from 20 July 2012 (Cm 8423).

Job offer with a salary of £150,000 or more

78A. In order for the applicant to be awarded points for a job offer with a salary of £150,000 or more, the Certificate of Sponsorship Checking Service entry must show that the applicant's gross annual salary (including such allowances as are specified as acceptable for this purpose in paragraph 79 of this Appendix) to be paid by the Sponsor is £150,000 or higher.

[Job offer passes Resident Labour Market Test or an exemption applies

78B. (a) In order for the applicant to be awarded points for a job offer that passes the resident labour market test... , the Certificate of Sponsorship Checking Service entry must:

(i) indicate that the Sponsor has met the requirements of that test, as set out in (c) below, in respect of the job, and

(ii) contain full details of when and where the job was advertised, and any advertisement reference numbers, including the Jobcentre Plus or JobCentre online vacancy reference number, if paragraph 2 of Appendix J specify that the job must have been advertised in Jobcentre Plus or JobCentre online.

(b) In order for the applicant to be awarded points for a job offer where an exemption from the resident labour market test applies:

(i) the appropriate salary, as determined by paragraphs 79 to 79D of this Appendix, must be at least £150,000 per year,

(ii) the job offer is to continue working as a Doctor or Dentist in training, under the same NHS Training Number which was assigned to the applicant for previous lawful employment as a Doctor or Dentist in Training in the UK, or

(iii) the job offer is as a Doctor in Speciality Training where the applicant's salary and the costs of his training are being met by the government of another country under an agreement with that country and the United Kingdom Government,

and the Certificate of Sponsorship Checking Service entry must provide full details of why an exemption applies.

(c) The requirements of the Resident Labour Market Test are:

(i) The Sponsor must have advertised the post in the specified media for the job, as set out in paragraph 2 of Appendix J.

(ii) If the job and the Resident Labour Market Test satisfy the milkround provisions set out in the Codes of Practice in Appendix J, the advertisements must have run for at least 28 days during the 48 month period immediately before the date the Sponsor assigned the Certificate of Sponsorship to the applicant.

(iii) If the job appears on the list of PhD-level occupation codes, as stated in the Codes of Practice in Appendix J, and (ii) does not apply, the advertisements must have run for at least 28 days during the 12 month period immediately before the date that the Sponsor assigned the Certificate of Sponsorship to the applicant.

(iv) If (ii) and (iii) do not apply, the advertisements must have run for at least 28 days during the 6 month period immediately before the date the Sponsor assigned the Certificate of Sponsorship to the applicant.

(v) The advertisements must have stated:

(1) the job title,

(2) the main duties and responsibilities of the job (job description),

(3) the location of the job,

(4) an indication of the salary package or salary range or terms on offer,

(5) the skills, qualifications and experience required for the job, and

(6) the closing date for applications, unless it is part of the Sponsor's rolling recruitment programme, in which case the advertisement should show the period of the recruitment programme.

(vi) The Sponsor must be able to show that no suitable settled worker is available to fill the job.

(vii) Settled workers will not be considered unsuitable on the basis that they lack qualifications, experience or skills (including language skills) that were not specifically requested in the job advertisement.]

Note: Paragraph 78B substituted from20 July 2012 (Cm 8423). Words deleted from sub-para (a) from 6 September 2012 (HC 565).

Post-Study Work

78C. In order for the applicant to be awarded points for post-study work:

(a) the applicant must be applying for leave to remain,

[(b) the applicant must:

(i) have current entry clearance, leave to enter or leave to remain which has not expired, as:

(1) a Tier 1 (Post-Study Work) Migrant,

(2) a Participant in the International Graduates Scheme (or its predecessor, the Science and Engineering Graduates Scheme),

(3) a Participant in the Fresh Talent: Working in Scotland Scheme, or

(ii) The applicant must meet the requirements of paragraphs 245HD(b)(ii) and 245HD(d) of these Rules.]

Note: Sub-paragraph (b) substituted from 6 April 2012 with savings for applications made before that date (HC 1888).

Continuing to work in the same job for the same Sponsor

78D. In order for the applicant to be awarded points for continuing to work in the same job for the same Sponsor:

(a) the applicant must be applying for leave to remain,

(b) the applicant must have entry clearance or leave to remain as:

(i) a Tier 2 (General) Migrant,

(ii) a Qualifying Work Permit Holder,

(iii) a Representative of an Overseas Newspaper, News Agency or Broadcasting Organisation,

(iv) a Member of the Operational Ground Staff of an Overseas-owned Airline or

(v) a Jewish Agency Employee,

[(c)] the Sponsor must be the same employer:

(i) as the Sponsor on the previous application that was granted, in the case of an applicant whose last grant of leave was as a Tier 2 (General) Migrant,

(ii) that the work permit was issued to, in the case of an applicant whose last grant of leave was as a Qualifying Work Permit Holder,

(iii) for whom the applicant was working or stated he was intending to work when last granted leave, in the case of an applicant whose last grant of leave was a Representative of an Overseas Newspaper, News Agency or Broadcasting Organisation, a Member of the Operational Ground Staff of an Overseas-owned Airline, or a Jewish Agency Employee.

[(d)] the job that the Certificate of Sponsorship Checking Service entry records the applicant as having been engaged to do must be the same job:

(i) in respect of which the Certificate of Sponsorship that led to the previous grant was issued, in the case of an applicant whose last grant of leave was as a Tier 2 (General) Migrant,

(ii) in respect of which the previous work permit was issued, in the case of an applicant whose last grant of leave was as a Qualifying Permit Holder, or

(iii) that the applicant was doing, or intended to do, when he received his last grant of leave, in the case of an applicant whose last grant of leave was a Representative of an Overseas Newspaper, News Agency or Broadcasting Organisation, a Member of the Operational Ground Staff of an Overseas- owned Airline, or a Jewish Agency Employee.

Note: Sub-paragraphs (c) and (d) renumbered from 6 April 2012 with savings for applications made before that date (HC 1888).

Appropriate salary

79. The points awarded for appropriate salary will be based on the applicant's gross annual salary to be paid by the Sponsor,... subject to the following conditions:

(i) Points will be awarded based on basic pay (excluding overtime);

(ii) Allowances, such as London weighting, will be included in the salary for the awarding of points where they are part of the guaranteed salary package and would be paid to a local settled worker in similar circumstances;

(iii) Other allowances and benefits, such as bonus or incentive pay, travel and subsistence (including travel to and from the applicant's home country), will not be included.

Note: Words in the opening sentence deleted from 5 September 2012 (HC 565). NB: the said deletion is based on para 105 of HC 565 which refers to para 79E which does not exist; it appears the intention is to refer to para 79..

79A. No points will be awarded if the salary referred to in paragraph 79 above is less than £20,000 per year, unless the applicant is applying for leave to remain and has, or last had entry clearance, leave to enter or leave to remain as:

(i) a Qualifying Work Permit Holder,

(ii) a Representative of an Overseas Newspaper, News Agency or Broadcasting Organisation,

(iii) a Member of the Operational Ground Staff of an Overseas-owned Airline

(iv) a Jewish Agency Employee, or

(v) a Tier 2 (General) Migrant under the Rules in place before 6 April 2011.

79B. No points will be awarded for appropriate salary if the salary referred to in paragraph 79 above is less than the appropriate rate for the job as stated in [the Codes of Practice in Appendix J], unless the applicant is an Established Entertainer as defined in paragraph 6 of these rules.

Note: Words in square brackets substituted from 20 July 2012 (Cm 8423).

79C. Where the applicant is paid hourly, the appropriate salary consideration will be based on earnings up to a maximum of 48 hours a week, even if the applicant works for longer than this. For example, an applicant who works 60 hours a week for £8 per hour be considered to have a salary of £19,968 (8x48x52) and not £25,960 (8x60x52), and will therefore not be awarded points for appropriate salary.

79D. No points will be awarded for appropriate salary if the applicant does not provide a valid Certificate of Sponsorship reference number with his application.

Tier 2 (General) limit

Overview

80. The Secretary of State shall be entitled to limit the number of Certificates of Sponsorship available to be allocated to Sponsors in any specific period under the Tier 2 (General) limit referred to in paragraph 77B(a) above.

[80A. The Tier 2 (General) limit for the specific periods 6 April 2012 to 5 April 2013 and 6 April 2013 to 5 April 2014 is 20,700 Certificates of Sponsorship in each year.]

Note: Paragraph 80A substituted from 6 April 2012 except for applications made but not decided before that date (Cm 8337).

80B. The process by which Certificates of Sponsorship shall be allocated to Sponsors under the Tier 2 (General) limit is set out in paragraphs 80C to 84A and Tables 11B and 11C below.

80C. A Sponsor must apply to the Secretary of State for a Certificate of Sponsorship.

80D. Available points for an application for a Certificate of Sponsorship are shown in Table 11B. No application will be granted unless it scores a minimum of 30 points under the heading "Type of Job" and a minimum of 2 points under the heading "Salary on Offer".

80E. Notes to accompany Table 11B appear below the table.

Table 11B Applications for Certificates of Sponsorship under the Tier 2 (General) limit

Type of job	Points	Salary on offer	Points
Shortage Occupation	75	£20,000–£20,999.99	2
PhD-level occupation code and job passes Resident Labour Market Test [or an exemption applies as set out in paragraph 78B]	50	£21,000 – £21,999.99	3
Job passes Resident Labour Market Test	30	£22,000 – £22,999.99	4
		£23,000 – £23,999.99	5
		£24,000 – £24,999.99	6
		£25,000 – £25,999.99	7
		£26,000 – £26,999.99	8
		£27,000 – £27,999.99	9
		£28,000 – £31,999.99	10
		£32,000 – £45,999.99	15
		£46,000 – £74,999.99	20
		£75,000 – £99,999.99	25
		£100,000 – £149,999.99	30

Note: Words in square brackets inserted from 6 April 2012 with savings for applications made before that date (HC 1888).

Notes

81. Points may only be scored for one entry in each column.

[81A. No points will be awarded under the heading "Type of Job" unless the job described in the Sponsor's application for a Certificate of Sponsorship:

(a) appears on:

(i) the list of occupations skilled to National Qualifications Framework level 6 or above, as stated in [the Codes of Practice in Appendix J], or

[(ii) one of the following creative sector occupations skilled to National Qualifications Framework level 4 or above:

(1) 3411 Artists,

(2) 3412 Authors, writers,

(3) 3413 Actors, entertainers,

(4) 3414 Dancers and choreographers, or

(5) 3422 Designers, product, clothing-related,

or]

(b) is skilled to National Qualifications Framework level 4 or above, and appears on [the Shortage Occupation List in Appendix K.]

Note: Paragraph 81A substituted from 14 June 2012 except for applications made but not decided before that date (Cm 8337). Words in square brackets substituted from 20 July 2012 (Cm 8423).

81B. In order for the Sponsor's application to be awarded points for a job in a shortage occupation, the job must, at the time the application for a Certificate of Sponsorship is decided, appear on [the Shortage Occupation List in Appendix K] and contracted working hours must be for at least 30 hours a week. Furthermore, if the UK Border Agency list of shortage occupations indicates that the job appears on the 'Scotland only' shortage occupation list, the job must be for employment in Scotland.

Note: Words in square brackets substituted from 20 July 2012 (Cm 8423).

81C. In order for the Sponsor's application to be awarded points for a job in a PhD-level occupation code, the job must be in an occupation code which appears on the list of PhD-level occupation codes as stated in [the Codes of Practice in Appendix J.] The Sponsor's application must also meet the requirements of paragraph 81D.

Note: Words in square brackets substituted from 20 July 2012 (Cm 8423)

[81D. In order for the Sponsor's application to be awarded points for a job that passes the resident labour market test or an exemption applies, the Sponsor must certify that it has met the requirements of that test, as defined [in paragraph 78B of this Appendix,] in respect of the job, or that one of the exemptions set out in paragraph 78B of this Appendix applies.]

Note: Paragraph 81D substituted from 6 April 2012 with savings for applications made before that date (HC 1888). Words in square brackets substituted from 20 July 2012 (Cm 8423).

81E. The points awarded under the heading 'Salary on Offer' will be based on the gross annual salary on offer to be paid by the Sponsor, as stated in the Sponsor's application, subject to the following conditions:

(i) Points will be awarded based on basic pay (excluding overtime);

(ii) Allowances, such as London weighting, will be included in the salary for the awarding of points where they are part of the guaranteed salary package and would be paid to a local settled worker in similar circumstances;

(iii) Other allowances and benefits, such as bonus or incentive pay, travel and subsistence (including travel to and from the applicant's home country), will not be included.

81F. No points will be awarded for the salary on offer if the salary referred to in paragraph 81E above is less than the appropriate rate for the job as stated in [the Codes of Practice in Appendix J.]

Note: Words in square brackets substituted from 20 July 2012 (Cm 8423).

81G. Where the salary on offer will be paid hourly, the salary on offer will be calculated on the basis of earnings up to a maximum of 48 hours a week, even if the jobholder works for longer than this.

Monthly allocations

82. The Tier 2 (General) limit will be divided into monthly allocations.

82A. There will be a monthly allocation specifying the number of Certificates of Sponsorship available to be allocated in respect of applications for Certificates of Sponsorship received during each application period. The provisional monthly allocation, subject to the processes set out in paragraphs 83 to 84a below, in respect of each application period is set out in table 11C below.

82B. Applications by Sponsors for Certificates of Sponsorship will be accepted for consideration against each monthly allocation in the relevant application period as set out in table 11C below.

82C. An application that would fall to be considered as having been received in a particular application period may be deferred for consideration as if it had been received in the following application period if the Secretary of State considers that the information stated in the application requires verification checks, and may be refused if the information cannot be verified or is confirmed as false. If the verification checks are prolonged due to the failure of the sponsor to co-operate with the verification process such that the application cannot be considered as if it had been received in the next monthly allocation period, the application will be refused.

82D. These provisional monthly allocations may be adjusted according to the processes set out in paragraphs 83 to 84A in the notes below the table.

Table 11C Certificates of Sponsorship under the Tier 2 (General) limit available to be allocated each month (subject to the processes set out at paragraphs 83 to 84A)

Tier 2 (General) limit for the year 6 April 2012 to 5 April 2013

Application Period	Provisional monthly allocation
6 March 2012 – 5 April 2012	1,725
6 April 2012 – 5 May 2012	1,725
6 May 2012 – 5 June 2012	1,725
6 June 2012 – 5 July 2012	1,725
6 July 2012 – 5 August 2012	1,725
6 August 2012 – 5 September 2012	1,725
6 September 2012 – 5 October 2012	1,725
6 October 2012 – 5 November 2012	1,725
6 November 2012 – 5 December 2012	1,725
6 December 2012 – 5 January 2013	1,725

6 January 2013 – 5 February 2013	1,725
6 February 2013 – 5 March 2013	1,725

Tier 2 (General) limit for the year 6 April 2013 to 5 April 2014

Application Period	Provisional monthly allocation
6 March 2013 – 5 April 2013	1,725
6 April 2013 – 5 May 2013	1,725
6 May 2013 – 5 June 2013	1,725
6 June 2013 – 5 July 2013	1,725
6 July 2013 – 5 August 2013	1,725
6 August 2013 – 5 September 2013	1,725
6 September 2013 – 5 October 2013	1,725
6 October 2013 – 5 November 2013	1,725
6 November 2013 – 5 December 2013	1,725
6 December 2013 – 5 January 2014	1,725
6 January 2014 – 5 February 2014	1,725
6 February 2014 – 5 March 2014	1,725

Note: Table 11C substituted from 6 April 2012 except for applications made but not decided before that date (Cm 8337).

Notes

83. In paragraphs 83A to 84A below:

(a) number of applications means the number of applications by Sponsors for a Certificate of Sponsorship under the Tier 2 (General) limit in one of the monthly periods set out in Table 11C above.

(b) "monthly allocation" means the monthly allocation for that period as set out in Table 11C above, including if applicable any adjustment according to the processes set out in these paragraphs following the assigning of Certificates of Sponsorship under the Tier 2 (General) limit in the previous monthly period.

83A. Subject to paragraph 83E below, if the number of applications is equal to or less than the monthly allocation:

(a) all applications by Sponsors which score 32 points or more from the points available in Table 11B above will be granted, and

(b) if the number of applications granted under (a) above is less than the monthly allocation, the next monthly allocation will be increased by a number equivalent to the Certificates of Sponsorship remaining for allocation in the undersubscribed current month.

83B. Subject to paragraph 83E below, if the number of applications is greater than the monthly allocation:

(a) The minimum points level at which applications for Certificates of Sponsorship will be granted will be calculated as follows:

(i) if the number of applications scoring 32 points or more is no more than 100 greater than the monthly allocation, all applications which score 32 points or more will be granted.

(ii) if the number of applications scoring 32 points or more is more than 100 greater than the monthly allocation, X (being both the number of points scored in Table 11B above and the minimum number of points required for an application to be granted) will be increased by 1 point incrementally until the number of applications scoring X points is:

(1) less than or equal to the monthly allocation; or

(2) no more than 100 greater than the monthly allocation;whichever results in the higher value of X, at which stage all applications which score X points or more will be granted.

(b) 'if the number of applications granted under (a) above is less than the monthly allocation, the number remaining under the monthly allocation will be added to the next monthly allocation.

(c) 'if the number of applications granted under (a) above is more than the monthly allocation, the number by which the monthly allocation is exceeded will be subtracted from the next monthly allocation.

83C. If a Sponsor is allocated one or more Certificates of Sponsorship under the Tier 2 (General) limit which it then elects not to assign to a migrant it may return them to the Secretary of State and the Secretary of State will subsequently add such Certificates of Sponsorship to the following monthly allocation.

83D. If:

(i) a Sponsor is allocated one or more Certificates of Sponsorship under the Tier 2 (General) limit; and

(ii) the application(s) by the Sponsor scored points from Table 11C for a job in a shortage occupation; and

(iii) the Sponsor has not assigned the Certificate(s) of Sponsorship to a migrant(s); and

(iv) the job(s) in question no longer appear on the list of shortage occupations published by the UK Border Agency,

the Certificate(s) of Sponsorship in question will be cancelled and the Secretary of State will subsequently add such Certificates of Sponsorship to the following monthly allocation.

83E. With regard to the final monthly allocation under the Tier 2 (General) limit [for 6 April to 5 April each year, to which the application period of 6 February to 5 March relates:]

(i) Paragraphs 83A(b), 83B(b) and 83B(c) do not apply to this monthly allocation, such that no adjustments will be made to the next monthly allocation, and

(ii) references to "more than 100 greater than the monthly allocation" in paragraphs 83B(a)(ii) to (iii) are amended to "greater than the monthly allocation", such that [the total Tier 2 (General) limit in the period 6 April to 5 April each year] will not be exceeded.

Note: Words in square brackets substituted from 6 April 2012 except for applications made but not decided before that date (Cm 8337).

84. The Secretary of State is entitled (but not required) to grant an application for a Certificate of Sponsorship under the Tier 2 (General) limit exceptionally outside of the processes set out in paragraphs 82A to 83B above if:

(a) the application is considered by the Secretary of State to require urgent treatment when considered in line with the Tier 2 (Sponsor) guidance published on the UK Border Agency website, and

(b) the application scores enough points from Table 11B above that it would have met the requirements to be granted under the previous monthly allocation.

84A. For each Certificate of Sponsorship application granted under the urgent treatment process set out in paragraph 84 above:

(i) the current monthly allocation for granting Certificates of Sponsorship further to requests for urgent treatment will be reduced by one, if the current monthly allocation has not yet been reached; or

(ii) in all other cases, the subsequent monthly allocation for granting Certificates of Sponsorship further to requests for urgent treatment will be reduced by one.]

Note: Paragraphs 73 to 84A substituted from 6 April 2011 with savings for applications made before that date (HC863).

Attributes for Tier 2 (Ministers of Religion) Migrants

85. An applicant applying for entry clearance or leave to remain as a Tier 2 (Ministers of Religion) Migrant must score 50 points for attributes.

86. Available points are shown in Table 12 below.

87. Notes to accompany Table 12 appear below that table.

Table 12

Criterion	Points
Certificate of Sponsorship	50

Notes

88. In order to obtain points for sponsorship. the applicant will need to provide a valid Certificate of Sponsorship reference number in this category.

[89. A Certificate of Sponsorship reference number will only be considered to be valid for the purposes of this subcategory if:

(a) the number supplied links to a Certificate of Sponsorship Checking Service entry that names the applicant as the Migrant and confirms that the Sponsor is sponsoring him as a Tier 2 (Minister of Religion) Migrant, and

(b) the Sponsor is an A-rated Sponsor, unless:

(1) the application is for leave to remain, and

(2) the applicant has, or was last granted, leave as a Tier 2 (Minister of Religion) Migrant, a Minister of Religion, Missionary or Member of a Religious Order, and

(3) the applicant is applying to work for the same employer named on the Certificate of Sponsorship which led to his last grant of leave or, in the case of an applicant whose last grant of leave was as a Minister of Religion, Missionary or Member of a Religious Order, the same employer for whom the applicant was working or stated he was intending to work when last granted leave.]

Note: Paragraph 89 substituted from 21 April 2011, except for applications made but not decided before that date (HC 908).

90. The sponsor must have assigned the Certificate of Sponsorship reference number to the migrant no more than 3 months before the application is made and the reference number must not have been cancelled by the sponsor or by the United Kingdom Border Agency since then.

[91. The migrant must not previously have applied for entry clearance, leave to enter or leave to remain using the same Certificate of Sponsorship reference number, if that application was either approved or refused (not rejected as an invalid application, declared void or withdrawn).]

Note: Paragraph 91 substituted from 6 April 2012 except for applications made but not decided before that date (HC 1888).

92. In addition, the Certificate of Sponsorship Checking Service entry [must]:

[(a) confirm that the applicant is being sponsored to perform religious duties, which:

(i) must be work which is within the Sponsor's organisation, or directed by the Sponsor's organisation,

(ii) may include preaching, pastoral work and non pastoral work, and

[(iii) must not involve mainly non-pastoral duties, such as school teaching, media production, domestic work, or administrative or clerical work, unless the role is a senior position in the Sponsor's organisation, and]

(b) provide an outline of the duties in (a),

(c) if the Sponsor's organisation is a religious order, confirm that the applicant is a member of that order,

(d) confirm that the applicant will receive pay and conditions at least equal to those given to settled workers in the same role, that the remuneration complies with or is exempt from National Minimum Wage regulations, and provide details of the remuneration,

(e) confirm that the requirements of the resident labour market test, [as set out in paragraph 92A below,] in respect of the job, have been complied with, unless the applicant is applying for leave to remain and the Sponsor is the same Sponsor as in his last grant of leave,]

[e] the migrant:

(i) is qualified to do the job in respect of which he is seeking leave as a Tier 2 (Minister of Religion) Migrant,

(ii) intends to base himself in the UK, and

(iii) will comply with the conditions of his leave, if his application is successful, and

[(f)] the sponsor will maintain or accommodate the migrant.

Note: Word in square brackets, sub-para (a) and numbering substituted from 6 April 2012 except for applications made but not decided before that date (HC 1888). Sub-paragraph (a)(iii) inserted and words in square brackets in first sub-para (e) substituted from 20 July 2012 (Cm 8423).

[92A. To confirm that the Resident Labour Market Test has been passed and for points to be awarded, the Certificate of Sponsorship Checking Service entry must confirm:

(a) That the role is supernumerary, such that it is over and above the Sponsor's normal staffing requirements and if the person filling the role was not there, it would not need to be filled by anyone else, with a full explanation of why it is supernumerary; or

(b) That the Sponsor holds national records of all available individuals, details of those records and confirmation that the records show that no suitable settled worker is available to fill the role; or

(c) That a national recruitment search was undertaken, including the following details:

(i) Where the role was advertised, which must be at least one of the following:

(1) a national form of media appropriate to the Sponsor's religion or denomination,

(2) the Sponsor's own website, if that is how the Sponsor usually reaches out to its community on a national scale, that is where it normally advertises vacant positions, and the pages containing the advertisement are free to view without paying a subscription fee or making a donation, or

(3) Jobcentre Plus (or in Northern Ireland, JobCentre Online) or in the employment section of a national newspaper, if there is no suitable national form of media appropriate to the Sponsor's religion or denomination;

(ii) any reference numbers of the advertisements;

(iii) the period the role was advertised for, which must include at least 28 days during the 6 month period immediately before the date the Sponsor assigned the Certificate of Sponsorship to the applicant; and

(iv) confirmation that no suitable settled workers are available to be recruited for the role.]

Note: Paragraph 92A inserted from 20 July 2012 (Cm 8423).

Attributes for Tier 2 (Sportsperson) Migrants

93. An applicant applying for entry clearance or leave to remain as a Tier 2 (Sportsperson) Migrant must score 50 points for attributes.

94. Available points are shown in Table 13 below,

95. Notes to accompany Table 13 appear below that table.

Table 13

Criterion	Points
Certificate of Sponsorship	50

Notes

96. In order to obtain points for sponsorship, the applicant will need to provide a valid Certificate of Sponsorship reference number for sponsorship in this subcategory.

[97. A Certificate of Sponsorship reference number will only be considered to be valid for the purposes of this subcategory if:

(a) the number supplied links to a Certificate of Sponsorship Checking Service entry that names the applicant as the Migrant and confirms that the sponsor is sponsoring him as a Tier 2 (Sportsperson) Migrant, and

(b) the Sponsor is an A-rated Sponsor, unless:

(1) the application is for leave to remain, and

(2) the applicant has, or was last granted, leave as a Tier 2 (Sportsperson) Migrant or a Qualifying Work Permit Holder, and

(3) the applicant is applying to work for the same employer named on the Certificate of Sponsorship or Work Permit document which led to his last grant of leave.]

Note: Paragraph 97 substituted from 21 April 2011 with savings for applications made before that date (HC 908).

98. The sponsor must have assigned the Certificate of Sponsorship reference number to the migrant no more than 3 months before the application is made and the reference number must not have been cancelled by the sponsor or by the United Kingdom Border Agency since then.

[99. The migrant must not previously have applied for entry clearance, leave to enter or leave to remain using the same Certificate of Sponsorship reference number, if that application was either approved or refused (not rejected as an invalid application, declared void or withdrawn).]

Note: Paragraph 99 substituted from 6 April 2012 except for applications made but not decided before that date (HC 1888).

100. In addition the Certificate of Sponsorship Checking Service entry must confirm that the migrant:

(a) is qualified to do the job in question

(b) has been endorsed by the Governing Body for his Sport (that is, the organisation which is [specified in Appendix M] as being the Governing Body for the sport in question),

[(c) the endorsement referred to in (b) above must confirm that the player or coach is internationally established at the highest level whose employment will make a significant contribution to the development of his sport at the highest level in the UK, and that the post could not be filled by a suitable settled worker,]

[(d)] intends to base himself in the UK, and

[(e)] will comply with the conditions of his leave, if his application is successful.

Note: Sub-paragraph (c) inserted and sub-paras (d) and (e) renumbered from 6 April 2011 except for applications made before that date (HC 863). Words in square brackets in (b) substituted from 20 July 2012 (Cm 8423).

Attributes for Tier 5 (Youth Mobility Scheme) Temporary Migrants

101. An applicant applying for entry clearance as a Tier 5 (Youth Mobility Scheme) Temporary Migrant must score 40 points for attributes.

102. Available points are shown in Table 14 below.

103. Notes to accompany Table 14 below.

Table 14

Criterion	Points
Citizen of a country [or rightful holder of a passport issued by a territory listed] in Appendix G or Is a British Overseas Citizen, British Territories Overseas Citizen or British National (Overseas.)	30
Will be 18 or over when his entry clearance becomes valid for use and was under the age of 31 on the date his application was made.	10

Note: Words in square brackets in Table 14 inserted from 1 January 2012 (HC 1693).

Notes

[104. The applicant must provide a valid passport as evidence of all of the above.]

Note: Paragraph 104 substituted from 20 July 2012 (Cm 8423).

Attributes for Tier 5 (Temporary Worker) Migrants

105. An applicant applying for entry clearance or leave enter or remain as a Tier 5 (Temporary Worker) Migrant must score 30 points for attributes.

106. Available points are shown in Table 15 below.

107. Notes to accompany Table 15 appear below in that table.

Table 15

Criterion	Points awarded
Holds a Tier 5 (Temporary Worker) Certificate of Sponsorship	30

Notes

108. In order to meet the 'holds a Certificate of Sponsorship' requirement, the applicant will provide a valid Certificate of Sponsorship reference number for sponsorship in this category.

109. A Certificate of Sponsorship reference number will only be considered to be valid if the number supplied links to a Certificate of Sponsorship Checking Service reference that names the applicant as the migrant and confirms that the sponsor is sponsoring him as a Tier 5(Temporary Worker) Migrant in the subcategory indicated by the migrant in his application for entry clearance or leave.

109A. A Certificate of Sponsorship reference number will only be considered to be valid if:

(a) the sponsor assigned the reference number to the migrant no more than 3 months before the application for entry clearance or leave to remain is made, unless the migrant is applying for leave to enter and has previously been granted leave to enter using the same Certificate of Sponsorship reference number,

(b) the application for entry clearance or leave to remain is made no more than 3 months before the start date of the employment as stated on the Certificate of Sponsorship,

(c) that reference number must not have been cancelled by the sponsor or by the United Kingdom Border Agency since it was assigned[, and

(d) the Sponsor is an A-rated Sponsor, unless the application is for leave to remain and the applicant has, or was last granted, leave as a Tier 5 Migrant, an Overseas Government Employee or a Qualifying Work Permit Holder.]

Note: Sub-paragraph (d) inserted from 21 April 2011 with savings for applications made before that date (HC 908).

[110. The migrant must not previously have applied for entry clearance or leave to remain using the same Certificate of Sponsorship reference number, if that application was either approved or refused (not rejected as an invalid application, declared void or withdrawn).

111. In addition, a Certificate of Sponsorship reference number will only be considered to be valid:

(a) where the Certificate of Sponsorship Checking Service entry shows that the Certificate of Sponsorship has been issued in the Creative and Sporting subcategory to enable the applicant to work as a sportsperson, if:

(i) the Certificate of Sponsorship Checking Service entry shows that the applicant has been endorsed by the Governing Body for his sport (that is, the organisation which is [specified in Appendix M] as being the Governing Body for the sport in question), and

(ii) the endorsement referred to in (i) above confirms that the player or coach is internationally established at the highest level and/or will make a significant contribution to the development of his sport at the highest level in the UK, and that the post could not be filled by a suitable settled worker.

(b) where the Certificate of Sponsorship Checking Service entry shows that the Certificate of Sponsorship has been issued in the Creative and Sporting subcategory to enable the applicant to work as a creative worker, if the entry confirms [that the Sponsor has taken into account the needs of the resident labour market in that field, as set out in the creative sector Codes of Practice in Appendix J, and] that the work could not be carried out by a suitable settled worker,

(c) where the Certificate of Sponsorship Checking Service entry shows that the Certificate of Sponsorship has been issued in the Charity Workers subcategory, if the work the applicant is being sponsored to do is:

(i) voluntary fieldwork directly related to the purpose of the charity which is sponsoring him,

(ii) not paid (except reasonable expenses outlined in section 44 of the National Minimum Wage Act), and

(iii) not a permanent position,

(d) where the Certificate of Sponsorship Checking Service entry shows that the Certificate of Sponsorship has been issued in the Religious Workers subcategory, if the entry confirms:

(i) that the applicant is being sponsored to perform religious duties, which:

(1) must be work which is within the Sponsor's organisation, or directed by the Sponsor's organisation,

(2) may include preaching, pastoral work and non pastoral work, and

(ii) an outline of the duties in (i),

(iii) if the Sponsor's organisation is a religious order, that the applicant is a member of that order;

(iv) that the applicant will receive pay and conditions at least equal to those given to settled workers in the same role,

(v) that the remuneration complies with or is exempt from National Minimum Wage regulations, and provides details of the remuneration,

[(vi) that the requirements of the resident labour market test, as set out in paragraph 92A of this Appendix, in respect of the job, have been complied with, unless the applicant is applying for leave to remain and the Sponsor is the same Sponsor as in his last grant of leave.]

(e) where the Certificate of Sponsorship Checking Service entry shows that the Certificate of Sponsorship has been issued in the Government Authorised Exchange subcategory, if the entry confirms that the work, volunteering or job shadowing the applicant is being sponsored to do:

(i) meets the requirements of the individual exchange scheme, [as set out in Appendix N,]

(ii) does not fill a vacancy in the workforce,

(iii) is skilled to National Qualifications Framework level 3, as stated in [the Codes of Practice in Appendix J], unless the applicant is being sponsored under an individual exchange scheme set up as part of the European Commission's Lifelong Learning Programme,

(iv) conforms with all relevant UK and EU legislation, such as the National Minimum Wage Act and the Working Time Directive.

(f) where the Certificate of Sponsorship Checking Service entry shows that the Certificate of Sponsorship has been issued in the International Agreement subcategory, if the entry confirms that applicant is being sponsored:

(i) for a purpose covered by the UK's commitments in respect of the admission of persons engaged in the supply of a service under the General Agreement on Trade in Services and similar trade agreements, or

(ii) as an employee of an overseas government, or

(iii) as an employee of an international organisation established by international treaty signed by the UK or European Union, or

(iv) as a private servant in a diplomatic household under the provisions of the Vienna Convention on Diplomatic Relations, 1961, and confirms the name of the individual who is employing them.]

> **Note:** Paragraphs 110–111 substituted from 6 April 2012 except for applications made but not decided before that date (HC 1888). Words in square brackets substituted from 20 July 2012 (Cm 8423).

112. Points will not be awarded for a Tier 5 (Temporary Worker) Certificate of Sponsorship where the claimed basis for its issuance are the provisions under Mode 4 of the General Agreement on Trade in Services relating to intra-corporate transfers.

Attributes for Tier 4 (General) Students

113. An applicant applying for entry clearance or leave to remain as a Tier 4 (General) Student must score 30 points for attributes.

114. Available points are shown in Table 16 below.

115. Notes to accompany Table 16 appear below that table.

Table 16

Criterion	Points awarded
Confirmation of Acceptance for Studies	30

Notes

[115A. In order to obtain points for a Confirmation of Acceptance for Studies, the applicant must provide a valid Confirmation of Acceptance for Studies reference number.]

> **Note:** Paragraph 115A inserted from 21 April 2011 except for applications made but not decided before that date (HC 908).

Tier 4 Interim Limit

115B. The Secretary of State shall be entitled to limit the number of Confirmations of Acceptance for Studies allocated to any specific Sponsor in any one period.

> **Note:** Paragraph 115B inserted from 21 April 2011 except for applications made but not decided before that date (HC 908).

115C. The limit on the number of Confirmations of Acceptance for Studies allocated to specific Sponsors shall be known as the Tier 4 Interim Limit.

Note: Paragraph 115C inserted from 21 April 2011 except for applications made but not decided before that date (HC 908).

[115CA. The interim limit implemented by HC908 and effective in relation to Tier 4 between 21 April 2011 and 5 April 2012 shall be known as the Former Interim Limit.]

Note: Paragraph 115CA inserted from 6 April 2012 except for applications made but not decided before that date (HC 1888).

115D. The Tier 4 Interim Limit will apply from [6 April 2012 to 31 December 2012] (inclusive) (the 'Tier 4 interim Limit Period').

Note: Paragraph 115D inserted from 21 April 2011 except for applications made but not decided before that date (HC 908). Words in square brackets substituted from 6 April 2012 except for applications made but not decided before that date (HC 1888).

115E. The Tier 4 interim limit will be applied to any Tier 4 sponsor that does not satisfy both of the following criteria throughout the Tier 4 Interim Limit Period:
    (i) has Highly Trusted Sponsor status; and
    (ii) is subject to and holds a valid and satisfactory full institutional inspection, review or audit by one of the following bodies:
    (a) the Bridge Schools Inspectorate; or
    (b) the Education and Training Inspectorate; or
    (c) Estyn; or
    (d) [Education Scotland]; or
    (e) the Independent Schools Inspectorate; or
    (f) Ofsted; or
    (g) the Quality Assurance Agency for Higher Education; or
    (h) the Schools Inspection Service;
  or is not:
    (iii) the Foundation Programme office;
    (iv) the Yorkshire and Humber Strategic Health Authority;
    (v) a Tier 4 Sponsor that applied for a Tier 4 Sponsor licence on or after 21 April 2011 and meets the requirements of (ii) (but not (i)) above [and has yet to receive a first decision on its application for Highly Trusted Sponsor status;]
    [(vi) an overseas higher education institution which has Highly Trusted Sponsor status] [or
    (vii) a licensed sponsor, who did not have a licence on 5 April 2012, and was granted a licence on or after 6 April 2012 and has yet to receive a first decision on its application for Highly Trusted Sponsor status.]

Note: Paragraph 115E inserted from 21 April 2011 except for applications made but not decided before that date (HC 908). Sub-paragraph (vi) inserted from 4 July 2011 except for applications made but not decided before that date (HC 1148). Words in square brackets in sub-para (d) substituted from 31 October 2011 (HC 1511). Sub-paragraph (vii) inserted from 4 July 2012 except for applications made but not decided before that date (HC 1888).

115F. A Tier 4 Sponsor who does not satisfy the requirements of paragraph 115E and is therefore subject to the Tier 4 Interim Limit is known as a Limited Sponsor.

Note: Paragraph 115F inserted from 21 April 2011 except for applications made but not decided before that date (HC 908).

[115FA. No Confirmations of Acceptance for Studies will be allocated to a Limited Sponsor where:
    (i) the Limited Sponsor did not apply for inspection, review or audit by the appropriate specified body by the relevant deadline, as listed below:

Specified body	Deadline
Quality Assurance Agency	9 September 2011
Independent Schools Inspectorate	9 September 2011
Bridge Schools Inspectorate	7 October 2011
Schools Inspection Service	7 October 2011
Educations Scotland	11 November 2011

or
    (ii) the Limited Sponsor applied by the deadline specified in (i) above, and failed to meet the required standard to obtain a full institutional audit, inspection or review; or
    (iii) the Limited Sponsor applied for Highly Trusted Sponsor status on two occasions and has not been granted Highly Trusted Sponsor status.

Note: Paragraph 115FA inserted from 6 April 2012 except for applications made but not decided before that date (HC 1888).

115FB. A Limited Sponsor that is allocated no Confirmations of Acceptance for Studies further to paragraph 115FA is known as a Legacy Sponsor.]

Note: Paragraph 115FB inserted from 6 April 2012 except for applications made but not decided before that date (HC 1888).

[115G. All Confirmations of Acceptance for Studies allocated by the Secretary of State to Limited Sponsors prior to [6 April 2012] and which have not been assigned to an applicant for entry clearance, leave to enter or leave to remain under Tier 4 prior to [6 April 2012] are withdrawn and the only Confirmations of Acceptance for Studies allocated to a Limited Sponsor are the Confirmations of Acceptance for Studies allocated in accordance with paragraph 115H below.]

Note: Paragraph 115G inserted from 21 April 2011 except for applications made but not decided before that date (HC 908). Words in square brackets inserted from 6 April 2012 except for applications made but not decided before that date (HC 1888).

[115H. The Tier 4 Interim Limit will be calculated as follows:

(i) A Limited Sponsor who has that status as at 6 April 2012 will be allocated:

(a) where the Limited Sponsor was subject to the Former Tier 4 Interim Limit for the entirety of the period 21 April 2011 to 5 April 2012, a number of Confirmations of Acceptance for Studies equal to three quarters of the number of Confirmations of Acceptance for Studies allocated to that Limited Sponsor for the period 21 April 2011 to 5 April 2012;

(b) where the Limited Sponsor had a Tier 4 Sponsor Licence for only part of the period 21 April 2011 to 5 April 2012, and was subject to the Former Tier 4 Interim Limit from the date on which it was granted a sponsor licence, a number of Confirmations of Acceptance for Studies equal to:

(i) the number of Confirmations of Acceptance for Studies allocated to that Limited Sponsor for the period it was licenced between 21 April 2011 to 5 April 2012;

(ii) multiplied by the appropriate factor such that the figure in (i) is equal to the number of Confirmations of Acceptance for Studies that would have been granted to that Limited Sponsor for a period of 9 months;

(c) where the Limited Sponsor had a Tier 4 Sponsor Licence for the entirety of the period 21 April 2011 to 5 April 2012 and was subject to the Former Tier 4 Interim Limit for only part of that period, a number of Confirmations of Acceptance for Studies equal to:

(i) the number of Confirmations of Acceptance for Studies allocated to that Limited Sponsor under the Tier 4 Interim Limit;

(ii) multiplied by the appropriate factor such that the figure in (i) is equal to the number of Confirmations of Acceptance for Studies that would have been granted to that Limited Sponsor for a period of 9 months;

(d) where the calculation in paragraphs (a) to (c) results in 0 or a negative number, the Limited Sponsor will be allocated 0 Confirmations of Acceptance for Studies under the Tier 4 Interim Limit;

(e) where the calculation in paragraphs (a) to (c) does not result in a whole number, the Limited Sponsor will be allocated a number of Confirmations of Acceptance for Studies equal to the nearest whole number (fractions will be rounded up to the nearest whole number).

(ii) a Limited Sponsor who acquires that status after 6 April 2012 will be allocated a number of Confirmations of Acceptance for Studies:

(a) equal to the result of the calculation appropriate for the Limited Sponsor's circumstances as set out in 115H(i) above;

(b) subject where appropriate to a reduction equal to the number of Confirmations of Acceptance for Studies assigned by the Limited Sponsor to Tier 4 Migrants since 6 April 2012 which were used for an application for entry clearance, leave to enter or leave to remain since 6 April 2012; and

(c) divided by the appropriate factor such that the figure resulting from (a) and (b) is proportionate to the period of the Tier 4 Interim Limit remaining.]

Note: Paragraph 115H inserted from 21 April 2011 with savings for applications made before that date (HC 908), substituted from 6 April 2012 with savings for applications made before that date (HC 1888).

115I. A Limited Sponsor will, on provision to the UK Border Agency of evidence that it meets the criteria set out in paragraph 115E above, be exempt from the Tier 4 Interim Limit from the date the UK Border Agency provides written confirmation that it is so exempt.]

Note: Paragraph 115I inserted from 21 April 2011 except for applications made but not decided before that date (HC 908).

116. A Confirmation of Acceptance for Studies will only be considered to be valid if:

(a) it was issued no more than 6 months before the application is made,

(b) the application for entry clearance or leave to remain is made no more than 3 months before the start date of the course of study as stated on the Confirmation of Acceptance for Studies,

(c) the sponsor has not withdrawn the offer since the Confirmation of Acceptance for Studies was issued,

(d) it was issued by an institution with a Tier 4 (General) Student Sponsor Licence,

[(da) where the application for entry clearance or leave to remain is for the applicant to commence a new course of study, not for completion of a course already commenced by way of re-sitting examinations or repeating a module of a course, the Sponsor must hold an A-rated or Highly Trusted Sponsor Licence][, and must not be a Legacy Sponsor,]

[(db) where the Confirmation of Acceptance for Studies is issued by a Legacy Sponsor or a B-rated sponsor, the Confirmation of Acceptance for Studies will only be valid if it is issued for completion of a course already commenced by way of re-sitting examinations or repeating a module of a course and the Confirmation of Acceptance for Studies must be for the same course as the course for which the last period of leave was granted to study with that same sponsor,]

(e) the institution must still hold such a licence at the time the application for entry clearance or leave to remain is determined[,

(ea) the migrant must not previously have applied for entry clearance, leave to enter or leave to remain using the same Confirmation of acceptance for studies reference number where that application was either approved or refused (not rejected as an invalid application[, declared void] or withdrawn),]

[(f) it contains the following mandatory information:

(i) the applicant's:

(1) name,

(2) date of birth,

(3) gender,

(4) nationality, and

(5) passport number;

(ii) the course:

(1) title,

(2) level,

(3) start and end dates, and

(4) hours per week, including confirmation that the course is full-time;

(iii) confirmation if the course is one in which the applicant must hold a valid Academic Technology Approval Scheme clearance certificate from the Counter-Proliferation Department of the Foreign and Commonwealth Office;

(iv) confirmation if the course is a recognised Foundation Programme for post-graduate doctors or dentists, and requires a certificate from the Postgraduate Dean;

(v) the main study address;

(vi) details of how the Tier 4 Sponsor has assessed the applicant's English language ability including, where relevant, the applicant's English language test scores in all four components (reading, writing, speaking and listening);

(vii) details of any work placements relating to the course;

(viii) accommodation, fees and boarding costs;

(ix) details of any partner institution, if the course will be provided by an education provider that is not the Tier 4 Sponsor; and

(x) the name and address of the overseas higher education institution, if the course is part of a study abroad programme.]

[,and]

[(g) if it was not issued for a course of studies, it was issued for a full-time, salaried, elected executive position as a student union sabbatical officer to an applicant who is part-way through their studies or who is being sponsored to fill the position in the academic year immediately after their graduation.]

Note: Sub-paragraph (g) inserted from 23 July 2010 (HC 382). Sub-paragraphs (da) and (ea) inserted from 21 April 2011 except for applications made but not decided before that date (HC 908). Sub-paragraph 116(db) and words in square brackets in sub-paras (da) and (ea) inserted from 6 April 2012 except for applications made but not decided before that date (HC 1888). Sub-paragraph (f) substituted from 6 September 2012 (HC 565).

117. A Confirmation of Acceptance for Studies reference number will only be considered to be valid if:

(a) the number supplied links to a Confirmation of Acceptance for Studies Checking Service entry that names the applicant as the migrant and confirms that the sponsor is sponsoring him in the Tier 4 category indicated by the migrant in his application for leave to remain (that is, as a Tier 4 (General) Student or a Tier 4 (Child) Student), and

[(b) that reference number must not have been withdrawn or cancelled by the Sponsor or the UK Border Agency since it was assigned.]

Note: Sub-paragraph (b) substituted from 21 April 2011 except for applications made but not decided before that date (HC 908).

[118. No points will be awarded for a Confirmation of Acceptance for Studies unless:

(a) the applicant supplies, as evidence of previous qualifications, [the specified documents, as set out in paragraph 120-SD(a), that the applicant] used to obtain the offer of a place on a course from the Sponsor [unless the applicant is sponsored by a Highly Trusted sponsor, is a national of one of the countries [or the rightful holder of a qualifying passport issued by one of the relevant competent authorities, as appropriate] listed in appendix H, and is applying for entry clearance in his country of nationality [or in the territory related to the passport he holds, as appropriate,] or leave to remain in the UK. The UK Border Agency reserves the right to request the specified documents from these applicants. The application will be refused if the specified documents are not provided in accordance with the request made,] and]

[(b)] [One] of the requirements in (i) to (iii) below is met:

(i) the course is degree level study and the Confirmation of Acceptance for Studies has been assigned by a Sponsor which is a Recognised Body or a body in receipt of funding as a higher education institution from the Department for Employment and Learning in Northern Ireland, the Higher Education Funding Council for England, the Higher Education Funding Council for Wales, or the Scottish Funding Council, and:

(1) the applicant is a national of one of the following countries: Antigua and Barbuda; Australia; The Bahamas; Barbados; Belize; Canada; Dominica; Grenada; Guyana; Jamaica; New Zealand; St Kitts and Nevis; St Lucia; St Vincent and the Grenadines; Trinidad and Tobago; United States of America, and provides the specified documents [set out in paragraph 120-SD(b)]; or

(2) has obtained an academic qualification (not a professional or vocational qualification), which is deemed by UK NARIC to meet or exceed the recognised standard of a Bachelor's or Master's degree or a PhD in the UK, from an educational establishment in one of the following countries: Antigua and Barbuda; Australia; The Bahamas; Barbados; Belize; Dominica; Grenada; Guyana; Ireland; Jamaica; New Zealand; St Kitts and Nevis; St Lucia; St Vincent and The Grenadines; Trinidad and Tobago; the UK; the USA, and provides the specified documents [set out in paragraph 120-SD(a)]; or

(3) the applicant has successfully completed a course as a Tier 4 (Child) Student (or under the student rules that were in force before 31 March 2009, where the student was granted permission [to] stay whilst he was under 18 years old) which:

        i. was at least six months in length, and

        ii. ended within two years of the date the sponsor assigned the Confirmation of Acceptance for Studies; or

(4) the Confirmation of Acceptance for Studies Checking service entry confirms that the applicant has a knowledge of English equivalent to level B2 of the Council of Europe's Common European Framework for Language Learning in all four components (reading, writing, speaking and listening), or above,

    or

(ii) the course is degree level study and the Confirmation of Acceptance for Studies has been assigned by a Sponsor which is not a Recognised Body or is not a body in receipt of funding as a higher education institution from the Department for Employment and Learning in Northern Ireland, the Higher Education Funding Council for England, the Higher Education Funding Council for Wales, or the Scottish Funding Council, and:

(1) the applicant is a national of one of the following countries: Antigua and Barbuda; Australia; The Bahamas; Barbados; Belize; Canada; Dominica; Grenada; Guyana; Jamaica; New Zealand; St Kitts and Nevis; St Lucia; St Vincent and the Grenadines; Trinidad and Tobago; United States of America, and provides the specified documents [set out in paragraph 120-SD(b)]; or

(2) has obtained an academic qualification (not a professional or vocational qualification), which is deemed by UK NARIC to meet or exceed the recognised standard of a Bachelor's or Master's degree or a PhD in the UK, from an educational establishment in one of the following countries: Antigua and Barbuda; Australia; The Bahamas; Barbados; Belize; Dominica; Grenada; Guyana; Ireland; Jamaica; New Zealand; St Kitts and Nevis; St Lucia; St Vincent and The Grenadines; Trinidad and Tobago; the UK; the USA, and provides the specified documents[set out in paragraph 120-SD(a)]; or

(3) the applicant has successfully completed a course as a Tier 4 (Child) Student (or under the student rules that were in force before 31 March 2009, where the student was granted permission [to] stay whilst he was under 18 years old) which:

        i. was at least six months in length, and

        ii. ended within two years of the date the sponsor assigned the Confirmation of Acceptance for Studies; or

(4) the applicant provides an original English language test certificate from an English language test provider approved by the Secretary of State for these purposes, [as listed in Appendix O,] which is within its validity date, and clearly shows:

i. the applicant's name,

ii. that the applicant has achieved or exceeded level B2 of the Council of Europe's Common European Framework for Language Learning in all four components (reading, writing, speaking and listening), unless exempted from sitting a component on the basis of the applicant's disability, and

iii. the date of the award,

or

(iii) the course is for below degree level study and:

(1) the applicant is a national of one of the following countries: Antigua and Barbuda; Australia; The Bahamas; Barbados; Belize; Canada; Dominica; Grenada; Guyana; Jamaica; New Zealand; St Kitts and Nevis; St Lucia; St Vincent and the Grenadines; Trinidad and Tobago; United States of America, and provides the specified documents [set out in paragraph 120-SD(b)]; or

(2) has obtained an academic qualification (not a professional or vocational qualification), which is deemed by UK NARIC to meet or exceed the recognised standard of a Bachelor's or Master's degree or a PhD in the UK, from an educational establishment in one of the following countries: Antigua and Barbuda; Australia; The Bahamas; Barbados; Belize; Dominica; Grenada; Guyana; Ireland; Jamaica; New Zealand; St Kitts and Nevis; St Lucia; St Vincent and The Grenadines; Trinidad and Tobago; the UK; the USA, and provides the specified documents [set out in paragraph 120-SD(a); or

(3) the applicant has successfully completed a course as a Tier 4 (Child) Student (or under the student rules that were in force before 31 March 2009, where the student was granted permission [to] stay whilst he was under 18 years old) which:

i. was at least six months in length, and

ii. ended within two years of the date the sponsor assigned the Confirmation of Acceptance for Studies; or

(4) the applicant provides an original English language test certificate from an English language test provider approved by the Secretary of State for these purposes, [as listed in Appendix O,] which is within its validity date, and clearly shows:

i. the applicant's name,

ii. that the applicant has achieved or exceeded level B1 of the Council of Europe's Common European Framework for Language Learning in all four components (reading, writing, speaking and listening), unless exempted from sitting a component on the basis of the applicant's disability, and

iii. the date of the award.]

Note: Paragraph 118 substituted from 12 August 2010 (HC 382). Sub-paragraph (c) inserted from 21 April 2011 except for applications made but not decided before that date (HC 908). Words in 2nd square brackets in sub-para (a) inserted from 4 July 2011 except for applications made but not decided before that date (HC 1148). Words in subsequent square brackets in sub-para (a) inserted from 31 October 2011 (HC 1511). Sub-paragraph (b) deleted and first words in square brackets in sub-para (c) substituted and words in square brackets in (c)(i)(3), (c)(ii)(3) and (c)(iii)(3) inserted from 6 April 2012 except for applications made but not decided before that date (HC 1888). Sub-paragraph (c) renumbered as (b) from 6 April 2012 except for applications made but not decided before that date (HC 1888). Words in first square brackets in sub-para (a) substituted and words in square brackets in (b) inserted form 20 July 2012 (Cm 8423).

119. If the applicant is re-sitting examinations or repeating a module of a course, the applicant must not previously have re-sat the same examination or repeated the same module more than once, unless the sponsor is a Highly Trusted Sponsor. If this requirement is not met then no points will be awarded for the Confirmation of Acceptance for Studies, unless the sponsor is a highly trusted sponsor.

[120. Points will only be awarded for a Confirmation of Acceptance for Studies [. . .] (even if all the requirements in paragraphs 116 to 119 above are met) if the course in respect of which it is issued meets each of the following requirements:

(a) The course must meet the following minimum academic requirements:

(i) for applicants applying to study in England, Wales or Northern Ireland, the course must be at National Qualifications Framework (NQF) / Qualifications and Credit Framework (QCF) level 3 or above if the sponsor is a Highly Trusted Sponsor; or

(ii) for applicants applying to study in England, Wales or Northern Ireland, the course must be at National Qualifications Framework (NQF) / Qualifications and Credit Framework (QCF) level 4 or above if the Sponsor is an A-rated Sponsor or a B-rated Sponsor; or

(iii) for applicants applying to study in Scotland, the course must be accredited at Level 6 or above in the Scottish Credit and Qualifications Framework (SCQF) by the Scottish Qualifications Authority and the Sponsor must be a Highly Trusted Sponsor; or

(iv) for applicants applying to study in Scotland, the course must be accredited at Level 7 or above in the Scottish Credit and Qualifications Framework (SCQF) by the Scottish Qualifications Authority if the Sponsor is an A-rated Sponsor or B-rated Sponsor; or

(v) the course must be a short-term Study Abroad Programme in the United Kingdom as part of the applicant's qualification at an overseas higher education institution, and that qualification must be confirmed as the same as a United Kingdom degree level by the National Recognition Information Centre for the United Kingdom (UK NARIC); or

(vi) the course must be an English language course at level B2 or above of the Common European Framework of Reference for Languages; or

(vii) the course must be a recognised Foundation Programme for postgraduate doctors or dentists;

(b) The Confirmation of Acceptance for Studies must be for a single course of study except where the Confirmation of Acceptance for Studies is:

(i) issued by a Sponsor which is a Recognised Body or a body in receipt of funding as a higher education institution from the Department for Employment and Learning in Northern Ireland, the Higher Education Funding Council for England, the Higher Education Funding Council for Wales,

or the Scottish Funding Council to cover both a pre-sessional course of no longer than three months' duration and a course of degree level study at that Sponsor; and

(ii) the applicant has an unconditional offer of a place on a course of degree level study at that Sponsor; and

(iii) the course of degree level study commences no later than one month after the end date of the pre-sessional course.

(c) The course must, except in the case of a pre-sessional course, lead to an approved qualification [as defined in (cb) below].

[(ca) If a student is specifically studying towards an Association of Certified Chartered Accountants (ACCA) qualification or an ACCA Foundations in Accountancy

(FIA) qualification, the sponsor must be an ACCA approved learning partner - student tuition (ALP-st) at either Gold or Platinum level.]

[(cb) An approved qualification as one that is:

(1) validated by Royal Charter,

(2) awarded by a body that is on the list of recognised bodies produced by the Department for Business, Innovation and Skills,

(3) recognised by one or more recognised bodies through a formal articulation agreement with the awarding body,

(4) in England, Wales and Northern Ireland, on the Register of Regulated Qualifications (http://register.ofqual.gov.uk/) at National Qualifications Framework (NQF) / Qualifications and Credit Framework (QCF) level 3 or above,

(5) in Scotland, accredited at Level 6 or above in the Scottish Credit and Qualifications Framework (SCQF) by the Scottish Qualifications Authority,

(6) an overseas qualification that UK NARIC assesses as valid and equivalent to National Qualifications Framework (NQF) / Qualifications and Credit Framework (QCF) level 3 or above, or

(7) covered by a formal legal agreement between a UK-recognised body and another education provider or awarding body. An authorised signatory for institutional agreements within the recognised body must sign this. The agreement must confirm the recognised body's own independent assessment of the level of the Tier 4 Sponsor's or the awarding body's programme compared to the National Qualifications Framework (NQF) / Qualifications and Credit Framework (QCF) or its equivalents. It must also state that the recognised body would admit any student who successfully completes the Tier 4 Sponsor's or the awarding body's named course onto a specific or a range of degree-level courses it offers.]

(d) Other than when the applicant is on a course-related work placement or a pre-sessional course, all study that forms part of the course must take place on the premises of the sponsoring educational institution or an institution which is a partner institution of the migrant's Sponsor.

(e) The course must meet one of the following requirements:

(i) be a full time course of degree level study that leads to an approved qualification [as defined in (cb) above];

(ii) be an overseas course of degree level study that is recognised as being equivalent to a UK Higher Education course and is being provided by an overseas Higher Education Institution; or

(iii) be a full time course of study involving a minimum of 15 hours per week organized daytime study and, except in the case of a pre-sessional course, lead to an approved qualification, below bachelor degree level [as defined in (cb) above]

[(f) Where the student is following a course of below degree level study including course-related work placement, the course can only be offered by a Highly Trusted Sponsor. If the course contains a course-related work placement, any period that the applicant will be spending on that placement must not exceed one third of the total length of the course spent in the United Kingdom except:

(i) where it is a United Kingdom statutory requirement that the placement should exceed one third of the total length of the course; or

(ii) where the placement does not exceed one half of the total length of the course undertaken in the UK and the student is following a course of degree level study and is either:

(a) sponsored by a Sponsor that is a Recognised Body or a body in receipt of public funding as a higher education institution from the Department of Employment and Learning in Northern Ireland, the Higher Education Funding Council for England, the Higher Education Funding Council for Wales or the Scottish Funding Council; or

(b) sponsored by an overseas higher education institution to undertake a short-term Study Abroad Programme in the United Kingdom.]

Note: Paragraph 120 inserted from 21 April 2011 except for applications made but not decided before that date (HC 908). Sub-paragraph (ca) inserted from 4 July 2011 except for applications made but not decided before that date (HC 1148) and then substituted from 6 September 2012 (HC 565). Words deleted, sub-para (f) substituted, previous para 120 deleted and para 120A renumbered as para 120 from 6 April 2012 except for applications made but not decided before that date (HC 1888). Sub-paragraph (cb) inserted, words substituted in (c) and (e) from 20 July 2012 (Cm 8423).

[Specified documents

120-SD. Where paragraphs 118 to 120 of this Appendix refer to specified documents, those specified documents are as follows:

(a) In the case of evidence relating to previous qualifications, the applicant must provide, for each qualification, either:

(i) The original certificate(s) of qualification, which clearly shows:

(1) the applicant's name,

(2) the title of the award,

(3) the date of the award, and

(4) the name of the awarding institution;

(ii) The original transcript of results, which clearly shows:

(1) the applicant's name,

(2) the name of the academic institution,

(3) their course title, and

(4) confirmation of the award;

or

(iii) If the applicant's Tier 4 sponsor has assessed the applicant by using one or more references, and the Confirmation of Acceptance for Studies Checking Service entry includes details of the references assessed, the original reference(s) (or a copy, together with an original letter from the Tier 4 sponsor confirming it is a true copy of the reference they assessed), which must contain:

(1) the applicant's name,

(2) confirmation of the type and level of course or previous experience; and dates of study or previous experience,

(3) date of the letter, and

(4) contact details of the referee.

(b) In the case of evidence of the applicant's nationality, the specified documents are the applicant's current valid original passport or travel document. If the applicant is unable to provide this, the UK Border Agency may exceptionally consider this requirement to have been met where the applicant provides full reasons in the passport section of the application form, and either:

(1) a current national identity document, or

(2) an original letter from his home government or embassy, on the letter-headed paper of the government or embassy, which has been issued by an author-ised official of that institution and confirms the applic' full name, date of birth and nationality.]

Note: Paragraph 120-SD inserted from 20 July 2012 (Cm 8423).

[120A]. [(a)] Points will only be awarded for a valid Confirmation of acceptance for studies [. . .] (even if all the requirements in paragraphs 116 to 120A above are met) if the sponsor has confirmed that the course for which the Confirmation of acceptance for studies has been assigned represents academic progress from previous study [as defined in (b) below] undertaken during the last period of leave as a Tier 4 (General) student or as a student, [where the applicant has had such leave] except where:

    (i) the applicant is re-sitting examinations or repeating modules in accordance with paragraph 119 above, or

    (ii) the applicant is making a first application to move to a new institution to com-plete a course commenced elsewhere.]

    [(b) For a course to represent academic progress from previous study, the course must:

    (i) be above the level of the previous course for which the applicant was granted leave as a Tier 4 (General) Student or as a Student, or

    (ii) involve further study at the same level, which the Tier 4 Sponsor confirms as complementing the previous course for which the applicant was granted leave as a Tier 4 (General) Student or as a Student.]

Note: Paragraph 120B inserted from 21 April 2011 except for applications made but not decided before that date (HC 1148). Words omitted and paragraph renumbered as 120A from 6 April 2012 except for applications made but not decided before that date (HC 1888). Words in square brackets in (a) and sub-para (b) inserted form 20 July 2012 (Cm 8423).

Attributes for Tier 4 (Child) Students

121. An applicant applying for entry clearance or leave to remain as a Tier 4 (Child) Student must score 30 points for attributes.

122. Available points are show in Table 17 below.

123. Notes to accompany Table 17 appear below that table.

[123A. In order to obtain points for a Confirmation of Acceptance for Studies, the applicant must provide a valid Confirmation of of Acceptance for Studies reference number.]

Note: Paragraph 123A inserted from 6 April 2012 except for applications made but not decided before that date (HC 1888).

Table 17

Criterion	Points awarded
Confirmation of Acceptance for Studies	30

Notes

124. A Confirmation of Acceptance for Studies will be considered to be valid only if:

(a) where the applicant is under 16, it was issued by an independent, fee paying school,

(b) it was issued no more than 6 months before the application is made,

(c) the application for entry clearance or leave to remain is made no more than 3 months before the start date of the course of study as stated on the Confirmation of Acceptance for Studies,

(d) the sponsor has not withdrawn the offer since the Confirmation of Acceptance for Studies was issued,

(e) it was issued by an institution with a Tier 4 (Child) Student Sponsor Licence,

(f) the institution must still hold such a licence at the time the application for entry clearance or leave to remain is determined, and[,

(fa) the migrant must not previously have applied for entry clearance, leave to enter or leave to remain using the same Confirmation of Acceptance for Studies reference number, if that application was either approved or refused (not rejected as an invalid application[, declared void] or withdrawn), and]

(g) it contains such information as is specified as mandatory in guidance published by the United Kingdom Border Agency.

Note: Sub-paragraph (fa) inserted from 21 April 2011 except for applications made but not decided before that date (HC 908). Words in square brackets in sub-para (fa) inserted from 6 April 2012 except for applications made but not decided before that date (HC 1888).

125. A Confirmation of Acceptance for Studies reference number will only be considered to be valid if:

(a) the number supplied links to a Confirmation of Acceptance for Studies Checking Service entry that names the applicant as the migrant and confirms that the sponsor is sponsoring him in the Tier 4 category indicated by the migrant in his application for leave to remain (that is, as a Tier 4 (General) Student or a Tier 4 (Child) Student), and

[(b) that reference number must not have been withdrawn or cancelled by the sponsor or the UK Border Agency since it was assigned.]

Note: Sub-paragraph (b) substituted from 21 April 2011 except for applications made but not decided before that date (HC 908).

[125A. Points will only be awarded for a Confirmation of acceptance for studies if the applicant:

(a) supplies, as evidence of previous qualifications, [the specified documents set out in paragraph 125-SD] that the applicant used to obtain the offer of a place on a course from the sponsor,

(b) is sponsored by a Highly Trusted Sponsor, is a national of one of the countries [or the rightful holder of a qualifying passport issued by one of the relevant competent authorities, as appropriate,] listed in appendix H and is applying for entry clearance in his country of nationality [or in the territory related to the passport he holds, as appropriate,] or leave to remain in the UK. The UK Border agency reserves the right to request the specified documents [set out in paragraph 125-SD] from these applicants. The application will be refused if the specified documents are not provided in accordance with the request made] [, or

(c) where the application for entry clearance or leave to remain is for the applicant to commence a new course of study, not for completion of a course already commenced by way of re-sitting examinations or repeating a module of a course, the Sponsor must hold an A-rated or Highly Trusted Sponsor Licence and must not be a Legacy Sponsor,

(d) where the Confirmation of Acceptance for Studies is issued by a Legacy Sponsor or a B-rated sponsor, the Confirmation of Acceptance for Studies will only be valid if it is issued for completion of a course already commenced by way of re-sitting examinations or repeating a module of a course and the Confirmation of Acceptance for Studies must be for the same course as the course for which the last period of leave was granted to study with that same sponsor.]

Note: Paragraph 125A inserted from 4 July 2011 except for applications made but not decided before that date (HC 1148). Words in square brackets in sub-para (b) inserted from 31 October 2011 (HC 1511). Sub-paragraph (c) inserted from 6 April 2012 except for applications made but not decided before that date (HC 1888). Words in third square brackets in (b) and square brackets in (a) substituted from 20 July 2012 (Cm 8423).

[Specified documents

125-SD. Where paragraph 125 of this Appendix refers to specified documents evidence relating to previous qualifications, those specified documents are:

  (i) The original certificate(s) of qualification, which clearly shows:
    (1) the applicant's name,
    (2) the title of the award,
    (3) the date of the award, and
    (4) the name of the awarding institution;
  (ii) The original transcript of results, which clearly shows:
    (1) the applicant's name,
    (2) the name of the academic institution,
    (3) their course title, and
    (4) confirmation of the award;]

Note: Paragraph 125-SD inserted from 20 July 2012 (Cm 8423).

126. Points will not be awarded under Table 17 unless the course that the student will be pursuing meets one of the following requirements:

(a) be taught in accordance with the National Curriculum,
(b) be taught in accordance with the National Qualification Framework (NQF),
(c) be accepted as being of equivalent academic status to (a) or (b) above by Ofsted (England), the Education and Training Inspectorate (Northern Ireland), [Education Scotland] (Scotland) or Estyn (Wales),
(d) be provided as required by prevailing independent school education inspection standards.

[(e) is a single course of study, except where the Confirmation of Acceptance for Studies is:

(i) issued by an independent school to cover both a pre-sessional course and a course at an independent school; and

(ii) the applicant has an unconditional offer of a place at the independent school; and

(iii) the duration of the pre-sessional course and period of study at the independent school does not exceed the maximum period of entry clearance or leave to remain that can be granted under paragraphs 245ZZB and 245ZZD of the immigration rules.]

Note: Sub-paragraph (e) inserted from 21 April 2011 except for applications made but not decided before that date (HC 908). Words in square brackets in sub-para (c) substituted from 31 October 2011 (HC 1511).

* This is an external website, for which the Home Office is not responsible.]

Note: Appendix A inserted from 29 February 2008 (HC 321). Subsequent amendments of this Appendix embodied in the text are as follows.

Amendments by HC 607 from 30 June 2008: Attributes for Tier 1 (Entrepreneur) Migrants, Attributes for Tier 1 (Entrepreneur) Migrants, Attributes for Tier 1 (Investor) Migrants and Attributes for Tier 1 (Post-study Work) Migrants inserted; paras 5, 6, 11(b), 11(d), 22, 24 and 25 amended; para 27(a)(iii) inserted; Table 3 and Table 4 amended.

Amendments by HC 1113 (with effect from 27 November 2008: paragraphs 1A and 1B inserted; para 2 amended; para 16(h) amended; para 16(k) inserted; Table 2A amended; Table 6(c) amended; Table 7(a) amended; Table 8 amended; paras 59 to 111 inserted.

Amendments by Cm 7701 from 31 October 2009: para 10(a) amended; para 11 deleted; para 12 amended; Table 9 amended.

Amendments by HC 120 from 22 February 2010: Table 16 substituted; para 116 amended; para 120 amended; Table 17 substituted; para 124 amended. Other amendments by HC 120 from 1 January 2010: para 119 amended; para 124 amended.

Amendments by HC 314 from 31 March 2009: Table 8(b)(ii) amended; para 47 deleted; Table 9 amended; para 67 substituted; paras 72, 74, 77(a), 81 and 109 amended; para 109A inserted; Table 11 amended; paras 112 to 116 inserted.

Amendments by HC 439 from 6 April 2010: Table 1 substituted; Table 2 substituted; Table 3 substituted; Table 4 substituted; Table 9 amended; para 54 amended; paras 56 and 57 deleted; Table 10 substituted; para 61(a)(ii) and 61(b)(ii) amended; paras 65, 69, 72, 75 to 77 substituted; Table 11 substituted; para 81 amended; para 83(d) substituted; para 84 deleted; para 119 substituted; paras 120(a) and 120(iii)(d) amended.

Amendments by HC 59 from 19 July 2010: para 1 substituted; para 1A amended; the third section of Table 2 amended.

Subsequent amendments are identified in the notes after the amended paragraph/table.

[APPENDIX B
ENGLISH LANGUAGE

1. An applicant applying as a Tier 1 Migrant or Tier 2 Migrant must have 10 points for English language, unless applying:

(i) for entry clearance as a Tier 1 (Exceptional Talent) Migrant

(ii) for entry clearance or leave to remain as a Tier 1 (Investor) Migrant

(iii) for entry clearance as a Tier 2 (Intra-Company Transfer) Migrant

(iv) for a grant of leave to remain as a Tier 2 (Intra-Company Transfer) Migrant that would not extend his total stay in this category beyond 3 years.

2. The levels of English language required are shown in Table 1.

3. Available points for English language are shown in Table 2.

4. Notes to accompany the tables are shown below each table.

Table 1 Level of English language required to score points

Tier 1 Row	Category	Applications	Level of English language required
A	Tier 1 (General)	Entry clearance and leave to remain	A knowledge of English equivalent to level C1 or above of the Council of
B	Tier 1 (Entrepreneur)	Entry clearance and leave to remain	Europe's Common European Framework for Language Learning
C	Tier 1 (Graduate Entrepreneur)	Leave to remain	A knowledge of English equivalent level B1 or above
D	Tier 1 (Exceptional Talent)	Leave to remain	of the Council of Europe's Common European Framework for Language Learning

Tier 2 Row	Category	Applications	Level of English language required
E	Tier 2 (Minister of equivalent Religion)	Entry clearance and leave to remain	A knowledge of English to level B2 or above of the Council of Europe's Common European Framework for Language Learning
F	Tier 2 (General)	Entry clearance and Leave to remain, other than the cases in paragraph 5 below Learning	A knowledge of English equivalent to level B1 or above of the Council of Europe's Common European Framework for Language Learning
G	Tier 2 (Intra-Company to Transfer)	Leave to remain, other than the cases in paragraph 1(iv) above.	A knowledge of English equivalent level A1 or above of the Council of Europe's Common European Framework for Language Learning

| H | Tier 2 (General) | Leave to remain cases in paragraph 5 below | A knowledge of English equivalent level A1 or above of the Council of Europe's Common European Framework for Language Learning |
| I | Tier 2 (Sportsperson) | Entry clearance and leave to remain | |

Notes

5. An applicant applying for leave to remain as a Tier 2 (General) Migrant must have competence of English to a level A1 or above as set out in Table 1 above if:

(i) he previously had leave as:

(1) a Tier 2 (General) Migrant under the rules in place before 6 April 2011,

(2) a Qualifying Work Permit Holder,

(3) a representative of an overseas newspaper, news agency or Broadcasting organisation,

(4) a Member of the Operational Ground Staff of an Overseas-owned Airline, or

(5) a Jewish Agency Employee,

and

(ii) he has not been granted leave to remain in any other routes, or entry clearance or leave to enter in any route, since the grant of leave referred to in (i) above.

Table 2 Points available for English language

Factor	Points
National of a majority English speaking country	10
Degree taught in English	10
Passed an English language test	10
Met requirement in a previous grant of leave	10
Transitional arrangements	10

Notes

National of a majority English speaking country

6. 10 points will only be awarded for being a national of a majority English speaking country if the applicant has the relevant level of English language shown in Table 1 and:

(i) is a national of one of the following countries:

Antigua and Barbuda
Australia
The Bahamas

Barbados
Belize
Canada
Dominica
Grenada
Guyana
Jamaica
New Zealand
St Kitts and Nevis
St Lucia
St Vincent and the Grenadines
Trinidad and Tobago
USA,
and

[(ii) provides his current valid original passport or travel document to show that this requirement is met. If the applicant is unable to do so, the UK Border Agency may exceptionally consider this requirement to have been met where the applicant provides full reasons in the passport section of the application form, and either:

(1) a current national identity document, or

(2) an original letter from his home government or embassy, on the letter-headed paper of the government or embassy, which has been issued by an authorised official of that institution and confirms the applicant's full name, date of birth and nationality.]

Note: Sub-paragraph (ii) substituted from 20 July 2012 (Cm 8423).

Degree taught in English

7. 10 points will be awarded for a degree taught in English if the applicant has the relevant level of English language shown in Table 1 and:

(i) has obtained an academic qualification (not a professional or vocational qualification) which either:

(1) is deemed by UK NARIC to meet the recognised standard of a Bachelor's degree (not a Master's degree or a PhD) in the UK, and UK NARIC has confirmed that the degree was taught or researched in English to level C1 of the Council of Europe's Common European Framework for Language learning or above; or

(2) is deemed by UK NARIC to meet or exceed the recognised standard of a Bachelor's or Master's degree or a PhD in the UK, and is from an educational establishment in one of the following countries:

Antigua and Barbuda
Australia
The Bahamas
Barbados
Belize
Dominica
Grenada
Guyana

Ireland
Jamaica
New Zealand
St Kitts and Nevis
St Lucia
St Vincent and The Grenadines
Trinidad and Tobago
the UK
the USA,

and

[(ii) provides the following specified documents to show he has the qualification:

(1) the original certificate of the award, or

(2) if the applicant is awaiting graduation having successfully completed the qualification, or no longer has the certificate and the awarding institution is unable to provide a replacement, an academic transcript (or original letter in the case of a PhD qualification) from the awarding institution on its official headed paper, which clearly shows:

(a) the applicant's name,

(b) the name of the awarding institution,

(c) the title of the award,

(d) confirmation that the qualification has been or will be awarded, and

(e) the date that the certificate will be issued (if the applicant has not yet graduated) or confirmation that the institution is unable to reissue the original certificate or award.]

Note: Sub-paragraph (ii) substituted from 20 July 2012 (Cm 8423).

8. If the applicant is required to have competence of English to level A1 as set out in Table 1 above (rows G to I) , 10 points will be awarded for a degree taught in English if the applicant has the relevant level of English language shown in Table 1 and:

(i) has obtained an academic qualification (not a professional or vocational qualification) which is deemed by UK NARIC to meet or exceed the recognised standard of a Bachelor's or Master's degree or a PhD in the UK,

[(ii) provides the specified documents in paragraph 7(ii) evidence to show that he has the qualification, and

(iii) provides provide an original letter from the awarding institution on its official headed paper, which clearly shows:

(1) the applicant's name,

(2) the name of the awarding institution,

(3) the title of the award,

(4) the date of the award, and

(5) confirmation that the qualification was taught in English.]

Note: Sub-paragraph (ii) and (iii) substituted from 20 July 2012 (Cm 8423).

9. An applicant for leave to remain as a Tier 1 (Graduate Entrepreneur) can only score the required 10 points for English language by having a qualification taught in English and scoring 75 points under Table 10, Appendix A.

Passed an English language test

10. 10 points will only be awarded for passing an English language test if the applicant has the relevant level of English language shown in Table 1 and provides an original English language test document from an English language test provider approved by the Secretary of State for these purposes, [as listed in Appendix O] which is within its validity date and clearly shows:

(1) the applicant's name,

(2) the qualification obtained, which must meet or exceed the relevant level shown in Table 1 in all four components (reading, writing, speaking and listening), unless the applicant was exempted from sitting a component on the basis of his disability, and

(3) the date of the award.

Note: Words in square brackets inserted from 20 July 2012 (Cm 8423).

Met requirement in a previous grant of leave

11. Subject to paragraph 14 below, 10 points will be awarded for meeting the requirement in a previous grant of leave if the applicant:

(i) has ever been granted leave as a Tier 1 (General) Migrant or a Tier 1 (Entrepreneur) Migrant or Business person, or

(ii) has ever been granted leave as a Highly Skilled Migrant under the Rules in place on or after 5 December 2006.

12. Subject to paragraph 14 below, where the application falls under rows D to I of Table 1 above, 10 points will be awarded for meeting the requirement in a previous grant of leave if the applicant has ever been granted:

(i) leave as a Minister of Religion (not as a Tier 2 (Minister of Religion) Migrant) under the Rules in place on or after 19 April 2007, or

(ii) leave as a Tier 2 (Minister of Religion) Migrant, provided that when he was granted that leave he obtained points for English language for being a national of a majority English speaking country, a degree taught in English, or passing an English language test.

13. Subject to paragraph 14 below, where the application falls under row D or rows F to I of table 1 above, 10 points will be awarded for meeting the requirement in a previous grant of leave if the applicant has ever been granted:

(i) leave as a Tier 2 (General) Migrant under the Rules in place on or after 6 April 2011, provided that when he was granted that leave he obtained points for having a knowledge of English equivalent to level B1 of the Council of Europe's Common European Framework for Language Learning or above, or

(ii) leave to remain as a Tier 1 (Exceptional Talent) Migrant.

14. Where the application falls under rows G to I of table 1 above, 10 points will be awarded for meeting the requirement in a previous grant of leave if the applicant has ever been granted:

(i) leave as a Minister of Religion (not as a Tier 2 (Minister of Religion) Migrant) under the Rules in place on or after 23 August 2004,

(ii) leave as a Tier 2 Migrant, provided that when he was granted that leave he obtained points for English language for being a national of a majority English speaking country, a degree taught in English, or passing an English language test.

15. No points will be awarded for meeting the requirement in a previous grant of leave if false representations were made or false documents or information were submitted (whether or not to the applicant's knowledge) in relation to the requirement in the application for that previous grant of leave.

Transitional arrangements

16. 10 points will be awarded for English language if the applicant:

(a) is applying for leave to remain as a Tier 2 (General) or a Tier 2 (Intra-Company Transfer) Migrant, and

(b) has previously been granted entry clearance, leave to enter or leave to remain as:

(i) a Jewish Agency Employee,

(ii) a Member of the Operational Ground Staff of an Overseas-owned Airline,

(iii) a Minister of Religion, Missionary or Member of a Religious Order,

(iv) a Qualifying Work Permit Holder,

(v) a Representative of an Overseas Newspaper, News Agency or Broadcasting Organisation,

and

(c) has not been granted leave in any categories other than Tier 2 (General), Tier 2 (Intra-Company Transfer) and those listed in (b) above under the Rules in place since 28 November 2008.

17. 10 points will be awarded for English language if the applicant:

(a) is applying for leave to remain as a Tier 2 (Minister of Religion) Migrant,

(b) has previously been granted entry clearance, leave to enter and/or leave to remain as a Minister of Religion, Missionary or Member of a Religious Order, and

(c) has not been granted leave in any categories other than Tier 2 (Minister of Religion) and those listed in (b) above under the Rules in place since 28 November 2008.

18. 10 points will be awarded for English language if the applicant:

(a) is applying for leave to remain as a Tier 2 (Sportsperson) Migrant,

(b) has previously been granted entry clearance, leave to enter and/or leave to remain as a Qualifying Work Permit Holder, and

(c) has not been granted leave in any categories other than Tier 2 (Sportsperson) and as a Qualifying Work Permit Holder under the Rules in place since 28 November 2008.]

Note: Appendix B substituted from 6 April 2012 except for applications made but not decided before that date (HC 1888).

Appendix C
Maintenance (funds)

[**1A.** In all cases where an applicant is required to obtain points under Appendix C, the applicant must meet the requirements listed below:

(a) the applicant must have the funds specified in the relevant part of Appendix C at the date of the application;

[(b) if the applicant is applying as a Tier 1 Migrant, a Tier 2 Migrant or a Tier 5 (Temporary Worker) Migrant, the applicant must have had the funds referred to in (a) above for a consecutive 90-day period of time, unless applying as a Tier 1 (exceptional Talent) Migrant or a Tier 1 (investor) Migrant;

(c) if the applicant is applying as a Tier 4 Migrant, the applicant must have had the funds referred to in (a) above for a consecutive 28-day period of time;

[(ca) if the applicant is applying for entry clearance or leave to remain as a Tier 4 Migrant, he must confirm that the funds referred to in (a) above are:

(i) available in the manner specified in paragraph 13 below for his use in studying and living in the UK; and

(ii) that the funds will remain available in the manner specified in paragraph 13 below unless used to pay for course fees and living costs;]

(d) if the funds were obtained when the applicant was in the UK, the funds must have been obtained while the applicant had valid leave and was not acting in breach of any conditions attached to that leave;

(e) where the funds are in one or more foreign currencies, the applicant must have the specified level of funds when converted to pound sterling (£) using the spot exchange rate which appears on www.oanda.com* for the date of the application;

(f) where the applicant is applying as a Tier 1 Migrant, a Tier 2 Migrant or a Tier 5 Migrant, the funds must have been under his own control on the date of the application and for the period specified in (b) above; and

(g) where the application is made at the same time as applications by the partner or child of the applicant (such that the applicant is a relevant Points Based System migrant for the purposes of paragraph 319AA), each applicant must have the total requisite funds specified in the relevant parts of Appendices C and E. If each applicant does not individually meet the requirements of Appendices C and / or E, as appropriate, all the applications (the application by the relevant Points Based System Migrant and applications as the partner or child of that relevant Points Based System Migrant) will be refused.]

[(h) The end date of the 90-day and 28-day periods referred to in (b) and (c) above will be taken as the date of the closing balance on the most recent of the specified documents [(where specified documents from two or more accounts are submitted, this will be the end date for the account that most favours the applicant)], and must be no earlier than 31 days before the date of application.]

[(i) No points will be awarded where the specified documents show that the funds are held in a financial institution listed in Appendix P as being an institution with which the UK Border Agency is unable to make satisfactory verification checks.]

[(j) Maintenance must be in the form of cash funds. Other accounts or financial instruments such as shares, bonds, pension funds etc, regardless of notice period are not acceptable.

(k) If the applicant wishes to rely on a joint account as evidence of available funds, the applicant (or for children under 18 years of age, the applicant's parent or legal guardian who is legally present in the United Kingdom) must be named on the account as one of the account holders.]

Note: Paragraph 1A substituted from 23 July 2010 (HC 382). Sub-paragraphs (f) to (h) inserted from 6 April 2011 except for applications made but not decided before that date (HC 863). Sub-paragraphs (b) to (c) substituted and (ca) and (i) inserted from 4 July 2011 except for applications made but not decided before that date (HC 1148). Sub-paragraph (i) inserted from 6 April 2012 except for applications made but not decided before that date (HC 1888). Sub-paragraph (j) substituted, sub-para (e) deleted and former (f)–(j) renumbered as (e) to (i); sub-paras (j)–(k) inserted from 20 July 2012 (Cm 8423). Words in sub-para (h) inserted from 6 September 2012 (HC 565).

1B. In all cases where Appendix C or Appendix E states that an applicant is required to provide specified documents, the specified documents are:

(a) Personal bank or building society statements which satisfy the following requirements:

(i) The statements must cover:

(1) a consecutive 90-day period of time, if the applicant is applying as a Tier 1 Migrant, a Tier 2 Migrant a Tier 5 (Temporary Worker) Migrant, or the Partner or Child of a Relevant Points Based System Migrant in any of these categories,

(2) a single date within 31 days of the date of the application, if the applicant is applying as a Tier 5 (Youth Mobility Scheme) Migrant, or

(3) a consecutive 28-day period of time, if the applicant is applying as a Tier 4 Migrant or the Partner or Child of a Relevant Points Based System Migrant who is a Tier 4 Migrant

(ii) The most recent statement must be dated no earlier than 31 days before the date of the application;

(iii) The statements must clearly show:

(1) the name of:

_i. the applicant,

_ii the applicant's parent(s) or legal guardian's name, if the applicant is applying as Tier 4 Migrant,

_iii. the name of the Relevant Points-Based System Migrant, if the applicant is applying as a Partner or Child of a Relevant Points-Based System Migrant, or

_iv. the name of the applicant's other parent who is legally present in the UK, if the applicant is applying as a Child of a Relevant Points-Based System Migrant,

(2) the account number,

(3) the date of each statement,

(4) the financial institution's name,

(5) the financial institution's logo,

(6) any transactions during the specified period, and

(7) that the funds in the account have been at the required level throughout the specified period;

(iv) The statements must be either:

(1) printed on the bank's or building society's letterhead,

(2) electronic bank or building society statements from an online account, accompanied by a supporting letter from the bank or building society, on company headed paper, confirming the statement provided is authentic, or

(3) electronic bank or building society statements from an online account, bearing the official stamp of the bank or building society on every page,

(v) The statements must not be mini-statements from automatic teller machines (ATMs);

or

(b) A building society pass book which satisfies the following requirements:

(i) The building society pass book must cover:

(1) a consecutive 90-day period of time, if the applicant is applying as a Tier 1 Migrant, a Tier 2 Migrant a Tier 5 (Temporary Worker) Migrant, or the Partner or Child of a Relevant Points Based System Migrant in any of these categories,

(2) a single date within 31 days of the date of the application, if the applicant is applying as a Tier 5 (Youth Mobility Scheme) Migrant, or

(3) a consecutive 28-day period of time, if the applicant is applying as a Tier 4 Migrant or the Partner or Child of a Relevant Points Based System Migrant who is a Tier 4 Migrant

(ii) The period covered by the building society pass book must end no earlier than 31 days before the date of the application;

(iii) The building society pass book must clearly show:

the name of:

_i. the applicant,

_ii the applicant's parent(s) or legal guardian's name, if the applicant is applying as Tier 4 Migrant,

_iii. the name of the Relevant Points-Based System Migrant, if the applicant is applying as a Partner or Child of a Relevant Points-Based System Migrant, or

_iv. the name of the applicant's other parent who is legally present in the UK, if the applicant is applying as a Child of a Relevant Points-Based System Migrant,

(2) the account number,

(3) the building society's name and logo,

(4) any transactions during the specified period, and

(5) that there have been enough funds in the applicant's account throughout the specified period; or

(c) A letter from the applicant's bank or building society, or a letter from a financial institution regulated by the Financial Services Authority or, for overseas accounts, the official regulatory body for the country in which the institution operates and the funds are located, which satisfies the following requirements:

(i) The letter must confirm the level of funds and that they have been held for:

(1) a consecutive 90-day period of time, if the applicant is applying as a Tier 1 Migrant, a Tier 2 Migrant a Tier 5 (Temporary Worker) Migrant, or the Partner or Child of a Relevant Points Based System Migrant in any of these categories,

(2) a single date within 31 days of the date of the application, if the applicant is applying as a Tier 5 (Youth Mobility Scheme) Migrant, or

(3) a consecutive 28-day period of time, if the applicant is applying as a Tier 4 Migrant or the Partner or Child of a Relevant Points Based System Migrant who is a Tier 4 Migrant;

(ii) The period covered by the letter must end no earlier than 31 days before the date of the application;

(iii) The letter must be dated no earlier than 31 days before the date of the application;

(iv) The letter must be on the financial institution's letterhead or official stationery;

(v) The letter must clearly show:

(1) the name of:

_i. the applicant,

_ii the applicant's parent(s) or legal guardian's name, if the applicant is applying as Tier 4 Migrant, _iii. the name of the Relevant Points-Based System Migrant, if the applicant is applying as a Partner or Child of a Relevant Points-Based System Migrant, or

_iv. the name of the applicant's other parent who is legally present in the UK, if the applicant is applying as a Child of a Relevant Points-Based System Migrant,

(2) the account number,

(3) the date of the letter,

(4) the financial institution's name and logo,

(5) the funds held in the applicant's account, and

(5) confirmation that there have been enough funds in the applicant's account throughout the specified period;

(d) If the applicant is applying as Tier 4 Migrant, an original loan letter from a financial institution regulated by either the Financial Services Authority or, in the case of overseas accounts, the official regulatory body for the country the institution is in and where the money is held, which is dated no more than 6 months before the date of the application and clearly shows:

(1) the applicant's name,

(2) the date of the letter,

(3) the financial institution's name and logo,

(4) the money available as a loan,

(5) for applications for entry clearance, that the loan funds are or will be available to the applicant before he travels to the UK, unless the loan is an academic or student loan from the applicant's country's national government and will be released to the applicant on arrival in the UK, and

(6) there are no conditions placed upon the release of the loan funds to the applicant, other than him making a successful application as a Tier 4 Migrant.]

Note: Paragraph 1B inserted from 20 July 2012 (Cm 8423).

Tier 1 Migrants

[1. An applicant applying for entry clearance or leave to remain as a Tier 1 Migrant must score 10 points for funds, unless applying as a Tier 1 (Exceptional Talent) Migrant or a Tier 1 (Investor) Migrant.]

Note: Paragraph 1 substituted from 4 July 2011 with savings for applications made but not decided before that date (HC 1148).

2. 10 points will only be awarded if an applicant:

(a) applying for entry clearance, has the level of funds shown in the table below and provides the specified documents [in paragraph 1B above], or

Level of funds	Points
[£3,100]	10

(b) applying for leave to remain, has the level of funds shown in the table below and provides the specified documents [in paragraph 1B above].

Level of funds	Points
[£900]	10

Note: Figures in the tables above substituted from 14 June 2012 except for applications made but not decided before that date (HC 1888). Words in square brackets inserted from 20 July 2012 (Cm 8423).

3. ...

Tier 2 Migrants

4. An applicant applying for entry clearance or leave to remain as a Tier 2 Migrant must score 10 points for Funds.

5. 10 points will only be awarded if:

(a) the applicant has the level of funds shown in the table below and provides the specified documents [in paragraph 1B above], or

Level of funds	Points awarded
[£900]	10

(b) the applicant has...entry clearance, leave to enter or leave to remain as:
  (i) a Tier 2 Migrant
  (ii) a Jewish Agency Employee
  (iii) A member of the Operational Ground Staff of an Overseas-owned Airline,
  (iv) a Minister of Religion, Missionary or Member of a Religious Order,
  (v) a Representative of an Overseas Newspaper, News Agency or Broadcasting Organisation, or
  (vi) a Work Permit Holder, or
[(c)] the sponsor is an A rated sponsor and has certified on the Certificate of sponsorship that, should it become necessary, it will maintain and accommodate the migrant up to the end of the first month of his employment. The sponsor may limit the amount of the undertaking but any limit must be at least [£900]. Points will only be awarded if the applicant provides a valid Certificate of sponsorship reference number with his application.]

Note: Sub-paragraph (d) substituted from 6 April 2011 except for applications made but not decided before that date (HC 863). Sub-paragraph (d) renumbered as (c), (previous (c) deleted) from 6 April 2012, and figures substituted from 14 June 2012 except for applications made but not decided before those dates (HC 1888). Words in square brackets inserted from 20 July 2012 (Cm 8423).

Tier 5 (Youth Mobility) Temporary Migrants

6. An applicant applying for entry clearance as a Tier 5 (Youth Mobility) Temporary Migrant must score 10 points for funds.

7. 10 points will only be awarded if an applicant has the level of funds shown in the table below and provides the specified documents [in paragraph 1B above].

Level of funds	Points awarded
[£1,800]	10

Note: Amount substituted from 6 April 2012 except for applications made but not decided before that date (HC 1888). Words in square brackets inserted from 20 July 2012 (Cm 8423).

Tier 5 (Temporary Worker) Migrants

8. A migrant applying for entry clearance or leave to remain as a Tier 5 (Temporary Worker) Migrant must score 10 points for funds.

9. 10 points will only be awarded if an applicant has the level of funds shown in the table below and provides the specified documents [in paragraph 1B above]:

Criterion	Points awarded
Meets one of the following criteria:	10
• Has [£900]; or	
• The sponsor is an A rated Sponsor and the Certificate of Sponsorship Checking Service confirms that the sponsor has certified that the applicant will not claim public funds during his period of leave as a Tier 5 (Temporary Worker) Migrant. [Points will only be awarded if the applicant provides a valid Certificate of Sponsorship reference number with his application.]	

Note: Words in last square brackets inserted from 26 April 2011 except for applications made but not decided before that date (HC 863). Amount in table substituted from 14 June 2012 except for applications made but not decided before that date (HC 1888). Words in first square brackets inserted from 20 July 2012 (Cm 8423).

Tier 4 (General) Students

10. A Tier 4 (General) Student must score 10 points for funds.

[**11.** 10 points will only be awarded if the funds shown in the table below are available in the manner specified in paragraph 13 [and 13A] below to the applicant. The applicant must either:

(a) provide the specified documents [in paragraph 1B above] to show that the funds are available to him, or

(b) where the applicant is sponsored by a Highly Trusted sponsor, is a national of one of the countries [or the rightful holder of a qualifying passport issued by one of the relevant competent authorities, as appropriate,] listed in Appendix H, and is applying for entry clearance in his country of nationality [or in the territory related to the passport he holds, as appropriate,] or leave to remain in the UK, confirm that the funds are available to him in the specified manner. The UK Border Agency reserves the right to request the specified documents [in paragraph 1B above] from these applicants to support this confirmation. The application will be refused if the specified documents are not provided in accordance with the request made.]

Criterion	Points
If studying in inner London:	10
i) Where the applicant does not have an established presence studying in the United Kingdom, the applicant must have funds amounting to the full course fees for the first academic year of the course, or for the entire course if it is less than a year long, plus [£1,000] for each month of the course up to a maximum of nine months.	

ii) Where the applicant has an established presence studying in the United Kingdom, the applicant must have funds amounting to the course fees required either for the remaining academic year if the applicant is applying part-way through, or for the next academic year if the applicant will continue or commence a new course at the start of the next academic year, or for the entire course if it is less than a year long, plus [£1,000] for each month of the course up to a maximum of two months.

If studying in outer London and elsewhere in the United Kingdom	10

iii) Where the applicant does not have an established presence studying in the United Kingdom, the applicant must have funds amounting to the full course fees for the first academic year of the course, or for the entire course if it is less than a year long, plus [£800] for each month of the course up to a maximum of nine months.

iv) Where the applicant has an established presence studying in the United Kingdom, the applicant must have funds amounting to the course fees required either for the remaining academic year if the applicant is applying part-way through, or for the next academic year if the applicant will continue or commence a new course at the start of the next academic year, or for the entire course if it is less than a year long, plus [£800] for each month of the course up to a maximum of two months.

Note: Paragraph 11 substituted from 4 July 2011 except for applications made but not decided before that date (HC 1148). Words in first square brackets in (b) inserted from 31 October 2011 (HC 1511). Other words inserted and amounts in table substituted from 6 April 2012 except for applications made but not decided before that date (HC 1888). Words in square brackets in (a) and last square brackets in (b) inserted from 20 July 2012 (Cm 8423).

Notes

12. An applicant will be considered to be studying in [inner London] if the institution, or branch of the institution, at which the applicant will be studying is situated "in any of the London boroughs of Camden, City of London, Hackney, Hammersmith and Fulham, Haringey, Islington, Kensington and Chelsea, Lambeth, Lewisham, Newham Southwark, Tower Hamlets, Wandsworth, or Westminster. If the applicant will be studying at more than one site, one or more of which is in [inner London] and one or more outside, then the applicant will be considered to be studying in [inner London] if the applicant's . . . { Confirmation of Acceptance for Studies} states that the applicant will be spending the majority of time studying at a site or sites situated in [inner London].

Note: Word 'inner' in square brackets substituted from 6 April 2011 except for applications made but not decided before that date (HC 863). Same words substituted again from 21 April 2011 except for applications made but undecided before that date (HC 908). Other word in square brackets substituted from 20 July 2012 (Cm 8423).

[**12A.** If the length of the applicant's course includes a part of a month, the time will be rounded up to the next full month.]

Note: Paragraph 12A inserted from 21 April 2011 except for applications made but not decided before that date (HC 908).

[**13.** Funds will be available to the applicant only where the specified documents show [or, where permitted by these rules, the applicant confirms that] the funds are held or provided by:

    (i) the applicant (whether as a sole or joint account holder); and/or

    (ii) the applicant's parent(s) or legal guardian(s), and the parent(s) or legal guardian(s) have provided written consent that their funds may be used by the applicant in order to study in the UK; and/or

    (iii) an official financial sponsor which must be Her Majesty's Government, the applicant's home government, the British Council or any international organisation, international company, University or Independent school.]

Note: Paragraph 13 substituted from 21 April 2011 except for applications made but undecided before that date (HC 908). Words in square brackets inserted from 4 July 2011 except for applications made but not decided before that date (HC 1148).

[**13A.** In assessing whether the requirements of Appendix C, paragraph 11 are met, where an applicant pays a deposit on account to the sponsor for accommodation costs the maximum amount that will be offset against the total maintenance requirement to be met is £1,000 irrespective of the actual amount of the deposit paid.]

Note: Paragraph 13A inserted from 4 July 2011 (HC 1148), and substituted from 6 April 2012 except for applications made but not decided before that date (HC 1888).

[**13B.** If the applicant is relying on the provisions in paragraph 13(ii) above, he must provide:

    (a) one of the following original (or notarised copy) documents:

        (i) his birth certificate showing names of his parent(s),

        (ii) his certificate of adoption showing the names of both parent(s) or legal guardian, or

        (iii) a Court document naming his legal guardian;
        and

    (b) a letter from his parent(s) or legal guardian, confirming:

        (1) the relationship between the applicant and his parent(s) or legal guardian, and

        (2) that the parent(s) or legal guardian give their consent to the applicant using their funds to study in the UK.

Note: Paragraph 13B inserted from 20 July 2012 (Cm 8423).

13C. If the applicant has already paid all or part of the course fees to his Tier 4 Sponsor:

    (a) the Confirmation of Acceptance for Studies Checking Service entry must confirm details of the fees already paid; or

(b) the applicant must provide an original paper receipt issued by the Tier 4 Sponsor, confirming details of the fees already paid.

Note : Paragraph 13C inserted from 20 July 2012 (Cm 8423)

13D. If the applicant has an official financial sponsor as set out in paragraph 13(iii) above:

(a) the Confirmation of Acceptance for Studies Checking Service entry must confirm details of the official financial sponsorship, if it is the Tier 4 Sponsor who is the official financial sponsor; or

(b) the applicant must provide a letter of confirmation from his official financial sponsor, on official letter-headed paper or stationery of that organisation and bearing the official stamp of that organisation, which clearly shows:

(1) the applicant's name,

(2) the name and contact details of the official financial sponsor,

(3) the date of the letter,

(4) the length of the official financial sponsorship, and

(5) the amount of money the official financial sponsor is giving to the applicant, or a statement that the official financial sponsor will cover all of the applicant's fees and living costs.]

Note: Paragraph 13D inserted from 20 July 2012 (Cm 8423).

[**14.** An applicant will have an established presence studying in the UK if the applicant has current entry clearance, leave to enter or leave to remain as a Tier 4 migrant, student or as a Postgraduate doctor or dentist and at the date of application:

(i) has finished a single course that was at least six months long within the applicant's last period of entry clearance, leave to enter or leave to remain, or

(ii) is applying for continued study on a single course where the applicant has completed at least six months of that course.]

Note: Paragraph 14 substituted from 21 April 2011 except for applications made but undecided before that date (HC 908).

Tier 4 (Child) Students

15. A Tier 4 (Child) Student must score 10 points for funds.

[**16.** 10 points will only be awarded if the funds shown in the table below are available in the manner specified in paragraph 21 [and 21A] below to the applicant. The applicant must either:

(a) provide the specified documents [in paragraph 1B above] to show that the funds are available to him, or

(b) where the applicant is sponsored by a Highly Trusted Sponsor, is a national of one of the countries [or the rightful holder of a qualifying passport issued by one of the relevant competent authorities, as appropriate,] listed in Appendix H, and is applying for entry clearance in his country of nationality [or in the territory related to the passport he holds, as appropriate,] or leave to remain in the UK, confirm that the funds are available to him in the specified manner. The UK Border Agency reserves the right to request the specified documents [in paragraph 1B above] from these applicants to support this confirmation. The application will be refused if the specified documents are not provided in accordance with the request made.]

Level of funds	Points
Where the child is (or will be) studying at a residential independent school: sufficient funds are available to the applicant to pay boarding fees (being course fees plus board/lodging fees) for an academic year.	10
Where the child is (or will be) studying at a non-residential independent school and is in a private foster care arrangement (see notes below) or staying with and cared for by a close relative (see notes below): sufficient funds are available to the applicant to pay school fees for an academic year, the foster carer or relative (who must meet the requirements specified in paragraph 19 of this Appendix] has undertaken to maintain and accommodate the child for the duration of the course, and that foster carer or relative has funds equivalent to at least [£550] per month, for up to a maximum of nine months, to support the child while he is in the United Kingdom.	10
Where the child is (or will be) studying at a non-residential independent school, is under the age of 12 and is (or will be) accompanied by a parent, sufficient funds are available to the applicant to pay school fees for an academic year, plus: if no other children are accompanying the applicant and the parent, [£1,500 per month of stay] up to a maximum of nine months; or if other children are accompanying the applicant and the parent, [£1,500 per month, plus £600] per month for each additional child, up to a maximum of nine months.	10
Where the child is aged 16 or 17 years old and is living independently and studying in inner London: i) Where the applicant does not have an established presence studying in the United Kingdom, the applicant must have funds amounting to the full course fees for the first academic year of the course, or for the entire course if it is less than a year long, plus [£900] for each month of the course up to a maximum of nine months. ii) Where the applicant has an established presence studying in the United Kingdom, the applicant must have funds amounting to the course fees required either for the remaining academic year if the applicant is applying part-way through, or for the next academic year if the applicant will continue or commence a new course at the start of the next academic year, or for the entire course if it is less than a year long, plus [£900] for each month of the course up to a maximum of two months.	10

Where the child is aged 16 or 17 years old, is living independently and studying in outer London or elsewhere in the United Kingdom:	10
iii) Where the applicant does not have an established presence studying in the United Kingdom, the applicant must have funds amounting to the full course fees for the first academic year of the course, or for the entire course if it is less than a year long, plus [£700] for each month of the course up to a maximum of nine months.	
iv) Where the applicant has an established presence studying in the United Kingdom, the applicant must have funds amounting to the course fees required either for the remaining academic year if the applicant is applying part-way through, or for the next academic year if the applicant will continue or commence a new course at the start of the next academic year, or for the entire course if it is less than a year long, plus [£700] for each month of the course up to a maximum of two months.	

Note: Paragraph 16 substituted from 4 July 2011 except for applications made but not decided before that date (HC 1148). Words in square brackets in sub-para (b) inserted from 31 October 2011 (HC 1511). Words in first square brackets and amounts in square brackets substituted from 6 April 2012 except for applications made but not decided before that date (HC 1888). Words in square brackets in (a) and third square brackets in (b) inserted from 20 July 2012 (Cm 8423).

Notes

17. Children (under 16, or under 18 if disabled) are privately fostered when they are cared for on a full-time basis by a person or persons aged 18 or over, who are not their parents or a close relative, for a period of 28 days or more.

18. A close relative is a grandparent, brother, sister, step-parent, uncle (brother or half-brother of the child's parent) or aunt (sister or half-sister of the child's parent) who is aged 18 or over.

[**19.** The care arrangement made for the child's care in the UK must comply with the following requirements:

(a) In all cases, the applicant must provide a letter from their parent(s) or legal guardian, confirming:

(1) the relationship between the parent(s) or legal guardian and the applicant,

(2) that the parent(s) or legal guardian have given their consent to the application,

(3) that the parent(s) or legal guardian agrees to the applicant's living arrangements in the UK, and

(4) if the application is for entry clearance, that the parent(s) or legal guardian agrees to the arrangements made for the applicant's travel to and reception in the UK,

(5) if a parent(s) or legal guardian has legal custody or sole responsibility for the applicant,

(6) that each parent or legal guardian with legal custody or responsibility for the applicant agrees to the contents of the letter, and signs the letter, and

(7) the applicant's parent(s) or legal guardian's consent to the applicant travelling to and living in the UK independently, if the applicant is 16 or 17 years old and living independently.

(b) If the applicant is under 16 years old or is not living in the UK independently, the applicant must provide:

(i) a written letter of undertaking from his intended carer confirming the care arrangement, which clearly shows:

(1) the name, current address and contact details of the intended carer,

(2) the address where the carer and the applicant will be living in the UK if different from the intended carer's current address,

(3) confirmation that the accommodation offered to the applicant is a private address, and not operated as a commercial enterprise, such as a hotel or a youth hostel,

(4) the nature of the relationship between the applicant's parent(s) or legal guardian and the intended carer,

(5) that the intended carer agrees to the care arrangements for the applicant,

(6) that the intended carer has at least £550 per month (up to a maximum of nine months) available to look after and accommodate the applicant for the length of the course,

(7) a list of any other people that the intended carer has offered support to, and

(8) the carer's signature and date of the undertaking;

(ii) A letter from his parent(s) or legal guardian, which confirms the care arrangement and clearly shows:

and

(1) the nature of parent(s) or legal guardian's relationship with the intended carer,

(2) the address in the UK where the applicant and the intended carer will be living,

(3) that the parent(s) or legal guardian support the application, and authorise the intended carer to take responsibility for the care of the applicant during his stay in the UK; and

(iii) The intended carer's original (or notarised copy, although the UK Border Agency reserves the right to request the original):

(1) current UK or European Union passport,

(2) current passport or travel document to confirm that they are allowed to stay in the UK, or

(3) certificate of naturalisation.

(c) If the applicant is staying in a private foster care arrangement, he must receive permission from the private foster carer's UK local authority, as set out in the Children (Private Arrangements for Fostering) Regulations 2005.

(d) If the applicant is staying in a private foster care arrangement and is under 16 years old, he must provide:

(i) A copy of the letter of notification from his parent(s), legal guardian or intended carer to the UK local authority, confirming that the applicant will be in the care of a private foster carer while in the UK, and

(ii) The UK local authority's confirmation of receipt, confirming that the local authority has received notification of the foster care arrangement.

Note: Paragraph 19 substituted from 20 July 2012 (Cm 8423).

[**19A.** (a) An applicant will be considered to be studying in inner London if the institution, or branch of the institution, at which the applicant will be studying is situated in any of the London boroughs of Camden, City of London, Hackney, Hammersmith and Fulham, Haringey, Islington, Kensington and Chelsea, Lambeth, Lewisham, Newham Southwark, Tower Hamlets, Wandsworth, or Westminster.

(b) If the applicant will be studying at more than one site, one or more of which is in inner London and one or more outside, then the applicant will be considered to be studying in inner London if the applicant's Confirmation of Acceptance for Studies states that the applicant will be spending the majority of time studying at a site or sites situated in inner London.]

Note: Paragraph 19A inserted from 20 July 2012 (Cm 8423).

[**20.** If the length of the applicant's course includes a part of a month, the time will be rounded up to the next full month.

21. Funds will be available to the applicant only where the specified documents show [or, where permitted by these rules, the applicant confirms that] the funds are held or provided by:

(i) the applicant (whether as a sole or joint account holder); and/or

(ii) the applicant's parent(s) or legal guardian(s), and the parent(s) or legal guardian(s) have provided written consent that their funds may be used by the applicant in order to study in the UK; and/or

(iii) an official financial sponsor which must be Her Majesty's Government, the applicant's home government, the British Council or any international organisation, international company, University or independent school.

Note: Words in square brackets inserted from 4 July 2011 except for applications made but not decided before that date (HC 1488).

[**21A.** In assessing whether the requirements of Appendix C, paragraph 11 are met, where an applicant pays a deposit on account to the sponsor for accommodation costs the maximum amount that will be offset against the total maintenance requirement to be met is £1,000 irrespective of the actual amount of the deposit paid.]

Note: Paragraph 21A inserted from 4 July 2011 and substituted from 6 April 2012 except for applications made before that date (HC 1888).

[**21B.** If the applicant has already paid all or part of the course fees to his Tier 4 Sponsor:

(a) the Confirmation of Acceptance for Studies Checking Service entry must confirm details of the fees already paid; or

(b) the applicant must provide an original paper receipt issued by the Tier 4 Sponsor, confirming details of the fees already paid.

Note: Paragraph 21B inserted from 20 July 2012 (Cm 8423).

21C. If the applicant has an official financial sponsor as set out in paragraph 21(iii) above:

(a) the Confirmation of Acceptance for Studies Checking Service entry must confirm details of the official financial sponsorship, if it is the Tier 4 Sponsor who is the official financial sponsor; or

(b) the applicant must provide a letter of confirmation from his official financial sponsor, on official letter-headed paper or stationery of that organisation and bearing the official stamp of that organisation, which clearly shows:

(1) the applicant's name,

(2) the name and contact details of the official financial sponsor,

(3) the date of the letter,

(4) the length of the official financial sponsorship, and

(5) the amount of money the official financial sponsor is giving to the applicant, or a statement that the official financial sponsor will cover all of the applicant's fees and living costs.]

Note: Paragraph 21C inserted from 20 July 2012 (Cm 8423).

22. An applicant will have an established presence studying in the UK if the applicant has current entry clearance, leave to enter or leave to remain as a Tier 4 migrant or student and at the date of application:

(i) has finished a single course that was at least six months long within the applicant's last period of entry clearance, leave to enter or leave to remain, or

(ii) is applying for continued study on a single course where the applicant has completed at least six months of that course.]

Note: Appendix C inserted from 29 February 2008 (HC 321) and substituted from 30 June 2008 (HC 607). Paragraph 1A and paras 4 to 9 inserted and para 3 deleted from 27 November 2008 (HC 1113). Words omitted from para 5(b) and words inserted in para 5(d) from 1 March 2009 (HC 314). Paragraphs 10 to 18 inserted from 1 March 2009 (HC 314) with paras 14 to 18 being subsequently renumbered as 15 to 19 from 6 April 2010 (HC 439). Words inserted in para 12 from 1 October 2009 (Cm 7701). Words omitted from para 12 from 1 January 2010 (HC 120). Table following para 11 substituted from 6 April 2010 (HC 439). Paragraph 14 inserted from 6 April 2010 (HC 439). Table following para 16 substituted from 6 April 2010 (HC 439). Paragraph 20 inserted from 6 April 2010 (HC 439). Paragraph 20 substituted by paras 20 to 22 from 21 April 2011 except for applications made but undecided before that date (HC 908).

APPENDIX D

IMMIGRATION RULES FOR LEAVE TO ENTER AS A
HIGHLY SKILLED MIGRANT AS AT 31 MARCH 2008, AND IMMIGRATION
RULES FOR LEAVE TO REMAIN AS A HIGHLY SKILLED MIGRANT
AS AT 28 FEBRUARY

Requirements for an extension of stay as a highly skilled migrant

135A. The requirements to be met by a person seeking leave to enter as a highly skilled migrant are that the applicant:

(i) must produce a valid document issued by the Home Office confirming that he meets, at the time of the issue of that document, the criteria specified by the Secretary of State for entry to the United Kingdom under the Highly Skilled Migrant Programme; and

(ii) intends to make the United Kingdom his main home; and

(iii) is able to maintain and accommodate himself and any dependants adequately without recourse to public funds; and

(iv) holds a valid United Kingdom entry clearance for entry in this capacity.

Leave to enter as a highly skilled migrant

135B. A person seeking leave to enter the United Kingdom as a highly skilled migrant may be admitted for a period not exceeding 2 years, subject to a condition prohibiting Employment as a Doctor in Training, (unless the applicant has submitted with this application a valid Highly Skilled Migrant Programme Approval Letter, where the application for that approval letter was made on or before 6 February 2008), provided the Immigration Officer is satisfied that each of the requirements of paragraph 135A is met and that the application does not fall for refusal under paragraph 135HA.

Refusal of leave to enter as a highly skilled migrant

135C. Leave to enter as a highly skilled migrant is to be refused if the Immigration Officer is not satisfied that each of the requirements of paragraph 135A is met or if the application falls for refusal under paragraph 135HA.

135D. The requirements for an extension of stay as a highly skilled migrant for a person who has previously been granted entry clearance or leave in this capacity, are that the applicant:

(i) entered the United Kingdom with a valid United Kingdom entry clearance as a highly skilled migrant, or has previously been granted leave in accordance with paragraphs 135DA–135DH of these Rules; and

(ii) has achieved at least 75 points in accordance with the criteria specified in Appendix 4 of these Rules, having provided all the documents which are set out in Appendix 5 (Part I) of these Rules which correspond to the points which he is claiming; and

(iii) (a) has produced an International English Language Testing System certificate issued to him to certify that he has achieved at least band 6 competence in English; or

(b) has demonstrated that he holds a qualification which was taught in English and which is of an equivalent level to a UK Bachelor's degree by providing both documents which are set out in Appendix 5 (Part II) of these Rules; and

(iv) meets the requirements of paragraph 135A(ii)–(iii).

135DA. The requirements for an extension of stay as a highly skilled migrant for a work permit holder are that the applicant:

(i) entered the United Kingdom or was given leave to remain as a work permit holder in accordance with paragraphs 128 to 132 of these Rules; and

(ii) meets the requirements of paragraph 135A (i)–(iii).

135DB. The requirements for an extension of stay as a highly skilled migrant for a student are that the applicant:

(i) entered the United Kingdom or was given leave to remain as a student in accordance with paragraphs 57 to 62 of these Rules; and

(ii) has obtained a degree qualification on a recognised degree course at either a United Kingdom publicly funded further or higher education institution or a bona fide United Kingdom private education institution which maintains satisfactory records of enrolment and attendance; and

(iii) has the written consent of his official sponsor to remain as a highly skilled migrant if he is a member of a government or international scholarship agency sponsorship and that sponsorship is either ongoing or has recently come to an end at the time of the requested extension; and

(iv) meets the requirements of paragraph 135A(i)–(iii).

135DC. The requirements for an extension of stay as a highly skilled migrant for a postgraduate doctor or postgraduate dentist are that the applicant:

(i) entered the United Kingdom or was given leave to remain as a postgraduate doctor or a postgraduate dentist in accordance with paragraphs 70 to 75 of these Rules; and

(ii) has the written consent of his official sponsor to such employment if he is a member of a government or international scholarship agency sponsorship and that sponsorship is either ongoing or has recently come to an end at the time of the requested extension; and

(iii) meets the requirements of paragraph 135A(i)–(iii).

135DD. The requirements for an extension of stay as a highly skilled migrant for a working holidaymaker are that the applicant:

(i) entered the United Kingdom as a working holidaymaker in accordance with paragraphs 95 to 96 of these Rules; and

(ii) meets the requirements of paragraph 135A(i)–(iii).

135DE. The requirements for an extension of stay as a highly skilled migrant for a participant in the Science and Engineering Graduates Scheme or International Graduates Scheme are that the applicant:

(i) entered the United Kingdom or was given leave to remain as a participant in the Science and Engineering Graduates Scheme or International Graduates Scheme in accordance with paragraphs 135O to 135T of these Rules; and

(ii) meets the requirements of paragraph 135A(i)–(iii).

135DF. The requirements for an extension of stay as a highly skilled migrant for an innovator are that the applicant:

(i) entered the United Kingdom or was given leave to remain as an innovator in accordance with paragraphs 210A to 210E of these Rules; and

(ii) meets the requirements of paragraph 135A(i)–(iii).

135DG. Deleted.

135DH. The requirements for an extension of stay as a highly skilled migrant for a participant in the Fresh Talent: Working in Scotland scheme are that the applicant:

(i) entered the United Kingdom or was given leave to remain as a Fresh Talent: Working in Scotland scheme participant in accordance with paragraphs 143A to 143F of these Rules; and

(ii) has the written consent of his official sponsor to such employment if the studies which led to him being granted leave under the Fresh Talent: Working in Scotland scheme in accordance with paragraphs 143A to 143F of these Rules, or any studies he has subsequently undertaken, were sponsored by a government or international scholarship agency; and

(iii) meets the requirements of paragraph 135A(i)–(iii).

Extension of stay as a highly skilled migrant

135E. An extension of stay as a highly skilled migrant may be granted for a period not exceeding 3 years, provided that the Secretary of State is satisfied that each of the requirements of paragraph 135D, 135DA, 135DB, 135DC, 135DD, 135DE, 135DF or 135DH is met and that the application does not fall for refusal under paragraph 135HA.

Refusal of extension of stay as a highly skilled migrant

135F. An extension of stay as a highly skilled migrant is to be refused if the Secretary of State is not satisfied that each of the requirements of paragraph 135D, 135DA, 135DB,

135DC, 135DD, 135DE, 135DF or 135DH is met or if the application falls for refusal under paragraph 135HA.

Additional grounds for refusal for highly skilled migrants

135HA. An application under paragraphs 135A-135H of these Rules is to be refused, even if the applicant meets all the requirements of those paragraphs, if:

(i) the applicant submits any document which, whether or not it is material to his application, is forged or not genuine, unless the Immigration Officer or Secretary of State is satisfied that the applicant is unaware that the document is forged or not genuine; or

(ii) the Immigration Officer or Secretary of State has cause to doubt the genuineness of any document submitted by the applicant and, having taken reasonable steps to verify the document, has been unable to verify that it is genuine.

Note: Appendix D inserted from 29 February 2008 (HC321).

[Appendix E

Maintenance (funds) for the family of [Relevant Points Based System Migrants]

A sufficient level of funds must be available to an applicant applying as the Partner or Child of a [Relevant Points Based System Migrant]. A sufficient level of funds will only be available if the requirements below are met.

[(aa) Paragraphs 1A and 1B of Appendix C also apply to this Appendix.]

[(a) Where the application is connected to a Tier 1 Migrant (other than a Tier 1 (Investor) Migrant) [or a Tier 1 (Exceptional Talent) Migrant] who is outside the UK or who has been in the UK for a period of less than 12 months, there must be [£1,800] in funds.]

[(b) Where:

(i) paragraph (a) does not apply, and

(ii) the application is connected to a Relevant Points Based System Migrant who is not a Tier 1 (Investor) Migrant[, a Tier 1 (Exceptional Talent) Migrant] or a [Tier 4 (General) Student] there must be [£600] in funds.]

[(ba) (i) Where the application is connected to a [Tier 4 (General) Student]:

(1) if the [Tier 4 (General) Student] is studying in [inner London (as defined in paragraph 12 of Appendix C)], there must be [£600] in funds for each month for which the applicant would, if successful, be granted leave under paragraph 319D(a), up to a maximum of [£5,400] [or],

(2) if the [Tier 4 (General) Student] is not studying in inner] London, there must be [£450] in funds for each month for which the applicant would, if successful, be granted leave under paragraph 319D(a), up to a maximum of [£4,050] [, and in each case

(3) the applicant must confirm that the funds referred to in (1) or (2) above are:

(i) available in the manner specified in paragraph (f) below for use in living costs in the UK; and

(ii) that the funds will remain available in the manner specified in paragraph (f) below unless used to pay for living costs.]

(c) Where the applicant is applying as the Partner of a [Relevant Points Based System Migrant], the relevant amount of funds must be available to either the applicant or the [Relevant Points Based System Migrant].

(d) Where the applicant is applying as the Child of a [Relevant Points Based System Migrant], the relevant amount of funds must be available to the applicant, the [Relevant Points Based System Migrant], or the applicant's other parent who is lawfully present in the UK or being granted entry clearance, or leave to enter or remain, at the same time.

(e) Where the [Relevant Points Based System Migrant] is applying for entry clearance or leave to remain at the same time as the applicant, the amount of funds available to the applicant must be in addition to the level of funds required separately of the [Relevant Points Based System Migrant].

[(f) in all cases, the funds in question must be available to:

    (i) the applicant, or

    (ii) where he is applying as the partner of a relevant Points Based System Migrant, either to him or to that relevant Points Based System Migrant, or

    (iii) where he is applying as the child of a relevant Points Based System Migrant, either to him, to the relevant Points Based System Migrant or to the child's other parent who is lawfully present in the UK or being granted entry clearance, or leave to enter or remain, at the same time;

(g) the funds in question must have been available to the person referred to in [(f)] above [on the date of the application and] for:

    (i) a consecutive 90-day period of time, [...], if the applicant is applying as the Partner or Child of a Tier 1 Migrant (other than a Tier 1 (Investor) Migrant), [or a Tier 1 (Exceptional Talent) Migrant] a Tier 2 Migrant or a Tier 5 (Temporary Worker) Migrant;

    (ii) a consecutive 28-day period of time, [...], if the applicant is applying as the Partner or Child of a [Tier 4 (General) Student];

(h) if the funds in question were obtained when the person referred to in [(f)] above was in the UK, the funds must have been obtained while that person had valid leave and was not acting in breach of any conditions attached to that leave; and

    (i) in the following cases, sufficient funds will be deemed to be available where all of the following conditions are met:

        (1) the relevant Points Based System Migrant to whom the application is connected has, or is being granted, leave as a Tier 2 Migrant,

        (2) the Sponsor of that relevant Points Based System Migrant is A-rated, and

        [(3) that Sponsor has certified on the Certificate of Sponsorship that, should it become necessary, it will maintain and accommodate the dependants of the relevant Points Based System Migrant up to the end of [the first month of the dependant's leave, if granted]. The undertaking may be limited provided the limit is at least [£600] per dependant. If the relevant Points Based System Migrant is applying at the same time as the applicant, points will only be awarded if the relevant Points Based system Migrant provides a valid Certificate of Sponsorship reference number with his application.]

[(ia) Sufficient funds will not be deemed to be available to the Partner or Child if the specified documents, as set out in paragraph 1B of Appendix C, show that the funds are held in a financial institution listed in Appendix P as being an institution with which the UK Border Agency is unable to make satisfactory verification checks.]

[(j) in all cases the applicant must provide the specified documents] [as set out in paragraph 1B of Appendix C][, unless the applicant is applying at the same time as the Relevant Points Based System Migrant who is a Tier 4 (General) Student sponsored by a Highly Trusted Sponsor, is a national of one of the countries [or the rightful holder of a qualifying passport issued by one of the relevant competent authorities, as appropriate,] listed in appendix H, and is applying for entry clearance in his country of nationality [or in the territory related to the passport he holds, as appropriate,] or leave to remain in the UK and the applicant is also a national of the same country, and confirms these requirements are met, in which case the specified documents shall not be required. The UK Border Agency reserves the right to request the specified documents from these applicants. The application will be refused if the specified documents are not provided in accordance with the request made.]

[(k) Where the funds are in one or more foreign currencies, the applicant must have the specified level of funds when converted to pound sterling (£) using the spot exchange rate which appears on www.oanda.com* for the date of the application.

(l) Where the application is one of a number of applications made at the same time as a partner or child of a relevant Points Based System Migrant (as set out in paragraphs 319(a) and 319(f)) each applicant, including the relevant Points Based System Migrant if applying at the same time, must have the total requisite funds specified in the relevant parts of appendices C and E. If each applicant does not individually meet the requirements of appendices C and / or E, as appropriate, all the applications (the application by the relevant Points Based System Migrant and applications as the partner or child of that relevant Points Based System Migrant) will be refused.]

[(m) The end date of the 90-day and 28-day periods referred to in (g) above will be taken as the date of the closing balance on the most recent of the specified documents [(where specified documents from two or more accounts are submitted, this will be the end date for the account that most favours the applicant)], [as set out in paragraph 1B of Appendix C] and must be no earlier than 31 days before the date of application.]

[(n) If:

(i) the Relevant Points-Based System Migrant is a Tier 4 (General) Student who has official financial sponsorship as set out in paragraph 13(iii) of Appendix C, and

(ii) this sponsorship is intended to cover costs of the Relevant Points-Based System Migrant's family member(s),

the applicant must provide a letter of confirmation from the Tier 4 (General) Student's official financial sponsor which satisfies the requirements in paragraph 13D of Appendix C, and confirms that the sponsorship will cover costs of the applicant in addition to costs of the Relevant Points-Based System Migrant.]

Note: Appendix E inserted from 29 February 2008 (HC 321). Paragraph (ea) inserted from 30 June 2008 (HC 607). Paragraphs (a) and (b) substituted and para (ba) inserted from 31 March 2009 (HC 314). Paragraphs (ea) and (eb) deleted, and para (f) substituted from 23 July 2010 (HC 382). Word in first square brackets in sub-paras (g) and (h) substituted from 20 August 2010 (Cm 7929). Other words in square brackets in sub-paras (a), (b)(ii), (g) and sub-paras (k) and (l) inserted, sub-para (i)(3) substituted from 6 April 2011 except for applications made but not decided before that date (HC 863). Words in square brackets in sub-para (j) inserted from 31 October 2011 (HC 1511). 'Tier 4 (General) Student' in (b)(ii), (ba)(i) and (g)(ii) and 'inner London (as defined in paragraph 12 of Appendix C)' substituted; sub-paras (ba)(i)(3), (ia), the word 'inner' in ((ba)(i)(2) and words in square brackets in (j) inserted from 4 July 2011 except for applications made but not decided before that date (HC 1148). Amounts in (a), (b)(ii) and (i) (3) substituted from 14 June 2012 except for applications made but not decided before that date (HC 1888). Other amounts in (ba), and words in square brackets in (i)(3) substituted; sub-para (m) and words in square brackets in (g) inserted and other words in (g)(i), (ii) and (ia) deleted from 6 April 2012 except for applications made but not decided before that date (HC 1888). Sub-paragraph (ia) substituted, words in second square brackets in (j) and square brackets in (m) and sub-paras (aa) and (n) inserted from 20 July 2012 (Cm 8423). Words inserted in sub-para (m) from 6 September 2012 (HC 565).

Appendix F

Immigration rules relating to Highly Skilled Migrants, the International Graduates Scheme, the Fresh Talent: Working in Scotland Scheme, Businesspersons, Innovators, Investors and Writers, Composers and Artists as at 29 June 2008

Highly skilled migrants

Requirements for leave to enter the United Kingdom as a highly skilled migrant

135A. The requirements to be met by a person seeking leave to enter as a highly skilled migrant are that the applicant:

(i) must produce a valid document issued by the Home Office confirming that he meets, at the time of the issue of that document, the criteria specified by the Secretary of State for entry to the United Kingdom under the Highly Skilled Migrant Programme; and

(ii) intends to make the United Kingdom his main home; and

(iii) is able to maintain and accommodate himself and any dependants adequately without recourse to public funds; and

(iv) holds a valid United Kingdom entry clearance for entry in this capacity; and

(v) if he makes an application for leave to enter on or after 29 February 2008, is not applying in India.

Immigration Officers at port should not refuse entry to passengers on the basis that they applied in India, if those passengers have a valid entry clearance for entry in this capacity.

Leave to enter as a highly skilled migrant

135B. A person seeking leave to enter the United Kingdom as a highly skilled migrant may be admitted for a period not exceeding 2 years, subject to a condition prohibiting Employment as a Doctor in Training (unless the applicant has submitted with this application a valid Highly Skilled Migrant Programme Approval Letter, where the application for that approval letter was made on or before 6 February 2008), provided the Immigration Officer is satisfied that each of the requirements of paragraph 135A is met and that the application does not fall for refusal under paragraph 135HA.

Refusal of leave to enter as a highly skilled migrant

135C. Leave to enter as a highly skilled migrant is to be refused if the Immigration Officer is not satisfied that each of the requirements of paragraph 135A is met or if the application falls for refusal under paragraph 135HA.

International Graduates Scheme

Requirements for leave to enter as a participant in the International Graduates Scheme

135O. The requirements to be met by a person seeking leave to enter as a participant in the International Graduates Scheme are that he:

(i) has successfully completed and obtained either:

(a) a recognised UK degree (with second class honours or above) in a subject approved by the Department for Education and Skills for the purposes of the Science and Engineering Graduates scheme, completed before 1 May 2007; or

(b) a recognised UK degree, Master's degree, or PhD in any subject completed on or after 1 May 2007; or

(c) a postgraduate certificate or postgraduate diploma in any subject completed on or after 1 May 2007;

at a UK education institution which is a recognised or listed body.

(ii) intends to seek and take work during the period for which leave is granted in this capacity;

(iii) can maintain and accommodate himself and any dependants without recourse to public funds;

(iv) completed his degree, Master's degree, PhD or postgraduate certificate or diploma, in the last 12 months;

(v) if he has previously spent time in the UK as a participant in the Science and Engineering Graduates Scheme or International Graduates Scheme, is not seeking leave to enter to a date beyond 12 months from the date he was first given leave to enter or remain under the Science and Engineering Graduates Scheme or the International Graduates Scheme;

(vi) intends to leave the United Kingdom if, on expiry of his leave under this scheme, he has not been granted leave to remain in the United Kingdom in accordance with paragraphs 128–135, 200–210H or 245A–245G of these Rules;

(vii) has the written consent of his official sponsor to enter or remain in the United Kingdom under the Science and Engineering Graduates Scheme or International Graduates Scheme if his approved studies, or any studies he has subsequently undertaken, were sponsored by a government or international scholarship agency; and

(viii) holds a valid entry clearance for entry in this capacity except where he is a British National (Overseas), a British overseas territories citizen, a British Overseas citizen, a British protected person or a person who under the British Nationality Act 1981 is a British subject.

Leave to enter as a participant in the International Graduates Scheme

135P. A person seeking leave to enter the United Kingdom as a participant in the International Graduates Scheme may be admitted for a period not exceeding 12 months provided he is able to produce to the Immigration Officer, on arrival, a valid United Kingdom entry clearance for entry in this capacity.

Refusal of leave to enter as a participant in the International Graduates Scheme

135Q. Leave to enter as a participant in the International Graduates Scheme is to be refused if the Immigration Officer is not satisfied that each of the requirements of paragraph 135O is met.

Requirements for leave to remain as a participant in the International Graduates Scheme

135R. The requirements to be met by a person seeking leave to remain as a participant in the International Graduates Scheme are that he:

(i) meets the requirements of paragraph 135O(i) to (vii); and

(ii) has leave to enter or remain as a student or as a participant in the Science and Engineering Graduates Scheme or International Graduates Scheme in accordance with paragraphs 57–69L or 135O–135T of these Rules;

(iii) would not, as a result of an extension of stay, remain in the United Kingdom as a participant in the International Graduates Scheme to a date beyond 12 months from the date on which he was first given leave to enter or remain in this capacity or under the Science and Engineering Graduates Scheme.

Leave to remain as a participant in the International Graduates Scheme

135S. Leave to remain as a participant in the International Graduates Scheme may be granted if the Secretary of State is satisfied that the applicant meets each of the requirements of paragraph 135R.

Refusal of leave to remain as a participant in the International Graduates Scheme

135T. Leave to remain as a participant in the International Graduates Scheme is to be refused if the Secretary of State is not satisfied that each of the requirements of paragraph 135R is met.

Requirements for leave to enter the United Kingdom as a Fresh Talent: Working in Scotland scheme participant

143A. The requirements to be met by a person seeking leave to enter as a Fresh Talent: Working in Scotland scheme participant are that the applicant:

(i) has been awarded:

(a) a HND, by a Scottish publicly funded institution of further or higher education, or a Scottish bona fide private education institution; or

(b) a recognised UK undergraduate degree, Master's degree or PhD or postgraduate certificate or diploma, by a Scottish education institution which is a recognised or listed body; and

(ii) has lived in Scotland for an appropriate period of time whilst studying for the HND, undergraduate degree, Master's degree or PhD or postgraduate certificate or diploma referred to in (i) above; and

(iii) intends to seek and take employment in Scotland during the period of leave granted under this paragraph; and

(iv) is able to maintain and accommodate himself and any dependants adequately without recourse to public funds; and

(v) has completed the HND, undergraduate degree, Master's degree or PhD or postgraduate certificate or diploma referred to in (i) above in the last 12 months; and

(vi) intends to leave the United Kingdom if, on expiry of his leave under this paragraph, he has not been granted leave to remain in the United Kingdom as:

(a) a work permit holder in accordance with paragraphs 128–135 of these Rules; or

(b) a Tier 1 (General) Migrant; or

(c) a person intending to establish themselves in business in accordance with paragraphs 200–210 of these Rules; or

(d) an innovator in accordance with paragraphs 210A-210H of these Rules; and

(vii) has the written consent of his official sponsor to enter or remain in the United Kingdom as a Fresh Talent: Working in Scotland scheme participant, if the studies which led to his qualification under (i) above (or any studies he has subsequently undertaken) were sponsored by a government or international scholarship agency; and

(viii) if he has previously been granted leave as either:

(a) a Fresh Talent: Working in Scotland scheme participant in accordance with this paragraph; and/or

(b) a participant in the Science and Engineering Graduates Scheme or International Graduates Scheme in accordance with paragraphs 135O-135T of these Rules is not seeking leave to enter under this paragraph which, when amalgamated with any previous periods of leave granted in either of these two categories, would total more than 24 months; and

(ix) holds a valid entry clearance for entry in this capacity except where he is a British National (Overseas), a British overseas territories citizen, a British Overseas citizen, a British protected person or a person who under the British Nationality Act 1981 is a British subject.

Leave to enter as a Fresh Talent: Working in Scotland scheme participant

143B. A person seeking leave to enter the United Kingdom as a Fresh Talent: Working in Scotland scheme participant may be admitted for a period not exceeding 24 months provided the Immigration Officer is satisfied that each of the requirements of paragraph 143A is met.

Refusal of leave to enter as a Fresh Talent: Working in Scotland scheme participant

143C. Leave to enter as a Fresh Talent: Working in Scotland scheme participant is to be refused if the Immigration Officer is not satisfied that each of the requirements of paragraph 143A is met.

Requirements for an extension of stay as a Fresh Talent: Working in Scotland scheme participant

143D. The requirements to be met by a person seeking an extension of stay as a Fresh Talent: Working in Scotland scheme participant are that the applicant:

(i) meets the requirements of paragraph 143A (i) to (vii); and

(ii) has leave to enter or remain in the United Kingdom as either:

(a) a student in accordance with paragraphs 57–69L of these Rules; or

(b) a participant in the Science and Engineering Graduates Scheme or International Graduates Scheme in accordance with paragraphs 135O–135T of these Rules; or

(c) a Fresh Talent: Working in Scotland scheme participant in accordance with paragraphs 143A–143F of these Rules; and

(iii) if he has previously been granted leave as either:

(a) a Fresh Talent: Working in Scotland scheme participant in accordance with paragraphs 143A–143F of these Rules; and/or

(b) a Science and Engineering Graduates Scheme or International Graduates Scheme participant in accordance with paragraphs 135O–135T of these Rules is not seeking leave to remain under this paragraph which, when amalgamated with any previous periods of leave granted in either of these two categories, would total more than 24 months.

Extension of stay as a Fresh Talent: Working in Scotland scheme participant

143E. An extension of stay as a Fresh Talent: Working in Scotland scheme participant may be granted for a period not exceeding 24 months if the Secretary of State is satisfied that each of the requirements of paragraph 143D is met.

Refusal of an extension of stay as a Fresh Talent: Working in Scotland scheme participant

143F. An extension of stay as a Fresh Talent: Working in Scotland scheme participant is to be refused if the Secretary of State is not satisfied that each of the requirements of paragraph 143D is met.

Persons intending to establish themselves in business

Requirements for leave to enter the United Kingdom as a person intending to establish himself in business

200. For the purpose of paragraphs 201–210 a business means an enterprise as:
—a sole trader; or
—a partnership; or
—a company registered in the United Kingdom.

201. The requirements to be met by a person seeking leave to enter the United Kingdom to establish himself in business are:

(i) that he satisfies the requirements of either paragraph 202 or paragraph 203; and

(ii) that he has not less than £200,000 of his own money under his control and disposable in the United Kingdom which is held in his own name and not by a trust or other investment vehicle and which he will be investing in the business in the United Kingdom; and

(iii) that until his business provides him with an income he will have sufficient additional funds to maintain and accommodate himself and any dependants without recourse to employment (other than his work for the business) or to public funds; and

(iv) that he will be actively involved full time in trading or providing services on his own account or in partnership, or in the promotion and management of the company as a director; and

(v) that his level of financial investment will be proportional to his interest in the business; and

(vi) that he will have either a controlling or equal interest in the business and that any partnership or directorship does not amount to disguised employment; and

(vii) that he will be able to bear his share of liabilities; and

(viii) that there is a genuine need for his investment and services in the United Kingdom; and

(ix) that his share of the profits of the business will be sufficient to maintain and accommodate himself and any dependants without recourse to employment (other than his work for the business) or to public funds; and

(x) that he does not intend to supplement his business activities by taking or seeking employment in the United Kingdom other than his work for the business; and

(xi) that he holds a valid United Kingdom entry clearance for entry in this capacity.

202. Where a person intends to take over or join as a partner or director an existing business in the United Kingdom he will need, in addition to meeting the requirements at paragraph 201, to produce:

    (i) a written statement of the terms on which he is to take over or join the business; and

    (ii) audited accounts for the business for previous years; and

    (iii) evidence that his services and investment will result in a net increase in the employment provided by the business to persons settled here to the extent of creating at least 2 new full time jobs.

203. Where a person intends to establish a new business in the United Kingdom he will need, in addition to meeting the requirements at paragraph 201 above, to produce evidence:

    (i) that he will be bringing into the country sufficient funds of his own to establish a business; and

    (ii) that the business will create full time paid employment for at least 2 persons already settled in the United Kingdom.

Leave to enter the United Kingdom as a person seeking to establish himself in business

204. A person seeking leave to enter the United Kingdom to establish himself in business may be admitted for a period not exceeding 2 years with a condition restricting his freedom to take employment provided he is able to produce to the Immigration Officer, on arrival, a valid United Kingdom entry clearance for entry in this capacity.

Refusal of leave to enter the United Kingdom as a person seeking to establish himself in business

205. Leave to enter the United Kingdom as a person seeking to establish himself in business is to be refused if a valid United Kingdom entry clearance for entry in this capacity is not produced to the Immigration Officer on arrival.

Requirements for an extension of stay in order to remain in business

206. The requirements for an extension of stay in order to remain in business in the United Kingdom are that the applicant can show:

    (i) that he entered the United Kingdom with a valid United Kingdom entry clearance as a businessman; and

    (ii) audited accounts which show the precise financial position of the business and which confirm that he has invested not less than £200,000 of his own money directly into the business in the United Kingdom; and

    (iii) that he is actively involved on a full time basis in trading or providing services on his own account or in partnership or in the promotion and management of the company as a director; and

    (iv) that his level of financial investment is proportional to his interest in the business; and

    (v) that he has either a controlling or equal interest in the business and that any partnership or directorship does not amount to disguised employment; and

(vi) that he is able to bear his share of any liability the business may incur; and

(vii) that there is a genuine need for his investment and services in the United Kingdom; and

(viii) (a) that where he has established a new business, new full time paid employment has been created in the business for at least 2 persons settled in the United Kingdom; or

(b) that where he has taken over or joined an existing business, his services and investment have resulted in a net increase in the employment provided by the business to persons settled here to the extent of creating at least 2 new full time jobs; and

(ix) that his share of the profits of the business is sufficient to maintain and accommodate him and any dependants without recourse to employment (other than his work for the business) or to public funds; and

(x) that he does not and will not have to supplement his business activities by taking or seeking employment in the United Kingdom other than his work for the business.

206A. The requirements for an extension of stay as a person intending to establish himself in business in the United Kingdom for a person who has leave to enter or remain for work permit employment are that the applicant:

(i) entered the United Kingdom or was given leave to remain as a work permit holder in accordance with paragraphs 128 to 133 of these Rules; and

(ii) meets each of the requirements of paragraph 201 (i)–(x).

206B. The requirements for an extension of stay as a person intending to establish himself in business in the United Kingdom for a highly skilled migrant are that the applicant:

(i) entered the United Kingdom or was given leave to remain as a highly skilled migrant in accordance with paragraphs 135A to 135F of these Rules; and

(ii) meets each of the requirements of paragraph 201 (i)–(x).

206C. The requirements for an extension of stay as a person intending to establish himself in business in the United Kingdom for a participant in the Science and Engineering Graduates Scheme or International Graduates Scheme are that the applicant:

(i) entered the United Kingdom or was given leave to remain as a participant in the Science and Engineering Graduates Scheme or International Graduates Scheme in accordance with paragraphs 135O to 135T of these Rules; and

(ii) meets each of the requirements of paragraph 201 (i)–(x).

206D. The requirements for an extension of stay as a person intending to establish himself in business in the United Kingdom for an innovator are that the applicant:

(i) entered the United Kingdom or was given leave to remain as an innovator in accordance with paragraphs 210A to 210F of these Rules; and

(ii) meets each of the requirements of paragraph 201 (i)–(x).

206E. The requirements for an extension of stay as a person intending to establish himself in business in the United Kingdom for a student are that the applicant:

(i) entered the United Kingdom or was given leave to remain as a student in accordance with paragraphs 57 to 62 of these Rules; and

(ii) has obtained a degree qualification on a recognised degree course at either a United Kingdom publicly funded further or higher education institution or a bona fide United Kingdom private education institution which maintains satisfactory records of enrolment and attendance; and

(iii) has the written consent of his official sponsor to such self employment if he is a member of a government or international scholarship agency sponsorship and that sponsorship is either ongoing or has recently come to an end at the time of the requested extension; and

(iv) meets each of the requirements of paragraph 201 (i)–(x).

206F. The requirements for an extension of stay as a person intending to establish himself in business in the United Kingdom for a working holidaymaker are that the applicant:

(i) entered the United Kingdom or was given leave to remain as a working holiday-maker in accordance with paragraphs 95 to 100 of these Rules; and

(ii) has spent more than 12 months in total in the UK in this capacity; and

(iii) meets each of the requirements of paragraph 201 (i)–(x).

206G. The requirements for an extension of stay as a person intending to establish himself in business in the United Kingdom in the case of a person who has leave to enter or remain as a Fresh Talent: Working in Scotland scheme participant are that the applicant:

(i) entered the United Kingdom or was given leave to remain as a Fresh Talent: Working in Scotland scheme participant in accordance with paragraphs 143A to 143F of these Rules; and

(ii) has the written consent of his official sponsor to such employment if the studies which led to him being granted leave under the Fresh Talent: Working in Scotland scheme in accordance with paragraphs 143A to 143F of these Rules, or any studies he has subsequently undertaken, were sponsored by a government or international scholarship agency; and

(iii) meets each of the requirements of paragraph 201 (i)–(x).

206H. The requirements for an extension of stay as a person intending to establish himself in business in the United Kingdom for a postgraduate doctor or dentist are that the applicant:

(i) entered the United Kingdom or was given leave to remain as a postgraduate doctor or dentist in accordance with paragraphs 70 to 75 of these Rules; and

(ii) has the written consent of his official sponsor to such self employment if he is a member of a government or international scholarship agency sponsorship and that sponsorship is either ongoing or has recently come to an end at the time of the requested extension; and

(iii) meets each of the requirements of paragraph 201 (i)–(x).

206I. The requirements for an extension of stay as a person intending to establish himself in business in the United Kingdom for a Tier 1 (General) Migrant are that the applicant:

(i) entered the United Kingdom or was given leave to remain as a Tier 1 (General) Migrant; and

(ii) meets each of the requirements of paragraph 201 (i)–(x).

Extension of stay in order to remain in business

207. An extension of stay in order to remain in business with a condition restricting his freedom to take employment may be granted for a period not exceeding 3 years at a time provided the Secretary of State is satisfied that each of the requirements of paragraph 206, 206A, 206B, 206C, 206D, 206E, 206F, 206G, 206H or 206I is met.

Refusal of extension of stay in order to remain in business

208. An extension of stay in order to remain in business is to be refused if the Secretary of State is not satisfied that each of the requirements of paragraph 206, 206A, 206B, 206C, 206D, 206E, 206F, 206G, 206H or 206I is met.

Innovators

Requirements for leave to enter the United Kingdom as an innovator

210A. The requirements to be met by a person seeking leave to enter as an innovator are that the applicant:

    (i) is approved by the Home Office as a person who meets the criteria specified by the Secretary of State for entry under the innovator scheme at the time that approval is sought under that scheme;

    (ii) intends to set up a business that will create full-time paid employment for at least 2 persons already settled in the UK; and

    (iii) intends to maintain a minimum five per cent shareholding of the equity capital in that business, once it has been set up, throughout the period of his stay as an innovator; and

    (iv) will be able to maintain and accommodate himself and any dependants adequately without recourse to public funds or to other employment; and

    (v) holds a valid United Kingdom entry clearance for entry in this capacity.

Leave to enter as an innovator

210B. A person seeking leave to enter the United Kingdom as an innovator may be admitted for a period not exceeding 2 years, provided the Immigration Officer is satisfied that each of the requirements of paragraph 210A is met.

Refusal of leave to enter as an innovator

210C. Leave to enter as an innovator is to be refused if the Immigration Officer is not satisfied that each of the requirements of paragraph 210A is met.

Requirements for an extension of stay as an innovator

210D. The requirements for an extension of stay in the United Kingdom as an innovator, in the case of a person who was granted leave to enter under paragraph 210A, are that the applicant:

    (i) has established a viable trading business, by reference to the audited accounts and trading records of that business; and

    (ii) continues to meet the requirements of paragraph 210A (i) and (iv); and has set up a business that will create full-time paid employment for at least 2 persons already settled in the UK; and

    (iii) has maintained a minimum five per cent shareholding of the equity capital in that business, once it has been set up, throughout the period of his stay.

210DA. The requirements for an extension of stay in the United Kingdom as an innovator, in the case of a person who has leave for the purpose of work permit employment are that the applicant:

    (i) entered the United Kingdom or was given leave to remain as a work permit holder in accordance with paragraphs 128 to 132 of these Rules; and

    (ii) meets the requirements of paragraph 210A (i)–(iv).

210DB. The requirements for an extension of stay in the United Kingdom as an innovator in the case of a person who has leave as a student are that the applicant:

(i) entered the United Kingdom or was given leave to remain as a student in accordance with paragraphs 57 to 62 of these Rules; and

(ii) has obtained a degree qualification on a recognised degree course at either a United Kingdom publicly funded further or higher education institution or a bona fide United Kingdom private education institution which maintains satisfactory records of enrolment and attendance; and

(iii) has the written consent of his official sponsor to remain under the Innovator category if he is a member of a government or international scholarship agency sponsorship and that sponsorship is either ongoing or has recently come to an end at the time of the requested extension; and

(iv) meets the requirements of paragraph 210A (i)–(iv).

210DC. The requirements to be met for an extension of stay as an innovator, for a person who has leave as a working holidaymaker are that the applicant:

(i) entered the United Kingdom as a working holidaymaker in accordance with paragraphs 95 to 96 of these Rules; and

(ii) meets the requirements of paragraph 210A (i)–(iv).

210DD. The requirements to be met for an extension of stay as an innovator, for a postgraduate doctor, postgraduate dentist or trainee general practitioner are that the applicant:

(i) entered the United Kingdom or was given leave to remain as a postgraduate doctor, postgraduate dentist or trainee general practitioner in accordance with paragraphs 70 to 75 of these Rules; and

(ii) has the written consent of his official sponsor to remain under the innovator category if he is a member of a government or international scholarship agency sponsorship and that sponsorship is either ongoing or has recently come to an end at the time of the requested extension; and

(iii) meets the requirements of paragraph 210A (i)–(iv).

210DE. The requirements to be met for an extension of stay as an innovator, for a participant in the Science and Engineering Graduate Scheme or International Graduates Scheme are that the applicant:

(i) entered the United Kingdom or was given leave to remain as a participant in the Science and Engineering Graduate Scheme or International Graduates Scheme in accordance with paragraphs 135O to 135T of these Rules; and

(ii) meets the requirements of paragraph 210A (i)–(iv).

210DF. The requirements to be met for an extension of stay as an innovator, for a highly skilled migrant are that the applicant:

(i) entered the United Kingdom or was given leave to remain as a highly skilled migrant in accordance with paragraphs 135A to 135E of these Rules; and

(ii) meets the requirements of paragraph 210A (i)–(iv).

Requirements for leave to enter the United Kingdom as an investor

224. The requirements to be met by a person seeking leave to enter the United Kingdom as an investor are that he:

(i) (a) has money of his own under his control in the United Kingdom amounting to no less than £1 million; or

(b) (i) owns personal assets which, taking into account any liabilities to which he is subject, have a value exceeding £2 million; and

(ii) has money under his control in the United Kingdom amounting to no less than £1 million, which may include money loaned to him provided that it was loaned by a financial institution regulated by the Financial Services Authority; and

(ii) intends to invest not less than £750,000 of his capital in the United Kingdom by way of United Kingdom Government bonds, share capital or loan capital in active and trading United Kingdom registered companies (other than those principally engaged in property investment and excluding investment by the applicant by way of deposits with a bank, building society or other enterprise whose normal course of business includes the acceptance of deposits); and

(iii) intends to make the United Kingdom his main home; and

(iv) is able to maintain and accommodate himself and any dependants without taking employment (other than self employment or business) or recourse to public funds; and

(v) holds a valid United Kingdom entry clearance for entry in this capacity.

Leave to enter as an investor

225. A person seeking leave to enter the United Kingdom as an investor may be admitted for a period not exceeding 2 years with a restriction on his right to take employment, provided he is able to produce to the Immigration Officer, on arrival, a valid United Kingdom entry clearance for entry in this capacity.

Refusal of leave to enter as an investor

226. Leave to enter as an investor is to be refused if a valid United Kingdom entry clearance for entry in this capacity is not produced to the Immigration Officer on arrival.

Requirements for an extension of stay as an investor

Extension of stay as an investor

227. The requirements for an extension of stay as an investor are that the applicant:

(i) entered the United Kingdom with a valid United Kingdom entry clearance as an investor; and

(ii) (a) has money of his own under his control in the United Kingdom amounting to no less than £1 million; or

(b) (i) owns personal assets which, taking into account any liabilities to which he is subject, have a value exceeding £2 million; and

(ii) has money under his control in the United Kingdom amounting to no less than £1 million, which may include money loaned to him provided that it was loaned by a financial institution regulated by the Financial Services Authority; and

(iii) has invested not less than £750,000 of his capital in the United Kingdom on the terms set out in paragraph 224 (ii) above and intends to maintain that investment on the terms set out in paragraph 224 (ii); and

(iv) has made the United Kingdom his main home; and

(v) is able to maintain and accommodate himself and any dependants without taking employment (other than his self employment or business) or recourse to public funds.

227A. The requirements to be met for an extension of stay as an investor, for a person who has leave to enter or remain in the United Kingdom as a work permit holder are that the applicant:

(i) entered the United Kingdom or was granted leave to remain as a work permit holder in accordance with paragraphs 128 to 133 of these Rules; and

(ii) meets the requirements of paragraph 224 (i)–(iv).

227B. The requirements to be met for an extension of stay as an investor, for a person in the United Kingdom as a highly skilled migrant are that the applicant:

(i) entered the United Kingdom or was granted leave to remain as a highly skilled migrant in accordance with paragraphs 135A to 135F of these Rules; and

(ii) meets the requirements of paragraph 224 (i)–(iv).

227C. The requirements to be met for an extension of stay as an investor, for a person in the United Kingdom to establish themselves or remain in business are that the applicant:

(i) entered the United Kingdom or was granted leave to remain as a person intending to establish themselves or remain in business in accordance with paragraphs 201 to 208 of these Rules; and

(ii) meets the requirements of paragraph 224 (i)–(iv).

227D. The requirements to be met for an extension of stay as an investor, for a person in the United Kingdom as an innovator are that the applicant:

(i) entered the United Kingdom or was granted leave to remain as an innovator in accordance with paragraphs 210A to 210F of these Rules; and

(ii) meets the requirements of paragraph 224 (i)–(iv).

227E. The requirements to be met for an extension of stay as an investor, for a person in the United Kingdom as a Tier 1 (General) Migrant are that the applicant:

(i) entered the United Kingdom or was granted leave to remain as a Tier 1 (General) Migrant; and

(ii) meets the requirements of paragraph 224 (i)–(iv).

228. An extension of stay as an investor, with a restriction on the taking of employment, may be granted for a period not exceeding 3 years at a time of 3 years, provided the Secretary of State is satisfied that each of the requirements of paragraph 227, 227A, 227B, 227C, 227D or 227E is met.

Refusal of extension of stay as an investor

229. An extension of stay as an investor is to be refused if the Secretary of State is not satisfied that each of the requirements of paragraph 227, 227A, 227B, 227C, 227D or 227E is met.

Writers, composers and artists

Requirements for leave to enter the United Kingdom as a writer, composer or artist

232. The requirements to be met by a person seeking leave to enter the United Kingdom as a writer, composer or artist are that he:

(i) has established himself outside the United Kingdom as a writer, composer or artist primarily engaged in producing original work which has been published (other than exclusively in newspapers or magazines), performed or exhibited for its literary, musical or artistic merit; and

    (ii) does not intend to work except as related to his self employment as a writer, composer or artist; and

    (iii) has for the preceding year been able to maintain and accommodate himself and any dependants from his own resources without working except as a writer, composer or artist; and

    (iv) will be able to maintain and accommodate himself and any dependants from his own resources without working except as a writer, composer or artist and without recourse to public funds; and

    (v) holds a valid United Kingdom entry clearance for entry in this capacity.

Leave to enter as a writer, composer or artist

233. A person seeking leave to enter the United Kingdom as a writer, composer or artist may be admitted for a period not exceeding 2 years, subject to a condition restricting his freedom to take employment, provided he is able to produce to the Immigration Officer, on arrival, a valid United Kingdom entry clearance for entry in this capacity.

Refusal of leave to enter as a writer, composer or artist

234. Leave to enter as a writer, composer or artist is to be refused if a valid United Kingdom entry clearance for entry in this capacity is not produced to the Immigration Officer on arrival.

Requirements for an extension of stay as a writer, composer or artist

235. The requirements for an extension of stay as a writer, composer or artist are that the applicant:

    (i) entered the United Kingdom with a valid United Kingdom entry clearance as a writer, composer or artist; and

    (ii) meets the requirements of paragraph 232 (ii)–(iv).

Extension of stay as a writer, composer or artist

236. An extension of stay as a writer, composer or artist may be granted for a period not exceeding 3 years with a restriction on his freedom to take employment, provided the Secretary of State is satisfied that each of the requirements of paragraph 235 is met.

Refusal of extension of stay as a writer, composer or artist

237. An extension of stay as a writer, composer or artist is to be refused if the Secretary of State is not satisfied that each of the requirements of paragraph 235 is met.

IMMIGRATION RULES AS AT 26 NOVEMBER 2008 RELATING TO
ROUTES DELETED ON 27 NOVEMBER 2008

A. Requirements for leave to enter as an overseas qualified nurse or midwife

69M. The requirements to be met by a person seeking leave to enter as an qualified nurse or midwife are that the applicant:

(i) has obtained confirmation from the Nursing and Midwifery Council that he is eligible:

(a) for admission to the Overseas Nurses Programme; or

(b) to undertake a period of supervised practice; or

(c) to undertake an adaptation programme leading to registration as a midwife; and

(ii) as been offered:

(a) a supervised practice placement through an education provider that is recognised by the Nursing and Midwifery Council; or

(b) a supervised practice placement in a setting approved by the Nursing and Midwifery Council; or

(c) a midwifery adaptation programme placement is a setting approved by the Nursing and Midwifery Council; and

(iii) did not obtain acceptance of the offer referred to in paragraph 69 (ii) by misrepresentation; and

(iv) is able and intends to undertake the supervised practice placement or midwife adaptation programme; and

(v) does not intend to engage in business or take employment, except

(a) in connection with the supervised practice placement or midwife adaptation programme; or

(b) part-time work of a similar nature to the work undertaken on the supervised practice placement or midwife adaptation programme; and

(vi) is able to maintain and accommodate himself and any dependants without recourse to public funds.

Leave to enter the United Kingdom as an overseas qualified nurse or midwife

69N. Leave to enter the United Kingdom as an overseas qualified nurse or midwife may be granted for a period not exceeding 18 months, provided the Immigration Officer is satisfied that each of the requirements of paragraph 69M is met.

Refusal of leave to enter as an overseas qualified nurse or midwife

69O. Leave to enter the United Kingdom as an overseas qualified nurse or midwife is to be refused if the Immigration Officer is not is satisfied that each of the requirements of paragraph 69M is met.

*B. Requirements for an extension of stay as an overseas
qualified nurse or midwife*

69P. The requirements to be met by a person seeking an extension of stay as an overseas qualified nurse or midwife are that the applicant:

(i) has leave to enter or remain in the United Kingdom as a prospective student in accordance with paragraphs 82–87 of these Rules; or

(ii) has leave to enter or remain in the United Kingdom as a student in accordance with paragraphs 57 to 69L of these Rules; or

(iii) (a) has leave to enter or remain in the United Kingdom as a work permit holder in accordance with paragraphs 128 to 135 of these Rules; or

C. Requirements for leave to enter the United Kingdom to take the PLAB Test

75A. The requirements to be met by a person seeking leave to enter in order to take the PLAB Test are that the applicant:

(iv) intends to leave the United Kingdom at the end of his leave granted under this paragraph unless he is successful in the PLAB Test and granted leave to remain:

(c) as a work permit holder for employment in the United Kingdom as a doctor in accordance with paragraphs 128 to 135.

Requirements for an extension of stay in order to take the PLAB Test

75D. The requirements for an extension of stay in the United Kingdom in order to take the PLAB Test are that the applicant:

(iv) intends to leave the United Kingdom at the end of his leave granted under this paragraph unless he is successful in the PLAB Test and granted leave to remain:

(c) as a work permit holder for employment in the United Kingdom as a doctor in accordance with paragraphs 128 to 135; and

Requirements for leave to enter to undertake a clinical or dental observer post

75G. The requirements to be met by a person seeking leave to enter to undertake a clinical attachment or dental observer post are that the applicant:

(iv) intends to leave the United Kingdom at the end of his leave granted under this paragraph unless he is granted leave to remain:

(b) as a work permit holder for employment in the United Kingdom as a doctor or dentist in accordance with paragraphs 128 to 135; and

Requirements for an extension of stay in order to undertake a clinical attachment or dental observer post

75K. The requirements to be met by a person seeking an extension of stay to undertake a clinical attachment or dental observer post are that the applicant:

(iv) intends to leave the United Kingdom at the end of his period of leave granted under this paragraph unless he is granted leave to remain:

(b) as a work permit holder for employment in the United Kingdom as a doctor or dentist in accordance with paragraphs 128 to 135; and

D. Definition of an 'au pair' placement

88. For the purposes of these Rules an 'au pair' placement as an arrangement whereby a young person:

(a) comes to the United Kingdom for the purpose of learning the English language; and

(b) lives for a time as a member of an English speaking family with appropriate opportunities for study; and

(c) helps in the home for a maximum of 5 hours per day in return for a reasonable allowance and with two free days a week.

Requirements for leave to enter as an 'au pair'

89. The requirements to be met by a person seeking leave to enter the United Kingdom as an 'au pair' are that he:

 (i) is seeking entry for the purpose of taking up an arranged placement which can be shown to fall within the definition set out in paragraph 88; and

 (ii) is aged between 17 and 27 inclusive or was so aged when first given leave to enter this category; and

 (iii) is unmarried and is not a civil partner; and

 (iv) is without dependants; and

 (v) is a national of one of the following countries: Andorra, Bosnia-Herzegovina, Croatia, The Faroes, Greenland, Macedonia, Monaco, San Marino or Turkey; and

 (vi) does not intend to stay in the United Kingdom for more than 2 years as an 'au pair'; and

 (vii) intends to leave the United Kingdom on completion of his stay as an 'au pair'; and

 (viii) if he has previously spent time in the United Kingdom as an 'au pair', is not seeking leave to enter to a date beyond 2 years from the date on which he was first given leave to enter the United Kingdom in this capacity; and

 (ix) is able to maintain and accommodate himself without recourse to public funds.

Leave to enter as an 'au pair'

90. A person seeking leave to enter the United Kingdom as an 'au pair' may be admitted for a period not exceeding 2 years with a prohibition on employment except as an 'au pair' provided the Immigration Officer is satisfied that each of the requirements of paragraph 89 is met. (A non-visa national who wishes to ascertain in advance whether a proposed 'au pair' placement is likely to meet the requirements of paragraph 89 is advised to obtain an entry clearance before travelling to the United Kingdom.)

Refusal of leave to enter as an 'au pair'

91. An application for leave to enter as an 'au pair' is to be refused if the Immigration Officer is not satisfied that each of the requirements of paragraph 89 is met.

E. Working Holidaymakers

Requirements for leave to enter as a working holidaymaker

95. The requirements to be met by a person seeking leave to enter the United Kingdom as a working holidaymaker are that he:

 (i) is a national or citizen of a country listed in Appendix 3 of these Rules, or a British Overseas Citizen; a British Overseas Territories Citizen; or a British National; and

(ii) is aged between 17 and 30 inclusive or was so aged at the date of his application for leave to enter; and

(iii) (a) is unmarried and is not a civil partner; or

(b) is married to, or the civil partner of, a person who meets the requirements of this paragraph and the parties to the marriage or civil partnership intend to take a working holiday together; and

(iv) has the means to pay for his return or onward journey; and

(v) is able and intends to maintain and accommodate himself without recourse to public funds; and

(vi) is intending only to take employment incidental to a holiday, and not to engage in business, or to provide services as a professional sportsperson, and in any event not to work for more than 12 months during his stay; and

(vii) does not have dependent children any of whom are 5 years of age or over or who will reach 5 years of age before the applicant completes his working holiday; and

(viii) intends to leave the UK at the end of his working holiday: and

(ix) has not spent time in the United Kingdom on a previous working holidaymaker entry clearance; and

(x) holds a valid United Kingdom entry clearance, granted for a limited period not exceeding 2 years, for entry in this capacity.

Leave to enter as a working holidaymaker

96. A person seeking to enter the United Kingdom as a working holidaymaker may be admitted provided he is able to produce on arrival a valid United Kingdom entry clearance granted for a period not exceeding 2 years for entry in this capacity.

Refusal of leave to enter as a working holidaymaker

97. Leave to enter as a working holidaymaker is to be refused if a valid United Kingdom entry clearance for entry in this capacity is not produced to the Immigration Officer on arrival.

F. Children of working holidaymakers

Requirements for leave to enter or remain as the child of a working holidaymaker

101. The requirements to be met by a person seeking leave to enter or remain in the United Kingdom as the child of a working holidaymaker are that:

(i) he is the child of a parent admitted to, and currently present in, the United Kingdom as a working holidaymaker; and

(ii) he is under the age of 5 and will leave the United Kingdom before reaching that age; and

(iii) he can and will be maintained and accommodated adequately without recourse to public funds or without his parent(s) engaging in employment except as provided by paragraph 95 above; and

(iv) both parents are being or have been admitted to the United Kingdom, save where:

(a) the parent he is accompanying or joining is his sole surviving parent; or

(b) the parent he is accompanying or joining has had sole responsibility for his upbringing; or

(c) there are serious and compelling family or other considerations which make exclusion from the United Kingdom undesirable and suitable arrangements have been made for his care; and

(v) he holds a valid United Kingdom entry clearance for entry in this capacity or, if seeking leave to remain, was admitted with a valid United Kingdom entry clearance for entry in this capacity, and is seeking leave to a date not beyond the date to which his parent(s) have leave to enter in the working holidaymaker category.

Leave to enter or remain as the child of a working holidaymaker

102. A person seeking to enter the United Kingdom as the child of working holidaymaker/s must be able to produce on arrival a valid United Kingdom entry clearance for entry in this capacity.

Refusal of leave to enter or remain as the child of a working holidaymaker

103. Leave to enter or remain in the United Kingdom as the child of a working holidaymaker is to be refused if, in relation to an application for leave to enter, a valid United Kingdom entry clearance for entry in this capacity is not produced to the Immigration Officer on arrival or, in the case of an application for leave to remain, the applicant was not admitted with a valid United Kingdom entry clearance for entry in this capacity or is unable to satisfy the Secretary of State that each of the requirements of paragraph 101 (i)–(iv) is met.

G. Requirements for leave to enter as a teacher or language assistant under an approved exchange scheme

110. The requirements to be met by a person seeking leave to enter the United Kingdom as a teacher or language assistant on an approved exchange scheme are that he:

(i) is coming to an educational establishment in the United Kingdom under an exchange scheme approved by the Department for Education and Skills, the Scottish or Welsh Office of Education or the Department of Education, Northern Ireland, or administered by the British Council's Education and Training Group or the League for the Exchange of Commonwealth Teachers; and

(ii) intends to leave the United Kingdom at the end of his exchange period; and

(iii) does not intend to take employment except in the terms of this paragraph; and

(iv) is able to maintain and accommodate himself and any dependants without recourse to public funds; and

(v) holds a valid United Kingdom entry clearance for entry in this capacity.

Leave to enter as a teacher or language assistant under an exchange scheme

111. A person seeking leave to enter the United Kingdom as a teacher or language assistant under an approved exchange scheme may be given leave to enter for a period not exceeding 12 months provided he is able to produce to the Immigration Officer, on arrival, a valid United Kingdom entry clearance for entry in this capacity.

Refusal of leave to enter as a teacher or language assistant under an approved exchange scheme

112. Leave to enter the United Kingdom as a teacher or language assistant under an approved exchange scheme is to be refused if a valid United Kingdom entry clearance for entry in this capacity is not produced to the Immigration Officer on arrival.

Requirements for extension of stay as a teacher or language assistant under an approved exchange scheme

113. The requirements for an extension of stay as a teacher or language assistant under an approved exchange scheme are that the applicant:

(i) entered the United Kingdom with a valid United Kingdom entry clearance as a teacher or language assistant; and

(ii) is still engaged in the employment for which his entry clearance was granted; and

(iii) is still required for the employment in question, as certified by the employer; and

(iv) meets the requirements of paragraph 110 (ii)–(iv); and

(v) would not, as a result of an extension of stay, remain in the United Kingdom as an exchange teacher or language assistant for more than 2 years from the date on which he was first given leave to enter the United Kingdom in this capacity.

Extension of stay as a teacher or language assistant under an approved exchange scheme

114. An extension of stay as a teacher or language assistant under an approved exchange scheme may be granted for a further period not exceeding 12 months provided the Secretary of State is satisfied that each of the requirements of paragraph 113 is met.

Refusal of extension of stay as a teacher or language assistant under an approved exchange scheme

115. An extension of stay as a teacher or language assistant under an approved exchange scheme is to be refused if the Secretary of State is not satisfied that each of the requirements of paragraph 113 is met.

H. Requirements for leave to enter for Home Office approved training or work experience

116. The requirements to be met by a person seeking leave to enter the United Kingdom for Home Office approved training or work experience are that he:

(i) holds a valid work permit from the Home Office issued under the Training and Work Experience Scheme; and

(ii) [Paragraph deleted]

(iii) is capable of undertaking the training or work experience as specified in his work permit; and

(iv) intends to leave the United Kingdom on the completion of his training or work experience; and

(v) does not intend to take employment except as specified in his work permit; and

(vi) is able to maintain and accommodate himself and any dependants adequately without recourse to public funds; and

(vii) holds a valid United Kingdom entry clearance for entry in this capacity except where he holds a work permit valid for 6 months or less or he is a British National (Overseas), a British overseas territories citizen, a British Overseas citizen, a British protected person or a person who under the British Nationality Act 1981 is a British subject.

Leave to enter for Home Office approved training or work experience

117. A person seeking leave to enter the United Kingdom for the purpose of approved training or approved work experience under the Training or Work Experience Scheme may be admitted to the United Kingdom for a period not exceeding the period of training or work experience approved by the Home Office for this purpose(as specified in his work permit), subject to a condition restricting him to that approved employment, provided he is able to produce to the Immigration Officer, on arrival, a valid United Kingdom entry clearance for entry in this capacity or, where entry clearance is not required, provided the Immigration Officer is satisfied that each of the requirements of paragraph 116(i)–(vi) is met.

Refusal of leave to enter for Home Office approved training or work experience

118. Leave to enter the United Kingdom for Home Office approved training or work experience under the Training and Work Experience scheme is to be refused if a valid United Kingdom entry clearance for entry in this capacity is not produced to the Immigration Officer on arrival or, where entry clearance is not required, if the Immigration Officer is not satisfied that each of the requirements of paragraph 116(i)–(vi) is met.

Requirements for extension of stay for Home Office approved training or work experience

119. The requirements for an extension of stay for Home Office approved training or work experience are that the applicant:

(i) entered the United Kingdom with a valid work permit under paragraph 117 or was admitted or allowed to remain in the United Kingdom as a student; and

(ii) has written approval from the Home Office for an extension of stay in this category; and

(iii) meets the requirements of paragraph 116(ii)–(vi).

Extension of stay for Home Office approved training or work experience

120. An extension of stay for approved training or approved work experience under the Training and Work Experience scheme may be granted for a further period not exceeding the extended period of training or work experience approved by the Home Office for this purpose (as specified in his work permit), provided that in each case the Secretary of State is satisfied that the requirements of paragraph 119 are met. An extension of stay is to be subject to a condition permitting the applicant to take or change employment only with the permission of the Home Office.

Refusal of extension of stay for Home Office approved training or work experience

121. An extension of stay for approved training or approved work experience under the Training and Work Experience scheme is to be refused if the Secretary of State is not satisfied that each of the requirements of paragraph 119 is met.

I. Representatives of overseas newspapers, news agencies and broadcasting organisations

Requirements for leave to enter as a representative of an overseas newspaper, news agency or broadcasting organisation

136. The requirements to be met by a person seeking leave to enter the United Kingdom as a representative of an overseas newspaper, news agency or broadcasting organisation are that he:

(i) has been engaged by that organisation outside the United Kingdom and is being posted to the United Kingdom on a long term assignment as a representative; and

(ii) intends to work full time as a representative of that overseas newspaper, news agency or broadcasting organisation; and

(iii) does not intend to take employment except within the terms of this paragraph; and

(iv) can maintain and accommodate himself and any dependants adequately without recourse to public funds; and

(v) holds a valid United Kingdom entry clearance for entry in this capacity.

Leave to enter as a representative of an overseas newspaper, newsagency or broadcasting organisation

137. A person seeking leave to enter the United Kingdom as a representative of an overseas newspaper, news agency or broadcasting organisation may be admitted for a period not exceeding 2 years, provided he is able to produce to the Immigration Officer, on arrival, a valid United Kingdom entry clearance for entry in this capacity.

Refusal of leave to enter as a representative of an overseas newspaper, news agency or broadcasting organisation

138. Leave to enter as a representative of an overseas newspaper, news agency or broadcasting organisation is to be refused if a valid United Kingdom entry clearance for entry in this capacity is not produced to the Immigration Officer on arrival.

Requirements for an extension of stay as a representative of an overseas newspaper, news agency or broadcasting organisation

139. The requirements for an extension of stay as a representative of an overseas newspaper, news agency or broadcasting organisation are that the applicant:

(i) entered the United Kingdom with a valid United Kingdom entry clearance as a representative of an overseas newspaper, news agency or broadcasting organisation; and

(ii) is still engaged in the employment for which his entry clearance was granted; and

(iii) is still required for the employment in question, as certified by his employer; and

(iv) meets the requirements of paragraph 136 (ii)–(iv).

Extension of stay as a representative of an overseas newspaper, news agency or broadcasting organisation

140. An extension of stay as a representative of an overseas newspaper, news agency or broadcasting organisation may be granted for a period not exceeding 3 years provided the Secretary of State is satisfied that each of the requirements of paragraph 139 is met.

Refusal of extension of stay as a representative of an overseas newspaper, news agency or broadcasting organisation

141. An extension of stay as a representative of an overseas newspaper, news agency or broadcasting organisation is to be refused if the Secretary of State is not satisfied that each of the requirements of paragraph 139 is met.

J. Private servants in diplomatic households

Requirements for leave to enter as a private servant in a diplomatic household

152. The requirements to be met by a person seeking leave to enter the United Kingdom as a private servant in a diplomatic household are that he:

(i) is aged 18 or over; and

(ii) is employed as a private servant in the household of a member of staff of a diplomatic or consular mission who enjoys diplomatic privileges and immunity within the meaning of the Vienna Convention on Diplomatic and Consular Relations or a member of the family forming part of the household of such a person; and

(iii) intends to work full time as a private servant within the terms of this paragraph; and

(iv) does not intend to take employment except within the terms of this paragraph; and

(v) can maintain and accommodate himself and any dependants adequately without recourse to public funds; and

(vi) holds a valid United Kingdom entry clearance for entry in this capacity.

Leave to enter as a private servant in a diplomatic household

153. A person seeking leave to enter the United Kingdom as a private servant in a diplomatic household may be given leave to enter for a period not exceeding 12 months provided he is able to produce to the Immigration Officer, on arrival, a valid United Kingdom entry clearance for entry in this capacity.

Refusal of leave to enter as a private servant in a diplomatic household

154. Leave to enter as a private servant in a diplomatic household is to be refused if a valid United Kingdom entry clearance for entry in this capacity is not produced to the Immigration Officer on arrival.

Requirements for an extension of stay as a private servant in a diplomatic household

155. The requirements for an extension of stay as a private servant in a diplomatic household are that the applicant:

(i) entered the United Kingdom with a valid United Kingdom entry clearance as a private servant in a diplomatic household; and

(ii) is still engaged in the employment for which his entry clearance was granted; and

(iii) is still required for the employment in question, as certified by the employer; and

(iv) meets the requirements of paragraph 152 (iii)–(v).

Extension of stay as a private servant in a diplomatic household

156. An extension of stay as a private servant in a diplomatic household may be granted for a period not exceeding 12 months at a time provided the Secretary of State is satisfied that each of the requirements of paragraph 155 is met.

Refusal of extension of stay as a private servant in a diplomatic household

157. An extension of stay as a private servant in a diplomatic household is to be refused if the Secretary of State is not satisfied that each of the requirements of paragraph 155 is met.

K. Overseas government employees

Requirements for leave to enter as an overseas government employee

160. For the purposes of these Rules an overseas government employee means a person coming for employment by an overseas government or employed by the United Nations Organisation or other international organisation of which the United Kingdom is a member.

161. The requirements to be met by a person seeking leave to enter the United Kingdom as an overseas government employee are that he:

(i) is able to produce either a valid United Kingdom entry clearance for entry in this capacity or satisfactory documentary evidence of his status as an overseas government employee; and

(ii) intends to work full time for the government or organisation concerned; and

(iii) does not intend to take employment except within the terms of this paragraph; and

(iv) can maintain and accommodate himself and any dependants adequately without recourse to public funds.

Leave to enter as an overseas government employee

162. A person seeking leave to enter the United Kingdom as an overseas government employee may be given leave to enter for a period not exceeding 2 years, provided he is able, on arrival, to produce to the Immigration Officer a valid United Kingdom entry clearance for entry in this capacity or satisfy the Immigration Officer that each of the requirements of paragraph 161 is met.

Refusal of leave to enter as an overseas government employee

163. Leave to enter as an overseas government employee is to be refused if a valid United Kingdom entry clearance for entry in this capacity is not produced to the Immigration Officer on arrival or if the Immigration Officer is not satisfied that each of the requirements of paragraph 161 is met.

Requirements for an extension of stay as an overseas government employee

164. The requirements to be met by a person seeking an extension of stay as an overseas government employee are that the applicant:

(i) was given leave to enter the United Kingdom under paragraph 162 as an overseas government employee; and

(ii) is still engaged in the employment in question; and

(iii) is still required for the employment in question, as certified by the employer; and

(iv) meets the requirements of paragraph 161 (ii)–(iv).

Extension of stay as an overseas government employee

165. An extension of stay as an overseas government employee may be granted for a period not exceeding 3 years provided the Secretary of State is satisfied that each of the requirements of paragraph 164 is met.

Refusal of extension of stay as an overseas government employee

166. An extension of stay as an overseas government employee is to be refused if the Secretary of State is not satisfied that each of the requirements of paragraph 164 is met.

L. Requirements for leave to enter as a minister of religion, *missionary, or member of a religious order*

170. The requirements to be met by a person seeking leave to enter the United Kingdom as a minister of religion, missionary or member of a religious order are that he:

i) (a) if seeking leave to enter as a Minister of Religion has either been working for at least one year as a minister of religion in any of the 5 years immediately prior to the date on which the application is made or, where ordination is prescribed by a religious faith as the sole means of entering the ministry, has been ordained as a minister of religion following at least one year's full time or two years' part time training for the ministry; or

(b) if seeking leave to enter as a missionary has been trained as a missionary or has worked as a missionary and is being sent to the United Kingdom by an overseas organisation; or

(c) if seeking leave to enter as a member of a religious order is coming to live in a community maintained by the religious order of which he is a member and, if intending to teach, does not intend to do so save at an establishment maintained by his order; and

(ii) intends to work full time as a minister of religion, missionary or for the religious order of which he is a member; and

(iii) does not intend to take employment except within the terms of this paragraph; and

(iv) can maintain and accommodate himself and any dependants adequately without recourse to public funds; and

(iva) if seeking leave as a Minister of Religion can produce an International English Language Testing System certificate issued to him to certify that he has achieved level 6 competence in spoken and written English and that it is dated not more than two years prior to the date on which the application is made.

(v) holds a valid United Kingdom entry clearance for entry in this capacity.

Leave to enter as a minister of religion, missionary, or member of a religious order

171. A person seeking leave to enter the United Kingdom as a minister of religion, missionary or member of a religious order may be admitted for a period not exceeding 2 years provided he is able to produce to the Immigration Officer, on arrival, a valid United Kingdom entry clearance for entry in this capacity.

Refusal of leave to enter as a minister of religion, missionary or member of a religious order

172. Leave to enter as a minister of religion, missionary or member of a religious order is to be refused if a valid United Kingdom entry clearance for entry in this capacity is not produced to the Immigration Officer on arrival.

Requirements for an extension of stay as a minister of religion where entry to the United Kingdom was granted in that capacity

173. The requirements for an extension of stay as a minister of religion, where entry to the United Kingdom was granted in that capacity, missionary or member of a religious order are that the applicant:

(i) entered the United Kingdom with a valid United Kingdom entry clearance as a minister of religion, missionary or member of a religious order; and

(ii) is still engaged in the employment for which his entry clearance was granted; and

(iii) is still required for the employment in question as certified by the leadership of his congregation, his employer or the head of his religious order; and

(iv) (a) if he entered the United Kingdom as a minister of religion, missionary or member of a religious order in accordance with sub paragraph (i) prior to 23 August 2004 meets the requirements of paragraph 170(ii)–(iv); or

(b) if he entered the United Kingdom as a minister of religion, missionary or member of a religious order in accordance with sub paragraph (i), on or after 23 August 2004 but prior to 19 April 2007, or was granted leave to remain in accordance with paragraph 174B between those dates, meets the requirements of paragraph 170 (ii)–(iv), and if a minister of religion met the requirement to produce an International English Language Testing System certificate certifying that he achieved level 4 competence in spoken English at the time he was first granted leave in this capacity; or

(c) if he entered the United Kingdom as a minister of religion, missionary or member of a religious order in accordance with sub paragraph (i) on or after 19 April 2007, or was granted leave to remain in accordance with paragraph 174B on or after that date, meets the requirements of paragraph 170 (ii)–(iv), and if a Minister of Religion met the requirement to produce an International English Language Testing System certificate certifying that he achieved level 6 competence in spoken and written English at the time he was first granted leave in this capacity.

Extension of stay as a minister of religion, missionary or member of a religious order

174. An extension of stay as a minister of religion, missionary or member of a religious order may be granted for a period not exceeding 3 years provided the Secretary of State is satisfied that each of the requirements of paragraph 173 is met.

Requirements for an extension of stay as a minister of religion where entry to the United Kingdom was not granted in that capacity

174A. The requirements for an extension of stay as a minister of religion for an applicant who did not enter the United Kingdom in that capacity are that he:

(i) entered the United Kingdom, or was given an extension of stay, in accordance with these Rules, except as a minister of religion or as a visitor under paragraphs 40–56 of these Rules, and has spent a continuous period of at least 12 months here pursuant to that leave immediately prior to the application being made; and

(ii) has either been working for at least one year as a minister of religion in any of the 5 years immediately prior to the date on which the application is made (provided that, when doing so, he was not in breach of a condition of any subsisting leave to enter or remain) or, where ordination is prescribed by a religious faith as the sole means of entering the ministry, has been ordained as a minister of religion following at least one year's full-time or two years part-time training for the ministry; and

(iii) is imminently to be appointed, or has been appointed, to a position as a minister of religion in the United Kingdom and is suitable for such a position, as certified by the leadership of his prospective congregation; and

(iv) meets the requirements of paragraph 170 (ii)–(iva).

Extension of stay as a minister of religion where leave to enter was not granted in that capacity

174B. An extension of stay as a minister of religion may be granted for a period not exceeding 3 years at a time provided the Secretary of State is satisfied that each of the requirements of paragraph 174A is met.

Refusal of extension of stay as a minister of religion, missionary or member of a religious order

175. An extension of stay as a minister of religion, missionary or member of a religious order is to be refused if the Secretary of State is not satisfied that each of the requirements of paragraph 173 or 174A is met.

M. *Refusal of indefinite leave to remain for a minister of religion, missionary or member of a religious order*

177. Indefinite leave to remain in the United Kingdom for a minister of religion, missionary or member of a religious order is to be refused if the Secretary of State is not satisfied that each of the requirements of paragraph 176 is met.

177A. For the purposes of these Rules: Visiting religious workers and religious workers in non-pastoral roles:

(i) a visiting religious worker means a person coming to the UK for a short period to perform religious duties at one or more locations in the UK;

(ii) a religious worker in a non-pastoral role means a person employed in the UK by the faith he is coming here to work for, whose duties include performing religious rites within the religious community, but not preaching to a congregation.

Requirements for leave to enter the United Kingdom as a visiting religious worker or a religious worker in a non-pastoral role

177B. The requirements to be met by a person seeking leave to enter as a visiting religious worker or a religious worker in a non-pastoral role are that the applicant:

(i) (a) if seeking leave to enter as a visiting religious worker:

(i) is an established religious worker based overseas; and

(ii) submits a letter(s) from a senior member or senior representative of one or more local religious communities in the UK confirming that he is invited to perform religious duties as a visiting religious worker at one or more locations in the UK and confirming the expected duration of that employment; and

(iii) if he has been granted leave as a visiting religious worker in the last 12 months, is not seeking leave to enter which, when amalgamated with his previous periods of leave in this category in the last 12 months, would total more than 6 months; or

(b) if seeking leave to enter as a religious worker in a non-pastoral role:

(i) has at least one year of full time training or work experience, or a period of part- time training or work experience equivalent to one year full time training or work experience, accrued in the five years preceding the application in the faith with which he has employment in the UK; and

(ii) can show that, at the time of his application, at least one full-time member of staff of the local religious community which the applicant is applying to join in the UK has a sufficient knowledge of English; and

(iii) submits a letter from a senior member or senior representative of the local religious community which has invited him to the UK, confirming that he has been offered employment as religious worker in a non-pastoral role in that religious community, and confirming the duration of that employment; and

(ii) does not intend to take employment except as a visiting religious worker or religious worker in a non-pastoral role, whichever is the basis of his application; and

(iii) does not intend to undertake employment as a Minister of Religion, Missionary or Member of a Religious Order, as described in paragraphs 169–177 of these Rules; and

(iv) is able to maintain and accommodate himself and any dependants without recourse to public funds, or will, with any dependants, be maintained and accommodated adequately by the religious community employing him; and

(v) intends to leave the UK at the end of his leave in this category; and

(vi) holds a valid entry clearance for entry in this capacity except where he is a British National (Overseas), a British overseas territories citizen, a British Overseas citizen, a British protected person or a person who under the British Nationality Act 1981 is a British subject.

Leave to enter as a visiting religious worker or a religious worker in a non-pastoral role

177C. Leave to enter the United Kingdom as a visiting religious worker or a religious worker in a non-pastoral role may be granted:

(a) as a visiting religious worker, for a period not exceeding 6 months; or

(b) as a religious worker in a non-pastoral role, for a period not exceeding 12 months; provided the Immigration Officer is satisfied that each of the requirements of paragraph 177B is met.

Refusal of leave to enter as a visiting religious worker or a religious worker in a non-pastoral role

177D. Leave to enter as a visiting religious worker or a religious worker in a non pastoral role is to be refused if the Immigration Officer is not satisfied that each of the requirements of paragraph 177B is met.

Requirements for an extension of stay as a visiting religious worker or a religious worker in a non pastoral role

177E. The requirements to be met by a person seeking an extension of stay as a visiting religious worker or a religious worker in a non-pastoral role are that the applicant:

(i) entered the United Kingdom with a valid entry clearance in this capacity or was given leave to enter as a visiting religious worker or a religious worker in a non-pastoral role; and

(ii) intends to continue employment as a visiting religious worker or a religious worker in a non-pastoral role; and

(iii) if seeking an extension of stay as a visiting religious worker:

(a) meets the requirement of paragraph 177B(i)(a)(i) above; and

(b) submits a letter from a senior member or senior representative of one or more local religious communities in the UK confirming that he is still wanted to perform religious duties as a visiting religious worker at one or more locations in the UK and confirming the expected duration of that employment; and

(c) would not, as the result of an extension of stay, be granted leave as a visiting religious worker which, when amalgamated with his previous periods of leave in this category in the last 12 months, would total more than 6 months; or

(iv) if seeking an extension of stay as a religious worker in a non-pastoral role:

(a) meets the requirements of paragraph 177B(i)(b)(i) and (ii); and

(b) submits a letter from a senior member or senior representative of the local religious community for which he works in the UK confirming that his employment as a religious worker in a non-pastoral role in that religious community will continue, and confirming the duration of that employment; and

(c) would not, as the result of an extension of stay, remain in the UK for a period of more than 24 months as a religious worker in a non-pastoral role; and

(v) meets the requirements of paragraph 177B (ii) to (v).

Extension of stay as a visiting religious worker or a religious worker in a non-pastoral role

177F. An extension of stay as a visiting religious worker or a religious worker in a non-pastoral role may be granted:

(a) as a visiting religious worker, for a period not exceeding 6 months; or

(b) as a religious worker in a non-pastoral role, for a period not exceeding 24 months;

if the Secretary of State is satisfied that each of the requirements of paragraph 177E is met.

Refusal of an extension of stay as a visiting religious worker or a religious worker in a non pastoral role

177G. An extension of stay as a visiting religious worker or a religious worker in a non-pastoral role is to be refused if the Secretary of State is not satisfied that each of the requirements of paragraph 177E is met.

N. *Airport based operational ground staff of overseas-owned airlines*

Requirements for leave to enter the United Kingdom as a member of the operational ground staff of an overseas-owned airline

178. The requirements to be met by a person seeking leave to enter the United Kingdom as a member of the operational ground staff of an overseas owned airline are that he:

(i) has been transferred to the United Kingdom by an overseas-owned airline operating services to and from the United Kingdom to take up duty at an international airport as station manager, security manager or technical manager; and

(ii) intends to work full time for the airline concerned; and

(iii) does not intend to take employment except within the terms of this paragraph; and

(iv) can maintain and accommodate himself and any dependants without recourse to public funds; and

(v) holds a valid United Kingdom entry clearance for entry in this capacity.

Leave to enter as a member of the operational ground staff of an overseas owned airline

179. A person seeking leave to enter the United Kingdom as a member of the operational ground staff of an overseas owned airline may be given leave to enter for a period not exceeding 2 years, provided he is able to produce to the Immigration Officer, on arrival, a valid United Kingdom entry clearance for entry in this capacity.

Refusal of leave to enter as a member of the operational ground staff of an overseas owned airline

180. Leave to enter as a member of the operational ground staff of an overseas owned airline is to be refused if a valid United Kingdom entry clearance for entry in this capacity is not produced to the Immigration Officer on arrival.

Requirements for an extension of stay as a member of the operational ground staff of an overseas owned airline

181. The requirements to be met by a person seeking an extension of stay as a member of the operational ground staff of an overseas owned airline are that the applicant:

    (i) entered the United Kingdom with a valid United Kingdom entry clearance as a member of the operational ground staff of an overseas owned airline; and

    (ii) is still engaged in the employment for which entry was granted; and

    (iii) is still required for the employment in question, as certified by the employer; and

    (iv) meets the requirements of paragraph 178 (ii)–(iv).

Extension of stay as a member of the operational ground staff of an overseas owned airline

182. An extension of stay as a member of the operational ground staff of an overseas owned airline may be granted for a period not exceeding 3 years, provided the Secretary of State is satisfied that each of the requirements of paragraph 181 is met.

Refusal of extension of stay as a member of the operational ground staff of an overseas owned airline

183. An extension of stay as a member of the operational ground staff of an overseas owned airline is to be refused if the Secretary of State is not satisfied that each of the requirements of paragraph 181 is met.

O. Retired persons of independent means

Requirements for leave to enter the United Kingdom as a retired person of independent means

263. The requirements to be met by a person seeking leave to enter the United Kingdom as a retired person of independent means are that he:

    (i) is at least 60 years old; and

    (ii) has under his control and disposable in the United Kingdom an income of his own of not less than £25,000 per annum; and

    (iii) is able and willing to maintain and accommodate himself and any dependants indefinitely in the United Kingdom from his own resources with no assistance from any other person and without taking employment or having recourse to public funds; and

    (iv) can demonstrate a close connection with the United Kingdom; and

    (v) intends to make the United Kingdom his main home; and

    (vi) holds a valid United Kingdom entry clearance for entry in this capacity.

Leave to enter as a retired person of independent means

264. A person seeking leave to enter the United Kingdom as a retired person of independent means may be admitted subject to a condition prohibiting employment for a period not exceeding 5 years, provided he is able to produce to the Immigration Officer, on arrival, a valid United Kingdom entry clearance for entry in this capacity.

Refusal of leave to enter as a retired person of independent means

265. Leave to enter as a retired person of independent means is to be refused if a valid United Kingdom entry clearance for entry in this capacity is not produced to the Immigration Officer on arrival.

Requirements for an extension of stay as a retired person of independent means

266. The requirements for an extension of stay as a retired person of independent means are that the applicant:

 (i) entered the United Kingdom with a valid United Kingdom entry clearance as a retired person of independent means; and

 (ii) meets the requirements of paragraph 263 (ii)–(iv); and

 (iii) has made the United Kingdom his main home.

Extension of stay as a retired person of independent means

266A. The requirements for an extension of stay as a retired person of independent means for a person in the United Kingdom as a work permit holder are that the applicant:

 (i) entered the United Kingdom or was granted leave to remain as a work permit holder in accordance with paragraphs 128 to 133 of these Rules; and

 (ii) meets the requirements of paragraph 263 (i)–(v).

266B. The requirements for an extension of stay as a retired person of independent means for a person in the United Kingdom as a highly skilled migrant are that the applicant:

 (i) entered the United Kingdom or was granted leave to remain as a highly skilled migrant in accordance with paragraphs 135A to 135F of these Rules; and

 (ii) meets the requirements of paragraph 263 (i)–(v).

266C. The requirements for an extension of stay as a retired person of independent means for a person in the United Kingdom to establish themselves or remain in business are that the applicant:

 (i) entered the United Kingdom or was granted leave to remain as a person intending to establish themselves or remain in business in accordance with paragraphs 201 to 208 of these Rules; and

 (ii) meets the requirements of paragraph 263 (i)–(v).

266D. The requirements for an extension of stay as a retired person of independent means for a person in the United Kingdom as an innovator are that the applicant:

 (i) entered the United Kingdom or was granted leave to remain as an innovator in accordance with paragraphs 210A to 210F of these Rules; and

 (ii) meets the requirements of paragraph 263 (i)–(v).

266E. The requirements for an extension of stay as a retired person of independent means for a person in the UK as a Tier 1 (General) Migrant, Tier 1 (Entrepreneur) Migrant or Tier 1 (Investor) Migrant are that the applicant:

 (i) entered the UK or was granted leave to remain as a Tier 1 (General) Migrant, Tier 1 (Entrepreneur) Migrant or Tier 1 (Investor) Migrant; and

 (ii) meets the requirements of paragraphs 263(i)–(v).

267. An extension of stay as a retired person of independent means, with a prohibition on the taking of employment, may be granted so as to bring the person's stay in this category up to a maximum of 5 years in aggregate, provided the Secretary of State is satisfied that each of the requirements of paragraph 266 is met. An extension of stay as a retired person of independent means, with a prohibition on the taking of employment, may be granted for a maximum period of 5 years, provided the Secretary of State is satisfied that each of the requirements of paragraph 266A, 266B, 266C, 266D or 266E is met.

Refusal of extension of stay as a retired person of independent means

268. An extension of stay as a retired person of independent means is to be refused if the Secretary of State is not satisfied that each of the requirements of paragraph 266, 266A, 266B, 266C, 266D or 266E is met.

Indefinite leave to remain for a retired person of independent means

269. Indefinite leave to remain may be granted, on application, to a person admitted as a retired person of independent means provided he:

 (i) has spent a continuous period of 5 years in the United Kingdom in this capacity; and

 (ii) has met the requirements of paragraph 266 throughout the 5 year period and continues to do so.

Refusal of indefinite leave to remain for a retired person of independent means

270. Indefinite leave to remain in the United Kingdom for a retired person of independent means is to be refused if the Secretary of State is not satisfied that each of the requirements of paragraph 269 is met.

IMMIGRATION RULES AS AT 30 MARCH 2009 RELATING TO STUDENTS, STUDENT NURSES, STUDENTS RE-SITTING AN EXAMINATION, STUDENTS WRITING-UP A THESIS, POSTGRADUATE DOCTORS OR DENTISTS, SABBATICAL OFFICERS AND APPLICANTS UNDER THE SECTORS-BASED SCHEME

Specified forms and procedures for applications or claims in connection with immigration

34B. Where an application form is specified, it must be sent by prepaid post to the United Kingdom Border Agency of the Home Office, or submitted in person at a public enquiry office of the United Kingdom Border Agency of the Home Office, save for the following exceptions:

(i) an application may not be submitted at a public enquiry office of the United Kingdom Border Agency of the Home Office if it is an application for:

(f) limited leave to remain as a Tier 5 (Temporary Worker) Migrant.

Requirements for leave to enter as a student

57. The requirements to be met by a person seeking leave to enter the United Kingdom as a student are that he:

(i) has been accepted for a course of study, or a period of research, which is to be provided by or undertaken at an organisation which is included on the Register of Education and Training Providers, and is at either;

(a) a publicly funded institution of further or higher education which maintains satisfactory records of enrolment and attendance of students and supplies these to the United Kingdom Border Agency when requested; or

(b) a bona fide private education institution; or

(c) an independent fee paying school outside the maintained sector which maintains satisfactory records of enrolment and attendance of students and supplies these to the United Kingdom Border Agency when requested; and

(ii) is able and intends to follow either:

(a) a recognised full-time degree course or postgraduate studies at a publicly funded institution of further or higher education; or

(b) a period of study and/or research in excess of 6 months at a publicly funded institution of higher education where this forms part of an overseas degree course; or

(c) a weekday full-time course involving attendance at a single institution for a minimum of 15 hours organised daytime study per week of a single subject, or directly related subjects; or

(d) a full-time course of study at an independent fee paying school; and

(iii) if under the age of 16 years is enrolled at an independent fee paying school on a full time course of studies which meets the requirements of the Education Act 1944; and

(iv) if he has been accepted to study externally for a degree at a private education institution, he is also registered as an external student with the UK degree awarding body; and

(v) he holds a valid Academic Technology Approval Scheme (ATAS) clearance certificate from the Counter-Proliferation Department of the Foreign and Commonwealth Office which relates to the course, or area of research, he intends to undertake and the institution at which he wishes to undertake it; if he intends to undertake either,

(i) postgraduate studies leading to a Doctorate or Master's degree by research in one of the disciplines listed in paragraph 1 of Appendix 6 to these Rules; or

(ii) postgraduate studies leading to a taught Masters degree in one of the disciplines listed in paragraph 2 of Appendix 6 to these Rules; or

(iii) a period of study or research, as described in paragraph 57(ii)(b), in one of the disciplines listed in paragraph 1 or 2 of Appendix 6 to these Rules, that forms part of an overseas postgraduate qualification; and

(vi) intends to leave the United Kingdom at the end of his studies; and

(vii) does not intend to engage in business or to take employment, except part-time or vacation work undertaken with the consent of the Secretary of State; and

(viii) is able to meet the costs of his course and accommodation and the maintenance of himself and any dependants without taking employment or engaging in business or having recourse to public funds; and

(ix) holds a valid United Kingdom entry clearance for entry in this capacity.

Leave to enter as a student

58. A person seeking leave to enter the United Kingdom as a student may be admitted for an appropriate period depending on the length of his course of study and his means, and with a condition restricting his freedom to take employment, provided he is able to produce to the Immigration Officer on arrival a valid United Kingdom entry clearance for entry in this capacity.

Refusal of leave to enter as a student

59. Leave to enter as a student is to be refused if the Immigration Officer is not satisfied that each of the requirements of paragraph 57 is met.

Requirements for an extension of stay as a student

60. The requirements for an extension of stay as a student are that the applicant:

(i)(a) was last admitted to the United Kingdom in possession of a valid student entry clearance in accordance with paragraphs 57–62 or valid prospective student entry clearance in accordance with paragraphs 82–87 of these Rules; or

(b) has previously been granted leave to enter or remain in the United Kingdom to re-sit an examination in accordance with paragraphs 69A–69F of these Rules; or

(c) if he has been accepted on a course of study at degree level or above, has previously been granted leave to enter or remain in the United Kingdom in accordance with paragraphs 87A–87F, 128–135, 135O–135T and 143A to 143F or 245V to 245ZA of these Rules; or

(d) has valid leave as a student in accordance with paragraphs 57–62 of these Rules; and

(ii) meets the requirements for admission as a student set out in paragraph 57 (i)-(viii); and

(iii) has produced evidence of his enrolment on a course which meets the requirements of paragraph 57; and

(iv) can produce satisfactory evidence of regular attendance during any course which he has already begun; or any other course for which he has been enrolled in the past; and

(v) can show evidence of satisfactory progress in his course of study including the taking and passing of any relevant examinations; and

(vi) would not, as a result of an extension of stay, spend more than 2 years on short courses below degree level (ie courses of less than 1 years duration, or longer courses broken off before completion); and

(vii) has not come to the end of a period of government or international scholarship agency sponsorship, or has the written consent of his official sponsor for a further period of study in the United Kingdom and satisfactory evidence that sufficient sponsorship funding is available.

Extension of stay as a student

61. An extension of stay as a student may be granted, subject to a restriction on his freedom to take employment, provided the Secretary of State is satisfied that the applicant meets each of the requirements of paragraph 60.

Refusal of extension of stay as a student

62. An extension of stay as a student is to be refused if the Secretary of State is not satisfied that each of the requirements of paragraph 60 is met.

Student nurses

Definition of student nurse

63. For the purposes of these Rules the term student nurse means a person accepted for training as a student nurse or midwife leading to a registered nursing qualification.

Requirements for leave to enter as a student nurse

64. The requirements to be met by a person seeking leave to enter the United Kingdom as a student nurse are that the person:

(i) comes within the definition set out in paragraph 63 above; and

(ii) has been accepted for a course of study in a recognised nursing educational establishment offering nursing training which meets the requirements of the Nursing and Midwifery Council;

(iii) did not obtain acceptance on the course of study referred to in (ii) above by misrepresentation;

(iv) is able and intends to follow the course; and

(v) does not intend to engage in business or take employment except in connection with the training course; and

(vi) intends to leave the United Kingdom at the end of the course; and

(vii) has sufficient funds available for accommodation and maintenance for himself and any dependants without engaging in business or taking employment (except in connection with the training course) or having recourse to public funds. The possession of a Department of Health bursary may be taken into account in assessing whether the student meets the maintenance requirement.

Leave to enter the United Kingdom as a student nurse

65. A person seeking leave to enter the United Kingdom as a student nurse may be admitted for the duration of the course, with a restriction on his freedom to take employment, provided the Immigration Officer is satisfied that each of the requirements of paragraph 64 is met.

Refusal of leave to enter as a student nurse

66. Leave to enter as a student nurse is to be refused if the Immigration Officer is not satisfied that each of the requirements of paragraph 64 is met.

Requirements for an extension of stay as a student nurse

67. The requirements for an extension of stay as a student nurse are that the applicant:

(i) was last admitted to the United Kingdom in possession of a valid student entry clearance, or valid prospective student entry clearance in accordance with paragraphs 82 to 87 of these Rules, if he is a person specified in Appendix 1 to these Rules; and

(ii) meets the requirements set out in paragraph 64 (i)–(vii); and

(iii) has produced evidence of enrolment at a recognised nursing educational establishment; and

(iv) can provide satisfactory evidence of regular attendance during any course which he has already begun; or any other course for which he has been enrolled in the past; and

(v) would not, as a result of an extension of stay, spend more than 4 years in obtaining the relevant qualification; and

(vi) has not come to the end of a period of government or international scholarship agency sponsorship, or has the written consent of his official sponsor for a further period of study in the United Kingdom and evidence that sufficient sponsorship funding is available.

Extension of stay as a student nurse

68. An extension of stay as a student nurse may be granted, subject to a restriction on his freedom to take employment, provided the Secretary of State is satisfied that the applicant meets each of the requirements of paragraph 67.

Refusal of extension of stay as a student nurse

69. An extension of stay as a student nurse is to be refused if the Secretary of State is not satisfied that each of the requirements of paragraph 67 is met.

Re-sits of examinations

Requirements for leave to enter to re-sit an examination

69A. The requirements to be met by a person seeking leave to enter the United Kingdom in order to re-sit an examination are that the applicant:

(i) (a) meets the requirements for admission as a student set out in paragraph 57(i)–(viii); or

(b) met the requirements for admission as a student set out in paragraph 57 (i)-(iii) in the previous academic year and continues to meet the requirements of paragraph 57 (iv)–(viii), save, for the purpose of paragraphs (i)(a) or (b) above, where leave was last granted in accordance with paragraphs 57–62 of these Rules before 30 November 2007, the requirements of paragraph 57(v) do not apply; and

(ii) has produced written confirmation from the education institution or independent fee paying school which he attends or attended in the previous academic year that he is required to re-sit an examination; and

(iii) can provide satisfactory evidence of regular attendance during any course which he has already begun; or any other course for which he has been enrolled in the past; and

(iv) has not come to the end of a period of government or international scholarship agency sponsorship, or has the written consent of his official sponsor for a further period of study in the United Kingdom and satisfactory evidence that sufficient sponsorship funding is available; and

 (v) has not previously been granted leave to re-sit the examination.

Leave to enter to re-sit an examination

69B. A person seeking leave to enter the United Kingdom in order to re-sit an examination may be admitted for a period sufficient to enable him to re-sit the examination at the first available opportunity with a condition restricting his freedom to take employment, provided the Immigration Officer is satisfied that each of the requirements of paragraph 69A is met.

Refusal of leave to enter to re-sit an examination

69C. Leave to enter to re-sit an examination is to be refused if the Immigration Officer is not satisfied that each of the requirements of paragraph 69A is met.

Requirements for an extension of stay to re-sit an examination

69D. The requirements for an extension of stay to re-sit an examination are that the applicant:

 (i) was admitted to the United Kingdom with a valid student entry clearance if he was then a visa national; and

 (ii) meets the requirements set out in paragraph 69A (i)–(v).

Extension of stay to re-sit an examination

69E. An extension of stay to re-sit an examination may be granted for a period sufficient to enable the applicant to re-sit the examination at the first available opportunity, subject to a restriction on his freedom to take employment, provided the Secretary of State is satisfied that the applicant meets each of the requirements of paragraph 69D.

Refusal of extension of stay to re-sit an examination

69F. An extension of stay to re-sit an examination is to be refused if the Secretary of State is not satisfied that each of the requirements of paragraph 69D is met.

Writing up a thesis

Requirements for leave to enter to write up a thesis

69G. The requirements to be met by a person seeking leave to enter the United Kingdom in order to write up a thesis are that the applicant:

 (i) (a) meets the requirements for admission as a student set out in paragraph 57(i)–(viii); or

  (b) met the requirements for admission as a student set out in paragraph 57 (i)-(iii) in the previous academic year and continues to meet the requirements of paragraph 57 (iv)–(viii) save, for the purpose of paragraphs (i)(a) or (b) above, where leave was last granted in accordance with paragraphs 57–62 of these Rules before 30 November 2007, the requirements of paragraph 57(v) do not apply; and

(ii) can provide satisfactory evidence that he is a postgraduate student enrolled at an education institution as either a full time, part time or writing up student; and

(iii) can demonstrate that his application is supported by the education institution; and

(iv) has not come to the end of a period of government or international scholarship agency sponsorship, or has the written consent of his official sponsor for a further period of study in the United Kingdom and satisfactory evidence that sufficient sponsorship funding is available; and

(v) has not previously been granted 12 months leave to write up the same thesis.

Leave to enter to write up a thesis

69H. A person seeking leave to enter the United Kingdom in order to write up a thesis may be admitted for 12 months with a condition restricting his freedom to take employment, provided the Immigration Officer is satisfied that each of the requirements of paragraph 69G is met.

Refusal of leave to enter to write up a thesis

69I. Leave to enter to write up a thesis is to be refused if the Immigration Officer is not satisfied that each of the requirements of paragraph 69G is met.

Requirements for an extension of stay to write up a thesis

69J. The requirements for an extension of stay to write up a thesis are that the applicant:

(i) was admitted to the United Kingdom with a valid student entry clearance if he was then a visa national; and

(ii) meets the requirements set out in paragraph 69G (i)–(v).

Extension of stay to write up a thesis

69K. An extension of stay to write up a thesis may be granted for 12 months subject to a restriction on his freedom to take employment, provided the Secretary of State is satisfied that the applicant meets each of the requirements of paragraph 69J.

Refusal of extension of stay to write up a thesis

69L. An extension of stay to write up a thesis is to be refused if the Secretary of State is not satisfied that each of the requirements of paragraph 69J is met.

Postgraduate doctors, dentists and trainee general practitioners

Requirements for leave to enter the United Kingdom as a postgraduate doctor or dentist

70. The requirements to be met by a person seeking leave to enter the UK as a postgraduate doctor or dentist are that the applicant:

(i) has successfully completed and obtained a recognised UK degree in medicine or dentistry from either:

(a) a UK publicly funded institution of further or higher education; or

(b) a UK bona fide private education institution which maintains satisfactory records of enrolment and attendance; and

(ii) has previously been granted leave:

(a) in accordance with paragraphs 57 to 69L of these Rules for the final academic year of the studies referred to in (i) above; and

(b) as a student under paragraphs 57 to 62 of these Rules for at least one other academic year (aside from the final year) of the studies referred to in (i) above; and

(iii) holds a letter from the Postgraduate Dean confirming he has a full-time place on a recognised Foundation Programme; and

(iv) intends to train full time in his post on the Foundation Programme; and

(v) is able to maintain and accommodate himself and any dependants without recourse to public funds; and

(vi) intends to leave the United Kingdom if, on expiry of his leave under this paragraph, he has not been granted leave to remain in the United Kingdom as:

(a) a doctor or dentist undertaking a period of clinical attachment or a dental observer post in accordance with paragraphs 75G to 75M of these Rules; or

(b) a Tier 2 Migrant;

(c) a Tier 1 (General) Migrant or Tier (1) (Entrepreneur) Migrant; and

(vii) if his study at medical school or dental school, or any subsequent studies he has undertaken, were sponsored by a government or international scholarship agency, he has the written consent of his sponsor to enter or remain in the United Kingdom as a postgraduate doctor or dentist; and

(viii) if he has not previously been granted leave in this category has completed his medical or dental degree in the 12 months preceding this application; and

(ix) if he has previously been granted leave as a postgraduate doctor or dentist, is not seeking leave to enter to a date beyond 3 years from that date on which he was first granted leave to enter or remain in this category; and

(x) holds a valid entry clearance for entry in this capacity except where he is a British National (Overseas), a British Overseas Territories Citizen, a British Overseas Citizen, a British Protected Person or a person who under the British Nationality Act 1981 is a British Subject.

Leave to enter as a postgraduate doctor or dentist

71. Leave to enter the United Kingdom as a postgraduate doctor or dentist may be granted for the duration of the Foundation Programme, for a period not exceeding 26 months, provided the Immigration Officer is satisfied that each of the requirements of paragraph 70 is met.

Refusal of leave to enter as a postgraduate doctor or dentist

72. Leave to enter as a postgraduate doctor or dentist is to be refused if the Immigration Officer is not satisfied that each of the requirements of paragraph 70 is met.

Requirements for an extension of stay as a postgraduate doctor or dentist

73. The requirements to be met by a person seeking an extension of stay as a postgraduate doctor or dentist are that the applicant:

    (i) meets the requirements of paragraph 70 (i)–(vii); and

    (ii) has leave to enter or remain in the United Kingdom as either:

        (a) a student in accordance with paragraphs 57 to 69L of these Rules; or

        (b) as a postgraduate doctor or dentist in accordance with paragraphs 70 to 75 of these Rules; or

        (c) as a doctor or dentist undertaking a period of clinical attachment or a dental observer post in accordance with paragraphs 75G to 75M of these Rules.

    (iii) if he has not previously been granted leave in this category, has completed his medical or dental degree in the last 12 months;

    (iv) would not, as a result of an extension of stay, remain in the United Kingdom as a postgraduate doctor or dentist to a date beyond 3 years from the date on which he was first given leave to enter or remain in this capacity.

Extension of stay as a postgraduate doctor or dentist

74. An extension of stay as a postgraduate doctor or dentist may be granted for the duration of the Foundation Programme, for a period not exceeding 3 years, provided the Secretary of State is satisfied that each of the requirements of paragraph 73 is met.

Refusal of an extension of stay as a postgraduate doctor or dentist

75. An extension of stay as a postgraduate doctor or dentist is to be refused if the Secretary of State is not satisfied that each of the requirements of paragraph 73 is met.

Requirements for leave to enter the United Kingdom to take the PLAB Test

75A. The requirements to be met by a person seeking leave to enter in order to take the PLAB Test are that the applicant:

    (i) is a graduate from a medical school and intends to take the PLAB Test in the United Kingdom; and

    (ii) can provide documentary evidence of a confirmed test date or of his eligibility to take the PLAB Test; and

    (iii) meets the requirements of paragraph 41 (iii)–(vii) for entry as a visitor; and

    (iv) intends to leave the United Kingdom at the end of his leave granted under this paragraph unless he is successful in the PLAB Test and granted leave to remain:

        (a) as a postgraduate doctor or trainee general practitioner in accordance with paragraphs 70 to 75; or

        (b) to undertake a clinical attachment in accordance with paragraphs 75G to 75M of these Rules [; or]

Leave to enter to take the PLAB Test

75B. A person seeking leave to enter the United Kingdom to take the PLAB Test may be admitted for a period not exceeding 6 months, provided the Immigration Officer is satisfied that each of the requirements of paragraph 75A is met.

Refusal of leave to enter to take the PLAB Test

75C. Leave to enter the United Kingdom to take the PLAB Test is to be refused if the Immigration Officer is not satisfied that each of the requirements of paragraph 75A is met.

Requirements for an extension of stay in order to take the PLAB Test

75D. The requirements for an extension of stay in the United Kingdom in order to take the PLAB Test are that the applicant:

(i) was given leave to enter the United Kingdom for the purposes of taking the PLAB Test in accordance with paragraph 75B of these Rules; and

(ii) intends to take the PLAB Test and can provide documentary evidence of a confirmed test date; and

(iii) meets the requirements set out in paragraph 41 (iii) (vii); and

(iv) intends to leave the United Kingdom at the end of his leave granted under this paragraph unless he is successful in the PLAB Test and granted leave to remain:

(a) as a postgraduate doctor or trainee general practitioner in accordance with paragraphs 70 to 75; or

(b) to undertake a clinical attachment in accordance with paragraphs 75G to 75M of these Rules; or

(v) would not as a result of an extension of stay spend more than 18 months in the United Kingdom for the purpose of taking the PLAB Test.

Extension of stay to take the PLAB Test

75E. A person seeking leave to remain in the United Kingdom to take the PLAB Test may be granted an extension of stay for a period not exceeding 6 months, provided the Secretary of State is satisfied that each of the requirements of paragraph 75D is met.

Refusal of extension of stay to take the PLAB Test

75F. Leave to remain in the United Kingdom to take the PLAB Test is to be refused if the Secretary of State is not satisfied that each of the requirements of paragraph 75D is met.

Requirements for leave to enter to undertake a clinical attachment or dental observer post

75G. The requirements to be met by a person seeking leave to enter to undertake a clinical attachment or dental observer post are that the applicant:

(i) is a graduate from a medical or dental school and intends to undertake a clinical attachment or dental observer post in the United Kingdom; and

(ii) can provide documentary evidence of the clinical attachment or dental observer post which will:

(a) be unpaid; and

(b) only involve observation, not treatment, of patients; and

(iii)   meets the requirements of paragraph 41 (iii)–(vii) of these Rules; and

(iv)   intends to leave the United Kingdom at the end of his leave granted under this paragraph unless he is granted leave to remain:

(a)   as a postgraduate doctor, dentist or trainee general practitioner in accordance with paragraphs 70 to 75;

(v)   if he has previously been granted leave in this category, is not seeking leave to enter which, when amalgamated with those previous periods of leave, would total more than 6 months.

Leave to enter to undertake a clinical attachment or dental observer post

75H. A person seeking leave to enter the United Kingdom to undertake a clinical attachment or dental observer post may be admitted for the period of the clinical attachment or dental observer post, up to a maximum of 6 weeks at a time or 6 months in total in this category, provided the Immigration Officer is satisfied that each of the requirements of paragraph 75G is met.

Refusal of leave to enter to undertake a clinical attachment or dental observer post

75J. Leave to enter the United Kingdom to undertake a clinical attachment or dental observer post is to be refused if the Immigration Officer is not satisfied that each of the requirements of paragraph 75G is met.

Requirements for an extension of stay in order to undertake a clinical attachment or dental observer post

75K. The requirements to be met by a person seeking an extension of stay to undertake a clinical attachment or dental observer post are that the applicant:

(i)   was given leave to enter or remain in the United Kingdom to undertake a clinical attachment or dental observer post or:

(a)   for the purposes of taking the PLAB Test in accordance with paragraphs 75A to 75F and has passed both parts of the PLAB Test;

(b)   as a postgraduate doctor, dentist or trainee general practitioner in accordance with paragraphs 70 to 75; or

(c)   as a work permit holder for employment in the UK as a doctor or dentist in accordance with paragraphs 128 to 135; and

(ii)   is a graduate from a medical or dental school and intends to undertake a clinical attachment or dental observer post in the United Kingdom; and

(iii)   can provide documentary evidence of the clinical attachment or dental observer post which will:

(a)   be unpaid; and

(b)   only involve observation, not treatment, of patients; and

(iv)   intends to leave the United Kingdom at the end of his period of leave granted under this paragraph unless he is granted leave to remain:

(a)   as a postgraduate doctor, dentist or trainee general practitioner in accordance with paragraphs 70 to 75; or

(v)   meets the requirements of paragraph 41 (iii)–(vii) of these Rules; and

(vi) if he has previously been granted leave in this category, is not seeking an extension of stay which, when amalgamated with those previous periods of leave, would total more than 6 months.

Extension of stay to undertake a clinical attachment or dental observer post

75L. A person seeking leave to remain in the United Kingdom to undertake a clinical attachment or dental observer post up to a maximum of 6 weeks at a time or 6 months in total in this category, may be granted an extension of stay for the period of their clinical attachment or dental observer post, provided that the Secretary of State is satisfied that each of the requirements of paragraph 75K is met.

Refusal of extension of stay to undertake a clinical attachment or dental observer post

75M. Leave to remain in the United Kingdom to undertake a clinical attachment or dental observer post is to be refused if the Secretary of State is not satisfied that each of the requirements of paragraph 75K is met.

Requirements for leave to enter as a prospective student

82. The requirements to be met by a person seeking leave to enter the United Kingdom as a prospective student are that he:

(i) can demonstrate a genuine and realistic intention of undertaking, within 6 months of his date of entry:

(b) a supervised practice placement or midwife adaptation course which would meet the requirements for an extension of stay as an overseas qualified nurse or midwife under paragraphs 69P to 69R of these Rules; and

(ii) intends to leave the United Kingdom on completion of his studies or on the expiry of his leave to enter if he is not able to meet the requirements for an extension of stay:

(b) as an overseas qualified nurse or midwife in accordance with paragraph 69P of these Rules; and

Student unions' sabbatical officers

Requirements for leave to enter as a sabbatical officer

87A. The requirements to be met by a person seeking leave to enter the United Kingdom as a sabbatical officer are that the person:

(i) has been elected to a full-time salaried post as a sabbatical officer at an educational establishment at which he is registered as a student;

(ii) meets the requirements set out in paragraph 57 (i)–(ii) or met the requirements set out in paragraph 57 (i)–(ii) in the academic year prior to the one in which he took up or intends to take up sabbatical office; and

(iii) does not intend to engage in business or take employment except in connection with his sabbatical post; and

(iv) is able to maintain and accommodate himself and any dependants adequately without recourse to public funds; and

(v) at the end of the sabbatical post he intends to:

   (a) complete a course of study which he has already begun; or

   (b) take up a further course of study which has been deferred to enable the applicant to take up the sabbatical post; or

   (c) leave the United Kingdom; and

(vi) has not come to the end of a period of government or international scholarship agency sponsorship, or has the written consent of his official sponsor to take up a sabbatical post in the United Kingdom; and

(vii) has not already completed 2 years as a sabbatical officer.

Leave to enter the United Kingdom as a sabbatical officer

87B. A person seeking leave to enter the United Kingdom as a sabbatical officer may be admitted for a period not exceeding 12 months on conditions specifying his employment provided the Immigration Officer is satisfied that each of the requirements of paragraph 87A is met.

Refusal of leave to enter the United Kingdom as a sabbatical officer

87C. Leave to enter as a sabbatical officer is to be refused if the Immigration Officer is not satisfied that each of the requirements of paragraph 87A is met.

Requirements for an extension of stay as a sabbatical officer

87D. The requirements for an extension of stay as a sabbatical officer are that the applicant:

(i) was admitted to the United Kingdom with a valid student entry clearance if he was then a visa national; and

(ii) meets the requirements set out in paragraph 87A (i)–(vi); and

(iii) would not, as a result of an extension of stay, remain in the United Kingdom as a sabbatical officer to a date beyond 2 years from the date on which he was first given leave to enter the United Kingdom in this capacity.

Extension of stay as a sabbatical officer

87E. An extension of stay as a sabbatical officer may be granted for a period not exceeding 12 months on conditions specifying his employment provided the Secretary of State is satisfied that the applicant meets each of the requirements of paragraph 87D.

Refusal of extension of stay as a sabbatical officer

87F. An extension of stay as a sabbatical officer is to be refused if the Secretary of State is not satisfied that each of the requirements of paragraph 87D is met.

Requirements for leave to enter the United Kingdom for the purpose of employment under the Sectors-Based Scheme

135I. The requirements to be met by a person seeking leave to enter the United Kingdom for the purpose of employment under the Sectors-Based Scheme are that he:

(i) holds a valid Home Office immigration employment document issued under the Sectors-Based Scheme; and

(ii) is aged between 18 and 30 inclusive or was so aged at the date of his application for leave to enter; and

(iii) is capable of undertaking the employment specified in the immigration employment document; and

(iv) does not intend to take employment except as specified in his immigration employment document; and

(v) is able to maintain and accommodate himself adequately without recourse to public funds; and

(vi) intends to leave the United Kingdom at the end of his approved employment; and

(vii) holds a valid United Kingdom entry clearance for entry in this capacity.

Leave to enter for the purpose of employment under the Sectors-Based Scheme

135J. A person seeking leave to enter the United Kingdom for the purpose of employment under the Sectors-Based Scheme may be admitted for a period not exceeding 12 months (normally as specified in his work permit), subject to a condition restricting him to employment approved by the Home Office, provided the Immigration Officer is satisfied that each of the requirements of paragraph 135I is met.

Refusal of leave to enter for the purpose of employment under the Sectors-Based Scheme

135K. Leave to enter the United Kingdom for the purpose of employment under the Sectors-Based Scheme is to be refused if the Immigration Officer is not satisfied that each of the requirements of paragraph 135I is met.

Requirements for an extension of stay for Sectors-Based employment

135L. The requirements for an extension of stay for Sectors-Based employment are that the applicant:

(i) entered the United Kingdom with a valid Home Office immigration employment document issued under the Sectors-Based Scheme and;

(ii) has written approval from the Home Office for the continuation of his employment under the Sectors-Based Scheme; and

(iii) meets the requirements of paragraph 135I (ii)–(vi); and

(iv) would not, as a result of the extension of stay sought, remain in the United Kingdom for Sectors-Based Scheme employment to a date beyond 12 months from the date on which he was given leave to enter the United Kingdom on this occasion in this capacity.

Extension of stay for Sectors-Based Scheme employment

135M. An extension of stay for Sectors-Based Scheme employment may be granted for a period not exceeding the period of approved employment recommended by the Home Office provided the Secretary of State is satisfied that each of the requirements of paragraph 135L are met. An extension of stay is to be subject to a condition restricting the applicant to employment approved by the Home Office.

Refusal of extension of stay for Sectors-Based Scheme employment

135N. An extension of stay for Sectors-Based Scheme employment is to be refused if the Secretary of State is not satisfied that each of the requirements of paragraph 135L is met.

245ZG. Period and conditions of grant

(b) The cases referred to in paragraph (a) are those where the applicant has, or was last granted, entry clearance, leave to enter or leave to remain as:

(iii) a Minister of Religion, Missionary or Member of a Religious Order, provided he is still working for the same employer.

Attributes for Tier 1 (Investor) Migrants

47. A regulated financial institution is one which is regulated by the appropriate regulatory body for the country in which the financial institution operates. For example, where a financial institution does business in the UK, the appropriate regulator is the Financial Services Authority.

[Immigration Rules as at 5 April 2012 relating to Overseas qualified nurses or midwives, Seasonal agricultural workers, Work permit employment, Multiple Entry work permit Employment, and Tier 1 (Post Study Work) Migrants

Overseas qualified nurse or midwife

Requirements for leave to enter as an overseas qualified nurse or midwife

69M. Deleted on 27 November 2008 by paragraph 39 of Statement of Changes HC 1113 except insofar as relevant to paragraph 69P.

Leave to enter the United Kingdom as an overseas qualified nurse or midwife

69N. DELETED.

Refusal of leave to enter as an overseas qualified nurse or midwife

69O. DELETED.

Requirements for an extension of stay as an overseas qualified nurse or midwife

69P. The requirements to be met by a person seeking an extension of stay as an overseas qualified nurse or midwife are that the applicant:

(i)–(iii) Deleted by HC 1113

(iv) has leave to enter or remain as an overseas qualified nurse or midwife in accordance with paragraphs 69M–69R of these Rules; and

(v) meets the requirements set out in paragraph 69M (i)–(vi); and

(vi) can provide satisfactory evidence of regular attendance during any previous period of supervised practice or midwife adaptation course; and

(vii) if he has previously been granted leave:

(a) as an overseas qualified nurse or midwife under paragraphs 69M–69R of these Rules, or

(b) to undertake an adaptation course as a student nurse under paragraphs 63–69 of these Rules; and is not seeking an extension of stay in this category which, when amalgamated with those previous periods of leave, would total more than 18 months; and

(viii) if his previous studies, supervised practice placement or midwife adaptation programme placement were sponsored by a government or international scholarship agency, he has the written consent of his official sponsor to remain in the United Kingdom as an overseas qualified nurse or midwife.

Extension of stay as an overseas qualified nurse or midwife

69Q. An extension of stay as an overseas qualified nurse or midwife may be granted for a period not exceeding 18 months, provided that the Secretary of State is satisfied that each of the requirements of paragraph 69P is met.

Refusal of extension of stay as an overseas qualified nurse or midwife

69R. An extension of stay as an overseas qualified nurse or midwife is to be refused if the Secretary of State is not satisfied that each of the requirements of paragraph 69P is met.

Seasonal agricultural workers

Requirements for leave to enter as a seasonal agricultural worker

104. The requirements to be met by a person seeking leave to enter the United Kingdom as a seasonal agricultural worker are that he:

(i) is a student in full time education aged 18 or over; and

(ii) holds an immigration employment document in the form of a valid Home Office work card issued by the operator of a scheme approved by the Secretary of State; and

(iii) intends to leave the United Kingdom at the end of his period of leave as a seasonal worker; and

(iv) does not intend to take employment except as permitted by his work card and within the terms of this paragraph; and

(v) is not seeking leave to enter on a date less than 3 months from the date on which an earlier period of leave to enter or remain granted to him in this capacity expired; and

(vi) is able to maintain and accommodate himself without recourse to public funds.

Leave to enter as a seasonal agricultural worker

105. A person seeking leave to enter the United Kingdom as a seasonal agricultural worker may be admitted with a condition restricting his freedom to take employment for

a period not exceeding 6 months providing the Immigration Officer is satisfied that each of the requirements of paragraph 104 is met.

Refusal of leave to enter as a seasonal agricultural worker

106. Leave to enter the United Kingdom as a seasonal agricultural worker is to be refused if the Immigration Officer is not satisfied that each of the requirements of paragraph 104 is met.

Requirements for extension of stay as a seasonal agricultural worker

107. The requirements for an extension of stay as a seasonal agricultural worker are that the applicant:

(i) entered the United Kingdom as a seasonal agricultural worker under paragraph 105; and

(ii) meets the requirements of paragraph 104 (iii)–(vi); and

(iii) would not, as a result of an extension of stay sought, remain in the United Kingdom as a seasonal agricultural worker beyond 6 months from the date on which he was given leave to enter the United Kingdom on this occasion in this capacity.

Extension of stay as a seasonal agricultural worker

108. An extension of stay as a seasonal agricultural worker may be granted with a condition restricting his freedom to take employment for a period which does not extend beyond 6 months from the date on which he was given leave to enter the United Kingdom on this occasion in this capacity, provided the Secretary of State is satisfied that the applicant meets each of the requirements of paragraph 107.

Refusal of extension of stay as a seasonal worker

109. An extension of stay as a seasonal worker is to be refused if the Secretary of State is not satisfied that each of the requirements of paragraph 107 is met.

Work permit employment

Requirements for leave to enter the United Kingdom for work permit employment

128. The requirements to be met by a person coming to the United Kingdom to seek or take employment (unless he is otherwise eligible for admission for employment under these Rules or is eligible for admission as a seaman under contract to join a ship due to leave British waters) are that he:

(i) holds a valid Home Office work permit; and

(ii) is not of an age which puts him outside the limits for employment; and

(iii) is capable of undertaking the employment specified in the work permit; and

(iv) does not intend to take employment except as specified in his work permit; and

(v) is able to maintain and accommodate himself and any dependants adequately without recourse to public funds; and

(vi) in the case of a person in possession of a work permit which is valid for a period of 12 months or less, intends to leave the United Kingdom at the end of his approved employment; and

(vii) holds a valid United Kingdom entry clearance for entry in this capacity except where he holds a work permit valid for 6 months or less or he is a British National (Overseas), a British overseas territories citizen, a British Overseas citizen, a British protected person or a person who under the British Nationality Act 1981 is a British subject.

Leave to enter for work permit employment

129. A person seeking leave to enter the United Kingdom for the purpose of work permit employment may be admitted for a period not exceeding the period of employment approved by the Home Office (as specified in his work permit), subject to a condition restricting him to that approved employment, provided he is able to produce to the Immigration Officer, on arrival, a valid United Kingdom entry clearance for entry in this capacity or, where entry clearance is not required, provided the Immigration Officer is satisfied that each of the requirements of paragraph 128(i)–(vi) is met.

Refusal of leave to enter for employment

130. Leave to enter for the purpose of work permit employment is to be refused if a valid United Kingdom entry clearance for entry in this capacity is not produced to the Immigration Officer on arrival or, where entry clearance is not required, if the Immigration Officer is not satisfied that each of the requirements of paragraph 128(i)–(vi) is met.

Requirements for an extension of stay for work permit employment

131. The requirements for an extension of stay to seek or take employment (unless the applicant is otherwise eligible for an extension of stay for employment under these Rules) are that the applicant:

(i) entered the United Kingdom with a valid work permit under paragraph 129; and

(ii) has written approval from the Home Office for the continuation of his employment; and

(iii) meets the requirements of paragraph 128 (ii)–(v).

131A. The requirements for an extension of stay to take employment (unless the applicant is otherwise eligible for an extension of stay for employment under these Rules) for a student are that the applicant:

(i) entered the United Kingdom or was given leave to remain as a student in accordance with paragraphs 57 to 62 of these Rules; and

(ii) has obtained a degree qualification on a recognised degree course at either a United Kingdom publicly funded further or higher education institution or a bona fide United Kingdom private education institution which maintains satisfactory records of enrolment and attendance; and

(iii) holds a valid Home Office immigration employment document for employment; and

(iv) has the written consent of his official sponsor to such employment if he is a member of a government or international scholarship agency sponsorship and that sponsorship is either ongoing or has recently come to an end at the time of the requested extension; and

(v) meets each of the requirements of paragraph 128 (ii) to (vi).

131B. The requirements for an extension of stay to take employment (unless the applicant is otherwise eligible for an extension of stay for employment under these Rules) for a student nurse overseas qualified nurse or midwife, postgraduate doctor or postgraduate dentist are that the applicant:

(i) entered the United Kingdom or was given leave to remain as a student nurse in accordance with paragraphs 63 to 69 of these Rules; or

(ia) entered the United Kingdom or was given leave to remain as an overseas qualified nurse or midwife in accordance with paragraphs 69M to 69R of these Rules; and

(ii) entered the United Kingdom or was given leave to remain as a postgraduate doctor or a postgraduate dentist in accordance with paragraphs 70 to 75 of these Rules; and

(iii) holds a valid Home Office immigration employment document for employment as a nurse, doctor or dentist; and

(iv) has the written consent of his official sponsor to such employment if he is a member of a government or international scholarship agency sponsorship and that sponsorship is either ongoing or has recently come to an end at the time of the requested extension; and

(v) meets each of the requirements of paragraph 128 (ii) to (vi).

131C. The requirements for an extension of stay to take employment for a Science and Engineering Graduate Scheme or International Graduates Scheme participant are that the applicant:

(i) entered the United Kingdom or was given leave to remain as a Science and Engineering Graduate Scheme or International Graduates Scheme participant in accordance with paragraphs 135O to 135T of these Rules; and

(ii) holds a valid Home Office immigration employment document for employment; and

(iii) meets each of the requirements of paragraph 128 (ii) to (vi).

131D. The requirements for an extension of stay to take employment (unless the applicant is otherwise eligible for an extension of stay for employment under these Rules) for a working holidaymaker are that the applicant:

(i) entered the United Kingdom as a working holidaymaker in accordance with paragraphs 95 to 96 of these Rules; and

(ii) he has spent more than 12 months in total in the UK in this capacity; and

(iii) holds a valid Home Office immigration employment document for employment in an occupation listed on the Work Permits (UK) shortage occupations list; and

(iv) meets each of the requirements of paragraph 128 (ii) to (vi).

131E. The requirements for an extension of stay to take employment for a highly skilled migrant are that the applicant:

(i) entered the United Kingdom or was given leave to remain as a highly skilled migrant in accordance with paragraphs 135A to 135E of these Rules; and

(ii) holds a valid work permit; and

(iii) meets each of the requirements of paragraph 128(ii) to (vi).

131F. The requirements for an extension of stay to take employment (unless the applicant is otherwise eligible for an extension of stay for employment under these Rules) for an Innovator are that the applicant:

(i) entered the United Kingdom or was given leave to remain as an Innovator in accordance with paragraphs 210A to 210E of these Rules; and

(ii) holds a valid Home Office immigration employment document for employment; and

(iii) meets each of the requirements of paragraph 128(ii) to (vi).

131G. The requirements for an extension of stay to take employment (unless the applicant is otherwise eligible for an extension of stay for employment under these Rules) for an individual who has leave to enter or leave to remain in the United Kingdom to take the PLAB Test or to undertake a clinical attachment or dental observer post are that the applicant:

(i) entered the United Kingdom or was given leave to remain for the purposes of taking the PLAB Test in accordance with paragraphs 75A to 75F of these Rules; or

(ii) entered the United Kingdom or was given leave to remain to undertake a clinical attachment or dental observer post in accordance with paragraphs 75G to 75M of these Rules; and

(iii) holds a valid Home Office immigration employment document for employment as a doctor or dentist; and

(iv) meets each of the requirements of paragraph 128 (ii) to (vi).

131H. The requirements for an extension of stay to take employment (unless the applicant is otherwise eligible for an extension of stay for employment under these Rules) in the case of a person who has leave to enter or remain as a Fresh Talent: Working in Scotland scheme participant are that the applicant:

(i) entered the United Kingdom or was given leave to remain as a Fresh Talent: Working in Scotland scheme participant in accordance with paragraphs 143A to 143F of these Rules; and

(ii) holds a valid Home Office immigration employment document for employment in Scotland; and

(iii) has the written consent of his official sponsor to such employment if the studies which led to him being granted leave under the Fresh Talent: Working in Scotland scheme in accordance with paragraphs 143A to 143F of these Rules, or any studies he has subsequently undertaken, were sponsored by a government or international scholarship agency; and

(iv) meets each of the requirements of paragraph 128 (ii) to (vi).

131I. The requirements for an extension of stay to take employment for a Tier 1 Migrant are that the applicant:

(i) entered the UK or was given leave to remain as a Tier 1 Migrant, and

(ii) holds a valid work permit; and

(iii) meets each of the requirements of paragraph 128(ii) to (vi).

Extension of stay for work permit employment

132. An extension of stay for work permit employment may be granted for a period not exceeding the period of approved employment recommended by the Home Office provided the Secretary of State is satisfied that each of the requirements of paragraphs 131, 131A, 131B, 131C, 131D, 131E, 131F, 131G, 131H or 131I is met. An extension of stay is to be subject to a condition restricting the applicant to employment approved by the Home Office.

133. An extension of stay for employment is to be refused if the Secretary of State is not satisfied that each of the requirements of paragraphs 131, 131A, 131B, 131C, 131D, 131E, 131F, 131G, 131H or 131I is met (unless the applicant is otherwise eligible for an extension of stay for employment under these Rules).

Multiple Entry work permit employment

Requirements for leave to enter for Multiple Entry work permit employment

199A. The requirements to be met by a person coming to the United Kingdom to seek or take Multiple Entry work permit employment are that he:

   (i) holds a valid work permit;

  (ii) is not of an age which puts him outside the limits for employment;

 (iii) is capable of undertaking the employment specified in the work permit;

 (iv) does not intend to take employment except as specified in his work permit;

  (v) is able to maintain and accommodate himself adequately without recourse to public funds; and

 (vi) intends to leave the United Kingdom at the end of the employment covered by the Multiple Entry work permit and holds a valid United Kingdom Entry clearance for entry into this capacity excepts where he holds a work permit valid for 6 months or less or he is a British National (Overseas), a British overseas territories citizen, a British Overseas citizen, a British protected person or a person who under the British Nationality Act 1981 is a British subject.

Leave to enter for Multiple Entry work permit employment

199B. A person seeking leave to enter the United Kingdom for the purpose of Multiple Entry work permit employment may be admitted for a period not exceeding 2 years provided that the Immigration Officer is satisfied that each of the requirements of paragraph 199A are met.

Refusal of leave to enter for Multiple Entry work permit employment

199C. Leave to enter for the purpose of Multiple Entry work permit employment is to be refused if the Immigration Officer is not satisfied that each of the requirements of paragraph 199A is met.

Tier 1 (Post-Study Work) Migrants

245F. Purpose

The purpose of this route is to encourage international graduates who have studied in the UK to stay on and do skilled or highly skilled work.

245FA. Entry to the UK

All migrants arriving in the UK and wishing to enter as a Tier 1 (Post-Study Work) Migrant must have a valid entry clearance for entry under this route. If they do not have a valid entry clearance, entry will be refused.

245FB. Requirements for entry clearance

To qualify for entry clearance as a Tier 1 (Post-Study Work) Migrant, an applicant must meet the requirements listed below. If the applicant meets these requirements, entry clearance will be granted. If the applicant does not meet these requirements, the application will be refused.

Requirements:

(a) The applicant must not fall for refusal under the general grounds for refusal.

(b) The applicant must not previously have been granted entry clearance or leave to remain as a Tier 1 (Post-Study Work) Migrant as a Participant in the International Graduates Scheme (or its predecessor, the Science and Engineering Graduates Scheme), or as a Participant in the Fresh Talent: Working in Scotland Scheme.

(c) The applicant must have a minimum of 75 points under paragraphs 66 to 72 of Appendix A.

(d) The applicant must have a minimum of 10 points under paragraphs 1 to 3 of Appendix B.

(e) The applicant must have a minimum of 10 points under paragraphs 1 to 2 of Appendix C.

(f) If:

   (i) the studies that led to the qualification for which the applicant obtains points under paragraphs 66 to 72 of Appendix A were sponsored by a Government or international scholarship agency, and

   (ii) those studies came to an end 12 months ago or less the applicant must provide the unconditional written consent of the sponsoring Government or agency to the application and must provide the specified documents to show that this requirement has been met.

245FC. Period and conditions of grant

Entry clearance will be granted for a period of 2 years and will be subject to the following conditions:

(a) no recourse to public funds,

(b) registration with the police, if this is required by paragraph 326 of these Rules, and

(c) no Employment as a Doctor or Dentist in Training, unless the applicant has obtained a degree in medicine or dentistry at bachelor's level or above from a UK institution that is a UK recognised or listed body, or which holds a sponsor licence under Tier 4 of the Points Based System.

245FD. Requirements for leave to remain

To qualify for leave to remain as a Tier 1 (Post-Study Work) Migrant, an applicant must meet the requirements listed below. Subject to paragraph 245FE(a)(i), if the applicant meets these requirements, leave to remain will be granted. If the applicant does not meet these requirements, the application will be refused.

Requirements:

(a) The applicant must not fall for refusal under the general grounds for refusal, and must not be an illegal entrant.

(b) The applicant must not previously have been granted entry clearance or leave to remain as a Tier 1 (Post-Study Work) migrant.

(c) The applicant must have a minimum of 75 points under paragraphs 66 to 72 of Appendix A.

(d) The applicant must have a minimum of 10 points under paragraphs 1 to 3 of Appendix B.

(e) The applicant must have a minimum of 10 points under paragraphs 1 to 2 of Appendix C.

(f) The applicant must have, or have last been granted, entry clearance, leave to enter or leave to remain:

(i) as a Participant in the Fresh Talent: Working in Scotland Scheme,

(ii) as a Participant in the International Graduates Scheme (or its predecessor, the Science and Engineering Graduates Scheme),

(iii) as a Student, provided the applicant has not previously been granted leave in any of the categories referred to in paragraphs (i) and (ii) above,

(iv) as a Student Nurse, provided the applicant has not previously been granted leave in any of the categories referred to in paragraphs (i) and (ii) above,

(v) as a Student Re-Sitting an Examination, provided the applicant has not previously been granted leave in any of the categories referred to in paragraphs (i) and (ii) above,

(vi) as a Student Writing Up a Thesis, provided the applicant has not previously been granted leave as a Tier 1 Migrant or in any of the categories referred to in paragraphs (i) and (ii) above,

(vii) as a Tier 4 Migrant, provided the applicant has not previously been granted leave as a Tier 1 (Post-Study Work) Migrant or in any of the categories referred to in paragraphs (i) and (ii) above, or

(viii) as a Postgraduate Doctor or Dentist, provided the applicant has not previously been granted leave as a Tier 1 (Post-Study Work) Migrant or in any of the categories referred to in paragraphs (i) and (ii) above.

(g) An applicant who has, or was last granted leave as a Participant in the Fresh Talent: Working in Scotland Scheme must be a British National (Overseas), British overseas territories citizen, British Overseas citizen, British protected person or a British subject as defined in the British Nationality Act 1981.

(h) If:

(i) the studies that led to the qualification for which the applicant obtains points under paragraphs 66 to 72 of Appendix A were sponsored by a Government or international scholarship agency, and

(ii) those studies came to an end 12 months ago or less the applicant must provide the unconditional written consent of the sponsoring Government or agency to the application and must provide the specified documents to show that this requirement has been met.

245FE. Period and conditions of grant

(a) Leave to remain will be granted:

(i) for a period of the difference between 2 years and the period of the last grant of entry clearance, leave to enter or remain, to an applicant who has or was last granted leave as a Participant in the Fresh Talent: Working in Scotland Scheme, as a Participant in the International Graduates Scheme (or its predecessor the Science and Engineering Graduates Scheme). If this calculation results in no grant of leave then leave to remain is to be refused;

(ii) for a period of 2 years, to any other applicant.

(b) Leave to remain under this route will be subject to the following conditions:
   (i) no access to public funds,
   (ii) registration with the police, if this is required by paragraph 326 of these Rules, and
   (iii) no Employment as a Doctor or Dentist in Training, unless the applicant:
      (1) has obtained a primary degree in medicine or dentistry at bachelor's level or above from a UK institution that is a UK recognised or listed body, or which holds a sponsor licence under Tier 4 of the Points Based System; or
      (2) has, or has last been granted, entry clearance, leave to enter or leave to remain that was not subject to any condition restricting him from taking employment as a Doctor in Training, and has been employed during that leave as a Doctor in Training; or
      (3) has, or has last been granted, entry clearance, leave to enter or leave to remain that was not subject to any condition restricting him from taking employment as a Dentist in Training, and has been employed during that leave as a Dentist in Training.

Appendix A
Attributes for Tier 1 (Post-Study Work) Migrants

66. An applicant applying for entry clearance or leave to remain as a Tier 1 (Post-Study Work) Migrant must score 75 points for attributes.

67. Available points are shown in Table 10.

68. Notes to accompany the table appear below the table.

Table 10

Qualifications	Points
The applicant has been awarded:	20
(a) a UK recognised bachelor or postgraduate degree, or	
(b) a UK postgraduate certificate in education or Professional Graduate Diploma of Education, or	
(c) a Higher National Diploma ('HND') from a Scottish institution.	
(a) The applicant studied for his award at a UK institution that is a UK recognised or listed body, or which holds a sponsor licence under Tier 4 of the Points Based System, or	20
(b) If the applicant is claiming points for having been awarded a Higher National Diploma from a Scottish Institution, he studied for that diploma at a Scottish publicly funded institution of further or higher education, or a Scottish bona fide private education institution which maintains satisfactory records of enrolment and attendance.	
The Scottish institution must:	
(i) be on the list of Education and Training Providers list on the Department of Business, Innovation and Skills website, or	
(ii) hold a Sponsor licence under Tier 4 of the Points Based System.	

The applicant's periods of UK study and/or research towards his eligible award were undertaken whilst he had entry clearance, leave to enter or leave to remain in the UK that was not subject to a restriction preventing him from undertaking a course of study and/or research.	20
The applicant made the application for entry clearance or leave to remain as a Tier 1 (Post-Study Work) Migrant within 12 months of obtaining the relevant qualification or within 12 months of completing a United Kingdom Foundation Programme Office affiliated Foundation Programme as a postgraduate doctor or dentist.	15
The applicant is applying for leave to remain and has, or was last granted, leave as a Participant in the International Graduates Scheme (or its predecessor, the Science and Engineering Graduates Scheme) or as a Participant in the Fresh Talent: Working in Scotland Scheme.	75

Qualification: notes

69. Specified documents must be provided as evidence of the qualification and, where relevant, completion of the United Kingdom Foundation Programme Office affiliated Foundation Programme as a postgraduate doctor or dentist.

70. A qualification will have been deemed to have been 'obtained' on the date on which the applicant was first notified in writing, by the awarding institution, that the qualification had been awarded.

71. If the institution studied at is removed from one of the relevant lists referred to in Table 10, or from the Tier 4 Sponsor Register, no points will be awarded for a qualification obtained on or after the date the institution was removed from the relevant list or from the Tier 4 Sponsor Register.

72. To qualify as an HND from a Scottish institution, a qualification must be at level 8 on the Scottish Credit and Qualifications Framework.]

Note: Appendix F inserted from 30 June 2008 (HC 607). Immigration rules as at 26 November 2008 relating to routes deleted on 27 November 2008 were inserted into Appendix F from 27 November 2008 (HC 1113). Immigration rules as at 30 March 2009 relating to Students, Student Nurses, Students Re-sitting an Examination, Students Writing Up a Thesis, Postgraduate Doctors or Dentists, Sabbatical Officers and applicants under the Sectors-Based Scheme were inserted into Appendix F from 31 March 2009 (HC 314). Immigration rules as at 5 April 2012 relating to Overseas qualified nurses or midwives, Seasonal Agricultural workers, Work permit employment, Multiple Entry work permit Employment, and Tier 1 (Post Study Work) Migrants inserted from 6 April 2012 (HC 1888).

[Appendix FM
Family Members

This Appendix applies to applications under this route made on or after 9 July 2012 and to applications under Part 8 as set out in the Statement of Changes laid on 13 June 2012 (HC 194), except as otherwise set out at paragraphs A277–A280.

The sections of this Appendix are set out in the following order –

General

Section GEN: General

Family life as a partner

Section EC-P: Entry clearance as a partner

Section S-EC: Suitability-entry clearance

Section E-ECP: Eligibility for entry clearance as a partner

Section D-ECP: Decision on application for entry clearance as a partner

Section R-LTRP: Requirements for limited leave to remain as a partner

Section S-LTR: Suitability-leave to remain

Section E-LTRP: Eligibility for limited leave to remain as a partner

Section D-LTRP: Decision on application for limited leave to remain as a partner

Section R-ILRP: Requirements for indefinite leave to remain (settlement) as a partner

Section E-ILRP: Eligibility for indefinite leave to remain as a partner

Section D-ILRP: Decision on application for indefinite leave to remain as a partner

Exception

Section EX: Exception

Bereaved partner

Section BPILR: Indefinite leave to remain (settlement) as a bereaved partner

Section E-BPILR: Eligibility for indefinite leave to remain as a bereaved partner

Section D-BPILR: Decision on application for indefinite leave to remain as a bereaved partner

Victim of domestic violence

Section DVILR: Indefinite leave to remain (settlement) as a victim of domestic violence

Section E-DVILR: Eligibility for indefinite leave to remain as a victim of domestic violence

Section D-DVILR: Decision on application for indefinite leave to remain as a victim of domestic violence

Family life as a child of a parent with limited leave as a partner or parent

Section EC-C: Entry clearance as a child

Section E-ECC: Eligibility for entry clearance as a child

Section D-ECC: Decision on application for entry clearance as a child

Section R-LTR-C: Requirements for leave to remain as a child

Section E-LTRC: Eligibility for leave to remain as a child

Section D-LTRC: Decision on application for leave to remain as a child

Family life as a parent

Section EC-PT: Entry clearance as a parent

Section E-ECPT: Eligibility for entry clearance as a parent

Section D-ECPT: Decision on application for entry clearance as a parent

Section R-LTRPT: Requirements for limited leave to remain as a parent

Section E-LTRPT: Eligibility for limited leave to remain as a parent

Section D-LTRPT: Decision on application for limited leave to remain as a parent

Section R-ILRPT: Requirements for indefinite leave to remain (settlement) as a parent

Section E-ILRPT: Eligibility for indefinite leave to remain as a parent

Section D-ILRPT: Decision on application for indefinite leave to remain as a parent

Adult dependent relatives

Section EC-DR: Entry clearance as an adult dependent relative

Section E-ECDR: Eligibility for entry clearance as an adult dependent relative

Section D-ECDR: Decision on application for entry clearance as an adult dependent relative

Section R-ILRDR: Requirements for indefinite leave to remain as an adult dependent relative

Section E-ILRDR: Eligibility for indefinite leave to remain as an adult dependent relative

Section D-ILRDR: Decision on application for indefinite leave to remain as an adult relative

General

Section GEN: General

Purpose

GEN.1.1. This route is for those seeking to enter or remain in the UK on the basis of their family life with a person who is a British Citizen, is settled in the UK, or is in the UK with limited leave as a refugee or person granted humanitarian protection. It sets out the requirements to be met and, in considering applications under this route, it reflects how, under Article 8 of the Human Rights Convention, the balance will be struck between the right to respect for private and family life and the legitimate aims of protecting national security, public safety and the economic well-being of the UK; the prevention of disorder and crime; the protection of health or morals; and the protection of the rights and freedoms of others. It also takes into account the need to safeguard and promote the welfare of children in the UK.

Definitions

GEN.1.2. For the purposes of this Appendix 'partner' means–
   (i) the applicant's spouse;
   (ii) the applicant's civil partner;
   (iii) the applicant's fiancé(e) or proposed civil partner; or
   (iv) a person who has been living [together] with the applicant in a relationship akin to a marriage or civil partnership for at least two years prior to the date of application, unless the context otherwise requires.

   Note: Word inserted in sub-para (iv) from 6 September 2012 (HC 565).

GEN.1.3. For the purposes of this Appendix–
   (a) 'application for leave to remain' also includes an application for variation of leave to enter or remain by a person in the UK;
   (b) references to a person being present and settled in the UK also include a person who is being admitted for settlement on the same occasion as the applicant; and
   (c) references to a British Citizen in the UK also include a British Citizen who is coming to the UK with the applicant as their partner or parent.

GEN.1.4. In this Appendix 'specified' means specified in [{Appendix}FM-SE, unless otherwise stated].

   Note: Words in square brackets substituted from 20 July 2012 (Cm 8423). Word in curly brackets substituted from 6 September 2012 (HC 565).

GEN.1.5. If the Entry Clearance Officer, or Secretary of State, has reasonable cause to doubt the genuineness of any document submitted in support of an application, and having taken reasonable steps to verify the document, is unable to verify that it is genuine, the document will be discounted for the purposes of the application.

GEN.1.6. For the purposes of paragraph E-ECP.4.1.(a); E-LTRP.4.1.(a); E- ECPT.4.1(a) and E-LTRPT.5.1.(a) the applicant must be a national of Antigua and Barbuda; Australia; the Bahamas; Barbados; Belize; Canada; Dominica; Grenada; Guyana; Jamaica; New Zealand; St Kitts and Nevis; St Lucia; St Vincent and the Grenadines; Trinidad and Tobago; or the United States of America.

GEN.1.7. In this Appendix references to paragraphs are to paragraphs of this Appendix unless the context otherwise requires.

GEN.1.8. Paragraphs 277–280, 289AA, 295AA and 296 of Part 8 of these Rules shall apply to this Appendix.

[GEN.1.9. In this Appendix [(a)] the requirement to make a valid application will not apply when the Article 8 claim is raised:

   [(i)] as part of an asylum claim, or as part of a further submission in person after an asylum claim has been refused;
   [(ii)] where a migrant is in immigration detention;
   [(iii)] where removal directions have been set pending an imminent removal;
   [(iv)] in an appeal; or
   [(v)] in response to a (one stop) notice issued under section 120 of the Nationality, Immigration and Asylum Act 2002] [; and

   (b) where the Article 8 claim is raised in any of the circumstances specified in paragraph GEN.1.9.(a) the requirements of paragraphs R-LTRP.1.1.(c) and R-LTRPT.1.1.(c) are not met.]

Note: Paragraph GEN 1.9 inserted from 20 July 2012 (Cm 8423). Amendments in square brackets inserted from 6 September 2012 (HC 565).

Leave to enter

GEN.2.1. The requirements to be met by a person seeking leave to enter the UK under this route are that the person—

(a) must have a valid entry clearance for entry under this route; and

(b) must produce to the Immigration Officer on arrival a valid national passport or other document satisfactorily establishing their identity and nationality.

GEN.2.2. If a person does not meet the requirements of paragraph GEN.2.1. entry will be refused.

Family life with a Partner

Section EC-P: Entry clearance as a partner

EC-P.1.1. The requirements to be met for entry clearance as a partner are that—

(a) the applicant must be outside the UK;

(b) the applicant must have made a valid application for entry clearance as a partner;

(c) the applicant must not fall for refusal under any of the grounds in Section S-EC: Suitability-entry clearance; and

(d) the applicant must meet all of the requirements of Section E-ECP:

Eligibility for entry clearance as a partner.

Section S-EC: Suitability-entry clearance

S-EC.1.1. The applicant will be refused entry clearance on grounds of suitability if any of paragraphs S-EC.1.2. to 1.7. apply.

S-EC.1.2. The Secretary of State has personally directed that the exclusion of the applicant from the UK is conducive to the public good.

S-EC.1.3. The applicant is at the date of application the subject of a deportation order.

S-EC.1.4. The exclusion of the applicant from the UK is conducive to the public good because they have been convicted of an offence for which they have been sentenced to imprisonment for at least 12 months.

S-EC.1.5. The exclusion of the applicant from the UK is conducive to the public good,,, because, for example, the applicant's conduct (including convictions which do not fall within paragraph S-EC.1.4.), character, associations, or other reasons, make it undesirable to grant them entry clearance.

Note: Word deleted from para SE-C 1.5 from 6 September 2012 (HC 565).

[S-EC.1.6. The applicant has failed without reasonable excuse to- [comply with requirements to]

[(a)] attend an interview;

[(b)] provide ... information;

[(c)] provide ... physical data; or

[(d)] undergo a medical examination or provide a medical report ...]

Note: Paragraph S-EC.1.6. substituted from 20 July 2012 (Cm 8423). Amendments in square brackets inserted and words deleted from 6September 2012 (HC 565).

S-EC.1.7. It is undesirable to grant entry clearance to the applicant for medical reasons.

S-EC.2.1. The applicant will normally be refused on grounds of suitability if any of paragraphs S-EC.2.2. to 2.4. apply.

S-EC.2.2. Whether or not to the applicant's knowledge—

(a) false information, representations or documents have been submitted in relation to the application (including false information submitted to any person to obtain a document used in support of the application); or

(b) there has been a failure to disclose material facts in relation to the application.

S-EC.2.3. One or more relevant NHS body has notified the Secretary of State that the applicant has failed to pay charges in accordance with the relevant NHS regulations on charges to overseas visitors and the outstanding charges have a total value of at least £1000.

S-EC.2.4. A maintenance and accommodation undertaking has been requested or required under paragraph 35 of these Rules or otherwise and has not been provided.

Section E-ECP: Eligibility for entry clearance as a partner

E-ECP.1.1. To meet the eligibility requirements for entry clearance as a partner all of the requirements in paragraphs E-ECP.2.1. to 4.2. must be met.

Relationship requirements

E-ECP.2.1. The applicant's partner must be—
(a) a British Citizen in the UK; or[, subject to GEN.1.3.(c)
(b) present and settled in the UK; or[, subject to GEN.1.3.(b)
(c) in the UK with refugee leave or with humanitarian protection.

E-ECP.2.2. The applicant must be aged 18 or over at the date of application.

E-ECP.2.3. The partner must be aged 18 or over at the date of application.

E-ECP.2.4. The applicant and their partner must not be within the prohibited degree of relationship.

E-ECP.2.5. The applicant and their partner must have met in person.

E-ECP.2.6. The relationship between the applicant and their partner must be genuine and subsisting.

E-ECP.2.7. If the applicant and partner are married or in a civil partnership it must be a valid marriage or civil partnership, as specified.

E-ECP.2.8. If the applicant is a fiancé(e) or proposed civil partner they must be seeking entry to the UK to enable their marriage or civil partnership to take place.

E-ECP.2.9. Any previous relationship of the applicant or their partner must have broken down permanently, unless it is a relationship which falls within paragraph 278(i) of these Rules.

E-ECP.2.10. The applicant and partner must intend to live together permanently in the UK.

Financial requirements

E-ECP.3.1. The applicant must provide specified evidence, from the sources listed in paragraph E-ECP.3.2., of—

(a) a specified gross annual income of at least—
  (i) £18,600;
  (ii) an additional £3,800 for the first child; and
  (iii) an additional £2,400 for each additional child; alone or in combination with
(b) specified savings of-
  (i) £16,000; and
  (ii) additional savings of an amount equivalent to 2.5 times the amount which is the difference between the gross annual income from the sources listed in paragraph E-ECP.3.2.(a)–(d) and the total amount required under paragraph E-ECP.3.1.(a); or
(c) the requirements in paragraph E-ECP.3.3.being met.
In this paragraph "child" means a dependent child of the applicant who is—
(a) under the age of 18 years, or who was under the age of 18 years when they were first granted entry under this route;
(b) applying for entry clearance as a dependant of the applicant, or has limited leave to enter or remain in the UK;
(c) not a British Citizen or settled in the UK; and
(d) not an EEA national with a right to be admitted under the Immigration (EEA) Regulations 2006.

E-ECP.3.2. When determining whether the financial requirement in paragraph E- ECP.3.1. is met only the following sources will be taken into account—
(a) income of the partner from specified employment or self-employment, which, in respect of a partner returning to the UK with the applicant, can include specified employment or self-employment overseas and in the UK;
(b) specified pension income of the applicant and partner;
(c) any specified maternity allowance or bereavement benefit received by the partner in the UK;
(d) other specified income of the applicant and partner; and
(e) specified savings of the applicant and partner.

E-ECP.3.3. The requirements to be met under this paragraph are—
(a) the applicant's partner must be receiving one or more of the following—
  (i) disability living allowance;
  (ii) severe disablement allowance;
  (iii) industrial injury disablement benefit;
  (iv) attendance allowance; or
  (v) carer's allowance; and
(b) the applicant must provide...evidence that their partner is able to maintain and accommodate themselves, the applicant and any dependants adequately in the UK without recourse to public funds.

Note: Word deleted from 20 July 2012 (Cm 8423).

E-ECP.3.4. The applicant must provide...evidence that there will be adequate accommodation, without recourse to public funds, for the family, including other family members who are not included in the application but who live in the same household, which the family own or occupy exclusively: accommodation will not be regarded as adequate if—
(a) it is, or will be, overcrowded; or
(b) it contravenes public health regulations.

Note: Word deleted from 20 July 2012 (Cm 8423).

English language requirement

E-ECP.4.1. The applicant must provide specified evidence that they—

(a) are a national of a majority English speaking country listed in paragraph [GEN.1.6.];

(b) have passed an English language test in speaking and listening at a minimum of level A1 of the Common European Framework of Reference for Languages with a provider approved by the UK Border Agency;

(c) have an academic qualification recognised by NARIC UK to be equivalent to the standard of a Bachelor's or Master's degree or PhD in the UK, which was taught in English; or

(d) are exempt from the English language requirement under paragraph E- ECP.4.2.

Note : Number in square brackets substituted from 20 July 2012 (Cm 8423).

E-ECP.4.2. The applicant is exempt from the English language requirement if at the date of application—

(a) the applicant is aged 65 or over;

(b) the applicant has a disability (physical or mental condition) which prevents the applicant from meeting the requirement; or

(c) there are exceptional circumstances which prevent the applicant from being able to meet the requirement prior to entry to the UK.

Section D-ECP: Decision on application for entry clearance as a partner

D-ECP.1.1. If the applicant meets the requirements for entry clearance as a partner the applicant will be granted entry clearance for an initial period not exceeding 33 months, and subject to a condition of no recourse to public funds; or, where the applicant is a fiancé(e) or proposed civil partner, the applicant will be granted entry clearance for a period not exceeding 6 months, and subject to a condition of no recourse to public funds and a prohibition on employment.

D-ECP.1.2. Where the applicant does not meet the requirements for entry clearance as a partner the application will be refused.

Section R-LTRP: Requirements for limited leave to remain as a partner

R-LTRP.1.1. The requirements to be met for limited leave to remain as a partner are—

(a) the applicant and their partner must be in the UK;

(b) the applicant must have made a valid application for limited leave to remain as a partner; and either

(c) (i) the applicant must not fall for refusal under Section S-LTR: Suitability leave to remain; and

(ii) the applicant must meet all of the requirements of Section E-LTRP: Eligibility for leave to remain as a partner; and

(iii) paragraph EX.1. has not been applied; or

(d) (i) the applicant [must not fall for refusal under] Section S-LTR: Suitability leave to remain; and

[(ii) the applicant meets the requirements of paragraphs E-LTRP.1.2.–1.12. and E-LTRP.2.1.;] and

(iii) paragraph EX.1. applies.

Note: Words substituted in sub-para (d)(i) and sub-para (d)(ii) substituted from 6 September 2012 (HC 565).

Section S-LTR: Suitability-leave to remain

S-LTR.1.1. The applicant will be refused limited leave to remain on grounds of suitability if any of paragraphs.

S-LTR.1.2. to 1.7. apply.

S-LTR.1.2. The applicant is at the date of application the subject of a deportation order.

S-LTR.1.3. The presence of the applicant in the UK is not conducive to the public good because they have been convicted of an offence for which they have been sentenced to imprisonment for at least 4 years.

S-LTR.1.4. The presence of the applicant in the UK is not conducive to the public good because they have been convicted of an offence for which they have been sentenced to imprisonment for less than 4 years but at least 12 months.

S-LTR.1.5. The presence of the applicant in the UK is not conducive to the public good because, in the view of the Secretary of State, their offending has caused serious harm or they are a persistent offender who shows a particular disregard for the law.

S-LTR.1.6. The presence of the applicant in the UK is not conducive to the public good because their conduct (including convictions which do not fall within paragraphs S-LTR.1.3. to 1.5.), character, associations, or other reasons, make it undesirable to allow them to remain in the UK.

[S-LTR.1.7. The applicant has failed without reasonable excuse to- [comply with a requirement to]

   [(a)] attend an interview;
   [(b)] provide... information;
   [(c)] provide... physical data; or
   [(d)] undergo a medical examination or provide a medical report.

Note: Paragraph S-LTR.1.6. substituted from 20 July 2012 (Cm 8423). Amendments in square brackets inserted and words deleted from 6 September 2012 (HC 565).

S-LTR.2.1. The applicant will normally be refused on grounds of suitability if any of paragraphs S-LTR.2.2. to 2.4. apply.

S-LTR.2.2. Whether or not to the applicant's knowledge—

   (a) false information, representations or documents have been submitted in relation to the application (including false information submitted to any person to obtain a document used in support of the application); or

   (b) there has been a failure to disclose material facts in relation to the application.

S-LTR.2.3. One or more relevant NHS body has notified the Secretary of State that the applicant has failed to pay charges in accordance with the relevant NHS regulations on charges to overseas visitors and the outstanding charges have a total value of at least £1000.

S-LTR.2.4. A maintenance and accommodation undertaking has been requested under paragraph 35 of these Rules and has not been provided.

S-LTR.3.1. When considering whether the presence of the applicant in the UK is not conducive to the public good any legal or practical reasons why the applicant cannot presently be removed from the UK must be ignored.

Section E-LTRP: Eligibility for limited leave to remain as a partner

E-LTRP.1.1. To qualify for limited leave to remain as a partner all of the requirements of paragraphs E-LTRP.1.2. to 4.2. must be met.

Relationship requirements

E-LTRP.1.2. The applicant's partner must be—
  (a) a British Citizen in the UK;
  (b) present and settled in the UK; or
  (c) in the UK with refugee leave or as a person with humanitarian protection.

E-LTRP.1.3. The applicant must be aged 18 or over at the date of application.

E-LTRP.1.4. The partner must be aged 18 or over at the date of application.

E-LTRP.1.5. The applicant and their partner must not be within the prohibited degree of relationship.

E-LTRP.1.6. The applicant and their partner must have met in person.

E-LTRP.1.7. The relationship between the applicant and their partner must be genuine and subsisting.

E-LTRP.1.8. If the applicant and partner are married or in a civil partnership it must be a valid marriage or civil partnership, as specified.

E-LTRP.1.9. Any previous relationship of the applicant or their partner must have broken down permanently, unless it is a relationship which falls within paragraph 278(i) of these Rules.

E-LTRP.1.10. The applicant and their partner must intend to live together permanently in the UK [and, in any application for further leave to remain as a partner (except where the applicant is in the UK as a fiancé(e) or proposed civil partner) and in any application for indefinite leave to remain as a partner, the applicant must provide evidence that, since entry clearance as a partner was granted under paragraph D-ECP1.1. or since the last grant of limited leave to remain as a partner, the applicant and their partner have lived together in the UK or there is good reason, consistent with a continuing intention to live together permanently in the UK, for any period in which they have not done so].

  Note: Words in square brackets inserted from 6 September 2012 (HC 565).

E-LTRP.1.11. If the applicant is in the UK with leave as a fiancé(e) or proposed civil partner [and the marriage or civil partnership did not take place during that period of leave] there must be good reason why... and evidence that it will take place within the next 6 months.

  Note: Words deleted and words in square brackets inserted from 6 September 2012 (HC 565).

[E-LTRP.1.12. The applicant's partner cannot be the applicant's fiancé(e) or proposed civil partner, unless the applicant was granted entry clearance as that person's fiancé(e) or proposed civil partner.]

  Note: Paragraph E-LTRP.1.12. inserted from 6 September 2012 (HC 565).

Immigration status requirements

E-LTRP.2.1. The applicant must not be in the UK—

    (a) as a visitor;

    (b) with valid leave granted for a period of 6 months or less, unless that leave is as a fiancé(e) or proposed civil partner; or

    (c) on temporary admission.

E-LTRP.2.2. The applicant must not be in the UK in breach of immigration laws (disregarding any period of overstaying for a period of 28 days or less), unless paragraph EX.1. applies.

Financial requirements

E-LTRP.3.1. The applicant must provide specified evidence, from the sources listed in paragraph E-LTRP.3.2., of—

    (a) a specified gross annual income of at least—

        (i) £18,600;

        (ii) an additional £3,800 for the first child; and

        (iii) an additional £2,400 for each additional child;

    alone or in combination with

    (b) specified savings of—

        (i) £16,000;and

        (ii) additional savings of an amount equivalent to 2.5 times the amount which is the difference between the gross annual income from the sources listed in paragraph E-LTRP.3.2.(a)-(f) and the total amount required under paragraph E-LTRP.3.1.(a); or

    (c) the requirements in paragraph E-LTRP.3.3.being met,

    unless paragraph EX.1. applies.

In this paragraph "child" means a dependent child of the applicant who is—

    (a) under the age of 18 years, or who was under the age of 18 years when they were first granted entry under this route;

    (b) applying for entry clearance or is in the UK as a dependant of the applicant;

    (c) not a British Citizen or settled in the UK; and

    (d) not an EEA national with a right to remain in the UK under the Immigration (EEA) Regulations 2006.

E-LTRP.3.2. When determining whether the financial requirement in paragraph E- LTRP.3.1. is met only the following sources may be taken into account—

    (a) income of the partner from specified employment or self-employment;

    (b) income of the applicant from specified employment or self-employment unless they are working illegally; (c) specified pension income of the applicant and partner;

    (d) any specified maternity allowance or bereavement benefit received by the applicant and partner in the UK;

    (e) other specified income of the applicant and partner;

    (f) income from the sources at (b), (d) or (e) of a dependent child of the applicant under paragraph E-LTRP.3.1. who is aged 18 years or over; and

    (g) specified savings of the applicant, partner and a dependent child of the applicant under paragraph E-LTRP.3.1. who is aged 18 years or over.

E-LTRP.3.3. The requirements to meet this paragraph are—

    (a) the applicant's partner must be receiving one or more of the following—

        (i) disability living allowance;

    (ii) severe disablement allowance;

   (iii) industrial injury disablement benefit;

   (iv) attendance allowance; or

    (v) carer's allowance; and

  (b) the applicant must provide…evidence that their partner is able to maintain and accommodate themselves, the applicant and any dependants adequately in the UK without recourse to public funds.

Note: Word deleted from 20 July 2012 (Cm 8423).

E-LTRP.3.4. The applicant must provide…evidence that there will be adequate accommodation, without recourse to public funds, for the family, including other family members who are not included in the application but who live in the same household, which the family own or occupy exclusively[, unless paragraph EX.1. applies]: accommodation will not be regarded as adequate if—

  (a) it is, or will be, overcrowded; or

  (b) it contravenes public health regulations.

Note: Word deleted from 20 July 2012 (Cm 8423). Words inserted from 6 September 2012 (HC 565).

English language requirement

E-LTRP.4.1. If the applicant has not met the requirement in a previous application for leave as a partner, the applicant must provide specified evidence that they—

  (a) are a national of a majority English speaking country listed in paragraph [GEN.1.6.];

  (b) have passed an English language test in speaking and listening at a minimum of level A1 of the Common European Framework of Reference for Languages with a provider approved by the UK Border Agency;

  (c) have an academic qualification recognised by NARIC UK to be equivalent to the standard of a Bachelor's or Master's degree or PhD in the UK, which was taught in English; or

  (d) are exempt from the English language requirement under paragraph E- LTRP.4.2;
       unless paragraph EX.1. applies.

Note: Number in square brackets substituted from 20 July 2012 (Cm 8423).

E-LTRP.4.2. The applicant is exempt from the English language requirement if at the date of application—

  (a) the applicant is aged 65 or over;

  (b) the applicant has a disability (physical or mental condition) which prevents the applicant from meeting the requirement; or

  (c) there are exceptional circumstances which prevent the applicant from being able to meet the requirement.

Section D-LTRP: Decision on application for limited leave to remain as a partner

D-LTRP.1.1. If the applicant meets the requirements in paragraph R-LTRP.1.1.(a) to (c) for limited leave to remain as a partner the applicant will be granted limited leave to remain for a period not exceeding 30 months, and subject to a condition of no recourse to public funds, and they will be eligible to apply for settlement after[a continuous period of at least 60 months with such leave or in the UK with entry clearance as a partner under paragraph D-ECP1.1. (excluding in all cases any period of entry clearance or limited leave as a fiancé(e) or proposed civil partner)]; or, if paragraph E-LTRP.1.11. applies, the applicant will be granted limited leave for a period not exceeding 6 months and subject to a condition of no recourse to public funds and a prohibition on employment.

Note: Words in square brackets substituted from 6 September 2012 (HC 565).

D-LTRP.1.2. If the applicant meets the requirements in paragraph R-LTRP.1.1.(a), (b) and (d) for limited leave to remain as a partner they will be granted leave to remain for a period not exceeding 30 months, and will be eligible to apply for settlement after [a continuous period of at least 120 months with such leave, with limited leave as a partner under paragraph D-LTRP.1.1., or in the UK with entry clearance as a partner under paragraph D-ECP1.1. (excluding in all cases any period of entry clearance or limited leave as a fiancé(e) or proposed civil partner)], or, if paragraph E-LTRP.1.11. applies, the applicant will be granted limited leave for a period not exceeding 6 months and subject to a condition of no recourse to public funds and a prohibition on employment.

Note: Words in square brackets substituted from 6 September 2012 (HC 565).

D-LTRP.1.3. If the applicant does not meet the requirements for limited leave to remain as a partner the application will be refused.

Section R-ILRP: Requirements for indefinite leave to remain (settlement) as a partner

[R]-ILRP.1.1. The requirements to be met for indefinite leave to remain as a partner are that—

(a) the applicant and their partner must be in the UK;

(b) the applicant must have made a valid application for indefinite leave to remain as a partner;

(c) the applicant must not fall for refusal under any of the grounds in Section S-LTR: Suitability-leave to remain;

(d) the applicant must meet all of the requirements of Section E-LTRP: Eligibility for leave to remain as a partner (but in applying paragraph E- LTRP.3.1.(b)(ii) delete the words "2.5 times"); and

(e) the applicant must meet all of the requirements of Section E-ILRP: Eligibility for indefinite leave to remain as a partner.

Note: Error in numeration corrected from 6 September 2012 (HC 565).

Section E-ILRP: Eligibility for indefinite leave to remain as a partner

E-ILRP.1.1. To meet the eligibility requirements for indefinite leave to remain as a partner all of the requirements of paragraphs E-ILRP.1.2. to 1.6. must be met.

E-ILRP.1.2. The applicant must be in the UK with valid leave to remain as a partner (disregarding any period of overstaying for a period of 28 days or less).

E-ILRP.1.3. The applicant must have completed a continuous period of at least 60 months with limited leave as a partner under paragraph R-LTRP.1.1.(a) to (c) [or in the UK with entry clearance as a partner under paragraph D-ECP.1.1.], or a continuous period of at least 120 months with limited leave as a partner under paragraph R-LTR.P.1.1(a), (b) and (d) [or in the UK with entry clearance as a partner under paragraph D-ECP.1.1.],or a continuous period of at least 120 months with limited leave as a partner under a combination of these paragraphs.

Note: Words in square brackets inserted from 6 September 2012 (HC 565).

E-ILRP.1.4. In calculating the periods under paragraph E-ILRP.1.3. only the periods when the applicant's partner is the same person as the applicant's partner for the previous period of limited leave shall be taken into account.

E-ILRP.1.5. The applicant must at the date of application have no unspent convictions.

E-ILRP.1.6. The applicant must have sufficient knowledge of the English language and sufficient knowledge about life in the UK in accordance with the requirements of paragraphs 33B to 33G of these Rules.

Section D-ILRP: Decision on application for indefinite leave to remain as a partner

D-ILRP.1.1. If the applicant meets all of the requirements for indefinite leave to remain as a partner the applicant will be granted indefinite leave to remain.

D-ILRP.1.2. If the applicant does not meet the requirements for indefinite leave to remain as a partner only for one or both of the following reasons-

(a) the applicant has an unspent conviction;

(b) the applicant has not met the requirements of paragraphs 33B to 33G of these Rules, the applicant will be granted further limited leave to remain as a partner for a period not exceeding 30 months, and subject to a condition of no recourse to public funds.

D-ILRP.1.3. If the applicant does not meet the requirements for indefinite leave to remain as a partner, or further limited leave to remain as a partner under paragraph D- ILRP.1.2., the application will be refused[, unless paragraph EX.1. applies. Where paragraph EX.1. applies, the applicant will be granted further limited leave to remain as a partner for a period not exceeding 30 months under paragraph D- LTRP.1.2].

Note: Words in square brackets inserted from 6 September 2012 (HC 565).

Section EX: Exception

EX.1. This paragraph applies if

(a) (i) the applicant has a genuine and subsisting parental relationship with a child who-

(aa) is under the age of 18 years;

(bb) is in the UK;

(cc) is a British Citizen or has lived in the UK continuously for at least the 7 years immediately preceding the date of application; and

(ii) it would not be reasonable to expect the child to leave the UK; or

(b) the applicant has a genuine and subsisting relationship with a partner who is in the UK and is a British Citizen, settled in the UK or in the UK with refugee leave or humanitarian protection, and there are insurmountable obstacles to family life with that partner continuing outside the UK.

Bereaved partner

Section BPILR: Indefinite leave to remain (settlement) as a bereaved partner

BPILR.1.1. The requirements to be met for indefinite leave to remain in the UK as a bereaved partner are that-

(a) the applicant must be in the UK;

(b) the applicant must have made a valid application for indefinite leave to remain as a bereaved partner;

(c) the applicant must not fall for refusal under any of the grounds in Section S-LTR: Suitability-leave to remain; and

(d) the applicant must meet all of the requirements of Section E-BPILR: Eligibility for indefinite leave to remain as a bereaved partner.

Section E-BPILR: Eligibility for indefinite leave to remain as a bereaved partner

E-BPILR.1.1. To meet the eligibility requirements for indefinite leave to remain as a bereaved partner all of the requirements of paragraphs E-BPILR1.2. to 1.5. must be met.

E-BPILR.1.2. The applicant's last grant of limited leave must have been as-

(a) a partner (other than a fiancé(e) or proposed civil partner) of a British Citizen or a person settled in the UK; or

(b) a bereaved partner.

E-BPILR.1.3. The person who was the applicant's partner at the time of the last grant of limited leave as a partner must have died.

E-BPILR.1.4. At the time of the partner's death the relationship between the applicant and the partner must have been genuine and subsisting and each of the parties must have intended to live permanently with the other in the UK.

E-BPILR.1.5. The applicant must at the date of application have no unspent convictions.

Section D-BPILR: Decision on application for indefinite leave to remain as a bereaved partner

D-BPILR.1.1. If the applicant meets all of the requirements for indefinite leave to remain as a bereaved partner the applicant will be granted indefinite leave to remain.

D-BPILR.1.2. If the applicant does not meet the requirements for indefinite leave to remain as a bereaved partner only because the applicant has an unspent conviction, the applicant will be granted further limited leave to remain for a period not exceeding 30 months, and subject to a condition of no recourse to public funds.

D-BPILR.1.3. If the applicant does not meet the requirements for indefinite leave to remain as a bereaved partner, or limited leave to remain as a bereaved partner under paragraph D-BPILR.1.2., the application will be refused.

Victim of domestic violence

Section DVILR: Indefinite leave to remain (settlement) as a victim of domestic violence

DVILR.1.1. The requirements to be met for indefinite leave to remain in the UK as a victim of domestic violence are that—
(a) the applicant must be in the UK;
(b) the applicant must have made a valid application for indefinite leave to remain as a victim of domestic violence;
(c) the applicant must not fall for refusal under any of the grounds in Section S-LTR: Suitability-leave to remain; and
(d) the applicant must meet all of the requirements of Section E-DVILR: Eligibility for indefinite leave to remain as a victim of domestic violence.

Section E-DVILR: Eligibility for indefinite leave to remain as a victim of domestic violence

E-DVILR.1.1. To meet the eligibility requirements for indefinite leave to remain as a victim of domestic violence all of the requirements of paragraphs E-DVILR.1.2. to 1.4. must be met.

E-DVILR.1.2. The applicant's last grant of limited leave must have been—
(a) as a partner (other than a fiancé(e) or proposed civil partner) of a British Citizen or a person settled in the UK;
(b) granted to enable access to public funds pending an application under DVILR.; or
(c) granted under paragraph D-DVILR.1.2.

E-DVILR.1.3. The applicant must provide . . . evidence that during the last period of limited leave as a partner the applicant's relationship with their partner broke down permanently as a result of . . . domestic violence.

> **Note:** Word after 'provide' deleted from 20 July 2012 (Cm 8423) and other words deleted from 6 September 2012 (HC 565).

E-DVILR1.4. The applicant must at the date of application have no unspent convictions.

Section D-DVILR: Decision on application for indefinite leave to remain as a victim of domestic violence

D-DVILR.1.1. If the applicant meets all of the requirements for indefinite leave to remain as a victim of domestic violence the applicant will be granted indefinite leave to remain.

D-DVILR.1.2. If the applicant does not meet the requirements for indefinite leave to remain as a victim of domestic violence only because the applicant has an unspent conviction the applicant will be granted further limited leave to remain for a period not exceeding 30 months.

D-DVILR.1.3. If the applicant does not meet the requirements for indefinite leave to remain as a victim of domestic violence, or further limited leave to remain under paragraph D-DVILR.1.2. the application will be refused.

Family life as a child of a person with limited leave as a partner or parent

This route is for a child whose parent is applying for entry clearance or leave, or who has limited leave, as a partner or parent. For further provision on a child seeking to enter or remain in the UK for the purpose of their family life see Part 8 of these Rules.

Section EC-C: Entry clearance as a child

EC-C.1.1. The requirements to be met for entry clearance as a child are that-
  (a) the applicant must be outside the UK;
  (b) the applicant must have made a valid application for entry clearance as a child;
  (c) the applicant must not fall for refusal under any of the grounds in Section S-EC: Suitability for entry clearance; and
  (d) the applicant must meet all of the requirements of Section E-ECC: Eligibility for entry clearance as a child.

Section E-ECC: Eligibility for entry clearance as a child

E-ECC.1.1. To meet the eligibility requirements for entry clearance as a child all of the requirements of paragraphs E-ECC.1.2. to 2.4. must be met.

Relationship requirements

E-ECC.1.2. The applicant must be under the age of 18 at the date of application.

E-ECC.1.3. The applicant must not be married or in a civil partnership.

E-ECC.1.4. The applicant must not have formed an independent family unit.

E-ECC.1.5. The applicant must not be leading an independent life.

E-ECC.1.6. One of the applicant's parents must be in the UK with limited leave to enter or remain, or be applying, or have applied for, entry clearance, as] a partner or a parent under this Appendix (referred to in this section as the 'applicant's parent').

Note: Words in square brackets substituted from 6 September 2012 (HC 565).

Financial requirement

E-ECC.2.1. The applicant must provide specified evidence, from the sources listed in paragraph E-ECC.2.2[, of].-
  (a) a specified gross annual income of at least
    (i) £18,600;
    (ii) an additional £3,800 for the first child; and
    (iii) an additional £2,400 for each additional child; alone or in combination with
  (b) specified savings of-
    (i) £16,000;and
    (ii) additional savings of an amount equivalent to 2.5 times the amount which is the difference between the gross annual income from the sources listed in paragraph E-ECC.2.2.(a)-(f) and the total amount required under paragraph E-ECC.2.1.(a); or
  (c) the requirements in paragraph E-ECC.2.3. being met.

In this paragraph "child" means the applicant and any other dependent child of the applicant's parent who is—

(a) under the age of 18 years, or who was under the age of 18 years when they were first granted entry under this route;

(b) in the UK;

(c) not a British Citizen or settled in the UK; and

(d) not an EEA national with a right to remain in the UK under the Immigration (EEA) Regulations 2006.

Note: Word in square brackets inserted from 6 September 2012 (HC 565).

E-ECC.2.2. When determining whether the financial requirement in paragraph E-ECC.2.1. is met only the following sources may be taken into account-

(a) income of the applicant's parent's partner from specified employment or self-employment [, which, in respect of an applicant's parent's partner returning to the UK with the applicant, can include specified employment or self-employment overseas and in the UK;]

(b) income of the applicant's parent from specified employment or self- employment if they are in the UK unless they are working illegally;

(c) specified pension income of the applicant's parent and that parent's partner;

(d) any specified maternity allowance or bereavement benefit received by the applicant's parent and that parent's partner in the UK;

(e) other specified income of the applicant's parent and that parent's partner...;

(f) income from the sources at (b), (d) or (e) of a dependent child of the applicant's parent under paragraph E-ECC.2.1. who is aged 18 years or over; and

(g) specified savings of the applicant's parent, that parent's partner and a dependent child of the applicant's parent under paragraph E-ECC.2.1. who is aged 18 years or over.

Note: Words in square brackets in sub-para (a) inserted and words deleted from sub-para (e) from 6 September 2012 (HC 565).

E-ECC.2.3. The requirements to be met under this paragraph are-

(a) the applicant's parent's partner must be receiving one or more of the following-

(i) disability living allowance;

(ii) severe disablement allowance;

(iii) industrial injury disablement benefit;

(iv) attendance allowance; or

(v) carer's allowance; and

(b) the applicant must provide... evidence that their parent's partner is able to maintain and accommodate themselves, the applicant's parent, the applicant and any dependants adequately in the UK without recourse to public funds.

Note: Word deleted from 20 July 2012 (Cm 8423).

E-EEC.2.4. The applicant must provide... evidence that there will be adequate accommodation, without recourse to public funds, for the family, including other family members who are not included in the application but who live in the same household, which the family own or occupy exclusively: accommodation will not be regarded as adequate if-

(a) it is, or will be, overcrowded; or

(b) it contravenes public health regulations.

Note: Word deleted from 20 July 2012 (Cm 8423).

Section D-ECC: Decision on application for entry clearance as a child

D-ECC.1.1. If the applicant meets the requirements for entry clearance as a child they will be granted entry clearance of a duration which will expire at the same time as the leave granted to the applicant's parent, and subject to a condition of no recourse to public funds.

D-ECC.1.2. If the applicant does not meet the requirements for entry clearance as a child the application will be refused.

Section R-LTR-C: Requirements for leave to remain as a child

R-LTR-C.1.1. The requirements to be met for leave to remain as a child are that-
   (a) the applicant must be in the UK;
   (b) the applicant must have made a valid application for leave to remain as a child;
   (c) the applicant must not fall for refusal under any of the grounds in Section S-LTR: Suitability-leave to remain; and
   (d) the applicant must meet all of the requirements of Section E-LTRC: Eligibility for leave to remain as a child.

Section E-LTRC: Eligibility for leave to remain as a child

E-LTRC.1.1. To qualify for limited leave to remain as a child all of the requirements of paragraphs E-LTRC.1.2. to 2.4. must be met.

Relationship requirements

E-LTRC.1.2. The applicant must be under the age of 18 at the date of application or when first granted leave as a child under this route.

E-LTRC.1.3. The applicant must not be married or in a civil partnership.

E-LTRC.1.4. The applicant must not have formed an independent family unit.

E-LTRC.1.5. The applicant must not be leading an independent life.

E-LTRC.1.6. One of the applicant's parents must be in the UK with leave to enter or remain as, or have applied for leave to remain or indefinite leave to remain as, a partner or a parent under this Appendix (referred to in this section as the 'applicant's parent').

Financial requirements

E-LTRC.2.1. The applicant must provide specified evidence, from the sources listed in paragraph E-LTRC.2.2., of -
   (a) a specified gross annual income of at least-
      (i) £18,600;
      (ii) an additional £3,800 for the first child; and
      (iii) an additional £2,400 for each additional child; alone or in combination with
   (b) specified savings of-
      (i) £16,000;and
      (ii) additional savings of an amount equivalent to 2.5 times (or if the parent is applying for indefinite leave to remain 1 times) the amount which is the difference between the

gross annual income from the sources listed in paragraph E-LTRC.2.2.(a)-(f) and the total amount required under paragraph E-LTRC.2.1.(a); or

(c) the requirements in paragraph E-LTRC.2.3. being met. In this paragraph 'child' means the applicant and any other dependent child of the applicant's parent who is—

(i) under the age of 18 years, or who was under the age of 18 years when they were first granted entry under this route;

(ii) in the UK;

(iii) not a British Citizen or settled in the UK; and

(iv) not an EEA national with a right to remain in the UK under the Immigration (EEA) Regulations 2006.

E-LTRC.2.2. When determining whether the financial requirement in paragraph E-LTRC.2.1. is met only the following sources may be taken into account—

(a) income of the applicant's parent's partner from specified employment or self-employment;

(b) income of the applicant's parent from specified employment or self-employment;

(c) specified pension income of the applicant's parent and that parent's partner;

(d) any specified maternity allowance or bereavement benefit received by the applicant's parent and that parent's partner in the UK;

(e) other specified income of the applicant's parent and that parent's partner...;

(f) income from the sources at (b), (d) or (e) of a dependent child of the applicant's parent under paragraph E-LTRC.2.1. who is aged 18 years or over; and

(g) specified savings of the applicant's parent, that parent's partner and a dependent child of the applicant's parent under paragraph E-ECC.2.1. who is aged 18 years or over.

Note: Words deleted from sub-para (e) from 6 September 2012 (HC 565).

E-LTRC.2.3. The requirements to be met under this paragraph are-

(a) the applicant's parent's partner must be receiving one or more of the following—

(i) disability living allowance;

(ii) severe disablement allowance;

(iii) industrial injury disablement benefit;

(iv) attendance allowance; or

(v) carer's allowance; and

(b) the applicant must provide...evidence that their parent's partner is able to maintain and accommodate themselves, the applicant's parent, the applicant and any dependants adequately in the UK without recourse to public funds.

Note: Word deleted from 20 July 2012 (Cm 8423).

E-LTRC2.4. The applicant must provide...evidence that there will be adequate accommodation in the UK, without recourse to public funds, for the family, including other family members who are not included in the application but who live in the same household, which the family own or occupy exclusively: accommodation will not be regarded as adequate if-

(a) it is, or will be, overcrowded; or

(b) it contravenes public health regulations.

Note: Word deleted from 20 July 2012 (Cm 8423).

Section D-LTRC: Decision on application for leave to remain as a child

D-LTRC.1.1. If the applicant meets the requirements for leave to remain as a child the applicant will be granted leave to remain of a duration which will expire at the same time as the leave granted to the applicant's parent, and subject to a condition of no recourse to public funds, and if the applicant's parent is granted indefinite leave to remain the applicant will be granted indefinite leave to remain.

D-LTRC.1.2. If the applicant does not meet the requirements for leave to remain as a child the application will be refused.

Family life as a parent of a child in the UK

Section EC-PT: Entry clearance as a parent of a child in the UK

EC-PT.1.1. The requirements to be met for entry clearance as a parent are that—

(a) the applicant must be outside the UK;

(b) the applicant must have made a valid application for entry clearance as a parent;

(c) the applicant must not fall for refusal under any of the grounds in Section S-EC: Suitability–entry clearance; and

(d) the applicant must meet all of the requirements of Section E-ECPT: Eligibility for entry clearance as a parent.

Section E-ECPT: Eligibility for entry clearance as a parent

E-ECPT.1.1. To meet the eligibility requirements for entry clearance as a parent all of the requirements in paragraphs E-ECPT.2.1. to 4.2. must be met.

Relationship requirements

E-ECPT.2.1. The applicant must be aged 18 years or over.

E-ECPT.2.2. The child of the applicant must be—

(a) under the age of 18 years at the date of application;

(b) living in the UK; and

(c) a British Citizen or settled in the UK.

E-ECPT.2.3. Either—

(a) the applicant must have sole parental responsibility for the child; or

(b) the parent or carer with whom the child normally lives must be—

(i) a British Citizen in the UK or settled in the UK;

(ii) not the partner of the applicant; and

(iii) the applicant must not be eligible to apply for entry clearance as a partner under this Appendix.

E-ECPT.2.4.

(a) The applicant must provide.. evidence that they have either—

(i) sole parental responsibility for the child; or

(ii) access rights to the child; and

(b) The applicant must provide . . . evidence that they are taking, and intend to continue to take, an active role in the child's upbringing.

Note: Word deleted from sub-para (b) deleted from 20 July 2012 (Cm 8423). Word deleted from sub-para (a) from 6 September 2012 (HC 565).

Financial requirements

E-ECPT.3.1. The applicant must provide.... evidence that they will be able to adequately maintain and accommodate themselves and any dependants in the UK without recourse to public funds.

Note: Word deleted from 20 July 2012 (Cm 8423).

E-ECPT.3.2. The applicant must provide...evidence that there will be adequate accommodation in the UK, without recourse to public funds, for the family, including other family members who are not included in the application but who live in the same household, which the family own or occupy exclusively: accommodation will not be regarded as adequate if—
  (a) it is, or will be, overcrowded; or
  (b) it contravenes public health regulations.

Note: Word deleted from 20 July 2012 (Cm 8423).

English language requirement

E-ECPT.4.1. The applicant must provide specified evidence that they—
  (a) are a national of a majority English speaking country listed in paragraph [GEN.1.6.];
  (b) have passed an English language test in speaking and listening at a minimum of level A1 of the Common European Framework of Reference for Languages with a provider approved by the UK Border Agency;
  (c) have an academic qualification recognised by NARIC UK to be equivalent to the standard of a Bachelor's or Master's degree or PhD in the UK, which was taught in English; or
  (d) are exempt from the English language requirement under paragraph E- ECPT.4.2.

Note: Number in square brackets inserted from 20 July 2012 (Cm 8423).

E-ECPT.4.2. The applicant is exempt from the English language requirement if at the date of application—
  (a) the applicant is aged 65 or over;
  (b) the applicant has a disability (physical or mental condition) which prevents the applicant from meeting the requirement; or
  (c) there are exceptional circumstances which prevent the applicant from being able to meet the requirement prior to entry to the UK.

Section D-ECPT: Decision on application for entry clearance as a parent

D-ECPT.1.1. If the applicant meets the requirements for entry clearance as a parent they will be granted entry clearance for an initial period not exceeding 33 months, and subject to a condition of no recourse to public funds.

D-ECPT.1.2. If the applicant does not meet the requirements for entry clearance as a parent the application will be refused.

Section R-LTRPT: Requirements for limited leave to remain as a parent

R-LTRPT.1.1. The requirements to be met for limited leave to remain as a parent are-
    (a) the applicant and the child must be in the UK;
    (b) the applicant must have made a valid application for limited leave to remain as a parent; and either
    (c) (i) the applicant must not fall for refusal under Section S-LTR: Suitability leave to remain; and
        (ii) the applicant must meet all of the requirements of Section E- LTRPT: Eligibility for leave to remain as a parent, and
        (iii) paragraph EX.1. has not been applied; or
    (d) (i) the applicant [must not fall for refusal under]Section S-LTR: Suitability leave to remain; and
        [(ii) the applicant meets the requirements of paragraphs E-LTRPT.2.2–2.4. and E-LTRPT.3.1.] and
        (iii) paragraph EX.1. applies.

    Note: Sub-paragraph (d)(ii) substituted from 6 September 2012 (HC 565).

Section E-LTRPT: Eligibility for limited leave to remain as a parent

E-LTRPT.1.1. To qualify for limited leave to remain as a parent all of the requirements of paragraphs E-LTRPT.2.2. to 5.2. must be met.

Relationship requirements

E-LTRPT.2.2. The child of the applicant must be—
    (a) under the age of 18 years at the date of application;
    (b) living in the UK; and
    (c) a British Citizen or settled in the UK[; or
    (d) has lived in the UK continuously for at least the 7 years immediately preceding the date of application and paragraph EX.1. applies.]

    Note: Sub-paragraph (d) inserted from sub-para (e) from 6 September 2012 (HC 565).

E-LTRPT.2.3. Either—
    (a) the applicant must have sole parental responsibility for the child; or
    (b) the parent or carer with whom the child normally lives must be—
        (i) a British Citizen in the UK or settled in the UK;
        (ii) not the partner of the applicant; and
        (iii) the applicant must not be eligible to apply for leave to remain as a partner under this Appendix.
E-LTRPT.2.4. (a) The applicant must provide...evidence that they have either—
        (i) sole parental responsibility for the child ; or
        (ii) access rights to the child; and

(b) The applicant must provide...evidence that they are taking, and intend to continue to take, an active role in the child's upbringing.

Note: Words deleted from 20 July 2012 (Cm 8423).

Immigration status requirement

E-LTRPT.3.1. The applicant must not be in the UK—
(a) as a visitor;
(b) with valid leave granted for a period of 6 months or less;
(c) on temporary admission.

E-LTRPT.3.2. The applicant must not be in the UK in breach of immigration laws, (disregarding any period of overstaying for a period of 28 days or less), unless paragraph EX.1. applies.

Financial requirements

E-LTRPT.4.1. The applicant must provide...evidence that they will be able to adequately maintain and accommodate themselves and any dependants in the UK without recourse to public funds[, unless paragraph EX.1. applies].

Note: Word deleted from 20 July 2012 (Cm 8423). Words inserted from 6 September 2012 (HC 565).

E-LTRPT.4.2. The applicant must provide...evidence that there will be adequate accommodation in the UK, without recourse to public funds, for the family, including other family members who are not included in the application but who live in the same household, which the family own or occupy exclusively[, unless paragraph EX.1. applies]: accommodation will not be regarded as adequate if—
(a) it is, or will be, overcrowded; or
(b) it contravenes public health regulations.

Note: Word deleted from 20 July 2012 (Cm 8423). Words inserted from 6 September 2012 (HC 565).

English language requirement

E-LTRPT.5.1. The applicant must provide specified evidence that they—
(a) are a national of a majority English speaking country listed in paragraph [GEN.1.6.];
(b) have passed an English language test in speaking and listening at a minimum of level A1 of the Common European Framework of Reference for Languages with a provider approved by the UK Border Agency;
(c) have an academic qualification recognised by NARIC UK to be equivalent to the standard of a Bachelor's or Master's degree or PhD in the UK, which was taught in English; or
(d) are exempt from the English language requirement under paragraph E- LTRPT.5.2. [, unless paragraph EX.1. applies.]

Note: Number in square brackets substituted from 20 July 2012 (Cm 8423). Words inserted from sub-para (e) from 6 September 2012 (HC 565).

E-LTRPT.5.2. The applicant is exempt from the English language requirement if at the date of application-

(a) the applicant is aged 65 or over;

(b) the applicant has a disability (physical or mental condition) which prevents the applicant from meeting the requirement; or

(c) there are exceptional circumstances which prevent the applicant from being able to meet the requirement.

Section D-LTRPT: Decision on application for limited leave to remain as a parent

D-LTRPT.1.1. If the applicant meets the requirements in paragraph LTRPT.1.1. (a) to (c) for limited leave to remain as a parent the applicant will be granted limited leave to remain for a period not exceeding 30 months, and subject to a condition of no recourse to public funds, and they will be eligible to apply for settlement after [a continuous period of at least 60 months with such leave or in the UK with entry clearance as a parent under paragraph D-ECPT.1.1.]

Note: Words inserted from 6 September 2012 (HC 565).

D-LTRPT.1.2. If the applicant meets the requirements in paragraph LTRPT.1.1. (a), (b) and (d) for limited leave to remain as a parent they will be granted leave to remain for a period not exceeding 30 months, and will be eligible to apply for settlement after [a continuous period of at least 120 months with such leave, with limited leave as a parent under paragraph D-LTRPT.1.1., or in the UK with entry clearance as a parent under paragraph D-ECPT.1.1].

Note: Words inserted from 6 September 2012 (HC 565).

D-LTRPT.1.3. If the applicant does not meet the requirements for limited leave to remain as a parent the application will be refused.

Section R-ILRPT: Requirements for indefinite leave to remain (settlement) as a parent

R-ILRPT.1.1. The requirements to be met for indefinite leave to remain as a parent are that—

(a) the applicant must be in the UK;

(b) the applicant must have made a valid application for indefinite leave to remain as a parent;

(c) the applicant must not fall for refusal under any of the grounds in Section S-LTR: Suitability-leave to remain;

(d) the applicant must meet all of the requirements of Section E-LTRPT: Eligibility for leave to remain as a parent; and

(e) the applicant must meet all of the requirements of Section E-ILRPT: Eligibility for indefinite leave to remain as a parent.

Section E-ILRPT: Eligibility for indefinite leave to remain as a parent

E-ILRPT.1.1. To meet the eligibility requirements for indefinite leave to remain as a parent all of the requirements of paragraphs E-ILRPT.1.2. to 1.5. must be met.

E-ILRPT.1.2. The applicant must be in the UK with valid leave to remain as a parent (disregarding any period of overstaying for 28 days or less).

E-ILRPT.1.3. The applicant must have completed a continuous period of at least 60 months with limited leave as a parent under paragraph R-LTRPT.1.1.(a) to (c) [or in the UK with entry clearance as a parent under paragraph D-ECPT.1.1.,] or a continuous period of at least 120 months with limited leave [as] a parent, under paragraphs R-LTRPT.1.1(a), (b) and (d) [or in the UK with entry clearance as a parent under paragraph D-ECPT.1.1.,] or a continuous period of at least 120 months with limited leave as a [partner] under a combination of these paragraphs.

Note: Words inserted/substituted from 6 September 2012 (HC 565).

E-ILRPT.1.4. The applicant must at the date of application have no unspent convictions.

E-ILRPT.1.5. The applicant must have sufficient knowledge of the English language and sufficient knowledge about life in the UK in accordance with the requirements of paragraphs 33B to 33G of these Rules.

Section D-ILRPT: Decision on application for indefinite leave to remain as a parent

D-ILRPT.1.1. If the applicant meets all of the requirements for indefinite leave to remain as a parent the applicant will be granted indefinite leave to remain.

D-ILRPT.1.2. If the applicant does not meet the requirements for indefinite leave to remain as a parent only for one or both of the following reasons—

(a) the applicant has an unspent conviction; or

(b) the applicant has not met the requirements of paragraphs 33B to 33G of these Rules, the applicant will be granted further limited leave to remain as a parent for a period not exceeding 30 months, and subject to a condition of no recourse to public funds.

D-ILRPT.1.3. If the applicant does not meet the requirements for indefinite leave to remain as a parent, or further limited leave to remain under paragraph D-ILRPT.1.2., the application will be refused[, unless paragraph EX.1. applies. Where paragraph EX.1. applies, the applicant will be granted further limited leave to remain as a parent for a period not exceeding 30 months under paragraph D- LTRPT.1.2.]

Note: Words inserted from 6 September 2012 (HC 565).

Adult Dependent Relative

Section EC-DR: Entry clearance as an adult dependent relative

EC-DR.1.1. The requirements to be met for entry clearance as an adult dependent relative are that—

(a) the applicant must be outside the UK;

(b) the applicant must have made a valid application for entry clearance as an adult dependent relative;

(c) the applicant must not fall for refusal under any of the grounds in Section S-EC: Suitability for entry clearance; and

(d) the applicant must meet all of the requirements of Section E-ECDR: Eligibility for entry clearance as an adult dependent relative.

Section E-ECDR: Eligibility for entry clearance as an adult dependent relative

E-ECDR.1.1. To meet the eligibility requirements for entry clearance as an adult dependent relative all of the requirements in paragraphs E-ECDR.2.1. to 3.2. must be met.

Relationship requirements

E-ECDR.2.1. The applicant must be the—
(a) parent aged 18 years or over;
(b) grandparent;
(c) brother or sister aged 18 years or over; or
(d) son or daughter aged 18 years or over
of a person ('the sponsor') who is in the UK.

E-ECDR.2.2. If the applicant is the sponsor's parent or grandparent they must not be in a subsisting relationship with a partner unless that partner is also the sponsor's parent or grandparent and is applying for entry clearance at the same time as the applicant.

E-ECDR.2.3. The sponsor must at the date of application be—
(a) aged 18 years or over; and
(b) (i) a British Citizen in the UK; or
(ii) present and settled in the UK; or
(iii) in the UK with refugee leave or humanitarian protection.

E-ECDR.2.4. The applicant or, if the applicant and their partner are the sponsor's parents or grandparents, the applicant's partner, must as a result of age, illness or disability require long-term personal care to perform everyday tasks.

E-ECDR.2.5. The applicant or, if the applicant and their partner are the sponsor's parents or grandparents, the applicant's partner, must be unable, even with the practical and financial help of the sponsor, to obtain the required level of care in the country where they are living, because—
(a) it is not available and there is no person in that country who can reasonably provide it; or
(b) it is not affordable.

Financial requirements

E-ECDR.3.1. The applicant must provide...evidence that they can be adequately maintained, accommodated and cared for in the UK by the sponsor without recourse to public funds.

Note: Word deleted from 20 July 2012 (Cm 8423).

E-ECDR.3.2. If the applicant's sponsor is a British Citizen or settled in the UK, the applicant must provide an undertaking signed by the sponsor confirming that the applicant will have no recourse to public funds, and that the sponsor will be responsible for their maintenance, accommodation and care, for a period of 5 years from the date the applicant enters the UK if they are granted indefinite leave to enter.

Section D-ECDR: Decision on application for entry clearance as an adult dependent relative

D-ECDR.1.1. If the applicant meets the requirements for entry clearance as an adult dependent relative of a British Citizen or person settled in the UK they will be granted indefinite leave to enter.

D-ECDR.1.2. If the applicant meets the requirements for entry clearance as an adult dependent relative and the sponsor has limited leave the applicant will be granted limited leave of a duration which will expire at the same time as the sponsor's limited leave, and subject to a condition of no recourse to public funds. If the sponsor applies for further limited leave, the applicant may apply for further limited leave of the same duration, if the requirements in EC-DR.1.1.(c) and (d) continue to be met, and subject to no recourse to public funds.

D-ECDR.1.3. If the applicant does not meet the requirements for entry clearance as an adult dependent relative the application will be refused.

Section R-ILRDR: Requirements for indefinite leave to remain as an adult dependent relative.

R-ILRDR.1.1. The requirements to be met for indefinite leave to remain as an adult dependent relative are that—

(a) the applicant is in the UK;

(b) the applicant must have made a valid application for indefinite leave to remain as an adult dependent relative;

(c) the applicant must not fall for refusal under any of the grounds in Section S-LTR: Suitability-leave to remain; and

(d) the applicant must meet all of the requirements of Section E-ILRDR: Eligibility for indefinite leave to remain as an adult dependent relative.

Section E-ILRDR: Eligibility for indefinite leave to remain as an adult dependent relative

E-ILRDR.1.1. To qualify for indefinite leave to remain as an adult dependent relative all of the requirements of paragraphs E-ILRDR.1.2. to 1.6. must be met.

E-ILRDR.1.2. The applicant must be in the UK with valid leave to remain as an adult dependent relative (disregarding any period of overstaying for a period of 28 days or less).

E-ILRDR.1.3. The applicant's sponsor must at the date of application be—

(a) present and settled in the UK; or

(b) in the UK with refugee leave or as a person with humanitarian protection and have made an application for indefinite leave to remain.

E-ILRDR.1.4. The applicant must provide.... evidence that they can be adequately maintained, accommodated and cared for in the UK by the sponsor without recourse to public funds.

Note: Word deleted from 20 July 2012 (Cm 8423).

E-ILRDR.1.5. The applicant must provide an undertaking signed by the sponsor confirming that the applicant will have no recourse to public funds, and that the sponsor will be responsible for their maintenance, accommodation and care, for a period ending 5 years from the date the applicant entered the UK with limited leave as an adult dependent relative.

E-ILRDR.1.6. To qualify for indefinite leave to remain the applicant must not at the date of application have any unspent convictions.

Section D-ILRDR: Decision on application for indefinite leave to remain as an adult dependent relative

D-ILRDR.1.1. If the applicant meets the requirements for indefinite leave to remain as an adult dependent relative and the applicant's sponsor is settled in the UK, the applicant will be granted indefinite leave to remain as an adult dependent relative.

D-ILRDR.1.2. If the applicant does not meet the requirements for indefinite leave to remain as an adult dependent relative because the applicant has an unspent conviction, the applicant will be granted further limited leave to remain as an adult dependent relative for a period not exceeding 30 months, and subject to a condition of no recourse to public funds.

D-ILRDR.1.3. If the applicant's sponsor has made an application for indefinite leave to remain and that application is refused, the applicant's application for indefinite leave to remain will be refused. If the sponsor is granted limited leave, the applicant will be granted further limited leave as an adult dependent relative of a duration which will expire at the same time as the sponsor's further limited leave, and subject to a condition of no recourse to public funds.

D-ILRDR.1.4. Where an applicant does not meet the requirements for indefinite leave to remain, or further limited leave to remain under paragraphs D-ILRDR.1.2. or 1.3., the application will be refused.

Deportation and Removal

Where the Secretary of State or an immigration officer is considering deportation or removal of a person who claims that their deportation or removal from the UK would be a breach of the right to respect for private and family life under Article 8 of the Human Rights Convention that person may be required to make an application under this Appendix or paragraph 276ADE, but if they are not required to make an application Part 13 of these Rules will apply.]

Note: Appendix FM inserted from 9 July 2012 for applications made on or after that date (HC 194).

[Appendix FM-SE
Family Members – Specified Evidence

A. This Appendix sets out the specified evidence applicants need to provide to meet the requirements of rules contained in Appendix FM [and, where those requirements are also contained in other rules and unless otherwise stated, the specified evidence applicants need to provide to meet the requirements of those rules].

Note: Words inserted from 6 September 2012 (HC 565).

B. Where evidence is not specified by Appendix FM, but is of a type covered by this Appendix, the requirements of this Appendix shall apply.

C. In this Appendix references to paragraphs are to paragraphs of this Appendix unless the context otherwise requires.

Evidence of Financial Requirements [under Appendix FM]

Note: Words inserted in heading from 6 September 2012 (HC 565).

[A1. To meet the financial requirement under paragraphs E-ECP.3.1., E-LTRP.3.1., E- ECC.2.1. and E-LTRC.2.1. of Appendix FM, the applicant must meet:

(a) The level of financial requirement applicable to the application under Appendix FM; and

(b) The requirements specified in Appendix FM and this Appendix as to:

(i) The permitted sources of income and savings;

(ii) The time periods and permitted combinations of sources applicable to each permitted source relied upon; and

(iii) The evidence required for each permitted source relied upon.]

Note: Paragraph A1 inserted from 6 September 2012 (HC 565).

1. In relation to evidencing the financial requirements in Appendix FM the following general provisions shall apply:

(a) ... bank statements must:

(i) be from a financial institution regulated by the appropriate regulatory body for the country in which that institution is operating.

(ii) not be from a financial institution on the list of excluded institutions in Appendix P of these rules.

(iii) [in relation to personal bank statements] be only in the name of:

(1) the applicant's partner, the applicant or both as appropriate; or

(2) if the applicant is a child the applicant parent's partner, the applicant's parent or both as appropriate; or

(3) if the applicant is an adult dependent relative, the applicant's sponsor [or the applicant],

unless otherwise stated.

(b) [Promises of third party support will not be accepted. Third party support will only be accepted in the form of]:

(i) maintenance payments from a former partner of an applicant in relation to the applicant and former partner's child or children [or in relation to the applicant];

(ii) income from a dependent child who has turned 18, remains in the same UK household as the applicant and continues to be counted towards the financial requirement under Appendix FM; ...

(iii) [gift of cash savings (whose source must be declared)] evidenced at paragraph 1(a)(iii), provided that the cash savings have been held by the person or persons at paragraph 1(a)(iii) for at least 6 months prior to the date of application and are under their control [; and

(iv) a maintenance grant or stipend associated with undergraduate study or post-graduate study or research.]

(c) The employment income of an applicant will only be taken into account if they are in the UK, aged 18 years or over and working legally[, and prospective employment income will not be taken into account (except that of an applicant's partner or parent's partner who is returning to employment or self-employment in the UK at paragraphs E-ECP.3.2.(a) and E-ECC.2.2.(a) of Appendix FM).]

(d) All income and savings must be lawfully derived.

(e) Savings must be held in cash.

(f) Income or cash savings in a foreign currency will be converted to pounds sterling using the closing spot exchange rate which appears on www.oanda.com* on the date of application.

(g) Where there is income or cash savings in different foreign currencies, each will be converted into pounds sterling before being added together, and then added to any UK income or savings to give a total amount.

(h) All documentary evidence must be original, unless otherwise stated.

(i) Evidence of profit from the sale of a business, property, investment, bond, stocks, shares or other asset will:

(i) not be accepted as evidence of income, but

(ii) the associated funds will be accepted as cash savings subject to the requirements of this Appendix and Appendix FM.

(j) Where a document is not in English or Welsh, the original must be accompanied by a certified translation by a professional translator. This translation must include details of the translator's credentials and confirmation that it is an accurate translation of the original document. It must also be dated and include the original signature of the translator.

(k) [Entry Clearance Officer or Secretary of State] should normally refuse an application which does not provide the evidence specified in this Appendix. However, where document(s) have been submitted, but not as specified, and the [Entry Clearance Officer or Secretary of State] considers that, if the specified document(s) were submitted, it would result in a grant of leave, they should contact the applicant or their representative in writing or otherwise to request the document(s) be submitted within a reasonable timeframe. Examples of documents submitted not as specified include:

a) A document missing from a series, e.g. a bank statement;

b) A document in the wrong format; or

c) A document that is a copy rather than the original.

[(l) Where the gross (pre-tax) amount of any income cannot be properly evidenced, the net (post-tax) amount will be counted, including towards a gross income requirement.]

If the applicant does not submit the document(s) as requested, the caseworker may refuse the application. Where the specified document(s) cannot be supplied (e.g. because they are not available in a particular country or have been permanently lost), the caseworker has discretion not to apply the requirement for the specified document(s) or to request alternative or additional information or documents be submitted by the applicant.

Note: Words deleted from sub-para (a) and (b)(ii), words inserted in sub-para (a)(iii), words substituted in sub-para (b), words inserted in sub-para (b)(i), words substituted in sub-para (b)(iii), sub-para (b)(iv) inserted, words inserted in sub-para (c), words substituted in sub-para (k) and sub-para (l) inserted from 6 September 2012 (HC 565).

2. In respect of salaried employment in the UK, all of the following evidence must be provided:

(b) The P60 for the relevant period or periods [of employment relied on] (if issued).

(c) Wage slips covering:

(i) a period of 6 months prior to the date of application if the applicant has been employed by their current employer for at least 6 months; or

(ii) [any period of salaried employment in the] period of 12 months prior to the date of application if the applicant has been employed by their current employer for less than 6 months.

(d) A letter from the employer[(s) who issued the payslips at paragraph 2(c)] confirming:

(i) the person's employment and gross annual salary;

(ii) the length of their employment;

(iii) the period over which they have been or were paid the level of salary relied upon in the application; and

(iv) the type of employment (permanent, fixed-term contract or agency).

(e) A signed contract of employment [for employment currently held].

(f) Monthly personal bank statements corresponding to the same period[(s)] as the wage slips at paragraph 2(c), showing that the salary has been paid into an account in the name of the person or in the name of the person and their partner jointly.

Note: Words in square brackets in sub-paras (b), (c)(ii), (d), (e) and (f) inserted from 6 September 2012 (HC 565).

3. In respect of salaried employment outside of the UK, evidence should be a reasonable equivalent to that set out in paragraph 2.

4. In respect of a job offer in the UK [(for an applicant's partner or parent's partner returning to salaried employment in the UK at paragraphs E-ECP.3.2.(a) and E-ECC.2.2.(a) of Appendix FM)] a letter from the employer must be provided:

(a) confirming the job offer, the gross annual salary and the starting date of the employment which must be within 3 months of the applicant's partner's return to the UK; or

(b) enclosing a signed contract of employment, which must have a starting date within 3 months of the applicant's partner's return to the UK.

Note: Words in square brackets substituted from 6 September 2012 (HC 565).

5. In respect of statutory or contractual maternity, paternity or adoption pay in the UK all of the following must be provided:

(a) A P60 for the relevant period or periods [of employment relied on] prior to commencement of the maternity, paternity or adoption leave (if issued).

(b) Wage slips covering:

(i) a period of 6 months prior to the commencement of the maternity, paternity or adoption leave, if the applicant has been employed by their current employer for at least 6 months; or

(ii) [any period of salaried employment in the] period of 12 months prior to the commencement of the maternity, paternity or adoption leave, if the applicant has been employed by their current employer for less than 6 months.

(c) A letter from the employer confirming:

(i) the length of the person's employment;

(ii) the gross annual salary and the period over which it has been paid at this level;

(iii) the entitlement to maternity, paternity or adoption leave; and

(iv) the date of commencement and the end-date of the maternity, paternity or adoption leave.

Note: Words in square brackets inserted/substituted from 6 September 2012 (HC 565).

6. In respect of statutory or contractual sick pay in the UK all of the following must be provided:

(a) A P60 for the relevant period or periods [of employment relied on] prior to the commencement of the sick leave (if issued).

(b) Wage slips covering:

    (i) a period of 6 months prior to the commencement of the sick leave, if the applicant has been employed by their current employer for at least 6 months; or,

    (ii) [any period of salaried employment in the] period of 12 months prior to the commencement of the sick leave, if the applicant has been employed by their current employer for less than 6 months.

(c) A letter from employer confirming:

    (i) the length of the person's employment;

    (ii) the gross annual salary and the period over which it has been paid at this level;

    (iii) that the person is in receipt of statutory or contractual sick pay; and

    (iv) the date of commencement of the sick leave.

Note: Words in square brackets inserted/substituted from 6 September 2012 (HC 565).

7. In respect of self-employment in the UK as a partner, as a sole trader or in a franchise all of the following must be provided:

(a) Evidence of the amount of tax payable, paid and unpaid for the last financial year.

(b) The latest:

    (i) annual self-assessment tax return to HMRC;

    (ii) Statement of Account (SA300 or SA302); and,

    (iii) the same for the previous financial year if the latest return does not show the necessary level of gross income, but the average of the last 2 financial years does.

(c) Proof of registration with HMRC as self-employed. This evidence must be either an original or a certified copy of the registration documentation issued by HMRC.

(d) Each partner's Unique Tax Reference Number (UTR) and/or the UTR of the partnership or business.

(e) Where the person holds or held a separate business bank account(s), monthly bank statements for the same 12-month period as the tax return(s).

(f) Monthly personal bank statements for the same 12-month period as the tax return(s) showing that the income from self-employment has been paid into an account in the name of the person or in the name of the person and their partner jointly.

(g) Evidence of ongoing self-employment through:

    (i) evidence of payment of Class 2 National Insurance contributions (for self-employed persons); or,

    (ii) current Appointment Reports from Companies House (for Directors).

(h) One of the following documents must also be submitted:

    (i) The organisation's latest annual audited accounts with:

        (1) the name of the accountant clearly shown; and,

        (2) the accountant must be a member of an accredited accounting body [specified in paragraph 19(g)(ii) of Appendix A of these rules];

(ii) A certificate of VAT registration and the latest VAT return confirming the VAT registration number, if turnover is in excess of £73,000;

(iii) Evidence to show appropriate planning permission or local planning authority consent is held to operate the type/class of business at the trading address (where this is a local authority requirement); or

(iv) A franchise agreement signed by both parties.

(i) The document referred to in paragraph [7](h)(iv) must be provided if the organisation is a franchise.

Note: Words in square brackets inserted/substituted from 6 September 2012 (HC 565).

8. In respect of self-employment outside of the UK, evidence should be a reasonable equivalent to that set out in paragraph 7.

9. In respect of self-employment in a limited company based in the UK all of the following must be provided:

(b) Evidence of registration with the Registrar of Companies at Companies House.

(c) Latest Notice to file a Company Tax Return – CT603 and Company Tax Return – CT600 (both parts must be supplied).

(d) The organisation's latest audited annual accounts with:

(i) the name of the accountant clearly shown; and

(ii) the accountant must be a member of an accredited accounting body [specified in paragraph 19(g)(ii) of Appendix A of these rules].

(e) Monthly corporate/business bank statements covering the same 12-month period as the tax return(s).

(f) Monthly personal bank statements covering the same 12-month period as the tax return(s) showing that the income from self-employment has been paid into an account in the name of the person or in the name of the person and their partner jointly.

(g) Evidence of ongoing self-employment through:

(i) evidence of payment of Class 2 National Insurance contributions (for self-employed persons); or,

(ii) current Appointment Reports from Companies House (for Directors),

(h) One of the following documents must also be provided:

(i) A certificate of VAT registration and the latest VAT return confirming the VAT registration number, if turnover is in excess of £73,000.

(ii) Proof of ownership or lease of business premises.

(iii) Original proof of registration with HMRC as an employer for the purposes of PAYE and National Insurance, proof of PAYE reference number and Accounts Office reference number. This evidence may be in the form of a certified copy of the documentation issued by HMRC.

(iv) Proof of registration with the London Stock Exchange or with an international stock exchange approved by the Financial Services Authority in the UK.

(i) The document referred to in paragraph 9(h)(iv) must be provided for a company registered on the London Stock Exchange or an FSA-approved international stock exchange.

Note: Words in square brackets in sub-para (d)(ii) inserted from 6 September 2012 (HC 565).

10. In respect of non-employment income all the following evidence, in relation to the form of income relied upon, must be provided:

(a) To evidence property rental income:

(i) Confirmation that [the person or the person and their partner jointly] own the property for which the rental income is received, through:

    (1) The title deeds of the property; or

    (2) A mortgage statement.

  (ii) Monthly personal bank statements for the 12-month period prior to the date of application showing the rental income was paid into an account in the name of the person or of the person and their partner jointly.

  (iii) A rental agreement or contract.

(b) To evidence dividends or other income from investments, stocks, shares, bonds or trust funds:

  (i) A certificate showing proof of ownership and the amount(s) of any investment(s).

  (ii) A portfolio report (for a financial institution regulated by the Financial Services Authority in the UK).

  (iii) Monthly personal bank statements for the 12-month period prior to the date of application showing that the income relied upon was paid into an account in the name of the person or of the person and their partner jointly.

(c) To evidence interest from savings:

  (i) Monthly personal bank statements for the 12-month period prior to the date of application showing the amount of the savings held and that the interest was paid into an account in the name of the person or of the person and their partner jointly.

(d) To evidence maintenance payments (from a former partner to maintain their and the applicant's child or children [or the applicant]):

  (i) Evidence of a maintenance agreement through any of the following:

    (1) A court order;

    (2) Written voluntary agreement; or

    (3) Child Support Agency documentation.

  (ii) Monthly personal bank statements for the 12-month period prior to the date of application showing the income relied upon was paid into an account in the name of the applicant.

(e) To evidence a pension:

  (i) Official documentation from:

    (1) HMRC (in respect of the Basic State Pension and the Additional or Second State Pension);

    (2) An overseas pension authority; or

    (3) A pension company, confirming pension entitlement and amount.

  (ii) At least one [monthly personal bank statement in the 12-month period prior to the date of application] showing payment of the pension into the person's account.

(f) To evidence UK Maternity Allowance, Bereavement Allowance, Bereavement Payment and Widowed Parent's Allowance:

  (i) Department for Work and Pensions documentation confirming [the person or their partner] is or was in receipt of the benefit [in the 12-month period prior to the date of application].

  (ii) Monthly personal bank statements for the 12-month period prior to the date of application showing the income was paid into the person's account.

[(g) To evidence a maintenance grant or stipend (not a loan) associated with undergraduate study or postgraduate study or research:

  (i) Documentation from the body or company awarding the grant or stipend confirming that the person is currently in receipt of the grant or stipend or will be within

3 months of the date of application, confirming that the grant orstipend will be paid for a period of at least 12 months from the date of application or from the date on which payment of the grant or stipend will commence, and confirming the annual amount of the grant or stipend.

(ii) Monthly personal bank statements for any part of the 12-month period prior to the date of the application during which the person has been in receipt of the grant or stipend showing the income was paid into the person's account.]

Note: Sub-paragraph (g) inserted and other words in square brackets inserted/substituted from 6 September 2012 (HC 565).

11. In respect of cash savings the following must be provided:

(a) Monthly personal bank statements showing the cash savings have been held in an account in the name of the person or of the person and their partner jointly for at least 6 months prior to the date of application.

[(b) A declaration by the account holder(s) of the source(s) of the cash savings.]

Note: Subparagraph (b) inserted from 6 September 2012 (HC 565).

[**11A.** In respect of cash savings:

(a) The savings may be held in any form of bank/savings account, provided that the account allows the savings to be accessed immediately (with or without a penalty for withdrawing funds without notice). This can include, for those of retirement age, savings held in a pension savings account which can be immediately withdrawn.

(b) Paid out competition winnings or a legacy which has been paid can contribute to cash savings.]

Note: Paragraph 11A inserted from 6 September 2012 (HC 565).

12. Where the applicant's partner is in receipt of Carer's Allowance, Disability Living Allowance, Severe Disablement Allowance, Industrial Injuries Disablement Benefit or Attendance Allowance, all the following must be provided:

(a) Official documentation from the Department for Work and Pensions confirming the entitlement and the amount received.

(b) At least one [monthly personal bank statement in the 12-month period prior to the date of application] showing payment of the benefit or allowance into the person's account.

Note: Words inserted in sub-para (b) from 6 September 2012 (HC 565).

[**12A.** Where the financial requirement the applicant must meet under Appendix FM relates to adequate maintenance, paragraphs 2 to 12 apply only to the extent and in the manner specified by this paragraph. Where such a financial requirement applies, the applicant must provide the following evidence:

(a) Where the current salaried employment in the UK of the applicant or their partner, parent, parent's partner or sponsor is relied upon:

(i) A letter from the employer confirming the employment, the gross annual salary and the annual salary after income tax and National Insurance contributions have been paid, how long the employment has been held, and the type of employment (permanent, fixed-term contract or agency).

(ii) Wage slips covering the period of 6 months prior to the date of application or such shorter period as the current employment has been held.

(iii) Monthly personal bank statement covering the same period as the wage slips, showing that the salary has been paid into an account in the name of the person or in the name of the person and their partner jointly.

(b) Where statutory or contractual maternity, paternity, adoption or sick pay in the UK of the applicant or their partner, parent, parent's partner or sponsor are relied upon, paragraph 5(b)(i) and (c) or paragraph 6(b)(i) and (c) apply as appropriate.

(c) Where self-employment in the UK of the applicant or their partner, parent, parent's partner or sponsor is relied upon, paragraph 7 or 9 applies as appropriate.

(d) Where the non-employment income of the applicant or their partner, parent, parent's partner or sponsor is relied upon, paragraph 10 applies and paragraph 10(f) shall apply as if it referred to any UK welfare benefit or tax credit relied upon and to HMRC as well as Department for Work and Pensions documentation.

(e) Where the cash savings of the applicant or their partner, parent, parent's partner or sponsor are relied upon, paragraphs 11 and 11A apply.

(f) The monthly housing and Council Tax costs for the accommodation in the UK in which the applicant (and any other family members who are or will be part of the same household) lives or will live if the application is granted.

(g) Where the applicant is an adult dependent relative applying for entry clearance, the applicant must in addition provide details of the care arrangements in the UK planned for them by their sponsor (which can involve other family members in the UK), of the cost of these arrangements and of how that cost will be met by the sponsor.]

Note: Paragraph 12A inserted from 6 September 2012 (HC 565).

Calculating Gross Annual Income [under Appendix FM]

Note: Heading amended from 6 September 2012 (HC 565).

13. Based on evidence that meets the requirements of this Appendix, and can be taken into account with reference to the applicable provisions of Appendix FM, gross annual income under paragraphs E-ECP.3.1., E-LTRP.3.1., E-ECC.2.1. and E-LTRC.2.1. will be calculated in the following ways:

(a) Where the person is in salaried employment in the UK at the date of application and has been employed by their current employer for at least 6 months, their gross annual income will be the total of:

(i) The gross annual salary from their employment as it was at its lowest level in the 6 months prior to the date of application;

(ii) The gross amount of any specified non-employment income [other than pension income] received by them or their partner in the 12 months prior to the date of application; and

(iii) The gross annual income from a UK or foreign State pension or a private pension received by them or their partner.

(b) Where the person is in salaried employment in the UK at the date of application and has been employed by their current employer for less than 6 months, their gross annual income will be the total of:

(i) The gross annual salary from employment as it was at the date of application;

(ii) The gross amount of any specified non-employment income [other than pension income] received by them or their partner in the 12 months prior to the date of application; and

(iii) The gross annual income from a UK or foreign State pension or a private pension received by them or their partner.

[In addition, the requirements of paragraph 15 must be met].

(c) Where the person is the applicant's partner, is in salaried employment outside of the UK at the date of application, has been employed by their current employer for at least 6 months, and is returning to the UK to take up salaried employment in the UK starting within 3 months of their return, the person's gross annual income will be calculated:

(i) On the basis set out in paragraph 13(a); and also

(ii) On that basis but substituting for the gross annual salary at paragraph 13(a)(i) the gross annual salary in the salaried employment in the UK to which they are returning.

(d) Where the person is the applicant's partner, has been in salaried employment outside of the UK within 12 months of the date of application, and is returning to the UK to take up salaried employment in the UK starting within 3 months of their return, the person's gross annual income will be calculated:

(i) On the basis set out in paragraph 13(a) but substituting for the gross annual salary at paragraph 13(a)(i) the gross annual salary in the salaried employment in the UK to which they are returning; and also

(ii) On the basis set out in paragraph 15(b).

(e) Where the person is self-employed, their gross annual income will be the total of their gross income from their self-employment, from any salaried employment they have had, from specified non-employment income received by them or their partner, and from income from a UK or foreign State pension or a private pension received by them or their partner, in the last full financial year or as an average of the last two full financial years.

(f) Where the person is self-employed, they cannot combine their gross annual income at paragraph 13(e) with specified savings in order to meet the level of income required under Appendix FM.

[(g) Where the person is not relying on income from salaried employment or self-employment, their gross annual income will be the total of:

(i) The gross amount of any specified non-employment income (other than pension income) received by them or their partner in the 12 months prior to the date of application; and

(ii) The gross annual income from a UK or foreign State pension or a private pension received by them or their partner.]

Note: Sub-paragraph (g) and words in square brackets in sub-paras (a) and (b) inserted from 6 September 2012 (HC 565).

14. Where the requirements of this Appendix and Appendix FM are met by the combined income or cash savings of more than one person, the income or the cash savings must only be counted once unless stated otherwise.

15. In respect of paragraph 13(b) [and paragraph 13(d)], the provisions in this paragraph also apply:

(a) In order to evidence the level of gross annual income required by Appendix FM, the person must meet the requirements in paragraph 13(b) [or paragraph 13(d)(i)]; and

(b) The person must also meet the level of gross annual income required by Appendix FM on the basis that their income is the total of:

(i) The gross income from salaried employment earned by the person in the 12 months prior to the date of application;

(ii) The gross amount of any specified non-employment income [other than pension income] received by the person or their partner in the 12 months prior to the date of application;

(iii) The gross amount received from a UK or foreign State pension or a private pension by the person or their partner in the 12 months prior to the date of application; and

(iv) ...

(v) The person cannot combine the gross annual income at paragraph 15(b)(i)-[(iii)] with specified savings in order to meet the level of income required.

Note: Words in square brackets inserted and sub-para (b)(iv) deleted from 6 September 2012 (HC 565).

16. Where a person is in receipt of maternity, paternity, adoption or sick pay, this paragraph applies:

(a) the relevant date for considering the length of employment with their current employer will be the date that the maternity, paternity, adoption or sick leave commenced and not the date of application; and

(b) the relevant period for calculating income from their salaried employment will be the period prior to the commencement of the maternity, paternity, adoption or sick pay and not the date of application.

17. If a person is an equity partner, for example in a law firm, the income they draw from the partnership will be treated as salaried employment for the purposes of this Appendix and Appendix FM.

18. When calculating income from salaried employment under paragraphs [12A and] 13 to 16, this paragraph applies:

(a) Basic pay, skills-based allowances, and UK location-based allowances will be counted as income provided that:

(i) They are contractual; and

(ii) Where these allowances make up more than 30% of the total salary, only the amount up to 30% is counted.

(b) Overtime, commission-based pay and bonuses will be counted as income.

(c) UK and overseas travel, subsistence and accommodation allowances, and allowances relating to the cost of living overseas will not be counted as income.

Note: Words in square brackets inserted from 6 September 2012 (HC 565).

19. When calculating income from self-employment under[paragraphs 12A and 13(e)], this paragraph applies:

(a) There must be evidence of ongoing self-employment at the date of application.

(b) Where the self-employed person is a sole trader or is in a partnership or franchise agreement, the income will be:

(i) the gross taxable profits from their share of the business; and

(ii) allowances or deductable expenses which are not taxed will not be counted towards income.

(c) Where the self-employed person has set up their own registered company and is listed as a director of that company, the income that can be counted will be any income drawn from the post-tax profits of the company.

Note: Words in square brackets inserted from 6 September 2012 (HC 565).

20. When calculating income from specified non-employment sources[paragraphs 12A and 13 to 15], this paragraph applies:

(a) Assets or savings must be in the name of the person, or jointly with their partner.

(b) [Any asset or savings on which income is based] must be held [or owned] by the person at the date of application.

(c) Any rental income from property, in the UK or overseas, must be from a property that is:

    (i) owned by the person;

    (ii) not their main residence; and

    (iii) if ownership of the property is shared with a third party, only income received from their share of the property can be counted.

(d) Equity in a property cannot be used to meet the financial requirement.

Note: Words in square brackets inserted/substituted from 6 September 2012 (HC 565).

[**20A.** When calculating the gross annual income from pension under paragraph 13, the gross annual amount of any pension received may be counted where the pension has become a source of income at least 28 days prior to the date of application.]

Note: Paragraph 20A inserted from 6 September 2012 (HC 565).

21. When calculating income under paragraphs 13 to 16, the following sources will not be counted:

(a) Loans and credit facilities.

(b) Income-related benefits: Income Support, income-related Employment and Support Allowance, Pension Credit, Housing Benefit, Council Tax Benefit and income-based Jobseeker's Allowance.

(c) The following contributory benefits: contribution-based Jobseeker's Allowance, contribution-based Employment and Support Allowance and Incapacity Benefit.

(d) Child Benefit.

(e) Working Tax Credit.

(f) Child Tax Credit.

(g) Any other source of income not specified in this appendix.

Evidence of Marriage or Civil Partnerships

22. A claim to have been married in the United Kingdom must be evidenced by a marriage certificate.

23. A claim to be divorced in the United Kingdom must be evidenced by a decree absolute from a civil court.

24. A civil partnership in the United Kingdom must be evidenced by a civil partnership certificate.

25. The dissolution of a civil partnership in the UK must be evidenced by a final order of civil partnership dissolution from a civil court.

26. Marriages, civil partnerships or evidence of divorce or dissolution from outside the UK must be evidenced by a reasonable equivalent to the evidence detailed in paragraphs 22 to 25, valid under the law in force in the relevant country.

Evidence of English Language Requirements

27. Evidence of passing an English language test in speaking and listening must take the form of either:

(a) a certificate that:

(i) is from an English language test provider approved by the Secretary of State for these purposes as specified in Appendix O of these rules

(ii) is a test approved by the Secretary of State for these purposes as specified in Appendix O of these rules

(iii) shows the applicant's name;

(iv) shows the qualification obtained (which must meet or exceed level A1 of the Common European Framework of Reference); and,

(v) shows the date of award.

Or,

(b) a print out of the online score from a PTE (Pearson) test which:

(i) is a test approved by the Secretary of State for these purposes as specified in Appendix O of these rules;

(ii) can be used to show that the qualification obtained (which must meet or exceed level A1 of the Common European Framework of Reference); and,

(iii) is from an English language test provider approved by the Secretary of State for these purposes as specified in Appendix O of these rules.

28. The evidence required to show that a person is a citizen or national of a majority English speaking country is a valid passport or travel document, unless paragraphs 29 and 30 apply. A dual national may invoke either of their nationalities.

29. If the applicant has not provided their passport or travel document other evidence of nationality can be supplied in the following circumstances only (as indicated by the applicant on their application form):

(a) where the passport has been lost or stolen;

(b) where the passport has expired and been returned to the relevant authorities; or

(c) where the passport is with another part of the UK Border Agency.

30. Alternative evidence as proof of nationality, if acceptable, must be either:

(a) A current national identity document; or

(b) An original letter from the applicant's Home Government or Embassy confirming the applicant's full name, date of birth and nationality.

31. Evidence of an academic qualification (recognised by NARIC UK to be equivalent to the standard of a Bachelor's or Master's degree or PhD in the UK) and was taught in English must be either:

(a) A certificate issued by the relevant institution confirming the award of the academic qualification showing:

(i) the applicant's name;

(ii) the title of award;

(iii) the date of award;

(iv) the name of the awarding institution; and,

(v) that the qualification was taught in English.

Or,

(b) If the applicant is awaiting graduation or no longer has the certificate and cannot get a new one, the evidence must be:

(i) an original academic reference from the institution awarding the academic qualification that;

(1) is on official letter headed paper;

(2) shows the applicant's name;

(3) shows the title of award;

(4) confirms that the qualification was taught in English;

(5) explains when the academic qualification has been, or will be awarded; and

(6) states either the date that the certificate will be issued (if the applicant has not yet graduated) or confirms that the institution is unable to re-issue the original certificate of award.

or

(ii) an original academic transcript that

(1) is on official letter headed paper

(2) shows the applicant's name;

(3) the name of the academic institution;

(4) the course title;

(5) confirms that the qualification was taught in English; and,

(6) provides confirmation of the award.

32. If the qualification was taken in one of the following countries, it will be assumed for the purpose of paragraph 31 that it was taught in English: Antigua and Barbuda, Australia, the Bahamas, Barbados, Belize, Dominica, Grenada, Guyana, Ireland, Jamaica, New Zealand, St Kitts and Nevis, St Lucia, St Vincent and the Grenadines, Trinidad and Tobago, the UK, the USA.

Adult dependent relatives

33. Evidence of the family relationship between the applicant(s) and the sponsor should take the form of birth or adoption certificates, or other documentary evidence.

34. Evidence that, as a result of age, illness or disability, the applicant requires long-term personal care should take the form of:

(a) Medical evidence that the applicant's physical or mental condition means that they cannot perform everyday tasks; and

(b) This must be from a doctor or other health professional.

35. Evidence that the applicant is unable, even with the practical and financial help of the sponsor in the UK, to obtain the required level of care in the country where they are living should be from:

(a) a central or local health authority;

(b) a local authority; or

(c) a doctor or other health professional.

36. If the applicant's required care has previously been provided through a private arrangement, the applicant must provide details of that arrangement and why it is no longer available.]

Note: Appendix FM–SE inserted from 20 July 2012 (Cm 8423).

[**37.** If the applicant's required level of care is not, or is no longer, affordable because payment previously made for arranging this care is no longer being made, the applicant must provide records of that payment and an explanation of why that payment cannot continue. If financial support has been provided by the sponsor or other close family in the UK, the applicant must provide an explanation of why this cannot continue or is no longer sufficient to enable the required level of care to be provided.]

Note: Words in square brackets inserted from 6 September 2012 (HC 565).

[APPENDIX G
COUNTRIES AND TERRITORIES PARTICIPATING IN THE
TIER 5 YOUTH MOBILITY SCHEME AND ANNUAL ALLOCATIONS OF
PLACES FOR 2012

Countries and Territories with Deemed Sponsorship Status:
- Australia – 32,500 places
- Canada – 5,000 places
- Japan – 1,000 places
- New Zealand – 10,000 places
- Monaco – 1,000 places

Countries and Territories without Deemed Sponsorship Status:
- Taiwan – 1,000 places]
- [South Korea – 500 places]

Note: Appendix G inserted from 1 January 2012 (HC 1693). South Korea inserted from 9 July 2012, with savings for applications made but not decided before that date (HC 194).

[APPENDIX H
[APPLICANTS WHO] ARE SUBJECT TO
DIFFERENT DOCUMENTARY REQUIREMENTS UNDER TIER 4 OF THE
POINTS BASED SYSTEM

[An applicant will be subject to different documentary requirements under Tier 4 of the Points Based System where he is a national of one of the following countries and he is applying for entry clearance in his country of nationality or leave to remain in the UK:]

Argentina
Australia
{Botswana}
[...]
Brunei
Canada
Chile
Croatia
[...]
Japan
{Malaysia}
New Zealand
Singapore
South Korea
[...]
Trinidad and Tobago
United States of America

Where an applicant is a dual national, and only one of their nationalities is listed above, he will be able to apply using the different documentary requirements that apply to these nationals, provided he is applying either for entry clearance in his country of nationality listed above or for leave to remain in the UK.

[An applicant will be subject to different documentary requirements under Tier 4 of the Points Based System where he is the rightful holder of one of the following passports, which has been issued by the relevant competent authority, and where he is applying for leave to remain in the UK or for entry clearance in the territory related to the passport he holds:

British National (Overseas)

Hong Kong

Taiwan (those who hold a passport issued by Taiwan that includes the number of the identification card issued by the competent authority in Taiwan).

Where an applicant is the rightful holder of a passport issued by a relevant competent authority listed above and also holds another passport or is the national of a country not listed above, he will be able to apply using the different documentary requirements that apply to rightful holders of those passports listed in this Appendix provided he is applying either for entry clearance in the territory related to the passport he holds or for leave to remain in the UK.]

Note: Appendix H inserted from 4 July 2011 with savings for applications made but not decided before that date (HC 1148). Words in square brackets inserted and other words omitted from 31 October 2011 (HC 1511). 'Malaysia' and 'Botswana' inserted from 1 October 2012 (HC 565).

[Appendix I
Pay requirements which the Secretary of State intends to apply to applications for indefinite leave to remain from Tier 2 (General) and Tier 2 (Sportspersons) migrants made on or after 6 April 2016. The Immigration Rules are subject to change and applicants will need to meet the Rules in force at the date of application. However, it is the Secretary of State's intention that these rules, as they relate to pay, will replace paragraph 245HF from that date.

245HF. Requirements for indefinite leave to remain as a Tier 2 (General) or Tier 2 (Sportsperson) Migrant

To qualify for indefinite leave to remain as a Tier 2 (General) Migrant or Tier 2 (Sportsperson) Migrant an applicant must meet the requirements listed below. If the applicant meets these requirements, indefinite leave to remain will be granted. If the applicant does not meet these requirements, the application will be refused.

Requirements:

(a) The applicant must not have one or more unspent convictions within the meaning of the Rehabilitation of Offenders Act 1974.

(b) The applicant must not fall for refusal under the general grounds for refusal, and must not be an illegal entrant.

(c) The applicant must have spent a continuous period of 5 years lawfully in the UK, in any combination of the following categories of which the most recent period must have been spent with leave as a Tier 2 Migrant either:

(i) as a Tier 1 Migrant, other than a Tier 1 (Post Study Work) Migrant,

(ii) as a Tier 2 (General) Migrant, a Tier 2 (Minister of Religion) Migrant or a Tier 2 (Sportsperson) Migrant.

(d) The Sponsor that issued the Certificate of Sponsorship that led to the applicant's last grant of leave must certify in writing:

(i) that he still requires the applicant for the employment in question, and

(ii) subject to sub-paragraph (iii), in the case of a Tier 2 (General) or Tier 2 (Sportsperson) Migrant applying for settlement, that they are being paid for the employment in question either:

(1) at or above the appropriate rate for the job, as stated in [the Codes of Practice in Appendix J], or

(2) a gross annual salary of £35,000 per annum,

whichever is higher, where the appropriate rate or salary includes basic pay and allowances as set out in paragraph 79E or paragraph 100A of Appendix A.

(iii) where a Tier 2 (General) Migrant applying for settlement is recorded (at the time of application for settlement) by the Certificate of Sponsorship Checking Service as being sponsored to do a job that either:

(1) appears on [the Shortage Occupation List in Appendix K], or has appeared on that list during any time the applicant was being sponsored to do that job and during the continuous period of 5 years referred to in paragraph (c) above, or

(2) appears on [the occupations skilled to PhD-level as stated in the Codes of Practice in Appendix J], or has appeared on that list during any time the applicant was being sponsored to do that job and during the continuous period of 5 years referred to in paragraph (c) above, sub paragraph (d)(ii) does not apply and the Sponsor that issued the Certificate of Sponsorship for the employment in question must certify that the Tier 2 (General) migrant applying for Indefinite Leave to Remain is being paid at or above the appropriate rate for the job as stated in [the Codes of Practice in Appendix J], where the appropriate rate or salary includes basic pay and allowances as set out in paragraph 79E of Appendix A.

[(e) The applicant provides the specified documents in paragraph 245HF-SD to evidence the sponsor's certification in subsection (d)(ii).]

(f) The applicant must have sufficient knowledge of the English language and sufficient knowledge about life in the United Kingdom, in accordance with paragraph 33BA of these Rules, unless the applicant is under the age of 18 or aged 65 or over at the time the application is made.

Note: Sub-para (e) substituted from 6 September 2012 (HC 565).

245HG. Requirements for indefinite leave to remain as a Tier 2 (Minister of Religion) Migrant

To qualify for indefinite leave to remain as a Tier 2 (Minister of Religion) Migrant, an applicant must meet the requirements listed below. If the applicant meets these requirements, indefinite leave to remain will be granted. If the applicant does not meet these requirements, the application will be refused.

Requirements:

(a) The applicant must not have one or more unspent convictions within the meaning of the Rehabilitation of Offenders Act 1974.

(b) The applicant must not fall for refusal under the general grounds for refusal, and must not be an illegal entrant.

(c) The applicant must have spent a continuous period of 5 years lawfully in the UK, in any combination of the following categories of which the most recent period must have been spent with leave as a Tier 2 Migrant (Minister of Religion):

(i) as a Tier 1 Migrant, other than a Tier 1 (Post Study Work) Migrant, or

(ii) as a Tier 2 (General) Migrant, a Tier 2 (Minister of Religion) Migrant or a Tier 2 (Sportsperson) Migrant,

(d) The Sponsor that issued the Certificate of Sponsorship that led to the applicant's last grant of leave must certify in writing that he still requires the applicant for the employment in question, and

(e) The applicant must have sufficient knowledge of the English language and sufficient knowledge about life in the United Kingdom, in accordance with paragraph 33BA of these Rules, unless the applicant is under the age of 18 or aged 65 or over at the time the application is made.

2. In Appendix A – Attributes, after 79D insert: 79E. Appropriate salary for indefinite leave to remain

An applicant applying for Indefinite Leave to Remain under paragraph 245HF is expected to demonstrate that he is being paid either at or above the appropriate rate for the job, as stated in [the Codes of Practice in Appendix J], or a gross annual salary of £35,000 per annum, whichever is higher. The appropriate rate or £35,000 will be based on the applicant's gross annual salary to be paid by the Sponsor, as recorded in the Certificate of Sponsorship Checking Service entry to which the applicant's Certificate of Sponsorship reference number relates, subject to the following conditions:

(i) Salary will be based on basic pay (excluding overtime);

(ii) Allowances, such as London weighting, will be included in the salary where they are part of the guaranteed salary package and would be paid to a local settled worker in similar circumstances;

(iii) Other allowances and benefits, such as a bonus or incentive pay, travel expenses and subsistence (including travel to and from the applicant's home country), will not be included.

3. In Appendix A – Attributes, after paragraph 100 insert: Appropriate salary for indefinite leave to remain

100A.

An applicant applying for Indefinite Leave to Remain under 245HF is expected to demonstrate that he is being paid either at or above the appropriate rate for the job, as stated in [the Codes of practice in Appendix J], or a gross annual salary of £35,000 per annum, whichever is higher. The appropriate rate or £35,000 will be based on the applicant's gross annual salary to be paid by the Sponsor, as recorded in the Certificate of Sponsorship Checking Service entry to which the applicant's Certificate of Sponsorship reference number relates, subject to the following conditions:

(i) Salary will be based on basic pay (excluding overtime);

(ii) Allowances, such as London weighting, will be included in the salary where they are part of the guaranteed salary package and would be paid to a local settled worker in similar circumstances;

(iii) Other allowances and benefits, such as a bonus or incentive pay, travel expenses and subsistence (including travel to and from the applicant's home country), will not be included.

Note: Appendix I inserted by (HC 1888), commencement from a date to be notified, expected to be 6 April 2016. Words in square brackets substituted from 20 July 2012 (Cm 8423).

[APPENDIX J
CODES OF PRACTICE FOR TIER 2 SPONSORS, TIER 5 SPONSORS
AND EMPLOYERS OF WORK PERMIT HOLDERS

1. Where Part 5, Part 6A or Appendix A of these Rules impose such a requirement, migrants must be paid the appropriate salary rates stated in this Appendix. The stated salary rates are per year and based on a 37½-hour working week unless otherwise stated. They should be pro-rated for other working patterns.

2. (a) Where Appendix A of these Rules requires that the job passes the Resident Labour Market Test and (c) does not apply, the job that the Certificate of Sponsorship Checking Service entry records that the migrants is being sponsored to do must have been advertised in Jobcentre Plus (or JobCentre Online if the job is based in Northern Ireland), and at least one of the following:

    (i) any national newspapers, or
    (ii) any of the following websites:
        (1) www.reed.co.uk,
        (2) www.totaljobs.com,
        (3) www.monster.co.uk,
        (4) www.jobserve.com,
        (5) www.jobsite.co.uk,
        (6) www.fish4.co.uk/iad/jobs,
        (7) jobs.guardian.co.uk,
        (8) ijobs.independent.co.uk,
        (9) jobs.telegraph.co.uk, or
        (10) jobs.timesonline.co.uk,
  or
    (iii) if the Sponsor is a multi-national or global organisation, or has over 250 permanent employees in the UK, the Sponsor's own website, or
    (iv) if the entry for the occupation in Tables 1 to 4 below lists other media, in any one or more of the listed media for that occupation.

(b) The media in (i) to (iii) above cannot be used for advertising the creative sector jobs in Table 5; only the media stated in Table 5 may be used.

(c) Where the entry for the occupation in Tables 1 to 4 below lists "Milkround" as an alternative medium, the requirement for the job to be advertised in Jobcentre Plus or JobCentre Online does not apply, providing:

    (i) recruitment activity for the job has taken place through annual recruitment visits to at least 3 UK universities,
    (ii) the job has been advertised on at least one of the following websites:
        (1) www.jobs.ac.uk,
        (2) www.milkround.com, or
        (3) www.prospects.ac.uk,
    and
    (iii) the job has been advertised in at least one of the media listed in (a).

(d) The requirement for the job to be advertised in Jobcentre Plus or JobCentre Online does not apply to:

    (i) jobs where the appropriate salary, as determined by paragraphs 79 to 79D of Appendix A, is at least [£70,000] per year,
    (ii) jobs where there will be stock exchange disclosure requirements, or

(iii) jobs in the PhD-level occupation codes set out in Table 1.

These jobs must still satisfy the other requirements of the Resident Labour Market Test, where it applies.

3. PhD-level occupation codes are set out in Table 1.

4. Occupations skilled to National Qualifications Framework level 6 or above are set out in Table 2.

5. Occupations skilled to National Qualifications Framework level 4 or above are set out in Table 3.

6. Occupations skilled to National Qualifications Framework level 3 or above are set out in Table 4.

7. Creative sector codes of practice, as referred to in Tables 1 to 4, are set out in Table 5.

8. Where stated in Tables 1 to 5, only those specific jobs stated within each Standard Occupational Classification code or creative sector field are considered to be skilled to the required level.

Table 1: Occupations skilled to PhD-level

SOC Code and Description	Appropriate salary ratew	Resident Labour Market Test–additional media
1137 Research and development managers	£17.42 per hour	Professional journals: Any of the following publications: • Nature • New Scientist Milkround Internet: Any of the following websites: • www.jobs.ac.uk • www.naturejobs.com • www.newscientistjobs.com Head-hunters (without national advertising), for jobs where the annual salary is at least £40,000
2111 Chemists	£13.39 per hour	Professional journals: Any of the following publications: • Nature • New Scientist Milkround Internet: Any of the following websites: • www.jobs.ac.uk • www.naturejobs.com • www.newscientistjobs.com Head-hunters (without national advertising), for jobs where the annual salary is at least £40,000

SOC Code and Description	Appropriate salary ratew	Resident Labour Market Test–additional media
2112 Biological scientists and research chemists	• Posts at Agenda for Change band 5 or equivalent: £20,710 • Posts at Agend a for Change band 6 or equivalent: £24,831 • Posts at Agenda for Change band 7 or equivalent: £29,789 • Posts at Agenda for Change band 8 or equivalent: £37,996	Professional journals: Any of the following publications: • The Biomedical Scientist • Nature • New Scientist Milkround Internet: Any of the following websites: • www.jobs.nhs.uk • www.wales.nhs.uk/jobs/ • www.jobs.scot.nhs.uk • www.n-i.nhs.uk • www.careerscene.com • www.naturejobs.com • www.newscientistjobs.com • www.nhsclinicalscientists.info/ • www.healthjobsuk.com Head-hunters (without national advertising), for jobs where the annual salary is at least £40,000
2113 Physicists, geologists and meteorologists	£15.33 per hour	Professional journals: Any of the following publications: • Nature • New Scientist • Geology Today Milkround Internet: Any of the following websites: • www.acenetrecruit.co.uk • www.jobs.ac.uk • www.naturejobs.com • www.newscientistjobs.com Head-hunters (without national advertising), for jobs where the annual salary is at least £40,000
2311 Higher education teaching professionals	£23,499	Professional journals: The following publication: • Times Higher Education Supplement Milkround Internet: Any of the following websites: • www.jobs.ac.uk • www.timeshighereducation.co.uk • www.schoolsrecruitment.dcsf.gov.uk • www.theeducationjob.com Head-hunters (without national advertising), for jobs where the annual salary is at least £40,000

SOC Code and Description	Appropriate salary ratew	Resident Labour Market Test–additional media
2321 Scientific researchers	£15,641	Professional journals: Any of the following publications: • Nature • New Scientist • Times Higher Education Supplement Milkround Internet: Any of the following websites: • www.jobs.ac.uk • www.naturejobs.com • www.newscientistjobs.com • www.timeshighereducation.co.uk Head-hunters (without national advertising), for jobs where the annual salary is at least £40,000 'Named researchers' pass the resident labour market test as they will not be filling established posts or displacing resident workers. 'Named researchers' are defined as those whose employment is linked to specific research grants awarded to Higher Education Institutions or Research Institutes by external organisations. They will be named specifically on the research grant because their knowledge and expertise in the relevant field means they are the only person able to undertake the research. If they are unable to come to the UK the research grant would be cancelled. Sponsors must, on request, provide a copy of the grant papers naming the individual to demonstrate that the resident labour market test has been met.
2322 Social science researchers	£15,641	Professional journals: The following publication: • Times Higher Education supplement Milkround Internet: Any of the following websites: • www.jobs.ac.uk • www.timeshighereducation.co.uk Head-hunters (without national advertising), for jobs where the annual salary is at least £40,000 'Named researchers' pass the resident labour market test as they will not be filling established posts or displacing resident workers. 'Named researchers' are defined as those whose employment is linked to specific research grants awarded to Higher Education Institutions or Research Institutes by external organisations. They will be named specifically on the research grant because their knowledge and expertise in the relevant field means they are the only person able to undertake the research. If they are unable to come to the UK the research grant would be cancelled.

SOC Code and Description	Appropriate salary ratew	Resident Labour Market Test–additional media
		Sponsors must, on request, provide a copy of the grant papers naming the individual to demonstrate that the resident labour market test has been met.
2329 Researchers not elsewhere classified	£15,641	Professional journals: Any of the following publications: • Nature • Times Higher Education Supplement Milkround Internet: Any of the following websites: • www.jobs.ac.uk • www.naturejobs.com • www.timeshighereducation.co.uk Head-hunters (without national advertising), for jobs where the annual salary is at least £40,000 'Named researchers' pass the resident labour market test as they will not be filling established posts or displacing resident workers. 'Named researchers' are defined as those whose employment is linked to specific research grants awarded to Higher Education Institutions or Research Institutes by external organisations. They will be named specifically on the research grant because their knowledge and expertise in the relevant field means they are the only person able to undertake the research. If they are unable to come to the UK the research grant would be cancelled. Sponsors must, on request, provide a copy of the grant papers naming the individual to demonstrate that the resident labour market test has been met.

Table 2: Occupations skilled to National Qualifications Framework level 6 or above

SOC Code and Description	Appropriate salary rate	Resident Labour Market Test – additional media
All occupations in Table 1	As stated in Table 1	As stated in Table 1
1111 Senior officials in national government	£22.57 per hour	Milkround Internet: The following website: • www.civilservice.gov.uk Head-hunters (without national advertising), for jobs where the annual salary is at least £40,000
1112 Directors and chief executives of major organisations	£38.58 per hour	Milkround Internet: Any of the following websites: • www.chairtyjob.co.uk • www.ft.com

SOC Code and Description	Appropriate salary rate	Resident Labour Market Test – additional media
		• www.seniorsalesjobs.co.uk
		Head-hunters (without national advertising), for jobs where the annual salary is at least £40,000
1113 Senior officials in local government	£15.46 per hour	Milkround
		Head-hunters (without national advertising), for jobs where the annual salary is at least £40,000
1114 Senior officials of special interest organisations	£13.86 per hour	Milkround
		Head-hunters (without national advertising), for jobs where the annual salary is at least £40,000
1121 Production, works and maintenance managers	£13.95 per hour	Milkround
		Head-hunters (without national advertising), for jobs where the annual salary is at least £40,000
1122 Managers in construction	• Starting salary: £21,000 (for a 40 hour week) • Managers with 2 to 5 years' experience: £27,000 (for a 40 hour week)	Professional journals: Any of the following publications: • Construction Manager • Building • Building Services Journal • Construction New • Contracts Journal Milkround Internet: Any of the following websites: • www.acenetrecruit.co.uk • www.careerstructure.com • www.constructionjobsnet.co.uk • www.justconstruction.net • www.construction-manager.co.uk • www.icwgb.org (Clerk Of Works jobs only) • myjobscotland.gov.uk Head-hunters (without national advertising), for jobs where the annual salary is at least £40,000
1123 Managers in mining and energy	£18.59 per hour	Milkround
		Head-hunters (without national advertising), for jobs where the annual salary is at least £40,000
1131 Financial managers and chartered secretaries	• Financial manager (London): £33.65 per hour	Professional journals: Any of the following publications: • PASS Magazine • Accountancy Age • Chartered Secretary Magazine • The Law Gazette

SOC Code and Description	Appropriate salary rate	Resident Labour Market Test – additional media
	• Financial manager (rest of England and Wales): £24.03 per • Financial manager (Scotland): £19.23 per hour • Financial manager (London): £21.63 per hour • Financial manager (rest of England and Wales): £16.82 per hour • Financial manager (Scotland): £9.61 per hour • Company secretary: £22.11 per hour • Credit manager: £14.42 per hour • Investment banker: £24.03 per hour	• The Economist Tier 2 Section K Occupational Codes of Practice - Version 06/12: Valid from 14/06/2012 Page 9 of 28 • Accountancy Magazine • Third Sector • Credit Today Internet: Any of the following websites: • www.accaglobal.com • www.accountancyage.com • www.ccrmagazine.co.uk • www.chambersandpartners.com • www.charteredsecretary.net • www.cimaglobal.com • www.cipfa.org.uk • www.cityjobs.com • www.credittoday.net • www.efinancialcareers.co.uk • www.ft.com • www.hays.co.uk/legal • www.icaew.co.uk • www.icai.ie • www.icas.org.uk • www.icm.org.uk • www.icsaorg.uk • www.jobsatthebank.co.uk • www.lawgazette.co.uk • www.lgcplus.com • www.localgov.co.uk • www.passmagazine.com • www.thirdsector.co.uk Head-hunters (without national advertising), for jobs where the annual salary is at least £40,000
1132 Marketing and sales managers	£15.88 per hour	Professional journals: Any of the following publications: • Marketing Week • Campaign • Marketing Milkround Internet: Any of the following websites: • www.brandrepublic.com • www.marketingweek.co.uk Head-hunters (without national advertising), for jobs where the annual salary is at least £40,000

SOC Code and Description	Appropriate salary rate	Resident Labour Market Test – additional media
1133 Purchasing managers	£17.04 per hour	Professional journals: Any of the following publications: • Supply Management • The Hobsons GET Directory Milkround Internet: Any of the following websites: • www.supplymanagement.com • www.cips-gpa.com • www.supplychainonline.co.uk Head-hunters (without national advertising), for jobs where the annual salary is at least £40,000
1134 Advertising and public relations managers	£15.81 per hour	Professional journals: Any of the following publications: • Campaign • Marketing Week • Media Week • PR Week • Creative Review • Press Gazette • Advertising Age • Profile Extra Milkround Internet: Any of the following websites: • www.ipa.co.uk • www.brandrepublic.com/campaign • www.marketingweek.co.uk • www.brandrepublic.com/mediaweek • www.prweekjobs.co.uk • www.ciprjobs.co.uk • www.pressgazette.co.uk • www.mad.co.uk Head-hunters (without national advertising), for jobs where the annual salary is at least £40,000
1135 Personnel, training and industrial relations managers	£16.03 per hour	Professional journals: Any of the following publications: • People Management • Personnel Today • Training & Coaching Today Milkround Internet: Any of the following websites: • www2.peoplemanagement.co.uk • www.personneltoday.com • www.trainingzone.co.uk Head-hunters (without national advertising), for jobs where the annual salary is at least £40,000

SOC Code and Description	Appropriate salary rate	Resident Labour Market Test – additional media
1136 Information and communication technology managers	• IT director or IS director:£83,200 • MIS manager or IT manager: £44,700 • Systems development manager: £41,600 • Computer services manager: £43,600 • Software manager or programming manager: £40,500 • Operations manager: £41,600 • Technical support manager: £39,000 • Communications network manager: £41,600 • Office systems manager or helpdesk manager: £34,100 • Senior business analyst: £43,600 • Business analyst: £31,200 • Development director (computer and video games): £50,000 • Executive producer (computer and video games): £40,000 • Producer (computer and video games): £28,000 • QA manager (computer and video games): £25,000 • Design director (computer and video games): £50,000 • Lead designer (computer and video games): £30,000 • Technical director (computer and video games): £60,000 • Programming manager (computer and video games): £50,000 • Art director (computer and video	Professional journals: Any of the following publications: • Computer Weekly • Computing Magazine • PC Pro • Develop Magazine (games jobs only) • Edge Magazine (games jobs only) Milkround Internet: Any of the following websites: • www.cwjobs.co.uk • www.developmag.com (games jobs only) • www.edge-online.com (games jobs only) • www.gamesindustry.biz (games jobs only) • myjobscotland.gov.uk Head-hunters (without national advertising), for jobs where the annual salary is at least £40,000

SOC Code and Description	Appropriate salary rate	Resident Labour Market Test – additional media
	games): £45,000 • Art manager or lead artist (computer and video games): £35,000 • Outsource manager (computer and video games): £25,000	
1141 Quality assurance managers	• IT and Internet sector: £49,500 • Banking, insurance and finance sector: £44,000 • Health and medicine sector: £40,800 • Engineering and manufacturing sector: £38,500 • Retail and wholesale sector: £33,000 • All other sectors: £14.88 per hour	Professional journals: Any of the following publications: • New Scientist • Quality Today • Qualityworld Milkround Internet: Any of the following websites: • www.beechwoodrecruit.com • www.bindt.org • www.jonlee.co.uk • www.newscientistjobs.com • www.thecqi.org • www.ukas.com Head-hunters (without national advertising), for jobs where the annual salary is at least £40,000
1151 Financial institution managers	£15.33 per hour	Milkround Head-hunters (without national advertising), for jobs where the annual salary is at least £40,000
1161 Transport and distribution managers	£12.60 per hour	Milkround
1172 Police officers (inspectors and above)	• Inspectors: £43,320 • Chief Inspectors: £47,949 • Super-intendents: £56,274 • Chief Super-intendents: £67,200	Professional journals: Any of the following publications: • Police Review • Police Professional Internet: Any of the following websites: • www.policecouldyou.co.uk • www.allpolicejobs.co.uk • www.police-information.co.uk • www.bluelinejobs.co.uk • www.policeoracle.com • Local Government websites
1173 Senior officers in fire, ambulance, prison and related services	£15.46 per hour	Milkround Head-hunters (without national advertising), for jobs where the annual salary is at least £40,000

SOC Code and Description	Appropriate salary rate	Resident Labour Market Test – additional media
1181 Hospital and health service managers	£17.64 per hour	Professional journals: The following publication: • Health Service Journal Milkround Internet: Any of the following websites: • www.jobs.nhs.uk • www.wales.nhs.uk/jobs • www.jobs.scot.nhs.uk • www.n-i.nhs.uk • www.hsj.co.uk • www.healthjobsuk.com Head-hunters (without national advertising), for jobs where the annual salary is at least £40,000
1182 Pharmacy managers	• Pharmacy technician team manager (band 7 or equivalent): £29,789 • Pharmacist team manager (band 8 or equivalent): £37,996	Professional journals: Any of the following publications: • The Pharmaceutical Journal • Chemist & Druggist • New Scientist Milkround Internet: Any of the following websites: • www.jobs.nhs.uk • www.wales.nhs.uk/jobs/ • www.jobs.scot.nhs.uk • www.n-i.nhs.uk • www.pharmj.com • www.chemistanddruggist.co.uk • www.newscientistjobs.com • www.healthjobsuk.com Head-hunters (without national advertising), for jobs where the annual salary is at least £40,000
1184 Social services managers	• Social worker team manager (band 7 or equivalent): £29,789 • Senior practitioner (band 7 or equivalent): £29,789 • Principle practitioner (band 8a or equivalent): £37,996 • Social work locality service manager (band 8a or equivalent): £37,996 • Social care programme manager (band 8b or equivalent): £44,258	Professional journals: Any of the following publications: • Community Care Magazine • Professional Social Work • Social Work Today Milkround Internet: Any of the following websites: • www.baswjobs.com • www.communitycare.co.uk/jobs • www.ecarers.com • www.jobs.nhs.uk • www.wales.nhs.uk/jobs/ • www.jobs.scot.nhs.uk • www.lgjobs.com • www.healthjobsuk.com

SOC Code and Description	Appropriate salary rate	Resident Labour Market Test – additional media
	• Assistant director social services (band 8b or equivalent): £44,258 • Director of social work (band 8c or equivalent): £53,256	• myjobscotland.gov.uk Head-hunters (without national advertising), for jobs where the annual salary is at least £40,000
1212 Natural environment and cconservation managers	£12.94 per hour	Internet: The following website: • myjobscotland.gov.uk
2121 Civil engineers	• New graduate (1st year after graduation): £20,770 • Civil engineers undertaking on the job training: £22,800 • Participate in project work: £23,000 • Project management: £35,000 • Senior project management: £41,042 • Civil engineering not project based: £39,000 • Manager / Director: £54,000 • Managing director / Chief executive officer: £70,000	Professional journals: Any of the following publications: • Building magazine • The Engineer • New Civil Engineer • The Structural Engineer - IstructE: • Transportation Professional • Construction News • Contract Journal Milkround Internet: Any of the following websites: • www.acenetrecruit.co.uk • www.building.co.uk • www.thecareerengineer.com • www.careersinconstruction.com • www.cnplus.co.uk • www.constructor.co.uk • www.earthworks-jobs.com • www.istructe.org/thestructuralengineer/ • www.iht.org/jiht/ • www.justengineers.net • www.nce.co.uk • www.oilandgasjobsearch.com • www.oilcareers.com • myjobscotland.gov.uk Head-hunters (without national advertising), for jobs where the annual salary is at least £40,000
2122 Mechanical engineers	• New graduate: £23,000 • Other jobs: £14.52 per hour	Professional journals: The following publication: • Engineering magazine Milkround Internet: Any of the following websites: • www.acenetrecruit.co.uk • www.thecareerengineer.com • www.engineersonthenet.com

SOC Code and Description	Appropriate salary rate	Resident Labour Market Test – additional media
		• www.jimfinder.com • www.oilandgasjobsearch.com • www.oilcareers.com
		Head-hunters (without national advertising), for jobs where the annual salary is at least £40,000
2123 Electrical engineers	• New graduate: £23,000 • Other jobs: £16.27 per hour	Professional journals: Any of the following publications: • Electronics Weekly • Engineering magazine • Engineering Technology Milkround Internet: Any of the following websites: • www.acenetrecruit.co.uk • www.thecareerengineer.com • www.electronicsweekly.com/jobs • www.engineersonthenet.com • www.hays.co.uk • www.theiet.org/jobs • www.jimfinder.com • www.oilandgasjobsearch.com • www.oilcareers.com Head-hunters (without national advertising), for jobs where the annual salary is at least £40,000
2124 Electronics engineers	• New graduate: £23,000 • Other jobs: £17.46 per hour	Professional journals: Any of the following publications: • Engineering Magazine • Electronics Weekly • Engineering and Technology Milkround Internet: Any of the following websites: • www.thecareerengineer.com • www.electronicsweekly.com/jobs • www.engineeringnet.co.uk • www.engineersonthenet.com • www.theiet.org/jobs • www.jimfinder.com Head-hunters (without national advertising), for jobs where the annual salary is at least £40,000
2125 Chemical engineers	• New Graduate: £25,400 • Non-chartered chemical engineer: £26,500 • Chartered chemical engineer: £36,000	Professional journals: Any of the following publications: • The Chemical Engineer (TCE) • Engineering magazine • Nature • New Scientist

SOC Code and Description	Appropriate salary rate	Resident Labour Market Test – additional media
		Milkround
		Internet: Any of the following websites: • www.chempeople.com • www.engineeringnet.co.uk • www.thecareerengineer.com • www.engineersonthenet.com • www.gradcracker.com • www.jimfinder.com • www.naturejobs.com • www.newscientistjobs.com • www.tcetoday.com
		Head-hunters (without national advertising), for jobs where the annual salary is at least £40,000
2126 Design and development engineers	£14.40 per hour	Milkround
		Head-hunters (without national advertising), for jobs where the annual salary is at least £40 000
2127 Production and process engineers	£12.78 per hour	Milkround
		Head-hunters (without national advertising), for jobs where the annual salary is at least £40,000
2128 Planning and quality control engineers	• New graduate: £23,000 • Other jobs: £12.62 per hour	Professional journals: Any of the following publications: • Nature • New Scientist
		Milkround
		Internet: Any of the following websites: • www.naturejobs.com • www.newscientistjobs.com
		Head-hunters (without national advertising), for jobs where the annual salary is at least £40,000
2129 Engineering professionals not elsewhere classified	• New graduate: £23,000 • Other jobs: £14.76 per hour	Professional journals: Any of the following publications: • Nature • New Scientist
		Milkround
		Internet: Any of the following websites: • www.naturejobs.com • www.newscientistjobs.com
		Head-hunters (without national advertising), for jobs where the annual salary is at least £40,000

SOC Code and Description	Appropriate salary rate	Resident Labour Market Test – additional media
2131 IT strategy and planning professionals	• Management consultant or systems consultant: £67,600 • Network pre or post-sales support consultant: £36,400 • Projects manager: £39,000 • Web designer: £26,000 • Senior games designer (computer and video games): £27,000 • Games designer (computer and video games): £20,000	Professional journals: Any of the following publications: • Computer Weekly • Computing Magazine • PC Pro • Develop Magazine (games jobs only) • Edge Magazine (games jobs only) Milkround Internet: Any of the following websites: • www.cwjobs.co.uk • www.developmag.com (games jobs only) • www.edge-online.com (games jobs only) • www.gamesindustry.biz (games jobs only) Head-hunters (without national advertising), for jobs where the annual salary is at least £40,000
2132 Software professionals	• Project leader or senior systems analyst: £41,600 • Systems analyst: £31,200 • Senior test analyst: £33,200 • Senior network communications analyst or engineer: £41,300 • Network communications analyst or engineer: £29,100 • Senior network support engineer: £31,200 • Test analyst: £28,000 • Systems auditor: £34,600 • Training officer or lecturer: £36,300 • Technical author: £32,200 • Development team leader: £41,600 • Senior systems developer: £37,400 • Systems developer: £31,200 • Analyst programmer: £29,100 • Graduate developer: £22,300	Professional journals: Any of the following publications: • Computer Weekly • Computing Magazine • PC Pro • Develop Magazine (games jobs only) • Edge Magazine (games jobs only) Milkround Internet: Any of the following websites: • www.cwjobs.co.uk • www.developmag.com (games jobs only) • www.edge-online.com (games jobs only) • www.gamesindustry.biz (games jobs only) • myjobscotland.gov.uk Head-hunters (without national advertising), for jobs where the annual salary is at least £40,000

SOC Code and Description	Appropriate salary rate	Resident Labour Market Test – additional media
	• Senior programmer: £31,200	
	• Programmer: £26,000	
	• Systems architect or systems planner: £46,800	
	• Systems programmer: £31,200	
	• Senior software engineer: £37,400	
	• Software engineer: £30,100	
	• Software communications engineer: £36,400	
	• Software test engineer: £31,200	
	• Operations analyst: £27,000	
	• Hardware engineer: £20,800	
	• Engine programmer (computer and video games): £25,000	
	• Graphics programmer (computer and video games): £25,000	
	• Audio programmer (computer and video games): £25,000	
	• Network programmer (computer and video games): £30,000	
	• Gameplay programmer (computer and video games): £25,000	
	• Special effects programmer (computer and video games): £25,000	
	• Senior artist (computer and video games): £25,000	
	• Graphic artist (computer and video games): £20,000	
	• Special effects artist (computer and video games): £25,000	

SOC Code and Description	Appropriate salary rate	Resident Labour Market Test – additional media
	• Technical artist (computer and video games): £25,000 • Animator (computer and video games): £20,000	
2211 Medical practitioners	• Foundation year 1 (F1): £21,391 • Foundation year 2 (F2): £26,532 • Pre-registration house officer: £21,391 • House officer: £21,391 • Senior house officer: £26,532 • Speciality registrar (StR): £29,411 • Senior registrar: £29,364 • Speciality Doctor: £36,443 • Senior chief medical officer: £44,059 • Staff grade practitio-ner: £32,547 • Associate specialist: £35,977 • Consultant (new contract): £71,822	Professional journals: Any of the following publications: • British Medical Journal • GMC News • Hospital Doctor • The Lancet Internet: Any of the following websites: • www.jobs.nhs.uk • www.wales.nhs.uk/jobs/ • www.jobs.scot.nhs.uk • www.n-i.nhs.uk • www.healthjobsuk.com • www.doctors.net.uk
2212 Psychologists	• Posts at Agenda for Change band 4 or equivalent: £17,732 • Posts at Agenda for Change band 5 or equivalent: £20,710 • Posts at Agenda for Change band 6 or equivalent: £24,831 • Posts at Agenda for Change band 7 or equivalent: £29,789 • Posts at Agenda for Change band 8 or equivalent: £37,996	Professional journals: Any of the following publications: • British Medical Journal • The Psychologist Milkround Internet: Any of the following websites: • www.jobs.nhs.uk • www.wales.nhs.uk/jobs/ • www.jobs.scot.nhs.uk • www.n-i.nhs.uk/index/.php?link=jobs • www.psychapp.co.uk/ • www.mentalhealthjobs.co.uk/ • www.healthjobsuk.com
2213 Pharmacists / pharmacologists	• Pharmacy technician (band 4 or equivalent): £17,732	Professional journals: Any of the following publications: • The Pharmaceutical Journal

SOC Code and Description	Appropriate salary rate	Resident Labour Market Test – additional media
	• Pre-registration pharmacists (band 5 or equivalent): £20,710 • Pharmacist entry level (band 5 or equivalent): £20,710 • Pharmacist (Band 6 or equivalent): £24,831 • Pharmacist specialist (Band 7 or equivalent): £29,789 • Pharmacist advanced (Band 8a-b or equivalent): £37,996 • Pharmacist consultant (Band 8b-d or equivalent): £44,258	• Chemist & Druggist • The New Scientist Milkround Internet: Any of the following websites: • www.jobs.nhs.uk • www.wales.nhs.uk/jobs/ • www.jobs.scot.nhs.uk • www.n-i.nhs.uk/index/.php?link=jobs • www.healthjobsuk.com • www.pharmacytraining.nhs.uk • www.nes.scot.nhs.uk • www.psni.org.uk/
2214 Ophthalmic opticians	**Private sector:** • Pre-registration: £11,500 • Registered optometrists (starting salary): £26,000 • Registered optometrists with five years experience: £39,000 **Public sector:** • Optometrist pre-registration (band 4): £17,732 • Optometrist (band 6): £24,831 • Optometrist specialist (band 7): £29,789 • Optometrist principal (band 8A): £37,996 • Optometrist consultant, head of service (band 8C): £53,256	Professional journals: Any of the following publications: • Optometry Today • Optician Milkround Internet: Any of the following websites: • www.jobs.nhs.uk • www.wales.nhs.uk/jobs/ • www.jobs.scot.nhs.uk • www.n-i.nhs.uk • www.opticianjobs.net • www.healthjobsuk.com Head-hunters (without national advertising), for jobs where the annual salary is at least £40,000
2215 Dental practitioners	• Vocational dental practitioner: £28,752 • Community dental officer band 1: £33,768 • Senior dental officer: £47,215 • Assistant clinical director: £64,122 • Clinical director: £62,741	Professional journals: The following publication: • British Dental Journal (BDJ) Internet: Any of the following websites: • www.bdjjobs.co.uk • www.jobs.nhs.uk • www.wales.nhs.uk/jobs/ • www.jobs.scot.nhs.uk

SOC Code and Description	Appropriate salary rate	Resident Labour Market Test – additional media
	• Senior house officer (SHO), hospital dental services: £27,116 • Specialist Registrar (SpR), hospital dental services: £30,231 • Consultant, hospital dental services: £82,590	• www.n-i.nhs.uk • www.healthjobsuk.com
2216 Veterinarians	• Newly qualified veterinary surgeon: £30,700 • Veterinary surgeon with five years' experience: £36,000 • Veterinary surgeon with twenty years' experience: £42,000	Professional journals: Any of the following publications: • Farmers Weekly • The Veterinary Record • Veterinary Times Milkround Internet: Any of the following websites: • www.fwi.co.uk/jobs • www.vetrecordjobs.com • www.vbd.co.uk
2312 Further education teaching professionals	**England** • Unqualified lecturer: £18,030 • Qualified lecturer: £22,857 • Advanced teaching and training lecturer: £34,587 **Scotland** £15.03 per hour **Wales** • Instructor, demonstrator and associate lecturer: £16,932 • Main grade lecturer: £20,257 • Upper pay spine lecturer: £31,875 **Northern Ireland** • Lecturer: £21,072 • Senior lecturer: £30,552 • Principal lecturer: £37,662	Professional journals: The following publication: • Times Educational Supplement Milkround Internet: Any of the following websites: • www.fecareers.co.uk • www.fejobs.com • www.jobs.ac.uk • www.teachFE.com • www.tes.co.uk • www.theeducationjob.com Head-hunters (without national advertising), for jobs where the annual salary is at least £40,000
2313 Education officers, school inspectors	• School inspector in England: £58,169 • School inspector in Scotland (grade C2): £43,094	Professional journals: Any of the following publications: • The Times Educational Supplement • Golwg - National Welsh publication Milkround

SOC Code and Description	Appropriate salary rate	Resident Labour Market Test – additional media
	• School inspector in Wales (grade 6): £51,500 • School inspector in Northern Ireland (grade 6): £46,400 • Other posts: £14.46 per hour	Internet: Any of the following websites: • www.tes.co.uk • www.jobsgopublic.com • www.lgjobs.com/ • www.civilservice.gov.uk • www.scotland.gov.uk • www.theeducationjob.com • myjobscotland.gov.uk
2314 Secondary education teaching professionals	**Inner London** • Unqualified teacher: £19,007 • Qualified teacher: £25, 000 • Head teacher, other school leader: £42,559 **Outer London** • Unqualified teacher: £17,953 • Qualified teacher: £24,000 • Head teacher, other school leader: £38,634 **London fringe** • Unqualified teacher: £16,106 • Qualified teacher: £21,619 • Head teacher, other school leader: £36,781 **Elsewhere in England and Wales** • Unqualified teacher: £15,113 • Qualified teacher: £20,627 • Head teacher, other school leader: £35,794 **Scotland** • Probationer: £20,427 • Unpromoted teacher: £24,501 • Chartered teacher: £33,588 • Principal teacher £35,523 • Head teacher, deputy head teacher: £40,290 **Northern Ireland** • Qualified teacher: £20,627 • Leadership Group: £35,794	Professional journals: The following publication: • Times Educational Supplement Milkround Internet: Any of the following websites: • www.eteach.com • www.schoolsrecruitment.education.gov.uk • www.tes.co.uk • www.theeducationjob.com • myjobscotland.gov.uk

SOC Code and Description	Appropriate salary rate	Resident Labour Market Test – additional media
	These salary rates are based the following definitions of a full time teacher: • **England, Wales and Northern Ireland:** Full time teachers are expected to work 195 days a year (190 of these must be working with pupils) .• **Scotland:** Full time teachers are expected to work 35 hours a week, 195 days a year over 39 weeks, with 5 days for in-service training	
2315 Primary and nursery education teaching professionals	**Inner London** • Unqualified teacher: £19,007 • Qualified teacher: £25,000 • Head teacher, other school leader: £42,559 **Outer London** • Unqualified teacher: £17,953 • Qualified teacher: £24,000 • Head teacher, other school leader: £38,634 **London fringe** • Unqualified teacher: £16,106 • Qualified teacher: £21,619 • Head teacher, other school leader: £36,781 **Elsewhere in England and Wales** • Unqualified teacher: £15,113 • Qualified teacher: £20,627 • Head teacher, other school leader: £35,794 **Scotland** • Probationer: £20,427	Professional journals: The following publication: • Times Educational Supplement Milkround Internet: Any of the following websites: • www.eteach.com • www.schoolsrecruitment.education.gov.uk • www.tes.co.uk • www.theeducationjob.com • myjobscotland.gov.uk

SOC Code and Description	Appropriate salary rate	Resident Labour Market Test – additional media
	• Unpromoted teacher: £24,501 • Chartered teacher: £33,588 • Principal teacher £35,523 • Head teacher, deputy head teacher: £40,290 **Northern Ireland** • Qualified teacher: £20,627 • Leadership Group: £35,794 These salary rates are based the following definitions of a full time teacher: • **England, Wales and Northern Ireland:** Full time teachers are expected to work 195 days a year (190 of these must be working with pupils). • **Scotland:** Full time teachers are expected to work 35 hours a week, 195 days a year over 39 weeks, with 5 days for in-service training	
2316 Special needs education teaching professionals	**Inner London** • Unqualified teacher: £19,007 • Qualified teacher: £25,000 • Head teacher, other school leader: £42,559 **Outer London** • Unqualified teacher: £17,953 • Qualified teacher: £24,000 • Head teacher, other school leader: £38,634 **London fringe** • Unqualified teacher: £16,106 • Qualified teacher: £21,619 • Head teacher, other school leader: £36,781	Professional journals: Any of the following publications: • Guardian Educational Supplement • Times Educational Supplement Milkround Internet: Any of the following websites: • www.eteach.com • www.schoolsrecruitment.education.gov.uk • www.tes.co.uk • www.scotsman.com • www.theherald.co.uk/jobs • www.theeducationjob.com • myjobscotland.gov.uk

SOC Code and Description	Appropriate salary rate	Resident Labour Market Test – additional media
	Elsewhere in England and Wales • Unqualified teacher: £15,113 • Qualified teacher: £20,627 • Head teacher, other school leader: £35,794 **Scotland** • Probationer: £20,427 • Unpromoted teacher: £24,501 • Chartered teacher: £33,588 • Principal teacher £35,523 • Head teacher, deputy head teacher: £40,290 **Northern Ireland** • Qualified teacher: £20,627 • Leadership Group: £35,794 These salary rates are based the following definitions of a full time teacher: • **England, Wales and Northern Ireland:** Full time teachers are expected to work 195 days a year (190 of these must be working with pupils). • **Scotland:** Full time teachers are expected to work 35 hours a week, 195 days a year over 39 weeks, with 5 days for in-service training **Further education – England** • Unqualified lecturer: £18,030 • Qualified lecturer: £22,857 • Advanced teaching and training lecturer: £34,587	

SOC Code and Description	Appropriate salary rate	Resident Labour Market Test – additional media
	Further education – Scotland • All posts: £16.34 per hour **Further education – Wales** • Instructor, demonstrator and associate lecturer: £16,932 • Main grade lecturer: £20,257 • Upper pay spine lecturer: £31,875 **Further education – Northern Ireland** • Lecturer: £21,072 • Senior lecturer: £30,552 • Principal lecturer: £37,662	
2317 Registrars and senior administrators of educational establishments	£13.02 per hour	Professional journals: The following publication: • Times Higher Education Supplement Milkround Internet: Any of the following websites: • www.jobs.ac.uk • www.schoolsrecruitment.education.gov.uk • www.timeshighereducation.co.uk • www.theeducationjob.com
2319 Teaching professionals not elsewhere classified	£13.22 per hour	Milkround Internet: Any of the following websites: • www.schoolsrecruitment.education.gov.uk • www.theeducationjob.com
2411 Solicitors and lawyers, judges and coroners	**Solicitors and Lawyers (Greater London)** • Trainee solicitor: £18,121 • Newly qualified solicitor or lawyer: £39,000 • Solicitor or lawyer with 3 years' experience: £47,000 • Newly qualified in-house solicitor or lawyer: £45,000	Professional journals: Any of the following publications: • The Law Society Gazette • Legal Week • The Lawyer • Scottish Law Gazette • The Scots Law Times Milkround Internet: Any of the following websites: • www.lawgazette.co.uk • www.journalonline.co.uk • www.legalweek.com • www.thelawyer.com • www.lawsociety.org.uk • www.lawscot.org.uk

SOC Code and Description	Appropriate salary rate	Resident Labour Market Test – additional media
	• In-house solicitor or lawyer with 3 years' experience: £65,000	• www.totallylegal.com Head-hunters (without national advertising), for jobs where the annual salary is at least £40,000
	Solicitors and Lawyers (Scotland) • Trainee solicitor: £14,000 • Qualified solicitor: £20,000 • Equity partner: £114,000 • Trainee, Crown Prosecution Service: £17,888 • Qualified Crown prosecutor: £30,138 • Principal prosecutor: £37,522	
	Solicitors and Lawyers (elsewhere in the UK) • Trainee solicitor (England outside Greater London): £16,650 • Trainee solicitor (Wales): £17,171 • Newly qualified solicitor or lawyer: £23,000 • Solicitor or lawyer with 3 years' experience: £28,000 • Newly qualified in-house solicitor or lawyer: £25,000 • In-house solicitor or lawyer with 3 years' experience: £35,000	
	Coroners and Judges (throughout the UK) • Coroners: £68,000 • Group 7 judges: £88,109 • Group 6 judges: £106,812 • Group 5 judges: £133,100 • Group 4 judges: £140,875	

SOC Code and Description	Appropriate salary rate	Resident Labour Market Test – additional media
	• Group 3 judges: £188,900 • Group 2 judges: £198,700 • Group 1 judges: £205,700	
2419 Legal professionals not elsewhere classified	£13.73 per hour	Milkround Internet: The following website: • myjobscotland.gov.uk Head-hunters (without national advertising), for jobs where the annual salary is at least £40,000
2421 Chartered and certified accountants	• ACCA Part 1 qualified: £14,000 • ACCA Part 2 qualified: £17,000 • ACCA Part 3 qualified: £20,000 • Trainee in public practice, Foundation: £13,000 • Trainee in public practice, Advanced: £16,000 • Newly fully qualified: £27,000 • Fully qualified with post- qualification experience: £33,000	Professional journals: Any of the following publications: • Accounting & Business • Accounting, Auditing & Accountability • Financial Accountant Milkround Internet: Any of the following websites: • www.accaglobal.com • www.efinancialcareers.co.uk • www.ifaorg.uk • myjobscotland.gov.uk Head-hunters (without national advertising), for jobs where the annual salary is at least £40,000
2422 Management accountants	£15.81 per hour	Professional journals: Any of the following publications: • Accountancy • Accountancy Age Milkround Internet: Any of the following websites: • www.accountancyagejobs.com • www.accountancyjobsonline.co.uk • www.accountingweb.co.uk • www.cimaglobal.com • www.efinancialcareers.co.uk • www.totallyfinancial.com Head-hunters (without national advertising), for jobs where the annual salary is at least £40,000

SOC Code and Description	Appropriate salary rate	Resident Labour Market Test – additional media
2423 Management consultants, actuaries, economists and statisticians	• Actuaries: £42,500 • Consultants: £43,000 • Other jobs: £15.20 per hour	Professional journals: Any of the following publications: **Management Consultants** • Consulting Magazine • The Economist • Management Consultancy Magazine • People Management • Top Consultant **Actuaries** • The Actuary **Economists** • The Business Economist • The Economist **Statisticians** • Health Service Journal • New Scientist • RSS News • Times Educational Supplement Milkround Internet: Any of the following websites: • www.consultingmag.com • www.economist.com • www.bestcompaniesguide.co.uk • www.exec-appointments.com • www.top-consultant.com • www.actuaries.org.uk (for actuary jobs only) • www.efinancialcareers.co.uk • www.thesupplycurve.com (for economist and statistician jobs only) • www.hsj.co.uk (for healthcare statisticians only) • www.newscientistjobs.com (for statisticians only) • www.pharmiweb.com (for healthcare statisticians only) • www.tes.co.uk (for education statisticians only) Head-hunters (without national advertising), for jobs where the annual salary is at least £40,000
2431 Architects	• Part 1: £17,000 (for a 35 hour week) • Part 2: £21,000 (for a 35 hour week) • Part 3: £27,000 (for a 35 hour week) • New graduate (newly registered): £29,000 (for a 35 hour week)	Professional journals: Any of the following publications: • Architects (RIBA Directory of Practise) • Architects Journal • Architectural Review • Building • Building Design • Perspective

SOC Code and Description	Appropriate salary rate	Resident Labour Market Test – additional media
	• Architect with 3-5 years' experience: £34,000 (for a 35 hour week) • Senior architect £36,000: (for a 35 hour week)	Tier 2 Section F Occupational Codes of Practice - Version 06/12: Valid from 14/06/2012. Page 17 of 37 • RIBA Journal • The Chartered Architect (Scotland) • TARGETjobs Construction & Building Services • TARGETjobs Property • Touchstone (Wales) Milkround (Part 1 and Part 2 architects only) Internet: Any of the following websites: • www.arb.org.uk • www.architecturecentre.net • www.arplus.com • www.ajplus.co.uk • www.building.co.uk • www.bd4jobs.co.uk • www.careersinconstruction.com • www.ribajournal.com • www.ribaappointments.com • myjobscotland.gov.uk Head-hunters (without national advertising), for jobs where the annual salary is at least £40,000
2432 Town planners	£20,000	Professional journals: The following publication: • Planning Milkround Internet: Any of the following websites: • Local government websites • www.planningresource.co.uk • www.lgtalent.com • myjobscotland.gov.uk Head-hunters (without national advertising), for jobs where the annual salary is at least £40,000
2433 Quantity surveyors	• New graduate: £17,000 • Chartered surveyor: £25,000 • Associate surveyor: £35,000	Professional journals: Any of the following publications: • Building • Construction News • Contract Journal • Estates Gazette • GET Engineering • Inside Careers: Engineering & Technology • TARGETjobs Construction & Building Services

SOC Code and Description	Appropriate salary rate	Resident Labour Market Test – additional media
		• TARGETjobs Engineering • TARGETjobs Quantity Surveying & Building Surveying including Commercial Management • Local Government Jobs • Opportunities: the Public Sector Recruitment Weekly • Property Week • QS Week • RICS Business • RICS Directory • RICS Construction Journal
		Milkround
		Internet: Any of the following websites: • Websites of the professional journals above • www.ricsrecruit.com • www.careersinconstruction.com • www.building4jobs.co.uk • www.lgjobs.com • myjobscotland.gov.uk
		Head-hunters (without national advertising), for jobs where the annual salary is at least £40,000
2434 Chartered surveyors (not quantity surveyors)	• New graduate: £18,500 • Fully qualified: £35,000	Professional journals: Any of the following publications: • Building • Construction News • Surveyor • Property Week • Estates Gazette • Building Engineer
		Tier 2 Section F Occupational Codes of Practice - Version 06/12: Valid from 14/06/2012. Page 19 of 37 • Town & Country Planning • New Builder • RICS Journals • RICS Business
		Milkround
		Internet: Any of the following websites: • Websites of the professional journals above • www.lgjobs.com • www.macdonaldandcompany.com • www.planningresource.co.uk • www.matchtech.com • www.tedrecruitment.com

SOC Code and Description	Appropriate salary rate	Resident Labour Market Test – additional media
		• www.ricsrecruit.com • myjobscotland.gov.uk Head-hunters (without national advertising), for jobs where the annual salary is at least £40,000
2441 Public service administrative professionals	£19.17 per hour	Milkround Internet: The following website: • www.civilservice.gov.uk Head-hunters (without national advertising), for jobs where the annual salary is at least £40,000
2442 Social workers	• Social worker entry level (band 5 or equivalent): £20,710 • Social worker (band 6 or equivalent): £24,831 • Social worker specialist or team manager (band 7 or equivalent): £29,789	Professional journals: Any of the following publications: • Community Care Magazine • Professional Social Work • Social Work Today Milkround Internet: Any of the following websites: • www.baswjobs.com • www.communitycare.co.uk/jobs • www.ecarers.com • www.lgjobs.com • www.jobs.nhs.uk • www.jobs.scot.nhs.uk • www.wales.nhs.uk/jobs/ • www.n-i.nhs.uk • www.healthjobsuk.com • myjobscotland.gov.uk Head-hunters (without national advertising), for jobs where the annual salary is at least £40,000
2443 Probation officers	£13.29 per hour	Professional journals: The following publication: • Probation Bulletin Milkround Internet: Any of the following websites: • www.justice.gov.uk • www.pbni.org.uk • Local authority websites Head-hunters (without national advertising), for jobs where the annual salary is at least £40,000

SOC Code and Description	Appropriate salary rate	Resident Labour Market Test – additional media
2451 Librarians	£9.71 per hour	Professional journals: Any of the following publications: • Library and Information Gazette • Managing Information **Milkround** Internet: Any of the following websites: • www.cilip.org.uk • lisjobnet.com/lisjobnet • myjobscotland.gov.uk Head-hunters (without national advertising), for jobs where the annual salary is at least £40,000
2452 Archivists and curators	£12.03 per hour	Professional journals: The following publication: • ARC Recruitment / ARC Recruitment Plus Milkround Internet: Any of the following websites: • www.archives.org.uk • www.mla.gov.uk/aboutus/jobs Head-hunters (without national advertising), for jobs where the annual salary is at least £40,000
3211 Nurses	• Supervised practice nurse (band 3 or equivalent): £15,190 Points will be awarded for the guaranteed annual salary that will be paid when the applicant achieves Nursing and Midwifery Council registration, provided he has a guaranteed job offer from his Sponsor on completion of the supervised practice placement. If the applicant has not achieved NMC registration after nine months, his leave may be curtailed. • Qualified nurse (band 5 or equivalent): £20,710 • District nurse (band 6 or equivalent): £24,831	Professional journals: Any of the following publications: • Nursing Times • Nursing Standard Internet: Any of the following websites: • www.jobs.nhs.uk • www.wales.nhs.uk/jobs/ • www.jobs.scot.nhs.uk • www.n-i.nhs.uk • www.nurses.co.uk • www.staffnurse.com • www.healthjobsuk.com

SOC Code and Description	Appropriate salary rate	Resident Labour Market Test – additional media
	• Community psychiatric nurse (band 6 or equivalent): £24,831 • Community mental nurse (band 6 or equivalent): £24,831 • Nurse specialist (band 6 or equivalent): £24,831 • Nurse team leader (band 6 or equivalent): £24,831 • Specialist theatre nurse (band 6 or equivalent): £24,831 • Nurse team manager (band 7 or equivalent): £29,789 • Nurse advanced (band 7 or equivalent): £29,789 • Nurse consultant (band 8 or equivalent): £37,996 • Modern matron (band 8 or equivalent): £37,996	
3212 Midwives	• Supervised practice midwife (band 3 or equivalent): £15,190 Points will be awarded for the guaranteed annual salary that will be paid when the applicant achieves Nursing and Midwifery Council registration, provided he has a guaranteed job offer from his Sponsor on completion of the supervised practice placement. If the applicant has not achieved NMC registration after nine months, his leave may be curtailed. • Midwife entry level (band 5 or equivalent): £20,710	Professional journals: Any of the following publications: • Nursing Times • Nursing Standard Internet: Any of the following websites: • www.jobs.nhs.uk • www.wales.nhs.uk/jobs/ • www.jobs.scot.nhs.uk • www.n-i.nhs.uk • www.healthjobsuk.com

SOC Code and Description	Appropriate salary rate	Resident Labour Market Test – additional media
	• Community, hospital, integrated midwife (band 6 or equivalent): £24,831 • Midwife higher level or team manager (band 7 or equivalent): £29,789 • Midwife consultant (band 8 or equivalent): £37,996	
3214 Medical radiographers	• Clinical support worker higher level (radiography): £15,190 • Assistant practitioner (radiography): £17,732 • Radiographer (therapeutic): £20,710 • Radiographer (diagnostic): £20,710 • Radiographer specialist (diagnostic therapeutic): £24,831 • Radiographer advanced: £29,789 • Radiographer specialist (reporting sonographer): £29,789 • Radiographer team manager: £29,789 • Radiographer principal: £37,996 • Radiographer consultant (therapy): £37,996 • Radiographer consultant (diagnostic): £44,258	Professional journals: Any of the following publications: • Synergy news • RAD Magazine Internet: Any of the following websites: • www.jobs.nhs.uk • www.wales.nhs.uk/jobs/ • www.jobs.scot.nhs.uk • www.n-i.nhs.uk • www.healthjobsuk.com
3215 Chiropodists	• Clinical support worker higher level (band 3 or equivalent): £15,190 • Technician or assistant practitioner (band 4 or equivalent): £17,732 • Podiatrist (band 5 or equivalent): £20,710	Professional journals: Any of the following publications: • Podiatry Now • The Chiropody Review Internet: Any of the following websites: • www.jobs.nhs.uk • www.wales.nhs.uk/jobs/ • www.jobs.scot.nhs.uk • www.n-i.nhs.uk • www.healthjobsuk.com

SOC Code and Description	Appropriate salary rate	Resident Labour Market Test – additional media
	• Podiatrist specialist (band 6 or equivalent): £24,831 • Principal podiatrist or head of service (band 7 or equivalent): £29,789 • Registrar or consultant surgeon (band 7 or equivalent): £29,789 • Consultant surgeon head of service (band 8 or equivalent): £37,996	
3221 Physiotherapists	• Assistant practitioner (band 4 or equivalent): £17,732 • Physiotherapist (band 5 or equivalent): £20,710 • Physiotherapist specialist (band 6 or equivalent): £24,831 • Physiotherapist team manager (band 7 or equivalent): £29,789 • Consultant or principal physiotherapist (band 8 or equivalent): £36,996	Professional journals: Any of the following publications: • Frontline • Therapy Weekly Internet: Any of the following websites: • www.jobs.nhs.uk • www.wales.nhs.uk/jobs/ • www.jobs.scot.nhs.uk • www.n-i.nhs.uk • www.healthjobsuk.com • www.csp.org.uk • www.healthjobsuk.com
3222 Occupational therapists	• Occupational therapist (band 5 or equivalent): £20,710 • Occupational therapist specialist (band 6 or equivalent): £24,831 • Occupational therapist advanced (band 7 or equivalent): £29,789 • Principal or consultant occupational therapist (band 8 or equivalent): £37,996	Professional journals: Any of the following publications: • British Journal of Occupational Therapy • Occupational Therapy News Internet: Any of the following websites: • www.jobs.nhs.uk • www.wales.nhs.uk/jobs/ • www.jobs.scot.nhs.uk • www.n-i.nhs.uk • www.occupationaltherapist.com • www.healthjobsuk.com
3223 Speech and language therapists	• Posts at Agenda for Change band 5 or equivalent: £20,710 • Posts at Agenda for Change band 6 or equivalent: £24,831	Professional journals: The following publication: • Royal College of Speech and Language Therapists Bulletin Internet: Any of the following websites: • www.jobs.nhs.uk

SOC Code and Description	Appropriate salary rate	Resident Labour Market Test – additional media
	• Posts at Agenda for Change band 7 or equivalent: £29,789 • Posts at Agenda for Change band 8 or equivalent: £37,996	• www.wales.nhs.uk/jobs/ • www.jobs.scot.nhs.uk • www.n-i.nhs.uk • www.rcslt.org • www.healthjobsuk.com
3229 Therapists not elsewhere classified	£ 13.38 per hour	Internet: Any of the following websites: • www.jobs.nhs.uk • www.wales.nhs.uk/jobs/ • www.jobs.scot.nhs.uk • www.n-i.nhs.uk • www.healthjobsuk.com
3415 Musicians • Musicians must be established in the industry as a musician. Whether the level of the musician is appropriate should be determined by the Sponsor in consultation with relevant representatives of the industry in the UK. Evidence of this consultation must be retained by the Sponsor. Recognised representatives are: • Musicians Union • Association of British Orchestras • The Society of London Theatre • Theatrical Management Association	Payment should be commensurate with industry standards; the salary should be at least at the level of appropriate UK rates and of at least the minimum salary for Tier 2 of £20,000. The salary must also meet National Minimum Wage regulations.	Internet: Any of the following websites: • www.abo.org.uk • www.musicalchairs.info • www.thestage.co.uk Head-hunters (without national advertising), for jobs where the annual salary is at least £40,000

SOC Code and Description	Appropriate salary rate	Resident Labour Market Test – additional media
3416 Arts officers, producers and directors • Arts officers, producers and directors must be established in the relevant industry at the highest level. Examples include producers and directors in theatre or opera. Whether the level of the job is appropriate should be determined by the sponsor in consultation with relevant representatives of the industry in the United Kingdom Evidence of this consultation must be retained by the sponsor. Recognised representatives are: • Broadcasting entertainment cinematograph and theatre union (BECTU) • Equity • Independent Theatre Council(ITC) • Nationa l Campaign for the Arts (NCA) • Producers alliance for cinema and television (PACT)	Payment should be commensurate with the relevant industry standards in the United Kingdom and of at least the minimum salary for Tier 2 of £20,000	Details of the Resident Labour Market Test requirements for arts officers, producers and directors in the film industry are set out in the creative sector code of practice in Table 5. Arts officer roles and producer/director roles in theatre and opera must be advertised in accordance with standard industry practice through at least one of the following: • Arts Professional • Gig incorporating International Arts Manager • The Stage • www.artsjobsonline.com • www.jobs.guardian.co.uk

SOC Code and Description	Appropriate salary rate	Resident Labour Market Test – additional media
• Production Guild • Society of London Theatre (SOLT) • Theatrical Management Association (TMA)		
3431 Journalists, newspaper and periodical editors	• Journalist with 1-2 years' experience: £18,000 • Journalist with 3-5 years' experience: £24,000 • Journalist with 5-10 years' experience: £30,000 • Journalist with more than 10 years' experience: £40,000	Professional journals: Any of the following publications: • Press Gazette • Haymarket Publishing (Media Week) Internet: Any of the following websites: • Benn's Media Directory • Hold the Front Page • Media UK - internet directory • Newspaper Society (lists groups with in-company training schemes) • Press Gazette • Writers and Artists Yearbook Head-hunters (without national advertising), for jobs where the annual salary is at least £40,000
3432 Broadcasting associate professionals • Broadcasting associate professionals who work in the television industry must be established at the highest level in the television industry. Whether the level of the job is appropriate should be determined by the Sponsor following consultation with the relevant representatives of the industry in the UK.	Payment should be commensurate with the relevant industry standards in the United Kingdom and of at least the minimum salary for Tier 2 of £20,000	Details of the Resident Labour Market Test requirements for broadcasting associate professionals who work in the television industry are set out in the creative sector code of practice in Table 5. No other media for other jobs

SOC Code and Description	Appropriate salary rate	Resident Labour Market Test – additional media
Evidence of this consultation must be retained by the Sponsor. Representatives are: • Broadcasting entertainment cinematograph and theatre union (BECTU) • Producers alliance for cinema and television (PACT) • The Production Guild		
3433 Public relations officers	• Information officer: £16,000 • Senior information officer: £26,000 • Press officer: £22,000 • Senior press officer: £32,000 • Public relations consultant: £36,300 • Publicity assistant: £16,000	Internet: Any of the following websites: • PR Week • Press Gazette • PRCA Yearbook • Chartered Institute of Public Relations (CIPR) • Hollis Publishing Ltd • myjobscotland.gov.uk Head-hunters (without national advertising), for jobs where the annual salary is at least £40,000
3512 Aircraft pilots and flight engineers	• Fixed wing commercial jet pilots: £34,000 per annum • Helicopter pilots: £30,000 per annum	Professional journals: Any of the following publications: • Pilot Magazine • Flight International • Flyer • Aviation Week Milkround (through air training schools) Internet: Any of the following websites: • www.pilotweb.aero • www.ppjn.com • www.flightinternational.com • www.aviationnow.com • www.balpaorg Head-hunters (without national advertising), for jobs where the annual salary is at least £40,000

SOC Code and Description	Appropriate salary rate	Resident Labour Market Test – additional media
3532 Brokers	£15.93 per hour	Professional journals: Any of the following publications: • Insurance Age • Insurance Brokers Monthly • Insurance Day • Insurance Times • The Insurance Week • Professional Broking Milkround Internet: Any of the following websites: • www.broking.co.uk • www.efinancialcareers.com • www.ft.com • www.insurancejobs.co.uk • www.insurancetimes.co.uk • www.jobsfinancial.com Head-hunters (without national advertising), for jobs where the annual salary is at least £40,000
3534 Finance and investment analysts / advisers	£13.86 per hour	Milkround Internet: Any of the following websites: • www.efinancialcareers.com • www.ft.com • www.jobsfinancial.com Head-hunters (without national advertising), for jobs where the annual salary is at least £40,000
3535 Taxation experts	£13.31 per hour	Milkround Internet: Any of the following websites: • www.hmrc.gov.uk • www.efinancialcareers.com Head-hunters (without national advertising), for jobs where the annual salary is at least £40,000
3565 Inspectors of factories, utilities and trading standards	£13.03 per hour	Milkround Head-hunters (without national advertising), for jobs where the annual salary is at least £40,000
3568 Environmental health officers	£13.23 per hour	Professional journals: Any of the following publications: • Environmental Health Practitioner - CIEH • Environmental Health News - CIEH • Environmental Health News • Environmental Health Scotland

SOC Code and Description	Appropriate salary rate	Resident Labour Market Test – additional media
		Milkround
		Internet: The following website: • www.ehn-jobs.com

Table 3: Occupations skilled to National Qualifications Framework level 4 or above

SOC Code and Description	Appropriate salary rate	Resident Labour Market Test – additional media
All occupations in Table 1	As stated in Table 1	As stated in Table 1
All occupations in Table 2	As stated in Table 2	As stated in Table 2
1142 Customer care managers	£12.51 per hour	Professional journals: Any of the following publications: • Customer First • Customer Strategy Milkround Internet: Any of the following websites: • www.icsjobsboard.com • myjobscotland.gov.uk Head-hunters (without national advertising), for jobs where the annual salary is at least £40,000
1152 Office managers	£11.64 per hour	Professional journals: Any of the following publications: • Professional Manager • Management Today Milkround Internet: The following website: • myjobscotland.gov.uk Head-hunters (without national advertising), for jobs where the annual salary is at least £40,000
1174 Security managers	£12.53 per hour	Milkround Head-hunters (without national advertising), for jobs where the annual salary is at least £40,000
1183 Healthcare practice managers	• Practice Management (small practice): £20,710 • Practice Manager (group practice): £24,831	Professional journals: The following publication: • Health Service Journal Milkround Internet: Any of the following websites: • www.jobs.nhs.uk • www.wales.nhs.uk/jobs/ • www.jobs.scot.nhs.uk

SOC Code and Description	Appropriate salary rate	Resident Labour Market Test – additional media
		• www.n-i.nhs.uk • www.firstpracticemanagement.co.uk • www.hsj.co.uk • www.healthjobsuk.com
		Head-hunters (without national advertising), for jobs where the annual salary is at least £40,000
1185 Residential and day care managers	£11.43 per hour	Professional journals: Any of the following publications: • Community Care • Opportunities • Professional Social Work • Social Work Today Milkround Internet: Any of the following websites: • www.baswjobs.com • www.communitycare.co.uk/jobs • www.ecarers.com • www.lgjobs.com • www.greatsocialcare.co.uk • www.jobsgopublic.com/socialcarecareers • www.opportunities.co.uk • www.healthjobsuk.com • myjobscotland.gov.uk Head-hunters (without national advertising), for jobs where the annual salary is at least £40,000
1219 Managers in animal husbandry, forestry and fishing not elsewhere classified	• Fish farm managers: £18,000 • Forestry managers: £25,000 • Racehorse trainers: £25,000 • Assistant racehorse trainers: £15,000	Professional journals: Any of the following publications: • Fish Farmer (Fish farm manager jobs only) • Fish farming International (Fish farm manager jobs only) • Forestry Journal (Forestry manager jobs only) • Racing Post (Racehorse training jobs only) • Horse and Hound (Racehorse training jobs only) • Horse and Rider (Racehorse training jobs only) Internet: Any of the following websites: • www.britishtrout.co.uk (Fish farm manager jobs only) • www.ifm.org.uk (Fish farm manager jobs only)

SOC Code and Description	Appropriate salary rate	Resident Labour Market Test – additional media
		• www.environment-agency.gov.uk (Fish farm manager jobs only) • www.arbjobs.com (Forestry manager jobs only) • www.forestry.gov.uk (Forestry manager jobs only) • www.forestserviceni.gov.uk (Forestry manager jobs only) • www.animal-job.co.uk (Animal husbandry management jobs only) • www.racingpost.com (Racehorse training jobs only) • www.horseandhound.co.uk (Racehorse training jobs only) • www.horseandrideruk.com (Racehorse training jobs only) • www.biaza.org.uk (Zoo manager jobs only) • www.zoonewsdigest.com (Zoo manager jobs only) • www.countryside-jobs.com • www.land-force.com • www.defiragov.uk • www.LGjobs.com • www.newscientistjobs.co.uk Head-hunters (without national advertising), for zoo manager jobs where the annual salary is at least £40,000
1222 Conference and exhibition managers	• Conference manager: £20,000 • Events manager: £19,000 • Hospitality manager: £18,600	Professional journals: Any of the following publications: • Caterer & Hotelkeeper • Hospitality Magazine (The Magazine for Hospitality Management Professionals) Internet: Any of the following websites: • www.caterer.com
1231 Property, housing and land managers	£12.53 per hour	No other media
1235 Recycling and refuse disposal managers	£12.76 per hour	No other media
1239 Managers and proprietors in other services not elsewhere classified	£10.55 per hour	No other media

SOC Code and Description	Appropriate salary rate	Resident Labour Market Test – additional media
3121 Architectural technologists and town planning technicians	• Town planning technicians: £10.99 per hour • Junior architectural technologist: £14,000 • Technologist with 3-5 years experience: £20,500 • Senior technologist: £29,000 (annual salaries, based on an average of 40 hours per week)	Professional journals: Any of the following publications: **Architectural technologists** • Architects (RIBA Directory of Practices) • Architectural Review • Architectural Technology • The Architectural Technology Careers Handbook • Building Design Magazine • Management Today • RIBA Journal • TARGETjobs Construction & Building Services **Town planning technicians** • Estates Gazette • Building • Planning • Contract Journal • Opportunities: the Public Sector Recruitment Weekly • Local Government Jobs Internet: Any of the following websites: • Websites of the professional journals above • www.ribaappointments.com (architectural technologists) • info.architectsjournal.co.uk (architectural technologists) • www.ciat.org.uk/en/careers/ (architectural technologists) • www.ciob.org.uk/topics/foaas (architectural technologists) • www.rias.org.uk (architectural technologists) • www.lgjobs.com (town planning technicians) • jobs.planningresource.co.uk (town planning technicians) • www.acenetrecruit.co.uk
3123 Building inspectors	£13.31 per hour	Professional journals: Any of the following publications: • Building • Building Control Journal • Building Engineer • Construction News

SOC Code and Description	Appropriate salary rate	Resident Labour Market Test – additional media
		Internet: Any of the following websites: • www.building4jobs.com • www.careersinconstruction.com • www.propertyweek.com • www.propertyjobs.co.uk
3131 IT operations technicians	• Senior systems administrator: £33,200 • Systems administrator: £28,000 • Network controller or network administrator: £26,000 • Network support engineer: £27,000 • Webmaster or web administrator: £28,000 • Asset manager (computer and video games): £20,000	Professional journals: Any of the following publications: • Computer Weekly • Computing Magazine • PC Pro • Develop Magazine (games jobs only) • Edge Magazine (games jobs only) Internet: Any of the following websites: • www.cwjobs.co.uk • www.developmag.com (games jobs only) • www.edge-online.com (games jobs only) • www.gamesindustry.biz (games jobs only)
3213 Paramedics	• Posts at Agenda for Change band 5 or equivalent: £20,710 • Posts at Agenda for Change band 6 or equivalent: £24,831	Professional journals: Any of the following publications: • Ambulance UK • British Paramedic Association Internet: Any of the following websites: • www.jobs.nhs.uk • www.wales.nhs.uk/jobs/ • www.jobs.scot.nhs.uk • www.n-i.nhs.uk • www.healthjobsuk.com
3218 Medical and dental technicians	• Posts at agenda for change band 3 or equivalent: £15,190 • Posts at agenda for change band 4 or equivalent: £17,732 • Posts at agenda for change band 5 or equivalent: £20,710 • Posts at agenda for change band 6 or equivalent: £24,831 • Posts at agenda for change band 7 or equivalent: £29,789	Professional journals: Any of the following publications: • The Dental Technician • Dental Guide • Medical Laboratory World Internet: Any of the following websites: • www.jobs.nhs.uk • www.wales.nhs.uk/jobs/ • www.jobs.scot.nhs.uk • www.n-i.nhs.uk • www.healthjobsuk.com

SOC Code and Description	Appropriate salary rate	Resident Labour Market Test – additional media
3319 Protective service associate professionals not elsewhere classified	£11.49 per hour	No other media
3411 Artists • Animators in film and television must be established in the industry at the highest level and meet the requirement of the Tier 2 and 5 creative code of practice for workers in film and television	• Artists: £9.98 per hour • Animators: Payment commensurate with the relevant industry standards in the United Kingdom and of at least the minimum salary for Tier 2 of £20,000	Head-hunters (without national advertising), for artists where the annual salary is at least £40,000 Details of the Resident Labour Market Test requirements for animators within film and television are set out in the creative sector code of practice for workers in film and television in Table 5.
3412 Authors, writers • Scriptwriters in the film and television industry must be established at the highest level in the industry. Whether the level of the job is appropriate should be determined by the sponsor following consultation with the Writers' Guild of Great Britain. Evidence of this consultation must be retained by the sponsor.	• Authors and writers: £11.21 per hour • Payment of scriptwriters should be commensurate with the relevant industry standards in the United Kingdom and at least at the level of appropriate rates as on the writers' guild of Great Britain website and of at least the minimum salary for Tier 2 of £20,000.	Head-hunters (without national advertising), for authors and writers where the annual salary is at least £40,000 Details of the Resident Labour Market Test requirements for scriptwriters in the film and television industry are set out in the creative sector code of practice for workers in film and television in Table 5.
3413 Actors, entertainers	Payment should be commensurate with industry standards and of at least the minimum salary for Tier 2 of £20,000. For jobs	Details of the Resident Labour Market Test requirements for actors and entertainers in film and television, and in the theatre and opera are set out in the creative sector code of practice in Table 5. No other media for other roles

SOC Code and Description	Appropriate salary rate	Resident Labour Market Test – additional media
• The minimum level required for the job of an actor working in theatre, opera, film and television is that he has to be established in the industry as an actor. • The minimum level for the job of entertainer working in theatre, opera, film and television is that he should either have performed at the highest level and have established a reputation in his profession or be engaged to perform or do work which only he can do. Whether the level of the job is appropriate should be determined by the Sponsor by consulting with the relevant representatives of the industry in the United Kingdom Evidence of this consultation must be retained by the Sponsor. Recognised representatives are: **Theatre** • Equity	which are covered by the Tier 2 and 5 creative codes of practice for performers in theatre or opera or performers in film and television, details on the agreed minimum salaries are set out in Table 5. For other entertainers, the salary should be at least at the level of appropriate UK rates in this sector as on the Equity website and of at least the minimum salary for Tier 2 of £20,000. The salary must also meet the National Minimum Wage Regulations.	

SOC Code and Description	Appropriate salary rate	Resident Labour Market Test – additional media
• Independent Theatre Council (ITC) • National Campaign for the Arts (NCA) • Society of London Theatre (SOLT) • Theatrical Management Association (TMA) **Film and television** • Equity • Producers Alliance for Cinema and Television (PACT)		
3414 Dancers and choreographers • Dancers and choreographers must be established at the highest level in the relevant industry as a dancer or choereographer. Whether the level of the job is appropriate should be determined by the Sponsor in consultation with relevant representatives of the industry in the UK.	Payment of dancers and choreographers should be commensurate with the relevant industry standards and of at least the minimum salary for Tier 2 of £20,000. More details on the agreed minimum salaries for dancers following: in ballet, dance forms other than ballet, and in theatre or opera are set out in the creative sector code of practice in Table 5. Payment of choreographers must be at least at the level of appropriate United Kingdom rates in this sector as stated on the Equity website.	Details of the Resident Labour Market Test requirements for dancers are set out in the creative sector code of practice in Table 5. Choreographer roles must be advertised in accordance with standard industry practice through at least one of the following: • Dance agencies • The Stage • Dance Europe • Juice • The Spotlight Link • Equity's Job Information Service

SOC Code and Description	Appropriate salary rate	Resident Labour Market Test – additional media
Evidence of this consultation must be retained by the sponsor. Recognised representatives are: • Equity • Independent Theatre Council (ITC) • National Campaign for the Arts (NCA) • Society of London Theatre (SOLT) • Theatrical Management Association (TMA)		
3422 Product, clothing and related designers	• Product designer: £25,537 (based on a 44 hour week) • Fashion designer: £22,000 (based on a 40 hour week) • Textile designer: £25,000 (based on a 40 hour week)	Professional journals: Any of the following publications: • Drapers • Design Week • The Designer Tier 2 Section C Occupational Codes of Practice - Version: 06/12: Valid from 14/06/2012 Page 27 of 75 • Blueprint • Crafts • Creative Review • Textile Horizons • Textile Month • New Design • RIBA Journal (interior or furniture designers only) • Fashion Weekly (fashion designers only) • Fashion Business International (fashion designers only) • I.D. Magazine (furniture designers only) Internet: Any of the following websites: • www.mad.co.uk (interior designers only) • www.theappointment.co.uk (fashion designers only)

SOC Code and Description	Appropriate salary rate	Resident Labour Market Test – additional media
		• www.designcouncil.org.uk (fashion designers only) • www.retailcareers.co.uk (fashion designers only) • www.retailchoice.com (fashion designers only) • www.inretail.co.uk (fashion designers only) • www.coroflot.com (product designers only) • www.jimfinder.com (product designers only) • www.justengineers.net (product designers only) • www.thecareerengineer.com (product designers only) • www.retailcareers.co.uk (furniture designers only) • www.cabinet-maker.co.uk (furniture designers only) • www.thebcfa.com (furniture designers only) • www.csd.org.uk • www.newdesignmagazine.co.uk Head-hunters (without national advertising), for jobs where the annual salary is at least £40,000
3442 Sports officials	£9.11 per hour	Head-hunters (without national advertising), for jobs where the annual salary is at least £40,000
3513 Ship and hovercraft officers	No data available, appropriate rate considered to have been met where the application meets the minimum Tier 2 salary of £20,000.	Milkround Head-hunters (without national advertising), for jobs where the annual salary is at least £40,000
3531 Estimators, valuers and assessors	£11.03 per hour	Professional journals: The following publication: • Lloyd's List (for Marine Surveyors) Milkround Internet: Any of the following websites: • www.shiptalk.com (for Marine Surveyors) • www.marine-jobs.co.uk (for Marine Surveyors) • www.nautilusint.org (for Marine Surveyors)

SOC Code and Description	Appropriate salary rate	Resident Labour Market Test – additional media
		Head-hunters (without national advertising), for jobs where the annual salary is at least £40,000
3537 Financial and accounting technicians	£13.09 per hour	Professional journals: Any of the following publications: • Accounting & Business • Accounting, Auditing & Accountability • Financial Accountant Milkround Internet: Any of the following websites: • www.accaglobal.com • www.ifa.org.uk Head-hunters (without national advertising), for jobs where the annual salary is at least £40,000
3539 Business and related associate professionals not elsewhere classified	£11.00 per hour	Milkround Head-hunters (without national advertising), for jobs where the annual salary is at least £40,000
3541 Buyers and purchasing officers	£11.44 per hour	Professional journals: Any of the following publications: • Campaign (for media buyers) • Creative Review (for media buyers) • Drapers (for retail fashion buyers) • Marketing (for media buyers) • Marketing Week (for media buyers) • Media Week (for media buyers) • Retail Week (for retail buyers) • Supply Management Milkround Internet: Any of the following websites: • www.theappointment.co.uk • www.careersinfoodanddrink.co.uk • www.cips-gpa.com • www.hays.co.uk • www.inretail.co.uk • www.ipa.co.uk • www.jobsinretail.co.uk • www.mad.co.uk • www.retailcareers.co.uk • www.retailchoice.com • www.retail-week.com • www.supplymanagement.com • www.talismanretail.co.uk

SOC Code and Description	Appropriate salary rate	Resident Labour Market Test – additional media
		Head-hunters (without national advertising), for jobs where the annual salary is at least £40,000
3543 Marketing associate professionals	£11.01 per hour	Milkround
		Head-hunters (without national advertising), for jobs where the annual salary is at least £40,000
3551 Conservation and environmental protection officers	£12.07 per hour	Professional journals: Any of the following publications: • In Practice • New Scientist Milkround Internet: Any of the following websites: • www.acre-resources.co.uk • www.ccw.gov.uk • www.countryside-jobs.com • www.environment-agency.gov.uk • www.environmentjobs.co.uk • www.groundwork.org.uk • www.growing-careers.com • www.ieem.org.uk • www.land-force.com • www.lgjobs.com • www.newscientistjobs.com • www.ntjobs.org.uk • www.sepa.org.uk Head-hunters (without national advertising), for jobs where the annual salary is at least £40,000
3561 Public service associate professionals	£11.43 per hour	Milkround
		Head-hunters (without national advertising), for jobs where the annual salary is at least £40,000
3564 Careers advisers and vocational guidance specialists	£11.90 per hour	Milkround
		Head-hunters (without national advertising), for jobs where the annual salary is at least £40,000
3566 Statutory examiners	£11.69 per hour	Milkround
		Head-hunters (without national advertising), for jobs where the annual salary is at least £40,000

SOC Code and Description	Appropriate salary rate	Resident Labour Market Test – additional media
3567 Occupational hygienists and safety officers (health and safety)	£12.57 per hour	Milkround Internet: Any of the following websites: • www.jobs.nhs.uk • www.wales.nhs.uk/jobs/ • www.jobs.scot.nhs.uk • www.n-i.nhs.uk • www.healthjobsuk.com Head-hunters (without national advertising), for jobs where the annual salary is at least £40,000

Table 4: Occupationns skilled to National Qualifications Framework level 3 or above

SOC Code and Description	Appropriate salary rate	Resident Labour Market Test – additional media
All occupations in Table 1	As stated in Table 1	As stated in Table 1
All occupations in Table 2	As stated in Table 2	As stated in Table 2
All occupations in Table 3	As stated in Table 3	As stated in Table 3
1162 Storage and warehouse managers	£10.03 per hour	Professional journals: Any of the following publications: • Logistics Manager • Storage Handling Distribution • Warehouse Milkround Internet: Any of the following websites: • www.bjdgroup.com • www.careersinlogistics.co.uk • www.ciltuk.org.uk • jobs.foodmanufacture.co.uk • www.mvp-search.com • www.supplychainrecruit.com Head-hunters (without national advertising), for jobs where the annual salary is at least £40,000
1163 Retail and wholesale managers	£8.18 per hour	Professional journals: Any of the following publications: • The Appointment • The Grocer • Retail Week

SOC Code and Description	Appropriate salary rate	Resident Labour Market Test – additional media
		Milkround Internet: Any of the following websites: • www.theappointment.co.uk • jobs.thegrocer.co.uk • www.inretail.co.uk • www.jobsinretail.co.uk • www.retailcareers.co.uk • www.retailmoves.com • www.retail-week.com • www.talkingretail.com Head-hunters (without national advertising), for jobs where the annual salary is at least £40,000
1211 Farm managers	£9.26 per hour	Professional journals: Any of the following publications: • Farmers Guardian • Farmers Weekly • Farming Life • Poultry World • The Scottish Farmer • Harper's Wine & Spirit TradeReview (for viticulturist jobs only) Internet: Any of the following websites: • www.farmersguardian.com • www.fwi.co.uk • www.growing-careers.com • www.harpers.co.uk (for viticulturist jobs) • www.land-force.com • www.thescottishfarmer.co.uk
1221 Hotel and accommodation managers	• Hotel general manager (4-star and above): £25,000 • Hotel general manager (3-star and below): £19,700 • Hotel reception manager(4-star and above): £17,000 • Hotel reception manager(3-star and below): £15,000 • Front of house manager: £23,000	Professional journals: Any of the following publications: • Caterer & Hotelkeeper • Hospitality Magazin(The Magazine for Hospitality Management Professionals) Internet: The following website: • www.caterer.com

SOC Code and Description	Appropriate salary rate	Resident Labour Market Test – additional media
1223 Restaurant and catering managers -**ONLY** the following jobs in this occupation code: • Restaurant manager or catering manager • Banqueting manager • Fast food restaurant manager • Hotel food and beverage manager • Assistant restaurant manager, establishments with 80 or more covers (covers being the maximum number of customers that can be seated at any one time)	• Restaurant manager: £18,000 • Banqueting manager or catering manager: £18,000 • Fast food restaurant manager: £18,000 • Hotel food and beverage manager: £16,000 • Assistant restaurant manager, establishment with 80 or more covers: £7.21 per hour	Professional journals: Any of the following publications: • Caterer & Hotelkeeper • Hospitality Magazine (The Magazine for Hospitality Management Professionals) Internet: The following website: • www.caterer.com
1224 Publicans and managers of licensed premises -**ONLY** the following jobs in this occupation code: • Publican • Licensee or pub manager	• Publican: £25,000 • Licensee or pub manager: £17,000	Professional journals: Any of the following publications: • Caterer & Hotelkeeper • Hospitality Magazine (The Magazine for Hospitality Management Professionals) Internet: The following website: • www.caterer.com
1225 Leisure and sports managers	• Leisure centre manager or sports centre manager: £25,000 • Riding school manager: £20,000	Professional journals: The following publication: • Horse and Hound (Riding school managers only)

SOC Code and Description	Appropriate salary rate	Resident Labour Market Test – additional media
		Internet: Any of the following websites: • www.leisureopportunities.co.uk • British Horse Society (Riding school managers only) • Horse and Hound (Riding school managers only) • Leisure Jobs • Leisure Opportunities • www.equinetourism.co.uk (Riding school managers only)
1226 Travel agency managers	£9.27 per hour	Professional journals: Any of the following publications: • ABTA Magazine • Travel Trade Gazette UK and Ireland • Travel Weekly Internet: Any of the following websites: • www.abta.com • www.e-tid.com • www.newfrontiers.co.uk • www.tandtrecruitsolutions.co.uk • www.traveljobsearch.com • www.traveltradejobs.com • www.travelweekly.co.uk • www.ttglive.com • www.uksp.co.uk
1232 Garage managers and proprietors	£10.35 per hour	Professional journals: Any of the following publications: • Automotive News • Motor Industry Magazine • Motor Trader • AM (Automotive Management) Internet: Any of the following websites: • www.autojob.co.uk • www.motor.org.uk/magazine • www.am-online.com
1233 Hairdressing and beauty salon managers and proprietors	£8.65 per hour	Professional journals: Any of the following publications: • Health & Beauty Salon • Professional Beauty • International Therapist • Hairdresser's Journal Internet: Any of the following websites: • www.hji.co.uk • www.leisurejobs.co.uk

SOC Code and Description	Appropriate salary rate	Resident Labour Market Test – additional media
1234 Shopkeepers and whole-sale / retail dealers	£6.57 per hour	Professional journals: Any of the following publications: • The Appointment • The Grocer • Retail Week Internet: Any of the following websites: • www.retail-week.com • www.theappointment.co.uk
3111 Laboratory technicians	£8.36 per hour	Professional journals: Any of the following publications: • Nature • New Scientist Milkround Internet: Any of the following websites: • www.jobs.ac.uk • www.naturejobs.com • www.newscientistjobs.com Head-hunters (without national advertising), for jobs where the annual salary is at least £40,000
3112 Electrical / electronics technicians	£10.56 per hour	No other media
3113 Engineering technicians	£12.56 per hour	Professional journals: The following publication: • The Engineer Internet: Any of the following websites: • www.acenetrecruit.co.uk • www.theengineer.co.uk • www.engineeringjobsnet.co.uk
3114 Building and civil engineering technicians	• New entrant civil engineering technician: £17,000 • New entrant building technician: £14,500 • Civil engineering technician with 3-5 years experience: £20,000 • Building technician with 3-5 years experience: £17,000	Professional journals: Any of the following publications: • Building • Building Design • Civic and Public Building Specifier • Construction News • Contract Journal • Forum for the Built Environment. • New Civil Engineer • Public Sector Building • RIBA Journal • The Builder • The Builder Magazine • The Engineer

SOC Code and Description	Appropriate salary rate	Resident Labour Market Test – additional media
	• Senior building or civil engineering technician: £25,000 (annual salaries, based on an average of 40 hours per week)	• The Structural Engineer Internet: Any of the following websites: • www.acenetrecruit.co.uk • www.engineeringjobsnet.co.uk • www.icerecruit.com • www.theengineer.co.uk
3115 Quality assurance technicians	£9.80 per hour	No other media
3119 Science and engineering technicians not elsewhere classified	£9.49 per hour	Professional journals: Any of the following publications: • Nature • New Scientist Internet: Any of the following websites: • www.naturejobs.com • www.newscientistjobs.com
3122 Draughtspersons	£10.36 per hour	Professional journals: Any of the following publications: • Architects Journal • Contracts Journal Internet: Any of the following websites: • www.acenetrecruit.co.uk • info.architectsjournal.co.uk • www.engineeringjobs.co.uk
3132 IT user support technicians -**ONLY** the following jobs in this occupation code: • Senior PC support analyst • Senior PC support • Technical pre- or post-sales support • Senior database administrator or analyst • Database administrator or analyst	• Senior PC support analyst: £26,000 • Senior PC support: £24,900 • Technical pre- or post- sales support: £41,600 • Senior database administrator or analyst: £41,600 • Database administrator or analyst: £31,200	Professional journals: Any of the following publications: • Computer Weekly • Computing Magazine • PC Pro Internet: Any of the following websites: • www.cwjobs.co.uk
3216 Dispensing opticians	• Qualified dispensing optician: £18,000 • Practice managers: £30,000	Professional journals: Any of the following publications: • Optician • Optometry Today

SOC Code and Description	Appropriate salary rate	Resident Labour Market Test – additional media
	• Dispensing opticians with a specialist qualification in contact lens fitting: £30,000	Internet: Any of the following websites: • www.jobs.nhs.uk • www.wales.nhs.uk/jobs/ • www.jobs.scot.nhs.uk • www.n-i.nhs.uk • www.abdo.org.uk • www.opticianjobs.net
3217 Pharmaceutical dispensers -**ONLY** the following jobs in this occupation code: • Pharmacy technician posts at NHS Agenda for Change band 4 or equivalent or above	• Pharmacy technician (band 4 or equivalent): £17,732 • Pharmacy technician higher level (band 5 or equivalent): £20,710	Professional journals: The following publication: • Pharmaceutical Journal Internet: Any of the following websites: • www.pjonline.com • www.jobs.nhs.uk • www.wales.nhs.uk/jobs/ • www.jobs.scot.nhs.uk • www.n-i.nhs.uk • www.healthjobsuk.com
3231 Youth and community workers	£10.31 per hour	Professional journals: The following publications: • Children and Young People Now Internet: Any of the following websites: • www.cypnow.co.uk • myjobscotland.gov.uk
3232 Housing and welfare officers	£10.03 per hour	Professional journals: Any of the following publications: • Community Care • Inside Housing Internet: Any of the following websites: • www.housingnews.co.uk • www.insidehousing.co.uk
3312 Police officers (sergeant and below)	£14.53 per hour	No other media
3313 Fire service officers (leading fire officer and below)	£12.72 per hour	No other media
3421 Graphic designers	£9.79 per hour	Professional journals: Any of the following publications: • Blueprint • Campaign • Creative Review • Design Week • Eye

SOC Code and Description	Appropriate salary rate	Resident Labour Market Test – additional media
		• Grafik • The Designer • New Design Internet: The following website: • www.csd.org.uk Head-hunters (without national advertising), for jobs where the annual salary is at least £40,000
3434 Photographers and audio-visual equipment operators -**ONLY** the following jobs in this occupation code: • Audio visual technician • Senior audio visual technician • Photographer • Press photographer (regional) • Press photographer (National) • Film technician • Sound recordist • Camera operator(film, television production)	• Audio visual technician: £16,000 • Senior audio visual technician: £20,000 • Photographer: £20,000 • Press photographer (regional): £15,000 • Press photographer (national): £20,000 • Film technician: £16,000 • Sound recordist: £18,000 • Camera operator (film, television production): £14,000	Professional journals: Any of the following publications: • Ariel - BBC • Broadcast • Zerb - Guild of Television Cameramen • Press Gazette • British Journal of Photography Internet: Any of the following websites: • BBC Jobs • Grapevine Jobs • Ariel (BBC internal publication) • Press Gazette • British Journal of Photography • Freelance Photographer's Market Handbook • Benn's Media Directory • Hold the Front Page • Creative Opportunities • PACT Directory of Independent Producers Head-hunters (without national advertising), for jobs where the annual salary is at least £40,000
3443 Fitness instructors	£6.83 per hour	No other media
3449 Sports and fitness occupations not elsewhere classified	No data available, appropriate rate considered to have been met where the application meets the Tier 2 minimum salary of £20,000	Head-hunters (without national advertising), for jobs where the annual salary is at least £40,000
3511 Air traffic controllers	£21.32 per hour	Professional journals: Any of the following publications: • Air Traffic Management • Flight International Internet: Any of the following websites: • www.flightglobal.com • www.nats.co.uk

SOC Code and Description	Appropriate salary rate	Resident Labour Market Test – additional media
3520 Legal associate professionals	£9.94 per hour	Milkround Head-hunters (without national advertising), for jobs where the annual salary is at least £40,000
3533 Insurance underwriters	£11.44 per hour	Professional journals: Any of the following publications: • Insurance Age • Insurance Day • Insurance Times • The Insurance Week • Post Magazine Milkround Internet: Any of the following websites: • www.efinancialcareers.com • www.ft.com • www.insurancejobs.co.uk • www.insurancetimes.co.uk • www.jobsfinancial.com • www.postonline.co.uk Head-hunters (without national advertising), for jobs where the annual salary is at least £40,000
3536 Importers, exporters	£9.24 per hour	Professional journals: Any of the following publications: • International Freight Weekly • Air Cargo News Milkround Internet: Any of the following websites: • aircargonews.net • www.careersinlogistics.co.uk • www.ifw-net.com Head-hunters (without national advertising), for jobs where the annual salary is at least £40,000
3542 Sales representatives	£9.20 per hour	Milkround Head-hunters (without national advertising), for jobs where the annual salary is at least £40,000
3544 Estate agents, auctioneers	£9.12 per hour	Milkround Head-hunters (without national advertising), for jobs where the annual salary is at least £40,000
3552 Countryside and park rangers	£8.40 per hour	Professional journals: The following publication: • The Environment Post

SOC Code and Description	Appropriate salary rate	Resident Labour Market Test – additional media
		Milkround
		Internet: Any of the following websites: • www.countryside-jobs.com • www.environmentjob.co.uk • www.growing-careers.com • www.land-force.com • www.lgjobs.com • www.wildlifetrusts.org • myjobscotland.gov.uk
		Head-hunters (without national advertising), for jobs where the annual salary is at least £40,000
3562 Personnel and industrial relations officers	£9.71 per hour	Milkround
		Head-hunters (without national advertising), for jobs where the annual salary is at least £40,000
3563 Vocational and industrial trainers and instructors	£10.44 per hour	Milkround
		Head-hunters (without national advertising), for jobs where the annual salary is at least £40,000
4111 Civil Service executive officers	£10.97 per hour	No other media
4114 Officers of non-governmental organisations	£9.56 per hour	No other media
4134 Transport and distribution clerks	£8.95 per hour	No other media
4137 Market research interviewers	£7.00 per hour	No other media
4214 Company secretaries	£7.02 per hour	No other media
4215 Personal assistants and other secretaries	£8.81 per hour	No other media
5111 Farmers -**ONLY** the following jobs in this occupation code: • Herd managers	• Farming jobs in England and Wales: £7.39 per hour • Farming jobs in Scotland: £7.14 per hour	Professional journals: Any of the following publications: • Farmers Guardian • Farmers Weekly • Farming Life • The Scottish Farmer

SOC Code and Description	Appropriate salary rate	Resident Labour Market Test – additional media
• Livestock breeders • Pig breeders • Agricultural contractor jobs that require an NQF level 3 in Agricultural Crop Production, Mixed Farming or Livestock Production, or an NPTC Advanced National Certificate in Agriculture	• Farming jobs in Northern Ireland: £6.98 per hour	Internet: Any of the following websites: • www.farmersguardian.com • www.fwi.co.uk • www.growing-careers.com • www.land-force.com
5112 Horticultural trades -**ONLY** the following jobs in this occupation code: • Horticultural foreman • Horticultural nursery supervisor • Horticultural technician • Nursery stock production technician or specialist	• Horticultural foreman or nursery supervisor: £40,000 • Horticultural technician: £25,000 • Nursery stock production technician or specialist: £25,000	Professional journals: The following publication: • The Horticulturalist Internet: Any of the following websites: • www.bloominggoodjobs.com • www.growing-careers.com • www.land-force.com • www.LGjobs.com
5113 Gardeners and groundsmen / groundswomen -**ONLY** the following jobs in this occupation code: • Gardening Team Supervisor or Manager • Head Greenkeeper	• Head greenkeeper - London (30 mile radius): £33,593 • Head greenkeeper - South East England, Essex, Hertfordshire: £32,289 • Head greenkeeper - Rest of United Kingdom: £29,822 • Ground manager: £28,100	Professional journals: Any of the following publications: • Greenkeeper International • Greenkeeping • The Groundsman • Horticulture Week • The Horticulturist • Leisure Manager • Nurseryman and Garden Centre • Pitchcare • The Plantsman • Professional Landscaper and Groundsman • Recreation Management

SOC Code and Description	Appropriate salary rate	Resident Labour Market Test – additional media
• Landscaper jobs,where the job requires a Registration of Land-Based Operatives (ROLO) Gold Card • Ground Managers and Head Grounds-person • Garden Desi-gner(although the majority of these jobs are self-employed)	• Head groundsper-son: £23,965 • Deputy head groundsperson: £19,160 • Other jobs in this occupation code: £6.96 per hour	Internet: Any of the following websites: • www.bali.co.uk • www.bigga.org.uk (Head greenkeepers only) • www.gscl.co.uk • www.growing-careers.com • www.iog.org • www.land-force.com • www.leisureopportunities.co.uk • www.LGtalent.com • www.LGjobs.com • www.pitchcare.com
5119 Agricultural and fishing trades not elsewhere classified -**ONLY** the following jobs in this occupa-tion code: • Fishing vessel skippers in inshore areas, and limited and unlimited offshore areas • Fishing ves-sel mates in unlimited offshore areas • Forest officers and forest or woodland managers • Supervising tree surgeons and supervis-ing arbori-culturists / arborists • Head game-keepers, head river keepers and head ghillies	• Horseracing stable staff: £6.61 per hour • Other jobs in this occupation: £7.55 per hour	Professional journals: Any of the following publications: • The Chartered Forester (Forest / wood-land manager jobs only) • Forestry Journal (Forest / woodland manager jobs only) • Quarterly Journal of Forestry (Forest / woodland manager jobs only) • Scottish Forestry (Forest / woodland manager jobs only) • Keeping the Balance (Gamekeeper and river keeper / ghillie jobs only) • Countryman's Weekly (Gamekeeper and river keeper / ghillie jobs only) • Deer (Gamekeeper and river keeper / ghillie jobs only) • Sporting Shooter (Gamekeeper and river keeper / ghillie jobs only) • Horse and Hound (Horse racing and performance horse jobs only) • Horse and Rider (Horse racing and performance horse jobs only) • Racing Post (Horse racing and perfor-mance horse jobs only) Internet: Any of the following websites: • www.seafish.org (Fishing vessel jobs only) • www.arbjobs.com (Forestry related jobs only) • www.charteredforesters.org (Forestry related jobs only)

SOC Code and Description	Appropriate salary rate	Resident Labour Market Test – additional media
• Head lad and travelling head lad for horseracing stables. • Head groom for horseracing stables and performance horse stud farms • Competition groom • Stud hand, stallion handler, foaling specialists in performance horse • stud farms • Head riding instructor • Work rider		• www.countryside-jobs.com (Forestry related jobs only) • www.forestryjournal.co.uk (Forestry related jobs only) • www.trees.org.uk (Forestry related jobs only) • www.nationalgamekeepers.org.uk (Gamekeeper and river keeper / ghillie jobs only) • www.shootinguk.co.uk (Gamekeeper and river keeper / ghillie jobs only) • www.horseandhound.co.uk (Horse racing and performance horse jobs only) • www.horseandrideruk.com (Horse racing and performance horse jobs only) • www.racingpost.com (Horse racing and performance horse jobs only)
5211 Smiths and forge workers	• Farriers: £30,000 based on a 40 hour week • Blacksmiths: £15,000, based on a 37 hour week	Professional journals: The following publication: • Forge Magazine Internet: Any of the following websites: • www.farrier-reg.gov.uk • www.forgemagazine.co.uk • www.land-force.com
5212 Moulders, core makers, die casters -**ONLY** the following jobs in this occupation code: • Jobs which require an engineering technician registered with the Engineering Council • Jobs which require an NQF level 3 qualification in Materials Processing and Finishing • Foundry or casting shop foremen	• Moulder: £9.28 per hour • Core Maker: £9.64 per hour • Die Caster: £7.62 per hour	Professional journals: Any of the following publications: • Foundry Trade Journal • Cast Metal and Diecasting Times Internet: The following website: • www.icme.org.uk

SOC Code and Description	Appropriate salary rate	Resident Labour Market Test – additional media
5213 Sheet metal workers	£9.30 per hour	No other media
5214 Metal plate workers, ship-wrights, riveters -**ONLY** the following jobs in this occupation code: • Jobs which require successful completion of the National Apprenticeship Scheme for Engineering Construction (NASEC) • Jobs which require successful completion of an Advanced Modern Apprenticeship in fabrication or welding	£9.59 per hour	Professional journals: Any of the following publications: • The Engineer • Engineering Internet: Any of the following websites: • www.theengineer.co.uk • www.engineeringnet.co.uk
5215 Welding trades -**ONLY** the following jobs in this occupation code: • High integrity pipe welders where the job requires three or more years related on-the-job experience • Welding fore-man • Welding engineer or consultant • Welding fitter • Welding super-visor • Welding tech-nician	• High integrity pipe welder: £11.91 per hour • Other welding trades: £8.66 per hour	Professional journals: Any of the following publications: • Materials World • NDT News • Professional Engineering • Welding & Cutting Internet: Any of the following websites: • www.bindt.org • www.engineeringjobsnet.co.uk • www.justengineers.net • ndtcabin.com • www.oilcareers.com • www.theengineer.co.uk • www.ukwelder.com

SOC Code and Description	Appropriate salary rate	Resident Labour Market Test – additional media
• Jobs that require a completed Modern Apprenticeship with NQF level 3 in Fabrication and Welding at level 3, Welding (Pipework) at level 3 or Welding (Plate) at level 3 and a completed Welder Approval Test		
5216 Pipe fitters -**ONLY** the following jobs in this occupation code: • All Pipe fitter/ welder jobs that require an Engineering Services Gold SKILLcard in Heating and Ventilation Fitting / Welding	£11.61 per hour	Internet: Any of the following websites: • www.apexes.co.uk • www.buildingservicesjobs.co.uk • www.careersinconstruction.com
5221 Metal machining setters and setter-operators	£9.69 per hour	No other media
5222 Tool makers, tool fitters and markers-out	£9.34 per hour	No other media
5223 Metal working production and maintenance fitters -**ONLY** the following jobs in this occupation code: • Aircraft engineers	£9.96 per hour	Professional journals: Any of the following publications: • Flight International (aircraft engineers only) • Association of Licensed Aircraft Engineers Tech-Log (licensed aircraft engineers only) Internet: Any of the following websites: • www.justengineers.net

SOC Code and Description	Appropriate salary rate	Resident Labour Market Test – additional media
• Fitter, turner or millwright jobs that require a completed Engineering Advanced Apprenticeship with an NQF level 3 qualification in Engineering Maintenance or Engineering Technology and Maintenance • licensed and military certifying engineer / inspector technician • airframe fitter		• www.theengineer.co.uk/Jobs/Aerospace.htm • www.engineeringjobsnet.co.uk
5224 Precision instrument makers and repairers	£8.97 per hour	No other media
5231 Motor mechanics, auto engineers	£8.51 per hour	No other media
5232 Vehicle body builders and repairers	£8.67 per hour	No other media
5233 Auto electricians	No data available, appropriate rate considered to have been met where the application meets the Tier 2 minimum salary of £20,000	No other media
5234 Vehicle spray painters	£8.72 per hour	No other media
5241 Electricians, electrical fitters -**ONLY** the following jobs in this occupation code:	**London** • Electrician (or equivalent specialist grade) £13.28 per hour	Professional journals: The following publication: • Electrical and Mechanical Contractor Internet: The following website: • www.emconline.co.uk

SOC Code and Description	Appropriate salary rate	Resident Labour Market Test – additional media
• Electricians, as defined by the joint industry board (JIB) or the Scottish joint industry board (SJIB) grading definitions • Approved electricians, as defined by the JIB / SJIB grading definitions • Technicians, as defined by the JIB / SJIB grating definitions	• Approved electrician (or equivalent specialist grade) £14.49 per hour • Technician (or equivalent specialist grade) £16.41 per hour **Elsewhere in England, Wales and Northern Ireland** • Electrician (or equivalent specialist grade) £11.86 per hour • Approved electrician (or equivalent specialist grade) £12.94 per hour • Technician (or equivalent specialist grade) £14.65 per hour **Scotland** • Electrician (or equivalent specialist grade) £10.93 per hour • Approved electrician (or equivalent specialist grade) £12.00 per hour • Technician (or equivalent specialist grade) £13.70 per hour	
5242 Telecommunications engineers	£12.10 per hour	No other media
5243 Lines repairers and cable jointers -**ONLY** the following jobs in this occupation code: • LE1-equivalent line workers and cable jointers (Chargehands or Leadhands)	£12.33 per hour	Professional journals: The following publication: • Utility week Internet: Any of the following websites: • www.utilityjobsearch.com • www.justutilities.net
5244 TV, video and audio engineers	£7.89 per hour	No other media

SOC Code and Description	Appropriate salary rate	Resident Labour Market Test – additional media
5245 Computer engineers, installation and maintenance	£9.97 per hour	No other media
5249 Electrical / electronics engineers not elsewhere classified	£10.12 per hour	No other media
5311 Steel erectors	£8.79 per hour	No other media
5312 Bricklayers, masons -**ONLY** the following jobs in this occupation code: • Architectural Stone Carver • Stonemason • Bricklayer, where the job requires NQF level 3 in Bricklaying or Trowel Trades	£23,000 (for a 39 hour week)	Professional journals: Any of the following publications: • Architects Journal • The Builder Magazine • The Builder • Building • Building Design • Civic and Public Building Specifier • Contract Journal • Construction Management • Construction Europe • Construction News • Forum for the Built Environment. • International Construction • Natural Stone Specialist • Public Sector Building • RIBA Journal • Dabs Magazine Internet: Any of the following websites: • Websites of the professional journals above • www.constructionjobsnet.co.uk • www.namm.org.uk
5313 Roofers, roof tilers and slaters	£8.36 per hour	No other media
5314 Plumbers, heating and ventilating engineers	£10.51 per hour	No other media
5319 Construction trades not elsewhere classified	£9.39 per hour	No other media

SOC Code and Description	Appropriate salary rate	Resident Labour Market Test – additional media
5411 Weavers and knitters	No data available, the appropriate rate is considered to have been met where the application meets the Tier 2 minimum salary of £20,000	No other media
5412 Upholsterers	£7.25 per hour	No other media
5413 Leather and related trades	£7.16 per hour	No other media
5414 Tailors and dressmakers -**ONLY** the following jobs in this occupation code: • Bespoke or handcraft tailor jobs that require a completed Bespoke Tailoring Apprenticeship leading to an NQF level 3 in Bespoke Cutting and Tailoring • Jobs that require a completed Modern Apprenticeship in Handicraft Tailoring leading to an NQF level 3 in Apparel Manufacturing Technology.	• Bespoke or handcraft tailor (Saville Row level tailoring, London): £40,000 • Bespoke or handcraft tailor (elsewhere in the United Kingdom): £20,000 • Dressmaker: £20,000	Professional journals: Any of the following publications: • Drapers • Textile Month • Textile Horizons Internet: The following websites: • www.drapersonline.com
5419 Textiles, garments and related trades not elsewhere classified -**ONLY** the following jobs in this occupation code:	• Pattern Cutter £18,000 • Pattern Grader £16,000	Professional journals: Any of the following publications: • Drapers • Textile Horizons • Textile Month • Textiles

SOC Code and Description	Appropriate salary rate	Resident Labour Market Test – additional media
• Jobs that require Licentiateship (LTI) or Associateship (Ctext ATI) of the Textile Institute • Pattern cutter jobs that require an ABC Level 3 Certificate in Pattern Cutting or an NQF level 3 in Apparel Technology • Head pattern grader • Pattern grader jobs that require a completed Advanced Apprenticeship in Textiles		
5421 Originators, compositors and print preparers	£8.39 per hour	No other media
5422 Printers	£10.15 per hour	No other media
5423 Bookbinders and print finishers	£7.28 per hour	No other media
5424 Screen printers -**ONLY** the following jobs in this occupation code:	£6.25 per hour	Professional journals: Any of the following publications: • Artyfacts: Vacancies Bulletin • a-n Magazine • Printmaking Today • Creative Opportunities • MAiLOUT • ArtsJobs • FESPA World • Sign World • ImageReports • Print Week • Printing World • Screen Process & Digital Imaging • The Print Business

SOC Code and Description	Appropriate salary rate	Resident Labour Market Test – additional media
• Jobs that require a completed Modern Apprenticeship with an NQF 3 in Machine Printing, or an NQF level 3 in Printmaking Skills, Screen Printing or Screen Printing Skills.		Internet: Any of the following websites: • www.a-n.co.uk • www.artscouncil.org.uk • www.cellopress.co.uk • www.mailout.co • www.jobsinprint.com • www.printmaker.co.uk/pmc • jobs.printweek.com • jobs.tes.co.uk • www.timeshighereducation.co.uk
5431 Butchers, meat cutters	£9.00 per hour	No other media
5432 Bakers, flour confectioners	£6.95 per hour	No other media
5433 Fishmongers, poultry dressers -**ONLY** the following jobs in this occupation code: • Manual filleters of frozen fish, where the job requires an individual with three or more years' related on-the-job paid experience • Machine-trained operatives in the fish processing industry, where the job requires an individual with three or more years' related on-the-job paid experience	£7.21 per hour	Professional journals: Any of the following publications: • Meat Trades Journal • Food Trader for Butchers • Food Manufacture Internet: The following website: • www.foodmanjobs.co.uk

SOC Code and Description	Appropriate salary rate	Resident Labour Market Test – additional media
• Quality controllers in the fish processing industry, where the job requires an individual with three or more years' related on-the-job paid experience.		
5434 Chefs, cooks -**ONLY** the following jobs in this occupation code: • Skilled chef positions where the pay is at least equal to the appropriate salary rates shown and the job requires three or more years relevant experience	• Head chef: £9.62 per hour • Second chef: £8.65 per hour • Other skilled chef: £8.45 per hour(The above rates apply after any deductions for accommodation, meals etc.Any overtime must also be paid at the above rates.)	Professional journals: Any of the following publications: • Caterer & Hotelkeeper • Hospitality Magazine (The Magazine for Hospitality Management Professionals) Internet: Any of the following websites: • www.caterer.com • www.caterweb.co.uk
5491 Glass and ceramics makers, decorators and finishers	£8.25 per hour	No other media
5492 Furniture makers, other craft woodworkers	£7.64 per hour	No other media
5493 Pattern makers (moulds)	No data available, appropriate rate considered to have been met where the application meets the Tier 2 minimum salary of £20,000	No other media
5494 Musical instrument makers and tuners	No data available, appropriate rate considered *to* have been met where the application meets the Tier 2 minimum salary of £20,000	No other media

SOC Code and Description	Appropriate salary rate	Resident Labour Market Test – additional media
5495 Goldsmiths, silversmiths, precious stone workers	£20,000	Professional journals: Any of the following publications: • The Jeweller • Jewellery Focus • Retail Jeweller Internet: Any of the following websites: • www.a-n.co.uk • benchpeg.com • www.bja.org.uk • www.jackson-maine.com • www.jewelleryjobs.com • www.jeweller-recruitment.co.uk
5496 Floral arrangers, florists **-ONLY** the following jobs in this occupation code: • Florist managers and shop managers who manage purchasing and relationships with suppliers, manage and develop staff, and ensure that the business meets health and safety standards and other legal requirements • Senior floristsand floral designers who manage the production and design of formal displays	• Florist managers: £12.34 per hour • Senior florists and floral designers: £7.80 per hour	Professional journals: The following publication: • The Florist and Wholesale Buyer
5499 Hand craft occupations not elsewhere classified	£7.21 per hour	No other media

SOC Code and Description	Appropriate salary rate	Resident Labour Market Test – additional media
6111 Nursing auxiliaries and assistants -**ONLY** the following jobs in this occupation code: • Posts at NHS Agenda for Change band 3 or equivalent or above	• Posts at Agenda for Change band 3 or equivalent: £15,190 • Posts at Agenda for Change band 4 or equivalent: £17,732	Professional journals: Any of the following publications: • Nursing Times • Nursing Standard Internet: Any of the following websites: • nursingstandard.rcnpublishing.co.uk • www.jobs.nhs.uk • www.wales.nhs.uk/jobs/ • www.jobs.scot.nhs.uk • www.n-i.nhs.uk • www.healthjobsuk.com
6113 Dental nurses -**ONLY** the following jobs in this occupation code: • Registered dental nursing posts that require registration with the General Dental Council (GDC). Dental nurse is a protected title.	• Dental Nurse Entry level (band 3 or equivalent): £15,190 • Dental Nurse (band 4 or equivalent): £17,732 • Dental Nurse Team Leader (band 5 or equivalent): £20,710 • Dental Nurse specialist (band 5 or equivalent): £20,710 • Dental Nurse Team Manager (band 6 or equivalent): £24,831 • Dental Nurse Tutor (band 6 or equivalent): £24,831	Professional journals: Any of the following publications: • British Dental Nurses Journal • Dental Nursing • Dental Practice • The Probe Internet: Any of the following websites: • www.jobs.nhs.uk • www.wales.nhs.uk/jobs/ • www.jobs.scot.nhs.uk • www.n-i.nhs.uk • www.badn.org.uk/ • www.healthjobsuk.com
6114 Houseparents and residential wardens	£8.20 per hour	No other media
6115 Care assistants and home carers -**ONLY** the following jobs in this occupation code: • In **England** and **Northern Ireland**, skilled senior care worker positions where the job:-includes supervisory responsibilities (see below); and-requires at least	• Applications where the applicant has, or has previously had, leave as a work permit holder to work as a senior care worker: £7.02 per hour • All other applications: £7.80 per hour	Internet: The following website: • www.healthjobsuk.com

SOC Code and Description	Appropriate salary rate	Resident Labour Market Test – additional media
a relevant NQF level 2 or equivalent qualification in care; and-requires two or more years relevant experience. (The two years experience does not include experience gained whilst on a work placement studying for a qualification.)		
• In **Scotland**, skilled senior care worker positions where the job:-includes supervisory responsibilities (see below); and-requires at least a relevant NQF level 3 or equivalent qualification in care; and - requires registration with the Scottish Social Services Council as a Supervisor (This may need to be done after entry to the United Kingdom but must be done before starting work).		
• In **England**, **Northern Ireland** and **Scotland**, 'supervisory responsibilities'		

SOC Code and Description	Appropriate salary rate	Resident Labour Market Test – additional media
requires that, as part of their regular daily duties, the individual will have responsibility for front line supervision and monitoring of care workers and care assistants, be in charge of a shift of workers and take responsibility for the smooth running of the service whilst they are on duty. They will respond to emergencies and provide guidance and support to care workers. • In **Wales,** skilled senior care worker positions where the job:-requires working at NQF level 3(Functions and job responsibilities will depend on the size of provision and the staffing structure and must bee stablished by the sponsor.) ;and-requires at least a relevant NQF level 3 or equivalent		

SOC Code and Description	Appropriate salary rate	Resident Labour Market Test – additional media
qualification in care; and - requires registration with the Care Council for Wales as an Assistant Manager / Senior Care Worker / Senior Care Officer / Senior Care Assistant(This may need to be done after entry to the United Kingdom but must be done before starting work).		
6121 Nursery nurses -**ONLY** the following jobs in this occupation code: • Nursery nurse /practitioner • Nursery supervisor • Nursery room leader • Montessori teacher	£6.00 per hour	Professional journals: The following publication: • Nursery World Milkround Internet: Any of the following websites: • www.cypnowjobs.co.uk • www.lgjobs.com • www.nurseryworldjobs.co.uk
6123 Playgroup leaders / assistants -**ONLY** the following jobs in this occupation code: • Playgroup leader • Playgroup supervisor	£6.90 per hour	Professional journals: The following publication: • Nursery World Milkround Internet: Any of the following websites: • www.cypnowjobs.co.uk • www.lgjobs.com • www.nurseryworldjobs.co.uk
6131 Veterinary nurses	£6.26 per hour	Professional journals: The following publication: • The Veterinary Record Internet: Any of the following websites: • www.synergyvets.com

SOC Code and Description	Appropriate salary rate	Resident Labour Market Test – additional media
		• www.vetsandnursesjobline.com
		Head-hunters (without national advertising), for jobs where the annual salary is at least £40,000
6214 Air travel assistants	£8.87 per hour	No other media
6215 Rail travel assistants	£10.91 per hour	No other media
7125 Merchandisers and window dressers	£6.10 per hour	No other media
8124 Energy plant operatives	£10.31 per hour	No other media
8126 Water and sewerage plant operatives	£9.64 per hour	No other media
8215 Driving instructors	No data available,appropriate rate considered to have been met where the application meets the Tier 2 minimum salary of £20,000.	No other media
8217 Seafarers (merchant navy); barge, lighter and boat operatives -**ONLY** the following jobs in this occupation code: • Merchant navy master • Merchant navy chief officer • Merchant navy 2nd officer • Merchant navy 3rd officer • Merchant navy chief engineer officer • Merchant navy 2nd engineer officer	• Merchant navy master: £40,000 • Merchant navy chief officer: £34,000 • Merchant navy 2nd officer: £26,000 • Merchant navy 3rd officer: £23,000 • Merchant navy chief engineer officer: £60,000 • Merchant navy 2nd engineer officer: £40,000 • Merchant navy 3rd engineer officer: £28,000 • Merchant navy 4th engineer officer: £24,000 • Officer of the watch: £20,000 • Chief mate: £30,000 • Ship master: £40,000	Professional journals: Any of the following publications: • Nautilus UK Telegraph • Lloyd's List Internet: The following website • www.lloydslist.com

SOC Code and Description	Appropriate salary rate	Resident Labour Market Test – additional media
• Merchant navy 3rd engineer officer • Merchant navy 4th engineer officer • Officer of the watch • Chief mate • Ship master		
9119 Fishing and agriculture related occupations not elsewhere classified -**ONLY** the following jobs in this occupation code: • Sheep Shearers with a recognised qualification equivalent to British Wool Marketing Board (BWMB) Bronze, Silver or Gold Seal • Chick sexers (vent sexers)	• Sheep shearer: 65p per sheep (a highly skilled shearer will be able to shear up to 400 sheep a day, making potential daily earnings of £260) • Chick sexer (vent sexer): £30,000 per annum (based on a rate of £3.00 per 100 chicks examined)	Professional journals: Any of the following publications: • Farmers Weekly (sheep shearers only) • Poultry World (chick sexers only) Internet: Any of the following websites: • www.nfu.org.uk • www.land-force.com
9224 Waiters, Waitresses -**ONLY** the following jobs in this occupation code: • Head waiter or waitress, establishments with 80 or more covers (covers being the maximum number of customers that can be seated at any one time) • Sommelier	• Head waiter or waitress: £18,000 • Sommelier: £18,000	Professional journals: Any of the following publications: • Caterer & Hotelkeeper • Hospitality Magazine (The Magazine for Hospitality Management Professionals) Internet: Any of the following websites: • www.caterer.com • www.caterweb.co.uk

Table 5: Creative sector codes of practice

Ballet	
Appropriate salary rate	Payment should be commensurate with industry standards set out at: www.equity.org.uk; www.itc-arts.org; www.solt.co.uk; and www.tmauk.org.
Exemptions from advertising for those deemed to be making an additional contribution to the UK labour market	**1. The dancer is required for continuity** The applicant has worked for a period of one month or more during the past year on the same production outside the EEA prior to coming to the UK. The 'same production' means one which is largely the same in terms of direction and design as the production outside the EEA. The Sponsor must be able to supply proof that the dancer is currently working, or has worked, on the same production outside the EEA and has done so, or did so, for at least one month during the past year, e.g. contract of employment, press cuttings, cast list. **2. The dancer has international status** The applicant is internationally famous in their field. (This is different to being well-known only in one country.). The Sponsor must be able to supply proof that the dancer has international status, e.g. press cuttings, awards, publicity material, television/radio interviews, programmes. **3. The dancer is engaged by a unit company** A unit company is a ballet company which exists in a country outside the EEA and has put on at least one production in that country. The Sponsor must be able to supply proof that the company has put on at least one production in its home country, e.g. press cuttings, awards, publicity material, television/radio interviews, programmes; and proof that the applicant is engaged by the unit company for the production in the UK, e.g. contract of employment. **4. The dancer is recruited from a specified school for a specified company** The applicant is recruited from: (a) the English National Ballet School for English National Ballet; (b) the Royal Ballet School for the Royal Ballet; or (c) the Royal Ballet School or Elmhurst School for Dance for Birmingham Royal Ballet. The Sponsor must be able to supply proof that, at the time of recruitment, the applicant was or recently had been a student at the school concerned, e.g. a letter of confirmation from the school, and proof that the applicant has been engaged by the company concerned, e.g. contract of employment, letter of confirmation from the company.
Required advertising media for other posts	At least one of: • The Stage • Dance Europe • The Spotlight Link • Dancing Times • Equity's Job Information Service

Dancers (in dance forms other than ballet	
Appropriate salary rate	Payment should be commensurate with industry standards set out at: www.equity.org.uk; www.itc-arts.org; www.solt.co.uk; and www.tmauk.org.

Exemptions from advertising for those deemed to be making an additional contribution to the UK labour market	**1. The dancer is required for continuity** The applicant has worked for a period of one month or more during the past year on the same production outside the EEA prior to it coming to the UK. The 'same production' means one which is largely the same in terms of direction and design as the production outside the EEA. The Sponsor must be able to supply proof that the dancer is currently working or has worked on the same production outside the EEA and has done so, or did so, for at least one month during the past year, e.g. contract of employment, press uttings, cast list. **2. The dancer has international status** The applicant is internationally famous in their field. (This is different to being well-known only in one country.) The Sponsor must be able to supply proof that the dancer has international status, e.g. press cuttings, awards, publicity material, television/radio interviews, programmes. **3. The dancer is engaged by a unit company** A unit company is a dance company which exists in a country outside the EEA and has put on at least one production in that country. The Sponsor must be able to supply proof that the company has put on at least one production in its home country, e.g. press cuttings, awards, publicity material, television/radio interviews, programmes; and proof that the individual is engaged by the unit company for the production in the UK, e.g. contract of employment. **4. The dancer performs in a certain style unlikely to be available in the EEA** It would not be reasonable to expect the sponsor to engage an EEA national because a style is required which would be unlikely to be available in the EEA labour force. The Sponsor must be able to supply proof that: (a) a certain style is required; and (b) the individual performs in that style, e.g. press cuttings, awards, publicity material, proof of training.
Required advertising media for other posts	At least one of: • Dance agencies • The Stage • Dance Europe • Juice • The Spotlight Link • Equity's Job Information Service

Performers in film and television

Appropriate salary rate	Payment should be at least at the level of the appropriate UK market rates, which can be obtained from Equity at www.equity.org.uk or from 020 767 00246. No worker may be paid less than the national minimum wage.
Exemptions from advertising for those deemed to be making an additional	**1. The work is for continuity** The Sponsor must be able to supply proof that the overseas national has worked on, or will be working on the same production overseas for at least one month. Where a Sponsor wishes to issue a Certificate of Sponsorship for reasons of continuity involving a performer that has worked on the same piece of work overseas for less than one month, the Sponsor must

contribution to the UK labour market notify Equity at least 5 working days prior to the issuing of the certificate with details of the filming schedules. This is in order to verify that the migrant is being genuinely engaged for reasons of continuity. Sponsors may issue Certificates of Sponsorship for performers to enter the UK to undertake post-production work only and provided that such post-production work solely relates to their own role in the film or TV production. For such Certificate of Sponsorship, neither the one month requirement nor prior notice to Equity procedure applies. The Sponsor must be able to supply documentary proof that the performer has worked on, or will be working on, the same production outside the UK for at least a month e.g. contracts, press cuttings, cast lists, etc.

2. The performer has international status
The Sponsor must be able to provide proof the applicant is known internationally, or they has demonstrable international box-office appeal e.g. press cuttings, awards, accolades, publicity material, television/radio interviews, film and TV credits; or documentary proof that the performer has demonstrable international box-office appeal through international box office figures for films they have starred in or led as a principal performer.

3. Highly specialist or unusual roles
For certain highly specialist or unusual roles, it may not be possible or reasonable to recruit from the EEA because the role requires specific or specialist attributes, including but not limited to: physical appearance; physical talent and linguistic or vocal skills. In such circumstances, where appropriate, Sponsors should first attempt to conduct searches in the EEA as set out in category 3 to a reasonable degree. However, it is recognised that the extent of such searches within the EEA shall be proportionate to the rarity and specialty of the attributes of the role. The Sponsor must be able to provide proof:
• that the role requires certain highly specialist attributes; and
• that the performer possesses those attributes; and
• of the casting process and casting considerations; and
• of reasonable and appropriate searches in the EEA (if applicable); and
• a list of any EEA candidates who were unavailable at the required time.

4. Featured guest in an entertainment programme, or subject of a factual programme
The applicant must be a featured guest on an entertainment programme or subject of a factual programme. For example, actors, comedians or other performers booked to appear on a chat show or a professional variety show, or scheduled to be subject of an arts programme or documentary. The Sponsor must be able to provide:
• A formal letter from the broadcaster or producer or copy of the relevant section of the commissioning agreement confirming the reason the migrant is required (e.g. to feature in an entertainment programme); and
• The name of the programme concerned; and
• Details of any recording or filming schedules.

5. Performers who are tied to the finance of the production
The applicant must be necessary to a production because the finance is contingent on the particular performer being cast in the film or TV production. The Sponsor must be able to provide a formal letter of confirmation from the production's principal financier.

6. Performers who do not meet the key criteria but who are commercially important

The applicant must be commercially important to the production. This may be demonstrated by a formal letter in support from a principal financier, or distributor. The Sponsor must give prior notice to Equity providing supporting evidence detailing: description of the role and film, and the reasons why advertising was not appropriate and a letter in support. The sponsor must provide Equity with:

• the details of the performer(s) required, role, description of the production; and

• the reasons why the role has not been advertised; and,

• a formal letter in support of the migrant from a financier or distributor; and

• if the performer is an up-and-coming performer, or cast to appeal to a particular overseas audience, then evidence of their CV, reviews, previous work, awards/accolades, and/or evidence of audience appeal would be required.

7. International Co-productions

Sponsors issuing CoSs to performers taking part in international co-productions structured under one of the UK's bilateral co-production treaties, or under the European Convention on Cinematographic Co-Production, need to provide the following evidence:

• Provisional approval from the UK Film Council certification department that the film is being structured as an official co-production; or

• Interim certification from the UK Film Council Certification Department.

Required advertising media for other posts	• A resident labour search in accordance with standard industry practice, which will normally involve engagement of casting agents within the EEA and contacting performers' agents, and may include advertising on Equity's job information service or Spotlight magazine.
Additional evidence required for stunt performers	The sponsor must also demonstrate that the applicant possesses the equivalent qualifications, skills and competence to UK industry standards. This may be demonstrated by either 1) a reference in support from a UK-based expert with demonstrable knowledge of the UK stunt industry; or 2) evidence of competence at a level equivalent to UK industry standards.

Performers in theatre or opera

Appropriate salary rate	Payment should be commensurate with industry standards set out at: www.equity.org.uk; www.itc-arts.org; www.solt.co.uk; and www.tmauk.org.
Exemptions from advertising for those deemed to be making an additional contribution to the UK labour market	**1. The performer is required for continuity** The applicant has worked for a period of one month or more during the past year, on the same production outside the EEA prior to it coming to the UK. The 'same production' means one which is largely the same in terms of direction and design as the production outside the EEA. The Sponsor must be able to provide proof that the performer is currently working, or has worked, on the same production outside the EEA and has done so, or did so, for at least one month during the past year, e.g. contract of employment, ress cuttings, cast list.

2. The performer has international status

The applicant is internationally famous in his field. (This is different to being well-known only in one country.) The Sponsor must be able to provide proof that the performer has international status, e.g. press cuttings, awards, publicity material, television/radio interviews, programmes.

3. The performer is engaged by a unit company

A unit company is a theatre or opera company which exists in a country outside the EEA and has put on at least one production in that country. The Sponsor must be able to provide proof that the company has put on at least one production in its home country, e.g. press cuttings, awards, publicity material, television/radio interviews, programmes; and proof that the individual is engaged by the unit company for the production in the UK, e.g. contract of employment.

4. The performer has a certain attribute unlikely to be available in the EEA

The role requires an attribute which would be unlikely to be available in the EEA labour force, e.g. a certain physical appearance, physical talent, or linguistic or vocal skill. The Sponsor must be able to provide proof that (a) the role requires a certain attribute; and (b) the individual has that attribute.

5. The performer is the subject of an exchange under one of the UK theatre industry's exchange programmes

The applicant satisfies the requirements of either of the exchange programmes with the United States and Australia operated by the theatre industry. Sponsors wishing to use this category must contact Equity in the first instance: Stephen Spence at sspence@equity.org.uk or on 020 76700233.

Required advertising media for other posts	At least one of: • The Stage • PCR • Spotlight • agents • Equity's Job Information Service

Workers in film and television

Appropriate salary rate	Payment of migrant workers in all cases must not be below the UK market rates found on the PACT and BECTU websites at www.pact.co.uk and www.bectu.org.uk. No worker may be paid less than the national minimum wage.
Exemptions from advertising for those deemed to be making an additional contribution to the UK labour market	**1. The worker is a Senior Creative Grade** The applicant must possess the skills and experience of a Senior Creative Grade for the following roles: • Producer • Director • Director of Photography (Cinematographer) • Production Designer • Costumer Designer • Hair/Make Up Supervisor • Editor • Composer • Visual Effects Supervisor • Sound Designer • Script Writer

The Sponsor must be able to provide documentary proof that the worker has the skills and experience in that role e.g. film and TV credits, qualifications, CV, press cuttings, awards, accolades, publicity material, television/radio interviews.

2. The worker is required for production continuity

The applicant must be providing significant creative input and have worked on or will be working in a post involving creative input on the same piece of work overseas for at least one month. The sponsor must demonstrate that the applicant has a direct working relationship with a Senior Creative Grade as listed in Category 1. For example, a first assistant editor might work directly with an Editor on the same piece of work overseas. No more than one additional worker may be sponsored in addition to a Senior Creative Grade, other than in exceptional circumstances, where there is a case based on production continuity. Sponsors must be able to provide:
• Evidence that the role involves creative input and the worker possesses the skills and qualifications for the role, e.g. copies of qualifications, CV, credits, press cuttings, awards, accolades; and
• Evidence that the worker is currently, or has worked on, or will be working on the same production outside the UK for at least a month and evidence of current working relationship with a key Creative grade in Category 1 i.e. contracts, letters of engagement, casting lists, CV, references in support, credits, press cuttings; and
• In the circumstances where more than one additional worker is sponsored, the case must be set out in supporting documentation from the Sponsor.

3. Other key creative workers

The applicant must be providing key creative input and has a significant previous working relationship with a Senior Creative Grade as listed in Category 1. A "significant" previous working relationship entails an established pattern of joint working on a number of previous productions rather than isolated or random examples. No more than one additional worker may be sponsored in addition to a Senior Creative Grade, other than in exceptional circumstances, where there is a creative case.

The UK Border Agency will notify BECTU promptly of the issuing of certificates of sponsorship for camera, editing and grip grades, and 1st Assistant Directors and BECTU may request sight of the evidence in support for such grades.

The UK Border Agency will notify the Production Guild promptly of the issuing of certificates of sponsorship for the following grades: Executive Producer (when providing the functions of a Line Producer or Financial Controller/Production Accountant), Line Producer, Co-Producer, 1st Assistant Director, Unit Production Manager, Production Supervisor, Financial Controller, Production Accountant and the Production Guild may request sight of the evidence in support for such roles.

Sponsors must be able to provide:
• Evidence that the applicant is in a creative or technical role and possesses the skills and qualifications for the role, e.g. copies of qualifications, CV, credits, press cuttings, awards, accolades etc; and
• Evidence of the applicant's previous working relationship with a key Creative Grade in category 1 e.g. CV, references in support, credits, press cuttings; and

• In the circumstances where more than one additional worker is sponsored per Department head, the case must be set out in a supporting documentation from the Sponsor.

4. The role is highly specialist, where advertising is demonstrably not appropriate

For certain highly specialist roles, it would not be reasonable to expect an employer to undertake a resident labour market search. One example would be a role which requires particular attributes considered unlikely to be available from the resident labour force, for example where the role involves the application of highly specialist skills or new technology or proprietary technology or special effect, or unique knowledge. The Sponsor must be able to provide documentary proof that it would not be reasonable to expect the sponsor to undertake a resident labour market search e.g. in relation to above example, proof that the role requires certain highly specialised skills e.g. job description; and that the applicant possesses those skills e.g. qualifications, CV, credits. For all roles under this category, UKBA will notify BECTU promptly of the issuing of certificates of sponsorship and BECTU may request sight of the evidence in support for such grades.

5. International Co-productions

Sponsors issuing certificates of sponsorship to workers taking part in international co-productions structured under one of the UK's bilateral co-production treaties, or under the European Convention on Cinematographic Co-Production, need to provide the following evidence:
• Provisional approval from the UK Film Council certification department that the film is being structured as an official co-production; or
• Interim certification from the UK Film Council Certification Department.

Required advertising media for other posts	• **For roles where formal advertising is not the usual industry practice for recruiting for a particular role:** For these roles, the sponsor must carry out suitable and reasonable searches of the resident labour market, such as contacting agents, organisations, diary services or semi-formal worker networks. Where such informal recruitment methods are used, the sponsor must demonstrate a reasonable period within which it has searched the resident labour market, this should be for a least a period of two weeks.

• **Where formal advertising is usual for a role:**
For these roles, the sponsor must advertise the role to suitably qualified resident workers in an appropriate journal, newspaper, website or online directory. The choice of advertising medium should be appropriate for the particular role. The following advertising media may be appropriate: searching relevant online directories such as the Knowledge Online, Production Base, or through industry organisations such as the Production Guild. Other forms of advertising may be appropriate depending on the type of role. For longer terms contracts advertisements in Guardian Media, Broadcast, Screen International, Marketing Week would be appropriate.
Under this category, in the case of camera, editing and grip grades, and 1st Assistant Directors, the UK Border Agency shall promptly notify BECTU of the issuing of certificates of sponsorship and BECTU may request sight of the evidence of the steps to search for resident labour for these roles.
Under this category, in the case of Executive Producer (when providing the functions of a Line Producer or Financial Controller/Production Accountant) Line Producer, Co-Producer, 1st Assistant Director, Unit Production Manager, Production Supervisor, Financial Controller, Production

	Accountant grades, the UK Border Agency will promptly notify the Production Guild of the issuing of a certificate of sponsorship and the Production Guild may request sight of the evidence in support for such roles.
Additional evidence required for Personal Assistants to Directors and Producers of international status	Sponsors may issue a Certificate of Sponsorship to a single, non-technical,non-creative personal assistant who supports a Director or Producer under category 1, who have demonstrable international status i.e. are known worldwide for international box office success. The Sponsor must notify BECTU promptly of the issuing of a certificate under this category for a PA to a Director and must notify the Production Guild promptly of the issuing of a certificate for a PA to a Producer. They may request sight of the evidence in support for such roles. Sponsors issuing certificates to migrants under this category must be able to supply proof that: • the migrant has a significant previous working relationship with the Director or Producer (a "significant" previous working relationship entails an established pattern of joint working on a number of previous productions rather than isolated or random examples); and • the migrant works only as a personal assistant to the Director/Producer and does not undertake creative or technical duties; and • the Director or Producer is of international status i.e. known worldwide , or they have demonstrable box-office appeal worldwide. • the worker has the skills and experience in that role e.g. a reference in support from the Director or Producer, film and TV credits, qualifications, and CV • the Director or Producer has international status e.g. press cuttings, awards,—accolades, publicity material, television/radio interviews, film and TV credits; or, documentary proof that they have demonstrable worldwide box-office appeal through box office figures for films they have led.

Note: Appendix J inserted from 20 July 2012 (Cm 8423).

Appendix K
Shortage Occupation List

Note: Appendix K inserted from 20 July 2012 (Cm 8423).

1. Where these Rules refer to jobs which appear on the Shortage Occupation List, this means only those specific jobs within each Standard Occupational Classification code stated in Tables 1 and 2 below and, where stated, where the further specified criteria are met.

2. Jobs which appear on the United Kingdom Shortage Occupation List are set out in Table 1.

3. Jobs which appear on the Scotland Only Shortage Occupation List are set out in Table 2.

Table 1: United Kingdom Shortage Occupation List

Related occupation title and Standard Occupational Classification code	Job titles included on the United Kingdom Shortage Occupation List and further specified criteria
Directors and chief executives of major organisations (1112)	ONLY the following jobs in this occupation code: • the following jobs in the decommissioning and waste management areas of the nuclear industry: – managing director – programme director – site director
Production, works and maintenance managers (1121)	ONLY the following job in this occupation code: • project manager in the electricity transmission and distribution industry
Managers in mining and energy (1123)	ONLY the following jobs in this occupation code: • site manager in the electricity transmission and distribution industry
Biological scientists and biochemists (2112)	ONLY the following jobs in this occupation code: • cardiac physiologist • clinical neurophysiologist • clinical vascular scientist • respiratory physiologist • sleep physiologist A voluntary register for Sleep Physiologists (also known as Respiratory Physiologists) and Clinical Physiologists is held by the Registration Council for Clinical Physiologists (RCCP). If an individual is a member of the RCCP, the sponsor must retain evidence of their registration and provide it to UK Border Agency on Request. Sponsors must retain evidence of the individual's HPC registration and provide this to the UK Border Agency on request. (Registration may need to be done after the individual has entered the United Kingdom but must be done before starting work).

Physicists, geologists and meteorologists (2113)	**ONLY** the following jobs in this occupation code: • hydro geologist • geophysicist • geoscientist • geophysical specialist • engineering geophysicist • engineering geomorphologist • geologist • geochemist • environmental scientist • technical services manager in the decommissioning and waste areas of the nuclear industry • nuclear medicine scientist • radiotherapy physicist • staff working in diagnostic radiology (including magnetic resonance imaging)
Civil engineers (2121)	**ONLY** the following jobs in this occupation code: • geotechnical design engineer • geotechnical specialist • reservoir panel engineer • rock mechanics engineer • soil mechanics engineer • geomechanics engineer • mining geotechnical engineer • mining and coal engineer • wells engineer • tunnelling engineer • petroleum engineer • drilling engineer • completions engineer • fluids engineer • reservoir engineer • offshore and subsea engineer • control and instrument engineer • process safety engineer
Mechanical engineers (2122)	**ONLY** the following job in this occupation code: • mechanical engineer in the aerospace sector
Electrical engineers (2123)	**ONLY** the following jobs in this occupation code: • all electrical engineers in the oil and gas industry • the following jobs in the electricity transmission and distribution industry: – power system engineer – control engineer – protection engineer
Chemical engineers (2125)	**ALL** jobs in this occupation code

Design and development engineers (2126)	**ONLY** the following jobs in this occupation code: • design engineer in the electricity transmission and distribution industry • simulation development engineer
Production and process engineers (2127)	**ONLY** the following jobs in this occupation code: • manufacturing engineer (process planning) in the aerospace sector • technical services representative in the aerospace sector

Planning and quality control engineers (2128)	**ONLY** the following jobs in this occupation code:
	• the following jobs in the electricity transmission and distribution industry:
	  − planning / development engineer
	  − quality, health, safety and environment (QHSE) engineer

Engineering professionals (not elsewhere classified (2129)	**ONLY** the following jobs in this occupation code:
	• geoenvironmental specialist
	• geoenvironmental engineer
	• contaminated land engineer
	• landfill engineer
	• metallurgical / mineral processing engineer
	• the following jobs in the aerospace sector:
	  − aerothermal engineer
	  − stress engineer
	  − chief of engineering
	  − advance tool and fixturing engineer
	• the following jobs in the decommissioning and waste management areas of the nuclear industry:
	  − operations manager
	  − decommissioning specialist manager
	  − project / planning engineer
	  − radioactive waste manager
	  − radiological protection advisor
	• the following jobs in the electricity transmission and distribution industry:
	  − project engineer
	  − proposals engineer

Software professionals (2132)	**ONLY** the following jobs in this occupation code:
	• the following jobs in visual effects and 2D / 3D computer animation for film, television or video games:
	  − software developer
	  − systems engineer
	  − shader writer

Medical practitioners (2211)	**ONLY** the following jobs in this occupation code:
	• Consultants in the following specialities:
	  – clinical neurophysiology
	  – emergency medicine
	  – genito-urinary medicine
	  – haematology
	  – neurology
	  – occupational medicine
	• Consultants in the following specialities of psychiatry:
	  – forensic psychiatry
	  – general psychiatry
	  – learning disabilities psychiatry
	  – old age psychiatry
	• Non-consultant, non-training, medical staff posts in the following specialities:
	  – anaesthetics
	  – paediatrics
	  – general medicine specialities delivering acute care services (intensive care medicine, general internal medicine (acute))
	  – emergency medicine
	  – general surgery
	  – obstetrics and gynaecology
	  – trauma and orthopaedic surgery
	• ST4 level trainees in paediatrics

Secondary education teaching professionals (2314)	**ONLY** the following jobs in this occupation code: • secondary education teachers in the subjects of maths or pure sciences (physics and / or chemistry)
Special needs education teaching professionals (2316)	**ONLY** the following jobs in this occupation code: • all teaching posts in special schools
Management consultants, actuaries, economists and statisticians (2423)	**ONLY** the following jobs in this occupation code: • qualified actuaries working in the life assurance, general insurance, and health and care sectors
Social workers (2442)	**ONLY** the following job in this occupation code: • social worker in children's and family services

Engineering Technicians (3113)	**ONLY** the following job in this occupation code:
	• the following jobs in the electricity transmission and distribution industry:
	  – commissioning engineer
	  – substation electrical engineer

Nurses (3211)	**ONLY** the following jobs in this occupation code: • specialist nurse working in operating theatres • operating department practitioner • specialist nurse working in neonatal intensive care units Sponsors must retain evidence of the individual's provisional / full NMC registration and provide this to the UK Border Agency on request.
Medical radiographers (3214)	**ONLY** the following jobs in this occupation code: • HPC-registered diagnostic radiographer • HPC-registered therapeutic radiographer • sonographer Sponsors must retain evidence of the individual's HPC registration and provide this to the UK Border Agency on request. (Registration may need to be done after the individual has entered the United Kingdom but must be done before starting work).
Medical and dental technicians (3218)	**ONLY** the following jobs in this occupation code: • nuclear medicine technologist • radiotherapy technologist
Artists (3411)	**ONLY** the following job in this occupation code: • animator in visual effects and 2D / 3D computer animation for film, television or video games

Dancers and choreographers (3414)	**ONLY** the following jobs in this occupation code:
	• skilled classical ballet dancers who meet the standard required by internationally recognised United Kingdom ballet companies (e.g. Birmingham Royal Ballet, English National Ballet, Northern Ballet Theatre, The Royal Ballet and Scottish Ballet). The company must either:
	  – have performed at or been invited to perform at venues of the calibre of the Royal Opera House, Sadler's Wells or Barbican, either in the United Kingdom or overseas; or
	  – attract dancers and/or choreographers and other artists from other countries; or
	  – be endorsed as being internationally recognised by a United Kingdom industry body such as the Arts Councils (of England, Scotland and/or Wales)
	• skilled contemporary dancers who meet the standard required by internationally recognised United Kingdom contemporary dance companies (e.g. Shobana Jeyasingh Dance Company, Scottish Dance Theatre and Rambert Dance Company). The company must either:

– have performed at or been invited to perform at venues of the calibre of Sadler's Wells, the Southbank Centre or The Place, either in the United Kingdom or overseas; or

– attract dancers and/or choreographers and other artists from all over the world; or

– be endorsed as being internationally recognised by a United Kingdom industry body such as the Arts Councils (of England, Scotland and/or Wales)

Musicians (3415)	**ONLY** the following job in this occupation code: • skilled orchestral musicians who meet the standard required by internationally recognised United Kingdom orchestras (e.g. London Symphony Orchestra, London Philharmonic Orchestra, Philharmonia Orchestra, and Royal Philharmonic Orchestra)
Arts officers, producers and directors (3416)	**ONLY** the following jobs in this occupation code: • the following roles within visual effects and 2D / 3D computer animation for film, television or video games: – 2D supervisor – 3D supervisor – computer graphics supervisor – producer – production manager – technical director – visual effects supervisor
Graphic designers (3421)	**ONLY** the following jobs in this occupation code: • the following roles within visual effects and 2D / 3D computer animation for film, television or video games: – compositing artist – matte painter – modeller – rigger – stereo artist – texture artist
Buyers and purchasing officers (3541)	**ONLY** the following job in this occupation code: • manufacturing engineer (purchasing) in the aerospace sector

Welding trades (5215)	**ONLY** the following job in this occupation code: • high integrity pipe welder where the job requires three or more years relevant experience Sponsors must retain references from the individual's past employer(s) detailing three or more years' relevant experience and provide these to the UK Border Agency on request. Sponsors must also retain relevant evidence to enable them to justify the following: 1) - Why does the job require someone with at least five years' previous experience in a role of at least equivalent status? What elements of the job require this experience and why? 2) - Why could the job not be carried out to the required standard by someone with less experience? 3) - How would you expect a settled worker to gain this experience before being appointed to the post?
Metal working production and maintenance fitters (5223)	**ONLY** the following job in this occupation code: • licensed and military certifying engineer / inspector technician
Line repairers and cable jointers (5243)	**ONLY** the following job in this occupation code: • overhead linesworker in the electricity transmission and distribution industry, working on high voltage lines that carry at least 275,000 volts

Chefs, cooks (5434)	**ONLY** the following job in this occupation code:
	• skilled chef where:
	  – the pay is at least £28,260 per year after deductions for accommodation, meals etc; **and**
	  – the job requires five or more years relevant experience in a role of at least equivalent status to the one they are entering; **and**
	  – the job is not in either a fast food outlet, a standard fare outlet, or an establishment which provides a take-away service; **and**
	  – the job is in one of the following roles:
	    o executive chef-limited to one per establishment
	    o head chef-limited to one per establishment
	    o sous chef-limited to one for every four kitchen staff per establishment
	    o specialist chef-limited to one per speciality per establishment
	
	A fast food outlet is one where food is prepared in bulk for speed of service, rather than to individual order.

A standard fare outlet is one where the menu is designed centrally for outlets in a chain / franchise, rather than by a chef or chefs in the individual restaurant. Standard fare outlets also include those where dishes and / or cooking sauces are bought in ready-made, rather than prepared from fresh / raw ingredients.

Sponsors must retain references from the individual's past employer(s) detailing five or more years' relevant experience in a role of at least equivalent status and provide these to the UK Border Agency on request.

Sponsors must also retain relevant evidence to enable them to justify the following:

1) - Why does the job require someone with at least five years' previous experience in a role of at least equivalent status? What elements of the job require this experience and why?
2) - Why could the job not be carried out to the required standard by someone with less experience?
3) - How would you expect a settled worker to gain this experience before being appointed to the post?

Table 2: Scotland Only Shortage Occupation List

Related occupation title and Standard Occupational Classification code	Job titles included on the United Kingdom Shortage Occupation List and further specified criteria
All	**ALL** job titles and occupations on the United Kingdom Shortage Occupation List
Medical practitioners (2211)	**ONLY** the following jobs in this occupation code: • **ALL** jobs on the UK shortage occupation list • ST3, ST5 and ST6 level trainees in paediatrics* • Staff grade and Associate Specialist (SAS) doctors in paediatrics • consultants in paediatrics

* ST4 level trainees in paediatrics are included on the UK shortage occupation list.

APPENDIX L
DESIGNATED COMPETENT BODY CRITERIA FOR TIER 1 (EXCEPTIONAL TALENT) APPLICATIONS

Criteria for endorsement by The Royal Society, The Royal Academy of Engineering or The British Academy

Note: Appendix L inserted from 20 July 2012 (Cm 8423).

1. The applicant must:

(a) satisfy all of the mandatory "Exceptional Talent (world leader)" criteria, and at least one of the qualifying criteria, in the table below, or

(b) satisfy all of the "Exceptional Promise (potential world leader)" criteria in the table below.

Exceptional Talent (world leader) Mandatory	Exceptional Promise (potential world leader) Mandatory
The applicant must: • Be an actve researcher in a relevant field, typically within a university, research institute or within industry; • Have a PhD or equivalent research experience; experience[(including industrial research;] • Provide a [dated] letter of personal personal recommendation from an eminent person resident in the UK who is familiar with his work and his contribution to his field, and is qualified to assess his claim to be a he world leader in his field; • Meet one or more of the following Qualifying Criteria.	The applicant must: • Be an active researcher in a relevant field, typically within a university, research institute or within industry; • Have a PhD or equivalent research • Provide a [dated] letter of recommendation from an eminent person resident in the UK who is familiar with his work and his contribution to his field, and is qualified to assess his claim that has the potential to be a world leader in his field; • Be at an early stage in his career; • Have been awarded, hold, or have held in the past five years, a prestigious UK-based Research Fellowship, or an international Fellowship [or advanced research post] judged by the competent bodies to be of equivalent standing.
Qualifying • Be a member of his national academy or a foreign member of academies of other countries (in particular any of the UK national academies);	

- Have been awarded a prestigious internationally recognised prize;
- Provide a written recommendation from a reputable UK organisation concerned with research in his field. The [dated] letter must be written by an authorised senior member of the organisation, such as a Chief Executive, Vice-Chancellor or similar, on official paper.

Note: Words in square brackets in Table inserted from 1 October 2012 (HC 565).

2. The applicant must provide the following documents:

(a) A completed Designated Competent Bodies' Tier 1 (Exceptional Talent) application form;

(b) A short curriculum vitae outlining his career and publication history (of no more than 3 A4 sides in length,…);

(c) A mandatory letter of recommendation from an eminent person resident in the UK who is familiar with his work and his contribution to his field, and is qualified to assess his claim to be a world leader or a potential world leader in his field. The letter should [be dated and] include details of how the eminent person knows the applicant; the applicant's achievements in the specialist field, and how in the opinion of the eminent person the applicant exhibits exceptional talent; how the applicant would benefit from living in the UK; and the contribution they would make to UK research excellence and to wider society.

(d) Evidence in relation to at least one of the qualifying criteria listed above.

Note: Words inserted in sub-para (c) from 1 October 2012 (HC 565).

3. The documents in paragraph 2 above must be:

(a) Hard copy,

(b) Printed (not hand-written), and

(c) Written in English or accompanied by authorised English translations.

4. When assessing applicants the Designated Competent Bodies will take into consideration the following:

(a) The applicant's track record/career history (including his international standing, the significance of his publications, prizes and research funding awarded, patents, and the impact of past innovation activity, in a company, academia or as an individual);

(b) The strength of the supporting statements in the letter of personal recommendation, and evidence in relation to qualifying criteria, including a written recommendation from a reputable UK organisation concerned with research in the applicant's field (if relevant);

(c) The expected benefits of the applicant's presence in the UK in terms of the contribution to UK research excellence and to wider society, including potential economic benefits from exploitation of intellectual capital; and

(d) The additional factors in the table below.

Exceptional Talent (world leader)	Exceptional Promise (potential world leader)
• Whether the applicant is the winner of a prestigious prize or award; • Whether the applicant has secured significant funding for his work in the past ten years; • Whether the applicant is regarded as a world leader in your field.	• Whether the applicant has provided evidence sufficient to demonstrate that he has the potential to be a future world leader in the field; • The level of additional funding secured during or following tenure of a relevant fellowship; • Whether he can provide evidence of a relevant prize or award for early career researchers; • The significance of his contribution to his field relative to his career stage.

Criteria for endorsement by The Arts Council

5. Unless the applicant's work is in the film, television, animation, post production and visual effects industry, the applicant must provide evidence that his work is of exceptional quality and has international recognition (this is different from being known in one country). This must consist of no more than ten documents in total (such documents can include for example, web links) to support two or more of the following:

(1) examples of significant media recognition, articles or reviews from national publications or broadcasting companies in at least one country other than his country of residence. Event listings or advertisements are not acceptable.

(2) international awards for excellence e.g. The Booker Prize, Grammy Award; and/ or domestic awards in another country e.g. Tony Award. It remains for the Arts Council to judge whether a particular award provides appropriate evidence of international recognition in his field.

(3) proof of appearances, performances or exhibitions in contexts which are recognised as internationally significant in his field and/or extensive international distribution and audiences for his work.

6. If the applicant's work is in the film, television, animation, post production and visual effects industry, the applicant must:

(a) (i) Have, within the last five years from the year of application, received a Nomination for an Academy Award, BAFTA, Golden Globe or Emmy Award,

or

(ii) At any time, have won an Academy Award, BAFTA, Golden Globe or Emmy Award,

and

(b) provide:

(i) full details of the production nominated/award including category and year of nomination/ award,

(ii) evidence of his involvement if the nomination/award was as part of a group, and

(iii) the credit he received for the nomination/ award

7. The applicant must provide 2 letters of endorsement from established arts/cultural organisations, institutions or companies with a national or international reputation. At least 1 of these should be from a UK body and both should be on headed notepaper and signed by the author. Acceptable organisations would be those which work with many international artists each year and are widely acknowledged as possessing expertise in their field.

8. The letters of endorsement referred to in paragraph 7 must:

(a) Be written on headed paper by an authorised member of the organisation such as the Chief Executive, Artistic Director or Chair,

(b) Include details of the author's credentials (for example, a CV/resume) and how they know the applicant (personal relationship or reputation),

(c) Detail the applicant's achievements in their specialist field and how in the opinion of the author they exhibit exceptional talent,

(d) Describe how the applicant would benefit from living in the UK and the contribution they could make to the cultural life of the nation, and

(e) Include full contact details of the author including personal email address and direct telephone number so that personal contact can be made.

9. The documents in paragraph 5 to 8 above must be:

(a) Hard copy,

(b) Printed (not hand-written), and

(c) Written in English or accompanied by authorised English translations.

10. When assessing applicants, The Arts Council will review the documentation and letters of endorsement provided and make an assessment of the extent to which they provide clear evidence that the applicant meets the stated criteria. Film, television, animation, post production and visual effects applications will be referred to Pact (the UK trade association for independent feature film, television, digital, children's and animation media companies), for review and recommendation.

Note: Appendix L inserted from 20 July 2012 (Cm 8423).

[Appendix M
Sports Governing Bodies for Tier 2 (Sportsperson) and Tier 5 (Temporary Worker - Creative and Sporting) applications

1. Applicants in these categories must be endorsed by the relevant Governing Body from the table below, and the Certificate of Sponsorship Checking Service entry relating to the application must confirm this endorsement.

Sport	Governing body
Archery	Grand National Archery Society
Athletics	UK Athletics
Badminton	Badminton England
Badminton	Badminton Scotland

Baseball	BaseballSoftball UK
Basketball	Basketball England
Basketball	Basketball Ireland
Boxing	British Boxing Board of Control
Canoeing	British Canoe Union
Chinese Martial Arts	British Council for Chinese Martial Arts
Cricket	ECB
Cricket	Cricket Scotland
Cricket	Cricket Ireland
Curling	Royal Caledonian Curling Club
Cycling	British Cycling
Equestrianism	British Horse Society
Fencing	British Fencing
Field Hockey England	England Hockey
Field Hockey Scotland	Scottish Hockey Union
Field Hockey Wales	Welsh Hockey Union
Field Hockey Ireland	Irish Hockey Association
Football England	The Football Association
Football Scotland	Scottish Football Association
Football Wales	The Football Association of Wales
Football Northern Ireland	Irish Football Association
Gymnastics	British Gymnastics
Handball	British Handball Association
Ice Hockey	Ice Hockey (UK)
Ice Skating	National Ice Skating Association of Great Britain and Northern Ireland
Jockeys and Trainers	British Horseracing Authority
Judo	British Judo Association
Kabbadi	England Kabaddi Federation (UK) Registered
Lacrosse	English Lacrosse
Motorcycling (except speedway)	Auto-cycle Union

Motorsports	The Royal Automobile Club Motor Sports Association Ltd
Netball	Welsh Netball Association
Netball	England Netball
Polo	Hurlingham Polo Association
Rowing	British Rowing
Rugby League	Rugby Football League
Rugby Union England	Rugby Football Union
Rugby Union Scotland	Scottish Rugby Union
Rugby Union Wales	Welsh Rugby Union
Rugby Union Ireland	Ulster Rugby
Shooting	British Shooting
Snooker	World Snooker
Speedway	British Speedway Promoters Association
Squash and racketball	England Squash and Racketball
Swimming, water polo, diving and synchronised Swimming	British Swimming
Table Tennis	English Table Tennis Federation
Tennis	Lawn Tennis Association
Triathlon	British Triathlon
Volleyball England	Volleyball England
Water Skiing	British Water Ski
Wrestling	British Wrestling Association

Note: Appendix M inserted from 20 July 2012 (Cm 8423).

[Appendix N
Approved Tier 5 Government Authorised Exchange Schemes

Note: Appendix N inserted from 20 July 2012 (Cm 8423). Entry for Korean Teacher Exchange Programme inserted and entries relating to Mandarin teachers programme amended from 6 September 2012 (HC 565).

Name of scheme	Scheme summary	Name of overarching body (Sponsor)	Type of Scheme	Area of UK covered
AIESEC Internships	The scheme is part of AIESEC's global exchange programme in which 4,000 graduates participate every year. It develops the leadership skills of recent graduates from overseas, with typically at least a years' experience in Management (marketing, finance, sales), Technical (IT, engineering) and Development (charity) through work with UK companies and organisations.	AIESEC	Work Experience Programme Maximum 12 months	All UK
American Institute for Foreign Study (AIFS)	A programme for US undergraduate education majors and postgraduate students run jointly with the Institute of Education, with whom they spend an initial four weeks and followed by around 10 weeks undertaking placements working with teachers in English secondary schools.	AIFS (UK) Ltd	Work Experience Programme Maximum 12 months	England

Bar Council	The scheme is an umbrella for three types of programmes; involving overseas law overseas students and lawyers undertaking pupillages (both funded and unfunded) and mini pupillages within barristers chambers and other legal training programmes.	Bar Council	Work Experience Programme Maximum 12 months	All UK
BNSC Satellite KHTT Programme	A secondment programme for employees of foreign space agencies to undertake practical training and work experience working alongside specialist UK staff	British National Space Centre (DBIS)	Research & Training Programmes Maximum 24 months	All UK
BOND Business Internships	The British Overseas Industrial Placement scheme (BOND) is UK Trade & Investment initiative whereby high quality professionals, selected through the British Council offices overseas, are assigned to UK companies for up to a year. Participants gain an understanding of UK business practices and	British Council	Work Experience Programme Maximum 12 months	All UK

	the programme aims to foster links between them and the British business community.			
British Council-Speak European	This programme will provide practical on-the-job training to a group of mid- career government employee from Serbia working in key departments of the central government, as well as in local self-government institutions.	British Council	Work Experience Programme Maximum 12 months	All UK
Broadening Horizons	The Broadening Horizons scheme brings to the UK Taiwanese teachers who are professionally qualified to teach Mandarin as a second language, to provide children at participating schools with a unique opportunity to study Mandarin Chinese and to explore the culture of Taiwan, which also brings benefits to teachers and language assistants.	The Sir Bernard Lovell Language School	Work Experience Programme Maximum 12 months	England

BUNAC Blue Card Internships - 'Intern in Britain'	BUNAC has over forty years experience of running international work programmes and the Blue Card Internships scheme provides a well-controlled pathway for a wide range of organisations in the UK to offer and to benefit from work experience opportunities (internships) for eligible students and recent graduates.	BUNAC	Work Experience Programme Maximum 12 months	All UK
Cabinet Office Interchange Programme		Cabinet Office	Work Experience Programme Maximum 12 months	All UK
Chatham House Fellowship	The scheme provides opportunities, generally for those who are overseas government employees and normally for a year, to undertake research relevant to their government position.	The Royal Institute of International Affairs (Chatham House)	Research & Training Programmes Maximum 24 months	All UK
Chevening Programme	The programme includes scholars and researchers attending the UK Environment Programme's World Conservation Monitoring Centre in Cambridge,	Association of Commonwealth Universities (ACU)	Research & Training Programmes Maximum 24 months	All UK

	the Oxford Centre for Islamic Studies and the Clore Leadership programme.			
City Fellowships Scheme	The scheme aims to strengthen Anglo-American financial relations by bringing young minority financiers from the US to the City of London to work at Goldman Sachs and Morgan Stanley	Sponsors for Educational Opportunity (SEO) London	Work Experience Programme Maximum 12 months	All UK
Commonwealth Exchange Programme	The programme offers teachers the opportunity to work in different education systems, exchange ideas and knowledge and observe teaching practices in another country. Teachers exchange positions and homes with those from Australia, Canada or New Zealand for between one term and one year. Exchanges to Canada take place from September to August; those to Australia and New Zealand run from January to December.	Commonwealth Youth Exchange Council (CYEC)	Work Experience Programme Maximum 12 months	All UK
Commonwealth Scholarships and Fellowships Plan	This is an annual scheme made available to developing Commonwealth countries by the Commonwealth	British Council	Research & Training Programmes Maximum 24 months	All UK

	Scholarships Commission. Participants undertake academic, medical or professional research fellowships.			
Competition Commission/US Federal Trade Commission scheme	A work exchange scheme with the USA, primarily with the Federal Trade Commission and the Journal of Economists, to promote cooperation and mutual understanding with the objective of learning from one another's expertise in competition regulation.	Competition Commission	Work Experience Programme Maximum 12 months	All UK
Defence Academy		Defence Academy	Research & Training Programmes Maximum 24 months	All UK
Encouraging Dynamic Global Entrepreneurs (EDGE)	EDGE is a unique business development and entrepreneurial programme involving undergraduates from Scottish and overseas universities and 5th and 6 year school pupils, working in consultancy teams implementing key business development for companies, providing experiential learning for students and businesses.	Scottish Enterprise	Work Experience Programme Maximum 12 months	Scotland

| Erasmus | Erasmus is a European Commission educational exchange programme for Higher Education students and teachers. It aims to increase student mobility within Europe through opportunities for work and study and promotes transnational co-operation projects among universities across Europe. Erasmus Mundus is for joint cooperation and mobility programmes for postgraduate students, researchers and staff. | British Council Wales British Council Scotland British Council British Council Northern Ireland | Work Experience Programme Maximum 12 months | All UK |
| EU/China Managers Exchange and Training Programme (METP) | The programme is co-funded by the EU and the People's Republic of China with the aim of training Chinese and EU business managers, especially in small and medium sized companies, in their languages, culture and business practices and to build networks. | Manchester Metropolitan University | Work Experience Programme Maximum 12 months | All UK |

European Voluntary Service, (Youth in Action Programme)	Part of the European Union's Youth in Action Programme, funded by the European Commission, the EVS scheme offers people aged 18-30 the opportunity to undertake voluntary work placements in the social, cultural, environmental and sports sectors for a period of two to twelve months. Placements of two weeks to two months are also available.	British Council	Work Experience Programme Maximum 12 months	All UK
Finance Ministries and Central Banks schemes	The schemes includes secondments by employees of other Central Banks and Financial Institutions, research fellowships and PhD research internships for economists who will undertake placements with the Bank of England for between one and 18 months duration.	H. M. Treasury	Research & Training Programmes Maximum 24 months	England
Food Standards Australia and New Zealand	A secondment programme for government bodies, to promote cooperation and mutual understanding; with the objective of learning from one another's expertise in food safety.	Food Standards Agency	Work Experience Programme Maximum 12 months	All UK

Foreign & Commonwealth Office		Foreign & Commonwealth Office	Work Experience Programme Maximum 12 months	All UK
Foreign Language Assistants Programme	Working with partner organisations overseas to provide opportunities for young people to work as language assistants both in the UK, the programme aims to improve both the language ability of the assistants and students in addition to expanding their cultural awareness.	British Council British Council Northern Ireland British Council Scotland British Council Wales	Work Experience Programme Maximum 12 months	All UK
Fullbright UK/ US Teacher Exchange Programme	Run by the British Council in collaboration with the US Department of State the programme offers outstanding UK teachers the opportunity to trade places with Teachers can spend the autumn term or one full academic year teaching in the United States. Exchanges involve elementary and secondary schools, including community and further education colleges throughout the US.	British Council British Council Northern Ireland British Council Scotland British Council Wales	Work Experience Programme Maximum 12 months	All UK

Glasgow Caledonian University International exchange programme	To offer students through the exchange programme, work experience, cultural diversity and personal development to strengthen their employability.	Glasgow Caledonian University	Work Experience Programme Maximum 12 months	Scotland
Grundtvig	Grundtvig, part of the European Commission's Lifelong Learning Programme, aims to strengthen the European dimension in adult education and lifelong learning. Funding is open to any organisation based in one of the countries participating in the programme involved in adult education. The programme funds a range of activities: assistantships, in-service training, learner workshops, visits & exchanges	Ecorys UK Ltd	Work Experience Programme Maximum 12 months	All UK
Highways Agency Scheme	The scheme is intended to honour the historic and future commitments to facilitating the sharing of experience,	Highways Agency	Work Experience Programme Maximum 12 months	All UK

	scientific information, technology, working practice and organisational cultures between Highways Agency and similar administrations outside of the EEA.			
HMC Projects in Central and Eastern Europe- Teachers' Work Exchange Scheme	This scheme offers teachers from Central and Eastern Europe a year of work experience in UK independent schools to enable them to experience the UK educational system	HMC Central and Eastern European Projects	Work Experience Programme Maximum 12 months	All UK
HMRC Exchange Scheme	The scheme facilitates the sharing of experience, working practices and organisational cultures between HMRC and tax, customs and similar administrations outside the EEA.	HM Revenue & Customs	Work Experience Programme Maximum 12 months	All UK
IAESTE	IAESTE UK provides science, engineering and applied arts graduates with training experience relevant to their studies through work placements	British Council British Council Northern Ireland British Council Scotland British Council Wales	Work Experience Programme Maximum 12 months	England Northern Ireland Wales Scotland
International Cross-Posting Programme for Kazakhstan		UK Trade & Investment	Work Experience Programme Maximum 12 months	All UK

International Defence and Security Scheme (IDSS)	The aim of the IDSS scheme is to share knowledge, experience and best practice between the UK and foreign defence, aerospace, security and space industries in cooperative programmes.	ADS Group	Work Experience Programme Maximum 12 months	All UK
International Exchange Programme (UK) Ltd	Providing international training and career development through guided practical work experience across the environmental and land based sector. Programmes monitored and industry endorsed via individuals IntSCA personal development programme, encouraging continued skills progression.	IEPUK Ltd	Work Experience Programme Maximum 12 months	All UK
International Fire and Rescue Training Scheme		The Fire Service College Executive Agency of the Department of Communities and Local Government (DCLG)	Research & Training Programmes Maximum 24 months	England with scope to include devolved administrations if required.
International Horticulture Scheme	This Tier 5 Government Authorised Scheme is an international horticultural and education skills development and exchange scheme designed to develop practical skills and to further academic studies within the designated establishments of the	Lantra	Work Experience Programme Maximum 12 months	Gardens or establishments linked to the Royal Botanic Gardens, Kew the Royal Horticultural Society's Gardens

	Royal Botanic Gardens, Kew and the Royal Horticultural Society.			
International Internship Scheme	A scheme for young people and future business leaders from outside the EEA to experience working for UK companies in the UK working environment which, as they develop in their careers.	Fragomen LLP	Work Experience Programme Maximum 12 months	All UK
International Science and Innovation Unit		International Science and Innovation Unit	Work Experience Programme Maximum 12 months	All UK
International Optometrists Scheme	Scheme for Registration for optometry graduates with a 2.2 degree or above. The Scheme ensures they have the knowledge and skills to enter the General Optical Council's (GOC) Register and practise optometry without supervision.	College of Optometrists	Research & Training Programmes Maximum 24 months	All UK
Jiangsu Centre for Chinese Studies in Essex	To promote the teaching and learning of Mandarin and an appreciation of Chinese culture in Essex schools and to the wider local community, including businesses; underpin the links of friendship, education, culture and business between the County of Essex and the Province of Jiangsu.	Essex County Council	Work Experience Programme Maximum 12 months	England

Korean Teacher Exchange Programme	The scheme contributes to the DfE objective of strengthening maths teaching in schools.	Institute of Education University of London	Work Experience Programme Maximum 12 months	All UK
Law Society Tier 5 scheme for migrant lawyers.	This scheme for migrant lawyers is open to law firms based in England and Wales. It covers placements, internships and secondments offered to lawyers and law students from other countries coming to the UK for primarily non-economic purposes for limited periods to share knowledge, experience and best practice.	The Law Society of England and Wales.	Work Experience Programme Maximum 12 months	England and Wales
Leonardo da Vinci	Leonardo is part of the European Commission's Lifelong Learning Programme. UK organisations work with European partners to exchange best practice, increase staff expertise and develop learners' skills. The programme is open to any organisation involved in vocational training in the countries participating in the programme and includes activities such as mobility projects, preparatory visits and transfer of Innovation.	Ecorys Ltd	Work Experience Programme Maximum 12 months	All UK

London Organising Committee of the Olympic & Paralympic Olympic Games (LOCOG)	Secondment programme for employees of future Organising Committees, allowing them to undertake practical training and work experience working alongside London 2012 staff. They will then cascade this learning back to their home Organising Committee.		Work Experience Programme Maximum 12 months	All UK
Lord Chancellor's Training Scheme for Young Chinese Lawyers	The programme is organised to enable the Chinese lawyers to obtain practical experience in commercial law, litigation and court procedure as well as the management of a legal practice.	British Council	Work Experience Programme Maximum 12 months	All UK
Mandarin Teaching Programme (Scotland)	The programme supports the teaching and learning of Mandarin Chinese and teaching about China through the Confucius Institute. The scheme supports the Government's purpose of providing sustainable economic growth whilst also	University of Edinburgh	Work Experience Programme Maximum 12 months	Scotland

	contributing to a number of stated National Outcomes, one of which is that young people are successful learners, confident individuals, effective contributors and responsible citizens. The scheme is also valued for the links Scottish institutions can build with China, one of Scotland's key partner countries.			
Mandarin Teachers Programme (Scotland - Strathclyde University)	Mandarin teachers will come to Scotland to support teaching and learning Mandarin Chinese and teaching about China in Confucius classroom hubs around Scotland.	Strathclyde University (Scotland's National Centre for Languages)	Work Experience Programme Maximum 12months	Scotland
Medical Training Initiative	The scheme allows postgraduate medical graduates to undertake a fixed period of training or development in the UK, normally within the NHS. It covers all schemes and arrangements sponsored or administered by the Medical	Academy of Medical Royal Colleges	Research & Training Programmes Maximum 24 months	All UK

	Royal Colleges and similar organisations for the training of overseas doctors. MTI placements are temporary, time limited and require the approval of the employer and the local Postgraduate Dean of the relevant Medical Royal College.			
Medical Training Initiative for Dentistry	International Training Fellows: The Faculty of Dental Surgery (FDS) of the Royal College of Surgeons of England is able to sponsor suitably qualified postgraduate dentists to come to the UK for clinical training in an approved hospital training post.	The Royal College of Surgeons of England	Research & Training Programmes Maximum 24 months	England
Mountbatten Programme		Mountbatten Institute	Work Experience Programme Maximum 12 months	All UK
National Assembly for Wales Intern Programme	The scheme enables students from Ohio University to undertake intern placements for up to three months with Assembly Members.	The National Assembly for Wales	Work Experience Programme Maximum 12 months	Wales

National Policing Improvement Agency (NPIA)	To support the NPIA in establishing a UK Police Training and Development Exchange Scheme, aligned to one of their core strategic aims of improving international police training & development partnerships in order to increase shared good practice, improve interoperability and enhance the impact of UK international policing assistance aligned to HMG security and development priorities.	National Policing Improvement Agency (NPIA)	Work Experience Programme Maximum 12 months	All UK
NHS Tayside International Staff Exchange Scheme	The scheme aims to share different ways of working and approaches to care needs. This would provide an insight in to how different health systems operate and use this to develop local services.	NHS Tayside	Work Experience Programme Maximum 12 months	All UK
NIM China Secondee Programme		LGC Ltd	Work Experience Programme Maximum 12 months	All UK
NPL Guest Worker and Secondment Scheme	This reciprocal scheme aims to encourage closer collaboration between UK and overseas	National Physical Laboratory (NPL) Management Limited	Research & Training Programmes Maximum 24 months	England

	organisations interested in metrology by allowing scientists, industrial experts and students to undertake placements with the NPL.			
Overseas Fellows Post	The opportunity is accredited by the Postgraduate Medical Education and Training Board and approved by the Royal College of Surgeons of Edinburgh International Medical Graduate Sponsorship Scheme.	National Health Service (NHS) Highland	Research & Training Programmes Maximum 24 months	Scotland
REX Programme	The REX programme enables highly qualified teachers from Japan to work on a temporary basis in countries where English is spoken to teach Japanese language and culture.	Ceredigion County Council	Work Experience Programme Maximum 12 months	All UK
Royal Pharmaceutical Society International pre-registration scheme.	Pre-registration placements are supernumerary training positions, under the supervision of a pre-registration tutor, which enables the pre-registration trainee pharmacist to undergo training as mandated by the General Pharmaceutical Council (GPhC).	Royal Pharmaceutical Society	Research & Training Programmes Maximum 24 months	All UK

Sponsored Researchers	A scheme to enable higher education institutions to recruit sponsored researchers, visiting academics giving lectures, acting as examiners or working on supernumerary research collaborations. Institutions do not need individual support from the Department for Business, Innovation and Skills to operate a scheme.	Higher Education institutions	Research & Training Programmes Maximum 24 months	All UK
Sponsored Scientific Researcher Initiative	This scheme enables organisations to engage overseas postgraduate scientists in formal research projects and/or collaborations within an internationally recognised Host institute/ laboratory for sharing knowledge, experience and best practice, and enabling the individual to experience the social and cultural life of the United Kingdom.	RCUK Shared Service Centre	Research & Training Programmes Maximum 24 months	All UK

The Ofgem International Staff Exchange Scheme	A scheme to promote cooperation and mutual understanding between Ofgem and similar regulatory agencies overseas.	Office of Gas & Electricity Markets (Ofgem)	Work Experience Programme Maximum 12 months	England
Tier 5 interns scheme	Designed for employers, the Tier 5 intern programme is a government approved scheme which allows graduates and undergraduates from countries outside the EEA to gain intern experience working within UK industry and provides organisations with the scope to deploy the brightest and best talent on key initiatives and learn skills they can take back to their home country.	GTI Recruiting Solutions	Work Experience Programme Maximum 12 months	All UK
UK-China Graduate Work Experience Programme	The programme brings together UK and Chinese employers and their top graduates giving graduates an insight into life in another country and employers the chance to build relationships with the UK and China's top talent. Graduates.	GTI Recruiting Solutions	Work Experience Programme Maximum 12 months	England

	take part in work placements with companies. For employers the programme is a way to access the UK and China's most promising talent, develop cultural links and raise the company's profile.			
UK-India Education and Research Initiative	This five year initiative is designed to facilitate education and research cooperation between the two countries through collaboration between schools; professional and technical skills; HE research and graduate work experience.	British Council British N Ireland Council Wales British Council Scotland British Council N Ireland	Research & Training Programmes Maximum 24 months	England Wales Scotland N Ireland
UK-India Graduate Work Experience Programme	Managed by GTI Recruiting Solutions on behalf of the UK India Education and Research Initiative, the programme gives Indian graduates the opportunity to take part in salaried internships with companies in the UK and a greater understanding of UK people, society and way of life.	GTI Recruiting Solutions	Work Experience Programme Maximum 12 months	All UK

US-UK Education Commission (aka The US-UK Fulbright Commission)	To foster mutual understanding between the US and the UK through academic exchange by the awarding of merit based scholarships.	The US-UK Education Commission (aka The US-UK Fulbright Commission)	Research & Training Programmes Maximum 24 months	All UK
Welsh Language Teaching Programme in Patagonia	The scheme aims to strengthen the use of Welsh in Patagonia by bringing Patagonians to Wales to improve their language fluency and bilingual environments. Participants are either teachers, tutors or those suitable to work in activities which develop the use of Welsh in the wider social and business situations.	British Council Wales	Work Experience Programme Maximum 12 months	Wales

[APPENDIX O

LIST OF ENGLISH LANGUAGE TESTS THAT HAVE BEEN {APPROVED BY THE UK BORDER AGENCY FOR ENGLISH LANGUAGE REQUIREMENTS FOR LIMITED LEAVE TO ENTER OR REMAIN UNDER THE IMMIGRATION RULES}

{Only the level(s) of test specified for each test are approved}

Border Agency's requirements

English language Test	Awarded by	Levels covered by test	Test validity	Documents required with application
Cambridge English: Key (also known as Key English Test)	Cambridge ESOL	A1 A2 B1	No expiry	Certificate Statement of Results Candidate ID number + Candidates secret number (applicants should provide Statement of Entry if possible)

Cambridge English: Preliminary (also known as Preliminary English Test)	Cambridge ESOL	A2 B1 B2	No expiry	Certificate Statement of Results Candidate ID number + Candidates secret number (applicants should provide Statement of Entry if possible)
Cambridge English: First (also known as First Certificate in English)	Cambridge ESOL	B1 B2 C1	No expiry	Certificate Statement of Results Candidate ID number + Candidates secret number (applicants should provide Statement of Entry if possible)
Cambridge English: Advanced (also known as Certificate in Advanced English)	Cambridge ESOL	B2 C1 C2	No expiry	Certificate Statement of Results Candidate ID number + Candidates secret number (applicants should provide Statement of Entry if possible)
Cambridge English: Proficiency (also known as Certificate of Proficiency in English)	Cambridge ESOL	C1 C2	No expiry	Certificate Statement of Results Candidate ID number + Candidates secret number (applicants should provide Statement of Entry if possible)
Cambridge English: Business Preliminary (also known as Business English Certificate Preliminary)	Cambridge ESOL	A2 B1 B2	No expiry	Certificate Statement of Results Candidate ID number + Candidates secret number (applicants should provide Statement of Entry if possible)

Cambridge English: Business Vantage (also known as Business English Certificate Vantage)	Cambridge ESOL	B1 B2 C1	No expiry	Certificate Statement of Results Candidate ID number + Candidates secret number (applicants should provide Statement of Entry if possible)
Cambridge English: Business Higher (also known as Business English Certificate Higher)	Cambridge ESOL	B2 C1 C2	No expiry	Certificate Statement of Results Candidate ID number + Candidates secret number (applicants should provide Statement of Entry if possible)
Cambridge English Legal (also known as International Legal English Certificate)	Cambridge ESOL	B2 C1	No expiry	Certificate Statement of Results Candidate ID number + Candidates secret number (applicants should provide Statement of Entry if possible)
Cambridge English: Financial (also known as International Certificate in Financial English)	Cambridge ESOL	B2 C1	No expiry	Certificate Statement of Results Candidate ID number + Candidates secret number (applicants should provide Statement of Entry if possible)
ESOL Skills for Life Entry 1	Cambridge ESOL	A1	No expiry	Certificate Statement of Results for each component (reading, writing, speaking, listening) Name of test centre

ESOL Skills for Life Entry 2	Cambridge ESOL	A2	No expiry	Certificate Statement of Results for each component (reading, writing, speaking, listening) Name of test centre
ESOL Skills for Life Entry 3	Cambridge ESOL	B1	No expiry	Certificate Statement of Results for each component (reading, writing, speaking, listening) Name of test centre
ESOL Skills for Life Level 1	Cambridge ESOL	B2	No expiry	Certificate Statement of Results for each component (reading, writing, speaking, listening) Name of test centre
ESOL Skills for Life Level 2	Cambridge ESOL	C1	No expiry	Certificate Statement of Results for each component (reading, writing, speaking, listening) Name of test centre
BULATS Online (certificated version) Only tests taken with Certifying BULATS Agents detailed on the BULATS website: www. bulats.org/ certificated-bulats/ certificated-bulats-online	Cambridge ESOL	A1 A2 B1 B2 C1 C2	2 years	Certificate Test report form for each component (reading, writing, speaking, listening) Name of test centre Country where test was taken

IELTS (Academic and General Training)	Cambridge ESOL	B1 B2 C1 C2	2 years	Test Report Form
City & Guilds International Speaking and Listening IESOL Diploma at A1 level	City & Guilds	A1 (spouse/ partner)	No expiry	**One** of the following document combinations: **(1)** 'International Speaking and Listening IESOL Diploma' certificate **OR** **(2)** ISESOL certificate **Plus** IESOL Listening (A1)* certificate
City & Guilds International ESOL (IESOL) Diploma	City & Guilds	A1 (spouse/ partner)	No expiry	**One** of the following document combinations: **(1)** IESOL Diploma certificate **Plus** IESOL notification of candidate results sheet **OR** **(2)** ISESOL certificate **Plus** IESOL certificate **Plus** IESOL notification of candidate results sheet **OR** **(3)** ISESOL certificate **Plus** IESOL notification of candidate results sheet

City & Guilds International ESOL (IESOL) Diploma	City & Guilds	A1 (all other categories) A2 B1 B2 C1 C2	No expiry	**One** of the following document combinations: **(1)** IESOL Diploma certificate **Plus** IESOL notification of candidate results sheet **OR** **(2)** ISESOL certificate **Plus** IESOL certificate **Plus** IESOL notification of candidate results sheet
TOEIC	Educational Testing Service (ETS)	A1 A2 B1 B2 C1	2 years	Score report
TOEFL iBT Test	Educational Testing Service (ETS)	A1-B1 B1 B2 C1	2 years	Score Report
Pearson Test of English Academic (PTE Academic)	Pearson	A1 A2 B1 B2 C1 C2	2 years	Print-out of online score report. Scores must also be sent to the UK Border Agency online. Pearson does not issue paper certificates
Entry Level Certificate in ESOL Skills for Life	Trinity College London	A1 A2 B1	For UK immigration purposes, the tests are valid for 2 years only	Summary slip and certificate

Level 1 Certificate in ESOL Skills for life	Trinity College London	B2	For UK immigration purposes, the tests are valid for 2 years only	Summary slip and certificate
Level 2 Certificate in ESOL Skills for life	Trinity College London	C1	For UK immigration purposes, the tests are valid for 2 years only	Summary slip and certificate
Integrated Skills in English	Trinity College London	A2 B1 B2 C1 C2	For UK immigration purposes, the tests are valid for 2 years only	Summary slip and certificate
Graded Examinations in Spoken English	Trinity College London	A1	For UK immigration purposes, the tests are valid for 2 years only	Certificate

Note: Appendix O inserted from 20 July 2012 (Cm 8423).

[APPENDIX P

LISTS OF FINANCIAL INSTITUTIONS THAT DO NOT SATISFACTORILY
VERIFY FINANCIAL STATEMENTS, OR WHOSE FINANCIAL STATEMENTS
ARE ACCEPTED

1. An institution may be included on the relevant list of those that do not satisfactorily verify financial statements if:

(a) on the basis of experience, that it does not verify financial statements to the UK Border Agency's satisfaction in more than 50 per cent of a sample of cases; or

(b) it does not participate in specified schemes or arrangements in the country of origin, where the UK Border Agency trusts the verification checks provided by banks that do participate in those schemes.

2. An institution may be (but is not required to be) included on the relevant list of those whose financial statements are accepted if it:

(a) is an international banks;

(b) is a national bank with a UK private banking presence;

(c) is a regulated national or state bank that provides a core banking service; or

(d) has a history of providing satisfactory verification checks to the UK Border Agency.

3. The addition or removal of each institution to or from the relevant lists will be considered on its own facts.

4. An applicant will not satisfy any requirement in these Rules which requires him to provide documents if those documents relate to a financial institution on a list of those that do not satisfactorily verify financial statements.

5. Where stated in the tables below, the 'effective date' is the date from which the UK Border Agency will not accept financial statements relating to the stated institution.

6. The UK Border Agency will continue to verify financial information from other institutions on a case-by-case basis, and may refuse applications on the basis of these individual checks.

7. The following lists have been established and are set out below:

(i) Financial institutions in Cameroon whose financial statements are accepted, set out in Table 1;

(ii) Financial institutions in India that do not satisfactorily verify financial statements, set out in Table 2;

(iii) Financial institutions in India whose financial statements are accepted, set out in Table 3;

(iv) Financial institutions in Ghana whose financial statements are accepted, set out in Table 4;

(v) Financial institutions in Pakistan that do not satisfactorily verify financial statements, set out in Table 5;

(vi) Financial institutions in Pakistan whose financial statements are accepted, set out in Table 6;

(vii) Financial institutions in Iran that do not satisfactorily verify financial statements, set out in Table 7;

(viii) Financial institutions in Iran whose financial statements are accepted, set out in Table 8;

(ix) Financial institutions in the Philippines that do not satisfactorily verify financial statements, set out in Table 9;

(x) Financial institutions in the Philippines whose financial statements are accepted, set out in Table 10.

Table 1: Financial institutions whose financial statements are accepted - Cameroon

Name of Financial Institution
Standard Chartered Bank Cameroun
Banque Atlantique du Cameroun
BGFI Bank Cameroun
United Bank for Africa Cameroun Plc
National Financial Credit Bank
Union Bank of Cameroon Ltd
Commercial Bank of Cameroon
Citibank NA Cameroon
Afriland First Bank
SGCB
Credit Agricole (CA-SCB)
BICEC
Ecobank Cameroun (EBC)

Table 2: Financial Institutions that do not satisfactorily verify financial statements - India

AP Mahajans Co-operative Urban Bank Ltd	24 November 2011
AP Janata Co-operative Urban Bank Ltd	24 November 2011
AP RajaRajeswari Mahila Co-Operative	24 November 2011
Abhinandan Urban Co-operative Bank Ltd	24 November 2011
Abhinav Sahakari Bank Ltd	24 November 2011
Abhivriddhi Mahila Sahakara Bank	24 November 2011
Abhyudaya Mahila Urban Co-operative Bank Ltd	24 November 2011
Abiramam Co-Op Urban Bank Ltd	24 November 2011
Accountant General's Office Employees Co-opera	24 November 2011
ACE Co-operative Bank Ltd	24 November 2011
Adarniya P.D. Patil Saheb Sahakari Bank Ltd	24 November 2011
Adarsh Co-operative Bank Ltd	24 November 2011
Adarsh Co-operative Urban Bank Ltd	24 November 2011
Adarsh Mahila Mercantile Co-operative Bankltd	24 November 2011
Adarsh Mahila Nagari Sahakari Bank Ltd	24 November 2011
Adarsha Pattana Souharda Sahakara Bank	24 November 2011

Adhyapaka Urban Co-operative Bank Ltd	24 November 2011
Adoor Co-operative Urban Bank Ltd	24 November 2011
Agartala Co-Op Urban Bank Ltd	24 November 2011
Agra Zilla Sahakari Bank Ltd	24 November 2011
Agrasen Co-operative Urban Bank Ltd	24 November 2011
Agroha Co-operative Urban Bank Ltd	24 November 2011
Ahilyadevi Urban Co-Operative Bank Ltd	24 November 2011
Ahmedabad District Central Co-operative Bank Ltd	24 November 2011
Ahmednagar District Central Co-operative Bank Ltd	24 November 2011
Ahmednagar Merchants' Co-operative Bank Ltd	24 November 2011
Ahmednagar Shahar Sahakari Bank Ltd	24 November 2011
Ahmednagar Zilla Prathamik Shikshak Saha.Bank	24 November 2011
Ajantha Urban Co-operative Bank Ltd	24 November 2011
Ajara Urban Co-operative Bank Ltd	24 November 2011
Ajinkyatara Mahila Sahakari Bank Ltd	24 November 2011
Ajinkyatara Sahakari Bank Ltd	24 November 2011
Ajmer Central Co-operative Bank Ltd	24 November 2011
Ajmer Urban Co-Op Bank Ltd	24 November 2011
Akhand Anand Co-Operative Bank Ltd	24 November 2011
Akkamahadevi Mahila Sahakari Bank	24 November 2011
Akki-Alur Urban Co-operative Bank Ltd	24 November 2011
Akola District Central Co-operative Bank Ltd	24 November 2011
Akola Merchant Co-operative Bank Ltd	24 November 2011
Alappuzha District Co-operative Central Bank Ltd	24 November 2011
Alavi Co-Op Bank Ltd	24 November 2011
Alibag Co-operative Urban Bank Ltd	24 November 2011
Aligarh Zilla Sahakari Bank Ltd	24 November 2011
Allahabad District Central Co-operative Bank Ltd	24 November 2011
Allahabad UP Gramin Bank	24 November 2011
Alleppey Urban Co-operative Bank Ltd	24 November 2011
Almel Urban Co-operative Bank Ltd	24 November 2011
Almora Urban Co-operative Bank Ltd	24 November 2011
Almora Zilla Sahakari Bank Ltd	24 November 2011
Alnavar Urban Co-operative Bank Ltd	24 November 2011
Alwar Central Co-operative Bank Ltd	24 November 2011
Alwar Urban Co-Op Bank Ltd	24 November 2011

Alwaye Urban Co-operative Bank Ltd	24 November 2011
Amalapuram Co-operative Town Bank Ltd	24 November 2011
Amalner Co-operative Urban Bank Ltd	24 November 2011
Aman Sahakari Bank Ltd	24 November 2011
Amanath Co-operative Bank Ltd	24 November 2011
Amarnath Co-operative Bank Ltd	24 November 2011
Ambajogai Peoples Co-operative Bank Ltd	24 November 2011
Ambala Central Co-operative Bank Ltd	24 November 2011
Ambarnath Jai-Hind Cooperative Bank Ltd	24 November 2011
Ambasamudram Co-Op Urban Bank Ltd	24 November 2011
Ambica Mahila Sahakari Bank Ltd	24 November 2011
Ameer Urban Co-operative Bank Ltd	24 November 2011
Ammapet Urban Co-Op Bank Ltd	24 November 2011
Amod Nagric Co-op. Bank Ltd	24 November 2011
Amravati District Central Co-operative Bank Ltd	24 November 2011
Amreli Jilla Madhyasth Sahakari Bank Maryadit	24 November 2011
Amreli Nagrik Sahakari Bank Ltd	24 November 2011
Amritsar Central Co-operative Bank Ltd	24 November 2011
Anand Mercantile Co-Op Bank Ltd	24 November 2011
Ananda Co-operative Bank Ltd	24 November 2011
Anandeshwari Nagrik Sahakarti bank	24 November 2011
Ananthasayanam Co-operative Bank Ltd	24 November 2011
Anantnag Central Co-operative Bank Ltd	24 November 2011
Anantpur co-op Town Bank Ltd	24 November 2011
Andersul Urban Co-operative Bank Ltd	24 November 2011
Andhra Bank Employees Co-Op Bank Ltd	24 November 2011
Andhra Pradesh Grameena Vikas Bank	24 November 2011
Andhra Pradesh Mahesh Co-Op Urban Bank Ltd	24 November 2011
Andhra Pragathi Grameena Bank	24 November 2011
Angul United Central Co-operative Bank Ltd	24 November 2011
Ankaleshwar Udyognagar Co-Operative Bank Ltd	24 November 2011
Ankola Urban Co-operative Bank Ltd	24 November 2011
Anna Sahaeb Magar Sahakari Bank	24 November 2011
Anuradha Urban Co-operative Bank Ltd	24 November 2011
Apani Sahakari Bank Ltd	24 November 2011
Apna Sahakari Bank Ltd	24 November 2011

Appasaheb Birnale Sahakari Bank Ltd	24 November 2011
Arantangi Co-Op Town Bank Ltd	24 November 2011
Arcot Co-operative Urban Bank Ltd	24 November 2011
Arihant Urban Co-Operative Bank	24 November 2011
Ariyalur Co-Op Urban Bank Ltd	24 November 2011
Arjun Urban Co-operative Bank Ltd	24 November 2011
Arkonam Co-Op Urban Bank Ltd	24 November 2011
Army Base Work-Shop Credit Co-operative	24 November 2011
Arni Co-Operative Town Bank Ltd	24 November 2011
Aroodhjyoti Pattan Sahakara Bank Niyamith,	24 November 2011
Arrah-Buxer District Central Co-operative Bank Ltd	24 November 2011
Arsikere Urban Co-operative Bank Ltd	24 November 2011
Aruna Sahakara Bank Niyamitha	24 November 2011
Arunachal Pradesh Rural Bank	24 November 2011
Arvind Sahakari Bank Ltd	24 November 2011
Arya Vaishya Co-operative Bank Ltd	24 November 2011
Aryapuram Co-operative Urban Bank Ltd	24 November 2011
Aryavart Gramin Bank	24 November 2011
Ashok Nagri Sahakari Bank Ltd	24 November 2011
Ashok Sahakari Bank Ltd	24 November 2011
Ashoknagar Co-operative Bank Ltd	24 November 2011
Ashta People's Co-op. Bank Ltd	24 November 2011
Aska Central Co-operative Bank Ltd	24 November 2011
Assam Gramin Vikash Bank	24 November 2011
Astha Mahila Nagrik Sahakari Bank	24 November 2011
Attur Town Co-Op Bank Ltd	24 November 2011
Aurangabad District Central Co-operative Bank Ltd	24 November 2011
Aurangabad District Co-operative Bank Ltd	24 November 2011
AVB Employees' Co-operative Credit Society & Bank	24 November 2011
Azad Co-operative Bank Ltd	24 November 2011
Azamgarh District Central Co-operative Bank Ltd	24 November 2011
B.Komarapalayam Co op Urban Bank Limited	24 November 2011
Bagalkot Central Co-operative Bank Ltd	24 November 2011
Bagalkot Urban Co-operative Bank Ltd	24 November 2011
Baghat Urban Coop Bank Limited Solan.	24 November 2011
Bahraich District central Co-operative Bank Ltd	24 November 2011

Bailhongal Merchants' Co-operative Bank Ltd	24 November 2011
Bailhongal Urban Co-operative Bank Ltd	24 November 2011
Baitarani Gramya Bank	24 November 2011
Bajirao Appa Sahakari Bank Ltd	24 November 2011
Balangir District Central Co-operative Bank Ltd	24 November 2011
Balasore Coop. Urban Bank Ltd	24 November 2011
Balasore District Central Co-operative Bank Ltd	24 November 2011
Balgeria Central Co-operative Bank Ltd	24 November 2011
Balitikuri Co-operative Bank Limited	24 November 2011
Ballia District Central Co-operative Bank Ltd	24 November 2011
Ballia-Etawah Gramin Bank	24 November 2011
Bally Co-operative Bank Limited	24 November 2011
Balotra Urban Coop. Bank Ltd	24 November 2011
Balsinor Nagarik Sahakari Bank Ltd	24 November 2011
Balusseri Co-operative Urban Bank Ltd	24 November 2011
Banaras Mercantile Co-operative Bank Ltd	24 November 2011
Banaskantha District Central Co-operative Bank Ltd	24 November 2011
Banaskantha Mercantile co-op Bank Limited	24 November 2011
Banda District Central Co-operative Bank Ltd	24 November 2011
Banda Urban Co-operative Bank Ltd	24 November 2011
Bangalore City Co-operative Bank Ltd	24 November 2011
Bangalore District and Bangalore Rural	24 November 2011
Bangiya Gramin Vikash Bank	24 November 2011
Bank Jogindra Central Co-operative Bank Ltd	24 November 2011
Banki District Central Co-operative Bank Ltd	24 November 2011
Bankura District Central Co-operative Bank Ltd	24 November 2011
Banswara Central Co-operative Bank Ltd	24 November 2011
Bapatla Co-operative Urban Bank Ltd	24 November 2011
Bapuji Co-operative Bank Ltd	24 November 2011
Bapunagar Maahilaa Co-Operative Bank Ltd	24 November 2011
Barabanki District Central Co-operative Bank Ltd	24 November 2011
Baramati Co-op. Bank Ltd	24 November 2011
Baramulla Central Co-operative Bank Ltd	24 November 2011
Baran Nagarik Sahakari Bank Limited	24 November 2011
Baranagar Co-operative Bank Limited	24 November 2011
Bardoli Nagrik Sahakari Bank Ltd	24 November 2011

Bareilly Zilla Sahakari Bank Ltd	24 November 2011
Baripada Urban Co op Bank Limited	24 November 2011
Barmer Central Co-operative Bank Ltd	24 November 2011
Baroda City co-op bank Limited	24 November 2011
Baroda District Central Co-operative Bank Ltd	24 November 2011
Baroda Gujarat Gramin Bank	24 November 2011
Baroda Rajasthan Gramin Bank	24 November 2011
Baroda Trader's Co op Bank Ltd	24 November 2011
Baroda Uttar Pradesh Gramin Bank	24 November 2011
Basaveshwar Sahakar Bank	24 November 2011
Basoda Nagrik Sahakari Bank	24 November 2011
Bassein Catholic Co-operative Bank Ltd	24 November 2011
Basti District Central Co-operative Bank Ltd	24 November 2011
Batlagundu Co op Urban Bank Limited	24 November 2011
Bavla Nagarik Sahakari Bank Limited	24 November 2011
Bayad Nagarik Sahakari Bank Ltd	24 November 2011
Beawar Urban Cooperative Bank Ltd	24 November 2011
Bechraji Nagarik Sahakari Bank Ltd	24 November 2011
Bedkihal Urban Co-operative Bank Ltd	24 November 2011
Beed District Central Co-operative Bank Ltd	24 November 2011
Begusarai District Central Co-operative Bank Ltd	24 November 2011
Begusarai District Central Co-operative Bank Ltd	24 November 2011
Behrampore District Central Co-operative Bank Ltd	24 November 2011
Belgaum District Central Co-operative Bank Ltd	24 November 2011
Belgaum District Revenue Employees' Co-operati	24 November 2011
Belgaum Industrial Co-operative Bank Ltd	24 November 2011
Belgaum Zilla Rani Channamma Mahila Sahakari	24 November 2011
Bellad Bagewadi Urban Souharda Sahakari Bank	24 November 2011
Bellary District Co-operative Central Bank Ltd	24 November 2011
Bellary Urban Co-operative Bank Ltd	24 November 2011
Belur Urban Co-operative Bank Ltd	24 November 2011
Berhampur Co-Operative Urban Bank Ltd,	24 November 2011
Betul Nagarik Sahakari Bank	24 November 2011
Bhabhar Vibhag Nagarik sahakari Bank Limited	24 November 2011
Bhadgaon Peoples Co-operative Bank	24 November 2011
Bhadohi Urban Co-operative Bank Ltd	24 November 2011

Bhadradri Co-Operative Urban Bank Ltd	24 November 2011
Bhadran People's Co op Bank Ltd	24 November 2011
Bhagalpur Central Co-operative Bank Ltd	24 November 2011
Bhagini Nivedita Sahakari Bank Ltd	24 November 2011
Bhagyodaya co-op Bank Limited	24 November 2011
Bhagyodaya Friends Urban Co-operative Bank Ltd	24 November 2011
Bhandara District Central Co-operative Bank Ltd	24 November 2011
Bhandari Co-op Bank Ltd	24 November 2011
Bharat Co-operative Bank (Mumbai) Ltd	24 November 2011
Bharat Heavy Electricals Employees Co op Bank	24 November 2011
Bharat Urban Co-operative Bank Ltd	24 November 2011
Bharath Co-operative Bank Limited	24 November 2011
Bharathiya Sahakara Bank	24 November 2011
Bharati Sahakari Bank Limited	24 November 2011
Bharatpur Central Co-operative Bank Ltd	24 November 2011
Bharatpur Urban Co-Op Bank Ltd	24 November 2011
Bhatinda Central Co-operative Bank Ltd	24 November 2011
Bhatkal Urban Co-operative Bank Limited	24 November 2011
Bhatpara Naihati Co-operative Bank Limited	24 November 2011
Bhausaheb Birajdar Nagari Sahakari Bank Ltd	24 November 2011
Bhavana Rishi Co-Operative Urban Bank Ltd	24 November 2011
Bhavanagar District Central Co-operative Bank Ltd	24 November 2011
Bhavani Sahakari Bank Limited	24 November 2011
Bhavani Urban Co-operative Bank Ltd	24 November 2011
Bhavanikudal Co op Urban Bank Limited	24 November 2011
Bhavasar Kshatriya Co-operative Bank Ltd	24 November 2011
Bhavnagar Mahila Nagarik Sahakari Bank Ltd	24 November 2011
Bhawanipatna Central Co-operative Bank Ltd	24 November 2011
Bhilai Nagarik Sahakari Bank	24 November 2011
Bhilwara Central Co-operative Bank Ltd	24 November 2011
Bhilwara Mahila Urban Co-op. Bank Ltd	24 November 2011
Bhilwara Urban Co op Bank Limited	24 November 2011
Bhimashankar Nagari Sahakari Bank Ltd	24 November 2011
Bhimavaram Co-op Urban Bank Limited	24 November 2011
Bhind Nagarik Sahakari Bank	24 November 2011
Bhinger Urban Co-operative Bank Limited	24 November 2011

Bhiwani Central Co-operative Bank Ltd	24 November 2011
Bhopal District Central Co-operative Bank Ltd	24 November 2011
Bhopal Nagarik Sahakari Bank Limited	24 November 2011
Bhuj Commercial Co op Bank Ltd	24 November 2011
Bhuj Mercantile Co-operative Bank Ltd	24 November 2011
Bhupathiraju Co op Credit Bank Limited	24 November 2011
Bhusawal People's Co-op. Bank Ltd	24 November 2011
Bicholim Urban Co-operative Bank Limited	24 November 2011
Bidar District Central Co-operative Bank Ltd	24 November 2011
Bidar Mahila Urban Co-operative Bank Ltd,	24 November 2011
Big Kancheepuram Co op Town Bank Limited	24 November 2011
Bihar Kshetriya Gramin Bank	24 November 2011
Bijapur District Central Co-operative Bank Ltd	24 November 2011
Bijapur District Mahila Co-operative Bank Ltd	24 November 2011
Bijapur Mahalaxmi Urban Co-operative Bank Ltd	24 November 2011
Bijapur Sahakari Bank	24 November 2011
Bijapur Zilla Sarkari Naukarara Sahakari Bank	24 November 2011
Bijnor Jilla Sahakari Bank Ltd	24 November 2011
Bijnor Urban Co-operative Bank Ltd	24 November 2011
Bikaner Central Co-operative Bank Ltd	24 November 2011
Bilagi Pattan Sahakari Bank	24 November 2011
Birbhum District Central Co-operative Bank Ltd	24 November 2011
Birdeo Sahakari Bank Ltd	24 November 2011
Bodeli Urban Co op Bank Ltd	24 November 2011
Bombay Mercantile Co-operative Bank Limited	24 November 2011
Borsad Nagarik Sahakari Bank Ltd	24 November 2011
Botad Peoples Co-Operative Bank Ltd	24 November 2011
Boudh Central Co-operative Bank Ltd	24 November 2011
Brahmadeodada Mane Sahakari Bank Ltd	24 November 2011
Brahmawart Commercial Co-operative Bank Ltd	24 November 2011
Bramhapuri Urban Co-operative Bank Ltd	24 November 2011
Broach District Central Co-operative Bank Ltd	24 November 2011
Budaun Zilla Sahakari Bank Ltd	24 November 2011
Budge-Budge Nangi Co-operative Bank Ltd	24 November 2011
Buldhana District Central Co-operative Bank Ltd	24 November 2011
Bundi Central Co-operative Bank Ltd	24 November 2011

Bundi Urban Co op Bank Limited	24 November 2011
Burdwan Central Co-operative Bank Ltd	24 November 2011
Business Co-operative Bank	24 November 2011
Calicut Co-operative Urban Bank Ltd	24 November 2011
Cannanore Co-operative Urban Bank Ltd	24 November 2011
Cardamom Merchants Co-operative Bank Ltd	24 November 2011
Catholic Co-Operative Urban Bank Ltd	24 November 2011
Cauvery Kalpatharu Grameena Bank	24 November 2011
Chaitanya Co-Operative Urban Bank Ltd	24 November 2011
Chaitanya Godavari Grameena Bank	24 November 2011
Chaitanya Mahila Sahakari Bank Ltd	24 November 2011
Chamba Urban Coop. Bank Ltd	24 November 2011
Chamoli Zilla Sahakari Bank Ltd	24 November 2011
Chanasma Commercial Coop. Bank Ltd	24 November 2011
Chanasma Nagrik Sahakari Bank Ltd	24 November 2011
Chandgad Urban Coop. Bank Ltd	24 November 2011
Chandrapur District Central Co-operative Bank Ltd	24 November 2011
Chandraseniya Kayastha Prabhu Coop Bank Ltd	24 November 2011
Chandwad Merchant's Coop. Bank Ltd	24 November 2011
Changanacherry Co-operative Urban Bank Ltd	24 November 2011
Charda Nagrik Sahakari Bank Ltd	24 November 2011
Charminar Co-operative Urban Bank Ltd	24 November 2011
Chartered Sahakari Bank	24 November 2011
Chatrapur Coop. Bank Ltd	24 November 2011
Chembur Nagarik Sahakari Bank Ltd	24 November 2011
Chengalpattu Coop. Urban Bank Ltd	24 November 2011
Chennai Central Co-operative Bank Ltd	24 November 2011
Chennai Port Trust Employees Co-Op Bank Ltd	24 November 2011
Chennimalai Co-operative Urban Bank Ltd	24 November 2011
Cherpalcheri Co-operative Urban Bank Ltd	24 November 2011
Chhapi Nagrik Sahakari Bank Ltd	24 November 2011
Chhattisgarh Gramin Bank	24 November 2011
Chhopda Urban Co-operative Bank	24 November 2011
Chidambaram Coop. Urban Bank Ltd	24 November 2011
Chidambaranar District Central Co-operative Bank Ltd	24 November 2011
Chikmagalur District Central Co-operative Bank Ltd	24 November 2011

Chikmagalur Jilla Mahila Sahakara Bank	24 November 2011
Chikmagalur Pattana Sahakara Bank	24 November 2011
Chikmagalur-Kodagu Grameena Bank	24 November 2011
Chiplun Urban Coop. Bank Ltd	24 November 2011
Chitradurg District Central Co-operative Bank Ltd	24 November 2011
Chittoor Co-operative Town Bank Ltd	24 November 2011
Chittoor District Co-operative Bank Ltd	24 November 2011
Chittorgarh Central Co-operative Bank Ltd	24 November 2011
Chittorgarh Urban Co-operative Bank Ltd	24 November 2011
Chopda People's Urban Coop. Bank Ltd	24 November 2011
Choudeshwari Sahakari Bank Ltd	24 November 2011
Churu Central Co-operative Bank Ltd	24 November 2011
Churu Zilla Urban Coop. Bank Ltd	24 November 2011
Citizen Coop Bank Limited	24 November 2011
Citizen Co-op. Bank Ltd	24 November 2011
Citizen Co-operative Bank Ltd	24 November 2011
Citizen Credit Co-operative Bank Ltd	24 November 2011
Citizen Urban Co op Bank Limited	24 November 2011
Citizens' Urban Co-operative Bank Ltd	24 November 2011
City Co-operative Bank	24 November 2011
Coastal Urban Co-operative Bank Ltd	24 November 2011
Coimbatore City Coop. Bank Ltd	24 November 2011
Coimbatore District Central Co-opertive Bank Ltd	24 November 2011
Col R D Nikam Sainik Sahakari Bank Ltd	24 November 2011
Colour Merchants' Coop Bank Ltd	24 November 2011
Commercial Cooperative Bank Ltd	24 November 2011
Commercial Co-operative Bank Ltd	24 November 2011
Comptroller's Office Co-operative Bank Ltd	24 November 2011
Contai Co-operative Bank Ltd	24 November 2011
Coonoor Cooperative Urban Bank Ltd	24 November 2011
Coop. Bank Of Baroda Ltd	24 November 2011
Coop. Bank Of Rajkot Ltd	24 November 2011
Co-operative bank of Mehsana Ltd	24 November 2011
Cooperative City Bank Ltd	24 November 2011
Cooperative Urban Bank Ltd	24 November 2011
Cordite Factory Coop. Bank Ltd	24 November 2011

Cosmos Co-operative Urban Bank Ltd	24 November 2011
Cuddalore & Villipuram DCCB Employees Co-Op	24 November 2011
Cuddalore District Central Co-operative Bank Ltd	24 November 2011
Cuddapah District Central Co-operative Bank Ltd	24 November 2011
Cumbum Coop. Town Bank Ltd	24 November 2011
Cuttack United Central Co-operative Bank Ltd	24 November 2011
D Y Patil Sahakari Bank Ltd	24 November 2011
Dadasaheb Gajmal Co-op. Bank Ltd	24 November 2011
Dadasaheb Ramrao Patil Co-op. Bank Ltd	24 November 2011
Dahanu Road Janata Co-op. Bank Ltd	24 November 2011
Dahod Mercantile Co-op. Bank Ltd	24 November 2011
Dahod Urban Co-op. Bank Ltd	24 November 2011
Daivadnya Sahakara Bank	24 November 2011
Dakor Nagrik Sahakari Bank Ltd	24 November 2011
Dakshin Dinajpur (Balurghat) District Central Co-op. Bank Ltd	24 November 2011
Dakshina Kannada Jilla Mahila Co-operative Ban	24 November 2011
Dalmiapuram Empl.s' Co-op. Bank Ltd	24 November 2011
Dapoli Urban Co-op. Bank Ltd	24 November 2011
Darjeeling District Central Co-operative Bank Ltd	24 November 2011
Darus Salam Coop. Urban Bank Ltd	24 November 2011
Dattatraya Maharaj Kalambi Jaoli Sahakari Bank	24 November 2011
Daund Urban Co-Operative Bank Ltd	24 November 2011
Dausa Central Co-operative Bank Ltd	24 November 2011
Dausa Urban Co-Operative Bank Ltd	24 November 2011
Davangere Central Co-operative Bank Ltd	24 November 2011
Davangere Urban Co-operative Bank Ltd	24 November 2011
Davangere-Harihar Urban Sahakara Bank	24 November 2011
Dayalbagh Mahila Co-operative Bank Ltd	24 November 2011
Deccan Co-Operative Urban Bank Ltd	24 November 2011
Deccan Grameena Bank	24 November 2011
Deccan Merchants Co-op. Bank Ltd	24 November 2011
Deendayal Nagari Sahakari Bank Ltd	24 November 2011
Deepak Sahakari Bank Ltd	24 November 2011
Defence Accounts Co-operative Bank Ltd	24 November 2011
Dehradun District Central Co-operative Bank Ltd	24 November 2011
Delhi Nagrik Sehkari Bank Ltd	24 November 2011

Dena Gujarat Gramin Bank	24 November 2011
Deoghar Jamtara District Co-operative Central Bank Ltd	24 November 2011
Deogiri Nagari Sahakari Bank Ltd	24 November 2011
Deola Merchants' Coop Bank Ltd	24 November 2011
Deoria Kasia District Central Co-operative Bank Ltd	24 November 2011
Desaiganj Nagari Co-operative Bank	24 November 2011
Development Co-operative Bank Ltd	24 November 2011
Devgad Urban Co-op. Bank Ltd	24 November 2011
Devi Gayatri Co-operative Urban Bank Ltd	24 November 2011
Devyani Co-operative Bank Ltd	24 November 2011
Dhakuria Co-operative Bank Ltd	24 November 2011
Dhanashree Urban Co-operative Bank Ltd	24 November 2011
Dhanbad District Central Co-operative Bank Ltd	24 November 2011
Dhanera Mercantile Co-Operative Bank Ltd	24 November 2011
Dharampuri District Central Co-operative Bank Ltd	24 November 2011
Dharamvir Sambhaji Urban Co-operative Bank Ltd	24 November 2011
Dharapuram Coop Urban Bank Limited	24 November 2011
Dharmaj Peoples' Co-op. Bank Ltd	24 November 2011
Dharmapuri Co-op. Town Bank Ltd	24 November 2011
Dharmavaram Co-op. Town Bank Ltd	24 November 2011
Dhinoj Nagrik Sahakari Bank Ltd	24 November 2011
Dholpur Urban Co-op. Bank Ltd	24 November 2011
Dhrangadhra Peoples' Co-op. Bank Ltd	24 November 2011
Dhule and Nandurbar Jilha Sarkari Nokaranchi	24 November 2011
Dhule Vikas Sahakari Bank Ltd	24 November 2011
Dhulia District Central Co-operative Bank Ltd	24 November 2011
Dilip Urban Co-operative Bank Ltd	24 November 2011
Dindigul Central Co-operative Bank Ltd	24 November 2011
Dindigul Urban Coop Bank Ltd	24 November 2011
District Central Co-operative Bank Ltd, Bulandshahar	24 November 2011
District Co-operative Bank Ltd, Sitapur	24 November 2011
Dombivli Nagari Sahakari Bank Ltd	24 November 2011
Dr. Annasahab Chaugule Co-op. Bank Ltd	24 November 2011
Dr. Babasaheb Ambedkar Nagari Sahakari Bank	24 November 2011
Dr. Babasaheb Ambedkar Sahakari Bank Ltd	24 November 2011
Dr. Babasaheb Ambedkar Urban Co-operativeBank	24 November 2011

Dr. Jaiprakash Mundada Urban Co-operative Bank	24 November 2011
Dr. Shivajirao Patil Nilangekar Urban Co-operative	24 November 2011
Dumka District Co-operative Central Bank Ltd	24 November 2011
Dungarpur Central Co-operative Bank Ltd	24 November 2011
Durga Co-op. Urban Bank Ltd	24 November 2011
Durgapur Mahila Co-Operative Bank Ltd	24 November 2011
Durgapur Steel Peoples' Co-operative Bank Ltd	24 November 2011
Durg-Rajnandgaon Gramin Bank	24 November 2011
Dwarakadas Mantri Nagari Sahakari Bk. Ltd	24 November 2011
Eastern & North East Frontier Railway Co-operative	24 November 2011
Eenadu Co-Operative Urban bank Ltd	24 November 2011
Ellaquai Dehati Bank	24 November 2011
Eluri Co-operative Urban Bank Ltd	24 November 2011
Eluru Co-op. Urban Bank Ltd	24 November 2011
Eluru District Central Co-operative Bank Ltd	24 November 2011
Ernakulam District Co-operative Central Bank Ltd	24 November 2011
Erode Co-operative Urban Bank Ltd	24 November 2011
Erode District Central Co-operative Bank Ltd	24 November 2011
Etah District Co-operative Bank Ltd	24 November 2011
Etah Urban Co-operative Urban Bank Ltd	24 November 2011
Etawah Urban Co-operative Bank Ltd	24 November 2011
Etawah Zilla Sahakari Bank Ltd	24 November 2011
Excellent Co-operative Bank Ltd	24 November 2011
Faiz Mercantile Co-operative Bank Ltd	24 November 2011
Faizabad co-operative District Bank Ltd	24 November 2011
Faridabad Central Co-operative Bank Ltd	24 November 2011
Faridcot Central Co-operative Bank Ltd	24 November 2011
Farrukhabad District Central Co-operative Bank Ltd	24 November 2011
Fatehabad Central Co-operative Bank Ltd	24 November 2011
Fatehgarh Sahib Central Co-operative Bank Ltd, Sirhind	24 November 2011
Fathehpur District Central Co-operative Bank Ltd	24 November 2011
Fazilka Central Co-operative Bank Ltd	24 November 2011
Feroke Co-operative Urban Bank Ltd	24 November 2011
Ferozepur Central Co-operative Bank Ltd	24 November 2011
Financial Co-Operative Bank Ltd	24 November 2011
Gadchiroli District Central Co-operative Bank Ltd	24 November 2011

Gadhinglaj Urban Co op Bank Limited	24 November 2011
Gandevi People's Co op Bank Limited	24 November 2011
Gandhi Coop Urban Bank Ltd	24 November 2011
Gandhi Gunj Co-operative Bank Ltd	24 November 2011
Gandhibag Sahakari Bank Ltd	24 November 2011
Gandhidham Co op Bank Limited	24 November 2011
Gandhidham Mercantile Co-op. Bk. Ltd	24 November 2011
Gandhinagar Nagarik Co op Bank Limited	24 November 2011
Gandhinagar Urban Co-operative Bank Ltd	24 November 2011
Ganesh Sahakari Bank Ltd	24 November 2011
Ganga Mercantile Urban Co-operative Bank Ltd	24 November 2011
Ganganagar Kendriya Sahakari Bank Ltd	24 November 2011
Ganraj Nagri Sahakari Bank Ltd	24 November 2011
Gauhati Co-op. Urban Bank Ltd	24 November 2011
Gautam Sahakari Bank Ltd	24 November 2011
Gayatri Co-operative Urban Bank Ltd	24 November 2011
George Town Co op Bank Limited	24 November 2011
Ghaziabad District Central Co-operative Bank Ltd	24 November 2011
Ghaziabad Urban Co-operative Bank Ltd	24 November 2011
Ghazipur District Co-operative Bank Ltd	24 November 2011
Ghazipur Urban Co-operative Bank Ltd	24 November 2011
Ghoghamba Vibhag Nagarik Sahakari Bank Limite	24 November 2011
Ghoti Marchants Co-op. Bank Ltd	24 November 2011
Giridh District Central Co-operative Bank Ltd	24 November 2011
Goa Urban Co-operative Bank Limited	24 November 2011
Gobichettipalyam Co op Urban Bank Limited	24 November 2011
Godavari Laxmi Co-op. Bank Ltd	24 November 2011
Godavari Urban Co-op. Bank Ltd	24 November 2011
Godhra City Co op Bank Limited	24 November 2011
Godhra Urban Co op Bank Limited	24 November 2011
Gokak Urban Co-operative Credit Bank Ltd	24 November 2011
Gokul Co-operative Urban Bank Ltd	24 November 2011
Gomthi Nagariya Sahkari Bank Ltd	24 November 2011
Gondal Nagarik Sahakari Bank Limited	24 November 2011
Gondia District Central Co-operative Bank Ltd	24 November 2011
Gooty Coop Town Bank Ltd	24 November 2011

Gopalganj District Central Co-operative Bank Ltd	24 November 2011
Gopinath Patil Parsik Janata Sahakari Bank Ltd	24 November 2011
Gorakhpur Zilla Sahakari Bank Ltd	24 November 2011
Government Employees Co-operative Bank Ltd,	24 November 2011
Gozaria Nagrik Sahakari Bank Ltd	24 November 2011
Graduates' Co-operative Bank Ltd	24 November 2011
Grain Merchants' Co-operative Bank Ltd	24 November 2011
Greater Bombay Co-operative Bank Limited	24 November 2011
Guardian Souharda Sahakari Bank	24 November 2011
Gudiwada Co-op. Urban bank Ltd	24 November 2011
Gudiyattam Co-Operative Urban Bank Ltd	24 November 2011
Gujarat Ambuja Co-operative Bank Ltd	24 November 2011
Gujarat Mercantile Co-Operative Bank Ltd	24 November 2011
Gulbarga District Central Co-operative Bank Ltd	24 November 2011
Gulshan Mercantile Urban Co-operative Bank Ltd	24 November 2011
Gumla Simdga District Central Co-operative Bank Ltd	24 November 2011
Guna District Central Co-operative Bank Ltd	24 November 2011
Guntur Coop Urban Bank Ltd	24 November 2011
Guntur District Co-operative Bank Ltd	24 November 2011
Guntur Women Co-op Urban Bank Ltd	24 November 2011
Gurdaspur Central Co-operative Bank Ltd	24 November 2011
Gurgaon Central Co-operative Bank Ltd	24 November 2011
Gurgaon Gramin Bank	24 November 2011
Guruvayur Co-operative Urban Bank Ltd	24 November 2011
Hadgali Urban Co-operative Bank Ltd	24 November 2011
Hadoti Kshetriya Gramin Bank	24 November 2011
Halol Mercantile Coop Bank Limited	24 November 2011
Halol Urban Coop Bank Limited	24 November 2011
Hamirpur District Co-operative Bank Ltd	24 November 2011
Hanamasagar Urban Co-operative Bank Ltd	24 November 2011
Hangal Urban Co-operative Bank Ltd	24 November 2011
Hansot Nagrik Sahakari Bank Limited	24 November 2011
Hanumanthanagar Co-operative Bank Ltd	24 November 2011
Hardoi District Co-operative Bank Ltd	24 November 2011
Hardoi Urban Co-operative Bank Ltd	24 November 2011
Harihareshwar Sahakari Bank Ltd	24 November 2011

Harij Nagrik Sahakari Bank Ltd	24 November 2011
Haryana Gramin Bank	24 November 2011
Hassan District Central Co-operative Bank Ltd	24 November 2011
Hasti Co-operative Bank Ltd	24 November 2011
Haveli Sahakari Bank Maryadit.	24 November 2011
Haveri Urban Co-operative Bank Limited	24 November 2011
Hazaribagh District Central Co-operative Bank Ltd	24 November 2011
Himachal Gramin Bank	24 November 2011
Himatnagar Nagrik Sahakari Bank Limited	24 November 2011
Hindu Co-operative Bank Ltd	24 November 2011
Hindustan Coop Bank Limited	24 November 2011
Hindustan Co-operative Bank Ltd	24 November 2011
Hindustan Shipyard Staff Coop. Bank Ltd	24 November 2011
Hira Sugar Employees' Co-operative Bank Ltd	24 November 2011
Hiriyur Urban Co-operative Bank Ltd	24 November 2011
Hissar District Central Co-operative Bank Ltd	24 November 2011
Hissar Urban Coop Bank Limited	24 November 2011
Honavar Urban Co-operative Bank Ltd	24 November 2011
Hoogly District Central Co-operative Bank Ltd	24 November 2011
Hoshiarpur Central Co-operative Bank Ltd	24 November 2011
Hospet Co-operative City Bank Ltd	24 November 2011
Hotel Industrialists Co-operative Bank Ltd	24 November 2011
Howrah District Central Co-operative Bank Ltd	24 November 2011
Hubli Urban Co-operative Bank Limited	24 November 2011
Hukeri Urban Co-operative Bank Ltd	24 November 2011
Hutatma Sahakari Bank Ltd	24 November 2011
Hyderabad District Central Co-operative Bank Ltd	24 November 2011
Ichalkaranji Merchants Co-op Bank Ltd	24 November 2011
Idar Nagrik Sahakari Bank Ltd	24 November 2011
Idukki District Co-operative Central Bank Ltd	24 November 2011
Ilayangudi Coop Urban Bank Ltd	24 November 2011
Ilkal Co-operative Bank Ltd	24 November 2011
Imperial Urban Co-operative Bank Ltd	24 November 2011
Imperial Urban Cooperative Bank Ltd	24 November 2011
Imphal Urban Coop Bank Ltd	24 November 2011
Income Tax Department Co-operative Bank Ltd	24 November 2011

Indapur Urban Co-operative Bank Ltd	24 November 2011
Independence Co-operative Bank Ltd	24 November 2011
Indian Mercantile Co-operative Bank Ltd	24 November 2011
Indira Mahila Nagari Sahakari Bank Ltd	24 November 2011
Indira Mahila Sahakari Bank Ltd	24 November 2011
Indore Premier Co-operative Bank Ltd	24 November 2011
Indraprastha Sehkari Bank Limited	24 November 2011
Indrayani Co-operative Bank Ltd	24 November 2011
Industrial Cooperative Bank Ltd	24 November 2011
Innespeta Coop urban Bank Ltd	24 November 2011
Innovative Co-operative Urban Bank Ltd	24 November 2011
Integral Urban co-operative Bank Ltd	24 November 2011
Irinjalakuda Town Co-Operative Bank Ltd	24 November 2011
Islampur Urban Cooperative Bank Ltd	24 November 2011
J&K Grameen Bank	24 November 2011
Jagruti Co-operative Bank Ltd	24 November 2011
Jagruti Co-operative Urban Bank Ltd	24 November 2011
Jai Bhawani Sahakari Bank Ltd	24 November 2011
Jai Hind Urban Co-operative Bank Ltd	24 November 2011
Jai Kalimata Mahila Urban Co-Operative Bank Ltd	24 November 2011
Jain Co-operative Bank Ltd	24 November 2011
Jain Sahakari Bank Ltd	24 November 2011
Jaipur Central Co-operative Bank Ltd	24 November 2011
Jaipur Thar Gramin Bank	24 November 2011
Jaisalmer Central Co-operative Bank Ltd	24 November 2011
Jalana District Central Co-operative Bank Ltd	24 November 2011
Jalaun District Co-operative Bank Ltd	24 November 2011
Jalgaon District Central Co-operative Bank Ltd	24 November 2011
Jalgaon Janata Sahakari Bank Ltd	24 November 2011
Jalgaon Merchants' Sahakari Bank Ltd	24 November 2011
Jalgaon People's Co-operative Bank Ltd	24 November 2011
Jalna Merchants Co-operative Bank Ltd	24 November 2011
Jalore Central Co-operative Bank Ltd	24 November 2011
Jalore Nagarik Sahakari Bank Ltd	24 November 2011
Jalpaiguri Central Co-operative Bank Ltd	24 November 2011
Jamia Co-operative Bank Ltd	24 November 2011

Jamkhandi Urban Co-operative Bank Ltd	24 November 2011
Jamkhed Merchants Co-operative Bank Ltd	24 November 2011
Jammu Central Co-operative Bank Ltd	24 November 2011
Jamnagar District Central Co-operative Bank Ltd	24 November 2011
Jamnagar mahila Sahakari Bank Ltd	24 November 2011
Jamnagar People's Coop Bank Ltd	24 November 2011
Jampeta Co-operative Urban Bank Ltd	24 November 2011
Janakalyan Co-Operative Bank Ltd	24 November 2011
Janakalyan Sahakari Bank Ltd	24 November 2011
Janalaxmi Co-operative Bank Ltd	24 November 2011
Janaseva Sahakari (Borivli) Bank Ltd	24 November 2011
Janaseva Sahakari Bank Ltd	24 November 2011
Janata Coop. Bank Ltd	24 November 2011
Janata Coop. Bank Ltd Godhra	24 November 2011
Janata Sahakari Bank Limited	24 November 2011
Janata Sahakari Bank Limited	24 November 2011
Janata Sahakari Bank Ltd	24 November 2011
Janata Sahakari Bank Ltd	24 November 2011
Janata Urban Co-operative Bank Ltd	24 November 2011
Janatha Seva Co-operative Bank Ltd	24 November 2011
Jankalyan Urban Co-operative Bank Ltd	24 November 2011
Janseva Co-operative Bank Ltd	24 November 2011
Janseva Nagari Sahakari Bank	24 November 2011
Jansewa Urban Co-operative Bank Ltd	24 November 2011
Jath Urban Coop Bank Ltd	24 November 2011
Jaunpur Zilla Sahakari Bank Ltd	24 November 2011
Jawahar Sahakari Bank Ltd	24 November 2011
Jawahar Urban Coop Bank Ltd	24 November 2011
Jay Tuljabhavani Urban Co-operative Bank Ltd	24 November 2011
Jayprakash Narayan Nagari Sahakari Bank Ltd	24 November 2011
Jaysingpur Udgaon Sahakari Bank Ltd	24 November 2011
Jeypore coop Urban Bank Ltd	24 November 2011
Jhabua Dhar Kshetriya Gramin Bank	24 November 2011
Jhajjar Central Co-operative Bank Ltd	24 November 2011
Jhalawar Central Co-operative Bank Ltd	24 November 2011
Jhalawar Nagarik Sahakari Bank Ltd	24 November 2011

Jhalod Urban Coop Bank Ltd	24 November 2011
Jharkhand Gramin Bank	24 November 2011
Jhunjhunu Central Co-operative Bank Ltd	24 November 2011
Jijamata Mahila Nagri Sahakari Bank Ltd	24 November 2011
Jijamata Mahila Sahakari Bank Ltd	24 November 2011
Jijau Commercial Co-operative Bank Ltd	24 November 2011
Jilla Sahakari Kendriya Bank Maryadit	24 November 2011
Jind Central Co-operative Bank Ltd	24 November 2011
Jivan Commercial Coop Bank Ltd	24 November 2011
Jivhaji Sahakari Bank Ltd	24 November 2011
Jodhpur Central Co-operative Bank Ltd	24 November 2011
Jodhpur Nagarik Sahakari Bank Ltd	24 November 2011
Jolarpet Coop Urban Bank Ltd	24 November 2011
Jowai Co-Operative Urban Bank Ltd	24 November 2011
Jubilee Hills Mercantile Co-Operative Urban Bank	24 November 2011
Jugalkishor Tapdia - Shri Mahesh Urban Co-opera	24 November 2011
Jullunder Central Co-operative Bank Ltd	24 November 2011
Junagadh Commercial Coop Bank Ltd	24 November 2011
Junagadh District Central Co-operative Bank Ltd	24 November 2011
Kachchh District Central Co-operative Bank Ltd	24 November 2011
Kaduthuruthy Urban Co-operative Bank Ltd	24 November 2011
Kagal Co-op. Bank Ltd	24 November 2011
Kaira District Central Co-operative Bank Ltd	24 November 2011
Kaithal Central Co-operative Bank Ltd	24 November 2011
Kakatiya Co-operative Urban Bank Ltd	24 November 2011
Kakinada Co-op. Town Bank Ltd	24 November 2011
Kakinada Co-operative Central Bank Ltd	24 November 2011
Kalghatgi Urban Co-operative Bank Ltd	24 November 2011
Kalinga Gramya Bank	24 November 2011
Kallappanna Awade Ichalkaranji Janata Sahakari Bank Ltd	24 November 2011
Kallidaikurichi Coop Urban Bank Limited	24 November 2011
Kalol Nagarik Sahakari Bank Ltd	24 November 2011
Kalol Urban Co-op. Bank Ltd	24 November 2011
Kalpavruksha Co-operative Bank Ltd	24 November 2011
Kalupur Commercial Coop. Bank Ltd	24 November 2011
Kalwan Marchants' Co-op. Bank Ltd	24 November 2011

Kalyan Cooperative Bank Ltd	24 November 2011
Kalyan Janata Sahakari Bank Ltd	24 November 2011
Kalyansagar Urban Co-operative Bank Ltd	24 November 2011
Kamala Co-operative Bank Ltd	24 November 2011
Kamaraj Coop Town Bank Ltd	24 November 2011
Kamuthi Coop Urban Bank Ltd	24 November 2011
Kanaka Mahalakshmi Co-operative Bank Ltd	24 November 2011
Kanaka Pattana Sahakara Bank	24 November 2011
Kanara District Central Co-operative Bank Ltd	24 November 2011
Kancheepuram Central co-operative Bank Ltd	24 November 2011
Kangra Central Co-operative Bank Ltd	24 November 2011
Kankaria Maninagar Nagarik Sahakari Bank Ltd	24 November 2011
Kannur (Cannanore) District Cooperative Central Bank Ltd	24 November 2011
Kanpur Zilla Sahakari Bank Ltd	24 November 2011
Kanyakumari District Central Co-operative Bank Ltd	24 November 2011
Kapadwanj Peoples' Co-op. Bank Ltd	24 November 2011
Kapurthala Central Co-operative Bank Ltd	24 November 2011
Karad Janata Sahakari Bank Ltd	24 November 2011
Karad Urban Co-operative Bank Ltd	24 November 2011
Karaikudi Coop. Town Bank Ltd	24 November 2011
Karamana Co-operative Urban Bank Ltd	24 November 2011
Karan Urban Cooperative Bank Ltd	24 November 2011
Karimnagar Coop. Urban Bank Ltd	24 November 2011
Karimnagar District co-operative Bank Ltd	24 November 2011
Karjan Nagarik Sahakari Bank Ltd	24 November 2011
Karmala Urban Co-op. Bank Ltd	24 November 2011
Karnal Central Co-operative Bank Ltd	24 November 2011
Karnala Nagari Sahakari Bank Ltd	24 November 2011
Karnataka Central Co-operative Bank Ltd	24 November 2011
Karnataka Co-operative Bank Ltd	24 November 2011
Karnataka Rajya Kaigarika Vanijya Sahakara Bank	24 November 2011
Karnataka Vikas Grameena Bank	24 November 2011
Karnavathi Co-operative Bank Ltd	24 November 2011
Karunagapalli Taluk Urban Co-operative Bank Ltd	24 November 2011
Karuntattankudi Dravidian Coop Bank Ltd	24 November 2011
Karur Town Coop. Bank Ltd	24 November 2011

Karwar Urban Co-operative Bank Ltd	24 November 2011
Kasaragod District Co-operative Central Bank Ltd	24 November 2011
Kasargod Co-operative Town Bank Ltd	24 November 2011
Kashi Gomti Samyut Gramin Bank	24 November 2011
Kashipur Urban Co-opeerative Bank Ltd	24 November 2011
Kasundia Co-operative Bank Ltd	24 November 2011
Katihar District Central Co-operative Bank Ltd	24 November 2011
Kattappana Urban Co-operative Bank Ltd	24 November 2011
Kaujalgi Urban Co-operative Bank Ltd	24 November 2011
Kaveripatnam Coop Town Bank Ltd	24 November 2011
Kavita Urban Co-Operative Bank Ltd	24 November 2011
Kedarnath Urban Co-operative Bank Ltd	24 November 2011
Kempegowda Pattana Souharda Sahakara Bank	24 November 2011
Kendrapara Urban Coop Bank Ltd	24 November 2011
Keonjhar Central Co-operative Bank Ltd	24 November 2011
Kerala Mercantile Co-operative Bank Ltd	24 November 2011
Khagaria District Central Co-operative Bank Ltd	24 November 2011
Khalilabad Nagar Sahkari Bank Ltd	24 November 2011
Khambhat Nagrik Sahakari Bank Ltd	24 November 2011
Khammam District Co-operative Central Bank Ltd	24 November 2011
Khanapur Co-operative Bank Ltd	24 November 2011
Khardah Co-operative Bank Ltd	24 November 2011
Kheda Peoples' Co-op. Bank Ltd	24 November 2011
Khedbrahma Nagrik Sahakari Bank Ltd	24 November 2011
Kheralu Nagarik Sahakari Bank Ltd	24 November 2011
Khurda Central Co-operative Bank Ltd	24 November 2011
Kisan Nagri Sahakari Bank	24 November 2011
Kittur Channamma Mahila Sahakari Bank	24 November 2011
Kodagu District Central Co-operative Bank Ltd	24 November 2011
Kodagu Zilla Mahila Sahakara Bank	24 November 2011
Kodaikanal Coop. Urban Bank Ltd	24 November 2011
Kodinar Nagarik Sahakari Bank Ltd	24 November 2011
Kodinar Taluka Co-operative Banking Union Ltd	24 November 2011
Kodoli Urban Co-op. Bank Ltd	24 November 2011
Kodungallur Town Co-operative Urban Bank Ltd	24 November 2011
Kohinoor Sahakari Bank Ltd	24 November 2011

Koilkuntla Co-Operative Town Bank Ltd	24 November 2011
Kokan Mercantile Co-op. Bank Ltd	24 November 2011
Kokan Prant Sahakari Bank Ltd	24 November 2011
Kolar District Central Co-opertive Bank Ltd	24 November 2011
Kolhapur District Central Co-operative Bank Ltd	24 November 2011
Kolhapur Mahila Sahakari Bank Ltd	24 November 2011
Kolhapur Urban Co-op. Bank Ltd	24 November 2011
Kolikata Mahila Co-Operative Bank Ltd	24 November 2011
Kolkata Police Co-operative Bank Ltd	24 November 2011
Kollam District Co-operative Central Bank Ltd	24 November 2011
Konark Urban Co-operative Bank Ltd	24 November 2011
Konnagar Samabaya Bank Ltd	24 November 2011
Konoklota Mahila Urban Co-operative Bank Ltd	24 November 2011
Kopargaon Peoples' Co-operative Bank Ltd	24 November 2011
Koraput Central Co-operative Bank Ltd	24 November 2011
Kosamba Mercantile Co-op. Bank Ltd	24 November 2011
Kota Central Co-operative Bank Ltd	24 November 2011
Kota Mahila Nagarik Sahakari Bank Ltd	24 November 2011
Kota Nagarik Sahakari Bank Ltd	24 November 2011
Koteshwara Sahakari Bank	24 November 2011
Kottakal Co-operative Urban Bank Ltd	24 November 2011
Kottayam Co-operative Urban Bank Ltd	24 November 2011
Kottayam District Co-operative Central Bank Ltd	24 November 2011
Kovilpatti Co-operative Bank Ltd	24 November 2011
Kovvur Coop. Urban Bank Ltd	24 November 2011
Koyana Sahakari Bank Ltd	24 November 2011
Kozhikode District Co-operative Central Bank Ltd	24 November 2011
Kranti Co-Operative Urban Bank Ltd	24 November 2011
Krishna District Co-operative Central Bank Ltd	24 November 2011
Krishna Grameena Bank	24 November 2011
Krishna Pattana Sahakar Bank	24 November 2011
Krishna Urban Co-operative Bank Ltd	24 November 2011
Krishna Valley Co-operative Bank Ltd	24 November 2011
Krishnagiri Urban Coop. Bank Ltd	24 November 2011
Krushiseva Urban Co-operative Bank Ltd	24 November 2011
Kshetriya Kisan Gramin Bank	24 November 2011

Kukarwada Nagrik Sahakari Bank Ltd	24 November 2011
Kulitalai Coop Urban Bank Limited	24 November 2011
Kumbakonam Central Co-operative Bank Ltd	24 November 2011
Kumbakonam Coop. Urban Bank Ltd	24 November 2011
Kumbhi Kasari Sahakari Bank Ltd	24 November 2011
Kumta Urban Co-operative Bank Ltd	24 November 2011
Kunbi Sahakari Bank Ltd	24 November 2011
Kuppam Coop.Town Bank Ltd	24 November 2011
Kurla Nagrik Sahakari Bank Ltd	24 November 2011
Kurmanchal Nagar Sahkari Bank Ltd	24 November 2011
Kurnool District Central co-operative Bank Ltd	24 November 2011
Kurukshetra Central Co-operative Bank Ltd	24 November 2011
Kurukshetra Urban Co-op. Bank Ltd	24 November 2011
Kushtagi Pattana Sahakari Bank	24 November 2011
Kutch Co-operative Bank Ltd	24 November 2011
Kutch Mercantile Co-operative Bank Ltd	24 November 2011
Kuttiady Co-operative Urban Bank Ltd	24 November 2011
L.I.C. of India Staff Co-operative Bank Ltd	24 November 2011
L.I.C.Employees' Coop Bank Ltd	24 November 2011
Lakhimpur-Kheri District Co-operative Bank Ltd	24 November 2011
Lakhvad Nagrik Sahakari Bank Limited	24 November 2011
Lala Urban Coop Bank Limited	24 November 2011
Lalbaug Co-Operative Bank Ltd	24 November 2011
Lalgudi Coop Urban Bank Limited	24 November 2011
Lalitpur District Central Co-operative Bank Ltd	24 November 2011
Langpi Dehangi Rural Bank	24 November 2011
Lasalgaon Merchant's Coop. Bank Ltd	24 November 2011
Latur District Central Co-operative Bank Ltd	24 November 2011
Laxmi Co-operative Bank Ltd	24 November 2011
Laxmi Co-operative Bank Ltd,	24 November 2011
Laxmi Urban Co-operative Bank Ltd	24 November 2011
Laxmi Vishnu Sahakari Bank Ltd	24 November 2011
Liberal Co-operative Bank Ltd	24 November 2011
Liluah Co-operative Bank Limited	24 November 2011
Limbasi Urban Coop Bank Limited	24 November 2011
Limdi Urban Coop Bank Limited	24 November 2011

Little Kancheepuram Coop Urban Bank Limited	24 November 2011
Lokapavani Mahila Sahakari Bank	24 November 2011
Lokmangal Co-operative Bank Ltd	24 November 2011
Lokneta Dattaji Patil Sahakari Bank Ltd	24 November 2011
Lokseva Sahakari Bank Ltd	24 November 2011
Lokvikas Nagari Sahakari Bank Ltd	24 November 2011
Lonavla Sahakari Bank Ltd	24 November 2011
Lucknow University Adm.Staff Primary Co-operative	24 November 2011
Lucknow Urban Co-operative Bank Limited	24 November 2011
Ludhiana Central Co-operative Bank Ltd	24 November 2011
Lunawada Nagrik Sahakari Bank Limited	24 November 2011
Lunawada People's Coop Bank Ltd	24 November 2011
M.D.Pawar Peoples Co-operative Bank Ltd	24 November 2011
M.S. Co-Operative Bank Ltd	24 November 2011
Madanapalle Co-Op. Town Bank Ltd	24 November 2011
Madgaum Urban Co-op Bank Ltd	24 November 2011
Madhavpura Mercantile Co-Op Bank Ltd	24 November 2011
Madheshwari Urban Development Co-operative	24 November 2011
Madhya Bharat Gramin Bank	24 November 2011
Madhya Bihar Gramin Bank	24 November 2011
Madikeri Town Co-operative Bank Ltd	24 November 2011
Madura Sourashtra Co-Op Bank Ltd	24 November 2011
Madurai District Central Co-operative Bank Ltd	24 November 2011
Madurantakam Co-Op Urban Bank Ltd	24 November 2011
Magadh District Central Co-operative Bank Ltd	24 November 2011
Maha.Mantralaya & Allied Offices Coop Bank Ltd	24 November 2011
Mahabaleshwar Urban Co-op Bank Ltd	24 November 2011
Mahabhairab Co-Operative Urban Bank Ltd	24 November 2011
Mahabubanagar District Co-operative Central Bank Ltd	24 November 2011
Mahakaushal Kshetriya Gramin Bank	24 November 2011
Mahalakshmi Co-operative Bank Ltd	24 November 2011
Mahalaxmi Co-operative Bank Ltd	24 November 2011
Mahalingpur Urban Co-Op Bank Ltd	24 November 2011
Mahamedha Urban Co-operative Bank Ltd	24 November 2011
Mahanagar Co-operative Bank Ltd	24 November 2011
Mahanagar Co-Operative Urban Bank Ltd	24 November 2011

Maharaja Co-operative Urban Bank Ltd	24 November 2011
Maharana Pratap Co-Operative Urban Bank Ltd	24 November 2011
Maharashtra Gramin Bank	24 November 2011
Maharashtra Nagari Sahakari Bank	24 November 2011
Mahatma Fule District Urban Co-operative Bank	24 November 2011
Mahatma Fule Urban Co-oprative Bank Ltd	24 November 2011
Mahaveer Co-operative Bank Ltd	24 November 2011
Mahaveer Co-Operative Urban Bank Ltd	24 November 2011
Mahendragarh Central Co-operative Bank Ltd	24 November 2011
Mahesh Sahakari Bank Ltd	24 November 2011
Mahesh Urban Co-operative Bank Ltd	24 November 2011
Mahila Co-operative Bank Ltd	24 November 2011
Mahila Co-Operative Nagrik Bank Ltd	24 November 2011
Mahila Sahakari Bank Ltd	24 November 2011
Mahoba Urban Co-operative Bank Ltd	24 November 2011
Mahudha Nagrik Sahakari Bank Ltd	24 November 2011
Mainpuri District Co-operative Bank Ltd	24 November 2011
Makarpura Industrial Estate Co-op Bank Ltd	24 November 2011
Malad Sahakari Bank Ltd	24 November 2011
Malappuram District Co-operative Central Bank Ltd	24 November 2011
Malda District Central Co-operative Bank Ltd	24 November 2011
Malegaon Merchants Co-op Bank Ltd	24 November 2011
Mallapur Urban Co-operative Bank Ltd	24 November 2011
Malleswaram Co-operative Bank Ltd	24 November 2011
Malpur Nagrik Sahakari Bank Ltd	24 November 2011
Malviya Urban Co-operative Bank Ltd	24 November 2011
Malwa Gramin Bank	24 November 2011
Manapparai Town Co-Op Bank Ltd	24 November 2011
Mandal Nagarik Sahakari Bank Ltd	24 November 2011
Mandapeta Co-Operative Town Bank Ltd	24 November 2011
Mandi Urban Co-op. Bank Ltd	24 November 2011
Mandvi Mercantile Co-operative Bank Ltd	24 November 2011
Mandvi Nagrik Sahakari Bank Ltd	24 November 2011
Mandya City Co-operative Bank Ltd	24 November 2011
Mandya District Central Co-operative Bank Ltd	24 November 2011
Mangal Cooperative Bank Ltd	24 November 2011

Mangaldai Nagar Samabai Bank Ltd	24 November 2011
Mangalore Catholic Co-operative Bank Ltd	24 November 2011
Mangalore Co-operative Town Bank Ltd	24 November 2011
Maninagar Co-Op Bank Ltd	24 November 2011
Manipal Co-operative Bank Ltd	24 November 2011
Manipur Rural Bank	24 November 2011
Manipur Women's Co-op. Bank Ltd	24 November 2011
Manjeri Co-operative Urban Bank Ltd	24 November 2011
Manjra Mahila Urban Co-operative Bank Ltd	24 November 2011
Manmad Urban Co-operative Bank Ltd	24 November 2011
Manmandhir Co-Op Bank Ltd	24 November 2011
Mannargudi Co-Op Urban Bank Ltd	24 November 2011
Manndeshi Mahila Sahakari Bank Ltd	24 November 2011
Manorama Urban Co-operative Bank Ltd	24 November 2011
Mansa Central Co-operative Bank Ltd	24 November 2011
Mansa Nagrik Sahakari Bank Ltd	24 November 2011
Mansarovar Urban Co-operative Bank Ltd	24 November 2011
Mansingh Co-operative Bank Ltd	24 November 2011
Mantha Urban Co-operative Bank Ltd	24 November 2011
Manvi Pattana Souharda Sahakari Bank	24 November 2011
Manwath Urban Co-Operative Bank Ltd	24 November 2011
Mapusa Urban Co-operative Bank of Goa Ltd	24 November 2011
Maratha Co-operative Urban Bank Ltd	24 November 2011
Maratha Sahakari Bank Ltd	24 November 2011
Markandey Nagari Sahakari Bank Ltd	24 November 2011
Marketyard Commercial Cooperative Bank Ltd	24 November 2011
Marwar Ganganagar Bikaner Gramin Bank	24 November 2011
Masulipatanam Co-Op Urban Bank Ltd	24 November 2011
Mathura Zilla Sahakari Bank Ltd	24 November 2011
Matoshri Mahila Sahakari Bank Ltd	24 November 2011
Mattancherry Mahajanik Co-operative Urban Bank	24 November 2011
Mattancherry Sarvajanik Co-operative Bank Ltd	24 November 2011
Mayani Urban Co-op. Bank Ltd	24 November 2011
Mayuram Co-Op Urban Bank Ltd	24 November 2011
Mayurbhanj Central Co-operative Bank Ltd	24 November 2011
Mechanical Department Primary Co-operative Bank	24 November 2011

Medak District Co-operative Central Bank Ltd	24 November 2011
Meenachil East Urban Co-operative Bank Ltd	24 November 2011
Meerut District Co-operative Bank Ltd	24 November 2011
Meghalaya Rural Bank	24 November 2011
Megharaj Nagrik Sahakari Bank Ltd	24 November 2011
Mehmadabad Urban People's Co-Op Bank Ltd	24 November 2011
Mehsana District central Co-operative Bank Ltd	24 November 2011
Mehsana Jilla Panchayat Karmachari Co op Bank	24 November 2011
Mehsana Mahila Sahakari Bank Ltd	24 November 2011
Mehsana Nagrik Sahakari Bank Ltd	24 November 2011
Mehsana Urban Co-Op Bank Ltd	24 November 2011
Melur Co-Op Urban Bank Ltd	24 November 2011
Memon Co-op Bank Ltd	24 November 2011
Mercantile Cooperative Bank Ltd	24 November 2011
Mercantile Urban Co-operative Bank Ltd	24 November 2011
Merchants' Co-operative Bank Ltd	24 November 2011
Merchants' Liberal Co-operative Bank Ltd	24 November 2011
Merchants' Souharda Sahakara Bank	24 November 2011
Merchants' Urban Co-operative Bank Ltd,	24 November 2011
Mettupalayam Co-Op Urban Bank Ltd	24 November 2011
Mewar Anchalik Gramin Bank	24 November 2011
Millath Co-operative Bank Ltd	24 November 2011
Mirzapur Urban Co-operative Bank Ltd	24 November 2011
Mirzapur Zilla Sahakari Bank Ltd	24 November 2011
Mizoram Rural Bank	24 November 2011
Mizoram Urban Co-Op Development Bank Ltd	24 November 2011
Modasa Nagrik Sahakari Bank Ltd	24 November 2011
Model Co-op. Bank Ltd	24 November 2011
Model Co-Operative Urban Bank Ltd	24 November 2011
Modern Co-op. Bank Ltd	24 November 2011
Moga Central Co-operative Bank Ltd	24 November 2011
Mogaveera Co-op. Bank Ltd	24 November 2011
Mohol Urban Co-operative Bank Ltd	24 November 2011
Moirang Primary Coop Bank Ltd	24 November 2011
Monghyr-Jamui District Central Co-operative Bank Ltd	24 November 2011
Moradabad Zilla Sahakari Bank Ltd	24 November 2011

Moti Urban Cooperative Bank Ltd	24 November 2011
Motihari District Central Co-operative Bank Ltd	24 November 2011
Mudalgi Co operative Bank Ltd,	24 November 2011
Mudgal Urban Co-operative Bank Ltd	24 November 2011
Mudhol Co-Operative Bank Ltd	24 November 2011
Mugberia District Central co-operative Bank Ltd	24 November 2011
Mukkuperi Co-Op Urban Bank Ltd	24 November 2011
Muktai Co-op. Bank Ltd	24 November 2011
Muktsar Central Co-operative Bank Ltd	24 November 2011
Mula Sahakari Bank Ltd	24 November 2011
Mulgund Urban Souharda Co-operative Bank Ltd	24 November 2011
Mumbai District Central Co-operative Bank Lt	24 November 2011
Mumbai Mahanager Palika Shikshan VibhagSaha	24 November 2011
Municipal Coop Bank Ltd	24 November 2011
Municipal Cooperative Bank Ltd	24 November 2011
Murshidabad District Central Co-opertive Bank Ltd	24 November 2011
Musiri Urban Co-operative Bank Ltd	24 November 2011
Muslim Cooperative Bank Ltd	24 November 2011
Muvattupuzha Urban Co-operative Bank Ltd	24 November 2011
Muzaffarnagar District Co-operative Bank Ltd	24 November 2011
Muzaffarrur District Central Co-operative Bank Ltd	24 November 2011
Mysore Co-operative Bank Ltd	24 November 2011
Mysore District central Co-operative Bank Ltd	24 November 2011
Mysore Merchant's Co-operative Bank Ltd	24 November 2011
Mysore Silk Cloth Merchants' Co-operative Bank	24 November 2011
Mysore Zilla Mahila Sahakara Bank	24 November 2011
Niyamitha. N.E. Rly.Emp.Multi State Pri.Co-operative Bank	24 November 2011
Nabagram People's Co-operative Credit Bank Ltd	24 November 2011
Nadapuram Co-operative Urban Bank Ltd	24 November 2011
Nadia District Central Co-operative Bank Ltd	24 November 2011
Nadiad People's Coop. Bank Ltd	24 November 2011
Nagaland Rural Bank	24 November 2011
Nagar Sahakari Bank Ltd	24 November 2011
Nagar Urban Co-operative Bank Ltd	24 November 2011
Nagar Vikas Sahkari Bank Ltd	24 November 2011
Nagarik Sahakari Bank Ltd	24 November 2011

Nagarik Samabay Bank Ltd	24 November 2011
Nagaur Central Co-operative Bank Ltd	24 November 2011
Nagaur Urban Coop. Bank Ltd	24 November 2011
Nagina Urban Co-operative Bank Ltd	24 November 2011
Nagnath Urban Co-operative Bank Ltd	24 November 2011
Nagpur District Central Co-operative Bank Ltd	24 November 2011
Nagpur Mahanagarpalika Karmachari Sahahakari	24 November 2011
Nagpur Nagrik Sahakari Bank Ltd	24 November 2011
Nagrik Sahkari Bank Ltd	24 November 2011
Nainital Almora Kshetriya Gramin Bank	24 November 2011
Nainital District Co-operative Bank Ltd	24 November 2011
Nakodar Hindu Coop. Bank Ltd	24 November 2011
Nalanda District Central Co-operative Bank Ltd	24 November 2011
Nalbari Urban Co-operative Bank Ltd	24 November 2011
Nalgaonda District Co-operative Central Bank Ltd	24 November 2011
Namakkal Coop. Urban Bank Ltd	24 November 2011
Nandani Sahakari Bank Ltd	24 November 2011
Nanded District Central Co-operative Bank Ltd	24 November 2011
Nandgaon Urban Co-operative Ltd	24 November 2011
Nandurbar Merchants' Co-op Ltd	24 November 2011
Narayanaguru Urban Co-operative Bank Ltd,	24 November 2011
Narmada Malwa Gramin Bank	24 November 2011
Naroda Nagrik Coop. Bank Ltd	24 November 2011
Nasik District Central Co-operative Bank Ltd	24 November 2011
Nasik District Industrial & Mercantile Co-op Bank	24 November 2011
Nasik Jilha Mahila Sahakari Bank Ltd	24 November 2011
Nasik Merchant's Co-operative Bank Ltd	24 November 2011
Nasik Road Deolali Vyapari Sahakari Bank Ltd	24 November 2011
Nasik Zilla Girna Sahakari Bank Ltd	24 November 2011
Nasik Zilla Mahila Vikas Sahakari Bank Ltd	24 November 2011
Nasik Zilla Sar & Par Karmachari Sah Bank	24 November 2011
National Co-operative Bank Ltd	24 November 2011
National Co-operative Bank Ltd	24 November 2011
National Insurance Emp. Co-operative Cr.& Bank	24 November 2011
National Mercantile Co-operative Bank Ltd	24 November 2011
National Urban Co-operative Bank Ltd	24 November 2011

National Urban Co-operative Bank Ltd	24 November 2011
Nav Jeevan Coop Bank	24 November 2011
Navabharat Co-operative Urban Bank Ltd	24 November 2011
Navakalyan Co-operative Bank Ltd	24 November 2011
Naval Dockyard Coop Bank Ltd	24 November 2011
Navanagara Urban Co-operative Bank Ltd	24 November 2011
Navanirman Co-Operative Urban Bank Ltd	24 November 2011
Navapur Mercantile Co-operative Bank Ltd	24 November 2011
Navi Mumbai Co-operative Bank Ltd	24 November 2011
Navnirman Coop.Bank Ltd	24 November 2011
Navsarjan Industrial Co-Operative Bank Ltd	24 November 2011
Nawadh Central Co-operative Bank Ltd	24 November 2011
Nawanagar Coop. Bank Ltd	24 November 2011
Nawanshahr Central Co-operative Bank Ltd	24 November 2011
Nayagarh Central Co-operative Bank Ltd	24 November 2011
Nazareth Urban Coop. Bank Ltd	24 November 2011
Nedumangad Co-operative Urban Bank Ltd	24 November 2011
Needs of Life Coop Bank Ltd	24 November 2011
Neela Krishna Co-operative Urban Bank Ltd	24 November 2011
Neelachal Gramya Bank	24 November 2011
Nehru Nagar Co-operative Bank Ltd	24 November 2011
Nellai Nagar Coop. Urban Bank Ltd	24 November 2011
Nellore Coop. Urban Bank Ltd	24 November 2011
Nellore District Co-operative Central Bank Ltd	24 November 2011
Nemmara Co-operative Urban Bank Ltd	24 November 2011
Nesargi Urban Co-operative Credit Bank Ltd	24 November 2011
New Agra Urban Co-operative Bank Ltd	24 November 2011
New India Co-operative Bank Ltd	24 November 2011
New Urban Co-operative Bank Ltd	24 November 2011
Neyyattinkara Co-operative Bank Ltd	24 November 2011
Nicholson Coop. Town Bank Ltd	24 November 2011
Nidhi Co-Operative Bank Ltd	24 November 2011
Nilambur Co-operative Urban Bank Ltd	24 November 2011
Nileshwar Co-operative Urban Bank Ltd	24 November 2011
Nilgiries Central Co-operative Bank Ltd	24 November 2011
Nilkanth Urban Coop Bank Ltd	24 November 2011

Nipani Urban Souharda Sahakari Bank	24 November 2011
Niphad Urban Coop. Bank Ltd	24 November 2011
Nirmal Urban Co-operative Bank Ltd	24 November 2011
Nishigandha Sahakari Bank Ltd	24 November 2011
Nizamabad District Co-operative Central Bank Ltd	24 November 2011
NKGSB Co-operative Bank Ltd	24 November 2011
Noble Co-operative Bank Ltd	24 November 2011
Noida Commercial Co-operative Bank Ltd	24 November 2011
North Arcot Ambedkar District Central Co-operative Bank Ltd	24 November 2011
North Malabar Gramin Bank	24 November 2011
Northern Railway Primary Co-operative Bank Ltd	24 November 2011
Nutan Nagari Sahakari Bank Ltd	24 November 2011
Nutan Nagarik Sahakari Bank Ltd	24 November 2011
Nyayamitra Sahakari Bank	24 November 2011
Ode Urban Coop Bank Ltd	24 November 2011
Ojhar Merchants Coop Bank Ltd	24 November 2011
Omalur Urban Co-Operative Bank Ltd	24 November 2011
Om-Datta Chaitanya Sahakari Bank Ltd	24 November 2011
Omerga Janata Sahakari Bank Ltd	24 November 2011
Omkar Nagriya Sahkari Bank Ltd	24 November 2011
Ordinance Equip. Factory Prarambhik Sahkari Bk	24 November 2011
Osmanabad District Central Co-operative Bank Ltd	24 November 2011
Osmanabad Janata Sahakari Bank Ltd	24 November 2011
Ottapalam Co-operative Urban Bank Ltd	24 November 2011
Pachhapur Urban Co-operative Bank Ltd	24 November 2011
Pachora People's Co-op. Bank Ltd	24 November 2011
Padmaavati Co-Operative Urban Bank Ltd	24 November 2011
Padmashri Dr Vithalrao Vikhe Patil Co-operative	24 November 2011
Padra Nagar Nagrik Sahakari Bank Ltd	24 November 2011
Padukkottai Central Co-operative Bank Ltd	24 November 2011
Pala Urban Co-operative Bank Ltd	24 November 2011
Palakkad District Co-operative Central Bank Ltd	24 November 2011
Palamoor Co-operative Urban Bank Ltd	24 November 2011
Palani Coop. Urban Bank Ltd	24 November 2011
Palanpur People's Co-Op Bank Ltd	24 November 2011
Palayamkottai Urban Coop Bank Ltd	24 November 2011

Palghat Co-operative Urban Bank Ltd	24 November 2011
Pali Central Co-operative Bank Ltd	24 November 2011
Pali Urban Cooperative Bank Ltd	24 November 2011
Pallavan Grama Bank	24 November 2011
Pallikonda Coop. Urban Bank Ltd	24 November 2011
Palus Sahakari Bank Ltd	24 November 2011
Panchkula Central Co-operative Bank Ltd	24 November 2011
Panchkula Urban Co-Op Bank Ltd	24 November 2011
Panchmahals District Central Co-operative Bank Ltd	24 November 2011
Panchsheel Mercantile Coop. Bank Ltd	24 November 2011
Pandharpur Marchant's Co-op. Bank Ltd	24 November 2011
Pandharpur Urban Co-operative Bank Ltd	24 November 2011
Pandyan Grama Bank	24 November 2011
Panipat Central Co-operative Bank Ltd	24 November 2011
Panipat Urban Co-Op Bank Ltd	24 November 2011
Panvel Co-op. Urban Bank Ltd	24 November 2011
Papanasam Coop. Urban Bank Ltd	24 November 2011
Paramakudi Coop. Urban Bank Ltd	24 November 2011
Parbhani District Central Co-operative Bank Ltd	24 November 2011
Parner Taluka Sainik Sahakari Bank Ltd	24 November 2011
Parshwanath Co-operative Bank Ltd	24 November 2011
Parvatiya Gramin Bank	24 November 2011
Parwanoo Urban Co-operative Bank Ltd	24 November 2011
Paschim Banga Gramin Bank	24 November 2011
Patan Co-op. Bank Ltd	24 November 2011
Patan Nagarik Sahakari Bank Ltd	24 November 2011
Patan Urban Co-operative Bank Ltd	24 November 2011
Patdi Nagrik Sahakari Bank Ltd	24 November 2011
Pathanamthitta District Co-operative Central Bank Ltd	24 November 2011
Patiala Central Co-operative Bank Ltd	24 November 2011
Patliputra Central Co-operative Bank Ltd	24 November 2011
Pattukottai Coop. Urban Bank Ltd	24 November 2011
Pavana Sahakari Bank Ltd	24 November 2011
Payangadi Urban Co-operative Bank Ltd	24 November 2011
Payyanur Co-operative Town Bank Ltd	24 November 2011
Payyoli Co-operative Urban Bank Ltd	24 November 2011

Pen Co-op. Urban Bank Ltd	24 November 2011
Peoples Co-operative Bank Ltd	24 November 2011
People's Co-operative Bank Ltd	24 November 2011
People's Urban Co-operative Bank Ltd	24 November 2011
Periyakulam Coop. Urban Bank Ltd	24 November 2011
Pij People's Co-Op Bank Ltd	24 November 2011
Pilibhit District Co-operative Bank Ltd	24 November 2011
Pimpalgaon Merchants' Co-op. Bank Ltd	24 November 2011
Pimpri Chinchwad Sahakari Bank	24 November 2011
Pioneer Urban Co-operative Bank Ltd	24 November 2011
Pioneer Urban Co-operative Bank Ltd	24 November 2011
Pithorgarh Zilla Sahakari Bank Ltd	24 November 2011
Pochampally Co-Operative Urban Bank Ltd	24 November 2011
Pollachi Coop. Urban Bank Ltd	24 November 2011
Ponani Co-operative Urban Bank Ltd	24 November 2011
Pondicherry Coop. Urban Bank Ltd	24 November 2011
Ponnampet Town Co-operative Bank	24 November 2011
Poona Marchant's Co-op. Bank Ltd	24 November 2011
Poornawadi Nagrik Sahakari Bank	24 November 2011
Porbandar Commercial Co-Op Bank Ltd	24 November 2011
Porbandar Vibhagiya Nagarik Sahakari Bank Ltd	24 November 2011
Postal & R.M.S. Employees' Coop Bank Ltd	24 November 2011
Pragathi Co-operative Bank Ltd	24 November 2011
Pragathi Gramin Bank	24 November 2011
Pragathi Sahakara Bank	24 November 2011
Pragati Coop Bank Ltd	24 November 2011
Pragati Sahakari Bank Ltd	24 November 2011
Pragati Urban Co-operative Bank Ltd	24 November 2011
Prakasam District Co-operative Central Bank Ltd	24 November 2011
Prakasapuram Coop. Urban Bank Ltd	24 November 2011
Pratap Coop Bank Ltd	24 November 2011
Pratapgarh Jilla Sahakari Bank Ltd	24 November 2011
Prathama Bank	24 November 2011
Prathamik Shikshak Sahakari bank Ltd	24 November 2011
Prathamik Shikshak Sahakari Bank Ltd	24 November 2011
Pravara Sahakari Bank Ltd	24 November 2011

Premier Automobile Employees' Co-op. Bank Ltd	24 November 2011
Prerna Co-operative Bank Ltd	24 November 2011
Prime Co-operative Bank Ltd	24 November 2011
Pritisangam Sahakari Bank Ltd	24 November 2011
Priyadarshani Mahila Nagri Sahakari Bank Ltd	24 November 2011
Priyadarshani Nagari Sahakari Bank Ltd	24 November 2011
Priyadarshani Urban Co-operative Bank Ltd	24 November 2011
Priyadarshini Mahila Coop Bank Ltd	24 November 2011
Priyadarshini Mahila Sahakari Bank Ltd	24 November 2011
Priyadarshini Mahila Urban Sahakari Bank	24 November 2011
Priyadarshini Urban Co-Operative Bank Ltd	24 November 2011
Proddatur Co-Op Town Bank Ltd	24 November 2011
Progressive Coop Bank Ltd	24 November 2011
Progressive Mercantile Coop Bank Ltd	24 November 2011
Progressive Urban Co-operative Bank Ltd	24 November 2011
Pudukottai Coop.Town Bank Ltd	24 November 2011
Puduvai Bharathiar Grama Bank	24 November 2011
Pune Cantonment Sahakari Bank Ltd	24 November 2011
Pune District Central Co-operative Bank Ltd	24 November 2011
Pune Municipal Corporation Servants Co-operative	24 November 2011
Pune Sahakari Bank Ltd	24 November 2011
Pune Urban Co-op. Bank Ltd	24 November 2011
Punjab & Maharashtra Co-operative Bank Ltd	24 November 2011
Punjab Gramin Bank	24 November 2011
Purasawalkam Coop. Bank Ltd	24 November 2011
Puri Urban Co-op. Bank Ltd	24 November 2011
Purnea District Central Co-operative Bank Ltd	24 November 2011
Purulia Central Co-operative Bank Ltd	24 November 2011
Purvanchal Gramin Bank	24 November 2011
Pusad Urban Co-operative Bank Ltd	24 November 2011
Puttur Co-operative Town Bank Ltd	24 November 2011
Quilon Co-operative Urban Bank Ltd	24 November 2011
R.B.I. Employees' Co-op Credit Bank Ltd	24 November 2011
R.S. Co-operative Bank Ltd	24 November 2011
Raddi Sahakara Bank	24 November 2011
Radhasoami Urban Co-operative Bank Ltd	24 November 2011

Rae Bareli District Co-operative Bank Ltd	24 November 2011
Rahimatpur Sahakari Bank Ltd	24 November 2011
Raichur City Urban Co-operative Bank Ltd	24 November 2011
Raichur District Central Co-operative Bank Ltd	24 November 2011
Raigad District Central Co-operative Bank Ltd	24 November 2011
Raigad Sahakari Bank Ltd	24 November 2011
Raiganj Central Co-operative Bank Ltd	24 November 2011
Railway Co-operative Bank Ltd	24 November 2011
Railway Employees' Coop Bank Ltd	24 November 2011
Railway Employees'Coop Banking Soc Ltd	24 November 2011
Railway Shramik Sahakari Bank Ltd	24 November 2011
Raj Laxmi Mahila Urban Co-Operative Bank Ltd	24 November 2011
Rajadhani Co-Operative Bank Ltd	24 November 2011
Rajajinagar Co-operative Bank Ltd	24 November 2011
Rajapalayam Co-Op Urban Bank Ltd	24 November 2011
Rajapur Sahakari Bank Ltd	24 November 2011
Rajapur Urban Cooperative Bank Ltd	24 November 2011
Rajarambapu Sahakari Bank Ltd	24 November 2011
Rajarshi Shahu Government Servants' Co-op. Bank	24 November 2011
Rajarshi Shahu Sahakari Bank	24 November 2011
Rajasthan Gramin Bank	24 November 2011
Rajasthan Urban Co-Operative Bank Ltd	24 November 2011
Rajdhani Nagar Sahkari Bank Ltd	24 November 2011
Rajgurunagar Sahakari Bank Ltd	24 November 2011
Rajiv Gandhi Sahakari Bank Ltd	24 November 2011
Rajkot Commercial Cooperative Bank Ltd	24 November 2011
Rajkot Nagrik Sahakari Bank Ltd	24 November 2011
Rajkot Peoples Co-Operative Bank Ltd	24 November 2011
Rajlaxmi Urban Co-operative Bank Ltd	24 November 2011
Rajmata Urban Co-operative Bank Ltd	24 November 2011
Rajpipla Nagrik Sahakari Bank Ltd	24 November 2011
Rajputana Mahila Urban Co-op Bank Ltd	24 November 2011
Rajsamand Urban Co-operative Bank Ltd	24 November 2011
Rajula Nagrik Sahakari Bank Ltd	24 November 2011
Ramakrishna Mutually Aided Co-operative	24 November 2011
Ramanagaram Urban Co-operative Bank Ltd	24 November 2011

Ramanathapuram Co-Op Urban Bank Ltd	24 November 2011
Ramanathapuram District Central Co-operative Bank Lt	24 November 2011
Rameshwar Co-operative Bank Ltd	24 November 2011
Ramgarhia Co-operative Bank Ltd	24 November 2011
Rampur District Co-operative Bank Ltd	24 November 2011
Ramrajya Sahakari Bank Ltd	24 November 2011
Ranaghat People's Bank Ltd	24 November 2011
Ranchi-Khunti Central Co-operative Bank Ltd	24 November 2011
Rander People's Co-Op Bank Ltd	24 November 2011
Randheja Commercial Co-Op Bank Ltd	24 November 2011
Ranga Reddy Co-operative Urban Bank Ltd	24 November 2011
Raniganj Co-operative Bank Ltd	24 November 2011
Ranilaxmibai Urban Co-operative Bank Ltd	24 November 2011
Ranipet Town Co-Op Bank Ltd	24 November 2011
Ranuj Nagrik Sahakari Bank Ltd	24 November 2011
Rasipuram Co-Op Urban Bank Ltd	24 November 2011
Ratanchand Shaha Sahakari Bank Ltd	24 November 2011
Ratnagiri District Central Co-operative Bank Ltd	24 November 2011
Ratnagiri Urban Co-operative Bank Ltd	24 November 2011
Raver People's Co-op. Bank Ltd	24 November 2011
Ravi Commercial Urban Co-operative Bank Ltd	24 November 2011
Rayat Sevak Co-op. Bank Ltd	24 November 2011
Rendal Sahakari Bank Ltd	24 November 2011
Repalle Co-Op Bank Ltd	24 November 2011
Reserve Bank Employees' Coop Bank Ltd	24 November 2011
Reserve Bank Employees' Co-operative Bank Ltd	24 November 2011
Revdanda Co-op. Urban bank Ltd	24 November 2011
Rewari Central Co-operative Bank Ltd	24 November 2011
Rewa-Sidhi Gramin Bank	24 November 2011
Rohika Central Co-opertive Bank Ltd	24 November 2011
Rohtak Central Co-operative Bank Ltd	24 November 2011
Ron Taluka Primary Teachers' Co-operative	24 November 2011
Ropar Central Co-operative Bank Ltd	24 November 2011
Rukhmini Nagari Sahakati Bank Ltd	24 November 2011
Rupee Co-operative Bank Ltd	24 November 2011
Rushikulya Gramya Bank	24 November 2011

Sabarkantha District Central Co-operative Bank Ltd	24 November 2011
Sachin Industrial Co-Operative Bank Ltd	24 November 2011
Sadalga Urban Souharda Sahakari Bank	24 November 2011
Sadguru Gahininath Urban Co-op. Bank Ltd	24 November 2011
Sadhana Sahakari Bank Ltd	24 November 2011
Sadhana Sahakari Bank Ltd	24 November 2011
Saharanpur District Co-operative Bank Ltd	24 November 2011
Sahasrarjun Seva Kalyan Co-operative Bank Ltd	24 November 2011
Sahebrao Deshmukh Co-op. Bank Ltd	24 November 2011
Sahyadri Mahila Urban Co-operative Bank Ltd	24 November 2011
Sahyadri Sahakari Bank Ltd	24 November 2011
Sai Nagari Sahakari Bank	24 November 2011
Saibaba Janata Sahakari Bank Ltd	24 November 2011
Saibaba Nagari Sahakari Bank	24 November 2011
Saidapet Co op Bank Ltd	24 November 2011
Salal Sarvodaya Nagrik Sahakari Bank Ltd	24 November 2011
Salem District Central Co-operative Bank Ltd	24 November 2011
Salem Urban Co op Bank Ltd	24 November 2011
Salur Cooperative Urban Bank Ltd	24 November 2011
Samarth Sahakari Bank	24 November 2011
Samarth Sahakari Bank Ltd	24 November 2011
Samarth Urban Co-Operative Bank Ltd	24 November 2011
Samastipur District Central Co-operative Bank Ltd	24 November 2011
Samastipur Kshetriya Gramin Bank	24 November 2011
Samata Co-operative Development Bank Ltd	24 November 2011
Samata Sahakari Bank Ltd	24 November 2011
Samatha Mahila Co-Operative Urban Bank Ltd	24 November 2011
Sambalpur District Central Co-operative Bank Ltd	24 November 2011
Sampada Sahakari Bank Ltd	24 November 2011
Samruddhi Co-operative Bank Ltd	24 November 2011
Sandur Pattana Souharda Sahakari Bank	24 November 2011
Sangamner Merchant's Co op Bank Ltd	24 November 2011
Sanghamitra Co-Operative Urban Bank Ltd	24 November 2011
Sangli District Central Co-operative Bank Ltd	24 November 2011
Sangli District Primary Teacher's Co op Bank Ltd	24 November 2011
Sangli Sahakari Bank Ltd	24 November 2011

Sangli Urban Co-operative Bank Ltd	24 November 2011
Sangola Urban Co-operative Bank Ltd	24 November 2011
Sangrur Central Co-operative Bank Ltd	24 November 2011
Sankari Co op Urban Bank Ltd	24 November 2011
Sankheda Nagarik Sahakari Bank Ltd	24 November 2011
Sanmathi Sahakari Bank Ltd	24 November 2011
Sanmitra Mahila Nagri Sahakari Bank	24 November 2011
Sanmitra Sahakari Bank	24 November 2011
Sanmitra Sahakari Bank Ltd	24 November 2011
Sanmitra Urban Co-operative Bank Ltd	24 November 2011
Sant Motiram Maharaj Nagari Sahakari Bank Ltd	24 November 2011
Sant Sopankaka Sahakari Bank	24 November 2011
Santrampur Urban Co op Bank Ltd	24 November 2011
Saptagiri Grameena Bank	24 November 2011
Sarangpur Co op Bank Limited	24 November 2011
Saraspur Nagarik Co op Bank Limited	24 November 2011
Saraswat Co-operative Bank Ltd	24 November 2011
Saraswathi Sahakari Bank Ltd	24 November 2011
Sardar Bhiladwala Pardi Peoples Coop Bank Ltd	24 November 2011
Sardar Vallabhbhai Sahakari Bank Limited	24 November 2011
Sardarganj Mercantile Coop Bank Ltd	24 November 2011
Sardargunj Mercantile Coop Bank Ltd	24 November 2011
Sarjerao-Dada Naik Shirala Sahakari Bank Ltd	24 November 2011
Sarsa People's Co op Bank Limited	24 November 2011
Sarva UP Gramin Bank	24 November 2011
Sarvodaya Commercial Coop Bank Ltd	24 November 2011
Sarvodaya Co-operative Bank Ltd	24 November 2011
Sarvodaya Nagrik Sahakari Bank Ltd	24 November 2011
Sarvodaya Sahakari Bank Ltd	24 November 2011
Sarvodaya Sahakari Bank Ltd	24 November 2011
Sasaram Bhabua Central Co-operative Bank Ltd	24 November 2011
Satana Merchants' Co-op. Bank Ltd	24 November 2011
Satara District Central Co-operative Bank Ltd	24 November 2011
Satara Sahakari Bank Ltd	24 November 2011
Sathamba People's Co op Bank Ltd	24 November 2011
Satpura Narmada Kshetriya	24 November 2011

Satyamangalam Co op Urban Bank Ltd	24 November 2011
Satyashodhak Sahakari Bank Ltd	24 November 2011
Saurashtra Co op Bank Ltd	24 November 2011
Saurashtra Gramin Bank	24 November 2011
Savanur Urban Co-operative Bank Ltd	24 November 2011
Sawai Madhopur Central Co-operative Bank Ltd	24 November 2011
Sawai Madhopur Urban Co-operative Bank Ltd	24 November 2011
Sawantwadi Urban Co-op. Bank Ltd	24 November 2011
Secunderabad Co-Operative Urban Bank Ltd	24 November 2011
Secunderabad Mercantile Co-operative Urban Bank	24 November 2011
Seva Vikas Coop Bank Ltd	24 November 2011
Sevalia Urban Co op Bank Ltd	24 November 2011
Seven Hills Co-Operative Urban Bank Ltd	24 November 2011
Shahada People's Co-operative Bank Ltd	24 November 2011
Shahjahanpur District Central Co-operative Bank Ltd	24 November 2011
Shalini Sahakari Bank Ltd	24 November 2011
Shamrao Vithal Co-operative Bank Ltd	24 November 2011
Shankar Nagari Sahakari Bank Ltd	24 November 2011
Shankarrao Chavan Nagri Sahakari Bank	24 November 2011
Shankerrao Mohite-Patil Sahakari Bank Ltd	24 November 2011
Sharad Nagari Sahakari Bank Ltd	24 November 2011
Sharad Sahakari Bank Ltd	24 November 2011
Sharda Gramin Bank	24 November 2011
Shatabdi Mahila Sahakari Bank Ltd	24 November 2011
Shedbal Urban Co-operative Bank Ltd	24 November 2011
Shevapet Urban Coop Bank Ltd	24 November 2011
Shiggaon Urban Co-operative Bank Ltd	24 November 2011
Shihori Nagarik Sahakari Bank Ltd	24 November 2011
Shikshak Sahakari Bank Ltd	24 November 2011
Shillong Co op Urban Bank Ltd	24 November 2011
Shimla Urban Co op Bank Ltd	24 November 2011
Shimoga Arecanut Mandy Merchants Co-operative	24 November 2011
Shimoga District Central Co-operative Bank Ltd	24 November 2011
Shimsha Sahakara Bank	24 November 2011
Shirpur Merchants Co-op. Bank Ltd	24 November 2011
Shirpur Peoples Co-operative Bank Ltd	24 November 2011

Shiva Sahakari Bank	24 November 2011
Shivaji Nagari Sahakari Bank Ltd	24 November 2011
Shivajirao Bhosale Sahakari Bank Ltd	24 November 2011
Shivalik Mercantile Co-operative Bank Ltd	24 November 2011
Shivam Sahakari Bank Ltd	24 November 2011
Shivdaulat Sahakari Bank Ltd	24 November 2011
Shivneri Sahakari Bank Ltd	24 November 2011
Shivparvati Mahila Nagari Sahakari Bank Ltd	24 November 2011
Shivshakti Urban Co-op BnkLtd	24 November 2011
Sholapur District Central Co-operative Bank Ltd	24 November 2011
Sholavandan Urban Coop Bank Ltd	24 November 2011
Sholinghur Co op Urban Bank Ltd	24 November 2011
Shoranur Co-operative Urban Bank Ltd	24 November 2011
Shree Agrasen Co-operative Bank Ltd	24 November 2011
Shree Baria Nagarik Sahakari Bank Ltd	24 November 2011
Shree Basaveshwar Co-operative Bank Ltd	24 November 2011
Shree Basaveshwar Urban Co-operative Bank Ltd	24 November 2011
Shree Bhadran Mercantile Cooperative Bank Ltd	24 November 2011
Shree Bharat Coop Bank Ltd	24 November 2011
Shree Bhavnagar Nagrik Sahakari Bank Limited	24 November 2011
Shree Botad Mercantile Co op Bank Ltd	24 November 2011
Shree Coop. Bank Ltd	24 November 2011
Shree Dhandhuka Janta Sahakari Bank Ltd	24 November 2011
Shree Dharati Cooperative Bank Ltd	24 November 2011
Shree Gajanan Lokseva Sahakari Bank Ltd	24 November 2011
Shree Gajanan Maharaj Urban Co-operative Bank	24 November 2011
Shree Gajanan Urban Co-operative Bank Ltd	24 November 2011
Shree Govardhansingji Raghuvashi Sahakari Bank	24 November 2011
Shree Kadi Nagrik Sahakari Bank Ltd	24 November 2011
Shree Lathi Vibhagiya Sahakari Bank Ltd	24 November 2011
Shree Laxmi Coop Bank Ltd	24 November 2011
Shree Laxmi Mahila Sahakari Bank Ltd	24 November 2011
Shree Laxmi Mahila Sahakari Bank Ltd	24 November 2011
Shree Lodhra Nagrik Sahakari Bank Ltd	24 November 2011
Shree Mahabaleshwar Co operative Bank Ltd	24 November 2011
Shree Mahalaxmi Mercantile Coop Bk Ltd	24 November 2011

Shree Mahalaxmi Urban Co-operative Credit Bank	24 November 2011
Shree Mahavir Sahakari Bank	24 November 2011
Shree Mahayogi Lakshmamma Co-Operative Ban	24 November 2011
Shree Mahesh Co-operative Ltd	24 November 2011
Shree Mahuva Nagrik Sahakari Bank Ltd	24 November 2011
Shree Murugharajendra Co-operative Bank	24 November 2011
Shree Panchaganga Nagari Sahakari Bank Ltd	24 November 2011
Shree Parswanth Co-Operative Bank Ltd	24 November 2011
Shree Samarth Sahakari Bank Ltd	24 November 2011
Shree Savarkundla Nagrik Sahakari Bank Ltd	24 November 2011
Shree Savli Nagrik Sahakari Bank Ltd	24 November 2011
Shree Sidhhi Vinayak Nagari Sahakari Bank Ltd	24 November 2011
Shree Talaja Nagarik Sahakari Bank Limited	24 November 2011
Shree Tukaram Co-operative Bank Ltd	24 November 2011
Shree Vardhaman Sahakari Bank Ltd	24 November 2011
Shree Virpur Urban Sahakari Bank Ltd	24 November 2011
Shree Vyas Dhanvarsha Sahakari Bank Ltd	24 November 2011
Shree Warana Sahakari Bank Ltd	24 November 2011
Shree Yugprabhav Sahakari Bank Limited	24 November 2011
Shreeji Bhatia Co-operative Bank Ltd	24 November 2011
Shreenath Coop Bank Ltd	24 November 2011
Shreeram Sahakari Bank Ltd	24 November 2011
Shreyas Gramin Bank	24 November 2011
Shri Adinath Co-Operative Bank Ltd	24 November 2011
Shri Anand Co-operative Bank Ltd	24 November 2011
Shri Anand Nagari Sahakari Bank Ltd	24 November 2011
Shri Arihant Co-operative Bank Ltd	24 November 2011
Shri Babasaheb Deshmukh Sahakari Bank Ltd	24 November 2011
Shri Balaji Co-op Bank Ltd	24 November 2011
Shri Balbhim Coop Bank Ltd	24 November 2011
Shri Basaveshwar Sahakari Bank	24 November 2011
Shri Bhagasara Nagrik Sahakari Bank Limited	24 November 2011
Shri Bhailalbhai Contractor Smarak Co-operative	24 November 2011
Shri Bharat Urban Coop Bank Ltd	24 November 2011
Shri Bhausaheb Thorat Amrutvahini Sahakari Bank	24 November 2011
Shri Chatrapati Shivaji Maharaj Sahakari Bank	24 November 2011

Shri Chhani Nagrik Sahakari Bank Limited	24 November 2011
Shri Chhatrapati Rajarshi Shahu Urban Co-operative	24 November 2011
Shri Chhatrapati Urban Co-operative Bank Ltd	24 November 2011
Shri Gajanan Nagari Sahakari Bank Ltd	24 November 2011
Shri Ganesh Sahakari Bank Ltd	24 November 2011
Shri Gurudev Brahmanand Pattana Sahakara Bank	24 November 2011
Shri Gurusiddheshwar Co-operative Bank Ltd	24 November 2011
Shri Janata Sahakari Bank Ltd	24 November 2011
Shri Kadasiddeshwar Pattan Sahakari Bank	24 November 2011
Shri Kanyaka Nagari Sahakari Bank Ltd	24 November 2011
Shri Lakshmi Krupa Urban Cooperative Bank Ltd	24 November 2011
Shri Laxmi Sahakari Bank Ltd	24 November 2011
Shri Mahalaxmi Coop Bank Ltd	24 November 2011
Shri Mahalaxmi Pattan Sahakara Bank	24 November 2011
Shri Mahant Shivayogi Sahakari Bank Ltd	24 November 2011
Shri Mahaveer Urban Co-Operative Bank Ltd	24 November 2011
Shri Mahila Sewa Sahakari Bank Ltd	24 November 2011
Shri Morbi Nagrik Sahakari Bank Ltd	24 November 2011
Shri Nrusingh Saraswati sahakari Bank Ltd	24 November 2011
Shri Patneshwar Urban Cooperative Bank Ltd	24 November 2011
Shri Rajkot District Central Co-operative Bank Ltd	24 November 2011
Shri Rukmini Sahakari Bank Ltd	24 November 2011
Shri Sai Urban Co-operative Bank Ltd	24 November 2011
Shri Satyavijay Sahakari Bank Ltd	24 November 2011
Shri Shadakshari Shivayogi Siddharameshwar	24 November 2011
Shri Shantappanna Mirji Urban Co-operative Bank	24 November 2011
Shri Sharada Sahakari Bank Ltd	24 November 2011
Shri Sharan Veereshwar Sahakari Bank	24 November 2011
Shri Shiddheshwar Co-operative Bank Ltd	24 November 2011
Shri Shivaji Sahakari Bank Ltd	24 November 2011
Shri Shivayogi Murughendra Swami Urban Co-op	24 November 2011
Shri Shiveshwar Nagri Sahakari Bank Ltd	24 November 2011
Shri Siddeshwar Co-operative Bank Ltd	24 November 2011
Shri Swami Samarth Sahakari Bank Ltd	24 November 2011
Shri Swami Samarth Urban Co-operative Bank Ltd	24 November 2011
Shri Veer Pulikeshi Co-operative Bank Ltd	24 November 2011

Shri Veershaiv Co op Bank Ltd	24 November 2011
Shri Vijay Mahantesh Co-operative Bank Limited	24 November 2011
Shri Vinayak Sahakari Bank Limited	24 November 2011
Shri Vyankatesh Co-operative Bank Ltd	24 November 2011
Shri Yashwant Sahakari Bank Ltd	24 November 2011
Shrikrishna Co-operative Bank Ltd	24 November 2011
Shrimant Malojiraje Sahakari Bank Ltd	24 November 2011
Shripatrao Dada Sahakari Bank Ltd	24 November 2011
Shriram Urban Co-operative Bank Ltd	24 November 2011
Shushruti Souharda Sahakara Bank Niyamita	24 November 2011
Siddaganga Urban Co-operative Bank Ltd	24 November 2011
Siddarthnagar District Co-operative Bank Ltd	24 November 2011
Siddharth Sahakari Bank Maryadit	24 November 2011
Siddheshwar Sahakari Bank Ltd	24 November 2011
Siddheshwar Urban Co-operative Bank	24 November 2011
Siddhi Cooperative Bank Ltd	24 November 2011
Sihor Mercantile Co op Bank Ltd	24 November 2011
Sihor Nagrik Sahakari Bank Ltd	24 November 2011
Sikar Central Co-operative Bank Ltd	24 November 2011
Sikar Urban Co Op Bank Ltd	24 November 2011
Sind Co-Operative Urban Bank Ltd	24 November 2011
Sindgi Urban Co-operative Bank Ltd	24 November 2011
Sindhudurg District Central Co-operative Bank Ltd	24 November 2011
Sindhudurg Sahakari Bank Ltd	24 November 2011
Singhbhum District Central Co-operative Bank Ltd	24 November 2011
Sinor Nagrik Sahakari Bank Ltd	24 November 2011
Sir M Vishweshwaraiah Sahakar Bank Niyamitha	24 November 2011
Sir M.Visvesvaraya Co-operative Bank Ltd	24 November 2011
Sircilla Co op Urban bank Limited	24 November 2011
Sirkali Co op Urban Bank Ltd	24 November 2011
Sirohi Central Co-operative Bank Ltd	24 November 2011
Sirsa Central Co-operative Bank Ltd	24 November 2011
Sirsi Urban Sahakari Bank Ltd	24 November 2011
Sitamarhi Central Co-operative Bank Ltd	24 November 2011
Sivagangai (Pasumpon) District Central Co-operative Bank Ltd	24 November 2011
Sivakasi Co op Urban Bank Ltd	24 November 2011

Siwan Co-operative Central Bank Ltd	24 November 2011
Smriti Nagrik Sahakari Bank Maryadit., Mandsau	24 November 2011
Sojitra Co-operative Bank Ltd	24 November 2011
Solapur Janata Sahakari Bank Ltd	24 November 2011
Solapur Nagri Audhyogik Sahakari Bank	24 November 2011
Solapur Siddheshwar Sahakari Bank Ltd	24 November 2011
Solapur Social Urban Co-op Bank Ltd	24 November 2011
Sonbhadra Nagar Sahkari Bank Ltd	24 November 2011
Sonepat Central Co-operative Bank Ltd	24 November 2011
Sonpeth Nagri Sahakari Bank	24 November 2011
Soubhagya Mahila Souharda Sahakar Bank	24 November 2011
South Canara District Central Co-operative Bank Ltd	24 November 2011
South Kanara Government Officers' Co-operative	24 November 2011
South Malabar Gramin Bank	24 November 2011
Sree Anjaneya Co-operative Bank Ltd	24 November 2011
Sree Bhyraveshwara Sahakara Bank Niyamitha	24 November 2011
Sree Chaitanya Co-Operative Bank Ltd	24 November 2011
Sree Charan Souharda Co-operative Bank Ltd	24 November 2011
Sree Co-operative Urban Bank Ltd	24 November 2011
Sree Harihareshwara Urban Co-operative Bank Ltd	24 November 2011
Sree Narayana Guru Co-op. Bank Ltd	24 November 2011
Sree Subramanyeswara Co-operative Bank Ltd	24 November 2011
Sree Thyagaraja Co-operative Bank Ltd	24 November 2011
Sreenidhi Souharda Sahakari Bank Niyamitha,	24 November 2011
Sreenivasa Padmavatthi Co-Operative Urban Bank	24 November 2011
Sri Amba Bhavani Urban Co-operative Bank Ltd	24 November 2011
Sri Balaji Urban Co-operative Bank Ltd	24 November 2011
Sri Banashankari Mahila Co-operative Bank Ltd	24 November 2011
Sri Basaveshwar Pattana Sahakari Bank Niyamit	24 November 2011
Sri Basaveshwar Sahakar Bank Niyamitha	24 November 2011
Sri Basaveshwara Pattana Sahakara Bank	24 November 2011
Sri Basaveswar Co-operative Bank Ltd	24 November 2011
Sri Bhagavathi Co-operative Bank Ltd	24 November 2011
Sri Bharathi Co-op. Urban Bank Ltd	24 November 2011
Sri Channabasavaswamy Souharda Pattana Saha	24 November 2011
Sri Durgadevi Mahila Sahakari Bank Ltd	24 November 2011

Sri Ganapathi Urban Co-operative Bank Ltd	24 November 2011
Sri Ganesh Co-operative Bank Ltd	24 November 2011
Sri Gavisiddeshwar Urban Co-operative Bank Ltd	24 November 2011
Sri Gayatri Co-Operative Urban Bank Ltd	24 November 2011
Sri Gokarnanath Co-operative Bank Ltd	24 November 2011
Sri Guru Raghavendra Sahakara Bank	24 November 2011
Sri Kalahasti Co-operative Town Bank Ltd	24 November 2011
Sri Kalidasa Sahakara Bank	24 November 2011
Sri Kamalambika Co op Urban Bank Ltd	24 November 2011
Sri Kannikaparameshwari Co-operative Bank Ltd	24 November 2011
Sri Kanyakaparameswari Co-operative Bank Ltd	24 November 2011
Sri Krishnarajendra Co-operative Bank Ltd	24 November 2011
Sri Lakshmi Mahila Sahakara Bank	24 November 2011
Sri Lakshminarayana Co-operative Bank Ltd	24 November 2011
Sri Laxminarayana Coop Urban Bank Ltd	24 November 2011
Sri Mahatma Basaveshwar Co-Operative Bank	24 November 2011
Sri Mallikarjuna Pattana Sahakari Bank	24 November 2011
Sri Parshwanatha Sahakara Bank	24 November 2011
Sri Rama Co-operative Bank Ltd	24 November 2011
Sri Revana Siddeshwar Pattana Sahakara Bank	24 November 2011
Sri Seetharaghava Souharda Sahakara Bank	24 November 2011
Sri Sharada Mahila Co-operative Bank Ltd	24 November 2011
Sri Sharadamba Mahila Cooperative Urban Bank	24 November 2011
Sri Sharanabasaveshwar Pattana Sahakar Bank	24 November 2011
Sri Siddarameshwara Sahakara Bank	24 November 2011
Sri Sudha Co-operative Bank Ltd	24 November 2011
Sri Vasavamba Co-operative Bank Ltd	24 November 2011
Sri Veerabhadreshwar Co-operative Bank Ltd	24 November 2011
Srikakulam Co-op. Urban Bank Ltd	24 November 2011
Srikakulam District Co-operative Central Bank Ltd	24 November 2011
Srimatha Mahila Sahakari Bank	24 November 2011
Sriramnagar Pattana Sahakar Bank	24 November 2011
Srirangam Co op Urban Bank Ltd	24 November 2011
Srivilliputtur Co op Urban Bank Ltd	24 November 2011
Stambhadri Co-operative Urban Bank Ltd	24 November 2011
State Transport Coop Bank Ltd	24 November 2011

State Transport Employees' Coop Bank Ltd	24 November 2011
Sterling Urban Co-Operative Bank Ltd	24 November 2011
Subramanianagar Coop Urban Bank Ltd	24 November 2011
SUCO Souharda Sahakari Bank Ltd	24 November 2011
Sudha Co-operative Urban Bank Ltd	24 November 2011
Suleimani Coop. Bank Ltd	24 November 2011
Sultanpur Zilla Sahakari Bank Ltd	24 November 2011
Sultan's Battery Co-operative Urban Bank Ltd	24 November 2011
Sumerpur Mercantile Urban Co-operative Bank Ltd	24 November 2011
Sundargarh Central Co-operative Bank Ltd	24 November 2011
Sundarlal Sawji Urban Co-operative Bank Ltd	24 November 2011
Surat District Central Co-operative Bank Ltd	24 November 2011
Surat Mercantile Coop Bank Ltd	24 November 2011
Surat Nagrik Sahakari Bank Ltd	24 November 2011
Surat National Coop Bank Ltd	24 November 2011
Surat Peoples Coop Bank Ltd	24 November 2011
Surendranagar District Central Co-operative Bank Ltd	24 November 2011
Surguja Kshetriya Gramin Bank	24 November 2011
Sutlej Kshetriya Gramin Bank	24 November 2011
Suvarna Co-operative Bank Ltd	24 November 2011
Suvarnayug Sahakari Bank Ltd	24 November 2011
Suvikas Peoples Co-Operative Bank Ltd	24 November 2011
Swami Samarth Sahakari Bank Ltd	24 November 2011
Swami Vivekanand Sahakari Bank	24 November 2011
Swarna Bharathi Sahakara Bank	24 November 2011
Swarna Co-Operative Urban Bank Ltd	24 November 2011
Swasakthi Mercantile Co-Operative Urban Bank	24 November 2011
Swatantrya Senani	24 November 2011
Tadpatri Coop Town Bank Ltd	24 November 2011
Talikoti Sahakari Bank	24 November 2011
Taliparamba Co-operative Urban Bank Ltd	24 November 2011
Talod Nagarik Sahakari Bank Ltd	24 November 2011
Tambaram Coop Urban Bank Ltd	24 November 2011
Tamilnadu Circle Postal Co-Op Bank Ltd	24 November 2011
Tamilnadu Industrial Co-operative Bank	24 November 2011
Tamluk-Ghatal Central Co-operative Bank Ltd	24 November 2011
Tandur Mahila Co-operative Bank Ltd	24 November 2011

Tanur Co-operative Urban Bank Ltd	24 November 2011
Tarapur Co-Op Urban Bank Ltd	24 November 2011
Tasgaon Urban Co-operative Bank Ltd	24 November 2011
Tavaragera Pattana Souharda Sahakar Bank	24 November 2011
Teachers' Co-operative Bank Ltd	24 November 2011
Tehri Garhwal District Co-operative Bank Ltd	24 November 2011
Tellicherry Co-operative Urban Bank Ltd	24 November 2011
Tenali Co-Op Urban Bank Ltd	24 November 2011
Terna Nagari Sahakari Bank Ltd	24 November 2011
Textile Co-op. Bank of Surat Ltd	24 November 2011
Textile Co-operative Bank Ltd	24 November 2011
Textile Manufacturers' Co-operative Bank	24 November 2011
Textile Traders' Coop Bank Ltd	24 November 2011
Thane Bharat Sahakari Bank Ltd	24 November 2011
Thane District Central Co-operative Bank Ltd	24 November 2011
Thane Janata Sahakari Bank Ltd	24 November 2011
Thanjavur Central Co-operative Bank Ltd	24 November 2011
Thanjavur Public Servants'Coop Bank Ltd	24 November 2011
Thasra Peoples' Co-Op Bank Ltd	24 November 2011
The Adilabad District Central Co-operative Bank Ltd	24 November 2011
The Adinath Co-operative Bank Ltd	24 November 2011
The Agrasen Nagari Sahakari Bank Ltd	24 November 2011
The Akola Janata Commercial Co-operative Bank Ltd	24 November 2011
The Akola Urban Co-operative Bank Ltd	24 November 2011
The Amravati Merchants' Co-operative Bank Ltd	24 November 2011
The Amravati People's Co-operative Bank Ltd	24 November 2011
The Amravati Zilla Mahila Sahakari Bank Ltd	24 November 2011
The Amravati Zilla-Parishad Shikshak Sahakari	24 November 2011
The Anantapur District Central Co-operative Bank Ltd	24 November 2011
The Andaman and Nicobar State Co-operative Bank Ltd	24 November 2011
The Andhra Pradesh State Co-operative Bank Ltd	24 November 2011
The Anjangaon Surji Nagari Sahakari Bank Ltd	24 November 2011
The Annasaheb Savant Co-Op. Urban Bank	24 November 2011
The Arunachal Pradesh State Co-operative Apex Bank Ltd	24 November 2011
The Assam Co-operative Apex Bank Ltd	24 November 2011
The Associate Co-operative Bank Ltd	24 November 2011
The Aurangabad District Industrial & Urban Co-op	24 November 2011

The Badagara Co-operative Urban Bank Ltd	24 November 2011
The Baidyabati Sheoraphuli Co-operative Bank	24 November 2011
The Bank Employees' Co-operative Bank Ltd	24 November 2011
The Bankura Town Co-operative Bank Limited	24 November 2011
The Bantra Co-operative Bank Limited	24 November 2011
The Bhagyalakshmi Mahila Sahakari Bank Ltd	24 November 2011
The Bhandara Urban Co-operative Bank Ltd	24 November 2011
The Bihar Awami Co-operative Bank Ltd	24 November 2011
The Bihar State Co-operative Bank Ltd	24 November 2011
The Bishnupur Town Co-operative Bank Limited	24 November 2011
The Boral Union Co-operative Bank Limited	24 November 2011
The Chandigarh State Co-operative Bank Ltd	24 November 2011
The Chhattisgarh RajyaSahakari Bank Maryadit	24 November 2011
The Chikhli Urban Co-operative Bank Ltd	24 November 2011
The Chitnavispura Sahakari Bank Ltd	24 November 2011
The Citizen Co operative Bank Limited	24 November 2011
The Citizen Co-operative Bank Ltd	24 November 2011
The Citizens' Co-operative Bank Ltd	24 November 2011
The Delhi State Co-operative Bank Ltd	24 November 2011
The Devika Urban Co-operative Bank Ltd	24 November 2011
The Dr. Panjabrao Deshmukh Urban Co-operative	24 November 2011
The Eastern Railway Employees' Co-operative Bank	24 November 2011
The Ghadchiroli Nagari Sahakari Bank	24 November 2011
The Ghatal Peoples' Co-operative Bank Ltd	24 November 2011
The Goa State Co-operative Bank Ltd	24 November 2011
The Gujarat Industrial Co-operative Bank Ltd	24 November 2011
The Gujarat Rajya Karmachari Cooperative Bank	24 November 2011
The Gujarat State Co-operative Bank Ltd	24 November 2011
The Haryana State Co-opertive Apex Bank Ltd	24 November 2011
The Himachal Pradesh State Co-operative Bank Ltd	24 November 2011
The Hooghly Co-operative Credit Bank Limited	24 November 2011
The Jalna People's Co-operative Bank Ltd	24 November 2011
The Jambusar People's Coop Bank Ltd	24 November 2011
The Jammu and Kashmir State Co-operative Bank Ltd	24 November 2011
The Jamshedpur Urban Co-operative Bank Ltd	24 November 2011
The Janata Commercial Co-operative Bank Ltd	24 November 2011
The Jaynagar Mozilpur Peoples' Co-operative Bank	24 November 2011

The Kalna Town Credit Co-operative Bank Ltd	24 November 2011
The Kangra Co-operative Bank Ltd	24 November 2011
The Kapol Co-operative Bank Ltd	24 November 2011
The Karnataka State Co-operative Apex Bank Ltd	24 November 2011
The Kashmir Mercantile Co-operative Bank Ltd	24 November 2011
The Kerala State Co-operative Bank Ltd	24 November 2011
The Keshav Sehkari Bank Ltd	24 November 2011
The Khamgaon Urban Co-operative Bank Ltd	24 November 2011
The Khatra Peoples' Co-operative Bank Ltd	24 November 2011
The Khattri Co-operative Urban Bank Ltd	24 November 2011
The Koylanchal Urban Co-operative Bank Ltd	24 November 2011
The Krishnagar City Co-operative Bank Ltd	24 November 2011
The Latur Urban Co-operative Bank Ltd	24 November 2011
The Madhya Pradesh Rajya Sahakari Bank Maryadit	24 November 2011
The Maharashtra State Co-operative Bank Ltd	24 November 2011
The Mahila Urban Co-operative Bank Ltd	24 November 2011
The Mahila Vikas Co-operative Bank Ltd	24 November 2011
The Malkapur Urban Co-operative Bank Ltd	24 November 2011
The Manipur State Co-operative Bank Ltd	24 November 2011
The Meghalaya Co-operative Apex Bank Ltd	24 November 2011
The Mehkar Urban Co-operative Bank Ltd	24 November 2011
The Midnapore People's Co-operative Bank Ltd	24 November 2011
The Mizoram Co-operative Apex Bank Ltd	24 November 2011
The Muzzaffarpur District Central Co-operative Bank Ltd	24 November 2011
The Nabadwip Co-operative Credit Bank Ltd	24 November 2011
The Nabapalli Co-operative Bank Ltd	24 November 2011
The Nagaland State Co-operative Bank Ltd	24 November 2011
The Nagarik Shakari Bank Maryadit, Jhabua	24 November 2011
The Nanded Merchant's Co-operative Bank Ltd	24 November 2011
The Nandura Urban Co-operative Bank Ltd	24 November 2011
The Navodaya Urban Co-operative Bank Ltd	24 November 2011
The Orissa State Co-operative Bank Ltd	24 November 2011
The Panihati Co-operative Bank Ltd	24 November 2011
The Pondichery State Co-opertive Bank Ltd	24 November 2011
The Prerna Nagari Sahakari Bank Ltd	24 November 2011
The Punjab State Co-operative Bank Ltd	24 November 2011
The Raipur Urban Mercantile Co-operative Bank	24 November 2011

The Rajasthan State Co-operative Bank Ltd	24 November 2011
The Sahyog Urban Co-operative Bank Ltd	24 November 2011
The Santragachi Co-operative Bank Ltd	24 November 2011
The Shibpur Co-operative Bank Ltd	24 November 2011
The Sikkim State Co-operative Bank Ltd	24 November 2011
The Social Coop Bank Ltd	24 November 2011
The Sonepat Urban Co-op. Bank Ltd	24 November 2011
The Suri Friends' Union Co-operative Bank Ltd	24 November 2011
The Sutex Co operative Bank Ltd	24 November 2011
The Tamil Nadu State Apex Co-operative Bank Ltd	24 November 2011
The Tapindu Urban Co-operative Bank Ltd	24 November 2011
The Tripura State Co-operative Bank Ltd	24 November 2011
The Udgir Urban Co-operative Bank Ltd	24 November 2011
The Union Co-operative Bank Ltd	24 November 2011
The Urban Co-operative Bank Ltd	24 November 2011
The Uttar Pradesh Co-operative Bank Ltd	24 November 2011
The Uttaranchal Rajya Sahakari Bank Ltd	24 November 2011
The Uttarpara Co-operative Bank Ltd	24 November 2011
The V.S.V. Co-operative Bank Ltd	24 November 2011
The Vaidyanath Urban Co-operative Bank Ltd	24 November 2011
The Vaijapur Merchants Co-operative Bank	24 November 2011
The Vaish Co-operative Adarsh Bank Ltd	24 November 2011
The Vaish Co-operative Commercial Bank Ltd	24 November 2011
The Vaish Co-operative New Bank Ltd	24 November 2011
The Vardhman Co-operative Bank Ltd	24 November 2011
The Washim Urban Co-operative Bank Limited	24 November 2011
The West Bengal State Co-operative Bank Ltd	24 November 2011'
The Yavatmal Mahila Sahakari Bank Ltd	24 November 2011
The Yavatmal Urban Co-operative Bank Ltd	24 November 2011
Thiruvaikuntam Co op Urban Bank Ltd	24 November 2011
Thiruvalluvar Town Co-Op Bank Ltd	24 November 2011
Thiruvananthapuram District Co-operative Central Bank Ltd	24 November 2011
Thiruvannamali Sambuvarayar District Central	24 November 2011
Thodupuzha Urban Co-operative Bank Ltd	24 November 2011
Thrissur District Co-operative Central Bank Ltd	24 November 2011
Thyagarayanagar Co-Op Bank Ltd	24 November 2011
Tindivanam Co-Op Urban Bank Ltd	24 November 2011

Tiruchendoor Co-Op Urban Bank Ltd	24 November 2011
Tiruchengode Co-Op Urban Bank Ltd	24 November 2011
Tiruchirapalli City Co-Op Bank Ltd	24 November 2011
Tiruchirapalli District Central Co-operative Bank Ltd	24 November 2011
Tiruchirapalli Hirudayapuram Co-Op Credit Bank	24 November 2011
Tirukoilur Co-Op Urban Bank Ltd	24 November 2011
Tirumala Co-op. Urban Bank Ltd	24 November 2011
Tirumangalam Co-Op Urban Bank Ltd	24 November 2011
Tirunelveli Central Co-operative Bank Ltd	24 November 2011
Tirunelveli Junction Co-Op Urban Bank Ltd	24 November 2011
Tirupati Co-Op Bank Ltd	24 November 2011
Tirupati Urban Co-operative Bank Ltd	24 November 2011
Tirupattur Urban Co-operative Bank Ltd	24 November 2011
Tiruppur Coop Urban Bank Ltd	24 November 2011
Tirur Urban Co-operative Bank Ltd	24 November 2011
Tiruturaipundi Co-Op Urban Bank Ltd	24 November 2011
Tiruvalla East Co-operative Bank Ltd	24 November 2011
Tiruvalla Urban Co-operative Bank Ltd	24 November 2011
Tiruvallur Co-Op Urban Bank Ltd	24 November 2011
Tiruvannamalai Co-Op Urban Bank Ltd	24 November 2011
Tiruvathipuram Coop Urban Bank Ltd	24 November 2011
Tonk Central Co-operative Bank Ltd	24 November 2011
Town Co-operative Bank Ltd	24 November 2011
Transport Coop Bank Ltd, Indore	24 November 2011
Trichur Urban Co-operative Bank Ltd	24 November 2011
Tripura Gramin Bank	24 November 2011
Trivandrum Co-operative Urban Bank Ltd	24 November 2011
Tumkur District Central Co-operative Bank Ltd	24 November 2011
Tumkur Grain Merchants Co-operative Bank Ltd	24 November 2011
Tumkur Pattana Sahakara Bank	24 November 2011
Tumkur Veerashaiva Co-operative Bank Ltd	24 November 2011
Tura Urban Co-Op Bank Ltd	24 November 2011
Tuticorin Co-Op Bank Ltd	24 November 2011
Tuticorin Melur Co-Op Bank Ltd	24 November 2011
Twin Cities Co-operative Urban Bank Ltd	24 November 2011
U.P. Civil Secretriat Primary Co-operative Bank	24 November 2011
U.P. Postal Primary Co-operative Bank Ltd	24 November 2011

Udaipur Central Co-operative Bank Ltd	24 November 2011
Udaipur Mahila Samridhhi Urban Coop Bk Ltd	24 November 2011
Udaipur Mahila Urban Co-Op Bk. Ltd	24 November 2011
Udaipur Urban Co-Op Bank Ltd	24 November 2011
Udamalpet Co-operative Bank Ltd	24 November 2011
Udhagmandlam Co-Op Urban Bank Ltd	24 November 2011
Udhana Citizen Co-operative Bank Ltd	24 November 2011
Udupi Co-operative Town Bank Ltd	24 November 2011
Udyam Vikas Sahakari Bank Ltd	24 November 2011
Ujjain Audhyogik Vikas Nagrik Sahkari Bank	24 November 2011
Ujjain Nagarik Sahakari Bank Maryadit, Ujjain	24 November 2011
Ujjain Paraspar Sahakari Bank Maryadit	24 November 2011
Uma Co-operative Bank Ltd	24 November 2011
Umiya Urban Co-operative Bank	24 November 2011
Umreth Urban Co-Op Bank Ltd	24 November 2011
Una Peoples' Co-Op Bank Ltd	24 November 2011
Unava Nagrik Sahakari Bank Ltd	24 November 2011
Union Co-Op Bank Limited Naroda	24 November 2011
United Commercial Co-operative Bank Ltd	24 November 2011
United Co-Op Bank Ltd	24 November 2011
United Co-operative Bank Limited	24 November 2011
United India Co-operative Bank Ltd	24 November 2011
United Mercantile Co-operative Bank Ltd	24 November 2011
United Puri Nimpara Central Co-operative Bank Ltd	24 November 2011
Universal Co-operative Urban Bank Ltd	24 November 2011
Unjha Nagarik Sahakari Bank Ltd	24 November 2011
Uravakonda Co-Op Town Bank Ltd	24 November 2011
Urban Co-Op Bank Limited	24 November 2011
Urban Co-Op Bank Limited Cuttack	24 November 2011
Usilampatti Co-Op Urban Bank Ltd	24 November 2011
Uthamapalayam Coo-Op. Urban Bank Ltd	24 November 2011
Utkal Co-Op Banking Soc Ltd	24 November 2011
Utkal Gramya Bank	24 November 2011
Uttar Banga Kshetriya Gramin Bank	24 November 2011
Uttar Bihar Gramin Bank	24 November 2011
Uttarakhand co-op. Bank LTD	24 November 2011
Uttaranchal Gramin Bank	24 November 2011

Uttarkashi Zilla Sahakari Bank Ltd	24 November 2011
Uttarsanda Peoples' Coop Bank Ltd	24 November 2011
V.I.S.L. Employees' Co-operative Bank Ltd	24 November 2011
Vadali Nagrik Sahakari Bank Ltd	24 November 2011
Vadnagar Nagrik Sahakari Bank Limited	24 November 2011
Vaijanath Appa Saraf Marathwada Nagari Sahaka	24 November 2011
Vaikom Urban Co-operative Bank Limited	24 November 2011
Vaishali District Central Co-operative Bank Ltd	24 November 2011
Vaishali Urban Co-op. Bank Ltd	24 November 2011
Vaishya Nagari Sahakari Bank Ltd	24 November 2011
Vaishya Sahakari Bank Ltd	24 November 2011
Vallabh Vidhyanagar Commercial Co op Bank Ltd	24 November 2011
Valmiki Urban Co-operative Bank Ltd	24 November 2011
Valparai Co-Operative Urban Bank Ltd	24 November 2011
Valsad District Central Co-operative Bank Ltd	24 November 2011
Valsad Mahila Nagrik Sahakari Bank Ltd	24 November 2011
Vananchal Gramin Bank	24 November 2011
Vani Co-operative Urban Bank Ltd	24 November 2011
Vani Merchants Co-operative Bank Ltd	24 November 2011
Vaniyambadi Town Coop Bank Ltd	24 November 2011
Varachha Co-operative Bank Ltd	24 November 2011
Varaganeri Coop Bank Ltd	24 November 2011
Varanashi District Central Co-operative Bank Ltd	24 November 2011
Vardhaman (Mahila) Co-Op Urban Bank Ltd	24 November 2011
Vasai Janata Sahakari Bank Ltd	24 November 2011
Vasai Vikas Sahakari Bank Ltd	24 November 2011
Vasantdada Nagari Sahakari Bank Ltd	24 November 2011
Vasavi Coop Urban Bank Limited	24 November 2011
Vasundhara Mahila Nagari Sahakari Bank Ltd	24 November 2011
Veershaiva Co-op Bank Ltd	24 November 2011
Veershaiva Sahakari Bank Ltd	24 November 2011
Vejalpur Nagarik Sahakari Bank Ltd	24 November 2011
Vellala Coop Bank Ltd	24 November 2011
Vellore Coop Town Bank Ltd	24 November 2011
Velur Coop Urban Bank Ltd	24 November 2011
Vepar Udhyog Vikas Sahakari Bank Limited	24 November 2011
Veraval Mercantile Coop Bank Limited	24 November 2011

Veraval Peoples' Coop Bank Limited	24 November 2011
Vidharbha Kshetriya Gramin Bank	24 November 2011
Vidharbha Merchants Urban Co-operative Bank	24 November 2011
Vidisha Bhopal Kshetriya Vidya Sahakari Bank Ltd	24 November 2011
Vidyanand Co-operative Bank Ltd	24 November 2011
Vidyasagar Central Co-operative Bank Ltd	24 November 2011
Vijapur Nagrik Sahakari Bank Limited	24 November 2011
Vijay Commercial Coop Bank Limited	24 November 2011
Vijay Coop Bank Limited	24 November 2011
Vikas Co-operative Bank Ltd	24 November 2011
Vikas Sahakari Bank Ltd	24 November 2011
Vikas Souharda Co-operative Bank Ltd	24 November 2011
Vikas Urban Co-operative Bank	24 November 2011
Vikramaditya Nagarik Sahakari Bank Maryadit,	24 November 2011
Villupuram Coop Urban Bank Limited	24 November 2011
Villupuram District Central Co-operative Bank Ltd	24 November 2011
Vima Kamgar Co-operative Bank Ltd	24 November 2011
Virajpet Pattana Sahakara Bank	24 November 2011
Viramgam Mercantile Coop Bank Limited	24 November 2011
Viravanallur Coop Urban Bank Ltd	24 November 2011
Virudhunagar Coop Urban Bank Ltd	24 November 2011
Virudhunagar District Central Co-operative Bank Ltd	24 November 2011
Visakhapatnam Co-op. Bank Ltd	24 November 2011
Vishakapatnam District Co-operative Central Bank Ltd	24 November 2011
Vishwakalyan Sahakara Bank	24 November 2011
Vishwakarma Nagari Sahakari Bank Ltd	24 November 2011
Vishwakarma Sahakara Bank	24 November 2011
Vishwanathrao Patil Murgud Sahakari Bank Ltd	24 November 2011
Vishwas Co-operative Bank Ltd Vishweshwar Sahakari Bank Ltd	24 November 2011
Visveshvaraya Grameena Bank Vita Merchants Coop Bank Ltd	24 November 2011
Vita Urban Co-operative Bank Ltd	24 November 2011
Vitthal Nagari Sahari Bank Ltd	24 November 2011
Vivekanada Nagarik Sahakari Bank Maryad.,Shuj	24 November 2011
Vriddhachalam Coop Urban Bank Ltd	24 November 2011
Vyankateshwara Sahakari Bank Ltd	24 November 2011
Vyapari Sahakari Bank Ltd	24 November 2011
Vyaparik Audhyogik Sahakari Bank Maryadit	24 November 2011

Vyavasayik Evam Audhyogik Sah.Bk.Maryadit.	24 November 2011
Vyavsaik Sahakari Bank Maryadit, Raipur	24 November 2011
Vysya Co-operative Bank Ltd	24 November 2011
Waghodia Urban Coop Bank Ltd	24 November 2011
Wai Urban Coop Bank Ltd	24 November 2011
Wainganga Krishna Gramin Bank	24 November 2011
Walchandnagar Sahakari Bank Ltd	24 November 2011
Wana Nagrik Sahakari Bank Ltd Wani Nagari Sahakari Bank Ltd	24 November 2011
Warangal District Co-operative Central Bank Ltd	24 November 2011
Warangal Urban Coop Bank Ltd	24 November 2011
Wardha District Ashirwad Mahila Nagari Sahakari	24 November 2011
Wardha District Central Co-operative Bank Ltd	24 November 2011
Wardha Nagari Sahakari Adhikosh (Bank)	24 November 2011
Wardha Zilla Parishad Employees (Urban) Co-op	24 November 2011
Wardhaman Urban Co-operative Bank Ltd	24 November 2011
Warud Urban Co-operative Bank Ltd	24 November 2011
Women's Co-operative Bank Ltd	24 November 2011
Wynad District Co-operative Central Bank Ltd	24 November 2011
Yadagiri Lakshmi Narasimha Swamy Co-op.Urban	24 November 2011
Yadrav Co-operative Bank Ltd	24 November 2011
Yamuna Nagar Central Co-operative Bank Ltd	24 November 2011
Yaragatti Urban Co-operative Credit Bank Ltd	24 November 2011
Yashwant Co-op. Bank Ltd	24 November 2011
Yashwant Nagari Sahakari Bank Ltd	24 November 2011
Yavatmal District Central Co-operative Bank Ltd	24 November 2011
Yawal Peoples Co-op Bank Ltd	24 November 2011
Yemmiganur Co-op.Town Bank Ltd	24 November 2011
Yeola Merchants Coop Bank Ltd	24 November 2011
Yeshwant Urban Co-operative Bank Ltd	24 November 2011
Youth Development Coop Bank Ltd	24 November 2011
Zilla Sahakari Bank Ltd, Garhwal	24 November 2011
Zilla Sahakari Bank Ltd, Haridwar	24 November 2011
Zilla Sahakari Bank Ltd, Jhansi	24 November 2011
Zilla Sahakari Bank Ltd, Lucknow	24 November 2011
Zilla Sahakari Bank Ltd, Mau	24 November 2011
Zilla Sahakari Bank Ltd, Unnao	24 November 2011
Zoroastrian Co-operative Bank Ltd	24 November 2011

Table 3: Financial institutions whose financial statements are accepted – India

Name of Financial Institution
Scheduled Commercial Banks – India
Abu Dhabi Commercial Bank Ltd
American Express Bank Ltd
Arab Bangladesh Bank Limited
Allahabad Bank
Andhra Bank
Antwerp Diamond Bank N.V.
Axis Bank Ltd
Bank Internasional Indonesia
Bank of America N.A.
Bank of Bahrain & Kuwait BSC
Barclays Bank Plc
BNP PARIBAS
Bank of Ceylon
Bharat Overseas Bank Ltd
Bank of Baroda
Bank of India
Bank of Maharashtra
Canara Bank
Central Bank of India
Calyon Bank
Citibank N.A.
Cho Hung Bank
Chinatrust Commercial Bank Ltd
Centurion Bank of Punjab Limited
City Union Bank Ltd
Coastal Local Area Bank Ltd
Corporation Bank
Catholic Syrian Bank Ltd
Deutsche Bank AG
Development Credit Bank Ltd
Dena Bank
IndusInd Bank Limited
ICICI Bank
IDBI Bank Limited
Indian Bank

Indian Overseas Bank
Industrial Development Bank of India
ING Vysya Bank
J P Morgan Chase Bank, National Association
Krung Thai Bank Public Company Limited
Kotak Mahindra Bank Limited
Karnataka Bank
Karur Vysya Bank Limited.
Lord Krishna Bank Ltd
Mashreqbank psc
Mizuho Corporate Bank Ltd
Oman International Bank S A O G
Oriental Bank of Commerce
Punjab & Sind Bank
Punjab National Bank
Societe Generale
Sonali Bank
Standard Chartered Bank
State Bank of Mauritius Ltd
SBI Commercial and International Bank Ltd
State Bank of Bikaner and Jaipur
State Bank of Hyderabad
State Bank of India
State Bank of Indore
State Bank of Mysore
State Bank of Patiala
State Bank of Saurashtra
State Bank of Travancore
Syndicate Bank
The Bank of Nova Scotia
The Bank of Tokyo-Mitsubishi, Ltd
The Development Bank of Singapore Ltd. (DBS Bank Ltd)
The Hongkong & Shanghai Banking Corporation Ltd
Tamilnad Mercantile Bank Ltd
The Bank of Rajasthan Limited
The Dhanalakshmi Bank Limited
The Federal Bank Ltd
The HDFC Bank Ltd
The Jammu & Kashmir Bank Ltd

The Nainital Bank Ltd
The Sangli Bank Ltd
The South Indian Bank Ltd
The Ratnakar Bank Ltd
The Royal Bank of Scotland N.V.
The Lakshmi Vilas Bank Ltd
UCO Bank
Union Bank of India
United Bank Of India
Vijaya Bank
Yes Bank

Table 4: Financial institutions whose financial statements are accepted – Ghana

Name of Financial Institution
Standard Chartered Bank Ghana Limited
Ghana Commercial Bank Limited
The Trust Bank Ltd
SG-SSB Ltd UT Bank Ltd
International Commercial Bank Ltd
uniBank Ghana Ltd
National Investment Bank
Agricultural Development Bank Ltd
Prudential Bank Ltd
Merchant Bank (Ghana) Ltd
Ecobank Ghana Ltd
CAL Bank Ltd
HFC Bank Ltd
United bank for Africa (Ghana) Ltd
Stanbic
Bank of Baroda (Ghana) Ltd
Zenith Bank (Ghana) Ltd
Guaranty Trust bank (Ghana) Ltd
Fidelity Bank Ltd
First Atlantic Merchant Bank Ltd
Bank of Africa (Ghana) Ltd

| BSIC Ghana Ltd |
| Access bank Ghana Ltd |
| Barclays Bank of Ghana Ltd |
| Energy Bank (Ghana) Ltd |
| ARB Apex Bank |
| Citibank NA Ghana Representative office |
| Ghana International Bank Plc |

Table 5: Financial Institutions that do not satisfactorily verify financial statements – Pakistan

Name of financial institution	Effective date
Government Post Office Region Islamabad	24 November 2011
Government Post Office Region Karachi	24 November 2011
Government Post Office Region Lahore	24 November 2011

Table 6: Financial institutions whose financial statements are accepted – Pakistan

Name of Financial Institution
Al-Baraka Islamic Banking B.S.C. (E.C)
Allied Bank Limited
American Express Bank Limited
Askari Bank Limited
Bank Al-Falah
Bank Al-Habib
Bank of Ceylon
Bank Khyber
Bank of Tokyo Mitsubishi Limited
Barclays
Burj Bank
Citibank
Credit Agricole Indosuez (The Global French Bank)
Deutsche Bank A.G.
Doha Bank
Dubai Islamic Bank

Faysal Bank
First Women Bank
GPO Abbottabad
GPO Charsadda
GPO Gujar Khan
GPO Haripur
GPO Jhelum
GPO Kotli
GPO Mardan
GPO Mirpur
GPO Multan
GPO Nowshera
GPO Peshawar
GPO Swabi
GPO Swat
Habib bank A.G Zurich
Habib Bank Limited
Habib Metropolitan Bank
Industrial Development Bank of Pakistan (IDBP)
International Finance Investment & Commerce Bank Limited
JS bank
KASB Bank
Khushhali Bank
Mashreq Bank P.S.C
Meezan Bank
Muslim Commercial Bank (MCB)
National Bank of Pakistan
National Investment Bank (NIB)
National Investment Trust Limited (NIT)
National Savings Abbottabad
National Savings Bahawalpur
National Savings Faisalabad
National Savings Gujranwala
National Savings Hyderabad
National Savings Islamabad
National Savings Karachi
National Savings Lahore

National Savings Multan
National Savings Peshawar
National Savings Quetta
National Savings Sukkur
Oman International Bank S.O.A.G
Pak Kuwait Investment Company (Pvt) Limited
Pak Libya Holding Company (Pvt) Limited
Pak Oman Investment Company (PVT) Limited
Pakistan Industrial Credit & Investment Corporation Limited
Punjab Provincial Corporative Bank (PPCB)
Rupali Bank Limited
Samba Bank Limited
Saudi Pak Industrial & Agricultural Investment Company (Pvt) Limited
Silk Bank Limited
Sindh Bank
SME BANK
Soneri Bank
Standard Chartered Bank
Summit Bank
The Bank of Azad Jammu & Kashmir (Bank of AJK)
The Bank of Punjab
The First Micro Finance Bank Ltd
Trust Bank
United Bank Limited
Zarai Taraqiati Bank Limited (ZTBL)

Table 7: Financial Institutions that do not satisfactorily verify financial statements – Iran

Name and address of financial institution	Effective date
en Bank:	6 May 2012
Head Office, No.24, Esfandiyar Blvd., Valiasr Ave., Tehran, Iran, Tel: +98 21 8233 0000	
Building #2, No.51, Jahan Koodak Crossroad, Africa Blvd., Tehran, Iran, Tel: +98 21 8461 0000	

Mellat:	6 May 2012

Head office, # 327 Taleghani Ave, Tehran 15817 Iran, Tel: +98 21 82961

Main Branch, 21 82962090 , 21 82962440, FAX: + 98 21 82962702

Main Branch 21 82962720 / TLX: 226313 bkntir

Melli:	6 May 2012

Bank Melli Iran Central Depts, Ferdowsi Ave. P.O. Box: 11365-123 Tehran, Iran Tel: +98 +21- 23583303, Fax: +98 +21- 26403760

Tejarat:	6 May 2012

Bank Tejarat, Esfahan Br., Main Office of Bank Tejarat, Museum of Sheikh Bahayee Ave. & Abuzar St. junction, Zip Code: 8134877151 Tel.: (0311) 2341036, Tlx.: 312104, Fax: (0311) 2341039

Ghavvamin:	6 May 2012

Head Office: No. 252, Milad Tower Beginning of Africa Blvd., Argentin Sq., 151490 Tehran, Iran. Tel: +98 21 88643000, Fax: +98 21 88784021

Bank Keshavarzi (Agri Bank):	6 May 2012

General Management & Head Office No 129, Patric Lumumba St, Jalal-Al-Ahmad Expressway, P.O.Box: 14155/6395, Tehran, Iran. Tel : +98 21 825 0135, Fax : +98 21 826 2313, Tlx : 212058 ADBI-IR

Bank Sedarat:	6 May 2012

Bank Saderat Iran, Sepehr Tower, Somayeh street, P.O. Box 15745 - 631, Tehran, Iran. Tel : 009821 - 8829469, Fax 009821 - 8839534

Saman Bank:	6 May 2012

Building no.1 no879. Kaledge Junction, Engheleb St., Tehran, Iran. Tel : +982166959050 Building No2: No1543. Tarkesh Dooz Al, Parkway-Valiasr St, Tehran, Iran. Tel: +982126210926-31

Fereshtegan (No info found)	6 May 2012 6
Samenolaemeh (No info found)	May 2012 6
Samenolhojaj:	May 2012

Next to Shahid Eisavi Alley, Ghiam Shomali St., Nabard St., Pirouzi St. Tel : 33195774

Bank Maskan:	6 May 2012

PO Box 11365/5699, No 247 3rd Floor Fedowsi Ave, Cross Sarhang Sakhaei St, Tehran, Iran

Table 8: Financial Institutions whose financial statements are accepted – Iran

Name and address of Financial Institution
Pasargad:
No. 430, Mirdamad Blvd., Tehran, 1969774511, Iran. Tel :+98(21)82890
Parsian:
No.4, Zarafshan St., Shahid Farahzadi Blvd, Shahrak.Ghods, Tehran, Iran. Tel:(+ 9821) 88502024

Table 9: Financial Institutions that do not satisfactorily verify financial statements – Philippines

Name of financial institution	Address of financial institution	Effective date
1st Macro Bank, Inc. (A Rural Bank)	B. Morcilla & P. Herrera Sts., Pateros City	24 November 2011
1st Macro Bank, Inc. (A Rural Bank)	B. Morcilla & P. Herrera Sts., Pateros City	24 November 2011
1st Valley Bank, Inc. (A Rural Bank)	Baroy, Lanao del Norte	24 November 2011
5 Speed Rural Bank, Inc.	J. P. Rizal St., Poblacion, Padre Garcia, Batangas	24 November 2011
A B Capital and Investment Corporation	Unit 1008, 10F Tower I & Exchange Plaza, Ayala Triangle, Ayala Avenue, Makati City	24 November 2011
Advantage Bank Corp. (A Microfinance-Oriented Rural Bank)	Stop Over Commercial Complex, Mac Arthur Highway (Namkwang Road) corner Gerona-Pura Road, Brgy. Abagon, Gerona, Tarlac	24 November 2011
Agri-Business Rural Bank, Inc.	Poblacion, Solano, Nueva Vizcaya	24 November 2011
Agricom Rural Bank (Sta. Maria,Bulacan), Inc.	F. Santiago cor. A. Morales Sts. Poblacion, Sta. Maria, Bulacan	24 November 2011
Agusan Norte – Butuan City Coop RB	UCCP Bldg., R. Calo St., Butuan City, Agusan del Norte	24 November 2011
Air Materiel Wing Savings & Loan Association, Inc. (AMWSLAI)	AMWSLAI Bldg. Cor. Boni Serrano and 18th Avenue, Murphy, Cubao, Quezon City	24 November 2011
Aliaga Farmers Rural Bank (Nueva Ecija), Inc.	Poblacion West III, Aliaga, Nueva Ecija	24 November 2011

AMA Bank (A Rural Bank)	311 Shaw Blvd., Mandaluyong, Metro Manila	24 November 2011
Anilao Bank (Rural Bank of Anilao (Iloilo), Inc.	Poblacion, Anilao, Iloilo	24 November 2011
Armed Forces of the Phils. Savings & Loan Association, Inc. (AFPSLAI)	AFPSLA Bldg. EDSA Cor. Col. Bonny Serrano, Camp. Aguinaldo, Quezon City	24 November 2011
Arsenal Savings and Loan Association, Inc.	Camp Gen. Antonio Luna, Limay, Bataan	24 November 2011
Asian Consumers Bank (A Rural Bank), Inc.	Basista, Pangasinan	24 November 2011
Asiatrust Development Bank	ATDB Bldg., 1424 Quezon Avenue, 1100 Quezon City	24 November 2011
ASLA Savings & Loan Association, Inc.	G/F Makati Stock Exchange Ayala Avenue, Makati City	24 November 2011
Aspac Rural Bank, Inc.	M. L. Quezon National Highway, 6015 Pusok, Lapu-lapu City, Cebu	24 November 2011
Aurorabank (A Microfinance-Oriented Rural Bank), Inc.	Rizal St., Brgy. 5, Poblacion, Baler, Aurora	24 November 2011
Baclaran Rural Bank, Inc.	83 Redemptorist Rd., Baclaran, Parañaque City	24 November 2011
Bagong Bangko Rural ng Malabang, Inc.	Chinatown, Malabang, Lanao del Sur	24 November 2011
Baguio Vendors Savings & Loan Association, Inc.	2/F BPI Family Bank Building, Malcolm Square, Baguio City	24 November 2011
Balanga Rural Bank, Inc.	Don Manuel Banzon Ave., Doña Francisca Subdivision, Balanga City, Bataan	24 November 2011
Baliuag Rural Bank, Inc.	Baliuag, Bulacan	24 November 2011
Banco Alabang, Inc. (A Rural Bank)	Ground Floor, Minerva Building, National Road, Putatan, Muntinlupa	24 November 2011
Banco Bakun, Inc. (A Rural Bank)	Antamok Tram, Ucab, Itogon, Benguet	24 November 2011
Banco Batangan, Inc. (A Rural Bank)	J.P. Rizal, Taysan, Batangas	24 November 2011
Banco Carmona, Inc., A Rural Bank	J.M. Loyal St., Carmona, Cavite	24 November 2011
Banco de Arevalo, Inc. (A Rural Bank)	Concordia, Sibunag, Guimaras	24 November 2011
Banco de Mindoro, Inc. (A Rural Bank)	Calapan, Oriental Mindoro	24 November 2011

Banco Dingras (Comm. RB Dingras, Inc.)	Madamba, Dingras, Ilocos Norte 2913	24 November 2011
Banco Dipolog, Inc., A Rural Bank	Calibo St., Dipolog City, Zamboanga Del Norte	24 November 2011
Banco Makiling, A Rural Bank, Inc.	Brgy. Poblacion 2, Sto. Tomas, Batangas	24 November 2011
Banco Maximo, Inc. (A Rural Bank)	E. Binghay St., Baliwagan, Balamban, 6041 Cebu	24 November 2011
Banco ng Masa, Inc. (A Microfinance-Oriented Rural Bank)	East Mart, National Highway, Calatagan, Batangas	24 November 2011
Banco Rural de General Tinio (BRGT), Inc.	Poblacion, Gen. Tinio, Nueva Ecija	24 November 2011
Banco Rural de Isla Cordova, Inc.	San Miguel, Cordova, 6017 Cebu	24 November 2011
Banco San Juan, Inc.	71 N. Domingo St., San Juan City (Exec. Office: BSJ Centre Guadalupe Mansion, J.P. Rizal Ext., Makati City)	24 November 2011
Banco Sual (A Rural Bank), Inc.	Poblacion Sual, Pangasinan	24 November 2011
Bangko Buena Consolidated, Inc. (A Rural Bank)	23 Valeria & Rizal Sts., Iloilo City	24 November 2011
Bangko Carrascal, Inc. (A Rural Bank), Inc.	Arreza cor Cervantes St Embarcadero, Carrascal, Surigao del Sur	24 November 2011
Bangko Kabayan (A Rural Bank), Inc.	Santiago St., Poblacion, Ibaan, Batangas	24 November 2011
Bangko Mabuhay (RB of Tanza, Inc.)	Tanza, Cavite	24 November 2011
Bangko Magsaysay (Isabela), Inc. – A Rural Bank	Saguday, Quirino	24 November 2011
Bangko Pangasinan – A Rural Bank, Inc.	Perez Boulevard, Dagupan City	24 November 2011
Bangko Pasig (Rural Bank), Inc.	G/F Hanston Bldg.,Ruby Road, Ortigas Centre, Pasig City	24 November 2011
Bangko Rural ng Magarao (Camarines Sur), Inc.	San Pantaleon, Magarao, Camarines Sur	24 November 2011
Bangko Rural ng Pasacao, Inc.	Sta. Rosa del Sur, Pasacao, 4417, Camarines Sur	24 November 2011
BANGKO RURAL NG SAN TEODORO	VVBG Building Poblacion San Teodoro Oriental Mindoro	24 November 2011

Bangko Rural ng Tagoloan, Inc.	Jacinto St. Poblacion, Tagoloan, Misamis Oriental	24 November 2011
Bank of Florida, Inc. (A Rural Bank)	Dolores, 2000 City of San Fernando, Pampanga	24 November 2011
Bank of Makati (A Rural Bank), Inc.	44 Sen. Gil J. Puyat Ave., Bgy. Isidro, Makati City	24 November 2011
Bank One Savings and Trust Corporation	4201 R. Magsaysay Blvd., Sta. Mesa, Manila 1016	24 November 2011
Banko Nuestra Sra. del Pilar, Inc. (A Rural Bank)	678 McArthur H-way, San Simon, Pampanga	24 November 2011
Bannawag Rural Bank, Inc.	Camilio Osias Street, Balaoan, La Union	24 November 2011
Basa Air Base Savings & Loan Associatiom, Inc.	Basa Air Base, Floridablanca, Pampanga	24 November 2011
Bataan Cooperative Bank	Capitol Compound, Balanga, Bataan	24 November 2011
Bataan Development Bank	Aguirre St., Balanga, Bataan, 2100 Bataan	24 November 2011
Bataan Savings and Loan Association, Inc.	33 Rizal St., Dinalupihan, Bataan 2110	24 November 2011
Batanes Government Employees Savings & Loan, Inc.	1588 Santana St., Brgy. Kaychanarianan, Basco, Batanes	24 November 2011
Batangas Rural Bank for Coop., Inc.	Pastor Ave., New Public Market, Cuta, Batangas City	24 November 2011
Baybank, Inc. (A Rural Bank)	Baganga, Davao Oriental	24 November 2011
Benguet Centre Bank, Inc. A Rural Bank	Poblacion, Sablan, Benguet	24 November 2011
BHF Rural Bank, Inc.	A.V. Fernandez Ave., Mayombo District, Dagupan City	24 November 2011
Bicol Teachers Savings & Loan Association, Inc.	Rm. 203 PVLB Bldg., 4 Peñaranda St, Legazpi City	24 November 2011
Biñan Rural Bank, Inc.	J. Gonzales St., Biñan, Laguna	24 November 2011
Binangonan Rural Bank, Inc.	135 Baltazar St., Layunan, Binangonan, Rizal	24 November 2011
BIR Savings & Loan Association, Inc.	1st Flr. DPC Bldg., BIR Nat'l. Office Compound, Diliman, Quezon City	24 November 2011
Bolbok Rural Bank, Inc.	Mojica Street, Poblacion, San Juan, Batangas	24 November 2011
Bottlers Employees Savings & Loan Association, Inc.	7/F ACE Bldg., Dela Rosa cor. Rada Sts., Legaspi Village, Makati City	24 November 2011

Bridgeway Rural Banking Corp.	Botolan Agora Complex, Batonlapoc, Botolan, Zambales 2202	24 November 2011
Builders Rural Bank, Inc.	410 J.P. Rizal St., Sto. Niño, Marikina City	24 November 2011
Bukidnon Bank, INC (RB of Kalilangan)	Poblacion, Kalilangan, Bukidnon	24 November 2011
Business and Consumers Bank (A Dev't. Bank)	BCB Building, Simon Ledesma St., Jaro, Iloilo City	24 November 2011
Butuan City Rural Bank, Inc.	A. D. Curato St., Butuan City, Agusan del Norte	24 November 2011
Cabanatuan City Rural Bank, Inc.	1068 Burgos Ave., Cabanatuan City, Nueva Ecija	24 November 2011
Cagsawa Rural Bank, Inc.	T. Perez Street, Daraga, Albay	24 November 2011
Camiling Rural Bank, Inc.	Quezon Avenue, Camiling, Tarlac	24 November 2011
Cantilan Bank, Inc. (A Rural Bank)	Cantilan, Surigao del Sur	24 November 2011
Capitol City Bank, Inc., A Rural Bank	Governor's Drive, Trece Martires City, Cavite	24 November 2011
Capiz Settlers Cooperative Rural Bank, Inc.	Elemar Bldg., San Roque Ext., Roxas City 5800	24 November 2011
Card Bank, Inc. (A Microfinance Rural Bank)	20 M. L. Quezon, City Subd. , San Pablo City, Laguna	24 November 2011
Card SME Bank, Inc. A Thrift Bank	Gen. Malvar Ave., Poblacion II, Sto. Tomas, Batangas	24 November 2011
Cavite Naval Base Savings and Loan Association,Inc. (CNBSLAI)	Fort San Felipe, Cavite City	24 November 2011
Cavite Rural Banking Corporation	M.H. del Pilar cor. Kiamzon Sts, Silang, Cavite	24 November 2011
CDCP Employees Savings & Loan Association, Inc.	PNCC Complex, EDSA – Reliance Street, Mandaluyong City	24 November 2011
Cebu International Finance Corporation	8th Floor, CIFC Towers, J. Luna Avenue cor. Humabon St., NRA, 6000 Cebu City	24 November 2011
Cebuana Lhuillier Rural Bank, Inc.	160 Zapote Rd., Bacoor, Cavite	24 November 2011
Central Equity Rural Bank	121 Don Placido Campos Avenue, Dasmariñas, Cavite	24 November 2011
Central Visayas Rural Bank, Inc.	Real St., Dumaguete City 6200, Negros Oriental	24 November 2011

Century Rural Bank Inc.(RB of Babak Inc.)	Babak District, Island Garden City of Samal, 8119 Davao del Norte	24 November 2011
Century Savings Bank Corporation	232 Shaw Blvd. cor. Oranbo Drive, Pasig City 1601	24 November 2011
Certified Savings & Loan Association, Inc.	3/F SGV Bldg., 6760 Ayala Ave., 1226 Makati City	24 November 2011
Citizen's Rural Bank (Cabiao), Inc.	San Juan North, Cabiao, Nueva Ecija 3107	24 November 2011
City Savings Bank	City Savings Bank Financial Plaza cor. Osmena Boulevard. and P. Burgos St., 6000 Cebu City	24 November 2011
Citystate Savings Bank, Inc.	Citystate Centre Building, 709 Shaw Blvd., Oranbo, Pasig City 1600	24 November 2011
Classic Rural Bank, Inc.	Evangelista St., Batangas City	24 November 2011
Community Bank (RB of Alfonso, Inc.)	Mabini St., Alfonso, Cavite	24 November 2011
Community RB of Naawan, Inc.	Magsaysay St., Naawan, Misamis Oriental	24 November 2011
Community Rural Bank of Catmon, Inc.	684 Corazon, Catmon, Cebu	24 November 2011
Community Rural Bank of Clarin, Inc.	Clarin, Misamis Occidental	24 November 2011
Community Rural Bank of Dapitan City, Inc.	Andres Bonifacio St., Dapitan City 7101 Zamboanga del Norte	24 November 2011
Community Rural Bank of Magallon, Inc.	Moises Padilla, Negros Occidental	24 November 2011
Community Rural Bank of Magsaysay, Inc.	Poblacion, Magsaysay, Davao del Sur	24 November 2011
Community Rural Bank of Medellin, Inc.	Jose Rizal St., Poblacion, Medellin, Cebu City	24 November 2011
Community Rural Bank of Romblon, Inc.	Bagong Lipunan, Bry. 1 Romblon, Romblon	24 November 2011
Community Rural Bank of San Felipe, Inc	West Feria, San Felipe, Zambales	24 November 2011
Community Rural Bank of San Gabriel, Inc.	Poblacion, San Gabriel, La Union	24 November 2011
Composite Wing Savings and Loan Association, Inc. (CWSLAI)	Lot 13, Blk. 87, Phase 5, A. Luna St., AFP Officers Village, Fort Bonifacio, Taguig City	24 November 2011
Cooperative Bank of Agusan del Sur	Quezon St., Brgy.2, San Francisco, Agusan del Sur	24 November 2011

Cooperative Bank of Aurora	Avenida Aurora, San Luis, Aurora	24 November 2011
Cooperative Bank of Benguet	JC 225 Central Pico, La Trinidad, Benguet	24 November 2011
Cooperative Bank of Cagayan	Diversion Road, San Gabriel, Tuguegarao City, Cagayan	24 November 2011
Cooperative Bank of Camarines Norte	Governor Panotes Ave.,Daet, Camarines Norte	24 November 2011
Cooperative Bank of Cavite	Capitol Rd., Trece Martires City, Cavite	24 November 2011
Cooperative Bank of Cebu	52-A Andres Abellana Ext., Guadalupe, Cebu City	24 November 2011
Cooperative Bank of Cotabato	CBC Bldg 1, Lanao Kidapawan City, North Cotabato	24 November 2011
Cooperative Bank of Ilocos Norte	Municipal Public Market Brgy #3, San Pablo, San Nicolas, Ilocos Norte 290	24 November 2011
Cooperative Bank of Iloilo	Bonifacio Drive, 5000 Iloilo City	24 November 2011
Cooperative Bank of La Union	Dona Toribia Aspiras Road, Consolacion, Agoo, La Union	24 November 2011
Cooperative Bank of Leyte-Leyte Coop RB	Pongos Hotel Annex, Bonifacio St. cor. Lopez Jaena St., Ormoc City	24 November 2011
Cooperative Bank of Misamis Oriental	Provincial Capitol Compound, Cagayan de Oro City	24 November 2011
Cooperative Bank of Mt. Province	Ground Floor, Diocesan, Bontoc, Mt. Province	24 November 2011
Cooperative Bank of Negros Oriental	Cervantes St.,Dumaguete City	24 November 2011
Cooperative Bank of Nueva Vizcaya	Burgos St. cor.Gaddang Sts., Quirino Solano, Bayombong, Nueva Vizcaya	24 November 2011
Cooperative Bank of Palawan	Junction I, National Highway, Brgy. San Miguel,Puerto Princesa City, Palawan	24 November 2011
Cooperative Bank of Pampanga, Inc.	McArthur Highway, Dolores, San Fernando, Pampanga	24 November 2011
Cooperative Bank of Quezon Province	Granja cor. L. Guinto Sts. Lucena City, Quezon	24 November 2011
Cooperative Bank of Surigao del Sur	Mangagoy, Bislig, Surigao del Sur	24 November 2011
Cooperative Bank of Tarlac, Inc.	Macabulos Drive, San Roque, Tarlac City	24 November 2011

Cooperative Bank of Zambales	Zambales Livelihood Bldg., Magsaysay Ave., Iba, Zambales	24 November 2011
Cooperative Rural Bank of Bohol, Inc.	C.P.Garcia East Ave., Tagbilaran City	24 November 2011
Cooperative Rural Bank of Bukidnon, Inc.	San Victores St., Malaybalay City, Bukidnon	24 November 2011
Cooperative Rural Bank of Bulacan, Inc.	Banga 1st, Plaridel, 3004 Bulacan	24 November 2011
Cooperative Rural Bank of Davao del Sur, Inc.	Luna St., Digos City, Davao del Sur (8002)	24 November 2011
Cooperative Rural Bank of Zamboanga del Norte	484 Gen. Luna and Balintawak Sts., Dipolog City, Zamboanga del Norte	24 November 2011
Cordillera Bank (A Rural Bank), Inc.	M. Crisologo St., Vigan City, Ilocos Sur 2700	24 November 2011
Cordillera Savings Bank, Inc.	No. 31 Mena Crisologo St., Vigan, 2700 Ilocos Sur	24 November 2011
Country Rural Bank of Taguig, Inc.	10 Gen Luna St., Tuktukan, Taguig, Metro Manila	24 November 2011
Countryside Coop Rural Bank of Batangas	Capitol Hills, Batangas City, Batangas	24 November 2011
Countryside Rural Bank of Palauig (Zambales), Inc.	Palauig, Zambales	24 November 2011
Crown Bank, Inc. (A Rural Bank)	San Vicente, Apalit, Pampanga	24 November 2011
CSFirst Bank, INC. -A Rural Bank	J.P. Rizal St., Poblacion Sur, Bayambang, 2423 Pangasinan	24 November 2011
Cuyapo Rural Bank, Inc.	No. 2 Quezon St., Cuyapo, Nueva Ecija	24 November 2011
D' Asian Hills Bank (A Rural Bank)	2/F DAHBI Centre, Fortich St., Malaybalay City, Bukidnon	24 November 2011
De La O Rural Bank, Inc.	San Jose St., Pangil, Laguna	24 November 2011
Delmont Bank, Inc. (RB of San Jose del Monte)	Quirino H-way, Tungkong Mangga, San Jose Del Monte, Bulacan	24 November 2011
DEPW Savings & Loan Association, Inc.	Room 358 City Hall Bldg., Ermita, Manila	24 November 2011
DER Savings & Loan Association, Inc. (DERSALA)	Rm. 410, 5-storey Blsg., BSP Complex, A Mabini St., Malate, Manila	24 November 2011
Diamond Rural Bank, Inc.	2 Kayang St., Baguio City	24 November 2011
Dumaguete City Development Bank	Dr. Vicente Locsin cor. Cervantes Sts., Dumagute City	24 November 2011

Dumaguete Rural Bank, Inc.	San Jose St., Dumaguete City, Negros Oriental	24 November 2011
Dungganon Bank, Inc. (A Microfinance Thrift Bank)	NTWTF Bldg., 102 San Sebastian St. Bacolod City, Negros Occidental	24 November 2011
Earist Savings & Loan Association, Inc.	Nagtahan, Sampaloc, Manila	24 November 2011
East Coast Rural Bank, Inc. (RB Hagonoy)	G. Panganiban St., Sto. Niño, Hagonoy, Bulacan	24 November 2011
Eastern Rizal Rural Bank Inc. (Jala-Jala Rural Bank)	C. Villaran St.,Jala-Jala, Rizal	24 November 2011
EIB Savings Bank, Inc.	Cebu South Road, Brgy Bulacao, Talisay City, Cebu	24 November 2011
Emerald Rural Bank, Inc.	Lot 12-A, Area-D, Sapang Palay, San Jose Del Monte City, Bulacan	24 November 2011
Empire Rural Bank, Inc.	C.M. Recto Ave., Lipa City	24 November 2011
Enterprise Bank, Inc. A Rural Bank	Lianga 8307, Surigao del Sur	24 November 2011
Enterprise Capital Bank (Rural Bank of Taguig)	Amber Place, 19 Bayani Road, Fort Bonifacio, 1630 Taguig City, Metro Manila	24 November 2011
Entrepreneur Rural Bank A.	Mabini St., San Pedro, Laguna	24 November 2011
Equicom Savings Bank, Inc.	G/F Renaissance Condominium, 215 Salcedo St., Legaspi Village, Makati City	24 November 2011
Faculty Savings & Loan Association of Adamson University, Inc.	900 San Marcelino St., Ermita, Manila	24 November 2011
Far Eastern Bank (A Rural Bank), Inc.	Brgy. 7 Market Site, Dolores, Eastern Samar	24 November 2011
Farm Bank (A Rural Bank) – Farmer's Bank of Capiz, Inc.	5800 Roxas City, Capiz	24 November 2011
Farmers Rural Bank, Inc.	J.P. Rizal St., Poblacion, Lian, Batangas	24 November 2011
Farmers Savings and Loan Bank, Inc.	McArthur Highway, Wakas, Bocaue, Bulacan	24 November 2011
Fernando Air Base Savings & Loan Association, Inc. (FABSLAI)	Fernando Air Base, Lipa City, Batangas	24 November 2011
Fil-Agro Rural Bank, Inc.	McArthur Highway, Poblacion, Marilao, Bulacan	24 November 2011

Filidian Rural Bank, Inc.	#6 Circumferencial Rd., Brgy. Dalig, Antipolo, Rizal	24 November 2011
Filipino Savers Bank, Inc. (A Rural Bank)	457 Tandang Sora Avenue, Quezon City	24 November 2011
Finman Rural Bank, Inc.	360 Dr. Sixto Antonio, Caniogan, Pasig City	24 November 2011
First Agro-Industrial Rural Bank, Inc.	Dela Viña cor. J. Lequin Sts., Cantecson, Bogo City, 6010 Cebu	24 November 2011
First Community Bank, Inc. (A Rural Bank)	101 JP & Heritage Square, Burgos St., Bacolod City	24 November 2011
First Integrity Bank, Inc. (Rural Bank of Bailen)	Calle Real, Brgy. Poblacion I, General E. Aguinaldo, Cavite 4124	24 November 2011
First Isabela Cooperative Bank, Inc.	Minante I, Cauayan City Public Mkt, Cauayan City (Executive Address: National Hi-way , Minante 1, Cauayan City, Isabela)	24 November 2011
First Malayan Leasing & Finance Corporation	20th Floor GT Tower International, Ayala Avenue corner HV dela Costa	24 November 2011
First Metro Investment Corporation	5th Floor Grepalife Building, 221 Sen. Gil Puyat Avenue, 1200 Makati City	24 November 2011
First Midland Rural Bank, Inc.	FM RBI Bldg., Dessa, New Lucena, 5005 Iloilo	24 November 2011
First Mindoro Microfinance Rural Bank, INC.	Poblacion, Bongabong, Oriental Mindoro	24 November 2011
First Naga Bank (A Rural Bank)	Villa Grande Homes, Conception Grande, Naga City	24 November 2011
First Provincial Bank, Inc. (A Rural Bank)	MacArthur Highway, Brgy. Ligtasan, Tarlac City	24 November 2011
First State Rural Bank, Inc.	cor. Lopez Jaena & Sta. Ana Sts., Bacolod City	24 November 2011
First Tagum Rural Bank , Inc.	Bonifacio cor. Rizal Sts., Tagum City, Davao del Norte	24 November 2011
First United Farmers Rural Bank, Inc.	Bgy Callos, Sta. Cruz, Laguna	24 November 2011
Forestry Savings & Loan Association, Inc.	DENR – Forest Management Bureau Bldg. Visayas Avenue, Diliman, Q.C.	24 November 2011

Frontier Rural Bank, Inc.	New Road, Basak, Lapu-Lapu City, Davao del Norte	24 November 2011
Gateway Rural Bank, Inc.	McArthur Highway, Wawa, Balagtas, Bulacan	24 November 2011
GM BANK OF LUZON, INC. (A RURAL BANK)	Maharlika Highway, Brgy. Dimasalang, Cabanatuan City, Nueva Ecija	24 November 2011
Golden Rural Bank of the Philippines, Inc.	National Hi-way, Cabaruan, Cauayan City, Isabela	24 November 2011
Grand-Agri Rural Bank, Inc.	Luis Palad St., Tayabas, Quezon	24 November 2011
Green Bank (Rural Green Bank of Caraga)	Montilla Blvd., Butuan City, Agusan del Norte	24 November 2011
GSIS Bayanihan Savings & Loan Association, Inc.	Level 2A GSIS Bldg. Financial Centre, Roxas Blvd., Pasay City	24 November 2011
GSIS Family Bank, A Thrift Bank	2/F AIC Grande Tower, Sapphire & Garnet Rds., Ortigas Ctr., Pasig City	24 November 2011
Guagua Rural Bank, Inc.	Plaza Burgos, Guagua, Pampanga	24 November 2011
Guagua Savers Bank (A Rural Bank), Inc.	Plaza Burgos, Sto. Cristo, Guagua, Pampanga	24 November 2011
Gulf Bank, Inc. (RB of Lingayen, Inc.)	#3 Avenida Rizal East, Lingayen, Pangasinan	24 November 2011
Highland Rural Bank, Inc. (RB Kapangan, Inc.)	Lomon, Kapangan, Benguet	24 November 2011
Hiyas Banking Corporation (A Thrift Bank)	Gov. Fortunato F. Halili Ave., Bagbaguin, Sta. Maria, Bulacan	24 November 2011
Iligan City Public School Teachers Savings & Loan Association, Inc.	Roxas Avenue, Iligan City	24 November 2011
Ilocandia Community Bank, Inc.	Pasuquin, Ilocos Norte	24 November 2011
Ilocos Sur Cooperative Bank	National Highway, Bagani Campo, Candon, Ilocos Sur	24 November 2011
Iloilo City Development Bank	G/F Dolores O. Tan Bldg. Valeria St. Iloilo City	24 November 2011
Imus Rural Bank, Inc.	Imus, Cavite	24 November 2011
Innovative Rural Bank, Inc. (A Rural Bank)	Pililia, Rizal	24 November 2011
Insular Rural Bank, Inc.	Acme Bldg., Alabang-Zapote Rd., Las Piñas City	24 November 2011

Inter-Asia Development Bank	J.P. Rizal Avenue corner Mahogany Market Street , 4120 Tagaytay City	24 November 2011
Isla Lipana & Co- Employees Savings & Loan Association, Inc.	29/F Philamlife Towers, 8767 Paseo de Roxas, Makati City	24 November 2011
Janiuay Rural Bank, Inc.	Janiuay, Iloilo	24 November 2011
Jemba Savings & Loan Association, Inc.	c/o Johnson & Johnson (Phils.), Inc., Bo. Ibayo, Edison Road, Parañaque City	24 November 2011
Judiciary Savings & Loan Association, Inc. (JUSLAI)	Court of Appeals Building, Ma. Orosa St., Ermita, Manila	24 November 2011
Kaluyagan Rural Bank, Inc.	Mabini St., San Carlos City, 2420 Pangasinan	24 November 2011
Kap. Kawani ng Quezon City Hall	7/F Main Bldg., Quezon City Hall, Diliman, 1101 Quezon City	24 November 2011
Katipunan Bank, Inc. (A Rural Bank)	Quezon Avenue, cor. Aguilar St., Dipolog City, Zamboanga del Norte	24 November 2011
Key Rural Bank, Inc.	San Antonio, Nueva Ecija	24 November 2011
Koronadal Rural Bank, Inc.	Alunan Avenue, Koronadal City, South Cotabato	24 November 2011
La Consolacion Rural Bank, Inc.	Landayan, San Pedro, Laguna	24 November 2011
Lagawe Highlands Rural Bank	JDT Bldg., Poblacion East, Lagawe, Ifugao	24 November 2011
Laguna Prestige Banking Corporation, (A Rural Bank)	J.P. Rizal St. cor. F. Limcaoco St. Cabuyao Laguna	24 November 2011
Lapu-Lapu Rural Bank, Inc.	Sta. Catalina St., Poblacion II, Carcar, 1019 Cebu	24 November 2011
LBC Development Bank	809 J.P. Rizal cor. F. Zobel St., 1200 Makati City	24 November 2011
Legazpi Savings Bank, Inc.	G/F AB Silverscreen Entertainment Centre, Alonzo cor. Magallanes Sts., 4500 Legazpi City	24 November 2011
Lemery Savings and Loan Bank, Inc.	Ilustre Avenue, Lemery, Batangas 4209	24 November 2011
Lepanto Savings & Loan Association, Inc.	Lepanto, Mankayan, Benguet	24 November 2011
Liberty Savings Bank Inc.	McArthur Highway, Calvario, Meycauayan, Bulacan	24 November 2011

Life Bank – Rural Bank of Maasin (Iloilo), Inc.	Taft St., Maasin, Iloilo	24 November 2011
Life Savings Bank, Inc.	Units 13-14 Marieta Arcade, Marcos Highway corner A. Tuazon, Cainta, Rizal	24 November 2011
Limcoma Rural Bank, Inc.	Makalintal Avenue, Poblacion 2, San Jose, Batangas	24 November 2011
Lipa Bank, Inc. (A Rural Bank)	65 T.M. Kalaw St., Lipa City, Balayan, Batangas	24 November 2011
LUDB Bank, Inc. (A Rural Bank)	San Fernando City, La Union	24 November 2011
Luzon Development Bank	Paciano Rizal St., Mayapa, Calamba City, Laguna	24 November 2011
Mactan Air Base Savings & Loan Association, Inc. (MABSLAI)	Mactan Benito Ebuen Air Base, 6015 Lapu-Lapu City	24 November 2011
Mactan Rural Bank, Inc.	Patalinghug Ave.,Pajo, Lapu-Lapu City	24 November 2011
Maharlika Rural Bank, Inc.	Sta. Cruz, Zambales	24 November 2011
Malacañang Savings & Loan Association, Inc.	MESLA Office, J. P. Rizal Street	24 November 2011
Malarayat Rural Bank, Inc.	G.A. Solis, Lipa City, Batangas	24 November 2011
Malasiqui Progressive Savings and Loan Bank, Inc.	Quezon Blvd. Ext., Malasiqui, Pangasinan 2421	24 November 2011
Malaybalay Rural Bank, Inc.	Judge Murillo St., Malaybalay City , Bukidnon	24 November 2011
Mallig Plains Rural Bank, Inc.	Centro, Mallig, Isabela	24 November 2011
Manila Teacher's Savings & Loan Association, Inc.	918 UN Ave. Ermita, Manila	24 November 2011
Mantrasco Employees Savings & Loan Association, Inc.	2278 Priscilla Building I, Don Chino Roces Extension, Makati City	24 November 2011
Maritime Savings and Loan Association, Inc.	E. Aguinaldo Highway, Molino, Bacoor, Cavite 4102	24 November 2011
Mariwasa Employees Savings & Loan Association, Inc.	Bo. Rosario, Pasig City	24 November 2011
Masagana Rural Bank (Nueva Ecija), Inc.	Gen. Natividad, Nueva Ecija	24 November 2011
Masantol Rural Bank, Inc.	Masantol, Pampanga	24 November 2011
Masuwerte Rural Bank of Bacoor, Inc.	Giron Arcade, Zapote, Bacoor, Cavite	24 November 2011

Mead Johnson Nutrition Employees Savings and Loan Association, Inc.	2309 BMS Bldg., Pasong Tamo Extension, Makati City	24 November 2011
Mega Rural Bank, Inc.	C.M. Recto St., Brgy. IX, Lucena City	24 November 2011
Meralco Savings & Loan Association (MESALA)	Operations Building, Meralco Centre, Ortigas Avenue, Pasig City	24 November 2011
Merchants Savings and Loan Association, Inc.	46F Yuchengco Tower, RCBC Plaza, 6819 Ayala Avenue, Makati City	24 November 2011
Metro South Cooperative Bank	MSCB Bldg., 4718 Eduque St., Makati Ave., Makati City	24 November 2011
Metrobank Card Corporation (A Finance Co.)	12th floor, MCC Centre 6778 Ayala Avenue, Makati City	24 November 2011
Metro-Cebu Public Savings Bank	Tabunok, Talisay, Cebu	24 November 2011
Microfinance Maximum Savings Bank (Maxbank)	No. 54 Barangay Sabang, Puerto Galera, 5203 Oriental Mindoro	24 November 2011
Millenium Bank, Inc. (A Rural Bank)	Del Pilar St., Cabanatuan City	24 November 2011
Misamis Occidental Cooperative Bank	Sen. J. Oxamis St.., Pob. I, Oroquieta City, Misamis Occidental	24 November 2011
Money Mall Rural Bank, Inc. (Com. RB Cuambog, Inc.)	8807 Poblacion Mabini, Compostela Valley Province	24 November 2011
Mt. Carmel Rural Bank, Inc.	J. M. Kalaw St., Lipa City, Batangas	24 November 2011
Multinational Investment Bancorporation	22/F Multinational Bancorporation Centre 6805 Ayala Avenue Makati City	24 November 2011
Multi-Savings & Loan Association, Inc.	7th Floor, Unit 705 Pryce Centre Building 1179 Chino Roces Avenue Corner Bagtikan St., Makati City	24 November 2011
Municipal Rural Bank of Libmanan, Inc.	Poblacion, Libmanan, Camarines Sur	24 November 2011
Municipal Rural Bank of Poblacion, Nabua, Inc.	Nabua, Camarines Sur	24 November 2011
Muntinlupa Savings & Loan Association, Inc.	ARBAR Bldg., 2nd Floor, Bruger Subdivision, Putatan, Muntinlupa City	24 November 2011

MVSM Bank (A Rural Bank Since 1953) INC.	341 J. P. Rizal St., Sto. Nino, Marikina City	24 November 2011
N2/NISF Military Personnel & Civilian Employees Savings & Loan Association, Inc. (N2/NISF MPCESLAI)	Bonifacio Naval Station, Fort Bonifacio, Makati City	24 November 2011
National Teachers & Employees Cooperative Bank	Corner M.J. Cuenco and Juan Luna Avenues, Mabolo, Cebu City	24 November 2011
NBI Savings & Loan Association, Inc.	NBI Building, Taft Avenue, Manila	24 November 2011
Negros Cooperative Bank	North Capitol Road, Bacolod City	24 November 2011
New Covenant Bank, Inc. (A Rural Bank)	Poblacion, Dingalan, Aurora	24 November 2011
New Rural Bank of Agoncillo, Inc.	Poblacion, Agoncillo, Batangas	24 November 2011
New Rural Bank of Binalbagan, Inc.	Binalbagan, Negros Occidental	24 November 2011
New Rural Bank of San Leonardo (Nueva Ecija), Inc.	#41 Magsaysay Sur Maharlika Highway, Cabanatuan City, Nueva Ecija, Philippines	24 November 2011
New Rural Bank of Tagkawayan, Inc.	No. 30 Lagdameo Blvd., Tagkawayan, Quezon, Zip Code 4321	24 November 2011
New Rural Bank of Victorias, Inc.	GF VCY Centre, Hilado Extension, Capitol Shopping Centre, Bacolod City, Negros Occidental	24 November 2011
NIA Savings & Loan Association, Inc.	4/F Building A, NIA Building Complex, EDSA, Quezon City	24 November 2011
North Pacific Banking Corp. (A Rural Bank)	NWTF Building, Poblacion I, Sta. Maria, Isabela (Mailing Address: La Patria Bldg. Cabaruan, Cauayan City, Isabela)	24 November 2011
Northpoint Development Bank, Inc.	BR Building III, National Road, Brgy. Landayan, San Pedro, Laguna, 4023	24 November 2011
NPC Savings & Loan Association, Inc.	Quezon Avenue – BIR Road, Diliman, Quezon City	24 November 2011
Occidental Mindoro Cooperative Bank	615 Lapu-Lapu, San Jose, Occidental Mindoro	24 November 2011

Occidental Mindoro Rural Bank, Inc.	Lubang, Occidental Mindoro	24 November 2011
One Network Rural Bank, Inc.	Km. 9 Sasa, Davao City 8000	24 November 2011
Opportunity Kauswagan Bank, Inc. (A Microfinance TB)	A & L Bldg., E. Lopez St., Jaro, Iloilo City, 5000	24 November 2011
Optimum Development Bank, Inc.	Upper Ground Floor, Metropolis Star Mall, Alabang, Muntinlupa City	24 November 2011
Oriental Tamaraw Rural Bank of Naujan, Inc.	Pinagsabangan II, Naujan, Oriental Mindoro	24 November 2011
Orix Metro Leasing and Finance Corporation	21F GT Tower International, Ayala Avenue corner HV Dela Costa St., Salcedo Village, Makati City	24 November 2011
Ormon Bank (RB of Mulanay, Inc.)	Bay, Laguna	24 November 2011
Own Bank, The Rural Bank of Cavite City, Inc.	505 Burgos Ave., Caridad, 4100 Cavite City	24 November 2011
Pacific Ace Savings Bank	Retail 1 Lot 6 Time Square Complex, Subic Bay Freeport Zone, Olongapo City	24 November 2011
PAL Employees Savings & Loan Association (PESALA)	PAL Gate 1 Nichols City Andrews Ave., Pasay City	24 November 2011
Pampanga Development Bank	McArthur Highway, Dolores, San Fernando City, 2000 Pampanga	24 November 2011
Pangasinan Bank (A Rural Bank)	Mangaldan, Pangasinan	24 November 2011
Panguil Bay Rural Bank	Ozamis City, Misamis Occidental	24 November 2011
Partner Rural Bank (Cotabato), Inc.	Pigkawayan, North Cotabato	24 November 2011
Peñafrancia Rural Bank of Calabanga, Inc.	Del Carmen, Calabanga, Camarines Sur	24 November 2011
Penbank, Inc. (A Private Development Bank) (Formerly: Peninsula Rural Bank, Inc.)	3/F PenBank Centre, Santiago Blvd., Gen. Santos City	24 November 2011
People's Bank of Caraga, Inc.	National Highway Barangay 5, San Francisco, Agusan del Sur	24 November 2011

People's Rural Bank (Gen. Santos City), Inc.	Plaza Nova, I.Santiago Blvd., Gen. Santos City, South Cotabato	24 November 2011
Philippine Coast Guard Savings & Loan Association, Inc. (PCGSLAI)	Muelle Industria, Farola Compound, Binondo, Manila	24 November 2011
Philippine Depository and Trust Corp	37th/F Tower I, The Enterprise Centre, 6766 Ayala Avenue corner P. de Roxas, Makati City	24 November 2011
Philippine Navy Savings & Loan Association, Inc. (PNSLAI)	Bonifacio Naval Station, Fort Bonifacio, Taguig City	24 November 2011
Philippine Postal Savings Bank	Postalbank Centre, Liwasang Bonifacio, Ermita, Mla.	24 November 2011
Philippine Rural Banking Corp. (PR Bank)	Alingay Centre, Rizal cor Canciller Ave., Cauayan City, Isabela	24 November 2011
Philippine Savings & Loan Association, Inc.	4 Junquera Extension, Cebu City	24 November 2011
Philippine SME Bank, Inc., A Rural Bank	OCSBldg. M. L. Quezon St., Cabancalan, Mandaue City, Cebu	24 November 2011
Philippine Trust Company	Philtrust Bank Bldg., 1000 U.N. Ave. cor. San Marcelino St., Paco, Manila 1004	24 November 2011
Philnabank Employees Savings & Loan Association, Inc.	2/F PNB Financial Centre, Roxas 24 November 2011 Blvd., Pasay City	24 November 2011
Philtrust Company Employees Savings & Loan Association, Inc.	United Nations Avenue – San & Marcelino Street, Manila	24 November 2011
Phimco Employees Savings & Loan Association, Inc.	Phimco Compound, F. Manalo St., Punta, Sta. Ana, Manila	24 November 2011
PlanBank-Rural Bank of Canlubang Planters, Inc.	National Highway, Halang, Calamba, Laguna	24 November 2011
Port Community Savings & Loan Association, Inc.	Mezzanine Floor, PPA Bldg., A. Bonifacio Drive, South Harbor, Port Area, Manila	24 November 2011
Premiere Development Bank	EDSA cor. Magallanes Ave., Makati City 1200	24 November 2011
Pres. Jose P. Laurel Rural Bank, Inc.	Pres. Laurel Highway, Tanauan City, Batangas 4232	24 November 2011
Pride Star Development Bank, Inc.	Batangan Plaza, Kumintang Ibaba, Batangas City	24 November 2011

Producers Savings Bank Corporation	17/F One San Miguel Bldg., Shaw Blvd cor San Miguel Ave., Ortigas Centre, 1605 Pasig City	24 November 2011
Professional Regulation Commission Savings & Loan Association, Inc.	2/F PRC Annex Bldg., P. Paredes St., Sampaloc, Manila	24 November 2011
Progress Savings and Loan Association, Inc.	Poblacion, Subic, 2209 Zambales	24 November 2011
Progressive Bank, Inc.	Brgy. Luta Norte, Malvar, Batangas	24 November 2011
Progressive Bank, Inc. (Progressive-A Rural Bank Inc.)	Poblacion, Balasan, Iloilo	24 November 2011
Providence Rural Bank, Inc.	Banco Agricola Bldg., Aglipay St., Dugo, Camalaniugan, Cagayan	24 November 2011
Provident Rural Bank of Sta. Cruz, Inc.	Quezon Avenue, Callios, Sta. Cruz, Laguna	24 November 2011
Public Safety Savings & Loan Association, Inc. (PSSLAI)	G/F Kiangan Hall, Camp Crame, Quezon city	24 November 2011
Quezon Capital Rural Bank, Inc.	Perez cor C.M.Recto, Lucena City	24 November 2011
Quezon Coconut Producers Savings and Loan Bank, Inc.	Cor. Gov. Guinto & Enriquez Sts., Lucena City	24 November 2011
Quezon Traders Rural Bank of Candelaria, Inc.	Cabuñag St., Candelaria, Quezon	24 November 2011
Racso's Bank, Inc. (A Rural Bank)	Guimbal, Iloilo	24 November 2011
Rang-ay Bank (A Rural Bank), Inc.	#67 Gov. Luna St., San Fernando, La Union	24 November 2011
RB of Doña Remedios Trinidad, Inc.	Poblacion Doña Remedios Trinidad, Bulacan	24 November 2011
RB of Pres. Manuel A. Roxas, Inc.	Pres. M. A. Roxas, Zamb. del Norte	24 November 2011
RBG Imperial Bank, Inc. (A Rural Bank)	Gerona St., Guimbal, 5022 Iloilo	24 November 2011
RBT Bank, Inc., A Rural Bank	Rizal St., Poblacion, Talisayan, 9012 Misamis Oriental	24 November 2011
RGC Employees Savings & Loan Association, Inc.	Asahi Glass Compound, Brgy. Pinagbuhatan, Pasig City	24 November 2011
Rizal Rural Bank, Inc.	227 Rizal Ave., Taytay, Rizal	24 November 2011
RNG Coastal Bank, Inc. (A Rural Bank)	Talamban Mart, Cabancalan Road, Talamban, Cebu City	24 November 2011

Rodriguez Rural Bank, Inc.	Unit A, GF, Rayle Bldg,, 52 Dr. Sixto Antonio, Kapasigan, Pasig City	24 November 2011
RPP Savings & Loan Association, Inc.	Finance Bldg., Resins Inc., E. Rodriguez Jr. Ave., Bagong Ilog, Pasig City	24 November 2011
Rural Bank of Abucay, Inc.	Abucay, Bataan	24 November 2011
Rural Bank of Agoo, Inc.	Agoo, La Union	24 November 2011
Rural Bank of Alabat, Inc.	Alabat, Quezon	24 November 2011
Rural Bank of Alabel, Inc.	Aldevinco St., Alabel, Sarangani	24 November 2011
Rural Bank of Alaminos (Laguna), Inc.	99 Rizal St., Alaminos, Laguna	24 November 2011
Rural Bank of Alaminos (Pangasinan), Inc.	Quezon Avenue, City of Alaminos, Pangasinan	24 November 2011
Rural Bank of Alicia, Inc.	Alicia, Isabela	24 November 2011
Rural Bank of Alimodian, Inc.	Alimodian, Iloilo	24 November 2011
Rural Bank of Alitagtag, Inc.	Poblacion, Alitagtag, Batangas	24 November 2011
Rural Bank of Altavas, Inc.	Gen. Luna St., Altavas, Aklan	24 November 2011
Rural Bank of Amadeo (Cavite), Inc.	A. Mabini St., Amadeo, Cavite	24 November 2011
Rural Bank of Amlan, Inc.	Poblacion, Amlan, Negros Oriental	24 November 2011
Rural Bank of Anda, Inc.	Anda, Pangasinan	24 November 2011
Rural Bank of Angadanan, Inc.	Angadanan, Isabela	24 November 2011
Rural Bank of Angat, Inc.	M.A. Fernando St., Poblacion, Angat, Bulacan	24 November 2011
Rural Bank of Angeles, Inc.	1229 Sto. Entierro St.,Angeles City, Pampanga	24 November 2011
Rural Bank of Angono, Inc.	M.L. Quezon Ave.,Angono, Rizal	24 November 2011
Rural Bank of Antipolo, Inc.	53 J. Sumulong St., Antipolo City 1870 Rizal	24 November 2011
Rural Bank of Apalit, Inc.	San Vicente, Apalit, Pampanga	24 November 2011
Rural Bank of Aritao, Inc.	Aritao, Nueva Vizcaya	24 November 2011
Rural Bank of Atimonan, Inc.	111 Quezon St., Poblacion, Atimonan, Quezon	24 November 2011
Rural Bank of Bacnotan, Inc.	Bacnotan, La Union	24 November 2011
Rural Bank of Baco, Inc.	Baco, Oriental Mindoro	24 November 2011

Rural Bank of Bacolod City, Inc.	74-76 Narra Ave.,CSC, Bacolod City, Negros Occidental	24 November 2011
Rural Bank of Bacong (Negros Oriental), Inc.	V. Locsin St., Dumaguete City, Negros Oriental	24 November 2011
Rural Bank of Badiangan, Inc.	Badiangan, Iloilo	24 November 2011
Rural Bank of Bagabag, Inc.	Bagabag, Nueva Vizcaya	24 November 2011
Rural Bank of Bagac, Inc.	G/F Dilig Bldg-2, Don Manuel Banzon Ave., Balanga City, Bataan	24 November 2011
Rural Bank of Baguio, Inc.	91 Sessions Road, Baguio City	24 November 2011
Rural Bank of Balete, Inc.	Poblacion, Balete, Aklan (5614)	24 November 2011
Rural Bank of Balingasag, Inc.	Poblacion, Balingasag, Misamis Oriental	24 November 2011
Rural Bank of Balungao, Inc.	Balungao, Pangasinan	24 November 2011
Rural Bank of Bambang, Inc.	Bambang, Nueva Vizcaya	24 November 2011
Rural Bank of Banayoyo, Inc.	Poblacion, Banayoyo, 2708 Ilocos Sur	24 November 2011
Rural Bank of Banga, Inc.	Rosal St., Banga, Aklan	24 November 2011
Rural Bank of Bangar, Inc.	Bangar, La Union	24 November 2011
Rural Bank of Bansud, Inc.	Bansud, Oriental Mindoro	24 November 2011
Rural Bank of Barili, Inc.	H. Alquisola St., Barili, Cebu	24 November 2011
Rural Bank of Barotac Nuevo, Inc.	L. Araneta St., Barotac Nuevo, Iloilo	24 November 2011
Rural Bank of Barotac Viejo, Inc.	Zulueta Drive, Poblacion, Barotac Viejo, 5011 Iloilo	24 November 2011
Rural Bank of Basay, Inc.	Gov. M. Perdices Street Dumaguete City Negros Oriental	24 November 2011
Rural Bank of Basey, Inc.	Serafin Marabut St., Brgy Loyo, Basey, Samar	24 November 2011
Rural Bank of Batac, Inc.	Batac, Ilocos Norte	24 November 2011
Rural Bank of Bato, Inc.	482 Juan Luna St., Bato, Leyte 6525	24 November 2011
Rural Bank of Bauang, Inc.	Bauang, La Union	24 November 2011
Rural Bank of Bay, Inc.	Bay, Laguna	24 November 2011
Rural Bank of Bayambang, Inc.	Bayambang, Pangasinan	24 November 2011
Rural Bank of Bayawan, Inc.	807 H. Bollos St.,Bayawan City, Negros Oriental	24 November 2011

Rural Bank of Bayombong, Inc.	National Road, 3700 Bayombong, Nueva Vizcaya	24 November 2011
Rural Bank of Benito Soliven, Inc.	Amity Building, National Highway, Cauayan, Isabela	24 November 2011
Rural Bank of Bogo, Inc.	P. Rodriguez St., Bogo, Cebu	24 November 2011
Rural Bank of Bolinao, Inc.	Poblacion, Bolinao, Pangasinan	24 November 2011
Rural Bank of Bonifacio, Inc.	Bonifacio, Misamis Occidental	24 November 2011
Rural Bank of Bontoc, Inc.	Bontoc, Mountain Province	24 November 2011
Rural Bank of Borongan, Inc.	Borongan, Eastern Samar	24 November 2011
Rural Bank of Brookes Point, Inc.	Brooke's Point, Palawan	24 November 2011
Rural Bank of Bucay, Inc.	South Poblacion, Bucay, Abra (2805)	24 November 2011
Rural Bank of Buenavista, Inc.	Buenavista, Agusan del Norte	24 November 2011
Rural Bank of Bugasong, Inc.	5704 Bugasong, Antique	24 November 2011
Rural Bank of Buguias, Inc.	Buguias, Benguet	24 November 2011
Rural Bank of Burauen, Inc.	San Ramon St., Burauen, Leyte	24 November 2011
Rural Bank of Bustos, Inc.	National H-way, Bonga Manor, Bustos, Bulacan	24 November 2011
Rural Bank of Caba (La Union), Inc.	Sobrepeña Bldg., Natl H-way, Caba, La Union	24 November 2011
Rural Bank of Cabadbaran, Inc.	Cabadbaran, Agusan del Norte	24 November 2011
Rural Bank of Cabangan, Inc.	Cabangan, Zambales	24 November 2011
Rural Bank of Cabatuan (Iloilo), Inc.	Cabatuan, Iloilo	24 November 2011
Rural Bank of Cabugao, Inc.	Cabugao, Ilocos Sur	24 November 2011
Rural Bank of Cadiz, Inc.	Cabahug St.,Cadiz, Negros Occidental	24 November 2011
Rural Bank of Cainta, Inc.	Cainta, Rizal	24 November 2011
Rural Bank of Calaca, Inc.	Poblacion, Calaca, Batangas	24 November 2011
Rural Bank of Calamba, Inc.	Calamba, Laguna	24 November 2011
Rural Bank of Calasiao, Inc.	Calasiao, Pangasinan	24 November 2011
Rural Bank of Calauan, Inc.	Rizal Ave.,Calauan, Laguna	24 November 2011
Rural Bank of Calbayog City, Inc.	82 T. Bugallon St., Calbayog City, Western Samar	24 November 2011
Rural Bank of Calinog, Inc.	Calinog, Iloilo	24 November 2011
Rural Bank of Caloocan, Inc.	571 A. Mabini St., Caloocan City	24 November 2011

Rural Bank of Calubian, Inc.	Poblacion, Calubian, Leyte	24 November 2011
Rural Bank of Camalig, Inc.	2/F Camalig Bank Building Penaranda Street 4500 Legaspi City	24 November 2011
Rural Bank of Candelaria (Quezon), Inc.	Corner Cabunag & Bustamante Streets, Candelaria, Quezon	24 November 2011
Rural Bank of Candelaria (Zambales), Inc.	Candelaria, Zambales	24 November 2011
Rural Bank of Capalonga, Inc.	J.P. Rizal St., Poblacion, Capalonga, Camarines Norte	24 November 2011
Rural Bank of Cardona, Inc.	Cardona, Rizal	24 November 2011
Rural Bank of Casiguran, Inc.	Jose Angara Avenue, Poblacion 4, Casiguran 3204 Aurora	24 November 2011
Rural Bank of Catubig, Inc.	Poblacion Catubig, Northern Samar	24 November 2011
Rural Bank of Cauayan (Isabela), Inc.	Don Jose Canciller Avenue, Cauayan City, 3305 Isabela	24 November 2011
Rural Bank of Cavinti, Inc.	Cavinti, Laguna	24 November 2011
Rural Bank of Cebu South, Inc. (Sibonga RB)	Poblacion, Pardo, Cebu City	24 November 2011
Rural Bank of Central Pangasinan, Inc.	Corporate Office: Chuson Bldg., McArthur Highway, Calasiao, Pangasinan	24 November 2011
Rural Bank of Claveria, Inc.	Poblacion, Claveria, Cagayan	24 November 2011
Rural Bank of Compostela (Comval), Inc.	J.P. Laurel St.Compostela, Compostela Valley	24 November 2011
Rural Bank of Cotabato, Inc.	EC Tanghal Building No. 5 Don Roman Vilo Street, Cotabato City	24 November 2011
Rural Bank of Cuartero, Inc.	Cuartero, Capiz	24 November 2011
Rural Bank of Cuenca, Inc.	Marasigan St., Cuenca, Batangas	24 November 2011
Rural Bank of Cuyo, Inc.	Mendoza St., Bancal, 5318 Cuyo, Palawan	24 November 2011
Rural Bank of Dasmariñas, Inc.	19 Camerino Ave., Dasmarinas, Cavite	24 November 2011
Rural Bank of Datu Paglas, Inc.	Datu Paglas, Maguindanao	24 November 2011
Rural Bank of Digos, Inc.	2964 Rizal Avenue, Digos City, Davao del Sur	24 November 2011
Rural Bank of Dolores (Quezon), Inc.	Silangan, Dolores, Quezon	24 November 2011

Rural Bank of Donsol, Inc.	4715 Donsol, Sorsogon	24 November 2011
Rural Bank of Dulag, Inc.	Kempis St., Poblacion, Dulag, Leyte 6505	24 November 2011
Rural Bank of Dumangas, Inc.	Dumangas, Iloilo	24 November 2011
Rural Bank of Dupax , Inc.	Dupax Del Norte 3706 Nueva Vizcaya	24 November 2011
Rural Bank of El Salvador, Inc.	National Highway, Poblacion, El Salvador, Misamis Oriental	24 November 2011
Rural Bank of Escalante, Inc.	North Avenue, Escalante City, Negros Occidental (6124)	24 November 2011
Rural Bank of Gainza, Inc.	Poblacion, Gainza, Camarines Sur	24 November 2011
Rural Bank of Galimuyod, Inc.	Poblacion, Galimuyod, 2709 Ilocos Sur	24 November 2011
Rural Bank of Gandara, Inc.	Gandara, Western Samar	24 November 2011
Rural Bank of Gattaran, Inc.	National High-way, Centro Norte, Gattaran, Cagayan	24 November 2011
Rural Bank of General Luna, Inc.	Ester St., Poblacion, Luna, Quezon	24 November 2011
Rural Bank of General Trias, Inc.	Tejero, Gen. Trias, Cavite	24 November 2011
Rural Bank of Gigaquit, Inc.	San Isidro, Gigaquit, Surigao del Norte (8409)	24 November 2011
Rural Bank of Gingoog, Inc.	Lupod-Guno St.,Gingoog, 9014 Misamis Oriental	24 November 2011
Rural Bank of Gitagum, Inc.	Poblacion, Gitagum, Misamis Oriental	24 November 2011
Rural Bank of Gloria, Inc.	Poblacion Gloria, Oriental Mindoro	24 November 2011
Rural Bank of Goa, Inc.	San Jose St., Goa, Camarines Sur 4422	24 November 2011
Rural Bank of Guihulngan, Inc.	Guihulngan, Negros Oriental	24 November 2011
Rural Bank of Guinobatan, Inc.	Guinobatan, Albay	24 November 2011
Rural Bank of Guiuan, Inc.	Sta. Cruz, Guiuan, Eastern Samar	24 November 2011
Rural Bank of Hagonoy, Inc.	Guihing, Hagonoy, 8006 Davao del Sur	24 November 2011
Rural Bank of Hermosa, Inc.	Burgos St. Poblacion, Hermosa, Bataan (2111)	24 November 2011

Rural Bank of Hilongos,Inc.	R.V. Villaflores St., Hilongos 6524 Leyte	24 November 2011
Rural Bank of Hindang, Inc.	Poblacion, Hindang, Leyte	24 November 2011
Rural Bank of Hinundayan, Inc.	Poblacion, Hinundayan, Southern Leyte	24 November 2011
Rural Bank of Ibajay, Inc.	National Road, Poblacion, Ibajay, Aklan	24 November 2011
Rural Bank of Iligan City, Inc.	Gen. E. Aguinaldo St., Iligan City, Lanao del Norte	24 November 2011
Rural Bank of Ilog, Inc.	Dancalan, Ilog, Negros Occidental	24 November 2011
Rural Bank of Iloilo City, Inc.	Luna St., La Paz, Iloilo City	24 November 2011
Rural Bank of Infanta, Inc.	Corner Velasco & Mabini Streets, Infanta, Quezon	24 November 2011
Rural Bank of Initao, Inc.	Poblacion, Initao, 9022 Misamis Oriental	24 November 2011
Rural Bank of Irosin, Inc.	San Julian, Irosin, Sorsogon	24 November 2011
Rural Bank of Itogon, Inc.	1993 Public Bldg., Km 5 Pico, La Trinidad, Benguet	24 November 2011
Rural Bank of Jaen, Inc.	Jaen, Nueva Ecija	24 November 2011
Rural Bank of Jamindan, Inc.	Jamindan, Capiz	24 November 2011
Rural Bank of Javier, Inc.	Zone II Real St., Javier, Leyte	24 November 2011
Rural Bank of Jimenez, Inc.	Rizal Street, Jimenez 7204 Misamis Occidental	24 November 2011
Rural Bank of Jordan, Inc.	5045 Wharf Area, Jordan, Guimaras	24 November 2011
Rural Bank of Jose Panganiban, Inc.	Poblacion Jose Panganiban, Camarines Norte	24 November 2011
Rural Bank of Kabasalan, Inc.	7005 Kabasalan,Zambaonga Sibugay	24 November 2011
Rural Bank of Kapalong, Inc.	Kapalong, Davao del Norte	24 November 2011
Rural Bank of Karomatan, Inc.	Crossing Tubod, 9215 Karomatan, Lanao del Norte	24 November 2011
Rural Bank of Kawit, Inc.	Kawit, Cavite	24 November 2011
Rural Bank of Kiamba, Inc.	Poblacion, Kiamba, Sarangani	24 November 2011
Rural Bank of Kibawe, Inc.	Kibawe, Bukidnon	24 November 2011
Rural Bank of Kinogitan, Inc.	Poblacion, Kinogitan, Misamis Oriental 9010	24 November 2011
Rural Bank of Kolambugan, Inc.	Cabili St., Kolambugan 9207 Lanao del Norte	24 November 2011

Rural Bank of La Paz (Tarlac), Inc.	Corner J. Catalan and Burgos Streets., La Paz, Tarlac	24 November 2011
Rural Bank of La Trinidad, Inc.	JC 105 Solis Building, Pico, La Trinidad, Benguet	24 November 2011
Rural Bank of Labason, Inc.	7117 Rizal Avenue, Labason, Zamboanga del Norte	24 November 2011
Rural Bank of Labrador, Inc.	Labrador, Pangasinan	24 November 2011
Rural Bank of Lanuza, Inc.	Carmen, Surigao del Sur	24 November 2011
Rural Bank of Larena, Inc.	Larena, Siquijor	24 November 2011
Rural Bank of Lebak, Inc.	Lebak, Sultan Kudarat	24 November 2011
Rural Bank of Leganes, Inc.	Quintin Salas St., Poblacion, Leganes, Iloilo	24 November 2011
Rural Bank of Lemery (Batangas), Inc.	Ilustre Avenue, Lemery, Batangas	24 November 2011
Rural Bank of Liloy, Inc.	7115 Liloy, Zamboanga del Norte	24 November 2011
Rural Bank of Limay, Inc.	Nat'l Rd.Townsite, Limay, Bataan	24 November 2011
Rural Bank of Lipa City, Inc.	J.P. Rizal St., Lipa City, Batangas	24 November 2011
Rural Bank of Lobo, Inc.	Poblacion, Lobo, Batangas (Mailing Address: P. Torres cor. G.A. Solis Sts. Lipa City, 4217 Batangas)	24 November 2011
Rural Bank of Loboc, Inc.	Poblacion, Loboc, Bohol	24 November 2011
Rural Bank of Loon, Inc.	Across Loon Municipal Bldg., National Highway, Loon, Bohol	24 November 2011
Rural Bank of Lopez Jaena, Inc.	Lopez Jaena, Misamis Occidental	24 November 2011
Rural Bank of Loreto, Inc.	Purok 1, Rizal St., Poblacion, San Jose, Province of Dinagat Islands	24 November 2011
Rural Bank of Lubao, Inc.	Lubao, Pampanga	24 November 2011
Rural Bank of Lucban, Inc.	103 Rizal St.,Lucban, Quezon	24 November 2011
Rural Bank of Luisiana, Inc.	Luisiana, Laguna	24 November 2011
Rural Bank of Lumban, Inc.	National Highway, Brgy. Lewin, Lumban, Laguna	24 November 2011
Rural Bank of Luna (Isabela), Inc.	National Highway, Harana, Luna, Isabela	24 November 2011
Rural Bank of Luna (Kalinga-Apayao), Inc.	San Isidro, Luna, Apayao	24 November 2011

Rural Bank of Luna (La Union), Inc.	Luna, La Union	24 November 2011
Rural Bank of Lupao, Inc.	Lupao, Nueva Ecija	24 November 2011
Rural Bank of Ma-ao, Inc.	Sta. Cecilia St., Bago City, Negros Occidental	24 November 2011
Rural Bank of Maasin (So. Leyte), Inc.	E.Rafols St., Maasin City, Southern Leyte	24 November 2011
Rural Bank of Mabalacat, Inc.	107 Mac-Arthur Highway, Dau, Mabalacat, 2010 Pampanga	24 November 2011
Rural Bank of Mabini (Batangas), Inc.	Castillo Ave., Poblacion, Mabini, Batangas	24 November 2011
Rural Bank of Mabitac, Inc. (Fortune Bank)	J. Rizal St.,Mabitac, Laguna	24 November 2011
Rural Bank of Maddela, Inc.	E. Mangaoil Building, Poblacion Norte, Maddela, Quirino	24 November 2011
Rural Bank of Madridejos, Inc.	Poblacion, Madridejos, Cebu	24 November 2011
Rural Bank of Magdalena, Inc.	10 E. Jacinto St.,Magdalena, Laguna	24 November 2011
Rural Bank of Magsingal, Inc.	Magsingal, Ilocos Sur	24 November 2011
Rural Bank of Mahaplag, Inc.	6512 Mahaplag, Leyte	24 November 2011
Rural Bank of Maigo, Inc.	Maigo, Lanao del Norte	24 November 2011
Rural Bank of Majayjay, Inc.	P. Zamora St., Majayjay, 4005 Laguna	24 November 2011
Rural Bank of Makato, Inc.	Mayor Paterio Tirol St., Poblacion, Makato, Aklan	24 November 2011
Rural Bank of Malinao (Aklan), Inc.	Poblacion, Malinao, Aklan	24 November 2011
Rural Bank of Malitbog, Inc.	Poblacion, Malitbog, Southern Leyte	24 November 2011
Rural Bank of Malolos, Inc.	Pariancillo St., Sto. Niño, City of Malolos, Bulacan	24 November 2011
Rural Bank of Mambusao, Inc.	Mambusao, Capiz	24 November 2011
Rural Bank of Manapla, Inc.	Crossing Ubos, Manapla, Negros Occidental	24 November 2011
Rural Bank of Mandaue, Inc.	A. Del Rosario St., Centro Mandue City	24 November 2011
Rural Bank of Mangaldan, Inc.	Mangaldan, Pangasinan	24 November 2011

Rural Bank of Manolo Fortich, Inc.	Manolo Fortich, Bukidnon	24 November 2011
Rural Bank of Manukan, Inc.	Poblacion, Manukan, Zamboanga del Norte	24 November 2011
Rural Bank of Maragondon, Inc.	Maragondon, Cavite	24 November 2011
Rural Bank of Marayo (Negros Occidental), Inc.	Cortez St., Pontevedra, Negros Occidental	24 November 2011
Rural Bank of Maria Aurora, Inc.	Maria Aurora, Aurora	24 November 2011
Rural Bank of Marilag (Sta. Maria,Laguna), Inc.	Real Velasquez St., Sta. Maria, 4005 Laguna	24 November 2011
Rural Bank of Matag-ob, Inc.	McArthur St., Matag-ob, 6532 Leyte	24 November 2011
Rural Bank of Mati, Inc.	Mati, Davao Oriental	24 November 2011
Rural Bank of Mauban, Inc.	Quezon St., Mauban, Quezon	24 November 2011
Rural Bank of Mawab, Inc.	Poblacion, Mawab, Compostela Valley	24 November 2011
Rural Bank of Medina, Inc.	Poblacion, Medina, Misamis Oriental	24 November 2011
Rural Bank of Mendez, Inc.	145 J.P. Rizal St., Mendez, Cavite	24 November 2011
Rural Bank of Mexico, Inc.	Mexico, Pampanga	24 November 2011
Rural Bank of Miagao, Inc.	Noble St.,Miagao, Iloilo	24 November 2011
Rural Bank of Midsayap, Inc.	Quezon Ave., Midsayap, North Cotabato	24 November 2011
Rural Bank of M'lang, Inc.	Magsaysay Ave., Poblacion A, M'lang, North Cotabato	24 November 2011
Rural Bank of Montalban, Inc.	J.P. Rizal Ave.,Manggahan Rodriguez, Montalban, Rizal	24 November 2011
Rural Bank of Montevista, Inc.	National Highway, Montevista, Compostela Valley (Mailing Address: Old DXDN Building., Mabini Street, Tagum City, Davao Del Norte 8100)	24 November 2011
Rural Bank of Nabunturan, Inc.	Echavez St., Nabunturan, Compostela Valley	24 November 2011
Rural Bank of Nagcarlan, Inc.	Nagcarlan, Laguna	24 November 2011
Rural Bank of Naguilian (La Union) Inc.	Naguilian Highway, Natividad, Naguilian, La Union	24 November 2011
Rural Bank of Naic, Inc.	No. 16 Nazareno St., Bgy. Nazareno, Naic, Cavite	24 November 2011

Rural Bank of Nasugbu, Inc.	Poblacion, Nasugbu, Batangas	24 November 2011
Rural Bank of Naval, Inc.	964 Burgos St., Naval, Biliran	24 November 2011
Rural Bank of New Corella, Inc.	New Corella, Davao del Norte	24 November 2011
Rural Bank of New Washington, Inc.	Magsaysay Ave., Poblacion,New Washington, Aklan	24 November 2011
Rural Bank of Norala, Inc.	9508 Poblacion, Norala, South Cotabato	24 November 2011
Rural Bank of Ocampo, Inc.	Poblacion, Ocampo, Camarines Sur	24 November 2011
Rural Bank of Odiongan, Inc.	Poblacion, Odiongan, Romblon	24 November 2011
Rural Bank of Ormoc City, Inc.	Mabini St., Ormoc City, Leyte	24 November 2011
Rural Bank of Oroquieta, Inc.	Barrientos St., Oroquieta City, Misamis Occidental	24 November 2011
Rural Bank of Oslob, Inc.	Poblacion, 6025 Oslob, Cebu	24 November 2011
Rural Bank of Oton, Inc.	Mabini St., Oton, Iloilo	24 November 2011
Rural Bank of Padre Burgos (Southern Leyte), Inc.	Padre Burgos, Southern Leyte	24 November 2011
Rural Bank of Padre Garcia, Inc.	Mabini St., Poblacion, Padre Garcia, Batangas	24 November 2011
Rural Bank of Paete, Inc.	Rizal cor. Quesada Sts., Paete, 4016 Laguna	24 November 2011
Rural Bank of Pagadian, Inc.	Pagadian, Zamboanga del Sur	24 November 2011
Rural Bank of Pagbilao, Inc.	Poblacion, Pagbilao, Quezon	24 November 2011
Rural Bank of Pagsanjan, Inc.	National Highway, Pagsanjan, 4008 Laguna	24 November 2011
Rural Bank of Pamplona (Camarines Sur), Inc.	Maharlika Highway, Tambo, Pamplona, Camarines Sur	24 November 2011
Rural Bank of Pamplona (Negros Oriental), Inc.	Pamplona, Negros Oriental	24 November 2011
Rural Bank of Pana-on, Inc.	Pana-on, Misamis Occidental	24 November 2011
Rural Bank of Panay, Inc.	Poblacion, Panay, Capiz	24 November 2011
Rural Bank of Pandi, Inc.	Poblacion, Pandi, Bulacan	24 November 2011
Rural Bank of Pangil, Inc.	Pangil, Laguna	24 November 2011
Rural Bank of Paracale, Inc.	Paracale, Camarines Norte	24 November 2011
Rural Bank of Pavia, Inc.	Cor. Hendriana-Sumakwel Sts., Poblacion, Pavia, Iloilo	24 November 2011
Rural Bank of Pilar (Bataan), Inc.	Rizal St., Poblacion, Pilar, Bataan	24 November 2011

Rural Bank of Pilar (Sorsogon), Inc.	G/F Roces Bldg., Poblacion, Pilar, Sorsogon	24 November 2011
Rural Bank of Pinamalayan, Inc.	Pinamalayan, Oriental Mindoro	24 November 2011
Rural Bank of Placer (Surigao del Norte), Inc.	Km. 1, National Highway, Surigao City	24 November 2011
Rural Bank of Plaridel (Bulacan), Inc.	Plaridel, Bulacan	24 November 2011
Rural Bank of Plaridel (Misamis Occidental), Inc.	Plaridel, Misamis Occidental	24 November 2011
Rural Bank of Pola, Inc.	Pola, Oriental Mindoro	24 November 2011
Rural Bank of Polomolok, Inc.	Polomolok, South Cotabato	24 November 2011
Rural Bank of Porac, Inc.	General Luna St., Congatba, Porac, Pampanga	24 November 2011
Rural Bank of Pototan, Inc.	T. Magbanua Street, Pototan Iloilo, 5008	24 November 2011
Rural Bank of Pozorrubio, Inc.	Pozorrubio, Pangasinan	24 November 2011
Rural Bank of Pres. Quirino, Inc.	National Highway, Pres. Quirino, 9804 Sultan Kudarat	24 November 2011
Rural Bank of Puerto Galera, Inc.	Poblacion Puerto Galera, Oriental Mindoro 5203	24 November 2011
Rural Bank of Pura, Inc.	Pura, Tarlac	24 November 2011
Rural Bank of Quezon (Nueva Ecija), Inc.	T. Joson Ave., Dulong Bayan, Quezon, Nueva Ecija 3113	24 November 2011
Rural Bank of Ragay, Inc.	Poblacion, Ragay, Camarines Sur	24 November 2011
Rural Bank of Ramon, Inc,	121 National Road, Bugallon Proper, Ramon, Isabela	24 November 2011
Rural Bank of Reina Mercedes, Inc.	Reina Mercedes, Isabela	24 November 2011
Rural Bank of Rizal (Kalinga), Inc.	Rizal, Kalinga-Apayao	24 November 2011
Rural Bank of Rizal (Laguna), Inc.	Rizal, Laguna	24 November 2011
Rural Bank of Rizal (Z.N.), Inc.	Rizal, Zamboanga del Norte 7104	24 November 2011
Rural Bank of Rosario (La Union), Inc.	Rosario, La Union	24 November 2011
Rural Bank of Roxas (Oriental Mindoro), Inc.	Roxas, Oriental Mindoro	24 November 2011

Rural Bank of Sagada, Inc.	Poblacion Sagada, Mountain Province	24 November 2011
Rural Bank of Sagay (Negros Occidental), Inc.	Poblacion, Sagay City, Negros Occidental	24 November 2011
Rural Bank of Salcedo, Inc.	Poblacion, Salcedo, Ilocos Sur	24 November 2011
Rural Bank of Salinas, Inc.	Marsella St., Rosario, Cavite	24 November 2011
Rural Bank of Salug, Inc.	7114 Salug, Zamboanga del Norte	24 November 2011
Rural Bank of Sampaloc, Inc.	Poblacion, Sampaloc, Quezon	24 November 2011
Rural Bank of San Agustin, Inc.	Masaya Centro, San Agustin 3314 Isabela	24 November 2011
Rural Bank of San Antonio (Quezon), Inc.	J. C. Wagan Avenue, Poblacion, San Antonio, Quezon	24 November 2011
Rural Bank of San Enrique, Inc.	Salvacion corner San Juan Sts., Passi City, Iloilo	24 November 2011
Rural Bank of San Fabian, Inc.	San Fabian, Pangasinan	24 November 2011
Rural Bank of San Fernando (Camarines Sur), Inc.	Bonifacio St., San Fernando, Camarines Sur	24 November 2011
Rural Bank of San Fernando (Cebu), Inc.	Poblacion, San Fernando, Cebu	24 November 2011
Rural Bank of San Jacinto, Inc.	San Jacinto, Masbate	24 November 2011
Rural Bank of San Jose (Camarines), Inc.	Poblacion San Jose, Camarines Sur 4423	24 November 2011
Rural Bank of San Juan (Southern Leyte), Inc.	6611 San Juan, Southern Leyte	24 November 2011
Rural Bank of San Lorenzo Ruiz (Siniloan), Inc.	Siniloan, Laguna	24 November 2011
Rural Bank of San Luis (Batangas), Inc.	San Luis, Batangas	24 November 2011
Rural Bank of San Luis (Pampanga), Inc.	F. Carlos St., Sta. Cruz Pob. San Luis, Pampanga	24 November 2011
Rural Bank of San Manuel (Isabela), Inc.	San Manuel, Isabela	24 November 2011
Rural Bank of San Marcelino, Inc.	Agpalo St., Central, San Marcelino, Zambales	24 November 2011
Rural Bank of San Mateo (Isabela), Inc.	Poblacion, San Mateo, Isabela	24 November 2011
Rural Bank of San Miguel (Iloilo), Inc.	San Raymundo St., Poblacion, San Miguel, Iloilo	24 November 2011

Rural Bank of San Narciso (Zambales), Inc.	Fontimayor St., Bgy Libertad, San Narciso, Zambales	24 November 2011
Rural Bank of San Nicolas (Pangasinan), Inc.	Rizal St., Poblacion, San Nicolas, 2447 Pangasinan	24 November 2011
Rural Bank of San Pascual, Inc.	345 M.H. del Pilar cor Navarette St. Brgy. Arkong Bato, Valenzuela City	24 November 2011
Rural Bank of San Quintin, Inc.	Poblacion, San Quintin, 2444 Pangasinan	24 November 2011
Rural Bank of San Rafael (Bulacan), Inc.	San Rafael, Bulacan	24 November 2011
Rural Bank of San Vicente, Inc.	San Vicente, Camarines Norte	24 November 2011
Rural Bank of Sanchez Mira, Inc.	Centro I, Sanchez Mira, Cagayan	24 November 2011
Rural Bank of Santa Catalina, Inc.	Caranoche St., Sta. Catalina, 6220 Negros Oriental	24 November 2011
Rural Bank of Santiago de Libon, Inc.	San Francisco St., Libon, Albay	24 November 2011
Rural Bank of Sapian, Inc.	Poblacion, Sapian, Capiz	24 November 2011
Rural Bank of Sasmuan, Inc.	San Nicolas II, Sasmuan, 2004 Pampanga	24 November 2011
Rural Bank of Seven Lakes, Inc.	M. Paulino St., San Pablo City	24 November 2011
Rural Bank of Siaton, Inc.	Poblacion, Siaton, Negros Oriental	24 November 2011
Rural Bank of Sibalom, Inc.	Sibalom, Antique	24 November 2011
Rural Bank of Sibulan, Inc.	Poblacion, Sibulan, Negros Oriental	24 November 2011
Rural Bank of Silay City, Inc.	Corner Eusebio and G. Gamboa Streets Brgy. 3 6116 Silay City	24 November 2011
Rural Bank of Siocon, Inc.	183-C Ong Bldg.,Governor Alvarez Avenue, Zamboanga City	24 November 2011
Rural Bank of Sipocot, Inc.	Poblacion Sipocot, Camarines Sur	24 November 2011
Rural Bank of Socorro, Inc.	Poblacion, Socorro, Oriental Mindoro	24 November 2011
Rural Bank of Solano, Inc.	Gaddang St.,Solano, Nueva Vizcaya	24 November 2011
Rural Bank of Sta. Barbara (Iloilo), Inc.	Sta. Barbara, Iloilo	24 November 2011

Rural Bank of Sta. Elena, Inc.	Sta. Elena, Camarines Norte	24 November 2011
Rural Bank of Sta. Fe (Romblon), Inc.	Poblacion, Sta. Fe, Tablas Island, Romblon	24 November 2011
Rural Bank of Sta. Ignacia, Inc. (Signa Bank)	Poblacion East, Sta. Ignacia, Tarlac	24 November 2011
Rural Bank of Sta. Magdalena, Inc.	Rural Bank Bldg., Brgy. 3, Poblacion, Sta. Magdalena, Sorsogon	24 November 2011
Rural Bank of Sta. Maria (Ilocos Sur) Inc.	Col. S. Reyes Ave., Pob Sur, Sta. Maria, Ilocos Sur	24 November 2011
Rural Bank of Sta. Rosa (Laguna), Inc.	City of Sta. Rosa, Laguna	24 November 2011
Rural Bank of Sta. Rosa de Lima, Inc.	#7 Burgos St., Poblacion Sur, Paniqui, Tarlac	24 November 2011
Rural Bank of Sto. Domingo (Nueva Ecija), Inc.	D. Noriel St., Hulo, Sto. Domingo, Nueva Ecija	24 November 2011
Rural Bank of Sto. Tomas (Davao), Inc.	Magsaysay Ave., Poblacion, Sto. Tomas, Davao del Norte	24 November 2011
Rural Bank of Sudipen, Inc.	2520 Sudipen, La Union	24 November 2011
Rural Bank of Taal, Inc.	F. Agoncillo St., Taal, Batangas	24 November 2011
Rural Bank of Tabuk, Inc.	Tabuk, Kalinga	24 November 2011
Rural Bank of Taft, Inc.	Real St., Taft, Eastern Samar	24 November 2011
Rural Bank of Tagaytay City, Inc.	Tagaytay City, Cavite	24 November 2011
Rural Bank of Talisay (Batangas), Inc.	Gen. A. Laurel St., Talisay, Batangas	24 November 2011
Rural Bank of Talisay (Cebu), Inc.	Tabunoc, Talisay, Cebu	24 November 2011
Rural Bank of Talisay (Negros Occidental), Inc.	Talisay, Negros Occidental	24 November 2011
Rural Bank of Talugtog, Inc.	Poblacion, Talugtug 3118 Nueva Ecija	24 November 2011
Rural Bank of Tandag, Inc.	Tandag, Surigao del Sur	24 November 2011
Rural Bank of Tangub, Inc.	Lorenzo Tan St.,Tangub City, Misamis Occidental	24 November 2011
Rural Bank of Tanjay, Inc.	639 Magallanes St., Tanjay City, 6204 Negros Oriental	24 November 2011
Rural Bank of Tayabas, Inc.	No.62 Gen. Luna St., Tayabas, Quezon	24 November 2011
Rural Bank of Taysan, Inc. (Banco Batangas)	Taysan, Batangas	24 November 2011
Rural Bank of Teresa, Inc.	Teresa, Rizal	24 November 2011

Rural Bank of Tibiao, Inc.	Tibiao, Antique	24 November 2011
Rural Bank of Tigaon, Inc.	Poblacion, Tigaon, Camarines Sur	24 November 2011
Rural Bank of Tigbauan, Inc.	Tigbauan, Iloilo	24 November 2011
Rural Bank of Tudela, Inc.	Sibas, Tudela, Misamis Occidental	24 November 2011
Rural Bank of Tumauini, Inc.	National Highway, Poblacion, Tumauini, Isabela	24 November 2011
Rural Bank of Valencia (Bukidnon), Inc.	Valencia, Bukidnon	24 November 2011
Rural Bank of Valencia (Negros Or.), Inc.	Larena St., Valencia, Negros Oriental	24 November 2011
Rural Bank of Victoria (Oriental Mindoro), Inc.	Poblacion, Victoria, Oriental Mindoro	24 November 2011
Rural Bank of Victoria, Inc.	Victoria, Tarlac	24 November 2011
Rural Bank of Villaverde, Inc.	Bintawan Norte, 3710 Villaverde, Nueva Vizcaya	24 November 2011
Rural Bank of Villaviciosa, Inc.	National Road, Poblacaion, Villaviciosa, Abra 2811	24 November 2011
Rural Bank of Zarraga, Inc.	Zarraga, Iloilo	24 November 2011
Sadiri Rural Bank, Inc.	Poblacion, San Juan, 2731 Ilocos Sur	24 November 2011
Salug Valley Rural Bank, Inc.	Mabini St.,Maloloy-on, Molave, Zamboanga del Sur	24 November 2011
Sampaguita Savings Bank, Inc.	No. 10 J. Luna St., Poblacion, San Pedro, Laguna	24 November 2011
San Bartolome Rural Bank, Inc.	San Pedro I, Magalang, Pampanga	24 November 2011
San Fernando Rural Bank, Inc.	Consunji St., Brgy. Sto. Rosario, San Fernando City, Pampanga	24 November 2011
San Francisco Del Monte Rural Bank, Inc.	958-964 Del Monte Ave., Quezon City	24 November 2011
Sarangani Rural Bank, Inc.	P. Acharon Blvd.,General Santos City, Polomolok, South Cotabato	24 November 2011
Savings & Loan Association of Government Auditors, Inc.	COA Bldg., Mariano Marcos Avenue, Quezon City	24 November 2011
Savings & Loan Association of Mataas na Kahoy, Inc.	Barangay IV, V Templo Avenue, Mataas na Kahoy, Batangas	24 November 2011
Savings & Loan Association of Power Employees, Inc.	c/o NPC-MRC, Ma. Cristina, Iligan City	24 November 2011

Savings &n Loan Association of P & G Phil. Employees, Inc.	20/F 6750 Ayala Office Tower, Ayala Avenue, 1200 Makati City	24 November 2011
Saviour Rural Bank, Inc.	Olongapo Highway cor. Osmeña St., Sta. Cruz, Lubao, Pampanga	24 November 2011
Science Savings & Loan Association, Inc.	SSLAI Bldg., DOST Compound, Gen. Santos Ave., Bicutan, Taguig, Metro Manila	24 November 2011
Second Rural Bank of Meycauayan, Inc.	Meycauayan, Bulacan	24 November 2011
Second Rural Bank of San Luis (Pampanga), Inc.	Barangay Santo Cristo, Guagua, Pampanga	24 November 2011
Second Rural Bank of Valenzuela, Inc.	Polo, Valenzuela City, Metro Manila	24 November 2011
Secured Bank, Inc. (A Rural Bank)	Capt. Vicente Rosa St., Cogon, Cagayan de Oro City	24 November 2011
Shell Employees Savings & Loan Association, Inc.	3/F Shell House Bldg., 156 Valero St., Salcedo Village, Makati City	24 November 2011
Shell Refinery Employees Savings & Loan Association, Inc.	Tabangao, Batangas City	24 November 2011
Shoe Mart Savings & Loan Association, Inc.	Bldg. 104 Bay Boulevard, SM Central Business Park, Bay City, Pasay City	24 November 2011
Siam Bank (CRB of Lugait Inc.)	Cagayan de Oro City, Misamis Oriental	24 November 2011
Siargao Bank, Inc. (A Rural Bank) RB of Dapa, Inc.	Jose C. Sering Bldg., Capitol Road, Surigao City	24 November 2011
Silahis Bank Inc. (A Rural Bank)	452 Mc Arthur Highway, Balagtas, Bulacan	24 November 2011
Silangan Savings and Loan Bank, Inc.	J. P. Rizal St., Silang, 4118 Cavite	24 November 2011
Smart Bank (A Rural Bank), Inc.	Madrigal Business Centre, Alabang, Muntinlupa City	24 November 2011
Sorsogon Provincial Cooperative Bank	B. Flores St., Sorsogon City, Sorsogon	24 November 2011
South Bank, Inc. (A Rural Bank)	Rodelsa Hall, R.N. Pelaez Blvd., Kauswagan, Cagayan de Oro City	24 November 2011
Southeast Country Bank, Inc. – RB of Camaligan, Inc.	Sto. Domingo St., Camaligan, Camarines Sur	24 November 2011

Southern Leyte Cooperative Bank	Rafols St., Tunga-tunga, Maasin, Southern Leyte	24 November 2011
Southern Luzon Teachers Savings & Loan Association, Inc. (SLTSLAI)	Alday Street, Candelaria, Quezon	24 November 2011
Southernside Savings & Loan Association, Inc.	SMS Compound, Camella Homes IV, Poblacion, 1776 Muntinlupa City	24 November 2011
St. Michael Rural Bank, Inc.	Herminia Bldg., Espinosa St. cor. Rizal St., Tarlac City, Tarlac	24 November 2011
Sta. Maria Rural Bank (Bulacan), Inc.	Sta. Maria, Bulacan	24 November 2011
State Investment Trust, Inc.	333 3F Juan Luna Street, 1006 Binondo, Manila	24 November 2011
Sterling Bank of Asia, Inc. (A Savings Bank)	Sterling Bank Corporate Centre, Greenhills, San Juan City	24 November 2011
Sto. Niño Rural Bank, Inc.	Ternate, Cavite	24 November 2011
Sto. Rosario Rural Bank (Batangas), Inc.	J.P. Rizal St., P.Garcia, Batangas	24 November 2011
Sugbuanon Rural Bank, Inc.	Dr. Ramon Arcenas Bldg., Osmeña Blvd., Cebu City	24 November 2011
Summit Bank (Rural Bank of Tublay, Inc.)	Acop, Tublay, Benguet (Exec. Office – #35 Lim Ting Bldg., Diego Silang St., Baguio City)	24 November 2011
Summit Rural Bank of Lipa City, Inc.	Morada Ave., Lipa City, Batangas	24 November 2011
Sunrise Rural Bank, Inc.	Zuno St., Rosario, Batangas	24 November 2011
Supreme Court Savings & Loan Association, Inc. (SCSLAI)	Padre Faure, Manila	24 November 2011
Surigao City Evergreen Rural Bank, Inc.	No. 03337 Borromeo St., Surigao City, Surigao del Norte	24 November 2011
Surigao Officials & Employees Savings & Loan Association	Rizal Street, 8400 Surigao City, Surigao del Norte	24 November 2011
Surigaonon Rural Banking Corporation	J.P. Rizal corner Gemina Sts., 8400 Surigao City	24 November 2011
Synergy Rural Bank, Inc.	No. 5 Kap. Simeon Luz St., Brgy. 4, Lipa City, Batangas 4217	24 November 2011

Tamaraw Rural Bank, Inc.	M.H. Del Pilar cor. Magsaysay Sts., San Jose, Occidental Mindoro	24 November 2011
Tanay Rural Bank, Inc.	F.T. Catapusan St., Brgy. Plaza Aldea, Tanay, Rizal	24 November 2011
Telecommunications Savings & Loan Association, Inc.	Bureau of Telecommunications Bldg., A. Roces Avenue, Quezon City	24 November 2011
The Country Bank, Inc. (RB Bongabong, Inc.)	Poblacion Bongabong, Oriental Mindoro	24 November 2011
The Palawan Bank (Palawan Development Bank, Inc.)	167 Rizal Ave., Puerto Princesa City, Palawan 5300	24 November 2011
Tiaong Rural Bank, Inc.	Doña Tating St., Pob. I, Tiaong, Quezon	24 November 2011
Tong Yang Savings Bank, Inc.	G / F Chatham House Condominium, 116 Valero cor. Herrera Sts. , Salcedo Village, 1227 Makati City	24 November 2011
Tower Development Bank	G/F Rockavilla Bldg., Poblacion, Guiguinto, Bulacan	24 November 2011
Towncall Rural Bank, Inc.	G/F Towncall Bldg., Maharlika Highway, Cabanatuan City	24 November 2011
Toyota Financial Services Philippines Corporation (TFSPH)	32F GT Tower International, Ayala Avenue corner HV Dela Costa St., Salcedo Village, Makati City	24 November 2011
Toyota Motor Philippines Savings & Loan Association, Inc. (TMPSLAI)	Santa Rosa-Tagaytay Road, Santa Rosa, Laguna	24 November 2011
Turumba Rural Bank of Pakil, Inc.	36 Tavera Street, Pakil, Laguna	24 November 2011
Unilink Bank Inc. (A Rural Bank)	Km. 39 Nat'l H-way, Balibago, Sta. Rosa, Laguna	24 November 2011
United Consumers Rural Bank, Inc.	National Highway, Centro, Aurora, Isabela	24 November 2011
United Overseas Bank Philippines	17/F Pacific Star Building, Sen. Gil J. Puyat Ave. cor. Makati Ave., Makati City 1200	24 November 2011
United People's Rural Bank, Inc.	Nadres St., Candelaria, 4323 Quezon	24 November 2011
Unity Bank (A Rural Bank), Inc.	V. Tiomico St., San Fernando, Pampanga	24 November 2011

Universal Rural Bank of Lopez, Inc.	San Francisco Street, Brgy. Talolong, Lopez, Quezon	24 November 2011
University of Luzon Savings & Loan Association	Perez Boulevard, Dagupan City, Pangasinan	24 November 2011
University Savings Bank	1497 Dapitan cor. Alfredo St., Sampaloc, Manila	24 November 2011
Unlad Rural Bank of Noveleta, Inc.	Poblacion, Noveleta, Cavite	24 November 2011
Upland Rural Bank of Dalaguete (Cebu), Inc.	Legaspi St., Poblacion, Dalaguete, 6022 Cebu	24 November 2011
Utility Bank, Inc. (A Rural Bank)	J. P. Rizal St., Bauan, Batangas	24 November 2011
Valiant Rural Bank, Inc.	41 Mabini St., Iloilo City	24 November 2011
Vigan Banco Rural, Incorporada	Vigan, Ilocos Sur	24 November 2011
Village Bank, Inc. (A Thrift Bank)	Centro I, Orani, Bataan	24 November 2011
Vision Bank, Inc.- A Rural Bank (Microfinance)	Libod Poblacion, Bato, Catanduanes	24 November 2011
Vizcaya Bank, A Rural Bank, Inc.	Gen. Luna St., Solano, 3709 Nueva Vizcaya	24 November 2011
Water and Sewerage Savings & Loan Association, Inc.	MWSS Complex, Katipunan Road, Balara, Quezon City	24 November 2011
Wealth Bank – A Development Bank	Taft Financial Centre, Cardinal Rosales Ave., Cebu Bus. Park, Cebu City 6000	24 November 2011
Women's Rural Bank, Inc.	Carandang Street, Poblacion, Rosario, Batangas	24 November 2011
Wyeth Suaco Employees Savings & Loan Association, Inc.	2236 Chino Roces Ave., Makati City	24 November 2011
Xavier-Punla Rural Bank, Inc.	Sayre Highway, Poblacion, Pangantucan, Bukidnon 8717	24 November 2011
Xavier-Tibod Bank, Inc. (Microfinance Rural Bank)	Pabayo St., Divisoria, Cagayan De Oro City	24 November 2011
Zambales Rural Bank (Zambank)-RB Castillejos	#6, 20th St., East Bajac-Bajac, Olongapo City	24 November 2011
Zamboanga City Rural Bank, Inc.	Tomas Claudio St., Zamboanga City	24 November 2011

Table 10: Financial institutions whose financial statements are accepted – Philippines

Name and address of Financial Institution
ABN Amro Bank: LKG Tower 6801 Ayala Avenue 1200, Makati City, Manila
Al-Amanah Islamic Bank: PHIDCO A. Building Veterans Avenue, Zamboanga City
Allied Banking Corporation: Allied Banking Centre, 6754 Ayala Ave. cor. Legaspi St., Makati City
Allied Savings Bank: Allied Bank Centre, 6754 Ayala Ave. cor. Legaspi St., Makati City
Asia United Bank: JN Bldg., Joy Nastalg Centre, 17 ADB Avenue, Ortigas Centre, Pasig City 1605
Australia & New Zealand Banking Group (ANZ): 9F Metrobank Card Corp. Centre, 6778 Ayala Avenue, Makati City
Banco de Oro Unibank, Inc: BDO Corporate Centre, 7899 Makati Avenue, Makati City
Bangkok Bank Public Co Ltd: 10th Floor Tower II The Enterprise Centre 6766 Ayala Avenue, Makati City
Bank of America, N.A: 27/F Philamlife Tower, 8767 Paseo de Roxas, Makati City 1226
Bank of China (Limited – Manila Branch): 36/F Philamlife Tower, 8767 Paseo de Roxas, Makati City
Bank of Commerce: San Miguel Properties Centre (SMPC), No. 7 Saint Francis Street, Mandaluyong City 1550
Bank of the Philippine Islands: BPI Bldg., Ayala Avenue cor. Paseo de Roxas, Makati City 0720
Bank of Tokyo-Mitsubishi: 15/F Makati Sky Plaza Building, 6788 Ayala Avenue, Makati City 1226
BDO Elite Savings Bank, Inc: 11th Floor Net Cube 3rd Avenue 30th Street Global City (Mailing address: BDO Corporate Centre, 7899 Makati Avenue, Makati City)
BDO Private Bank: 27 / F Tower One and Exchange Plaza, Ayala Triangle, Ayala Avenue, Makati City 1226
BPI Capital Corporation: 8th Floor 8753 BPI Building, Ayala Avenue corner Paseo de Roxas, Makati City
BPI Card Finance Corporation: BPI Card Centre, 8753 Paseo de Roxas, Makati City
BPI Direct Savings Bank: 8th Floor BPI Card Centre, 8753 Paseo de Roxas, Makati City 0720
BPI Family Savings Bank: BPI FSB Centre, Paseo de Roxas cor. dela Rosa Sts., Makati City
BPI Globe BanKo, Inc., A Savings Bank: G/F Greentop Condominium Bldg., Ortigas Avenue, North Greenhills, San Juan, Metro Manila
BPI Leasing Corporation: 8th Floor Ayala Wing, BPI Building, Ayala Ave., cor Paseo de Roxas, Makati City

China Banking Corporation: 8745 Paseo de Roxas cor. Villar St., Makati City 1226

China Bank Savings, Inc: VGP Centre Bldg., 6772 Ayala Avenue, 1226 Makati City

China Trust (Phils) Commercial Bank: 16th to 19th Floors, Fort Legend Towers, 31st Street cor. 3rd Ave., Bonifacio Global City, Taguig City

Citibank N.A: 9F Citibank Tower, 8741 Paseo de Roxas St., Makati City 1226

Citibank Savings, Inc: 19th Floor, Citibank Square, 1 Eastwood Avenue, Eastwood City, Libis, Quezon City

Deutsche Bank AG: 26/F Ayala Tower One, Ayala Triangle, Ayala Ave., Makati City 1274

Development Bank of the Philippines (DBP): Sen. Gil. J. Puyat Avenue corner Makati Avenue Makati City

East West Bank: 20/F PBCom Tower, Ayala Avenue, Salcedo Village, Makati City 1226

Export and Industry Bank: Export Bank Plaza, Export Drive cor. Chino Roces cor. Sen Gil Puyat Ave., Makati City 1200

First Consolidated Bank: C.P. Garcia North Ave., Taloto District, Tagbilaran

Hongkong and Shanghai Banking Corporation: HSBC Centre, 3058 Fifth Avenue West, Bonifacio Global City, Taguig City 1634

HSBC Savings Bank (Phils) Inc: G/F Peninsula Court, 8735 Paseo de Roxas cor. Makati Ave., Makati City

ING Bank (Internationale Nederlanden Groep Bank N.V. – Manila Branch): 21/F Tower One & Exchange Plaza, Ayala Triangle, Ayala Avenue, Makati City

ISLA Bank (A Thrift Bank), Inc: G/F & 2/F Glass Tower, 115 C. Palanca, Jr. Legaspi Village 1229 Makati City

JP Morgan Chase Bank: 31/F Philamlife Tower, 8767 Paseo de Roxas, Makati City 1229

Korea Exchange Bank: 33/F Citibank Tower, 8741 Paseo de Roxas St., Salcedo Village, Makati City

Land Bank of the Philippines: Land Bank Plaza Bldg., 1598 M. H. Del Pilar cor. Dr. J. Quintos Sts., Malate, Manila 1004

Malayan Bank Savings and Mortgage Bank: Majalco Building., cor. Benavidez & Trasierra Streets, Legaspi Village, Makati City

Maybank Philippines, Inc: Legaspi Towers, 300 Roxas Blvd. cor. Vito Cruz St., Malate, Manila 1004

Mega International Commercial Bank: 3/F Pacific Star Bldg., Sen. Gil J. Puyat Ave. cor. Makati Ave., Makati City 1200

Metropolitan Bank and Trust Company: Metrobank Plaza, Sen. Gil J. Puyat Ave., Makati City 1200

Mizuho Corporate Bank Ltd: 26/F Citibank Tower, Valero cor. Villar Sts., Salcedo Village, Makati City

Philippine Bank of Communications: 5/F PBCom Tower, 6795 Ayala Avenue, Makati City 1200

Philippine Business Bank: 350 cor 8th and Rizal Ave., Grace Park, 1403 Caloocan City

Philippine National Bank: PNB Financial Centre, Pres. Diosdado Macapagal Blvd., Pasay City 1305

Philippine Savings Bank: 3rd Floor, PSBank Centre, 777 Paseo de Roxas cor. Sedeño St., Makati City 1226

Philippine Veterans Bank: PVB Bldg. 101V.A. Rufino cor. Dela Rosa Sts., Legaspi Village, Makati City 1229

Planters Development Bank: Plantersbank Bldg., 314 Sen. Gil Puyat Extension, Makati City 1200

Queen City Development Bank: Queenbank Financial Centre, Sky City Tower, Mapa St., Iloilo City

RCBC Capital Corporation: 7th Floor Yuchengco Tower, RCBC Plaza, 6819 Ayala Avenue Makati City 0727

RCBC Savings Bank, Inc: Pacific Place Bldg., Pearl Drive, Ortigas Centre, 1600 Pasig City (Executive office: 18/F Philippine Stock Exchange Centre, West Tower, Exchange Road, Ortigas Centre, Pasig City)

Rizal Commercial Banking Corporation: 46th Floor, Yuchengco Tower, RCBC Plaza, 6819 Ayala Avenue, Makati City 0727

Robinsons Bank Corporation: 17/F Galleria Corporate Centre, EDSA cor. Ortigas Avenue, 1110 Quezon City

Security Bank Corporation: Security Bank Centre, 6776 Ayala Ave., Makati City 0719

Standard Chartered Bank: The Sky Plaza, 6788 Ayala Ave., Makati City 1226

The Real Bank: 7/F President Tower, 81 Timog Avenue, Diliman, Quezon City

UCPB Leasing and Finance Corporation (ULFC): 14F UCPB Building, Makati enue, Makati City

UCPB Savings Bank: 18th Flr. UCPB Bldg., Makati Avenue, Makati City 1200

Unionbank of the Philippines: Unionbank Plaza Building, Meralco Ave., cor. Onyx & Sapphire Roads, Pasig City 1605

United Coconut Planters Bank: UCPB Bldg., 7907 Makati Ave., Makati City 0728

World Partner's Bank (A Thrift Bank): 72 Mabini Street, San Pedro, Laguna

Note: Appendix O inserted from 20 July 2012 (Cm 8423).

[Appendix Q

Statement of Written Terms and Conditions of employment required in paragraph 245ZO(f)(ii) and paragraph 245ZQ (e)(ii)

Statement of the terms and conditions of employment of an overseas domestic worker in a diplomatic household in the United Kingdom

This form must be completed and signed by the employer, signed by the overseas domestic worker and submitted with the entry clearance application or with the leave to remain application as required by paragraphs 245ZO (f) (ii) and 245ZQ (e) (ii) of the Immigration Rules

Please complete this form in capitals

Name of employee:

Name of employer:

1. Job Title:

2. Duties/Responsibilities:

3. Date of start of employment in the UK:

4. Employer's address in the UK:

5. Employee's address in the UK
   (if different from 4 please explain):

6. Employee's place of work in the UK
   (if different from 4 please explain):

7. Rate of Pay per week/month:

Note: By signing this document, the employer is declaring that the employee will be paid in accordance with the National Minimum Wage Act 1998 and any Regulations made under it for the duration of the employment.

8. Hours of work per day/week:

Free periods per day:
Free periods per week:

9. Sleeping accommodation:

10. Holidays:

11. Ending the employment:

Employee must give .... weeks notice if he/she decides to leave his/her job.

Employee is entitled to .... weeks notice if the employer decides to dismiss him/her.

Employee is employed on a fixed-term contract until (date) [if applicable].

Signed .... Date .... (Employer)

I confirm that my conditions of employment are as described above:

Signed .... Date ....   (Employee)]

Note: Appendix Q inserted from 6 September 2012 (HC 565).

[Appendix R

List of recognised festivals for which entry by amateur and professional entertainer visitors is permitted

Aberdeen International Youth Festival
Aldeburgh Festival and Snape Proms
Alnwick International Music Festival
Barbican Festivals (Summer, Autumn 1, Autumn 2, Only Connect).
Bath International Music Festival
BBC Proms
Belfast Festival at Queens
Bestival
Billingham International Folklore Festival
Birmingham International Jazz Festival
Breakin' Convention
Brighton Festival
Brighton Fringe
Brouhaha International Festival
Cambridge Folk Festival
Camp Bestival
Celtic Connections Festival
Cheltenham Festivals (Jazz/Science/Music/Literature)
City of London Festival
DaDa
Dance Umbrella
Edinburgh Festival Fringe
Edinburgh International Festival
Edinburgh International Jazz and Blues Festival
Edinburgh Military Tattoo
Festival Republic-Reading, Leeds, Latitude,
Glyndebourne

Greenbelt Festival
Hay Festival
Huddersfield Contemporary Music Festival
London Jazz
Live Nation (Wireless, Download, Hard Rock Calling)
Llangollen International Music Eisteddfod
London International Festival of Theatre
London 2012 Festival
Norfolk and Norwich Festival
Salisbury International Arts Festival
Southbank Centre (Meltdown)
T in the Park
V Festivals
WOMAD Festival]

Note: Appendix R inserted from 6 September 2012 (HC 565).

APPENDIX S

HIGHLY SKILLED MIGRANTS PROGRAMME (HSMP) – QUALIFYING FOR INDEFINITE LEAVE TO REMAIN AFTER FOUR YEARS CONTINUOUS RESIDENCE

1. In this appendix, all references to the Highly Skilled Migrants Programme refer to the scheme of that name that operated until 7 November 2006.

2. Paragraphs 4 – 16 of this appendix cover migrants who:

    a. Received a Highly Skilled Migrants Programme approval letter issued on the basis of an application made before 3 April 2006; and,

    b. Were granted Entry Clearance or Leave to Remain on the basis of that letter; and,

    c. Fall into one of the following five categories:

        i. Have already settled in the United Kingdom under Highly Skilled Migrants Programme or Tier 1 (General) on the basis of having completed five years continuous residence in a qualifying category.

        ii. Have completed four years continuous residence in the United Kingdom in a qualifying category.

        iii. Are coming up to having completed four years continuous residence in the United Kingdom in a qualifying category.

        iv. Had applied for Indefinite Leave to Remain after four years, were refused, and either;

            1. won an appeal against the refusal decision and were then granted permission to stay; or

            2. did not appeal the refusal decision or their appeal was dismissed.

        v. Those who have completed four years continuous residence in the United Kingdom in a qualifying category and have submitted an application for Further Leave to Remain (FLR)

3. Paragraph 17 of this appendix covers migrants who:

    a. Received a Highly Skilled Migrants Programme approval letter issued on the basis of an application made between 3 April 2006 and 7 November 2006; and

b. Were granted Entry Clearance or Leave to Remain on the basis of that letter.

Requirements for Indefinite Leave to Remain under the terms of this appendix for those groups covered by paragraph 2 of this appendix.

4. The requirements for Indefinite Leave to Remain for a person qualifying for consideration under this appendix are that they:

a. have spent a continuous period of four years lawfully in the United Kingdom, of which the most recent period must have been spent with leave as a highly skilled migrant, and the remainder must be made up of leave as a highly skilled migrant, leave as a work permit holder (under paragraphs 128 to 133 of the Immigration Rules), leave as an Innovator (under paragraphs 210A to 210F of the Immigration Rules) or leave as a Tier 1 (General) migrant;

b. had applied to enter onto the Highly Skilled Migrants Programme before the qualifying period for Indefinite Leave to Remain was increased from four to five years on 3 April 2006, and was successful in that application;

c. have throughout the period of five years maintained and accommodated themselves and any dependants adequately without recourse to public funds; and,

d. are lawfully economically active in the United Kingdom in employment, self-employment or a combination of both.

Those who have already settled in the United Kingdom under Highly Skilled Migrants Programme or Tier 1 (General) on the basis of having spent completed five years continuous residence in the UK in a qualifying category

5. These migrants gained an initial grant of one year's leave under the Highly Skilled Migrants Programme requirements, then extended their initial year grant by a further three years, and were subsequently required to make a second extension application in order to have completed five years continuous residence in the UK.

Those who have completed four years continuous residence in the United Kingdom in a qualifying category

6. These migrants gained an initial grant of one year's leave under the Highly Skilled Migrants Programme requirements, then extended their initial year grant by a further three years, and were subsequently required to make a second extension application in order for them to complete the fifth years' continuous residence in the United Kingdom.

7. Migrants will be allowed to apply for Indefinite Leave to Remain after they have completed four years qualifying residence.

8. The requirements for Indefinite Leave to Remain will be those described in paragraph 4 of this appendix.

Those who are coming up to having completed four years continuous residence in the United Kingdom in a qualifying category

9. These migrants gained an initial grant of one year's leave under the Highly Skilled Migrants Programme requirements, or a grant of two years where their application was

made before 3 April 2006 but not approved until after this date, and then extended their initial year grant by either three or four years.

10. The migrants described in the paragraph above will be allowed to apply for Indefinite Leave to Remain after they have completed four years qualifying residence.

11. The requirements for Indefinite Leave to Remain will be those described in paragraph 4 of this appendix.

Those who applied for settlement after four years, were refused, and either won an appeal against the refusal decision and were then granted permission to stay, or did not appeal the refusal decision or their appeal was dismissed

12. These migrants will be entitled to apply for their original Indefinite Leave to Remain application to be reviewed under the requirements set out in paragraph 4 of this appendix.

13. If the migrant meets the requirements of paragraph 4 of this appendix their leave will be varied to Indefinite Leave to Remain under the Highly Skilled Migrants Programme.

Those who have completed four years continuous residence in the United Kingdom in a qualifying category and have submitted an application for Further Leave to Remain

14. These migrants gained an initial grant of one year's leave under the Highly Skilled Migrants Programme requirements, then extended their initial year grant by a further three years, and have now made a second extension application in order to complete five years continuous residence in the United Kingdom.

15. The migrants described in the paragraph above will be invited to vary their application to an Indefinite Leave to Remain application under the terms of this appendix.

16. The requirements for Indefinite Leave to Remain will be those described in paragraph 4 of this appendix.

Requirements for Indefinite Leave to Remain under the terms of this appendix, for those groups covered by paragraph 3 of this appendix.

17. The requirements for Indefinite Leave to Remain for a person qualifying for consideration under this appendix are that they:

a. have spent a continuous period of five years lawfully in the United Kingdom, of which the most recent period must have been spent with leave as a highly skilled migrant, and the remainder must be made up of leave as a highly skilled migrant, leave as a work permit holder (under paragraphs 128 to 133 of the Immigration Rules), leave as an Innovator (under paragraphs 210A to 210F of the Immigration Rules) or leave as a Tier 1 (General) migrant;

b. had applied to enter onto the Highly Skilled Migrants Programme between 03 April 2006, and 7 November 2006 and was successful in that application;

c. have throughout the period of five years maintained and accommodated themselves and any dependants adequately without recourse to public funds; and

d. are lawfully economically active in the United Kingdom in employment, self-employment or a combination of both.

General Grounds for Refusal

18. Where the migrant falls for refusal under the General Grounds for Refusal in paragraphs 320-322 of the Immigration Rules, their application should be refused even if it otherwise qualifies under the terms of this appendix.

Dependants

19. The immigration status of dependants of migrants in the categories covered by this appendix will follow that of the principal applicant

APPENDIX T –

TUBERCULOSIS SCREENING

PART 1 – APPLICABLE COUNTRIES

Migrants applying to enter the UK for more than six months from the countries listed below must present at the time of application a valid medical certificate issued by a medical practitioner listed in Part 2 of this Appendix confirming that they have undergone screening for active pulmonary tuberculosis and that such tuberculosis is not present in the applicant.

Bangladesh
Burkina Faso
Cambodia
Côte d'Ivoire
Eritrea
Ghana
India
Kenya
Laos
Niger
Pakistan
Somalia
Sudan
Tanzania
Togo
Thailand

Applicants from Burkina Faso, Cote d'Ivoire, Niger, Togo are screened in Ghana, those from Eritrea and Somalia are screened in Kenya and those from Laos are screened in Thailand

PART 2 – LIST OF SCREENING CLINICS

Migrants applying to enter the UK for more than six months from the countries listed in Part 1 of this Appendix must present at the time of application a valid medical certificate issued by a medical practitioner from a medical clinic listed below confirming that they have undergone screening for active pulmonary tuberculosis and that such tuberculosis is not present in the applicant.

Bangladesh

DHAKA – International Organisation for Migration (IOM)
Migration Health Assessment Clinic (MHAC)
Prescription Point Ltd. (3rd floor)
House 105, Road 12, Block E, Banani
Dhaka 1213, Bangladesh

SYLHET – International Organisation for Migration (IOM)
Migration Health Assessment Clinic (MHAC)
Medi-Aid Heart Centre
South Dorga Gate (Near Minar)
Dorga Moholla, Sylhet – 3100, Bangladesh

Cambodia

PHNOM PENH – International Organisation for Migration (IOM)
No.31, Street 71 Sangkat Boeun Keng Kang 1 Khan Cham Car Morn Phnom Penh,
Cambodia
Tel: +855 12 900 131 Fax: +855 23 21 64 23

Ghana

ACCRA – International Organisation for Migration (IOM)
17 Ridge Road
Roman Ridge
Tel: 030-7010251/53/54

India

ANDHRA PRADESH:
Centre for Migration Medicine (CMM)
#3-6-20, Street#19,
Himayatnagar,
Hyderabad, AP-500029
Tel: (040) 29806789/ Mob: 08500777000
Email: CMM.UK@MigrationMedicine.com

GYD Diagnostics & Reference Laboratories Pvt Ltd
6-1-126 & 127/4,
Padmarao Nagar, (lane opposite Gharounda supermarket),
Secunderabad, Andhra Pradesh, 500 025
Tel: (040) 42414142/ 43/ 44

BANGALORE:
Elbit Medical Diagnostic Ltd
1 & ½ Indian Express Building Queens Road,
Bangalore -560 001
Tel: (080) 40570000 / 41132461

Fortis Hospital
154/9 Bannerghatta Road,
Opp IIM-B
Bangalore -560076
Tel: (080) 66214166/66214444

CHANDIGARH:
Kansal Clinic
Kothi No.4, Phase 2,
Sector-54 Nr. Bassi Theatre,
SAS Nagar, 160 047,
Chandigarh
Tel: (0172) 2225124 / 2273587

National Medical and Dialysis Centre
516, Sector 10 –D
(opposite Hotel Mountain View)
Chandigarh
Tel: (0172)-6652000/Mob: 08427661909

New Diagnostic Centre
Sector 20C,
Tribune Road,
Chandigarh

Max Super Special Speciality Hospital
New Civil Hospital,
Ph IV, Mohali, Punjab -160055
Tel: (0172)-6652000/Mob: 08427661909

CHENNAI:
Osler Diagnostics (Pvt) Ltd.
2 Maloney Road,
T Nagar,
Chennai 600017
Tel: (044) 2434 6424/ 5881/ (044) 2432 2189

The Apollo Heart Centre
156 Greams Road,
Chennai 600006
Tel: (044) 60601066 / 28296916/ Mob: 09551011666

GUJARAT:
Apollo Hospitals International Ltd
Plot No.1 A, Bhat GIDC Estate, Ahmedabad
Gujarat, 382 428
Tel: (079) 66701800

Saviour Hospital
(Near Bharat Petrol Pump),
Lakhudi Circle Stadium Road,
Navrangpura,
Ahmedabad 380014
Tel: (079) 61908080/61908000/Mob: 09824053196

Apollo Clinic
Mann Complex
Opp. Shree Ram Petrol Pump
Anand Mahal Road, Adajan
Surat 395009
Tel: (0261) 2790202

GUWAHATI:
The Apollo Clinic
Kanchan Road, Bora Service,
G S Road, Guwahati
Tel: (0361) 2461473 / 2461474

KERALA:
Kerala Institute of Medical Sciences (KIMS)
P.B. No 1, Anayara, Thiruvananthapuram,
Kerala, 695 029
Tel: (0471) 3041312

KOLKATA:
Apollo Gleneagles Hospital Ltd
58 Canal Circular Road,
Kolkata 700054
Tel: (033) 23202122 / 23202040

Pulse Diagnostics Pty Ltd
75 Sarat Bose Road,
Kolkata 700019
Tel: (033) 24546142 / 21492603

LUCKNOW:
Medical Clinic
122 Faizabad Road,
(near Indira Bridge)
Lucknow 226007
Tel: (0522) 2324656 / 2336629

National X-ray Clinic
195/104 Jagat Narain Road,
Lucknow 226 003
Tel: (0522) 2253845

LUDHIANA:
Dr Har Kamal Bagga/ Dr Wahiguru Pal Singh
3791/3A Jagjit Nagar Pakhowal Road,
Ludhiana 141 001, Punjab
Tel: (0161) 2459403/ Mob: 09814001200
Mob: (0161) 2458403/Mob: 91-09872266666

Dr U S Sidhu
82-A, SARABHA NAGAR,
Near PVR Cinema/Malhar Road,
Ludhiana 141 001, Punjab
Tel: 09779750340 (preferred contact) / (0161)-2450340

Dr Harminder Singh Pannu
B2412, Krishna Nagar, Opp. Aarti Cinema,
Ferozepur Road, 141 001
Tel: (0161) 2409036 / 2408108
S.P.S Apollo Hospitals
Sherpur Chowk,
G.T Road
Ludhiana 141 003
Tel: (0161) 6617100 / 6617111/ 6617222

Super X-ray Clinic
2353/2 Krishana Nagar,
Ferozepur Road,
(near Aarti Cinema)
Ludhiana 141 001
Tel: (0161) 240 8031 / 4629231

MUMBAI:
Lilavati Hospital
A-791, Bandra Reclamation,
Bandra West, 400 050
Tel: (022) 26568000. Ext. no 8248 / 8283
Direct line 26568248
Email Id: visa@lilavatihospital.com

Clinical Diagnostic Centre, South Mumbai
A-2 Ben Nevis,
Bhulabhai Desai Road, Next to Tata Garden,
Mumbai400 036
Tel: (022) 61196200/ 23684764/ 65
Contact Person: Ms Theresa Ferrao

Clinical Diagnostic Centre, North Mumbai
A403 Floral Deck Plaza, C Cross Road, MIDC,
Opp. Seepz near Rolta Bhavan, Andheri (east),
Mumbai-400093
Tel: (022) 61196300 / 66972352/ 53
Contact Person: M Phadtare

Rele Clinic
10 AA, Gita Building,
'A' Wing, Second Floor,
Pandita Ramabai Road,
Gamdevi, Mumbai 400 007
Tel: (022) 23613737 / 23613838

Insight Health Scan,
Geeta Building Pandit Ramabai Road, Grant Road,
Mumbai -400007
Tel: (022) 23694191/ 23695344

NAGPUR:
Sanjiwani Chikitsa Kendra
Opposite City Post Office
Itwari
Nagpur 440 002
Tel: (071 2) 276 9494/ 2422996 / Mob: 09422102590

Sarda Imaging Clinic
70 Central Avenue
(near the Gandhi statue)
Itwari
Nagpur 440 002
Tel: (0712) 2766384 / 2769715 / 6612668

NEW DELHI:
Max Medcentre
N-110, Panchsheel Park
New Delhi 110 021
Tel: (011) 26499870 / Mob: 8800334457

Sadhu Vaswani Mission Medical Centre
4/27, Shanti Niketan
New Delhi 110 021
Tel: (011) 24111562/ 2411 4316/ 24111693

PUNE
Ruby Hall Clinic
40, Sassoon Road,
411 001 Pune
Tel: (020) 6645 5242 / 6645 5286 / 2616 3391

Kenya

NAIROBI – International Organisation for Migration (IOM)
Doctors' Plaza Annex Nairobi Hospital Compound
Nairobi, Kenya
Tel: 00254 20 2718559 Fax: 00254 20 2718096

Pakistan

ISLAMABAD – International Organisation for Migration (IOM) SUB OFFICE
Khurmrial Centre (Behind PTCL Head Quarter),
G-8/4 Islamabad.
Call Centre for appointments: UAN: +92 51 111 466 472

LAHORE – International Organisation for Migration (IOM) SUB OFFICE
1 – Ali Block, New Garden Town, Lahore.
Call Centre for appointments: UAN: +92 51 111 466 472

KARACHI – International Organisation for Migration (IOM) SUB OFFICE
House # F-8/1, KDA Scheme I, Tipu Sultan Road,
Adjacent to Main Karsaz Road, Karachi
Call Centre for appointments: UAN: +92 51 111 466 472

MIRPUR – International Organisation for Migration (IOM) SUB OFFICE
House # 6, Sector D/4, F2 Road, Block West,
Mirpur, Azad Kashmir.
Call Centre for appointments: UAN: +92 51 111 466 472

Sudan

KHARTOUM – International Organisation for Migration (IOM)
IOM Sudan Mission, Amarat, Street 47, House 18, Block 11 OE
PO Box 8322, Khartoum, Sudan
Tel: +249983570802
Fax: +24983569094

Tanzania

DAR ES SALAAM – International Organisation for Migration (IOM)
Slip Road, off Chole, Plot #1365 – Msasani,
PO Box 9270 Dar es Salaam, Tanzania
Tel: +255222602913
Fax: +255222602782

Thailand

BANGKOK – International Organisation for Migration (IOM)
8th Floor, Kasemkij Bldg, 120 Silom Road,
Bangrak District, Bangkok 10500 Thailand
Tel: +66 2 234 7950
Fax: +66 2 234 7956

Note: Appendix T inserted from 6 September 2012 (HC 565).

STATUTORY INSTRUMENTS

Immigration (Control of Entry through Republic of Ireland) Order 1972
(SI 1972, No. 1610)

1. This Order may be cited as the Immigration (Control of Entry through Republic of Ireland) Order 1972 and shall come into operation on 1 January 1973.

2.—(1) In this Order—

'the Act' means the Immigration Act 1971; and

'visa national' means a person who, in accordance with the immigration rules, is required on entry into the United Kingdom to produce a passport or other document of identity endorsed with a United Kingdom visa and includes a stateless person.

(2) In this Order any reference to an Article shall be construed as a reference to an Article of this Order and any reference in an Article to a paragraph as a reference to a paragraph of that Article.

(3) The Interpretation Act 1889 shall apply to the interpretation of this Order as it applies to the interpretation of an Act of Parliament.

3.—(1) This Article applies to—

(a) any person (other than a citizen of the Republic of Ireland) who arrives in the United Kingdom on an aircraft which began its flight in that Republic if he entered that Republic in the course of a journey to the United Kingdom which began outside the common travel area and was not given leave to land in that Republic in accordance with the law in force there;

(b) any person (other than a person to whom sub-paragraph (a) of this paragraph applies) who arrives in the United Kingdom on a local journey from the Republic of Ireland if he satisfies any of the following conditions, that is to say—

(i) he is a visa national who has no valid visa for his entry into the United Kingdom;

(ii) he entered that Republic unlawfully from a place outside the common travel area;

(iii) he entered that Republic from a place in the United Kingdom and Islands after entering there unlawfully, [or if he had a limited leave to enter or remain there, after the expiry of the leave, provided that in either case] he has not subsequently been given leave to enter or remain in the United Kingdom or any of the Islands; or

(iv) he is a person in respect of whom directions have been given by the Secretary of State for him not to be given entry to the United Kingdom on the ground that his exclusion is conducive to the public good.

(2) In relation only to persons to whom this Article applies, the Republic of Ireland shall be excluded from section 1(3) of the Act (provisions relating to persons travelling on local journeys in the common travel area).

Note: Words in square brackets in Art 3(1)(b)(iii) inserted by SI 1979/730.

4.—(1) Subject to paragraph (2), this Article applies to [any person who does not have the right of abode in the United Kingdom under section 2 of the Act] and is not a citizen of the Republic of Ireland and who enters the United Kingdom on a local journey from the Republic of Ireland after having entered that Republic—

(a) on coming from a place outside the common travel area; or

(b) after leaving the United Kingdom whilst having a limited leave to enter or remain there which has since expired.

(2) This Article shall not apply to any person [who arrives in the United Kingdom with leave to enter or remain in the United Kingdom which is in force but which was given to him before arrival or] who requires leave to enter the United Kingdom by virtue of Article 3 or section 9(4) of the Act.

(3) A person to whom this Article applies by virtue only of paragraph (1)(a) shall, unless he is a visa national who has a visa containing the words 'short visit', be subject to the restriction and to the condition set out in paragraph (4).

(4) The restriction and the condition referred to in paragraph (3) are—
(a) the period for which he may remain in the United Kingdom shall not be more than three months from the date on which he entered the United Kingdom; and
[(b) unless he is a national of a state which is a member of the European Economic Community, he shall not engage in any occupation for reward; and
(c) unless he is a national of a state which is a member of the European Economic Community other than [Portugal or Spain] he shall not engage in any employment.]

(5) In relation to a person who is a visa national and has a visa containing the words 'short visit' the restriction and the conditions set out in paragraph (6) shall have effect instead of the provisions contained in paragraph (4).

(6) The restriction and the conditions referred to in paragraph (5) are—
(a) the period for which he may remain in the United Kingdom shall not be more than one month from the date on which he entered the United Kingdom;
(b) he shall not engage in any occupation for reward or any employment; and
(c) he shall, unless he is under the age of 16 years, be required to register with the police.

(7) The preceding provisions of this Article shall have effect in relation to a person to whom this Article applies by virtue of sub-paragraph (b) of paragraph (1) (whether or not he is also a person to whom this Article applies by virtue of subparagraph (a) thereof) as they have effect in relation to a person to whom this Article applies by virtue only of the said subparagraph (a), but as if for the references in paragraphs (4) and (6) to three months and one month respectively there were substituted a reference to seven days.

Note: Words in square brackets in Art 4(1) substituted by SI 1982/1028. Words in square brackets in Art 4(2) inserted by SI 2000/1776 from 30 July 2000. Art 4(4)(b) and (c) substituted by SI 1980/1859. Words in square brackets in Art 4(4)(c) inserted by SI 1985/1854.

Immigration (Exemption from Control) Order 1972
(SI 1972, No. 1613)

---

1. This Order may be cited as the Immigration (Exemption from Control) Order 1972 and shall come into operation on 1 January 1973.
2.—(1) In this Order—
'the Act' means the Immigration Act 1971; and

'consular employee' and 'consular officer' have the meanings respectively assigned to them by Article 1 of the Vienna Convention on Consular Relations as set out in Schedule 1 to the Consular Relations Act 1968.

(2) In this Order any reference to an Article or to the Schedule shall be construed as a reference to an Article of this Order or, as the case may be, to the Schedule thereto and any reference in an Article to a paragraph as a reference to a paragraph of that Article.

(3) In this Order any reference to an enactment is a reference to it as amended, and includes a reference to it as applied, by or under any other enactment and any reference to an instrument made under or by virtue of any enactment is a reference to any such instrument for the time being in force.

(4) The Interpretation Act 1889 shall apply to the interpretation of this Order as it applies to the interpretation of an Act of Parliament.

3.—(1) The following persons shall be exempt from any provision of the Act relating to those who are not [British citizens], that is to say:—

(a) any consular officer in the service of any of the states specified in the Schedule (being states with which consular conventions have been concluded by Her Majesty);

(b) any consular employee in such service as is mentioned in sub-paragraph (a) of this paragraph; and

(c) any member of the family of a person exempted under sub-paragraph (a) or (b) of this paragraph forming part of his household.

(2) In paragraph (1) and in Article 4 any reference to a consular employee shall be construed as a reference to such an employee who is in the full-time service of the state concerned and is not engaged in the United Kingdom in any private occupation for gain.

Note: Words in square brackets in Art 3(1) substituted by SI 1982/1649.

4. The following persons shall be exempt from any provision of the Act relating to those who are not [British citizens] except any provision relating to deportation, that is to say:—

(a) unless the Secretary of State otherwise directs, any member of the government of a country or territory outside the United Kingdom and Islands who is visiting the United Kingdom on the business of that government;

(b) any person entitled to immunity from legal process with respect to acts performed by him in his official capacity under any Order in Council made under section 3(1) of the Bretton Woods Agreements Act 1945 (which empowers Her Majesty by Order in Council to make provision relating to the immunities and privileges of the governors, executive directors, alternates, officers and employees of the International Monetary Fund and the International Bank for Reconstruction and Development);

(c) any person entitled to immunity from legal process with respect to acts performed by him in his official capacity under any Order in Council made under section 3(1) of the International Finance Corporation Act 1955 (which empowers Her Majesty by Order in Council to make provision relating to the immunities and privileges of the governors, directors, alternates, officers and employees of the International Finance Corporation);

(d) any person entitled to immunity from legal process with respect to acts performed by him in his official capacity under any Order in Council made under section 3(1) of the International Development Association Act 1960 (which empowers Her Majesty by Order in Council to make provision relating to the immunities and privileges of the governors, directors, alternates, officers and employees of the International Development Association);

(e) any person (not being a person to whom section 8(3) of the Act applies) who is the representative or a member of the official staff of the representative of the government of a country to which section 1 of the Diplomatic Immunities (Conferences with Commonwealth Countries and Republic of Ireland) Act 1961 applies (which provides for representatives of certain Commonwealth countries and their staff attending conferences in the United Kingdom to be entitled to diplomatic immunity) so long as he is included in a list complied and published in accordance with that section;

(f) any person on whom any immunity from jurisdiction is conferred by any Order in Council made under section 12(1) of the Consular Relations Act 1968 (which empowers Her Majesty by Order in Council to confer on certain persons connected with the service of the government of Commonwealth countries or the Republic of Ireland all or any of the immunities and privileges which are conferred by or may be conferred under that Act on persons connected with consular posts);

(g) any person (not being a person to whom section 8(3) of the Act applies) on whom any immunity from suit and legal process is conferred by any Order in Council made under section 1(2), 5(1) or 6(2) of the International Organisations Act 1968 (which empower Her Majesty by Order in Council to confer certain immunities and privileges on persons connected with certain international organisations and international tribunals and on representatives of foreign countries and their staffs attending certain conferences in the United Kingdom) except any such person as is mentioned in section 5(2)(c) to (e) of the said Act of 1968 [or by any Order in Council continuing to have effect by virtue of section 12(5) of the said Act of 1968];

(h) any consular officer (not being an honorary consular officer) in the service of a state other than such a state as is mentioned in the Schedule;

(i) any consular employee in such service as is mentioned in paragraph (h);

[(j) any officer or servant of the Commonwealth Secretariat falling within paragraph 6 of the Schedule to the Commonwealth Secretariat Act 1966 (which confers certain immunities on those members of the staff of the Secretariat who are not entitled to full diplomatic immunity);]

[(k) any person on whom any immunity from suit and legal process is conferred by the European Communities (Immunities and Privileges of the North Atlantic Salmon Conservation Organisation) Order 1985 (which confers certain immunities and privileges on the representatives and officers of the North Atlantic Salmon Conservation Organisation);]

[(l) any member of the Hong Kong Economic and Trade Office as defined by paragraph 8 of the Schedule to the Hong Kong Economic and Trade Office Act 1996,]

[(m)

(i) Any member or servant of the Independent International Commission on Decommissioning ('the Commission') established under an Agreement between the Government of the United Kingdom of Great Britain and Northern Ireland and the Government of the Republic of Ireland concluded on 26 August 1997,

(ii) in sub-paragraph (i) above, 'servant' includes any agent of or person carrying out work for or giving advice to the Commission,

(n) any member of the family of a person exempted under any of the preceding paragraphs forming part of his household.']

[(o) any person falling within Article 4A below.]

[**4A.** —(1) In relation to the court ('the ICC') established by the Rome Statute of the International Criminal Court done at Rome on 17 July 1998 ('the Rome Statute');

(a) except in so far as in any particular case the exemption given by this Article is waived by the State or intergovernmental organisation they represent,

(i) any representative of a State party to the Rome Statute attending meetings of the Assembly or one of its subsidiary organs,

(ii) any representative of another State attending meetings of the Assembly or one of its subsidiary organs as an observer, and

(iii) any representative of a State or of an intergovernmental organisation invited to a meeting of the Assembly or one of its subsidiary organs,

while exercising their official functions and during their journey to and from the place of the meeting;

(b) except in so far as in any particular case the exemption given by this Article is waived by the State they represent, any representative of a State participating in the proceedings of the ICC while exercising their official functions and during their journeys to and from the place of the proceedings of the ICC;

(c) except in so far as in any particular case the exemption given by this Article is waived by an absolute majority of the judges, any judge and the Prosecutor, when engaged on or with respect to the business of the ICC;

(d) except in so far as in any particular case the exemption given by this Article is waived by the Prosecutor, any Deputy Prosecutor, when engaged on or with respect to the business of the ICC;

(e) except in so far as in any particular case the exemption given by this Article is waived by the Presidency, the Registrar, when engaged on or with respect to the business of the ICC;

(f) except in so far as in any particular case the exemption given by this Article is waived by the Registrar, the Deputy Registrar, so far as necessary for the performance of his functions;

(g) except in so far as in any particular case the exemption given by this Article is waived by the Prosecutor, any member of the staff of the office of the Prosecutor, so far as necessary for the performance of their functions;

(h) except in so far as in any particular case the exemption given by this Article is waived by the Registrar, any member of the staff of the Registry, so far as necessary for the performance of their functions;

(i) except in so far as in any particular case the exemption given by this Article is waived by the Presidency and subject to the production of the certificate under seal of the Registrar provided to counsel and persons assisting defence counsel upon appointment, counsel and any person assisting defence counsel, so far as necessary for the performance of their functions;

(j) except in so far as in any particular case the exemption given by this Article is waived by the Presidency and subject to the production of a document provided by the ICC certifying that the person's appearance before the ICC is required by the ICC and specifying a time period during which such appearance is necessary, any witness, to the extent necessary for their appearance before the ICC for the purposes of giving evidence;

(k) except in so far as in any particular case the exemption given by this Article is waived by the Presidency and subject to the production of a document provided by the ICC certifying the participation of the person in the proceedings of the ICC and specifying a time period for that participation, any victim, to the extent necessary for their appearance before the ICC;

(l) except in so far as in any particular case the exemption given by this Article is waived by the head of the organ of the ICC appointing the person and subject to the production of a document provided by the ICC certifying that the person is performing functions for the ICC and specifying a time period during which those functions will last, any expert performing functions for the ICC, to the extent necessary for the exercise of those functions;

(m) any member of the family of a person exempted under any of paragraphs (c) to (h) above forming part of their household.

(2) In paragraph (1) above:

'the Assembly' means the assembly of State parties to the Rome Statute;

'the Presidency' means the organ of the ICC composed of the president and the first and second vice-presidents of the ICC elected in accordance with Article 38, paragraph 1, of the Rome Statute;

'the Prosecutor' and 'Deputy Prosecutors' mean the prosecutor and deputy prosecutors respectively elected by the assembly of State parties to the Rome Statute in accordance with Article 42, paragraph 4, of the Rome Statute;

'the Registrar' and 'the Deputy Registrar' mean the registrar and deputy registrar respectively elected by the ICC in accordance with Article 43, paragraph 4, of the Rome Statute.]

Note: First words in square brackets Art 4 substituted by SI 1982/1649. Words in square brackets Art 4(g) added by SI 1977/693. Article 4(j) substituted by SI 1977/693. Article 4(k) substituted by SI 1985/1809. Art 4(l) substituted by SI 1402/1997. Art 4(m) substituted by SI 2207/1997. Article 4(o) and Art 4A inserted from a date to be appointed (SI 2004/3171).

5.—(1) Subject to the provisions of this Article the following persons who are not [British citizens] shall, on arrival in the United Kingdom, be exempt from the provisions of section 3(1)(a) of the Act (which requires persons who are not [British citizens] to obtain leave to enter the United Kingdom), that is to say—

(a) any citizen of the United Kingdom and Colonies who holds a passport issued to him in the United Kingdom and Islands and expressed to be a British Visitor's Passport;

(b) any Commonwealth citizen who is included in a passport issued in the United Kingdom by the Government of the United Kingdom or in one of the Islands by the Lieutenant-Governor thereof which is expressed to be a Collective Passport;

(c) any Commonwealth citizen or citizen of the Republic of Ireland returning to the United Kingdom from an excursion to France or Belgium [or the Netherlands] who holds a valid document of identity issued in accordance with arrangements approved by the United Kingdom Government and in a form authorised by the Secretary of State and enabling him to travel on such an excursion without a passport;

(d) any Commonwealth citizen who holds a British seaman's card or any citizen of the Republic of Ireland if (in either case) he was engaged as a member of the crew of a ship in a place within the common travel area and, on arrival in the United Kingdom, is, or is to be, discharged from his engagement;

(e) any person who, having left the United Kingdom after having been given a limited leave to enter, returns to the United Kingdom within the period for which he had leave as a member of the crew of an aircraft under an engagement requiring him to leave on that or another aircraft as a member of its crew within a period exceeding seven days.

(2) Paragraph (1) shall not apply so as to confer any exemption on any person against whom there is a deportation order in force or who has previously entered the United Kingdom unlawfully and has not subsequently been given leave to enter or remain in the United Kingdom and sub-paragraphs (d) and (e) of that paragraphs shall not apply to a person who is required by an immigration officer to submit to examination in accordance with Schedule 2 to the Act.

(3) In this Article any reference to a Commonwealth citizen shall be construed as including a reference to a British protected person and in paragraph (1)(d) 'British seaman's card'

means a valid card issued under any regulations in force under section 70 of the Merchant Shipping Act 1970 or any card having effect by virtue of the said regulations as a card so issued and 'holder of a British seaman's card' has the same meaning as in the said regulations.

Note: Words in square brackets in Art 5(1) substituted by SI 1982/1649. Words in square brackets in Art 5(1)(c) added by SI 1975/617.

6.—(1) For the purposes of section 1(1) of the British Nationality Act 1981 (which relates to acquisition of British citizenship by birth in the United Kingdom), a person to whom a child is born in the United Kingdom on or after 1 January 1983 is to be regarded (notwithstanding the preceding provisions of this Order) as settled in the United Kingdom at the time of the birth if—

(a) he would fall to be so regarded but for his being at that time entitled to an exemption by virtue of this Order; and

(b) immediately before he became entitled to that exemption he was settled in the United Kingdom; and

(c) he was ordinarily resident in the United Kingdom from the time when he became entitled to that exemption to the time of the birth;

but this Article shall not apply if at the time of the birth the child's father or mother is a person on whom any immunity from jurisdiction is conferred by or under the Diplomatic Privileges Act 1964.

(2) Expressions used in this Article shall be construed in accordance with section 50 of the British Nationality Act 1981.

Note: Article 6 added by SI 1982/1649.

Articles 3 and 4   SCHEDULE

STATES WITH WHICH CONSULAR CONVENTIONS HAVE BEEN CONCLUDED BY HER MAJESTY

Austria	Japan
Belgium	Mexico
Bulgaria	[Mongolia]
[Czechoslovakia]	Norway
Denmark	Poland
France	Romania
[German Democratic Republic]	Sweden
Greece	Spain
Federal Republic of Germany	Union of Soviet Socialist Republics
Hungary	United States of America
Italy	Yugoslavia

Note: Words in square brackets in the Sch added by SI 1977/693.

The Channel Tunnel (International Arrangements) Order 1993
(SI 1993 No.1813)

Note: The Channel Tunnel (International Arrangements) includes provisions modifying the application of specified statutory provisions in specified circumstances. Only the text relevant to the modification of statutes and statutory instruments included in this book are reproduced.

Citation and commencement

1. ...

Note: Order in force from 2 August 1993 being the date notified in the London, Edinburgh and Belfast Gazettes.

Interpretation

2. ...

Application of international articles

3. ...

[Application of supplementary articles

3A. ...

4.— Application of enactments

(1) All frontier control enactments [except those relating to transport and road traffic controls] shall for the purpose of enabling officers belonging to the United Kingdom to carry out frontier controls extend to France within a control zone.

[(1A) All frontier control enactments relating to transport and road traffic controls shall for the purpose of enabling officers belonging to the United Kingdom to carry out such controls extend to France within the control zone in France within the tunnel system.]

[(1B) All immigration control enactments shall, for the purpose of enabling immigration officers to carry out immigration controls, extend to France within a supplementary control zone.]

[(1C) The Race Relations Act 1976 shall apply to the carrying out by immigration officers of their functions in a control zone or a supplementary control zone outside the United Kingdom as it applies to the carrying out of their functions within the United Kingdom.]

[(2–4] ...

Note: Paras (2)-(4) concern processing of data. Words inserted in para (1) and para (1A) inserted from 2 October 1996 (SI 1996/2283). Para (1B) inserted from 25 May 2001 (SI 2001/1544). Para (1C) inserted from 10 December 2001 (SI 2001/3707).

Role of the Office of Rail Regulation

4A. ...

Application of criminal law

5. ...

Persons boarding a through train

5A. ...

Powers of officers and supplementary controls

6. ...

7.— Enactments modified

(1) Without prejudice to the generality of [articles 4(1), 4(1B) and 5(1)], the frontier control enactments mentioned in Schedule 4 shall–

    (a) in their application to France by virtue of article 4(1) [or article 4(1B)], and

    (b) in their application to the United Kingdom–

        (i) within the tunnel system, and

        (ii) elsewhere for the authorised purposes,

have effect with the modifications set out in Schedule 4.

[(1A) Nothing in paragraph (1)(b)(ii) implies the existence of a supplementary control zone in the station of London-Waterloo on British Territory.]

(2) ...

(3) ...

[(3A) ...

(4) ...

Note: Paras (2)–(3A) concern the application of the Firearms Act 1968. Para 4 concerns transport and road traffic controls. Words inserted in para (1) from 25 May 2001 (SI 2001/1544). Para (1A) inserted from 14 November 2007 (SI 2007/2907).

SCHEDULE 1

EXPRESSIONS DEFINED

SCHEDULE 2

INTERNATIONAL ARTICLES

SCHEDULE 2A

SUPPLEMENTARY ARTICLES

SCHEDULE 3

POWERS OF OFFICERS

Article 4   SCHEDULE 4

ENACTMENTS MODIFIED

(1) In this paragraph "the 1971 Act" means the Immigration Act 1971.

(2) In section 3 of the 1971 Act (general provision for regulation and control)–

(a) after subsection (4) insert–

"(4A) For the purposes of subsection (4) above a person seeking to leave the United Kingdom through the tunnel system who is refused admission to France shall be treated as having gone to a country outside the common travel area."

; and

(b) after subsection (7) insert–

"(7A) Any reference in an Order in Council under subsection (7) above to embarking or being about to embark shall be construed as including a reference to leaving or seeking to leave the United Kingdom through the tunnel system."

(3) In section 4 of the 1971 Act (administration of control) in subsection (2)(b)–

(a) for the words "the United Kingdom by ship or aircraft" substitute ", or seeking to arrive in or leave, the United Kingdom through the tunnel system"; and

(b) for the words after "arrive as" substitute "members of the crews of through trains or shuttle trains".

(4) In section 8 of the 1971 Act (exceptions for seamen etc.) in subsection (1)–

(a) for the words from "of a ship" to "its crew" substitute "of a through train or shuttle train under an engagement requiring him to leave within seven days as a member of the crew of that or another such train"; and

(b) for the words "departure of the ship or aircraft" substitute "departure of the through train or shuttle train".

(5) In section 11 of the 1971 Act (construction of references to entry etc.)–

(a) in subsection (1)–

(i) for the words "by ship or aircraft" substitute "through the tunnel system", and

(ii) for the words from "he disembarks" to "immigration officer" substitute–

"(a) he leaves any control area designated under paragraph 26 of Schedule 2 to this Act, or

(b) he remains on a through train after it has ceased to be such a control area";

(b) omit subsections (2) and (3); and

(c) in subsection (4) omit the words after "section 1(3)".

(6) In section 13 of the 1971 Act (appeals against exclusion from United Kingdom) in subsection (3) omit the words "at a port of entry and".

(7) In section 24 of the 1971 Act (illegal entry and similar offences)–

(a) in subsection (1)(f) for the words from "disembarks" to "aircraft" substitute "leaves a train in the United Kingdom"; and

(b) in subsection (1)(g) for the word "embarks" substitute "leaves or seeks to leave the United Kingdom through the tunnel system".

(8) In section 25 of the 1971 Act (assisting illegal entry and harbouring)–

[...]

(b) for subsection (6) substitute–

"(6) Where a person convicted on indictment of an offence under subsection (1) above is at the time of the offence–

(a) the owner or one of the owners of a through train, shuttle train or vehicle used or intended to be used in carrying out the arrangements in respect of which the offence is committed; or

(b) a director or manager of a company which is the owner or one of the owners of any such train or vehicle; or

(c) the train manager of any such train;

then subject to subsections (7) and (8) below the court before which he is convicted may order the forfeiture of the train or vehicle.

In this subsection (but not in subsection (7) below)–

"owner"in relation to a train or vehicle which is the subject of a hire-purchase agreement includes the person in possession of it under that agreement, and in relation to a train, includes a charterer; and

"vehicle"includes a railway vehicle capable of being uncoupled from a train and a road vehicle carried on a train.";

(c) in subsection (7)–

(i) for the words "ship or aircraft", wherever occurring, substitute "train",

(ii) omit paragraph (a), and

(iii) omit the words from "In this subsection" to "in respect of the aircraft"; and

(d) in subsection (8) for the words "ship, aircraft", wherever occurring, substitute "train".

(9) In section 27 of the 1971 Act (offences by persons connected with ships etc.)–

(a) in paragraph (a)–

(i) for the words "captain of a ship or aircraft" substitute "train manager of a through train or shuttle train", and

(ii) in sub-paragraph (i) for the word "disembark" substitute "leave the train";

(b) in paragraph (b)–

(i) for the words "as owner or agent of a ship or aircraft" substitute "as, or as agent of, a person operating an international service",

(ii) in sub-paragraph (i) for the words from "the ship" to "port of entry" substitute "a through train to stop at a place other than a terminal control point [or an international station]"; and

(c) in paragraph (c)–

(i) for the words from "as owner" to "port" substitute "as, or as agent of, a person operating an international service, or as an occupier or person concerned with the management of a terminal control point [or of an international station]", and

(ii) for the words "the embarkation or disembarkation of passengers" substitute "persons arriving or seeking to arrive in, or leaving or seeking to leave, the United Kingdom through the tunnel system".

[(9A) In section 28A of the 1971 Act (arrest without warrant), in subsection (3) after the words "immigration officer" insert "or a constable".]

(10) In section 33 of the 1971 Act (interpretation)–

(a) in subsection (1)–

(i) omit the definitions of "airport" and "port",

(ii) in the definition of "crew" after the word "captain," insert "and in relation to a through train or a shuttle train, means all persons on the train who are actually employed in its service or working, including the train manager,", and

(iii) in the definition of "illegal entrant" after the words "unlawfully entering or seeking" insert "(whether or not he has arrived in the United Kingdom)"; and

(b) [in subsection (3) for the words "ports of entry for purposes of this Act" substitute "international stations for purposes of this Act shall be such railway stations as may from time to time be designated by order of the Secretary of State".]

(11) In Schedule 2 to the 1971 Act (administrative provisions as to control on entry etc.)—

(a) in paragraph 1(4) and where first occurring in paragraph 1(5) for the words "ship or aircraft" substitute "through train or shuttle train";

(b) in paragraph 1(5) for the words after "vehicle" substitute
"which–
(a) is in a control zone in France within the tunnel system, or
(b) has arrived in, or is seeking to leave, the United Kingdom through the tunnel system.";

(c) in paragraph 2(1) for the words from "in the United Kingdom" to "seeking to enter the United Kingdom)" substitute ", or who are seeking to arrive, in the United Kingdom through the tunnel system";

[(d) after paragraph 2(1) insert—
"(1A) The power conferred by sub-paragraph (1) is exercisable—
(a) as respects persons who have arrived in the United Kingdom, in a control area, and
(b) as respects persons seeking to arrive in the United Kingdom (who may first be questioned to ascertain whether they are seeking to do so), in a control zone in France or Belgium, or in a supplementary control zone in France.";]

(e) in paragraph 2(3)[after the words "further examination" insert "(or, if examined by an immigration officer in a supplementary control zone, may be required to submit to a [further examination before or after arrival] in the United Kingdom)" and]–
(i) for the words "crew of a ship or aircraft" substitute "crew of a through train or shuttle train",
(ii) after the words "joining a ship or aircraft" insert "or a shuttle train or through train", and
(iii) after the words "intended ship or aircraft" insert "or train";

[(ea) after paragraph 2A(1) insert—
"(1A) This paragraph also applies to a person who seeks to arrive in the United Kingdom and who is in a control zone in France or Belgium, or in a supplementary control zone in France.";
and after paragraph 2A(5) insert—
"(5A) A person examined by an immigration officer under this paragraph in a supplementary control zone may be required to submit to a [further examination before or after arrival] in the United Kingdom.";]

(eb) in paragraph 2A(6)–
(i) [after the words "sub-paragraph (5)" insert "or sub-paragraph (5A)"] for the words "crew of a ship or aircraft" substitute "crew of a through train or shuttle train";
(ii) after the words "joining a ship or aircraft" insert "or a shuttle train or through train"; and
(iii) after the words "intended ship or aircraft", insert "or train";]

(f) in paragraph 3(1) and (2) for the words "embarking or seeking to embark in the United Kingdom" substitute "leaving or seeking to leave the United Kingdom through the tunnel system";

(g) in paragraph 5–
(i) for the words from "requiring passengers" to "such passengers" substitute "requiring persons, or any class of persons, arriving in or leaving, or seeking to arrive in or leave, the United Kingdom through the tunnel system", and
(ii) for the words after "and for requiring" substitute "persons operating international services to supply such cards to those persons.";

(h) in paragraph 8(1)–

(i) after the words "in the United Kingdom" insert "through the tunnel system", and

(ii) for the words after "sub-paragraph (2) below" substitute

"give the person operating the international service by which he arrived ("the carrier") directions requiring the carrier–

(a) to remove him from the United Kingdom through the tunnel system; or

(b) to make arrangements for his removal from the United Kingdom in any ship or aircraft specified or indicated in the directions to a country or territory so specified, being either–

(i) a country of which he is a national or citizen; or

(ii) a country or territory in which he has obtained a passport or other document of identity; or

(iii) the country from which he departed for the United Kingdom; or

(iv) a country or territory to which there is reason to believe he will be admitted.";

(i) after paragraph 8(1) insert–

"(1A) Where a person seeking to arrive in the United Kingdom through the tunnel system is refused leave to enter and is then in a control zone in France within the tunnel system, an immigration officer may give the Concessionaires directions requiring them to secure that the person is taken out of the control zone to a place where he may be accepted back by the competent French authorities as provided in Article 18 of the international articles.";

(j) in paragraph 8(2)–

(i) for the words "sub-paragraph (1)(b) or (a)" substitute "sub-paragraph (1)", and

(ii) for the words "the owners or agents in question" substitute "the carrier";

(k) in paragraph 9 for the words after "an immigration officer" substitute
"may–

(a) if the illegal entrant has arrived in the United Kingdom, give such directions in respect of him as in a case within sub-paragraph (1) of paragraph 8 above are authorised by that sub-paragraph, or

(b) if the illegal entrant is in a control zone in France within the tunnel system, give such directions in respect of him as in a case within sub-paragraph (1A) of paragraph 8 above are authorised by that sub-paragraph. ";

(l) in paragraph 10(1)–

(i) omit the words from "either" to "or (b)",

(ii) for the words "owners or agents of any ship or aircraft" substitute "person operating the international service by which he arrived", and

(iii) for the words "paragraph 8(1)(c)" substitute "paragraph 8(1)";

(m) in paragraph 11 after the words "ship or aircraft" insert "or through train or shuttle train";

(n) in paragraph 13 omit sub-paragraph (1) and in sub-paragraph (2)–

(i) for the words "crew of a ship or aircraft, and either" substitute "crew of a through train or shuttle train, and",

(ii) omit the words from "or (B)" to "do so", and

(iii) for the words after "an immigration officer may" substitute–

"(a) give the train manager of the train in which that person ("the crew member") arrived directions requiring the train manager to remove him from the United Kingdom in that train; or

(b) give the person operating the international service on which that train is engaged directions requiring that person to remove the crew member from the United Kingdom in any train specified or indicated in the directions, being a train engaged on that international service; or

(c) give that person directions requiring him to make arrangements for the removal of the crew member from the United Kingdom in any ship or aircraft or through train or shuttle train specified in the directions to a country or territory so specified, being either–

(i) a country of which he is a national or citizen; or

(ii) a country or territory in which he has obtained a passport or other document of identity; or

(iii) the country from which he departed for the United Kingdom; or

(iv) a country or territory in which he was engaged as a member of the crew of the through train or shuttle train in which he arrived in the United Kingdom; or

(v) a country or territory to which there is reason to believe he will be admitted.";

(o) in paragraph 15 after the words "ship or aircraft" insert "or through train or shuttle train";

(p) in paragraph 16–

(i) in sub-paragraph (2) for the words "his removal in pursuance of" substitute "the taking of any action in respect of him required by",

(ii) for sub-paragraph (3) substitute–

"(3) A person may under the authority of an immigration officer be removed for detention under this paragraph–

(a) from a vehicle in a control zone in the tunnel system in France; or

(b) from a train or vehicle in which he arrives in the United Kingdom through the tunnel system."

, and

(iii) after sub-paragraph (4) insert–

"(5) Where a person has under paragraph 11 or 15 above been placed on a through train or shuttle train sub-paragraph (4) of this paragraph has effect with the substitution–

(a) for the word "captain", wherever occurring, of the words "train manager"; and

(b) for the words "ship or aircraft", wherever occurring, of the word "train"; and

(c) for the word "disembarking", of the words "leaving the train".";

(q) in paragraphs 19(1) and 20(1) for the words "owners or agents of the ship or air-craft in" substitute "person operating the international service by"; [...]

(r) for paragraphs 26 and 27 substitute–

"26.—(1) Persons operating international services shall not, without the approval of the Secretary of State, arrange for any through train to stop for the purpose of enabling passengers to leave it except at a terminal control point.

(2) The Secretary of State may from time to time give written notice to persons operating international services designating all or any through trains as control areas while they are within any area in the United Kingdom specified in the notice or while they constitute a control zone.

(3) The Secretary of State may from time to time give written notice designating a control area–

(a) to the Concessionaires as respects any part of the tunnel system in the United Kingdom or of a control zone within the tunnel system in France, or

(b) to any occupier or person concerned with the management of a terminal control point in the United Kingdom.

(4) A notice under sub-paragraph (2) or (3) above may specify conditions and restrictions to be observed in a control area, and any person to whom such a notice is given shall take all reasonable steps to secure that any such conditions or restrictions are observed.

[27.—(1) The train manager of a through train or shuttle train arriving in the United Kingdom—

(a) shall take such steps as may be necessary to secure that persons, other than members of the crew who may lawfully enter the United kingdom by virtue of section 8(1) of this Act, do not leave the train except in accordance with any arrangements approved by an immigration officer; and

(b) where persons are to be examined by an immigration officer on the train, shall take such steps as may be necessary to secure that they are ready for examination.

(2) The Secretary of State may by order require, or enable an immigration officer to require, the train manager of a through train or shuttle train or a person operating an international service or his agent to supply—

(a) a passenger list showing the names and nationality or citizenship of passengers arriving or leaving on board the train; and

(b) particulars of members of the crew of the train.

(3) An order under sub-paragraph (2) may relate—

(a) to all through trains or shuttle trains arriving or expected to arrive in the United Kingdom;

(b) to all through trains or shuttle trains leaving or expected to leave the United Kingdom.

(4) An order under sub-paragraph (2)—

(a) may specify the time at which or period during which information is to be provided,

(b) may specify the form and manner in which information is to be provided,

(c) shall be made by statutory instrument, and

(d) shall be subject to annulment in pursuance of a resolution of either House of Parliament.".]

[(s) In paragraph 27B (passenger information)–

(i) in sub-paragraph (1) for the words "ships or aircraft" substitute "through trains or shuttle trains";

(ii) in sub-paragraph (2) for the words "owner or agent ("the carrier")" of a ship or aircraft" substitute "person operating an international service or his agent ("the carrier")";

(iii) in sub-paragraph (3)(a) for the words "ship or particular aircraft" substitute "train";

(iv) in sub-paragraph (3)(b) and (c) for the words "ships or aircraft" substitute "trains"; and

(v) in sub-paragraphs (4) and (9) for the words "ship or aircraft", wherever occurring, substitute "train"; [...]

[(vi) in sub-paragraph (9A) for "voyage or flight" substitute "international service" and for the words "ship or aircraft" substitute "through train or shuttle train"; and]

(t) In paragraph 27C (notification of non-EEA arrivals)–

(i) in sub-paragraph (1)–

(a) for the words "owner or agent ("the carrier") of a ship or aircraft" substitute "person operating an international service other than a shuttle service or his agent ("the carrier")", and

(b) for the second occurrence of the words "ship or aircraft" substitute "through train";

(ii) in sub-paragraph (2)(a) for the words "ship or particular aircraft" substitute "through train";

(iii) in sub-paragraph (2)(b) and (c) for the words "ships or aircraft" substitute "through trains"; and

(iv) in sub-paragraphs (6), (7) and (9) for the words "ship or aircraft" substitute "through trains".]

(12) In Schedule 3 to the 1971 Act (supplementary provisions as to deportation)–

(a) in paragraph 1(1) after the words "any person" insert "who arrived in the United Kingdom through the tunnel system";

(b) in paragraph 1(2) after sub-paragraph (b) insert–

"(bb) directions to the person operating the international service by which the person in question arrived ("the carrier") requiring the carrier to make arrangements for the removal of the person in question through the tunnel system; or"

; and

(c) in paragraph 1(4) after the word "voyage" insert "or journey".

Note: Words omitted from para 1(8) from 25 May 2001 (SI 2001/1544). Words inserted in para 1(9)(b)(ii) and 1(9)(c)(i) from 1 July 1994 (SI 1994/1405). Para 1(9A) inserted from 25 May 2001 (SI 2001/1544). Para 1(10)(iii)(b) inserted from 1 July 1994 (SI 1994/1405). Para 1(11)(d) substituted and words inserted in para 1(11)(e) from 25 May 2001 (SI 2001/1544). Para 1(11)(ea) and (eb) inserted from 30 July 2000 (SI 2000/1775). Words substituted in para 1(11)(ea) from 10 December 2001 (SI 2001/3707). Words substituted in para 1(11)(eb) from 25 May 2001 (SI 2001/1544). Words omitted from para 1(11)(q) from 28 April 2000 (SI 2000/913). Words substituted in para 1(11)(r) and words inserted in para 1(11)(s) from 2 January 2008 (SI 2007/3579). Para 1(11)(s) inserted from 28 April 2000 (SI 2000/913).

[2A. In the Immigration and Asylum Act 1999 in section 141 (fingerprinting)—

(a) in subsection (7)(a) for "on his arrival in the United Kingdom" substitute "in a control zone or a supplementary control zone";

(b) in subsection (9)(b) for his "removal or deportation from the United Kingdom" substitute "his leaving a control zone or a supplementary control zone".]

Note: Para 2A inserted from 26 October 2006 (SI 2006/2626).

[3A. In the Immigration, Asylum and Nationality Act 2006—

(a) in section 32 (passenger and crew information: police powers)—

(i) in subsection (1) for "ships and aircraft" substitute "through trains and shuttle trains";

(ii) in subsections (2) and (3) for "owner or agent of a ship or aircraft" substitute "person operating an international service or his agent";

(iii) in subsection (5)(a)(iii) for "a voyage or flight" substitute "an international service"; and

(iv) in subsection (6)(b) for "ships or aircraft" substitute "through trains or shuttle trains";

(b) in section 34 (offence) the reference to section 32 includes a reference to that provision as modified by paragraph (a);

(c) in section 36 (duty to share information)—

(i) in subsection (4) for "ship or aircraft", wherever occurring, substitute "through train or shuttle train"; and

(ii) in subsection (4) for "flights or voyages" substitute "international services";

(d) in section 37 (information sharing: code of practice) the references to section 36 include references to that provision as modified by paragraph (c);

(e) in section 38 (disclosure of information for security purposes) in subsection (4)—

(i) for "ship or aircraft", wherever occurring, substitute "through train or shuttle train"; and

(ii) for "flights or voyages" substitute "international services"; and

(f) in section 39 (disclosure to law enforcement agencies) the reference to section 32 includes a reference to that provision as modified by paragraph (a).]

Note: Para 3A inserted from 2 January 2008 (SI 2007/3579).

[4. In the Immigration (Leave to Enter and Remain) Order 2000—

(a) in article 4(2)—

(i) after the words "arrives in the United Kingdom", insert "or enters a control zone in France or Belgium, or a supplementary control zone in France, seeking to arrive in the United Kingdom through the tunnel system";

(ii) after the words "before arrival", insert "or entry into the control zone or supplementary control zone"; and

(iii) after the words "date of arrival", insert "or entry into the control zone or supplementary control zone";

(b) in article 4(3)—

(i) after the words "on arrival in the United Kingdom", insert "or entry into a control zone in France or Belgium, or a supplementary control zone in France, seeking to arrive in the United Kingdom through the tunnel system"; and

(ii) after the words "before arrival", insert "or entry into the control zone or supplementary control zone"; and

(c) in article 6(2)(a) after the words "arrives in the United Kingdom", insert "or enters a control zone in France or Belgium, or a supplementary control zone in France, seeking to arrive in the United Kingdom through the tunnel system".]

Note: Para 4 substituted from 25 May 2001 (SI 200/1544).

[5. In the [Immigration (European Economic Area) Regulations 2006] [...] —

(a) after [regulation 11(2)] insert—

"(3) Any passport, identity card, family permit, [residence card or permanent residence card] which is required to be produced under this regulation as a condition for admission to the United Kingdom ("the required documents") may, for the same purpose, be required to be produced in a control zone or a supplementary control zone.";

[(b) in regulations 11(4) and 19(2) after the word "arrival" and in regulations 20(4) and (5) after the words "United Kingdom" insert "or the time of his production of the required documents in a control zone or a supplementary control zone".]]

Note: Para 5 inserted from 10 December 2001 (SI 2001/3707). Words substituted from 30 April 2006 (SI 2006/1003 Schedule 5).

SCHEDULE 5

AMENDMENTS OF ENACTMENTS AND INSTRUMENTS

...

The Asylum Support Regulations 2000
(SI 2000, No. 704)

Arrangement of Regulations
General

Contributions

16. Contributions

Recovery of sums by Secretary of State

17. Recovery where assets become realisable
17A. Recovery of asylum support
18. Overpayments: method of recovery

Breach of conditions and suspension and discontinuation of support

19. Breach of conditions: decision whether to provide support
20. Suspension or discontinuation of support
20A. Temporary support
21. Effect of previous suspension or discontinuation

Notice to quit

22. Notice to quit

Meaning of 'destitute' for certain other purposes

23. Meaning of 'destitute' for certain other purposes

SCHEDULE

GENERAL

Citation and commencement

1. These Regulations may be cited as the Asylum Support Regulations 2000 and shall come into force on 3 April 2000.

Interpretation

2.—(1) In these Regulations—

'the Act' means the Immigration and Asylum Act 1999;

'asylum support' means support provided under section 95 of the Act;

'dependant' has the meaning given by paragraphs (4) and (5);

'the interim Regulations' means the Asylum Support (Interim Provisions) Regulations 1999;

'married couple' means a man and woman who are married to each other and are members of the same household; and

'unmarried couple' means a man and woman who, though not married to each other, are living together as if married.

[(2) The period prescribed under section 94(3) of the Act (day on which a claim for asylum is determined) for the purposes of Part VI of the Act is 28 days where paragraph (2A) applies, and 21 days in any other case.

(2A) This paragraph applies where:

(a) the Secretary of State notifies the claimant that his decision is to accept the asylum claim;

(b) the Secretary of State notifies the claimant that his decision is to reject the asylum claim but at the same time notifies him that he is giving him limited leave to enter or remain in the United Kingdom; or

(c) an appeal by the claimant against the Secretary of State's decision has been disposed of by being allowed.]

(3) Paragraph (2) does not apply in relation to a case to which the interim Regulations apply (for which case, provision corresponding to paragraph (2) is made by regulation 2(6) of those Regulations).

(4) In these Regulations 'dependant', in relation to an asylum-seeker, a supported person or an applicant for asylum support, means, subject to paragraph (5), a person in the United Kingdom ('the relevant person') who—

(a) is his spouse;

(b) is a child of his or of his spouse, is dependant on him and is, or was at the relevant time, under 18;

(c) is a member of his or his spouse's close family and is, or was at the relevant time, under 18;

(d) had been living as part of his household—

(i) for at least six of the twelve months before the relevant time, or

(ii) since birth,

and is, or was at the relevant time, under 18;

(e) is in need of care and attention from him or a member of his household by reason of a disability and would fall within sub-paragraph (c) or (d) but for the fact that he is not, and was not at the relevant time, under 18;

(f) had been living with him as a member of an unmarried couple for at least two of the three years before the relevant time;

(g) is living as part of his household and was, immediately before 6 December 1999 (the date when the interim Regulations came into force), receiving assistance from a local authority under section 17 of the Children Act 1989;

(h) is living as part of his household and was, immediately before the coming into force of these Regulations, receiving assistance from a local authority under—

(i) section 22 of the Children (Scotland) Act 1995; or

(ii) Article 18 of the Children (Northern Ireland) Order 1995; or

(i) has made a claim for leave to enter or remain in the United Kingdom, or for variation of any such leave, which is being considered on the basis that he is dependant on the asylum-seeker;

and in relation to a supported person, or an applicant for asylum support, who is himself a dependant of an asylum-seeker, also includes the asylum-seeker if in the United Kingdom.

(5) Where a supported person or applicant for asylum support is himself a dependant of an asylum-seeker, a person who would otherwise be a dependant of the supported person, or of the applicant, for the purposes of these Regulations is not such a dependant unless he is also a dependant of the asylum-seeker or is the asylum-seeker.

(6) In paragraph (4), 'the relevant time', in relation to the relevant person, means—

(a) the time when an application for asylum support for him was made in accordance with regulation 3(3); or

(b) if he has joined a person who is already a supported person in the United Kingdom and sub-paragraph (a) does not apply, the time when he joined that person in the United Kingdom.

(7) Where a person, by falling within a particular category in relation to an asylum-seeker or supported person, is by virtue of this regulation a dependant of the asylum-seeker or supported person for the purposes of these Regulations, that category is also a prescribed category for the purposes of paragraph (c) of the definition of 'dependant' in section 94(1) of the Act and, accordingly, the person is a dependant of the asylum-seeker or supported person for the purposes of Part VI of the Act.

(8) Paragraph (7) does not apply to a person who is already a dependant of the asylum-seeker or supported person for the purposes of Part VI of the Act because he falls within either of the categories mentioned in paragraphs (a) and (b) of the definition of 'dependant' in section 94(1) of the Act.

(9) Paragraph (7) does not apply for the purposes of any reference to a 'dependant' in Schedule 9 to the Act.

Note: Regulation 2(2) substituted from 8 April 2002 (SI 2002/472).

Initial application for support

Initial application for support: individual and group applications

3.—(1) Either of the following—
  (a) an asylum-seeker, or
  (b) a dependant of an asylum-seeker,
may apply to the Secretary of State for asylum support.

(2) An application under this regulation may be—
  (a) for asylum support for the applicant alone; or
  (b) for asylum support for the applicant and one or more dependants of his.

(3) The application must be made by completing in full and in English the form for the time being issued by the Secretary of State for the purpose; and any form so issued shall be the form shown in the Schedule to these Regulations or a form to the like effect.

[(4) The application may not be entertained by the Secretary of State—
  (a) where it is made otherwise than in accordance with paragraph (3); or
  (b) where the Secretary of State is not satisfied that the information provided is complete or accurate or that the applicant is co-operating with enquiries made under paragraph (5).]

(5) The Secretary of State may make further enquiries of the applicant about any matter connected with the application.

[(5A) Where the Secretary of State makes further enquiries under paragraph (5) the applicant shall reply to those enquiries within five working days of his receipt of them.

(5B) The Secretary of State shall be entitled to conclude that the applicant is not co-operating with his enquiries under paragraph (5) if he fails, without reasonable excuse, to reply within the period prescribed by paragraph (5A).

(5C) In cases where the Secretary of State may not entertain an application for asylum support he shall also discontinue providing support under section 98 of the Act.]

(6) Paragraphs (3) and (4) do not apply where a person is already a supported person and asylum support is sought for a dependant of his for whom such support is not already provided (for which case, provision is made by regulation 15).

[(7) For the purposes of this regulation, working day means any day other than a Saturday, a Sunday, Christmas Day, Good Friday or a day which is a bank holiday under section 1 of the Banking and Financial Dealings Act 1971 in the locality in which the applicant is living.]

Note: Sub-paragraphs (5A), (5B), (5C) and (7) inserted from 5 February 2005, SI 2005/11.

Persons excluded from support

4.—(1) The following circumstances are prescribed for the purposes of subsection (2) of section 95 of the Act as circumstances where a person who would otherwise fall within subsection (1) of that section is excluded from that subsection (and, accordingly, may not be provided with asylum support).

(2) A person is so excluded if he is applying for asylum support for himself alone and he falls within paragraph (4) by virtue of any sub-paragraph of that paragraph.

(3) A person is so excluded if—

(a) he is applying for asylum support for himself and other persons, or he is included in an application for asylum support made by a person other than himself;

(b) he falls within paragraph (4) (by virtue of any sub-paragraph of that paragraph); and

(c) each of the other persons to whom the application relates also falls within paragraph (4) (by virtue of any sub-paragraph of that paragraph).

(4) A person falls within this paragraph if at the time when the application is determined—

(a) he is a person to whom interim support applies; or

(b) he is a person to whom social security benefits apply; or

(c) he has not made a claim for leave to enter or remain in the United Kingdom, or for variation of any such leave, which is being considered on the basis that he is an asylum-seeker or dependent on an asylum-seeker.

(5) For the purposes of paragraph (4), interim support applies to a person if—

(a) at the time when the application is determined, he is a person to whom, under the interim Regulations, support under regulation 3 of those Regulations must be provided by a local authority;

(b) sub-paragraph (a) does not apply, but would do so if the person had been determined by the local authority concerned to be an eligible person; or

(c) sub-paragraph (a) does not apply, but would do so but for the fact that the person's support under those Regulations was (otherwise than by virtue of regulation 7(1) (d) of those Regulations) refused under regulation 7, or suspended or discontinued under regulation 8, of those Regulations;

and in this paragraph 'local authority', 'local authority concerned' and 'eligible person' have the same meanings as in the interim Regulations.

(6) For the purposes of paragraph (4), a person is a person to whom social security benefits apply if he is—

(a) a person who by virtue of regulation 2 of the Social Security (Immigration and Asylum) Consequential Amendments Regulations 2000 is not excluded by section 115(1) of the Act from entitlement to—

(i) income-based jobseeker's allowance under the Jobseekers Act 1995; or

(ii) income support, housing benefit or council tax benefit under the Social Security Contributions and Benefits Act 1992;

(b) a person who, by virtue of regulation 2 of the Social Security (Immigration and Asylum) Consequential Amendments Regulations (Northern Ireland) 2000 is not excluded by section 115(2) of the Act from entitlement to—

(i) income-based jobseeker's allowance under the Jobseekers (Northern Ireland) Order 1995; or

(ii) income support or housing benefit under the Social Security Contributions and Benefits (Northern Ireland) Act 1992;

(7) A person is not to be regarded as falling within paragraph (2) or (3) if, when asylum support is sought for him, he is a dependant of a person who is already a supported person.

(8) The circumstances prescribed by paragraphs (2) and (3) are also prescribed for the purposes of section 95(2), as applied by section 98(3), of the Act as circumstances where a person who would otherwise fall within subsection (1) of section 98 is excluded from that subsection (and, accordingly, may not be provided with temporary support under section 98).

(9) For the purposes of paragraph (8), paragraphs (2) and (3) shall apply as if any reference to an application for asylum support were a reference to an application for support under section 98 of the Act.

Determining whether persons are destitute

Determination where application relates to more than one person, etc.

5.—(1) Subject to paragraph (2), where an application in accordance with regulation 3(3) is for asylum support for the applicant and one or more dependants of his, in applying section 95(1) of the Act the Secretary of State must decide whether the applicant and all those dependants, taken together, are destitute or likely to become destitute within the period prescribed by regulation 7.

(2) Where a person is a supported person, and the question falls to be determined whether asylum support should in future be provided for him and one or more other persons who are his dependants and are—

(a) persons for whom asylum support is also being provided when that question falls to be determined; or

(b) persons for whom the Secretary of State is then considering whether asylum support should be provided,

in applying section 95(1) of the Act the Secretary of State must decide whether the supported person and all those dependants, taken together, are destitute or likely to become destitute within the period prescribed by regulation 7.

Income and assets to be taken into account

6.—(1) This regulation applies where it falls to the Secretary of State to determine for the purposes of section 95(1) of the Act whether—

(a) a person applying for asylum support, or such an applicant and any dependants of his, or

(b) a supported person, or such a person and any dependants of his, is or are destitute or likely to become so within the period prescribed by regulation 7.

(2) In this regulation 'the principal' means the applicant for asylum support (where paragraph (1)(a) applies) or the supported person (where paragraph (1)(b) applies).

(3) The Secretary of State must ignore—

(a) any asylum support, and

(b) any support under section 98 of the Act, which the principal or any dependant of his is provided with or, where the question is whether destitution is likely within a particular period, might be provided with in that period.

(4) But he must take into account—

(a) any other income which the principal, or any dependant of his, has or might reasonably be expected to have in that period;

(b) any other support which is available to the principal or any dependant of his, or might reasonably be expected to be so available in that period; and

(c) any assets mentioned in paragraph (5) (whether held in the United Kingdom or elsewhere) which are available to the principal or any dependant of his otherwise than by way of asylum support or support under section 98, or might reasonably be expected to be so available in that period.

(5) Those assets are—

(a) cash;

(b) savings;

(c) investments;

(d) land;

(e) cars or other vehicles; and

(f) goods held for the purpose of a trade or other business.

(6) The Secretary of State must ignore any assets not mentioned in paragraph (5).

Period within which applicant must be likely to become destitute

7. The period prescribed for the purposes of section 95(1) of the Act is—

(a) where the question whether a person or persons is or are destitute or likely to become so falls to be determined in relation to an application for asylum support and sub-paragraph (b) does not apply, 14 days beginning with the day on which that question falls to be determined;

(b) where that question falls to be determined in relation to a supported person, or in relation to persons including a supported person, 56 days beginning with the day on which that question falls to be determined.

Adequacy of existing accommodation

8.—(1) Subject to paragraph (2), the matters mentioned in paragraph (3) are prescribed for the purposes of subsection (5)(a) of section 95 of the Act as matters to which the Secretary of State must have regard in determining for the purposes of that section whether the accommodation of—

(a) a person applying for asylum support, or

(b) a supported person for whom accommodation is not for the time being provided by way of asylum support, is adequate.

(2) The matters mentioned in paragraph (3)(a) and (d) to (g) are not so prescribed for the purposes of a case where the person indicates to the Secretary of State that he wishes to remain in the accommodation.

(3) The matters referred to in paragraph (1) are—

(a) whether it would be reasonable for the person to continue to occupy the accommodation;

(b) whether the accommodation is affordable for him;

(c) whether the accommodation is provided under section 98 of the Act, or otherwise on an emergency basis, only while the claim for asylum support is being determined;

(d) whether the person can secure entry to the accommodation;

(e) where the accommodation consists of a moveable structure, vehicle or vessel designed or adapted for human habitation, whether there is a place where the person is entitled or permitted both to place it and reside in it;

(f) whether the accommodation is available for occupation by the person's dependants together with him;

(g) whether it is probable that the person's continued occupation of the accommodation will lead to domestic violence against him or any of his dependants.

(4) In determining whether it would be reasonable for a person to continue to occupy accommodation, regard may be had to the general circumstances prevailing in relation to housing in the district of the local housing authority where the accommodation is.

(5) In determining whether a person's accommodation is affordable for him, the Secretary of State must have regard to—

(a) any income, or any assets mentioned in regulation 6(5) (whether held in the United Kingdom or elsewhere), which is or are available to him or any dependant of his otherwise than by way of asylum support or support under section 98 of the Act, or might reasonably be expected to be so available;

(b) the costs in respect of the accommodation; and

(c) the person's other reasonable living expenses.

(6) In this regulation—

(a) 'domestic violence' means violence from a person who is or has been a close family member, or threats of violence from such a person which are likely to be carried out; and

(b) 'district of the local housing authority' has the meaning given by section 217(3) of the Housing Act 1996.

(7) The reference in paragraph (1) to subsection (5)(a) of section 95 of the Act does not include a reference to that provision as applied by section 98(3) of the Act.

Essential living needs

9. —(1) The matter mentioned in paragraph (2) is prescribed for the purposes of subsection (7)(b) of section 95 of the Act as a matter to which the Secretary of State may not have regard in determining for the purposes of that section whether a person's essential living needs (other than accommodation) are met.

(2) That matter is his personal preference as to clothing (but this shall not be taken to prevent the Secretary of State from taking into account his individual circumstances as regards clothing).

(3) None of the items and expenses mentioned in paragraph (4) is to be treated as being an essential living need of a person for the purposes of Part VI of the Act.

(4) Those items and expenses are—

(a) the cost of faxes;

(b) computers and the cost of computer facilities;

(c) the cost of photocopying;

(d) travel expenses, except the expense mentioned in paragraph (5);

(e) toys and other recreational items;

(f) entertainment expenses.

(5) The expense excepted from paragraph (4)(d) is the expense of an initial journey from a place in the United Kingdom to accommodation provided by way of asylum support or (where accommodation is not so provided) to an address in the United Kingdom which has been notified to the Secretary of State as the address where the person intends to live.

(6) Paragraph (3) shall not be taken to affect the question whether any item or expense not mentioned in paragraph (4) or (5) is, or is not, an essential living need.

(7) The reference in paragraph (1) to subsection (7)(b) of section 95 of the Act includes a reference to that provision as applied by section 98(3) of the Act and, accordingly, the reference in paragraph (1) to 'that section' includes a reference to section 98.

Provision of support

Kind and levels of support for essential living needs

10.—(1) This regulation applies where the Secretary of State has decided that asylum support should be provided in respect of the essential living needs of a person.

[(2) As a general rule, asylum support in respect of the essential living needs of that person may be expected to be provided weekly in the form of [cash, equal to] the amount shown in the second column of the following table opposite the entry in the first column which for the time being describes that person, [...].

Table

Qualifying couple	£72.52
Lone parent aged 18 or over	£43.94
Single person aged 25 or over (where the decision to grant support was made prior to 5th October 2009 and the person reached age 25 prior to that date)	£42.62
Any other single person aged 18 or over	£36.62
Person aged at least 16 but under 18 (except a member of a qualifying couple)	£39.80
Person aged under 16	£52.96.

(3) In paragraph (1) and the provisions of paragraph (2) preceding the table, 'person' includes 'couple'.

(4) In this regulation—

(a) 'qualifying couple' means a married or unmarried couple at least one of whom is aged 18 or over and neither of whom is aged under 16;

(b) 'lone parent' means a parent who is not a member of a married or unmarried couple;

(c) 'single person' means a person who is not a parent or a member of a qualifying couple; and

(d) 'parent' means a parent of a relevant child, that is to say a child who is aged under 18 and for whom asylum support is provided.

(5) Where the Secretary of State has decided that accommodation should be provided for a person (or couple) by way of asylum support, and the accommodation is provided in a form which also meets other essential living needs (such as bed and breakfast, or half or full board), the amounts shown in the table in paragraph (2) shall be treated as reduced accordingly.

(6) ...

Note: Regulation 10(6) omitted from 8 April 2002 (SI 2002/472). Regulation 10(2) substituted from 7 April 2005 (SI 2003/755). Words in square brackets in reg 10(2) substituted from 4 June 2004 (SI 2004/1313). Table substituted from 18 April 2011 (SI 2011/907).

[Additional support for pregnant women and children under 3

10A.—(1) In addition to the [cash support which the Secretary of State may be expected to provide weekly as] described in regulation 10(2), in the case of any pregnant woman or child aged under 3 for whom the Secretary of State has decided asylum support should be provided, there shall, as a general rule, be added to the [cash support] for any week the amount shown in the second column of the following table opposite the entry in the first column which for the time being describes that person.

(2) In this regulation, 'pregnant woman' means a woman who has provided evidence to satisfy the Secretary of State that she is pregnant.]

Pregnant woman	£3.00
Child aged under 1	£5.00
Child aged at least 1 and under 3	£3.00

Note: Regulation 10A inserted from 3 March 2003 (SI 2003/241). Words in square brackets substituted from 4 June 2004 (SI 2004/1313).

Additional single payments in respect of essential living needs

11.—(1) ...

Note: Regulation 11 revoked from 4 June 2004 (SI 2004/1313), save to enable the Secretary of State to make a payment to a person whose qualifying period ends on or before that date.

(6) Where a person is, in the opinion of the Secretary of State, responsible without reasonable excuse for a delay in the determination of his claim for asylum, the Secretary of State may treat any qualifying period as extended by the period of delay.

Note: Words in square brackets in reg 11(1) inserted from 8 April 2002 (SI 2002/472).

Income and assets to be taken into account in providing support

12.—(1) This regulation applies where it falls to the Secretary of State to decide the level or kind of asylum support to be provided for—

(a) a person applying for asylum support, or such an applicant and any dependants of his.

(b) a supported person, or such a person and any dependants of his.

(2) In this regulation 'the principal' means the applicant for asylum support (where paragraph (1)(a) applies) or the supported person (where paragraph (1)(b) applies).

(3) The Secretary of State must take into account—

(a) any income which the principal or any dependant of his has or might reasonably be expected to have,

(b) support which is or might reasonably be expected to be available to the principal or any dependant of his, and

(c) any assets mentioned in regulation 6(5) (whether held in the United Kingdom or elsewhere) which are or might reasonably be expected to be available to the principal or any dependant of his, otherwise than by way of asylum support.

Accommodation

13.—(1) The matters mentioned in paragraph (2) are prescribed for the purposes of subsection (2)(b) of section 97 of the Act as matters to which regard may not be had when exercising the power under section 95 of the Act to provide accommodation for a person.

(2) Those matters are—

(a) his personal preference as to the nature of the accommodation to be provided; and

(b) his personal preference as to the nature and standard of fixtures and fittings; but this shall not be taken to prevent the person's individual circumstances, as they relate to his accommodation needs, being taken into account.

Services

14.—(1) The services mentioned in paragraph (2) may be provided or made available by way of asylum support to persons who are otherwise receiving such support, but may be so provided only for the purpose of maintaining good order among such persons.

(2) Those services are—

(a) education, including English language lessons,

(b) sporting or other developmental activities.

Change of circumstances

Change of circumstances

15.—(1) If a relevant change of circumstances occurs, the supported person concerned or a dependant of his must, without delay, notify the Secretary of State of that change of circumstances.

(2) A relevant change of circumstances occurs where a supported person or a dependant of his—

(a) is joined in the United Kingdom by a dependant or, as the case may be, another dependant, of the supported person;

(b) receives or gains access to any money, or other asset mentioned in regulation 6(5), that has not previously been declared to the Secretary of State;

(c) becomes employed;

(d) becomes unemployed;

(e) changes his name;

(f) gets married;

(g) starts living with a person as if married to that person;

(h) gets divorced;

(i) separates from a spouse, or from a person with whom he has been living as if married to that person;

(j) becomes pregnant;

(k) has a child;

(l) leaves school;

(m) starts to share his accommodation with another person;

(n) moves to a different address, or otherwise leaves his accommodation;

(o) goes into hospital;

(p) goes to prison or is otherwise held in custody;

(q) leaves the United Kingdom; or

(r) dies.

(3) If, on being notified of a change of circumstances, the Secretary of State considers that the change may be one—

(a) as a result of which asylum support should be provided for a person for whom it was not provided before, or

(b) as a result of which asylum support should no longer be provided for a person, or

(c) which may otherwise affect the asylum support which should be provided for a person, he may make further enquiries of the supported person or dependant who gave the notification.

(4) The Secretary of State may, in particular, require that person to provide him with such information as he considers necessary to determine whether, and if so, what, asylum support should be provided for any person.

Contributions

Contributions

16.—(1) This regulation applies where, in deciding the level of asylum support to be provided for a person who is or will be a supported person, the Secretary of State is required to take into account income, support or assets as mentioned in regulation 12(3).

(2) The Secretary of State may—

(a) set the asylum support for that person at a level which does not reflect the income, support or assets; and

(b) require from that person payments by way of contributions towards the cost of the provision for him of asylum support.

(3) A supported person must make to the Secretary of State such payments by way of contributions as the Secretary of State may require under paragraph (2).

(4) Prompt payment of such contributions may be made a condition (under section 95(9) of the Act) subject to which asylum support for that person is provided.

Recovery of sums by Secretary of State

Recovery where assets become realisable

17.—(1) This regulation applies where it appears to the Secretary of State at any time (the relevant time)—

(a) that a supported person had, at the time when he applied for asylum support, assets of any kind in the United Kingdom or elsewhere which were not capable of being realised; but

(b) that those assets have subsequently become, and remain, capable of being realised.

(2) The Secretary of State may recover from that person a sum not exceeding the recoverable sum.

(3) Subject to paragraph (5), the recoverable sum is a sum equal to whichever is the less of—

(a) the monetary value of all the asylum support provided to the person up to the relevant time; and

(b) the monetary value of the assets concerned.

(4) As well as being recoverable as mentioned in paragraph 11(2)(a) of Schedule 8 to the Act, an amount recoverable under this regulation may be recovered by deduction from asylum support.

(5) The recoverable sum shall be treated as reduced by any amount which the Secretary of State has by virtue of this regulation already recovered from the person concerned (whether by deduction or otherwise) with regard to the assets concerned.

[Recovery of asylum support

17A.—(1) The Secretary of State may require a supported person to refund asylum support if it transpires that at any time during which asylum support was being provided for him he was not destitute.

(2) If a supported person has dependants, the Secretary of State may require him to refund asylum support if it transpires that at any time during which asylum support was being provided for the supported person and his dependants they were not destitute.

(3) The refund required shall not exceed the monetary value of all the asylum support provided to the supported person or to the supported person and his dependants for the relevant period.

(4) In this regulation the relevant period is the time during which asylum support was provided for the supported person or the supported person and his dependants and during which he or they were not destitute.

(5) If not paid within a reasonable period, the refund required may be recovered from the supported person as if it were a debt due to the Secretary of State.]

Note: Regulation 17A inserted from 5 April 2005 (SI 2005/11).

Overpayments: method of recovery

18. As well as being recoverable as mentioned in subsection (3) of section 114 of the Act, an amount recoverable under subsection (2) of that section may be recovered by deduction from asylum support.

Breach of conditions and suspension and discontinuation of support

Breach of conditions: decision whether to provide support

19.—(1) When deciding—

(a) whether to provide, or to continue to provide, asylum support for any person or persons, or

(b) the level or kind of support to be provided for any person or persons, the Secretary of State may take into account [the extent to which a] relevant condition has been complied with.

[(2) A relevant condition is one which makes the provision of asylum support subject to actual residence by the supported person or a dependant of his for whom support is being provided in a specific place or location.]

Note: Words in square brackets in paras (1) and (2) substituted from 5 February 2005 (SI 2005/11).

[Suspension or discontinuation of support

20.—(1) Asylum support for a supported person and any dependant of his or for one or more dependants of a supported person may be suspended or discontinued if—

(a) support is being provided for the supported person or a dependant of his in collective accommodation and the Secretary of State has reasonable grounds to believe that the supported person or his dependant has committed a serious breach of the rules of that accommodation;

(b) the Secretary of State has reasonable grounds to believe that the supported person or a dependant of his for whom support is being provided has committed an act of seriously violent behaviour whether or not that act occurs in accommodation provided by way of asylum support or at the authorised address or elsewhere;

(c) the supported person or a dependant of his has committed an offence under Part VI of the Act;

(d) the Secretary of State has reasonable grounds to believe that the supported person or any dependant of his for whom support is being provided has abandoned the authorised address without first informing the Secretary of State or, if requested, without permission;

(e) the supported person has not complied within a reasonable period, which shall be no less than five working days beginning with the day on which the request was received by him, with requests for information made by the Secretary of State and which relate to the supported person's or his dependant's eligibility for or receipt of asylum support including requests made under regulation 15;

(f) the supported person fails, without reasonable excuse, to attend an interview requested by the Secretary of State relating to the supported person's or his dependant's eligibility for or receipt of asylum support;

(g) the supported person or, if he is an asylum seeker, his dependant, has not complied within a reasonable period, which shall be no less than ten working days beginning with the day on which the request was received by him, with a request for information made by the Secretary of State relating to his claim for asylum;

(h) the Secretary of State has reasonable grounds to believe that the supported person or a dependant of his for whom support is being provided has concealed financial resources and that the supported person or a dependant of his or both have therefore unduly benefited from the receipt of asylum support;

(i) the supported person or a dependant of his for whom support is being provided has not complied with a reporting requirement;

(j) the Secretary of State has reasonable grounds to believe that the supported person or a dependant of his for whom support is being provided has made a claim for asylum ('the first claim') and before the first claim has been determined makes or seeks to make a further claim for asylum not being part of the first claim in the same or a different name; or

(k) the supported person or a dependant of his for whom support is being provided has failed without reasonable excuse to comply with a relevant condition.

(2) If a supported person is asked to attend an interview of the type referred to in paragraph (1)(f) he shall be given no less than five working days notice of it.

(3) Any decision to discontinue support in the circumstances referred to in paragraph (1) above shall be taken individually, objectively and impartially and reasons shall be given. Decisions will be based on the particular situation of the person concerned and particular regard shall be had to whether he is a vulnerable person as described by Article 17 of Council Directive 2003/9/EC of 27 January 2003 laying down minimum standards for the reception of asylum seekers.

(4) No person's asylum support shall be discontinued before a decision is made under paragraph (1).

(5) Where asylum support for a supported person or his dependant is suspended or discontinued under paragraph (1)(d) or (i) and the supported person or his dependant are traced or voluntarily report to the police, the Secretary of State or an immigration officer, a duly motivated decision based on the reasons for the disappearance shall be taken as to the reinstatement of some or all of the supported person's or his dependant's or both of their asylum support.

(6) For the purposes of this regulation—

(a) the authorised address is—

(i) the accommodation provided for the supported person and his dependants (if any) by way of asylum support; or

(ii) if no accommodation is so provided, the address notified by the supported person to the Secretary of State in his application for asylum support or, where a change of address has been notified to the Secretary of State under regulation 15 or under the Immigration Rules or both, the address for the time being so notified;

(b) 'collective accommodation' means accommodation which a supported person or any dependant of his for whom support is being provided shares with any other supported person and includes accommodation in which only facilities are shared;

(c) 'relevant condition' has the same meaning as in regulation 19(2);

(d) 'reporting requirement' is a condition or restriction which requires a person to report to the police, an immigration officer or the Secretary of State and is imposed under—

(i) paragraph 21 of Schedule 2 to the Immigration Act 1971 (temporary admission or release from detention);

(ii) paragraph 22 of that Schedule; or

(iii) paragraph 2 or 5 of Schedule 3 to that Act (pending deportation).

(e) 'working day' has the same meaning as in regulation 3(7) save that the reference to the applicant shall be a reference to the supported person or his dependant.]

Note: Regulation 20 substituted from 5 February 2005 (SI 2005/11).

[Temporary Support

20A. Regulations 19 and 20 shall apply to a person or his dependant who is provided with temporary support under section 98 of the Act in the same way as they apply to a person and his dependant who is in receipt of asylum support and any reference to asylum support in regulations 19 and 20 shall include a reference to temporary support under section 98.]

Note: Regulation 20A inserted from 5 April 2005 (SI 2005/11).

Effect of previous suspension or discontinuation

21.—(1) [Subject to regulation 20(5) where—]
   (a) an application for asylum support is made,
   (b) the applicant or any other person to whom the application relates has previously had his asylum support suspended or discontinued under regulation 20, and
   (c) there has been no material change of circumstances since the suspension or discontinuation,

the application need not be entertained unless the Secretary of State considers that there are exceptional circumstances which justify its being entertained.

(2) A material change of circumstances is one which, if the applicant were a supported person, would have to be notified to the Secretary of State under regulation 15.

(3) This regulation is without prejudice to the power of the Secretary of State to refuse the application even if he has entertained it.

Note: Words in square brackets in para (1) substituted from 5 February 2005 (SI 2005/11).

Notice to quit

Notice to quit

22.—(1) If—
   (a) as a result of asylum support, a person has a tenancy or licence to occupy accommodation,
   (b) one or more of the conditions mentioned in paragraph (2) is satisfied, and
   (c) he is given notice to quit in accordance with paragraph (3) or (4),

his tenancy or licence is to be treated as ending with the period specified in that notice, regardless of when it could otherwise be brought to an end.

(2) The conditions are that—
   (a) the asylum support is suspended or discontinued as a result of any provision of regulation 20;
   (b) the relevant claim for asylum has been determined;
   (c) the supported person has ceased to be destitute; or
   (d) he is to be moved to other accommodation.

(3) A notice to quit is in accordance with this paragraph if it is in writing and—
   (a) in a case where sub-paragraph (a), (c) or (d) of paragraph (2) applies, specifies as the notice period a period of not less than seven days; or
   (b) in a case where the Secretary of State has notified his decision on the relevant claim for asylum to the claimant, specifies as the notice period a period at least as long as whichever is the greater of—
      (i) seven days; or

(ii) the period beginning with the date of service of the notice to quit and ending with the date of determination of the relevant claim for asylum (found in accordance with section 94(3) of the Act).

(4) A notice to quit is in accordance with this paragraph if—
(a) it is in writing;
(b) it specifies as the notice period a period of less than seven days; and
(c) the circumstances of the case are such that that notice period is justified.

Meaning of 'destitute' for certain other purposes

Meaning of 'destitute' for certain other purposes

23.—(1) In this regulation 'the relevant enactments' means—
(a) section 21(1A) of the National Assistance Act 1948;
(b) section 45(4A) of the Health Services and Public Health Act 1968;
(c) paragraph 2(2A) of Schedule 8 to the National Health Service Act 1977;
(d) sections 12(2A), 13A(4) and 13B(3) of the Social Work (Scotland) Act 1968;
(e) sections 7(3) and 8(4) of the Mental Health (Scotland) Act 1984; and
(f) Articles 7(3) and 15(6) of the Health and Personal Social Services (Northern Ireland) Order 1972.

(2) The following provisions of this regulation apply where it falls to an authority, or the Department, to determine for the purposes of any of the relevant enactments whether a person is destitute.

(3) Paragraphs (3) to (6) of regulation 6 apply as they apply in the case mentioned in paragraph (1) of that regulation, but as if references to the principal were references to the person whose destitution or otherwise is being determined and references to the Secretary of State were references to the authority or (as the case may be) Department.

(4) The matters mentioned in paragraph (3) of regulation 8 (read with paragraphs (4) to (6) of that regulation) are prescribed for the purposes of subsection (5)(a) of section 95 of the Act, as applied for the purposes of any of the relevant enactments, as matters to which regard must be had in determining for the purposes of any of the relevant enactments whether a person's accommodation is adequate.

(5) The matter mentioned in paragraph (2) of regulation 9 is prescribed for the purposes of subsection (7)(b) of section 95 of the Act, as applied for the purposes of any of the relevant enactments, as a matter to which regard may not be had in determining for the purposes of any of the relevant enactments whether a person's essential living needs (other than accommodation) are met.

(6) Paragraphs (3) to (6) of regulation 9 shall apply as if the reference in paragraph (3) to Part VI of the Act included a reference to the relevant enactments.

(7) The references in regulations 8(5) and 9(2) to the Secretary of State shall be construed, for the purposes of this regulation, as references to the authority or (as the case may be) Department.

SCHEDULE

Regulation 3(3)

...

The Immigration (Leave to Enter and Remain) Order 2000

(SI 2000, No. 1161)

PART I

GENERAL

1. Citation, commencement and interpretation

(1) This Order may be cited as the Immigration (Leave to Enter and Remain) Order 2000.

(2) Articles 1 to 12, 14 and 15(1) of this Order shall come into force on 28 April 2000 or, if later, on the day after the day on which it is made and articles 13 and 15(2) shall come into force on 30 July 2000.

(3) In this Order—

'the Act' means the Immigration Act 1971;

['ADS Agreement with China' means the Memorandum of Understanding on visa and related issues concerning tourist groups from the People's Republic of China to the United Kingdom as an approved destination, signed on 21 January 2005;]

'control port' means a port in which a control area is designated under paragraph 26(3) of Schedule 2 to the Act;

['convention travel document' means a travel document issued pursuant to Article 28 of the Refugee Convention, except where that travel document was issued by the United Kingdom Government;]

'the Immigration Acts' means:
(a) the Act;
(b) the Immigration Act 1988;
(c) the Asylum and Immigration Appeals Act 1993;
(d) the Asylum and Immigration Act 1996; and
(e) the Immigration and Asylum Act 1999.

['Refugee Convention' means the Convention relating to the Status of Refugees done at Geneva on 28 July 1951 and its Protocol;]

'responsible third party' means a person appearing to an immigration officer to be:
(a) in charge of a group of people arriving in the United Kingdom together or intending to arrive in the United Kingdom together;
(b) a tour operator;
(c) the owner or agent of a ship, aircraft, train, hydrofoil or hovercraft;
(d) the person responsible for the management of a control port or his agent; or
(e) an official at a British Diplomatic Mission or at a British Consular Post or at the office of any person outside the United Kingdom and Islands who has been authorised by the Secretary of State to accept applications for entry clearance;

'tour operator' means a person who, otherwise than occasionally, organises and provides holidays to the public or a section of it; and 'visit visa' means an entry clearance granted for the purpose of entry to the United Kingdom as a visitor under the immigration rules.

Note: Words in first square brackets inserted from 1 April 2005 (SI 2005/1159). Other words in square brackets inserted from 27 February 2004 (SI 2004/475).

PART II
ENTRY CLEARANCE AS LEAVE TO ENTER

2. Entry clearance as Leave to Enter

Subject to article 6(3), an entry clearance which complies with the requirements of article 3 shall have effect as leave to enter the United Kingdom to the extent specified in article 4, but subject to the conditions referred to in article 5.

3. Requirements

[(1) Subject to paragraph (4), an entry clearance shall only have effect as leave to enter if it complies with the requirements of this article.]

(2) The entry clearance must specify the purpose for which the holder wishes to enter the United Kingdom.

(3) The entry clearance must be endorsed with:
  (a) the conditions to which it is subject; or
  (b) a statement that it is to have effect as indefinite leave to enter the United Kingdom.

[(4) Subject to paragraph (5), an entry clearance shall not have effect as leave to enter if it is endorsed on a convention travel document.

(5) An entry clearance endorsed on a convention travel document before 27 February 2004 shall have effect as leave to enter.]

Note: Article 3(1) substituted and Art 3(4) and (5) inserted from 27 February 2004 (SI 2004/475).

4. Extent to which entry clearance is to be leave to enter

(1) A visit visa, [(other than a visit visa granted pursuant to the ADS Agreement with China) unless endorsed with a statement that it is to have effect as a single-entry visa] during its period of validity, shall have effect as leave to enter the United Kingdom on an unlimited number of occasions, in accordance with paragraph (2).

(2) On each occasion the holder arrives in the United Kingdom, he shall be treated for the purposes of the Immigration Acts as having been granted, before arrival, leave to enter the United Kingdom for a limited period beginning on the date of arrival, being:
  (a) six months if six months or more remain of the visa's period of validity; or
  (b) the visa's remaining period of validity, if less than six months.

[(2A) A visit visa granted pursuant to the ADS Agreement with China endorsed with a statement that it is to have effect as a dual-entry visa, shall have effect as leave to enter the United Kingdom on two occasions during its period of validity, in accordance with paragraph (2B).

(2B) On arrival in the United Kingdom on each occasion, the holder shall be treated for the purposes of the Immigration Acts as having been granted, before arrival, leave to enter the United Kingdom for a limited period, being the period beginning on the date on which the holder arrives in the United Kingdom and ending on the date of expiry of the entry clearance.]

(**3**) In the case of [any form of entry clearance to which this paragraph applies], it shall have effect as leave to enter the United Kingdom on one occasion during its period of validity; and, on arrival in the United Kingdom, the holder shall be treated for the purposes of the Immigration Acts as having been granted, before arrival, leave to enter the United Kingdom:

(a) in the case of an entry clearance which is endorsed with a statement that it is to have effect as indefinite leave to enter the United Kingdom, for an indefinite period; or

(b) in the case of an entry clearance which is endorsed with conditions, for a limited period, being the period beginning on the date on which the holder arrives in the United Kingdom and ending on the date of expiry of the entry clearance.

[(**3A**) Paragraph (3) applies to—

(a) a visit visa (other than a visit visa granted pursuant to the ADS Agreement with China) endorsed with a statement that it is to have effect as a single entry visa;

(b) a visit visa granted pursuant to the ADS Agreement with China unless endorsed with a statement to the effect that it is to have effect as a dual entry visa; and

(c) any other form of entry clearance.]

(**4**) In this article 'period of validity' means the period beginning on the day on which the entry clearance becomes effective and ending on the day on which it expires.

Note: Words in square brackets inserted from 1 April 2005 (SI 2005/1159). Paras (2) and (3) have effect in a form modified by and in circumstances specified by the Channel Tunnel (International Arrangements) Order (SI 1993/1813) as amended by SIs 1994/1405, 2000/913, 2001/178, 2001/3707, 2006/1003 and 2007/3759.

5. Conditions

An entry clearance shall have effect as leave to enter subject to any conditions, being conditions of a kind that may be imposed on leave to enter given under section 3 of the Act, to which the entry clearance is subject and which are endorsed on it.

6. Incidental, supplementary and consequential provisions

(**1**) Where an immigration officer exercises his power to cancel leave to enter under paragraph 2A(8) of Schedule 2 to the Act or article 13(7) below in respect of an entry clearance which has effect as leave to enter, the entry clearance shall cease to have effect.

(**2**) If the holder of an entry clearance—

(a) arrives in the United Kingdom before the day on which it becomes effective; or

(b) seeks to enter the United Kingdom for a purpose other than the purpose specified in the entry clearance, an immigration officer may cancel the entry clearance.

(**3**) If the holder of an entry clearance which does not, at the time, have effect as leave to enter the United Kingdom seeks leave to enter the United Kingdom at any time before his departure for, or in the course of his journey to, the United Kingdom and is refused leave to enter under article 7, the entry clearance shall not have effect as leave to enter.

Note: Para (2)(a) has effect in a form modified by and in circumstances specified by the Channel Tunnel (International Arrangements) Order (SI 1993/1813) as amended by SIs 1994/1405, 2000/913, 2001/178, 2001/3707, 2006/1003 and 2007/3759.

PART III

FORM AND MANNER OF GIVING AND REFUSING
LEAVE TO ENTER

7. Grant and refusal of leave to enter before arrival in the United Kingdom

(1) An immigration officer, whether or not in the United Kingdom, may give or refuse a person leave to enter the United Kingdom at any time before his departure for, or in the course of his journey to, the United Kingdom.

(2) In order to determine whether or not to give leave to enter under this article (and, if so, for what period and subject to what conditions), an immigration officer may seek such information, and the production of such documents or copy documents, as an immigration officer would be entitled to obtain in an examination under paragraph 2 or 2A of Schedule 2 to the Act.

(3) An immigration officer may also require the person seeking leave to supply an up to date medical report.

(4) Failure by a person seeking leave to supply any information, documents, copy documents or medical report requested by an immigration officer under this article shall be a ground, in itself, for refusal of leave.

8. Grant or refusal of leave otherwise than by notice in writing

(1) [Subject to paragraph (5),] a notice giving or refusing leave to enter may, instead of being given in writing as required by section 4(1) of the Act, be given as follows.

(2) The notice may be given by facsimile or electronic mail.

(3) In the case of a notice giving or refusing leave to enter the United Kingdom as a visitor, it may be given orally, including by means of a telecommunications system.

(4) In paragraph (3), 'leave to enter the United Kingdom as a visitor' means leave to enter as a visitor under the immigration rules for a period not exceeding six months, subject to conditions prohibiting employment and recourse to public funds (within the meaning of the immigration rules).

[(5) No notice shall be given where a person is given leave to enter the United Kingdom by passing through an automated gate in accordance with article 8A.]

Note: Words in square brackets inserted from 25 March 2010 (SI 2010/957).

[Automatic grant of leave

8A.—(1) An immigration officer may authorise a person to be a person who may obtain leave to enter the United Kingdom by passing through an automated gate.

(2) Such an authorisation may—

(a) only authorise a person to obtain leave to enter the United Kingdom as one of the categories of person under the immigration rules mentioned in paragraph (5);

(b) set out the conditions of use for an automated gate;

(c) list the automated gates for which the authorisation is valid;

(d) remain in force for up to 24 months; and

(e) be varied or withdrawn at any time, with or without notice being given to the person.

(3) Where a person passes through an automated gate—

(a) having been authorised under paragraph (1) as a person who may obtain leave to enter the United Kingdom by passing through an automated gate;

(b) in accordance with the conditions of use for an automated gate;

(c) which is an automated gate for which the authorisation is valid; and

(d) while the authorisation remains in force; the person shall be given leave to enter the United Kingdom for six months as the category of person under the immigration rules for which the person has been authorised under paragraph (1).

(4) Such leave shall be subject to conditions prohibiting employment and recourse to public funds (within the meaning of the immigration rules).

(5) The categories of person under the immigration rules mentioned in this paragraph are—

(a) a general visitor;

(b) a business visitor;

(c) an academic visitor;

(d) a sports visitor;

(e) an entertainer visitor;

(f) a person seeking leave to enter as a visitor for private medical treatment;

(g) a person seeking leave to enter as the parent of a child at school in the United Kingdom.]

Note: Article 8A inserted from 25 March 2010 (SI 2010/957).

9. Grant or refusal of leave by notice to a responsible third party

(1) Leave to enter may be given or refused to a person by means of a notice given (in such form and manner as permitted by the Act or this Order for a notice giving or refusing leave to enter) to a responsible third party acting on his behalf.

(2) A notice under paragraph (1) may refer to a person to whom leave is being granted or refused either by name or by reference to a description or category of persons which includes him.

10. Notice of refusal of leave

(1) Where a notice refusing leave to enter to a person is given under article 8(3) or 9, an immigration officer shall as soon as practicable give to him a notice in writing stating that he has been refused leave to enter the United Kingdom and stating the reasons for the refusal.

(2) Where an immigration officer serves a notice under the Immigration (Appeals) Notices Regulations 1984 or under regulations made under paragraph 1 of Schedule 4 to the Immigration and Asylum Act 1999 in respect of the refusal, he shall not be required to serve a notice under paragraph (1).

(3) Any notice required by paragraph (1) to be given to any person may be delivered, or sent by post to—

(a) that person's last known or usual place of abode; or

(b) any address provided by him for receipt of the notice.

11. Burden of proof

Where any question arises under the Immigration Acts as to whether a person has leave to enter the United Kingdom and he alleges that he has such leave by virtue of a notice given under article 8(3) or 9, [or by virtue of article 8A,] the onus shall lie upon him to show the manner and date of his entry into the United Kingdom.

Note: Words in square brackets inserted from 25 March 2010 (SI 2010/957).

12.—(1) This article applies where—

(a) an immigration officer has commenced examination of a person ('the applicant') under paragraph 2(1)(c) of Schedule 2 to the Act (examination to determine whether or not leave to enter should be given);

(b) that examination has been adjourned, or the applicant has been required (under paragraph 2(3) of Schedule 2 to the Act) to submit to a further examination, whilst further inquiries are made (including, where the applicant has made an asylum claim, as to the Secretary of State's decision on that claim); and

(c) upon the completion of those inquiries, an immigration officer considers he is in a position to decide whether or not to give or refuse leave to enter without interviewing the applicant further.

(2) Where this article applies, any notice giving or refusing leave to enter which is on any date thereafter sent by post to the applicant (or is communicated to him in such form or manner as is permitted by this Order) shall be regarded, for the purposes of the Act, as having been given within the period of 24 hours specified in paragraph 6(1) of Schedule 2 to the Act (period within which notice giving or refusing leave to enter must be given after completion of examination).

PART IV

LEAVE WHICH DOES NOT LAPSE ON TRAVEL OUTSIDE COMMON TRAVEL AREA

13.—(1) In this article 'leave' means—

(a) leave to enter the United Kingdom (including leave to enter conferred by means of an entry clearance under article 2); and

(b) leave to remain in the United Kingdom.

(2) Subject to paragraph (3), where a person has leave which is in force and which was:

(a) conferred by means of an entry clearance (other than a visit visa) under article 2; or

(b) given by an immigration officer or the Secretary of State for a period exceeding six months,

such leave shall not lapse on his going to a country or territory outside the common travel area.

(3) Paragraph (2) shall not apply:

(a) where a limited leave has been varied by the Secretary of State; and

(b) following the variation the period of leave remaining is six months or less.

(4) Leave which does not lapse under paragraph (2) shall remain in force either indefinitely (if it is unlimited) or until the date on which it would otherwise have expired (if limited), but—

(a) where the holder has stayed outside the United Kingdom for a continuous period of more than two years, the leave (where the leave is unlimited) or any leave then remaining (where the leave is limited) shall thereupon lapse; and

(b) any conditions to which the leave is subject shall be suspended for such time as the holder is outside the United Kingdom.

(5) For the purposes of paragraphs 2 and 2A of Schedule 2 to the Act (examination by immigration officers, and medical examination), leave to remain which remains in force under this article shall be treated, upon the holder's arrival in the United Kingdom, as leave to enter which has been granted to the holder before his arrival.

(6) Without prejudice to the provisions of section 4(1) of the Act, where the holder of leave which remains in force under this article is outside the United Kingdom, the Secretary of State may vary that leave (including any conditions to which it is subject) in such form and manner as permitted by the Act or this Order for the giving of leave to enter.

(7) Where a person is outside the United Kingdom and has leave which is in force by virtue of this article, that leave may be cancelled:

(a) in the case of leave to enter, by an immigration officer; or

(b) in the case of leave to remain, by the Secretary of State.

(8) In order to determine whether or not to vary (and, if so, in what manner) or cancel leave which remains in force under this article and which is held by a person who is outside the United Kingdom, an immigration officer or, as the case may be, the Secretary of State may seek such information, and the production of such documents or copy documents, as an immigration officer would be entitled to obtain in an examination under paragraph 2 or 2A of Schedule 2 to the Act and may also require the holder of the leave to supply an up to date medical report.

(9) Failure to supply any information, documents, copy documents or medical report requested by an immigration officer or, as the case may be, the Secretary of State under this article shall be a ground, in itself, for cancellation of leave.

(10) Section 3(4) of the Act (lapsing of leave upon travelling outside the common travel area) shall have effect subject to this article.

PART V

CONSEQUENTIAL AND TRANSITIONAL PROVISIONS

14. Section 9(2) of the Act (further provisions as to common travel area: conditions applicable to certain arrivals on a local journey) shall have effect as if, after the words 'British Citizens', there were inserted 'and do not hold leave to enter or remain granted to them before their arrival'.

15. —(1) Article 12 shall apply where an applicant's examination has begun before the date that article comes into force, as well as where it begins on or after that date.

(2) Article 13 shall apply with respect to leave to enter or remain in the United Kingdom which is in force on the date that article comes into force, as well as to such leave given after that date.

The Immigration (Removal Directions) Regulations 2000
(SI 2000, No. 2243)

1. Citation and commencement

These Regulations may be cited as the Immigration (Removal Directions) Regulations 2000 and shall come into force on 2 October 2000.

2. Interpretation

(1) In these Regulations—

'the Act' means the Immigration and Asylum Act 1999;

'aircraft' includes hovercraft;

'captain' means master (of a ship) or commander (of an aircraft);

'international service' has the meaning given by section 13(6) of the Channel Tunnel Act 1987;

'ship' includes every description of vessel used in navigation; and

'the tunnel system' has the meaning given by section 1(7) of the Channel Tunnel Act 1987.

(2) In these Regulations, a reference to a section number is a reference to a section of the Act.

3. Persons to whom directions may be given

For the purposes of section 10(6)(a) (classes of person to whom directions may be given), the following classes of person are prescribed—

    (a) owners of ships;

    (b) owners of aircraft;

    (c) agents of ships;

    (d) agents of aircraft;

    (e) captains of ships about to leave the United Kingdom;

    (f) captains of aircraft about to leave the United Kingdom; and

    (g) persons operating an international service.

4. Requirements that may be imposed by directions

(1) For the purposes of section 10(6)(b) (requirements that may be imposed by directions), the following kinds of requirements are prescribed—

    (a) in the case where directions are given to a captain of a ship or aircraft about to leave the United Kingdom, a requirement to remove the relevant person from the United Kingdom in that ship or aircraft;

    (b) in the case where directions are given to a person operating an international service, a requirement to make arrangements for the removal of the relevant person through the tunnel system;

(c) in the case where directions are given to any other person who falls within a class prescribed in regulation 3, a requirement to make arrangements for the removal of the relevant person in a ship or aircraft specified or indicated in the directions; and

(d) in all cases, a requirement to remove the relevant person in accordance with arrangements to be made by an immigration officer.

(2) Paragraph (1) only applies if the directions specify that the relevant person is to be removed to a country or territory being—

(i) a country of which he is a national or citizen; or

(ii) a country or territory to which there is reason to believe that he will be admitted.

(3) Paragraph (1)(b) only applies if the relevant person arrived in the United Kingdom through the tunnel system.

(4) 'Relevant person' means a person who may be removed from the United Kingdom in accordance with section 10(1).

The Asylum (Designated Safe Third Countries) Order 2000
(SI 2000, No. 2245)

1. This Order may be cited as the Asylum (Designated Safe Third Countries) Order 2000 and shall come into force on 2 October 2000.

2. The Asylum (Designated Countries of Destination and Designated Safe Third Countries) Order 1996 is hereby revoked.

3. The following countries are designated for the purposes of section 12(1)(b) of the Immigration and Asylum Act 1999 (designation of countries other than EU Member States for the purposes of appeal rights):

Canada

Norway

Switzerland

United States of America.

The Immigration (Leave to Enter) Order 2001
(SI 2001, No. 2590)

1.—(1) This Order may be cited as the Immigration (Leave to Enter) Order 2001 and shall come into force on the day after the day on which it is made.

(2) In this Order—

(a) 'the 1971 Act' means the Immigration Act 1971; and

(b) 'claim for asylum' and 'the Human Rights Convention' have the meanings assigned by section 167 of the Immigration and Asylum Act 1999.

Note: Commencement 18 July 2001.

2.—(1) Where this article applies to a person, the Secretary of State may give or refuse him leave to enter the United Kingdom.

(2) This article applies to a person who seeks leave to enter the United Kingdom and who—
    (a) has made a claim for asylum; or
    (b) has made a claim that it would be contrary to the United Kingdom's obligations under the Human Rights Convention for him to be removed from, or required to leave, the United Kingdom.

(3) This article also applies to a person who seeks leave to enter the United Kingdom for a purpose not covered by the immigration rules or otherwise on the grounds that those rules should be departed from in his case.

(4) In deciding whether to give or refuse leave under this article the Secretary of State may take into account any additional grounds which a person has for seeking leave to enter the United Kingdom.

(5) The power to give or refuse leave to enter the United Kingdom under this article shall be exercised by notice in writing to the person affected or in such manner as is permitted by the Immigration (Leave to Enter and Remain) Order 2000.

3. In relation to the giving or refusing of leave to enter by the Secretary of State under article 2, paragraphs 2 (examination by immigration officers, and medical examination), 4 (information and documents), 7(1), (3) and (4) (power to require medical examination after entry), 8 (removal of persons refused leave to enter), 9 (removal of illegal entrants) and 21 (temporary admission of persons liable to detention) of Schedule 2 to the 1971 Act shall be read as if references to an immigration officer included references to the Secretary of State.

4.—(1) This article applies where—
    (a) an immigration officer has commenced examination of a person ('the applicant') under paragraph 2(1)(c) of Schedule 2 to the 1971 Act (examination to determine whether or not leave to enter should be given);
    (b) that examination has been adjourned, or the applicant has been required (under paragraph 2(3) of Schedule 2 to the Immigration Act 1971) to submit to a further examination;
    (c) the Secretary of State subsequently examines the applicant or conducts a further examination in relation to him; and
    (d) the Secretary of State thereafter gives or refuses the applicant leave to enter.

(2) Where this article applies, the notice giving or refusing leave to enter shall be regarded for the purposes of the 1971 Act as having been given within the period of 24 hours specified in paragraph 6(1) of Schedule 2 to that Act (period within which notice giving or refusing leave to enter must be given after completion of examination by an immigration officer).

The Immigration (Entry Otherwise than by Sea or Air) Order 2002
(SI 2002, No. 1832)

---

1. This Order may be cited as the Immigration (Entry Otherwise than by Sea or Air) Order 2002 and shall come into force on the day after the day on which it is made.

Note: Commencement 17 July 2002.

2.—(1) This article applies where—

(a) a person who requires leave to enter the United Kingdom by virtue of section 9(4) of the Immigration Act 1971 or by virtue of article 3 of the Immigration (Control of Entry through Republic of Ireland) Order 1972; or

(b) a person in respect of whom a deportation order is in force, has entered or is seeking to enter the United Kingdom from the Republic of Ireland.

(2) Where this article applies, paragraphs 8, 9 and 11 of Schedule 2 to the Immigration Act 1971 shall have effect in relation to persons entering or seeking to enter the United Kingdom on arrival otherwise than by ship or aircraft as they have effect in the case of a person arriving by ship or aircraft, with the modifications set out in the Schedule to this Order.

3. Article 2 shall apply where an illegal entrant entered the United Kingdom before the date when this Order comes into force, as well as where he entered the United Kingdom on or after that date.

(3) Article 2 shall not apply where a person has arrived in, but not entered, the United Kingdom before the date on which this Order comes into force.

Article 2(2)   SCHEDULE

MODIFICATIONS TO SCHEDULE 2 OF THE IMMIGRATION ACT 1971

1. In this Schedule 'Schedule 2' means Schedule 2 to the Immigration Act 1971.

2. For paragraph 8 of Schedule 2, substitute:

'**8.**—(1) Where a person arriving in the United Kingdom is refused leave to enter, an immigration officer or the Secretary of State may give the owners or agents of any train, vehicle, ship or aircraft directions requiring them to make arrangements for that person's removal from the United Kingdom in any train, vehicle, ship or aircraft specified or indicated in the direction to a country or territory so specified being—

(a) a country of which he is a national or citizen; or

(b) a country or territory in which he has obtained a passport or other document of identify; or

(c) a country or territory in which he embarked for the United Kingdom; or

(d) a country or territory to which there is reason to believe that he will be admitted.

(2) The costs of complying with any directions given under this paragraph shall be defrayed by the Secretary of State.'.

3. In paragraph 9(1) of Schedule 2:

(a) after 'immigration officer', insert 'or the Secretary of State'; and

(b) after 'authorised by paragraph 8(1)', insert 'and the costs of complying with any directions given under this paragraph shall be defrayed by the Secretary of State'.

4. In paragraph 11 of Schedule 2, after 'on board any', insert 'train, vehicle,'.

The British Nationality (General) Regulations 2003
(SI 2003, No. 548)

Arrangement of Regulations

Part I. General

Part II. Registration and Naturalisation

Part III. Renunciation and Deprivation

Part IV. Supplemental

Schedules

PART I
GENERAL

Citation and commencement

1. These Regulations may be cited as the British Nationality (General) Regulations 2003 and shall come into force on 1 April 2003.

Interpretation

2.—(1) In these Regulations, the following expressions have the meanings hereby assigned to them, that is to say—

'the Act' means the British Nationality Act 1981;

'applicant' in relation to an application made on behalf of a person not of full age or capacity means that person;

'High Commissioner' means, in relation to a country mentioned in Schedule 3 to the Act, the High Commissioner for Her Majesty's Government in the United Kingdom appointed to that country, and includes the acting High Commissioner.

(2) In the application of the provisions of regulation 6(2) [6(3), 6A(1), (3) and (5), paragraph 3 of Schedule 3] [...] where a function of the Secretary of State under the Act is exercised by the Lieutenant-Governor of any of the Islands by virtue of arrangements made under section 43(1) of the Act, any reference in those provisions to the Secretary of State shall be construed as a reference to the Lieutenant-Governor.

Note: Words in square brackets inserted from 1 January 2004 (SI 2003/3158), words omitted from 3 December 2007 (SI 2007/3137).

PART II
REGISTRATION AND NATURALISATION

Applications

3. Any application for registration as a British citizen, British Overseas citizen or British subject or for a certificate of naturalisation as a British citizen shall—

    (a) be made to the appropriate authority specified in regulation 4; and

    (b) satisfy the requirements of Part I and, if made on behalf of a person not of full age or capacity, Part II of Schedule 1 and such further requirements, if any, as are specified in relation thereto in Schedule 2.

Authority to whom application is to be made

4.—(1) Except as provided by paragraphs (2) and (3), the authority to whom an application is to be made is as follows:

    (a) if the application is in Great Britain or Northern Ireland, to the Secretary of State at the Home Office;

    (b) if the applicant is in any of the Islands, to the Lieutenant-Governor;

    (c) if the applicant is in a British overseas territory, to the Governor;

    (d) if the applicant is in a country mentioned in Schedule 3 to the Act, to the High Commissioner or, if there is no High Commissioner, to the Secretary of State at the Home Office;

(e) if the applicant is elsewhere, to any consular officer, any established officer in the Diplomatic Service of Her Majesty's Government in the United Kingdom or any person authorised by the Secretary of State in that behalf.

(2) The authority to whom an application under section 4(5) of the Act (acquisition by registration: British overseas territories citizens, etc), on grounds of Crown Service under the government of a British overseas territory or service as a member of a body established by law in a British overseas territory, is to be made is in all cases the Governor of that territory.

(3) The authority to whom an application under section 5 of the Act (acquisition by registration: nationals for purposes of the [EU] Treaties) is to be made is in all cases the Governor of Gibraltar.

Persons not of full age or capacity

5. An application may be made on behalf of someone not of full age or capacity by his father or mother or any person who has assumed responsibility for his welfare.

[Knowledge of language and life in the United Kingdom

5A.—(1) A person has sufficient knowledge of the English language and sufficient knowledge about life in the United Kingdom for the purpose of an application for naturalisation as a British citizen under section 6 of the Act if—

[(a)   (i) he has attended a course at an accredited college;

(ii) the course used teaching materials derived from the document entitled 'Citizenship Materials for ESOL Learners';

(iii) he has demonstrated relevant progress in accordance with paragraph (2); and

(iv) he has attained a relevant qualification; or]

(b) he has passed the test known as the 'Life in the UK Test' administered by an educational institution or other person approved for this purpose by the Secretary of State; or

(c) in the case of a person who is ordinarily resident outside the United Kingdom, a person designated by the Secretary of State certifies in writing that he has sufficient knowledge of the English language and sufficient knowledge about life in the United Kingdom for this purpose [; or

(d) the Secretary of State has previously accepted that he has sufficient knowledge of language and sufficient knowledge about life in the United Kingdom when granting the person Indefinite Leave to Remain].

[(2) A person has demonstrated relevant progress if he meets the requirements of paragraph (3) or (4)].

[(3) The requirements in respect of a relevant qualification awarded or authenticated by a body which is recognised by the Office of Qualifications and Examinations Regulation under section 132 of the Apprenticeships, Skills, Children and Learning Act 2009 are that the person provides evidence to the Secretary of State that—

(a) prior to his commencing a course of study leading to a relevant qualification an ESOL assessment was undertaken by a suitably qualified person to assess his level of language ability; and

(b) he has successfully completed a course of study leading to a relevant qualification; and

(c) having been assessed in accordance with paragraph (a) as being below Entry 1, he has attained a relevant qualification at Entry 1, 2 or 3; or

(d) having been assessed in accordance with paragraph (a) as being at Entry 1, he has attained a relevant qualification at Entry 2 or 3; or

(e) having been assessed in accordance with paragraph (a) as being at Entry 2, he has attained a relevant qualification at Entry 3.

(4) The requirements in respect of a relevant qualification approved by the Scottish Qualifications Authority are that the person provides evidence to the Secretary of State that—

(a) prior to his commencing a course of study leading to a relevant qualification an ESOL assessment was undertaken by a suitably qualified person to assess his level of language ability; and

(b) he has successfully completed a course of study leading to a relevant qualification; and

(c) having been assessed in accordance with paragraph (a) as being below Access 2, he has attained a relevant qualification at Access 2 or 3 or at Intermediate 1 level; or

(d) having been assessed in accordance with paragraph (a) at Access 2, he has attained a relevant qualification at Access 3 or Intermediate 1 level; or

(e) having been assessed in accordance with paragraph (a) at Access 3, he has attained a relevant qualification at Intermediate 1 level.

(5) In this regulation:

(a) an 'accredited college' is:

(i) a publicly funded college that is subject to inspection by the Office for Standards in Education, Children's Services and Skills (if situated in England), the Education and Training Inspectorate (if situated in Northern Ireland), Her Majesty's Inspectorate of Education (if situated in Scotland), Estyn (if situated in Wales), or an inspection programme that has been approved by the Island's Government (if situated in the Channel Islands or Isle of Man); or

(ii) a private college accredited by Accreditation UK, the British Accreditation Council, the Accreditation Body for Language Services, the Accreditation Service for International Colleges;

(b) a 'relevant qualification' is:

(i) an ESOL qualification in speaking and listening which is awarded or authenticated by a body which is recognised by the Office of Qualifications and Examinations Regulation (Ofqual) under section 132 of the Apprenticeships, Skills, Children and Learning Act 2009 and is determined by Ofqual as being at Entry Level; or

(ii) one National Qualifications Unit in ESOL at Access 2, Access 3 or Intermediate 1 level approved by the Scottish Qualifications Authority;

(c) a 'suitably qualified person' is a person who is deemed suitably qualified by the institution in which the assessment is undertaken.]]

Note: Regulation 5A substituted from 1 November 2005 (SI 2005/2785). Regulation 5A(1)(a) substituted, reg 5A(1(d) inserted, reg 5A(2) substituted and regs 5(3)–5(5) inserted from 7 April 2010 (SI 2010/785).

[Citizenship oaths and pledges

6.—(1) Where a citizenship oath or pledge is required by section 42 of the Act to be made by an applicant for registration or for a certificate of naturalisation, it shall be administered in accordance with the requirements of Schedule 3.

(2) If, on an application for a registration or for a certificate of naturalisation by an applicant who is required to make a citizenship oath or pledge, the Secretary of State decides that the registration should be effected or the certificate should be granted, he shall cause notice in writing of the decision to be given to the applicant.

(3) The requirement to make a citizenship oath or pledge shall be satisfied within three months of the giving of the notice referred to in paragraph (2) or such longer time as the Secretary of State may allow.

(4) Any notice required by paragraph (2) to be given to an applicant may be given—

(a) in any case where the applicant's whereabouts are known, by causing the notice to be delivered to him personally or by sending it to him by post;

(b) in a case where the applicant's whereabouts are not known, by sending it by post in a letter addressed to him at his last known address.

(5) In this regulation, references to the requirement to make a citizenship oath or pledge include the requirement to make a citizenship oath and pledge at a citizenship ceremony.

Arrangements for, and conduct of, citizenship ceremonies

6A.—(1) The Secretary of State may designate or authorise a person to exercise a function (which may include a discretion) in connection with a citizenship ceremony or a citizenship oath or pledge, and the reference in paragraph (3)(b) to 'designated person' shall be construed accordingly.

(2) Each local authority (within the meaning of section 41(3B) of the Act) shall—

(a) make available, or make arrangements for, premises at which citizenship ceremonies may be conducted; and

(b) arrange for citizenship ceremonies to be conducted with sufficient frequency so as to enable applicants in their area who are required to make a citizenship oath and pledge at a citizenship ceremony to meet the time limit laid down by regulation 6(3).

(3) Where an applicant is required by section 42 of the Act to make a citizenship oath and pledge at a citizenship ceremony, the Secretary of State shall—

(a) issue to the applicant an invitation in writing to attend a citizenship ceremony (a 'ceremony invitation');

(b) notify the applicant of the local authority or designated person which the applicant should contact to arrange attendance at a citizenship ceremony (the 'relevant authority'); and

(c) notify the relevant authority of his decision in relation to the applicant.

(4) An applicant who has arranged attendance at a citizenship ceremony shall bring with him to the ceremony his ceremony invitation; and if the applicant fails to do so, the person conducting the ceremony may refuse admittance to, or participation in, the ceremony if he is not reasonably satisfied as to the identity of the applicant.

(5) Where an applicant makes the relevant citizenship oath and pledge at a citizenship ceremony as required by section 42 of the Act—

(a) the person conducting the ceremony shall grant to the applicant a certificate of registration or naturalisation, duly dated with the date of the ceremony; and

(b) the relevant authority shall notify the Secretary of State in writing within 14 days of the date of the ceremony that the applicant has made the relevant citizenship oath and pledge at a citizenship ceremony and the date on which the ceremony took place.

(6) In this regulation, 'the person conducting the ceremony' is the person who administers the citizenship oath and pledge at the citizenship ceremony in accordance with paragraph 3 of Schedule 3.]

Note: Regulation 6 substituted from 1 January 2004 (SI 2003/3158).

[Certificates of naturalisation

7. A certificate of naturalisation shall include the following information relating to the person to whom the certificate is being granted—
   (a) full name;
   (b) date of birth; and
   (c) place and country of birth.]

Note: Regulation 7 substituted from 3 December 2007 (SI 2007/3137).

PART III
RENUNCIATION AND DEPRIVATION

Declarations of renunciation

8. Any declaration of renunciation of British citizenship, British Overseas citizenship or the status of a British subject shall—
   (a) be made to the appropriate authority specified in regulation 9; and
   (b) satisfy the requirements of Schedule 5.

Authority to whom declaration of renunciation is to be made

9. The authority to whom a declaration of renunciation is to be made is as follows:

   (a) if the declarant is in Great Britain or Northern Ireland, to the Secretary of State at the Home Office;
   (b) if the declarant is in any of the Islands, to the Lieutenant-Governor;
   (c) if the declarant is in a British overseas territory, to the Governor;
   (d) if the declarant is in a country mentioned in Schedule 3 to the Act, to the High Commissioner or, if there is no High Commissioner, to the Secretary of State at the Home Office;
   (e) if the declarant is elsewhere, to any consular officer, any established officer in the Diplomatic Service of Her Majesty's Government in the United Kingdom or any person authorised by the Secretary of State in that behalf.

Notice of proposed deprivation of citizenship

10.—(1) Where it is proposed to make an order under section 40 of the Act depriving a person of a citizenship status, the notice required by section 40(5) of the Act to be given to that person may be given—

   (a) in a case where that person's whereabouts are known, by causing the notice to be delivered to him personally or by sending it to him by post;
   (b) in a case where that person's whereabouts are not known, by sending it by post in a letter addressed to him at his last known address.

(2) If a notice required by section 40(5) of the Act is given to a person appearing to the Secretary of State or, as appropriate, the Governor or Lieutenant-Governor to represent the person to whom notice under section 40(5) is intended to be given, it shall be deemed to have been given to that person.

(3) A notice required to be given by section 40(5) of the Act shall, unless the contrary is proved, be deemed to have been given—

(a) where the notice is sent by post from and to a place within the United Kingdom, on the second day after it was sent;

(b) where the notice is sent by post from or to a place outside the United Kingdom, on the twenty-eighth day after it was sent, and

(c) in any other case on the day on which the notice was delivered.

Cancellation of registration of person deprived of citizenship

11. Where an order has been made depriving a person who has a citizenship status by virtue of registration (whether under the Act or under the former nationality Acts) of that citizenship status, the name of that person shall be removed from the relevant register.

Cancellation of certificate of naturalisation in case of deprivation of citizenship

12. Where an order has been made depriving a person who has a citizenship status by virtue of the grant of a certificate of naturalisation (whether under the Act or under the former nationality Acts) of that citizenship status, the person so deprived or any other person in possession of the relevant certificate of naturalisation shall, if required by notice in writing given by the authority by whom the order was made, deliver up the said certificate to such person, and within such time, as may be specified in the notice; and the said certificate shall thereupon be cancelled or amended.

PART IV
SUPPLEMENTAL

Evidence

13. A document may be certified to be a true copy of a document for the purpose of section 45(2) of the Act by means of a statement in writing to that effect signed by a person authorised by the Secretary of State, the Lieutenant-Governor, the High Commissioner or the Governor in that behalf.

[Manner of signifying parental consent to registration

14. Where a parent, in pursuance of section 3(5)(c) or 4D(3) of the Act, consents to the registration of a person as a British citizen under subsection 3(5) or section 4D, the consent shall be expressed in writing and signed by the parent.]

Note: Regulation 14 substituted from 13 January 2010 (SI 2009/3363).

Revocation

15. The British Nationality (General) Regulations 1982 are hereby revoked.

Regulation 3   SCHEDULE 1

GENERAL REQUIREMENTS AS RESPECTS APPLICATIONS

PART I

ALL APPLICATIONS

1. An application shall be made in writing and shall state the name, address and date and place of birth of the applicant.

2. An application shall contain a declaration that the particulars stated therein are true.

PART II

APPLICATIONS BY PERSONS NOT OF FULL AGE OR CAPACITY

3. An application in respect of someone not of full age or capacity made by another person on his behalf shall state that that is the case and the name and address of that person.

4. An application made by a person on behalf of someone not of full age or capacity shall indicate the nature of that person's connection with him and, if that person has any responsibility for him otherwise than as a parent, the nature of that responsibility and the manner in which it was assumed.

Regulation 3   SCHEDULE 2

PARTICULAR REQUIREMENTS AS RESPECTS APPLICATIONS

Application under section 1(3) of the Act

1. An application under section 1(3) of the Act shall contain information showing:
[(a)] that the applicant's father or mother became a British citizen, or became settled in the United Kingdom, after the applicant's birth [; and
(b) where the applicant is aged 10 or over, that he is of good character.]

Note : Words in square brackets inserted from 3 December 2007 (SI 2007/3137).

Application under section 1(3A) of the Act

1A. An application under section 1(3A) shall contain information showing—
(a) that the applicant's father or mother became a member of the armed forces after the applicant's birth; and
(b) where the applicant is aged 10 or over, that he is of good character.]

Note: Paragraph 1A inserted from 13 January 2010 (SI 2009/3363).

Application under section 1(4) of the Act

2. An application under section 1(4) of the Act shall contain information showing:
[(a)] that the applicant possesses the requisite qualifications in respect of residence
[; and

(b) where the applicant is aged 10 or over, that he is of good character.]

Note: Words in square brackets inserted from 3 December 2007 (SI 2007/3137).

3. If the applicant was absent from the United Kingdom on more than 90 days in all in any one of the first 10 years of his life and it is desired that the application should nevertheless be considered under section 1(7) of the Act, it shall specify the special circumstances to be taken into consideration.

Application under section 3(2) of the Act

4. An application under section 3(2) of the Act shall contain information showing—
(a) that the applicant's father or mother ('the parent in question') was a British citizen by descent at the time of the applicant's birth;
(b) that the father or mother of the parent in question—
(i) was a British citizen otherwise than by descent at the time of the birth of the parent in question; or
(ii) became a British citizen otherwise than by descent at commencement; or
(iii) would have become a British citizen otherwise than by descent at commencement but for his or her death;
(c) either—
(i) that the parent in question possesses the requisite qualifications in respect of residence; or
(ii) that the applicant was born stateless.

5. ...

Note : Paragraph 5 omitted from 13 January 2010 (SI 2009/3363).

Application under section 3(5) of the Act

6. An application under section 3(5) of the Act shall contain information showing—
(a) that the applicant's father or mother was a British citizen by descent at the time of the applicant's birth;
(b) that the applicant and his father and mother possess the requisite qualifications in respect of residence;
(c) that the consent of the applicant's father and/or mother (as required by section 3(5)(c) and (6) of the Act) has been signified in accordance with regulation 14 and, if the consent of one parent only has been signified, the reason for that fact [; and
(d) where the applicant is aged 10 or over, that he is of good character.]

Note: Words in square brackets inserted from 3 December 2007 (SI 2007/3137).

Application under section 4(2) of the Act

7.—(1) An application under section 4(2) of the Act shall contain information showing—
(a) that the applicant is a British overseas territories citizen, a British Overseas citizen, a British subject under the Act or a British protected person;

(b) that the applicant possesses the requisite qualifications in respect of residence, freedom from immigration restrictions and compliance with the immigration laws [; and

(c) where the applicant is aged 10 or over, that he is of good character.]

(2) If the applicant does not possess the requisite qualifications in respect of residence, freedom from immigration restrictions and compliance with the immigration laws and it is desired that the application should nevertheless be considered under section 4(4) of the Act, it shall specify the special circumstances to be taken into consideration.

Note : Words in square brackets inserted from 3 December 2007 (SI 2007/3137).

Application under section 4(5) of the Act

8.—(1) An application under section 4(5) of the Act shall contain information showing—

(a) that the applicant is a British overseas territories citizen, a British Overseas citizen, a British subject under the Act or a British protected person;

(b) that the applicant possesses the requisite qualifications in respect of service [; and

(c) where the applicant is aged 10 or over, that he is of good character.]

(2) The application shall specify the special circumstances to be taken into consideration.

Note : Words in square brackets inserted from 3 December 2007 (SI 2007/3137).

Application under section 4A of the Act

9. An application under section 4A of the Act shall contain information showing—

(a) that the applicant is a British overseas territories citizen who is not such a citizen by virtue only of a connection with the Sovereign Base Areas of Akrotiri and Dhekelia;

(b) that the applicant has not ceased to be a British citizen as a result of a declaration of renunciation [; and

(c) where the applicant is aged 10 or over, that he is of good character].

Note : Words in square brackets inserted from 3 December 2007 (SI 2007/3137).

[Application under section 4B of the Act

10. An application under section 4B of the Act shall contain information showing—

(a) that the applicant is a British Overseas citizen, a British subject under the Act, a British protected person or a British National (Overseas) and does not have any other citizenship or nationality; and

(b) (i) in the case of an application made by virtue of subsection (1)(a), (b) or (c), that the applicant has not, after 4th July 2002, renounced, voluntarily relinquished or lost through action or inaction, any citizenship or nationality; or

(ii) in the case of an application made by virtue of subsection (1)(d), that the applicant has not, after 19th March 2009, renounced, voluntarily relinquished or lost through action or inaction, any citizenship or nationality].

Note: Paragraph 10 substituted from 13 January 2010 (SI 2009/3363).

[Application under section 4C of the Act

11. An application under section 4C of the Act shall contain information showing—

(a) that the applicant was born before 1 January 1983;

(b) that the applicant would at some time before 1 January 1983 have become a citizen of the United Kingdom and Colonies—

(i) under section 5 or 12(2) of, or paragraph 3 of Schedule 3 to, the British Nationality Act 1948 if (as the case may be) that section or paragraph provided for citizenship by descent from a mother in the same terms as it provided for citizenship by descent from a father and if references in that provision to a father were references to the applicant's mother; or

(ii) under section 12(2), (3), (4) or (5) of the British Nationality Act 1948 if a provision of the law at some time before 1 January 1949, which provided for a nationality status to be acquired by descent from a father, provided in the same terms for its acquisition by descent from a mother and if references in that provision to a father were references to the applicant's mother;

(c) that immediately before 1st January 1983 the applicant would have had the right of abode in the United Kingdom by virtue of section 2 of the Immigration Act 1971 had he become a citizen of the United Kingdom and Colonies as described in either sub-paragraph (b)(i) or (ii) above; and

(d) that he is of good character.]

Note : Paragraph 11 substituted from 13 January 2010 (SI 2009/3363).

[Application under section 4D of the Act

11A.—(1) An application under section 4D of the Act shall contain information showing—

(a) that the applicant's father or mother was a member of the armed forces and serving outside of the United Kingdom and qualifying territories at the time of the applicant's birth;

(b) that the consent of the applicant's father and/or mother (as required by section 4D(3) and (4) of the Act) has been signified in accordance with regulation 14 and, if the consent of one parent only has been signified, the reason for that fact; and

(c) where the applicant is aged 10 or over, that he is of good character.

(2) If the application is made without the consent of the applicant's father and/or mother and it is desired that the application should nevertheless be considered under section 4D(5) of the Act, it shall specify the special circumstances to be taken into consideration.]

Note : Paragraph 11A inserted from 13 January 2010 (SI 2009/3363).

Application under section 5 of the Act

12. An application under section 5 of the Act shall contain information showing

[(a)] that the applicant is a British overseas territories citizen who falls to be treated as a national of the United Kingdom for the purposes of the {EU}Treaties [; and

(b) where the applicant is aged 10 or over, that he is of good character.]

Note : Words in square brackets inserted from 3 December 2007 (SI 2007/3137).

Application under section 6(1)

13.—(1) An application under section 6(1) of the Act shall contain information showing—

(a) that the applicant possesses the requisite qualifications in respect of residence or Crown service, freedom from immigration restrictions, compliance with the immigration laws, good character, knowledge of language [, knowledge about life in the United Kingdom] and intention with respect to residence or occupation in the event of a certificate of naturalisation being granted to him;

(b) that the applicant is of full capacity.

(2) If the applicant does not possess the requisite qualifications in respect of residence, freedom from immigration restrictions, compliance with the immigration laws and knowledge of language and it is desired that the application should nevertheless be considered under paragraph 2 of Schedule 1 to the Act, it shall specify the special circumstances to be taken into consideration.

[(3) If the applicant is not of full capacity and it is desired that the requirement of full capacity be waived in accordance with section 44A of the Act (waiver of requirement for full capacity), the application shall specify why it would be in the applicant's best interests for the requirement to be waived in his case.]

Note: Words in square brackets substituted from 1 May 2006 (SI 2005/2785). Sub-paragraph (3) inserted from 3 December 2007 (SI 2007.3137).

Application under section 6(2) of the Act

14.—(1) An application under section 6(2) of the Act shall contain information showing—

(a) that the applicant is married to a British citizen;

(b) that the applicant possesses the requisite qualifications in respect of residence, freedom from immigration restrictions, compliance with the [immigration laws, good character, knowledge of language and knowledge about life in the United Kingdom].

(c) that the applicant is of full capacity.

(2) If the applicant does not possess the requisite qualifications in respect of residence and compliance with the immigration laws and it is desired that the application should nevertheless be considered under paragraph 4 of Schedule 1 to the Act, it shall specify the special circumstances to be taken into consideration.

(3) If the applicant does not possess the requisite qualifications in respect of residence and it is desired that the application should nevertheless be considered under paragraph 4(d) of Schedule 1 to the Act on the grounds of marriage to a person who is serving in Crown Service under the government of the United Kingdom or other designated service, it shall specify the nature of the service and contain information showing that recruitment for that service took place in the United Kingdom.

[(4) If the applicant is not of full capacity and it is desired that the requirement of full capacity be waived in accordance with section 44A of the Act (waiver of requirement for full capacity), the application shall specify why it would be in the applicant's best interests for the requirement to be waived in his case.]

Note: Words in square brackets substituted from 1 May 2006 (SI 2005/2785). Sub-paragraph (4) inserted from 3 December 2007 (SI 2007/3137).

Application under section 10(1) of the Act

15. An application under section 10(1) of the Act shall contain information showing—

(a) that the applicant renounced citizenship of the United Kingdom and Colonies;

(b) that at the time when he renounced it the applicant was, or was about to become, a citizen of a country mentioned in section 1(3) of the British Nationality Act 1948;

(c) that the applicant could not have remained or become such a citizen but for renouncing it or had reasonable cause to believe that he would be deprived of his citizenship of that country unless he renounced it;

(d) that the applicant possessed the requisite qualifying connection with the United Kingdom immediately before commencement or was married before commencement to a person who possessed the requisite qualifying connection with the United Kingdom immediately before commencement or would if living have possessed such a connection;

(e) that the applicant has not previously been registered under section 10(1) of the Act [; and

(f) where the applicant is aged 10 or over, that he is of good character].

Note: Sub-paragraph (f) inserted from 3 December 2007 (SI 2007/3137).

Application under section 10(2) of the Act

16. [(1)] An application under section 10(2) of the Act shall contain information showing—

(a) that the applicant has renounced citizenship of the United Kingdom and Colonies and his reason for so doing;

(b) that the applicant possesses the requisite qualifying connection with the United Kingdom or has been married to a person who has, or would if living have, such a connection;

(c) that the applicant is of full capacity [; and

(d) where the applicant is aged 10 or over, that he is of good character];

[(2) If the applicant is not of full capacity and it is desired that the requirement of full capacity be waived in accordance with section 44A of the Act (waiver of requirement for full capacity), the application shall specify why it would be in the applicant's best interests for the requirement to be waived in his case.]

Note: Words in square brackets inserted from 3 December 2007 (SI 2007/3137).

Application under section 13(1) of the Act

17. [(1)] An application under section 13(1) of the Act shall contain information showing—

(a) that the applicant has renounced British citizenship;

(b) that, at the time when he renounced it, the applicant had or was about to acquire some other citizenship or nationality;

(c) that the renunciation of British citizenship was necessary to enable him to retain or acquire that other citizenship or nationality;

(d) that the applicant has not previously been registered under section 13(1) of the Act;

(e) that the applicant is of full capacity [; and

(f) where the applicant is aged 10 or over, that he is of good character];

[(2) If the applicant is not of full capacity and it is desired that the requirement of full capacity be waived in accordance with section 44A of the Act (waiver of requirement for full capacity), the application shall specify why it would be in the applicant's best interests for the requirement to be waived in his case.]

Note: Words in square brackets inserted from 3 December 2007 (SI 2007/3137).

Application under section 13(3) of the Act

18. [(1)] An application under section 13(3) of the Act shall contain information showing—

(a) that the applicant has renounced British citizenship and his reason for so doing;

(b) that the applicant is of full capacity [; and

(c) where the applicant is aged 10 or over, that he is of good character.]

[(2) If the applicant is not of full capacity and it is desired that the requirement of full capacity be waived in accordance with section 44A of the Act (waiver of requirement for full capacity), the application shall specify why it would be in the applicant's best interests for the requirement to be waived in his case.]

Note: Words in square brackets inserted from 3 December 2007 (SI 2007/3137).

Application under paragraph 3 of Schedule 2 to the Act

19.—(1) An application under paragraph 3 of Schedule 2 to the Act shall contain information showing—

(a) that the applicant is and always has been stateless;

(b) that the applicant seeks British citizenship and possesses the requisite qualifications in respect of residence.

(2) If the applicant does not possess the requisite qualifications in respect of residence and it is desired that the application should nevertheless be considered under paragraph 6 of Schedule 2 to the Act, it shall specify the special circumstances to be taken into consideration.

Application under paragraph 4 of Schedule 2

20.—(1) An application under paragraph 4 of Schedule 2 to the Act shall contain information showing—

(a) that the applicant is and always has been stateless;

(b) in respect of both the father and mother of the applicant, which of the following statuses, namely, British citizenship, British overseas territories citizenship, British Overseas citizenship or the status of a British subject under the Act, was held at the time of the applicant's birth;

(c) that the applicant possesses the requisite qualifications in respect of residence;

(d) if more than one of the statuses mentioned in sub-paragraph (b) above are available to the applicant, which status or statuses is or are wanted.

(2) If the applicant does not possess the requisite qualifications in respect of residence and it is desired that the application should nevertheless be considered under paragraph 6 of Schedule 2 to the Act, it shall specify the special circumstances to be taken into consideration.

Application under paragraph 5 of Schedule 2

21. An application under paragraph 5 of Schedule 2 to the Act shall contain information showing—

(a) that the applicant is and always has been stateless;

(b) if he was not born at a place which is at the date of the application within the United Kingdom and British overseas territories—

(i) that the applicant's mother was a citizen of the United Kingdom and Colonies at the time of his birth; or

(ii) that he possesses the requisite qualifications in respect of parentage or residence and parentage;

(c) that the applicant seeks British citizenship or British Overseas citizenship and that that citizenship is available to the applicant in accordance with paragraph 5(2) of Schedule 2 to the Act.

Regulation 6   Schedule 3

Administration of [Citizenship Oath or Pledge]

1. Subject to [paragraphs 2 and 3] [a citizenship oath or pledge] shall be administered by one of the following persons:

(a) in England and Wales or Northern Ireland—any justice of the peace, commissioner for oaths or notary public;

(b) in Scotland—any sheriff principal, sheriff, justice of the peace or notary public;

(c) in the Channel Islands, the Isle of Man or any British overseas territory—any judge of any court of civil or criminal jurisdiction, any justice of the peace or magistrate, or any person for the time being authorised by the law of the place where the applicant, declarant or deponent is, to administer an oath for any judicial or other legal purpose;

(d) in any country mentioned in Schedule 3 to the Act of which Her Majesty is Queen, or in any territory administered by the government of any such country—any person for the time being authorised by the law of the place where the deponent is to administer an oath for any judicial or other legal purpose, any consular officer or any established officer of the Diplomatic Service of Her Majesty's Government in the United Kingdom;

(e) elsewhere—any consular officer, any established officer of the Diplomatic Service of Her Majesty's Government in the United Kingdom or any person authorised by the Secretary of State in that behalf.

2. If the deponent is serving in Her Majesty's naval, military or air forces, the oath [or pledge] may be administered by any officer holding a commission in any of those forces, whether the oath [or pledge] is made […] in the United Kingdom or elsewhere.

[3. Where a citizenship oath and pledge is required by section 42 of the Act to be made at a citizenship ceremony, it shall be administered at the ceremony:

(a) in the case of a ceremony held in England, Wales or Scotland, by a registrar (within the meaning of section 41(3B) of the Act); and

(b) in the case of a ceremony held elsewhere, by a person authorised to do so by the Secretary of State.]

Note: Words in square brackets substituted and inserted, and words omitted from 1 January 2004 (SI 2003/3158).

| Regulation 7 | SCHEDULE 4 |

....

Note: Schedule 4 revoked from 3 December 2007 (SI 2007/3137).

| Regulation 8 | SCHEDULE 5 |

REQUIREMENTS AS RESPECTS DECLARATIONS OF RENUNCIATION

1. A declaration shall be made in writing and shall state the name, address, date and place of birth of the declarant.

2. A declaration shall contain information showing that the declarant—

(a) is a British citizen, British Overseas citizen or British subject, as the case may be;

(b) is of full age or, if not, has been married;

(c) is of full capacity;

(d) will, after the registration of the declaration, have or acquire some citizenship or nationality other than British citizenship, British Overseas citizenship or British subject status, as the case may be.

[**2A.** If the declarant is not of full capacity and it is desired that the requirement of full capacity be waived in accordance with section 44A of the Act (waiver of requirement for full capacity), the declaration shall specify why it would be in the applicant's best interests for the requirement to be waived in his case.]

Note: Paragraph 2A inserted from 3 December 2007 (SI 2007/3137).

3. A declaration shall contain a declaration that the particulars stated therein are true.

The Immigration (Notices) Regulations 2003
(SI 2003, No. 658)

Citation and commencement

1. These Regulations may be cited as the Immigration (Notices) Regulations 2003 and shall come into force on the 1 April 2003.

Interpretation

2. In these Regulations—

'the 1971 Act' means the Immigration Act 1971;

'the 1997 Act' means the Special Immigration Appeals Commission Act 1997;

'the 1999 Act' means the Immigration and Asylum Act 1999;

'the 2002 Act' means the Nationality, Immigration and Asylum Act 2002;

'decision-maker' means—

    (a) the Secretary of State;

    (b) an immigration officer;

    (c) an entry clearance officer;

['EEA decision' has the same meaning as in regulation 2(1) of the Immigration (European Economic Area) Regulations 2006];

'entry clearance officer' means a person responsible for the grant or refusal of entry clearance;

'immigration decision' has the same meaning as in section 82(2) [and (3A)] of the 2002 Act;

'minor' means a person who is under 18 years of age;

'notice of appeal' means a notice in the appropriate prescribed form in accordance with the rules for the time being in force under section 106(1) of the 2002 Act;

'Procedure Rules' means rules made under section 106(1) of the 2002 Act;

'representative' means a person who appears to the decision-maker—

    (a) to be the representative of a person referred to in regulation 4(1) below; and

    (b) not to be prohibited from acting as a representative by section 84 of the 1999 Act.

Note: Definition of 'EEA Decision' substituted from16 July 2012 (SI 2012/1547). Other words in square brackets inserted from 1 August 2008 (SI 2008/1819).

Transitional provision

3. These Regulations apply to a decision to make a deportation order which, by virtue of paragraph 12 of Schedule 15 of the 1999 Act,—

    (a) is appealable under section 15 of the 1971 Act (appeals in respect of deportation orders); or

    (b) would be appealable under section 15 of the 1971 Act, but for section 15(3) (deportation conducive to public good), and is appealable under section 2(1)(c) of the 1997 Act (appeal to Special Immigration Appeals Commission against a decision to make a deportation order).

Notice of decisions

4.—(1) Subject to regulation 6, the decision-maker must give written notice to a person of any immigration decision or EEA decision taken in respect of him which is appealable.

(2) The decision-maker must give written notice to a person of the relevant grant of leave to enter or remain if, as a result of that grant, a right of appeal arises under section 83(2) of the 2002 Act.

[(**2A**) The decision-maker must give written notice to a person of a decision that they are no longer a refugee if as a result of that decision a right of appeal arises under section 83A(2) of the 2002 Act.]

(**3**) If the notice is given to the representative of the person, it is to be taken to have been given to the person.

Note: Paragraph (2A) inserted from 31 August 2006 (SI 2006/2168).

Contents of notice

5.—[(**1**) A notice given under regulation 4(1)—

(a) is to include or be accompanied by a statement of the reasons for the decision to which it relates; and

(b) if it relates to an immigration decision specified in section 82(2)(a), (g), (h), [(ha),] (i), (ia) [,(j) or (3A)] of the 2002 Act—

(i) shall state the country or territory to which it is proposed to remove the person; or

(ii) may, if it appears to the decision-maker that the person to whom the notice is to be given may be removable to more than one country or territory, state any such countries or territories.]

(**2**) A notice given under regulation 4(2) is to include or be accompanied by a statement of the reasons for the rejection of the claim for asylum.

[(**2A**) A notice given under regulation 4(2A) is to include or be accompanied by a statement of the reasons for the decision that the person is no longer a refugee.]

(**3**) Subject to paragraph (6), the notice given under regulation 4 shall also include, or be accompanied by, a statement which advises the person of—

(a) his right of appeal and the statutory provision on which his right of appeal is based;

(b) whether or not such an appeal may be brought while in the United Kingdom;

(c) the grounds on which such an appeal may be brought; and

(d) the facilities available for advice and assistance in connection with such an appeal.

(**4**) Subject to paragraph (6), the notice given under regulation 4 shall be accompanied by a notice of appeal which indicates the time limit for bringing the appeal, the address to which it should be sent or may be taken by hand and a fax number for service by fax.

(**5**) Subject to paragraph (6), where the exercise of the right is restricted by an exception or limitation by virtue of a provision of Part 5 of the 2002 Act, the notice given under regulation 4 shall include or be accompanied by a statement which refers to the provision limiting or restricting the right of appeal.

(**6**) The notice given under regulation 4 need not comply with paragraphs (3); (4) and (5) where a right of appeal may only be exercised on the grounds referred to in section 84(1)(b), (c) or (g) of the 2002 Act by virtue of the operation of section 88(4), [88A(3),] [89(2)], 90(4), 91(2), 98(4) or (5) of that Act.

(**7**) Where notice is given under regulation 4 and paragraph (6) applies, if the person claims in relation to the immigration decision or the EEA decision that—

(a) the decision is unlawful by virtue of section 19B of the Race Relations Act 1976 (discrimination by public authorities);

(b) the decision is unlawful under section 6 of the Human Rights Act 1998 (public authority not to act contrary to the Human Rights Convention) as being incompatible with the person's Convention rights; or

(c) removal of the person from the United Kingdom in consequence of the immigration decision would breach the United Kingdom's obligations under the Refugee Convention or would be unlawful under section 6 of the Human Rights Act 1998 as being incompatible with the person's Convention rights, the decision-maker must as soon as practicable re-serve the notice of decision under regulation 4 and paragraph (6) of this regulation shall not apply.

(8) Where a notice is re-served under paragraph (7), the time limit for appeal under the Procedure Rules shall be calculated as if the notice of decision had been served on the date on which it was re-served.

Note: Paragraph (1) substituted from 31 August 2006 (SI 2006/2168). Words in second square brackets in para (1) inserted from 1 August 2008 (SI 2008/1819). Paragraph (2A) inserted from 1 December 2007 (SI 2007/3187). Other words in square brackets in paras (1) and (6) inserted from 1 April 2008 (SI 2008/684).

Certain notices under the 1971 Act deemed to comply with the regulations

6.—(1) This regulation applies where the power to—
(a) refuse leave to enter; or
(b) vary leave to enter or remain in the United Kingdom;
is exercised by notice in writing under section 4 of (administration of control), or paragraph 6(2) (notice of decisions of leave to enter or remain) of Schedule 2 to, the 1971 Act.

(2) If—
(a) the statement required by regulation 5(3) is included in or accompanies that notice; and
(b) the notice is given in accordance with the provision of regulation 7; the notice is to be taken to have been given under regulation 4(1) for the purposes of these Regulations.

Service of notice

7.—(1) A notice required to be given under regulation 4 may be—
(a) given by hand;
(b) sent by fax;
(c) sent by postal service in which delivery or receipt is recorded to—
  (i) an address provided for correspondence by the person or his representative; or
  (ii) where no address for correspondence has been provided by the person, the last-known or usual place of abode or place of business of the person or his representative [;
  [(c) sent electronically;
(d) sent by document exchange to a document exchange number or address;
(e) sent by courier; or
(f) collected by the person who is the subject of the decision or their representative.]

(2) Where—
(a) a person's whereabouts are not known; and

(b) (i) no address has been provided for correspondence and the decision-maker does not know the last-known or usual place of abode or place of business of the person; or

(ii) the address provided to the decision-maker is defective, false or no longer in use by the person; and

(c) no representative appears to be acting for the person,

the notice shall be deemed to have been given when the decision-maker enters a record of the above circumstances and places the signed notice on the relevant file.

(3) Where a notice has been given in accordance with paragraph (2) and then subsequently the person is located, he shall be given a copy of the notice and details of when and how it was given as soon as is practicable.

(4) Where a notice is sent by post in accordance with paragraph (1)(c) it shall be deemed to have been served, unless the contrary is proved,—

(a) on the second day after it was posted if it is sent to a place within the United Kingdom;

(b) on the twenty-eighth day after it was posted if it is sent to a place outside the United Kingdom.

(5) For the purposes of paragraph (4) the period is to be calculated—

(a) excluding the day on which the notice is posted; and

(b) in the case of paragraph (4)(a), excluding any day which is not a business day.

(6) In this regulation, 'business day' means any day other than Saturday or Sunday, a day which is a bank holiday under the Banking and Financial Dealings Act 1971 in the part of the United Kingdom to which the notice is sent, Christmas Day or Good Friday.

(7) A notice given under regulation 4 may, in the case of a minor who does not have a representative, be given to the parent, guardian or another adult who for the time being takes responsibility for the child.

Note: Words in square brackets in paragraph (1) inserted from 1 April 2008 (SI 2008/684)

...

The Immigration (Passenger Transit Visa) Order 2003
(SI 2003, No. 1185)

Citation, commencement and interpretation

1. This order may be cited as the Immigration (Passenger Transit Visa) Order 2003 and shall come into force on 2 May 2003.

2. —(1) Subject to paragraph (4), in this Order a 'transit passenger' means a person to whom [paragraph (2), (3) or [(3B)]] applies and who on arrival in the United Kingdom passes through another country or territory without entering the United Kingdom.

(2) This paragraph applies to a person who is a citizen or national of a country or territory listed in Schedule 1 to this order.

(3) This paragraph applies to a person holding a travel document issued by:

    (a) the purported 'Turkish Republic of Northern Cyprus';

    (b) the former Socialist Republic of Yugoslavia;

    (c) the former Federal Republic of Yugoslavia; or

    (d) the former Zaire.

[(3B) This paragraph applies to a person who holds a passport issued by the Republic of Venezuela that does not contain biometric information held in an electronic chip.]

(4) A person to whom paragraph (2), (3) or [(3B)]]applies will not be a transit passenger if he:

    (a) has the right of abode in the United Kingdom under the Immigration Act 1971;

    (b) is a national of an EEA State; or

    (c) in the case of a national or citizen of the People's Republic of China, holds a passport issued by either the Hong Kong Special Administrative Region or the Macao Special Administrative Region.

(5) In [this Order] 'EEA State' means a country which is a contracting party to the Agreement on the European Economic Area signed at Oporto on 2 May 1992 as adjusted by the Protocol signed at Brussels on 17 March 1993.

Note: Words in square brackets in paragraphs (1) and (4) substituted from 3 March 2009, (SI 2009/198); '(3B)' in paragraphs (1) and (4) substituted from 18 May 2009 (SI 2009/1233).

Paragraph (3B) inserted from 18 May 2009 and para (3A) deleted from 1 July 2009 (SI 2009/1229).

Requirement for a transit passenger to hold a transit visa

3. [Subject to article 3A, a] transit passenger is required to hold a transit visa.]

[Exemption from the requirement for a transit passenger to hold a transit visa

3A.—(1) A transit passenger is not required to hold a transit visa if he holds or a person with whom he arrives in the United Kingdom holds on his behalf:

    (a) a valid visa for entry to Canada or the United States of America and a valid airline ticket for travel via the United Kingdom [as part of a journey] from another country or territory to the country in respect of which the visa is held;

    [(b) a valid airline ticket for travel via the United Kingdom as part of a journey from Canada or the United States of America to another country or territory, provided that the transit passenger does not seek to travel via the United Kingdom on a date more than six months from the date on which he last entered Canada or the United States of America with a valid visa for entry to that country or territory;]

    (c) a valid USA I-551 Permanent Resident Card issued on or after 21 April 1998;

    (d) a valid Canadian Permanent Resident Card issued on or after 28 June 2002;

    (e) a valid common format Category D visa for entry to an EEA State;

    (f) a valid common format residence permit issued by an EEA State pursuant to Council Regulation (EC) No. 1030/2002;

    (g) a diplomatic or service passport issued by the People's Republic of China; or

    (h) a diplomatic or official passport issued by India.

    [(i) a diplomatic or official passport issued by Vietnam.]

(2) … .]

Method of application for a transit visa

4. An application for a transit visa may be made to any British High Commission, Embassy or Consulate which accepts such applications.

Revocations

5. The Orders specified in Schedule 2 to this Order are hereby revoked.

Article 2   [SCHEDULE 1

COUNTRIES OR TERRITORIES WHOSE NATIONALS OR CITIZENS NEED TRANSIT VISAS

Afghanistan	Gambia	Rwanda
Albania	Ghana	Senegal
Algeria	India	Serbia and Montenegro
Angola	Iran	Sierra Leone
Bangladesh	Iraq	Somalia
Belarus	Ivory Coast	[South Africa]
[Bolivia]	[Jamaica]	[South Sudan]
Burma	[Kenya]	Sri Lanka
Burundi	Lebanon	Sudan
Cameroon	[Lesotho]	[Swaziland]
Colombia	Liberia	[Syria]
Democratic Republic of the	[Libya]	[Tanzania]
Congo	[Malawi]	Turkey
Ecuador	Moldova	Uganda
[Egypt]	Nepal	Vietnam
Eritrea	Nigeria	[Yemen]
Ethiopia	Pakistan	Zimbabwe].
Former Yugoslav Republic of Macedonia	Palestinian Territories People's Republic of China	

Note: Words in square brackets in Arts 2 and 3, and Schedule substituted, and Art 3A inserted from 1 October 2003 (SI 2003/2628). Words in square brackets in Art 3A (1)(a) and (1)(i) and Schedule inserted and Art 3A revoked from 13 May 2004 (SI 2004/1304). 'Kenya' inserted into Schedule from 2 March 2006 (SI 2006/493). 'Jamaica' inserted from 3 March 2009, (SI 2009/198). 'Bolivia' inserted from 18 May 2009, other countries inserted from 1 July 2009 (SI 2009/1229). Yemen inserted from 14 July 2011 (SI 2011/1553). South Sudan inserted from 10 February 2012 (SI 2012/116). Egypt, Libya and Syria inserted from 3 April 2012 (SI 2012/771).

Article 5   SCHEDULE 2

REVOCATIONS

...

The Immigration and Asylum Act 1999 (Part V Exemption: Relevant Employers) Order 2003
(SI 2003, No. 3214)

Citation and commencement

1. This Order may be cited as the Immigration and Asylum Act 1999 (Part V Exemption: Relevant Employers) Order 2003 and shall come into force on 1 January 2004.

Interpretation

2. In this Order—

'the Act' means the Immigration and Asylum Act 1999;

'immigration advice' and 'immigration services' have the same meanings as in section 82 of the Act;

'work permit' has the same meaning as in section 33(1) of the Immigration Act 1971;

'immediate family' means a person's spouse, and children below eighteen years of age;

'EEA national' means a person to whom the [Immigration (European Economic Area) Regulations 2006] apply;

'family member of an EEA national' has the same meaning as in the Immigration (European Economic Area) Regulations 2006.

Note: Words in square brackets inserted from 30 April 2006 (SI 2006/1003).

Exemption of relevant employers

3.—(1) Subject to paragraph (2), the following category of person is hereby specified for the purposes of section 84(4)(d) of the Act (provision of immigration services), namely, a person who provides immigration advice or immigration services free of charge to an employee or prospective employee who—

(a) is the subject of an application for a work permit submitted by the prospective employer;

(b) has been granted a work permit entitling him to work with the employer; or

(c) is an EEA national or the family member of an EEA national,

where the immigration advice or immigration services are restricted to matters which concern that employee or prospective employee or his immediate family.

(2) For the purposes of paragraph (1), the person providing the immigration advice or immigration services must be the employer or prospective employer of the person receiving the advice or services, or an employee of that employer acting as such.

The Immigration (Claimant's Credibility) Regulations 2004

(SI 2004, No. 3263)

Citation and commencement

1. These Regulations may be cited as the Immigration (Claimant's Credibility) Regulations 2004 and shall come into force on the 1 January 2005.

Interpretation

2. In these Regulations—

'the 2004 Act' means the Asylum and Immigration (Treatment of Claimants, etc) Act 2004;

'representative' means a person who appears to the decision-maker—

(a) to be the representative of a person; and

(b) not to be prohibited from acting as a representative by section 84 of the Immigration and Asylum 1999 Act.

Manner of notifying immigration decision

3.—(1) For the purpose of section 8(5) of the 2004 Act a person may be notified of an immigration decision in any of the following ways—

(a) orally, including by means of a telecommunications system;

(b) in writing given by hand; or

(c) in writing

(i) sent by fax to a fax number;

(ii) sent by electronic mail to an electronic mail address; or

(iii) delivered or sent by postal service to an address,

provided for correspondence by the person or his representative.

(2) Where no fax number, electronic mail or postal address for correspondence has been provided by the person, notice of an immigration decision under paragraph (1)(c) may be delivered or sent by postal service to the last known or usual place of abode or place of business of the person or his representative.

(3) Notice given in accordance with paragraph (1) or (2) to the representative of the person, is to be taken to have been given to the person.

(4) In the case of a minor who does not have a representative, notice given in accordance with paragraph (1) or (2) to the parent, guardian or another adult who for the time being takes responsibility for the minor is taken to have been given to the minor.

Presumptions about receipt of notice

4.—(1) For the purpose of section 8(5) of the 2004 Act notice of an immigration decision shall, unless the contrary is proved, be treated as received;

(a) where the notice is sent by postal service in which delivery or receipt is recorded to an address, on the recorded date of delivery or receipt, or on the second day after the day it was posted, whichever is the earlier;

(b) in any other case in which the notice is sent by postal service on the second day after the day it was posted; or

(c) in any other case, on the day and time that it was communicated orally, given by hand or sent by electronic mail or fax.

(2) For the purposes of determining the second day after a notice is posted under paragraph (1) (a) and (b) any day which is not a business day shall be excluded.

(3) In this regulation 'business day' means any day other than Saturday or Sunday, a day which is a bank holiday under the Banking and Financial Dealings Act 1971 in the part of the United Kingdom from or to which the notice is sent, Christmas Day or Good Friday.

The Asylum Seekers (Reception Conditions) Regulations 2005
(SI 2005, No. 7)

Citation and commencement

1.—(1) These Regulations may be cited as the Asylum Seekers (Reception Conditions) Regulations 2005 and shall come into force on 5 February 2005.

(2) These Regulations shall only apply to a person whose claim for asylum is recorded on or after 5 February 2005.

Interpretation

2.—(1) In these Regulations—

(a) 'the 1999 Act' means the Immigration and Asylum Act 1999;

(b) 'asylum seeker' means a person who is at least 18 years old who has made a claim for asylum which has been recorded by the Secretary of State but not yet determined;

(c) 'claim for asylum' means a claim made by a third country national or a stateless person that to remove him or require him to leave the United Kingdom would be contrary to the United Kingdom's obligations under the Convention relating to the Status of Refugees done at Geneva on 28 July 1951 and its Protocol;

(d) 'family members' means, in so far as the family already existed in the country of origin, the following members of the asylum seeker's family who are present in the United Kingdom and who are asylum seekers or dependants on the asylum seeker's claim for asylum:

(i) the spouse of the asylum seeker or his unmarried partner in a stable relationship;

(ii) the minor child of the couple referred to in paragraph (2)(d)(i) or of the asylum seeker as long as the child is unmarried and dependent on the asylum seeker;

(e) 'Immigration Acts' has the same meaning as in section 44 of the Asylum and Immigration (Treatment of Claimants, etc.) Act 2004; and

(f) 'third country national' means a person who is not a national of a member State.

(2) For the purposes of these Regulations—

(a) a claim is determined on the date on which the Secretary of State notifies the asylum seeker of his decision on his claim or, if the asylum seeker appeals against the Secretary of State's decision, the date on which that appeal is disposed of; and

(b) an appeal is disposed of when it is no longer pending for the purposes of the Immigration Acts.

Families

3.—(1) When the Secretary of State is providing or arranging for the provision of accommodation for an asylum seeker and his family members under section 95 or 98 of the 1999 Act, he shall have regard to family unity and ensure, in so far as it is reasonably practicable to do so, that family members are accommodated together.

(2) Paragraph (1) shall only apply to those family members who confirm to the Secretary of State that they agree to being accommodated together.

(3) This regulation shall not apply in respect of a child when the Secretary of State is providing or arranging for the provision of accommodation for that child under section 122 of the 1999 Act.

Provisions for persons with special needs

4.—(1) This regulation applies to an asylum seeker or the family member of an asylum seeker who is a vulnerable person.

(2) When the Secretary of State is providing support or considering whether to provide support under section 95 or 98 of the 1999 Act to an asylum seeker or his family member who is a vulnerable person, he shall take into account the special needs of that asylum seeker or his family member.

(3) A vulnerable person is—

(a) a minor;

(b) a disabled person;

(c) an elderly person;

(d) a pregnant woman;

(e) a lone parent with a minor child; or

(f) a person who has been subjected to torture, rape or other serious forms of psychological, physical or sexual violence;

who has had an individual evaluation of his situation that confirms he has special needs.

(4) Nothing in this regulation obliges the Secretary of State to carry out or arrange for the carrying out of an individual evaluation of a vulnerable person's situation to determine whether he has special needs.

Asylum support under section 95 or 98 of the 1999 Act

5.—(1) If an asylum seeker or his family member applies for support under section 95 of the 1999 Act and the Secretary of State thinks that the asylum seeker or his family member is eligible for support under that section he must offer the provision of support to the asylum seeker or his family member.

(2) If the Secretary of State thinks that the asylum seeker or his family member is eligible for support under section 98 of the 1999 Act he must offer the provision of support to the asylum seeker or his family member.

Tracing family members of unaccompanied minors

6.—(1) So as to protect an unaccompanied minor's best interests, the Secretary of State shall endeavour to trace the members of the minor's family as soon as possible after the minor makes his claim for asylum.

(2) In cases where there may be a threat to the life or integrity of the minor or the minor's close family, the Secretary of State shall take care to ensure that the collection, processing and circulation of information concerning the minor or his close family is undertaken on a confidential basis so as not to jeopardise his or their safety.

(3) For the purposes of this regulation—

(a) an unaccompanied minor means a person below the age of eighteen who arrives in the United Kingdom unaccompanied by an adult responsible for him whether by law or custom and makes a claim for asylum;

(b) a person shall be an unaccompanied minor until he is taken into the care of such an adult or until he reaches the age of 18 whichever is the earlier;

(c) an unaccompanied minor also includes a minor who is left unaccompanied after he arrives in or enters the United Kingdom but before he makes his claim for asylum.

The Immigration and Asylum (Provision of Accommodation to Failed Asylum-Seekers) Regulations 2005
(SI 2005, No. 930)

Citation and commencement

1.—(1) These Regulations may be cited as the Immigration and Asylum (Provision of Accommodation to Failed Asylum-Seekers) Regulations 2005 and shall come into force on 31 March 2005.

(2) These Regulations apply to a person who is receiving accommodation when these Regulations come into force to the same extent as they apply to a person provided with accommodation after these Regulations come into force.

Interpretation

2. In these Regulations—

'the 1999 Act' means the Immigration and Asylum Act 1999;

'destitute' is to be construed in accordance with section 95(3) of the 1999 Act; and

'reporting requirement' means a condition or restriction which requires a person to report to the police, an immigration officer or the Secretary of State, and is imposed under—

  (a) paragraph 21 of Schedule 2 to the Immigration Act 1971 (temporary admission or release from detention),

  (b) paragraph 22 of that Schedule, or

  (c) paragraph 2 or 5 of Schedule 3 to that Act (pending deportation).

Eligibility for and provision of accommodation to a failed asylum-seeker

3.—(1) Subject to regulations 4 and 6, the criteria to be used in determining the matters referred to in paragraphs (a) and (b) of section 4(5) of the 1999 Act in respect of a person falling within section 4(2) or (3) of that Act are—

  (a) that he appears to the Secretary of State to be destitute, and

  (b) that one or more of the conditions set out in paragraph (2) are satisfied in relation to him.

  (2) Those conditions are that—

  (a) he is taking all reasonable steps to leave the United Kingdom or place himself in a position in which he is able to leave the United Kingdom, which may include complying with attempts to obtain a travel document to facilitate his departure;

  (b) he is unable to leave the United Kingdom by reason of a physical impediment to travel or for some other medical reason;

  (c) he is unable to leave the United Kingdom because in the opinion of the Secretary of State there is currently no viable route of return available;

  (d) he has made an application for judicial review of a decision in relation to his asylum claim—

    (i) in England and Wales, and has been granted permission to proceed pursuant to Part 54 of the Civil Procedure Rules 1998,

    (ii) in Scotland, pursuant to Chapter 58 of the Rules of the Court of Session 1994 or

    (iii) in Northern Ireland, and has been granted leave pursuant to Order 53 of the Rules of Supreme Court (Northern Ireland) 1980; or

  (e) the provision of accommodation is necessary for the purpose of avoiding a breach of a person's Convention rights, within the meaning of the Human Rights Act 1998.

Community activities: general

4.—(1) Where the Secretary of State so determines, the continued provision of accommodation to a person falling within section 4(2) or (3) of the 1999 Act is to be conditional upon that person's performance of or participation in such community activity as is described in this regulation and is from time to time notified to the person in accordance with regulation 5.

(2) In making the determination referred to in paragraph (1), regard will be had to the following matters—

(a) the length of time that he believes the person will continue to be eligible for accommodation,

(b) the arrangements that have been made for the performance of or participation in community activities in the area in which the person is being provided with accommodation,

(c) any relevant health and safety standards which are agreed between the Secretary of State and a person with whom he has made arrangements for the provision of community activities in the person's area,

(d) whether the person is in the Secretary of State's belief unable to perform or participate in community activities because of a physical or mental impairment or for some other medical reason,

(e) whether the person is in the Secretary of State's belief unable to perform or participate in community activities because of a responsibility for the care of a dependant child or of a dependant who because of a physical or mental impairment is unable to look after himself, and

(f) any relevant information provided to the Secretary of State, regarding the person's suitability to perform or participate in particular tasks, activities or a range of tasks or activities.

(3) Paragraph (1) does not apply in relation to a person who is under the age of 18.

(4) No condition on the continued provision of accommodation will require a person to perform or participate in community activities for more than 35 hours in any week, including the weekend.

Community activities: Relevant information

5. A notice under regulation 4(1) falls within this regulation if it contains the following information—

(a) the task, activity or range of tasks or activities in the area in which the person lives which are to be performed or participated in as community activities,

(b) the geographical location at which the community activities will be performed or participated in,

(c) the maximum number of hours per week that the person will be expected to perform or participate in community activities, where it is possible for the Secretary of State to so specify, and

(d) the date upon which the task, activity or range of tasks or activities to be performed or participated in as community activities will commence and, where it is possible for the Secretary of State to so specify, the length of time such community activities will last.

Other conditions on continued provision of accommodation

6.—(1) The continued provision of accommodation to a person falling within section 4(2) or (3) of the 1999 Act is to be subject to such other conditions falling within paragraph (2) as—

(a) the Secretary of State may from time to time determine, and

(b) are set out in a notice to that person in writing.

(2) A condition falls within this paragraph to the extent that it relates to—

  (a) complying with specified standards of behaviour,

  (b) complying with a reporting requirement,

  (c) complying with a requirement—

    (i) to reside at an authorised address, or

    (ii) if he is absent from an authorised address without the permission of the Secretary of State, to ensure that that absence is for no more than seven consecutive days and nights or for no more than a total of fourteen days and nights in any six month period, or

  (d) complying with specified steps to facilitate his departure from the United Kingdom.

The Immigration (European Economic Area) Regulations 2006
(SI 2006, No. 1003)

CONTENTS

PART 1

INTERPRETATION ETC

Citation and commencement

1. These Regulations may be cited as the Immigration (European Economic Area) Regulations 2006 and shall come into force on 30 April 2006.

General interpretation

2.—(1) In these Regulations—

'the 1971 Act' means the Immigration Act 1971;
'the 1999 Act' means the Immigration and Asylum Act 1999;
'the 2002 Act' means the Nationality, Immigration and Asylum Act 2002;

['the Accession Regulations' means the Accession (Immigration and Worker Registration) Regulations 2004;]

['civil partner' does not include—

(a) a party to a civil partnership of convenience; or

(b) the civil partner ("C") of a person ("P") where a spouse, civil partner or durable partner of C or P is already present in the United Kingdom;]

'decision maker' means the Secretary of State, an immigration officer or an entry clearance officer (as the case may be);

['deportation order' means an order made pursuant to regulation 24(3);]

['derivative residence card' means a card issued to a person, in accordance with regulation 18A, as proof of the holder's derivative right to reside in the United Kingdom as at the date of issue;]

'document certifying permanent residence' means a document issued to an EEA national, in accordance with regulation 18, as proof of the holder's permanent right of residence under regulation 15 as at the date of issue;

['durable partner' does not include the durable partner ("D") of a person ("P") where a spouse, civil partner or durable partner of D or P is already present in the United Kingdom and where that marriage, civil partnership or durable partnership is subsisting;]

['EEA decision' means a decision under these Regulations that concerns—

(a) a person's entitlement to be admitted to the United Kingdom;

(b) a person's entitlement to be issued with or have renewed, or not to have revoked, a registration certificate, residence card, derivative residence card, document certifying permanent residence or permanent residence card;

(c) a person's removal from the United Kingdom; or

(d) the cancellation, pursuant to regulation 20A, of a person's right to reside in the United Kingdom;]

'EEA family permit' means a document issued to a person, in accordance with regulation 12, in connection with his admission to the United Kingdom;

'EEA national' means a national of an EEA State [who is not also a United Kingdom national;]

'EEA State' means—

(a) a member State, other than the United Kingdom;

(b) Norway, Iceland or Liechtenstein; or

(c) Switzerland;

'entry clearance' has the meaning given in section 33(1) of the 1971 Act;

'entry clearance officer' means a person responsible for the grant or refusal of entry clearance;

['exclusion order' means an order made under regulation 19(1B)];

'immigration rules' has the meaning given in section 33(1) of the 1971 Act;

'military service' means service in the armed forces of an EEA State;

'permanent residence card' means a card issued to a person who is not an EEA national, in accordance with regulation 18, as proof of the holder's permanent right of residence under regulation 15 as at the date of issue;

'registration certificate' means a certificate issued to an EEA national, in accordance with regulation 16, as proof of the holder's right of residence in the United Kingdom as at the date of issue;

'relevant EEA national' in relation to an extended family member has the meaning given in regulation 8(6); 'residence card' means a card issued to a person who is not an EEA national, in accordance with regulation 17, as proof of the holder's right of residence in the United Kingdom as at the date of issue;

'spouse' does not include—

[(a) a party to a marriage of convenience; or

(b) the spouse ("S") of a person ("P") where a spouse, civil partner or durable partner of S or P is already present in the United Kingdom;]

'United Kingdom national' means a person who falls to be treated as a national of the United Kingdom for the purposes of the[EU] Treaties.

(2) Paragraph (1) is subject to paragraph 1(a) of Schedule 4 (transitional provisions).

[(3) Section 11 of the 1971 Act (construction of references to entry)(4) shall apply for the purpose of determining whether a person has entered the United Kingdom for the purpose of these Regulations as it applies for the purpose of determining whether a person has entered the United Kingdom for the purpose of that Act.]

Note: Paragraph (3) and definitions of 'deportation order' and 'exclusion order' inserted from 1 June 2009 (SI 1009/1117). Definition of 'Accession Regulations' inserted from 1 May 2011 (SI 2011/544). Definitions of 'derivative residence card' and 'durable partner' inserted and definitions of 'civil partner', 'spouse' and 'EEA decision' amended from 16 July 2012 (SI 2012/1547). Definition of 'EEA national' amended from 16 October 2012 (SI 2012/1547).

Continuity of residence

3.—(1) This regulation applies for the purpose of calculating periods of continuous residence in the United Kingdom under regulation 5(1) and regulation 15.

(2) Continuity of residence is not affected by—

(a) periods of absence from the United Kingdom which do not exceed six months in total in any year;

(b) periods of absence from the United Kingdom on military service; or

(c) any one absence from the United Kingdom not exceeding twelve months for an important reason such as pregnancy and childbirth, serious illness, study or vocational training or an overseas posting.

(3) But continuity of residence is broken if a person is removed from the United Kingdom under [these Regulations].

Note: Words in square brackets substituted from 1 June 2009 (SI 1009/1117).

'Worker', 'self-employed person', 'self-sufficient person' and 'student'

4.—(1) In these Regulations—

(a) 'worker' means a worker within the meaning of[Article 45 of the Treaty on the Functioning of the European Union];

(b) 'self-employed person' means a person who establishes himself in order to pursue activity as a self-employed person in accordance with[Aticle 49 of Treaty on the Functioning of the European Union];

(c) 'self-sufficient person' means a person who has—

(i) sufficient resources not to become a burden on the social assistance system of the United Kingdom during his period of residence; and

(ii) comprehensive sickness insurance cover in the United Kingdom;

(d) 'student' means a person who—

[(i) is enrolled, for the principal purpose of following a course of study (including vocational training), at a public or private establishment which is—

(aa) financed from public funds; or

(bb) otherwise recognised by the Secretary of State as an establishment which has been accredited for the purpose of providing such courses or training within the law or administrative practice of the part of the United Kingdom in which the establishment is located;]

(ii) has comprehensive sickness insurance cover in the United Kingdom; and

(iii) assures the Secretary of State, by means of a declaration, or by such equivalent means as the person may choose, that he has sufficient resources not to become a burden on the social assistance system of the United Kingdom during his period of residence.

(2) For the purposes of paragraph (1)(c), where family members of the person concerned reside in the United Kingdom and their right to reside is dependent upon their being family members of that person—

(a) the requirement for that person to have sufficient resources not to become a burden on the social assistance system of the United Kingdom during his period of residence shall only be satisfied if his resources and those of the family members are sufficient to avoid him and the family members becoming such a burden;

(b) the requirement for that person to have comprehensive sickness insurance cover in the United Kingdom shall only be satisfied if he and his family members have such cover.

(3) For the purposes of paragraph (1)(d), where family members of the person concerned reside in the United Kingdom and their right to reside is dependent upon their being family members of that person, the requirement for that person to assure the Secretary of State that he has sufficient resources not to become a burden on the social assistance system of the United Kingdom during his period of residence shall only be satisfied if he assures the Secretary of State that his resources and those of the family members are sufficient to avoid him and the family members becoming such a burden.

[(4) For the purposes of paragraphs (1)(c) and (d) and paragraphs (2) and (3), the resources of the person concerned and, where applicable, any family members, are to be regarded as sufficient if—

(a) they exceed the maximum level of resources which a United Kingdom national and his family members may possess if he is to become eligible for social assistance under the United Kingdom benefit system; or

(b) paragraph (a) does not apply but, taking into account the personal situation of the person concerned and, where applicable, any family members, it appears to the decision maker that the resources of the person or persons concerned should be regarded as sufficient.]

[(5) For the purpose of regulation 15A(2) references in this regulation to "family members" includes a "primary carer" as defined in regulation 15A(7).]

Note: Paragraph (4) substituted from 2 June 2011 (SI 2011/1247). Words in square brackets in para 4(1)(a) and (b) substituted from 1 August 2012 (SI 2012/1809). Para (1)(d) substituted and para 5 inserted from 16 July 2012 (SI 2012/1547)'Worker or self-employed person who has ceased activity'.

5.—(1) In these Regulations, 'worker or self-employed person who has ceased activity' means an EEA national who satisfies the conditions in paragraph (2), (3), (4) or (5).

(2) A person satisfies the conditions in this paragraph if he—

(a) terminates his activity as a worker or self-employed person and—

(i) has reached the age at which he is entitled to a state pension on the date on which he terminates his activity; or

(ii) in the case of a worker, ceases working to take early retirement;

(b) pursued his activity as a worker or self-employed person in the United Kingdom for at least twelve months prior to the termination; and

(c) resided in the United Kingdom continuously for more than three years prior to the termination.

(3) A person satisfies the conditions in this paragraph if—

(a) he terminates his activity in the United Kingdom as a worker or self-employed person as a result of a permanent incapacity to work; and

(b) either—

(i) he resided in the United Kingdom continuously for more than two years prior to the termination; or

(ii) the incapacity is the result of an accident at work or an occupational disease that entitles him to a pension payable in full or in part by an institution in the United Kingdom.

(4) A person satisfies the conditions in this paragraph if—

(a) he is active as a worker or self-employed person in an EEA State but retains his place of residence in the United Kingdom, to which he returns as a rule at least once a week; and

(b) prior to becoming so active in that EEA State, he had been continuously resident and continuously active as a worker or self-employed person in the United Kingdom for at least three years.

(5) A person who satisfies the condition in paragraph (4)(a) but not the condition in paragraph (4)(b) shall, for the purposes of paragraphs (2) and (3), be treated as being active and resident in the United Kingdom during any period in which he is working or self-employed in the EEA State.

(6) The conditions in paragraphs (2) and (3) as to length of residence and activity as a worker or self-employed person shall not apply in relation to a person whose spouse or civil partner is a United Kingdom national.

(7) [Subject to regulation 7A(3), for the purposes of this regulation—]

(a) periods of inactivity for reasons not of the person's own making;

(b) periods of inactivity due to illness or accident; and

(c) in the case of a worker, periods of involuntary unemployment duly recorded by the relevant employment office,

shall be treated as periods of activity as a worker or self-employed person, as the case may be.

Note: Words in square brackets in para (7) substituted from 1 May 2011 (SI 2011/544).

'Qualified person'

6.—(1) In these Regulations, 'qualified person' means a person who is an EEA national and in the United Kingdom as—

(a) a jobseeker;

(b) a worker;

(c) a self-employed person;

(d) a self-sufficient person; or

(e) a student.

(2) [Subject to regulation 7A(4), a person who is no longer working shall not cease to be treated as a worker for the purpose of paragraph (1)(b) if—]

(a) he is temporarily unable to work as the result of an illness or accident;

(b) he is in duly recorded involuntary unemployment after having been employed in the United Kingdom, provided that he has registered as a jobseeker with the relevant employment office and—

(i) he was employed for one year or more before becoming unemployed;

(ii) he has been unemployed for no more than six months; or

(iii) he can provide evidence that he is seeking employment in the United Kingdom and has a genuine chance of being engaged;

(c) he is involuntarily unemployed and has embarked on vocational training; or

(d) he has voluntarily ceased working and embarked on vocational training that is related to his previous employment.

(3) A person who is no longer in self-employment shall not cease to be treated as a self-employed person for the purpose of paragraph (1)(c) if he is temporarily unable to pursue his activity as a self-employed person as the result of an illness or accident.

(4) For the purpose of paragraph (1)(a), 'jobseeker' means a person who enters the United Kingdom in order to seek employment and can provide evidence that he is seeking employment and has a genuine chance of being engaged.

Note: Words in square brackets in para (2) substituted from 1 May 2011 (SI 2011/544).

Family member

7.—(1) Subject to paragraph (2), for the purposes of these Regulations the following persons shall be treated as the family members of another person—

(a) his spouse or his civil partner;

(b) direct descendants of his, his spouse or his civil partner who are—

(i) under 21; or

(ii) dependants of his, his spouse or his civil partner;

(c) dependent direct relatives in his ascending line or that of his spouse or his civil partner;

(d) a person who is to be treated as the family member of that other person under paragraph (3).

(2) A person shall not be treated under paragraph (1)(b) or (c) as the family member of a student residing in the United Kingdom after the period of three months beginning on the date on which the student is admitted to the United Kingdom unless—

(a) in the case of paragraph (b), the person is the dependent child of the student or of his spouse or civil partner; or

(b) the student also falls within one of the other categories of qualified persons mentioned in regulation 6(1).

(3) Subject to paragraph (4), a person who is an extended family member and has been issued with an EEA family permit, a registration certificate or a residence card shall be

treated as the family member of the relevant EEA national for as long as he continues to satisfy the conditions in regulation 8(2), (3), (4) or (5) in relation to that EEA national and the permit, certificate or card has not ceased to be valid or been revoked.

(4) Where the relevant EEA national is a student, the extended family member shall only be treated as the family member of that national under paragraph (3) if either the EEA family permit was issued under regulation 12(2), the registration certificate was issued under regulation 16(5) or the residence card was issued under regulation 17(4).

[Application of the Accession Regulations

7A.—(1) This regulation applies to an EEA national who was an accession State worker requiring registration on 30th April 2011 ('an accession worker').

(2) In this regulation—

'accession State worker requiring registration' has the same meaning as in regulation 1(2)(d) of the Accession Regulations;

'legally working' has the same meaning as in regulation 2(7) of the Accession Regulations.

(3) In regulation 5(7)(c), where the worker is an accession worker, periods of involuntary unemployment duly recorded by the relevant employment office shall be treated only as periods of activity as a worker—

(a) during any period in which regulation 5(4) of the Accession Regulations applied to that person; or

(b) when the unemployment began on or after 1st May 2011.

(4) Regulation 6(2) applies to an accession worker where he—

(a) was a person to whom regulation 5(4) of the Accession Regulations applied on 30th April 2011; or

(b) became unable to work, became unemployed or ceased to work, as the case maybe, on or after 1st May 2011.

(5) For the purposes of regulation 15, an accession worker shall be treated as having resided in accordance with these Regulations during any period before 1st May 2011 in which the accession worker—

(a) was legally working in the United Kingdom; or

(b) was a person to whom regulation 5(4) of the Accession Regulations applied.

(6) Subject to paragraph (7), a registration certificate issued to an accession worker under regulation 8 of the Accession Regulations shall, from 1st May 2011, be treated as if it was a registration certificate issued under these Regulations where the accession worker was legally working in the United Kingdom for the employer specified in that certificate on—

(a) 30th April 2011; or

(b) the date on which the certificate is issued where it is issued after 30th April 2011.

(7) Paragraph (6) does not apply—

(a) if the Secretary of State issues a registration certificate in accordance with regulation 16 to an accession worker on or after 1st May 2011; and

(b) from the date of registration stated on that certificate.]

Note: Regulation 7A inserted from 1 May 2011 (SI 2011/544). To the extent necessary for the purpose of reg 7A the Accession (Immigration and Worker Registration) Regulations 2004

(SI 2004/1219 as amended) continue in force, subject to amendment, after repeal from 1 May 2011 (SI 2011/544).

'Extended family member'

8.—(1) In these Regulations 'extended family member' means a person who is not a family member of an EEA national under regulation 7(1)(a), (b) or (c) and who satisfies the conditions in paragraph (2), (3), (4) or (5).

(2) A person satisfies the condition in this paragraph if the person is a relative of an EEA national, his spouse or his civil partner and—

(a) the person is residing in [a country other than the United Kingdom] in which the EEA national also resides and is dependent upon the EEA national or is a member of his household;

(b) the person satisfied the condition in paragraph (a) and is accompanying the EEA national to the United Kingdom or wishes to join him there; or

(c) the person satisfied the condition in paragraph (a), has joined the EEA national in the United Kingdom and continues to be dependent upon him or to be a member of his household.

(3) A person satisfies the condition in this paragraph if the person is a relative of an EEA national or his spouse or his civil partner and, on serious health grounds, strictly requires the personal care of the EEA national, his spouse or his civil partner.

(4) A person satisfies the condition in this paragraph if the person is a relative of an EEA national and would meet the requirements in the immigration rules (other than those relating to entry clearance) for indefinite leave to enter or remain in the United Kingdom as a dependent relative of the EEA national were the EEA national a person present and settled in the United Kingdom.

(5) A person satisfies the condition in this paragraph if the person is the partner of an EEA national (other than a civil partner) and can prove to the decision maker that he is in a durable relationship with the EEA national.

(6) In these Regulations 'relevant EEA national' means, in relation to an extended family member, the EEA national who is or whose spouse or civil partner is the relative of the extended family member for the purpose of paragraph (2), (3) or (4) or the EEA national who is the partner of the extended family member for the purpose of paragraph (5).

Note: Words substituted in para (2)(a) from 2 June 2011 (SI 2011/1247).

Family members of United Kingdom nationals

9.—(1) If the conditions in paragraph (2) are satisfied, these Regulations apply to a person who is the family member of a United Kingdom national as if the United Kingdom national were an EEA national.

(2) The conditions are that—

(a) the United Kingdom national is residing in an EEA State as a worker or self-employed person or was so residing before returning to the United Kingdom; and

(b) if the family member of the United Kingdom national is his spouse or civil partner, the parties are living together in the EEA State or had entered into the marriage or civil partnership and were living together in that State before the United Kingdom national returned to the United Kingdom.

(3) Where these Regulations apply to the family member of a United Kingdom national the United Kingdom national shall be treated as holding a valid passport issued by an EEA State for the purpose of the application of regulation 13 to that family member.

'Family member who has retained the right of residence'

10.—(1) In these Regulations, 'family member who has retained the right of residence' means, subject to paragraph (8), a person who satisfies the conditions in paragraph (2), (3), (4) or (5).

(2) A person satisfies the conditions in this paragraph if—

[(a) he was a family member of a qualified person or of an EEA national with a permanent right residence when that person died;]

(b) he resided in the United Kingdom in accordance with these Regulations for at least the year immediately before the death of the qualified person [or the EEA national with a permanent right of residence]; and

(c) he satisfies the condition in paragraph (6).

(3) A person satisfies the conditions in this paragraph if—

(a) he is the direct descendant of—

(i) a qualified person [or an EEA national with a permanent right of residence] who has died;

(ii) a person who ceased to be a qualified person on ceasing to reside in the United Kingdom; or

(iii) the person who was the spouse or civil partner of the qualified person [or the EEA national with a permanent right of residence] mentioned in sub-paragraph (i) when he died or is the spouse or civil partner of the person mentioned in sub-paragraph (ii); and

(b) he was attending an educational course in the United Kingdom immediately before the qualified person [or the EEA national with a permanent right of residence] died or ceased to be a qualified person and continues to attend such a course.

(4) A person satisfies the conditions in this paragraph if the person is the parent with actual custody of a child who satisfies the condition in paragraph (3).

(5) A person satisfies the conditions in this paragraph if—

[(a) he ceased to be a family member of a qualified person or of an EEA national with a permanent right of residence on the termination of the marriage or civil partnership of that person;]

(b) he was residing in the United Kingdom in accordance with these Regulations at the date of the termination;

(c) he satisfies the condition in paragraph (6); and

(d) either—

(i) prior to the initiation of the proceedings for the termination of the marriage or the civil partnership the marriage or civil partnership had lasted for at least three years and the parties to the marriage or civil partnership had resided in the United Kingdom for at least one year during its duration;

(ii) the former spouse or civil partner of the qualified person [or the EEA national with a permanent right of residence] has custody of a child of the qualified person;

[(a) he ceased to be a family member of a qualified person or of an EEA national with a permanent right of residence on the termination of the marriage or civil partnership of that person;]

(iv) the continued right of residence in the United Kingdom of the person is warranted by particularly difficult circumstances, such as he or another family member having been a victim of domestic violence while the marriage or civil partnership was subsisting.

(6) The condition in this paragraph is that the person—

(a) is not an EEA national but would, if he were an EEA national, be a worker, a self-employed person or a self-sufficient person under regulation 6; or

(b) is the family member of a person who falls within paragraph (a).

(7) In this regulation, 'educational course' means a course within the scope of Article 12 of Council Regulation (EEC) No. 1612/68 on freedom of movement for workers.

(8) A person with a permanent right of residence under regulation 15 shall not become a family member who has retained the right of residence on the death or departure from the United Kingdom of the qualified person [or the EEA national with a permanent right of residence] or the termination of the marriage or civil partnership, as the case may be, and a family member who has retained the right of residence shall cease to have that status on acquiring a permanent right of residence under regulation 15.

Note: Paras 2(a), 5(a) and 5(d)(iii) substituted and words inserted in paras 2(b), 3(a)(iii), 3(b), 5(d)(ii), 8 and 3(a)(i) from 16 July 2012 (SI 2012/1547).

PART 2

EEA RIGHTS

Right of admission to the United Kingdom

11.—(1) An EEA national must be admitted to the United Kingdom if he produces on arrival a valid national identity card or passport issued by an EEA State.

(2) A person who is not an EEA national must be admitted to the United Kingdom if he is a family member of an EEA national, a family member who has retained the right of residence[, a person who meets the criteria in paragraph (5)] or a person with a permanent right of residence under regulation 15 and produces on arrival—

(a) a valid passport; and

(b) an EEA family permit, a residence card[, a derivative residence card] or a permanent residence card.

(3) An immigration officer may not place a stamp in the passport of a person admitted to the United Kingdom under this regulation who is not an EEA national if the person produces a residence card or permanent residence card.

(4) Before an immigration officer refuses admission to the United Kingdom to a person under this regulation because the person does not produce on arrival a document mentioned in paragraph (1) or (2), the immigration officer must give the person every reasonable opportunity to obtain the document or have it brought to him within a reasonable period of time or to prove by other means that he is—

(a) an EEA national;

(b) a family member of an EEA national with a right to accompany that national or join him in the United Kingdom;

[(ba) a person who meets the criteria in paragraph (5); or]

(c) a family member who has retained the right of residence or a person with a permanent right of residence under regulation 15.

[(5) A person ("P") meets the criteria in this paragraph where—

(a) P previously resided in the United Kingdom pursuant to regulation 15A(3) and would be entitled to reside in the United Kingdom pursuant to that regulation were P in the country;

(b) P is accompanying an EEA national to, or joining an EEA national in, the United Kingdom and P would be entitled to reside in the United Kingdom pursuant to regulation 15A(2) were P and the EEA national both in the United Kingdom;

(c) P is accompanying a person ("the relevant person") to, or joining the relevant person in, the United Kingdom and—

(i) the relevant person is residing, or has resided, in the United Kingdom pursuant to regulation 15A(3); and

(ii) P would be entitled to reside in the United Kingdom pursuant to regulation 15A(4) were P and the relevant person both in the United Kingdom.

(d) P is accompanying a person who meets the criteria in (b) or (c) ("the relevant person") to the United Kingdom and—

(i) P and the relevant person are both—

(aa) seeking admission to the United Kingdom in reliance on this paragraph for the first time; or

(bb) returning to the United Kingdom having previously resided there pursuant to the same provisions of regulation 15A in reliance on which they now base their claim to admission; and

(ii) P would be entitled to reside in the United Kingdom pursuant to regulation 15A(5) were P and the relevant person there.]

[(6) Paragraph (7) applies where—

(a) a person ("P") seeks admission to the United Kingdom in reliance on paragraph (5)(b) or (c); and

(b) if P were in the United Kingdom, P would have a derived right of residence by virtue of regulation 15A(7)(b)(ii).]

[(7) Where this paragraph applies a person ("P") will only be regarded as meeting the criteria in paragraph (5)(b) or (c) where P—

(a) is accompanying the person with whom P would on admission to the United Kingdom jointly share care responsibility for the purpose of regulation 15A(7)(b)(ii); or

(b) has previously resided in the United Kingdom pursuant to regulation 15A(2) or (4) as a joint primary carer and seeks admission to the United Kingdom in order to reside there again on the same basis.]

(8) But this regulation is subject to regulations 19(1) and (2).

Issue of EEA family permit

12. —(1) An entry clearance officer must issue an EEA family permit to a person who applies for one if the person is a family member of an EEA national and—

(a) the EEA national—

(i) is residing in the UK in accordance with these Regulations; or

(ii) will be travelling to the United Kingdom within six months of the date of the application and will be an EEA national residing in the United Kingdom in accordance with these Regulations on arrival in the United Kingdom; and

[(b) the family member will be accompanying the EEA national to the United Kingdom or joining the EEA national there.]

[(**1A**) An entry clearance officer must issue an EEA family permit to a person who applies and provides proof that, at the time at which he first intends to use the EEA family permit, he—

(a) would be entitled to be admitted to the United Kingdom by virtue of regulation 11(5); and

(b) will (save in the case of a person who would be entitled to be admitted to the United Kingdom by virtue of regulation 11(5)(a)) be accompanying to, or joining in, the United Kingdom any person from whom his right to be admitted to the United Kingdom under regulation 11(5) will be derived.]

[(**1B**) An entry clearance officer must issue an EEA family permit to a family member who has retained the right of residence.]

(**2**) An entry clearance officer may issue an EEA family permit to an extended family member of an EEA national who applies for one if—

(a) the relevant EEA national satisfies the condition in paragraph (1)(a);

(b) the extended family member wishes to accompany the relevant EEA national to the United Kingdom or to join him there; and

(c) in all the circumstances, it appears to the entry clearance officer appropriate to issue the EEA family permit.

(**3**) Where an entry clearance officer receives an application under paragraph (2) he shall undertake an extensive examination of the personal circumstances of the applicant and if he refuses the application shall give reasons justifying the refusal unless this is contrary to the interests of national security.

(**4**) An EEA family permit issued under this regulation shall be issued free of charge and as soon as possible.

(**5**) But an EEA family permit shall not be issued under this regulation if the applicant or the EEA national concerned [is subject to a deportation or exclusion order] {is not entitled to be admitted to the United Kingdom as a result of regulation 19(1A) or falls to be excluded in accordance with regulation 19(1B)}

[(**6**) An EEA family permit will not be issued under this regulation to a person ("A") who is the spouse, civil partner or durable partner of a person ("B") where a spouse, civil partner or durable partner of A or B holds a valid EEA family permit.]

Note: Paragraph (1)(b) substituted from 2 June 2011 (SI 2011/1247). Words in square brackets in para (5) inserted from 1 June 2009 (SI 2009/1117). Paras (1A) and (1B) inserted, words in curly brackets in para (5) substituted and para (6) inserted from 16 July 2012 (SI 2012/1547).

Initial right of residence

13.—(**1**) An EEA national is entitled to reside in the United Kingdom for a period not exceeding three months beginning on the date on which he is admitted to the United Kingdom provided that he holds a valid national identity card or passport issued by an EEA State.

(**2**) A family member of an EEA national [or a family member who has retained the right of residence who is] residing in the United Kingdom under paragraph (1) who is not himself an EEA national is entitled to reside in the United Kingdom provided that he holds a valid passport.

[(**3**) An EEA national or his family member who becomes an unreasonable burden on the social assistance system of the United Kingdom will cease to have a right to reside under this regulation.]

[(4) A person who otherwise satisfies the criteria in this regulation will not be entitled to reside in the United Kingdom under this regulation where the Secretary of State has made a decision under regulation 19(3)(b), 20(1) or 20A(1).]

Note: Words inserted in para (2), para 3 substituted and para (4) inserted from 16 July 2012 (SI 2012/1547).

Extended right of residence

14.—(1) A qualified person is entitled to reside in the United Kingdom for so long as he remains a qualified person.

(2) A family member of a qualified person residing in the United Kingdom under paragraph (1) or of an EEA national with a permanent right of residence under regulation 15 is entitled to reside in the United Kingdom for so long as he remains the family member of the qualified person or EEA national.

(3) A family member who has retained the right of residence is entitled to reside in the United Kingdom for so long as he remains a family member who has retained the right of residence.

(4) A right to reside under this regulation is in addition to any right a person may have to reside in the United Kingdom under regulation 13 or 15.

[(5) A person who otherwise satisfies the criteria in this regulation will not be entitled to a right to reside in the United Kingdom under this regulation where the Secretary of State has made a decision under regulation 19(3)(b), 20(1) or 20A(1).]

Note: Para (5) substituted from 16 July 2012 (SI 2012/1547).

Permanent right of residence

15.—(1) The following persons shall acquire the right to reside in the United Kingdom permanently—

(a) an EEA national who has resided in the United Kingdom in accordance with these Regulations for a continuous period of five years;

(b) a family member of an EEA national who is not himself an EEA national but who has resided in the United Kingdom with the EEA national in accordance with these Regulations for a continuous period of five years;

(c) a worker or self-employed person who has ceased activity;

(d) the family member of a worker or self-employed person who has ceased activity;

(e) a person who was the family member of a worker or self-employed person where—

(i) the worker or self-employed person has died;

(ii) the family member resided with him immediately before his death; and

(iii) the worker or self-employed person had resided continuously in the United Kingdom for at least the two years immediately before his death or the death was the result of an accident at work or an occupational disease;

(f) a person who—

(i) has resided in the United Kingdom in accordance with these Regulations for a continuous period of five years; and

(ii) was, at the end of that period, a family member who has retained the right of residence.

[(**1A**) Residence in the United Kingdom as a result of a derivative right of residence does not constitute residence for the purpose of this regulation;]

(**2**) [The] right of permanent residence under this regulation shall be lost only through absence from the United Kingdom for a period exceeding two consecutive years.

[(**3**) A person who satisfies the criteria in this regulation will not be entitled to a permanent right to reside in the United Kingdom where the Secretary of State has made a decision under regulation 19(3)(b), 20(1) or 20A(1).]

Note: Para (1A) inserted, words substituted in para (2) and para (3) substituted from 16 July 2012 (SI 2012/1547).

[15A. Derivative right of residence

(**1**) A person ("P") who is not entitled to reside in the United Kingdom as a result of any other provision of these Regulations and who satisfies the criteria in paragraph (2), (3), (4) or (5) of this regulation is entitled to a derivative right to reside in the United Kingdom for as long as P satisfies the relevant criteria.

(**2**) P satisfies the criteria in this paragraph if—
(a) P is the primary carer of an EEA national ("the relevant EEA national"); and
(b) the relevant EEA national—
(i) is under the age of 18;
(ii) is residing in the United Kingdom as a self-sufficient person; and
(iii) would be unable to remain in the United Kingdom if P were required to leave.

(**3**) P satisfies the criteria in this paragraph if—
(a) P is the child of an EEA national ("the EEA national parent");
(b) P resided in the United Kingdom at a time when the EEA national parent was residing in the United Kingdom as a worker; and
(c) P is in education in the United Kingdom and was in education there at a time when the EEA national parent was in the United Kingdom.

(**4**) P satisfies the criteria in this paragraph if—
(a) P is the primary carer of a person meeting the criteria in paragraph (3) ("the relevant person"); and
(b) the relevant person would be unable to continue to be educated in the United Kingdom if P were required to leave.

(**5**) P satisfies the criteria in this paragraph if—
(a) P is under the age of 18;
(b) P's primary carer is entitled to a derivative right to reside in the United Kingdom by virtue of paragraph (2) or (4);
(c) P does not have leave to enter, or remain in, the United Kingdom; and
(d) requiring P to leave the United Kingdom would prevent P's primary carer from residing in the United Kingdom.

(**6**) For the purpose of this regulation—
(a) "education" excludes nursery education; and
(b) "worker" does not include a jobseeker or a person who falls to be regarded as a worker by virtue of regulation 6(2).

(7) P is to be regarded as a "primary carer" of another person if

  (a) P is a direct relative or a legal guardian of that person; and

  (b) P—

    (i) is the person who has primary responsibility for that person's care; or

    (ii) shares equally the responsibility for that person's care with one other person who is not entitled to reside in the United Kingdom as a result of any other provision of these Regulations and who does not have leave to enter or remain.

(8) P will not be regarded as having responsibility for a person's care for the purpose of paragraph (7) on the sole basis of a financial contribution towards that person's care.

(9) A person who otherwise satisfies the criteria in paragraph (2), (3), (4) or (5) will not be entitled to a derivative right to reside in the United Kingdom where the Secretary of State has made a decision under regulation 19(3)(b), 20(1) or 20A(1).]

Note: Regulation 15A inserted from 16 July 2012 (SI 2012/1547).

[15B. Continuation of a right of residence

(1) This regulation applies during any period in which, but for the effect of regulation 13(4), 14(5), 15(3) or 15A(9), a person ("P") who is in the United Kingdom would be entitled to reside here pursuant to these Regulations.

(2) Where this regulation applies, any right of residence will (notwithstanding the effect of regulation 13(4), 14(5), 15(3) or 15A(9)) be deemed to continue during any period in which—

  (a) an appeal under regulation 26 could be brought, while P is in the United Kingdom, against a relevant decision (ignoring any possibility of an appeal out of time with permission); or

  (b) an appeal under regulation 26 against a relevant decision, brought while P is in the United Kingdom, is pending (within the meaning of section 104 of the 2002 Act).

(3) Periods during which residence pursuant to regulation 14 is deemed to continue as a result of paragraph (2) will not constitute residence for the purpose of regulation 15 unless and until—

  (a) a relevant decision is withdrawn by the Secretary of State; or

  (b) an appeal against a relevant decision is allowed and that appeal is finally determined (within the meaning of section 104 of the 2002 Act).

(4) Periods during which residence is deemed to continue as a result of paragraph (2) will not constitute residence for the purpose of regulation 21(4)(a) unless and until—

  (a) a relevant decision is withdrawn by the Secretary of State; or

  (b) an appeal against a relevant decision is allowed and that appeal is finally determined (within the meaning of section 104 of the 2002 Act).

(5) A "relevant decision" for the purpose of this regulation means a decision pursuant to regulation 19(3)(b), 20(1) or 20A(1) which would, but for the effect of paragraph (2), prevent P from residing in the United Kingdom pursuant to these Regulations.]

Note: Regulation 15B inserted from 16 July 2012 (SI 2012/1547).

PART 3
RESIDENCE DOCUMENTATION

Issue of registration certificate

16.—(1) The Secretary of State must issue a registration certificate to a qualified person immediately on application and production of—

(a) a valid identity card or passport issued by an EEA State;

(b) proof that he is a qualified person.

(2) In the case of a worker, confirmation of the worker's engagement from his employer or a certificate of employment is sufficient proof for the purposes of paragraph (1)(b).

(3) The Secretary of State must issue a registration certificate to an EEA national who is the family member of a qualified person or of an EEA national with a permanent right of residence under regulation 15 immediately on application and production of—

(a) a valid identity card or passport issued by an EEA State; and

(b) proof that the applicant is such a family member.

(4) The Secretary of State must issue a registration certificate to an EEA national who is a family member who has retained the right of residence on application and production of—

(a) a valid identity card or passport; and

(b) proof that the applicant is a family member who has retained the right of residence.

(5) The Secretary of State may issue a registration certificate to an extended family member not falling within regulation 7(3) who is an EEA national on application if—

(a) the relevant EEA national in relation to the extended family member is a qualified person or an EEA national with a permanent right of residence under regulation 15; and

(b) in all the circumstances it appears to the Secretary of State appropriate to issue the registration certificate.

(6) Where the Secretary of State receives an application under paragraph (5) he shall undertake an extensive examination of the personal circumstances of the applicant and if he refuses the application shall give reasons justifying the refusal unless this is contrary to the interests of national security.

(7) A registration certificate issued under this regulation shall state the name and address of the person registering and the date of registration and shall be issued free of charge.

(8) [But this regulation is subject to regulations 7A(6) and 20(1).]

Note: Paragraph (8) substituted from 1 May 2011 (SI 2011/544).

Issue of residence card

17.—(1) The Secretary of State must issue a residence card to a person who is not an EEA national and is the family member of a qualified person or of an EEA national with a permanent right of residence under regulation 15 on application and production of—

(a) a valid passport; and

(b) proof that the applicant is such a family member.

(2) The Secretary of State must issue a residence card to a person who is not an EEA national but who is a family member who has retained the right of residence on application and production of—

(a) a valid passport; and

(b) proof that the applicant is a family member who has retained the right of residence.

(3) On receipt of an application under paragraph (1) or (2) and the documents that are required to accompany the application the Secretary of State shall immediately issue the applicant with a certificate of application for the residence card and the residence card shall be issued no later than six months after the date on which the application and documents are received.

(4) The Secretary of State may issue a residence card to an extended family member not falling within regulation 7(3) who is not an EEA national on application if—

(a) the relevant EEA national in relation to the extended family member is a qualified person or an EEA national with a permanent right of residence under regulation 15; and

(b) in all the circumstances it appears to the Secretary of State appropriate to issue the residence card.

(5) Where the Secretary of State receives an application under paragraph (4) he shall undertake an extensive examination of the personal circumstances of the applicant and if he refuses the application shall give reasons justifying the refusal unless this is contrary to the interests of national security.

(6) A residence card issued under this regulation may take the form of a stamp in the applicant's passport and shall be [...] valid for—

(a) five years from the date of issue; or

(b) in the case of a residence card issued to the family member or extended family member of a qualified person, the envisaged period of residence in the United Kingdom of the qualified person,

whichever is the shorter.

[(6A) A residence card issued under this regulation shall be entitled 'Residence card of a family member of an EEA national' or 'Residence card of a family member who has retained the right of residence', as the case may be.]

(7) A residence card issued under this regulation shall be issued free of charge.

(8) But this regulation is subject to regulation 20(1) and (1A)].

Note: Words omitted from paragraph (6), paragraph (6A) inserted and words in square brackets in paragraph (8) substituted from 1 June 2009 (SI 2009/1117).

Issue of a document certifying permanent residence and a permanent residence card

18.—(1) The Secretary of State must issue an EEA national with a permanent right of residence under regulation 15 with a document certifying permanent residence as soon as possible after an application for such a document and proof that the EEA national has such a right is submitted to the Secretary of State.

(2) The Secretary of State must issue a person who is not an EEA national who has a permanent right of residence under regulation 15 with a permanent residence card no

later than six months after the date on which an application for a permanent residence card and proof that the person has such a right is submitted to the Secretary of State.

(3) Subject to paragraph (5) [...], a permanent residence card shall be valid for ten years from the date of issue and must be renewed on application.

(4) A document certifying permanent residence and a permanent residence card shall be issued free of charge.

(5) A document certifying permanent residence and a permanent residence card shall cease to be valid if the holder ceases to have a right of permanent residence under regulation 15.

[(6) But this regulation is subject to regulation 20.]

Note: Words omitted from paragraph (3) and paragraph (6) inserted from 1 June 2009 (SI 2009/1117).

[18A. Issue of a derivative residence card

(1) The Secretary of State must issue a person with a derivative residence card on application and on production of—
    (a) a valid identity card issued by an EEA State or a valid passport; and
    (b) proof that the applicant has a derivative right of residence under regulation 15A.

(2) On receipt of an application under paragraph (1) the Secretary of State must issue the applicant with a certificate of application as soon as possible.

(3) A derivative residence card issued under paragraph (1) may take the form of a stamp in the applicant's passport and will be valid until—
    (a) a date five years from the date of issue; or
    (b) any other date specified by the Secretary of State when issuing the derivative residence card.

(4) A derivative residence card issued under paragraph (1) must be issued free of charge and as soon as practicable.

(5) But this regulation is subject to regulations 20(1) and 20(1A).]

Note: Regulation 18A inserted from 16 July 2012 (SI 2012/1547).

PART 4

REFUSAL OF ADMISSION AND REMOVAL ETC

Exclusion and removal from the United Kingdom

19.—(1) A person is not entitled to be admitted to the United Kingdom by virtue of regulation 11 if his exclusion is justified on grounds of public policy, public security or public health in accordance with regulation 21.

[(1A) A person is not entitled to be admitted to the United Kingdom by virtue of regulation 11 if that person is subject to a deportation or exclusion order.

(1B) If the Secretary of State considers that the exclusion of an EEA national or the family member of an EEA national is justified on the grounds of public policy, public security or public health in accordance with regulation 21 the Secretary of State may make an order for the purpose of these Regulations prohibiting that person from entering the United Kingdom.]

(2) A person is not entitled to be admitted to the United Kingdom as the family member of an EEA national under regulation 11(2) unless, at the time of his arrival—

(a) he is accompanying the EEA national or joining him in the United Kingdom; and

(b) the EEA national has a right to reside in the United Kingdom under these Regulations.

[(3) Subject to paragraphs (4) and (5), an EEA national who has entered the United Kingdom or the family member of such a national who has entered the United Kingdom may be removed if –

(a) that person does not have or ceases to have a right to reside under these Regulations; or

(b) the Secretary of State has decided that the person's removal is justified on grounds of public policy, public security or public health in accordance with regulation 21.]

(4) A person must not be removed under paragraph (3) as the automatic consequence of having recourse to the social assistance system of the United Kingdom.

(5) A person must not be removed under paragraph (3) if he has a right to remain in the United Kingdom by virtue of leave granted under the 1971 Act unless his removal is justified on the grounds of public policy, public security or public health in accordance with regulation 21.

Note : Paragraph (1A) and (1B) inserted and paragraph (3) substituted from 1 June 2009 (SI 2009/1117).

Refusal to issue or renew and revocation of residence documentation

20.—(1) The Secretary of State may refuse to issue, revoke or refuse to renew a registration certificate, a residence card, a document certifying permanent residence or a permanent residence card if the refusal or revocation is justified on grounds of public policy, public security or public health.

[(1A) {A decision under regulation 19(3) to remove a person from the United Kingdom will (save during any period in which a right of residence is deemed to continue as a result of regulation 15B(2)) invalidate} a registration certificate, residence card, document certifying permanent residence or permanent residence card held by that person or an application made by that person for such a certificate, card or document.]

(2) The Secretary of State may revoke a registration certificate or a residence card or refuse to renew a residence card if the holder of the certificate or card has ceased to have a right to reside under these Regulations.

(3) The Secretary of State may revoke a document certifying permanent residence or a permanent residence card or refuse to renew a permanent residence card if the holder of the certificate or card has ceased to have a right of permanent residence under regulation 15.

(4) An immigration officer may, at the time of a person's arrival in the United Kingdom—

(a) revoke that person's residence card if he is not at that time the family member of a qualified person or of an EEA national who has a right of permanent residence under regulation 15, a family member who has retained the right of residence or a person with a right of permanent residence under regulation 15;

(b) revoke that person's permanent residence card if he is not at that time a person with a right of permanent residence under regulation 15.

(5) [An entry clearance officer or immigration officer may at any time revoke a person's] EEA family permit if—

(a) the revocation is justified on grounds of public policy, public security or public health; or

(b) the person is not at that time the family member of an EEA national with the right to reside in the United Kingdom under these Regulations or is not accompanying that national or joining him in the United Kingdom.

(6) Any action taken under this regulation on grounds of public policy, public security or public health shall be in accordance with regulation 21.

Note: Paragraph (1A) inserted and words in square brackets in para (5) substituted from 1 June 2009 (SI 2009/1117). Words in curly brackets in para (1A) substituted from 16 July 2012 (SI 2012/1547).

[20A. Cancellation of a right of residence

(1) Where the conditions in paragraph (2) are met the Secretary of State may cancel a person's right to reside in the United Kingdom pursuant to these Regulations.

(2) The conditions in this paragraph are met where—

(a) a person has a right to reside in the United Kingdom as a result of these Regulations;

(b) the Secretary of State has decided that the cancellation of that person's right to reside in the United Kingdom is justified on grounds of public policy, public security or public health in accordance with regulation 21;

(c) the circumstances are such that the Secretary of State cannot make a decision under regulation 20(1); and

(d) it is not possible for the Secretary of State to remove the person from the United Kingdom pursuant to regulation 19(3)(b).]

Note: Regulation 20A inserted from 16 July 2012 (SI 2012/1547).

Decisions taken on public policy, public security and public health grounds

21.—(1) In this regulation a 'relevant decision' means an EEA decision taken on the grounds of public policy, public security or public health.

(2) A relevant decision may not be taken to serve economic ends.

(3) A relevant decision may not be taken in respect of a person with a permanent right of residence under regulation 15 except on serious grounds of public policy or public security.

(4) A relevant decision may not be taken except on imperative grounds of public security in respect of an EEA national who—

(a) has resided in the United Kingdom for a continuous period of at least ten years prior to the relevant decision; or

(b) is under the age of 18, unless the relevant decision is necessary in his best interests, as provided for in the Convention on the Rights of the Child adopted by the General Assembly of the United Nations on 20th November 1989.

(5) Where a relevant decision is taken on grounds of public policy or public security it shall, in addition to complying with the preceding paragraphs of this regulation, be taken in accordance with the following principles—

(a) the decision must comply with the principle of proportionality;

(b) the decision must be based exclusively on the personal conduct of the person concerned;

(c) the personal conduct of the person concerned must represent a genuine, present and sufficiently serious threat affecting one of the fundamental interests of society;

(d) matters isolated from the particulars of the case or which relate to considerations of general prevention do not justify the decision;

(e) a person's previous criminal convictions do not in themselves justify the decision.

(6) Before taking a relevant decision on the grounds of public policy or public security in relation to a person who is resident in the United Kingdom the decision maker must take account of considerations such as the age, state of health, family and economic situation of the person, the person's length of residence in the United Kingdom, the person's social and cultural integration into the United Kingdom and the extent of the person's links with his country of origin.

(7) In the case of a relevant decision taken on grounds of public health—

(a) a disease that does not have epidemic potential as defined by the relevant instruments of the World Health Organisation or is not a disease [listed in Schedule 1 to the Health Protection (Notification) Regulations 2010] shall not constitute grounds for the decision; and

(b) if the person concerned is in the United Kingdom, diseases occurring after the three month period beginning on the date on which he arrived in the United Kingdom shall not constitute grounds for the decision.

Note: Words substituted (England, Scotland and Northern Ireland only) in para (7)(a) from 6 April 2010 (SI 2010/708) and (Wales) from 26 July 2010 (SI 2010/1593)

[21A. Application of Part 4 to persons with a derivative right of residence

(1) Where this regulation applies Part 4 of these Regulations applies subject to the modifications listed in paragraph (3).

(2) This regulation applies where a person—

(a) would, notwithstanding Part 4 of these Regulations, have a right to be admitted to, or reside in, the United Kingdom by virtue of a derivative right of residence arising under regulation 15A(2), (4) or (5);

(b) holds a derivative residence card; or

(c) has applied for a derivative residence card.

(3) Where this regulation applies Part 4 applies in relation to the matters listed in paragraph (2) as if—

(a) references to a matter being "justified on grounds of public policy, public security or public health in accordance with regulation 21" referred instead to a matter being "conducive to the public good";

(b) the reference in regulation 20(5)(a) to a matter being "justified on grounds of public policy, public security or public health" referred instead to a matter being "conducive to the public good";

(c) references to "the family member of an EEA national" referred instead to "a person with a derivative right of residence";

(d) references to "a registration certificate, a residence card, a document certifying permanent residence or a permanent residence card" referred instead to "a derivative residence card";

(e) the reference in regulation 19(1A) to a deportation or exclusion order referred also to a deportation or exclusion order made under any provision of the immigration Acts.

(f) regulation 20(4) instead conferred on an immigration officer the power to revoke a derivative residence card where the holder is not at that time a person with a derivative right of residence; and

(g) regulations 20(3), 20(6) and 21 were omitted.]

Note: Regulation 21A inserted from 16 July 2012 (SI 2012/1547).

PART 5

PROCEDURE IN RELATION TO EEA DECISIONS

Person claiming right of admission

22.—(1) This regulation applies to a person who claims a right of admission to the United Kingdom under regulation 11 as—

(a) a person, not being an EEA national, who is a family member of an EEA national, a family member who has retained the right of residence[, a person who has a derivative right of residence] or a person with a permanent right of residence under regulation 15; or

[(b) an EEA national, where there is reason to believe that he may fall to be excluded under regulation 19(1) or (1A).]

(2) A person to whom this regulation applies is to be treated as if he were a person seeking leave to enter the United Kingdom under the 1971 Act for the purposes of paragraphs 2, 3, 4, 7, 16 to 18 and 21 to 24 of Schedule 2 to the 1971 Act (administrative provisions as to control on entry etc), except that—

(a) the reference in paragraph 2(1) to the purpose for which the immigration officer may examine any persons who have arrived in the United Kingdom is to be read as a reference to the purpose of determining whether he is a person who is to be granted admission under these Regulations;

(b) the references in paragraphs 4(2A), 7 and 16(1) to a person who is, or may be, given leave to enter are to be read as references to a person who is, or may be, granted admission under these Regulations; and

(c) a medical examination is not to be carried out under paragraph 2 or paragraph 7 as a matter of routine and may only be carried out within three months of a person's arrival in the United Kingdom.

(3) For so long as a person to whom this regulation applies is detained, or temporarily admitted or released while liable to detention, under the powers conferred by Schedule 2 to the 1971 Act, he is deemed not to have been admitted to the United Kingdom.

Note : Paragraph (1)(b) substituted from 1 June 2009 (SI s009/1117). Words inserted in para 1(a) from 16 July 2012 (SI 2012/1547)

Person refused admission

23.—(1) This regulation applies to a person who is in the United Kingdom and has been refused admission to the United Kingdom—

(a) because he does not meet the requirement of regulation 11 (including where he does not meet those requirements because his EEA family permit, residence card[, derivative residence card] or permanent residence card has been revoked by an immigration officer in accordance with regulation 20); or

(b) in accordance with regulation [19(1), (1A) or (2)].

(2) A person to whom this regulation applies, is to be treated as if he were a person refused leave to enter under the 1971 Act for the purpose of paragraphs 8, 10, 10A, 11, 16 to 19 and 21 to 24 of Schedule 2 to the 1971 Act, except that the reference in paragraph 19 to a certificate of entitlement, entry clearance or work permit is to be read as a reference to an EEA family permit, residence card[, derivative residence card] or a permanent residence card.

Note : Words in square brackets in paragraph (1)(b) substituted from 1 June 2009 (SI 2009/1117). Wo)rds inserted in para 1(a) and para (2) from 16 july 2012 (SI 2012/1547).

Person subject to removal

24.—[(1) If there are reasonable grounds for suspecting that a person is someone who may be removed from the United Kingdom under [regulation 19(3)(b)], that person may be detained under the authority of {the Secretary of State] pending a decision whether or not to remove the person under that regulation, and paragraphs 17 and 18 of Schedule 2 to the 1971 Act shall apply in relation to the detention of such a person as those paragraphs apply in relation to a person who may be detained under paragraph 16 of that Schedule.]

(2) [Where a decision is taken to remove a person] under regulation 19(3)(a), the person is to be treated as if he were a person to whom section 10(1)(a) of the 1999 Act applied, and section 10 of that Act (removal of certain persons unlawfully in the United Kingdom) is to apply accordingly.

(3) [Where a decision is taken to remove a person] under regulation 19(3)(b), the person is to be treated as if he were a person to whom section 3(5)(a) of the 1971 Act (liability to deportation) applied, and section 5 of that Act (procedure for deportation) and Schedule 3 to that Act (supplementary provision as to deportation) are to apply accordingly.

(4) A person who enters the United Kingdom in breach of a deportation or exclusion order shall be removable as an illegal entrant under Schedule 2 to the 1971 Act and the provisions of that Schedule shall apply accordingly].

(5) Where such a deportation order is made against a person but he is not removed under the order during the two year period beginning on the date on which the order is made, the Secretary of State shall only take action to remove the person under the order after the end of that period if, having assessed whether there has been any material change in circumstances since the deportation order was made, he considers that the removal continues to be justified on the grounds of public policy, public security or public health.

(6) A person to whom this regulation applies shall be allowed one month to leave the United Kingdom, beginning on the date on which he is notified of the decision to remove him, before being removed pursuant to that decision except—

(a) in duly substantiated cases of urgency;

(b) where the person is detained pursuant to the sentence or order of any court;

(c) where a person is a person to whom regulation 24(4) applies.

[(7) Paragraph (6) of this regulation does not apply where a decision has been taken under regulation 19(3) on the basis that the relevant person—

(a) has ceased to have a derivative right of residence; or

(b) is a person who would have had a derivative right of residence but for the effect of a decision to remove under regulation 19(3)(b).]

Note : Words in square brackets substituted from 1 June 2009 (SI 2009/1117). Para (1) amended and para (7) inserted from 16 July 2012 (SI 2012/1547).

[**24A.**—(1) A deportation or exclusion order shall remain in force unless it is revoked by the Secretary of State under this regulation.

(2) A person who is subject to a deportation or exclusion order may apply to the Secretary of State to have it revoked if the person considers that there has been a material change in the circumstances that justified the making of the order.

(3) An application under paragraph (2) shall set out the material change in circumstances relied upon by the applicant and may only be made whilst the applicant is outside the United Kingdom.

(4) On receipt of an application under paragraph (2), the Secretary of State shall revoke the order if the Secretary of State considers thatthe criteria for making such an order are no longer satisfied].

(5) The Secretary of State shall take a decision on an application under paragraph (2) no later than six months after the date on which the application is received.]

Note: Regulation (24A) inserted from 1 June 2009 (SI 2009/1117). Words substituted in para (4) from 16 July 2012 (SI 2012/1547).

PART 6
APPEALS UNDER THESE REGULATIONS

Interpretation of Part 6

25.—(1) In this Part—

...

['Asylum claim' has the meaning given in section 113(1) of the 2002 Act;]

'Commission' has the same meaning as in the Special Immigration Appeals Commission Act 1997;

...

['Human rights claim' has the meaning given in section 113(1) of the 2002 Act.]

(2) For the purposes of this Part, and subject to paragraphs (3) and (4), an appeal is to be treated as pending during the period when notice of appeal is given and ending when the appeal is finally determined, withdrawn or abandoned.

(3) An appeal is not to be treated as finally determined while a further appeal may be brought; and, if such a further appeal is brought, the original appeal is not to be

treated as finally determined until the further appeal is determined, withdrawn or abandoned.

(4) A pending appeal is not to be treated as abandoned solely because the appellant leaves the United Kingdom.

Note: Words omitted from 15 February 2010 (SI 2010/21) and from 16 July 2012 (SI 2012/1547). Definitions of 'asylum claim' and 'human rights claim' inserted from 16 July 2012 (SI 2012/1547).

Appeal rights

26.—(1) Subject to the following paragraphs of this regulation, a person may appeal under these Regulations against an EEA decision.

(2) If a person claims to be an EEA national, he may not appeal under these Regulations unless he produces a valid national identity card or passport issued by an EEA State.

[(3) If a person claims to be a family member who has retained the right of residence or the family member or relative of an EEA national he may not appeal under these Regulations unless he produces—

(a) a valid national identity card issued by an EEA State or a passport; and

(b) either—

(i) an EEA family permit;

(ii) proof that he is the family member or relative of an EEA national; or

(iii) in the case of a person claiming to be a family member who has retained the right of residence, proof that he was a family member of the relevant person.]

[3A] If a person claims to be a person with a derivative right of residence he may not appeal under these Regulations unless he produces a valid national identity card issued by an EEA State or a passport, and either—

(a) an EEA family permit; or

(b) proof that—

(i) where the person claims to have a derivative right of residence under regulation 15A(2), he is a direct relative or guardian of an EEA national who is under the age of 18;

(ii) where the person claims to have a derivative right of residence under regulation 15A(3), he is the child of an EEA national;

(iii) where the person claims to have a derivative right of residence under regulation 15A(4), he is a direct relative or guardian of the child of an EEA national;

(iv) where the person claims to have a derivative right of residence under regulation 15A(5), he is under the age of 18 and is a dependant of a person satisfying the criteria in (i) or (iii).]

(4) A person may not bring an appeal under these Regulations on a ground certified under paragraph (5) or rely on such a ground in an appeal brought under these Regulations.

(5) The Secretary of State or an immigration officer may certify a ground for the purposes of paragraph (4) if it has been considered in a previous appeal brought under these Regulations or under section 82(1) of the 2002 Act.

(6) Except where an appeal lies to the Commission, an appeal under these Regulations lies to the [First-tier Tribunal].

(7) The provisions of or made under the 2002 Act referred to in Schedule 1 shall have effect for the purposes of an appeal under these Regulations to the [First-tier Tribunal] in accordance with that Schedule.

Note: Words in square brackets in paras (6) and (7) substituted from 15 February 2010 (SI 2010/21). Para (3) substituted and para (3A) inserted from 16 july 2012 (SI 2012/1547).

Out of country appeals

27.—(1) Subject to paragraphs (2) and (3), a person may not appeal under regulation 26 whilst he is in the United Kingdom against an EEA decision—

(a) to refuse to admit him to the United Kingdom;

[(aa) to make an exclusion order against him;]

(b) to refuse to revoke a deportation [or exclusion] order made against him;

(c) to refuse to issue him with an EEA family permit;

{(ca) to revoke, or to refuse to issue or renew any document under these Regulations where that decision is taken at a time when the relevant person is outside the United Kingdom; or}

[(d) to remove him from the United Kingdom after he has entered the United Kingdom in breach of a deportation or exclusion order].

(2) [Paragraphs (1)(a) and (aa) do not apply where the person is in the United Kingdom and]

(a) the person held [a valid EEA family permit, registration certificate, residence card, {derivative residence card,} document certifying permanent residence or permanent residence card], a registration certificate, a residence card, a document certifying permanent residence or a permanent residence card on his arrival in the United Kingdom or can otherwise prove that he is resident in the United Kingdom;

(b) the person is deemed not to have been admitted to the United Kingdom under regulation 22(3) but at the date on which notice of the decision to refuse to admit him is given he has been in the United Kingdom for at least 3 months; [or]

{(c) has made an asylum or human rights claim (or both), unless the Secretary of State has certified that the claim or claims is or are clearly unfounded.} {(3) Paragraph (1)(d) does not apply where the person has made an asylum or human rights claim (or both), unless the Secretary of State has certified that the claim or claims is or are clearly unfounded.}

Note: Para (1)(aa) and words in square brackets in paras (1)(b) and (2)(c) inserted and other words in square brackets substituted from 1 June 2009 (SI 2009/1117). Para (1)(ca) inserted, words in para (2) inserted and paras (2)(c) and (3) substituted from 16 July 2012 (SI 2012/1547).

Appeals to the Commission

28.—(1) An appeal against an EEA decision lies to the Commission where paragraph (2) or (4) applies.

(2) This paragraph applies if the Secretary of State certifies that the EEA decision was taken—

(a) by the Secretary of State wholly or partly on a ground listed in paragraph (3); or

(b) in accordance with a direction of the Secretary of State which identifies the person to whom the decision relates and which is given wholly or partly on a ground listed in paragraph (3).

(3) The grounds mentioned in paragraph (2) are that the person's exclusion or removal from the United Kingdom is—

(a) in the interests of national security; or

(b) in the interests of the relationship between the United Kingdom and another country.

(4) This paragraph applies if the Secretary of State certifies that the EEA decision was taken wholly or partly in reliance on information which in his opinion should not be made public—

(a) in the interests of national security;

(b) in the interests of the relationship between the United Kingdom and another country; or

(c) otherwise in the public interest.

(5) In paragraphs (2) and (4) a reference to the Secretary of State is to the Secretary of State acting in person.

(6) Where a certificate is issued under paragraph (2); or (4); in respect of a pending appeal to the [First-tier Tribunal or Upper Tribunal] the appeal shall lapse.

(7) An appeal against an EEA decision lies to the Commission where an appeal lapses by virtue of paragraph (6).

(8) The Special Immigration Appeals Commission Act 1997 shall apply to an appeal to the Commission under these Regulations as it applies to an appeal under section 2 of that Act to which subsection (2) of that section applies (appeals against an immigration decision) but paragraph (i) of that subsection shall not apply in relation to such an appeal.

Note: Words in square brackets substituted from 15 February 2010 (SI 2010/21)

Effect of appeals to the [First-tier Tribunal or Upper Tribunal]

29.—(1) This Regulation applies to appeals under these Regulations made to the [First-tierTribunal or Upper Tribunal].

(2) If a person in the United Kingdom appeals against an EEA decision to refuse to admit him to the United Kingdom, any directions for his removal from the United Kingdom previously given by virtue of the refusal cease to have effect, except in so far as they have already been carried out, and no directions may be so given while the appeal is pending.

(3) If a person in the United Kingdom appeals against an EEA decision to remove him from the United Kingdom, any directions given under section 10 of the 1999 Act or Schedule 3 to the 1971 Act for his removal from the United Kingdom are to have no effect, except in so far as they have already been carried out, while the appeal is pending.

(4) But the provisions of Part I of Schedule 2, or as the case may be, Schedule 3 to the 1971 Act with respect to detention and persons liable to detention apply to a person appealing against a refusal to admit him or a decision to remove him as if there were in force directions for his removal from the United Kingdom, except that he may not be detained on board a ship or aircraft so as to compel him to leave the United Kingdom while the appeal is pending.

(5) In calculating the period of two months limited by paragraph 8(2) of Schedule 2 to the 1971 Act for—

(a) the giving of directions under that paragraph for the removal of a person from the United Kingdom; and

(b) the giving of a notice of intention to give such directions, any period during which there is pending an appeal by him is to be disregarded.

(6) If a person in the United Kingdom appeals against an EEA decision to remove him from the United Kingdom, a deportation order is not to be made against him under section 5 of the 1971 Act while the appeal is pending.

(7) Paragraph 29 of Schedule 2 to the 1971 Act (grant of bail pending appeal) applies to a person who has an appeal pending under these Regulations as it applies to a person who has an appeal pending under section 82(1) of the 2002 Act.

Note: Words in square brackets substituted from 15 February 2010 (SI 2010/21).

PART 7
GENERAL

Effect on other legislation

30. Schedule 2 (effect on other legislation) shall have effect.

Revocations, transitional provisions and consequential amendments

31. —(1) The Regulations listed in column 1 of the table in Part 1 of Schedule 3 are revoked to the extent set out in column 3 of that table, subject to Part 2 of that Schedule and to Schedule 4.

(2) Schedule 4 (transitional provisions) and Schedule 5 (consequential amendments) shall have effect.

Regulation 26(7)   SCHEDULE 1

APPEALS TO THE [FIRST-TIER TRIBUNAL OR UPPER TRIBUNAL]

[1.] The following provisions of, or made under, the 2002 Act have effect in relation to an appeal under these Regulations to the [First-tier Tribunal or Upper Tribunal] Asylum and Immigration Tribunal as if it were an appeal against an immigration decision under section 82(1) of that Act:

section 84(1), except paragraphs (a) and (f);

sections 85 to 87;

…;

section 105 and any regulations made under that section; and

section 106 and any rules made under that section.

[2. Tribunal Procedure Rules have effect in relation to appeals under these Regulations.]

Note: Words in square brackets substituted, other words omitted and paragraph 2 inserted from 15 February 2010 (SI 2010/21).

Regulation 30   SCHEDULE 2

EFFECT ON OTHER LEGISLATION

Leave under the 1971 Act

1.—**(1)** In accordance with section 7 of the Immigration Act 1988, a person who is admitted to or acquires a right to reside in the United Kingdom under these Regulations shall not require leave to remain in the United Kingdom under the 1971 Act during any period in which he has a right to reside under these Regulations but such a person shall require leave to remain under the 1971 Act during any period in which he does not have such a right.

(2) [Subject to sub-paragraph (3),] Where a person has leave to enter or remain under the 1971 Act which is subject to conditions and that person also has a right to reside under these Regulations, those conditions shall not have effect for as long as the person has that right to reside.

[**(3)** Where the person mentioned in sub-paragraph (2) is an accession State national subject to worker authorisation working in the United Kingdom during the accession period and the document endorsed to show that the person has leave is an accession worker authorisation document, any conditions to which that leave is subject restricting his employment shall continue to apply. **(4)** In sub-paragraph (3)—

(a) 'accession period' has the meaning given in regulation 1(2)(c) of the Accession (Immigration and Worker Authorisation) Regulations 2006;

(b) 'accession State national subject to worker authorisation' has the meaning given in regulation 2 of those Regulations; and

(c) 'accession worker authorisation document' has the meaning given in regulation 9(2) of those Regulations.]

Persons not subject to restriction on the period for which they may remain

2.—**(1)** For the purposes of the 1971 Act and the British Nationality Act 1981, a person who has a permanent right of residence under regulation 15 shall be regarded as a person who is in the United Kingdom without being subject under the immigration laws to any restriction on the period for which he may remain.

(2) But a qualified person, the family member of a qualified person[, a person with a derivative right of residence] and a family member who has retained the right of residence shall not, by virtue of that status, be so regarded for those purposes.

Carriers' liability under the 1999 Act

3. For the purposes of satisfying a requirement to produce a visa under section 40(1)(b) of the 1999 Act (charges in respect of passenger without proper documents), 'a visa of the required kind' includes an EEA family permit, a residence card[, a derivative residence card] or a permanent residence card required for admission under regulation 11(2).

Appeals under the 2002 Act and previous immigration Acts

4.—**(1)** The following EEA decisions shall not be treated as immigration decisions for the purpose of section 82(2) of the 2002 Act (right of appeal against an immigration decision)—

(a) a decision that a person is to be removed under regulation 19(3)(a) by way of a direction under section 10(1)(a) of the 1999 Act (as provided for by regulation 24(2));

(b) a decision to remove a person under regulation 19(3)(b) by making a deportation order under section 5(1) of the 1971 Act (as provided for by regulation 24(3));

(c) a decision to remove a person mentioned in regulation 24(4) by way of directions under paragraphs 8 to 10 of Schedule 2 to the 1971 Act.

(**2**) A person who has been issued with a registration certificate, residence card, [derivative residence card,] a document certifying permanent residence or a permanent residence card under these Regulations or a registration certificate under the Accession (Immigration and Worker Registration) Regulations 2004, [or an accession worker card under the Accession (Immigration and Worker Authorisation) Regulations 2006,] or a person whose passport has been stamped with a family member residence stamp, shall have no right of appeal under section 2 of the Special Immigration Appeals Commission Act 1997 or section 82(1) of the 2002 Act. Any existing appeal under those sections of those Acts or under the Asylum and Immigration Appeals Act 1993, the Asylum and Immigration Act 1996 or the 1999 Act shall be treated as abandoned.

(**3**) Subject to paragraph (4), a person may appeal to the [First-tier Tribunal] under section 83(2) of the 2002 Act against the rejection of his asylum claim where—

(a) that claim has been rejected, but

(b) he has a right to reside in the United Kingdom under these Regulations.

(**4**) Paragraph (3) shall not apply if the person is an EEA national and the Secretary of State certifies that the asylum claim is clearly unfounded.

(**5**) The Secretary of State shall certify the claim under paragraph (4) unless satisfied that it is not clearly unfounded.

(**6**) In addition to the national of a State which is a contracting party to the Agreement referred to in section 84(2) of the 2002 Act, a Swiss national shall also be treated as an EEA national for the purposes of section 84(1)(d) of that Act.

(**7**) An appeal under these Regulations against an EEA decision (including an appeal made on or after 1 April 2003 which is treated as an appeal under these Regulations under Schedule 4 but not an appeal made before that date) shall be treated as an appeal under section 82(1) of the 2002 Act against an immigration decision for the purposes of section 96(1)(a) of the 2002 Act.

(**8**) Section 120 of the 2002 Act shall apply to a person if an EEA decision has been taken or may be taken in respect of him and, accordingly, the Secretary of State or an immigration officer may by notice require a statement from that person under subsection (2) of that section and that notice shall have effect for the purpose of section 96(2) of the 2002 Act.

(**9**) In sub-paragraph [(2)], 'family member residence stamp' means a stamp in the passport of a family member of an EEA national confirming that he is the family member of an accession State worker requiring registration [or an accession State national subject to worker authorisation working in the United Kingdom] with a right of residence under these Regulations as the family member of that worker; and in this sub- paragraph 'accession State worker requiring registration' has the same meaning as in regulation 2 of the Accession (Immigration and Worker Registration) Regulations 2004 [and 'accession State national subject to worker authorisation' has the meaning given in regulation 2 of the Accession (Immigration and Worker Authorisation) Regulations 2006].

Note: Words in paragraph 4(3) substituted from 15 February 2010 (SI 2010/21). Words inserted in paras 2(2), 3 and 4(2) inserted and para 2(9) amended from 16 July 2012 (SI 2012/1547). Other words in square brackets in Schedule 2 inserted from 1 January 2007, (SI 2006/3317).

Regulation 31(2)   SCHEDULE 3

REVOCATIONS AND SAVINGS

PART 1

TABLE OF REVOCATIONS

...

PART 2

SAVINGS

1. The—

(a) Immigration (Swiss Free Movement of Persons) (No. 3) Regulations 2002 are not revoked insofar as they apply the 2000 Regulations to posted workers; and

(b) the 2000 Regulations and the Regulations amending the 2000 Regulations are not revoked insofar as they are so applied to posted workers;

and, accordingly, the 2000 Regulations, as amended, shall continue to apply to posted workers in accordance with the Immigration (Swiss Free Movement of Persons) (No. 3) Regulations 2002.

2. In paragraph 1, 'the 2000 Regulations' means the Immigration (European Economic Area) Regulations 2000 and 'posted worker' has the meaning given in regulation 2(4)(b) of the Immigration (Swiss Free Movement of Persons) (No. 3) Regulations 2002.

Regulation 31(2)   SCHEDULE 4

TRANSITIONAL PROVISIONS

Interpretation

1. In this Schedule—

(a) the '2000 Regulations' means the Immigration (European Economic Area) Regulations 2000 and expressions used in relation to documents issued or applied for under those Regulations shall have the meaning given in regulation 2 of those Regulations;

(b) the 'Accession Regulations' means the Accession (Immigration and Worker Registration) Regulations 2004.

Existing documents

2.—(1) An EEA family permit issued under the 2000 Regulations shall, after 29 April 2006, be treated as if it were an EEA family permit issued under these Regulations.

(2) Subject to paragraph (4), a residence permit issued under the 2000 Regulations shall, after 29 April 2006, be treated as if it were a registration certificate issued under these Regulations.

(3) Subject to paragraph (5), a residence document issued under the 2000 Regulations shall, after 29 April 2006, be treated as if it were a residence card issued under these Regulations.

(4) Where a residence permit issued under the 2000 Regulations has been endorsed under the immigration rules to show permission to remain in the United Kingdom indefinitely it shall, after 29 April 2006, be treated as if it were a document certifying permanent residence issued under these Regulations and the holder of the permit shall be treated as a person with a permanent right of residence under regulation 15.

(5) Where a residence document issued under the 2000 Regulations has been endorsed under the immigration rules to show permission to remain in the United Kingdom indefinitely it shall, after 29 April 2006, be treated as if it were a permanent residence card issued under these Regulations and the holder of the permit shall be treated as a person with a permanent right of residence under regulation 15.

(6) Paragraphs (4) and (5) shall also apply to a residence permit or residence document which is endorsed under the immigration rules on or after 30 April 2006 to show permission to remain in the United Kingdom indefinitely pursuant to an application for such an endorsement made before that date.

Outstanding applications

3.—(1) An application for an EEA family permit, a residence permit or a residence document made but not determined under the 2000 Regulations before 30 April 2006 shall be treated as an application under these Regulations for an EEA family permit, a registration certificate or a residence card, respectively.

(2) But the following provisions of these Regulations shall not apply to the determination of an application mentioned in sub-paragraph (1)—

(a) the requirement to issue a registration certificate immediately under regulation 16(1); and

(b) the requirement to issue a certificate of application for a residence card under regulation 17(3).

Decisions to remove under the 2000 Regulations

4.—(1) A decision to remove a person under regulation 21(3)(a) of the 2000 Regulations shall, after 29 April 2006, be treated as a decision to remove that person under regulation 19(3)(a) of these Regulations.

(2) A decision to remove a person under regulation 21(3)(b) of the 2000 Regulations, including a decision which is treated as a decision to remove a person under that regulation by virtue of regulation 6(3)(a) of the Accession Regulations, shall, after 29 April 2006, be treated as a decision to remove that person under regulation 19(3)(b) of these Regulations.

(3) A deportation order made under section 5 of the 1971 Act by virtue of regulation 26(3) of the 2000 Regulations shall, after 29 April 2006, be treated as a deportation made under section 5 of the 1971 Act by virtue of regulation 24(3) of these Regulations.

Appeals

5.—(1) Where an appeal against an EEA decision under the 2000 Regulations is pending immediately before 30 April 2006 that appeal shall be treated as a pending appeal against the corresponding EEA Decision under these Regulations.

(2) Where an appeal against an EEA decision under the 2000 Regulations has been determined, withdrawn or abandoned it shall, on and after 30 April 2006, be treated as an appeal against the corresponding EEA decision under these Regulations which has been determined, withdrawn or abandoned, respectively.

(3) For the purpose of this paragraph—

(a) a decision to refuse to admit a person under these Regulations corresponds to a decision to refuse to admit that person under the 2000 Regulations;

(b) a decision to remove a person under regulation 19(3)(a) of these Regulations corresponds to a decision to remove that person under regulation 21(3)(a) of the 2000 Regulations;

(c) a decision to remove a person under regulation 19(3)(b) of these Regulations corresponds to a decision to remove that person under regulation 21(3)(b) of the 2000 Regulations, including a decision which is treated as a decision to remove a person under regulation 21(3)(b) of the 2000 Regulations by virtue of regulation 6(3)(a) of the Accession Regulations;

(d) a decision to refuse to revoke a deportation order made against a person under these Regulations corresponds to a decision to refuse to revoke a deportation order made against that person under the 2000 Regulations, including a decision which is treated as a decision to refuse to revoke a deportation order under the 2000 Regulations by virtue of regulation 6(3)(b) of the Accession Regulations;

(e) a decision not to issue or renew or to revoke an EEA family permit, a registration certificate or a residence card under these Regulations corresponds to a decision not to issue or renew or to revoke an EEA family permit, a residence permit or a residence document under the 2000 Regulations, respectively.

[6. Periods of residence prior to the entry into force of these Regulations

(1) Any period during which a person ("P"), who is an EEA national, carried out an activity or was resident in the United Kingdom in accordance with the conditions in subparagraph (2) or (3) is to be treated as a period during which the person carried out that activity or was resident in the United Kingdom in accordance with these Regulations for the purpose of calculating periods of activity and residence there under.

(2) P carried out an activity, or was resident, in the United Kingdom in accordance with this subparagraph where such activity or residence was at that time in accordance with—

(a) the 2000 Regulations;

(b) the Immigration (European Economic Area) Order 1994(5) ("the 1994 Order"); or

(c) where such activity or residence preceded the entry into force of the 1994 Order, any of the following Directives which was at the relevant time in force in respect of the United Kingdom—

   (i) Council Directive 64/221/EEC;

   (ii) Council Directive 68/360/EEC);

   (iii) Council Directive 72/194/EEC);

   (iv) Council Directive 73/148/EEC;

(v) Council Directive 75/34/EEC;

(vi) Council Directive 75/35/EEC;

(vii) Council Directive 90/364/EEC;

(viii) Council Directive 90/365/EEC; and

(ix) Council Directive 93/96/EEC.

(3) P carried out an activity or was resident in the United Kingdom in accordance with this subparagraph where P—

(a) had leave to enter or remain in the United Kingdom; and

(b) would have been carrying out that activity or residing in the United Kingdom in accordance with these Regulations had the relevant state been an EEA State at that time and had these Regulations at that time been in force.

(4) Any period during which P carried out an activity or was resident in the United Kingdom in accordance with subparagraph (2) or (3) will not be regarded as a period during which P carried out that activity or was resident in the United Kingdom in accordance with these Regulations where it was followed by a period—

(a) which exceeded two consecutive years and for the duration of which P was absent from the United Kingdom; or

(b) which exceeded two consecutive years and for the duration of which P's residence in the United Kingdom—

(i) was not in accordance with subparagraph (2) or (3); or

(ii) was not otherwise in accordance with these Regulations.

(5) The relevant state for the purpose of subparagraph (3) is the state of which P is, and was at the relevant time, a national.]

Note: Para 6 substituted from 16 July 2012 (SI 2012/1547).

Regulation 31(2)   SCHEDULE 5
                          CONSEQUENTIAL AMENDMENTS

...

The Immigration (European Economic Area) (Amendment) Regulations 2012
(SI 2012, No. 1547)

Citation

1. These Regulations may be cited as the Immigration (European Economic Area) (Amendment) Regulations 2012.

2–4...

Note: Articles 2-4 and Schedules 1 and 2 amend the Immigration (European Economic Area) Regulations 2006 (SI 2006/1003) and make consequential amendments.

Schedule 3
Transitional Provisions

Interpretation

1. In this Schedule—

(a) the "2006 Regulations" means the Immigration (European Economic Area) Regulations 2006; and

(b) the terms "EEA family permit", "EEA State", "family member", "registration certificate" and "residence card" have the meanings given in regulation 2(1) of the 2006 Regulations.

Amendments to the definition of EEA national

2.—(1) Where the right of a family member ("F") to be admitted to, or reside in, the United Kingdom pursuant to the 2006 Regulations depends on the fact that a person ("P") is an EEA national, P will, notwithstanding the effect of paragraph 1(d) of Schedule 1 to these Regulations, continue to be regarded as an EEA national for the purpose of the 2006 Regulations where the criteria in subparagraphs (2), (3) or (4) are met and for as long as they remain satisfied in accordance with subparagraph (5).

(2) The criterion in this subparagraph is met where F was on 16th July 2012 a person with a permanent right to reside in the United Kingdom under the 2006 Regulations.

(3) The criteria in this subparagraph are met where F—

(a) was on the 16th July 2012 a person with a right to reside in the United Kingdom under the 2006 Regulations; and

(b) on the 16th October 2012—

(i) held a valid registration certificate or residence card issued under the 2006 Regulations;

(ii) had made an application under the 2006 Regulations for a registration certificate or residence card which had not been determined; or

(iii) had made an application under the 2006 Regulations for a registration certificate or residence card which had been refused and in respect of which an appeal under regulation 26 could be brought while the appellant is in the United Kingdom (excluding the possibility of an appeal out of time with permission) or was pending (within the meaning of section 104 of the Nationality, Immigration and Asylum Act 2002(19)).

(4) The criteria in this sub-paragraph are met where F—

(a) had, prior to the 16th July 2012, applied for an EEA family permit pursuant to regulation 12 of the 2006 Regulations; or

(b) has applied for and been refused an EEA family permit and where, on the 16th July 2012, an appeal under regulation 26 against that decision could be brought (excluding the possibility of an appeal out of time with permission) or was pending (within the meaning of section 104 of the 2002 Act).

(5) Where met, the criteria in subparagraph (2), (3) and (4) remain satisfied until the occurrence of the earliest of the following events—

(a) the date six months after an EEA family permit has been issued if F has not within that period been admitted to the United Kingdom;

(b) the date on which an appeal against a decision referred to in subparagraph (3)(b) (iii) or (4)(b) can no longer be brought (ignoring the possibility of an appeal out of time with permission) where no such appeal has been brought;

(c) the date on which any appeal against a decision referred to in sub-paragraph (3)
(b)(iii) or (4)(b) is finally determined, is withdrawn or is abandoned (within the meaning
of section 104 of the 2002 Act) (save where the outcome of the appeal process is that the
document in question falls to be granted);

(d) the date on which F ceases to be the family member of an EEA national; or

(e) the date on which a right of permanent residence under regulation 15 of the 2006
Regulations is lost in accordance with regulation 15(2) of those Regulations.

(6) P will only continue to be regarded as an EEA national for the purpose of considering the position of F under the 2006 Regulations.

Note: Schedule 3 in force from 16 July 2012 (article 2).

The British Nationality (Proof of Paternity)
Regulations 2006
(SI 2006, No. 1496)

1. These Regulations may be cited as the British Nationality (Proof of Paternity)
Regulations 2006 and shall come into force on 1 July 2006.

2. The following requirements are prescribed as to proof of paternity for the purposes
of section 50(9A)(c) of the British Nationality Act 1981—

(a) the person must be named as the father of the child in a birth certificate issued
within one year of the date of the child's birth; or

(b) the person must satisfy the Secretary of State that he is the father of the child.

3. The Secretary of State may determine whether a person is the father of a child
for the purpose of regulation 2(b), and for this purpose the Secretary of State may have
regard to any evidence which he considers to be relevant, including, but not limited
to—

(a) DNA test reports; and

(b) court orders.

The Immigration (Provision of Physical Data)
Regulations 2006
(SI 2006, No. 1743)

Citation, commencement and interpretation

1. These Regulations may be cited as the Immigration (Provision of Physical Data)
Regulations 2006 and shall come into force on the day after they are made.

2. In these Regulations:

['accreditation card' means an Olympic Identity and Accreditation Card or a Paralympic Identity and Accreditation Card issued by the London Organising Committee of the Olympic Games and Paralympic Games Limited;]

'application' means:

(a) an application for entry clearance;

(b) an application for leave to enter the United Kingdom where the person seeking leave to enter presents a Convention travel document endorsed with an entry clearance for that journey to the United Kingdom;

[(c) an application for leave to enter the United Kingdom made during the period commencing on 30th March 2012 and ending on 8th November 2012 where the person seeking leave to enter holds an accreditation card and would be required to obtain a visa to enter the United Kingdom under Appendix 1 to the immigration rules were that person not exempted from that requirement in accordance with the provisions of paragraph 2 of that Appendix applicable to holders of accreditation cards; or

(d) an application for leave to remain in the United Kingdom made during the period commencing on 30th March 2012 and ending on 8th November 2012 where—

(i) the person has been granted leave to enter the United Kingdom following an application mentioned in paragraph (c);

(ii) an authorised person did not require a record of the person's fingerprints and photograph of the person's face to accompany that application for leave to enter; and

(iii) the person seeking leave to remain holds an accreditation card and would have been required to obtain a visa to enter the United Kingdom under Appendix 1 to the immigration rules were that person not exempted from that requirement in accordance with the provisions of paragraph 2 of that Appendix applicable to holders of accreditation cards;]

'Convention travel document' means a travel document issued pursuant to Article 28 of the Refugee Convention, except where that travel document was issued by the United Kingdom Government;

['immigration rules' means rules made under section 3(2) of the Immigration Act 1971;]

'Refugee Convention' means the Convention relating to the Status of Refugees done at Geneva on 28 July 1951 and its Protocol.

Note: Definitions of 'accreditation card' and 'immigration rules' inserted and definition of 'application' amended from 30 March 2012 (SI 2011/1779).

Power for an authorised person to require an individual to provide a record of his fingerprints and a photograph of his face

3. Subject to regulations 4 and 5, an authorised person may require an individual who makes an application to provide a record of his fingerprints and a photograph of his face.

Provision in relation to applicants under the age of sixteen

4.—(1) An applicant under the age of sixteen shall not be required to provide a record of his fingerprints or a photograph of his face except where the authorised person is satisfied that the fingerprints or the photograph will be taken in the presence of a person aged eighteen or over who is—

(a) the child's parent or guardian; or

(b) a person who for the time being takes responsibility for the child.

(2) The person mentioned in paragraph (1)(b) may not be—

(a) an officer of the Secretary of State who is not an authorised person;

(b) an authorised person; or

(c) any other person acting on behalf of an authorised person as part of a process specified under regulation 6(2).

(3) An authorised person shall not require a person under the age of sixteen to provide a record of his fingerprints or a photograph of his face unless his decision to do so has been confirmed by a person designated for the purpose by the Secretary of State.

(4) This regulation shall not apply if the authorised person reasonably believes that the applicant is aged sixteen or over.

Provision in relation to section 141 of the Immigration and Asylum Act 1999

5. An applicant shall not be required to provide a record of his fingerprints or a photograph of his face under regulation 3 if he is a person to whom section 141 of the Immigration and Asylum Act 1999 applies, during the relevant period within the meaning of that section.

Process by which the applicant's fingerprints and photograph may be obtained and recorded

6.—(1) An authorised person who requires an individual to provide a record of his fingerprints or a photograph of his face under regulation 3 may require that individual to submit to any process specified in paragraph (2).

(2) A process by which the individual who makes the application:

(a) attends a British Diplomatic mission or British Consular post where a record of his fingerprints or a photograph of his face is taken;

(b) attends a Diplomatic mission or Consular post of another State where a record of his fingerprints or a photograph of his face is taken by an official of that State on behalf of an authorised person; or

[(c) attends any other place nominated by an authorised person where a record of his fingerprints or a photograph of his face is taken by an authorised person or by a person on behalf of an authorised person.]

Note: Paragraph 2(c) substituted from 30 March 2012 (SI 2011/1779).

Consequences of failure to comply with these Regulations

7.—(1) Subject to paragraphs (2) and (3), where an individual does not provide a record of his fingerprints or a photograph of his face in accordance with a requirement imposed under these Regulations, his application may be treated as invalid.

(2) An application shall not be treated as invalid under paragraph (1) if it is for leave to enter the United Kingdom where the person seeking leave to enter presents a

Convention travel document endorsed with an entry clearance for that journey to the United Kingdom.

(3) Where an application is of a type described in paragraph (2) and the applicant does not provide a record of his fingerprints or a photograph of his face in accordance with a requirement imposed under these Regulations, that application may be refused.

Destruction of information

8. Subject to regulation 9, any record of fingerprints, photograph, copy of fingerprints or copy of a photograph held by the Secretary of State pursuant to these Regulations must be destroyed by the Secretary of State at the end of ten years beginning with the date on which the original record or photograph was provided.

9. If an applicant proves that he is—

(a) a British citizen; or

(b) a Commonwealth citizen who has a right of abode in the United Kingdom as a result of section 2(1)(b) of the Immigration Act 1971,any record of fingerprints, photograph, copy of fingerprints or copy of a photograph held by the Secretary of State pursuant to these Regulations must be destroyed as soon as reasonably practicable.

10.—(1) The Secretary of State must take all reasonably practicable steps to secure:

(a) that data held in electronic form which relate to any record of fingerprints or photograph which have to be destroyed in accordance with regulation 8 or 9 are destroyed or erased; or

(b) that access to such data is blocked.

(2) The applicant to whom the data relates is entitled, on written request, to a certificate issued by the Secretary of State to the effect that he has taken the steps required by paragraph (1).

(3) A certificate issued under paragraph (2) must be issued within three months of the date on which the request was received by the Secretary of State.

Revocation and transitional provisions

11.—(1) ...

(2) For the purposes of paragraph (3) only, 'application' means an application within the meaning of regulation 2 of the Immigration (Provision of Physical Data) Regulations 2003 (the '2003 Regulations').

(3) Where a person made an application before these Regulations came into force, the 2003 Regulations will continue to apply for the purposes of that application as if they had not been revoked by paragraph (1).

The Immigration (Continuation of Leave) (Notices) Regulations 2006
(SI 2006, No. 2170)

Citation and Commencement

1. These Regulations may be cited as the Immigration (Continuation of Leave) (Notices) Regulations 2006 and shall come into force on 31 August 2006.

Decision on an application for variation of leave

2. For the purpose of section 3C of the Immigration Act 1971 an application for variation of leave is decided—

(a) when notice of the decision has been given in accordance with regulations made under section 105 of the Nationality, Immigration and Asylum Act 2002; or where no such notice is required,

(b) when notice of the decision has been given in accordance with section 4(1) of the Immigration Act 1971.

The Refugee or Person in Need of International Protection (Qualification) Regulations 2006
(SI 2006, No. 2525)

Citation and commencement

1.—(1) These Regulations may be cited as The Refugee or Person in Need of International Protection (Qualification) Regulations 2006 and shall come into force on 9 October 2006.

(2) These Regulations apply to any application for asylum which has not been decided and any immigration appeal brought under the Immigration Acts (as defined in section 64(2) of the Immigration, Asylum and Nationality Act 2006) which has not been finally determined.

Interpretation

2. In these Regulations—

'application for asylum' means the request of a person to be recognised as a refugee under the Geneva Convention;

'Geneva Convention' means the Convention Relating to the Status of Refugees done at Geneva on 28 July 1951 and the New York Protocol of 31 January 1967;

'immigration rules' means rules made under section 3(2) of the Immigration Act 1971;

'persecution' means an act of persecution within the meaning of Article 1(A) of the Geneva Convention;

'person eligible for humanitarian protection' means a person who is eligible for a grant of humanitarian protection under the immigration rules;

'refugee' means a person who falls within Article 1(A) of the Geneva Convention and to whom regulation 7 does not apply;

'residence permit' means a document confirming that a person has leave to enter or remain in the United Kingdom whether limited or indefinite;

'serious harm' means serious harm as defined in the immigration rules;

'person' means any person who is not a British citizen.

Actors of persecution or serious harm

3. In deciding whether a person is a refugee or a person eligible for humanitarian protection, persecution or serious harm can be committed by:

(a) the State;

(b) any party or organisation controlling the State or a substantial part of the territory of the State;

(c) any non-State actor if it can be demonstrated that the actors mentioned in paragraphs (a) and (b), including any international organisation, are unable or unwilling to provide protection against persecution or serious harm.

Actors of protection

4.—(1) In deciding whether a person is a refugee or a person eligible for humanitarian protection, protection from persecution or serious harm can be provided by:

(a) the State; or

(b) any party or organisation, including any international organisation, controlling the State or a substantial part of the territory of the State.

(2) Protection shall be regarded as generally provided when the actors mentioned in paragraph (1)(a) and (b) take reasonable steps to prevent the persecution or suffering of serious harm by operating an effective legal system for the detection, prosecution and punishment of acts constituting persecution or serious harm, and the person mentioned in paragraph (1) has access to such protection.

(3) In deciding whether a person is a refugee or a person eligible for humanitarian protection the Secretary of State may assess whether an international organisation controls a State or a substantial part of its territory and provides protection as described in paragraph (2).

Act of persecution

5.—(1) In deciding whether a person is a refugee an act of persecution must be:

(a) sufficiently serious by its nature or repetition as to constitute a severe violation of a basic human right, in particular a right from which derogation cannot be made under Article 15 of the Convention for the Protection of Human Rights and Fundamental Freedoms; or

(b) an accumulation of various measures, including a violation of a human right which is sufficiently severe as to affect an individual in a similar manner as specified in (a).

(2) An act of persecution may, for example, take the form of:

(a) an act of physical or mental violence, including an act of sexual violence;

(b) a legal, administrative, police, or judicial measure which in itself is discriminatory or which is implemented in a discriminatory manner;

(c) prosecution or punishment, which is disproportionate or discriminatory;

(d) denial of judicial redress resulting in a disproportionate or discriminatory punishment;

(e) prosecution or punishment for refusal to perform military service in a conflict, where performing military service would include crimes or acts falling under regulation 7.

(3) An act of persecution must be committed for at least one of the reasons in Article 1(A) of the Geneva Convention.

Reasons for persecution

6.—(1) In deciding whether a person is a refugee:

(a) the concept of race shall include consideration of, for example, colour, descent, or membership of a particular ethnic group;

(b) the concept of religion shall include, for example, the holding of theistic, non-theistic and atheistic beliefs, the participation in, or abstention from, formal worship in private or in public, either alone or in community with others, other religious acts or expressions of view, or forms of personal or communal conduct based on or mandated by any religious belief;

(c) the concept of nationality shall not be confined to citizenship or lack thereof but shall include, for example, membership of a group determined by its cultural, ethnic, or linguistic identity, common geographical or political origins or its relationship with the population of another State;

(d) a group shall be considered to form a particular social group where, for example:

(i) members of that group share an innate characteristic, or a common background that cannot be changed, or share a characteristic or belief that is so fundamental to identity or conscience that a person should not be forced to renounce it, and

(ii) that group has a distinct identity in the relevant country, because it is perceived as being different by the surrounding society;

(e) a particular social group might include a group based on a common characteristic of sexual orientation but sexual orientation cannot be understood to include acts considered to be criminal in accordance with national law of the United Kingdom;

(f) the concept of political opinion shall include the holding of an opinion, thought or belief on a matter related to the potential actors of persecution mentioned in regulation 3 and to their policies or methods, whether or not that opinion, thought or belief has been acted upon by the person.

(2) In deciding whether a person has a well-founded fear of being persecuted, it is immaterial whether he actually possesses the racial, religious, national, social or political characteristic which attracts the persecution, provided that such a characteristic is attributed to him by the actor of persecution.

Exclusion

7.—(1) A person is not a refugee, if he falls within the scope of Article 1D, 1E or 1F of the Geneva Convention.

(2) In the construction and application of Article 1F(b) of the Geneva Convention:

(a) the reference to serious non-political crime includes a particularly cruel action, even if it is committed with an allegedly political objective;

(b) the reference to the crime being committed outside the country of refuge prior to his admission as a refugee shall be taken to mean the time up to and including the day on which a residence permit is issued.

(3) Article 1F(a) and (b) of the Geneva Convention shall apply to a person who instigates or otherwise participates in the commission of the crimes or acts specified in those provisions.

The Immigration (Certificate of Entitlement to Right of Abode in the United Kingdom) Regulations 2006
(SI 2006, No. 3145)

Citation, commencement and interpretation

1. These Regulations may be cited as the Immigration (Certificate of Entitlement to Right of Abode in the United Kingdom) Regulations 2006 and shall come into force on 21 December 2006.

2. In these Regulations—

'the 1971 Act' means the Immigration Act 1971;

'the 1981 Act' means the British Nationality Act 1981;

'the 2002 Act' means the Nationality, Immigration and Asylum Act 2002;

['the 2008 Act' means the Human Fertilisation and Embryology Act 2008;]

'appropriate authority' means the authority to whom an application for a certificate of entitlement must be made, as determined in accordance with regulation 3;

'certificate of entitlement' means a certificate, issued in accordance with these Regulations, that a person has the right of abode in the United Kingdom;

'Governor', in relation to a territory, includes the officer for the time being administering the government of that territory;

'High Commissioner' means, in relation to a country mentioned in Schedule 3 to the 1981 Act, the High Commissioner for Her Majesty's Government in the United Kingdom appointed to that country, and includes the acting High Commissioner; and

'passport' includes a document which relates to a national of a country other than the United Kingdom and which is designed to serve the same purpose as a passport.

Note: Definition of '2008 Act' inserted from 1 September 2009 (SI 2009/1892).

Authority to whom an application must be made

3. An application for a certificate of entitlement must be made—

(a) if the applicant is in the United Kingdom, to the Secretary of State for the Home Department;

[(b) if the applicant is in any of the Channel Islands or the Isle of Man, to the Lieutenant-Governor or the Secretary of State for the Home Department;]

(c) if the applicant is in a British overseas territory, to the Governor;

(d) if the applicant is in a country mentioned in Schedule 3 to the 1981 Act, to the High Commissioner, or, if there is no High Commissioner, to the Secretary of State for the Home Department; and

(e) if the applicant is elsewhere, to any consular officer, any established officer in the Diplomatic Service of Her Majesty's Government in the United Kingdom or any other person authorised by the Secretary of State in that behalf.

Note: Regulation 3(b) substituted from 12 December 2011 (SI 2011/2682).

Form of application

[4.—(1) Subject to paragraph (2), an application for a certificate of entitlement must be accompanied by—

(a) the applicant's passport or travel document;

(b) two photographs of the applicant taken no more than 6 months prior to making the application; and

(c) the additional documents which are specified in the right-hand column of the Schedule in respect of an application of a description specified in the corresponding entry in the left hand column.

(2) The requirement in paragraph (1)(c) may be waived in relation to a particular document if the appropriate authority—

(a) is satisfied that it is appropriate to do so in light of the facts of the particular case; and

(b) is otherwise satisfied that the applicant has a right of abode in the United Kingdom.]

Note: Regulation 4 substituted from 12 December 2011 (SI 2011/2682).

5. A passport produced by or on behalf of a person is valid for the purposes of regulation 4 if it—

(a) relates to the person by whom or on whose behalf it is produced;

(b) has not been altered otherwise than by or with the permission of the authority who issued it; and

(c) was not obtained by deception.

Issue of certificate of entitlement

6. A certificate of entitlement will only be issued where the appropriate authority is satisfied that the applicant—

(a) has a right of abode in the United Kingdom under section 2(1) of the 1971 Act;

[(b) is not a person who holds:

(i) a United Kingdom passport describing him as a British citizen,

(ii) a United Kingdom passport describing him as a British subject with the right of abode in the United Kingdom, or

(iii) a certificate of entitlement;]

(c) is not a person whose exercise of his right of abode is restricted under section 2 of the Immigration Act 1988 (restrictions on exercise of right of abode in cases of polygamy); and

(d) is not a person who is deprived of his right of abode by an order under section 2A of the 1971 Act.

7. A certificate of entitlement is to be issued by means of being affixed to the passport or travel document of the applicant.

Note: Regulation 6(b) substituted from 12 December 2011 (SI 2011/2682).

Expiry and revocation of certificate of entitlement

8. A certificate of entitlement shall cease to have effect on the expiry of the passport or travel document to which it is affixed.

9. A certificate of entitlement may be revoked by the Secretary of State for the Home Department, an immigration officer, a consular officer or a person responsible for the grant or refusal of entry clearance, where the person who revokes the certificate is satisfied that the person in possession of the certificate (whether or not this is the person to whom the certificate was issued)—

(a) does not have the right of abode in the United Kingdom under section 2(1) of the 1971 Act;

[(b) is the holder of:

(i) a United Kingdom passport describing him as a British citizen,

(ii) a United Kingdom passport describing him as a British subject with the right of abode in the United Kingdom,

(iii) another certificate of entitlement;]

(c) is a person whose exercise of his right of abode is restricted under section 2 of the Immigration Act 1988; or

(d) is a person who is deprived of his right of abode by an order under section 2A of the 1971 Act.

Note: Regulation 9(b) substituted from 12 December 2011 (SI 2011/2682).

Savings

10. The effect of a certificate described in section 10(6) of the 2002 Act is that it will cease to have effect on the expiry of the passport or travel document to which it is affixed.

SCHEDULE

Additional documents which must accompany an application for a certificate of entitlement

[REGULATION 4(I)(C)]

Basis of application	Documents
Applicant was registered or naturalised as a British citizen on or after 1st January 1983	Applicant's registration or naturalisation certificate
Applicant was born in the United Kingdom before 1st January 1983	Applicant's full birth certificate, showing parents' details
Applicant was registered or naturalised as a citizen of the United Kingdom and Colonies in the United Kingdom before 1st January 1983	Applicant's registration or naturalisation certificate
Applicant is a Commonwealth (not British) citizen born before 1st January 1983 to a parent who was born in the United Kingdom	(i) Applicant's full birth certificate showing parents' details; and (ii) Parent's full UK birth certificate
Applicant is a female Commonwealth citizen who was married before 1st January 1983 to a man with right of abode in the United Kingdom	(i) Applicant's marriage certificate; and (ii) Evidence of applicant's husband's right of abode, eg passport or UK birth certificate
Applicant was born in the United Kingdom or the Falkland Islands on or after 1st January 1983, or in another qualifying British overseas territory on or after 21st May 2002	(i) Applicant's full birth certificate showing parents' details; (ii) Evidence of either parent's British citizenship or settled status at time of applicant's birth, eg a passport describing the relevant parent as a British citizen or indicating that he or she then had indefinite leave to remain; and [(iii) Parents' marriage or civil partnership certificate (if claiming through father or if claiming through woman who is a parent of the applicant by virtue of section 42 or 43 of the 2008 Act.]
Applicant was born outside the United Kingdom and the Falkland Islands on or after 1st January 1983, or outside the United Kingdom and any qualifying	(i) Applicant's full birth certificate showing parents' details;

British overseas territory on or after 21st May 2002, to a parent born in the United Kingdom or the Falkland Islands (or, on/after 21 May 2002, any qualifying British overseas territory) or to a parent registered or naturalised in the United Kingdom prior to the applicant's birth

[(ii) Parents' marriage or civil partnership certificate (if claiming through father or if claiming through woman who is a parent of the applicant by virtue of section 42 or 43 of the 2008 Act);] and

(iii) Parents' full birth certificate, registration or naturalisation certificate

---

Applicant was born outside the United Kingdom and the Falkland Islands on or after 1st January 1983, or outside the United Kingdom and any qualifying British overseas territory on or after 21 May 2002, to a parent who, at the time of the birth, was a British citizen in service to which section 2(1)(b) of the British Nationality Act 1981 applies

(i) Applicant's full birth certificate;

[(ii) Parents' marriage or civil partnership certificate (if claiming through father or if claiming through woman who is a parent of the applicant by virtue of section 42 or 43 of the 2008 Act);] and

(iii) Evidence of parent's relevant employment at the time of the birth, eg a letter from the employer

---

Applicant was adopted in the United Kingdom, a qualifying British overseas territory, or otherwise under the terms of the Hague Convention on Intercountry Adoption(1)

(i) Applicant's adoption certificate; and

(ii) Evidence of adoptive parents' citizenship and, if a Convention adoption, of their place of habitual residence at the time of the adoption, eg in respect of citizenship, a passport, and in respect of habitual residence at the time of the Convention adoption, the adoption certificate

---

Applicant was a citizen of the United Kingdom and Colonies and was ordinarily resident in the United Kingdom for a continuous period of 5 years before 1st January 1983 and was settled in the United Kingdom at the end of that period

(i) Evidence of citizenship of the United Kingdom and Colonies, eg a passport or certificate of naturalisation or registration; and

(ii) Evidence of settlement and 5 years' ordinary residence in the UK before 1983, eg, passport, P60s, details of National Insurance contributions, DSS claims, employers' letters

---

Applicant was a citizen of the United Kingdom and Colonies and had a parent who was born, adopted, registered or naturalised in the United Kingdom prior to the applicant's birth/adoption

(i) Applicant's full birth certificate or adoption certificate;

[(ii) Parents' marriage or civil partnership certificate (if claiming through father or if claiming through woman who is a parent of the applicant by virtue of section 42 or 43 of the 2008 Act);] and

Applicant was a citizen of the United Kingdom and Colonies and had a grandparent born, adopted, registered or naturalised in the United Kingdom before the applicant's parent's birth/adoption	(iii) Parent's full birth certificate, adoption, registration or naturalisation certificate
	(i) Parents' marriage certificate (if claiming through father);
	[(ii) Parents' marriage or civil partnership certificate (if claiming through father or if claiming through woman who is a parent of the applicant by virtue of section 42 or 43 of the 2008 Act);]
	(iii) Applicant's full birth certificate or adoption certificate;
	(iv) Grandparents' marriage certificate (if claiming through grandfather); and
	(v) Grandparent's full birth certificate, adoption, registration or naturalisation certificate.

Note: Schedule amended from 1 September 2009 by SI 2009/1892 and from 12 December 2011 by SI 2011/2682.

The Accession (Immigration and Worker Authorisation) Regulations 2006
(SI 2006, No. 3317)

PART I
GENERAL

Citation, commencement, interpretation and consequential amendments

1.—(1) These Regulations may be cited as the Accession (Immigration and Worker Authorisation) Regulations 2006 and shall come into force on 1 January 2007. (2) In these Regulations—

(a) 'the 1971 Act' means the Immigration Act 1971;

(b) 'the 2006 Regulations' means the Immigration (European Economic Area) Regulations 2006;

(c) 'accession period' means the period beginning on 1 January 2007 and ending on[31 December 2013];

(d) 'accession State national subject to worker authorisation' has the meaning given in regulation 2;

(e) 'accession worker authorisation document' shall be interpreted in accordance with regulation 9(2);

(f) 'authorised category of employment' means a category of employment listed in the first column of the table in Schedule 1;

(g) 'authorised family member' has the meaning given in regulation 3;

(h) 'civil partner' does not include a party to a civil partnership of convenience;

(i) 'EEA State' means—

(i) a member State, other than the United Kingdom;

(ii) Norway, Iceland or Liechtenstein;

(iii) Switzerland;

(j) 'employer' means, in relation to a worker, the person who directly pays the wage or salary of that worker;

(k) 'family member' shall be interpreted in accordance with regulation 7 of the 2006 Regulations;

(l) 'highly skilled person' has the meaning given in regulation 4;

(m) 'immigration rules' means the rules laid down as mentioned in section 3(2) of the 1971 Act applying on 1 January 2007;

(n) 'letter of approval under the work permit arrangements' has the meaning given in paragraph 1(b) of Schedule 1;

(o) 'registration certificate' means a certificate issued in accordance with regulation 16 of the 2006 Regulations;

(p) 'relevant requirements' means, in relation to an authorised category of employment, the requirements set out in the second column of the table in Schedule 1 for that category;

(q) 'Sectors Based Scheme' has the meaning given in paragraph 1(f) of Schedule 1;

(r) 'spouse' does not include a party to a marriage of convenience;

(s) 'student' has the meaning given in regulation 4(1)(d) of the 2006 Regulations;

(t) 'worker' means a worker within the meaning of[Article 45 of the Treaty on the Functioning of the European Union], and 'work' and 'working' shall be construed accordingly.

(3) Schedule 2 (consequential amendments) shall have effect.

Note: Regulation 1(2)(c) amended from 30 December 2011 (SI 2011/2816). Words substituted in para (2)(t) from 1 August 2012 (SI 2012/1809).

'Accession State national subject to worker authorisation'

2.—(1) Subject to the following paragraphs of this regulation, in these Regulations 'accession State national subject to worker authorisation' means a national of Bulgaria or Romania.

[(2) A national of Bulgaria or Romania is not an accession State national subject to worker authorisation if on 31 December 2006 he had leave to enter or remain in the United Kingdom under the 1971 Act that was not subject to any condition restricting his employment or he is given such leave after that date.]

(3) A national of Bulgaria or Romania is not an accession State national subject to worker authorisation if he was legally working in the United Kingdom on 31 December 2006 and had been legally working in the United Kingdom without interruption throughout the period of 12 months ending on that date.

(4) A national of Bulgaria or Romania who legally works in the United Kingdom without interruption for a period of 12 months falling partly or wholly after 31 December 2006 shall cease to be an accession State national subject to worker authorisation at the end of that period of 12 months.

(5) A national of Bulgaria or Romania is not an accession State national subject to worker authorisation during any period in which he is also a national of—

   (a) the United Kingdom; or

   (b) an EEA State, other than Bulgaria or Romania.

[(5A) A national of Bulgaria or Romania is not an accession State national subject to worker authorisation during any period in which that national is the spouse, civil partner or child under 18 of a person who has leave to enter or remain in the United Kingdom under the 1971 Act that allows that person to work in the United Kingdom.]

(6) A national of Bulgaria or Romania is not an accession State national subject to worker authorisation during any period in which he is the spouse or civil partner of a national of the United Kingdom or of a person settled in the United Kingdom.

[(6A) A national of Bulgaria or Romania is not an accession State national subject to worker authorisation during any period in which he is a member of a mission or other person mentioned in section 8(3) of the 1971 Act (member of a diplomatic mission, the family member of such a person, or a person otherwise entitled to diplomatic immunity), other than a person who, under section 8(3A) of that Act, does not count as a member of a mission for the purposes of section 8(3).]

(7) A national of Bulgaria or Romania is not an accession State national subject to worker authorisation during any period in which he has a permanent right of residence under regulation 15 of the 2006 Regulations.

[(8) A national of Bulgaria or Romania is not an accession State national subject to worker authorisation during any period in which he is a family member of —

   (a) an EEA national who has a right to reside in the United Kingdom under the 2006 Regulations, other than —

     (i) an accession State national subject to worker authorisation; or

     (ii) a person who is not an accession State national subject to worker authorisation solely by virtue of being the family member of a person mentioned in sub-paragraph (b) [or a worker mentioned in paragraph (8A)]; or

   (b) an accession State national subject to worker authorisation who has a right to reside under regulation 14(1) of the 2006 Regulations by virtue of being a self-employed person, a self-sufficient person or a student falling within sub-paragraph (c), (d) or (e) of regulation 6(1) of those Regulations ('qualified person').]

[(8A) A national of Bulgaria or Romania is not an accession State national subject to worker authorisation during any period in which that national is the spouse, civil partner or descendant of an accession State national subject to worker authorisation who has a right to reside under regulation 14(1) of the 2006 Regulations by virtue of being a worker falling within sub-paragraph (b) of regulation 6(1) of those Regulations ('qualified person') provided that, in the case of a descendant, the descendant is under 21 or dependent on the accession State national subject to worker authorisation.]

(9) A national of Bulgaria or Romania is not an accession State national subject to worker authorisation during any period in which he is a highly skilled person and holds a registration certificate that includes a statement that he has unconditional access to the United Kingdom labour market.

[(**10**) A national of Bulgaria or Romania is not an accession State national subject to worker authorisation during any period in which he is in the United Kingdom as a student and—

(a) holds a registration certificate that includes a statement that he is a student who may work in the United Kingdom whilst a student in accordance with the condition set out in paragraph (10A); and

(b) complies with that condition.

(**10A**) The condition referred to in paragraph (10) is that the student shall not work for more than 20 hours a week unless —

(a) he is following a course of vocational training and is working as part of that training; or

(b) he is working during his vacation.

(**10B**) A national of Bulgaria or Romania who ceases to be a student at the end of his course of study is not an accession State national subject to worker authorisation during the period of four months beginning with the date on which his course ends provided he holds a registration certificate that was issued to him before the end of the course that includes a statement that he may work during that period.]

(**11**) A national of Bulgaria or Romania is not an accession State national subject to worker authorisation during any period in which he is a posted worker.

(**12**) For the purposes of paragraphs (3) and (4) of this regulation—

(a) a person working in the United Kingdom during a period falling before 1 January 2007 was working legally in the United Kingdom during that period if—

(i) he had leave to enter or remain in the United Kingdom under the 1971 Act for that period, that leave allowed him to work in the United Kingdom, and he was working in accordance with any condition on that leave restricting his employment; or

[(ia) he was exempt from the provisions of the 1971 Act by virtue of section 8(3) of that Act; or]

(ii) he was entitled to reside in the United Kingdom for that period under the Immigration (European Economic Area) Regulations 2000 or the 2006 Regulations without the requirement for such leave;

(b) a person working in the United Kingdom on or after 1 January 2007 is legally working during any period in which he—

(i) falls within paragraphs (5) to [(10B)]; or

(ii) holds an accession worker authorisation document and is working in accordance with the conditions set out in that document;

(c) a person shall be treated as having worked in the United Kingdom without interruption for a period of 12 months if he was legally working in the United Kingdom at the beginning and end of that period and any intervening periods in which he was not legally working in the United Kingdom do not, in total, exceed 30 days.

(**13**) In this regulation—

(a) 'posted worker' means a worker who is posted to the United Kingdom, within the meaning of Article 1(3) of Directive 96/71/EC concerning the posting of workers, by an undertaking established in an EEA State;

(b) the reference to a person settled in the United Kingdom shall be interpreted in accordance with section 33(2A) of the 1971 Act.

Note: Paragraphs (2) and (10) substituted from 16 March 2007 (SI 2007/475). For the purpose of paragraphs (10) and (10B), a statement in a registration certificate issued before 16 March 2007 that the holder of the certificate is a student who has access to the United Kingdom labour market for 20 hours a week, shall, on or after that date, be treated as if it were a statement that the holder of the certificate is a student who may work in the United Kingdom whilst a student in accordance with the condition set out in reg 2(10A) of those Regulations and who, on ceasing to be a student, may work during the period referred to in reg 2(10B) of those Regulations. Paragraphs (6A) and (12)(a)(ia) inserted and paragraph (8) substituted from 19 November 2007 (SI 2007/3012). Paragraphs (5A), (8A) and words in square brackets in paragraph (8)(a) (ii) inserted from 2 October 2009 (SI 2009/2426).

Authorised family member

[3. A person is an authorised family member for the purpose of these Regulations if that person is the family member of an accession State national subject to worker authorisation who has a right to reside in the United Kingdom under regulation 14(1) of the 2006 Regulations as a worker, unless –

(a) the worker is only authorised to work under these Regulations by virtue of holding an accession worker card issued in accordance with regulation 11 pursuant to an application as an authorised family member; or

(b) the family member is the spouse or civil partner of the worker or a descendant of the worker who is under 21 or dependent on the worker].

Note: Regulation 3 substituted from 2 October 2009 (SI 2009/2426).

'Highly skilled person'

4.—(1) In these Regulations 'highly skilled person' means a person who—

(a) meets the criteria specified by the Secretary of State for the purpose of paragraph 135A(i) [of the immigration rules (entry to the United Kingdom under the Highly Skilled Migrant Programme) and applying on 1 January 2007, other than the criterion requiring a proficiency in the English language; or

(b) has been awarded one of the following qualifications and applies for a registration certificate or submits a registration certificate to the Secretary of State under regulation 7(4) within 12 months of being awarded the qualification—

[(i) a Higher National Diploma awarded by a relevant institution in Scotland; or

(ii) a degree, postgraduate certificate or postgraduate diploma awarded by a relevant institution in the United Kingdom.]

(2) In paragraph (1)(b), 'relevant institution' means an institution that is financed from public funds or included on the Department for Education and Skills' Register of Education and Training Providers on 1 January 2007.

Note: Sub-paragraph (b)(i)–(ii) substituted from 19 November 2007 (SI 2007/3012).

Derogation from provisions of [EU] law relating to workers

5. Regulations 6, 7 and 9 derogate during the accession period from[Article 45 of the Treaty on the Functioning of the European Union], Articles 1 to 6 of Regulation (EEC) No. 1612/68 on freedom of movement for workers within the Community and Council Directive 2004/38/EC on the right of citizens of the Union and their family members to move and reside freely within the territory of the Member States.

Note: Words substituted in square brackets substituted from 1 August 2012 (SI 2012/1809).

PART 2

IMMIGRATION

Right of residence of an accession State national subject to worker authorisation

6.—(1) An accession State national subject to worker authorisation shall, during the accession period, only be entitled to reside in the United Kingdom in accordance with the 2006 Regulations, as modified by this regulation.

(2) An accession State national subject to worker authorisation who is seeking employment in the United Kingdom shall not be treated as a jobseeker for the purpose of the definition of 'qualified person' in regulation 6(1) of the 2006 Regulations and such a person shall be treated as a worker for the purpose of that definition only during a period in which he holds an accession worker authorisation document and is working in accordance with the conditions set out in that document.

(3) Regulation 6(2) of the 2006 Regulations shall not apply to an accession State national subject to worker authorisation who ceases to work.

Issuing registration certificates and residence cards to nationals of Bulgaria and Romania and their family members during the accession period

7.—(1) Subject to paragraph (2), an accession State national subject to worker authorisation shall not be treated as a qualified person for the purposes of regulations 16 and 17 of the 2006 Regulations (issue of registration certificates and residence cards) during the accession period unless he falls within sub-paragraphs (c), (d) or (e) of regulation 6(1) of the 2006 Regulations.

(2) The Secretary of State shall issue a registration certificate to an accession State national subject to worker authorisation on application if he is satisfied that the applicant—

(a) is seeking employment in the United Kingdom; and

(b) is a highly skilled person.

(3) Where the Secretary of State issues a registration certificate during the accession period to a Bulgarian or Romanian national under paragraph (2) or in any case where he is satisfied that the Bulgarian or Romanian national is not an accession State national subject to worker authorisation [(other than solely by virtue of falling within paragraph (10) or (10B) of regulation 2)], the registration certificate shall include a statement that the holder of the certificate has unconditional access to the United Kingdom labour market.

(4) A Bulgarian or Romanian national who holds a registration certificate that does not include a statement that he has unconditional access to the United Kingdom labour market may, during the accession period, submit the certificate to the Secretary of State for the inclusion of such a statement.

(5) The Secretary of State shall re-issue a certificate submitted to him under paragraph (4) with the inclusion of a statement that the holder has unconditional access to the United Kingdom labour market if he is satisfied that the holder—

(a) is a highly skilled person; or

(b) has ceased to be an accession State national subject to worker authorisation other than solely by virtue of falling within [paragraph (10) or (10B) of regulation 2].

(6) A registration certificate issued to a Bulgarian or Romanian student during the accession period shall include a statement that the holder of the certificate is a student who [may work in the United Kingdom whilst a student in accordance with the condition set out in regulation 2 (10A) and who, on ceasing to be a student, may work during the period referred to in regulation 2(10B)] unless it includes a statement under paragraph (3) or (5) that the holder has unconditional access to the United Kingdom labour market.

(7) But this regutlation is subject to regulation 20 of the 2006 Regulations (power to refuse to issue and to revoke registration certificates).

Note: Words in square brackets in para (3) inserted and in paragraphs (5) and (6) substituted from 16 March 2007 (SI 2007/475).

Transitional provisions to take account of the application of the 2006 Regulations to nationals of Bulgaria and Romania and their family members on 1 January 2007

8.—(1) Where before 1 January 2007 directions have been given for the removal of a Bulgarian or Romanian national or the family member of such a national under paragraphs 8 to 10A of Schedule 2 to the 1971 Act or section 10 of the 1999 Act, those directions shall cease to have effect on and after that date.

(2) Where before 1 January 2007 the Secretary of State has made a decision to make a deportation order against a Bulgarian or Romanian national or the family member of such a national under section 5(1) of the 1971 Act—

(a) that decision shall, on and after 1 January 2007, be treated as if it were a decision under regulation 19(3)(b) of the 2006 Regulations; and

(b) any appeal against that decision, or against the refusal of the Secretary of State to revoke the deportation order, made under section 63 of the 1999 Act or section 82(2)(j) or (k) of the 2002 Act before 1 January 2007, shall, on or after that date, be treated as if it had been made under regulation 26 of the 2006 Regulations.

(3) In this regulation—

(a) 'the 1999 Act' means the Immigration and Asylum Act 1999;

(b) 'the 2002 Act' means the Nationality, Immigration and Asylum Act 2002;

(c) any reference to the family member of a Bulgarian or Romanian national is a reference to a person who on 1 January 2007 acquires a right to reside in the United Kingdom under the 2006 Regulations as the family member of a Bulgarian or Romanian national.

PART 3
ACCESSION STATE WORKER AUTHORISATION

Requirement for an accession State national subject to worker authorisation to be authorised to work

9.—(1) An accession State national subject to worker authorisation shall only be authorised to work in the United Kingdom during the accession period if he holds an accession worker authorisation document and is working in accordance with the conditions set out in that document.

(2) For the purpose of these Regulations, an accession worker authorisation document is—

(a) a passport or other travel document endorsed before 1 January 2007 to show that the holder has leave to enter or remain in the United Kingdom under the 1971 Act, subject to a condition restricting his employment in the United Kingdom to a particular employer or category of employment;

(b) a seasonal agricultural work card, except where the holder of the card has a document mentioned in sub-paragraph (a) giving him leave to enter the United Kingdom as a seasonal agricultural worker; or

(c) an accession worker card issued in accordance with regulation 11.

(3) But a document shall cease to be treated as an accession worker authorisation document under paragraph (2)—

(a) in the case of a document mentioned in paragraph (2)(a), at the end of the period for which leave to enter or remain is given;

(b) in the case of a seasonal agricultural work card, at the end of the period of six months beginning with the date on which the holder of the card begins working for the agricultural employer specified in the card;

(c) in the case of an accession worker card, on the expiry of the card under regulation 11(7).

(4) For the purpose of this regulation—

(a) 'seasonal agricultural work card' means a Home Office work card issued by the operator of a seasonal agricultural workers scheme approved by the Secretary of State for the purpose of paragraph 104(ii) of the immigration rules;

(b) the reference to a travel document other than a passport is a reference to a document which relates to a national of Bulgaria or Romania and which is designed to serve the same purpose as a passport.

Application for an accession worker card

10.—(1) An application for an accession worker card may be made by an accession State national subject to worker authorisation who wishes to work for an employer in the United Kingdom if—

(a) the employment concerned falls within an authorised category of employment; or

(b) the applicant is an authorised family member.

(2) The application shall be in writing and shall be made to the Secretary of State.

(3) The application shall state—

(a) the name, address, and date of birth of the applicant;

(b) the name and address of the employer for whom the applicant wishes to work; and

(c) unless the applicant is an authorised family member, the authorised category of employment covered by the application.

(4) The application shall be accompanied by—

(a) the applicant's national identity card or passport; and

(b) two passport size photographs of the applicant.

(5) Where the applicant is not an authorised family member, the application shall, in addition to the documents required by paragraph (4), be accompanied by—

(a) where the relevant requirements for the authorised category of employment specified in the application require the applicant to hold a letter of approval under the work permit arrangements, that letter;

(b) where sub-paragraph (a) does not apply, a letter from the e~~i~~
in the application confirming that the applicant has an offer of empl~~c~~
employer; and

(c) any other proof that the applicant wishes to provide to establish that ~~no~~
relevant requirements.

(6) Where the applicant is an authorised family member, the application shall, in addition to the documents required by paragraph (4), be accompanied by—

(a) a letter from the employer specified in the application confirming that the applicant has an offer of employment with the employer; and

(b) proof that the applicant is an authorised family member.

(7) In this regulation 'address' means, in relation to an employer which is a body corporate or partnership, the head or main office of that employer.

Issuing an accession worker card etc

11.—(1) Subject to paragraph (2), the Secretary of State shall issue an accession worker card pursuant to an application made in accordance with regulation 10 if he is satisfied that the applicant is an accession State national subject to worker authorisation who—

(a) is an authorised family member; or

(b) meets the relevant requirements for the authorised category of employment covered by the application.

(2) The Secretary of State shall not issue an accession worker card if he has decided to remove the applicant from the United Kingdom under regulation 19(3)(b) of the 2006 Regulations (removal on grounds of public policy, public security or public health).

(3) An accession worker card issued under this regulation to an authorised family member shall include a condition restricting the applicant's employment to the employer specified in the application.

(4) An accession worker card issued under this regulation pursuant to an application that was accompanied by a letter of approval under the work permit arrangements shall include the following conditions—

(a) a condition restricting the applicant's employment to the employer specified in the application and any secondary employer; and

(b) a condition restricting him to the type of employment specified in the letter of approval under the work permit arrangements.

(5) In any other case, an accession worker card issued under this regulation shall include the following conditions—

(a) a condition restricting the applicant's employment to the employer specified in the application; and

(b) a condition restricting him to the authorised category of employment specified in the application.

(6) An accession worker card issued under this regulation shall include a photograph of the applicant and shall set out—

(a) the name, nationality and date of birth of the applicant;

(b) the name and address of the employer specified in the application;

(c) the conditions required by paragraph (3), (4) or (5), as the case may be; and

(d) the date on which the card was issued.

(7) An accession worker card shall expire if the holder of the card ceases working for the employer specified in the application.

(8) Where the Secretary of State is not satisfied as mentioned in paragraph (1) or where paragraph (2) applies, he shall refuse the application and issue a notice of refusal setting out the reasons for the refusal.

(9) An accession worker card or notice of refusal issued under this regulation shall be sent to the applicant by post together with the identity card or passport that accompanied the application.

(10) In this regulation, 'secondary employer' means, in relation to an applicant, an employer who is not specified in his application and who employs the applicant for no more than 20 hours a week when the applicant is not working for the employer who is specified in the application.

Unauthorised employment of accession State national – employer offence

12.—(1) Subject to paragraphs (2) and (3), an employer who employs an accession State national subject to worker authorisation during the accession period shall be guilty of an offence if—

(a) the employee does not hold an accession worker authorisation document; or

(b) the employee's accession worker authorisation document is subject to conditions that preclude him from taking up the employment.

(2) Subject to paragraph (4), in proceedings under this regulation it shall be a defence to prove that before the employment began there was produced to the employer a document that appeared to him to be a registration certificate issued to the worker and—

(a) the registration certificate contained a statement that the worker has unconditional access to the United Kingdom labour market; or

[(b) the registration certificate contained a statement that the worker is a student who may work in the United Kingdom whilst a student in accordance with the condition set out in regulation 2(10A) and who, on ceasing to be a student, may work during the period referred to in regulation 2(10B), and the employer has not employed that worker otherwise than in accordance with that condition or during that period.]

(3) Subject to paragraph (4), in proceedings under this regulation it shall be a defence to prove that before the employment began there was produced to the employer a document that appeared to him to be an accession worker authorisation document that authorised the worker to take up the employment.

(4) The defence afforded by paragraph (2) and (3) shall not be available in any case where the employer—

(a) did not take and retain a copy of the relevant document; or

(b) knew that his employment of the worker constituted an offence under this regulation.

(5) A person guilty of an offence under this regulation shall be liable on summary conviction to a fine not exceeding level 5 on the standard scale.

(6) Where an offence under this regulation committed by a body corporate is proved to have been committed with the consent or connivance of, or to be attributable to any neglect on the part of—

(a) any director, manager, secretary or other similar officer of the body corporate; or

(b) any person purporting to act in such a capacity,he, as well as the body corporate, shall be guilty of an offence and shall be liable to be proceeded against and punished accordingly.

(7) Where the affairs of a body corporate are managed by its members, paragraph (6) shall apply in relation to acts and defaults of a member in connection with his functions of management as if he were a director of the body corporate.

(8) Where an offence under this regulation is committed by a partnership (other than a limited partnership) each partner shall be guilty of an offence and shall be liable to be proceeded against and punished accordingly.

(9) Paragraph (6) shall have effect in relation to a limited partnership as if—

(a) a reference to a body corporate were a reference to a limited partnership; and

(b) a reference to an officer of the body corporate were a reference to a partner.

(10) An offence under this regulation shall be treated as—

(a) a relevant offence for the purpose of sections 28B and 28D of the 1971 Act (search, entry and arrest);

(b) an offence under Part III of that Act (criminal proceedings) for the purposes of sections 28E, 28G and 28H of that Act (search after arrest); and

(c) an offence referred to in section 28AA of that Act (arrest with warrant).

Note: Words in square brackets substituted from 16 March 2007 (SI 2007/475). For the purpose of paragraph (2), a statement in a registration certificate issued before 16 March 2007 that the holder of the certificate is a student who has access to the United Kingdom labour market for 20 hours a week, shall, on or after that date, be treated as if it were a statement that the holder of the certificate is a student who may work in the United Kingdom whilst a student in accordance with the condition set out in reg 2 (10A) of those Regulations and who, on ceasing to be a student, may work during the period referred to in reg 2(10B) of those Regulations.

Unauthorised working by accession State national—employee offence

13.—(1) Subject to paragraph

(2) an accession State national subject to worker authorisation who works in the United Kingdom during the accession period shall be guilty of an offence if—

(a) he does not hold an accession worker authorisation document; or

(b) he is working in breach of the conditions set out in his accession worker authorisation document.

(2) A person guilty of an offence under this regulation shall be liable on summary conviction to a fine not exceeding level 5 on the standard scale or imprisonment for not more than three months, or both.

(3) A constable or immigration officer who has reason to believe that a person has committed an offence under this regulation may give that person a notice offering him the opportunity of discharging any liability to conviction for that offence by payment of a penalty in accordance with the notice.

(4) The penalty payable in pursuance of a notice under paragraph (3) is £1000 and shall be payable to the Secretary of State.

(5) Where a person is given a notice under paragraph (3) in respect of an offence—

(a) no proceedings may be instituted for that offence before the expiration of the period of twenty one days following the date of the notice; and

(b) he may not be convicted of that offence if before the expiration of that period he pays the penalty in accordance with the notice.

(6) A notice under paragraph (3) must give such particulars of the circumstances alleged to constitute the offence as are necessary for giving reasonable information of the offence.

(7) A notice under paragraph (3) must also state—

(a) the period during which, by virtue of paragraph (5), proceedings will not be instituted for the offence;

(b) the amount of the penalty; and

(c) that the penalty is payable to the Secretary of State at the address specified in the notice.

(8) Without prejudice to payment by any other method, payment of a penalty in pursuance of a notice under paragraph (3) may be made by pre-paying and posting a letter containing the amount of the penalty (in cash or otherwise) to the Secretary of State at the address specified in the notice.

(9) Where a letter is sent in accordance with paragraph (8) payment is to be regarded as having been made at the time at which that letter would be delivered in the ordinary course of post.

Deception—employee offence

14.—(1) A person is guilty of an offence if, by means which include deception by him, he obtains or seeks to obtain an accession worker card.

(2) A person guilty of an offence under this regulation shall be liable on summary conviction to a fine not exceeding level 5 on the standard scale or imprisonment for not more than three months, or both.

Offences under regulations 13 and 14—search, entry and arrest

15. An offence under regulation 13 or 14 shall be treated as—

(a) a relevant offence for the purpose of sections 28B and 28D of the 1971 Act (search, entry and arrest);

(b) an offence under Part III of that Act (criminal proceedings) for the purpose of sections 28E, 28G and 28H of that Act (search after arrest); and

(c) an offence under section 24(1)(b) of that Act for the purpose of sections 28A, 28CA and 28FA of that Act (arrest without warrant, entry of business premises to arrest and search for personal records).

SCHEDULE 1

REGULATION 1(2)

AUTHORISED CATEGORIES OF EMPLOYMENT AND
RELEVANT REQUIREMENTS

Authorised category of employment	Relevant requirements in relation to authorised category of employment
Authorised categories of employment requiring a letter of approval under the work permit arrangements	
Employment under the Sectors Based Scheme	The applicant—(1) holds a letter of approval under the work permit arrangements issued under the Sectors-Based Scheme; and
	(2) is capable of undertaking the employment specified in that letter.
Training or work experience	The applicant—(1) holds a letter of approval under the work permit arrangements issued under the Training and Work Experience Scheme; and
	(2) is capable of undertaking the training or work experience as specified in that letter.
Work permit employment	The applicant—(1) holds a letter of approval under the work permit arrangements issued in relation to work permit employment; and
	(2) is capable of undertaking the employment specified in that letter.
Other authorised categories of employment	
Airport-based operational ground staff of an overseas airline	The applicant has been transferred to the United Kingdom by an overseas-owned airline operating services to and from the United Kingdom to take up duty at an international airport as station manager, security manager or technical manager.
Au pair placement	The applicant—(1) has and intends to take up an offer of an au pair placement;
	(2) is aged between 17 to 27 inclusive;
	(3) is unmarried and is not in a civil partnership; and
	(4) is without dependants.
Domestic worker in a private household	The applicant—(1) is over 18;
	(2) has been employed for at least a year outside the United Kingdom as a domestic worker under the same roof as his employer or in a household that the employer uses for himself on a regular basis; and
	(3) intends to be so employed by that employer in the United Kingdom.

Minister of religion, missionary or member of a religious order	The applicant—(1) if a minister of religion—
	(a) has either been working for at least one year as a minister of religion in any of the five years immediately prior to the date on which the application for the worker accession card is made or, where ordination is prescribed by a religious faith as the sole means of entering the ministry, has been ordained as a minister of religion following at least one year's full time or two years' part time training for the ministry; and
	(b) holds an International English Language Testing System Certificate issued to him to certify that he has achieved level 4 competence in spoken English, and the Certificate is dated not more than two years prior to the date on which the application for an accession worker card is made;
	(2) if a missionary, has been trained as a missionary or has worked as a missionary and is being sent or has been sent to the United Kingdom by an overseas organisation;
	(3) if a member of a religious order, is living or coming to live in a community maintained by the religious order of which he is a member and, if intending to teach, does not intend to do so save at an establishment maintained by his order; and
	(4) intends to work in the United Kingdom as a minister of religion, missionary or for the religious order of which he is a member.
Overseas government employment	The applicant intends to work in the United Kingdom for an overseas government or the United Nations or other international organisation of which the United Kingdom is a member.
Postgraduate doctors, dentists and trainee general practitioners	The applicant—(1) is a graduate from a medical or dental school who is eligible for provisional or limited registration with the General Medical Council or General Dental Council and intends to work in the United Kingdom as a doctor or dentist as part of his training; or
	(2) is a doctor, dentist or trainee general practitioner eligible for full or limited registration with the General Medical Council or the General Dental Council and intends to work in the United Kingdom as part of his postgraduate training or general practitioner training in a hospital or the Community Health Services.

Private servant in a diplomatic household	The applicant—(1) is over 18; and (2) intends to work in the United Kingdom as a private servant in the household of a member of staff of a diplomatic or consular mission who enjoys diplomatic privileges and immunity within the meaning of the Vienna Convention on Diplomatic Relations.
Representative of an overseas newspaper, news agency or broadcasting organisation	The applicant has been engaged by an overseas newspaper, news agency or broadcasting organisation outside the United Kingdom and is being posted to the United Kingdom by that newspaper, agency or organisation to act as its representative.
Sole representative	The applicant—(1) has been employed outside the United Kingdom as a representative of a firm that has its headquarters and principal place of business outside the United Kingdom and has no branch, subsidiary or other representative in the United Kingdom; (2) intends to work as a senior employee with full authority to take operational decisions on behalf of the overseas firm for the purpose of representing it in the United Kingdom by establishing and operating a registered branch or wholly owned subsidiary of that overseas firm; and (3) is not a majority shareholder in that overseas firm.
Teacher or language assistant	The applicant intends to work at an educational establishment in the United Kingdom under an exchange scheme approved by the Department for Education and Skills, the Scottish or Welsh Office of Education or the Department of Education, Northern Ireland, or administered by the British Council's Education and Training Group.
Overseas qualified nurses	The applicant—(1) has obtained confirmation from the Nursing and Midwifery Council that he is eligible for admission to the Overseas Nurses Programme; and (2) has been offered and intends to take up a supervised practice placement through an education provider that is recognised by the Nursing and Midwifery Council or a midwifery adaptation programme placement in a setting approved by that Council.

1. In this Schedule—

(a) 'au pair placement' means an arrangement whereby a young person—

(i) comes to the United Kingdom for the purpose of learning English;

(ii) lives for a time as a member of an English speaking family with appropriate opportunities for study; and

(iii) helps in the home for a maximum of 5 hours per day in return for an allowance and with two free days per week;

(b) 'letter of approval under the work permit arrangements' means a letter issued by the Secretary of State under the work permit arrangements stating that employment by the employer specified in the letter of the person so specified for the type of employment so specified satisfies the labour market criteria set out in those arrangements;

(c) 'member of a religious order' means a person who lives in a community run by that order;

(d) 'minister of religion' means a religious functionary whose main regular duties comprise the leading of a congregation in performing the rites and rituals of the faith and in preaching the essentials of the creed;

(e) 'missionary' means a person who is directly engaged in spreading a religious doctrine and whose work is not in essence administrative or clerical;

(f) 'Sectors Based Scheme' means the scheme established by the Secretary of State for the purpose of paragraph 135I(i) of the immigration rules (requirements for leave to enter the United Kingdom for the purpose of employment under the Sectors Based Scheme);

(g) 'Training and Work Experience Scheme' means the scheme established by the Secretary of State for the purpose of paragraph 116(i) of the immigration rules (requirement for leave to enter the United Kingdom for approved training or work experience);

(h) 'work permit arrangements' means the arrangements published by the Secretary of State setting out the labour market criteria to be applied for the purpose of issuing the work permits referred to in paragraphs 116(i) (Training and Work Experience Scheme) and 128(i) of the immigration rules and the immigration employment document referred to in paragraph 135I(i) (Sectors Based Scheme) of the immigration rules;

(i) 'work permit employment' means a category of employment covered by the work permit arrangements, other than employment covered by the Sectors Based Scheme and the Training and Work Experience Scheme.

SCHEDULE 2

REGULATION 1(3)

CONSEQUENTIAL AMENDMENTS

…

The Immigration (Leave to Remain) (Prescribed Forms and Procedures) Regulations 2007
(SI 2007, No. 882)

Citation, commencement and interpretation

1. These Regulations may be cited as the Immigration (Leave to Remain) (Prescribed Forms and Procedures) Regulations 2007 and shall come into force on 2 April 2007.

2. In these Regulations:

'asylum claimant' means a person making a claim for asylum which has not been determined or has been granted;

'claim for asylum' has the meaning given in section 94(1) of the Immigration and Asylum Act 1999, and a claim for asylum is taken to be determined—

(a) on the day on which the Secretary of State notifies the claimant of his decision on the claim,

(b) if the claimant has appealed against the Secretary of State's decision, on the day on which the appeal is disposed of, or

(c) if the claimant has brought an in-country appeal against an immigration decision under section 82 of the Nationality, Immigration and Asylum Act 2002 or section 2 of the Special Immigration Appeals Commission Act 1997, on the day on which the appeal is disposed of; 'dependant', in respect of a person, means—

(a) the spouse, civil partner, unmarried partner or same sex partner, or

(b) a child under the age of eighteen,

of that person; and

'public enquiry office' means a public enquiry office of the Border and Immigration Agency of the Home Office.

Prescribed forms

3.—(1) Subject to paragraph (2), the form set out in Schedule 1 is prescribed for an application for limited or indefinite leave to remain in the United Kingdom as:

(a) a business person,

(b) a sole representative,

(c) a retired person of independent means,

(d) an investor, or

(e) an innovator,for the purposes of the immigration rules.

(2) Paragraph (1) does not apply to an application for limited or indefinite leave to remain in the United Kingdom as a business person where the application is made under the terms of a European Community Association Agreement.

4. The form set out in Schedule 2 is prescribed for an application for limited leave to remain in the United Kingdom:

(a) for work permit employment,

(b) as a seasonal agricultural worker,

(c) for the purpose of employment under the Sectors Based Scheme, or

(d) for Home Office approved training or work experience, for the purposes of the immigration rules.

5. The form set out in Schedule 3 is prescribed for an application for limited leave to remain in the United Kingdom as a highly skilled migrant for the purposes of the immigration rules.

6. The form set out in Schedule 4 is prescribed for an application for limited leave to remain in the United Kingdom as:

(a) the spouse or civil partner of a person present and settled in the United Kingdom, or

(b) the unmarried partner or same sex partner of a person present and settled in the United Kingdom, for the purposes of the immigration rules.

7. The form set out in Schedule 5 is prescribed for an application for limited leave to remain in the United Kingdom:

(a) as a student,

(b) as a student nurse,

(c) to re-sit an examination,

(d) to write up a thesis,

(e) as a student union sabbatical officer, or

(f) as a prospective student, for the purposes of the immigration rules.

8 The form set out in Schedule 6 is prescribed for an application for limited leave to remain in the United Kingdom as a participant in the [International Graduates Scheme] for the purposes of the immigration rules.

Note: Words in square brackets inserted from 1 May 2007 (SI 2007/1122).

9. The form set out in Schedule 7 is prescribed for an application for limited leave to remain in the United Kingdom as a participant in the Fresh Talent: Working in Scotland Scheme for the purposes of the immigration rules.

10.—(1) The form set out in Schedule 8 is prescribed for an application for limited leave to remain in the United Kingdom as:

(a) a visitor,

(b) a visitor seeking to undergo or continue private medical treatment,

(c) a postgraduate doctor or dentist or a trainee general practitioner,

(d) an au pair,

(e) a teacher or language assistant under an approved exchange scheme,

(f) a representative of an overseas newspaper, news agency or broadcasting organisation,

(g) a private servant in a diplomatic household,

(h) a domestic worker in a private household,

(i) an overseas government employee,

(j) a minister of religion, missionary or member of a religious order,

(k) a visiting religious worker or a religious worker in a non-pastoral role,

(l) a member of the operational ground staff of an overseas-owned airline,

(m) a person with United Kingdom ancestry,

(n) a writer, composer or artist,

(o) an overseas qualified nurse or midwife, or

(p) the spouse, civil partner or child of an armed forces member who is exempt from immigration control under section 8(4) of the Immigration Act 1971, for the purposes of the immigration rules.

(2) Subject to paragraph (3), the form set out in Schedule 8 is prescribed for an application for limited leave to remain in the United Kingdom for any other reason or purpose for which provision is made in the immigration rules but which is not covered by the forms prescribed by regulations 3 to 9.

(3) Paragraph (2) does not apply to an application for limited leave to remain in the United Kingdom where:

(a) the application is made under the terms of a European Community Association Agreement, or

(b) the basis on which the application is made is that the applicant is an asylum claimant or a dependant of an asylum claimant.

11. The form set out in Schedule 9 is prescribed for an application for indefinite leave to remain in the United Kingdom as:

(a) the spouse or civil partner of a person present and settled in the United Kingdom, or

(b) the unmarried partner or same sex partner of a person present and settled in the United Kingdom, for the purposes of the immigration rules.

12. The form set out in Schedule 10 is prescribed for an application for indefinite leave to remain in the United Kingdom as:

(a) the child under the age of eighteen of a parent, parents or relative present and settled in the United Kingdom,

(b) the adopted child under the age of eighteen of a parent or parents present and settled in the United Kingdom, or

(c) the parent, grandparent or other dependent relative of a person present and settled in the United Kingdom, for the purposes of the immigration rules.

13. The form set out in Schedule 11 is prescribed for an application for indefinite leave to remain in the United Kingdom as a victim of domestic violence.

14.—(1) The form set out in Schedule 12 is prescribed for an application for indefinite leave to remain in the United Kingdom:

(a) as a work permit holder,

(b) as a highly skilled migrant,

(c) as a representative of an overseas newspaper, news agency or broadcasting organisation,

(d) as a private servant in a diplomatic household,

(e) as a domestic worker in a private household,

(f) as an overseas government employee,

(g) as a minister of religion, missionary or member of a religious order,

(h) as a member of the operational ground staff of an overseas-owned airline,

(i) as a person with United Kingdom ancestry,

(j) as a writer, composer or artist,

(k) on the basis of long residence in the United Kingdom, or

(l) as a foreign or Commonwealth citizen discharged from HM Forces, for the purposes of the immigration rules.

(2) Subject to paragraph (3), the form set out in Schedule 12 is prescribed for an application for indefinite leave to remain in the United Kingdom for any other reason or purpose for which provision is made in the immigration rules but which is not covered by the forms prescribed by regulations 11, 12 or 13.

(3) Paragraph (2) does not apply to an application for indefinite leave to remain in the United Kingdom where:

(a) the application is made under the terms of a European Community Association Agreement,

(b) the basis on which the application is made is that the applicant is an asylum claimant or a dependant of an asylum claimant.

15. An application for leave to remain in the United Kingdom which is made by a person ('the main applicant') on a form prescribed by any of the regulations 3 to 14 above may include an application in respect of any person applying for leave to remain in the United Kingdom as a dependant of the main applicant.

Prescribed procedures

16.—(1) The following procedures are prescribed in relation to an application for which a form is prescribed by regulations 3 to 14:

(a) the form shall be signed and dated by the applicant, save that where the applicant is under the age of eighteen, the form may be signed and dated by the parent or legal guardian of the applicant on behalf of the applicant;

(b) the application shall be accompanied by such documents and photographs as specified in the form; and

(c) each part of the form shall be completed as specified in the form.

(2) The following procedures are prescribed in relation to delivery of an application for which a form is prescribed:

(a) in relation to an application for which a form is prescribed by regulation 3, the application shall be sent by prepaid post or by courier to the Border and Immigration Agency of the Home Office; it may not be submitted in person at a public enquiry office,

(b) in relation to an application for which a form is prescribed by regulation 4, the application shall be:

(i) sent by prepaid post or by courier to Work Permits (UK) at the Border and Immigration Agency of the Home Office, or

(ii) submitted in person at the Croydon public enquiry office (but no other public enquiry office),

(c) in relation to an application for which a form is prescribed by regulation 5, the application shall be sent by prepaid post or by courier to Work Permits (UK) at the Border and Immigration Agency of the Home Office, and may not be submitted in person at a public enquiry office,

(d) in relation to an application for which a form is prescribed by regulations 6 to 12 and regulation 14, the application shall be:

(i) sent by prepaid post to the Border and Immigration Agency of the Home Office, or

(ii) submitted in person at a public enquiry office,

(e) in relation to an application for which a form is prescribed by regulation 13, the application shall be sent by prepaid post to the Border and Immigration Agency of the Home Office; it may not be submitted in person at a public enquiry office.

17.—(1) A failure to comply with any of the requirements of regulation 16(1) to any extent will only invalidate an application if:

(a) the applicant does not provide, when making the application, an explanation for the failure which the Secretary of State considers to be satisfactory,

(b) the Secretary of State notifies the applicant, or the person who appears to the Secretary of State to represent the applicant, of the failure within 28 days of the date on which the application is made, and

(c) the applicant does not comply with the requirements within a reasonable time, and in any event within 28 days, of being notified by the Secretary of State of the failure.

(2) For the purposes of this regulation, the date on which the application is made is:

(a) in the case of an application sent by post, the date of posting,

(b) in the case of an application submitted in person, the date on which the application is delivered to, and accepted by, a public enquiry office, and

(c) in the case of an application sent by courier, the date on which the application is delivered to Work Permits (UK) at the Border and Immigration Agency of the Home Office.

Revocation and transitional provision

18.—(1) ...

(2) ...

(3) An application made on a form prescribed by the Immigration (Leave to Remain) (Prescribed Forms and Procedures) Regulations 2006 shall be deemed to have been made on the corresponding form prescribed by these Regulations if made within 21 days of these Regulations coming into force for the purposes of section 31A of the Immigration Act 1971.

Note: Paragraphs (1) and (2) revoke SI 2006/1421, SI 2006/1548, SI 2006/2889.

SCHEDULES

...

The Asylum (Procedures) Regulations 2007
(SI 2007, No. 3187)

Citation and commencement

1. These Regulations may be cited as the Asylum (Procedures) Regulations 2007 and shall come into force on 1 December 2007.

Interpretation

2. In these Regulations –

'the 1997 Act' means the Special Immigration Appeals Commission Act 1997);

'the 2002 Act' means the Nationality, Immigration and Asylum Act 2002;

'asylum claim' and 'human rights claim' have the meanings given to them in section 113 of the 2002 Act.

Designation of States or parts of States for the purposes of section 94 of the 2002 Act

3. ....

Note: Amends s 94 Nationality, Immigration and Asylum Act 2002.

European Common List of Safe Countries of Origin

4. ....

Note: Amends s 94 Nationality, Immigration and Asylum Act 2002.

Interpreters

5.—(1) Paragraph (2) applies where a person who has made an asylum or a human rights claim (or both)—

(a) appeals under section 82, 83 or 83A of the 2002 Act or section 2 of the 1997 Act, and

(b) by virtue of Rules made under section 106 of the 2002 Act or sections 5 and 8 of the 1997 Act is entitled to the services of an interpreter for the purposes of bringing his appeal.

(2) The Secretary of State shall defray the costs of providing the interpreter.

(3) Paragraph (5) applies where a person who has made an asylum claim or a human rights claim (or both) is party to –

(a) an appeal under section 103B, 103C or 103E of the 2002 Act, or

(b) an appeal under section 7 of the 1997 Act.

(4) Paragraph (5) also applies where a person who has made an asylum or a human rights claim (or both) makes –

(a) an application to the supervisory jurisdiction of the Court of Session made by petition for judicial review,

(b) an application under section 31 of the Supreme Court Act 1981, or

(c) an application under section 18 of the Judicature (Northern Ireland) Act 1978.

(5) The person mentioned in paragraphs (3) and (4) shall be entitled to the services of an interpreter for the purposes of the appeal or application —

(a) when giving evidence, and

(b) in such other circumstances as the court hearing the appeal or application considers it necessary.

(6) Where a person is entitled to the services of an interpreter under paragraph (5), the Secretary of State shall defray the costs of providing such interpreter.

Amendment to the Immigration (Notices) Regulations 2003

6. ....

Note: Amends SI 2003/658.

The Immigration (Restrictions on Employment) Order 2007

(SI 2007, No. 3290)

Citation, commencement and interpretation

1. This order may be cited as the Immigration (Restrictions on Employment) Order 2007 and shall come into force on 29 February 2008.

2. In this order—

'the 2006 Act' means the Immigration, Asylum and Nationality Act 2006; and

'document' means an original document.

Excuse from paying civil penalty

3.—(1) To the extent provided for by paragraph (2) an employer is excused from paying a penalty under section 15 of the 2006 Act if —

(a) the employee or prospective employee produces to the employer any of the documents or combinations of documents described in list A in the Schedule to this Order; and

(b) the employer complies with the requirements set out in article 6 of this order.

(2) An employer will be excused under this article from paying a penalty under section 15 of the 2006 Act—

(a) for the duration of the employment, if the document or combination of documents is produced prior to the commencement of employment; or

(b) subject to article 5, for the remainder of the employment, if the document or combination of documents is produced after the employment has commenced.

4.—(1) To the extent provided for by paragraph (2) an employer is excused from paying a penalty under section 15 of the 2006 Act if —

(a) the employee or prospective employee produces to the employer any of the documents or combination of documents described in list B in the Schedule to this Order; and

(b) the employer complies with the requirements set out in article 6 of this Order.

(2) Subject to article 5 an employer will be excused under this article from paying a penalty under section 15 of the 2006 Act for a period of twelve months, beginning with the date on which the employee produced the document or combination of documents.

5. An employer is excused from paying a penalty under section 15 of the 2006 Act by virtue of article 3(2)(b) and article 4(2) only if prior to the commencement of employment the employee produced to the employer any of the documents or combination of documents described in the Schedule to this Order.

6. The requirements in relation to any documents or combinations of documents produced by an employee pursuant to articles 3 or 4 of this order are that—

(a) the employer takes all reasonable steps to check the validity of the document;

(b) the copy or copies are retained securely by the employer for a period of not less than two years after the employment has come to an end;

(c) if a document contains a photograph, the employer has satisfied himself that the photograph is of the prospective employee or employee;

(d) if a document contains a date of birth, the employer has satisfied himself that the date of birth is consistent with the appearance of the prospective employee or employee;

(e) the employer takes all other reasonable steps to check that the prospective employee or employee is the rightful owner of the document;

(f) if the document is not a passport or other travel document the employer retains a copy of whole of the document in a format which cannot be subsequently altered; [...]

[(g) if the document is a passport or other travel document (which is not in the form of a card), the employer retains a copy of the following pages of that document in a format which cannot be subsequently altered—

(i) the front cover;

(ii) any page containing the holder's personal details including nationality;

(iii) any page containing the holder's photograph;

(iv) any page containing the holder's signature;

(v) any page containing the date of expiry; and

(vi) any page containing information indicating the holder has an entitlement to enter or remain in the UK and undertake the work in question; and

(h) if the document is a travel document in the form of a card, the employer retains a copy of the whole of that document in a format which cannot be subsequently altered].

Note: Paragraph (g) substituted from 24 November 2009 (SI 2009/2908).

7. Nothing in this Order permits employers to retain documents produced by an employee for the purposes of articles 3 or 4 for any period longer than is necessary for the purposes of ensuring compliance with article 6.

Objections

8. The manner prescribed in which the notice of objection must be given is that it must contain—

(a) the reference number of the notice given under section 15(2) of the 2006 Act;

(b) the name and contact address of the employer;

(c) the name and contact address of the employee in respect of whom the penalty was issued;

(d) the full grounds of objection;

(e) where the employer requests permission to pay by instalments, full details of the employer's ability to pay the penalty;

(f) confirmation and details of any appeal made by the employer to a County Court or Sheriff Court on the basis that the employer is not liable to the penalty, he is excused payment by virtue of section 15(3) of the 2006 Act, or that the amount of the penalty is too high; and

(g) any documents to be relied upon in support of the objection.

9. The prescribed period within which a notice of objection must be given for the purposes of section 16(3)(d) of the 2006 Act is 28 days, beginning with the date specified in the penalty notice as the date upon which it is given.

10. The period prescribed for the purposes of section 16(5)(b) of the 2006 Act within which the Secretary of State must inform the objector of his decision is 28 days, beginning with the date on which the notice of objection was given to the Secretary of State.

Codes of Practice

11. The code of practice entitled 'Civil Penalties for Employers', issued by the Secretary of State under section 19(1) of the 2006 Act shall come into force on 29 February 2008.

12. The code of practice entitled 'Guidance for Employers on the Avoidance of Unlawful Discrimination in Employment Practice While Seeking to Prevent Illegal Working', issued by the Secretary of State under section 23(1) of the 2006 Act shall come into force on 29 February 2008.

Articles 3 and 4   SCHEDULE
                                         LIST A

1. [An ID Card (issued to the holder under the Identity Cards Act 2006(3)) or] a passport showing that the holder, or a person named in the passport as the child of the holder, is a British citizen or a citizen of the United Kingdom and Colonies having the right of abode in the United Kingdom.

2. An ID Card (issued to the holder under the Identity Cards Act 2006), a national identity card or a passport which has the effect of identifying the holder, or a person named in the passport as the child of the holder, as a national of the European Economic Area or Switzerland.]

3. A residence permit, registration certificate or document certifying or indicating permanent residence issued by the Home Office or the Border and Immigration Agency to a national of a European Economic Area country or Switzerland.

4. A permanent residence card issued by the Home Office or the Border and Immigration Agency to the family member of a national of a European Economic Area country or Switzerland.

5. A Biometric Immigration Document issued by the Border and Immigration Agency to the holder which indicates that the person named in it is allowed to stay indefinitely in the United Kingdom, or has no time limit on their stay in the United Kingdom.

6. A passport or other travel document endorsed to show that the holder is exempt from immigration control, is allowed to stay indefinitely in the United Kingdom, has the right of abode in the United Kingdom, or has no time limit on their stay in the United Kingdom.

7. An Immigration Status Document issued by the Home Office or the Border and Immigration Agency to the holder with an endorsement indicating that the person named in it is allowed to stay indefinitely in the United Kingdom or has no time limit on their stay in the United Kingdom, when produced in combination with an official document giving the person's permanent National Insurance Number and their name issued by a Government agency or a previous employer.

8. A full birth certificate issued in the United Kingdom which includes the name(s) of at least one of the holder's parents, when produced in combination with an official document giving the person's permanent National Insurance Number and their name issued by a Government agency or a previous employer.

9. A full adoption certificate issued in the United Kingdom which includes the name(s) of at least one of the holder's adoptive parents when produced in combination with an official document giving the person's permanent National Insurance Number and their name issued by a Government agency or a previous employer.

10. A birth certificate issued in the Channel Islands, the Isle of Man or Ireland, when produced in combination with an official document giving the person's permanent National Insurance Number and their name issued by a Government agency or a previous employer.

11. An adoption certificate issued in the Channel Islands, the Isle of Man or Ireland, when produced in combination with an official document giving the person's permanent National Insurance Number and their name issued by a Government agency or a previous employer.

12. A certificate of registration or naturalisation as a British citizen, when produced in combination with an official document giving the person's permanent National Insurance Number and their name issued by a Government agency or a previous employer.

13. A letter issued by the Home Office or the Border and Immigration Agency to the holder which indicates that the person named in it is allowed to stay indefinitely in the United Kingdom when produced in combination with an official document giving the person's permanent National Insurance Number and their name issued by a Government agency or a previous employer.

Note: Words in square brackets in paragraph 1 inserted and paragraph 2 substituted from 24 November 2009 (SI 2009/2908).

List B

1. A passport or travel document endorsed to show that the holder is allowed to stay in the United Kingdom and is allowed to do the type of work in question, provided that it does not require the issue of a work permit.

2. A Biometric Immigration Document issued by the Border and Immigration Agency to the holder which indicates that the person named in it can stay in the United Kingdom and is allowed to do the work in question.

3. A work permit or other approval to take employment issued by the Home Office or the Border and Immigration Agency when produced in combination with either a passport or another travel document endorsed to show the holder is allowed to stay in the United Kingdom and is allowed to do the work in question, or a letter issued by the Home Office or the Border and Immigration Agency to the holder or the employer or prospective employer confirming the same.

4. A certificate of application issued by the Home Office or the Border and Immigration Agency to or for [a person who has applied under regulation 18A(1) of the Immigration (European Economic Area) Regulations 2006, or to or for] a family member of a national of a European Economic Area country or Switzerland stating that the holder is permitted to take employment which is less than 6 months old when produced in combination with evidence of verification by the Border and Immigration Agency Employer Checking Service.

5. A residence card or document issued by the Home Office or the Border and Immigration Agency to a family member of a national of a European Economic Area country or Switzerland.

6. An Application Registration Card issued by the Home Office or the Border and Immigration Agency stating that the holder is permitted to take employment, when produced in combination with evidence of verification by the Border and Immigration Agency Employer Checking Service.

7. An Immigration Status Document issued by the Home Office or the Border and Immigration Agency to the holder with an endorsement indicating that the person named in it can stay in the United Kingdom, and is allowed to do the type of work in question, when produced in combination with an official document giving the person's permanent National Insurance Number and their name issued by a Government agency or a previous employer.

8. A letter issued by the Home Office or the Border and Immigration Agency to the holder or the employer or prospective employer, which indicates that the person named in it can stay in the United Kingdom and is allowed to do the work in question when produced in combination with an official document giving the person's permanent National Insurance Number and their name issued by a Government agency or a previous employer.

Note: Words inserted in para 4 of List B from 16 July 2012 (SI 2012/1547).

The Immigration and Asylum (Provision of Services or Facilities) Regulations 2007
(SI 2007, No. 3627)

Citation and commencement

1. These Regulations may be cited as the Immigration and Asylum (Provision of Services or Facilities) Regulations 2007 and shall come into force on 31 January 2008.

Interpretation

2. In these Regulations—

'the 1999 Act' means the Immigration and Asylum Act 1999;

'ante-natal eligible period' means the period from eight weeks before the expected date of birth to the date of birth;

'child' means an individual who is less than 18 years old;

'destitute' is to be construed in accordance with section 95(3) of the 1999 Act;

'full birth certificate' means a birth certificate issued in the United Kingdom, which specifies the names of the child's parents;

'immigration officer' means a person appointed as an immigration officer under paragraph 1(1) of Schedule 2 to the Immigration Act 1971;

'maternity payment' means a payment of £250 made by the Secretary of State to a person supported under section 95 or section 98 of the 1999 Act to help with the costs arising from the birth of a child;

'mother' means a woman who is a supported person and who has provided evidence to satisfy the Secretary of State that she has given birth to a child;

'post-natal eligible period' means the period from the date of the birth to six weeks after the birth;

'pregnant woman' means a woman who is a supported person who has provided evidence to satisfy the Secretary of State that she is pregnant;

'provider' means a person providing facilities for the accommodation of persons by arrangement with the Secretary of State under section 4 of the 1999 Act;

'qualified person' has the same meaning as in section 84(2) of the 1999 Act;

'qualifying journey' means where—

(a) a single journey of a distance of not less than three miles; or

(b) where there is a specified need, a single journey of a distance of less than three miles; 'specified need' means where—

(a) the supported person is unable or virtually unable to walk a distance of up to three miles by reason of a physical impediment or for some other reason; or

(b) the supported person has one or more child dependants—

(i) aged under five; or

(ii) who are unable or virtually unable to walk a distance of up to three miles by reason of a physical impediment or for some other reason;

'supported person' means a person who is being provided with accommodation under section 4 of the 1999 Act and who is destitute; and

'voluntary sector partner' means an organisation funded by the Secretary of State to deliver aspects of asylum support services.

Travel

3.—(1) The Secretary of State may supply, or arrange for the supply of, facilities for travel for a qualifying journey to a supported person to—

(a) receive healthcare treatment, provided that the supported person has provided evidence that the qualifying journey is necessary; or

(b) register a birth.

(2) Subject to paragraph (3), if the Secretary of State supplies, or arranges for the supply of, facilities for travel for a qualifying journey to a supported person under paragraph (1) then, if necessary, the Secretary of State may also supply, or arrange for the supply of, facilities for travel for that qualifying journey to—

(a) one or more dependants of that supported person; and

(b) in the case of a supported person who is a child—

(i) a parent or guardian of that supported person or a person who for the time being takes parental responsibility for that supported person; and

(ii) if the parent, guardian or person who for the time being takes parental responsibility for that supported person himself has dependants then one or more of his dependants.

(3) The Secretary of State may only supply, or arrange for the supply of, facilities for travel under paragraph (2) to persons who are supported persons.

Birth certificates

4. The Secretary of State may arrange for the provision to a supported person of his child's full birth certificate.

Telephone calls and letters

5.—(1) The Secretary of State may supply, or arrange for the supply of, facilities to make telephone calls—

(a) regarding medical treatment or care,

(b) to a qualified person,

(c) to a court or tribunal,

(d) to a voluntary sector partner,

(e) to a citizens advice bureau,

(f) to a local authority,

(g) to an immigration officer, or

(h) to the Secretary of State,

to a supported person aged 18 or over.

(2) The Secretary of State may supply, or arrange for the supply of, stationery and postage for correspondence—

(a) regarding medical treatment or care,

(b) to a qualified person,

(c) to a court or tribunal,

(d) to a voluntary sector partner,

(e) to a citizens advice bureau,

(f) to a local authority,

(g) to an immigration officer, or

(h) to the Secretary of State,

to a supported person aged 18 or over.

One-off supply of vouchers for pregnant women and new mothers

6.—(1) During the ante-natal eligible period, on application, the Secretary of State may supply, or arrange for the supply of, vouchers redeemable for goods to the value of £250 in respect of each expected child to a pregnant woman.

(2) In a case where such support has not been provided under paragraph (1), during the post-natal eligible period, on application, the Secretary of State may supply, or arrange for the supply of, vouchers redeemable for goods to the value of £250 in respect of each new born child to a mother.

(3) Paragraphs (1) and (2) shall not apply if a maternity payment has been made in respect of the child in question.

Additional weekly vouchers for pregnant women and children under three

7.—(1) For the duration of the pregnancy, on application, the Secretary of State may supply, or arrange for the supply of, vouchers redeemable for goods or services to the value of £3 per week to a pregnant woman.

(2) Until the first birthday of a child who is a supported person, on application, the Secretary of State may supply, or arrange for the supply of, vouchers redeemable for goods or services to the value of £5 per week to him.

(3) From the day after the first birthday of a child who is a supported person, until the third birthday, on application, the Secretary of State may supply, or arrange for the supply of, vouchers redeemable for goods or services to the value of £3 per week to him.

Additional weekly vouchers for clothing for children

8. Until the sixteenth birthday of a child who is a supported person, on application, the Secretary of State may supply, or arrange for the supply of, vouchers redeemable for clothing to the value of £5 per week to him.

Exceptional specific needs

9.—(1) If the Secretary of State is satisfied that a supported person has an exceptional need for:

(a) facilities for travel,

(b) facilities to make telephone calls,

(c) stationery and postage, or

(d) essential living needs,she may provide for that need, notwithstanding that the conditions for the supply of those services or facilities referred to respectively in regulations 3, 5, and 6 are not satisfied.

(2) In determining what are or are not to be treated as essential living needs, the Secretary of State shall have regard to regulations made under section 95(7) of the 1999 Act.

The Immigration, Asylum and Nationality Act 2006 (Commencement No. 8 and Transitional and Saving Provisions) Order 2008

2008 No. 310 (C. 10)

Citation and interpretation

1.—(1) This Order may be cited at the Immigration, Asylum and Nationality Act 2006 (Commencement No. 8 and Transitional and Saving Provisions) Order 2008.

(2) In this Order—
'the 2006 Act' means the Immigration, Asylum and Nationality Act 2006;
'the 2002 Act' means the Nationality, Immigration and Asylum Act 2002;
'the 1999 Act' means the Immigration and Asylum Act 1999;
'the 1996 Act' means the Asylum and Immigration Act 1996; and
'immigration rules' means rules made under section 3(2) of the Immigration Act 1971.

Commencement

2.—(1) Subject to article 5 the following provisions of the 2006 Act shall come into force on 29 February 2008—
(a) sections 15 to 18 to the extent to which they are not already in force (penalty for employment of adult subject to immigration control);
(b) sections 21 and 22 (offence of employing adult subject to immigration control);
(c) section 24 (employment of adult subject to immigration control: temporary admission);
(d) section 26 (repeal); and
(e) in Schedule 3, the entries relating to the 1996 Act.

(2) The following provisions of the 2006 Act shall come into force on 29 February 2008—
(a) section 50(3)(a) (repeal); and
(b) in Schedule 3, the entries relating to section 31A of the Immigration Act 1971.

3. The following provisions of the 2006 Act shall come in to force on 1 April 2008—
(a) subject to article 4, section 4 (entry clearance);
(b) section 33 (freight information: police powers) for the purposes of making an order under subsection (5)(a); and
(c) section 47 (removal: person with statutorily extended leave).

Saving and Transitional Provision

4. Notwithstanding the commencement of section 4 of the 2006 Act and the substitution of section 88A of the 2002 Act and section 23 of the 1999 Act, section 4(1) (appeals: entry clearance) and section 4(2) of the 2006 Act (monitoring refusals of entry clearance) shall have effect only so far as they relate to applications of a kind identified in immigration rules as requiring to be considered under a 'Points Based System' [and applications

made for the purpose of entering the United Kingdom as a visitor, including applications made for the purpose of visiting a person of a class or description prescribed by regulations for the purpose of section 88A(1)(a)(3) of the 2002 Act].

5.—(1) Notwithstanding the commencement of section 26 of the 2006 Act (repeal) the following provisions and instruments continue to have effect in relation to employment which commenced before 29th February 2008, including employment which continued on or after that date—

(a) sections 8 (restrictions on employment) and 8A (code of practice) of the 1996 Act;

(b) any Code of Practice in force immediately before 29 February 2008 under section 8A of the 1996 Act;

(c) the Immigration (Restrictions on Employment) Order 2004; and

(d) the Immigration (Restrictions on Employment) (Code of Practice) Order 2001.

(2) Sections 15 to 18, 21, 22, 24, 25 and 26 of the 2006 Act are of no effect in relation to employment of a kind mentioned in paragraph (1).

Note: Words inserted in article 4 from 9 July 2012 (SI 2012/1531).

The Appeals from the Upper Tribunal to the
Court of Appeal Order 2008
2008 No. 2834

1. This Order may be cited as the Appeals from the Upper Tribunal to the Court of Appeal Order 2008 and shall come into force on 3 November 2008.

2. Permission to appeal to the Court of Appeal in England and Wales or leave to appeal to the Court of Appeal in Northern Ireland shall not be granted unless the Upper Tribunal or, where the Upper Tribunal refuses permission, the relevant appellate court, considers that—

(a) the proposed appeal would raise some important point of principle or practice; or

(b) there is some other compelling reason for the relevant appellate court to hear the appeal.

The Immigration (Biometric Registration)
Regulations 2008
SI 2008 No. 3048

Made	*24th November 2008*
Coming into force	*25th November 2008*

CONTENTS

Citation, commencement and interpretation

1. These Regulations may be cited as the Immigration (Biometric Registration) Regulations 2008 and shall come into force on the day after the day on which they are made.

[**2.** In these Regulations—

'Certificate of Travel' means a travel document issued in the United Kingdom at the discretion of the Secretary of State to persons who have been formally and, in the view of the Secretary of State, unreasonably refused a passport by their own authorities and who have—

(a) been refused recognition as a refugee or as a stateless person but have been granted discretionary leave to remain or humanitarian protection; or

(b) been granted indefinite leave to enter or remain;

'Convention travel document' means a travel document issued pursuant to Article 28 of the Geneva Convention;

'dependant' means a spouse, a civil partner, an unmarried or same sex partner, or a child;

'Geneva Convention' means the Convention relating to the Status of Refugees done at Geneva on 28th July 1951 and the New York Protocol of 31st January 1967;

'humanitarian protection' means protection granted in accordance with paragraph 339C of the immigration rules;

'immigration rules' means the rules for the time being laid down as mentioned in section 3(2) of the Immigration Act 1971(a);

'leave to remain' means limited or indefinite leave to remain in the United Kingdom given in accordance with the provisions of the Immigration Act 1971 or the immigration rules;

'refugee' means a person who falls within Article 1(A) of the Geneva Convention and to whom regulation 7 of the Refugee or Person in Need of International Protection (Qualification) Regulations 2006 does not apply(b);

'Stateless Convention' means the Convention relating to the Status of Stateless Persons done at New York on 28th September 1954; and

'Stateless Person's Travel Document' means a travel document issued pursuant to Article 28 of the Stateless Convention.]

Note: Regulation 2 substituted from 28 February 2012 (SI 2012/594).

Requirement to apply for a biometric immigration document

[3.—(1) Subject to paragraph (6), a person subject to immigration control must apply for the issue of a biometric immigration document where he—

(a) satisfies the condition in paragraph (2); or

(b) is a person falling within paragraph (3).

(2) The condition is that whilst in the United Kingdom the person makes an application—

(a) for limited leave to remain for a period which, together with any preceding period of leave to enter or remain, exceeds a cumulative total of 6 months leave in the United Kingdom;

(b) for indefinite leave to remain;

(c) to replace a stamp, sticker or other attachment in a passport or other document which indicated that he had been granted limited or indefinite leave to enter or remain in the United Kingdom;

(d) to replace a letter which indicated that he had been granted limited or indefinite leave to enter or remain in the United Kingdom;

(e) to be recognised as a refugee or a person in need of humanitarian protection;

(f) to be recognised as a stateless person in accordance with Article 1 of the Stateless Convention;

(g) for a Convention Travel Document, Stateless Person's Travel Document or a Certificate of Travel and does not already hold a valid biometric immigration document; or

(h) as the dependant of a person who is making an application in accordance with subparagraph (a), (b), (e) or (f).

(3) Subject to paragraph (4), a person falls within this paragraph if he has been notified on or after 1st December 2012 that the Secretary of State has decided to grant him—

(a) limited leave to remain for a period which, together with any preceding period of leave to enter or remain, exceeds a cumulative total of 6 months leave in the United Kingdom; or

(b) indefinite leave to remain.

(4) A person does not fall within paragraph (3) if—

(a) he was required to apply for a biometric immigration document in respect of his application for that leave; or

(b) he was required to apply for a biometric immigration document in respect of any application mentioned in paragraph (2).

(5) Where a person is required to apply for a biometric immigration document, that application must be made on the form or in the manner specified for that purpose (if one is specified) in the immigration rules.

(6) These Regulations do not apply to a person who applies for or is granted leave to remain in accordance with paragraphs 56R and 56U of the immigration rules (Olympic or Paralympic Games Family Member Visitor or an Olympic or Paralympic Games Family Member Child Visitor).]

Note: Regulation 3 substituted from 28 February 2012 (SI 2012/594).

[**Specified categories**

4 ...

Note: Regulation 4 omitted from 28 February 2012 (SI 2012/594).

Power for an authorised person to require a person to provide biometric information

5.—(1) Subject to regulation 7, where a person makes an application for the issue of a biometric immigration document in accordance with regulation 3, an authorised person may require him to provide a record of his fingerprints and a photograph of his face.

(2) Where an authorised person requires a person to provide biometric information in accordance with paragraph (1), the person must provide it.

Power for the Secretary of State to use and retain existing biometric information

6.—(1) This regulation applies where —

(a) a person makes an application for the issue of a biometric immigration document in accordance with regulation 3; and

(b) the Secretary of State already has a record of the person's fingerprints or a photograph of the person's face in his possession (for whatever reason).

(2) Where this regulation applies the Secretary of State may use or retain that information for the purposes of these Regulations.

Provision in relation to persons under the age of sixteen

7.—(1) A person under the age of sixteen ('the child') must not be required to provide a record of his fingerprints or a photograph of his face in accordance with regulation 5 except where the authorised person is satisfied that the fingerprints or the photograph will be taken in the presence of a person aged eighteen or over who is —

(a) the child's parent or guardian; or

(b) a person who for the time being takes responsibility for the child.

(2) The person mentioned in paragraph (1)(b) may not be —

    (a) an officer of the Secretary of State who is not an authorised person;

    (b) an authorised person; or

    (c) any other person acting on behalf of an authorised person under regulation 8(2)(d).

(3) This regulation does not apply if the authorised person reasonably believes that the person who is to be fingerprinted or photographed is aged sixteen or over.

Process by which a person's fingerprints and photograph may be obtained and recorded

8.—(1) An authorised person who requires a person to provide a record of his fingerprints or a photograph of his face under regulation 5 may require the person to submit to any process, or any combination of processes, specified in paragraph (2).

(2) An authorised person may —

    (a) require a person to make an appointment before a specified date, which the person must attend, to enable a record of his fingerprints or a photograph of his face to be taken;

    (b) specify the date, time and place for the appointment;

    (c) specify any documents which the person must bring to the appointment, or action which the person must take, to confirm his appointment and identity;

    [(d) require a person to attend premises before a specified date where a record of his fingerprints or a photograph of his face is taken by a person on behalf of an authorised person; and

    (e) specify any documents which the person must bring to the premises, or action which the person must take to confirm his identity.]

(3) An authorised person may require a record of fingerprints or photograph to be of a particular specification.

(4) Where an authorised person requires a person to submit to any process, or any combination of processes, in accordance with paragraph (1), the person must submit to it.

Note: Sub-paragraph (2)(d) substituted and 2(e) inserted from 28 February 2012 (SI 2012/594).

Use and retention of biometric information

9. Subject to regulations 10 and 11, the Secretary of State may use a record of a person's fingerprints or a photograph of a person's face provided in accordance with these Regulations —

    (a) in connection with the exercise of a function by virtue of the Immigration Acts;

    (b) in connection with the control of the United Kingdom's borders;

    (c) in connection with the exercise of a function related to nationality;

    (d) in connection with the prevention, investigation, or prosecution of an offence;

    (e) for a purpose which appears to the Secretary of State to be required in order to protect national security;

    (f) in connection with identifying victims of an event or situation which has caused loss of human life or human illness or injury;

    (g) for the purpose of ascertaining whether any person has failed to comply with the law or has gained, or sought to gain, a benefit or service, or has asserted an entitlement, to which he is not by law entitled.

10. Subject to regulation 11, any record of a person's fingerprints or his photograph, or any copy of them, held by the Secretary of State pursuant to these Regulations must be destroyed if the Secretary of State thinks it is no longer likely to be of use in accordance with regulation 9.

11. If a person proves that he is —

(a) a British citizen; or

(b) a Commonwealth citizen who has a right of abode in the United Kingdom as a result of section 2(1)(b) of the Immigration Act 1971 (statement of right of abode in the United Kingdom).

Any record of the person's fingerprints or his photograph, or any copy of them, held by the Secretary of State pursuant to these Regulations must be destroyed as soon as reasonably practicable.

12.—(1) The Secretary of State must take all reasonably practicable steps to secure —

(a) that data held in an electronic form which relate to any record of fingerprints or photograph which has to be destroyed in accordance with regulation 10 or 11 are destroyed or erased; or

(b) that access to such data is blocked.

(2) The person to whom the data relate is entitled, on written request, to a certificate issued by the Secretary of State to the effect that he has taken the steps required by paragraph (1).

(3) A certificate issued under paragraph (2) must be issued within three months of the date on which the request was received by the Secretary of State.

Issue of a biometric immigration document

13.—(1) The Secretary of State may issue a biometric immigration document to a person who has applied in accordance with regulation 3, provided the Secretary of State has decided to—

[(a) grant limited leave to remain to the person for a period which, together with any preceding period of leave to enter or remain, exceeds a cumulative total of 6 months leave in the United Kingdom; or

(b) grant indefinite leave to remain to the person; or

(c) issue or replace a document to the person following an application mentioned in regulation 3(2)(c), (d) or (g).]

(2) A biometric immigration document begins to have effect on the date of issue.

(3) A biometric immigration document ceases to have effect on one of the dates specified in paragraph (4), whichever date occurs earliest.

(4) The specified dates are —

(a) the date that the person's leave to remain ceases to have effect, including where the leave to remain is varied, cancelled or invalidated, or is to lapse;

(b) in the case of a biometric immigration document which was issued to a person aged [sixteen] or over, the date after the expiry of ten years beginning with the date of issue; or

(c) in the case of a biometric immigration document which was issued to a person aged under [sixteen], the date after the expiry of five years beginning with the date of issue.

Note: Sub-paragraphs (1)(a)–(c) substituted/inserted from 28 February 2012 (SI 2012/594). Words in square brackets in paragraph (4) substituted from 31 March 2009, but without effect to biometric immigration documents issued before that date, (SI 2009/819).

Requirement to surrender documents connected with immigration and nationality

14.—(1) On issuing the biometric immigration document, the Secretary of State may require the surrender of other documents connected with immigration or nationality.

(2) Where the Secretary of State requires the surrender of other documents, the person must comply with the requirement.

Content of a biometric immigration document

15.—(1) A biometric immigration document may contain some or all of the following information on the face of the document—
  (a) the title of the document;
  (b) the document number;
  (c) the name of the holder;
  (d) the holder's date of birth;
  (e) the holder's place of birth;
  (f) the holder's nationality;
  (g) the sex of the holder;
  (h) the period of leave to remain which the person is granted;
  (i) the class of leave to remain which the person is granted;
  (j) any conditions to which the limited leave to remain is subject or remarks relating to those conditions;
  (k) the place and date of issue of the document;
  (l) the period for which the document is valid;
  (m) the holder's facial image;
  (n) the signature of the holder;
  (o) a machine readable code;
  (p) a hologram;
  (q) an emblem of the United Kingdom and the words 'United Kingdom';
  (r) the symbol of the International Civil Aviation Organization denoting a machine readable travel document which contains a contactless microchip; and
  (s) any additional security features.

(2) A biometric immigration document may contain some or all of the following within a radio frequency electronic microchip embedded in the document—
  (a) any of the information specified in paragraph (1)(a) to (m);
  (b) information relating to a record of any two of the holder's fingerprints; and
  (c) any additional security features.

Surrender of a biometric immigration document

16.—(1) The Secretary of State may require the surrender of a biometric immigration document as soon as reasonably practicable if he thinks that —
  (a) information provided in connection with the document was or has become false, misleading or incomplete;
  (b) the document (including any information recorded in it) has been altered, damaged or destroyed (whether deliberately or not);
  (c) an attempt has been made (whether successfully or not) to copy the document or to do anything to enable it to be copied;

(d) the document should be re-issued (whether because the information recorded in it requires alteration or for any other reason);

(e) the holder's leave to remain is to be varied, cancelled or invalidated, or is to lapse;

(f) a person has acquired the biometric immigration document without the consent of the holder or of the Secretary of State;

(g) the document has ceased to have effect under regulation 13(3) or has been cancelled under regulation 17; [...]

(h) the holder has died.

[(i) the holder has failed to produce a valid passport or travel document when required to do so by an immigration officer; or

(j) the holder has proved that he is a British citizen or a Commonwealth citizen who has a right of abode in the United Kingdom as a result of section 2(1)(b) of the Immigration Act 1971 (statement of right of abode in the United Kingdom).]

(2) Where a person is required to surrender the biometric immigration document under paragraph (1), the person must comply with the requirement.

Note: Sub-paragraphs (1)(i)–(j) inserted from 31 March 2009 (SI 2009/819).

Cancellation of a biometric immigration document

17. The Secretary of State may cancel a biometric immigration document if he thinks that—

(a) information provided in connection with the document was or has become false, misleading or incomplete;

(b) the document has been lost or stolen;

(c) the document (including any information recorded in it) has been altered, damaged or destroyed (whether deliberately or not);

(d) an attempt has been made (whether successfully or not) to copy the document or to do anything to enable it to be copied;

(e) a person has failed to surrender the document when required to do so under regulation [16(a) to (f), (h), (i) or (j);]

(f) the document should be re-issued (whether because the information recorded in it requires alteration or for any other reason);

(g) a person has acquired the biometric immigration document without the consent of the holder or of the Secretary of State; [...]

(h) the holder has died [or

(i) the holder has proved that he is a British citizen or a Commonwealth citizen who has a right of abode in the United Kingdom as a result of section 2(1)(b) of the Immigration Act 1971 (statement of right of abode in the United Kingdom).]

Note: Words in square brackets substituted and inserted from 31 March 2009 (SI 2009/819).

Requirement for the holder of a document to notify the Secretary of State

18. The holder of a biometric immigration document must notify the Secretary of State as soon as reasonably practicable if he —

(a) knows or suspects that information provided in connection with the document was or has become false, misleading or incomplete;

(b) knows or suspects that the document has been lost or stolen;

(c) knows or suspects that the document (including any information recorded in it) has been altered or damaged (whether deliberately or not);

(d) was given leave to enter or remain in the United Kingdom in accordance with a provision of the immigration rules and knows or suspects that owing to a change of his circumstances he would no longer qualify for leave under that provision; or

(e) knows or suspects that another person has acquired the biometric immigration document without his consent or the consent of the Secretary of State.

Requirement to apply for a replacement biometric immigration document

19.—(1) A person who has been issued with a biometric immigration document under regulation 13(1) is required to apply for a replacement biometric immigration document where his original document—
(a) has been cancelled under [paragraphs (a) to (g) of] regulation 17; or
(b) has ceased to have effect under regulation 13(4)(b) or (c).

(2) A person required to apply for a biometric immigration document under paragraph (1) must do so within 3 months beginning with the date that the original document was cancelled or ceased to have effect.

Note: Words in square brackets inserted from 31 March 2009 (SI 2009/819).

Application of these Regulations to a person who is required to apply for a replacement biometric immigration document

20.—(1) These Regulations apply to a person who makes an application for a biometric immigration document in accordance with regulation 19 just as they apply to a person who makes an application for a document in accordance with regulation 3, with the modification in paragraph (2).

(2) The Secretary of State may issue a biometric immigration document to a person who has applied in accordance with regulation 19, provided the person has limited leave to remain.

Requirement to use a biometric immigration document

21.—(1) The holder of a biometric immigration document must provide his document to an immigration officer or the Secretary of State, as applicable—
(a)   where he is examined by an immigration officer under paragraph 2, 2A or 3 of Schedule 2 to the Immigration Act 1971;
(b)   where he is examined by an immigration officer under Article 7(2) of the Immigration (Leave to Enter and Remain) Order 2000;
(c)   where he is examined by the Secretary of State under Article 3 of the Immigration (Leave to Enter) Order 2001;
[(d)   where he makes an application for entry clearance, leave to enter or leave to remain;
(da)   where he makes an application to be recognised as a refugee, as a person in need of humanitarian protection, or as a stateless person in accordance with Article 1 of the Stateless Convention;

(db) where he applies as a dependant of a person who makes an application mentioned in sub-paragraph (d) or (da);

(dc) where he makes an application for a Convention Travel Document, Stateless Person's Travel Document or a Certificate of Travel;(e) when his dependant makes an application—

(i) for entry clearance, leave to enter, leave to remain; or

(ii) to be recognised as a refugee, as a person in need of humanitarian protection, or as a stateless person in accordance with Article 1 of the Stateless Convention;]

(f) when he is the sponsor under the immigration rules of a person who seeks entry clearance, leave to enter or leave to remain in the United Kingdom.

(2) Where the holder of a biometric immigration document attends premises to take a test known under the immigration rules as the 'Life in the UK Test', he must provide his document to the representative of the educational institution, or other person, who is administering the test.

(3) The holder of a biometric immigration document must provide his document to a prospective employer or employer—

(a) prior to the commencement of his employment; and

(b) [where he has limited leave to remain,] on the anniversary of the date that the document was first produced, provided he is still working for that employer on that date.

[(4) Where the holder of a biometric immigration document makes—

(a) an application for a certificate of entitlement under section 10 of the Nationality, Immigration and Asylum Act 2002(a) that a person has the right of abode in the United Kingdom;

(b) an application for a letter or other document confirming a person's immigration or nationality status or that a person is not a British citizen;

(c) an application for naturalisation as a British citizen under section 6(1) or (2) of the British Nationality Act 1981(b), or as a British overseas territories citizen under section 18(1) or (2) of that Act; or

(d) an application for registration under any provision of the British Nationality Act 1981, he must provide his biometric immigration document to the Secretary of State or a person acting on behalf of the Secretary of State in connection with that application.]

Note: Sub-paragraphs (1)(d)–(e) substituted/inserted, words inserted in sub-para (3)(b) and para (4) inserted from 28 February 2012 (SI 2012/594).

Requirement to provide information for comparison

22.—(1) A person who provides a biometric immigration document in accordance with [regulation 21] is required to provide biometric information for comparison with biometric information provided in connection with the application for the document.

(2) Where the document is provided to an authorised person, the authorised person may require the provision of the information in a specified form.

(3) Regulation 8 applies to a person required to provide information under paragraph (1) as it applies to a person who is required to provide biometric information under regulation 5.

Note: Words substituted in para (1) from 28 February 2012 (SI 2012/594).

Consequences of a failure to comply with a requirement of these Regulations

[**23.**—(1) Subject to paragraphs (3) and (4), where a person who is required to make an application for the issue of a biometric immigration document fails to comply with a requirement of these Regulations, the Secretary of State—

(a) may take any, or any combination, of the actions specified in paragraph (2); and

(b) must consider giving a notice under section 9 of the UK Borders Act 2007.

(2) The actions specified are to—

(a) refuse an application for a biometric immigration document;

(b) treat the person's application for leave to remain as invalid;

(c) refuse the person's application for leave to remain; and

(d) cancel or vary the person's leave to enter or remain.

(3) Where a person is required to apply for a biometric immigration document under regulation 3(2)(a) or (b) or as a dependant of a person who has made an application in accordance with regulation 3(2)(a) or (b) and fails to comply with a requirement of these Regulations, the Secretary of State—

(a) must refuse the person's application for a biometric immigration document;

(b) must treat the person's application for leave to remain as invalid; and

(c) may cancel or vary the person's leave to enter or remain.

(4) Where a person is required to apply for a biometric immigration document under regulation 3(2)(e), (f) or (g) or as the dependant of a person who has made an application in accordance with regulation 3(2)(e) or (f) and fails to comply with a requirement of these Regulations the Secretary of State—

(a) may refuse the application for a biometric immigration document; and

(b) must consider giving a notice under section 9 of the UK Borders Act 2007.

(5) Where any person apart from a person referred to in paragraph (1), (3) or (4) fails to comply with a requirement of these Regulations, the Secretary of State must consider giving a notice under section 9 of the UK Borders Act 2007.

(6) The Secretary of State may designate an adult as the person responsible for ensuring that a child complies with the requirements of these Regulations.]

Note: Regulation 23 substituted from 28 February 2012 (SI 2012/594).

Revocation and transitional provisions

24.—(1) Subject to paragraph (2), the Immigration (Biometric Registration) (Pilot) Regulations 2008 are revoked.

(2) The Immigration (Biometric Registration) (Pilot) Regulations 2008 continue to apply to a person who was required to apply for a biometric immigration document in accordance with regulation 3 of those Regulations before the coming into force of these Regulations, subject to paragraph (3).

(3) These Regulations apply to any application for leave to remain falling within regulation 3 of these Regulations, which is made by a person referred to in paragraph (2) on or after the coming into force of these Regulations.

The Appeals (Excluded Decisions) Order 2009
2009 No. 275

Citation and commencement

1. This Order may be cited as the Appeals (Excluded Decisions) Order 2009 and comes into force on 1 April 2009.

[Excluded decisions

2. For the purposes of section 11(1) of the Tribunals, Courts and Enforcement Act 2007, the following decisions of the First-tier Tribunal are excluded decisions—

(a) a decision under section 103 of the Immigration and Asylum Act 1999 (appeals); and

(b) a decision under paragraphs 22, 23, 24, 29, 30, 31, 32 and 33 of Schedule 2 to the Immigration Act 1971.]

Note: Article 2 substituted from 15 February 2010 (SI 2010/41).

3. For the purposes of sections 11(1) and 13(1) of the Tribunals, Courts and Enforcement Act 2007, the following decisions of the First-tier Tribunal or the Upper Tribunal are excluded decisions—

(a) ...
(b) ...
(c) ...
(d) ...
(e) ...
(f) ...
(g) ...
(h) ...
(i) ...
(j) ...
(k) ...
(l) ...

[(m) any procedural, ancillary or preliminary decision made in relation to an appeal against a decision under section 40A of the British Nationality Act 1981, section 82, 83 or 83A of the Nationality, Immigration and Asylum Act 2002, or regulation 26 of the Immigration (European Economic Area) Regulations 2006.]

Note: Paragraphs (a)–(l) not relevant to immigration law. Paragraph (m) inserted from 15 February 2010 (SI 2010/41).

Revocations

4. ...

The Immigration and Asylum Act 1999
(Part V Exemption: Licensed Sponsors Tiers 2 and 4) Order 2009
SI 2009 No. 506

Citation and Commencement

1. This Order may be cited as the Immigration and Asylum Act 1999 (Part V Exemption: Licensed Sponsors Tiers 2 and 4) Order 2009 and shall come into force on 31 March 2009.

Interpretation

2. In this Order—

'the Act' means the Immigration and Asylum Act 1999;

'immediate family' means a Tier 2 or Tier 4 migrant's spouse, civil partner, unmarried partner, same-sex partner, dependant child under 18 or parent of a Tier 4 (Child) Student;

'immigration advice' and 'immigration services' have the same meanings as in section 82 of the Act;

'immigration rules' means rules made under section 3(2) of the Immigration Act 1971;

'licensed sponsor' means a person who has been granted a sponsor licence;

'Points based system' means the points-based system under Part 6A of the immigration rules;

'sponsor licence' means a licence granted by the Secretary of State to a person who, by virtue of such a grant, is licensed as a Sponsor under Tiers 2, 4 or 5 of the Points Based System;

'Tier 2 migrant' means a migrant who (i) makes an application of a kind identified in the immigration rules as requiring to be considered under 'Tier 2' of the immigration rules' points-based system or (ii) has been granted leave under the relevant paragraphs of the immigration rules;

'Tier 4 migrant' means a migrant who (i) makes an application of a kind identified in the immigration rules as requiring to be considered under 'Tier 4' of the immigration rules' points-based system or (ii) has been granted leave under the relevant paragraphs of the immigration rules;

Exemption of licensed sponsors

3.—(1) Subject to paragraphs (2) and (3) and for the purposes of section 84(4)(d) of the Act the following persons shall be specified, namely persons who are licensed sponsors of Tier 2 and Tier 4 migrants and who provide immigration advice or immigration services free of charge to those migrants or their immediate family.

(2) The immigration advice or services given must be restricted to matters relating to the migrant's application under Tier 2 or Tier 4 of the Points-based system or to an application for entry clearance, leave to enter or leave to remain made by that person's immediate family and which is dependent on the migrant's application under Tier 2 or Tier 4 of the Points-based system.

(3) For the purposes of paragraph (1), the person providing the immigration advice or immigration services must be the licensed sponsor.

The Transfer of Functions of the Asylum and Immigration Tribunal Order 2010
2010 No. 21

Citation and commencement

1. This Order may be cited as the Transfer of Functions of the Asylum and Immigration Tribunal Order 2010 and comes into force on 15th February 2010.

Transfer of functions and abolition of tribunal

2.—(1) The functions of the Asylum and Immigration Tribunal are transferred to the First-tier Tribunal.

(2) The Asylum and Immigration Tribunal is abolished.

Transfer of persons into the First-tier Tribunal and the Upper Tribunal

3. …

Transfer of Rules

4. The Asylum and Immigration Tribunal (Procedure) Rules 2005 and the Asylum and Immigration Tribunal (Procedure) (Fast-track) Rules 2005 have effect as if they were Tribunal Procedure Rules.

Consequential and transitional provisions

…

SCHEDULE 4
Transitional and saving provisions

Appeals and applications for bail

1. An appeal under section 40A of the British Nationality Act 1981, section 82, 83 or 83A of the 2002 Act or regulation 26 of the Immigration (European Economic Area) Regulations 2006, or an application for bail under Schedule 2 to the Immigration Act 1971, made to the Asylum and Immigration Tribunal before 15 February 2010 but not determined before that date shall continue as an appeal or application before the First-tier Tribunal.

Section 103A applications

2. An application for review made to the Asylum and Immigration Tribunal under section 103A of the 2002 Act and Schedule 2 to the 2004 Act before 15 February 2010 but

not determined before that date shall continue as an application to the First-tier Tribunal for permission to appeal to the Upper Tribunal under section 11 of the 2007 Act.

3. Where the Asylum and Immigration Tribunal or the appropriate court has made an order for reconsideration under section 103A of the 2002 Act before 15 February 2010, but reconsideration has not taken place before that date, the order for reconsideration shall be treated as an order granting permission to appeal to the Upper Tribunal under section 11 of the 2007 Act and sections 12 and 13 of the 2007 Act shall apply.

4. Where the reconsideration of an appeal by the Asylum and Immigration Tribunal under section 103A of the 2002 Act has commenced before 15 February 2010 but has not been determined, the reconsideration shall continue as an appeal to the Upper Tribunal under section 12 of the 2007 Act and section 13 of the 2007 Act shall apply.

5. An application for review made to the appropriate court under section 103A of the 2002 Act before 15 February 2010 but not determined before that date shall continue as an application for review under section 103A of the 2002 Act.

6. An order for reconsideration made by the appropriate court on or after 15 February 2010 which, if it had been made before that date would have been for reconsideration by the Asylum and Immigration Tribunal, shall be treated as an order granting permission to appeal to the Upper Tribunal under section 11 of the 2007 Act and sections 12 and 13 of the 2007 Act shall apply.

Section 103C references

7. A reference made by the appropriate court to the appropriate appellate court under section 103C of the 2002 Act before 15 February 2010 shall continue to be considered as a reference under section 103C of the 2002 Act.

8. A case remitted or restored by the appropriate appellate court on or after 15 February 2010 which, if it had been remitted or restored before that date would have been remitted to the Asylum and Immigration Tribunal or restored to the appropriate court, shall be remitted to the Upper Tribunal and sections 12 and 13 of the 2007 Act shall apply.

Section 103B and 103E applications

9. An application for permission to appeal to the appropriate appellate court made to the Asylum and Immigration Tribunal under section 103B or 103E of the 2002 Act before 15 February 2010 but not determined before that date shall continue as an application to the Upper Tribunal for permission to appeal to the relevant appellate court under section 13 of the 2007 Act.

10. An application for permission to appeal to the appropriate appellate court made to that court under section 103B or 103E of the 2002 Act before 15 February 2010 but not determined before that date shall continue as an application for permission to appeal to the appropriate appellate court under section 103B or 103E of the 2002 Act.

11. An appeal which is proceeding before the appropriate appellate court under section 103B or 103E of the 2002 Act before 15 February 2010 but which is not determined before that date shall continue as an appeal to the appropriate appellate court under section 103B or 103E of the 2002 Act.

12. A case remitted by the appropriate appellate court on or after 15 February 2010 which, if it had been remitted before that date would have been remitted to the Asylum and Immigration Tribunal, shall be remitted to the Upper Tribunal and sections 12 and 13 of the 2007 Act shall apply.

Time limits

13.—(1) Where the time period for making an appeal or application has begun but not expired before 15 February 2010, in the case of—

(a) an appeal to the Asylum and Immigration Tribunal under section 40A of the British Nationality Act 1981. section 82, 83 or 83A of the 2002 Act or regulation 26 of the Immigration (European Economic Area) Regulations 2006, an appeal may be made within that period to the First-tier Tribunal;

(b) an application to the Asylum and Immigration Tribunal for review under section 103A of the 2002 Act and Schedule 2 to the 2004 Act, an application for permission to appeal to the Upper Tribunal under section 11 of the 2007 Act may be made within that period to the First-tier Tribunal;

(c) an application to the appropriate court for review under section 103A of the 2002 Act, an application may be made within that period under section 103A of the 2002 Act to the appropriate court;

(d) an application to the Asylum and Immigration Tribunal for permission to appeal to the appropriate appellate court under section 103B or 103E of the 2002 Act, an application for permission to appeal to the relevant appellate court under section 13 of the 2007 Act may be made within that period to the Upper Tribunal; and

(e) an application to the appropriate appellate court for permission to appeal to that court under section 103B or 103E of the 2002 Act, an application for permission to appeal to the relevant appellate court under section 13 of the 2007 Act may be made within that period to that court.

(2) Where an appeal or application mentioned in sub-paragraphs (1)(a) to (e) is made after the time period in question has expired, it must be made and decided in accordance with the relevant procedural rules or other enactments, as they apply on and after the transfer date.

(3) Where an appeal or application has been determined by the Asylum and Immigration Tribunal before the transfer date but the determination has not been served on the parties before that date, the determination shall be treated as if it were a determination of the First-tier Tribunal or (if it follows reconsideration) a determination of the Upper Tribunal, as the case may be, and the determination may be served accordingly.

(4) Sub-paragraph (3) applies, subject to any necessary modifications, to any other decision of the Asylum and Immigration Tribunal that has been made but not served before the transfer date.

General

14.—(1) This paragraph applies where proceedings are commenced or continued in the First-tier Tribunal or the Upper Tribunal by virtue of the provisions of this Schedule.

(2) The First-tier Tribunal or Upper Tribunal, as the case may be, may give any direction to ensure that the proceedings are dealt with fairly and, in particular, may apply any provision in procedural rules which applied to the proceedings before 15 February 2010.

(3) In sub-paragraph (2) "procedural rules" includes any provision (whether called rules or not) regulating practice or procedure before the Asylum and Immigration Tribunal.

(4) Any direction or order given or made in the proceedings which is in force immediately before 15 February 2010 remains in force on and after that date as if it were a direction or order of the First-tier Tribunal or Upper Tribunal, as the case may be, and may be varied accordingly.

(5) A time period which has started to run before15 February 2010 and which has not expired shall continue to apply.

15. Any procedural, ancillary or preliminary matter before the Asylum and Immigration Tribunal before 15 February 2010 may, on or after that date, be considered by the First-tier Tribunal or the Upper Tribunal, as the case may be, as appropriate.

16.—(1) This paragraph applies when—

(a) the Asylum and Immigration Tribunal has started to reconsider or has reconsidered an appeal before 15 February 2010, but has not produced a determination before that date; and

(b) the reconsideration of the appeal continues as an appeal to the Upper Tribunal by virtue of paragraph 4.

(2) A member of the Asylum and Immigration Tribunal who was hearing or otherwise considering the appeal may take all such steps as the member considers necessary to determine the appeal and produce a determination on or after 15 February 2010.

17. In any judicial review proceedings before the High Court, the Court of Session or the High Court of Northern Ireland before 15 February 2010 where a matter could be remitted to the Asylum and Immigration Tribunal, on or after that date the matter may be remitted to the First-tier Tribunal or the Upper Tribunal as the court considers appropriate.

18. Staff appointed to the Asylum and Immigration Tribunal before 15 February 2010 are to be treated on and after that date, for the purpose of any enactment, as if they had been appointed by the Lord Chancellor under section 40(1) of the Tribunals, Courts and Enforcement Act 2007 (tribunal staff and services).

Saving provisions

19. In accordance with the provisions of this Schedule, sections 87(3) and (4), 103A, 103B, 103C and 103E of the 2002 Act, shall continue to apply to proceedings to which paragraphs 5, 7, 10 to 12 and 13(1)(c) and (2) (in relation to sub-paragraph (1)(c)) apply as if the repeals in Schedule 1 in respect of those sections of the 2002 Act had not been made.

20. Section 103D of the 2002 Act and the Community Legal Service (Asylum and Immigration Appeals) Regulations 2005 ("the 2005 Regulations") (legal aid funding arrangements) shall continue to apply to proceedings to which paragraphs 2 to 8 and 13(1) (b), (c) and (2) (in relation to sub-paragraphs (1)(b) to (e)) apply until the proceedings are finally determined —

(a) as if the repeals in Schedule 1 in respect of sections 103A and 103D of the 2002 Act and rule 33 of the Asylum and Immigration Tribunal (Procedure) Rules 2005 ("the 2005 Rules"), and the repeals and revocations in Schedule 3 in respect of paragraph 30 of Schedule 2 to the 2004 Act and the 2005 Regulations had not been made;

(b) as if the references to the Tribunal in section 103D of the 2002 Act, paragraph 30 of Schedule 2 to the 2004 Act, the 2005 Regulations and rule 33 of the 2005 Rules were references to the First-tier Tribunal or the Upper Tribunal as appropriate, and the references to the appropriate court and the High Court were references to the Upper Tribunal where appropriate; and

(c) subject to any necessary modifications to the 2005 Regulations and the 2005 Rules.

Interpretation

21. In this Schedule—

'appropriate court' means—

(i) in relation to an appeal decided in England or Wales, the High Court;

(ii) in relation to an appeal decided in Scotland, the Outer House of the Court of Session; and

(iii) in relation to an appeal decided in Northern Ireland, the High Court of Northern Ireland;

'appropriate appellate court' means—

(iv) in relation to an appeal decided in England or Wales, the Court of Appeal;

(v) in relation to an appeal decided in Scotland, the Inner House of the Court of Session; and

(vi) in relation to an appeal decided in Northern Ireland, the Court of Appeal of Northern Ireland;

'the 2002 Act' means the Nationality, Immigration and Asylum Act 2002;

'the 2004 Act' means the Asylum and Immigration (Treatment of Claimants, etc.) Act 2004(; and

'the 2007 Act' means the Tribunals, Courts and Enforcement Act 2007.

The First-tier Tribunal (Immigration and Asylum Chamber) Fees Order 2011
2011 No. 2841

Citation and commencement

1. This Order may be cited as the First-tier Tribunal (Immigration and Asylum Chamber) Fees Order 2011 and shall come into force on the day after the date on which it is made.

Interpretation

2. In this Order—

'an immigration or asylum matter' means a matter in respect of which functions are allocated to the Immigration and Asylum Chamber of the First-tier Tribunal under article 5 of the First-tier Tribunal and Upper Tribunal (Chambers) Order 2010(b);

'appellant' means any person identified in the notice of appeal as appealing in relation to an immigration and asylum matter to the First-tier Tribunal;

'BACS' means the method of payment known as 'Banks Automated Clearing System' by which money is transferred from one bank in the United Kingdom to another by means of an automated system;

'international money transfer' means a method of payment by which money is transferred from a bank account outside the United Kingdom to a bank account in the United Kingdom by means of an automated system;

'the 1971 Act' means the Immigration Act 1971;

'the 1999 Act' means the Immigration and Asylum Act 1999;

'the 2002 Act' means the Nationality, Immigration and Asylum Act 2002.

Fees for appeals

3.—(1) A fee is payable in respect of an appeal to the First-tier Tribunal where the appeal relates to an immigration or asylum matter and the decision against which the appeal is made was taken on or after the coming into force of this Order.

(2) The fee is payable by or in respect of each appellant on the date on which the Notice of Appeal is given.

(3) The fee payable is—

(a) where the appellant consents to the appeal being determined without a hearing, £80; or

(b) where the appellant does not consent to the appeal being determined without a hearing, £140.

(4) Subject to paragraph (5), where after making payment in accordance with paragraph (3)(a), the appellant withdraws their consent to the appeal being determined without a hearing, the difference between the amounts specified in subparagraphs (a) and (b) of paragraph (3) ('the balance') becomes payable on the withdrawal of that consent.

(5) The balance referred to in paragraph (4) ceases to be payable if the Tribunal decides that the appeal can be justly determined without a hearing.

(6) This article is subject to articles 5, 6 and 7.

Method of paying fee

4.—(1) The fee payable must be paid by one of the following methods—

(a) credit card;

(b) debit card;

(c) BACS; or

(d) international money transfer.

(2) For the purposes of enabling payment to be made by or in respect of the appellant—

(a) authorisation to take payment and details of the credit or debit card, or

(b) an undertaking by or on behalf of each appellant to pay by BACS or an international money transfer, must be provided at the same time as the giving of the notice of appeal or the subsequent withdrawal of their consent to the appeal being determined without a hearing (as the case may be).

Exemption from fees

5.—(1) No fee is payable for—
    (a) an appeal against a decision made under—
        (i) section 2A of the 1971 Act(d) (deprivation of right of abode);
        (ii) section 5(1) of the 1971 Act (a decision to make a deportation order);
        (iii) paragraphs 8, 9,10, 10A or 12(2) of Schedule 2 to the 1971 Act(a) (a decision that an illegal entrant, any family or seaman and aircrew is or are to be removed from the United Kingdom by way of directions);
        (iv) section 40 of the British Nationality Act 1981(b) (deprivation of citizenship);
        (v) section 10(1) of the 1999 Act (removal of certain persons unlawfully in the United Kingdom);
        (vi) section 76 of the 2002 Act (revocation of indefinite leave to enter or remain in the United Kingdom);
        (vii) section 47 of the Immigration, Asylum and Nationality Act 2006(d) (removal: persons with statutorily extended leave);
        (viii) regulation 19(3) of the Immigration (European Economic Area) Regulations 2006 (a decision to remove an EEA national or the family member of such a national); or

    (b) an appeal to which Part 2 of the Asylum and Immigration Tribunal (Fast Track Procedure) Rules 2005 applies.

(2) No fee is payable where, at the time the fee would otherwise become payable, the appellant is, under the 1999 Act—
    (a) a 'supported person' as defined in section 94(1); or
    (b) provided with temporary support under section 98.

(3) No fee is payable where, for the purpose of proceedings before the Tribunal, the appellant is in receipt of—
    (a) funding provided by the Legal Services Commission, established under section 1 of the Access to Justice Act 1999, as part of the Community Legal Service;
    (b) legal aid under Part 2 of the Legal Aid, Advice and Assistance (Northern Ireland) Order 1981; or
    (c) civil legal aid or advice and assistance under the Legal Aid (Scotland) Act 1986.

(4) No fee is payable where the appellant is the person for whose benefit services are provided by a local authority under section 17 of the Children Act 1989.

(5) Where by any convention, treaty or other instrument entered into by Her Majesty with any foreign power it is provided that no fee is required to be paid in respect of any proceedings, the fees specified in this Order are not payable in respect of those proceedings.

Power to defer payment in certain cases

6. The Lord Chancellor may defer payment of a fee where the appeal is brought on the grounds that the removal of the appellant from, or a requirement for the appellant to leave, the United Kingdom would breach the United Kingdom's obligations under either—
    (a) the Convention relating to the Status of Refugees done at Geneva on 28 July 1951 and the Protocol to the Convention; or
    (b) article 21 of Directive 2004/83/EC of the European Parliament and Council of 29 April 2004.

Reduction or remission of fees

7. A fee specified in this Order may be reduced or remitted where the Lord Chancellor is satisfied that there are exceptional circumstances which justify doing so.

Certificate of fee satisfaction

8.—(1) The Lord Chancellor must issue a certificate of fee satisfaction if satisfied that—

(a) the appropriate fee payable under article 3 has been paid;

(b) in view of an undertaking given by or on behalf of the appellant, payment will be promptly made by BACS or an international money transfer;

(c) no fee is payable;

(d) payment is to be deferred in accordance with article 6; or

(e) the appellant has, at the time a fee would otherwise be payable under article 3, applied for the fee to be reduced or remitted in accordance with article 7.

(2) The issuing of such a certificate is without prejudice to the power to recover the amount of any payable fee or part of such fee which remains unpaid and unremitted.

(3) The Lord Chancellor may revoke a certificate of fee satisfaction and if a certificate is revoked, the Tribunal shall be notified accordingly.

Refunds

9.—(1) Subject to paragraph (2) —

(a) where the fee payable under article 3(3)(b) has been paid but the appeal is determined without a hearing, the difference between the amounts specified in article 3(3)(a) and 3(3)(b) may be refunded; and

(b) where a fee has been paid which the Lord Chancellor, if all the circumstances had been known, would have reduced or remitted under article 7, the fee or the amount by which the fee would have been reduced, as the case may be, shall be refunded.

(2) No refund will be made under this article unless the appellant applies in writing to the Lord Chancellor within 6 months of the date the fee becomes payable.

(3) The Lord Chancellor may extend the period of 6 months mentioned in paragraph (2) if the Lord Chancellor considers there is a good reason for the application being made after the end of the period of 6 months.

The Immigration Appeals (Family Visitor) Regulations 2012
2012 No. 1532

The Secretary of State, in exercise of the powers conferred by sections 88A(1)(a), 2(a) and (c) and 112(1) and (3) of the Nationality, Immigration and Asylum Act 2002(1), makes the following Regulations:

Citation and commencement

1. These Regulations may be cited as the Immigration Appeals (Family Visitor) Regulations 2012 and shall come into force on 9th July 2012.

Class or description of person to be visited

2.—(1) A person ("P") is of a class or description prescribed for the purposes of section 88A(1)(a) of the Nationality, Immigration and Asylum Act 2002 (entry clearance), if—

    (a) the applicant for entry clearance ("A") is a member of the family of P; and

    (b) P's circumstances match those specified in regulation 3.

(2) For the purposes of paragraph (1), A is a member of the family of P if A is the—

    (a) spouse, civil partner, father, mother, son, daughter, grandfather, grandmother, grandson, granddaughter, brother or sister;

    (b) father-in-law, mother-in-law, brother-in-law or sister-in-law;

    (c) son-in-law or daughter-in-law; or

    (d) stepfather, stepmother, stepson, stepdaughter, stepbrother or stepsister;of P.

(3) For the purposes of paragraph (1), A is also a member of the family of P if A is the partner of P.

(4) In this regulation, A is the partner of P if—

    (a) A and P have been in a relationship that is akin to a marriage or civil partnership for at least the two years before the day on which A's application for entry clearance was made; and

    (b) such relationship is genuine and subsisting.

(5) In this regulation—

    (a) "father-in-law of P" includes the father of P's civil partner;

    (b) "mother-in-law of P" includes the mother of P's civil partner;

    (c) "brother-in-law of P" includes the brother of P's civil partner;

    (d) "sister-in-law of P" includes the sister of P's civil partner;

    (e) "son-in-law of P" includes the son of P's civil partner;

    (f) "daughter-in-law of P" includes the daughter of P's civil partner;

    (g) "stepfather of P" includes the person who is the civil partner of A's father (but is not A's parent);

    (h) "stepmother of P" includes the person who is the civil partner of A's mother (but is not A's parent);

    (i) "stepson of P" includes the person who is the son of A's civil partner (but is not A's son);

    (j) "stepdaughter of P" includes the person who is the daughter of A's civil partner (but is not A's daughter);

    (k) "stepbrother of P" includes the person who is the son of the civil parent of A's parent (but is not the son of either of A's parents); and

    (l) "stepsister of P" includes the person who is the daughter of the civil partner of A's parent (but is not the daughter of either of A's parents).

Circumstances of the person to be visited

3. The circumstances of P mentioned in regulation 2(1)(b) are that P–

(a) is settled in the United Kingdom as defined in paragraph 6(2) of the immigration rules;

(b) has been granted asylum in the United Kingdom under paragraph 334(3) of the immigration rules; or

(c) has been granted humanitarian protection in the United Kingdom under paragraph 339C(4) of the immigration rules.

Transitional provision

4. These Regulations apply only to an application for entry clearance made on or after the day on which they come into force.

The Immigration, Asylum and Nationality Act 2006 (Commencement No. 8 and Transitional and Saving Provisions) (Amendment) Order 2012
2012 No. 1531 (C. 57)

The Secretary of State, in exercise of the powers conferred by section 62 of the Immigration, Asylum and Nationality Act 2006(1), makes the following Order:

Citation and commencement

1. This Order may be cited as the Immigration, Asylum and Nationality Act 2006 (Commencement No. 8 and Transitional and Saving Provisions) (Amendment) Order 2012 and shall come into force on 9th July 2012.

Amendment of the Immigration, Asylum and Nationality Act 2006 (Commencement No. 8 and Transitional and Saving Provisions) Order 2008

2. ...

Note: Article 2 amends art 4 of SI 2008/310.

Saving provision

3. Notwithstanding the substitution of section 88A of the Nationality, Immigration and Asylum Act 2002 for section 90 of that Act, section 90 and the Immigration Appeals (Family Visitor) Regulations 2003 continue to have effect in relation to an appeal brought in respect of an application for entry clearance made before 9th July 2012.

EUROPEAN MATERIALS

Consolidated Version of the Treaty on the Functioning of the European Union*

PART TWO
NON-DISCRIMINATION AND CITIZENSHIP OF THE UNION

Article 18
(ex Article 12 TEC)

Within the scope of application of the Treaties, and without prejudice to any special provisions contained therein, any discrimination on grounds of nationality shall be prohibited.

The European Parliament and the Council, acting in accordance with the ordinary legislative procedure, may adopt rules designed to prohibit such discrimination.

Article 19
(ex Article 13 TEC)

1. Without prejudice to the other provisions of the Treaties and within the limits of the powers conferred by them upon the Union, the Council, acting unanimously in accordance with a special legislative procedure and after obtaining the consent of the European Parliament, may take appropriate action to combat discrimination based on sex, racial or ethnic origin, religion or belief, disability, age or sexual orientation.

2. By way of derogation from paragraph 1, the European Parliament and the Council, acting in accordance with the ordinary legislative procedure, may adopt the basic principles of Union incentive measures, excluding any harmonisation of the laws and regulations of the Member States, to support action taken by the Member States in order to contribute to the achievement of the objectives referred to in paragraph 1.

Article 20
(ex Article 17 TEC)

1. Citizenship of the Union is hereby established. Every person holding the nationality of a Member State shall be a citizen of the Union. Citizenship of the Union shall be additional to and not replace national citizenship.

2. Citizens of the Union shall enjoy the rights and be subject to the duties provided for in the Treaties. They shall have, *inter alia*:

   (a) the right to move and reside freely within the territory of the Member States;

(b) the right to vote and to stand as candidates in elections to the European Parliament and in municipal elections in their Member State of residence, under the same conditions as nationals of that State;

(c) the right to enjoy, in the territory of a third country in which the Member State of which they are a nationals is not represented, the protection of the diplomatic and consular authorities of any Member State on the same conditions as the nationals of that State;

(d) the right to petition the European Parliament, to apply to the European Ombudsman, and to address the institutions and advisory bodies of the Union in any of the Treaty languages and to obtain a reply in the same language.

These rights shall be exercised in accordance with the conditions and limits defined by the Treaties and by the measures adopted thereunder.

Article 21

(ex Article 18 TEC)

1. Every citizen of the Union shall have the right to move and reside freely within the territory of the Member States, subject to the limitations and conditions laid down in the Treaties and by the measures adopted to give them effect.

2. If action by the Union should prove necessary to attain this objective and the Treaties have not provided the necessary powers, the European Parliament and the Council, acting in accordance with the ordinary legislative procedure, may adopt provisions with a view to facilitating the exercise of the rights referred to in paragraph 1.

3. For the same purposes as those referred to in paragraph 1 and if the Treaties have not provided the necessary powers, the Council, acting in accordance with a special legislative procedure, may adopt measures concerning social security or social protection. The Council shall act unanimously after consulting the European Parliament.

PART THREE

TITLE IV

Free Movement of Persons, Services and Capital

CHAPTER 1
WORKERS

Article 45

(ex Article 39 TEC)

1. Freedom of movement for workers shall be secured within the Union.

2. Such freedom of movement shall entail the abolition of any discrimination based on nationality between workers of the Member States as regards employment, remuneration and other conditions of work and employment.

3. It shall entail the right, subject to limitations justified on grounds of public policy, public security or public health:

(a) to accept offers of employment actually made;

(b) to move freely within the territory of Member States for this purpose;

(c) to stay in a Member State for the purpose of employment in accordance with the provisions governing the employment of nationals of that State laid down by law, regulation or administrative action;

(d) to remain in the territory of a Member State after having been employed in that State, subject to conditions which shall be embodied in regulations to be drawn up by the Commission.

4. The provisions of this Article shall not apply to employment in the public service.

Article 46

(ex Article 40 TEC)

The European Parliament and the Council shall, acting in accordance with the ordinary legislative procedure and after consulting the Economic and Social Committee, issue directives or make regulations setting out the measures required to bring about freedom of movement for workers, as defined in Article 45, in particular:

(a) by ensuring close cooperation between national employment services;

(b) by abolishing those administrative procedures and practices and those qualifying periods in respect of eligibility for available employment, whether resulting from national legislation or from agreements previously concluded between Member States, the maintenance of which would form an obstacle to liberalisation of the movement of workers;

(c) by abolishing all such qualifying periods and other restrictions provided for either under national legislation or under agreements previously concluded between Member States as imposed on workers of other Member States conditions regarding the free choice of employment other than those imposed on workers of the State concerned;

(d) by setting up appropriate machinery to bring offers of employment into touch with applications for employment and to facilitate the achievement of a balance between supply and demand in the employment market in such a way as to avoid serious threats to the standard of living and level of employment in the various regions and industries. EN C 83/66 Official Journal of the European Union 30.3.2010.

Article 47

(ex Article 41 TEC)

Member States shall, within the framework of a joint programme, encourage the exchange of young workers.

Article 48

(ex Article 42 TEC)

The European Parliament and the Council shall, acting in accordance with the ordinary legislative procedure, adopt such measures in the field of social security as are necessary to provide freedom of movement for workers; to this end, they shall make arrangements to secure for employed and self- employed migrant workers and their dependants:

(a) aggregation, for the purpose of acquiring and retaining the right to benefit and of calculating the amount of benefit, of all periods taken into account under the laws of the several countries;

(b) payment of benefits to persons resident in the territories of Member States.

Where a member of the Council declares that a draft legislative act referred to in the first subparagraph would affect important aspects of its social security system, including its scope, cost or financial structure, or would affect the financial balance of that system, it may request that the matter be referred to the European Council. In that case, the ordinary legislative procedure shall be suspended. After discussion, the European Council shall, within four months of this suspension, either:

(a) refer the draft back to the Council, which shall terminate the suspension of the ordinary legislative procedure; or

(b) take no action or request the Commission to submit a new proposal; in that case, the act originally proposed shall be deemed not to have been adopted.

CHAPTER 3
SERVICES

Article 56

(ex Article 49 TEC)

Within the framework of the provisions set out below, restrictions on freedom to provide services within the Union shall be prohibited in respect of nationals of Member States who are established in a Member State other than that of the person for whom the services are intended.

The European Parliament and the Council, acting in accordance with the ordinary legislative procedure, may extend the provisions of the Chapter to nationals of a third country who provide services and who are established within the Union.

Article 57

(ex Article 50 TEC)

Services shall be considered to be 'services' within the meaning of the Treaties where they are normally provided for remuneration, in so far as they are not governed by the provisions relating to freedom of movement for goods, capital and persons.

'Services' shall in particular include:

(a) activities of an industrial character;

(b) activities of a commercial character;

(c) activities of craftsmen;

(d) activities of the professions.

Without prejudice to the provisions of the Chapter relating to the right of establishment, the person providing a service may, in order to do so, temporarily pursue his activity in the Member State where the service is provided, under the same conditions as are imposed by that State on its own nationals.

Article 58

(ex Article 51 TEC)

1. Freedom to provide services in the field of transport shall be governed by the provisions of the Title relating to transport.

2. The liberalisation of banking and insurance services connected with movements of capital shall be effected in step with the liberalisation of movement of capital. EN C 83/70 Official Journal of the European Union 30.3.2010.

Article 59

(ex Article 52 TEC)

1. In order to achieve the liberalisation of a specific service, the European Parliament and the Council, acting in accordance with the ordinary legislative procedure and after consulting the Economic and Social Committee, shall issue directives.

2. As regards the directives referred to in paragraph 1, priority shall as a general rule be given to those services which directly affect production costs or the liberalisation of which helps to promote trade in goods.

Article 60

(ex Article 53 TEC)

The Member States shall endeavour to undertake the liberalisation of services beyond the extent required by the directives issued pursuant to Article 59(1), if their general economic situation and the situation of the economic sector concerned so permit.

To this end, the Commission shall make recommendations to the Member States concerned.

Article 61

(ex Article 54 TEC)

As long as restrictions on freedom to provide services have not been abolished, each Member State shall apply such restrictions without distinction on grounds of nationality or residence to all persons providing services within the meaning of the first paragraph of Article 56.

Article 62

(ex Article 55 TEC)

The provisions of Articles 51 to 54 shall apply to the matters covered by this Chapter.

TITLE V

Area of Freedom, Security and Justice

CHAPTER 1
GENERAL PROVISIONS

Article 67

(ex Article 61 TEC and ex Article 29 TEU)

1. The Union shall constitute an area of freedom, security and justice with respect for fundamental rights and the different legal systems and traditions of the Member States.

2. It shall ensure the absence of internal border controls for persons and shall frame a common policy on asylum, immigration and external border control, based on solidarity between Member States, which is fair towards third-country nationals. For the purpose of this Title, stateless persons shall be treated as third-country nationals.

3. The Union shall endeavour to ensure a high level of security through measures to prevent and combat crime, racism and xenophobia, and through measures for coordination and cooperation between police and judicial authorities and other competent authorities, as well as through the mutual recognition of judgments in criminal matters and, if necessary, through the approximation of criminal laws.

4. The Union shall facilitate access to justice, in particular through the principle of mutual recognition of judicial and extrajudicial decisions in civil matters. EN 30.3.2010 Official Journal of the European Union C 83/73.

Article 68

The European Council shall define the strategic guidelines for legislative and operational planning within the area of freedom, security and justice.

Article 69

National Parliaments ensure that the proposals and legislative initiatives submitted under Chapters 4 and 5 comply with the principle of subsidiarity, in accordance with the arrangements laid down by the Protocol on the application of the principles of subsidiarity and proportionality.

Article 70

Without prejudice to Articles 258, 259 and 260, the Council may, on a proposal from the Commission, adopt measures laying down the arrangements whereby Member States, in collaboration with the Commission, conduct objective and impartial evaluation of the implementation of the Union policies referred to in this Title by Member States' authorities, in particular in order to facilitate full application of the principle of mutual recognition. The European Parliament and national Parliaments shall be informed of the content and results of the evaluation.

Article 71

(ex Article 36 TEU)

A standing committee shall be set up within the Council in order to ensure that operational cooperation on internal security is promoted and strengthened within the Union. Without prejudice to Article 240, it shall facilitate coordination of the action of Member States' competent authorities. Representatives of the Union bodies, offices and agencies concerned may be involved in the proceedings of this committee. The European Parliament and national Parliaments shall be kept informed of the proceedings.

Article 72

(ex Article 64(1) TEC and ex Article 33 TEU)

This Title shall not affect the exercise of the responsibilities incumbent upon Member States with regard to the maintenance of law and order and the safeguarding of internal security.

Article 73

It shall be open to Member States to organise between themselves and under their responsibility such forms of cooperation and coordination as they deem appropriate between the competent departments of their administrations responsible for safeguarding national security. EN C 83/74 Official Journal of the European Union 30.3.2010.

Article 74

(ex Article 66 TEC)

The Council shall adopt measures to ensure administrative cooperation between the relevant departments of the Member States in the areas covered by this Title, as well as between those departments and the Commission. It shall act on a Commission proposal, subject to Article 76, and after consulting the European Parliament.

Article 75

(ex Article 60 TEC)

Where necessary to achieve the objectives set out in Article 67, as regards preventing and combating terrorism and related activities, the European Parliament and the Council, acting by means of regulations in accordance with the ordinary legislative procedure, shall define a framework for administrative measures with regard to capital movements and payments, such as the freezing of funds, financial assets or economic gains belonging to, or owned or held by, natural or legal persons, groups or non-State entities.

The Council, on a proposal from the Commission, shall adopt measures to implement the framework referred to in the first paragraph.

The acts referred to in this Article shall include necessary provisions on legal safeguards.

Article 76

The acts referred to in Chapters 4 and 5, together with the measures referred to in Article 74 which ensure administrative cooperation in the areas covered by these Chapters, shall be adopted:

(a) on a proposal from the Commission, or

(b) on the initiative of a quarter of the Member States.

CHAPTER 2
POLICIES ON BORDER CHECKS, ASYLUM AND IMMIGRATION

Article 77

(ex Article 62 TEC)

1. The Union shall develop a policy with a view to:

(a) ensuring the absence of any controls on persons, whatever their nationality, when crossing internal borders; EN 30.3.2010 Official Journal of the European Union C 83/75;

(b) carrying out checks on persons and efficient monitoring of the crossing of external borders;

(c) the gradual introduction of an integrated management system for external borders.

2. For the purposes of paragraph 1, the European Parliament and the Council, acting in accordance with the ordinary legislative procedure, shall adopt measures concerning:

(a) the common policy on visas and other short-stay residence permits;

(b) the checks to which persons crossing external borders are subject;

(c) the conditions under which nationals of third countries shall have the freedom to travel within the Union for a short period;

(d) any measure necessary for the gradual establishment of an integrated management system for external borders;

(e) the absence of any controls on persons, whatever their nationality, when crossing internal borders.

3. If action by the Union should prove necessary to facilitate the exercise of the right referred to in Article 20(2)(a), and if the Treaties have not provided the necessary powers, the Council, acting in accordance with a special legislative procedure, may adopt provisions concerning passports, identity cards, residence permits or any other such document. The Council shall act unanimously after consulting the European Parliament.

4. This Article shall not affect the competence of the Member States concerning the geographical demarcation of their borders, in accordance with international law.

Article 78

(ex Articles 63, points 1 and 2, and 64(2) TEC)

1. The Union shall develop a common policy on asylum, subsidiary protection and temporary protection with a view to offering appropriate status to any third-country national requiring international protection and ensuring compliance with the principle of *non-refoulement*. This policy must be in accordance with the Geneva Convention of 28 July 1951 and the Protocol of 31 January 1967 relating to the status of refugees, and other relevant treaties.

2. For the purposes of paragraph 1, the European Parliament and the Council, acting in accordance with the ordinary legislative procedure, shall adopt measures for a common European asylum system comprising:

(a) a uniform status of asylum for nationals of third countries, valid throughout the Union;

(b) a uniform status of subsidiary protection for nationals of third countries who, without obtaining European asylum, are in need of international protection;

(c) a common system of temporary protection for displaced persons in the event of a massive inflow;

(d) common procedures for the granting and withdrawing of uniform asylum or subsidiary protection status;

(e) criteria and mechanisms for determining which Member State is responsible for considering an application for asylum or subsidiary protection;

(f) standards concerning the conditions for the reception of applicants for asylum or subsidiary protection;

(g) partnership and cooperation with third countries for the purpose of managing inflows of people applying for asylum or subsidiary or temporary protection.

3. In the event of one or more Member States being confronted by an emergency situation characterised by a sudden inflow of nationals of third countries, the Council, on a proposal from the Commission, may adopt provisional measures for the benefit of the Member State(s) concerned. It shall act after consulting the European Parliament.

Article 79

(ex Article 63, points 3 and 4, TEC)

1. The Union shall develop a common immigration policy aimed at ensuring, at all stages, the efficient management of migration flows, fair treatment of third-country nationals residing legally in Member States, and the prevention of, and enhanced measures to combat, illegal immigration and trafficking in human beings.

2. For the purposes of paragraph 1, the European Parliament and the Council, acting in accordance with the ordinary legislative procedure, shall adopt measures in the following areas:

(a) the conditions of entry and residence, and standards on the issue by Member States of long-term visas and residence permits, including those for the purpose of family reunification;

(b) the definition of the rights of third-country nationals residing legally in a Member State, including the conditions governing freedom of movement and of residence in other Member States;

(c) illegal immigration and unauthorised residence, including removal and repatriation of persons residing without authorisation;

(d) combating trafficking in persons, in particular women and children.

3. The Union may conclude agreements with third countries for the readmission to their countries of origin or provenance of third-country nationals who do not or who no longer fulfil the conditions for entry, presence or residence in the territory of one of the Member States. EN 30.3.2010 Official Journal of the European Union C 83/77.

4. The European Parliament and the Council, acting in accordance with the ordinary legislative procedure, may establish measures to provide incentives and support for the action of Member States with a view to promoting the integration of third-country nationals residing legally in their territories, excluding any harmonisation of the laws and regulations of the Member States.

5. This Article shall not affect the right of Member States to determine volumes of admission of third-country nationals coming from third countries to their territory in order to seek work, whether employed or self-employed....

Regulation (EEC) No. 1612/68 of the Council of 15 October 1968
on freedom of movement for workers within the Community

THE COUNCIL OF THE EUROPEAN COMMUNITIES,

Having regard to the Treaty establishing the European Economic Community, and in particular Article 49 thereof;

Having regard to the proposal from the Commission;

Having regard to the Opinion of the European Parliament;

Having regard to the Opinion of the Economic and Social Committee;

Whereas freedom of movement for workers should be secured within the Community by the end of the transitional period at the latest; whereas the attainment of this objective entails the abolition of any discrimination based on nationality between workers of the Member States as regards employment, remuneration and other conditions of work and employment, as well as the right of such workers to move freely within the Community in order to pursue activities as employed persons subject to any limitations justified on grounds of public policy, public security or public health;

Whereas by reason in particular of the early establishment of the customs union and in order to ensure the simultaneous completion of the principal foundations of the Community, provisions should be adopted to enable the objectives laid down in Articles 48 and 49 of the Treaty in the field of freedom of movement to be achieved and to perfect measures adopted successively under Regulation No 15 on the first steps for attainment of freedom of movement and under Council Regulation No 38/64/EEC of 25 March 1964 on freedom of movement for workers within the Community;

Whereas freedom of movement constitutes a fundamental right of workers and their families; whereas mobility of labour within the Community must be one of the means by which the worker is guaranteed the possibility of improving his living and working conditions and promoting his social advancement, while helping to satisfy the requirements of the economies of the Member States; whereas the right of all workers in the Member States to pursue the activity of their choice within the Community should be affirmed;

Whereas such right must be enjoyed without discrimination by permanent, seasonal and frontier workers and by those who pursue their activities for the purpose of providing services;

Whereas the right of freedom of movement, in order that it may be exercised, by objective standards, in freedom and dignity, requires that equality of treatment shall be ensured in fact and in law in respect of all matters relating to the actual pursuit of activities as employed persons and to eligibility for housing, and also that obstacles to the mobility of workers shall be eliminated, in particular as regards the worker's right to be joined by his family and the conditions for the integration of that family into the host country;

Whereas the principle of non-discrimination between Community workers entails that all nationals of Member States have the same priority as regards employment as is enjoyed by national workers;

Whereas it is necessary to strengthen the machinery for vacancy clearance, in particular by developing direct co-operation between the central employment services and also between the regional services, as well as by increasing and co-ordinating the exchange of information in order to ensure in a general way a clearer picture of the labour market; whereas workers wishing to move should also be regularly informed of living and working conditions; whereas, furthermore, measures should be provided for the case where a Member State undergoes or foresees disturbances on its labour market which may seriously threaten the standard of living and level of employment in a region or an industry; whereas for this purpose the exchange of information, aimed at discouraging workers from moving to such a region or industry, constitutes the method to be applied in the first place but, where necessary, it should be possible to strengthen the results of such exchange of information by temporarily suspending the above-mentioned machinery, any such decision to be taken at Community level;

Whereas close links exist between freedom of movement for workers, employment and vocational training, particularly where the latter aims at putting workers in a position to take up offers of employment from other regions of the Community; whereas such links make it necessary that the problems arising in this connection should no longer be studied in isolation but viewed as inter-dependent, account also being taken of the problems of employment at the regional level; and whereas it is therefore necessary to direct the efforts of Member States towards co-ordinating their employment policies at Community level;

Whereas the Council, by its Decision of 15 October 1968 made Articles 48 and 49 of the Treaty and also the measures taken in implementation thereof applicable to the French overseas departments;

HAS ADOPTED THIS REGULATION:

PART I

EMPLOYMENT AND WORKERS' FAMILIES

TITLE I
Eligibility for Employment

Article 1

1. Any national of a Member State, shall, irrespective of his place of residence, have the right to take up an activity as an employed person, and to pursue such activity, within the territory of another Member State in accordance with the provisions laid down by law, regulation or administrative action governing the employment of nationals of that State.

2. He shall, in particular, have the right to take up available employment in the territory of another Member State with the same priority as nationals of that State.

Article 2

Any national of a Member State and any employer pursuing an activity in the territory of a Member State may exchange their applications for and offers of employment, and may conclude and perform contracts of employment in accordance with the provisions in force laid down by law, regulation or administrative action, without any discrimination resulting therefrom.

Article 3

1. Under this Regulation, provisions laid down by law, regulation or administrative action or administrative practices of a Member State shall not apply:

—where they limit application for and offers of employment, or the right of foreign nationals to take up and pursue employment or subject these to conditions not applicable in respect of their own nationals; or

—where, though applicable irrespective of nationality, their exclusive or principal aim or effect is to keep nationals of other Member States away from the employment offered.

This provision shall not apply to conditions relating to linguistic knowledge required by reason of the nature of the post to be filled.

2. There shall be included in particular among the provisions or practices of a Member State referred to in the first subparagraph of paragraph 1 those which:

(a) prescribe a special recruitment procedure for foreign nationals;

(b) limit or restrict the advertising of vacancies in the press or through any other medium or subject it to conditions other than those applicable in respect of employers pursuing their activities in the territory of that Member State;

(c) subject eligibility for employment to condition of registration with employment offices or impede recruitment of individual workers, where persons who do not reside in the territory of that State are concerned.

Article 4

1. Provisions laid down by law, regulation or administrative action of the Member States which restrict by number or percentage the employment of foreign nationals in

any undertaking, branch of activity or region, or at a national level, shall not apply to nationals of the other Member States.

2. When in a Member State the granting of any benefit to undertakings is subject to a minimum percentage of national workers being employed, nationals of the other Member States shall be counted as national workers, subject to the provisions of the Council Directive of 15 October 1963.

Article 5

A national of a Member State who seeks employment in the territory of another Member State shall receive the same assistance there as that afforded by the employment offices in that State to their own nationals seeking employment.

Article 6

1. The engagement and recruitment of a national of one Member State for a post in another Member State shall not depend on medical, vocational or other criteria which are discriminatory on grounds of nationality by comparison with those applied to nationals of the other Member State who wish to pursue the same activity.

2. Nevertheless, a national who holds an offer in his name from an employer in a Member State other than that of which he is a national may have to undergo a vocational test, if the employer expressly requests this when making his offer of employment.

TITLE II
Employment and Equality of Treatment

Article 7

1. A worker who is a national of a Member State may not, in the territory of another Member State, be treated differently from national workers by reason of his nationality in respect of any conditions of employment and work, in particular as regards remuneration, dismissal, and should he become unemployed, reinstatement or re-employment;

2. He shall enjoy the same social and tax advantages as national workers.

3. He shall also, by virtue of the same right and under the same conditions as national workers, have access to training in vocational schools and retraining centres.

4. Any clause of a collective or individual agreement or of any other collective regulation concerning eligibility for employment, employment remuneration and other conditions of work or dismissal shall be null and void in so far as it lays down or authorises discriminatory conditions in respect of workers who are nationals of the other Member States.

Article 8

1. A worker who is a national of a Member State and who is employed in the territory of another Member State shall enjoy equality of treatment as regards membership of trade unions and the exercise of rights attaching thereto, including the right to vote; [and to be

eligible for the administration or management posts of a trade union,] he may be excluded from taking part in the management of bodies governed by public law and from holding an office governed by public law. Furthermore, he shall have the right of eligibility for workers' representative bodies in the undertaking. The provisions of this Article shall not affect laws or regulations in certain Member States which grant more extensive rights to workers coming from the other Member States.

2. ...

Note: Article 8 amended by EEC 312/76.

Article 9

1. A worker who is a national of a Member State and who is employed in the territory of another Member State shall enjoy all the rights and benefits accorded to national workers in matters of housing, including ownership of the housing he needs.

2. Such worker may, with the same right as nationals, put his name down on the housing lists in the region in which he is employed, where such lists exist; he shall enjoy the resultant benefits and priorities.If his family has remained in the country whence he came, they shall be considered for this purpose as residing in the said region, where national workers benefit from a similar presumption.

TITLE III
Workers' Families

Article 10

...

Note: Article 10 repealed from 30 April 2006 (Directive 2004/38, Art 38).

Article 11

...

Note: Article 11 repealed from 30 April 2006 (Directive 2004/38, Art 38).

Article 12

The children of a national of a Member State who is or has been employed in the territory of another Member State shall be admitted to that State's general educational, apprenticeship and vocational training courses under the same conditions as the nationals of that State, if such children are residing in its territory.

Member States shall encourage all efforts to enable such children to attend these courses under the best possible conditions.

PART II
CLEARANCE OF VACANCIES AND APPLICATIONS FOR EMPLOYMENT

TITLE I

Co-operation between the Member States and with the Commission

Article 13

1. The Member States or the Commission shall instigate or together undertake any study of employment or unemployment which they consider necessary for securing freedom of movement for workers within the Community.

The central employment services of the Member States shall co-operate closely with each other and with the Commission with a view to acting jointly as regards the clearing of vacancies and applications for employment within the Community and the resultant placing of workers in employment.

2. To this end the Member States shall designate specialist services which shall be entrusted with organising work in the fields referred to above and co-operating with each other and with the departments of the Commission.

The Member States shall notify the Commission of any change in the designation of such services; the Commission shall publish details thereof for information in the *Official Journal of the European Communities.*

Article 14

1. The Member States shall send to the Commission information on problems arising in connection with the freedom of movement and employment of workers and particulars of the state and development of employment.

[2. The Commission, taking the utmost account of the opinion of the Technical Committee, shall determine the manner in which the information referred to in paragraph 1 is to be drawn up.]

3. In accordance with the procedure laid down by the Commission [taking the utmost account of the opinion of the Technical Committee,] the specialist service of each Member State shall send to the specialist services of the other Member States and to the European Co-ordination Office such information concerning living and working conditions and the state of the labour market as is likely to be of guidance to workers from the other Member States. Such information shall be brought up to date regularly.

The specialist services of the other Member States shall ensure that wide publicity is given to such information, in particular by circulating it among the appropriate employment services and by all suitable means of communication for informing the workers concerned.

Note: Amended by EEC 2434/92.

TITLE II

Machinery for Vacancy Clearance

[**Article 15**

1. The specialist service of each Member State shall regularly send to the specialist services of the other Member States and to the European Co-ordination Office:
    (a) details of vacancies which could be filled by nationals of other Member States;

(b) details of vacancies addressed to non-Member States;

(c) details of applications for employment by those who have formally expressed a wish to work in another Member State;

(d) information, by region and by branch of activity, on applicants who have declared themselves actually willing to accept employment in another country.

The specialist service of each Member State shall forward this information to the appropriate employment services and agencies as soon as possible.

2. The details of vacancies and applications referred to in paragraph 1 shall be circulated according to a uniform system to be established by the European Coordination Office in collaboration with the Technical Committee. If necessary, the European Co-ordination Office may adapt this system in collaboration with the Technical Committee.]

Note: Substituted by EEC 2434/92.

[Article 16

1. Any vacancy within the meaning of Article 15 communicated to the employment services of a Member State shall be notified to and processed by the competent employment services of the other Member States concerned. Such services shall forward to the services of the first Member State the details of suitable applications.

2. The applications for employment referred to in Article 15(1)(c) shall be responded to by the relevant services of the Member States within a reasonable period, not exceeding one month.

3. The employment services shall grant workers who are nationals of the Member States the same priority as the relevant measures grant to nationals *vis-a-vis* workers from non-Member States.]

Note: Substituted by EEC 2434/92.

Article 17

1. The provisions of Article 16 shall be implemented by the specialist services. However, in so far as they have been authorised by the central services and in so far as the organisation of the employment services of a Member State and the placing techniques employment make it possible:

(a) the regional employment services of the Member States shall:

(i) on the basis of the [details] referred to in Article 15, on which appropriate action will be taken, directly bring together and clear vacancies and applications for employment;

(ii) establish direct relations for clearance:

— of vacancies offered to a named worker;

— of individual applications for employment sent either to a specific employment service or to an employer pursuing his activity within the area covered by such a service;

— where the clearing operations concern seasonal workers who must be recruited as quickly as possible;

[(b) the services territorially responsible for the border regions of two or more Member States shall regularly exchange data relating to vacancies and applications for employment in their area and, acting in accordance with their arrangements with the other employment services of their countries, shall directly bring together and clear vacancies and applications for employment.

If necessary, the services territorially responsible for border regions shall also set up cooperation and service structures to provide:

— users with as much practical information as possible on the various aspects of mobility, and

— management and labour, social services (in particular public, private or those of public interest) and all institutions concerned, with a framework of coordinated measures relating to mobility;]

(c) official employment services which specialise in certain occupations or specific categories of persons shall co-operate directly with each other.

2. The Member States concerned shall forward to the Commission the list, drawn up by common accord, of services referred to in paragraph 1; the Commission shall publish such list, and any amendment thereto, in the Official Journal of the European Communities.

Note: Amended by EEC 2434/92.

Article 18

Adoption of recruiting procedures as applied by the implementing bodies provided for under agreements concluded between two or more Member States shall not be obligatory.

TITLE III
Measures for controlling the balance of the labour market

Article 19

[1. On the basis of a report from the Commission drawn up from information supplied by the Member States, the latter and the Commission shall at least once a year analyse jointly the results of Community arrangements regarding vacancies and applications.]

2. The Member States shall examine with the Commission all the possibilities of giving priority to nationals of Member States when filling employment vacancies in order to achieve a balance between vacancies and applications for employment within the Community. They shall adopt all measures necessary for this purpose.

[3. Every two years the Commission shall submit a report to the European Parliament, the Council and the Economic and Social Committee on the implementation of Part II of this Regulation, summarising the information required and the data obtained from the studies and research carried out and highlighting any useful points with regard to developments on the Community's labour market.]

Note: Amended by EEC 2434/92.

Article 20

. . .

Note: Deleted by EEC 2434/92.

Title IV

European Co-ordination Office

Article 21

The European Office for Co-ordinating the Clearance of Vacancies and Applications for Employment, established within the Commission (called in this Regulation the 'European Co-ordination Office'), shall have the general task of promoting vacancy clearance at Community level. It shall be responsible in particular for all the technical duties in this field which, under the provisions of this Regulation, are assigned to the Commission, and especially for assisting the national employment services.

It shall summarise the information referred to in Articles 14 and 15 and the data arising out of the studies and research carried out pursuant to Article 13, so as to bring to light any useful facts about foreseeable developments on the Community labour market; such facts shall be communicated to the specialist services of the Member States and to the Advisory and Technical Committees.

Article 22

1. The European Co-ordination Office shall be responsible, in particular, for:

(a) co-ordinating the practical measures necessary for vacancy clearance at Community level and for analysing the resulting movements of workers;

(b) contributing to such objectives by implementing, in co-operation with the Technical Committee, joint methods of action at administrative and technical levels;

(c) carrying out, where a special need arises, and in agreement with the specialist services, the bringing together of vacancies and applications for employment for clearance by these specialist services.

2. It shall communicate to the specialist services vacancies and applications for employment sent directly to the Commission, and shall be informed of the action taken thereon.

Article 23

The Commission may, in agreement with the competent authority of each Member State, and in accordance with the conditions and procedures which it shall determine on the basis of the Opinion of the Technical Committee, organise visits and assignments for officials of other Member States, and also advanced programmes for specialist personnel.

Part III

Committees for Ensuring Close Co-operation Between the Member States in Matters Concerning the Freedom of Movement of Workers and Their Employment

TITLE I
The Advisory Committee

Article 24

The Advisory Committee shall be responsible for assisting the Commission in the examination of any questions arising from the application of the Treaty and measures taken in pursuance thereof, in matters concerning freedom of movement of workers and their employment.

Article 25

The Advisory Committee shall be responsible in particular for:

(a) examining problems concerning freedom of movement and employment within the framework of national manpower policies, with a view to co-ordinating the employment policies of the Member States at Community level, thus contributing to the development of the economies and to an improved balance of the labour market;

(b) making a general study of the effects of implementing this Regulation and any supplementary measures;

(c) submitting to the Commission any reasoned proposals for revising this Regulation;

(d) delivering, either at the request of the Commission or on its own initiative, reasoned opinions on general questions or on questions of principle, in particular on exchange of information concerning developments in the labour market, on the movement of workers between Member States, on programmes or measures to develop vocational guidance and vocational training which are likely to increase the possibilities of freedom of movement and employment, and on all forms of assistance to workers and their families, including social assistance and the housing of workers.

Article 26

1. The Advisory Committee shall be composed of six members for each Member State, two of whom shall represent the government, two the trade unions and two the employers' associations.

2. For each of the categories referred to in paragraph 1, one alternate member shall be appointed by each Member State.

3. The term of office of the members and their alternates shall be two years. Their appointments shall be renewable. On expiry of their term of office, the members and their alternates shall remain in office until replaced or until their appointments are renewed.

Article 27

The members of the Advisory Committee and their alternates shall be appointed by the Council which shall endeavour, when selecting representatives of trade unions and employers' associations, to achieve adequate representation on the Committee of the various economic sectors concerned.

The list of members and their alternates shall be published by the Council for information in the *Official Journal of the European Communities*.

Article 28

The Advisory Committee shall be chaired by a member of the Commission or his alternate. The Chairman shall not vote. The Committee shall meet at least twice a year. It shall be convened by its Chairman, either on his own initiative, or at the request of at least one third of the members. Secretarial services shall be provided for the Committee by the Commission.

Article 29

The chairman may invite individuals or representatives of bodies with wide experience in the field of employment or movement of workers to take part in meetings as observers or as experts. The Chairman may be assisted by expert advisers.

Article 30

1. An opinion delivered by the Committee shall not be valid unless two thirds of the members are present.

2. Opinions shall state the reasons on which they are based; they shall be delivered by an absolute majority of the votes validly cast; they shall be accompanied by a written statement of the views expressed by the minority, when the latter so requests.

Article 31

The Advisory Committee shall establish its working methods by rules of procedure which shall enter into force after the Council, having received an opinion from the Commission, has given its approval. The entry into force of any amendment that the Committee decides to make thereto shall be subject to the same procedure.

Title II
The Technical Committee

Article 32

The Technical Committee shall be responsible for assisting the Commission to prepare, promote and follow up all technical work and measures for giving effect to this Regulation and any supplementary measures.

Article 33

The Technical Committee shall be responsible in particular for:

(a) promoting and advancing co-operation between the public authorities concerned in the Member States on all technical questions relating to freedom of movement of workers and their employment;

(b) formulating procedures for the organisation of the joint activities of the public authorities concerned;

(c) facilitating the gathering of information likely to be of use to the Commission and for the studies and research provided for in this Regulation, and encouraging exchange of information and experience between the administrative bodies concerned;

(d) investigating at a technical level the harmonisation of the criteria by which Member States assess the state of their labour markets.

Article 34

1. The Technical Committee shall be composed of representatives of the Governments of the Member States. Each Government shall appoint as member of the Technical Committee one of the members who represent it on the Advisory Committee.

2. Each government shall appoint an alternate from among its other representatives—members or alternates—on the Advisory Committee.

Article 35

The Technical Committee shall be chaired by a member of the Commission or his representative. The Chairman shall not vote. The Chairman and the members of the Committee may be assisted by expert advisers.

Secretarial services shall be provided for the Committee by the Commission.

Article 36

The proposals and opinions formulated by the Technical Committee shall be submitted to the Commission, and the Advisory Committee shall be informed thereof. Any such proposals and opinions shall be accompanied by a written statement of the views expressed by the various members of the Technical Committee, when the latter so request.

Article 37

The Technical Committee shall establish its working methods by rules of procedure which shall enter into force after the Council, having received an opinion from the Commission, has given its approval. The entry into force of any amendment which the Committee decides to make thereto shall be subject to the same procedure.

PART IV

TRANSITIONAL AND FINAL PROVISIONS

TITLE I

Transitional provisions

Article 38

Until the adoption by the Commission of the uniform system referred to in Article 15(2), the European Co-ordination Office shall propose any measures likely to be of use in drawing up and circulating the returns referred to in Article 15(1).

Article 39

The rules of procedure of the Advisory Committee and the Technical Committee in force at the time of entry into force of this Regulation shall continue to apply.

Article 40

Until the entry into force of the measures to be taken by Member States in pursuance of the Council Directive of 15 October 1968 and where, under the measures taken by the Member States in pursuance of the Council Directive of 25 March 1964 the work permit provided for in Article 22 of Regulation No 38/64/EEC is necessary to determine the period of validity and extension of the residence permit, written confirmation of engagement from the employer or a certificate of employment stating the period of employment may be substituted for such work permit. Any written confirmation by the employer or certificate of employment showing that the worker has been engaged for an indefinite period shall have the same effect as that of a permanent work permit.

Article 41

If, by reason of the abolition of the work permit, a Member State can no longer compile certain statistics on the employment of foreign nationals, such Member State may, for statistical purposes, retain the work permit in respect of nationals of the other Member States until new statistical methods are introduced, but no later than 31 December 1969. The work permit must be issued automatically and must be valid until the actual abolition of work permits in such Member State.

TITLE II
Final Provisions

Article 42

1. This Regulation shall not affect the provisions of the Treaty establishing the European Coal and Steel Community which relate to workers with recognised qualifications in coalmining or steelmaking, nor those of the Treaty establishing the European Atomic Energy Community which deal with eligibility for skilled employment in the field of nuclear energy, nor any measures taken in pursuance of those Treaties.

Nevertheless, this Regulation shall apply to categories of workers referred to in the first sub-paragraph and to members of their families in so far as their legal position is not governed by the above-mentioned Treaties or measures.

2. This Regulation shall not affect measures taken in accordance with Article 51 of the Treaty.

3. This Regulation shall not affect the obligations of Member States arising out of:

— special relations or future agreements with certain non-European countries or territories, based on institutional ties existing at the time of the entry into force of this Regulation; or

— agreements in existence at the time of the entry into force of this Regulation with certain non-European countries or territories, based on institutional ties between them.

Workers from such countries or territories who, in accordance with this provision, are pursuing activities as employed persons in the territory of one of those Member States may not invoke the benefit of the provisions of this Regulation in the territory of the other Member States.

Article 43

Member States shall, for information purposes, communicate to the Commission the texts of agreements, conventions or arrangements concluded between them in the manpower field between the date of their being signed and that of their entry into force.

Article 44

The Commission shall adopt measures pursuant to this Regulation for its implementation. To this end it shall act in close cooperation with the central public authorities of the Member States.

Article 45

The Commission shall submit to the Council proposals aimed at abolishing, in accordance with the conditions of the Treaty, restrictions on eligibility for employment of workers who are nationals of Member States, where the absence of mutual recognition of diplomas, certificates or other evidence of formal qualifications may prevent freedom of movement for workers.

Article 46

The administrative expenditure of the Committees referred to in Part III shall be included in the budget of the European Communities in the section relating to the Commission.

Article 47

This Regulation shall apply to the territories of the Member States and to their nationals, without prejudice to Articles 2, 3, 10 and 11.

Article 48

Regulation No 38/64/EEC shall cease to have effect when this Regulation enters into force.

This Regulation shall be binding in its entirety and directly applicable in all Member States.

Done at Luxembourg, 15 October 1968.

Note: Annex deleted by EEC 2434/92.

Council Directive 2001/55/EC
of 20 July 2001

on minimum standards for giving temporary protection in the event of a mass influx of displaced persons and on measures promoting a balance of efforts between Member States in receiving such persons and bearing the consequences thereof

Note: Entered into force on 7 August 2001 (Article 33).

THE COUNCIL OF THE EUROPEAN UNION,

Having regard to the Treaty establishing the European Community, and in particular point 2(a) and (b) of Article 63 thereof,
Having regard to the proposal from the Commission[1],
Having regard to the opinion of the European Parliament[2],
Having regard to the opinion of the Economic and Social Committee[3],
Having regard to the opinion of the Committee of the Regions[4],
Whereas:

(1) The preparation of a common policy on asylum, including common European arrangements for asylum, is a constituent part of the European Union's objective of establishing progressively an area of freedom, security and justice open to those who, forced by circumstances, legitimately seek protection in the European Union.

(2) Cases of mass influx of displaced persons who cannot return to their country of origin have become more substantial in Europe in recent years. In these cases it may be necessary to set up exceptional schemes to offer them immediate temporary protection.

(3) In the conclusions relating to persons displaced by the conflict in the former Yugoslavia adopted by the Ministers responsible for immigration at their meetings in London on 30 November and 1 December 1992 and Copenhagen on 1 and 2 June 1993, the Member States and the Community institutions expressed their concern at the situation of displaced persons.

(4) On 25 September 1995 the Council adopted a Resolution on burden-sharing with regard to the admission and residence of displaced persons on a temporary basis[5], and, on 4 March 1996, adopted Decision 96/198/JHA on an alert and emergency procedure for burden-sharing with regard to the admission and residence of displaced persons on a temporary basis[6].

[1] OJ C 311 E, 31.10.2000, p 251.
[2] Opinion delivered on 13 March 2001 (not yet published in the Official Journal).
[3] OJ C 155, 29.5.2001, p. 21.
[4] Opinion delivered on 13 June 2001 (not yet published in the Official Journal).
[5] OJ C 262, 7.10.1995, p. 1.
[6] OJ L 63, 13.3.1996, p. 10.

(5) The Action Plan of the Council and the Commission of 3 December 1998[7] provides for the rapid adoption, in accordance with the Treaty of Amsterdam, of minimum standards for giving temporary protection to displaced persons from third countries who cannot return to their country of origin and of measures promoting a balance of effort between Member States in receiving and bearing the consequences of receiving displaced persons.

(6) On 27 May 1999 the Council adopted conclusions on displaced persons from Kosovo. These conclusions call on the Commission and the Member States to learn the lessons of their response to the Kosovo crisis in order to establish the measures in accordance with the Treaty.

(7) The European Council, at its special meeting in Tampere on 15 and 16 October 1999, acknowledged the need to reach agreement on the issue of temporary protection for displaced persons on the basis of solidarity between Member States.

(8) It is therefore necessary to establish minimum standards for giving temporary protection in the event of a mass influx of displaced persons and to take measures to promote a balance of efforts between the Member States in receiving and bearing the consequences of receiving such persons.

(9) Those standards and measures are linked and interdependent for reasons of effectiveness, coherence and solidarity and in order, in particular, to avert the risk of secondary movements. They should therefore be enacted in a single legal instrument.

(10) This temporary protection should be compatible with the Member States' international obligations as regards refugees. In particular, it must not prejudge the recognition of refugee status pursuant to the Geneva Convention of 28 July 1951 on the status of refugees, as amended by the New York Protocol of 31 January 1967, ratified by all the Member States.

(11) The mandate of the United Nations High Commissioner for Refugees regarding refugees and other persons in need of international protection should be respected, and effect should be given to Declaration No 17, annexed to the Final Act to the Treaty of Amsterdam, on Article 63 of the Treaty establishing the European Community which provides that consultations are to be established with the United Nations High Commissioner for Refugees and other relevant international organisations on matters relating to asylum policy.

(12) It is in the very nature of minimum standards that Member States have the power to introduce or maintain more favourable provisions for persons enjoying temporary protection in the event of a mass influx of displaced persons.

(13) Given the exceptional character of the provisions established by this Directive in order to deal with a mass influx or imminent mass influx of displaced persons from third countries who are unable to return to their country of origin, the protection offered should be of limited duration.

(14) The existence of a mass influx of displaced persons should be established by a Council Decision, which should be binding in all Member States in relation to the displaced persons to whom the Decision applies. The conditions for the expiry of the Decision should also be established.

---

[7] OJ C 19, 20.1.1999, p. 1.

(15) The Member States' obligations as to the conditions of reception and residence of persons enjoying temporary protection in the event of a mass influx of displaced persons should be determined. These obligations should be fair and offer an adequate level of protection to those concerned.

(16) With respect to the treatment of persons enjoying temporary protection under this Directive, the Member States are bound by obligations under instruments of international law to which they are party and which prohibit discrimination.

(17) Member States should, in concert with the Commission, enforce adequate measures so that the processing of personal data respects the standard of protection of Directive 95/46/EC of the European Parliament and the Council of 24 October 1995 on the protection of individuals with regard to the processing of personal data and on the free movement of such data[8].

(18) Rules should be laid down to govern access to the asylum procedure in the context of temporary protection in the event of a mass influx of displaced persons, in conformity with the Member States' international obligations and with the Treaty.

(19) Provision should be made for principles and measures governing the return to the country of origin and the measures to be taken by Member States in respect of persons whose temporary protection has ended.

(20) Provision should be made for a solidarity mechanism intended to contribute to the attainment of a balance of effort between Member States in receiving and bearing the consequences of receiving displaced persons in the event of a mass influx. The mechanism should consist of two components. The first is financial and the second concerns the actual reception of persons in the Member States.

(21) The implementation of temporary protection should be accompanied by administrative cooperation between the Member States in liaison with the Commission.

(22) It is necessary to determine criteria for the exclusion of certain persons from temporary protection in the event of a mass influx of displaced persons.

(23) Since the objectives of the proposed action, namely to establish minimum standards for giving temporary protection in the event of a mass influx of displaced persons and measures promoting a balance of efforts between the Member States in receiving and bearing the consequences of receiving such persons, cannot be sufficiently attained by the Member States and can therefore, by reason of the scale or effects of the proposed action, be better achieved at Community level, the Community may adopt measures in accordance with the principle of subsidiarity as set out in Article 5 of the Treaty. In accordance with the principle of proportionality as set out in that Article, this Directive does not go beyond what is necessary in order to achieve those objectives.

(24) In accordance with Article 3 of the Protocol on the position of the United Kingdom and Ireland, annexed to the Treaty on European Union and to the Treaty establishing the European Community, the United Kingdom gave notice, by letter of 27 September 2000, of its wish to take part in the adoption and application of this Directive.

(25) Pursuant to Article 1 of the said Protocol, Ireland is not participating in the adoption of this Directive. Consequently and without prejudice to Article 4 of the aforementioned Protocol, the provisions of this Directive do not apply to Ireland.

---

[8] OJ L 281, 23.11.1995, p. 31.

(26) In accordance with Articles 1 and 2 of the Protocol on the position of Denmark, annexed to the Treaty on European Union and to the Treaty establishing the European Community, Denmark is not participating in the adoption of this Directive, and is therefore not bound by it nor subject to its application,

HAS ADOPTED THIS DIRECTIVE:

CHAPTER I
GENERAL PROVISIONS

Article 1

The purpose of this Directive is to establish minimum standards for giving temporary protection in the event of a mass influx of displaced persons from third countries who are unable to return to their country of origin and to promote a balance of effort between Member States in receiving and bearing the consequences of receiving such persons.

Article 2

For the purpose of this Directive:

(a) 'temporary protection' means a procedure of exceptional character to provide, in the event of a mass influx or imminent mass influx of displaced persons from third countries who are unable to return to their country of origin, immediate and temporary protection to such persons, in particular if there is also a risk that the asylum system will be unable to process this influx without adverse effects for its efficient operation, in the interests of the persons concerned and other persons requesting protection;

(b) 'Geneva Convention' means the Convention of 28 July 1951 relating to the status of refugees, as amended by the New York Protocol of 31 January 1967;

(c) 'displaced persons' means third-country nationals or state-less persons who have had to leave their country or region of origin, or have been evacuated, in particular in response to an appeal by international organisations, and are unable to return in safe and durable conditions because of the situation prevailing in that country, who may fall within the scope of Article 1A of the Geneva Convention or other international or national instruments giving international protection, in particular:

(i) persons who have fled areas of armed conflict or endemic violence;

(ii) persons at serious risk of, or who have been the victims of, systematic or generalised violations of their human rights;

(d) 'mass influx' means arrival in the Community of a large number of displaced persons, who come from a specific country or geographical area, whether their arrival in the Community was spontaneous or aided, for example through an evacuation programme;

(e) 'refugees' means third-country nationals or stateless persons within the meaning of Article 1A of the Geneva Convention;

(f) 'unaccompanied minors' means third-country nationals or stateless persons below the age of eighteen, who arrive on the territory of the Member States unaccompanied by an adult responsible for them whether by law or custom, and for as long as they are not effectively taken into the care of such a person, or minors who are left unaccompanied after they have entered the territory of the Member States;

(g) 'residence permit' means any permit or authorisation issued by the authorities of a Member State and taking the form provided for in that State's legislation, allowing a third country national or a stateless person to reside on its territory;

(h) 'sponsor' means a third-country national enjoying temporary protection in a Member State in accordance with a decision taken under Article 5 and who wants to be joined by members of his or her family.

Article 3

1. Temporary protection shall not prejudge recognition of refugee status under the Geneva Convention.

2. Member States shall apply temporary protection with due respect for human rights and fundamental freedoms and their obligations regarding non-refoulement.

3. The establishment, implementation and termination of temporary protection shall be the subject of regular consultations with the Office of the United Nations High Commissioner for Refugees (UNHCR) and other relevant international organisations.

4. This Directive shall not apply to persons who have been accepted under temporary protection schemes prior to its entry into force.

5. This Directive shall not affect the prerogative of the Member States to adopt or retain more favourable conditions for persons covered by temporary protection.

CHAPTER II
DURATION AND IMPLEMENTATION OF TEMPORARY PROTECTION

Article 4

1. Without prejudice to Article 6, the duration of temporary protection shall be one year. Unless terminated under the terms of Article 6(1)(b), it may be extended automatically by six monthly periods for a maximum of one year.

2. Where reasons for temporary protection persist, the Council may decide by qualified majority, on a proposal from the Commission, which shall also examine any request by a Member State that it submit a proposal to the Council, to extend that temporary protection by up to one year.

Article 5

1. The existence of a mass influx of displaced persons shall be established by a Council Decision adopted by a qualified majority on a proposal from the Commission, which shall also examine any request by a Member State that it submit a proposal to the Council.

2. The Commission proposal shall include at least:
(a) a description of the specific groups of persons to whom the temporary protection will apply;
(b) the date on which the temporary protection will take effect;
(c) an estimation of the scale of the movements of displaced persons.

3. The Council Decision shall have the effect of introducing temporary protection for the displaced persons to which it refers, in all the Member States, in accordance with the provisions of this Directive. The Decision shall include at least:

(a) a description of the specific groups of persons to whom the temporary protection applies;

(b) the date on which the temporary protection will take effect;

(c) information received from Member States on their reception capacity;

(d) information from the Commission, UNHCR and other relevant international organisations.

4. The Council Decision shall be based on:

(a) an examination of the situation and the scale of the movements of displaced persons;

(b) an assessment of the advisability of establishing temporary protection, taking into account the potential for emergency aid and action on the ground or the inadequacy of such measures;

(c) information received from the Member States, the Commission, UNHCR and other relevant international organisations.

5. The European Parliament shall be informed of the Council Decision.

Article 6

1. Temporary protection shall come to an end:

(a) when the maximum duration has been reached; or

(b) at any time, by Council Decision adopted by a qualified majority on a proposal from the Commission, which shall also examine any request by a Member State that it submit a proposal to the Council.

2. The Council Decision shall be based on the establishment of the fact that the situation in the country of origin is such as to permit the safe and durable return of those granted temporary protection with due respect for human rights and fundamental freedoms and Member States' obligations regarding non-refoulement. The European Parliament shall be informed of the Council Decision.

Article 7

1. Member States may extend temporary protection as provided for in this Directive to additional categories of displaced persons over and above those to whom the Council Decision provided for in Article 5 applies, where they are displaced for the same reasons and from the same country or region of origin. They shall notify the Council and the Commission immediately.

2. The provisions of Articles 24, 25 and 26 shall not apply to the use of the possibility referred to in paragraph 1, with the exception of the structural support included in the European Refugee Fund set up by Decision 2000/596/EC[9], under the conditions laid down in that Decision.

---

[9] OJ L 252, 6.10.2000, p. 12.

CHAPTER III

OBLIGATIONS OF THE MEMBER STATES TOWARDS PERSONS ENJOYING TEMPORARY PROTECTION

Article 8

1. The Member States shall adopt the necessary measures to provide persons enjoying temporary protection with residence permits for the entire duration of the protection. Documents or other equivalent evidence shall be issued for that purpose.

2. Whatever the period of validity of the residence permits referred to in paragraph 1, the treatment granted by the Member States to persons enjoying temporary protection may not be less favourable than that set out in Articles 9 to 16.

3. The Member States shall, if necessary, provide persons to be admitted to their territory for the purposes of temporary protection with every facility for obtaining the necessary visas, including transit visas. Formalities must be reduced to a minimum because of the urgency of the situation. Visas should be free of charge or their cost reduced to a minimum.

Article 9

The Member States shall provide persons enjoying temporary protection with a document, in a language likely to be understood by them, in which the provisions relating to temporary protection and which are relevant to them are clearly set out.

Article 10

To enable the effective application of the Council Decision referred to in Article 5, Member States shall register the personal data referred to in Annex II, point (a), with respect to the persons enjoying temporary protection on their territory.

Article 11

A Member State shall take back a person enjoying temporary protection on its territory, if the said person remains on, or, seeks to enter without authorisation onto, the territory of another Member State during the period covered by the Council Decision referred to in Article 5. Member States may, on the basis of a bilateral agreement, decide that this Article should not apply.

Article 12

The Member States shall authorise, for a period not exceeding that of temporary protection, persons enjoying temporary protection to engage in employed or self-employed activities, subject to rules applicable to the profession, as well as in activities such as educational opportunities for adults, vocational training and practical workplace experience. For reasons of labour market policies, Member States may give priority to EU citizens and citizens of States bound by the Agreement on the European Economic Area and also to legally resident third-country nationals who receive unemployment benefit. The general law in force in the Member States applicable to remuneration, access to social security systems relating to employed or self-employed activities and other conditions of employment shall apply.

Article 13

1. The Member States shall ensure that persons enjoying temporary protection have access to suitable accommodation or, if necessary, receive the means to obtain housing.

2. The Member States shall make provision for persons enjoying temporary protection to receive necessary assistance in terms of social welfare and means of subsistence, if they do not have sufficient resources, as well as for medical care. Without prejudice to paragraph 4, the assistance necessary for medical care shall include at least emergency care and essential treatment of illness.

3. Where persons enjoying temporary protection are engaged in employed or self-employed activities, account shall be taken, when fixing the proposed level of aid, of their ability to meet their own needs.

4. The Member States shall provide necessary medical or other assistance to persons enjoying temporary protection who have special needs, such as unaccompanied minors or persons who have undergone torture, rape or other serious forms of psychological, physical or sexual violence.

Article 14

1. The Member States shall grant to persons under 18 years of age enjoying temporary protection access to the education system under the same conditions as nationals of the host Member State. The Member States may stipulate that such access must be confined to the state education system.

2. The Member States may allow adults enjoying temporary protection access to the general education system.

Article 15

1. For the purpose of this Article, in cases where families already existed in the country of origin and were separated due to circumstances surrounding the mass influx, the following persons shall be considered to be part of a family:

(a) the spouse of the sponsor or his/her unmarried partner in a stable relationship, where the legislation or practice of the Member State concerned treats unmarried couples in a way comparable to married couples under its law relating to aliens; the minor unmarried children of the sponsor or of his/her spouse, without distinction as to whether they were born in or out of wedlock or adopted;

(b) other close relatives who lived together as part of the family unit at the time of the events leading to the mass influx, and who were wholly or mainly dependent on the sponsor at the time.

2. In cases where the separate family members enjoy temporary protection in different Member States, Member States shall reunite family members where they are satisfied that the family members fall under the description of paragraph 1(a), taking into account the

wish of the said family members. Member States may reunite family members where they are satisfied that the family members fall under the description of paragraph 1(b), taking into account on a case by case basis the extreme hardship they would face if the reunification did not take place.

3. Where the sponsor enjoys temporary protection in one Member State and one or some family members are not yet in a Member State, the Member State where the sponsor enjoys temporary protection shall reunite family members, who are in need of protection, with the sponsor in the case of family members where it is satisfied that they fall under the description of paragraph 1(a). The Member State may reunite family members, who are in need of protection, with the sponsor in the case of family members where it is satisfied that they fall under the description of paragraph 1(b), taking into account on a case by case basis the extreme hardship which they would face if the reunification did not take place.

4. When applying this Article, the Member States shall take into consideration the best interests of the child.

5. The Member States concerned shall decide, taking account of Articles 25 and 26, in which Member State the reunification shall take place.

6. Reunited family members shall be granted residence permits under temporary protection. Documents or other equivalent evidence shall be issued for that purpose. Transfers of family members onto the territory of another Member State for the purposes of reunification under paragraph 2, shall result in the withdrawal of the residence permits issued, and the termination of the obligations towards the persons concerned relating to temporary protection, in the Member State of departure.

7. The practical implementation of this Article may involve cooperation with the international organisations concerned.

8. A Member State shall, at the request of another Member State, provide information, as set out in Annex II, on a person receiving temporary protection which is needed to process a matter under this Article.

Article 16

1. The Member States shall as soon as possible take measures to ensure the necessary representation of unaccompanied minors enjoying temporary protection by legal guardianship, or, where necessary, representation by an organisation which is responsible for the care and well-being of minors, or by any other appropriate representation.

2. During the period of temporary protection Member States shall provide for unaccompanied minors to be placed:
    (a) with adult relatives;
    (b) with a foster-family;
    (c) in reception centres with special provisions for minors, or in other accommodation suitable for minors;
    (d) with the person who looked after the child when fleeing.

The Member States shall take the necessary steps to enable the placement. Agreement by the adult person or persons concerned shall be established by the Member States. The views of the child shall be taken into account in accordance with the age and maturity of the child.

CHAPTER IV

ACCESS TO THE ASYLUM PROCEDURE IN THE CONTEXT OF
TEMPORARY PROTECTION

Article 17

1. Persons enjoying temporary protection must be able to lodge an application for asylum at any time.

2. The examination of any asylum application not processed before the end of the period of temporary protection shall be completed after the end of that period.

Article 18

The criteria and mechanisms for deciding which Member State is responsible for considering an asylum application shall apply. In particular, the Member State responsible for examining an asylum application submitted by a person enjoying temporary protection pursuant to this Directive, shall be the Member State which has accepted his transfer onto its territory.

Article 19

1. The Member States may provide that temporary protection may not be enjoyed concurrently with the status of asylum seeker while applications are under consideration.

2. Where, after an asylum application has been examined, refugee status or, where applicable, other kind of protection is not granted to a person eligible for or enjoying temporary protection, the Member States shall, without prejudice to Article 28, provide for that person to enjoy or to continue to enjoy temporary protection for the remainder of the period of protection.

CHAPTER V

RETURN AND MEASURES AFTER TEMPORARY PROTECTION HAS ENDED

Article 20

When the temporary protection ends, the general laws on protection and on aliens in the Member States shall apply, without prejudice to Articles 21, 22 and 23.

Article 21

1. The Member States shall take the measures necessary to make possible the voluntary return of persons enjoying temporary protection or whose temporary protection has ended. The Member States shall ensure that the provisions governing voluntary return of persons enjoying temporary protection facilitate their return with respect for human dignity.

The Member State shall ensure that the decision of those persons to return is taken in full knowledge of the facts. The Member States may provide for exploratory visits.

2. For such time as the temporary protection has not ended, the Member States shall, on the basis of the circumstances prevailing in the country of origin, give favourable consideration to requests for return to the host Member State from persons who have enjoyed temporary protection and exercised their right to a voluntary return.

3. At the end of the temporary protection, the Member States may provide for the obligations laid down in Chapter III to be extended individually to persons who have been covered by temporary protection and are benefiting from a voluntary return programme. The extension shall have effect until the date of return.

Article 22

1. The Member States shall take the measures necessary to ensure that the enforced return of persons whose temporary protection has ended and who are not eligible for admission is conducted with due respect for human dignity.

2. In cases of enforced return, Member States shall consider any compelling humanitarian reasons which may make return impossible or unreasonable in specific cases.

Article 23

1. The Member States shall take the necessary measures concerning the conditions of residence of persons who have enjoyed temporary protection and who cannot, in view of their state of health, reasonably be expected to travel; where for example they would suffer serious negative effects if their treatment was interrupted. They shall not be expelled so long as that situation continues.

2. The Member States may allow families whose children are minors and attend school in a Member State to benefit from residence conditions allowing the children concerned to complete the current school period.

CHAPTER VI
SOLIDARITY

Article 24

The measures provided for in this Directive shall benefit from the European Refugee Fund set up by Decision 2000/596/EC, under the terms laid down in that Decision.

Article 25

1. The Member States shall receive persons who are eligible for temporary protection in a spirit of Community solidarity. They shall indicate—in figures or in general terms—their capacity to receive such persons. This information shall be set out in the Council Decision referred to in Article 5. After that Decision has been adopted, the Member States may indicate additional reception capacity by notifying the Council and the Commission. This information shall be passed on swiftly to UNHCR.

2. The Member States concerned, acting in cooperation with the competent international organisations, shall ensure that the eligible persons defined in the Council Decision referred to in Article 5, who have not yet arrived in the Community have expressed their will to be received onto their territory.

3. When the number of those who are eligible for temporary protection following a sudden and massive influx exceeds the reception capacity referred to in paragraph 1, the Council shall, as a matter of urgency, examine the situation and take appropriate action, including recommending additional support for Member States affected.

Article 26

1. For the duration of the temporary protection, the Member States shall cooperate with each other with regard to transferral of the residence of persons enjoying temporary protection from one Member State to another, subject to the consent of the persons concerned to such transferral.

2. A Member State shall communicate requests for transfers to the other Member States and notify the Commission and UNHCR. The Member States shall inform the requesting Member State of their capacity for receiving transferees.

3. A Member State shall, at the request of another Member State, provide information, as set out in Annex II, on a person enjoying temporary protection which is needed to process a matter under this Article.

4. Where a transfer is made from one Member State to another, the residence permit in the Member State of departure shall expire and the obligations towards the persons concerned relating to temporary protection in the Member State of departure shall come to an end. The new host Member State shall grant temporary protection to the persons concerned.

5. The Member States shall use the model pass set out in Annex I for transfers between Member States of persons enjoying temporary protection.

Chapter VII
Administrative Cooperation

Article 27

1. For the purposes of the administrative cooperation required to implement temporary protection, the Member States shall each appoint a national contact point, whose address they shall communicate to each other and to the Commission. The Member States shall, in liaison with the Commission, take all the appropriate measures to establish direct cooperation and an exchange of information between the competent authorities.

2. The Member States shall, regularly and as quickly as possible, communicate data concerning the number of persons enjoying temporary protection and full information on the national laws, regulations and administrative provisions relating to the implementation of temporary protection.

Chapter VIII
Special Provisions

Article 28

1. The Member States may exclude a person from temporary protection if:

(a) there are serious reasons for considering that:

(i) he or she has committed a crime against peace, a war crime, or a crime against humanity, as defined in the international instruments drawn up to make provision in respect of such crimes;

(ii) he or she has committed a serious non-political crime outside the Member State of reception prior to his or her admission to that Member State as a person enjoying temporary protection. The severity of the expected persecution is to be weighed against the nature of the criminal offence of which the person concerned is suspected. Particularly cruel actions, even if committed with an allegedly political objective, may be classified as serious non-political crimes. This applies both to the participants in the crime and to its instigators;

(iii) he or she has been guilty of acts contrary to the purposes and principles of the United Nations;

(b) there are reasonable grounds for regarding him or her as a danger to the security of the host Member State or, having been convicted by a final judgment of a particularly serious crime, he or she is a danger to the community of the host Member State.

2. The grounds for exclusion referred to in paragraph 1 shall be based solely on the personal conduct of the person concerned. Exclusion decisions or measures shall be based on the principle of proportionality.

Chapter IX
Final Provisions

Article 29

Persons who have been excluded from the benefit of temporary protection or family reunification by a Member State shall be entitled to mount a legal challenge in the Member State concerned.

Article 30

The Member States shall lay down the rules on penalties applicable to infringements of the national provisions adopted pursuant to this Directive and shall take all measures necessary to ensure that they are implemented. The penalties provided for must be effective, proportionate and dissuasive.

Article 31

1. Not later than two years after the date specified in Article 32, the Commission shall report to the European Parliament and the Council on the application of this Directive in

the Member States and shall propose any amendments that are necessary. The Member States shall send the Commission all the information that is appropriate for drawing up this report.

2. After presenting the report referred to at paragraph 1, the Commission shall report to the European Parliament and the Council on the application of this Directive in the Member States at least every five years.

Article 32

1. The Member States shall bring into force the laws, regulations and administrative provisions necessary to comply with this Directive by 31 December 2002 at the latest. They shall forthwith inform the Commission thereof.

2. When the Member States adopt these measures, they shall contain a reference to this Directive or shall be accompanied by such reference on the occasion of their official publication. The methods of making such a reference shall be laid down by the Member States.

Article 33

This Directive shall enter into force on the day of its publication in the *Official Journal of the European Communities.*

Article 34

This Directive is addressed to the Member States in accordance with the Treaty establishing the European Community.

Done at Brussels, 20 July 2001.

For the Council
The President
J. VANDE LANOTTE

Council Directive 2003/9/EC
of 27 January 2003
laying down minimum standards for the reception of asylum seekers

Note: Entered into force on 6 February 2003 (Article 27).

THE COUNCIL OF THE EUROPEAN UNION,

Having regard to the Treaty establishing the European Community, and in particular point (1)(b) of the first sub-paragraph of Article 63 thereof,

Having regard to the proposal from the Commission[10],

Having regard to the opinion of the European Parliament[11],

Having regard to the opinion of the Economic and Social Committee[12],

Having regard to the opinion of the Committee of the Regions[13],

Whereas:

(1) A common policy on asylum, including a Common European Asylum System, is a constituent part of the European Union's objective of progressively establishing an area of freedom, security and justice open to those who, forced by circumstances, legitimately seek protection in the Community.

(2) At its special meeting in Tampere on 15 and 16 October 1999, the European Council agreed to work towards establishing a Common European Asylum System, based on the full and inclusive application of the Geneva Convention relating to the Status of Refugees of 28 July 1951, as supplemented by the New York Protocol of 31 January 1967, thus maintaining the principle of non-refoulement.

(3) The Tampere Conclusions provide that a Common European Asylum System should include, in the short term, common minimum conditions of reception of asylum seekers.

(4) The establishment of minimum standards for the reception of asylum seekers is a further step towards a European asylum policy.

(5) This Directive respects the fundamental rights and observes the principles recognised in particular by the Charter of Fundamental Rights of the European Union. In particular, this Directive seeks to ensure full respect for human dignity and to promote the application of Articles 1 and 18 of the said Charter.

(6) With respect to the treatment of persons falling within the scope of this Directive, Member States are bound by obligations under instruments of international law to which they are party and which prohibit discrimination.

(7) Minimum standards for the reception of asylum seekers that will normally suffice to ensure them a dignified standard of living and comparable living conditions in all Member States should be laid down.

(8) The harmonisation of conditions for the reception of asylum seekers should help to limit the secondary movements of asylum seekers influenced by the variety of conditions for their reception.

(9) Reception of groups with special needs should be specifically designed to meet those needs.

(10) Reception of applicants who are in detention should be specifically designed to meet their needs in that situation.

(11) In order to ensure compliance with the minimum procedural guarantees consisting in the opportunity to contact organisations or groups of persons that provide legal assistance, information should be provided on such organisations and groups of persons.

---

[10] OJ C 213 E, 31.7.2001, p. 286.
[11] Opinion delivered on 25 April 2002 (not yet published in the Official Journal).
[12] OJ C 48, 21.2.2002, p. 63.
[13] OJ C 107, 3.5.2002, p. 85.

(12) The possibility of abuse of the reception system should be restricted by laying down cases for the reduction or withdrawal of reception conditions for asylum seekers.

(13) The efficiency of national reception systems and cooperation among Member States in the field of reception of asylum seekers should be secured.

(14) Appropriate coordination should be encouraged between the competent authorities as regards the reception of asylum seekers, and harmonious relationships between local communities and accommodation centres should therefore be promoted.

(15) It is in the very nature of minimum standards that Member States have the power to introduce or maintain more favourable provisions for third-country nationals and stateless persons who ask for international protection from a Member State.

(16) In this spirit, Member States are also invited to apply the provisions of this Directive in connection with procedures for deciding on applications for forms of protection other than that emanating from the Geneva Convention for third country nationals and stateless persons.

(17) The implementation of this Directive should be evaluated at regular intervals.

(18) Since the objectives of the proposed action, namely to establish minimum standards on the reception of asylum seekers in Member States, cannot be sufficiently achieved by the Member States and can therefore, by reason of the scale and effects of the proposed action, be better achieved by the Community, the Community may adopt measures in accordance with the principles of subsidiarity as set out in Article 5 of the Treaty. In accordance with the principle of proportionality, as set out in that Article, this Directive does not go beyond what is necessary in order to achieve those objectives.

(19) In accordance with Article 3 of the Protocol on the position of the United Kingdom and Ireland, annexed to the Treaty on European Union and to the Treaty establishing the European Community, the United Kingdom gave notice, by letter of 18 August 2001, of its wish to take part in the adoption and application of this Directive.

(20) In accordance with Article 1 of the said Protocol, Ireland is not participating in the adoption of this Directive. Consequently, and without prejudice to Article 4 of the aforementioned Protocol, the provisions of this Directive do not apply to Ireland.

(21) In accordance with Articles 1 and 2 of the Protocol on the position of Denmark, annexed to the Treaty on European Union and to the Treaty establishing the European Community, Denmark is not participating in the adoption of this Directive and is therefore neither bound by it nor subject to its application,

HAS ADOPTED THIS DIRECTIVE:

CHAPTER I
PURPOSE, DEFINITIONS AND SCOPE

Article 1

Purpose

The purpose of this Directive is to lay down minimum standards for the reception of asylum seekers in Member States.

Article 2

Definitions

For the purposes of this Directive:

(a) 'Geneva Convention' shall mean the Convention of 28 July 1951 relating to the status of refugees, as amended by the New York Protocol of 31 January 1967;

(b) 'application for asylum' shall mean the application made by a third-country national or a stateless person which can be understood as a request for international protection from a Member State, under the Geneva Convention. Any application for international protection is presumed to be an application for asylum unless a third-country national or a stateless person explicitly requests another kind of protection that can be applied for separately;

(c) 'applicant' or 'asylum seeker' shall mean a third country national or a stateless person who has made an application for asylum in respect of which a final decision has not yet been taken;

(d) 'family members' shall mean, in so far as the family already existed in the country of origin, the following members of the applicant's family who are present in the same Member State in relation to the application for asylum:

(i) the spouse of the asylum seeker or his or her unmarried partner in a stable relationship, where the legislation or practice of the Member State concerned treats unmarried couples in a way comparable to married couples under its law relating to aliens;

(ii) the minor children of the couple referred to in point (i) or of the applicant, on condition that they are unmarried and dependent and regardless of whether they were born in or out of wedlock or adopted as defined under the national law;

(e) 'refugee' shall mean a person who fulfils the requirements of Article 1(A) of the Geneva Convention;

(f) 'refugee status' shall mean the status granted by a Member State to a person who is a refugee and is admitted as such to the territory of that Member State;

(g) 'procedures' and 'appeals', shall mean the procedures and appeals established by Member States in their national law;

(h) 'unaccompanied minors' shall mean persons below the age of eighteen who arrive in the territory of the Member States unaccompanied by an adult responsible for them whether by law or by custom, and for as long as they are not effectively taken into the care of such a person; it shall include minors who are left unaccompanied after they have entered the territory of Member States;

(i) 'reception conditions' shall mean the full set of measures that Member States grant to asylum seekers in accordance with this Directive;

(j) 'material reception conditions' shall mean the reception conditions that include housing, food and clothing, provided in kind, or as financial allowances or in vouchers, and a daily expenses allowance;

(k) 'detention' shall mean confinement of an asylum seeker by a Member State within a particular place, where the applicant is deprived of his or her freedom of movement;

(l) 'accommodation centre' shall mean any place used for collective housing of asylum seekers.

Article 3

Scope

1. This Directive shall apply to all third country nationals and stateless persons who make an application for asylum at the border or in the territory of a Member State as long as they are allowed to remain on the territory as asylum seekers, as well as to family members, if they are covered by such application for asylum according to the national law.

2. This Directive shall not apply in cases of requests for diplomatic or territorial asylum submitted to representations of Member States.

3. This Directive shall not apply when the provisions of Council Directive 2001/55/EC of 20 July 2001 on minimum standards for giving temporary protection in the event of a mass influx of displaced persons and on measures promoting a balance of efforts between Member States in receiving such persons and bearing the consequences thereof[14] are applied.

4. Member States may decide to apply this Directive in connection with procedures for deciding on applications for kinds of protection other than that emanating from the Geneva Convention for third-country nationals or stateless persons who are found not to be refugees.

Article 4

More favourable provisions

Member States may introduce or retain more favourable provisions in the field of reception conditions for asylum seekers and other close relatives of the applicant who are present in the same Member State when they are dependent on him or for humanitarian reasons insofar as these provisions are compatible with this Directive.

CHAPTER II
GENERAL PROVISIONS ON RECEPTION CONDITIONS

Article 5

Information

1. Member States shall inform asylum seekers, within a reasonable time not exceeding fifteen days after they have lodged their application for asylum with the competent authority, of at least any established benefits and of the obligations with which they must comply relating to reception conditions.

Member States shall ensure that applicants are provided with information on organisations or groups of persons that provide specific legal assistance and organisations that might be able to help or inform them concerning the available reception conditions, including health care.

---

[14] OJ L 212, 7.8.2001, p. 12.

2. Member States shall ensure that the information referred to in paragraph 1 is in writing and, as far as possible, in a language that the applicants may reasonably be supposed to understand. Where appropriate, this information may also be supplied orally.

Article 6

Documentation

1. Member States shall ensure that, within three days after an application is lodged with the competent authority, the applicant is provided with a document issued in his or her own name certifying his or her status as an asylum seeker or testifying that he or she is allowed to stay in the territory of the Member State while his or her application is pending or being examined.   If the holder is not free to move within all or a part of the territory of the Member State, the document shall also certify this fact.

2. Member States may exclude application of this Article when the asylum seeker is in detention and during the examination of an application for asylum made at the border or within the context of a procedure to decide on the right of the applicant legally to enter the territory of a Member State. In specific cases, during the examination of an application for asylum, Member States may provide applicants with other evidence equivalent to the document referred to in paragraph 1.

3. The document referred to in paragraph 1 need not certify the identity of the asylum seeker.

4. Member States shall adopt the necessary measures to provide asylum seekers with the document referred to in paragraph 1, which must be valid for as long as they are authorised to remain in the territory of the Member State concerned or at the border thereof.

5. Member States may provide asylum seekers with a travel document when serious humanitarian reasons arise that require their presence in another State.

Article 7

Residence and freedom of movement

1. Asylum seekers may move freely within the territory of the host Member State or within an area assigned to them by that Member State. The assigned area shall not affect the unalienable sphere of private life and shall allow sufficient scope for guaranteeing access to all benefits under this Directive.

2. Member States may decide on the residence of the asylum seeker for reasons of public interest, public order or, when necessary, for the swift processing and effective monitoring of his or her application.

3. When it proves necessary, for example for legal reasons or reasons of public order, Member States may confine an applicant to a particular place in accordance with their national law.

4. Member States may make provision of the material reception conditions subject to actual residence by the applicants in a specific place, to be determined by the Member States. Such a decision, which may be of a general nature, shall be taken individually and established by national legislation.

5. Member States shall provide for the possibility of granting applicants temporary permission to leave the place of residence mentioned in paragraphs 2 and 4 and/or the assigned area mentioned in paragraph 1. Decisions shall be taken individually, objectively and impartially and reasons shall be given if they are negative.

The applicant shall not require permission to keep appointments with authorities and courts if his or her appearance is necessary.

6. Member States shall require applicants to inform the competent authorities of their current address and notify any change of address to such authorities as soon as possible.

Article 8

Families

Member States shall take appropriate measures to maintain as far as possible family unity as present within their territory, if applicants are provided with housing by the Member State concerned. Such measures shall be implemented with the asylum seeker's agreement.

Article 9

Medical screening

Member States may require medical screening for applicants on public health grounds.

Article 10

Schooling and education of minors

1. Member States shall grant to minor children of asylum seekers and to asylum seekers who are minors access to the education system under similar conditions as nationals of the host Member State for so long as an expulsion measure against them or their parents is not actually enforced. Such education may be provided in accommodation centres.

The Member State concerned may stipulate that such access must be confined to the State education system.

Minors shall be younger than the age of legal majority in the Member State in which the application for asylum was lodged or is being examined. Member States shall not withdraw secondary education for the sole reason that the minor has reached the age of majority.

2. Access to the education system shall not be postponed for more than three months from the date the application for asylum was lodged by the minor or the minor's parents. This period may be extended to one year where specific education is provided in order to facilitate access to the education system.

3. Where access to the education system as set out in paragraph 1 is not possible due to the specific situation of the minor, the Member State may offer other education arrangements.

Article 11

Employment

1. Member States shall determine a period of time, starting from the date on which an application for asylum was lodged, during which an applicant shall not have access to the labour market.

2. If a decision at first instance has not been taken within one year of the presentation of an application for asylum and this delay cannot be attributed to the applicant, Member States shall decide the conditions for granting access to the labour market for the applicant.

3. Access to the labour market shall not be withdrawn during appeals procedures, where an appeal against a negative decision in a regular procedure has suspensive effect, until such time as a negative decision on the appeal is notified.

4. For reasons of labour market policies, Member States may give priority to EU citizens and nationals of States parties to the Agreement on the European Economic Area and also to legally resident third-country nationals.

Article 12

Vocational training

Member States may allow asylum seekers access to vocational training irrespective of whether they have access to the labour market.

Access to vocational training relating to an employment contract shall depend on the extent to which the applicant has access to the labour market in accordance with Article 11.

Article 13

General rules on material reception conditions and health care

1. Member States shall ensure that material reception conditions are available to applicants when they make their application for asylum.

2. Member States shall make provisions on material reception conditions to ensure a standard of living adequate for the health of applicants and capable of ensuring their subsistence. Member States shall ensure that that standard of living is met in the specific situation of persons who have special needs, in accordance with Article 17, as well as in relation to the situation of persons who are in detention.

3. Member States may make the provision of all or some of the material reception conditions and health care subject to the condition that applicants do not have sufficient means to have a standard of living adequate for their health and to enable their subsistence.

4. Member States may require applicants to cover or contribute to the cost of the material reception conditions and of the health care provided for in this Directive, pursuant to the provision of paragraph 3, if the applicants have sufficient resources, for example if they have been working for a reasonable period of time.

If it transpires that an applicant had sufficient means to cover material reception conditions and health care at the time when these basic needs were being covered, Member States may ask the asylum seeker for a refund.

5. Material reception conditions may be provided in kind, or in the form of financial allowances or vouchers or in a combination of these provisions.

Where Member States provide material reception conditions in the form of financial allowances or vouchers, the amount thereof shall be determined in accordance with the principles set out in this Article.

Article 14

Modalities for material reception conditions

1. Where housing is provided in kind, it should take one or a combination of the following forms:

(a) premises used for the purpose of housing applicants during the examination of an application for asylum lodged at the border;

(b) accommodation centres which guarantee an adequate standard of living;

(c) private houses, flats, hotels or other premises adapted for housing applicants.

2. Member States shall ensure that applicants provided with the housing referred to in paragraph 1(a), (b) and (c) are assured:

(a) protection of their family life;

(b) the possibility of communicating with relatives, legal advisers and representatives of the United Nations High Commissioner for Refugees (UNHCR) and non-governmental organisations (NGOs) recognised by Member States. Member States shall pay particular attention to the prevention of assault within the premises and accommodation centres referred to in paragraph 1(a) and (b).

3. Member States shall ensure, if appropriate, that minor children of applicants or applicants who are minors are lodged with their parents or with the adult family member responsible for them whether by law or by custom.

4. Member States shall ensure that transfers of applicants from one housing facility to another take place only when necessary. Member States shall provide for the possibility for applicants to inform their legal advisers of the transfer and of their new address.

5. Persons working in accommodation centres shall be adequately trained and shall be bound by the confidentiality principle as defined in the national law in relation to any information they obtain in the course of their work.

6. Member States may involve applicants in managing the material resources and non-material aspects of life in the centre through an advisory board or council representing residents.

7. Legal advisors or counsellors of asylum seekers and representatives of the United Nations High Commissioner for Refugees or non-governmental organisations designated by the latter and recognised by the Member State concerned shall be granted access to accommodation centres and other housing facilities in order to assist the said asylum seekers. Limits on such access may be imposed only on grounds relating to the security of the centres and facilities and of the asylum seekers.

8. Member States may exceptionally set modalities for material reception conditions different from those provided for in this Article, for a reasonable period which shall be as short as possible, when:

— an initial assessment of the specific needs of the applicant is required,

— material reception conditions, as provided for in this Article, are not available in a certain geographical area,

— housing capacities normally available are temporarily exhausted,

— the asylum seeker is in detention or confined to border posts. These different conditions shall cover in any case basic needs.

Article 15

Health care

1. Member States shall ensure that applicants receive the necessary health care which shall include, at least, emergency care and essential treatment of illness.

2. Member States shall provide necessary medical or other assistance to applicants who have special needs.

Chapter III

Reduction or Withdrawal of Reception Conditions

Article 16

Reduction or withdrawal of reception conditions

1. Member States may reduce or withdraw reception conditions in the following cases:
    (a) where an asylum seeker:
    — abandons the place of residence determined by the competent authority without informing it or, if requested, without permission, or
    — does not comply with reporting duties or with requests to provide information or to appear for personal interviews concerning the asylum procedure during a reasonable period laid down in national law, or
    — has already lodged an application in the same Member State.

When the applicant is traced or voluntarily reports to the competent authority, a duly motivated decision, based on the reasons for the disappearance, shall be taken on the reinstallation of the grant of some or all of the reception conditions;

    (b) where an applicant has concealed financial resources and has therefore unduly benefited from material reception conditions.

If it transpires that an applicant had sufficient means to cover material reception conditions and health care at the time when these basic needs were being covered, Member States may ask the asylum seeker for a refund.

2. Member States may refuse conditions in cases where an asylum seeker has failed to demonstrate that the asylum claim was made as soon as reasonably practicable after arrival in that Member State.

3. Member States may determine sanctions applicable to serious breaching of the rules of the accommodation centres as well as to seriously violent behaviour.

4. Decisions for reduction, withdrawal or refusal of reception conditions or sanctions referred to in paragraphs 1, 2 and 3 shall be taken individually, objectively and impartially and reasons shall be given. Decisions shall be based on the particular situation of the person concerned, especially with regard to persons covered by Article 17, taking into

account the principle of proportionality. Member States shall under all circumstances ensure access to emergency health care.

5. Member States shall ensure that material reception conditions are not withdrawn or reduced before a negative decision is taken.

Chapter IV
Provisions for Persons with Special Needs

Article 17

General principle

1. Member States shall take into account the specific situation of vulnerable persons such as minors, unaccompanied minors, disabled people, elderly people, pregnant women, single parents with minor children and persons who have been subjected to torture, rape or other serious forms of psychological, physical or sexual violence, in the national legislation implementing the provisions of Chapter II relating to material reception conditions and health care.

2. Paragraph 1 shall apply only to persons found to have special needs after an individual evaluation of their situation.

Article 18

Minors

1. The best interests of the child shall be a primary consideration for Member States when implementing the provisions of this Directive that involve minors.

2. Member States shall ensure access to rehabilitation services for minors who have been victims of any form of abuse, neglect, exploitation, torture or cruel, inhuman and degrading treatment, or who have suffered from armed conflicts, and ensure that appropriate mental health care is developed and qualified counselling is provided when needed.

Article 19

Unaccompanied minors

1. Member States shall as soon as possible take measures to ensure the necessary representation of unaccompanied minors by legal guardianship or, where necessary, representation by an organisation which is responsible for the care and well-being of minors, or by any other appropriate representation. Regular assessments shall be made by the appropriate authorities.

2. Unaccompanied minors who make an application for asylum shall, from the moment they are admitted to the territory to the moment they are obliged to leave the host Member State in which the application for asylum was made or is being examined, be placed:
   (a) with adult relatives;
   (b) with a foster-family;
   (c) in accommodation centres with special provisions for minors;
   (d) in other accommodation suitable for minors.

Member States may place unaccompanied minors aged 16 or over in accommodation centres for adult asylum seekers.

As far as possible, siblings shall be kept together, taking into account the best interests of the minor concerned and, in particular, his or her age and degree of maturity. Changes of residence of unaccompanied minors shall be limited to a minimum.

3. Member States, protecting the unaccompanied minor's best interests, shall endeavour to trace the members of his or her family as soon as possible. In cases where there may be a threat to the life or integrity of the minor or his or her close relatives, particularly if they have remained in the country of origin, care must be taken to ensure that the collection, processing and circulation of information concerning those persons is undertaken on a confidential basis, so as to avoid jeopardising their safety.

4. Those working with unaccompanied minors shall have had or receive appropriate training concerning their needs, and shall be bound by the confidentiality principle as defined in the national law, in relation to any information they obtain in the course of their work.

Article 20

Victims of torture and violence

Member States shall ensure that, if necessary, persons who have been subjected to torture, rape or other serious acts of violence receive the necessary treatment of damages caused by the aforementioned acts.

CHAPTER V
APPEALS

Article 21

Appeals

1. Member States shall ensure that negative decisions relating to the granting of benefits under this Directive or decisions taken under Article 7 which individually affect asylum seekers may be the subject of an appeal within the procedures laid down in the national law. At least in the last instance the possibility of an appeal or a review before a judicial body shall be granted.

2. Procedures for access to legal assistance in such cases shall be laid down in national law.

CHAPTER VI
ACTIONS TO IMPROVE THE EFFICIENCY OF THE RECEPTION SYSTEM

Article 22

Cooperation

Member States shall regularly inform the Commission on the data concerning the number of persons, broken down by sex and age, covered by reception conditions and provide full information on the type, name and format of the documents provided for by Article 6.

Article 23

Guidance, monitoring and control system

Member States shall, with due respect to their constitutional structure, ensure that appropriate guidance, monitoring and control of the level of reception conditions are established.

Article 24

Staff and resources

1. Member States shall take appropriate measures to ensure that authorities and other organisations implementing this Directive have received the necessary basic training with respect to the needs of both male and female applicants.

2. Member States shall allocate the necessary resources in connection with the national provisions enacted to implement this Directive.

CHAPTER VII
FINAL PROVISIONS

Article 25

Reports

By 6 August 2006, the Commission shall report to the European Parliament and the Council on the application of this Directive and shall propose any amendments that are necessary.

Member States shall send the Commission all the information that is appropriate for drawing up the report, including the statistical data provided for by Article 22 by 6 February 2006.

After presenting the report, the Commission shall report to the European Parliament and the Council on the application of this Directive at least every five years.

Article 26

Transposition

1. Member States shall bring into force the laws, regulations and administrative provisions necessary to comply with this Directive by 6 February 2005. They shall forthwith inform the Commission thereof.

When the Member States adopt these measures, they shall contain a reference to this Directive or shall be accompanied by such a reference on the occasion of their official publication. Member States shall determine how such a reference is to be made.

2. Member States shall communicate to the Commission the text of the provisions of national law which they adopt in the field relating to the enforcement of this Directive.

Article 27

Entry into force

This Directive shall enter into force on the day of its publication in the *Official Journal of the European Union*.

Article 28

Addresses

This Directive is addressed to the Member States in accordance with the Treaty establishing the European Union.

Done at Brussels, 27 January 2003.

For the Council
The President
G. PAPANDREOU

25.2.2003 L 50/1 Official Journal of the European Union EN

I

(Acts whose publication is obligatory)

Council Regulation

(EC) No. 343/2003 of 18 February 2003

establishing the criteria and mechanisms for determining the Member State responsible for examining an asylum application lodged in one of the Member States by a third-country national

THE COUNCIL OF THE EUROPEAN UNION,

Having regard to the Treaty establishing the European Community; and in particular Article 63, first paragraph, point (1)(a),

Having regard to the proposal from the Commission[15],

Having regard to the opinion of the European Parliament[16],

Having regard to the opinion of the European Economic and Social Committee[17],

Whereas:

(1) Common policy on asylum, including a Common European Asylum System, is a constituent part of the European Union's objective of progressively establishing an area

---

[15] Article amended by the Treaty of Nice.
[16] Article amended by the Treaty of Nice.
[17] OJ C 125, 27.5.2002, p. 28.

of freedom, security and justice open to those who, forced by circumstances, legitimately seek protection in the Community.

(2) The European Council, at its special meeting in Tampere on 15 and 16 October 1999, agreed to work towards establishing a Common European Asylum System, based on the full and inclusive application of the Geneva Convention relating to the Status of Refugees of 28 July 1951, as supplemented by the New York Protocol of 31 January 1967, thus ensuring that nobody is sent back to persecution, i.e. maintaining the principle of non-refoulement. In this respect, and without affecting the responsibility criteria laid down in this Regulation, Member States, all respecting the principle of non-refoulement, are considered as safe countries for third-country nationals.

(3) The Tampere conclusions also stated that this system should include, in the short term, a clear and workable method for determining the Member State responsible for the examination of an asylum application.

(4) Such a method should be based on objective, fair criteria both for the Member States and for the persons concerned. It should, in particular, make it possible to determine rapidly the Member State responsible, so as to guarantee effective access to the procedures for determining refugee status and not to compromise the objective of the rapid processing of asylum applications.

(5) As regards the introduction in successive phases of a common European asylum system that should lead, in the longer term, to a common procedure and a uniform status, valid throughout the Union, for those granted asylum, it is appropriate at this stage, while making the necessary improvements in the light of experience, to confirm the principles underlying the Convention determining the State responsible for examining applications for asylum lodged in one of the Member States of the European Communities[18], signed in Dublin on 15 June 1990 (hereinafter referred to as the Dublin Convention), whose implementation has stimulated the process of harmonising asylum policies.

(6) Family unity should be preserved in so far as this is compatible with the other objectives pursued by establishing criteria and mechanisms for determining the Member State responsible for examining an asylum application.

(7) The processing together of the asylum applications of the members of one family by a single Member State makes it possible to ensure that the applications are examined thoroughly and the decisions taken in respect of them are consistent. Member States should be able to derogate from the responsibility criteria, so as to make it possible to bring family members together where this is necessary on humanitarian grounds.

(8) The progressive creation of an area without internal frontiers in which free movement of persons is guaranteed in accordance with the Treaty establishing the European Community and the establishment of Community policies regarding the conditions of entry and stay of third country nationals, including common efforts towards the management of external borders, makes it necessary to strike a balance between responsibility criteria in a spirit of solidarity.

(9) The application of this Regulation can be facilitated, and its effectiveness increased, by bilateral arrangements between Member States for improving communications between competent departments, reducing time limits for procedures or simplifying the processing

---

[18] OJ C 254, 19.8.1997, p. 1.

of requests to take charge or take back, or establishing procedures for the performance of transfers.

(10) Continuity between the system for determining the Member State responsible established by the Dublin Convention and the system established by this Regulation should be ensured. Similarly, consistency should be ensured between this Regulation and Council Regulation (EC) No 2725/2000 of 11 December 2000 concerning the establishment of 'Eurodac' for the comparison of fingerprints for the effective application of the Dublin Convention[19].

(11) The operation of the Eurodac system, as established by Regulation (EC) No 2725/2000 and in particular the implementation of Articles 4 and 8 contained therein should facilitate the implementation of this Regulation.

(12) With respect to the treatment of persons falling within the scope of this Regulation, Member States are bound by obligations under instruments of international law to which they are party.

(13) The measures necessary for the implementation of this Regulation should be adopted in accordance with Council Decision 1999/468/EC of 28 June 1999 laying down the procedures for the exercise of implementing powers conferred on the Commission[20].

(14) The application of the Regulation should be evaluated at regular intervals.

(15) The Regulation observes the fundamental rights and principles which are acknowledged in particular in the Charter of Fundamental Rights of the European Union[21]. In particular, it seeks to ensure full observance of the right to asylum guaranteed by Article 18.

(16) Since the objective of the proposed measure, namely the establishment of criteria and mechanisms for determining the Member State responsible for examining an asylum application lodged in one of the Member States by a third country national, cannot be sufficiently achieved by the Member States and, given the scale and effects, can therefore be better achieved at Community level, the Community may adopt measures in accordance with the principle of subsidiarity as set out in Article 5 of the Treaty. In accordance with the principle of proportionality, as set out in that Article, this Regulation does not go beyond what is necessary in order to achieve that objective.

(17) In accordance with Article 3 of the Protocol on the position of the United Kingdom and Ireland, annexed to the Treaty on European Union and to the Treaty establishing the European Community, the United Kingdom and Ireland gave notice, by letters of 30 October 2001, of their wish to take part in the adoption and application of this Regulation.

(18) In accordance with Articles 1 and 2 of the Protocol on the position of Denmark, annexed to the Treaty on European Union and to the Treaty establishing the European Community, Denmark does not take part in the adoption of this Regulation and is not bound by it nor subject to its application.

(19) The Dublin Convention remains in force and continues to apply between Denmark and the Member States that are bound by this Regulation until such time an agreement allowing Denmark's participation in the Regulation has been concluded,

HAS ADOPTED THIS REGULATION:

[19] OJ L 316, 15.12.2000, p. 1.
[20] OJ L 184, 17.7.1999, p. 23.
[21] OJ C 364, 18.12.2000, p. 1.

CHAPTER I
SUBJECT-MATTER AND DEFINITIONS

Article 1

This Regulation lays down the criteria and mechanisms for determining the Member State responsible for examining an application for asylum lodged in one of the member States by a third-country national.

Article 2

For the purposes of this Regulation:

(a) 'third-country national' means anyone who is not a citizen of the Union within the meaning of Article 17(1) of the Treaty establishing the European Community;

(b) 'Geneva Convention' means the Convention of 28 July 1951 relating to the status of refugees, as amended by the New York Protocol of 31 January 1967;

(c) 'application for asylum' means the application made by a third-country national which can be understood as a request for international protection from a Member State, under the Geneva Convention. Any application for international protection is presumed to be an application for asylum, unless a third-country national explicitly requests another kind of protection that can be applied for separately;

(d) 'applicant' or 'asylum seeker' means a third country national who has made an application for asylum in respect of which a final decision has not yet been taken;

(e) 'examination of an asylum application' means any examination of, or decision or ruling concerning, an application for asylum by the competent authorities in accordance with national law except for procedures for determining the Member State responsible in accordance with this Regulation;

(f) 'withdrawal of the asylum application' means the actions by which the applicant for asylum terminates the procedures initiated by the submission of his application for asylum, in accordance with national law, either explicitly or tacitly;

(g) 'refugee' means any third-country national qualifying for the status defined by the Geneva Convention and authorised to reside as such on the territory of a Member State;

(h) 'unaccompanied minor' means unmarried persons below the age of eighteen who arrive in the territory of the Member States unaccompanied by an adult responsible for them whether by law or by custom, and for as long as they are not effectively taken into the care of such a person; it includes minors who are left unaccompanied after they have entered the territory of the Member States;

(i) 'family members' means insofar as the family already existed in the country of origin, the following members of the applicant's family who are present in the territory of the Member States:

(i) the spouse of the asylum seeker or his or her unmarried partner in a stable relationship, where the legislation or practice of the Member State concerned treats unmarried couples in a way comparable to married couples under its law relating to aliens;

(ii) the minor children of couples referred to in point (i) or of the applicant, on condition that they are unmarried and dependent and regardless of whether they were born in or out of wedlock or adopted as defined under the national law;

(iii) the father, mother or guardian when the applicant or refugee is a minor and unmarried;

(j) 'residence document' means any authorisation issued by the authorities of a Member State authorising a third-country national to stay in its territory, including the documents substantiating the authorisation to remain in the territory under temporary protection arrangements or until the circumstances preventing a removal order from being carried out no longer apply, with the exception of visas and residence authorisations issued during the period required to determine the responsible Member State as established in this Regulation or during examination of an application for asylum or an application for a residence permit;

(k) 'visa' means the authorisation or decision of a Member State required for transit or entry for an intended stay in that Member State or in several Member States. The nature of the visa shall be determined in accordance with the following definitions:

(i) 'long-stay visa' means the authorisation or decision of a Member State required for entry for an intended stay in that Member State of more than three months;

(ii) 'short-stay visa' means the authorisation or decision of a Member State required for entry for an intended stay in that State or in several Member States for a period whose total duration does not exceed three months;

(iii) 'transit visa' means the authorisation or decision of a Member State for entry for transit through the territory of that Member State or several Member States, except for transit at an airport;

(iv) 'airport transit visa' means the authorisation or decision allowing a third-country national specifically subject to this requirement to pass through the transit zone of an airport, without gaining access to the national territory of the Member State concerned, during a stopover or a transfer between two sections of an international flight.

Chapter II
General Principles

Article 3

1. Member States shall examine the application of any third-country national who applies at the border or in their territory to any one of them for asylum. The application shall be examined by a single Member State, which shall be the one which the criteria set out in Chapter III indicate is responsible.

2. By way of derogation from paragraph 1, each Member State may examine an application for asylum lodged with it by a third-country national, even if such examination is not its responsibility under the criteria laid down in this Regulation. In such an event, that Member State shall become the Member State responsible within the meaning of this Regulation and shall assume the obligations associated with that responsibility. Where appropriate, it shall inform the Member State previously responsible, the Member State conducting a procedure for determining the Member State responsible or the Member State which has been requested to take charge of or take back the applicant.

3. Any Member State shall retain the right, pursuant to its national laws, to send an asylum seeker to a third country, in compliance with the provisions of the Geneva Convention.

4. The asylum seeker shall be informed in writing in a language that he or she may reasonably be expected to understand regarding the application of this Regulation, its time limits and its effects.

Article 4

1. The process of determining the Member State responsible under this Regulation shall start as soon as an application for asylum is first lodged with a Member State.

2. An application for asylum shall be deemed to have been lodged once a form submitted by the applicant for asylum or a report prepared by the authorities has reached the competent authorities of the Member State concerned. Where an application is not made in writing, the time elapsing between the statement of intention and the preparation of a report should be as short as possible.

3. For the purposes of this Regulation, the situation of a minor who is accompanying the asylum seeker and meets the definition of a family member set out in Article 2, point (i), shall be indissociable from that of his parent or guardian and shall be a matter for the Member State responsible for examining the application for asylum of that parent or guardian, even if the minor is not individually an asylum seeker. The same treatment shall be applied to children born after the asylum seeker arrives in the territory of the Member States, without the need to initiate a new procedure for taking charge of them.

4. Where an application for asylum is lodged with the competent authorities of a Member State by an applicant who is in the territory of another Member State, the determination of the Member State responsible shall be made by the Member State in whose territory the applicant is present. The latter Member State shall be informed without delay by the Member State which received the application and shall then, for the purposes of this Regulation, be regarded as the Member State with which the application for asylum was lodged. The applicant shall be informed in writing of this transfer and of the date on which it took place.

5. An asylum seeker who is present in another Member State and there lodges an application for asylum after withdrawing his application during the process of determining the Member State responsible shall be taken back, under the conditions laid down in Article 20, by the Member State with which that application for asylum was lodged, with a view to completing the process of determining the Member State responsible for examining the application for asylum. This obligation shall cease, if the asylum seeker has in the meantime left the territories of the Member States for a period of at least three months or has obtained a residence document from a Member State.

CHAPTER III
HIERARCHY OF CRITERIA

Article 5

1. The criteria for determining the Member State responsible shall be applied in the order in which they are set out in this Chapter.

2. The Member State responsible in accordance with the criteria shall be determined on the basis of the situation obtaining when the asylum seeker first lodged his application with a Member State.

Article 6

Where the applicant for asylum is an unaccompanied minor, the Member State responsible for examining the application shall be that where a member of his or her family is legally present, provided that this is in the best interest of the minor. In the absence of a family member, the Member State responsible for examining the application shall be that where the minor has lodged his or her application for asylum.

Article 7

Where the asylum seeker has a family member, regardless of whether the family was previously formed in the country of origin, who has been allowed to reside as a refugee in a Member State, that Member State shall be responsible for examining the application for asylum, provided that the persons concerned so desire.

Article 8

If the asylum seeker has a family member in a Member State whose application has not yet been the subject of a first decision regarding the substance, that Member State shall be responsible for examining the application for asylum, provided that the persons concerned so desire.

Article 9

1. Where the asylum seeker is in possession of a valid residence document, the Member State which issued the document shall be responsible for examining the application for asylum.

2. Where the asylum seeker is in possession of a valid visa, the Member State which issued the visa shall be responsible for examining the application for asylum, unless the visa was issued when acting for or on the written authorisation of another Member State. In such a case, the latter Member State shall be responsible for examining the application for asylum. Where a Member State first consults the central authority of another Member State, in particular for security reasons, the latter's reply to the consultation shall not constitute written authorisation within the meaning of this provision.

3. Where the asylum seeker is in possession of more than one valid residence document or visa issued by different Member States, the responsibility for examining the application for asylum shall be assumed by the Member States in the following order:

(a) the Member State which issued the residence document conferring the right to the longest period of residency or, where the periods of validity are identical, the Member State which issued the residence document having the latest expiry date;

(b) the Member State which issued the visa having the latest expiry date where the various visas are of the same type;

(c) where visas are of different kinds, the Member State which issued the visa having the longest period of validity, or, where the periods of validity are identical, the Member State which issued the visa having the latest expiry date.

4. Where the asylum seeker is in possession only of one or more residence documents which have expired less than two years previously or one or more visas which have expired less than six months previously and which enabled him actually to enter the territory of

a Member State, paragraphs 1, 2 and 3 shall apply for such time as the applicant has not left the territories of the Member States. Where the asylum seeker is in possession of one or more residence documents which have expired more than two years previously or one or more visas which have expired more than six months previously and enabled him actually to enter the territory of a Member State and where he has not left the territories of the Member States, the Member State in which the application is lodged shall be responsible.

5. The fact that the residence document or visa was issued on the basis of a false or assumed identity or on submission of forged, counterfeit or invalid documents shall not prevent responsibility being allocated to the Member State which issued it. However, the Member State issuing the residence document or visa shall not be responsible if it can establish that a fraud was committed after the document or visa had been issued.

Article 10

1. Where it is established, on the basis of proof or circumstantial evidence as described in the two lists mentioned in Article 18(3), including the data referred to in Chapter III of Regulation (EC)No 2725/2000, that an asylum seeker has irregularly crossed the border into a Member State by land, sea or air having come from a third country, the Member State thus entered shall be responsible for examining the application for asylum. This responsibility shall cease 12 months after the date on which the irregular border crossing took place.

2. When a Member State cannot or can no longer be held responsible in accordance with paragraph 1, and where it is established, on the basis of proof or circumstantial evidence as described in the two lists mentioned in Article 18(3), that the asylum seeker—who has entered the territories of the Member States irregularly or whose circumstances of entry cannot be established—at the time of lodging the application has been previously living for a continuous period of at least five months in a Member State, that Member State shall be responsible for examining the application for asylum. If the applicant has been living for periods of time of at least five months in several Member States, the Member State where this has been most recently the case shall be responsible for examining the application.

Article 11

1. If a third-country national enters into the territory of a Member State in which the need for him or her to have a visa is waived, that Member State shall be responsible for examining his or her application for asylum.

2. The principle set out in paragraph 1 does not apply, if the third-country national lodges his or her application for asylum in another Member State, in which the need for him or her to have a visa for entry into the territory is also waived. In this case, the latter Member State shall be responsible for examining the application for asylum.

Article 12

Where the application for asylum is made in an international transit area of an airport of a Member State by a third-country national, that Member State shall be responsible for examining the application.

Article 13

Where no Member State responsible for examining the application for asylum can be designated on the basis of the criteria listed in this Regulation, the first Member State with which the application for asylum was lodged shall be responsible for examining it.

Article 14

Where several members of a family submit applications for asylum in the same Member State simultaneously, or on dates close enough for the procedures for determining the Member State responsible to be conducted together, and where the application of the criteria set out in this Regulation would lead to them being separated, the Member State responsible shall be determined on the basis of the following provisions:

(a) responsibility for examining the applications for asylum of all the members of the family shall lie with the Member State which the criteria indicate is responsible for taking charge of the largest number of family members;

(b) failing this, responsibility shall lie with the Member State which the criteria indicate is responsible for examining the application of the oldest of them.

CHAPTER IV

HUMANITARIAN CLAUSE

Article 15

1. Any Member State, even where it is not responsible under the criteria set out in this Regulation, may bring together family members, as well as other dependent relatives, on humanitarian grounds based in particular on family or cultural considerations. In this case that Member State shall, at the request of another Member State, examine the application for asylum of the person concerned. The persons concerned must consent.

2. In cases in which the person concerned is dependent on the assistance of the other on account of pregnancy or a new-born child, serious illness, severe handicap or old age, Member States shall normally keep or bring together the asylum seeker with another relative present in the territory of one of the Member States, provided that family ties existed in the country of origin.

3. If the asylum seeker is an unaccompanied minor who has a relative or relatives in another Member State who can take care of him or her, Member States shall if possible unite the minor with his or her relative or relatives, unless this is not in the best interests of the minor.

4. Where the Member State thus approached accedes to the request, responsibility for examining the application shall be transferred to it.

5. The conditions and procedures for implementing this Article including, where appropriate, conciliation mechanisms for settling differences between Member States concerning the need to unite the persons in question, or the place where this should be done, shall be adopted in accordance with the procedure referred to in Article 27(2).

Chapter V

Taking Charge and Taking Back

Article 16

1. The Member State responsible for examining an application for asylum under this Regulation shall be obliged to:

(a) take charge, under the conditions laid down in Articles 17 to 19, of an asylum seeker who has lodged an application in a different Member State;

(b) complete the examination of the application for asylum;

(c) take back, under the conditions laid down in Article 20, an applicant whose application is under examination and who is in the territory of another Member State without permission;

(d) take back, under the conditions laid down in Article 20, an applicant who has withdrawn the application under examination and made an application in another Member State;

(e) take back, under the conditions laid down in Article 20, a third-country national whose application it has rejected and who is in the territory of another Member State without permission.

2. Where a Member State issues a residence document to the applicant, the obligations specified in paragraph 1 shall be transferred to that Member State.

3. The obligations specified in paragraph 1 shall cease where the third-country national has left the territory of the Member States for at least three months, unless the third-country national is in possession of a valid residence document issued by the Member State responsible.

4. The obligations specified in paragraph 1(d) and (e) shall likewise cease once the Member State responsible for examining the application has adopted and actually implemented, following the withdrawal or rejection of the application, the provisions that are necessary before the third-country national can go to his country of origin or to another country to which he may lawfully travel.

Article 17

1. Where a Member State with which an application for asylum has been lodged considers that another Member State is responsible for examining the application, it may, as quickly as possible and in any case within three months of the date on which the application was lodged within the meaning of Article 4(2), call upon the other Member State to take charge of the applicant. Where the request to take charge of an applicant is not made within the period of three months, responsibility for examining the application for asylum shall lie with the Member State in which the application was lodged.

2. The requesting Member State may ask for an urgent reply in cases where the application for asylum was lodged after leave to enter or remain was refused, after an arrest for an unlawful stay or after the service or execution of a removal order and/or where the asylum seeker is held in detention. The request shall state the reasons warranting an urgent reply and the period within which a reply is expected. This period shall be at least one week.

3. In both cases, the request that charge be taken by another Member State shall be made using a standard form and including proof or circumstantial evidence as described in the two lists mentioned in Article 18(3) and/or relevant elements from the asylum seeker's statement, enabling the authorities of the requested Member State to check whether it is responsible on the basis of the criteria laid down in this Regulation. The rules on the preparation of and the procedures for transmitting requests shall be adopted in accordance with the procedure referred to in Article 27(2).

Article 18

1. The requested Member State shall make the necessary checks, and shall give a decision on the request to take charge of an applicant within two months of the date on which the request was received.

2. In the procedure for determining the Member State responsible for examining the application for asylum established in this Regulation, elements of proof and circumstantial evidence shall be used.

3. In accordance with the procedure referred to in Article 27(2) two lists shall be established and periodically reviewed, indicating the elements of proof and circumstantial evidence in accordance with the following criteria:

(a) Proof:

(i) This refers to formal proof which determines responsibility pursuant to this Regulation, as long as it is not refuted by proof to the contrary.

(ii) The Member States shall provide the Committee provided for in Article 27 with models of the different types of administrative documents, in accordance with the typology established in the list of formal proofs.

(b) Circumstantial evidence:

(i) This refers to indicative elements which while being refutable may be sufficient, in certain cases, according to the evidentiary value attributed to them.

(ii) Their evidentiary value, in relation to the responsibility for examining the application for asylum shall be assessed on a case-by-case basis.

4. The requirement of proof should not exceed what is necessary for the proper application of this Regulation.

5. If there is no formal proof, the requested Member State shall acknowledge its responsibility if the circumstantial evidence is coherent, verifiable and sufficiently detailed to establish responsibility.

6. Where the requesting Member State has pleaded urgency, in accordance with the provisions of Article 17(2), the requested Member State shall make every effort to conform to the time limit requested. In exceptional cases, where it can be demonstrated that the examination of a request for taking charge of an applicant is particularly complex, the requested Member State may give the reply after the time limit requested, but in any case within one month. In such situations the requested Member State must communicate its decision to postpone a reply to the requesting Member State within the time limit originally requested.

7. Failure to act within the two-month period mentioned in paragraph 1 and the one-month period mentioned in paragraph 6 shall be tantamount to accepting the request, and entail the obligation to take charge of the person, including the provisions for proper arrangements for arrival.

Article 19

1. Where the requested Member State accepts that it should take charge of an applicant, the Member State in which the application for asylum was lodged shall notify the applicant of the decision not to examine the application, and of the obligation to transfer the applicant to the responsible Member State.

2. The decision referred to in paragraph 1 shall set out the grounds on which it is based. It shall contain details of the time limit for carrying out the transfer and shall, if necessary, contain information on the place and date at which the applicant should appear, if he is travelling to the Member State responsible by his own means. This decision may be subject to an appeal or a review. Appeal or review concerning this decision shall not suspend the implementation of the transfer unless the courts or competent bodies so decide on a case by case basis if national legislation allows for this.

3. The transfer of the applicant from the Member State in which the application for asylum was lodged to the Member State responsible shall be carried out in accordance with the national law of the first Member State, after consultation between the Member States concerned, as soon as practically possible, and at the latest within six months of acceptance of the request that charge be taken or of the decision on an appeal or review where there is a suspensive effect. If necessary, the asylum seeker shall be supplied by the requesting Member State with a laissez passer of the design adopted in accordance with the procedure referred to in Article 27(2). The Member State responsible shall inform the requesting Member State, as appropriate, of the safe arrival of the asylum seeker or of the fact that he did not appear within the set time limit.

4. Where the transfer does not take place within the six months' time limit, responsibility shall lie with the Member State in which the application for asylum was lodged. This time limit may be extended up to a maximum of one year if the transfer could not be carried out due to imprisonment of the asylum seeker or up to a maximum of eighteen months if the asylum seeker absconds.

5. Supplementary rules on carrying out transfers may be adopted in accordance with the procedure referred to in Article 27(2).

Article 20

1. An asylum seeker shall be taken back in accordance with Article 4(5) and Article 16(1)(c), (d) and (e) as follows:

(a) the request for the applicant to be taken back must contain information enabling the requested Member State to check that it is responsible;

(b) the Member State called upon to take back the applicant shall be obliged to make the necessary checks and reply to the request addressed to it as quickly as possible and under no circumstances exceeding a period of one month from the referral. When the request is based on data obtained from the Eurodac system, this time limit is reduced to two weeks;

(c) where the requested Member State does not communicate its decision within the one month period or the two weeks period mentioned in subparagraph (b), it shall be considered to have agreed to take back the asylum seeker;

(d) a Member State which agrees to take back an asylum seeker shall be obliged to readmit that person to its territory. The transfer shall be carried out in accordance with the national law of the requesting Member State, after consultation between the Member

States concerned, as soon as practically possible, and at the latest within six months of acceptance of the request that charge be taken by another Member State or of the decision on an appeal or review where there is a suspensive effect;

(e) the requesting Member State shall notify the asylum seeker of the decision concerning his being taken back by the Member State responsible. The decision shall set out the grounds on which it is based. It shall contain details of the time limit on carrying out the transfer and shall, if necessary, contain information on the place and date at which the applicant should appear, if he is travelling to the Member State responsible by his own means. This decision may be subject to an appeal or a review. Appeal or review concerning this decision shall not suspend the implementation of the transfer except when the courts or competent bodies so decide in a case-by-case basis if the national legislation allows for this. If necessary, the asylum seeker shall be supplied by the requesting Member State with a laissez-passer of the design adopted in accordance with the procedure referred to in Article 27(2). The Member State responsible shall inform the requesting Member State, as appropriate, of the safe arrival of the asylum seeker or of the fact that he did not appear within the set time limit.

2. Where the transfer does not take place within the six months' time limit, responsibility shall lie with the Member State in which the application for asylum was lodged. This time limit may be extended up to a maximum of one year if the transfer or the examination of the application could not be carried out due to imprisonment of the asylum seeker or up to a maximum of eighteen months if the asylum seeker absconds.

3. The rules of proof and evidence and their interpretation, and on the preparation of and the procedures for transmitting requests, shall be adopted in accordance with the procedure referred to in Article 27(2).

4. Supplementary rules on carrying out transfers may be adopted in accordance with the procedure referred to in Article 27(2).

Chapter VI

Administrative Cooperation

Article 21

1. Each Member State shall communicate to any Member State that so requests such personal data concerning the asylum seeker as is appropriate, relevant and non-excessive for:

(a) the determination of the Member State responsible for examining the application for asylum;

(b) examining the application for asylum;

(c) implementing any obligation arising under this Regulation.

2. The information referred to in paragraph 1 may only cover:

(a) personal details of the applicant, and, where appropriate, the members of his family (full name and where appropriate, former name; nicknames or pseudonyms; nationality, present and former; date and place of birth);

(b) identity and travel papers (references, validity, date of issue, issuing authority, place of issue, etc.);

(c) other information necessary for establishing the identity of the applicant, including fingerprints processed in accordance with Regulation (EC) No 2725/2000;

(d) places of residence and routes travelled;

(e) residence documents or visas issued by a Member State;

(f) the place where the application was lodged;

(g) the date any previous application for asylum was lodged, the date the present application was lodged, the stage reached in the proceedings and the decision taken, if any.

3. Furthermore, provided it is necessary for the examination of the application for asylum, the Member State responsible may request another Member State to let it know on what grounds the asylum seeker bases his application and, where applicable, the grounds for any decisions taken concerning the applicant. The Member State may refuse to respond to the request submitted to it, if the communication of such information is likely to harm the essential interests of the Member State or the protection of the liberties and fundamental rights of the person concerned or of others. In any event, communication of the information requested shall be subject to the written approval of the applicant for asylum.

4. Any request for information shall set out the grounds on which it is based and, where its purpose is to check whether there is a criterion that is likely to entail the responsibility of the requested Member State, shall state on what evidence, including relevant information from reliable sources on the ways and means asylum seekers enter the territories of the Member States, or on what specific and verifiable part of the applicant's statements it is based. It is understood that such relevant information from reliable sources is not in itself sufficient to determine the responsibility and the competence of a Member State under this Regulation, but it may contribute to the evaluation of other indications relating to the individual asylum seeker.

5. The requested Member State shall be obliged to reply within six weeks.

6. The exchange of information shall be effected at the request of a Member State and may only take place between authorities whose designation by each Member State has been communicated to the Commission, which shall inform the other Member States thereof.

7. The information exchanged may only be used for the purposes set out in paragraph 1. In each Member State such information may, depending on its type and the powers of the recipient authority, only be communicated to the authorities and courts and tribunals entrusted with:

(a) the determination of the Member State responsible for examining the application for asylum;

(b) examining the application for asylum;

(c) implementing any obligation arising under this Regulation.

8. The Member State which forwards the information shall ensure that it is accurate and up-to-date. If it transpires that that Member State has forwarded information which is inaccurate or which should not have been forwarded, the recipient Member States shall be informed thereof immediately. They shall be obliged to correct such information or to have it erased.

9. The asylum seeker shall have the right to be informed, on request, of any data that is processed concerning him. If he finds that this information has been processed in breach of this Regulation or of Directive 95/46/EC of the European Parliament and the Council of 24 October 1995 on the protection of individuals with regard to the processing of personal data and on the free movement of such data[22], in particular because it is incomplete

---

[22] OJ L281, 23.11.1995, p. 31.

or inaccurate, he is entitled to have it corrected, erased or blocked. The authority correcting, erasing or blocking the data shall inform, as appropriate, the Member State transmitting or receiving the information.

10. In each Member State concerned, a record shall be kept, in the individual file for the person concerned and/or in a register, of the transmission and receipt of information exchanged.

11. The data exchanged shall be kept for a period not exceeding that which is necessary for the purposes for which it is exchanged.

12. Where the data is not processed automatically or is not contained, or intended to be entered, in a file, each Member State should take appropriate measures to ensure compliance with this Article through effective checks.

Article 22

1. Member States shall notify the Commission of the authorities responsible for fulfilling the obligations arising under this Regulation and shall ensure that those authorities have the necessary resources for carrying out their tasks and in particular for replying within the prescribed time limits to requests for information, requests to take charge of and requests to take back asylum seekers.

2. Rules relating to the establishment of secure electronic transmission channels between the authorities mentioned in paragraph 1 for transmitting requests and ensuring that senders automatically receive an electronic proof of delivery shall be established in accordance with the procedure referred to in Article 27(2).

Article 23

1. Member States may, on a bilateral basis, establish administrative arrangements between themselves concerning the practical details of the implementation of this Regulation, in order to facilitate its application and increase its effectiveness. Such arrangements may relate to:

(a) exchanges of liaison officers;

(b) simplification of the procedures and shortening of the time limits relating to transmission and the examination of requests to take charge of or take back asylum seekers;

2. The arrangements referred to in paragraph 1 shall be communicated to the Commission. The Commission shall verify that the arrangements referred to in paragraph 1(b) do not infringe this Regulation.

CHAPTER VII
TRANSITIONAL PROVISIONS AND FINAL PROVISIONS

Article 24

1. This Regulation shall replace the Convention determining the State responsible for examining applications for asylum lodged in one of the Member States of the European Communities, signed in Dublin on 15 June 1990 (Dublin Convention).

2. However, to ensure continuity of the arrangements for determining the Member State responsible for an application for asylum, where an application has been lodged after the date mentioned in the second paragraph of Article 29, the events that are likely to entail the responsibility of a Member State under this Regulation shall be taken into consideration, even if they precede that date, with the exception of the events mentioned in Article 10(2).

3. Where, in Regulation (EC) No 2725/2000 reference is made to the Dublin Convention, such references shall be taken to be a reference made to this Regulation.

Article 25

1. Any period of time prescribed in this Regulation shall be calculated as follows:

(a) where a period expressed in days, weeks or months is to be calculated from the moment at which an event occurs or an action takes place, the day during which that event occurs or that action takes place shall not be counted as falling within the period in question;

(b) a period expressed in weeks or months shall end with the expiry of whichever day in the last week or month is the same day of the week or falls on the same date as the day during which the event or action from which the period is to be calculated occurred or took place. If, in a period expressed in months, the day on which it should expire does not occur in the last month, the period shall end with the expiry of the last day of that month;

(c) time limits shall include Saturdays, Sundays and official holidays in any of the Member States concerned.

2. Requests and replies shall be sent using any method that provides proof of receipt.

Article 26

As far as the French Republic is concerned, this Regulation shall apply only to its European territory.

Article 27

1. The Commission shall be assisted by a committee.

2. Where reference is made to this paragraph, Articles 5 and 7 of Decision 1999/468/EC shall apply. The period laid down in Article 5(6) of Decision 1999/468/EC shall be set at three months.

3. The Committee shall draw up its rules of procedure.

Article 28

At the latest three years after the date mentioned in the first paragraph of Article 29, the Commission shall report to the European Parliament and the Council on the application of this Regulation and, where appropriate, shall propose the necessary amendments. Member States shall forward to the Commission all information appropriate for the preparation of that report, at the latest six months before that time limit expires. Having submitted that report, the Commission shall report to the European Parliament and the Council on the application of this Regulation at the same time as it submits reports on the implementation of the Eurodac system provided for by Article 24(5) of Regulation (EC) No 2725/2000.

Article 29

This Regulation shall enter into force on the 20th day following that of its publication in the Official Journal of the European Union. It shall apply to asylum applications lodged as from the first day of the sixth month following its entry into force and, from that date, it will apply to any request to take charge of or take back asylum seekers, irrespective of the date on which the application was made. The Member State responsible for the examination of an asylum application submitted before that date shall be determined in accordance with the criteria set out in the Dublin Convention. This Regulation shall be binding in its entirety and directly applicable in the Member States in conformity with the Treaty establishing the European Community.

Done at Brussels, 18 February 2003.

For the Council
The President
N. CHRISTODOULAKIS

Commission Regulation (EC) No. 1560/2003
of 2 September 2003

laying down detailed rules for the application of Council Regulation (EC) No. 343/2003 establishing the criteria and mechanisms for determining the Member State responsible for examining an asylum application lodged in one of the Member States by a third-country national

Note: Entered into force on 6 September 2003 (Article 23).

THE COMMISSION OF THE EUROPEAN COMMUNITIES,

Having regard to the Treaty establishing the European Community,

Having regard to Council Regulation (EC) No 343/2003 of 18 February 2003 establishing the criteria and mechanisms for determining the Member State responsible for examining an asylum application lodged in one of the Member States by a third-country national[23], and in particular Article 15(5), Article 17(3), Article 18(3), Article 19(3) and (5), Article 20(1), (3) and (4) and Article 22(2) thereof,

---

[23] OJ L 50, 25.2.2003, p. 1.

Whereas:

(1) A number of specific arrangements must be established for the effective application of Regulation (EC) No 343/2003. Those arrangements must be clearly defined so as to facilitate cooperation between the authorities in the Member States competent for implementing that Regulation as regards the transmission and processing of requests for the purposes of taking charge and taking back, requests for information and the carrying out of transfers.

(2) To ensure the greatest possible continuity between the Convention determining the State responsible for examining applications for asylum lodged in one of the Member States of the European Communities[24], signed in Dublin on 15 June 1990, and Regulation (EC) No 343/2003, which replaces that Convention, this Regulation should be based on the common principles, lists and forms adopted by the committee set up by Article 18 of that Convention, with the inclusion of amendments necessitated by the introduction of new criteria, the wording of certain provisions and of the lessons drawn from experience.

(3) The interaction between the procedures laid down in Regulation (EC) No 343/2003 and the application of Council Regulation (EC) No 2725/2000 of 11 December 2000 concerning the establishment of 'Eurodac' for the comparison of fingerprints for the effective application of the Dublin Convention[25] must be taken into account.

(4) It is desirable, both for the Member States and the asylum seekers concerned, that there should be a mechanism for finding a solution in cases where Member States differ over the application of the humanitarian clause in Article 15 of Regulation (EC) No 343/2003.

(5) The establishment of an electronic transmission network to facilitate the implementation of Regulation (EC) No 343/2003 means that rules must be laid down relating to the technical standards applicable and the practical arrangements for using the network.

(6) Directive 95/46/EC of the European Parliament and of the Council of 24 October 1995 on the protection of individuals with regard to the processing of personal data and on the free movement of such data[26] applies to processing carried out pursuant to the present Regulation in accordance with Article 21 of Regulation (EC) No 343/2003.

(7) In accordance with Articles 1 and 2 of the Protocol on the position of Denmark annexed to the Treaty on European Union and to the Treaty establishing the European Community, Denmark, which is not bound by Regulation (EC) No 343/2003, is not bound by the present Regulation or subject to its application, until such time as an agreement allowing it to participate in Regulation (EC) No 343/2003 is reached.

(8) In accordance with Article 4 of the Agreement of 19 January 2001 between the European Community and the Republic of Iceland and the Kingdom of Norway concerning the criteria and mechanisms for establishing the State responsible for examining an application for asylum lodged in a Member State or in Iceland or Norway[27], this Regulation is to be applied by Iceland and Norway as it is applied by the Member States of the European Community.Consequently, for the purposes of this Regulation, Member States also include Iceland and Norway.

---

[24] OJ C 254, 19.8.1997, p. 1.
[25] OJ L 316, 15.12.2000, p. 1.
[26] OJ L 281, 23.11.1995, p. 31.
[27] OJ L 93, 3.4.2001, p. 40.

(9) It is necessary for the present Regulation to enter into force as quickly as possible to enable Regulation (EC) No 343/2003 to be applied.

(10) The measures set out in this Regulation are in accordance with the opinion of the Committee set up by Article 27 of Regulation (EC) No 343/2003,

HAS ADOPTED THIS REGULATION:

TITLE I

Procedures

CHAPTER I

PREPARATION OF REQUESTS

Article 1

Preparation of requests for taking charge

1. Requests for taking charge shall be made on a standard form in accordance with the model in Annex I. The form shall include mandatory fields which must be duly filled in and other fields to be filled in if the information is available. Additional information may be entered in the field set aside for the purpose.

The request shall also include:

(a) a copy of all the proof and circumstantial evidence showing that the requested Member State is responsible for examining the application for asylum, accompanied, where appropriate, by comments on the circumstances in which it was obtained and the probative value attached to it by the requesting Member State, with reference to the lists of proof and circumstantial evidence referred to in Article 18(3) of Regulation (EC) No 343/2003, which are set out in Annex II to the present Regulation;

(b) where necessary, a copy of any written declarations made by or statements taken from the applicant.

2. Where the request is based on a positive result (hit) transmitted by the Eurodac Central Unit in accordance with Article 4(5) of Regulation (EC) No 2725/2000 after comparison of the asylum seeker's fingerprints with fingerprint data previously taken and sent to the Central Unit in accordance with Article 8 of that Regulation and checked in accordance with Article 4(6) of that Regulation, it shall also include the data supplied by the Central Unit.

3. Where the requesting Member State asks for an urgent reply in accordance with Article 17(2) of Regulation (EC) No 343/2003, the request shall describe the circumstances of the application for asylum and shall state the reasons in law and in fact which warrant an urgent reply.

Article 2

Preparation of requests for taking back

Requests for taking back shall be made on a standard form in accordance with the model in Annex III, setting out the nature of the request, the reasons for it and the provisions of Regulation (EC) No 343/2003 on which it is based.

The request shall also include the positive result (hit) transmitted by the Eurodac Central Unit, in accordance with Article 4(5) of Regulation (EC) No 2725/2000, after comparison of the applicant's fingerprints with fingerprint data previously taken and sent to the Central Unit in accordance with Article 4(1) and (2) of that Regulation and checked in accordance with Article 4(6) of that Regulation.

For requests relating to applications dating from before Eurodac became operational, a copy of the fingerprints shall be attached to the form.

CHAPTER II
REACTION TO REQUESTS

Article 3

Processing requests for taking charge

1. The arguments in law and in fact set out in the request shall be examined in the light of the provisions of Regulation (EC) No 343/2003 and the lists of proof and circumstantial evidence which are set out in Annex II to the present Regulation.

2. Whatever the criteria and provisions of Regulation (EC) No 343/2003 that are relied on, the requested Member State shall, within the time allowed by Article 18(1) and (6) of that Regulation, check exhaustively and objectively, on the basis of all information directly or indirectly available to it, whether its responsibility for examining the application for asylum is established. If the checks by the requested Member State reveal that it is responsible under at least one of the criteria of that Regulation, it shall acknowledge its responsibility.

Article 4

Processing of requests for taking back

Where a request for taking back is based on data supplied by the Eurodac Central Unit and checked by the requesting Member State, in accordance with Article 4(6) of Regulation (EC) No 2725/2000, the requested Member State shall acknowledge its responsibility unless the checks carried out reveal that its obligations have ceased under the second subparagraph of Article 4(5) or under Article 16(2), (3) or (4) of Regulation (EC) No 343/2003. The fact that obligations have ceased on the basis of those provisions may be relied on only on the basis of material evidence or substantiated and verifiable statements by the asylum seeker.

Article 5

Negative reply

1. Where, after checks are carried out, the requested Member State considers that the evidence submitted does not establish its responsibility, the negative reply it sends to the requesting Member State shall state full and detailed reasons for its refusal.

2. Where the requesting Member State feels that such a refusal is based on a misappraisal, or where it has additional evidence to put forward, it may ask for its request to be

re-examined. This option must be exercised within three weeks following receipt of the negative reply. The requested Member State shall endeavour to reply within two weeks. In any event, this additional procedure shall not extend the time limits laid down in Article 18(1) and (6) and Article 20(1)(b) of Regulation (EC) No 343/2003.

Article 6

Positive reply

Where the Member State accepts responsibility, the reply shall say so, specifying the provision of Regulation (EC) No 343/2003 that is taken as a basis, and shall include practical details regarding the subsequent transfer, such as contact particulars of the department or person to be contacted.

CHAPTER III
TRANSFERS

Article 7
Practical arrangements for transfers

1. Transfers to the Member State responsible may be carried out in one of the following ways:

(a) at the request of the asylum seeker, by a certain specified date;

(b) by supervised departure, with the asylum seeker being accompanied to the point of embarkation by an official of the requesting Member State, the responsible Member State being notified of the place, date and time of the asylum seeker's arrival within an agreed time limit;

(c) under escort, the asylum seeker being accompanied by an official of the requesting Member State or by a representative of an agency empowered by the requesting Member State to act in that capacity and handed over to the authorities in the responsible Member State.

2. In the cases referred to in paragraph 1(a) and (b), the applicant shall be supplied with the laissez-passer referred to in Article 19(3) and Article 20(1)(e) of Regulation (EC) No 343/2003, a model of which is set out in Annex IV to the present Regulation, to allow him to enter the Member State responsible and to identify himself on his arrival at the place and time indicated to him at the time of notification of the decision on taking charge or taking back by the Member State responsible.

In the case referred to in paragraph 1(c), a laissez-passer shall be issued if the asylum seeker is not in possession of identity documents. The time and place of transfer shall be agreed in advance by the Member States concerned in accordance with the procedure set out in Article 8.

3. The Member State making the transfer shall ensure that all the asylum seeker's documents are returned to him before his departure, given into the safe keeping of members of the escort to be handed to the competent authorities of the Member State responsible, or sent by other appropriate means.

Article 8

Cooperation on transfers

1. It is the obligation of the Member State responsible to allow the asylum seeker's transfer to take place as quickly as possible and to ensure that no obstacles are put in his way. That Member State shall determine, where appropriate, the location on its territory to which the asylum seeker will be transferred or handed over to the competent authorities, taking account of geographical constraints and modes of transport available to the Member State making the transfer. In no case may a requirement be imposed that the escort accompany the asylum seeker beyond the point of arrival of the international means of transport used or that the Member State making the transfer meet the costs of transport beyond that point.

2. The Member State organising the transfer shall arrange the transport for the asylum seeker and his escort and decide, in consultation with the Member State responsible, on the time of arrival and, where necessary, on the details of the handover to the competent authorities. The Member State responsible may require that three working days' notice be given.

Article 9

Postponed and delayed transfers

1. The Member State responsible shall be informed without delay of any postponement due either to an appeal or review procedure with suspensive effect, or physical reasons such as ill health of the asylum seeker, non-availability of transport or the fact that the asylum seeker has withdrawn from the transfer procedure.

2. A Member State which, for one of the reasons set out in Article 19(4) and Article 20(2) of Regulation (EC) No 343/2003, cannot carry out the transfer within the normal time limit of six months provided for in Article 19(3) and Article 20(1)(d) of that Regulation, shall inform the Member State responsible before the end of that time limit. Otherwise, the responsibility for processing the application for asylum and the other obligations under Regulation (EC) No 343/2003 falls to the former Member State, in accordance with Article 19(4) and Article 20(2) of that Regulation.

3. When, for one of the reasons set out in Article 19(4) and Article 20(2) of Regulation (EC) No 343/2003, a Member State undertakes to carry out the transfer after the normal time limit of six months, it shall make the necessary arrangements in advance with the Member State responsible.

Article 10

Transfer following an acceptance by default

1. Where, pursuant to Article 18(7) or Article 20(1)(c) of Regulation (EC) No 343/2003 as appropriate, the requested Member State is deemed to have accepted a request to take charge or to take back, the requesting Member State shall initiate the consultations needed to organise the transfer.

2. If asked to do so by the requesting Member State, the Member State responsible must confirm in writing, without delay, that it acknowledges its responsibility as a result of its failure to reply within the time limit. The Member State responsible shall take the necessary steps to determine the asylum seeker's place of arrival as quickly as possible and, where applicable, agree with the requesting Member State the time of arrival and the practical details of the handover to the competent authorities.

CHAPTER IV
HUMANITARIAN CLAUSE

Article 11

Situations of dependency

1. Article 15(2) of Regulation (EC) No 343/2003 shall apply whether the asylum seeker is dependent on the assistance of a relative present in another Member State or a relative present in another Member State is dependent on the assistance of the asylum seeker.

2. The situations of dependency referred to in Article 15(2) of Regulation (EC) No 343/2003 shall be assessed, as far as possible, on the basis of objective criteria such as medical certificates. Where such evidence is not available or cannot be supplied, humanitarian grounds shall be taken as proven only on the basis of convincing information supplied by the persons concerned.

3. The following points shall be taken into account in assessing the necessity and appropriateness of bringing together the persons concerned:
    (a) the family situation which existed in the country of origin;
    (b) the circumstances in which the persons concerned were separated;
    (c) the status of the various asylum procedures or procedures under the legislation on aliens under way in the Member States.

4. The application of Article 15(2) of Regulation (EC) No 343/2003 shall, in any event, be subject to the assurance that the asylum seeker or relative will actually provide the assistance needed.

5. The Member State in which the relatives will be reunited and the date of the transfer shall be agreed by the Member States concerned, taking account of:
    (a) the ability of the dependent person to travel;
    (b) the situation of the persons concerned as regards residence, preference being given to bringing the asylum seeker together with his relative where the latter already has a valid residence permit and resources in the Member State in which he resides.

Article 12

Unaccompanied minors

1. Where the decision to entrust the care of an unaccompanied minor to a relative other than the mother, father or legal guardian is likely to cause particular difficulties, particularly where the adult concerned resides outside the jurisdiction of the Member State in which the minor has applied for asylum, cooperation between the competent authorities in the Member States, in particular the authorities or courts responsible for the protection

of minors, shall be facilitated and the necessary steps taken to ensure that those authorities can decide, with full knowledge of the facts, on the ability of the adult or adults concerned to take charge of the minor in a way which serves his best interests. Options now available in the field of cooperation on judicial and civil matters shall be taken account of in this connection.

2. The fact that the duration of procedures for placing a minor may lead to a failure to observe the time limits set in Article 18(1) and (6) and Article 19(4) of Regulation (EC) No 343/2003 shall not necessarily be an obstacle to continuing the procedure for determining the Member State responsible or carrying out a transfer.

Article 13

Procedures

1. The initiative of requesting another Member State to take charge of an asylum seeker on the basis of Article 15 of Regulation (EC) No 343/2003 shall be taken either by the Member State where the application for asylum was made and which is carrying out a procedure to determine the Member State responsible, or by the Member State responsible.

2. The request to take charge shall contain all the material in the possession of the requesting Member State to allow the requested Member State to assess the situation.

3. The requested Member State shall carry out the necessary checks to establish, where applicable, humanitarian reasons, particularly of a family or cultural nature, the level of dependency of the person concerned or the ability and commitment of the other person concerned to provide the assistance desired.

4. In all events, the persons concerned must have given their consent.

Article 14

Conciliation

1. Where the Member States cannot resolve a dispute, either on the need to carry out a transfer or to bring relatives together on the basis of Article 15 of Regulation (EC) No 343/2003, or on the Member State in which the persons concerned should be reunited, they may have recourse to the conciliation procedure provided for in paragraph 2 of this Article.

2. The conciliation procedure shall be initiated by a request from one of the Member States in dispute to the Chairman of the Committee set up by Article 27 of Regulation (EC) No 343/2003. By agreeing to use the conciliation procedure, the Member States concerned undertake to take the utmost account of the solution proposed.

The Chairman of the Committee shall appoint three members of the Committee representing three Member States not connected with the matter. They shall receive the arguments of the parties either in writing or orally and, after deliberation, shall propose a solution within one month, where necessary after a vote.

The Chairman of the Committee, or his deputy, shall chair the discussion. He may put forward his point of view but he may not vote.

Whether it is adopted or rejected by the parties, the solution proposed shall be final and irrevocable.

CHAPTER V

COMMON PROVISIONS

Article 15

Transmission of requests

1. Requests, replies and all written correspondence between Member States concerning the application of Regulation (EC) No 343/2003 shall where possible be sent through the 'DubliNet' electronic communications network, set up under Title II of the present Regulation.

By way of derogation from the first subparagraph, correspondence between the departments responsible for carrying out transfers and competent departments in the requested Member State regarding the practical arrangements for transfers, time and place of arrival, particularly where the asylum seeker is under escort, may be transmitted by other means.

2. Any request, reply or correspondence emanating from a National Access Point, as referred to in Article 19, shall be deemed to be authentic.

3. The acknowledgement issued by the system shall be taken as proof of transmission and of the date and time of receipt of the request or reply.

Article 16

Language of communication

The language or languages of communication shall be chosen by agreement between the Member States concerned.

Article 17

Consent of the persons concerned

1. For the application of Articles 7 and 8, Article 15(1) and Article 21(3) of Regulation (EC) No 343/2003, which require the persons concerned to express a desire or give consent, their approval must be given in writing.

2. In the case of Article 21(3) of Regulation (EC) No 343/2003, the applicant must know for what information he is giving his approval.

TITLE II

Establishment of the 'Dublinet' Network

CHAPTER I

TECHNICAL STANDARDS

Article 18

Establishment of 'DubliNet'

1. The secure electronic means of transmission referred to in Article 22(2) of Regulation (EC) No 343/2003 shall be known as 'DubliNet'.

2. DubliNet is based on the use of the generic IDA services referred to in Article 4 of Decision No 1720/1999/EC[28].

Article 19

National Access Points

1. Each Member State shall have a single designated National Access Point.

2. The National Access Points shall be responsible for processing incoming data and transmitting outgoing data.

3. The National Access Points shall be responsible for issuing an acknowledgement of receipt for every incoming transmission.

4. The forms of which the models are set out in Annexes I and III and the form for the request of information set out in Annex V shall be sent between National Access Points in the format supplied by the Commission. The Commission shall inform the Member States of the technical standards required.

CHAPTER II
RULES FOR USE

Article 20

Reference number

1. Each transmission shall have a reference number making it possible unambiguously to identify the case to which it relates and the Member State making the request. That number must also make it possible to determine whether the transmission relates to a request for taking charge (type 1), a request for taking back (type 2) or a request for information (type 3).

2. The reference number shall begin with the letters used to identify the Member State in Eurodac. This code shall be followed by the number indicating the type of request, according to the classification set out in paragraph 1.

If the request is based on data supplied by Eurodac, the Eurodac reference number shall be included.

Article 21

Continuous operation

1. The Member States shall take the necessary steps to ensure that their National Access Points operate without interruption.

2. If the operation of a National Access Point is interrupted for more than seven working hours the Member State shall notify the competent authorities designated pursuant to

---

[28] OJ L 203, 3.8.1999, p. 9.

Article 22(1) of Regulation (EC) No 343/2003 and the Commission and shall take all the necessary steps to ensure that normal operation is resumed as soon as possible.

3. If a National Access Point has sent data to a National Access Point that has experienced an interruption in its operation, the acknowledgement of transmission generated by the IDA generic services shall be used as proof of the date and time of transmission. The deadlines set by Regulation (EC) No 343/2003 for sending a request or a reply shall not be suspended for the duration of the interruption of the operation of the National Access Point in question.

TITLE III

Transitional and Final Provisions

Article 22

Laissez-passer produced for the purposes of the dublin convention

Laissez-passer printed for the purposes of the Dublin Convention shall be accepted for the transfer of applicants for asylum under Regulation (EC) No 343/2003 for a period of no more than 18 months following the entry into force of the present Regulation.

Article 23

Entry into Force

This Regulation shall enter into force on the day following that of its publication in the *Official Journal of the European Union.*
This Regulation shall be binding in its entirety and directly applicable in all Member States.

Done at Brussels, 2 September 2003.

For the Commission
António VITORINO
Member of the Commission

Council Directive 2004/83/EC
of 29 April 2004

on minimum standards for the qualification and status of third-country nationals or stateless persons as refugees or as persons who otherwise need international protection and the content of the protection granted

Note: Entered into force on 20 October 2004 (Article 39). Implemented 10 October 2006 (Article 38).

THE COUNCIL OF THE EUROPEAN UNION,

Having regard to the Treaty establishing the European Community, and in particular points 1(c), 2(a) and 3(a) of Article 63 thereof,

Having regard to the proposal from the Commission[29],

Having regard to the opinion of the European Parliament[30],

Having regard to the opinion of the European Economic and Social Committee[31],

Having regard to the opinion of the Committee of the Regions[32],

Whereas:

(1) A common policy on asylum, including a Common European Asylum System, is a constituent part of the European Union's objective of progressively establishing an area of freedom, security and justice open to those who, forced by circumstances, legitimately seek protection in the Community.

(2) The European Council at its special meeting in Tampere on 15 and 16 October 1999 agreed to work towards establishing a Common European Asylum System, based on the full and inclusive application of the Geneva Convention relating to the Status of Refugees of 28 July 1951 (Geneva Convention), as supplemented by the New York Protocol of 31 January 1967 (Protocol), thus affirming the principle of non-refoulement and ensuring that nobody is sent back to persecution.

(3) The Geneva Convention and Protocol provide the cornerstone of the international legal regime for the protection of refugees.

(4) The Tampere conclusions provide that a Common European Asylum System should include, in the short term, the approximation of rules on the recognition of refugees and the content of refugee status.

(5) The Tampere conclusions also provide that rules regarding refugee status should be complemented by measures on subsidiary forms of protection, offering an appropriate status to any person in need of such protection.

(6) The main objective of this Directive is, on the one hand, to ensure that Member States apply common criteria for the identification of persons genuinely in need of international protection, and, on the other hand, to ensure that a minimum level of benefits is available for these persons in all Member States.

(7) The approximation of rules on the recognition and content of refugee and subsidiary protection status should help to limit the secondary movements of applicants for asylum between Member States, where such movement is purely caused by differences in legal frameworks.

(8) It is in the very nature of minimum standards that Member States should have the power to introduce or maintain more favourable provisions for third-country nationals or stateless persons who request international protection from a Member State, where such a request is understood to be on the grounds that the person concerned is either a refugee within the meaning of Article 1(A) of the Geneva Convention, or a person who otherwise needs international protection.

[29] OJ C 51 E, 26.2.2002, p. 325.
[30] OJ C 300 E, 11.12.2003, p. 25.
[31] OJ C 221, 17.9.2002, p. 43.
[32] OJ C 278, 14.11.2002, p. 44.

(9) Those third country nationals or stateless persons, who are allowed to remain in the territories of the Member States for reasons not due to a need for international protection but on a discretionary basis on compassionate or humanitarian grounds, fall outside the scope of this Directive.

(10) This Directive respects the fundamental rights and observes the principles recognised in particular by the Charter of Fundamental Rights of the European Union. In particular this Directive seeks to ensure full respect for human dignity and the right to asylum of applicants for asylum and their accompanying family members.

(11) With respect to the treatment of persons falling within the scope of this Directive, Member States are bound by obligations under instruments of international law to which they are party and which prohibit discrimination.

(12) The 'best interests of the child' should be a primary consideration of Member States when implementing this Directive.

(13) This Directive is without prejudice to the Protocol on asylum for nationals of Member States of the European Union as annexed to the Treaty Establishing the European Community.

(14) The recognition of refugee status is a declaratory act.

(15) Consultations with the United Nations High Commissioner for Refugees may provide valuable guidance for Member States when determining refugee status according to Article 1 of the Geneva Convention.

(16) Minimum standards for the definition and content of refugee status should be laid down to guide the competent national bodies of Member States in the application of the Geneva Convention.

(17) It is necessary to introduce common criteria for recognising applicants for asylum as refugees within the meaning of Article 1 of the Geneva Convention.

(18) In particular, it is necessary to introduce common concepts of protection needs arising *sur place*; sources of harm and protection; internal protection; and persecution, including the reasons for persecution.

(19) Protection can be provided not only by the State but also by parties or organisations, including international organisations, meeting the conditions of this Directive, which control a region or a larger area within the territory of the State.

(20) It is necessary, when assessing applications from minors for international protection, that Member States should have regard to child-specific forms of persecution.

(21) It is equally necessary to introduce a common concept of the persecution ground 'membership of a particular social group'.

(22) Acts contrary to the purposes and principles of the United Nations are set out in the Preamble and Articles 1 and 2 of the Charter of the United Nations and are, amongst others, embodied in the United Nations Resolutions relating to measures combating terrorism, which declare that 'acts, methods and practices of terrorism are contrary to the purposes and principles of the United Nations' and that 'knowingly financing, planning and inciting terrorist acts are also contrary to the purposes and principles of the United Nations'.

(23) As referred to in Article 14, 'status' can also include refugee status.

(24) Minimum standards for the definition and content of subsidiary protection status should also be laid down. Subsidiary protection should be complementary and additional to the refugee protection enshrined in the Geneva Convention.

(25) It is necessary to introduce criteria on the basis of which applicants for international protection are to be recognised as eligible for subsidiary protection. Those criteria should be drawn from international obligations under human rights instruments and practices existing in Member States.

(26) Risks to which a population of a country or a section of the population is generally exposed do normally not create in themselves an individual threat which would qualify as serious harm.

(27) Family members, merely due to their relation to the refugee, will normally be vulnerable to acts of persecution in such a manner that could be the basis for refugee status.

(28) The notion of national security and public order also covers cases in which a third country national belongs to an association which supports international terrorism or supports such an association.

(29) While the benefits provided to family members of beneficiaries of subsidiary protection status do not necessarily have to be the same as those provided to the qualifying beneficiary, they need to be fair in comparison to those enjoyed by beneficiaries of subsidiary protection status.

(30) Within the limits set out by international obligations, Member States may lay down that the granting of benefits with regard to access to employment, social welfare, health care and access to integration facilities requires the prior issue of a residence permit.

(31) This Directive does not apply to financial benefits from the Member States which are granted to promote education and training.

(32) The practical difficulties encountered by beneficiaries of refugee or subsidiary protection status concerning the authentication of their foreign diplomas, certificates or other evidence of formal qualification should be taken into account.

(33) Especially to avoid social hardship, it is appropriate, for beneficiaries of refugee or subsidiary protection status, to provide without discrimination in the context of social assistance the adequate social welfare and means of subsistence.

(34) With regard to social assistance and health care, the modalities and detail of the provision of core benefits to beneficiaries of subsidiary protection status should be determined by national law. The possibility of limiting the benefits for beneficiaries of subsidiary protection status to core benefits is to be understood in the sense that this notion covers at least minimum income support, assistance in case of illness, pregnancy and parental assistance, in so far as they are granted to nationals according to the legislation of the Member State concerned.

(35) Access to health care, including both physical and mental health care, should be ensured to beneficiaries of refugee or subsidiary protection status.

(36) The implementation of this Directive should be evaluated at regular intervals, taking into consideration in particular the evolution of the international obligations of Member States regarding non-refoulement, the evolution of the labour markets in the Member States as well as the development of common basic principles for integration.

(37) Since the objectives of the proposed Directive, namely to establish minimum standards for the granting of international protection to third country nationals and stateless persons by Member States and the content of the protection granted, cannot be sufficiently achieved by the Member States and can therefore, by reason of the scale and

effects of the Directive, be better achieved at Community level, the Community may adopt measures, in accordance with the principle of subsidiarity as set out in Article 5 of the Treaty. In accordance with the principle of proportionality, as set out in that Article, this Directive does not go beyond what is necessary in order to achieve those objectives.

(38) In accordance with Article 3 of the Protocol on the position of the United Kingdom and Ireland, annexed to the Treaty on European Union and to the Treaty establishing the European Community, the United Kingdom has notified, by letter of 28 January 2002, its wish to take part in the adoption and application of this Directive.

(39) In accordance with Article 3 of the Protocol on the position of the United Kingdom and Ireland, annexed to the Treaty on European Union and to the Treaty establishing the European Community, Ireland has notified, by letter of 13 February 2002, its wish to take part in the adoption and application of this Directive.

(40) In accordance with Articles 1 and 2 of the Protocol on the position of Denmark, annexed to the Treaty on European Union and to the Treaty establishing the European Community, Denmark is not taking part in the adoption of this Directive and is not bound by it or subject to its application,

HAS ADOPTED THIS DIRECTIVE,

CHAPTER I
GENERAL PROVISIONS

Article 1

Subject matter and scope

The purpose of this Directive is to lay down minimum standards for the qualification of third country nationals or stateless persons as refugees or as persons who otherwise need international protection and the content of the protection granted.

Article 2

Definitions

For the purposes of this Directive:

(a) 'international protection' means the refugee and subsidiary protection status as defined in (d) and (f);

(b) 'Geneva Convention' means the Convention relating to the status of refugees done at Geneva on 28 July 1951, as amended by the New York Protocol of 31 January 1967;

(c) 'refugee' means a third country national who, owing to a well-founded fear of being persecuted for reasons of race, religion, nationality, political opinion or membership of a particular social group, is outside the country of nationality and is unable or, owing to such fear, is unwilling to avail himself or herself of the protection of that country, or a stateless person, who, being outside of the country of former habitual residence for the same reasons as mentioned above, is unable or, owing to such fear, unwilling to return to it, and to whom Article 12 does not apply;

(d) 'refugee status' means the recognition by a Member State of a third country national or a stateless person as a refugee;

(e) 'person eligible for subsidiary protection' means a third country national or a stateless person who does not qualify as a refugee but in respect of whom substantial grounds have been shown for believing that the person concerned, if returned to his or her country of origin, or in the case of a stateless person, to his or her country of former habitual residence, would face a real risk of suffering serious harm as defined in Article 15, and to whom Article 17(1) and (2) do not apply, and is unable, or, owing to such risk, unwilling to avail himself or herself of the protection of that country;

(f) 'subsidiary protection status' means the recognition by a Member State of a third country national or a stateless person as a person eligible for subsidiary protection;

(g) 'application for international protection' means a request made by a third country national or a stateless person for protection from a Member State, who can be understood to seek refugee status or subsidiary protection status, and who does not explicitly request another kind of protection, outside the scope of this Directive, that can be applied for separately;

(h) 'family members' means, insofar as the family already existed in the country of origin, the following members of the family of the beneficiary of refugee or subsidiary protection status who are present in the same Member State in relation to the application for international protection:

— the spouse of the beneficiary of refugee or subsidiary protection status or his or her unmarried partner in a stable relationship, where the legislation or practice of the Member State concerned treats unmarried couples in a way comparable to married couples under its law relating to aliens,

— the minor children of the couple referred to in the first indent or of the beneficiary of refugee or subsidiary protection status, on condition that they are unmarried and dependent and regardless of whether they were born in or out of wedlock or adopted as defined under the national law;

(i) 'unaccompanied minors' means third-country nationals or stateless persons below the age of 18, who arrive on the territory of the Member States unaccompanied by an adult responsible for them whether by law or custom, and for as long as they are not effectively taken into the care of such a person; it includes minors who are left unaccompanied after they have entered the territory of the Member States;

(j) 'residence permit' means any permit or authorisation issued by the authorities of a Member State, in the form provided for under that State's legislation, allowing a third country national or stateless person to reside on its territory;

(k) 'country of origin' means the country or countries of nationality or, for stateless persons, of former habitual residence.

Article 3

More favourable standards

Member States may introduce or retain more favourable standards for determining who qualifies as a refugee or as a person eligible for subsidiary protection, and for determining the content of international protection, insofar as those standards are compatible with this Directive.

Chapter II

Assessment of Applications for International Protection

Article 4

Assessment of facts and circumstances

1. Member States may consider it the duty of the applicant to submit as soon as possible all elements needed to substantiate the application for international protection. In cooperation with the applicant it is the duty of the Member State to assess the relevant elements of the application.

2. The elements referred to in paragraph 1 consist of the applicant's statements and all documentation at the applicant's disposal regarding the applicant's age, background, including that of relevant relatives, identity, nationality(ies), country(ies) and place(s) of previous residence, previous asylum applications, travel routes, identity and travel documents and the reasons for applying for international protection.

3. The assessment of an application for international protection is to be carried out on an individual basis and includes taking into account:

(a) all relevant facts as they relate to the country of origin at the time of taking a decision on the application; including laws and regulations of the country of origin and the manner in which they are applied;

(b) the relevant statements and documentation presented by the applicant including information on whether the applicant has been or may be subject to persecution or serious harm;

(c) the individual position and personal circumstances of the applicant, including factors such as background, gender and age, so as to assess whether, on the basis of the applicant's personal circumstances, the acts to which the applicant has been or could be exposed would amount to persecution or serious harm;

(d) whether the applicant's activities since leaving the country of origin were engaged in for the sole or main purpose of creating the necessary conditions for applying for international protection, so as to assess whether these activities will expose the applicant to persecution or serious harm if returned to that country;

(e) whether the applicant could reasonably be expected to avail himself of the protection of another country where he could assert citizenship.

4. The fact that an applicant has already been subject to persecution or serious harm or to direct threats of such persecution or such harm, is a serious indication of the applicant's well-founded fear of persecution or real risk of suffering serious harm, unless there are good reasons to consider that such persecution or serious harm will not be repeated.

5. Where Member States apply the principle according to which it is the duty of the applicant to substantiate the application for international protection and where aspects of the applicant's statements are not supported by documentary or other evidence, those aspects shall not need confirmation, when the following conditions are met:

(a) the applicant has made a genuine effort to substantiate his application;

(b) all relevant elements, at the applicant's disposal, have been submitted, and a satisfactory explanation regarding any lack of other relevant elements has been given;

(c) the applicant's statements are found to be coherent and plausible and do not run counter to available specific and general information relevant to the applicant's case;

(d) the applicant has applied for international protection at the earliest possible time, unless the applicant can demonstrate good reason for not having done so; and

(e) the general credibility of the applicant has been established.

Article 5

International protection needs arising *Sur place*

1. A well-founded fear of being persecuted or a real risk of suffering serious harm may be based on events which have taken place since the applicant left the country of origin.

2. A well-founded fear of being persecuted or a real risk of suffering serious harm may be based on activities which have been engaged in by the applicant since he left the country of origin, in particular where it is established that the activities relied upon constitute the expression and continuation of convictions or orientations held in the country of origin.

3. Without prejudice to the Geneva Convention, Member States may determine that an applicant who files a subsequent application shall normally not be granted refugee status, if the risk of persecution is based on circumstances which the applicant has created by his own decision since leaving the country of origin.

Article 6

Actors of persecution or serious harm

Actors of persecution or serious harm include:

(a) the State;

(b) parties or organisations controlling the State or a substantial part of the territory of the State;

(c) non-State actors, if it can be demonstrated that the actors mentioned in (a) and (b), including international organisations, are unable or unwilling to provide protection against persecution or serious harm as defined in Article 7.

Article 7

Actors of protection

1. Protection can be provided by:

(a) the State; or

(b) parties or organisations, including international organisations, controlling the State or a substantial part of the territory of the State.

2. Protection is generally provided when the actors mentioned in paragraph 1 take reasonable steps to prevent the persecution or suffering of serious harm, *inter alia*, by operating an effective legal system for the detection, prosecution and punishment of acts constituting persecution or serious harm, and the applicant has access to such protection.

3. When assessing whether an international organisation controls a State or a substantial part of its territory and provides protection as described in paragraph 2, Member States shall take into account any guidance which may be provided in relevant Council acts.

Article 8

Internal protection

1. As part of the assessment of the application for international protection, Member States may determine that an applicant is not in need of international protection if in a part of the country of origin there is no well-founded fear of being persecuted or no real risk of suffering serious harm and the applicant can reasonably be expected to stay in that part of the country.

2. In examining whether a part of the country of origin is in accordance with paragraph 1, Member States shall at the time of taking the decision on the application have regard to the general circumstances prevailing in that part of the country and to the personal circumstances of the applicant.

3. Paragraph 1 may apply notwithstanding technical obstacles to return to the country of origin.

CHAPTER III

QUALIFICATION FOR BEING A REFUGEE

Article 9

Acts of persecution

1. Acts of persecution within the meaning of article 1 A of the Geneva Convention must:

(a) be sufficiently serious by their nature or repetition as to constitute a severe violation of basic human rights, in particular the rights from which derogation cannot be made under Article 15(2) of the European Convention for the Protection of Human Rights and Fundamental Freedoms; or

(b) be an accumulation of various measures, including violations of human rights which is sufficiently severe as to affect an individual in a similar manner as mentioned in (a).

2. Acts of persecution as qualified in paragraph 1, can, *inter alia*, take the form of:

(a) acts of physical or mental violence, including acts of sexual violence;

(b) legal, administrative, police, and/or judicial measures which are in themselves discriminatory or which are implemented in a discriminatory manner;

(c) prosecution or punishment, which is disproportionate or discriminatory;

(d) denial of judicial redress resulting in a disproportionate or discriminatory punishment;

(e) prosecution or punishment for refusal to perform military service in a conflict, where performing military service would include crimes or acts falling under the exclusion clauses as set out in Article 12(2);

(f) acts of a gender-specific or child-specific nature.

3. In accordance with Article 2(c), there must be a connection between the reasons mentioned in Article 10 and the acts of persecution as qualified in paragraph 1.

Article 10

Reasons for persecution

1. Member States shall take the following elements into account when assessing the reasons for persecution:

(a) the concept of race shall in particular include considerations of colour, descent, or membership of a particular ethnic group;

(b) the concept of religion shall in particular include the holding of theistic, non-theistic and atheistic beliefs, the participation in, or abstention from, formal worship in private or in public, either alone or in community with others, other religious acts or expressions of view, or forms of personal or communal conduct based on or mandated by any religious belief;

(c) the concept of nationality shall not be confined to citizenship or lack thereof but shall in particular include membership of a group determined by its cultural, ethnic, or linguistic identity, common geographical or political origins or its relationship with the population of another State;

(d) a group shall be considered to form a particular social group where in particular:

— members of that group share an innate characteristic, or a common background that cannot be changed, or share a characteristic or belief that is so fundamental to identity or conscience that a person should not be forced to renounce it, and

— that group has a distinct identity in the relevant country, because it is perceived as being different by the surrounding society;

depending on the circumstances in the country of origin, a particular social group might include a group based on a common characteristic of sexual orientation. Sexual orientation cannot be understood to include acts considered to be criminal in accordance with national law of the Member States. Gender related aspects might be considered, without by themselves alone creating a presumption for the applicability of this Article;

(e) the concept of political opinion shall in particular include the holding of an opinion, thought or belief on a matter related to the potential actors of persecution mentioned in Article 6 and to their policies or methods, whether or not that opinion, thought or belief has been acted upon by the applicant.

2. When assessing if an applicant has a well-founded fear of being persecuted it is immaterial whether the applicant actually possesses the racial, religious, national, social or political characteristic which attracts the persecution, provided that such a characteristic is attributed to the applicant by the actor of persecution.

Article 11

Cessation

1. A third country national or a stateless person shall cease to be a refugee, if he or she:

(a) has voluntarily re-availed himself or herself of the protection of the country of nationality; or

(b) having lost his or her nationality, has voluntarily reacquired it; or

(c) has acquired a new nationality, and enjoys the protection of the country of his or her new nationality; or

(d) has voluntarily re-established himself or herself in the country which he or she left or outside which he or she remained owing to fear of persecution; or

(e) can no longer, because the circumstances in connection with which he or she has been recognised as a refugee have ceased to exist, continue to refuse to avail himself or herself of the protection of the country of nationality;

(f) being a stateless person with no nationality, he or she is able, because the circumstances in connection with which he or she has been recognised as a refugee have ceased to exist, to return to the country of former habitual residence.

2. In considering points (e) and (f) of paragraph 1, Member States shall have regard to whether the change of circumstances is of such a significant and non-temporary nature that the refugee's fear of persecution can no longer be regarded as well-founded.

Article 12

Exclusion

1. A third country national or a stateless person is excluded from being a refugee, if:

(a) he or she falls within the scope of Article 1 D of the Geneva Convention, relating to protection or assistance from organs or agencies of the United Nations other than the United Nations High Commissioner for Refugees. When such protection or assistance has ceased for any reason, without the position of such persons being definitely settled in accordance with the relevant resolutions adopted by the General Assembly of the United Nations, these persons shall ipso facto be entitled to the benefits of this Directive;

(b) he or she is recognised by the competent authorities of the country in which he or she has taken residence as having the rights and obligations which are attached to the possession of the nationality of that country; or rights and obligations equivalent to those.

2. A third country national or a stateless person is excluded from being a refugee where there are serious reasons for considering that:

(a) he or she has committed a crime against peace, a war crime, or a crime against humanity, as defined in the international instruments drawn up to make provision in respect of such crimes;

(b) he or she has committed a serious non-political crime outside the country of refuge prior to his or her admission as a refugee; which means the time of issuing a residence permit based on the granting of refugee status; particularly cruel actions, even if committed with an allegedly political objective, may be classified as serious non-political crimes;

(c) he or she has been guilty of acts contrary to the purposes and principles of the United Nations as set out in the Preamble and Articles 1 and 2 of the Charter of the United Nations.

3. Paragraph 2 applies to persons who instigate or otherwise participate in the commission of the crimes or acts mentioned therein.

CHAPTER IV

REFUGEE STATUS

Article 13

Granting of refugee status

Member States shall grant refugee status to a third country national or a stateless person, who qualifies as a refugee in accordance with Chapters II and III.

Article 14

Revocation of, ending of or refusal to renew refugee status

1. Concerning applications for international protection filed after the entry into force of this Directive, Member States shall revoke, end or refuse to renew the refugee status of a third country national or a stateless person granted by a governmental, administrative, judicial or quasi-judicial body, if he or she has ceased to be a refugee in accordance with Article 11.

2. Without prejudice to the duty of the refugee in accordance with Article 4(1) to disclose all relevant facts and provide all relevant documentation at his/her disposal, the Member State, which has granted refugee status, shall on an individual basis demonstrate that the person concerned has ceased to be or has never been a refugee in accordance with paragraph 1 of this Article.

3. Member States shall revoke, end or refuse to renew the refugee status of a third country national or a stateless person, if, after he or she has been granted refugee status, it is established by the Member State concerned that:

(a) he or she should have been or is excluded from being a refugee in accordance with Article 12;

(b) his or her misrepresentation or omission of facts, including the use of false documents, were decisive for the granting of refugee status.

4. Member States may revoke, end or refuse to renew the status granted to a refugee by a governmental, administrative, judicial or quasi-judicial body, when:

(a) there are reasonable grounds for regarding him or her as a danger to the security of the Member State in which he or she is present;

(b) he or she, having been convicted by a final judgement of a particularly serious crime, constitutes a danger to the community of that Member State.

5. In situations described in paragraph 4, Member States may decide not to grant status to a refugee, where such a decision has not yet been taken.

6. Persons to whom paragraphs 4 or 5 apply are entitled to rights set out in or similar to those set out in Articles 3, 4, 16, 22, 31 and 32 and 33 of the Geneva Convention insofar as they are present in the Member State.

CHAPTER V

QUALIFICATION FOR SUBSIDIARY PROTECTION

Article 15

Serious harm

Serious harm consists of:

(a) death penalty or execution; or

(b) torture or inhuman or degrading treatment or punishment of an applicant in the country of origin; or

(c) serious and individual threat to a civilian's life or person by reason of indiscriminate violence in situations of international or internal armed conflict.

Article 16

Cessation

1. A third country national or a stateless person shall cease to be eligible for subsidiary protection when the circumstances which led to the granting of subsidiary protection status have ceased to exist or have changed to such a degree that protection is no longer required.

2. In applying paragraph 1, Member States shall have regard to whether the change of circumstances is of such a significant and non-temporary nature that the person eligible for subsidiary protection no longer faces a real risk of serious harm.

Article 17

Exclusion

1. A third country national or a stateless person is excluded from being eligible for subsidiary protection where there are serious reasons for considering that:

(a) he or she has committed a crime against peace, a war crime, or a crime against humanity, as defined in the international instruments drawn up to make provision in respect of such crimes;

(b) he or she has committed a serious crime;

(c) he or she has been guilty of acts contrary to the purposes and principles of the United Nations as set out in the Preamble and Articles 1 and 2 of the Charter of the United Nations;

(d) he or she constitutes a danger to the community or to the security of the Member State in which he or she is present.

2. Paragraph 1 applies to persons who instigate or otherwise participate in the commission of the crimes or acts mentioned therein.

3. Member States may exclude a third country national or a stateless person from being eligible for subsidiary protection, if he or she prior to his or her admission to the Member State has committed one or more crimes, outside the scope of paragraph 1, which would be punishable by imprisonment, had they been committed in the Member State concerned, and if he or she left his or her country of origin solely in order to avoid sanctions resulting from these crimes.

CHAPTER VI
SUBSIDIARY PROTECTION STATUS

Article 18

Granting of subsidiary protection status

Member States shall grant subsidiary protection status to a third country national or a stateless person eligible for subsidiary protection in accordance with Chapters II and V.

Article 19

Revocation of, ending of or refusal to renew subsidiary protection status

1. Concerning applications for international protection filed after the entry into force of this Directive, Member States shall revoke, end or refuse to renew the subsidiary protection status of a third country national or a stateless person granted by a governmental, administrative, judicial or quasi-judicial body, if he or she has ceased to be eligible for subsidiary protection in accordance with Article 16.

2. Member States may revoke, end or refuse to renew the subsidiary protection status of a third country national or a stateless person granted by a governmental, administrative, judicial or quasi-judicial body, if after having been granted subsidiary protection status, he or she should have been excluded from being eligible for subsidiary protection in accordance with Article 17(3).

3. Member States shall revoke, end or refuse to renew the subsidiary protection status of a third country national or a stateless person, if:

(a) he or she, after having been granted subsidiary protection status, should have been or is excluded from being eligible for subsidiary protection in accordance with Article 17(1) and (2);

(b) his or her misrepresentation or omission of facts, including the use of false documents, were decisive for the granting of subsidiary protection status.

4. Without prejudice to the duty of the third country national or stateless person in accordance with Article 4(1) to disclose all relevant facts and provide all relevant documentation at his/her disposal, the Member State, which has granted the subsidiary protection status, shall on an individual basis demonstrate that the person concerned has ceased to be or is not eligible for subsidiary protection in accordance with paragraphs 1, 2 and 3 of this Article.

CHAPTER VII
CONTENT OF INTERNATIONAL PROTECTION

Article 20

General rules

1. This Chapter shall be without prejudice to the rights laid down in the Geneva Convention.

2. This Chapter shall apply both to refugees and persons eligible for subsidiary protection unless otherwise indicated.

3. When implementing this Chapter, Member States shall take into account the specific situation of vulnerable persons such as minors, unaccompanied minors, disabled people, elderly people, pregnant women, single parents with minor children and persons who have been subjected to torture, rape or other serious forms of psychological, physical or sexual violence.

4. Paragraph 3 shall apply only to persons found to have special needs after an individual evaluation of their situation.

5. The best interest of the child shall be a primary consideration for Member States when implementing the provisions of this Chapter that involve minors.

6. Within the limits set out by the Geneva Convention, Member States may reduce the benefits of this Chapter, granted to a refugee whose refugee status has been obtained on the basis of activities engaged in for the sole or main purpose of creating the necessary conditions for being recognised as a refugee.

7. Within the limits set out by international obligations of Member States, Member States may reduce the benefits of this Chapter, granted to a person eligible for subsidiary protection, whose subsidiary protection status has been obtained on the basis of activities engaged in for the sole or main purpose of creating the necessary conditions for being recognised as a person eligible for subsidiary protection.

Article 21

Protection from refoulement

1. Member States shall respect the principle of non-refoulement in accordance with their international obligations.

2. Where not prohibited by the international obligations mentioned in paragraph 1, Member States may refoule a refugee, whether formally recognised or not, when:

(a) there are reasonable grounds for considering him or her as a danger to the security of the Member State in which he or she is present; or

(b) he or she, having been convicted by a final judgement of a particularly serious crime, constitutes a danger to the community of that Member State.

3. Member States may revoke, end or refuse to renew or to grant the residence permit of (or to) a refugee to whom paragraph 2 applies.

Article 22

Information

Member States shall provide persons recognised as being in need of international protection, as soon as possible after the respective protection status has been granted, with access to information, in a language likely to be understood by them, on the rights and obligations relating to that status.

Article 23

Maintaining family unity

1. Member States shall ensure that family unity can be maintained.

2. Member States shall ensure that family members of the beneficiary of refugee or subsidiary protection status, who do not individually qualify for such status, are entitled to claim the benefits referred to in Articles 24 to 34, in accordance with national procedures and as far as it is compatible with the personal legal status of the family member.

In so far as the family members of beneficiaries of subsidiary protection status are concerned, Member States may define the conditions applicable to such benefits.

In these cases, Member States shall ensure that any benefits provided guarantee an adequate standard of living.

3. Paragraphs 1 and 2 are not applicable where the family member is or would be excluded from refugee or subsidiary protection status pursuant to Chapters III and V.

4. Notwithstanding paragraphs 1 and 2, Member States may refuse, reduce or withdraw the benefits referred therein for reasons of national security or public order.

5. Member States may decide that this Article also applies to other close relatives who lived together as part of the family at the time of leaving the country of origin, and who were wholly or mainly dependent on the beneficiary of refugee or subsidiary protection status at that time.

Article 24

Residence permits

1. As soon as possible after their status has been granted, Member States shall issue to beneficiaries of refugee status a residence permit which must be valid for at least three years and renewable unless compelling reasons of national security or public order otherwise require, and without prejudice to Article 21(3).

Without prejudice to Article 23(1), the residence permit to be issued to the family members of the beneficiaries of refugee status may be valid for less than three years and renewable.

2. As soon as possible after the status has been granted, Member States shall issue to beneficiaries of subsidiary protection status a residence permit which must be valid for at least one year and renewable, unless compelling reasons of national security or public order otherwise require.

Article 25

Travel document

1. Member States shall issue to beneficiaries of refugee status travel documents in the form set out in the Schedule to the Geneva Convention, for the purpose of travel outside their territory unless compelling reasons of national security or public order otherwise require.

2. Member States shall issue to beneficiaries of subsidiary protection status who are unable to obtain a national passport, documents which enable them to travel, at least when serious humanitarian reasons arise that require their presence in another State, unless compelling reasons of national security or public order otherwise require.

Article 26

Access to employment

1. Member States shall authorise beneficiaries of refugee status to engage in employed or self-employed activities subject to rules generally applicable to the profession and to the public service, immediately after the refugee status has been granted.

2. Member States shall ensure that activities such as employment-related education opportunities for adults, vocational training and practical workplace experience are offered to beneficiaries of refugee status, under equivalent conditions as nationals.

3. Member States shall authorise beneficiaries of subsidiary protection status to engage in employed or self-employed activities subject to rules generally applicable to the profession and to the public service immediately after the subsidiary protection status has been granted. The situation of the labour market in the Member States may be taken into account, including for possible prioritisation of access to employment for a limited period of time to be determined in accordance with national law. Member States shall ensure that the beneficiary of subsidiary protection status has access to a post for which the beneficiary has received an offer in accordance with national rules on prioritisation in the labour market.

4. Member States shall ensure that beneficiaries of subsidiary protection status have access to activities such as employment-related education opportunities for adults, vocational training and practical workplace experience, under conditions to be decided by the Member States.

5. The law in force in the Member States applicable to remuneration, access to social security systems relating to employed or self-employed activities and other conditions of employment shall apply.

Article 27

Access to education

1. Member States shall grant full access to the education system to all minors granted refugee or subsidiary protection status, under the same conditions as nationals.

2. Member States shall allow adults granted refugee or subsidiary protection status access to the general education system, further training or retraining, under the same conditions as third country nationals legally resident.

3. Member States shall ensure equal treatment between beneficiaries of refugee or subsidiary protection status and nationals in the context of the existing recognition procedures for foreign diplomas, certificates and other evidence of formal qualifications.

Article 28

Social welfare

1. Member States shall ensure that beneficiaries of refugee or subsidiary protection status receive, in the Member State that has granted such statuses, the necessary social assistance, as provided to nationals of that Member State.

2. By exception to the general rule laid down in paragraph 1, Member States may limit social assistance granted to beneficiaries of subsidiary protection status to core benefits

which will then be provided at the same levels and under the same eligibility conditions as nationals.

Article 29

Health care

1. Member States shall ensure that beneficiaries of refugee or subsidiary protection status have access to health care under the same eligibility conditions as nationals of the Member State that has granted such statuses.

2. By exception to the general rule laid down in paragraph 1, Member States may limit health care granted to beneficiaries of subsidiary protection to core benefits which will then be provided at the same levels and under the same eligibility conditions as nationals.

3. Member States shall provide, under the same eligibility conditions as nationals of the Member State that has granted the status, adequate health care to beneficiaries of refugee or subsidiary protection status who have special needs, such as pregnant women, disabled people, persons who have undergone torture, rape or other serious forms of psychological, physical or sexual violence or minors who have been victims of any form of abuse, neglect, exploitation, torture, cruel, inhuman and degrading treatment or who have suffered from armed conflict.

Article 30

Unaccompanied minors

1. As soon as possible after the granting of refugee or subsidiary protection status Member States shall take the necessary measures, to ensure the representation of unaccompanied minors by legal guardianship or, where necessary, by an organisation responsible for the care and well-being of minors, or by any other appropriate representation including that based on legislation or Court order.

2. Member States shall ensure that the minor's needs are duly met in the implementation of this Directive by the appointed guardian or representative. The appropriate authorities shall make regular assessments.

3. Member States shall ensure that unaccompanied minors are placed either:
    (a) with adult relatives; or
    (b) with a foster family; or
    (c) in centres specialised in accommodation for minors; or
    (d) in other accommodation suitable for minors.

In this context, the views of the child shall be taken into account in accordance with his or her age and degree of maturity.

4. As far as possible, siblings shall be kept together, taking into account the best interests of the minor concerned and, in particular, his or her age and degree of maturity. Changes of residence of unaccompanied minors shall be limited to a minimum.

5. Member States, protecting the unaccompanied minor's best interests, shall endeavour to trace the members of the minor's family as soon as possible. In cases where there may be a threat to the life or integrity of the minor or his or her close relatives, particularly if they have remained in the country of origin, care must be taken to ensure that the

collection, processing and circulation of information concerning those persons is undertaken on a confidential basis.

6. Those working with unaccompanied minors shall have had or receive appropriate training concerning their needs.

Article 31

Access to accommodation

The Member States shall ensure that beneficiaries of refugee or subsidiary protection status have access to accommodation under equivalent conditions as other third country nationals legally resident in their territories.

Article 32

Freedom of movement within the member state

Member States shall allow freedom of movement within their territory to beneficiaries of refugee or subsidiary protection status, under the same conditions and restrictions as those provided for other third country nationals legally resident in their territories.

Article 33

Access to integration facilities

1. In order to facilitate the integration of refugees into society, Member States shall make provision for integration programmes which they consider to be appropriate or create pre-conditions which guarantee access to such programmes.

2. Where it is considered appropriate by Member States, beneficiaries of subsidiary protection status shall be granted access to integration programmes.

Article 34

Repatriation

Member States may provide assistance to beneficiaries of refugee or subsidiary protection status who wish to repatriate.

CHAPTER VIII
ADMINISTRATIVE COOPERATION

Article 35

Cooperation

Member States shall each appoint a national contact point, whose address they shall communicate to the Commission, which shall communicate it to the other Member States.

Member States shall, in liaison with the Commission, take all appropriate measures to establish direct cooperation and an exchange of information between the competent authorities.

Article 36

Staff

Member States shall ensure that authorities and other organisations implementing this Directive have received the necessary training and shall be bound by the confidentiality principle, as defined in the national law, in relation to any information they obtain in the course of their work.

CHAPTER IX
FINAL PROVISIONS

Article 37

Reports

1. By 10 April 2008, the Commission shall report to the European Parliament and the Council on the application of this Directive and shall propose any amendments that are necessary. These proposals for amendments shall be made by way of priority in relation to Articles 15, 26 and 33. Member States shall send the Commission all the information that is appropriate for drawing up that report by 10 October 2007.

2. After presenting the report, the Commission shall report to the European Parliament and the Council on the application of this Directive at least every five years.

Article 38

Transposition

1. The Member States shall bring into force the laws, regulations and administrative provisions necessary to comply with this Directive before 10 October 2006. They shall forthwith inform the Commission thereof. When the Member States adopt those measures, they shall contain a reference to this Directive or shall be accompanied by such a reference on the occasion of their official publication. The methods of making such reference shall be laid down by Member States.

2. Member States shall communicate to the Commission the text of the provisions of national law which they adopt in the field covered by this Directive.

Article 39

Entry into force

This Directive shall enter into force on the twentieth day following that of its publication in the *Official Journal of the European Union*.

Article 40

Addressees

This Directive is addressed to the Member States in accordance with the Treaty establishing the European Community.

Done at Luxembourg, 29 April 2004.

For the Council
The President
M. McDOWELL

Directive 2004/38/EC of the European Parliament and of the Council
of 29 April 2004

on the right of citizens of the Union and their family members to move and reside freely within the territory of the Member States amending Regulation (EEC) No 1612/68 and repealing Directives 64/221/EEC, 68/360/EEC, 72/194/EEC, 73/148/EEC, 75/34/EEC, 75/35/EEC, 90/364/EEC, 90/365/EEC and 93/96/EEC

(Text with EEA relevance)

Note: Entered into force on 30 April 2004 (Article 41). To be implemented by 30 April 2006 (Article 40).

THE EUROPEAN PARLIAMENT AND THE COUNCIL OF
THE EUROPEAN UNION,

Having regard to the Treaty establishing the European Community, and in particular Articles 12, 18, 40, 44 and 52 thereof,
Having regard to the proposal from the Commission[33],
Having regard to the Opinion of the European Economic and Social Committee[34],
Having regard to the Opinion of the Committee of the Regions[35],
Acting in accordance with the procedure laid down in Article 251 of the Treaty[36],

[33] OJ C 270 E, 25.9.2001, p. 150.
[34] OJ C 149, 21.6.2002, p. 46.
[35] OJ C 192, 12.8.2002, p. 17.
[36] Opinion of the European Parliament of 11 February 2003 (OJ C 43 E, 19.2.2004, p. 42), Council Common Position of 5 December 2003 (OJ C 54 E, 2.3.2004, p. 12) and Position of the European Parliament of 10 March 2004 (not yet published in the Official Journal).

Whereas:

(1) Citizenship of the Union confers on every citizen of the Union a primary and individual right to move and reside freely within the territory of the Member States, subject to the limitations and conditions laid down in the Treaty and to the measures adopted to give it effect.

(2) The free movement of persons constitutes one of the fundamental freedoms of the internal market, which comprises an area without internal frontiers, in which freedom is ensured in accordance with the provisions of the Treaty.

(3) Union citizenship should be the fundamental status of nationals of the Member States when they exercise their right of free movement and residence. It is therefore necessary to codify and review the existing Community instruments dealing separately with workers, self-employed persons, as well as students and other inactive persons in order to simplify and strengthen the right of free movement and residence of all Union citizens.

(4) With a view to remedying this sector-by-sector, piecemeal approach to the right of free movement and residence and facilitating the exercise of this right, there needs to be a single legislative act to amend Council Regulation (EEC) No 1612/68 of 15 October 1968 on freedom of movement for workers within the Community[37], and to repeal the following acts: Council Directive 68/360/EEC of 15 October 1968 on the abolition of restrictions on movement and residence within the Community for workers of Member States and their families[38], Council Directive 73/148/EEC of 21 May 1973 on the abolition of restrictions on movement and residence within the Community for nationals of Member States with regard to establishment and the provision of services[39], Council Directive 90/364/EEC of 28 June 1990 on the right of residence[40], Council Directive 90/365/EEC of 28 June 1990 on the right of residence for employees and self-employed persons who have ceased their occupational activity[41] and Council Directive 93/96/EEC of 29 October 1993 on the right of residence for students[42].

(5) The right of all Union citizens to move and reside freely within the territory of the Member States should, if it is to be exercised under objective conditions of freedom and dignity, be also granted to their family members, irrespective of nationality. For the purposes of this Directive, the definition of 'family member' should also include the registered partner if the legislation of the host Member State treats registered partnership as equivalent to marriage.

(6) In order to maintain the unity of the family in a broader sense and without prejudice to the prohibition of discrimination on grounds of nationality, the situation of those persons who are not included in the definition of family members under this Directive, and who therefore do not enjoy an automatic right of entry and residence in the host Member State, should be examined by the host Member State on the basis of its own national legislation, in order to decide whether entry and residence could be granted to such persons, taking into consideration their relationship with the Union citizen or

---

[37] OJ L 257, 19.10.1968, p. 2. Regulation as last amended by Regulation (EEC) No 2434/92 (OJ L 245, 26.8.1992, p. 1).

[38] OJ L 257, 19.10.1968, p. 13. Directive as last amended by the 2003 Act of Accession.

[39] OJ L 172, 28.6.1973, p. 14.

[40] OJ L 180, 13.7.1990, p. 26.

[41] OJ L 180, 13.7.1990, p. 28.

[42] OJ L 317, 18.12.1993, p. 59.

any other circumstances, such as their financial or physical dependence on the Union citizen.

(7) The formalities connected with the free movement of Union citizens within the territory of Member States should be clearly defined, without prejudice to the provisions applicable to national border controls.

(8) With a view to facilitating the free movement of family members who are not nationals of a Member State, those who have already obtained a residence card should be exempted from the requirement to obtain an entry visa within the meaning of Council Regulation (EC) No 539/2001 of 15 March 2001 listing the third countries whose nationals must be in possession of visas when crossing the external borders and those whose nationals are exempt from that requirement[43] or, where appropriate, of the applicable national legislation.

(9) Union citizens should have the right of residence in the host Member State for a period not exceeding three months without being subject to any conditions or any formalities other than the requirement to hold a valid identity card or passport, without prejudice to a more favourable treatment applicable to job-seekers as recognised by the case-law of the Court of Justice.

(10) Persons exercising their right of residence should not, however, become an unreasonable burden on the social assistance system of the host Member State during an initial period of residence. Therefore, the right of residence for Union citizens and their family members for periods in excess of three months should be subject to conditions.

(11) The fundamental and personal right of residence in another Member State is conferred directly on Union citizens by the Treaty and is not dependent upon their having fulfilled administrative procedures.

(12) For periods of residence of longer than three months, Member States should have the possibility to require Union citizens to register with the competent authorities in the place of residence, attested by a registration certificate issued to that effect.

(13) The residence card requirement should be restricted to family members of Union citizens who are not nationals of a Member State for periods of residence of longer than three months.

(14) The supporting documents required by the competent authorities for the issuing of a registration certificate or of a residence card should be comprehensively specified in order to avoid divergent administrative practices or interpretations constituting an undue obstacle to the exercise of the right of residence by Union citizens and their family members.

(15) Family members should be legally safeguarded in the event of the death of the Union citizen, divorce, annulment of marriage or termination of a registered partnership. With due regard for family life and human dignity, and in certain conditions to guard against abuse, measures should therefore be taken to ensure that in such circumstances family members already residing within the territory of the host Member State retain their right of residence exclusively on a personal basis.

(16) As long as the beneficiaries of the right of residence do not become an unreasonable burden on the social assistance system of the host Member State they should not be

---

[43] OJ L 81, 21.3.2001, p. 1. Regulation as last amended by Regulation (EC) No 453/2003 (OJ L 69, 13.3.2003, p. 10).

expelled. Therefore, an expulsion measure should not be the automatic consequence of recourse to the social assistance system. The host Member State should examine whether it is a case of temporary difficulties and take into account the duration of residence, the personal circumstances and the amount of aid granted in order to consider whether the beneficiary has become an unreasonable burden on its social assistance system and to proceed to his expulsion. In no case should an expulsion measure be adopted against workers, self-employed persons or job-seekers as defined by the Court of Justice save on grounds of public policy or public security.

(17) Enjoyment of permanent residence by Union citizens who have chosen to settle long term in the host Member State would strengthen the feeling of Union citizenship and is a key element in promoting social cohesion, which is one of the fundamental objectives of the Union. A right of permanent residence should therefore be laid down for all Union citizens and their family members who have resided in the host Member State in compliance with the conditions laid down in this Directive during a continuous period of five years without becoming subject to an expulsion measure.

(18) In order to be a genuine vehicle for integration into the society of the host Member State in which the Union citizen resides, the right of permanent residence, once obtained, should not be subject to any conditions.

(19) Certain advantages specific to Union citizens who are workers or self-employed persons and to their family members, which may allow these persons to acquire a right of permanent residence before they have resided five years in the host Member State, should be maintained, as these constitute acquired rights, conferred by Commission Regulation (EEC) No 1251/70 of 29 June 1970 on the right of workers to remain in the territory of a Member State after having been employed in that State[44] and Council Directive 75/34/EEC of 17 December 1974 concerning the right of nationals of a Member State to remain in the territory of another Member State after having pursued therein an activity in a self-employed capacity[45].

(20) In accordance with the prohibition of discrimination on grounds of nationality, all Union citizens and their family members residing in a Member State on the basis of this Directive should enjoy, in that Member State, equal treatment with nationals in areas covered by the Treaty, subject to such specific provisions as are expressly provided for in the Treaty and secondary law.

(21) However, it should be left to the host Member State to decide whether it will grant social assistance during the first three months of residence, or for a longer period in the case of job-seekers, to Union citizens other than those who are workers or self-employed persons or who retain that status or their family members, or maintenance assistance for studies, including vocational training, prior to acquisition of the right of permanent residence, to these same persons.

(22) The Treaty allows restrictions to be placed on the right of free movement and residence on grounds of public policy, public security or public health. In order to ensure a tighter definition of the circumstances and procedural safeguards subject to which Union citizens and their family members may be denied leave to enter or may be expelled, this Directive should replace Council Directive 64/221/EEC of 25 February 1964 on the coordination of

---

[44] OJ L 142, 30.6.1970, p. 24.
[45] OJ L 14, 20.1.1975, p. 10.

special measures concerning the movement and residence of foreign nationals, which are justified on grounds of public policy, public security or public health[46].

(23) Expulsion of Union citizens and their family members on grounds of public policy or public security is a measure that can seriously harm persons who, having availed themselves of the rights and freedoms conferred on them by the Treaty, have become genuinely integrated into the host Member State. The scope for such measures should therefore be limited in accordance with the principle of proportionality to take account of the degree of integration of the persons concerned, the length of their residence in the host Member State, their age, state of health, family and economic situation and the links with their country of origin.

(24) Accordingly, the greater the degree of integration of Union citizens and their family members in the host Member State, the greater the degree of protection against expulsion should be. Only in exceptional circumstances, where there are imperative grounds of public security, should an expulsion measure be taken against Union citizens who have resided for many years in the territory of the host Member State, in particular when they were born and have resided there throughout their life. In addition, such exceptional circumstances should also apply to an expulsion measure taken against minors, in order to protect their links with their family, in accordance with the United Nations Convention on the Rights of the Child, of 20 November 1989.

(25) Procedural safeguards should also be specified in detail in order to ensure a high level of protection of the rights of Union citizens and their family members in the event of their being denied leave to enter or reside in another Member State, as well as to uphold the principle that any action taken by the authorities must be properly justified.

(26) In all events, judicial redress procedures should be available to Union citizens and their family members who have been refused leave to enter or reside in another Member State.

(27) In line with the case-law of the Court of Justice prohibiting Member States from issuing orders excluding for life persons covered by this Directive from their territory, the right of Union citizens and their family members who have been excluded from the territory of a Member State to submit a fresh application after a reasonable period, and in any event after a three year period from enforcement of the final exclusion order, should be confirmed.

(28) To guard against abuse of rights or fraud, notably marriages of convenience or any other form of relationships contracted for the sole purpose of enjoying the right of free movement and residence, Member States should have the possibility to adopt the necessary measures.

(29) This Directive should not affect more favourable national provisions.

(30) With a view to examining how further to facilitate the exercise of the right of free movement and residence, a report should be prepared by the Commission in order to evaluate the opportunity to present any necessary proposals to this effect, notably on the extension of the period of residence with no conditions.

(31) This Directive respects the fundamental rights and freedoms and observes the principles recognised in particular by the Charter of Fundamental Rights of the European

---

[46] OJ 56, 4.4.1964, p. 850. Directive as last amended by Directive 75/35/EEC (OJ 14, 20.1.1975, p. 14).

Union. In accordance with the prohibition of discrimination contained in the Charter, Member States should implement this Directive without discrimination between the beneficiaries of this Directive on grounds such as sex, race, colour, ethnic or social origin, genetic characteristics, language, religion or beliefs, political or other opinion, membership of an ethnic minority, property, birth, disability, age or sexual orientation,

HAVE ADOPTED THIS DIRECTIVE:

CHAPTER I
GENERAL PROVISIONS

Article 1

Subject

This Directive lays down:

(a) the conditions governing the exercise of the right of free movement and residence within the territory of the Member States by Union citizens and their family members;

(b) the right of permanent residence in the territory of the Member States for Union citizens and their family members;

(c) the limits placed on the rights set out in (a) and (b) on grounds of public policy, public security or public health.

Article 2

Definitions

For the purposes of this Directive:

(1) 'Union citizen' means any person having the nationality of a Member State;

(2) 'Family member' means:

(a) the spouse;

(b) the partner with whom the Union citizen has contracted a registered partnership, on the basis of the legislation of a Member State, if the legislation of the host Member State treats registered partnerships as equivalent to marriage and in accordance with the conditions laid down in the relevant legislation of the host Member State;

(c) the direct descendants who are under the age of 21 or are dependants and those of the spouse or partner as defined in point (b);

(d) the dependent direct relatives in the ascending line and those of the spouse or partner as defined in point (b);

(3) 'Host Member State' means the Member State to which a Union citizen moves in order to exercise his/her right of free movement and residence.

Article 3

Beneficiaries

1. This Directive shall apply to all Union citizens who move to or reside in a Member State other than that of which they are a national, and to their family members as defined in point 2 of Article 2 who accompany or join them.

2. Without prejudice to any right to free movement and residence the persons concerned may have in their own right, the host Member State shall, in accordance with its national legislation, facilitate entry and residence for the following persons:

(a) any other family members, irrespective of their nationality, not falling under the definition in point 2 of Article 2 who, in the country from which they have come, are dependants or members of the household of the Union citizen having the primary right of residence, or where serious health grounds strictly require the personal care of the family member by the Union citizen;

(b) the partner with whom the Union citizen has a durable relationship, duly attested.

The host Member State shall undertake an extensive examination of the personal circumstances and shall justify any denial of entry or residence to these people.

CHAPTER II
RIGHT OF EXIT AND ENTRY

Article 4

Right of exit

1. Without prejudice to the provisions on travel documents applicable to national border controls, all Union citizens with a valid identity card or passport and their family members who are not nationals of a Member State and who hold a valid passport shall have the right to leave the territory of a Member State to travel to another Member State.

2. No exit visa or equivalent formality may be imposed on the persons to whom paragraph 1 applies.

3. Member States shall, acting in accordance with their laws, issue to their own nationals, and renew, an identity card or passport stating their nationality.

4. The passport shall be valid at least for all Member States and for countries through which the holder must pass when travelling between Member States. Where the law of a Member State does not provide for identity cards to be issued, the period of validity of any passport on being issued or renewed shall be not less than five years.

Article 5

Right of entry

1. Without prejudice to the provisions on travel documents applicable to national border controls, Member States shall grant Union citizens leave to enter their territory with a valid identity card or passport and shall grant family members who are not nationals of a Member State leave to enter their territory with a valid passport.

No entry visa or equivalent formality may be imposed on Union citizens.

2. Family members who are not nationals of a Member State shall only be required to have an entry visa in accordance with Regulation (EC) No 539/2001 or, where appropriate, with national law. For the purposes of this Directive, possession of the valid residence card referred to in Article 10 shall exempt such family members from the visa requirement.

Member States shall grant such persons every facility to obtain the necessary visas. Such visas shall be issued free of charge as soon as possible and on the basis of an accelerated procedure.

3. The host Member State shall not place an entry or exit stamp in the passport of family members who are not nationals of a Member State provided that they present the residence card provided for in Article 10.

4. Where a Union citizen, or a family member who is not a national of a Member State, does not have the necessary travel documents or, if required, the necessary visas, the Member State concerned shall, before turning them back, give such persons every reasonable opportunity to obtain the necessary documents or have them brought to them within a reasonable period of time or to corroborate or prove by other means that they are covered by the right of free movement and residence.

5. The Member State may require the person concerned to report his/her presence within its territory within a reasonable and non-discriminatory period of time. Failure to comply with this requirement may make the person concerned liable to proportionate and non-discriminatory sanctions.

CHAPTER III
RIGHT OF RESIDENCE

Article 6

Right of residence for up to three months

1. Union citizens shall have the right of residence on the territory of another Member State for a period of up to three months without any conditions or any formalities other than the requirement to hold a valid identity card or passport.

2. The provisions of paragraph 1 shall also apply to family members in possession of a valid passport who are not nationals of a Member State, accompanying or joining the Union citizen.

Article 7

Right of residence for more than three months

1. All Union citizens shall have the right of residence on the territory of another Member State for a period of longer than three months if they:

(a) are workers or self-employed persons in the host Member State; or

(b) have sufficient resources for themselves and their family members not to become a burden on the social assistance system of the host Member State during their period of residence and have comprehensive sickness insurance cover in the host Member State; or

(c) — are enrolled at a private or public establishment, accredited or financed by the host Member State on the basis of its legislation or administrative practice, for the principal purpose of following a course of study, including vocational training; and

— have comprehensive sickness insurance cover in the host Member State and assure the relevant national authority, by means of a declaration or by such equivalent means as they may choose, that they have sufficient resources for themselves and their family members not to become a burden on the social assistance system of the host Member State during their period of residence; or

(d) are family members accompanying or joining a Union citizen who satisfies the conditions referred to in points (a), (b) or (c).

2. The right of residence provided for in paragraph 1 shall extend to family members who are not nationals of a Member State, accompanying or joining the Union citizen in the host Member State, provided that such Union citizen satisfies the conditions referred to in paragraph 1(a), (b) or (c).

3. For the purposes of paragraph 1(a), a Union citizen who is no longer a worker or self-employed person shall retain the status of worker or self-employed person in the following circumstances:

(a) he/she is temporarily unable to work as the result of an illness or accident;

(b) he/she is in duly recorded involuntary unemployment after having been employed for more than one year and has registered as a job-seeker with the relevant employment office;

(c) he/she is in duly recorded involuntary unemployment after completing a fixed-term employment contract of less than a year or after having become involuntarily unemployed during the first twelve months and has registered as a job-seeker with the relevant employment office. In this case, the status of worker shall be retained for no less than six months;

(d) he/she embarks on vocational training. Unless he/she is involuntarily unemployed, the retention of the status of worker shall require the training to be related to the previous employment.

4. By way of derogation from paragraphs 1(d) and 2 above, only the spouse, the registered partner provided for in Article 2(2)(b) and dependent children shall have the right of residence as family members of a Union citizen meeting the conditions under 1(c) above. Article 3(2) shall apply to his/her dependent direct relatives in the ascending lines and those of his/her spouse or registered partner.

Article 8

Administrative formalities for union citizens

1. Without prejudice to Article 5(5), for periods of residence longer than three months, the host Member State may require Union citizens to register with the relevant authorities.

2. The deadline for registration may not be less than three months from the date of arrival. A registration certificate shall be issued immediately, stating the name and address of the person registering and the date of the registration. Failure to comply with the registration requirement may render the person concerned liable to proportionate and non-discriminatory sanctions.

3. For the registration certificate to be issued, Member States may only require that

— Union citizens to whom point (a) of Article 7(1) applies present a valid identity card or passport, a confirmation of engagement from the employer or a certificate of employment, or proof that they are self-employed persons;

— Union citizens to whom point (b) of Article 7(1) applies present a valid identity card or passport and provide proof that they satisfy the conditions laid down therein;

— Union citizens to whom point (c) of Article 7(1) applies present a valid identity card or passport, provide proof of enrolment at an accredited establishment and of comprehensive sickness insurance cover and the declaration or equivalent means referred to in point (c) of Article 7(1). Member States may not require this declaration to refer to any specific amount of resources.

4. Member States may not lay down a fixed amount which they regard as 'sufficient resources' but they must take into account the personal situation of the person concerned. In all cases this amount shall not be higher than the threshold below which nationals of the host Member State become eligible for social assistance, or, where this criterion is not applicable, higher than the minimum social security pension paid by the host Member State.

5. For the registration certificate to be issued to family members of Union citizens, who are themselves Union citizens, Member States may require the following documents to be presented:

(a) a valid identity card or passport;

(b) a document attesting to the existence of a family relationship or of a registered partnership;

(c) where appropriate, the registration certificate of the Union citizen whom they are accompanying or joining;

(d) in cases falling under points (c) and (d) of Article 2(2), documentary evidence that the conditions laid down therein are met;

(e) in cases falling under Article 3(2)(a), a document issued by the relevant authority in the country of origin or country from which they are arriving certifying that they are dependants or members of the household of the Union citizen, or proof of the existence of serious health grounds which strictly require the personal care of the family member by the Union citizen;

(f) in cases falling under Article 3(2)(b), proof of the existence of a durable relationship with the Union citizen.

Article 9

Administrative formalities for family members who are not nationals of a member state

1. Member States shall issue a residence card to family members of a Union citizen who are not nationals of a Member State, where the planned period of residence is for more than three months.

2. The deadline for submitting the residence card application may not be less than three months from the date of arrival.

3. Failure to comply with the requirement to apply for a residence card may make the person concerned liable to proportionate and non-discriminatory sanctions.

Article 10

Issue of residence cards

1. The right of residence of family members of a Union citizen who are not nationals of a Member State shall be evidenced by the issuing of a document called 'Residence card of

a family member of a Union citizen' no later than six months from the date on which they submit the application. A certificate of application for the residence card shall be issued immediately.

2. For the residence card to be issued, Member States shall require presentation of the following documents:

(a) a valid passport;

(b) a document attesting to the existence of a family relationship or of a registered partnership;

(c) the registration certificate or, in the absence of a registration system, any other proof of residence in the host Member State of the Union citizen whom they are accompanying or joining;

(d) in cases falling under points (c) and (d) of Article 2(2), documentary evidence that the conditions laid down therein are met;

(e) in cases falling under Article 3(2)(a), a document issued by the relevant authority in the country of origin or country from which they are arriving certifying that they are dependants or members of the household of the Union citizen, or proof of the existence of serious health grounds which strictly require the personal care of the family member by the Union citizen;

(f) in cases falling under Article 3(2)(b), proof of the existence of a durable relationship with the Union citizen.

Article 11

Validity of the residence card

1. The residence card provided for by Article 10(1) shall be valid for five years from the date of issue or for the envisaged period of residence of the Union citizen, if this period is less than five years.

2. The validity of the residence card shall not be affected by temporary absences not exceeding six months a year, or by absences of a longer duration for compulsory military service or by one absence of a maximum of twelve consecutive months for important reasons such as pregnancy and childbirth, serious illness, study or vocational training, or a posting in another Member State or a third country.

Article 12

Retention of the right of residence by family members in the event of death or departure of the union citizen

1. Without prejudice to the second subparagraph, the Union citizen's death or departure from the host Member State shall not affect the right of residence of his/her family members who are nationals of a Member State.

Before acquiring the right of permanent residence, the persons concerned must meet the conditions laid down in points (a), (b), (c) or (d) of Article 7(1).

2. Without prejudice to the second subparagraph, the Union citizen's death shall not entail loss of the right of residence of his/her family members who are not nationals of a Member State and who have been residing in the host Member State as family members for at least one year before the Union citizen's death.

Before acquiring the right of permanent residence, the right of residence of the persons concerned shall remain subject to the requirement that they are able to show that they are workers or self-employed persons or that they have sufficient resources for themselves and their family members not to become a burden on the social assistance system of the host Member State during their period of residence and have comprehensive sickness insurance cover in the host Member State, or that they are members of the family, already constituted in the host Member State, of a person satisfying these requirements. 'Sufficient resources' shall be as defined in Article 8(4). Such family members shall retain their right of residence exclusively on a personal basis.

3. The Union citizen's departure from the host Member State or his/her death shall not entail loss of the right of residence of his/her children or of the parent who has actual custody of the children, irrespective of nationality, if the children reside in the host Member State and are enrolled at an educational establishment, for the purpose of studying there, until the completion of their studies.

Article 13

Retention of the right of residence by family members in the event of divorce, annulment of marriage or termination of registered partnership

1. Without prejudice to the second subparagraph, divorce, annulment of the Union citizen's marriage or termination of his/her registered partnership, as referred to in point 2(b) of Article 2 shall not affect the right of residence of his/her family members who are nationals of a Member State.

Before acquiring the right of permanent residence, the persons concerned must meet the conditions laid down in points (a), (b), (c) or (d) of Article 7(1).

2. Without prejudice to the second subparagraph, divorce, annulment of marriage or termination of the registered partnership referred to in point 2(b) of Article 2 shall not entail loss of the right of residence of a Union citizen's family members who are not nationals of a Member State where:

(a) prior to initiation of the divorce or annulment proceedings or termination of the registered partnership referred to in point 2(b) of Article 2, the marriage or registered partnership has lasted at least three years, including one year in the host Member State; or

(b) by agreement between the spouses or the partners referred to in point 2(b) of Article 2 or by court order, the spouse or partner who is not a national of a Member State has custody of the Union citizen's children; or

(c) this is warranted by particularly difficult circumstances, such as having been a victim of domestic violence while the marriage or registered partnership was subsisting; or

(d) by agreement between the spouses or partners referred to in point 2(b) of Article 2 or by court order, the spouse or partner who is not a national of a Member State has the right of access to a minor child, provided that the court has ruled that such access must be in the host Member State, and for as long as is required.

Before acquiring the right of permanent residence, the right of residence of the persons concerned shall remain subject to the requirement that they are able to show that they are workers or self-employed persons or that they have sufficient resources for themselves and their family members not to become a burden on the social assistance system of the host

Member State during their period of residence and have comprehensive sickness insurance cover in the host Member State, or that they are members of the family, already constituted in the host Member State, of a person satisfying these requirements. 'Sufficient resources' shall be as defined in Article 8(4).

Such family members shall retain their right of residence exclusively on personal basis.

Article 14

Retention of the right of residence

1. Union citizens and their family members shall have the right of residence provided for in Article 6, as long as they do not become an unreasonable burden on the social assistance system of the host Member State.

2. Union citizens and their family members shall have the right of residence provided for in Articles 7, 12 and 13 as long as they meet the conditions set out therein.

In specific cases where there is a reasonable doubt as to whether a Union citizen or his/her family members satisfies the conditions set out in Articles 7, 12 and 13, Member States may verify if these conditions are fulfilled. This verification shall not be carried out systematically.

3. An expulsion measure shall not be the automatic consequence of a Union citizen's or his or her family member's recourse to the social assistance system of the host Member State.

4. By way of derogation from paragraphs 1 and 2 and without prejudice to the provisions of Chapter VI, an expulsion measure may in no case be adopted against Union citizens or their family members if:

    (a) the Union citizens are workers or self-employed persons, or

    (b) the Union citizens entered the territory of the host Member State in order to seek employment.

In this case, the Union citizens and their family members may not be expelled for as long as the Union citizens can provide evidence that they are continuing to seek employment and that they have a genuine chance of being engaged.

Article 15

Procedural safeguards

1. The procedures provided for by Articles 30 and 31 shall apply by analogy to all decisions restricting free movement of Union citizens and their family members on grounds other than public policy, public security or public health.

2. Expiry of the identity card or passport on the basis of which the person concerned entered the host Member State and was issued with a registration certificate or residence card shall not constitute a ground for expulsion from the host Member State.

3. The host Member State may not impose a ban on entry in the context of an expulsion decision to which paragraph 1 applies.

CHAPTER IV

RIGHT OF PERMANENT RESIDENCE

SECTION I

Eligibility

Article 16

General Rule for Union Citizens and their Family Members

1. Union citizens who have resided legally for a continuous period of five years in the host Member State shall have the right of permanent residence there. This right shall not be subject to the conditions provided for in Chapter III.

2. Paragraph 1 shall apply also to family members who are not nationals of a Member State and have legally resided with the Union citizen in the host Member State for a continuous period of five years.

3. Continuity of residence shall not be affected by temporary absences not exceeding a total of six months a year, or by absences of a longer duration for compulsory military service, or by one absence of a maximum of twelve consecutive months for important reasons such as pregnancy and childbirth, serious illness, study or vocational training, or a posting in another Member State or a third country.

4. Once acquired, the right of permanent residence shall be lost only through absence from the host Member State for a period exceeding two consecutive years.

Article 17

Exemptions for persons no longer working in the host Member State and their family members

1. By way of derogation from Article 16, the right of permanent residence in the host Member State shall be enjoyed before completion of a continuous period of five years of residence by:

(a) workers or self-employed persons who, at the time they stop working, have reached the age laid down by the law of that Member State for entitlement to an old age pension or workers who cease paid employment to take early retirement, provided that they have been working in that Member State for at least the preceding twelve months and have resided there continuously for more than three years.

If the law of the host Member State does not grant the right to an old age pension to certain categories of self-employed persons, the age condition shall be deemed to have been met once the person concerned has reached the age of 60;

(b) workers or self-employed persons who have resided continuously in the host Member State for more than two years and stop working there as a result of permanent incapacity to work.

If such incapacity is the result of an accident at work or an occupational disease entitling the person concerned to a benefit payable in full or in part by an institution in the host Member State, no condition shall be imposed as to length of residence;

(c) workers or self-employed persons who, after three years of continuous employment and residence in the host Member State, work in an employed or self-employed capacity in another Member State, while retaining their place of residence in the host Member State, to which they return, as a rule, each day or at least once a week.

For the purposes of entitlement to the rights referred to in points (a) and (b), periods of employment spent in the Member State in which the person concerned is working shall be regarded as having been spent in the host Member State.

Periods of involuntary unemployment duly recorded by the relevant employment office, periods not worked for reasons not of the person's own making and absences from work or cessation of work due to illness or accident shall be regarded as periods of employment.

2. The conditions as to length of residence and employment laid down in point (a) of paragraph 1 and the condition as to length of residence laid down in point (b) of paragraph 1 shall not apply if the worker's or the self-employed person's spouse or partner as referred to in point 2(b) of Article 2 is a national of the host Member State or has lost the nationality of that Member State by marriage to that worker or self-employed person.

3. Irrespective of nationality, the family members of a worker or a self-employed person who are residing with him in the territory of the host Member State shall have the right of permanent residence in that Member State, if the worker or self-employed person has acquired himself the right of permanent residence in that Member State on the basis of paragraph 1.

4. If, however, the worker or self-employed person dies while still working but before acquiring permanent residence status in the host Member State on the basis of paragraph 1, his family members who are residing with him in the host Member State shall acquire the right of permanent residence there, on condition that:

(a) the worker or self-employed person had, at the time of death, resided continuously on the territory of that Member State for two years; or

(b) the death resulted from an accident at work or an occupational disease; or

(c) the surviving spouse lost the nationality of that Member State following marriage to the worker or self-employed person.

Article 18

Acquisition of the right of permanent residence by certain family members who are not nationals of a Member State

Without prejudice to Article 17, the family members of a Union citizen to whom Articles 12(2) and 13(2) apply, who satisfy the conditions laid down therein, shall acquire the right of permanent residence after residing legally for a period of five consecutive years in the host Member State.

SECTION II
Administrative Formalities

Article 19

Document certifying permanent residence for Union citizens

1. Upon application Member States shall issue Union citizens entitled to permanent residence, after having verified duration of residence, with a document certifying permanent residence.

2. The document certifying permanent residence shall be issued as soon as possible.

Article 20

Permanent residence card for family members who are not nationals of a Member State

1. Member States shall issue family members who are not nationals of a Member State entitled to permanent residence with a permanent residence card within six months of the submission of the application. The permanent residence card shall be renewable automatically every ten years.

2. The application for a permanent residence card shall be submitted before the residence card expires. Failure to comply with the requirement to apply for a permanent residence card may render the person concerned liable to proportionate and non-discriminatory sanctions.

3. Interruption in residence not exceeding two consecutive years shall not affect the validity of the permanent residence card.

Article 21

Continuity of residence

For the purposes of this Directive, continuity of residence may be attested by any means of proof in use in the host Member State. Continuity of residence is broken by any expulsion decision duly enforced against the person concerned.

CHAPTER V

PROVISIONS COMMON TO THE RIGHT OF RESIDENCE AND THE RIGHT OF PERMANENT RESIDENCE

Article 22

Territorial scope

The right of residence and the right of permanent residence shall cover the whole territory of the host Member State. Member States may impose territorial restrictions on the right of residence and the right of permanent residence only where the same restrictions apply to their own nationals.

Article 23

Related rights

Irrespective of nationality, the family members of a Union citizen who have the right of residence or the right of permanent residence in a Member State shall be entitled to take up employment or self-employment there.

Article 24

Equal treatment

1. Subject to such specific provisions as are expressly provided for in the Treaty and secondary law, all Union citizens residing on the basis of this Directive in the territory

of the host Member State shall enjoy equal treatment with the nationals of that Member State within the scope of the Treaty. The benefit of this right shall be extended to family members who are not nationals of a Member State and who have the right of residence or permanent residence.

2. By way of derogation from paragraph 1, the host Member State shall not be obliged to confer entitlement to social assistance during the first three months of residence or, where appropriate, the longer period provided for in Article 14(4)(b), nor shall it be obliged, prior to acquisition of the right of permanent residence, to grant maintenance aid for studies, including vocational training, consisting in student grants or student loans to persons other than workers, self-employed persons, persons who retain such status and members of their families.

Article 25

General provisions concerning residence documents

1. Possession of a registration certificate as referred to in Article 8, of a document certifying permanent residence, of a certificate attesting submission of an application for a family member residence card, of a residence card or of a permanent residence card, may under no circumstances be made a precondition for the exercise of a right or the completion of an administrative formality, as entitlement to rights may be attested by any other means of proof.

2. All documents mentioned in paragraph 1 shall be issued free of charge or for a charge not exceeding that imposed on nationals for the issuing of similar documents.

Article 26

Checks

Member States may carry out checks on compliance with any requirement deriving from their national legislation for non-nationals always to carry their registration certificate or residence card, provided that the same requirement applies to their own nationals as regards their identity card. In the event of failure to comply with this requirement, Member States may impose the same sanctions as those imposed on their own nationals for failure to carry their identity card.

CHAPTER VI

RESTRICTIONS ON THE RIGHT OF ENTRY AND THE RIGHT OF RESIDENCE ON GROUNDS OF PUBLIC POLICY, PUBLIC SECURITY OR PUBLIC HEALTH

Article 27

General principles

1. Subject to the provisions of this Chapter, Member States may restrict the freedom of movement and residence of Union citizens and their family members, irrespective of

nationality, on grounds of public policy, public security or public health. These grounds shall not be invoked to serve economic ends.

2. Measures taken on grounds of public policy or public security shall comply with the principle of proportionality and shall be based exclusively on the personal conduct of the individual concerned. Previous criminal convictions shall not in themselves constitute grounds for taking such measures. The personal conduct of the individual concerned must represent a genuine, present and sufficiently serious threat affecting one of the fundamental interests of society. Justifications that are isolated from the particulars of the case or that rely on considerations of general prevention shall not be accepted.

3. In order to ascertain whether the person concerned represents a danger for public policy or public security, when issuing the registration certificate or, in the absence of a registration system, not later than three months from the date of arrival of the person concerned on its territory or from the date of reporting his/her presence within the territory, as provided for in Article 5(5), or when issuing the residence card, the host Member State may, should it consider this essential, request the Member State of origin and, if need be, other Member States to provide information concerning any previous police record the person concerned may have. Such enquiries shall not be made as a matter of routine. The Member State consulted shall give its reply within two months.

4. The Member State which issued the passport or identity card shall allow the holder of the document who has been expelled on grounds of public policy, public security, or public health from another Member State to re-enter its territory without any formality even if the document is no longer valid or the nationality of the holder is in dispute.

Article 28

Protection against expulsion

1. Before taking an expulsion decision on grounds of public policy or public security, the host Member State shall take account of considerations such as how long the individual concerned has resided on its territory, his/her age, state of health, family and economic situation, social and cultural integration into the host Member State and the extent of his/her links with the country of origin.

2. The host Member State may not take an expulsion decision against Union citizens or their family members, irrespective of nationality, who have the right of permanent residence on its territory, except on serious grounds of public policy or public security.

3. An expulsion decision may not be taken against Union citizens, except if the decision is based on imperative grounds of public security, as defined by Member States, if they:
    (a) have resided in the host Member State for the previous ten years; or
    (b) are a minor, except if the expulsion is necessary for the best interests of the child, as provided for in the United Nations Convention on the Rights of the Child of 20 November 1989.

Article 29

Public health

1. The only diseases justifying measures restricting freedom of movement shall be the diseases with epidemic potential as defined by the relevant instruments of the World

Health Organisation and other infectious diseases or contagious parasitic diseases if they are the subject of protection provisions applying to nationals of the host Member State.

2. Diseases occurring after a three-month period from the date of arrival shall not constitute grounds for expulsion from the territory.

3. Where there are serious indications that it is necessary, Member States may, within three months of the date of arrival, require persons entitled to the right of residence to undergo, free of charge, a medical examination to certify that they are not suffering from any of the conditions referred to in paragraph 1. Such medical examinations may not be required as a matter of routine.

Article 30

Notification of decisions

1. The persons concerned shall be notified in writing of any decision taken under Article 27(1), in such a way that they are able to comprehend its content and the implications for them.

2. The persons concerned shall be informed, precisely and in full, of the public policy, public security or public health grounds on which the decision taken in their case is based, unless this is contrary to the interests of State security.

3. The notification shall specify the court or administrative authority with which the person concerned may lodge an appeal, the time limit for the appeal and, where applicable, the time allowed for the person to leave the territory of the Member State. Save in duly substantiated cases of urgency, the time allowed to leave the territory shall be not less than one month from the date of notification.

Article 31

Procedural safeguards

1. The persons concerned shall have access to judicial and, where appropriate, administrative redress procedures in the host Member State to appeal against or seek review of any decision taken against them on the grounds of public policy, public security or public health.

2. Where the application for appeal against or judicial review of the expulsion decision is accompanied by an application for an interim order to suspend enforcement of that decision, actual removal from the territory may not take place until such time as the decision on the interim order has been taken, except:
— where the expulsion decision is based on a previous judicial decision; or
— where the persons concerned have had previous access to judicial review; or
— where the expulsion decision is based on imperative grounds of public security under Article 28(3).

3. The redress procedures shall allow for an examination of the legality of the decision, as well as of the facts and circumstances on which the proposed measure is based. They shall ensure that the decision is not disproportionate, particularly in view of the requirements laid down in Article 28.

4. Member States may exclude the individual concerned from their territory pending the redress procedure, but they may not prevent the individual from submitting his/her

defence in person, except when his/her appearance may cause serious troubles to public policy or public security or when the appeal or judicial review concerns a denial of entry to the territory.

Article 32

Duration of exclusion orders

1. Persons excluded on grounds of public policy or public security may submit an application for lifting of the exclusion order after a reasonable period, depending on the circumstances, and in any event after three years from enforcement of the final exclusion order which has been validly adopted in accordance with Community law, by putting forward arguments to establish that there has been a material change in the circumstances which justified the decision ordering their exclusion.

The Member State concerned shall reach a decision on this application within six months of its submission.

2. The persons referred to in paragraph 1 shall have no right of entry to the territory of the Member State concerned while their application is being considered.

Article 33

Expulsion as a penalty or legal consequence

1. Expulsion orders may not be issued by the host Member State as a penalty or legal consequence of a custodial penalty, unless they conform to the requirements of Articles 27, 28 and 29.

2. If an expulsion order, as provided for in paragraph 1, is enforced more than two years after it was issued, the Member State shall check that the individual concerned is currently and genuinely a threat to public policy or public security and shall assess whether there has been any material change in the circumstances since the expulsion order was issued.

CHAPTER VII
FINAL PROVISIONS

Article 34

Publicity

Member States shall disseminate information concerning the rights and obligations of Union citizens and their family members on the subjects covered by this Directive, particularly by means of awareness-raising campaigns conducted through national and local media and other means of communication.

Article 35

Abuse of rights

Member States may adopt the necessary measures to refuse, terminate or withdraw any right conferred by this Directive in the case of abuse of rights or fraud, such as marriages of convenience. Any such measure shall be proportionate and subject to the procedural safeguards provided for in Articles 30 and 31.

Article 36

Sanctions

Member States shall lay down provisions on the sanctions applicable to breaches of national rules adopted for the implementation of this Directive and shall take the measures required for their application. The sanctions laid down shall be effective and proportionate. Member States shall notify the Commission of these provisions not later than . . .* and as promptly as possible in the case of any subsequent changes.

Article 37

More favourable national provisions

The provisions of this Directive shall not affect any laws, regulations or administrative provisions laid down by a Member State which would be more favourable to the persons covered by this Directive.

Article 38

Repeals

1. Articles 10 and 11 of Regulation (EEC) No 1612/68 shall be repealed with effect from . . .*.

2. Directives 64/221/EEC, 68/360/EEC, 72/194/EEC, 73/148/EEC, 75/34/EEC, 75/35/EEC, 90/364/EEC, 90/365/EEC and 93/96/EEC shall be repealed with effect from . . .*.

3. References made to the repealed provisions and Directives shall be construed as being made to this Directive.

Article 39

Report

No later than . . . † the Commission shall submit a report on the application of this Directive to the European Parliament and the Council, together with any necessary proposals, notably on the opportunity to extend the period of time during which Union citizens and their family members may reside in the territory of the host Member State without any conditions. The Member States shall provide the Commission with the information needed to produce the report.

Article 40

Transposition

1. Member States shall bring into force the laws, regulations and administrative provisions necessary to comply with this Directive by . . .*.

---

* Two years from the date of entry into force of this Directive.
† Four years from the date of entry into force of this Directive.

When Member States adopt those measures, they shall contain a reference to this Directive or shall be accompanied by such a reference on the occasion of their official publication. The methods of making such reference shall be laid down by the Member States.

2. Member States shall communicate to the Commission the text of the provisions of national law which they adopt in the field covered by this Directive together with a table showing how the provisions of this Directive correspond to the national provisions adopted.

Article 41

Entry into force

This Directive shall enter into force on the day of its publication in the *Official Journal of the European Union*.

Article 42

Addresses

This Directive is addressed to the Member States.

Done at Strasbourg, 29 April 2004.

For the European Parliament	For the Council
The President	The President
P. COX	M. McDOWELL

Council Directive 2005/85/EC
of 1 December 2005

on minimum standards on procedures in Member States for granting and withdrawing refugee status

THE COUNCIL OF THE EUROPEAN UNION,

Having regard to the Treaty establishing the European Community, and in particular point (1)(d) of the first paragraph of Article 63 thereof,

Having regard to the proposal from the Commission[47],

Having regard to the opinion of the European Parliament[48],

Having regard to the opinion of the European Economic and Social Committee[49],

[47] OJ C 62, 27.2.2001, p. 231 and OJ C 291, 26.11.2002, p. 143.
[48] OJ C 77, 28.3.2002, p. 94.
[49] OJ C 193, 10.7.2001, p. 77. Opinion delivered following non-compulsory consultation.

Whereas:

(1) A common policy on asylum, including a Common European Asylum System, is a constituent part of the European Union's objective of establishing progressively an area of freedom, security and justice open to those who, forced by circumstances, legitimately seek protection in the Community.

(2) The European Council, at its special meeting in Tampere on 15 and 16 October 1999, agreed to work towards establishing a Common European Asylum System, based on the full and inclusive application of the Geneva Convention of 28 July 1951 relating to the status of refugees, as amended by the New York Protocol of 31 January 1967 (Geneva Convention), thus affirming the principle of non-refoulement and ensuring that nobody is sent back to persecution.

(3) The Tampere Conclusions provide that a Common European Asylum System should include, in the short term, common standards for fair and efficient asylum procedures in the Member States and, in the longer term, Community rules leading to a common asylum procedure in the European Community.

(4) The minimum standards laid down in this Directive on procedures in Member States for granting or withdrawing refugee status are therefore a first measure on asylum procedures.

(5) The main objective of this Directive is to introduce a minimum framework in the Community on procedures for granting and withdrawing refugee status.

(6) The approximation of rules on the procedures for granting and withdrawing refugee status should help to limit the secondary movements of applicants for asylum between Member States, where such movement would be caused by differences in legal frameworks.

(7) It is in the very nature of minimum standards that Member States should have the power to introduce or maintain more favourable provisions for third country nationals or stateless persons who ask for international protection from a Member State, where such a request is understood to be on the grounds that the person concerned is a refugee within the meaning of Article 1(A) of the Geneva Convention.

(8) This Directive respects the fundamental rights and observes the principles recognised in particular by the Charter of Fundamental Rights of the European Union.

(9) With respect to the treatment of persons falling within the scope of this Directive, Member States are bound by obligations under instruments of international law to which they are party and which prohibit discrimination.

(10) It is essential that decisions on all applications for asylum be taken on the basis of the facts and, in the first instance, by authorities whose personnel has the appropriate knowledge or receives the necessary training in the field of asylum and refugee matters.

(11) It is in the interest of both Member States and applicants for asylum to decide as soon as possible on applications for asylum. The organisation of the processing of applications for asylum should be left to the discretion of Member States, so that they may, in accordance with their national needs, prioritise or accelerate the processing of any application, taking into account the standards in this Directive.

(12) The notion of public order may cover a conviction for committing a serious crime.

(13) In the interests of a correct recognition of those persons in need of protection as refugees within the meaning of Article 1 of the Geneva Convention, every applicant should, subject to certain exceptions, have an effective access to procedures, the opportunity to cooperate and properly communicate with the competent authorities so as to present the relevant facts of his/her case and sufficient procedural guarantees to pursue his/her case throughout all stages of the procedure. Moreover, the procedure in which an application for asylum is examined should normally provide an applicant at least with the right to stay pending a decision by the determining authority, access to the services of an interpreter for submitting his/her case if interviewed by the authorities, the opportunity to communicate with a representative of the United Nations High Commissioner for Refugees (UNHCR) or with any organisation working on its behalf, the right to appropriate notification of a decision, a motivation of that decision in fact and in law, the opportunity to consult a legal adviser or other counsellor, and the right to be informed of his/her legal position at decisive moments in the course of the procedure, in a language he/she can reasonably be supposed to understand.

(14) In addition, specific procedural guarantees for unaccompanied minors should be laid down on account of their vulnerability. In this context, the best interests of the child should be a primary consideration of Member States.

(15) Where an applicant makes a subsequent application without presenting new evidence or arguments, it would be disproportionate to oblige Member States to carry out a new full examination procedure. In these cases, Member States should have a choice of procedure involving exceptions to the guarantees normally enjoyed by the applicant.

(16) Many asylum applications are made at the border or in a transit zone of a Member State prior to a decision on the entry of the applicant. Member States should be able to keep existing procedures adapted to the specific situation of these applicants at the border. Common rules should be defined on possible exceptions made in these circumstances to the guarantees normally enjoyed by applicants. Border procedures should mainly apply to those applicants who do not meet the conditions for entry into the territory of the Member States.

(17) A key consideration for the well-foundedness of an asylum application is the safety of the applicant in his/her country of origin. Where a third country can be regarded as a safe country of origin, Member States should be able to designate it as safe and presume its safety for a particular applicant, unless he/she presents serious counter-indications.

(18) Given the level of harmonisation achieved on the qualification of third country nationals and stateless persons as refugees, common criteria for designating third countries as safe countries of origin should be established.

(19) Where the Council has satisfied itself that those criteria are met in relation to a particular country of origin, and has consequently included it in the minimum common list of safe countries of origin to be adopted pursuant to this Directive, Member States should be obliged to consider applications of persons with the nationality of that country, or of stateless persons formerly habitually resident in that country, on the basis of the rebuttable presumption of the safety of that country. In the light of the political importance of the designation of safe countries of origin, in particular in view of the implications of an assessment of the human rights situation in a country of origin and its implications for the policies of the European Union in the field of external relations, the

Council should take any decisions on the establishment or amendment of the list, after consultation of the European Parliament.

(20) It results from the status of Bulgaria and Romania as candidate countries for accession to the European Union and the progress made by these countries towards membership that they should be regarded as constituting safe countries of origin for the purposes of this Directive until the date of their accession to the European Union.

(21) The designation of a third country as a safe country of origin for the purposes of this Directive cannot establish an absolute guarantee of safety for nationals of that country. By its very nature, the assessment underlying the designation can only take into account the general civil, legal and political circumstances in that country and whether actors of persecution, torture or inhuman or degrading treatment or punishment are subject to sanction in practice when found liable in the country concerned. For this reason, it is important that, where an applicant shows that there are serious reasons to consider the country not to be safe in his/her particular circumstances, the designation of the country as safe can no longer be considered relevant for him/her.

(22) Member States should examine all applications on the substance, i.e. assess whether the applicant in question qualifies as a refugee in accordance with Council Directive 2004/83/EC of 29 April 2004 on minimum standards for the qualification and status of third country nationals or stateless persons as refugees or as persons who otherwise need international protection and the content of the protection granted[50], except where the present Directive provides otherwise, in particular where it can be reasonably assumed that another country would do the examination or provide sufficient protection. In particular, Member States should not be obliged to assess the substance of an asylum application where a first country of asylum has granted the applicant refugee status or otherwise sufficient protection and the applicant will be readmitted to this country.

(23) Member States should also not be obliged to assess the substance of an asylum application where the applicant, due to a connection to a third country as defined by national law, can reasonably be expected to seek protection in that third country. Member States should only proceed on this basis where this particular applicant would be safe in the third country concerned. In order to avoid secondary movements of applicants, common principles for the consideration or designation by Member States of third countries as safe should be established.

(24) Furthermore, with respect to certain European third countries, which observe particularly high human rights and refugee protection standards, Member States should be allowed to not carry out, or not to carry out full examination of asylum applications regarding applicants who enter their territory from such European third countries. Given the potential consequences for the applicant of a restricted or omitted examination, this application of the safe third country concept should be restricted to cases involving third countries with respect to which the Council has satisfied itself that the high standards for the safety of the third country concerned, as set out in this Directive, are fulfilled. The Council should take decisions in this matter after consultation of the European Parliament.

---

[50] OJ L 304, 30.9.2004, p. 12.

(25) It follows from the nature of the common standards concerning both safe third country concepts as set out in this Directive, that the practical effect of the concepts depends on whether the third country in question permits the applicant in question to enter its territory.

(26) With respect to the withdrawal of refugee status, Member States should ensure that persons benefiting from refugee status are duly informed of a possible reconsideration of their status and have the opportunity to submit their point of view before the authorities can take a motivated decision to withdraw their status. However, dispensing with these guarantees should be allowed where the reasons for the cessation of the refugee status is not related to a change of the conditions on which the recognition was based.

(27) It reflects a basic principle of Community law that the decisions taken on an application for asylum and on the withdrawal of refugee status are subject to an effective remedy before a court or tribunal within the meaning of Article 234 of the Treaty. The effectiveness of the remedy, also with regard to the examination of the relevant facts, depends on the administrative and judicial system of each Member State seen as a whole.

(28) In accordance with Article 64 of the Treaty, this Directive does not affect the exercise of the responsibilities incumbent upon Member States with regard to the maintenance of law and order and the safeguarding of internal security.

(29) This Directive does not deal with procedures governed by Council Regulation (EC) No 343/2003 of 18 February 2003 establishing the criteria and mechanisms for determining the Member State responsible for examining an asylum application lodged in one of the Member States by a third-country national[51].

(30) The implementation of this Directive should be evaluated at regular intervals not exceeding two years.

(31) Since the objective of this Directive, namely to establish minimum standards on procedures in Member States for granting and withdrawing refugee status cannot be sufficiently attained by the Member States and can therefore, by reason of the scale and effects of the action, be better achieved at Community level, the Community may adopt measures, in accordance with the principle of subsidiarity as set out in Article 5 of the Treaty. In accordance with the principle of proportionality, as set out in that Article, this Directive does not go beyond what is necessary in order to achieve this objective.

(32) In accordance with Article 3 of the Protocol on the position of the United Kingdom and Ireland, annexed to the Treaty on European Union and to the Treaty establishing the European Community, the United Kingdom has notified, by letter of 24 January 2001, its wish to take part in the adoption and application of this Directive.

(33) In accordance with Article 3 of the Protocol on the position of the United Kingdom and Ireland, annexed to the Treaty on European Union and to the Treaty establishing the European Community, Ireland has notified, by letter of 14 February 2001, its wish to take part in the adoption and application of this Directive.

(34) In accordance with Articles 1 and 2 of the Protocol on the position of Denmark, annexed to the Treaty on European Union and to the Treaty establishing the European

---

[51] OJ L 50, 25.2.2003, p. 1.

Community, Denmark does not take part in the adoption of this Directive and is not bound by it or subject to its application,

HAS ADOPTED THIS DIRECTIVE:

CHAPTER I
GENERAL PROVISIONS

Article 1

Purpose

The purpose of this Directive is to establish minimum standards on procedures in Member States for granting and withdrawing refugee status.

Article 2

Definitions

For the purposes of this Directive:

(a) 'Geneva Convention' means the Convention of 28 July 1951 relating to the status of refugees, as amended by the New York Protocol of 31 January 1967;

(b) 'application' or 'application for asylum' means an application made by a third country national or stateless person which can be understood as a request for international protection from a Member State under the Geneva Convention. Any application for international protection is presumed to be an application for asylum, unless the person concerned explicitly requests another kind of protection that can be applied for separately;

(c) 'applicant' or 'applicant for asylum' means a third country national or stateless person who has made an application for asylum in respect of which a final decision has not yet been taken;

(d) 'final decision' means a decision on whether the third country national or stateless person be granted refugee status by virtue of Directive 2004/83/EC and which is no longer subject to a remedy within the framework of Chapter V of this Directive irrespective of whether such remedy has the effect of allowing applicants to remain in the Member States concerned pending its outcome, subject to Annex III to this Directive;

(e) 'determining authority' means any quasi-judicial or administrative body in a Member State responsible for examining applications for asylum and competent to take decisions at first instance in such cases, subject to Annex I;

(f) 'refugee' means a third country national or a stateless person who fulfils the requirements of Article 1 of the Geneva Convention as set out in Directive 2004/83/EC;

(g) 'refugee status' means the recognition by a Member State of a third country national or stateless person as a refugee;

(h) 'unaccompanied minor' means a person below the age of 18 who arrives in the territory of the Member States unaccompanied by an adult responsible for him/her whether by law or by custom, and for as long as he/she is not effectively taken into the care of such a person; it includes a minor who is left unaccompanied after he/she has entered the territory of the Member States;

(i) 'representative' means a person acting on behalf of an organisation representing an unaccompanied minor as legal guardian, a person acting on behalf of a national organisation which is responsible for the care and well-being of minors, or any other appropriate representation appointed to ensure his/her best interests;

(j) 'withdrawal of refugee status' means the decision by a competent authority to revoke, end or refuse to renew the refugee status of a person in accordance with Directive 2004/83/EC;

(k) 'remain in the Member State' means to remain in the territory, including at the border or in transit zones, of the Member State in which the application for asylum has been made or is being examined.

Article 3

Scope

1. This Directive shall apply to all applications for asylum made in the territory, including at the border or in the transit zones of the Member States, and to the withdrawal of refugee status.

2. This Directive shall not apply in cases of requests for diplomatic or territorial asylum submitted to representations of Member States.

3. Where Member States employ or introduce a procedure in which asylum applications are examined both as applications on the basis of the Geneva Convention and as applications for other kinds of international protection given under the circumstances defined by Article 15 of Directive 2004/83/EC, they shall apply this Directive throughout their procedure.

4. Moreover, Member States may decide to apply this Directive in procedures for deciding on applications for any kind of international protection.

Article 4

Responsible authorities

1. Member States shall designate for all procedures a determining authority which will be responsible for an appropriate examination of the applications in accordance with this Directive, in particular Articles 8(2) and 9. In accordance with Article 4(4) of Regulation (EC) No 343/2003, applications for asylum made in a Member State to the authorities of another Member State carrying out immigration controls there shall be dealt with by the Member State in whose territory the application is made.

2. However, Member States may provide that another authority is responsible for the purposes of:

(a) processing cases in which it is considered to transfer the applicant to another State according to the rules establishing criteria and mechanisms for determining which State is responsible for considering an application for asylum, until the transfer takes place or the requested State has refused to take charge of or take back the applicant;

(b) taking a decision on the application in the light of national security provisions, provided the determining authority is consulted prior to this decision as to whether the applicant qualifies as a refugee by virtue of Directive 2004/83/EC;

(c) conducting a preliminary examination pursuant to Article 32, provided this authority has access to the applicant's file regarding the previous application;

(d) processing cases in the framework of the procedures provided for in Article 35(1);

(e) refusing permission to enter in the framework of the procedure provided for in Article 35(2) to (5), subject to the conditions and as set out therein;

(f) establishing that an applicant is seeking to enter or has entered into the Member State from a safe third country pursuant to Article 36, subject to the conditions and as set out in that Article.

3. Where authorities are designated in accordance with paragraph 2, Member States shall ensure that the personnel of such authorities have the appropriate knowledge or receive the necessary training to fulfil their obligations when implementing this Directive.

Article 5

More favourable provisions

Member States may introduce or maintain more favourable standards on procedures for granting and withdrawing refugee status, insofar as those standards are compatible with this Directive.

CHAPTER II
BASIC PRINCIPLES AND GUARANTEES

Article 6

Access to the procedure

1. Member States may require that applications for asylum be made in person and/or at a designated place.

2. Member States shall ensure that each adult having legal capacity has the right to make an application for asylum on his/her own behalf.

3. Member States may provide that an application may be made by an applicant on behalf of his/her dependants. In such cases Member States shall ensure that dependent adults consent to the lodging of the application on their behalf, failing which they shall have an opportunity to make an application on their own behalf. Consent shall be requested at the time the application is lodged or, at the latest, when the personal interview with the dependent adult is conducted.

4. Member States may determine in national legislation:

(a) the cases in which a minor can make an application on his/her own behalf;

(b) the cases in which the application of an unaccompanied minor has to be lodged by a representative as provided for in Article 17(1)(a);

(c) the cases in which the lodging of an application for asylum is deemed to constitute also the lodging of an application for asylum for any unmarried minor.

5. Member States shall ensure that authorities likely to be addressed by someone who wishes to make an application for asylum are able to advise that person how and where

he/she may make such an application and/or may require these authorities to forward the application to the competent authority.

Article 7

Right to remain in the Member State pending the examination of the application

1. Applicants shall be allowed to remain in the Member State, for the sole purpose of the procedure, until the determining authority has made a decision in accordance with the procedures at first instance set out in Chapter III. This right to remain shall not constitute an entitlement to a residence permit.

2. Member States can make an exception only where, in accordance with Articles 32 and 34, a subsequent application will not be further examined or where they will surrender or extradite, as appropriate, a person either to another Member State pursuant to obligations in accordance with a European arrest warrant[52] or otherwise, or to a third country, or to international criminal courts or tribunals.

Article 8

Requirements for the examination of applications

1. Without prejudice to Article 23(4)(i), Member States shall ensure that applications for asylum are neither rejected nor excluded from examination on the sole ground that they have not been made as soon as possible.

2. Member States shall ensure that decisions by the determining authority on applications for asylum are taken after an appropriate examination. To that end, Member States shall ensure that:

(a) applications are examined and decisions are taken individually, objectively and impartially;

(b) precise and up-to-date information is obtained from various sources, such as the United Nations High Commissioner for Refugees (UNHCR), as to the general situation prevailing in the countries of origin of applicants for asylum and, where necessary, in countries through which they have transited, and that such information is made available to the personnel responsible for examining applications and taking decisions;

(c) the personnel examining applications and taking decisions have the knowledge with respect to relevant standards applicable in the field of asylum and refugee law.

3. The authorities referred to in Chapter V shall, through the determining authority or the applicant or otherwise, have access to the general information referred to in paragraph 2(b), necessary for the fulfilment of their task.

4. Member States may provide for rules concerning the translation of documents relevant for the examination of applications.

---

[52] Council Framework Decision 2002/584/JHA of 13 June 2002 on the European arrest warrant and the surrender procedures between Member States (OJ L 190, 18.7.2002, p. 1).

Article 9

Requirements for a decision by the determining authority

1. Member States shall ensure that decisions on applications for asylum are given in writing.

2. Member States shall also ensure that, where an application is rejected, the reasons in fact and in law are stated in the decision and information on how to challenge a negative decision is given in writing.

Member States need not state the reasons for not granting refugee status in a decision where the applicant is granted a status which offers the same rights and benefits under national and Community law as the refugee status by virtue of Directive 2004/83/EC. In these cases, Member States shall ensure that the reasons for not granting refugee status are stated in the applicant's file and that the applicant has, upon request, access to his/her file.

Moreover, Member States need not provide information on how to challenge a negative decision in writing in conjunction with a decision where the applicant has been provided with this information at an earlier stage either in writing or by electronic means accessible to the applicant.

3. For the purposes of Article 6(3), and whenever the application is based on the same grounds, Member States may take one single decision, covering all dependants.

Article 10

Guarantees for applicants for asylum

1. With respect to the procedures provided for in Chapter III, Member States shall ensure that all applicants for asylum enjoy the following guarantees:

(a) they shall be informed in a language which they may reasonably be supposed to understand of the procedure to be followed and of their rights and obligations during the procedure and the possible consequences of not complying with their obligations and not cooperating with the authorities. They shall be informed of the time-frame, as well as the means at their disposal for fulfilling the obligation to submit the elements as referred to in Article 4 of Directive 2004/83/EC. This information shall be given in time to enable them to exercise the rights guaranteed in this Directive and to comply with the obligations described in Article 11;

(b) they shall receive the services of an interpreter for submitting their case to the competent authorities whenever necessary. Member States shall consider it necessary to give these services at least when the determining authority calls upon the applicant to be interviewed as referred to in Articles 12 and 13 and appropriate communication cannot be ensured without such services. In this case and in other cases where the competent authorities call upon the applicant, these services shall be paid for out of public funds;

(c) they shall not be denied the opportunity to communicate with the UNHCR or with any other organisation working on behalf of the UNHCR in the territory of the Member State pursuant to an agreement with that Member State;

(d) they shall be given notice in reasonable time of the decision by the determining authority on their application for asylum. If a legal adviser or other counsellor is legally representing the applicant, Member States may choose to give notice of the decision to him/her instead of to the applicant for asylum;

(e) they shall be informed of the result of the decision by the determining authority in a language that they may reasonably be supposed to understand when they are not assisted or represented by a legal adviser or other counsellor and when free legal assistance is not available. The information provided shall include information on how to challenge a negative decision in accordance with the provisions of Article 9(2).

2. With respect to the procedures provided for in Chapter V, Member States shall ensure that all applicants for asylum enjoy equivalent guarantees to the ones referred to in paragraph 1(b), (c) and (d) of this Article.

Article 11

Obligations of the applicants for asylum

1. Member States may impose upon applicants for asylum obligations to cooperate with the competent authorities insofar as these obligations are necessary for the processing of the application.

2. In particular, Member States may provide that:

(a) applicants for asylum are required to report to the competent authorities or to appear before them in person, either without delay or at a specified time;

(b) applicants for asylum have to hand over documents in their possession relevant to the examination of the application, such as their passports;

(c) applicants for asylum are required to inform the competent authorities of their current place of residence or address and of any changes thereof as soon as possible. Member States may provide that the applicant shall have to accept any communication at the most recent place of residence or address which he/she indicated accordingly;

(d) the competent authorities may search the applicant and the items he/she carries with him/her;

(e) the competent authorities may take a photograph of the applicant; and

(f) the competent authorities may record the applicant's oral statements, provided he/she has previously been informed thereof.

Article 12

Personal interview

1. Before a decision is taken by the determining authority, the applicant for asylum shall be given the opportunity of a personal interview on his/her application for asylum with a person competent under national law to conduct such an interview.

Member States may also give the opportunity of a personal interview to each dependent adult referred to in Article 6(3).

Member States may determine in national legislation the cases in which a minor shall be given the opportunity of a personal interview.

2. The personal interview may be omitted where:

(a) the determining authority is able to take a positive decision on the basis of evidence available; or

(b) the competent authority has already had a meeting with the applicant for the purpose of assisting him/her with completing his/her application and submitting the essential information regarding the application, in terms of Article 4(2) of Directive 2004/83/EC; or

(c) the determining authority, on the basis of a complete examination of information provided by the applicant, considers the application to be unfounded in cases where the circumstances mentioned in Article 23(4)(a), (c), (g), (h) and (j) apply.

3. The personal interview may also be omitted where it is not reasonably practicable, in particular where the competent authority is of the opinion that the applicant is unfit or unable to be interviewed owing to enduring circumstances beyond his/her control. When in doubt, Member States may require a medical or psychological certificate.

Where the Member State does not provide the applicant with the opportunity for a personal interview pursuant to this paragraph, or where applicable, to the dependant, reasonable efforts shall be made to allow the applicant or the dependant to submit further information.

4. The absence of a personal interview in accordance with this Article shall not prevent the determining authority from taking a decision on an application for asylum.

5. The absence of a personal interview pursuant to paragraph 2(b) and (c) and paragraph 3 shall not adversely affect the decision of the determining authority.

6. Irrespective of Article 20(1), Member States, when deciding on the application for asylum, may take into account the fact that the applicant failed to appear for the personal interview, unless he/she had good reasons for the failure to appear.

Article 13

Requirements for a personal interview

1. A personal interview shall normally take place without the presence of family members unless the determining authority considers it necessary for an appropriate examination to have other family members present.

2. A personal interview shall take place under conditions which ensure appropriate confidentiality.

3. Member States shall take appropriate steps to ensure that personal interviews are conducted under conditions which allow applicants to present the grounds for their applications in a comprehensive manner. To that end, Member States shall:

(a) ensure that the person who conducts the interview is sufficiently competent to take account of the personal or general circumstances surrounding the application, including the applicant's cultural origin or vulnerability, insofar as it is possible to do so; and

(b) select an interpreter who is able to ensure appropriate communication between the applicant and the person who conducts the interview. The communication need not necessarily take place in the language preferred by the applicant for asylum if there is another language which he/she may reasonably be supposed to understand and in which he/she is able to communicate.

4. Member States may provide for rules concerning the presence of third parties at a personal interview.

5. This Article is also applicable to the meeting referred to in Article 12(2)(b).

Article 14

Status of the report of a personal interview in the procedure

1. Member States shall ensure that a written report is made of every personal interview, containing at least the essential information regarding the application, as presented by the applicant, in terms of Article 4(2) of Directive 2004/83/EC.

2. Member States shall ensure that applicants have timely access to the report of the personal interview. Where access is only granted after the decision of the determining authority, Member States shall ensure that access is possible as soon as necessary for allowing an appeal to be prepared and lodged in due time.

3. Member States may request the applicant's approval of the contents of the report of the personal interview.

Where an applicant refuses to approve the contents of the report, the reasons for this refusal shall be entered into the applicant's file.

The refusal of an applicant to approve the contents of the report shall not prevent the determining authority from taking a decision on his/her application.

4. This Article is also applicable to the meeting referred to in Article 12(2)(b).

Article 15

Right to legal assistance and representation

1. Member States shall allow applicants for asylum the opportunity, at their own cost, to consult in an effective manner a legal adviser or other counsellor, admitted or permitted as such under national law, on matters relating to their asylum applications.

2. In the event of a negative decision by a determining authority, Member States shall ensure that free legal assistance and/or representation be granted on request, subject to the provisions of paragraph 3.

3. Member States may provide in their national legislation that free legal assistance and/or representation is granted:

(a) only for procedures before a court or tribunal in accordance with Chapter V and not for any onward appeals or reviews provided for under national law, including a rehearing of an appeal following an onward appeal or review; and/or

(b) only to those who lack sufficient resources; and/or

(c) only to legal advisers or other counsellors specifically designated by national law to assist and/or represent applicants for asylum; and/or

(d) only if the appeal or review is likely to succeed.

Member States shall ensure that legal assistance and/or representation granted under point (d) is not arbitrarily restricted.

4. Rules concerning the modalities for filing and processing requests for legal assistance and/or representation may be provided by Member States.

5. Member States may also:

(a) impose monetary and/or time-limits on the provision of free legal assistance and/or representation, provided that such limits do not arbitrarily restrict access to legal assistance and/or representation;

(b) provide that, as regards fees and other costs, the treatment of applicants shall not be more favourable than the treatment generally accorded to their nationals in matters pertaining to legal assistance.

6. Member States may demand to be reimbursed wholly or partially for any expenses granted if and when the applicant's financial situation has improved considerably or if the decision to grant such benefits was taken on the basis of false information supplied by the applicant.

Article 16

Scope of legal assistance and representation

1. Member States shall ensure that a legal adviser or other counsellor admitted or permitted as such under national law, and who assists or represents an applicant for asylum under the terms of national law, shall enjoy access to such information in the applicant's file as is liable to be examined by the authorities referred to in Chapter V, insofar as the information is relevant to the examination of the application.

Member States may make an exception where disclosure of information or sources would jeopardise national security, the security of the organisations or person(s) providing the information or the security of the person(s) to whom the information relates or where the investigative interests relating to the examination of applications of asylum by the competent authorities of the Member States or the international relations of the Member States would be compromised. In these cases, access to the information or sources in question shall be available to the authorities referred to in Chapter V, except where such access is precluded in cases of national security.

2. Member States shall ensure that the legal adviser or other counsellor who assists or represents an applicant for asylum has access to closed areas, such as detention facilities and transit zones, for the purpose of consulting that applicant. Member States may only limit the possibility of visiting applicants in closed areas where such limitation is, by virtue of national legislation, objectively necessary for the security, public order or administrative management of the area, or in order to ensure an efficient examination of the application, provided that access by the legal adviser or other counsellor is not thereby severely limited or rendered impossible.

3. Member States may provide rules covering the presence of legal advisers or other counsellors at all interviews in the procedure, without prejudice to this Article or to Article 17(1)(b).

4. Member States may provide that the applicant is allowed to bring with him/her to the personal interview a legal adviser or other counsellor admitted or permitted as such under national law.

Member States may require the presence of the applicant at the personal interview, even if he/she is represented under the terms of national law by such a legal adviser or counsellor, and may require the applicant to respond in person to the questions asked.

The absence of a legal adviser or other counsellor shall not prevent the competent authority from conducting the personal interview with the applicant.

Article 17

Guarantees for unaccompanied minors

1. With respect to all procedures provided for in this Directive and without prejudice to the provisions of Articles 12 and 14, Member States shall:

(a) as soon as possible take measures to ensure that a representative represents and/ or assists the unaccompanied minor with respect to the examination of the application. This representative can also be the representative referred to in Article 19 of Directive 2003/9/EC of 27 January 2003 laying down minimum standards for the reception of asylum seekers[53];

(b) ensure that the representative is given the opportunity to inform the unaccompanied minor about the meaning and possible consequences of the personal interview and, where appropriate, how to prepare himself/herself for the personal interview. Member States shall allow the representative to be present at that interview and to ask questions or make comments, within the framework set by the person who conducts the interview.

Member States may require the presence of the unaccompanied minor at the personal interview, even if the representative is present.

2. Member States may refrain from appointing a representative where the unaccompanied minor:

(a) will in all likelihood reach the age of maturity before a decision at first instance is taken; or

(b) can avail himself, free of charge, of a legal adviser or other counsellor, admitted as such under national law to fulfil the tasks assigned above to the representative; or

(c) is married or has been married.

3. Member States may, in accordance with the laws and regulations in force on 1 December 2005, also refrain from appointing a representative where the unaccompanied minor is 16 years old or older, unless he/she is unable to pursue his/her application without a representative.

4. Member States shall ensure that:

(a) if an unaccompanied minor has a personal interview on his/her application for asylum as referred to in Articles 12, 13 and 14, that interview is conducted by a person who has the necessary knowledge of the special needs of minors;

(b) an official with the necessary knowledge of the special needs of minors prepares the decision by the determining authority on the application of an unaccompanied minor.

5. Member States may use medical examinations to determine the age of unaccompanied minors within the framework of the examination of an application for asylum.

In cases where medical examinations are used, Member States shall ensure that:

(a) unaccompanied minors are informed prior to the examination of their application for asylum, and in a language which they may reasonably be supposed to understand,

---

[53] OJ L 31, 6.2.2003, p. 18.

of the possibility that their age may be determined by medical examination. This shall include information on the method of examination and the possible consequences of the result of the medical examination for the examination of the application for asylum, as well as the consequences of refusal on the part of the unaccompanied minor to undergo the medical examination;

(b) unaccompanied minors and/or their representatives consent to carry out an examination to determine the age of the minors concerned; and

(c) the decision to reject an application for asylum from an unaccompanied minor who refused to undergo this medical examination shall not be based solely on that refusal.

The fact that an unaccompanied minor has refused to undergo such a medical examination shall not prevent the determining authority from taking a decision on the application for asylum.

6. The best interests of the child shall be a primary consideration for Member States when implementing this Article.

Article 18

Detention

1. Member States shall not hold a person in detention for the sole reason that he/she is an applicant for asylum.

2. Where an applicant for asylum is held in detention, Member States shall ensure that there is a possibility of speedy judicial review.

Article 19

Procedure in case of withdrawal of the application

1. Insofar as Member States provide for the possibility of explicit withdrawal of the application under national law, when an applicant for asylum explicitly withdraws his/her application for asylum, Member States shall ensure that the determining authority takes a decision to either discontinue the examination or reject the application.

2. Member States may also decide that the determining authority can decide to discontinue the examination without taking a decision. In this case, Member States shall ensure that the determining authority enters a notice in the applicant's file.

Article 20

Procedure in the case of implicit withdrawal or abandonment of the application

1. When there is reasonable cause to consider that an applicant for asylum has implicitly withdrawn or abandoned his/her application for asylum, Member States shall ensure that the determining authority takes a decision to either discontinue the examination or reject the application on the basis that the applicant has not established an entitlement to refugee status in accordance with Directive 2004/83/EC.

Member States may assume that the applicant has implicitly withdrawn or abandoned his/her application for asylum in particular when it is ascertained that:

(a) he/she has failed to respond to requests to provide information essential to his/her application in terms of Article 4 of Directive 2004/83/EC or has not appeared for a personal interview as provided for in Articles 12, 13 and 14, unless the applicant demonstrates within a reasonable time that his/her failure was due to circumstances beyond his control;

(b) he/she has absconded or left without authorisation the place where he/she lived or was held, without contacting the competent authority within a reasonable time, or he/she has not within a reasonable time complied with reporting duties or other obligations to communicate.

For the purposes of implementing these provisions, Member States may lay down time-limits or guidelines.

2. Member States shall ensure that the applicant who reports again to the competent authority after a decision to discontinue as referred to in paragraph 1 of this Article is taken, is entitled to request that his/her case be reopened, unless the request is examined in accordance with Articles 32 and 34.

Member States may provide for a time-limit after which the applicant's case can no longer be re-opened.

Member States shall ensure that such a person is not removed contrary to the principle of non-refoulement.

Member States may allow the determining authority to take up the examination at the stage where it was discontinued.

Article 21

The role of UNHCR

1. Member States shall allow the UNHCR:

(a) to have access to applicants for asylum, including those in detention and in airport or port transit zones;

(b) to have access to information on individual applications for asylum, on the course of the procedure and on the decisions taken, provided that the applicant for asylum agrees thereto;

(c) to present its views, in the exercise of its supervisory responsibilities under Article 35 of the Geneva Convention, to any competent authorities regarding individual applications for asylum at any stage of the procedure.

2. Paragraph 1 shall also apply to an organisation which is working in the territory of the Member State concerned on behalf of the UNHCR pursuant to an agreement with that Member State.

Article 22

Collection of information on individual cases

For the purposes of examining individual cases, Member States shall not:

(a) directly disclose information regarding individual applications for asylum, or the fact that an application has been made, to the alleged actor(s) of persecution of the applicant for asylum;

(b) obtain any information from the alleged actor(s) of persecution in a manner that would result in such actor(s) being directly informed of the fact that an application has been made by the applicant in question, and would jeopardise the physical integrity of the applicant and his/her dependants, or the liberty and security of his/her family members still living in the country of origin.

CHAPTER III
PROCEDURES AT FIRST INSTANCE

Section I

Article 23
Examination procedure

1. Member States shall process applications for asylum in an examination procedure in accordance with the basic principles and guarantees of Chapter II.

2. Member States shall ensure that such a procedure is concluded as soon as possible, without prejudice to an adequate and complete examination.

Member States shall ensure that, where a decision cannot be taken within six months, the applicant concerned shall either:

(a) be informed of the delay; or

(b) receive, upon his/her request, information on the time-frame within which the decision on his/her application is to be expected. Such information shall not constitute an obligation for the Member State towards the applicant concerned to take a decision within that time-frame.

3. Member States may prioritise or accelerate any examination in accordance with the basic principles and guarantees of Chapter II, including where the application is likely to be well-founded or where the applicant has special needs.

4. Member States may also provide that an examination procedure in accordance with the basic principles and guarantees of Chapter II be prioritised or accelerated if:

(a) the applicant, in submitting his/her application and presenting the facts, has only raised issues that are not relevant or of minimal relevance to the examination of whether he/she qualifies as a refugee by virtue of Directive 2004/83/EC; or

(b) the applicant clearly does not qualify as a refugee or for refugee status in a Member State under Directive 2004/83/EC; or

(c) the application for asylum is considered to be unfounded:

(i) because the applicant is from a safe country of origin within the meaning of Articles 29, 30 and 31, or

(ii) because the country which is not a Member State, is considered to be a safe third country for the applicant, without prejudice to Article 28(1); or

(d) the applicant has misled the authorities by presenting false information or documents or by withholding relevant information or documents with respect to his/her identity and/or nationality that could have had a negative impact on the decision; or

(e) the applicant has filed another application for asylum stating other personal data; or

(f) the applicant has not produced information establishing with a reasonable degree of certainty his/her identity or nationality, or it is likely that, in bad faith, he/she has destroyed or disposed of an identity or travel document that would have helped establish his/her identity or nationality; or

(g) the applicant has made inconsistent, contradictory, improbable or insufficient representations which make his/her claim clearly unconvincing in relation to his/her having been the object of persecution referred to in Directive 2004/83/EC; or

(h) the applicant has submitted a subsequent application which does not raise any relevant new elements with respect to his/her particular circumstances or to the situation in his/her country of origin; or

(i) the applicant has failed without reasonable cause to make his/her application earlier, having had opportunity to do so; or

(j) the applicant is making an application merely in order to delay or frustrate the enforcement of an earlier or imminent decision which would result in his/her removal; or

(k) the applicant has failed without good reason to comply with obligations referred to in Article 4(1) and (2) of Directive 2004/83/EC or in Articles 11(2)(a) and (b) and 20(1) of this Directive; or

(l) the applicant entered the territory of the Member State unlawfully or prolonged his/her stay unlawfully and, without good reason, has either not presented himself/herself to the authorities and/or filed an application for asylum as soon as possible, given the circumstances of his/her entry; or

(m) the applicant is a danger to the national security or public order of the Member State, or the applicant has been forcibly expelled for serious reasons of public security and public order under national law; or

(n) the applicant refuses to comply with an obligation to have his/her fingerprints taken in accordance with relevant Community and/or national legislation; or

(o) the application was made by an unmarried minor to whom Article 6(4)(c) applies, after the application of the parents or parent responsible for the minor has been rejected and no relevant new elements were raised with respect to his/her particular circumstances or to the situation in his/her country of origin.

Article 24

Specific procedures

1. Member States may provide for the following specific procedures derogating from the basic principles and guarantees of Chapter II:

(a) a preliminary examination for the purposes of processing cases considered within the framework set out in Section IV;

(b) procedures for the purposes of processing cases considered within the framework set out in Section V.

2. Member States may also provide a derogation in respect of Section VI.

Section II

Article 25

Inadmissible applications

1. In addition to cases in which an application is not examined in accordance with Regulation (EC) No 343/2003, Member States are not required to examine whether the

applicant qualifies as a refugee in accordance with Directive 2004/83/EC where an application is considered inadmissible pursuant to this Article.

2. Member States may consider an application for asylum as inadmissible pursuant to this Article if:

(a) another Member State has granted refugee status;

(b) a country which is not a Member State is considered as a first country of asylum for the applicant, pursuant to Article 26;

(c) a country which is not a Member State is considered as a safe third country for the applicant, pursuant to Article 27;

(d) the applicant is allowed to remain in the Member State concerned on some other grounds and as result of this he/she has been granted a status equivalent to the rights and benefits of the refugee status by virtue of Directive 2004/83/EC;

(e) the applicant is allowed to remain in the territory of the Member State concerned on some other grounds which protect him/her against refoulement pending the outcome of a procedure for the determination of status pursuant to point (d);

(f) the applicant has lodged an identical application after a final decision;

(g) a dependant of the applicant lodges an application, after he/she has in accordance with Article 6(3) consented to have his/her case be part of an application made on his/her behalf, and there are no facts relating to the dependant's situation, which justify a separate application.

Article 26

The concept of first country of asylum

A country can be considered to be a first country of asylum for a particular applicant for asylum if:

(a) he/she has been recognised in that country as a refugee and he/she can still avail himself/herself of that protection; or

(b) he/she otherwise enjoys sufficient protection in that country, including benefiting from the principle of non-refoulement;

provided that he/she will be re-admitted to that country.

In applying the concept of first country of asylum to the particular circumstances of an applicant for asylum Member States may take into account Article 27(1).

Article 27

The safe third country concept

1. Member States may apply the safe third country concept only where the competent authorities are satisfied that a person seeking asylum will be treated in accordance with the following principles in the third country concerned:

(a) life and liberty are not threatened on account of race, religion, nationality, membership of a particular social group or political opinion;

(b) the principle of non-refoulement in accordance with the Geneva Convention is respected;

(c) the prohibition of removal, in violation of the right to freedom from torture and cruel, inhuman or degrading treatment as laid down in international law, is respected; and

(d) the possibility exists to request refugee status and, if found to be a refugee, to receive protection in accordance with the Geneva Convention.

2. The application of the safe third country concept shall be subject to rules laid down in national legislation, including:

(a) rules requiring a connection between the person seeking asylum and the third country concerned on the basis of which it would be reasonable for that person to go to that country;

(b) rules on the methodology by which the competent authorities satisfy themselves that the safe third country concept may be applied to a particular country or to a particular applicant. Such methodology shall include case-by-case consideration of the safety of the country for a particular applicant and/or national designation of countries considered to be generally safe;

(c) rules in accordance with international law, allowing an individual examination of whether the third country concerned is safe for a particular applicant which, as a minimum, shall permit the applicant to challenge the application of the safe third country concept on the grounds that he/she would be subjected to torture, cruel, inhuman or degrading treatment or punishment.

3. When implementing a decision solely based on this Article, Member States shall:

(a) inform the applicant accordingly; and

(b) provide him/her with a document informing the authorities of the third country, in the language of that country, that the application has not been examined in substance.

4. Where the third country does not permit the applicant for asylum to enter its territory, Member States shall ensure that access to a procedure is given in accordance with the basic principles and guarantees described in Chapter II.

5. Member States shall inform the Commission periodically of the countries to which this concept is applied in accordance with the provisions of this Article.

Section III

Article 28

Unfounded applications

1. Without prejudice to Articles 19 and 20, Member States may only consider an application for asylum as unfounded if the determining authority has established that the applicant does not qualify for refugee status pursuant to Directive 2004/83/EC.

2. In the cases mentioned in Article 23(4)(b) and in cases of unfounded applications for asylum in which any of the circumstances listed in Article 23(4)(a) and (c) to (o) apply, Member States may also consider an application as manifestly unfounded, where it is defined as such in the national legislation.

Article 29

Minimum common list of third countries regarded as safe countries of origin

1. The Council shall, acting by a qualified majority on a proposal from the Commission and after consultation of the European Parliament, adopt a minimum common list of third countries which shall be regarded by Member States as safe countries of origin in accordance with Annex II.

2. The Council may, acting by a qualified majority on a proposal from the Commission and after consultation of the European Parliament, amend the minimum common list by adding or removing third countries, in accordance with Annex II. The Commission shall examine any request made by the Council or by a Member State to submit a proposal to amend the minimum common list.

3. When making its proposal under paragraphs 1 or 2, the Commission shall make use of information from the Member States, its own information and, where necessary, information from UNHCR, the Council of Europe and other relevant international organisations.

4. Where the Council requests the Commission to submit a proposal for removing a third country from the minimum common list, the obligation of Member States pursuant to Article 31(2) shall be suspended with regard to this third country as of the day following the Council decision requesting such a submission.

5. Where a Member State requests the Commission to submit a proposal to the Council for removing a third country from the minimum common list, that Member State shall notify the Council in writing of the request made to the Commission. The obligation of this Member State pursuant to Article 31(2) shall be suspended with regard to the third country as of the day following the notification to the Council.

6. The European Parliament shall be informed of the suspensions under paragraphs 4 and 5.

7. The suspensions under paragraphs 4 and 5 shall end after three months, unless the Commission makes a proposal before the end of this period, to withdraw the third country from the minimum common list. The suspensions shall in any case end where the Council rejects a proposal by the Commission to withdraw the third country from the list.

8. Upon request by the Council, the Commission shall report to the European Parliament and the Council on whether the situation of a country on the minimum common list is still in conformity with Annex II. When presenting its report, the Commission may make such recommendations or proposals as it deems appropriate.

Article 30

National designation of third countries as safe countries of origin

1. Without prejudice to Article 29, Member States may retain or introduce legislation that allows, in accordance with Annex II, for the national designation of third countries other than those appearing on the minimum common list, as safe countries of origin for the purposes of examining applications for asylum. This may include designation of part of a country as safe where the conditions in Annex II are fulfilled in relation to that part.

2. By derogation from paragraph 1, Member States may retain legislation in force on 1 December 2005 that allows for the national designation of third countries, other than those appearing on the minimum common list, as safe countries of origin for the purposes of examining applications for asylum where they are satisfied that persons in the third countries concerned are generally neither subject to:

    (a) persecution as defined in Article 9 of Directive 2004/83/EC; nor

    (b) torture or inhuman or degrading treatment or punishment.

3. Member States may also retain legislation in force on 1 December 2005 that allows for the national designation of part of a country as safe, or a country or part of a country as safe for a specified group of persons in that country, where the conditions in paragraph 2 are fulfilled in relation to that part or group.

4. In assessing whether a country is a safe country of origin in accordance with paragraphs 2 and 3, Member States shall have regard to the legal situation, the application of the law and the general political circumstances in the third country concerned.

5. The assessment of whether a country is a safe country of origin in accordance with this Article shall be based on a range of sources of information, including in particular information from other Member States, the UNHCR, the Council of Europe and other relevant international organisations.

6. Member States shall notify to the Commission the countries that are designated as safe countries of origin in accordance with this Article.

Article 31

The safe country of origin concept

1. A third country designated as a safe country of origin in accordance with either Article 29 or 30 may, after an individual examination of the application, be considered as a safe country of origin for a particular applicant for asylum only if:

(a) he/she has the nationality of that country; or

(b) he/she is a stateless person and was formerly habitually resident in that country;

and he/she has not submitted any serious grounds for considering the country not to be a safe country of origin in his/her particular circumstances and in terms of his/her qualification as a refugee in accordance with Directive 2004/83/EC.

2. Member States shall, in accordance with paragraph 1, consider the application for asylum as unfounded where the third country is designated as safe pursuant to Article 29.

3. Member States shall lay down in national legislation further rules and modalities for the application of the safe country of origin concept.

Section IV

Article 32

Subsequent application

1. Where a person who has applied for asylum in a Member State makes further representations or a subsequent application in the same Member State, that Member State may examine these further representations or the elements of the subsequent application in the framework of the examination of the previous application or in the framework of the examination of the decision under review or appeal, insofar as the competent authorities can take into account and consider all the elements underlying the further representations or subsequent application within this framework.

2. Moreover, Member States may apply a specific procedure as referred to in paragraph 3, where a person makes a subsequent application for asylum:

(a) after his/her previous application has been withdrawn or abandoned by virtue of Articles 19 or 20;

(b) after a decision has been taken on the previous application. Member States may also decide to apply this procedure only after a final decision has been taken.

3. A subsequent application for asylum shall be subject first to a preliminary examination as to whether, after the withdrawal of the previous application or after the decision referred to in paragraph 2(b) of this Article on this application has been reached, new elements or findings relating to the examination of whether he/she qualifies as a refugee by virtue of Directive 2004/83/EC have arisen or have been presented by the applicant.

4. If, following the preliminary examination referred to in paragraph 3 of this Article, new elements or findings arise or are presented by the applicant which significantly add to the likelihood of the applicant qualifying as a refugee by virtue of Directive 2004/83/EC, the application shall be further examined in conformity with Chapter II.

5. Member States may, in accordance with national legislation, further examine a subsequent application where there are other reasons why a procedure has to be re-opened.

6. Member States may decide to further examine the application only if the applicant concerned was, through no fault of his/her own, incapable of asserting the situations set forth in paragraphs 3, 4 and 5 of this Article in the previous procedure, in particular by exercising his/her right to an effective remedy pursuant to Article 39.

7. The procedure referred to in this Article may also be applicable in the case of a dependant who lodges an application after he/she has, in accordance with Article 6(3), consented to have his/her case be part of an application made on his/her behalf. In this case the preliminary examination referred to in paragraph 3 of this Article will consist of examining whether there are facts relating to the dependant's situation which justify a separate application.

Article 33

Failure to appear

Member States may retain or adopt the procedure provided for in Article 32 in the case of an application for asylum filed at a later date by an applicant who, either intentionally or owing to gross negligence, fails to go to a reception centre or appear before the competent authorities at a specified time.

Article 34

Procedural rules

1. Member States shall ensure that applicants for asylum whose application is subject to a preliminary examination pursuant to Article 32 enjoy the guarantees provided for in Article 10(1).

2. Member States may lay down in national law rules on the preliminary examination pursuant to Article 32. Those rules may, *inter alia*:

(a) oblige the applicant concerned to indicate facts and substantiate evidence which justify a new procedure;

(b) require submission of the new information by the applicant concerned within a time-limit after he/she obtained such information;

(c) permit the preliminary examination to be conducted on the sole basis of written submissions without a personal interview.

The conditions shall not render impossible the access of applicants for asylum to a new procedure or result in the effective annulment or severe curtailment of such access.

3. Member States shall ensure that:

(a) the applicant is informed in an appropriate manner of the outcome of the preliminary examination and, in case the application will not be further examined, of the reasons for this and the possibilities for seeking an appeal or review of the decision;

(b) if one of the situations referred to in Article 32(2) applies, the determining authority shall further examine the subsequent application in conformity with the provisions of Chapter II as soon as possible.

Section V

Article 35

Border procedures

1. Member States may provide for procedures, in accordance with the basic principles and guarantees of Chapter II, in order to decide at the border or transit zones of the Member State on applications made at such locations.

2. However, when procedures as set out in paragraph 1 do not exist, Member States may maintain, subject to the provisions of this Article and in accordance with the laws or regulations in force on 1 December 2005, procedures derogating from the basic principles and guarantees described in Chapter II, in order to decide at the border or in transit zones as to whether applicants for asylum who have arrived and made an application for asylum at such locations, may enter their territory.

3. The procedures referred to in paragraph 2 shall ensure in particular that the persons concerned:

(a) are allowed to remain at the border or transit zones of the Member State, without prejudice to Article 7;

(b) are be [sic] immediately informed of their rights and obligations, as described in Article 10(1)(a);

(c) have access, if necessary, to the services of an interpreter, as described in Article 10(1)(b);

(d) are interviewed, before the competent authority takes a decision in such procedures, in relation to their application for asylum by persons with appropriate knowledge of the relevant standards applicable in the field of asylum and refugee law, as described in Articles 12, 13 and 14;

(e) can consult a legal adviser or counsellor admitted or permitted as such under national law, as described in Article 15(1); and

(f) have a representative appointed in the case of unaccompanied minors, as described in Article 17(1), unless Article 17(2) or (3) applies.

Moreover, in case permission to enter is refused by a competent authority, this competent authority shall state the reasons in fact and in law why the application for asylum is considered as unfounded or as inadmissible.

4. Member States shall ensure that a decision in the framework of the procedures provided for in paragraph 2 is taken within a reasonable time. When a decision has not been

taken within four weeks, the applicant for asylum shall be granted entry to the territory of the Member State in order for his/her application to be processed in accordance with the other provisions of this Directive.

5. In the event of particular types of arrivals, or arrivals involving a large number of third country nationals or stateless persons lodging applications for asylum at the border or in a transit zone, which makes it practically impossible to apply there the provisions of paragraph 1 or the specific procedure set out in paragraphs 2 and 3, those procedures may also be applied where and for as long as these third country nationals or stateless persons are accommodated normally at locations in proximity to the border or transit zone.

Section VI

Article 36

The European safe third countries concept

1. Member States may provide that no, or no full, examination of the asylum application and of the safety of the applicant in his/her particular circumstances as described in Chapter II, shall take place in cases where a competent authority has established, on the basis of the facts, that the applicant for asylum is seeking to enter or has entered illegally into its territory from a safe third country according to paragraph 2.

2. A third country can only be considered as a safe third country for the purposes of paragraph 1 where:

(a) it has ratified and observes the provisions of the Geneva Convention without any geographical limitations;

(b) it has in place an asylum procedure prescribed by law;

(c) it has ratified the European Convention for the Protection of Human Rights and Fundamental Freedoms and observes its provisions, including the standards relating to effective remedies; and

(d) it has been so designated by the Council in accordance with paragraph 3.

3. The Council shall, acting by qualified majority on a proposal from the Commission and after consultation of the European Parliament, adopt or amend a common list of third countries that shall be regarded as safe third countries for the purposes of paragraph 1.

4. The Member States concerned shall lay down in national law the modalities for implementing the provisions of paragraph 1 and the consequences of decisions pursuant to those provisions in accordance with the principle of non-refoulement under the Geneva Convention, including providing for exceptions from the application of this Article for humanitarian or political reasons or for reasons of public international law.

5. When implementing a decision solely based on this Article, the Member States concerned shall:

(a) inform the applicant accordingly; and

(b) provide him/her with a document informing the authorities of the third country, in the language of that country, that the application has not been examined in substance.

6. Where the safe third country does not re-admit the applicant for asylum, Member States shall ensure that access to a procedure is given in accordance with the basic principles and guarantees described in Chapter II.

7. Member States which have designated third countries as safe countries in accordance with national legislation in force on 1 December 2005 and on the basis of the criteria in paragraph 2(a), (b) and (c), may apply paragraph 1 to these third countries until the Council has adopted the common list pursuant to paragraph 3.

CHAPTER IV

PROCEDURES FOR THE WITHDRAWAL OF REFUGEE STATUS

Article 37

Withdrawal of refugee status

Member States shall ensure that an examination to withdraw the refugee status of a particular person may commence when new elements or findings arise indicating that there are reasons to reconsider the validity of his/her refugee status.

Article 38

Procedural rules

1. Member States shall ensure that, where the competent authority is considering withdrawing the refugee status of a third country national or stateless person in accordance with Article 14 of Directive 2004/83/EC, the person concerned shall enjoy the following guarantees:

(a) to be informed in writing that the competent authority is reconsidering his or her qualification for refugee status and the reasons for such a reconsideration; and

(b) to be given the opportunity to submit, in a personal interview in accordance with Article 10(1)(b) and Articles 12, 13 and 14 or in a written statement, reasons as to why his/her refugee status should not be withdrawn.

In addition, Member States shall ensure that within the framework of such a procedure:

(c) the competent authority is able to obtain precise and up-to-date information from various sources, such as, where appropriate, from the UNHCR, as to the general situation prevailing in the countries of origin of the persons concerned; and

(d) where information on an individual case is collected for the purposes of reconsidering the refugee status, it is not obtained from the actor(s) of persecution in a manner that would result in such actor(s) being directly informed of the fact that the person concerned is a refugee whose status is under reconsideration, nor jeopardise the physical integrity of the person and his/her dependants, or the liberty and security of his/her family members still living in the country of origin.

2. Member States shall ensure that the decision of the competent authority to withdraw the refugee status is given in writing. The reasons in fact and in law shall be stated in the decision and information on how to challenge the decision shall be given in writing.

3. Once the competent authority has taken the decision to withdraw the refugee status, Article 15, paragraph 2, Article 16, paragraph 1 and Article 21 are equally applicable.

4. By derogation to paragraphs 1, 2 and 3 of this Article, Member States may decide that the refugee status shall lapse by law in case of cessation in accordance with Article

11(1)(a) to (d) of Directive 2004/83/EC or if the refugee has unequivocally renounced his/her recognition as a refugee.

Article 39

The right to an effective remedy

1. Member States shall ensure that applicants for asylum have the right to an effective remedy before a court or tribunal, against the following:

(a) a decision taken on their application for asylum, including a decision:

(i) to consider an application inadmissible pursuant to Article 25(2),

(ii) taken at the border or in the transit zones of a Member State as described in Article 35(1),

(iii) not to conduct an examination pursuant to Article 36;

(b) a refusal to re-open the examination of an application after its discontinuation pursuant to Articles 19 and 20;

(c) a decision not to further examine the subsequent application pursuant to Articles 32 and 34;

(d) a decision refusing entry within the framework of the procedures provided for under Article 35(2);

(e) a decision to withdraw refugee status pursuant to Article 38.

2. Member States shall provide for time-limits and other necessary rules for the applicant to exercise his/her right to an effective remedy pursuant to paragraph 1.

3. Member States shall, where appropriate, provide for rules in accordance with their international obligations dealing with:

(a) the question of whether the remedy pursuant to paragraph 1 shall have the effect of allowing applicants to remain in the Member State concerned pending its outcome;

(b) the possibility of legal remedy or protective measures where the remedy pursuant to paragraph 1 does not have the effect of allowing applicants to remain in the Member State concerned pending its outcome. Member States may also provide for an ex officio remedy; and

(c) the grounds for challenging a decision under Article 25(2)(c) in accordance with the methodology applied under Article 27(2)(b) and (c).

4. Member States may lay down time-limits for the court or tribunal pursuant to paragraph 1 to examine the decision of the determining authority.

5. Where an applicant has been granted a status which offers the same rights and benefits under national and Community law as the refugee status by virtue of Directive 2004/83/EC, the applicant may be considered as having an effective remedy where a court or tribunal decides that the remedy pursuant to paragraph 1 is inadmissible or unlikely to succeed on the basis of insufficient interest on the part of the applicant in maintaining the proceedings.

6. Member States may also lay down in national legislation the conditions under which it can be assumed that an applicant has implicitly withdrawn or abandoned his/

her remedy pursuant to paragraph 1, together with the rules on the procedure to be followed.

CHAPTER VI
GENERAL AND FINAL PROVISIONS

Article 40

Challenge by public authorities

This Directive does not affect the possibility for public authorities of challenging the administrative and/or judicial decisions as provided for in national legislation.

Article 41

Confidentiality

Member States shall ensure that authorities implementing this Directive are bound by the confidentiality principle as defined in national law, in relation to any information they obtain in the course of their work.

Article 42

Report

No later than 1 December 2009, the Commission shall report to the European Parliament and the Council on the application of this Directive in the Member States and shall propose any amendments that are necessary. Member States shall send the Commission all the information that is appropriate for drawing up this report. After presenting the report, the Commission shall report to the European Parliament and the Council on the application of this Directive in the Member States at least every two years.

Article 43

Transposition

Member States shall bring into force the laws, regulations and administrative provisions necessary to comply with this Directive by 1 December 2007. Concerning Article 15, Member States shall bring into force the laws, regulations and administrative provisions necessary to comply with this Directive by 1 December 2008. They shall forthwith inform the Commission thereof.

When Member States adopt those provisions, they shall contain a reference to this Directive or shall be accompanied by such a reference on the occasion of their official publication. The methods of making such reference shall be laid down by Member States.

Member States shall communicate to the Commission the text of the provisions of national law which they adopt in the field covered by this Directive.

Article 44

Transition

Member States shall apply the laws, regulations and administrative provisions set out in Article 43 to applications for asylum lodged after 1 December 2007 and to procedures for the withdrawal of refugee status started after 1 December 2007.

Article 45

Entry into force

This Directive shall enter into force on the 20th day following its publication in the *Official Journal of the European Union*.

Article 46

Addressees

This Directive is addressed to the Member States in conformity with the Treaty establishing the European Community.

Done at Brussels, 1 December 2005.

For the Council
The President
Ashton of UPHOLLAND

ANNEX I

Definition of 'determining authority'

When implementing the provision of this Directive, Ireland may, insofar as the provisions of section 17(1) of the *Refugee Act* 1996 (as amended) continue to apply, consider that:

— 'determining authority' provided for in Article 2(e) of this Directive shall, insofar as the examination of whether an applicant should or, as the case may be, should not be declared to be a refugee is concerned, mean the *Office of the Refugee Applications Commissioner*; and

— 'decisions at first instance' provided for in Article 2(e) of this Directive shall include recommendations of the *Refugee Applications Commissioner* as to whether an applicant should or, as the case may be, should not be declared to be a refugee.

Ireland will notify the Commission of any amendments to the provisions of section 17(1) of the *Refugee Act* 1996 (as amended).

ANNEX II

Designation of safe countries of origin for the purposes of Articles 29 and 30(1)

A country is considered as a safe country of origin where, on the basis of the legal situation, the application of the law within a democratic system and the general political circumstances, it can be shown that there is generally and consistently no persecution as defined in Article 9 of Directive 2004/83/EC, no torture or inhuman or degrading treatment or punishment and no threat by reason of indiscriminate violence in situations of international or internal armed conflict.

In making this assessment, account shall be taken, *inter alia*, of the extent to which protection is provided against persecution or mistreatment by:

(a) the relevant laws and regulations of the country and the manner in which they are applied;

(b) observance of the rights and freedoms laid down in the European Convention for the Protection of Human Rights and Fundamental Freedoms and/or the International Covenant for Civil and Political Rights and/or the Convention against Torture, in particular the rights from which derogation cannot be made under Article 15(2) of the said European Convention;

(c) respect of the non-refoulement principle according to the Geneva Convention;

(d) provision for a system of effective remedies against violations of these rights and freedoms.

ANNEX III

Definition of 'applicant' or 'applicant for asylum'

When implementing the provisions of this Directive Spain may, insofar as the provisions of '*Ley 30/1992 de Régimen jurídico de las Administraciones Públicas y del Procedimiento Administrativo Común*' of 26 November 1992 and '*Ley 29/1998 reguladora de la Jurisdicción Contencioso-Administrativa*' of 13 July 1998 continue to apply, consider that, for the purposes of Chapter V, the definition of 'applicant' or 'applicant for asylum' in Article 2(c) of this Directive shall include 'recurrente' as established in the abovementioned Acts.

A '*recurrente*' shall be entitled to the same guarantees as an 'applicant' or an 'applicant for asylum' as set out in this Directive for the purposes of exercising his/her right to an effective remedy in Chapter V.

Spain will notify the Commission of any relevant amendments to the abovementioned Act.

IV (NOTICES)

Notices From European Union Institutions and Bodies
European Parliament Council Commission
Charter of Fundamental Rights of the European Union
(2007/C 303/01) EN
C 303/2 Official Journal of the European Union 14.12.2007

The European Parliament, the Council and the Commission solemnly proclaim the following text as the Charter of Fundamental Rights of the European Union.

CHARTER OF FUNDAMENTAL RIGHTS OF THE EUROPEAN UNION

Preamble

The peoples of Europe, in creating an ever closer union among them, are resolved to share a peaceful future based on common values.

Conscious of its spiritual and moral heritage, the Union is founded on the indivisible, universal values of human dignity, freedom, equality and solidarity; it is based on the principles of democracy and the rule of law. It places the individual at the heart of its activities, by establishing the citizenship of the Union and by creating an area of freedom, security and justice.

The Union contributes to the preservation and to the development of these common values while respecting the diversity of the cultures and traditions of the peoples of Europe as well as the national identities of the Member States and the organisation of their public authorities at national, regional and local levels; it seeks to promote balanced and sustainable development and ensures free movement of persons, services, goods and capital, and the freedom of establishment.

To this end, it is necessary to strengthen the protection of fundamental rights in the light of changes in society, social progress and scientific and technological developments by making those rights more visible in a Charter.

This Charter reaffirms, with due regard for the powers and tasks of the Union and for the principle of subsidiarity, the rights as they result, in particular, from the constitutional traditions and international obligations common to the Member States, the European Convention for the Protection of Human Rights and Fundamental Freedoms, the Social Charters adopted by the Union and by the Council of Europe and the case-law of the Court of Justice of the European Union and of the European Court of Human Rights. In this context the Charter will be interpreted by the courts of the Union and the Member States with due regard to the explanations prepared under the authority of the Praesidium of the Convention which drafted the Charter and updated under the responsibility of the Praesidium of the European Convention.

Enjoyment of these rights entails responsibilities and duties with regard to other persons, to the human community and to future generations.

The Union therefore recognises the rights, freedoms and principles set out hereafter.

TITLE I
DIGNITY

ARTICLE 1
HUMAN DIGNITY

Human dignity is inviolable. It must be respected and protected.

ARTICLE 2

RIGHT TO LIFE

1. Everyone has the right to life.

2. No one shall be condemned to the death penalty, or executed.

ARTICLE 3

RIGHT TO THE INTEGRITY OF THE PERSON

1. Everyone has the right to respect for his or her physical and mental integrity.

2. In the fields of medicine and biology, the following must be respected in particular:

- the free and informed consent of the person concerned, according to the procedures laid down by law;

- the prohibition of eugenic practices, in particular those aiming at the selection of persons;

- the prohibition on making the human body and its parts as such a source of financial gain;

- the prohibition of the reproductive cloning of human beings.

ARTICLE 4

PROHIBITION OF TORTURE AND INHUMAN OR DEGRADING TREATMENT OR PUNISHMENT

No one shall be subjected to torture or to inhuman or degrading treatment or punishment.

ARTICLE 5

PROHIBITION OF SLAVERY AND FORCED LABOUR

1. No one shall be held in slavery or servitude.

2. No one shall be required to perform forced or compulsory labour.

3. Trafficking in human beings is prohibited.

TITLE II

FREEDOMS

ARTICLE 6

RIGHT TO LIBERTY AND SECURITY

Everyone has the right to liberty and security of person.

ARTICLE 7

RESPECT FOR PRIVATE AND FAMILY LIFE

Everyone has the right to respect for his or her private and family life, home and communications.

ARTICLE 8

PROTECTION OF PERSONAL DATA

1. Everyone has the right to the protection of personal data concerning him or her.

2. Such data must be processed fairly for specified purposes and on the basis of the consent of the person concerned or some other legitimate basis laid down by law. Everyone has the right of access to data which has been collected concerning him or her, and the right to have it rectified.

3. Compliance with these rules shall be subject to control by an independent authority.

ARTICLE 9

RIGHT TO MARRY AND RIGHT TO FOUND A FAMILY

The right to marry and the right to found a family shall be guaranteed in accordance with the national laws governing the exercise of these rights.

ARTICLE 10

FREEDOM OF THOUGHT, CONSCIENCE AND RELIGION

1. Everyone has the right to freedom of thought, conscience and religion. This right includes freedom to change religion or belief and freedom, either alone or in community with others and in public or in private, to manifest religion or belief, in worship, teaching, practice and observance.

2. The right to conscientious objection is recognised, in accordance with the national laws governing the exercise of this right.

ARTICLE 11

FREEDOM OF EXPRESSION AND INFORMATION

1. Everyone has the right to freedom of expression. This right shall include freedom to hold opinions and to receive and impart information and ideas without interference by public authority and regardless of frontiers.

2. The freedom and pluralism of the media shall be respected.

ARTICLE 12
FREEDOM OF ASSEMBLY AND OF ASSOCIATION

1. Everyone has the right to freedom of peaceful assembly and to freedom of association at all levels, in particular in political, trade union and civic matters, which implies the right of everyone to form and to join trade unions for the protection of his or her interests.

2. Political parties at Union level contribute to expressing the political will of the citizens of the Union.

ARTICLE 13
FREEDOM OF THE ARTS AND SCIENCES

The arts and scientific research shall be free of constraint. Academic freedom shall be respected.

ARTICLE 14
RIGHT TO EDUCATION

1. Everyone has the right to education and to have access to vocational and continuing training.

2. This right includes the possibility to receive free compulsory education.

3. The freedom to found educational establishments with due respect for democratic principles and the right of parents to ensure the education and teaching of their children in conformity with their religious, philosophical and pedagogical convictions shall be respected, in accordance with the national laws governing the exercise of such freedom and right.

ARTICLE 15
FREEDOM TO CHOOSE AN OCCUPATION AND RIGHT
TO ENGAGE IN WORK

1. Everyone has the right to engage in work and to pursue a freely chosen or accepted occupation.

2. Every citizen of the Union has the freedom to seek employment, to work, to exercise the right of establishment and to provide services in any Member State.

3. Nationals of third countries who are authorised to work in the territories of the Member States are entitled to working conditions equivalent to those of citizens of the Union.

ARTICLE 16

FREEDOM TO CONDUCT A BUSINESS

The freedom to conduct a business in accordance with Union law and national laws and practices is recognised.

ARTICLE 17

RIGHT TO PROPERTY

1. Everyone has the right to own, use, dispose of and bequeath his or her lawfully acquired possessions. No one may be deprived of his or her possessions, except in the public interest and in the cases and under the conditions provided for by law, subject to fair compensation being paid in good time for their loss. The use of property may be regulated by law in so far as is necessary for the general interest.

2. Intellectual property shall be protected.

ARTICLE 18

RIGHT TO ASYLUM

The right to asylum shall be guaranteed with due respect for the rules of the Geneva Convention of 28 July 1951 and the Protocol of 31 January 1967 relating to the status of refugees and in accordance with the Treaty on European Union and the Treaty on the Functioning of the European Union (hereinafter referred to as 'the Treaties').

ARTICLE 19

PROTECTION IN THE EVENT OF REMOVAL, EXPULSION OR EXTRADITION

1. Collective expulsions are prohibited.

2. No one may be removed, expelled or extradited to a State where there is a serious risk that he or she would be subjected to the death penalty, torture or other inhuman or degrading treatment or punishment.

TITLE III

EQUALITY

ARTICLE 20

EQUALITY BEFORE THE LAW

Everyone is equal before the law.

ARTICLE 21

NON-DISCRIMINATION

1. Any discrimination based on any ground such as sex, race, colour, ethnic or social origin, genetic features, language, religion or belief, political or any other opinion, membership of a national minority, property, birth, disability, age or sexual orientation shall be prohibited.

2. Within the scope of application of the Treaties and without prejudice to any of their specific provisions, any discrimination on grounds of nationality shall be prohibited.

ARTICLE 22

CULTURAL, RELIGIOUS AND LINGUISTIC DIVERSITY

The Union shall respect cultural, religious and linguistic diversity.

ARTICLE 23

EQUALITY BETWEEN WOMEN AND MEN

Equality between women and men must be ensured in all areas, including employment, work and pay.

The principle of equality shall not prevent the maintenance or adoption of measures providing for specific advantages in favour of the under-represented sex.

ARTICLE 24

THE RIGHTS OF THE CHILD

1. Children shall have the right to such protection and care as is necessary for their well-being. They may express their views freely. Such views shall be taken into consideration on matters which concern them in accordance with their age and maturity.

2. In all actions relating to children, whether taken by public authorities or private institutions, the child's best interests must be a primary consideration.

3. Every child shall have the right to maintain on a regular basis a personal relationship and direct contact with both his or her parents, unless that is contrary to his or her interests.

ARTICLE 25

THE RIGHTS OF THE ELDERLY

The Union recognises and respects the rights of the elderly to lead a life of dignity and independence and to participate in social and cultural life.

ARTICLE 26

INTEGRATION OF PERSONS WITH DISABILITIES

The Union recognises and respects the right of persons with disabilities to benefit from measures designed to ensure their independence, social and occupational integration and participation in the life of the community.

TITLE IV

SOLIDARITY

ARTICLE 27

WORKERS' RIGHT TO INFORMATION AND CONSULTATION WITHIN THE UNDERTAKING

Workers or their representatives must, at the appropriate levels, be guaranteed information and consultation in good time in the cases and under the conditions provided for by Union law and national laws and practices.

ARTICLE 28

RIGHT OF COLLECTIVE BARGAINING AND ACTION

Workers and employers, or their respective organisations, have, in accordance with Union law and national laws and practices, the right to negotiate and conclude collective agreements at the appropriate levels and, in cases of conflicts of interest, to take collective action to defend their interests, including strike action.

ARTICLE 29

RIGHT OF ACCESS TO PLACEMENT SERVICES

Everyone has the right of access to a free placement service.

ARTICLE 30

PROTECTION IN THE EVENT OF UNJUSTIFIED DISMISSAL

Every worker has the right to protection against unjustified dismissal, in accordance with Union law and national laws and practices.

ARTICLE 31

FAIR AND JUST WORKING CONDITIONS

1. Every worker has the right to working conditions which respect his or her health, safety and dignity.

2. Every worker has the right to limitation of maximum working hours, to daily and weekly rest periods and to an annual period of paid leave.

ARTICLE 32

PROHIBITION OF CHILD LABOUR AND PROTECTION OF YOUNG PEOPLE AT WORK

The employment of children is prohibited. The minimum age of admission to employment may not be lower than the minimum school-leaving age, without prejudice to such rules as may be more favourable to young people and except for limited derogations.

Young people admitted to work must have working conditions appropriate to their age and be protected against economic exploitation and any work likely to harm their safety, health or physical, mental, moral or social development or to interfere with their education.

ARTICLE 33

FAMILY AND PROFESSIONAL LIFE

1. The family shall enjoy legal, economic and social protection.

2. To reconcile family and professional life, everyone shall have the right to protection from dismissal for a reason connected with maternity and the right to paid maternity leave and to parental leave following the birth or adoption of a child.

ARTICLE 34

SOCIAL SECURITY AND SOCIAL ASSISTANCE

1. The Union recognises and respects the entitlement to social security benefits and social services providing protection in cases such as maternity, illness, industrial accidents, dependency or old age, and in the case of loss of employment, in accordance with the rules laid down by Union law and national laws and practices.

2. Everyone residing and moving legally within the European Union is entitled to social security benefits and social advantages in accordance with Union law and national laws and practices.

3. In order to combat social exclusion and poverty, the Union recognises and respects the right to social and housing assistance so as to ensure a decent existence for all those who lack sufficient resources, in accordance with the rules laid down by Union law and national laws and practices.

ARTICLE 35

HEALTH CARE

Everyone has the right of access to preventive health care and the right to benefit from medical treatment under the conditions established by national laws and practices. A high level of human health protection shall be ensured in the definition and implementation of all the Union's policies and activities.

ARTICLE 36

ACCESS TO SERVICES OF GENERAL ECONOMIC INTEREST

The Union recognises and respects access to services of general economic interest as provided for in national laws and practices, in accordance with the Treaties, in order to promote the social and territorial cohesion of the Union.

ARTICLE 37

ENVIRONMENTAL PROTECTION

A high level of environmental protection and the improvement of the quality of the environment must be integrated into the policies of the Union and ensured in accordance with the principle of sustainable development.

ARTICLE 38

CONSUMER PROTECTION

Union policies shall ensure a high level of consumer protection.

TITLE V
CITIZENS' RIGHTS

ARTICLE 39

RIGHT TO VOTE AND TO STAND AS A CANDIDATE AT ELECTIONS TO THE EUROPEAN PARLIAMENT

1. Every citizen of the Union has the right to vote and to stand as a candidate at elections to the European Parliament in the Member State in which he or she resides, under the same conditions as nationals of that State.

2. Members of the European Parliament shall be elected by direct universal suffrage in a free and secret ballot.

ARTICLE 40

RIGHT TO VOTE AND TO STAND AS A CANDIDATE AT MUNICIPAL ELECTIONS

Every citizen of the Union has the right to vote and to stand as a candidate at municipal elections in the Member State in which he or she resides under the same conditions as nationals of that State.

ARTICLE 41
RIGHT TO GOOD ADMINISTRATION

1. Every person has the right to have his or her affairs handled impartially, fairly and within a reasonable time by the institutions, bodies, offices and agencies of the Union.

2. This right includes:

- the right of every person to be heard, before any individual measure which would affect him or her adversely is taken;

- the right of every person to have access to his or her file, while respecting the legitimate interests of confidentiality and of professional and business secrecy;

- the obligation of the administration to give reasons for its decisions.

3. Every person has the right to have the Union make good any damage caused by its institutions by its servants in the performance of their duties, in accordance with the general principles common the laws of the Member States.

4. Every person may write to the institutions of the Union in one of the languages of the Treaties and must have an answer in the same language.

ARTICLE 42
RIGHT OF ACCESS TO DOCUMENTS

Any citizen of the Union, and any natural or legal person residing or having its registered office in a Member State, has a right of access to documents of the institutions, bodies, offices and agencies of the Union, whatever their medium.

ARTICLE 43
EUROPEAN OMBUDSMAN

Any citizen of the Union and any natural or legal person residing or having its registered office in a Member State has the right to refer to the European Ombudsman cases of maladministration in the activities of the institutions, bodies, offices or agencies of the Union, with the exception of the Court of Justice of the European Union acting in its judicial role.

ARTICLE 44
RIGHT TO PETITION

Any citizen of the Union and any natural or legal person residing or having its registered office in a Member State has the right to petition the European Parliament.

ARTICLE 45
FREEDOM OF MOVEMENT AND OF RESIDENCE

1. Every citizen of the Union has the right to move and reside freely within the territory of the Member States.

2. Freedom of movement and residence may be granted, in accordance with the Treaties, to nationals of third countries legally resident in the territory of a Member State.

ARTICLE 46

DIPLOMATIC AND CONSULAR PROTECTION

Every citizen of the Union shall, in the territory of a third country in which the Member State of which he or she is a national is not represented, be entitled to protection by the diplomatic or consular authorities of any Member State, on the same conditions as the nationals of that Member State.

TITLE VI

JUSTICE

ARTICLE 47

RIGHT TO AN EFFECTIVE REMEDY AND TO A FAIR TRIAL

Everyone whose rights and freedoms guaranteed by the law of the Union are violated has the right to an effective remedy before a tribunal in compliance with the conditions laid down in this Article.

Everyone is entitled to a fair and public hearing within a reasonable time by an independent and impartial tribunal previously established by law. Everyone shall have the possibility of being advised, defended and represented.

Legal aid shall be made available to those who lack sufficient resources in so far as such aid is necessary to ensure effective access to justice.

ARTICLE 48

PRESUMPTION OF INNOCENCE AND RIGHT OF DEFENCE

Everyone who has been charged shall be presumed innocent until proved guilty according to Respect for the rights of the defence of anyone who has been charged shall be guaranteed.

ARTICLE 49

PRINCIPLES OF LEGALITY AND PROPORTIONALITY OF CRIMINAL OFFENCES AND PENALTIES

1. No one shall be held guilty of any criminal offence on account of any act or omission which did not constitute a criminal offence under national law or international law at the time when it was committed. Nor shall a heavier penalty be imposed than the one that was applicable at the time the criminal offence was committed. If, subsequent to the commission of a criminal offence, the law provides for a lighter penalty, that penalty shall be applicable.

2. This Article shall not prejudice the trial and punishment of any person for any act or omission which, at the time when it was committed, was criminal according to the general principles recognised by the community of nations.

3. The severity of penalties must not be disproportionate to the criminal offence.

ARTICLE 50
RIGHT NOT TO BE TRIED OR PUNISHED TWICE IN CRIMINAL PROCEEDINGS FOR THE SAME CRIMINAL OFFENCE

No one shall be liable to be tried or punished again in criminal proceedings for an offence for which he or she has already been finally acquitted or convicted within the Union in accordance with the law.

TITLE VII
GENERAL PROVISIONS GOVERNING THE INTERPRETATION AND APPLICATION OF THE CHARTER

ARTICLE 51
FIELD OF APPLICATION

1. The provisions of this Charter are addressed to the institutions, bodies, offices and agencies of the Union with due regard for the principle of subsidiarity and to the Member States only when they are implementing Union law. They shall therefore respect the rights, observe the principles and promote the application thereof in accordance with their respective powers and respecting the limits of the powers of the Union as conferred on it in the Treaties.

2. The Charter does not extend the field of application of Union law beyond the powers of the Union or establish any new power or task for the Union, or modify powers and tasks as defined in the Treaties.

ARTICLE 52
SCOPE AND INTERPRETATION OF RIGHTS AND PRINCIPLES

1. Any limitation on the exercise of the rights and freedoms recognised by this Charter must be provided for by law and respect the essence of those rights and freedoms. Subject to the principle of proportionality, limitations may be made only if they are necessary and genuinely meet objectives of general interest recognised by the Union or the need to protect the rights and freedoms of others.

2. Rights recognised by this Charter for which provision is made in the Treaties shall be exercised under the conditions and within the limits defined by those Treaties.

3. In so far as this Charter contains rights which correspond to rights guaranteed by the Convention for the Protection of Human Rights and Fundamental Freedoms, the meaning and scope of those rights shall be the same as those laid down by the said Convention. This provision shall not prevent Union law providing more extensive protection.

ARTICLE 53
LEVEL OF PROTECTION

Nothing in this Charter shall be interpreted as restricting or adversely affecting human rights and fundamental freedoms as recognised, in their respective fields of application, by Union law and international law and by international agreements to which the Union or all the Member States are party, including the European Convention for the Protection of Human Rights and Fundamental Freedoms, and by the Member States' constitutions.

ARTICLE 54
PROHIBITION OF ABUSE OF RIGHTS

Nothing in this Charter shall be interpreted as implying any right to engage in any activity or to perform any act aimed at the destruction of any of the rights and freedoms recognised in this Charter or at their limitation to a greater extent than is provided for herein.

The above text adapts the wording of the Charter proclaimed on 7 December 2000, and will replace it as from the date of entry into force of the Treaty of Lisbon.

Done at Strasbourg on the twelfth day of December in the year two thousand and seven.

Note: The Charter became law once the Lisbon Treaty came into force on 1 December 2009. See Article 51 above, Article 6 of Treaty of Europe and Protocol 30 below for limited application of the Charter generally.

Protocol (No 30)
On the Application of the Charter of Fundamental Rights of the European Union to Poland and to the United Kingdom

THE HIGH CONTRACTING PARTIES,

WHEREAS in Article 6 of the Treaty on European Union, the Union recognises the rights, freedoms and principles set out in the Charter of Fundamental Rights of the European Union,

WHEREAS the Charter is to be applied in strict accordance with the provisions of the aforementioned Article 6 and Title VII of the Charter itself,

WHEREAS the aforementioned Article 6 requires the Charter to be applied and interpreted by the courts of Poland and of the United Kingdom strictly in accordance with the explanations referred to in that Article,

WHEREAS the Charter contains both rights and principles,

WHEREAS the Charter contains both provisions which are civil and political in character and those which are economic and social in character,

WHEREAS the Charter reaffirms the rights, freedoms and principles recognised in the Union and makes those rights more visible, but does not create new rights or principles,

RECALLING the obligations devolving upon Poland and the United Kingdom under the Treaty on European Union, the Treaty on the Functioning of the European Union, and Union law generally,

NOTING the wish of Poland and the United Kingdom to clarify certain aspects of the application of the Charter,

DESIROUS therefore of clarifying the application of the Charter in relation to the laws and administrative action of Poland and of the United Kingdom and of its justiciability within Poland and within the United Kingdom,

REAFFIRMING that references in this Protocol to the operation of specific provisions of the Charter are strictly without prejudice to the operation of other provisions of the Charter,

REAFFIRMING that this Protocol is without prejudice to the application of the Charter to other Member States,

REAFFIRMING that this Protocol is without prejudice to other obligations devolving upon Poland and the United Kingdom under the Treaty on European Union, the Treaty on the Functioning of the European Union, and Union law generally,

HAVE AGREED UPON the following provisions, which shall be annexed to the Treaty on European Union and to the Treaty on the Functioning of the European Union:

Article 1

1. The Charter does not extend the ability of the Court of Justice of the European Union, or any court or tribunal of Poland or of the United Kingdom, to find that the laws, regulations or administrative provisions, practices or action of Poland or of the United Kingdom are inconsistent with the fundamental rights, freedoms and principles that it reaffirms.

2. In particular, and for the avoidance of doubt, nothing in Title IV of the Charter creates justiciable rights applicable to Poland or the United Kingdom except in so far as Poland or the United Kingdom has provided for such rights in its national law.

Article 2

To the extent that a provision of the Charter refers to national laws and practices, it shall only apply to Poland or the United Kingdom to the extent that the rights or principles that it contains are recognized in the law or practices of Poland or of the United Kingdom.

INTERNATIONAL MATERIALS

UNHCR Handbook on Procedures and Criteria for Determining Refugee Status

under the 1951 Convention and the 1967 Protocol relating to the Status of Refugees

Office of the United Nations High Commissioner for Refugees

Reedited Geneva, January 1992.

TABLE OF CONTENTS

PART TWO

ANNEXES

FOREWORD

I) Refugee status, on the universal level, is governed by the 1951 Convention and the 1967 Protocol relating to the Status of Refugees. These two international legal instruments have been adopted within the framework of the United Nations. At the time of republishing this Handbook 110 states have become parties to the Convention or to the Protocol or to both instruments.

II) These two international legal instruments are applicable to persons who are refugees as therein defined. The assessment as to who is a refugee, i.e. the determination of refugee status under the 1951 Convention and the 1967 Protocol, is incumbent upon the Contracting State in whose territory the refugee applies for recognition of refugee status.

III) Both the 1951 Convention and the 1967 Protocol provide for co-operation between the Contracting States and the Office of the United Nations High Commissioner for Refugees. This co-operation extends to the determination of refugee status, according to arrangements made in various Contracting States.

IV) The Executive Committee of the High Commissioner's Programme at its twenty-eighth session requested the Office of the High Commissioner 'to consider the possibility of issuing—for the guidance of Governments—a handbook relating to procedures and criteria for determining refugee status'. The first edition of the Handbook was issued by my Division in September 1979 in response to this request by the Executive Committee. Since then the Handbook has been regularly reprinted to meet the increasing demands of government officials, academics, and lawyers concerned with refugee problems. The present edition updates information concerning accessions to the international refugee instruments including details of declarations on the geographical applicability of the 1951 Convention and 1967 Protocol.

V) The segment of this Handbook on the criteria for determining refugee status breaks down and explains the various components of the definition of refugee set out in the 1951 Convention and the 1967 Protocol. The explanations are based on the knowledge accumulated by the High Commissioner's Office over some 25 years, since the entry into force of the 1951 Convention on 21 April 1954. The practice of States is taken into account as are exchanges of views between the Office and the competent authorities of Contracting States, and the literature devoted to the subject over the last quarter of a century. As the Handbook has been conceived as a practical guide and not as a treatise on refugee law, references to literature etc. have purposely been omitted.

VI) With respect to procedures for the determination of refugee status, the writers of the Handbook have been guided chiefly by the principles defined in this respect by the Executive Committee itself. Use has naturally also been made of the knowledge available concerning the practice of States.

VII) The Handbook is meant for the guidance of government officials concerned with the determination of refugee status in the various Contracting States. It is hoped that it will also be of interest and useful to all those concerned with refugee problems.

Michel Moussalli

Director of International Protection
Office of the United Nations
High Commissioner for Refugees

Introduction

International Instruments Defining the Term 'Refugee'

A. Early Instruments (1921–1946)

1. Early in the twentieth century, the refugee problem became the concern of the international community, which, for humanitarian reasons, began to assume responsibility for protecting and assisting refugees.

2. The pattern of international action on behalf of refugees was established by the League of Nations and led to the adoption of a number of international agreements for their benefit. These instruments are referred to in Article 1A(1) of the 1951 Convention relating to the Status of Refugees (see paragraph 32 below).

3. The definitions in these instruments relate each category of refugees to their national origin, to the territory that they left and to the lack of diplomatic protection by their former

home country. With this type of definition 'by categories' interpretation was simple and caused no great difficulty in ascertaining who was a refugee.

4. Although few persons covered by the terms of the early instruments are likely to request a formal determination of refugee status at the present time, such cases could occasionally arise. They are dealt with below in Chapter II, A. Persons who meet the definitions of international instruments prior to the 1951 Convention are usually referred to as 'statutory refugees'.

B. 1951 Convention relating to the Status of Refugees

5. Soon after the Second World War, as the refugee problem had not been solved, the need was felt for a new international instrument to define the legal status of refugees. Instead of ad hoc agreements adopted in relation to specific refugee situations, there was a call for an instrument containing a general definition of who was to be considered a refugee. The Convention relating to the Status of Refugees was adopted by a Conference of Plenipotentiaries of the United Nations on 28 July 1951, and entered into force on 21 April 1954. In the following paragraphs it is referred to as 'the 1951 Convention'. (The text of the 1951 Convention will be found in Annex II.)

C. 1967 Protocol relating to the Status of Refugees

6. According to the general definition contained in the 1951 Convention, a refugee is a person who:

'As a result of events occurring before 1 January 1951 and owing to well-founded fear of being persecuted ... is outside his country of nationality . . .'

7. The 1951 dateline originated in the wish of Governments, at the time the Convention was adopted, to limit their obligations to refugee situations that were known to exist at that time, or to those which might subsequently arise from events that had already occurred. [The 1951 Convention also provides for the possibility of introducing a geographic limitation (see paragraphs 108 to 110 below).]

8. With the passage of time and the emergence of new refugee situations the need was increasingly felt to make the provisions of the 1951 Convention applicable to such new refugees. As a result, a Protocol relating to the Status of Refugees was prepared. After consideration by the General Assembly of the United Nations, it was opened for accession on 31 January 1967 and entered into force on 4 October 1967.

9. By accession to the 1967 Protocol, States undertake to apply the substantive provisions of the 1951 Convention to refugees as defined in the Convention, but without the 1951 dateline. Although related to the Convention in this way, the Protocol is an independent instrument, accession to which is not limited to States parties to the Convention.

10. In the following paragraphs, the 1967 Protocol relating to the Status of Refugees is referred to as 'the 1967 Protocol'. (The text of the Protocol will be found in Annex III.)

11. At the time of writing, 78 States are parties to the 1951 Convention or to the 1967 Protocol or to both instruments. (A list of the States parties will be found in Annex IV.)

D. Main provisions of the 1951 Convention and the 1967 Protocol

12.— The 1951 Convention and the 1967 Protocol contain three types of provisions:

(i) Provisions giving the basic definition of who is (and who is not) a refugee and who, having been a refugee, has ceased to be one. The discussion and interpretation of these provisions constitute the main body of the present Handbook, intended for the guidance of those whose task it is to determine refugee status.

(ii) Provisions that define the legal status of refugees and their rights and duties in their country of refuge. Although these provisions have no influence on the process of determination of refugee status, the authority entrusted with this process should be aware of them, for its decision may indeed have far-reaching effects for the individual or family concerned.

(iii) Other provisions dealing with the implementation of the instruments from the administrative and diplomatic standpoint. Article 35 of the 1951 Convention and Article II of the 1967 Protocol contain an undertaking by Contracting States to co-operate with the Office of the United Nations High Commissioner for Refugees in the exercise of its functions and, in particular, to facilitate its duty of supervising the application of the provisions of these instruments.

E. Statute of the Office of the United Nations High Commissioner for Refugees

13. The instruments described above under A-C define the persons who are to be considered refugees and require the parties to accord a certain status to refugees in their respective territories.

14. Pursuant to a decision of the General Assembly, the Office of the United Nations High Commissioner for Refugees ('UNHCR') was established as of 1 January 1951. The Statute of the Office is annexed to Resolution 428(V), adopted by the General Assembly on 14 December 1950. According to the Statutes the High Commissioner is called upon— *inter alia*—to provide international protection, under the auspices of the United Nations, to refugees falling within the competence of his Office.

15. The Statute contains definitions of those persons to whom the High Commissioner's competence extends, which are very close to, though not identical with, the definition contained in the 1951 Convention. By virtue of these definitions the High Commissioner is competent for refugees irrespective of any dateline [see paragraphs 35 and 36 below] or geographic limitation. [See paragraphs 108 to 110 below.]

16. Thus, a person who meets the criteria of the UNHCR Statute qualifies for the protection of the United Nations provided by the High Commissioner, regardless of whether or not he is in a country that is a party to the 1951 Convention or the 1967 Protocol or whether or not he has been recognised by his host country as a refugee under either of these instruments. Such refugees, being within the High Commissioner's mandate, are usually referred to as 'mandate refugees'.

17. From the foregoing, it will be seen that a person can simultaneously be both a mandate refugee *and* a refugee under the 1951 Convention or the 1967 Protocol. He may, however, be in a country that is not bound by either of these instruments, or he may be excluded from recognition as a 'Convention refugee' by the application of the dateline or the geographic limitation. In such cases he would still qualify for protection by the High Commissioner under the terms of the Statute.

18. The above mentioned Resolution 428(V) and the Statute of the High Commissioner's Office call for co-operation between Governments and the High Commissioner's Office in dealing with refugee problems. The High Commissioner is designated as the authority charged with providing international protection to refugees, and is required inter alia to promote the conclusion and ratification of international conventions for the protection of refugees, and to supervise their application.

19. Such co-operation, combined with his supervisory function, forms the basis for the High Commissioner's fundamental interest in the process of determining refugee status under the 1951 Convention and the 1967 Protocol. The part played by the High Commissioner is reflected, to varying degrees, in the procedures for the determination of refugee status established by a number of Governments.

F. Regional instruments relating to refugees

20. In addition to the 1951 Convention and the 1967 Protocol, and the Statute of the Office of the United Nations High Commissioner for Refugees, there are a number of regional agreements, conventions and other instruments relating to refugees, particularly in Africa, the Americas and Europe. These regional instruments deal with such matters as the granting of asylum, travel documents and travel facilities, etc. Some also contain a definition of the term 'refugee', or of persons entitled to asylum.

21. In Latin America, the problem of diplomatic and territorial asylum is dealt with in a number of regional instruments including the Treaty on International Penal Law, (Montevideo, 1889); the Agreement on Extradition, (Caracas, 1911); the Convention on Asylum, (Havana, 1928); the Convention on Political Asylum, (Montevideo, 1933); the Convention on Diplomatic Asylum, (Caracas, 1954); and the Convention on Territorial Asylum, (Caracas, 1954).

22. A more recent regional instrument is the Convention Governing the Specific Aspects of Refugee Problems in Africa, adopted by the Assembly of Heads of State and Government of the Organization of African Unity on 10 September 1969. This Convention contains a definition of the term 'refugee', consisting of two parts: the first part is identical with the definition in the 1967 Protocol (i.e. the definition in the 1951 Convention without the dateline or geographic limitation). The second part applies the term 'refugee' to:

'every person who, owing to external aggression, occupation, foreign domination or events seriously disturbing public order in either part or the whole of his country of origin or nationality, is compelled to leave his place of habitual residence in order to seek refuge in another place outside his country of origin or nationality'.

23. The present Handbook deals only with the determination of refugee status under the two international instruments of universal scope: the 1951 Convention and the 1967 Protocol.

G. Asylum and the treatment of refugees

24. The Handbook does not deal with questions closely related to the determination of refugee status e.g. the granting of asylum to refugees or the legal treatment of refugees after they have been recognized as such.

25. Although there are references to asylum in the Final Act of the Conference of Plenipotentiaries as well as in the Preamble to the Convention, the granting of asylum is not dealt with in the 1951 Convention or the 1967 Protocol. The High Commissioner has always pleaded for a generous asylum policy in the spirit of the Universal Declaration of Human Rights and the Declaration on Territorial Asylum, adopted by the General Assembly of the United Nations on 10 December 1948 and on 14 December 1967 respectively.

26. With respect to the treatment within the territory of States, this is regulated as regards refugees by the main provisions of the 1951 Convention and 1967 Protocol (see paragraph 12(ii) above). Furthermore, attention should be drawn to Recommendation E contained in the Final Act of the Conference of Plenipotentiaries which adopted the 1951 Convention:

'The Conference

Expresses the hope that the Convention relating to the Status of Refugees will have value as an example exceeding its contractual scope and that all nations will be guided by it in granting so far as possible to persons in their territory as refugees and who would not be covered by the terms of the Convention, the treatment for which it provides.'

27. This recommendation enables States to solve such problems as may arise with regard to persons who are not regarded as fully satisfying the criteria of the definition of the term 'refugee'.

PART ONE
CRITERIA FOR THE DETERMINATION OF REFUGEE STATUS

CHAPTER I
GENERAL PRINCIPLES

28. A person is a refugee within the meaning of the 1951 Convention as soon as he fulfils the criteria contained in the definition. This would necessarily occur prior to the time at which his refugee status is formally determined. Recognition of his refugee status does not therefore make him a refugee but declares him to be one. He does not become a refugee because of recognition, but is recognized because he is a refugee.

29. Determination of refugee status is a process which takes place in two stages. Firstly, it is necessary to ascertain the relevant facts of the case. Secondly, the definitions in the 1951 Convention and the 1967 Protocol have to be applied to the facts thus ascertaine(d).

30. The provisions of the 1951 Convention defining who is a refugee consist of three parts, which have been termed respectively 'inclusion', 'cessation' and 'exclusion' clauses.

31. The inclusion clauses define the criteria that a person must satisfy in order to be a refugee. They form the positive basis upon which the determination of refugee status is made. The so-called cessation and exclusion clauses have a negative significance; the former indicate the conditions under which a refugee ceases to be a refugee and the latter enumerate the circumstances in which a person is excluded from the application of the 1951 Convention although meeting the positive criteria of the inclusion clauses.

Chapter II
Inclusion Clauses

A. Definitions

(1) Statutory Refugees

32. Article 1A(1) of the 1951 Convention deals with statutory refugees, i.e. persons considered to be refugees under the provisions of international instruments preceding the Convention. This provision states that:

> 'For the purposes of the present Convention, the term 'refugee' shall apply to any person who:(1) Has been considered a refugee under the Arrangements of 12 May 1926 and 30 June 1928 or under the Conventions of 28 October 1933 and 10 February 1938, the Protocol of 14 September 1939 or the Constitution of the International Refugee Organization;Decisions of non-eligibility taken by the International Refugee Organization during the period of its activities shall not prevent the status of refugees being accorded to persons who fulfil the conditions of paragraph 2 of this section.'

33. The above enumeration is given in order to provide a link with the past and to ensure the continuity of international protection of refugees who became the concern of the international community at various earlier periods. As already indicated (para 4 above), these instruments have by now lost much of their significance, and a discussion of them here would be of little practical value. However, a person who has been considered a refugee under the terms of any of these instruments is automatically a refugee under the 1951 Convention. Thus, a holder of a so-called 'Nansen Passport' ['Nansen Passport': a certificate of identity for use as a travel document, issued to refugees under the provisions of pre-war instruments] or a 'Certificate of Eligibility' issued by the International Refugee Organization must be considered a refugee under the 1951 Convention unless one of the cessation clauses has become applicable to his case or he is excluded from the application of the Convention by one of the exclusion clauses. This also applies to a surviving child of a statutory refugee.

(2) General definition in the 1951 Convention

34. According to article 1A(2) of the 1951 Convention the term 'refugee' shall apply to any person who:

> 'As a result of events occurring before 1 January 1951 and owing to well-founded fear of being persecuted for reasons of race, religion, nationality, membership of a particular social group or political opinion, is outside the country of his nationality and is unable or, owing to such fear, is unwilling to avail himself of the protection of that country; or who, not having a nationality and being outside the country of his former habitual residence as a result of such events, is unable or, owing to such fear, is unwilling to return to it.'

This general definition is discussed in detail below.

B. Interpretation of terms

(1) 'Events occurring before 1 January 1951'

35. The origin of this 1951 dateline is explained in paragraph 7 of the Introduction. As a result of the 1967 Protocol this dateline has lost much of its practical significance. An interpretation of the word 'events' is therefore of interest only in the small number of States parties to the 1951 Convention that are not also party to the 1967 Protocol. [See Annex IV.]

36. The word 'events' is not defined in the 1951 Convention, but was understood to mean 'happenings of major importance involving territorial or profound political changes as well as systematic programmes of persecution which are after-effects of earlier changes'. [UN Document E/1618 page 39.] The dateline refers to 'events' as a result of which, and not to the date on which, a person becomes a refugee, nor does it apply to the date on which he left his country. **A refugee may have left his country before or after the datelines,** provided that his fear of persecution is due to 'events' that occurred before the dateline or to after-effects occurring at a later date as a result of such events. [*loc. cit.*]

(2) 'well founded fear of being persecuted'

(a) General analysis

37. The phrase 'well-founded fear of being persecuted' is the key phrase of the definition. It reflects the view of its authors as to the main elements of refugee character. It replaces the earlier method of defining refugees by categories (i.e. persons of a certain origin not enjoying the protection of their country) by the general concept of 'fear' for a relevant motive. Since fear is subjective, the definition involves a subjective element in the person applying for recognition as a refugee. Determination of refugee status will therefore primarily require an evaluation of the applicant's statements rather than a judgement on the situation prevailing in this country of origin.

38. To the element of fear—a state of mind and a subjective condition—is added the qualification 'well-founded'. This implies that it is not only the frame of mind of the person concerned that determines his refugee status, but that this frame of mind must be supported by an objective situation. The term 'well-founded fear' therefore contains a subjective and an objective element, and in determining whether well-founded fear exists, both elements must be taken into consideration.

39. It may be assumed that, unless he seeks adventure or just wishes to see the world, a person would not normally abandon his home and country without some compelling reason. There may be many reasons that are compelling and understandable, but only one motive has been singled out to denote a refugee. The expression 'owing to well-founded fear of being persecuted'—for the reasons stated—by indicating a specific motive automatically makes all other reasons of escape irrelevant to the definition. It rules out such persons as victims of famine or natural disaster, unless they also have well-founded fear of persecution for one of the reasons stated. Such other motives may not, however, be altogether irrelevant to the process of determining refugee status, since all the circumstances need to be taken into account for a proper understanding of the applicant's case.

40. An evaluation of the subjective element is inseparable from an assessment of the personality of the applicant, since psychological reactions of different individuals may

not be the same in identical conditions. One person may have strong political or religious convictions, the disregard of which would make his life intolerable; another may have no such strong convictions. One person may make an impulsive decision to escape; another may carefully plan his departure.

41. Due to the importance that the definition attaches to the subjective element, an assessment of credibility is indispensable where the case is not sufficiently clear from the facts on record. It will be necessary to take into account the personal and family background of the applicant, his membership of a particular racial, religious, national, social or political group, his own interpretation of his situation, and his personal experiences—in other words, everything that may serve to indicate that the predominant motive for his application is fear. Fear must be reasonable. Exaggerated fear, however, may be well-founded if, in all the circumstances of the case, such a state of mind can be regarded as justified.

42. As regards the objective element, it is necessary to evaluate the statements made by the applicant. The competent authorities that are called upon to determine refugee status are not required to pass judgement on conditions in the applicant's country of origin. The applicant's statements cannot, however, be considered in the abstract, and must be viewed in the context of the relevant background situation. A knowledge of conditions in the applicant's country of origin—while not a primary objective—is an important element in assessing the applicant's credibility. In general, the applicant's fear should be considered well-founded if he can establish, to a reasonable degree, that his continued stay in his country of origin has become intolerable to him for the reasons stated in the definition, or would for the same reasons be intolerable if he returned there.

43. These considerations need not necessarily be based on the applicant's own personal experience. What, for example, happened to his friends and relatives and other members of the same racial or social group may well show that his fear that sooner or later he also will become a victim of persecution is well-founded. The laws of the country of origin, and particularly the manner in which they are applied, will be relevant. The situation of each person must, however, be assessed on its own merits. In the case of a well-known personality, the possibility of persecution may be greater than in the case of a person in obscurity. All these factors, e.g. a person's character, his background, his influence, his wealth or his outspokenness, may lead to the conclusion that his fear of persecution is 'well-founded'.

44. While refugee status must normally be determined on an individual basis, situations have also arisen in which entire groups have been displaced under circumstances indicating that members of the group could be considered individually as refugees. In such situations the need to provide assistance is often extremely urgent and it may not be possible for purely practical reasons to carry out an individual determination of refugee status for each member of the group. Recourse has therefore been had to so-called 'group determination' of refugee status, whereby each member of the group is regarded *prima facie* (i.e. in the absence of evidence to the contrary) as a refugee.

45. Apart from the situations of the type referred to in the preceding paragraph, an applicant for refugee status must normally show good reason why he individually fears persecution. It may be assumed that a person has well-founded fear of being persecuted if he has already been the victim of persecution for one of the reasons enumerated in the 1951 Convention. However, the word 'fear' refers not only to persons who have actually been persecuted, but also to those who wish to avoid a situation entailing the risk of persecution.

46. The expressions 'fear of persecution' or even 'persecution' are usually foreign to a refugee's normal vocabulary. A refugee will indeed only rarely invoke 'fear of persecution' in these terms, though it will often be implicit in his story. Again, while a refugee may have very definite opinions for which he has had to suffer, he may not, for psychological reasons, be able to describe his experiences and situation in political terms.

47. A typical test of the well-foundedness of fear will arise when an applicant is in possession of a valid national passport. It has sometimes been claimed that possession of a passport signifies that the issuing authorities do not intend to persecute the holder, for otherwise they would not have issued a passport to him. Though this may be true in some cases, many persons have used a legal exit from their country as the only means of escape without ever having revealed their political opinions, a knowledge of which might place them in a dangerous situation vis-à-vis the authorities.

48. Possession of a passport cannot therefore always be considered as evidence of loyalty on the part of the holder, or as an indication of the absence of fear. A passport may even be issued to a person who is undesired in his country of origin, with the sole purpose of securing his departure, and there may also be cases where a passport has been obtained surreptitiously. In conclusion, therefore, the mere possession of a valid national passport is no bar to refugee status.

49. If, on the other hand, an applicant, without good reason, insists on retaining a valid passport of a country of whose protection he is allegedly unwilling to avail himself, this may cast doubt on the validity of his claim to have 'well-founded fear'. Once recognized, a refugee should not normally retain his national passport.

50. There may, however, be exceptional situations in which a person fulfilling the criteria of refugee status may retain his national passport—or be issued with a new one by the authorities of his country of origin under special arrangements. Particularly where such arrangements do not imply that the holder of the national passport is free to return to his country without prior permission, they may not be incompatible with refugee status.

(b) Persecution

51. There is no universally accepted definition of 'persecution', and various attempts to formulate such a definition have met with little success. From Article 33 of the 1951 Convention, it may be inferred that a threat to life or freedom on account of race, religion, nationality, political opinion or membership of a particular social group is always persecution. Other serious violations of human rights—for the same reasons—would also constitute persecution.

52. Whether other prejudicial actions or threats would amount to persecution will depend on the circumstances of each case, including the subjective element to which reference has been made in the preceding paragraphs. The subjective character of fear of persecution requires an evaluation of the opinions and feelings of the person concerned. It is also in the light of such opinions and feelings that any actual or anticipated measures against him must necessarily be viewed. Due to variations in the psychological make-up of individuals and in the circumstances of each case, interpretations of what amounts to persecution are bound to vary.

53. In addition, an applicant may have been subjected to various measures not in themselves amounting to persecution (e.g. discrimination in different forms), in some cases combined with other adverse factors (e.g. general atmosphere of insecurity in the country

of origin). In such situations, the various elements involved may, if taken together, produce an effect on the mind of the applicant that can reasonably justify a claim to well-founded fear of persecution on 'cumulative grounds'. Needless to say, it is not possible to lay down a general rule as to what cumulative reasons can give rise to a valid claim to refugee status. This will necessarily depend on all the circumstances, including the particular geographical, historical and ethnological context.

(c) Discrimination

54. Differences in the treatment of various groups do indeed exist to a greater or lesser extent in many societies. Persons who receive less favourable treatment as a result of such differences are not necessarily victims of persecution. It is only in certain circumstances that discrimination will amount to persecution. This would be so if measures of discrimination lead to consequences of a substantially prejudicial nature for the person concerned, e.g. serious restrictions on his right to earn his livelihood, his right to practise his religion, or his access to normally available educational facilities.

55. Where measures of discrimination are, in themselves, not of a serious character, they may nevertheless give rise to a reasonable fear of persecution if they produce, in the mind of the person concerned, a feeling of apprehension and insecurity as regards his future existence. Whether or not such measures of discrimination in themselves amount to persecution must be determined in the light of all the circumstances. A claim to fear of persecution will of course be stronger where a person has been the victim of a number of discriminatory measures of this type and where there is thus a cumulative element involved. [See also paragraph 53.]

(d) Punishment

56. Persecution must be distinguished from punishment for a common law offence. Persons fleeing from prosecution or punishment for such an offence are not normally refugees. It should be recalled that a refugee is a victim—or potential victim—of injustice, not a fugitive from justice.

57. The above distinction may, however, occasionally be obscured. In the first place, a person guilty of a common law offence may be liable to excessive punishment, which may amount to persecution within the meaning of the definition. Moreover, penal prosecution for a reason mentioned in the definition (for example, in respect of 'illegal' religious instruction given to a child) may in itself amount to persecution.

58. Secondly, there may be cases in which a person, besides fearing prosecution or punishment for a common law crime, may also have 'well-founded fear of persecution'. In such cases the person concerned is a refugee. It may, however, be necessary to consider whether the crime in question is not of such a serious character as to bring the applicant within the scope of one of the exclusion clauses. [See paragraphs 144 to 156.]

59. In order to determine whether prosecution amounts to persecution, it will also be necessary to refer to the laws of the country concerned, for it is possible for a law not to be in conformity with accepted human rights standards. More often, however, it may not be the law but its application that is discriminatory. Prosecution for an offence against 'public order', e.g. for distribution of pamphlets, could for example be a vehicle for the persecution of the individual on the grounds of the political content of the publication.

60. In such cases, due to the obvious difficulty involved in evaluating the laws of another country, national authorities may frequently have to take decisions by using their own national legislation as a yardstick. Moreover, recourse may usefully be had to the principles set out in the various international instruments relating to human rights, in particular the International Covenants on Human Rights, which contain binding commitments for the States parties and are instruments to which many States parties to the 1951 Convention have acceded.

(e) Consequences of unlawful departure or unauthorized stay outside country of origin

61. The legislation of certain States imposes severe penalties on nationals who depart from the country in an unlawful manner or remain abroad without authorization. Where there is reason to believe that a person, due to his illegal departure or unauthorized stay abroad is liable to such severe penalties his recognition as a refugee will be justified if it can be shown that his motives for leaving or remaining outside the country are related to the reasons enumerated in Article 1A(2) of the 1951 Convention (see paragraph 66 below).

(f) Economic migrants distinguished from refugees

62. A migrant is a person who, for reasons other than those contained in the definition, voluntarily leaves his country in order to take up residence elsewhere. He may be moved by the desire for change or adventure, or by family or other reasons of a personal nature. If he is moved exclusively by economic considerations, he is an economic migrant and not a refugee.

63. The distinction between an economic migrant and a refugee is, however, sometimes blurred in the same way as the distinction between economic and political measures in an applicant's country of origin is not always clear. Behind economic measures affecting a person's livelihood there may be racial, religious or political aims or intentions directed against a particular group. Where economic measures destroy the economic existence of a particular section of the population (e.g. withdrawal of trading rights from, or discriminatory or excessive taxation of, a specific ethnic or religious group), the victims may according to the circumstances become refugees on leaving the country.

64. Whether the same would apply to victims of general economic measures (i.e. those that are applied to the whole population without discrimination) would depend on the circumstances of the case. Objections to general economic measures are not by themselves good reasons for claiming refugee status. On the other hand, what appears at first sight to be primarily an economic motive for departure may in reality also involve a political element, and it may be the political opinions of the individual that expose him to serious consequences, rather than his objections to the economic measures themselves.

(g) Agents of persecution

65. Persecution is normally related to action by the authorities of a country. It may also emanate from sections of the population that do not respect the standards established by the laws of the country concerned. A case in point may be religious intolerance,

amounting to persecution, in a country otherwise secular, but where sizeable fractions of the population do not respect the religious beliefs of their neighbours. Where serious discriminatory or other offensive acts are committed by the local populace, they can be considered as persecution if they are knowingly tolerated by the authorities, or if the authorities refuse, or prove unable, to offer effective protection.

(3) 'for reasons of race, religion, nationality, membership of a particular social group or political opinion'

(a) General analysis

66. In order to be considered a refugee, a person must show well-founded fear of persecution for one of the reasons stated above. It is immaterial whether the persecution arises from any single one of these reasons or from a combination of two or more of them. Often the applicant himself may not be aware of the reasons for the persecution feared. It is not, however, his duty to analyse his case to such an extent as to identify the reasons in detail.

67. It is for the examiner, when investigating the facts of the case, to ascertain the reason or reasons for the persecution feared and to decide whether the definition in the 1951 Convention is met with in this respect. It is evident that the reasons for persecution under these various headings will frequently overlap. Usually there will be more than one element combined in one person, e.g. a political opponent who belongs to a religious or national group, or both, and the combination of such reasons in his person may be relevant in evaluating his well-founded fear.

(b) Race

68. Race, in the present connexion, has to be understood in its widest sense to include all kinds of ethnic groups that are referred to as 'races' in common usage. Frequently it will also entail membership of a specific social group of common descent forming a minority within a larger population. Discrimination for reasons of race has found worldwide condemnation as one of the most striking violations of human rights. Racial discrimination, therefore, represents an important element in determining the existence of persecution.

69. Discrimination on racial grounds will frequently amount to persecution in the sense of the 1951 Convention. This will be the case if, as a result of racial discrimination, a person's human dignity is affected to such an extent as to be incompatible with the most elementary and inalienable human rights, or where the disregard of racial barriers is subject to serious consequences.

70. The mere fact of belonging to a certain racial group will normally not be enough to substantiate a claim to refugee status. There may, however, be situations where, due to particular circumstances affecting the group, such membership will in itself be sufficient ground to fear persecution.

(c) Religion

71. The Universal Declaration of Human Rights and the Human Rights Covenant proclaim the right to freedom of thought, conscience and religion, which right includes the

freedom of a person to change his religion and his freedom to manifest it in public or private, in teaching, practice, worship and observance.

72. Persecution for 'reasons of religion' may assume various forms, e.g. prohibition of membership of a religious community, of worship in private or in public, of religious instruction, or serious measures of discrimination imposed on persons because they practise their religion or belong to a particular religious community.

73. Mere membership of a particular religious community will normally not be enough to substantiate a claim to refugee status. There may, however, be special circumstances where mere membership can be a sufficient ground.

(d) Nationality

74. The term 'nationality' in this context is not to be understood only as 'citizenship'. It refers also to membership of an ethnic or linguistic group and may occasionally overlap with the term 'race'. Persecution for reasons of nationality may consist of adverse attitudes and measures directed against a national (ethnic, linguistic) minority and in certain circumstances the fact of belonging to such a minority may in itself give rise to well-founded fear of persecution.

75. The co-existence within the boundaries of a State of two or more national (ethnic, linguistic) groups may create situations of conflict and also situations of persecution or danger of persecution. It may not always be easy to distinguish between persecution for reasons of nationality and persecution for reasons of political opinion when a conflict between national groups is combined with political movements, particularly where a political movement is identified with a specific 'nationality'.

76. Whereas in most cases persecution for reason of nationality is feared by persons belonging to a national minority, there have been many cases in various continents where a person belonging to a majority group may fear persecution by a dominant minority.

(e) Membership of a particular social group

77. A 'particular social group' normally comprises persons of similar background, habits or social status. A claim to fear of persecution under this heading may frequently overlap with a claim to fear of persecution on other grounds, i.e. race, religion or nationality.

78. Membership of such a particular social group may be at the root of persecution because there is no confidence in the group's loyalty to the Government or because the political outlook, antecedents or economic activity of its members, or the very existence of the social group as such, is held to be an obstacle to the Government's policies.

79. Mere membership of a particular social group will not normally be enough to substantiate a claim to refugee status. There may, however, be special circumstances where mere membership can be a sufficient ground to fear persecution.

(f) Political opinion

80. Holding political opinions different from those of the Government is not in itself a ground for claiming refugee status, and an applicant must show that he has a fear of persecution for holding such opinions. This pre-supposes that the applicant holds opinions

not tolerated by the authorities, which are critical of their policies or methods. It also presupposes that such opinions have come to the notice of the authorities or are attributed by them to the applicant. The political opinions of a teacher or writer may be more manifest than those of a person in a less exposed position. The relative importance or tenacity of the applicant's opinions—in so far as this can be established from all the circumstances of the case—will also be relevant.

81. While the definition speaks of persecution 'for reasons of political opinion' it may not always be possible to establish a causal link between the opinion expressed and the related measures suffered or feared by the applicant. Such measures have only rarely been based expressly on 'opinion'. More frequently, such measures take the form of sanctions for alleged criminal acts against the ruling power. It will, therefore, be necessary to establish the applicant's political opinion, which is at the root of his behaviour, and the fact that it has led or may lead to the persecution that he claims to fear.

82. As indicated above, persecution 'for reasons of political opinion' implies that an applicant holds an opinion that either has been expressed or has come to the attention of the authorities. There may, however, also be situations in which the applicant has not given any expression to his opinions. Due to the strength of his convictions, however, it may be reasonable to assume that his opinions will sooner or later find expression and that the applicant will, as a result, come into conflict with the authorities. Where this can reasonably be assumed, the applicant can be considered to have fear of persecution for reasons of political opinion.

83. An applicant claiming fear of persecution because of political opinion need not show that the authorities of his country of origin knew of his opinions before he left the country. He may have concealed his political opinion and never have suffered any discrimination or persecution. However, the mere fact of refusing to avail himself of the protection of his Government, or a refusal to return, may disclose the applicant's true state of mind and give rise to fear of persecution. In such circumstances the test of well-founded fear would be based on an assessment of the consequences that an applicant having certain political dispositions would have to face if he returned. This applies particularly to the so-called refugee '*sur place*'. [See paragraphs 94 to 96.]

84. Where a person is subject to prosecution or punishment for a political offence, a distinction may have to be drawn according to whether the prosecution is for political *opinion* or for politically-motivated acts. If the prosecution pertains to a punishable act committed out of political motives, and if the anticipated punishment is in conformity with the general law of the country concerned, fear of such prosecution will not in itself make the applicant a refugee.

85. Whether a political offender can also be considered a refugee will depend upon various other factors. Prosecution for an offence may, depending upon the circumstances, be a pretext for punishing the offender for his political opinions or the expression thereof. Again, there may be reason to believe that a political offender would be exposed to excessive or arbitrary punishment for the alleged offence. Such excessive or arbitrary punishment will amount to persecution.

86. In determining whether a political offender can be considered a refugee, regard should also be had to the following elements: personality of the applicant, his political opinion, the motive behind the act, the nature of the act committed, the nature of the prosecution and its motives; finally, also, the nature of the law on which the prosecution is based. These elements may go to show that the person concerned has a fear of persecution

and not merely a fear of prosecution and punishment—within the law—for an act committed by him.

(4) 'is outside the country of his nationality'

(a) General analysis

87. In this context, 'nationality' refers to 'citizenship'. The phrase 'is outside the country of his nationality' relates to persons who have a nationality, as distinct from stateless persons. In the majority of cases, refugees retain the nationality of their country of origin.

88. It is a general requirement for refugee status that an applicant who has a nationality be outside the country of his nationality. There are no exceptions to this rule. International protection cannot come into play as long as a person is within the territorial jurisdiction of his home country. [In certain countries, particularly in Latin America, there is a custom of 'diplomatic asylum', i.e. granting refuge to political fugitives in foreign embassies. While a person thus sheltered may be considered to be outside his country's *jurisdiction*, he is not outside its territory and cannot therefore be considered under the terms of the 1951 Convention. The former notion of the 'extraterritoriality' of embassies has lately been replaced by the term 'inviolability' used in the 1961 Vienna Convention on Diplomatic Relations.]

89. Where, therefore, an applicant alleges fear of persecution in relation to the country of his nationality, it should be established that he does in fact possess the nationality of that country. There may, however, be uncertainty as to whether a person has a nationality. He may not know himself, or he may wrongly claim to have a particular nationality or to be stateless. Where his nationality cannot be clearly established, his refugee status should be determined in a similar manner to that of a stateless person, i.e. instead of the country of his nationality, the country of his former habitual residence will have to be taken into account. [See paragraphs 101 to 105.]

90. As mentioned above, an applicant's well-founded fear of persecution must be in relation to the country of his nationality. As long as he has no fear in relation to the country of his nationality, he can be expected to avail himself of that country's protection. He is not in need of international protection and is therefore not a refugee.

91. The fear of being persecuted need not always extend to the whole territory of the refugee's country of nationality. Thus in ethnic clashes or in cases of grave disturbances involving civil war conditions, persecution of a specific ethnic or national group may occur in only one part of the country.

In such situations, a person will not be excluded from refugee status merely because he could have sought refuge in another part of the same country, if under all the circumstances it would not have been reasonable to expect him to do so.

92. The situation of persons having more than one nationality is dealt with in paragraphs 106 and 107 below.

93. Nationality may be proved by the possession of a national passport. Possession of such a passport creates a *prima facie* presumption that the holder is a national of the country of issue, unless the passport itself states otherwise. A person holding a passport showing him to be a national of the issuing country, but who claims that he does not possess that country's nationality, must substantiate his claim, for example, by showing

that the passport is a so-called 'passport of convenience' (an apparently regular national passport that is sometimes issued by a national authority to non-nationals). However, a mere assertion by the holder that the passport was issued to him as a matter of convenience for travel purposes only is not sufficient to rebut the presumption of nationality. In certain cases, it might be possible to obtain information from the authority that issued the passport. If such information cannot be obtained, or cannot be obtained within reasonable time, the examiner will have to decide on the credibility of the applicant's assertion in weighing all other elements of his story.

(b) Refugees '*sur place*'

94. The requirement that a person must be outside his country to be a refugee does not mean that he must necessarily have left that country illegally, or even that he must have left it on account of well-founded fear. He may have decided to ask for recognition of his refugee status after having already been abroad for some time. A person who was not a refugee when he left his country, but who becomes a refugee at a later date, is called a refugee '*sur place*'.

95. A person becomes a refugee '*sur place*' due to circumstances arising in his country of origin during his absence. Diplomats and other officials serving abroad, prisoners of war, students, migrant workers and others have applied for refugee status during their residence abroad and have been recognized as refugees.

96. A person may become a refugee '*sur place*' as a result of his own actions, such as associating with refugees already recognized, or expressing his political views in his country of residence. Whether such actions are sufficient to justify a well-founded fear of persecution must be determined by a careful examination of the circumstances. Regard should be had in particular to whether such actions may have come to the notice of the authorities of the person's country of origin and how they are likely to be viewed by those authorities.

(5) '*and is unable or, owing to such fear, is unwilling to avail himself of the protection of that country*'

97. Unlike the phrase dealt with under (6) below, the present phrase relates to persons who have a nationality. Whether unable or unwilling to avail himself of the protection of his Government, a refugee is always a person who does not enjoy such protection.

98. Being *unable* to avail himself of such protection implies circumstances that are beyond the will of the person concerned. There may, for example, be a state of war, civil war or other grave disturbance, which prevents the country of nationality from extending protection or makes such protection ineffective. Protection by the country of nationality may also have been denied to the applicant. Such denial of protection may confirm or strengthen the applicant's fear of persecution, and may indeed be an element of persecution.

99. What constitutes a refusal of protection must be determined according to the circumstances of the case. If it appears that the applicant has been denied services (e.g., refusal of a national passport or extension of its validity, or denial of admittance to the home territory) normally accorded to his co-nationals, this may constitute a refusal of protection within the definition.

100. The term *unwilling* refers to refugees who refuse to accept the protection of the Government of the country of their nationality. [UN Document E/1618, page 39.] It is qualified by the phrase 'owing to such fear'. Where a person is willing to avail himself of the protection of his home country, such willingness would normally be incompatible with a claim that he is outside that country 'owing to well-founded fear of persecution'. Whenever the protection of the country of nationality is available, and there is no ground based on well-founded fear for refusing it, the person concerned is not in need of international protection and is not a refugee.

> *(6) 'or who, not having a nationality and being outside the country of his former habitual residence as a result of such events, is unable or, owing to such fear, is unwilling to return to it'*

101. This phrase, which relates to stateless refugees, is parallel to the preceding phrase, which concerns refugees who have a nationality. In the case of stateless refugees, the 'country of nationality' is replaced by 'the country of his former habitual residence', and the expression 'unwilling to avail himself of the protection...' is replaced by the words 'unwilling to return to it'. In the case of a stateless refugee, the question of 'availment of protection' of the country of his former habitual residence does not, of course, arise. Moreover, once a stateless person has abandoned the country of his former habitual residence for the reasons indicated in the definition, he is usually unable to return.

102. It will be noted that not all stateless persons are refugees. They must be outside the country of their former habitual residence for the reasons indicated in the definition. Where these reasons do not exist, the stateless person is not a refugee.

103. Such reasons must be examined in relation to the country of 'former habitual residence' in regard to which fear is alleged. This was defined by the drafters of the 1951 Convention as 'the country in which he had resided and where he had suffered or fears he would suffer persecution if he returned'. [*loc. cit.*]

104. A stateless person may have more than one country of former habitual residence, and he may have a fear of persecution in relation to more than one of them. The definition does not require that he satisfies the criteria in relation to all of them.

105. Once a stateless person has been determined a refugee in relation to 'the country of his former habitual residence', any further change of country of habitual residence will not affect his refugee status.

> *(7) Dual or multiple nationality*

Article 1A(2), paragraph 2, of the 1951 Convention:

> 'In the case of a person who has more than one nationality, the term 'the country of his nationality' shall mean each of the countries of which he is a national, and a person shall not be deemed to be lacking the protection of the country of his nationality if, without any valid reason based on well-founded fear, he has not availed himself of the protection of one of the countries of which he is a national.'

106. This clause, which is largely self-explanatory, is intended to exclude from refugee status all persons with dual or multiple nationality who can avail themselves of the protection of at least one of the countries of which they are nationals. Wherever available, national protection takes precedence over international protection.

107. In examining the case of an applicant with dual or multiple nationality, it is necessary, however, to distinguish between the possession of a nationality in the legal sense and the availability of protection by the country concerned. There will be cases where the applicant has the nationality of a country in regard to which he alleges no fear, but such nationality may be deemed to be ineffective as it does not entail the protection normally granted to nationals. In such circumstances, the possession of the second nationality would not be inconsistent with refugee status. As a rule, there should have been a request for, and a refusal of, protection before it can be established that a given nationality is ineffective. If there is not explicit refusal of protection, absence of a reply within reasonable time may be considered a refusal.

(8) Geographical scope

108. At the time when the 1951 Convention was drafted, there was a desire by a number of States not to assume obligations the extent of which could not be foreseen. This desire led to the inclusion of the 1951 dateline, to which reference has already been made (paragraphs 35 and 36 above). In response to the wish of certain Governments, the 1951 Convention also gave to Contracting States the possibility of limiting their obligations under the Convention to persons who had become refugees as a result of events occurring in Europe.

109. Accordingly, Article 1B of the 1951 Convention states that:

> '(1) For the purposes of this Convention, the words "events occurring before 1 January 1951" in Article 1, Section A, shall be understood to mean either
>> (a) "events occurring in Europe before 1 January 1951", or
>> (b) "events occurring in Europe and elsewhere before 1 January 1951";
>
> and each Contracting State shall make a declaration at the time of signature, ratification or accession, specifying which of these meanings it applies for the purposes of its obligations under this Convention.
>
> (2) Any Contracting State which has adopted alternative (a) may at any time extend its obligations by adopting alternative (b) by means of a notification addressed to the Secretary-General of the United Nations.'

110. Of the States parties to the 1951 Convention, at the time of writing 9 still adhere to alternative (a), 'events occurring in Europe'. [See Annex IV.] While refugees from other parts of the world frequently obtain asylum in some of these countries, they are not normally accorded refugee status under the 1951 Convention.

CHAPTER III
CESSATION CLAUSES

A. General

111. The so-called 'cessation clauses' (Article 1C(1) to (6) of the 1951 Convention) spell out the conditions under which a refugee ceases to be a refugee. They are based on the consideration that international protection should not be granted where it is no longer necessary or justified.

112. Once a person's status as a refugee has been determined it is maintained unless he comes within the terms of one of the cessation clauses. [In some cases refugee status may continue even though the reasons for such status have evidently ceased to exist. Cf sub-sections (5) and (6) (paragraphs 135 to 139 below).] This strict approach towards the determination of refugee status results from the need to provide refugees with the assurance that their status will not be subject to constant review in the light of temporary changes—not of a fundamental character—in the situation prevailing in their country of origin.

113. Article 1C of the 1951 Convention provides that:

'This Convention shall cease to apply to any person falling under the terms of section A if:

(1) He has voluntarily re-availed himself of the protection of the country of his nationality; or

(2) Having lost his nationality, he has voluntarily re-acquired it; or

(3) He has acquired a new nationality, and enjoys the protection of the country of his new nationality; or

(4) He has voluntarily re-established himself in the country which he left or outside which he remained owing to fear of persecution; or

(5) He can no longer, because the circumstances in connexion with which he has been recognised as a refugee have ceased to exist, continue to refuse to avail himself of the protection of the country of his nationality;Provided that this paragraph shall not apply to a refugee falling under section A(1) of this Article who is able to invoke compelling reasons arising out of previous persecution for refusing to avail himself of the protection of the country of nationality;

(6) Being a person who has no nationality he is, because the circumstances in connexion with which he has been recognized as a refugee have ceased to exist, able to return to the country of his former habitual residence;Provided that this paragraph shall not apply to a refugee falling under section A(1) of this Article who is able to invoke compelling reasons arising out of previous persecution for refusing to return to the country of his former habitual residence.'

114. Of the six cessation clauses, the first four reflect a change in the situation of the refugee that has been brought about by himself, namely:

(1) voluntary re-availment of national protection;

(2) voluntary re-acquisition of nationality;

(3) acquisition of a new nationality;

(4) voluntary re-establishment in the country where persecution was feared.

115. The last two cessation clauses, (5) and (6), are based on the consideration that international protection is no longer justified on account of changes in the country where persecution was feared, because the reasons for a person becoming a refugee have ceased to exist.

116. The cessation clauses are negative in character and are exhaustively enumerated. They should therefore be interpreted restrictively, and no other reasons may be adduced by way of analogy to justify the withdrawal of refugee status. Needless to say, if a refugee, for whatever reasons, no longer wishes to be considered a refugee, there will be no call for continuing to grant him refugee status and international protection.

117. Article 1C does not deal with the cancellation of refugee status. Circumstances may, however, come to light that indicate that a person should never have been recognized as a refugee in the first place; e.g. if it subsequently appears that refugee status was obtained by a misrepresentation of material facts, or that the person concerned possesses another nationality, or that one of the exclusion clauses would have applied to him had all the relevant facts been known. In such cases, the decision by which he was determined to be a refugee will normally be cancelled.

B. Interpretation of terms

(1) *Voluntary Re-availment of national protection*

Article 1C(1) of the 1951 Convention:

'He has voluntarily re-availed himself of the protection of the country of his nationality;'

118. This cessation clause refers to a refugee possessing a nationality who remains outside the country of his nationality. (The situation of a refugee who has actually returned to the country of his nationality is governed by the fourth cessation clause, which speaks of a person having 're-established' himself in that country.) A refugee who has voluntarily re-availed himself of national protection is no longer in need of international protection. He had demonstrated that he is no longer 'unable or unwilling to avail himself of the protection of the country of his nationality'.

119. This cessation clause implies three requirements:
   (a) voluntariness: the refugee must act voluntarily;
   (b) intention: the refugee must intend by his action to re-avail himself of the protection of the country of his nationality;
   (c) re-availment: the refugee must actually obtain such protection.

120. If the refugee does not act voluntarily, he will not cease to be a refugee. If he is instructed by an authority, e.g. of his country of residence, to perform against his will an act that could be interpreted as a re-availment of the protection of the country of his nationality, such as applying to his Consulate for a national passport, he will not cease to be a refugee merely because he obeys such an instruction. He may also be constrained, by circumstances beyond his control, to have recourse to a measure of protection from his country of nationality. He may, for instance, need to apply for a divorce in his home country because no other divorce may have the necessary international recognition. Such an act cannot be considered to be a 'voluntary re-availment of protection' and will not deprive a person of refugee status.

121. In determining whether refugee status is lost in these circumstances, a distinction should be drawn between actual re-availment of protection and occasional and incidental contacts with the national authorities. If a refugee applies for and obtains a national passport or its renewal, it will, in the absence of proof to the contrary, be presumed that he intends to avail himself of the protection of the country of his nationality. On the other hand, the acquisition of documents from the national authorities, for which non-nationals would likewise have to apply—such as a birth or marriage certificate—or similar services, cannot be regarded as a re-availment of protection.

122. A refugee requesting protection from the authorities of the country of his nationality has only 're-availed' himself of that protection when his request has actually been granted. The most frequent case of 're-availment of protection' will be where the refugee wishes to return to his country of nationality. He will not cease to be a refugee merely by applying for repatriation. On the other hand, obtaining an entry permit or a national passport for the purposes of returning will, in the absence of proof to the contrary, be considered as terminating refugee status. [The above applies to a refugee who is still outside his country. It will be noted that the fourth cessation clause provides that any refugee will cease to be a refugee when he has voluntarily 're-established' himself in his country or nationality or former habitual residence.] This does not, however, preclude assistance being given to the repatriant—also by UNHCR—in order to facilitate his return.

123. A refugee may have voluntarily obtained a national passport, intending either to avail himself of the protection of his country of origin while staying outside that country, or to return to that country. As stated above, with the receipt of such a document he normally ceases to be a refugee. If he subsequently renounces either intention, his refugee status will need to be determined afresh. He will need to explain why he changed his mind, and to show that there has been no basic change in the conditions that originally made him a refugee.

124. Obtaining a national passport or an extension of its validity may, under certain exceptional conditions, not involve termination of refugee status (see paragraph 120 above). This could for example be the case where the holder of a national passport is not permitted to return to the country of his nationality without specific permission.

125. Where a refugee visits his former home country not with a national passport but, for example, with a travel document issued by his country of residence, he has been considered by certain States to have re-availed himself of the protection of his former home country and to have lost his refugee status under the present cessation clause. Cases of this kind should, however, be judged on their individual merits. Visiting an old or sick parent will have a different bearing on the refugee's relation to his former home country than regular visits to that country spent on holidays or for the purpose of establishing business relations.

(2) Voluntary re-acquisition of nationality

Article 1C(2) of the 1951 Convention:

'Having lost his nationality, he has voluntarily re-acquired it;'

126. This clause is similar to the preceding one. It applies to cases where a refugee, having lost the nationality of the country in respect of which he was recognized as having well-founded fear of persecution, voluntarily re-acquires such nationality.

127. While under the preceding clause (Article 1C(1)) a person having a nationality ceases to be a refugee if he re-avails himself of the protection attaching to such nationality, under the present clause (Article 1C(2)) he loses his refugee status by reacquiring the nationality previously lost. [In the majority of cases a refugee maintains the nationality of his former home country. Such nationality may be lost by individual or collective measures of deprivation of nationality. Loss of nationality (statelessness) is therefore not necessarily implicit in refugee status.]

128. The re-acquisition of nationality must be voluntary. The granting of nationality by operation of law or by decree does not imply voluntary re-acquisition, unless the nationality has been expressly or impliedly accepted. A person does not cease to be a refugee merely because he could have re-acquired his former nationality by option, unless this option has actually been exercised. If such former nationality is granted by operation of law, subject to an option to reject, it will be regarded as a voluntary reacquisition if the refugee, with full knowledge, has not exercised this option; unless he is able to invoke special reasons showing that it was not in fact his intention to reacquire his former nationality.

(3) Acquisition of a new nationality and protection

Article 1C(3) of the 1951 Convention:

'He has acquired a new nationality and enjoys the protection of the country of his new nationality;'

129. As in the case of the re-acquisition of nationality, this third cessation clause derives from the principle that a person who enjoys national protection is not in need of international protection.

130. The nationality that the refugee acquires is usually that of the country of his residence. A refugee living in one country may, however, in certain cases, acquire the nationality of another country. If he does so, his refugee status will also cease, provided that the new nationality also carries the protection of the country concerned. This requirement results from the phrase 'and enjoys the protection of the country of his new nationality'.

131. If a person has ceased to be a refugee, having acquired a new nationality, and then claims well-founded fear in relation to the country of his new nationality, this creates a completely new situation and his status must be determined in relation to the country of his new nationality.

132. Where refugee status has terminated through the acquisition of a new nationality, and such new nationality has been lost, depending on the circumstances of such loss, refugee status may be revived.

(4) Voluntary re-establishment in the country where persecution was feared

Article 1C(4) of the 1951 Convention:

'He has voluntarily re-established himself in the country which he left or outside which he remained owing to fear of persecution;'

133. This fourth cessation clause applies both to refugees who have a nationality and to stateless refugees. It relates to refugees who, having returned to their country of origin or previous residence, have not previously ceased to be refugees under the first or second cessation clauses while still in their country of refuge.

134. The clause refers to 'voluntary re-establishment'. This is to be understood as return to the country of nationality or former habitual residence with a view to permanently residing there. A temporary visit by a refugee to his former home country, not with a national passport but, for example, with a travel document issued by his country of residence, does not constitute 're-establishment' and will not involve loss of refugee status under the present clause. [See paragraph 125 above.]

(5) Nationals whose reasons for becoming a refugee have ceased to exist

Article 1C(5) of the 1951 Convention:

'He can no longer, because the circumstances in connexion with which he has been recognized as a refugee have ceased to exist, continue to refuse to avail himself of the protection of the country of his nationality;Provided that this paragraph shall not apply to a refugee falling under section A(1) of this Article who is able to invoke compelling reasons arising out of previous persecution for refusing to avail himself of the protection of the country of nationality;'

135. 'Circumstances' refer to fundamental changes in the country, which can be assumed to remove the basis of the fear of persecution. A mere—possibly transitory—change in the facts surrounding the individual refugee's fear, which does not entail such major changes of circumstances, is not sufficient to make this clause applicable. A refugee's status should not in principle be subject to frequent review to the detriment of his sense of security, which international protection is intended to provide.

136. The second paragraph of this clause contains an exception to the cessation provision contained in the first paragraph. It deals with the special situation where a person may have been subjected to very serious persecution in the past and will not therefore cease to be a refugee, even if fundamental changes have occurred in his country of origin. The reference to Article 1A(1) indicates that the exception applies to 'statutory refugees'. At the time when the 1951 Convention was elaborated, these formed the majority of refugees. The exception, however, reflects a more general humanitarian principle, which could also be applied to refugees other than statutory refugees. It is frequently recognized that a person who—or whose family—has suffered under atrocious forms of persecution should not be expected to repatriate. Even though there may have been a change of régime in his country, this may not always produce a complete change in the attitude of the population, nor, in view of his past experiences, in the mind of the refugee.

(6) Stateless Persons whose reasons for becoming a refugee have ceased to exist

Article 1C(6) of the 1951 Convention:

> 'Being a person who has no nationality he is, because the circumstances in connexion with which he has been recognized as a refugee have ceased to exist, able to return to the country of his former habitual residence;Provided that this paragraph shall not apply to a refugee falling under section A(1) of this Article who is able to invoke compelling reasons arising out of previous persecution for refusing to return to the country of his former habitual residence.'

137. This sixth and last cessation clause is parallel to the fifth cessation clause, which concerns persons who have a nationality. The present clause deals exclusively with stateless persons who are able to return to the country of their former habitual residence.

138. 'Circumstances' should be interpreted in the same way as under the fifth cessation clause.

139. It should be stressed that, apart from the changed circumstances in his country of former habitual residence, the person concerned must be *able* to return there. This, in the case of a stateless person, may not always be possible.

CHAPTER IV
EXCLUSION CLAUSES

A. General

140. The 1951 Convention, in Section D, E and F of Article 1, contains provisions whereby persons otherwise having the characteristics of refugees, as defined in Article 1, Section A, are excluded from refugee status. Such persons fall into three groups. The first group (Article 1D) consists of persons already receiving United Nations protection or assistance; the second group (Article 1E) deals with persons who are not considered to be in need of international protection; and the third group (Article 1F) enumerates the categories of persons who are not considered to be deserving of international protection.

141. Normally it will be during the process of determining a person's refugee status that the facts leading to exclusion under these clauses will emerge. It may, however, also happen that facts justifying exclusion will become known only after a person has been recognized as a refugee. In such cases, the exclusion clause will call for a cancellation of the decision previously taken.

B. Interpretation of terms

(1) *Persons Already Receiving United Nations Protection or Assistance*

Article 1D of the 1951 Convention:

> 'This Convention shall not apply to persons who are at present receiving from organs or agencies of the United Nations other than the United Nations High Commissioner for Refugees protection or assistance.
>
> When such protection or assistance has ceased for any reason, without the position of such persons being definitively settled in accordance with the relevant resolutions adopted by the General Assembly of the United Nations, these persons shall *ipso facto* be entitled to the benefits of this Convention.'

142. Exclusion under this clause applies to any person who is in receipt of protection or assistance from organs or agencies of the United Nations, other than the United Nations High Commissioner for Refugees. Such protection or assistance was previously given by the former United Nations Korean Reconstruction Agency (UNKRA) and is currently given by the United Nations Relief and Works Agency for Palestine Refugees in the Near East (UNRWA). There could be other similar situations in the future.

143. With regard to refugees from Palestine, it will be noted that UNRWA operates only in certain areas of the Middle East, and it is only there that its protection or assistance are given. Thus, a refugee from Palestine who finds himself outside that area does not enjoy the assistance mentioned and may be considered for determination of his refugee status under the criteria of the 1951 Convention. It should normally be sufficient to establish that the circumstances which originally made him qualify for protection or assistance from UNRWA still persist and that he has neither ceased to be a refugee under one of the cessation clauses nor is excluded from the application of the Convention under one of the exclusion clauses.

(2) *Persons not Considered to be in need of international protection*

Article 1E of the 1951 Convention:

> 'This Convention shall not apply to a person who is recognized by the competent authorities of the country in which he has taken residence as having the rights and obligations which are attached to the possession of the nationality of that country.'

144. This provision relates to persons who might otherwise qualify for refugee status and who have been received in a country where they have been granted most of the rights normally enjoyed by nationals, but not formal citizenship. (They are frequently referred to as 'national refugees'.) The country that has received them is frequently one where the population is of the same ethnic origin as themselves. [In elaborating this exclusion clause, the drafters of the Convention had principally in mind refugees of German extraction having arrived in the Federal Republic of Germany who were recognized as possessing the rights and obligations attaching to German nationality.]

145. There is no precise definition of 'rights and obligations' that would constitute a reason for exclusion under this clause. It may, however, be said that the exclusion operates if a person's status is largely assimilated to that of a national of the country. In particular he must, like a national, be fully protected against deportation or expulsion.

146. The clause refers to a person who has 'taken residence' in the country concerned. This implies continued residence and not a mere visit. A person who resides outside the country and does not enjoy the diplomatic protection of that country is not affected by the exclusion clause.

(3) Persons not considered to be deserving of international protection

Article 1F of the 1951 Convention:

'The provisions of this Convention shall not apply to any person with respect to whom there are serious reasons for considering that:
(a) he has committed a crime against peace, a war crime, or a crime against humanity, as defined in the international instruments drawn up to make provision in respect of such crimes;
(b) he has committed a serious non-political crime outside the country of refuge prior to his admission to that country as a refugee;
(c) he has been guilty of acts contrary to the purposes and principles of the United Nations.'

147. The pre-war international instruments that defined various categories of refugees contained no provisions for the exclusion of criminals. It was immediately after the Second World War that for the first time special provisions were drawn up to exclude from the large group of then assisted refugees certain persons who were deemed unworthy of international protection.

148. At the time when the Convention was drafted, the memory of the trials of major war criminals was still very much alive, and there was agreement on the part of States that war criminals should not be protected. There was also a desire on the part of States to deny admission to their territories of criminals who would present a danger to security and public order.

149. The competence to decide whether any of these exclusion clauses are applicable is incumbent upon the Contracting State in whose territory the applicant seeks recognition of his refugee status. For these clauses to apply, it is sufficient to establish that there are 'serious reasons for considering' that one of the acts described has been committed. Formal proof of previous penal prosecution is not required. Considering the serious consequences of exclusion for the person concerned, however, the interpretation of these exclusion clauses must be restrictive.

(a) War crimes, etc.

'(a) he has committed a crime against peace, a war crime or a crime against humanity, as defined in the international instruments drawn up to make provision in respect of such crimes.'

150. In mentioning crimes against peace, war crimes or crimes against humanity, the Convention refers generally to 'international instruments drawn up to make provision in respect of such crimes'. There are a considerable number of such instruments dating from the end of the Second World War up to the present time. All of them contain definitions of what constitute 'crimes against peace, war crimes and crimes against humanity'. The most comprehensive definition will be found in the 1945 London Agreement and Charter of the International Military Tribunal. The definitions contained in the above-mentioned London Agreement and a list of other pertinent instruments are given in Annexes V and VI.

(b) Common crimes

'(b) he has committed a serious non-political crime outside the country of refuge prior to his admission to that country as a refugee.'

151. The aim of this exclusion clause is to protect the community of a receiving country from the danger of admitting a refugee who has committed a serious common crime. It also seeks to render due justice to a refugee who has committed a common crime (or crimes) of a less serious nature or has committed a political offence.

152. In determining whether an offence is 'non-political' or is, on the contrary, a 'political' crime, regard should be given in the first place to its nature and purpose i.e. whether it has been committed out of genuine political motives and not merely for personal reasons or gain. There should also be a close and direct causal link between the crime committed and its alleged political purpose and object. The political element of the offence should also outweigh its common-law character. This would not be the case if the acts committed are grossly out of proportion to the alleged objective. The political nature of the offence is also more difficult to accept if it involves acts of an atrocious nature.

153. Only a crime committed or presumed to have been committed by an applicant 'outside the country of refuge prior to his admission to that country as a refugee' is a ground for exclusion. The country outside would normally be the country of origin, but it could also be another country, except the country of refuge where the applicant seeks recognition of his refugee status.

154. A refugee committing a serious crime in the country of refuge is subject to due process of law in that country. In extreme cases, Article 33 paragraph 2 of the Convention permits a refugee's expulsion or return to his former home country if, having been convicted by a final judgement of a 'particularly serious' common crime, he constitutes a danger to the community of his country of refuge.

155. What constitutes a 'serious' non-political crime for the purposes of this exclusion clause is difficult to define, especially since the term 'crime' has different connotations in different legal systems. In some countries the word 'crime' denotes only offences of a serious character. In other countries it may comprise anything from petty larceny to murder. In the present context, however, a 'serious' crime must be a capital crime or a very grave punishable act. Minor offences punishable by moderate sentences are not grounds for exclusion under Article 1F(b) even if technically referred to as 'crimes' in the penal law of the country concerned.

156. In applying this exclusion clause, it is also necessary to strike a balance between the nature of the offence presumed to have been committed by the applicant and the degree of persecution feared. If a person has well-founded fear of very severe persecution, e.g. persecution endangering his life or freedom, a crime must be very grave in order to exclude him. If the persecution feared is less serious, it will be necessary to have regard to the nature of the crime or crimes presumed to have been committed in order to establish whether the applicant is not in reality a fugitive from justice or whether his criminal character does not outweigh his character as a *bona fide* refugee.

157. In evaluating the nature of the crime presumed to have been committed, all the relevant factors—including any mitigating circumstances—must be taken into account. It is also necessary to have regard to any aggravating circumstances as, for example, the fact that the applicant may already have a criminal record. The fact that an applicant convicted of a serious non-political crime has already served his sentence or has been granted a pardon or has benefited from an amnesty is also relevant. In the latter case, there is a presumption that the exclusion clause is no longer applicable, unless it can be shown that, despite the pardon or amnesty, the applicant's criminal character still predominates.

158. Considerations similar to those mentioned in the preceding paragraphs will apply when a crime—in the widest sense—has been committed as a means of, or concomitant with, escape from the country where persecution was feared. Such crimes may range from the theft of a means of locomotion to endangering or taking the lives of innocent people. While for the purposes of the present exclusion clause it may be possible to overlook the fact that a refugee, not finding any other means of escape, may have crashed the border in a stolen car, decisions will be more difficult where he has hijacked an aircraft, i.e. forced its crew, under threat of arms or with actual violence, to change destination in order to bring him to a country of refuge.

159. As regards hijacking, the question has arisen as to whether, if committed in order to escape from persecution, it constitutes a serious non-political crime within the meaning of the present exclusion clause. Governments have considered the unlawful seizure of aircraft on several occasions within the framework of the United Nations, and a number of international conventions have been adopted dealing with the subject. None of these instruments mentions refugees. However, one of the reports leading to the adoption of a resolution on the subject states that 'the adoption of the draft Resolution cannot prejudice any international legal rights or duties of States under instruments relating to the status of refugees and stateless persons'. Another report states that 'the adoption of the draft Resolution cannot prejudice any international legal rights or duties of States with respect to asylum'. [Reports of the Sixth Committee on General Assembly resolutions 2645 (XXV) United Nations document A/8716, and 2551 (XXIV), United Nations document A/7845.]

160. The various conventions adopted in this connexion [Convention on Offences and Certain Other Acts Committed on Board Aircraft, Tokyo, 14 September 1963; Convention for the Suppression of Unlawful Seizure of Aircraft, the Hague, 16 December 1970; Convention for the Suppression of Unlawful Acts against the Safety of Civil Aviation, Montreal, 23 September 1971] deal mainly with the manner in which the perpetrators of such acts have to be treated. They invariably give Contracting States the alternative of extraditing such persons or instituting penal proceedings for the act on their own territory, which implies the right to grant asylum.

161. While there is thus a possibility of granting asylum, the gravity of the persecution of which the offender may have been in fear, and the extent to which such fear is well-founded, will have to be duly considered in determining his possible refugee status under the 1951 Convention. The question of the exclusion under Article 1F(b) of an applicant who has committed an unlawful seizure of an aircraft will also have to be carefully examined in each individual case.

(c)   Acts Contrary to the purposes and principles of the United Nations

'(c) he has been guilty of acts contrary to the purposes and principles of the United Nations.'

162. It will be seen that this very generally-worded exclusion clause overlaps with the exclusion clause in Article 1F(a); for it is evident that a crime against peace, a war crime or a crime against humanity is also an act contrary to the purposes and principles of the United Nations. While Article 1F(c) does not introduce any specific new element, it is intended to cover in a general way such acts against the purposes and principles of the United Nations that might not be fully covered by the two preceding exclusion clauses. Taken in conjunction with the latter, it has to be assumed, although this is not specifically stated, that the acts covered by the present clause must also be of a criminal nature.

163. The purposes and principles of the United Nations are set out in the Preamble and Articles 1 and 2 of the Charter of the United Nations. They enumerate fundamental principles that should govern the conduct of their members in relation to each other and in relation to the international community as a whole. From this it could be inferred that an individual, in order to have committed an act contrary to these principles, must have been in a position of power in a member State and instrumental to his State's infringing these principles. However, there are hardly any precedents on record for the application of this clause, which, due to its very general character, should be applied with caution.

CHAPTER V
SPECIAL CASES

A. War refugees

164. Persons compelled to leave their country of origin as a result of international or national armed conflicts are not normally considered refugees under the 1951 Convention or 1967 Protocol. [In respect of Africa, however, see the definition in Article 1(2) of the OAU Convention concerning the Specific Aspects of Refugee Problems in Africa, quoted in paragraph 22 above.] They do, however, have the protection provided for in other international instruments, e.g. the Geneva Conventions of 1949 on the Protection of War Victims and the 1977 Protocol additional to the Geneva Conventions of 1949 relating to the protection of Victims of International Armed Conflicts. [See Annex VI, items (6) and (7).]

165. However, foreign invasion or occupation of all or part of a country can result—and occasionally has resulted—in persecution for one or more of the reasons enumerated in the 1951 Convention. In such cases, refugee status will depend upon whether the applicant is able to show that he has a 'well-founded fear of being persecuted' in the occupied territory and, in addition, upon whether or not he is able to avail himself of the protection of his government, or of a protecting power whose duty it is to safeguard the interests of his country during the armed conflict, and whether such protection can be considered to be effective.

166. Protection may not be available if there are no diplomatic relations between the applicant's host country and his country of origin. If the applicant's government is itself in exile, the effectiveness of the protection that it is able to extend may be open to question. Thus, every case has to be judged on its merits, both in respect of well-founded fear of persecution and of the availability of effective protection on the part of the government of the country of origin.

B. Deserters and persons avoiding military service

167. In countries where military service is compulsory, failure to perform this duty is frequently punishable by law. Moreover, whether military service is compulsory or not, desertion is invariably considered a criminal offence. The penalties may vary from country to country, and are not normally regarded as persecution. Fear of prosecution and punishment for desertion or draft-evasion does not in itself constitute well-founded fear of persecution under the definition. Desertion or draft-evasion does not, on the other hand, exclude a person from being a refugee, and a person may be a refugee in addition to being a deserter or draft-evader.

168. A person is clearly not a refugee if his only reason for desertion or draft-evasion is his dislike of military service or fear of combat. He may, however, be a refugee if his desertion or evasion of military service is concomitant with other relevant motives for leaving or remaining outside his country, or if he otherwise has reasons, within the meaning of the definition, to fear persecution.

169. A deserter or draft-evader may also be considered a refugee if it can be shown that he would suffer disproportionately severe punishment for the military offence on account of his race, religion, nationality, membership of a particular social group or political opinion. The same would apply if it can be shown that he has well-founded fear of persecution on these grounds above and beyond the punishment for desertion.

170. There are, however, also cases where the necessity to perform military service may be the sole ground for a claim to refugee status, i.e. when a person can show that the performance of military service would have required his participation in military action contrary to his genuine political, religious or moral convictions, or to valid reasons of conscience.

171. Not every conviction, genuine though it may be, will constitute a sufficient reason for claiming refugee status after desertion or draft-evasion. It is not enough for a person to be in disagreement with his government regarding the political justification for a particular military action. Where, however, the type of military action, with which an individual does not wish to be associated, is condemned by the international community as contrary to basic rules of human conduct, punishment for desertion or draft-evasion could, in the light of all other requirements of the definition, in itself be regarded as persecution.

172. Refusal to perform military service may also be based on religious convictions. If an applicant is able to show that his religious convictions are genuine, and that such convictions are not taken into account by the authorities of his country in requiring him to perform military service, he may be able to establish a claim to refugee status. Such a claim would, of course, be supported by any additional indications that the applicant or his family may have encountered difficulties due to their religious convictions.

173. The question as to whether objection to performing military service for reasons of conscience can give rise to a valid claim to refugee status should also be considered in the light of more recent developments in this field. An increasing number of States have introduced legislation or administrative regulations whereby persons who can invoke genuine reasons of conscience are exempted from military service, either entirely or subject to their performing alternative (i.e. civilian) service. The introduction of such legislation or administrative regulations has also been the subject of recommendations by international agencies. [Cf Recommendation 816 (1977) on the Right of Conscientious Objection to Military Service, adopted at the Parliamentary Assembly of the Council of Europe at its Twenty-ninth Ordinary Session (5–13 October 1977).] In the light of these developments, it would be open to Contracting States, to grant refugee status to persons who object to performing military service for genuine reasons of conscience.

174. The genuineness of a person's political, religious or moral convictions, or of his reasons of conscience for objecting to performing military service, will of course need to be established by a thorough investigation of his personality and background. The fact that he may have manifested his views prior to being called to arms, or that he may already have encountered difficulties with the authorities because of his convictions, are relevant considerations. Whether he has been drafted into compulsory service or joined the army as a volunteer may also be indicative of the genuineness of his convictions.

C. Persons having resorted to force or committed acts of violence

175. Applications for refugee status are frequently made by persons who have used force or committed acts of violence. Such conduct is frequently associated with, or claimed to be associated with, political activities or political opinions. They may be the result of individual initiatives, or may have been committed within the framework of organized groups. The latter may either be clandestine groupings or political cum military organizations that are officially recognized or whose activities are widely acknowledged. [A number of liberation movements, which often include an armed wing, have been officially recognized by the General Assembly of the United Nations. Other liberation movements have only been recognized by a limited number of governments. Others again have no official recognition.] Account should also be taken of the fact that the use of force is an aspect of the maintenance of law and order and may—by definition—be lawfully resorted to by the police and armed forces in the exercise of their functions.

176. An application for refugee status by a person having (or presumed to have) used force, or to have committed acts of violence of whatever nature and within whatever context, must in the first place—like any other application—be examined from the standpoint of the inclusion clauses in the 1951 Convention (paragraphs 32–110 above).

177. Where it has been determined that an applicant fulfils the inclusion criteria, the question may arise as to whether, in view of the acts involving the use of force or violence committed by him, he may not be covered by the terms of one or more of the exclusion clauses. These exclusion clauses which figure in Article 1F(a) to (c) of the 1951 Convention, have already been examined (paragraphs 147 to 163 above).

178. The exclusion clause in Article 1F(a) was originally intended to exclude from refugee status any person in respect of whom there were serious reasons for considering that he has 'committed a crime against peace, a war crime, or a crime against humanity' in an official capacity. This exclusion clause is, however, also applicable to persons who have committed such crimes within the framework of various non-governmental groupings, whether officially recognized, clandestine or self-styled.

179. The exclusion clause in Article 1F(b), which refers to 'a serious non-political crime', is normally not relevant to the use of force or to acts of violence committed in an official capacity. The interpretation of this exclusion clause has already been discussed. The exclusion clause in Article 1F(c) has also been considered. As previously indicated, because of its vague character, it should be applied with caution.

180. It will also be recalled that, due to their nature and the serious consequences of their application to a person in fear of persecution, the exclusion clauses should be applied in a restrictive manner.

Chapter VI
The Principle of Family Unity

181. Beginning with the Universal Declaration of Human Rights, which states that 'the family is the natural and fundamental group unit of society and is entitled to protection by society and the State', most international instruments dealing with human rights contain similar provisions for the protection of the unit of a family.

182. The Final Act of the Conference that adopted the 1951 Convention:

'Recommends Governments to take the necessary measures for the protection of the refugee's family, especially with a view to:

(1) Ensuring that the unity of the refugee's family is maintained particularly in cases where the head of the family has fulfilled the necessary conditions for admission to a particular country.

(2) The protection of refugees who are minors, in particular unaccompanied children and girls, with special reference to guardianship and adoption.' [See Annex I.]

183. The 1951 Convention does not incorporate the principle of family unity in the definition of the term refugee. The above-mentioned Recommendation in the Final Act of the Conference is, however, observed by the majority of States, whether or not parties to the 1951 Convention or to the 1967 Protocol.

184. If the head of a family meets the criteria of the definition, his dependants are normally granted refugee status according to the principle of family unity. It is obvious, however, that formal refugee status should not be granted to a dependant if this is incompatible with his personal legal status. Thus, a dependant member of a refugee family may be a national of the country of asylum or of another country, and may enjoy that country's protection. To grant him refugee status in such circumstances would not be called for.

185. As to which family members may benefit from the principle of family unity, the minimum requirement is the inclusion of the spouse and minor children. In practice, other dependants, such as aged parents of refugees, are normally considered if they are living in the same household. On the other hand, if the head of the family is not a refugee, there is nothing to prevent any one of his dependants, if they can invoke reasons on their own account, from applying for recognition as refugees under the 1951 Convention or the 1967 Protocol. In other words, the principle of family unity operates in favour of dependants, and not against them.

186. The principle of the unity of the family does not only operate where all family members become refugees at the same time. It applies equally to cases where a family unit has been temporarily disrupted through the flight of one or more of its members.

187. Where the unity of a refugee's family is destroyed by divorce, separation or death, dependants who have been granted refugee status on the basis of family unity will retain such refugee status unless they fall within the terms of a cessation clause; or if they do not have reasons other than those of personal convenience for wishing to retain refugee status; or if they themselves no longer wish to be considered as refugees.

188. If the dependant of a refugee falls within the terms of one of the exclusion clauses, refugee status should be denied to him.

PART TWO
PROCEDURES FOR THE DETERMINATION OF REFUGEE STATUS

A. General

189. It has been seen that the 1951 Convention and the 1967 Protocol define who is a refugee for the purposes of these instruments. It is obvious that, to enable States parties to the Convention and to the Protocol to implement their provisions, refugees have to be identified. Such identification, i.e. the determination of refugee status, although mentioned in the 1951 Convention (cf. Article 9), is not specifically regulated. In particular, the Convention does not indicate what type of procedures are to be adopted for the determination of refugee status. It is therefore left to each Contracting State to establish the procedure that it considers most appropriate, having regard to its particular constitutional and administrative structure.

190. It should be recalled that an applicant for refugee status is normally in a particularly vulnerable situation. He finds himself in an alien environment and may experience serious difficulties, technical and psychological, in submitting his case to the authorities of a foreign country, often in a language not his own. His application should therefore be examined within the framework of specially established procedures by qualified personnel having the necessary knowledge and experience, and an understanding of an applicant's particular difficulties and needs.

191. Due to the fact that the matter is not specifically regulated by the 1951 Convention, procedures adopted by States parties to the 1951 Convention and to the 1967 Protocol vary considerably. In a number of countries, refugee status is determined under formal procedures specifically established for this purpose. In other countries, the question of refugee status is considered within the framework of general procedures for the admission of aliens. In yet other countries, refugee status is determined under informal arrangements, or *ad hoc* for specific purposes, such as the issuance of travel documents.

192. In view of this situation and of the unlikelihood that all States bound by the 1951 Convention and the 1967 Protocol could establish identical procedures, the Executive Committee of the High Commissioner's Programme, at its twenty-eighth session in October 1977, recommended that procedures should satisfy certain basic requirements. These *basic requirements*, which reflect the special situation of the applicant for refugee status, to which reference has been made above, and which would ensure that the applicant is provided with certain essential guarantees, are the following:

(i) The competent official (e.g. immigration officer or border police officer) to whom the applicant addresses himself at the border or in the territory of a Contracting State should have clear instructions for dealing with cases which might come within the purview of the relevant international instruments. He should be required to act in accordance with the principle of *non-refoulement* and to refer such cases to a higher authority.

(ii) The applicant should receive the necessary guidance as to the procedure to be followed.

(iii) There should be a clearly identified authority—wherever possible a single central authority—with responsibility for examining requests for refugee status and taking a decision in the first instance.

(iv) The applicant should be given the necessary facilities, including the services of a competent interpreter, for submitting his case to the authorities concerned. Applicants should also be given the opportunity, of which they should be duly informed, to contact a representative of UNHCR.

(v) If the applicant is recognized as a refugee, he should be informed accordingly and issued with documentation certifying his refugee status.

(vi) If the applicant is not recognized, he should be given a reasonable time to appeal for a formal reconsideration of the decision, either to the same or to a different authority, whether administrative or judicial, according to the prevailing system.

(vii) The applicant should be permitted to remain in the country pending a decision on his initial request by the competent authority referred to in paragraph (iii) above, unless it has been established by that authority that his request is clearly abusive. He should also be permitted to remain in the country while an appeal to a higher administrative authority or to the courts is pending. [Official Records of the General Assembly, Thirty-second Session, Supplement No. 12 (A/32/12/Add.1), paragraph 53(6)(e).]

193. The Executive Committee also expressed the hope that all States parties to the 1951 Convention and the 1967 Protocol that had not yet done so would take appropriate steps to establish such procedures in the near future and give favourable consideration to UNHCR participation in such procedures in appropriate form.

194. Determination of refugee status, which is closely related to questions of asylum and admission, is of concern to the High Commissioner in the exercise of his function to provide international protection for refugees. In a number of countries, the Office of the High Commissioner participates in various forms, in procedures for the determination of refugee status. Such participation is based on Article 35 of the 1951 Convention and the corresponding Article II of the 1967 Protocol, which provide for co-operation by the Contracting States with the High Commissioner's Office.

B. Establishing the facts

(1) Principles and methods

195. The relevant facts of the individual case will have to be furnished in the first place by the applicant himself. It will then be up to the person charged with determining his status (the examiner) to assess the validity of any evidence and the credibility of the applicant's statements.

196. It is a general legal principle that the burden of proof lies on the person submitting a claim. Often, however, an applicant may not be able to support his statements by documentary or other proof, and cases in which an applicant can provide evidence of all his statements will be the exception rather than the rule. In most cases a person fleeing from persecution will have arrived with the barest necessities and very frequently even without personal documents. Thus, while the burden of proof in principle rests on the applicant, the duty to ascertain and evaluate all the relevant facts is shared between the applicant and the examiner. Indeed, in some cases, it may be for the examiner to use all the means at his disposal to produce the necessary evidence in support of the application. Even such independent research may not, however, always be successful and there may also be statements that are not susceptible of proof. In such cases, if the applicant's account appears credible, he should, unless there are good reasons to the contrary, be given the benefit of the doubt.

197. The requirement of evidence should thus not be too strictly applied in view of the difficulty of proof inherent in the special situation in which an applicant for refugee status finds himself. Allowance for such possible lack of evidence does not, however, mean that unsupported statements must necessarily be accepted as true if they are inconsistent with the general account put forward by the applicant.

198. A person who, because of his experiences, was in fear of the authorities in his own country may still feel apprehensive vis-à-vis any authority. He may therefore be afraid to speak freely and give a full and accurate account of his case.

199. While an initial interview should normally suffice to bring an applicant's story to light, it may be necessary for the examiner to clarify any apparent inconsistencies and to resolve any contradictions in a further interview, and to find an explanation for any misrepresentation or concealment of material facts. Untrue statements by themselves are not a reason for refusal of refugee status and it is the examiner's responsibility to evaluate such statements in the light of all the circumstances of the case.

200. An examination in depth of the different methods of fact-finding is outside the scope of the present Handbook. It may be mentioned, however, that basic information is frequently given, in the first instance, by completing a standard questionnaire. Such basic information will normally not be sufficient to enable the examiner to reach a decision, and one or more personal interviews will be required. It will be necessary for the examiner to gain the confidence of the applicant in order to assist the latter in putting forward his case and in fully explaining his options and feelings. In creating such a climate of confidence it is, of course, of the utmost importance that the applicant's statements will be treated as confidential and that he be so informed.

201. Very frequently the fact-finding process will not be complete until a wide range of circumstances has been ascertained. Taking isolated incidents out of context may be misleading. The cumulative effect of the applicant's experience must be taken into account. Where no single incident stands out above the others, sometimes a small incident may be 'the last straw'; and although no single incident may be sufficient, all the incidents related by the applicant taken together, could make his fear 'well-founded' (see paragraph 53 above).

202. Since the examiner's conclusion on the facts of the case and his personal impression of the applicant will lead to a decision that affects human lives, he must apply the criteria in a spirit of justice and understanding and his judgement should not, of course, be influenced by the personal consideration that the applicant may be an 'undeserving case'.

(2) Benefit of the doubt

203. After the applicant has made a genuine effort to substantiate his story there may still be a lack of evidence for some of his statements. As explained above (paragraph 196), it is hardly possible for a refugee to 'prove' every part of his case and, indeed, if this were a requirement the majority of refugees would not be recognized. It is therefore frequently necessary to give the applicant the benefit of the doubt.

204. The benefit of the doubt should, however, only be given when all available evidence has been obtained and checked and when the examiner is satisfied as to the applicant's general credibility. The applicant's statements must be coherent and plausible, and must not run counter to generally known facts.

(3) Summary

205. The process of ascertaining and evaluating the facts can therefore be summarized as follows:

(a) The *applicant* should:

(i) Tell the truth and assist the examiner to the full in establishing the facts of his case.

(ii) Make an effort to support his statements by any available evidence and give a satisfactory explanation for any lack of evidence. If necessary he must make an effort to procure additional evidence.

(iii)   Supply all pertinent information concerning himself and his past experience in as much detail as is necessary to enable the examiner to establish the relevant facts. He should be asked to give a coherent explanation of all the reasons invoked in support of his application for refugee status and he should answer any questions put to him.

(b) The *examiner* should:

(i) Ensure that the applicant presents his case as fully as possible and with all available evidence.

(ii) Assess the applicant's credibility and evaluate the evidence (if necessary giving the applicant the benefit of the doubt), in order to establish the objective and the subjective elements of the case.

(iii) Relate these elements to the relevant criteria of the 1951 Convention, in order to arrive at a correct conclusion as to the applicant's refugee status.

C. Cases giving rise to special problems in establishing the facts

(1) Mentally disturbed persons

206. It has been seen that in determining refugee status the subjective element of fear and the objective element of its well-foundedness need to be established.

207. It frequently happens that an examiner is confronted with an applicant having mental or emotional disturbances that impede a normal examination of his case. A mentally disturbed person may, however, be a refugee, and while his claim cannot therefore be disregarded, it will call for different techniques of examination.

208. The examiner should, in such cases, whenever possible, obtain expert medical advice. The medical report should provide information on the nature and degree of mental illness and should assess the applicant's ability to fulfil the requirements normally expected of an applicant in presenting his case (see paragraph 205(a) above). The conclusions of the medical report will determine the examiner's further approach.

209. This approach has to vary according to the degree of the applicant's affliction and no rigid rules can be laid down. The nature and degree of the applicant's 'fear' must also be taken into consideration, since some degree of mental disturbance is frequently found

in persons who have been exposed to severe persecution. Where there are indications that the fear expressed by the applicant may not be based on actual experience or may be an exaggerated fear, it may be necessary, in arriving at a decision, to lay greater emphasis on the objective circumstances, rather than on the statements made by the applicant.

210. It will, in any event, be necessary to lighten the burden of proof normally incumbent upon the applicant, and information that cannot easily be obtained from the applicant may have to be sought elsewhere, e.g. from friends, relatives and other persons closely acquainted with the applicant, or from his guardian, if one has been appointed. It may also be necessary to draw certain conclusions from the surrounding circumstances. If, for instance, the applicant belongs to and is in the company of a group of refugees, there is a presumption that he shares their fate and qualifies in the same manner as they do.

211. In examining his application, therefore, it may not be possible to attach the same importance as is normally attached to the subjective element of 'fear', which may be less reliable, and it may be necessary to place greater emphasis on the objective situation.

212. In view of the above considerations, investigation into the refugee status of a mentally disturbed person will, as a rule, have to be more searching than in a 'normal' case and will call for a close examination of the applicant's past history and background, using whatever outside sources of information may be available.

(2) Unaccompanied minors

213. There is no special provision in the 1951 Convention regarding the refugee status of persons under age. The same definition of a refugee applies to all individuals, regardless of their age. When it is necessary to determine the refugee status of a minor, problems may arise due to the difficulty of applying the criteria of 'well-founded fear' in his case. If a minor is accompanied by one (or both) of his parents, or another family member on whom he is dependent, who requests refugee status, the minor's own refugee status will be determined according to the principle of family unity (paragraphs 181 to 188 above).

214. The question of whether an unaccompanied minor may qualify for refugee status must be determined in the first instance according to the degree of his mental development and maturity. In the case of children, it will generally be necessary to enrol the services of experts conversant with child mentality. A child—and for that matter, an adolescent—not being legally independent should, if appropriate, have a guardian appointed whose task it would be to promote a decision that will be in the minor's best interests. In the absence of parents or of a legally appointed guardian, it is for the authorities to ensure that the interests of an applicant for refugee status who is a minor are fully safeguarded.

215. Where a minor is no longer a child but an adolescent, it will be easier to determine refugee status as in the case of an adult, although this again will depend upon the actual degree of the adolescent's maturity. It can be assumed that—in the absence of indications to the contrary—a person of 16 or over may be regarded as sufficiently mature to have a well-founded fear of persecution. Minors under 16 years of age may normally be assumed not to be sufficiently mature. They may have fear and a will of their own, but these may not have the same significance as in the case of an adult.

216. It should, however, be stressed that these are only general guidelines and that a minor's mental maturity must normally be determined in the light of his personal, family and cultural background.

217. Where the minor has not reached a sufficient degree of maturity to make it possible to establish well-founded fear in the same way as for an adult, it may be necessary to have greater regard to certain objective factors. Thus, if an unaccompanied minor finds himself in the company of a group of refugees, this may—depending on the circumstances—indicate that the minor is also a refugee.

218. The circumstances of the parents and other family members, including their situation in the minor's country of origin, will have to be taken into account. If there is reason to believe that the parents wish their child to be outside the country of origin on grounds of well-founded fear of persecution, the child himself may be presumed to have such fear.

219. If the will of the parents cannot be ascertained or if such will is in doubt or in conflict with the will of the child, then the examiner, in cooperation with the experts assisting him, will have to come to a decision as to the well-foundedness of the minor's fear on the basis of all the known circumstances, which may call for a liberal application of the benefit of the doubt.

Conclusions

220. In the present Handbook an attempt has been made to define certain guidelines that, in the experience of UNHCR, have proved useful in determining refugee status for the purposes of the 1951 Convention and the 1967 Protocol relating to the Status of Refugees. In so doing, particular attention has been paid to the definitions of the term 'refugee' in these two instruments, and to various problems of interpretation arising out of these definitions. It has also been sought to show how these definitions may be applied in concrete cases and to focus attention on various procedural problems arising in regard to the determination of refugee status.

221. The Office of the High Commissioner is fully aware of the shortcomings inherent in a Handbook of this nature, bearing in mind that it is not possible to encompass every situation in which a person may apply for refugee status. Such situations are manifold and depend upon the infinitely varied conditions prevailing in countries of origin and on the special personal factors relating to the individual applicant.

222. The explanations given have shown that the determination of refugee status is by no means a mechanical and routine process. On the contrary, it calls for specialized knowledge, training and experience and—what is more important—an understanding of the particular situation of the applicant and of the human factors involved.

223. Within the above limits it is hoped that the present Handbook may provide some guidance to those who in their daily work are called upon to determine refugee status.

Annex I

Excerpt from the final act of the United Nations Conference of Plenipotentiaries on the Status of Refugees and Stateless Persons (United Nations Treaty Series, vol. 189, p. 37)
IV

The Conference adopted unanimously the following recommendations:

A.

'The Conference,

Considering that the issue and recognition of travel documents is necessary to facilitate the movement of refugees, and in particular their resettlement,

Urges Governments which are parties to the Inter-Governmental Agreement on Refugee Travel Documents signed in London 15 October 1946, or which recognize travel documents issued in accordance with the Agreement, to continue to issue or to recognize such travel documents, and to extend the issue of such documents to refugees as defined in article 1 of the Convention relating to the Status of Refugees or to recognize the travel documents so issued to such persons, until they shall have undertaken obligations under article 28 of the said Convention.'

B.

'The Conference,

Considering that the unity of the family, the natural and fundamental group of society, is an essential right of the refugee, and that such unity is constantly threatened, and

Noting with satisfaction that, according to the official commentary of the ad hoc Committee on Statelessness and Related Problems the rights granted to a refugee are extended to members of his family,

Recommends Governments to take the necessary measures for the protection of the refugee's family, especially with a view to:
(1) Ensuring that the unity of the refugee's family is maintained particularly in cases where the head of the family has fulfilled the necessary conditions for admission to a particular country,
(2) The protection of refugees who are minors, in particular unaccompanied children and girls, with special reference to guardianship and adoption.'

C.

'The Conference,

Considering that, in the moral, legal and material spheres, refugees need the help of suitable welfare services, especially that of appropriate non-governmental organizations,

Recommends Governments and inter-governmental bodies to facilitate, encourage and sustain the efforts of properly qualified organizations.'

D.

'The Conference,

Considering that many persons still leave their country of origin for reasons of persecution and are entitled to special protection on account of their position,

Recommends that Governments continue to receive refugees in their territories and that they act in concert in a true spirit of international co-operation in order that these refugees may find asylum and the possibility of resettlement.'

E.

'The Conference,

Expresses the hope that the Convention relating to the Status of Refugees will have value as an example exceeding its contractual scope and that all nations will be guided by it in granting so far as possible to persons in their territory as refugees and who would not be covered by the terms of the Convention, the treatment for which it provides.'

ANNEX II
1951 CONVENTION RELATING TO THE STATUS OF REFUGEES (UNITED NATIONS TREATY SERIES, VOL. 189, P. 137)

PREAMBLE
THE HIGH CONTRACTING PARTIES

Considering that the Charter of the United Nations and the Universal Declaration of Human Rights approved on 10 December 1948 by the General Assembly have affirmed the principle that human beings shall enjoy fundamental rights and freedoms without discrimination,

Considering that the United Nations has, on various occasions, manifested its profound concern for refugees and endeavoured to assure refugees the widest possible exercise of these fundamental rights and freedoms,

Considering that it is desirable to revise and consolidate previous international agreements relating to the status of refugees and to extend the scope of and the protection accorded by such instruments by means of a new agreement,

Considering that the grant of asylum may place unduly heavy burdens on certain countries, and that a satisfactory solution of a problem of which the United Nations has recognized the international scope and nature cannot therefore be achieved without international co-operation,

Expressing the wish that all States, recognizing the social and humanitarian nature of the problem of refugees, will do everything within their power to prevent this problem from becoming a cause of tension between States,

Noting that the United Nations High Commissioner for Refugees is charged with the task of supervising international conventions providing for the protection of Refugees, and recognizing that the effective co-ordination of measures taken to deal with this problem will depend upon the co-operation of States with the High Commissioner,

Have agreed as follows.

CHAPTER I
GENERAL PROVISIONS

Article 1 Definition of the term 'Refugee'

A. For the purposes of the present Convention, the term 'refugee' shall apply to any person who:

(1) Has been considered a refugee under the Arrangements of 12 May 1926 and 30 June 1928 or under the Conventions of 28 October 1933 and 10 February 1938, the Protocol of 14 September 1939 or the Constitution of the International Refugee Organization;

Decisions of non-eligibility taken by the International Refugee Organization during the period of its activities shall not prevent the status of refugee being accorded to persons who fulfil the conditions of paragraph 2 of this section;

(2) As a result of events occurring before 1 January 1951 and owing to wellfounded fear of being persecuted for reasons of race, religion, nationality, membership of a particular social group or political opinion, is outside the country of his nationality and is unable or, owing to such fear, is unwilling to avail himself of the protection of that country; or who, not having a nationality and being outside the country of his former habitual residence as a result of such events, is unable or, owing to such fear, is unwilling to return to it.

In the case of a person who has more than one nationality, the term 'the country of his nationality' shall mean each of the countries of which he is a national, and a person shall not be deemed to be lacking the protection of the country of his nationality if, without any valid reason based on well-founded fear, he has not availed himself of the protection of one of the countries of which he is a national.

B. (1) For the purposes of this Convention, the words 'events occurring before 1 January 1951' in Article 1, Section A, shall be understood to mean either:

(a) 'events occurring in Europe before 1 January 1951' or

(b) 'events occurring in Europe or elsewhere before 1 January 1951' and each Contracting State shall make a declaration at the time of signature, ratification or accession, specifying which of these meanings it applies for the purpose of its obligations under this Convention.

(2) Any Contracting State which has adopted alternative (a) may at any time extend its obligations by adopting alternative (b) by means of a notification addressed to the Secretary-General of the United Nations.

C. This Convention shall cease to apply to any person falling under the terms of Section A if:

(1) He has voluntarily re-availed himself of the protection of the country of his nationality; or

(2) Having lost his nationality, he has voluntarily re-acquired it; or

(3) He has acquired a new nationality, and enjoys the protection of the country of his new nationality; or

(4) He has voluntarily re-established himself in the country which he left or outside which he remained owing to fear of persecution; or

(5) He can no longer, because the circumstances in connexion with which he has been recognized as a refugee have ceased to exist, continue to refuse to avail himself of the protection of the country of his nationality;

Provided that this paragraph shall not apply to a refugee falling under section A(1) of this Article who is able to invoke compelling reasons arising out of previous persecution for refusing to avail himself of the protection of the country of nationality;

(6) Being a person who has no nationality he is, because the circumstances in connexion with which he has been recognized as a refugee have ceased to exist, able to return to the country of his former habitual residence;

Provided that this paragraph shall not apply to a refugee falling under section A(1) of this Article who is able to invoke compelling reasons arising out of previous persecution for refusing to return to the country of his former habitual residence.

D. This Convention shall not apply to persons who are at present receiving from organs or agencies of the United Nations other than the United Nations High Commissioner for Refugees protection or assistance.

When such protection or assistance has ceased for any reason, without the position of such persons being definitively settled in accordance with the relevant resolutions adopted by the General Assembly of the United Nations, these persons shall *ipso facto* be entitled to the benefits of this Convention.

E. This Convention shall not apply to a person who is recognized by the competent authorities of the country in which he has taken residence as having the rights and obligations which are attached to the possession of the nationality of that country.

F. The provisions of this Convention shall not apply to any person with respect to whom there are serious reasons for considering that:

(a) he has committed a crime against peace, a war crime, or a crime against humanity, as defined in the international instruments drawn up to make provision in respect of such crimes;

(b) he has committed a serious non-political crime outside the country of refuge prior to his admission to that country as a refugee;

(c) he has been guilty of acts contrary to the purposes and principles of the United Nations.

Article 2 General obligations

Every refugee has duties to the country in which he finds himself, which require in particular that he conform to its laws and regulations as well as to measures taken for the maintenance of public order.

Article 3 Non-discrimination

The Contracting States shall apply the provisions of this Convention to refugees without discrimination as to race, religion or country of origin.

Article 4 Religion

The Contracting States shall accord to refugees within their territories treatment at least as favourable as that accorded to their nationals with respect to freedom to practise their religion and freedom as regards the religious education of their children.

Article 5 Rights granted apart from this Convention

Nothing in this Convention shall be deemed to impair any rights and benefits granted by a Contracting State to refugees apart from this Convention.

Article 6 The term 'in the same circumstances'

For the purpose of this Convention, the term 'in the same circumstances' implies that any requirements (including requirements as to length and conditions of sojourn or residence) which the particular individual would have to fulfil for the enjoyment of the right in question, if he were not a refugee, must be fulfilled by him, with the exception of requirements which by their nature a refugee is incapable of fulfilling.

Article 7 Exemption from reciprocity

1. Except where this Convention contains more favourable provisions, a Contracting State shall accord to refugees the same treatment as is accorded to aliens generally.

2. After a period of three years' residence, all refugees shall enjoy exemption from legislative reciprocity in the territory of the Contracting States.

3. Each Contracting State shall continue to accord to refugees the rights and benefits to which they were already entitled, in the absence of reciprocity, at the date of entry into force of this Convention for that State.

4. The Contracting States shall consider favourably the possibility of according to refugees, in the absence of reciprocity, rights and benefits beyond those to which they are entitled according to paragraphs 2 and 3, and to extending exemption from reciprocity to refugees who do not fulfil the conditions provided for in paragraphs 2 and 3.

5. The provisions of paragraphs 2 and 3 apply both to the rights and benefits referred to in articles 13, 18, 19, 21 and 22 of this Convention and to rights and benefits for which this Convention does not provide.

Article 8 Exemption from exceptional measures

With regard to exceptional measures which may be taken against the person, property or interests of nationals of a foreign State, the Contracting States shall not apply such measures to a refugee who is formally a national of the said State solely on account of such nationality. Contracting States which, under their legislation, are prevented from applying the general principle expressed in this article, shall, in appropriate cases, grant exemptions in favour of such refugees.

Article 9 Provisional measures

Nothing in this Convention shall prevent a Contracting State, in time of war or other grave and exceptional circumstances, from taking provisionally measures which it considers to be essential to the national security in the case of a particular person, pending a determination by the Contracting State that that person is in fact a refugee and that the continuance of such measures is necessary in his case in the interests of national security.

Article 10 Continuity of residence

1. Where a refugee has been forcibly displaced during the Second World War and removed to the territory of a Contracting State, and is resident there, the period of such enforced sojourn shall be considered to have been lawful residence within that territory.

2. Where a refugee has been forcibly displaced during the Second World War from the territory of a Contracting State and has, prior to the date of entry into force of this Convention, returned there for the purpose of taking up residence, the period of residence before and after such enforced displacement shall be regarded as one uninterrupted period for any purposes for which uninterrupted residence is required.

Article 11 Refugee seamen

In the case of refugee regularly serving as crew members on board a ship flying the flag of a Contracting State, that State shall give sympathetic consideration to their establishment on its territory and the issue of travel documents to them on their temporary admission to its territory particularly with a view to facilitating their establishment in another country.

CHAPTER II
JURIDICAL STATUS

Article 12 Personal status

1. The personal status of a refugee shall be governed by the law of the country of his domicile or, if he has no domicile, by the law of the country of his residence.

2. Rights previously acquired by a refugee and dependent on personal status, more particularly rights attaching to marriage, shall be respected by a Contracting State, subject to compliance, if this be necessary, with the formalities required by the law of that State, provided that the right in question is one which would have been recognized by the law of that State had he not become a refugee.

Article 13 Movable and immovable property

The Contracting States shall accord to a refugee treatment as favourable as possible and, in any event, not less favourable than that accorded to aliens generally in the same circumstances as regards the acquisition of movable and immovable property and other rights pertaining thereto, and to leases and other contracts relating to movable and immovable property.

Article 14 Artistic Rights and industrial property

In respect of the protection of industrial property, such as inventions, designs or models, trade marks, trade names, and of rights in literary, artistic and scientific works, a refugee shall be accorded in the country in which he has his habitual residence the same protection as is accorded to nationals of that country. In the territory of any other Contracting State, he shall be accorded the same protection as is accorded in that territory to nationals of the country in which he has habitual residence.

Article 15 Right of association

As regards non-political and non-profit-making associations and trade unions the Contracting States shall accord to refugees lawfully staying in their territory the most favourable treatment accorded to nationals of a foreign country, in the same circumstances.

Article 16 Access to courts

1. A refugee shall have free access to the courts of law on the territory of all Contracting States.

2. A refugee shall enjoy in the Contracting State in which he has his habitual residence the same treatment as a national in matters pertaining to access to the Courts, including legal assistance and exemption from *cautio judicatum solvi*.

3. A refugee shall be accorded in the matters referred to in paragraph 2 in countries other than that in which he has his habitual residence the treatment granted to a national of the country of his habitual residence.

CHAPTER III
GAINFUL EMPLOYMENT

Article 17 Wage-earning employment

1. The Contracting State shall accord to refugees lawfully staying in their territory the most favourable treatment accorded to nationals of a foreign country in the same circumstances, as regards the right to engage in wage-earning employment.

2. In any case, restrictive measures imposed on aliens or the employment of aliens for the protection of the national labour market shall not be applied to a refugee who was already exempt from them at the date of entry into force of this Convention for the Contracting States concerned, or who fulfils one of the following conditions:

(a) He has completed three years' residence in the country;

(b) He has a spouse possessing the nationality of the country of residence. A refugee may not invoke the benefits of this provision if he has abandoned his spouse;

(c) He has one or more children possessing the nationality of the country of residence.

3. The Contracting States shall give sympathetic consideration to assimilating the rights of all refugees with regard to wage-earning employment to those of nationals, and in particular of those refugees who have entered their territory pursuant to programmes of labour recruitment or under immigration schemes.

Article 18 Self-employment

The Contracting States shall accord to a refugee lawfully in their territory treatment as favourable as possible and, in any event, not less favourable than that accorded to aliens generally in the same circumstances, as regards the right to engage on his own account in agriculture, industry, handicrafts and commerce and to establish commercial and industrial companies.

Article 19 Liberal professions

1. Each Contracting State shall accord to refugees lawfully staying in their territory who hold diplomas recognized by the competent authorities of that State, and who are desirous of practising a liberal profession, treatment as favourable as possible and, in any event, not less favourable than that accorded to aliens generally in the same circumstances.

2. The Contracting States shall use their best endeavours consistently with their laws and constitutions to secure the settlement of such refugees in the territories, other than the metropolitan territory, for whose international relations they are responsible.

Chapter IV
Welfare

Article 20 Rationing

Where a rationing system exists, which applies to the population at large and regulates the general distribution of products in short supply, refugees shall be accorded the same treatment as nationals.

Article 21 Housing

As regards housing, the Contracting States, insofar as the matter is regulated by laws or regulations or is subject to the control of public authorities, shall accord to refugees lawfully staying in their territory treatment as favourable as possible and, in any event, not less favourable than that accorded to aliens generally in the same circumstances.

Article 22 Public education

1. The Contracting States shall accord to refuges the same treatment as is accorded to nationals with respect to elementary education.

2. The Contracting States shall accord to refugees treatment as favourable as possible, and, in any event, not less favourable than that accorded to aliens generally in the same circumstances, with respect to education other than elementary education and, in particular, as regards access to studies, the recognition of foreign school certificates, diplomas and degrees, the remission of fees and charges and the award of scholarships.

Article 23 Public relief

The Contracting States shall accord to refugees lawfully staying in their territory the same treatment with respect to public relief and assistance as is accorded to their nationals.

Article 24 Labour legislation and social security

1. The Contracting States shall accord to refugees lawfully staying in their territory the same treatment as is accorded to nationals in respect of the following matters:

(a) In so far as such matters are governed by laws or regulations or are subject to the control of administrative authorities: remuneration, including family allowances where these form part of remuneration, hours of work, overtime arrangements, holidays with pay, restrictions on home work, minimum age of employment, apprenticeship and training, women's work and the work of young persons, and the enjoyment of the benefits of collective bargaining;

(b) Social security (legal provisions in respect of employment injury, occupational diseases, maternity, sickness, disability, old age, death, unemployment, family responsibilities and any other contingency which, according to national laws or regulations, is covered by a social security scheme), subject to the following limitations:

(i) There may be appropriate arrangements for the maintenance of acquired rights and rights in course of acquisition;

(ii) National laws or regulations of the country of residence may prescribe special arrangements concerning benefits or portions of benefits which are payable wholly out of public funds, and concerning allowances paid to persons who do not fulfil the contribution conditions prescribed for the award of a normal pension.

2. The right to compensation for the death of a refugee resulting from employment injury or from occupational disease shall not be affected by the fact that the residence of the beneficiary is outside the territory of the Contracting State.

3. The Contracting States shall extend to refugees the benefits of agreements concluded between them, or which may be concluded between them in the future, concerning the maintenance of acquired rights and rights in the process of acquisition in regard to social security, subject only to the conditions which apply to nationals of the States signatory to the agreements in question.

4. The Contracting States will give sympathetic consideration to extending to refugees so far as possible the benefits of similar agreements which may at any time be in force between such Contracting States and non-contracting States.

Chapter V
Administrative Measures

Article 25 Administrative assistance

1. When the exercise of a right by a refugee would normally require the assistance of authorities of a foreign country to whom he cannot have recourse, the Contracting States in whose territory he is residing shall arrange that such assistance be afforded to him by their own authorities or by an international authority.

2. The authority or authorities mentioned in paragraph 1 shall deliver or cause to be delivered under their supervision to refugees such documents or certifications as would normally be delivered to aliens by or through their national authorities.

3. Documents or certifications so delivered shall stand in the stead of the official instruments delivered to aliens by or through their national authorities, and shall be given credence in the absence of proof to the contrary.

4. Subject to such exceptional treatment as may be granted to indigent persons, fees may be charged for the services mentioned herein, but such fees shall be moderate and commensurate with those charges to nationals for similar services.

5. The provisions of this article shall be without prejudice to articles 27 and 28.

Article 26 Freedom of movement

Each Contracting State shall accord to refugees lawfully in its territory the right to choose their place of residence and to move freely within its territory, subject to any regulations applicable to aliens generally in the same circumstances.

Article 27 Identity papers

The Contracting States shall issue identity papers to any refugee in their territory who does not possess a valid travel document.

Article 28 Travel documents

1. The Contracting States shall issue to refugees lawfully staying in their territory travel documents for the purpose of travel outside their territory unless compelling reasons of national security or public order otherwise require, and the provisions of the Schedule to this Convention shall apply with respect to such documents. The Contracting States may issue such a travel document to any other refugee in their territory; they shall in particular give sympathetic consideration to the issue of such a travel document to refugees in their territory who are unable to obtain a travel document from the country of their lawful residence.

2. Travel documents issued to refugees under previous international agreements by parties thereto shall be recognized and treated by the Contracting States in the same way as if they had been issued pursuant to this article.

Article 29 Fiscal charges

1. The Contracting States shall not impose upon refugees duties, charges or taxes, of any description whatsoever, other or higher than those which are or may be levied on their nationals in similar situations.

2. Nothing in the above paragraph shall prevent the application to refugees of the laws and regulations concerning charges in respect of the issue to aliens of administrative documents including identity papers.

Article 30 Transfer of assets

1. A Contracting State shall, in conformity with its laws and regulations permit refugees to transfer assets which they have brought into its territory, to another country where they have been admitted for the purposes of resettlement.

2. A Contracting State shall give sympathetic consideration to the application of refugees for permission to transfer assets wherever they may be and which are necessary for their resettlement in another country to which they have been admitted.

Article 31 Refugees unlawfully in the country of refuge

1. The Contracting States shall not impose penalties, on account of their illegal entry or presence, on refugees who, coming directly from a territory where their life or freedom was threatened in the sense of Article 1, enter or are present in their territory without authorization, provided they present themselves without delay to the authorities and show good cause for their illegal entry or presence.

2. The Contracting States shall not apply to the movements of such refugees restrictions other than those which are necessary and such restrictions shall only be applied until their status in the country is regularized or they obtain admission into another country. The Contracting States shall allow such refugees a reasonable period and all the necessary facilities to obtain admission into another country.

Article 32 Expulsion

1. The Contracting States shall not expel a refugee lawfully in their territory save on grounds of national security or public order.

2. The expulsion of such a refugee shall be only in pursuance of a decision reached in accordance with due process of law. Except where compelling reasons of national security otherwise require, the refugee shall be allowed to submit evidence to clear himself, and to appeal to and be represented for the purpose before competent authority or a person or persons specially designated by the competent authority.

3. The Contracting States shall allow such a refugee a reasonable period within which to seek legal admission into another country. The Contracting States reserve the right to apply during that period such internal measures as they may deem necessary.

Article 33 Prohibition of expulsion or return ('refoulement')

1. No Contracting State shall expel or return ('refouler') a refugee in any manner whatsoever to the frontiers of territories where his life or freedom would be threatened on account of his race, religion, nationality, membership of a particular social group or political opinion.

2. The benefit of the present provision may not, however, be claimed by a refugee whom there are reasonable grounds for regarding as a danger to the security of the country in which he is, or who, having been convicted by a final judgement of a particularly serious crime, constitutes a danger to the community of that country.

Article 34 Naturalization

The Contracting States shall as far as possible facilitate the assimilation and naturalization of refugees. They shall in particular make every effort to expedite naturalization proceedings and to reduce as far as possible the charges and costs of such proceedings.

CHAPTER VI
EXECUTORY AND TRANSITORY PROVISIONS

Article 35 Co-operation of the national authorities with the United Nations

1. The Contracting States undertake to co-operate with the Office of the United Nations High Commissioner for Refugees, or any other agency of the United Nations which may succeed it, in the exercise of its functions, and shall in particular facilitate its duty of supervising the application of the provisions of this Convention.

2. In order to enable the Office of the High Commissioner or any other agency of the United Nations which may succeed it, to make reports to the competent organs of the United Nations, the Contracting States undertake to provide them in the appropriate form with information and statistical data requested concerning:

    (a) the condition of refugees,
    (b) the implementation of this Convention, and
    (c) laws, regulations and decrees which are, or may hereafter be, in force relating to refugees.

Article 36 Information on national legislation

The Contracting States shall communicate to the Secretary-General of the United Nations the laws and regulations which they may adopt to ensure the application of this Convention.

Article 37 Relation to previous conventions

Without prejudice to article 28, paragraph 2, of this Convention, this Convention replaces, as between parties to it, the Arrangements of 5 July 1922, 31 May 1924, 12 May 1926, 30 June 1928 and 30 July 1935, the Conventions of 28 October 1933 and 10 February 1938, the Protocol of 14 September 1939 and the Agreement of 15 October 1946.

CHAPTER VII
FINAL CLAUSES

Article 38 Settlement of disputes

Any dispute between parties to this Convention relating to its interpretation or application, which cannot be settled by other means, shall be referred to the International Court of Justice at the request of any one of the parties to the dispute.

Article 39 Signature, ratification and accession

1. This Convention shall be opened for signature at Geneva on 28 July 1951 and shall thereafter be deposited with the Secretary-General of the United Nations. It shall be open for signature at the European Office of the United Nations from 28 July to 31 August 1951 and shall be reopened for signature at the Headquarters of the United Nations from 17 September 1951 to 31 December 1952.

2. This Convention shall be open for signature on behalf of all States Members of the United Nations, and also on behalf of any other State invited to attend the Conference of Plenipotentiaries on the Status of Refugees and Stateless Persons or to which an invitation to sign will have been addressed by the General Assembly. It shall be ratified and the instruments of ratification shall be deposited with the Secretary-General of the United Nations.

3. This Convention shall be open from 28 July 1951 for accession by the States referred to in paragraph 2 of this Article. Accession shall be effected by the deposit of an instrument of accession with the Secretary-General of the United Nations.

Article 40 Territorial application clause

1. Any State may, at the time of signature, ratification or accession, declare that this Convention shall extend to all or any of the territories for the international relations of which it is responsible. Such a declaration shall take effect when the Convention enters into force for the States concerned.

2. At any time thereafter any such extension shall be made by notification addressed to the Secretary-General of the United Nations and shall take effect as from the ninetieth day after the day of receipt by the Secretary-General of the United Nations of this notification, or as from the date of entry into force of the Convention for the State concerned, whichever is the later.

3. With respect to those territories to which this Convention is not extended at the time of signature, ratification or accession, each State concerned shall consider the possibility of taking the necessary steps in order to extend the application of this Convention to such

territories, subject where necessary for constitutional reasons, to the consent of the governments of such territories.

Article 41 Federal clause

In the case of a Federal or non-unitary State, the following provisions shall apply:

(a) With respect to those articles of this Convention that come within the legislative jurisdiction of the federal legislative authority, the obligations of the Federal Government shall to this extent be the same as those of Parties which are not Federal States,

(b) With respect to those articles of this Convention that come within the legislative jurisdiction of constituent States, provinces or cantons which are not, under the constitutional system of the federation, bound to take legislative action, the Federal Government shall bring such articles with a favourable recommendation, to the notice of the appropriate authorities of States, provinces or cantons at the earliest possible moment.

(c) A Federal State Party to this Convention shall, at the request of any other Contracting State transmitted through the Secretary-General of the United Nations, supply a statement of the law and practice of the Federation and its constituent units in regard to any particular provision of the Convention showing the extent to which effect has been given to that provision by legislative or other action.

Article 42 Reservations

1. At the time of signature, ratification or accession, any State may make reservations to articles of the Convention other than to articles 1, 3, 4, 16(1), 33, 36 to 46 inclusive.

2. Any State making a reservation in accordance with paragraph 1 of this article may at any time withdraw the reservation by a communication to that effect addressed to the Secretary-General of the United Nations.

Article 43 Entry into force

1. This Convention shall come into force on the ninetieth day following the day of deposit of the sixth instrument of ratification or accession.

2. For each State ratifying or acceding to the Convention after the deposit of the sixth instrument of ratification or accession, the Convention shall enter into force on the ninetieth day following the day of deposit by such State of its instrument of ratification or accession.

Article 44 Denunciation

1. Any Contracting State may denounce this Convention at any time by a notification addressed to the Secretary-General of the United Nations.

2. Such denunciation shall take effect for the Contracting State concerned one year from the date upon which it is received by the Secretary-General of the United Nations.

3. Any State which has made a declaration or notification under article 40 may, at any time thereafter, by a notification to the Secretary-General of the United Nations, declare that the Convention shall cease to extend to such territory one year after the date of receipt of the notification by the Secretary-General.

Article 45 Revision

1. Any Contracting State may request revision of this Convention at any time by a notification addressed to the Secretary-General of the United Nations.

2. The General Assembly of the United Nations shall recommend the steps, if any, to be taken in respect of such request.

Article 46 Notifications by the Secretary-General of the United Nations

The Secretary-General of the United Nations shall inform all Members of the United Nations and non-member States referred to in article 39:

(a)   of declarations and notifications in accordance with Section B of Article 1;
(b)   of signatures, ratifications and accessions in accordance with article 39;
(c)   of declarations and notifications in accordance with article 40;
(d)   of reservations and withdrawals in accordance with article 42;
(e)   of the date on which this Convention will come into force in accordance with article 43;
(f)   of denunciations and notifications in accordance with article 44;
(g)   of requests for revision in accordance with article 45.

In faith whereof the undersigned, duly authorized, have signed this Convention on behalf of their respective Governments,

Done at Geneva, this twenty-eighth day of July, one thousand nine hundred and fifty-one, in a single copy, of which the English and French texts are equally authentic and which shall remain deposited in the archives of the United Nations, and certified true copies of which shall be delivered to all Members of the United Nations and to the non-member States referred to in article 39.

Schedule

Paragraph 1

1. The travel document referred to in article 28 of this Convention shall be similar to the specimen annexed hereto.

2. The document shall be made out in at least two languages, one of which shall be in English or French.

Paragraph 2

Subject to the regulations obtaining in the country of issue, children may be included in the travel document of a parent or, in exceptional circumstances, of another adult refugee.

Paragraph 3

The fees charged for issue of the document shall not exceed the lowest scale of charges for national passports.

Paragraph 4

Save in special or exceptional cases, the document shall be made valid for the largest possible number of countries.

Paragraph 5

The document shall have a validity of either one or two years, at the discretion of the issuing authority.

Paragraph 6

1. The renewal or extension of the validity of the document is a matter for the authority which issued it, so long as the holder has not established lawful residence in another territory and resides lawfully in the territory of the said authority. The issue of a new document is, under the same conditions, a matter for the authority which issued the former document.

2. Diplomatic or consular authorities, specially authorized for the purpose, shall be empowered to extend, for a period not exceeding six months, the validity of travel documents issued by their Governments.

3. The Contracting States shall give sympathetic consideration to renewing or extending the validity of travel documents or issuing new documents to refugees no longer lawfully resident in their territory who are unable to obtain a travel document from the country of their lawful residence.

Paragraph 7

The Contracting States shall recognize the validity of the documents issued in accordance with the provisions of article 28 of this Convention.

Paragraph 8

The competent authorities of the country to which the refugee desires to proceed shall, if they are prepared to admit him and if a visa is required, affix a visa on the document of which he is the holder.

Paragraph 9

1. The Contracting States undertake to issue transit visas to refugees who have obtained visas for a territory of final destination.

2. he issue of such visas may be refused on grounds which would justify refusal of a visa to any alien.

Paragraph 10

The fees for the issue of exit, entry or transit visas shall not exceed the lowest scale of charges for visas on foreign passports.

Paragraph 11

When a refugee has lawfully taken up residence in the territory of another Contracting State, the responsibility for the issue of a new document, under the terms and conditions of article 28, shall be that of the competent authority of that territory, to which the refugee shall be entitled to apply.

Paragraph 12

The authority issuing a new document shall withdraw the old document and shall return it to the country of issue, if it is stated in the document that it should be so returned; otherwise it shall withdraw and cancel the document.

Paragraph 13

1. ach Contracting State undertakes that the holder of a travel document issued by it in accordance with article 28 of this Convention shall be readmitted to its territory at any time during the period of its validity.

2. Subject to the provisions of the preceding sub-paragraph, a Contracting State may require the holder of the document to comply with such formalities as may be prescribed in regard to exit from or return to its territory.

3. The Contracting States reserve the right, in exceptional cases, or in cases where the refugee's stay is authorized for a specific period, when issuing the document, to limit the period during which the refugee may return to a period of not less than three months.

Paragraph 14

Subject only to the terms of paragraph 13, the provisions of this Schedule in no way affect the laws and regulations governing the conditions of admission to, transit through, residence and establishment in, and departure from, the territories of the Contracting States.

Paragraph 15

Neither the issue of the document nor the entries made thereon determine or affect the status of the holder, particularly as regards nationality.

Paragraph 16

The issue of the document does not in any way entitle the holder to the protection of the diplomatic or consular authorities of the country of issue, and does not confer on these authorities a right of protection.

ANNEX

Specimen Travel Document

The document will be in booklet form (approximately 15 × 10 centimetres).
It is recommended that it be so printed that any erasure or alteration by chemical or other means can be readily detected, and that the words 'Convention of 28 July 1951' be printed in continuous repetition on each page, in the language of the issuing country.

(Cover of booklet)

TRAVEL DOCUMENT
(Convention of 28 July 1951)

No.

(1)
TRAVEL DOCUMENT
(Convention of 28 July 1951)

This document expires on_____
unless its validity is extended or renewed._____
Name_____
Forename(s)_____
Accompanied by_____child (children)
1. This document is issued solely with a view to providing the holder with a travel document which can serve in lieu of a national passport. It is without prejudice to and in no way affects the holder's nationality.
2. The holder is authorized to return to_____
_____[state here the country whose authorities are issuing the document] on or before_____unless some
later date is hereafter specified.
[The period during which the holder is allowed to return must not be less than three months]
3. Should the holder take up residence in a country other than that which issued the present document, he must, if he wishes to travel again, apply to the competent authorities of his country of residence for a new document. [The old travel document shall be withdrawn by the authority issuing the new document and returned to the authority which issued it.][1]

(This document contains   pages, exclusive of cover.)

[1] The sentence in brackets to be inserted by Governments which so desire.

(2)
Place and date of birth
Occupation
Present residence
* Maiden name and forename(s) of wife
* Name and forename(s) of husband

Description

Height_____
Hair_____
Colour of eyes_____
Nose_____
Shape of face_____
Complexion_____

Special peculiarities_____

Children accompanying holder_____

_____

_____

_____

_____

* Strike out whichever does not apply.

(This document contains   pages, exclusive of cover).

_____

(3)

Photograph of holder and stamp of issuing authority
Finger-prints of holder (if required)

Signature of holder Sex_____

(This document contains   pages, exclusive of cover).

_____

(4)

1. This document is valid for the following countries:

_____

_____

_____

_____

2. Document or documents on the basis of which the present document is issued:

_____

_____

_____

Issued at_____

DateDate_____

Signature and stamp of authority
issuing the document:

Fee paid

(This document contains   pages, exclusive of cover).

(5)

Extension or renewal of validity

Fee paid:

From_____

To_____

Done at_____ Date_____

Signature and stamp of authority extending
or renewing the validity of the document:

_____

Extension or renewal of validity

Fee paid:

From_____

To_____

Done at _____ Date_____

Signature and stamp of authority extending
or renewing the validity of the document:

(This document contains   pages, exclusive of cover.)

_____

(6)

Extension or renewal of validity

Fee paid:

From_____

To_____

Done at _____ Date_____

Signature and stamp of authority extending
or renewing the validity of the document:

_____

Extension or renewal of validity

Fee paid:

From_____

To_____

Done at _____ Date_____

Signature and stamp of authority extending
or renewing the validity of the document:

(This document contains   pages, exclusive of cover.)

_____

(7–32)

Visas

The name of the holder of the document must be repeated in each visa.

(This document contains   pages, exclusive of cover.)

_____

ANNEX III

1967 PROTOCOL RELATING TO THE STATUS OF REFUGEES
(UNITED NATIONS, TREATY SERIES, VOL 606, P 267)

The States Parties to the present protocol,

Considering that the Convention relating to the Status of Refugees done at Geneva on 28 July 1951 (hereinafter referred to as the Convention) covers only those persons who have become refugees as a result of events occurring before 1 January 1951,

Considering that new refugee situations have arisen since the Convention was adopted and that the refugees concerned may therefore not fall within the scope of the Convention,

Considering that it is desirable that equal status should be enjoyed by all refugees covered by the definition in the Convention irrespective of the dateline 1 January 1951,

Have agreed as follows:

Article I General provision

1. The States Parties to the present Protocol undertake to apply articles 2 to 34 inclusive of the Convention to refugees as hereinafter defined.

2. For the purpose of the present Protocol, the term 'refugee' shall, except as regards the application of paragraph 3 of this article, mean any person within the definition of article 1 of the Convention as if the words 'As a result of events occurring before 1 January 1951 and...' and the words '... as a result of such events', in article 1A(2) were omitted.

3. The present Protocol shall be applied by the States Parties hereto without any geographic limitation, save that existing declarations made by States already Parties to the Convention in accordance with article 1B(1)(a) of the Convention, shall, unless extended under article 1B(2) thereof, apply also under the present Protocol.

Article II Co-operation of the national authorities with the United Nations

1. The States Parties to the present Protocol undertake to co-operate with the Office of the United Nations High Commissioner for Refugees, or any other agency of the United Nations which may succeed it, in the exercise of its functions, and shall in particular facilitate its duty of supervising the application of the provisions of the present Protocol.

2. In order to enable the Office of the High Commissioner, or any other agency of the United Nations which may succeed it, to make reports to the competent organs of the United Nations, the States Parties to the present Protocol undertake to provide them with the information and statistical data requested, in the appropriate form, concerning:

    (a) The condition of refugees;
    (b) The implementation of the present Protocol;
    (c) Laws, regulations and decrees which are, or may hereafter be, in force relating to refugees.

Article III Information on national legislation

The States Parties to the present Protocol shall communicate to the Secretary-General of the United Nations the laws and regulations which they may adopt to ensure the application of the present Protocol.

Article IV Settlement Of Disputes

Any dispute between States Parties to the present Protocol which relates to its interpretation or application and which cannot be settled by other means shall be referred to the International Court of Justice at the request of any one of the parties to the dispute.

Article V Accession

The present Protocol shall be open for accession on behalf of all States Parties to the Convention and of any other State Member of the United Nations or member of any of the specialized agencies or to which an invitation to accede may have been addressed by the General Assembly of the United Nations. Accession shall be effected by the deposit of an instrument of accession with the Secretary-General of the United Nations.

Article VI Federal clause

In the case of a Federal or non-unitary State, the following provisions shall apply:

(a) With respect to those articles of the Convention to be applied in accordance with article 1, paragraph 1, of the present Protocol that come within the legislative jurisdiction of the federal legislative authority, the obligations of the Federal Government shall to this extent be the same as those of States Parties which are not Federal States;

(b) With respect to those articles of the Convention to be applied in accordance with article I, paragraph 1, of the present Protocol that come within the legislative jurisdiction of constituent States, provinces or cantons which are not, under the constitutional system of the federation, bound to take legislative action, the Federal Government shall bring such articles with a favourable recommendation to the notice of the appropriate authorities of States, provinces or cantons at the earliest possible moment;

(c) A Federal State Party to the present Protocol shall, at the request of any other State Party hereto transmitted through the Secretary-General of the United Nations, supply a statement of the law and practice of the Federation and its constituent units in regard to any particular provision of the Convention to be applied in accordance with article I, paragraph 1, of the present Protocol, showing the extent to which effect has been given to that provision by legislative or other action.

Article VII Reservations and Declarations

1. At the time of accession, any State may make reservations in respect of article IV of the present Protocol and in respect of the application in accordance with article I of the present Protocol of any provisions of the Convention other than those contained in articles 1, 3, 4, 16(1) and 33 thereof, provided that in the case of a State Party to the Convention reservations made under this article shall not extend to refugees in respect of whom the Convention applies.

2. Reservations made by States Parties to the Convention in accordance with article 42 thereof shall, unless withdrawn, be applicable in relation to their obligations under the present Protocol.

3. Any State making a reservation in accordance with paragraph 1 of this article may at any time withdraw such reservation by a communication to that effect addressed to the Secretary-General of the United Nations.

4. Declarations made under article 40, paragraphs 1 and 2, of the Convention by a State Party thereto which accedes to the present Protocol shall be deemed to apply in respect of the present Protocol, unless upon accession a notification to the contrary is addressed by the State Party concerned to the Secretary-General of the United Nations. The provisions of article 40, paragraphs 2 and 3, and of article 44, paragraph 3, of the Convention shall be deemed to apply *mutatis mutandis* to the present Protocol.

Article VIII Entry into force

1. The present Protocol shall come into force on the day of deposit of the sixth instrument of accession.

2. For each State acceding to the Protocol after the deposit of the sixth instrument of accession, the Protocol shall come into force on the date of deposit by such State of its instrument of accession.

Article IX Denunciation

1. Any State Party hereto may denounce this Protocol at any time by a notification addressed to the Secretary-General of the United Nations.

2. Such denunciation shall take effect for the State Party concerned one year from the date on which it is received by the Secretary-General of the United Nations.

Article X Notifications by the Secretary-General of the United Nations

The Secretary-General of the United Nations shall inform the States referred to in article V above of the date of entry into force, accessions, reservations and withdrawals of reservations to and denunciations of the present Protocol, and of declarations and notifications relating hereto.

Article XI Deposit in the Archives of the Secretariat of the United Nations

A copy of the present Protocol, of which the Chinese, English, French, Russian and Spanish texts are equally authentic, signed by the President of the General Assembly and by the Secretary-General of the United Nations, shall be deposited in the archives of the Secretariat of the United Nations. The Secretary-General will transmit certified copies thereof to all States Members of the United Nations and to the other States referred to in article V above.

Annex IV

Convention relating to the Status of Refugees of 28 July 1951

(Entry into force—22 April 1954)

Protocol relating to the Status of Refugees of 31 January 1967

(Entry into force—4 October 1967)

List of States Parties

States parties to the 1951 UN Convention: 106
States parties to the 1967 Protocol: 107
States parties to both the 1951 Convention and the 1967 Protocol: 103
States parties to either one or both of these instruments: 110

I. Africa

Algeria
Angola
Benin
Botswana
Burkina Faso
Burundi
Cameroon
Cape Verde(P)
Central African Republic
Chad
Congo
Djibouti
Egypt
Equatorial Guinea
Ethiopia
Gabon

Gambia
Ghana
Guinea
Guinea Bissau
Ivory Coast
Kenya
Lesotho
Liberia
Madagascar(C)*
Malawi
Mali
Mauritania
Morocco
Mozambique
Niger
Nigeria

Rwanda
Sao Tome and Principe
Senegal
Seychelles
Sierra Leone
Somalia
Sudan
Swaziland(P)
Togo
Tunisia
Uganda
United Republic of Tanzania
Zaire
Zambia
Zimbabwe

II. Americas

Argentina
Dominican Republic
Panama
Belize
Ecuador
Paraguay
Bolivia
El Salvador

Peru
Brazil
Guatemala
Suriname
Canada
Haiti
United States of America(P)
Chile

Jamaica
Uruguay
Colombia
Nicaragua
Venezuela(P)
Costa Rica

III. Asia

China	Philippines	Japan
Israel	Iran (Islamic Republic of)	Yemen

IV. Europe

Austria	Luxembourg	Switzerland
Czechoslovakia	Romania	Ireland
France[3]	Holy See	Norway
Belgium	Malta*	Turkey*
Denmark[2]	Spain	Italy
Germany, Federal Republic of[4]	Hungary*	Poland
	Monaco(C)*	United Kingdom[6]
Cyprus	Sweden	Liechtenstein
Finland	Iceland	Portugal
Greece	Netherlands[5]	Yugoslavia

V. Oceania

Australia[1]	Samoa(C)	Papua New Guinea
New Zealand	Fiji	Tuvalu

* The five States marked with an asterisk – Hungary, Madagascar, Malta, Monaco and Turkey – have made a declaration in accordance with Article 1(B) 1 of the 1951 Convention to the effect that the words 'events occurring before 1 January 1951' in Article 1, Section A should be understood to mean 'events occurring *in Europe* before 1 January 1951'. All other States Parties apply the Convention without geographical limitation. The following two States have expressly maintained their declarations of geographical limitation with regard to the 1951 Convention upon acceding to the 1967 Protocol: Malta and Turkey. Madagascar and Monaco have not yet adhered to the 1967 Protocol.

'(C)': the three States marked with a 'C' are Parties to the 1951 Convention only.

'(P)': the four States marked with a 'P' are Parties to the 1967 Protocol only.

1 Australia extended application of the Convention to Norfolk Island.

2 Denmark declared that the Convention was also applicable to Greenland.

3 France declared that the Convention applied to all territories for the international relations of which France was responsible.

4 The Federal Republic of Germany made a separate declaration stating that the Convention and the Protocol also applied to Land Berlin.

5 The Netherlands extended application of the Protocol to Aruba.

6 The United Kingdom extended application of the Convention to the following territories for the conduct of whose international relations the Government of the United Kingdom is responsible:

Channel Islands, Falkland Islands (Malvinas), Isle of Man, St. Helena.

The United Kingdom declared that its accession to the Protocol did not apply to Jersey, but extended its application to Montserrat.

ANNEX V

EXCERPT FROM THE CHARTER OF THE INTERNATIONAL
MILITARY TRIBUNAL*

Article 6

'The Tribunal established by the Agreement referred to in Article 1 hereof for the trial and punishment of the major war criminals of the European Axis countries shall have the power to try and punish persons who, acting in the interests of the European Axis countries, whether as individuals or as members of organisations, committed any of the following crimes.

The following acts, or any of them, are crimes coming within the jurisdiction of the Tribunal for which there shall be individual responsibility:

(a) Crimes against peace: namely, planning, preparation, initiation or waging of a war of aggression, or a war in violation of international treaties, agreements or assurances, or participation in a common plan or conspiracy for the accomplishment of any of the foregoing;

(b) War crimes: namely, violations of the laws or customs of war. Such violations shall include, but not be limited to, murder, ill-treatment or deportation to slave labour or for any other purpose, of civilian population of or in occupied territory, murder or ill-treatment of prisoners of war or persons on the seas, killing of hostages, plunder of public or private property, wanton destruction of cities, towns or villages, or devastation not justified by military necessity;

(c) Crimes against humanity: namely, murder, extermination, enslavement, deportation and other inhumane acts committed against any civilian population, before or during the war; or persecutions on political, racial or religious grounds in execution of or in connection with any crime within the jurisdiction of the Tribunal, whether or not in violation of the domestic law of the country where perpetrated.

Leaders, organisers, instigators and accomplices participating in the formulation or execution of a common plan or conspiracy to commit any of the foregoing crimes are responsible for all acts performed by any persons in execution of such plan.'

Note: *See 'The Charter and Judgement of the Nürnberg Tribunal: History and Analysis' Appendix II—United Nations General Assembly—International Law Commission 1949 (A/CN.4/5 of 3 March 1949).

ANNEX VI

INTERNATIONAL INSTRUMENTS RELATING TO
ARTICLE 1F(A) OF THE 1951 CONVENTION

The main international instruments which pertain to Article 1F(a) of the 1951 Convention are as follows:

(1) the London Agreement of 8 August 1945 and Charter of the International Military Tribunal;

(2) Law No. 10 of the Control Council for Germany of 20 December 1945 for the Punishment of Persons Guilty of War Crimes, Crimes against Peace and Crimes against Humanity;

(3) United Nations General Assembly Resolution 3(1) of 13 February 1946 and 95(1) of 11 December 1946 which confirm war crimes and crimes against humanity as they are defined in the Charter of the International Military Tribunal of 8 August 1945;

(4) Convention on the Prevention and Punishment of the Crime of Genocide of 1948 (Article III); (entered into force 12 January 1951);

(5) Convention of the Non-Applicability of Statutory Limitations of War Crimes and Crimes Against Humanity of 1968 (entered into force 11 November 1970);

(6) Geneva Conventions for the protection of victims of war of 12 August 1949 (Convention for the protection of the wounded, and sick, Article 50; Convention for the protection of wounded, sick and shipwrecked, Article 51; Convention relative to the treatment of prisoners of war, Article 130; Convention relative to the protection of civilian persons, Article 147);

(7) Additional Protocol to the Geneva Conventions of 12 August 1949 Relating to the Protection of Victims of International Armed Conflicts (Article 85 on the repression of breaches of this Protocol).

The above text was reproduced by kind permission of UNHCR. Permission for any further reproduction should be requested from UNHCR.

Convention for the Protection of Human Rights and Fundamental Freedoms
as amended by Protocol No. 11
Rome, 4.XI.1950

The text of the Convention had been amended according to the provisions of Protocol No. 3 (ETS No. 45), which entered into force on 21 September 1970, of Protocol No. 5 (ETS No. 55), which entered into force on 20 December 1971 and of Protocol No. 8 (ETS No. 118), which entered into force on 1 January 1990, and comprised also the text of Protocol No. 2 (ETS No. 44) which, in accordance with Article 5, paragraph 3 thereof, had been an integral part of the Convention since its entry into force on 21 September 1970. All provisions which had been amended or added by these Protocols are replaced by Protocol No. 11 (ETS No. 155), as from the date of its entry into force on 1 November 1998. As from that date, Protocol No. 9 (ETS No. 140), which entered into force on 1 October 1994, is repealed and Protocol No. 10 (ETS No. 146) has lost its purpose.

Protocol
Protocols: No. 4 | No. 6 | No. 7
No. 12 | No. 13 | No. 14

The governments signatory hereto, being members of the Council of Europe,

Considering the Universal Declaration of Human Rights proclaimed by the General Assembly of the United Nations on 10th December 1948;

Considering that this Declaration aims at securing the universal and effective recognition and observance of the Rights therein declared;

Considering that the aim of the Council of Europe is the achievement of greater unity between its members and that one of the methods by which that aim is to be pursued is the maintenance and further realisation of human rights and fundamental freedoms;

Reaffirming their profound belief in those fundamental freedoms which are the foundation of justice and peace in the world and are best maintained on the one hand by an effective political democracy and on the other by a common understanding and observance of the human rights upon which they depend;

Being resolved, as the governments of European countries which are like-minded and have a common heritage of political traditions, ideals, freedom and the rule of law, to take the first steps for the collective enforcement of certain of the rights stated in the Universal Declaration,

Have agreed as follows:

Article 1 Obligation to respect human rights[1]

The High Contracting Parties shall secure to everyone within their jurisdiction the rights and freedoms defined in Section I of this Convention.

Section I—Rights and Freedoms[1]

Article 2 Right to life[1]

1. Everyone's right to life shall be protected by law. No one shall be deprived of his life intentionally save in the execution of a sentence of a court following his conviction of a crime for which this penalty is provided by law.

2. Deprivation of life shall not be regarded as inflicted in contravention of this article when it results from the use of force which is no more than absolutely necessary:

    (a) in defence of any person from unlawful violence;

    (b) in order to effect a lawful arrest or to prevent the escape of a person lawfully detained;

    (c) in action lawfully taken for the purpose of quelling a riot or insurrection.

Article 3 Prohibition of torture[1]

No one shall be subjected to torture or to inhuman or degrading treatment or punishment.

Article 4 Prohibition of slavery and forced labour[1]

1. No one shall be held in slavery or servitude.

2. No one shall be required to perform forced or compulsory labour.

3. For the purpose of this article the term 'forced or compulsory labour' shall not include:

---

[1] Heading added according to the provisions of Protocol No. 11 (ETS No. 155).

(a) any work required to be done in the ordinary course of detention imposed according to the provisions of Article 5 of this Convention or during conditional release from such detention;

(b) any service of a military character or, in case of conscientious objectors in countries where they are recognised, service exacted instead of compulsory military service;

(c) any service exacted in case of an emergency or calamity threatening the life or well-being of the community;

(d) any work or service which forms part of normal civic obligations.

Article 5 Right to liberty and security[1]

1. Everyone has the right to liberty and security of person. No one shall be deprived of his liberty save in the following cases and in accordance with a procedure prescribed by law:

(a) the lawful detention of a person after conviction by a competent court;

(b) the lawful arrest or detention of a person for non-compliance with the lawful order of a court or in order to secure the fulfilment of any obligation prescribed by law;

(c) the lawful arrest or detention of a person effected for the purpose of bringing him before the competent legal authority on reasonable suspicion of having committed an offence or when it is reasonably considered necessary to prevent his committing an offence or fleeing after having done so;

(d) the detention of a minor by lawful order for the purpose of educational supervision or his lawful detention for the purpose of bringing him before the competent legal authority;

(e) the lawful detention of persons for the prevention of the spreading of infectious diseases, of persons of unsound mind, alcoholics or drug addicts or vagrants;

(f) the lawful arrest or detention of a person to prevent his effecting an unauthorised entry into the country or of a person against whom action is being taken with a view to deportation or extradition.

2. Everyone who is arrested shall be informed promptly, in a language which he understands, of the reasons for his arrest and of any charge against him.

3. Everyone arrested or detained in accordance with the provisions of paragraph 1.c of this article shall be brought promptly before a judge or other officer authorised by law to exercise judicial power and shall be entitled to trial within a reasonable time or to release pending trial. Release may be conditioned by guarantees to appear for trial.

4. Everyone who is deprived of his liberty by arrest or detention shall be entitled to take proceedings by which the lawfulness of his detention shall be decided speedily by a court and his release ordered if the detention is not lawful.

5. Everyone who has been the victim of arrest or detention in contravention of the provisions of this article shall have an enforceable right to compensation.

Article 6 Right to a fair trial[1]

1. In the determination of his civil rights and obligations or of any criminal charge against him, everyone is entitled to a fair and public hearing within a reasonable time by an independent and impartial tribunal established by law. Judgement shall be pronounced publicly but the press and public may be excluded from all or part of the trial in

the interests of morals, public order or national security in a democratic society, where the interests of juveniles or the protection of the private life of the parties so require, or to the extent strictly necessary in the opinion of the court in special circumstances where publicity would prejudice the interests of justice.

2. Everyone charged with a criminal offence shall be presumed innocent until proved guilty according to law.

3. Everyone charged with a criminal offence has the following minimum rights:

(a) to be informed promptly, in a language which he understands and in detail, of the nature and cause of the accusation against him;

(b) to have adequate time and facilities for the preparation of his defence;

(c) to defend himself in person or through legal assistance of his own choosing or, if he has not sufficient means to pay for legal assistance, to be given it free when the interests of justice so require;

(d) to examine or have examined witnesses against him and to obtain the attendance and examination of witnesses on his behalf under the same conditions as witnesses against him;

(d) to have the free assistance of an interpreter if he cannot understand or speak the language used in court.

Article 7 No Punishment without law[1]

1. No one shall be held guilty of any criminal offence on account of any act or omission which did not constitute a criminal offence under national or international law at the time when it was committed. Nor shall a heavier penalty be imposed than the one that was applicable at the time the criminal offence was committed.

2. This article shall not prejudice the trial and punishment of any person for any act or omission which, at the time when it was committed, was criminal according to the general principles of law recognised by civilised nations.

Article 8 Right to respect for private and family life[1]

1. Everyone has the right to respect for his private and family life, his home and his correspondence.

2. There shall be no interference by a public authority with the exercise of this right except such as is in accordance with the law and is necessary in a democratic society in the interests of national security, public safety or the economic well-being of the country, for the prevention of disorder or crime, for the protection of health or morals, or for the protection of the rights and freedoms of others.

Article 9 Freedom of thought, conscience and religion[1]

1. Everyone has the right to freedom of thought, conscience and religion; this right includes freedom to change his religion or belief and freedom, either alone or in community with others and in public or private, to manifest his religion or belief, in worship, teaching, practice and observance.

2. Freedom to manifest one's religion or beliefs shall be subject only to such limitations as are prescribed by law and are necessary in a democratic society in the interests of public

safety, for the protection of public order, health or morals, or for the protection of the rights and freedoms of others.

Article 10 Freedom of expression[1]

1. Everyone has the right to freedom of expression. This right shall include freedom to hold opinions and to receive and impart information and ideas without interference by public authority and regardless of frontiers. This article shall not prevent States from requiring the licensing of broadcasting, television or cinema enterprises.

2. The exercise of these freedoms, since it carries with it duties and responsibilities, may be subject to such formalities, conditions, restrictions or penalties as are prescribed by law and are necessary in a democratic society, in the interests of national security, territorial integrity or public safety, for the prevention of disorder or crime, for the protection of health or morals, for the protection of the reputation or rights of others, for preventing the disclosure of information received in confidence, or for maintaining the authority and impartiality of the judiciary.

Article 11 Freedom of assembly and association[1]

1. Everyone has the right to freedom of peaceful assembly and to freedom of association with others, including the right to form and to join trade unions for the protection of his interests.

2. No restrictions shall be placed on the exercise of these rights other than such as are prescribed by law and are necessary in a democratic society in the interests of national security or public safety, for the prevention of disorder or crime, for the protection of health or morals or for the protection of the rights and freedoms of others. This article shall not prevent the imposition of lawful restrictions on the exercise of these rights by members of the armed forces, of the police or of the administration of the State.

Article 12 Right to marry[1]

Men and women of marriageable age have the right to marry and to found a family, according to the national laws governing the exercise of this right.

Article 13 Right to an effective remedy[1]

Everyone whose rights and freedoms as set forth in this Convention are violated shall have an effective remedy before a national authority notwithstanding that the violation has been committed by persons acting in an official capacity.

Article 14 Prohibition of discrimination[1]

The enjoyment of the rights and freedoms set forth in this Convention shall be secured without discrimination on any ground such as sex, race, colour, language, religion, political or other opinion, national or social origin, association with a national minority, property, birth or other status.

Article 15 Derogation in time of emergency[1]

1. In time of war or other public emergency threatening the life of the nation any High Contracting Party may take measures derogating from its obligations under this Convention to the extent strictly required by the exigencies of the situation, provided that such measures are not inconsistent with its other obligations under international law.

2. No derogation from Article 2, except in respect of deaths resulting from lawful acts of war, or from Articles 3, 4 (paragraph 1) and 7 shall be made under this provision.

3. Any High Contracting Party availing itself of this right of derogation shall keep the Secretary General of the Council of Europe fully informed of the measures which it has taken and the reasons therefor. It shall also inform the Secretary General of the Council of Europe when such measures have ceased to operate and the provisions of the Convention are again being fully executed.

Article 16 Restrictions on political activity of aliens[1]

Nothing in Articles 10, 11 and 14 shall be regarded as preventing the High Contracting Parties from imposing restrictions on the political activity of aliens.

Article 17 Prohibition of abuse of rights[1]

Nothing in this Convention may be interpreted as implying for any State, group or person any right to engage in any activity or perform any act aimed at the destruction of any of the rights and freedoms set forth herein or at their limitation to a greater extent than is provided for in the Convention.

Article 18 Limitation on use of restrictions on rights[1]

The restrictions permitted under this Convention to the said rights and freedoms shall not be applied for any purpose other than those for which they have been prescribed.

Section II—European Court of Human Rights[2]

Article 19 Establishment of the Court

To ensure the observance of the engagements undertaken by the High Contracting Parties in the Convention and the Protocols thereto, there shall be set up a European Court of Human Rights, hereinafter referred to as 'the Court'. It shall function on a permanent basis.

Article 20 Number of judges

The Court shall consist of a number of judges equal to that of the High Contracting Parties.

---

[2] New Section II according to the provisions of Protocol No. 11 (ETS No. 155).

Article 21 Criteria for office

1. The judges shall be of high moral character and must either possess the qualifications required for appointment to high judicial office or be jurisconsults of recognised competence.

2. The judges shall sit on the Court in their individual capacity.

3. During their term of office the judges shall not engage in any activity which is incompatible with their independence, impartiality or with the demands of a full-time office; all questions arising from the application of this paragraph shall be decided by the Court.

Article 22 Election of judges

1. The judges shall be elected by the Parliamentary Assembly with respect to each High Contracting Party by a majority of votes cast from a list of three candidates nominated by the High Contracting Party.

2. The same procedure shall be followed to complete the Court in the event of the accession of new High Contracting Parties and in filling casual vacancies.

Article 23 Terms of office

1. The judges shall be elected for a period of six years. They may be re-elected. However, the terms of office of one-half of the judges elected at the first election shall expire at the end of three years.

2. The judges whose terms of office are to expire at the end of the initial period of three years shall be chosen by lot by the Secretary General of the Council of Europe immediately after their election.

3. In order to ensure that, as far as possible, the terms of office of one-half of the judges are renewed every three years, the Parliamentary Assembly may decide, before proceeding to any subsequent election, that the term or terms of office of one or more judges to be elected shall be for a period other than six years but not more than nine and not less than three years.

4. In cases where more than one term of office is involved and where the Parliamentary Assembly applies the preceding paragraph, the allocation of the terms of office shall be effected by a drawing of lots by the Secretary General of the Council of Europe immediately after the election.

5. A judge elected to replace a judge whose term of office has not expired shall hold office for the remainder of his predecessor's term.

6. The terms of office of judges shall expire when they reach the age of 70.

7. The judges shall hold office until replaced. They shall, however, continue to deal with such cases as they already have under consideration.

Article 24 Dismissal

No judge may be dismissed from his office unless the other judges decide by a majority of two-thirds that he has ceased to fulfil the required conditions.

Article 25 Registry and legal secretaries

The Court shall have a registry, the functions and organisation of which shall be laid down in the rules of the Court. The Court shall be assisted by legal secretaries.

Article 26 Plenary Court

The plenary Court shall:

(a) elect its President and one or two Vice-Presidents for a period of three years; they may be re-elected;

(b) set up Chambers, constituted for a fixed period of time;

(c) elect the Presidents of the Chambers of the Court; they may be re-elected;

(d) adopt the rules of the Court; and

(e) elect the Registrar and one or more Deputy Registrars.

Article 27 Committees, Chambers and Grand Chamber

1. To consider cases brought before it, the Court shall sit in committees of three judges, in Chambers of seven judges and in a Grand Chamber of seventeen judges. The Court's Chambers shall set up committees for a fixed period of time.

2. There shall sit as an ex officio member of the Chamber and the Grand Chamber the judge elected in respect of the State Party concerned or, if there is none or if he is unable to sit, a person of its choice who shall sit in the capacity of judge.

3. The Grand Chamber shall also include the President of the Court, the Vice-Presidents, the Presidents of the Chambers and other judges chosen in accordance with the rules of the Court. When a case is referred to the Grand Chamber under Article 43, no judge from the Chamber which rendered the judgment shall sit in the Grand Chamber, with the exception of the President of the Chamber and the judge who sat in respect of the State Party concerned.

Article 28 Declarations of inadmissibility by committees

A committee may, by a unanimous vote, declare inadmissible or strike out of its list of cases an application submitted under Article 34 where such a decision can be taken without further examination. The decision shall be final.

Article 29 Decisions by chambers on admissibility and merits

1. If no decision is taken under Article 28, a Chamber shall decide on the admissibility and merits of individual applications submitted under Article 34.

2. A Chamber shall decide on the admissibility and merits of inter-State applications submitted under Article 33.

3. The decision on admissibility shall be taken separately unless the Court, in exceptional cases, decides otherwise.

Article 30 Relinquishment of jurisdiction to the Grand Chamber

Where a case pending before a Chamber raises a serious question affecting the interpretation of the Convention or the protocols thereto, or where the resolution of a question before the Chamber might have a result inconsistent with a judgment previously delivered by the Court, the Chamber may, at any time before it has rendered its judgment, relinquish jurisdiction in favour of the Grand Chamber, unless one of the parties to the case objects.

Article 31 Powers of the Grand Chamber

The Grand Chamber shall:

(a) determine applications submitted either under Article 33 or Article 34 when a Chamber has relinquished jurisdiction under Article 30 or when the case has been referred to it under Article 43; and

(b) consider requests for advisory opinions submitted under Article 47.

Article 32 Jurisdiction of the Court

1. The jurisdiction of the Court shall extend to all matters concerning the interpretation and application of the Convention and the protocols thereto which are referred to it as provided in Articles 33, 34 and 47.

2. In the event of dispute as to whether the Court has jurisdiction, the Court shall decide.

Article 33 Inter-State cases

Any High Contracting Party may refer to the Court any alleged breach of the provisions of the Convention and the protocols thereto by another High Contracting Party.

Article 34 Individual applications

Chart of Declarations under former Articles 25 and 46 of the ECHR
The Court may receive applications from any person, non-governmental organisation or group of individuals claiming to be the victim of a violation by one of the High Contracting Parties of the rights set forth in the Convention or the protocols thereto. The High Contracting Parties undertake not to hinder in any way the effective exercise of this right.

Article 35 Admissibility criteria

1. The Court may only deal with the matter after all domestic remedies have been exhausted, according to the generally recognised rules of international law, and within a period of six months from the date on which the final decision was taken.

2. The Court shall not deal with any application submitted under Article 34 that:

(a) is anonymous; or

(b) is substantially the same as a matter that has already been examined by the Court or has already been submitted to another procedure of international investigation or settlement and contains no relevant new information.

3. The Court shall declare inadmissible any individual application submitted under Article 34 which it considers incompatible with the provisions of the Convention or the protocols thereto, manifestly ill-founded, or an abuse of the right of application.

4. The Court shall reject any application which it considers inadmissible under this Article. It may do so at any stage of the proceedings.

Article 36 Third party intervention

1. In all cases before a Chamber or the Grand Chamber, a High Contracting Party one of whose nationals is an applicant shall have the right to submit written comments and to take part in hearings.

2. The President of the Court may, in the interest of the proper administration of justice, invite any High Contracting Party which is not a party to the proceedings or any person concerned who is not the applicant to submit written comments or take part in hearings.

Article 37 Striking out applications

1. The Court may at any stage of the proceedings decide to strike an application out of its list of cases where the circumstances lead to the conclusion that:
    (a) the applicant does not intend to pursue his application; or
    (b) the matter has been resolved; or
    (c) for any other reason established by the Court, it is no longer justified to continue the examination of the application.
However, the Court shall continue the examination of the application if respect for human rights as defined in the Convention and the protocols thereto so requires.

2. The Court may decide to restore an application to its list of cases if it considers that the circumstances justify such a course.

Article 38 Examination of the case and friendly settlement proceedings

1. If the Court declares the application admissible, it shall:
    (a) pursue the examination of the case, together with the representatives of the parties, and if need be, undertake an investigation, for the effective conduct of which the States concerned shall furnish all necessary facilities;
    (b) place itself at the disposal of the parties concerned with a view to securing a friendly settlement of the matter on the basis of respect for human rights as defined in the Convention and the protocols thereto.

2. Proceedings conducted under paragraph 1(b) shall be confidential.

Article 39 Finding of a friendly settlement

If a friendly settlement is effected, the Court shall strike the case out of its list by means of a decision which shall be confined to a brief statement of the facts and of the solution reached.

Article 40 Public hearings and access to documents

1. Hearings shall be in public unless the Court in exceptional circumstances decides otherwise.

2. Documents deposited with the Registrar shall be accessible to the public unless the President of the Court decides otherwise.

Article 41 Just satisfaction

If the Court finds that there has been a violation of the Convention or the protocols thereto, and if the internal law of the High Contracting Party concerned allows only partial reparation to be made, the Court shall, if necessary, afford just satisfaction to the injured party.

Article 42 Judgments of Chambers

Judgments of Chambers shall become final in accordance with the provisions of Article 44, paragraph 2.

Article 43 Referral to the Grand Chamber

1. Within a period of three months from the date of the judgment of the Chamber, any party to the case may, in exceptional cases, request that the case be referred to the Grand Chamber.

2. A panel of five judges of the Grand Chamber shall accept the request if the case raises a serious question affecting the interpretation or application of the Convention or the protocols thereto, or a serious issue of general importance.

3. If the panel accepts the request, the Grand Chamber shall decide the case by means of a judgment.

Article 44 Final Judgments

1. The judgment of the Grand Chamber shall be final.

2. The judgment of a Chamber shall become final:

(a) when the parties declare that they will not request that the case be referred to the Grand Chamber; or

(b) three months after the date of the judgment, if reference of the case to the Grand Chamber has not been requested; or

(c) when the panel of the Grand Chamber rejects the request to refer under Article 43.

3. The final judgment shall be published.

Article 45 Reasons for judgments and decisions

1. Reasons shall be given for judgments as well as for decisions declaring applications admissible or inadmissible.

2. If a judgment does not represent, in whole or in part, the unanimous opinion of the judges, any judge shall be entitled to deliver a separate opinion.

Article 46 Binding force and execution of judgments

1. The High Contracting Parties undertake to abide by the final judgment of the Court in any case to which they are parties.

2. The final judgment of the Court shall be transmitted to the Committee of Ministers, which shall supervise its execution.

Article 47 Advisory opinions

1. The Court may, at the request of the Committee of Ministers, give advisory opinions on legal questions concerning the interpretation of the Convention and the protocols thereto.

2. Such opinions shall not deal with any question relating to the content or scope of the rights or freedoms defined in Section I of the Convention and the protocols thereto, or with any other question which the Court or the Committee of Ministers might have to consider in consequence of any such proceedings as could be instituted in accordance with the Convention.

3. Decisions of the Committee of Ministers to request an advisory opinion of the Court shall require a majority vote of the representatives entitled to sit on the Committee.

Article 48 Advisory jurisdiction of the Court

The Court shall decide whether a request for an advisory opinion submitted by the Committee of Ministers is within its competence as defined in Article 47.

Article 49 Reasons for advisory opinions

1. Reasons shall be given for advisory opinions of the Court.

2. If the advisory opinion does not represent, in whole or in part, the unanimous opinion of the judges, any judge shall be entitled to deliver a separate opinion.

3. Advisory opinions of the Court shall be communicated to the Committee of Ministers.

Article 50 Expenditure on the Court

The expenditure on the Court shall be borne by the Council of Europe.

Article 51 Privileges and immunities of judges

The judges shall be entitled, during the exercise of their functions, to the privileges and immunities provided for in Article 40 of the Statute of the Council of Europe and in the agreements made thereunder.

Section III Miscellaneous provisions[1,3]

Article 52 Inquiries by the Secretary General[1]

On receipt of a request from the Secretary General of the Council of Europe any High Contracting Party shall furnish an explanation of the manner in which its internal law ensures the effective implementation of any of the provisions of the Convention.

---

[3] The articles of this Section are renumbered according to the provisions of Protocol No. 11 (ETS No. 155).

Article 53 Safeguard for existing human rights[1]

Nothing in this Convention shall be construed as limiting or derogating from any of the human rights and fundamental freedoms which may be ensured under the laws of any High Contracting Party or under any other agreement to which it is a Party.

Article 54 Powers of the committee of ministers[1]

Nothing in this Convention shall prejudice the powers conferred on the Committee of Ministers by the Statute of the Council of Europe.

Article 55 Exclusion of other means of dispute settlement[1]

The High Contracting Parties agree that, except by special agreement, they will not avail themselves of treaties, conventions or declarations in force between them for the purpose of submitting, by way of petition, a dispute arising out of the interpretation or application of this Convention to a means of settlement other than those provided for in this Convention.

Article 56 Territorial application[1]

1. [4]Any State may at the time of its ratification or at any time thereafter declare by notification addressed to the Secretary General of the Council of Europe that the present Convention shall, subject to paragraph 4 of this Article, extend to all or any of the territories for whose international relations it is responsible.

2. The Convention shall extend to the territory or territories named in the notification as from the thirtieth day after the receipt of this notification by the Secretary General of the Council of Europe.

3. The provisions of this Convention shall be applied in such territories with due regard, however, to local requirements.

4. [4]Any State which has made a declaration in accordance with paragraph 1 of this article may at any time thereafter declare on behalf of one or more of the territories to which the declaration relates that it accepts the competence of the Court to receive applications from individuals, non-governmental organisations or groups of individuals as provided by Article 34 of the Convention.

Article 57 Reservations[1]

1. Any State may, when signing this Convention or when depositing its instrument of ratification, make a reservation in respect of any particular provision of the Convention to the extent that any law then in force in its territory is not in conformity with the provision. Reservations of a general character shall not be permitted under this article.

2. Any reservation made under this article shall contain a brief statement of the law concerned.

---

[4] Text amended according to the provisions of Protocol No. 11 (ETS No. 155).

Article 58 Denunciation[1]

1. A High Contracting Party may denounce the present Convention only after the expiry of five years from the date on which it became a party to it and after six months' notice contained in a notification addressed to the Secretary General of the Council of Europe, who shall inform the other High Contracting Parties.

2. Such a denunciation shall not have the effect of releasing the High Contracting Party concerned from its obligations under this Convention in respect of any act which, being capable of constituting a violation of such obligations, may have been performed by it before the date at which the denunciation became effective.

3. Any High Contracting Party which shall cease to be a member of the Council of Europe shall cease to be a Party to this Convention under the same conditions.

4. [4]The Convention may be denounced in accordance with the provisions of the preceding paragraphs in respect of any territory to which it has been declared to extend under the terms of Article 56.

Article 59 Signature and ratification[1]

1. This Convention shall be open to the signature of the members of the Council of Europe. It shall be ratified. Ratifications shall be deposited with the Secretary General of the Council of Europe.

2. The present Convention shall come into force after the deposit of ten instruments of ratification.

3. As regards any signatory ratifying subsequently, the Convention shall come into force at the date of the deposit of its instrument of ratification.

4. The Secretary General of the Council of Europe shall notify all the members of the Council of Europe of the entry into force of the Convention, the names of the High Contracting Parties who have ratified it, and the deposit of all instruments of ratification which may be effected subsequently.

Done at Rome this 4th day of November 1950, in English and French, both texts being equally authentic, in a single copy which shall remain deposited in the archives of the Council of Europe. The Secretary General shall transmit certified copies to each of the signatories.

Convention Relating to the Status of Stateless Persons
(New York, September 28, 1954)

PREAMBLE

The High Contracting Parties,

Considering that the Charter of the United Nations and the Universal Declaration of Human Rights approved on 10 December 1948 by the General Assembly of the United Nations have affirmed the principle that human beings shall enjoy fundamental rights and freedoms without discrimination,

Considering that the United Nations has, on various occasions, manifested its profound concern for stateless persons and endeavoured to assure stateless persons the widest possible exercise of these fundamental rights and freedoms,

Considering that only those stateless persons who are also refugees are covered by the Convention relating to the Status of Refugees of 28 July 1951, and that there are many stateless persons who are not covered by that Convention,

Considering that it is desirable to regulate and improve the status of stateless persons by an international agreement.

Have agreed as follows:

CHAPTER I
GENERAL PROVISIONS

Article 1 Definition of the term 'Stateless Person'

1. For the purpose of this Convention, the term 'stateless person' means a person who is not considered as a national by any State under the operation of its law.

2. This Convention shall not apply:

(i) To persons who are at present receiving from organs or agencies of the United Nations other than the United Nations High Commissioner for Refugees protection or assistance so long as they are receiving such protection or assistance;

(ii) To persons who are recognized by the competent authorities of the country in which they have taken residence as having the rights and obligations which are attached to the possession of the nationality of that country;

(iii) To persons with respect to whom there are serious reasons for considering that:

(a) They have committed a crime against peace, a war crime, or a crime against humanity, as defined in the international instruments drawn up to make provisions in respect of such crimes;

(b) They have committed a serious non-political crime outside the country of their residence prior to their admission to that country;

(c) They have been guilty of acts contrary to the purposes and principles of the United Nations.

Article 2 General obligations

Every stateless person has duties to the country in which he finds himself, which require in particular that he conform to its laws and regulations as well as to measures taken for the maintenance of public order.

Article 3 Non-discrimination

The Contracting States shall apply the provisions of this Convention to stateless persons without discrimination as to race, religion or country of origin.

Article 4 Religion

The Contracting States shall accord to stateless persons within their territories treatment at least as favourable as that accorded to their nationals with respect to freedom to practise their religion and freedom as regards the religious education of their children.

Article 5 Rights granted apart from this convention

Nothing in this Convention shall be deemed to impair any rights and benefits granted by a Contracting State to stateless persons apart from this Convention.

Article 6 The term 'in the same circumstances'

For the purpose of this Convention, the term 'in the same circumstances' implies that any requirements (including requirements as to length and conditions of sojourn or residence) which the particular individual would have to fulfil for the enjoyment of the right in question, if he were not a stateless person, must be fulfilled by him, with the exception of requirements which by their nature a stateless person is incapable of fulfilling.

Article 7 Exemption from reciprocity

1. Except where this Convention contains more favourable provisions, a Contracting State shall accord to stateless persons the same treatment as is accorded to aliens generally.

2. After a period of three years' residence, all stateless persons shall enjoy exemption from legislative reciprocity in the territory of the Contracting States.

3. Each Contracting State shall continue to accord to stateless persons the rights and benefits to which they were already entitled, in the absence of reciprocity, at the date of entry into force of this Convention for that State.

4. The Contracting States shall consider favourably the possibility of according to stateless persons, in the absence of reciprocity, rights and benefits beyond those to which they are entitled according to paragraphs 2 and 3, and to extending exemption from reciprocity to stateless persons who do not fulfil the conditions provided for in paragraphs 2 and 3.

The provisions of paragraphs 2 and 3 apply both to the rights and benefits referred to in Articles 13, 18, 19, 21 and 22 of this Convention and to rights and benefits for which this Convention does not provide.

Article 8 Exemption from exceptional measures

With regard to exceptional measures which may be taken against the person, property or interests of nationals or former nationals of a foreign State, the Contracting States shall not apply such measures to a stateless person solely on account of his having previously possessed the nationality of the foreign State in question. Contracting States which, under their legislation, are prevented from applying the general principle expressed in this Article shall, in appropriate cases, grant exemptions in favour of such stateless persons.

Article 9 Provisional measures

Nothing in this Convention shall prevent a Contracting State, in time of war or other grave and exceptional circumstances, from taking provisionally measures which it considers to be essential to the national security in the case of a particular person, pending a determination by the Contracting State that that person is in fact a stateless person and that the continuance of such measures is necessary in his case in the interests of national security.

Article 10 Continuity of residence

1. Where a stateless person has been forcibly displaced during the Second World War and removed to the territory of a Contracting State, and is resident there, the period of such enforced sojourn shall be considered to have been lawful residence within that territory.

2. Where a stateless person has been forcibly displaced during the Second World War from the territory of a Contracting State and has, prior to the date of entry into force of this Convention, returned there for the purpose of taking up residence, the period of residence before and after such enforced displacement shall be regarded as one uninterrupted period for any purpose for which uninterrupted residence is required.

Article 11 Stateless seamen

In the case of stateless persons regularly serving as crew members on board a ship flying the flag of a Contracting State, that State shall give sympathetic consideration to their establishment on its territory and the issue of travel documents to them or their temporary admission to its territory particularly with a view to facilitating their establishment in another country.

CHAPTER II

JURIDICAL STATUS

Article 12 Personal status

1. The personal status of a stateless person shall be governed by the law of the country of his domicile or, if he has no domicile, by the law of the country of his residence.

2. Rights previously acquired by a stateless person and dependent on personal status, more particularly rights attaching to marriage, shall be respected by a Contracting State, subject to compliance, if this be necessary, with the formalities required by the law of that State, provided that the right in question is one which would have been recognized by the law of that State had he not become stateless.

Article 13 Movable and immovable property

The Contracting States shall accord to a stateless person treatment as favourable as possible and, in any event, not less favourable than that accorded to aliens generally in the same circumstances, as regards the acquisition of movable and immovable property and other rights pertaining thereto, and to leases and other contracts relating to movable and immovable property.

Article 14 Artistic rights and industrial property

In respect of the protection of industrial property, such as inventions, designs or models, trade marks, trade names, and of rights in literary, artistic and scientific works, a stateless person shall be accorded in the country in which he has his habitual residence the same protection as is accorded to nationals of that country. In the territory of any other Contracting State, he shall be accorded the same protection as is accorded in that territory to nationals of the country in which he has his habitual residence.

Article 15 Right of association

As regards non-political and non-profit-making associations and trade unions the Contracting States shall accord to stateless persons lawfully staying in their territory treatment as favourable as possible, and in any event, not less favourable than that accorded to aliens generally in the same circumstances.

Article 16 Access to Courts

1. A stateless person shall have free access to the Courts of Law on the territory of all Contracting States.

2. A stateless person shall enjoy in the Contracting State in which he has his habitual residence the same treatment as a national in matters pertaining to access to the Courts, including legal assistance and exemption from *cautio judicatum solvi*.

3. A stateless person shall be accorded in the matters referred to in paragraph 2 in countries other than that in which he has his habitual residence the treatment granted to a national of the country of his habitual residence.

CHAPTER III
GAINFUL EMPLOYMENT

Article 17 Wage-earning employment

1. The Contracting States shall accord to stateless persons lawfully staying in their territory treatment as favourable as possible and, in any event, not less favourable than that accorded to aliens generally in the same circumstances, as regards the right to engage in wage-earning employment.

2. The Contracting States shall give sympathetic consideration to assimilating the rights of all stateless persons with regard to wage-earning employment to those of nationals, and in particular of those stateless persons who have entered their territory pursuant to programmes of labour recruitment or under immigration schemes.

Article 18 Self-employment

The Contracting States shall accord to a stateless person lawfully in their territory treatment as favourable as possible and, in any event, not less favourable than that accorded to aliens generally in the same circumstances, as regards the right to engage on his own account in agriculture, industry, handicrafts and commerce and to establish commercial and industrial companies.

Article 19 Liberal professions

Each Contracting State shall accord to stateless persons lawfully staying in their territory who hold diplomas recognized by the competent authorities of that State, and who are desirous of practising a liberal profession, treatment as favourable as possible and, in any event, not less favourable than that accorded to aliens generally in the same circumstances.

CHAPTER IV
WELFARE

Article 20 Rationing

Where a rationing system exists, which applies to the population at large and regulates the general distribution of products in short supply, stateless persons shall be accorded the same treatment as nationals.

Article 21 Housing

As regards housing, the Contracting States, in so far as the matter is regulated by laws or regulations or is subject to the control of public authorities, shall accord to stateless persons lawfully staying in their territory treatment as favourable as possible and, in any event, not less favourable than that accorded to aliens generally in the same circumstances.

Article 22 Public education

1. The Contracting States shall accord to stateless persons the same treatment as is accorded to nationals with respect to elementary education.

2. The Contracting States shall accord to stateless persons treatment as favourable as possible and, in any event, not less favourable than that accorded to aliens generally in the same circumstances, with respect to education other than elementary education and, in particular, as regards access to studies, the recognition of foreign school certificates, diplomas and degrees, the remission of fees and charges and the award of scholarships.

Article 23 Public relief

The Contracting States shall accord to stateless persons lawfully staying in their territory the same treatment with respect to public relief and assistance as is accorded to their nationals.

Article 24 Labour legislation and social security

1. The Contracting States shall accord to stateless persons lawfully staying in their territory the same treatment as is accorded to nationals in respect of the following matters:

(a) In so far as such matters are governed by laws or regulations or are subject to the control of administrative authorities: remuneration, including family allowances where these form part of remuneration, hours of work, overtime arrangements, holidays with pay, restrictions on home work, minimum age of employment, apprenticeship and training, women's work and the work of young persons, and the enjoyment of the benefits of collective bargaining;

(b) Social security (legal provisions in respect of employment injury, occupational diseases, maternity, sickness, disability, old age, death, unemployment, family responsibilities and any other contingency which, according to national laws or regulations, is covered by a social security scheme), subject to the following limitations:

(i) There may be appropriate arrangements for the maintenance of acquired rights and rights in course of acquisition;

(ii) National laws or regulations of the country of residence may prescribe special arrangements concerning benefits or portions of benefits which are payable wholly out of public funds, and concerning allowances paid to persons who do not fulfil the contribution conditions prescribed for the award of a normal pension.

2. The right to compensation for the death of a stateless person resulting from employment injury or from occupational disease shall not be affected by the fact that the residence of the beneficiary is outside the territory of the Contracting State.

3. The Contracting States shall extend to stateless persons the benefits of agreements concluded between them, or which may be concluded between them in the future, concerning the maintenance of acquired rights and rights in the process of acquisition in regard to social security, subject only to the conditions which apply to nationals of the States signatory to the agreements in question.

4. The Contracting States will give sympathetic consideration to extending to stateless persons so far as possible the benefits of similar agreements which may at any time be in force between such Contracting States and non-Contracting States.

CHAPTER V

ADMINISTRATIVE MEASURES

Article 25 Administrative assistance

1. When the exercise of a right by a stateless person would normally require the assistance of authorities of a foreign country to whom he cannot have recourse, the Contracting State in whose territory he is residing shall arrange that such assistance be afforded to him by their own authorities.

2. The authority or authorities mentioned in paragraph 1 shall deliver or cause to be delivered under their supervision to stateless persons such documents or certifications as would normally be delivered to aliens by or through their national authorities.

3. Documents or certifications so delivered shall stand in the stead of the official instruments delivered to aliens by or through their national authorities, and shall be given credence in the absence of proof to the contrary.

4. Subject to such exceptional treatment as may be granted to indigent persons, fees may be charged for the services mentioned herein, but such fees shall be moderate and commensurate with those charged to nationals for similar services.

5. The provisions of this article shall be without prejudice to Articles 27 and 28.

Article 26 Freedom of movement

Each Contracting State shall accord to stateless persons lawfully in its territory the right to choose their place of residence and to move freely within its territory, subject to any regulations applicable to aliens generally in the same circumstances.

Article 27 Identity papers

The Contracting States shall issue identity papers to any stateless person in their territory who does not possess a valid travel document.

Article 28 Travel documents

The Contracting States shall issue to stateless persons lawfully staying in their territory travel documents for the purpose of travel outside their territory, unless compelling reasons of national security or public order otherwise require, and the provisions of the Schedule to this Convention shall apply with respect to such documents. The Contracting States may issue such a travel document to any other stateless person in their territory; they shall in particular give sympathetic consideration to the issue of such a travel document to stateless persons in their territory who are unable to obtain a travel document from the country of their lawful residence.

Article 29 Fiscal charges

1. The Contracting States shall not impose upon stateless persons duties, charges or taxes, of any description whatsoever, other or higher than those which are or may be levied on their nationals in similar situations.

2. Nothing in the above paragraph shall prevent the application to stateless persons of the laws and regulations concerning charges in respect of the issue to aliens of administrative documents including identity papers.

Article 30 Transfer of assets

1. A Contracting State shall, in conformity with its laws and regulations, permit stateless persons to transfer assets which they have brought into its territory, to another country where they have been admitted for the purpose of resettlement.

2. A Contracting State shall give sympathetic consideration to the application of stateless persons for permission to transfer assets wherever they may be and which are necessary for their resettlement in another country to which they have been admitted.

Article 31 Expulsion

1. The Contracting States shall not expel a stateless person lawfully in their territory save on grounds of national security or public order.

2. The expulsion of such a stateless person shall be only in pursuance of a decision reached in accordance with due process of law. Except where compelling reasons of national security otherwise require, the stateless person shall be allowed to submit evidence to clear himself, and to appeal to and be represented for the purpose before the competent authority or a person or persons specially designated by the competent authority.

3. The Contracting States shall allow such a stateless person a reasonable period within which to seek legal admission into another country. The Contracting States reserve the right to apply during that period such internal measures as they may deem necessary.

Article 32 Naturalization

The Contracting States shall as far as possible facilitate the assimilation and naturalization of stateless persons. They shall in particular make every effort to expedite naturalization proceedings and to reduce as far as possible the charges and costs of such proceedings.

CHAPTER VI

FINAL CLAUSES

...

UNITED KINGDOM OF GREAT BRITAIN AND NORTHERN IRELAND

'I have the honour further to state that the Government of the United Kingdom deposit the present instrument of ratification on the understanding that the combined effects of Articles 36 and 38 permit them to include in any declaration or notification made under paragraph 1 of Article 36 or paragraph 2 of Article 36 respectively any reservation consistent with Article 38 which the Government of the territory concerned might desire to make.'

'When ratifying the Convention relating to the Status of Stateless Persons which was opened for signature at New York on September 28, 1954, the Government of the United Kingdom have deemed it necessary to make certain reservations in accordance with paragraph 1 of Article 38 thereof the text of which is reproduced below:—

(1) The Government of the United Kingdom of Great Britain and Northern Ireland understand Articles 8 and 9 as not preventing them from taking in time of war or other grave and exceptional circumstances measures in the interests of national security in the case of a stateless person on the ground of his former nationality. The provisions of Article 8 shall not prevent the Government of the United Kingdom of Great Britain and Northern Ireland from exercising any rights over property or interests which they may acquire or have acquired as an Allied or Associated Power under a Treaty of Peace or other agreement or arrangement for the restoration of peace which has been or may be completed as a result of the Second World War. Furthermore, the provisions of Article 8 shall not affect the treatment to be accorded to any property or interests which at the date of entry into force of this Convention for the United Kingdom of Great Britain and Northern Ireland are under the control of the

Government of the United Kingdom of Great Britain and Northern Ireland by reason of a state of war which exists or existed between them and any other state.

(2) The Government of the United Kingdom of Great Britain and Northern Ireland in respect of such of the matters referred to in sub-paragraph (b) of paragraph 1 of Article 24 as fall within the scope of the National Health Service, can only undertake to apply the provisions of that paragraph so far as the law allows.

(3) The Government of the United Kingdom of Great Britain and Northern Ireland cannot undertake to give effect to the obligations contained in paragraphs 1 and 2 of Article 25 and can only undertake to apply the provisions of paragraph 3 so far as the law allows.'

Convention Against Torture and Other Cruel, Inhuman or Degrading Treatment or Punishment

(United Nations Headquarters, New York, 4 February 1985)

Note: Articles 1–4 only.

The States Parties to this Convention,

Considering that, in accordance with the principles proclaimed in the Charter of the United Nations, recognition of the equal and inalienable rights of all members of the human family is the foundation of freedom, justice and peace in the world,

Recognizing that those rights derive from the inherent dignity of the human person,

Considering the obligation of States under the Charter, in particular Article 55, to promote universal respect for, and observance of, human rights and fundamental freedoms,

Having regard to Article 5 of the Universal Declaration of Human Rights and Article 7 of the International Covenant on Civil and Political Right, both of which provide that no one shall be subjected to torture or to cruel, inhuman or degrading treatment or punishment,

Having regard also to the Declaration on the Protection of All Persons from Being Subjected to Torture and Other Cruel, Inhuman or Degrading Treatment or Punishment, adopted by the General Assembly on 9 December 1975,

Desiring to make more effective the struggle against torture and other cruel, inhuman or degrading treatment or punishment throughout the world,

Have agreed as follows:

PART I

Article 1

1. For the purposes of this Convention, the term 'torture' means any act by which severe pain or suffering, whether physical or mental, is intentionally inflicted on a person for such purposes as obtaining from him or a third person information or a confession, punishing him for an act he or a third person has committed or is suspected of having committed, or intimidating or coercing him or a third person, or for any reason based on discrimination of any kind, when such pain or suffering is inflicted by or at the instigation

of or with the consent or acquiescence of a public official or other person acting in an official capacity. It does not include pain or suffering arising only from, inherent in or incidental to lawful sanctions.

2. This article is without prejudice to any international instrument or national legislation which does or may contain provisions of wider application.

Article 2

1. Each State Party shall take effective legislative, administrative, judicial or other measures to prevent acts of torture in any territory under its jurisdiction.

2. No exceptional circumstances whatsoever, whether a state of war or a threat of war, internal political instability or any other public emergency, may be invoked as a justification of torture.

3. An order from a superior officer or a public authority may not be invoked as a justification of torture.

Article 3

1. No State Party shall expel, return (*'refouler'*) or extradite a person to another State where there are substantial grounds for believing that he would be in danger of being subjected to torture.

2. For the purpose of determining whether there are such grounds, the competent authorities shall take into account all relevant considerations including, where applicable, the existence in the State concerned of a consistent pattern of gross, flagrant or mass violations of human rights.

Article 4

1. Each State Party shall ensure that all acts of torture are offences under its criminal law. The same shall apply to an attempt to commit torture and to an act by any person which constitutes complicity or participation in torture.

2. Each State Party shall make these offences punishable by appropriate penalties which take into account their grave nature.

Convention on the Rights of the Child

**Adopted and opened for signature, ratification and
accession by General Assembly
resolution 44/25 of 20 November 1989
entry into force 2 September 1990, in accordance with article 49**

PREAMBLE

The States Parties to the present Convention,

Considering that, in accordance with the principles proclaimed in the Charter of the United Nations, recognition of the inherent dignity and of the equal and inalienable rights of all members of the human family is the foundation of freedom, justice and peace in the world,

Bearing in mind that the peoples of the United Nations have, in the Charter, reaffirmed their faith in fundamental human rights and in the dignity and worth of the human person, and have determined to promote social progress and better standards of life in larger freedom,

Recognizing that the United Nations has, in the Universal Declaration of Human Rights and in the International Covenants on Human Rights, proclaimed and agreed that everyone is entitled to all the rights and freedoms set forth therein, without distinction of any kind, such as race, colour, sex, language, religion, political or other opinion, national or social origin, property, birth or other status,

Recalling that, in the Universal Declaration of Human Rights, the United Nations has proclaimed that childhood is entitled to special care and assistance,

Convinced that the family, as the fundamental group of society and the natural environment for the growth and well-being of all its members and particularly children, should be afforded the necessary protection and assistance so that it can fully assume its responsibilities within the community,

Recognizing that the child, for the full and harmonious development of his or her personality, should grow up in a family environment, in an atmosphere of happiness, love and understanding,

Considering that the child should be fully prepared to live an individual life in society, and brought up in the spirit of the ideals proclaimed in the Charter of the United Nations, and in particular in the spirit of peace, dignity, tolerance, freedom, equality and solidarity,

Bearing in mind that the need to extend particular care to the child has been stated in the Geneva Declaration of the Rights of the Child of 1924 and in the Declaration of the Rights of the Child adopted by the General Assembly on 20 November 1959 and recognized in the Universal Declaration of Human Rights, in the International Covenant on Civil and Political Rights (in particular in articles 23 and 24), in the International Covenant on Economic, Social and Cultural Rights (in particular in article 10) and in the statutes and relevant instruments of specialized agencies and international organizations concerned with the welfare of children,

Bearing in mind that, as indicated in the Declaration of the Rights of the Child, "the child, by reason of his physical and mental immaturity, needs special safeguards and care, including appropriate legal protection, before as well as after birth",

Recalling the provisions of the Declaration on Social and Legal Principles relating to the Protection and Welfare of Children, with Special Reference to Foster Placement and Adoption Nationally and Internationally; the United Nations Standard Minimum Rules for the Administration of Juvenile Justice (The Beijing Rules); and the Declaration on the Protection of Women and Children in Emergency and Armed Conflict,

Recognizing that, in all countries in the world, there are children living in exceptionally difficult conditions, and that such children need special consideration,

Taking due account of the importance of the traditions and cultural values of each people for the protection and harmonious development of the child,

Recognizing the importance of international cooperation for improving the living conditions of children in every country, in particular in the developing countries,

Have agreed as follows:

PART I

Article 1

For the purposes of the present Convention, a child means every human being below the age of eighteen years unless under the law applicable to the child, majority is attained earlier.

Article 2

1. States Parties shall respect and ensure the rights set forth in the present Convention to each child within their jurisdiction without discrimination of any kind, irrespective of the child's or his or her parent's or legal guardian's race, colour, sex, language, religion, political or other opinion, national, ethnic or social origin, property, disability, birth or other status.

2. States Parties shall take all appropriate measures to ensure that the child is protected against all forms of discrimination or punishment on the basis of the status, activities, expressed opinions, or beliefs of the child's parents, legal guardians, or family members.

Article 3

1. In all actions concerning children, whether undertaken by public or private social welfare institutions, courts of law, administrative authorities or legislative bodies, the best interests of the child shall be a primary consideration.

2. States Parties undertake to ensure the child such protection and care as is necessary for his or her well-being, taking into account the rights and duties of his or her parents, legal guardians, or other individuals legally responsible for him or her, and, to this end, shall take all appropriate legislative and administrative measures.

3. States Parties shall ensure that the institutions, services and facilities responsible for the care or protection of children shall conform with the standards established by competent authorities, particularly in the areas of safety, health, in the number and suitability of their staff, as well as competent supervision.

Article 4

States Parties shall undertake all appropriate legislative, administrative, and other measures for the implementation of the rights recognized in the present Convention. With regard to economic, social and cultural rights, States Parties shall undertake such measures to the maximum extent of their available resources and, where needed, within the framework of international co-operation.

Article 5

States Parties shall respect the responsibilities, rights and duties of parents or, where applicable, the members of the extended family or community as provided for by local custom, legal guardians or other persons legally responsible for the child, to provide, in a manner consistent with the evolving capacities of the child, appropriate direction and guidance in the exercise by the child of the rights recognized in the present Convention.

Article 6

1. States Parties recognize that every child has the inherent right to life.

2. States Parties shall ensure to the maximum extent possible the survival and development of the child.

Article 7

1. The child shall be registered immediately after birth and shall have the right from birth to a name, the right to acquire a nationality and. as far as possible, the right to know and be cared for by his or her parents.

2. States Parties shall ensure the implementation of these rights in accordance with their national law and their obligations under the relevant international instruments in this field, in particular where the child would otherwise be stateless.

Article 8

1. States Parties undertake to respect the right of the child to preserve his or her identity, including nationality, name and family relations as recognized by law without unlawful interference.

2. Where a child is illegally deprived of some or all of the elements of his or her identity, States Parties shall provide appropriate assistance and protection, with a view to re-establishing speedily his or her identity.

Article 9

1. States Parties shall ensure that a child shall not be separated from his or her parents against their will, except when competent authorities subject to judicial review determine, in accordance with applicable law and procedures, that such separation is necessary for the best interests of the child. Such determination may be necessary in a particular case such as one involving abuse or neglect of the child by the parents, or one where the parents are living separately and a decision must be made as to the child's place of residence.

2. In any proceedings pursuant to paragraph 1 of the present article, all interested parties shall be given an opportunity to participate in the proceedings and make their views known.

3. States Parties shall respect the right of the child who is separated from one or both parents to maintain personal relations and direct contact with both parents on a regular basis, except if it is contrary to the child's best interests.

4. Where such separation results from any action initiated by a State Party, such as the detention, imprisonment, exile, deportation or death (including death arising from any cause while the person is in the custody of the State) of one or both parents or of the child, that State Party shall, upon request, provide the parents, the child or, if appropriate, another member of the family with the essential information concerning the whereabouts of the absent member(s) of the family unless the provision of the information would be detrimental

to the well-being of the child. States Parties shall further ensure that the submission of such a request shall of itself entail no adverse consequences for the person(s) concerned.

Article 10

1. In accordance with the obligation of States Parties under article 9, paragraph 1, applications by a child or his or her parents to enter or leave a State Party for the purpose of family reunification shall be dealt with by States Parties in a positive, humane and expeditious manner. States Parties shall further ensure that the submission of such a request shall entail no adverse consequences for the applicants and for the members of their family.

2. A child whose parents reside in different States shall have the right to maintain on a regular basis, save in exceptional circumstances personal relations and direct contacts with both parents. Towards that end and in accordance with the obligation of States Parties under article 9, paragraph 1, States Parties shall respect the right of the child and his or her parents to leave any country, including their own, and to enter their own country. The right to leave any country shall be subject only to such restrictions as are prescribed by law and which are necessary to protect the national security, public order (ordre public), public health or morals or the rights and freedoms of others and are consistent with the other rights recognized in the present Convention.

Article 11

1. States Parties shall take measures to combat the illicit transfer and non-return of children abroad.

2. To this end, States Parties shall promote the conclusion of bilateral or multilateral agreements or accession to existing agreements.

Article 12

1. States Parties shall assure to the child who is capable of forming his or her own views the right to express those views freely in all matters affecting the child, the views of the child being given due weight in accordance with the age and maturity of the child.

2. For this purpose, the child shall in particular be provided the opportunity to be heard in any judicial and administrative proceedings affecting the child, either directly, or through a representative or an appropriate body, in a manner consistent with the procedural rules of national law.

Article 13

1. The child shall have the right to freedom of expression; this right shall include freedom to seek, receive and impart information and ideas of all kinds, regardless of frontiers, either orally, in writing or in print, in the form of art, or through any other media of the child's choice.

2. The exercise of this right may be subject to certain restrictions, but these shall only be such as are provided by law and are necessary:

(a) For respect of the rights or reputations of others; or

(b) For the protection of national security or of public order (ordre public), or of public health or morals.

Article 14

1. States Parties shall respect the right of the child to freedom of thought, conscience and religion.

2. States Parties shall respect the rights and duties of the parents and, when applicable, legal guardians, to provide direction to the child in the exercise of his or her right in a manner consistent with the evolving capacities of the child.

3. Freedom to manifest one's religion or beliefs may be subject only to such limitations as are prescribed by law and are necessary to protect public safety, order, health or morals, or the fundamental rights and freedoms of others.

Article 15

1. States Parties recognize the rights of the child to freedom of association and to freedom of peaceful assembly.

2. No restrictions may be placed on the exercise of these rights other than those imposed in conformity with the law and which are necessary in a democratic society in the interests of national security or public safety, public order (ordre public), the protection of public health or morals or the protection of the rights and freedoms of others.

Article 16

1. No child shall be subjected to arbitrary or unlawful interference with his or her privacy, family, home or correspondence, nor to unlawful attacks on his or her honour and reputation.

2. The child has the right to the protection of the law against such interference or attacks.

Article 17

States Parties recognize the important function performed by the mass media and shall ensure that the child has access to information and material from a diversity of national and international sources, especially those aimed at the promotion of his or her social, spiritual and moral well-being and physical and mental health.

To this end, States Parties shall:

 (a) Encourage the mass media to disseminate information and material of social and cultural benefit to the child and in accordance with the spirit of article 29;

 (b) Encourage international co-operation in the production, exchange and of such information and material from a diversity of cultural, national and international sources;

 (c) Encourage the production and dissemination of children's books;

 (d) Encourage the mass media to have particular regard to the linguistic needs of the child who belongs to a minority group or who is indigenous;

 (e) Encourage the development of appropriate guidelines for the protection of the child from information and material injurious to his or her well-being, bearing in mind the provisions of articles 13 and 18.

Article 18

1. States Parties shall use their best efforts to ensure recognition of the principle that both parents have common responsibilities for the upbringing and development of the child. Parents or, as the case may be, legal guardians, have the primary responsibility for the upbringing and development of the child. The best interests of the child will be their basic concern.

2. For the purpose of guaranteeing and promoting the rights set forth in the present Convention, States Parties shall render appropriate assistance to parents and legal guardians in the performance of their child-rearing responsibilities and shall ensure the development of institutions, facilities and services for the care of children.

3. States Parties shall take all appropriate measures to ensure that children of working parents have the right to benefit from child-care services and facilities for which they are eligible.

Article 19

1. States Parties shall take all appropriate legislative, administrative, social and measures to protect the child from all forms of physical or mental violence, injury or abuse, neglect or negligent treatment, maltreatment or exploitation, including sexual abuse, while in the care of parent(s), legal guardian(s) or any other person who has the care of the child.

2. Such protective measures should, as appropriate, include effective procedures for the establishment of social programmes to provide necessary support for the child and for those who have the care of the child, as well as for other forms of prevention and for identification, reporting, referral, investigation, treatment and follow-up of instances of child maltreatment described heretofore, and, as appropriate, for judicial involvement.

Article 20

1. A child temporarily or permanently deprived of his or her family environment, or in whose own best interests cannot be allowed to remain in that environment, shall be entitled to special protection and assistance provided by the State.

2. States Parties shall in accordance with their national laws ensure alternative care for such a child.

3. Such care could include, inter alia, foster placement, kafalah of Islamic law, adoption or if necessary placement in suitable institutions for the care of children. When considering solutions, due regard shall be paid to the desirability of continuity in a child's upbringing and to the child's ethnic, religious, cultural and linguistic background.

Article 21

States Parties that recognize and/or permit the system of adoption shall ensure that the best interests of the child shall be the paramount consideration and they shall:

(a) Ensure that the adoption of a child is authorized only by competent authorities who determine, in accordance with applicable law and procedures and on the basis of all pertinent and reliable information, that the adoption is permissible in view of the child's status concerning parents, relatives and legal guardians and that, if required, the persons concerned have given their informed consent to the adoption on the basis of such counselling as may be necessary;

(b) Recognize that inter-country adoption may be considered as an alternative means of child's care, if the child cannot be placed in a foster or an adoptive family or cannot in any suitable manner be cared for in the child's country of origin;

(c) Ensure that the child concerned by inter-country adoption enjoys safeguards and standards equivalent to those existing in the case of national adoption;

(d) Take all appropriate measures to ensure that, in inter-country adoption, the placement does not result in improper financial gain for those involved in it;

(e) Promote, where appropriate, the objectives of the present article by concluding bilateral or multilateral arrangements or agreements, and endeavour, within this framework, to ensure that the placement of the child in another country is carried out by competent authorities or organs.

Article 22

1. States Parties shall take appropriate measures to ensure that a child who is seek refugee status or who is considered a refugee in accordance with applicable international or domestic law and procedures shall, whether unaccompanied or accompanied by his or her parents or by any other person, receive appropriate protection and humanitarian assistance in the enjoyment of applicable rights set forth in the present Convention and in other international human rights or humanitarian instruments to which the said States are Parties.

2. For this purpose, States Parties shall provide, as they consider appropriate, co-operation in any efforts by the United Nations and other competent intergovernmental organizations or nongovernmental organizations co-operating with the United Nations to protect and assist such a child and to trace the parents or other members of the family of any refugee child in order to obtain information necessary for reunification with his or her family. In cases where no parents or other members of the family can be found, the child shall be accorded the same protection as any other child permanently or temporarily deprived of his or her family environment for any reason, as set forth in the present Convention.

Article 23

1. States Parties recognize that a mentally or physically disabled child should enjoy a full and decent life, in conditions which ensure dignity, promote self-reliance and facilitate the child's active participation in the community.

2. States Parties recognize the right of the disabled child to special care and shall encourage and ensure the extension, subject to available resources, to the eligible child and those responsible for his or her care, of assistance for which application is made and which is appropriate to the child's condition and to the circumstances of the parents or others caring for the child.

3. Recognizing the special needs of a disabled child, assistance extended in accordance with paragraph 2 of the present article shall be provided free of charge, whenever possible, taking into account the financial resources of the parents or others caring for the child,

and shall be designed to ensure that the disabled child has effective access to and receives education, training, health care services, rehabilitation services, preparation for employment and recreation opportunities in a manner conducive to the child's achieving the fullest possible social integration and individual development, including his or her cultural and spiritual development.

4. States Parties shall promote, in the spirit of international cooperation, the exchange of appropriate information in the field of preventive health care and of medical, psychological and functional treatment of disabled children, including dissemination of and access to information concerning methods of rehabilitation, education and vocational services, with the aim of enabling States Parties to improve their capabilities and skills and to widen their experience in these areas. In this regard, particular account shall be taken of the needs of developing countries.

Article 24

1. States Parties recognize the right of the child to the enjoyment of the highest attainable standard of health and to facilities for the treatment of illness and rehabilitation of health. States Parties shall strive to ensure that no child is deprived of his or her right of access to such health care services.

2. States Parties shall pursue full implementation of this right and, in particular, shall take appropriate measures:

(a) To diminish infant and child mortality;

(b) To ensure the provision of necessary medical assistance and health care to all children with emphasis on the development of primary health care;

(c) To combat disease and malnutrition, including within the framework of primary health care, through, *inter alia*, the application of readily available technology and through the provision of adequate nutritious foods and clean drinking-water, taking into consideration the dangers and risks of environmental pollution;

(d) To ensure appropriate pre-natal and post-natal health care for mothers;

(e) To ensure that all segments of society, in particular parents and children, are informed, have access to education and are supported in the use of basic knowledge of child health and nutrition, the advantages of breastfeeding, hygiene and environmental sanitation and the prevention of accidents;

(f) To develop preventive health care, guidance for parents and family planning education and services.

3. States Parties shall take all effective and appropriate measures with a view to abolishing traditional practices prejudicial to the health of children.

4. States Parties undertake to promote and encourage international co-operation with a view to achieving progressively the full realization of the right recognized in the present article. In this regard, particular account shall be taken of the needs of developing countries.

Article 25

States Parties recognize the right of a child who has been placed by the competent authorities for the purposes of care, protection or treatment of his or her physical or mental health, to a periodic review of the treatment provided to the child and all other circumstances relevant to his or her placement.

Article 26

1. States Parties shall recognize for every child the right to benefit from social security, including social insurance, and shall take the necessary measures to achieve the full realization of this right in accordance with their national law.

2. The benefits should, where appropriate, be granted, taking into account the resources and the circumstances of the child and persons having responsibility for the maintenance of the child, as well as any other consideration relevant to an application for benefits made by or on behalf of the child.

Article 27

1. States Parties recognize the right of every child to a standard of living adequate for the child's physical, mental, spiritual, moral and social development.

2. The parent(s) or others responsible for the child have the primary responsibility to secure, within their abilities and financial capacities, the conditions of living necessary for the child's development.

3. States Parties, in accordance with national conditions and within their means, shall take appropriate measures to assist parents and others responsible for the child to implement this right and shall in case of need provide material assistance and support programmes, particularly with regard to nutrition, clothing and housing.

4. States Parties shall take all appropriate measures to secure the recovery of maintenance for the child from the parents or other persons having financial responsibility for the child, both within the State Party and from abroad. In particular, where the person having financial responsibility for the child lives in a State different from that of the child, States Parties shall promote the accession to international agreements or the conclusion of such agreements, as well as the making of other appropriate arrangements.

Article 28

1. States Parties recognize the right of the child to education, and with a view to achieving this right progressively and on the basis of equal opportunity, they shall, in particular:

   (a) Make primary education compulsory and available free to all;

   (b) Encourage the development of different forms of secondary education, including general and vocational education, make them available and accessible to every child, and take appropriate measures such as the introduction of free education and offering financial assistance in case of need;

   (c) Make higher education accessible to all on the basis of capacity by every appropriate means;

   (d) Make educational and vocational information and guidance available and accessible to all children;

   (e) Take measures to encourage regular attendance at schools and the reduction of drop-out rates.

2. States Parties shall take all appropriate measures to ensure that school discipline is administered in a manner consistent with the child's human dignity and in conformity with the present Convention.

3. States Parties shall promote and encourage international cooperation in matters relating to education, in particular with a view to contributing to the elimination of ignorance and illiteracy throughout the world and facilitating access to scientific and technical knowledge and modern teaching methods. In this regard, particular account shall be taken of the needs of developing countries.

Article 29

1. States Parties agree that the education of the child shall be directed to:

(a) The development of the child's personality, talents and mental and physical abilities to their fullest potential;

(b) The development of respect for human rights and fundamental freedoms, and for the principles enshrined in the Charter of the United Nations;

(c) The development of respect for the child's parents, his or her own cultural identity, language and values, for the national values of the country in which the child is living, the country from which he or she may originate, and for civilizations different from his or her own;

(d) The preparation of the child for responsible life in a free society, in the spirit of understanding, peace, tolerance, equality of sexes, and friendship among all peoples, ethnic, national and religious groups and persons of indigenous origin;

(e) The development of respect for the natural environment.

2. No part of the present article or article 28 shall be construed so as to interfere with the liberty of individuals and bodies to establish and direct educational institutions, subject always to the observance of the principle set forth in paragraph 1 of the present article and to the requirements that the education given in such institutions shall conform to such minimum standards as may be laid down by the State.

Article 30

In those States in which ethnic, religious or linguistic minorities or persons of indigenous origin exist, a child belonging to such a minority or who is indigenous shall not be denied the right, in community with other members of his or her group, to enjoy his or her own culture, to profess and practise his or her own religion, or to use his or her own language.

Article 31

1. States Parties recognize the right of the child to rest and leisure, to engage in play and recreational activities appropriate to the age of the child and to participate freely in cultural life and the arts.

2. States Parties shall respect and promote the right of the child to participate fully in cultural and artistic life and shall encourage the provision of appropriate and equal opportunities for cultural, artistic, recreational and leisure activity.

Article 32

1. States Parties recognize the right of the child to be protected from economic exploitation and from performing any work that is likely to be hazardous or to interfere with

the child's education, or to be harmful to the child's health or physical, mental, spiritual, moral or social development.

2. States Parties shall take legislative, administrative, social and educational measures to ensure the implementation of the present article. To this end, and having regard to the relevant provisions of other international instruments, States Parties shall in particular:

(a) Provide for a minimum age or minimum ages for admission to employment;

(b) Provide for appropriate regulation of the hours and conditions of employment;

(c) Provide for appropriate penalties or other sanctions to ensure the effective enforcement of the present article.

Article 33

States Parties shall take all appropriate measures, including legislative, administrative, social and educational measures, to protect children from the illicit use of drugs and psychotropic substances as defined in the relevant international treaties, and to prevent the use of children in the illicit production and trafficking of such substances.

Article 34

States Parties undertake to protect the child from all forms of sexual exploitation and sexual abuse. For these purposes, States Parties shall in particular take all appropriate national, bilateral and multilateral measures to prevent:

(a) The inducement or coercion of a child to engage in any unlawful sexual activity;

(b) The exploitative use of children in prostitution or other unlawful sexual practices;

(c) The exploitative use of children in pornographic performances and materials.

Article 35

States Parties shall take all appropriate national, bilateral and multilateral measures to prevent the abduction of, the sale of or traffic in children for any purpose or in any form.

Article 36

States Parties shall protect the child against all other forms of exploitation prejudicial to any aspects of the child's welfare.

Article 37

States Parties shall ensure that:

(a) No child shall be subjected to torture or other cruel, inhuman or degrading treatment or punishment. Neither capital punishment nor life imprisonment without possibility of release shall be imposed for offences committed by persons below eighteen years of age;

(b) No child shall be deprived of his or her liberty unlawfully or arbitrarily. The arrest, detention or imprisonment of a child shall be in conformity with the law and shall be used only as a measure of last resort and for the shortest appropriate period of time;

(c) Every child deprived of liberty shall be treated with humanity and respect for the inherent dignity of the human person, and in a manner which takes into account the needs of persons of his or her age. In particular, every child deprived of liberty shall be separated from adults unless it is considered in the child's best interest not to do so and shall have the right to maintain contact with his or her family through correspondence and visits, save in exceptional circumstances;

(d) Every child deprived of his or her liberty shall have the right to prompt access to legal and other appropriate assistance, as well as the right to challenge the legality of the deprivation of his or her liberty before a court or other competent, independent and impartial authority, and to a prompt decision on any such action.

Article 38

1. States Parties undertake to respect and to ensure respect for rules of international humanitarian law applicable to them in armed conflicts which are relevant to the child.

2. States Parties shall take all feasible measures to ensure that persons who have not attained the age of fifteen years do not take a direct part in hostilities.

3. States Parties shall refrain from recruiting any person who has not attained the age of fifteen years into their armed forces. In recruiting among those persons who have attained the age of fifteen years but who have not attained the age of eighteen years, States Parties shall endeavour to give priority to those who are oldest.

4. In accordance with their obligations under international humanitarian law to protect the civilian population in armed conflicts, States Parties shall take all feasible measures to ensure protection and care of children who are affected by an armed conflict.

Article 39

States Parties shall take all appropriate measures to promote physical and psychological recovery and social reintegration of a child victim of: any form of neglect, exploitation, or abuse; torture or any other form of cruel, inhuman or degrading treatment or punishment; or armed conflicts. Such recovery and reintegration shall take place in an environment which fosters the health, self-respect and dignity of the child.

Article 40

1. States Parties recognize the right of every child alleged as, accused of, or recognized as having infringed the penal law to be treated in a manner consistent with the promotion of the child's sense of dignity and worth, which reinforces the child's respect for the human rights and fundamental freedoms of others and which takes into account the child's age and the desirability of promoting the child's reintegration and the child's assuming a constructive role in society.

2. To this end, and having regard to the relevant provisions of international instruments, States Parties shall, in particular, ensure that:

(a) No child shall be alleged as, be accused of, or recognized as having infringed the penal law by reason of acts or omissions that were not prohibited by national or international law at the time they were committed;

(b) Every child alleged as or accused of having infringed the penal law has at least the following guarantees:

(i) To be presumed innocent until proven guilty according to law;

(ii) To be informed promptly and directly of the charges against him or her, and, if appropriate, through his or her parents or legal guardians, and to have legal or other appropriate assistance in the preparation and presentation of his or her defence;

(iii) To have the matter determined without delay by a competent, independent and impartial authority or judicial body in a fair hearing according to law, in the presence of legal or other appropriate assistance and, unless it is considered not to be in the best interest of the child, in particular, taking into account his or her age or situation, his or her parents or legal guardians;

(iv) Not to be compelled to give testimony or to confess guilt; to examine or have examined adverse witnesses and to obtain the participation and examination of witnesses on his or her behalf under conditions of equality;

(v) If considered to have infringed the penal law, to have this decision and any measures imposed in consequence thereof reviewed by a higher competent, independent and impartial authority or judicial body according to law;

(vi) To have the free assistance of an interpreter if the child cannot understand or speak the language used;

(vii) To have his or her privacy fully respected at all stages of the proceedings.

3. States Parties shall seek to promote the establishment of laws, procedures, authorities and institutions specifically applicable to children alleged as, accused of, or recognized as having infringed the penal law, and, in particular:

(a) The establishment of a minimum age below which children shall be presumed not to have the capacity to infringe the penal law;

(b) Whenever appropriate and desirable, measures for dealing with such children without resorting to judicial proceedings, providing that human rights and legal safeguards are fully respected.

4. A variety of dispositions, such as care, guidance and supervision orders; counselling; probation; foster care; education and vocational training programmes and other alternatives to institutional care shall be available to ensure that children are dealt with in a manner appropriate to their well-being and proportionate both to their circumstances and the offence.

Article 41

Nothing in the present Convention shall affect any provisions which are more conducive to the realization of the rights of the child and which may be contained in:

(a) The law of a State party; or

(b) International law in force for that State.

INDEX